International Directory of
COMPANY
HISTORIES

International Directory of
COMPANY HISTORIES

VOLUME 55

Editor

Tina Grant

ST. JAMES PRESS®

Detroit • New York • San Diego • San Francisco • Cleveland • New Haven, Conn. • Waterville, Maine • London • Munich

International Directory of Company Histories, Volume 55

Tina Grant, Editor

Project Editor
Miranda H. Ferrara

Editorial
Erin Bealmear, Joann Cerrito, Jim Craddock, Stephen Cusack, Peter M. Gareffa, Kristin Hart, Melissa Hill, Margaret Mazurkiewicz, Carol A. Schwartz, Christine Tomassini, Michael J. Tyrkus

Imaging and Multimedia
Randy Bassett, Dean Dauphinais, Robert Duncan, Lezlie Light

Manufacturing
Rhonda Williams

LIBRARY OF CONGRESS CATALOG NUMBER 89-190943

ISBN: 1-55862-485-6

BRITISH LIBRARY CATALOGUING IN PUBLICATION DATA

International directory of company histories. Vol. 55
I. Tina Grant
33.87409

Printed in the United States of America
10 9 8 7 6 5 4 3 2 1

CONTENTS _____

Preface . . . . page vii
List of Abbreviations ix

Company Histories

Academy of Television Arts &
   Sciences, Inc. 3
Acorn Products, Inc. 6
Air Wisconsin Airlines Corporation 10
Alloy, Inc. 13
Amerada Hess Corporation 16
American Eagle Outfitters, Inc. 21
Andrx Corporation 25
Arrow Air Holdings Corporation 28
ASC, Inc. 31
Atlantic Coast Airlines Holdings, Inc. 35
Autoroutes du Sud de la France SA 38
Bain & Company 41
Bandai Co., Ltd. 44
Banknorth Group, Inc. 49
Bénéteau SA 54
Big 5 Sporting Goods Corporation 57
Bilfinger & Berger AG 60
BMC Software, Inc. 64
Bobit Publishing Company 68
Buck Consultants, Inc. 71
Bulley & Andrews, LLC 74
Bureau Veritas SA 77
C & S Wholesale Grocers, Inc. 80
Calvin Klein, Inc. 84
Carlson Wagonlit Travel 89
CarMax, Inc. 93
The Carriage House Companies, Inc. 96
The Christian Science Publishing Society . . . 99
Coach USA, Inc. 103
Cogent Communications Group, Inc. 107
Conn-Selmer, Inc. 111
Daiwa Securities Group Inc. 115
The Detroit Lions, Inc. 119

Devro plc 122
The Doctors' Company 125
The Dress Barn, Inc. 129
Duncan Toys Company 132
Ellen Tracy, Inc. 136
Empresas Polar SA 139
Faultless Starch/Bon Ami Company 142
Faygo Beverages Inc. 146
G. Leblanc Corporation 149
The Gap, Inc. 153
The George F. Cram Company, Inc. 158
George S. May International Company 161
The Great Atlantic & Pacific Tea
   Company, Inc. 164
Greene, Tweed & Company 170
Groupe Alain Manoukian 173
Groupe Soufflet SA 176
Grupo Dragados SA 179
Guittard Chocolate Company 183
Haci Omer Sabanci Holdings A.S. 186
Halliburton Company 190
HCI Direct, Inc. 196
Head N.V. 199
Home Interiors & Gifts, Inc. 202
Home Products International, Inc. 205
Hoshino Gakki Co. Ltd. 208
Huntington Learning Centers, Inc. 212
Imatra Steel Oy Ab 215
Ingersoll-Rand Company Ltd. 218
International Airline Support Group, Inc. . . . 223
Israel Chemicals Ltd. 226
IVAX Corporation 230
J.F. Shea Co., Inc. 234
Jazz Basketball Investors, Inc. 237

Kuwait Petroleum Corporation 240

Landmark Communications, Inc. 244

Lebhar-Friedman, Inc. 250

Lonely Planet Publications Pty Ltd. 253

MAPICS, Inc. 256

MasTec, Inc. 259

McWane Corporation 264

The Metropolitan Museum of Art 267

MTR Foods Ltd. 271

National Organization for Women, Inc. 274

Noodles & Company, Inc. 277

Norwich & Peterborough Building
     Society 280

Noven Pharmaceuticals, Inc. 283

Observer AB 286

ODL, Inc. 290

Patterson-UTI Energy, Inc. 293

Penford Corporation 296

PennWell Corporation 300

Peterson American Corporation 304

Pochet SA 307

Professional Bull Riders Inc. 310

Public Service Company of
     New Hampshire 313

Red Spot Paint & Varnish Company 319

Rockford Products Corporation 323

Ron Tonkin Chevrolet Company 326

Royal & Sun Alliance Insurance
     Group plc 329

San Francisco Baseball Associates, L.P. 340

SHV Holdings N.V. 344

Silhouette Brands, Inc. 348

Staples, Inc. 351

Stonyfield Farm, Inc. 357

Stussy, Inc. 361

Swift & Company 364

Tenet Healthcare Corporation 368

Tokyo Gas Co., Ltd. 372

The Tussauds Group 376

Viskase Companies, Inc. 379

Warwick Valley Telephone Company 382

Weil, Gotshal & Manges LLP 385

Index to Companies 389

Index to Industries 593

Geographic Index 631

Notes on Contributors 667

PREFACE

The St. James Press series *The International Directory of Company Histories (IDCH)* is intended for reference use by students, business people, librarians, historians, economists, investors, job candidates, and others who seek to learn more about the historical development of the world's most important companies. To date, *IDCH* has covered over 6,050 companies in 55 volumes.

Inclusion Criteria

Most companies chosen for inclusion in *IDCH* have achieved a minimum of US$25 million in annual sales and are leading influences in their industries or geographical locations. Companies may be publicly held, private, or nonprofit. State-owned companies that are important in their industries and that may operate much like public or private companies also are included. Wholly owned subsidiaries and divisions are profiled if they meet the requirements for inclusion. Entries on companies that have had major changes since they were last profiled may be selected for updating.

The *IDCH* series highlights 10% private and nonprofit companies, and features updated entries on approximately 45 companies per volume.

Entry Format

Each entry begins with the company's legal name, the address of its headquarters, its telephone, toll-free, and fax numbers, and its web site. A statement of public, private, state, or parent ownership follows. A company with a legal name in both English and the language of its headquarters country is listed by the English name, with the native-language name in parentheses.

The company's founding or earliest incorporation date, the number of employees, and the most recent available sales figures follow. Sales figures are given in local currencies with equivalents in U.S. dollars. For some private companies, sales figures are estimates and indicated by the abbreviation *est.* The entry lists the exchanges on which a company's stock is traded and its ticker symbol, as well as the company's NAIC codes.

Entries generally contain a *Company Perspectives* box which provides a short summary of the company's mission, goals, and ideals, a *Key Dates* box highlighting milestones in the company's history, lists of *Principal Subsidiaries, Principal Divisions, Principal Operating Units, Principal Competitors,* and articles for *Further Reading.*

American spelling is used throughout *IDCH*, and the word "billion" is used in its U.S. sense of one thousand million.

Sources

Entries have been compiled from publicly accessible sources both in print and on the Internet such as general and academic periodicals, books, annual reports, and material supplied by the companies themselves.

Cumulative Indexes

IDCH contains three indexes: the **Index to Companies**, which provides an alphabetical index to companies discussed in the text as well as to companies profiled, the **Index to Industries**, which allows researchers to locate companies by their principal industry, and the **Geographic Index**, which lists companies alphabetically by the country of their headquarters. The indexes are cumulative and specific instructions for using them are found immediately preceding each index.

Suggestions Welcome

Comments and suggestions from users of *IDCH* on any aspect of the product as well as suggestions for companies to be included or updated are cordially invited. Please write:

> The Editor
> *International Directory of Company Histories*
> St. James Press
> 27500 Drake Rd.
> Farmington Hills, Michigan 48331-3535

AB	Aktiebolag (Finland, Sweden)
AB Oy	Aktiebolag Osakeyhtiot (Finland)
A.E.	Anonimos Eteria (Greece)
AG	Aktiengesellschaft (Austria, Germany, Switzerland, Liechtenstein)
A.O.	Anonim Ortaklari/Ortakligi (Turkey)
ApS	Amparteselskab (Denmark)
A.Š.	Anonim Širketi (Turkey)
A/S	Aksjeselskap (Norway); Aktieselskab (Denmark, Sweden)
Ay	Avoinyhtio (Finland)
B.A.	Buttengewone Aansprakeiijkheid (The Netherlands)
Bhd.	Berhad (Malaysia, Brunei)
B.V.	Besloten Vennootschap (Belgium, The Netherlands)
C.A.	Compania Anonima (Ecuador, Venezuela)
C. de R.L.	Compania de Responsabilidad Limitada (Spain)
Co.	Company
Corp.	Corporation
CRL	Companhia a Responsabilidao Limitida (Portugal, Spain)
C.V.	Commanditaire Vennootschap (The Netherlands, Belgium)
G.I.E.	Groupement d'Interet Economique (France)
GmbH	Gesellschaft mit beschraenkter Haftung (Austria, Germany, Switzerland)
Inc.	Incorporated (United States, Canada)
I/S	Interessentselskab (Denmark); Interesentselskap (Norway)
KG/KGaA	Kommanditgesellschaft/Kommanditgesellschaft auf Aktien (Austria, Germany, Switzerland)
KK	Kabushiki Kaisha (Japan)
K/S	Kommanditselskab (Denmark); Kommandittselskap (Norway)
Lda.	Limitada (Spain)
L.L.C.	Limited Liability Company (United States)
Ltd.	Limited (Various)
Ltda.	Limitada (Brazil, Portugal)
Ltee.	Limitee (Canada, France)
mbH	mit beschraenkter Haftung (Austria, Germany)
N.V.	Naamloze Vennootschap (Belgium, The Netherlands)
OAO	Otkrytoe Aktsionernoe Obshchestve (Russia)
OOO	Obschestvo s Ogranichennoi Otvetstvennostiu (Russia)
Oy	Osakeyhtiö (Finland)
PLC	Public Limited Co. (United Kingdom, Ireland)
Pty.	Proprietary (Australia, South Africa, United Kingdom)
S.A.	Société Anonyme (Belgium, France, Greece, Luxembourg, Switzerland, Arab speaking countries); Sociedad Anónima (Latin America [except Brazil], Spain, Mexico); Sociedades Anônimas (Brazil, Portugal)
SAA	Societe Anonyme Arabienne
S.A.R.L.	Sociedade Anonima de Responsabilidade Limitada (Brazil, Portugal); Société à Responsabilité Limitée (France, Belgium, Luxembourg)
S.A.S.	Societá in Accomandita Semplice (Italy); Societe Anonyme Syrienne (Arab speaking countries)
Sdn. Bhd.	Sendirian Berhad (Malaysia)
S.p.A.	Società per Azioni (Italy)
Sp. z.o.o.	Spólka z ograniczona odpowiedzialnoscia (Poland)
S.R.L.	Società a Responsabilità Limitata (Italy); Sociedad de Responsabilidad Limitada (Spain, Mexico, Latin America [except Brazil])
S.R.O.	Spolecnost s Rucenim Omezenym (Czechoslovakia
Ste.	Societe (France, Belgium, Luxembourg, Switzerland)
VAG	Verein der Arbeitgeber (Austria, Germany)
YK	Yugen Kaisha (Japan)
ZAO	Zakrytoe Aktsionernoe Obshchestve (Russia)

ABBREVIATIONS FOR CURRENCY

$	United States dollar	KD	Kuwaiti dinar
£	United Kingdom pound	L	Italian lira
¥	Japanese yen	LuxFr	Luxembourgian franc
A$	Australian dollar	M$	Malaysian ringgit
AED	United Arab Emirates dirham	N	Nigerian naira
B	Thai baht	Nfl	Netherlands florin
B	Venezuelan bolivar	NIS	Israeli new shekel
BFr	Belgian franc	NKr	Norwegian krone
C$	Canadian dollar	NT$	Taiwanese dollar
CHF	Switzerland franc	NZ$	New Zealand dollar
COL	Colombian peso	P	Philippine peso
Cr	Brazilian cruzado	PLN	Polish zloty
CZK	Czech Republic koruny	PkR	Pakistan Rupee
DA	Algerian dinar	Pta	Spanish peseta
Dfl	Netherlands florin	R	Brazilian real
DKr	Danish krone	R	South African rand
DM	German mark	RMB	Chinese renminbi
E£	Egyptian pound	RO	Omani rial
Esc	Portuguese escudo	Rp	Indonesian rupiah
EUR	Euro dollars	Rs	Indian rupee
FFr	French franc	Ru	Russian ruble
Fmk	Finnish markka	S$	Singapore dollar
GRD	Greek drachma	Sch	Austrian schilling
HK$	Hong Kong dollar	SFr	Swiss franc
HUF	Hungarian forint	SKr	Swedish krona
IR£	Irish pound	SRls	Saudi Arabian riyal
ISK	Icelandic króna	TD	Tunisian dinar
J$	Jamaican dollar	W	Korean won
K	Zambian kwacha		

International Directory of

COMPANY
HISTORIES

Academy of Television Arts & Sciences, Inc.

5220 Lankershim Boulevard
North Hollywood, California 91601
U.S.A.
Telephone: (818) 754-2800
Web site: http://www.emmys.org

Not-For-Profit Company
Founded: 1948
NAIC: 813920 Professional Organizations

Located in North Hollywood, California, The Academy of Television Arts & Sciences, Inc. (ATAS) is a not-for-profit corporation best known for its annual Emmy Awards ceremony, honoring the best that primetime television has to offer. A rival group based in New York, The National Academy of Television Arts & Sciences (NATAS), awards Emmys for daytime programming, sports, news, and documentaries. The Academy also hosts seminars related to broadcasting and emerging technologies, sponsors student internships, is responsible for a hall of fame, maintains a television archive with the University of California, Los Angeles (UCLA) and a library at the University of Southern California (USC), and publishes a newsletter as well as *Emmy*, a bi-monthly general interest magazine dedicated to the television industry. Membership in the Academy is based on peer groups—such as performers, writers, and directors—which are responsible for determining eligibility requirements. Each peer group has two representatives on the Board of Governors and is responsible for overseeing the operation of the Academy. Members of individual peer groups also determine the winner of Emmys within their area of expertise.

Academy Founded During Television's Infancy

The man most responsible for the foundation of the Academy of Television Arts & Sciences was Syd Cassyd, a Teaneck, New Jersey, native. While serving with the Army Signal Corps during World War II, he worked as a film editor with renowned Hollywood film director Frank Capra. He then moved to Los Angeles after the war, finding work as a grip on the Paramount Pictures lot as well as reporting for *Film World* and television trade publications *TV World* and *Boxoffice*. At the time, televi-

sion was still very much in its embryonic stages: CBS had made the first commercial broadcasts in 1939, but it was not until February 12, 1946 that the first broadcast was transmitted by way of coaxial cable from New York to Washington, D.C., thus establishing the foundation for network television. Cassyd realized that the new medium had a bright future and might benefit from having an organization similar to the Academy of Motion Picture Arts and Sciences. He also looked to the French Academy of Sciences and the National Academy of Science in Washington for inspiration, envisioning a television academy where position papers could be exchanged and ideas freely debated. Cassyd first discussed his concept with UCLA professor Paul Sheets, president of the Audio-Visual Educational Association of America, as well as Klaus Landsberg, Paramount's TV Engineer. He then organized an exploratory meeting, held on November 14, 1946 in the offices of Federal Communications Commission (FCC) attorney S.R. Rabinof, who also ran a television school, American Television Laboratories. Also in attendance was Sam Nathanson, a film distributor; Harmon Stevens, a Michigan radio station owner; Morrie Goldman, a cartoon director; schoolteacher Orville Engstrom; and Russell Furse, who worked for Telefilm, Inc. in public relations. Over the next few weeks the group met three more times in Rabinof's offices, agreeing that in order to achieve some measure of credibility they needed to attract a well-known personality to chair the organization and serve as a public face. Cassyd, the initial chairman, asked Edgar Bergen, the famous ventriloquist and comedian, to take over the post. Bergen, who was quite interested in pursuing a career in television, agreed. On January 7, 1947, the Academy held its first official meeting, attended by 37 television professionals and hosted by Bergen, who was quickly elected the first president and proceeded to turn the meeting into a performance, entertaining his colleagues with a puppet made from a handkerchief wrapped around his fist. Over the course of the next year, Bergen entertained ever larger audiences, as the number of professionals attending Academy meetings grew steadily. According to Cassyd, by the fifth meeting the group boasted 250 members. The Academy was officially incorporated on January 28, 1948, its stated aim "to promote the cultural, educational and research aims of television."

In order to gain some publicity for the new organization, as well as lend a degree of credibility to the new medium, the

Company Perspectives:

The Academy of Television Arts & Sciences—founded one month after network television was born in 1946—is a nonprofit corporation devoted to the advancement of tele-communications arts and sciences and to fostering creative leadership in the telecommunications industry.

Academy decided to present awards to recognize outstanding work in television, in very much the same way the Oscars did for the film industry. It was not necessarily an obvious decision, in light of the situation with radio, an extremely popular medium at its height, which never created an awards program to honor its work. Designing an appropriate trophy and naming it proved somewhat difficult, but the Academy at least had the Oscar statuette to emulate. Cassyd suggested the award be called "Ike," an allusion to the television iconoscope tube, but "Ike" was too well identified with Dwight D. Eisenhower, the famous World War II general and future president of the United States. Harry Lubcke, president of the Society of Television Engineers, offered an alternative in "Immy," the nickname for the early image orthicon camera. Immy would later become Emmy, which Academy members felt was more appropriate for the female statuette that won an industry design competition. The winner out of 48 entrants was a television engineer for Cascade Pictures named Louis McManus, who used his wife, Dorothy, as a model for a winged woman holding aloft a massive atom. It was considered to be an appropriate symbol of the Academy, the wings representing the muse of art and the atom the technical aspirations of the new medium. The Emmy was then produced, as it has ever since, by the R.S. Owens Company in Chicago. Each statuette, made out of copper, nickel, silver, and gold, weighed four and three-quarter pounds.

First Emmys Awarded in 1949

The first Emmy award ceremony, honoring the 1948 season, was a modest affair, a 600-person banquet held at the Hollywood Athletic Club in Los Angeles on January 25, 1949. There were few celebrities in attendance and participants recalled that most parked their own cars, a far different atmosphere from the stretch limousines and staged introductions in the decades to come. Most of the people attending the first Emmys were Academy members. While radio and film heavyweights of the day chose to ignore the importance of television, local politicians were quick to embrace the Emmy awards. California Governor Earl Warren, Los Angeles Mayor Fletcher Bowron, as well as city councilmen and a county supervisor were in attendance. In many ways, the first Emmy was very much a local affair. It was broadcast on local station KTSL, the audience quite small. There were no more than 50,000 television sets in Los Angeles and only one million nationwide. There were five awards given out that night, and only programs produced in Los Angeles County and aired over the four television stations in the area were eligible. As a result, New York critics regarded the Emmys as a provincial affair not worth noting. For that matter, the Emmys received little attention from the Los Angeles media. The first Emmy ever awarded, for Most Outstanding Personality, went to Shirley Dinsdale, a 20-year-old ventriloquist who performed with her puppet, Judy Splinters, five days a week in a 15-minute broadcast on KTLA. The Most Popular Program of 1948 was "Pantomime Quiz," a charades game played by celebrities. McManus was also recognized that night for his design of the Emmy symbol. Instead of an Emmy, however, he was given a plaque.

The Emmys quickly caught on, as evidenced by the aggressive campaigning for the award that began to take place in 1949. The competition was also opened up by changing the requirements so that any television program was eligible as long as it aired on a Los Angeles television station, meaning that kinescope programming could now be considered. Because there would not be coast-to-coast transmissions via microwave until 1951, the fledgling networks had to rely on the kinescope process, which reproduced a program for later showing by filming directly off a television screen, then making prints. The Best Kinescope Show of 1949 was Milton Berle's *Texaco's Star Theater,* produced in New York. Another New Yorker, Ed Wynn, won the Emmy as Most Outstanding Live Personality. The second Emmy production was marred somewhat because the names of the winners leaked out earlier in the day, although most of the recipients offered an appropriate measure of surprise, if not astonishment, upon hearing their names announced. All told, the second award ceremony featured more of the fanfare expected of a faux-Academy Awards affair.

There was no assurance, however, that the Emmys and the Academy were securely established. Other TV awards cropped up during the 1950s, including ones sponsored by *TV Guide, Look* magazine, and the Sylvania electronics company, but it was the challenge of legendary showman and Broadway columnist Ed Sullivan that would have a more lasting effect. Sullivan personalized a growing rivalry between Los Angeles and New York over control of the new medium. Although Hollywood dominated the film industry, most television programming at this time originated in New York. In 1950, Sullivan launched his own television awards, the Michaels, which he hosted and staged in Manhattan until 1953. Ironically, neither Sullivan nor the Academy issued awards in 1954, the Academy concluding that the show was simply too expensive to produce. The situation changed in 1955 when the television networks decided the Emmys were worth showing nationwide. In order to incorporate the important contributions of New Yorkers, as well as outmaneuver Sullivan, the Academy elected to simulcast the ceremony from both Los Angeles and New York, a difficult technological feat in the days before satellite transmissions. The Emmy simulcast continued until 1971, becoming something of a tradition. Never knowing when the screen might go blank for minutes at a time actually piqued the interest of viewers and the Emmy awards broadcast enjoyed very high ratings.

Unable to beat the Academy, Sullivan now demanded that he be allowed to join it. Creating a "Committee of 50" New York television heavyweights, he petitioned the Academy for an East Coast chapter, which was granted in June 1955. Still not satisfied, he began advocating the creation of an entirely new academy, one that would designate both Los Angeles and New York as the founding chapters. Sullivan's lobbying efforts finally paid off in 1957 and the original Academy was superceded by a new organization, the National Academy of Television Arts and Sciences. Sullivan was also named its first president. The rivalry between the two coasts only intensified as the

Emmys almost turned into a sporting contest, with both cities keeping score on how many statuettes they took home. With the demise of live primetime dramas produced in New York, the balance of power tilted increasingly in the direction of Los Angeles in the 1960s, and the New York portion of the Emmy telecast was essentially reduced to news awards. By 1968, the news winners were not invited to accept their Emmys on stage but rather were relegated to rising from their seats en masse and having the statuettes delivered to their tables. Local NASTA chapters were also organized in such cities as Chicago, Atlanta, Seattle, and Washington, D.C.—all nurtured by the New York chapter as a way to counterbalance Hollywood's growing power. In the late 1960s, the Academy formed a foundation in order to establish a television archive, and the site chosen for the repository was the University of the City of Los Angeles. NASTA's New York co-headquarters was shut down in 1970, and a year later the New York portion of the Emmy telecast was eliminated by NBC to save money. A separate primetime Emmy awards telecast for New York news awards was tried in 1973 and 1974, but poor ratings forced its cancellation.

The "Divorce" of 1976

As the most powerful chapter of NASTA, Los Angeles began to question why Academy members in middle America should have an equal say on peer-based awards. The schism between Hollywood and the rest of the organization reached a head in 1976 when New York and the smaller chapters joined forces to defeat a Hollywood-backed candidate for the presidency. Angered, the Los Angeles chapter sued for the dissolution of the Academy, which led to "the divorce." After a year of legal wrangling a settlement was reached, resulting in the organization splitting into two academies. New York-based NASTA would be responsible for daytime, sports, news, international, and local Emmy awards, while a newly formed ASTA retained the more prestigious primetime Emmy telecast. Bitterness lingered between the two sides, as both pursued their separate agendas. ASTA launched its magazine, *Emmy*, in 1978, then reestablished the foundation in 1988 to pursue fund raising activities and to operate and expand upon the Academy's educational programs. In the late 1990s, the foundation established a library at the University of Southern California.

The primetime Emmy awards ceremony, however, remained the Academy's most visible function and continued to have its share of unusual moments. In 1981, the awards were boycotted by both the Screen Actors Guild and the American Federation of Radio and Television Artists as part of a strike against the network. None of the emcees appeared and only one actor, Powers Booth, showed up to accept his Emmy. Due to the terrorist attacks of September 11, 2001, the Emmys were twice postponed.

The long-term practice of rotating the Emmy telecast between ABC, CBS, and NBC was disrupted in 1987 when the new FOX network sought to gain credibility by outbidding the established networks for the broadcast rights to the ceremony for the next three years. Ratings were poor on FOX, which lacked the nationwide coverage of the other networks. ABC then became the sole network of the Emmys from 1990 to 1992, after which the Academy decided to return to its "wheel" concept of alternating networks, with FOX now included in the rotation. This arrangement was once again threatened in the fall of 2002 when cable giant HBO presented the Academy with a five-year $50 million offer for the Emmys. In the preceding weeks, the Academy had attempted to negotiate a richer deal with the networks, arguing that the show was worth more than what the broadcasters were paying. The networks increased only the annual license fee from $3 million to $3.3 million, a mere fraction of ABC's seven-year $350 million contract for the Oscars. Faced with losing the Emmy awards to cable, the networks were angered at first, with CBS even threatening to boycott the ceremony, but in the end they countered HBO's offer with a $52 million eight-year agreement that called for a $5.5 million fee for the first four years and $7.5 million for the final four years. Although the Academy took less money than HBO had offered, it was clearly pleased with its new deal.

The rivalry between ATAS and NATAS cooled as new leadership, uninvolved in the divorce of the 1970s, took over. At the very least, the two sides had to work together in order to keep the Emmys vital in a changing media landscape. For instance, in 2002 NATAS wanted to create a Latin Emmys for Spanish-language programming but needed ATAS to sign off on the idea. Cassyd, who died in 2000, maintained that reunification of the Academy was inevitable. The heads of the rival groups were at least on speaking terms and began to hold meetings to discuss common concerns. Whether this thawing out would one day lead to a full reconciliation, however, remained to be seen.

Principal Subsidiaries

Academy of Television Arts & Sciences Foundation.

Principal Competitors

National Academy of Television Arts and Sciences.

Further Reading

Albinak, Paige, "The Emmy Goes ... Nowhere," *Broadcasting & Cable*, November 18, 2002, p. 6.

Milano, Valerie, Natalie Casale, and Dom Serafini, "If the Emmy Wins an Award, Who Gets It?," *Video Age International*, January 1, 2001, p. 1.

O'Neil, Thomas, *The Emmys*, New York: Berkeley, 1998, 642 p.

Schlosser, Joe, "Emmy's Parents to Remarry?," *Broadcasting & Cable*, August 27, 2001, p. 16.

—Ed Dinger

Acorn Products, Inc.

390 West Nationwide Boulevard
Columbus, Ohio 43215
U.S.A.
Telephone: (614) 222-4400
Fax: (614) 221-8397
Web site: http://www.uniontools.com

Public Company
Incorporated: 1890 as Union Fork & Hoe Company
Employees: 450
Sales: $91.2 million (2002)
Stock Exchanges: NASDAQ
Ticker Symbol: ACRN
NAIC: 333112 Lawn and Garden Tractor and Home
   Lawn and Garden Equipment Manufacturing; 332212
   Hand and Edge Tool Manufacturing; 551112 Offices
   of Other Holding Companies

Toolmaker Acorn Products, Inc. came into existence in the early 1990s as a result of a merger between Vision Hardware Group, Inc.—the parent company of tool wholesaler Union-Tools, Inc.—and an affiliate of the investment company TCW Group, Inc. UnionTools is Acorn's primary operating subsidiary and source of the company's revenues. UnionTools is one of America's top three manufacturers of non-power lawn and garden tools, such as hoes, shovels, rakes, and hand tools. In addition to selling tools under its own brand names, which include Union, Razor-Back, Perfect Cut, and Yard 'n Garden, the company makes private label tools for retailers such as Sears, Roebuck and Co. and Ace Hardware Corporation. Although Acorn has been struggling to achieve profitability during the late 1990s and early years of the new millennium, it has recently shifted its focus away from its traditional base of retailers to direct-to-consumer marketing in hopes of boosting its fortunes.

Early Years

Acorn Products traces its roots back to several pre-Revolutionary American enterprises, including lumber mills in Appalachia and steel plants in New York and Ohio. In 1890, George Durell merged these operations together, establishing a headquarters in Columbus, Ohio, and naming the new, unified concern the Union Fork & Hoe Company. Using forged steel and ash wood, Union manufactured and sold a basic set of tools including forks, hoes, rakes, and repair handles for such tools. The company took a significant step forward in 1913 when it partnered with catalogue giant Sears, Roebuck and Co. to manufacture tools under Sears' Craftsman brand, an alliance that would continue into the twenty-first century. In 1936, Union made another significant move when it introduced its first line of branded tools under the Razor-Back name. The Razor-Back shovel, in particular, proved to be a major seller for the company, and the Razor-Back brand as a whole became well respected in the professional hand tools field.

Prior to World War II, farmers and other agricultural workers were the primary consumers of Union's products. With the increasing mechanization of farming in the postwar years, however, Union and other hand tools makers began to shift their focus to the nascent home gardening market. This change reflected not so much an alteration in product offerings—Union and its competitors continued to focus on non-power hand tools—but rather was a consequence of the fact that their traditional farming customers were now having to use larger and non-manual equipment to do their jobs.

Vision Hardware Group Assumes Control: 1986–93

Union remained firmly in family control until 1986, when Ed Durell, a descendant of company founder George, sold the company to Vision Hardware Group, Inc. Vision Hardware was a Commerce, California-based holding company founded by Jack Corwin, who had formerly worked in the corporate finance division of Drexel Burnham Lambert. Vision Hardware's portfolio was comprised of a stable of steady-performing hardware companies, which included VSI Fasteners, Inc., McGuire-Nicholas Co., and Buffalo Tool Co., in addition to Union. To this conglomeration, Union brought its core product line of long-handled tools; McGuire-Nicholas, which was launched in the 1930s to make leather aprons for tradesmen, had evolved into a manufacturer of leather, canvas, and synthetic fabric tool holders

6

Company Perspectives:

Columbus, Ohio-based UnionTools is a leading manufacturer and marketer of non-powered lawn and garden tools in North America. For more than a century, UnionTools has been a leader and innovator in design and manufacturing techniques that improve tool life and performance.

and work aprons; Buffalo Tools made implements for the automotive trade; and VSI Fasteners produced and distributed packaged fasteners and chain. This diversification performed well for Vision Hardware. The group's 1989 sales topped $210 million, with Union Fork & Hoe accounting for $70 million of that total.

But this steady, stable industry was about to experience some significant upheaval. From their early years through much of the 1980s, tool manufacturers had never focused on pitching their products directly to consumers, since it was conventional wisdom across the industry that retail customers did not pay attention to or care about the brand names affixed to the shovels, hoes, rakes, or other hardware equipment they were buying. Rather, they tended to purchase tools according to price or, more importantly, what their local hardware store had available. In this environment, tool manufacturers concentrated simply on selling their goods to retailers and generally left the consumer out of the equation. A new pattern began to emerge in the late 1980s, however. Sales in the manual tools sector began to flatten, forcing tool producers to scramble for new methods of boosting sales. In addition, so-called "do-it-yourselfers" began to account for a greater share of sales in the sector. Middle-class homeowners began to undertake home repair and gardening as a hobby, and their buying patterns were far different from those of the contractors and other professionals who had long formed the core of the industry's end-users. Finally, independent hardware stores began to be pushed out of business by giant discount retailers, such as Wal-Mart Stores, Inc., and Home Depot, Inc. As these megastores carried a multitude of brands and models all at once—rather than the one or two items that a small store might stock—tool makers could no longer rely on mere shelf presence to move their offerings. It became imperative for tool makers to distinguish their products from their rivals' on the shelves.

These factors prompted the major players in the industry to revamp their strategies. According to *Selected Federal Filings Newswires*, Union's new business plan was designed to take it from being "a manufacturing-oriented industrial company to a marketing-oriented products company." New President and CEO Gabe Mihaly, who had taken the reigns of the company in 1991, was in charge of overseeing the shift. In keeping with this new philosophy, Mihaly strove to broaden the company's appeal by changing Union Fork & Hoe's name to the broader UnionTools in 1992. Mihaly also led the company's drive to launch new products, enter new segments of the market, and improve the perception of its brand. The company was not alone in these efforts. In the early 1990s, as the *Central Pennsylvania Business Journal* explained, True Temper, then one of UnionTool's chief competitors, unveiled new product lines and embarked on a major advertising campaign that touted its tools were "made in America."

In 1992, UnionTools received a major boost when O.M. Scott & Sons Co. selected the company to manufacture, market, and distribute a new line of tools bearing the Scotts name. Scotts was one of the most recognizable brands in the lawncare industry, but it had never ventured into tools. UnionTools saw two opportunities in this licensing agreement. Not only would it see an immediate increase in sales, but it could also reap longer-term rewards from its association with the Scotts name. "Union-Tools never has had a national brand name" of its own, a UnionTools marketing director told the *Columbus Dispatch* for August 15, 1992. "Now we have the strongest name in the lawn and garden field."

Financial Struggles: 1992–97

The Scotts licensing agreement, however, was not enough to solve Vision Hardware's problems. As the entire U.S. economy floundered in the early 1990s—and the tool business slumped along with it—Vision Hardware struggled to fund the expansion its new brand-building business plan required. A solution appeared in November of 1993, when Vision Hardware was acquired by an investment fund managed by an affiliate of TCW Group, Inc., an investment management company that oversaw $44 billion of capital for institutional and individual investors. As part of the deal, Vision Hardware received $12.5 million in capital, which would allow it to enhance its product lines and expand into new markets. After Vision Hardware was bought out, the holding company—seeking a more consumer-friendly name—changed its name to Acorn Products, Inc.

The infusion of capital failed to revivify the newly christened Acorn Products. The company—including UnionTools—continued to lose money throughout the mid-1990s, despite the introduction of new product lines, such as the Lady Gardener line of tools designed specifically for women. To compensate, Acorn borrowed heavily from TCW. In a cost-cutting effort, Acorn Products also shed its poorest-performing subsidiary, VSI Fasteners, in December of 1996. This move generated an additional $6.9 million of operating capital for Acorn Products. Encouraged by this boost to its bottom line, Acorn shifted gears and snapped up a new subsidiary barely two months later when it purchased an injection-molding facility from one of its suppliers. The plant would produce plastic handles and parts needed for UnionTools' products. Acorn Products declared it a sound purchase, since it felt that vertical integration of this sort would help the company achieve operating efficiencies. Nevertheless, in fiscal year 1996, Acorn Products reported a drop in both sales and profits, citing consolidation in the retail industry and unseasonably cold spring weather that stalled sales of its gardening equipment.

Acorn Products tried to fight its way out of these doldrums in 1997. In an effort to pare down its considerable debt, the company went public in June 1997 with an initial stock offering of 3.25 million shares. (Oaktree Capital Management LLC and Trust Company of the West together became Acorn Products' majority shareholders.) With the $41 million generated by the stock sale, Acorn Products planned to repay debt and redeem preferred stock held by TCW. A few months later, Acorn Products sold its McGuire-Nicholas subsidiary to Kirkland Messin LLC for $4.7 million. The company touted these divestments as part of a practical strategy that would let Acorn

<table>
<tr><td colspan="2">**Key Dates:**</td></tr>
<tr><td>**1890:**</td><td>George Durell founds Union Fork & Hoe Company.</td></tr>
<tr><td>**1913:**</td><td>Union Fork & Hoe begins making the Craftsman line of tools for Sears, Roebuck and Co.</td></tr>
<tr><td>**1936:**</td><td>Union Fork & Hoe introduces its Razor-Back line of tools.</td></tr>
<tr><td>**1986:**</td><td>Vision Hardware Group acquires Union Fork & Hoe.</td></tr>
<tr><td>**1993:**</td><td>Vision Hardware merges with an affiliate of TCW Group, Inc. and changes its name to Acorn Products, Inc.; Union Fork & Hoe changes its name to UnionTools, Inc.</td></tr>
<tr><td>**1997:**</td><td>Acorn lists itself on the NASDAQ exchange with an initial public offering.</td></tr>
<tr><td>**2000:**</td><td>Acorn closes UnionTools' Columbus manufacturing plant and moves those operations to Kentucky.</td></tr>
</table>

Products focus predominantly on UnionTools' core product line. An Acorn Products spokesperson told *The Daily Reporter* that the reason for Acorn's problems with both McGuire-Nicholas and VMI Fasteners was that the relationship between the parent company and its subsidiaries "did not mesh" and declared that the problem would not be repeated in future acquisitions. Acorn Products reported a net loss of $9.9 million for fiscal year 1997.

Turbulent Times and Growing Pains: 1997 and Beyond

The year 1998 saw Acorn Products expanding into new areas and bolstering its presence in the manual tools business. After going public, Acorn Products worked to improve its relationship with key retailers such as Sears and Home Depot. Recognizing that its best bet for profitability was to become a dependable supplier to these major chains, Acorn Products revamped its manufacturing processes and inventory controls to serve the volume and delivery needs of these retail titans. Acorn Products also continued to build its brand through marketing and product development. As the company's director of investor relation told the *Daily Reporter*, "A shovel is a shovel is a shovel. If we can show [consumers] why it's better to buy the more expensive brand of shovel, if that fits their needs, we've succeeded." He added, "We've worked very hard to consumerize the product."

Alongside this effort to promote its core product lines more strenuously, Acorn Products moved into new areas of operations as well. Most significantly, the company decided to become a player in the watering products industry. In February 1998, Acorn Products purchased the Minnesota-based H.B. Sherman Manufacturing Company for $3.1 million. Sherman, which manufactured and marketed hose attachments and related products such as spray nozzles, sprinklers, and couplings, had earned $4.1 million the previous year. A few months later, Acorn Products bought Thompson Manufacturing Company for $6.65 million. Like Sherman, Thompson was a consumer-oriented hose attachment products company. "We are excited by the prospect of combining the product lines of Thompson and Sherman into a watering products subsidiary and building

these businesses with the sales and marketing skills and extensive distribution network of UnionTools," Acorn Products president Mihaly announced in a press release. Reflecting this importance of these new acquisitions, the company established a separate division to oversee their management.

A turning point came in 1998 for Mihaly as well. He had gone out on a limb when he declared that 1998 would be a "key year" for Acorn. After going public, divesting unprofitable subsidiaries, and entering new segments of the market, the company had to return to profitability. Unfortunately, it did not. In fact, 1998 sales fell again. In response, Acorn Products announced that it was closing its Columbus manufacturing facility and consolidating production at UnionTools' factory in Frankfort, New York. It also restructured its entire cast of senior management. By September 1999, Mihaly had been replaced as president and CEO by Cory Meyer, who announced yet another shift in strategy. Pledging that it would rededicate itself to its core products (specifically long-handled tools), Acorn Products sold its fledgling watering division to L.R. Nelson Corporation. "Our customers have come to expect industry leadership from us, and we will continue to provide this leadership by focusing on long-handled tools, wheelbarrows, pruning, and striking tools," Meyer said by way of an explanation in a press release. Nevertheless, the company still foundered. Sales for fiscal year 2000 fell 1.5 percent to $116.6 million, and another net loss—this one of $14 million—was reported. The year 2001 was even more disappointing, as the company lost $15.7 million on sales of $93.5 million.

Although Acorn Product's reputation as a manufacturer of top-flight tools remained undiminished, the company's bottom-line prospects were uncertain. In April 2002, Acorn defaulted on its loans from previous lenders but was able to work out a financial restructuring the preserved the company. President Meyer remained optimistic about the company's future. In July 2002, he announced that Acorn Products had completed its financial restructuring. As part of this plan, the firm would close its Columbus, Ohio, distribution center in favor of a facility in Louisville, Kentucky, where the municipal government had offered an attractive set of tax incentives. "We feel we have rewarded the trust put in us by customers, vendors, and associates," he told the *Columbus Dispatch* for July 3, 2002. It remained to be seen whether the shareholders would be similarly rewarded.

Principal Subsidiaries

UnionTools, Inc.

Principal Competitors

Ames Tools; True Temper Hardware Co.; The Black & Decker Corporation.

Further Reading

"Acorn Products IPO: Bought Molding Facility in 1997," *Selected Federal Filings Newswires*, April 22, 1997.
Allen, Robert M., Jr., "Quick Response: The Consumer's Handshake with Manufacturing at UnionTools," *National Productivity Review*, June 1, 1995.

Datres, Nancy, "Hardware Maker Kicks Off New Line and New Management Style," *Central Pennsylvania Business Journal*, July 1, 1991.

Franklin, Peter, "Tool Line Coming from Scotts, UnionTools," *Columbus Dispatch*, August 15, 1992.

Montooth, Michael, "With Eye on Weather, Acorn Focuses on Business," *Daily Reporter*, October 3, 1997.

Niquette, Mark, "Acorn Will Move Jobs as Part of Restructuring," *Columbus Dispatch*, July 3, 2002.

Sheban, Jeffrey, "Acorn Expects Stock Offering Will Sprout Growth," *Columbus Dispatch*, June 21, 1997.

—Rebecca Stanfel

Air Wisconsin Airlines Corporation

W6390 Challenger Drive, Suite 203
Appleton, Wisconsin 54914
U.S.A.
Telephone: (920) 739-5123
Toll free: (888) 354-4505
Fax: (920) 739-1325
Web site: http://www.airwis.com

Private Company
Incorporated: 1965
Employees: 2,900
Sales: $409 million (2001 est.)
NAIC: 481111 Scheduled Passenger Air Transportation;
488190 Other Support Activities for Air Transportation

Air Wisconsin Airlines Corporation is a leading regional airline in the United States. It operates 325 United Express flights a day to 45 destinations from hubs in Denver and Chicago, and in 2002 began flying feeder routes to Atlanta for AirTran Airways. The company expected to raise its regional jet fleet to 95 by the end of 2003, when it would be operating 100 flights a day for AirTran.

Origins

Air Wisconsin was created in August 1965 to provide an air link to Chicago from its hometown of Appleton, Wisconsin. The company went public in 1970 and was consistently profitable for more than two decades after.

Air Wisconsin grew rapidly to become a premier regional airline. In some ways it revolutionized the industry. Its pioneering code share arrangements created a new marketing tool that eventually would come to be used by nearly all scheduled airlines of any size around the world.

By 1985, Air Wisconsin had become the country's largest regional airline. In July 1985, the carrier became a United Express affiliate of United Airlines. The arrangement gave Air Wisconsin access to United's all-important computer reserva-tions system. Before working with United, it had a marketing agreement with American Airlines.

Early Regional Jets in the 1980s

The workhorse of Air Wisconsin's fleet was the 50-seat de Havilland of Canada DHC-7, or Dash 7. Air Wisconsin also pioneered, in the mid-1980s, the regional jet concept—i.e., using smaller jet aircraft, in this case the 100-seat British Aerospace BAe 146, to replace turboprops on short routes. This efficient jet was also quiet enough to allow Air Wisconsin to reinstate jet service to noise-sensitive communities such as New Haven, Connecticut, one of its first routes to the East Coast. The jets also boasted high enough performance to operate from high-altitude airports with runways too short for larger airliners, like Aspen.

Mississippi Valley Airlines (MVA) merged with Air Wisconsin in 1985. The two had combined annual revenues of $115 million and together served two million passengers a year. Both airlines had mutually complementary schedules centered on Chicago's O'Hare airport. Air Wisconsin had 700 employees before the merger, and MVA had 530. There was no commonality in the fleets, with MVA operating a mixed bag of turboprops, and Air Wisconsin adding another jet type, the BAC 111. MVA brought additional maintenance capacity to the merger.

Air Wisconsin had a disappointing year in 1989, and blamed United Airlines for taking its most profitable routes, such as Milwaukee-Chicago. Air Wisconsin attempted to diversify by expanding into the Washington, D.C. market.

Changing Ownership in the 1990s

The 1990 acquisition of Aspen Airways (for an estimated $9 million) made Air Wisconsin one of the country's largest regional airlines. Aspen offered seasonal routes to the ski destination from a handful of departure cities.

The first Gulf War and the following recession soon strained the airline industry. Air Wisconsin lost more than $31 million in 1991. In 1992, United Airlines bought Air Wis Services Inc., Air Wisconsin's parent company, for more than $300 million in cash (about $74 million) and assumed liabilities. American Air-

Company Perspectives:

Built on a foundation of exceptional quality and reliability, Air Wisconsin Airlines Corporation prides itself on the strength of its customer service and the dedication to excellence by its employees. With a continued focus on those strengths, the company looks optimistically to the future.

Key Dates:

1965: Air Wisconsin is formed to link Appleton hometown with Chicago.
1970: The company goes public.
1985: Air Wisconsin merges with MVA, becoming a United Express affiliate.
1990: Aspen Airways is acquired.
1992: United Airlines buys Air Wisconsin.
1993: Air Wisconsin jet operations are spun off as a private company (AWAC).
1998: AWAC buys MAX; the company begins operating Canadair Regional Jets.
2001: AWAC gives Bombardier a $2.4 billion RJ order.
2002: AWAC begins flying for Air Tran; main client United files for bankruptcy.

lines had offered to pay Air Wis $150 million for its landing slots at O'Hare. Most of the slots were unrestricted, allowing the owner to fly any size aircraft to any destination. United prevailed in spite of an antitrust suit by American.

Air Wisconsin's Chicago turboprop operations were sold to a regional affiliate of TWA, and other turboprops were transferred to other United Express carriers, making Air Wisconsin an all-jet operation. It also sold Air Wisconsin's Dulles-based operations to Atlantic Coast Airlines, Inc., another United Express affiliate.

In 1993, CJT Holdings, Inc. bought Air Wisconsin's jet operations, which then amounted to a dozen BAe 146 jets, for about $6 million. The O'Hare landing slots were not included in the deal. The Denver hub would be the chief source of the company's growth in the next few years.

The newly independent company, which employed about 550 people, was named Air Wisconsin Airlines Corporation (AWAC). Geoffrey T. Crowley, formerly of Presidential Airways, the Trump Shuttle, and Northwest, led the buyout group and became AWAC's president and CEO. The AWAC buyout was complicated somewhat by the buyout of United by its employees, which happened about the same time.

Some big things happened for AWAC in 1998. That April, it took over several United Express routes out of Denver from Mesa Air Group, which was dropped by United for alleged poor service. AWAC acquired Mountain Air Express (MAX) shortly after, again adding turboprop planes (four Dornier 328s) to its fleet. AWAC paid $1.5 million for MAX, formerly a unit of bankrupt Western Pacific Airlines.

AWAC also was introducing a new regional jet, the Canadair RJ. It ordered four in June 1998 for $84 million; the first two arrived in December. Company president Geoffrey Crowley noted that these were Air Wisconsin's first brand-new aircraft. The new RJs were smaller than the four-engine BAe 146s the company continued to operate, and they had a greater range (1,000 miles) and were more comfortable than turboprops.

In negotiating a new agreement between Air Wis and United, Crowley, who formerly managed Northwest's relations with regional carriers, changed the payment arrangement so that Air Wis received a fixed fare for each passenger carried, rather than a percentage of the total fare based on the passenger's ultimate destination, which could be quite small if the passenger were connecting to a long flight on United. The new arrangement was seen as beneficial for both carriers. Revenues were $140 million for 1998, producing income of $3.5 million. The airline carried about two million passengers that year.

Optimism, Uncertainty Beyond 2001

In 2001, AWAC gave Bombardier its largest regional jet order to date, placing 51 firm orders, 24 conditional orders, and options for another 75 Canadair RJs. The deal, made with the help of Canadian government financing, was valued at $2.4 billion.

Air Wisconsin's 105,000-square-foot maintenance hangar in Appleton, Wisconsin was traded for a much smaller one owned by Gulfstream Aerospace Corp. in late 2001. Air Wis was planning a $6 million maintenance base for its RJs at Mitchell International Airport in Milwaukee. The company was also the anchor tenant for a new pilot training center near Denver International Airport.

Like most airlines, Air Wisconsin was affected by the drop in air travel following the September 11, 2001 terrorist attacks on the United States. Passenger traffic was halved in the next couple of months, and the company cut 10 percent of its workforce of 3,000 employees.

In September 2002, AWAC announced a new marketing campaign to provide feeder traffic to Atlanta for budget carrier AirTran Airways under the name AirTran JetConnect. Air Wis planned to be operating 100 flights a day for AirTran by the end of 2003.

The future of United Airlines, which filed for bankruptcy protection in December 2002, was certain to influence the course of Air Wisconsin and other United Express carriers. United asked for court permission to lower its payments to the regionals; matters such as these were still being decided into the spring of 2003.

At the same time, Air Wisconsin's Fairchild Dornier 328 turboprops were being phased out. As late as 2001, the company had been operating 23 of the planes. United contracted Mesa Air Group to replace Air Wisconsin's turboprop service on affected Denver-based routes.

Principal Operating Units

AirTran JetConnect; United Express.

Principal Competitors

Atlantic Coast Airlines, Inc.; Frontier Airlines; Mesa Air Group, Inc.; Midwest Express Airlines; Rocky Mountain Airways.

Further Reading

"Air Wisconsin Becomes UAL Subsidiary After Acquisition Plan Approval," *Aviation Week & Space Technology,* February 10, 1992, p. 35.

"Air Wisconsin Is Being Sought," *New York Times,* November 14, 1987, p. 38.

"Air Wisconsin Losing Routes to Mesa Air," *Milwaukee Journal Sentinel,* February 28, 2003, p. 3D.

"Air Wisconsin Purchases Aspen Airways for Estimated $9 Million," *Aviation Week & Space Technology,* May 7, 1990, p. 95.

Alexander, Keith L., "United Tries to Cut Airline Partner Fees; Regional Carriers Are Part of the Plan," *Washington Post,* December 21, 2002, p. E3.

Baldo, Anthony, "Air Wisconsin, UAL Merger Approved," *Mergers & Acquisitions Report,* January 27, 1992, p. 1.

——, "Can UAL Make Merger with Air Wisconsin Work?," *Mergers & Acquisitions Report,* February 17, 1992, p. 3.

——, "UAL Is Growing Impatient with Air Wisconsin," *Mergers & Acquisitions Report,* November 18, 1991, p. 3.

Barrett, Rick, "Orlando, Fla.-Based Airline Makes Flight Agreement with Air Wisconsin," *Milwaukee Journal Sentinel,* September 28, 2002.

Branch, John, "Colorado Springs Airline Likely to Be Bought by Air Wisconsin," *Gazette* (Colorado Springs), February 14, 1998.

Davis, Jerry C., "Air Wisconsin 'Marries' United," *Chicago Sun-Times,* May 21, 1986, p. 70.

Feyder, Susan, "CJT Holdings Completes Acquisition of Wisconsin-Based Commuter Airline," *Star Tribune* (Minneapolis), December 30, 1993, p. 1D.

Gertzen, Jason, "Air Wisconsin to Cut 10 Percent of Work Force," *Milwaukee Journal Sentinel,* October 3, 2001.

Griffin, Greg, "Risk of Pilot Strike Hovers Over Aspen; Town's Tourism Depends on Air Wisconsin," *Denver Post,* August 5, 2001, p. K1.

——, "Stage Set for Aviator Walkout; Mediators Fail to Unite Air Wisconsin, Pilots," *Denver Post,* July 11, 2001.

Kaye, Ken, "Commuter Turns Professional Pilot," *Sun Sentinel* (Fort Lauderdale), October 9, 1991, p. 3.

Lank, Avrum D., "Air Wis Wins by Flying Under the Radar: To Customers, Line Looks Like United; to Industry, Method Was Cutting-Edge," *Milwaukee Journal Sentinel,* March 15, 1998, p. 1.

——, "Air Wisconsin to Buy Four Canadair Jets," *Milwaukee Journal Sentinel,* June 24, 1998.

——, "Air Wisconsin to Cut Back Maintenance Operation in Appleton," *Milwaukee Journal Sentinel,* May 19, 2001.

Leger, Kathryn, "Bombardier Snags $2.4B Order from U.S. Airline: Air Wisconsin; Government Helps Out with Low-Cost Loan," *National Post,* April 17, 2001, p. C17.

Lewis, Arnold, "Air Wisconsin Seals Deal, But . . . ," *Business & Commercial Aviation,* March 1994, p. 70.

Lundy, Dave, "Exec Working to Revamp OAG's Thinking," *Chicago Sun-Times,* February 27, 2003, p. 52.

Mulholland, Megan, "Jets Will Strengthen Air Wisconsin's Denver Route," *Post-Crescent,* December 24, 1998.

Ott, James, "Air Wisconsin Uses New Aircraft to Enter Noise-Sensitive Markets," *Aviation Week & Space Technology,* January 7, 1985.

Pulley, Brett, and James P. Miller, "UAL to Acquire Air Wis Services for $72.7 Million," *Wall Street Journal,* September 18, 1991, p. B7.

Shifrin, Carole A., "Air Wisconsin, Mississippi Valley Agree in Principle on Merger," *Aviation Week & Space Technology,* February 4, 1985, p. 30.

Sobie, Brendan, "Air Wisconsin Retires 328s; Others Look to Fill Void in Denver," *Air Transport Intelligence,* February 26, 2003.

Williamson, Richard, "Air Wisconsin Gets Right Down to Business on Max; Officials of New Owner in Springs for Transition," *Denver Rocky Mountain News,* February 17, 1998, p. 4B.

——, "Carrier Looking at Max Planes; Air Wisconsin Could Take Over Mesa Cities," *Denver Rocky Mountain News,* February 13, 1998, p. 1B.

—Frederick C. Ingram

Alloy, Inc.

115 West 26th Street, 11th Floor
New York, New York 10001
U.S.A.
Telephone: (212) 244-4307
Toll Free: (888) 452-5569
Fax: (212) 244-4311
Web site: http://www.alloy.com

Public Company
Incorporated: 1996
Employees: 948
Sales: $165.6 million (2001)
Stock Exchanges: NASDAQ
Ticker Symbol: ALOY
NAIC: 452910 Warehouse Clubs and Superstores;
    518111 Internet Service Providers

Alloy, Inc. is a multimedia marketing services company that targets the fastest-growing demographic in the United States, Generation Y, or those between the ages of 10 and 24. Alloy uses direct mail catalogs, Web sites, print media, promotional events, and on-campus marketing programs to attract its audience, generating revenue from products and services sold to the youth markets from offering advertisers access to Alloy's target market. The company's Web sites include alloy.com and ccs-strength.com, designed for teen girls and teen boys, respectively. The company's catalogs include *Alloy, CCS,* and *Strength.* Alloy possesses a database containing detailed information about roughly ten million consumers classified within Generation Y.

Origins

When Alloy entered the business world, the company's founders, Matthew C. Diamond and James K. Johnson, were only slightly older than the age group that would dictate the success of their entrepreneurial creation. Diamond received his undergraduate degree from the University of North Carolina in 1991. Johnson attended Hamilton College, earning a B.A. in history in 1989. During the early 1990s, the pair worked for

General Electric Co., holding various financial and business development positions at the massive conglomerate. Diamond left General Electric in 1994 to attend the Harvard Graduate School of Business, where he earned his M.B.A. in 1996. When Alloy was incorporated in 1996, Diamond was 27 years old and Johnson was 28 years old. They were two members of Generation X attempting to entice the constituents of Generation Y.

Alloy's business strategy centered on winning the minds and wallets of the roughly 55 million 10- to 24-year-olds who composed Generation Y in 1996. According to the United States Census Bureau, the demographic popularly defined as Generation Y was expected to reach 63.5 million people by 2015, outpacing the growth of the general population by nearly 20 percent. During the late 1990s, Generation Y accounted for $250 billion in annual disposable income, 70 percent of which was deemed discretionary, according to Diamond's and Johnson's estimates. By positioning Alloy as a brand, the founders hoped to garner as much as they could of the $175 billion up for grabs. As the primary tool to communicate the Alloy brand, Diamond and Johnson selected the Internet, the electronic superhighway populated by Generation Y.

Generation Y was the first generation to grow up with the Internet as part of daily life. Like Generation Y itself, the Internet was growing rapidly during the late 1990s, developing into an economic force popularly referred to as e-commerce, or electronic-commerce. Industry sources projected exponential growth of e-commerce during Alloy's formative years, particularly in relation to the company's target audience. Teen online spending was expected to increase from less than $100 million in 1996 to $1.3 billion by 2002. During the same period, the number of teens and college-age students who accessed the Internet at least twice a week for an hour or more was expected to more than double.

As part of the Internet's maturation during the early 1990s, the number of community Web sites increased. Community Web sites, like the site launched by Diamond and Johnson, served as online destinations for like-minded users, providing a gathering point tailored to the particular interests of a particular group. Community Web sites also could act as e-commerce hubs, serving as a single site offering products and services related to a particular group that could also draw the business of third-party marketers wishing to reach a particular group. Diamond and Johnson intended to create such a hub, designing it to attract Generation Y and the companies wishing to market products to Generation Y.

After incorporating Alloy in January 1996, Diamond and Johnson launched their community Web site, alloy.com, in August 1996. Alloy.com offered visitors free e-mail; a channel containing celebrity gossip, horoscopes, and other teen-oriented news items; a shopping channel; an entertainment channel; a chat channel; a sports channel; and a fashion channel, as well as a number of other features designed to attract Generation Y. A majority of the features and services on the Web site were accessible by all visitors, but some of the services required visitors to register. With the information gleaned from registrations, Alloy was able to compile a database of names that could be used to attract advertisers and sponsors to place their business on alloy.com.

Alloy.com represented the first of many media platforms Alloy launched during its first several years of business. Eventually, as the company developed into a multimedia teen marketer, Diamond and Johnson extended their reach into other mediums, either launching or acquiring a spectrum of media properties, including catalogs, magazines, books, and display media boards. Alloy.com was the first company property, however, and, as such, it bore the burden of serving as the lone source of income for the nascent company. By the end of its truncated, inaugural year, alloy.com had only generated a pittance of revenue for the company, a mere $25,000. During that same time span, from August 1996 to the end of January 1997, Alloy accumulated $118,000 in losses. In the years ahead, Alloy would continue to remain unprofitable—not an uncommon financial record for an Internet-reliant company—but its ability to generate revenue improved greatly once Diamond and Johnson began developing Alloy's business beyond the Internet.

1997 Launch of Catalog Unleashes Financial Growth

Throughout much of 1997, Alloy, dependent entirely on alloy.com, generated negligible sales figures. The turning point in the company's financial magnitude occurred after the launch of the first *Alloy* catalog in August 1997, one year after the debut of alloy.com. In later manifestations, the typical *Alloy* catalog ranged between 72 and 96 pages, featuring approximately 400

items, including apparel, footwear, and room furnishings. Initially, the merchandise available from an *Alloy* catalog was geared for both boys and girls, but as the company developed, both alloy.com and *Alloy* catalogs were designed exclusively for the female members of Generation Y. (Pre-teen, teenage, and college-age males would be given their own domains, both online and offline, once Alloy's expansion began in earnest).

Although Diamond and Johnson later would stress building advertising and sponsorship revenue, initially the company derived almost all of its revenue from the sale of merchandise. Thanks primarily to the distribution of *Alloy*, the company recorded $1.8 million in revenue by the end of January 1998, a significant increase from the $25,000 collected the previous year. The losses had mounted, however, driven upwards by the escalating marketing costs the company was incurring. The $1.8 million registered in sales for the year was coupled with a loss of nearly $1.9 million. The following year, the company's operations gained momentum, snowballing financially in two opposite directions. The financial totals for 1998, which included the first month of 1999, revealed an impressive gain in revenue to $10.2 million, driven by a 460 percent jump in merchandise sales, but the increase was tempered by a loss of $6.36 million.

Alloy's losses were not unexpected, particularly in an era notorious for unprofitable e-commerce enterprises. Profits and revenue increases would arrive, according the business plan mapped out by Diamond and Johnson, when Alloy flowered into a genuine multimedia marketer, and its properties could serve not only as a convergence point for Generation Y but also for the commercial interests in pursuit of Generation Y.

The development of the described enterprise began in earnest not long after Alloy turned to Wall Street. In March 1999, Alloy filed with the Securities and Exchange Commission (SEC) for an initial public offering (IPO) of stock. In May 1999, Alloy completed the offering, issuing 3.7 million shares of common stock at $15 per share, marking its debut as a publicly-traded concern. By the end of the summer, the company had launched its first advertising campaign on television, a $1 million expenditure that saw the Alloy name broadcast on ESPN, Fox, and, primarily, on MTV.

In December 1999, Alloy followed up on the television advertising campaign with the acquisition of Celebrity Sightings, LLC. Based in Marina del Ray, Celebrity Sightings operated a Web site featuring an online magazine revolving around teen celebrities. The following month, Alloy acquired 17th Street Acquisition Corp., a New York-based developer and producer of media properties for teens. As the company that had produced best-selling teenage books such as *Roswell High*, *Fearless*, and *Sweet Valley High*, 17th Street was embraced by Diamond. In a January 17, 2000, interview with *Publishers Weekly*, he referred to the acquisition, saying it "represents another step toward our long-term goal of expanding Alloy's multimedia platform."

The cost of expanding Alloy's multimedia platform continued to increase the company's annual losses, although revenues swelled. After completing the acquisition of 17th Street, Alloy announced its financial totals for the previous year. Revenues,

Key Dates:

1996: Alloy is founded by two former General Electric Co. employees.
1997: The first *Alloy* catalog is distributed in August.
1999: Alloy completes its initial public offering of stock.
2000: Alloy acquires CCS, Inc.
2001: Dan's Competition, Inc. is acquired.
2002: Alloy acquires Market Place Media.

driven by a 180 percent increase in merchandise sales, reached $28.2 million. One source of revenue that would become increasingly important in the coming years delivered its first meaningful contribution in 1999. The company's in-house advertising sales group, benefiting from an increased number of visitors to alloy.com, was able to leverage the popularity of the Web site to substantially increase Alloy's advertising and sponsorship revenue. Efforts to cultivate commercial relationships, which began in 1998 and generated $100,000, produced nearly $3 million in revenue in 1999. For the year, however, the company's losses widened, increasing from a deficit of $6.4 million to a deficit of $14.9 million.

Expansion Campaign Begins in 2000

Alloy's management pressed ahead in 2000, making an important acquisition that complemented the company's increasingly popular alloy.com site. In March 2000, an independent survey firm recorded 1.1 million unique visitors to alloy.com, up substantially from the 263,000 visitors recorded in April 1999. From these visitors, Alloy obtained detailed information on 1.7 million teens who had registered to receive the company's weekly electronic magazine. To this growing database, the company added another, acquiring Kubic Marketing, Inc. in July 2000. Kubic owned CCS, Inc., a leading direct marketer to teenage boys that possessed a database with 1.5 million names. Once CCS was acquired, Alloy's catalogs and Web sites became gender specific, with the Alloy brand built around Generation Y girls, and CCS, through ccs.com and *CCS* catalog, serving as a brand for Generation Y boys.

At a time when most e-commerce firms were resigned to treading water, Alloy pursued expansion aggressively. Diamond believed the economic and market conditions provided an opportunity for the company to acquire other firms, which led to a buying spree that began in December 2000. The company purchased Triple Dot Communications, Inc., a marketing services company the helped other companies identify the members of Generation Y. In February 2001, Alloy acquired *Strength* magazine, a skateboarding lifestyle publication that the company subsequently melded with CCS, creating ccs-strength.com. The following month, Alloy purchased Carnegie Communications, Inc., a publisher and Web site operator that provided information on colleges and universities to teens. In July 2001, Alloy reached an agreement to acquire CASS Communications, a leading owner of rights to sell advertisements in college campus newspapers across the country.

In the fall of 2001, the company completed a flurry of acquisitions. In October, Alloy purchased Dan's Competition, Inc., a direct marketer that offered BMX biking equipment and related apparel. The $38 million deal, a combination of cash and stock, was expected to add as much as $15 million in annual revenue to Alloy's balance sheet. In November, the company acquired Target Marketing & Promotions, which spearheaded promotional marketing programs and media merchandising efforts for clients such as Hasbro, Jose Cuervo, Frito-Lay, and Cadbury-Schweppes. Under Alloy's control, Target Marketing worked with Triple Dot to create and execute marketing strategies. Alloy also acquired the 360 Youth division of MarketSource Corp., which was perceived by industry pundits as a strategic complement to the company's acquisition of CASS Communications. Generating an estimated $16 million in annual sales, 360 Youth provided marketing services targeted toward teens and college-age men and women.

As Alloy celebrated its fifth anniversary and prepared for the future, its management could take pride in the company's performance. Unlike most e-commerce firms, the company was a success story, a status underscored by the announcement of financial figures in 2002. During the first quarter of the year, Alloy posted a profit, registering $2.5 million in net income, which represented a considerable swing from the $10.3 million loss the company reported for the same period in 2001. On the heels of the encouraging news, the company completed another acquisition, presumably not the last purchase it would complete during through the first decade of the 21st century. In July, Alloy acquired Market Place Media, which focused on marketing to college students, multicultural audiences, and the military. With $48 million in annual revenues, Market Place was added to Alloy's 360 Youth media and marketing services operation.

Principal Subsidiaries

360 Youth Inc.; Target Marketing and Promotions, Inc.; Private Colleges and Universities, Inc.

Principal Competitors

AOL Time Warner Inc.; Bolt, Inc.; PRIMEDIA, Inc.

Further Reading

Benjamin, Ericka, "Alloy Online Inc.," *Venture Capital Journal*, May 1, 1999.
Curan, Catherine, "Alloy Boasts Profits, but Dilutes Value," *Crain's New York Business*, August 12, 2002, p. 3.
"Goleta, Calif., Ad Firm Will Meld with Generation Y Marketing Company," *Knight Ridder/Tribune Business News*, July 24, 2002.
Johnson, Greg, "Alloy Buys MarketSource Unit," *Daily Deal*, November 27, 2001, p. 4.
Milliot, Jim, "Internet Company Buys 17th Street Productions," *Publishers Weekly*, January 17, 2000, p. 14.
Rountree, Kristen, "Target Teams with Triple Dot," *ADWEEK New England Advertising Week*, November 19, 2001, p. 5.
Seckler, Valerie, "Alloy Adding 360 Youth to Mix," *WWD*, November 28, 2001, p. 11.

—Jeffrey L. Covell

Amerada Hess Corporation

1185 Avenue of the Americas
New York, New York 10036
U.S.A.
Telephone: (212) 997-8500
Fax: (212) 536-8390
Web site: http://www.hess.com

Public Company
Incorporated: 1920 as Amerada Corporation
Employees: 10,838
Sales: $11.9 billion (2002)
Stock Exchanges: New York
Ticker Symbol: AHC
NAIC: 213112 Support Activities for Oil and Gas
    Operations; 211111 Crude Petroleum and Natural Gas
    Extraction; 32411 Petroleum Refineries

Amerada Hess Corporation operates as a leading integrated oil and gas concern involved in exploration, production, refining, energy marketing, and retail marketing through a chain of over 1,000 Hess gas stations in the eastern U.S. The company and partner Petroleos de Venezuela S.A. operate the Hovensa refinery in St. Croix, one of the largest refineries in the world with an operating capacity of 500,000 barrels a day. The majority of the firm's exploration and production takes place in the United States, the United Kingdom, Norway, North and West Africa, and Southeast Asia. During 2001, the company's proved reserves reached 1.4 billion barrels of oil equivalent. Nearly 90 percent of Amerada's capital spending is related to the search, development, and production of crude oil and natural gas.

Origins

The Amerada Hess story begins with the English oil entrepreneur Lord Cowdray, who early in 1919 set up the Amerada Corporation to explore for petroleum in the United States, Canada, and Central America. At this time, Everette DeGolyer, a geophysicist and engineer with a record of important technical innovations, was made Amerada's first vice-president and general manager. DeGolyer repeatedly stressed the importance of both geological competence and the then-newly evolving technologies of gravimetric and seismic reflection exploration, arguing that Amerada's ultimate success lay in making accurate and timely scientific estimates and appraisals of oil well production, as well as in the equally difficult economic estimates of oil market futures.

The company's first operations centered on wildcat and development fields in Kansas, Oklahoma, Texas, Louisiana, and Alabama. As well as having ties to the Mexican Eagle Oil Company, Amerada Corporation by 1920 controlled two subsidiaries, Goodrich Oil Company and Cameron Oil Company. Early successes were in major fields in Kansas, such as the Urschel, and in Oklahoma (the Osage, Seminole, Cromwell, and others). In 1923, DeGolyer was one of the first and most vocal advocates for systematic, as opposed to guesswork, exploration for certain kinds of oil traps around salt domes, frequently found in the Gulf of Mexico states. After state, congressional, and private rumblings about the large land and financial holdings of foreign-controlled oil companies in the United States, between 1924 and 1926 Lord Cowdray sold Amerada stock on the United States market at $26 a share, principally through the Rycade Corporation, to fund the acquisition of oil field holdings in Texas.

As many explorationists and historians acknowledge, much of the drama and success of the Amerada Corporation before and during the Depression was tied closely to its pioneering use of geophysical exploration methods. In 1922, DeGolyer conducted what was apparently the first survey of an oil deposit at the famous Spindletop Salt Dome in Texas using advanced geophysical techniques. To further develop and perfect these methods, in 1925, after oil's recovery from approximately 50 cents to $3 a barrel, DeGolyer together with J. Clarence Karcher organized a subsidiary company, Geophysical Research Corporation (GRC) of New Jersey, which established numerous patents and which eventually spawned Geophysical Service, Incorporated, now Texas Instruments. Pioneering many early joint ventures, Amerada's first major success in new field prospecting by geophysical methods came with the discovery of the Nash dome, along with ten others elsewhere, on a lease held by

Company Perspectives:

Our vision is to be the leading independent, integrated oil and gas company delivering superior financial returns with long-term profitable growth. We strive to be the leading independent in each of our businesses, to maximize shareholder value through superior financial performance, and to be in the top one-third of oil companies based on returns on capital employed.

Louisiana Land and Exploration Company (LL&E), systematically exploring over three million acres of south Louisiana swamps in a fraction of the time of prior surveys. GRC undertook another major survey for Amerada Corporation in 1927 and 1928, finding oil deposits in the Wilcox sands, which had been missed by many other major and independent oil companies. DeGolyer's innovations and discoveries led to his becoming president in 1929, and in 1930 chairman of the board of Amerada. Notwithstanding continued exploration successes because of geophysical innovations developed during the Depression, in 1932 DeGolyer resigned from the company to continue work as an independent consultant and exploration company.

After extensive joint seismic exploration survey in 1933, Amerada and Stanolind Oil & Gas made the first discoveries in the famous Katy, Texas, oil and gas fields. Further extension surveys led to other discoveries near Houston, Texas. In 1945, Amerada was responsible for finding another major reservoir in the west Texas Permian Basin. The history of the famous North Dakota Williston Basin oil fields emerged into geological and public attention when Amerada, between 1951 and 1953, completed major reconnaissance seismic surveys leading to an important wildcat discovery, in the Nesson anticline.

Mergers and Growth: 1940s–60s

In 1941, Amerada Corporation merged with its principal operating subsidiary and became Amerada Petroleum Corporation. Throughout the World War II period, Amerada operated exclusively within the United States and Canada. In December 1948, Amerada Petroleum Corporation, Continental Oil Company (now Conoco), and Ohio Oil Company (now Marathon) formed the Conorada Petroleum Corporation. Conorada was charged with petroleum exploration outside the United States and Canada, and negotiated major concessions in Egypt around the Qatiara Depression near the Libyan border. In January 1963, Amerada acquired the stock interests of Conorada held by Conoco and Marathon, becoming full owner of Conorada. In 1964, Amerada joined with Marathon, Continental, and Shell to form the major Oasis petroleum consortium in Libya, reportedly holding half of Libyan production—estimated at one million barrels a day—and paying only 30 cents a barrel in taxes compared to Exxon's 90 cents.

In 1950, Amerada became active in petroleum pipelining and refining. By 1954, Amerada Petroleum Corporation was one of a group of small producers that sold its output at the wellhead. On July 15, 1966, *Fortune* magazine reported that since 1957 Amerada Petroleum had ranked first in profit margin on crude oil and natural gas, holding full or partial interest in over six million acres in both the United States and Canada, and some 68 million acres overseas. During this period, Amerada Petroleum had been producing natural gas in the North Sea in partnership with Standard Oil Company of Indiana. In spring 1966, Leon Hess bought nearly 10 percent of Amerada's outstanding common stock from the Bank of England, which had acquired it during World War II.

Shortly before World War II, Leon Hess had initiated expansion of his father's original fuel oil business. His father, Mores Hess, founded the small business in 1925. In the late 1930s, Leon Hess refocused the business to post-refinery residual oil, usually treated as waste and used as fuel only for large boilers and utility operations. Hess apparently recognized that as power companies and industrial consumers progressively switched from coal to oil, residual oil had the potential to become a profitable commodity. Hess subsequently created a tank-truck fleet specifically designed to transport residual oil to power plants. The trucks were equipped with heaters that kept the oil hot and thus still useful. Adding more distribution depots and a provision terminal, Hess was able to underbid his competition for a variety of federal fuel contracts, a traditional source of significant revenue throughout the company's history. It is probable that Hess's own World War II experience in the army as a petroleum supply officer was a notable source of his later ideas about organization and discipline in business.

The late 1940s marked the start of Hess's first large profits from residual oil sales, serving customers such as Public Service Electric & Gas. Hess competed on a tight price basis, establishing large stations at prime locations close to refineries and depots and pioneering gasoline sales without services. After a period of further expansion through debt, in early 1962 the high debt-to-equity ratio forced Hess to take his company public by means of a merger with the Cletrac Corporation. Under terms of the May 1962 merger, the new company became Hess Oil & Chemical Corporation, with Hess becoming CEO and chief stockholder.

At this point, all of Hess's operations were exclusively in refining, transportation, distribution, and retailing. Because of the opportunities, and possible vulnerability, Hess considered a merger with a larger integrated independent oil company. The Amerada-Hess merger that ultimately ensued has generally been acknowledged as an extremely well-planned and well-timed success, resulting in a sizable gain in crude supply coupled with a dramatic reduction in federal income tax liabilities at a time when oil prices were low and expected to remain so. At the time of the merger, Amerada Petroleum had no debt and had proven oil reserves exceeding 500 million barrels in the United States and 750,000 barrels in Libya through the Oasis consortium. Hess made an initial purchase of Amerada stock in 1966. Amerada's chairman tried to stop the takeover, first by an arranged merger with Ashland Oil, then later by an agreement with Phillips Petroleum. By offering a notable over-market price, Hess invested more than $250 million in what *Fortune,* in January 1970, called "one of Hess's most dangerous gambles." In spring 1969, Phillips withdrew from the contest for ownership, and despite a May 1969 suit filed in federal district court to nullify the merger, Amerada's stockholders approved it by an overwhelming margin.

Key Dates:

1919: Lord Cowdray establishes the Amerada Corp. to explore for petroleum.

1933: Amerada and Stranolind Oil make the first discoveries in the Katy, Texas, oil and gas fields.

1941: Amerada merges with its principal subsidiary to form Amerada Petroleum Corp.

1962: Leon Hess takes his company public as Hess Oil & Chemical Corp.

1966: Leon Hess purchases nearly 10 percent of Amerada's common stock.

1969: Hess and Amerada merge to form the Amerada Hess Corporation.

1985: Monsanto Oil Company is acquired.

1998: Amerada sells a 50 percent interest in its U.S. Virgin Islands refinery.

2001: The company acquires Triton Energy Ltd.

Because of what several analysts consider some surprising similarities in strategy and outlook, the two companies integrated so smoothly that the new Amerada Hess Corporation rapidly pursued an aggressive and successful exploration program. In May 1970, Amerada Hess drilled the first successful wildcat well in Prudhoe Bay on Alaska's North Slope. In mid-1971, Amerada Hess was one of seven oil companies invited by the Canadian government to explore the building of pipelines from oil fields in Alaska's North Slope through Canada to the United States. In September 1974, the U.S. Department of the Interior reported that the company was the first to apply for permits to unload supertankers from the Trans-Alaska Pipeline.

Between 1966 and 1967, the Hess Oil & Chemical Corporation built a refinery on St. Croix in the Virgin Islands. In late 1967, plans had been approved—following negotiations involving Hess, the local government, and the U.S. Department of the Interior—on a ten-year plan to promote economic development in the Virgin Islands by U.S. industry, reciprocally permitting Hess the right to ship 15,000 barrels per day of finished oil products made from foreign crude to the U.S. mainland. The reported rationale was the need for cost-efficient heating oil in the northeastern United States, where Hess was a major refiner and fuel dealer to the government and industry. Some adverse attention and controversy arose following Secretary of the Interior Stewart L. Udall's announcement that a similar proposal by the Coastal States Gas Producing Company had been finally rejected in favor of Hess. In November 1970, Amerada Hess was charged by the U.S. Interior Department with import-rules violation from claims that it had made no significant expenditures for upgrading its Virgin Island facilities and employee quota and apparently had not paid the agreed-upon royalty of 50 cents per barrel to the local development and conservation fund. By 1979, the company's St. Croix refinery output was reported as 700,000 barrels per day, the world's largest. A longtime supplier of jet and fuel oil to the Defense Supply Agency, the Defense Logistics Agency, and the Defense Fuel Supply center, Amerada Hess had also long been a chief supplier of residual and fuel oil to numerous community power and light companies. In April 1975, Amerada Hess was one of several oil companies charged by the Federal Energy Administration with pricing violations. In August 1978, Amerada Hess was one of five firms convicted on federal charges of fixing retail gasoline prices.

Oil Embargos and Other Crises: 1970s–80s

In 1973, Amerada Hess received permission from U.S. President Richard Nixon's Office of Emergency Preparedness to import an extra six million barrels per day of heating oil to ease the nation's shortages but received some unfavorable notice by selling primarily to the East instead of the more energy-needy Midwest regions. With the prices of crude oil increasing threefold in less than six months, Amerada Hess received notable profits. Net reported earnings of $133 million in 1971 increased to $246 million in 1973, and to $577 million by 1980. On July 16, 1979, *Business Week* magazine reported Amerada Hess as being among the biggest gainers of the United States's oil entitlements program, established in 1974 to equalize costs between domestic refineries supplied by lower-priced domestic sources and those depending on higher-priced foreign imports.

Including its role as major partner—with Hunt, Getty, and Louisiana Land and Exploration Company—on the Alaska North Slope, between 1973 and 1979 Amerada Hess invested more than $1.2 billion in exploration and production. In the early 1970s, Amerada Hess was one of many companies negotiating with Portugal for oil and gas exploration concessions in and off the shore of Angola, and later Gabon. In 1975, Amerada Hess and Mississippi Chemical Corporation initiated a five-year joint venture of exploration and evaluation in southern Mississippi and Alabama. In 1981, Petro-Canada initiated the operation of drill ships off Labrador on behalf of a consortium including Amerada Minerals Corporation of Canada Ltd., with considerable exploration success continuing through 1984, when it also made major natural discoveries offshore of Grand Isle, Louisiana, and further Alaskan strikes off Seal Island in 1986. In 1985, Amerada Hess acquired Monsanto Oil Company in the United Kingdom and it became a wholly owned subsidiary.

In response to U.S. President Ronald Reagan's June 1986 deadlines, Amerada Hess officially ended its Libyan operations. Although after January 1989 U.S. oil companies had U.S. government approval to resume activities there, because of the instability in the Middle East the future of such activities remained uncertain. In 1987, Amerada Hess and Chevron were reported as the top U.S. crude and product importers of the year. In August 1989, Amerada Hess acquired for $911 million a 37 percent interest in major offshore oil and gas properties in the northern Gulf of Mexico from the TXP Operating Company, a Texas limited partnership affiliated with the Transco Energy Company, increasing Amerada Hess's total natural gas reserves by 25 percent. Included were major efforts at development and production in the North Sea Scott and Rob Roy fields. Natural gas was reported in 1990 to make up approximately half the company's total hydrocarbon reserves. In September 1990, Amerada Minerals Corporation of Canada acquired assets from Placer Cego Petroleum Ltd. in Alberta and British Columbia. Amerada Hess Norge A/S maintained 25 percent interests in several major offshore fields.

In December 1989, the company settled its part in a 13-year suit brought by the state of Alaska concerning the North Slope oil pipeline. More notably, Amerada Hess survived apparent takeover plans in the mid-1980s. In late 1988, despite much published speculation about the flaws in corporate management, the company's overall picture remained strong. Its trend was considered uncertain, however, because its five-year record was reported to be among the lowest for the entire petroleum industry. The clear trend of reserve acquisitions in the United States, Canada, and overseas reportedly pushed company debt to approximately 45 percent of total capital.

Staying Financially Fit: Early to Mid-1990s

A major goal for Amerada Hess in the 1990s included substantial reduction in overall debt levels. Because the company was no longer the leading innovator in developing geophysical exploration technologies or wildcatting as it was from the 1920s to the 1940s, at least some of its successes depended on continued joint efforts with major partners, notably in improved subsurface development of established fields. Amerada Hess has long been an advocate of domestic oil decontrol and comprehensive national energy policy. Amerada Hess is, in several published opinions, cited as a successful example of the trend toward increased economies via vertical integration.

Low oil prices and the costs of compliance with federal pollution control regulations hampered Amerada Hess's profitability throughout the 1990s. Net income dropped from $483 million in 1990 to only $7.5 million in 1992, and in 1993 and 1995 Amerada Hess suffered staggering net losses of $268 and $394 million, respectively. Its decision to pump $1.1 billion into the upgrade of its St. Croix refinery—damaged by Hurricane Hugo in 1989—was partly to blame, but Amerada Hess's vast network of East Coast storage facilities also imposed burdensome inventory costs when oil supplies were abundant, as they were throughout the decade. Between 1989 and 1993 alone, Amerada Hess's $7.3 billion in capital expenditures was three times higher than the total for 1984–88, and by the end of 1993 the tab for developing its North Sea oilfields and the St. Croix refinery upgrade totaled more than $42 billion. In 1993, the company finished construction on its Central Area Transmission System pipeline between the North Sea and the United Kingdom. However, by the end of 1995, Amerada Hess's stock had been unable to regain its high of four years earlier, and a decade and a half separated it from its earnings peak of 1980. In the words of *Forbes* magazine, Amerada Hess was "visibly bleeding."

In May 1994, Leon Hess retired after six decades at the company's helm—he died in 1999—and a year later his son John was named chairman and CEO. As production began at Amerada Hess's new South Scott oil field in the North Sea, John Hess announced his intention to sell off marginal properties, consolidate the company's U.S. exploration and production operations in Houston, downsize its workforce, and reduce the company's debt. In 1995, he initiated a top-down review of the company's operations to reassess its strategy and prospects. With the goal of producing 500,000 barrels of crude oil a day by the end of the century, John Hess began building the company's hydrocarbon reserves and production through acquisitions, continued its debt reduction efforts, laid off some 20 percent of his workforce, and disposed of non-core properties, including the company's Canadian subsidiary, which alone had accounted for 10 percent of its assets.

Now reduced to its core operations—primarily in the North Sea and the Gulf of Mexico—Amerada Hess moved into the Brazilian market in 1996 in a joint venture with Petrobas, and in 1997 pursued the Venezuelan market through negotiations with Petroleos de Venezuela S.A. It also gained stakes in oil fields in Thailand and the Falkland Islands and explored oil development prospects in Namibia. On the marketing side, it expanded its 548-store East Coast HESS gas station chain by acquiring 66 Pick Kwik retail stores in Florida and four Sears outlets in New York, and in 1997 initiated a gas retail marketing venture in the United Kingdom.

Repositioning in the Late 1990s and Beyond

By 1997, the "first phase" of Amerada Hess's "repositioning" program was announced as complete. Net income for 1996 had rebounded more than $1 billion from 1995's loss, to $660 million, and Amerada Hess's debt-to-capitalization ratio had been cut by almost $800 million to 36.4 percent. With $1 billion worth of exploration and production properties jettisoned, five new high-return oil and gas fields fully developed, and a commitment to streamline its administrative operations by adopting SAP's enterprise planning software, Amerada viewed its goal of moving into the top one-third of U.S. oil companies by the year 2000 with some optimism.

As Amerada Hess pressed on to achieve that goal, it faced some distinct challenged. Profits at its St. Croix refinery began to dwindle during the mid-1990s, prompting the firm to seek out a partner. As such, Amerada Hess sold a 50 percent interest in the Virgin Island refinery to Petroleos de Venezuela in 1998, creating the Hovensa LLC joint venture. That same year, oil prices began dropping off. In an attempt to bolster profits, Amerada Hess launched yet another aggressive cost cutting campaign, slashing capital spending by 38 percent and cutting 20 percent of its U.S. and UK exploration workforce. During 1998, revenues fell and the firm reported a net loss of $459 million, due in part to the sale of several assets. During 1999, however, both profits and revenues rebounded. The company sold off pipeline and terminal holdings in the Southeast and also various Gulf Coast terminals. By this time, over $2 billion of non-core assets had been sold and operating costs had been reduced by $100 million. Overall, Amerada Hess reported a rise in net income to $438 million while revenue climbed to $7.4 billion.

Under the leadership of John Hess, Amerada Hess entered the new century intent on securing its position as a leading independent, integrated energy company. The company's main focus centered on exploration and production, while marketing and refining remained secondary concerns. During 2000, Amerada Hess attempted to strengthen its international holdings when it made a play for Lasmo, a British exploration and production firm. The company offered Lasmo $3.5 billion in cash and stock. However, its plans were thwarted when Italy-based ENI S.p.A. came in with a higher offer.

Amerada Hess's failed merger attempt did little to dampen its acquisition strategy, and in 2001 the company set its sights on Triton Energy Ltd., an international exploration and production company focused on the West African, Latin American, and Southeast Asian regions. The $3.2 billion merger was completed in August 2001 and was expected to increase company production from 425,000 barrels of oil equivalent (BOE) per day to 535,000 BOE per day. The deal also gave Amerada Hess access to Triton's lucrative assets in Equatorial Guinea and Gabon. The firm added additional international holdings to its arsenal during 2002, including three deepwater tracts in the offshore regions of Senegal, Gambia, and Guinea-Bissau.

During 2002, energy prices fell and global economies weakened. Amerada Hess's financial situation faltered as a result, with revenues falling by 11 percent over the previous year. The firm also reported a net loss of $218 million just one year after securing a net income of $914 million—the second-highest in its history. While economic conditions did indeed play a role in Amerada Hess's fluctuating financial results, the majority of the company's loss stemmed from a $530 million charge related to the write-down of its Ceiba oil field, which proved to be less fertile than expected. This field was part of the Triton purchase and left analysts speculating as whether the merger would be as lucrative as Amerada had hoped in the years to come.

Economies across the globe remained in a state of instability during early 2003 due to the looming threat of a possible U.S. war against Iraq. Rumors began to surface that Amerada Hess could be a possible takeover target during the next round of oil consolidation. Nevertheless, the company maintained that its goal was to be the leading independent, integrated oil and gas company.

Principal Subsidiaries

Triton Energy Ltd.; Amerada Hess Ltd. (United Kingdom); Hess Oil Virgin Islands Corporation; Hess Energy Trading Company LLC; Amerada Hess Denmark ApS; Amerada Hess Gas Limited (United Kingdom); Amerada Hess Norge A/S (Norway); Amerada Hess GEEA Ltd. (Cayman Islands); Amerada Hess Production Gabon; Amerada Hess Ltd. (Thailand); Tioga Gas Plant Inc.; Jamestown Insurance Co. Ltd. (Bermuda); Hygrade Operators Inc.

Principal Competitors

BP plc; ConocoPhillips; Exxon Mobil Corporation.

Further Reading

"Amerada Hess Pursues Specific Opportunities Upstream, Downstream," *Petroleum Finance Week*, February 21, 2000.

"Amerada Hess Spreads Wings in Hunt for African Oil," *Oil Daily*, May 24, 2002.

"Charge Swallows Hess Results; Exxon Shines," *Oil Daily*, January 31, 2003.

Easton, Thomas, "Boot the Coach?," *Forbes*, December 4, 1995, p. 64.

"ENI Snatches Lasmo From Amerada Hess," *Oil Daily*, December 22, 2000.

Ingham, John, and Lynne Feldman, *Contemporary American Business Leaders*, Westport, Conn.: Greenwood Press, 1990.

Jaffe, Thomas, "Amerada, Mon Amour," *Forbes*, July 19, 1993, p. 254.

Kovski, Alan, "PDVSA to Buy 50 Percent Stake in Hess' St. Croix Plant," *Oil Daily*, February 4, 1998, p. 1.

Marcial, Gene G., "Whispers About Hess," *Business Week*, March 11, 2002.

Norman, James, "Hess Makeover Pays Off Despite Wall Street Doubts," *Platt's Oilgram News*, July 27, 1999.

"Refiner Seeks Oil for Troubled Waters," *Crain's New York Business*, January 21, 2002, p. 4.

Tinkle, Lon, *Mr. De: A Biography of Everette Lee DeGolyer*, Boston: Little, Brown, 1972.

Wetuski, Jodi, "Triton Will Do," *Oil and Gas Investor*, August 2001, p. 65.

—Gerardo G. Tango
—updates: Paul S. Bodine and Christina M. Stansell

American Eagle Outfitters, Inc.

150 Thorn Hill Drive
Warrendale, Pennsylvania 15086-7528
U.S.A.
Telephone: (724) 776-4857
Fax: (724) 779-5585
Web site: http://www.ae.com

Public Company
Incorporated: 1993
Employees: 10,892
Sales: $1.5 billion (2002)
Stock Exchanges: NASDAQ
Ticker Symbol: AEOS
NIAC: 448190 Other Clothing Stores; 448150 Clothing
    Accessories Stores

American Eagle Outfitters, Inc. (AE) is a chain of mall-based stores that sells casual, outdoor-inspired fashion apparel. With nearly 700 shops in the United States and Canada, AE enjoyed average annual sales increases of 35 percent from 1996 to 2001. This growth rate earned AE a ranking of 63rd among *Fortune* magazine's list of fastest growing companies. American Eagle generated record net income of $105.5 million in fiscal 2001 (ended February 2, 2002). Retail outlets in regional shopping malls account for the vast majority of sales, but the company also sells its gear via a website and its "magalog"—a combination lifestyle magazine and catalog. AE's Canadian operations include the Thrifty's/Bluenotes chain, as well as Bramear shops and National Logistics Services, a distribution arm. The company also operates a small distribution center, Eagle Trading, in Mexico.

The vast majority of the chain's sales are generated from private label brands—American Eagle Outfitters, AE, and AE Supply; this focus on private-label merchandise was launched through a 1992 repositioning and was intended to differentiate American Eagle from its mall competitors, such as The Limited, The Gap, and Abercrombie & Fitch. To keep up with the latest fashion trends, the company employs an in-house design team, whose merchandise designs are then manufactured to specifica-

tion by outside vendors or by American Eagle's manufacturing subsidiary, Prophecy Ltd. This private-label/in-house design system enables American Eagle to keep tight control of quality and hold prices down. Customer credit is offered through an American Eagle Outfitters credit card.

Approximately 26 percent of the company's stock is owned by the Schottenstein family, whose Schottenstein Stores Corp. is a large privately held company based in Columbus, Ohio, with numerous retail holdings. Jay L. Schottenstein acted as CEO of American Eagle from 1992 to 2002, when he stepped aside to make room for co-CEOs Roger S. Markfield and James V. O'Donnell. Schottenstein remained as chairman of the board.

1977 Debut

When American Eagle Outfitters was launched in 1977, it was part of Silvermans Menswear, Inc., a retailing company whose flagship was the Silvermans chain, which sold young men's apparel and accessories and was founded in McKees Rocks, Pennsylvania (near Pittsburgh), in 1904. The Silverman family owned and operated Silvermans Menswear, and by the mid-1970s two brothers—in the third generation of Silvermans in the family business—were running things: Jerry Silverman, president and CEO, and Mark Silverman, executive vice-president and COO. The Silverman brothers believed that they needed more than one concept to continue growing their company—that the addition of other chains would then enable them to operate more than one store in the same mall. They thus opened the first American Eagle Outfitters store in 1977, positioning it as a seller of brand-name leisure apparel, footwear, and accessories for men and women, with an emphasis on merchandise geared toward outdoor sports, such as hiking, mountain climbing, and camping. American Eagle quickly established itself as a mall store able to attract an unusually wide array of shoppers, although its "rugged" offerings were geared more toward men. And with a nationally distributed mail-order catalog supporting the retail units, the new chain quickly became a key competitor not only to such established retailers as The Gap but also to such venerable catalogers as L.L. Bean and Lands End.

In 1980, Silvermans Menswear changed its name to Retail Ventures, Inc. (RVI). That same year, the Silvermans ran into

---

Company Perspectives:

American Eagle Outfitters is a leading lifestyle retailer that designs, markets, and sells its own brand of relaxed, versatile clothing for 16- to 34-year-olds, providing high-quality merchandise at affordable prices. AE's lifestyle collection includes casual basics like khakis, cargos, and jeans; fashion tops like rugbys, polos, and graphic T's; and functional items like swimwear, outerwear, footwear and accessories.

---

some financial difficulties and sold a 50 percent stake in RVI to the Schottenstein family. The Schottensteins owned Schottenstein Stores, a retailing giant based in Columbus, Ohio. Schottenstein Stores was founded in the early 20th century by E.L. Schottenstein when he opened the first Value City Department Store, a discount department store chain which by the early 21st century included DSW Shoe Warehouse and Filene's Basement.

In 1985, RVI launched three more new chains: His Place and Go Places, concepts similar to that of Silvermans, and Help-Ur-Self, a bulk food store. The following year the company spent $8 million to expand its headquarters, adding 25,000 square feet to its office space and 146,000 square feet to its 119,000-square-foot distribution center. Also in 1986 RVI added 34 new stores to its existing 200. Many of these were American Eagle units, as the company began that year to concentrate more of its resources on American Eagle, which was achieving rapid sales growth, than on Silvermans, whose sales were being hurt from increasing competition, particularly from discount chains.

This shift in emphasis culminated in early 1989 when RVI announced a major restructuring in which it sold its Silvermans, His Place, and Go Places chains—a total of 125 stores—to Merry-Go-Round Enterprises Inc., a Towson, Maryland-based operator of 430 mall-based clothing stores, including Merry-Go-Round, Cignal, and Attivo. RVI also spun off to the Silverman family the 11-store Help-Ur-Self chain, which had performed reasonably well but was not considered synergistic with American Eagle. RVI was thus left with American Eagle Outfitters—now with 137 stores in 36 states and sales of $125 million—as its single focus. The company planned to aggressively expand its sole remaining chain by as many as 120 stores over the following three years. It began to implement this plan but only after The Gap had approached RVI in early 1989 about buying American Eagle and after negotiations to do so had fallen through.

The Early 1990s

Although the chain clearly had potential for growth, in the midst of the recessionary early 1990s American Eagle was saddled with dated inventory that brought low profit margins. With brand-name apparel increasingly being offered by various clothing chains, catalogers, and discounters, American Eagle was facing increasing competition. High management turnover also contributed to the chain's difficulties during this period.

By mid-1991 American Eagle had grown to 153 stores—not nearly the expansion rate envisioned two years earlier—and sales had stagnated. For the fiscal year ending in July 1991, sales were

$144.3 million, a minuscule increase over the $142.4 million of the previous year. Worse yet, the chain posted a net loss of $8.9 million for the year. In a deal designed to position American Eagle for renewed growth, the Schottenstein family bought the 50 percent of RVI owned by the Silverman family, giving the Schottensteins full control of the company and its only chain. Jay L. Schottenstein became the new chairman and CEO of RVI, replacing Mark Silverman, while Sam Forman was brought in as president and COO. Forman had been CEO of Kuppenheimer Clothiers. The Schottensteins also hired Roger Markfield as president and "chief merchant." Formerly of Macy's and the Gap, Markfield helped AEO find its target customer.

Under its new ownership and leadership, the chain was repositioned in 1992 to focus on private-label casual apparel for men and women, while retaining the outdoor-oriented look for which it was best known. It hired its own cadre of designers and began developing its own sources of merchandise. The private label strategy was intended to position American Eagle merchandise as value priced. The company also began opening American Eagle outlet stores to reduce its inventory of out-of-season and branded clothing items.

Going Public in 1994

American Eagle's 1994 fiscal year was its best year to date, evidence that the repositioning was working. Sales for the year were $199.7 million, while net income was a healthy $11.9 million. In the midst of this successful year, RVI announced that it would go public through an initial public offering (IPO). In November 1993 an American Eagle Outfitters, Inc. subsidiary was established and it was under this name that RVI and the American Eagle chain emerged in April 1994, with a listing on the NASDAQ stock exchange and with the Schottenstein family maintaining roughly a 60 percent stake in the new company and Forman about 10 percent. American Eagle went public as a 167-store chain with nine outlet stores and locations in 34 states.

Much of the approximate $37 million raised through the IPO was almost immediately poured back into the company for an aggressive program of expansion and renovation. From July through December of 1994 alone, 55 new stores were opened. At the one-year anniversary of the IPO, nearly 90 new stores had been added. Unfortunately, several of these new locations were unprofitable from the time they opened their doors, and it became apparent that the chain had expanded too rapidly.

Adding to the confusion at this time was a rapid succession of management changes. In early 1995, Forman was named vice-chairman, with Robert G. Lynn, a one-time president and CEO of F.W. Woolworth Co., becoming vice-chairman and COO and Roger S. Markfield being promoted to president and chief merchandising officer. Lynn, however, left the company in December 1995 over reported management differences. Later that same month, George Kolber took over Lynn's vice-chairman and COO spots.

Forman, meanwhile, sold his 10 percent stake in American Eagle in early 1995. Later that year he resigned from his position as vice-chairman following his purchase of 32 American Eagle outlet stores in 18 states for between $14 million and $16 million. The company had decided to divest the outlets in

Key Dates:

1977:	American Eagle Outfitters (AE) is launched as segment of Silvermans Menswear, Inc.
1991:	AE grows to 153 stores.
1992:	The company focuses on private-label merchandise.
1993:	American Eagle Outfitters, Inc. is incorporated.
1994:	AE goes public with a listing on the NASDAQ stock exchange.
2000:	AE steps up its promotional campaign, gaining exposure for its clothing on the television series ''Dawson's Creek'' and in teen-oriented movies.
2001:	AE generates record net income of $105.5 million.

order to concentrate on its mall locations, and it subsequently closed its remaining seven outlet stores. Forman signed a licensing agreement with American Eagle, whereby the outlets he purchased would operate under the American Eagle Outlets name and would sell merchandise made specifically for the outlets. Through all of these changes, Jay Schottenstein continued in his role of chairman and CEO.

Repositioned Again in 1996

The year 1996 was a transitional one for American Eagle as it cut back drastically on its expansion plans in order to reposition the chain once again. In search of higher-margin merchandise to offer, Markfield and Kolber determined that the chain had to sell more women's apparel, which is typically more profitable. The leaders also decided to completely divorce American Eagle of its once-eclectic range of customers and target the lucrative youth market—ages 16 to 34—through a younger and hipper feel to the clothing and in the chain's marketing. The company launched a ''magalog,'' a catalog of merchandise that also included editorial content of interest to this key demographic, including music and book reviews, feature stories, horoscopes, and advice columns. Finally, American Eagle would strongly emphasize value pricing through a commitment to private label merchandise. Remaining at the chain's core was its venerable rugged, outdoorsy style.

For fiscal 1996 (the first year of the company's new fiscal year, which now ended at the end of January), about 98 percent of the company's sales were generated from its private label brands, American Eagle Outfitters, AE, and AE Supply. Women's clothing, meantime—which in fiscal 1995 had accounted for only 30 percent of sales—accounted for 47 percent of sales by that time.

If 1996 was a transitional year for American Eagle, then the transition went exceedingly well, as 1997 turned into a breakout year. For the year, sales increased 24.3 percent to a record $405.7 million, while net income more than tripled, going from $5.9 million in 1996 to $19.5 million in 1997. Comparable store sales were very strong, increasing 15.1 percent in 1997 compared to the previous year.

In addition to opening 32 new stores in 1997, American Eagle that year also for the first time began manufacturing its own clothing through the acquisition of Prophecy Ltd., a New

York-based contract apparel maker which had been majority owned by the Schottenstein family. This move toward further vertical integration was in keeping with the chain's desire to control costs and maintain quality. The terms of the purchase were $900,000 in cash plus a contingency payment of up to $700,000.

Early 1998 was a busy period for American Eagle as it introduced the AE Clear Card, the first clear credit card. By the end of 1999, the card accounted for 14 percent of total sales. The company also began to open new stores outside of enclosed malls, in airports, strip malls, and other locales. AE also undertook a West Coast expansion that year, with openings in Seattle and Tacoma, Washington as well as Portland, Oregon. AE also launched a Web site to appeal to the chain's youth-oriented customer base. The company envisioned its Internet outlet not so much as a primary sales vehicle, but more as a way for customers to ''preshop'' and for the company to track geographic areas that were ripe for retail expansion.

The company's growth strategies were well-timed, as AE rode a rising tide in the young men's clothing business. During the late 1990s, the U.S. teen population—AE's key demographic—expanded more rapidly than the general populace. Women's Wear Daily, a clothing industry periodical, called AE ''one of the hottest retailers in the country,'' citing it as ''a case study on how to build a brand.'' The renewed strength of American Eagle was also evident in two separate three-for-two stock splits, which occurred during the first five months of 1998. AE posted record results that fiscal year, as earnings increased more than 175 percent to $54.1 million on a 44.8 percent increase in sales, to $587.6 million.

AEO's success garnered the attention of upscale competitor Abercrombie & Fitch, which brought three lawsuits over the course of four years accusing AEO of ''intentionally and systematically copying'' everything from the paper its catalog was printed on to editorial content and product names like ''vintage sweatshirts'' and ''field jerseys.'' American Eagle won each case, some by outright dismissal.

Having successfully repositioned its brand, AEO moved to fine-tune in-house efficiencies in the latter years of the 1990s. The company instituted a new computer system that would separate inventory and personnel management from sales transactions. Capturing up-to-the-minute information on fast and slow moving merchandise gave the company the ability to refine production schedules in line with demand. More efficient distribution meant that the company could keep up with the fast-changing tastes of U.S. teens. In 2000, AE announced its plans to open a distribution center near Kansas City, Missouri, to support its growth plans for the Western United States.

The company continued to hone its marketing strategy as well, becoming the official costumer for the television series *Dawson's Creek* and inking a deal with Dimension Films to provide the wardrobe for no fewer than four of its teen-oriented films in the years to come. AE subsequently signed a deal to provide clothing to the 10th anniversary season of MTV's *Road Rules* reality series as well. The company soon added national television advertising, primarily via cable.

Writing for *WWD*, Jennifer Weitzman attributed AE's success to its sole focus on the teen market, noting that the appeal to a particular clique—in this case, "jock-prep"—differentiated it from stores like the Gap, which had a broader pull. The pitfall of this niche marketing strategy was the fickle nature of teen tastes; if AE were to fall out of favor, it would have a difficult time regaining its following.

The company reached a milestone at the end of the 20th century, crossing the $1 billion sales mark in fiscal 2000 (the year ended February 2, 2000).

New Century, New Country

In 2000, American Eagle made a bold move into the Canadian market with the purchase of the a 172-store chain and its warehouse operations from Dylex Limited for $74 million. Like AE, the 115-store Thriftys chain offered "Bluenotes" private-label clothing at locations in major shopping malls. The acquisition provided an opportunity for AE to quickly convert the majority of these stores to its own format. By early 2002, it had made 46 such changes. As American Eagle CFO Laura Weil told Mortgage Banking, "It would have taken years to build up this kind of store location portfolio any other way."

The company chalked up another year of record earnings in fiscal 2001, with a net income of $105.5 million on sales of $1.37 billion. Despite a recession, sales continued to grow in fiscal 2002, increasing 6.7 percent to $1.5 billion. However, the Bluenotes/Thriftys operations proved a drag on results, with sales for that segment of the company falling 5.7 percent for the period.

After ten years at the helm, Jay L. Schottenstein relinquished the chief executive office to Roger S. Markfield and James V. O'Donnell, who served as co-CEOs beginning in December 2002. By early 2003, American Eagle appeared to be weathering the recession quite handsomely, but its new leaders faced the ongoing challenges of converting the remaining Canadian operations to the AE format, as well as continuing to correctly gauge the finicky tastes of North America's youth.

Principal Subsidiaries

Prophecy Ltd.; Eagle Trading (Mexico).

Principal Competitors

The Gap, Inc.; Eddie Bauer, Inc.; Abercrombie & Fitch Co.

Further Reading

"American Eagle Buys Canadian Clothier," *Pittsburgh Business Times*, September 1, 2000, p. 49.

"American Eagle Outfitters Inc. Wins Abercrombie & Fitch Lawsuit in U.S. Court of Appeals," *Market News Publishing*, February 26, 2002.

Benson, Betsy, "Retail Ventures Plans Restructuring: New Focus on American Eagle Outfitters Unit," *Pittsburgh Business Times*, February 27, 1989.

Davis, Jim, "American Eagle Lands $40 million Distribution Center in Lawrence, Kan.," *Pittsburgh Business Times*, March 31, 2000, p. 10.

Fitzpatrick, Dan, "New Lines Pace American Eagle Comeback Bid," *Pittsburgh Business Times*, December 30, 1996, pp. 1 + .

Gallagher, Jim, "Gap Won't Buy American Eagle," *Pittsburgh Post Gazette*, March 18, 1989.

Lewis, David, "American Eagle Outfitters Revamps Site, Eyes High Sales Growth," *InternetWeek*, March 26, 2001, p. 70.

Much, Marilyn, "Retailer Moves into New Venues, Cyberspace," *Investor's Business Daily*, January 30, 1998, p. A3.

Palmieri, Jean, "American Eagle Makes a Name For Itself," *WWD*, December 9, 1998, p. 4.

——, "American Eagle Spreading Wings on West Coast," *Daily News Record*, June 5, 1998, p. 23.

Phillips, Jeff, "Schottensteins Buy 153 Stores," *Business First of Columbus*, June 3, 1991, pp. 1 + .

Scardio, Emily, "Specialty Rules," *DSN Retailing Today*, February 11, 2002, p. A6.

Walters, Rebecca, "American Eagle Going Public," *Business First of Columbus*, March 21, 1994.

Warson, Albert, "U.S. Retailers are SOLD ON Canada," *Mortgage Banking*, July 2001, p. 73.

Weitzman, Jennifer, "Outfitters' Net Results Diverge," *WWD*, August 19, 2002, p. 7.

——, " 'Tribal' Looks Lead Teen Retailers," *WWD*, March 16, 2001, p. 21.

Young, Vicki M., "A&F Sues American Eagle," *WWD*, June 3, 1998, p. 2.

——, "American Eagle Builds New Nests," *WWD*, August 18, 1999, p. 12.

Zimmermann, Kim Ann, "American Eagle Gets Lean at POS," *WWD*, March 10, 1999, p. 17.

—David E. Salamie
—update: April D. Gasbarre

Andrx Corporation

4955 Orange Drive
Davie, Florida 33314
U.S.A.
Telephone: (954) 584-0300
Fax: (954) 217-4327
Web site: http://www.andrx.com

Public Company
Incorporated: 1992 as Andrx Pharmaceuticals, Inc.
Employees: 1,837
Sales: $771 million (2002)
Stock Exchanges: NASDAQ
Ticker Symbol: ADRX
NAIC: 325412 Pharmaceutical Preparation Manufacturing

Andrx Corporation, operating out of Davie, Florida, is a pharmaceutical company that uses timed-release drug delivery technologies to create generic versions of popular brand-name drugs whose patents have expired. To fund its research efforts the company operates a generic drug distribution business, selling products manufactured by third parties to some 14,000 independent pharmacies and regional chains. This distribution arm, named Anda, also helps the company keep close tabs on developments in the generic pharmaceutical industry and serves as a sales platform for both generic drugs as well as original branded drugs using the company's timed-release technology— a more recent emphasis at Andrx. Cash realized from drug distribution also helps pay Andrx's considerable legal bills. Because major pharmaceutical firms zealously attempt to maintain a tight grip over their high-selling branded drugs, Andrx is involved in lengthy and expensive litigation on a continual basis.

Founding Andrx: 1992

Andrx's founder, Alan P. Cohen, a registered pharmacist, first became involved in the distribution of generic drugs in 1984 when he founded Best Generics, Inc., which he then sold in 1988 to Miami-based Ivax Corp., a generic pharmaceutical company. He continued to serve as president of Best until June 1990. In August 1992 he incorporated a new company, naming

it Andrx Pharmaceuticals, Inc. His goal was not to directly compete against generic manufacturers like Ivax, but to work with brand-name pharmaceutical companies to develop generic products using timed-release technologies, which Cohen recognized held significant advantages over prior dosage mechanisms. Rather than taking several doses of a medication each day, for example, a patient might take a single timed-release dose, the effects of which would be automatically produced throughout the day. Moreover, Cohen understood that the technology was expensive and difficult to master and that many pharmaceutical companies would want to team up with Andrx rather than invest in starting their own in-house operations. To help fund the necessary research and development, Cohen also established Andrx's generic drug distribution business, a complementary activity with which he was well familiar.

To help him run Andrx, Cohen recruited two former colleagues at Ivax. One, Dr. Chih-Ming J. Chen, had been director of product development at Ivax, where he headed a research team involved in timed-release drug mechanisms. After graduating from The Ohio State University in 1981, Chen worked at both Bristol-Myers and Berlex Labs. In January 1992 he started his own company, ASAN Labs, Inc., which in November 1992 he sold to Andrx after agreeing to work with Cohen and become Andrx's chief scientist, as well as a director of the company. It was at this point that Andrx Pharmaceutical changed its name to Andrx Corporation and launched its generic drug distribution business. Another Ivax executive, Dr. Elliot F. Hahn, then joined the company in February 1993. Serving as vice-president of scientific affairs at Ivax, Hahn handled product licensing and oversaw the maintenance of intellectual property. He now became president of Andrx and a director of the company. With Hahn's arrival, Andrx began developing generic timed-release drugs using its proprietary delivery technologies.

Andrx soon began establishing development and licensing agreements with other pharmaceuticals. The first contract involved Ivax, signed in June 1993, to develop a generic version of the drug K-Dur. Later in the year, Andrx signed development and licensing agreements with California-based Watson Pharmaceuticals Inc. to develop generic versions of Verelan and Sudafed. Andrx also established international relationships, in

July 1993 signing a deal with Yung Shin Pharmaceutical to develop generic versions of Cardizem CD, Seldane, and K-Dur for marketing in Taiwan, China, and parts of southeast Asia. In January 1994 Andrx landed another Taiwan-based partner, Purzer Pharmaceutical Co., to produce a generic version of Dilacor as well as some over-the-counter products for distribution in Russia and Asia. To help fuel its growth, Andrx also prepared to make a initial public offering (IPO) of stock. The company had two very strong trends in its favor: the sale of generic drugs was growing at an average rate in excess of 30 percent per year and the market for controlled release drugs, which totaled $4 billion in 1993, was estimated to grow to $15 billion by the end of the decade. Scheduled for March 1994, the IPO was canceled, however, due to poor market conditions. Although Andrx could have gone public at the time, the price would have been lower than management envisioned and the company opted to find alternative funding. In July 1994 Andrx received $6 million in cash from Circa Pharmaceuticals Inc. and established a joint venture called Ancirc to develop up to six generic timed-release products. A year later Watson acquired Circa, then further strengthened its ties with Andrx by making equity investments in the company, acquiring a 16 percent stake, as well as warrants to purchase additional shares of common stock, at a total cost of nearly $21.6 million.

Revenues grew at a steady clip for Andrx, due almost entirely to its generic drug distribution business, which was enjoying success in penetrating the generic market. During its first full year in operation the company posted sales of nearly $5.7 million, followed by $25.9 million in 1994 and $50.5 million in 1995. The company's losses also kept pace while Andrx developed its own generic drugs to manufacture: the net loss for 1993 topped $2 million, followed by another $3.1 million in 1994 and $5.2 million in 1995. Tangible progress on the generic drug development side of the business was made later in 1995 when Andrx submitted Abbreviated New Drug Applications (ANDAs) to the U.S. Food and Drug Administration (FDA) for generic versions of Cardizem CD and Dilacor, which in 1995 had combined sales of more than $870 million. Moreover, Andrx had a dozen other generics in the pipeline, the brand name equivalents of which had combined U.S. sales of some $3 billion in 1995. Years of patent litigation would ensue, however, before Andrx could actually sell any of its drugs. The salary of scientists and lawyers were both regarded as developmental costs for the company. By law the brand drug patent holder had the right to challenge ANDAs, file suit for patent infringement, and gain 30 months time in which to sell the drug while the two sides fought in court. With a lot of money at stake, and a lot of expensive legal talent available to major pharmaceuticals, firms such as Andrx faced a difficult task in getting their products to market.

Going Public: 1996

Despite this uncertainty, Andrx finally went public in June 1996, selling 2.53 million shares of common stock at $12 per share, and in the end netted $27.4 million. Also in 1996 Andrx established Cybear, a venture designed to serve as an Internet Service Provider and Application Services Provider for the healthcare industry. Among Cybear's capabilities would be hospital messaging, purchasing, eligibility verification, claims processing, lab results, and prescription writing. At the end of the year Andrx posted revenues of $86.7 million and a net loss of $4 million, which represented a positive step in light of the company's 1995 loss of $5.2 million.

In 1997 Andrx continued its efforts to receive FDA approval on ANDAs for timed-release generic drug equivalents of brand name drugs, including Cardizem CD, a Hoechst Marion Roussel drug. Ancirc also submitted ANDAs for two generics. More importantly, Andrx was finally able to manufacture a product, a generic version of Dilacor that the company began selling in the fourth quarter of the year after the FDA granted final approval. Before the end of the year Andrx was able to post net sales of $3.3 million. When compared to the growth in revenues in the generic drug distribution business, which enjoyed an increase of $59.5 million over the previous year, these sales were negligible but represented a major step in the company's development and move toward profitability. The company also looked to expand beyond generic drugs and started a program to produce its own brand drugs, which offered much higher profit margins. For the year Andrx generated revenues of $149.7 million and a net loss of $7.6 million, but the company had clearly turned a corner.

Andrx continued to submit ANDAs in 1998 and further engaged in litigation with pharmaceutical companies attempting to fend off generics. Of particular importance was the April acceptance by the FDA of an Andrx ANDA for a generic version of Prilosec, the top-selling prescription drug in the country, marketed as the "purple pill" and used to treat heartburn, ulcers, acid reflux disease, and a variety of other chronic gastrointestinal conditions. In addition to U.S. sales of $2 billion, Prilosec boasted worldwide sales of $4 billion. The patent for the drug's active ingredient, held by AstraZeneca, was set to expire in April 2001, and Andrx was preparing the way to market its generic equivalent at that time, although with such high stakes involved the company anticipated a vigorous legal challenge from the patent holder. Andrx also became involved in legal difficulties of a different sort. In October 1998 it learned that it was being investigated by the Federal Trade Commission. In question was an agreement with Aventis that paid Andrx $10 million each quarter for not marketing its generic equivalent of Cardizem CD, a deal that grew out of the company's patent litigation. The question was whether this agreement violated antitrust legislation, as the FTC began to look into the matter on an industry-wide basis. Although Andrx maintained that new competitors were not prevented from entering the market, the FTC ultimately concluded in 2001 that the agreement had blocked entry. Moreover, 15 states launched a suit against Andrx and Aventis claiming $100 million in compensation for the higher prices consumers had to pay because there was no generic version of Cardizem CD on the market.

In October 1998 Andrx posted its first profitable quarter, and for the year the company produced a net profit of nearly $8.4

Key Dates:

1992: Andrx is founded.
1996: Company goes public.
1997: First generic product is manufactured and marketed.
2001: Founder Alan P. Cohen steps down as CEO.
2002: First brand drug, Altocor, is manufactured and marketed.

million on revenues of more than $247 million. Investors, however, focused on the problems with the FTC and litigation that delayed Andrx from marketing its generic drugs, both of which had an adverse impact on the price of the company's stock. Andrx continue to persevere in 1999, entering into a significant product development agreement with Bayer and receiving ANDA approval for generic versions of the drugs Oruvail, Wellbutrin SR, Zyban, and K-Dur. Andrx also resolved one of its lawsuits and began to market its generic version of Cardizem CD. As a result of these positive developments, the price of the company's stock soared, on its way to topping $100 per share in early 2000, leading to a two-for-one split. Revenues for 1999 totaled nearly $476 million, and net profits jumped to more than $94 million. In March 2000 Andrx received tentative approval for its generic version of Prilosec, which served as a lead-in to a secondary stock offering in May 2000, when the company was able to raise approximately $235 million. The situation with Prilosec also concerned some analysts who maintained serious reservations about Andrx. Not only was patent holder AstraZeneca vigorously defending its rights in courts, there was some question about the market for Prilosec once Andrx was able to sell its version. AstraZeneca was already selling a drug called Nexium, positioning it as the replacement for Prilosec, which it had stopped actively promoting. Andrx countered that Nexium was only effective as a heartburn treatment and that Prilosec would continue to be a major prescription drug. The company also downplayed the possibility that Prilosec might even go over-the-counter.

A number of concerns in 2001 led to a drop in the price of Andrx stock, which fell from a high of $76.52 to the low $20s. Not only were investors troubled about the state of the Prilosec generic, they were concerned about changes in management. In October of that year Cohen resigned as CEO, replaced by Hahn on an interim basis, and Chen soon announced that he was leaving, too. Nevertheless, the company continued to prepare for future growth, especially as it looked forward to marketing its own brand drugs. In 2001 Andrx acquired CTEX Pharmaceuticals, a sales and marketing company; Armstrong Pharmaceuticals, makers of pharmaceutical aerosols; and the Entex line of cough and cold products.

New CEO, New Focus on Brand Drugs: 2002

In June 2002 a new CEO took over, Richard J. Lane, an executive with experience at Bristol-Myers Squibb and Merck. He quickly reassured shareholders that prospects for the company remained promising. Several months after he took office the Prilosec matter was finally resolved when Andrx and AstraZeneca agreed to share in the profits of the Prilosec generic developed by the Kudco unit of Schwarz Pharma. Under Lane's leadership Andrx also began to sell off its stake in Cybear, which had lost more than $35 million in 2001. The CEO was also very supportive of the company's move into brand drugs to augment its generic program. By marketing both generic and brand drugs Lane hoped that Andrx would be able to post revenues between $1.5 billion and $2 billion by 2007. Andrx's first brand drug, Altocor, a timed-release form of the anti-cholesterol drug lovastatin, went on sale in 2002. To help bolster its manufacturing capabilities, Andrx in January 2003 bought a 500,000-square-foot, Morrisville, North Carolina plant for $28 million and made plans to invest another $85 million in upgrades. According to Lane in an interview with *Chemical Week,* "We believe that this facility, together with our existing facilities, will enable Andrx to meet market demand for our current and new product introductions well into the future." With some 30 generics and one brand drug in the pipeline awaiting FDA approval, Andrx would very likely need that extra capacity.

Principal Subsidiaries

Anda, Inc.; Andrx Pharmaceuticals, Inc.; CTEX Pharmaceuticals, Inc.; Cybear Inc.; Valmed Pharmaceutical, Inc.

Principal Competitors

Biovail Corporation; Mylan Laboratories Inc.; Elan Corporation, plc; Elite Pharmaceuticals, Inc.

Further Reading

Alpert, Bill, "Dirty Tricks of the Land of Generic Drugs," *Barron's,* March 11, 2002, p. T1.

Fakler, John T., "ANDRX: Stock Makes a Stunning Turnaround," *South Florida Business Journal,* March 10, 2000, p. 29.

Gibbs, Lisa, "Bitter Pills," *Florida Trend,* December 2002, p. 74.

Miller, Susan R., "Time Is Ripe for Andrx's Line of Timed-Release Drugs," *South Florida Business Journal,* July 26, 1996, p. 3A.

Scott, Alex, "Andrx Purchases Pharma from Bristol-Myers," *Chemical Week,* January 22, 2003, p. 21.

Singer, Glenn, "Davie, Fla.-Based Andrx Markets with Generics, Brand-Name Drugs," *South Florida Sun-Sentinel,* October 14, 2002, p. 1.

——, "Davie, Fla.-Based Drug Maker Projects Bright Outlook," *South Florida Sun-Sentinel,* July 20, 2002, p. 1.

—Ed Dinger

Arrow Air Holdings Corporation

200 N.W. 62 Avenue, Building 711
P.O. Box 523726
Miami, Florida 33152
U.S.A.
Telephone: (305) 871-3116
Toll Free: (800) 871-3370
Fax: (305) 526-0933
Web site: http://www.arrowair.com

Private Company
Incorporated: 1947
Employees: 1026
Sales: $148 million (2001)
NAIC: 481111 Scheduled Passenger Air Transportation;
481212 Nonscheduled Chartered Freight Air
Transportation

Arrow Air Holdings Corporation owns Arrow Air, Inc., which is the fourth largest cargo airline in the United States and is based at Miami International Airport. Clientele includes freight forwarders, the United States Postal Service, and the U.S. Department of Defense, although the company stopped flying military personnel in the mid-1980s. Arrow dominates the air cargo market between the United States and Latin America and the Caribbean. The carrier operates 135 flights a week to 29 destinations in the region and has a hub in San Juan, Puerto Rico. Arrow carries nearly 150,000 tons of freight a year.

California Origins

Arrow Air founder George Batchelor was born of Native American ancestry in Shawnee, Oklahoma in 1901. He became a pilot, and the loss of his first wife and son in a plane crash did not stop him from moving to Compton, California, in 1947 and establishing Arrow Air.

Batchelor's aircraft brokering business was more lucrative than this secondary airline, reported the *Miami Herald.* In his first deal, Batchelor bought a DC-3 in Hawaii for $10,000 and resold it for a $15,000 profit. The airline stopped scheduled operations in 1953 in what Batchelor saw as an anti-competitive regulatory environment. However, Batchelor continued leasing aircraft, often with crews, to other small airlines.

Batchelor moved Arrow Air to South Florida in 1964. By this time, he was with his third wife. Considered a pioneer in both south Florida's aviation industry and in the Latin American air cargo market, Batchelor would amass a considerable fortune and donate much of it to homeless and children's causes before dying in July 2002.

Relaunched in 1981

On May 26, 1981, Arrow Air relaunched as a charter airline under Miami's Batchelor Enterprises, whose aviation operations included fixed-base operator (FBO) Batch Air and International Air Leases, Inc., Arrow's parent company. (Batch Air eventually became owned by an employee group and was sold to Greenwich Air in 1987 for more than $30 million.) Arrow added scheduled services in April 1982, beginning with California-Montego Bay.

Low fares were causing the company to lose money. In October 1984, it canceled several routes, including Tampa-London. At the same time, the company reoriented its route structure from an east-west alignment to a north-south one, reported *Aviation Week & Space Technology.* San José, Puerto Rico, where the company was building a new hub, was the center of the scheduled network, and by the end of 1985 Arrow Air was connecting the destination with Montreal, New York, Philadelphia, Boston, Baltimore, Orlando, and Miami. In 1985, more than one million people flew Arrow to 245 destinations in 72 countries.

Arrow was operating McDonnell Douglas DC-10 and DC-8 aircraft. Like other start-ups, Arrow contracted some functions to other airlines. United Airlines trained its crews in Denver, and Florida Air supplemented Batch-Air's maintenance work.

The company was approved for military charters in 1984, and in October 1985 won a $13.8 million contract with the Department of Defense. This accounted for only a small segment of Arrow's revenues. Most of its business came from scheduled service from Canada and the East Coast to Puerto

<table>
<tr><td>

Company Perspectives:

Mission: to provide a safe, reliable, and profitable air freight transportation system that meets the changing needs of its customers with courteous and efficient service; to provide a growth oriented workplace that recognizes the interests, rights, and ideas of its employees and offers career advancement opportunities; and to provide a corporate environment that encourages ethical behavior and compliance with all regulations and laws.

</td></tr>
</table>

Rico and Mexico. Commercial charters accounted for another 20 percent or so.

In carrying out its military flights, the airline experienced a large-scale disaster and its first fatal accident. On December 12, 1985, one of the company's DC-8s crashed after takeoff in Gander, Newfoundland, killing 248 soldiers of the 101st Airborne Division and eight of Arrow's flight crew personnel. The flight had originated in Cairo and had taken on fuel in Gander after stopping in Cologne, West Germany. The accident resulted in a great deal of unfavorable media coverage and government scrutiny for the airline. Arrow filed for Chapter 11 bankruptcy reorganization in February 1986, laying off 400 employees. However, operations continued.

Haberly Leads a Turnaround: 1987–94

Named president of Arrow Air in 1987, Richard L. Haberly is credited with turning the company around. (Arrow attained profitability in 1990.) Haberly had begun his aviation career loading baggage for United Airlines, later entering the company's management-training program. He also spent ten years with the Flying Tiger cargo airline.

Arrow's wet lease business—the practice of hiring out planes complete with crews and fuel—began to pick up again. In 1989, Arrow began leasing a DC-8 to Lot Polish Airlines for a Warsaw-New York-Chicago route. It also provided a plane to the Airline of the Marshall Islands. In early 1991, Arrow was again carrying U.S. troops, this time for the military buildup preceding the war in the Persian Gulf.

Arrow boasted a 98 percent on-time rate and a high degree of customer loyalty. Rates for Latin American cargo fell 15 percent in the early 1990s as U.S. passenger airlines United and American paid increased attention to that market. After a few profitable years, Arrow posted losses in 1992 and 1993. Richard Haberly was succeeded as Arrow president in June 1994 by Jonathan D. Batchelor, son of chairman and company founder George Batchelor. Haberly left to take over the ailing cargo airline Florida West.

In the mid-1990s, Arrow's fleet numbered 18 aircraft—DC-8's and Boeing 727's (two of which were configured for passengers). Many of the planes were acquired from bankrupt Eastern Airlines. The company dropped the 727's and began leasing Lockheed L-1011 widebody jets in 1996, when its fleet numbered just nine planes. By this time, charters for other airlines were accounting for half of Arrow's business.

Grounded in 1995

Market conditions were not Arrow's only worries. The FAA grounded Arrow in March 1995, charging the carrier had improperly documented maintenance. A company spokesman countered that the grounding was unfair and was related simply to the FAA's request that Arrow print out a hard copy of its fleet records, which were stored electronically. Company officials blamed the affair on a disgruntled employee who had been fired for theft.

Arrow contracted other carriers to handle its business during the crisis. British Airways, for example, handled the route between Columbus, Ohio, and Glasgow, Scotland. Arrow also laid off 368 of its 587 employees. During the shutdown, Arrow lost $3.5 million, plus another $1.5 million in FAA fines.

The FAA allowed the company to begin flying cargo again in June 1995. Soon, Arrow was carrying more international freight at Miami International than any other carrier. It was connecting San Juan to the Northeast via Hartford, Connecticut; to the Midwest via Columbus, Ohio; and to the Southeast via Atlanta.

A restructuring in June 1996 placed Terence Fensome as president and CEO of Arrow Air. Jonathan Batchelor soon took over again as president, but in July 1998 relinquished that role for the positions of chairman and CEO as Guillermo J. "Willy" Cabeza became president and chief operating officer. Cabeza had been vice-president of operations at Arrow.

Arrow failed to profit from the upswing in the economy in 1997. It lost $15.1 million for the year on revenues of $88.3 million. The company had posted losses of $11.3 million in 1996 on revenues of $61.1 million.

Arrow started a new weekly service from Houston to Peru and Ecuador in February 1998. Houston was billing itself as a "Gateway to Latin America" to compete with Miami, which handled 85 percent of cargo traffic to the region. Arrow revenues were $87 million in fiscal 1998.

A Merger and a Bankruptcy: 1999–2000

After a few difficult years, Arrow was acquired by Fine Air Services in early 1999 (the deal was finalized in April) from International Air Leases Inc. for $115 million. Frank and Barry Fine, owners of Fine Air, planned to keep Arrow's brand name viable and continued to emphasize scheduled, rather than charter, cargo service. Included in the purchase were 13 DC-8 aircraft, four L-1011's, 130 jet engines, and spare parts. The buy gave Arrow access to Fine's 133,000-square-foot refrigerated distribution facility for handling perishables, which made up the bulk of Latin American cargo.

Unfortunately, Fine Air had its own set of woes resulting from a fatal crash of one of its DC-8's in August 1997. This scuttled Fine's planned $123 million initial public offering. Rising fuel costs, a downturn in the Latin American market, and debt left over from its Arrow Air acquisition combined to make the airline unflyable. Fine lost $108 million in 2000 on revenues of $152 million, and another $36 million on 2001 revenues of $148 million.

Key Dates:

1947: Arrow Air is launched.
1953: Passenger operations are terminated.
1981: Arrow Air reestablishes passenger operations.
1985: A military charter flight crashes in Greenland, taking 256 lives.
1999: Fine Air Services acquires Arrow Air.
2002: Fine Air emerges from bankruptcy as a subsidiary of Arrow Air; AGI is acquired.

The company filed for bankruptcy on September 27, 2000, and subsequently merged with Arrow Air, Inc., leaving behind the Fine Air Services name. The Fine brothers would no longer control the company. It emerged from Chapter 11 in May 2002 as a unit of Arrow Air Holdings Corp., a Greenwich, Connecticut, investment group led by Dort Cameron. Richard L. Haberly returned to rebuild the airline.

Revenues were $148 million in 2001, when Arrow had about 800 employees in Miami and another 200 in other locations. The fleet had grown to 16 DC-8's and two L-1011's; the carrier had also begun leasing a pair of DC-10's.

Haberly Returns in 2002

Former Arrow president Richard Haberly returned to the company after restoring Florida West to profitability. Haberly, noted as a turnaround specialist, had his work cut out for him. The new Arrow was losing $3 million a month, reported *Traffic World* in early 2002, yet Haberly aimed to have it breaking even by year-end.

The withdrawal of Grupo TACA's freighters from the market provided Haberly with an opportunity to expand services in Central America with some east-west routes. He also aimed Arrow to re-enter the charter business and to diversify geographically via partnerships with airlines such as Atlas Air, Lloyd Aeroeo Boliviano, and Air Global International (AGI). AGI had been formed in 2001 and leased two Boeing 747's to carry cargo to South America. Its routes complemented those of Arrow Air, which acquired AGI in March 2002, keeping its brand name active and its CEO Frank Visconti in place. Operationally, Arrow Air planned to retire its L-1011 by 2003 and replace its dozen DC-8's with Boeing 767's a few years after.

Principal Subsidiaries

Arrow Air Inc.

Principal Competitors

Amerijet International; Challenge Air Cargo Inc.; Federal Express Corporation; United Parcel Service; Varig Brazilian Airlines.

Further Reading

Armbruster, William, "Arrow Air Acquires AGI," *Journal of Commerce Online*, February 14, 2003.

"Arrow Air Halts Service, Files for Bankruptcy," *Aviation Week & Space Technology*, February 17, 1986, p. 36.

Burgess, Lisa, "Arrow Air Lashes Out at FAA Charges; Agency Finds Fleet Unsafe," *Journal of Commerce*, March 21, 1995, p. 2B.

Davies, Frank, "Miami-Based Arrow Air Agrees to Pay Penalty," *Miami Herald*, April 27, 1998.

"Fine Air Services Agrees to Buy a Rival for $115 Million," *New York Times*, Company News, February 12, 1999, p. 2.

Hemlock, Doreen, "Cargo Firms Fight Costly War on Crooks; Thefts, Drugs Cause Boost in Security," *Sun Sentinel* (Fort Lauderdale), March 15, 1998, p. 1F.

——, "Miami Air-Cargo Firm's Woes Are Unique, But Fuel Costs Are Industry-Wide Bane," *Sun-Sentinel* (Fort Lauderdale), September 29, 2000.

Imse, Ann, "Military Ban Includes Airline with DIA Flights," *Denver Rocky Mountain News*, February 16, 1996.

"Investors Submit New Plan of Reorganization for Miami-Based Carrier," *Miami Herald*, March 30, 2002.

Kjelgaard, Chris, "Arrow Air Operation to Stay Separate Under Fine Air," *Air Transport Intelligence*, February 13, 1999.

Krause, Kristin S., "Changes at Arrow Air; Cabeza Named President & COO; Batchelor Becomes Chairman, CEO," *Traffic World*, July 6, 1998, p. 21.

——, "Fine, Arrow Merger Complete," *Traffic World*, April 19, 1999, p. 57.

——, "He's Back; Haberly Returns to Arrow Air to Pull Airline from Brink Once More," *Traffic World*, June 17, 2002, p. 21.

Lee, Richard, "Arrow Reports Few Post-Crash Cancellations," *Travel Weekly*, December 26, 1985, p. 1.

"Line's History: Swift Growth and Setbacks," *Travel Weekly*, December 26, 1985, p. 45.

Matthews, Carole, "Lift Flourishes for Produce Industry," *Air Cargo World*, October 1994, pp. 10ff.

Max, K.J., "Fine Looks to Replace DC-8s," *Flight International*, October 20, 1999, p. 20.

Moreno, Jenalia, "Houston Gets Direct Route to South America with Arrow Air," *Houston Chronicle*, February 3, 1998.

Ott, James, "Flight Data Recorder Examined After Arrow Air DC-8 Crash," *Aviation Week & Space Technology*, December 23, 1985, p. 30.

Parezo, Stephen, "Return Trip: Arrow Air Will Look Just Fine with a More Global Reach as Far as Richard Haberly Is Concerned," *Air Cargo World*, July 2002, p. 10.

"Philanthropist, Aviation Pioneer George Batchelor Dies at 81," *Miami Herald*, July 31, 2002.

"Restructuring at Arrow Air Puts Fensome in Top Spot," *Journal of Commerce*, June 24, 1996, p. 2B.

Sterman, David, "The Benefits of Arrow Air's Restructuring and Service to Latin Markets," *Air Cargo World*, April 1996, p. 16.

"Veteran Team Has New Ideas for Miami Air Cargo Company," *Miami Herald*, June 3, 2002.

Zisser, Melinda, "Arrow Air to Re-Enter Passenger Charter Business," *South Florida Business Journal*, April 9, 1993, p. 3A.

—Frederick C. Ingram

ASC, Inc.

One Sunroof Center
Southgate, Michigan 48195
U.S.A.
Telephone: (734) 285-4911
Fax: (734) 246-0501
Web site: http://www.ascglobal.com

Wholly Owned Subsidiary of Questor Management Co.
LLC
Incorporated: 1965 as American Sunroof Company
Employees: 1,000
Sales: $406 million (2001 est.)
NAIC: 336399 All Other Motor Vehicle Parts
Manufacturing; 336360 Motor Vehicle Seating and
Interior Trim Manufacturing

ASC, Inc. is a designer and manufacturer of specialty products for the auto industry. The firm is a top producer of sunroofs and also makes convertible tops, interior trim for trucks, and prototype and concept cars. Other activities include installation of entertainment systems and vehicle enhancement packages. ASC works for many of the major auto makers in the United States and abroad, and also makes products for the aftermarket. Following the sudden death of company founder Heinz Prechter in 2001, the firm was sold to Questor Management Co. LLC of Southfield, Michigan.

Early Years

ASC was founded in Los Angeles in 1965 as the American Sunroof Company by Heinz Prechter, a 21-year-old West German immigrant. Prechter, who had been raised in a village in Bavaria and learned mechanical skills in his uncle's car repair shop, had driven a cab until he saved enough money to come to America. He started his small firm in a two-car garage rented from famed custom car builder George Barris. While the idea of cutting a hole in the roof of a brand-new car and replacing it with a window was not appealing to everyone, Prechter found enough interested parties to give him a steady business. Though sunroofs were already popular in Europe, he was one of the first

to put them in American cars. When word of his company spread, he began traveling the United States to do conversions for customers around the country.

Prechter's reputation for quality work eventually came to the attention of the Ford Motor Co., which asked him to come to Detroit to install sunroofs in custom Lincoln cars that were being built for the likes of President Lyndon Johnson. He used a former car wash to perform these conversions at first, with Ford shipping vehicles to Prechter for the installation process. After a few months, he was asked to add sunroofs to some models of the 1968 Mercury Cougar XR-7, making it the first U.S. car to offer a sunroof as a factory option.

Prechter's firm began growing rapidly. During the 1970s, the company started producing kits for factory installation of sunroofs by the auto industry, developed the first glass panel sunroof, and created the first simulated convertible top. By 1978, American Sunroof had managed more than 40 projects, modified over 1.6 million vehicles, and provided more than 300,000 sunroof kits for factory installation.

Drop in U.S. Auto Sales Has Devastating Impact: 1979

A sharp decline in domestic auto sales that followed the Iranian hostage crisis of 1979 wreaked havoc with American Sunroof, and Prechter was forced to cut his workforce from 2,300 to 500 to keep from going under. He subsequently began to turn an eye toward international sales and also sought out other areas to invest in, including real estate, newspaper publishing, and a savings and loan bank.

In 1982, the company revised its corporate structure and took the shortened name of ASC, Incorporated. During the year, the firm began producing the Buick Riviera convertible as part of a resurgence of interest in the open body style, which had earlier been discontinued industry-wide due to dwindling sales.

In 1986, ASC began to supply convertible tops for the sporty Chevrolet Corvette, and the following year the company bought a leading supplier of interior trim for heavy trucks, Aeromotive Systems Co. The firm was also starting to make custom and

Company Perspectives:

With a very proud tradition spanning decades as a worldwide, value driven innovator, ASC, Incorporated is proud to provide the automotive industry with Specialty Customization and innovative specialty systems, state-of-the-art open air systems. Internationally recognized for its solid commitment to product quality and excellence, ASC continues to build on its reputation as a world leader in automotive enhancement technology.

limited-production vehicles, and in 1987 built the Buick GNX, the world's fastest car from 0 to 60 miles per hour.

The year 1988 saw ASC begin working with the German carmaker Porsche to build model 944 convertible Cabrios at a newly built plant in Heilbron, West Germany. ASC now expected to perform 3,500 to 4,000 conversions per year. The company also bought a small German coachmaking firm, Karrosseriewerke Weinsberg GmbH, which was renamed ASC/Weinsberg. Other acquisitions during 1988 included Pioneer Engineering and Manufacturing Co. and sister company Troy Design Group, auto design and engineering firms which expanded ASC's specialty vehicle manufacturing capabilities significantly. Because the company had labor costs as much as 20 percent below those of the American Big 3 automakers, it was able to offer a viable alternative for production of low-volume specialty vehicles.

In 1989, ASC began working with Dodge to build the first production convertible pickup truck, the Dakota. The company was also given the green light by Seat, a Spanish automaker owned by Volkswagen, to build a convertible version of its Ibiza model. In 1990, ASC announced it would partner with Modern Engineering of Warren, Michigan, to design and build specialty vehicles.

During these years, CEO Heinz Prechter continued to explore other business ventures, many of which were based in the so-called Downriver area south of Detroit, a heavily industrial, blue-collar community. He purchased the *Wyandotte News-Herald* and Mellus newspapers, which were later renamed Heritage Newspapers, acquired the Ramada Inn in Southgate (next to ASC's headquarters), and assisted in the financial bailout of the famed London Chop House in Detroit. Prechter also helped broaden the scope of the Detroit Auto Show, which evolved from a mostly local-based event into the North American International Auto Show. Another pursuit was lobbying government officials for such things as new roads and a second bridge across the Detroit River. Prechter's political activity was not confined to the local area, however, and he also helped raise $10 million to promote the Republican Party's "Contract with America" and coordinated a 1992 trip to Asia by President George Bush and a group of business leaders. Prechter had known Bush since the mid-1970s and had raised $1 million for his 1988 presidential campaign. He was later chosen to serve as chairman of the President's Export Council.

By 1992, ASC had grown to employ almost 3,000 worldwide and was operating plants around North America and in South Korea and Germany. It had revenues of an estimated $400 million. Construction of a new 115,000 square foot plant was begun in Columbus, Ohio, during the year to house all of the firm's sunroof production, transferring work from sites in Gibraltar, Michigan, and Youngshon, Korea. ASC had a new contract to build Honda Accord sunroofs, and much of the space was dedicated to this work, along with putting sunroofs in several Chrysler Corp. models. Honda had been making Accords at a plant in nearby Marysville, Ohio, since 1982.

In late 1993, ASC announced it would soon begin to work with General Motors to produce convertibles at an idle GM plant in Lansing, Michigan, for the so-called J-cars, the Chevrolet Cavalier and Pontiac Sunbird. The 50–50 joint venture was later named GENASYS. Fifteen thousand vehicles were expected to be produced each year by 180 workers. The year 1993 also saw the Aeromotive subsidiary partner with Freightliner to develop the FLD 170 sleeper cab.

Prechter Names New CEO; Company Restructured: 1995

In January 1995, Heinz Prechter gave the job of CEO to his newly hired chief operating officer, Donald Barefoot. He retained the job of chairman and also remained in place as CEO and president of the GENASYS venture. Prechter had reportedly decided to make the move to give him more time to devote to his political interests, as well as because recurrent bouts of depression sometimes interfered with his work.

Barefoot was taking over a company that appeared to be in decline. ASC had recently lost the contract to make convertible tops for Corvettes as well as a bid to supply Toyota with 100,000 sunroofs for the 1997 Camry, and had also ceased supplying convertible tops for the Saab 900. In 1995 and 1996, the firm was restructured and its staff trimmed, both on the manufacturing level and at the corporate headquarters in Southgate. The firm's four divisions—American Sunroof Co., ASC Convertible Systems Co., Automobile Specialty Co., and Aeromotive Systems Co.—were given more control over their own operations as well. ASC also sold a manufacturing plant in Owosso, Michigan, to Talon Automotive Group during this time. The company's original-equipment sunroof work was down from several years earlier, but it had nearly a quarter of the U.S. market for convertible top production. Other firms were aggressively entering the field, and ASC's restructuring moves were partly a response to this challenge.

In April 1997, having significantly improved ASC's fortunes, CEO Barefoot resigned and was replaced by Lawrence Doyle, a former General Electric executive. Prechter praised the departing Barefoot's efforts at making the company more organized and productive, telling Automotive News, "Until Don came, the company was floundering because I was running it from my hip pocket." At Barefoot's departure, ASC was again doing $400 million in business, up by a third from 1995, and the leaner company had one-third fewer employees. Following Doyle's installation, he too reorganized the company, combining the sunroof and convertible top divisions into one unit, American Sunroof Co. A new division, Aeromotive Services Co., was also formed to design prototype automobiles such as the Toyota Solara.

and also introduced new entertainment systems for GM minivans. In 2001, the company created ASC Vehicle Technologies to design and build vehicles out of a new facility in Oak Park, Michigan.

Key Dates:

1965: Heinz Prechter comes to Los Angeles from Germany and starts an auto sunroof company.
1967: Prechter moves to Detroit and begins installing sunroofs for Ford.
1970s: Sunroof kits and simulated convertible tops are introduced by the rapidly growing firm.
1982: The firm is renamed ASC, Inc.
1987: The company buys truck trim manufacturer Aeromotive Systems Co.
1988: Two specialty vehicle firms and a German coachbuilder are acquired.
1995: GENASYS joint sunroof venture is formed with General Motors.
1997: Prechter Holdings becomes the parent of ASC; two new joint ventures are formed.
1999: JPE, Inc. is bought with Kojaian Holdings and renamed ASC Exterior Technologies.
2001: Founder Heinz Prechter dies; a joint sunroof venture is formed with Inalfa Industries.
2002: ASC is sold to Questor Management Co. LLC.

Death of Heinz Prechter: 2001

In July 2001, company founder Heinz Prechter took his own life in his Grosse Ile Township home. He had suffered from bipolar disorder for many years. Before his death he had been working on plans to sell off his business interests with his wife Waltraud, and the cattle ranch and newspapers were sold during the fall. In May 2002, a deal was reached to sell ASC to Jay Alix's Questor Management Co. LLC. Included in the sale were ASC Holdings, Inc. and its stake in the ASCET business, automotive engineering firm Triad Services Group, Inc., Prechter's remaining real estate and hotel holdings, and a home-building company in Florida that he also owned. Questor specialized in investing in companies, boosting their value, and reselling them, and it was expected that ASC would go on the block again within five years. In September 2002, former DiamlerChrysler executive Paul Wilbur was named CEO of ASC.

The year 2002 saw a new joint venture, American Sunroof Inalfa, launched with Inalfa Industries, which became the second largest maker of aftermarket sunroofs worldwide. The company was also producing convertible systems for the Toyota Solara, Mitsubishi Eclipse, Chevy Camaro, Pontiac Firebird, and BMW Z3 at this time, and the 2003 Chevrolet SSR convertible truck would soon bring additional work in this area.

Having spearheaded their introduction to the United States, ASC, Incorporated remained one of the leading manufacturers of sunroofs in North America. The company had also branched out into designing and building specialty vehicles, manufacturing truck trim, and installing convertible tops and entertainment systems. The recent death of founder Heinz Prechter, and the company's subsequent sale to Questor, had brought relatively few changes, and ASC continued to work with top carmakers like General Motors and Toyota to supply a range of specialty products.

Other efforts of 1997 included formation of A Y Manufacturing, Ltd., a joint sunroof-making venture with Yachiyo, and Trim Systems, LLC, a joint venture between ASC's truck trim division (the former Aeromotive Systems) and Hidden Creek Industries. The company suffered another blow during the year when Chrysler Corporation announced it was changing sunroof suppliers for its popular Cirrus/Stratus models, dropping ASC to give the work to a new concern, Webasto Sunroofs Inc.

The year 1997 also saw Heinz Prechter create a new corporate entity called Prechter Holdings to own ASC and his other business interests. These now included the Heritage Media Group, which owned 12 suburban weekly newspapers in Michigan; Heritage Development, a real estate investment firm; Heritage Beef and Cattle, which operated a 10,000-acre cattle ranch in Texas; and Heritage Networks, an investment firm. Prechter and his wife also ran a charitable organization, the World Heritage Foundation, which contributed to the Downriver community, education, the arts, and the promotion of cultural exchange between the United States and Germany.

In 1998, ASC opened a new vehicle design and engineering facility in Warren, Michigan, and began producing vehicle enhancement packages for the Chevy Trailblazer and Pontiac WS6, as well as an entertainment system for the Oldsmobile Silhouette Premier. The following year, a new manufacturing facility was opened in Kitchener, Ontario, Canada, for production of the Toyota Solara convertible, along with one in Bloomington, Illinois, to produce convertible tops for the Mitsubishi Eclipse. Prechter and real estate executive C. Michael Kojaian also banded together to buy JPE, Inc., an auto trim and heavy truck brake manufacturer, renaming it ASC Exterior Technologies, Inc. (ASCET). The company retained its publicly traded status.

In 2000, ASC opened a new technical center in Munich, Germany, to develop open-air systems for European vehicles,

Principal Subsidiaries

ASC Composite Systems; ASC Vehicle Technologies; ASC Creative Services; ASC Open Air Systems; ASC Specialty Vehicles; ASC Technologies; ASC Holdings, Inc.

Principal Competitors

Bestop, Inc.; Dura Convertible Systems, Inc.; ArvinMeritor, Inc.; Webasto Sunroofs Inc.; Delphi Corporation.

Further Reading

Bailey, Laura, and Dietderich, Andrew, " 'He Touched Every Person He Met'," *Crain's Detroit Business*, July 16, 2001, p. 21.
Barkholz, David, "ASC Seeks Big 3 Contract to Build Specialty Car," *Automotive News*, December 19, 1988, p. 4.
——, "Faces: Heinz Prechter, ASC Corp.," *Crain's Detroit Business*, February 27, 1995, p. A60.
Carney, Susan, "Prechter Assets Sold Off," *Detroit News*, May 7, 2002.

Chappell, Lindsay, "Death Ends Prechter's Story of an Entrepreneur," *Automotive News*, July 9, 2001, p. 2.

Diem, William R., and Max Gates, "Trading on Good Will; ASC's Heinz Prechter has the Ear of the President," *Automotive News*, March 9, 1992, p. 3.

Fleming, Al, "Sky's The Limit; The Prospects are Sizzling for Installations of Sunroofs in Cars, Sport-Utilities and Vans," *Automotive News*, June 22, 1992, p. 6i.

Kosdrosky, Terry, and Robert Ankeny, "Prechter's Death Stuns; Business Leaders, Politicians Feel the Loss," *Crain's Detroit Business*, July 9, 2001, p. 1.

McCracken, Jeffrey, "JPE Becomes ASCET: Prechter, Kojaian Holding Companies Invest in Supplier," *Crain's Detroit Business*, May 31, 1999, p. 1.

Ramirez, Charles E., "GM and ASC May Expand Niche Operations," *Automotive News*, December 6, 1993, p. 4.

Renaux, Jean-Jacques, "He'll Do More than Slice Porsches; Prechter Expects Additional Work for New Plant in Germany," *Automotive News*, April 11, 1988, p. 46.

Sedgwick, David, "New ASC Chief Revamps Company to Stress Technical Development," *Automotive News*, June 9, 1997, p. 33.

Sherefkin, Robert, "Alix-Led Fund Set to Buy ASC; Questor Also Acquiring Other Prechter Holdings," *Crain's Detroit Business*, May 6, 2002, p. 1.

Strong, Michael, and Jennete Smith, "Heirs Continue Prechter Plan to Shed Nonauto Holdings," *Crain's Detroit Business*, November 12, 2001, p. 3.

—Frank Uhle

Atlantic Coast Airlines Holdings, Inc.

45200 Business Court
Dulles, Virginia 20166
U.S.A.
Telephone: (703) 650-6000
Fax: (703) 650-6299
Web site: http://www.atlanticcoast.com

Public Company
Incorporated: 1991 as Atlantic Coast Airlines, Inc.
Employees: 3,992
Sales: $760.52 million (2002)
Stock Exchanges: NASDAQ
Ticker Symbol: ACAI
NAIC: 481111 Scheduled Passenger Air Transportation;
   488190 Other Support Activities for Air Transportation

Atlantic Coast Airlines Holdings, Inc. (ACAI) is the parent company for the regional airline that shares its name. Atlantic Coast Airlines (ACA) operates feeder routes for major airlines. Much of its growth has come from its role as the United Express affiliate operating from Chicago's O'Hare Airport and Dulles Airport in Washington, D.C. ACA also flies as under the Delta Connection banner from La Guardia in New York and Logan in Boston.

Origins

The story of Atlantic Coast Airlines begins with WestAir Commuter Airlines Inc., the United Airlines Inc. regional partner operating in California and the Pacific Northwest in the late 1980s. According to the *Washington Times,* Fresno-based WestAir was the country's largest regional airline holding company.

In December 1989, United asked WestAir to hastily put together a new operation on the other side of the country to replace a partner that suddenly went out of business, four-year-old Presidential Airways. The new WestAir unit would be using the United Express name, which had been sullied in the East by the flight cancellations and other disruptions that attended Presidential's bankruptcy.

The Atlantic Coast division's first day of operations was December 15, 1989, just 11 days after the call from United. Company lore recalls tales of the mostly Californian staffers stepping into one of the D.C. area's coldest winters. After a couple of weeks at a Holiday Inn, a two-room office was set up in Sterling, Virginia. The company had 50 employees at the time.

The division started with six Brasilian-made turboprop aircraft on six routes. By the end of 1990, it was carrying 480 passengers a day; the fleet of 23 aircraft connected 23 cities.

High tech companies in the Dulles corridor provided a lot of demand for ACA flights linking smaller communities, notes the *Washington Post.* One important early route was to Jacksonville, Florida, where AOL maintained a training center. Columbus, Ohio, became an important destination after AOL acquired CompuServe Inc. Raleigh, in the heart of North Carolina's Research Triangle, was another important destination for techies.

ACA Spun Off in 1991

In 1991, WestAir Holdings Inc. faced its own set of financial troubles and in October sold off the fledgling Atlantic Coast division to a group of investors lead by C. Edward Acker, a veteran of Pan Am World Airways Inc., Branniff, and Air Florida. Acker's group paid $22.7 million for ACA. Kerry B. Skeen, a senior vice-president at WestAir, was named president in 1992 and became CEO three years later. A native of Georgia, Skeen had started his aviation career with a seven-month stint as a janitor for Delta Air Lines Inc.

ACA went public on the NASDAQ exchange in 1993. While United Airlines lost nearly a billion dollars in 1992, ACA, like most regionals, had not been affected to the same degree as the majors by the post-Gulf War recession. Ever expanding, ACA began originating flights at Newark and Orlando (following United's expansion into Florida) as well as Dulles, where it had more daily departures than any other airline, including the majors.

Employment at ACA doubled in 1993 alone, as ACA took over many north-south flights that United abandoned that February. United also sold ACA the Dulles-based operations of its Air

Company Perspectives:

The same values and principals that guided the early years of the company are the ones that have forged our current— and future—successes: a strong spirit of excitement about growth and new opportunities; an appreciation of the creative challenge of working in an environment where cost-consciousness, efficiency, and maximum productivity are paramount; determination to succeed, even in the face of incredible obstacles; and a strong sense of the value of providing excellent service to our partners, passengers, employees, and shareholders. Although ACA is a company made up of people from a wide range of backgrounds, experiences, and cultures, anyone who values teamwork, loves new challenges, and possesses an inner drive to succeed is always welcome on the ACA team. Everyone at ACA is of equal importance. The work of the person loading baggage on the ramp is of equal worth to the work of the captain in the cockpit. The clerical work of processing invoices is as important as the work of a station supervisor. We have no special groups. There are no unimportant positions. Every job is vital to the continued success of ACA, because working together, there is nothing we cannot do.

Wisconsin subsidiary, another feeder line that it had acquired one year earlier. There were also discussions between United and its unions over the possibility of United buying ACA.

The next year was a particularly difficult one for the carrier. On January 7, one of its planes crashed in Ohio, killing five people. A particularly nasty winter caused ACA to cancel 18 percent of its flights in the first seven weeks of 1994. The company spent the next few months coping with the effect of the winter on revenues and the strain of growing so quickly the previous year. It made some layoffs and simplified its fleet by returning its 12 Embraer Brasilia turboprops to Mesa Airlines in exchange for a dozen British Aerospace (BAe) Jetstream 31 aircraft. BAe also provided a $20 million capital infusion. The new hubs at Orlando and Newark, where ACA faced a fare war with the short-lived Continental Lite, were all but abandoned. Nevertheless, ACA posted a $25 million loss for the year, though a turnaround was well in evidence by mid-1995.

First Jets in 1997

By 1996, ACA was operating 52 planes. The airline's first jets began to arrive in 1997, soon after ACA placed an order for a dozen of Bombardier's Canadair Regional Jet (CRJ). United lagged behind its competitors in having its regional partners switch to regional jets. ACA's first CRJ arrived before United and its pilots' union had formally approved it for the United Express program, and so was delivered in ACA's own blue and white livery.

The new jets powered rapid expansion. ACA had 2,000 employees in 1998; staff had quadrupled in just six years. The company celebrated the opening of its new $10 million maintenance hangar at Washington-Dulles (IAD), the hub of its route network. A regional concourse opened at IAD the next year.

ACA had established a second regional jet hub at United's own home base of Chicago O'Hare (ORD), where an entire concourse was eventually dedicated just to ACA's United Express operations. Another major construction project was the company's new headquarters in Dulles, Virginia. ACA earned $30.4 million on revenue of $289.9 million in 1998.

Connecting with Delta in 2000

Yet another exciting development was announced in October 1999: the beginning of ACA's partnership with Delta. ACA Delta Connection was launched using small Fairchild-Dornier 328JET aircraft rather than the Canadair jets.

Skeen succeeded Ed Ackers as chairman upon his retirement in 2000 as Tom Moore became president. The Delta operations were known as Atlantic Coast Jet during their first year. The first flights originated at New York LaGuardia before routes from Boston and Cincinnati were added.

There was still more expansion on the United Express side. In November 2000, ACA announced it was tripling these operations and confirmed a conditional order for 27 Canadair regional jets worth $594 million. Just a couple of months later, ACA ordered 145 Fairchild Dornier 328JETs for its Delta Connection operations, a commitment worth $1.75 billion. However, ACA cancelled this order in February 2002 after Fairchild went insolvent and gave Bombardier another $870 million worth of business.

In March 2001, United offered to sell ACA Allegheny, Piedmont, and PSA as part of its acquisition of US Airways. The US Airways buy was scuttled by antitrust regulators, but ACA still reached an arrangement to operate these regionals.

A new ten-year contract signed with United in 2001 gave ACA a fixed fee for every United Express flight it operated, rather than ACA having to share revenue with United. As a result, ACA was much less affected by the effects of 9/11 than was United. ACA's net income was $34 million for 2001, and the company was expanding even as United scaled back its own operations by a fifth.

United Airlines accounted for 85 percent of ACA's revenues; UAL's bankruptcy had the potential to greatly affect ACA's fortunes. ACA and Air Wisconsin, both of which had many new planes on order, asked the bankruptcy court to force United to decide on renewing their contracts by February 28, 2003, but this request was denied. UAL's recovery depended on regional jets, and ACA's financial health was dependent on UAL staying in business. ACA could lose a great deal of business were UAL's planes to be grounded by a strike or financial reasons.

ACA's 100th regional jet was delivered in 2002 as the carrier grew to a total fleet of 130 planes. Employment had more than doubled, to 4,800, in four years, as ACA carried 22,000 people a day on 600 daily flights to 68 destinations. The company expected to have an all-jet fleet of 154 aircraft by 2004.

ACA posted a profit of $34.3 million on revenues of $583 million in 2001. These figures rose to $39.3 million and $760.5 million in 2002. Although ACA weathered the post-9/11

Key Dates:

1989: WestAir hastily forms an Atlantic Coast division to handle United Express traffic.
1991: WestAir sells off its Atlantic Coast division.
1993: ACA goes public on NASDAQ exchange.
1997: ACA's first jets are delivered.
1998: The company opens a maintenance hangar at Washington-Dulles.
2000: ACA Delta Connection lifts off.

industry turmoil well, concern over the war in Iraq in early 2003 caused Wall Street to abandon ACAI along with all the other airline stocks, observed the *Washington Post*. Concern over UAL's future was another factor.

Principal Operating Units

ACA/Delta Connection; ACA/United Express.

Principal Competitors

AirTran Holdings, Inc.; American Eagle; Comair, Inc.; US Airways Group, Inc.

Further Reading

"Atlantic Coast Airlines," *Investors Chronicle*, May 3, 2002.
Bary, Andrew, "Signs of Turbulence," *Barron's*, April 8, 2002, p. 17.
Behr, Peter, "Atlantic Coast Airlines to Fly Jets from Dulles," *Washington Post*, November 19, 1997, p. C10.
——, "Atlantic Coast to Build Facility at Dulles," *Washington Post*, April 18, 1997, p. G1.
Craver, Richard, "US Airways-United Merger May Bring Winston-Salem, N.C.-Based Airline New Owner," *High Point Enterprise* (North Carolina), March 5, 2001.
De Lollis, Barbara, "United Partner Atlantic Coast Soars," *USA Today*, February 18, 2002, p. B5.
Field, David, "Atlantic Coast Airlines Takes Over Flights Shed by United at Dulles," *Washington Times*, October 21, 1992, p. C3.
——, " 'Feeders' Continue to Expand at Dulles," *Washington Times*, January 11, 1993, p. B4.
——, "Troubled Atlantic Coast Sees Savings in Smaller Planes," *Washington Times*, July 19, 1994, p. B7.
Hassler, David, "Bombardier Jet Buyer May Stall on Deliveries: Atlantic Coast Says Partner United's Woes Must Be Solved," *National Post* (Toronto), March 4, 2003, p. FP8.
Hinden, Stan, "Regional Airline Ready to Land Its Stock," *Washington Post*, July 12, 1993, p. F29.
Knight, Jerry, "Small Airline Has Chance to Soar Again," *Washington Post*, February 10, 2003, p. E1.
Levere, Jane L., "Delta and US Airways Will Soon Face Competition in the New York-Washington Air Shuttle Market," *New York Times*, July 16, 1997, p. D5.
Merrion, Paul, "Small Jet Firms Go on Rough UAL Ride," *Crain's Chicago Business*, February 17, 2003, p. 3.
Phillips, Don, "Airline Plans Second Hub at O'Hare," *Washington Post*, December 18, 1997, p. E1.
Sauder, Rick, "Airline to Expand Commuter Service," *Richmond Times-Dispatch*, March 31, 1993, Bus. Sec.
Silcoff, Sean, "Bombardier Wins $870M Order: Closer Look at Fairchild," *National Post* (Toronto), June 5, 2002, p. FP4.
——, "U.S. Airline to Get EDC Cash to Buy Bombardier Planes," *National Post* (Toronto), October 24, 2002, p. FP5.
Stoughton, Stephanie, "Dulles Carrier Taking Off, But Not on Ego Trip," *Washington Post*, January 1, 1998, p. V5.
Swoboda, Frank, "Atlantic Coast May Use Own Name on Jets," *Washington Post*, June 4, 1997, p. C13.
Swoboda, Frank, and Sarah Schafer, "From Dulles: A New High-Tech Link," *Washington Post*, November 1, 1999.
Tomesco, Frédéric, "Bombardier Bags Order for 27 Jets: Atlantic Move Follows Its Deal with UAL," *Gazette* (Montreal), November 30, 2000, p. E3.
Weintraub, Richard M., "Atlantic Coast Airlines Strains Under the Weather," *Washington Post*, February 22, 1994, p. E1.
——, "Local Airline Reports Wider Quarterly Loss," *Washington Post*, April 27, 1994, p. F2.
——, "Va. Airline Takes Steps to Cut Costs," *Washington Post*, July 19, 1994, p. C1.

—Frederick C. Ingram

Autoroutes du Sud de la France SA

100 avenue de Suffren
75015 Paris Cedex 15
France
Telephone: (+33) 1-47-53-37-00
Fax: (+33) 1-47-53-39-36
Web site: http://www.asf.fr

Public Company
Incorporated: 1957 as Autoroutes de la Vallée du Rhône
Employees: 8,277
Sales: EUR 2.10 billion ($2.05 billion)(2002)
Stock Exchanges: Euronext Paris
Ticker Symbol: ASF
NAIC: 237310 Highway, Street, and Bridge Construction

Autoroutes du Sud de la France SA (ASF) is that country's largest operator of toll roads. The nearly 2,800 kilometers of roadway under ASF's control also make it the second-largest toll road operator in Europe, behind Italy's Autostrade, and number three worldwide. The company, together with primary subsidiary Escota, holds long-term concessions for its roadways, which were also constructed under its auspices, extending through to 2032. Concessions for an additional 300 kilometers of French controlled-access highway, expected to be completed during the first decade of the 21st century, give the company a solid base for revenue growth. At the same time, ASF, which, together with subsidiary Escota, traditionally has operated in France's southern and western regions, has begun to compete for concessions elsewhere, both within France and internationally. ASF has also signaled its interest in expanding into a the multi-modal market, particularly in the development of a railway link. Nearly all of ASF's revenues, which topped EUR 2.1 billion in 2002, come from toll collections; fiber optic networking provisions and other telecom fees, such as antenna placements, as well fees from service area operators, contributed less than 2 percent to the company's revenues. ASF went public on the Euronext Paris exchange in 2002 in one of the year's largest and most successful European IPOs. The company remains held at some 50 percent by the French govern-

ment. Chairman Bernard Val and CEO Jacques Tavernier have successfully overseen ASF's transition from government entity to privately operated company.

Building France's Freeways in the 1950s

The development of Europe's freeway system began in the early 1900s as automobiles began to achieve higher speeds and became more widespread. Among the earliest high-speed roadways was a ten-kilometer stretch built in Berlin, begun in 1909 but not completed until 1921. However, that roadway's use was limited to racing and road-testing vehicles. Italy became the site of the next development in freeway construction techniques, that of elevated crossings, devised by Strade et Cave founder and Mussolini supporter Piero Puricelli. Puricelli's company completed what many consider as the first true freeway in 1924, opening an 85-kilometer ''autostrada'' between Milan and Varese. The autostrada also marked another innovation: that of the toll road.

France, which had long boasted a national network of roads built under the auspices of Napoleon, began preparations for the development of its own freeway network in the late 1920s, focusing at first on the region around Paris. In 1935, the creation of a national freeway system granted official government approval. In that year, construction began on the country's first autoroute, as the French freeway system was to be called, along a 20-kilometer route between the Paris Saint-Cloud tunnel and the town of Orgeval.

The start of World War II and the subsequent German occupation of France, however, put a temporary end to the country's freeway development. Nonetheless, the Saint Cloud-Orgeval roadway was put in service by the occupying forces. After the completion of repairs, that roadway was officially opened for civil traffic in 1946, marking the start of the first true French autoroute.

France was long to play catch up with its European neighbors in the development of a national freeway system. Until the mid-1950s, the French government had attempted to finance autoroute construction itself. In 1955, however, the government abandoned that model and instead converted its planned freeway system, at least temporarily, into a toll road network. By then, France's autoroute system represented just 77 kilometers, compared to more than 3,000 kilometers in Germany. As part of its new legislation, the French government decided to create a number of semi-public companies that would take over the construction and operation of the country's toll-based autoroute system.

The first of the new generation of autoroute companies began operations in 1956, when the Société de l'Autoroute d'Estérel Côte d'Azur, or Escota, was granted the concession to build the country's A8 roadway between Aix and Nice. The following year, however, saw the creation of a new company, Société d'Autoroutes de la Vallée du Rhône, destined to become the country's largest autoroute operator under the name of Autoroutes du Sud de la France. Also in 1957, the various European countries met to define common technical characteristics for the extended European freeway network.

The creation of semi-public companies and the use of tolls permitted France to more than double its freeway network by 1960. In that year, the French government imposed the toll-road system on a permanent basis. This action helped stimulate autoroute construction, and by the mid-1960s the country counted more than seven semi-public toll-road companies, which had put more than 650 kilometers of roadway into service. That number was to top 1,500 kilometers by the end of the decade.

Nevertheless, a movement for a reform of legislation governing the French autoroute system had been building through the 1960s. This movement gained significant impetus in 1970 when a snowstorm stranded some 6,000 vehicles on the A7 autoroute. By the beginning of the following year, reforms of the system had gotten underway. A chief feature of the new reforms was a liberalization of the market, enabling the formerly government run business to operate as more or less private companies. At the same time, the law allowed a number of new, non-government-owned business to enter the sector, including Cofiroute, which won concessions in the country's central western region, and ACOBA, which operated along the Basque coast. The reforms also led many of the existing roadway operators to change names, including the SAVR, which adopted the new name of Autoroutes du Sud de la France (ASF) in 1973.

ASF continued to build out its network—its concessions later placed as the largest of the French autoroute groups—while adapting new features and services to its roadway already in service. In 1975, ASF inaugurated its first automated entry lanes. The following year, the company debuted its first "village" rest area, the Village Catalan along the A9 roadway. ASF's rest areas, which offered typical rest stop amenities, often became destinations in and of themselves, helping to make the autoroute system even more attractive to travelers who

more and more turned from the country's toll-free national road system to the higher speed autoroute network.

In 1981, ASF completed its 1,000th kilometer of roadway, along the A62 autoroute, representing nearly one-fifth of the total French autoroute system then in service. Two years later, the company's rest area operations boasted the first "multimodal" rest area, in Port Lauragais, open not only to autoroute travelers but also to marine traffic along the Canal du Midi.

World-leading Public Toll-road Group in the 21st Century

An attempt to do away with tolls on France's autoroute network, spearheaded by the socialist government that came to power in 1980, was defeated in the face of the enormous financial effort needed to construct and maintain the country's roadway system. Meanwhile, a decade of economic turmoil, sparked by the Oil Embargo of the early 1970s, had brought most of the privately run autoroute companies to bankruptcy. Most of these were converted into government-owned entities—with Cofiroute remaining the sole privately held survivor—by the end of the 1980s. As a result, ASF itself gained in scope, taking over the A63 roadway developed by ACOBA, in 1991.

New reform in 1994 brought about a reformation of the French autoroute system as the government regrouped its autoroute business around three major regional poles, with ASF becoming responsible for most of the southern part of the country. As a result of the reorganization, Escota, which by then had nearly 550 kilometers of roadway completed, was placed under ASF's control.

ASF continued to add new services to its autoroute network, including automatic lanes for trucks in 1990, then began testing an electronic toll collection system in Toulouse in 1993. The company also continued to expand its network, building its 2000th kilometer in 2000. By then, ASF was the clear leader in the French autoroute system, with concessions totaling 34 percent of the entire national autoroute network and a 37 percent share of total autoroute revenues. Where the other government-held autoroute operators struggled against losses, ASF remained highly profitable.

The 21st century, however, was to mark the beginning of a new era for ASF. Under pressure from the European Union, the French government agreed to enact a number of changes in 2001, including the introduction of value-added taxes, a move which slashed more than EUR 110 million from ASF's profits. The French government also agreed to open up bidding for new highway concessions to the wider European pool, which in turn led the way to the creation of a number of new, privately held companies that began to compete for a share of the French roadway pool.

ASF itself moved to take advantage of the new opportunities available to it in the European Union, tendering bids for roadway concessions in Ireland and Greece in 2001. Meanwhile, further reforms were being put into place in the French autoroute sector, including the end of the financial system that had allowed the autoroute companies to finance construction of new roadway sections through the toll receipts gained on their existing network.

Key Dates:

1935: Construction begins on the first French autoroute between Paris Saint-Cloud and Orgeval.

1946: Saint-Cloud Orgeval autoroute is opened to civilian traffic.

1955: The French government adopts legislation placing the development, maintenance, and operation of the country's autoroute network under the control of quasi-governmental companies.

1956: Escota becomes the first of the new autoroute companies, beginning construction of the Nice-Aix autoroute.

1957: Autoroutes de la Vallée du Rhône (SAVR) begins operations in southwestern France.

1973: SAVR changes its name to Autoroutes du Sud de la France (ASF).

1975: ASF introduces its first automated toll entry points.

1981: ASF completes 1,000 kilometers of autoroute.

1993: ASF begins testing automated payment systems in Toulouse.

1994: Under reorganization plan, ASF becomes the parent company to Escota, which continues to operate independently.

2000: ASF completes 2,000 kilometers of autoroute.

2002: The French government lists 49 percent of ASF on the Euronext Paris stock exchange, marking the one of the largest European IPOs of the year.

As a consequence, the French government announced its intention to privatize ASF, its largest and most profitable autoroute company, in 2002. While the economic downturn, and especially the depressed stock market, forced the government to cancel a number of other privatization projects, the move to list ASF proved more successful. Indeed, the ASF listing promised to be one of the largest European IPOs that year, and, given the company's steady, toll-based income, one of the most sought after.

The ASF IPO went ahead in March 2002, with shares selling at EUR 25 per share, nearly reaching the top of its proposed range, and pricing at a multiple of 24 times its estimated 2002 earnings. With 50 percent of the company up for sale, the listing was oversubscribed by some 18 times, driving up the share price by the end of its first day of trading. In all, the listing raised nearly EUR 2 billion for the French government.

By April 2002, ASF found itself sought after not only by investors but also by a joint-venture formed between French construction giants Vinci and Eiffage. Having gained a stake of more than 15 percent in ASF, both Vinci and Eiffage acknowledged their interest in expanding their holding in the autoroute operator. The French government was expected to sell off still more of its ASF shares in the near future. A link-up with Vinci appeared particularly attractive, given Vinci's 66 percent share of Cofiroute, and its roadway holdings elsewhere in the world, which included an 83 percent share of the Chile's Chillian-Collipuli highway and minor shares in roadways in Canada and Thailand.

By the end of 2002, ASF appeared to confirm its investors hopes as its revenues topped EUR 2.1 billion, with net profits of more than EUR 230 million. The near future appeared to hold bright prospects for the company: it still held concessions on more than 300 kilometers of highway, which were expected to be completed by the end of the 2000s, more or less guaranteeing continued revenue growth. At the same time, the company was expected to begin cost-cutting initiatives to continue to drive up profits. Meanwhile, ASF had begun to compete for new autoroute concessions elsewhere in France, a move that was expected to help the company expand beyond its core southern and western regional focus. Lastly, the opening of the European roadway network to international competition promised still more growth opportunities for ASF. As one of the primary builders of France's nearly 10,000-kilometer autoroute system, generally considered one of the world's most advanced roadway networks, ASF looked forward to a promising future.

Principal Subsidiaries

Escota SA.

Principal Competitors

Autostrade - Concessioni e Costruzioni Autostrade S.p.A; Autopistas Concesionaria Española, S.A.; Société des Autoroutes du Nord et de l'Est de la France; Compagnie Financière et Industrielle des Autoroutes S.A; Société des Autoroutes Esterel Côte d'Azur Provence Alpes S.A.; Société des Autoroutes Rhône-Alpes S.A.; Autoroutes et Tunnel du Mont Blanc; Ste Autoroutes Esterel Côte d'Azur Provence Alpes; Société des Autoroutes; Société de Construction des Autoroutes du Sud et de l'Ouest Sarl; Cofiroute SA.

Further Reading

Chaperon, Isabelle, "France Opts for Floatation of Road Group," *Financial Times*, January 28, 2002, p. 24.

"Driving Through the Storm: Best Global Equity Issue—Autoroutes du Sud de la France," *Euroweek*, January 24, 2003, p. 24.

Graham, Robert, and Mallet, Victor, "Motorways Sell-off Breaks New Ground," *Financial Times*, October 18, 2001, p. 14.

Lanchner, David, "All Roads Lead to ASF," *Institutional Investor International Edition*, January 2003, p. 47.

Minder, Raphael, "French Set for ASF Toll Road Windfall," *Financial Times*, March 15, 2002, p. 28.

Paisner, Guy, "Vinci Courts Government Over ASF," *Financial News*, June 7, 2002.

Tieman, Ross, "Scramble as France Floats Its Toll Roads," *Evening Standard*, March 28, 2002, p. 82.

—M. L. Cohen

Bain & Company

2 Copley Place
Boston, Massachusetts 02116
U.S.A.
Telephone: (617) 572-2000
Fax: (617) 572-2427
Web site: http://www.bain.com

Private Company
Incorporated: 1985
Employees: 2,800
Sales: $825 million (2001 est.)
NAIC: 541611 Administrative Management and General
Management Consulting Services

Boston-based Bain & Company is one of the world's leading corporate consulting companies, the pioneer in the concept that consultants should help implement strategies not just make recommendations. The Bain approach is often called relationship consulting, especially known for forging strong bonds with chief executive officers. For most of its history, the company has opted to take on a single client in a particular industry as a way of more fully aligning itself with the client's goals. More recently, Bain has begun accepting equity as part of its payment in order to again tie its own success to achieving tangible results for its clients. The partnership operates 27 offices around the world, employing some 2,800 people. Although Bain is primarily known for its work with Fortune 500 clients, it also consults with startups through its bainlab operation. More recently the firm has joined forces with several other companies to form BainNet in order to provide technology-based strategies. In addition, Bain has established a non-profit company, The Bridge Group, to assist other non-profits.

William Bain Turns to Consulting in 1960s

The founder of Bain & Company, William W. Bain, Jr., was born in Johnson City, Tennessee, the son of a food wholesaler. After earning a history degree in 1959 from Vanderbilt University, he went on to graduate school but soon took a position at a steel-fabricating company, where he not only helped to work up engineering studies but also made sales calls. Bain then returned

to Vanderbilt to become director of development, raising funds from alumni at a salary of $19,000 a year. When Vanderbilt began to think about establishing a business school, he asked for advice from alumnus Bruce Henderson, founder of the Boston Consulting Group, BCG. Henderson was so impressed with Bain, despite his lack of basic business knowledge, that he offered him a job with BCG and only a few weeks later, in 1967, Bain relocated to Massachusetts. He quickly rose through the ranks of BCG, becoming known for his hard work, attention to detail, and physically fit appearance. Within two years, he commanded a six-figure salary and rose to the position of vice-president, overseeing one of four BCG divisions, which began to generate a significant share of the firm's revenues. There was talk in the air that Bain was Henderson's likely heir apparent. His mentor, however, was not as ready to retire as Bain was eager to succeed him. In 1972, Bain unsuccessfully attempted to pressure Henderson into stepping down. Moreover, Bain was increasingly frustrated with the BCG's project-oriented approach, which emphasized issuing reports over achieving results. His idea was to assemble a thorough overview of a company and its competition then develop and implement a strategy to improve profitability of the entire business.

In 1973, Bain informed Henderson that he and colleague Patrick Graham were leaving to launch their own business, a software company. This announcement came the day before Henderson was scheduled to fly to Spain for a meeting. While dining that first night in Madrid, according to a 1987 *Fortune* profile, he was tracked down ''with an urgent call from his secretary. It seems the 'software company' was setting out to solicit BCG clients, although this is a point Bain disputes. Henderson caught the next flight back and frantically began rousting his consultants out of bed to get his firm's clients before Bain did. Recalls Henderson: 'It was war.' By the time the guns stopped firing, several week later, Bain and Graham had made off with seven of BCG's consultants and two of its biggest clients, Black & Decker and Texas Instruments.''

At first, Bain & Company set up shop in Bill Bain's Beacon Hill apartment, sharing a single telephone line, but soon established new offices in Boston as the business quickly proved successful in its novel approach to consulting: working directly with CEO's, taking on just one client in a particular industry,

---

Company Perspectives:

Bain's Business is making companies more valuable. We convert strategy and action into economic performance.

---

and getting deeply immersed in a company in order to develop and implement its strategies. It also developed a mystique, becoming known as "the KGB of consulting," its partners opting not to carry business cards and referring to clients by code names. Because Bain worked intensively with a small roster of clients, partners felt no need to market their services (almost taking pride in the fact), relying instead on referrals from the boardrooms of the corporate world. In some cases, the firm landed new clients by offering several weeks of work at no cost until proving the worth of their services. Offering top salaries, the company recruited top business school graduates, generally from Harvard or Stanford, who shared similar traits to Bill Bain: trim and fastidious about their appearance, bright and calculating, and utterly devoted to destroying the competition of their clients. These young associates became known as "Bainies," a reference to the Moonie cult and a comment on their zealousness and loyalty to Bill Bain.

Early 1990s See Discontent With Partnership Deed

In 1979, Bain opened a London office to serve European customers as the firm grew at a rapid pace, with revenues increasing at a rate of 40 to 50 percent a year. By the early 1980s, however, cracks began to appear. Although a partnership, the company was very much controlled by Bill Bain. According to *The New York Times,* one former partner called the partnership deed "not a bill of rights, but the rights of Bill." According to *Fortune,* "the partners were partners by courtesy only. They did not have rights to a specific percentage of the firm's earnings; rather, Bain parceled out profits at the end of the year as he saw fit. Partners could not easily argue with the split because most of them were never told what the firm earned. The partnership agreement did, however, contain a noncompete clause." In the early 1980s, the company began to suffer significant turnover in personnel. The often abrasive and invasive style of some Bain consultants also resulted in what one associate called "transplant-reject syndrome" and led to the loss of some clients, such as Texas Instruments, Black & Decker, and Monsanto. Nevertheless, Bain continued to grow and between 1980 and 1986 tripled its staff to meet the demanded for its services.

Despite criticism, Bain achieved some notable successes in the early 1980s. When National Steel hired Bain in 1981, it was the highest-cost steel producer, but by 1984, after applying Bain's recommendations that it simultaneously downsize and modernize, it became the lowest-cost producer, the first in the industry to adopt new continuous-casting technologies. Another success was Chrysler Corporation, which hired Bain in 1983 after a free, four-month study of an electrical wiring system. The firm went on to help Chrysler cut the price of the Omni/Horizon by $1,400 by packaging options in a way that reduced manufacturing configurations while retaining 99 percent of the options that customers wanted. Although these successes were tangible, some questioned how much value Bain, or any con-

sulting firm, actually provided its customers. All too often, according to conventional wisdom, consultants were brought in to write up a CEO's plan and be available to take the blame should it fail. To help aid its case that Bain added true value, the firm in 1983 created the "Bain Index" to measure the improved performance of clients' stocks against the Dow Jones industrial average. The goal of the firm was to increase values for its clients at a rate ten times its fees.

Rather than just rely on fees to provide growth, Bain began to look for direct investment in companies, which ultimately led to the acceptance of equity as part of its compensation, not only to more closely align its interest with the clients but also to reap the rewards of its successful strategies. In 1983, the firm acquired Salt Lake City-based Key Air Lines Inc., a local commuter carrier, and assigned several staff members to manage it. In 1984, it created Bain Capital, a limited partnership headed by W. Mitt Romney, son of politician George Romney, which invested in start-up companies and buyouts that could be readily improved. According to *The New York Times,* Bain Capital "has managed to steer clear of conflicts of interest by having Bain & Company retain veto power over investments. But it is not entirely a neutral operation." Nonetheless, Bain maintained that Bain Capital was not a sister company or a division but rather a completely separate company that simply shared a similar approach to producing results. The firm was, however, housed in the same building as Bain & Company and its employees shared the same cafeteria.

Bain Capital provided an investment opportunity for Bain partners who were becoming increasing disenchanted with the partnership agreement. In 1985, to help redress their longstanding grievances, Bain was incorporated, and over the course of the next two years Bill Bain and seven senior executives sold off 30 percent of their equity to two Employee Stock Ownership Plans (ESOP) for $200 million, the payout funded by debt that, because of the high valuation of the deals, saddled the firm with burdensome annual interest payments to the tune of $25 million. The price had been based on Bain's ability to maintain its strong growth, but the company soon endured a number of setbacks that prevented it from realizing those expectations. In 1987, the firm endured a public relations nightmare when it became entangled in a scandal involving one of its clients, Guinness plc, which had been one of Bain's notable success stories. The relationship began in 1981, at a time when Guinness shares were trading at penny stock levels after a decade of diversification efforts that took the company far from its core business. After selling off some 150 companies, Guinness' head, Ernest Saunders, then took Bain's advice and looked to move into the hard liquor market by acquiring two scot whiskey producers: Arthur Bell & Sons and Distillers Inc. By the end of fiscal 1986, Guinness and Bain were flying high, with the client posting profits of nearly $400 million, a six-fold increase since contracting Bain, while at the same time the company's stock reached a high of $5.75 per share. In December 1986, however, Britain's Department of Trade and Industry began to investigate the $3.8 billion stock acquisition of Distillers, masterminded by a "war cabinet" that included a Bain associate named Olivier Roux, who had been "lent" to Saunders and became one of his top aides. At issue were acts taken by Guinness to illegally inflate the price of its stock to fend off a competing offer from Argyll Group, including the charge that Guinness bought its own stock during the offering period and indemnified other companies against loss if they

Key Dates:
1973: Bain & Company is formed.
1979: A London office is opened.
1984: Bain Capital is formed.
1985: Bain is incorporated and an employee stock ownership plan is launched.
1991: Bill Bain relinquishes control.
1993: Orit Gadiesh is named chairman.
1999: Bainlab is established.
2000: The Bridge Group is incorporated.

purchased stock on behalf of Guinness. In the end, Saunders went to jail for his part in the scheme, and although Bain escaped unscathed legally, the revelation of the company's conduct in the affair led several top clients to drop the firm or to at least cut back on their contracts. Hurt further by a sluggish economy, in addition to its high debt service, Bain was forced to cut its staff by 10 percent in 1988. According to *Forbes,* there was now considerable friction between Bain professionals: ''Infighting became intense and the split between the graybeards and the young Turks grew as the younger partners worried their bonuses would get squeezed.'' To help revitalize the company's fortunes and make up for the defection of key rainmakers, Bain hired Peter Dawkins, a former U.S. Army general and Heisman Trophy winner for his college football exploits. Dawkins may have had impressive contacts in the corporate world, but he lacked experience in consulting and proved ill suited as the head of North American operations. Even more turmoil developed within the ranks of Bain, and many talented people opted to leave the company. In the fall of 1990, Bill Bain attempted to sell the company but found no buyer. Another 200 consultants were terminated, resulting in even more discontent from the younger partners. To bring peace to the situation, Mitt Romney was brought in to replace Bill Bain as the head the company. Moreover, the founding partners returned about $100 million to the firm by dissolving Bain Holdings, an investment fund that was partially funded by the ESOP. A recapitalization plan was also instituted by which the founding partners turned back the 70 percent stake in the company they held, so that the firm's 75 younger partners now owned 60 percent of the business and the ESOP the remaining 40 percent. Other than some stock in the ESOP, Bill Bain no longer owned any of the company that continued to bear his name.

New Leadership in 1993

Although Bain had ironed out its internal difficulties, it now faced the daunting task of convincing potential clients to contract its services when it had so clearly mismanaged its own affairs. A major step in the revitalization of Bain's fortunes came in 1993 when one of the younger partners, Orit Gadiesh, was named the new chairman, becoming the first female head of a major consulting firm. She had been a key player in preventing senior partners from abandoning the firm. Born in Israel, she earned a degree in psychology from Hebrew University, then spent two years in the Israeli army, serving in military intelli-

gence, before earning a degree from the Harvard Business School, where she graduated in the top 5 percent of her class despite the handicap of simultaneously mastering English. When Romney left to pursue politics, Gadiesh continued the revitalization of Bain that he had initiated. Financially, the company regained lost ground, and it loosened its guidelines so that it could work for more than one company in a particular industry, thereby making the firm less dependent on a limited roster of clients. Bain also began to expand the number of offices it maintained around the world. Finally, in the summer of 2000, Bain opened an office in New York City in an effort to accommodate talented people who wanted to work for the firm but preferred to live in New York.

To meet a changing business environment and to keep pace with rival consulting firms that were tending towards specialization, Bain began to adjust the services it offered in the late 1990s and early years of the new century. It looked to the Internet in 1999, establishing bainlab to serve as an incubator to help entrepreneurs with Internet-based business plans. Later, bainlab began to work with venture capital firms to help them improve the value of the Internet and technology companies in their portfolios. One of bainlab's first initiatives was Ideaforest.com, an online seller of arts and crafts products and kits. Also in 2000, Bain launched BainNet in conjunction with several high-tech companies to help clients implement technology-driven strategies. In that same year, Bain founded The Bridge Group to aid non-profit corporations, as well as to provide a place where Bain associates could take time out, up to six months, to do volunteer work. As the economy began to struggle in the early years of the new century, Bain, like other management consultant firms, attempted to change its approach, offering such specific services as managing supply chains and engendering the loyalty effect in customers. Nevertheless, Bain remained dedicated to the generalist approach to strategy consulting.

Principal Divisions

Bainlab; BainNet.

Principal Competitors

Booz Allen Hamilton Inc.; The Boston Consulting Group; McKinsey & Company; BearingPoint Inc.

Further Reading

Gallese, Liz Roman, ''Counselor to the King,'' *New York Times Magazine,* September 24, 1989.

Hammonds, Keith H., ''Can Bain Consultants Get Bain & Co. Out of This Jam?,'' *Business Week,* February 11, 1991, p. 52.

Hemp, Paul, ''Did Greed Destroy Bain & Co.?,'' *Boston Globe,* February 26, 1991.

Koselka, Rita, ''Physician Heal Thyself,'' *Forbes,* February 18, 1991, p. 67.

Perry, Nancy J., ''A Consulting Firm Too Hot to Handle?,'' *Fortune,* April 27, 1987, p. 91.

Rifkin, Glenn, ''Don't Ever Judge This Consultant by Her Cover,'' *New York Times,* May 1, 1994, p. 35.

—Ed Dinger

Bandai Co., Ltd.

2-5-4 Komagata, Taito-ku,
Tokyo 111-8081
Japan
Telephone: (+81) 3-3847-5005
Fax: (+81) 3-3847-5067
Web site: http://www.bandai.co.jp

Public Company
Incorporated: 1950
Employees: 895
Sales: ¥227.93 billion ($1.72 billion) (2002)
Stock Exchanges: Tokyo
Ticker Symbol: BNDCY
NAIC: 339932 Game, Toy, and Children's Vehicle
    Manufacturing

Bandai Co., Ltd. is the third-largest toy manufacturer in the world. The company is best known for products derived from popular television and comic book characters such as Power Rangers, Gundam, and Ultraman. These range from action figures and their accessories to video game software, clothing, and candy. The firm has also had success with faddish toys like the ''digital pets'' Tamagotchi and Digimon and other ventures that include selling toys in vending machines and providing digital content online and through cellphones. Other Bandai units make animated television programs and movies, design and manufacture amusement machines and amusement centers, make stationery, and sell, lease, and manage real estate properties. Based in Japan, where it is the number one toymaker, Bandai distributes its products worldwide.

Early Years

Bandai's roots date to post-World War II Japan, where Naoharu Yamashina, a war veteran who had lost an eye in combat, was struggling to make a living. The son of a rice retailer, Yamashina had studied business in high school, and after the war he began working for a textile wholesaler in Kanazawa run by his wife's brother. Business was slow, and when a neighbor told

him of the potential for success in toy sales, Yamashina convinced his employer to send him to Tokyo to try this new field. Putting in long hours there with his wife, he gradually built up a small toy distribution business.

In 1950, Yamashina took control of the toy distributorship and renamed it Bandai, which was derived from the Chinese phrase for ''things that are eternal.'' At this time the firm was mainly selling celluloid and metallic toys, along with rubber swimming rings.

Deciding to add an original product to its lineup, in September of 1950 Bandai introduced the Rhythm Ball, a beach ball with a bell inside. The Rhythm Ball initially suffered from a high rate of defects, but its quality was improved and the company soon added other products such as the metal B-26 Night Plane. In March 1951, Bandai began to export inexpensive toys like metal cars and planes to the United States and other foreign markets. The growing company built a new shipping and warehousing facility in the spring of 1953, and in the summer added research and development, product inspection, and transportation departments.

In early 1955, Bandai established a manufacturing facility, the Waraku Works, and during the summer began construction of a new Tokyo headquarters and introduced a new ''BC'' logo. The fall of 1955 saw the firm offer its first product guarantee for the Toyopet Crown model car. Bandai highlighted this in television commercials that began airing in 1958, which used the phrase, ''The Red Box means a BC-guaranteed toy.'' The following year a Cars of the World model line was launched, and the company's logo was redesigned to stress its emphasis on quality. In the early 1960s, Bandai began to establish direct overseas sales and opened an office in New York.

Character-Based Toys Debut in 1963

In 1963, Bandai introduced its first toy based on a children's television character, which was called Astroboy. The firm would go on to refine a strategy of helping to fund a new program's development and then sponsoring its episodes as they were broadcast, running ads for derivative products that might include action figures, toy vehicles, and costumes. Begin-

Company Perspectives:

The Bandai Group aspires to grow and develop as a company, fulfilling dreams and providing happiness to people around the world while making a positive contribution to society. The main tenets of our management philosophy are as follows. 1. Shareholder satisfaction: As well as honoring the trust of our shareholders by passing on profits and disclosing relevant information in a fair and appropriate manner, Bandai strives to continuously improve the company's business performance, aiming to maximize the value of its shares. 2. Customer satisfaction: Bandai is committed to developing and supplying products and services that meet the needs of the times, to enhancing the quality of people's lives, and to making an ongoing contribution to the world's cultural richness. 3. Job satisfaction for employees: Bandai believes that human resources are the key to corporate growth and development, and we respect the professional aspirations and ambitions of our employees. Careful to ensure that the right employee is in the right job, we carry out impartial and rigorous staff assessments, we and do all we can to help employees augment their skills and to maintain staff morale at a high level. 4. Good corporate citizenship: Bandai is fully aware of our role and duties as a corporate member of society and is fully committed to our policy of environmental responsibility. 5. Flexible and pragmatic management: In line with our global perspective, Bandai keeps closely in touch with changing trends and adapts management infrastructure in accordance with the needs of the times.

ning in 1966, Bandai found success with toys based on Ultraman, a giant, caped, metal-skinned hero who fired laser beams and battled monsters. The live-action program and some of its related toys were later imported to the United States, though their impact there was slight. Other Bandai character products were taken from manga, the serial comic books which were hugely popular in Japan. To keep up with a growing demand for its toys, Bandai built the Toy Town Manufacturing Complex, which opened in October of 1965.

In the latter half of the 1960s, the company had hits with Water Motor, Thunderbird, and Naughty Flipper toys, as well as Crazy Foam. In the fall of 1969, Bandai formed a Travel Services unit and acquired an additional factory in Shimizu City, where it would manufacture plastic model toys such as the World Car, Thunderbird 2, and Beetle series.

The firm established Tonka Japan in 1970 in a marketing tie-up with that company, and a year later it added a Models unit and created Popy as a manufacturer of character toys. In 1975, Bandai again changed its logo and trademark designs as part of the launch of a new worldwide marketing effort. Ties were established in October of that year with U.S. model maker Monogram, and in 1976 toy giant Mattel began selling Bandai's Mazinger Z action figures in the United States under the brand name ''Shogun.'' Bandai entered the publishing business in the fall of 1976 with ''The Moving Picture Book,'' later formally establishing Bandai Publishing as a subsidiary.

In November of 1976, the company opened a new factory for Popy toys and in April of 1977 began marketing encapsulated toys in vending machines. During the same year, the firm founded its first overseas manufacturing entity, Bandai (H.K.) Co., Ltd., in Hong Kong. In 1978, Bandai America, Inc. was formed to market the company's toys in the United States, and the following year the B-AI Electronics and B-AI Mibu units were formed.

Makoto Yamashina Takes Control of Firm: 1980

In 1980, Naoharu Yamashina's son took over the job of president from his father, who continued to serve as board chairman. 35-year old Makoto Yamashina, who had a degree in economics from Keio University, had originally worked at a publishing firm, where he wanted to become an editor. When he was instead assigned to sell encyclopedias, he left to join his father at Bandai.

After taking over as president, the aggressive younger Yamashina fired many of his father's senior executives and replaced them with people closer to his own age. This was a shocking move to many in the ''lifetime employment'' culture of Japan, but Makoto Yamashina was interested in operating his company in a different way, modeled more on the U.S. style. He also began making changes to the traditional distribution pattern for toys, dealing directly with large retail chains rather than selling to them through middlemen.

Shortly after he took control, Bandai launched its Gundam toy line, based on a cartoon program about futuristic warriors. The series was popular, and, like Ultraman, Gundam became a long-term moneymaker for the company. In 1981, the firm marketed its first candy products and expanded to Europe, opening French and Italian subsidiaries. These were followed in 1982 by Dutch, British, and Australian branches. The year 1982 also saw Bandai form a department to develop and create original animation and film projects, and a new subsidiary, Emotion, which began to open video shops in Japan. In 1983, the company added an apparel department, founded a division called A.E. Planning (later Bandai Visual), and launched its first original feature film, *Daros,* which came out in the fall.

Gobots Invade America: 1984

In 1984, Bandai had another go at the U.S. market with toys called Gobots, which were Americanized versions of the popular Machine Robo line that had been available in Japan and elsewhere for several years. Gobots were mechanical creatures that could change into vehicles and fight battles against a series of evil counterparts. Despite the best efforts of Bandai and Tonka, their U.S. distributor, the Gobots were ultimately displaced by the rival Transformers, which were marketed by toy giant Hasbro and based on a line made by a Bandai competitor. Transformers were larger, and their associated television program was perceived as better than one featuring the Gobots, while Tonka also had some problems supplying retailers with the toys when they began to sell. It would be almost a decade before Bandai would again make an impact in the U.S. market.

Meanwhile, the company had begun expanding its operations in Asia, opening a second plant in Hong Kong and forming

Key Dates:

1947: Naoharu Yamashina begins distributing toys in Tokyo for his brother-in-law.
1950: Yamashina takes over the business and renames it Bandai.
1950s: Bandai introduces its own toys and begins exporting cheap ones abroad.
1963: The company creates its first toys based on characters from a television program.
1971: The Popy character toy unit is formed.
1980: Yamashina's son Makoto is named president of the firm.
1984: Changeable Gobots toys are launched in United States but are outsold by Transformers.
1993: Power Rangers toys become a huge success in United States and other markets.
1996: Pippin game console and Tamagotchi virtual pets are introduced.
1997: Pippin and a proposed merger with Sega are abandoned; Makoto Yamashina steps down.
1999: A 5 percent stake in the firm is sold to Mattel Co.
2000: Digital content unit is spun off to create Bandai Networks Co., Inc.
2002: Ground is broken for the company's new 15-story headquarters in Tokyo.
2003: Bandai announces its plan to create a holding company structure by 2005.

a Chinese joint venture called the China Fuman Toy Company. Bandai was experiencing a sharp decline in sales at this time, with 1985 revenues of 70.7 billion yen ($495 million) down significantly from the previous year's figure of 84.5 billion yen. The company went public with a listing on the Tokyo Stock Exchange's Second Section in January of 1986, but due to the lingering sales downturn cancelled a secondary offering slated for early 1987. A line of products tied to a hit Japanese cartoon and comic book series, Dragon Ball, was one bright spot for the company, as was the Kitty Stick furry toy.

As part of its plan to move all manufacturing abroad, in March of 1987 the company formed a joint venture in Thailand, Bandai and K.C. Co., with Imperial Thai Toy. Bandai also moved the production and marketing staff of its overseas division from the firm's headquarters in Tokyo to its Hong Kong subsidiary. Other ventures aimed at strengthening the bottom line included branching out into non-toy areas such as health equipment and video sales. In the latter category, Bandai reached an agreement with the Walt Disney Company to market up to 150 of its video titles in Japan for a two year period.

In 1989, the company moved into a new headquarters building in Tokyo, and entered the music business by forming the Emotion label and establishing a relationship with the firm Apollon Music Industry. The year also saw opening of the Ultraman "Shot M78" retail outlet. In 1991, Bandai became 5 percent owner of a $200 million satellite-based video-on-demand startup called Entertainment Made Convenient, formed

a sales subsidiary in Taiwan, and began marketing Chara-Can, its first line of toys packaged with drinks.

Power Rangers Make American Debut: 1993

In 1993, Bandai had its biggest international success to date with toys based on the live-action show Mighty Morphin' Power Rangers (called Jyu Rangah in Japan when originally shown there). The series once again featured superheroes that battled the forces of evil. Unlike many such exports, the live-action Power Rangers show was partially reshot for North American broadcast, adding some non-Asian characters and increasing the ratio of females to males. Soon after its U.S. debut in August 1993 on the Fox network, the program became a surprise hit. Demand for Power Rangers toys quickly outstripped their availability, leading to frantic scenes in stores as parents tried to secure them for their children.

Working to take advantage of this success, in March 1994 Bandai announced it would build factories in Vietnam and Mexico to increase output as well as to lower costs. The firm was hoping to triple production of Power Rangers toys and also add new items to the line, as a Power Rangers motion picture that was in the works was expected to keep interest in the characters high for the foreseeable future. Bandai was now focusing more and more on the international marketplace, as the Japanese toy market was shrinking due to a declining birthrate in that country.

Despite the company's success with Power Rangers, it experienced a sizable earnings loss for the year as the result of a February 1993 decision to end an agreement with Nintendo to market that company's video game equipment and software in Europe. Several of Bandai's regional subsidiaries experienced drastic revenue drops, and the firm was forced to write off billions of yen worth of outdated games and players, leading to a loss of $18.6 million for the fiscal year.

In its home country, Bandai's reach now extended beyond toys to such items as candy, clothing, shampoo, personal organizers, and word processors. An estimated 20 percent of toy-store shelf space in Japan was occupied by the firm's products. Bandai continued to sponsor a number of cartoon programs on television, notably Pretty Soldier Sailor Moon, in which five young girls used the power of the moon to combat aliens, and Crayon Shin-Chan, a program about a mischievous preschooler that was watched by viewers of all ages. The company launched about 60 new characters each year, and when one of them caught on marketing and manufacturing would be ramped up to flood stores with products. Bandai might introduce—and pull from the market—between 8,000 and 10,000 items per year, most of which only appeared in Japan. By this time the firm was manufacturing just a quarter of its own products, down from 45 percent in 1988, with the rest contracted out. Character-based items accounted for more than 80 percent of revenues. Other developments at this time included the purchase of majority ownership in Sunrise, one of Japan's top animation companies, and participation in a joint venture to build a theme park near Tokyo Disneyland.

In November 1994, Bandai took one of its biggest risks to date when it announced it would develop, with computer maker

Apple, a multimedia device that would plug into a television monitor and could be used for game play and Web browsing. To be called "Pippin," the product would retail for approximately $500, considerably less than a computer but more than a typical video-game player. It was to use CD-ROM discs that would also be playable on Apple computers. The machine could be upgraded with purchase of a keyboard and other peripherals for use as a word processor. Bandai subsequently formed three new U.S. subsidiaries to increase its presence in that country, including Bandai Digital Entertainment, Inc., which would market Pippin.

In March 1996, the Pippin Atmark, as it was now called, was introduced in Japan. Its $620 price tag was almost 25 percent higher than originally projected. Reviews were mixed, with a typical response being that the machine was overpriced as a video-game platform but under-equipped as a computer. Both Bandai and Apple had high hopes for Pippin, as the Power Rangers phenomenon was in decline and Apple was increasingly losing its market share to Windows-based equipment. Bandai officials admitted that the firm was not making money on Pippin players but expressed confidence that sales of software and subscriptions to a Bandai-owned online service would make it profitable.

Tamagotchi "Virtual Pet" Takes Japan By Storm: 1996

In November 1996, a toy designed by former housewife Aki Maita was launched which would become the company's next blockbuster hit. This was the Tamagotchi, an electronic egg-shaped device attached to a keychain. A small screen on the front displayed an image of a chicken-like creature, which would have to be "cared for" by manipulating several buttons. If it was not tended to, the creature would die; by pressing a button, another creature could be hatched. If cared for properly, the character could grow and change, "living" for up to several weeks. The toys quickly became popular in Japan, perhaps in part because they annoyed parents, who had to go to great lengths to secure them, after which they were often faced with babysitting the Tamagotchi when the child had other responsibilities.

By February 1997, Bandai was so far behind in filling orders that it issued a public apology, at the same time launching Tamagotchi version 2. Tamagotchis were so difficult to obtain that some Bandai employees reported being threatened with harm by Japanese "Yakuza" gangsters if they would not turn over copies of the toys, which were reportedly selling for as much as ¥50,000 on the black market, 25 times their list price. New variations were soon in development, including Tamapitchi, a pair of cellphones that could send an animated character from one device to another, enabling it to mate and create a third creature.

While all this was taking place, Bandai was also laying plans for an October 1997 merger with video game giant Sega, which would create an entertainment conglomerate on par with the Walt Disney Company. Bandai's employees showed strong opposition to the move, however, and industry analysts were not enthusiastic. In late May, Makoto Yamashina abruptly called off the deal, simultaneously tendering his resignation as head of the company. He was replaced by a Bandai veteran, Takashi Mogi, who had earlier helped salvage several troubled subsidiaries.

Along with the turmoil caused by the cancelled merger, Bandai was also suffering from the failure of Pippin, which was discontinued in March after total sales of just 42,000 units worldwide. The misfire would end up costing the company more than $200 million in write-offs.

Tamagotchi sales had now peaked in Japan, but the product's launch in the international market had just begun and it was proving to be nearly as successful abroad. Tamagotchi spinoff items such as clothes and video games were already in the pipeline, as was followup DigiMon, which could be connected to another toy for battles, the winner gaining some of the loser's strength. By the end of 1997, 40 million Tamagotchis had been sold worldwide. On a sad note, in October 1997 Bandai founder Naoharu Yamashina passed away at the age of 79.

In March 1998, the firm opened its first Ultraman Club, which contained shops and amusement machines. The club, one of a projected chain of ten, would be used in part for researching toy trends. A restructuring also took place in the spring which realigned the company into ten units that included Toys, Entertainment, Service, Production, and Images and Music. Other new developments of the year included formation of a U.S. home video division, creation of a line of character-based gardening tools, and the introduction of "Silent Shout," a lollipop which broadcast music into a consumer's head through vibrations in the candy's battery-powered handle. A popular toy of this period was the hyper yo-yo, which had a special bearing inside that allowed more complex movements than a standard yo-yo.

In the spring of 1999, Bandai introduced another new product, WonderSwan, a handheld electronic game toy which could be used by itself or connected to another unit or a computer. It had been designed by Gunpei Yokoi, creator of Nintendo's similar Game Boy. In the spring of 1999, the company also changed its top leadership, with Takeo Takaso becoming president and Yukimasa Sugiura CEO and chairman. Takashi Mogi had stepped down because of the company's poor recent financial performance, which came as the Tamagotchi craze burned itself out. Makoto Yamashina, who had been serving as chairman since stepping down as CEO, was named honorary chairman.

Mattel Buys into Bandai: July 1999

In the summer of 1999, Bandai announced it was selling a 5 percent stake in the firm to toy industry leader Mattel, Inc. as the first step in a new cooperative marketing agreement. Bandai would have the option of buying 5 percent of Mattel as well. The move gave Bandai its first presence in Latin America, while Mattel would be strengthened in Japan, where its prior efforts had met with little success. Bandai would continue to distribute its own toys to the United States in the short term. Other projected benefits of the union were mutual development of new toys and sales of Bandai products through a Web site Mattel was preparing to launch. Bandai had recently also joined with seven other companies to form a joint venture called e-Shopping Toys Corp. to sell toys on the Internet. Another joint venture was announced a few months later in which Bandai and Japan's other top three toy makers would produce robot toys. The company was now increasingly focusing on technology-based offerings, including robotic pets, video and computer games, and digital content provision.

Bandai's revenues were dropping off at this time, but reorganizing efforts were paying off with an increase in net earnings. For the fiscal year ending in March of 2000, the company reported sales of ¥208.62 billion ($1.91 billion) and net earnings of ¥1.28 billion, up from the previous year's loss of ¥16.4 billion.

In the spring of 2000, Bandai announced it would pay a bonus of ¥1 million for each baby an employee had after their second child. Japan's birth rate was at an all-time low, and Bandai's offer was the most generous to date of many that companies were making in an attempt to reverse this trend.

The fall of 2000 saw Bandai spin off a recently created cellphone and Internet content provider unit to create wholly owned subsidiary Bandai Networks Co., Inc. In January 2001, the firm sold a 50 percent stake it owned in Upper Deck Group, a California-based trading card maker. Upper Deck would continue to make cards featuring Bandai characters such as Gundam, which had only recently been introduced in the United States. The company also sold one of its Thai manufacturing plants and consolidated production there at a single facility near Bangkok, causing the loss of a number of jobs. A Chinese plant had been sold several years earlier.

Bandai's financial picture continued to improve in 2001, with numbers released in the spring for the preceding fiscal year showing profits jumping to ¥12.9 billion on sales of ¥217 billion. In July, a joint venture was formed with two Korean firms to create Bandai GV Co., which would develop online games for the Japanese market. The company also announced it would introduce a higher-priced line of capsuled toys, which included such items as a digital watch priced at ¥300. In the fall, the firm began offering shares of its Bandai Visual unit on the JASDAQ Stock Exchange and formed a joint venture in Korea with several Japanese and Korean firms called Daiwon Digital Broadcasting Co. Ltd. to broadcast animated programs via satellite under the name AniOne TV.

In March 2002, another joint venture, Bandai Channel Co., was launched to provide digital content to computers and video game terminals that would be based on characters such as Gundam. The fiscal year just ended proved to be the firm's best ever, with earnings hitting a record ¥21.99 billion ($170.7 million) on sales of ¥227.93 billion.

In the summer, Bandai bought Tsukuda Original Co.—a doll, toy and software maker—to help broaden the firm's offerings. The year 2002 also saw Bandai begin construction of a new ¥4 billion headquarters building in Tokyo. Built on land near the company's existing offices, it would feature a Bandai Museum exhibiting toys from the firm's entire 52-year history. The 15-story facility was expected to open in April 2005. In the fall of 2002, Bandai announced it would revive the Strawberry Shortcake line of toys, which had been popular in the United States during the 1980s. Thirty items were to be released, retailing at between $3 and $20. In January 2003, the recently-purchased Tsukuda Original was sold to Wakui Corporation. Shortly afterwards, Bandai announced that the firm's structure would be shifted to a holding company pattern over the next several years, with all of its various divisions spun off into wholly-owned subsidiaries.

After more than a half century, Bandai Co., Ltd. had grown to become the third-largest toy maker in the world. The firm continued to offer a wide range of character-based products as well as an ever-changing lineup of electronic toys, videos, video-games, clothing, capsuled items, and food. The multi-faceted firm was also increasingly expanding into the digital realm with the offerings of its Bandai Networks Co. unit and a series of joint ventures.

Principal Subsidiaries

Banpresto Co., Ltd.; Bandai Visual Co., Ltd.; Bandai Networks Co., Ltd.; Sunrise Inc.; Yutaka Co., Ltd.; Megahouse Corp.; Seika Co., Ltd.; Banalex Corp.; Plex Co., Ltd.; Bec Co., Ltd.; Seeds Co., Ltd.; Artpresto Co., Ltd.; Happinet Corp.; Bandai Logipal Inc.; Bandai America Inc. (U.S.); Bandai Entertainment Inc. (U.S.); Bandai S.A. (France); Bandai U.K. Ltd. (U.K.); Bandai Espana S.A. (Spain); Bandai (H.K.) Co., Ltd. (Hong Kong); Bandai Trading (Shanghai) Co., Ltd. (China); Bandai Korea Co., Ltd. (Korea); Hebei Wanrong Co., Ltd. (China); Bandai Industrial Co., Ltd. (Thailand); Banpresto (H.K.) Ltd. (Hong Kong); Bandai Logipal (H.K.) Ltd. (Hong Kong).

Principal Competitors

Hasbro, Inc.; Mattel, Inc.; Nintendo Co., Ltd.; SEGA Corp.; Takara Co., Ltd.; Tomy Co., Ltd.

Further Reading

"Bandai to Adopt Holding Company System by FY05," *Nikkei Report*, February 17, 2003.

Cody, Jennifer, "Power Rangers Take on the Whole World," *Wall Street Journal*, March 23, 1994, p. B1.

Dougherty, Philip A., "Gobots Set U.S. Invasion," *New York Times*, January 25, 1984, p. D15.

Eisenstodt, Gale, and Kerry A. Dolan, "Watch Out, Barbie," *Forbes*, January 2, 1995, p. 58.

Friedland, Jonathan, "Kid Stuff: Bandai Stays on Top of Japan's Toy Market," *Far Eastern Economic Review*, June 9, 1994, p. 61.

Hamilton, David P., "Sega, Bandai Cite Cultural Differences In Calling Off Billion-Dollar Merger," *Wall Street Journal*, May 28, 1997, p. B6.

"Japan's Bandai Posts Return to Profit After Reorganizing Its Operations," *Dow Jones Business News*, May 9, 2000.

Kunii, Irene M., "How Long Can Bandai Keep Those Cute Little Pets Alive?," *Business Week*, March 16, 1998, p. 29.

Lynch, Stephen, "Big in Japan (er, America) Japan's Hot Toys and Cartoons Have Caught on Here—And it Only Took 20 Years," *Orange County Register*, February 9, 2001, p. 1.

"NW: Bandai Stages Sharp Turnaround," *Nikkei Report*, August 12, 2002.

Ono, Yumiko, "Bandai Shares May Draw Power From Mattel Deal," *Asian Wall Street Journal*, July 26, 1999, p. 11.

Pollack, Andrew, "Is Pippin a Breakthrough or Outmoded on Arrival?," *New York Times*, March 14, 1996, p. D1.

——, "Naoharu Yamashina, Toy Maker, Dies at 79," *New York Times*, October 31, 1997, p. D23.

Sims, Calvin, "Japanese Workers Paid Baby Bonuses," *Globe and Mail*, May 31, 2000, p. A12.

—Frank Uhle

Banknorth Group, Inc.

Banknorth Group, Inc.

Two Portland Square
P.O. Box 9540
Portland, Maine 04112-9540
U.S.A.
Telephone: (207) 761-8500
Toll Free: (800) 462-3666
Fax: (207) 761-8534
Web site: http://www.banknorth.com

Public Company
Incorporated: 1852 as Portland Savings Bank
Employees: 6,000
Total Assets: $23.4 billion (2002)
Stock Exchanges: New York
Ticker Symbol: BNK
NAIC: 522110 Commercial Banking; 522120 Savings
    Institutions; 523110 Investment Banking and
    Securities Dealing; 524113 Direct Life Insurance
    Carrier; 551111 Office of Bank Holding Companies

One of the 30 largest commercial banking companies in the United States, Banknorth Group, Inc. is headquartered in Portland, Maine, and has banking divisions in six states throughout the Northeast. Banknorth is the third-largest banking company in New England. Through its banking subsidiary, Banknorth, N.A., the company operates as Peoples Heritage Bank in Maine, Bank of New Hampshire, Banknorth Massachusetts, Banknorth Connecticut, Banknorth Vermont, and Evergreen Bank in upstate New York. Banknorth operates in over 300 branches and more than 470 ATM's in the New England region. With total assets of $26 billion in 2003, Banknorth and its operating subsidiaries and divisions offer a range of commercial and consumer banking and financial services for individuals, businesses, and governments, including investment planning, money management, insurance, securities brokerage, leasing, merchant services, mortgage banking, and government banking.

19th-Century New England Roots

Banknorth Group traces its roots back to several prominent 19th-century New England banks, including Portland Savings Bank, Penobscot Savings Bank, and Waterville Savings Bank. Portland Savings Bank, one of New England's best-known mutual institutions, received its charter April 17, 1852. On July 3 of that year, Portland Savings opened its doors to receive its first transaction, a $100-dollar deposit. At that time, Millard Fillmore was president, and the bank could count Henry Wadsworth Longfellow as one of its customers. Its first office was situated in a one-room space on Middle Street and was open only on Wednesdays and Saturdays from 11:00 A.M. to 1:00 P.M. Its first president was Portland mayor Albion K. Parris, who was also a former Maine governor, U.S. senator and congressman, and justice of the Maine Supreme Court. After land speculation during the 1830s precipitated many bank failures in the East, it was helpful for the public's confidence to have such an upstanding citizen as Parris heading the new bank.

By 1856, Portland Savings' assets had grown from its initial deposit of $100 to $161,825, and in 1860 the bank made its first significant loan. To help finance a renovation of an old mansion into a hotel, the bank took a $10,000 mortgage that allowed its owners to remodel the renowned Preble House. Also that year, it loaned $20,000 for the completion of the Morse-Libby House, which exists today as Victoria Mansion, a national historic landmark that represents one of the finest examples of pre-Civil War architecture. At the bank's tenth anniversary in 1862, Portland Savings held $406,656 in deposits.

In 1866, a fire swept through Portland and destroyed Portland Savings, as well as all other banks in the city. Portland Savings purchased land on Exchange Street to build anew while occupying temporary office space in a store at Free and Cotton Streets. On May 1, 1867, it opened its doors in the new Exchange Street location, offering such services to its customers as the first safe deposit vault.

Throughout the late 19th century, Portland Savings played an integral role in developing industry in the greater Portland area by offering loans to Westbrook Manufacturing Company,

Company Perspectives:

Banknorth will be the premier community bank in the Northeast. Our goal is to maximize sustainable earnings. We operate primarily within the environment that we know well: the Northeastern United States. Our decisions are based on an understanding of the needs of customers and the demands of the marketplace. We strive to provide service that is timely, personal, and creative and that conforms with local ways of doing business. We are a responsible employer. We are a responsible corporate citizen. We strive for quality in everything we do.

Maine Central Railroad, Portland Street Railroad Company, Bath Iron Works, Berlin Mills, Portland Rolling Mill, Portland Steam Packet Company, and the Portland Company. Additionally, Portland Savings weathered several bank panics and runs to emerge with $7,424,851 in deposits by the end of the century. In 1906, Portland Savings opened its first branch bank in Monument Square, where it ultimately located its main office in March 1925.

During the tumultuous years of World War I, when many people bought savings bonds, deposits in the bank fell to $11,682,00 in 1918 from $14,161,00 in 1917. By the end of the decade, deposits were once again up. However, difficult times were ahead with the stock market crash of 1929. In 1922, the bank counted 30,881 individual depositors, yet by 1932 that number had fallen to 25,298. The bank endured the Great Depression by forming a real estate department to operate the properties of the many defaulted loans and encouraged borrowers to hang in until the bank could bail them out. Tenaciously holding on, Portland Savings had over $24,000,000 in deposits at the anniversary of its centennial in 1952 and $40,000,000 in 1958.

New England Bank Mergers: 1982–89

Big changes in Maine banks began in 1982 when the respected century-old mutual institutions Waterville Savings Bank, Penobscot Savings Bank of Bangor, and Heritage Savings Bank of Rockland merged to form Heritage Savings Bank. A year later, in 1983, Portland Savings Bank merged with Peoples Savings Bank of Lewiston-Auburn, Maine. This merger created Peoples Savings Bank, which then had assets of over $413 million and a net worth over $24 million, with 18 branch offices from Kittery to Fort Kent, Maine, forming the second-largest thrift institution in the state with the largest area of coverage. Two years later, in 1985, Peoples Bank merged with Heritage Savings Bank to create Peoples Savings Heritage Bank, the largest bank in Maine, with assets over $970 million, 33 branch offices, and 550 employees.

The bank's president, Weston L. Bonney, an alumnus of Bates College in Lewiston, Maine, had served as chairman of the board and director of the Bank of New England-Bay State in Lawrence, Massachusetts, as well as chief executive officer at Depositors Trust Co. in Lewiston. At the onset of the merger, Bonney maintained that Peoples Heritage would not be owned by out-of-state financial institutions, as had occurred with many other banks in Maine. Bonney emphasized the direction of Peoples Heritage in the *Portland Evening Express,* maintaining, ''We want to remain sensitive to our local communities.'' He further asserted that the bank would limit any single loan to $8 million. Bonney also speculated about Peoples' status as a mutual institution. Like all its predecessor banks, Peoples Heritage operated under the mutual system by which depositors own the bank and elected corporators and a board of directors to govern it. Bonney noted, ''If we grow faster than our earnings can be retained, it's always possible we might have to convert to a stock bank.''

Peoples Heritage announced plans to build new headquarters in 1986. With assets reaching over $1.049 billion and a growing staff, the bank needed a larger space than the Congress Street building, the offices Portland Savings had originally occupied in 1925. Scheduled to be completed in 1987, the new headquarters would be located in the Old Port's financial district in a ten-story, 190,000-square foot building.

True to Bonney's predictions in 1985, Peoples Heritage went public in 1986, forming Peoples Heritage Financial Group, with shares opening at $15 and quickly rising to $21 a share. At the completion of the bank's conversion from mutual to stock, Peoples Heritage had raised $135.5 million in equity by December 1986, having offered 9.2 million shares to depositors, employees, residents of Maine, and through underwriters to the general public. At the bank's first annual meeting as a publicly held company in 1987, the bank reported 1987 first-quarter profits of $4.7 million, a rise by 85 percent from the previous year. The bank looked to grow further through acquisitions of banks in other states. Peoples Heritage purchased the New Hampshire-based First National Bank of Portsmouth. The bank also diversified its $1 billion loan portfolio away from a focus on residential mortgages to aggressively pursue commercial real estate loans, small business loans, and consumer loans. Maintaining its focus on serving community needs, Peoples Heritage received high valuation reports from such research groups as Alex Brown & Sons, E.F. Hutton Equity Research, and Scottish Life Assurance Co.

Peoples Heritage acquired Oxford Bank and Trust Co. in Maine and First Coastal Banks Inc., a bank holding company with two subsidiaries in New Hampshire, between 1988 and 1989. By 1989, the bank had achieved status as the largest bank holding company based in Maine, beating out The One Bancorp. Peoples Heritage held assets of $2.8 billion and a record $6 million earnings during its third quarter amid an increasingly soft New England economy. The bank focused on controlling non-performing real estate loans that had become a detriment for many New England banks by late 1989.

Economic Downturn: 1989–93

In 1989, William J. Ryan, former president and chief executive officer of the Bank of New England North in Lowell, Massachusetts, was hired by Peoples Heritage to be groomed to replace Bonney as president in 1990. Officials remained cautiously optimistic about the bank's prospects and such analysts as Prudential-Bache Securities commended Peoples' ''lending restraint during the [real estate] boom,'' noting that such restraint ''could pay off dramatically during the bust.''

Key Dates:

1852: Portland Savings Bank receives a charter on April 17 and opens its doors on July 3 to receive its first deposit.

1869: Penobscot Savings Bank is incorporated.

1982: Waterville Savings Bank, Penobscot Savings Bank of Bangor, and Heritage Savings Bank of Rockland merge to form Heritage Savings Bank.

1983: Portland Savings Bank and Peoples Savings Bank of Lewiston-Auburn merge to form Peoples Savings Bank.

1985: Heritage Savings Bank and Peoples Savings Bank merge to form Peoples Heritage Savings Bank.

1986: Peoples Heritage goes public and forms Peoples Heritage Financial Group.

1993: The bank earns a $15.5 million profit to turn its profitability around.

1994: Peoples Heritage introduces Sunday banking hours and supermarket banking, one of first banks in New England to offer such services.

2000: The bank purchases Burlington, Vermont-based Banknorth, a bank with $4.4 billion in assets, and changes the name of its holding company from Peoples Heritage Financial Group, Inc. to Banknorth Group, Inc.

2001: Banknorth introduces online banking and Customer eCare, the bank's first step in online strategy to be executed over several years.

2002: The bank's divisions are consolidated under a single charter bank as Banknorth, N.A. and moves to the New York Stock Exchange.

2003: Banknorth is ranked on Forbes Platinum 400 list.

Cautious optimism soon gave way to a darker economic outlook. During the late 1980s and early 1990s, the recession in the real estate sector caused over 100 New England banks to fail, including such venerable institutions as Maine Savings and Maine National Bank. After its strong showing in late 1989, Peoples Heritage reported losses in earnings of $61.9 million in 1990 and $25 million in 1991. At 1989 year-end, Peoples Heritage reported $49.2 million in non-performing loans, and by end of first quarter 1990 the amount of non-performing loans had increased to $76.5 million, a rise of 55 percent. Stock in Peoples Heritage plunged from $18 a share in 1989 to $1.87 over the next several years. In April 1990, the bank doubled its reserves as a measure to cover possible future losses on bad loans. Most analysts viewed this action as prudent and characterized the bank's management as strong. John R. Hefferen of Alex Brown brokerage was quoted in the *Portland Press Herald* as stating, "I have the sense and think [Peoples] have the right people doing the right things, but . . . to a certain extent it's our of their hands. . . . They're trying to manage these problems as aggressively as possible, but the economy is truly the significant factor."

The company finally was able to show a small profit of $329,000 in the third quarter 1992, the first profit in two years. Ryan, the company's president and chief operating officer, related to the *Portland Press Herald,* "This quarter is a break-

through. We will build on that profitability for the next year or two." Three years later, in a speech to the Newcomen Society of the United States, Ryan summarized the bank's standing during those difficult years: "Success isn't measured by the position you're in, it's measured by the obstacles you overcome." Ryan also credited the Peoples Heritage Board of Directors and a loyal staff who worked without salary increases for as long as three years to withstand the downturn and ultimately emerge successful.

Successful Turnaround and Acquisitions: 1993–2003

By 1993, after years of losses, Peoples Heritage finally showed a significant profit of $15.5 million to clearly establish its turnaround. The bank raised $40 million in capital and was poised to expand its product base and develop its niche as a bank focusing on high-quality customer service. Peoples Heritage became the first Maine bank to offer Sunday banking hours and also the first bank in Maine to open full service branch offices in supermarkets. New accounts nearly doubled by 1994, with an average of 60,000 new accounts a year. According to Ryan, the bank aimed to meet the fiduciary responsibility of a public company while remaining independent. By 1995, Peoples Heritage stock traded at $19.25 a share, and the firm had established itself as one of the top ten companies in New England.

After gaining solid financial standing, Peoples began a move toward acquiring companies. In an interview with Lynn Fosse in the *Wall Street Corporate Reporter,* Ryan stated, "In 1993 we reviewed our strategy for the future and decided the best thing to do would be to grow the company outside Maine, taking the philosophy of community banking to other New England states." At that time, Peoples had approximately 90 percent of its assets in the state of Maine. At first, Peoples purchased companies in New Hampshire and Massachusetts, later expanding into Vermont, upstate New York, and Connecticut to diversify its geographic and product mix while also continuing to grow within the state of Maine. In 1996, Peoples acquired the Bank of New Hampshire, based in Manchester, and Family Bank of Haverhill in Massachusetts.

While acquiring a number of small to mid-sized companies, Peoples also set its sights on larger finds. In 1997, Peoples acquired the $3 billion company CFX Corp., based in Keene, New Hampshire, a deal that placed Peoples as the fourth largest banking company in New England. In 1999, the company purchased the $2 billion asset SIS Bancorp of Springfield, Massachusetts, a deal that also placed Peoples in Connecticut through its subsidiary Glastonbury Bank and Trust Co., which had branches throughout central Connecticut. Also in 1999, Peoples acquired the $4.4 billion asset Banknorth Group Inc. of Burlington, Vermont, for $780 million in stock. The deal also included Evergreen Bank of Glenn Falls, New York, which had been a subsidiary of Banknorth. Subsequently, Peoples took the Banknorth name. Ryan stated at the time, "Our new name will more clearly represent our presence in every New England state except Rhode Island and our entry into Upstate New York. We also hope to send the market a clear message that we are truly a commercial banking company and not a traditional thrift."

In 2001, Banknorth focused on creating a strong presence in Massachusetts. It announced plans to acquire Andover Bancorp

Inc. and MetroWest Bank, a pair of acquisitions that would add 32 branches in eastern Massachusetts and the wealthy northern suburbs of Boston, deposits of $2 billion, and assets of $3 billion to Banknorth. Banknorth paid $333 million in stock for Andover and $166 million in cash for MetroWest. In five years, Banknorth's presence in Massachusetts grew from no assets to becoming the fifth-largest bank in the state. These acquisitions typified Banknorth's strategy to purchase small, community banks that showed a clear, strategic fit and could seamlessly integrate into their own branch network.

In March 2002, Banknorth revealed plans to purchase at least ten more banks in Massachusetts, Connecticut, and upstate New York to achieve $30 billion in assets by 2005. Its first visible step in that direction was to announce a definitive agreement to purchase Ipswich Bancshares Inc. in Ipswich, Massachusetts, a northern Boston suburb, for $41 million in cash and stock. In August 2002, Banknorth announced it would purchase another North Shore bank, Warren Bancorp Inc. of Peabody, Massachusetts, for $122.6 million in cash and stock.

By 2002, Banknorth had acquired over 20 banks across six different states. Banknorth was the biggest bank in both Maine and New Hampshire, the second-largest in Vermont, and the fourth-largest in Massachusetts. The company broadened its scope in Connecticut when it purchased for $157 million Bancorp Connecticut Inc., the parent company of the 142-year-old Southington Savings Bank. Later in 2002, Banknorth announced plans to purchase the Connecticut holding company American Financial Holdings Inc., which was the parent of American Savings Bank, for $709.3 million in cash and stock. This deal, completed in early 2003, helped Banknorth leap from 14th in market share in the state of Connecticut to fifth. In the ten months from November 2001 to August 2002, Banknorth had spent over $1.5 billion in cash and shares of its own stock to acquire six banks. Banknorth's strategy with such aggressive acquisitions was to carefully weigh each acquisition before committing. According to company spokesman Brian Arsenault, "The property we purchase must add to our earnings within a year of being acquired by our company." Most analysts agreed that Banknorth's careful growth strategy paid off with the company showing no more debt despite its $1.5 billion spending.

Growing Insurance Operations

Concurrent with its aggressive bank acquisitions, Banknorth actively sought to expand its insurance operations, which in early 2000 were located in Maine, New Hampshire, and Massachusetts. In September 2000, through its subsidiary, Morse, Payson & Noyes (MPN), Banknorth purchased the Watson Group in Connecticut. Company spokesman Arsenault explained in *American Banker,* "Our strategy is to have an insurance agency in every market in which we provide banking services." In 2001, with the acquisitions of Andover Bancorp and MetroWest in Massachusetts, Banknorth's MPN Massachusetts offices were poised to benefit from cross-selling insurance products in the lucrative new bank branches in the northern Boston suburbs. MPN represented Banknorth's largest insurance operation, but it also had purchased a number of other smaller insurance companies. By July 2001, Banknorth's insurance unit had seven agencies in Maine, Massachusetts, New Hampshire, and Connecticut where the focus was to cross-sell personal, commercial, and disability insurance. By year-end 2001, the agencies had sold $400 million in insurance.

Banknorth's next step was to add insurance agencies in New York and Vermont. In mid-2002, Banknorth announced an intention to purchase Community Insurance Agencies Inc. of South Glen Falls, New York, making progress on its strategy to have insurance operations in each state where the company claims banking operations. Banknorth Insurance was closer to its goal of reaching $100 million in revenues by 2004.

Bright Outlook for the 21st Century

In January 2003, Banknorth CEO Ryan was interviewed for CNN's Stock of the Day, a feather in the cap of "a regional bank that's turned into a giant in the Northeast." Analysts are fond of relating the success stories of Banknorth, a company that follows a prudent and well-planned growth strategy. At the start of the 21st century, Banknorth intended to build on its successes by meeting the local needs of a community while still offering the services of larger banks. Ryan asserted in the CNN interview, "We think we want to stick within our knitting, and our knitting is New England. So I think we'll continue to grow in New England."

Principal Divisions

Banknorth Connecticut; Banknorth Massachusetts; Evergreen Bank; Peoples Heritage Bank; Bank of New Hampshire; Banknorth Vermont.

Principal Subsidiaries

Banknorth Investment Management Group; Banknorth Investment Planning Group; Banknorth Insurance Group; Banknorth Leasing.

Principal Competitors

FleetBoston; Citizens Bank; KeyCorp; Sovereign Bancorp.

Further Reading

Agosta, Veronica, "Banknorth Targets East Mass. in Pair of Bank Deals," *American Banker,* June 12, 2001, pp. 1–2.
——, "Banknorth to Acquire Warren of Mass," *American Banker,* August 9, 2002, p. 20.
Boyle, Harold J., "Portland Savings Bank Is 100 Years Old," *Portland Sunday Telegram,* May 4, 1952, pp. 1A, 16A.
Fosse, Lynn, "William J. Ryan, Chairman, President, Chief Executive Officer, Banknorth Group, Inc.: Interview," *Wall Street Corporate Reporter,* January 2, 2001.
Gjertsen, Lee Ann, "Banknorth Agency Deal to Get a Unit into New York," *American Banker,* May 20, 2002, p. 7.
Gormley, John H., Jr., "Peoples Nets First Profit in Two Years," *Portland Press Herald,* October 14, 1992, pp. 1A, 6B.
Huntington, Chris, and Pat Kiernan, "Stock of the Day: Banknorth CEO William Ryan, CNNfn," *The Money Gang,* January 13, 2003.
Irwin, Clark T., Jr., "Peoples Heritage Sets Profit, Growth Records," *Portland Press Herald,* April 29, 1987, p. 7.
Nelson, Scott Bernard, "Maine Bank Will Acquire Two in Massachusetts," *Boston Globe,* June 12, 2001.

——, "Portland, Maine-Based Banknorth Group to Acquire Connecticut-Based Firm," *Boston Globe*, August 23, 2002.

Pinto, Linda, "Portland, Maine-Based Banknorth Group to Acquire American Financial Holdings," *Connecticut Post*, August 24, 2002.

Porter, John W., "Bank OK, but Uneasy," *Portland Press Herald*, April 3, 1990, pp. 9, 17.

——, "Peoples CEO Urges Caution," *Portland Press Herald*, March 30, 1991, p. 5B.

Reosti, John, "Another Deal for Banknorth—This Time in Connecticut," *American Banker*, April 12, 2002, pp. 1–2.

Ryan, William J., *Peoples Heritage*, New York: The Newcomen Society of the United States, 1995.

Silvestrini, Marc, "Acquisition of New Britain, Conn.-Based Banking Firm Steps up Consolidation," *Waterbury Republican-American*, August 23, 2002.

——, "Financial Experts Analyze Portland, Maine-Based Bank's Acquisitions," *Waterbury Republican-American*, August 27, 2002.

Smith, Jeff, "Peoples Heritage Announces Loss," *Portland Press Herald*, April 18, 1990, pp. 1, 8.

Whiteman, Louis, "Maine Thrift to Buy Bank in Vermont for $780 Million," *American Banker*, June 3, 1999, pp. 1–2.

"William Ryan—Banknorth Group Inc.: CEO Interview," *Wall Street Transcript*, May 22, 2000.

—Elizabeth Henry

Bénéteau SA

Zone Industrielle des Mares, BP 66
85270 Saint-Hilaire-de-Riez
France
Telephone: (+33) 251605000
Fax: (+33) 251605010
Web site: http://www.beneteau.com

Public Company
Incorporated: 1884
Employees: 4,002
Sales: EUR 619.3 million ($600 million) (2002)
Stock Exchanges: Euronext Paris
Ticker Symbol: BEN
NAIC: 336611 Ship Building and Repairing

Bénéteau SA is the world's largest manufacturer of sailing yachts and pleasure craft, under the Bénéteau and Jeanneau names. Other well-known brand names in the Bénéteau stable include Waquiez, CNB (Construction Navales de Bordeaux), and catamaran maker Lagoon. Based in Saint-Hilaire-de-Riez, in France's Vendee region along the Atlantic coast, Bénéteau's sales are worldwide, representing more than two-thirds of its annual revenues of EUR 619 million per year. The United States, the site of the company's only international manufacturing facility, accounts for a significant share of Bénéteau's shares. The company also owns a majority stake in Polish motor yacht builder Ostroda, and has entered the Duboats joint venture with the United Arab Republic's Bin Zayed Group. In addition to its pleasure craft, Bénéteau also manufactures professional craft, including fishing boats and racing boats. A diversification drive undertaken during the lean years of the early 1990s has led Bénéteau into a number of related areas, including modular mobile homes, under the O'Hara brand, utilizing the company's expertise at creating comfort within confined spaces; and, through subsidiary Microcar, lightweight license-free automobiles, using Bénéteau's longstanding expertise in fiberglass manufacturing. Bénéteau, listed on the Euronext Paris Stock Exchange, remains controlled at more than 57 percent by the founding Bénéteau family. Annette Roux, granddaughter of the company's founder and chief architect of its success, remains company chairman, seconded by CEO and probable successor Bruno Cathelinais.

From Work to Pleasure in the 1960s

Benjamin Bénéteau had put to sea at the age of 12, before receiving training as a naval architect as part of France's navy before setting up his own small shipyard in Croix de Vie, in the Bay of Biscay, in 1884. Bénéteau established a family tradition in designing and building sail-based vessels—yet the company's production remained limited to fishing trawlers for nearly 80 years.

At the turn of the century, Bénéteau recognized the potential for adapting internal combustion engine designs, and by 1908 had proposed adding a motor to his trawlers. Yet fishermen rejected the idea, believing the engine noise would frighten off fish. Bénéteau nevertheless found a few takers for the proposed new vessel. In 1912, the first motor-equipped trawlers left the harbor—and returned far ahead of their sail-only counterparts, capturing the largest share of the market.

Throughout the first half of the 20th century, Bénéteau remained a small, if respected shipbuilder, then under the leadership of Bénéteau's son André. With orders outpacing production levels, the company had little interest in change through the 1950s. By the early 1960s, the company had grown to just 17 employees, including André Bénéteau's own five children, and especially son André and his younger sister Annette.

Stricken by the Spanish flu, and facing financial difficulties as a result of a crisis in the French fishing industry, André Bénéteau turned over leadership of the company to the team of André and Annette in 1964. The brother-sister team decided to launch the company into a new direction. While continuing to build its traditional wooden fishing boats, André Bénéteau set about designing a new type of boat. Using new fiberglass materials, Bénéteau designed the company's first pleasure craft, sailboats named the Fletan and the Guppy. Annette, who in that year married local businessman Louis-Claude Roux, took over the commercial side of the family business.

Bénéteau displayed models of its new sailboats at the Paris Boat Show in 1965 and promptly received an approach from a trio of boat shop owners located on the Brittany region coast, with orders that were to keep the company in production for the next six months. The company had, in fact, launched a revolution in pleasure boating, creating an affordable sailing product at a time when the French vacationer, enjoying years of economic prosperity, offered a huge demand. Annette Roux had quickly recognized the potential as well of developing a network of concessions for sales of its boating models.

The company quickly followed up its first successful models with a steady succession of innovative craft, boasting names such as the Galion, the Piranha, the Forban, and the Baroudeur. The Bénéteau name quickly became synonymous with French pleasure sailing, and also gained a reputation for quality construction. Bénéteau also extended its range into a growing new category of boating enthusiast, that of the pleasure fishing segment.

By the beginning of the 1970s, Bénéteau had succeeded in becoming one of the leading names in the French pleasure boating market. The company also had expanded into new boating categories, debuting the line of luxury combined motor-sail yachts, featuring an interior wheelhouse, called the Evasion 32, in 1973. The company also began building racing boats—and began winning races by the mid-1970s.

André Bénéteau had guided the company's boat designs into the mid-1970s and was to remain in charge of developing Bénéteau's motor craft. In 1976, however, the company hired on the first of a series of outside designers to conceive new generations of sailing craft. The first of these, the André Mauric-designed First 30, won the Paris Boat Show "Boat of the Year" award in 1978. The company next turned to Cees Van der Velden, who added the successful Flyer series. Meanwhile, André Bénéteau's Antares design became a highly popular fishing/cruising model.

Overcoming Crisis in the 1980s

Yet the First series remained the company's largest seller for the better part of a decade, raising the company to prominence beyond France to become one of the world's leading makers of sailing yachts. In 1981, the company extended the range with the launch of the First Evolution, which went on to win the World Half Ton Championship that year. The following year, the company received a new "Boat of the Year" award, with the launch of the Wizz model.

In 1984, the company went public, selling shares on the Paris Stock Exchange's Unlisted Securities Market. The Bénéteau family was to remain in control of the company, however, with more than 56 percent of shares held through a family holding company, and a further 8 percent of stock held directly by the company itself. Two years later, the company inaugurated one of the world's most modern boat-building plants at its Saint-Gilles-Croix-de-Vie home.

Bénéteau had long recognized the potential of the U.S. market, where the company's sail-based yachts had found a strong reception. In 1986, the company took a risk and opened its own U.S.-based shipbuilding yard, a replica of its main French facility, in the town of Marion, in South Carolina. Production there rose rapidly, and by 1990, the Marion facility had turned out its 1,000th boat.

Yet Bénéteau itself had nearly been sunk by an unexpected crisis. By 1986, the company had been forced to recall some 600 boats, including nearly all of its flagship First vessels, produced between 1983 and 1985. A supplier of a catalyst used to harden the paint on the vessels' hulls had replaced an ingredient with another, water-soluble ingredient—resulting in the hulls developing a condition called osmosis, described by Bénéteau more or less as the "cancer of plastic." Although Bénéteau later successfully sued the supplier, the company struggled to rebuild its reputation and its sales through the middle of the decade. By 1987, the company, which absorbed the costs of refitting its recalled vessels, was forced to report its first losses since the early 1960s.

By 1988, however, Bénéteau appeared to have overcome its crisis. In this the company was helped by the highly successful Oceanis range of yachts, designed around a concept of "the pleasure of the open sea," launched in 1986. The following year, the company's motor cruiser range gained in stature with the launch of a new generation of Flyer models, designed especially for the European market. That same year, the company won its latest Boat of the Year award with the launch of the First S, featuring designs from noted designer Philippe Starck. These events helped boost the company's sales past FFr 670 million (approximately EUR 100 million) by the end of 1988.

Acquisition and Diversification in the New Century

Bénéteau ran headlong into the international economic recession at the beginning of the 1990s, and especially into the crisis that hit the world yachting market, exacerbated by the outbreak of the first Persian Gulf War. By 1991, the company's revenues had dropped by some 30 percent, and Bénéteau was forced to lay off a number of its employees.

In order to counter the drop-off in sales in its core markets, Bénéteau decided to expand into new markets. In 1992 the company bought a shipyard in nearby Noirmoutier, where it began construction of smaller 20- to 25-meter craft. That year, also, the company acquired Construction Navale Bordeaux (CNB), a noted manufacturer of luxury yachts and service craft built from aluminum.

In 1995, Bénéteau took its expansion still further, launching an entirely new division: O'Hara Houses, a maker of portable and modular vacation homes (similar to mobile homes but more luxurious). Although that market seemed far removed from the

---

Key Dates:

1884: Benjamin Bénéteau founds his own shipyard and begins building wooden sail-based fishing boats.

1912: Bénéteau introduces the first motor-driven fishing boats.

1964: André Bénéteau and sister Annette Roux take over as head of the company and enter the fiberglass-based pleasure craft market.

1984: Bénéteau goes public on the Paris stock exchange.

1986: Bénéteau opens a new modern shipbuilding facility in France and establishes its first international facility, in South Carolina in the United States.

1992: The company acquires Construction Navale Bordeaux, a maker of aluminum-based fishing and service craft.

1995: The company acquires rival Jeanneau SA, doubling in size; the O'Hara Houses subsidiary is launched.

1997: The company acquires Wauquiez, a sailing yacht maker in France.

2001: The company acquires 57 percent of Ostroda, a maker of motor-driven boats in Poland.

2003: The company forms the Duboats joint venture with the Bin Zayed Group of United Arab Emirates to enter the Mideast market.

---

company's boat-building activities, it nonetheless made use of the company's long-held expertise at creating comfort within confined spaces.

With the yacht market picking up again at mid-decade, Bénéteau's next expansion move came as a defensive measure. By then, the company's main rival—and neighbor—Jeanneau SA had been forced into bankruptcy. Fearful that Jeanneau might fall under control of French inflatable craft specialist Zodiac, Bénéteau launched its own bid to acquire the bankrupt firm. In December 1995, the company's efforts were rewarded when it was given the go-ahead to acquire Jeanneau. That company, which began by building wooden dinghies in the 1957, had turned toward fiberglass boats at the beginning of the 1960s.

The acquisition more than doubled Bénéteau in size, making it far and away the world's leading manufacturer of luxury sailing yachts. Rather than absorb its new subsidiary, the company decided to maintain the Jeanneau brand and boating range alongside its own. Jeanneau also brought two additional operations to Bénéteau: the Lagoon branded line of racing boats, and its subsidiary Microcar, a maker of lightweight, license-less automobiles (a peculiarity of the French roadway, the class of automobile featured two-stroke engines with upper speed limits of 30 miles per hour). Again, Bénéteau found an extension of its manufacturing expertise—in this case, in the use of fiberglass materials—in a further diversification of its operations.

Bénéteau continued to build up its own boating line in the late 1990s, particularly with the launch of a new "ready-to-sail" concept that featured upgraded amenities as part of its

models' standard equipment. The company also launched a new nine-point "Sailing Contract" among its concessions, beginning in France, before extending the customer service program throughout Europe.

The company also continued making acquisitions, taking over another French sailing yacht maker, Wauquiez, which had been established in 1965. That brand promptly joined Bénéteau's growing stable of brands. Meanwhile, Bénéteau was preparing the launch of a number of new Bénéteau-branded models, including the large cruiser sailing yacht, the First 40.7, introduced in 1998, which was followed by the still larger First 47.7 in 1999. The company also debuted the Océanis Clipper 411, one of its most successful models, selling more than 1,000 by 2000.

Bénéteau enjoyed an upturn in the worldwide yacht market as it entered the new century, seeing its sales rise to more than EUR 570 million at the end of 2001, and again to nearly EUR 620 million for the 2002 year. The company continued to expand as well, beginning a new drive to add international operations. At the end of 2001, the company purchased a 57 percent stake in Poland's Ostrada, a maker of motor-driven cruising boats that had already acted as a subcontractor for Bénéteau in the past. The move was expected to enable Bénéteau to step up its presence in Northern Europe.

Despite the upheaval in the Persian Gulf at the beginning of 2003, Bénéteau targeted that region for future growth as well. In March 2003, the company formed a joint venture, Duboats, with the United Arab Emirates' Bin Zayed Group to develop sailing and motor craft for the Gulf markets. Approaching its 120th anniversary, Bénéteau had established itself as a clear leader in the international boating community.

Principal Subsidiaries

Chantiers Jeanneau; Microcar SA; Maisons O'Hara SA.

Principal Competitors

Brunswick Corporation; Chantiers de l'Atlantique; Groupe Zodiac; Polaris Industries Inc.; IZAR Construcciones Navales S.A.; Bass Pro L.P.; Genmar Holdings Inc.; Fiskars Oy Ab; BAE Systems Marine Ltd.; Arctic Cat Inc.; Fiberdome Inc.; Sanoyas Hishino Meisho Corporation; Morita Corporation; Triton Boat Company L.P.; Johnson Outdoors Inc.

Further Reading

Baudet, Marie-Beatrice, "Annette Roux, reine de la plaisance," *Le Monde,* December 7, 2000.

"Bénéteau Hoists Sails and Charts a Global Course," *Business Day,* July 16, 1999, p. 41.

"Beneteau: Les vents faiblissent, la Bourse s'inquiete," *Les Echos,* February 07, 2003, p. 11.

Mallet, Victor, "Steady Hand Guides the Tiller Through Choppiest of Seas," *Financial Times,* November 24, 2001, p. 18.

Schroeder, Peter, "Bénéteau to Maintain Separate Jeanneau Sail Line," *Boating Industry,* February 1996, p. 13.

—M. L. Cohen

Big 5 Sporting Goods Corporation

2525 East El Segundo Boulevard
El Segundo, California 90245
U.S.A.
Telephone: (310) 536-0611
Fax: (310) 297-7585
Web site: http://www.big5sportinggoods.com

Public Company
Incorporated: 1955 as United Merchandising Corporation
Employees: 6,327
Sales: $667.5 million (2002)
Stock Exchanges: NASDAQ
Ticker Symbol: BGFV
NAIC: 339920 Sporting and Athletic Goods
   Manufacturing

Big 5 Sporting Goods Corporation is an El Segundo, California-based regional chain of approximately 275 value-oriented sporting goods stores located in ten western states. While approximately 60 percent of outlets are found in California, Big 5 stores are also located in Arizona, Colorado, Idaho, Nevada, New Mexico, Oregon, Texas, Utah, and Washington. Big 5 is a niche player that is able to successfully compete against superstores by operating units in the 11,000-square-foot range generally located in strip centers, as opposed to the 40,000-square-foot freestanding big box operations of its larger rivals. Requiring less space, Big 5 is able to take a neighborhood approach and concentrate a number of stores in a particular market, which is then supported by weekly newspaper inserts and mailers, a marketing approach the company has successfully pursued for nearly 50 years. Big 5 also concentrates on offering superior customer service, which is enhanced by a limited selection of goods and low profile fixtures that allow customers to find what they are looking for and sales associates to spot customers in need of assistance. Rather than attempt to match the broad selection of goods that giant competitors can offer, Big 5 focuses on mid-price-point items from major brands such as Nike and Reebok and budget-priced merchandise for lesser brands such as Brooks, Pony, Spalding, and Riddell,

augmented by inventory acquired in closeouts. As a result of this approach, sales associates do not have to become knowledgeable about an excessive number of items, and Big 5 also greatly reduces its exposure to markdowns taken on more expensive shoes and apparel. If conditions warrant, individual stores have some latitude in adding higher-price-point merchandise. A Beverly Hills outlet, for example, carries Taylor Made golf clubs while the chain as a whole concentrates on value-priced golfing products from Spalding, Dunlop, Wilson, and Northwestern. Store managers, along with senior and mid-level management, have a direct incentive in making sure the Big 5 formula continues to work, sharing in the ownership of the company as the result of a 1997 recapitalization plan. In general, Big 5 is known for its conservative approach to business as well as a penchant for maintaining a low profile. Management rarely speaks with the press and avoids industry events sponsored by the major trade associations. The chain's buyers, however, attend trade shows, invariably focusing on opening price point products and a few mid-priced items.

Big 5 Founded in 1955

Big 5's parent company was formed in September 1955 as United Merchandising Corp. by Maurie and Harry Liff and the company's current Chairman Emeritus Robert W. Miller. They opened five stores in downtown Los Angeles, Burbank, Inglewood, Glendale, and San Jose. For a trade name they chose "Big 5 Stores," unconcerned that the name might not sound as appropriate should they one day expand the operation. In its early years, Big 5 concentrated on World War II army surplus items, as well as tents and air mattresses the company manufactured itself, plus assorted housewares and handtools. From the earliest days of the chain, Big 5 turned to print advertisements, making a regular practice of advertising on the back page of the *Los Angeles Times,* its customers growing accustomed to looking there for weekly specials. Other sporting goods aside from tents soon became part of the product mix, a natural for the highly active population of southern California. Sports merchandise became so popular that in 1963 management decided to specialize in it, and in December of that year changed its operating name to "Big 5 Sporting Goods."

Thrifty Acquires Big 5 in 1971

By March 1971, Big 5 had grown to 19 stores and entered the northern California market, at which point the company was merged with Thrifty Corporation, the West Coast's largest chain of drug stores. Big 5 operated as a subsidiary of Thrifty for the next 15 years. Then, in 1986, Pacific Enterprises, parent corporation of Southern California Gas Co., acquired Thrifty. With Robert Miller still at the helm of the company he helped found, Big 5 continued to prosper, by 1992 growing to 140 stores in California, Nevada (entered in 1978), and Washington (entered in 1984). To support its growth the company built a 440,000-square-foot, state-of-the-art distribution center twice the size of its previous facility. Pacific Enterprises' retail operations as a whole, however, endured mounting losses. In 1992, Pacific Enterprises decided to refocus on its core utility business and pay down debt by selling the 620-store Thrifty Drug Store chain and five other retail chains to an investment group headed by Los Angeles financier Leonard Green & Partners, a firm that specialized in management buyouts. In addition to Big 5, these assets included two other sporting goods subsidiaries, 83 MC Sporting Goods stores located in the Midwest and 52 Gart Brothers Sporting Goods stores in the Rocky Mountain states, as well as 40 Oregon B-Mart discount stores and 124 Pay 'n Save stores located in the Pacific Northwest, Hawaii, and Alaska. In a subsequent transaction to strengthen the Thrifty chain and allow it to retire some debt, Green formed a second investment group and along with a management group purchased Big 5 in a deal valued at $150 million. For the purpose of making this acquisition, Big 5 Holdings, Inc. and its parent, Big 5 Corporation, were established. Big 5 Holdings purchased all outstanding stock from Thrifty and merged with Big 5 Corporation, which then became the surviving entity.

Robert Miller stayed on as CEO and chairman of Big 5, while his son, Steve, retained his position as president and chief operating officer. They planned to continue to grow the chain, anticipating the addition of eight to ten stores each year. During the first year following the separation from Pacific Enterprises, Big 5 opened ten stores, followed by 15 in both 1993 and 1994, and 19 units in 1995 (including seven through acquisitions). During this period, it also closed four older stores. In the process of expansion, the chain entered new markets, such as Arizona and Idaho in 1993, and New Mexico, Oregon, and Texas in 1995. To support this growth, Big 5 installed and implemented new merchandising, distribution, and financial systems, allowing management to accomplish an inventory reduction strategy in 1995, a move instrumental in maintaining the company's ongoing fiscal health. To maintain strong growth at existing stores, the company also pursued a remodeling program. When California's economy slowed down in the mid-1990s, Big 5 cut back the pace of expansion, adding only four new stores in 1996. Annual revenue for the year reached $404.3 million with $4 million in net profits.

Management Acquires Controlling Stake in 1997

In November 1997, Miller led a management effort to control the destiny of the company, raising $250 million to acquire a controlling interest in Big 5 from Leonard Green. As a result, Leonard Green's ownership position fell from 67 percent to 36.2 percent. While still holding a sizeable interest in the business, the banking firm now took a less active role in the running of Big 5, although it retained seats on the board of directors. Having paid just $28.5 million in 1992 for its stake in Big 5, Leonard Green realized a windfall profit from the sporting goods chain, despite an economic environment during which the market value of major national chains dropped significantly. Senior management and Big 5 employees, in the meantime, saw their ownership position grow from just 14 percent to 55.3 percent. A significant portion of the chain's employees now had a personal interest in continuing to make Big 5's 40-year formula for success continue to work; this had become even more imperative because as a result of the buyout the chain was saddled with $173 million in long-term debt.

Although highly leveraged, Big 5 maintained its plan for expanding the chain. In 1997, 14 new stores were added, eight located in markets outside of California, bringing the total number of units in the chain to 210. In 1998, the company entered a new market in Utah, and during the year opened 12 new stores, one of which replaced an older unit. Big 5 added another 15 stores in 1999 and 15 in 2000 while closing 2 units, resulting in a total of 249 outlets in the chain. Revenues kept pace during this period, growing to $491.4 million in 1998, $514.3 million in 1999, and $571.5 million in 2000. Big 5's debt burden, however, adversely impacted profits, which dropped from $8.7 million in 1997 to $4.5 million in 1998, then improved to $5.8 million in 1999 and $11.1 million in 2000. Compared to the fortunes of publicly held competitors, Big 5's performance during these years was especially impressive. Since the heady days of the early 1990s, when several sporting goods chains went public, leading to a glut of new stores, many of Big 5's competitors had lapsed into bankruptcy or been forced to merge with better financed rivals.

During the late-1990s, Big 5 took steps to improve its information technology infrastructure. In 1999, the company launched a project to replace its decade-old point-of-sale registers and software with new hardware and a system based on a Micrsoft Windows NT operating system, a change that would allow it the flexibility of taking advantage of existing Windows applications while improving system speed and stability. Rollout of the point-of-sale systems was completed during 2000. Also in 1999, Big 5 implemented an electronic data interchange system (EDI) that dramatically cut down the time between ordering and receiving goods from participating vendors, in some cases reducing the cycle time from as long as three weeks to just three days. The move was actually initiated a year earlier by Nike, a major proponent of the technology, which encouraged Big 5 to start using EDI. Previously, Big 5 entered orders into a database system, then had a secretary spend two to three hours each day simply faxing purchase orders to individual vendors. On the other end of the fax machine the same data was entered into a computer a second time. Big 5's motivation for turning to EDI was essentially to avoid losing Nike as a vendor, but once the system was in place the company quickly realized

Key Dates:

1955: United Merchandising is formed using the trade name "Big 5 Stores."
1963: Operating name is changed to "Big 5 Sporting Goods" as the chain specializes in sporting goods.
1971: Thrifty Corp. acquires the chain.
1986: Thrifty is acquired by Pacific Enterprises.
1992: Big 5 is acquired in management-led buyout financed by Leonard Green & Partners.
1997: The company is recapitalized, with majority ownership passing to employees.
2002: Big 5 goes public.

a number of time-saving benefits. The company began using EDI to transmit insurance paperwork as well as employee withholding tax information to state governments. Big 5 also began to encourage its other vendors to come online in order to further magnify the benefits of the system.

In 2001, Big 5 entered a new market, Colorado, opening two stores. For the year, sales grew to nearly $622.5 million, with net income totaled almost $15 million. Management also made plans to take the company public, in the summer of 2001 filing for an initial public offering (IPO), hoping to raise as much as $115 million despite a difficult market for IPO's in recent months. Not only would Big 5 be able to relieve its debt burden, freeing up cash flow dedicated to servicing its debt and making the company less vulnerable to downturns in the economy, Leonard Green and its affiliate, Green Equity Investors, was looking to reduce its ownership position and further profit from its investment in the sporting goods chain. Big 5 enlisted Credit Suisse First Boston Corp. to underwrite the stock sale in association with U.S. Bancorp Piper Jaffray Inc., Jefferies & Co., and Stephens Inc. With the stock market adversely impacted by the terrorist attacks of September 11, 2001, the offering was postponed. It was finally held in June 2002 but proved somewhat disappointing. The company had established an expected price range of $14 to $16 per share but in the end had to settle for $13, resulting in $104.65 million raised. Moreover, when the stock began trading on the NASDAQ, the price showed almost no movement on the first day. It reached a high of $13.84 before closing at $13.17, leaving Big 5 with a market capitalization of little more than $280 million. Over the ensuing weeks, the stock continued to receive a lackluster response, prompting management to consider buying back some of the shares. Nonetheless, management planned to continue its strategy of controlled expansion, especially in markets beyond California. In the western states already served, Big 5 estimated it could backfill another 150 stores. To accommodate this growth, the company also made plans to replace its 12-year-old Fontana warehouse, setting up a satellite distribution center while it began looking at properties that could accommodate a new facility. Given that Big 5 had enjoyed ongoing success for nearly 50 years, there was every reason to believe that the chain would indeed have use for the additional warehouse space.

Principal Competitors

Foot Locker, Inc.; Gart Sports Company; The Sports Authority, Inc.; Sport Chalet Inc.

Further Reading

Pett, Laurence, "Big Five . . . on the Ball, Bat, Etc.," *Southern California Business*, January 1, 1989, p. 5.
Robinson-Jacobs, Karen, and Debora Vrana, "Big 5 Plans IPO," *Los Angeles Times*, August 23, 2001, p. C1.
Troy, Mike, "Big 5 Public Offering Raised $77 million," *DSN Retailing Today*, July 8, 2002, p. 5.
——, "California-based Big 5 Eyes Eastward Expansion," *Discount Store News*, May 11, 1998, p. 6.
——, "No Fancy Stuff: Big 5 Sticks to its Game Plan," *Discount Store News*, February 8, 1999, p. 21.

—Ed Dinger

BILFINGER BERGER

Bilfinger & Berger AG

Carl-Reiss-Platz 1-5
68165 Mannheim
Germany
Telephone: (49) 621-4590
Fax: (49) 621 459-2366
Web site: http://www.bilfingerberger.com

Public Company
Incorporated: 1975
Employees: 43,471
Sales: EUR 4.9 billion (2002)
Stock Exchanges: Frankfurt
Ticker Symbol: GBF
NAIC: 234110 Highway and Street Construction; 234120
Bridge and Tunnel Construction; 234910 Water,
Sewer, and Pipeline Construction; 234990 All Other
Heavy Construction; 233320 Commercial and
Institutional Building Construction

Bilfinger Berger AG operates as the second-largest general contractor in Germany, just behind competitor HOCHTIEF AG. With origins that date back to 1890, Bilfinger Berger has evolved from a heavy construction services firm to a global multi-service group involved in civil engineering, building and industrial construction activities, build-operate-transfer (BOT) projects, industrial and real estate services, and environmental services. The German industry experienced an upswing after German reunification in the early 1990s. It has since deteriorated dramatically, forcing Bilfinger Berger to focus heavily on diversification and international operations.

Origins

The company's structure is the result of the 1975 merger of Grün and Bilfinger A.G. and Julius Berger-Bauboag A.G. Founded in 1892, Grün and Bilfinger incorporated in 1906. Berger-Bauboag was itself the product of a 1969 merger. Bauboag was founded in 1890 as a public construction firm named Berlinische Bodengesellschaft; it built thousands of apartments and many banks, stores, and shopping centers. Julius Berger, also founded in 1890, incorporated in 1892 as Julius Berger-Civil Engineers.

In his first ten years in business, Julius Berger concentrated on railway, road, and bridge construction. He quickly earned a solid reputation with the government and received contracts for hundreds of miles of railways and roads. In 1893 alone he built 22 stretches of railroad across Germany. August Grün was co-director of a successful company with experience in water-related civil engineering projects. When Grün's partner left the firm in 1892, Paul Bilfinger, an engineer working for the government, stepped in. At that time the company already employed 250 people and had accumulated equipment and experience in a broad range of construction areas.

Growth and International Expansion: Early 1900s–30s

From the start of their partnership, Grün and Bilfinger bid on a wide variety of engineering projects. The firm entered the international arena in 1907 when it built a 45-mile stretch of railway in Hungary. In the same year, Berger's firm began work on jobs outside its previous focus, building a canal in Hamburg, a dam and power station in Blesen, and hydraulic control installations on several German rivers and canals. In 1909, the two firms collaborated on a project for the first time, widening the 61-mile Kiel Canal, an important shipping route connecting the North and Baltic Seas.

Both firms landed major foreign contracts in 1911. Grün and Bilfinger entered a joint venture with another enterprise to build ship-landing stages at Swakopmund. Julius-Berger won an international competition for the five-year contract to construct the five-mile Hauenstein Tunnel in Switzerland. By 1913, both firms had expanded their international activities to less developed countries. Grün and Bilfinger began excavation work in Tanga (German East Africa) and Cameroon in 1912, and Julius Berger began surveying for road projects in southwest Africa, Costa Rica, and Colombia the following year. Between that time and the firms' merger in 1975, their combined efforts accounted for a large share of the road, rail, bridge, and dam development in Africa, southwest and southeast Asia, and Central and South America. Both firms specialized in modernization of inter-city travel and efficient redirection of busy inner-city routes. The merged entity has continued the effort.

Julius Berger made a crucial move in 1914 when it launched its own mining activities. From then on the firm's standard practice in international contracts was to set up its own mining operations on or near each construction site. The firm would adapt its established formulas to fit the local supply. Julius Berger has saved millions of marks on materials over the years by collecting its own ores and soils instead of buying from suppliers.

Both firms frequently played vital roles in the German government's travel systems improvement plans. Along with their traditional work on roads and railways, the firms received several subway building contracts, beginning with one for the Berlin underground in 1915. They undertook many water-related jobs as well, including widening and re-channeling rivers, digging and dredging canals, and building locks and dams.

In the period between the world wars, both firms saw rapid growth in the international market. Among the larger projects Julius Berger engaged in during this time were the Trans-Persian railway in Iran (1923) and the Benha Bridge across the Nile in Egypt (1930). Among other projects, Grün and Bilfinger worked on a sewage system for Salonika, Greece (1926); reinforced concrete roads in the center of Montevideo, Uruguay (1926); an underground railway in Athens (1927); 16 miles of tunnels for a drainage system and subway in Buenos Aires (1928); and the Carioba Dam in Brazil (1934).

The burst of international activity declined to a near halt after 1935. The slowdown lasted through the end of World War II, but the two firms sustained themselves with work on the projects Adolf Hitler had begun in 1933 in an effort to ease unemployment in Germany. Hitler's programs included construction of the autobahns, a network of asphalt and concrete highways that would crisscross the nation. Both firms were at the top of the list of bidders, and they received several contracts. Many stretches of the autobahns called for long and high bridge sections, each requiring individual planning and, often, creative designs. The challenging requirements kept engineers who had been working in exotic locales and unusual terrain stimulated.

Finding Postwar Opportunities

During World War II, both Julius Berger and Grün and Bilfinger built several airports and naval installations. Like most other German companies, they spent the two years after the war clearing rubble, making emergency track and bridge repairs, and repairing damaged railway stations, roads, dikes, and housing and industrial properties.

By 1950, Julius Berger had resumed its activities abroad, building pumping stations in Egypt and the Managil Canal in the Sudan. Also in 1950, Grün and Bilfinger employed a new method in bridge building, using prestressed concrete for the first time on a railway bridge in Heilbronn. The method of pouring concrete around metal-cable frames quickly became the most popular and effective use of concrete, and is still common.

The German postwar administration hired both Julius Berger and Grün and Bilfinger to build series of telecommunications towers. The first went up in 1952, and the projects soon became a staple in the companies' logbooks. Between 1969 and 1977, they built a total of 18 of the structures. At the same time, the companies began constructing numerous hydro-electric power plants, usually in conjunction with a dam or barrage. Julius Berger was a leader in modifying the technology involved in hydro-electric power.

Both companies also continued to be innovators in bridge construction technology, and through the late 1950s were leaders in water-related engineering projects, building dams, bridges, port installations, locks, and power stations around the world. One of their biggest accomplishments during the era was a joint venture formed to build the 5.5-mile prestressed concrete Lake Maracaibo Bridge in Venezuela.

Creation of Bilfinger & Berger in 1975

After World War I, the Bauboag firm had changed its building focus from apartments to commercial and industrial structures. Through the 1950s and 1960s, it built stores and malls, universities, and industrial plants. Julius Berger wanted to enter the field, but rather than expand from within, it merged with Bauboag in 1969. The marriage was immediately successful; later the same year Julius Berger-Bauboag received contracts to build the National Library in Berlin and to do structural work at Munich's Olympic Stadium. The stadium job included a cycle-racing track, flyover access roads, and a new metropolitan train station.

In 1968, another joint effort would bring Grün and Bilfinger together with Julius Berger on a work site. The success of the project, a long autobahn tunnel in Hamburg, led in 1970 to Grün and Bilfinger acquiring a majority holding in Julius Berger-Bauboag. The two enterprises merged formally on December 29, 1975 and took the name Bilfinger & Berger Bau A.G.

Although a recession hit the international building industry in 1973, Bilfinger & Berger flourished throughout the 1970s. The two larger constituent companies began building nuclear power stations and offshore oil-drilling rigs early in the decade. In addition, the merged Bilfinger & Berger received sustained funding from the European Community and West Germany's Federal Ministry of Research and Technology to develop its innovative concrete articulated tower, which consists of a ball-and-socket joint between a drilling tower and its foundation on the ocean floor. The structure greatly reduces the stress caused by wind and waves. The firm also built some of Europe's largest sewage treatment plants during this time period.

Key Dates:

1890: Berlinische Bodengesellschaft (later known as Bauboag) is founded as a public construction firm.
1892: Grün and Bilfinger A.G. is established; Julius Berger-Civil Engineers incorporates.
1969: Julius Berger merges with Bauboag.
1970: Grün and Bilfinger purchase a majority interest in Julius Berger-Bauboag.
1975: Grün and Bilfinger and Julius Berger-Bauboag merge to form Bilfinger & Berger Bau AG.
1995: The German construction industry enters a period of decline.
2001: The company changes its name to Bilfinger Berger AG. ·

The international division of Bilfinger & Berger was very active during the 1970s and 1980s (its U.S. subsidiary is Fru-Con Corp. of Baldwin, Missouri). Some of the better known projects it worked were two nuclear power plants in Illinois (at Clinton and Baldwin), subway systems in Washington, D.C., and Atlanta, and the space shuttle launching complex in Vandenberg, California. The subsidiary Julius Berger Nigeria, Ltd., based in Lagos, modernized much of the transportation infrastructure in that country since 1970. The firm was also involved in the design and construction of the new Nigerian capital at Abuja. Bilfinger & Berger completed roadwork totaling over 330 miles in the Tripoli area in Libya in the past decade. Through the 1980s, projects abroad accounted for 60 percent to 70 percent of the firm's total construction volume.

By this time, Bilfinger & Berger was well known as a classical example of a successful civil engineering and construction firm. The company took on projects of all scales by solving the problems at hand efficiently, combining existing methods with its own creative new ideas wherever necessary. Its strong position in the industry served it well, especially in the early 1990s as German reunification took place.

Success Continues: 1990s and Beyond

In October 1990, East Germany and West Germany were reunited, creating the Federal Republic of Germany. The country ratified the Masstricht Treaty—this was the treaty that created the European Union—in 1993. The following year, Russian and Allied troops left Berlin and for the first time since World War II, leaving Berlin free of foreign occupation. These changes led to a boom for construction-related companies. Roads, housing, factories, and water systems needed to be upgraded in eastern Germany, creating solid business opportunities for Bilfinger & Berger. Parts of Eastern Europe, including Poland and the Czech Republic, also proved to be lucrative growth areas.

As the 1990s progressed, however, growth in the German and Western European construction markets slowed. Bilfinger & Berger began to consolidate its regional offices and launched a series of job cuts. It also stepped up its international expansion efforts, a strategy that continued into the new millennium. As many European countries began spending less on infrastructure

projects, governments began implementing new programs to encourage private company investment. One area of focus for Bilfinger Berger was build-operate-transfer (BOT) projects and private finance initiative (PFI) projects. These were typically public infrastructure projects that were funded by private companies. The private companies were then able to recover their investment through various tolls or charges. Through subsidiary Bilfinger Berger BOT, the company bid on concession projects related to transport infrastructure, public buildings, parking lots, and water and waste water treatment facilities. By 2002, the firm was bidding on projects in the United Kingdom and Australia. In its home country, it was also working on the Herren Tunnel, which would alleviate traffic problems on the Herrenbrücke bridge in Lübeck.

During 2001, the firm officially adopted the name Bilfinger Berger AG. As its competitors reported slumping sales and earnings, Bilfinger Berger charged ahead with positive financial results—a sure sign its diversification into infrastructure projects was paying off. In 2002, competitor Philipp Holzmann went under, catapulting the firm into the number two position among German general contractors. The company acquired construction services firm Rheinhold & Mahla AG that year along with Wolfferts Group, a building services engineering firm. Bilfinger Berger also eyed certain Holzmann assets as potential takeover targets. Some of the larger projects the company was involved in at this time included a 345 kilometer railway track between Taiwan's capital of Tapei and Kaohsiung; the Cross City Tunnel in Sydney, Australia's business district; a lock project on the Kanawha River in West Virginia; a lock project on the Nile in Egypt; and a highway that would link Goteborg and Oslo in Northern Europe.

The German construction industry remained in a depressed state during 2002. According to the General Association of the German Construction Industry, nearly 10,000 companies filed for bankruptcy that year and 75,000 jobs were cut. Having evolved into a multi-services group, Bilfinger Berger's bottom line was somewhat protected from the problems in its homeland and both sales and profits increased during 2002. The company remained focused on winning privately financed concession projects, international expansion, and providing integrated solutions for construction projects. With this strategy in place, Bilfinger Berger's management was confident it was on the right path to continue its success well into the future.

Principal Subsidiaries

Achatz GmbH Bauunternehmung; Bilfinger Berger Baustoffe GmbH; Bilfinger Berger Freiburg GmbH; Bilfinger Berger Vorspanntechnik GmbH; Bilfinger Berger Baugesellschaft m.b.H; A.W. Baulderstone Holdings Pty. Ltd. (Australia); Beijing Oulu Property Development Co. Ltd. (95%); Bilfinger Berger UK Ltd.; Fru-Con Holding Corporation (United States); Hydrobudowa-6 S.A. (Poland); Kin Ching China Ltd.; Razel S.A. (France); Bilfinger Berger BOT GmbH; Bilfinger Berger Umwelt GmbH.

Principal Competitors

Philipp Holzmann Group; Bau Holding Strabag AG; HOCHTIEF AG.

Further Reading

"Bilfinger Berger Bucks Construction Slump," *Handelsblatt*, September 4, 2001.

"Bilfinger Berger Continues Expansion Abroad," *AFX News*, May 27, 1997.

"Bilfinger Berger Eyes Acquisitions Worldwide," *Handelsblatt*, May 8, 2002.

"Bilfinger Berger Gains in Crisis," *Die Welt*, February 21, 2003.

"Bilfinger Takes Over Rheinhold & Mahla," *Handelsblatt*, June 7, 2002.

Harding, Ben, "Much Needed Shake-up in German Construction," *Acquisitions Monthly*, July 2002, p. 46.

Marray, Michael, "Green Fingers: Bilfinger Berger Wants to Make Deals Sprout in the UK and Australia," *Project Finance*, January 2002, p. 37.

Parkes, Christopher, "The European Market: German Construction Companies Prepare for Rebuilding of the East—Best Growth Prospects Are Beyond West Europe," *Financial Times*, June 15, 1992, p. 2.

Reina, Peter, "Global Wanderlust Helps Cushion German Firms' Problems at Home," *Engineering News Record*, August 14, 2000, p. 44.

—update: Christina M. Stansell

bmcsoftware

BMC Software, Inc.

2101 City West Boulevard
Houston, Texas 77042
U.S.A.
Telephone: (713) 918-8800
Fax: (713) 918-8000
Web site: http://www.bmc.com

Public Company
Incorporated: 1980
Employees: 6,335
Sales: $1.32 billion (2003)
Stock Exchanges: New York
Ticker Symbol: BMC
NAIC: 541511 Custom Computer Programming Services;
    511210 Software Publishers

BMC Software, Inc. is one of the world's largest developers and vendors of independent systems software. The company made its name with programs that increased the efficiency of IBM mainframe computer systems, and mainframes continue to constitute a sizable percentage of its sales. BMC also produces software for other computer systems, including Microsoft Windows NT and XP and the Linux operating systems. BMC products perform a variety of functions: monitoring and managing service levels; improving application responsiveness; minimizing system outages; automating systems maintenance tasks; assuring data availability, integrity, and recoverability; efficiently managing enterprise storage assets; increasing network performance; and administering business integrated scheduling, output management, and security. BMC is headquartered in Houston, Texas, in its own complex of four office buildings comprising over 1.5 million square feet of area. It also has offices in Austin, Texas; Waltham, Massachusetts; and San Jose, California. More than a third of BMC's 2003 revenues came from international sales. The company maintains offices throughout the world, including development offices in Tel Aviv, Israel; Aix en Provence, France; Frankfurt, Germany; Singapore; and, Pune, India. BMC licenses its software products to such firms as Intel Corporation, Hewlett-Packard, and Computer Associates. The company reached total revenues of $1.3 billion in 2002.

Late 1970s Origins

BMC Software began in the late 1970s as a partnership that did contract programming in the Houston area. The company took its name from the initials of the three partners: Scott Boulett, John Moores, Dan Cloer. By 1980, when it was incorporated, the 36-year-old Moores had become the company's CEO. As a programmer with Shell Oil, Moores realized that the software written for IBM mainframes, computers that dominated business and government at the time, could be much more efficient. With that in mind, Moores developed BMC's first product, the 3270 Optimizer, which sped up transmission by compressing data streams. To grow the young company, Moores paid top dollar to lure the best software developers and sales people to his firm. The strategy was successful, and new software poured out of BMC's development labs. Profit margins were unfortunately low due to the company's high salaries and generous benefit packages.

Another of Moores's innovations was marketing BMC software by telephone. Rather than send its sales staff out to meet personally with potential clients as other firms did, BMC sales people phoned database managers at target firms. Working in this way, they could pitch products directly to the individuals responsible for purchasing them, make many more sales calls in a day, and do it all for less money. Adding strength to the strategy, BMC designed its software packages specifically to make phone marketing easier. "We develop products that salesmen can explain in two or three minutes," BMC's Max Watson told the *Wall Street Journal*. The company worked on products for which it could make a clear, unambiguous claim—for example, that a particular program performed six to ten times faster than a comparable one by IBM.

In 1982, BMC's novel marketing methods and its IBM mainframe products attracted the attention of venture capitalist Jacqueline Morby. In BMC, she saw a company that was not living up to its potential, primarily because it was trying to develop too many products at the same time. For the next four

Company Perspectives:

Our heritage is helping our customers gain business advantage through more effective use of their IT groups. We continue that today by ensuring that our customers can confidently utilize new technology and application services to fundamentally change their business models.

years, Morby worked hard at introducing sound business practices at BMC. She persuaded Moores to cut back on new software development and to focus on the bottom line. By 1986, the company was earning profits equal to 20 percent of its revenues and a third of customers were from overseas.

In March 1988, BMC announced that in July it would make an initial public offering (IPO) of approximately three million shares of common stock on the NASDAQ. Company officials also hoped that the IPO would give the company visibility and prestige. The stock, which sold for between $9 and $11 a share, raised $27 million. Morby's initial investment had increased in value from $7 to $36 million. The company profited from the offering as well. By the end of 1988, its sales had skyrocketed by 50 percent from $93 million in 1987 to $139.5 million. Profits jumped even more, increasing by 55 percent from $20.3 million to $31.4 million. Over the next two years, BMC would go on the first of many buying sprees, acquiring companies and new products. In January 1989, it purchased Trimar Software Systems Ltd. and Trimar Software International Ltd., Toronto-based companies that produced IMS-VS Fast Path software products, for $4.5 million. One month later, it purchased the rights to CTOP and CTOP III products for $2 million in cash from H&W Computer Systems. By the beginning of 1991, it had also acquired Integrity Solutions, Inc. and the DB2 General Recovery Facility product.

Diversifying in the 1990s

By mid-1991, the *Wall Street Journal* could report that BMC was one of the most profitable and fastest-growing firms in the software field. It had 539 employees and net income of $31.4 million. BMC's stock had split once and was valued at $38.50 a share. Its telemarketing force was still going strong and their costs for sales and marketing were 20 to 40 percent less than competitors. The company continued to place the needs of its customers front and center, organizing regular focus groups to find out which problems needed fixing.

John Moores, the founder of BMC, had in the meantime become one of the richest men in the United States. In January 1992, Moores announced that he was retiring as BMC chairman in order to devote his time to philanthropy—he had already donated $51.4 million to his alma mater, the University of Houston, in October 1991—as well as other interests. When Moores gave up the day-to-day management of BMC in 1987, stepping down as CEO and president, Max Watson succeeded him. In 1992, Watson assumed the position of chairman as well. Soon after Moores left BMC, he founded a new software firm, Peregrine Systems, and started hiring software developers away from BMC, which responded in 1994 with a lawsuit against Peregrine and its former employees.

BMC was performing strongly in early 1992. Its stock had reached a high of $79 a share, and it had become one of the 20 largest software companies in the United States. By mid-1992, however, the situation had turned around. The stock's value had lost nearly 35 percent by July. For the next 12 months, the company was on a roller coaster ride. Although BMC had maintained strong growth through the early 1990s, in March 1993 its stock took another jarring hit on the NASDAQ when its value dropped by 20 percent. Few investors were surprised—by then the shares had acquired a reputation as one of the most volatile issues on the NASDAQ. Mainframes were an important reason for stock's fluctuations. By 1993, many analysts speculated that mainframe computers would soon be completely replaced by less expensive computer networks. These fears were largely unsupported by facts. BMC had managed to maintain a healthy annual growth rate of 40 percent while mainframe sales were getting sluggish. Nonetheless, in response BMC began to diversify its line of goods, in particular with software packages designed to expedite communications of mainframes in networks.

With its share price still falling in January 1994, BMC acquired privately owned Patrol Software of Redwood Shores, California. BMC paid $33.7 million for the company and an Australian affiliate. The acquisition represented a significant step away from the mainframe market. Patrol's software was designed to use so-called smart agent technology to continuously monitor computer networks for problems or potential problems. Chairman Max Watson was careful to point out that Patrol software did not represent a shift in BMC's essential market focus; instead, it was intended to serve as an adjunct to the company's still-successful mainframe business.

In 1993, BMC developed a new type of pact with its largest customers, styling these arrangements as "enterprise contracts." By March 1994, it had signed more than twenty such contracts with its largest clients. Frequently worth more than $1 million, enterprise contracts included large upgrade fees that were paid for at the time the original software was purchased. News of the deals caused another BMC slump on the NASDAQ. Wall Street was concerned that the contracts would result in increased fluctuations in BMC's quarterly revenues. In particular, they worried that the company was giving up future sales in exchange for booking revenue right away. In response, the company maintained that it had enterprise contracts with fewer than 10 percent of its total target market. It added that the contracts did not affect most BMC products or any yet-to-be-developed goods.

By 1996, it seemed that fears that mainframes were disappearing were unfounded, and BMC had reported sizable financial growth in fiscal 1995. Sales increased to $429 million over $345 in 1994, while profits jumped to $128 million from $103 million. In November 1996, BMC's stock split for the second time in a decade. In December, it announced plans to boost its Houston workforce by some 700 employees in the coming years. At the time, BMC employed about 1400 people worldwide. To house the new workers, BMC planned to construct a new ten-story office building next to the 20-story structure it already owned and operated on Houston's west side.

BMC's success at this juncture could be attributed in part to its recent attention to network computing. In 1996, network software, fueled in large measure by its purchase of Patrol in

Key Dates:

1980: BMC Software is founded.
1981: The company records more than $1 million in annual sales.
1984: The company opens its first international office in Frankfurt, Germany.
1988: The company makes an initial public stock offering.
1990: Integrity Solutions, Inc. is acquired.
1993: The company moves from Sugar Land to a new complex in Houston's Westchase area.
1999: *P.O.V.* magazine names BMC the nation's top employer.
2001: New CEO Robert Beauchamp institutes a company-wide reorganization plan.
2002: Remedy Software is acquired.

1994, accounted for half of BMC's new products and about 25 percent of its sales. "We've gone from being a mainframe software company to one that serves the entire enterprise," Max Watson told the *Houston Chronicle.* "We have not abandoned the mainframe, but we've taken the same valuable things we did before and spread them across many different computer platforms." Another factor in BMC's success was the modification of the tried and true telemarketing methods developed under John Moores. As it grew, the company found it needed staff who could call on clients personally. It therefore set up a worldwide system of sales offices. Around 1996, it began licensing its products for use by other companies for the first time. It soon boasted clients among the biggest companies in computing, including Hewlett-Packard, Intel, and even IBM, once BMC's main competitor.

Mainframe clients, far from declining, were as strong as ever. Mainframes, it turned out, were much better than networks at handling the large streams of data that companies were increasingly required to process. The renewed mainframe vogue was reflected in a 54 percent increase in BMC's profits for December 1998. The firm was healthy not only in financial terms. In summer 1999, *P.O.V.* magazine ranked BMC the top employer in the entire nation among those that "inspire employee happiness and loyalty while still finishing deep in the black." In addition to the company's competitive salaries and benefit packages, the magazine cited BMC's excellent stock options plan, the free food it provided to its workers every day, the firm's casual dress code, and perks like company basketball and volleyball courts.

BMC made three significant purchases as the 1990s drew to a close. In March 1999, it acquired Boole & Babbage, a San Jose, California-based software producer, for $900 million in stock. Analysts praised the merger for the compatibility of the two firms. Both served similar client-bases, large corporations and government agencies, with no significant overlap in product lines. Complementing BMC's software, which was meant to insure smooth cooperation between major applications, Boole's was designed to monitor the operations of computer networks. At the end of the same month, BMC acquired BGS Systems, Inc. of Waltham, Massachusetts, in a stock transaction worth

about $250 million. BGS developed programs to improve the performance of various business computer applications. Two weeks later, BMC paid about $675 million in cash for New Dimension Software, a Tel Aviv firm whose software was designed to schedule the operation of computer applications and manage security programs. New Dimension was made a fully owned subsidiary of BMC. The additions increased BMC's total annual revenues to approximately $1.3 billion and boosted its workforce to 5000 in 26 different countries.

Wall Street liked the developments at BMC. Over the course of 1999, the company's stock value increased a whopping 81 percent. Much of the interest was related to fears that the so-called Y2K bug was going to cause widespread serious computer problems in 2000. Companies and governments were scrambling to make sure their computer systems could survive the change in year and were buying lots of new software to do it. As 2000 finally rolled around, BMC stock was worth approximately $85 a share. When New Year's Day came and went with virtually no computer problems to speak of, BMC was left facing a morning after. Organizations that had bought and upgraded software at record levels in 1999 used their money for other purposes in 2000, and BMC sales fell drastically. In January 2000, BMC shares lost 36 percent of their value. In July, they dropped by another 50 percent. By October, the stock was selling for only $16.50 a share. BMC claimed that many of its customers were putting off new software purchases temporarily until the release of new IBM hardware at the end of 2000. Some analysts believed the problems were the aftermath of the acquisitions made in 1999. As if to belie that explanation, though, BMC continued to expand in 2000. In May, it acquired another Israeli software company, OptiSystems, for $70 million in cash. It was also in the midst of erecting two new office buildings to house its burgeoning operations in Houston.

Reorganizing in the 2000s

By early 2001, although stock prices had recovered slightly, the bad year had left its mark. Just after New Year's Day, Max Watson, BMC's longtime CEO and chairman, tendered his resignation. Watson's tenure was a good one. Under him, BMC grew from 500 employees and annual sales of less than $100 million in 1987 to over 7000 workers and $1.7 billion in sales. Watson was succeeded by BMC's senior vice-president of product management and development, Robert Beauchamp, who set changes in motion immediately. In March 2001, Beauchamp oversaw the move of BMC's stock to the New York Stock Exchange from the NASDAQ, the volatile market whose reputation had suffered from the Internet stock crash of 2000. The move, it was hoped, would increase BMC's market prestige and the stability of its stock. Beauchamp also introduced a reorganization plan that divided BMC into eleven separate business units, a strategy meant to streamline the sales and marketing forces which had been split among its various divisions and subsidiaries. Over the course of the year, BMC trimmed its workforce, eliminating mainly contract positions.

In November 2002, BMC spent $355 million in cash to purchase the Remedy Software assets of Peregrine Systems, Inc., which was going into bankruptcy. Peregrine was the company started by BMC's founder John Moores shortly after he left in the early 1990s. BMC was on an upswing as the 2002 fiscal year ended, posting profits in the second and fourth quarters. It was not enough to bring the company into the black for the entire year, however. Revenues dropped from $1.5 billion to $1.28 billion, while the firm's operating income fell from a $8.5 million loss in 2001 to a loss of $283.6 million in 2002. Net earnings also fell sharply, from $42.4 million in 2001 to a loss of $184.1 million the following year. Nevertheless, the gloomy financial results did not stop BMC from pursuing new acquisitions. In March 2003, it purchased Belgium's IT Masters, a developer and producer of computer systems management software, for $42 million.

Principal Subsidiaries

BMC Software India Private Limited (India); BMC Software Israel Ltd. (Israel); Evity, Inc.; New Dimension Software, Inc.; OptiSystems Solutions Ltd. (Israel).

Principal Competitors

International Business Machines Corporation; Computer Associates International, Inc.; Compuware Corporation; Network Associates Inc.; Hewlett-Packard Company.

Further Reading

Barnett, John, "More Houston Companies Get Wall Street Backing," *Houston Chronicle*, September 24, 1989.

Bivins, Ralph, "As BMC Grows, Others Join In," *Houston Chronicle*, August 30, 2000.

"BMC Software Files to Offer Initial 3 Million Common Shrs," *Dow Jones News Service*, July 18, 1988.

Boisseau, Charles, "BMC's Chairman Retiring—Founder, 47, Turns to Philanthropy," *Houston Chronicle*, January 21, 1992.

——, "BMC's Roller Coaster Stock Races Downward," *Houston Chronicle*, March 5, 1993.

Boslet, Mark, "BMC Software Sees Enterprise Contracts As Big Opportunities," *Dow Jones News Service*, August 30, 1994.

Davis, Michael, "BMC Software Takes $94.5 Million Loss," *Houston Chronicle*, January 25, 2002.

Fowler, Tom, "BMC Says Earnings Far Short of Forecast, 50% Shortfall Cited for Lagging U.S. Sales," *Houston Chronicle*, October 5, 2000.

——, "Watson Walking Away," *Houston Chronicle,* January 6, 2001.

Gordon, Buzzy, "BMC Acquires OptiSystems for $70m," *Jerusalem Post*, May 24, 2000.

Gupta, Udayan, "As Venture Capitalist, Morby Invests More Than Money," *Wall Street Journal*, December 9, 1988.

Hawkins, Lori, "BMC, Breaks Out of Its Software Shell," *Austin American-Statesman*, May 10, 1999.

McWilliams, Gary, "BMC Software Agrees to Buy Israeli Company," *Wall Street Journal*, March 9, 1999.

Schlegel, Darrin, "BMC Software Credits Cost-Cutting for Profit," *Houston Chronicle*, October 25, 2002.

——, "New Addition at BMC Gives Lift to Profits," *Houston Chronicle*, January 24, 2003.

Serju-Harris, Tricia, "BMC: Casual Atmosphere, Worker Perks Cited," *Houston Chronicle*, August 19, 1999.

——, "BMC Software Sees Stock Plummet," *Houston Chronicle*, January 6, 2000.

Silverman, Dwight, "BMC Sues Ex-Employees After Defection to Rival," *Houston Chronicle*, September 30, 1995.

—Gerald E. Brennan

Bobit Publishing Company

21061 South Western Avenue
Torrance, California 90501
U.S.A.
Telephone: (310) 533-2400
Fax: (310) 533-2500
Web site: http://www.bobit.com

Private Company
Incorporated: 1961
Employees: 100 (est.)
Sales: Not available.
NAIC: 511120 Periodical Publishers; 511130 Book
    Publishers; 561920 Convention and Trade Show
    Organizers

Bobit Publishing Company is a privately-held publisher of more than 20 business-to-business periodicals. Its publications are organized into the following groups: Auto, Automotive Aftermarket, Ground Transportation, Protection, and Beauty. The Auto Group's periodicals and publications are aimed at owners of car rental businesses, fleet managers, and similar businesses. They include *Auto Rental News, Automotive Fleet, Business Driver, Business Fleet, F&I Management & Technology, Fleet Association Directory, Fleet Financials,* and *Vehicle Remarketing.* The Automotive Aftermarket's periodicals serve the needs of businesses engaged in auto trim and restyling, mobile electronics, tire dealers, and truck and sport-utility vehicle (SUV) servicing. The Ground Transportation Group consists of three periodicals: *Limousine & Chauffeured Transportation, Metro,* and *School Bus Fleet.* Bobit also publishes *SBF Plus,* a newsletter for school bus fleet owners. The Protection Group includes *Police,* a magazine for law enforcement personnel, and *Security Sales & Integration* for security system installers and integrators. The Beauty Group includes *Nails,* a periodical for nail salons and technicians, and *Bella* for skin care professionals. Bobit also publishes *Death Row,* an annual reference book on capital punishment, and books on the security industry. Many of the company's periodicals are available online and have their own Web sites. Bobit also produces related e-newsletters for its target audiences and sponsors nearly ten annual transportation-related trade shows.

1960s Origins

Bobit Publishing Company was founded by Edward J. Bobit in 1961 in Glenview, Illinois, a suburb of Chicago. The company's first publication was *Automotive Fleet,* a magazine providing information to owners and operators of corporate fleets. Edward Bobit, a native of Michigan, graduated from Michigan State University in 1945 after serving two years in the U.S. Navy. After working for Dow Chemical Co., he took a position as sales manager at McGraw-Hill Inc., where he became interested in publishing. He worked for seven years at McGraw-Hill before launching Bobit Publishing Co.

In 1964, the company acquired two additional publications, *Metro* and *School Bus Fleet,* to strengthen its position in the transportation market. First published in 1904, *Metro* was devoted to surface public transportation and covered topics such as transit system operations, financing, motorcoach equipment and operations, urban transportation policies, and major system construction and rehabilitation of older transit systems. *School Bus Fleet* served the needs of school transportation professionals. It covered the management and maintenance of school bus fleets operated by public school districts, private schools, and other agencies and child care centers. Its audience included public operators as well as contract service providers.

1970s–80s: Relocation and Expansion

Bobit relocated in 1977 from the cold climate of Chicago to warmer weather in southern California, where it established an office in Redondo Beach. In 1979, the company launched *Security Sales,* a periodical serving the interests of security and alarm system installers and integrators. Another Bobit publication, *Police Product News,* began publication in 1976. The title was subsequently changed to *Police.*

During the 1980s, Bobit began producing trade shows as a way of providing the readers of its various periodicals with information on new products and services. Among the first trade shows produced by Bobit in the 1980s were the Limousine and

Company Perspectives:

Bobit Publishing Company's mission is to be a leading business-to-business media company that anticipates and meets customer needs with superior quality publications. We provide ancillary products and services, enabling our customers to attain maximum benefit from our industry knowledge. Quality is an important part of what Bobit Publishing Company does, whether it's a magazine, convention, or Web site. Embedded within the culture, every associate strives to make the best quality communication available. Bobit Publishing publications have won numerous Maggie Awards, a national acknowledgment for excellence in a publication. In addition, Eddy Awards are given out internally to publications that exhibit high editorial quality. Playfully named after our founder, Edward J. Bobit, the awards are presented annually to publications judged to be the best in a variety of categories.

Key Dates:

1961: Edward J. Bobit establishes Bobit Publishing Company in Glenview, Illinois, and launches *Automotive Fleet.*

1964: The company acquires two more ground transportation publications, *Metro* and *School Bus Fleet.*

1977: Bobit Publishing relocates to Redondo Beach, California.

1979: Bobit begins publishing *Security Sales.*

1983: Bobit launches three publications: *Limousine & Chauffeured Transportation, Mobile Electronics,* and *Nails.*

1999: Bobit acquires Security Press.

2000: Bobit acquires three automotive publications from Bill Communications: *Modern Tire Dealer, Auto Trim & Restyling,* and *Truck Accessory News.*

2002: Bobit launches *Bella,* a magazine for skin care professionals and spa and salon owners.

Chauffeured Transportation Show and a trade show on mobile electronics. These shows addressed the audiences of two publications that Bobit launched in 1983, *Limousine and Chauffeur* and *Mobile Electronics Retailer.*

Limousine and Chauffeur, which was renamed *Limousine & Chauffeured Transportation* in 1999, served the information needs of the limousine service industry with a circulation of about 10,000. *Mobile Electronics Retailer* reached automotive aftermarket electronics dealers with a controlled circulation of nearly 23,000. In 1999, the title was changed to *Mobile Electronics.* In 1983, Bobit also launched *Nails,* a magazine for nail technicians and salon owners with a controlled circulation of 50,000.

Later in the decade, Bobit expanded its presence among auto rental companies with the introduction in 1988 of *Auto Rental News,* a bi-monthly with a controlled circulation of 17,000. The company also began publishing *Fleet Financials* three times a year to provide additional data to fleet owners.

Periodical Web Sites and Electronic Newsletters: 1990s

Bobit continued to enhance its communications with its target audiences in the 1990s by launching Web sites for most of its periodicals. It also began publishing e-mail newsletters that complemented its print publications. By the end of the decade, Bobit was producing about 15 e-mail newsletters for readers of publications such as *Automotive Fleet, Auto Rental News, Business Fleet, Limousine & Chauffeured Transportation, Metro,* and *Nails.*

In the early 1990s, Bobit became involved with the publication of *Death Row,* a comprehensive reference book on capital punishment. The publication was the result of Bobit family member Bonnie Bobit's interest in the subject. After graduating from Arizona State University, she took on a part-time position as editor of the book, which was first published in 1989. She soon became its full-time editor and associate publisher and began hosting a weekly radio show called "Live from Death Row," which was broadcast on COPNET Radio. She also contributed a monthly column to *Crime Magazine* and has reported on capital punishment for BBC Radio One.

Bobit Publishing continued to produce new trade shows during the 1990s. In 1996, it launched the Conference of Automotive Remarketers (CAR). Aimed at the entire pre-owned vehicle market, CAR attracted businesses and individuals involved in vehicle remarketing, vehicle manufacturing, automotive financing, auto auctions, resale dealers, and remarketing suppliers.

By the mid-1990s, Bobit was publishing 15 business-to-business periodicals. Its top titles included *Metro Magazine,* with a circulation of 17,500, for public transit and charter bus owners and operators; *Security Sales,* with a circulation of 23,500, for security alarm businesses; and *Auto Rental News,* with a circulation of 16,000, for the car and truck rental industry.

1999 and Beyond

Bobit expanded its presence among security and alarm dealers and installers with the purchase of Security Press in mid-1999. Based in Lake Placid, New York, Security Press published reference and educational materials on sales and marketing management for security and alarm dealers.

In January 2000, Bobit launched a new periodical, *Business Fleet.* The quarterly began with a controlled circulation of 100,000 industry executives. The magazine was targeted at the commercial small fleet market, which included fleets of between 10 and 50 vehicles. Bobit felt this was a growing market that advertisers, including vehicle lessors and manufacturers' dealers, would be interested in reaching. The magazine also provided valuable information in its editorial content, which covered topics such as factory and dealer programs, funding opportunities, fuel management, driver safety, and similar subjects.

Later in the year Bobit acquired three automotive publications from Bill Communications, a unit of media giant VNU-USA Inc. The acquisition included *Modern Tire Dealer,* an Akron, Ohio-based publication that was first published in 1919.

Two other periodicals were also included in the acquisition: *Auto Trim & Restyling News,* a monthly publication first published in the early 1950s that Bill Communications acquired from Shore-Varrone, Inc., and *Truck Accessory News,* a bi-monthly spin-off from *Auto Trim & Restyling News* that began publication in 1994. *Truck Accessory News* was subsequently renamed *Truck & SUV Performance.* The acquisition gave Bobit a total of 20 business-to-business periodicals.

In mid-2002, Bobit launched a new magazine for skin care professionals and spa and salon owners. Titled *Bella,* the new bi-monthly began with a controlled circulation of 27,000. It combined advertising for new products with relevant editorial content. Among the topics covered in the magazine were retail developments, new products, and discoveries and technical advances in skin care.

As part of its trade show and exposition business, Bobit also provided management services to national associations. In February 2002, Bobit was selected by the National Limousine Association to provide management services to its membership. According to Bobit's Web site, the company's trade show business was its fastest-growing business segment.

With more than 20 business-to-business periodicals, Bobit Publishing occupies a well-established niche among business-to-business publishers. Over the years it has cultivated its audience by providing them with a variety of information sources about their businesses, including trade shows, expositions, Web sites, and e-mail newsletters. The privately-held company remains a family-owned business with Edward Bobit as its chairman and CEO. A new generation of Bobits working at the company are being groomed to lead the company in the future.

Principal Competitors

Chilton Co.; Hearst Business Publishing; Randall Publishing Co.; Shore-Varrone, Inc.; Vance Publishing Corp.

Further Reading

''Bill Comm. Sells Automotive Group to Bobit Publishing,'' *Business Publisher,* April 17, 2000, p. 4.

''Bobit Publishing Acquires Bill Communications Automotive Group,'' *Write News,* April 14, 2000.

''Bobit Publishing Launches Mag for Salon and Spa Professionals,'' *Business Publisher,* June 17, 2002, p. 3.

''Bobit to Launch 'Business Fleet' Magazine in January,'' *Business Publisher,* November 17, 1999, p. 3.

Hochwald, Lambeth, ''Cloudy with Bursts of Creativity,'' *Folio,* March 1, 1996, p. 35.

''Security Press Sold to Bobit Publishing Co.,'' *Business Publisher,* July 31, 1999, p. 5.

—David P. Bianco

Buck Consultants, Inc.

1 Pennsylvania Plaza
New York, New York 10119-4798
U.S.A.
Telephone: (212) 330-1000
Fax: (212) 695-4184
Web site: http://www.buckconsultants.com

*Wholly Owned Subsidiary of Mellon Financial
    Corporation*
Founded: 1916 as George B. Buck, Consulting Actuary
Employees: 3,000
Operating Revenues: $416 million (2000)
NAIC: 541612 Human Resources and Executive Search
    Consulting Services

A subsidiary of Mellon Financial Corporation, Buck Consultants, Inc. is the oldest benefits consulting firm in the United States and boasts a rich history of its own. Located in New York City, Buck offers a wide range of consulting and outsourcing services. Originally focused on pension funds, Buck now provides consulting on a full range of compensation and benefits programs intended to attract, motivate, reward, and, most importantly, retain talented employees. The company also helps companies develop and implement an effective human resources strategy. In recent years, Buck has become increasingly more involved in offering technologies to aid a company in its human resources programs. Not only can it help clients choose appropriate vendors, it has the capability to set up Web site and intranet systems, help to integrate hardware and software, and develop custom technology solutions. Moreover, the company can manage the processes for a client, hosting it on Buck's own systems, thus allowing Buck to offer end-to-end IT solutions—from developing a strategy to implementing and running it. Buck also provides outsourcing and insourcing solutions for clients' human resources and benefits programs. The company maintains 50 offices located in 15 countries.

George B. Buck: 20th-Century Innovator

The company's founder, George Burton Buck, was a pioneer in the development of modern employee pension funds and also played a minor role in the computer revolution. Born in Baltimore in 1891, Buck earned a Bachelor of Law degree from George Washington University. After being admitted to the Bar of the District of Columbia, he became involved in the actuarial discipline of the life insurance business, which used statistics to determine life expectancy and calculate annuity premiums—pivotal considerations in the life insurance as well as the pension field, into which Buck moved and made his reputation. In 1912, he helped to found Brown & Buck Consulting Actuaries, the first company to specialize in setting up and valuing employee benefit funds. His first major achievement came a year later when he produced the first actuarial report for the New York City Police Pension Fund. In 1914, he was hired by the city to serve as the working actuary on its committee on pensions, his work leading to the New York City Teachers' Retirement System became the first governmental plan in America to adopt the reserve basis for employer contributions.

Buck's interest in statistics led to his 1915 invention of the Hollerith keypunch verifier, an important addition to the Hollerith Keypunch Machine, the first electro-mechanical punch card system, an important building block in the development of the computer. It was invented by a Census Bureau statistician named Herman Hollerith in the aftermath of the 1880 census, which was not completed until 1887 and prompted fears that the 1890 census would not be completed before 1900. Hollerith drew on the automatic weaving machine that relied on a pasteboard method and designed a 3×5 card, a card punch apparatus, sorting box, and counter. Information was recorded by punching holes in the card then tabulated by passing the cards over a vat of mercury as pins pressed down on the cards. If a pin passed through a punched hole and touched the mercury, it created a electrical contact that moved mechanical counters. Although crude by today's standards, Hollerith's invention allowed the 1890 census to be completed in just three years. In 1903, he left the Census Bureau to start his own company, which in 1911 merged with two other firms to create the Computing-Tabulating-Recording Company. Buck's invention provided a way to double-check the work of the keypunch operators. He patented the device, then sold it to the Computing-Tabulating-Recording Company, where the verifier became a standard part of the punch-card system that was the basis of the early computer. In 1924, the Computing-Tabulating-Recording Company changed its name to International Business Machines, better known today by its initials, IBM.

Company Origins in 1916

Buck launched a new business in 1916, George B. Buck, Consulting Actuary, located in the Wall Street area of Lower Manhattan. He continued to reveal an innovative spirit, becoming a pioneer in the development of methods to determine sound financial reserves for retirement plans. Buck's basic premise was that people could retire with an income of half-pay if they contributed some of their earnings during their careers, 4 to 6 percent, and it was matched by their employer and interest earnings met assumptions. In 1916, Buck was named the actuary for the City of New York, providing much needed guidance for retirement plans for policemen, firemen, teachers, and other municipal employees. He would serve in this capacity until 1956. Because of his success in New York City, other actuaries began to open similar consulting firms to work on government and private pension plans. Buck also served for many years on the New York State Pension Commission and was influential in the establishment of the State Employees Retirement System and the State Teachers Retirement System. In 1920, he became chairman of the Board of Actuaries of the United States Civil Service Retirement and Disability Fund, covering federal civil service employees, a post which he held until his death 41 years later. Buck also represented the Railroad Brotherhoods on the actuarial advisory committee mandated by the Railroad Retirement Act.

Buck's son, George B. Buck, Jr., joined the company in 1938 after graduating from Dartmouth University and would work there for the rest of his life (aside from service in the Navy during World War II, when he commanded an escort destroyer). Buck Consultants also began to take on private industry as clients, in 1940 adding U.S. Steel and Ford. By now, it became the leading consulting firm in a number of industries, including glass, steel, aluminum, tobacco, and banking. It ultimately grew into of the world's largest consulting firm specializing in retirement, fringe, and disability programs for 1,000 clients, which included such major companies as the United States Steel Corporation, the Shell Oil Company, and the American Telephone and Telegraph Corporation. In 1958, George B. Buck, Jr. succeeded his father when he was named administrative head of the partnership. Three years later, in April 1961, George B. Buck, Sr. died of a heart attack at the age of 69. His son, however, would run the firm for only ten years. After suffering several minor heart attacks early in 1968 he was put on a limited work week. He reportedly suffered from periodic pain and worried about his health, then in the early morning hours of July 5, 1968, while spending a weekend with his family on his yacht, he was found dead in the stateroom by his wife after having

apparently committed suicide. A revolver was found next to the body but he left no note.

The partnership carried on the George B. Buck tradition. In 1970, it broadened its purview to include the entire range of employee benefits. In the 1980s, it expanded internationally, opening 21 offices around the world. Despite this growth, by 1992 the firm, now called Buck Consultants, had been surpassed by other companies and ranked just 24 among the nation's management consulting firms, with revenues of $157.1 million. Nevertheless, the firm's future looked promising due to the recent trend of major corporations to outsource the maintenance of employee pension and retirement benefit plans, especially desirable for companies that experienced a series of mergers and faced the arduous task of tracking employee records through these changes. As part of an effort to grow externally, in 1994 the company made an offer to acquire rival Towers Perrin, the eighth largest management consulting firm, roughly four times its size. The bid was immediately rejected, although there remained some speculation that the two sides might fashion a merger, which could have resulted in the creation of an industry powerhouse.

The combination never materialized and Buck Consultants looked for other opportunities to improve its position. In 1996, it paid $20.3 million to acquire the W.F. Corroon unit of London-based insurer Willis Corroon Group PLC., a move that helped in both the U.S. and British markets by adding offices in key cities. As a result, Buck Consulting became America's seventh largest benefits consultant and the world's eighth largest, with annual revenues of $197 million and offices in 16 countries. It served more than 5,000 corporate clients and the pension and other benefits plans of some ten million active and retired employees, the assets of which totaled $400 billion.

1997 Acquisition by Mellon Bank

In late 1996, Buck Consultants announced that it reached a tentative deal with Mellon Bank Corp., a client of 50 years, that in one stroke would once again elevate it into the top ranks of benefits consulting firms. The $200 million acquisition was not completed until July 1997, when 300 principals in Buck Consultants who were the shareholders of the employee-owned company agreed to the transaction. It appeared to be a good fit for both parties. Mellon in recent years had pursued a strategy of buying non-bank financial companies that would provide steady revenue in spite of downturns in the economy. Mellon subsidiary Dreyfus Corp. (acquired in 1994) offered investment services, in particular mutual funds, much of which were related to retirement plans, while Boston Co. (acquired in 1993) provided administrative and custodial services for both pension plans and institutional investors. In order to take full advantage of the large amounts of money flowing into retirement plans, especially 401(k) plans, Mellon wanted to offer total outsourcing solutions to clients, a one-stop shopping approach to attract new customers who were now beginning to demand a full package of services before awarding their 401(k) business. Rather than incurring the cost and difficulty of hiring its own actuarial experts and other necessary specialists in order to provide outside consulting and actuarial services, Mellon opted to acquire Buck Consultants. Moreover, Mellon gained cross-selling opportunities with desirable clients of Buck Consultants, and the firm's presence in 16 other countries gave Mellon entry into

Key Dates:

1912: George B. Buck, Sr. forms the first company to specialize in employee benefit funds.
1916: George B. Buck, Consulting Actuary is established.
1958: George B. Buck, Jr. is named administrative head of the firm.
1970: The company expands its services to offer a full range of employee benefits.
1997: Buck Consultants is acquired by Mellon Bank Corp.
2001: Mellon's acquires Unifi Network, adding PricewaterhouseCoopers' consulting unit to Buck.

new markets for its other investment service businesses. For Buck Consultants, becoming part of the Mellon family of financial companies provided it with resources beyond mere cash to allow it to better compete in an increasingly competitive field. According to terms of the transaction, Buck Consultants remained under the direction of its current management team and operated independently from other Mellon businesses. As a result, its clients would not be forced to bundle their businesses with other Mellon units—a provision to guard against the erosion of its customer base.

Folded into Mellon's Human Resources Services unit, Buck Consultants continued to operate in much the same manner as before the merger. Unlike some rival consulting firms, it chose not to expand into providing investment advice to its clients, services that normally involved charging performance fees as well as fees based on the amount of assets under advice. Buck Consultants opted instead to maintain its independence and objectivity on the strategic aspect of setting up funds, for which it would continue to charge a fixed fee. Instead, Buck Consultants looked for new areas in which to expand, especially the new technologies, which were becoming ever more important in human resources programs. In 2001, it acquired a major interest in LiveWireMedia, a St. Louis company which since 1999 had been providing it with the capability of creating electronic total compensation reports, intranet and Internet sites, and employee self-service applications for a variety of human resources and benefits programs. Later in 2001, Buck Consultants acquired iQuantic, Inc., a San Francisco-based consulting firm that provided a chance to do business with the technology-based companies in which it specialized. IQuantic offered particular expertise in the area of equity-based pay programs, an area of expansion for Buck Consultants, and was also an industry leader in survey services and conferences. With satellite offices in Boston, Chicago, Denver, Kansas City, and Pittsburgh, iQuantic (now operating as iQuantic Buck, a Mellon Consulting Company) added $15 million in annual revenues. Furthermore, in 2001 Buck Consultants, in an effort to supplement its technology push as well as strengthen Mellon's West Coast presence, acquired Harbor Technology Group, an Oakland,

California-based technology human resources consulting firm that specialized in creating Internet-based systems for Fortune 500 companies. The four-year-old company now operated as Buck Harbor Technologies, Inc., a Mellon Consulting Company. To cap off an active 2001, Buck Consultants positioned itself for even more significant growth when an agreement was reached by Mellon to acquire the Unifi Network, the human resourcing and consulting units of PricewaterhouseCoopers. It was a move in keeping with a trend of major accounting firms to divest themselves of their consulting business in wake of the Enron scandal and demise of the Arthur Anderson accounting firm. The $275 million cash deal closed in early 2002 when the outsourcing business was combined with Mellon Employee Benefit Solutions and the consulting business, with $100 million in annual revenues, was added to Buck Consultants. In particular, the new assets would greatly increase its benefits and human resources outsourcing business, an area in which Buck Consultants had lagged behind the competition and one that was expected to experience strong growth in the future. For both parties, it was a significant move. Buck Consulting needed the client base that Unifi provided, while Unifi's growth was stifled by Securities and Exchange Commission rules that prevented it from providing human resources outsourcing for audit clients of PricewaterhouseCoopers. Moreover, as a result of the Unifi purchase, Mellon became the world's fourth largest provider of human resources consulting and administration services. As Mellon continued to break away from its roots in traditional banking, Buck Consultants, with its strong heritage, would likely continue to play a significant role in the transformation of its corporate parent.

Principal Subsidiaries

iQuantic Buck; Buck Harbor Technologies, Inc.

Principal Competitors

March & McLennan Companies Inc.; Drake Beam Morin, Inc.

Further Reading

Chase, Brett, "High Hopes at Mellon for Pension Business Bought This Month in Little-Noticed Deal," *American Banker*, July 10, 1997, p. 9.

Kapiloff, Howard, "Mellon Buying Nation's Oldest Benefits Consultancy," *American Banker*, December 31, 1996, p. 1.

Kazel, Robert, "Mellon Bank to Acquire Buck," *Business Insurance*, January 6, 1997, p. 1.

Massey, Steve, "Mellon Buys Buck Consultants," *Pittsburgh Post-Gazette*, December 31, 1996, p. B7.

Prince, Michael, "Mellon to Enlarge Benefit Consulting," *Business Insurance*, December 3, 2001, p. 1.

Spina, Phillip, "A New Mellon Emerging, Following Reorganization," *Pittsburgh Post-Gazette*, July 7, 2002, p. E3.

—Ed Dinger

Bulley & Andrews, LLC

1755 West Armitage Avenue
Chicago, Illinois 60622-1163
U.S.A.
Telephone: (773) 235-2433
Fax: (773) 235-2471
Web site: http://www.bulley.com

Private Company
Incorporated: 1906
Employees: 300
Sales: $150 million (2002 est.)
NAIC: 233000 Building, Developing, and General
   Contracting

Bulley & Andrews, LLC (B&A) is one of Chicago's largest and most respected general contracting companies, as well as one of the oldest contractors in the United States. Bulley concentrates on higher-end jobs, generally favoring private, corporate, or institutional clients over public projects. The firm's reputation for quality workmanship is reflected in the fact that three-quarters of its work comes from repeat customers. Bulley also owns The Meyne Company, a Chicago construction company with a similar approach and an almost as lengthy history. In addition, the company's B&A Telecom division is involved in the building of cellular towers and has grown into one of the nation's 25 largest telecom construction companies.

19th-Century Roots

One of the founders of B&A, Frederick Bulley, was born in Devonshire, England, in 1870, and raised in Canada, where be became skilled as a stonemason, learning from his father as an indentured apprentice at a starting salary of six cents an hour. According to family lore, his father was a stern taskmaster who did not feel that Bulley worked hard enough, an attitude that prompted Frederick Bulley to move to Chicago as a teenager. At first he built chimneys but soon became involved in the business of constructing brick foundations for houses that were being raised to a higher level to make them compatible with the city's new sewer lines. It was during work on one of these

projects in 1891, when he was 21 years old, that Bulley met the man who would become his longtime business partner, architect Alfred B. Andrews. A year younger than Bulley, Andrews had been born in Chicago and had studied architecture at Beloit College in Wisconsin. The two men decided to go into business together, becoming general contractors, the concept of which was a recent innovation. Because of their complementary skills, the partners could handle an entire project, from design to construction, although much of their early work was the result of Bulley's excellent reputation in Chicago for masonry. The young architect's chief contribution at this point was his ability to accurately estimate jobs, allowing the company to win bids in a highly competitive industry. B&A took on a wide range of projects, from small houses to factories and warehouses. The partners' dedication to quality workmanship and honesty ultimately allowed the firm to take on higher profile clients and much larger projects. B&A designed and built North Shore mansions, libraries, and private clubs. In 1906, the year the business was incorporated in Illinois, the firm began work on one of its most ambitious projects, a brick factory for Western Electric, manufacturers of telephone equipment, that was a full 200 yards long. In 1909 B&A built the Kenilworth Union Church, establishing a relationship that would last into the next century. Another major project of this period was the 22-story Transportation Building, completed in 1911. A year later B&A built the Lying-in Hospital for the University of Chicago, the first of some 500 commissions from the school over the ensuing decades.

B&A experienced several significant changes in the 1920s. Frederick Bulley's son, Allan, who had been born in 1899, joined the firm in 1922 after earning a degree from the University of Illinois. Two years later, Andrews decided to pursue other interests and sold his stake of the business to his partner of 33 years, leaving B&A a father and son affair. As he gained more influence, Allan Bulley shifted the direction of the company further away from residential projects and more solidly into commercial and institutional construction. It was also in 1924 that B&A moved into a new building designed and constructed by its own people. One of the most prominent contracts completed by the firm during the 1920s was the Chicago Riding School Building, a massive structure that not only stabled the horses of Chicago's wealthy, offering stables for more than 450 horses, but also featured one of the largest riding rings in the world and an observation hall that could seat 3,000, as well as provide access to bridle paths that laced the shoreline of Lake Michigan. Due to highway construction in the 1930s many of the paths were destroyed, leading to the demise of the facility, which over the years became home to an ice skating rink and bowling alley before being purchased by CBS in 1953 and converted into television studios. Also in the 1920s the company handled several projects for John Hertz. Some years earlier, when Hertz was making the transition from sports writer to transportation mogul, he was a tenant of Frederick Bulley, who briefly owned some rental properties. When Hertz, who owned a chauffeured livery business, was unable to pay his rent, Bulley offered encouragement and allowed the young entrepreneur to pay him back when he had the money. Hertz would go on to establish the Yellow Cab Company, the country's first reliable taxicab service, and Hertz Rent-A-Car. Forever grateful, he directed considerable work to B&A over the years. In the 1920s B&A completed several projects for Yellow Cab and Hertz's Chicago Motor Coach Company, and later Hertz hired the firm to construct riding stables in North Carolina and a fraternity in Ithaca, New York.

From Generation to Generation: 1930s–80s

Building strong relationships with customers that resulted in repeat business proved key to the firm's survival during the difficult years of the Depression in the 1930s. The firm's current chairman and CEO, Allan E. Bulley, Jr., was born in 1933 and claimed that as an infant he heard his father exclaim that if he ever became a builder he would starve to death. Nevertheless, the desire to work in the construction field was passed from generation to generation in the Bulley family. In 1939 Allan Bulley, Sr., became the head of the business, his father having been involved in the company for almost half a century.

In the 1940s, shortly after the United States was drawn into World War II, B&A participated in highly secretive building contracts at the University of Chicago at the behest of the War Department. One of the projects was the construction of a room where an old squash court had been located under the stands of Stagg Field, the only guidance offered to Bulley coming from an anonymous Washington official over a secure telephone line. Workers thought that the project was related to an advanced form of radar or perhaps poison gas, and it was only in the final days of the war, when the United States dropped an atomic bomb on Hiroshima, that they began to understand that they had been part of the Manhattan Project, the Army's top-secret effort to develop the world's first nuclear weapon. They had built the room that housed a self-sustaining reactor that produced the world's first atomic pile.

Allan Bulley, Sr., headed the company until 1970, and under his leadership during the 25 years following the end of World War II, B&A continued to specialize in large commercial and institutional construction contracts. The firm completed several projects for Chicago's St. Luke's Hospital, including the School of Nursing and the Morton Clinic Laboratory. Significant commercial ventures included the 60,000-square-foot Ray C. Ingersoll Research Center built for the Borg-Warner Corporation, a 100,000-square-foot headquarters for Standard Rate & Data Service Incorporated, a manufacturing plant and offices for A. Stein, Inc., and a 123,000-square-foot manufacturing facility and boiler house for Skil Corporation that won a pair of important industry awards.

A third generation of the Bulley family took charge of the firm in 1970 when Allan Bulley, Jr., succeeded his father. After graduating from Brown University, where he earned a degree in civil engineering, the younger Bulley went to work for the family business in 1956 and was now well prepared to continue the efforts of his grandfather and father, nurturing relationships with longtime customers while also taking steps to ensure the viability of the company as it met the challenge of changing times. During the 1970s B&A was involved in the high-profile task of replacing the ice rink at the Chicago Stadium, home of the Chicago Blackhawks professional hockey team. The company also took on a number of major projects for St. Francis Hospital, located in Evanston, Illinois. Hospital work continued to be important in the 1980s, when Bulley completed a number of contracts for Gottlieb Hospital in Melrose Park, Illinois, including a 70,000-square-foot Professional Medical Building and a health and fitness center.

It was also during the 1980s that Allan Bulley, Jr., took steps to position the firm for ongoing growth in an industry that was experiencing significant changes brought on by mergers and acquisitions. To expand its base of clients, B&A hired more project managers and beefed up its efforts in marketing and technology. A significant addition was Paul Hellerman, a man with a great deal of experience in major construction projects, hired in 1988. Hellerman played a major role in creating the type of project management teams that could successfully win and complete even larger projects. When Hellerman joined the company, B&A was generating annual revenues of $55 million; a dozen years later it would be posting revenues in excess of $125 million.

Acquisition of Gerhardt F. Meyne Company: 1991

In 1991 B&A grew through external means, acquiring Gerhardt F. Meyne Company, which was subsequently renamed The Meyne Company and operated as a division of B&A. Founded in 1906 by Gerhardt Meyne, who had no more than a grade school education, the firm was very similar to B&A. It was committed to quality workmanship that led to repeat business from such major clients as American National Bank, Central Steel and Wire, and McDonald's. B&A also underwent some managerial changes early in the decade; in 1992 Hellerman was elevated to the position of president and chief operating officer. Alan Bulley remain CEO but now assumed the chairmanship of the corporation, a newly created position. Also in 1992, a fourth generation from the Bulley family entered management when Allan E. Bulley, III was

Key Dates:

1891: Frederick Bulley and Alfred Andrews form partnership.
1906: Company incorporates.
1924: Andrews sells out to Bulley.
1939: Allan E. Bulley, Sr., takes over company from father.
1956: Allan E. Bulley, Jr., joins company.
1970: Allan E. Bulley, Jr., succeeds father as head of company.
1991: Gerhardt F. Meyne Company is acquired.
1993: Allan E. Bulley, III, becomes fourth generation involved in business.
2000: B&A Telecom division is formed.

named marketing director after earning an undergraduate degree from Yale University and a master's of management from Northwestern University.

During the decade of the 1990s, the firm continued to be involved in traditional areas of work. In 1994 it started work on an historical restoration effort for St. Mark's Episcopal Church, an Evanston, Illinois, structure originally built in 1890. B&A also continued to work for major financial institutions, including the Northern Trust Company, while the Meyne Company built a new computing laboratory at the University of Chicago. In addition, in the 1990s B&A became more heavily involved in the senior living area, including independent, assisted living, and skilled-care facilities. The company completed contracts for the Presbyterian Home in Evanston, Illinois, as well as One Arbor Lane, Geneva Place, James King Home, Kimble Fitness Center, and the Hazel Wright Manor. B&A also found a new market for its services in the mid-1990s. A Seattle-based con-

tractor, through a reference from a former employee, turned to B&A to help him construct five cellular towers in the Chicago area for AT&T. By the end of the first year the contract grew to 150 and B&A had a new lucrative revenue stream that led to the creation of a special project team focused on the telecommunications industry. After enjoying several profitable years in this sector, B&A in 2000 formed a separate division, B&A Telecom, which in addition to tower erection and traditional construction services also offered help with lightning protection, switch facilities, and cable and antenna installation.

As it entered a new century, B&A continued to maintain strong ties with traditional clients—Chicago-area hospitals, universities, churches, corporations, and financial institutions—as well as developing new areas of business, such as telecommunications. Moreover, the company was devoted to keeping up with the latest technological innovations in the construction field. B&A was one of the founding members of Gradebeam, a joint effort to use the Internet to automate a costly bidding process. In the end, however, B&A's greatest asset remained its oldest: a reputation for honesty and craftsmanship.

Principal Divisions

B&A Telecom; The Meyne Company.

Principal Competitors

James McHugh Construction Co.; McShane Construction Corporation; The Walsh Group.

Further Reading

Bulley, Allan E., Jr., ''Bulley & Andrews, LLC,'' Exton, Pa. and New York: Newcomen Society of the United States, 2001.

—Ed Dinger

Bureau Veritas SA

17 bis, place des Reflets
La Défense 2
92400 Courbevoie
France
Telephone: (+33) 01-42-91-52-91
Fax: (+33) 01-42-91-54-47
Web site: http://www.bureauveritas.com

Private Company
Incorporated: 1828 as Information Bureau for Maritime
   Insurers
Employees: 13,000
Sales: EUR 1.01 billion ($1 billion)(2002)
NAIC: 541380 Testing Laboratories; 541330 Engineering
   Services

Bureau Veritas SA is one of the world's leading companies providing QHSE (Quality, Health, Safety, and Environmental) testing, certification, and management services. The company's services range from its historic core of marine certification to consumer goods testing services to building and facilities inspection and certification and government services and industrial services. Based in the La Defense office park in Paris, France, Bureau Veritas is also one of that country's most international companies, with more than 550 offices and laboratories operating in more than 140 countries. The company's total customer base numbers more than 200,000, served through six geographically defined primary divisions: North America, Latin America, Europe, France, Africa, and Asia and the Middle East. France remains the company's single largest market, at 39 percent of sales; Europe adds nearly 20 percent to the company's total sales—which topped EUR 1 billion for the first time in 2002—while the Americas add another 20 percent to sales. Bureau Veritas has put on hold plans to go public at the turn of the century: principal shareholders remain Poincare Investissements and CGIP, which each hold the 32.6 percent of the company; individual shareholders, including members of the founding families, hold another 31 percent of the company.

Ship Insurance Certification in the 19th Century

Bureau Veritas evolved into one of the world's leading testing and certification companies in the 20th century. Veritas's roots, however, stemmed from the early part of the 19th century. The rise of international shipping routes and the growing numbers of private vessels plying the world's oceans corresponded with the development of the rise of the marine insurance industry. Insurers in turn required information about the vessels they were asked to insure in order to properly assess a vessel's insurance risk. While the forerunner to Lloyd's Register, which was long to remain Bureau Veritas's chief rival, had been publishing a ships' register since the mid-18th century, the European continent lacked a similar service.

In 1828, Louis van den Broek, Alexandre Delaye, and August Morel recognized the opportunity to set up an assessment service on the European continent, opening an office in Antwerp. Initially called Information Bureau for Maritime Insurers, the company's original motto—"to seek out the truth and tell it without fear or favor"—provided the basis for the name Bureau Veritas, adopted in 1829.

Bureau Veritas provided assessment services as to a vessel's seaworthiness, as well as the condition of its equipment and the quality of its crew. Insurers quickly picked up on the service, and by 1830 Bureau Veritas had already compiled a register of more than 10,000 vessels. In that year, the company opened an office in Paris. Two years later, Paris became the site of Bureau Veritas's headquarters.

Throughout the remainder of the 19th century, Bureau Veritas focused on its maritime market. By the turn of the century, however, the company had recognized that growing industrialization had given rise to similar quality, health, and safety assessment services among the world's industries. By 1910, those activities had grown sufficiently for the company to form a dedicated Industrial Division. That division was later to become the company's most important, accounting for more than a third of sales at the beginning of the 21st century.

Bureau Veritas became an officially recognized certification body for the French government. In 1922, the government turned over the assessment and certification of the country's

Key Dates:

1828: Information Bureau for Maritime Insurers set up in Antwerp to provide ship assessments for maritime insurance agencies.
1829: The company adopts the name of Bureau Veritas.
1832: Company headquarters move to Paris.
1910: An Industrial Division is formed.
1922: An Aeronautics Division is formed and takes over the aircraft certification concession for the French government.
1984: Bureau Veritas begins spinning off operations into subsidiaries, starting with government contracts operations.
1985: Tecnitas, a subsidiary dedicated to marine and offshore industries, is formed.
1986: Veritdatas, a specialist in computer security, is created.
1990: Veritas Auto is created to take over the company's automobile inspection operations.
1994: Veritas Auto is merged with the automobile inspection operations of Dekra, forming Dekra-Veritas.
1996: CGIP and Poincare Investissement acquire majority control of Bureau Veritas.
1998: ACTS Testing Labs of the United States is acquired.
2002: MTL and ACTS are merged to form MTL-ACTS; the company acquires IPM (Germany), Regspec (U.K.), US Laboratories Inc. (U.S.), and Aquarism (France).

aircraft, prompting Bureau Veritas to form a new dedicated Aeronautics Division. By the end of that decade, Bureau Veritas had created another dedicated division for the construction market, creating the Building and Facilities division in 1929.

Following World War II, Bureau Veritas's organization began to take on a more corporate form as the company's activities extended to include a wide range of consulting and engineering services. In the early 1980s, Bureau Veritas took a step closer toward adopting a full corporate model, regrouping a number of its activities into dedicated subsidiaries, starting in 1984. One of the first of these was its Contrats de Gouvernement unit, which took over the company's government services operations. In 1985, the company created Tecnitas, a subsidiary dedicated to the marine and offshore industries.

In 1986, the company created Véridatas, a subsidiary specialized in computer security applications. Two years later, Bureau Veritas spun off its certification operations into a dedicated subsidiary, Bureau Veritas Quality International (BVQI). That year, the company made two acquisitions as well, buying up Assistance Technique Aéronautique (ASII) and PKB.

Expansion in the New Century

By the beginning of the 1990s, Bureau Veritas had expanded into another area, that of the French automobile inspection market, building a nationally operating chain of inspection centers. In 1990, the company created a dedicated subsidiary for its automobile inspection activities, regrouped under the name Véritas Auto. Then, in 1994, the company formed a joint venture with another leading automobile inspection group, Dekra, forming Dekra-Veritas SA. The combined operation featured more than 1,100 inspection centers throughout France.

In 1996, Bureau Veritas paid FFr155 million to acquire fellow French company CEP (Controle et Prevention), the country's leading provider of building survey and industrial inspection services. In that year, also, Bureau Véritas found new owners, when investment firms CGIP and Poincare Investissements bought out majority control of the company from its founding families. The new owners, which each controlled 32.6 percent of the company, then began preparations for taking Bureau Veritas public in 1998. However, the volatility of international stock markets that year forced the company to put its IPO on hold, if only temporarily.

In the meantime, Bureau Veritas began something of a spending spree at the turn of the century. In 1998, the company acquired ACTS Testing Labs, based in Buffalo, New York. The acquisition enabled Bureau Véritas to enter a new business

market, that of consumer goods testing. The following year, Bureau Veritas made three more acquisitions, those of ATL Consulting Group Ltd., a UK-based engineering and management consulting company, and the U.S. firm of Unicon International, together with its subsidiary Neptunus, adding their specialized operations in the logistics and transportation markets.

Bureau Veritas's acquisition drive continued into 2000 with the purchases of Bio-Control, which specialized in the inspection of hospital equipment, and Germany's DASAzert, which had formerly operated as the aerospace certification body of Daimler Chrysler. In 2000, also, Bureau Veritas created a new division providing e-commerce certification services. The following year, the company boosted its aerospace component with the acquisition of a 70 percent share in the Raytheon's aerospace division.

Bureau Veritas sought a far larger prize in 2000 when it began a bid for Italian rival RINA (Registro Italiano Navale), which was then in negotiations with the American Bureau of Shipping. The company had also been making overtures to another rival, Germanischer Lloyd, with the possibility of forming, together with RINA, a European classification "supersociety." By February 2001, the company appeared to have worked out a merger agreement with RINA. In the end, however, talks with both RINA and Germanischer Lloyd broke down.

Bureau Veritas began looking elsewhere for acquisition possibilities. Thwarted in its attempt to build up its ships' registry wing, the company instead continued to broaden its range of activities. In 2001, the company purchased Merchandising Testing Laboratories, based in Amherst, Massachusetts. That company specialized in textile testing services and was combined with ACTS in 2002 to form MTL-ACTS.

In December 2001, Bureau Veritas purchased Plant Safety Ltd., an industrial inspection subsidiary of the UK's CGNU Plc. By then, the company had also made another significant acquisition, that of Laboratoire Centrale des Industries Electriques (LCIE). Founded in 1881, that company had grown to become the top French testing and certification body for the electrical and electronics industries.

Bureau Veritas paused in its acquisition drive at the beginning of 2002. By the mid-2002, however, the company had completed the first of four new acquisitions for the year—Germany's IPM (Ingenieurgesellschaft für Projektmanagement GmbH), which operated in the project management field. Next, Bureau Veritas paid some $83 million to acquire US Laboratories Inc., which provided quality control services to the construction, public works, defense, and aerospace industries, as well as related architectural and engineering services. The company also completed its acquisition of Regspec, a subsidiary of National Britannia, based in the United Kingdom, which specialized in the electrical safety market.

The company completed its acquisitions for 2002 with the purchase of Aquarism, a small French company set up in 1998 that specialized in inspections and quality control of water supply systems and other water engineering projects. Nevertheless, Bureau Veritas showed no signs of slowing down its external growth. In January 2003, the company added its latest acquisi-

tion, that of DIN VSB ZERT Zertifizierungsgeseelschaft GmbH, a German specialist in the railway sector. By then, Bureau Veritas had grown into one of France's most internationally operating companies, with subsidiaries in more than 140 countries and revenues topping EUR 1 billion.

Principal Subsidiaries

Bivac International; Tecnitas; MTL-ACTS; LCIE; CEP Industrie; Plant Safety Ltd.; Qualité France; Transcable; Unicon.

Principal Divisions

Industrial; Aeronautics; Building and Facilities.

Principal Competitors

Lloyd's Register of Shipping; Det Norske Veritas; American Bureau of Shipping; Registro Italiano Navale; Fortis NV.

Further Reading

Bridger, Chet, "Testing, Testing: Paris Firm Adds 30 Jobs Here in Restructuring," *Buffalo News,* July 10, 2002, p. B4.
"Bureau Veritas Boss Mulls 'supersociety'," *Lloyd's List Daily Commercial News,* October 25, 2000, p. 12.
"Bureau Veritas to Acquire US Laboratories," *New York Times,* August 10, 2002, p. C4.
"CGNU Sells Plant Safety to Bureau Veritas," *AFX UK,* December 17, 2001.
Linstedt, Sharon, "ACTS Testing Labs Acquired by Bureau Veritas in France," *Buffalo News,* May 13, 1998, p. B10.

—M. L. Cohen

C&S Wholesale Grocers

C & S Wholesale Grocers, Inc.

47 Old Ferry Road
Brattleboro, Vermont 05302
U.S.A.
Telephone: (802) 257-4371
Fax: (802) 257-6810
Web site: http://www.cswg.com

Private Company
Founded: 1918
Employees: 8,500
Sales: $9.5 billion (2002 est.)
NAIC: 424410 General Line Grocery Merchant
  Wholesalers

C & S Wholesale Grocers, Inc. is ranked the third largest grocery wholesaler behind Fleming and SuperValu in the United States and the largest grocery wholesaler in New England. A third-generation family-owned business, C & S distributes wholesale groceries to supermarket chains, independent stores, and military bases across the northeastern and midwestern United States. The company is headquartered in Vermont and maintains warehouse facilities in Connecticut, Massachusetts, Maryland, New Jersey, New York, Ohio, and Pennsylvania. C & S claims A & P, BJ's Wholesale Club, Safeway, and Shaw's among its numerous customers and projects annual sales of $11 billion.

Origins

In the early 1900s, the founder of C & S, Israel Cohen, worked in wholesale grocery in Worcester, Massachusetts. In 1918, he partnered with Abraham Siegel to found their own company, C & S Wholesale Grocers. At the start, the company employed three warehouse workers in its 5,000-square-foot building on Winter Street in Worcester and distributed 1,200 products to independent grocers.

C & S entered a highly competitive market at a time in which wholesale grocers were vying for the business of large numbers of independent neighborhood stores. After World War I, independent retail grocers began to form cooperatives to boost their

buying power, a strategy that in turn enabled wholesalers to consolidate orders and operate more efficiently. In 1921, as the company began to benefit from the new industry structure, Cohen bought out Siegel's share in the business.

Under Cohen's leadership, C & S distinguished itself from its competitors by focusing on the needs of its customers as its top priority. Whereas many wholesalers did not allow their customers much, if any, say in how they stocked store shelves, C & S salespeople listened to their customers and stocked shelves according to their needs. C & S also increased their speed of delivery through efficient warehouse procedures. In 1929, the Winter Street facility and its entire inventory was destroyed by a flood. The following year, the company moved to a warehouse space on Hygeia Street that was twice the size of the original facility.

Second Generation Success: 1945 to the 1970s

After serving as a B-24 navigator during World War II, Israel's son Lester, who had worked in the family business before the war, returned home. From his experience in the military, Lester recognized an opportunity to expand C & S by selling to military commissaries. Following the war, Lester secured the company's first government commissary contracts. By the year 2000, C & S would serve 27 East Coast military bases.

During the postwar years, when many other wholesalers entered the retail side of the grocery business, C & S maintained its focus on wholesale distribution. Lester introduced a roller system in the company's warehouse to increase speed and efficiency. The company's initial $200 purchase ultimately paid off when their delivery time improved, and they earned new customers.

By 1955, with Israel and Lester at the helm of C & S, the company grew into a successful mid-sized wholesale grocer operating out of a 35,000-square-foot warehouse. Lester carried on his father's tradition of making personalized service a priority and maintained close contact with customers. At this time, the elder Cohen passed executive power to his son.

Until the late 1950s, most grocery stores were still small independent businesses. Big D, an eight-chain supermarket, led the industry and heralded the move away from independent grocers to supermarket chains. C & S gained the Big D account in 1958 and was soon acquiring more large accounts. Sales soared to $2 million, and by 1963 the company moved to a still larger facility—the historic Pullman Street warehouse, where Pullman train cars had previously been housed. Utilization of both the truck and train loading docks at the facility increased the distribution capabilities of the company. C & S continued to grow throughout the 1960s and early 1970s. By 1974, annual sales for the company had reached $14 million. That same year, Rick Cohen, Lester's son, joined the company.

Third Generation Continues Growth: 1980s–90s

Although the Pullman Street warehouse had served the company well, by the late 1970s it was evident that the century-old facility could no longer accommodate the growing needs of modern food warehouse distribution to large supermarkets. Having been located in Massachusetts since its founding, Rick proposed C & S build a new facility outside their current locale where they would be close to interstate highways and new markets. In 1981, C & S opened a new 300,000-square-foot warehouse and distribution center in Brattleboro, Vermont.

The opening of this new facility, which was twice as large as the Pullman Street operation and the largest single structure in the state of Vermont, carried with it great sacrifice. In order to meet the costs of the expansion, employees took pay cuts on a temporary basis. The company set a $300 million sales goal to be reached in five years. The Brattleboro facility, with its modern capabilities, attracted the attention of such large customers as A & P, Edward's, Walbaum's, and Stop & Shop. C & S soon surpassed its goal, and employees wages were raised above previous standards.

Employee concerns were not overlooked at C & S. In 1987, when a group of warehouse workers approached Rick Cohen about frustrations regarding their jobs and management communication, Cohen listened. At the same time, he happened to be reading *Thriving on Chaos*, a best-selling book by management consultant Tom Peters. Following a week-long seminar with Peters and a tour by the author of the company's distribution center, Rick Cohen initiated self-managed warehouse teams in 1988. The premise behind this self-managed team approach was to empower workers by allowing them the poten-

tial to increase their wages through team productivity incentives. The teams were composed of three to eight workers. Each team coordinated every aspect of a customer's order from the time the order was placed to its delivery to the customer. Rather than reward individuals on the team, which can create counterproductive work practices, the team as a whole would be rewarded equally based on orders that were delivered successfully. Conversely, teams could be penalized for unsuccessfully delivered or damaged orders. The team approach induced cooperation among workers as well as reduced employee absenteeism, which dipped to under 3 percent within the program's first six months. Essentially, the self-managed teams eliminated the need for supervisors and placed control in the hands of employees. As Rick Cohen acknowledged in *U.S Distribution Journal* in September 1993, "We were cautious going into [self-managed teams], but it wasn't anything we were afraid of. The ideas came from the employees and we trusted them."

The new warehouse team structure quickly proved to be a success. Within six months of its inception, shipping volume increased by 35 percent and labor costs decreased by 20 percent. Bonuses earned by team employees increased their hourly wages. According to *U.S. Distribution Journal*, hourly wages in 1993 for strong teams could range between $14 and $16, far above the industry average of $9.87 for nonunion shop workers. With the success of the warehouse teams, C & S employees exercised additional empowerment through a variety of employee committees whose decisions influenced company policies, employment practices, and expenditures. The team-based incentive program was used in other areas of the company in addition to the warehouse. According to the company's Web site, by 2003 75 percent of C & S employees were either working on incentive pay or were members of a self-managed team. As Cohen acknowledged in *Ken Blanchard's Profiles of Success* in 1996, "Part of the reason this is working so well and continuing to motivate employees is that there is no cap on what a person can make. We publicize successes and we go over the company's profit and loss statements every week with all the employees. They now see how they affect the totals."

Innovation, Expansion, and Acquisition: 2000 and Beyond

C & S easily surpassed its $300-million-sales goal established when they first moved into the Brattleboro facility. By the end of the company's first decade in Brattleboro, annual sales had reached over $1 billion. The company began adding warehouse facilities in 1993 with the opening of a 350,000-square-foot warehouse in South Hatfield, Massachusetts. In 1994, C & S transferred their perishable operations to a 445,000-square-foot center in North Hatfield, Massachusetts. In 1996, C & S opened its largest facility, a one-million-square-foot distribution center in Windsor Locks, Connecticut. That same year, the company purchased one of the largest freezers in the world, a 347,000-square-foot freezer in Westfield, Massachusetts, that had a capacity of 15 million cubic feet. C & S plans to expand this freezer to increase its capacity to 22.7 million cubic feet and make it the largest freezer in the world. By 2003, C & S owned and operated 18 warehouses.

The opening of numerous warehouse and distribution facilities was necessitated by the increased customer contracts that

Key Dates:

1918: Israel Cohen partners with Abraham Siegel to found C & S Wholesale Grocers in Worcester, Massachusetts.

1929: The Blackstone River floods the C & S warehouse, destroying all of the company's inventory.

1930: Company opens new, larger warehouse in Worcester.

1940s: Lester Cohen, Israel's son, establishes contracts with U.S. military commissaries.

1955: C & S moves to larger warehouse facility in Worcester.

1958: The company lands the eight-store supermarket account Big D.

1963: C & S moves into a 200,000-square-foot former Pullman train facility with truck and train loading docks.

1974: Rick Cohen, Lester's son, joins the company.

1981: The company builds a 300,000-square-foot warehouse and distribution center in Brattleboro, Vermont.

1988: Rick Cohen initiates self-managed teams in the warehouse, increasing total volume shipped by 35 percent.

1996: The company opens one-million-square-foot warehouse in Windsor Locks, Connecticut.

2002: *Forbes* magazine ranks C & S the 11th largest privately held company in the United States.

amounted to an annual growth rate of 30 percent by 1996. In September of that year, C & S acquired Winter Hill Frozen Foods and Services of Westboro, Massachusetts, and, in 1997, the company took over the distribution of ice cream and frozen foods from New England Frozen Foods, adding 4,000 new stores. By the late 1990s, C & S showed steady sales growth, gaining the 25th ranking of the 500 largest private companies by *Forbes* magazine in 1998, 20th in 1999, and 18th in 2000. In 2002, C & S partnered with Tops Markets to add over one million square storage feet in Ohio and New York, pushing C & S to operate 26 facilities in eight states.

In late 1995, the financially troubled New Jersey and New York-based Grand Union Co. announced it would close its New Jersey centers. C & S proposed to take over distribution for the company's New York-area supermarkets. Five years later, in October 2000, C & S entered into new agreements with Grand Union Co. when it filed a third time in five years for bankruptcy protection. C & S agreed to a $300 million purchase of 185 of Grand Union's 197 stores as well as a distribution center in Orange County, New York. As Grand Union's chief creditor, with $7.8 million owed, C & S found itself in the unusual position of also being Grand Union's chief supplier, with $1 billion of $7 billion in annual sales to Grand Union. Additionally, C & S was the supplier to some of Grand Union's rivals such as Pathmark and ShopRite. Most industry specialists speculated that after the sale C & S would not run the stores but instead would resell them to supermarket chains in order to keep the third-party buyers as customers. After C & S won the bid to purchase Grand Union for $301.8 million, A & P charged C & S with conspiring with several supermarket chains, including Stop & Shop, Tops, Pathmark, Price Chopper, and Hannaford, to silence bids through secret deals. Kevin G. DeMarrais reported in the *Record* that A & P noted in its court filing, "Obviously concerned about the possibility of losing a substantial piece of its business, C & S undertook a plan to assure that it would continue to service the [Grand Union] stores, even after the [company] no longer owned them." Some observers speculated whether or not A & P's claim was based on sour grapes that they had not participated in the deal as well as the fact that this missed opportunity would accelerate their diminishing market share.

In early December 2000, a New Jersey bankruptcy judge ruled that C & S had operated under a joint bid that the company had not attempted to hide and that C & S had not violated federal laws. Following the favorable judgement, C & S had agreements to sell 102 of the Grand Union stores to third-party supermarkets and would temporarily run 83 stores under the Grand Union name. Several specialists wondered how C & S would fare in the retail world with virtually no experience operating stores. As negotiations neared conclusion in February 2001, C & S was left with 94 stores that would not be purchased by a third-party grocer. When the dust finally settled at the closing on March 3, C & S purchased 150 of 168 Grand Union supermarkets and would resell 95 of the 150 stores to six supermarket chains, including Stop & Shop and Pathmark. Many of the remaining stores would be sold to smaller food retailers and non-food retailers or would be faced with liquidations and closings. Union officials estimated that 1,400 workers would lose their jobs. C & S maintained that they would keep 30 stores open under the Grand Union name if they could prove to be profitable.

GU Family Markets, a subsidiary of C & S, was led by 30-year Grand Union veteran James J. Santamarina. While C & S sold or closed many stores in upstate New York, the company focused on revamping its two most promising Grand Union stores in Hoosick Falls and Glenmont, New York. By April 2002, the two updated stores opened with such attractions as artisan breads, sushi bars, and natural foods to compete with Price Chopper and Hannaford. Additionally, the Glenmont Grand Union added a Pride of New York section that featured products grown locally. Santamarina maintained that with GU Markets improved operations, they planned to renovate the 26 remaining Grand Union supermarkets in New York, Vermont, and Pennsylvania. By November 2002, however, GU Markets announced it would close its Glenmont store, largely due to increased competition from the new, nearby 56,000-square-foot Price Chopper. The 25 remaining GU Market stores were not closed.

Following the acquisition of Grand Union and the resultant widespread changes in wholesale grocery in the Northeast, C & S moved ahead with a definitive agreement in July 2001 with Grocery Haulers, Inc., a Brooklyn-based grocery wholesale supplier of Key Food Stores Co-Operative. C & S agreed to acquire certain assets of Grocery Haulers, which served 110 supermarkets. Growth in the company also produced the development of new facilities. In late 2001, C & S had begun construction on a state-of-the-art facility in York County, Pennsylvania. Scheduled to open in mid-2002, the two-million-square-foot project would include two warehouses and a maintenance building and would employ a staff of 200. In June 2002, C & S entered agreements with Tops Markets to purchase two of Tops' distribution centers in the Buffalo, New York, area and one in northeastern Ohio, all of which were staffed by union workers. C & S asserted union contracts would be honored at all three distribution centers with no planned layoffs.

By 2003, C & S had established itself as a major player in the wholesale grocer market as the third largest wholesaler in the United States and the largest in New England with projected annual sales to meet $11 billion. Despite its growth, the company prides itself in maintaining its goals of excellence in customer service and innovation set by Israel Cohen over eight decades ago.

Principal Divisions

GU Markets.

Principal Competitors

Di Giorgio; Fleming Companies; SUPERVALU; Penn Traffic.

Further Reading

"A & P Goes to Court over Grand Union Sale," *Food Institute Report*, November 27, 2000, p. 1.

Adkins, Sean, "C & S Wholesale Grocers Builds Distribution Center in York, Pa., Area," *York Daily Record*, November 12, 2001.

Boyer, Jeremy, "Operator of Albany, N.Y., Supermarket Plans to Close Store," *Times Union*, November 4, 2002.

"Bragging About Teams," *Ken Blanchard's Profiles of Success*, February 1996, p. 7.

DeMarrais, Kevin G., "Vermont Buyer to Sell Most Stores in Wayne, N.J.-Based Grocery Chain," *Record*, February 22, 2001.

Furfaro, Danielle T., "Brattleboro, Vt.-Based Grocery Company to Close Some Former Grand Union Stores," *Times Union*, February 22, 2001.

——, "Final Sales of 10 Grand Union Grocery Stores Are Up in the Air," *Times Union*, March 7, 2001.

——, "Two Grand Union Supermarkets in Albany, N.Y., Area Get Fresh Look," *Times Union*, April 29, 2002.

Glynn, Matt, "Tops Markets Sells Three Distribution Centers to Vermont Firm," *Buffalo News*, June 12, 2002.

Haarlander, Lisa, "Buying Food Warehouses Expands Wholesale Grocer's Presence in Western New York," *Buffalo News*, June 24, 2002.

Petreycik, Richard M., "The C & S Vision," *U.S. Distribution Journal*, September 15, 1993, pp. 37–40.

Philippidis, Alex, "Supermarkets Shake Up in Store Shuffle," *Westchester County Business Journal*, December 4, 2000, p. 1.

——, "ShopRite Operator Faces Fight over Cooperative," *Westchester County Business Journal*, December 11, 2000, p. 7.

——, "Teamsters Locals to Expand Boycott of Grand Union Co.," *Westchester County Business Journal*, December 25, 1995, p. 9.

Roberts, Ricardo, "A & P Balks as Grand Union Divests," *Mergers & Acquisitions Report*, December 4, 2000, p. 1.

—Elizabeth Henry

Calvin Klein

Calvin Klein, Inc.

205 West 39th Street
New York, New York 10018
U.S.A.
Telephone: (212) 719-2600
Fax: (212) 221-4541

*Wholly Owned Subsidiary of Phillips-Van Heusen
    Corporation*
Incorporated: 1967 as Calvin Klein Ltd.
Employees: 900
Sales: $170 million (2001 est.)
NAIC: 315232 Women's and Girls' Cut and Sew Blouse
    and Shirt Manufacturing; 315233 Women's and Girls'
    Cut and Sew Dress Manufacturing; 315234 Women's
    and Girls' Cut and Sew Suit, Coat, Tailored Jacket,
    and Skirt Manufacturing; 315999 Other Apparel
    Accessories and Other Apparel Manufacturing

Calvin Klein, Inc., designs, licenses, and, in some cases, produces clothing, accessories, fragrances, and home furnishings bearing the name of designer Calvin Klein. Since its inception, the company was a partnership between Klein and his childhood friend Barry Schwartz. Named by *Time* magazine in 1996 as one of the 25 most influential Americans, Klein made his impact not only by designing but also by marketing his wares through high visibility and often controversial advertisements created by the company's in-house agency, CRK Advertising. In 2002, worldwide retail sales of Calvin Klein products surpassed $3 billion. Most of these goods were manufactured and sold by other companies under license—licensed products account for over 90 percent of company revenue. After three years of shopping around for a buyer, Schwartz and Klein inked a deal with Phillips-Van Heusen Corporation, the largest shirtmaker in the United States. The $430 million transaction was completed in February 2003.

Rocketing to Stardom in the 1970s

Born and raised in New York City's borough of the Bronx, Calvin Richard Klein decided he wanted to be a fashion de-

signer at an early age. After graduating from the Fashion Institute of Technology in 1963, he worked for women's coat and suit manufacturers in Manhattan's garment district before opening his own business in 1968. A childhood friend, Barry Schwartz, loaned him $10,000 in start-up money and joined the firm a month later, after the family supermarket in Harlem that Schwartz had inherited was gutted in the riots that followed the assassination of Martin Luther King.

Klein rented a dingy showroom to exhibit a small line of samples. His big break came when a vice-president at Bonwit Teller stopped at the wrong floor of the building, liked what he saw, and invited Klein to bring his samples to the president's office. Klein wheeled the rack of clothes uptown personally and won an order of $50,000 (retail) on the spot. Bonwit's gave the merchandise impressive exposure, with window displays in its flagship Fifth Avenue store and full-page ads in the New York Times. Soon after, Calvin Klein was besieged by orders. The fledgling company booked $1 million worth of business in its first year, reaching sales volume of $5 million by 1971.

Klein mainly designed women's coats and two-piece suits until 1972, when he began concentrating on sporty sweaters, skirts, dresses, shirts, and pants that could be mixed and matched for a complete wardrobe. The clothing featured the simplicity of line, muted earth tones, and classic fabrics that characterized his work and gave it an air of understated elegance. Klein won a Coty American Fashion Critics Award—fashion's Oscar—in 1973. He received an unprecedented third consecutive Coty Award for women's wear in 1975 and, at age 32, was elected to the group's Hall of Fame. That fiscal year (ending June 30, 1975) the firm shipped $12 million worth of merchandise, including swimsuits and dresses. It earned another $2 million to $6 million from licensing furs, umbrellas, sheets, shoes, scarves, belts, dresses, sunglasses, suedes, and patterns. Klein not only designed every item carrying his name but closely watched every step of the production process.

Company revenues rose to $40 million in fiscal 1976 and a startling $90 million in 1977. Because its prices were generally below those of its two major competitors, Ralph Lauren and Anne Klein, the firm won the loyalty of young working women as well as older, wealthier buyers. Calvin Klein merchandise was so hot that the company could pick and choose among

Company Perspectives:

We believe our expertise in brand management, product design, sourcing, and other logistics provides us with the ability to successfully expand product offerings and distribution under the Calvin Klein brands while preserving the brands' prestige and global presence. As a result, we believe we have the opportunity to realize sales growth and enhanced profitability.

stores that wanted to carry the company's products and black-ball those that dared to try to return unsold goods. Seven hundred buyers and reporters were turned away from Klein's fall 1978 fashion show; the buyers who got in placed $28 million worth of orders within 48 hours.

Klein introduced his first menswear collection in 1978, telling the *New York Times Magazine* that he approached men's clothing "with the same philosophy as the women's. They're for Americans who like simple, comfortable but stylish clothes—but with nothing overscale or extreme." No less than 779 fabrics were used in the European-produced collection, which ranged from neckties to suits and overcoats. The production and sale of most of the men's clothing was licensed to Bidermann Industries. Also in 1978, Calvin Klein introduced his own line of fragrances and a complete makeup collection of 18 beauty and skin-care products that stressed neutral colors to give the face a natural effect. However, the lightweight, rosy perfume (at $85 an ounce) needed to anchor the collection never caught on with the public. The fragrance and cosmetics business was sold to Minnetonka, Inc. in 1980.

Calvin Klein jeans, by contrast, were to become the company's biggest hit. Klein's first attempt, in 1976, to capitalize on the designer-jeans craze—at $50 a pair—was a failure. The following year, however, his company cut a deal to design the product for Puritan Fashions Corp., the largest dress manufacturer in the world. Klein raised the groin in his jeans to accentuate the crotch and pulled the seam up between the buttocks to give the rear more shape. A Times Square billboard of model Patti Hansen on her hands and knees, her derriere arched skyward and the Calvin Klein label on her right hip visible, caused a sensation and remained in place for four years. By 1979, Calvin Klein was second to Gloria Vanderbilt in designer-jeans sales, with one-fifth of the market. A company spokesman observed, "The tighter they are, the better they sell."

The biggest lift to Calvin Klein's jeans was the television campaign directed by Richard Avedon that featured 15-year-old model/actress Brooke Shields provocatively posed in a skintight pair of Calvin Klein jeans. In the best-remembered spot, she pronounced, "Do you know what comes between me and my Calvins? Nothing." In another she declared, "I've got seven Calvins in my closet, and if they could talk, I'd be ruined." These suggestions of underage sexuality struck a public nerve and, following a flood of complaints, the New York flagship stations of all three networks banned the two ads from the air. Klein could shrug off the criticism because sales of his jeans were then climbing to two million pairs a month. He added a jeans-inspired collection that included shirts, skirts, and

jackets, also licensed to Puritan. These products accounted for about $100 million in sales in 1980.

Branching Out in the 1980s

In 1982, Calvin Klein entered the underwear business, once again exploiting the allure of youth in provocative poses to push the product. Photographer Bruce Weber's beefcake ads featured a brawny Olympic pole vaulter in various states of well-endowed undress. When the company rented space in 25 New York bus shelters to display advertising posters featuring the underwear, all 25 had their glass shattered and posters stolen overnight. The follow-up was predictable—a line of women's underwear featuring male-style briefs and boxer shorts that retained the fly front. Both campaigns were hits. The men's line was part of the Bidermann license, which lapsed in 1987, while the women's skivvies so outstripped Calvin Klein's own manufacturing capabilities that in 1984 this division was sold to Kayser Roth Corp., a unit of Gulf & Western Industries, for about $11.2 million. Calvin Klein continued to design and create advertising for women's underwear, later adding hosiery and sleepwear lines.

In 1982, Puritan Fashions—9 percent owned by Klein and Schwartz—had sales of $245.6 million, of which licensed Calvin Klein products accounted for about 94 percent, earning $15.6 million in royalties for the firm. However, Puritan's finances deteriorated as the designer-jeans boom ended and so, to protect their investment, in late 1983 Klein and Schwartz bought almost all the shares they did not already hold for $65.8 million in a leveraged buyout, with a Puritan subsidiary financing the purchase by taking out bank loans. The consolidated companies were renamed Calvin Klein Industries. After Puritan lost $11.3 million in 1984, Calvin Klein Industries placed $80 million in high-yield bonds (so-called junk bonds) through Michael Milken of Drexel Burnham Lambert Inc., mostly to keep Puritan afloat.

Registration statements filed with the Securities and Exchange Commission in connection with the junk bonds Calvin Klein issued afforded the public a rare look at the finances of the closely held enterprise. Calvin Klein Industries had 1984 revenue of $258.2 million and net income of $17.2 million, with Klein and Schwartz each collecting $12 million in salary, dividends, and other distributions. Puritan returned to profitability in 1985, earning $12.4 million. Nevertheless, Calvin Klein Industries had huge payments to make on its big junk-bond debt, and this financial problem seemed to be taking a toll on the designer. "Every color choice became life or death," he later told *Newsweek,* "because doing everything as well as possible meant survival." In 1988, he spent a month at the Hanley Hazelden Center in Minnesota to receive treatment for drug and alcohol addiction.

When Minnetonka launched a new perfume called Obsession—at $170 an ounce—in 1985, Calvin Klein created a heavy-breathing print and TV campaign that cost more than $17 million in ten months alone, followed by another $6 million campaign for Obsession for Men. One Weber print ad featured two nude men entwined around one female; another, a naked couple with their groins pressed together; a third, three naked women, limbs entangled. A survey ranked the Obsession ads as the most memorable print advertisements of the year for four

Key Dates:

1968: The Calvin Klein brand is launched.
1973: Klein wins his first Coty American Fashion Critics Award.
1979: Calvin Klein controls one-fifth of the designer jeans market.
1982: Klein enters the underwear business.
1985: A new perfume called Obsession is launched with a $17 million advertising campaign.
1989: A Unilever Co. subsidiary purchases the Calvin Klein cosmetics/fragrance line.
1994: A unisex fragrance, cKone, is introduced; the company's underwear business is licensed to Warnaco Group Inc.
2000: Klein files suit against Warnaco Group and its CEO Linda Wachner.
2003: Calvin Klein is acquired by Phillips-Van Heusen Corporation.

years in a row. TV commercials displayed a female model as the object of obsessive love by, in turn, a boy, a young man, an older man, and an older woman. Obsession quickly became the second-best selling fragrance in the world. Combined with Obsession for Men and a line of body products, sales broke the $100 million mark by the end of 1987.

To complement Obsession, an oriental fragrance, in 1988 Calvin Klein introduced a floral scent, dubbed Eternity, which was marketed in perfume, cologne, cologne-spray, and body-cream forms. Newly married to his second wife, Klein devised a softer $18 million promotional campaign based on the themes of spirituality, love, marriage, and commitment. By the end of its first year on the market, Eternity had grossed $35 million. Minnetonka (14 percent owned by the Calvin Klein Sport division) was sold in 1989, with the Calvin Klein cosmetics/fragrance line fetching $376.2 million from Unilever Co.'s Chesebrough-Pond's subsidiary. Also in 1989, Calvin Klein opened its first full-line free-standing store, in a Dallas suburb. Products included Calvin Klein Sport lines for men and women, women's and men's underwear and sleepwear, hosiery, shoes, outerwear, accessories, cosmetics, and fragrances.

Rescue and Resurgence in the 1990s

In 1991, Calvin Klein introduced a new silk-scarf collection licensed to Ray Strauss Unlimited. Also that year, the company resumed menswear, licensing it to Gruppo GFT, an Italian manufacturer. Eyewear and sunglasses bearing the designer's name, previously made by Starline Optical Corp., were licensed to Marchon Eyewear. The big story that year, however, was the introduction of Escape, a $115-an-ounce "fruity, floral" scent. "After work you get away," Klein explained regarding the concept. "You escape, and you do it with style." Escape proved a hit and was followed in 1993 by Escape for Men.

Despite sizable royalty payments from these and other products, Calvin Klein was falling into financial trouble in the new decade. The company's revenue dropped 13 percent in

1990, to $197 million, leading to a $4.3 million loss, the third time in five years the company had been in the red. The Puritan/Calvin Klein Sport division lost $14.2 million alone. Many younger women who could not afford the designer's flagship Collection line were not buying his clothes at all. A sexually suggestive insert for Calvin Klein Jeans in *Vanity Fair* in October 1991 failed to stimulate sales, prompting U.S. retailers to contend that Klein had fallen out of touch with their customers.

Calvin Klein, Inc. was restored to financial health partly through the efforts of David Geffen, the entertainment tycoon who was a long-time friend of the designer. Geffen purchased $62 million of the company's debt securities in 1992 at a discount and was repaid in 1993, when the company took out a $58 million loan from Citibank. The firm then paid off the Citibank loan by licensing the underwear business to Warnaco Group Inc. for $64 million. Warnaco also won the license for a new venture, men's accessories.

Undeterred by suggestions that with the end of the "decadent" 1980s sex no longer sold, Klein introduced a new line of underwear, including $16 fly-button shorts, in 1992 with ads featuring Marky Mark (Mark Wahlberg), a muscular rap star. The campaign proved successful with both young men and women, grossing $85 million for the company within 12 months. In 1994, a partnership later renamed Designer Holdings Ltd. bought Calvin Klein's fading jeans business for about $50 million. Calvin Klein introduced a khaki collection in 1996 and also licensed it to Designer Holdings, along with CK Calvin Klein Jeans Kids and CK Calvin Klein Kids Underwear, also introduced that year. Designer Holdings was acquired by Warnaco in 1997.

By 1995, when it opened a four-level, 22,000-square-foot minimalist-style emporium at Madison Avenue and East 60th Street in Manhattan, Calvin Klein had six stores in the United States. In addition, during 1993 and 1994, the company licensed Calvin Klein boutiques to operators in Barcelona, St. Moritz, Zurich, and Singapore and formed a partnership with four Japanese companies to create in-store shops there and to produce more licensed apparel. Four stores—in Manhattan, Dallas, Palm Beach and Costa Mesa, California—remained in 1997. The company also had an outlet store in Secaucus, New Jersey.

In 1994, Calvin Klein introduced cKone, a unisex fragrance that became another smash hit, grossing $60 million in its first three months. It was followed in 1996 by cKbe, promoted in a $20 million monochrome print and TV campaign directed by Richard Avedon that featured young models exposing lots of pierced and tattooed flesh. In a poll conducted by Louis Harris for *USA Today,* only 4 percent of the respondents expressed strong liking for the ads, while 57 percent said they disliked them. Advertising experts suggested that what was turning off the general public was precisely what was attracting the people who were buying the product, especially teenagers.

Advertisements for Calvin Klein jeans also continued to provoke controversy. Posters featuring a notably skinny model, Kate Moss, were festooned with stickers reading "Feed this woman" by a Boston-area group called Boycott Anorexic Marketing. The company ignored the group but was unable to shrug off the reaction, especially from Christian groups, created by its summer 1995 campaign for CK Jeans, featuring models who appeared to be teenagers in states of undress that, according to one writer, "suggested auditions for low-budget porn movies." For the first time the company retreated, pulling the ads, which the designer maintained had been "misunderstood. . . . People didn't get that it's about modern young people who have an independent spirit and do the things they want to and can't be told or sold." A U.S. Justice Department investigation ended without charges after federal agents determined that no minors were used in the ads.

The controversial ads did not offend the market for which the campaign was intended. CK Calvin Klein Jeans continued to be one of the strongest sellers among youths. "They want the Calvin Klein label," explained the executive editor of *Children's Business* in 1996. "Also at the point the children are over eight, they're pretty much deciding what they want to wear. . . . These lines . . . have the cachet that comes from the adult market." Later that year a Calvin Klein underwear ad showing a 20-year-old male model in very tight gray briefs, posed with his legs wide apart, was dropped by the company's own licensee, Warnaco. Also in 1996, a group of parent-led anti-drug groups called for a boycott of Calvin Klein products to protest a new ad campaign that they said glamorized heroin addiction. The magazine and television advertisements in question featured gaunt, glassy-eyed models to promote cKbe. In 1999, an underwear billboard in Times Square featuring two scantily clad young boys launched yet another round of controversy. The ad was eventually pulled after rumors surfaced that speculated on Klein's sexual orientation.

In 1995, Calvin Klein launched, under license, a home collection composed of sheets, towels, and tableware. By 1997, only the designer's signature Calvin Klein women's collection of apparel and accessories and the CK Calvin Klein bridge collections of less-expensive women's and men's apparel (except in Europe, the Middle East, and Japan) were being manufactured by the company itself. Of the company's $260 million in sales in 1996, $141 million came from its in-house products and $119 million from royalties and designer income. Of worldwide retail sales of $4.4 billion, apparel accounted for $2.7 billion, fragrances for $1.5 billion, and other products for $200 million. Net profits were $41 million.

During the late 1990s, Calvin Klein, Inc. was 43 percent owned by the designer and 43 percent owned by Schwartz, who was chairman and chief executive officer. The rest of the equity was held by family trusts. Gabriella Forte, a former Giorgio Armani executive, became the company's president in 1994 and was put in charge of day-to-day administration. The company was divided into three parts: the Calvin Klein collection, cK sportswear, and cK Jeans. In addition to apparel, each segment offered perfume, accessories, and housewares.

New Ownership in a New Century

During 1999, both Klein and Schwartz agreed that it was time to seek out expansion via a merger or an alliance. In October, the company hired investment firm Lazard Freres & Co. to organize a deal. With a billion dollar price tag however, Calvin Klein was unable to find a suitable partner. and in April

2000 the firm took itself off of the market. Klein commented on the process in a June 2000 *DNR* article, claiming that "a year ago we decided to explore strategic options for the company. We wanted to see how we can take the company to the next step. It gave us the opportunity to talk to various partners and explore opportunities and take the business to the next level." Klein went on to say, "We decided to remain a private company because we thought we could do it better on our own."

During that same time period, Klein filed suit against his largest licensee, the Warnaco Group Inc. and its CEO Linda Wachner. Claiming the firm had violated federal trademark laws and breached fiduciary duty and several contracts by distributing its jeans to low-end retailers, Klein hoped to strip Warnaco—on the brink of bankruptcy—of its licensing rights. Warnaco on the other hand, claimed that Klein had been fully aware of its distribution practices for years and they stood to lose millions if the suit favored Klein. In 1999, one-third of the company's revenues and cash flow was attributed to the sale of Calvin Klein jeans. Relations became even more strained between the two companies when Wachner filed a libel suit against Klein for comments made in several speeches and on the television show *Larry King Live*. The two appeared in court in January 2001 but came to an amicable resolution before the proceedings began.

In late 2002, Calvin Klein, Inc. caught the eye of Phillips-Van Heusen Corporation (PVH), a company looking to acquire a major brand. As the largest shirtmaker in the United States, PVH owned the Van Heusen, IZOD, and G.H Bass brands and had licensing agreements with Geoffrey Beene, Arrow, DKNY, and Kenneth Cole. Under the leadership of CEO Bruce Klatsky, PVH made a play for Calvin Klein and eventually won the battle. A 2002 *New York Times* article reported that the union would "give Van Heusen what Mr. Klatsky called the best-known apparel label in the world, and will give Calvin Klein, who will stay on with the new company, the financial resources to further expand his name in Asia and Europe. The purchase will also free the designer to worry more about aesthetics and less about production and bookkeeping."

Under the terms of the deal, Klein remained a design consultant for Calvin Klein, Inc. while PVH retained 100 percent ownership of the firm. The $430 million cash and stock deal also included royalty payments to Klein through 2018. Completed in February 2003, the acquisition marked a new era for the brand. For the first time, Klein did not have complete control over the products sold under his name, and his partner Schwartz had retired. After questionable behavior in March at a Knicks basketball game in New York was made public, Klein announced he was again seeking professional help for substance abuse. Both PVH management and Klein claimed it would not affect his role with the company.

In March 2003, Calvin Klein announced a licensing agreement with Vestimenta S.p.A. in which the Italy-based concern would manufacture and distribute the Calvin Klein Collection line. PVH also planned to launch a new Calvin Klein men's sportswear line in 2004. While Calvin Klein would no doubt continue as a leading brand for years to come, the results of its new ownership and management structure remained to be seen.

Principal Competitors

Donna Karan International Inc.; Polo Ralph Lauren Corporation; Tommy Hilfiger Corporation.

Further Reading

Agins, Teri, and Jeffrey A. Trachtenberg, "Calvin Klein Is Facing a Bid As Magic Touch Seems To Be Slipping," *Wall Street Journal*, November 22, 1991, pp. 1A, 9A.

Agins, Teri, "Shaken by a Series of Business Setbacks, Calvin Klein, Inc. Is Redesigning Itself," *Wall Street Journal*, March 21, 1994, pp. 1B, 4B.

Chambers, Andrea, "Calvin Klein's Romantic Season," *New York Times Magazine*, January 30, 1977, pp. 46–48.

Cowley, Susan Cheever, "Calvin Klein's Soft, Sexy Look," *Newsweek*, May 8, 1978, pp. 80–82, 84, 87.

Gaines, Steven, and Sharon Churcher, *Obsession: The Lives and Times of Calvin Klein*, New York: Birch Lane, 1994.

Gross, Michael, "The Latest Calvin," *New York*, August 8, 1988, pp. 20–29.

Ingrassia, Michele, "Calvin's World," *Newsweek*, September 11, 1995, pp. 60, 62–64, 66.

Kanner, Beatrice, "The New Calvinism," *New York*, September 17, 1984, pp. 31, 35–36.

Kaplan, James, "Triumph Calvinism," *New York*, September 18, 1995, pp. 46–52, 57, 101.

Lipke, David, and Courtney Colavita, "Vestimenta: CKI's New Strategic Partner," *Daily News Record*, March 3, 2003, p. 1A.

McQuade, Walter, "The Bruising Businessman Behind Calvin Klein," *Fortune*, November 17, 1980, pp. 106–108, 112, 116, 118.

Rozhon, Tracie, "Calvin Klein Selling His Company to Biggest Shirtmaker in the U.S.," *New York Times*, December 18, 2002, p. C1.

Ryan, Thomas J., "Calvin Won't Follow Ralph Onto the Big Board," *Daily News Record*, June 18, 1997, p. 17.

Steinhauer, Jennifer, "Firm Grasp of Fashion: Tenacious President Transforms Calvin Klein," *New York Times*, November 7, 1997, pp. 1D, 6D.

—Robert Halasz
—update: Christina M. Stansell

Carlson Wagonlit Travel

1405 Xenium Lane
Plymouth, Minnesota 55441
U.S.A.
Telephone: (763) 212-4000
Fax: (763) 212-2219
Web site: http://www.carlsonwagonlit.com

Private Company
Incorporated: 1994
Employees: 8,083
Sales: $11 billion (2001 est.)
NAIC: 561510 Travel Agencies; 561520 Tour Operators

With more than 3,000 offices in more than 140 countries, Carlson Wagonlit Travel (CWT) is the second-largest travel agency in the world. Although the combined name is relatively new, the company's roots go back to the oldest travel businesses in Europe and America. Wagonlit Travel's founder was the creator of the legendary Orient Express, while the Carlson Travel Network was based on Ask Mr. Foster Travel, one of the first travel agencies in the United States. Carlson also operates a separate, wholly-owned leisure and franchised travel agency network in North America under the Carlson Wagonlit Travel Associates name. In addition, Accor manages separate CWT Leisure operations in Europe.

Origins

Compagnie Internationale des Wagons-Lits et du Tourisme was founded in 1872 by Georges Nagelmakers, a Belgian, to market rides on railway sleeper cars (wagons-lits) of his own design. This culminated in the richly outfitted carriages of the legendary Orient Express, officially inaugurated in 1883. A network of Wagons-Lits travel agencies appeared in Europe in 1928.

Carlson Wagonlit's origins in the United States date back to the country's first travel agency. Ask Mr. Foster Travel began with a souvenir shop Ward Grenelle Foster opened in St. Augustine, Florida, in 1888. As a child in New York, Foster had been hospitalized for tuberculosis. While confined, he developed a passion for travel literature. He became sought after for travel advice, leading to a career as the father of the travel agency in the United States.

Foster started by publishing travel guides. During the 1920s, his travel agency grew to 70 offices in the United States. This era saw the professionalization of the business with the appearance of Foster Girls, who were dedicated to the travel business full time. Men did not begin working as travel agents in the United States until the 1940s.

Paxton Mendelssohn of Detroit bought Ask Mr. Foster in 1937. Within a few years, the outbreak of World War II curtailed leisure travel. After the war, demand was great—so great that the railroads did not need to advertise with Ask Mr. Foster, so the agency began to switch to a commission-based system.

Changing Hands in the 1970s

Peter Ueberroth, future Major League Baseball commissioner, acquired Ask Mr. Foster through his Los Angeles travel company, First Travel Corp., in 1972. Ueberroth paid $1 million for the agency, which had 29 branch offices. He placed his brother, John Ueberroth, in charge of its expansion.

In 1979, Ask Mr. Foster was sold to the Carlson Companies, Inc., which Curt Carlson had built up from a small trading stamp company to one of the biggest privately held firms in the United States. Ask Mr. Foster then had more than 100 branches and more than $100 million in sales a year.

Carlson entered the travel market just as deregulation of the airline industry was getting underway. With their newfound freedom, airlines introduced thousands of airfares using complex formulas to make the most profit from every flight. Corporations with large travel accounts turned to agencies like Ask Mr. Foster Travel to find the best deals and to provide reporting of travel expenses.

John Ueberroth remained with Ask Mr. Foster after it was acquired by Carlson and continued to direct its expansion. He eventually became president of Carlson Travel, which grew by

---

Company Perspectives:

Carlson Wagonlit Travel is one of the leading travel and expense management companies in the world, serving both corporate and leisure clients. Carlson Wagonlit created the first truly multinational presence for corporate travel management. Our global strength was enhanced when U.S.-based Carlson Travel Group and French-based Wagon-Lits merged to form Carlson Wagonlit Travel. Carlson Wagonlit continues to develop in key markets, including Asia Pacific and Latin America. With offices in more than 140 countries worldwide, Carlson Wagonlit is a true global leader in travel and expense management. As a worldwide leader in the corporate travel industry, Carlson Wagonlit offers our clients a comprehensive, resourceful, and, above all, forward-thinking approach to travel and expense management—all with an eye toward balancing corporate objectives with cost savings, personalized service, and quality.

---

acquisition through the first half of the 1980s, picking up Canada's P. Lawson Travel and leisure travel agencies Cartan Tours and First Tours. Carlson acquired a 70 percent holding in P. Lawson in 1983 and had acquired the remainder by 1992.

Mixing Corporate and Leisure Travel in the 1980s

By the mid-1980s, Carlson Travel Group had become one of the largest travel companies in the world by focusing on corporate sales. It had 600 offices and accounted for nearly half of Carlson Companies' 1986 revenues of $3.5 billion. The group's only near rival was American Express Travel Management Services. The company owned 18 agencies inside Neiman-Marcus department stores (Neiman-Marcus Travel Service) in addition to its Ask Mr. Foster units.

Company head John Ueberroth was trying to replicate this success on the leisure side of the market. CTN began an associates program from U.S. agencies in 1984. The number of participating agencies exceeded 600 in 1990. Ask Mr. Foster acquired Don Travel Service Inc. in 1986. This regional agency based in New York had annual sales of about $200 million.

Northwest and TWA's PARS computer reservations system was installed in 80 Ask Mr. Foster offices in early 1988. Carlson acquired Gelco Travel Management Service Inc., a unit of GE Capital, in the same year. Gelco, a $250 million travel company with 660 employees, was folded into Ask Mr. Foster.

Going Global in the 1990s

In 1990, Carlson Travel acquired a 76 percent interest in the A.T. Mays travel agency chain, the fourth-largest in the United Kingdom. A.T. Mays had more than 300 offices, more than 2,400 employees, and annual revenues of $576 million. It was eventually renamed Carlson Worldchoice. Mays was Carlson's first major overseas acquisition. A wave of consolidation had begun among travel agencies in the United States and United Kingdom.

The Ask Mr. Foster name was retired in April 1990, replaced by that of Carlson Travel Network. The new name conveyed both the connection to the Carlson-owned restaurants and hotels as well as the existence of a global distribution network. Also in 1990, operations at the company were restructured into commercial and retail sides, while computing and accounting operations were centralized at its Minneapolis headquarters. Carlson had acquired a company specializing in travel management software, CompuCheck Corp. Carlson Travel Network's system-wide revenues rose 42 percent to $5.1 billion in 1990.

Travis Tanner was named president of Carlson Travel Group, which included the Carlson Travel Network, in January 1993. He was returning to the unit after four years as head of Walt Disney Travel Co. Carlson Travel Network soon underwent a restructuring aimed at delegating more decision-making to local and regional offices. The unit had about 6,000 employees at the time.

The next year, in March 1994, Carlson Travel announced the merger of its business travel operations with those of Paris-based Wagonlit Travel (Compagnie Internationale des Wagon-Lits et du Tourisme), a unit of the Accor Group SA, a French tourism and business service conglomerate that also owned Novotel, Sofitel, and Motel 6 hotels and car rental agencies. Accor was the largest travel and hospitality company operating outside the United States.

A global travel enterprise, named Carlson Wagonlit Travel (CWT), was formed with annual revenues of $10.8 billion. This was large enough to re-take the industry lead from American Express Travel Related Services (TRS), which till then had been the largest travel company in the world with 1993 sales of $8 billion. Carlson's independent foreign franchises were not included in the deal. Carlson Wagonlit had 4,000 offices in 125 countries; 2,300 of these came from Carlson Travel. The combined operations booked 24 million airline and train tickets a year, plus seven million hotel stays and six million days of car rentals.

The merger made Carlson Wagonlit competitive for large multinational businesses, such as GE, that were beginning to switch to single vendors for their travel needs. The merger created new possibilities for monitoring global spending trends for these clients. The process of integrating Wagonlit Travel's information systems with Carlson Travel's was a five-year endeavor.

A London-based joint venture, Carlson Wagonlit Development Co., was created to develop markets in Australia, Singapore, and Hong Kong. Carlson and Accor agreed to each invest $45 million in the joint venture over three years.

Carlson Wagonlit soon unveiled a branded Visa credit card for 85,000 of its accounts, intensifying its competition with American Express (AmEx). In September 1994, AmEx leapfrogged Carlson Wagonlit in size by acquiring Thomas Cook Ltd.'s North American operations. Carlson Travel president described the consolidation trend in *Business Week*: "In 1985, you had to be national. In 1995, you have to be global."

CWT acquired Sweden's third-largest travel agency group, Resecenter, in October 1996. Resecenter had 1995 revenues of $90 million and 110 employees, compared to $13.3 billion for CWT, which had more than 20,000 employees.

Key Dates:

1872: Compagnie Internationale des Wagons-Lits et du Tourisme is founded.
1888: Ask Mr. Foster Travel is founded.
1972: Peter Ueberroth acquires Ask Mr. Foster.
1979: Carlson enters the travel market by purchasing Ask Mr. Foster Travel.
1983: Carlson Travel buys 70 percent of Canadian travel firm P. Lawson.
1990: Ask Mr. Foster becomes Carlson Travel Network.
1992: The remainder of P. Lawson is acquired.
1994: Carlson merges its business travel operations with Wagonlit Travel.
1998: Thomas Cook's British package holiday business merges with Carlson Wagonlit Travel.
2001: U.S. revenues fall due to lower commissions and wary travelers.

Expanding Online and in the UK in late 1990s

CWT introduced enQuest, its Internet-based travel agency in September 1997. Around the same time, it rolled out Mercavia, an extranet for providing travel agents with information that included video clips.

CWT's online debut lagged behind the Travelocity and American Express Travel on the Web by more than a year. The first online travel agency had been rolled out in 1995, and the field was already crowded, including offerings from Microsoft Corp. and other technology-based companies. However, CWT executives believed their bricks-and-mortar agencies offered unparalleled customer service opportunities.

CWT continued to expand in Britain. It acquired Inspirations, a packager of summer holidays, for £42 million. In October 1998, CWT merged the British package holiday interests of Thomas Cook with its own UK operations. This tied it for third place among UK tour operators. The merger also included Cook's travel businesses in Canada, Australia, and India, financial services operations, as well as Carlson's Caledonian and Peach Airways charter airlines and the tour operator Inspirations. Thomas Cook, which was owned by Westdeutsche Landesbank, had annual sales of more than £23 billion. It had been founded in 1841.

Jon Madonna, a former executive with the Travelers Group and KPMG Peat Marwick, replaced Travis Tanner as CWT CEO in late 1998. Tanner had left to join the Atlanta-based leisure start-up Luxury Travel Co. CWT was reorganizing around customers' needs, rather than geographical divisions.

Herve Gourio, president of Wagonlit Travel at the time of the merger with Carlson, returned to lead CWT after the departure of Madonna in October 2000.

Scaling Back After 2000

CWT cut several hundred positions in early 2001 due to a softening economy. CWT employed 15,000 people around the world, including 6,000 in North America. About 200 telephone reservationists were let go. Airlines were also suffering from a downturn in the travel business even before the September 11, 2001 terror attacks and were reducing commissions to travel agencies by as much as 60 percent. Overall revenues fell 8.3 percent in 2001, to $11 billion, mostly due to a slump in the U.S. market, which was down 20 percent.

In early 2003, Carlson Wagonlit announced a joint venture with China Air Service, the leading corporate travel management company in the People's Republic. A joint venture with the Japan Travel Bureau had been formed in 2001.

Principal Competitors

American Express Company; Kuoni Travel Holding Ltd.; Rosenbluth International; TUI AG; WorldTravel BTI.

Further Reading

Apgar, Sally, "Carlson Travel Announces Restructuring, Plans to Give More Decision-Making Power to Employees," *Star Tribune* (Minneapolis), Bus. Sec., October 19, 1993.

Apgar, Sally, and David Phelps, "President of Marketing Unit at Carlson Cos. Resigns," *Star Tribune* (Minneapolis), April 2, 1993, p. 1D.

"Carlson Group to Drop Ask Mr. Foster Name," *Aviation Daily*, February 15, 1990, p. 330.

"Carlson Travel Acquires A.T. Mays Group," *Aviation Daily*, January 2, 1990, p. 4.

"Carlson Travel Group Completes Acquisition of A.T. Mays Group," *Aviation Daily*, May 9, 1990, p. 270.

"Carlson Travel Network Adds 39 Agencies to Program," *Aviation Daily*, October 15, 1991, p. 86.

"Carlson Wagonlit Travel in Swedish Acquisition," *European Report* (Brussels), October 2, 1996, p. 1.

Churchill, David, "The Perks of the Job," *Times* (London), April 10, 1994.

"Commission Checks Wagon-Lits/Carlson Travel Merger Deal," *European Report* (Brussels), February 19, 1997.

Daneshkhu, Scheherazade, "Thomas Cook Finds That a Merger Is Even Better Than a Rest," *Financial Times* (London), October 7, 1998, p. 27.

Fedor, Liz, "Carlson Wagonlit Expected to Announced China Venture," *Star Tribune* (Minneapolis), January 16, 2003.

Field, David, "Titans of Travel: AmEx Follows Industry Trend with Cook Buy," *Washington Times*, October 4, 1994, p. B7.

Gaw, Jonathan, "Carlson Wagonlit to Travel Online," *Star Tribune* (Minneapolis), September 8, 1997, p. 1D.

Grant, Peter, "Travel Exec Seeks the Road to High Sales," *Crain's New York Business*, August 29, 1988, p. 6.

Jones, Del, "Big Business in Travel: Firms Write Own Ticket for Savings," *USA Today*, November 18, 1992, p. 1B.

"Les Echos: Carlson Wagonlit Travel Forecasts Slight Fall in Turnover in 2002 (Carlson Wagonlit Travel prevoit une legere baise de son activité en 2002)," *Financial Times World Media Abstracts*, March 14, 2002, p. 25.

Levy, Melissa, "Ex-Travelers, KPMG Executive to Head Carlson Wagonlit," *Star Tribune* (Minneapolis), December 18, 1998, p. 1D.

Marcotty, Josephine, "Tanner Returning to Carlson Travel," *Star Tribune* (Minneapolis), January 12, 1993, p. 3D.

Merrill, Ann, "Carlson Wagonlit 'Tweaking' Staff; Hundreds of Jobs Cut," *Star Tribune* (Minneapolis), March 22, 2001, p. 3D.

——, "Have Masks, Won't Travel," *Star Tribune* (Minneapolis), April 12, 2003.

"Oldest US Travel Agency Bolstered by Extensive Retooling in the '70s," *Journal of Commerce*, February 7, 1989, p. 5B.

Oslund, John J., "Carlson Travel Executive a Salesman at Heart," *Minneapolis Star and Tribune*, June 1, 1987, p. 2M.

"P. Lawson Sale," *Financial Post* (Toronto), August 16, 1988, p. 16.

Ross, Robert, "100 Years of Travel Advice: Many Clients Ask Mr. Foster Again and Again," *Sunday Patriot-News* (Harrisburg, Pa.), January 29, 1989, p. G7.

Schine, Eric, and Leah Nathans Spiro, "Survival of the Biggest," *Business Week*, September 26, 1994, p. 66.

Smithers, Rebecca, "Wagons Roll for Business Travel Giant," *Guardian* (Manchester), March 16, 1994, p. 116.

St. Anthony, Neal, "Carlson and Wagonlit to Merge Their Business Travel Operations," *Star Tribune* (Minneapolis), March 15, 1994, p. D1.

"Thomas Cook Poised to Merge with Holiday Rival," *Yorkshire Post*, October 7, 1998, p. 11.

Toy, Stewart, Corie Brown, and Gregory L. Miles, "The New Nepotism: Why Dynasties Are Making a Comeback," *Business Week*, April 4, 1988, p. 106.

Wilson, Linda and Joshua M. Greenbaum, "Merging Technologies; Travel Duo Charts Course—The Goal for Carlson Wagonlit Travel Is Integrated Global Data," *InformationWeek*, August 22, 1994, p. 40.

—Frederick C. Ingram

CarMax, Inc.

4900 Cox Road
Glen Allen, Virginia 23060
U.S.A.
Telephone: (804) 747-0422
Toll Free: (800) 922-7829
Fax: (804) 747-5848
Web site: http://www.carmax.com

Public Company
Incorporated: 1993 as CarMax Group
Employees: 5,910
Sales: $3.2 billion (2002)
Stock Exchanges: New York
Ticker Symbol: KMX
NAIC: 441120 Used Car Dealers

CarMax, Inc. operates a chain of used car lots and new car franchises. CarMax's used car lots are patterned after the mass-merchandising business model of its former parent company, Circuit City Stores, Inc., operating as "superstores." The company's stores typically contain roughly 500 used cars no more than six model years old. The prices of the vehicles are fixed in an effort to create a more relaxed sales atmosphere. CarMax operates 37 used car superstores and 17 new car franchises.

Origins

CarMax, industry observers noted at the time of its inception, triggered a revolution in used car retailing, sending tremors of fear among the legions of traditional, small-sized dealers and establishing a new business model that was quickly aped by others. The creation of the concept was the work of Richard Sharp and W. Austin Ligon. The corporate entity behind the formation of CarMax was Circuit City Stores, Inc. A 375-store, consumer electronics chain with $7 billion in sales during the early 1990s, Circuit City was led by Sharp. Ligon worked under Sharp, serving as Circuit City's senior vice-president of corporate planning. Together, the pair developed the CarMax concept, a business approach that drew its inspiration from the sprawling Circuit City chain and its "big-box" retail concept.

The story of CarMax's development began with a survey conducted in 1991. "We asked people who bought used and new cars about their shopping experience," Sharp explained in an October 23, 1995 interview with *Forbes*. "Not surprisingly, there were more dislikes than likes." Sharp looked at the $150 billion used car market and saw three qualities that convinced him the Circuit City approach to retailing could be grafted onto the used car market: first, the supply of used cars was abundant; second, the demand for used cars was consistent; and finally— perhaps most importantly—the management practices employed within the fragmented industry were unsophisticated. For two years, Sharp and Ligon worked on fine-tuning their concept, devoting much of their time to developing a process to monitor inventory and pricing. The two Circuit City executives concentrated on ways to determine precisely which make, model, and color of vehicles to stock on their proposed chain of lots, and when and how much to adjust prices. The strategy, like that of a Circuit City store, centered on a broad selection of merchandise, a high-volume business, economies of scale, and sharply honed management methods. "We can apply our expertise in electronics retailing to auto retailing," Sharp informed *Discount Store News* in a November 6, 1996 interview.

Sharp and Ligon were ready by 1993 to put their theories to the test. Using money from Circuit City to finance the startup, Sharp and Ligon opened their first superstore, a lot operating under the banner "CarMax: The Auto Superstore," in October 1993. The showroom, located in Richmond, Virginia, represented the first unit of the newly created CarMax Group, a wholly owned subsidiary of Circuit City. The Richmond lot served as the prototype of the other used car superstores that would follow in its wake: 500 cars were on display, each no more than five model years old, and each with no more than 70,000 miles on its odometer. Inside, the Richmond CarMax contained a service shop and salespeople offering a refreshing approach to used car sales. Prices on the vehicles were fixed, obviating the need for customers to negotiate the price of a prospective purchase. CarMax's "no-haggling" policy and the less adversarial atmosphere it created between salespeople and customers was complemented by computer kiosks delineating the lot's inventory and particular details about each vehicle.

As Sharp and Ligon pressed forward with their plan of applying the superstore concept to used car retailing, they knew the road ahead would be difficult. Neither executive anticipated the enterprise would generate a profit for several years—perhaps taking as long as the end of the 1990s. In the interim, substantial sums of money would need to be spent to establish a network of CarMax superstores and to bring the company to the point of critical mass where economies of scale and its sophisticated management practices would give the concept the advantages of a retail superstore. At the time Sharp and Ligon set out, the United States contained 42,000 used car dealers and 22,000 new car dealers who sold used cars received as trade-ins. Among this field, the average used car dealer generated $2 million a year, a total deemed too small to achieve economies of scale or to apply modern management methods.

By October 1995, two years after the first CarMax opened, the company had yet to generate a profit, recording $77 million in sales for the previous fiscal year. New superstore openings had lifted CarMax's unit count to four lots, with two superstores in Atlanta and one in Raleigh, North Carolina, having joined the fold. A fifth lot was expected to open in Charlotte, North Carolina, in early 1996, but Sharp had yet to decide whether to turn CarMax into a national chain. A final decision was expected to be made within 18 months on the matter of going national.

As CarMax pressed forward during the critical phase of its development, the company's progress was defined by escalating sales and mounting losses. By the end of the company's 1995 fiscal year, sales had increased substantially, soaring from $77 million to $304 million, which exceeded analysts' estimates of between $200 million and $278 million. CarMax's robust sales growth was pocked by a $7 million loss for the year, however, perpetuating speculation that the mass-merchandising approach to used car sales was not a sound business model. Few industry observers doubted whether CarMax could sell cars, but many pundits doubted whether the company could sell cars profitably. The one glaring problem with the chain, according to the business press, was its inability to secure volume discounts on the purchase of its used cars, an ability intrinsic to the success of the Circuit City chain. CarMax purchased its vehicles at the same auctions attended by independent dealers and paid roughly the same price an independent dealer paid. Without the benefits of volume purchasing, CarMax faced a difficult road to profitability.

The solution to CarMax's cashflow problem, as proposed by Sharp and Ligon, was the physical expansion of the chain. The company opened its fifth and sixth lots in 1996 and announced ambitious expansion plans. In 1997, Sharp and Ligon planned to open between 8 and 10 lots, with new openings of between 15 and 20 stores for each year thereafter. The markets slated for expansion included Miami, Tampa, Dallas, Houston, Washington, D.C., Baltimore, Chicago, Los Angeles, San Francisco, and Tidewater, Virginia. The company projected an 80- to 90-unit chain by 2001.

By the mid-1990s, CarMax's expansion strategy included a new facet to the company's business. The company acquired its first new car franchise in 1996, a Chrysler-Plymouth-Jeep store located in Atlanta. Looking ahead, CarMax planned to open between 15 and 25 new car dealerships by 2002, stores that were to operate alongside the company's used car dealerships.

Late 1990s Expansion

The financial constraints of expanding in the face of persistent losses presented formidable obstacles to Sharp and Ligon. Although Circuit City had contributed to CarMax's startup, the company's financial assistance to CarMax essentially ended there. The arrangement kept Circuit City's financial health from being drained by CarMax's costly expansion program, forcing Sharp and Ligon to find other ways to secure capital. At the end of 1996, the pair proposed a new method of securing financing, announcing that Circuit City would sell a portion of the CarMax subsidiary to the public. The initial proposal called for offering between 15 and 20 percent of CarMax to the public, a stake that was expected to raise as much as $300 million. The offering was completed in February 1997, providing CarMax with fresh resources to finance its expansion and to repay its rising debt.

The proceeds gained from CarMax's public offering enabled the company to accelerate its expansion program. At the time of the offering, the company had seven superstores in operation, which generated nearly $450 million in revenues. By mid-1998, there were 23 superstores in operation, enabling the company to record $1.47 billion in sales for fiscal 1998. Despite the impressive gain in sales, the company continued to be hobbled by annual losses. CarMax lost $23.5 million in fiscal 1998, enough of a loss to prompt Sharp and Ligon to scale back expansion plans for 1999. Instead of opening between 15 and 20 stores in 1999, as originally planned, the company announced it would open 10 stores that year.

By the end of the decade, CarMax was nearing the moment of truth. "We've had to learn as we go along," Ligon explained in a July 12, 1999 interview with *Automotive News*. "We're going to hit about $2 billion in sales this year, which is about the critical mass we need to get to make a profit." Roughly six months later, when the financial results for fiscal 2000 were announced, something unprecedented in the history of CarMax occurred. For the year, the company generated $2.01 billion in revenues and a profit of $1.1 million, the first time CarMax ended a fiscal year in the black. The profit total was meager, but it suggested there was financial viability in the "big box" used car retailing concept. CarMax's progress in the coming years underscored the success of 2000, prompting critics to alter their assessment of the company's business strategy.

Profits and Independence in the 21st Century

Buoyed by the first annual profit in the company's history, Ligon focused on plans for the future. A national rollout of

Key Dates:
1993: The first CarMax used car lot opens in Richmond, Virginia.
1996: CarMax acquires its first new car franchise.
1997: A portion of CarMax is sold to the public.
1999: CarMax records its first annual profit.
2002: CarMax is spun off from Circuit City Stores.

CarMax superstores remained the company's long-term objective, a goal that was expected to require between 20 and 25 years to achieve. ''You can't do it any faster than that,'' Ligon informed *Automotive News* in a July 10, 2000 interview. More immediate plans called for a measured pace of expansion, as the company sought to add to the 40 new car franchises and used car superstores in operation at the beginning of the century. Despite the eventual goal of national expansion, initially the company planned to open new locations in markets where it already maintained a presence, focusing on markets with populations ranging between one and two million residents.

As CarMax's 10th anniversary approached, the company's financial results provided cause for celebration. In fiscal 2001, sales leaped to $2.5 billion, but the most impressive gain was achieved in CarMax's profit total, which by far eclipsed the symbolic $1.1 million recorded in 2000. Ligon expected to post between $40 million and $43 million in net income in 2001, but the company did better, posting $45.6 million in profits. In 2002, the results were equally as sanguine, as revenues swelled 28 percent to $3.2 billion and net income nearly doubled, jumping to $90.8 million.

Against the backdrop of vigorous financial growth, a new era at CarMax began. In the spring of 2002, Circuit City announced it intended to spin off its CarMax subsidiary into a separate, publicly traded company, part of the consumer electronics chain's plan to focus on its core business. The spinoff, completed in October 2002, created CarMax Inc., a corporate entity distinct from Circuit City with Ligon serving as its chief executive officer, a title he gained at the time of the spinoff. As CarMax prepared for its second decade of business, expectations for further financial growth were high. Ligon anticipated opening between six and eight used car superstores per year

through 2005, building on the 37 used car superstores and 17 new car franchises already in operation.

Principal Subsidiaries

CarMax Auto Finance.

Principal Competitors

AutoNation, Inc.; Hendrick Automotive Group; United Auto Group, Inc.

Further Reading

''Circuit City to Spin Off CarMax, Chain Will Focus on Electronics,'' *Chain Store Age Executive Fax,* March 1, 2002, p. 1.

Gilligan, Gregory J., ''Circuit City's CarMax Superstores Pass $300 Million in Yearly Sales,'' *Knight Ridder/Tribune Business News,* April 5, 1996.

——, ''Circuit City Stores to Sell Stake in CarMax Used-Car Chain,'' *Knight Ridder/Tribune Business News,* November 14, 1996.

Heller, Laura, ''Circuit City Restructures, Spins Off CarMax Unit,'' *DSN Retailing Today,* March 11, 2002, p. 3.

McLean, Bethany, ''Squeaky Wheels,'' *Fortune,* March 17, 1997, p. 202.

Rubinstein, Ed, ''Sharp Touts Potential of CarMax,'' *Discount Store News,* November 4, 1996, p. 6.

Rudnitsky, Howard, ''Would You Buy a Used Car from This Man?,'' *Forbes,* October 23, 1995, p. 52.

Sawyers, Arlena, ''CarMax Doubles Profit, Plans More Stores,'' *Automotive News,* April 8, 2002, p. 16.

——, ''CarMax Says It's Prepared to Fly Solo,'' *Automotive News,* November 4, 2002, p. 17.

——, ''CarMax's Ligon: Shoppers Are Happy, Profits Are Near,'' *Automotive News,* July 12, 1999, p. 32.

——, ''CarMax Speeds into Expansion Fast Lane,'' *Automotive News,* January 15, 2001, p. 69.

——, ''Slowdown Doesn't Faze CarMax,'' *Automotive News,* March 12, 2001, p. 8.

——, ''Though in the Black, CarMax Has No Expansion Plans,'' *Automotive News,* July 10, 2000, p. 34.

Wernle, Bradford, ''CarMax Sees Red, Slows Expansion Plans,'' *Automotive News,* June 15, 1998, p. 6.

——, ''CarMax's Strategy: Make Do with Lower Margins,'' *Automotive News,* December 2, 1996, p. 52.

—Jeffrey L. Covell

The Carriage House Companies, Inc.

196 Newton Street
Fredonia, New York 14063
U.S.A.
Telephone: (716) 673-1000
Toll Free: (800) 828-8915
Fax: (716) 679-7702
Web site: http//www.carriagehousecos.com

Wholly Owned Subsidiary of Ralcorp Holdings Inc.
Incorporated: 2000
Employees: 1,000
Sales: $451.5 million (2002)
NAIC: 311941 Mayonnaise, Dressing, and Other
    Prepared Sauce Manufacturing

Based in Fredonia, New York, The Carriage House Companies, Inc. is a subsidiary of Ralcorp Holdings Inc. One of the top store brand food suppliers in the United States, it is the largest supplier of store brand preserves and jellies, spoonable and pourable salad dressings and mayonnaise, and America's largest producer of table syrup. Carriage House is the third largest producer of peanut butter in the country in addition to being the leader in store brand peanut butter. Other products include pasta and pizza sauce, chocolate and other flavored syrups, barbecue sauce, Mexican sauces such as salsa, steak sauce and marinades, and chili, seafood, and cocktail sauces. The company also makes and markets Sauce Arturo, a gourmet sauce. Carriage House not only supplies product to its customers, it provides a variety of services. It helps to develop labels and offers assistance in marketing store brands. Manufacturing facilities are located in Fredonia and Dunkirk, New York; Buckner, Kentucky; Streator, Illinois; Kansas City, Kansas; and Los Angeles, San Jose, and Colusa County, California.

Origins in the 1994 Creation of Ralcorp

Carriage House is comprised of three major acquisitions made by Ralcorp Holdings: Martin Gillet Co., Red Wing Co., and product lines from Tobitt and Castleman Company. Each of these companies boast a rich history in the food industry. The assets of Ralcorp were the result of a 1994 spinoff by Ralston Purina Co., the pet food giant which over the years had acquired a mixed bag of other interests. After enduring a difficult fiscal 1992, Ralston initiated some cost-cutting measures and other strategies to support its stock price. In 1993, it offered a new class of stock in order to separate out the Ralston-Continental Baking Group. A short time later, management began to consider a tax-free spinoff of some human food interests. A plan was approved by Ralston's board of directors in September 1993, the new entity to be called Ralcorp Holdings. Its assets included several food segments: branded and private label cereals, including well-known Chex ready-to-eat cereals and the oat cereal business of recently acquired National Oats Co.; Beech-Nut brand baby food products, including cereal; and branded and private label crackers and cookies, including Ry-Krisp, Bremner crackers, and Chex Mix snacks. Although the spinoff was intended to primarily benefit the cereal business, Ralcorp also became the recipient of some assets that were even less complementary than baby food and snacks: the Breckenride and Keystone Colorado ski resorts and American Redemption Systems, a coupon redemption business. In addition to the two ski resorts and a coupon redemption center, Ralcorp facilities included five cereal plants, two cracker and cookie plants, and two baby food plants. All told, the businesses posted revenues of $902.8 million and net profits of $42.6 in fiscal 1993 (ended on September 30). Cereal provided the lion's share of sales, nearly $550 million, with the unbranded private-label cereal showing strong growth. The new company was also saddled with approximately $400 million in debt. According to *Business Week,* "Analysts suspects Ralston's cagey chairman, William P. Stiritz, of unloading a bunch of losers." Nevertheless, Ralston sought Securities and Exchange Commission (SEC) and Internal Revenue Service (IRS) approval for the tax-free spinoff, and once it passed scrutiny Ralcop began business as an independent company in April 1994. Under terms of the plan, Ralston shareholders received one share of Ralcorp for every three shares of Ralston Purina Group Stock they owned. Moreover, Ralcorp would not be able to shed any of its assets for two years in order to comply with tax laws.

Assuming the job of chief executive officer was Richard A. Pearce, who ran Ralston's human food businesses. He quickly took steps to cut costs and improve efficiency in order to boost profits and service the company's heavy debt load. He also invested in new plant technology in order to support the company's fast growing private label cereal business, a segment in which Ralcorp was dominant. Now Ralcorp would be better able to duplicate popular branded cereals, legally permissible because brand cereals relied on nonproprietary manufacturing processes. Only trademarks and names were protected. As a result, Ralcorp produced a version of Kix named Silly Spheres, Post Grape Nuts became Nutty Nuggets, and Kellogg's Apple Jacks were recast as Apple Dapples. Pierce targeted major cereals that had no store-brand equivalent, hoping to introduce as many as four knockoffs each year. It was a segment that offered a great deal of promise, the private label cereal segment growing at an 8 percent clip each year while branded cereals grew at just 3 percent. Because private label cereals were able to undercut the major brands by as much as $1 a box, and retailers were able to earn twice the profits as they did on brand cereals, Ralcorp had no worries about gaining shelf space. Nonetheless, private label cereal still only accounted for 6 percent of all cereal sales, and Ralcorp, despite being America's fourth-largest cereal maker, was still a small player in an industry dominated by such powerhouses as Kellogg's and General Mills. It they elected to slash prices on their cereals, Ralcorp faced a very serious challenge. Indeed, when in the spring of 1996 a price war in the breakfast cereal industry broke out, Ralcorp lacked the resources to effectively compete, especially with its branded products. As soon as the two-year IRS ban on selling assets expired in April of that year, the company began to unload some properties. It sold most of its interests in ski resorts, then in August 1996 announced that it was selling its Chex line of branded cereals and snacks to General Mills. In order to effectuate the transaction, Ralcorp spun off a new company under the same name with the remaining assets. Old Ralcorp then merged with General Mills, leaving the new Ralcorp with virtually no debt and some $500 million in annual revenues. Several weeks after the sale to General Mills was announced, Pearce resigned from the company.

Martin Gillet & Co. Acquired in 1999

Ralcorp's focus was now to build up its portfolio of private label food products. In 1997, it acquired the Wortz Company, a private label cracker and cookie maker. In 1998, Ralcorp acquired Flavor House, a private label and branded snack nut company; Sugar Kake Cookie Inc., a private label and branded cookie manufacturer; and Nutcracker Brands, Inc. a private label and value branded snack nut company. To help finance this expansion into private labels, Ralcorp sold Beech-Nut Nutrition Corporation in 1998 for $68 million in cash. In 1999, the company continued its buying spree, adding Southern Roasted Nuts, a private label snack nut company, and Ripon Foods, a private label and branded cookie company. It was also in March

1999 that Ralcorp diversified into new product lines when it purchased a private label salad dressing and mayonnaise company named Martin Gillet & Co., a significant step which eventually led to the creation of the Carriage House Companies.

Martin Gillet, founded in Baltimore, Maryland, in 1811, was originally a tea importer. The business remained under the control of the Gillet family for nearly 150 years. In the 1870s, it became the first company to move beyond the sale of traditional 40-pound chests of tea when it began to offer tea packed in quarter-pound, half-pound, and one-pound boxes. In 1955, Martin Gillet was sold to Joseph J. Katz, whose family owned it until Ralcorp's acquisition. Katz attempted some innovations of his own, such as the stringless tea bag he introduced in 1961, but eventually Martin Gillet exited the tea business in favor of mayonnaise and salad dressings, most of which was produced under a supermarket label or for food service or restaurant use, as well as the company's Our Family Recipe label. At the time of its acquisition, Martin Gillet was generating annual sales in the $70 million range. In addition to its general offices and a manufacturing facility located in Baltimore, the company also operated plants in Kansas City, Kansas, and Los Angeles, California.

Ralcorp continued to build its portfolio of private label food producers in 2000. It acquired Cascade Cookie Company, Inc. for $22 million, followed by the $31.5 million purchase of James P. Linette, Inc., a chocolate candy manufacturer that was subsequently integrated into Ralcorp's snack nut business. The most significant acquisition in 2000, and the tenth in just three and a half years, was The Red Wing Company, Inc., a $132.5 million deal. Based in Fredonia, New York, Red Wing not only produced private labels products that complemented Martin Gillet, such as spoonable spreads and pourable dressings, it also offered Ralcorp even greater diversity by creating a critical mass in the shelf-stable wet fill category of food products. Additional Red Wing private label products included peanut butter, preserves and jellies, honey, syrups, tomato-based sauces, barbeque sauces, and specialty sauces. Red Wing also brought with it cocktail mix products, including the Major Peters and Jero Bloody Mary mixes. By adding nearly $350 million in annual sales, the acquisition of Red Wing pushed Ralcorp's annual sales level beyond the $1 billion mark.

Red Wing was founded in 1912, originally a subsidiary of the Cudahy Packing Company that operated as a seasonal packer, producing juice from apples and grapes grown in western New York. It added ketchup in 1926 and jellies and preserves in 1930. The 1955 acquisition of the American Preserve Company of Philadelphia expanded Red Wing's product lines, which grew to include peanut butter in 1966, followed by salad dressing, mayonnaise, syrup, and barbecue sauce in the early 1970s. RHM Holdings (USA) acquired the company in 1977 and over the next 15 years added to the business. In 1990, the Indiana Division of Naas Foods, Inc. was merged into the operation. Naas was originally an upstate New York processor of dried apples, cider, and cider vinegar, and like Red Wing moved into ketchup in the 1920s. Because Indiana was the major producer of tomatoes at the time, the company soon moved its operations to Sunman, Indiana. In 1992, RHM acquired Sunstar Foods for its Red Wing subsidiary, a deal that brought with it a major plant in Streator, Illinois. Red Wing's

---

Key Dates:

1811: Martin Gillet Co. is founded in Baltimore, Maryland.
1912: The Red Wing Company is founded.
1994: Ralcorp is spun off from Ralston Purina.
1999: Ralcorp acquires Martin Gillet.
2000: Red Wing is acquired; Ralcorp forms Carriage House.
2002: Product lines of Torbitt & Castleman are acquired.

---

ownership changed hands in 1992 when its parent company was acquired by Tomkins PLC, a British conglomerate with interests in auto parts, firearms, and bakeries. When the company decided to concentrate on its automotive business, Red Wing became expandable and Ralcorp was able to acquire it.

Carriage House Created in 2000

Red Wing's New York facilities soon became a hub for Ralcorp's activity in the shelf-stable condiments category. Shortly after closing the Red Wing acquisition, management announced that it was closing the Martin Gillet salad dressing and mayonnaise plant in Baltimore and moving the operations to Red Wing's Dunkirk site, thus bringing to an end nearly two centuries of a presence in Baltimore for Martin Gillet. Most of the 195 jobs were transferred to Dunkirk, with a smaller number moving to Martin Gillet's factory in Kansas City. Ralcorp also expanded both the Dunkirk plant and the Fredonia, New York, operation, which added a warehouse. More importantly, Ralcorp formed The Carriage House Companies, Inc. to encompass the combined businesses of Martin Gillet and Red Wing, the headquarters of the subsidiary to be located at the Fredonia site.

Ralcorp soon added to Carriage House in January 2001 when it completed the $55.6 million acquisition of the wet products portion of The Torbitt & Castleman Company, LLC, a division with $80 million in annual sales. Like the other companies of Carriage House, Torbitt & Castleman boasted a long history. It was established in Louisville, Kentucky, in the 1870s as a small grocery wholesaler and eventually began to produce syrup. With the acquisition of land in Oldham County, Kentucky, the company expanded its operations, producing a full range of sauces and condiments for private labels, contract packaging, and the food service industries. Torbitt & Castleman

was then acquired by The Northern Group in the 1980s. The company's wet products were picked up by Carriage House included syrups, flavored syrups, jellies and jams, Mexican sauces, barbecue sauces, and other specialty sauces.

Carriage House posted revenues of $125.8 million in fiscal 2000, followed by $420.5 million in fiscal 2001, the increase mostly due to the timing of acquisitions. In fiscal 2002, the subsidiary generated sales of $451.5 million and contributed $13.5 million in profits to its corporate parent. With a weak economy, exacerbated by the loss of a major customer and increases in the cost of ingredients, the company faced a difficult short-term business climate, necessitating some cost-cutting steps. The situation appeared to grow even worse in November 2002 when Carriage House experienced a strike at its Fredonia and Dunkirk facilities following stalled contract talks with Local Union No. 266 of the National Conference of Fireman and Oilers, S.U.I.U. The strike of 540 union employees lasted less than a week, however, and both sides went back to working together to grow the business. Despite the adverse impact of a troubled economy in 2003, Carriage House appeared well positioned in the long run to become an even larger player in its private label niche.

Principal Subsidiaries

Martin Gillet Co.; The Red Wing Corporation.

Principal Competitors

General Mills Inc.; Aurora Foods Inc.; The J.M. Smucker Company.

Further Reading

Burns, Greg, ''A Froot Loop By Any other Name . . . Ralcorp's Private-label Cereals are Gobbling Market Share,'' *Business Week*, June 26, 1995, p. 72.
Glynn, Matt, ''Food Company to Expand Fredonia, N.Y., Operation,'' *Buffalo News*, August 12, 2000.
Linstedt, Sharon, ''Red Wing Adding 75 Jobs As Work Is Moved Here,'' *Buffalo News*, July 26, 2000, p. E1.
Salganik, William, ''Martin Gillet Will Close Baltimore Plant in December,'' *Baltimore Sun*, October 4, 2000.
Stroud, Jean, ''Ralston Plans New Company, new Stock,'' *St. Louis Post-Dispatch*, January 28, 1994, p 9D.

—Ed Dinger

The Christian Science Publishing Society

1 Norway Street
Boston, Massachusetts 02115-3195
U.S.A.
Telephone: (617) 450-2000
Toll Free: (800) 288-7090
Fax: (617) 450-2031
Web site: http://www.csmonitor.com

Nonprofit Corporation
Incorporated: 1897
Employees: 900
Sales: $98.3 million (2001)
NAIC: 511110 Newspaper Publishers; 511120 Periodical
   Publishers

The Christian Science Publishing Society is the nonprofit, independently run media arm of The First Church of Christ, Scientist—better known as Christian Science, a Boston-based religious sect that stresses spiritual healing. The Publishing Society is best known for its flagship venture, the *Christian Science Monitor,* a well-respected international daily newspaper that since its inception in 1908 has won numerous journalism awards. In addition to a book publishing program, the Publishing Society is responsible for the *Christian Science Journal,* devoted to providing readers with a better understanding of Christian Science; *Christian Science Quarterly,* offering weekly Bible lessons for self-study; *Christian Science Sentinel,* applying the tenets of Christian Science to world events; and the *Herald of Christian Science,* published in 13 languages and intended to share the message of Christian Science to a world audience. The Publishing Society also produces short-wave radio transmission of religious programming.

19th-Century Christian Science Movement

The founder of the Publishing Society, Mary Baker Eddy, was born Mary Morse Baker in 1821 and raised on a New Hampshire farm. (She took the last name Eddy in 1877 after marrying her third husband, Asa Gilbert Eddy.) As a child she suffered from an unknown nervous disorder that caused hysterical seizures and prevented her from attending school on a regular basis. Instead she was educated by her older brother, Albert, who taught her Hebrew, Greek, and Latin. She also took to writing poetry, and at a young age had her work appearing in periodicals. As a young adult she continued to endure tribulations with her father. At the age of 21 she married builder George Washington Glover and moved to Charleston, South Carolina, but shortly after she became pregnant her husband died from an illness, forcing her to return to New Hampshire, impoverished, to give birth to a son, who she would eventually have to give up. Continuing to suffer from nervous disorders and bouts of depression, which led to an abiding interest in methods of healing, she married in 1853 a homeopath and dentist named Dr. Daniel Patterson. Nine years later, at the outbreak of the Civil War, she was once again visited by misfortune. Patterson, visiting the Bull Run battlefield, was captured by Confederate troops and sent to a prison camp. Once again, Mrs. Eddy was destitute and forced to return home to live with her family as an invalid. Now 40 years of age, she reached a turning point. She turned to a Portland, Maine, mental healer, Dr. Phineas Parkhurst Quimby, who within three weeks cured her, essentially relying on the power of suggestion. Raised in a Congregational Church in New Hampshire, she viewed through a religious prism Quimby's system, which assumed that disease had a mental rather than physical cause. Her own beliefs were then crystallized in 1866, when after bedridden from a fall and three days of intensely reading the Bible, she reported experiencing a revelation. She was instantly cured, by what she called "Christian science," and was now completely devoted to promoting the truths that had been revealed to her: namely, that physical matter was illusory, and that to be well one had to come into harmony with the infinite Mind as revealed through Jesus Christ.

Within a few years, Mrs. Eddy had a group of followers and a number of practitioners who performed healing. Her beliefs were codified with the 1875 publication of *Science and Health* (after the original title, *The Science of Life,* was found to be already in use), which was financially backed by friends George Barry and Elizabeth Newhall. For the rest of her life Mrs. Eddy would continually revise and expand the book, as it took its place alongside the Bible as an essential study aide for The First

> ## Company Perspectives:
>
> *In an age of corporate conglomerates dominating news media, the* Monitor *combination of church ownership, a public-service mission, and commitment to covering the world (not to mention the fact that it was founded by a woman shortly after the turn of the century, when US women didn't yet have the vote!) gives the paper a uniquely independent voice in journalism.*

Church of Christ, Scientist, which she (as head) and her followers founded in Boston in 1879. The Church's present form dates to 1892 when it was reorganized. By the time of her death in 1910, combined editions of *Science and Health,* which targeted an educated middle-class audience, sold approximately 400,000 copies. It also made Mrs. Eddy wealthy and a celebrity.

In 1883 the Christian Scientist Association established the Christian Scientist Publishing Company and under Mrs. Eddy's influence became involved in magazines. Its first periodical was the *Journal of Christian Science,* which made its debut in April 1883 and was at first mostly written and edited by Mrs. Eddy. In 1885 the publication assumed its present name, the *Christian Science Journal.* Unlike *Science and Health,* the *Journal* was meant to appeal to lower-income, less educated readers, presenting Christian Science tenets in digestible form through testimonials, anecdotes, and letters to and from the editor. In 1890 Mrs. Eddy established another monthly magazine, *Christian Science Bible Lessons,* to provide weekly Bible lessons for church services and individual study. It was subsequently renamed *Christian Science Quarterly* and publication was cut back to a quarterly basis. It was also in 1890 that the Church printed a four-page leaflet of hymns, published by an entity called the Christian Science Publishing Society. In 1897 the Publishing Society was incorporated and obtained a state charter. In January 1898 the corporation sold all of its assets to Mrs. Eddy, the corporation was dissolved, and she subsequently set up the current Publishing Society as a Deed of Trust. The deed also provided independence for the three trustees of the Society, an arrangement that would become a matter of controversy in the years following Mrs. Eddy's death. Later in 1898 the *Christian Science Weekly* (soon renamed the *Christian Science Sentinel*) was founded. *Der Herold der Christian Science* premiered in 1903, a monthly and/or quarterly magazine of articles and testimonies of healing originally published in German.

Establishing the Christian Science Monitor *in 1908*

The Publishing Society's best known product, its daily newspaper, the *Christian Science Monitor,* was established in 1908 at the behest of Mrs. Eddy, who despite having retired from active involvement in the running of the Church nearly 20 years earlier still held considerable sway in the Church. She had entertained thoughts of starting a newspaper for some 25 years, disturbed by the tawdry yellow journalism practiced at the time. In 1906, at the age of 86, she and the rapidly emerging Christian Science church became the victim of that excess when Joseph Pulitzer's *New York World* launched a scathing crusade against her and *McClure's Magazine* published a virulent profile of

Mrs. Eddy. Suggesting that the wealthy elderly woman was either senile and being used by others, or was simply dead and replaced by an impostor, the *World* was not merely satisfied with making lurid claims. It managed to convince her son to sue for control of her estate, which led to a sensational trial in 1907. Although an interview with court-appointed officials short-circuited the suit, Mrs. Eddy was clearly upset by her treatment in the press. Another important factor in her decision to launch a newspaper was a letter she received from John L. Wright in March 1908. A journalist as well as Christian Scientist, he made the case that there was a deep need for a truly independent newspaper that would be "fair, frank and honest with the people on all subjects and under whatever pressure." On July 28, 1908 she sent a letter to the directors of the Church, followed by an August 8 note to the trustees of the Publishing Society, stating: "It is my request that you start a daily newspaper at once, and call it the *Christian Science Monitor.* Let there be no delay. The Cause demands that it be issued now." Despite the misgivings of the directors and trustees, Mrs. Eddy's request was fulfilled in an astonishingly short period of time. On November 25, 1908 the first issue of the *Monitor* was published, reflecting considerable direct input from Mrs. Eddy herself. She was consulted about the type to be used and instructed that a better quality paper be used. She also chose the publication's motto (and location of it): "First the blade, then the ear, then the full grain in the ear." She also defeated attempts to find a more commercial name for the newspaper. On the editorial page of the first issue she offered an insight into the naming of all the Publishing Society's major periodicals: "The first was The Christian Science Journal, designed to put on record the divine Science of Truth; the second I entitled Sentinel, intended to hold guard over Truth, Life and Love; the third, Der Herold der Christian Science, to proclaim the universal activity and availability of Truth; the next I named Monitor, to spread undivided the Science that operates unspent. The object of The Monitor is to injure no man, but to bless all mankind." Aside from the mention of Christian Science in its title, and one religious article that would run each day, the newspaper quickly gained a reputation for its independence and journalistic integrity and soon became a thriving enterprise.

Mrs. Eddy died in 1910 and without her presence the trustees of the Publishing Society and the directors of the Mother Church came into conflict. What became known as the Great Litigation lasted from 1917 to 1921, initiated after the trustees sued to stop the directors from interfering with their running of the Publishing Society. At issue legally was whether Mrs. Eddy's 1898 trust deed granted the trustees and the Publishing Society authority independent of the directors. Most Christian Scientists supported the directors, firmly believing the Publishing Society should unquestionably serve the needs of the Church, but in the end the courts agreed with the trustee's position that Mrs. Eddy clearly intended a double, balancing power structure between the two entities.

With the litigation settled, the Publishing Society continued to publish the works of Mrs. Eddy and the periodicals she was so instrumental in founding. The *Herald,* which began publishing a French edition in 1918, added other languages over the years, including the Scandinavian languages in 1930, Dutch in 1931, Spanish in 1946, Japanese and Indonesian in 1962, and Greek in 1964. *Christian Science Quarterly* also expanded to

Key Dates:

1875: Mary Baker Eddy publishes the first edition of *Science and Health.*
1897: The Christian Science Publishing Society is incorporated.
1898: The Publishing Society assets are sold to Mrs. Eddy, the corporation is dissolved, and a Deed of Trust is established.
1908: The *Christian Science Monitor* begins publication.
1961: Last year the *Monitor* is profitable.
1984: Monitor Radio is established.
1988: *World Monitor* begins publication.

more than a dozen languages over the years. The *Sentinel* changed formats in the 1940s, eschewing its original broadsheet presentation for a digest-size that became extremely popular. The *Monitor,* in the meantime, became the Publishing Society's most visible face to the world. It grew into an award-winning newspaper, ironically receiving a number of Pulitzer Prizes, endowed by Mrs. Eddy's former tormentor, Joseph Pulitzer. Rather than rely heavily on wire services for international coverage, the *Monitor* maintained correspondents around the world as well as throughout the United States. From a financial point of view the *Monitor* peaked in the 1950s, after which the growth of television, rising production costs, and the expense of maintaining an international operation made it impossible for the newspaper to turn a profit. Starting in 1962 it began operating at a loss, subsidized by the Publishing Society. By the mid-1970s the *Monitor* deficit reached $8 million, resulting in cutbacks that led to the resignation of a number of senior writers.

Instituting a New Media Strategy in the Early 1980s

In 1982 John Hoagland joined the Publishing Society as manager and developed a strategy of extending the *Monitor* brand to radio and television, with financial support from the Church. On the radio side, the Publishing Society established Monitor Radio in 1984, producing a one-hour weekend program distributed by National Public Radio. In October 1985 a daily show was introduced, with an early edition added in July 1989. A short-wave radio program was initiated in March 1987 with facilities located in Maine, South Carolina, and Saipan. From 1983 to 1985 the Publishing Society produced pilots for what became a 30-minute television news program relying on the *Monitor*'s news-gathering network. The show finally premiered in September 1988. The Publishing Society purchased a Boston television station (WQTV, channel 68) in 1986, with the original intent of operating it on a commercial basis. The strategy resulted in a larger audience share than anticipated and led to the investment of $14 million in syndicated programming. Management then decided to change course and converted WQTV into a noncommercial, public service station, essentially making it a laboratory for an even grander vision: the Monitor Channel, a cable television service. Not only was most of the syndicated programming shelved at the cost of $10 million, the Publishing Society had to buy out the contract of a high-priced consultant who had been hired to advise the station on commercial operations. Moreover, the executives involved in the na-

scent television operations were spending in a manner that was quite lavish in comparison to the way the Publishing Society traditionally had operated.

In 1988 the Publishing Society launched a news magazine, *World Monitor,* taking on such entrenched competition as *Time* and *Newsweek.* A nightly cable news program, "World Monitor," also debuted in September of that year. As a result of its rapid accumulation of media operations, the Publishing Society and the Church now faced a severe financial crunch. Although the *Monitor* remained the flagship product, on whose brand all the other ventures were dependent, it was the newspaper that was forced to hike its subscription price and accept cuts, while at the same time money was poured into television. According to Hoagland, the Publishing Society was committed to publishing the *Monitor* at a deficit. "But television will have to prove itself." Staff reductions as well as scaling back the size of the *Monitor* did not sit well with some of the newspaper's top editors, who in December 1988 resigned in protest. They were soon joined by several prominent staff writers.

Although the circulation of the *Monitor* fell following the changes, its losses also dropped, but this relative improvement did little to compensate for the mounting investments in the other media ventures. Furthermore, the Publishing Society elevated its television aspirations, deciding to launch a 24-hour, satellite-based cable programming network. In essence the directors of the Church and the trustees of the Publishing Society were gambling that television would turn profitable before they were pressured to back off. Because of Christian Scientists' beliefs, the service refused to accept pharmaceutical- or alcohol-related commercials, which handicapped its chances from the outset. By March 1992, however, the situation reached a tipping point, following press reports that the Church had borrowed $41.5 million from an employee pension fund and another $5 million from its trustee endowment in order to keep afloat its television operations, which now were consuming $1 million a week and already had cost the Church and Publishing Society a total of $250 million. Despite protestations from officials that the Monitor Channel remained on track to become profitable by 1996, prominent Church members brought enough pressure to bear that several leaders were forced to resign, the syndicated news was cancelled, and the cable service put up for sale. The *Monitor* and *World Monitor* were not affected, but WQTV was sold in 1993, while on the radio side the weekend program came to an end in June 1996 and, later, the daily shows were terminated as well. The short-wave radio facilities were eventually sold, leaving a limited slate of religious short-wave radio programming.

Several years passed before the Publishing Society and the Church recovered from their move into television. It was not until July 1998 that the Church was able to repay the pension funds. The *Monitor*'s circulation, which fell to a low of 75,000 in 1997 (a loss of 100,000 since 1988), rebounded to 90,000 in 1998. To help the newspaper stage a comeback, the Publishing Society renovated its newsroom and invested $500,000 in a national ad campaign. The *Monitor* also underwent a redesign, an attempt to appeal to a wider audience, and even looked into the possibility of home delivery rather than a reliance on the U.S. mail. The *Sentinel* also was redesigned in 1998. Although matters clearly were improving for the *Monitor* and other ventures of the Publishing Society, the world of media was changing rapidly, making it all but impossible that the organization could enjoy the kind of impact it once held. Nevertheless, it remained committed to fulfilling the mission laid out by its founder more than a century earlier.

Principal Operating Units

The Christian Science Monitor; Christian Science Quarterly; The Christian Science Journal; Christian Science Sentinel; The Herald of Christian Science.

Principal Competitors

The New York Times Company; The Washington Post Company.

Further Reading

Alster, Norm, ''Netty Douglass' Impossible Task,'' *Forbes,* September 17, 1990, p. 186.

Beam, Alex, ''Turmoil at the Monitor,'' *Boston Globe,* November 11, 1998, p. 73.

Biddle, Frederic M., and Alex Beam, ''Walkout by Editors at Monitor Creates a Crisis for Church,'' *Boston Globe,* November 22, 1988, p. 45.

Franklin, James L., ''Christian Science Media Officials Said Due to Depart,'' *Boston Globe,* April 13, 1992.

Gill, Gillian, *Mary Baker Eddy,* Reading, Mass.: Perseus Books, 1998.

Smith, Samantha T., ''Magazine Aims at Spiritual Yearnings,'' *Boston Business Journal,* April 24, 1998.

Symonds, William C., ''Is a Revival Under Way at the Christian Science Monitor?,'' *Business Week,* November 30, 1998, p. 42.

—Ed Dinger

Everywhere you need us most™

Coach USA, Inc.

One Riverway, Suite 500
Houston, Texas 77057
U.S.A.
Telephone: (713) 888-0104
Fax: (713) 888-0218
Web site: http://www.coachusa.com

Wholly-Owned Subsidiary of Stagecoach Group plc
Incorporated: 1995
Employees: 12,450
Sales: £682.3 million ($995.5 million)
NAIC: 485111 Mixed Mode Transit Systems

Although it has cornered a meager 2 percent share of the North American motorcoach business, Coach USA, Inc., can claim leadership of this highly fragmented, $40 billion industry. The company also ranks as one of the five largest private sector providers of commuter and transit motorcoach services in Canada and the United States. Headquartered in Houston, Texas, Coach USA also provides airport ground transportation, paratransit, taxi, and other related passenger ground transportation services. Altogether, its fleet encompassed about 7,600 motorcoaches, minibuses, and vans as well as 6,700 limousines and taxicabs. The company was acquired by Stagecoach Group plc, a Scottish transportation concern, in 1999. By 2003, Coach USA comprised about one-third of Stagecoach's business.

Origins As a Roll-Up: 1995

Founded in September 1995, Coach USA was the creation of a merchant banking firm, Notre Capital Ventures II, L.P. (Notre) a Houston, Texas-based organization recognized for its successful ''roll-ups,'' in which several choice smaller companies within a growth industry are identified and then combined to form one large company. Major funding is then established through the sale of stock. For a decade or more, principals at Notre had worked at various accounting and acquisition functions related to the waste industry, which had undergone extensive consolidation. That successful model was applied to roll-up ventures in other industries. The Notre group was responsible for the public offerings of U.S. Delivery Systems, Physicians Resource Group, Allwaste, Sanifill, and American Medical Response. They focused on industries that were very large, very fragmented, with businesses that were stable from a non-cyclical and profit margin standpoint. The criteria utilized by Notre for selecting individual companies within various industries has included profitability, sizable operations, a long track record, and demonstrated leadership and entrepreneurial management.

By the mid-1990s, the Notre management team identified the motorcoach industry as ''ripe for consolidation,'' according to Larry Plachno of the National Bus Trader. Within the United States the motorcoach industry primarily offered three types of services: recreation and excursion (charter, tour and sightseeing), commuter and transit, and regularly scheduled intercity service. In 1996, the highly fragmented industry accounted for approximately 5,000 motorcoach operators, which collectively generated roughly $20 billion in annual revenues. With the U.S. travel and tourism industry growing substantially, large organizations such as AAA and the American Association of Retired Persons, as well as convention organizers, were targeted by chartering companies as potential customers. Furthermore, due to the growing numbers of tourists from Europe and Asia, in particular, the motorcoach industry was viewed by the investors as a potentially lucrative market.

Notre management first opted to concentrate on motorcoach businesses that specialized in the charter and tour market, along with privatized transit and commuter service, rather than companies in the scheduled intercity bus service market. Also, they anticipated future expansion due to declining transit funding of capital intensive operations by state and local governments, which would eventually steer transit agencies to the more competitive privatized companies. Management forecast a scenario where sizable federal funding available for subsidizing commuter, transit, and ancillary services, such as paratransit services required under the Americans with Disabilities Act, would diminish. By merging a number of companies they could benefit by the large scale of their operations, qualifying them for lower equipment and insurance costs, financing costs, and other cost advantages.

Company Perspectives:

Coach USA is your one-stop-shop for all your ground transportation needs. Coach USA offers charter bus, airport shuttle, sightseeing, group tour, and taxi service in over 120 locations in the United States and Canada. Whether you need transportation for one person or 10,000 people, Coach USA can help you find a solution to any ground transportation challenge.

Going Public: 1996

Coach USA went public in May 1996, with an initial offering of 3,600,000 shares priced at $14 per share. Coach USA was formed with six initial "founding companies" which were well established in the motorcoach industry: Suburban Transit Corp. of New Brunswick, New Jersey; Gray Line of San Francisco, California; Leisure Time Tours in Mahway, New Jersey; Community Bus Lines in Passaic, New Jersey; Adventure Trails in Atlantic City, New Jersey; and Arrow Stage Line in Phoenix, Arizona. The acquisitions were valued at $88.4 million. Forty million passengers were accommodated annually by these companies equipped with a combined force of 760 coaches. Owners of the merging companies exchanged their corporate stock for stock in Coach USA, which gave the company ownership of equipment as well as the individual businesses. Coach USA espoused a decentralized management philosophy. Their arrangement allowed previous owners to continue as presidents of the acquired companies so that the new consolidated company gained from experienced management in localized operations. Almost half of the stock holdings were held by the founding companies following the consolidation. The individual companies, including most of the later acquisitions, were restructured as subsidiaries of Coach USA, retaining their original identities and operating practices.

Using Notre Capital's effective management model, the team was split into an operational management team and an acquisition management team. Heading the operations team, John Mercandante—industry veteran and prior owner of Adventure Trails—became the first Coach USA president and chief operating officer. Local operators continued to identify candidates for corporate management, who focused on the acquisition program and coordinated equipment sharing among the various companies, set safety standards, and conducted financing procedures and vendor contacts. This arrangement allowed entrepreneurs at the acquired companies to continue to deal with day-to-day operations, including customer relationships, equipment utilization, and local pricing. Former Arthur Anderson partner Richard H. Kristinik was named chairman and chief executive officer of the company, responsible for leading strategic initiatives and coordinating acquisition activities and negotiations. The company's executive management team consisted of eight professionals, including CFO Larry King, Senior Vice-President and Corporate Development Officer Frank Gallagher, and Senior Vice-President and General Counsel Doug Cerney.

As Kristinik told John O'Hanlon of the Wall Street Corporate Reporter, "We think our decentralized management philosophy is one of the keys to our success. It is a key for Coach USA being able to attract new companies to become part of Coach USA. . . . [An owner-operator] can sell his company, enjoy the benefit of selling his company at capital gains rates, and continue to be president of his company." Kristinik also stated that the decentralized management philosophy was also important in remaining close to the customer by keeping the "former owner-operator entrepreneur in his own backyard, serving the customer and growing the business."

In an effort to begin strengthening Coach USA's geographical position a second stock offering was made in November 1996, followed by the addition of six companies that were merged into Coach USA, including American Bus Lines Inc. of Miami, Gray Line and Texas Bus Lines of Houston, KT Contract Services of Las Vegas, and California Charter Inc. of Los Angeles and San Diego. The Yellow Cab Service companies of Houston and Austin, Texas, and Colorado Springs, Colorado, were also acquired during this time period.

Acquisitions Continue

Two months after the 3.1 million shares of common stock were sold at $25 a share, another round of acquisitions followed. Four new companies were added in December 1996. Their aggregate annualized revenues totaled $52 million, bringing Coach USA within the range of their projected $73 million of acquired revenue for 1997. By this time the company, with a fleet of approximately 1,700 coaches, was rivaling the Greyhound lines. The addition of Gray Line of Anaheim, California, which operated mainly in per capita sightseeing and tour and charter services in and around Disneyland, had given Coach USA a strong presence in California. The acquisition of Powder River Transportation opened up an entirely new area for the company, with substantial contract operations, including use of transit buses to accommodate the attractive employee shuttle business, as well as tour and charter business to major national parks in and around Wyoming and the Rocky Mountains, including Mt. Rushmore and Yellowstone. Another transit contract company, Progressive Transportation of New York, was added, offering commuter and transit services for small and medium-sized municipalities. The company acquired the Gray Line of Montreal and Quebec City, its first expansion outside the continental United States. As the premiere motorcoach and tour and charter company in the Montreal area, the Gray Line focused on per capita sightseeing and airport shuttle services, in addition to offering equipment repair and maintenance services to companies that offer tours and charters into Montreal and Quebec.

The company used a network of hotel lobby ticket counters, hotel concierges, and travel agents to sell sightseeing tours. Charter and tour services were provided on a fixed daily rate, based on mileage and hours of operation. Coach USA's charter and tour fleet vehicles were designed for comfort, featuring plush interiors with televisions and VCRs. Customers traveling in the San Francisco area could comfortably enjoy the sites while touring the Napa Valley wine country, the Monterey Peninsula tour, or the San Francisco city tour. Businesses, schools, and social organizations chartered Coach USA motorcoaches to visit sporting venues, ski resorts, and historical sites. International groups book trips from Niagara Falls to the

Key Dates:

1995: Coach USA is created out of several smaller companies by merchant banking firm Notre Capital Ventures II, L.P.

1996: Coach USA makes an initial public offering (IPO) in May and a second offering in November.

1997: Through acquisition and internal growth, Coach USA has built a fleet of 1,700 coaches.

1998: Coach USA holds the leadership position in the U.S. motorcoach industry.

1999: The company is acquired by Scotland-based Stagecoach Group plc.

2001: Cost-cutting measures are enacted to weather the downturn in tourist travel after the September 11 terrorist attacks.

2003: The company begins to focus on scheduled, transit, and sightseeing services, while scaling back its tour and charter services.

Rocky Mountains among the various other attractions. Large events serviced by the company have included the Super Bowl, Rose Bowl, the massive COMDEX trade show in Las Vegas, the Home Builders Association, Houston Livestock and Rodeo, Phoenix Open Golf Tournament, and the Arizona State Fair. In 1997, Coach's tour and charter businesses comprised 47 percent of company revenues. The company also provided special services to regions not served by airports or ground transportation, as in service between Colorado Springs to Denver, or other ski destinations, where customers travel from airline to coach without having to claim their bags. Additionally, the company provided service from airports in Atlantic City, Houston, Las Vegas, Los Angeles, Miami, and Philadelphia, transporting customers to casinos, hotels, cruise ships, and convention sites.

Due to the company's diverse operations, Coach USA was able to rotate its equipment according to specific need requirements. For example, a motorcoach used for the tour and charter business, where a customer may spend a week or more, should be a newer, more luxurious vehicle. When that same motorcoach was four or five years old it might be used in a commuter and transit operation, where its customers were simply going back and forth to work. When that same motorcoach was eight or nine years old, it might be effectively used in an airport shuttle operation, according to industry analyst Anthony Gallo, interviewed in the *Wall Street Corporate Reporter.* Coaches on commuter routes could be used on mid-day routes nearby at times when commuter bussing was not needed. Coach USA increased profits by closely considering the logistics of optimizing its equipment.

By 1997, the company claimed approximately 52 percent of the U.S. industry's commuter and transit business. They boasted operations in Seattle, Houston, Los Angeles, New York, and San Francisco. For the most part, the company had fixed routes serviced on a daily basis. Some of Coach USA's commuter service motorcoaches were owned by a state or municipal transit authority and provided to the company at a nominal rent; sometimes they were even given to the company.

Contracts to provide these services were generally won through a bidding process which challenged companies to demonstrate significant guaranteed cost savings. Typically, a contract was structured so that the municipality carried the risk of delivering ridership levels, while the service provider was responsible for its own costs. In the highly competitive municipal transit market, average savings from these privatized operations ran in the 30 percent range.

Two of Coach's key transit contract competitors in the late 1990s were Laidlaw and Ryder. The three companies also competed for contracts that provide accessible transportation to the disabled (paratransit services), in addition to competing for potential acquisitions. Within the United States, Laidlaw's annual revenues from non-school bus operations averaged $300 million. Their tour and charter business generated about $40 million annually, compared to Coach USA's revenues of approximately $200 million in that sector. Ryder had neither tour nor charter services but accounted for approximately $150 million of transit dollars annually. Ryder had not been as aggressive in its acquisitions as the other two major competing companies. Neither competitor was considered a substantial threat to Coach USA's dominance.

By late 1998, Coach USA had completed more than 70 acquisitions since its IPO in May 1996. It had also surpassed $900 million in assets and now led the motorcoach industry in the United States. CEO Richard Kristinik announced his retirement in 1998 and was succeeded by CFO Larry King.

By 1999, Coach USA had about 9,000 buses operating in 35 states, Canada, and Mexico. Coach USA's success attracted the attention of a Scottish company that had begun to consolidate the global motorcoach business. The Stagecoach Group plc had itself been founded in 1980 by Brian Souter and Ann Gloag. Starting with two buses, the brother and sister had amassed one of the biggest rail and bus groups in the world, with 20,000 vehicles and almost 45,000 employees by 2001. Stagecoach's reach extended to New Zealand, Scandinavia, Portugal, Hong Kong, and China, as well as the United Kingdom and Canada. That July, Stagecoach acquired Coach USA for over $1.8 billion, or $42 per share. Stagecoach also took on some $630 million in debt held by Coach USA. Frank Gallagher, director of Stagecoach, assumed the role of CEO at Coach USA.

Notwithstanding all of the acquisitions Coach USA had made over its short history, the U.S. motorcoach industry remained highly fragmented, with an estimated 5,000 players, and Coach commanded just a 2 percent market share. With its balance sheet cleared of debt, Coach USA was free to continue its growth via acquisition, albeit at a somewhat slower pace. At least 11 acquisitions were made in 1999, five more in 2000, and another seven in 2001.

Under its new ownership, Coach USA also worked to grow its existing operations. In 2000, the company announced a partnership with Six Flags Theme Parks whereby Coach would offer special rates to the amusement park's customers. Coach USA also set up a network of routes to service hotels and resorts near the Disneyland theme park in California. The UK influence soon began to be evidenced by Coach USA's introduction of double-decker buses to key tourist markets like San Diego, New

York, and Chicago. According to the 2002 Stagecoach annual report, the parent company was "encouraged by the way Coach USA was moving forward prior to September 11."

September 11: Tragedy Brings Challenges

The terrorist attacks of September 11, 2001, made a lasting impact on both the business and leisure travel industries, the very basis of Coach USA's business. The downturn in ridership in the immediate aftermath of the incident forced the company to reduce its Houston headquarters staff by 40 percent, eliminate 10 percent of all non-driver employees, and take 330 busses off the road. By the end of 2001, Coach USA had cut costs by $25 million.

Although the company was at that time Stagecoach's largest division, contributing one-third of revenues, its sales fell 5 percent during fiscal 2002 (ended April 30, 2002). Net income declined by more than one-third during the period, proving a serious drag on the parent company's earnings. As a result, in 2002 Stagecoach Group—in the person of CEO Brain Souter—started a "full business review" of its newest and biggest subsidiary, with a primary goal of cutting costs. By 2003, the company had already begun to focus on scheduled ("line run"), transit, and sightseeing services, while scaling back its reliance on tour and charter services. Coach USA's roadmap to the future would depend on Brian Souter's appraisal of the business.

Principal Competitors

Carey International Inc.; BostonCoach; Laidlaw Inc.; The Hertz Corporation.

Further Reading

Apte, Angela, "Acquisition of Coach USA Offers U.S. Growth For British Company," *Houston Business Journal*, June 18, 1999, p. 4.

Brooks, George, "If You Could Love Only One . . . ," *Equities*, December 7, 1997, pp. 11–12.

Gannon, Joyce, "Coach USA of Texas to Buy Yellow Cab of Pittsburgh, Sister Firm," *Knight-Ridder/Tribune Business News*, December 10, 1997.

Hollahan, Terry, "Regional Hub Launched By Coach USA," *Memphis Business Journal*, August 27, 1999, p. 1.

O'Hanlon, John, "Consolidating the Industry," *Wall Street Corporate Reporter*, October 6, 1997, pp. 1–4.

Perin, Monica, "Founding CEO of Coach Hits the Road," *Houston Business Journal*, November 13, 1988, p. 6.

Pfeffer, Sally, "Adventure-Seeking Retirees Pump Money Into Economy," *Business Journal-Milwaukee*, December 22, 2000, p. 21.

Plachno, Larry, "Coach USA," *National Bus Trader*, April 1997, pp. 1–4.

Rodrigues, Tanya, "Company Branches Out with Double-Decker Buses," *San Diego Business Journal*, March 18, 2002, p. 13.

Welsh, Gordon, Leslie Davis, and Cliff Henke, "Big U.K. Companies Still Show Interest in U.S.," *Metro*, September-October 2000, p. 86.

—Terri Mozzone
—update: April Gasbarre

cogent
COMMUNICATIONS

Optical Internet

Cogent Communications Group, Inc.

1015 31st Street Northwest
Washington, D.C. 20007
U.S.A.
Telephone: (202) 295-4200
Toll Free: (877) 926-4368
Fax: (202) 338-8798
Web site: http://www.cogentco.com

Public Company
Incorporated: 1999 as Cogent Communications, Inc.
Employees: 200
Sales: $51.9 million (2002)
Stock Exchanges: American
Ticker Symbol: COI
NAIC: 513310 Wired Telecommunications Carriers;
    514191 Online Information Services

For companies involved in transmitting high-speed Internet-based data, the so-called "last mile" is considered the most difficult. The phrase refers to the final link of connectivity between a customer and the high-speed optical network that connects it to the Internet. Since Cogent Communications Group, Inc. owns its own network, it specializes in making that last-mile connection and, more specifically, in providing high-speed Internet access to businesses located in multi-tenant buildings in the central business districts of major U.S. cities.

Cogent provides its high-speed services through its own facilities-based national optical network, known as an Internet backbone, that connects to its customers' own local area networks (LANs) through metropolitan fiber rings. Cogent created its national network in 2000, acquiring the rights to dark fiber, or unused fiber-optic strands, that connected large cities. Through an agreement with Circuit City Stores, Inc., Cogent used Cisco's equipment to light or activate those strands of dark fiber, making them capable of carrying Internet protocol (IP) data at capacity up to 80 Gbps. Within the cities it services, Cogent acquires dark fiber rings known as metro rings. Cogent then acquires the rights to make the fiber connections linking the customer to its metro rings, the so-called "last mile." Cogent's flat-rate pricing model garnered national attention for its low rates, which were $1,000 per month for 100 Mbps service and $10,000 per month for 1 Gbps service.

Offering Low-Cost Internet-Based Data Transmission: 1999–2000

The company was founded as Cogent Communications, Inc. in August 1999 by David Schaeffer. Schaeffer was a serial entrepreneur who had founded several companies before launching Cogent, including Mercury Message Paging and Pathnet, Inc., a broadband telecommunications provider that he established in 1995. He served as Pathnet's CEO from 1995 to 1997 and as its chairman from 1997 to 1999. Schaeffer severed his association with Pathnet in 1999, and afterwards in 2001 Pathnet filed for bankruptcy under Chapter 11 of the U.S. Bankruptcy Code.

Cogent's business plan was to offer high-speed Internet access over its own IP data-only network, thus bypassing the traditional voice-based networks operated by the Regional Bell Operating Companies (RBOCs). Cogent planned to reduce the cost to transport bandwidth by two orders of magnitude, or 99 percent, and offer it at radically reduced prices while still making a profit. The company's initial product was 100 Mbps of Internet access on a non-oversubscribed basis at $1,000 per month. The service was initially offered in 13 major U.S. markets.

During 2000 Cogent successfully completed two rounds of venture capital financing. In the first round, completed in February, the company raised $26 million from a group of venture capital firms, including Jerusalem Venture Partners, Worldview Technology Partners, Oak Investment Partners, Boulder Ventures, and C. Blair Asset Management. James Wei of Worldview Technology Partners and Erel Margalit of Jerusalem Venture Partners subsequently joined Cogent's board of directors. The second round of funding, completed in July, was led by Oak Investment Partners and raised an additional $90 million. Ed Glassmeyer, founder of Oak Investment Partners, joined Cogent's board of directors.

Company Perspectives:

The Cogent solution offers the unique combination of higher quality at a lower price. Data-only network technology combined with end-to-end network ownership allows Cogent to offer ultra-high speed Internet access at prices never before offered in the industry.

Cogent established significant partnerships in the first half of 2000. In March the company announced it had selected Cisco Systems to build its high-speed optical network. Under the $280 million contract, Cisco would provide all the technology necessary to construct a nationwide network optimized for Internet traffic. The network, Cogent's IP backbone, would connect 13 cities using OC-192 long-haul Dense Wavelength-Division Multiplexing (DWDM) and use OC-48 metro DWDM connections within each city. Cisco's technology would allow Cogent to offer high-capacity Internet access at 100 Mbps, 100 times faster than a T-1 connection, directly to business customers situated in major metropolitan areas at less than the cost of a T-1 line. In a separate agreement announced in April, Cisco was selected to provide real-time end-to-end monitoring of Cogent's network infrastructure and service-level agreement (SLA) management through its Cisco Info Center monitoring and diagnostics tool.

Another significant partnership was with Williams Communications Group. In April Cogent announced a long-term agreement with Williams to lease its nationwide dark fiber backbone totaling more than 12,400 route miles and to obtain access to Williams' network services. As a result of the agreement, which was valued at $215 million, Cogent would be able to activate and operate a nationwide OC-192 backbone that would transmit data at speeds of 10 Gbps and scalable to 640 Gbps. A third partnership with Metromedia Fiber Networks gave Cogent the rights to purchase single-fiber rings in 50 major metropolitan markets. Metromedia was in the process of building an optical network using more than 29,000 miles of fiber to connect 67 cities in North America and Europe.

As a result of these agreements, Cogent was able to announce in November 2000 that it had lit up or activated its all-optical, national facilities-based network. The initial activation included the company's national IP backbone and four cities: New York, Chicago, Philadelphia, and Washington, D.C., with service to begin January 1, 2001. One of Cogent's first customers in the Washington, D.C., area was the American Gas Association, which noted that Cogent provided it with 100 times the bandwidth of its current T-1 service at about two-thirds of the cost.

Expanding Service to Additional U.S. Cities: 2001

Cogent began offering all-optical, non-oversubscribed 100 Mbps Internet access capability for $1,000 per month to multi-tenant commercial properties in the cities it serviced in January 2001. While Cogent's pricing undercut that of T-1 service, the company was also competing with DSL service. Commercial customers could order DSL service of up to 7 Mbps from Qwest

Communications International, Inc. or Verizon Communications Inc. for between $190 and $400 a month. For many small and medium-size businesses, that was sufficient capacity. Cogent promoted the view that DSL, being a copper-based technology, offered a low-quality connection and would soon be outpaced by market demand. By February 2001 Cogent had attracted some 2,800 customers for its low-cost service.

Cogent enhanced its network's reliability in January 2001 through an agreement with American Power Conversion Corporation. Cogent selected the company to provide power solutions that would guarantee uninterrupted service over Cogent's network.

With service now available in four major cities, Cogent's next task was to sign access agreements with the owners of large commercial buildings in those cities' central business districts. In addition, Cogent began signing agreements with fiber-optic companies that had already established access to commercial properties in those cities. An agreement with New York-based FiberNet Telecom Group gave Cogent the right to use FiberNet's existing connections to commercial properties to provide high-speed Internet access in New York City. A deal with Rudin Management Company, one of the largest privately held real estate firms in New York City, gave Cogent the rights to equip 16 commercial properties totaling 10 million square feet. As part of the agreement, Cogent's New York hub would be located in one of Rubin's properties at 32 Sixth Avenue.

At the end of March 2001 Cogent announced a national co-location agreement with Switch and Data, which operated 34 co-location centers in the United States. Switch and Data's co-location centers, called Convergent Network Centers (CNCs), offered a variety of networking infrastructure for telecommunications providers to deliver broadband services and applications. Located in urban centers, the CNCs enabled providers to quickly and cost-effectively enter new markets and deploy their services. Under its agreement with Switch and Data, Cogent gained access to 12 of Switch and Data's CNCs in 10 major metropolitan centers.

Around this time Cogent underwent a corporate reorganization. Cogent Communications Group, Inc. was formed to become the parent company of Cogent Communications, Inc. Effective March 14, 2001, Cogent exchanged all of its outstanding shares for an equal number of shares of Cogent Communications Group and became a wholly owned subsidiary of Cogent Communications Group.

In April 2001 Cogent announced that it would expand its network capacity to 80 Gbps due to larger than anticipated customer demand. With each OC-192 wavelength operating at 10 Gbps, Cogent began work to add seven additional wavelengths to increase its network capacity. The expansion was completed in November 2001. Around this time Cogent also received the first preferred service provider designation from Cisco Systems, its new IP + Optical Cisco Powered Network designation. Over the past year Cogent had received some $310 million in vendor financing from Cisco.

With its fiber-optic IP backbone and multiple metropolitan area network stretching some 17,400 miles, Cogent announced in May 2001 that it had secured access to its 525th building, representing more than 161 million square feet of commercial office space. Cogent had been successful in signing contracts with large real estate firms in major cities, including Rudin Management, The Trump Group, The Lurie Company, Jamison Properties, Crescent Real Estate Equities Co., and Carlyle Realty, among others. These contracts enabled Cogent to approach individual tenants to sell them high-speed Internet access.

Cogent continued to add service to more cities in 2001. In June it added service to its 10th urban market, Santa Clara, California. Within each city it served, Cogent also established one or more hub offices. Other cities serviced by Cogent included Dallas, Denver, Kansas City, Boston, and San Francisco, in addition to its original four cities of New York, Chicago, Philadelphia, and Washington, D.C.

In July 2001 an agreement with Level 3 Communications, Inc. gave Cogent access to Level 3 data centers and other buildings in 18 major business markets. The deal expanded Cogent's depth in those 18 markets and enabled service provider customers to connect with Cogent in Level 3's co-location centers. Later that month Cogent launched its service in Dallas and Houston and set up hub sites in both cities. By the end of July Cogent had gained access agreements to more than 50 multi-tenant office buildings and co-location centers in Dallas, including six of the city's 10 tallest buildings. Another agreement with TXU Communications gave Cogent fiber access to 20 additional buildings in downtown Dallas. Through its agreement with TXU, Cogent was able to offer customers high-speed Internet connectivity within 60 days in those buildings.

In August 2001 Cogent introduced its Value Added Services Program. Through the program customers could gain access to a select group of vendors who provided value-added services compatible with Cogent's high bandwidth Internet connectivity. Unlike many other Internet service providers (ISPs), Cogent did not offer additional bundled services along with its Internet connections. Rather, the company remained focused on providing customers with low-cost, high-speed fiber-optic access to the Internet. Around this time Cogent introduced service in Los Angeles, its 12th market.

In September 2001 Cogent acquired the assets of NetRail, a Tier One ISP that was in bankruptcy. Cogent planned to continue service to NetRail's customers and integrate its service into Cogent's national backbone. NetRail provided Cogent with crucial peering relationships that allowed Cogent to become a Tier One ISP and exchange traffic with other providers on a settlement-free basis. Cogent's new Tier One status enabled it to offer cost-effective Ethernet Internet access to small and medium-size businesses in major metropolitan markets. In November the company announced it had completed the upgrade of its system to handle Internet access up to 80 Gbps. By the end of 2001 the company had reached its goal of serving 20 cities by adding service to Atlanta, Orlando, Tampa, Jacksonville, Miami, San Diego, Sacramento, and Seattle.

Another significant acquisition involved Allied Riser Communications Corp., a financially troubled ISP based in Dallas. Completed in February 2002, the acquisition gave Cogent more potential customers through networks that Allied Riser had already installed in large office buildings in the United States and Canada. Following the merger-acquisition, Allied Riser became a wholly owned subsidiary of Cogent, with Allied Riser's shareholders receiving equivalent shares of Cogent. Since Allied Riser was a publicly traded company, Cogent became a public company when the transaction was finalized, and Cogent was subsequently listed on the American Stock Exchange. Around this time Cogent announced that it had landed more than $200 million in additional venture capital financing, including significant equipment financing from Cisco Systems. At the time Cogent had about 4,000 customers.

Acquiring Financially Troubled Competitors: 2002–03

Once Cogent's acquisition of Allied Riser was completed, the company's stock began trading on the American Stock Exchange on February 5, 2002. Later that month Cogent announced it would acquire, for $10 million, the major U.S. operating assets of PSINet Inc., an ISP in bankruptcy. PSINet was established in 1989 and was the first company to provide commercial Internet access. Included in the U.S. assets Cogent acquired from PSINet were its customer base, backbone network, associated equipment, three co-location facilities, and rights to intellectual property. Cogent planned to support and build on PSINet's brand name by continuing to offer PSINet services. In October Cogent announced it had upgraded PSINet's three data centers located in Los Angeles, New York, and Herndon, Virginia.

Other ISPs specializing in high-speed Internet access for businesses were also filing for bankruptcy. At the end of March 2002 competitor Yipes Communications filed for Chapter 11 protection. In April Cogent acquired a portfolio of real estate access agreements from OnSite Access, Inc., a high-speed communications provider that had been in Chapter 11 for nearly a year. Most of the access agreements pertained to buildings in New York City, with others located in cities serviced by Cogent.

In the second half of 2002 Cogent was selected by Merit Network, Inc. to deliver ultra-high speed Internet access to all 13 of Michigan's publicly funded universities. In September Cogent acquired key assets from New York-based FiberCity Networks, including its customer base and building access agreements. Following the acquisition FiberCity ceased operations. Cogent entered the Canadian market in October by opening an office in Toronto. Service in Canada would be delivered by Shared Technologies of Canada, a wholly owned subsidiary that Cogent obtained as part of its acquisition of Allied Riser Communications. Cogent made another acquisition in February 2003 when it purchased the ISP business of Fiber Network Solutions, Inc. (FNSI). Based in Columbus, Ohio, FNSI was an Internet access and co-location service provider to businesses in Ohio, Michigan, and Pennsylvania. As part of the deal Cogent acquired five co-location facilities, including those located in Columbus, Pittsburgh, and Detroit.

At the beginning of 2003 Cogent adjusted its marketing plans to reach small and medium-size companies that did not need Cogent Classic service of 100 Mbps of bandwidth for $1,000 a month. In January the company launched a 500 Kbps service for $249 a month that competed directly with DSL service. According to Cogent CEO and Chairman David Schaeffer, ''We did an awful lot of market research and discovered only 45 percent of the tenants in our on-network buildings would be good candidates for our Cogent Classic service. The rest were too small to need that much bandwidth, but of that remaining 55 percent, we discovered about 40 percent fell squarely in the DSL space.'' Cogent's 500 Kbps service enabled it to compete with DSL carriers without having to make similar capital investments. Another benefit that distinguished Cogent's new service from DSL was that customers gained access to Cogent's entire network.

While Cogent had made several acquisitions that provided new revenue streams, the company continued to operate at a loss in 2002. For 2001 Cogent had an operating loss of $61.1 million and revenue of only $3 million. For 2002 Cogent's sales rose significantly, to $51.9 million. However, losses also rose, this time to $91.8 million. Schaeffer forecast that the company would achieve a positive cashflow sometime in 2004. Meanwhile, Cogent was surviving on venture capital financing.

Principal Subsidiaries

Allied Riser Communications Corp.; Cogent Communications, Inc.; Shared Technologies of Canada.

Principal Competitors

AT&T Corp.; Cable & Wireless plc; Genuity Inc.; Sprint Corp.; WorldCom Inc.

Further Reading

Allen, Doug, ''Yipes Bankruptcy: A Vacuum for RBOCs to Fill?,'' *Network Magazine,* May 1, 2002, p. 18.

Barrett, Brendan, ''Big Winners?,'' *Washington Techway,* September 3, 2001, p. 22.

Brown, Patricia, ''Cheap Ideas—Cogent Moves to Tackle Burgeoning Market Niche Through Inexpensive Service,'' *Tele.com,* November 27, 2000, p. 35.

Carlson, Caron, ''Fast Ethernet for a Grand,'' *eWeek,* November 20, 2000, p. 38.

''Cogent Brings All-Optical Network to the Table,'' *Boardwatch Magazine,* March 2002, p. 24.

''Cogent Communications,'' *Washington Techway,* February 18, 2002, p. 22.

''Cogent Communications Acquires US PSINet's U.S. Operations,'' *High-Speed Internet Access,* April 2002, p. 11.

''Cogent Communications and Level 3 Sign Fiber Agreement,'' *Fiber Optics Business,* August 31, 2001, p. 10.

''Cogent Communications Launches Metro-Loop High-Speed Data Transport Service,'' *High-Speed Internet Access User,* May-June 2001, p. 19.

''Cogent Communications to Acquire Dallas-Based Internet Service Provider,'' *Knight-Ridder/Tribune Business News,* August 30, 2001.

''Cogent Connects Colleges,'' *Fiber Optics Weekly Update,* August 30, 2002, p. 2.

''Cogent Doesn't Want Your Infrastructure,'' *ISP Business News,* February 26, 2001.

''Cogent Speeds up Its Service,'' *ISP Business,* May 2001, p. 14.

''Cogent Woos Small Companies with Scaled-Down Service,'' *Telephony,* January 27, 2003.

''Download: Going Against the Grain,'' *Telephony,* March 6, 2000.

''Extending Ethernet's Reach,'' *Telephony,* March 10, 2003.

''Fiber Fuels Future for Cogent,'' *ISP Business News,* September 18, 2000.

''FiberNet Telecom Group,'' *Washington Business Journal,* January 26, 2001, p. 29.

Hakala, David, and Joseph Panettieri, ''Do Go into the Light,'' *Sm@rt Reseller,* March 20, 2000, p. 26.

Hardy, Stephen, ''Carrier Throws Optical Bandwidth at Quality-of-Service Problem,'' *Lightwave,* May 2000, p. 31.

Kady, Martin, II, ''Cogent Keeps Things Humming in Dicey Telecom Field,'' *Washington Business Journal,* November 17, 2000, p. 36.

——, ''Cogent to Land $200M,'' *Washington Business Journal,* August 31, 2001, p. 1.

''The Merger Route to Going Public,'' *Mergers & Acquisitions Journal,* October 2001, p. 14.

Miller, Elizabeth Starr, ''The Last Mile's Still the Hardest,'' *Interactive Week,* October 8, 2001, p. 44.

''Promises Made, Promises Kept,'' *Telephony,* July 9, 2001, p. 30.

Sweeney, Dan, ''Cogent Informants Spill All,'' *America's Network,* June 1, 2002, p. 16.

Woolley, Scott, ''Cogent or Crazy?,'' *Forbes,* April 2, 2001, p. 126.

—David P. Bianco

Conn-Selmer, Inc.

600 Industrial Parkway
Elkhart, Indiana 46516
U.S.A.
Telephone: (574) 522-1675
Fax: (574) 295-5405
Web site: http://www.conn-selmer.com

Wholly Owned Subsidiary of Steinway Musical
*   Instruments, Inc.*
Incorporated: 1874 as C.G. Conn Co.
Employees: 2,000 (est.)
Sales: $184 million (2001)
NAIC: 339992 Musical Instrument Manufacturing

Conn-Selmer, Inc. is the largest manufacturer of wind instruments in the United States. The company makes and distributes many prominent brands of musical instruments, including C.G. Conn and Selmer brasswinds, Artley flutes, King band instruments, Bach trumpets, and instruments made under the names Emerson, Glaesel, Scherl & Roth, Musser, and Wm. Lewis & Son. Many of these are historic brands with a cherished reputation among both professional and amateur musicians. Conn and Selmer were both leading wind instrument manufacturers based in Elkhart, Indiana, since the early years of the 20th century. Both went through a series of ownership changes and made acquisitions of smaller companies. In 2000, Selmer's parent company, Steinway Musical Instruments, bought United Musical Instruments, formerly known as C.G. Conn. After the acquisition, the parent combined the two subsidiaries to create Conn-Selmer, Inc.

From Horse Collar Pads to Vulcanized Mouthpieces

The C.G. Conn Company was founded by Charles Gerard Conn, a skilled musician, band leader, inventor, entrepreneur, and politician. Conn was born in 1844, and as a young man lived in Buchanan, Michigan. A series of accidents led to his invention of an improved trumpet mouthpiece. Conn allegedly broke a finger while at work at the local horse collar pad factory. He was the Buchanan town band leader, and the injury made it impossi-

ble for him to play his violin. So he switched to cornet, which had been his secondary instrument, and quickly became a very good player. While playing in a traveling band, he got in a fight and received another career-changing blow, this one to the lip. Apparently the pain of playing his cornet with a swollen, tender lip gave Conn the idea for a rubber-rimmed mouthpiece. This happened around 1871. Shortly thereafter, Conn and his wife moved to Elkhart, Indiana, where Conn pursued various lines of work that included peddling a healthful ointment, engraving silverware, making rubber stamps, and inventing and selling sewing machine parts. Possibly in collaboration with his former boss at the Buchanan horse collar pad factory, Conn found a way to vulcanize rubber directly onto metal, and in 1874 he produced his first rubber-rimmed trumpet mouthpiece. Conn went into business making and selling a variety of musical instrument mouthpieces, working first out of a small second-story space over a drugstore and later opening his own brass foundry. He took out several patents for his mouthpieces in the United States as well as in Canada, England, France, and Belgium.

In 1876, Conn invited a French musical instrument maker, Eugene Victor Jean Baptiste Dupont, to join him in Elkhart. The two began working on improved brass instruments, hoping to create a "perfect" cornet. Dupont left the company after three years, but the C.G. Conn Co. continued to grow, making all kinds of wind instruments as well as mouthpieces. By 1878, the company had a large factory, and Conn had become a major employer in Elkhart. He was elected mayor of Elkhart in 1880 at the age of 36. The factory burned down in 1883, and Conn considered moving his business to Ohio. However, the town persuaded him to stay, and the company rebuilt in Elkhart. Conn's factory produced an estimated 10 percent of all goods made in Elkhart, and by the late 1880s the business employed as many as 300 workers, many of them skilled laborers brought in from France and England. At that time, Conn declared his musical instrument factory the largest of its kind in the world. Many well-known professional musicians endorsed Conn's instruments, which bore the brand name "Wonder."

After rebuilding the Elkhart factory, Conn also acquired a factory in Worcester, Massachusetts, that had belonged to the Isaac Fiske instrument manufacturing company. The company

---

Company Perspectives:

The company's mission is to provide the finest band and orchestra instruments, products, and services in the world, representing the best value in all categories in which we profitably compete.

---

began making a greater variety of instruments. Conn produced the first U.S.-made saxophone in 1888, and the firm began putting out a line of flutes, piccolos, and clarinets. Conn continued to be involved in politics. He founded a newspaper, the *Elkhart Truth,* in 1889, and was elected to the Indiana state legislature that year. He was elected to the U.S. Congress in 1892 and served one term. He also bought the capital city newspaper the *Washington Times.* He served on the military staff of Indiana's governor as well and was given the rank of Colonel. He was called Colonel Conn for the rest of his life. His political activities did not seem to distract Conn from running his business. Conn opened a retail store in New York City in 1897, and around this time the company began producing ''Wonder'' violins. Conn also acquired a mandolin factory in New York and then combined it with his Elkhart violin-making division. The company also began making portable reed organs and debuted the Sousaphone, an instrument designed for bandleader John Phillip Sousa.

The Roaring Twenties through World War II

The C.G. Conn factory burned to the ground for a second time in 1910. Conn rebuilt again, this time putting up an impressive Spanish mission-style structure. The factory was up and running again in only four months, and Conn put out a new brand, ''New Invention,'' that temporarily replaced the older ''Wonder'' lines. Five years later, Colonel Conn retired. He sold the business for $1 million to Carl Diamond Greenleaf, a flour miller from Ohio. Greenleaf had no background in musical instrument manufacture, yet he immediately brought improvements to the Conn plant. By 1917, the factory had been significantly upgraded and retooled, and it now employed some 550 workers. Greenleaf instituted new technology and quality control, leading to a more consistent product. The factory began turning out as many as 2,500 instruments a month.

Through the 1920s, C.G. Conn Ltd., as it was then called, increased its production of the popular new jazz instrument, the saxophone. The company produced saxophones in a wide pitch range, including odd instruments such as the contrabass sarrusophone and a combination saxophone, English horn, and heckelphone called the Conn-O-Sax. Conn also produced saxophones in vivid colors such as purple, green, and white-and-gold. During the 1920s, Carl Greenleaf also owned a part-interest in another Elkhart saxophone maker, the Buescher Company. The company made other acquisitions in the 1920s as well. For a short time it owned a half-interest in H. & A. Selmer, the company it would join with in 2000 to form the present Conn-Selmer, Inc. Conn also owned the Elkhart Band Instrument Company between 1923 and 1927 and ran the Continental Music Company, which was a wholesale division, and the Pan American Band Instrument Company, which made

instruments for student players. Conn acquired a percussion manufacturer, Leedy Co., in 1927. When the stock market crashed in 1929, many musical instrument companies were hurt. Fortunately, Conn had the cash reserves to buy up its rivals at this time. It acquired drum-maker Ludwig & Ludwig in 1930, as well as the accordion-maker Soprani Company and the musical instrument division of Carl Fischer.

During the 1920s, Conn opened music stores across the United States and Canada. The company founded a Conn National School of Music in Chicago in 1923 and helped put together the first National Band Contest in Chicago that year. Carl Greenleaf wanted to promote student music programs, though he did not want this to be seen as his way of creating a school instrument market for his company. Greenleaf helped develop the National Music Camp at Interlochen, Michigan, founded by Joseph Maddy in 1923. C.G. Conn Ltd. donated $10,000 towards building the camp. Greenleaf also supported the development of experimental electronic instruments and acoustic devices. C.G. Conn Ltd. ran an experimental laboratory from 1923 to 1940 and developed the first electronic tuning device and the Stroboconn, the first device for visual measurement of sound.

During World War II, the Conn factory was completely converted to wartime manufacturing. The company put out compasses, altimeters, and other measuring devices used by the military. It had a few orders for musical instruments required by military bands, but because all its machinery had been retooled, these instruments had to be made the old-fashioned way, by hand. Meanwhile, other smaller competitors were allowed to continue to make instruments during the war. After the war ended, it took Conn some time to revert back to instrument manufacturing, and it lost business to these smaller rivals. Its long-time leader, Carl Greenleaf, retired in 1949, though his family still owned Conn.

Because of problems with getting back to peacetime production, the company lost sway in the world of band instruments. Conn was also put back to work for the military during the Korean War. During the 1950s, the company sold off its subsidiaries and began making different kinds of instruments. The company produced the world's first all-electronic organ in 1946, known as the Connsonata organ. Electric organ sales became increasingly important to the company through the 1950s. By the mid-1950s, sales and profits from organs exceeded that from all other instruments combined. Organ sales grew by about 40 percent a year in the early to mid-1950s. By 1958, Conn's total sales were over $14 million, with more than half of that coming from organs. The company also produced pianos after the war. In 1940, Conn bought the Haddorff Piano Company, in Rockford, Illinois. The next year it picked up Chicago's Staube Piano Company. Conn made pianos in Rockford through the 1950s, and in 1964 bought the Janssen Piano Company. Conn made pianos until 1970, when the division was sold. Leland B. Greenleaf, son of Carl Diamond Greenleaf, took over the presidency of the company in 1958. (Carl Greenleaf died in 1959 at the age of 82.) During Leland Greenleaf's tenure, Conn began acquiring again. It bought the Artley Company, a major flute manufacturer, in 1959, and built the Artley division a new factory in Elkhart in 1963. The company also built another factory for its organ division and moved its school music division to facilities in Nogales, Arizona.

Key Dates:

1874: C.G. Conn founds Elkhart company to make rubber-rimmed mouthpieces.
1915: Colonel Conn sells the business to flour miller Carl Greenleaf.
1946: Conn invents the first all-electronic organ.
1969: The company is sold to publisher Crowell Collier Macmillan.
1980: Daniel Henkin buys Conn from Macmillan and brings the company's headquarters back to Elkhart.
1985: The company is sold to Skäne Gripen and renamed United Musical Instruments (UMI).
1990: Bernhard Muskantor buys UMI from Skäne Gripen.
2000: UMI is sold to Steinway Musical Instruments.
2002: UMI is combined with Steinway's Selmer division to become Conn-Selmer, Inc.

A Series of Owners: 1969–85

By the late 1960s, business conditions did not seem rosy at C.G. Conn. Its earnings were flat, and Leland Greenleaf, in his sixties, was thinking about retirement. Greenleaf was apparently considering selling the company when he received an offer from the Kernal Company, a Wall Street investment firm. Unwilling to sell to Kernal, Greenleaf began negotiating with another suitor in late 1968. In April 1969, the deal went through, and C.G. Conn was sold to Crowell Collier and Macmillan, Inc. for around $35 million. Crowell Collier Macmillan was a publishing company, and it had no background in running a musical instrument manufacturing business. Macmillan made a series of drastic changes at Conn. It moved the company headquarters out of Elkhart to Oak Brook, Illinois, while the organ division was moved to another Chicago suburb, Carol Stream. Some of the manufacturing was moved to Japan, while the reed instrument division moved to the former school music division facility in Nogales, Arizona. Conn's brasswind factory was sold to its rival and one-time partner Selmer, while an older Elkhart facility went to Coachman Industries. All these moves left Conn decentralized. By 1980, Conn had divisions or subsidiaries in several Chicago suburbs as well as in Texas, Arizona, Ohio, Indiana, Georgia, and Mexico. The company continued to be unprofitable through the 1970s, and Conn's reputation as a manufacturer suffered.

In 1980, Macmillan sold C.G. Conn Ltd. and its various subsidiaries to Daniel Henkin. Henkin had worked for Conn in the 1960s but left in 1970 to own and manage the historic Elkhart flute manufacturer K.G. Gemeinhardt. Henkin sold Gemeinhardt to Columbia Broadcasting System (CBS) in 1977, and three years later he plunged his capital into Conn. The purchase included the Slingerland Drum Co., flute maker Artley, Inc., a case manufacturing company and a music distributing business, two Mexican manufacturing subsidiaries, and other far-flung divisions. In May 1981, Henkin moved Conn's corporate headquarters back to Elkhart, an event celebrated with a week of elaborate entertainment. In 1981, Conn acquired the W.T. Armstrong Co., a woodwind manufacturer, and Henkin brought out new product lines, including the Henkin clarinet

and the Severinsen trumpet, named for the leader of the *Tonight Show* band, Doc Severinsen. Henkin hoped to rebuild Conn and to bring it back to its Elkhart glory days. The company made another acquisition in 1985, the King Musical Instruments company, but then Henkin abruptly sold C.G. Conn to a Swedish conglomerate, Skäne Gripen.

United Musical Instruments in the 1980s–90s

Skäne Gripen AB was a large Swedish company with interests in many areas. It had a small music division, having bought Sweden's largest musical instrument distributorship, Muskantor Musik AB, in 1982. Bernhard Muskantor, head of this family company, took a seat on Skäne Gripen's board when the conglomerate bought him out, and he directed the company to purchase Conn from Henkin in October 1985. Conn was renamed United Musical Instruments, or UMI. It consisted of C.G. Conn, its recent acquisitions King Musical Instruments and Armstrong Woodwinds, the Cleveland stringed instrument company Scherl & Roth, Benge Professional Brasses, and Artley Woodwinds. The Swedish company did not buy the Slingerland Drum Co., and other divisions were quickly sold or consolidated. UMI also encompassed the Swedish companies Muskantor Musik and two music retailers. In 1987, UMI bought a 50 percent interest in a German percussion instrument manufacturer, Sonor GmbH. While sales at UMI during 1989 were estimated at $80 million, Skäne Gripen's sales were over $1 billion, and the large company decided to shed its smaller subsidiaries and concentrate on a few main business lines. So UMI was sold to its chairman, Bernhard Muskantor, in 1990.

Shortly after the sale, UMI made another acquisition in Europe, buying up an Austrian instrument maker called Musica GmbH. Now the company had two Swedish subsidiaries; a Danish subsidiary, Anders Hoeg AS; and a Norwegian subsidiary, Starton AS, as well as its new Austrian company and its half-interest in Germany's Sonor. The company seemed about evenly split between European and U.S. markets. In November 1990, UMI's U.S. president, Tom Burzycki, resigned and moved to the Selmer Company. Selmer, based in Elkhart, had followed a somewhat similar trajectory to Conn's. After long years as a leading brasswind manufacturer, it had concentrated on the school music market almost exclusively since the late 1960s, when it was owned by the television manufacturer Magnavox. Magnavox sold it to Philips Electronics in 1975, and then in 1989 it changed hands again, going to an investment firm called Integrated Resources. Burzycki's move to Selmer was unexpected, but he was quickly replaced by Robert Palmer as president and Rocco Giglio as vice-chairman.

There were more changes in the musical instrument industry over the next decade. In the United States, UMI continued to sell well-known band instrument names, including Conn, King, Artley, and Benge, as well as Scherl & Roth, Hermann Beyer, and Otto Bruckner stringed instruments. It had three manufacturing plants, one in Elkhart, one in Nogales, Arizona, and one in the Cleveland suburb of Eastlake, Ohio. Meanwhile, its fellow band instrument maker Selmer was sold again in 1993 after its parent, Integrated Resources, went into bankruptcy. Its new owner was the investment firm Kirkland & Messina. Selmer then made a major move in 1995 and acquired Steinway & Sons, undoubtedly the best-known name in piano manufacturing. In order not to lose the prestigious name, the parent company was then named Steinway Musical Instruments, Inc., holding its two subsidiaries, Steinway & Sons and the Selmer Company.

Putting everything together, Steinway Musical Instruments then bought the U.S. assets of UMI in 2000. The company paid Bernhard Muskantor roughly $85 million for the company he had managed for 15 years. This gave Steinway two stables of brass instrument brands, along with UMI's string manufacturers. The Selmer and UMI lines overlapped somewhat, but Selmer had more sales of trumpets and trombones, while UMI's strength was in its bass brass instruments. The two companies integrated slowly, operating separately for two years. In 2002, Steinway combined Selmer and UMI into the present Conn-Selmer, Inc. This had long been the dream of Thomas Burzycki, who had been president of UMI before leaving for Selmer in 1990. Burzycki retired in December 2002, declaring that his work was done now that the two companies were under one roof. Conn-Selmer was now not only one of the world's largest band instrument makers, but it had brought together almost all the historic Elkhart-based instrument companies. Conn-Selmer, Inc. was still reorganizing in 2002 and 2003, working on its manufacturing processes and negotiating with its labor union. Sales for 2001 were around $183.6 million, which represented an increase of almost 25 percent over the previous year. The company faced a fairly flat market in band instruments and stiff competition from manufacturers of professional-grade instruments. Nevertheless, as the company moved slowly to bring together its Conn and Selmer units, it felt it had good prospects for increasing market share in the future. Conn-Selmer's new president in 2003 was John M. Stoner, Jr., who came to the company from Ames True Temper, Inc., a leading manufacturer of lawn and garden tools.

Principal Competitors

G. Leblanc Corporation; Yamaha Corporation.

Further Reading

Banks, Margaret Downie, *A Brief History of the Conn Company (1874–Present)*, Vermillion, S.D.: National Music Museum, 1997.

''Bernhard Muskantor on the Future of United Musical Instruments,'' *Music Trades*, June 1990, p. 88.

''Conn-Selmer Created from Merger of Selmer & UMI,'' *Music Trades*, November 2002, p. 30.

''Musical Chairs in Elkhart,'' *Music Trades*, November 1990, p. 62.

''Muskantor Acquires United Musical Instruments,'' *Music Trades*, November 1989, p. 24.

Sibley, John, ''Electric Organs Playing a Sales Crescendo,'' *New York Times*, March 26, 1959, p. 43.

''Steinway Beats Earnings Projections,'' *Music Trades*, April 2002, p. 38.

''Steinway to Pay $85M for United Musical Instruments,'' *Music Trades*, September 2000, p. 28.

''Stoner to Head Conn-Selmer, Burzycki Retires,'' *Music Trades*, December 2002, p. 159.

''UMI & Selmer: A Long and Shared History,'' *Music Trades*, September 2000, p. 30.

''UMI Poised for Growth in Europe,'' *Music Trades*, October 1990, p. 26.

Wilke, Gerd, ''2 Bidders Raise Offer for Conn,'' *New York Times*, October 18, 1968, p. 67.

—A. Woodward

Daiwa Securities Group Inc.

6-4, Otemachi 2-chome
Chiyoda-ku
Tokyo 100-8101
Japan
Telephone: (03) 3243-2100
Fax: (03) 3242-0955
Web site: http://www.daiwa.co.jp

Public Company
Incorporated: 1943
Employees: 11,483
Total Assets: ¥7.8 trillion ($58.8 billion) (2002)
Stock Exchanges: Tokyo Osaka Nagoya London Paris
    Frankfurt Brussels
Ticker Symbol: 8601
NAIC: 551111 Offices of Bank Holding Companies;
    523110 Investment Banking and Securities Dealing;
    523120 Securities Brokerage

Daiwa Securities Group Inc.—formerly known as Daiwa Securities Co. Ltd.—operates as Japan's second-largest securities firm. Through its subsidiaries, the company is involved in retail and wholesale securities, asset management, consulting, and venture capital. During the 1990s, Japan's financial industry began to restructure and deregulate, prompting Daiwa Securities to adopt a holding company structure. The firm also teamed up with Sumitomo Bank—now known as Sumitomo Mitsui Banking Corporation—to form a wholesaling securities joint venture. Daiwa Securities celebrated its 100th anniversary during 2002, just as an economic slowdown and a weakening securities market forced brokerage commissions and revenues to plummet.

Early History: 1902–40s

Daiwa Securities Company was incorporated in 1943 as a merger between the Fujimoto Bill Broker & Securities Company and the Nippon Trust Bank. The company's origins date back to 1902, when Sibei Fujimoto entered the bill-brokering business at a time when Japan's securities industry was still in its infancy. In 1907, the company entered the banking business and took the name Fujimoto Bill Broker and Bank, to reflect its expanded services. World War I brought tremendous growth to the Japanese economy. Export demand skyrocketed and stock trading increased, as did the number of corporate and government bond issues. As a result, the Fujimoto organization grew quickly.

After the war and throughout the 1920s, Fujimoto engaged in both banking and securities brokering. Bond trading reached new highs, and as the Japanese economy became more complex, stock trading set records too. However, a number of financial catastrophes rocked the economy in the later 1920s. In 1927, a run on the banks sent shock waves through the financial community. Dozens of banks and securities dealers collapsed, but Fujimoto, due to prudent management, survived intact. The Depression which followed the collapse of the New York Stock Exchange in 1929 brought about changes in the laws regarding Japanese financial institutions. Fujimoto was forced to give up the banking business, so in 1933 the Fujimoto Bill Broker & Securities Company was established in compliance with these new government regulations.

The 1930s were a time of great political turmoil in Japan. By the end of the decade, the country was at war with China. Increased demand for war-related goods accelerated economic expansion. The stock market was active and prices went up. As the Japanese government began to issue bonds to fuel the war, it also exercised greater control over the markets. Nonetheless, Fujimoto continued to profit from its underwriting and brokerage activities. By 1941, Japan had entered World War II. The war had a positive impact on the Japanese economy until 1943, when Japan's military success began to falter. The market responded accordingly and stock prices plummeted. Fujimoto Bill Broker & Securities Company decided to combine forces with another financial institution. On December 27, 1943, it merged with the Nippon Trust Bank to form a new entity, the Daiwa Securities Company.

After the war, the occupation forces halted all securities trading on the exchanges and restructured the Japanese economy and political system. Daiwa survived by trading non-defense-related industry securities over the counter at its offices until 1949, when the exchanges were reopened.

Company Perspectives:

We the Daiwa Securities Group are committed to acting as our client's best partner and promote their financial well-being. In order to achieve this, we shall redefine currently accepted best practice drawing on the following three core values: we shall provide products and services that exceed expectations; we shall bring the full strength of the group to bear; and we shall continually challenge the limits of financial best practice.

Entering New Markets: 1950s–60s

Throughout the next decade Japan's economy, and Daiwa with it, flourished. The Korean War created tremendous demand for Japanese goods, and the economy began the steady climb which continued almost uninterrupted through the 1980s.

In 1951, Daiwa entered the investment trust business. Investment trusts were a very popular savings instrument among the Japanese. Within eight years Daiwa's investment trust activity had grown so large that a separate company had to be set up to handle its business. The Daiwa Investment Trust and Management Company, Ltd. opened its doors in 1959. During the 1950s, Daiwa's underwriting and brokerage activities made it one of Japan's most successful financial companies. Daiwa's innovative philosophy was characterized by its motto, adopted in 1957: "Scrupulous as well as daring."

The early 1960s were a period of growth for Daiwa, both at home and abroad. Encountering stiff competition from other securities dealers in Japan, Daiwa began to look overseas for new opportunities. Japanese companies had begun to issues stocks on foreign exchanges, and Daiwa actively pursued the underwriting of these issues. In 1964, Daiwa established an office in London. Later that year, the Japanese stock market experienced the worst panic since before the war. Daiwa Securities was hit hard by the panic, as was the rest of the securities industry. The recession lasted through 1965 and prompted the Ministry of Finance to implement tighter restrictions on securities-company licensing, primarily requiring that companies acquire separate licenses for underwriting and for retailing. It was a technicality that affected small dealers but had little impact on Daiwa's operations.

By the end of 1965, the Japanese economy had bounced back. Daiwa established the Daiwa Securities Research Institute to forecast trends in the economy and analyze specific industries and companies. In 1967, the Japanese government liberalized Japanese capital markets, giving Daiwa an opportunity to solicit more foreign investments. By the early 1970s, considerable capital was flowing both in and out of Japan.

International Expansion: 1970s–80s

During the early 1970s, Daiwa's international sector saw the greatest growth. In 1970, Daiwa Securities (Hong Kong) Ltd. was established, followed by Daiwa Singapore Ltd. and a representative office in Paris in 1972. A year later, Daiwa Europe N.V. was incorporated in Amsterdam. The company also set up a subsidiary to handle asset management services in 1973, the Daiwa International Capital Management Company, Ltd. (DICAM). DICAM worked closely with the Daiwa Securities Research Institute to offer investment advice to its international customers.

During the 1970s, the bond market in Japan exploded. Beginning in 1970, foreign government bonds denominated in yen took the Japanese market by storm. These so-called "samurai bonds" increased in popularity throughout the decade. A secondary market for bonds soon developed that was accompanied by an influx of Japanese government, particularly municipal, bond issues. Between 1970 and 1975, bond sales in Japan tripled.

In 1978, Daiwa (Switzerland) Ltd. was incorporated. Together with its operations in the United Kingdom, the Netherlands, France, and West Germany, Daiwa had a firm base on the European continent that proved to be invaluable during the 1980s. The European appetite for Japanese stocks and bonds, combined with surplus Japanese capital available for foreign investment, made Daiwa a major dealer in the European market by the late 1970s.

Throughout the first half of the 1980s, Daiwa's earnings were staggering. The fact that Japan still allowed fixed commissions on security trades made Japanese brokers like Daiwa the most profitable in the world. Many new kinds of bonds appeared in the mid-1980s, when the Japanese Ministry of Finance approved substantial changes in the capital market regulations. Colorful names like "shogun bonds," "sushi bonds," and "geisha bonds" denoted a variety of issues, some in yen, some in foreign currencies. These new investment vehicles were, in effect, completely new product lines for Daiwa Securities.

Under pressure from abroad, mainly the United States, the Japanese continued to deregulate their capital markets. Daiwa was suddenly subject to competition from huge American investment banking firms like Morgan Stanley, First Boston, and Salomon Brothers on their home turf. At the same time, Japanese banks became active in securities trading. But Daiwa, with its close ties to institutional investors, was not as affected by the new competition as were other Japanese dealers who relied heavily on retail activities.

The company saw its future in U.S. markets. By the mid-1980s, Daiwa had become a large dealer in U.S. treasury notes. However, virtually all of its customers were Japanese. The company's U.S. subsidiary, Daiwa Securities America Inc., struggled to build a domestic base in the United States to ensure its success in those markets, but, like other Japanese securities companies, had only measured success. Part of the problem was the reluctance of U.S. corporations to develop close ties with foreign investment bankers. Another was that Japanese dealers were sluggish in reacting when American underwriting opportunities did arise; key decisions always had to be cleared with top management in Tokyo.

Daiwa was the first of the large Japanese securities companies to give its American employees authority to make underwriting decisions on the spot. Daiwa Securities America had an American vice-chairman. In addition, the subsidiary's U.S. employees outnumbered their Japanese co-workers six to one. These characteristics made Daiwa more attractive to Americans

---

Key Dates:

1907: Fujimoto Bill Broker and Bank enters the banking business.

1933: Fujimoto is forced to give up its banking business and forms Fujimoto Bill Broker & Securities Company.

1943: Fujimoto Bill Broker & Securities and Nippon Trust Bank merge to form Daiwa Securities Company.

1951: Daiwa enters the investment trust business.

1959: Daiwa Investment Trust and Management Company Ltd. is created.

1964: The firm establishes an office in London.

1986: The company is designated a primary dealer in U.S. government securities.

1998: Daiwa Securities SB Capital Markets Co. is formed in an alliance with Sumitomo Bank.

1999: Daiwa Securities Group Inc. is created to act as a holding company.

---

than other Japanese houses, but the company still had trouble competing with American investment bankers.

Daiwa's weak base in the United States was compounded by the stock market crash of October 1987. Many Japanese investors were scared out of the stock market. In 1988, Daiwa cut its U.S. staff by 7 percent but remained determined to position itself in the American market. In the late 1980s, Daiwa diversified its services in the United States, initiating mergers and acquisition services both at home and in the U.S. The company was designated a primary dealer in U.S. government securities in 1986. It became increasingly active in commodities futures trading in 1988 and became a member of the Chicago Board of Trade. By the end of the decade, American attitudes toward Japanese securities firms were changing. The sheer size of Daiwa and other large Japanese dealers had finally attracted the attention of American investors and issuers.

Daiwa Securities' growth in the 1980s was astounding. It was still considerably smaller than its rival Nomura Securities, but Daiwa's progressive attitude regarding its American operations and its historically stronger ties to institutional investors helped it close the gap. At the time, Daiwa had the most experience in international markets of any Japanese securities house, an important edge as securities markets became more and more global—by 1990, the firm was listed on seven stock exchanges in Europe.

Deregulation Leads to Changes: 1990s and Beyond

As the Japanese economy slowed during the early 1990s, many of the region's banks and brokerage houses saw profits plummet. As such, Japan's Ministry of Finance began to slowly deregulate its financial sector. Considered a crucial step in restoring the country's economy, Japanese deregulation came after global competitors had already revamped their financial sectors. A November 1994 *Business Week* article stated that "at stake is the global competitiveness of Japan's financial industry. Unless the country can restore the health of its banks and

brokers, they will be hard-pressed to do battle with U.S. and European rivals that have been expanding around the globe at a furious clip." In 1996, Japan announced its "Big Bang," a deregulation plan that would reform its financial system and open its industry to foreign competition by 2001.

Early deregulation allowed securities firms to enter the trust banking sector and allowed commercial banks into the bond underwriting market. While Daiwa worked to take advantage of new opportunities brought on by deregulation, the company faced an embarrassing scandal that threatened to take a toll on company profits. In 1997, after the firm had denied any wrongdoing, Daiwa was named in a corporate racketeering scandal. The company paid a sokaiya, or corporate extortionist, not to reveal certain information during annual meetings. In September of that year, Daiwa's chairman and president stepped down along with seven directors, leaving Yoshinari Hari to clean up the company's illegal activities. As a result of its involvement, Daiwa faced penalties including a four-month suspension of various business activities.

As Daiwa reported losses in 1998 and 1999 due to both the scandal and increased competition, the company continued to position itself for future deregulation. It teamed up with The Sumitomo Bank Ltd. in 1998 to create Daiwa Securities SB Capital Markets, a joint venture focused on providing securities services for corporate customers. Sumitomo Bank merged with The Sakura Bank Ltd. to create Sumitomo Mitsui Banking Corporation in 2001. At the time of the deal, Daiwa Securities SB acquired Sakura Securities, and its name was changed to Daiwa Securities SMBC Co. Ltd.

Meanwhile, Daiwa launched a sweeping restructuring effort that would allow the company to focus on its core businesses. On the international front, the company's main business lines were organized into Japanese equities, non-Japanese equities, Japanese-related international bonds, investment banking, asset securitization, and asset management. All in all, the company planned to shut down 12 overseas offices. As part of the restructuring effort, Daiwa also announced its plan to adopt a holding company structure. In April 1999, Daiwa Securities Group Inc. was established and became the first listed Japanese holding company. Under the new structure, Daiwa Securities Co. became the Group's retail service arm, while wholesale operations fell under control of Daiwa Securities SMBC.

As Daiwa entered the new century, both commissions and net income increased. During 2001, the company added a new facet to its strategy—adopting a new image. As such, Daiwa launched an aggressive re-branding campaign that had three core values as its focal point: exceptional customer orientation, seamless services building on group synergy, and continuous innovation.

Daiwa's centennial celebration in 2002 was overshadowed by a weak global economy and a lackluster Japanese securities market. The firm posted a net loss of ¥130 billion during fiscal 2002, due in part to the disposal of various properties. Nevertheless, Daiwa management remained optimistic about its future, hoping to eventually be the market leader in developing and offering products and services. With 100 years of experience under its belt, Daiwa felt it was well positioned to handle economic downturns and increased competition brought on by changes in Japan's financial sector.

Principal Subsidiaries

Daiwa Securities Co. Ltd.; Daiwa Securities SMBC Co. Ltd. (60%); Daiwa Asset Management Co. Ltd.; Daiwa Institute of Research Ltd.; Daiwa SB Investments Ltd.; Daiwa Securities Business Center Co. Ltd.; The Daiwa Real Estate Co. Ltd.; NIF Ventures Co. Ltd.; Daiwa Securities America Inc.; Daiwa Securities Trust Company; Daiwa Securities Trust & Banking Europe plc.

Principal Competitors

Merrill Lynch & Co Inc.; Nikko Cordial Corporation; Nomura Holdings Inc.

Further Reading

"Bad Omens for Japan's Big Four," *Financial Times London*, October 24, 1997, p. 25.

"Daiwa Securities Forms Japan's 1st Listed Holding Firm," *Japan Economic Newswire*, April 25, 1999.

A History of Japan's Postwar Securities Industry, Tokyo: Japanese Securities Research Institute, 1984.

Ishibashi, Asako, "New Finance Allies Seek Little Help for Abroad," *Nikkei Weekly*, August 3, 1998, p. 1.

"Japanese Securities Firms: Once There Were Four," *Economist*, September 27, 1997, p. 80.

"Making a Virtue of Modesty," *Financial Times London*, October 1, 1997, p. 28.

Neff, Robert, "The Big Bang, Japanese-Style," *Business Week*, November 21, 1994.

Tamura, Atsushi, "Brokers Shift Focus Away From Stocks," *Nikkei Weekly*, January 27, 2003.

Tett, Gillian, "Japanese Brokerages Show Severe Downturn," *Financial Times London*, January 20, 1998, p. 24.

——, "Scandal Takes Its Toll on Nomura," *Financial Times London*, July 18, 1997, p. 23.

Wagsstyl, Stefan, "Daiwa Securities Aims for a Wider Global Dimension," *Financial Times London*, December 6, 1989, p. 39.

—update: Christina M. Stansell

The Detroit Lions, Inc.

222 Republic Drive
Allen Park, Michigan 48101
U.S.A.
Telephone: (313) 216-4000
Fax: (313) 216-4226
Web site: http://www.detroitlions.com

Private Company
Incorporated: 1930 as the Portsmouth Spartans
Employees: 200
Sales: $116 million (2002 est.)
NAIC: 711211 Sports Teams and Clubs

The Detroit Lions, Inc. operates the Motor City's representative in the National Football League. In almost 70 years of play, the team has won four league championships and reached the post-season playoffs ten other times. A dozen Lions' stars have been inducted into the Professional Football Hall of Fame, including Dutch Clark, Bobby Layne, Doak Walker, and Lem Barney, and recent stars such as Barry Sanders are in line to join them. The team is owned by William Clay Ford, former vice-chairman of the Ford Motor Company.

Beginnings

The Detroit Lions football team traces its origins to 1930, when the Portsmouth, Ohio, Spartans came into being as a member of the ten-year-old National Football League. The Spartans played well but the organization struggled financially, being based in an area that had been hit hard by the Great Depression. In 1934, the Spartans were sold to a group of Detroiters headed by George A. Richards, owner of a string of radio stations that included Detroit's powerful WJR. They paid $7,952.08 to cover the team's debts as well as a $15,000 NFL franchise fee. Investors numbered more than two dozen and included several prominent auto industry and department store executives.

After the sale, the team was moved north to Detroit, and Richards and company changed its name to the Lions, inspired by the moniker of the city's popular baseball team, the Tigers. For uniform colors they chose blue and silver and had the refurbished bus which was purchased for the team repainted to match. On the field, the Lions kept three-year Spartans coach Potsy Clark and many of his players, including quarterback Dutch Clark (no relation), a future Hall of Famer. For mascots, the Detroit zoo provided the team with two lion cubs, appropriately named "Grid" and "Iron," which traveled with the players to games.

The Lions were not the first professional football team in Detroit, nor its first NFL-affiliated one. Earlier, there had been the Heralds of 1920, charter members of the NFL's predecessor organization; the Panthers of 1925–26; and the Wolverines of 1928. These teams had failed to find an audience, however, and each had subsequently folded. In 1934, the Lions were given a much warmer reception, and during the team's first season crowds averaging 11,000 per game came out to see them play at University of Detroit Stadium, which was rented for $400 a week. Ticket prices ranged from 40 cents to $2. A Detroit tradition was established the first season when a game played on Thanksgiving day drew a standing-room only crowd of 26,000. The team posted an impressive record of ten wins and three losses for the year, but despite this success the organization recorded a net loss of more than $28,000 on receipts of $115,000.

The Lions went all the way to the top in their second season to win the NFL championship, bringing Detroit a rare pro sports "triple crown" in conjunction with the World Series win of the Tigers and the Stanley Cup victory of hockey's Red Wings. Average home game attendance for 1935 topped 13,000. At the end of 1936, coach Potsy Clark, whose relationship with owner George Richards was strained, left to be replaced by Dutch Clark. The latter exited just two years later when he, too, found the autocratic Richards difficult to deal with.

Playing at Briggs Stadium Starting in 1938

Attendance continued to grow during the mid-1930s, and by 1937 the Lions were attracting 19,000 fans to an average game. A deal was struck the following year for the team to move into the Tigers' home of Briggs Stadium, which could seat 55,000 patrons and which was available during the fall football season.

Key Dates:

1930: The Portsmouth, Ohio, Spartans football team is formed.

1934: The Spartans become the Detroit Lions after being sold to a syndicate of Detroit businessmen.

1935: The team wins its first National Football League (NFL) championship.

1938: The Lions begin playing games at Briggs Stadium, home of the Detroit Tigers baseball club.

1940: Chicago department store executive Fred Mandel buys the franchise for $225,000.

1948: A group of Detroit businessmen purchases team from Mandel for $165,000.

1952–53: Lions win back-to-back NFL championships.

1957: The team wins its fourth NFL championship.

1964: William Clay Ford pays $4.5 million to become the sole owner of the franchise.

1975: The Lion's games are moved to the newly-built Pontiac Silverdome, 30 miles north of Detroit.

1990s: The Lions reach the playoffs six times during the decade but fail to win an NFL title.

2002: The team plays its first season at new Ford Field in downtown Detroit.

In 1940, after a recruitment scandal in which the Lions were fined $5,000 for tampering with the college draft, George Richards sold the franchise to Chicago department store executive Fred Mandel for $225,000. The war years saw the team hobbled by the military draft, with a number of players including star running back Byron "Whizzer" White joining the service for the duration. The year 1942 was a particular disaster as the Lions posted a 0–11 record and scored only 38 points during the entire season. After several coaching changes, the team settled in 1943 on Gus Dorais, who had formerly helmed the University of Detroit team. By 1945, the Lions had returned to form and took second place in the NFL Western division with a 7-3 record. The team also resumed the practice of playing a game on Thanksgiving day, which had been suspended during the war-clouded years of 1939–44.

After the war, the Lions faced the disappointing news that several star players were not coming back, including Whizzer White, who quit football to finish work on his Yale law degree (he would later serve on the U.S. Supreme Court), and Harry "Hippity" Hopp, who signed to play with a team in Buffalo, New York. The Lions' record for 1946 plunged to 1–10, and then improved slightly in 1947 to 3–9. In 1948, after first attempting to dismiss Dorais without giving him his full severance pay, Mandel paid him $100,000 to exit. A week later, he sold the team for $165,000 to a group of Detroit area businessmen led by D. Lyle Fife, head of an electrical products firm, and Edwin J. Anderson, president of Goebel Brewing Co. A new head coach, Bo McMillin, was named, and Anderson was appointed vice-president, then president a year later. The year 1948 also saw the Lions break the color barrier with the signing of the team's first African-American players, receiver Bob Mann and back Mel Groomes. Other stars of the 1940s included two future Hall of Famers—linebacker Alex Wojciechowicz and halfback Bill Dudley.

Dominating the NFL in the 1950s

In 1950, Lions management replaced head coach McMillin with his assistant, Buddy Parker. With Parker in charge, and with the help of recently acquired players like quarterback Bobby Layne, lineman Lou Creekmur, and halfback/kicker Doak Walker (all future Hall of Famers), the team won back-to-back league championships in 1952 and 1953 and then won again in 1957, each time defeating the Cleveland Browns for top honors. The 1957 championship, a lopsided 59–14 victory, was won under coach George Wilson, who had succeeded Parker just before the season began. Other stars of this era included defensive lineman Les Bingaman, receiver Cloyce Box, halfback Bob Hoernschemeyer, and future Hall of Fame linebacker Joe Schmidt. By now attendance figures were at an all-time high, with season ticket sales topping 40,000. The franchise had finally become profitable, having gone into the black for the first time in 1951.

In 1961, a fight for control of the Lions erupted between Fife and Anderson, which resulted in the latter relinquishing the job of president to director William Clay Ford, though he stayed on as general manager. More trouble came in 1963 when the Lions organization and six players were reprimanded by football commissioner Pete Rozelle for gambling on NFL games; the team was fined $4,000 and five of the players $2,000 each. A sixth player, star lineman Alex Karras, was suspended for a year.

On January 10, 1964, William Clay Ford became the Lions' sole owner when he purchased all outstanding shares of the team's stock for $4.5 million. Ford, the son of Ford Motor Company head Edsel Ford and chairman of the automaker's design committee, took the titles of president and chairman. The following year he appointed Harry Gilmer to replace George Wilson as head coach. Gilmer's tenure was brief, however, and recently retired star Joe Schmidt was named to the post in 1967, the same year that Edwin Anderson was replaced by Russ Thomas as general manager. That year also saw the NFL and rival organization the American Football League (AFL) agree to play a new championship game, the Super Bowl. The two leagues later joined forces in a reconfigured NFL, with the AFL becoming known as the American Football Conference (AFC) and the NFL the National Football Conference (NFC). Detroit would henceforth be a member of the Central Division of the NFC.

In 1970, the Lions returned to the playoffs for the first time since 1957, though they lost in the opening round to Dallas. Two years later, coach Schmidt resigned and was replaced by Don McCafferty. After McCafferty died of a heart attack during the summer of 1974, the job went to Rick Forzano. Stars of this era included cornerback Lem Barney (later inducted into the Hall of Fame), quarterback Greg Landry, and running back Mel Farr.

Move to Pontiac Silverdome in 1975

As far back as the 1950s, the Lions had begun seeking a larger stadium to accommodate their growing legion of fans, and the effort continued throughout the 1960s. After plans for several Detroit locations fell through, a deal was reached with the city of Pontiac to build a $55.7 million domed stadium there. In August 1975, the Lions' new home, a half-hour north of Detroit, was dedicated. The 80,000 seat Pontiac Silverdome was the largest stadium in the world with an inflatable domed fiberglass roof. The venue also featured more than 100 VIP suites and other modern amenities.

Seeking to improve the team's performance, in 1978 the Lions named yet another new head coach, Monte Clark. Bouncing back from an embarrassing 2–14 record in 1979, Clark led the team to the playoffs in the strike-shortened year of 1982 and again in 1983, though the Lions failed to make the Super Bowl each time. The front office let Clark and his entire coaching staff go at the end of the 1984 season, replacing them with a group headed by Darryl Rogers. In November 1988, Rogers too was fired and replaced by defensive coordinator Wayne Fontes.

Under Fontes, the Lions had their best season in franchise history, winning 12 of 16 games in 1991. The team's efforts to "restore the roar" had been spurred on by a tragedy in November when guard Mike Utley suffered a neck injury and was paralyzed from the chest down during a game with Los Angeles. The Lions won their first post-season contest but were denied entry into the Super Bowl with a loss in the second. The year 1991 also saw the team establish Detroit Lions Charities, a non-profit organization which donated funds for a variety of civic and educational purposes in Michigan.

After a 5–11 year in 1992, the Lions made it to the playoffs in 1993, 1994, and 1995, helped by the stellar play of running back Barry Sanders. Each time, however, they were frustrated in their goal of reaching the Super Bowl. At the end of a disappointing 1996 season, Fontes was dismissed and replaced by Bobby Ross. Under Ross, the Lions again made the playoffs in 1997 and 1999, though they lost in the first round each time. The team's success in the latter year had come despite the absence of Sanders, who retired just before the season began. Ross himself was sacked part way through the 2000 season, and interim coach Gary Moeller finished out the year.

Construction of Ford Field in the Late 1990s

During the latter half of the 1990s, the organization had once again begun thinking about finding a new stadium. The Silverdome was losing its luster, and the ravaged city of Detroit was now beginning to rebound, with new economic development taking place in its partially abandoned downtown area. With the Tigers already planning to build an elaborate new stadium there, a deal was worked out to fund construction of one for the Lions. The projected cost of $315 million would be paid with city and county contributions of $115 million, a $100 million interest-free loan from the NFL, $40 million from the Ford Motor Co. for naming rights, $10 million from other corporations, and $50 million from the Ford family. By this time William Clay Ford, Jr., the owner's son, had joined the organization and was serving as its vice-chairman.

Once the funding was set, construction of the enclosed 65,000 seat Ford Field began in November of 1999. The stadium, which featured 140 luxury boxes, incorporated part of the historic Hudson Co. warehouse into its design, and stores, restaurants, offices, and locker rooms would be located there. Season tickets for eight games in the new field cost between $300 and $650. The move did not sit well with the city of Pontiac, however, which asserted that the Lions should not only pay for breaking their lease on the Silverdome, good through 2005, but also for loss of income and prestige to Pontiac and its

business community. Construction bonds amounting to $14 million had yet to be paid off as well. After a lawsuit was filed, in 2001 the Lions agreed to settle the claims for $26 million.

Meanwhile, determined to bring home another long sought-after championship, in January of 2001 Ford named former player and sportscaster Matt Millen to the newly created posts of president and CEO. He replaced executive vice-president and chief operating officer Chuck Schmidt, who had headed the organization since Russ Thomas's retirement in 1989. Two weeks after taking charge, Millen chose San Francisco 49ers offensive coordinator Marty Mornhinweg for the job of head coach. Despite the renewed focus on fielding a winning team, the 2001 season proved to be one of the Lions' worst ever. After losing their first 12 games, the team finished 2–14 for the year.

Hoping that the new stadium would inspire a return to form, in 2002 the Lions began playing at Ford Field, whose cost had ultimately mushroomed to $500 million. The team had also recently begun using a new $20 million headquarters and training facility in suburban Allen Park. The Lions, now members of the newly-created North division of the NFL, unfortunately showed scant improvement for the year, posting just three wins against 13 losses. In January 2003, Mornhinweg was dismissed and replaced by former boss Steve Mariucci, who had himself just been fired as head coach of the San Francisco 49ers. Former Michigander Mariucci had a strong track record, and once again the Lions and their fans expressed hope that the team's fortunes would turn around under a new leader.

After nearly three-quarters of a century operating as a professional football team, the Detroit Lions were struggling with several years of disappointing results and fan apathy. The move to new Ford Field in downtown Detroit had improved morale, but the team's unimpressive performance on the field remained the cause of much hand-wringing both in and out of the organization. Professional sports is a cyclical business, however, and with time the Lions' fortunes were sure to improve, just as the city of Detroit itself was rebounding from decades of decay.

Principal Competitors

Chicago Bears Football Club, Inc.; Minnesota Vikings Football Club, Inc.; The Green Bay Packers, Inc.; Cleveland Browns LLC.

Further Reading

Brasier, L.L., "Pontiac Sues Over Lions Move," *Detroit Free Press*, December 6, 2000.
Dow, Bill, "An Ode to the Former Lions Dens," *Detroit Free Press*, August 21, 2002.
Lage, Larry, "Lions Land Mariucci as Coach," *Detroit News*, February 4, 2003.
Lam, Tina, "Ford Field Expected to Add Luster to a City Center Used to Being Dark," *Detroit Free Press*, November 17, 1999.
——, "NFL Loan to Help Pay for Lions' Next Home," *Detroit Free Press*, May 26, 2000.
McDiarmid, Hugh, Jr., "Lions, Pontiac Settle Lawsuit," *Detroit Free Press*, November 29, 2001.
Murray, Mike, ed. *Lions Pride: 60 Years of Detroit Lions Football*. Dallas: Taylor Publishing Company, 1993.

—Frank Uhle

Devro plc

Gartterry Road, Moodiesburn, Chryston
Glasgow, G69 OJE
United Kingdom
Telephone: (44) 1236-879-191
Fax: (44) 1236-811-005
Web site: http:www.devro.plc.uk

Public Company
Incorporated: 1960 as Devro Inc.
Employees: 3,072
Sales: $302.2 million (2001)
Stock Exchanges: London
Ticker Symbol: DVO
NAIC: 325188 All Other Basic Inorganic Chemical
    Manufacturing

Based in Glasgow, Scotland, Devro plc is the world's largest supplier of collagen products to the food industry. Collagen is a natural protein found in the connective tissue of cowhide, which the company uses to make casings for sausages, hot dogs, and similar products, as well as film for packaging ham, salami, and other processed meats. In addition, Devro produces collagen as a commodity for the medical and cosmetic markets. The company maintains manufacturing facilities in Scotland, Australia, the Czech Republic, and South Carolina in the United States. Sales offices are located in Scotland, Germany, New Zealand, Australia, Japan, Hong Kong, the Czech Republic, and the United States.

Origins in 1950s Johnson & Johnson Research

Devro owes its existence to the research efforts of Johnson & Johnson, the New Jersey-based multinational manufacturer of healthcare products. Johnson & Johnson was established in 1885 to produce packaged, antiseptic surgical dressing, and over the ensuing decades it developed such well-known products as Band-Aid brand adhesive bandages and Johnson's Baby Cream. In the 1950s Johnson & Johnson researchers began looking for an absorbent, flexible material to be used in a new type of surgical suture; their search led to experiments with collagen.

Not only did collagen show promise as a suture material, the research team realized that it had other potential uses, including the unlikely application to sausage casings. For hundreds of years sausages and similar foods relied on the cleansed intestines of sheep, cows, or pigs. Casings made out of reconstituted collagen were a revolutionary improvement over animal gut because in addition to being edible and hygienic they were of consistent quality and could be produced in long, compressed slugs, allowing processors to quickly produce varying lengths of meat products. Moreover, collagen casings were strong and durable, able to withstand the pressure of meat blasted into them, as well as possessing qualities that allowed them to be frozen or fried without breaking. The raw material was created from the corium collagen layer of cowhide, sandwiched between the grain leather and the cow's layer of flesh and fat. The corium split was a byproduct of tanneries, produced by the removal of the grain layer before producing leather. This split was then washed and processed in large rotating drums, resulting in collagen fiber that was further refined until it reached a suitable state and could be used in various applications.

Johnson & Johnson had a longstanding practice of forming subsidiaries to be responsible for specific product lines once they reached a certain size. For instance, a 1930s birth control pill evolved into the Ortho Pharmaceutical Corporation, and in 1949 the company's suture business became Ethicon. In 1960 Johnson & Johnson established a separate collagen business, which it named Devro after the unit responsible for the collagen project: "Development and Research Organization." Although the application of collagen for sutures never became a commercial success, collagen casings found a ready and eager marketplace.

Devro began production of casings in 1963 in Somerville, New Jersey. In 1964 the subsidiary opened a second factory in Moodiesburn, Scotland, and another Scotland facility was built in 1976 in Bellshill. Devro in the late 1970s began to target the Asian market in the hope of substituting collagen casings for the traditional pig intestines used for Chinese sausages. In order to serve a potentially large Asian market, Devro opened a large manufacturing plant in Bathurst, Australia. Cracking the Asian market, however, proved problematic and would remain a desirable yet elusive market for the next 20 years.

Completion of LBO in 1991

Devro was a profitable niche business, the leader in the edible collagen sausage casings market, yet by the mid-1980s Johnson & Johnson began looking to sell Devro as part of an effort to focus its attention on its core healthcare assets. It appeared that in January 1990 the parent company had a buyer in a group of investors led by Devro's president, Christopher B. Chaffey, but the deal fell through. By now the subsidiary was posting nearly $120 million in annual revenues and generating operating income of close to $30 million. Finally in May 1991 Johnson & Johnson found a buyer in a management team led by Frank de Angeli, a Johnson & Johnson executive. The $173 million purchase was arranged by Charterhouse Development Capital Ltd. with backing from eight international institutional investors. Another syndicate of nine international banks, including the First National Bank of Chicago, Industrial Bank of Japan, and Royal Bank of Scotland, provided more than $115 million in loans and revolving credits to secure the deal.

Devro's headquarters were moved to Moodiesburn, Scotland, where the company would be suitably positioned to carry out management's goal of concentrating on European markets—as well as a continued emphasis on the Far East. To pay off some of the debt incurred from the buyout, Devro was taken public, floated on the London Stock Exchange, where it began trading in June 1993. The transition was not without incident, however. The man hired as the chief executive to replace a retiring de Angeli and take the company public did not have the confidence of the City, the London investment community, and he was paid off even before assuming the job. He was replaced by Graeme Alexander, who had been in charge of marketing. Soon after he took over as CEO and Devro completed its initial public offering, Alexander and his management team assessed the state of the company in order to determine a future direction and reassure shareholders that a one-product company was a safe investment. To position Devro as a collagen company would have meant becoming fully committed to such areas as food additives, cosmetics, and biomedical. Instead they decided to focus on other types of casings, and in this regard in 1994 began to study Chicago-based Teepak International, which not only produced collagen casings but also noncollagen synthetic casings using cellulous and fibrous food materials. Teepak recorded revenues of $60.9 million in 1994, while Devro International and its U.S.-based subsidiary, Devro North America, combined for $169.5 million in sales. Established in 1933, Teepak had a significant history in the casings industry. It developed its first cellulose casings in 1934, followed by the 1944 introduction of the Wienie-Pak.

In March 1995 Devro reached an agreement to acquire Teepak for $135 million in cash and the assumption of $155 million in debt. The deal was contingent upon securing approval from the Federal Trade Commission (FTC), which soon showed concern that the merger might violate antitrust laws because it would likely result in higher costs for collagen casings in the United States where there would now be no competition. After nine months Devro and the FTC finally reached a settlement that permitted the acquisition of Teepak in exchange for the divestiture of Devro North America. In January 1996 the acquisition was finally completed, and in August of that year the Devro North America business (composed of the Somerville, New Jersey manufacturing plant and a finishing plant in Ontario, Canada) was sold to Nitta Gelatin, part of Japan's Nitta family of companies, resulting in the creation of Nitta Casings. The reported purchase price was $26 million.

Following the merger with Teepak, the company changed its name to Devro-Teepak. Included in the transaction was a 56 percent interest in a Czech casing maker, Cutisin, which operated two manufacturing plants and a sales office in the Czech Republic. Over the few years Devro increased its stake in Cutisin, totaling 96 percent by 2000, with the ultimate intention of owning the entire business. The Teepak deal also brought with it a manufacturing facility in Belgium, finishing operations in The Netherlands and the Czech Republic, and sales offices in Switzerland, Russia, and the Czech Republic. Although Devro gave up its New Jersey plant, it gained Teepak's Danville, Illinois, factory as well as a Sandy Run, South Carolina, manufacturing facility and finishing plants in Kansas City, Missouri; Atlanta, Georgia; and Scarborough, Canada—in addition to sales offices in Chicago and Miami. The first year following the Teepak acquisition Devro posted strong results, despite an outbreak of Bovine spongiform encephalopathy (BSE), commonly known as Mad Cow disease, in England. Because of the connection between collagen and cattle, Devro was quick to turn to non-British hides, a move that reassured customers and prevented any serious erosion in business. Overall the company appeared well positioned for strong ongoing growth, as management focused on the Asia-Pacific market and Eastern Europe, where demand was strong in Russia and other former Soviet states. Moreover, traditional gut sausage skins still accounted for more than half of all casings sold around the world, providing considerable room for growth in collagen casings.

Stock Price Peaks in May 1998

To investors Devro was well regarded, and because of its large market share and high margin the company was deemed to be immune from the normal fluctuations of the food industry. Its dominant position also was thought to be assured because of the large investment that would be required for a competitor to match Devro's production facilities and gain entry to the industry. As a result, investors bid up the price of Devro's shares, which peaked in May 1998. Then management issued profits warnings in back-to-back months, prompting a dramatic slide in the price of the stock. Management cited a number of reasons for the shortfall, which was mostly limited to the cellulose casing business. Poor economic conditions in Latin America, Southeast Asia, and Eastern Europe, as well as sluggishness in parts of Western Europe, and poor weather in England that

Key Dates:

1960: Devro is formed as a Johnson & Johnson subsidiary.
1964: Company opens a plant in Scotland.
1979: A plant is opened in Australia.
1991: The company undergoes a management buyout.
1996: Teepak International is acquired.
2001: The Teepak assets are sold.

resulted in fewer barbecues, were cited as reasons. In addition, the company's margins were hurt by the strong performance of sterling in relation to the mark and yen.

The situation grew so poor for Devro that by 1999 the company became the subject of takeover rumors, including the possibility that Alexander might take the company private. After some six months of intense speculation, Alexander finally insisted that there was no truth to the rumors of management taking the company private. Instead Devro continued a restructuring effort launched earlier in the year. Matters only worsened in 2000 when BSE was discovered on the Continent, as was listeria in hot dogs in the U.S. market. Although Devro's products were considered safe and passed health regulations, many customers simply refused to purchase casings made from collagen drawn from British herds. As a result Devro was forced to buy source collagen from the United States and Australia at a much higher cost. Many consumers in Europe simply stopped eating meat. An outbreak of foot-and-mouth disease in 2001 in the United Kingdom only served to exacerbate an already difficult business environment for Devro.

With BSE and foot-and-mouth crippling its business, Devro had to cut back on production. More important, management decided to focus on collagen and sell off its interests in cellulose. It proved difficult to find a buyer, however, and it was not until August 2001 that Devro was able to announce that it was selling its cellulose and fibrous food casing business to Lake Pacific Partners, LLC, a Chicago-based private equity firm in a $48 million deal, of which $7.2 million was in cash and the balance in assumed liabilities. Lake Pacific was established in 2000 by William R. Voss, the former chairman and CEO of National

Nutrition Group, and Terry E. Sebastian, a senior vice-president of the company. Together they raised $100 million to invest in small- to mid-sized food and consumer products companies. Lake Pacific created a holding company, Teepak LLC, to buy the Devro assets and established a headquarters in Lisle, Illinois.

Devro endured a difficult 2001, but with a worldwide economic climate worsening in the ensuing months, 2002 proved to be another difficult year. In an effort to cut costs and improve profits, Devro initiated a restructuring of its operations, allowing for more local autonomy by setting up regional businesses in the Americas, Europe, and the Asia-Pacific region. One positive development in 2002 was the announcement that the company had developed the world's first casing made from pork collagen, a product long requested by pork sausage makers who been forced to rely on beef or lamb collagen casings. The long-term fate of Devro, however, was uncertain. In early 2002 the company appeared to be in the sights of a mysterious buyer. A Swiss-registered company named Acomita Investment, named after a town in New Mexico, began buying up large blocks of shares of Devro stock, prompting press speculations of a takeover. It was generally assumed that Acomita was a front for a food group bidder.

Principal Subsidiaries

Devro (Scotland) Limited; Devro Holdings Limited; Devro New Holdings Limited: Devro Acquisition Corporation.

Principal Competitors

Nitta Casings Inc.; Viscofan S.A.; Viskase Companies, Inc.

Further Reading

"Bangers and Panache," *Director,* November 1995, p. 104.
Buxton, James, "Devro Shares Slip on Warning as Hot Dog Sales Slide," *Financial Times,* November 27, 1998, p. 24.
Cunningham, Sara, "Beauty Is Skin Deep for Devro's Chief," *Times,* February 15, 1997, p. 29.
"Devro-Teepak Has Meat Casings Industry All Wrapped Up," *Food Trade Review,* November 2000, p. 747.
Turpin, Andrew, "At Full Strength," *Director,* November 1997, p. 118.

—Ed Dinger

The Doctors' Company

185 Greenwood Road
Napa, California 94558-0900
U.S.A.
Telephone: (707) 226-0100
Fax: (707) 226-0111
Web site: http://www.thedoctors.com

Private Company
Incorporated: 1976
Employees: 320
Total Assets: $266.9 million (2001)
NAIC: 524128 Other Direct Insurance (Except Life,
    Health, and Medical)Carriers

Founded in 1976, The Doctors' Company is the original, and one of the nation's largest, physician owned and operated medical liability insurers. The Doctors' Company is the premier company in the TDC Group, which includes six wholly owned subsidiaries, formed to expand and diversify TDC's policy offerings. With ten regional offices around the country, the TDC Group provides services to its 35,000 member-policyholders in all 50 states. The TDC Group insures individual doctors, nurses, technicians, and other health care professionals; it also writes policies for small group practices, larger medical groups, clinics, and hospitals.

Origins

The Doctors' Company was founded in response to a crisis in the availability of medical liability insurance that began in the early 1970s. Just as the public's attitude toward health care was becoming increasingly consumer oriented, advances in medicine were leading to more sophisticated medical practices. Patients' demand for perfection increased; at the same time, doctors confronted a higher margin for error in treatment. Dissatisfied "customers" became more inclined to pursue legal action against their physicians, and a flood of malpractice suits ensued: in California, malpractice suits filed between 1970 and 1975 accounted for 80 percent of all such suits filed in the first three-quarters of the 20th century. By 1975, malpractice insurance premiums had skyrocketed and many commercial insurance providers were even concluding that medical practice constituted an uninsurable risk. Some relief was anticipated with the California State Legislature's passage of the Medical Injury Compensation Reform Act (MICRA), which served to rebalance the scales between plaintiffs' and defendants' rights.

The California Physicians' Crisis Committee (CPCC) was formed to take action for medical liability reform, and in 1976 some members of the executive committee of the CPCC founded The Doctors' Company, the first doctor-owned provider of medical liability insurance. The founders saw several advantages inherent in a business model where doctors provide coverage for doctors. As a member-owned company, TDC was able to focus on satisfying the needs of its member-policyholders without having to respond to the competing demands of outside stockholders. Furthermore, with their medical training and first-hand experience, TDC's founders saw themselves as uniquely qualified to assess risk across the spectrum of medical practices and to represent and advocate for their clients in negotiations and legal settings.

Still, TDC's founders recognized that medical expertise alone would not guarantee the company's success; they took pains to fortify TDC's infrastructure with staff members possessing legal and insurance expertise and committed themselves to conservative fiscal policies. Also, while TDC often lauded doctors as everyday heroes, the company did not delude itself with the idea that all doctors were alike in their professionalism. As part of TDC's no-nonsense attitude toward liability coverage, doctor-applicants were rigorously screened to determine their qualifications, modes of practice, and level of competence. Whereas a commercial insurer would likely approve any doctor who belonged to a medical society or to a hospital staff, TDC scrutinized its applicants much more stringently. Applicants deemed to be practicing beyond the scope of their qualifications or taking on other unnecessary risks were charged higher premiums, required to rein in their practices, or rejected for coverage altogether.

As TDC's founders predicted, MICRA did gradually alleviate the crisis in California. By reconstituting the balance between plaintiffs' and defendants' rights, MICRA reinvigorated the defense of capricious and baseless malpractice suits, thereby facilitating the quick and equitable settlement of legitimate ones. Claims costs began to drop significantly. By 1977, when TDC was still less than a year old, the company had established $14 million in assets and was able to redistribute the benefits of lower claims costs to its 2,600 member-policyholders in the form of a $500,000 dividend. Based on the MICRA model, TDC recognized that continued advocacy for liability (or tort) reform was critical to the success of the company; therefore, commitment to this legal advocacy became an essential and ongoing component of the company's business.

Expansion and Diversification: 1980s–90s

The Doctors' Company was quick to recognize that the company would only achieve limited success if it did not seek to extend its services beyond the borders of California. In order to do this successfully, the company would also have to export the MICRA model of tort reform to other states. TDC had begun to lay the groundwork for tort reform efforts in other states as early as 1977. By 1979, TDC had gained authorization to offer its medical liability coverage in Nevada, Wyoming, and Montana. By 1986, medical malpractice liability laws had been reformed in Nevada, Montana, and Washington. During these years the original MICRA legislation also came under fire in California. The Doctors' Company defended it vigorously. In 1986, TDC played a key role in derailing an attempt by the plaintiff's bar to overturn MICRA.

The Doctors' Company ushered in a new president in 1985. Manuel S. Puebla, then a 40-year veteran of the insurance industry, brought on board a wealth of experience with medical liability underwriting and claims and regulatory issues, plus the proven ability to foster business development and facilitate government relations.

By 1989, TDC had been authorized to offer its coverage in 37 states, and the company was well equipped to mobilize its forces for liability reform. The company's Board of Governors endorsed the formation of the first doctors' political action committee (DOPAC) and work began to develop an effective legislative contact system. By 1990, TDC's Government Relations Department was exerting pressure for liability reform on both state and federal levels. TDC maintained a high level of advocacy for tort reform throughout the 1990s, with the awareness that, as the U.S. tort system would inevitably influence foreign judicial systems as well, TDC would one day be positioned to offer its insurance services internationally.

One of the notable strengths of The Doctors' Company was that it managed to be fiscally disciplined and assertively growth oriented at the same time. In the 1980s, TDC created several wholly owned subsidiaries to pursue opportunities to expand its offerings. In 1980, TDC established The Doctors' Life Insurance Company (TDLIC) to offer life insurance policies to doctors. In 1984, The Doctors' Company Insurance Services (TDCIS) was established for the primary purpose of making agency licensure available in states where TDC offered insurance coverage other than medical malpractice policies. TDC formed three new subsidiaries in 1989: Professional Underwriters Liability Insurance Company (PULIC), Bernard Warschaw Insurance Sales Agency, Inc. (Warschaw), and Underwriter for the Professions Insurance Company (UFTP). PULIC was established to offer malpractice insurance to health care professionals who were hard to place—that is, unlikely to qualify for regular malpractice insurance from TDC or another medical liability provider due to disproportionate exposure or nonstandard risks. Similarly, TDC acquired the Bernard Warschaw Agency to create specially tailored coverage for individual applicants bearing nonstandard loss profiles. Once an applicant was accepted by the Warschaw subsidiary, he or she was covered either by TDC or by PULIC. UFTP was established to expand the TDC Group's ability to offer coverage to a range of non-medical professions.

As part of its broad-based diversification strategy, TDC also established two strategic business units, TDC*Re* and Alternative Risks, in 1995 and 1996, respectively, both designed to tap tributary revenue streams. TDC*Re* was created to substantiate TDC's reinsurance business function. This unit developed into a significant revenue source for TDC, accounting for approximately 16 percent of total TDC premium by 1999. Alternative Risks was a body created to pursue new revenues for TDC from alternative, reduced-risk sources. TDC's efforts to diversify proved visionary: by 1997, over 20 percent of TDC's premium revenue was coming from niche insurance markets outside the medical malpractice arena. Moreover, during the five year period between 1994 and 1999, TDC managed to nearly double its surplus (the reserve funds it used to pay claims).

In the mid-1990s, the market began to flood with opportunistic insurance carriers eager to capitalize on the favorable climate for medical malpractice policy underwriting. Increased competition resulted in a flurry of lower and lower premium offerings. TDC viewed these aggressive pricing strategies as short sighted and transparent grabs for market share. Despite market pressures, and even while some if its own members complained that the company's pricing structure was outdated, TDC maintained its commitment to the fair and stable pricing policy that had always underpinned the company's fiscal strength, refusing to succumb to the price-cutting game. It was not long before TDC was vindicated for its conservatism. By the late 1990s, many of TDC's competitors were placed under regulatory supervision and even liquidated after it was revealed that their surpluses had fallen too low to cover their claims.

In 1997, P.I.E. Mutual Insurance Company of Ohio, a once-reputable physician-owned carrier whose high volume of premiums had constituted nearly 70 percent of Ohio's medical malpractice insurance business in 1994, revealed that it was facing grave financial difficulties. P.I.E.'s stated mission had

Key Dates:

1976: The Doctors' Company (TDC) is founded in Santa Monica, California.

1979: TDC expands to offer coverage in four additional western states.

1980: TDC forms The Doctors' Life Insurance Company, a wholly owned subsidiary.

1989: TDC forms three wholly owned subsidiaries: Professional Underwriters Liability Insurance Company (PULIC); Bernard Warschaw Insurance Sales Agency, Inc. (Warschaw); and Underwriter for the Professions Insurance Company (UFTP).

1994: TDC launches the first federal Doctors' Political Action Committee (DOPAC).

1995: TDC formalizes its reinsurance functions by establishing a separate strategic business unit called TDC*Re*.

1997: TDC assumes responsibility for renewing policies formerly underwritten by then-collapsing P.I.E. Mutual Insurance Company of Ohio.

1999: TDC opens its ninth regional office in Florida; TDC also revises its mission statement to emphasize diversification efforts.

2001: TDC is the first national physician-owned and -operated insurance provider to celebrate its 25th anniversary.

been to sell liability insurance to doctors at cost, and the company was known for offering highly competitive prices, but by the end of 1997 its stability was jeopardized by a sharply diminished surplus due, in large part, to precipitous underwriting losses. The Ohio Department of Insurance placed P.I.E. under regulatory supervision and advised P.I.E.'s policyholders to begin looking for new coverage. Ultimately, TDC received the distinction of being the only carrier endorsed by ODI to create a professional liability program specifically to enroll physicians who had been insured by P.I.E. The situation with P.I.E. offered TDC the opportunity to establish a strong presence in the Ohio, which would become an important launching ground for the company's planned East Coast expansion.

TDC got a similar business opportunity in 1999 when a Florida insurer, Caduceus Self Insurance Fund, Inc., announced that it did not have sufficient funds to pay its claims. Interestingly, Caduceus was a physician-owned company that had also been founded during the national insurance crisis of 1976. Unlike TDC, however, the Florida company had a history of undercutting its competitors with aggressively low premium rates. Here again, TDC had the opportunity to benefit from a competitor's short-sighted fiscal policies. TDC entered into an affiliation agreement with Caduceus to enroll its members when their policies with the Florida company expired. To properly serve its new members and continue regional expansion in the Southeast, TDC opened its ninth regional office in Florida that year.

By the late 1990s, The Doctors' Company had developed a superior record of claims defense. The company consistently resolved 80 percent of claims against its doctor-insureds without indemnity payments and without damaging reports being filed with the National Practitioner Data Bank. Furthermore, of the small percentage of litigated claims that went to trial, TDC secured favorable results for its doctor-insureds 80 percent of the time. As a result of these new ventures in the Midwest and the Southeast, and the expansion that ensued from them, TDC's policyholders enjoyed the added benefits of an enlarged risk-sharing pool and a broadened premium base. Nevertheless, even with TDC's exemplary record and the real and symbolic victories of the P.I.E. and Caduceus bailouts, the company faced fiercely competitive market conditions as it headed into the 21st century.

Increased Competition in the 21st Century

In an effort to adapt to market pressures, The Doctors' Company revised its mission statement in 1999 to reflect the accelerated pace of its diversification strategy. More than ever, TDC saw it as essential to extend liability insurance to a wider pool of policyholders, even those outside the medical profession. One of TDC's efforts to make its services accessible to a broader spectrum of policyholders involved revising its pricing structure to more accurately calibrate premium with loss experience. To further protect itself from the instability of the market and the ever-increasing range of professional liabilities, TDC remained vigilant in its efforts to maintain strong reserves-to-surplus and premium-to-surplus ratios. At the end of 2000, with $500.1 million in reserves, $381.1 million in surplus, and $255 million in written premium, TDC was keeping these ratios well below regulatory standards.

TDC launched a major effort to improve its technology beginning in 1998. After years of preparation, the company introduced a new computer system in 2000. TDC also perceived that member demand for electronic services would only continue to increase and thus looked for ways to offer its members greater access to real-time business transactions as well as state-of-the-art security to protect their privacy. In 1999, the company introduced TDC Easy Quote and Application Online to its Web site to meet the needs of prospective members looking for a quick and easy way to estimate a premium for customized policy and apply for coverage. In another move to embrace technology, in 2000 TDC developed a collaborative program with iScribe, Inc., where TDC doctors would receive a discount on their insurance premiums if they adopted iScribe's wireless, handheld, electronic prescribing technology.

Advances in technology posed problems for the medical community too, however. Electronic tools such as e-mail promised to transform relationships between doctors and patients, and while there were many benefits to this convenient means of communication, there were also legal risks. In 2000, The Doctors' Company joined a group of more than 30 medical societies and other malpractice carriers in forming a committee to examine liability issues related to online communication. The committee, called the eRisk Working Group for Healthcare, developed a set of guidelines to protect doctors from liability. Released in 2002, these guidelines included strong recommendations for getting informed consent from patients before using e-mail and for using only encrypted and authentication-secured messaging systems.

True to the eRisk Group's recommendations, in 2002 TDC made a significant commitment to protecting the privacy of its members when it contracted Symantec Corporation, a world leader in Internet security, to provide the company with a range of products to protect its Web site and its internal network against current and future security threats. The move to protect policyholders' information from hackers was commensurate with TDC's ongoing commitment to provide its members with the most dependable service in the industry.

In 2001, the market for medical liability insurance was still plagued by tumult. Insurance analyst A.M. Best had issued a rash of downgrades to overly aggressive, poorly performing carriers; other carriers announced plans to discontinue medical-malpractice coverage altogether, citing the unpredictability and too-high risk of the business. While so many companies floundered, TDC was named to the Ward's 50 Benchmark Group for the sixth time and a third consecutive year. Ward Financial Group was a Cincinnati-based consulting firm that specialized in the insurance industry. In compiling its top-50 list, Ward analyzed the overall performances of more than 4,000 insurance companies over a five-year period. That year, The Doctors' Company was the first national physician-owned and -operated insurance provider to celebrate its 25th anniversary.

Principal Subsidiaries

The Doctors' Management Company (TDMC); Professional Underwriters Liability Insurance Company (PULIC); Bernard Warschaw Insurance Sales Agency, Inc. (Warschaw); Underwriter for the Professions Insurance Company (UFTP); The Doctors' Company Insurance Services (TDCIS); The Doctors' Life Insurance Company (TDLIC).

Principal Competitors

CNA Financial; FPIC Insurance; ProAssurance.

Further Reading

Baldwin, Gary, "Group Cautions Physicians About Online Liability," *American Banker-Bond Buyer*, March, 2001, p. 6.

"The Doctors' Company Protects Network with Symantec Managed Security Services," *Business Wire*, March 13, 2002.

"Malpractice Policies That Earn Profits," *Business Week*, March 21, 1977, p. 37

Miller, Susan R., "A Bitter Pill," *Palm Beach Daily Business Review*, September 2, 1999.

Solov, Diane, "P.I.E. to Move Policies to California Insurer," *Plain Dealer*, November 21, 1997, p. 1C

"TDC Named to Ward's 50 Benchmark Group of Insurers," *Business Wire*, September 10, 1999.

—Erin Brown

The Dress Barn, Inc.

30 Dunnigan Drive
Suffern, New York 10901
U.S.A.
Telephone: (845) 369-4500
Fax: (845) 369-4829
Web site: http://www.dressbarn.com

Public Company
Incorporated: 1962
Employees: 8,900
Sales: $717.1 million (2001)
Stock Exchanges: NASDAQ
Ticker Symbol: DBRN
NAIC: 5621 Women's Clothing Stores

The Dress Barn, Inc. ranks among the U.S.'s largest specialty women's clothing retailers, with over 750 stores throughout the country. The chain caters to career-oriented women in the middle-range income bracket. In the early years of the 21st century, Dress Barn transformed itself from a discounter into ''a value-priced specialty retailer'' offering its own private label clothing. The company also shifted its focus from careerwear to casualwear, with the latter accounting for 65 percent of sales by the end of 2002. Still operated by the founding Jaffe family in 2003, The Dress Barn has store units positioned throughout 43 states under the names Dress Barn and Dress Barn Woman (specializing in women's plus-sized apparel), with the vast majority of locations offering the full range of sizes.

Early Years

The beginnings of The Dress Barn can be traced to 1962, when Elliot Jaffe was working as a merchandising manager for Macy's Department Store in Connecticut. He approached his wife, Roslyn, with an idea for a women's discounted apparel store, and the two decided to begin planning a test store. Knowing that they needed a reliable source of income to support their children, Jaffe retained his job at Macy's as he and Roslyn worked after-hours to open the first Dress Barn store later that year in Stamford, Connecticut.

According to Jaffe, the first store was marked by numerous retail errors, such as the lack of convenient parking nearby, the lack of dressing rooms for customers, and the existence of stairs that customers had to climb in order to access the store. Despite these shortcomings, however, the new store was an immediate success. In fact, it was so successful that less than a year after its grand opening, Jaffe was able to leave his job at Macy's to focus solely on the operations of their new enterprise. Meanwhile, Roslyn had begun planning the preparation and introduction of a second store nearby. In March 1963, the second store unit was opened, and The Dress Barn store chain was born.

Increased sales demands at the two Dress Barn stores soon prompted the Jaffes to begin searching for another store location and a new warehouse in the Stamford area. Previously, The Dress Barn's warehousing, receiving, and distribution operations had been done from the first store's basement, which could only be accessed using a narrow flight of stairs. After searching the area for a new location that would lend itself to more efficient operations, the Jaffes chose an old barn in Stamford, a choice well-suited to the company's name. This barn was renovated to become the company's third store as well as its distribution center.

In mid-1966, the company's holdings were incorporated as Dress Barn, Inc. Throughout the rest of the decade, the company experienced calculated and planned growth under the watchful eye of Jaffe and his expanding management team. They made sure that the business was not expanded too quickly, in order to maintain available capital and avoid sinking all resources into the company at once. Meanwhile, stores were added to the chain sporadically at a rate consistent with the company's increase in earnings.

Growth in the 1970s–80s

By the 1970s, after almost a decade of steady growth and expansion, The Dress Barn, Inc. was composed of almost 20 store units. The company was large enough to have gained the buying power to bring in products from big-name designers, such as Liz Claiborne, Calvin Klein, and Jones New York. Dress Barn continued to focus on selling this apparel to career-oriented women at discounted prices, usually 20 to 50 percent lower than those of its department store competition. Meanwhile, the chain continued to expand through the opening of new stores and the acquisition of other chains, such as Pants Corral and Off the Rax.

On May 3, 1983, Dress Barn went public, offering its stock for $23 per share. Half of the shares were sold publicly, while the other half was retained by management insiders. The money earned through the public offering gave Dress Barn added capital with which to expand and grow while also incurring added responsibility for the company to perform well for all of its new owners.

By July 1984, Dress Barn owned and operated 100 stores throughout the United States, holdings which marked a 30 percent increase from the year before. By the end of 1984, the company possessed 157 stores, after the acquisition of 46 Off the Rax stores, eight stores from The Gap, and the addition of three new Dress Barn stores.

The year 1985 saw the company begin to earn national recognition, as *Forbes* magazine ranked Dress Barn number 42 out of the Top-200 Small Companies in the United States. The following year, *Business Week* listed Dress Barn as number 26 of the country's Top-200 Hot Growth Companies. By that point in time, the company was operating over 200 stores throughout the United States, with high concentrations in the Atlantic Northeast, the Midwest, and California.

Two years later, Dress Barn's store count had increased almost 50 percent to 307, spread throughout 26 states. The company was clearly achieving success in the discount women's apparel niche that it had created for itself and decided to build on that by entering the market for plus-sized women's clothing. In 1989, Dress Barn Woman was introduced, targeting plus-sized women from the same basic demographic segment as the original Dress Barn stores. Most new Dress Barn Woman store units were placed in areas nearby existing Dress Barn stores to capitalize on Dress Barn's name recognition factor.

Struggle and Success in the 1990s

At the beginning of the decade, Dress Barn received further recognition of its achievements in the retail market when it was awarded the High-Performance Retailer Award from Management Horizons, a division of Price Waterhouse. The award was based on four consecutive years of performance highs for the company. Also in 1990, Dress Barn purchased JRL Consulting Corporation for $2.56 million.

The 1990s saw the company continue to enter new markets in the United States through the opening of new stores and the acquisition of existing chains. In 1993, Dress Barn added 21 new women's apparel stores purchased from Country Miss. At that point, the company was operating hundreds of Dress Barn and Dress Barn Woman stores, as well as numerous combination units.

Dress Barn, which had traditionally marketed its women's apparel at discounted prices, suffered a hit to its earnings potential in the early 1990s when many department stores began to introduce their own moderately priced, private-label clothing lines. Dress Barn's sales advantage was diminished by this trend, which was reflected by the company's annual profit margins. Another detriment to Dress Barn's sales potential was the fact that a few of its own suppliers, such as Jones Apparel Group, also moved into the discounted apparel market through the introduction of their own factory outlet stores.

Despite its hardships, however, Dress Barn continued to achieve increased sales figures each year in the first half of the 1990s. Its continued growth prompted the company to begin searching for a larger and more advanced headquarters and distribution location. In 1994, the company moved into a new facility in Suffern, New York. The state-of-the-art facility handled all distribution and warehousing needs, while also housing the company's executive offices. Also in 1994, Dress Barn issued its own credit card to the public, and soon thereafter over half a million cards were in circulation.

From 1995 through 1996 the company opened an impressive number of new stores, 136 in all. Most new stores being introduced were combination Dress Barn/Dress Barn Woman stores, a decision which allowed the company to reach both target groups while using less space and capital. The chain eventually peaked at some 775 stores, but this number dropped to 680 by mid-1998 due to closures of poorly performing stores. The retrenchment paid off when Dress Barn earned a record $40.2 million on sales of $598.2 million in 1998.

New Century, New Strategy

At the turn of the 21st century, Dress Barn was facing an ominous trend. While the chain had long focused on careerwear—suits, dresses, and blazers—the influence of "casual Fridays" was being felt throughout the work week. The shift impacted Dress Barn's bottom line in 1999, when sales increased 3 percent to $616 million but net income fell 17.1 percent to $33.3 million.

The company created a comprehensive plan to reverse its slide in profitability for 2000. One key component of the repositioning was an increase in private-label clothing, which promised higher profit margins. Over the next two years, Dress Barn's in-house brand grew from 40 percent of its offerings to 100 percent. During this period the company also expanded its lines to include shoe and petites departments as well as jewelry and casualwear. As stated in its 2002 10-K report, Dress Barn "shifted its focus from structured, career looks to softer outfit dressings and assortments." By the end of 2002, sportswear accounted for about 65 percent of sales. The company hoped that this mix of clothing for both workdays and weekend wear

Key Dates:

1962: Elliot Jaffe and his wife Roslyn open the first Dress Barn store in Stamford, Connecticut.
1963: A second store is opened.
1966: The company incorporates as The Dress Barn, Inc.
1983: The Dress Barn goes public.
1985: The company owns and operates 200 stores throughout the United States.
1989: Dress Barn Woman, targeting plus-sized women, is introduced.
1990: Dress Barn is acquired by JRL Consulting Corporation.
2000: Dress Barn begins a changeover to sell exclusively its own private-label brand of women's wear.
2002: Dress Barn's new line of sportswear accounts for 65 percent of sales.
2003: The company announces plans to resume Internet sales.

would make its stores "one-stop shopping" destinations for working women. New store openings hewed to a "combo" format, encompassing both Dress Barn and Dress Barn Woman merchandise. Although the company continued to open additional locations, it also shuttered poorly-performing stores.

A new marketing campaign encompassed a brand makeover, advertising push, and a foray into cataloging. The company launched its first catalog in September 1999, hoping to "extend the reach of the brand to both existing store markets and non-store markets." Dress Barn hoped to put 10 million catalogs under the noses of existing and potential customers over the course of 2000. However, losses in both the catalog and e-commerce divisions brought an end to those outlets in November 2001. The company planned to resume Internet sales during fiscal 2003.

Dress Barn also hoped to shift its appeal to a "younger-feeling" customer in part by refining the name to "dressbarn," a format that subtly reflected a more casual image. As Elliot Jaffe told *WWD* in November 2000, "We intend to promote Dress Barn as a brand and a lifestyle, not just a label, to differentiate ourselves from our competition." One thing that would not change was Dress Barn's longstanding commitment to customer service.

The changes produced mixed results over the ensuing two years. Annual sales increased by $100 million, to $717.1 million,

by the end of fiscal 2002 (July 27), but net income only grew by $4.6 million, from $33.3 million in 1999 to $37.9 million in 2002. During this period, the retailer chalked up its best quarterly performances ever, with a net income of $13.4 million on $177.3 million in sales in the final period of fiscal 2002.

That year David Jaffe succeeded his father as CEO, with the elder Jaffe remaining as chairman. The Jaffes were "cautiously optimistic" about Dress Barn's future, setting a goal of $1 billion in sales and announcing an expansion into California.

Principal Competitors

Charming Shoppes, Inc.; Deb Shops Inc.; Burlington Coat Factory Warehouse Corporation; Ross Stores Inc.

Further Reading

Blair, Adam, "Dress Barn's Catalog and E-Commerce Mix," *WWD*, August 18, 1999, p. 16.

Brammer, Rhonda, "Recovery in Store: Sizing Up Small Caps," *Barron's*, August 1, 1994, p. 19.

Coletti, Richard J., "Spaghetti Straps: How a Top Niche Player in the Rag Trade Is Coping with the Campeau Crunch," *Financial World*, March 20, 1990, p. 56.

Dress Barn 35th Anniversary Video, Suffern, N.Y.: Dress Barn, Inc., 1997.

"Dress Barn Reports Best Quarter Ever," *WWD*, September 18, 2000, p. 46.

Duff, Mike, "Dress Barn Spells Out Plan for 2000," *Discount Store News*, January 24, 2000, p. 3.

——, "Dress Barn Tailors 2002 Growth Plan to Include Entry into California Market," *DSN Retailing Today*, January 7, 2002, p. 6.

"Jaffe Rises at Dress Barn," *WWD*, September 5, 2001, p. 12.

Power, Denise, "Dress Barn's Dramatic Upgrade," *WWD*, December 22, 1999, p. 16.

Reda, Susan, "Dress Barn: Opens Doors in New Markets, New Formats," *Stores*, August 1992, p. 19.

Seaton, Jay, "Brand Recognition Is a Springboard," *Communications News*, July 2000, p. 66.

Solnik, Claude, "Dress Barn Makes Big Pitch at Shoes," *Footwear News*, May 25, 1998, p. 2.

Weitzman, Jennifer, "Cost Control, Margins Boost Dress Barn Net," *WWD*, September 19, 2002, p. 17.

——, "Dress Barn Comps, Sales Down," *WWD*, December 2, 2002, p. 16.

——, Specialty Stores Ride a Strong Profit Wave," *WWD*, November 17, 2000, p. 2.

—Laura E. Whiteley
—update: April D. Gasbarre

Duncan Toys Company

15981 Valplast Road
Middlefield, Ohio 44062
U.S.A.
Telephone: (440) 632-1631
Toll Free: (800) 232-3474
Fax: (440) 632-1581
Web site: http://www.yo-yo.com

*Wholly Owned Division of Flambeau Products
    Corporation*
Incorporated: 1929
Employees: 100
Sales: $20 million (2002 est.)
NAIC: 339932 Game, Toy, and Children's Vehicle
    Manufacturing

Duncan Toys Company is the number one manufacturer of yo-yos in the world. The firm produces a wide variety of styles, ranging from simple plastic beginner's models and reproductions of classic wooden designs to "high-tech" modern yo-yos with special inner bearings that allow performance of advanced tricks. Duncan also makes spin tops under the Wizzzer and Tetra Tops brand names and markets instructional videos and other yo-yo related items. The company is owned by Flambeau Products Corporation, which purchased the Duncan name and goodwill after the firm went bankrupt in the mid-1960s. In 2001, Duncan acquired Playmaxx, Inc., a leading competitor that had been founded in 1976 by former company owner Donald F. Duncan, Jr.

1920s Beginnings

The founding of Duncan Toys dates to the late 1920s, but the yo-yo itself goes back thousands of years. Though its exact origin is unknown, depictions of people using yo-yo like toys appeared in ancient Greece and Egypt, and a related toy, the Diabolo, was long known in China. It would later show up in the mid-1600s in the Netherlands and then in the late 1700s in India, France, and England, where it was called a chucki, a bandalore, and a quiz, respectively. It also made its way to the United States, where in 1866 James L. Haven and Charles Hettrick received a patent for an "improved bandalore." Another country where the toy was familiar was the Philippines, where it was typically carved from a single piece of wood and called a yo-yo. Translated from that country's Tagalog language, the name meant "come-come."

The story of Duncan Toys begins with a native of Vintarilocos Norte, Philippines, named Pedro Flores. In 1915, at the age of 16, Flores emigrated to the United States, where several years later he attended San Francisco's High School of Commerce. After briefly studying law in the Bay Area, he moved south to Santa Barbara, where he ended up working a series of odd jobs. It was there, while employed as a bellboy, that he hit upon the idea of marketing the toy he had played with as a child in the Philippines.

In early 1928, Flores approached some wealthy Filipino immigrants in Los Angeles to ask for financial assistance but was turned down. Undaunted, he decided to go it alone and on June 9, 1928 formed the Yo-Yo Manufacturing Company. Within several weeks he had made a dozen handmade yo-yos, and by November had produced more than 2,000. Interest in the toy began to spread, and during the month he won financial backing from James and Daniel Stone of Los Angeles. With their help, he was able to purchase equipment to boost production, and by the spring of 1929 more than 100,000 yo-yos had been made.

The toy's popularity was now growing rapidly, due primarily to yo-yo spinning contests which Flores had begun sponsoring in late 1928. Contestants would try to see who could keep a yo-yo going up and down the longest, throw and return a yo-yo the farthest, or perform the most "perfect spins" in a five-minute period. The contests soon spread from coast to coast, boosting the popularity and sales of the yo-yo. By the end of 1929, Flores was employing 600 workers at three factories and producing thousands of yo-yos per day.

Flores' yo-yos, which cost between 15 cents and $1.50, incorporated a new feature, the slip-string, which allowed the yo-yo to "sleep" or keep spinning when the string was fully extended. Competitors soon began to appear, and on July 22, 1930 he trademarked the name "Flores Yo-Yo," a fact which was highlighted in the company's slogan, "If it isn't a Flores, it isn't a yo-yo." Some Flores yo-yos bore the notation that the company had applied for a patent, but in fact the bandalore patent of 1866 already covered the basic design.

Flores Sells Out to Donald Duncan: 1930

One of Flores' keenest competitors was Donald F. Duncan, an entrepreneur who had already found success with the Good Humor ice cream bar, and who had formed his own yo-yo company in 1929. He would also later start a firm that manufactured most of the parking meters sold in the U.S. In 1930, Duncan bought out Flores for a sum estimated at more than $250,000, and the Donald F. Duncan Yo-Yo Company began selling Flores yo-yos along with its own models. Pedro Flores was hired to promote the firm by sponsoring yo-yo contests around the country, which now featured many new competitive categories.

Donald Duncan was as good, if not better than Flores at marketing, and his promotional acumen helped boost the sales of yo-yos even further. A cross-promotion with the Hearst newspaper chain would prove to be particularly successful. Duncan arranged to get free advertisements from Hearst to promote the firm's yo-yo contests in exchange for limiting participation to players who had sold three subscriptions to a Hearst paper. In one such promotion in Philadelphia, Duncan reportedly sold 3 million yo-yos in 30 days.

The company also had a group of expert yo-yo players who traveled the country and gave demonstrations at places like candy stores to stimulate sales. The men, typically Filipinos, played up the "exotic" origin of the toy by telling stories of the yo-yos supposed use as a weapon in the Philippines, as well as carving pictures of birds and palm trees on the sides of the wooden yo-yos children bought. Other publicity was achieved through the use of paid celebrities like the children of the "Our Gang" movie shorts in ads, as well by the media's publication of photographs that caught stars like Mary Pickford, Bing Crosby, and Lou Gehrig playing with yo-yos.

During the 1930s, Duncan offered a variety of different yo-yo designs, including the fixed string "O-Boy" beginners model, the tournament Gold Seal version, and even a tin whistling yo-yo. Distribution was expanded internationally during the decade, helped by events like the World Yo-Yo Competition, which was held for the first time in London in 1932. The 1930s were a golden era for the toy, although sales fell off during World War II.

In 1946, Duncan built a new yo-yo factory in the small town of Luck, Wisconsin, where there was a large supply of hard maple, the main ingredient in the firm's product. In 1950, the

company introduced a new model, the plastic Electric Yo-Yo, which lit up courtesy of a battery-powered light inside. It was only briefly produced, but in 1954 Duncan began making a regular production plastic model, the junior-sized Pony Boy. This yo-yo was made of polystyrene and had a BB inside that rattled. A short time later, the firm introduced the Imperial, made of tennite plastic, which duplicated the dimensions of the classic wood Model 77 that had been in production since 1929. The Imperial would go on to become the world's best-selling yo-yo. Several years later Duncan also introduced the wooden Butterfly model, which was a standard yo-yo turned inside out, giving the player a wider slot to catch the string in. The company was now also marketing wooden spin tops.

In 1957, Donald F. Duncan retired and gave control of the company to his sons Donald, Jr. and Jack. He would sell a sister firm, Duncan Parking Meter Corporation, in 1959. By this time, Duncan completely dominated the yo-yo market, producing an estimated 85 percent of the toys made.

In 1959, Duncan began running its first television commercials, which debuted in Philadelphia. After they went on the air, sales there quickly increased from $20,000 to $100,000, and the company soon extended the campaign to more cities. A number of different designs were introduced during this period, including versions shaped like sports balls and a planet as well as multicolor plastic models with embedded glitter. The latter series, known as Mardi Gras, was intended to appeal to girls, who were under-represented in the ranks of yo-yo aficionados. By 1962, yo-yo sales were at an all-time high, and Duncan's annual revenues rose to an estimated $7 million from $2 million several years earlier. In 1963, the company sold a record 33 million yo-yos.

Lawsuit Leads to Bankruptcy in 1965

Duncan's competition was heating up, however, and the firm became embroiled in a protracted court battle with the Royal Tops Manufacturing Co., which had been founded in 1937 by a former Duncan demonstrator, Joe Radovan. Duncan sued Royal over the latter's use of the name "yo-yo," asserting that it was an exclusive trademark. In 1965, Royal won the case, but neither company benefited from the victory as legal costs forced both into bankruptcy. The most recent yo-yo craze had faded by the time the suit was settled, helping to seal Duncan's fate.

In 1967, the company's yo-yo turning lathes were sold to Fred Strombeck, who used them to manufacture the "Medalist" brand wooden yo-yo, and in 1968 Flambeau Products Corporation bought the Duncan name and good will. Flambeau had made plastic yo-yos for the firm since 1955 and had retained the company's molds.

The reconstituted Duncan soon began to introduce new models, including the Jewel, the butterfly-style light-up Satellite, the fuzz-covered Velvet, the slimline Professional, and later the Wheels series, designed to look like various muscle-car wheels. The early 1970s saw sales begin to take off once again, and Duncan revived the practice of hiring demonstrators to travel the country performing yo-yo tricks.

The technical side of yo-yo design saw a number of new developments during the 1970s and 1980s, though most of the

Key Dates:

1928: Pedro Flores starts making yo-yos in Santa Barbara, California.

1929: Entrepreneur Donald F. Duncan forms a rival yo-yo company.

1930: Duncan buys out Flores and acquires the trademark on yo-yo name.

1930s: Duncan becomes the dominant yo-yo maker through the use of contests and demonstrators.

1946: The firm builds a new yo-yo factory in Luck, Wisconsin.

1954: The first line of plastic yo-yos is introduced.

1957: Donald F. Duncan passes control of the company to his sons Don, Jr. and Jack.

1963: Yo-yo sales hit a peak; Duncan sells 33 million during the year.

1965: The company loses a lawsuit over yo-yo trademark and declares bankruptcy.

1968: Flambeau Products Corp. buys the Duncan name and resumes production.

1970s: Duncan adds new models and sends out demonstrators as yo-yo sales rebound.

1990: ''Return of the Yo-Yo'' exhibit tours shopping malls.

1995: A TV ad campaign and a middle-school yo-yo science program spark a new sales boom.

1997: The company buys the rights to market the Wizzzer, the world's most popular spin top.

2001: High-tech yo-yo maker Playmaxx, Inc. is acquired.

ideas came from outside of Duncan. In 1976, Donald F. Duncan, Jr. founded a firm which later became known as Playmaxx to market a high quality plastic yo-yo called the ProYo, which had a weighted rim and brass axle that yielded longer spin times. In 1980, inventor Michael Caffrey patented an internal clutch mechanism, and in 1985 a Swedish firm introduced a yo-yo with a ball bearing transaxle that would later revolutionize yo-yo play. Duncan itself brought out the World Class model, a butterfly-shaped yo-yo which had metal weight rings and a teflon-coated axle for longer sleep times, but did not keep it in production.

''Return of the Yo-Yo'': Late 1980s

Despite these improvements, yo-yo sales were in decline, with just 500,000 sold industry-wide in 1985. That year saw Duncan lure one of the firm's former marketing executives out of retirement to help boost sales. Clyde Mortensen had worked for the company during its heyday of the early 1960s, and he soon turned to the medium that had brought success more than two decades ago—television. In February 1986, Duncan began running 30-second spots on youth-oriented cable television networks, including Nickelodeon and USA. Sales soon tripled, and the ad campaign was expanded.

The yo-yo revival was also influenced by other factors. In 1985, yo-yos were in the public eye when an astronaut played with a yellow plastic Duncan Imperial aboard the Space Shuttle Discovery, making it the first yo-yo in space. The following

year comedian Tommy Smothers introduced his trick-performing ''Yo-Yo Man'' character on Johnny Carson's *Tonight Show,* which he reprised in 1987 on the Smothers Brothers' weekly television program. An instructional video subsequently released by Smothers sold an estimated 200,000 copies.

In 1990, Duncan sponsored an exhibition called ''Return of the Yo-Yo'' that traveled to shopping malls around the United States for more than a year. The Duncan Family Collection was exhibited and professional yo-yo demonstrators appeared at the opening of each stop of the tour. The Duncan collection would later become a central part of the National Yo-Yo Museum in Chico, California. Sales of yo-yos were now booming, with an estimated 12 million sold during 1990, the majority of which bore the Duncan logo. Other developments of this time period included the reappearance of yo-yo contests and the founding of the American Yo-Yo Association and other yo-yo fan groups. The company was now producing 11,000 of the toys each day, which were typically sold through large retailers like Wal-Mart and Kmart.

Another Revival in the Mid-1990s

As had happened before, the new yo-yo craze soon faded, and sales became stagnant. In 1993, Duncan hired yo-yo inventor Michael Caffrey, a one-time company demonstrator and cofounder of competitor Yomega, to head the firm's marketing and sales department. In 1995, he returned to the firm's proven sales-boosting strategy and introduced a new television commercial known as ''Video Boy,'' which was intended to position yo-yos as an alternative to video games. Caffrey also added a new marketing wrinkle of his own by devising an educational program called ''Teaching Science With the Yo-Yo.'' Written with the assistance of a college physics professor and a middle-school science teacher, it used yo-yos to teach basic principles about rotational physics and kinetic energy. Duncan was soon distributing a teacher's guide and series of five lessons to 80,000 sixth-grade classrooms and offering yo-yos at low prices for educational use.

By 1996, Duncan's sales were approaching 5 million yo-yos for the year, which yielded $5 million in revenues—an improvement of 50 percent over 1994. Playing up its heritage, in 1996 Duncan released its first wooden yo-yo since the 1960s, a reissue of the 1955 Super Tournament model, which was available in five colors and came packaged with a reproduction of the company's 1955 Yo-Yo Trick Book.

The yo-yo boom continued to grow in 1997, with Duncan's output lagging behind demand, even with its Columbus, Indiana, plant running 24 hours a day, seven days per week. A second production line was subsequently opened at Flambeau Products' Middlefield, Ohio, headquarters. Demand for yo-yos was not confined to the United States, and Duncan reported strong sales in foreign markets such as Australia, England, and Japan. In the last-named country, Duncan sold one million yo-yos in just two months' time. The year 1997 also saw Duncan sign a licensing agreement with Coca-Cola—for which it produced 18 different yo-yo designs using the beverage maker's logo—and acquire the rights to make the Wizzzer, a toy top that had a friction motor inside to make it spin faster. The 30-year old toy had previously been marketed by several other companies, including Mattel, and was considered the world's best-selling top. It was priced at $3.95, just a dollar more than Duncan's most basic yo-yo.

Nineteen ninety-eight was another banner year for yo-yos, with total sales for the industry reaching an estimated $35 million, of which Duncan's share was 65 percent. The firm's top competitor, Yomega, was having success with high-tech yo-yos like its Brain and Fireball models, which incorporated many newer design features, and in the fall of 1999 Duncan introduced a new line of yo-yos with take-apart bodies and ball-bearing transaxles. These included the Imperial-shaped Ballistic, which had an adjustable weight system and interchangeable graphics; the light-up, Imperial-shaped ORB; and the open-face, uniquely shaped Avenger. These would form the basis of the company's "Hardcore" line, which later added other models.

The year 2000 saw Duncan further expand its high-tech offerings with acquisition of the German Mondial design from CameYo. The $100 aluminum yo-yo was touted by the company as the most advanced model ever produced. It featured a self-lubing ball-bearing and an adjustable string gap. Duncan was now marketing its yo-yos more aggressively than ever, using a controversial television commercial that featured people holding their yo-yo (middle) fingers toward the camera. This commercial was run on sports programs and during wrestling shows. Though complaints were received from a number of family groups, the company's sales continued to rise. Duncan was also using traditional promotional methods, hiring talented yo-yo players like Steve Brown and Chris Neff to criss-cross the country doing demonstrations.

In 2001, Duncan introduced the Freehand model, an extra-wide butterfly shaped yo-yo which was the first one that could be used without being tied to a player's hand. Freehand-style play had been invented by Steve Brown, and his picture was used on the package. In December 2001, Duncan bought Playmaxx, Inc., makers of high-tech yo-yos like the ProYo, Bumble Bee, and Cold Fusion models. A number of patents held by Playmaxx were acquired in the deal. Steve Brown himself received a patent during the year for his own freehand counterweight system, which was assigned to Flambeau Products.

Nearly 75 years after it was founded, Duncan Toys Co. had come full circle, going from leading the yo-yo industry, to bankruptcy, and then back again. The yo-yo itself had evolved from a simple child's toy into a high-tech product with a number of variations, and Duncan's offerings covered the entire range of yo-yo styles.

Principal Competitors

Yomega Corporation; Royal Tops Manufacturing Company.

Further Reading

Berg, Eric N., "In a World of Space-Age Toys, A Return of String and Spool," *New York Times*, April 14, 1991, p. 1A.

"Donald Duncan, 78; Promoter of Yo-Yo and Parking Meter," *New York Times*, May 16, 1971, p. 74.

Greenberg, Herb, "Around the World: Yo-Yo Shortages," *Fortune*, June 23, 1997, p. 40.

Hannon, Kerry, "Nostalgic Yo-Yos Spin into Record Popularity," *USA Today*, December 28, 1998, p. 3B.

Kawa, Barry, "Yo-Yos Back in the Swing," *Plain Dealer*, July 12, 1999, p. 1B.

McClellan, April, "Up-and-Down Trends No Worry to Spin Doctors," *Plain Dealer*, September 1, 2002, p. B4.

Meisenheimer, Lucky, MD, "Pedro Flores," *American Yo-Yo Association Newsletter*, September 1997.

Munno, Greg, "Yo-Yos on a Climb," *Plain Dealer*, May 24, 1996, p. 1C.

Payne, Melanie, "Duncan Toys Cashes in as Yo-Yo Mania Spreads Across America," *Akron Beacon Journal*, July 23, 1997.

Rubin, Sylvia, "Just Say Yo." *San Francisco Chronicle*, March 23, 1990, p. B3.

—Frank Uhle

Ellen Tracy, Inc.

575 7th Avenue
New York, New York 10018
U.S.A.
Telephone: (212) 944-6999
Toll Free: (800) 925-7979
Fax: (212) 398-1678
Web site: http://www.ellentracy.com

Wholly Owned Subsidiary of Liz Claiborne, Inc.
Incorporated: 1949
Employees: 200 (est.)
Sales: $171 million (2001 est.)
NAIC: 315232 Women's and Girls' Cut and Sew Blouse
and Shirt Manufacturing; 315233 Women's and Girls'
Cut and Sew Dress Manufacturing; 315234 Women's
and Girls' Cut and Sew Suit, Coat, Tailored Jacket,
and Skirt Manufacturing

Ellen Tracy, Inc., which originally made blouses, is now a leading maker of bridge apparel—clothing that falls in between high-price designer lines and lower-priced labels. Located on Manhattan's Seventh Avenue, Ellen Tracy is especially adept at producing quality garments suitable for the professional woman, workhorse items that complement a wardrobe for many years despite changing styles. Its Company Ellen Tracy label produces casual clothing aimed at a younger market. In addition, Ellen Tracy has licensed agreements for shoes, hosiery, belts, eyewear, and a home collection. The company was acquired in 2002 by Liz Claiborne, Inc. and became a wholly owned subsidiary of that company.

Launching the Company in 1949

Herbert Gallen established Ellen Tracy in 1949. He grew up in Patterson, New Jersey, the grandson of a silk mill owner and son of a fabric manufacturer. Ironically, he never planned to become involved in the apparel industry. After graduating from high school, he went to work for an uncle who owned more than two-dozen auto supply stores. Gallen ran his own store before serving a stint in the army, and was still involved in the auto parts business during World War II. Because of wartime restrictions, fabric became difficult to acquire and he recognized a chance to take advantage of his Patterson connections to move into the apparel industry. With fabric procured from a friend, he produced several sample blouses, which he then took to the major department stores located on Manhattan's 34th Street. He visited Franklin Simon and immediately sold every blouse he had, a successful launch of a new business. For the next few years he produced plain-looking blouses, using his wife's name, Betty Barr, for a label. Along with a sales manager he opened a showroom on Third Avenue that also served as a warehouse and shipping point for the blouses he had produced in Manhattan. In 1949, with financial backing from a partner named Mike Brawer, Gallen formed a new company, which he called Ellen Tracy, a name he made up in the belief that a women's line should feature a woman's name.

Ellen Tracy blouses sold $28.50 to $30 a dozen at wholesale to such customers as Oppenheim Collins, B. Altman, and Macy's. As the business began to grow, Gallen hired more people, moved to a larger showroom, and opened a warehouse in Hackensack, New Jersey. Manhattan production also was supplemented by contractors in Pennsylvania. It was not until the early 1960s that the company began to do some manufacturing overseas. Gallen was very much a hands-on owner, involved in all aspects of the business, earning a reputation as a perfectionist. He hired a designer to produce more attractive garments, and over the course of a dozen years went through several designers before hiring a recent college graduate named Linda Allard who over the next 40 years would be instrumental in helping him build Ellen Tracy into an important bridge label.

Allard grew up on a farm in Doylestown, Ohio, her father a civil engineer and her mother a first grade teacher and 4-H Club adviser. By age ten she was designing outfits for her paper dolls. Along with her two sisters she learned to sew from their mother, who refused to accept anything less than excellent work. Years later Allard recalled, "If I sewed a seam and it wasn't exactly to her liking, I had to rip it out until it was perfect in her eyes." As a teenager she began to make her own clothes and although she knew she wanted to involve her life in some way with clothing she was simply unaware that fashion school was an option. Instead she went to Kent State University after winning a fine arts scholarship. There she was able to take a few pattern-making courses, but her art curriculum was essentially geared toward producing school teachers, which held no appeal for Allard. For a senior-year project she held her first fashion show and assembled a portfolio of photographs, revealing both a drive to succeed as well as ingenuity. To find models she approached friends, offering to make an outfit they could keep if they participated in the show, not to mention bought the fabric. She also received a glimpse of New York after winning a month-long internship with *Mademoiselle* in a guest editor contest.

After graduating from Kent State, with $200 from her parents in her purse, Allard took the Greyhound bus to New York, checked into a women's hotel, and began to search for a job in the fashion industry. She assumed it would be a short-term career, followed by marriage and a life devoted to raising a family. With no contacts and little knowledge, she naively went door-to-door in Manhattan's garment district asking if anyone was in need of an assistant designer. No one was interested, including Ellen Tracy at first. After three weeks, with her money all but exhausted and facing the prospect of returning home, she was asked to return to Ellen Tracy to interview with Gallen. His designer at the time was Dorothy Avazian, who according to Gallen had recently angered him: "She showed me things I didn't like, and the sales manager said there was a girl who was here earlier in the week, and we called her in." Allard's memory of their meeting was vivid: "It was 2 p.m. on September 27, 1962, a fateful day. I sat across from Mr. Gallen and it happened to be a really lousy, New York, rainy, drenched day. I think he felt I was desperate for a job. He looked at my portfolio and asked, 'How much money would you like to make?' Well, I hadn't even thought about that. So I said, 'I would like to make $50 a week.' He said, 'Sorry, but if you'll take $60, you can have a job.' "

Linda Allard Becoming Head Designer in 1964

Allard became Avazian's assistant and learned the technical side of the garment industry before being allowed to try her hand at designing. After Avazian quit in 1964, Gallen asked Allard if she was interested in taking over the collection, and despite a fear of failure she accepted, becoming director of design. Ellen Tracy at this point was still devoted to the business of producing quality blouses, as well as shirtwaist dresses. It was also a time when women's work attire was a suit, hat, gloves, and high heels, but the 1960s, a decade that produced a wide range of social changes, would soon see a more youthful, casual approach to fashion, one that a young designer like Linda Allard would be well able to exploit. The first move into sportswear for Ellen Tracy was a white ottoman peacoat with brass buttons and sailor pants that Allard designed. The blazer was a major departure for the label, as well as being expensive,

yet it sold by the thousands and established Ellen Tracy in the junior sportswear sector.

The maturation of the Ellen Tracy label reflected both Allard's life and a changing society. As an increasing number of its junior customers joined the workforce, and in the 1970s more women began to enter the ranks of management, Allard started to design suitable clothing, which in many ways was the kind of apparel she, occupying a similar place in the business world, wanted to wear. She and Ellen Tracy grew along with their customers, creating a strong bond. She also learned a practical lesson from Gallen: "He said we were in business to make money and not to make a press statement." It was advice she followed; for the runway she might cut the clothes in one way, but they were always shipped in a more wearable, modest version. The clothes were to serve the customer, not the ego of the designer. To keep in touch with customers and maintain relevance of the line, both she and Gallen made periodic trips around the country to visit stores that carried the Ellen Tracy line and receive direct feedback. As the company's manufacturing moved overseas, Gallen and Allard also made regular extended trips to Hong Kong. Eventually Ellen Tracy also turned to China, South Korea, and other parts of the world to produce their garments, without losing sight of maintaining high quality.

In 1979 Ellen Tracy moved beyond junior sportswear, becoming involved in the designer-sportswear category. In 1983 the company added a petite division, and a year later, with designer names becoming an important aspect of marketing apparel, Allard's name was added to the Ellen Tracy label. It was also around this time that the bridge category began to emerge in the fashion industry and Ellen Tracy found a natural niche within it. The company added a dress division in 1985, then in 1986 made its first attempt at licensing the Ellen Tracy name, a deal for scarves with Collection XIIX Ltd. As would be the case with subsequent licensing arrangements, Allard provided a major influence over accessories bearing the Ellen Tracy name, making sure they complemented the apparel and exercising final approval. During this period the label was supported by advertising campaigns that in 1983 featured model Carol Alt and in 1987 a young Cindy Crawford.

1991 Launch of Company Ellen Tracy

With its core customer growing older, Ellen Tracy in 1991 launched a new line, Company Ellen Tracy, to appeal to a younger market and offer casual weekend attire rather than more formal, business clothing. Although much smaller in scale than the original line, it proved popular with customers. The success of Company also led to the addition of plus sizes in spring 1993. In 1992 Ellen Tracy made an attempt to enter the fragrance business, signing a licensing agreement with Revlon. Despite being accepted by customers, the perfume was soon discontinued when Revlon elected to focus on the mass market and eliminated prestige product lines. Ellen Tracy grew internally at a steady pace, yet Gallen never showed any interest in acquisitions. The label was also very much a domestic business, with attempts to penetrate the European markets never successful. Nonetheless, Ellen Tracy topped $200 million in annual revenues during the 1990s. It was a solid performer in stores, had a loyal customer base, and attracted a number of suitors who believed that the company held tremendous promise.

Key Dates:

1949: Herbert Gallen establishes Ellen Tracy, Inc. to manufacture blouses.
1964: Linda Allard becomes design director and moves
the business into junior sportswear.
1984: Allard's name is added to the label.
1991: Company Ellen Tracy label is added.
2000: Gallen and Allard marry.
2002: Ellen Tracy is sold to Liz Claiborne, Inc.

Gallen turned down several offers, but as he approached 80 years of age he began to take bids more seriously.

In 1995 rumors circulated that Ellen Tracy would soon be sold and by October a deal was signed, with Boston-based investment firm, Bain Capital Group, agreeing to pay an undisclosed amount. As part of the transaction, executive Jay Margolis was to be brought in as chief operating officer with the expectation of ultimately replacing Gallen. Margolis was well respected in the fashion industry, having previously served as vice-chairman of Liz Claiborne as well as vice-chairman and president of Tommy Hilfiger. Gallen told the press, however, that Margolis would have to prove himself before taking over. Several weeks later Margolis opted to become chairman and CEO of Esprit de Corp, a struggling junior sportswear company. The sale of Ellen Tracy to Bain Capital was subsequently called off, although both parties maintained that Margolis's change of heart played no role in the decision, instead calling it a "mutual decision."

Gallen and Allard continued to run Ellen Tracy, with the elderly majority owner showing no signs of relinquishing power. In 1996 the company awarded a three-year license for footwear to Intershoe Inc. for both of its major lines. Gallen chose Intershoe as a partner because of its international reach, which supported his goal of growing Ellen Tracy's international business so that within five years it would match domestic sales. Later in the year the company also signed a licensing agreement with Roma, a Norman M. Morris Corp. division, to produce belts under the Ellen Tracy labels. It took another stab at fragrances in 1998, licensing the Ellen Tracy label to Cosmopolitan Cosmetics, a well-respected company that also made and marketed cosmetics and fragrances for such major names as Gucci, Rochas, Anna Sui, and Charles Jourdan. When the fragrance premiered in March 2000 it was an immediate hit with consumers, prompting the launch of ancillary products.

Also in 1998 Ellen Tracy signed licensing deals for eyewear with Viva International Group and outerwear with Listeff Fashions. All told, 1998 proved to be a highly successful year for Ellen Tracy, due in large part to the introduction of the Ellen Tracy Club, which rewarded customers for paying full price for its garments: members received a $100 gift certificate toward regular-priced apparel for every $1,000 spent. In this way, Ellen Tracy was able to overcome the bridge category's habit of attracting customers through markdowns, as well as build brand loyalty. A newsletter sent to some 20,000 club members also reinforced the bond with customers, sharing developments at Ellen Tracy as well as giving out such prizes as free New York shopping trips.

A widower for several years, Gallen at the age of 84 in March 2000 married Allard, who at the age of 59 had never married. She continued to use her name professionally and there were no apparent changes in how Ellen Tracy operated, the two enjoying a long-term and well-established working relationship. They recognized that the lines had blurred between their two major brands and took steps to tie the two collections together. In many ways it was simply a recognition that Ellen Tracy customers were already mixing and matching apparel between the two lines. A more significant change took place in September 2002 when Gallen finally sold the business to Liz Claiborne for $170 million in cash and the assumption of $10 million in debt, a move that not only allowed him to plan his estate but also ensure that Ellen Tracy would outlive him. Moreover, Claiborne had the financial resources to take Ellen Tracy to another level. Gallen stayed on as chairman and continued to exert a major influence on the business, while Allard retained her position as Design Director.

Brought in as president to provide day-to-day management of the subsidiary was Glenn McMahon, former president of Kenneth Cole women's sportswear at Liz Claiborne, which now boasted some two dozen brands and annual revenues of nearly $3.5 billion. With the backing of its corporate parent, Ellen Tracy was poised for significant growth, with plans for more licensing agreements (jewelry and handbags being likely candidates), international expansion, and the possible opening of Ellen Tracy specialty stores in key markets.

Principal Competitors

Ann Taylor; Bernard Chaus; Jones Apparel.

Further Reading

Gottschalk, Mary, "Behind the Ellen Tracy Name for 30 Years, Designer Kept Label Thriving," *Record,* September 3, 1992, p. b05.
Hatfield, Julie, "The Real Ellen Tracy at Work," *Boston Globe,* September 5, 1994, p. 38.
Jeannin, Judy, "The Quiet Man for 50 Years," *The Record,* July 25, 1999, p. L01.
Larson, Kristin, "The Claiborne Era Commences," *WWD,* October 23, 2002, p. S19.
Lockwood, Lisa, "Captain Gallen's Voyage," *WWD,* October 23, 2002, p. S2.
Thompson, Lynne, "Material Girl," *Inside Business,* September 2001, p. 41.
Wilson, Eric, "A Company Woman," *WWD,* October 23, 2002, p. S6.

—Ed Dinger

Empresas Polar SA

4ta. Transv. De los Cortijos de Lourdes
Centro Empresarial Polar, Piso 1
Caracas 1070
Venezuela
Telephone: (212) 203-111
Fax: (212) 202-7210
Web site: http://www.empresas-polar.com

Private Company
Incorporated: 1941
Employees: 18,000
Sales: $2.5 billion (2002 est.)
NAIC: 311919 Other Snack Food Manufacturing; 312130
    Wineries; 312120 Breweries; 312111 Soft Drink
    Manufacturing; 311999 All Other Miscellaneous Food
    Manufacturing

Empresas Polar SA operates as Venezuela's largest private industrial conglomerate, manufacturing and distributing a wide variety of food products and beverages, including beer, soft drinks, juice, corn flours, rice, pastas, margarines, corn oil, cheese spreads, jellies, tuna fish, and frozen sea food. Beer accounts for over half of company sales; subsidiary Cerveceria Polar is the 17th largest beer company in the world. Empresas also has key investments in Venezuela's oil, petrochemical, and banking industries. Third-generation Lorenzo Mendoza was named CEO in 1999. In 2002, he was listed as one of the richest men in the world by *Fortune* magazine.

Origins and Growth: 1940s–70s

Dr. Lorenzo Mendoza Fleury, a Venezuelan lawyer, inherited a soap factory from his family during the late 1930s. Although this factory proved to be a financial failure, Fleury established a business style worthy of future success; he soon sold the soap factory in pursuit of a more profitable industry. The search ended in 1941 when he established a brewery in Antimano, a suburb of Caracas. The rapid expansion that followed is the legacy of Mendoza Fleury's far-sighted decision.

The Antimano facility enjoyed sufficient success so that by 1950 a second brewery, Cerveceria de Oriente, could be established in the Venezuelan city of Barcelona. A year later, production demand required the construction of a new brewery with large scale capacity. Also located in Caracas, this establishment eventually became the headquarters for all Polar's activities. The company trademark, a polar bear looking across a body of blue water, emerged from this facility. In 1954, the firm also began its initial expansion into the food sector when it created Refinadora de Maiz Venezolana C.A.

By 1960, at a time when large Venezuelan corporations lacked confidence in the country's beleaguered economy and thus turned their attention to overseas markets, Cerveceria Polar decided instead to expand at home. This decision marked a significant turning point in establishing Polar as the pre-eminent Venezuelan brewery. Soon Cerveceria Modelo, the company's newest brewery, was in operation in Maracaibo in western Venezuela.

During the following decade, Cerveceria Polar captured 50 percent of the domestic market. The continual pursuit of product stability and production quality required adaptation to climatic conditions and the eventual automation of all Polar's activities.

Beer sales tripled during the 1970s. To maximize existing capacity, the company introduced a number of improvements in the production process. They included the implementation of high-gravity brewing, first fermenting wort of 14 percent extract and then correcting this to 11.3 percent extract. Three week cycles of fermentation and storage followed this process. Tight production schedules were maintained.

By the end of the decade, yet another brewery, Cerveceria Polar del Centro, began operations in the city of San Joaquin. A major innovation, signifying a technological breakthrough in the brewing process, was initiated at this site: the San Joaquin facility became the first brewery in the world to use a one-tank system with cylinder-conical tanks from the start of production. The efficiency of the process marked the end for the company of the kind of beer supply shortages which had occurred in the past. The small Antimano brewery had now outlived its usefulness and was duly closed.

Cerveceria's Brewing Process

In the 1980s, Cerveceria Polar's brewing process began with water, supplied by municipal sources, that was passed through sand and activated carbon filters and then decarbonated by weak-acid ion exchangers. Since Venezuela's climate precluded the cultivation of malt or hops, these supplies were imported from countries as diverse as Canada, Finland, Czechoslovakia, and Australia. Pre-cooked rice flakes were used as an adjunct, and wort was extracted by the infusion mashing method and lautering. Flavor stability was guaranteed through the separation of the hot trub.

The fermentation process followed over the next 21 days. Except at the Caracas brewery, where conventional fermentation continued, all other Polar facilities used cylinder-conical tanks. Fermentation occurred at 11 to 14 degrees Celsius. Then, after reducing total diacetyl to under .1 mg/liter, the beer was cooled until it reached 1 degree Celsius.

Automation at the Cerveceria Polar breweries took the form of milling, mashing, lautering, and wort boiling. Later, automation was used for filtration and cleaning. The company also planned to automate the one-tank fermentation process promises to increase production capacity. The bottling process, using both European and U.S. equipment, involved two different size glass bottles and standard aluminum cans. Once in the containers, the beer was pasteurized in tunnel pasteurizers.

Cerveceria Polar conducted its operations with careful attention to water conservation and environmental protection—the recycling of condensates, the use of air coolants for diesel engines, and the condensation of exhaust steam. Waste water was treated with activated sludge to eliminate 95 percent of the organic load. In an attempt to extend their environmental activities, the company began to demineralized treated waste so that it could be reused for indirect processes. Polar worked in close cooperation with Venezuelan universities in conducting research on uses for sludge produced in waste water treatment. Possible uses for the sludge ranged from improving sandy soils to forming an ingredient in cattle feed.

During this time period, research and development at Polar concentrated on process innovation. Numerous laboratory tests involved investigations into methods of improving beer flavor stability. Venezuela's climate subjects the country to year-round sunshine; high temperatures cause product variability. At Polar laboratories a method was devised to deal with this problem peculiar to tropical climates. A simple means of measuring oxygen content in the bottles eliminated flavor instability. The method has subsequently been adopted by other breweries around the world.

Distribution of Polar products took place under the direction of eight wholly-owned regional distributors, and Polar beer could be found in even the most remote regions of Venezuela. Although transportation conditions were at times precarious, Polar succeeded in the consistent delivery of its products.

Polar also operated its own in-house advertising agency, Cadesa, which directed a highly effective campaign using patriotic messages. A popular example is the short film entitled "Traveling with Polar." Here viewers share in the celebration of images of national scenery and cultural heritage.

By 1984, Cerveceria Polar controlled an 85 percent share of its domestic marketplace. New areas of expansion included the production of alcohol-free malt beverages and the penetration of overseas markets. The establishment of a food division signaled Polar's attempt to become a more diversified business. Prior to their use of rice flakes, the company had used imported cornflakes as an adjunct to the brewing process. Corn, however, was an indigenous crop to Venezuela. Instead of continuing to import, Polar purchased a small local corn mill to produce cornflakes. This operation was the precursor of Polar's food divisions, which now produced corn oil, animal feed, and the traditional Venezuelan "arepa," a type of corn-based pancake. During the mid-1980s, over 500,000 tons of corn were processed annually. The company subsequently expanded into other agricultural activities, including poultry farms, pork production, and slaughterhouses.

Over the course of its history, Polar acquired several subsidiaries to augment company growth—Superenvases Envalic, a manufacturer of two-piece aluminum cans; Plasticos Metalgrafica, a manufacturer of plastic beer cases; and Industria Metalgrafica, producers of crown corks. All three of these subsidiaries supplied products not only to Polar but also to industry competitors. In 1988, Polar acquired nine food processing companies from U.S.-based TLC Group, an investment firm that had purchased the international food operations of Beatrice Companies in 1987. Included in the deal was Industrias Savoy, which came to be known as Savoy Brands International.

Expansion Continues: 1990s and Beyond

During the 1990s, the company—now known as Empresas Polar—continued its acquisition strategy and focused on restructuring company operations in order to position itself as a major industrial conglomerate. In 1993, the firm entered the soft drink market when it acquired Golden Cup. It gained a much stronger presence in that sector in 1996 when it teamed up with PepsiCo Inc. to bottle and market PepsiCo products. PepsiCo had entered the Venezuelan market in the 1940s and had remained a market leader over competitor Coca-Cola until 1996, when its bottler Cisneros prematurely terminated its contract and went with Coca-Cola. A *Financial Times London* article asked PepsiCo CEO Roger Enrico about Cisneros' abrupt departure, to which he replied that "a big red truck full of money showed up on the door step and our partner decided to get in and

Key Dates:

1941: Lorenzo Mendoza Fleury establishes a brewery in Antimano, a suburb of Caracas.

1951: A large-scale capacity brewery is constructed in Caracas.

1954: The firm expands into the food sector.

1988: Industrias Savoy is acquired.

1993: The company enters the soft drink market with the purchase of Golden Cup.

1996: Empresas teams up with PepsiCo Inc.

1998: The company forms a joint venture with Frito-Lay Inc.

2001: Empresas acquires 98.2 percent of competitor Mavesa S.A.

drive away with it.'' PepsiCo instantly lost its 80 percent market share and as a result sued Cisneros for breaking their contract, which should have lasted until 2003. The anti-trust agency in Venezuela fined the new partners $1.9 million for violating anti-monopoly regulations. Nevertheless, the partnership was approved and left PepsiCo scrambling to find a new distributor.

Empresas Polar jumped at the chance to secure a stronger foothold in the soft drink industry and partnered with PepsiCo to form Sociedad Productora de Refrescos y Sabores (Sopresa), a joint venture that manufactured and distributed PepsiCo products throughout Venezuela. By 2000, Sopresa had six production facilities and 55 distribution warehouses, and its products were found in over 200,000 stores. Empresas' next move came in 1998 when it created a 50–50 joint venture with Frito-Lay Inc., PepsiCo's snack food division. The venture manufactured and distributed products in Venezuela, Chile, Columbia, Ecuador, Guatemala, Honduras, Panama, Peru, and El Salvador.

During 1999, third-generation Lorenzo Mendoza was named CEO. Under his leadership, Empresas began to restructure company operations, creating distinct company divisions. The company also began to bolster its existing business lines with a goal of securing a larger share of the Latin American food and beverage industry. The company prospered amid a weak Venezuelan economy. In 1999, it purchased a 7.5 percent stake in Backus & Johnston, Peru's largest brewer. By 2001, its stake had increased to 25 percent. During that year, Empresas acquired a 98.2 percent stake in competitor Mavesa S.A., a Venezuelan food manufacturer traded on the New York Stock Exchange. The $500 million deal signaled Empresas' determination to continue its growth well into the new century.

Principal Operating Units

Beer and Malt Beverages; Foods; Soft Drinks.

Principal Competitors

Cisneros Group; Grupo Empresarial Bavaria.

Further Reading

Castano, Ivan, ''Venezuela's Polar Buys Mavesa for $500M,'' *Daily Deal*, March 28, 2001.

Dolan, Kerry A., ''The Beer Baron,'' *Forbes*, July 5, 1999, p. 198.

Galloway, Jennifer, ''Quenching Corporate Thirst,'' *LatinFinance*, December 2002, p. 22.

Hoag, Christine, ''Empresas Polar Reports Record Sales Rise,'' *Financial Times London*, October 2, 1998, p. 17.

Mann, Joe, ''Venezuelan Brewer Expands,'' *Financial Times London*, June 21, 1988, p. 27.

''PepsiCo Begins South American Marathon,'' *Financial Times London*, December 13, 1996, p. 29.

''Polar Doubles Up,'' *LatinFinance*, September 2001.

Rousch, Chris, ''Pepsi Finds Bottler in Venezuela,'' *Atlanta Journal and Constitution*, November 14, 1996, p. 2F.

—update: Christina M. Stansell

Faultless Starch/Bon Ami Company

1025 West 8th Street
Kansas City, Missouri 64101
U.S.A.
Telephone: (816) 842-1230
Fax: (816) 842-3417
Web site: http://www.faultless.com

Private Company
Incorporated: 1887 as Beaham & Moffit
Employees: Not available.
Sales: $35 million (1996 est.)
NAIC: 325611 Soap and Other Detergent Manufacturing;
325612 Polish and Other Sanitation Good
Manufacturing

Faultless Starch/Bon Ami Company is a manufacturer of consumer and commercial cleaners and laundry products. Its two major brands are Faultless Starch, a line of starch and sizing products sold across the United States and in 30 countries worldwide, and Bon Ami cleansers. Faultless Starch claims about one-third of U.S. market share and 10 percent of the worldwide market in laundry starches. Bon Ami is the third most popular brand of powdered cleansers in the United States, where it holds a 5 percent market share. Bon Ami is known as an environmentally friendly product, and it is the preferred household cleanser for people with chemical sensitivity. The company also makes a line of Kleen King metal cleaners and the Magic brand line of laundry starches and sizing. Faultless Starch/Bon Ami also distributes a line of garden tools, including the Garden Weasel tiller, and a line of scented candles and room sprays. The company operates manufacturing plants and a distribution center in Kansas City, Missouri, and one factory in nearby Humansville, Missouri. Tracing its roots back to the late 19th century, it has been continuously operated by members of the founding Beaham family since that time.

Origins of Faultless Starch

The Faultless Starch Company was a family-owned business in Kansas City since the late 19th century. It began when Major Thomas G. Beaham moved to Kansas City from Zanesville, Ohio, in 1886. Once there, he bought a part ownership in a tea, coffee, and spice company called Smith & Moffit. This company became Beaham & Moffit the next year. Sometime after that, Beaham & Moffit bought up the formula for a dry laundry starch called Faultless Starch from the Bosworth Manufacturing Company. In 1891, Beaham & Moffit changed its name to reflect its leading product and thus became the Faultless Starch Company. Faultless Starch won wide popularity in the Midwest. It not only saved women the labor of making their own laundry starch but was also used as baby powder and bath powder. Traveling salesmen brought Faultless Starch into the West and Southwest. One Texas salesman added a premium to his starch boxes, bundling them with reading primers. This became a widespread practice, and the series of 36 Faultless Starch primers were used as school texts throughout the West. The company distributed the primers until the 1930s, and many Americans learned to read using the free Faultless Starch booklets.

The company incorporated in 1902, and in 1903 built a new factory in Kansas City after an earlier facility was destroyed by flood. Faultless Starch made nothing but dry laundry starch for the next 50 years. It remained in the hands of the Beaham family, and it operated out of its 1903 plant until 1968. The company advertised widely, especially on the radio in the 1940s. Its commercial jingle became so popular that marching bands played it during halftime at football games. Then, in 1960, the company brought out a new product that proved wildly successful, at least for a time. This was an aerosol starch. Faultless worked with a company called Arthur D. Little, Inc. to develop a laundry starch that could be sprayed from an aerosol can. The resulting product was very easy to use. Faultless Spray-On Starch debuted in 1960 and had the same sort of impact as the company's first packaged starch. Consumers flocked to it because it was so much easier to use than the powder version. In 1964, the company brought out Faultless Fabric Finish, followed in 1965 by Faultless Hot Iron Cleaner. In 1968, it came out with another new product, Faultless Spray Pre-Wash. That year, the company branched into a new market with its purchase of the Kleen King Company, a maker of metal cleaning products.

Aerosol starch made a big impression on the U.S. market. Sales grew quickly, and for several years during the 1960s aerosol starch was one of the leading growth categories in U.S. supermarkets. It was also popular abroad. In the mid-1960s, Faultless licensed a West German company to make the spray starch in that country. With the advent of wash-and-wear fabrics after 1970, however, Faultless sales began to fall off as consumers flocked to polyester, acrylic, and poly-cotton blends, all billed as easy-care, wrinkle-free fabrics. In 1968, Faultless had realized that it was too dependent on its core product, and it had branched into cleaners with the Kleen King line. In 1971, the company made another attempt to diversify and picked up the Bon Ami Company. Bon Ami was a cleanser that at one point held a 70 percent market share in the United States, a venerable brand even older than Faultless Starch. However, after its founding family gave up control of the company, it had been through several unscrupulous owners, and the brand had dropped out of sight.

Origins of Bon Ami

Bon Ami soap was first made in 1886, the same year Major Beaham showed up in Kansas City. It was initially manufactured by the J.T. Robertson Soap Company of Manchester, Connecticut. Robertson's company was attempting to duplicate a very popular brand name soap of the 1880s, Sapolio, which was made from tallow and finely ground quartz. The quartz mined in the Northeast was always found with feldspar, a softer mineral. To separate out the quartz, workers pounded it with heavy hammers called cobbing hammers. The soft feldspar was left behind and considered a waste product, but Robertson thought a soap could be made using the leftover feldspar. He interested a neighbor, Gurdon Hicks Childs, who had a grist mill that could be used to grind the feldspar. The two brought out Bon Ami brand household soap in 1886 under the aegis of the Robertson Soap Co. In 1892, the son and nephew of Gurdon Hicks Childs formed their own company, Childs & Childs, and purchased the exclusive rights to Bon Ami soap. By 1896, the brand was ubiquitous in the Northeast. The company changed its name to Bon Ami Co. in 1897. It continued to be run by members of the Childs family. Bon Ami used a logo of a yellow chick, with the slogan ''Hasn't Scratched Yet!'' (This referred to the fact, known to people familiar with chickens, that newborn chicks do not scratch the ground for food for two or three days. Unlike harsher cleansers, Bon Ami, being mild, did not scratch surfaces such as porcelain.) Around 1900, the yellow chick was re-imagined by artist Ben Austrian, a famous painter of the era, whose entire career was based on paintings of chickens and other birds. Bon Ami's logo and slogan became one of the most enduring examples of American advertising.

The company did well. In 1915, Bon Ami Co. was listed on the New York Stock Exchange. It reorganized so it had a

manufacturing subsidiary, Orford Soap Co., in 1915, and in 1922 opened a Canadian subsidiary, Canada Bon Ami Ltd. In 1930, the company formed another overseas subsidiary, Bon Ami Co. of Australia, Ltd. The Bon Ami brand enjoyed a large market share and little competition. Even throughout the Great Depression, Bon Ami Co. continued to pay its stockholders dividends, one of only 16 New York Stock Exchange companies that did so. After World War II, the company did pick up some serious rivals. Colgate brought out its Ajax cleanser in 1947, and Procter & Gamble came out with Comet in 1956. These were brands backed by major companies, and 50 years later they are the two leading powdered cleansers. Bon Ami's market share had been as high as 70 percent when Ajax and Comet were starting out.

In 1953, Eversley Childs died at the age of 87. Son of one of the founders of Bon Ami, he had worked for the company for over 60 years and eventually served as its chairman. On his death, the remaining members of the Childs family cashed out, and Bon Ami Co. was then run by a group of investors with ties to the grocery business. In 1955, Bon Ami was acquired by United Dye & Chemical Corp., a company controlled by a mysterious businessman named Alexander Guterma. Guterma claimed to have been born in Russia on the eve of the Revolution. His name at one time may have been Guterman, though he also at times used the name Sandy McSande. After drifting through China and the Philippines, he arrived in the United States in 1950 with plans to farm exotic plants that could be used for textile fibers. Through a series of quasi-legal mergers, Guterma built his Florida ramie farm into an up-and-coming conglomerate, and by 1956 he was chairman of an unprecedented three New York Stock Exchange companies. Guterma was hailed as a financial genius when he burst onto the scene in 1950; by 1958 he had been indicted for fraud. While in control of Bon Ami, Guterma had managed to wring $3 million (the company's entire cash holdings) from the company in fraudulent transactions involving the sale of television advertising rights. Then, in 1957, Guterma arranged for the sale of Bon Ami by United Dye to a convicted forger named Sortiris (Sonny) Fassoulis. Fassoulis immediately had Bon Ami spend over $1.3 million to buy some extremely limited television rights to a packet of old British films. Fassoulis, of course, owned the company that sold the film rights. Under the sway of these two con men, Bon Ami began to falter, and in 1958 the New York Stock Exchange threatened to delist its stock. Unfortunately, Fassoulis and Guterma were not the last shady characters to take a piece out of Bon Ami. In 1958, investor R. Paul Weesner gained control of the company and became its chairman. By 1962, the company was considered to have made a remarkable recovery from its previous mishandling. That year, however, the company received a hostile takeover offer from a Chicago company, Tel-A-Sign, Inc. Bon Ami's refusal of Tel-A-Sign's offer precipitated more charges of wrongdoing at the company, this time levied by Tel-A-Sign's attorney, Roy M. Cohn. (Cohn was known as one of the nation's leading anti-communists and had worked as assistant to Senator Joseph McCarthy from 1953 to 1954.) Cohn claimed that Weesner and others had misused funds and taken kickbacks, charges Weesner characterized as ''unfounded'' and ''filthy.'' Nevertheless, Weesner was soon charged with taking $550,000 in corporate funds. The company's chairman had billed the company for personal items,

Key Dates:

1886: Major Beaham goes into business in Kansas City; Bon Ami soap is first produced.
1891: Beaham's company changes its name to Faultless Starch Co.
1892: Childs & Childs buys exclusive rights to Bon Ami.
1915: Bon Ami Co. goes public.
1954: The Childs family sells off its Bon Ami holdings.
1955: United Dye acquires Bon Ami.
1957: Bon Ami comes under the control of Sonny Fassoulis.
1958: R. Paul Weesner gains control of Bon Ami.
1960: Faultless debuts spray-on starch.
1963: Bon Ami is sold to Lestoil Products.
1971: Faultless buys Bon Ami Co. for $1 million.
1974: The company name is changed to Faultless Starch/ Bon Ami Co.
1983: The company begins distributing garden tools.
1997: Faultless/Bon Ami acquires Magic brand of starch and sizing.

including a custom-built cage for his pet macaw, which cost $1,581. In 1963, the company changed hands yet again, falling to Lestoil Products, Inc.

Through all these troubles, the company spent less and less on advertising. In the early 1950s, it spent about $1 million annually on advertising, mostly on television. By 1970, its entire advertising budget was just under $200,000. Comet and Ajax had steadily gained market share, while Bon Ami's dwindled. When Faultless Starch Co. bought the company in 1971 for about $1 million, market share was around 1 percent. At least two-thirds of grocery stores in the United States did not stock Bon Ami, and even its competitors thought the company had gone out of business.

A New Start in the 1970s

The president of Faultless Starch was Gordon T. Beaham III, great-grandson of the company's founder. According to an interview with the *New York Times* (April 19, 1972), Beaham promised to give the Bon Ami brand "the tender loving care which it hasn't had in the last 25 years." The starch market was contracting by as much as 10 to 15 percent a year, according to Beaham's estimate, and his company needed to push a second product line to balance this out. Beaham saw unique characteristics in Bon Ami that the leading cleansers did not have. Besides being backed by huge companies with impressive advertising budgets, the leading cleansers had an advantage with consumers because they contained a host of "modern" ingredients that Bon Ami lacked, namely bleaches, disinfectants, perfumes, and dyes. Beaham hoped to turn this around and make Bon Ami stand out as a simpler, safer, old-fashioned cleanser. Chlorine and phosphates had been singled out by environmentalists as harmful chemicals, and Bon Ami had never had these ingredients. Beaham also hoped that Bon Ami would fit in with consumers who were keen on health and fitness. As the least abrasive cleanser on the market, Bon Ami required more "el-

bow grease," and Beaham speculated that health-conscious consumers would not mind this. Beaham wrote a letter that was printed in the 1974 *Whole Earth Catalog* explaining that Bon Ami was environmentally safe. That year, the company also changed its name to Faultless Starch/Bon Ami Co. Beaham stressed environmentalism as a selling point for his products and as a philosophy. He later became chairman of the National Parks and Conservation Association.

By 1983, Bon Ami's market share had risen from about 1 percent the year Faultless took it over to about 5 percent. The brand was distributed in approximately 95 percent of the nation's grocery stores, up from 35 percent a decade earlier. Yet effective advertising for the brand was still difficult. Though Beaham had hoped to raise market share to around 15 percent, in 1983 he told *Forbes* (September 12, 1983) that maintaining the 5 percent level was "like pushing water uphill." The company spent close to $1 million on advertising for Bon Ami in 1982, mostly on magazine ads, yet Bon Ami was afraid to call too much attention to itself and thus rouse the interest of Colgate-Palmolive and Procter & Gamble, its well-heeled competitors. So it tried some more unusual marketing routes. For example, the company sponsored a tour in the early 1980s for a woman who had written a book about living with chemical sensitivities. The author, Debra Lynn Dadd, touted Bon Ami as the only cleanser people with this problem could use.

Growth in the 1980s–90s

The company's sales in the early 1980s stood at around $15 million. Laundry starch began to return to popularity in the late 1970s, when fashions changed to include more natural textiles and a more finished look. Faultless Starch/Bon Ami Co. brought out several laundry starch line extensions in the 1980s, including Lemon Starch, Lite Starch, Heavy Starch, and Wrinkle Remover. The company also found receptive markets overseas. Faultless Starch was popular in the Arab world, where men starched their white headdresses. The company also commanded a large military market, because people in uniform needed starch for maintaining crisp creases. Both the domestic and export business seemed to be thriving for Faultless Starch during the 1980s. By the mid-1990s, sales for the company were estimated at around $35 million. The company had begun exporting the Faultless line to Russia and China, and now commanded some 10 percent of the global market for laundry starch.

Faultless Starch/Bon Ami Co. also added to its product roster in the 1980s and 1990s. In the early 1980s, it began distributing a German-made adjustable garden tool called the Garden Weasel. It began making garden statues out of recycled metal at a Humansville, Missouri, factory in the mid-1990s and selling them through nurseries. In the 1990s, the company also brought out a new line of cleaners, Steel Glo. Steel Glo was meant to clean fine cookware safely and was prized by cooks for the polish it gave to stainless steel. In 1997, the company acquired a new brand of laundry starch and sizing called Magic.

The neighborhood around the company's oldest manufacturing plant was swept by fire in 1998. In addition to rebuilding its own plant, Faultless Starch/Bon Ami Co. spearheaded rebuilding efforts in the surrounding district, a rather dilapidated industrial area known as the West Bottoms. The company hoped to restore the neighborhood, which was full of historic buildings.

In 2002, Faultless Starch/Bon Ami Co. was still owned and managed by members of the founding Beaham family. The fifth generation of the family was now in place, with David Beaham as president. Both its main product lines had weathered great changes over more than one hundred years on the market. Faultless Starch adapted technologically, with the transition to spray starch, and then maintained itself even through a drastically shrinking market in the 1970s. Though Bon Ami had almost gone out of business at one point, it now holds a respectable third place in the cleanser market.

Principal Competitors

Colgate-Palmolive Company; Procter & Gamble Company; CPC International Inc.

Further Reading

"Bon Ami Attacks Cohn Firm's Suit," *New York Times*, September 1, 1962, p. 29.

"Bon Ami Faces Ouster," *New York Times*, May 2, 1958, p. 39.

"Bon Ami Now Scratches for Soap Market Share," *New York Times*, March 21, 1983, pp. D1, D7.

"Court Rules Out Bon Ami Receiver," *New York Times*, September 12, 1962, p. 51.

Davis, Jim, "Faultless Sees Rise of West Bottoms," *Kansas City Business Journal*, December 25, 1998, p. 1.

Dorfman, John R., "Peep, Peep," *Forbes*, September 12, 1983, p. 206.

Dougherty, Philip H., "Advertising: Bon Ami's Plans," *New York Times*, April 19, 1972, p. 74.

"Eversley Childs, Industrialist, 87," *New York Times*, December 21, 1953, p. 31.

Gilmore, Casey, "No Junkyard Dogs Here," *Kansas City Business Journal*, September 16, 1994, p. 52.

Hammer, Alexander, "Control of Bon Ami Co. Sought by Tel-A-Sign, Inc., of Chicago," *New York Times*, July 26, 1962, p. 33.

"Lestoil Acquires Bon Ami Control," *New York Times*, August 27, 1963, p. 41.

Lilley, Valerie, "Keeping the Crease," *Kansas City Business Journal*, May 17, 1996, p. 13.

Wise, T.A., "The World of Alexander Guterma," *Fortune*, December 1959, pp. 144–64.

—A. Woodward

Faygo Beverages Inc.

3579 Gratiot Avenue
Detroit, Michigan 48207-1829
U.S.A.
Telephone: (313) 925-1600
Toll Free: (800) 347-6591
Fax: (313) 925-6311
Web site: http://www.faygo.com

Wholly Owned Subsidiary of National Beverage
  Corporation
Incorporated: 1907 as Feigenson Brothers Bottling
  Works
Employees: 550
Sales: $100 million (2002 est.)
NAIC: 312111 Soft Drink Manufacturing

Faygo Beverages Inc. is a regional soft drink bottling company based in Detroit, Michigan, that distributes its products to stores in 33 states, with Michigan, Ohio, Indiana, and western Pennsylvania its primary sales area. In addition to sodas, Faygo also makes non-carbonated sweetened fruit-flavored drinks and seltzer waters. Faygo products are sold at a lower price than national brands, and many flavors are directly inspired by popular competitors such as Mountain Dew, Dr. Pepper, Vernors, and Canada Dry Ginger Ale. The company was purchased in 1987 by National Beverage Corporation of Florida, which also owns West Coast soda maker Shasta and several other beverage companies.

Beginnings

Faygo was founded by two brothers, Ben and Perry Feigenson, who had immigrated to Detroit, Michigan, from their native Russia. Trained as bakers, the Feigensons adapted the flavorings of some of their cake frostings and, under the name Feigenson Brothers Bottling Works, began to bottle strawberry, fruit punch, and grape-flavored soft drinks in November 1907. They would manufacture a batch of drinks, then close the production line and take their products around on a horse-drawn wagon to sell them, as the beverages contained no preservatives and were best consumed fresh. They charged three cents for one soda, and a nickel for two. In the winter, when beverage sales dropped, they also sold bread and fish to make ends meet. To save money the brothers and their families lived above the small bottling plant.

Over the next decade the soda business grew, and the Feigensons were soon able to buy their own homes. They also hired their first employees and bought a second horse-drawn wagon for deliveries. New flavors were added, including Sassafras Soda and Lithiated Lemon, which used lithium salt as a flavoring agent. Taking a cue from the sound the carbonated beverages made when a bottle was opened, they also began calling their products "pop." The company's success was such that a new plant was needed, and one was built on Beaubien Street in Detroit.

In 1921 the firm abbreviated its name to "Faygo" because it fit more easily on the bottles. The Feigenson brothers also purchased their first delivery truck and began to make home deliveries in 1923. A vanilla flavored soft drink, a seltzer water, "Ace Hi" (an imitation of the popular soda NeHi), and the destined-to-be classic Rock & Rye flavor were introduced during the 1920s as well. Rock & Rye, a fruity, spicy soda, took its name from the popular jazz-age drink of Rye whiskey served over a "rock" of sugar. In 1935 Faygo moved its operations to a larger bottling plant on Gratiot Avenue in Detroit.

The 1940s was a decade of transition for the company. The postwar years saw a new generation of Feigensons enter the business when Perry's son Mort and his cousin Phil joined the firm. Television was also beginning to take hold with Americans, and the company decided to begin advertising in the new medium. Faygo hired the Detroit-based W.B. Doner Co. to create the spots. New flavors developed during the decade included chocolate creme, a richer-tasting root beer, and Uptown, a lemon-lime soda inspired by 7 Up.

Television Leading the Way
to Greater Success: 1950s–70s

The early 1950s saw an increase in television advertising and the debuts of animated characters The Faygo Kid and

Herkimer the Bottle Blower. Spots featuring the former used the memorable tagline, "Remember Black Bart? Which way did he go? Which way did he go? He went for Faaaaygoooooo!" In ads featuring Herkimer, the character changed from tired to energetic after taking a sip of the fizzy beverage. The Faygo Kid ad was later inducted into the Advertising Hall of Fame. The company also sponsored the popular children's program of comic Soupy Sales, who pitched the company's soda with the line, "George Washington may be the father of our country, but Faygo's the pop." The television advertising went over well, and Faygo solidified its position as a leading beverage maker in Michigan and several surrounding states. In other developments of the 1950s the company upgraded its manufacturing plant and installed new water treatment equipment. More flavors were also created, including Black Cherry and Faygo Tango, an imitation of the popular grapefruit-flavored Squirt.

A new line of "Royal" flavors was introduced in the early 1960s, which sold for a slightly higher price. One of these, Royal Hawaiian Pineapple Orange, turned out to be a near disaster for the company on its initial run. The pineapple extract used in the flavoring, which was obtained from the Dole company, had not been sterilized, and a few days after the product hit the stores bottles began to explode on shelves and at the factory. The flavor extract had turned rancid and was generating a buildup of gas in the bottles that caused their tops to shoot off. Faygo quickly recalled the product, and Dole supplied enough sterilized juice to cover the company's losses. After the problem had been corrected, the flavor went on to become a popular one. Other new varieties of the early 1960s included Frosh (a Fresca imitation), Moonshine (inspired by Mountain Dew), Dr. Mort (like Dr. Pepper, and named after Mort Feigenson, by now the company's president), an apple-flavored soda called Eve, a ginger beer named Faygo Brau, and a nonalcoholic, wine-like soda called Chateaux Faygeaux. As with many other flavors that were introduced over the years, a number eventually fell by the wayside, Frosh being the most durable (though Moonshine and Dr. Mort were both revived years later). The 1960s also saw Faygo introduce a full line of artificially sweetened diet sodas, which soon came to account for half the firm's revenues. At the end of the decade the company changed the name of one of its original and most popular flavors, Strawberry Soda, to Redpop.

Faygo began advertising its products on broadcasts of Detroit Tigers baseball games in 1965. As the geographic reach of the ads exceeded the company's distribution, the firm's ad agency duly tried to have the spots canceled on stations that were beyond its service area. When they were unable to do so, they suggested that Faygo try distributing its soda to these places. The company took up the challenge, and in so doing created a new distribution method. Rather than trucking its products to each individual store, the firm now began to ship much of its output directly to the warehouses of wholesale food brokers. Faygo also ramped up production of disposable containers for use by its more distant customers. The move paid off, helping sales jump from $6 million in 1966 to $20.4 million in 1971.

A new series of television ads that began airing in the early 1970s spawned a hit song of sorts for the company. The spots featured a character named Great Gildersleeve singing a song called "Remember When You Were a Kid," while riding on the boat that took Detroiters to Bob-lo Island, an amusement park on the Detroit River. Viewers began requesting a copy of the song, and the recording was pressed on 45 rpm records, 75,000 of which were sold for 25 cents each. The company's diet soft drink line also remained popular, and Detroit Lions football player-turned actor Alex Karras was signed as its spokesperson. Faygo's advertising presence remained strong, with 4 percent of gross revenues typically channeled into this area.

New Deposit Law Causing Problems: Mid-1970s

In the mid-1970s Michigan passed a beverage container deposit law which drastically affected the company's fortunes when it was implemented in 1978. Betting that the public would prefer returnable cans, Faygo geared up for its production by adding new production lines. But glass returnables, which got a strong push from Pepsi and Coke, turned out to be the choice of consumers, and Faygo had problems switching its plant back to bottles. The company's bottom line took a hit for several years before the situation was resolved.

Faygo had retained ad agency W.B. Doner since the late 1940s, but in 1975 decided to look elsewhere after what seemed to be a creative dry spell. The company went through five firms before returning to Doner in 1980. The agency soon came up with spots for Faygo's diet line that featured nationally known comedienne Joan Rivers. Though her fee was considerably higher than what the company had previously paid for talent, the expense was approved by Mort Feigenson, and the spots did well for the firm. Feigenson prided himself on getting the most for his advertising dollar, and was insistent on making Faygo's ads look as good as those of national competitors such as Coke and Pepsi.

Sale of Business to TreeSweet: 1986

As the second generation of Feigensons neared retirement age, they began to take stock of the company's future. Regional bottlers around the United States were in serious decline (dropping from 10,000 in the 1930s to less than 2,500 in 1983), and Faygo was facing increasing marginalization in the beverage marketplace. Though the company's products were frequently equal in quality to the big names, Faygo generally attracted customers by selling for a lower price and offering knock-offs of many popular national drinks. In 1986 the Feigenson family decided to sell the business to TreeSweet, a Texas-based juice maker, who initially vowed to make Faygo a national brand. However, a few months later TreeSweet sold the firm to National Beverage Corp. of Fort Lauderdale, Florida, a holding company which had been formed in 1985 to buy Shasta Beverages from Sara Lee Foods. California-based Shasta, like Faygo, was a regional soft drink bottler with a long history. Shasta had been the first company to put soft drinks in cans, which it

Key Dates:

1907:	Ben and Perry Feigenson begin bottling soft drinks in Detroit.
1921:	Company changes name to Faygo.
1935:	Operations move to larger plant on Gratiot Avenue.
1950s:	Use of animated television spots helps boost sales.
1960s:	Company introduces diet soft drinks, which soon comprise half of sales.
1961:	Royal line is introduced; Orange Pineapple flavor is recalled after bottles burst.
1965:	Distribution expands after ads begin to run on Detroit Tigers' broadcasts.
1978:	Michigan container deposit bill is passed; Faygo has difficulty adapting.
1986:	Feigenson family sells business to TreeSweet Companies.
1987:	TreeSweet sells Faygo to National Beverage Corp.
1996:	Ohana non-carbonated beverage line is introduced.
2001:	New logo and nostalgic line of glass-bottled sodas debut.

pioneered in 1954. Under National Beverage, Faygo was mostly left to continue on its own path.

The mid-1980s also saw Faygo introduce a line of flavored carbonated bottled water, which became popular, especially in Michigan. The beverage marketplace grew increasingly diversified during the 1990s, and the company introduced a number of new products, including a line of non-carbonated drinks in 1996. Dubbed Ohana, it initially offered Punch, Mango Punch, Lemon Iced Tea, Lemonade, and Kiwi-Strawberry flavors. The following year, 1997, marked Faygo's 90th anniversary, and the company published a special recipe book in celebration that included dishes that used Faygo sodas as ingredients. By this time the company's sales were estimated at $100 million, and Faygo claimed a 12 percent share of the soda market in Michigan. The firm's beverages were still mainly produced at its Gratiot plant, which had expanded over the years to 300,000 square feet through the incorporation of adjacent bottling facilities once owned by Pepsi and Coke. The stitched-together factory was limiting the company's output, however, and a new site was being sought. Faygo sodas were also produced in 11 other plants around the country as needed, distribution extending to 33 states by this time. While continuing to ship in bulk to chainstore warehouses, the company maintained more than 50 trucks to deliver to smaller outlets.

In 1998 Faygo introduced a web site that offered its beverages for sale by mail to homesick midwesterners. The late 1990s also saw the company receive a spate of unanticipated publicity from the nationally popular Detroit shock-rap group Insane Clown Posse, who featured lyrics about Faygo in their songs and sprayed audiences with shaken bottles of Faygo soda.

Faygo's logo and packaging were redesigned in 2001 for the second time in a decade. The new look was a softer, more nostalgic one that capitalized on the firm's long history and good-time image. In the summer of 2001 a line of retro-styled 16 ounce glass-bottled sodas was also introduced. Sold at a premium price, the bottles (in a limited number of flavors) utilized the company's 1950s logo design. By this time glass bottles had declined to only 1 percent of the total market, down from nearly 9 percent a decade earlier, with plastic bottles and cans accounting equally for the majority of containers used.

Nearly a century after it was founded, Faygo continued to produce flavorful, moderately priced beverages for customers around the Midwest and Middle Atlantic. While it would likely never be a national presence in the highly competitive soft drink marketplace, the trend away from cola drinks boded well for the flavor-focused company. Its proud regional heritage and unique offerings such as Redpop and Rock & Rye earned it a warm spot in the hearts of both loyal, longtime consumers and a new generation of converts.

Principal Competitors

The Coca-Cola Company; PepsiCo, Inc.; Dr. Pepper/Seven Up, Inc.; Cott Corporation.

Further Reading

Deierlein, Robert, "The Mouse That Roared: Taking a Different Approach in Many Areas Pays off for Faygo," *Beverage World*, May 1990, p. 60.
Haldane, Neal, "Faygo Brings Back Glass Bottles for Pop," *Detroit News*, June 5, 2001.
Hansell, Betty, "Profile: Mort Feigenson, President, Faygo Beverages, Inc.," *Detroit Free Press*, March 7, 1983, p. 1B.
Hunter, George, "Flavors, Prices Give Faygo an Edge in a Glutted Market," *Detroit News*, August 28, 1997, p. 1B.
"Revised Strategy: Stay Alive or Dive Were Faygo's Options," *Michigan Business*, December, 1986, p. 31.
Rudolph, Barbara, "Bottle Scars," *Forbes*, February 15, 1982, p. 76.
Stearns, Patty Lanoue, "Faygo Flavor Wizard Helps Detroit's Historic Pop Bottler Create the Fizz of the Future," *Detroit Free Press*, August 30, 1995, p. 1F.
Stopa, Marsha, "Seeks Site in City for New Plant," *Crain's Detroit Business*, August 4, 1997, p. 3.
Walsh, Tom, "Faygo Chugs Along," *Detroit Free Press*, October 10, 2002.
Wernle, Bradford, "Quick Moves Make Faygo a Pop Star," *Crain's Detroit Business*, September 20, 1993, p. 3.

—Frank Uhle

LeblanC ◉

G. Leblanc Corporation

7001 Leblanc Avenue
Kenosha, Wisconsin 53141
U.S.A.
Telephone: (262) 658-1644
Fax: (262) 658-2824
Web site: http://www.gleblanc.com

Private Company
Incorporated: 1946 as Leblanc USA
Employees: 500
Sales: $65 million (2001 est.)
NAIC: 339992 Musical Instrument Manufacturing

The G. Leblanc Corporation is one of the world's leading makers of woodwind and brass instruments. The company manufactures instruments under the brand names Leblanc, Noblet, Normandy, Vito, Holton, Martin, and Courtois. Leblanc's Holton subsidiary is the world's largest maker of French horns, and makes other brass instruments as well. Leblanc's Martin subsidiary is known for an esteemed line of trumpets, and specializes in smaller brasses. Leblanc also manufactures instrument cases and woodwind mouthpieces. Leblanc operates three factories in the United States, in Kenosha and Elkhorn, Wisconsin, and one plant in La Couture-Boussey, France. The company was originally set up as a joint venture with a French company, Leblanc S.A. Leblanc S.A. was one of the oldest corporations in France, tracing its roots back to 1750. Leblanc USA purchased a majority interest in the French company in 1989, then acquired the entire firm in 1993. Leblanc has been a key promoter of school music programs in the United States from the 1950s onward. The company manufactured an improved line of instruments for beginning students and helped establish the type of instrument rental practice that is now an industry standard. The company helped organize the school musical instrument sales industry, and its efforts led to the founding of the National Association of School Music Dealers.

18th-Century French Antecedents

The G. Leblanc Corporation harks back to the reign of Louis XV in France. The king promoted music at his court, leading to a new French musical instrument industry. The firm of Ets. D. Noblet was founded in 1750 in La Couture-Boussey to make woodwind instruments. Noblet was known for its clarinets and helped make France a European center for woodwind manufacturing. Members of the Noblet family operated the company until 1904. In that year, the last Noblet died without an heir, so the firm passed to Georges Leblanc. Leblanc was also a member of an illustrious family of woodwind makers, thought to be the best at his craft in all France. His firm, G. Leblanc Cie., was centered in Paris. Leblanc continued to manufacture the Noblet line of clarinets at La Couture-Boussey, while making improvements to Leblanc instruments in his Paris workshop. The business was a family affair. While Georges fought in World War I, his wife Clemence managed the factory. Later his son Leon greatly expanded and improved the business. The Leblanc family also worked with Charles Houvenaghel, a famed acoustic scientist. Houvenaghel and Leblanc set up an acoustical research laboratory, the first of its kind, and applied their research to instrument manufacture. Leblanc and Houvenaghel designed new clarinets in unusual ranges. They eventually made a line of clarinets ranging from the piccolo-like sopranino to the extremely low octo-contrabass—a whole clarinet choir, with a greater pitch spread than a string orchestra.

Leon Leblanc took his company's scientific principles even farther. Leon was a gifted clarinetist who took the top prize at the Paris Conservetoire as a young man. Although he could have had a great career as a performer, Leon chose to stay with the family business and apply his musical insight to instrument manufacture. He dedicated his life to bringing acoustical, mechanical, and musical improvements to woodwind instruments. Although Leblanc's instruments were almost entirely handmade, Leon Leblanc insisted that the craftsmen follow careful measurements. "Music is an art, but it is still governed by the laws of science," he declared (*Music Trades,* July 1996). As a result, Leblanc instruments were more consistent than those that had come before. The company continued to strive for consistent quality, ease of playability, and mechanical innovation, throughout its history.

Postwar Beginnings of the American Firm

G. Leblanc Cie. had worked with an American distributor since 1921. It gave exclusive rights to U.S. distribution to Walter Gretsch, who ran the large musical instrument company Gretsch & Brenner. Although the Leblanc family had strong personal ties to Walter Gretsch, the arrangement had many problems. The Leblanc instruments came from France by sea, and arrived in New York in terrible shape, out of tune and sticky from two weeks of exposure to damp and cold. Gretsch sold the instruments in this condition, much to the distress of the French manufacturer. But because Gretsch handled many product lines, he did not devote particular care to the Leblanc clarinets, and he did not have the time to acclimate and recondition the imports. Thus, the Leblancs were already thinking of an alternative to this distributorship when they met a young U.S. soldier in 1945. This was Vito Pascucci.

Pascucci grew up in Kenosha, Wisconsin, the son of Italian immigrants of modest means. His family had a musical bent, and Vito began playing the trumpet as a young boy. By the time he was 12, he was traveling to Chicago on weekends for lessons. After his lesson, he used to stop in at the Chicago Musical Instrument Company and watch the repairmen. When he was a teenager, he began repairing instruments in the back of a music store run by his older brother, Ben. In 1943, Pascucci was drafted into the army. He applied to join the army band, and was given a spot as the band repairman. Pascucci's band included three former members of the Cleveland Symphony, and with this kind of competition, he could not make it as a trumpet player. But later the famed swing band leader Glenn Miller began putting together his own army band. He snagged the symphony players, and they recommended he take Vito Pascucci as well. When Pascucci got a letter ordering him to report to the Glenn Miller band, he thought it was a hoax. Pascucci spent days trying to get the letter authenticated. He had no idea how Miller would have heard of him. When they finally met, Pascucci recalled that Miller treated him like a nonentity. But Pascucci had a chance to show his skills when a bandmate came to him with a smashed trumpet that he needed to be able to play the next morning. Pascucci worked all night and repaired the damaged trumpet with only a broomstick. Miller was impressed, and they began having lunch together every day. They became good friends, and came up with a plan to launch a chain of Glenn Miller Music Stores when the war was over. They planned to import European instruments, which were of better quality than U.S.-made ones.

Glenn Miller's plane disappeared over the English Channel on December 15, 1944. Pascucci was crushed at the loss of his friend. Nevertheless, he went on with plans he and Miller had made, and arranged to visit musical instrument factories in France. He wanted to meet the maker of Noblet clarinets, because he had seen those instruments at the Chicago Musical Instruments store he used to haunt as a child. Someone directed him to the Leblanc factory in La Couture-Boussey, where he met Georges and Leon Leblanc. The family had suffered during the German occupation. The Leblancs had had to trade clarinets for food in order to survive. The factory was down to only 20 workers, and raw materials were virtually non-existent. But the family instantly took to the young American repairman, showing him the workshop and teaching him some new skills. When he told the Leblancs about the Glenn Miller Music Stores idea, they instead asked him to distribute their instruments in the United States. Pascucci was taken aback. He felt that he did not know enough about business to take on such a responsibility. But the Leblancs liked him and trusted him. He left the factory with a duffel bag full of clarinets, and Leon Leblanc promised to meet him in the United States when the war was over.

Leblanc kept his promise and wired Pascucci to come to New York in 1946. The first order of business was to sever the firm's relationship with Gretsch & Brenner. Walter Gretsch had died, and the Leblanc business contract had passed to his daughter Gertrude. Gertrude happened to be married to John Jacob Astor, one of the wealthiest men in the country. Pascucci could not believe Leblanc would choose him, a poor Wisconsin boy, to run the U.S. distributorship, rather than the Astors. But all this worked out, and Pascucci entered a 50–50 partnership with G. Leblanc Cie., forming Leblanc USA in May 1946. Although Leblanc had wanted Pascucci to work in New York, where the musical instruments import business was centered, Pascucci insisted on returning to his hometown. So he signed a lease for a tiny storefront in Kenosha. He began by taking in the Leblanc instruments and making them playable, something Walter Gretsch had never bothered to do. Demand for musical instruments was on the rise, with the war over and a return to peacetime activities. With the baby boom that followed the war, school music programs also grew quickly, and Leblanc USA began supplying inexpensive instruments for beginners.

Expansion in the 1960s

The school market was the best opportunity for the young company, as the country's school-age population swelled. The company began importing inexpensive, durable instruments that were easy to play. It began in the 1950s with a line of metal clarinets. But plastic clarinets were already popular, so the firm abandoned metal and began making plastic student instruments. Demand was so great that the French factory could not supply enough. So Leblanc USA began manufacturing its own instruments for the first time, forming the plastic bodies and fitting them with French-made keys. This new line was given the name "Vito." Eventually the entire "Vito" clarinet line was made in Kenosha, including the keys. The small factory expanded in 1953, and then again several times in the 1960s.

Key Dates:

1750: Noblet is established in France.
1904: Noblet passes the business to the Leblanc family.
1921: Leblanc begins distribution of clarinets in the United States.
1946: Pascucci founds Leblanc USA in Kenosha.
1964: The company acquires the Frank Holton Company.
1971: The company acquires the Martin Band Instrument Company.
1989: A 65 percent interest in the French parent is acquired.
1993: A U.S. firm completes the acquisition of Leblanc S.A.
2000: Leon Leblanc dies; the U.S. plants are expanded and upgraded.

Leblanc worked to tame the school music industry, which had been a highly fractured market. In 1950 the company hired a music educator, Ernest Moore, to work on educational programs and materials for music teachers. Leblanc was the first wind instrument manufacturer to hire a music educator, and it continued to keep the post filled with distinguished pedagogues up to the present time. Leblanc also began organizing monthly meetings for musical instrument dealers, giving them a chance to compare notes and discuss ways to improve the business. The dealers who met under Leblanc's auspices adopted a rent-to-own policy, whereby students rented an instrument for a year and the payments could be put toward an eventual purchase. This became the standard way the student music industry worked, and it made sense for both the students and the instrument dealers. Some of the dealers who had met at the Leblanc meetings later organized the professional group the National Association of School Music Dealers.

By the late 1950s, Leblanc had become a major player in the school music industry. But its product line was limited to woodwinds. In 1964 the company acquired the Frank Holton Company, a maker of brass instruments. Holton was founded in Chicago in 1898 by a former trombonist with the John Philip Sousa band. In 1917 Holton moved to Elkhorn, Wisconsin. Leblanc bought the company, gaining its dominant Collegiate brand of student brass instruments. Under Leblanc's management, the Holton company began improving its French horn manufacturing. The firm developed a prized line of French horns, valued by professional players around the world. Holton eventually became the world's largest manufacturer of French horns. It also makes trombones, euphoniums, and other large horns.

Leblanc diversified further in 1968, when it bought The Woodwind Company. This was a small company that specialized in making woodwind mouthpieces. Around the same time it also bought an instrument case manufacturer, the Bublitz Case Company. Bublitz was based in Elkhart, Indiana. In 1971 Leblanc bought another Elkhart company, the Martin Band Instrument Company. Martin was the oldest band instrument manufacturer in the country, excepting the time it had been closed down for the Great Chicago Fire. It made a line of brass instruments, including the Martin Committee trumpet, an instrument still prized by jazz players today. Leblanc closed down Martin's Elkhart plant and moved manufacturing to a new facility in Kenosha. Leblanc also cut the overlap between its two brass subsidiaries by concentrating the making of trumpets and other small horns at Martin and letting Holton specialize in the larger instruments.

Leblanc expanded its facilities to make room for the new product lines and updated the Elkhorn and Kenosha factories. Leblanc constantly improved the technology it used to build instruments, following Leon Leblanc's dictum that science governed music. The firm designed and built much of the machinery it needed to automate the manufacturing process. Pascucci also insisted that the factory be a pleasant place to work, despite the prevalence of machines. Workers looked through glass walls into a garden, and quiet hallways were hung with paintings. Pascucci himself continued to innovate, developing new manufacturing methods as well as new models and new instruments. The company prepared for five years before it began making a new instrument, the descant horn, in the 1970s. By 1980, Leblanc had become the third largest manufacturer of wind instruments in the United States.

Buying the French Firm in the 1980s

In 1975 Pascucci's son Leon (named for Leon Leblanc) joined the company, beginning as vice-president for advertising. The younger Pascucci contributed to the striking interior design of the Leblanc headquarters, and became known for staging beautiful exhibits at industry trade shows. He seemed to have the artistry and flair that was vital to the firm's image. In the 1980s, Vito Pascucci began thinking of buying out the French firm. Leon Leblanc, born in 1900, was an elderly man with no heirs. It seemed natural that Pascucci would take over. He and his son would continue to run the company along the lines Leblanc had established. Pascucci began seriously negotiating the sale in 1986. Leblanc himself was all for giving Pascucci control. But the transaction involved selling one of the oldest businesses in France to an American, and this was difficult for the French government to abide. When Pascucci made his first inquiries, the French Ministry of Trade told him that odds were 100 to one against his ever buying Leblanc.

Over the next three years Pascucci made more than 20 trips to Paris to meet with French government officials. Because of the age of its Noblet subsidiary, Leblanc was considered a national treasure. Pascucci finally won approval to buy 65 percent of Leblanc S.A., as the French company was then known. But the deal was so sensitive that the French prime minister, Francois Mitterand, had to okay it. After the purchase, the Leblanc company sent a survey to clarinetists all over the world, asking their input for future clarinet models. The company then brought out a new line of improved instruments, which were made at the French factory in La Couture-Boussey. In 1991, Leon Pascucci became president of G. Leblanc Corporation. In 1993, the U.S. firm completed its acquisition of Leblanc S.A., acquiring the remaining 35 percent of the company. The new legal arrangements made little difference to how the company operated. The French factory employed about 100 workers, and the U.S. factories about 400. Overall sales were estimated at $37.5 million.

New Technology in the 2000s

Leon Pascucci was credited with continuing the drive toward automation at the company. This meant not only in the factory areas but in accounting and sales. Pascucci also served as president of the National Association of Band Instrument Manufacturers, an industry group that helped raise money for school music programs. He also helped the city of Kenosha raise funds for a bandshell on the Lake Michigan shore, and sustained the community band and orchestra. In 2000, the company began a multimillion dollar expansion. The main Kenosha plant doubled in size, and the company brought in scores of new machines. The firm stopped using toxic materials, such as brass cleaners, in favor of environmentally sound and efficient processes like sonic buffers. Leon Leblanc died that year, at the age of 99. The company was still operating on the principles he had laid out, with mechanical efficiency wedded to artistic production. In 2001 the G. Leblanc Corporation was given an ''Industry World Leadership'' award by the Wisconsin Manufacturers & Commerce association, the state's largest business group. The award noted the bold steps the company had taken in implementing new technology.

In 2003 the company's French factory was damaged by a suspicious fire. The ancient La Couture-Boussey plant suffered more than $3 million of damage, but volunteer fire fighters put out the flames before the building was destroyed. Although some inventory was lost, the factory's valuable stock of antique hardwood was not harmed. The factory was back in production about two months after the fire.

Principal Subsidiaries

Frank Holton Company; Martin Band Instrument Company; Woodwind Company; Bublitz Case Company.

Principal Competitors

Conn-Selmer, Inc.; Yamaha Corporation.

Further Reading

Bednarek, David I., ''G. Leblanc Strives for Perfect Pitch,'' *Milwaukee Journal,* June 20, 1993, p. B1.

Dunn, Michael J., III, ''The Musical World of G. Leblanc,'' *Wisconsin Trails,* Summer 1980, p. 35.

''Improving Productivity and Quality, Pursuing the Perfect Clarinet,'' *Music Trades,* July 2000, p. 162.

''Leblanc Turns 50,'' *Music Trades,* July 1996, p. 134.

''Leblanc U.S. Buys Leblanc Paris,'' *Music Trades,* June 1989, p. 34.

''Leon Pascucci Named Leblanc CEO,'' *Music Trades,* December 2001, p. 145.

''U.S./French Collaboration at Leblanc Yields New Pro Clarinets,'' *Music Trades,* January 1991, p. 53.

—A. Woodward

Gap Inc.

The Gap, Inc.

2 Folsom Street
San Francisco, California 94105
U.S.A.
Telephone: (650) 952-4400
Fax: (415) 427-2553
Web site: http://www.gap.com

Public Company
Incorporated: 1969 as The Gap Stores, Inc.
Employees: 169,000
Sales: $14.4 billion (2003)
Stock Exchanges: New York
Ticker Symbol: GPS
NAIC: 448140 Family Clothing Stores

Founded as a single store by Donald G. Fisher and wife Doris, The Gap, Inc. has evolved into a major retail company with well known brands, including its namesake, Banana Republic, and Old Navy. The firm sells a variety of casual-style and urbane chic clothing to men, women, and children in over 4,250 stores across the United States and in Canada, France, Japan, Germany, and the United Kingdom. The Gap flourished through the 1980s and 1990s under the leadership of Millard ''Mickey'' Drexler but has battled tough times in the early years of the new century. Drexler retired in 2002, and Paul Pressler was named CEO while Fisher remained chairman.

Capitalizing on the Generation Gap: 1969–75

Donald Fisher was not of the generation to whom The Gap owes its popularity. A member of a family that made its home in California for generations, Fisher was 40 years old and a successful real estate developer in 1969 when he took note of a new trend among the city's increasingly disaffected youth. Blue jeans, for years made chiefly by Levi Strauss & Co. for laborers and outdoorsmen, were suddenly becoming a part of the counterculture's standard costume. Durable, cheap, comfortable, and acceptably offbeat, jeans were the perfect uniform for a generation of young people anxious to demonstrate its antipathy to corporate America.

Fisher was said to have conceived of The Gap when he was unable to find the right size of Levi's in a department store in Sacramento, California. He realized that jeans had become more popular than current merchandising outlets could accommodate, and like hamburgers, stereo equipment, and gasoline, they could be sold through a chain of small stores devoted solely to that product. With the help of his wife, Doris, Fisher opened a shop near San Francisco State University in one of his own buildings, offering a combination of records and jeans. Their intention was to attract jeans customers by means of the records, but at first no one noticed the jeans, and Fisher was driven close to bankruptcy. In desperation, he placed ads in local newspapers announcing the sale of ''four tons'' of jeans at rock-bottom prices, and the clothes were soon gone. To emphasize the youthful ambiance of his new store, Fisher named it The Gap, an allusion to a then hot topic, the Generation Gap.

When Fisher incorporated his business as The Gap Stores, Inc., it was an immediate success. Although the Fishers had no experience in retailing, their stores' combination of jeans, low prices, and wide selection proved irresistible to the huge market of 14- to 25-year-olds. Fisher added new outlets in San Francisco and was soon enjoying the benefits of chain store merchandising: centralized buying and advertising, excellent name recognition, and uniform pricing. Initially, The Gap Stores' buying program was singularly uncomplicated, as the stores carried only one product, jeans by Levi Strauss & Co. The stores were brightly painted, often orange, filled with circular metal display racks known as ''rounders,'' and usually enlivened by rock and roll music. To hold down rental costs, the Fishers kept stores small—about 3,000 to 4,000 square feet. They located most of their stores in shopping centers, many of them enclosed in malls.

Two years after opening its first stores, The Gap's sales were running at $2.5 million annually, and the Fishers converted the company into a public corporation, though they retained the great majority of stock. With extraordinary celerity, they opened stores across the United States while maintaining tight control over the critical accounting, purchasing, and marketing functions of what was soon a sizable corporation. In five years, sales had increased almost 50-fold, to $97 million, and the number of stores had grown to 186, spread over 21 states. Analysts credited the company's success to the Fishers' observance of a few cardinal rules of retailing: Gap stores replaced its stock with maximum speed; its prices were low and stayed that way; big sellers were kept on the rack until they stopped moving, rather than being retired in favor of new styles simply for the sake of novelty; and only a few items were stocked—jeans, shirts, light jackets—each offered in its complete range of colors and sizes, ensuring a minimum of disappointed customers.

The company's growth was also made possible by the extensive national advertising of Levi Strauss, which provided 100 percent of The Gap's merchandise during its early years. Such dependence on a single supplier had obvious dangers, however, and around 1973 The Gap began marketing several labels of its own, as well as national brands other than Levi's. These proved crucial to the company's short- and long-term health; by 1975 Gap stores generated $100 million in net sales.

Ups and Downs: 1976–80

By 1976, the Fishers were ready to make their first substantial public stock offering. The company's spectacular growth had attracted widespread interest, and its offering of 1.2 million shares sold quickly at $18 per share in May. Coincidentally, however, the retail industry went into a steep slide, which, when combined with The Gap's large expenditures for new stores, pushed the company into the red for the final quarter of its fiscal year, ending July 31. The value of the newly issued stock fell to $7.25, prompting nine separate class-action suits from outraged stock purchasers who alleged that the Fishers had tried to dump their holdings before The Gap announced its bad news. These charges came despite the fact that the Fishers sold only about 10 percent of their holdings during the period in question. Rather than wage endless litigation, The Gap settled the suits in 1979 for a total of $5.8 million, or 40 cents per share, and did its best to mend its frayed relations with Wall Street.

By the end of the 1970s, the company could pay such a figure without undue strain. Adding between 50 and 80 stores annually, The Gap pushed its sales to $307 million in 1980 and was close to achieving nationwide representation. The jeans market was no longer quite so straightforward, however. Members of the great wave of youngsters who had come of age wearing blue jeans in the 1970s were now older, wealthier, and more conservative, and the Fishers were busily attempting to break out of the jeans niche by expanding The Gap's selection of clothing. Several experimental chains featuring upscale fash-

ions were essayed and brought together under the Taggs name but later liquidated because they were unprofitable. Gap stores were enlarged to handle increasing amounts of what became known as casual wear and were frequently moved outside of shopping centers to freestanding locations, where space was plentiful and rent lower per square foot.

Along with the search for a line of clothes to appeal to an older clientele, the Fishers also faced Levi Strauss & Co.'s decision to supply big mass marketers such as Sears and J.C. Penney with its jeans. Levi's were now sold everywhere, underscoring The Gap's need to develop a label and look of its own. The company's own brands, created during the 1970s, generated about 45 percent of Gap sales in 1980, with Levi's adding an equal amount and other national brands making up the balance. Considering that ten years earlier essentially all of The Gap's sales were Levi Strauss & Co. products, the 1980 figures represented an achievement, but it was clear that if the company were to avoid inundation by the rising tide of jeans discounters it would have to fashion a new, exclusively Gap image.

Mickey Comes to Town: 1981–86

To accomplish this task, Donald Fisher hired Millard "Mickey" Drexler as president in 1983. Drexler, then 40, had just solved a similar problem with AnnTaylor, creating a more chic image for the chain and quadrupling sales in the bargain. Drexler was born in the Bronx to a family with roots in the garment business and by age 23 was a buyer for Bloomingdale's. After a stint at Macy's, he became president of Ann-Taylor in 1980, where his work caught the eye of Donald Fisher, who was contemplating the future of The Gap. Drexler accepted the job as president at the end of 1983 (sales $480 million) and was given a block of stock that would make him one of the country's wealthiest retail executives.

Drexler immediately began The Gap's wholesale transformation, in spite of the company's currently excellent financial status. The new president found little that he liked; proliferating competition in jeans and The Gap's youthful marketing image had forced the company into a price-driven volume business. Its orange-painted stores were cluttered with rounders displaying merchandise of many labels that Drexler later described to the *New York Times* as "trendy but not tasteful ... well, just plain ugly." Worst of all, most consumers perceived The Gap as strictly for teenagers at a time when people who grew up in the 1960s were developing more upmarket tastes. It would be difficult to overcome The Gap's 15-year tradition as the place where kids went to pick up a pair of Levi's.

Drexler began by eliminating all private label brands but one: Gap. Levi Strauss products were kept but relegated to the background; henceforth, The Gap would be known not only as a store, but as a line of clothes as well. Drexler created a large in-house design staff to develop clothes that would be casual, simple, made of natural fibers, and more clearly differentiated by gender than were jeans. The look was informal but classic—still denim-based but including a variety of shirts, skirts, blouses, and sweaters in assorted colors and weaves. It was clothing for people who wanted to look and feel young without appearing slovenly or rebellious, a description that fit a vast number of U.S. consumers in the 1980s.

Key Dates:

1969: Don and Doris Fisher open their first store in San Francisco, California.
1976: The company offers 1.2 million shares to the public.
1983: Millard Drexler is named president; the firm acquires Banana Republic.
1986: The first GapKids store is opened.
1987: The first international store is opened in London.
1990: BabyGap is launched.
1994: The Old Navy brand is established.
1997: The Gap Web site debuts.
2002: Drexler retires; Paul Pressler is named CEO.

Gap stores were substantially revamped. Neutral grays and white replaced the garish orange, and the ubiquitous rounders gave way to shelves of neatly folded clothing under soft lighting. The company's advertising, as devised by Drexler's longtime colleague, Magdalena (Maggie) Gross, shifted from radio and television to upscale magazines and newspapers and featured older models engaged in familiar, outdoor activities that were not necessarily connected with the youth culture.

A few years later, Gross launched the ''Individuals of Style'' campaign, a series of black and white portraits of both famous and unknown subjects by a team of celebrated photographers. The ads stressed style, not The Gap, whose clothes did not always appear in all of the photos, and they were enormously successful in helping to change the public's perception of the company. The Gap came to mean good taste of an informal variety, and the brand name Gap soon acquired the cachet needed if the company were to compete with other retailers of casual wear such as Benetton and The Limited. In addition, the word ''stores'' was dropped from the company's name.

Drexler's revolution at The Gap cost a good deal of money, and financial results for 1984 were poor, with profits down 43 percent to $12.2 million. By the middle of the following year, however, it was clear he had pulled off something of a miracle. Gross revenue, profits, and same-store sales were all up; more importantly, the company had fresh energy and a merchandising focus that could carry it for years to come. In the meantime, The Gap had acquired a number of other retail chains, for better and worse. Foremost among these was Banana Republic, founded in 1979 by another California husband and wife team, Melvyn and Patricia Ziegler.

The two-store chain of safari and travel clothing outfits, bought by The Gap in 1983, had a well-established catalogue business. After its acquisition and the introduction of private-label clothing lines, Banana Republic's sales doubled each year through the mid-1980s but slowed quickly thereafter. Despite the mixed results of the Banana Republic acquisition, the company continued to seek out other chain stores. Pottery Barn was a housewares chain of about 30 stores in New York and California; after several problematic years, it was liquidated in 1986. That same year, Drexler sought to fill another clothing need of the baby boomer generation with the debut of GapKids, featuring comfortable, durable clothes for the children of par-

ents who shopped at Gap stores. The concept was a huge success, and along with Banana Republic (which peaked in the late 1980s with revenue of more than $250 million a year) figured largely in The Gap's long-range planning.

The Gap Continues Its Climb: 1987–96

By 1987, The Gap decided to try its wares outside the United States, and its first international store was opened in London. Additional stores soon sprang up throughout the United Kingdom, Canada, and France. Unfortunately, stateside, Banana Republic's safari gear bubble burst, and it became a money-losing liability. The Gap also tested the higher end of the clothing market with Hemisphere, a nine-store chain of upscale U.S. sportswear with European styling. Created in 1987, the same year the company broke $1 billion in sales, Hemisphere offered elegant fashions but soon ran afoul of a severe recession. Disposed of only two years later, neither the Hemisphere mistake or the demise of Pottery Barn was serious enough to cause more than a few tremors at the parent company, whose spectacular rebirth in the Drexler era left ample room for such experimentation.

In 1990, as Banana Republic searched for secure footing, GapKids prospered and launched a new venture, babyGap. Like its sibling, babyGap was a phenomenal success and became a popular attraction in GapKids stores. For the start of a new decade, The Gap was looking very good indeed: a stock split occurred in September, and at year-end the company's 1,092 stores pulled in $1.9 billion in sales with net earnings of $144.5 million. In the early 1990s, Banana Republic was busy refocusing its image while GapKids and babyGap flourished. Overall, though, revenue, net income, and return-on-equity were all outstanding ($2.5 billion, $229.8 million, and 40.2 percent respectively due to another stock split in June) in 1991 and virtually every year since Drexler's program had taken effect in 1985. The Gap's transition from a discount jeans warehouse to a sleek fashion arbiter was not altogether painless, yet the result had been more successful than Donald and Doris Fisher ever imagined. In 1991, the Fisher family still held more than 40 percent of the company, which now operated more than 1,216 stores in the United States, Canada, and the United Kingdom, with plans to expand total sales area by 15 percent annually. Not only had The Gap followed its Baby Boomer clientele as they grew older and wealthier, it provided for their children, too. GapKids was the fastest-growing segment of the company as a whole, with most of the more than 223 GapKids stores housing a babyGap department for infants and toddlers.

Though 1992 marked a dip in profits and sales growth due to slower turnover and increased competition, the company addressed these problems by turning away from unisex clothing to more gender-specific items. Along with refurbishing stores and placing more emphasis on women, The Gap came back with record numbers in 1993 and a new franchise, originally called Gap Warehouse, because for some it had become increasingly cool not to spend money on clothes (i.e., the ''grunge'' and ''slacker'' looks). Lacking the trademark flare associated with the company, Drexler hired an outside to firm to come up with a new name to no avail. Then when strolling in Paris with colleagues, Drexler saw the perfect moniker for the down-market stores painted on a building: Old Navy. Hence Old Navy Clothing Company, with stores nearly twice as big as other Gap stores, filled with sturdy, value-priced (20 to 30 percent lower) clothing for the entire family. Despite the circumstances of its birth, Old Navy became another Gap sensation.

Banana Republic, meanwhile, was gaining ground with urbane elegance as a hip alternative to The Gap's casualness. To shore up its product line, the upscale clothier initiated a shop-within-a-shop concept, featuring different collections, jewelry, and leather accessories. By 1994, there were 1,507 Gap-owned stores (188 were Banana Republic) contributing to the company's $3.72 billion in sales. Within a year, there were 1,680 stores—210 Banana Republic, 902 Gap, 437 GapKids, and 131 Old Navy. International stores had surged from 1994's 124 (72 in Canada, 49 in the United Kingdom, and 3 in France) to 91 in Canada, 55 in the United Kingdom, 12 in France, 4 in Japan, and 2 in Germany in 1995. Likewise, The Gap's statistics were robust: a two-for-one stock split paid out dividends in March; sales leapt 18 percent to nearly $4.4 billion; and net earnings rose 11 percent to $354 million over the previous year's $320 million.

Banana Republic, once a blemish on the perfect Gap picture, had blossomed with more new products, including footwear, personal care items, a sharper focus on women, and five new stores in Canada. At the same time, Old Navy increased its market share by doubling in size, exceeding the company's hopes for its newest division, while Gap and GapKids lost some of their momentum, although babyGap maintained its prominence. New directions for GapKids and babyGap included plush toys, other non-clothing items, and freestanding babyGap stores; The Gap debuted GapScents and continued to broaden its age range and clothing lines to include work attire. Yet perhaps the biggest news of 1995 was Donald Fisher's decision to relinquish his duties as CEO of The Gap, Inc. His successor was Mickey Drexler, who added the responsibilities of CEO to those of president. Fisher remained chairman, however, and still kept a hand in running the company he founded nearly 30 years before.

By 1996, The Gap's dominance of the fashion scene was fixed; consumers of all ages could find something in one of its stores. The industry even honored the company in the April issue of *Elle* when such high-brow designers as Giorgio Armani, Nino Cerruti, Carolina Herrera, Todd Oldham, and Cynthia Rowley paid ''tribute to the little company that became master of the universe.'' Though it began with a singular purpose, The Gap, with its burgeoning cluster of stores and subsidiaries, changed fashion for not only baby boomers but for generations to come. The Gap's success was in no small part due to Donald Fisher's and Mickey Drexler's business acuity, especially through vertical integration. By keeping the design, manufacture, inspection, packaging, shipment, display, advertising, and ultimate sale of every item with its name in-house, The Gap maintained exceptional quality and consistency in an increasingly erratic marketplace. If The Gap's clientele was not quite as broad as some department stores or mass marketers, its sophistication and ever-growing consumer base more than made up for it. The Gap—its name formerly a quirky play on generational unrest—came to mean the ultimate in fashion and taste for both younger and older generations.

Late 1990s and Beyond

By the late 1990s, Drexler felt The Gap had strayed too far into the trendy genre and was losing customers as a result. As such, he retooled The Gap's image in 1997, emphasizing a return to simplicity and the company's most basic offerings—pocket tee's, jeans, and khakis. Long-time advertising director Maggie Gross left the firm after Drexler pulled the plug on a print campaign that did not gel with The Gap's new basic image. That year, the firm went back to television advertising with commercials that highlighted Gap Easy Fit jeans featuring well-known celebrities that included Lena Horne, LL Cool J, and Luscious Jackson. In 1998, the firm launched another round of highly successful television commercials—this time the star being its line of khaki pants. The company also began its foray into e-tailing and introduced gap.com along with gapkids.com and babygap.com. Banana Republic and Old Navy began catering to online shoppers shortly thereafter.

Thanks to Drexler's efforts, The Gap grew at a rapid clip during the latter half of the 1990s, securing record sales and earnings. In 1997, sales at Old Navy surpassed $1 billion while overall company sales grew to $6.5 billion. Sales climbed to $9 billion the following year, bolstered by the opening of 356 new stores. The company could now claim that one new store opened each day. In 1999, 570 new stores were added to the company's arsenal as net earnings exceeded $1.1 billion. According to the *National Post,* the company had grown by 24,000 percent from 1984 to 1999. Drexler's reign at The Gap had become one of the retail industry's amazing success stories.

The new century, however, brought with it rocky times for the 30-year-old retailer. During 2000, the company opened 731 new units and sales grew to $13.6 billion. On the other hand, net income fell to $877 million while comparable store sales fell by 5 percent. In April 2000, sales began declining. Disaster struck in 2001 when the company posted a $7.7 million loss. ''Simply put,'' wrote Anne Kingston of the *National Post,* ''The Gap has lost its groove. Its merchandising is unfocused and it has lost ground to competitors. The formula that made it great no longer has the same currency. More damningly, Gap Inc. has alienated shoppers.''

Indeed, the company was losing market share in the over-30 category and was having difficulty appealing to a younger audience. The Gap had also come under fire for its labor practices in third-world countries. Various labor groups claimed The Gap advocated sweatshop labor overseas. In response, the company created a global monitoring program to supervise factory conditions where its clothes were manufactured.

Not surprisingly, Drexler announced his retirement during 2002. He later took a job to head up rival J. Crew Group Inc. After Drexler's departure, Fisher began his search for a new leader, one whose management style could catapult The Gap back into the upper echelon of retail fashion. Paul Pressler, an executive from Walt Disney Co., was tapped to revive the company just as Drexler had been called up to do in the 1980s. Pressler began to implement a series of sweeping corporate changes focused on customer research, strategic planning, new advertising, and store closures. Net income for fiscal 2002 bounced back to $477 million; however, Pressler knew he had his work cut out for him. The retail environment in 2003 remained fiercely competitive, prices were down, and the economy remained questionable. Despite these distinct challenges, both Pressler and Fisher were convinced that The Gap and its brands would carry on as a mainstay in the retail fashion world in the years to come.

Principal Operating Units

Gap; GapKids; babyGap; Banana Republic; Old Navy Clothing Company.

Principal Competitors

Abercrombie & Fitch Stores Inc.; American Eagle Outfitters Inc.; Spiegel Inc.

Further Reading

Abend, Jules, "Widening the Gap," *Stores*, November 1985.

Barmash, Isidore, "Gap Finds Middle Road to Success," *New York Times*, June 24, 1991.

Bensimon, Giles, "How They Learned to Stop Worrying and Love The Gap," *Elle*, April 1996.

Caminiti, Susan, "Will Old Navy Fill the Gap?," *Fortune*, March 18, 1996.

"Gap Lands in Japan," *WWD*, November 9, 1995.

Karr, Arnold J., "Gap's Sales Drop: What Happened?," *WWD*, September 1, 2000, p 2.

Kingston, Anne, "Bridging the Gap," *National Post*, May 4, 2002.

Munk, Nina, "Gap Gets It," *Fortune*, August 3, 1998.

Sellers, Patricia, "Gap's New Guy Upstairs," *Fortune*, April 14, 2003, p. 110.

Shabi, Rachel, "Gap or Crap? A High Street Brand Under Pressure," *New Statesman*, June 17, 2002, p 24.

Smith, Stephanie D., "Changing of the Guard," *Money*, April 1, 2003, p. 61.

Van Meter, Jonathan, "Fast Fashion: Americans Want Clothing That Is Quick and Easy; The Gap Made a Billion Giving It to Them," *Vogue*, May 1990.

Weitzman, Jennifer, "Gap Inc.'s Dire Years: 24 Declining Months and More on the Way," *WWD*, May 9, 2002, p. 1.

—Jonathan Martin
—updates: Taryn Benbow-Pfalzgraf
and Christina M. Stansell

The George F. Cram Company, Inc.

301 South LaSalle Street
Indianapolis, Indiana 46201
U.S.A.
Telephone: (317) 635-5564
Toll Free: (800) 227-4199
Fax: (317) 687-2845
Web site: http://www.georgefcram.com

Private Company
Incorporated: 1921
Employees: 90
Sales: $19.3 million (2000)
NAIC: 511199 All Other Publishers

Indianapolis-based The George F. Cram Company, Inc. is one of the nation's leading publishers and manufacturers of maps, atlases, globes, and related commercial and educational supplies. Its line of products include globes designed as gifts, world and decorator globes for home and office, home educator maps and programs, educational globes and maps, cultural and historical maps, state maps, curriculum material for the classroom, and social studies materials, including CDs, videos, and atlases. The company has been primarily owned and directed by the Douthit family since 1966, when family patriarch Loren B. Douthit began directing its fortunes as company president and majority stockholder. William L. Douthit took over Cram's reins when Loren Douthit died in 1996.

1867–1920: Evolution of a Map and Atlas Publisher

The George F. Cram Company traces its ancestry back to 1867, when a merchant named Rufus Blanchard, originally from Massachusetts, took his nephew George F. Cram into business with him in Evanston, Illinois, near Chicago. Prior to that, back East, Blanchard had prospered through the sale of globes, maps, and books, but after the Civil War had moved to the Midwest. He brought Cram into the trade as a partner.

Cram, who was born on May 20, 1842, was fairly young at the time. He had served in the Union Army during the Civil War, and, reportedly, had a role as a cartographer for General Ulysses S. Grant. He also wrote several letters while serving under General William T. Sherman and participating in that military commander's celebrated "march to the sea." Years later, Cram's biography and letters would command enough historical interest to find their way into print.

The company of the uncle and nephew, which sold maps and atlases, was named Blanchard & Cram. However, in 1869, Cram took full control of the firm, renamed it George F. Cram, and moved it to Chicago, where, initially, it was a supply house for traveling book salesmen. The great Chicago fire of 1871 destroyed that business, however, and when Cram re-established the company as the Cram Map Depot, he reverted to producing and selling maps and atlases, which he had been doing in his partnership with Blanchard.

By 1875, the Cram Map Depot had begun publishing a wide range of atlases, including its Atlas of the World series. It was a series that, with several modifications and revisions, would remain in print for over 70 years. It was also the core business of the company right through World War I and the 1920s.

1921–65: Merging to Become a Major Globe Manufacturer

In 1921, Cram, at 79, sold the company to E.A. Peterson, who merged it with his own business, the National Map Company. National had previously been Scarborough Company and was originally established in Boston in 1882, but when it merged with Cram, the business moved to East Georgia Street in Indianapolis, Indiana. In 1928, the year in which George F. Cram died, Peterson changed the firm's name to The George F. Cram Company.

It was not until the early 1930s that Cram began making globes, what would become one of the company's core products. These were made for both the home and school markets and came in a range of sizes from 8″ to 16″ in diameter. The product line included Cram's Universal Terrestrial Globes, political globes featuring a choice of sizes and different mountings. The company also produced a series dubbed Cram's Unrivaled Terrestrial Globes, as well as lighted globes.

In 1936, Loren B. Douthit began his long career with the company, initially working as school sales field manager. Over the next several years he rose through the business, becoming president and majority shareholder in 1966.

In 1940, Cram copyrighted and produced its Self-Revising Globe. With the world at war, the company realized that the restoration of peace would bring geopolitical changes, so it began selling globes with the guaranty that it would supply new map sections for globe owners who, following simple instructions, could update their globes.

Cram introduced one of its best-selling globes, the Tuffy Globe, in 1958. Cram manufactured the globes to hold up under reasonable wear, hence the suggestive name. The Tuffy line would prove very popular. It would also evolve through several versions and eventually carry a ten-year guarantee against the hazards of normal use, even by rambunctious children. The line would also reflect changing techniques in globe making. Models still in production in the next century were vacuum formed and injection molded, and thereafter marketed with the promise that they would not chip, dent, or peel.

1966–89: New Leadership and a Period of Vigorous Growth

In 1966, ownership of the company again changed hands when Loren B. Douthit and other family members bought a controlling interest in the business. Loren became president, and two years later, in 1968, he moved the company to South La Salle Street in Indianapolis, where it would remain into the next century. At about the same time, Douthit expanded the company's educational division, which produced not just globes and maps but also learning programs.

Cram faced difficult times, however, in the late 1960s and 1970s. The educational market started to dry up when geography lost its appeal to students and its status as a core subject in many school curricula slipped. The Soviet Union's successful launch of Sputnik in 1957 brought in its wake a new focus on math and science and, by the 1960s, schools, with their wide-swinging educational pendula, were soon turning out Johnnys who not only could not read or write but who could not locate New York on unmarked world maps, never mind London, Tokyo, Rome, or Rio de Janeiro.

William and John Douthit, Loren's two sons, assumed control of the day-to-day operations of the company when their father retired in July 1978, though Loren remained the titular head of the business as its board chairman. Under their leadership, Cram entered a period of fairly vigorous growth. Also, by the late 1980s, Cram's business market had undergone a major though gradual shift that had started in the 1960s. In 1963, it was selling more than 85 percent of its products to schools, and though that market remained central in the company's expansion, by 1989 commercial sales accounted for almost half of the company's business. In fact, the 1980s were strong growth years for the firm.

One good piece of luck came in 1982, when Target, then a 392-store chain of Dayton Hudson Corporation of Minneapolis, Minnesota, set out to find some new, low-priced Christmas items. Although Cram had been trying to sell items to Target, it was not pursuing that chain's business very vigorously. Neither were its competitors, however. In fact, one of them, Replogle Globes, Inc. of Chicago, was not even trying. The result was, to the company's surprise, that Target placed an order for over 25,000 globes with Cram, a giant order by the company's standards at the time. To fill it, Cram took a considerable risk. Douthit more than doubled his production staff, and even then had to work them many overtime hours to get the job done.

The result was a healthy growth-run by Cram. Its total business tripled between 1983 and 1989, and it enjoyed a particularly strong year in 1988, when sales rose by nearly 30 percent over the previous year. The company also left behind a rather stodgy reputation. Its customers helped encourage it to employ a more modern look, using, for example, bolder colors on its globes and more attractive packaging. The changes made Cram more competitive with Replogle and helped gain it a larger market share. Also, Cram was helped when, in 1987, Rand McNally completely exited the globe-making business. Between 1983 and 1989, Cram's production of globes increased five-fold, reaching close to 500,000 units per year. By that time, its globes were picked up for sale by several large retailers, including Venture, Child World, and Ames. As a result, retail store sales reached about 45 percent of the company's business.

Despite the tilting in its market axis towards increased commercial sales, the company's educational sales soared upward in the same period. One business boon was the 1988 introduction of a major new product: a primary map that blended activity and landscape panels. Cram experienced an enviable miscalculation when an anticipated 18-month supply of the maps sold out long before more were scheduled for printing. By 1988, Cram had also undertaken expansion through the acquisition of other companies. In January of that year it purchased American Geographic, a maker of large-scale state maps and specialty products; before buying that Michigan-based firm Cram had acquired two other companies: Visual Craft, an Illinois manufacturer of overhead transparencies; and Starlight Manufacturing, a metal spinning and stamping company located in Indianapolis.

1990 and Beyond: Expansion

Expansion continued into the 1990s, starting in 1991, when the company acquired Southwinds Publication. Southwinds, located in Florida, was a publisher of desk map programs. In the following year, Cram also purchased Rath Globe.

With the dissolution of the former Soviet Union in 1992, updating world maps and globes became a priority project for cartographers. Cram quickly produced a color globe, reputedly

Key Dates:

1867: Company is founded as Blanchard & Cram in Evanston, Illinois.

1869: Firm becomes George F. Cram Company with George as sole owner; company moves to Chicago.

1871: Great Chicago fire destroys the business; company is re-established as Cram Map Depot.

1921: Edward Peterson buy the company and merges it with his National Map Company of Indianapolis.

1928: After Cram's death, Peterson changes the company name to The George F. Cram Company.

1932: Cram begins manufacturing globes.

1937: Loren B. Douthit begins employment with Cram.

1966: Douthit becomes president and majority shareholder of the company.

1978: Douthit retires and his sons William and John assume leadership of Cram.

1988: Cram acquires American Geographic, Visual Craft, and Starlight Manufacturing.

1991: Company purchases Southwind Publications and introduces the first Vacuum-Formed Illuminated Globe.

2002: Company earns Export Achievement Certificate from the U.S. Department of Commerce.

the first to depict the 15 countries once more independent of the Soviet hegemony.

Cram's guiding genius since the 1960s, Loren Douthit, died in March 1996. William L. Douthit, his son, then became the company's CEO and chairman. The following June, in a cooperative venture with Berkeley, California-based Eureka Cartography, Cram produced the first digital vacuum-formed globe for Explore Technology. Vacuum-formed, illuminated globes had first appeared on the scene in 1991, when World Book, Inc. introduced them to the market.

In the following year, 1997, the company acquired the personal letters of George F. Cram, written to the founder's mother and uncles during the Civil War. Three years later, in a collection edited by Jennifer Cain Bohrnstedt, the letters were issued by the Northern Illinois University Press. That year, the company celebrated its 130th anniversary. It also introduced its all-new and original Explorer political maps of the world and the United States for the educational market. Once again, too, it partnered with Eureka Cartography, this time to produce and market the first fiberglass globes.

Starting in the 1990s and expanding in the new century, Cram tapped into foreign markets for an increasing percentage of its sales. By 2002, it was printing globes in English, Spanish, French, and Mandarin Chinese, and it was exporting them to almost 25 countries. The company's success in expanding into global markets earned the recognition of the U.S. Department of Commerce, which in May 2002 awarded the company with an Export Achievement Certificate. The company was the first Indiana firm to received the honor. Cram had begun working with the U.S. Commercial Service, an agency of the Department of Commerce, in 2001, and as a result had entered nine markets that generated sales of $350,000. Although foreign sales only accounted for about 12 percent of the company's revenue, Cram's prospects for increasing global sales over the next several years looked very good.

Principal Competitors

1-World Globes; Herff Jones, Inc.; National Geographic Society Inc.; Rand McNally Company; Replogle Globes; The World of Maps, Inc.

Further Reading

Cram, George F., *Soldiering with Sherman: Civil War letters of George F. Cram*, edited by Jennifer Cain Bohrnstedt, DeKalb.: Northern Illinois University Press, 2000.

Davis, Andrea M., ''Global Focus Pays Off for Cram,'' *Indiana Business Journal*, May 20, 2002, p.1.

Harris, John, ''Global Warfare,'' *Forbes*, October 16, 1989, p. 120.

Kronemyer, Bob, ''Going Global,'' *Indiana Business Magazine*, October 2000, p. 17.

Stewart, William B., ''The World According to Cram,'' *Indiana Business Magazine*, September 1989, p. 24.

—John W. Fiero

George S. May International Company

303 South Northwest Highway
Park Ridge, Illinois 60068-4255
U.S.A.
Telephone: (847) 825-8806
Fax: (847) 825-7937
Web site: http://www.georgesmay.com

Private Company
Employees: 1,200 (est.)
Sales: $116 million (2000 est.)
NAIC: 541611 Administrative Management and General
Management Consulting Services

George S. May International Company, with its headquarters located in the Chicago suburb of Park Ridge, Illinois, is a family-owned management consulting firm dedicated primarily to serving small and medium-sized companies in a wide range of industries. Most of its clients generate less than $100 million in annual sales and have fewer than 100 employees. May helps these businesses to improve their overall operations by offering assistance in a variety of areas, including profit engineering, human capital management, operational effectiveness, customer relations management, and technology management. May prides itself on completing assignments within an agreed upon time, making it necessary to service a large number of clients. Since the company's founding in 1925, May has advised over 350,000 businesses and usually maintains about 275 active accounts. This high turnover rate requires that the company pursue an aggressive and carefully coordinated marketing program, which starts with a centralized telemarketing effort. Using area business listings, May telemarketers cold call potential clients, informing them that May representatives will soon be in their area. If the businessperson is interested in a meeting, May will dispatch a salesperson within 48 hours. The goal at this stage is simply to sell May's diagnostic survey instrument to assess the company's condition. A May consultant then visits the client to offer bottom-line solutions; more detailed advice and specific projects can then be contracted. May projects generally last less than two months.

1920s Company Origins

George Storr May, the company founder, was born on a farm in the east central Illinois town of Windsor in 1890. The self-sufficiency of farm life led to a love for mechanical and technical matters and helped to nurture a talent for problem solving. Nevertheless, May was uninterested in becoming either a farmer or a teacher, despite earning a degree from Eastern Illinois States Teachers College. Instead, he pursued a business career, and at first worked as a Bible salesman, following the sawdust trail of legendary baseball-player-turned-evangelist Billy Sunday and selling into newly revived communities Sunday left in his wake. May then tried to put his problem solving skills to use by becoming a freelance consultant on short-term jobs. He found permanent work as an efficiency expert for a wholesale tailoring company, a job he enjoyed, but due to poor economic conditions in the aftermath of World War I he was laid off. May decided to start his own company to work as a business management consult and in 1924 mailed letters to a number of Chicago businesses offering his services as a business problem solver. Eventually he landed his first assignment with Chicago Flexible Shaft Company, today's Sunbeam Corporation. With that job in hand he established the George S. May Company on February 1, 1925, and initially focused on large companies.

May generated sales of $10,000 in the first year, but within three years, during the economic boom of the Roaring Twenties, the company was billing $250,000. Business was so strong that May expanded to both coasts, opening offices in both New York City and San Francisco in 1929, the same year that the stock market crash ushered in the Great Depression of the 1930s. Despite the difficult economic climate, May persevered, recovered lost business, and by 1937 increased annual revenues to more than $1 million. It was also during the 1930s that George May became involved in the game of golf, becoming a legendary promoter of the professional game while at the same time promoting his advisory firm.

May Becomes Involved in Golf in 1930s

In 1936, a fire destroyed the clubhouse of the Tam O'Shanter Country Club in the Chicago suburb of Niles and

> ### Company Perspectives:
>
> *Over the past 77 years, we've helped nearly 500,000 businesses in over 3,000 business categories spanning the full spectrum of manufacturing, wholesale, retail, construction, health care, and service industries.*

bankrupted the owners. May acquired a controlling interest in the golf club and over the next several years invested more than $500,000 to renovate and operate the facility. He also became involved in sponsoring golf tournaments in 1941, due in large part to dissatisfaction with his experience at the 1940 U.S. Open held at Cleveland's Canterbury Country Club. Following the 1940 Chicago Open held at Tam O'Shanter, May made a splash by announcing he would sponsor a new tournament in 1941, the Tam O'Shanter Open, offering the largest purse in professional golf: $15,000. While Canterbury had charged $3.30 a ticket, he would only charge $1. When the tournament was finally staged, May revealed a number of other unprecedented innovations, much of which are taken for granted today. He provided grandstands at key locations, as well as shortwave radio broadcasts so that fans could follow events happening elsewhere on the course. He also sold hot dogs, soda, and beer after the fashion of other sporting events. Moreover, he hosted a dance after the tournament and made slot machines available. Around 41,000 spectators attended the tournament, 23,000 on the final day alone, many having never attended a golf tournament before. Those more familiar with the reverence expected of golf galleries hardly knew what to make of the boisterous atmosphere May brought to the game. The *Saturday Evening Post* wrote: "All told, it was a cross between a county fair and a good airplane crash."

George May was just getting started with his foray into golf, which would include staging major tournaments for women. In the process, he built up the name recognition of his firm as well as fashioning a recognizable persona for himself. According to a 1943 *Time* magazine profile, May "advertises his personality by wearing $32 shirts, lurid handkerchiefs, and horse-blanket striped suits." In 1945, he launched the Tam O'Shanter World Championship, offering a total purse of $60,000 in war bonds, with the winner receiving $13,600. At the time, few tournaments offered purses of $10,000, and the standard winner's share was $2,000. By introducing big-money tournaments, May was instrumental in the rise of modern professional golf. Before his arrival, golfers simply did not expect to make a living at the sport. At the same time, May continued to introduce innovations. He was the first to mount large scoreboards that relied on shortwave radio communication to provide up-to-the-minute results. He was the first to allow club members to use golf carts and to install telephones at each tee for member use. He was, however, unsuccessful in forcing players to wear numbers so that fans could make use of scorecards, which he would be able to sell. His association with the Tam O'Shanter Country Club did not come without adverse publicity. Golf purists were upset over some of May's innovations and subjected him to criticism that portrayed him as little more than a carnival barker. May did not improve his image by arranging to have one player in his tournament compete wearing a mask and billing him as "The

Masked Marvel" or by paying a Scottish golfer to play wearing kilts. He was also criticized after making a playing exception for heavyweight boxing champion Joe Louis. A less savory episode occurred in 1951 when a Chicago grand jury recommended that he be held in contempt for refusing to produce financial records of the country club as part of an inquiry into whether organized crime was operating the slot machines. Later in the year, he refused to testify before a United States Senate committee investigating the relationship between gangsters and his club, and he was cited for contempt. In October 1952, he was exculpated of the contempt charge when a federal judge ruled that he was constitutionally protected against self-incrimination.

May's greatest moment in golf came in July 1953 when The Tam O'Shanter World Championship became the first tournament to be nationally televised. By now, the winner's share of the tournament had grown to $25,000, an amount higher than the total purse of every other professional tournament. Fledgling network ABC became interested in the event because of the large prize and offered to do a one-hour broadcast of the final round if May paid $32,000. Although television was still in its infancy, May understood the publicity value of televising the tournament, both in terms of the people watching on television and the print coverage of the broadcast. An estimated 1 million watched as a single camera located above the grandstand on the 18th green followed the conclusion of the tournament. There were only ten minutes left in the broadcast when golfer Lew Worsham, trailing by one shot, made a miraculous 115-yard eagle to overtake the leader and win the $25,000. It made great television and immediately showed the potential for golf on the medium. Not to be upstaged, May immediately stepped onto the green to announce that the winning share of the 1954 tournament would be doubled to $50,000, plus the winner would also have the chance to play 50 exhibitions to promote his consulting company at $1,000 each. Following in May's footsteps, the U.S. Open was nationally televised for the first time in 1954 and the Masters in 1956. Ironically, May stopped sponsoring golf tournaments after 1958 when he declined to meet the player's demand for even more money. He continued to operate the country club until his death, his wife eventually selling the property to a developer in the late 1960s.

While May was beginning his flirtation with golf just before the United States entered World War II, his company was expanding beyond the borders, working for Canadian clients whose country was already involved in the fight and were attempting to be as efficient as possible in their contributions to the war effort. This work proved invaluable for May, which subsequently consulted with the U.S. government and companies involved in the war effort once the United States was drawn into World War II. In 1943, revenues grew to $3 million, and by the time the war was over in 1945 the company was billing more than $6 million a year. It was at this point that George May initiated a significant shift in direction for the company in light of the changes that he anticipated would occur in the postwar business world. He believed that instead of focusing on large corporations the company should target the many small and medium size companies that arose to meet the challenge of the war effort. To achieve this new strategy, the company had to expand at a significant rate, and by 1950 it employed 500 people. Only 2 percent of the company's clients were now

Key Dates:

1925: George S. May founds a management consultant firm.
1929: The company opens offices in New York and San Francisco.
1936: May acquires Tam O'Shanter Country Club.
1953: May promotes the first nationally televised golf tournament.
1962: George May dies.
1990: Raymond Margolies retires after serving 18 years as president.
2002: Israel Kushnir replaces Donald J. Fletcher, who served 12 years as president.

larger corporations. May also became a truly international firm in the postwar years after it expanded into Europe, which had to be rebuilt following several years of fighting. Many Western European businesses were eager to improve their operations and turned to May, the first company to provide management consulting services on the continent. In the 1950s, the company opened offices in such cities as Dusseldorf, Germany; Milan, Italy; and Paris, France. As the transportation systems recovered and communication capabilities improved, there was less need for a network of offices and eventually May's European operations were consolidated in Milan.

Leadership Changes in the 1960s

On March 12, 1962, George May died of a heart at the Tam O'Shanter Country Club at the age of 71. He was survived by his wife Alice, his son Dale, and daughters Dorothy and Jean. Together they inherited all the shares of stock of the company May founded. Raymond Margolies, who had been with May for 13 years, was named the new president. He remained at the helm for 18 years, during which time the business continued to grow at such a steady rate that the company initiated a number of moves and expansions. The exodus from downtown Chicago to Park Ridge, Illinois, occurred in 1966.

Margolies retired in 1990, replaced by Donald J. Fletcher, who had 23 years service in May's Management Service Department. Under Fletcher's watch the company exceeded the $100 million mark in annual sales. All the while, the company continued to keep pace with the times. In the early years of the Internet, May established a Web site that offered small business owners and managers research data, management tips, and information on the latest business trends. Later on, the company offered Web-based software training for businesses looking to improve the computer skills of their employees. In 2000, May launched operations in Mexico and also acquired a building next to its headquarters in Park Ridge to establish the George S. May Training Center, in effect creating a corporate campus for the company at its main site. In 2002, Fletcher was replaced as May's president by Israel Kushnir, who had previously been associated with the company for 21 years. With strong continuity in management over its history and a strong track record, there was every reason to believe that May would continue to thrive in the foreseeable future.

Principal Divisions

Headquarters American; Western American Division; Worldwide Operations.

Principal Competitors

International Profit Associates, Inc.; McKinsey & Company; Bain & Company.

Further Reading

Dobrian, Joseph, "Golf Grows Up," *American Heritage*, 2002, p. 4.
"George S, May: Missionary Selling 101," *Consultants News*, February 1, 1997, p. 9.
Purkey, Mike, "The Barnum of Golf," *Golf Magazine*, December 1, 1995, p. 82.
Oloroso, Arsenio, Jr., "Small-Time Consulting: An Untapped Market Most Firms Ignore," *Crain's Chicago Business*, July 12, 1993, p. 15.

—Ed Dinger

The Great Atlantic & Pacific Tea Company, Inc.

2 Paragon Drive
Montvale, New Jersey 07645-1718
U.S.A.
Telephone: (201) 573-9700
Fax: (201) 571-8719
Web site: http://www.aptea.com

Public Subsidiary of Tengelmann Group
Incorporated: 1902
Employees: 79,000
Sales: $10.97 billion (2002)
Stock Exchanges: New York
Ticker Symbol: GAP
NAIC: 445110 Supermarkets and Other Grocery (Except
Convenience) Stores

The Great Atlantic & Pacific Tea Company, Inc. (A&P) is one of the dozen largest grocery store operators in North America. At its peak in the 1930s, A&P was the largest grocery chain in the United States, with 15,709 stores from coast to coast; in the early 21st century, however, it operated fewer than 700 stores in a little more than a dozen states and in the Canadian province of Ontario. The main states in which the company operates are New York, Michigan, New Jersey, Connecticut, Maryland, Pennsylvania, and Louisiana. Store brands include A&P, The Barn Markets, Dominion, Farmer Jack, Food Basics, Food Emporium, Sav-A-Center, Super Foodmart, Super Fresh, Ultra Food & Drug, and Waldbaum's. The company announced in early 2003 that it was exploring the sale of its Kohl's chain in Wisconsin. The company also manufactures and distributes coffee under the brand names Eight O' Clock, Bokar, and Royale—though this business too was up for sale in 2003. Tengelmann Group, a German retailer, has held a majority interest in A&P since 1979.

Early History: From Tea Merchant
to Cash-and-Carry Grocery Chain

In 1859 George Huntington Hartford and George Francis Gilman formed a partnership. Using Gilman's connections as an established grocer and the son of a wealthy shipowner, Hartford purchased coffee and tea from clipper ships on the waterfront docks of New York City. By eliminating brokers, Hartford and Gilman were able to sell their wares at "cargo prices." Initially, the operation was strictly a mail-order affair. But the enterprise proved so successful that Hartford and Gilman opened a series of stores under the name Great American Tea Company. The first of these, which opened in 1861, soon became a landmark on Vesey Street in New York City. By 1869 there were 11 such stores.

The company's appeal to the 19th-century consumer was enhanced by the lavish storefronts and Chinese-inspired interiors that Gilman designed: inside the Chinese paneled walls, cockatoos greeted customers, who brought their purchases to a pagoda-shaped cash desk. Outside, the red-and-gold storefronts were illuminated by dozens of gas lights that formed a giant "T," and on Saturdays customers were treated to the music of a live brass band.

Despite the company's extravagant trappings, its success was largely due to its innovative strategy of offering savings and incentives to the consumer. A&P's "club plan" (introduced in 1866), which encouraged the formation of clubs to make bulk mail-order sales for an additional one-third discount, was so successful that by 1886 hundreds of such clubs had been formed. Pioneering the concept of private labels and house brands, The Great American Tea Company introduced its own inexpensive tea and coffee blends, continuing to direct its efforts at the price-conscious consumer. In 1882 Eight O'Clock Breakfast Coffee was introduced; the Eight O'Clock blend remained a hallmark house brand into the early 21st century.

In 1869 the company became The Great Atlantic & Pacific Tea Company, to commemorate the joining of the first transcontinental railroad and to separate its retail stores from its mail-order operations. A&P's gradual national expansion began shortly thereafter. The company established a foothold in the Midwest in the aftermath of the Chicago Fire of 1871, when A&P sent staff and food to help the devastated city, and stayed to open stores in the region. By 1876 the company had become the first significant grocery chain, having reached the 100-store mark.

Careful thought and planning were given to A&P's expansion. New store openings were complemented by promotions

Company Perspectives:

Our mission at The Great Atlantic & Pacific Tea Company is to be the "Supermarket of Choice" . . . the place where people choose to shop, choose to work, and choose to invest.

and premiums. In the Midwest and the South, new stores gave away items such as crockery and lithographs in order to attract customers, and in other areas, showy "Teams of Eight" became legendary symbols of A&P. The brainchild of the flamboyant John Hartford, parades of teams of eight horses decorated with spangled harnesses and gold-plated bells drew red and gold vehicles through the towns; the person who best guessed the weight of the team was awarded $500 in gold.

In 1878, after Gilman's retirement, Hartford gained full control of the business. His two sons, George and John, were each apprenticed at the age of 16. Years later, a writer in the *Saturday Evening Post* observed that "in discussing the two brothers, tea company employees seldom get beyond the differences between the two." The older brother, who became known as Mr. George, earned a reputation as the "inside man" because of his concern for the books, and was considered to be the "conservative, bearish influence in the business." The younger, flamboyant Mr. John was described as an "old-school actor-manager." He was well-suited for his responsibility for promotions and premiums and generally ensured a "personal touch" in each of A&P's stores, which by 1900 numbered nearly 200 and generated $5.6 million in annual sales. Mr. John was also responsible for A&P peddlers, who by 1910 were carrying A&P products along 5,000 separate routes into rural areas in easily recognized red-and-black A&P wagons.

Responding to a dramatic rise in the cost of living in the first decade of the 20th century, when food prices increased by 35 percent, Mr. John devised the first cash-and-carry A&P Economy Store, which opened its doors in Jersey City, New Jersey, in 1912. Initially dismissed by both George, Jr., and George, Sr., economy stores obviated the problem of capital depletion posed by premiums, credit, and delivery. The cash-and-carry stores followed a simple formula—$3,000 was allotted for equipment, groceries, and working capital. Only one man was needed to run an economy store, and he was expected to adhere strictly to Mr. John's "Manual for Managers of Economy Stores," which outlined, in meticulous detail, how to run the stores. Among other things, Mr. John insisted that all the stores have the same goods at the same location; A&P legend has it that Mr. John could find the beans in any of his stores— blindfolded.

The Chain's Peak Years: 1920s–30s

When George Hartford, Sr., died in 1917, George, Jr., became chairman of A&P, while John Hartford became president. By 1925, A&P had 14,000 economy stores, with sales of $440 million, marking one of the greatest retail expansions ever. At this point, the company's national expansion was so far-reaching that A&P had to be divided into five geographical divisions to decentralize management.

During the 1920s, A&P continued to diversify, opening bakeries and pastry and candy shops. It also expanded its manufacturing facilities to produce its own Anne Page brand products and set up a corporation to buy coffee directly from Colombia and Brazil. "Combination stores" added hitherto unheard-of meat counters to the grocery chain and, when lines at these counters became a problem, A&P devised a system to make prepackaged meats available to customers, who had never before been offered such a convenience. At the same time, A&P introduced food-testing laboratories to maintain quality standards in its manufactured products. In 1929 when the stock market crashed, causing other retail companies to fold, merge, or sell out in the subsequent Great Depression, A&P was so firmly established and soundly managed that it was virtually unaffected. Sales reached the $1 billion mark in 1929, and the following year the chain's store count peaked at 15,709 outlets. Responding to consumers' needs, A&P began publishing literature with money-saving tips and recipes. The public's reception of these publications prompted the company to begin publishing *Woman's Day* magazine in 1937, at two cents per issue.

The 1930s marked the advent of supermarkets in the United States. The Hartfords found the supermarket idea distasteful and were slow to respond to the trend, but as A&P began to lose market share, they were swayed and opened their first such outlet in Braddock, Pennsylvania, in 1937. The following year, supermarkets represented 5 percent of A&P's stores—and 23 percent of its business. By 1939, the total number of A&P stores had dropped to 9,100, of which 1,100 were supermarkets, and A&P's sales had regained the level they first achieved in 1930. However, the company's size, though smaller than the 15,000 stores it had at its height in 1934, was a distinct liability. In 1936, the Robinson-Patman Act was passed, marking the beginning of the antitrust woes that shook A&P's hegemony. Anti-chainstore legislation, passed at the instigation of small independent grocers who claimed chains practiced unfair competition, imposed severe taxes and regulations on A&P and other chains, limiting pricing and other competitive advantages afforded to them by virtue of their size and purchasing power. Restrictions were based simply on store numbers, hitting A&P particularly hard. The company sought to redeem its damaged public image by publicizing its sense of corporate responsibility to consumers, producers, and employees. The loss of a suit in 1949, however, imposed limitations on A&P's purchasing practices that were more severe than any others in the industry. With this final blow, the company's position as an esteemed industry leader disintegrated.

Declining Fortunes at Mid-Century

In 1950 Ralph Burger, who had started at A&P in 1911 as an $11-a-week clerk, became president of the company. Much of A&P's early success had been due to Mr. George and Mr. John's scrupulous attention to the business, or, in Mr. John's term, to "the art of basketwatching." As the *Saturday Evening Post* article on the Hartfords had concluded in 1931, "who will watch the baskets after the Hartfords are gone? Neither has any children and although the 10 grandchildren get their due shares of income from the family trust, the direct line of shrewd vigilance will be broken." Burger remained loyal to the Hartford brothers even after their deaths, John in 1951 and George in

Key Dates:

1859: George Huntington Hartford and George Francis Gilman form The Great American Tea Company to sell discount tea via mail order.
1861: First store opens in New York City.
1869: Company is renamed The Great Atlantic & Pacific Tea Company (A&P).
1882: The Eight O'Clock house brand of coffee is introduced.
1912: First cash-and-carry A&P Economy Store opens its doors.
1925: A&P is operating 14,000 economy stores, generating $440 million in sales.
1930: Chain reaches its all-time store count peak of 15,709.
1937: With the opening of the first A&P supermarket, the chain begins transitioning to the innovative new grocery format.
1957: Family control of the company ends, and A&P is taken public.
1974: Company headquarters are moved from New York City to Montvale, New Jersey.
1979: Tengelmann Group, a West German retailer, purchases majority control of a financially troubled A&P.
1980: James Wood is appointed chairman and CEO and initiates a major restructuring.
1986: Company gains leading position in New York metropolitan area through the acquisitions of the Waldbaum and Shopwell/Food Emporium chains.
1989: Company makes an unsuccessful bid for Gateway Corporation, a major U.K. grocery operator, but succeeds in acquiring the Detroit-based Farmer Jack chain.
1998: Christian Haub is named CEO of A&P; revitalization program is launched.
2002: Retail operations are divided into two operating units: A&P U.S. and A&P Canada.

1957. With George's death, family control of A&P did in fact end and the company was taken public, but Burger, as president not only of A&P, but also of the Hartford Foundation, the charity to which the Hartfords had willed their A&P shares and which owned more than one-third of the company's shares, retained control of A&P. He ran the company, if not imaginatively, then at least reasonably successfully, until his death in 1969. At that point, despite its dusty image, A&P was still the grocery-industry leader, with sales of well over $5 billion a year—more than twice its closest competitor.

With the end of Burger's tenure, and the Hartford heirs' disinclination to enter business, A&P had no clear line of management succession. The "direct line of shrewd vigilance" was indeed broken, and management continued to change throughout the 1970s. The company's direction foundered so much that A&P, once an innovative industry leader, was no longer able even to follow the lead of its competitors. Failing to capitalize on suburban development and to accommodate changing consumer tastes, A&P's sales dropped and its reputation suffered serious injury. A&P's once "resplendent emporiums" were now perceived as antiquated, inefficient, and run-down.

1970s and 1980s: New Management, Closures, Renovations, and Acquisitions

In 1973, as A&P reported $51 million in losses and Safeway took its place as the largest food retailer in the country, Jonathan L. Scott was hired from Albertson's, marking the first time in history that A&P had looked outside its ranks for management. Scott's attempt to revive A&P by closing stores and cutting labor costs only resulted in more dissatisfied customers, and more losses. Finally, in 1979, the Tengelmann Group, a major West German retailer, bought 52.5 percent of A&P's stock. By this point, the A&P chain, which had consisted of more than 4,000 stores in the 1960s, was down to about 1,500 locations.

The Tengelmann Group appointed James Wood, the former CEO of the Grand Union Company, as chairman and CEO of A&P, in 1980. Wood's reputation as a turnaround manager underwent a trial by fire, but his radical restructuring of the company was later lauded by analysts as "an outstanding success." By 1982, close to 40 percent of the company's stores had been shut down. In addition, virtually all manufacturing facilities had been eliminated (the coffee-roasting plants were the exception). Management had won labor concessions in key markets, and the company returned to profitability. Between 1986 and 1990, A&P's earnings grew an average of 27 percent annually. With a formidable cashflow, Wood initiated an aggressive capital-spending program to rejuvenate the store base, develop new store formats, and make prudent acquisitions.

While some markets were abandoned, others were the focus of store recycling and expansion. High-growth areas (such as Phoenix, Arizona, and southern California) were avoided in favor of markets in which A&P's presence was firmly established amidst a stable and slow-growing population (such as Philadelphia, New York, and Detroit). Concentrating efforts in the most promising areas of its six major operating regions—the Northeast, the New York metropolitan area, the mid-Atlantic states, the South, the Midwest, and Ontario, Canada—the company had the flexibility to tailor store formats, product mixes, service, and pricing to local customer bases.

Initially, tens of millions of dollars were spent to remodel and expand 85 percent of A&P's extant stores to give them a more up-to-date presentation, rid the company of its tarnished reputation, and add service departments to accommodate consumers' changed tastes. Improved sales allowed the company to begin to undertake new-store construction by 1985: the "new" A&P aimed for an upscale, service-oriented image and catered to one-stop shoppers. Two new store formats addressed different market niches: Futurestores stressed A&P's broad variety of quality products, and Sav-A-Centers took a strong promotional approach by offering warehouse prices.

Wood also focused on growth through the purchase of regional chains, permitting A&P to establish itself as the top food retailer in certain regional markets without the risk and expense of building new facilities and establishing a market niche. Initial purchases included 17 Stop & Shop stores in New

Jersey, purchased in 1981 and converted to the A&P name; the Kohl's grocery chain in Wisconsin, bought in 1983; 20 Pantry Price Stores in Virginia, acquired in 1984; and 92 Dominion stores in Ontario, Canada, brought onboard in 1985. The Waldbaum and Shopwell/Food Emporium acquisitions in 1986 combined to make A&P the market leader in the New York metropolitan area, where the company had its strongest presence, and its 1989 acquisition of Borman's, a Detroit-area chain, resulted in a majority share of the Detroit market.

After the company's restructuring under James Wood, operating income per store more than doubled. Emphasizing high profit margin departments—full service delis, cheese shops, fresh seafood, and floral departments, for example—the company departed radically from low-price generic product offerings. In 1988, Master Choice, a private-brand label of specialty chocolates, pastas, sauces, and herbal teas was introduced in order to compete with what industry experts considered the real competition: restaurants and fast-food chains.

In 1989 A&P made a bid for Gateway Corporation, the third largest grocery chain in Britain. Gateway would have offered A&P a whole new arena for growth, one that was of considerable interest to Erivan Haub, Tengelmann's owner, who wished to shore up his European retailing empire in preparation for the unification of the common market in 1992. The Gateway bid ultimately failed. A&P also had trouble with another international venture, its $250 million acquisition of 70 Miracle Food Mart stores in Ontario in 1990. Ontario was soon hit by recession, as were A&P's other major markets in the United States, and sales fell in the Canadian stores by 5 percent the next year.

Continuing Struggles in the 1990s

A&P's acquisitions had given the company top market share in many cities. Its 1989 acquisition of Farmer Jack in Detroit, and its earlier purchases of Kohl's in Milwaukee and Waldbaum's in New York put it in the top spot in these major markets. But the company had trouble hanging on to its market share. Its stores averaged half the size of newly built supermarkets, and many were old and run-down. Waldbaum's in New York was cited in 1991 as the worst of all area grocery chains for numerous problems with rodents and cockroaches. The company was slow to respond, and Waldbaum's sanitation record improved only slightly the next year. Earnings for the company dropped from $151 million in 1990 to $71 million in 1991. Then sales for fiscal 1992 fell a shocking $1.1 billion, and the company was in the red, losing $189.5 million. By 1993, stores run by A&P had lost market share in six major markets. Faced with a poor economy and declining profits, the company cut back the amount it was spending on renovations.

A&P decided to focus its marketing efforts on a new store brand product line in 1993. Chairman Wood had sold or closed most of the company's store brand manufacturing plants in the 1980s, but A&P thought it was time to emphasize cost-cutting store brands again. The company consolidated nine different private labels into one—America's Choice—that would be found at all its different chains. Some 3,500 private label items were consolidated into 1,600 America's Choice items, which were promoted on television in major market areas.

A&P also remodeled more than 100 stores in 1993 and built 20 new ones. Analysts frequently noted that A&P could spend much more on remodeling, and on opening bigger stores. In 1994 A&P upped its capital spending 40 percent, to $340 million, and announced that it would concentrate on opening 50,000- to 60,000-square-foot stores, on par with its competitors'. But the company was still plagued with problems. Its Ontario chains, Miracle Food Mart and Ultra Mart, were closed by a 14 week-strike during 1993–94. A&P had attempted to lower its labor costs by cutting wages and relying on more part-time workers, setting off the strike. A&P finally settled with the unions, but the long strike had given Ontario customers plenty of time to build loyalty to competitive stores. A&P's Atlanta stores also faltered. The company bought 40 stores in the Atlanta area in 1993 in order to fight back competitors who were opening new stores in the area. The Atlanta stores, however, lost money and only began to show a profit in the fourth quarter of fiscal 1994.

The company gained a new president in 1994, Christian Haub, the 29-year-old son of Erivan Haub, the principal owner of A&P's majority owner Tengelmann Group. This was the first time a member of the Haub family had direct involvement with managing A&P. Haub planned to improve the image of A&P stores by emphasizing cleanliness, checkout service, and other highly visible areas of customer service. More than this, the company opened 16 new stores in 1994–95, remodeled or expanded 55 more, and closed 87 stores. According to Haub, A&P planned to open 50 stores a year after 1996. The company put aside $1.5 billion for store development over the next five years. Problems with the Canadian stores seemed to be improving by 1996. That, coupled with excellent results from the company's Michigan stores, helped A&P post a 28 percent increase in profits for the fiscal year ending in February 1997.

During 1997 Haub was promoted to president and co-CEO and then became sole CEO in May 1998, with Wood remaining chairman. Haub soon launched a new revitalization effort. In December 1998 A&P announced that it would shut 127 smaller, underperforming stores. The closures were designed to enable the company to concentrate on its better performing outlets in its strongest markets—those in which it had the potential to be the number one or number two player. A&P subsequently exited from the Richmond, Virginia, and Atlanta markets. The company also said that it would, over the next three years, open as many as 200 larger-format superstores and modernize 225 existing stores. The closed stores were expected to generate one-time cost savings of $90 million and lead to improved overall profitability. In turn, rising profits would place A&P in a better position to pursue acquisitions at a time when the supermarket industry was undergoing a significant consolidation wave. Restructuring charges of about $120 million led A&P to post a net loss of $67.2 million for the fiscal year ending in February 1999.

The store closures left A&P with three core markets: the Northeast, the Midwest (principally Michigan and Wisconsin), and Ontario. The company identified New Orleans as a fourth core area and in 1999 acquired six Schwegmann stores there that were later rebranded under the Sav-A-Center name. In addition to budgeting $400 million for capital improvements, A&P also set aside another $250 million for a second phase of the restructuring program involving the installation of a state-of-the-art computer system. This effort, launched in 2000, was designed to improve efficiencies throughout the company's entire supply chain and operations, from manufacturing through checkout. Between 90 and 95 percent of the firm's computer systems were to be replaced.

Early 2000s: A Stalled Turnaround

Following several executive defections in 2000, including that of the COO, Elizabeth Culligan was brought onboard as executive vice-president and COO in early 2001 (she was promoted to president and COO about a year later). Culligan was a former executive at Nabisco Holdings Corp., and her background in food manufacturing made her an unconventional choice to head up a major food retailer. In the middle of that year, Christian Haub was named chairman and CEO, bringing an end to Wood's long A&P tenure. In November the company announced the closure of another 39 underperforming supermarkets, most of which had been opened during the previous five years in what A&P now said was a "flawed" program of expansion. Investors reacted positively both to the closure plan and to the frank admission of past failure, and the company's stock began to rise.

In a hopeful sign for the company, A&P posted a profit for the fourth quarter of fiscal 2002, its first quarter in the black since the first quarter of 2000. The turnaround soon began stalling out, however, hampered by the stagnating U.S. economy and stepped-up competition in the company's main markets. A&P encountered a further setback in the middle of 2002 when it was forced to restate its financial results for the previous three fiscal years because of problems with the way it was accounting for inventory in certain regions and with vendor allowances—payments made by manufacturers to retailers for promoting their products in stores. The company's stock began declining, reaching an all-time low in October 2002, the same month that Culligan tendered her resignation.

At that same time, A&P announced that it was dividing its retail operations into two operating units: A&P U.S. and A&P Canada. A&P officials felt that its chains within the two countries were in markedly different operational situations. The Canadian chains, under the direction of Brian Piwek, had been successfully turned around and had entered a growth phase. By contrast, there was still much work to be done to turn the U.S. chains into competitive and consistently profitable properties. In fact, many of the programs that had been instrumental in the Canadian turnaround were to be transferred to the U.S. operations. For example, the Canadian A&P and Dominion chains had placed large emphasis on high-quality fresh foods and customer service. A&P had also developed a successful low-price/limited-assortment format in Canada under the Food Basics banner; the format was already being tested in the United States, and in December 2002 the company announced that it would convert 120 of its 700 stores to the Food Basics format. Management too was shifted to the south, Piwek having been named president and CEO of A&P U.S. Eric Claus took a similar position with A&P Canada. Claus came to A&P from Co-op Atlantic, a New Brunswick-based retail and wholesale food company, where he was president and CEO. Both Piwek and Claus began reporting directly to Haub, who added the title of president to his other duties.

These moves came as A&P was in increasingly dire straits. For the first nine months of the fiscal year ending in February 2003, the company suffered losses of $172 million. Burdened with more than $900 million in long-term debt as of late 2002, the company needed to raise cash and cut costs. During the first three months of 2003, A&P entered into several agreements to sell 17 stores in northern New England. These divestments would mark A&P's exit from Massachusetts and New Hampshire, reducing its New England operations to just its stores in Connecticut. In February 2003 the company reached an agreement to sell seven Kohl's stores in Madison, Wisconsin, and also said that it was seeking to sell the remaining Kohl's stores, which were located in the Milwaukee area. These latest store divestments would reduce the number of company stores to about 650. A&P also confirmed that it was exploring the sale of its Eight O'Clock coffee business. In an effort to be more competitive in the Detroit market, A&P lowered prices permanently at its Farmer Jack stores, replacing the need for customers to use a savings club card for weekly sales specials. Whether these moves would be sufficient to stabilize A&P's precarious financial position remained to be seen.

Principal Subsidiaries

A&P Wine and Spirits, Inc.; ANP Sales Corp.; APW Produce Company, Inc.; APW Supermarket Corporation; APW Supermarkets, Inc.; Big Star, Inc.; The Great Atlantic and Pacific Tea Company, Limited (Canada); Borman's, Inc.; Compass Foods, Inc.; Family Center, Inc.; Food Basics, Inc.; Futurestore Food Markets, Inc.; Gerard Avenue, Inc.; The Great Atlantic & Pacific Tea Company of Vermont, Inc.; Kwik Save Inc.; Limited Foods, Inc.; LO-LO Discount Stores, Inc.; Montvale Holdings, Inc.; Richmond, Incorporated; St. Pancras Company Limited (Bermuda); Shopwell, Inc.; Southern Development, Inc.; Super Fresh Food Markets, Inc.; Super Fresh Food Markets of Maryland, Inc.; Super Fresh/Sav-A-Center, Inc.; Super Fresh Food Markets of Virginia, Inc.; Super Market Service Corp.; Super Plus Food Warehouse, Inc.; Supermarket Distribution Service Corp.; Supermarket Distributor Service-Florence, Inc.; Supermarket Distribution Services, Inc.; Supermarket Systems, Inc.; Tea Development Co., Inc.; The South Dakota Great Atlantic & Pacific Tea Company, Inc.; Transco Service-Milwaukee, Inc.; Waldbaum, Inc.; W.S.L. Corporation; 2008 Broadway, Inc.

Principal Operating Units

A&P U.S.; A&P Canada.

Principal Competitors

Wal-Mart Stores, Inc.; The Kroger Co.; Safeway Inc.; Albertson's, Inc.; Loblaw Companies Limited; Meijer, Inc.; Sobeys Inc.; Wakefern Food Corporation; Giant Food Inc.; Ahold USA, Inc.; Shaw's Supermarkets, Inc.; Pathmark Stores, Inc.; Wegmans Food Markets, Inc.

Further Reading

"A&P Looks Like Tengelmann's Vietnam," *Business Week,* February 1, 1982, pp. 42+.
"A&P: Story of a Turnaround," *Chain Store Age,* September 1983, pp. 49+.

Bernstein, Peter W., "A&P Calls in a Reliever," *Fortune,* June 2, 1980, p. 66.

Biesada, Alexandra, "The Golden Coattails," *Financial World,* October 27, 1992, pp. 30–31.

Blyskal, Jeff, "Auf Wiedersehen, A&P?," *Forbes,* August 3, 1981, pp. 48+.

"Can Jonathan Scott Save A&P?," *Business Week,* May 19, 1975, p. 128.

DeMarrais, Kevin G., "A&P Girds for Merger Battles; Building 200 Stores, Shutting Down 127," *Hackensack (N.J.) Record,* December 9, 1998, p. A1.

——, "A&P Looks for a Fresh Start," *Hackensack (N.J.) Record,* November 5, 2000, p. B1.

——, "A&P Planning to Convert Stores to Food Basics," *Hackensack (N.J.) Record,* December 5, 2002, p. B1.

——, "A&P Selling Wisconsin Supermarkets, May Shed Coffee Business," *Hackensack (N.J.) Record,* February 26, 2003, p. B1.

——, "Great Expectations: Everything Is A-OK at A&P Stores Again with New Executive Minding P's and Q's," *Hackensack (N.J.) Record,* February 10, 2002, p. B1.

——, "Taking Stock, A&P to Close 39 Stores," *Hackensack (N.J.) Record,* November 15, 2001, p. B1.

——, "Troubled A&P's Chief Quits in Management Shake-up," *Hackensack (N.J.) Record,* October 30, 2002, p. B1.

DeNitto, Emily, "Private Labels Bounce Back into Favor at A&P," *Advertising Age,* September 27, 1993, p. 12.

Doebele, Justin, "Prosperity Around the Corner?," *Forbes,* February 22, 1999, pp. 124, 126.

Dowdell, Stephen, "A&P Is on Fresh Path to Growth in Future," *Supermarket News,* July 31, 1995, pp. 13+.

Eklund, Christopher S., "How A&P Fattens Profits by Sharing Them," *Business Week,* December 22, 1986, p. 44.

Garry, Michael, "A&P Strikes Back," *Progressive Grocer,* February 1994, pp. 32–37.

Grieves, Robert T., "Back to the Future," *Forbes,* May 30, 1988, pp. 116+.

Hager, Bruce, "Trouble Stalks the Aisles at A&P," *Business Week,* September 23, 1991, pp. 60–61.

Hamstra, Mark, "A&P Sets Big Rollout of Food Basics," *Supermarket News,* December 9, 2002, p. 1.

——, "Imported from Canada: A&P Turnaround Effort," *Supermarket News,* November 4, 2002, p. 1.

Hoyt, Edwin P., *That Wonderful A&P!,* New York: Hawthorne Books, 1969, 279 p.

Kansas, Dave, "A&P Seeking to Add Another Dash of Retailing Magic," *Wall Street Journal,* May 28, 1993, p. 4B.

Klokis, Holly, "A&P's Wood: Still Intrigued by the Challenge," *Chain Store Age,* June 1987, pp. 19+.

Lazo, Shirley A., "Woes Up North Lead to an A&P Slash," *Barron's,* December 12, 1994, p. 39.

Loeffelholz, Suzanne, "Hobson's Choice for A&P," *Financial World,* December 13, 1988, p. 18.

Marcial, Gene G., "Spicing Things Up at the A&P," *Business Week,* February 1, 1999, p. 112.

Merwin, John, "GAP's Credibility," *Forbes,* June 4, 1984, pp. 72+.

Naik, Gautall, "A&P, Hoping for a Comeback, to Stress Bigger Stores, Private-Label Promotion," *Wall Street Journal,* June 3, 1994, p. A7A.

Orgel, David, "A&P to Close 127 Units, Put Emphasis on Superstores," *Supermarket News,* December 14, 1998, p. 1.

Paikert, Charles, "A&P Awaits Results of Major Surgery," *Chain Store Age,* September 1982, pp. 26+.

"Portrait of a Survivor: America's First Grocery Chain Has Proved an Enduring Fixture—Through Good Times and Bad," *Supermarket News,* December 19, 1994, pp. 10+.

"Price and Price," *Forbes,* October 29, 1979, p. 98.

"Rebound All Over Again?," *Forbes,* March 16, 1992, p. 172.

Rothman, Andrea, "A&P Is Thriving—So Why Is James Wood Still Around?," *Business Week,* April 10, 1989, pp. 90+.

Sachar, Laura, "An Englishman's Cup of Tea," *Financial World,* August 11, 1987, pp. 32+.

Saporito, Bill, "A&P: Grandma Turns a Killer," *Fortune,* April 23, 1990, pp. 207+.

——, "Just How Good Is the Great A&P?," *Fortune,* March 16, 1987, pp. 92+.

Schifrin, Matthew, "Too Sharp a Knife?," *Forbes,* March 1, 1993, pp. 44–45.

"Taking the Long View," *Progressive Grocer,* May 1994, pp. 131–33.

Tracy, Eleanor Johnson, "How A&P Got Creamed," *Fortune,* January 1973, p. 103.

Walsh, William I., *The Rise and Decline of The Great Atlantic and Pacific Tea Company,* Secaucus, N.J.: L. Stuart, 1986, 254 p.

Wilson, Marianne, "A&P's Great Expectations," *Chain Store Age,* April 1999, pp. 36–39.

Zwiebach, Elliot, "A&P Begins Selling Stores to Offset Debt," *Supermarket News,* February 17, 2003, p. 1.

——, "A&P Sees Store Development As Growth Key," *Supermarket News,* July 20, 1998, p. 5.

——, "A&P's Turnaround Effort Stalls in Weak Economy," *Supermarket News,* August 5, 2002, p. 1.

—updates: A. Woodward and David E. Salamie

Greene, Tweed & Company

2075 Detwiler Road
Kulpsville, Pennsylvania 19443
U.S.A.
Telephone: (215) 256-9521
Fax: (215) 256-0189

Private Company
Incorporated: 1903
Employees: 1,200
Sales: $185 million (2002 est.)
NAIC: 332911 Industrial Valve Manufacturing

A private company located in the small town of Kulpsville, Pennsylvania, Greene, Tweed & Company is one of the world's leading manufacturers of specialty seals and engineered plastic components. Its products are used in a wide range of applications in the aerospace and defense, chemical, petrochemical, oilfield equipment manufacturing, industrial hydraulics, pharmaceutical, medical, biotechnology, and semiconductor industries. While many competitors in recent years have chosen to concentrate on standardized products that can be produced in high volumes, Greene, Tweed has prospered by focusing on high performance applications.

Origins in 1863

In May 1863, in the midst of the Civil War, Greene, Tweed & Co. opened for business in a small office on Murray Street in Lower Manhattan. It was established by brothers J. Ashton Greene and John W. Greene, along with partner Henry A. Tweed. At first the firm acted as a distributor of wholesale hardware and mill supplies. It performed no manufacturing, although several products were produced according to specifications by others and bore the Greene, Tweed brand. By the end of the war in 1865, the company traded throughout the Union states and quickly set out to extend its reach to all of the 35 states and ten territories comprising the United States. Greene, Tweed also expanded its product lines beyond general hardware to more specialize hardware used in shipbuilding, as well as leather goods such as buggy whips, harnessing, and leather belting. In addition, leather was used to help seal the water

pumps of the day. "Packings" would evolve to keep pace with changing technologies and remains a mainstay of the company to the present day.

An important turning point for Greene, Tweed occurred in 1873 when it began purchasing packings for resale from another New York company called Manhattan Packing Manufacturing Co. Highly unusual for the period, Manhattan Packing boasted a woman, Eliza D. Murfey, as its founder and principal partner. It was also known for its innovative internally-lubricated packing, marketed as "Manhattan" packing. By 1880, Greene, Tweed's mill supplies business was devoted to packings; in 1889, the company bought out Murfey and her partner and became directly involved in manufacturing.

Greene, Tweed underwent some ownership changes, with Henry Tweed selling out due to poor health. Willard H. Platt, a man with a background in dry goods, bought into the business and for a time operated as a co-partner with John W. Greene. In 1903, the business was incorporated and under this arrangement the major stockholders became John W. Greene, J. Ashton Greene, and Willard H. Platt and his son, Willard R. Platt. In the meantime, the industrial equipment that relied on Greene, Tweed packings became more demanding, running at ever-higher temperatures. Engineers with the company began experimenting with asbestos yarn used in conjunction with the Manhattan internal lubricating method. The result of these efforts was a superior, albeit expensive, product. Almost as difficult as developing the new seal was finding an appropriate product name. It was the elder Platt, having just returned from a trip to the South, who suggested Palmetto, noting that the asbestos packing reminded him of the braided look of a palmetto tree trunk. The name stuck and is still used by a Greene, Tweed Company—Palmetto, Inc.

Henry Demarest Spurs Sales in Early 1900s

In 1899, Greene, Tweed began to procure most of its asbestos yarn from the newly formed Asbestos Fiber Spinning Co., located in North Wales, Pennsylvania, some 20 miles north of Philadelphia (a connection that ultimately led to Greene, Tweed's exodus from New York City). Although the company boasted the industry's highest quality seal in Palmetto, the prod-

Company Perspectives:

When Greene, Tweed products are at work, there's not much to see. And that's the way our customers like it.

uct was poorly promoted and because of its high price made little inroads in the market. It took an outsider named Henry S. Demarest to change that situation. A self-educated engineer, Demarest became familiar with Palmetto while serving as a purchasing agent for the Henry R. Worthington Co. Ignoring specific requests for Palmetto, he bought cheaper, older types of packing. After enduring ongoing complaints from the firm's engineers, he conducted his own test of Palmetto and was so impressed by the results that he paid a visit to Willard R. Platt. Learning that Platt was unwilling to spend any money to market Palmetto, and firmly convinced that the product held great potential, Demarest offered to promote and sell Palmetto at no salary. Instead, he would split the profits on the sales he generated. Platt agreed to the arrangement, and in 1901 Demarest began a long-term association with Greene, Tweed. He faced the challenge of convincing parsimonious purchasers to buy an expensive product, but he also knew that once they understood that they actually saved money in the long run they would become customers. His favorite ploy was to offer to pack the most troublesome pump in the plant with Palmetto at no charge. Donning coveralls over his suit, Demarest performed the work himself and simply left his business card. Invariably the purchasing agent called back to place an order, having seen for himself how well the seal worked and projected the long-term savings.

Demarest also established a network of distributors throughout the country, supported by catalogues he produced as well as direct-mail advertising, circulars, and advertisements in trade publications. While on vacation in Denmark in 1904, he also took time to set up distributorships in Denmark, Norway, Sweden, and Finland, creating a foothold in Europe. He established a distributorship in South Africa in 1910, then, following World War I, arranged for distribution in Japan, Korea, Formosa, and Manchuria. In the 1920s, he moved into China as well as South America. Palmetto received some unsolicited, albeit welcome, publicity in 1928 when newspapers noted that Palmetto was in service on the *City of New York,* the ship transporting Admiral Byrd to Antarctica, where he would make his famous flight over the South Pole.

Greene, Tweed's business was not confined to just Palmetto and other packings. The company produced a number of items brought to it by inventors and licensed to outside manufacturers. These products included an oil pump, buckles used on galoshes and raincoats, the first chain tong wrench, the first split-head rawhide hammer, and the "Favorite" reversible ratchet socket wrench. The Favorite line of wrenches would become mainstays for use in industry as well as the military for many years to come. In December 1919, Greene Tweed acquired Brabson Bros., makers of builders' hardware and brass goods. Although this business prospered for the next several years, in 1928 the brass plant was divested and the hardware lines eventually sold to Slaymaker Lock Co.

With the crash of the stock market in 1929 and the subsequent Great Depression, Greene, Tweed like many businesses

was severely tested. In December 1932, Willard R. Platt retired as head of the firm and responsibility fell upon Demarest, who at the age of 66 agreed to lead the company through this difficult period. Although he would only live a few more years, dying in July 1937, he succeeded in strengthening the company and leaving behind a solid management team. With another world war on the horizon, the company was well positioned to meet the challenge of supplying America's defense needs. The demand for packings of all types was immense, leading to Greene, Tweed's acquisition of the Asbestos Fiber Spinning Co. in order to secure all of its output. In addition, Greene, Tweed was able to transfer some operations from its overcrowded facilities in the Bronx to the more spacious plant in North Wales, Pennsylvania. The Bronx plant concentrated on braided packings and tools, producing vast quantities of rawhide hammers for aircraft makers and the U.S. Navy, and Favorite wrenches for use in tanks and the building of portable Bailey bridges. The Pennsylvania plant produced new rubber-content packings using asbestos cloth, instrumental in Navy ship boilers. The plant also manufactured GT rings, die-formed rings of neoprene-impregnated seals used in tanks and the recoil mechanism of .50-caliber machine guns.

Postwar Expansion

Following the war Greene, Tweed leased its Bronx facility and moved it manufacturing operations and administrative offices to North Wales. Changes brought by the war also placed new demands on packings, especially for synthetic rubber molded seals. Synthetic rubber had been used during the war as a substitute for natural rubber, but the manmade material resisted hydraulic fluids and was more temperature resistant than the leather packings that were standard in most hydraulic mechanisms. This development opened up a major new market for Greene, Tweed, which now devoted greater resources to the creation of molded packings. Although prepared to convert back to peacetime applications, the company would once again devote much of its resources to servicing the military with the advent of the Korean conflict in 1950. It not only supplied GT rings to restore old tanks to serviceable condition, it also developed special tools for submarines and mine-sweepers, including non-magnetic wrenches and hammers made out of stainless steel. GT rings would also be key elements in new weapons, such as the Polaris missile, which the U.S. Navy added to its arsenal in 1960.

During the 1960s, Greene, Tweed moved beyond its traditional business of manufacturing a variety of hardware products, mostly intended for domestic consumption, and transformed itself into an international provider of highly-engineered, high-performance seals and sealing systems. In 1964, the company took a major step when it became involved in the aerospace market after one of its GT rings was approved for use in the landing gear of the F-4 Phantom. Later, the seals would become part of the landing gear of the Boeing 747 jumbo jet. In order to keep pace with the rapid evolution of technology, Greene, Tweed made an early and highly expensive investment in a state-of-the-art computer system.

Move to Kulpsville in 1970s

As the 1970s opened, the demand for Greene, Tweed products was so great that the company outgrew its production capacity in North Wales and moved to a larger, more modern

Key Dates:

1863: Greene, Tweed & Co. is established as a hardware wholesaler.
1878: Company begins purchasing packings for resale.
1903: The business is incorporated.
1946: The manufacture of packings at Greene, Tweed aids the U.S. war effort.
1964: The company sells its GT rings to the aerospace industry.
1981: A German subsidiary is formed.
1986: A Japanese subsidiary is formed.
1995: The company opens a clean room to serve the semiconductor industry.

facility in nearby Kulpsville, Pennsylvania. By 1973, the company's administrative offices, as well as its engineering and research and development labs, would also make the move to Kulpsville. Greene, Tweed was now heavily involved in the aerospace industry. It patented an advanced T-shaped sealing assembly, which provided high performance and an extended life in a number of aerospace applications. The company was so well respected internationally that the French designers of the supersonic Concorde aircraft specified that GT rings be used in the craft's landing gear. Advances were also made in other areas. In 1978, Greene, Tweed received a patent on the RSA seal, which quickly became a standard feature of hydraulic cylinders in construction equipment manufactured around the world.

In the 1980s, Greene, Tweed produced its first ''capped'' seal, offering both long life and low-friction properties. The business was then strengthened by the creation of Enerlon, a custom blended material that greatly enhanced the performance of capped seals. The company also introduced a substance called Flouraz, a versatile elastomer that could operate at temperatures above 500 degrees Fahrenheit. Another innovation was Chemraz, a chemical-resistant elastomer, effective in temperatures that ranged from −20 degrees Fahrenheit to 450 degrees Fahrenheit. Its introduction opened up new opportunities in a number of industries, including hydrocarbon processing, semiconductor, and instrumentation.

To help serve its growing markets, Greene, Tweed took steps to grow its production capacity from within as well as through acquisitions—both domestically and internationally. In 1981, it bought Advantec, makers of PTFE seals and custom components. Later in the decade, in order to support the petroleum exploration, extraction, and processing market, Greene, Tweed opened a Houston, Texas, plant and warehouse. Overseas, the company established a subsidiary in West Germany in 1981, followed a year later by an operation in England and another in France in 1985. Greene, Tweed entered the Pacific Rim market in 1986, opening a company in Japan in 1986.

New Technologies in the 1990s and Beyond

With the need for seals evolving at an almost dizzying rate, Greene, Tweed stepped back in the late 1980s to assess its strengths and determine how to proceed in the final years of the century. The company's president, Phil Paino, told *Design News* a decade later that management concluded that Greene, Tweed excelled at high-performance, state-of-the art sealing-related products, and as a result the company elected to concentrate on industries where high performance was crucial, such as aerospace, semiconductor equipment, CPI, oil field equipment, and mobile equipment. As Paino stated, ''We focused on developing products that meet the increasing technological demands of these industries, providing sealing solutions where the cost of failure far exceeds the cost of the right seal.'' The strategy served the company well in the 1990s, when many of its competitors decided to focus on standardized products with the hope of enjoying higher-volume production runs and the resulting economies of scale. By staking out the high-performance area, Greene, Tweed not only found itself with far less direct competition, it once again enjoyed the marketing edge exploited by Demarest decades earlier, when he proved to customers that lower-cost seals did not actually provide the lowest-cost solution.

In the 1990s, Greene, Tweed was especially successful in serving the semiconductor industry. In 1995, the company built a clean room in Kulpsville but quickly outgrew its capacity and ultimately opened a factory in Selma, Texas. As a new century began, the need for specialized sealing solutions increased across all markets. To help maintain its creative edge, Greene, Tweed established an Incubator Group to develop new products and open up new business opportunities. Its engineers also worked concurrently with customer's engineers, taking advantage of the Internet to share data and ideas. With new 3D design capabilities, Greene, Tweed engineers were better able to determine where failure in a seal might occur, rather than examine a ruptured seal returned by the customer, as was the case only a few years earlier. From the earliest days of its history, Greene, Tweed displayed a willingness to embrace innovation, and that same spirit promised to keep the company in the vanguard of its industry.

Principal Competitors

CE Franklin Ltd.; T-3 Energy Services, Inc.; UMECO plc.

Further Reading

''Founded During the Civil War, Greene, Tweed & Co. Today Supplies Seals for Space Shuttle Columbia,'' *Hydaulic & Pneumatics*, March 1983, p. 82.
Greene, Tweed & Co. 1863–1963, Kulpsville, Pa.: Greene, Tweed & Co., 1964.
Paino, Phi, ''Engineers Work More With Customers Today,'' *Design News*, May 21, 2001, p. 110.
Peach, Laurie Ann, ''They Make Seals Big Deal,'' *Design News*, November 2, 1998, pp. 86–88.

—Ed Dinger

alain manoukian
Groupe Alain Manoukian

Domaine de Blanchelaine
BP 29 Mercurol
26 600 Tain l'Hermitage
France
Telephone: +33 (0)4 75 07 50 50
Fax: +33 (0)4 75 07 44 71
Web site: http://www.groupe-alain-manoukian.com

Public Company
Incorporated: 1973
Employees: 1,077
Sales: EUR 160.79 million ($150 million) (2001)
Stock Exchanges: Euronext Paris
Ticker Symbol: AMKN
NAIC: 4481120 Women's Clothing Stores; 448110
    Men's Clothing Stores

France's Groupe Alain Manoukian is a leading designer, distributor, and retailer of ready-to-wear fashions, with an emphasis on knitwear. The company operates an international network of more than 180 retail stores—some 120 of which are directly owned by the company, the remainder operated as "affiliates" under a franchise agreement. In addition to its retail network, Manoukian's fashions are distributed through a network of third-party retailers. Manoukian's operations remain heavily dominated by its French sales, which account for nearly 80 percent of revenues of more than EUR 160 million. The group has been expanding its international presence, however, particularly in Spain, Belgium, Portugal, Greece, and Switzerland, but also in the Far East, with stores in Japan, Hong Kong, Korea, and Singapore. Manoukian also operates an e-commerce capable web site. Long known for its fashions targeting the women's 30- to 40-year-old market segment, Alain Manoukian has expanded its reach at the turn of the century, boosting its menswear line to account for 10 percent of total sales. The company also has launched two new labels, Séda Manoukian, targeting the 20- to 30-year-old women's market, and the high-end Manoukian label, which targets the women's 40- to 55-year-old segment. Listed on the Euronext Paris Secondary Market, Alain Manoukian remains controlled at more than 63 percent by the Manoukian family. Founder Alain Manoukian, together with wife Danielle and son David, continue to occupy the company's top management positions.

Knitting a Fashion Empire in the 1970s

Alain Manoukian might have spent his career at his family's shoe manufacturing company in Romans, in France's Rhône Alpes region if it had not been for the design talents of his wife, Danielle. While Alain Manoukian worked at the modest shoe company, Danielle Manoukian opened a clothing shop at the beginning of the 1960s. Danielle Manoukian had come from a textile family, which made sweaters in Belgium. Manoukian began designing her own sweaters, selling them in her shop.

The Manoukians soon realized that Danielle Manoukian's designs had begun to outsell the other sweaters sold at the shop. Encouraged by the success of Manoukian's sweaters, Alain Manoukian decided to leave the family shoe business and set up his own company based on his wife's sweater designs. With financial backing from his parents, Manoukian opened the first Alain Manoukian store in November 1972 in the town of Colmar.

The Manoukians met with quick success through the 1970s as the company developed a full line of women's fashions, targeting the 30- to 40-year-old, mid-priced segment. While knitwear represented the company's largest sales segment, reaching more than 75 percent of its sales, Manoukian also developed a strong line of coordinated separates to accompany its knitwear designs.

From the start, the company focused on the design and distribution ends of its business, contracting out to third-party manufacturers for the actual production. As Manoukian told *Le Monde,* "When one is at the same time producer, designer and retailer, one loses his soul." Over the next decade the company built up a network of subcontractors in France, Belgium, and especially Italy.

The company grew quickly during the 1970s, becoming a noted name in French knitwear designs. Manoukian explained the reasons behind the company's success to *Le Monde:* "Our strength is that we are retailers first of all. A manufacturer closed in behind the walls of his factory can't recognize evolutions in fashion. Only distributors can 'scent' the customer's desires."

Company Perspectives:

As a very well known label, Alain Manoukian has all the attributes to continue developing and to become a European leader in medium- / top-of-the-range fashion. The Groupe Alain Manoukian, active in the French Stock Market since 1985 and with international presence in more than 28 countries, has always known how to adapt to changes taking place outside of the company and the ever-growing demands of the clientele. Since it started up, our company has been developing in order to remain at the top in a very competitive environment. It is thanks to the company-based culture that manifests itself through constant re-appraisal and research into how we can make improvements that the Groupe Alain Manoukian has known such success since its creation. And it is this culture and the enthusiasm of our teams which allows Alain Manoukian's products and the label itself to lead the targeted market at the start of the third millennium.

By the late 1970s, the Manoukians had begun to build a network of stores throughout France. In 1979, the company, seeking to increase its expansion, began developing a franchise network as well. By the early 1980s, Manoukian had expanded throughout much of France, opening its own stores—nearly 80 by the middle of the decade—as well as developing a 400-strong distribution network of franchises and third-party retailers. Supporting this growth was a FFr 50 million investment in a computerized distribution system.

With growing success in France, Manoukian turned toward international growth in the mid-1980s, a process begun in 1984, with store openings in Italy, Spain, and Switzerland. The United States became a prime target for growth, as the company opened stores in New York, Boston, Atlanta, Houston, and Dallas, among other places, including a flagship store on Manhattan's Madison Avenue. To finance its continued expansion, Manoukian went public in 1985, listing on the Lyons stock exchange's Secondary Market. The Manoukian family maintained control of the business, however, with 67 percent of its shares.

By 1986, Manoukian's stock price had more than quadrupled, while its revenues continued to grow strongly, topping FFr 426 million (the equivalent of EUR 65 million), prompting many to label the company the "French Benetton," in reference to the highly successful Italian clothing company. At the end of 1986, the company was poised to expand still further, when it granted a franchise license to Pennsylvania's Retail Concepts Inc. to open as many as 200 Alain Manoukian stores in the United States. To maintain competitive pricing in the United States, Manoukian began subcontracting its clothing manufacture in Hong Kong for the first time.

Restructuring for Growth in the New Century

Manoukian sought to build on its brand name during the 1980s, joining the trend toward designer licensing—the company rolled out a line of Manoukian fashion eyewear, and also sought to extend its name to a variety of accessories. Meanwhile, Alain Manoukian attempted to duplicate its success in womenswear with a line of men's fashions, debuting the com-

pany's first 200-piece menswear collection in 1988 and launching plans to open as many as 200 Manoukian men's stores in France, before rolling out the men's concept to Japan, Spain, and the United States.

Manoukian's enthusiasm for expansion spread to new targets at the end of the 1980s, including a drive into the children's wear market. The company also began making acquisitions, buying up La Sweaterie and Imperial Classic, as well as an extension into silk-printing with subsidiary Société d'Impressions et Nouveautés, moves that led the group into manufacturing for the first time.

Yet by the beginning of the 1990s, Manoukian's expansion appeared too ambitious, while its designs, described by some as outdated and overpriced, appeared to be falling from consumer favor. From profits of nearly FFr 29 million on sales of FFr 570 million in 1989, the company dropped into losses, to the tune of FFr 10 million on sales of FFr 650 million in 1990. Manoukian's difficulties continued into the following year, with sales dropping back to just FFr 615 million and losses of nearly FFr 8 million.

Manoukian began restructuring in 1992, simplifying its organizational structure and refocusing its operations around its core knitwear and womenswear lines. The company now returned to its origins as a retailer and distributor, a strategy that included transferring ownership of its retail chain, previously held directly by the Manoukian family, to the company. As part of the restructuring, the company sold off a number of its holdings, licensed out its children's clothing line, and pulled out of the U.S. market.

These moves helped Manoukian return to profitability by the end of 1992, posting profits of FFr 1.9 million on sales of slightly less than FFr 560 million. By the following year, the company had increased its profitability to more than FFr 23 million, despite a further drop in revenues to FFr 530 million. By then, Manoukian had taken steps to gain tighter control over its distribution network, beginning a program in 1993 of converting its franchises into "affiliates" placed under the company's direction. Manoukian also began a program of acquiring a number of its affiliate stores, doubling the size of its company-owned network by the end of the decade.

By the middle of the 1990s, Manoukian was once again on a growth track, with sales rising from EUR 77 million (approximately FFr 510 million) in 1996 to EUR 90 million in 1997 and then topping EUR 105 million in 1998—with a goal of topping the FFr 1 billion (EUR 150 million) mark by 2001. Part of the company's success came with the relaunch of its menswear collection, which rose to 6 percent of the group's sales by 1998. Manoukian, backed by statistics showing that 60 percent of men's clothing purchases are made by women, also rolled out a new retail concept, that of "mixed" stores, featuring both women's and men's clothing—and separate doors for each. The first mixed store opened in 1996, and by 1998 the company operated 15 mixed stores.

Manoukian meanwhile had continued acquiring affiliate stores, giving it more control over its distribution costs and enabling it to post profit gains as well. The company began investing in its domestic distribution network, launching a EUR 60 million spending program to acquire a number of its affiliates and other retail locations in order to boost its total selling

Key Dates:

1972: Alain Manoukian opens the first store based on Danielle Manoukian's sweater designs.
1979: Manoukian launches a franchise network.
1984: Manoukian begins international expansion, establishing company-owned and franchised stores.
1985: The company goes public with a listing on the Lyons Stock Exchange's Secondary Market, leading Manoukian to add children's and men's wear lines and to enter manufacturing for the first time.
1992: Losses force the company to restructure and refocus on core distribution operations.
1996: The company débuts the "mixed" clothing store concept, featuring women's and men's fashions in the same stores, with separate entrances for each department.
2001: The company launches e-commerce and business-to-business web sites.
2002: The company launches two new clothing lines, the high-end Manoukian Collection and the youth market Séda Manoukian.

surface area to 14,000 square meters. By the end of 1999, that operation had been completed in large part, as the company's French store network topped 100 stores, with an additional 31 affiliates. Internationally, Manoukian remained present, particularly in Spain, Portugal, Greece, and Japan, with an additional 100 franchised stores.

Yet Manoukian began building up its foreign holdings as well, particularly in Spain, where it made plans to add four new stores to its existing two by the end of 2001, and in Belgium, where the company added six new stores to its eight-store network in that country. At the turn of the century, the company's foreign sales were slated to reach 25 percent of its total turnover. The company's menswear also was building strongly, nearing 10 percent of total sales. By then, Manoukian had developed an additional retail format, for a series of new, large-scale "megastores" featuring 500 square meters of selling space, with the first of the new retail concept opening in Nantes, Mulhouse, and Lyon.

In 2001, Manoukian turned to a new market, that of the Internet, launching two new web sites. The first was an e-commerce site featuring more than 700 clothing items, and available in a number of languages. The second was a business-to-business site directed at potential suppliers, licensees, investors, and employees. The company's e-commerce and overall retail operations were supported by a EUR 6 million investment in order to consolidate all of the company's distribution and logistics operations into a single site. That investment was part of a EUR 18 million spending program in which Manoukian renovated a number of its existing stores, adding nine new stores and absorbing 14 of its affiliate stores.

Manoukian reached its goal of FFr 1 billion in turnover in 2000, a year ahead of schedule. The company's double-digit growth rates—12 percent between 2000 and 2001—easily outshone the overall clothing sector in France, which was stalling at growth rates of less than 2 percent per year. Yet by the end of 2001, Manoukian had become mired in the sluggish retail sector. The group managed a modest sales increase, of more than 4 percent; much of this growth, however, came through expansion of the group's retail network.

At the beginning of 2002, Manoukian took steps to revitalize its growth, setting a new goal of doubling its sales within six years and transforming itself into a global brand name. The company began a "reengineering" of its operations, including a restructuring of its management and other operations, designed to help it reach its goals. At the same time, the company moved to expand its retail offer. In 2002, the company launched two new clothing lines. The first, Manoukian Collection, targeted the high-end, 40- to 55-year-old women's market. The second, Séda Manoukian, targeted the younger 20- to 30-year-old women's segment.

The immediate effect of Manoukian's restructuring effort was a dip in profits, in part because of disruptions in the group's supply chain, which, coupled with a drop in sales, brought the group into losses by the end of the first half of 2002. The trend toward slowing sales was to continue through much of the year. Nonetheless, the Manoukian brand remained strong, with recognition rates as high as 97 percent in France, as the company looked forward to a return to growth in the new century.

Principal Subsidiaries

Alain Manoukian Belgium; Alain Manoukian España; Nederalma BV (Netherlands); SA Alain Manoukian; SA Alpek (Switzerland); SA Danly; SA Fam; SAM Services (U.S.A.); SA Funny et Cie; SA Soveprom.

Principal Competitors

Rallye S.A.; Redcats SA; Vivarte SA; La Redoute SA; ETAM Developpement SA; Damart S.A.; KDI SAS; Sephora SA; Dyn SA; Promod SA; Zara SA; Tati S.A.; Du Pareil Au Meme SA; Cesar Industries S.A.; Lafuma S.A.; Spot SA; Armand Thiery SA; Cooperative Agridis SA; Catimini International SAS.

Further Reading

"Alain Manoukian a marqué le pas en 2001," *Les Echos,* March 28, 2002, p. 13.
Christine, Robert Marie, "Manoukian le magnifique!," *Le Monde,* March 7, 1987.
"Groupe manoukian alain manoukian en croissance XXL," *Challenges,* October 1, 1999.
Lecoeur, Xavier, "Manoukian veut resserrer production et distribution," *Les Echos,* December 7, 1992, p. 13.

—M. L. Cohen

Groupe Soufflet SA

Quai Sarrail
BP 12
10402 Nogent sur Seine Cedex
France
Telephone: (+33) 3 25 39 41 11
Fax: (+33) 3 25 39 00 87
Web site: http://www.soufflet-group.com

Private Company
Incorporated: 1946 as Etablissements Soufflet SARL
Employees: 2,645
Sales: EUR 2.83 billion ($2.8 billion)(2001)
NAIC: 424510 Grain and Field Bean Merchant
Wholesalers

Groupe Soufflet SA is one of the world's leading agro-industrial groups with an emphasis on grain collection, cereal processing, production and export, malting, and related activities. The company, based in Nogent sur Seine, in the north of France, has established top positions in a number of its primary areas of operations: the company is the number one privately owned collecter of grains in France, the leading producer of flour in Europe, the world's sixth largest maltster, the number one corn processor in France, and the number three rice producer in France. The company has also established a strong presence in the French vineyard supply sector, as well as a leading presence in the industrial bakery market. Since the late 1980s, Soufflet has also expanded into the consumer market, launching its own brands, including Perliz rice products and the Vivien Paille brand of dried vegetables. In France, Soufflet operates some 130 grain collection silos, 11 grain mills, ten malting plants, five bakery products manufacturing facilities, a corn processing plant, and a plant for processing rice and dried vegetables. The company supports its international operations, which accounted for 56 percent of the company's EUR 2.8 billion in sales in 2001, with a network of foreign subsidiaries in the United Kingdom, the Netherlands, the United States, and Belgium. Since the late 1990s, Soufflet has moved into the Eastern European market, acquiring or establishing subsidiaries

in Russia, the Ukraine, Romania, Slovakia, Poland, and Hungary. In 2002, the company expanded its Eastern European position again with acquisitions in the Czech Republic. Soufflet remains controlled by the founding Soufflet family. Jean-Michel Soufflet, grandson of the founder, serves as CEO, while his father, Michel Soufflet, serves as chairman of the board.

Grain Depot at the Turn of the Century

Groupe Soufflet origins can be traced to the turn of the twentieth century, with the establishment of a grain depot at Nogent Sur Seine, in France's northern Champagne region. The depot functioned as a trading hub for farmers who brought their grain harvests for delivery to millers. Steady improvements in farming techniques and grain seed quality enabled France to assert itself not only as a major agricultural force on the European scene but worldwide as well. By the late 1930s, grain production had made steady gains, and in 1939 Jean Soufflet, who had taken over the grain business, constructed the company's first grain silo in Nogent.

Soufflet's ambitions went beyond collecting and selling cereals to include a broader range of services and products supporting the agricultural community. Over time, the company added such activities as the collection and distribution of seeds, as well as fertilizers and insecticides. The company also took an active role in researching and developing new farming and harvesting techniques to help farmers boost their production.

Following World War II, Soufflet incorporated his growing business under the name Etablissements Soufflet SARL. The company then entered into a period of growth, expanding beyond the Champagne region and adding new grain silos. By the 1990s, the company operated more than 100 silos throughout much of France, a number that climbed to more than 130 by the turn of the next century.

Diversification and Growth: 1950s–80s

In the 1950s, Soufflet began expanding beyond cereal trading, entering the market for malt production with the acquisition of the Nogent-based Grande Malterie in 1953. That activity was to become one of Soufflet's most important; as the company

Company Perspectives:

The Soufflet group runs its business within the food chain through the collection, the trading, and the transformation of cereal and other vegetable products in France and in the world. The mastery of the sector and the implementation of synergies in each area of its expertise ensures the group the returns necessary for its development. Its position and its spirit of leadership provide the company with a motor role for giving added value to products of the agricultural sector. The group has acquired in each of its sectors a leading position.

continued to expand, it built or acquired nine more malting plants in France to become one of the world's major malt producers, with more than 11 percent of the global market.

Jean Soufflet died in 1957, and the company's direction was taken over by his son Michel. Under this new generation, Soufflet gradually expanded into one of the world's top agro-industrial groups. Until the mid-1960s, nearly all of Soufflet's activity took place within France. In 1966, Michel Soufflet led the company in its first moves onto the international grain market. In order to support its new international growth objectives, the company built its own silo in the port of Rouen, which was then in the process of becoming a major hub for the world's grain shipping industry. By the middle of the 1970s, Soufflet had succeeded in developing a strong international component, underscored by the creation of a subsidiary in the United Kingdom in 1974. That subsidiary later grew to include three silos, including its own port silo.

Under Michel Soufflet, the company also stepped up its interest in the industrial side of the agricultural business. The company set up a dedicated technical department in 1970, working with farmers to continue to improve seed quality and production quantity. Soufflet itself was becoming interested in expanding its industrial operations beyond its malting facilities. In 1978, the company bought up a grain mill, a move that coincided with Soufflet's new strategy of becoming a major industrial group in the cereals sector. Soufflet quickly expanded those operations, building a network of some 11 mills in France and becoming the leading flour producer in Europe.

In the early 1980s, Soufflet followed its growing flour milling interests into a new sector, that of the industrial baking market. In 1983, Soufflet established its own bakery complex in the town of Terville, beginning production of frozen pastries and other baked goods. Soufflet's milling operations also led the company to become a prominent supplier to France's craft bakers, an industry later to be codified by French law. For that market, Soufflet developed recipes under a new brand name, Baguépi.

Soufflet continued its diversification into the late 1980s. In 1986, the company added maize milling, becoming the European leader with the purchase of Costimex, based in Strasbourg. Two years later, Soufflet added a rice and dried vegetable component when it acquired four processing and packaging plants. The company also constructed a purpose-built process-

ing facility for its new operations in Valenciennes that year. The move into rice and vegetables also led Soufflet into a new arena—that of the consumer foods market—as the company launched its own brands of Perliz rice products and Vivien Paille dried vegetables.

The following year, Soufflet turned to another new market, that of the French wine-growing industry. With the creation of a new subsidiary, Soufflet Vigne, the company began offering products and services geared toward supporting the French wine industry. For this, the company opened its own network of supply stores featuring tools, fertilizers, and other grape-specific growing products, as well as other vintner's needs, including bottles and caps. Over the next decade, Soufflet expanded its Soufflet Vigne store network to nearly 20 units, thereby covering all of the major French wine-producing regions.

The year 1989 marked as well an important step in Soufflet's international growth. In that year, the company acquired Belgian milling group Ceres. Founded near Brussels in 1889, Ceres had grown to become the leading flour milling group in its home market—nearly half of the country's craft bakers purchased exclusively from Ceres—before becoming an important supplier to the European market. The acquisition of Ceres enabled Soufflet to take the leading spot in the European flour milling market.

Agro-Industrial Leader: 1990s and Beyond

By the early 1990s, Soufflet's annual revenues had topped the equivalent of EUR 2.6 billion. The company had successfully assumed a place among the majors in the global cereals industry, taking the number three place in Europe and the number six place worldwide.

Soufflet boosted its industrial bakery division in 1992 with the acquisition of Grigny Frais, a subsidiary of the Casino supermarket group, then in the process of restructuring its holdings. Two years later, Soufflet made a still more important acquisition when it took control of French milling and malting group Pantin. That purchase gave Soufflet the leading position in France in both the milling and malting categories.

Soufflet continued to expand into the late 1990s, beginning construction of a new malting plant in Rouen for a cost of more than EUR 30 million in 1997. In that year, the company also expanded its milling business with the acquisition of Pornic-based Laraison Frères, adding that group's three mills operating in France's western region.

Until the later 1990s, Soufflet operations had remained largely focused on the European market—while exports had risen to some two-thirds of the company's revenues, its French operations remained the group's largest component. The arrival of the third generation of the Soufflet family, in the person of Jean-Michel Soufflet, who took over the managing director's position in 1997, heralded a new, more internationally focused growth strategy for the turn of the century.

Soufflet took a dual approach to stepping up its international operations. On the one hand, the company began establishing new trading subsidiaries, including in the United States and Poland, while also turning toward the Far East, opening a representative office in Singapore and entering into a distribu-

Key Dates:

1900: A grain depot is opened in Nogent sur Seine.
1939: Jean Soufflet constructs a grain silo in Nogent sur Seine.
1946: Etablissements Soufflet SARL is incorporated.
1953: The company acquires Grand Malterie and enters the malting industry.
1957: Michel Soufflet takes over as head of the family business.
1966: The company builds a port silo in Rouen dedicated to grain exports.
1974: A subsidiary in the United Kingdom is opened.
1978: A flour mill is acquired as company targets the agro-industrial market.
1983: The company begins industrial bakery operations.
1988: The company launches its own consumer brands: Perliz (rice) and Vivien Paille (dried vegetables).
1994: The company acquires Groupe Pantin and becomes the leading French flour miller and malting company.
1997: Jean-Michel Soufflet is named managing director; the company begins targeting international growth with the creation of trading subsidiaries in the United States and Poland.
2001: Jean-Michel Soufflet takes over as CEO.

tion agreement with Japan's Nichimen in 1998. On the other hand, Soufflet targeted the international expansion of its industrial infrastructure for its further growth.

For this, Soufflet turned to the Eastern European market. In 1997, Soufflet formed a 70–30 joint-venture partnership with beer brewer Baltika to build and operate a malting plant in St. Petersburg, Russia, tapping into the fast-growing demand for malt products in that country. The success of that joint-venture led the partners to begin construction of a second, larger malting plant in 1999, with a new expansion planned for the early 2000s. By then, Soufflet had begun to expand elsewhere in Eastern Europe, buying up five malting plants in Hungary, Poland, Romania and Slovakia in 1998. The company expanded its malting operations again in 2000 when it acquired the Czech Republic's Moravska Sladovna, then in bankruptcy.

Soufflet's expansion in the malting market helped buffer the company against the sudden collapse of its milling market—between 1997 and 2001, the company's flour exports dropped by nearly 50 percent. The chief cause of this drop came from the emergence of a number of the company's former customer markets, such as Egypt, as self-sufficient flour producers. At the same time, a number of other countries began exporting flour production for the first time, with countries such as Morocco and Turkey becoming strong competitors on the international flour trade market. In response, Soufflet restructured its own milling operations to focus more on higher-value specialty products.

In 2001, Michel Soufflet turned over direction of the company to his son Jean-Michel, remaining on as chairman of the company's board of directors. In nearly 50 years, Soufflet had built his family's business into one of the world's leading agro-industrial groups. Yet Soufflet showed no signs of slowing down in its growth. In 2002, the company announced its purchase of majority control of Obchodni Sladovny Prostejov, the largest malt producer in the Czech Republic.

Principal Subsidiaries

Carburants Soufflet ; CERAPRO; CERES (Belgium); J Soufflet SA; Malterie Soufflet Magyaroszag Kft (Hungary); Malterie Soufflet Saint Petersbourg; Malterie Soufflet Slovaquie; PROLAC; RAMEL; SEMA; SERAGRI; Slodownia Soufflet Polska; SOCOCER (Italy); SOCOMAC; Soufflet Alimentaire; Soufflet Agriculture; Soufflet Atlantique; Soufflet Espagne; Soufflet Hollande; Soufflet Négoce; Soufflet UK; Soufflet USA; Soufflet Malt Roumania Srl; Soufflet Ukraine.

Principal Competitors

Sumitomo Corp.; Nissho Iwai Corp.; SK Global Company Ltd.; ADM-Growmark Inc.; Cargill International S.A.; Cenex Harvest States Cooperatives.

Further Reading

"Franco-Russian Malt Plant Opens in St. Petersburg," *AgraFood East Europe*, June 2000, p. 41.
"Groupe Soufflet, Baltika to Open Malt House in June," *INTERFAX*, March 10, 2000.
"Le groupe Soufflet rachète le minotier Laraison Frères," *Les Echos*, September 5, 1997, p. 24.
"Malterie Soufflet Owns 75 pct of Shares of Obchodni Sladovny," *Czech News Agency*, April 09, 2002.
"Soufflet inaugure une malterie sur le port de Rouen," *La Tribune*, November 16, 1999, p. 28.
"Soufflet Is to Build Another Malt Plant in Russia," *Moskovskie Novosti*, June 13, 2000, p. 4.

—M. L. Cohen

Grupo Dragados SA

Avenida Tenerife 4-6
28700 Madrid
Spain
Telephone: (+34) 91-583-30-00
Fax: (+34) 91-583-21-22
Web site: http://www.dragados.com

Public Company
Incorporated: 1941 as Dragados y Construcciones
Employees: 51,536
Sales: EUR 5.89 billion ($5.8 billion)(2002)
Stock Exchanges: Madrid
Ticker Symbol: DRC
NAIC: 551112 Offices of Other Holding Companies;
237990 Other Heavy and Civil Engineering
Construction; 562111 Solid Waste Collection; 221310
Water Supply and Irrigation Systems; 221320 Sewage
Treatment Facilities; 541330 Engineering Services

Grupo Dragados SA is Spain's second-largest construction and engineering company; pending a merger with rival ACS (Actividades de Construcción y Servicios S.A.), the company stood to become one of the largest in all of Europe. Dragados operates under four primary divisions: Construction, the largest division, representing more than 53 percent of sales in 2002; Services, ranging from street cleaning to waste treatment to port services, which provides about 25 percent of the group's sales; Industrial, generating 17 percent of sales and grouping the company's industrial construction and engineering projects, as well as its telecommunications infrastructure operations and new technology businesses, including its Internet component; and Concessions, which includes an international array of toll road, airport, and railroad concessions. In addition, the company holds a 20 percent stake in real estate group Immobiliaria Urbis. Since the 1990s, Dragados has been making an effort to increase its international scope; foreign operations now account for some 20 percent of the group's sales. In 2002, Dragados posted revenues of more than EUR 5.5 billion. In that year, ACS made a surprise move to acquire a 23.5 percent stake in Dragados, just under the level at which Spanish law requires it

launch a full takeover attempt. Nonetheless, the smaller ACS was able to gain a majority on Dragados's board of directors, giving it effective control of the company. In 2003, ACS purchased an additional 10 percent and indicated its interest in completing a full merger with Dragados. Until that event, Dragados remains quoted on the Madrid Stock Exchange.

From Dredging Group to Major Construction Firm: 1940s–1970s

Dragados y Construcciones ("Dredging and Construction") was formed in 1941 as part of the effort to build the Port of Tarifa, in Cadiz, Spain. Dragados's work in that port consisted of constructing and placing reinforced concrete caissons. The company continued to build expertise in port and harbor dredging, construction, and services, becoming the leading Spanish group in that sector. Port services was also to provide the company with entry into international markets.

Dragados soon turned its dredging experience toward the construction of hydroelectric dams, working with various Spanish utilities, as well as the Spanish government, starting in 1945. The following year, Dragados went public, listing on the Madrid Stock Exchange.

By the 1950s, Dragados had become a diversified construction group, entering the railroad infrastructure market in 1951. The 1950s also marked the start of the group's industrial plant construction operations and its entry into water supply and wastewater systems. After joining in the construction of the Spanish-American army bases, in which the company became involved in paving operations, Dragados began competing for airport construction contracts, winning its first, for Hondarribia Airport in Guipuzcoa, in 1953. In 1960, the company added to its airport portfolio with the construction of the first runway capable of handling jet airplane traffic at Madrid's Barajas Airport. That same year, Dragados started its first subway construction job, building reinforced concrete tunnels for Madrid's new subway system.

The company's first move internationally came in 1965, when it won the contract to participate in the construction of Turkey's Kadinicik Dam. Over the following decades, Dragados's dam-building expertise helped it build a strong in-

Company Perspectives:

Our corporate identity, culture, and values are expressed in the following points that reflect 60 years of history and summarize our business objectives: To function as an international Group dedicated to Services and Construction with 1.) criteria to increase profitability and create value for the shareholder and a strategy promoting growth and diversification of activities and markets; 2.) the vocation of a leader capable of responding to society's needs and in permanent technological innovation and development; 3.) a reputation for quality, competitiveness, transparency, business ethics, risk prevention, and respect for the environment; 4.) client satisfaction as a continuous goal; 5.) an attitude of collaboration and confidence towards its suppliers; 6.) employees with initiative, who are motivated, identified with the company's project, and in constant professional development.

ternational component, with a portfolio of over 120 dam projects worldwide. Meanwhile, Dragados's diversification continued through the 1960s. In 1967, the group received its first concession to build a toll road, between Seville and Cadiz. Infrastructure projects later became a significant part of the group's growth. By the turn of the next century, the company had completed more than 2,500 kilometers of highways (including toll roads), another 4,000 kilometers of other roadways, and more than 1,500 bridges, a portfolio that established the group as one of the world's leading infrastructure companies.

Other highlights for the group in the 1960s included the construction of the Guadarrama Tunnel in 1962, the Belesar dam in 1968, and the La Almendra dam, the Huelva wharf, and the Cadiz Bay bridge, all completed in 1969. By the end of the 1960s, Dragados had become one of the top construction groups in Spain. It had also gained a major shareholder, the Banco Central, which helped finance the group's growth in the 1970s.

The new decade saw Dragados move beyond its infrastructure projects to add a new, industrial construction component, beginning with the building of the Amposta Field offshore oil platform in the Mediterranean in 1970. The company created a dedicated Industrial Plants division in 1975; the following year, that division received a major contract to build a 300-kilometer section of the Bilbao-Barcelona-Valencia gas pipeline.

With Spain's economy foundering on the economic slump of the mid-1970s, Dragados turned toward international operations, entering the Latin American, North African, and Middle Eastern markets for the first time. The company also expanded into other European markets, notably through Dragados Industrial and construction activities in the United Kingdom's North Sea offshore market. By the end of the decade, Dragados had also entered the Asian market, with the construction of a fertilizer plant in the Philippines.

Adding Services in the 1980s

Spain remained the company's main focus, however, as Dragados completed a number of major projects in the 1980s. These included a Navarro toll road suspension bridge over the

Ebro River; the Ramon y Cajal Hospital, completed in 1981; the Telecommunications Tower in Madrid in 1984, and the Aldeadavila power station in 1985. In that year, the company's industrial component began construction on a turnkey fertilizer plant for the Philippines' Philphos.

The opening of the company-managed solid urban waste recycling plant in the Canary Islands in 1986 marked Dragados' entry into the services market. In 1988, the company formalized its interest in the area by creating a new Services division. Dragados then began competing not only for water treatment and sewage construction contracts but for the management contracts as well. With the influx of infrastructure subsidies from Spain's 1986 entry into the European Union, Dragados quickly became a leader in the Spanish services market. One of the Services division's first major contracts was that for the provision of street-cleaning services for the city of Madrid. The following year, the company signed a contract to provide complete waste-management services for another Spanish city, Elche.

The year 1990 marked the company's first entry into the international concessions market when the company won concessions to provide maintenance services for nearly 1,000 kilometers of roadway around Buenos Aires, as well as a second contract to widen and manage a 360-kilometer stretch of Argentina's Route 2. In 1992, Dragados Concessions won a bid to construct and operate the new Teodoro Moscoso Bridge in Puerto Rico. Two years later, that division was awarded the contract to build a northern access road into Buenos Aires.

Construction nonetheless remained Dragados's primary business component. In 1992, that division completed the new Port of Alamillo, in time for Spain's hosting of the 1992 World Fair. The company also completed a new metal roof for Barcelona's St. Jordi Stadium that year. Meanwhile, the company's industrial construction component had also been expanding, acquiring a new subsidiary, Control y Aplicaciones, in 1991, and winning a number of new domestic and international contracts, including the 1992 turnkey contract for a new cement factory for Venezuela's Vencemos. In 1995, Dragados created a separate subsidiary for its industrial construction operations, Dragados Industrial SA.

Maneuvering for New Markets in the New Century

European Community infrastructure subsidies in Spain were slated to end in the early years of the 21st century. In response, Dragados, as well as the other major players in Spain's construction sector, began maneuvering to increase both their share of the domestic market, as well as to position themselves on the international front. As part of that effort, Dragados, which by then had taken the number two spot in the country, joined with number one FCC (Fomento y Construcciones y Contratas) to compete for international contracts in a number of joint ventures. The move was meant to evolve into an eventual merger; however, talks broke down, and by 1998 Dragados had pulled out of its joint ventures with FCC.

By then, Dragados had drafted a new strategy, Dragados Plan XXI, which called for the group to reduce its reliance on construction by diversifying its activities and boosting its international operations to as much as one-fourth of its total reve-

Key Dates:

1941: Dragados y Construcciones forms to dredge the Port of Tarifa.

1945: Dragados begins construction on its first hydroelectric dam projects.

1953: Dragados begins its first airport construction project at Hondarribia Airport in Guipuzcoa.

1965: The company begins its first international project with a contract to participate in the construction of Turkey's Kadinicik Dam.

1967: Dragados takes on its first toll road construction and management concession between Seville and Cadiz.

1970: The company begins industrial construction activities with Amposta Field offshore oil platform.

1975: A dedicated Industrial Plants division is created.

1988: A Services division is created as the company expands into waste and water treatment and other infrastructure services.

1995: A new subsidiary, Dragados Industrial, is formed.

1999: The company changes its name to Grupo Dragados.

2002: ACS makes surprise purchase of 23.5 percent of Dragados, effectively gaining control of the company.

nues. The company also reorganized its operations, and, in 1999, changed its name to Grupo Dragados. As part of its new strategy, the company adopted a five-point divisional structure, which included the Construction, Services, Concessions, Industrial, and Real Estate divisions.

In the meantime, Dragados continued to build up its impressive portfolio of worldwide contracts. In 1995, the company was awarded its first airport concession at Columbia's El Dorado Airport, followed by a contract to resurface and manage a 280-kilometer roadway along the coast of Ecuador in 1996. The company returned to Columbia the following year with a contract to improve and operate the 100-kilometer highway. In 1998, Dragados turned northward, with a concession to build and operate a the 195-kilometer toll road between Moncton and Fredericton in New Brunswick, Canada.

The company's industrial division was also scoring increasing success overseas. In 1995, the company began building a gas line across Morocco as part of the Metragaz pipeline linking North Africa and Europe. The company built the Automatic Hydrological Data System in the Tajo Basin in 1996, then won a turnkey contract for an oil refinery in Costa Rica. Dragados also took part in the Petronas Twin Towers project in Malaysia. In 1997, the company participated in the construction of the Oresund Bridge between Denmark and Sweden; the following year, Dragados Industrial began construction of sections of Chile's Pacific Gas Pipeline and parts of the Bolivia-Brazil gas pipeline.

Dragados also began expanding externally. In 1999, the company acquired a 45 percent stake in Sopol, based in Portugal, which gave it the leading position in the Spain's port and transport services sector. In 2000, the company moved to take a

piece of the e-commerce market, forming a partnership with Virtual Net to provide Internet and related services, then launching the B2B web portal E-difica. In that year, also, the company spun off part of its concessions operations, which were merged with Aumar to create Aurea Concesiones de Infrastructures. Dragados retained a 34 percent stake in the new, publicly listed company. Dragados then entered the Brazilian market with the acquisition of Via Engheneria, which was subsequently renamed as Via Dragados.

Dragados continued its reorganization in 2001, spinning off its real estate holdings into a merger with Immobiliaria Urbis. Dragados then took a 20 percent share of the enlarged Urbis. This move was in keeping with Dragados' newly defined strategic plan (Plan 2001–2004), which called for the company to maintain its construction operations at over 50 percent of its total revenues, while stepping up its international growth. As part of that plan, the company proposed to spend more than EUR 1 billion by 2002 to continue the diversification of its operations. Among the company's plans was the construction of its own broadband telecommunications network capable of reaching more than 19 million people.

Meanwhile, Spain's construction sector continued jockeying for position. In 2001, Dragados joined in the drive to consolidate the sector, launching merger talks with a smaller, private rival, Sacyr. When those talks fell through, Dragados headed north, launching a friendly takeover of the Netherlands' Hollandsche Beton Groep (HBG) for a cost of $655 million. The takeover doubled Dragados size, placing it as number three in Europe—behind France's Bouygues and Vinci. It also gave it an entry point into the Eastern European market, which was poised to receive the bulk of EC infrastructure spending in the new century. Nonetheless, the move was criticized for exposing Dragados to the mature Dutch and German markets.

While it was expanding internationally, Dragados was caught off-guard domestically. In April 2002, the company's major shareholder, Santander Central Hispano (SCH), which had inherited Banco Central's original stake in Dragados and built it up to 23.5 percent, agreed to sell its entire holding to smaller rival ACS. This move was heavily criticized—performed just a day before a Dragados annual meeting that might have prevented such an action, the deal limited ACS stake to just below the 24 percent level, which would have triggered an automatic takeover offer under Spanish law. Instead, ACS effectively gained control of Dragados, nominating seven of the company's 15-member board of directors. Meanwhile, minority shareholders were deprived of the opportunity to sell off their shares at the same premium price paid by ACS to SCH.

In June 2002, Dragados sold off HBG to Royal BAM NM for a little more than it had paid in a move designed to pave the way to a future merger between Dragados and ACS. By January 2003, the two sides appeared to move closer to a full-scale merger when ACS agreed to acquire another 10 percent of Dragados, appeasing minority shareholders. The merger of the two companies was expected to be completed by the end of that year, making the combined group one of the largest construction and engineering companies in Europe. Backed by Dragados's more than 60 years of experience, and its extensive portfolio of international projects and concessions, the combined company was certain to remain a major force in the global construction market.

Principal Subsidiaries

Dragados Obras y Proyectos SA; Dragados Industrial SA; Urbaser SA; Aurea Concesiones de Infraestructuras SA; Construcciones Especiales y Dragados SA; Dragados Moroc, S.A. (Morocco); Dragados Road (United Kingdom); Dragados y Construcciones Argentina SA (63%, Argentina); Dragados y Construcciones Venezuela SA (99.43%, Venezuela); Dravo SA (50%); Geotecnia y Cimientos SA; Integra MGSI, S.A. (46%); Sociedad General de Construçoes e Obras Públicas SA (50%); Tecsa; Empresa Constructora SA; VIA DRAGADOS SA (50%, Brazil).

Principal Competitors

Bouygues S.A.; Acciona S.A.; Balfour Beatty plc; Hochtief AG; ACS Actividades de Construcción y Servicios S.A.; Kvaerner plc.

Further Reading

Elkin, Mike, "Spain's Construction Firms Poised for Deals," *Daily Deal*, October 10, 2001.

Hoare, Michael, "Power Struggle for Dragados Draws Fire from Bankers," *Financial News*, April 22, 2002.

——, "Spanish Takeover Rules in the Spotlight," *Financial News*, April 29, 2002.

Levitt, Joshua, "ACS Seeks to Lift Dragados Stake," *Financial Times*, January 16, 2003, p. 28.

White, David, "Dragados Seeks Foreign Link After Merger Collapse," *Financial Times*, August 14, 1998, p. 16.

—M. L. Cohen

Guittard Chocolate Company

10 Guittard Road
Burlingame, California 94010
U.S.A.
Telephone: (650) 697-4427
Toll Free: (800) 468-2462
Fax: (650) 692-2761
Web site: http://www.guittard.com

Private Company
Incorporated: 1868
Employees: 240
Sales: $57.5 million (2001 est.)
NAIC: 311320 Chocolate and Confectionery
   Manufacturing from Cacao Beans; 311340
   Nonchocolate Confectionery Manufacturing

Guittard Chocolate Company is a leading manufacturer of chocolate for the confectionary, baking, and ice cream industries. The company has been family-owned for four generations and is the oldest independent chocolate company in the United States. (The Ghirardelli family sold their famous Bay Area chocolate company in 1960.) The company is one of only ten in the United States making chocolate from cacao beans. Most of the company's output consists of ten-pound blocks of several varieties of chocolate, as well as other confections, which are then resold by retail confectioners. The company produces a range of branded confectionary products, most notably its Smooth & Melty mints. The company's strongest sales areas are in the Midwest and the West. Company president Gary Guittard has attributed the company's longevity, as well as its ability to survive as an independent player in spite of widespread industry consolidation, to a unique balance of flexibility and consistency. As he told *Newsday,* ''We always say, 'Taste has memory.' '' The company prides itself on being quick to respond to the marketplace. However, some of Guittard's recipes, such as for Old Dutch milk chocolate, date back more than 100 years. The corporate headquarters is known for the potted cacao tree in its lobby.

Gold Rush Origins

Etienne Guittard learned his trade at his uncle's chocolate shop in Paris. In 1860, during the California gold rush, he sailed around from France to California (via the Cape Horn route). In lieu of currency, he carried with him traditional French style chocolate, a rare commodity in those days, to purchase supplies. His three years of prospecting in the Sierras did not pan out, and he returned to France to save up money for a new enterprise— supplying newly affluent miners with premium chocolate and other fine foods.

Guittard returned to San Francisco in 1868 and, with equipment imported from Europe, established the Guittard Chocolate Company on Sansome Street on the waterfront. He originally sold tea, coffee, spices, flavorings, and yeast in addition to the chocolate produced there. The company's importance in the community was indicated by its listing in the 1878 San Francisco telephone directory, which ran to one full page.

Horace C. Guittard, son of the founder, joined the company and took the helm upon Etienne Guittard's death in 1899. In 1906, an earthquake and fire razed the company's first building. The firm relocated to another building on Commercial Street. Ten years later, it moved again, this time to a larger factory on Main Street. By now, the company was exclusively devoted to chocolate. More expansions came in 1921 and 1936. Guittard began a long-standing relationship with its neighbor, See's Candy Shops Inc., immediately after World War II.

New Plant in 1955

Horace C. Guittard died in 1950 and was succeeded by his son, Horace Albert Guittard. The construction of the Embarcadero Freeway prompted the company to move again in 1955. It relocated to a state-of-the-art, 50,000-square-foot factory in Burlingame, south of San Francisco. With equipment imported from Switzerland and Germany, it was considered the most advanced plant of its kind in the United States. Using the continuous flow principles of the day, the machines ran full-time, supplying first-tier confectionery, ice cream, and pastry producers.

Horace A. Guittard was known for embracing automated production and for establishing a testing lab, which he staffed

Company Perspectives:

At Guittard, we feel customer satisfaction comes from personal relationships built day in and day out on product quality, reliability, responsibility, and integrity. Building long-term relationships with superior products is how we've been doing business for four Guittard generations. With more than a century of experience, we're able to help you make the most of your opportunities. We'll assist you with everything from the analysis of industry trends to technological support. So welcome to Guittard. As an award-winning, internationally renowned chocolate company, we think you'll find our products and service of special value. Your business is vital to us. That's why pleasing you is our most important goal.

Key Dates:

1868: Guittard Chocolate Company is founded in San Francisco by Etienne Guittard.
1899: Horace C. Guittard leads the company upon death of Etienne Guittard.
1906: The company's original building is destroyed in the San Francisco earthquake.
1916: The company relocates to Main Street.
1950: Horace A. Guittard succeeds his father as head of the company.
1955: New Embarcadero Freeway on San Francisco waterfront prompts the company's relocation to Burlingame.
1989: Gary Guittard succeeds his brother Horace as CEO.
2001: The company launches E. Guittard artisan line, a collection of vintage chocolate that includes blends and single-bean varietal chocolates.

with degreed scientists. A product could undergo 75 different checks before it was finished. Taste testing remained as important as ever, though.

Guittard would be at the forefront of industry trends. Company literature notes it was the first to introduce high quality chocolate chips as well as the first to offer them in large sizes. It also helped its customers capitalize on the truffles fad, and its Guittard Sweet Ground Chocolate found its way into many a café mocha during the cappuccino boom.

Fourth Generation in the Late 1980s

Horace A. Guittard's son Jay had joined the company in 1965. He supervised wholesale operations and became head of the company after his father's death in December 1988. Just six months later, he too died and was succeeded by his brother, Gary W. Guittard. The plant by then had grown to 100,000 square feet and employed 150 people.

Gary Guittard recalled a childhood steeped in cocoa. At the age of 12, he formed his own side venture selling tiny chocolate guitars to neighborhood merchants. He worked in the plant as a teenager but later pursued a brief, unsuccessful career in the advertising business. His father would not let him join the family firm until he had picked up some outside business experience, which he did by working four years at a bakery supplier and a food broker. He joined the family business in 1975. Before his brother's death, Gary had overseen the retail side.

Sales were estimated at about $100 million a year from the mid-1980s to 1990. Purchasers of Guittard's wholesale chocolate included Baskin-Robbins, Blue Chip Cookies, and See's Candy Shops Inc. The company also sold its own brand of chocolate chips for baking and other confectionary ingredients in grocery stores nationwide.

As had already occurred with coffee during the rise of Starbuck's, the U.S. consumer's taste in chocolate seemed to be leaning more towards darker, stronger flavors than those offered by companies producing domestic, mass-produced milk chocolate. In the coming years, Guittard would call upon its specialized experience as a chocolate maker to take advantage of this trend.

Expanded Product Lines in the Late 1990s and Beyond

By the late 1990s, consolidation had left Guittard as one of the only two independent wholesale chocolate suppliers in the country. The company now began developing a line of its own candy bars for retail sale, its first since the 1930s. Chocolates in the "E. Guittard Collection" were branded with the name of the company founder and were replicas of the salesmen's samples Gary Guittard had remembered as a child. Appropriately, these were given French names: L'Harmonie (Harmony), a 64 percent cacao dark chocolate blend, and Soleil d'Or (Golden Sun), a 38 percent milk chocolate blend. These were officially launched to the trade in 2001 and retailed nationwide the following year. At the same time, the company began selling by direct order a range of single-bean varietal chocolates made from different kinds of cacao beans from around the world. These included Colombian (trinitario beans), Sur del Lago (rare criollo beans), and Ecuador Nacional (a unique, zero acidity chocolate made from heirloom trinitario beans).

Theobroma cacao, which translates to mean food of the gods, was first experienced by Europeans in the 1500s. "It's a great learning experience to realize that chocolate from different areas does taste differently," Gary Guittard told *Professional Candy Buyer*. This was part of the new market of "varietal chocolate." It takes three to four times as long to make chocolate using traditional, artisanal methods, and Guittard was one of the few players with the resources to do it with any scale. Only ten companies in the United States were making chocolate from cacao beans by any method in 2003.

Principal Competitors

Ghirardelli Chocolate Co.; Godiva Chocolatier, Inc.; Lindt & Sprungli (USA) Inc.; Maxfield Candy Co.; Nestlé SA; Valhrona, Inc.

Further Reading

Aguirre, Mary Lou, "Sweet Dreams for Chocolatiers; Clovis-Based Company Makes the Transition from Hobby to Business with Plans for Growth," *Fresno Bee*, December 3, 1996, p. D1.

Amire, Roula, "It's All in the Beans at Guittard," *Candy Industry*, September 1998, pp. 26+.

Blatt, Jessica, "Single-Minded Chocolatier," *Food & Wine*, November 2002.

Carter, Sylvia, "Rich Family Tradition, Chocolate Bar None," *Newsday*, April 26, 2000, p. B11.

"Consistency and Quality Are Key at Guittard," *Candy Industry*, August 2000, p. 67.

Fulmer, Melinda, "Beyond Bittersweet; Chocolate Used to Be Simple. Now It's Estate-Grown Varietal, Blended . . . ," *Newsday*, October 23, 2002, p. B18.

——, "Raising the Bar; Chocolate Connoisseurs Following Wine and Coffee Trends," *Journal-Gazette* (Ft. Wayne, Ind.), June 5, 2002, p. 1D.

Gugino, Sam, "The Cream of Cocoa; Quality Chocolates Reward the Not-So-Sweet Tooth," *Wine Spectator Online*, February 28, 1998.

Guittard, Gary W., and Patricia R. Olsen, "I'm a Chocolate Maker's Son," *New York Times*, November 29, 2000, p. C12.

E. Guittard: From Plantation to Package, Burlingame, Calif.: Guittard, 2002.

Gary Guittard: President and CEO, Guittard Chocolate Company; Fourth Generation at the Helm of a Family Business, Burlingame, Calif.: Guittard, 2002.

The Guittard Chocolate Company: Four Generations of Master Chocolatiers, Burlingame, Calif.: Guittard, 2002.

"Guittard Is Happy to Play Guinea Pig," *Packaging Digest*, April 1985, pp. 30+.

"H.A. Guittard, Chocolate Manufacturer," *Orange County Register*, December 30, 1988, p. B8.

Hedges, Joyce, "Chips Sweeten Guittard's Business," *San Francisco Business Times*, September 3, 1990, pp. 1+.

Larsen, Elain, "A Chip Off the Old Block; Gary Guittard Is a Fourth-Generation Chocolate Maker," *San Francisco Examiner*, February 11, 2000, p. P1.

——, "Favorite Guittard Recipes," *San Francisco Examiner*, February 11, 2000, p. P7.

Magee, Patricia L., "Guittard Chocolate Adds that Gourmet Touch," *Candy Industry*, June 1985, pp. 50+.

Marzec, Michael, Jan Shaw, Clifford Carlsen, Huntley Paton, and Patrick Danner, "Top 100 Private Companies (San Francisco Area)," *San Francisco Business Times*, November 9, 1987, pp. 17+.

"Refining the Bar Market: Premium Chocolate Bars Are Stirring the Retail Mix and Consumers Are Responding," *Professional Candy Buyer*, May 2002, pp. 94+.

Saekel, Karola, "Love, and the Art of Chocolate; Guittard Delves into Artisanal Market," *San Francisco Chronicle*, February 12, 2003.

Silver, Marc, and Vicky Hallett, "The Power of the Dark Side of Chocolate," *U.S. News & World Report*, December 2, 2002, p. 63.

Unterman, Patricia, "Chocolate Chic," *San Francisco Examiner*, February 12, 2003.

—Frederick C. Ingram

SABANCI HOLDING

Haci Omer Sabanci Holdings A.S.

Sabanci Center 4
Levent
80745 Istanbul
Turkey
Telephone: (+90) 212-2816600
Fax: (+90) 212-2810272
Web site: http://www.sabanci.com.tr

Public Company
Employees: 31,380
Sales: $5.85 billion (2001)
Stock Exchanges: Istanbul
Ticker Symbol: SAHOL
NAIC: 313210 Broadwoven Fabric Mills; 115116 Farm
   Management Services; 326211 Tire Manufacturing
   (Except Retreading); 423110 Automobile and Other
   Motor Vehicle Merchant Wholesalers; 423690 Other
   Electronic Parts and Equipment Merchant
   Wholesalers; 424490 Other Grocery and Related
   Product Merchant Wholesalers; 518210 Data
   Processing, Hosting, and Related Services; 522298 All
   Other Non-Depository Credit Intermediation; 524113
   Direct Life Insurance Carriers; 551112 Offices of
   Other Holding Companies; 561520 Tour Operators

Haci Omer Sabanci Holdings A.S. is one of Turkey's largest companies, posting almost $6 billion in sales per year. Sabanci's holdings include some 75 companies—including 13 publicly listed companies—spanning a wide variety of industries. Many of Sanbanci's holdings are in joint-venture with large foreign firms created in the 1980s and 1990s. At the beginning of the new century, however, Sabanci began to reduce its emphasis on partnerships in favor of pursuing its own international expansion. Sabanci Holding is listed on the Istanbul Stock Exchange, although the company remains controlled at 85 percent by the founding Sabanci family. Nonetheless, the family has taken steps to reduce its direct participation in the company and its holdings since the late 1990s, increasingly turning over operational direction to professional managers.

Sharecropper to Industrialist in the 1930s

Born in 1906, Haci Omer Sabanci represented one of Turkey's greatest rags-to-riches stories. When Sabanci was five years old, his father died; at the age of 14, Sabanci left his village, Akçakaya, in the Kayseri region, to seek work in the cotton fields of Adana, reportedly making the entire 450-kilometer journey by foot. Sabanci found work as a worker on a cotton plantation. By 1925, Sabanci had begun sharecropping his own plot of land, and by 1932 Sabanci had saved up enough money to invest in a cotton gin, Çirçir Fabrikasi.

With the profits from that investment, Sabanci turned to vegetable oils in the 1943, buying a stake in Türk Nebati Yaglar Fabrikasi, founded in 1925 as the Glido Oil Factory and later to become known as Yagsa. Sabanci continued to seek out investments and in 1946 purchased a second vegetable oil factory. Sabanci grouped his vegetable oil businesses under a new company, Toroslar Trading Company, which formed the first cornerstone of the future Sabanci empire. Toroslar began producing margarine in 1957 under the name Kitchen Margarine; in 1967, the company introduced its Breakfast Margarine brand, which was followed by the launch of Evet margarine in 1973. In that year, Toroslar's name was changed to Marsa (the "sa," the initial letters of the word "Sanayi" was by then already a standard feature of Sabanci's company naming system).

By then, Sabanci had already become a diversified conglomerate. The 1950s had seen a period of strong growth for Sabanci's interests. In 1949, Sabanci acquired his first farm, Misirli, in Cukurova-Ceyhan. The following year, Sabanci established a combination flour mill and cotton ginning mill, Bossa, to process the company's crops. By 1951, Bossa's production had grown sufficiently to set up a textiles subsidiary, Bossa Textiles. Through the remainder of the decade, Sabanci, joined by his five sons, continued to add onto his farming, ginning, and textiles interests, acquiring three more farms, bringing the company's total acreage to 2,200 acres. The group launched Sapeska Textiles and Soil Products Manufacturing and Trading Inc. in 1958.

Another rising area for the group was the banking and insurance sector. Sabanci entered that market in 1948 with the

Key Dates:

1932: Haci Omer Sabanci buys a stake in a cotton ginning mill, Circir Fabrikasi.

1943: Sabanci buys a share of Turk Nebati Yaglar Fabrikasi, a manufacturer of vegetable oils.

1946: Sabanci acquires a second vegetable oil plant and forms Toroslar Trading Company (renamed Marsa in 1973).

1948: Sabanci forms Akbank in partnership with others.

1950: Sabanci sets up Bossa, a flour and cotton ginning mill.

1951: Bossa begins the production of textiles.

1966: Haci Omer Sabanci dies; the company is taken over by his five sons and is soon regrouped as Haci Omer Sabanci Holding.

1968: The Temsa vehicle manufacturing and distribution subsidiary is created.

1974: Company headquarters move to Istanbul.

1983: The company begins a licensing and manufacturing agreement with Komatsu and Mitsubishi through Temsa.

1997: Danonesa joint-venture with Groupe Danone is established.

1999: Sabanci University opens.

2000: Sabanci Museum opens.

launch of Akbank—named for Sabanci's home village—in a partnership with a shareholding group made up of people from the Adana and Kayseri regions. The Sabanci family controlled the majority of the bank and remained its major shareholder at 40 percent even after its later public offering. Akbank grew quickly, opening a branch in Istanbul by 1950; that city became the bank's headquarters in 1954. By the mid-1960s, Akbank operated more than 100 branch offices. In 1964, Akbank opened its first foreign office in Frankfurt, Germany, following the wave of Turkish "guest workers" emigrating to Germany, the Netherlands. and other European countries. Back home, Akbank's success led the Sabanci family to enter the insurance branch as well, founding Aksigorta AS in 1960, initially as a subsidiary to Akbank, growing it into the largest non-life insurance company in Turkey.

Sabanci invested in other areas as well. In 1949, he was behind the creation of the Erciyes Palas, a vast complex featuring a hotel, movie theater, shopping center, and restaurant in Adana. In 1954, Sabanci entered the building sector itself, launching the Oralitsa Construction Materials Trading company.

Billionaires in the 1980s

By the time Haci Omer Sabanci died in 1966, the family was already one of the Adana region's most prominent. Under Sabanci's five sons and other members of the Sabanci family, the company, reformed as Haci Omer Sabanci Holdings in 1967, was to become one of the largest corporations in all of Turkey.

Sabanci's sons inherited not only their father's business talents but also his wide-ranging interests. In 1966, the group launched SASA Synthetic Fibres Inc., which was followed by the creation of Istanbul Nylon Yarn Inc., later known as Insa, in 1967. These investments led the group to enter the plastics sector in 1971 with the launch of its Pilsa extruded PVC pipe manufacturing company. Another new area of business for the company was the commercial and construction vehicle sector, which Sabanci entered with the creation of Temsa Thermo Mechanical Equipment Inc. in 1968. That company began manufacturing buses as well as acting as a distributor for other truck, bus, and commercial vehicle brands.

The group entered yet another business area, that of cement manufacturing, with the creation of Akcimento Cement Inc. in 1967. Sabanci's interest in that sector was extended in 1972 with the launch of Cimsa, in Mersin, which began production of white cement in 1975 and later became the world's leading producer in that cement segment. By then, Sabanci Holding had stepped up its textiles operations as well, forming the Yunsa Carpet and Worsted Products, becoming one of the top five worsted fabrics companies in Europe and the largest in Turkey. The company's interests in textiles also led it into a related area, that of the production of cords for automotive tires, establishing Kordsa in 1973. From there, Sabanci moved into tires themselves, forming Lassa in 1974 in order to produce tires under license with Bridgestone.

In 1974, Sabanci moved its headquarters to Istanbul and continued to add to its growing empire. In 1976, the company founded its own electronics firm, BIMSA (for Sabanci International Business Information and Management Systems). The company created Cipas Cement Products in that year as well. Sabanci moved into aluminum in 1980 with the purchase of Nasas Aluminum Corp., and in that year also added paper supplies with through a new company, Donkasan.

By the end of the 1970s, Sabanci became interested in the international trade sector and launched new companies Exsa Handels GmbH in Frankfurt, Germany, in 1978 and Holsa Inc. in New York in 1980. Other international moves followed in the new decade with the launch of Ak International Bank (later Sabanci Bank) in London in 1981 and Universal Trading (Jersey) Ltd., which was also based in London.

Sabanci's growth during this period became marked by a long series of partnerships. Sabanci's position as one of Turkey's largest and most internationally oriented companies attracted the interest of a variety of foreign companies attempting to enter the Turkish market, and the company was able to conclude a number of strategic partnerships and joint-ventures to boost its domestic and international position. One of the first of these was with the Netherlands' Philips, which formed the joint-venture partnership Turk Philips with Sabanci in 1977. The two companies increased their relationship in 1985 with the creation of a second partnership, Turk Philips Illumination Industry and Trade Inc. That year, the company formed its first banking joint venture, with Banque National de Paris, forming BNP-Akbank.

The Temsa vehicle subsidiary also grew strongly through partnerships, notably with Komatsu and Mitsubishi, which enabled Sabanci to break the near-monopoly enjoyed in Turkey until then by France's Renault. Beginning in 1983 and extending throughout the decade, Sabanci signed a number of distribution, licensing, and manufacturing agreements with the two Japanese vehicle groups.

The year 1987 marked a new phase in Sabanci's growth as it formed a number of major partnerships, including the Dusa yarn manufacturing company, Sabanci's first partnership with DuPont. That year, the company formed the Beksa joint-venture with Belgium's Bekeart to produce steel cord and other products for the tire and other industries. In 1988, the company created Brisa in partnership with Bridgestone, which took over Sabanci's Lassa tire operation. In that year, also, Germany's Dresdner Bank joined the BNP-Akbank joint-venture, which was then renamed BNP-AK-Dresdner Bank.

By the end of the 1980s, Sabanci family holdings had passed the billion-dollar mark, making the Sabancis one of the richest in Turkey and establishing Sabanci Holding as one of the country's top privately held companies. Yet the 1990s were to prove to be a period of still stronger growth for the company.

Going It Alone in the 21st Century

Partnerships remained Sabanci's vehicle for expansion into the 1990s. In 1991, the company formed its Philsa joint-venture with Phillip Morris to manufacture cigarettes and other tobacco products for the Turkish market. That partnership led to a second joint-venture, this time between Sabanci's Marsa subsidiary and Philip-Morris's Kraft Foods, which jointed together to create the Marsa KLS Food Products Manufacturing company in 1993. That move expanded Sabanci's food production beyond margarine and oils into a wider variety of food products. In 1994, Sabanci took over the marketing and distribution of Philip Morris's cigarette brands when the two companies formed a new joint-venture, Philip Morrissa.

Sabanci, which had established a number of hotels during the 1990s, formed a joint-venture with Hilton Hotels International in 1993. The company also moved into automotive production and distribution with its Toyatosa joint-venture with Toyota in 1994. While joint-ventures remained an important part of Sabanci's expansion, the company meanwhile continued to develop its international trading network, notably with the opening of new Exsa subsidiaries in Spain, Italy, and Germany in 1995. The following year, as the Turkish government began a privatization program of the country's utilities sectors, Sabanci entered the energy market with the launch of its Enerjisa Energy Production subsidiary.

Food products gained prominence in Sabanci's holdings in the late 1990s, particularly with the formation of the Danonesa dairy and food products joint-venture with France's Danone in 1997. That year, also, the company made its first venture into retailing, joining with French hypermarket powerhouse Carrefour to form the Carrefoursa joint-venture, which took over Carrefour's single Istanbul hypermarket and set an objective to open up to 23 hypermarkets by 2002. The company also expected to help fill its hypermarket's shelves—in 1998, Danonesa became one of Turkey's leading food products groups with the acquisition of the Tikvesli Company. Another acquisition, this time of Birtat, followed in 1999.

Sabanci's relationship with DuPont deepened at the turn of the century with the joint acquisitions of a number of industrial yarn and cord producers in South America. The two companies then formed Dupontsa Polyester Europe in 2000, which led the way to the creation in 2001 of Dusa International LLC, "the world's leading global supplier of heavy decitex nylon industrial yarn and tire cord fabric," according to the company. Other significant joint-ventures of the time include the Sakosa industrial yarn and cord joint-venture with the U.S. company Koch and Mexico's Saba, formed in 1998, and the ready-to-wear clothing joint-venture with Britain's Arcadia, Giysa Sabanci, formed in 1999.

Sabanci was undergoing an internal transformation as it prepared to enter the new century. A McKinsey survey, which revealed that 80 percent of family-owned businesses in developing countries failed by the third-generation of family ownership, convinced the Sabanci family to transition its company to a more professional management structure. Part of that process began in 1997 when Sabanci Holding went public on the Istanbul Stock Exchange. While the Sabancis retained 85 percent of the company's shares, the move helped ease most of the Sabanci family out of the main management positions within the holding company and its subsidiaries.

The new management in turn took on a more conservative business approach. Whereas the company's previous investments and diversification decisions had been decided among the family, Sabanci now proceeded through conducting market research. The company also indicated its intention to streamline its extremely diversified holdings, exiting on number of areas of operations. Such was the case with its decision to end its joint-venture with Toyota in 2001, as well as the shutting down of its Philip Morris and Philips joint-ventures in the late 1990s. The company indicated that other sectors of operations, including its textiles holdings, were potentially sell-off candidates as well.

Sabanci's new management also prepared to reduce the company's reliance on its joint-ventures and instead to seek more of its domestic and international growth on its own. As part of that effort, the company began acquiring full control of some of its partnerships, such as Sakosa, which became fully owned by Sabanci in 2002. The company meanwhile targeted expansion of its tire and reinforcement-materials divisions—which, under Guler Sabanci, granddaughter of the company's founder, had grown into one of the sector's world leaders—with an entry into China and Indonesia in 2003.

Sabanci Holding by then had grown to a company with annual sales worth nearly $6 billion per year. The company took on a new CEO, Dr. Celal Metin, in April 2003. The Sabanci family in the meantime had turned its fortune to philanthropy. In 1999, the group opened its own private university, Sabanci University, promising low tuitions; under family head Sakip Sabanci, son of Haci Omer and company chairman, the group has also created the Sabanci Museum.

Principal Subsidiaries

Akbank (40%); Akçansa; Akkardansa; Aknet; Beksa (50%); Bossa; Brisa; Carrefoursa (50%); Çimsa; Danonesa (50%); Dönkasan; DuPontsa B.V. (50%); Dusa Interantional (50%); Exsa; Enerjisa; Exsa Deutschland; Exsa (UK) Ltd. (United Kingdom);

F. Hefti & Co. AG (Germany); Holsa Inc. (United States); I-Bimsa (50%); Insa; Karçimsa; Kraftsa (50%); Marsa KJS (50%); Olmuksa (50%); Oysa Nigde; Oysa Iskenderun; Philsa (25%); Philip Morissa (25%); Pilsa; Sapeksa; Sabanci Bank plc; Temsa; Turk Notka Net; Universal Trading (Jersey LTD); Yünsa.

Principal Operating Units

Banking and Insurance; Automotive; Tire and Reinforcement Materials; Chemicals; Cement; Food; Retailing; International Trade; Textiles.

Principal Competitors

Koç Holding A.S.; Compagnie Générale des Établissements Michelin.

Further Reading

Barham, John, "Europe: Conglomerates Rule the Roost in Turkey," *Financial Times*, August 21, 1997, p. 20.

Boulton, Leyla, "Power Is Passing to the Professionals—Slowly," *Financial Times*, November 22, 1999, p. 3.

Dannenberg, Nikki, "Sabanci Takes Koc to School," *Institutional Investor International Edition*, November 1998, p. 18.

Raleigh, Patrick, "Sabanci to Take KoSa's Stake in Tyre Cord JV: Turkish Group Takes Full Control of Polyester Fibre Maker," *European Rubber Journal*, January 2002, p. 12.

White, Liz, "DuPont and Sabanci Finalize Nylon JV," *European Rubber Journal*, February 2001, p. 3.

Rossant, Juliette, "Turkey's Tire Queen," *Forbes*, July 5, 1999, p. 190.

—M. L. Cohen

Halliburton Company

3600 Lincoln Plaza
500 North Akard Street
Dallas, Texas 75201-3391
U.S.A.
Telephone: (214) 978-2600
Fax: (214) 978-2611
Web site: http://www.halliburton.com

Public Company
Incorporated: 1924 as Halliburton Oil Well Cementing
    Company
Employees: 83,000
Sales: $12.49 billion (2002)
Stock Exchanges: New York
Ticker Symbol: HAL
NAIC: 213112 Support Activities for Oil and Gas
    Operations; 333132 Oil and Gas Field Machinery and
    Equipment Manufacturing; 541330 Engineering Services

Halliburton Company is a world leader in energy services, as well as engineering and construction. The company has two main business segments: the Halliburton Energy Services Group, which offers a broad range of services and products used in the exploration, development, and production of oil and gas, and the KBR—Engineering and Construction Group, which designs and constructs major projects, including liquefied natural gas plants, refining and processing plants, production facilities, and pipelines. Halliburton, which has operations in more than 100 countries, merged with Dresser Industries, Inc. in 1998 to create one of the largest energy services firm in the world. The company faced challenges in the new millennium, however, due to lingering asbestos claims and an SEC investigation related to changes in accounting practices that occurred in 1998—when U.S. Vice-President Dick Cheney was company CEO.

Early History

One of Halliburton's numerous service operations is oil well cementing. This process protects oil from contamination by underground water, strengthens the walls of a well, lessens the danger of explosions from high pressure oil and gas, and protects fresh water veins from contamination by oil. It was the first service offered by company founder Erle Palmer Halliburton.

Erle Halliburton learned the cementing technique in California during a period of employment with the Perkins Oil Well Cementing Company that began and ended in 1916. Fired for suggesting too many method changes, he decided to utilize the engineering and hydraulics he had learned in the U.S. Navy and go into the cementing business on his own. He borrowed a pump and wagon, pawned his wife's wedding ring to finance his venture, and moved to Burkburnett, Texas, to introduce his services to the oil industry. Halliburton's method met with little interest in Texas.

Undaunted, he transferred his operation to Oklahoma. There, his luck soon changed, bringing the need for additional equipment, a patent for his process, and efficient management. To cope with these needs and increasing demands for his service, in 1920 Halliburton organized the Halliburton Oil Well Cementing Company. One year later, 17 trucks carried his crews and equipment to drilling sites in Louisiana, Arkansas, and other oil-rich areas from a base in Wilson, Oklahoma, as well as from the new company headquarters in Duncan, Oklahoma. Part of this growing reputation came from uncompromisingly reliable service, which was enhanced by new equipment invented by Halliburton to meet the needs of each project. One creation that revolutionized the oil industry was the jet mixer, a mechanized mixer that did away with hand-mixing of the minimum 250 bags of cement and water slurry needed for each well. Because it could control the proportions of cement and water, it eliminated wasted slurry that would harden before it could be poured.

By 1922, the company owned $14,000 worth of equipment and was paying some of its cementers $300 monthly. Two years later, Halliburton, with his wife Vida as his partner, set out to expand. To finance this the couple converted their partnership into a corporation and offered a substantial interest in their business to other oil companies. Their trump card lay in their meticulous patenting of all new processes and devices, which had left the oil companies unable to have oil wells cemented without using Halliburton services. Company patents also covered processes designed for well recementing, a maintenance necessity that gave the Halliburtons relative independence from competitors.

In 1924, the Halliburton Oil Well Cementing Company became a corporation in Delaware. The Halliburtons held 52 percent of the stock, and the Magnolia, Texas, Gulf, Humble, Sun, Pure, and Atlantic oil companies jointly held 48 percent. So as to retain equal voting rights with their partners, the Halliburtons placed 4 percent of their stock in a voting trust.

By the time the company reached its ten-year milestone in 1929, research and development had improved processes and equipment to the point where a mixture made up of 2,500 sacks of cement could be injected into a well in 48 minutes. By 1929, the use of four new company planes made for speedy contract completion. Marking this important anniversary was the Halliburton entry into Canada, as well as offering for sale a wide range of oil well apparatus.

The 1930s saw automobile production soar from 2.3 million vehicles in 1931 to 4.5 million by 1940. Domestic oil heating became more popular, growing from 100,000 homes supplied in 1929 to two million by 1940. Both circumstances benefited the oil industry. As the decade ended, oil and gas were supplying 44.5 percent of the U.S. total energy requirements.

Halliburton's expansion kept pace with demand. In 1932, it opened four new branches, enabling it to send 75 cementing and well-testing crews to sites in seven states. The company introduced bulk cementing to replace hand-moving of heavy cement sacks. Eager to participate in the marine oil exploration taking place in the Gulf of Mexico, Halliburton also began to mount equipment on ships and barges.

In 1940, the Halliburtons bought Perkins Cementing Company, extending operations to the West Coast and the Rocky Mountain region. In the same year, the company established in Venezuela its first South American subsidiary. These two moves were profitable; just one year later, earnings reached $13.5 million, of which $2 million was net profit.

Soon after the Japanese attack on Pearl Harbor, the company began to make gun-mount bearings for the U.S. Navy at its Duncan shops. Other war material manufactured included parts for the B-29 bomber and jigs, fixtures, and dies for the Boeing airplane plant in Wichita, Kansas. Wartime contracts were lucrative, and when World War II ended in 1945 annual earnings had reached $25.7 million.

In 1948, Halliburton shares were offered on the New York Stock Exchange for the first time. Having split its shares on a four-to-one basis a year earlier, Halliburton was able to offer 600,000, to which the Atlantic Refining Company added a further 80,000 shares. Of these, 50,000 shares were offered to employees before the balance was offered to the public.

By the end of the 1940s, although well cementing and bulk cement sales accounted for about 70 percent of company revenues, there were other profitable undertakings, all supported by specially designed equipment. Electrical well services provided information on the types of formations penetrated by a drill; acidizing of geological formations increased oil flow; and specialized equipment deposited various cements and chemicals into wells. Most profitable of all was a new process called Hydrafrac, licensed exclusively to Halliburton for a period of time by its developer, the Stanolind Oil and Gas Company. Designed to increase well productivity, this method used jellied gasoline, which was pumped under pressure into the bottom of a well to split the rock formation. The resulting crack was then propped open with quantities of sand, making penetration of tight rock formations easier. The Hydrafrac process made it possible to rejuvenate many dwindling oil wells and reduced the number of sites necessary to drain a field. Hydrafrac's great success showed up in a surge in annual revenues at Halliburton: $57.2 million in 1949, increasing to $69.3 million the following year, and leaping to $92.6 million by 1951.

Diversifying and Expanding in the 1950s

Between 1950 and 1955, the company expanded in all directions. Drilling activity increased dramatically. The company had 7,000 employees, and drills probed to more than 4,000 feet in an average well, as compared to 3,600 feet five years earlier. Offered for rental as well as for sale, equipment then included formation testing tools to obtain fluids and pressure readings from oil-bearing rock, plus other new equipment used in well completion operations. Wall cleaners, depth measuring equipment, and production packers were other lines that drillers could rent or buy. Services provided by the company included electronic logging and sidewall wellcoring and the transporting of cement and fracturing sands to drilling sites from nearby Halliburton storage areas. Oil exploration in the Texas and Louisiana Gulf Coast areas was flourishing; 23 vessels as well as about $10 million worth of other equipment were available for offshore drilling purposes. There were almost 200 operating centers in the United States, as well as 32 service locations in Canada and subsidiaries in Venezuela and Peru. The company also had operations in Mexico, Saudi Arabia, Sumatra, Italy, Germany, Australia, and Cuba.

Research and development kept the company at the forefront of oil exploration technology. Costing $3 million in 1956 alone, it rewarded the company's efforts with a new composition for cementing deep wells and a method for making the fracturing sand radioactive, among other innovations. All of this was reflected in annual sales figures, which reached $152.4 million by the end of 1955 and produced net profits of $16.3 million.

Erle Halliburton died in 1957, after 28 years as company president and ten as chairman. Cited by the New York Times as one of the richest people in the United States, he left behind a fortune estimated at between $75 and $100 million—the days of a pawned wedding ring long gone.

The same year saw the acquisition of Welex Jet Services. Originally based in Fort Worth, Texas, Welex broadened the Halliburton line of electronic testing and logging services. Other companies were acquired during this time, including Jet Research Center and FreightMaster, a maker of rail car couplings.

Key Dates:

1920: Erle Halliburton organizes the Halliburton Oil Well Cementing Company.
1924: The company incorporates in order to expand.
1940: Perkins Cementing Company is acquired; a South American subsidiary is established.
1948: Halliburton goes public.
1962: Brown & Root Inc. becomes a company subsidiary.
1995: Dick Cheney is named chairman, CEO, and president.
1998: Halliburton merges with Dresser Industries Inc.
2002: The SEC investigates Halliburton's accounting practices; the company announces a $4 billion settlement related to asbestos claims.

The end of the war had brought an increased demand for oil. Due partly to freedom from wartime price controls and partly to the technological advancement that brought plastics, synthetic fibers, fertilizers, and other petrochemical products into daily life in the United States, these demands were willingly fed by the oil drillers. Production almost doubled between 1945 and 1954, reaching a level of 2.3 million barrels daily. Such overexpansion came to a head in 1957 when a slump followed, bringing with it a corresponding decrease in the demand for exploration equipment. The company's annual sales figures showed the trend of the time: its net income before taxes, $38 million in 1957, decreased to $27.6 million in 1958, rallied to $33.9 million the following year, only to sink once again to $26.9 million by 1960. Because Halliburton was chiefly a supplier of drilling-related services, however, recovery was relatively swift. These services, plus the equipment required to implement them, were needed both for the deeper wells then being drilled and for stimulation of existing sites.

Acquiring Brown & Root in 1962

Offsetting the oil exploration slump, Halliburton continued with its acquisition program. Otis Engineering Corporation joined the company in 1959. Brown & Root, Inc. became a Halliburton subsidiary in 1962. A firm internationally known for the construction of military bases, petrochemical plants, and offshore platforms, Brown & Root was a private subsidiary of the Brown Foundation. Other Brown subsidiaries acquired at the same time were Southwestern Pipe, a manufacturer of explosives and thin-walled pipe; Joe B. Hughes, a trucking business; and Highlands Insurance Company, chiefly concerned with casualty insurance. Together, the four new subsidiaries broadened Halliburton's product and service lines, giving the company entry into many overseas markets and providing ways to adapt Halliburton skills to new purposes. Two company staples quickly found new uses: blended cement was now sold for building projects and thin-walled pipes for playground equipment and bicycles.

By 1965, Halliburton's acquisitions program resulted in 16 units that were autonomous but closely coordinated into three main areas. One division was oil-field services and sales. The second was the engineering segment headed by Brown & Root, the focus of which was such international construction projects as bases in Saigon and parts of NASA's Manned Spacecraft Center near Houston. The third division, specialty sales and services to general industry, included power supply units and transformers for the electronics industry, missile cleaning for defense, and, through two subsidiaries, insurance. Earnings reflected the company's steady growth. 1960s total earnings of $181.5 million rose to $525.7 million by 1965.

In the 1960s, offshore oil exploration became a major activity. Successfully undertaken in the Gulf of Mexico since 1938, offshore drilling produced about 12,500 wells by 1970, accounting for approximately 15 percent of U.S. oil and 10 percent of its gas. Anticipating its participation in offshore activities, Halliburton equipped Brown & Root well, spending $100 million to ensure competitiveness. The company had developed an automated mixing system for drilling mud, a process that was used in offshore operations. Designed to cut costs by monitoring and controlling fluid density, the new system came in tandem with a 50 percent interest in IMC Drilling Mud, a company with special emphasis on overseas expansion.

In 1968, the company's marine capabilities were broadened further by the acquisition of Jackson Marine Corporation, a Texas company specializing in the construction of vessels for offshore petroleum exploration, and the purchase of an 80 percent interest in New Orleans-based Taylor Diving and Salvage Company. The latter company proved its worth within a year by developing an underwater chamber that could be lowered to depths of 600 feet, then pumped dry. It was used for the undersea repair of damaged pipes.

Offshore exploration proved lucrative, and by 1970 the company's net income reached $46.3 million, up from $33.1 million in 1965. Other profitable ventures were hydraulic cushioning for railroad cars, electronics and explosives for the defense and aerospace industries, plant and road construction, transportation, and pollution control.

Destined for permanent importance, concern for the environment had attracted national attention a year earlier after a well eruption in California's Santa Barbara channel spilled 10,000 barrels of oil. Outrage over the resulting 200-square-mile oil slick hampered offshore exploration, as well as the construction of oil refineries and nuclear power plants. As could be expected, oil imports rose.

Continued Prosperity in the 1970s

Nevertheless, Halliburton's profits steadily climbed. Total revenues of $1 billion in 1970 grew to $2.1 billion by 1973, despite the Arab oil embargo that led to huge OPEC price increases in 1974. Acquisitions giving the company new entry into overseas markets encouraged industrial variety. The reconditioning and stimulation of older wells then became more profitable than it had ever been before, especially as the equipment the company used for its own projects was not available on the open market. Lucrative as oil-field services were, however, they were now contributing a smaller proportion to the company's total revenues. A larger part came from construction projects like steel mills, paper mills, and municipal construction.

The Halliburton corporate structure was relatively simple. In the 1970s, although the company had 55,000 employees worldwide, the Dallas headquarters housed fewer than 30 people, and day-to-day activities were handled by each segment. Operations were still divided into three main segments: oil-field services and products, producing 46 percent of 1975's total earnings; engineering and construction, contributing a 51 percent share; and specialty services and products, responsible for the remaining 3 percent. Each of these three groups had several internal divisions, themselves divided into several hundred profit centers run by field managers. Headquarters kept in touch with these field managers in a monthly reporting system that monitored specified financial goals.

By 1975, Halliburton had 40 subsidiaries in all parts of the world, most of which were smoothly fitted into their appropriate company segments. The exception was Ebasco Services, acquired along with Vernon Graphics from Boise Cascade in 1973. Like Brown & Root, Ebasco's main business was the engineering and construction of fossil fuel and nuclear electric power plants. Its merger led to a Justice Department antitrust suit claiming unfair competition. This resulted in Ebasco's sale in 1976.

By 1977, price controls had drained enthusiasm for domestic oil exploration. Imports now cost a total of $45 million, as against $7.7 billion in 1973. Two years later, the situation changed. Instability in Iran and the higher prices imposed by OPEC countries now stimulated domestic production that would alleviate international oil shortages. Beginning in June 1979, price controls were to be phased out over 28 months, although they were replaced with a windfall-profits excise tax to keep prices high, a method of encouraging oil conservation.

All these developments, as well as the slowdown of offshore exploration in the North Sea, where most major discoveries had already been made, affected the oil supply business. Halliburton's total income in 1977, $660.2 million, reached $717.5 in 1978, sinking slightly to $648.2 in 1979.

Joint ventures in construction fields helped to offset the oil-field slowdown. In 1976, Brown & Root and Raymond International, a competitor, teamed up in a $22 million bridge construction project in Louisiana. A similar arrangement the same year paired Brown & Root and Norwegian Petroleum Consultants.

Competition Increases in the 1980s

It was the company's old faithful, oil well cementing, that formed the basis for post-slump recovery. By 1980, Halliburton was servicing 60 percent of the market. Its service of stimulation of existing wells to retrieve remaining oil was garnering a 50 percent share. In early 1981, all oil price controls were eliminated and well drilling increased proportionately. That year, 77,500 new wells appeared, as compared to about 48,500 in 1978.

The upward trend brought competition for Halliburton when Dresser Industries, Schlumberger Limited, and other industry giants began to diversify into the traditional Halliburton strongholds of cementing and stimulation. However, by keeping service prices at competitive levels, Halliburton's market share remained at its usual high level, and company strength in drilling muds and well logging operations continued to be a flexible guard against competition.

By 1980, the company's total revenues reached $8.3 billion. In 1982, an economic recession plus sharply lower oil prices began to affect the oil exploration industry and its suppliers. The slowdown showed in the total income figure for 1983, which was down to $1.2 billion. While many smaller companies were unable to withstand the hard times, Halliburton merely downsized, slashing its employee roll from 115,000 to 65,000 by 1986 and then to 48,600 workers by 1988. Nevertheless, this was not a smooth time for the company. A lawsuit alleging that Brown & Root had mismanaged a south Texas nuclear power plant construction project cost a 1985 settlement of $750 million, producing a $340 million loss for the year.

The acquisitions program continued unabated. A 60 percent share of Geophysical Services, a maker of seismic analysis systems for oil exploration, was bought from Texas Instruments. Gearhart Industries joined the company lineup, and within a year its wireline services consolidated with Welex and its geophysical operations with Geophysical Services.

Research and development became even more active, including the development of horizontal drilling techniques. Spearheaded by the Geophysical Services unit, other research focused on continuous three-dimensional control for seismic surveys in offshore exploration.

As the 1980s drew to a close, Halliburton was engaged in about 40 other research and development projects. Streamlining for profitability, it had divested itself of its life insurance subsidiary, plus two other non-oil businesses. In 1989, its total revenues, showing assets of $4.2 billion, were $5.66 billion.

Restructuring and a Major Merger in the 1990s

Under the leadership of CEO Thomas Cruikshank, Halliburton in the early 1990s was contending with the effects of the sustained downturn in the U.S. oil industry, which had begun in 1986. After net income fell from $197 million in 1990 to $27 million in 1991, the company began a multi-year restructuring in 1992. A special charge of $264.6 million was recorded in that year for the first stages of the restructuring, which included the elimination of 3,000 jobs, including 26 vice-president slots. In July 1993, a significant act of streamlining took place when Halliburton merged its ten semi-autonomous energy services units, including Halliburton Services and Otis Engineering, into a single group called Halliburton Energy Services. Also created in 1993 was Brown & Root Energy Services, which combined all of Brown & Root's upstream oil and gas engineering and construction services. Later in the 1990s, Halliburton Energy Services and Brown & Root Energy Services were tied more closely together when they were placed within a newly formed Energy Group. Halliburton's engineering and construction activities (with the exception of upstream oil and gas) were likewise consolidated under a new Construction and Engineering Group.

At the same time, Halliburton shed additional non-core or underperforming units. It sold its health care cost management company for $24 million in September 1992, its troubled geophysical services and products unit to Western Atlas International Inc. for $190 million in January 1994, and its natural gas compression business to Tidewater Compression Service for $205 million in November 1994. In relation to its sale of the geophysical unit, Halliburton recorded a $301.8 million charge in 1993. In January 1996, in the last major divestment, the company spun off to shareholders Highlands Insurance, finally ridding itself of its last insurance unit. The only major acquisition of this period came in March 1993 when Smith International, Inc.'s Directional Drilling Systems and Services business was added for about $247 million in stock.

In late 1995, Dick Cheney, who had served as U.S. Secretary of Defense under President George H.W. Bush, was named chairman, CEO, and president of Halliburton, taking over the helm from the retiring Cruikshank. Cheney inherited a much leaner and more profitable company thanks to the Cruikshank-led restructuring (net income was $178 million in 1994) and quickly launched another round of acquisitions, perhaps the most ambitious in company history. In October 1996, Halliburton acquired Landmark Graphics Corp. for about $550 million in stock. Landmark, which became part of the Energy Group, was a provider of petroleum exploration and production information systems, software, and services. In April 1997, the company acquired OGC International plc—a provider of engineering, operations, and maintenance services, mainly to North Sea petroleum production companies—for about $118.3 million. In September of the same year, Halliburton spent about $360 million for NUMAR Corporation, a manufacturer of magnetic resonance imaging tools that evaluated subsurface rock formations in newly drilled oil and gas wells.

However, these deals paled in comparison to the multibillion dollar merger between Halliburton and Dresser Industries Inc. announced in February 1998. The deal was completed in September of that year and created one of the world's largest oil services firm, leaving just itself and competitor Schlumberger at the top of the industry. The merged company continued to operate under the Halliburton name and had three main business segments: the Energy Services Group, which included Halliburton Energy Services and Brown & Root Energy Services; the Engineering and Construction Group, which included Dresser's M.W. Kellogg business; and the Dresser Equipment Group business segment, which was eventually sold in 2001 for $1.55 billion.

"Once seen as badly trailing its competitors in areas such as directional drilling and drilling fluids," a 1999 *Forbes* article reported, "Halliburton now has everything it needs to win contracts for projects such as designing, building and operating systems to manage production from oilfields." In the same article, Cheney commented that "what we got was a significant improvement in our product lines," which was viewed as crucial to remaining competitive in the somewhat turbulent oil industry.

Challenges in the New Century

Halliburton's strength as a leading industry player was put to the test in the early years of the new century. Cheney resigned in 2000 to join running mate George W. Bush on the Republican ticket in the upcoming presidential election. David Lesar, named chairman and CEO, was left to deal with a barrage of asbestos claims as well as a Securities and Exchange (SEC) investigation.

Halliburton had been involved in asbestos-related litigation for years—since 1976 there had been 474,500 claims against the firm for its use of asbestos in certain products. The company and its subsidiaries—including various divisions of Dresser, Brown & Root, and Harbison-Walker, a refractory company spun off by Dresser in 1992—faced an onslaught of new claims in 2001 and 2002. Workers who had been exposed to asbestos numbered in the thousands. During 2001, a Baltimore jury awarded a group of plaintiffs $30 million, sending company stock to its lowest point in nine years. The following year, Halliburton was given an opportunity to put the litigation to rest. By agreeing to pay approximately $4.2 billion to settle all outstanding claims, Halliburton would be shielded from future asbestos litigation. Investors applauded the planned settlement and the firm's share price climbed from $9 to $21 per share.

However, just as the company appeared to be close to ending its legal woes, it faced yet another obstacle. During 2002, the SEC began an investigation into Halliburton's accounting practices. During 1998, when Cheney was in office, the company changed how it booked revenue related to cost overruns on billion-dollar contracts. Before 1998, the firm did not report revenue from cost overrun claims until that revenue was received. Then, in 1998, the firm began booking estimated payments it planned to receive in the future. For example, in 1998 the company booked $89 million in unpaid claims as pre-tax revenue.

While the change in the way the company booked certain revenue was legal, the firm neglected to report it to shareholders and the SEC for over a year. By making the change, Halliburton was able to meet earnings expectations for 1998—the year of the Dresser merger. Without it, earnings would have fallen short. The SEC began its investigation in May, forcing Halliburton to hand over nearly 200,000 accounting documents to prove that it had not inflated cost overrun claims.

At the same time, the faltering economy, falling oil prices, and a slowdown in North American gas production was wreaking havoc on Halliburton's bottom line. During 2002, the company reported an estimated loss of $984 million, compared to a net profit of $809 million secured in 2001. In response to difficult market conditions, Lesar launched a cost cutting effort and began selling off non-core assets. The company also realigned its businesses into two major groups—Halliburton Energy Services Group and KBR, the engineering and construction group—with hopes of eventually creating two independently run operating subsidiaries.

Lesar and his management teamed remained optimistic about Halliburton's future despite the challenges it faced related to the economic downturn. With an asbestos settlement on the horizon and rumors its SEC investigation would not lead to any legal action, Halliburton appeared to have made it through the worst.

Principal Operating Units

Energy Services Group; KBR Engineering & Construction.

Principal Competitors

Baker Hughes Inc.; Bechtel Group, Inc.; Schlumberger Ltd.

Further Reading

Antosh, Nelson, "Houston-Based Halliburton Posts $602 Million Loss in Fourth Quarter," *Houston Chronicle*, February 21, 2003.

"The Asbestos Monster: How Scary for Halliburton?," *Business Week*, December 24, 2001.

Basralian, Joseph, "Reveille in Dallas," *Financial World*, January 31, 1995, pp. 32–33.

Brown & Root Engineering, Houston: Brown & Root, Inc., 1990.

Dittrick, Paula, "Halliburton to Combine 10 Business Units to Create New Energy Services Organization," *Oil Daily*, June 17, 1993, p. 3.

Fisher, Daniel, "Mr. Outside Saves the Day," *Forbes*, January 11, 1999, p. 162.

Groom, Nichola, "SEC Turns Up Heat on Halliburton, Cheney," *National Post*, December 21, 2002, p. FP8.

Haley, J. Evetts, *Erle P. Halliburton: Genius with Cement*, Duncan, Okla., 1959.

"Halliburton Agrees to Buy Numar Corp. in $360 Million Deal," *Wall Street Journal*, June 11, 1997, p. C13.

Halliburton Company: Seventy-Five Years of Leadership, Dallas: Halliburton, 1994, 32 p.

"Halliburton Stock Plummets in Tailspin," *Oil Daily*, December 10, 2001.

Hogan, Rick, "Halliburton to Buy Landmark Graphics in $557 Million Deal," *Oil Daily*, July 2, 1996, pp. 1+.

Hudson, Rex, "A Brief History of Halliburton Services (1916–1977)," Halliburton corporate typescript, 1977.

Lipin, Steven, and Peter Fritsch, "Halliburton Agrees to Acquire Dresser," *Wall Street Journal*, February 26, 1998, p. A3.

Mack, Toni, "A Piece of the Action," *Forbes*, August 11, 1997, p. 60.

McWilliams, Gary, "Dick Cheney Ain't Studyin' War No More," *Business Week*, March 2, 1998, pp. 84–85.

Park, Andrew, and Lorraine Woellert, "Halliburton: Halfway Home?," *Business Week*, December 23, 2002.

Reifenberg, Anne, "Halliburton Co. Selects Cheney for 3 Top Posts," *Wall Street Journal*, August 11, 1995, p. B8.

Rodengen, Jeffrey L., *The Legend of Halliburton*, Fort Lauderdale, Fla.: Write Stuff Syndicate, 1996, 208 p.

"SEC Launches Halliburton Probe," *Oil Daily*, December 23, 2002.

Scism, Leslie, "Halliburton to Spin Off Insurance Unit in Plan Values at Up to $250 Million," *Wall Street Journal*, October 12, 1995, p. A8.

Wetuski, Jodi, "Halliburton to Separate Oil, Engineering Businesses," *Oil and Gas Investor*, May 2002, p. 80.

—Gillian Wolf

—updates: David E. Salamie and Christina M. Stansell

HCI Direct, Inc.

3050 Tillman Drive
Bensalem, Pennsylvania 19020
U.S.A.
Telephone: (215) 244-1777
Fax: (215) 244-0328
Web site: http://www.silkies.com

Private Company
Incorporated: 1974 as Hosiery Corporation of America
Employees: 200 (est.)
Sales: $180 million (2001)
NAIC: 315111 Sheer Hosiery Mills

HCI Direct, Inc. is a manufacturer of women's hosiery, under the Silkies brand, sold primarily through a direct mail marketing continuity program. Consumers are initially enticed by an offer of a free pair of hosiery in hopes of making them long-term, repeat customers. The Bensalem, Pennsylvania, company offers a variety of sheer panty hose as well as knee-highs, socks, and tights for girls. Over the years, HCI's sales approach has resulted in litigation initiated by both the Federal Trade Commission and a number of states, which have charged that the company's offer of free merchandise is intentionally deceptive. The company is also noteworthy for its failed attempts to go public in the 1990s. In addition to its Bensalem facility, HCI owns and operates a manufacturing plant in Newland, North Carolina.

1970s Origins

HCI Direct was originally called Hosiery Corporation of America (HCA), established in 1974 in Philadelphia, Pennsylvania, by businessman Jules "Sonny" Nelson, the son of poor immigrants. He started out with little but grew wealthy through mail-order ventures, the most successful of which was his hosiery business. In the early years, HCA relied on a variety of marketing efforts in addition to direct mailing, including cooperative advertising, package inserts, and newspaper ads. Nelson's wife Claire was part-owner of HCA and served as president. After 25 years of marriage, the couple separated, although

they never divorced. In 1980, they reached an agreement that paid Claire Nelson $1.8 million for her share of the company. During this difficult time for the Nelsons, an executive named Joseph Murphy was instrumental in keeping the business afloat. In 1981, as the health of Jules Nelson began to falter, Murphy officially took over as chief executive officer and chairman. At the same time, Jules Nelson was grooming the youngest of two adopted sons, Bryan D. Nelson, whom he hoped would one day take over the business.

When his father died of heart disease at the age of 56 in 1983, Bryan Nelson was 22 years old and, despite inheriting 97 percent of the voting stock, hardly ready to take control of HCA, a company generating $100 million in annual sales. Matters were further complicated when Claire Nelson sued for a share of HCA, resulting in a five-year legal battle that finally ended when she settled for $7 million and cash, a sprawling Bucks County estate, and title to several other properties. In the meantime, Bryan Nelson relied heavily on Murphy to run the company. According to insider accounts, the two men were close, with Murphy seeming to serve as a substitute father. Nevertheless, Nelson was afraid he might lose Murphy and in 1984 sold a 25 percent stake to him for just $1000. In addition, they signed a "buy-sell" agreement that required their shares to be sold back to the company in the event that either party died. According to HCA executive Ben Greber, as reported by the *Philadelphia Inquirer*, "Bryan knew that without Joe Murphy, the company would be down the tubes. And Joe wanted to make sure, naturally, that he would be protected if he stayed."

While the estate of Jules Nelson was being challenged and the young heir was working out a deal with the company's chief executive, HCA also dealt with Federal Trade Commission (FTC) litigation that had been initiated in 1982. As reported by the *Philadelphia Daily News,* the FTC charged that Hosiery Corp. had duped customers with low-priced come-on offers: "Mike Milgrom, a staff attorney for the Federal Trade Commission's Cleveland office, which covers Philadelphia, said the scheme worked this way: A person would receive one package of pantyhose in the mail. If the person liked the pantyhose, three additional pairs could be ordered at $1 each. 'The recipient was not told, however, that the company would continue to send

Company Perspectives:

For more than 25 years Silkies has been creating fabulous hosiery for women around the world. Thanks to our unique "at home" shopping experience, you're free from the hassle of running out of hosiery again. We deliver hosiery direct to your door, so you won't ever have to rummage through department store bins searching for the styles and shades you need. Silkies are available in all the styles, sizes and shades you want. They're guaranteed to be comfortable, fit perfectly and last a long time.

pantyhose at a higher price of $1.39 each until the person refused to pay for them,' Milgrom said. When that occurred Hosiery Corp. mailed the person a series of warning letters in which the company threatened to damage the person's credit rating.'' In August 1984, HCA agreed to pay a $200,000 fine and signed a consent decree that called for the company to change its practices, although it did not admit to any wrongdoing.

Despite running into some difficulty with its direct mail continuity program, HCA began to explore the possibility of focusing exclusively on this approach. Starting in the spring of 1988, the company initiated test programs and by 1991 decided to drop other forms of marketing. It also chose to focus on its core customers, women in their 40s. In 1990, it sold a subsidiary, MAQ Inc., a mail order company that sold home electronics and other items. In addition, HCA launched Meteor Publishing, a direct-mail publisher of romance novels. The history of the company was soon to take a twist worthy of fiction when the principal owner, 29-year-old Bryan Nelson, died under unusual circumstance.

Early 1990s Ownership Dispute

Nelson was a wealthy newlywed, having married 19-year-old Sarah Jannicky Nelson in the spring of 1991 after her freshman year in college. He was also an avid golfer, a morning regular at the Commonwealth National Country Club in Horsham, Pennsylvania. After completing the front nine one day, he was chatting outside the pro shop when he was stung by a yellow jacket. Several minutes later he lay unconscious as a Horsham Fire Company ambulance rushed him to Abington Memorial Hospital, where four days later he died. What happened during that hurried drive to the hospital would soon be the subject of litigation, as his young widow filed suit against the fire company and the two-man ambulance crew. According to the *Philadelphia Inquirer,* the suit charged that ''the workers, meaning to treat Nelson's allergic reaction to the bee sting with an intravenous bag of saline solution, grabbed the wrong bag. Nelson was given an overdose of an anesthetic called lidocaine, sending him into seizures and stopping his heart.''

Nelson was only unconscious for a day when it became apparent that he was likely to die. His wife, accompanied by her father and brother, searched the bedroom safe for a will, which would determine who would own HCA. A week later, Sarah Nelson was appointed to administer her husband's estate and reported that no will was found, which meant that under Penn-

sylvania law she was entitled to a little more than half of the estate, the balance going to Claire Nelson because the couple had no children. Murphy then moved to enforce the 1984 ''buy-sell'' agreement, calling in the stock. A few months later, he reached an agreement with Sarah's lawyers stipulating that HCA would purchase Bryan Nelson's stock for $4.3 million, about $1 million more than it was worth according to HCA accountants. However, Sarah Nelson unexpectedly changed lawyers and rejected the deal, and her new representatives went to court to void the 1984 ''buy-sell'' agreement. According to the *Philadelphia Inquirer,* ''Their petition essentially paints Nelson as a callow, trusting youth who was fleeced by a savvy elder. 'The effect of the [agreements] is that Joseph Murphy, for the nominal payment of $1,000, will have acquired rights to all of the stock in HCA, having a value in excess of $30 million,' the petition says. . . . Murphy and his lawyers smelled a conspiracy. Claire Nelson, they alleged, was back on the scene, scheming with Sarah. The widow and her mother-in-law had formed an 'illegal windfall profit scheme . . . which would operate in the same manner first used by Claire Nelson to extort millions of dollars from HCA and her estranged husband's estate,' Murphy's lawyers say in court documents.''

While this matter began to wend its way through the courts, ownership of HCA was further clouded in March 1992 when the elder adopted child, Jeffrey Nelson, a photographer living in Santa Fe, showed up with a copy of a 1985 will that gave him most of his brother's estate and 88 percent of his HCA stock, while awarding nothing to their mother. With only a copy in their possession, Jeffrey and his lawyers suggested that the original had been destroyed or hidden by Sarah and Claire, and asked that the court accept the copy as valid. Several months later, Jeffrey agreed to drop his efforts to push the 1985 will in exchange for being cut in on his brother's estate. Only a month later, however, in November 1992, Murphy produced another Bryan Nelson will, an original signed in 1984 that gave most of Nelson's stock to Murphy. Finally, in early 1994, HCA agreed to pay $7.85 million to Nelson's estate as part of a settlement in which the three Nelson family members agreed to drop any ownership claims on HCA. They were then left to split the estate among themselves, while HCA executives returned to running the company.

During the two years of litigation that embroiled the company, HCA closed its romance publishing venture and focused solely on its hosiery business. A few months after settling with the Nelson estate, the company was on the auction block, attracting considerable attention, although the asking price of $200 million scared off some suitors. In the end, the buyout firm of Kelso Equity Partners, L.P. of New York acquired a 71 percent controlling interest of HCA in a leveraged buyout.

HCA Enters British Market in 1995

HCA began testing the British market in 1995 and was pleased enough with the results that a year later it increased its UK efforts as part of a plan to grow the business internationally. By now, the company was shipping approximately 42 million pairs of hosiery a year, roughly double the business it was doing in 1991. During that five-year period, net revenues grew at a compound annual rate of 11.7 percent. It was a business, however, that faced challenges. The rising popularity of ''casual

---

Key Dates:

1974: Hosiery Corporation of America is founded.
1983: Jules Nelson dies, leaving controlling interest in the company to his son Bryan Nelson.
1991: Bryan Nelson dies.
1994: The company sold in a leveraged buyout.
1998: Enchantress Hosiery Corporation of Canada is acquired.
2002: The company requests Chapter 11 bankruptcy protection.

Fridays'' in the corporate world hurt sales, as did the growing tendency of women to wear longer skirts and pants. Moreover, while the retail price of hosiery had changed little over the years, the cost of raw materials increased, forcing manufacturers like HCA to invest in equipment that could produce hosiery less expensively. Over the course of several years, HCA spent $25 million upgrading its North Carolina manufacturing facilities. In the summer of 1996, it looked to take the company public in order to keep it funded well enough to compete in the low-margin, high-volume hosiery business. HCA also needed cash to make an acquisition of a company that officials never did identify, an effort that was eventually dropped. Due to poor market conditions, however, the initial public offering (IPO) was postponed and eventually dropped. In preparing for the offering, the board had offered stock options to 33 shareholders at below market prices. Because of the aborted acquisition and the costs of the failed IPO, HCA reported a loss of $4.3 million in 1996. The stock options alone resulted in a $23 million charge, the uncompleted IPO and acquisition accounting for another $1.6 million.

In January 1997, HCA once again faced scrutiny from the FTC, along with attorney generals from a dozen states, which began to review the company's promotional materials after receiving numerous complaints over the years. As described by *The Capital Times,* ''The company sends coupons offering a 'free' sample of 'Silkies' pantyhose, complete with a scratch off card allowing consumers to choose their size and shade. What wasn't obvious to a lot of consumers is that when you accept this 'free' offer, you are also agreeing to accept two more pairs that you must either buy or return to the company at your own expense.'' Moreover, some consumers had cards sent in by their friends, and when they did not pay for the unsolicited merchandise were told by HCA that the matter would be turned over to a collection agency. The states offered changes beyond those mandated by the 1984 injunction, including disclosures regarding initial and future shipments as well as a requirement that refunds be made under certain circumstances. To settle matters with the states, HCA agreed in July 1997 to pay $300,000, to be split among the states for refunds to customers. In addition, HCA agreed to make the terms of its offer more clear in future ads.

Between 1996 and 1999, HCA expanded its operations to Canada, Germany, and France. The move into Canada was accomplished through the 1998 acquisition of Enchantress Hosiery Corporation of Canada Ltd. at the cost of $3.9 million. Once again, the company took steps to make an initial public offering of stock, in the process of which, in 1999, HCA changed its name to HCI Direct. The hope was to repurchase preferred stock and pay down debt by selling 100 million shares at $15 to $17 each, but as was the case three years earlier the offering was ultimately cancelled.

With the start of the new century, HCI's business began to deteriorate, resulting in losses for both 2000 and 2001. In the early months of 2002, the company filed for Chapter 11 bankruptcy protection. Several weeks later, when a pre-packaged reorganization plan was approve by the U.S. Bankruptcy Court in Wilmington, Delaware, HCI emerged and the sum of $81 million in unsecured senior notes was exchanged for an 85 percent equity stake in the reorganized corporation. With its finances finally in order, HCI held onto its position as the third largest hosiery manufacturer in the United States. Nevertheles, the future of the company remained very much in question.

Principal Subsidiaries

Hosiery Corporation International.

Principal Competitors

Danskin, Inc.; Alba-Waldensian Inc.; Sara Lee Branded Apparel.

Further Reading

King, Larry, ''Hosiery Firm Pays Off Heirs of Man Who Died of Bee Sting,'' *Philadelphia Inquirer*, February 11, 1994.
——, ''Tangled Web of Wills Tees Off In Montgomery County,'' *Philadelphia Inquirer*, January 24, 1993.
Lowe, Frederick, ''$200G Fine for Hosiery,'' *Philadelphia Daily News*, August 15, 1984, p. 37.
Owens, Jennifer, ''Hosiery Corp.'s Loss Blamed on IPO Costs,'' *WWD*, April 7, 1997, p. 10.
Richards, Bob, '' 'Free' Pantyhose Deal Has A Serious Run In It,'' *Capital Times*, August 9, 1997. p. 1C.

—Ed Dinger

Head N.V.

Blaak 16
3011 TA Rotterdam
The Netherlands
Telephone: (+31) 10-214-1923
Fax: (+31) 10-401-6462
Web site: http:www.head.com

Public Company
Incorporated: 1950 as Head Ski Company, Inc.
Employees: 3,038
Sales: $387.5 million (2002)
Stock Exchanges: New York
Ticker Symbol: HED
NAIC: 339920 Sporting and Athletic Goods
    Manufacturing

With its headquarters located in Rotterdam, The Netherlands, Head N.V. is a multinational sporting goods manufacturer and marketer. Operations are organized into four divisions: Winter Sports, Racquet Sports, Diving, and Licensing. In addition to the Head brand, which is best known for ski and tennis products, the company also includes Penn, makers of tennis racquetball balls; Tyrolia ski bindings; Mares and Dacor, diving equipment manufacturers; and Blax and Generics snowboard equipment manufacturers. Head N.V. products are sold in more than 80 countries.

1930s Origins

The founder of Head N.V., Howard Head, was a frustrated writer turned engineer who eventually became an entrepreneur. Head was born in Philadelphia, Pennsylvania, in 1914, the son of a dentist. He aspired to become a screenwriter and enrolled at Harvard University to pursue that goal, but in his sophomore year changed his academic focus to engineering. After graduating with honors in 1936 with an engineering degree, Head nevertheless attempted to pursue a writing career, and over the course of the next three years he was fired from various low-paying jobs as a scriptwriter, reporter, and copywriter. He then took an aptitude test and, according to his recollections, suffered further humiliation when he scored the test's lowest aptitude for creative writing ever recorded. He did, however, earn the highest score then recorded for structural visualization, an ability to think in three dimensions that boded well for an engineering degree. In 1939, he went to work as a riveter for aircraft manufacturer Glenn L. Martin Company before securing a position as an engineer.

Head worked at Martin during the war years, when he became known for his fondness for poker and parties. He was still with the company in 1946 when his penchant for socializing led him to try skiing during an outing to Stowe, Vermont, an event that marked a turning point in his life. Despite being embarrassed by his efforts on the slopes, he was hooked on the sport and determined to improve his skill. Like many a beginner, he blamed the equipment for his poor performance, but unlike the vast majority of skiers, Head possessed the technical knowledge to make a convincing case. Skis at the time were long, heavy, and clumsy; they were also constructed of hickory wood, a material which easily lost its shape and created an unstable ride. Rather than simply devote himself to mastering the use of the traditional ski, Head boasted he could make a better, lighter, more efficient ski using metal and aircraft manufacturing techniques. He reasoned that if wood was such a superior material, why were airplanes no longer made out of it? Head bought a band saw for $250 and began designing skis in his spare time. His concept was not to simply make a metal ski, at which others had tried and failed. Rather, he looked to the metal-sandwich construction method of the aircraft industry, which developed during World War II when chemists created flexible, waterproof glues to bond aluminum and plywood. In 1947, Head launched his "honeycomb" ski project, so called because he envisioned a ski that was constructed of two layers of aluminum bonded to plywood sidewalls that encased a core of honeycomb plastic.

Head was so convinced that his future lay with ski design that in January 1948 he resigned from Martin to devote all his time to the development of a composite ski. With $6,000 in poker winnings, he founded Head Ski Company in Timonium, Maryland, and worked night and day to perfect his vision of the ideal, light-weight ski. The bonding process proved especially problematic, taking Head several months before he developed a technique of boiling the ski in oil in order to set the glue. After a year of effort he finally produced six pairs of composite skis, which he took to a Stowe, Vermont, resort and convinced ski instructors to test. All of his prototypes were broken within an hour on the Green Mountain slopes. Nonetheless, one of the professional skiers he enlisted, Neil Robinson, encouraged Head to keep trying and agreed to test new versions that Head would ship to him throughout the winter. By the end of the season, after Robinson returned a number of broken skis, Head produced a ski that was as strong as wood but at half the weight. It was far from perfect, however, and Head spent another three years engaged in developing the design, which suffered from two major drawbacks: the aluminum froze and collected snow on the bottom of the skis and the edges quickly became dull. To eliminate icing and improve sliding, Head coated the bottom of the skis with a special plastic, which he ultimately used to also cover the top and sides. To provide added strength, he replaced the honeycomb plastic core with plywood. Finally, to solve the problem of dull edges, he inlaid and bonded to the bottom of the ski long, sharp, steel strips. All told, Head worked through 40 different designs by 1950, when he finally watched a ski instructor carve up a hill with his composite skis and knew he had finally succeeded. He named his creation the "Standard," which he began to produce and sell for $85 a pair at a time when the market price for conventional skis was $25. In the end, his composite skis weighed nearly the same as conventional hickory ones, but they were also stronger, more flexible, and turned better. More importantly, the Standard allowed beginners like Head to participate in skiing, which was no longer the domain of the skilled athlete, many of whom called the Standard "cheaters."

Incorporation in 1950

In 1950, Head incorporated his business as Head Ski Company, Inc. To raise enough money to stay afloat, he had to sell 40 percent of the company for $60,000. His skis were not quickly embraced by the market, and it took several years of tireless promotion by Head to establish the expensive Standard as a status symbol product. According to company records, Head became the leading brand of ski sold in the United States and Europe by 1955. Convincing world class skiers to adopt composite skis took longer, but significant Olympic victories on Head skis during the 1960s sealed the fate of conventional hickory skis. Moreover, by possessing important patents covering metal ski construction, Head was well positioned to take advantage of the rising popularity of skiing while established ski manufacturers struggled to catch up.

Head attempted to diversify his business during the 1960s, adding an active wear division (Head Ski and Sports Wear) in 1966. In 1969, the company introduced a fiberglass/metal ski. It also became involved in the development of tennis rackets, once again fueled by Head's interest in a sport in which he hoped to improve his personal performance. As was the case with skis, tennis rackets had been constructed out of wood and not seen a major design change for 100 years. In 1968, Head launched a tennis division at the company, now named Head Sports Inc., and a year later introduced the first metal tennis racket at the U.S. Open. At the same time, Head was coming under pressure from a hostile takeover initiated by AMF Corp., a New York sporting goods conglomerate best known for its bowling products. Head was soon forced to sell his company to AMF in 1969 for $16 million, personally realizing $4.5 million in the deal. In retirement, he focused on his tennis game, which had shown little improvement even with a metal racket and numerous lessons. He bought a ball machine produced by a small Princeton, New Jersey, company named Prince Manufacturing Co. Frustrated with the machine's performance, he took it apart and assessed its design flaws. He soon purchased a controlling interest in the company and went on to develop the first oversized metal tennis racket, transforming Prince into a major tennis manufacturer and revolutionizing a second sport. Howard Head died in 1991 at the age of 76 from complications following quadruple-bypass surgery.

Under AMF control, Head Sports made two major acquisitions during the 1970s, adding Tyrolia, an Austrian maker of ski bindings and poles, and Mares, an Italian manufacturer of scuba gear. In 1985, AMF was acquired by Minneapolis-based Minstar Inc., controlled by corporate raider Irwin Jacobs, who earned the name "Irv the Liquidator" in the 1970s by dismantling Grain Belt Breweries and W.T. Grant & Co. In 1981, he picked up Minstar, a snowmobile company that had succumbed to bankruptcy after two consecutive years without snow but also included a sideline business in powerboats, which became Jacobs's focus. Minstar now began acquiring companies with attractive boating assets and in the process sold off non-boating interests to fuel continued growth. The largest of these transactions involved AMF, which in addition to Head Sports, Tyrolia, and Mares owned the Hatteras yacht business. During the four years that it was under Minstar management, Head Sports outsourced marketing and distribution of its products, leaving its Boulder, Colorado, manufacturing facility, where both skis and tennis rackets were produced, as the main operation. In 1987, the company diversified into athletic footwear, introducing a line of tennis shoes. A year later, all manufacturing was transferred from Boulder to a new state-of-the-art plant in Austria, resulting in the layoff of nearly 100 employees.

In March 1989, Minstar sold Head Sports, Tyrolia, and Mares in a leveraged buyout led by senior management of the three companies, backed primarily by Los-Angeles-based venture capitalist firm Freeman Spogli & Co. and to a lesser degree the Japanese firms of Nissho Iwai and J. Osawa & Co. Drawing on the initials of the three companies, the new business was renamed HTM. Head Sports was the largest of the entities, with annual revenues of $150 million, compared to Tyrolia's $100 million and Mares's $26 million. The Head Sport Boulder operation was now converted into a marketing and promotion, distribution, and customer service center for all three product lines.

New Ownership in 1993

Control of Head changed hands once again when in 1993 when Austria Tabak, the Austrian state-owned tobacco monop-

Key Dates:

1947: Howard Head begins designing the first metal ski.
1950: Head Ski Company, Inc. is founded.
1969: Head introduces the first aluminum tennis racket; the company is sold to AMF.
1985: Minstar acquires Head through AMF takeover.
1989: Management buys out Head, Tyrolia, and Mares, forming HTM.
1993: HTM is sold to Austria Tabak.
1995: Johan Eliasch gains control of HTM.
2000: Head N.V. is formed and taken public.

oly, acquired HTM as part of a European Union mandated diversification effort. It proved, however, to be a short-lived arrangement. Severely burdened by debt from the 1989 buyout, HTM, despite owning several strong brands, posted net losses of nearly $150 million for Tabak. In 1995, Swedish investor Johan Eliasch, known as a turnaround artist, convinced the Austrian government to sell HTM to him for less than $1 million as well as to honor a $120 million bailout package devised for Tabak.

Like Howard Head, Eliasch held an engineering degree, along with a master's degree from Stockholm Royal Institute of Technology, but unlike his predecessor he had been interested in business from an early age. His grandfather had been a major Swedish industrialist who, because he was afraid that easy wealth would adversely affect his heirs, stipulated that they could inherit their portions of his estate only upon reaching the age of 50, thus forcing Eliasch to earn a living. Both of Eliasch's parents were doctors, but it was business rather than medicine that held his interest. From the age of 12 he began buying stock. After training for a year with the German conglomerate Siemens in the early 1980s, Eliasch moved to New York, where he realized a quick profit by buying and turning around a small cards company. He then moved to London and along with several partners formed Tufton group, a private equity fund that raised money to buy troubled companies, restore them to financial health, and sell them. Tufton success stories included foot-products firm Scholl and film distributor Guild Entertainment. When his partners elected to become involved in shipping, Eliasch split from Tufton in 1991 and struck out on his own, establishing Equity Partners with minor interests held by Charles and Maurice Saatchi, who were better known for their global advertising business. One of Eliasch's first acquisitions was London Films, the famed production company founded by Sir Alexander Korda. Aside from a deep interest in cinema, Eliasch was also an avid skier and was well aware of the Head brand. When Head Sports came on the market in both 1989 and 1993, he had attempted to gain control of the business. He was finally successful in 1995.

Eliasch moved quickly to revitalize the fortunes of HTM. He cut overhead, eliminating 1,100 jobs, and discontinued two disappointing product lines, golf clubs and sports wear, which

had been responsible for most of the company's losses. With the product lines more focused, he directed the company's attention into three areas: winter sports, tennis, and scuba diving. A fourth division, licensing, was subsequently added. As a result of these changes, in 1997 revenues dropped 16 percent over the previous year, but the company was able to post a $4 million profit. Although an impressive start, Eliasch continued to be saddled with oppressive debt. In 1998, HTM defaulted on $190 million in debt, at an 8 percent interest rate, then negotiated a rescue package with Austrian and Japanese banks that forgave $72 million and lowered the interest rate to just 6 percent. Eliasch next floated a $100 million note to gain a financial cushion and began boosting the company's research and development budget in an effort to spur sales through innovation. In 1997, HTM introduced the first tennis racket made of titanium and graphite, which proved highly popular. It then developed the first computerized tennis racket, named Head Intelligence, which employed sensors to adjust the necessary power and in the process suppress about half of all vibrations, thus eliminating the cause of tennis elbow. On the skiing side of the business, new hourglass-shaped skis, designed to make sharp turns, also found a ready market. In addition, Eliasch looked to grow HTM through external means. In 1998, the company acquired Dacor, a diving industry pioneer, followed by the 1999 addition of Penn Tennis Balls and snowboard makers Blax and Generics.

In 2000, HTM was reorganized as Head N.V. was taken public, its initial offering netting the company more than $135 million. The company's shares began trading on both the Vienna Stock Exchange and New York Stock Exchange. As Head looked forward, it continued its emphasis on research and development while also pursuing external growth. The hope was to add new product lines to provide some diversification. In particular, management began to consider the fitness, bicycle, golf, and fishing sectors, with the goal of doubling the size of Head within five years.

Principal Divisions

Winters Sports; Racquet Sports; Diving; Licensing.

Principal Competitors

adidas-Salomon AG; Amer Group; NIKE.

Further Reading

Buckstein, Caryl, "Head Reorganization Looks to Double Company's Sales," *Boulder County Business Report*, April 1994, p. 20.

Landrum, Gene N., *Profiles of Genius: Thirteen Creative Men Who Changed the World,* Buffalo, New York: Prometheus Books, 1993, 263 p.

Lynn, Matthew, "Swede Proves Good Sport With Money," *Sunday Times*, February 7, 1999, p. 6.

McQuade, Walter, "Prince Triumphant," *Fortune*, February 22, 1982, p. 84.

Wherry, Rob, "Head's Up," *Forbes*, March 20, 2000, p. 264.

—Ed Dinger

Home Interiors & Gifts, Inc.

1649 Frankford Road West
Carrollton, Texas 75007
U.S.A.
Telephone: (972) 695-1000
Fax: (972) 695-1112
Web site: http://www.homeinteriors.com

Private Company
Incorporated: 1957
Employees: 2,400
Sales: $574.5 million (2002)
NAIC: 454390 Other Direct Selling Establishments

Home Interiors & Gifts, Inc. is one of the nation's leading home decor companies selling through private, in-home parties. The company sells a line of modestly priced interior decorations, principally small accent pieces such as shelves, mirrors, plaques, sconces, and figurines. A sales force of some 70,000 independent contractors, mostly women working part time, sell Home Interiors & Gifts products to their friends and neighbors. Independent contractors, known in the company as displayers, collect a commission on their own sales and then collect a smaller percentage in commission on the sales of people they have recruited to the company. The corporate structure is similar to Mary Kay Cosmetics, Avon, Shaklee, and Amway. Home Interiors & Gifts maintains corporate headquarters in Carrollton, Texas, and operates one Dallas-area warehouse and distribution center. The company's sales are mostly in the United States, but in the late 1990s Home Interiors began pushing into international markets. It now has significant representation in Mexico and makes sales in Puerto Rico as well. The firm was founded by Mary C. Crowley and its chief executive is Crowley's grandson Donald J. (Joey) Carter, Jr. Home Interiors was recapitalized in 1998 by members of the founder's family and the buyout firm Hicks, Muse, Tate & Furst. Hicks, Muse owns about 75 percent of the company.

A Gift for Selling

Mary C. Crowley founded Home Interiors & Gifts after years of struggling to make ends meet as a single mother of two children. She was born in 1915 and grew up mainly on her grandparents' Missouri wheat farm after her mother died when Crowley was an infant. When Crowley was older she went back and forth between her grandparents' home and that of her father, who had remarried, but she was unhappy under the regime of her stepmother. She married in 1932, while she was still a teenager, and lived with her husband in Sherman, Texas. She bore a son, Don, the next year, and a daughter, Ruthie, in 1935. Crowley's marriage, however, was strained. By the time she was 21, Crowley had separated from her husband and was on her own financially. She had little formal education, but her determination more than made up for this disadvantage. Though unemployment was rampant in 1937, with the country still in the grip of the Great Depression, Crowley had to find a job. Venturing into downtown Sherman, she evaluated all the stores. She decided the most impressive one was a department store, so she went in and informed the manager that she had chosen his store to be her new employer. Evidently bowled over by the young woman's confidence, the manager agreed to give her a one-day trial. She quickly proved her knack for selling, convincing customers to pick up four-cent spools of thread to bring their purchases up to an even dollar amount so they would not have to wait for their change. Crowley outsold the store's veteran employees and was given a permanent position.

Crowley's earnings at the department store came to $7 a week, which rose to $8 whenever she won the weekly bonus for best sales record. Even by Depression standards this was barely enough to support herself and two children. She began attending evening classes at Southern Methodist University to learn accounting in order to qualify for a better job. In the early 1940s, she worked for an insurance company and then became the bookkeeper for a furniture store. Though she had an office job, Crowley still loved the sales floor. She got her exposure to home decorating at the furniture store, where she frequently quizzed customers on what accessories they might want to go with their new chairs and sofas. Around this time, she met Mary Kay Eckman, who went on to found Mary Kay Cosmetics Co. Eckman was working for a company called Stanley Home Products, and she recruited Crowley to join her. Stanley Home Products was one of several companies that followed in the wake of Tupperware in the 1940s and sold directly to customers through home parties. Crowley began selling furniture waxes

Company Perspectives:

No nation, family, or business can become great unless it has a great purpose—a power that energizes, inspires, and builds people! The purpose of the company's structure is to provide a channel—a means whereby salespeople might use their creative skills to find identity and fulfillment in the achievement of homes decorated with Attraction Power— that is dedicated to the best in life, all under the direction of Almighty God.

and polishes for Stanley Home, and within five years she was the company's leading salesperson.

Crowley left Stanley Home Products in 1954 and began selling for a similar company called World Gift. World Gift specialized in accessories for the home, mostly decorative finishing touches such as shelves and candlesticks. Crowley worked for World Gift until 1957. By that time, she was a sales manager with 500 people working under her. She had become quite successful, but the company's owner held her back, putting a limit on the amount of commission women sales staff could make. The event that finally caused the split between Crowley and World Gift was a Christmas cocktail party. Crowley was a teetotaler, and she was enough put off by drinking in the office that she quit the company. She then put together her savings with loans from friends and started her own company, Home Interiors & Gifts. In the beginning, she did not have quite enough money to start her business and had to approach a bank for a loan of $6,000. Crowley recalled meeting plenty of resistance from bankers who could not fathom a corporation run by a woman. Not only was the company to be woman-owned, but its employees would all be women, mostly mothers and housewives working in their spare time. Nevertheless, Crowley's persuasive powers got her the loan, and the company was an immediate success. Crowley used her contacts at the manufacturers who supplied World Gift and arranged for her own unique line of home accessories.

Finding a Niche in the 1960s and 1970s

The new company found an under-served niche. Both its sales force and its customers were mostly women with children. They were often, like Crowley herself had been, women with little education, dependent on their husbands, and focused on their homes. Crowley understood what made these people tick. She knew not only what kind of decorations they liked, what colors were appealing, and what price range was affordable, but she had Bible-inspired philosophy that made a moral good out of home beautification. Many women who were conflicted about working outside the home were eager to work for Home Interiors. Crowley's recruits were willing to work part-time to make extra money, but they did not want to take time away from their families. Home Interiors' saleswomen, called displayers, arranged parties in the evenings, when their husbands could watch the children, or during the day, when kids were in school. The items in the Home Interiors line were for the most part moderately priced, and all sales were made on a cash-up-front basis. Crowley's message of optimism, her own success after many hard-luck years, and her choice of products that fit the taste and

lifestyles of her female clientele immediately attracted customers, many of whom in turn became displayers. The company was structured so that the displayers took a commission of about two-thirds of the price of the goods they sold. Another 10 percent went upstream to local and regional managers, and the rest went to corporate headquarters. Displayers often made only modest amounts, but they could collect points toward prizes such as mink coats, diamonds, and Hawaiian vacations. As displayers recruited more women to sell Home Interiors products, they also collected commissions from these people, enabling some Home Interiors managers to make impressive salaries.

Crowley worked closely with her family. She had remarried in 1948, and her second husband was enthusiastic about her career. Her son Don helped found the business and later became its chief executive officer. Crowley's daughter Ruthie headed an East Coast division of the company. By 1962, Home Interiors & Gifts had sales of $1 million. That year, Crowley was diagnosed with cancer. She fought two bouts of the disease and lived until 1987. Home Interiors continued to grow rapidly through the 1960s and 1970s. Crowley had made the company as much a people motivator as a business. She led business meetings with a mink-covered Bible in her lap and interspersed more mundane discussions with readings from the scriptures. She conveyed to her displayers that the success of the corporation was based on their personal success, a factor not measured entirely in money. "We believe a woman comes into this business to develop some part of her life, either financial, emotional, or educational," she told the *Saturday Evening Post* (April 1983). "To do that, she must look and act like a professional. We have a dress code and a behavior code. We offer training and help the girls set and meet their goals. It's our responsibility to assist them in becoming achievers and feeling like winners." Her own opulent lifestyle was an example for her "girls" to follow. In 1974, Crowley paid herself a salary of $1.6 million, a figure that was challenged by the Internal Revenue Service. When the case came before a U.S. Tax Court, the judge was completely swayed by Crowley and ruled that her compensation was clearly a legitimate business expense. She had a rare talent for motivating women, the judge concluded, and her leadership was irreplaceable.

By 1983, when the company celebrated its 25th anniversary, Home Interiors & Gifts had grown to a behemoth with $400 million in sales. Profit was estimated at over $20 million. Home Interiors oversaw some 38,000 displayers, still all women at that time. These women hosted over 100,000 decorating parties every single week. The average displayer worked part time and brought in only about $3,500 annually in commissions for herself. The price of the Home Interiors line remained modest, with most items going for $10 or $15. The most expensive item in the line was only $65 in 1983. However, the profit margin was high, and the business operated with virtually no debt. Mary Crowley made her mark nationwide. She was invited to the White House in 1977, one of only 20 business leaders asked to meet with President Carter. She won the Horatio Alger Award in 1978, celebrating her rags-to-riches story, and she served on the board of the American Cancer Society as well as on the board of the Billy Graham Evangelistic Association (the first woman board member). Crowley's son Don Carter, who was the principal stockholder in the company after his mother, had also enriched himself. In 1980, he spent $12 million to buy the National Basketball Association franchise team the Dallas Mavericks.

Key Dates:

1957:   Home Interiors & Gifts, Inc. is founded by Mary C.
        Crowley.
1962:   The company makes its first million in sales.
1987:   Mary Crowley dies.
1998:   The company is bought out by members of the
        Crowley family and Hicks, Muse, Tate & Furst.

Late 1980s: A Buyout Deferred

After Mary Crowley's death in 1987, Don Carter went on as president and CEO of the company. Sales continued to increase through the 1980s, and by the early 1990s the company had sales of over $850 million. The company had been growing from five to 10 percent a year, and by 1994 it had some 42,000 displayers working for it as independent contractors. Carter had amassed a huge portfolio of Texas real estate in the mid-1980s and ran that as a separate company. He was 61 in 1994, and he began planning the best way to pass the company on to his children. Knowing that estate taxes might make things difficult for his heirs, Carter decided to sell Home Interiors. At the same time, he wanted to retain some family control. Three of his children held executive positions at Home Interiors. In July 1994, the company announced that it had found a compatible buyer in the firm Hicks, Muse, Tate & Furst. Hicks, Muse was also based in Dallas, and its principal, Thomas Hicks, had become friends with Carter. Hicks, Muse had put together 25 buyout deals over the preceding five years, including the $390 million acquisition of the G. Heilemann Brewing Co. in 1993. The leveraged buyout of Home Interiors was to be Hicks, Muse's biggest deal yet, valued at $1 billion. The firm would own 51 percent of the company, and Carter family members would control 49 percent. Don Carter was to step down, but his children would remain in their jobs. Hicks, Muse would put up only $150 million toward the purchase, and the Carter family $73 million for their stake. The rest was to be borrowed or covered by the sale of junk bonds. The company would go from having no debt to owing hundreds of millions, but Home Interiors had enough cash flow to cover interest payments. The aim was to move Home Interiors into international markets to increase growth, and in several years take the company public. However, the deal did not go off that year. Don Carter instead invested some $20 million in another Hicks, Muse venture and sold Mr. Hicks a part-interest in the Dallas Mavericks. After praying about it, Carter called off the Home Interiors buyout. Carter was apparently nervous about some of the new owner's plans, including cutting administrative costs and moving into foreign markets. Carter also still wanted the company to be in family hands.

Four years later, Hicks, Muse got another shot at the company. This time, the landscape had changed somewhat. Revenue for 1997 had fallen to $468 million, a steep drop from 1994, when it had brought in over $850 million. Donald Carter was ready to retire, and he ceded the CEO and chairman position to his son, Donald J. (Joey) Carter, Jr. Joey, his brother Ronald, their sister Christi Carter Urschel, and company president Barbara Hammond were to own 15 percent of the company after a new buyout plan, this time valued at $920 million. Hicks, Muse ended up with 75 percent of the company, borrowing $350 million and floating a

$200 million bond offering. Hicks, Muse declared itself ecstatic to finally complete the deal that had slipped away four years earlier. Its long-term outlook for the company remained the same: trim costs, move into overseas markets, and eventually take the company public.

By 1999, the company had already moved into the Mexican market, where it had some 2,000 displayers. It had a small number of displayers selling Home Interiors goods in Puerto Rico as well. One major shift the new ownership made was to update the company's technology. To that end, Home Interiors consolidated its seven warehouses and distribution centers into one enormous, state-of-the-art facility in North Dallas. The new facility had automated order fulfillment and automated conveyors, something Home Interiors had done without for 40 years. The company also leased new corporate headquarters, and in 2002 bought up the assets of a bankrupt competitor, the Kansas City-based House of Lloyd. The company had sales of over $570 million in that year, creeping back towards its high point set in the mid-1990s. The outlook of the company changed with the buyout. Though Carter family members still ran Home Interiors, its goals were now much more quantifiable, with an eye towards Wall Street, than in Mary Crowley's day. The company's mission statement still spoke of serving God, ennobling women, and bringing Attraction Power to the home, much as Mary Crowley would have put it. However, as her grandson told the *Dallas Business Journal* (July 30, 1999), the company now wanted to "grow from moderate single-digit growth to double-digit growth," bespeaking a more tangible goal that was more likely to appeal to investors. The new owners had spoken openly about wanting to take the company public within three to five years. By 2002, no date had been set for the public offering.

Principal Competitors

Interiors, Inc.; Garden Ridge Corporation; Richmont Corporation.

Further Reading

Bagamery, Anne, "Please Make Me Feel Special," *Forbes*, March 28, 1983, p. 88.
Bodipo-Memba, Alejandro, "Hicks Muse Is to Get Control of Gift Maker," *Wall Street Journal*, April 24, 1998, p. B6.
Buckler, Arthur, "Hicks Muse Group Sets $1 Billion Buyout of Home Interiors in a Leveraged Plan," *Wall Street Journal*, July 13, 1994, p. A4.
"Dispute Deepens Over Sale of Bankrupt Gift Empire's Assets," *Knight Ridder/Tribune Business News*, December 4, 2002.
Goldstein, Tally, "Hicks Muse Taps Nations for Home Interiors Buyout Credit," *Bank Letter*, April 27, 1998, p. 1.
Miller, Holly G., "The First Lady of Home Interiors," *Saturday Evening Post*, April 1983, p. 58.
Myerson, Allen R., "From At-Home Parties to a $1 Billion Buyout," *New York Times*, July 13, 1994, p. D3.
——, "Purchase by Hicks, Muse Is Called Off," *New York Times*, October 22, 1994, pp. 39, 41.
Townsend, Lindsey, "Home Interiors & Gifts," *Dallas Business Journal*, February 25, 2000, p. 11C.
Vosburgh, Glenda, "Grand Vision: Home Interiors Makes a New Deal, Plans for Future Growth," *Dallas Business Journal*, July 30, 1999, p. 55.

—A. Woodward

Home Products International, Inc.

4501 West 47th Street
Chicago, Illinois 60632
U.S.A.
Telephone: (773) 890-1010
Fax: (773) 890-0523
Web site: http://www.hpii.com

Public Company
Incorporated: 1952 as Selfix, Inc.
Employees: 1,215
Sales: $249.7 million (2001)
Stock Exchanges: NASDAQ
Ticker Symbol: HOMZ
NAIC: 326100 Plastics Product Manufacturing

Home Products International, Inc. (HPI) is a leading maker of value-priced, non-electric consumer houseware products sold under the HOMZ brand. The Chicago-based company divides its business into five product categories. The largest, laundry management, accounts for more than one-third of all annual sales. The company manufactures a broad range of ironing boards, covers, and pads, as well as drying racks, clothes lines, clothes pins, laundry bags, hampers, and sorters. General storage is HPI's second largest product category, comprising plastic storage containers and stack drawer systems. Plastic clothes hangers are the primary items that make up the closet storage products category. Bathware products offers an assortment of plastic bath accessories and organizers, including soap dishes, shelves, towel bars, and shower organizers. Finally, the kitchen storage products category is mostly devoted to plastic food storage containers but also includes sinkware and wire organization products. Nearly half of all sales are attributed to three major customers: Wal-Mart, Kmart, and Target. Other important customers include Bed Bath & Beyond, Linens 'N Things, Staples, SAM's Club, Home Depot, and Lowe's.

1950s Origins

The origins of HPI date back to 1952 when a company named Selfix was started to produce a single, simple product: a plastic hook that could be fixed to a wall by wetting the dry glue on its back. The so-called "Wet 'n Set" application process is still used by some of HPI's products. By 1962, the limited Selfix line of plastic hooks was generating annual sales of $1 million. In that year, it was purchased by the husband and wife management team of Meyer ("Mike") and Norma Ragir. Together they would run the company for the next 30 years, adding hundreds of plastic housewares products, mostly for use in the bathroom. In the 1960s, Selfix expanded its sales beyond the United States, turning to the Latin American market, then in 1969 opened a Canadian subsidiary. Another subsidiary was launched in England in 1976 to serve Europe. The company's entry into the German market during the early 1980s proved difficult, leading to a net loss of $500,000 before the operation was shut down. Although Selfix was still selling its wares to more than 25 countries, annual revenues stalled around $17 million, and the company began to see profits decline. Nevertheless, Selfix was debt free, with $3 million in cash, and appeared well positioned for growth under the proper leadership.

In 1987, the aging Ragirs brought in a seasoned executive, 52-year-old Robert Mariani, to help revitalize their stagnant business. Although Mike Ragir would serve as chairman and CEO, Mariani was essentially given a free hand in shaping the future of the company. He was well experienced in growing small businesses, especially in the housewares industry. From 1971 to 1979, he had served as president of Acme Frame Products, improving annual revenues from $2 million to $20 million during that time. He then became president and CEO at Spartus Corp., a wall clock subsidiary of Kidde Consumer Durables Corp. Under his leadership, Spartus diversified into electronics, starting with clock radios and later adding digital clocks, travel alarms, portable audio products, combination TV/clock radios, and even venturing as far afield as telephones. As a result of Mariani's strategy, sales at Spartus grew from $25 million to $90 million during his tenure.

Mariani's goal at Selfix was, through acquisitions and the introduction of new products, to achieve annual revenues of $75 million within five years. To help fund this expansion Selfix planned to go public in July 1987, but when the initial public offering (IPO) market soured, and the opening price fell from an anticipated $13 a share to just $9, the Ragirs elected to cancel the offering, deciding instead to wait for better conditions.

Before then, however, the company doubled its research and development budget and brought out 32 new products. In February 1988, Selfix completed its first acquisition, paying close to $6 million for Shutters Inc., maker of decorative plastic house shutters with $5 million in annual revenues. Although not quite in keeping with the rest of Selfix's business, Shutters was a plastic consumer product that benefited somewhat from Selfix's ownership. Instead of relying on remodelers, lumberyards, and mobile home manufacturers, Shutters would now be able to sell its products through the mass merchandise channels of the parent company.

Going Public in 1983

Selfix renewed its effort to raise money in the equity market, completing an IPO of stock in October 1988, with a subsequent listing on the NASDAQ. Believing that Selfix was now well funded for expansion, Mariani upped his expectations, setting a goal of $100 million in annual revenues in the near future. He targeted the burgeoning home organization field as a major growth vehicle for the company. Early in 1989, Selfix launched its Space Works storage and shelving system, relying on a patented plastic locking mechanism, as a way to break into the category. A year later, the company introduced Spaceworks II, a complete line of plastic kitchen organizers. Furthermore, in 1990 Selfix made two acquisitions to bolster its growth in home organization. First it acquired Independent Products Co., a Pennsylvania-based plastic hanger manufacturer, then later in the year it bought the Orangeburg, New York-based Homecraft division of Dynacast Inc. Homecraft produced a wide variety of metal hooks, including hooks for hanging plants, baskets, picture frames, and even bicycles. Selfix also attempted to move beyond plastic and began to offer brass and wood fixtures for both the bath and kitchen, sourced in the Far East.

In September 1992, Mike Ragir died of leukemia at the age of 76. His wife Norma was named chairman and CEO, but Mariani continued to run the company on a day-to-day basis, and Selfix continued to follow his strategy of growing the business through product development and acquisition. Assimilating the company's three recent acquisitions, however, proved more difficult than anticipated. The move into brass and wood fixtures also failed, prompting the company to stick with the more familiar plastic products. All told, in 1992 Selfix lost nearly $800,000 while sales declined by 5 percent over the previous year. The company began to show signs of improvement after it shuttered some underutilized plants and introduced a new line of bedroom and play area organizers for children, which were well received by mass merchandisers. The Tidy Kids Juvenile Storage Organizers included the Bedside Buddy nightstand, Toy Chest Jr., and Shoe Store Jr., as well as several bathroom storage products.

Management Changes in the Mid-1990s

In February 1994, Selfix reached a major turning point when Norma Ragir died of a heart attack. Although Mariani had in effect been running the company for several years and her loss would not materially effect day-to-day operations, the Selfix board of directors took the opportunity to change management. Mariana's bid to become the new chair and CEO was rejected by the board, which instead named James Tennant to the open posts. Tennant, a Selfix board member for the past two years, was significantly younger at age 40 than Mariani, and his expertise was in marketing rather than finance. He came to Selfix after serving 14 years as president of FCB Direct, the direct marketing operation he founded for Foot Cone & Belding. Tennant's appointment at Selfix was well received on Wall Street. As expected, he announced that the company would now focus on aggressive marketing in addition to product innovation and growing international sales.

In August 1994, Mariani resigned the presidency of Selfix, a job he had held for seven years. Tennant established his own management team to implement his growth strategies for Selfix. A number of restructuring efforts were initiated that were not expected to pay off for a couple of years. Unprofitable products were eliminated, warehouses were reduced from five to just two, and the company invested heavily in research and development as well as in infrastructure. Selfix also sought new sales channels for its products, in particular home-centers like The Home Depot and Builders Square, and specialty channels like Bed, Bath and Beyond and Container Store. During this period, Tennant and his team had what Tennant told an interviewer was a "Moses sort-of-the-mountain meeting with our own product line and we felt that we had to understand what business we're in. The business we are in is space management. We help people organize the space that they have in their homes and at their office." Before coming to grips with this realization, however, Selfix found itself occasionally straying away from its core business. In 1995, for instance, the company briefly flirted with acquiring Studio RTA, a maker of ready-to-assemble computer furniture.

After two years in charge of Selfix, in which a net loss of $4 million in 1995 was succeeded by earnings of $806,000 a year later, Tennant launched the company on a cycle of expansion through acquisition, a move becoming increasingly more necessary as consolidation took place among retailers, which in turn put pressure on their vendors to provide support at a larger scale. In the words of one executive, it had become "big guys serving other big guys." Tennant's strategy was to target compatible companies that were leaders in their market segments but would stand to benefit from HPI's infrastructure and established sales channels. The first acquisition for Selfix was the $43 million stock and cash purchase of Tamor Plastics Corporation, a 50-year-old Massachusetts maker of plastic laundry baskets and other home storage and organization products. Not only did the Tamor deal triple Selfix's annual revenues to more than $120 million, there was little redundancy in their product lines. Moreover, the two businesses by combining their purchasing power would be able to save on resins and other raw materials. Before completing the transaction, Selfix was replaced on the NASDAQ by Home Products International, Inc., a new holding company to operate Selfix, Tamor, and Shutters.

<table>
<tr><td colspan="2">Key Dates:</td></tr>
<tr><td>1952:</td><td>Selfix, Inc. is founded as a plastic hook manufacturer.</td></tr>
<tr><td>1962:</td><td>Meyer and Norma Ragir acquire the company.</td></tr>
<tr><td>1988:</td><td>Selfix goes public.</td></tr>
<tr><td>1992:</td><td>Meyer Ragir dies.</td></tr>
<tr><td>1994:</td><td>Norma Ragir dies, resulting in a new management team.</td></tr>
<tr><td>1997:</td><td>Holding company Home Products International, Inc. is formed.</td></tr>
<tr><td>1998:</td><td>Seymour Housewares is acquired.</td></tr>
</table>

Tennant then became the chairman and CEO of HPI. In June 1997, the company issued a secondary offering of stock to help reduce the high level of debt it incurred from the Tamor deal.

Several months later, in January 1998, HPI completed another acquisition, a $100.7 million cash, stock, and debt deal to pick up Seymour Housewares, America's largest supplier of laundry care products, boasting the number one share in ironing boards, pads, and covers. Like other HPI subsidiaries, Seymour would operate independently, retaining its chief executive. The addition of Seymour added another $94 million in annual sales, and while providing significant diversification in household products, it also helped to further reduce HPI's total exposure to resin price volatility. Several months after the Seymour deal, HPI acquired Anchor Hocking Plastics and Plastics Inc. from Newell, which had received Anchor Hocking Plastics as part of the acquisition of Anchor Hocking 11 years earlier and now elected to sell off its plastics division because it no longer fit into its long-term plans. The addition of the Newell assets for $78 million in cash allowed HPI to make a strong entry into food storage, with Anchor Hocking Plastics selling its products to mass retailers. On the other hand, Plastics Inc., selling plastic serveware products through commercial channels, was not a natural fit for HPI. At the same time that it was arranging the Newell transaction, HPI was also finalizing a deal to buy the consumer storage line of Tenex Corp. for $16.4 million in cash, adding such product lines as plastic storage bins and rolling carts.

By the end of a very active 1998, HPI restructured its operation, splitting its subsidiaries between two "power platforms": storage and organization products—comprising Tenex, Anchor Hocking Plastics, and Tamor—and laundry-management, made up of Selfix and Seymour. Shutters no longer fit into the company's plans, and in January 1999 it was sold to the subsidiary's management team and a group of investors. Also in 1999, HPI acquired select assets from Austin Products, Inc., adding a number of plastic housewares products, including laundry baskets, tote caddys, crates, bins, and utility buckets. As a result of HPI's aggressive expansion, annual revenues grew at a dramatic rate, from $38.2 million in 1996 to more than $250 million in 1998 and close to $300 million in 1999. In the process, however, HPI took on considerable debt, and its stock was battered by investors. Despite strong cash flow, HPI, because of a poor perception on Wall Street, was not able to place a secondary offering of stock that would help reduce its debt load. The situation became so difficult that in December 1999 HPI retained First Union Securities Inc. to assess its strategic alternatives, essentially putting itself up for sale. Much larger players in the housewares industry, Corning and Newell Rubbermaid, were the likely suitors, but by May 2000, with no suitable bids in the offing, HPI elected not to sell. As a result, the price of HPI stock dipped below $7. Moreover, the company was crippled by the high cost of raw materials in 2000 when resin prices increased by more than 40 percent, a major factor in a $71.5 million loss for the year. Revenues, on the other hand, remained essentially flat. By September 2000, the price of HPI stock hovered around the $2 mark, making the company a potential takeover target.

HPI regrouped somewhat in 2001. It sold off Plastics Inc., whose serveware products were not part of the company's focus, for $71.25 million, which helped a great deal in lowering debt. HPI also took other cost-cutting steps, closing a plant in Leominister, Massachusetts, and eliminating about 15 percent of its workforce.

Unfortunately, a downturn in the economy hurt many of its customers, which in turn had an adverse effect on HPI. Smaller customers like Ames Department Stores and Bradlees filed for bankruptcy in 2001. For the year, revenues were down 16 percent, dipping below $250 million, but HPI was still able to post net income of $17 million. In January 2002, a more significant customer, Kmart, which owed HPI $5.7 million, filed for bankruptcy protection. With a large number of retailers suffering through tough economic times, HPI was not alone in downsizing its operations. When the company might be able to grow again, however, was very much an unanswered question.

Principal Subsidiaries

Home Products International—North American, Inc.

Principal Competitors

Knape & Vogt Manufacturing Company; Sterilite Corporation; Newell Rubbermaid Inc.

Further Reading

Edwin Darby, "Selfix Sticking to Growth Strategy," *Chicago Sun-Times*, September 22, 1998, p. 76.

Gallun, Alby F., "Eyeing High Costs, Debt Load, Investors Leave Home Prods," *Crain's Chicago Business*, September 11, 2000, p. 44.

——, "Home Products Looking at Rosier Picture," *Crain's Chicago Business*, December 2, 2001, p. 25.

Hill, Dawn, "Selfix to Buy Tamor," *HFN*, November 11, 1996, p. 57.

Kelt, Deborah C., "Selfix's Mass Market Moves," *HFD*, December 10, 1990. p. 82.

Meyer, Nancy, "Tennant: A New Generation at Selfix," *HFD*, April 25, 1994, p. 94.

Murphy, H. Lee, "Bathware Firm's New Prexy Maps Big Expansion Plans," *Crain's Chicago Business*, September 21, 1987, p. 24.

——, "Home Products Backs Up Name Change with Acquisition," *Crain's Chicago Business*, August 18, 1997, p. 39.

—Ed Dinger

Hoshino Gakki Co. Ltd.

No. 22, 3-CHOME
Shumoku-Cho
Higashi-Ku
Nagoya 461-8717
Japan
Telephone: (+81) 052 931-0381
Fax: (+81) 052 932-2684
Web site: http://www.hoshinogakki.co.jp

Private Company
Incorporated: 1908
Employees: 99
Sales: ¥20.68 billion ($175 million) (2001)
NAIC: 339992 Musical Instrument Manufacturing

Hoshino Gakki Co. Ltd. is best known for its two world-famous brands of musical products: Ibanez guitars and Tama drums. Both brands number among the best-selling and most-respected in their categories, although Hoshino itself manufactures only the Tama drum line through its Hoshino Gakki Hanbai and Hoshino Gakki Manufacturing subsidiaries. For the Ibanez brand, Hoshino provides research, design, and prototype construction support, while also handling worldwide distribution operations. Production of the wide range of Ibanez models is contracted out to third-party manufacturers, including Hoshino's primary and long-time partner in Japan, Fuji-Gen Gakki, which also produces guitars for Fender (notably the Squier line) and domestic brand Greco, as well as products for the Roland and Casio brands. Since the 1990s, Hoshino has contracted a growing portion of its guitar production to manufacturers in Korea and China. The company's U.S. subsidiary also produces custom-built and prototype guitars for the company's star endorsers. That subsidiary was also a partner in designing the theme restaurant On Stage Cleveland in partnership with the Rock and Roll Museum and HMSHost. The restaurant opened in 2001. The company has additionally stepped up its distribution presence in Europe, acquiring Serlui BV of the Netherlands, in 2002. Hoshino is led by Yoshihiro Hoshino, grandson of the private company's founder. In 2001, Hoshino total operations posted sales of approximately ¥20.68 billion ($175 million).

Western Music Pioneer in Turn-of-the-Century Japan

Hoshino Gakki was founded in 1908 by Matsujiro Hoshino in the city of Nagoya, Japan. Hoshino originally operated as a bookstore that also sold sheet music. This activity led the company into forming a wholesale business as well, and Hoshino began supplying music stores around Japan. Hoshino's sheet music distribution business quickly led the company into distributing musical instruments as well, and this activity became its main focus. Hoshino became particularly interested in Western music and musical instruments, which were just then beginning to enter the Japanese market. Hoshino later expanded its original shop into a series of instrument showrooms, becoming one of the first in the country to feature Western-style organs.

By 1929, Hoshino established its own musical instruments company, Hoshino Gakki Ten, which took over the company's wholesale distribution as well as import and export business. The rising demand for Western instruments led Hoshino Gakki Ten to begin producing its own musical instruments in 1935. Among the first of these was a Spanish-style guitar, which the company produced in order to capitalize on the sudden interest in the instrument following a Japanese tour by Andrés Segovia. Hoshino acquired the rights to label its guitar the Ibanez Salvadol, reasoning the Spanish-sounding name would prove more attractive as a brand. The company later acquired the Ibanez brand outright.

Hoshino's operations were completely destroyed by bombs during World War II. Following the war, Hoshino rebuilt, at first concentrating on its import and export business. In 1955, the company moved into a new headquarters building in Nagoya. In that year, Hoshino decided to focus its efforts on the booming overseas market and especially the markets in the United States and Europe, by then swept up in the early years of rock and roll. Hoshino's products were to remain absent from the Japanese market until the early 1980s.

Hoshino returned to manufacturing in 1962 with the establishment of TAMA Seisakusho Inc., which began producing electric guitars and guitar amplifiers, under the Ibanez and other brand names, as well as drums, largely under the Star brand name, introduced in 1965. Hoshino joined the tide of

Company Perspectives:

Hoshino Gakki Company started out in a period when Western music was still in its infancy in Japan. In the decades since then, a period of 94 years, we have kept step with Western music development in Japan. But the road has certainly not been an easy one. It was a period characterized by war and a long trail of difficult trials and obstacles. That Hoshino was able to emerge today as a leading instrument maker is due in large measure to our customers, lovers of fine music and fine musical instruments who entrusted their hopes and dreams to us. It's also due to the many people in the industry who, in both material and immaterial ways, have given us their unstinting support over the years. We want to express our sincere thanks to all these people. With the incredible variety of musical genres and forms now available, many new needs and demands have emerged in the area of musical instruments. In order to respond appropriately to those needs, Hoshino had to match up two totally different areas of technology: electronics with its quest for the newest sounds, and traditional instrument-making techniques, the crystallization of generations of sensitive craftsmanship. Today, Hoshino combines its 94 years of experience with a spirit of meeting future challenges as it dedicates itself to even greater efforts in research & development and product creation.

Japanese-made musical instruments then flooding Western markets as demand for electric and acoustic guitars skyrocketed in the 1960s. Many of Hoshino's guitars were sold through nontraditional channels, such as department stores and supermarkets. The company also used a variety of brand names for its products.

By the mid-1960s, however, Hoshino's manufacturing operation was unable to keep up with demand, and in 1966 the company turned to third-party manufacturers to build its guitars. Then, in 1970, Hoshino began a partnership with another manufacturer, Fuji-Gen Gakki, located in nearby Matsumoto. Fuji-Gen took over nearly all of the company's electric guitar manufacturing operations, while the TAMA subsidiary continued to make acoustic guitars and drums. Hoshino was to remain Fuji-Gen's main customer into the 21st century, accounting for half of its production. As Hoshino continued to focus on the export market, Fuji-Gen claimed the domestic market, launching its own brand of guitars, Greco, which were often based on Hoshino designs and became the leading high-end guitar brand in Japan.

If Japanese-built guitars were regarded as inferior quality, mass-produced products at the start of the 1960s, by the end of the decade a number of Japanese guitar makers, including Fuji-Gen, had boosted their quality levels to compete with, and even surpass, their American and European competitors. It was at this time that many of the more famous guitar makers, such as Fender and Gibson, had seen their own quality standards begin to slip, while their prices remained quite high. Meanwhile, copying designs among guitar makers—particularly as a number of guitar models, such as the Fender Stratocaster, Gibson

Les Paul, and Hofner "Beatle" bass, became well-known instruments—had become an industry mainstay, and Japanese guitar markets began to roll out their own copies, offering similar quality instruments that often sold for far less than the original guitar models.

Gaining a Reputation in the 1970s

Hoshino jumped on the bandwagon, launching its first new Ibanez-branded guitar, the 2020. The following year, the company launched its own Les Paul and Stratocaster models, also under the Ibanez brand. Supporting the company's drive to become a name brand guitar maker was the launch of a dedicated U.S. distribution subsidiary, Elger Inc., located near Philadelphia.

In 1972, Hoshino launched its own line of effects pedals, using the Maxon brand name for the Japanese market—marking a return to distribution activities in Japan—and the Ibanez name for the export market. Meanwhile, Ibanez guitars were quickly gaining in popularity as the company began to establish a reputation for the quality of its guitars, which continued to be low-priced copies of popular guitar models. Among the company's launches in the early 1970s were copies of the Fender Jazz bass guitar in 1972, the Gibson Flying V in 1973, the Gibson Double Neck SG in 1974, and the Rickenbacker bass in 1975. The company's Tama manufacturing operation meanwhile was also gaining a reputation for quality, particularly with the 1974 launches of the Royal Star and Imperial Star lines. That year marked the birth of the Tama brand of percussion instruments, although the company maintained the word "Star" in many of new its models. The success of both the Ibanez and Star lines led the company to open a dedicated distribution facility in Seto City in 1976.

By the mid-1970s, Hoshino set out to establish Ibanez as a premium-quality guitar brand. While continuing to produce copy guitars—the company's success in this market made it a target of a Gibson lawsuit—Hoshino began to develop its own guitar designs. Hoshino also jumped on another bandwagon, that of the professional endorsement models that had become popular since Fender hired Eric Clapton to play its guitars in the early 1970s.

During the 1970s, Hoshino stepped up its commitment to quality. As part of that effort, the company sought to go beyond copying other guitar designs and create an original design that would rival the world's legendary guitars. In the mid-1970s, the company met with Fuji-Gen to achieve this goal. The result was a highly innovative guitar, both in look and in technology, that became known as the Ibanez Iceman (and the Greco Mirage in Japan). The guitar was quickly picked up by a number of well-known artists, including Steve Miller and Rick Nielsen. Into the late 1970s, the company added more original designs, including the 2680 (which became known as the Bob Weir model, after the Grateful Dead guitarist) in 1977, which was followed in 1978 by the GB10 and GB20, named after George Benson, and the PS10, which became well-known as the guitar played by Kiss guitarist and singer Paul Stanley. The company also launched a line of MIDI-based guitars, and in 1978 expanded the Ibanez brand to include lines of banjos and mandolins, although these instruments were phased out in the early 1980s.

Key Dates:

1908: Matsujiro Hoshino sells sheet music, and soon begins distributing musical instruments and opening organ showrooms.

1929: Hoshino launches a manufacturing subsidiary, Hoshino Gakki Ten, to produce its own musical instruments.

1935: Hoshino begins production of Ibanez Salvadol brand Spanish guitars for the Japanese market.

1945: The Hoshino factory is destroyed by bombing during World War II.

1955: The company builds new headquarters in Nagoya and reorganizes as an export-only business.

1962: Hoshino begins manufacturing drums, guitars, and amplifiers for the export market.

1966: Hoshino turns over its guitar production to third-party manufacturers but continues to manufacture drums.

1971: Hoshino establishes a U.S. distribution subsidiary, Elger Inc., near Philadelphia.

1974: The Tama brand name is established for Hoshino's drum line.

1975: An original guitar design, the Iceman, is launched.

1980: Elger changes its name to Hoshino USA Inc.

1991: The company begins subcontracting some production to Korea and, later, China.

2001: Hoshino USA is named Company of the Year by *Music Trades Magazine.*

In 1980, Hoshino changed its U.S. subsidiary's name to Hoshino USA Inc. The following year, the company changed its own name to Hoshino Gakki Co. and established a new manufacturing subsidiary, Hoshino Gakki Mfg. Co., which took over the Tama Seisakusho operation. Tama had meanwhile been building up not only a reputation for quality but for innovation as well, offering a number of new hardware features, such as boomstands, memory locks, and especially double-braced stands, that were later to become industry standards. The Tama brand's real breakthrough, however, had come in 1977, with the release of the Superstar line. This was followed up in 1983 with the successful Artstar model, which became one of the company's best-selling and longest-lasting drum kits.

Premium Quality Instrument Maker for the New Century

In 1982, the company added a new subsidiary, Hoshino Gakki Hanbai, which took over manufacturing and distribution operations for the domestic market as Hoshino began promoting the Ibanez brand in Japan for the first time. The Ibanez brand stepped up its celebrity endorsement activity, building custom guitars for such noted artists as Lee Rittenour, Joe Pass, Steve Lukather, and Allan Holdsworth.

By the mid-1980s, Ibanez had more or less shaken its reputation as a guitar copier—the company had in fact lost the lawsuit brought by Gibson over its copies—and emerged as not only a quality brand but as a guitar innovator. The Japanese guitar industry was finally winning acknowledgment for its quality production, a development highlighted by the willingness of a number of noted brands, including Fender and Gibson, to begin producing certain of their own guitar models and brands in Japan. Meanwhile, guitar playing itself had been changing in the early 1980s, with a new generation of musicians adding new techniques that opened the market for technical innovations.

One of the most innovative of the new guitarists was Steve Vai, who had played with Frank Zappa. When Vai was known to be seeking new guitars—his own had been stolen while on tour—Ibanez leapt at the chance, offering not merely to supply Vai with guitars but also to design a new guitar according to Vai's own specifications. Vai agreed on the condition that the guitar would become a production model, because he wanted to be certain of having a ready supply of guitars. The result was the JEM guitar, the first models of which were launched in 1987.

The JEM guitar and the Vai endorsement instantly placed Ibanez on the worldwide guitar map, and the company now took its place among the world's top guitar makers. Ibanez carefully cultivated its reputation by hand-testing every one of its guitars, a practice that set it apart from many of its competitors. Tama too had risen to the top ranks, rivaling the Pearl, Sonor, and other leading drum brands. In 1988, Hoshino opened a new production facility in Seto City to help meet the demand for the Tama brand.

The rise of the yen against the dollar, coupled with the rising quality standards of Japanese guitars, which brought higher prices, led Hoshino to begin looking for alternative manufacturing markets at the beginning of the 1990s. Korea was fast becoming the newest site for guitar production; in 1991, Hoshino turned to that country, seeking manufacturers capable of matching Ibanez quality. Throughout the 1990s, as the Korean guitar market matured, Hoshino added manufacturers in China as well. The Japanese company continued to provide research, design, and prototype building, while its American subsidiary performed prototype and custom guitar designs for its celebrity endorsers, and its Fuji-Gen remained the manufacturer for its higher-end models. Hoshino's quality commitment extended across nearly all of its instruments—the company took charge of designing nearly all of the components for its guitar, even engineering the production molds used to manufacture the different parts.

Ibanez continued to pick up celebrity endorsers during the 1990s, notably Joe Satriani and Pat Metheny. Hoshino also continued to innovate, releasing its Ergodyne series, constructed from a new manmade material, Luthite, specially designed for its acoustic qualities. In 1995, the company issued an updated version of the Iceman, which had been out of production since the mid-1980s. In 1998, the company innovated again, launching a line of seven-string guitars.

Led by Yoshihiro Hoshino, grandson of the founder, Hoshino had emerged as an important force in both of its core musical instrument markets. The company's rising sales—its 2001 sales of nearly ¥21 billion ($175 million) represented a 28 percent increase over the previous year—and its commitment both to quality and to customer service led Hoshino USA to receive the *Music Trades Magazine* Company of the Year award for 2001. In that year, Hoshino boosted its U.S. profile with the opening of On Stage Cleveland in partnership with Cleveland's Rock and Roll Museum and HMSHost. The theme restaurant opened at the Cleveland airport in 2001. Hoshino also continued to expand its distribution reach, opening a dedicated European office in Kronberg, Germany in 1999. In 2002, the company acquired the Netherlands' Serlui BV, a major musical instruments distributor for that country.

Principal Subsidiaries

Hoshino Gakki Hanbai Co. Ltd.; Hoshino Gakki Mfg. Co. Ltd.; Hoshino USA Inc; Serlui BV (Netherlands).

Principal Competitors

Sony USA Inc.; Yamaha Corporation; Fender Musical Instruments Inc.; Roland Corporation; Peavey Electronics Inc.; Gibson Musical Instruments Inc.; C.F. Martin and Company Inc.; Avedis Zildjian Company Inc; Ludwig Industries Inc.

Further Reading

Hoggard, Brian, "Jim Donahue—Ibanez USA," *Musocafe*, October 16, 2000.
"Hoshino Gakki," *Music Trades Magazine*, April 2001.
Roesberg, Dieter, "90 Jahre Hoshino," *Gitarre & Bass*, April 1998.

—M. L. Cohen

Huntington Learning Centers, Inc.

496 Kinderkamack Road
Oradell, New Jersey 07649
U.S.A.
Telephone: (201) 261-8400
Fax: (201) 261-8460
Web site: http://www.huntingtonlearningcenter.com

Private Company
Incorporated: 1985
Employees: 60
Sales: $80 million (2002 est.)
NAIC: 611000 Educational Services

Privately owned Huntington Learning Centers, Inc. is the corporate entity that franchises Huntington Learning Centers, the oldest U.S. provider of a wide range of supplemental educational services for students in kindergarten through high school. A sister corporation, Huntington Learning Corp., operates company-owned units of the national chain, comprised by the end of 2002 of 214 units, 36 of which were company owned. Huntington offers personalized instruction in reading, writing, mathematics, phonics, and study skills, as well as preparation for such tests as the SAT. The company believes that many students are trapped in what it calls a cycle of frustration, in which poor performance hurts a child's confidence and leads to an increasing sense of failure. Huntington assesses a child's situation through a battery of proprietary diagnostic tests, then prescribes an individualized course of remedy and offers individualized attention from certified teachers, many of whom are full-time public and private school teachers. They help the child to develop basic study skills and systematically restore confidence in order to foster a desire to succeed. Huntington is owned by CEO Dr. Raymond Huntington and his wife Eileen, who is responsible for the operational side of the New Jersey-based business.

Early Years: 1970s

Supplemental education in the form of tutoring is an ancient endeavor, but it was not until 1970 that entrepreneurs began to develop the concept of multi-outlet tutoring. An early pioneer

was Kenneth Martyn, a professor of special education at California State University at Los Angeles, who became interested in helping students with reading problems after conducting a study on California's public school system. His business, The Reading Game, served both remedial and fast-track students, from kindergarten through 12th grade. He opened his first center in Huntington Beach, California, and soon added another 10 in the state before expanding into five other states. A tutor at one of these centers, former junior high art teacher Berry Fowler, decided to strike out on his own and in 1979 formed Achievement Centers Inc. in Portland, Oregon. He soon launched an aggressive effort to franchise his centers, an approach not embraced by Martyn, who franchised only a handful of Reading Game centers in order to maintain quality control. In 1981 Achievement Centers reorganized as Sylvan Learning Centers and was well on its way to becoming the dominant brand in the supplemental education field.

Two years prior to Fowler's start-up, on the other side of the country, Raymond and Eileen Huntington independently recognized the need for such services and established their own learning centers. Raymond Huntington received a doctorate in statistics in 1974 from Rutgers University, where he taught as both a graduate assistant and as an instructor before going to work for AT&T as a business analyst. His wife Eileen worked as a junior and senior high school teacher and took note of the large numbers of students who lacked basic study and reading skills. They lagged further and further behind their classmates, unable to receive the attention they needed from teachers who were stretched thin because of large class sizes. The Huntingtons were looking for a business opportunity and, concluding that there was a market for supplemental educational services, decided to launch Huntington Learning Centers.

To finance their start-up, according to Raymond Huntington, ''We hocked everything we had,'' and relied on personal lines of credit. They scraped together enough money to rent 1,700 square feet of space in an Ordell, New Jersey, office building and opened their first learning center. Huntington recalled those early days in a 1999 interview on CNNfn: ''It would be wonderful if we could say that we really had a business plan when we began, but our goal in the beginning was to do something that we felt really good about and over the years, the business has grown and the plan has evolved and the plan has changed. At the beginning though, there wasn't a business plan. There was just a desire to do what we felt was good and sure to make some money.'' What emerged was a three-step approach. The first goal was simple survival, the next was to establish a strong regional network, and the final goal was to take the business to a national level.

Growth During the Late 1970s and 1980s

As soon as the Huntingtons opened the doors of their first center in June 1977 they found an immediate demand for their services, so that the company's growth was little more than a function of keeping up with the level of interest. From the outset the company helped students ages five through 17, and with the introduction of test preparation coaching within the first few months of opening, Huntington Learning Centers essentially offered the same services as it would 25 years later. Demand was so strong that the Huntingtons opened a second outlet in Livingston, New Jersey, in 1978. In the beginning the couple shared all administrative and operational responsibilities and together gained a business education on the fly, sometimes learning by making mistakes. For instance, they had signed a three-year lease on their original office space but never thought to negotiate an option on future years. As the lease drew to a close they were surprised when the landlord informed them that they would have to move because an insurance company was ready to take over the space. As a result, the center was relocated to River Edge, New Jersey, in June 1980.

Over the first seven years in business the Huntingtons gradually expanded their chain of learning centers so that by 1985 they had a dozen outlets, all but one (located in Abbington, Pennsylvania) operating in New Jersey. With their first two goals met, they started to think about taking their business to the national level. It was also during this period that the Huntingtons first learned of Sylvan through an article in the *Wall Street Journal*. Sylvan, although founded two years after Huntington, was now a 200-unit chain with a presence in 39 states. Although both companies were pursuing similar educational goals, their approaches in some cases differed significantly. Sylvan guaranteed that students would exhibit a certain level of improvement or the center would provide additional instruction. The Huntingtons, on the other hand, believed that such an approach was inappropriate. A more significant divergence involved how the two companies chose to motivate their students. Sylvan rewarded correct answers with plastic tokens, redeemable for prizes in the ''Sylvan Store.'' Again, the Huntingtons viewed such a technique as inappropriate, opting instead to rely on praise and the satisfaction of success to motivate pupils.

Where Huntington and Sylvan agreed was on the use of franchising to grow the business. Rather than take on outside

investors to expand Huntington Learning Centers, the Huntingtons decided to let franchisees fund its growth. To move to this next stage of development, the business was reorganized with Huntington Learning Centers, Inc. created to handle the franchise operation and Huntington Learning Corp. to be responsible for the company-owned centers. The first franchise was sold to an attorney and his wife, who opened their learning center in 1985 in Langhorne, New Jersey. Huntington charged a $25,000 initial fee and an 8 percent royalty, the fee ultimately increasing to its 2002 level of $38,000. In its first year of franchising the company sold approximately 12 franchises. In the following two years, it sold 30 each year, then leveled off to between 10 and 20 franchises each year after that. In order to fuel the growth of company-owned units, the Huntingtons filed a registration with the Securities and Exchange Commission in July 1986 for an initial public offering of 1.1 million shares of common stock priced at $6 to $6.50 per share, but because of a lack of investor interest the offering never took place and Huntington Learning Centers remained a private company.

As the business grew, Raymond and Eileen Huntington began to separate their roles in the company and in the final years of the 1980s he began to focus his attention on administration while she concentrated on the operational side of the business. To support the increased number of learning centers and students, Huntington invested in a scheduling and billing-based computer system that was instrumental in securing the viability of the chain, which by the end of the decade was 100 units in size, 16 company owned. Huntington continued its growth in the 1990s, spurred in large part by an increasing nationwide concern that the public school system was all too often ineffective, sending to college and the general workforce high school graduates who lacked basic math and reading skills.

Overexpansion and Complications: Late 1990s

By the end of 1998 the Huntington chain was generating an estimated $52 million in annual revenues and was comprised of 174 units, 32 company owned. The company was particularly aggressive in moving into the Baltimore area, the home of Sylvan, which by contrast was now generating nearly $450 million in annual revenues. Huntington also launched an effort to substantially increase the number of company-owned centers, opening 17 in 1999 and another 20 in 2000. When the Huntingtons were interviewed by CNNfn in October 1999, the chain had reached the 200 level and they talked of an ''auspicious goal'' of having 650 franchised and company units by 2007. In 2000 Huntington added 20 company-owned centers but the expansion proved much too aggressive, and almost resulted in disaster for the owners. An advance of money from Huntington Learning Centers to Huntington Learning Corp. put the former in a position where it was unable to pay some creditors in a timely manner. One of the creditors, Baltimore advertising agency Trahan, Burden & Charles (TBC), had been contracted for services in September 2000 but was less than patient when Huntington began to default on its payments. Discussions about a payment plan fell apart and TBC's president and chief creative officer took drastic steps to resolve the matter. He first swore out a criminal complaint against Raymond Huntington, accusing him of intentionally passing a bad check in order to fraudulently obtain services from TBC.

Key Dates:

1977: First Huntington Learning Center opens in Oradell, New Jersey.
1978: Second center opens.
1980: Expired lease forces Oradell operation to move to River Edge, New Jersey.
1985: Huntington begins franchising.
1999: Huntington chain reaches 200 units.

Because TBC took the position that Huntington Learning Centers was a Maryland business, Raymond Huntington, who lived in New Jersey, was treated as a fugitive from Maryland and as a consequence was arrested and held at the Bergen County Jail in New Jersey for the purpose of extradition to Maryland. His attorneys intervened, however, and the Baltimore prosecutor dropped the criminal charges. TBC then joined with two other creditors—New York-based Jesse James Creative Inc. and Charlotte, North Carolina-based Avery Bell Advertising Inc. (Huntington's national advertising agency)—and seven days later filed a court petition to force Huntington into involuntary Chapter 7 bankruptcy, whereby the company's assets would be sold in order to meet its obligations. Huntington's lawyers argued that Maryland was the improper venue for the filing and sought a dismissal of the petition or to at least have the matter moved to New Jersey, arguing that Huntington Learning Centers had always been a profitable business and that TBC's "tactics have been so severe that they've really been an impediment rather than an assistance in resolving things between the two companies." By the time the court heard the motion in July, Jesse James Creative had been paid and Avery Bell was dropped from the case because it was actually a creditor of the sister company, Huntington Learning Corp. As a consequence, TBC was the sole remaining litigant. The judge, however, denied the motion and the case remained in Baltimore. Over the next two months Huntington was able to raise the necessary funds to pay off its debt to TBC and the two parties returned to court on September 11, 2001. With TBC paid in full, the petition was officially dropped. Because of the terrorist attacks that took place that morning in New York City and Washington D.C., the matter became the last order of business in the Baltimore courts for the day.

Huntington backed off on its aggressive growth strategy and sold a number of company-owned units, which decreased from 69 in 2000 to 36 in 2002. In the same period the number of franchises grew from 143 to 178. Prospects for the supplemental education market remained promising for the foreseeable future, especially in light of federal legislation mandating that chronically failing schools make supplemental educational services available to students. Huntington was already becoming involved with urban school districts, contracted to provide in-school services. While it was highly unlikely that Huntington would come close to reaching its ambitious goal of 650 centers by 2007, it was well positioned to take advantage of the poor state of public education in the United States. As Raymond Huntington commented to *Education Week* in January 2002, "What's nice about our business is that we can make money while helping kids."

Principal Competitors

Sylvan Learning Systems, Inc.; Kaplan, Inc.

Further Reading

Adler, Jerry, "The Tutor Age," *Newsweek,* March 30, 1998, p. 46.
Bowen, Ezra, "Teaching the Three Rs for Profit," *Time,* February 3, 1986, p. 70.
Miller, Bruce, "New Jersey Firm Seeks Dismissal, Change of Venue," *Daily Record,* July 16, 2001, p. A3.
Walsh, Mark, "Tutoring Services See Opportunity in New Law," *Education Week,* January 23, 2002, p. 19.

—Ed Dinger

✪ IMATRA STEEL

Imatra Steel Oy Ab

John Stenbergin ranta 2
P.O. Box 790
FIN-00101 Helsinki
Finland
Telephone: (+358) 9 70 95 300
Fax: (+358) 9 77 31 080
Web site: http://www.imatrasteel.com

Wholly Owned Division of Wärtsilä Corporation
Incorporated: 1991
Employees: 1,384
Sales: EUR 186 million ($148 million) (2001)
NAIC: 331513 Steel Foundries (Except Investment)

Imatra Steel Oy Ab is a specialist manufacturer of steel and steel components for the automotive and mechanical engineering industries. The company's products include low-alloy engineering-grade steel bars, produced at the main Imatra steel works, as well as forged engine blocks and front axles, crankshafts and camshafts, leaf springs and stabilizer bars, connecting rods, and components for steering columns. While many of these products are destined for the automobile market, more than 40 percent of Imatra's sales are generated through components for the heavy truck industry. Altogether, Imatra's automotive components products accounts for 65 percent of its total revenues of EUR 186 million. In addition to the main Imatra works, the company operates works at Billnäs and Kilsta in Finland, and, since 2002, at Ayr, Scotland. The company also operates sales and marketing subsidiaries in Norway, Germany, France, and the United Kingdom. Nearly all of Imatra Steel's revenues are generated in Europe, with clients including most of the major European automakers. Finland itself accounts for 15 percent of the group's sales, while the other Nordic countries represent 36 percent of revenues. The rest of Europe adds 46 percent of Imatra Steel's revenues. Imatra Steel is itself a subsidiary of Finnish shipping power plant manufacturing group Wärtsilä, a EUR 2 billion company listed on the Finnish stock exchange.

Finnish Ironworks Origins in the 17th Century

Formed in 1991 on the breakup of the Swedish-Finnish Ovako steel group jointly owned by Metra and SKF, the origins of the Imatra Steel group could be traced back to the early years of the Finnish and Swedish iron and steel industries. The core of Imatra stemmed from 1630, with the founding of the Antskog ironworks, one of the earliest in the Swedish kingdom, which included present-day Finland among its territorial holdings at the time.

In the 1640s, the owner of the Antskog works expanded, founding a new ironworks in the town of Fiskars. By 1647, the Fiskars works had come into the possession of Peter Thorwöste, originally from Holland, and in 1649 Thorwöste began casting and forging. This lay the foundation for the Fiskars company, which became better known for its scissors and other utensils at the turn of the 21st century.

Fiskars was to change ownership a number of times over the following century, and along the way had ceased iron production in favor of copper production. In 1822, however, the works was bought by pharmacist John Julin, who reoriented the company to iron production. In the early 1830s, Fiskars initiated fine forging operations, producing the cutlery and other utensils that were to make the company a brand name. Fiskars also became an early player in Finland's Industrial Revolution, inaugurating its own machine and engineering workshop in 1837. By the following year, the workshop had completed its first steamship engine.

The development of machinery and equipment, the laying of the Finnish railroad system, as well as the construction of bridges, led Fiskar to continue to expand its production in the middle of the 19th century. In 1890, the company acquired a bankrupt steel mill at Aminnefors, which Fiskars then renovated, installing new furnaces. The development of the internal combustion engine resulted in the creation of new machinery types and new motorized vehicles; it also led to a need for new types of components, including springs. By the end of World War I, the Aminnefors site had begun producing its own spring-grade steel, leading Fiskars to establish a factory dedicated to the production of springs, particularly for the railroad industry, in 1921.

In the 1920s, Fiskars continued to expand its steel production operations, buying up iron and steel works across Finland, including the Billnäs Bruks works, which remained a key part of the later Imatra group. In 1927, the company added its first springs for trucks. By 1964, the Billnäs site added a new plant dedicated to producing leaf springs.

Despite the years of economic and political turmoil, beginning with the Great Depression and extending through the end of World War II, Fiskars remained one of Finland's major corporations. Like many other companies of the era, Fiskars went on a spending spree in the 1960s, developing itself into a diversified conglomerate. By the end of that decade, however, Fiskars' expansion had cut deeply into its profits, and the company was forced to restructure its operations.

Setting up a Finnish Steel Group in the 1970s

In 1969, Fiskars agreed to spin off its steelmaking operations into a new company, Ovako Group, which was formed through the merger of Fiskars' holdings with those of fellow Finnish group Oy Vuoksenniska AB. That company had originated at the beginning of the century, with the establishment of Elektrometallurgiska AB, a producer of pig iron and other metals, in 1915. In 1933, Elektrometallurgiska merged with Vuoksenniska Oy, which had been founded in 1926 and had originally operated as a mechanical wood pulp processor.

Ovako remained a primary supplier of steel for Fiskars, while Fiskars retained a major Ovako (and later Wärtsilä) shareholder. In the late 1970s, as Fiskars continued to narrow its focus onto its core cutlery and utensils, the two company's agreed to transfer more of Fiskars holdings to Ovako, including the Billnäs Spring works. In that same year, Ovako expanded its operations again, adding the Dalsbruk Steel Works of the Finnish Wärtsilä Corporation, an industrial conglomerate with operations including a major ship power supply manufacturing unit.

While Ovako produced a range of steels and steel products—including nails, chains, and wire rods—the company began to emphasize its specialty steel products, especially its automotive and engineering components operations, including front axles for cars and trucks and heavy-duty springs. In 1981, the Billnäs site was overhauled in order to produce new parabol-

ic leaf spring designs. In 1984, Ovako purchased the leaf spring business from another company, Lesjoförs.

In 1986, Ovako merged with Sweden's SKF Group, forming the Ovako Steel Group. Ovako Steel quickly focused on the low-alloy specialty steel market and in 1987 sold off its commercial steel holdings to another Finnish steel producer, Rautaruukki. That year, Ovako's Billnäs unit began developing a new range of tubular stabilizer bars for the automotive industry. Ovako then began an aggressive acquisition campaign designed to transform it into a major steel maker, as well as extending its range into a variety of processed, low-alloy steel products. At the same time, the company began investing heavily in upgrading its steelworks in Imatra, Finland.

One of those acquisitions came in 1988, with the purchase of Sweden's Kilsta Smide, which specialized in die-forged components, including front axle beams and crankshafts. The Kilsta works stemmed from the mid-17th century and had begun producing drop-forged components for the automotive industry in 1914. Kilsta had begun producing die-forged components in the late 1950s and had launched production of heavy crankshafts and front axles in the early 1980s.

Specialized Steel Producer in the 21st Century

At the end of the 1980s, the holding company Metra Corporation was established, taking over such diversified, Finland-based interests as the Wärtsilä power business, Sanitec, a bathroom fixtures producer, locks producer Abloy—subsequently merged with Sweden's Assa to form Assa Abloy—and the 50 percent interest in Ovako not held by SKF.

By then, however, the Ovako Steel joint-venture had run into trouble. Its aggressive spending campaign of the late 1980s had saddled it with a huge debt burden just as the European steel market entered a lasting slump. As Ovako's losses mounted, Metra and SKF decided to call it a day, and at the end of 1991 the two partners agreed to break up Ovako Steel.

Metra took over that company's Finnish interests as well as two of its Swedish holdings, including the Kilsta works. Metra then placed these holdings into a newly established company, Imatra Steel, while SKF retained the remainder of Ovako.

In the early 1990s, Metra moved to focus Imatra's holdings around a core of Imatra Steel and its automotive and engineered components operations. In 1993, Imatra spun off its chain, nail, and cable rod operations in a management buyout. The new company was called OFA Oy.

By the mid-1990s, Imatra had established itself as a major supplier of specialized components to the European automotive industry. This position was reinforced with the launch of the company's Tapertec parabolic spring brand in 1996. In that year, the company also debuted its line of tubular stabilizers under the Benditec brand name. Then, in 1997, Imatra extended its automotive components range with the launch of the group's first steering components.

By then, Metra had succeeded in building up a number of globally competitive companies, including Assa Abloy, Sanitec, and, with the acquisition of the Sulzer diesel engine com-

Key Dates:

1630: Antskog iron works is founded.

1649: Fiskars iron works is founded.

1837: Fiskars begins forging industrial engineering components.

1914: Kilsta Smide, originally founded in mid-17th century, begins producing forged automotive components.

1915: Elektrometallurgiska AB, a producer of pig iron and other metals, is founded.

1921: Fiskars begins producing springs for the automotive industry, then buys Billnäs works.

1926: Vuoksenniska Oy, a mechanical wood pulp processor, is founded.

1927: Kilsta begins producing components for trucks.

1933: Elektrometallurgiska merges with Vuoksenniska Oy.

1964: Fiskars establishes Billnäs Spring Works to produce leaf springs.

1969: Fiskars merges its steel production operations with those of Vuoksenniska, forming the Ovako Steel Group.

1979: Fiskars sells its steel components operations, including Billnäs, to Ovako.

1986: Ovako merges with Sweden's SKF steel operations to form Ovako Steel Group joint-venture.

1987: Ovako sells off its commercial steel operations to focus on low-alloy steel production and components production.

1991: Metra and SKF agree to split up Ovako; Metra creates Imatra Steel.

1998: Metra breaks up, spinning off Assa Abloy and Sanitec, while keeping Wärtsilä and Imatra Steel operations.

2000: Metra changes its name to Wärtsilä, and Imatra Steel becomes a Wärtsilä division.

launched a EUR 21 million investment program designed to modernize Imatra Steel's production line, a move designed to step up production levels by some 10 percent by 2003.

Despite the sagging economy at the beginning of the new decade, Imatra Steel continued to look for growth opportunities, particularly for its automotive components operations. At the end of 2001, the company announced its acquisition of Scottish Stampings, based in Ayr, Scotland, which had been part of United Engineering Forgings. Imatra then set up a new subsidiary in Scotland, Imatra Stampings Ltd., for its new purchase. The addition of the Scottish operation, which specialized in front axles, boosted Imatra's position as one of the world's leading producers of forged components for the heavy truck industry. It also added some EUR 22 million to Imatra's revenues, which had neared EUR 195 million in 2000.

By the end of 2002, however, Imatra Steel had faced the consequences of the new economic downturn. With its revenues declining, dropping to EUR 186 million by the end of 2001, Imatra was forced to begin cutting costs, and at the end of 2002 announced its plans to shed some 90 jobs by 2004.

Principal Operating Units

Imatra Kilsta AB (Sweden); Imatra Stampings Ltd. (United Kingdom); Imatra Steel Norway; Imatra Steel Ltd. (United Kingdom); Imatra Stahl GmbH (Germany); Imatra Steel S.a.r.l. (France).

Principal Competitors

Arcelor S.A.; ThyssenKrupp Materials und Services AG; Ilva SpA; Aceralia Corporacion Siderurgica S.A.; Benteler AG; Rautaruukki Oyj; Georg Fischer AG; Imerys; Vallourec S.A.; Gonvarri Industrial S.A.; Babcock and Wilcox Co.; AvestaPolarit ABE AB; Lurgi Lentjes AG; Swiss Steel AG; Kuznetsk Steel Works Joint Stock Co.

Further Reading

"Imatra Steel Lays off 90," *Nordic Business Report*, November 12, 2002.

"Metra to Split into Three," *Financial Times*, May 12, 1998, p. 32.

"Wärtsilä's Imatra Steel Acquires Forge in Scotland," *Nordic Business Report*, November 6, 2001.

Wood, Peter, "Imatra Acquires Scottish Forge," *Steel Times International*, December 2001, p. 5.

—M. L. Cohen

pany, Wärtsilä NSD. In 1998, Metra announced its decision to break itself up, spinning off Assa Abloy and Sanitec as independent companies, although Metra maintained significant shareholding positions in both. By 2000, Metra, now refocused around its ship power supply business, changed its name to Wärtsilä.

If Wärtsilä's power supply business became the company's primary revenue producer, Imatra Steel remained an important part of the company's industrial holdings. As such, Wärtsilä

Ingersoll-Rand Company Ltd.

200 Chestnut Ridge Road
Woodcliff Lake, New Jersey 07675
U.S.A.
Telephone: (201) 573-0123
Toll Free: (800) 847-4041
Fax: (201) 573-3168
Web site: http://www.ingersoll-rand.com

Public Company
Incorporated: 1905
Employees: 56,000
Sales: $8.9 billion (2002)
Stock Exchanges: New York
Ticker Symbol: IR
NAIC: 333415 Air-Conditioning and Warm Air Heating
Equipment and Commercial and Industrial
Refrigeration Equipment Manufacturing; 333911
Pump and Pumping Equipment Manufacturing;
332991 Ball and Roller Bearing Manufacturing;
333912 Air and Gas Compressor Manufacturing;
333411 Air Purification Equipment Manufacturing;
333412 Industrial and Commercial Fan and Blower
Manufacturing; 333120 Construction Machinery
Manufacturing

Ingersoll-Rand Company Ltd. (IR) operates as a diversified machinery and industrial equipment concern catering to four markets—Climate Control, Industrial Solutions, Infrastructure, and Security and Safety. Through its 130 facilities across the globe, IR manufactures Schlage locks and security products, Thermo King transport temperature control equipment, Hussmann refrigeration equipment, Bobcat compact equipment, Club Car golf car and utility vehicles, PowerWorks microturbines, and its namesake industrial and construction equipment. U.S. operations account for the majority of company revenues—the remainder of company sales stem from business in Europe, the Asia Pacific region, Latin America, and Canada.

19th-Century Innovators

Ingersoll-Rand grew out of the efforts of four late 19th-century inventors. Simon Ingersoll, a farmer and inventor, patented a rock drill in 1871, then sold the rights to his patent; Henry Clark Sergeant improved upon Ingersoll's drill and persuaded businessman José F. de Navarro to invest in the idea; William Lawrence Saunders developed many diversified forms of the rock drill; and Addison Crittenden Rand also improved rock drills. Rand also was successful in persuading mining companies to substitute the new technology for the traditional hammer and chisel.

In 1870 inventor Simon Ingersoll, who worked at truck farming to support his family, accepted a contractor's commission to develop a drill that would work on rock. Ingersoll worked on the invention in a New York machine shop owned by entrepreneur José F. de Navarro. Ingersoll received a patent on the rock drill in 1871, but the new tool did not stand up to New York's rocky streets.

Henry Clark Sergeant, one of the partners in the machine shop, made an important change in the drill design. He separated the front head from the cylinder, since a drill in two pieces could better resist breakage. Sergeant then persuaded de Navarro to buy Ingersoll's patent, and de Navarro organized the Ingersoll Rock Drill Company in 1874, with Sergeant as its first president. Ingersoll, who was forced to sell most of his patents and work halfheartedly at farming to feed his family, died nearly destitute in 1894.

Henry Clark Sergeant, however, was able to turn ideas into profitable businesses. Sergeant had been inventing since he was a teenager, and had secured his first patent when he was 20. In 1868, at the age of 34, he had arrived in New York City where he started a machine shop that specialized in developing the ideas of other inventors. As the business grew, he took a partner and moved into de Navarro's shop. After de Navarro formed the Ingersoll Rock Drill Company, Sergeant worked for several years to improve Ingersoll's drill by using compressed air rather than steam to operate it.

In 1885 Sergeant developed a completely different rock drill and formed the Sergeant Drill Company to manufacture it. In

1888 he merged the two companies, becoming president of the Ingersoll-Sergeant Rock Drill Company. After several years he became a director and devoted himself to inventing.

At the same time Ingersoll was patenting his rock drill in 1871, Addison Crittenden Rand moved to New York City from Massachusetts. Rand's brother, Alfred T. Rand, had been instrumental in founding the Laflin & Rand Powder Company, a mining firm. Addison Rand had formed the Rand Drill Company to develop a rock drill and air-compressing machinery for his brother's company. Rand's firm developed the Little Giant tappet drill and the Rand Slugger drill and marketed them effectively, convincing mining companies to switch from hammer and chisel to rock drills with air compressors.

Rand was known for his paternalistic approach to business. He carefully selected his employees and trained them for skilled positions. Rand avoided unions, and was personally affronted when employees at his Tarrytown, New York, plant struck in 1886. The plant was shut down for a year before Rand would agree to a settlement.

The Formation of IR: 1905

In 1905 Michael P. Grace—a brother of William R. Grace, who founded W.R. Grace & Company—brought Ingersoll-Sergeant Drill Company and the Rand Drill Company together. The two companies had specialized in slightly different segments of the drill market—Ingersoll-Sergeant specialized in construction work while Rand focused on underground mining—and their interests were complementary. The new company was incorporated as the Ingersoll-Rand Company (IR) in June 1905 and billed itself as "the largest builder of air power machinery in the world." The Grace family owned the largest single block of stock, and a Grace has served on the IR board ever since.

William Lawrence Saunders became the first president of the company. Saunders, an engineer, had developed a compressed-air drilling apparatus for subaqueous use while in his 20s. The widely used invention made development of Russia's Baku oil fields possible. Saunders had inspected an underwater rock drilling and blasting project himself, diving down to it so he could design a subaqueous drill appropriate for the job. He was active in engineering societies, and established an award given by the American Institute of Mining and Metallurgical Engineers to recognize achievements in mining methods. He also established *Compressed Air,* the company's industrial trade journal, in 1896 and served as its editor. In addition, Saunders was a two-time mayor of North Plainfield, New Jersey.

As president of Ingersoll-Rand, Saunders expanded upon the company's original line of rock drills and air compressors. He promoted development of diverse types of these machines. He also led IR into related areas of the tool business. IR expanded into pneumatic tools in 1907 by acquiring the Imperial Pneumatic Tool Company of Athens, Pennsylvania. In 1909 the company bought the A.S. Cameron Steam Pump Works and entered the industrial pump business. In 1913 he added centrifugal pumps to IR's product list. Under Saunders IR also acquired the J. George Leyner Engineering Works Company. This firm had developed a small, hammer-type drill that could be operated by one man. IR began to produce the jackhammer in 1913, and it quickly became a popular item.

Advances Under the Leadership of Doubleday: 1913–55

Saunders moved to the board of directors in 1913 and was replaced as president by George Doubleday. Doubleday was determined to make Ingersoll-Rand the leader in its product areas—drills, air compressors, jackhammers, pneumatic tools, and industrial pumps. Doubleday led IR for 42 years.

Doubleday carefully adhered to the principles that Saunders had used to guide the company, using IR's four major plants in Phillipsburg, New Jersey; Easton and Athens, Pennsylvania; and Painted Post, New York, to handle increasing business. In these locations, IR was the major employer. Community life centered on the firm: many workers lived in company-owned houses, and community and school events were held in company buildings. Doubleday hired boys off the farm and trained them to become skilled machinists through a seven-year apprenticeship. These artisans accepted the company's credo of pride in personal work, and only a handful of quality-control specialists were needed. Doubleday charged a premium price for the high-quality machinery this system produced.

Little is known about the company itself under Doubleday or about Doubleday's personal life—he refused even to release a photograph of himself to the press—and he provided a bare minimum of information about IR. Under Doubleday the company never released a quarterly report and its annual report was a single folded sheet of paper containing only the figures the New York Stock Exchange required.

Advances were made in the firm's products during the Doubleday years, however. In 1933 IR introduced a new portable-compressor line, which was improved during the 1950s with the introduction of the revolutionary sliding-vane rotary portable unit. IR began to compete in the "big drill" field in 1947, when it introduced the Quarrymaster, which was used in quarrying, open-pit mining, and excavation. A self-propelled jumbo drill, the Drillmaster, was introduced in 1953, followed by the Downhole drill in 1955. Doubleday also purchased General Electric's centrifugal-compressor business in 1933, to become the leader in that sector of the business. In 1948 the company designed the first natural gas transmission centrifugal compressors.

When Doubleday retired in 1955 Ingersoll-Rand was indeed on sound financial footing. The company had more than $100 million in cash and no debt. With an operating profit margin of

Key Dates:

1905: Michael P. Grace acquires both Ingersoll-Sergeant and the Rand Drill Co.; the two companies merge together to form Ingersoll-Rand Co.
1933: The company acquires General Electric's centrifugal-compressor business.
1974: IR purchases Schlage Lock Company.
1986: A partnership is formed with Dresser Industries.
1995: IR purchases Clark Equipment Co.
1997: Newman Tonks Group plc and Thermal King are added to IR's holdings.
2000: Hussmann International Inc. is acquired.
2003: IR sells its Engineered Solutions business to The Timken Company.

37 percent and a net profit margin of 19 percent, it had paid a dividend every year since 1910, and return on stockholders' equity was 23 percent.

Doubleday had reached those impressive numbers, however, by abandoning the marketing orientation that he had originally brought to the job. By the end of his tenure he was 89 years old, and had become too conservative. The company's capital was the result of Doubleday's unwillingness to upgrade the company's plants to keep manufacturing costs low, to promote research and development to retain IR's technological edge, or to maintain sufficient foreign parts inventory to keep equipment running overseas. He also eschewed diversification outside of IR's basic product lines.

Doubleday died in 1955, and an interim management team followed his policies for another four years. Robert H. Johnson was named chairman of the company in 1959. At 58, Johnson had spent 35 years with the company he had joined as a salesman.

Changes Leading to Diversification: 1960s–70s

Johnson cut the company's premium prices to remain competitive. He also spent $25 million to increase parts inventories abroad, and thereby doubled sales overseas in five years; invested in research to promote a return to technological leadership; and increased spending for plant and equipment from an approximate average of $2 million a year to $15 million in 1965. Johnson put the company's excess cash—more than 65 percent of IR's total assets in 1966—to work through a policy of careful acquisitions. He invested, for example, in Lawrence Manufacturing Company, which specialized in producing mechanical moles for urban underground utility tunneling.

Johnson's successor as CEO, 52-year-old William L. Wearly, gave those policies new momentum. Wearly, who took the top position in 1967, was the first leader at IR who had not grown up with the company, another sign that it was leaving its conservative past behind. Wearly came to IR as a consultant in 1962 after leaving the presidency at Joy Manufacturing. With Wearly came a new generation of managers: President D. Wayne Hallstein was 49, while the four newest vice-presidents were under 44. The youth of the new management team was no accident; Johnson had decided that managers who were over 55

had been too thoroughly indoctrinated in the Doubleday method of doing business and bypassed them completely.

Wearly reaped the advantages of Johnson's investment in plant and equipment, which allowed Ingersoll-Rand to increase sales—especially abroad—because of increased manufacturing capacity. Wearly also increased capacity through overseas acquisitions in England, Italy, Canada, South Africa, and Australia.

Wearly then took IR into new, diversified areas to help offset the cyclical nature of the capital goods market. The acquisition of The Torrington Company in 1968, which brought needle and roller bearings, knitting needles, metal-forming machines, universal joints, and roller clutches to the company catalog, was especially important. So was Wearly's 1974 acquisition of the Schlage Lock Company, which produced locks, door hardware, and home and business security devices. Both acquisitions became consistent moneymakers for IR.

Wearly had clearly moved away from the company's tradition of operating paternalistic plants in small towns. By the early 1960s IR operated 36 plants in the United States and 17 abroad. One of them, its Roanoke, Virginia, plant, became the first factory in the country to use computerized direct numerical control of a production line. The plant used a computer to run machine tools and to automatically move parts from one tool to another on conveyer belts without human assistance. The new Roanoke facility took over much of the capacity of the old Athens, Pennsylvania, plant, which had been crippled by strikes and rising labor costs. In 1959 the company had threatened to leave Athens if the union did not make significant concessions on work methods, and IR had won the new five-year contract it wanted. A decade later those union concessions were not forthcoming, and the Athens plant was substantially bypassed—by a mechanized system instead of by other workers.

Overcoming Problems: 1970s–80s

Wearly's policies seemed destined to pay off in the early 1970s, when factors such as the search for new energy sources, Mideastern oil money, growing East-West trade, and Third World industrialization led to increased demand for almost all Ingersoll-Rand products. Five years later, the boom turned into a bust. Capital spending had slowed after the energy crisis of 1973. Coal and railroad strikes hurt the company because it was still a major supplier of coal-mining machinery. Wearly said that President Jimmy Carter's human rights emphasis hurt business in the Soviet Union and Brazil. All of these factors left IR with too much capacity and too much inventory.

Wearly retired in 1980 and Thomas Holmes, a 30-year employee, took over as CEO. Holmes convinced Clyde Folley, a member of Price Waterhouse's governing board who had worked on the IR account, to become chief financial officer. The two executives faced the global recession and resulting fall in earnings and sales, especially of oil drilling and construction equipment. Overall in 1983 IR lost $112 million, the first loss it had suffered since the 1930s.

As a result, the company closed 30 production plants and cut staff by one-third. The company's tight cash supply was spent only in the areas where returns were highest—bearings, locks, and tools—rather than on the traditional focus areas of the company—engineered equipment, coal mining equipment, and air compressors. Holmes and Folley tied management compensation to return on assets instead of sales to promote more efficient asset use, and centralized inventory controls.

Holmes, Folley, and Theodore Black then initiated joint ventures with competitors. One of the most important of these ventures was Dresser-Rand, a 50–50 partnership formed in 1986 with Dresser Industries, another major mining- and oil-equipment company. Almost immediately successful, Dresser-Rand turned a profit in only its second year of operation. In 1987 IR formed another joint venture in mining with B.R. Simmons. Folley said the joint ventures allowed the company to cut staff and losses while competing more effectively with Japanese and West German companies. Pooling talent also helped the firms stay current technologically.

IR had once again weathered recession by the time Holmes stepped down in 1988. His successor, Theodore Black, was able to focus on significant positive aspects of the company.

IR continued to emphasize new product development, introducing improved home air compressors, new papermaking technology, and a new type of camshaft in 1988. IR also continued to make appropriate acquisitions, including a Swedish company that designed waterjet cutting systems, a Canadian manufacturer of paving equipment, and a German maker of special-purpose hydraulic rock drills, in 1988. In 1990, the company purchased The Aro Corporation, one of its larger acquisitions of the period. IR continued to utilize state-of-the-art computerized production and design techniques. New techniques that utilize manufacturing cells to produce a product from start to finish with much less labor than a production line were able to produce more, higher-quality goods.

Another recession during the early 1990s barely registered on IR's balance sheet; 1991 profits fell 19 percent to $150.6 million, while the company's competitors posted losses—$404 million for Caterpillar Inc. and $36 million for The Timken Company. Part of the credit for IR's success was attributed to its geographical diversity. In the early 1980s only 30 percent of the company's sales were attributable to products manufactured outside the United States, but through a variety of acquisitions thereafter that percentage had increased to 70 percent by 1992. The Dresser-Rand partnership also was paying off huge dividends on the home front. The joint venture's sales exceeded $1.2 billion by 1991 and more than one-quarter (or $40 million) of IR's 1991 profits were generated from Dresser-Rand.

Dresser Industries and Ingersoll-Rand recognized another possible area of cooperation in 1991 within their then-competitive industrial pump manufacturing operations. The companies agreed in May of that year to combine their pump divisions into one organization that could better compete against competitors in Japan and Germany. The new firm would have annual sales of $800 million and 8,000 employees worldwide, and would dominate the pump manufacturing industry in the United States. The U.S. Justice Department initially opposed the joint venture under the Sherman Antitrust Act. Dresser and IR countered by contending that the Justice Department had to take the impact of foreign competition into account. After lengthy negotiations, in August 1992 the Justice Department agreed to let the merger go

through provided that the two companies divest about $10 million of their pump operations to mitigate its impact on domestic competition. The newly formed company was called Ingersoll-Dresser Pump Company and Ingersoll-Rand owned 51 percent of it.

Key Acquisitions: 1990s and Beyond

In September 1993, Black retired as chairman and CEO and was replaced by James E. Perrella, a 16-year veteran of the firm. Perrella continued to invest heavily in research and development, shelling out a record $154.6 million in 1994 alone, as well as to make strategic and significant acquisitions. Several smaller acquisitions in 1993 and 1994 served to increase IR's presence in the European market and brought additional complementary businesses into the company fold. These moves included the 1994 acquisitions of the France-based Montabert S.A., a manufacturer of hydraulic rock-breaking and drilling equipment, for $18.4 million and the Ecoair air compressor operation from MAN Gutehoffnungshütte AG for $10.6 million. In 1994 IR also invested $17.6 million in a joint venture with MAN to manufacture airends, an important component in certain industrial air compressors.

One of IR's most important acquisitions of this period came the following year when it purchased Clark Equipment Company, the South Bend, Indiana, manufacturer of small and medium-sized construction machines. Perrella was seeking a major acquisition—a firm that was first or second in its market with sales of $500 million to $1.5 billion—and Clark became a prime candidate. A Clark acquisition was seen as a particularly complementary one, given Clark's focus on construction and IR's construction-related lines, which comprised only about 18 percent of company sales prior to the takeover. Clark became an even more attractive target in early March 1995 when it sold its half-interest in VME Group N.V., an earthmoving equipment manufacturer, to its partner, Volvo AB, for $573 million.

Before the acquisition was completed, however, IR had to fend off Clark's management, which did not wish to relinquish control. After Clark's board rejected the first offer, IR made a hostile bid of $1.3 billion late in March. Clark then brought suit against IR, claiming that the takeover would violate antitrust laws; IR countered by taking steps to oust Clark's board at the annual meeting to be held in early May. In early April, Clark reluctantly accepted an increased offer of $1.5 billion, which many analysts viewed as fair. Through the acquisition, IR gained such Clark operations as Blaw-Knox, the world's leading manufacturer of asphalt road paving equipment; Melroe, the world leader in skid-steer loaders; and Club Car, the second largest golf car manufacturer in the world.

Perrella's tactics bode well for the company's finances. In 1995 sales reached a record $5.7 billion, an increase of 27 percent over the previous year. Operating income also grew at a significant clip. Several major acquisitions followed the Clark purchase. During 1997 IR bought Newman Tonks Group plc, an architectural hardware producer based in the United Kingdom. The firm also made a $2.56 billion cash purchase of Thermo King, a division of Westinghouse Electric Corp. that operated as the largest transport temperature control manufacturer in the United States.

By 1999, IR sales were nearing the $8 billion mark, a sign that the firm's acquisition strategy was indeed paying off. Perrella retired that year, leaving Herbert Henkel to take the helm. In a September 1999 *Forbes* article the new CEO remarked, "We have a good foundation. Now we have to build a skyscraper." Like his predecessor, Henkel made growth a key priority.

As such, IR continued to add to its product arsenal while making a few significant divestments. During 2000, the company sold its Ingersoll-Dresser pump business for $775 million and also rid itself of Corona Clipper, a hand tool manufacturer. In 2003, the company's engineered solutions arm was sold to The Timken Company for $840 million.

In June 2000 Hussmann International Inc.—a leading refrigeration manufacturer—became part of the IR family in a $1.7 billion deal. The firm also purchased lock manufacturer Kryptonite Corp., Netherlands-based Grenco Transportkoeling B.V., National Refrigeration Services Inc., Taylor Industries Inc., and several infrastructure-related firms.

During the early years of the new millennium IR made several internal changes. The company began an aggressive cost-cutting program in 2000 that included the closure of 20 manufacturing plants. The firm also reincorporated in Bermuda in a move that gave IR several tax advantages. At the same time, the company was hit by a slowdown in global economies, which began to take a toll on earnings. Nevertheless, IR appeared to be well positioned to withstand international economic downturns. With a diverse line of products and a solid business strategy in place, IR management felt it would progress well into the future.

Principal Subsidiaries

Aro International Corporation; Clark Equipment Company; Bobcat Corporation; Blaw-Knox Construction Equipment Corporation; Thermo King Enterprises Company; Club Car Inc.; Hussmann International, Inc.; IDP Acquisition, LLC; Ingersoll-Rand International Holding Corporation; Ingersoll-Rand International, Inc.; Ingersoll-Rand Transportation Services Company; Schlage Lock Company; Newman Tonks Holdings, Inc.; Steelcraft Holding Company; Taylor Industries, Inc.; Thermo King Corporation; The Torrington Company.

Principal Competitors

Caterpillar Inc.; Emerson Electric Company; York International Corporation.

Further Reading

Byrne, Harlan S., "Ingersoll-Rand: Leaner and Poised to Build Stronger Profits," *Barron's,* June 8, 1992, pp. 39–40.

Deutsch, Claudia H., "Ingersoll-Rand to Buy Westinghouse's Thermo King Unit," *New York Times,* September 16, 1997, p. D6.

"Ingersoll-Rand Acquires Kryptonite Corp.," *Doors and Hardware,* November 2001, p. 75.

"Ingersoll-Rand Seeks $1 Billion in Acquisitions," *Industrial Distribution,* March 2000, p. 32.

"Ingersoll-Rand to Acquire Hussmann," *Appliance,* July 2000, p. 16.

Johnson, James P., *New Jersey: A History of Ingenuity and Industry,* Northridge, Calif.: Windsor Publications, 1987.

Klebnikov, Paul, "A Traumatic Experience: Ingersoll-Rand Prospers Today Because It Stumbled So Badly a Few Years Ago," *Forbes,* January 18, 1993, pp. 83–84.

Koether, George, *The Building of Men, Machines, and a Company,* Woodcliff Lake, N.J.: Ingersoll, 1971.

Lipin, Steven, "Clark Accepts Ingersoll Bid of $1.5 Billion for Takeover," *Wall Street Journal,* April 10, 1995, pp. A3, A5.

Nelson, Brett, "Ingersoll-Rand Gets a Makeover," *Forbes,* September 6, 1999, p. 70.

—Ginger G. Rodriguez
—updates: David E. Salamie and Christina M. Stansell

I A S G

International Airline Support Group, Inc.

1954 Airport Road, Suite 200
Atlanta, Georgia 30341
U.S.A.
Telephone: (770) 455-7575
Fax: (770) 455-7550
Web site: http://www.iasgroup.com

Public Company
Incorporated: 1982
Employees: 29
Sales: $17.15 million (2002)
Stock Exchanges: American
Ticker Symbol: YLF
NAIC: 423860 Transportation Equipment and Supplies
(Except Motor Vehicles) Merchant Wholesalers

International Airline Support Group, Inc. (IASG) supplies operators with parts for older types of aircraft. Its main customers are cargo airlines using older aircraft such as the DC-9 and MD-80. The company diversified in the late 1990s by acquiring inventories of parts for regional aircraft, such as the Embraer Brasilia, and for the Boeing 747 jumbo jet. The company traditionally has acquired its inventories by buying used aircraft and disassembling them. This has proved very profitable in the past. However, IASG has suffered along with the airline industry following the terrorist attacks on the World Trade Center on September 11, 2001.

Globetrotting Origins

International Airline Support Group, Inc. was founded in 1982 by Richard R. Wellman, a scrap metal dealer, and his wife Lynda Wellman. Richard Wellman grew up in a working-class neighborhood of Detroit, recorded the *Wall Street Journal* in a 1992 article chronicling how much he enjoyed entrepreneurship. His involvement with aviation began in 1955, when he became a mechanic in the U.S. Air Force at the age of 17.

Upon leaving the air force, he worked for an air freight company. After this adventure, which involved shipping cadavers from Vietnam, he bought a share of his own cargo aircraft and used it to ship parts for the auto industry. This expanded into flying odd cargoes to far-flung corners of the world, noted the *Wall Street Journal*—tedious work that most other companies refused. This sometimes involved flying thousands of head of livestock to third world countries. Wellman also began trading aircraft and parts, a very lucrative sideline.

From 1975 to 1978, Wellman's planes carried air cargo on behalf of Air India. He then returned to the United States, exhausted from globetrotting and beleaguered by a new wave of competitors encroaching upon his market niche. He moved to Miami and became an employee of another air cargo service.

Soon, though, Wellman returned to his old side venture of selling parts. "The fun of it," Wellman told the *Wall Street Journal,* "is to take something other people think is junk and convert it into cash." He bought a used Boeing 707 and sold the nose gear for $23,000 before he had even towed it into its parking spot. Most of the planes IASG dealt with were no longer in production (DC-8 manufacturing ended in 1972; that of the DC-9 stopped ten years later), but newer aircraft often had some parts in common with the older planes, helping them maintain their value high. About 40 percent of the DC-9's parts were interchangeable with those of the DC-8.

International Airline Support Group (IASG) was formally launched in 1982. Wellman's wife Lynda handled the bookkeeping and became the corporation's secretary-treasurer. IASG began logging an annual profit in 1985 and grew rapidly into the 1990s. Revenue of $8 million for the 1989 fiscal year was nearly triple that of the year before, while net income rose to $487,000 from $55,000.

A major early customer, reported *Fortune* magazine, was the cargo airline Transafrik Corporation, based in Sao Tome and Principe. However, the agreement to purchase 17 aircraft from Northwest Airlines (11 DC-9's and six 727's) broadened IASG's customer base to include a handful of major cargo and passenger airlines in the United States. Before this, DC-8 parts had accounted for 85 percent of IASG's inventory. The 17 planes, Northwest's oldest, had an average value of $1 million each, according to one estimate.

Company Perspectives:

The marketplace is the driving force behind everything we do. IASG will be the best in each of its respective markets for the products and services we provide.

Going Public in 1990

IASG's initial public offering (IPO) in 1990 raised $2.4 million. Prior to the IPO, in October 20, 1989, a Delaware corporation called International Aircraft Support Group was formed. It was merged into the existing Florida corporation. The shares traded over the counter under the symbol "IASG."

About 70 percent of sales came from overseas. The company more than doubled its revenues in the fiscal year ending May 31, 1991, reaching $21.5 million. At the same time, profits tripled to $1.4 million. Revenues continued to rise in fiscal 1992, to $26.5 million, while net income hit $2 million. This led the *Miami Herald* to pronounce it Florida's second most profitable company. It had 60 employees at the time. The 1992 results were accredited to big gains in the domestic parts business and sales of whole aircraft and engines. IASG-Virgin Islands, Inc. (IASG-VI) was formed in July 1992 to promote international sales with tax benefits.

Throughout the 1980s and early 1990s, most major carriers were retiring their older, first generation airliners for more fuel efficient ones as well as for quieter models that could meet increasingly stringent noise regulations. According to IASG's Securities and Exchange Commission (SEC) filings, though, DC-8's equipped with "hush kits" to abate engine noise were among the cheapest aircraft to operate, making them particularly popular among cargo airlines and guaranteeing a market for DC-8 parts.

IASG joined International Aircraft Services, a leasing firm in Shannon, Ireland, in a joint venture in April 1990. The enterprise, called Seven Seas Leasing Ltd., leased and sold first generation airliners. Seven Seas was discontinued in June 1992 due to poor market conditions in the aircraft leasing business overseas. IASG also had a wholly owned subsidiary, Barnstorm, Inc., that traded and leased whole planes. Aircraft leasing increased to 10 percent of IASG revenues in the 1994 fiscal year.

In 1991, the company began leasing space for an aircraft and parts storage operation north of Dallas in Sherman. The company soon acquired three MD-80 airliners, a successor to the DC-9, which shared many of the same parts. The MD-80 was still in production at the time. IASG parted out its two MD-80's, acquired from Northwest Airlines, and leased a third.

In June 1993, the company established a subsidiary, International Airline Service Center, Inc. (IASC), in Sherman, Texas. IASC mainly performed maintenance checks on DC-9's and Boeing 727's. IASG provided IASC with the bulk of its business. However, the unit was never able to establish a substantial third party customer base, and it was sold off in May 1995. Later, IASC began refurbishing whole aircraft for resale. The unit also established a subsidiary of its own, Professional Avia-

tion Technical Services, Inc. (PATS), a provider of engineering services. IASG bought Brent Aviation, Inc., a tiny Texas air cargo operator, in November 1993. This was sold to a group of former employees in January 1995.

Revenues were about $33.5 million in fiscal 1993. Sales of jet parts slowed to half their normal rate. One joint venture, Aircraft Partners Limited, had been created to sell three aircraft. Its November 1993 bankruptcy plunged IASG, as the managing partner, into a financial crisis. Softness in the parts market removed any financial cushion.

In an effort to cut costs, the company let go 30 percent of its work force of 130 in February 1994 and dismissed its president, Dennis Young, at the same time. "It makes sense to not have a high-paid executive on top," said Young in the *Wall Street Journal.* Managers' salaries were also reduced by 20 percent. Meanwhile, the company's shares were delisted from the NASDAQ exchange.

1995 Turnaround

In 1995, Alexius A. Dyer III, head of the Barnstorm Leasing Inc. unit, was named president of IASG and charged with turning the company around. A new management team was installed. Employment was scaled back by more than half, from 60 to 25 employees. A recovery was well under way by fiscal 1996, when the company made a profit of $2.2 million on sales of $21 million.

IASG developed a specialty in McDonnell Douglas MD-80's and DC-9's, which had a significant number of interchangeable parts. It bought an inventory of these types of parts from Pt. Garuda Indonesia in May 1996 for $2.3 million. There were about 2,000 of these planes still in service in the mid-1990s, but the DC-9 was no longer in production. IASG also supplied parts for Boeing 727's, which were also out of production. *Fortune* magazine noted that IASG made an average profit of 200 percent on the price of a used plane by parting it out.

Move to Atlanta in 1997

IASG relocated its headquarters from Miami to Atlanta in February 1997. In April, the company's shares began trading on the American Stock Exchange (symbol: YLF). The company boasted 771 customers at the time, most of them domestic. Revenues were $21 million in the fiscal year ended May 31, 1997; profit was $1.7 million. That June, the company relocated its warehousing operation from Miami to a larger facility in Fort Lauderdale.

Changes in the aviation industry were helping propel the company's recovery. Company president Alexius A. Dyer III explained in the *Atlanta Business Chronicle:* "The world's commercial aircraft fleet is getting older and larger, and also more airlines are moving toward outsourcing their parts departments."

By this time, IASG was seeking to acquire other small companies in the fragmented aviation services industry. It was also aiming to expand into the market for regional airliner parts. IASG acquired an Airbus A300 in March 1998 for parts sales. A couple of months later, Mesa Air Group, which had recently been dropped as a United Airlines feeder airline, hired IASG

Key Dates:

1982: IASG is formed in Miami.
1990: IASG goes public.
1991: The company begins selling DC-9 parts and opens a new base in Sherman, Texas.
1992: IASG begins parting out Boeing 727's.
1995: Alexius Dyer brought in to turn around the troubled company.
1997: IASG relocates its headquarters to Atlanta from Miami and begins trading on the American Stock Exchange (AMEX).
1998: Airbus A300 is acquired.
1999: Comair's fleet of Brasilia turboprops is acquired.
2000: The company opens a sales office and distribution center in Europe.

to dispose of 20 Brasilia and 21 Jetstream J31 aircraft. Turboprop planes such as the Embraer Brasilia were being phased out by regional airlines in favor of small regional jets, which passengers found more comfortable. In the fall of 1999, IASG reached an agreement with Delta Air Lines' Comair unit to sell its Brasilia parts on consignment. On the other side of the spectrum, IASG also acquired a significant inventory of parts for the Boeing 747 jumbo jet.

In fiscal 1999, IASG invested $1.5 million for a 50 percent share in a joint venture called Air 41 LLC, formed to acquire twenty DC-9's from Scandinavian Airlines System (SAS) and then lease them back to SAS. These aircraft dropped in value following the September 11, 2001 terrorist attacks, and the venture was wrapped up in 2003.

Broadening Focus Beyond 2000

In 2000, IASG opened a sales office in France as well as a distribution center in the Netherlands, managed by KLM Aerospace Logistics Group. In Autumn 2000, IASG acquired an EMB-120 Brasilia turboprop, the first of the type to be converted to a freighter. IASG leased the plane to North-South Airways (NSA), an Atlanta-based charter carrier that IASG had acquired. While Embraer converted this first EMB-120 to a freighter itself, IASG ordered ten conversion kits, with options for ten more. A stock offering later reduced IASG's shareholding in NSA to 35 percent; by 2003, IASG's investment in NSA had been written off.

IASG soon acquired other regional airliners such as the de Havilland Dash-7 and Dash-8, the ATR-42, and the Dornier Do-328. In December 2002, the company announced the addition of parts for the Sikorsky S-76 helicopter. IASG's revenues were $21.5 million in fiscal 2001, with net earnings of $343,000, about a third that of the previous year. Revenues slipped to $17.2 million in fiscal 2002, producing an $8.5 million net loss.

Principal Competitors

AAR Corporation; Kellstrom Industries; The Memphis Group, Inc.; Volvo Aero Services.

Further Reading

Bowers, Brent, "The Thrill of It; Richard Wellman Has a Simple Reason for Being an Entrepreneur: It's Fun," *Wall Street Journal*, October 16, 1992, pp. R16–17.

Chuter, Andy, "Brasilia Conversion Enters Service in USA," *Flight International*, October 3, 2000.

"IASG to Disassemble A300 for Parts Sales," *Aviation Daily*, March 27, 1998, p. 510.

"International Airline Dismisses Its President Amid Restructuring," *Wall Street Journal*, February 16, 1994, p. B10.

"International Airline Support Group Reorganizing, Laying Off Workers," *Aviation Daily*, February 17, 1994, p. 272.

"International Airline Support Group Selling Comair Brasilia Parts," *Business & Commercial Aviation*, September 1999, p. 24.

"International Airline Support Group Terminates Joint Venture," *Aviation Daily*, June 29, 1992, p. 560.

"Mesa Hires Company to Dispose of WestAir Brasilias, Jetstream 31s; Announces More Personnel Changes," *Commuter/Regional Airline News*, May 18, 1998.

Murray, Brendan, "Plane Parts Firm Rebounds After Move," *South Florida Business Journal*, October 10, 1997, p. 6.

Neumeier, Shelley, "International Airline Support Group," *Fortune*, Companies to Watch, December 16, 1991, p. 106.

Phelps, David, "NWA Selling 17 Planes to Miami Firm," *Star Tribune* (Minneapolis), April 18, 1991, p. 1D.

Vyas, Rajiv, "Airline Parts Supplier Encountering Turbulence," *Atlanta Business Chronicle*, September 15, 2000, p. 8A.

Zisser, Melinda, "Air Firm Fires Exec; Cuts 40 Jobs," *South Florida Business Journal*, February 18, 1994, p. 1F.

—Frederick C. Ingram

Israel Chemicals Ltd.

Millenium Tower
23 Aranha Street
Tel-Aviv 61070
Israel
Telephone: (+972) 3-6844-401
Fax: (+972) 3-6844-428
Web site: http://www.israelchemicals.co.il

Public Company
Incorporated: 1968
Employees: 8,772
Sales: NIS 9.38 billion ($1.98 billion) (2002)
Stock Exchanges: Tel Aviv
Ticker Symbol: ICL
NAIC: 325188 All Other Inorganic Chemical
    Manufacturing; 325131 Inorganic Dye and Pigment
    Manufacturing; 325192 Cyclic Crude and Intermediate
    Manufacturing; 325311 Nitrogenous Fertilizer Manufac-
    turing; 325312 Phosphatic Fertilizer Manufacturing;
    325314 Fertilizer (Mixing Only) Manufacturing;
    325411 Medicinal and Botanical Manufacturing;
    424690 Other Chemical and Allied Products Merchant
    Wholesalers; 424910 Farm Supplies Merchant
    Wholesalers

Israel Chemicals Ltd. (ICL) is one of the world's leading producers of potash, bromine, and other mineral and chemical compounds. The company accounts for approximately 11 percent of total world potash production and 35 percent of world bromine production. It also produces more than 9 percent of the primary magnesium consumed by the markets of the West. More than 60 percent of the company's production come from its concessions in the Dead Sea (potash, bromine, salt, magnesium, and magnesium chloride) and the Negev Desert (phosphates and limestone). The company also operates potash mining concessions in England through subsidiary Cleveland Potash and in Spain through subsidiary Iberpotash, as well as maintaining manufacturing facilities in the United States, Chile, France, the Netherlands, Germany, China, and elsewhere. Inter-

national sales represent more than 90 percent of the company's total sales. Formerly owned by the Israeli government, ICL has been listed on the Tel Aviv Stock Exchange since the early 1990s. The majority of the company's stock is held, however, by the Ofer Group, which, through its investment company Israel Corporation, holds 52 percent of ICL's stock.

Government-Owned Mineral Concern in the 1970s

Israel Chemicals Ltd. stemmed from the mid-1970s combination of two important areas of Israel mineral production, that of phosphates from the Negev Desert and potash and other minerals from the rich Dead Sea basin. Negev Phosphates had been founded in 1952 for the purpose of mining phosphate rock from the Negev Desert. In 1966, another company was formed, Arad Chemical, which specialized in the production of phosphoric acid. Both companies were owned by the Israeli government, which formed a new holding company, Israel Chemicals Ltd., for these and other government-owned mineral companies operating in the Negev Desert. In 1975, ICL merged Negev Phosphates and Arad Chemical into a single company under the Negev Phosphates name. That year marked the consolidation of much of Israel's mineral production under the ICL umbrella. A significant addition to ICL was Dead Sea Works Ltd., one of the country's oldest mineral operations, predating the formation of the Israeli state itself.

Moshe Novomeysky had been an engineer in Siberia before emigrating to Palestine in the 1920s. There, Novomeysky recognized the vast mineral potential of the Dead Sea, particularly the possibility of producing bromine and potash (a potassium derivative) present in the Dead Sea water. Novomeysky was granted a concession for processing chemicals from the Dead Sea by the British authorities in 1927. Novomeysky founded Palestine Potash Ltd. in that year and began construction of a plant in Kalia, along the Dead Sea's northern shore.

Palestine Potash began producing bromine in 1931. The following year, the company launched potash production as well. By 1934, seeking expansion, Novomeysky decided to establish a new, larger plant in Sdom, on the southern shore of the Dead Sea. By 1936, when that plant began production, the company was turning out 80,000 tons of potash per year.

During the Israeli War of Independence, the Kalil site was destroyed. Production at the Sdom site was also interrupted and was not to resume again until 1954. By then, the company had taken on a new name, Dead Sea Works Ltd., and had come under the control of the Israeli government. The company's bromine production was placed under subsidiary Dead Sea Bromine. By the end of 1954, potash production had risen to more than 100,000 tons per year. Nevertheless, this was a relatively small scale of production, leaving the company operating at a loss.

In 1955, new managing director Moderchai Makleff, former General and Chief of Staff of the Israeli army, launched Dead Sea Works on a major expansion drive. Backed by the Israeli government, the Dead Sea Works expansion involved building a 20-kilometer dam across the Dead Sea, creating an evaporation bed of more than 100 square kilometers. Accompanying the construction of the dam was the development of a modern plant that produced potash using a hot crystallization process. This expansion enabled the company to boost its production to more than 400,000 tons per year in the early 1960s, more than 800,000 tons by the end of the decade, and more than 1.2 million tons by the early 1970s.

By then, Dead Sea Works had expanded into a new area, that of magnesium production, a byproduct of the potash production process. In 1970, the company founded a new enterprise, Dead Sea Periclase Ltd., which used brine from Dead Sea Works for its magnesium production. In 1975, Dead Sea Works and Dead Sea Periclase were merged into the newly expanded ICL.

ICL grew strongly in the late 1970s and early 1980s. In 1977, the company created a new subsidiary, Rotem, which began production of fertilizers and phosporic acid using phosphate rock mined from the Negev. That same year, ICL, in its first international move, acquired Germany specialty chemicals producer Giulini Chemie GmbH. Founded in 1823 in order to produce sulfuric acid from sulfur mined in Italy, that company had expanded into other chemical operations at the turn of the century, adding phosphate fertilizers, phosporic acid, and other compounds. In the second half of the 20th century, Giulini had continued its diversification, adding products ranging from pharmaceuticals to food additives to specialty chemicals used in the paper and footwear industries.

Meanwhile, Dead Sea Works, in conjunction with IMI (Tami) Institute for Research and Development, a government-owned body founded in 1964 and itself placed under ICL in 1975, had begun work on developing a new method for extracting potash using a cold crystallization process. That effort

paid off in 1980, and the company added new production facilities for the process. Initial production reached 400,000 tons per year, a figure that doubled by the middle of the decade.

Continuing its internationalization, ICL completed a new acquisition in 1982 when it acquired Amsterdam Fertilizers, or Amfert. The acquisition helped boost ICL's position in the European fertilizer market, giving it manufacturing capacity in the Netherlands and Germany as well as sales offices in France, Spain, and the United Kingdom.

Raw Materials to Finished Products Giant in the 1990s

During the 1980s, ICL began a shift from its position as a raw materials producer toward becoming a more vertically integrated producer of end products. As part of that movement, the company began making a series of new acquisitions designed to diversify its operation into related areas. Such was the case with its 1990 acquisition of Rami Ceramics, which produced specialty ceramics for the steel industry from two plants in Acre and Nazareth.

Yet ICL was also preparing for a still bigger change—that of becoming a private company. Calls for the privatization of Israel's industries had been building since the 1980s. ICL, as one of the country's largest government-owned companies, became a primary target for the privatization drive, particularly as Israel struggled through a currency crisis at the beginning of the 1990s. The privatization of the company nonetheless remained a contentious issue.

As a run-up to the privatization, however, ICL began to restructure parts of its operations. In 1989, Amfert was placed under phosphates group Rotem, which was then renamed Rotem Amfert Group. Then, in 1991, Rotem Amfert absorbed the Negev Phosphates operation, renaming itself Rotem Amfert Negev Ltd. and taking over all of ICL's phosphates production.

That same year, ICL launched an ambitious, $900 million, five-year investment program designed to step up phosphate production from 2.1 million tons to 2.5 million tons and bromine and bromine compound capacity to 200,000 tons per year. The company also began construction on a number of new manufacturing facilities, including a potassium sulfate facility capable of producing 150,000 tons per year, a new 100,000 tons-per-year magnesium chloride pellet production facility, a phosphate plant capable of production levels of one million tons per year, and an NPL fertilizer plant with a capacity of 50,000 tons per year.

ICL's public listing finally went through in 1992, as the Israeli government placed some 25 percent of the company on the Tel Aviv Stock Exchange. Control of the company and its decisions remained with the Israeli government, which considered ICL of vital interest to the Israeli state. At the same time, however, the government floated two ICL subsidiaries, Dead Sea Works and Fertilizers & Chemicals Ltd. Both remained, however, majority controlled by ICL.

ICL continued to expand through acquisitions and by entering new business areas. In 1992, subsidiary Giulini Chemie purchased German pharmaceutical company Philopharm, the maker of a product for the treatment of gastric disorders.

Key Dates:

1927: Moshe Novomeysky acquires a mineral concession for Dead Sea, founding Palestine Potash Ltd.
1931: Palestine Potash starts up bromine production in a plant built in Kalia.
1932: The company begins potash production
1934: A new plant is built in Sdom, on the Dead Sea's southern shore.
1952: Negev Phosphates is created to mine phosphate deposits in the Negev Desert.
1954: The company changes its name to Dead Sea Works Ltd., which becomes controlled by Israeli government.
1955: Dead Sea Works begins an expansion drive backed by the Israeli government.
1968: Israel Chemicals Ltd. (ICL) is created to group government-owned mineral companies.
1970: Dead Sea Periclase is founded.
1975: ICL absorbs Dead Sea Works and other companies.
1977: Rotem is created; Giulini Chemie (Germany) is acquired.
1982: Amsterdam Fertilizers (Netherlands) is acquired.
1989: Rotem and Amfert merge to create Rotem Amfert.
1991: Negev Phosphates merges into Rotem Amfert, forming Rotem Amfert Negev.
1992: Twenty-five percent of ICL is listed on the Tel Aviv Stock Exchange.
1995: Israel Corporation acquires nearly 25 percent of ICL from the Israeli government.
1996: Rotem Amfert Negev acquires BK Ladenburg, which is merged with Giulini to form BK Giulini.
1998: Dead Sea Works acquires Grupo Potasas of Spain, which is renamed Iberpotash.
1999: Ofer Brothers acquire a controlling stake in Israel Corporation, becoming the majority ICL shareholder.
2002: Cleveland Potash Ltd, based in the United Kingdom, is acquired; ICL Fertilizers is created.

Meanwhile, Rotem Amfert Negev entered a joint-venture with Chile's SQM to form NutriSi, marketing various fertilizer products that included mono-potassium phosphate (MKP) to the European market. The joint-venture, begun in 1993, led Rotem Amfert Negev to inaugurate a new MKP production plant the following year. Rotem Amfert Negev continued to expand that year, acquiring France's Penngar, which produced detergents for the dairy industry.

Public Chemicals Leader in the 21st Century

In 1994, the Israeli government announced its intention to float an additional 25 percent of ICL's shares, reducing its holding to below 50 percent. The government also proposed to list ICL's shares on the New York Stock Exchange but dropped that plan before the public offering in February 1995. The new offering turned over nearly 25 percent of the company to investment firm Israel Corporation, headed by Saul Eisenberg, which was also granted an option to acquire an additional 17 percent of ICL by 1997.

As a further step toward its full privatization, the company continued restructuring in 1995, regrouping ICL into three main groups: Dead Sea Works, which took over the company's Dead Sea minerals, pharmaceuticals, cosmetics, and energy products; Dead Sea Bromine, which was split off from Dead Sea Works to form the core of a new Bromine business unit that also incorporated Dead Sea Periclase and Rami Ceramics; and a new company, Rotem, which not only took over Rotem Amfert Negev but also Giulini Chemie and various other companies and businesses, including much of the ICL's international holdings.

ICL continued its acquisitions into the second half of the decade. In 1995, the company acquired U.S.-based Clearon Corp, which specialized in water treatment products. In 1996, Rotem strengthened its position in the German phosphates market through the purchase of BK Ladenburg Gesellschaft für Chemische Erzeugnisse. Founded in 1967, that company had come under control of Hoechst AG in 1990, producing phosphates for food additives, detergents, water treatments, and other markets. Following that acquisition, Rotem regrouped its German operations, merging BK Ladenburg with Giulini Chemie, creating BK Giulini.

Israel Corporation exercised its option to acquire a further stake in ICL, increasing its holding to 41.9 percent. The Israeli government, which by then had reduced its stake in ICL to just 31.5 percent, at last completed the privatization of the company in 1999 when it placed its entire holding in the company on the Tel Aviv Stock Exchange. Israel Corporation took that opportunity to increase its own holding in ICL to 52 percent—beating out Canadian rival Potash Corporation of Saskatchewan (PCS), which had been pursuing its international expansion at the end of the 1990s.

By then, ICL had itself outrun PCS when it acquired, through Dead Sea Works, Spanish potash company Grupo Potasas, based in Barcelona and the largest potash producer in Spain. That company was then renamed as Iberpotash. Dead Sea Works was expanding elsewhere as well, constructing a $450 million plant in China that was expected to produce up to 800,000 tons of potash per year using ICL's cold crystallization process. Dead Sea Works had also launched itself in a new direction, founding Dead Sea Magnesium and investing some $420 million to construct a magnesium production facility. The company guessed—correctly—that the automobile industry would increasingly turn to the use of magnesium alloys, which were both lightweight and less environmentally aggressive than traditional metals.

In 1999, ICL began a program of de-listing its publicly listed subsidiaries, beginning with Fertilizers & Chemicals Ltd. The following year, ICL reacquired all the outstanding shares of Dead Sea Works, Dead Sea Bromine, and Dead Sea Periclase. In the meantime, ICL itself had come under new ownership when Ofer Brothers Group, the largest privately owned company in Israel, acquired a controlling stake in Israel Corporation for $330 million—beating out a rival bid by PCS.

ICL's expansion continued into the next decade. In 2000, Rotem, through Rotem Amfert Negev, purchased Turkish phosphate producer Opal, which specialized in products for the feed market. That subsidiary was renamed as Rotem Turkey. Meanwhile, the company began shedding a number of non-core activities, including its stake in Dead Sea Laboratories, which marketed cosmetics and skin-care products under the Ahava brand name, sold off in 2001. In that year, the company also combined the marketing operations of Dead Sea Works and Rotem Amfert Negev, a move expected to cut costs while increasing service to customers.

In 2002, ICL enhanced its international profile with the purchase of Cleveland Potash Ltd., which operated potash mines in the United Kingdom, paying $45 million to Anglo American Plc. The purchase helped establish ICL as a major European potash producer and one of the largest in the world. Following that acquisition, ICL embarked on a new restructuring. The company created a new business unit, ICL Fertlizers, which combined nearly all of the company's fertilizer operations, including Dead Sea Works, Iberpotash, and Cleveland Potash, as well as Rotem and Fertilizers & Chemicals. Backed by its exclusive concession to the Dead Sea's minerals, but with a growing array of international operations, ICL had established itself as one of the world's leading specialty chemicals producers.

Principal Subsidiaries

Dead Sea Works Ltd.; Rotem Amfert Negev Ltd. (Netherlands); Cleveland Potash Ltd. (United Kingdom); Iberpotash S.A. (Spain); BK Giulini Chemie GmbH & Co. (Germany); Dead Sea Periclase Ltd.; Dead Sea Bromine Group; IDE Technologies Ltd. (50%); SQM (Chile).

Principal Competitors

IMC Global Inc.; Avecia Group plc; Agrium Inc.; Kali und Salz AG.

Further Reading

Alperowicz, Natasha, "Israel Chemicals Restructures Fertilizers and Specialties," *Chemical Week*, August 28, 2002, p. 16.

"ICL Buys Cleveland Potash," *Chemical Market Reporter*, May 6, 2002, p. 4.

"Israel Chemicals Buys Back Dead Sea Shares," *Chemical Week*, March 15, 2000, p. 8.

"Israeli Group Beats Out PCS in Bid for Israel Chemicals," *Chemical Week*, January 20, 1999, p. 25.

"Israel Sells Chemical Stake," *Privatisation International*, January 1999.

Machlis, Avi, "PCS Seeks Israel Chemicals Stake," *Financial Times*, January 11, 1999, p. 27.

—M. L. Cohen

IVAX Corporation

4400 Biscayne Boulevard
Miami, Florida 33137
U.S.A.
Telephone: (305) 575-6000
Toll Free: (800) 980-4829
Fax: (305) 575-6055
Web site: http://www.ivax.com

Public Company
Incorporated: 1985 as IVAX Inc.
Employees: 8,175
Sales: $1.19 billion (2002)
Stock Exchanges: American London
Ticker Symbol: IVX
NAIC: 325412 Pharmaceutical Preparation Manufacturing

IVAX Corporation develops, manufactures, markets, and distributes branded and brand-equivalent (generic) drugs and veterinary products. The firm's product line—which is found in over 70 countries around the world—includes branded drugs related to allergies, coughs and colds, and asthma, and nearly 400 generic prescription and over-the-counter drugs. The company is also involved in the development of pharmaceuticals designed to treat cancer, HIV, and various central nervous system diseases. With sales surpassing $1 billion, IVAX operates as one of the world's largest generic drug companies. IVAX Corporation is the creation of dermatologist and deal maker Dr. Philip Frost. Frost formed IVAX Inc. in 1987 as a holding company. Its principal subsidiary, IVACO Industries Inc., was an $11 million (in sales) specialty chemicals manufacturer based in New Jersey. IVAX also owned major shares of two small, ailing pharmaceutical companies. To the casual observer, IVAX may have seemed a rather odd organization with limited potential. However, Frost had big plans for the fledgling operation. In fact, many analysts also expected big things from Frost's peculiar venture based on his past successes.

1970s: Frost Lays the Foundation for IVAX

After finishing his residency at the University of Miami in the late 1960s, Frost's performance earned him a spot on the school's faculty. He left in 1970 to found the dermatology department at Miami Beach's Mt. Sinai Medical Center, where he served as chairman of the department until 1990. In addition to his professional activities during the 1970s, the high-energy Frost exercised his entrepreneurial bent through a variety of innovative ventures. Shortly after moving to Mt. Sinai, for example, Frost opened a fish farm in the everglades; a drought dried up the ponds and killed the fish, but the land appreciated in value, and Frost profited from the undertaking.

Of all Frost's business exploits, the one that would eventually garner him the greatest amount of respect (and profit) was his 1972 purchase of Key Pharmaceuticals, Inc. By 1972, Frost had created a number of medical-related inventions, such as his disposable biopsy punch, and he wanted to use Key as a vehicle to take his ideas to market. Frost and partner Michael Jaharis purchased the struggling Key for a paltry $100,000. Jaharis became the detail man, directing the day-to-day operations of the start-up enterprise, while Frost handled the big picture.

Rather than using Key to launch new products, Frost eventually decided to develop and market new delivery systems for proven drugs. He believed that he could eliminate the time, costs, and risk associated with developing entirely new drugs. True to his entrepreneurial nature, Frost kept an open mind about Key during the 1970s and early 1980s. He adjusted its goals and struck dozens of deals along the way with industry big-wigs like Pfizer Inc., Mitsubishi Chemical Industries Ltd., and several European drug companies. Largely as a result of Frost's savvy deal making, Key Pharmaceuticals went from $65,000 in losses in 1972 to a staggering $22.1 million in profits by 1984.

Frost's supreme deal related to Key transpired in March 1986. In a hurried transaction, pharmaceutical giant Schering-Plough purchased Key for an incredible $800 million. Because Frost and Jaharis still owned 30 percent of the company, Frost pocketed $150 million from the sale, cementing his position as

one of the wealthiest individuals in Miami. Frost also got a five-
year consulting contract with Schering that paid a cool half
million dollars annually. Importantly, Frost, without tipping off
Schering's management, negotiated a very favorable non-com-
pete clause with Schering's attorneys. It essentially allowed him
to remain active in the pharmaceutical industry, even if he
competed with Schering.

The Schering buyout came at an opportune time for Frost.
Although he had enjoyed transforming the company, by the
mid-1980s he was also itching to try his hand at a new type of
venture; rather than just market existing pharmaceuticals, he
wanted to create and sell new drugs, an activity that offered a
potentially greater opportunity for profit. Toward that end, Frost
started assembling IVAX. Besides purchasing Ivaco Inc., in
1986 he bought Diamedix, a medical diagnostic kit manufacturer, and Pharmedix, a pharmaceutical company. Ivaco was a
profitable company operating in a mature industry. Diamedix
and Pharmedix, in contrast, more closely resembled pre-1972
Key Pharmaceuticals—both were relatively small and losing
money when Frost purchased them. In December 1987, Frost
merged the three concerns into IVAX Corp.

Although IVAX's three companies were a strange mix, they
reflected a shrewd strategy conceived by Frost to make IVAX
into a major developer, manufacturer, and seller of proprietary
drugs. Frost planned to use Ivaco as a cash cow to fund capital-
intensive, pharmaceutical-related initiatives in a three-phase
growth strategy: First, IVAX would buy drugs that already had
passed the expensive and time-consuming regulatory approval
process. Second, cash flow from those drugs would be used to
purchase drugs that were not yet approved but had shown
promise in preliminary clinical trials. Finally, earnings from
those drugs would be devoted to the internal development of
new drugs by IVAX's own scientists.

Growth Through Acquisition:
Late 1980s–Early 1990s

IVAX maintained its general strategy in the late 1980s,
though Frost continued to seize new opportunities and adjust to
market changes. IVAX acquired several companies during its
first two full years of operation, including Baker Cummins
Pharmaceuticals Inc. and Harris Pharmaceuticals Ltd., and developed its existing businesses into more profitable enterprises.
By 1990, IVAX Corp.'s third full year of operation, the company had revenues of $60 million annually. It was still losing
money, but IVAX had positioned itself for future growth: it had
established a healthy cash flow and had plenty of money reserved for future acquisitions and development of new drugs.
Importantly, in 1990 IVAX acquired Norton Healthcare Ltd., a
leading British generic drug producer with more than 200 prod-

ucts. That purchase set the stage for IVAX's rampant growth
during the early 1990s.

Frost's love of, and knack for, cutting shrewd deals had been
a part of his personality since childhood. Born and raised in
Philadelphia, Frost developed a strong work ethic and an appreciation of salesmanship in his father's shoe store. "I always liked
that [selling shoes]," Frost reminisced in the May 1992 issue of
Florida Trend. "You know when you've done it right, and you
don't have to wait a long time to find that out." Aside from
business, another of Frost's interests and talents was science. As
a result of a scholarship offer, he enrolled in New York's Albert
Einstein College of Medicine following high school. Even there,
his bent for business came out. In fact, Frost was known by his
roommates for always knowing where the bargains were.

Norton Healthcare turned out to be a very good bargain for
IVAX. In 1991, IVAX's first full year of operation with Norton
under its corporate umbrella, IVAX achieved its first year of
profits. It earned $11.1 million on $181 million in sales. However, Frost made an even smarter purchase in December 1991
when he bought Goldline Laboratories Inc. Goldline was one of
the largest generic drug distributors in the United States, with
marketing networks reaching hospitals, nursing homes, retail
drug chains, and all other major sectors of the healthcare industry. It brought 490 employees and 1,600 new products to the
IVAX organization.

Generic drugs, which accounted for the majority of IVAX's
sales in the early 1990s, are basically molecular copies of
branded drugs. They perform the same function as the drugs
they mimic but do not benefit from patent protection. As a
result, they provide lower profit margins and are susceptible to
competing generic products. Although Goldline achieved prominence in the industry during the 1980s, bad press about generics contributed to the company's slide in the early 1990s. Goldline lost $20 million in 1990 and 1991. Nevertheless, Frost saw
potential in the lagging distributor and snapped it up. He jettisoned a troubled manufacturing plant and stepped up restructuring efforts. The results of his efforts were immediate, as Goldline began posting profits shortly after the acquisition.

Generic Success: 1992–93

Primarily as a result of its buyouts of Goldline and Norton,
IVAX's revenues spiraled upward in 1991 to $180 million and
then to a big-league $450 million in 1992. Furthermore, net
income rocketed to about $16 million in 1991 and then to
roughly $49 million in 1992. However, in 1993 Frost's acquisi-
tion of Goldline began to really pay off for IVAX. In August
1992, IVAX, through Goldline, introduced Verapamil, a breakthrough generic heart disease treatment priced 25 percent lower
than comparable brand name drugs. Massive demand made
Verapamil the largest selling generic in the history of the drug
industry. In 1993, in fact, IVAX captured revenues of $645
million, 23 percent of which were directly attributable to Verapamil. Furthermore, net income exploded to $85 million, a gain
of almost 75 percent over 1992.

Verapamil's staggering success during 1993 was augmented
by steady gains attained through numerous other product intro-

Key Dates:

1987: IVAX is established by Dr. Philip Frost.
1990: North Healthcare Ltd. is acquired.
1991: Frost purchases Goldline Laboratories Inc.
1994: McGaw Inc. and Zenith Laboratories Inc. are acquired.
1997: Merger plans with Bergen Brunswig fall through.
2001: Frost is given the National Ernst & Young Entrepreneur of the Year award.

ductions and acquisitions conducted by IVAX in the early 1990s. As sales and cash flow increased, in fact, the pace of Frost's purchases accelerated. In September 1992, for example, IVAX added H N Norton Co., a U.S. manufacturer of generic and over-the-counter drugs. Prior to that, in April, IVAX acquired Waverly Pharmaceutical Ltd., a European maker of eye drops, lens solutions, and other fluid health care products. That same month, IVAX branched out into veterinary products with its buyout of DVM Pharmaceuticals, Inc. In 1993, IVAX entered into two joint ventures in China to furnish pharmaceuticals to that massive market.

IVAX's dizzying acquisition pace was not limited to the pharmaceuticals industry. As Frost jetted around the globe in search of new deals, IVAX added a number of non-drug companies to its portfolio. In 1991, for instance, it bought Delta Biologicals S.r.l., an Italian manufacturer of diagnostic equipment. In 1992, IVAX bought out Flori Roberts, Inc., which sold a line of cosmetics for dark-skinned women. A more lucrative purchase was Frost's takeover of Johnson Products Co., Inc. in 1993. Johnson, a developer and marketer of African American personal care products, was recognized as one of the most successful black-owned businesses in the United States. IVAX also added to its original specialty chemicals division in 1993 with its purchase of Elf Atochem North America, Inc., a major producer of industrial cleaning and maintenance products.

IVAX's crowning acquisition was completed early in 1994, when it picked up McGaw Inc. for $440 million. California-based McGaw was the third-leading U.S. supplier of intravenous solutions and related equipment. The company brought 30 national distribution centers to the IVAX organization and represented a major new source of revenue. In fact, had IVAX owned McGaw during 1993 its total revenue would have been nearly $1 billion (as opposed to $645 million). A drawback of the merger was that it earned IVAX a risky credit rating. Credit analyst Standard & Poor's noted IVAX's heavy debt load, excessive use of equity financing, and heavy reliance on Verapamil, which was facing stiff competition from other generics in 1994.

Despite analyst's doubts concerning IVAX's long-term prospects, Frost and his management team viewed massive growth during the early 1990s as part of their original growth strategy. Indeed, now that IVAX had accumulated a mass of profitable, cash-producing holdings, including several pharmaceutical concerns, it was prepared to enter stage three of its long-term plan—the introduction of internally produced, proprietary drugs that would generate large profit margins. Even

without future plans for new drugs, IVAX was able to point to its (admittedly short) track record of success with its diversified core of businesses.

Going into 1994, IVAX continued to stress growth through acquisition and improvement of its existing holdings. It still had not introduced any of its own patented pharmaceuticals on a broad scale, but it had a pipeline of new drugs that it had been readying for market for several years. One of its most promising inventions was Elmiron, a drug that had already been approved in Canada as a treatment for a debilitating women's bladder disease. Elmiron was in the final stages of FDA approval early in 1994. Likewise, IVAX's Nalmefene, which could potentially treat a variety of afflictions, was also in the latter stages of development and was nearing FDA approval for some applications, such as reversal of drug overdoses. Other promising IVAX pharmaceuticals in 1994 included Ossirene, Azene, Naloxone, Scriptene, Nitric Oxide Vasodilator, and Taxol.

IVAX's long-term staying power remained a question going into the mid-1990s, but there was no uncertainty about the amazing short-term success the company had achieved since 1987. In less than seven years, IVAX had bolted from a awkward start-up to a $1 billion corporation listed in the Fortune 500. The personal success of IVAX's driving force, Frost, was just as impressive—Frost still owned nearly 20 percent of the company in 1994 and was serving as chairman, chief executive, and president.

Critics, citing IVAX's mediocre credit rating, feared that IVAX might end up like Frost's failed 1970s fish farm, or worse. However, Frost's past performance, combined with expected growth in the healthcare industry, indicated otherwise. In a February 1993 issue of *Miami Review,* analyst Richard M. Lilly asserted, "Phil Frost and the group around him, whatever their sins may have been, have created a more successful and more profitable company than anyone else in the business."

In July 1994, IVAX acquired the majority interest in Galena a.s., one of the oldest and best established pharmaceutical companies in Eastern Europe. A month later, IVAX announced the beginning of a merger with Zenith Laboratories, Inc. of Northvale, New Jersey. In October 1994, IVAX established a joint venture with Knoll AG and BASF AG for the manufacture and marketing of generic pharmaceutical products in Europe. With this joint venture and the acquisition of Galena and Zenith Laboratories, IVAX positioned itself as the world's largest international generic pharmaceutical company.

Frost made yet another effort to strengthen the company's hold on the generic market in 1995 by merging with Norway-based Hafslund Nycomed. The deal, which would have created a $2.5 billion company, fell through in November due to shareholder opposition. Despite the failed attempt, IVAX's financial growth continued its stellar pace. In 1995, the firm secured revenues of $1.3 billion while net income reached $114.8 million.

Overcoming Challenges: 1996 and Beyond

IVAX's strong position was soon challenged, however, and analyst doubts of the early 1990s began to ring true. During 1996, the pharmaceutical industry began to change shape. IVAX was forced to deal with major competition in the generics industry as well as a dramatic fall in prices. During 1996, the company posted a net loss of $160.8 million while revenues fell to $1.15 billion. The hard times continued in the following year when a second significant merger failed to come to fruition. In response to the changing industry environment, IVAX and drug wholesaler Bergen Brunswig Corp. had announced a $1.5 billion merger in late 1996. Bergen abruptly terminated the deal in March 1997. The company then filed a $50 million suit against IVAX claiming the firm had breached the merger agreement. IVAX denied the claim and the two went to court. The suit was settled in August 1997 for an undisclosed sum.

With two failed mergers under its belt, IVAX began to shift its focus to its core pharmaceuticals business. To help with the process, the company turned to industry veteran Robert Strauss, who was known for his turnaround of Cordis Corp. In May 1997, IVAX announced plans to name Strauss CEO at its upcoming annual meeting. Strauss' management style differed considerably from Frost's, however, and he soon resigned his post. David Bethune was named his replacement but left in 1998 to pursue other options.

Amid the management reshuffling, IVAX worked to restructure itself. The firm launched a cost cutting effort which included the sale of its McGaw subsidiary and various other non-core assets, jobs cuts, and the shuttering of several manufacturing facilities. It also toyed with the idea of changing its name to IVX Biosciences. The firm centered its drug development efforts on cancer treatments, respiratory-related drugs, and generic versions of proprietary drugs. With Frost maintaining both the CEO and chairman position, sales began a slow rebound. In 1998, the company secured revenues of $625.7 million and returned to profitability. In 1999, sales climbed to $656.4 million. During that year, the company received approval to market the proprietary anti-cancer drug Paxene.

IVAX's product pipeline began to strengthen, and it appeared that the firm had successfully overcome the hardships of the mid-1990s. Sales climbed to $793 million in 2000, and that year the company resumed its acquisition strategy with the purchases of Venezuelan firm Laboratorios Elmor S.A. and Wakefield Pharmaceuticals. IVAX continued to solidify its position in 2001 by acquiring Mexico-based Laboratorios Fustery S.A. de C.V., Indiana Protein Technologies, and Chile's largest pharmaceutical company, Laboratorio Chile S.A. During 2002, the firm also acquired Merck & Co.'s generic business in France. The firm's product line was bolstered by the acquisition of the proprietary intranasal steroid formulations of flunisolide hemihydrate used to treat allergic rhinitis under the brand names of Nasarel, Nasalide, Rhinalar, Syntaris, Locasyn, and Lokilan. IVAX also gained exclusive U.S. rights to QVAR, an asthma drug delivered in a metered dose inhaler with a non-ozone depleting propellant.

By 2001, sales had reached $1.2 billion. Frost's efforts to keep IVAX afloat in the highly competitive drug industry had paid off, and he had proved critics wrong. His business know-how was recognized that year when he was given the National Ernst & Young Entrepreneur of the Year award, an honor that placed him among upper echelon in the business world.

Despite the company's apparent turnaround, it continued to face slowing sales and declining prices. Nevertheless, Frost and his management team remained optimistic about IVAX's future. With promising new drugs in the company's pipeline and demand for its generic drugs expected to increase, IVAX appeared to be on track for future success.

Principal Subsidiaries

IVAX Pharmaceuticals Inc.; IVAX Laboratories; IVAX Research; DVM Pharmaceuticals Inc.; Indiana Protein Technologies; IVAX Pharmaceuticals UK; IVAX Pharmaceuticals SRO (Czech Republic); IVAX Drug Research Institute (Hungary); IVAX Scandinavia AB (Sweden); IVAX Argentina; Laboratorios Elmor S.A. (Venezuela); IVAX Mexico; Laboratorio Chile S.A.; IVAX Asia Limited (Hong Kong).

Principal Competitors

Barr Laboratories Inc.; Bristol-Myers Squibb Company; Teva Pharmaceuticals Industries Ltd.

Further Reading

Anderson, Veronica, "Bidder a Stark Contrast to Lagging Johnson," *Crain's Chicago Business*, June 21, 1993, p. 3.

Chandler, Michele, "Despite Losses, Miami-Based Drugmaker Ivax is Upbeat," *Miami Herald*, January 24, 1998.

——, "Ivax Chairman See Better Times Ahead for Pharmaceutical," *Miami Herald*, June 6 1998.

——, "Miami Drug Firm Ivax Corp. to Buy Mexican Pharmaceutical Company," *Miami Herald*, October 13, 2000.

Guinta, Peter, "Frost Is Building Another Drug Firm," *South Florida Business Journal*, December 7, 1987, p. 1.

Hagy, James R., "The Thrill of the Deal," *Florida Trend*, May 1992, p. 58.

Hensely, Scott, "Week in Healthcare: A Mysterious Breakup," *Modern Healthcare*, April 21, 1997.

Hosford, Christopher, "Following Frost's Footsteps," *South Florida Business Journal*, November 23, 1992, p. 1A.

"IVAX to Acquire Laboratorio Chile for $395 Million," *New York Times*, May 22, 2001.

Miller, Susan R., "Ivax's Elusive Cure," *Broward Daily Business Review*, November 12, 1997, p. A1.

Miracle, Barbara, and Janice G. Sharp, "The Florida CEO: Who Delivers—and Who Doesn't," *Florida Trend*, June 1994, p. 39.

Mowatt, Twig, "IVAX, Finally Has Seen the Competition," *Miami Daily Business Review*, April 4, 1994, p. A1.

Popolillo, Melissa C., "IVAX Moves Forward to Bolster Business Unit Sales Performance," *Drug Store News*, June 22, 1998, CP8.

Poppe, David, "IVAX Acquisitions, Not Development, Pay the Way," *Miami Review*, February 5, 1993, p. A12.

"Price Wars Behind IVAX's Higher Net Loss," *Medical Industry Today*, May 8, 1997.

Rubinger, Robert S., "United-Guardian to Market Products in Mainland China," *Business Wire*, June 2, 1993.

Sheridan, Mike, "Ivax '02 Profits Off 50% on Slower Sales," *Chemical News & Intelligence*, February 13, 2003.

Stieghorst, Tom, "IVAX Completes Buyout, Gains S&P Rating," *Sun-Sentinel*, March 29, 1994, p. D3.

—Dave Mote
—update: Christina M. Stansell

J.F. Shea Co., Inc.

655 Brea Canyon Road
Walnut, California 91789
U.S.A.
Telephone: (909) 594-9500
Fax: (909) 594-0957
Web site: http://www.jfshea.com

Private Company
Incorporated: 1881 as John F. Shea Plumbing Company
Employees: 150
Sales: $1.96 billion (2001)
NAIC: 237210 Land Subdivision; 233210 Single Family
Housing Construction

J.F. Shea Co., Inc. is one of the largest privately held construction companies in the United States. J.F. Shea comprises a collection of companies and divisions, including Shea Mortgage, Shea Properties, the Venture Capital Division, J.F. Shea Construction Inc., the Redding Division, Reed Manufacturing, and Shea Homes. Through Shea Homes, the company's primary business, J.F. Shea develops master-planned communities in California, Arizona, Colorado, and North Carolina.

Origins

J.F. Shea traces its corporate roots to the John F. Shea Plumbing Company, a plumbing contractor and wholesale supplier of plumbing equipment. The company was founded in Portland, Oregon, in 1881, by its namesake. With the establishment of his plumbing company, John Shea created a family business that would draw upon the talents of four generations of Shea family members—a legacy spanning more than a century—but the enduring strength of the company stemmed neither from the plumbing business, nor did it emanate from Portland. Instead, J.F. Shea's success and reputation was achieved in the construction industry, specifically in assisting in the construction of major civil engineering projects. The transformation from a plumbing business into a heavy construction business also included the company's relocation from the Pacific Northwest to northern California, the hub of J.F. Shea's operations for much of the 20th century.

J.F. Shea entered the construction business as an offshoot of its plumbing activities. During the 1910s, John Shea and his son Charlie formed the J.F. Shea Company, the abbreviated corporate title signaling the company's entrance into sewer construction. Not long after the company entered the sewer construction field, John Shea's other sons, Gilbert and Edmund, joined the family business.

One of the company's first large-scale projects was completed during the 1920s. During the decade, J.F. Shea constructed the Portland Seawall on the Willamette River. The company's connection to northern California was established during the decade as well, brought about through the construction of the Mokelumne pipeline, which transported water across central California to cities such as Oakland and Berkeley. The construction of the Mokelumne pipeline helped establish the company's reputation outside the Pacific Northwest, leading to its involvement in several of the largest civil engineering projects of the 20th century. During the 1930s, J.F. Shea built the foundation piers for the Golden Gate Bridge in San Francisco and assisted in the construction of the San Francisco-Oakland Bay Bridge. The company also served as the construction manager for the Hoover Dam, which ranked as the tallest dam in the United States when it was completed in 1936.

J.F. Shea's involvement in the massive construction projects of the 1930s gave the business a secure place within the heavy construction industry, but the company's promising new role in civil engineering was put on hold for much of the 1940s. The outbreak of World War II diverted the attention of nearly all types of businesses, forcing them to respond to the different conditions and demands of a country at war. J.F Shea spent the war years building liberty ships and shipyards. Construction activity of the type the company had become used to during the 1930s slowed, prompting management to invest in new industries, such as aluminum, magnesium, and cement.

Post-World War II Growth

The 1950s brought in the third generation of leaders at the company, John Shea and cousins Peter and Edmund. The three Sheas took command of the company's heavy construction operations during the 1950s, beginning the diversification and

Company Perspectives:

Built on a solid foundation, J.F. Shea Co., Inc. has inherited the family commitment to hard work and pride in a job well done. Today, the company upholds the ethics and principles established by John Shea more than a century ago.

expansion that eventually created the multifaceted collection of business interests that described the company's operations at the end of the 20th century. In 1957, the establishment of the Shea Sand and Gravel Plant marked the beginning of what became known as the J.F. Shea Redding Division, a supplier of aggregate materials to contractors and government agencies. As it matured, the Redding Division's business scope increased to embrace highway and bridge construction and repair work in northern California. Through a collection of gravel, asphalt, and concrete plants and quarries, the Redding Division produced construction materials and contracted for construction projects in northern California. During the 1950s, J.F. Shea also established Shasta Electric, a full-service electrical contractor offering services for commercial and industrial construction customers.

The diversification begun during the 1950s continued in earnest during the 1960s, as J.F. Shea followed the prevailing corporate trend of the era. Many companies sought to achieve financial consistency and stability by entering a range of businesses, thereby reducing dependence on the caprices of a single line of business. During the decade, J.F. Shea established Shea Homes, moving the company into residential housing construction—a business of vital importance to the company's financial well-being at the end of the 20th century. The company also divested its interests in the "smokestack" industries it had invested in during the 1940s. The money subsequently was diverted to high-technology investments, leading to the establishment in 1968 of the J.F. Shea Venture Capital Division. Through Venture Capital, J.F. Shea began investing in private start-up companies. Among the list of fledgling concerns aided by J.F. Shea were Compaq Computer Corporation, Brocade Corp., Exodus Corp., and Altera Corp.

Although the 1960s marked J.F. Shea's transformation into a diversified concern, the company continued to be a heavy construction firm at its core. The decade that saw the company delve into the venture capital business and into residential construction also included several major construction projects. J.F Shea constructed tunnels and stations for the San Francisco Bay Area Rapid Transit System, more commonly known as BART. J.F. Shea's contributions to BART helped the company secure another high-profile project during the 1970s, when it assisted in the construction of Metro, the subway system in Washington, D.C. The decade also saw the company broaden its business scope further. J.F. Shea established Shea Properties, the commercial and residential investment and management arm of the family business. Through Shea Properties, the company invested in and managed apartment buildings and commercial real estate, at first in California and then in Colorado. J.F. Shea also completed an acquisition during the 1970s, purchasing Reed Manufacturing, a producer of concrete guns and pumps used in civil, residential, and commercial construction projects.

During the 1980s, Shea Homes came to the fore, its growth fanned by the rapidly expanding real estate industry in California. Shea Homes began developing master-planned communities throughout California, registering enough success to warrant the establishment of a division in Arizona at the end of the decade. Meanwhile, aided by the same robust real estate market, Shea Properties substantially expanded its portfolio of retail and commercial properties.

1990s: Expansion of Homebuilding Operations Through Acquisitions

During the 1990s, J.F. Shea's fourth generation of family management—led by COO John, Jr., Ed, and Gil—spearheaded the company's geographic expansion. The company's residential construction business led the way during the decade, as Shea Homes developed into one of the largest privately held developers of residential communities in the United States. Before 1989, J.F. Shea's involvement in residential construction was limited to California markets, but an acquisition completed in the last year of the decade pushed the company beyond the Golden State's borders. In 1989, the company purchased Knoell Homes, a large-volume construction company that had built roughly 800 homes in Phoenix, Arizona, two years before its acquisition by J.F. Shea. The acquisition gave Shea Homes its Phoenix-based Arizona Division, an enterprise that served as a springboard for further geographic expansion

Initially, the Arizona Division fared poorly. By 1991, the number of sale closings in the Phoenix market had fallen to 324 homes, down substantially from the 800 closings recorded four years earlier. If it was any solace to Shea Homes' Phoenix-based executives, their troubles were shared by other homebuilders in the Phoenix area. The total number of new housing permits had fallen from 18,000 in the mid-1980s to 10,000 by the beginning of the 1990s, signaling the onset of a recessive real estate market. At this moment of vulnerability, Shea Homes' management team showed its mettle, turning the company's troubled state into a position of strength. Instead of retreating in the face of a contracting market, Shea Homes restructured its Arizona Division and launched an aggressive land-purchasing program in 1991. Land prices offered exceptional values, spurring management to purchase as much land as possible. The Arizona Division quickly put the purchased land to use. In a May 1994 interview with *Professional Builder and Remodeler,* a Shea Homes executive remarked, "We also put houses in the ground as quickly as possible with new plans. The timing was just right. The market was turning around." Thanks to the aggressive stance, the Arizona Division recorded a substantial surge in business, closing 1,337 homes in 1993. Between 1991 and 1993, the operation's market share in Phoenix increased from 2.7 percent to 7.4 percent.

As J.F. Shea entered the latter half of the 1990s, the actions of Shea Homes accounted for the major successes of the period. There were two important developments outside residential construction: Shea Mortgage, the home financing arm of the family enterprise, was established, and J.F. Shea Construction, the heavy construction arm, completed an acquisition of a southern California construction company; but the biggest news revolved around the acquisitions and expansion completed by Shea Homes. Shea Homes expanded its operating territory to include residential construction in Colorado, where the com-

Key Dates:

1881: John F. Shea Plumbing Company is founded.
1910s: Business is renamed J.F. Shea Company.
1989: Knoell Homes is acquired, moving J.F. Shea into the Arizona residential construction market.
1996: Shea Homes enters the Colorado homebuilding market.
1997: Mission Viejo Co. is acquired, greatly expanding homebuilding assets in Colorado and California.
1998: UDC Homes is purchased, giving Shea Homes the largest homebuilder in Phoenix.

pany entered the Denver market in 1996, and to North Carolina, where housing communities were developed in Charlotte. By the end of 1996, the company recorded $600 million in home sales, enough to make it the 23rd largest homebuilder in the United States. During the ensuing two years, the company's stature would increase substantially, as Shea Homes completed two pivotal acquisitions that increased its presence in California, Colorado, and Arizona.

In 1997, Shea Homes gave its fledgling Colorado homebuilding business a tremendous boost. The company reportedly paid $480 million for Mission Viejo Co., an acquisition that included two developments in southern California—Mission Viejo and Aliso Viejo—and a sprawling community in Colorado dubbed Highlands Ranch. The properties in southern California comprised 900 acres, while the Highlands Ranch property measured 22,000 acres, or seven square miles. Highlands Ranch, the prize asset of the acquisition, contained 14,800 homes, but at the time of the acquisition 3,600 acres remained to be developed, enough to build an additional 16,000 homes. With the addition of Mission Viejo Co., Shea Homes was able to sell more than 3,000 homes in 1997, generating more than $1 billion in residential construction revenue.

The acquisition of Mission Viejo Co. was followed by an equally prodigious purchase. In mid-1998, Shea Homes agreed to acquire UDC Homes, the largest homebuilder in Phoenix and one of the major developers of housing for seniors. Additionally, UDC owned lots for nearly 1,600 new homes in southern California. The acquisition of UDC drew praise from industry observers. One real estate analyst, in a July 11, 1998 interview with the *Los Angeles Times,* remarked: "Shea came through the tough [recessionary] times very strong, and they have been pursuing a brilliant strategy of expanding strategically into Colorado and Orange County. They've been able to go into these [new markets] and create more value than was previously there through intelligent planning, development, and marketing."

Combined, the acquisition of Mission Viejo and UDC represented a transaction value of nearly $1 billion. The magnitude

of the acquisitions left J.F. Shea primarily focused on the development of master-planned communities, although the company continued to operate as a heavy construction contractor. In the years after the two signal acquisitions, J.F. Shea attempted to acquire Del Webb Corp., a Phoenix-based builder of retirement homes. Against the wishes of Del Webb's management, J.F. Shea launched a $690 million bid for the Phoenix company, but the deal lapsed in November 2000. John F. Shea, the company's chairman and CEO, expressed a desire to resume what he termed "further constructive dialogue," according to the November 2, 2000 issue of *Business Wire,* but no definitive agreement had been reached by the end of 2002. That same year, Shea Homes, the main engine driving J.F. Shea's growth, gained a new leader. In January, Roy Humphreys announced his retirement, ending his 27-year tenure at the company. Humphreys joined Shea Homes in 1974 as an offsite coordinator for the Southern California division before being appointed as Shea Homes' president in 1980. Humphreys was replaced by Bert Selva, who joined Shea Homes in 1996 to head the company's Colorado operations. Selva was named president and chief executive officer in February 2002.

Principal Subsidiaries

Shea Homes; Shea Mortgage; Shea Properties; J.F. Shea Construction Inc.; Reed Manufacturing.

Principal Divisions

Venture Capital Division; Redding Division.

Principal Competitors

KB Home; Pulte Homes, Inc.; Tutor-Saliba Corporation.

Further Reading

Benderoff, Eric, "How to Position Product for Profit," *Professional Builder and Remodeler,* May 1994, p. 78.

Fulmer, Melinda, "Real Estate: Deal for Mission Viejo Co. Would Give Builder Control of Large Parcels in Orange County and Colorado," *Los Angeles Times,* August 2, 1997, p. D1.

McLeister, Editor, "Decentralization Gives Strength to Shea Homes," *Professional Builder,* December 1994, p. 68.

Rebchook, John, "California Home Builder Buys Highlands Ranch," *Rocky Mountain News,* September 3, 1997, p. 8B.

——, "Highlands Ranch Bought Calif. Home Builder Poised to Be Major Player in Colorado's Booming Market," August 2, 1997, p. 1B.

Sanchez, Jesus, "J.F. Shea Unit Plans to Acquire UDC Homes of Ariz.," *Los Angeles Times,* July 11, 1998, p. 4.

Strickland, Daryl, "Shea Properties Moving to New Aliso Viejo Park," *Los Angeles Times,* March 2, 2000, p. C4.

—Jeffrey L. Covell

Jazz Basketball Investors, Inc.

36 South State Street
Salt Lake City, Utah 84111-1401
U.S.A.
Telephone: (801) 325-2500
Fax: (801) 325-2562
Web site: http://www.nba.com/jazz

Wholly Owned Subsidiary of Larry H. Miller Group
Founded: 1974
Employees: 85
Sales: $87 million (2002)
NAIC: 711211 Sports Teams and Clubs; 711310
    Promoters of Performing Arts, Sports, and Similar
    Events with Facilities; 448150 Clothing Accessories
    Stores

Jazz Basketball Investors, Inc., owns the Utah Jazz, one of the most successful franchises in the National Basketball Association (NBA). Led since the late 1980s by forward Karl Malone and point guard John Stockton, the Jazz have appeared in the NBA playoffs every year since the 1985–86 season, including two trips to the finals in 1996–97 and 1997–98. More remarkably, the Jazz have consistently been among the NBA's attendance leaders, despite the fact that Salt Lake City is one of the smallest markets in the league. In 2001–2002 Utah drew 766,108 spectators, tenth in the NBA and better than much larger cities such as Boston, Detroit, and Atlanta. As the 2003–2004 season got underway, the team's popularity showed little sign of waning despite a rebuilding program anticipating the retirements of Malone and Stockton.

The 1970s in New Orleans

The Jazz basketball team was formed in early 1974 when the National Basketball Association awarded a franchise to the city of New Orleans. A group led by majority owner Sam Battistone and various local investors paid $6.15 million for the privilege of becoming the NBA's 18th member. The team's nickname was selected in a radio contest. The Jazz players who opened the

1974–75 season were largely veterans selected in the league expansion draft. However, they also included "Pistol" Pete Maravich, a player acquired in the Jazz's first trade, who quickly developed into one of the flashiest, most exciting performers in pro basketball. The Jazz named Scotty Robertson head coach, with former Lakers star Elgin Baylor as one of his assistants.

New Orleans had little basketball tradition, and it was common knowledge that, rather than joining the NBA, many in the city would have preferred a major league baseball franchise. A New Orleans television station aired the team's opening game— and was unable to sell a single minute of advertising. The Jazz lost that first game, and when the team finally played its home opener on October 24, 1974, it had a 0–4 win–loss record. Still, the town welcomed it with a celebration worthy of New Orleans. While jazzman Al Hirt blew his trumpet on court, 6,450 fans accompanied him on toy horns. Despite all the excitement, the Jazz lost its first home game too. The losing streak stretched out to ten games before the team finally managed a win against Portland in mid-November. A week later Robertson had been fired as coach and replaced by Butch van Breda Kolff, who for the next three years would be a popular fixture in New Orleans.

Coaching changes were not enough to make the young team a contender in the NBA. The Jazz's losing record continued under van Breda Kolff and under Elgin Baylor who replaced him in 1976. In fact, the Jazz would never have a winning season while they were in New Orleans. They seemed to be aiming at the playoffs in 1977–78, until a late season slump ended their hopes. While the Jazz were among the worst performing teams in the NBA, New Orleans warmed to the concept of its NBA team, and Jazz games were well-attended, consistently over the league average.

Canny promotional offers also helped the team realize single-game attendance records. Beginning in 1975, the Jazz played in New Orleans' mammoth Superdome, the largest venue in basketball. The team frequently attracted over 20,000 to the Dome and occasionally, against popular opponents like the Los Angeles Lakers or the Philadelphia 76ers, drew more than 30,000 fans.

However, playing in the Superdome also brought with it a host of challenges. Its seating capacity worked against the club

---

Company Perspectives:

The company's mission is to enhance the quality of life in Utah. As an organization we believe we must be part of the community and that we must give back to the community. We believe this can be accomplished through superior customer service and by our employees and players being of service and involved in charitable and community efforts. Winning on the court is what basketball is all about . . . but lifting and strengthening the community that supports you is what business should be about.

---

in some ways. Because fans knew that tickets would virtually always be available on the day of games, the Jazz found it exceedingly difficult to sell season tickets. In its last season in New Orleans, the club had only 2,600 season ticket holders. Large numbers of discount tickets also helped win capacity crowds in New Orleans which further suppressed income, as did the lack of luxury boxes and club seats, which had not yet been introduced in 1979.

Finally, the Superdome presented a greater challenge. It was a multipurpose arena that served a number of other events, such as major conventions and Mardi Gras celebrations, which tended to take precedence over Jazz basketball. Mardi Gras events, for example, would take over the Dome every year for over a month, forcing the Jazz to play on the road during that time. "A month on the road would put a crimp into anybody's won-lost record," Battistone told the *Times-Picayune*, "and we were facing that every year." Real problems would have developed had the Jazz gone into the playoffs while in New Orleans. There was no contingency plan at the Superdome, the team would have had to find another "home" court on which to play. "Teams have much more leverage today where they play," Lee Schlesinger, one of several local minority investors in the Jazz told the *Times-Picayune*. "We had no leverage. We had nowhere to go. I don't think the teams at that time, particularly in New Orleans, had any leverage. It was very difficult."

By the end of the 1978–79 season, the Jazz's difficult position in New Orleans was compounded by additional issues, including ticket taxes that were the highest in the nation and lukewarm support from government and business leaders, who—Jazz management sensed—were still hoping for a baseball franchise for the city.

In summer 1979, when majority owner Sam Battistone announced the decision to move the team to a new home in Salt Lake City, Utah, some New Orleans boosters felt that Battistone had sold the city out. Detractors maintained that the owner, who almost never visited New Orleans, simply wanted to move the team closer to his home in California, and that Salt Lake City, the capital of his Mormon faith, was a convenient choice. On the other hand, the team's proposal for the move, submitted to the NBA, claimed operating losses during its five-year tenure in New Orleans that totaled approximately $5 million. Other questions remained about the wisdom of the proposed move. At question was whether Salt Lake City, much smaller than New Orleans and home of another team (the Utah Stars) that had folded in 1975.

Moving to Salt Lake City in the 1980s

When the newly-christened Utah Jazz opened their first season in Salt Lake City's Salt Palace in 1979–80 few of the questions that surrounded the move had been answered. If anything, there were more. Pete Maravich would soon end his remarkable career. Elgin Baylor had been replaced by Tom Nissalke as head coach. The most important move made by the fledgling Utah team did not involve a player or coach, but rather the appointment of general manager, Frank Layden, who would prove instrumental in transforming the Jazz into a championship contender.

One of the first of Layden's inspired moves was to trade recently-acquired Spencer Haywood to the Los Angeles Lakers for versatile Adrian Dantley, who would soon fill Maravich's shoes as the team's scoring leader. Adding Darrell Griffith in the 1980 college draft, the Jazz put together a deadly scoring combo that averaged 51.3 points a game in 1980–81. The 1983 addition of Thurl Bailey and Bobby Hansen finally put the Jazz over the top—the team enjoyed its first winning season and its first trip to the NBA playoffs in 1983–84. Frank Layden, who by then was also coaching the Jazz, was named the NBA Coach of the Year.

After that season, the Jazz would rarely be absent from the playoffs, thanks in great measure to All-Star guard John Stockton, signed in 1984, and power forward Karl Malone in 1985.

Despite its steadily improving performance on the court, a significantly better arena lease, and a larger base of season ticket holders, the Utah Jazz remained in a precarious financial situation.

By 1985, after 11 years in the NBA, the team had lost a total of $17 million, and Sam Battistone began entertaining offers to sell the franchise. The most serious came from investors in Minnesota who planned to move the team there. The possibility of losing its second pro basketball team in a decade mobilized Salt Lake and its business community. In April 1985 Battistone's company, StratAmerica, announced that it had sold a 50 percent interest in the Jazz to Utah auto baron Larry H. Miller. Although the $8 million Battistone was asking was "well in excess of my net worth" Miller later recalled, he managed to raise the money in nine days. As part of the agreement, Miller also assumed 50 percent of the club's deferred compensation debt, which bailed the team out financially for a time. Through StratAmerica, Battistone continued to manage the team's day-to-day business for some time.

A year after the partial sale, Miller formed Jazz Basketball Investors, which acquired a loan package worth $3.6 million, and in October 1986, he bought the Jazz in full for $9 million and the assumption of all the team's outstanding debt. At the time Miller and Battistone turned down another offer from Minnesota buyers to purchase the Jazz for $25 million. One of Miller's first priorities upon assuming ownership was to put the team's business on solid ground. Using every tax loophole in the book and putting an end to questionable practices such as giving away thousands of free season tickets to area businesses every year, Miller managed to turn a $123,000 profit in 1987.

A key part of Miller's turnaround involved getting Salt Lake to see what a valuable asset it had in the Jazz. He warned

Key Dates:

1974: A group of New Orleans investors pays $6.15 for a franchise in the National Basketball Association.
1975: The New Orleans Jazz move from Municipal Stadium to the Superdome.
1979: The team moves to Salt Lake City.
1984: The Jazz have their first winning season.
1986: Larry H. Miller becomes the new owner of the Jazz.
1991: The team moves from Salt Palace to the new Delta Center.
2002: The company opens a state-of-the-art training facility in Salt Lake City.

community leaders that if the city lost a second basketball team it would likely never get another one. Salt Lake City, led by the chamber of commerce, responded. Corporate sponsors were signed on; season ticket sales soared.

A Basketball Powerhouse in the 1990s

The city helped the Jazz again two years later. When NBA player salaries soared following a new contract in 1988, Miller found that in order to meet his payroll, he needed the Jazz to play in a larger arena. With a waiting list of some 12,000 fans every game at the Salt Palace, Miller knew he could fill a larger venue. In 1990 the Salt Lake Redevelopment Agency floated $20 million in bonds to purchase the site. Miller, eschewing a trend in the 1980s and 1990s that saw communities footing the bill for private stadium and arenas, financed the construction of the Jazz's new Delta Center out of his own pocket, with $5 million of his own money and $66 million in funding from Japan's Sumitomo Trust and Banking Company Limited, which he borrowed. "I am against public subsidies of private enterprises," he later told the *Salt Lake Tribune*. The Jazz played their first game in the 19,000 seat Delta Center October 4,1991.

As owner, Miller put together an exemplary front office organization and showed an unusual ability for retaining talent. Miller forged solid relationships with stars Karl Malone and John Stockton, two of the all-time greats at their positions, proved himself a genial boss, and made Utah a pleasant enough home that neither Malone nor Stockton were tempted to test their true value on the free agent market. Nonetheless, the early 1990s tested Malone's resolve to stay. With the Jazz as playoff perennials, Malone took offense at the astronomical salaries commanded by phenoms new to the NBA. Miller was willing to renegotiate the veteran's contract to keep him in Utah, giving him in 1993 a package worth $28 million over a seven-year period. Miller extended Malone's contract again in 1999, a deal reportedly worth $16.5 million a season for Malone. In 1996, John Stockton—a two-time Olympic basketball gold medalist and the NBA's career leader in assists and steals—signed a new contract reportedly worth $15 million. With its no-trade clause, the deal seemed to guarantee that Stockton would finish his career with the Jazz.

The end of Jazz's 1996–97 season took on a storybook quality. Playing in the sixth game of the semi-final playoff round, Utah fought back from a 12-point deficit late in the game

to tie it with just seconds remaining. John Stockton took the inbounds pass and put the ball in the basket as the buzzer sounded, sending the team to the NBA Finals. Unfortunately, there they faced Michael Jordan's Chicago Bulls then at the peak of their form, and lost the last series. The Jazz made it to the Finals the following year as well, only to see the Bulls defeat them in six games once again.

Into the 2000s

In October 2002, the NBA approved the transfer of the Charlotte Hornets franchise to the Jazz's old home of New Orleans, and Larry Miller announced that he would be willing to sell the Jazz name back to New Orleans, a possibility of which Hornets management expressed interest.

In December 2002, Miller added another sports complex to his Jazz holdings. The club purchased an old furniture warehouse and converted it to a state-of-the-art training facility that included two NBA-sized courts with bleacher seating for more than 700 at each. The structure also included office space for some of Miller's other businesses. The cost of the renovation was $7 million.

The Utah Jazz's Larry Miller drew praise from NBA commissioner David Stern as an "A-plus" owner, who bought the club for $17 million in the mid-1980s and grew its value to about $200 by 2000. "He's not afraid to take chances, to follow his instincts," Jazz president told the *Salt Lake Tribune*. "That's what puts the Larry Millers of the world ahead of everyone else."

Principal Competitors

Utah Grizzlies Hockey Club; Utah Utes.

Further Reading

Cooper, Carrie, "JAZZ Training Facility," *Intermountain Contractor*, December 2002, p. 52.
"Deal Completed For Share of Jazz," *New York Times*, May 11, 1985.
Finney, Peter, "Former Jazzman James remembers 1970s NBA Hoopla," *Times-Picayune* (New Orleans), October 30, 2002, p. 1.
——, "It's a New Game This Time Around," *Times-Picayune* (New Orleans), October 31, 2002, p. 1.
"Jazz Name May Be For Sale," *Seattle Times*, October 9, 2002, p. D2.
Lewis, Michael C., "The Jazz—25 Years and Still Trying," *Salt Lake Tribune*, May 8, 1999, p. B1.
"New Arena Proposed For Jazz," *St. Louis Post-Dispatch*, February 15, 1989, p. 3D.
Oberbeck, Steven, "Utah Jazz Owner Renegotiates for Track Expansion," *Salt Lake Tribune*, September 5, 2002.
Smith, Jimmy, "Foul Timing," *Times-Picayune* (New Orleans), April 1, 2002, p. 1.
"Stratamerica Announces New $3.5 Million Financing Package," *Business Wire*, May 16, 1986.
"Stratamerica Completes $9 Million Sale of Utah Jazz Basketball Team to Larry H. Miller," *Business Wire*, October 1, 1986.
"Sumitomo Trust & Banking Closes $66 Million Loan For Construction Of New Home For Utah Jazz," *PR Newswire*, September 6, 1990.

—Gerald E. Brennan

مؤسسة البترول الكويتية
Kuwait Petroleum Corporation

Kuwait Petroleum Corporation

Salhia Complex
Fahed Al Salem Street
P.O. Box 26565
Safat 13126
Kuwait
Telephone: 965 240-0960
Fax: 965 240-7872
Web site: http://www.kpc.com.kw

State-Owned Company
Incorporated: 1980 as Kuwait Petroleum Company
Sales: KD9 billion ($28 billion) (2002 est.)
NAIC: 324110 Petroleum Refineries; 211111 Crude
    Petroleum and Natural Gas Extraction

Kuwait Petroleum Corporation (KPC) operates as a state-owned integrated oil and gas concern. Its operations include onshore and offshore upstream exploration and production, refining, marketing, retailing, petrochemical production, and marine transportation. Having successfully overcome the 1990 Iraqi invasion of its homeland, KPC spent most of the 1990s focused on international expansion. Through its subsidiaries, the firm markets over 300,000 barrels of crude oil per day in Western Europe and Thailand. Kuwait is home to the third largest oil reserve in the world, and KPC has reserves of 96.5 billion barrels of oil.

Early History: 1930s–40s

Although KPC was established only in January 1980, it took over a number of companies that had been active in Kuwait for much longer. The most important of these was the Kuwait Oil Company, which was incorporated in London on February 2, 1934, with an initial issued capital of £50,000 owned in equal shares by the Anglo-Persian Oil Company—later Anglo-Iranian Oil Company and then British Petroleum Company (BP)—and Gulf Oil Corporation of the United States. On December 23 of the same year, the ruler of Kuwait granted an exclusive concession to the Kuwait Oil Company (KOC), to explore for, produce, and market Kuwait's oil. The concession covered the whole country and was to last for 75 years. The formation of Kuwait Oil had been in part the result of a prolonged diplomatic dispute between Britain, the dominant power in the Middle East, and the United States, which supported U.S. oil companies' claims to participate in petroleum development in the region. The KOC formed part of a network of consortia of major U.K. and U.S. oil companies that controlled the Middle Eastern oil industry and that had made its first appearance in the Iraq Petroleum Company formed in 1928.

KOC began drilling for oil in 1936. Oil had been discovered in Iraq in 1927 and in Bahrain in 1932, and it was widely believed that Kuwait held equally good prospects. In May 1936, the first drilling began at Bahra, in north Kuwait, but eventually reached 7,950 feet without producing oil. Meanwhile, drilling had also started in October 1937, at Burgan, in south Kuwait. On the night of February 23, 1938, the drillers struck high-pressure oil in large quantities. This was the start of the Kuwait oil industry. Eight more wells were drilled at Burgan before July 1942, when all operations had to be suspended and all completed wells plugged with cement, because of the wartime emergency. After World War II ended in 1945, operations resumed, and in June 1946 the first Kuwaiti oil exports began.

Between 1946 and 1950 Kuwaiti oil production grew from 5.93 million barrels to 125.72 million barrels, making Kuwait the third-biggest Middle Eastern oil producer after Iran and Saudi Arabia. However, the real breakthrough came with the cessation of oil exports from Iran between 1951 and 1954 because of the dispute between the Iranian government and the Anglo-Iranian Oil Company. KOC rapidly increased Kuwaiti output to replace the Iranian crude. By 1955, it had 185 producing wells in operation in Kuwait, and annual production had reached nearly 400 million barrels, the highest output in the Middle East. Throughout almost all of the next 15 years, Kuwaiti oil production retained this leading position, until it was gradually overtaken by Saudi Arabia and Iran toward the end of the 1960s.

Oil transformed Kuwait. In the 1930s the country was largely desert, with most of its population of 70,000 concentrated around the mud-walled trading and fishing port of Kuwait town. An average annual rainfall of four inches and a lack of irrigation permitted little agriculture. Almost all food and all drinking water were imported, and the economy was based on pearl fishing, shipbuilding, and entrepôt trade. Oil revenues transformed the situation, especially after 1952 when it was agreed that the net profits of the industry would be shared evenly between Kuwait and the oil companies. By 1961, Kuwait, with a total population of 320,000, of whom only 50 percent were nationals, had one of the highest per capita incomes in the world. Nationals were given free medical treatment and free education, and the infrastructure of an advanced welfare state was created.

The Formation of OPEC: 1960

This wealth did nothing to reduce a growing irritation in Kuwait—and elsewhere—with Western control over its oil resources. The consortium system limited the bargaining power of host governments, for they faced only one producer. Iran's dispute in 1951 with the Anglo-Iranian Oil Company was just the first sign of general resentment at the system which spread throughout the Middle East in the 1950s and 1960s. In 1958, the Kuwaiti government granted a concession to the Arabian Oil Company, a Japanese venture in which the Kuwaiti government had a 10 percent shareholding. In 1960, Kuwait joined the Organization of Petroleum Exporting Countries (OPEC) as a founder member. OPEC's objective was to unify and coordinate the petroleum policies of its members and protect their interests against the Western oil companies. In the same year, the government organized the Kuwait National Petroleum Company (KNPC) as a joint enterprise owned 60 percent and 40 percent by the government and private sectors, respectively. For the next two decades, this element of private ownership distinguished KNPC from most other national oil companies in the Middle East. In 1962, KOC was made to relinquish 60 percent of the areas included in its concession to KNPC.

During the 1960s, the Kuwaiti government sought to increase the share of oil income staying in Kuwait, especially by promoting downstream development. The government attempted to persuade KOC to begin refining operations, but the company resisted. Economically, there was an overwhelming case for locating refineries near centers of consumption rather than of production, and the vast majority of new refining capacity installed in the decades after World War II was in Western Europe and the United States. However KOC, like the other Western oil companies in this period, underestimated the extent to which nationalist feelings were growing, even in conservative and pro-Western states such as Kuwait and Saudi Arabia. Kuwait also had a special interest in building refining capacity.

It would not only provide for technology transfer into Kuwait and create jobs, but by using advanced refinery technology it could counterbalance Kuwait's relatively weak export position, the result of its rather poor-quality crude oil. Eventually, KNPC decided to enter refining itself, and it started operating a refinery at Shuaiba—near the oil pipeline terminal—in 1968.

The Western oil consortia in the Middle East collapsed in the early 1970s during a dramatic restructuring of the industry. The most obvious manifestation of the restructuring was the huge rise in world oil prices in 1973. During the opening years of the 1970s, there was a rush of agreements designed to give producer-governments a stake in oil companies. In 1974, one such participation agreement transferred 60 percent of KOC's ownership to the state of Kuwait, the remaining 40 percent being divided equally between BP and Gulf Oil. In 1975, the Kuwaiti government took over this remaining 40 percent. In 1976, the Kuwait Oil Tanker Co. (KOTC), established in 1957 by private Kuwaiti interests, was converted to 49 percent state ownership, and it was fully nationalized in 1979. Also in 1976, a minority private sector shareholding in Petrochemical Industries Co. (PIC), established in 1963, was similarly bought out.

1980s Establishment of KPC

In January 1980, Kuwait Petroleum Company (KPC) was established as a holding company responsible for the overall management of this group of companies, together with the government's share of the capital of the Arabian Oil Company of Japan. Operations were rationalized, with KOC restricting its activities to exploration and production and KNPC to refining and distribution. In 1981, KPC established two new companies, the Kuwait Foreign Petroleum Exploration Company (KUFPEC)—a subsidiary empowered to undertake crude oil and natural gas exploration, development, and production operations outside Kuwait—and the Kuwait International Petroleum Investment Co., owned 70 percent by KPC and 30 percent by private Kuwaiti investors and empowered to engage in refining and petrochemical operations outside Kuwait.

KPC developed an ambitious strategy to integrate its oil industry from the well-head to the petrol pump in consumer countries. Considerable attention was given to expanding and upgrading Kuwait's refinery capacity, in order to enhance Kuwait's ability to respond rapidly to changes in the pattern of export demand. By 1983, the share of product exports in total oil exports was more than 40 percent by volume and more than 50 percent by value. By 1989, KPC had three modern refineries—the Mina Abdullah, Mina al-Ahmadi, and Shuaiba plants—and plans were being made to integrate their operations to attain the greatest possible economic efficiency. When the expanded Mina Abdullah refinery came on stream in February 1989, Kuwait had a refined-products capacity of over 700,000 barrels per day.

KPC's most dramatic move, however, was to expand overseas. In 1981, it acquired Santa Fe International, a California-based exploration-services company, for $2.5 billion. Santa Fe owned or operated, among other things, rig joint ventures in various regions, including the North Sea and Australia. It also had an engineering subsidiary, S.F. Braun. A more important step came in February 1983, when KPC purchased Gulf Oil's

Key Dates:

1934: The Kuwait Oil Company (KOC) incorporates.
1938: KOC strikes oil in south Kuwait.
1946: Kuwait begins exporting oil.
1960: Kuwait joins OPEC as a founding member; Kuwait National Petroleum Company (KNPC) is organized.
1975: The Kuwaiti government takes full control of KOC.
1980: Kuwait Petroleum Company (KPC) is established to act as a holding company.
1988: The firm launches is own brand—Q8—in Europe.
1990: The Iraqi invasion of Kuwait begins; an alternative head office is set up in the London premises of Kuwait Petroleum International.
1997: The Equate polyolefin plants opens.
2000: KPC is awarded $15.9 billion by the United Nations for damages related to the 1990 Iraqi invasion.

refining and marketing networks in the Benelux countries, adding those in Sweden and Denmark a month later. Under a further agreement with Gulf Oil in January 1984, KPC acquired 1,500 service stations and a 75 percent interest in a refinery at Bertonico, Italy, which had closed two years previously. In the following year, KPC purchased 53 of Elf Aquitaine's Belgian service stations, and in 1986 and 1987 KPC obtained access to 821 petrol stations in the United Kingdom by buying Hays Petroleum Services, an independent distributor, to which it added the 466-station network of Ultramar, a UK oil company. It also bought British Petroleum's oil-marketing subsidiary in Denmark. During 1988, KPC made several acquisitions in Italy, including a 25 percent equity interest in a petroleum-product pipeline in northern Italy and the purchase of Rol Oil, an independent company specializing in oil blending and distribution. During 1989, KPC acquired the UK oil-lubricants business Carless Lubricants. By 1989, through its London-based subsidiary Kuwait Petroleum International, KPC owned more than 4,500 petrol stations in seven countries, plus refineries in Rotterdam and in Gulfhaven, Denmark. In 1988, KPC launched its own brand—Q8—in Europe. Kuwaiti oil was transported to Europe by KOTC, which used large tankers to transport refined products as well as crude oil. By 1990, KOTC's fleet had 22 vessels, including three crude carriers, 14 product tankers, and five liquefied-gas tankers. Following a visit to Kuwait by the Thai energy minister in March 1989, it was agreed that KPC companies would explore for oil in Thailand and introduce Q8 petrol stations there. In the same year, another KPC subsidiary, Petrochemical Industries Company, moved into overseas petrochemicals, buying a 25 percent stake in Hoechst of West Germany.

In 1990, KPC had a downstream capacity in Western Europe of 450,000 barrels per day, or 25 percent of its crude-oil production in Kuwait. KPC's market shares in Europe included 24 percent in Denmark, 12 percent in Sweden, 7 percent in Belgium, 4.5 percent in the Netherlands, and 2.5 percent in the United Kingdom.

Although the construction of a retail network in Europe was at the heart of KPC's strategy in the 1980s, the company also was active in exploration activities in foreign countries through

its KUFPEC and Santa Fe subsidiaries. In 1984, KUFPEC acquired two petroleum concessions, in Bahrain and Tunisia. Offshore discoveries in Egypt and Indonesia were developed in 1985 and 1986, and in 1986 an agreement was signed to participate in the development of the Yacheng gas field in China.

Challenges in the 1980s

KPC was a remarkably successful national oil company. During the 1980s, it achieved a far greater degree of integration than any other OPEC producer, with the possible exception of Petroleos de Venezuela. KPC was the first—and by 1990 the only—state-owned oil company from the Third World to sell its oil under its own brand name and through its own service stations. However, there were problems. Some analysts considered that KPC had paid excessive amounts for some of its acquisitions, especially the purchase of Santa Fe in 1981. KPC's consolidated net profits were impressive—rising from $488.6 million in 1986–1987 to $606.9 million in 1987–1988—but it was likely that this disguised poor performance from certain downstream operations. KPC also faced resistance to its growth from established international oil companies, which partly explained its failure to penetrate the U.S. market in the 1980s. When, in 1984, KPC tried to purchase a refinery and around 4,000 petrol stations in the southeastern part of the United States from Chevron Corporation, it was outbid by Standard Oil Company of Ohio, which did not welcome its presence. Standard of Ohio was controlled by and later acquired by British Petroleum. More fundamentally, there was some conflict between the strategies of expanding refinery capacity within Kuwait and seeking to become an integrated oil major, which might dictate more refining operations nearer markets.

KPC's state ownership created political problems. KPC's attempts to buy downstream assets in Japan, for example, were blocked in part because it was owned by a foreign government. The Kuwait Investment Office's purchase of over 20 percent of British Petroleum's shares in 1988 as a consequence of Margaret Thatcher's privatization program was attacked on these grounds, and the Kuwaitis were forced to reduce their stake to 10 percent. At the time, there was speculation that this purchase was aimed at further advancing KPC's downstream integration strategy, because relations between the Kuwait Investment Office (KIO) and KPC were known to be close. KPC's greatest liability, however, was the geographical location of its home country. KPC relied entirely on sea transport through the Persian Gulf to export its oil, and during the Iran-Iraq War in the mid-1980s the resulting vulnerability of KPC was evident. A number of KOTC tankers were hit by Iranian raids, prompting the Kuwaitis to re-register some of their fleet in the United States and United Kingdom. However, this was a minor irritant and inconvenience compared to the Iraqi invasion and occupation of Kuwait in August 1990, which took place after a period of tension over Kuwait's reluctance to see an increase in oil prices.

The Iraqi Invasion of Kuwait

The Iraqi invasion devastated Kuwait, but it did not devastate KPC which, because of its international diversification strategy, survived. Senior staff of KPC escaped with the bulk of crucial management information intact, and within days had set up an alternative head office in the London premises of Kuwait Petroleum International. Saudi Arabia guaranteed KPI's European downstream commitment. In exile, KPC was granted immunity from the asset freeze which was imposed on Kuwait's overseas interests by the European Economic Community, the United States, and Japan, allowing it to continue normal commercial operations. Eight of KPC's ten directors were outside the country at the time of the Iraq invasion, enabling the company to continue functioning with a legal quorum. Shortly after the invasion, KPC's UK Lubricants business was relaunched as Kuwaiti Petroleum Lubricants. In October 1990, the diversification strategy was furthered when KIO acquired over 10 percent of the shares of the Singapore Petroleum Company, an oil-refining group. The continued vigor of KPC in the midst of the greatest crisis ever faced by Kuwait was a tribute to the strength of the business organization that had been created in a single decade.

The United States and its allies ousted Iraq from Kuwait during the Persian Gulf War. Allied forces led by the United States began their attack on Iraq in January 1991, and the war ended one month later. In the aftermath of the invasion, KPC was left to rebuild and recover from oil fires and damage. The oil concern recovered quickly, however, and was exporting oil products by June 1991. By early 1993, its refining capacity was nearing pre-invasion levels.

Development and Expansion: 1990s and Beyond

KPC spent the remaining years of the 1990s focused on its international expansion. Its upstream operations were bolstered by ventures in the South China Sea, Australia, Congo, Egypt, Indonesia, Tunisia, and Yemen. KPI expanded into Spain in 1992 and acquired BP's Luxembourg-based assets in 1994. The company also made key investments in Italy, Belgium, Sweden, and Thailand. In 1995, KPC re-entered the Italian refining market with the purchase of 300 service stations from Eni, Italy's state-owned chemicals firm. In 1998, 157 service stations in Belgium were acquired from British Petroleum Co. Encouraged by growth in the contract drilling market, KPC sold 31 percent of its Santa Fe International subsidiary in 1997, raising $997.5 million in one of the largest public offerings of the year.

Through its petrochemical development business, KPC was also involved in the development of the Equate facility, which was designed to reduce Kuwaiti dependence on oil production and refining. The Equate project was significant in several ways. It was the first major project to be completed in Kuwait since 1990, and it also marked the first joint venture between a local and international company in Kuwait. Owned by KPC's Petrochemical Industries Co. and Union Carbide Corp., Equate manufactured polyethylene, ethylene glycol, and polypropylene.

As KPC entered the new century, it was awarded $15.9 billion by the United Nations Compensation Commission for losses and damages related to the 1990 Iraqi invasion. The company's Santa Fe unit merged with Global Marine Inc. in a $3 billion deal to create Global Santa Fe Corp.—the world's second-largest offshore drilling contractor. KPC also made a significant move in 2001 when it announced plans to allow foreign oil companies to develop its oil fields in Northern Kuwait.

While KPC did indeed stand on stronger ground than it had just a decade ago, world events began to threaten its position.

The terrorist attacks of September 11, 2001, made crude oil prices fluctuate from $30 per barrel to just over $15 per barrel. The global economy also entered a downturn, with overall growth falling from 3.9 percent in 2000 to 1.5 percent between April 2001 and March 2002. Global demand for oil remained stagnant during this time period. According to KPC, this was the first time in twenty years that oil demand did not increase on an annual basis. KPC also faced hardships internally. In January 2002, an accident at a company facility caused the death of three employees and one fire fighter.

As KPC focused on workplace safety, environmental issues, and expansion, it faced yet another problem. Relations between the United States and Iraq had deteriorated and the United States was threatening military action. If a war broke out, the company's oil fields on the border of Iraq faced potential danger. Nevertheless, KPC had proven that it could overcome extreme hardships and appeared to be on track to handle future challenges.

Principal Subsidiaries

Kuwait Oil Co.; Kuwait National Petroleum Co.; Kuwait Oil Tanker Co.; Kuwait Foreign Petroleum Exploration Co.; Kuwait Petroleum International Ltd.; Kuwait Aviation Fueling Co.; Petrochemicals Industry Co.

Principal Competitors

Abu Dhabi National Oil Company; National Iranian Oil Company; Saudi Arabian Oil Company.

Further Reading

Chisholm, A.H.T., *The First Kuwait Oil Concession Agreement*, London: Frank Cass, 1975.
"Energy: Kuwaiti Products Return to Market," *Lloyd's List*, June 21, 1991, p. 2.
"Equate Kick Starts New Era in Kuwaiti Industry," *Middle East Economic Digest*, December 5, 1997, p. 6.
Evans, John, *OPEC, Its Member States and the World Energy Markets*, London: Longmans, 1986.
Harding, James, "Kuwait Petroleum to Pay Eni Dollars 500m for 300 Stations," *Financial Times London*, September 2, 1995, p. 9.
"KPC Chief Says Mideast Oil Secure Unless Directly Attacked," *Oil Daily*, October 9, 2001.
"Kuwait Introduces Oil Plan," *Oil Daily*, January 4, 2001.
"Kuwait Petroleum Expanding," *Journal of Commerce*, April 9, 1996, p. 7B.
Lippman, Thomas W., "A Global Company Without a Home," *Washington Post*, September 7, 1990, p. D1.
Luciani, Giacomo, *The Oil Companies and the Arab World*, London: Croom Helm, 1984.
"New Battle Brews Over Iraqi War Reparations," *Oil Daily*, June 29, 2000.
"Santa Fe Offering Hits a Gusher," *Houston Chronicle*, June 11, 1997, p. 2.
Stocking, George W., *Middle East Oil*, London: Allen Lane, 1970.
Thomas, David, and Jimmy Burns, "The Gulf War; Kuwaitis Prepare for the Ultimate Oil Disaster," *Financial Times London*, February 13, 1991, p. 3.

—Geoffrey Jones
—update: Christina M. Stansell

LANDMARK COMMUNICATIONS INC.

Landmark Communications, Inc.

150 West Brambleton Avenue
Norfolk, Virginia 23510-2075
U.S.A.
Telephone: (757) 446-2010
Toll Free: (800) 446-2004
Fax: (757) 446-2489
Web site: http://www.landmarkcom.com

Private Company
Incorporated: 1905 as Norfolk Newspapers Inc.
Employees: 5,000
Sales: $732 million (2001 est.)
NAIC: 511110 Newspaper Publishers; 511120 Periodical
    Publishers; 513111 Radio Networks; 513120
    Television Broadcasting; 513210 Cable Networks;
    514191 On-Line Information Services; 541850
    Display Advertising

Landmark Communications, Inc. owns a diverse array of media holdings. About 60 percent of the privately held firm's revenues come from its newspaper operations, which include three metropolitan dailies: the *Virginian-Pilot,* Norfolk, Virginia; the *News & Record,* Greensboro, North Carolina; and the *Roanoke Times,* Roanoke, Virginia. Landmark Community Newspapers, Inc. publishes more than 100 newspapers, shoppers, college sports publications, and special interest publications in the East, South, Midwest, and Southwest. Four of the community newspapers are dailies: the *Carroll County Times,* Westminster, Maryland; *Citrus County Chronicle,* Crystal River, Florida; *Los Alamos Monitor,* New Mexico; and *News-Enterprise,* Elizabethtown, Kentucky. Heading the company's cable programming businesses, which generate more than 30 percent of revenues, is The Weather Channel, which reaches 95 percent of the homes in the United States that have cable television, translating into a potential audience of 84 million. Landmark also owns a 50 percent stake in Pelmorex, Inc., a Canadian firm that runs The Weather Network and Meteo Media, which are, respectively, English-language and French-language equivalents of The Weather Channel in Canada. Less than 10 percent

of revenues derive from television broadcasting holdings, including KLAS-TV (Las Vegas), and WTVF-TV (Nashville), also known as NewsChannel 5 Network—both of which are CBS affiliates. Many of Landmark's operating units also operate web sites, and the company owns a one-third stake in InfiNet, which helps newspapers create and maintain an online presence (the other, equal, partners in this venture are Gannett Co., Inc. and Knight Ridder, Inc.). Landmark also owns 49.9 percent of Annapolis, Maryland-based Capital-Gazette Communications, Inc., publisher of the *Washingtonian* magazine and newspapers, including the *Annapolis Capital*; a 50 percent stake in Trader Publishing Company, publisher of hundreds of classified advertising publications in more than 170 U.S. cities (Cox Enterprises, Inc. owns the other half); and full ownership of Landmark Education Services, Inc., which operates three career schools focusing on allied health and information technology. Landmark Communications is owned by the Batten family and company executives.

Samuel Slover and the Founding of Norfolk Newspapers

Landmark was founded by Samuel Leroy Slover, an enterprising gentleman immersed in the Virginia newspaper business for 55 years. A native of Tennessee, Slover migrated to Virginia in 1900, hoping to change his fortune. He had been the 20-year-old business manager of the financially troubled *Knoxville Journal.* Despite his efforts, the paper went bankrupt and Slover, then 22, assumed its liabilities ($36,400) as a debt of honor. After arriving in Virginia, Slover sold ads for a New York trade journal before approaching the well-connected Joseph Bryan, owner of the *Richmond Times,* for a loan to purchase a newspaper in neighboring Norfolk. Bryan, aghast, refused the young man. Slover, undaunted, asked to sell advertising for the *Times.* When he received a second rejection, Slover tried another tack: what if he sold ads, on a commission basis, to area merchants who were not current clients? With this proposition, Bryan had nothing to lose and everything to gain, so he accepted the offer and was soon rewarded with a multitude of new advertisers.

It was then Bryan's turn to make an offer to Slover—rescue a Newport newspaper from going under within one year and gain half interest in its ownership. Samuel took the challenge, triumphed, and was named publisher of the *Newport News Times-Herald*. In 1909, relinquishing his title as publisher, Slover moved on to papers in Richmond, Petersburg, and other cities in southeast Virginia.

During the next several decades, he dominated the state's newspaper trade, owning outright or controlling six of Virginia's biggest papers. His *modus operandi* was to swoop in and rescue an ailing paper, nurse it from red to black ink, then move on. Through Slover's machinations, small, struggling papers were often merged together to create large, healthier ones, usually resulting in hyphenated names like two of Landmark's backbone publications, the *Virginian-Pilot* and the *Ledger-Star*.

By centering his company, Norfolk Newspapers Inc., near a major military installation, Slover capitalized on the region's immense growth, not only with newspapers, but other media as well. In 1930, as the Great Depression deepened, Slover took a gamble and purchased Norfolk's WTAR-AM, Virginia's first radio station, for $10,000. Though many had little faith in the sensibility of an aural medium and even less in another experimental medium, television, Slover believed in both and was later responsible for bringing Virginia its second television station.

Frank Batten, Taking Over in the 1950s

Throughout Slover's career, his exploits would prove both interesting and educational to his young nephew, Frank Batten, who joined the Slover household after the death of his father, Frank Batten, Sr., when the youngster was only two years old.

After serving in the merchant marines during World War II, Batten graduated from the University of Virginia in 1950 and received an M.B.A. from Harvard University in 1952. His initiation into the business world was fast and furious: he began as a reporter for the *Norfolk Ledger-Dispatch* (forerunner of the *Ledger-Star*), moved to the circulation and advertising departments of the *Ledger-Dispatch* and *Virginian-Pilot*, progressed to vice-president in 1953, and was appointed publisher by Slover at the age of 27 in 1954. Having absorbed much under the tutelage of his uncle and mentor, Batten learned the ropes in record time—accelerating his pivotal role in Norfolk Newspapers Inc., the forerunner of Landmark Communications. While Batten settled into his role as publisher of two of the area's most prosperous newspapers, Slover, 81, slowed down and contemplated retirement. He also sought to share the fruits of his illustrious career, by liberally offering stock to his employees. With Batten at the helm a mere five years, Samuel L. Slover died in 1959, at age 86, leaving Batten a vast legacy.

Like his uncle before him, Batten's prescience would firmly move Landmark into the future: just as Slover had envisioned the many possibilities of radio and television, Batten had been studying an extension of traditional television called "cable" programming. Batten considered cable a medium with vast potential and decided to invest in its promise. Within a year of his initial interest, in 1964, Batten acquired two cable franchises—one in Roanoke Rapids, North Carolina, and a second in Beckley, West Virginia. These two stations were the cornerstone for the development of the TeleCable Corporation, of Greensboro, North Carolina, which would eventually operate 21 cable systems in 15 states, reaching 740,000 subscribers nationwide. TeleCable's success led to a bountiful opportunity for Landmark stockholders in 1984, when it was spun off into an independent corporation. In late 1994, an offer of more than $1 billion in stock was made by rival TCI (Tele-Communications Inc.), the largest cable TV operator in the United States, to acquire TeleCable's assets. The deal was closed in January 1995.

In 1965, Batten further expanded the company by purchasing the *Greensboro Daily News, The Greensboro Record,* and a television station, WFMY-TV, all owned by the prominent Jeffress family. Landmark later combined the Greensboro papers into the *Greensboro News & Record,* which celebrated its centennial in 1990, and sold WFMY-TV. Two years after the Greensboro acquisitions, in 1967, Batten was named chairman of the board of Norfolk Newspapers, which at the same time changed its name to Landmark Communications, Inc. Within another two years, he was on the move again, this time acquiring the *Roanoke Times & World-News* in Virginia's third largest market (combined daily and Sunday circulation of over 240,000), bringing the Norfolk-based company's metro newspaper holdings to four. In the 1970s, Landmark also became home to community papers as well, including four dailies (*Carroll County Times, Citrus County Chronicle, News-Enterprise,* and *Los Alamos Monitor*); four triweeklies (the *Gazette, Lancaster News, Kentucky Standard,* and *Roane County News*); six semiweeklies; 21 weeklies; and 38 free "shoppers" available throughout the region and beyond.

In 1978 Landmark departed from its tradition of local and regional expansion by taking a leap to the West Coast, acquiring two television stations: KNTV in San Jose, for $24.5 million and KLAS-TV in Las Vegas, for $8 million. Though KNTV was later sold, KLAS, a CBS affiliate, became Las Vegas's top-ranked news station with 351,000 households, while another television acquisition, CBS-affiliate WTVF in Nashville, known as "NewsChannel 5" (purchased in 1992), delivered

Key Dates:

1900s–20s: Samuel Slover becomes publisher and half-owner of the *Newport News Times-Herald*; Slover takes over a string of Virginia papers through his company, Norfolk Newspapers Inc.

1954: Frank Batten, nephew of Slover, is named publisher of the *Norfolk Ledger-Dispatch* (later the *Ledger-Star*) and the flagship Norfolk Newspapers title, the *Virginian-Pilot*.

1964: Norfolk Newspapers enters the cable television field with the purchase of two cable franchises; these form the core of the TeleCable Corporation, which eventually operates 21 cable systems in 15 states, reaching 740,000 subscribers.

1965: The *Greensboro Daily News* and the *Greensboro Record* are acquired; they are later combined as the *Greensboro News & Record*.

1967: Batten is named chairman of the board of Norfolk Newspapers, which changes its name to Landmark Communications, Inc.

1969: Landmark buys its fourth metro daily paper, the *Roanoke Times & World News*.

1970s: Company begins buying a string of community newspapers.

1978: Las Vegas television station KLAS-TV is acquired.

1982: Landmark launches The Weather Channel, a 24-hour, national cable weather service.

1984: TeleCable is spun off to Landmark stockholders as an independent company.

1991: Trader Publishing Company, specializing in classified advertising publications, is established as a 50–50 joint venture with Cox Enterprises, Inc.

1992: Landmark acquires Nashville television station WTVF-TV, known as "NewsChannel 5."

1994: Company establishes InfiNet, an Internet service provider and developer of newspaper web sites.

1995: Tele-Communications Inc. pays more than $1 billion to acquire TeleCable; the *Ledger-Star* ceases publication.

1998: Batten is succeeded as company chairman by his son, Frank Batten, Jr.

2000: Trader Publishing acquires UAP, Inc., resulting in the merger of the two largest U.S. publishers of classified advertising publications.

award-winning specials and highly rated newscasts to 738,000 households. WTVF was also known for another distinction: the hiring of a college student in 1974 who went on to conquer the media industry—Oprah Winfrey.

Launching The Weather Channel in the 1980s

Three years later, still seeking opportunities to expand the company in both scope and value, Batten considered another leap—this one into the national broadcasting arena. In 1981 the Landmark think-tank developed what is probably regarded as the company's greatest achievement—a 24-hour cable weather service called "The Weather Channel." In less than 10 months,

plans progressed from paper to programming reality. "The Weather Channel was the most challenging task we had undertaken," Batten admitted. "It was Landmark's first national venture, with all the complexities of marketing and distribution a national enterprise must consider." Despite jitters and numerous naysayers from within and outside the industry, Landmark was determined to live up to its name while also providing the quality of the major networks. On May 2, 1982, The Weather Channel (TWC) officially debuted, with the expressed purpose of becoming "the nation's primary source of weather information."

Part of TWC's success was its universalization of the weather. Because everyone was affected by Mother Nature—an uncontrollable force—viewers could at least tune in, be informed, and prepare, which constituted a form of control in itself. Subscribers also appreciated TWC's format and flow: "Viewers can find a constantly varied presentation of scientific information, friendly advice, and spontaneous philosophy," said Andrew Ross, in his 1991 book, *Strange Weather: Culture, Science, and Technology in the Age of Limits*. Moreover, with programming Ross called "accessible, concrete displays of otherwise abstract weather events," viewers kept coming back for more, especially during catastrophic weather. Ratings skyrocketed during August 1991, as Hurricane Bob terrorized the coast; in March 1993 with the Northeast's unexpected blizzard; and again in December of the same year when heavy snow once again threatened the East Coast.

TWC became a staple of contemporary programming, with what Batten termed "one of the most loyal consumer audiences in television." Numbers proved him correct: at any given moment in the mid-1990s, 130,000 homes tuned in, while TWC programming was available to 56.7 million households that regularly watched its early morning and evening local forecasts, as well as a multitude of regular features (Boat & Beach Reports, Business Traveler's Reports, International Forecast, Michelin Drivers' Report, and Schoolday Forecast) and specials about weather-related health matters or seasonal hazards such as hurricanes and tornados. By 1995, TWC was available in 90 percent of all homes with cable television.

New Ventures in the 1990s

In 1990, Michael Eckert took over as president of what became Landmark's Video Networks and Enterprises Division. From 1991 through 1993, Paul FitzPatrick, formerly of C-Span, was The Weather Channel's president and chief operating officer. During that time, TWC's viewership increased from 48 million to 56.7 million. By 1994, TWC's staff of 325 employees (65 as on-camera meteorologists or OCMs) used over $20 million worth of specialized equipment to ply their trade, including the state-of-the-art Weather STAR system, implemented in late 1993. The STAR system allowed TWC to insert local forecasts for the United States' 750 weather zones, along with tags from local advertisers, into the channel's continuous transmission.

Once TWC was firmly into black ink, its skeptics and detractors were silenced; but just until Landmark's next national undertaking, The Travel Channel (TTC). Founded in 1987 by Trans World Airlines to help sell tickets, TTC was regarded as the bane of the cable industry for its blatant self-promotion; Landmark acquired a 97 percent share of TTC in 1992 for $50 million. Though TTC had never shown a profit and continued to lose $7 million annually, Landmark increased its stagnant viewership by 2.5 million during a concerted media campaign in 1993. Up to 20 million in 1994, Landmark hoped selling TWC and TTC as a team would bolster subscribers even more. Both the Travel and Weather channels won the attention of their peers and received cable ACE awards; in 1991 The Weather Channel was given the industry's highest programming accolade, the Golden ACE.

In April 1991 Landmark joined with Atlanta-based Cox Enterprises, Inc. to form Trader Publishing Company, a 50–50 joint venture that combined the classified advertising publications operations of Landmark Target Media and Cox's Trader Publications. Headquarters for Trader Publishing were established in Norfolk.

As the 1990s advanced, Landmark initiated the first of several new ventures, each in different directions. Mid-May of 1992 marked the acquisition of the nine-year-old Summary Scan! (renamed Promotion Information Management [PIM] in 1993), a tracking service of print media promotions (in-store circulars, coupons, direct mail, etc.) for packaged-goods manufacturers. Purchased from the Chicago-based Advertising Checking Bureau, PIM maintained offices in both Chicago and Overland Park, Kansas, selling its findings to customers on a weekly or monthly basis. Also in 1992, Landmark acquired Antique Trader Publications, which became a key part of Landmark Specialty Publications.

This year was also pivotal for personnel, as John O. Wynne was named corporate CEO in addition to his duties as Landmark's president; and E. Roger Williams joined The Travel Channel as president (and later CEO) after leaving ESPN. In 1994 Douglas Fox, formerly vice-president of marketing for the Times-Mirror Newspaper Group, was named COO for Landmark.

In the fall of 1993, further demonstrating its progressive nature and support of the underdog, Landmark's TeleCable Corp. was one of six cable operators agreeing to carry the new Fox network's programming in the fall of 1993. In June 1994, the company went online by forming a joint venture (70 percent ownership) with another Norfolk-based company, Wyvern Technologies Inc., to create InfiNet, a service bringing Virginia subscribers access to the Internet as well as establishing and maintaining web sites for newspapers and other media outlets. In the fall of 1994, The Weather Channel was in the news, too: CEO Michael Eckert announced plans for international expansion. A Spanish-language weather channel began serving the Latin American market in 1996, followed by a Portuguese channel for Brazil. These channels proved moderately successful, but a venture to develop several weather channels for the European market failed.

In February 1994, Travel, a London-based travel channel, was launched. In 1995, it served nearly one million cable households throughout the United Kingdom and all of Scandinavia. In May 1995, Landmark announced plans to expand further internationally by launching a new Travel Channel for Latin America, which would appeal, according to a press release, "not only to those who travel, but to those who are

interested in learning about the world." The new channel, based in Miami, began broadcasting later in the year. A further travel-related venture launched in 1995 was The Vacation Store. This was a mass-market travel agency that sold vacations nationwide, primarily at first through promotional programs that aired on The Travel Channel. The agency later ran such programs on other cable networks, such as Lifetime and Discovery.

Also in 1995, Landmark purchased full control of InfiNet and then sold a 50 percent stake in that venture to Knight-Ridder, Inc. InfiNet could now draw on the holdings and attempt to attract the subscribers of two major newspaper publishers. In February 1996 another leading newspaper publisher, Gannett Co., Inc., became an InfiNet partner. The three firms held equal one-third stakes in the venture, which was based in Norfolk.

Meantime, in August 1995, the number of Landmark metropolitan daily newspapers fell to three when the *Ledger-Star* ceased publication. Thus ended a decades-long run in which the *Ledger-Star* was Norfolk's afternoon newspaper and the *Virginian-Pilot* was the morning daily. The two papers, despite their common ownership, had been run independently and had maintained a fierce rivalry until 1982, when the staffs were combined in a cost-saving move precipitated by the declining fortunes of the newspaper industry. The differences between the two papers began to fade away, and circulation at the *Ledger-Star* went into a steep fall. By the end, circulation had plummeted to less than 10,000, compared to the more than 100,000 in the mid-1970s.

Late in 1996 Landmark expanded its international weather channel interests by purchasing a 50 percent stake in Pelmorex, Inc. This Canadian firm operated The Weather Network, a weather channel that reached 95 percent of the Canadian cable market, and a French-language weather channel called Meteo Media. Another 1996 development was Landmark's decision to begin divesting its travel-related holdings. In December of that year the company sold The Vacation Store to an investor group led by the agency's top executives. In the middle of the following year, after a prolonged search for a buyer, Landmark sold the troubled Travel Channel to Paxson Communications Corporation for $20 million in cash and $55 million in Paxson stock. Then in 1998 Travel Channel Latin America was sold to Discovery Communications Inc. Landmark retained ownership of Travel, its London-based travel channel.

In a somewhat incongruous development during this same period, Landmark purchased two publishers of travel guides at the same time that it was divesting The Vacation Store and the travel channels. In April 1997 the company bought The Insiders' Guides Inc., producer of a 45-title guidebook series from its headquarters in Manteo, North Carolina, and in October of that same year Landmark purchased Helena, Montana–based guidebook publisher Falcon Publishing Co. The two companies were merged, as Landmark hoped to grow the combined business by creating a new revenue stream in the form of paid advertising. This strategy did not work, and the business was soon deemed to be a noncore asset and was sold to Morris Communications Corporation in 2000.

Yet another new venture for Landmark was the formation in 1997 of American Outdoor Advertising Inc. This billboard advertisement subsidiary developed a network of 960 billboards in 11 southeastern states by the early 2000s. Landmark also began acquiring college sports fan magazines in 1997—starting with *The Cats' Pause,* a title focusing on the University of Kentucky—placing them within the Landmark Community Newspapers unit. In January of the next year, Frank Batten turned over control of Landmark Communications to his son, Frank Batten, Jr., who became chairman. The senior Batten remained involved at the company as chairman of the board's executive committee. Batten, Jr., had served as executive vice-president with responsibility for new ventures and new media since 1995. Prior to that, he had a four-year stint as president and publisher of the *Virginian-Pilot*—following precisely in his father's footsteps. Wynne continued in his capacity of president and CEO.

In early 1999 Landmark moved into the education field, specializing in career education. Company officials saw this as an extension of its core business of delivering information, because they viewed career education as a type of information business. Landmark Education Services, Inc. was created, and it bought Salt Lake City-based Certified Careers Institute, which focused on computer training. Schools focusing on allied health were later added. In another 1999 development, Landmark Specialty Publications, which included antiques and collectible titles such as *Antique Trader,* was sold to Krause Publications, Inc.

Early 2000s and Beyond

Landmark began the 2000s with two major acquisitions. Early in 2000, the company paid about $120 million to Litton Industries Inc. for its Weather Services International (WSI) unit. Using National Weather Service data, WSI packaged weather presentation systems for television stations (including The Weather Channel), the aviation industry, and the government. Later in 2000, Trader Publishing spent $520 million to acquire UAP, Inc., the U.S. classified advertising publication unit of London-based United News & Media plc. The deal combined the two largest U.S. publishers of classified advertising publications. UAP published 300 free advertising titles in 38 states. Landmark extended its hold on the Norfolk area media market through a third 2000 acquisition. The *Virginian-Pilot* bought Norfolk-based Military Newspapers of Virginia, Inc., publisher of several base-related newspapers that were distributed free of charge.

In 2001 Landmark ventured further into the Internet services sector by establishing Continental Broadband LLC. This Norfolk-headquartered company was a provider of fixed wireless Internet services for medium-sized businesses (fixed wireless being wireless broadband Internet service). A sharp drop in advertising in the wake of three circumstances—the bursting of the Internet bubble, the start of a prolonged recession in the United States, and the events of September 11, 2001—resulted in a decline in revenue for Landmark Communications from an estimated $805 million in 2000 to $732 million the following year.

At the beginning of 2002, Wynne retired as president and CEO. Decker Anstrom was named president and COO of Landmark. Anstrom had been president and CEO of The Weather Channel; before that, he had served as president of the National Cable Television Association, and he was thus the first Landmark president to have not spent the majority of his career with the company.

Alterations to the company's portfolio of businesses continued under the new president. In June 2002 Landmark sold its American Outdoor Advertising billboard subsidiary, which had been deemed a noncore asset, to Lamar Advertising Company. One month later, the company purchased a majority interest in Shorecliff Communications LLC. Headquartered in San Juan Capistrano, California, Shorecliff was a trade show enterprise specializing in industries related to telecommunications infrastructure. The firm produced two major trade shows, one serving the cellular tower industry and the other serving the fixed wireless industry. The investment in Shorecliff meshed well with the previous establishment of Continental Broadband, and Landmark's entrance into trade shows was not unexpected given that many media companies were heavily involved in the business.

In December 2002, meantime, Landmark elected to shut down its two weather channels in Latin America after six years of operating in the red. Deepening economic problems in the region contributed to the decision. In March 2003, however, The Weather Channel announced that it was developing a Spanish-language weather channel that would be aimed at the rapidly growing Hispanic population in the United States. The latter move exemplified Landmark's willingness to continue to pursue new, innovative ventures. While not all of the company's ventures proved successful, Landmark had managed over the 1980s and 1990s to add two major businesses—The Weather Channel and Trader Publishing—to its core operations in newspapers and television stations. Given the company's track record, successes of a similar magnitude seemed likely in the future.

Principal Subsidiaries

Continental Broadband LLC; KLAS-TV; Landmark Community Newspapers, Inc.; Landmark Education Services, Inc.; Landmark Travel Channel Limited (U.K.); *News & Record*; NewsChannel 5 Network; *Roanoke Times*; Shorecliff Communications LLC; *Virginian-Pilot*; The Weather Channel, Inc.

Principal Operating Units

Landmark Broadcasting; Landmark Communications; Landmark Publishing Group.

Principal Competitors

Media General, Inc.; Community Newspaper Holdings, Inc.; Knight Ridder, Inc.; Gannett Co., Inc.; Tribune Company; The Washington Post Company.

Further Reading

Batten, Frank, and Jeffrey L. Cruikshank, *The Weather Channel: The Improbable Rise of a Media Phenomenon,* Boston: Harvard Business School Press, 2002, 276 p.

Cunningham, Dwight, "School Spirit Pays Off Big-Time for Landmark Pubs," *Editor and Publisher,* December 18, 1999, p. 14.

Dinsmore, Christopher, "Landmark President and CEO to Pass Leadership Torch," *Norfolk (Va.) Virginian-Pilot,* May 23, 2001, p. D1.

——, "Landmark Sells Billboard Subsidiary," *Norfolk (Va.) Virginian-Pilot,* June 5, 2002, p. D1.

——, "Landmark to Close Second Business in Three Months," *Norfolk (Va.) Virginian-Pilot,* December 4, 2001, p. D1.

——, "Norfolk Publisher to Expand: Deal Would Make Trader Publisher One of the Largest Firms Based Here," *Norfolk (Va.) Virginian-Pilot,* May 10, 2000, p. D1.

——, "The Weather Channel Turns 20," *Norfolk (Va.) Virginian-Pilot,* May 2, 2002, p. D1.

"E. B. Jefress, 75, Dies," *New York Times,* May 24, 1961, p. 41.

Elliott, Stuart, "Defying the Skeptics, the Weather Channel Finds a Silver Lining in Mother Nature's Mood Swings," *New York Times,* June 9, 1993, p. D19.

——, "Seven Agencies Help Finance Study," *New York Times,* September 4, 1994, p. D15.

"Fates & Fortunes—John O. Wynne," *Broadcasting,* November 2, 1992, p. 77.

Garneau, George, "Another Way to Go Online," *Editor and Publisher,* June 24, 1995, p. 24.

——, "The Move to Alternative Delivery—A Success Story," *Editor and Publisher,* December 15, 1990, pp. 8–9.

Gersh, Debra, "Landmark Acquires Marcol," *Editor and Publisher,* August 19, 1989, pp. 13–14.

Gunther, Marc, "The Weather Channel: Hot Enough for Ya?," *Fortune,* October 25, 1999, pp. 46+.

Kolbert, Elizabeth, "Conflict, Fury, Highs, Lows and Humidity," *New York Times,* February 14, 1993, pp. 29, 38.

Linda, Kent, and Moss Gibbons, "Paxson Deal Puts End to Travel Nightmare," *Multichannel News,* June 23, 1997, p. 1.

Mayfield, Dave, "Gannett Buys Stake in InfiNet," *Norfolk (Va.) Virginian-Pilot,* February 15, 1996, p. D1.

——, "Knight-Ridder Buys into InfiNet," *Norfolk (Va.) Virginian-Pilot,* June 8, 1995, p. D1.

Meeks, Fleming, "What Brand Is Your Weather?," *Forbes,* October 23, 1994, p. 320.

Mehta, Stephanie N., "Small Fish Seek the Big As Internet Industry Consolidates," *Wall Street Journal,* June 24, 1994, p. B3.

Moses, Lucia, "Internet Access Business Loses Luster for Papers," *Editor and Publisher,* February 27, 1999, pp. 20–21.

"Other Fields Are Just As Green to Frank Batten," *Broadcasting,* July 19, 1982, p. 95.

Patsuris, Penelope, "Wild About the Weather," *TV Guide,* September 5, 1992, p. 24.

"Personals—John Wynne," *TV Digest,* October 26, 1992, p. 10.

"Promotion Information Management," *Advertising Age,* January 18, 1993, p. 38.

Robichaux, Mark, "If Snow Is Forecast, the Tour of Tahiti Will Be Irresistible," *Wall Street Journal,* January 16, 1992, p. B3.

Ross, Andrew, *Strange Weather: Culture, Science, and Technology in the Age of Limits,* London: Verso Press, 1991, pp. 237–46.

"Samuel L. Slover, Virginia Publisher" (obituary), *New York Times,* November 30, 1959, p. 31.

"Summary Scan! Sold," *Advertising Age,* May 18, 1992, p. 37.

Swift, Earl, "The Final Edition: The *Ledger-Star* Stops the Presses After 119 Years," *Norfolk (Va.) Virginian-Pilot,* August 25, 1995, p. A1.

Wagner, Lon, "Newspaper Leader Hands Company Over to Son," *Roanoke (Va.) Times & World News,* December 17, 1997, p. A13.

"The Weather Channel to Expand," *Adweek,* July 18, 1994, p. 12.

Williams, Debra Abe, "Taking a Safari on the Internet," *Advertising Age,* September 5, 1994, p. 14.

—Taryn Benbow-Pfalzgraf
—update: David E. Salamie

Lebhar-Friedman, Inc.

425 Park Avenue
New York, New York 10022
U.S.A.
Telephone: (212) 756-5000
Fax: (212) 207-8167
Web site: http://www.lf.com

Private Company
Incorporated: 1925
Employees: 400
Sales: $90 million (2002 est.)
NAIC: 511120 Periodical Publishers; 511130 Book
Publishers; 512230 Music Publishers; 561920
Convention and Trade Show Organizers; 511140
Database and Directory Publishers

Lebhar-Friedman, Inc. is the largest independent publisher of magazines and newspapers for the retail and foodservice industries. It also provides a wide range of other information products and services for its readers, including directories, executive fax and e-mail alerts, newsletters, databases, web sites, and trade shows and conferences. As of 2003 the company's principal periodicals included *Chain Store Age, DSN [Discount Store News] Retailing Today, Drug Store News, Nation's Restaurant News,* and *Home Channel News.* The company's directory publishing division, CSG [Chain Store Guides] Information Services, is based in Tampa, Florida, and produces industry-related directories based on a comprehensive database it maintains. The company also operates its own book publishing division, Lebhar-Friedman Books, and has a music publishing subsidiary, Largo Music, which owns and administers copyrights to musical compositions. Internationally, *Chain Store Age News* and *General Merchandiser* are published in Japan through the joint venture Diamond-Friedman. Another joint venture with Ediciones Y Estudios serves the growing Spanish distribution and advertising industries.

Early History: 1925–70

Lebhar-Friedman, Inc. was established in 1925 with the publication of the magazine *Chain Store Age.* Founded by Arnold Friedman, Godfrey M. Lebhar, and John Stern, *Chain Store Age* provided essential business information to the emerging industry of chain store retailers and their suppliers. Lebhar and Stern were publishing executives who provided financing, while Friedman served as editor and sales manager. As the retailing and foodservice industries grew during the 20th century, Lebhar-Friedman evolved into a multifaceted information company. The company remained privately held, and J. Roger Friedman succeeded his father as its president.

In the 1960s Lebhar-Friedman launched several new business-to-business periodicals aimed at different segments of the retail industry. In 1960 the company introduced *Drug Store News* under the title *Chain Store Age Drug Magazine.* Originally a monthly, it became a biweekly publication in 1978 providing information on new products and services, tips on store management, and similar topics to a circulation of 45,000 drug stores. Over the years Lebhar-Friedman introduced other targeted editions of *Chain Store Age* for specific retail markets, including *Chain Store Age Supermarkets* and others.

As discount stores became a new force in retailing, Lebhar-Friedman launched *Discount Store News* in 1962. Subsequently retitled *DSN Retailing Today,* the bimonthly periodical provided information on new products and services for discount store managers, along with articles on merchandising and operational methods and industry reports.

In 1964 Lebhar-Friedman held the inaugural SPECS: Store Planning, Equipment, Construction Services Seminars for retail headquarters executives from all retail segments. The trade show and seminars also were attended by suppliers and anyone involved in store construction, from product manufacturers to consultants and shopping center developers.

Lebhar-Friedman next turned its attention to the foodservice industry, where new developments such as fast-food and restaurant chains were taking place. In 1967 the company introduced *Nation's Restaurant News,* the newspaper of the foodservice industry. Originally published biweekly, it became a weekly in 1987 and was the leading source of information on new developments in foodservice. Its circulation grew to 90,000.

Lebhar-Friedman also began publishing industry-related directories that provided detailed individual company profiles, with key contact information and in-depth data. The 800- to 1,200-page directories also included statistical and graphic analyses of industry sectors, listings of major trade organizations and trade shows, trends, and other reference material. The directories were updated regularly, either annually or biennially.

Among the directories published by Lebhar-Friedman is the *Directory of Home Center Operators and Hardware Chains,* which was first published in 1948. It provided details on home centers, warehouses, and lumber and building materials cooperatives with more than $1 million in annual sales. In 1961 the company began publishing a directory of discount department stores, now titled *Directory of Discount and General Merchandise Stores.*

Targeting Other Retail Segments: 1970–90

In 1973 Lebhar-Friedman launched two new directories covering automotive supply chains and foodservice distributors. As the company's directory business grew, it established a subsidiary, CSG Information Services, in Tampa, Florida, for directory publishing and marketing.

In 1975 the company launched a new periodical for the home improvement industry. *National Home Center News* appeared 22 times a year and covered all aspects of the home improvement industry, including extended news coverage and industry statistics, along with special sections devoted to merchandising, marketing, operations, and similar topics. Lebhar-Friedman subsequently launched other periodicals for the home improvement industry, including *Homemarket Trends* and *Home Channel News.* In the mid-1970s Lebhar-Friedman established a joint venture in Japan, Diamond-Friedman, to publish *Chain Store Age News* and *General Merchandise.*

New periodicals introduced during the 1980s included *Food Merchandising for Non-Food Retailers,* which ceased publication in the 1990s; *Apparel Merchandising,* which was introduced in 1982; *Computer and Software News,* which was published from 1983 to 1989; and *Drug Store News: Continuing Education Quarterly,* which began targeting pharmacists in 1986.

The company also discontinued some of the targeted editions of its flagship publication, *Chain Store Age,* including *Chain Store Age Supermarkets* in 1983 and *Chain Store Age General Merchandise Trends* in 1988. Through surveys conducted by Lebhar-Friedman Research & Information Services, the company demonstrated the effectiveness of trade advertising in influencing purchase decisions. It also developed its own advertising campaigns to boost advertising in its business-to-business periodicals.

In 1987 Lebhar-Friedman reorganized to make way for the next generation under J. Roger Friedman's leadership. In that same year the company launched its first nonretail periodical, *Accounting Today.* The magazine was quickly recognized as a leading publication for the accounting profession. In 1994 Lebhar-Friedman sold *Accounting Today* to Faulkner & Gray, Inc., a New York City-based unit of Thomson Corporation.

One change instituted in the late 1980s by Lebhar-Friedman was to begin charging nonqualified individuals for subscriptions to its controlled circulation periodicals. It began by charging $25 a year for the biweekly *Discount Store News.* Within a couple of years there were 7,000 paid subscribers to the periodical, and the price had risen to $89. As a result, Lebhar-Friedman developed a similar pricing plan to charge nonqualified subscribers for its other controlled circulation periodicals.

Expanding Range of Information Products: 1990–2003

Responding to the globalization of the markets it served, Lebhar-Friedman formed a joint venture in 1995 with Corporate Intelligence, a London-based research firm. Corporate Intelligence offered a comprehensive range of retailing publications and services, including its proprietary online retailer database Euro-Retailnet. It also produced publications for the U.K. and pan-European markets, including *The Retail Rankings* and the *Retail Research Report.* The new London-based venture was called Corporate Intelligence on Retailing and combined the expertise and databases of both companies to produce published report and online services.

Lebhar-Friedman continued to expand its presence in providing information products and services to the United Kingdom and Europe. In 1998 it acquired the foodservice division of Marketpower, a market research firm based in London. The new division was renamed Foodservice Intelligence and reported to *Nation's Restaurant News* publisher James C. Doherty. Its principal products were market measurement and tracking services for the foodservice industry.

Lebhar-Friedman launched two new trade shows for the foodservice industry in the 1990s, MUFSO: MultiUnit Food Service Operators and FSTEC: Food Service Technology Show. Both served the audience of *Nation's Restaurant News.*

In 1998 Lebhar-Friedman announced that it was expanding its book publishing division, Lebhar-Friedman Books. It planned to produce about 24 titles annually that were focused on the niche retail industries served by the company's business-to-business periodicals. Among the topics to be covered were cookbooks and restaurant guides, retailing and management titles, educational training, and business history and biography.

In 1999 Lebhar-Friedman introduced *Menu,* a quarterly that provided fresh ideas for culinary professionals. Toward the end of 1999 the company acquired a minority interest in *Restaurants Asia,* which was published in Hong Kong.

In 2000 Lebhar-Friedman celebrated a century of retailing by hosting the Best of Century Awards at New York's Plaza Hotel. The event was attended by nearly 500 retailer and supplier executives. Later in 2000 Lebhar-Friedman and *Nation's Restaurant News* teamed with the Conrad N. Hilton College of Hotel and Restaurant Management at the University of Houston to inaugurate a restaurant management certification program.

Key Dates:

1925: Arnold Friedman, Godfrey M. Lebhar, and John Stern form Lebhar-Friedman, Inc. and launch *Chain Store Age.*

1960: Lebhar-Friedman begins publishing *Drug Store News.*

1962: The company begins publication of *Discount Store News,* which is later renamed *DSN Retailing Today.*

1964: *Chain Store Age* holds the first SPECS: Store Planning, Equipment, Construction Services Seminars trade show and exposition.

1967: *Nation's Restaurant News* is launched.

1975: Lebhar-Friedman introduces *National Home Center News.*

1980: Largo Music is established.

1982: *Apparel Merchandising* begins publication.

1989: Lebhar-Friedman begins to develop newsletters.

1998: The company expands its book publishing division.

1999: Lebhar-Friedman introduces *Menu,* a quarterly for culinary professionals.

2000: Company celebrates a century of retailing; teams with the University of Houston to inaugurate a restaurant management certification program.

The program consisted of four courses covering staffing, training, and supervision; customer service; sales and marketing; and law and litigation.

Responding to general weakness in the book market, Lebhar-Friedman scaled back its book publishing program in 2002. A list of 80 proposed titles was cut to eight, and the range of topics was limited to culinary subjects, including restaurant and dining guides. The company continued to publish its Chain Store Guide directories from its Tampa office. Approximately 15 directories were organized into three categories: Specialty Retailers and Distributors, Mass Merchandising, and Food Retailing and Foodservice.

Throughout its more than 75-year history, Lebhar-Friedman has remained focused on its core business of serving the information needs of retail executives and managers and their suppliers. The company's growth and diversification mirrored that of the retail industry itself in the 20th century. As a result, Lebhar-Friedman can rightly call itself, "The Voice of Retailing."

Principal Subsidiaries

Corporate Intelligence on Retailing (United Kingdom); Foodservice Intelligence (United Kingdom); Diamond-Friedman (Japan).

Principal Divisions

Lebhar-Friedman Books; Largo Music Publishing; CSG Information Services.

Principal Competitors

Bill Communications, Inc.; Business Research Publications, Inc.; E W A Publications; National Retail Foundation; National Retail Merchants Association; Retail Reporting Bureau.

Further Reading

"A Celebration for the Ages," *DSN Retailing Today,* May 8, 2000, p. 14.

"DiRoNA and Lebhar-Friedman Books Premiere New Dining Guide," *Nation's Restaurant News,* May 22, 2000, p. 284.

"Estes, Doll Named to Key L-F Posts," *Chain Store Age Supermarkets,* February 1983, p. 30.

Forseter, Murray, "Chain Store Age: Auld Lang Syne," *Chain Store Age – General Merchandise Trends,* January 1988, p. 5.

Friedman, J. Roger, "100 Years of Retailing," *Discount Store News,* April 17, 2000, p. 5.

——, "Retailing: The Heart of American Business," *Drug Store News,* July 11, 1994, p. 8.

"Lebhar-Friedman Buys Foodservice Division of Marketpower," *Nation's Restaurant News,* February 9, 1998, p. 4.

"Lebhar-Friedman Expands Its Book Publishing Division," *Nation's Restaurant News,* May 4, 1998, p. 8.

"Lebhar-Friedman Forms Publishing Partnership with London Firm," *Nation's Restaurant News,* May 1, 1995, p. 64.

"Mahler, ex-DrSN Publisher, to Develop L-F Newsletters," *Drug Store News,* May 1, 1989, p. 5.

"Make Non-Qualified Readers Pay," *Folio: The Magazine for Magazine Management,* October 1, 1991, p. 9.

"Mergers & Acquisitions," *Folio: The Magazine for Magazine Management,* March 1, 1994, p. 69.

"More Evidence That Trade Advertising Works," *Folio: The Magazine for Magazine Management,* March 1988, p. 38.

"Restaurants Asia," *Business Publisher,* November 30, 1999, p. 8.

"Univ. of Houston Hilton Hospitality School, Lebhar-Friedman Sponsor Program," *Nation's Restaurant News,* August 28, 2000, p. 81.

Zeitchik, Steven, "Lebhar-Friedman Condenses Book Program," *Publishers Weekly,* January 7, 2002, p. 13.

Zeldis, Nancy, "Staying on the Ball at Lebhar-Friedman," *Folio: The Magazine for Magazine Management,* April 1986, p. 51.

—David P. Bianco

Lonely Planet Publications Pty Ltd.

Locked Bag 1
Footscray, Victoria 3011
Australia
Telephone: (+61) 3-8379-8000
Fax: (+61) 3-8379-8111
Web site: http://www.lonelyplanet.com

Private Company
Incorporated: 1973
Employees: 400
Sales: A$82 million (2001)
NAIC: 511130 Book Publishing & Printing; 424920
  Book, Periodical and Newspaper Merchant
  Wholesalers; 511140 Database and Directory
  Publishers; 518111 Internet Service Providers

Lonely Planet Publications Pty Ltd. bills itself as a travel information publisher, producing guidebooks and a host of other related titles that offer frank and distinctive assessments of locations throughout the world. Lonely Planet maintains offices in Melbourne, Australia; Oakland, California; Paris, France; and London, England. The company has published more than 600 travel books and introduces roughly 25 new titles each year.

Origins

The partnership of Tony and Maureen Wheeler, the founders of Lonely Planet, began on a park bench in London in 1970. Tony Wheeler, in his mid-20s at the time, had earned a master's degree in automotive engineering at the London Business School. He sat on the park bench reading a car magazine. His soon-to-be wife sat next to him, reading a novel by Tolstoy, according to Tony Wheeler's recollection. The pair introduced themselves, struck up a conversation, and moved in with each other several days later. Tony Wheeler, born in Bournemouth, England, and Maureen Wheeler, a native of Ireland, were married a year later. The young couple flirted with a conventional lifestyle following their wedding, but wanderlust proved to have a stronger attraction than working in London. Tony Wheeler deferred accepting a well-paying job at Ford Motor

Co. and Maureen Wheeler left her job working for a London wine importer. "The plan was to get the travel bug out of our systems, then settle down for good," Tony Wheeler recalled in an October 1994 interview with *Smithsonian* magazine.

In 1972, the Wheelers embarked on what was supposed to be the last big adventure of their lives. They emptied their bank accounts and used the $1,400 they obtained to purchase a few maps and a used Austin minivan. With much dependent on the reliability of the $130 Austin, the Wheelers boarded a boat, crossed the English Channel, and began driving eastward. As the young couple began their trek, they observed a daily budget of $6, crossing Western Europe, the Balkans, Turkey, and into Iran. Once they arrived in Afghanistan, the next country in a dizzying itinerary, the Wheelers sold the Austin and resorted to any transportation mode made available to them. The couple traveled by bus, train, boat, and rickshaw, hitchhiking whenever the need arose. Impulse served as their guidebook, taking the Wheelers on a meandering course snaking through Pakistan, Kashmir, India, Nepal, Thailand, Malaysia, and Indonesia.

The itinerant Wheelers came to rest in Sydney, Australia, nine months after they left London. The journey left the couple virtually penniless, whittling their saving down to 27 cents. "Our original intent had been to find jobs in Sydney and work there for three or four months until we'd earned enough for plane tickets, then fly back to London and get on with our lives," Tony Wheeler explained in his October 1994 interview with *Smithsonian*. He found a marketing job at a pharmaceutical company, but the attempt to return to London soon was shelved. When other travelers heard of the Wheelers trip, they pressed the couple for details and advice. The interest convinced the Wheelers to write an account of their trip in guidebook form, a project neither one of them had entertained before or during the trip. They sat at the kitchen table in their small Sydney apartment and began writing their first travel guide. The effort was truly homespun, a hand-collated, trimmed, and stapled guidebook that was 96 pages long.

Lonely Planet Is Born: 1973

With the book completed, the Wheelers next needed a name for their kitchen-table company. The inspiration came from

Company Perspectives:

Lonely Planet is passionate about bringing people together, about understanding our world, and about people sharing experiences that enrich everyone's lives. We aim to inspire people to explore, have fun, and travel often. And we strive to provide travellers everywhere with reliable, comprehensive and independent travel information.

"Space Captain," a song by Joe Cocker and Leon Russell that contained the words "lovely planet." When he sang along to the song, Tony Wheeler had a habit of replacing "lovely" with "lonely," preferring his version of the lyrics even after Maureen Wheeler informed him of the mistake. Thus, Lonely Planet Publications became the name of the Wheelers' enterprise.

The 96-page travel book, which eventually became a collector's item, was entitled *Across Asia on the Cheap*, published in 1973. "It was a crude, totally handmade book," Tony Wheeler remembered in his October 1994 interview with *Smithsonian*, "but when we took it 'round to book shops in Melbourne and Sydney it was surprisingly easy to sell." The book sold for $1.80. The first printing sold out in ten days, necessitating another, larger print run. The second print run sold out as well, requiring another run. Within its first year on bookstore shelves, *Across Asia on the Cheap* sold 8,500 copies, prompting the Wheelers to plan a second adventure for the substance of the next Lonely Planet publication.

With the profits from their first travel guide, the Wheelers were able to finance their second trip throughout Asia. They purchased a 250cc Yamaha and rode the motorcycle through Indonesia, Burma, Malaysia, Laos, and Thailand. After spending a year gathering thorough information, the Wheelers spent the next three months in a $2-a-night Singapore hotel room, where the couple wrote their second guidebook, *South-East Asia on a Shoestring*, published in 1975. Reverently referred to as the "Yellow Bible" by its readers, *South-East Asia on a Shoestring* trumped the success of it predecessor, selling twice as many copies as *Across Asia on the Cheap*.

With *South-East Asia on a Shoestring*, Lonely Planet established several of its defining characteristics. The information within the guidebook was meticulously researched, conveyed to the reader in frank, sometimes witty prose. A Lonely Planet travel guide contained conventional and unconventional information, offering advice on hotels and restaurants as well as how to change money on the black market. Equally as important as how well the Wheelers did their work was where they did their work, particularly during Lonely Planet's formative years of development. They chose destinations that largely had escaped the attention of their competitors, focusing on countries, cities, and regions guidebook publishers such as Frommer's ignored. In an article he wrote for the July/August issue of *UNESCO Courier*, Tony Wheeler explained the importance of eschewing the world's more popular destinations. "We started with a very simple philosophy: we were the small time operator who couldn't compete head on with the big publishers in London or New York. So we would produce guidebooks to the places

nobody had ever thought of writing about. In retrospect, it was an amazingly clever idea. By the time the 'big guys' had woken up to the tourist boom that was taking off from airports all over the world, we had carved out a name for ourselves as publishers for the new destinations suddenly topping the statistics lists. This hard-won reputation gave us the stature to move on to the more established and familiar destinations."

The success of *South-East Asia on a Shoestring* firmly established Lonely Plant as a guidebook publisher, albeit a decidedly small publisher. Using Melbourne as the base of their operations, the Wheelers spent the latter half of the 1970s traveling in and writing about a series of countries, publishing travel guides for Nepal, Africa, New Zealand, and New Guinea. The books sold well, but the profits barely paid for the travel and publishing expenses incurred. Maureen Wheeler, in an October 1994 interview with *Smithsonian*, described their financial status in the years immediately following the publication of *South-East Asia on a Shoestring*: "We couldn't afford a decent car, the house we lived in didn't even have an indoor toilet, and the books remained pretty amateurish because we didn't have the money to do things as well as we should have. I didn't think Lonely Planet was ever really going to support the two of us." By the end of the 1970s, the Wheelers had published a dozen books, but the financial future of Lonely Planet remained uncertain. Certainty arrived at the beginning of the 1980s, when the publishing company's fervent yet limited readership shed the characteristics of a cult-like following.

Lonely Planet needed popularity on a higher level to ensure its survival and the Wheelers' financial well-being. The turning point in the publishing company's development occurred after the Wheelers decided in 1979 to write a guidebook for India, a project that quickly overwhelmed the Wheelers and the two writers they hired to help produce the book. In scope and scale, the travel guide to India eclipsed all other Lonely Planet titles preceding it. Once completed, the book was 700 pages long, nearly four times the length of the publisher's other books. The extra length demanded an increased price tag, but when the $10 copies of the India guidebook arrived in bookstores in 1980, the higher price did not deter buyers in the least. The book was an immediate success, selling 100,000 copies in its first print run and earning a prestigious British literary award hailing it as the best travel book of the year. Eventually, the book sold 500,000 copies, giving Lonely Planet financial stability for the future.

In the wake of the seminal success of the India guidebook, the Wheelers were able to expand the size of their operation both in terms of personnel and its physical presence. They could now afford to hire editors, cartographers, and writers, all of whom worked on a contract basis, to assist in the production of a steady stream of Lonely Planet publications. As the library of Lonely Planet books increased, giving coverage to nearly every corner of the world, a small network of Lonely Planet sales offices emerged. In 1984, an office was opened in San Francisco, followed by the establishment of an office in London six years later.

Maturity in the 1990s

Roughly 20 years after the first Lonely Planet books appeared in stores in Australia, Lonely Planet stood as one the most recognized names in travel guide publishing. By 1994, the

Key Dates:

1973: The publication of *Across Asia on the Cheap* spawns Lonely Planet Publications.
1975: The company's second book, *South-East Asia on a Shoestring,* is published.
1980: The success of a guidebook on India gives Lonely Planet financial security.
1984: A sales office in the United States is established.
1990: A sales office in the United Kingdom is opened.
1994: Lonely Planet launches its Web site.
2000: Lonely Planet begins to diversify aggressively.

company's staff had written and published 155 guide books, titles that were advertised as "travel survival kits." Offices in Australia, the United States, the United Kingdom, and France employed a full-time staff of 75 editors and cartographers, generating revenues exceeding $22 million a year.

As Lonely Planet pressed ahead during its third decade of existence, the company averaged annual sales growth of 24 percent. Part of the reason the company was able to maintain its momentum was its willingness to exploit new revenue-generating streams. In 1994, for instance, the company launched the Lonely Planet Web site, through which it fostered the development of a sizeable online community. To mark its 25th anniversary in 1998, the company published its first hardcover coffee-table book, *Chasing Rickshaws.* Another factor contributing to the unflagging strength of the company was the Wheelers' insistence that the tone and style of Lonely Planet books change to meet the changing tastes and needs of their readership. Travelers who were the Wheelers contemporaries during the 1970s had different life-styles and traveling desires by the 1990s. The Wheelers of the 1990s brought their children along on their adventures, took shorter trips, and stayed in more expensive accommodations than they had 25 years earlier. Lonely Planet guidebooks reflected the changes, ensuring that the publishing company did not lose touch with the demographic that had fueled its rise.

By its 25th anniversary, Lonely Planet had more than 350 titles in print, a total that was expanding by 20 to 25 new titles each year. "The thing that sets us apart from other travel guide companies is that right from the beginning, Tony Wheeler planted the seeds for worldwide distribution," explained the company's U.S. general manager in an October 12, 1998 interview with *Publishers Weekly.* "And that puts us in the unique position that we can publish a guidebook about almost any place in the world, and it will still make a reasonable return." Worldwide, Lonely Planet was generating annual sales in excess of $40 million, drawing 44 percent of the total from Europe, its largest market. North and South America ranked as the company's second-largest market, accounting for 36 percent of

sales. Next on the list was Australia, accounting for 20 percent of sales, with Asia and Africa accounting for the rest.

As Lonely Planet prepared for the future, a wealth of new products bearing the company's brand was expected to be unveiled. In 2000, the company marked the beginning of the new millennium by introducing seven new product categories. Included within the new breeds of Lonely Planet products were: *Healthy Travel,* a series of pocket guides on regional health issues; *World Food,* a series of pocket guides covering cuisine and culture; *Read This First,* a series listing pre-departure concerns for first-time travelers; and *Citysync,* which offered condensed palmtop versions of Lonely Planet guides for eight selected cities. In 2001, diversification continued when Lonely Planet published *Out to Eat: San Francisco 2001,* a restaurant guidebook. The success or failure of these new offerings would determine whether Lonely Planet evolved into a broadly-based publisher or stretched itself too thin. The Wheelers, emboldened by 30 years of success, awaited the challenge.

Principal Divisions

Lonely Planet Television; Lonely Planet Australia; Lonely Planet USA; Lonely Planet UK; Lonely Planet France; Lonely Planet Europe.

Principal Competitors

Berlitz International, Inc.; Random House; John Wiley & Sons, Inc.

Further Reading

Farmanfarmaian, Roxane, "Lonely Planet Celebrates 25th Anniversary," *Publishers Weekly.* October 12, 1998, p. 17.
——, "Lonely Planet Has Strong '99, Sees Gains in'00," *Publishers Weekly,* March 20, 2000, p. 17.
"Hitting the Road with a Lonely Planet Man," *Time International,* June 1, 1998, p. 6B.
Izon, Lucy, "New, Improved Guide to Russia," *Los Angeles Times,* May 5, 1996, p. 16.
Krakauer, John, "All They Really Wanted Was to Travel a Little," *Smithsonian,* October 1994, p. 132.
"Lonely Planet Releases First Cuba Guidebook," *Houston Chronicle,* January 19, 1997, p. 2.
Roether, Barbara, "Lonely Planet Adds Spanish Line," *Publishers Weekly,* March 5, 2001, p. 20.
Schuman, Michael, "The Not-So-Lonely Planet," *Forbes,* May 22, 1995, p. 104.
Symanovich, Steve, "Lonely Planet Roves a Hungry City," *San Francisco Business Times,* January 19, 2001, p. 50.
Wheeler, Tony, "Philosophy of a Guidebook Guru," *UNESCO Courier,* July-August 1999, p. 54.
"Words of Wisdom; Back to 'Lonely' Roots," *Advertiser,* June 23, 2001, p. M34.

—Jeffrey L. Covell

MAPICS, Inc.

1000 Windward Concourse Parkway
Alpharetta, Georgia 30005
U.S.A.
Telephone: (678) 319-8000
Fax: (678) 319-8455
Web site: http://www.mapics.com

Public Company
Incorporated: 1980 as Marcam Corporation
Employees: 450
Sales: $128.3 million (2002)
Stock Exchanges: NASDAQ
Ticker Symbol: MAPX
NAIC: 511210 Software Publishers

MAPICS, Inc. is a business application software and consulting company located in Alpharetta, Georgia, helping mid-sized manufacturers and corporate divisions to streamline and coordinate such business processes as manufacturing, customer service, engineering, supply chain planning, enterprise asset management, and financials. MAPICS has thousands of customers in more than 10,000 sites in 70 countries, and its applications are available in 19 languages. Major clients include Dukane Corp., Volvo Construction Equipment, Goodrich Corporation, and Honda Motor Co.

MAPICS Software Launched in Late 1970s

MAPICS is an acronym for Manufacturing, Accounting, Production, and Information Control System, the result of research and development that transformed early inventory tracking systems into material requirements planning (MRP). This concept was in turn expanded to include a wide range of business functions, allowing a manufacturer to manage, predict, and control its resources and investments. MAPICS was developed in 1977 by IBM's Atlanta Software Development Laboratory, also known as the Rainer Moore Lab in recognition of the facility's first director. The product, which debuted in 1978, was originally designed for use on the IBM System/34, which preceded the IBM AS/400 midrange computer. At first MAPICS

was devoted to such financial processes as accounts payable, accounts receivable, general ledger, and payroll, and only later did engineers build manufacturing applications around this core. MAPICS was geared towards discrete manufacturers, which assemble products from parts. (Process manufacturers rely on chemical reactions or deconstruct natural materials in order to create such products as foods, chemicals, and drugs.) Over the first 12 years, MAPICS built up a sizeable user base, IBM expanding the number of users by making it affordable, looking to profit instead from hardware sales. In 1992, when IBM decided to leave the applications business, it sought a suitable buyer of the product line, eventually settling on a small software developer based in Newton, Massachusetts, named Marcam Corporation.

Marcam was co-founded by Paul Margolis, who after earning a bachelors degree from Brown University and an MBA from Harvard Business School started his own electronics business, which he later sold. He then went to work for Ketron Corporation as a manufacturing manager before becoming a consultant, in which capacity he was involved in a number of MAPICS installations at electronic companies in the late 1970s. Marcam was founded in 1980 to service and support MAPICS customers and was successful three times in raising venture capital funds. In 1986, the company launched its own product, PRISM, designed to do for process manufacturers what MAPICS did for discrete manufacturers. In a world of rapid technological changes, Marcam attempted to get ahead of the curve in the late 1980s by investing heavily in research and development of new products, in particular those based on object/oriented programming, in the hopes of leapfrogging competition and emerging in a clear leadership position. To support this lengthy and expensive process, Marcam went public in August 1990.

Early 1990s Agreement between IBM and Marcam

In October 1992, IBM and Marcam announced they had reached an agreement on an alliance to develop, market, and support MRP applications. IBM received a 16 percent stake in Marcam, which in turn received exclusive worldwide marketing rights to the MAPICS software line for 25 years, with the option to buy the IBM subsidiary, Mapics, Inc. To support MAPICS,

Company Perspectives:

MAPICS is a visionary, global software company focused exclusively on delivering collaborative business applications and expert consulting services that help manufacturers become world class.

Marcam and IBM agreed to jointly staff an Atlanta facility with approximately 150 people. In reality, it was the same IBM personnel, now contracted to Marcam, which provided management of the operation.

Heading the new MAPICS Business Group for Marcam was the director of IBM's Atlanta Software Development Laboratory and the current CEO of MAPICS, Richard C. Cook. He originally went to work for IBM in 1967 as a programmer in an IBM factory located in Boca Raton, Florida. By writing programs, he became intimately familiar with a wide range of business functions, including production control, finance, and cost/profit analysis. Declining an opportunity to move to New York, he gained further experience by accepting lateral moves within the organization. Serving as director of site operations Cook was involved in the difficult task of establishing entire infrastructures. Later, he became director of manufacturing for IBM, and in this role he acquired a number of off-the-shelf products, one of which was MAPICS. He then became the director of the Atlanta Software Development lab in March 1990. After IBM granted the MAPICS rights to Marcam, Cook severed his ties to IBM after 25 years and convinced 127 colleagues to join him at Marcam. According to Cook, "During the first year I spent most of the time extricating myself from IBM's culture and adapting to what amounted to a start-up."

Because MAPICS and PRISM targeted different sets of customers, Margolis called the deal, which was completed in February 1993, "a marriage made in heaven." Marcam gained a steady revenue stream to help fund its costly research and development program, while MAPICS appeared to be a business now free of corporate shackles. According to a 1993 article in *MIDRANGE Systems* that relied on information from Cook, IBM had "commissioned an independent company to conduct a customer satisfaction survey of MAPICS and non-MAPICS users. It also has feedback from users attending COMMON [a MAPICS User Group conference]. Unfortunately, response previously didn't occur largely because decisions that benefited IBM as a whole often restricted advances to MAPICS. Freeing the MAPICS products from the slow moving hardware giant and placing it under the direction of a manufacturing applications software company like Marcam finally gives users cause for optimism. The brand managers—the people responsible for reviewing feedback from users and making product-specific recommendations—now work for the joint venture." IBM's inability to support MAPICS in a timely manner had opened the door to third-party companies to develop MAPICS products and services, business that the new MAPICS business group hoped to capture. When in June 1993 IBM and Marcam announced jointly the debut of 11 new modules (to augment 19 existing applications) as well as other enhancements, an improved MAPICS product received a positive response from users.

The future appeared bright for Marcam and its two-pronged business model. It was a one of only a handful of large players in an expanding and relatively fragmented industry. With a market share of just 6 percent, Marcam appeared to be well positioned to experience rapid growth. Marcam was so pleased with the performance of MAPICS that in September 1995 it exercised its option and bought out the IBM subsidiary. Not far from the surface, however, lay difficulties for MAPICS and its parent corporation. According to *MIDRANGE Systems* in August 1995, most MAPICS users "bought it as an IBM product known for its affordability at a time when IBM made its biggest profits from hardware sales. Marcam must make its profits from software sales and support contracts. This perception issue has caused disharmony with some users, who have expressed the feeling that if MAPICS begins to cost them as much as competitive products they plan to compare it with competitive products for new purchases or upgrades."

Late 1990s: MAPICS, Inc. Is Founded

Frustration was also mounting in Atlanta as it became increasingly more evident that anticipated synergy was never going to materialize. The two Marcam divisions did share the same sales channels or marketing and development philosophies. Reflecting on this period in a 2001 interview in *Strategic Finance,* Cook recalled, "MAPICS turned out to be a great deal for Marcam, which was losing tons of money. MAPICS was always profitable, with revenues of about $20 million a year, so we were a cash cow. However, we couldn't overcome 13 successive quarters of Marcam's losses, and by the fall of '96 we realized that our company would be dead by 1997 if we didn't do something drastic." Because Marcam was spending a great deal of money developing its object-oriented PROTEAN system for process manufacturers, profits suffered. Investors did not differentiate between the profitability of the two divisions, forcing down the price of Marcam stock. As a result, some potential customers of MAPICS were scared away, fearful about the long-term health of the vendor's corporate parent. According to Cook, he was unable to raise money from banks or venture capitalists: "We went to Marcam's board of directors and asked them to set us free so that MAPICS could survive. It was ugly, but the board agreed, and we hired lots of lawyers and accountants, spending an agonizing summer [of 1997] to finalize the deal. We borrowed $64 million from Bank of Boston and took over the parent, creating a subsidiary, Marcam Solutions, Inc. We took $25 million of our loan to pay off Marcam's debts and gave Marcam $39 million over two years as a divorce settlement." Marcam became MAPICS, Inc., which then made an initial public offering (IPO) under its new name. Investors bought 6.9 million shares at $9 each, well aware that the proceeds would be used by MAPICS to pay off the debts of Marcam Corporate to complete the split, but they were clearly confident that MAPICS would be a viable business on its own. Following the IPO, Marcam Solutions was spun-off in a tax-free distribution to shareholders of Marcam Corporation, buyers of the new offering excluded.

With the completion of this "reverse spin-out," Marcam Solutions remained headquartered in Newton, Massachusetts, with Michael J. Quinlan serving as CEO, having replaced Margolis in early 1996, while MAPICS choose to operate out of

Key Dates:

1978: MAPICS software debuts.
1980: Marcam Corporation is formed.
1993: IBM sells MAPICS rights to Marcam.
1997: Marcam changes its name to MAPICS, Inc.; other product lines are spun off as Marcam Solutions.

Atlanta with Cook named as its president. Both companies started with a clean slate, free of debt. MAPICS was especially interested in increasing its level of first-time users and devoted a good deal of its resources developing a version of MAPICS software that could be run on Windows NT, generally regarded as the chosen platform of the future. In the meantime, the company introduced a new release of MAPICS in early 1998, which served to drive license sales, while the company also beefed up its marketing staff and spent considerable sums in promoting itself and its products. In its first full year as an independent company, MAPICS posted nearly $130 million in revenues and a net profit of $18.7 million. Business was so strong that the company outgrew its 77,000 square feet of office space in metro Atlanta. In December 1998, it found 120,000 feet of new office space in nearby Alpharetta, Georgia.

Due to Y2K concerns, MAPICS experienced a slowdown in sales during 1999. Once through this rough patch, according to Cook, management "focused on an acceptable Windows alternative that wasn't a toy. First we had a make-or-buy decision. . . . Since we decided to buy rather than make we had five finalists with ERP backbones running on NT." Despite a softening economy, MAPICS elected in December 1999 to acquire Woburn, Massachusetts-based Pivotpoint for $48 million in cash, thereby adding Pivotpoint's Point.Man system, which allowed MAPICS to operate on UNIX, NT, and Linux platforms. In conjunction with Pivotpoint, MAPICS also looked to develop capabilities in e-business, which along with supply-chain management offered promising growth opportunities.

As the economy began to slow down in 2000, MAPICS experienced a decrease in licensing sales, the result of customers putting off investments. To trim costs, in August 2000 MAPICS cut its work force by 10 percent. In fiscal 2000, the company experienced a drop in revenues to $118.7 million and reported a net loss of $17.7 million. As the economy lapsed into recession, MAPICS lost an additional $27 million in 2001,

despite revenues growing to $138 million. With customers reluctant to purchase software, MAPICS and its competitors were forced to weather extremely difficult conditions. MAPICS, better positioned than most of its competitors, was able to take advantage of the situation and acquired one of its rivals, Frontstep, in a $28.6 million stock swap and the assumption of $20.1 million in debt. Frontstep's roots were as deep as MAPICS, founded in 1979 as MMS International by its chairman Larry Fox, who claimed in a 1995 interview that the inventory-control software business "started with one guy, 50 bucks and a computer." The company became known as Symix Computers Sytems before changing its name to Frontstep in 2000. After three consecutive years of losses, the company had little choice other than to join forces with another mid-sized company like MAPICS, which had a stronger balance sheet. After the acquisition was completed in February 2003, MAPICS reduced its work force by 23 percent, amounting to some 250 jobs. The company remained healthy and waited for economic conditions to improve, at which point manufacturers were expected to once again invest in managing-control software. It was also becoming clear that the market was maturing and that consolidation in the industry was starting to occur, with larger software companies able to command greater resources and likely to dominate. Whether MAPICS would emerge as one of these major players remained to be seen.

Principal Subsidiaries

Frontstep Inc.; Pivotpoint, Inc.

Principal Competitors

i2 Technologies, Inc.; PeopleSoft, Inc.; SAP AG.

Further Reading

Callaghan, Dennis, "MAPICS Turns 20, Looks Ahead," *MIDRANGE Systems*, November 14, 1997, p. 8.

Fulcher, Jim, "Two Heads Are Better Than One," *Manufacturing Systems*, June 1, 1997, p. 16.

Greene, Alice H., "MAPICS Direction Defined," *Manufacturing Systems*, June 1993, p. 15.

"Marcam to Separate Into Two ERP-Focused Companies," *Manufacturing Automation*, June 1, 1997.

Piturro, Marlene, "Bringing New Value and Technology to Old Manufacturing with MAPICS, Inc.," *Strategic Finance*, December 2001, p. 50.

—Ed Dinger

·MasTec

MasTec, Inc.

3155 Northwest 77th Avenue
Suite 110
Miami, Florida 33122-1205
U.S.A.
Telephone: (305) 599-1800
Fax: (305) 599-1572
Web site: http://www.mastec.com

Public Company
Founded: 1929 as Burnup & Sims Inc.
Employees: 8,500
Sales: $838.05 million (2002)
Stock Exchanges: New York
Ticker Symbol: MTZ
NAIC: 237130 Power and Communication Line and
Related Structures Construction; 237110 Water and
Sewer Line and Related Structures Construction;
237120 Oil and Gas Pipeline and Related Structures
Construction

The largest Hispanic-owned company in Florida, MasTec, Inc. is a leading specialty contractor focusing on end-to-end infrastructure services for telecommunications, energy, broadband, and intelligent traffic systems for a broad range of clients in the United States, Canada, and Brazil. The company has nearly 1,000 clients, none making up more than 10 percent of revenues. Besides corporate clientele, MasTec is also heavily involved with municipal, state, and federal agencies dealing with transportation, information technology, energy, and intelligent traffic systems. Beginning in 2001, MasTec was refocusing its business plan onto maintenance-related businesses and, ultimately, on the needs of residential premises. The company's marketing strategy, summarized by the tagline "Design, Build, Install, Maintain," is to emphasize that it monitors its end-to-end infrastructure services in order to increase market share in the fragmented infrastructure industry, and remakes itself according to the requirements of a rapidly changing industry.

1929–93: The Forerunners

In 1929 two unemployed carpenters—Russell Burnup and Riley V. Sims—founded Burnup & Sims (B&S) to provide design, construction, and maintenance services to the telephone and utilities industries. During the years of the Great Depression, the two established an office in West Palm Beach, Florida, and by 1936 had a small fleet of trucks and staff. The company's first telecommunications projects were undertaken the following year at Cape Canaveral, where it was responsible for burying 85 miles of cable.

B&S contributed to national defense during World War II by building airfields and telephone systems. After the war, the company became involved in the laying of underwater cable from Florida to Puerto Rico, and from there to Barbados, for such companies as AT&T and General Telephone. Projects then took on a greater geographical scope, as B&S established underground telecommunications systems and built radio towers in Costa Rica, Barbados, Trinidad-Tobago, and Venezuela.

In 1968 B&S went public, and sales of shares helped to raise capital for new, more ambitious projects. The company constructed the first fiber-optic link between Chicago and Washington, D.C. and, according to historian George P. Oslin in *The History of Telecommunications*, was noted for doing "a large and very profitable business installing cables for Cable TV." The advent of fiber optics in 1980 "meant a complete overhaul of phone systems everywhere," Katrina Burger wrote in the November 1997 issue of *Forbes* magazine. The company also operated a number of telecommunications subsidiaries as well as Floyd Theaters, Inc., a movie picture chain; Lectro Products, Inc., a CATV power-protection company; and Southeastern Printing, Inc., a printing business.

By the end of the decade, however, a poor economy, changes in utility spending, and aggressive competition for contracts brought tough years for B&S. Moreover, budgetary constrictions led certain telecommunications companies to postpone payments and to cut expenditures for plant construction and maintenance. By the end of fiscal 1993, losses at B&S amounted to $9.31 million, and senior management sought a buyer for the company.

Church & Tower of Florida, Inc. (CTF), incorporated in 1968 to construct and service telephone networks in Puerto Rico and Miami, overextended itself in Puerto Rico and could not build the telephone-infrastructure networks needed in Miami. When Miami-based CTF experienced financial difficulties, the company's owner asked his friend, Cuban immigrant Jorge L. Mas Canosa, to help save the business. In exchange for half ownership of CTF, Mas Canosa began to manage the company in 1969.

Eager to improve the business, Mas Canosa climbed down into ditches, manholes, and trenches to observe workers' construction methods. He listened to advice from telephone-company and government inspectors; he studied books about the most efficient and newest construction methods. As a result of these learning experiences, he transformed CTF into a fast-track, cost-effective construction program that won recognition for consistent professionalism and commitment to excellence. BellSouth Telecommunications, Inc. awarded CTF a long-term contract for projects in the greater Miami and Fort Lauderdale areas. By 1971 Mas Canosa had turned the failing company around; he then borrowed $50,000 and bought the remaining shares of the firm.

Jorge Mas, Mas Canosa's eldest son, began working at CTF in 1980 and became company president in 1984. At this time the development of new technologies and the removal of legal and regulatory barriers were laying the foundation for corporate alliances among the nation's largest telephone, CATV, computer, entertainment, and publishing businesses. Telephone companies were planning to invest billions of dollars to install fiber-optic systems to bring the new technologies to homes and businesses. A rapid increase in Florida's population was placing the existing telecommunications infrastructure under tremendous strain.

In 1990 Jorge Mas established a new subsidiary, Church & Tower, Inc. (CT), to engage in selected construction projects in the public and private sectors. For some time the Mas family had been thinking about taking the company public, but 1992 Hurricane Andrew's passage over southern Florida delayed the plans. The CTF Group, owner of a long-term maintenance contract with BellSouth, was responsible for reconstructing the damaged telecommunication infrastructure of Miami. In the wake of the hurricane, the senior managements of B&S and of the CTF Group realized their mutual interests. Employees from both companies began talking to each other; top management met and struck a deal.

1994: Founding of MasTec

On March 11, 1994—in a reverse acquisition—the privately owned Church & Tower Group acquired 65 percent of the outstanding common stock of publicly traded Burnup & Sims, Inc. The name of Burnup & Sims was changed to MasTec, Inc., the Church & Tower Group became a wholly owned subsidiary, and the senior management of the CTF Group took over leadership of the new entity; Jorge L. Mas Canosa became MasTec's chairman, and Jorge Mas was named president and chief executive officer. Mastec was now a regarded as a "minority business enterprise," publicly traded on NASDAQ under the symbol MASX.

At this time MasTec was one of the nation's leading companies of its kind and the fifth-largest Hispanic-owned public company. To express their entrepreneurial spirit as concisely as possible, MasTec's management adopted the former Burnup & Sims slogan "Opening the Lines of Communication" and added their own vision of the future: "Throughout the World."

Following the acquisition, one of President Jorge Mas' first moves was to express the company's philosophy of leadership in word and deed. In an introduction to the company's 1994 annual report, he asserted that "MasTec's improving performance and future capabilities are in large part due to the commitment of its 2,400 employee-owners . . . who work hard, work smart and complete their jobs on time and on budget." In April 1994 he had already set up this success-driven philosophy by distributing five shares of MasTec stock to each employee and encouraging all to invest in their company's benefits program.

Next, MasTec initiated a program for acquiring profitable, market-dominant companies in high-growth metropolitan areas nationwide. The first purchases were that of Designed Traffic Installation, Inc. (an installer of traffic control systems in southern Florida) and Buchanan Contracting Company, Inc. (the holder of two master contracts with BellSouth in Memphis, Tennessee, and Montgomery, Alabama.) Furthermore, Bell-South awarded MasTec contracts for telephone networks in Nashville and Franklin, Tennessee, as well as for networks in four of North Carolina's fastest-growing cities.

From the beginning and throughout MasTec's evolution as a provider of telecommunications services, long-term (master) contracts, such as those with BellSouth, and short-term contracts with alternate-access providers—such as MCI Telecommunications Corp. and US West Communications Services, Inc.—were the backbone of the company's business operations. The deregulation process had enabled alternate-access providers to enter the territory of the regional Bell operating companies, to build networks and sell services to high-volume users, such as those clustered in downtown office buildings and commerce parks. Several MasTec subsidiaries provided fast-track construction services to these competitive-access companies.

Another item on MasTec's business agenda for growth was to increase the Latin American presence it had acquired from the merger. By the mid-1990s many international telecommunication companies had been lured to South America by its improving economy and the privatization of telecommunications, including CATV services. These companies, however, had neither the personnel nor the in-country resources to implement system upgrades of the aging infrastructure for telecom-

Key Dates:

1929: Burnup & Sims (B&S), earliest forerunner of Mas-
Tec, is founded.
1968: Church & Tower of Florida, Inc. (CTF) enters the
infrastructure industry.
1969: Jorge L. Mas Canosa is hired to save failing CTF.
1994: In a reverse acquisition, CTF acquires 65 percent of
B&S, which changes its name to MasTec, Inc.
1996: Telecommunications Act removes barriers to competition.
1997: MasTec goes public; its stock is traded on the New
York Stock Exchange.
2000: MasTec revenue peaks at $1.33 billion.
2001: Economic downturn of telecom and cable markets
heavily impacts MasTec and restructuring begins.

munications. They needed the services of independent contractors who could apply cost-effective methods to the upgrade and
construction of these infrastructures. According to its 1994 annual report, President Jorge Mas believed that MasTec had ''the
cultural ties, management expertise and existing regional operations to serve these needs.''

Consequently, the company's international subsidiaries secured contracts for upgrading telephone networks in Guayaquil,
Ecuador; for building 35,000 telephone lines in San Salvador,
El Salvador; and for constructing fiber-optic facilities in Caracas, Venezuela. Furthermore, Video Cable Comunicacion, S.A.
awarded a design-build contract to MasTec Argentina, S.A. for
upgrading its CATV system in Buenos Aires from 30 channels
to 100. This is believed to have been the first contract of its kind
in Latin America. At year-end 1994 MasTec had met the
challenges of establishing itself as a new company; it reported a
net profit of $7.5 million on revenue of $111.29 million.

Mid-1990s Expansion and Reorganization

Management at MasTec decided to divest some B&S acquisitions not related to its core operations, specifically Floyd
Theaters, Lectro Products, and Southeastern Printing. The proceeds were used to reduce debt and finance the acquisition of
other companies related to MasTec's core business.

Among the acquisitions was Utility Line Maintenance, Inc.,
a company engaged in clearing right-of-ways for utilities in
southeastern United States. Church & Tower Fiber Tel, Inc.
then expanded its business to include installation of ''smart
highway'' systems (electronic systems that control highway
messaging and traffic signalization.) The acquisition of Tri-
Duct Corporation brought two more BellSouth master contracts
in Huntsville and Decatur, Alabama, thereby complementing
existing contracts in Montgomery, as well as in Memphis.
Consolidating administrative functions in these adjacent geographic areas reduced the company's operating expenses and
enhanced service capability in the region. MasTec won new
contracts to install telecommunications networks in the Dallas/
Fort Worth area; to manage construction for Metro Dade Water
& Sewer Authority's Pump Station Program; to install part of

MediaOne, Inc.'s new CATV network in metropolitan Atlanta;
and to develop and maintain infrastructure telephone services in
eastern Colorado for US West.

In its pursuit of international expansion, MasTec had to
compete with large international companies having significantly greater experience and resources. The company acquired
a 36 percent equity interest in Supercanal, S.A., a CATV
operator in Argentina, and equity interests ranging from 14
percent to 35 percent in four other companies. The company
also won a contract from The Virgin Islands Telephone Co. to
restore damaged telephone facilities on the island of St.
Thomas; and a contract from Tomen Corp., a leading Japanese
telecommunications company, for the construction of 35,000
telephone lines in Manila.

By the end of 1995 the company had combined the strengths
of its subsidiaries and organized its operations into three principal business segments: telecommunications and related construction services, CATV infrastructure construction and maintenance, and general construction services. That year MasTec's
revenues increased by some 57 percent, from $111.29 million in
1994 to $174.58 million in 1995.

As MasTec entered the second half of the 1990s, the telecommunications industry continued to undergo fundamental
changes. The U.S. Telecommunications Act of 1996, agreements among countries in the European Union, and continuing
privatization and regulatory initiatives in Latin America removed barriers to competition. Furthermore, growing customer
demand for better voice, video, and data telecommunications
emphasized the limited network bandwidth in sections of the
country. The U.S. government auctioned off radio-frequency
bandwidth for the creation of personal communications systems
(PCS): pure digital networks superior to the traditional analog-
cellular systems.

MasTec competed in the new markets created by these developments by concentrating on additional relevant acquisitions
and on expansion of its core telecommunications services. In a
major acquisition from Telefonica—the largest telecommunications infrastructure contractor in Spain—in 1996, MasTec
bought Sistemas e Instalaciones de Telecomunicacion, S.A.
(''Sintel''). This positioned MasTec to take advantage of the
increased competition anticipated in Europe and the rapid upgrading of telecommunications services expected in Latin
America. The purchase more than doubled the size of MasTec,
and gave it access to Sintel's established operations in Spain
and in Latin America.

Among other acquisitions during this time were the following: Harrison Wright Company, Inc., a telecommunications contractor with operations and BellSouth master contracts principally in Georgia and the Carolinas; Shanco Corporation and
Kennedy Cable Construction, Inc., CATV contractors providing
services to six southeastern states as well as to New Jersey and
New York. MasTec's subsidiaries installed a 370-mile fiber loop
for Telergy, Inc. in upstate New York and completed a fiber loop
for MCI Metro in Raleigh, North Carolina.

The limitations of analog networks propelled the upgrade
and installation of digital networks, which were more efficient.
MasTec increased its penetration into this market by combining

two subsidiaries—Carolina ComTec and Burnup & Sims Communications Services—to form a new company called MasTec ComTec, which brought single-project, turnkey, and maintenance solutions to the communications problems of Fortune 500 corporations, government agencies, colleges, universities, and medical institutions. MasTec ComTec installed both local area networks (LANs) and wide-area networks (WANs). The company was hired to fast-track construction of the enormous fiber-and-copper infrastructure of telecommunications equipment for the 1996 Olympic Village; to build LANs and WANs for the nationwide offices of a major stockbrokerage firm; and to install and maintain a bank holding company's consolidated voice, data, and video network.

Another subsidiary, MasTec Technologies Inc., was established in 1996 to provide management services of wireless networks. In little more than a year the company installed over 130 PCS tower-and-antenna sites for PCS companies, thereby establishing state-of-the-art wireless networks in southern Florida, Tampa, Orlando, and Phoenix. By year-end 1996 MasTec's revenues had increased 171 percent, from $174.58 million in 1995 to $472.8 million in 1996.

Late 1990s: Going Public and Meeting Demand

The Telecommunications Act unleashed a building boom in the telecommunications infrastructure industry—and MasTec prospered. In January 1997 the company announced a three-for-two stock split and on February 14 of that year began trading its common stock on the New York Stock Exchange. President Jorge Mas, in a company news bulletin released after the New York listing, declared that "MasTec's joining the world's premier exchange is a tribute to the dedication and hard work of its 7,000 employees worldwide. The fact that a company formed by Cuban exiles is able to trade among the Fortune 500 companies is living proof that the American dream is very much alive." MasTec celebrated by offering its employees a new stock-purchase program that enabled them to buy stock at a 15 percent discount.

Domestically, through its aggressive acquisition strategy, MasTec acted as a consolidator of thousands of mom-and-pop operators to create a national network of contractors that could provide service wherever it had clients. MasTec provided outside plant services to local exchange carriers—such as Bell South Telecommunications, Inc.; United Telephone of Florida, Inc.; and GTE Corp.—among others. By year-end 1997, MasTec had 20 multi-year master contracts with regional Bell operating companies and other local exchange carriers to meet all of their outside plant requirements according to stipulated costs per job and within a specific geographic areas.

MasTec Chairman Mas Canosa died in 1997; his son, Jorge, Jr., succeeded him. Newly acquired Sintel allowed MasTec to profit from the now deregulated Spanish market and establish itself in Latin America, primarily in the rapidly growing telecom markets of Argentina and Brazil. In July 1997 the company formed MasTec Inepar and held a 51 percent interest in the Brazilian company. By the end of the year, MasTec had acquired 16 domestic and three foreign companies. The following year, as part of a consolidation plan, MasTec sold 87 percent of Sintel and developed a company-wide marketing plan to emphasize the MasTec brand name.

A number of trends led to greater demand for MasTec's services in 1999. A need for greater bandwidth was prompted by increased reliance on personal computers; growth in telecommunications voice, video, and data traffic; electronic commerce; and transmission of high-quality information on the Internet. Furthermore, competition arose from consolidation and deregulation in the telecommunications industry, prompting the birth of new, integrated, geographically diverse companies that offered bundled services formerly available separately. In response, MasTec positioned itself to offer end-to-end solutions for the infrastructure needs of its clients. End-to-end projects started from a transmission point, such as the central office of a telephone company or cable television head-end and ran through aerial, underground cables or wireless transmission to the users' voice and data ports, computer terminals, cable outlets or cellular stations.

MasTec created a new service line that included voice and data network installations, power and gas distribution networks, telecommunications infrastructure projects, and intelligent transportation systems; the company was awarded millions of dollars in contracts for these lines. MasTec formed alliances with a number of companies; for example, it teamed up with Lucent Technologies to provide infrastructure solutions to the cable television industry, and also formed an alliance with Skanska U.S.A. to provide project management and telecommunications infrastructure services throughout North America. MasTec also acquired several external network service providers.

In 1999, Jorge, Jr., retired from day-to-day operations, remaining on-board as chairman. Joel-Tomas Citron was appointed president and CEO of MasTec. Although for a variety of reasons revenues slipped during this time, MasTec remained one of the fastest growing communication and energy infrastructure providers in the United States in 2000.

Contracts poured in. IBM chose MasTec to install and maintain services for its Rapid Network Deployment Program, a project that meant installing more than 1,200 medical kiosks in hospital emergency rooms. Comcast Cable Communications awarded MasTec a five-year contract to help build an advanced fiber-optic network in Comcast territories. The state of Florida chose MasTec to design and install an end-to-end fiber optic network along 2,200 miles of Florida's Turnpike and interstate highways. From the Texas Department of Transportation MasTec won a single contract totalling $740,000 to upgrade a lighting system along the main artery linking Galveston Island with the mainland. Acquisitions continued apace, and by 2000 MasTec reported record revenues of $1.33 billion, some $55.31 million of which came from Brazilian operations.

2001 and Beyond: Weathering a Downtown

MasTec derived a large amount of its revenue from telecommunications clients. However, as Rolf Boone observed in a 2002 article in the *Wenatchee Business Journal*, "a funny thing happened on the way to ever-expanding growth and revenue— the telecommunications bubble burst." In its 2001 annual report, MasTec management noted that "certain segments of the telecom industry suffered a severe downturn that resulted in a number of our clients filing for bankruptcy protection, or experiencing financial difficulties." Even clients not in financial difficulty began limiting capital expenditures for infrastructure projects.

MasTec began to consolidate its many subsidiaries into two major groups: MasTec North America, Inc. and MasTec Brazil, S.A. Still, for fiscal 2001 MasTec posted a loss of $92.35 million in revenue—due primarily to increases in bad debt expense of $182.2 million during the year. In August of that year, Citron resigned and was replaced as president and CEO by Austin J. Shanfelter. A new executive vice-president and CFO, Donald P. Weinstein, was named in January 2002.

Facing a market that had dried up, Shanfelter and Weinstein remained cautiously optimistic, reminding the public that MasTec had predicted the downtown and was making adjustments accordingly. The company's Project 2100 was introduced to streamline, downsize, and realize economies through strategic partnerships. Another key to the plan was in outsourcing much of the company's information technology functions. As a result, MasTec was refocused on telecom, broadband, intelligent traffic systems, and energy.

Financial results for 2002 were disappointing, with the company posting a net loss of $128.8 million on revenues of $838.1. While revenues were reportedly better than management had expected, the cost streamlining process had yet to produce satisfactory results. While analysts concurred that the industry was obviously weak, some also faulted MasTec for its financial results. Standard & Poor's downgraded the company's corporate bonds to junk-bond status. Other industry analysts, however, expected Project 2100 to bear fruit in the coming year and remained optimistic about the company's recovery. MasTec management was similarly hopeful, even confident, that the company was well-prepared to increase profits and cash flow.

Principal Subsidiaries

MasTec North America, Inc.; MasTec Brazil S.A.

Principal Competitors

Betchel Group, Inc.; Dycom Industries, Inc.; Level 3 Communications, Inc.; MYR Group, Inc.; SBA Communications Corporation.

Further Reading

Boone, Rolf, "MasTec Focusing on New Options for Cable News," *Wenatchee Business Journal,* October 2002, p. S4.

Burger, Katrina, "Somebody's Gotta do the Dirty Work," *Forbes,* November 17, 1997, p. 140.

Bussey, Jane, "Mas," *Miami Herald,* September 2, 1996, pp. 17, 21.

——, "Miami-Based Telecommunications-Infrastructure Builder Has Loss for Second Year," *Miami Herald,* March 11, 2003.

——, "S&P Downgrades MasTec Bonds," *Miami Herald,* March 18, 2003.

"CEO Interview: Donald Weinstein," *Wall Street Transcript Digest,* September 16, 2002.

Lunan, Charles, "MasTec Buys Firm in Spain," *Sun-Sentinel,* April 2, 1996, p. D2.

Oslin, George P., *The Story of Telecommunications,* Macon, Ga.: Mercer University Press, 1992, 507 pp.

"S&P Cuts MasTec Inc. [Bonds] to Junk Status," *Standard & Poor's Ratings Services,* March 18, 2003.

"Success in the Trenches: Utilities Share Costs and Benefits of Underground Joint Use," *Transmission & Distribution World,* December 1, p. 58.

Tubb, Maretta, "HydroExcavation Is Ideal for Texas Utility Job," *Underground Construction,* July 2002, pp. 44–46.

—Gloria A. Lemieux

McWane Corporation

2030 Inverness Center Parkway
Birmingham, Alabama 35242
U.S.A.
Telephone: (205) 414-3100
Fax: (205) 414-3180
Web sites: http://mh-valve.com;
          http://www.kennedyvalve.com;
          http://www.clowwatersystems.com;
          http://www.manchestertank.com;
          http://www.amerex-fire.com

Private Company
Incorporated: 1921 as McWane Cast Iron Pipe Co.
Employees: 5,000+
Sales: $1 billion (2002 est.)
NAIC: 331511 Iron Foundries; 332911 Industrial Valve
   Manufacturing; 332313 Plate Work Manufacturing;
   332919 Other Metal Valve and Pipe Fitting
   Manufacturing; 332996 Fabricated Pipe and Pipe
   Fitting Manufacturing; 331111 Iron and Steel Mills

Birmingham-based McWane Corporation is a holding company with an extensive network of interests in the manufacture of ductile iron pipe, water valves, pipe couplers, and fire hydrants, as well as an array of other products, including liquid propane (LPG) cylinders, fire extinguishers, and fire-suppression systems. A publicity-shy company ranking 441 on the *Forbes* list of private companies, McWane is largely owned by the McWane family, and former CEO Phillip McWane remains the company's chairman. The company is run by CEO John J. McMahon, Jr., and president Ruffner Page. Growing through acquisition, some of McWane's holdings were former competitors; others have taken McWane into different product markets and to new geographical regions of the United States as well as to Canada and overseas.

1920s Origins

The history of the McWane enterprise can be traced to 1921 in Birmingham Alabama, when James Ransom (J.R.) McWane left his post as president of the American Cast Iron Pipe Co. to establish his own business, McWane Cast Iron Pipe Co. The company prospered, and the city of Birmingham became known as a foundry and metal-casting hub. J.R. McWane reportedly helped finance the casting of a 56-foot metal sculpture of Vulcan, the god of fire and the forge, which was placed atop Red Mountain, overlooking the city of Birmingham.

McWane acquired Kennedy Valve of New York in 1925, and five years later McWane was reorganized as a holding company and reincorporated as McWane Inc., owner of Kennedy Valve and the McWane Cast Iron Pipe Co.

Kennedy Valve, one of the oldest companies in the McWane empire was founded as The Kennedy Valve Mfg. Co. in Elmira, New York, in 1877. Kennedy produced specialty valves and manufactured its first fire hydrants in the 1890s, spiral type hydrants that were manufactured until the 1930s, when the company adopted a new design.

An even older company, M&H Valve Company, was added to McWane's holdings in the 1980s, when McWane made a major expansion move through the acquisition of large, well-established companies. In 1984 it purchased M&H Valve Company, an Anniston, Alabama business that traced its origin back to 1854, when its founders, McNab and Harlin, started the company in New York City. M&H moved to Patterson, New Jersey, in 1872, seeking a larger facility. Over the next half century, M&H became an important name in various fields, but in the 1920s ran into both financial and familial problems which led to its breakup. In 1925, the division of the company that made cast iron valves was relocated to Anniston and incorporated as M&H Valve & Fitting Company. Although it struggled through the depression of the 1930s, it continued to grow. It also was bought and sold twice, first by the Walworth Valve Company of New York, which bought it in 1955, then by Dresser Industries, which bought it in 1961 and, in 1984, sold it to McWane.

It was in the next year, 1985, that McWane acquired Clow Corporation, purchasing all of its stock and making it a wholly-owned subsidiary. McWane retained two of Clow's operations: Clow Water Systems Company, with its plant in Coshocton, Ohio; and Clow Valve Company, with its valve plant in Oskaloosa, Iowa.

Key Dates:

1921: McWane Cast Iron Pipe Co. is founded.
1925: McWane forms its Kennedy Valve division.
1930: McWane Inc. is incorporated as a holding company for McWane Cast Iron Pipe and Kennedy Valve.
1984: McWane acquires the M and H Valve Co.
1985: Company purchases Clow Corporation.
1995: Company subsidiary Ransom Industries LP acquires Tyler Pipe unit from Tyler Corporation in Texas.
1999: McWane purchases Manchester Tank & Equipment and Amerex Corporation.
2000: McWane buys cylinder manufacturing plant from Trinity Industries Inc.

Clow Corporation was also a long-established business, one that traced its origin back to 1878, when it was founded as James B. Clow & Sons, a Chicago plumbing supply distributor and jobber of wrought iron pipe and other foundry products. In 1890, the company added fire hydrants and water work valves to its line when it became a distributor for the Eddy Valve Company of Waterford, New York. Its Ohio plant in Coshocton was begun in 1909. In 1922, that plant manufactured the first centrifugal cast iron pipe sold in the U.S. Then, in 1928, in order to acquire the rights to Dimitri Sensaud de Lavaud's process of casting iron pipe, Clow bought the National Cast Iron Pipe Company, located in Tarrant, Alabama. In the 1940s, Clow & Sons also acquired the Eddy Valve Company and the Iowa Valve Company of Oskaloosa, a move which helped further its expansion. To reflect its status as a national company, in 1967 James B. Clow & Sons changed its name to Clow Corporation. It continued to grow in the 1970s, acquiring Rich Manufacturing Company of Corona, California in 1972. That purchase added the wet barrel fire hydrant to Clow's line. In 1977, it also began producing ductile iron pipe.

After becoming subsidiaries of McWane Corporation, both Clow Water Systems and Clow Valve Company continued to operate as private entities. Clow Valve Company would also expand. In 1996 it would acquire the Waterworks Division of Long Beach Iron Works and add significantly to its fire hydrant line. It would also continue to operate the Oskaloosa and Corona plants.

McWane did not hold on to all of its acquired divisions or subsidiaries, even when profitable. In 1987, for example, it sold Waterworks Equipment Company, one of its divisions, to Davis Water & Waste Industries, Inc. At the time, Waterworks was operating in Nevada, Utah, and Arizona as a provider of water distribution equipment and supplies. Its net sales for 1986 were $24.0 million, and its assets were valued at approximately $6.7 million.

1990s: Renewed Expansion and Diversification

McWane's expansion continued in the 1990s. In 1995, after creating a holding subsidiary named Random Industries LP as the purchaser of record, it acquired one of its principal competitors, the Tyler Pipe Company of the Tyler Corporation. That company was founded in 1935 in Tyler, Texas, as the Tyler Iron and Foundry Company, and over its history expanded both its operations and product line. It also moved its main operation to Swan, Texas, just north of Tyler. In 1959, the company introduced the industry's first ten-foot soil pipe. Tyler's most notable innovation was its TY-SEAL compression gasket, a coupling device that virtually eliminated the use of molten lead joints for joining pipe sections. The compression gasket was introduced in 1961 and won general industry acceptance by 1963, the same year in which Tyler purchased Wade, Inc. and began marketing a full line of plumbing and drainage specification products. In 1964, the year in which Tyler purchased East Penn Foundry Company of Macungie, Pennsylvania, Tyler began producing No-Hub pipe and fittings. In 1968, then called Tyler Pipe Industries, the company became a subsidiary of Tyler Corporation.

President John McMahon of McWane described Tyler as "a good, old American foundry," one for which McWane as Ransom Industries paid $85 million. At the time Ransom purchased the company from Tyler Corporation, Tyler Pipe had foundries in Texas and Pennsylvania and a coupling/gasket manufacturing facility in Missouri. Like McWane, it made pressure fittings, but it had also just started generating castings for agriculture and automotive businesses. In 1996, Tyler Pipe acquired ANACO, giving it a West Coast market share and new products for its soil-pipe division. Ransom would go on to add a "sister" company for Tyler by acquiring the Union Foundry Co. of Anniston, Alabama, from the Mead Corporation. Union, in business since 1912, manufactured ductile iron pressure pipe fittings for the water and sewer industry. During its history it had various owners before McWane, Inc. bought it and reorganized it as a subsidiary of Ransom.

In 1999, McWane acquired two more companies: Manchester Tank & Equipment of Brentwood, Tennessee; and Amerex Corp of Trussville, Alabama. Manchester, founded in 1945 by Ed Reifschneider, was the largest North American manufacturer of cylinders and tanks for holding compressed air, propane, and various chemicals. At plants located in seven states, and in Australia and Canada, Manchester employed close to a 1,000 workers and produced over five million cylinder and tank units annually. In 1996, the Reifshneider family sold a majority of its shares to AEA Investors Inc. of New York. In turn, although the company was logging record sales, in 1999, AEA put Manchester up for sale.

According to Manchester's president, Darrel Reifshneider, Manchester fit well as a McWane subsidiary. He noted that McWane strongly supported "two-step distribution" and did not attempt to manage or interfere with the day-to-day operations of its divisions and subsidiaries. Instead, he said, "they supply the resources to help each of their divisions to grow, to achieve market expansion, both nationally and internationally." In fact, soon after its sale to McWane, Manchester signed a letter of intent to purchase APA Limited of Sydney, Australia for $15 million. APA Limited, a division of APA Industries Ltd., is a major manufacturer of gasoline tanks and propane cylinders. At least temporarily, the deal fell through, but Reifshneider indicated that an agreement with APA could eventually be ironed out, merging Manchester's Australian operation in the state of Victoria (Echua) with APA's. McWane also gave the green light to other Manchester expansion plans, including a 20 percent increase in the size of its 200/420 pound cylinder manufacturing plant in Virginia and its joint-venture agreement with Blue Rhino Corp. of Winston-Salem, North Carolina to build and operate a cylinder refurbishing plant in the Winston-Salem area.

Amerex Corp., the second major company that McWane acquired in 1999, was the world's largest manufacturer of fire extinguishers and fire-suppression equipment and systems. It was founded in 1971 by Ned Paine and his partner, George Baureis, who died in 1992. At the time of the sale, Amerex had 570 employees at its Trussville, Alabama plant, and the year before had grossed $80 million in revenue. In 1999, deciding to retire and sell the company, Paine stipulated that Amerex had to be sold to a local, family-run company, a provision that Mc-Wane, in Paine's estimate, fully met.

In the next year, 2000, McWane acquired the Cedartown, Georgia, LPG cylinder manufacturing facility from Trinity Industries Inc. of Dallas. Neither company disclosed the terms of the sale. The Cedartown plant produced 200 and 400 lb. DOT (Department of Transportation) cylinders for residential uses. In accordance with its usual policy, McWane elected to maintain Trinity's operation with the same management and workforce.

Challenges in the Early 2000s

In 2003, McWane became the focus of controversy when *The New York Times,* the PBS program *Frontline,* and the Canadian program *The Fifth Estate* made public the results of a nine-month study of the company's safety and environmental records. Citing a high number of sometimes fatal accidents and high pollution levels at some McWane plants, the findings suggested that McWane ran "a dangerous business." Specifically, investigators blamed the company's strict management style and an insistence on high productivity levels as fostering an atmosphere in which concern for worker safety and the environment was actively discouraged.

The notoriously private McWane family refused to be interviewed for the published story and broadcast, but management did issue a response indicating that it was financially committed to training programs that had dramatically improved working conditions at its plants. Management also noted that the steel industry itself was an inherently dangerous business, and that worker safety in the United States remained superior to that of other countries even at the expense of industry market share.

McWane remained unwilling to divulge information about its future prospects or plans. It has been a very successful company, however, and provides an array of products within an inherently stable industry. As its century-closing acquisitions indicated, McWane was still in a growth cycle.

Principal Subsidiaries

Atlantic States Cast Iron Pipe Co.; Clow Valve Company; Clow Water Systems Co.; Empire Coke Co.; Kennedy Valve; M and H Valve Co.; McWane Cast Iron Pipe Co.; Pacific States Cast Iron Pipe Company; Ransom Industries LP.

Principal Competitors

American Cast Iron Pipe Co.; Citation Corporation; Intermet Corporation; McJunkin Corporation.

Further Reading

Barstow, David, and Lowell Bergman, "Dangerous Business," *New York Times,* January 8, 2003, p. A1.

Chastain, Zane, "Reaching Higher," *LP Gas,* April 2000, p. 48.

Niolet, Benjamin, and Russell Hubbard, "50 Douse Fire at Pipe Company," *Birmingham News,* July 29, 2000.

"OSHA Cites New York Foundry for Alleged Safety and Health Violations; Proposes $603,600 Penalty," *OSHA National News Release,* July 14, 1995.

Park, Jennifer, "McWane Inc. Diversifies, Buys Local Amex Corp.," *Birmingham Business Journal,* December 31, 1999, p. 13.

——, "Paine Lets Go of the Amerex Reins," *Birmingham Business Journal,* December 10, 1999, p. 1.

Robertson, Scott, "McWane Seals Pipe Unit Deal," *American Metal Market,* December 5, 1995, p. 2.

"Tyler Corporation Announces Completion of Tyler Pipe Sale," *Southwest Newswire,* December 1, 1995.

—John W. Fiero

The Metropolitan Museum of Art

1000 Fifth Avenue
New York, New York 10028-0198
U.S.A.
Telephone: (212) 535-7710
Fax: (212) 570-3879
Web site: http://www.metmuseum.org

Non-Profit Corporation
Incorporated: 1870
Employees: Not available.
Operating Revenues: $241.35 million (2001)
NAIC: 712110 Museums

The Metropolitan Museum of Art ("The Met") is the non-profit organization that is responsible for the operation of one of the world's largest and most comprehensive art museums, visited by approximately five million people each year. Located in Central Park, the Met's two-million-square-foot main building is owned by the city of New York, while the collections are held for the benefit of the public by the corporation's trustees. In addition, the city pays for the museum's heat, light, and power, as well as funding a portion of the costs of maintenance and security. The corporation is responsible for its share of maintenance and security, plus the costs of acquisitions, conservation, special exhibitions, scholarly publications, and educational programs. The Met also receives an annual grant for basic operating expenses from the New York State Council on the Arts. Moreover, it receives funding through gifts and grants, endowment support, paid admissions, the selling of memberships, as well as ancillary income derived from merchandising, parking garage fees, auditorium admissions, and the museum's restaurants. Aside from its Central Park location, the Met owns and operates a branch museum, The Cloisters, located in northern Manhattan, one of the sites of the museum's Department of Medieval Art. Supplementing the Met's gift shop income are 13 satellite retail operations in the United States (with sales from the shop at Rockefeller Center ranking second to the museum itself) and 11 licensed shops around the world. Aside from the usual souvenirs of tee-shirts and post-cards, Met merchandise includes expensive reproductions of the artwork found in the museum.

19th Century Origins

Since its founding on the southern tip of Manhattan, New York City has been very much devoted to the making of money. It also grew to harbor aspirations for culture, or at least the accolades that were accorded a cultural center. A strong theatrical tradition was born during the Colonial period, and by the 1840s four different theaters were presenting opera. The Academy of Music, which opened in 1854, would become the hub of fashionable society. When it came to the appreciation of the fine arts, however, New Yorkers showed little interest. At the opera, at least, the wealthy had a venue where it could appreciate itself. The New York Historical Society, founded in 1804, which collected and displayed a limited amount of art, was as close to an art museum as the city had to offer. The only serious collector of American art in New York at the time was a wholesale grocery merchant named Luman Reed, who exhibited the pictures he purchased on the third floor of his home one day a week. After his death in 1841 his collection formed the basis of the New York Gallery of Fine Arts. This early attempt to create an art museum failed to maintain sufficient funding, however, and closed in 1854. The non-profit American Art Union, established on lower Broadway in 1838, provided a place for artists to display their work and charged the public a nominal admission fee. Following legal problems it closed its doors in 1852, but during its short history was instrumental in establishing New York as the country's most important marketplace for American Art. In 1859 the Cooper Union was established in New York for the Advancement of Science and Art. It offered a public reading room where collections of arts and artifacts were displayed, destined one day to become part of the Smithsonian Institution. During this period New York boasted a number of museums, as did most large cities, but they were devoted to natural science rather than the display of the fine arts. The popular dime museums of the 19th century, epitomized by P.T. Barnum's American Museum, also specialized in the exhibition of "curiosities." The idea of establishing a New York museum dedicated to the fine arts finally came to fruition in the years following the Civil War, prompted in large part by the success of the 1864 Metropolitan Art Fair, a charity auction that benefited the U.S. Sanitary Commission, ancestor of the American Red Cross.

The seeds for a major New York art museum were actually planted in Paris in 1866 during a Fourth of July luncheon at which John Jay, a prominent lawyer and the grandson of the first Chief Justice of the U.S. Supreme Court, commented in a post-meal speech that it was "time for the American people to lay the foundations of a National Institution and Gallery of Art." Among the Americans gathered that day were a number of New Yorkers who responded to Jay's call and that very night agreed to create such an institution in their native city.

Several were members of the Union League Club, which had been created to support Abraham Lincoln but was also involved in nonpolitical matters. The club referred the idea of a museum to its art committee, which deliberated for three years before recommending the establishment of a metropolitan art museum, provided that it was "free alike from bungling government officials and from the control of a single individual." A plan for the museum was then developed and legal documents drawn up, so that on January 31, 1870, the Board of Trustees for the new museum was selected, their numbers including merchants, lawyers, city officials, as well as a few practicing artists. On April 13, 1870, the New York Legislature agreed to incorporate the Met, mandating that it serve an educational mission to the public.

The Met's first president, railroad tycoon John Taylor Johnston, initiated a $250,000 fundraising campaign, but in the first year succeeded in raising only $110,000, the largest donation of $10,000 coming out of his own pocket. After a second year of effort, the Met was still $24,000 short of its goal, while at the same time Philadelphia and Boston were making great strides in funding their own museums. At this point the Met had no art and no place to display it. A permanent home for the Met would be provided by the city in the new Central Park, which many of the trustees considered too remote, preferring instead the present-day site of Bryant Park. City funding also paid for the construction of a building, which was begun in 1874. In the meantime, the Met secured its first collection of art, due to William T. Blodgett, a member of the executive committee, who on his own initiative bought three private collections of Dutch and Flemish paintings at the cost of $116,000. To display these works as well as other gifts and loans, in 1871 the museum leased a temporary home at 681 Fifth Avenue, a townhouse that had previously been the site of Dodworth's Dancing Academy.

Even before the Met opened its first exhibition, it began merchandising, selling $25 sets of Old Masters engravings. After two years the Met relocated downtown to West 14th Street, an area that was still a fashionable residential neighborhood. The move to the former Douglas Mansion was made necessary in large part by the purchase of the Cesnola Collection of antiquities in 1874, excavated by the American Counsul to Cyprus, and amateur archaeologist, General Luigi Palma di Cesnola. He sold a second collection to the Met in 1876, and three years later was hired to become the museum's first paid director. His reign would last 25 years.

A New Home in 1880

The Met's permanent building in Central Park opened in 1880 and was quickly found wanting. Over the next 100 years three master plans would be developed and abandoned for lack of funding, forcing the museum to make do with piecemeal improvements. (In 1888 the exhibition space was doubled by enlarging the southern end of the building; in 1894 a North Wing opened; in 1905 a Fifth Avenue facade was added; then in 1926 the present Fifth Avenue facade and entrance structure were completed.)

Although the Met now had a permanent home and city support for its upkeep, it still lacked the necessary funds to add to its collections and maintain them, as well as fulfill its educational mission. While many wealthy patrons donated art work to the museum, much was of inferior quality and more of a nuisance than a help. The Met made no secret that in most cases it preferred their patron's money over their art. When the museum received one of its most important bequests, however, it came from an entirely unexpected source. In 1901 New Jersey locomotive manufacturer Jacob S. Rogers, who had only been a supporter of the museum as a $10 per year member, died and left the bulk of his estate to the Met, totaling nearly $5 million. The result was an annual income of close to $200,000 that instantly transformed the institution into the richest museum in the world.

Cesnola died in 1904. The next day a new era began for the Met when famed banker J. Pierpont Morgan was named president of the corporation. With Sir Caspar Purdon Clarke serving as the museum's director, succeeded by his assistant Edward Robinson in 1910, the Met began to grow into a world-class organization supported by a strong professional staff. The publication of the Metropolitan Museum *Bulletin* began in 1905, and the Egyptian and Classical Departments were organized, as well as the Department of Decorative Arts. Over time other departments were spun off: Arms and Armor in 1912; Far Eastern Art in 1915; the American Wing in 1924; Near Eastern Art in 1932; and Medieval Art in 1933. Morgan was instrumental in naming other prominent millionaires to vacant board positions, an act that proved crucial as annual operating costs almost doubled to $362,000 during the eight years he served as president before his death in 1913. To make up the Met's budget deficit, Morgan simply bullied the board into making contributions. Despite his devotion to the museum, however, he left it no money in his will. A large portion of his wealth, which amounted to far less than anyone suspected, was tied up in his art collections. Much of Morgan's art was sold off to satisfy inheritance tax and other liabilities, and in the end just 40 percent came to the museum, albeit one of the most valuable bequests ever made to the Met.

The Met accumulated art at such a pace during the Morgan era that by 1915 the amount of city appropriations to maintain

Key Dates:

1870: The museum is incorporated.
1872: The first exhibition is presented in temporary quarters.
1880: The Central Park facility opens.
1904: J.P. Morgan becomes president of corporation.
1938: The Cloisters, a branch of the museum, opens.
1950: Annual attendance at the main museum reaches 2 million.
1970: A master plan for a major rebuilding project is announced.
1975: The Lehman Wing becomes first part of master plan to be completed.
1994: The major part of the master plan is completed, doubling the museum in size.

the collections had failed to keep pace, forcing the museum to turn to the public to raise additional funds. Nevertheless, the Met was able to acquire a considerable number of treasures that came available during the turbulence of World War I.

Despite increased funding from the city, the museum's money woes continued into the 1920s. By the end of the decade it boasted the highest attendance in its history, as well as its largest deficit. With the advent of the Great Depression, followed by the start of World War II, the Met struggled through the 1930s. Attendance fell off steadily as did memberships. City funding was cut from $501,495 in 1930 to $369,592 in 1939, although by the end of the decade it cost more to operate the museum, which now included the Cloisters, the northern Manhattan medieval museum created by John D. Rockefeller, Jr. Moreover, 17 years had passed since the last improvement had been made to the main Central Park facilities. The buildings were improperly heated and ventilated, and the galleries poorly lit and maintained. The museum, whose trustees in 1939 averaged 60 years of age, was becoming regarded as stodgy, and other institutions began to challenge the Met's preeminence. The Museum of Modern Art, for instance, was organized in large part because of the Met's disinterest in contemporary works.

To rejuvenate the Met and lead it into a new era, the trustees named Francis Henry Taylor to become the museum's new director in the fall of 1939. Taylor, who had introduced exciting new ideas while serving as the director of the Worcester Museum, was devoted to the goal of getting as many people as possible to attend the Met. He abolished the turnstiles and instituted free admission for every day of the week, thus ending 70 years of Monday and Friday pay days. Much of Taylor's plans for construction and rehabilitation, however, were interrupted by the United States' entry into World War II. A large portion of the museum's most treasured items, in fact, were stored in a Pennsylvania mansion during the first three years of the war, a precaution against German air raids. Following the war Taylor began to organize a series of exhibitions that attracted people who had never before visited an art museum. The American people in the post-war years began to visit all museums in record numbers, resulting in greater news coverage for exhibits, which

fueled even greater interest. By 1950 attendance at the Met's main museum reached 2 million, double the 1940 total.

Postwar Fundraising Challenges

One of Taylor's innovations was the opening of a restaurant in the Met, an idea that at the time occasioned scorn. Fundraising, however, proved not to be Taylor's strong suit. A 75th anniversary drive only netted a disappointing $1 million, one-fifth of its stated goal. The city agreed to help fund the costs of construction and rehabilitation of the museum buildings, but at only half of the total cost and none of the costs of installation. Moreover, it would budget no more than $1 million in a single year. Much needed renovations to the Met, as a result, had to be staggered. Finally in January 1954 remodeling was completed, and the Met featured six new period rooms and 95 renovated galleries. Despite this success, Taylor resigned as director of the Met by the end of the year, choosing to return to the Worcester Museum.

The Met was able to continue its acquisition of art through endowment funds earmarked for that purpose, and it was also able to take advantage of the liberal tax laws of the day that encouraged patrons to donate works to the museum in exchange for generous tax breaks. Raising money to air condition the galleries and fund much-needed construction, however, was difficult for director James Rorimer. The size of the Met collections had grown so large by now that only a small portion of it could be displayed.

Rorimer was replaced by Thomas Hoving, who was pivotal in transforming the Met into a business. He too created a master building plan for the Met, centered around its centennial celebration, but unlike his predecessors he was able to scrape together enough public and private money to achieve the goal, as well as to overcome strong opposition to the Met encroaching on Central Park land. He was so determined that he even threatened to take the Met's collections across the Hudson River to a new home in New Jersey. It was Hoving's search for income streams that resulted in the Met's parking garage, which became a important moneymaker for the museum. While construction of the master plan began he modernized the Met's merchandising, in particular growing a mail-order business, franchising sheets and other soft goods, as well as selling reproductions of choice clothing.

The first major part of the master plan to be completed was the Lehman Wing, which opened in 1975. Two years later Hoving resigned and would not see other phases completed, including the Sackler Wing in 1978, the American Wing in 1980, the Michael C. Rockefeller Wing in 1982, the Lila Acheson Wallace Wing in 1987, the Tisch Galleries in 1988, and the Henry R. Kravis Wing and Carroll and Milton Petrie European Sculpture Court in 1990.

With the completion of the 1970 master plan, the Met was now a massive facility with resources that rivaled or surpassed anything available elsewhere in the world. It was also an institution that required a constant flow of money, which was supplied by its well-run business operations. Fundraising reached a new magnitude in the mid-1990s when a booming economy resulted in unprecedented levels of donations to all of the arts. In 1995 the Met launched a $300 million capital campaign. The response was so strong that two years later the museum more than doubled its goal. By the end of the decade the Met had an annual budget in excess of $200 million, which it was more than capable of meeting through its different lines of funding, endowments, and income. The terrorist attack that struck New York on September 11, 2001, had an adverse impact on museum attendance, as it had on other city institutions dependent on tourism. Moreover, the Met would now incur increased security costs. Although cutbacks were clearly in order, and the museum faced its most difficult period in many years, there was little doubt that it would remain a strong and healthy institution, capable of fulfilling the mission set forth by its founders so many years ago.

Principal Competitors

Museum of Modern Art.

Further Reading

Cox, Meg, "At The Metropolitan Museum, Artwork Is to Be Seen, Bought—and Manufactured," *Wall Street Journal,* July 10, 1985, p. 1.

Hibbard, Howard, *The Metropolitan Museum of Art,* New York: Harper & Row, 1980, 592 p.

Hoving, Thomas, *Making the Mummies Dance: Inside the Metropolitan Museum of Art,* New York: Simon & Schuster, 1993, 447 p.

Lerman, Leo, *The Museum: One Hundred Years and the Metropolitan Museum of Art,* New York: Viking Press, 1969, 400 p.

Rosenbaum, Lee, "Museum Confronts an Altered Landscape," *Wall Street Journal,* October 11, 2001, p. A19.

Souccar, Miriam Kreinin, "Darkening Picture," *Crain's New York Business,* November 4, 2001, p. 3.

Tomkins, Calvin, *Merchants and Masterpieces: The Story of the Metropolitan Museum of Art,* New York: H. Holt, 1989, 415 p.

—Ed Dinger

SINCE 1924

THE PROMISE OF PURITY

MTR Foods Ltd.

2971, First Floor, Esturi Tower
K.R. Road, B.S.K Second Stage
Bangalore, 560 070
India
Telephone: (91) 80-676023
Fax: (91) 80-6760227
Web site: http://www.mtrfoods.com

Private Company
Incorporated: 1924 as Mavalli Tiffin Rooms
Sales: $26 million (2002 est.)
NAIC: 311991 Perishable Prepared Food Manufacturing

MTR Foods Ltd. is one of India's leading purveyors of packaged foods. Its products include a variety of vegetarian snack foods and chips, ready-to-eat meals, and partially pre-cooked meals, emphasizing the cuisine of southern India. Other products include pickles, vermicelli, and over 30 varieties of ice cream and ice cream cones. The company is one of only a few that sell packaged food nationwide. MTR Foods also exports canned foods to the United States in an arrangement with the grocery chain Kroger and sells spices in the United Kingdom through the British company Centura Foods. MTR products are also available in Australia, Singapore, Malaysia, and other Asian countries. In 2002, MTR Foods began opening franchised fast-food restaurants across India that served its vegetarian specialties. These are called MTR Super Shops. J.P. Morgan Partners owns a 28-percent share of MTR Foods. Another 14 percent of the company is owned by Magnus Capital Corporation, a venture capital group based in Mauritius. Chairman and company director Sadananda Maiya owns the remainder. MTR operates seven manufacturing facilities. The company is the first Indian processed food company to pass strict global food safety and hygiene standards, preparing the way for MTR's penetration into a broader export market in the 2000s.

Roots in a Popular Restaurant

MTR Foods Ltd. began as a single restaurant in Bangalore called Mavalli Tiffin Rooms. Tiffin is a word traced to colonial rule in India and refers to a light meal or lunch. Mavalli Tiffin Rooms opened in 1924 and was run by members of the Maiya family. The restaurant soon established itself as one of the city's hottest eating spots. It was a modest restaurant where diners paid a single price to a cashier in front and then sat down to a five-course vegetarian meal. The restaurant did not serve alcohol and took only cash. MTR, as the restaurant was known, had a reputation for savory food and high standards of hygiene. It became a favorite with politicians and movie stars, yet the restaurant showed no favoritism, and the VIP's waited in line like everybody else. The restaurant, which still exists but is not part of MTR Foods Ltd., also became a favorite dining spot for tourists in Bangalore. In 1951, MTR was one of the first Indian restaurants to introduce steam sterilization, furthering its reputation for cleanliness. The popular eatery later branched into catering.

Change was forced on the restaurant in 1975 during the State of Emergency declared by Prime Minister Indira Gandhi. Gandhi's rules for the emergency required every restaurant to conform to prices set by the government. The Maiya family felt unable to abide by the government price list. The prices were so low that the restaurant would have had to cut the quality of the food it offered. MTR had made its reputation on hygiene and cleanliness, and the owners felt that compromising the quality of the food they offered would have been disastrous. Rather than following that course, the family shut the restaurant. Its workers, many of whom had been with the restaurant for years, were suddenly unemployed. The Maiya family accommodated a few of them by offering them places in a small grocery store attached to the restaurant. At this point, Sadananda Maiya got the idea to expand the grocery by offering a bigger line of products under the MTR brand name.

Maiya was an electrical engineer by training, and he was able to bring together his skills with both food and technology to launch MTR Foods Ltd. He set the restaurant's former employees to work packaging a mix for the popular breakfast or snack pancake called rava idli. The MTR brand rava idli mix proved a good seller, and when the restaurant reopened after the State of Emergency was lifted in 1977, Maiya continued to manufacture the mix and ventured into other packaged foods as well. His company became MTR Foods Ltd., while the restau-

Key Dates:

1924: Mavalli Tiffin Rooms restaurant opens.
1975: Sadananda Maiya, a member of the founding family of the restaurant, branches into packaged food and founds MTR Foods Ltd.
1983: MTR begins its push into a wider regional market.
1994: The firm is reorganized and embarks on nationwide distribution.
2002: Super Shop restaurant chain debuts.

rant continued in the hands of other Maiya family members. MTR Foods began putting out other dry food mixes, as well as spices, special spice mixtures, and then pickles. The packaged food company built on the restaurant's reputation for purity.

A Dominant Regional Player in the 1980s

At first MTR Foods sold its packaged food through the MTR restaurant grocery. As the food mixes gained a following, the company persuaded other retailers in Bangalore to carry its products. Through the early 1980s, MTR distributed exclusively in Bangalore, selling at various department stores and major groceries. In 1983, MTR decided to press into other southern cities. It sent distributors to Madras, Hyderabad, and Vijayawada to introduce its products. The next year, the company made a major technical innovation. It began packaging its foods in what was called a polyester poly standy pack, the first of its kind in India. This was a high-quality plastic bag with a pyramidal base which enabled it to stand upright. The upright bags greatly increased the brand's visibility on store shelves.

Through the next ten years, MTR Foods worked on bolstering its reputation in southern India. It faced a slew of small competitors in a highly fragmented market. The only big food companies operating across India were Hindustan Lever Ltd., a subsidiary of Unilever, and the Swiss food giant Nestlé. The company consolidated its position in southern India and expanded its manufacturing facilities in and around Bangalore. MTR claimed to have leading market share in several product categories. Overall, however, the Indian packaged food market was still small. MTR was in a sense a pioneer, offering ready-to-eat food when such products were still a novelty and not entirely a necessity. In India, most food was cooked from scratch at home, and women had not yet started entering the workforce in significant numbers. MTR worked its way into being a respectably sized regional player in the 1980s, while the whole packaged foods market in India was valued at only around $30 million.

Big Changes in the 1990s

MTR began a push to become a more prominent company in the early 1990s. Beginning in 1993, the company increased the number of products it offered and actively sought out new markets. It pushed into more cities in southern India, where it eventually gained leading market share in every region that enjoyed a predominantly vegetarian cuisine. Market opportunities also increased in Bangalore, which had become the so-called Silicon Valley of India, the center of the country's booming information technology industry. MTR began providing lunches to workers at several prominent technology firms. By the end of the 1990s, Sadananda Maiya estimated that about 80 percent of Bangalore's high-tech workers were MTR consumers. Overall, the convenience food market in India was growing. As income levels rose and more women were holding jobs outside the home, packaged food boomed. The category was expected to triple in sales by the early years of the new century. MTR changed its structure in 1994 in order to accommodate future growth. The firm was broken into two divisions, one for its main food lines, spices, and vermicelli, and another to specialize in chips and other snacks. MTR also launched an export division. Sales at MTR grew as much as 40 percent annually in the late 1990s, and MTR planned to spread into more markets. Successful in southern India, MTR began penetrating into northern markets by 1998.

MTR launched a new product in 1998 in order to gain a nationwide following. This was its Softy ice cream cone. The ice cream market had long been dominated by big food companies, most prominently Hindustan Lever. MTR's new cone was an immediate hit. The company was able to price its ice cream competitively against Hindustan Lever and still maintain a high profit margin. In some cases, MTR was able to retail its frozen treats for half what Hindustan Lever charged. The company quickly expanded its ice cream portfolio, bringing out several sizes of packaged hard ice cream, some of which it sold to five-star hotels. MTR's reputation for purity evidently helped it pick up new customers.

The company also expanded its line of snack foods such as chips and fries. In addition, it brought out a new line of ready-to-eat meals based on North Indian recipes and entered an arrangement with another company to help with distribution in northern India. MTR also continued to upgrade its packaging technology. The company used a method that had been developed by India's defense department and eventually began supplying ready-to-eat food to the Indian Army. Its new packaging was called the retort pouch. The retort pouch was first developed in the 1970s and kept food safe with no refrigeration. The consumer simply dropped the unopened pouch in boiling water for a few minutes to heat the food. MTR's packaged meals were thus extremely easy to prepare and left virtually no cooking mess. The company brought 11 new prepared meals in retort pouches into the northern Indian market and debuted a smaller line of southern cuisine in the new packaging.

By the late 1990s, MTR also had plans to bring out a line of frozen food. The company proceeded slowly, because a distribution network for frozen food did not exist nationwide. Nonetheless, the company was thinking ahead, hoping to score big in the export market with frozen meals. By that time, the company was exporting some of its products to Australia, Singapore, and other Asian and Pacific countries. MTR saw great potential in exports and worked assiduously both to become a truly national presence in India and then a leading brand abroad. In 2002, the company received ISO 9002 certification, meaning it met globally recognized standards for food safety and hygiene. It also qualified under a similar global food safety program, the Hazard Analysis Critical Central Point. With these certifications, MTR had surmounted major barriers to export. It was able to get its foods into the United States through an arrangement with the grocery chain Kroger and began exporting cooking sauces to England. The company contemplated European markets as well, with a possible first venture in France.

The Vegetarian McDonald's

MTR Foods had made great strides since 1983, when it set it sights beyond Bangalore to become a major regional company. By 2001, the company still did 90 percent of its domestic business in its stronghold in southern India, yet the company fully expected to have half its sales earned in northern India within just a few more years. It had distribution in some 500 Indian towns and cities in that year and planned to reach over 800 locales by 2002. The company was also beginning to set foot in a global market that promised even greater sales. At the beginning of the 2000s, MTR took steps to ready itself for further growth. In 2000, the company raised cash by selling a 20 percent stake in itself to an investment group in Mauritius, Magnus Capital. Magnus was primarily run by Indian immigrants in Singapore. Chairman Maiya hired a new chief executive for MTR in 2001, bagging the former head of the beverage division of Hindustan Lever, Jayaraman Suresh. In 2002, Magnus Capital reduced its stake in MTR to 14 percent, and J.P. Morgan Partners, a division of J.P. Morgan Chase, paid $4 million for a 28 percent stake in the firm. This new infusion of cash was to fund MTR's most ambitious plan yet—to open a string of fast-food vegetarian restaurants. The company opened its first MTR Super Shop in Bangalore in 2002, with ten more planned for other Indian cities. The Super Shop was a combination restaurant/store that featured MTR brand ready-to-eat meals customers could buy and take home and a restaurant area where hot food was served. According to a profile in *Business Line* (March 22, 2001), the Super Shops were to be a "vegetarian replica of McDonald's." The company seemed to be completing a circle, from a modest restaurant to a packaged food manufacturer to a chain of franchised quick eating joints.

Revenue at MTR rose rapidly as its expansion rolled onwards. Sales stood at just under $9 million in fiscal 2001 and were expected to hit $26 million in fiscal 2002. Maiya and new CEO Suresh expected revenue to grow even more, passing $100 million by the middle of the decade if things went as planned. Exports were to account for 20 percent of revenue. This lavish growth did not seem unrealistic. The company had come far already and was now on the brink of even greater market penetration both inside India and abroad. MTR contemplated a public stock offering in 2003.

Principal Divisions

MTR Foods Ltd.; MTR Enterprises; MTR International; Sudarshan Enterprises.

Principal Competitors

Hindustan Lever Ltd.; Tasty Bite Eatables Ltd.; Nestlé S.A.

Further Reading

Ghangurde, Anju, "MTR Foods Offloads Minority Stake to Singapore Firm to Fund Expansion," *Indian Express Newspapers*, March 27, 2000.

"Indian Eatery Firm Embraces WTO Norms in Global Push," *Pakissan.com*, August 10, 2002.

Kurian, Boby, "India: A Ready Recipe," *Business Line*, March 22, 2001.

Rai, Saritha, "An Indian Food Company Expands," *New York Times*, November 27, 2002, pp. W1, W7.

Sethunath, K.P., "MTR's Recipe for Instant Success," *Indian Express Newspapers*, November 26, 2001.

—A. Woodward

National Organization for Women, Inc.

733 15th Street N.W., 2nd Floor
Washington, D.C. 20005-2112
U.S.A.
Telephone: (202) 331-0066
Fax: (202) 785-8576
Web site: http://www.now.org

Not-for-Profit Company
Incorporated: 1967
Employees: 30
Sales: Not available.
NAIC: 813319 Other Social Advocacy Organizations

The National Organization For Women, Inc., better known by its acronym NOW, is a Washington, D.C.-based organization with 500,000 members and 550 local chapters spread throughout the United States, pursuing both grassroots activism as well as national lobbying efforts to achieve equal treatment for women. A not-for-profit corporation, NOW is governed by a 42-member national board of directors, drawn from nine regional entities. NOW also includes state organizations, which focus on issues of local importance. The NOW Foundation serves as the educational and legal arm, pursuing policy initiatives and advocacy work. NOW/PAC is a political action committee that aids candidates for national office. A separate political action committee, NOW Equality PAC, focuses on local elections. The NOW Legal Defense and Education Fund, although established by NOW, is no longer directly affiliated with the organization.

Modern Women's Rights Movement Begins in 1960s

The roots of the American women's rights movement date to the mid-19th century with the focus on suffrage, or the right to vote, for women. In addition, activists such as Susan B. Anthony, Elizabeth Cady Stanton, and Sojourner Truth sought equality in the workplace and elsewhere. The right to vote was finally secured in 1920 but efforts on other fronts failed and the movement languished. Equal pay for women legislation was introduced in 1945—after women had proven themselves in a wide range of occupations when filling in for men who were serving in the military during World War II—but the provision was repeatedly defeated. In the postwar years, the significant presence of women in the workforce became accepted, but many women found their efforts at career advancement thwarted by gender discrimination, encountering the so-called "glass ceiling." As the 1960s began, women were once again spurred to take action and pursue equal treatment under the law in much the same ways that African Americans were pursuing civil rights.

A major spokesperson for the modern women's movement, and a founder of NOW, was author Betty Friedan. In the early 1960s, she lost her job as a newspaper reporter following a second maternity leave and turned to writing articles for women's magazines on a freelance basis. All too often she had her work edited so that references to a woman's life outside the home were virtually eliminated. What remained, she observed, was a fantasy of female domestic bliss, one heavily supported by the media, so that a woman's life had little meaning beyond love, marriage, and motherhood. She began interviewing housewives about the true state of their lives in the postwar years, resulting in a book she titled *The Feminine Mystique*. It was published in 1963 and quickly became a controversial bestseller while transforming Friedan into a celebrity and leader of the resurgent women's movement. Political pressure from women had achieved limited success with President Kennedy, who was compelled to establish a President's Commission on the Status of Women after failing to appoint more than a token number of women to his administration. The appointment of Eleanor Roosevelt as chair of the commission brought much needed attention to the endeavor, although she died a year before a report was released several months after the publication of *The Feminine Mystique*. Perhaps more important than the recommendations that resulted from the report, the President's commission led to the creation of state commissions, which in effect served to create a network of people devoted to advancing the status of women. Moreover, in 1963 federal equal pay legislation was finally passed and amended the Fair Labor Standards Act. A year later major Civil Rights legislation was passed which on the surface bolstered the rights of women but as implemented by the Equal Employment Opportunity Commission (EEOC) proved less than adequate to feminists such as Friedan, who came to believe that women needed a national organization to press their case in the same way African Americans had civil rights groups.

1966 Origins in a Hotel Room

It was at the Third National Conference of the Commission on the Status of Women (with representatives from the state commissions that grew out of the original President's Commission) held in June 1966 in Washington, D.C., that the desire for a national women's group came to fruition. Frustration with EEOC also came to a head when delegates were prohibited by conference rules from passing resolutions that called for the EEOC to enforce the sex discrimination provisions under its legal mandate. Attending as a writer and observer, Friedan invited a group of women to meet in her hotel room to discuss the idea of alternative strategies, although she arrived at the conference already convinced of the need for a national women's civil rights organization. The number of participants in this legendary meeting ranged from 15 to 20. What is not in dispute is that the discussion of alternative strategies quickly turned into an organizational meeting for the National Organization for Women, with the meaningful acronym of NOW, purportedly coined by Friedan. The meeting was contentious at times, with some of the attendees more cautious than others about launching a new organization before exploring alternatives. Supposedly at one point, Freidan tried to evict one of the skeptics from the room and failing to do so locked herself in the bathroom for 15 minutes. In any event, the participants agreed to form NOW, with some 28 people becoming the group's initial members, with a startup budget of just $140. The group's statement of purpose, which Friedan reportedly wrote on a napkin, called for NOW "to take action to bring women into full participation in the mainstream of American society now, exercising all the privileges and responsibilities thereof in truly equal partnership with men."

NOW held its organizing conference in October 1966 in Washington, D.C., attended by more than 300 men and women in the Washington Post Building. Elected as the first chairman of the group was Kathryn Clarenbach, while Friedan was named president despite her lack of administrative skills. Friedan's name recognition was a key asset in gaining media attention, and her large readership was likely to translate into NOW memberships. Both women served until 1970, but Clarenbach's contribution to the growth of NOW became overshadowed by Friedan's celebrity. Clarenbach not only possessed the organizational skills that Friedan lacked, but she was also well connected in academic circles and to a lesser extent in Washington, D.C. Moreover, she brought into the ranks of NOW leadership people possessing equally strong skills and connections. Much

of the longevity enjoyed by NOW is the result of this early decision to split the initial leadership between Friedan and Clarenbach.

NOW was incorporated as a not-for-profit in Washington, D.C., on February 10, 1967. The organization, despite the lack of paid staff members or a budget, quickly set about the task of organizing task forces to tackle the problems of women in the areas of employment, education, law, religion, politics, as well as their image in the media. Local chapters were also being founded around the country so that by the time of its second national conference, NOW grew to 1200 members. It was at this meeting that NOW formulated a "Bill of Rights for Women," which included the call for passage of an Equal Rights Amendment (ERA) to the Constitution and the repeal of all abortion laws. NOW, in fact, became the first national organization to advocate for the legalization of abortion. At this time, NOW very consciously avoided the subject of lesbianism within its ranks, which the group's leadership felt could tarnish the image of the organization with Main Street America. Not only did this tactic prove unsuccessful in controlling media coverage, it hurt the group's standing in the gay community. Other feminist groups that emerged in the 1960s were more radical and not as circumspect. There was WITCH (Women's International Terrorist Conspiracy from Hell), the Redstockings, Cell 16, and the October 17 Movement—now all but forgotten. To these feminists, NOW was too middle class, too cautious. Nevertheless, NOW pressed on, pursuing its goals and evolving with the times.

In 1970, NOW founded its Legal Defense and Education Fund. A year later, with membership totaling 15,000, NOW joined with other feminist groups to form the National Women's Political Caucus in order to become a more coordinated force in politics. Also in 1971, at its Fifth Annual Conference, NOW surprised many observers when it approved a resolution that acknowledged the "oppression of lesbians as a legitimate concern of feminism." Efforts by NOW and other groups on abortion rights culminated in the Supreme Court's landmark 1973 decision in *Roe v. Wade*, which legalized abortion. In that same year, NOW established a separate Public Information Office in New York, resulting in a marked increase in media attention for the organization and its activities. The office would operate until 1975, when budget constraints forced its closure. Nevertheless, the office was instrumental in helping NOW to outlive numerous other feminist organizations.

"Majority Caucus" Takes Control in 1975

In the mid-1970s, NOW faced an internal revolution instigated mostly by younger members who formed the "Majority Caucus" and wanted the organization to become actively involved in more radical issues. To them it was not enough to acknowledge that lesbians had legitimate grievances or to decry violence against women—they wanted action. Their slogan was "Out of the mainstream, into the revolution." In a bitterly contested election in 1975, the group, led by Eleanor Smeal, won a majority of seats on the executive committee and board of directors. Much of NOW's news coverage now focused on its internal riffs and many in the media opined that the organization might soon dissolve. Instead, NOW found its equilibrium and continued to pursue its agenda. In 1978, it declared a state of emergency on the ERA, which had failed to gain enough accep-

---

Key Dates:

1966: NOW is organized.
1967: NOW is incorporated.
1970: A legal defense fund for the organization is created.
1973: *Roe v. Wade* Supreme Court decision legalizes abortion.
1986: NOW Foundation is formed.
1992: NOW celebrates its 25th anniversary.
2003: NOW faces challenges from conservative women's groups, a Republican administration, and a Republican-controlled Congress.

---

tance at the state level to become added to the Constitution. Although proponents of the ERA were able to gain an extension on ratification, the amendment was narrowly defeated in 1982.

NOW's efforts in the ERA fight were not, however, without tangible benefit. The organization gained respect from politicians who recognized that NOW was able to work effectively within the system. In earlier years, candidates might ask that NOW avoid an endorsement, fearful it might hurt their chances of election, but now many began to actively seek the group's support. It was during the early 1980s that NOW coined the term "gender gap," noting how women had been less inclined to vote for Ronald Reagan in the 1980 election. It pushed the media to acknowledge the "gap," and in turn influence politicians, with the hope that women would be viewed as a distinct voting block. An endorsement from NOW and grassroots support, it was hoped, would become an important factor in future elections. Some 20 years later, the gender gap would continue to be invoked, although its origins were seldom recalled.

For all the revolutionary talk from its new leadership, NOW was still pursuing a mainstream approach to accomplishing its goals. By the early 1980s, it had a budget of more than $4 million, a far cry from the $140 it had in the bank just 15 years earlier. NOW did face a backlash, however, as well-financed conservative women's groups emerged to challenge it on a number of fronts. Moreover, with a conservative administration in power, the days of government activism for societal change were long past. The 1985 platform at NOW's National Conference called for a return to street demonstrations and marches, and in 1986 it organized the National Organization for Women Foundation as an education and litigation organization to fight for women's rights. In particular, the foundation employed a litigation strategy in its "Stop the Rescue Racket" project that sought to combat violence at abortion clinics and acts of anti-abortion terrorism. In 1987, NOW was instrumental in organizing nationwide opposition to the nomination of Robert Bork to the U.S. Supreme Court, but in general NOW was just another advocacy group, albeit a well-established one. With conservative women's groups directly opposing its positions, and other feminists charting their own course, NOW could not credibly maintain that it represented all women, a position implied when the group was formed in the mid-1960s.

Gains and Setbacks in the 1990s and Beyond

NOW was not without power and influence as it entered the 1990s. It began to establish high school chapters. In 1992, NOW's 25th year in existence, it organized what it maintained was the largest march and rally ever held in Washington, D.C., as 750,000 people turned out to support abortion rights. In that same year NOW supported a large number of men and women who won election to the U.S. Congress and to state legislatures, a reflection of the organization's commitment to electing influential people rather than just attempting to influence those in power. With the change in campaign finance laws and the rise of Political Action Committees, NOW formed PACs and raised money for them, both on the national and local levels. A legislative highlight of the decade was the 1994 passage of the federal Violence Against Women Act. A year later, to bring attention to the issue, NOW drew an estimated 250,000 people for rally on the Mall in Washington, D.C., focusing on the issue of violence against women. It organized a march in San Francisco in 1996 to support affirmative action, and later in the decade championed legislation and programs to help poor women who faced violence, as well as efforts to gain legal recognition for hate crimes based on gender or sexual orientation.

With the election of George W. Bush and Republican control of the Congress in the early years of the 21st century, NOW, like many progressive groups, faced a challenging period in the political wilderness. Rather than making progress on many of its issues, it was now fighting to hold onto hard-fought gains. In particular, 30 years after *Roe v. Wade*, NOW was worried about erosions in reproductive rights. The fate of the issues that NOW cared so much about may have been uncertain, but there was little doubt that the organization was strong, well entrenched, and likely to remain an influential voice in America for many years to come.

Principal Subsidiaries

NOW Foundation; NOW/PAC; NOW Equality PAC.

Principal Competitors

Independent Women's Forum; Concerned Women of America.

Further Reading

Carabillo, Toni, *The Feminist Chronicles*, Los Angeles: Women's Graphic, 1993, 306 p.
Barker-Plummer, Bernadette, "Producing Public Voice: Resource Mobilization and Media Access in the National Organization for Women," *Journalism and Mass Communication Quarterly*, Spring 2002, pp. 188–205.
Forman, Gayle, "The Nuts 'n' Bolts of NOW," *Ms Magazine*, July/August 1996.
Gabrels, Sara Terry, "The Changing Face of Feminism," *Christian Science Monitor*, July 20, 1998, p. 7.

—Ed Dinger

Noodles & Company, Inc.

4523 West 36th Place, Suite C
Boulder, Colorado 80212
U.S.A.
Telephone: (720) 214-1900
Fax: (720) 214-1934
Web site: http://www.noodles.com

Private Company
Incorporated: 1995
Employees: 2,000
Sales: $28.4 million (2001)
NAIC: 722211 Limited Service Restaurants

Noodles & Company, Inc. is a chain of global noodle shops offering a variety of noodle and pasta dishes influenced by Asian, European, and American flavors and prepared fresh-to-order in a hot sauté process. The company operates more than 56 restaurants in Colorado, Wisconsin, Minnesota, Illinois, Maryland, and Virginia. Noodles & Company provides a low cost meal in a fast-casual environment. Noodle dishes are priced under $6.00, with chicken breast, beef tenderloin, seared shrimp, or tofu available for less than $2.00 extra. Customers purchase their meals at the service counter and employees deliver food to the table in china bowls with silverware. Noodles & Company offers ten noodle dishes, six salads, and two soup flavors. Noodle dishes include Indonesian Peanut Sauté with rice noodles, Wok-Seared Lo Mein, and Roma Tomato Marinara with penne pasta. Japanese Pan Noodles is the most popular dish: udon noodles with broccoli, carrots, and shitake mushrooms sautéed in a pan heated to 450 degrees; the dish is flavored with ginger, garlic, and the company's sweet soy sauce and finished with fresh scallions and mung bean sprouts. Serving more than 25,000 bowls of hot noodles daily, the company's commitment to excellence is embodied in the motto, "Every guest, every bowl, every time."

Entrepreneurial Inspiration in 1993

As Aaron Kennedy walked down Hudson Street near his home in New York's Greenwich Village, the pleasure of dining at a Thai noodle shop inspired the notion of opening a restaurant that offered noodle dishes from all over Asia. The entrepreneur-

ial spirit struck like a lightning bolt as Kennedy expanded the idea, conceptualizing an international noodle shop which offered noodle and pasta dishes from around the world. Contemplating the idea further, Kennedy recognized that noodles are a familiar comfort food and common to most cultures; a global noodle shop would be original and have universal appeal.

Ten years experience as a brand manager for Pepsi Cola and Oscar Mayer Lunchables supported Kennedy's entrepreneurial inclinations. While employed at renowned design firms, he directed marketing programs for Coca Cola, Burger King, Swiss Army Products, The Limited clothing stores, and other major corporations. Though Kennedy did not have experience in the restaurant business, he possessed a unique concept and a willingness to learn.

After relocation to the Denver area, taking a position at a marketing design firm, Kennedy pursued his business idea. Kennedy, then 33 years old, searched through dozens of cookbooks, selecting several sample recipes from cuisines around the world. In 1994, Kennedy met chef Ross Kamens, formerly of the Aspen Lodge Resort, and hired him to consult on recipe and menu development. Kennedy, Kamens, and COO Joe Serafin met to cook and test recipes. In 1995, Kennedy founded The Noodle Shop Company, raising $250,000 in capital through 25 private investors, including family and friends, and a second mortgage on his home.

The first Noodles & Company restaurant opened in the Cherry Creek neighborhood southeast of downtown Denver in October 1995.

Kennedy chose the upscale shopping district because the location attracted educated, active, health-conscious consumers with disposable income. The menu consisted of nine noodle dishes, four salads, and two soup flavors. Noodles & Company offered a bowl of noodles for under $5.00 and a chicken or beef option for an additional $1.00. The 2,500-square-foot space provided seating for 50 customers in a plain setting. Food was prepared in advance and kept warm. Beverages included beer, wine, premium sodas, and specialty teas.

Noodles & Company generated $100,000 in revenues in 1995. Lunch comprised 45 percent of sales while dinner accounted for 55 percent of sales. With child-friendly food in the form of Wisconsin Macaroni and Cheese, the restaurant attracted families in the evening and experienced stronger business for dinner than many quick-casual restaurants. Take-out accounted for 32 percent of total sales.

Mid-1990s: Entrepreneurial Vision Matures

Though the Cherry Creek restaurant needed some improvement, Kennedy opened a second store in an entirely different market, near the University of Wisconsin in Madison where Kennedy received his MBA in Marketing Management. Kennedy's friend Tom Weigard, a real estate developer and owner of a Madison wine bar, joined the company at this time. With funds from additional private investment, Kennedy and Weigard opened the Madison store in March 1996.

The course of the company's development took a dramatic turn after a negative review of the restaurant appeared in the *Wisconsin State Journal* that April. The review deterred patronage of the shop and two months later sales covered only labor and food costs. Kennedy, Kamens, Weigard, and a team of consultants traveled to Madison to evaluate and reshape the concept. The "Redefine Noodles & Company" meeting began in Chicago where the group visited a handful of noodle shops, sampling various dishes and observing the food preparation process, hot sauté to order. Upon arrival at the Madison store, they found the atmosphere sterile and the pricing too low. Worse, the food proved substandard, just as the restaurant review stated.

While the team argued points of refinement, a rainstorm flooded the basement of the restaurant; they bailed water all night. From this prospect of disaster arose a new determination to make the business a success. Kennedy listed fifteen problems and the steps the company would take to resolve them. Kennedy hired two new managers, one with experience in fast food procedures and one with experience in fine dining. Kamens revamped the menu and reformulated recipes. He sought new food sources, such as a 50-year Japanese artisan master who made shanghai and udon noodles. Kamens determined a method of serving noodles that were not overcooked: prepared al dente, the noodles were shocked with cold water, stored at 38 degrees, and then cooked further during the hot sauté process. An architect on the team restructured the restaurant to allow for the hot sauté food preparation. With all problems resolved, the restaurant became profitable by fall and Noodles & Company opened a second store in Madison in May 1997.

Noodles & Company refined its brand concept further by hiring interior designers, graphic designers, and advertising professionals. For a savvy, urban look, new stores would blend an ochre and sage interior with warm lighting and wood tables, exposed ductwork, and a hand-troweled concrete service counter. The cost of opening a store ranged from $250,000 to $350,000 depending on seating, with each unit holding between 32 and 90 seats.

The company preferred corner locations with natural light and traffic visibility. Cooperation with other food service companies created "dining destinations" where the restaurants grouped together in a commercial district. Noodles & Company sought locations in downtown areas or in neighborhoods with a dense mix of residential housing and white-collar office buildings. The company defined its target market to account for level of education, population density, family size, and age of population.

With a polished brand concept, Noodles & Company opened new stores, though at a slow pace. The company raised $1 million in 1998 and $3.2 million in 1999, for a total of $5 million in private investment funds since the company's inception. In 1998, Noodles & Company opened stores in Boulder and Denver; a total of five stores generated $2.4 million in revenues. The company entered the Minneapolis market in September 1999, and the company's seventh store opened in Monona, in the Madison area, a month later. Noodles & Company recorded gross sales of $5.6 million in 1999, averaging approximately $1 million per store. Each store served approximately 500 customers per day, with a check average of $6.75 per person. Same store sales increased 31 percent for units open at least one year and surveys showed a repeat business rate of 30 percent weekly and 55 percent monthly.

Noodles & Company accelerated its rate of growth in 2000, opening ten stores. These included a unit in Fort Collins, Colorado, two units in the Denver metropolitan area, six in Minneapolis-St. Paul, and one each in Madison and Milwaukee. The company closed the year with 17 restaurants in operation and $13.5 million in revenues.

Early 2000s: Evolution and Expansion

Kennedy's experience with the first Madison store taught him to take a more analytical approach to business, so Noodles & Company instituted a continual review process. In 2000, the company formed the Culinary Steering Committee. The five members conducted customer surveys and in-store interviews and addressed customer suggestions. They determined what dishes needed refinement and acted as taste-testers. Kimberly Helouin, food scientist and sensory analyst, joined the company to manage food production at the central kitchen. In early 2001, Kamens returned as executive chef after a three-year hiatus. The company also hired a research and development chef and a quality assurance and support manager.

Refinements to the menu involved experimenting with changes to existing recipes and developing new recipes. The addition of sherry and fresh herbs improved the taste of Mushroom Stroganoff, resulting in increased sales of that item. Pesto Linguini became Pesto Cavatappi, cavatappi being a hollow, spiral noodle that holds the pesto sauce more effectively than

Key Dates:

1995: The first Noodles & Company restaurant opens in Denver.
1996: A negative review of the Madison, Wisconsin, store prompts the company to refine its concept.
1998: With five restaurants in operation, revenues reach $2.4 million.
2000: The company accelerates growth with ten new store openings.
2001: *Nation's Restaurant News* names Noodles & Company a "Hot Concept."
2002: A private offering of stock raises $10 million for facilities, working capital, and expansion.

linguini. To add variety to the menu, Noodles & Company created seasonal dishes. In winter 2001, the company introduced Buffalo Chili: ground buffalo meat, black beans, and kidney beans in a zesty tomato sauce, served over egg noodles. Roasted Tomato Cream, offered in spring 2002, combined fresh and roasted tomatoes in cream sauce, served over fettuccini noodles.

The appeal of the global noodle shop, serving light, freshly prepared comfort food, attracted attention from a variety of business interests. Continuum Partners, developer of 16 Market Square in downtown Denver, approached Kennedy to open a restaurant in the exquisite, new Northern Trust Bank building; Noodles & Company opened there in February 2001. *Nation's Restaurant News* recognized Noodles & Company with its "Hot Concepts" Award in May 2001. The success of the global noodle shop concept attracted investors and the company raised $3 million in a June 2001 private stock offering.

Noodles & Company met its goal of opening 20 new stores in 2001, for total of 37 noodle shops in operation. Besides adding new restaurants in existing markets, the company entered the Chicago market with stores openings in Wheaton, Naperville, and Deer Park Town Center. The company recorded sales of $28.4 million for 2001.

With plans to accelerate the rate of expansion, Noodles & Company hired executives with experience in large-scale business operations. Mary Beth Lewis, former CFO at Wild Oats, joined Noodles & Company in October 2001. In January, the company hired Key Keymer, former president of Sonic Corporation, to be president and co-CEO with Kennedy. A veteran of the fast food industry, Keymer's brought 22 years of executive experience with Taco Bell, Popeye's Friend Chicken, Boston Chicken, and Perkins Family Restaurants. In 2002, Noodles & Company opened 25 new restaurants, entering new markets in the Washington, D.C., area, with one store each in Arlington and Fairfax, Virginia, and one store in College Park, Maryland.

A greater concentration of Noodles & Company stores in the Denver-Boulder region, in metropolitan Chicago, and in Minneapolis-St. Paul made television advertising a viable means of promotion by the end of 2002. The company launched its first television advertising campaign in November, spending $13 million. The two commercials employed the tagline, "We're

going to get you." In "UFO," noodles danced down the ladder of a space ship that looked like the company's signature china bowl upside down. In "Snake Charmer," the quintessential snake charmer plays the flute, causing a noodle to rise from a Noodles & Company bowl. The noodle ensnares the snake charmer and lifts him into the air. The advertising campaign was intended to build brand recognition rather than to sell specific foods. Targeting 25- to 49-year olds, the commercials aired during prime time and late at night on ESPN, TLC, Nickelodeon, Animal Planet, Lifetime, NBC, and WB.

Kennedy decided to slow the company's rate of growth for 2003 due to a weak economy, expecting to open 30 restaurants. New markets under consideration for expansion included Dallas, Salt Lake City, and the Detroit-Ann Arbor area. A successful private placement of common stock in September 2002 raised $10 million for equipment and facilities purchase and leasing, as well as for working capital. In 2003, The Noodle Shop Company officially changed its name to Noodles & Company.

Principal Competitors

Brinker International, Inc.

Further Reading

Berta, Dina, "Noodles & Co.," *Nation's Restaurant News*, May 2001, p. 62.

Cebrzynski, Gregg, "Noodles & Company Takes to Airwaves, Rolls 1st TV Spots," *Nation's Restaurant News*, November 4, 2002, p. 14.

Conklin, Michele, "Restaurateur Uses His Noodle for Cherry Creek North Eatery," *Rocky Mountain News*, October 5, 1995, p. 65A.

"Former Sonic President to Take Helm at Noodles & Company," *Business Wire*, January 17, 2002.

Franklin, Jennifer, "Noodle Chain Plans Seven Metro Stores," *City Business* (Minneapolis-St. Paul), September 1999.

LaVecchia, Gina, "Going Bowling," *Restaurant Hospitality*, July 2000, p. 62.

Myers, Deborah J., "Noodles Keeps Its Big Bowl Restaurant Chain Moving into Bigger Local Headquarters," *Boulder Daily Camera*, April 5, 2002, p. E1.

Ochoa, Julio, "Noodles & Company Uses Financing to Expand into Louisville Location," *Boulder Daily Camera*, August 16, 2000, p. 1B.

O'Sullivan, Kate, "Trust but Verify," *Inc.*, April 2001.

——, "Using Your Noodle," *Inc.*, September 2001, p. 157.

Parker, Penny, "Entrepreneur Uses His Noodle," *Denver Post*, February 16, 1999, p. C1.

Quigley, Kelly, "Noodle Restaurant Chain Plans to Load up in Milwaukee," *Business Journal-Milwaukee*, November 5, 1999, p. 6.

Rebchook, John, "Noodles & Company Expands in Boulder," *Rocky Mountain News*, April 5, 2002, p. 5B.

Rogers, Monica, "The Zen of Noodles: Noodles & Company Menu Master Ross Kamens Never Stops Exploring New Ways to Prepare Pasta," *Chain Leader*, January 2002, p. 24.

Ruggless, Ron, "Noodles & Co. Plots Growth, Sparks Rocky Mountain Buzz," *Nation's Restaurant News*, December 6, 1999.

Sharos, David, "Eatery Owner Adds Naperville to Plate," *Chicago Tribune*, March 15, 2001.

Sneider, Julie, "Just Noodles," *Business Journal-Milwaukee*, December 7, 2001, p. S4.

—Mary Tradii

Norwich & Peterborough Building Society

Peterborough Business Park
Lynch Wood
Peterborough
Cambridgeshire PE2 6WZ
United Kingdom
Telephone: +44 845-300-6727
Fax: +44 173-337-2243
Web site: http://www.npbs.co.uk

Private Company
Incorporated: 1986
Employees: 891
Total Assets: £2.49 billion ($4.2 billion) (2002)
NAIC: 522292 Real Estate Credit; 522120 Savings
    Institutions

One of the largest of Britain's remaining mutual aid building societies, Norwich & Peterborough Building Society has set itself apart by offering a variety of niche products in addition to a full-range of banking services and banking products to its members. The member-based financial company is one of the early proponents of the so-called "green" mortgage, which provides loans and special interest rates for increasing energy efficiency and reducing the carbon dioxide emissions of new homes. Another of Norwich & Peterborough's products is its "carbon neutral" mortgage—the firm promises to plant 40 trees over a five-year period as a means of balancing out the carbon dioxide emissions of a typical home. While Norwich & Peterborough's target area remains the eastern region of England, the company has an international component as well, with an office on the island of Gibraltar, through which the company is able to offer "expatriate" mortgages for British homebuyers seeking pound-based mortgages for homebuilding and buying in Spain's Costa del Sol and other resort areas. Back at home, Norwich & Peterborough has become one of the British market's leading providers of self-build mortgages, which include support services for members building their own homes. The self-build market accounts for 10 percent of the building society's total annual lending portfolio. Commercial loans represent another 10 percent of the group's operations. Norwich & Peterborough services its customers through a network of 59 branch offices, a full-service web site, and a call center. The building society also operates subsidiaries offering brokering services, residential property valuing and surveying services, an insurance brokerage, and, in Gibraltar, an estate agency. These activities have helped the company build an asset base of nearly £2.5 billion by early 2003.

Mutual Aid in the 19th Century

The mutual aid-based building society movement had been responsible in large part for building residential England since the mid-19th century. Once a powerful force in the United Kingdom's financial market, with more than 1,700 individual building societies in existence at the beginning of the 20th century, the movement had barely survived into the 21st century, as most of the societies merged together to form a smaller number of larger operations, many of which later converted to full-fledged bank status, or went public with stock market listings. By the beginning of the 21st century, only 60-odd building societies remained. Many of these were quite small—the smallest had assets of only some £14 million. Norwich & Peterborough was to remain as one of the largest and vigorous of the country's building societies. Like the other holdouts, however, Norwich & Peterborough's strength lay in its commitment to providing local service. Yet Norwich & Peterborough also had established a reputation for innovative products and services.

The mutual aid movement was already a fixture in England by the beginning of the 19th century. Known as "terminating societies," a group of people, typically artisans employed in the same trade, or resident in the same village, joined together to pool their resources so that members were able to purchase land and build their own homes. The pool remained in existence only so long as necessary for the last member to build his home, at which point the society was "terminated."

The mutual aid societies formed by the relatively affluent artisan class were typically small groupings of just 30 or so members, and existed almost wholly for the purpose of directly assisting its members in building their own homes. The emer-

280

Company Perspectives:

Our Mission: To be the best independent regional building society in the UK. Our values: To create a business environment within which staff display initiative, maximise opportunity and provide our members and customers with a professional, prompt and caring service. To provide imaginative, competitive and high quality products and services. To maintain a strong financial position, providing security and stability in the interests of investors and mortgage customers.

gence of an entirely new population, the urban working class, during the Industrial Revolution, created a need for a different type of mutual aid society.

The lower relative wealth of individual workers was compensated by their growing numbers, as the British population shifted from a predominantly rural to increasingly urban base as people sought employment in the growing number of factories, construction sites, and shipyards appearing across the country. The concept of the mutual society in turn shifted to include the new working class. The new building societies now began providing loans—rather than the direct resources of the terminating society—and members were then expected to repay their loans.

This larger asset base also enabled building societies to begin paying interest on members' deposits, leading the new type of mutual aid society to launch secured savings facilities for its members as well. Building societies began providing more standard banking facilities, becoming mainstays of their local communities. As an added contrast to the earlier terminating society, many of the new building societies added the word ''permanent'' to their names. Such was the case with the earliest component of the later Norwich & Peterborough Building Society, which was founded in 1852 under the name Norwich and District Provident Permanent Benefit Building and Freehold Society.

As its name implied, the Norwich building society limited its membership for the most part to its surrounding region, a feature common among early building societies. Whereas many building societies originated as entities serving a local community, others represented the interests of specific communities. Such was the case with the Peterborough Provincial Benefit Building Society. The Peterborough society had been launched by a number of railway workers in 1860. The fast growth of the British railroad network had not only created large numbers of railroad workers, it had also led to a shortage of housing in the Peterborough area. The new building society enabled its members to construct their own homes in the region. Although originally limited to railroad employees, the Peterborough society soon became a regional fixture, and opened its membership to others in the Peterborough area.

Merger Movement at the End of the 20th Century

New legislation, particularly the Building Societies Act of 1874, provided more solid financial and legal foundations for the growth of the building society sector at the end of the 19th and beginning of the 20th centuries. The social climate of the time played a part in the movement's growth as well, as Britain saw the rise of strong workers unions, coupled with the growing prominence of the cooperative movement, and increasing demands for democratization of the British government. The building society fitted naturally within this climate and played an important role in safeguarding its members' savings, especially during turbulent economic times. By the dawn of the 20th century, the building society movement boasted more than 1,700 building societies in existence throughout the United Kingdom.

At the end of World War II, however, the economic situation in England had begun to change. Faced with growing competition from the country's large and powerful banks, and restrictive legislation that limited the types of products and services that building societies were allowed to offer, the movement saw the stirrings of a drive toward consolidation. By the 1960s, the number of individual building societies had dropped sharply, giving way to the emergence of a small number of large-scale building societies. By the beginning of the 1990s, only 100 building societies remained.

The Norwich building society had begun preparing for this transition since shortly after World War II, when it converted its legal status, reincorporating under the new name, Norwich Building Society. The Peterborough society also joined the industrywide transition, becoming the Peterborough Building Society by the 1960s. Peterborough then began to grow, joining the consolidation effort in 1967 when it merged with the King's Lynn Building Society.

Peterborough sought growth again at the beginning of the 1980s, adding the Stamford Building Society in 1980. The society grew once again in 1985 when it absorbed the Argyle Building Society. This acquisition helped Peterborough step up its asset portfolio, which neared £300 million at mid-decade.

In 1986, Peterborough and Norwich agreed to merge, creating one of the eastern region's largest building societies—and one of the top 20 building societies in the United Kingdom—Norwich & Peterborough Building Society. The new grouping represented assets of more than £450 million and included a newly established surveying and valuing arm, Hockleys Professional Limited, which was incorporated that year. The combined society also offered stockbroking, through subsidiary Waters Lunniss, which later became Norwich and Peterborough Sharedealing Services Ltd.

Norwich & Peterborough, though small compared with the country's largest banks, proved highly innovative. The social commitment that had been the basis of the mutual aid movement continued to play an important role in the new Norwich & Peterborough, particularly in its product development. As such, the company was one of the first in the country to go after the urban renewal market, setting up special ''dilapidated'' building mortgage products that offered attractive interest rates for rehabilitating rundown buildings.

In 1988, Norwich & Peterborough treated itself to a new home, opening a new headquarters in a greenfield business park outside Peterborough. Two years later, the company explored a new niche market, setting up a subsidiary operation to serve British citizens on the isle of Gibraltar. From there, Norwich &

Key Dates:

1852: The Norwich and District Provident Permanent Benefit Building and Freehold Society is established.
1860: Railway workers establish the Peterborough Provincial Benefit Building Society.
1874: The Building Societies Act is passed.
1967: Peterborough acquires the King's Lynn Building Society.
1980: Peterborough acquires the Stamford Building Society.
1985: Peterborough acquires the Argyle Building Society.
1986: Norwich and Peterborough merge to form the Norwich & Peterborough Building Society.
1990: Norwich & Peterborough opens an office in Gibraltar and begins offering pound-based mortgages to British expatriates in Spain.
1998: The first ''green'' mortgage is launched.
2000: The ''carbon neutral'' mortgage is launched.
2001: Norwich & Peterborough joins electronic intermediary service Mortgage Brain.
2002: Norwich & Peterborough joins electronic intermediary service Trigold.

Peterborough became interested in another growing new market of the 1990s, that of the growing number of British expatriates acquiring properties along Spain's Costa del Sol and other resort areas in the south of Spain. To serve this market, Norwich & Peterborough created new expatriate mortgage products, providing pound-based mortgages to overseas homeowners. The group also had been expanding its other products and services, including its sharebroking wing, which expanded in 1994 with the acquisition of a new office in Milton Keynes. That subsidiary grew to a network of nine offices by the end of the century.

Through the 1990s, Norwich & Peterborough remained an innovative mortgage provider. The building society was one of the first to cater to the self-build market, providing not only mortgages but support services for members building their own homes. As such, Norwich & Peterborough became one of the leading providers of self-build mortgages, which came to represent some 10 percent of the group's total assets.

By the late 1990s, Norwich & Peterborough's asset portfolio had risen by more than 300 percent, reaching £2 billion in 1998. In that year, the group became the first mainstream lender to offer so-called ''green'' mortgages, which provided incentive rates to encourage homebuilders to increase the energy efficiency of their homes. Norwich & Peterborough then prepared to launch a similar product for members acquiring existing buildings. In 2000, the group joined with Future Forests to promote a new ''carbon neutral'' mortgage, in which Norwich & Peterborough agreed to plant 40 new trees over a five-year period for each new mortgage.

These moves helped Norwich & Peterborough establish its reputation as one of the United Kingdom's most ecologically aware building societies, a description the group saw as befitting its legacy of social commitment. Meanwhile, the building society had not neglected its range of services, opening a call center and launching its first Internet site in 1998.

Branching Out in the Early 21st Century

At the dawn of the 21st century, Norwich & Peterborough began branching out in its efforts to attract additional customers. In 2001, the society signed on with Mortgage Brain, an intermediary service that enabled the electronic filing of mortgage applications, speeding up the application process. Norwich & Peterborough joined a second, similar service, Trigold, in 2002. These moves helped the society mark strong increases in its total assets, which neared £2.5 billion at the end of 2002, despite the prevailing economic uncertainty.

By then, the pool of building societies had continued to dwindle, as the largest building societies took advantage of new legislation granting greater flexibility in the financial industry by going public or converting to bank status. At the dawn of the new century, the United Kingdom counted slightly more than 60 remaining building societies, many of which remained quite small. As one of the largest of the remaining building societies, ranked at number 14, Norwich & Peterborough reaffirmed its commitment to its historic status. As the society's general manager told *Money Marketing:* ''We are staunchly mutual, which we believe gives us an advantage in terms of having competitive interest rates in mortgages and savings. We have no reason to change.'' Nonetheless, Norwich & Peterborough had by then earned its reputation as one of the industry's most innovative lenders.

Principal Subsidiaries

Norwich and Peterborough Sharedealing Services Limited; Norwich and Peterborough Insurance Brokers Ltd; Hockleys Professional Limited.

Principal Competitors

Abbey National PLC; Northern Rock PLC; Bradford and Bingley PLC; Britannia Building Society; Bristol and West PLC; Yorkshire Building Society; Lombard North Central PLC; Portman Building Society; Coventry Building Society; Skipton Building Society; Chelsea Building Society; Leeds and Holbeck Building Society; West Bromwich Building Society; Derbyshire Building Society.

Further Reading

Gallagher, Rosemary, ''Building Blocks of N&P Success,'' *Money Marketing,* June 27, 2002, p. 55.
Hunter, Teresa, and Paul Farrow, ''N&P Comes Top of Tessa League Table,'' *Daily Telegraph,* September 1, 2002.
Hunter, Teresa, ''Mortgage Lenders Prepare for Housing Downturn,'' *Daily Telegraph,* January 15, 2003.
Shaw, Annie, ''Societies Prune Their Branches,'' *Sunday Telegraph,* June 23, 2002, p. 3.
''Societies Pull Together to Keep the Business Mutual,'' *Daily Telegraph,* May 19, 2001.
''Society Branches Out with Tree Planting for New Loans,'' *Sunday Times,* July 16, 2000.

—M. L. Cohen

Noven Pharmaceuticals, Inc.

11960 Southwest 144 Street
Miami, Florida 33186
U.S.A.
Telephone: (305) 253-5099
Fax: (305) 251-1887
Web site: http://www.noven.com

Public Company
Incorporated: 1987
Employees: 252
Sales: $55.4 million (2002)
Stock Exchanges: NASDAQ
Ticker Symbol: NOVN
NAIC: 325410 Pharmaceutical and Medicine
  Manufacturing

Noven Pharmaceuticals, Inc. is a Miami-based company devoted to the development of transdermal drug delivery products. The company uses a small adhesive patch worn on a patient's skin to provide controlled delivery of a drug for a defined period of time, thereby improving patient compliance. Concentrating on the delivery of existing drugs, Noven has been able to focus its research and development efforts on improving transdermal technology, making Noven an industry leader and resulting in the development of much smaller patches that in addition to improving patient comfort allow for patch versions of drugs that would have previously been too large to wear. Noven's advanced technology also allows two drugs to be delivered on one small patch, such as its CombiPatch product that offers both estrogen and progestin to menopausal and post-menopausal women in the United States. Other Noven products, sold through its licensees, include Estalis, the European version of CombiPatch; Vivelle, an estrogen patch for the U.S. market; Menorest, an estrogen patch for the European market; Vivelle-Dot, the U.S. version of a later generation estrogen patch, the world's smallest; and Estradot, the European version of Vivelle-Dot. In addition, Noven directly markets DentiPatch, a product used by dentists as a preliminary anesthetic.

Development of Transdermal Technology: 1980s

From the beginning researchers faced three problems in developing a skin patch appropriate for the delivery of drugs: comfortable size, proper adhesion, and possible skin irritation. The first transdermals, produced in the 1980s, relied on a reservoir system that contained the drug in an alcohol solution. Although these patches effectively delivered a proper dosage of a prescribed drug, the alcohol caused skin irritation. The next generation of transdermals opted to solubilize the drug in an acrylic adhesive, resolving the problem of skin irritation, but leading to other complications. To make a patch small required more drugs and less adhesive, resulting in a product that did not stick very well to the skin. To maintain adhesion and still keep the patch to a reasonable size, researchers turned to a skin permeation enhancer, which once again resulted in problems with skin irritation. Despite the difficulties in working with transdermals, the technology offered great promise. One of the early researchers was Noven's cofounder, Steven Sablotsky, a University of Florida graduate with a degree in chemical engineering. While working with start-up Key Pharmaceuticals, he served as director of product and process development and was instrumental in the creation of a nitroglycerin transdermal patch, the Nitro-Dur II. As the result of its success with the product, Key was acquired by Schering-Plough in 1986. Noven's other cofounder was Sablotsky's cousin, Mitchell Goldberg, a New York City securities dealer. The two had grown up together, drifted apart because of their careers, but became reacquainted in 1986 when Sablotsky attended Goldberg's wedding. During this exciting period for Key, Sablotsky and Goldberg began to discuss the possibility of starting their own company to take advantage of the Nitro-Dur II by offering a second generation transdermal estrogen delivery product that relied on the adhesive method rather than a reservoir system. They founded their company in January 1987 and incorporated it in December 1987, with Sablotsky serving as president and chairman of the board and Goldberg as executive vice-president and director. Goldberg was responsible for business development, licensing, and corporate communications. The company name was a combination of letters from the first names of Steven Sablotsky and his wife, Noreen. Together the parties raised $250,000 in seed money from family and friends. Initially the

---

Company Perspectives:

Already a leader in the development of advanced drug delivery technologies, Noven Pharmaceutical's mission is to become the world's premier developer, manufacturer and marketer of transdermal drug delivery systems.

---

company was little more than Sablotsky working at the kitchen table in his East Kendall, Florida, home, but as the business began to take shape, Noven leased 20,000 square feet of space near the local Tamiami Airport.

Going Public: 1987

Operating with limited funds, Sablotsky and Goldberg looked to raise $1 million to fund Noven's research and development of transdermal, as well as transmucosal, drug delivery systems. They decided to take the company public, scheduling the offering for October 1987. Noven's investment banker advised the partners to hold off and to take a wait-and-see attitude. Then the stock market crashed. According to Sablotsky, his banker told him, ''Steve, you're on your own. I hope you didn't burn any bridges.'' The offering was postponed, not taking place until six months later. With so few companies now opting to go public, Noven was able to gain swift approval from the Securities and Exchange Commission. The company's research and development phase lasted until 1994, the initial focus on transdermal patches to deliver estrogen to menopausal and post-menopausal women, a potentially massive market as women of the baby boom generation began to enter menopause. Estrogen replacement offered a number of benefits for older women: lowering the risk of heart attack, preventing osteoporosis, and lessening palpitations and ''hot flashes.'' As a result, estrogen replacement therapy was expected to grow steadily over the ensuing years and transdermal delivery systems hoped to control a third of that market. Noven made quick strides in developing an estrogen patch and as early as 1989 the company was able to sign a worldwide licensing agreement, with the exception of Japan, for its transdermal estrogen delivery system. A year later, Noven reacquired the rights to the United States and Canada. During this initial stage, Noven posted revenues of $656,169 in 1989 and $1.1 million in 1990, with net losses of $87,904 and $186,863, respectively. In 1991 revenue dipped below $200,000 while losses topped $3 million. In need of a cash infusion, Noven attempted in September 1991 to sell itself for $47 million in stock to another south Florida pharmaceutical, Ivax Corporation. A month later, however, Ivax backed away from the deal due to the valuation of Noven's ''goodwill,'' the difference between the company's tangible assets and its potential. To this point Noven had no products on the market and had yet to file its first application with the Food and Drug Administration, although it had at least two products for which it was preparing paperwork. According to the *South Florida Business Journal,* ''under existing accounting principals and tax laws, Ivax would have been required to charge the 'goodwill' against revenue without having the benefits of corresponding tax deductions. Noven had so much 'goodwill' that Ivax could afford to buy the company using stock worth about $47 million then, but it could not risk the cost of paying taxes on the

amortized 'goodwill' for 40 years in the future, as accounting rules required.'' As a result, Ivax reluctantly decided not to proceed with the acquisition.

In the months after the failed merger with Ivax, Noven was able to secure much needed cash by signing licensing deals for its estrogen patch with two giant pharmaceuticals while retaining its freedom. Obtaining rights to the United States and Canada was Ciba-Geigy, which had been selling its own patch before concluding that Noven's product, named Vivelle for the North American market, was superior. Ciba decided to market Noven's patch as its own, acquiring warrants that would allow it to purchase a 7.6 percent stake in Noven. The French firm of Rhone-Poulenc Rorer (RPR) obtained rights to the rest of the world for the 10-day estrogen patch. To raise further cash, Noven held a secondary stock offering that netted $17.7 million. Because its licensees would require an overabundance of available product before marketing the estrogen patch, Noven had to expand its production capacity. Management considered moving the company to Pennsylvania, close to RPR's U.S. headquarters in Philadelphia, but officials in Dade County, Florida, were eager to keep Noven and offered a number of incentives to stay. Not only did Noven receive economic aid in labor recruitment and training, the county smoothed the way on zoning waivers and provided quick approval on water and sewage permits. As a consequence, Noven was able to purchase and lease a total of 100,000 square feet in three buildings located on 15 acres of land in South Dade County.

Noven was still an unprofitable business in June 1994, when it again tapped the equity market, raising $30.3 million by selling 2.25 million shares of stock at $13.50 per share, an amount that was $2 less than what the company had hoped for. Much of the funds went to purchase necessary equipment for a new manufacturing, distribution, and research facility. By now Noven had a number of other transdermal products in the pipeline, including patches for hormone replacement, cardiovascular disease, antifungal therapy, dental pain management, and asthma. In 1993 the company generated $4 million in revenues, posting a net loss of $3.3 million, and a year later had sales of $6 million and a net loss of nearly $5 million. In the fall of 1994 the company received FDA approval on its estrogen patch, and with the product finally able to enter the marketplace it appeared that Noven was on the verge of finally turning a profit, but a number of factors intervened to jeopardize the future of the company. In January 1995 another estrogen patch, produced by Berlex Laboratories, received FDA approval and it appeared that it would become available in the United States and Canada in the next three or four months.

Noven, on the other hand, was still nine to 12 months from being able to manufacture its patch in one of the company's new South Dade facilities, which was experiencing difficulty in gaining FDA approval. Ciba was reluctant to introduce the product unless it was certain of a steady supply, forcing Noven to start producing the patch at an existing facility for the European market and to build up sufficient inventory for eventual sales in North America. Noven officials were confident that their estrogen patch, designed to be used twice each week, was superior to the one developed by Berlex, which was to be worn for an entire week, resulting in problems with adhesion and skin irritation. Nevertheless, experience held that the product that

Key Dates:

1987: Company is founded by cousins Steven Sablotsky and Mitchell Goldberg.
1988: Initial public offering is completed.
1994: First product gains FDA approval.
1999: Noven posts first net profit.
2001: Steven Sablotsky resigns from the board.

launched first gained a significant market share. Essentially, Noven was forfeiting the advantage it had with Ciba, whose first-generation transdermal product had a monopoly on the estrogen patch market, generating $125 million in North American sales. Moreover, other companies were coming out with second-generation transdermal patches, so that Noven would have an even more difficult time entering the market. As a result investors lost confidence in the prospects of the company and Noven's stock languished in the $8 range, after hitting a high of $19.25 the previous year. Because of sales to Europe Noven was able to double its revenues over the previous year, logging sales of $12.1 million, but the company's net loss also grew to nearly $6.6 million.

Although Noven's new manufacturing plant had still not received FDA approval, Ciba (soon to become part of Novartis AG) decided in the spring of 1996 to finally start marketing Vivelle, after experiencing a 7 percent drop-off in sales of its older patch. This turn of events resulted in an surge of investor confidence, which would more than double the price of Noven stock. Such volatility in the price of the company's stock would be commonplace over the next few years. By the spring of 1997 the stock was again trading at the $8 level, due to lower levels of reorders as the company worked through its stockpile of estrogen patches. Noven hoped to improve its fortunes, and move closer to its elusive goal of profitability, when it introduced its second product, DentiPatch, in 1997. The adhesive strip filled with lidocain was designed to numb the mouth within two minutes and remain effective for 45 minutes, allowing a dentist to painlessly introduce a needle to the area. Although a positive step, Noven lost close to $9.6 million in 1997.

New CEO and Move to Profitability: Late 1990s, Early 2000s

In December 1997 Noven hired a seasoned executive, Robert C. Strauss, who was named president and chief executive officer as part of a transition to new management in early 1998. Not only did Sablotsky step down from these posts, he promised to ultimately resign as chairman of the company. Prior to joining Noven, Strauss served briefly as president and chief operating officer at Ivax, following 14 years of holding various executive positions with Cordis Corporation. Under his guidance Noven began to take significant strides toward profitability, due in large part to the introduction of new products that Sablotsky had been instrumental in developing. The company received FDA approval on the world's first combination patch, one that joined estrogen with progestin for menopausal women. In the late 1990s Noven also introduced Vivelle-dot and Estradot, much smaller estrogen patches that used the com-

pany's revolutionary Dot Matrix technology that ushered in a third generation of transdermal patches. Dot Matrix patches were able to achieve higher drug concentrations on the acrylic portion, resulting in smaller patches, because a silicone layer was added to provide adhesion. Because the silicone and acrylic did not compromise each other's functions, the patch offered drug delivery efficiency and was able to stick to the skin in spite of rigorous activities such as exercise and swimming.

Noven became profitable in 1999, earning $10.46 million on revenues of $31.6 million. The following year sales grew to nearly $43 million while the company posted a net profit of $19.6 million. One of the more exciting products Noven looked to market at the start of a new decade was a patch to treat Attention Deficit Hyperactivity Disorder (ADHD) with a 24-hour dose of methlyphenidate, the chemical name of the drugs Ritalin, Concerta, and Aderall. The company's position in the emerging transdermal market for this medication was bolstered by a patent it received on the patch. The product held great potential in a nearly $1 billion market. Investors bid up Noven's stock in anticipation of the company establishing a franchise in this area but when officials announced that the launch of the patch would be delayed by as much as a year while one more study was conducted, there was a general selloff—a continuation of the roller-coaster ride Noven's stock had experienced for the past decade.

In July 2001 Sablotsky fulfilled his pledge and resigned from Noven's board, and Strauss was elevated to the position of chairman in addition to maintaining his role as president and CEO. The business that Sablotsky had started from his kitchen table 15 years earlier was now very much established and profitable, a leader in transdermal technology. Noven continued to experience growing pains, especially abroad, but there was little doubt that the company was well-positioned for strong and sustained growth.

Principal Subsidiaries

Vivelle Ventures L.L.C.

Principal Competitors

ALZA Corporation; Amarin Corporation plc; Elan Corporation; Novavax, Inc.; Schering-Plough Corporation.

Further Reading

Bilodeau, Anne, "Noven Eyes Market Potential While Seeking FDA Approval," *South Florida Business Journal*, June 1, 1992, p. 4.
Eyerdam, Rick, "The Dreaded 'Goodwill' Continues to Confound," *South Florida Business Journal*, March 9, 1992, p. 1.
Hosford, Christopher, "Noven Deal One of Sweet Talk, Hard Incentives," *South Florida Business Journal*, February 12, 1993, p. 1.
Nesse, Leslie Kraft, "Noven Facing Competition in Estrogen-Patch Competition," *South Florida Business Journal*, January 13, 1995, p. 3B.
Sherrid, Pamela, "Will Boomer Women Defy Menopause," *U.S. News & World Report*, September 11, 2000, p. 70.
Tippet, Karen L., "Investors Lost Their Faith in Noven As U.S. Product Launch Hits Snag," *Wall Street Journal*, August 30, 1995, p. F2.

—Ed Dinger

Observer

Observer AB

Linnégatan 87
S-114 88 Stockholm
Sweden
Telephone: (+46) 8-507-410-00
Fax: (+46) 8-507-417-17
Web site: http://www.observergroup.com

Public Company
Incorporated: 2000
Employees: 2,506
Sales: SKr 1.69 billion ($194.36 million) (2002)
Stock Exchanges: Stockholm
Ticker Symbol: OBS
NAIC: 541820 Public Relations Agencies; 541910
   Marketing Research and Public Opinion Polling

Observer AB is the aptly named parent of a group of companies that focus on monitoring media in various countries for the purpose of evaluating and reporting on the success of a client corporation's or organization's media relations program. Through a series of international acquisitions, Observer AB grew from the dominant media monitoring organization in the Nordic region of Europe to become the world's leading media monitoring and intelligence organization. In addition, its Waymaker division provides services that help public relations and investor relations professionals develop, conduct, and evaluate communications campaigns with their constituent audiences.

Origins as a Division of Sifo Group: 1998–2000

Based in Stockholm, Sweden, Observer AB began as the Observer Media Intelligence division of the Sifo Group AB. In the late 1990s, Sifo Group had three divisions: Observer Media Intelligence, Sifo Research and Consulting, and SMG Consulting. Sifo Research and Consulting provided market research and consulting services. SMG Consulting focused on management and strategic consulting. Observer Media Intelligence's principal business involved media and market monitoring.

Sifo Group AB became a publicly traded stock company on the Stockholm Stock Exchange in September 1998. Previously,

Sifo Group was part of Scribona Group. When Sifo Group went public, its shares were distributed to Scribona's shareholders. At the beginning of 1999, the company had about 1,100 employees in Sweden, Norway, Denmark, Finland, Germany, and the Baltic states of Estonia, Lithuania, and Latvia. Sifo's annual sales for 1997 were SKr 723 million.

In 1998, Sifo Group expanded Sifo Research and Consulting through joint ventures and acquisitions. Sifo Research and Consulting had about 290 employees and was active in five areas: management of intangible assets, brand management, market development, media, and opinion and society. In September 1998, Sifo Research and Consulting and Telia Infomedia Response set up a joint venture called Defacto Inc., whose principal business was to provide reasonably priced customer surveys to small and medium-size companies. In October 1998, Sifo Group acquired Sverige Media from Infratest Burke AB. Sverige had an annual turnover of about SKr 10 million and specialized in media planning in Sweden. Following the acquisition, Sverige Media became part of Sifo Research and Consulting.

Sifo Group also made acquisitions on behalf of Observer Media Intelligence in 1998. In February of that year, the company acquired Word Report in Baden-Baden, Germany. Word Report was active in television monitoring and had about SKr 30 million in annual turnover. The acquisition complemented Observer Media Intelligence's existing operations in Germany, which were renamed Observer RTV Medienauswertungen. Observer Media Intelligence first established operations in Germany in 1997 with the acquisition of a traditional media monitoring business. In November, Sifo Group acquired Observer Eesti, a small media monitoring company with operations in Estonia, Latvia, and Lithuania. Its annual turnover was about SKr 2 million, and it had about ten employees. The acquisition represented a geographical expansion for Observer Media Intelligence.

For 1998, Sifo Group reported operating revenue of SKr 894.4 million, an increase of 24 percent over 1997. Observer Media Intelligence accounted for SKr 493.1 million, a 41 percent increase over the previous year. Internal growth in Observer Media Intelligence accounted for 18 percent of the growth and acquisitions for the rest. Sifo Research and Consulting had operating revenue of SKr 386.7 million, reflecting 10

Company Perspectives:

Observer is an attractive partner for international companies and organizations. The Observer Media Intelligence division has operations in the U.S.A., U.K., Canada, Sweden, Germany, Norway, Finland, Denmark, Portugal, Ireland, Estonia, Lithuania, and Latvia. Observer's services consist of comprehensive monitoring of press, news agencies, radio and TV, databases, and the Internet, as well as editorial and analytical services. The company currently monitors more than 45,000 channels of communication, such as newspapers and magazines, Web publications, broadcast, news services, press releases, Web sites, data bases, and other open sources. The mission of the Communications Tools division, Waymaker, is to offer solutions for the efficient, value enhancing communication with strategically important target groups. Essentially, this means helping clients to create and maintain relations with desired target groups such as journalists, analysts, and shareholders. The division offers services for the entire communication process, from selecting target groups to evaluating communication efforts.

percent growth in Sweden and a 6 percent decline in Norway. SMG Consulting had operating revenue of SKr 43 million, a 12 percent increase over 1997.

Sifo Group continued to expand both Sifo Research and Consulting and Observer Media Intelligence in 1999 through acquisitions and joint ventures. In January 1999, Sifo Group and Guide Konsult AB, one of Sweden's largest independent consulting firms, formed a new company to provide information technology (IT) solutions along with information and consulting services. In mid-1999, Sifo Group acquired Navigare Medical Marketing Research AB, a company that specialized in market studies in the medical field and also provided consulting services for pharmaceutical marketing. Its sales agents and project managers were highly trained in medical and pharmaceutical fields. In 1998, the company had sales of more than SKr 25 million. Following the acquisition, Navigare became part of Sifo Research and Consulting.

Sifo Group made two acquisitions on behalf of Observer Media Intelligence in 1999. The first took place in February 1999 and involved the acquisition of Pressfax OY, Finland's leading fax distributor and supplier of media data. The acquisition added three employees and annual sales of SKr 2.5 million. Pressfax became part of Observer Media Intelligence's BIT (Börslistans Informationstjänst) operations, which distributed financial information for public companies in Sweden. Pressfax was BIT's first international acquisition.

Sifo Group's second acquisition in 1999 for Observer Media Intelligence came at the end of the year and involved a much larger company. In December 1999, Sifo Group acquired Romeike Group, a media and market monitoring company based in London. According to the Sifo Group, Romeike Group was the world's largest media and market monitoring company in the world and at least three times larger than its nearest competitor in the United Kingdom. The company had about 500

employees and annual revenues of approximately SKr 350 million. Sifo Group acquired all of the shares of Romeike Group, financing the acquisition through a combination of short- and long-term debt financing, the issuance of new shares, and a rights offering to existing shareholders. The acquisition was supported by Sifo Group's principal shareholder, Investment AB Bure, which owned 50.1 percent of Sifo Group's shares and controlled 64.1 percent of the voting stock.

The acquisition of Romeike Group was a further step in Sifo Group's overall strategy of growth and internationalization. Following the acquisition, Sifo Group estimated that more than 70 percent of Observer Media Intelligence's revenue—and more than half of Sifo Group's revenue—would come from outside of Sweden. The company noted that even before the acquisition of Romeike Group, Observer Media Intelligence was Europe's leader in media and market monitoring and at least twice the size of its nearest competitors in all of its markets, including Sweden, Norway, Denmark, Finland, the Baltic states, and Germany.

Toward the end of 1999, Observer Media Intelligence obtained the exclusive rights to distribute English-language news about Nordic companies over Business Wire. As a result of the agreement, all English information distributed by BIT would also be posted through Business Wire to some 700,000 financial professionals, 850 online services, and various databases and Web sites around the world. In another transaction, Sifo Group expanded Observer Media Intelligence's presence in Germany by increasing its ownership of Argus Media from 50 percent to 86 percent, effective January 1, 2000. Argus Media was then merged into Germany's Observer RTV Medienauswertungen, giving it a market share of just over 40 percent.

For 1999, Sifo Group's operating revenue increased by 23 percent to Skr 1.09 billion, with operating revenue for comparable units rising by 11 percent. Observer Media Intelligence accounted for SKr 676.5 million in operating revenue, an increase of 37 percent that included 22 percent of internal growth. Sifo Research and Consulting had operating revenue of SKr 411.4 million, while SMG Consulting contributed operating revenue of SKr 42.7 million.

Sifo Group Becomes Observer AB in 2000

Toward the end of March 2000 Sifo Group agreed to sell Sifo Research and Consulting, along with the Sifo brand name, to Research International, a leading custom market research firm. Sifo Group received SKr 600 million for Sifo Research and Consulting and its brand name. The divestiture left Sifo Group with about 1,450 employees. At the same time Sifo Group announced it would focus its core business on media and market monitoring and undertake to change its name. Its other consulting division, SMG Consulting, was subsequently divested in March 2001.

Earlier in 2000, Sifo bolstered its presence in Internet measurement through an agreement with the U.S. monitoring company Media Metrix. Since 1997, Sifo had held the Nordic region's license for Media Metrix's RelevantKnowledge measurement method, which provided demographic data on a Web site's visitors. As part of the new agreement, Sifo transferred its

Key Dates:

1998: Sifo Group, formerly part of Scribona Group, becomes a publicly traded stock company on the Stockholm Stock Exchange.

1999: The Observer Media Intelligence division of Sifo Group acquires Romeike Group in the United Kingdom.

2000: Sifo Group sells its research and consulting division as well as the Sifo brand and changes its name to Observer AB.

2001: Observer AB embarks on an aggressive acquisitions policy.

ownership of its subsidiary Sifo Interactive Media, which had been part of Sifo Research and Consulting, to Media Metrix. In turn, Sifo became part owner of Media Metrix's European subsidiary, MMXI Europe. The sale of Sifo Research and Consulting included Sifo's interest in MMXI Europe.

Following the sale of Sifo Research and Consulting and the Sifo brand, Sifo Group changed its name to Observer AB effective June 6, 2000. The name change reflected the company's focus on its core business of media and market monitoring. Observer AB's strategy was to expand internationally through acquisitions while achieving internal growth of 10 to 15 percent annually. Immediately after becoming Observer AB in June, the company acquired the Norwegian media and monitoring company Imedia AS from its co-owners, Schibsted and Telenor. The acquisition added about 55 employees and was integrated with Observer Norway. Later in the year, the company divested a non-core business in the United Kingdom when it sold Hollis Directories to the British publisher Wilmington Group. Observer AB's media and market monitoring operations were organized under the company's Media Intelligence Division.

In September 2000, Observer AB formed a new Communications Division. The new division targeted clients in public relations and investor relations and provided them with a database of information on media and financial contacts as well as various types of electronic distribution solutions for their press releases, annual reports, and other communications. The Communications Division operated in the United Kingdom under the name Media Information and in Sweden, Finland, and Denmark as BIT. Later in the year, the Communications Division established international cooperation agreements with Bacon's Information, Inc. in the United States and Media Monitors in Australia, giving its clients distribution in the United States, Canada, Australia, and New Zealand.

For 2000, Observer AB reported operating revenue of SKr 1.13 billion. The Media Intelligence Division accounted for SKr 875.1 million, while Communications brought in SKr 210.8 million. Internal growth overall was approximately 20 percent.

Acquisitions and Financial Strategies: 2001 and Beyond

At the beginning of 2001, Observer AB introduced a stock option plan for all of its employees. Under the new incentive program, all employees with at least two years at the company were eligible to receive free stock options, which could then be exercised to purchase Observer shares. Management noted that the option program complemented existing incentive programs and was essential for the company to retain and recruit the right employees.

Observer AB embarked on an aggressive acquisitions program beginning in the first quarter of 2001 and continuing for the rest of the year. In March, it acquired Memorandum SA in Portugal and News Extracts in Ireland. Memorandum was Portugal's leading media and market monitoring company, with a network in southern Europe, including Spanish companies, as well as in Latin America. The acquisition represented Observer AB's first entry into those markets. For 2000 Memorandum had sales of about SKr 20 million and some 80 employees. News Extracts, founded in 1955, was Ireland's first press cutting and broadcast monitoring service. It was Ireland's leading media monitoring company and had operations in Dublin and Belfast, Northern Ireland. During the first quarter of 2001, Observer AB also established new operations in Germany for its Communications Division and divested SMG Consulting. The company also moved its headquarters from Sollentuna to Stockholm.

In May 2001, Observer AB acquired the News Online group and integrated the properties with the company's BIT operations in Scandinavia. The acquired News Online companies included Svenska Media, InformationsProjekt I Bara, and Info Media, which had operations in Norway and Sweden. Together, the News Online companies had sales of about SKr 22 million in 2000 and about 30 employees.

The series of acquisitions within the Communications Division resulted in a proliferation of brand names in different countries. Consequently, Observer AB decided to establish Waymaker as the single new brand for the Communications Division, which had operations in the United Kingdom, Norway, Germany, Sweden, Finland, and Denmark. Waymaker became the common brand for communications solutions for IR and PR professionals in all countries where it operated.

Observer AB made its entry into the North American market in August 2001 with the purchase of Bowdens Media Monitoring Ltd. of Toronto, Canada. Established in 1955, Bowdens was the oldest and largest media monitoring company in Canada. Bowdens had operations in seven Canadian cities, annual sales of SKr 125 million in 2000, and nearly 270 employees. At approximately the same time as it acquired Bowdens, Observer AB acquired Mediascan/CaisseChartier, a leading media monitoring service based in Montreal, Quebec. The company had annual sales of about SKr 40 million.

Before the end of 2001, Observer AB entered the United States market for media monitoring with the purchase of Bacon's Information, Inc. for $90 million. Observer AB acquired Bacon's from Primedia, Inc., which had acquired Bacon's in 1995 when Primedia was known as K-III Communications. Bacon's provided public relations professionals with a wide range of services, including media directories, a clipping service, a press release distribution service, and a media contacts list service.

Having completed six acquisitions in four new markets in 2001, Observer AB consolidated its position as the market leader in media and market monitoring. For 2001, the company reported operating revenue of SKr 1.39 billion, a 20 percent increase over 2000. Observer AB made no further acquisitions in 2002. It was focused on improving its operating margins and integrating its North American acquisitions. The company also strengthened its financial position by obtaining a $175 million multi-currency revolving credit facility from a syndicate of banks that included Nordea, SEB, Svenska Handelsbanken, Nykredit Bank, Bank of Nova Scotia, and HVB Bank Ireland.

While Observer AB admitted that recent acquisitions burdened its financial results for 2002, the company reported a 52 percent increase in operating profit before goodwill amortization for the first half of the year. For 2002, Observer AB's operating revenue rose to SKr 1.7 billion, a 25 percent increase over 2001. However, economic conditions forced the company to take action to cut costs, and it instituted an efficiency program to reduce costs by SKr 45 million. With no signs of increased demand, the company was focused on improving its operating margin. While there were no plans for immediate acquisitions, the company planned to raise funds for possible acquisitions through an issue of new shares and thus improve its debt-to-equity ratio, which stood at 94 percent in 2002.

Principal Divisions

Communications Tools; Media Intelligence.

Principal Subsidiaries

Bowdens Media Monitoring Ltd. (Canada); Observer Danmark A/S; Observer Eesti Oü (Estonia); Oy Observer Finland Ab; Waymaker Oy (Finland); Observer Argus Media GmbH (Germany); Waymaker GmbH (Germany); News Extracts Ltd. (Ireland); Observer Latvija SIA (Latvia); UAB Observer (Lithuania); Observer Norge AS (Norway); Memorandum (Portugal); Observer Sverige AB (Sweden); Waymaker AB (Sweden); Romeike Ltd. (United Kingdom); Romeike International (United Kingdom); Waymaker Ltd. (United Kingdom); Bacon's Information, Inc. (United States).

Principal Competitors

Business Wire; MediaMap, Inc.; PR Newswire Association Inc.

Further Reading

"Observer Divests Stake in SMG Consulting," *Nordic Business Report,* March 16, 2001.

"Observer Finalizes Acquisition of Bacon's of the US," *Business Wire,* November 29, 2001.

"Observer Reports 20% Increase in Operating Revenue," *Nordic Business Report,* February 19, 2002.

"Primedia Sells Bacon's Information to Observer AB," *Business Publisher,* November 17, 2001, p. 1.

"Primedia Will Sell Its Bacon Information Unit," *New York Times,* November 15, 2001, p. C4.

—David P. Bianco

ODL, Inc.

215 East Roosevelt Avenue
Zeeland, Michigan 49464
U.S.A.
Telephone: (616) 772-9111
Toll Free: (800) 253-3900
Fax: (616) 772-3840
Web site: http://www.odl.com

Private Company
Incorporated: 1951 as Zeeland Sash and Door
Employees: 1,250
Sales: $150 million (2002 est.)
NAIC: 321911 Wood Window and Door Manufacturing;
   332321 Metal Window and Door Manufacturing;
   337920 Blind and Shade Manufacturing; 332322
   Sheet Metal Work Manufacturing

ODL, Inc. is a leading manufacturer of decorative windows for doors and entryways, and also makes skylights, enclosed blinds, and retractable screens for doors. The firm's goods are sold to companies that integrate them into finished doors and other building products, and they also are available through home improvement retailers like Home Depot. ODL brands include Vista Skylights, Solar Flair Tubular Skylights, and EntryPoint window blinds and retractable screens, as well as windows that are made under the company's own name. The firm is owned by the Mulder family and run by Larry Mulder, the son of its founder.

1940s Beginnings

ODL traces its roots to March 1945 when Cyrus Mulder started a cabinetmaking shop at his home in Zeeland, Michigan. The small business, which later became known as Artcraft Novelty Shop, initially manufactured custom cabinets, wooden toys, and clothespins. In 1948 Mulder's brother Louis joined him and the two began making prefabricated windows and wooden exterior doors for the post-World War II homebuilding boom that was then in full swing.

Production of doors and windows soon became the Mulders' primary activity, and in 1951 the business was incorporated and renamed Zeeland Sash and Door. By then the firm also was making decorative windows for doors, which were known in the industry as doorlights.

The 1950s saw the company again change focus as the demand for doorlights outstripped its other offerings. In 1963 Zeeland Sash and Door was renamed Ottawa Door Lights, after the Michigan county in which Zeeland was located. Also in 1963 Cyrus Mulder's son Larry entered the family business on a full-time basis after he had quit college to get married.

At this time Ottawa Door Lights was still a small company, with only five employees and annual sales of just $65,000. To increase the firm's revenues, Larry Mulder began to work as a traveling sales representative, and also secured bank loans to help it expand. A few years later he and his brother Garvin would buy the business from their father.

During the mid-1960s Ottawa Door Lights began making windows for installation in the insulated steel doors then popular in home construction, and once again the company found itself with a new product that would shape its future. This new doorlight, the injection-molded polystyrene Uni-Guard Sash, proved so popular that the company opened a second plant to meet demand. The one-piece, gothic-inspired sash design had no joints like a wooden window frame, was not prone to cracking, and required no maintenance.

The 1970s saw the growing Ottawa Door Lights introduce a wide array of new products, including a thermal ventilating doorlight added in 1974 that could let air through a door without use of a screen. In 1976 the firm officially shortened its name to ODL, Inc. in acknowledgment of its by now national reach. During this time the company's sales volume was growing by 40 percent or more each year.

In 1977 the firm started a new subsidiary called ODL Profile, Inc., which would make sliding door tracks, trim strips, and other extruded plastic parts for use in office furniture, partitions, refrigerators, and automotive and lighting products. The company formed the new venture because it wanted to develop products that were not subject to the seasonal ebb and flow of the construction industry. Other new efforts of ODL at this time included production of energy-conserving doorlights and steel insulated sidelights as well as other products for steel insulated doors.

Moving into Skylights in 1979

Keeping up with new trends in home design, the firm created its first skylight for the residential market in 1979. ODL continued to make hardwood doors and various types of windows, which now used a number of different types of glass, including etched, ribbed, and beveled antique style designs.

In 1985 ODL began a round of acquisitions with the purchase of Gordon Skylight Company of Vista, California, a maker of flat dome skylights. In 1988 Red Boy Products of Boston, which made wood window grills, was purchased, and in 1991 the firm bought a Mexican company, Koamex Glass. The Hermosillo-based Koamex made decorative glass doorlights using a variety of techniques. Products added to the company's offerings during this era included oak and mahogany entry doors. A joint venture with the Chinese government also was announced, which involved the manufacture of doorlights in that country.

In the late 1980s residential home construction began slowing down, with new home ''starts'' dropping from 1.8 million in 1986 to 1 million in 1991. This period saw a shift toward purchases of existing homes, which new owners would often upgrade or modify. Chains of ''big box'' stores that catered to this trend, such as Home Depot and Builders' Square, sprang up to offer homeowners a wide array of do-it-yourself renovation products. Affected by the decline in home construction, ODL began developing a number of items for sale to the retail market.

Housing starts began to rise again in the early 1990s, and by 1994 stood at nearly 1.4 million. ODL's business began to pick up, and the firm was soon growing again at an annual rate of 15 percent, necessitating the expansion of one of its Zeeland plants and the hiring of 50 additional personnel.

By 1995 ODL was operating assembly plants or distribution centers in Allentown, Pennsylvania and Portland, Oregon, as well as in Atlanta, Dallas, and San Diego, in addition to three facilities in Zeeland. The firm was now taking in an estimated $85 million in revenues.

In 1997 ODL introduced a line of storage and organization products under the KeepTrak Universal Storage System name.

After conducting a number of focus groups and performing other research, the company had come up with an expandable grid system that could use hooks or drawers to hold items, depending on a user's needs. Price for the starter kit was less than $40, and a total of 15 different items were available. The move was made in part to help the company expand its presence in home center store chains.

Company CEO Larry Mulder ran a tight ship and was sometimes known as a gruff taskmaster, but he also took time off to enjoy a series of adventures outside of the workplace. He took his family on a 14-month sailing trip in 1973–74 that started in the Great Lakes and continued on to the Atlantic ocean and the Bahamas, leaving his brother to watch over the business. He later began hiking the Appalachian Trail, walking segments of the entire 2,159-mile route from Georgia to Maine in annual trips with his son or groups of children from his church in Holland, Michigan. In the summer of 1999 he finished the trek after 18 years of effort. In addition to his own activities, Mulder encouraged his employees to use their spare time to contribute to the community, and the firm and its staff were recognized by the state of Michigan for their work with the Habitat for Humanity organization.

Doubling the Size of the Firm in 2000

In early 2000 ODL made its largest acquisition to date when it purchased Doorlite, Inc. of Gallatin, Tennessee. Doorlite, also known as Western Reserve Products, was a manufacturer of decorative windows for doors with a factory in Mexico and distribution centers in Gallatin, Youngstown, Ohio, and Dallas. Doorlite's 600 employees would nearly double ODL's workforce, and the combined firms would account for an estimated $140 million in annual revenues. After the merger, Doorlite was renamed Western Reflections LLC and operated as a subsidiary of the company.

2000 also saw ODL expand again in Zeeland with a 7,800-square-foot addition to its main plant. The construction, which was assisted by a nearly $1 million, 12-year tax abatement, would add office space as well as an employee lobby and lunchroom. Fifteen new jobs would be created, bringing to 390 the total employed at the factory. The firm had added almost 50,000 square feet there over a two-year span. In 2001 ODL also added a division that would be devoted to manufacturing the company's new Solar Flair Tubular Skylight.

ODL was now offering a diverse, yet complementary product mix. The company made decorative windows for doors in a variety of designs in both clear and privacy-enhancing frosted styles. Matching windows were made for use in the entryway. The company also offered the Secure by Design line of laminated glass security windows which were highly impact-resistant. EntryPoint brand blinds and roller shades could be used in the entryway as well. Other products included Light-Touch Internal Blinds, which featured adjustable slatted blinds sealed inside window glass, and the space-saving EntryPoint retractable screen door that utilized a flexible sliding screen and a vertical roller unit mounted in the door frame.

ODL's skylight offerings included the Vista line, which featured a number of different designs including a severe

Key Dates:

1945: Cyrus Mulder founds a small cabinet making business in Zeeland, Michigan.
1948: The shop starts making doors and windows.
1951: Mulder incorporates the company and renames it Zeeland Sash and Door.
1963: The company name is changed to Ottawa Door Lights.
1976: The company shortens its name to ODL, Inc.
1979: ODL begins making skylights.
1985: The company acquires Gordon Skylight Company of Vista, California.
1988: ODL buys window grill maker Red Boy Products of Boston.
1991: The company purchases Koamex Glass of Hermosillo, Mexico.
2000: The acquisition of Doorlite, Inc. doubles the company's size.
2001: A new division is formed to manufacture Solar Flair Tubular Skylights.

weather model. The firm's Solar Flair Tubular Skylight utilized a small bubble-shaped glass roof opening that was connected to a tube made of highly reflective material, which extended down to the ceiling of a room. It could transmit up to 95 percent of the gathered light into the house. Other items such as wooden doors and storage and organizing systems had been dropped from the company's product mix by this time. Although mostly sold in the United States, ODL products were available in other countries, including Canada and England.

In 2003, nearly 60 years after it was founded, ODL, Inc. had earned a name as a leading manufacturer of door and entryway windows, skylights, and other building products. The firm's reputation for innovation and quality were well known within the industry, and it looked toward continued growth and success in the years to come.

Principal Subsidiaries

Western Reflections LLC.

Principal Competitors

Andersen Corporation; JELD-WEN, Inc.; Pella Corporation; Hunter Douglas N.V.

Further Reading

Goldbogen, Jessica, "ODL Enters Storage, Organization Market," *HFN: The Weekly Newspaper for the Home Furnishing Network,* February 17, 1997, p. 77.

"Holland Hiker Nears End of Trail," *Holland Sentinel,* August 19, 1999.

Leith, Scott, "Building Products Company Acquires Rival," *Grand Rapids Press,* January 25, 2000, p. B5.

McCarthy, Tom, "Mulder Helped Firm Take Off by Staying Out of Clouds," *Grand Rapids Press,* August 2, 1987.

"ODL Again Expanding Zeeland Headquarters," *Holland Sentinel,* June 25, 2000.

"ODL Doubles Sales Volume in Past Two Years," *Holland Sentinel,* January 19, 1978.

"ODL Inc. Acquires Competitor to Expand Capacity," *Holland Sentinel,* January 30, 2000.

"ODL, Inc. Leads the Way in Building Products Industry," *Holland Sentinel,* November 22, 2000.

"ODL, Incorporated Celebrates 50 Years of Growth," *Holland Chamber News,* June, 1995, pp. 4–5.

"ODL Offers Flexible Storage with Keep Trak Universal System," *DIY Week,* January 10, 1997, p. S15.

"Room for Improvements," *Glass Age,* April 1, 1999, p. 88.

Veverka, Amber, "Home Construction Activity Has Companies Adding On," *Grand Rapids Press,* July 17, 1994, p. F1.

—Frank Uhle

Patterson-UTI Energy, Inc.

4510 Lamesa Highway
Snyder, Texas 79549
U.S.A.
Telephone: (915) 574-6300
Fax: (915) 574-6390
Web site: http://www.patenergy.com

Public Company
Incorporated: 1978 as Patterson Drilling Company, Inc.
Employees: 4,607
Sales: $528 million (2002)
Stock Exchanges: NASDAQ
Ticker Symbol: PTEN
NAIC: 213111 Drilling Oil and Gas Wells

Operating out of Snyder, Texas, Patterson-UTI Energy, Inc. is North America's second largest onshore contract drilling company, offering services to major and independent oil and natural gas producers in the Permian Basin of west Texas and southeast New Mexico, south Texas, east Texas, Oklahoma, the Gulf Coast regions of Texas and Louisiana, the Gulf of Mexico, and western Canada. The company is the result of a 2001 merger of equals between Patterson Energy, Inc. and Houston-based UTI Energy Corp., with Patterson becoming the surviving entity. As of December 31, 2002, the company owns a fleet of 324 rigs, which are made up of the structure (hoists and derricks), power sources, and ancillary items such as pumps, blowout preventers, pipe, and other equipment needed to drive a drill bit into rock to depths as much as 30,000 feet. The vast majority of Patterson-UTI's rigs, 286, are mechanical rigs, and the remaining 38 are SCR electrical rigs. In addition, Patterson-UTI offers drilling fluids and completion fluids to customers in order to control pressure while drilling for oil or natural gas wells. Pressure pumping services are provided in the Appalachian Basin to complete new wells and stimulate old ones. The company is also involved in a minor way in the development and exploration of oil and natural gas. Services are contracted in three different ways. Daywork contracts, Patterson-UTI's most common arrangement, are negotiated on a per-day rate for a drilling rig and crew, which the customer is

responsible for supervising, and additional lump sums are paid for the mobilization and demobilization of the drilling rig. Under footage contracts Patterson-UTI drills a well for a customer at a fixed rate per foot. Although the risks are greater under this arrangement, if the project is completed ahead of schedule, the company realizes a higher profit than under a daywork contract. A turnkey contract is the riskiest, and potentially most rewarding, contract under which Patterson does business, requiring that the company provide services, supplies, and equipment not called for in a footage contract and the assumption of such risks as blowouts, fires, and the cratering of the well bore. In addition, payment in the form of a fixed fee is only received when the work is completed, requiring Patterson to bear considerable up-front costs that it may not recoup. As a consequence, Patterson-UTI is involved in relatively few turnkey operations.

Early Years: 1970s–80s

Patterson Energy was originally Patterson Drilling Company, Inc., a business founded by Cloyce A. Talbott and A. Glenn Patterson in 1978. Patterson earned a business degree from Angelo State University in 1970. The older of the partners was Talbott, a west Texas native who earned a degree in Petroleum Engineering from Texas Tech University in 1958. Upon graduation he worked four years for Standard Oil Company of Texas before striking out on his own, forming Snyder Well Servicing, acting as both president and co-owner. The business evolved into a drilling company, ultimately becoming Texas International. Patterson Drilling started out as a small land-based drilling company, with just nine drilling rigs. In 1984 it changed its name to Patterson Energy, although it continued to do business as Patterson Drilling. During difficult times, the company managed to survive into the 1990s, when better days arrived for the energy sector. By the summer of 1992, as it prepared for an initial public offering (IPO), Patterson owned and operated just 11 drilling rigs, with two other rigs jointly owned by an affiliated entity. The company also had two wholly owned subsidiaries, Patterson Petroleum, Inc. and Patterson Petroleum Trading Company, Inc. The offering was a modest one, intended to raise just $5 million, proceeds of which were intended to pay off the company's $3 million in long-term debt as well as support limited gas and oil exploration efforts.

Consolidation of Contract Drilling Operations: 1990s

At the start of the 1990s the land-based drilling rig business was highly fragmented, stocked with numerous companies similar in size to Patterson. Houston-based Nabors Industries was especially aggressive in making acquisitions, helping to set off a wave of consolidation in the industry, which was now enjoying boom times due to rising U.S. oil and gas prices that stimulated drilling activity and resulted in high dayrates. Moreover, drillers began to enjoy the benefit of cost reductions due to advances in technology. Like Nabors, which grew into the largest provider of contract land drilling services, Patterson following its IPO pursued a strategy of growth through acquisition. Its first significant acquisition deal came in July 1994 when it bought Questor Drilling Corp. in a $6.4 million cash and stock transaction. In July 1996 Patterson used stock to acquire Tucker Drilling Company. All told, in the four years following its IPO Patterson increased the size of its drilling fleet from 13 to 46. The company picked up the pace in 1997, growing to 87 rigs by mid-year. The year was highlighted by the purchase of Wes-Tex Drilling Co. and its 21 drilling rigs for $25 million in cash plus stock and warrants for a total deal worth approximately $35.4 million. In 1998 Patterson completed three more important acquisitions. Lone Star Mud, Inc. was bought for just under $13 million in cash and stock in January 1998, followed in February by the $42.2 million merger of Robertson Onshore Drilling with a Patterson subsidiary, and in September by the $3.5 million purchase of Tejas Drilling Fluids, Inc.

Acquisitions, the UTI Merger, and Plans for the Future: 2000s

A drop in oil and gas prices curtailed domestic drilling activities and the merger trend among drilling rig operators, but once the oil services market bottomed out in February 1999, Patterson renewed its quest for greater size and greater profitability. In the early months of 2000 the company was especially active on the acquisition front, picking up two competitors. In March 2000 the company bought four rigs from Wek Drilling when it paid $7.2 million in cash and stock, followed in June by the acquisition of High Valley Drilling in a stock transaction, which added eight drilling rigs. Patterson, through a subsidiary, then acquired Ambar, Inc. in October 2000 for $11.6 million in cash. At the start of 2001 the company agreed to an even larger transaction, which closed early in 2001: a $36.2 million cash and stock purchase of Jones Drilling Corp., a Duncan, Oklahoma, outfit that had been in business since the mid-1950s. As a result of these and lesser acquisitions, Patterson now owned 152 drilling rigs (138 operable) involved in projects spread across Oklahoma, Texas, New Mexico, Utah, and Louisiana. It was the second largest land-based oil and gas contract driller, trailing only Nabors Industries, which had 373 operable rigs. Because of the disparity in size, Patterson was a weak second, but in Febru-

ary 2001 the company took a bold step to challenge Nabors when it reached a deal, one that was three years in the making, to merge with the third largest oil and gas contract driller, UTI Energy, with its 150 drilling rigs, of which 144 were operable.

UTI, which also went public in 1993, was a diversified onshore oilfield services company whose chairman, Mark Siegel, also headed Los Angeles-based REMY Capital Partners III, UTI's largest shareholder. The company had been formed in 1986 and commenced business after acquiring operating subsidiaries from UGI Corporation, drawing on their initials to form its name: Universal Well Services, Union Supply Company, Triad Drilling Company, and International Petroleum Services Company. The oldest, Union, had been in the business of providing oilfield supplies and repair services since 1939. The oldest subsidiary devoted to contract drilling was Triad, commencing operations in 1947. Starting in 1995 UTI decided to focus on expanding its share of the consolidating land drilling industry. As a consequence, in September 1995 the company sold off its oilfield distribution business and began to acquire small independent drilling contractors, with a mind toward gaining access to new markets and establishing regional bases of operation. After one year, UTI's fleet consisted of 27 rigs, but by September 1997 the company had grown to 82 rigs, highlighted by the acquisition of Quarles Drilling. As was the case with Patterson, UTI was especially aggressive in 1999. In April of that year, the company paid $13 million for Norton Drilling Services, and in the same week, in conjunction with REMY Capital, UTI acquired Fracmaster Ltd., a former highflying Canadian oil service company that had fallen on difficult times, due in large part to Russian joint ventures that went sour when that country's finances collapsed. Once boasting a market capitalization of $700 million, Fracmaster was now only able to command a valuation of $95 million. UTI continued to expand its fleet even as it was finishing the final touches on its merger with Patterson Drilling. In January 2001 it paid $13.6 million for six more rigs, the result of three separate transactions.

For both Patterson Drilling and UTI, a merger of equals made a great deal of sense. Talbott and Siegel became acquainted in 1995, often competed over the same deals, and on several occasions discussed the possibility of merging their companies. By the time they agreed to a $1.34 billion stock swap, Paterson and UTI had reached a point where small acquisitions no longer provided enough value to shareholders and both executives believed that their companies were undervalued. According to industry analyst Jim Wicklund of the Dallas firm of Dain Rauscher Wessels, "The combined company now stands out as a strong No. 2, with significant operating leverage, whereas before there were three companies slugging it out for the same spot in investors' portfolios." With a market capitalization of $2.6 billion, Patterson-UTI controlled about 20 percent of the U.S. market of land-based drilling rigs.

Siegel assumed the chairmanship of Patterson-UTI with Talbott serving as chief executive officer. Because of low oil prices in 2001 and a slowdown in drilling activity, demand for drilling rigs fell, forcing the company to layoff between 500 and 1,000 workers, according to published reports. While 80 percent of its rigs had been in operation, now just 65 were under contract. Nevertheless, Patterson-UTI remained optimistic that the dip in activity was just another cycle in the oil and gas

Key Dates:

1978: Patterson Drilling Company is formed.
1984: Patterson Drilling changes its name to Patterson Energy.
1993: Patterson Energy and UTI Energy both go public.
1995: UTI elects to focus on contract drilling field.
2001: Patterson and UTI merge to form second largest contract drilling firm in North America.

business, and in December 2001 the company made its first post-merger acquisition, paying $13.5 million in cash plus stock and warrants for Cleere Drilling Company and its 17 drilling rigs. Explaining the move in light of a difficult business environment, Siegel publicly commented, ''With our strong cash position and $100 million line of credit, we have positioned Patterson-UTI to be able to respond quickly and selectively to unique situations that may arise in the marketplace. We believe that the Cleere assets represent such an opportunity, and are a good fit with out current operations and market coverage.'' In addition, the acquisition brought with it 28 rig-moving trucks and other equipment as well as executive talent in the form of Kirk Cleere, longtime head of Cleere Drilling. Despite a drop-off in business, Patterson-UTI completed its first year posting excellent results. Consolidated income for fiscal 2001 totaled nearly $990 million, compared to $513 million the year before. Net income grew from $37.2 million in 2000 to more than $164 million in 2001. However, the effects of a downturn in the economy and a decrease in drilling activity was felt in 2002. Day rates for a rig, which had peaked in July 2001 at $15,000 a day, fell to a breakeven level of $6,500. As a result, revenues in 2002 dropped to $528 million and net income to less than $2.2 million. Nonetheless, investors bid up the company's stock in recognition of Patterson-UTI's underlying strength. In a June 2002 analysis of the company, *Business Week* wrote, ''Sure, the

fate of the Snyder (Tex.) company . . . is pegged to an economic recovery, but even if natural gas prices don't budge from here, the company's profits could balloon.'' Once the drilling cycle ran its course and commodity prices rose, Patterson-UTI was well positioned to once again thrive in what Talbott described as ''a pretty good environment.'' In a *Wall Street Transcript* interview he went on to say, ''The market has consolidated down to fewer rig owners. It's better than it used to be. We have more sanity in pricing now than there used to be because of less competitors.'' The number of competitors was likely to decline even further in the coming years, with Patterson-UTI hoping to add 30 to 40 rigs per year.

Principal Subsidiaries

Ambar Drilling Fluids LP; International Petroleum Service Company; Patterson Petroleum Trading Company; Suits Drilling Company; Universal Well Services; UTI Drilling Canada Inc.; UTICO, Inc.

Principal Competitors

Grey Wolf, Inc.; Helmerich & Payne, Inc.; Nabors Industries, Inc.

Further Reading

Antosh, Nelson, ''Texas Firms Set to Form No. 2 Driller,'' *Houston Chronicle,* February 6, 2001, p. 1.

Coghlan, Keely, ''Patterson, UTI to Merge in $1.34 Billion Deal,'' *Oil Daily,* February 6, 2001, p. 1.

Hovanesian, Mara Der, ''An Oil Patch Darling,'' *Business Week,* June 3, 2002, p. 97.

Robinson, Rick, ''Snyder, Texas-Based Drilling Company to Acquire Houston Firm,'' *Daily Oklahoman,* February 14, 2001.

Snow, Nick, ''Patterson and UTI Will Combine to Become the Nation's Second Largest Land Driller,'' *Petroleum Finance Week,* February 12, 2001.

—Ed Dinger

Penford Corporation

7094 South Revere Parkway
Englewood, Colorado 80112
U.S.A.
Telephone: (303) 649-1900
Toll Free: (800) 204-7369
Fax: (303) 649-1700
Web site: http://www.penx.com

Public Company
Incorporated: 1983
Employees: 700
Sales: $231 million (2002)
Stock Exchanges: NASDAQ
Ticker Symbol: PENX
NAIC: 311211 Flour Milling; 325199 All Other Basic
    Organic Chemical Manufacturing; 311999 All Other
    Miscellaneous Food Manufacturing

Penford Corporation develops, produces, and markets specialty natural-based ingredients for industrial and food applications. The company uses carbohydrate chemistry to develop functional starch-based ingredients for applications in several markets, including papermaking, textiles, and food products. The company focuses on three business segments. The first two, industrial and food ingredients, encompass broad categories of end-market users and are primarily served by the company's U.S. operations. The company's operations in Australia and New Zealand comprise the third segment, which focuses primarily on the food ingredient business, although the industrial market is also becoming a growth area. Penford's specialty products for industrial applications are made with carbohydrate-based starches that possess binding and film-forming attributes. The products are designed to improve the strength, quality, and efficiencies in the manufacture of coated and uncoated paper and paper packaging products. These products are based principally on ethylated and cationic starches. The company uses ethylated starches to produce coatings and binders, providing strength and printability to fine white, magazine, and catalog

paper. Cationic and other liquid starches are used primarily in the paper-forming process in paper production, providing strong bonding of paper fibers. Penford's products provide a cost-effective alternative to more synthetic ingredients. In addition, the company produces starches for food applications, which are used in coatings to provide crispness, improved taste and texture, and increased product life for such items as French fries sold in fast-food restaurants. The company uses food-grade starch products as moisture binders to reduce fat levels, modify texture and improve color and consistency in a variety of foods, including whole and processed meats, dry powdered mixes and other food and bakery products.

Company Beginnings: 1895–1919

The company's origins date to 1895, when the incorporation of the Iowa Mill & Elevator Company was amended to become Douglas & Company. The change was made by brothers Walter D. and George B. Douglas, who shared their father's interest in the milling industry. Their father, George Douglas, Sr. was a Scottish immigrant who came to America to build railroads. After settling down in Cedar Rapids, Iowa, he invested in various business ventures, one of which was Northstar Milling, the 1874 predecessor of Quaker Oats. George B. was involved in the Northstar Mill and Walter in the Iowa Mill and Elevator Company, a linseed milling business. In 1895, the brothers assumed control of the Iowa Mill & Elevator Company, amended the company's incorporation, and changed its name to Douglas & Company. The Douglas brothers sold the mill four years later in 1899, seeing their future in corn milling. In 1903, they formed the Douglas Starch Works in Cedar Rapids, Iowa, the largest starch industry west of the Mississippi River. The Douglas Starch Works processed 6,000 bushels of corn a day and produced consumer goods, including food products, soap stock, brewer's grits, and paper ingredients. In May 1919, a massive explosion of unknown origin destroyed the entire plant, killing 48 workers. Stockholders subsequently pulled their money out of the insurance settlements until only the Douglas interest remained. Despite this setback, George B. Douglas managed to keep the business together until he sold it to Penick & Ford, Ltd., in December 1919.

Penick & Ford/Bedford Era: 1920–65

Penick & Ford was founded by William Snydor Penick and his brother-in-law, James Polk Ford, who formed a partnership in Shreveport, Louisiana, to sell barreled syrups and molasses in canned form. With increasing sales of corn syrup and can syrups, the monopolistic Corn Products Refining Company purchased a 25 percent stake in Penick & Ford. Nevertheless, in 1913, the Corn Products Refining Company was forced to divest its interest in Penick & Ford after a Supreme Court ruling resulting from President Theodore Roosevelt's trust-busting campaign. The interest was subsequently acquired by F.T. (Fred) Bedford, son of E.T. Bedford, who ran the Corn Products Refining Company. But F.T. Bedford was determined to build his own company. After purchasing the Douglas plant, F.T. Bedford incorporated it as Penick & Ford, Ltd on February 7, 1920. As a result, by 1921 the newly rebuilt plant was producing corn syrup. When the company quickly came under financial duress due to a precipitous drop in the price of sugar, a key ingredient in the production of syrup, Bedford converted most of its production to starch. By 1922, the company made a complete recovery, wielding 30,000 bushels a day, and by 1923 began paying preferred dividends to shareholders. In subsequent years throughout the 1920s and 1930s, the company prospered by producing numerous private labels—Brer Rabbit Molasses, Brer Rabbit Syrup, Penick Syrup, Penick Salad Oil, Douglas Starch, Penford Corn Syrup, Penford Corn Sugar, and Douglas Feed. Under Bedford's direction, the company further diversified by acquiring other grocery lines, such as Vermont Maid Syrup in 1928 and My-T-Fine Desserts in 1934.

In 1921, Penick & Ford hired J.D. Widmer, an émigré from Switzerland who instituted the company's first research and development program. With the grocery business booming, Widmer saw the vital importance of research and development in creating new products. Initially a technical director for F.T. Bedford's newly acquired Douglas plant, he later rose to become company president in 1952. Widmer developed several innovative processes, including a method of recovering corn by-products (corn gluten for feed), furthered advances in the production of crystalline dextrose and corn oil, and patented the bottling-up process, which became the industry standard. Widmer also hired several innovative chemists with considerable knowledge of the paper industry. In the 1940s, the company began manufacturing and supplying oxidized starches for paper applications. The company's chemists also innovated a dry starch from normal dent corn that performed as well as potato or tapioca starches. The process led to the development and patenting of Penford Gums, which commanded a major share of the dry starch specialty market in the paper industry.

Despite these innovative developments, throughout the 1950s and early 1960s the company largely maintained a conservative business approach. Rather than risk capital to develop and introduce new products to its grocery line, the company elected to acquire other businesses, such as New Orleans Coffee Co., W.H. Cargill Co., R.B. Davis Co., Six O'Clock Foods, and Illinois Foods Products Co. Nonetheless, the company proved profitable enough, with steadily improving sales each year.

The R.J. Reynolds/Univar Era: 1965–71

In 1963, Penick & Ford took a dramatic turn with the deaths of its dominant stockholders, including Joseph Jones and his wife, Eugene Penick Jones, William Penick, and F.T. Bedford. With a leadership gap and mediocre growth rate, the company was acquired in 1965 by the R.J. Reynolds Tobacco Company. Penick & Ford offered R.J. Reynolds opportunities for increased sales in grocery lines, which comprised about 40 percent of Penick & Ford's business. Nonetheless, because of concerns by the Federal Trade Commission that R.J Reynolds would compel its boxboard suppliers to buy only Penick & Ford starch, and because of pressure by the U.S. Justice Department, R.J. Reynolds decided to sell the bulk starch and syrup segments of the business in 1971 to VWR United (later renamed the Univar Corporation). The sale included the Cedar Rapids corn starch and syrup plant, three potato starch plants in Idaho, and one potato starch plant in Colorado. In the late 1970s, the company's corn syrup business was downsized and idled, but the Univar Corporation continued producing a full line of specialty starches.

The Penwest Era: 1984–98

On March 1, 1984, the Univar Corporation spun off its manufacturing divisions, including Penick & Ford, which was producing specialty chemical products for the paper, food, and textile industries, and Great Western Malting Company, a manufacturer of brewers malt for the beer industry, into a separate, independent, publicly-held corporation. Univar had first incorporated these manufacturing operations as a subsidiary company under the name Penwest, Ltd. on September 20, 1983, for the purpose of carrying out the divestiture. On November 19, 1987, the Penick & Ford division was renamed Penford Products Company. The two operating divisions served the company well for five years as Great Western generated positive cash flow, which was reinvested in Penick & Ford's faster growing specialty products. On March 13, 1989, the company sold Great Western to focus exclusively on its growing expertise in value-added carbohydrate chemistry for the specialty products industry. Proceeds from the sale were used to pay down debt, repurchase shares, and make two strategic acquisitions—the Alpha Biochemical Company in 1990 and the Penwest Pharmaceutical Company in 1991. Alpha Biochemical enabled the company to augment its potato starch business, while Penwest Pharmaceuticals provided entry to the pharmaceutical ingredients area. With these two acquisitions, the company began to focus exclusively on carbohydrate chemistry, leading to the strengthening of its market positions for specialty chemical products. The largest payoff came with the development of a highly modified starch

Key Dates:

1903: The Douglas brothers form Douglas Starch Works in Cedar Rapids, Iowa.

1919: Douglas Starch Works is sold to Penick & Ford, Ltd.

1965: Penick & Ford is purchased by R.J. Reynolds Tobacco Company.

1971: R.J. Reynolds sells Penick & Ford to the Univar Corporation.

1984: Penick & Ford and Great Western Malting, set up as divisions of Penwest Ltd., are spun off from Univar.

1989: Great Western is divested.

1997: The company changes its name to Penford Corporation.

1998: Penwest Pharmaceuticals Co. is divested.

2002: Penford relocates headquarters to Denver, Colorado.

for use in papermaking, especially in the coated and uncoated free sheet sectors. The consequent rise in demand for the company's products led to corporate profits nearly tripling from 1985 to 1991. During the same period, the company's stock rose from $5 to $37 per share.

In 1991, Penford Food Ingredients Company was established as a division of Penford Products to develop, manufacture, and market specialty carbohydrate-based ingredients to the food and confectionary industries. These ingredients comprised food grade potato and tapioca starch products as well as dextrose-based products, including specialty dried corn syrup. The division's modified starches were used in coatings to provide crispness, improved taste and texture, and increased product life for goods such as french fries sold in fast food restaurants. In addition, the division's food-grade products were used as moisture binders to reduce fat levels, modify texture and improve color and consistency in a variety of food applications.

The Penford Corporation Era: 1984–2002

Between 1992 and 1998, the company reported mostly flat profits as the paper industry fell into an extended recession. The company responded by sharply increasing investment in commercial applications in pharmaceuticals and foods for its carbohydrate technology. At the same time, on October 9, 1997, the company announced that it was spinning off 100 percent of the stock of its pharmaceuticals subsidiary to its shareholders. The sale of Penwest Pharmaceuticals was designed to foster growth of its Penford Products division as well as the company's specialty paper, chemical, and food ingredients businesses. The tax-free distribution to shareholders was completed on August 31, 1998. Following the announcement to divest its pharmaceuticals operation, on October 20, 1997, the company changed its name to the Penford Corporation. Because the divestiture essentially split the company in two, Penford's stock immediately fell by nearly half its value to little more than $13 a share. In addition, after spinning off Penwest Pharmaceuticals as a separate company, Penford experienced depressed sales in 1999, forcing it to layoff 20 employees in the paper-making division.

In April 2000, the company entered into a strategic product development alliance with Dow Chemical Company's Emulsion Polymers global business for coated paper and other applications. The agreement provided for Penford to license its patented starch copolymer (SCP) technology to Dow, which was interested in developing new products for its coated paper customers. Penford saw such alliances as key to developing its science into new growth areas. Other alliances included partnerships with Process Chemicals in textiles, Swedish-based Lyckeby Starkelsen in global food-grade potato starch applications, as well as an emerging relationship with Novartis in the world of biological sciences. Penford also announced in April 2000 that it would construct a new $4.7 million research and applications facility in Cedar Rapids, Iowa. The company considered this investment a significant expansion of its ability to develop new ingredient products for customers.

On September 29, 2000, the company completed the acquisition of Starch Australasia Limited from Goodman Fielder Limited for $54.5 million in cash. Starch Australasia, renamed Penford Australia Limited, was Australia's sole producer of corn starch products and a world leader in the research, development, and commercialization of starch based products. The acquisition, with two manufacturing facilities in Australia and one in New Zealand, provided Penford with new opportunities to develop and produce specialty carbohydrate-based ingredient systems for the food products, paper, and textile industries. Penford immediately added a product line of high growth potential, food-grade corn starch products to its portfolio of offerings, which up until the acquisition included primarily potato-based products. The acquisition also gave Penford expanded access to global markets in Asia and Africa. The addition of new operating facilities in Australia and New Zealand complemented Penford's four North American manufacturing operations, including its corn wet milling plant in Cedar Rapids, Iowa, and facilities in Idaho Falls, Idaho, Richland, Washington, and Plover, Wisconsin, which produced modified potato starches. Penford Australia brought with it fiscal 2000 revenues of approximately $70 million and 300 employees.

In fiscal 2000, the company's sales totaled $158.1 million, an increase of only $3 million or 1.9 percent compared to $155.1 million in 1999. The slight increase came primarily from higher company-wide sales volume of specialty starches and starch-based ingredients. Nevertheless, pricing pressure and lower corn costs pertaining to certain paper ingredient products dampened overall sales growth. In 2001, product sales of $205.1 million increased $46.9 million or 29.7 percent over sales of the previous year. The dramatic increase was largely attributed to the acquisition of Penford Australia and higher sales of specialty starch products to the food industry.

In January 2001, Penford and Minneapolis-based Cargill Corporation announced a joint venture to combine their industrial starch businesses in North America. The companies intended to create an enhanced specialty-starch ingredient manufacturing and distribution business with estimated annual sales of about $200 million focusing primarily on the paper and textile industry. The joint venture was also anticipated to generate significant cost-efficiencies. The two companies anticipated creating a limited liability corporation with Penford as managing partner. Nonetheless, on May 4, 2001, the companies called off the proposed joint venture after discussions failed to produce a final agreement.

In January 2002, Penford announced a strategic restructuring of business operations, including the relocation of its corporate headquarters from Bellevue, Washington, to Denver, Colorado. Penford's decision to move its corporate headquarters aimed to consolidate senior management, which was spread among Bellevue, Denver, and Iowa. Denver was the base of its food ingredients business and was more centrally located to its customers in the paper business. As part of the restructuring, Penford's board of directors named Thomas D. Malkoski to serve as the company's new CEO, replacing Jeffrey T. Cook. Before joining Penford, Malkoski was president and CEO of North American operations for Griffith Laboratories, a specialty food ingredients business. Under Malkoski, the company continued to focus on expanding sales of specialty food and industrial ingredients, which served to enhance Penford's growth prospects. As a result, on June 24, 2002, Penford announced that it had been selected on a preliminary basis to join the Russell 3000 Index, reflecting the growth in its market capitalization. This was a promising sign amidst a protracted economic downturn that began in late 2000 and extended into 2003. By the end of 2002, the company had reported overall sales of some $231 million compared to $226 million in 2001. These results appeared to presage further growth ahead even in the most difficult of economic times.

Principal Subsidiaries

Penford Products Company; Penford Food Ingredients Company; Penford Holdings Pty. Ltd. (Australia); Penford Australia Ltd.; Penford New Zealand Ltd.; Penford Export Corporation (U.S. Virgin Islands).

Principal Competitors

Cargill, Inc.; Archer Danils Midland Corporation; ConAgra, Inc.; British Petroleum Company plc.

Further Reading

Alwyn, Scott, "Penford, Cargill Form Joint Venture," *Seattle Times*, January 18, 2001.

Fitzpatrick, Tamra, "Bellevue-Based Penford Corp. Reports Weak Profit, Cuts Jobs, *Seattle Times*, March 24, 1999.

Ford, George C., "Bellevue-Based Firm Acquires Australian Starch Company for $58 Million," *Gazette*, September 4, 2000.

"Penford Corporation to Acquire Starch Australasia—Acquisition Immediately Enhances Penford's Revenue and Earnings Outlook," *PR Newswire*, August 29, 2000.

Virgin, Bill, "Penford Moving to Denver," *Seattle Post*, January 5, 2002.

——, "Penwest is Splitting into 2 Firms," *Seattle Post-Intelligencer*, 1997.

Wilheim, Steven, "Penford Poised for Growth On Starchy Diet," *Puget Sound Business Journal*, 1998.

—Bruce Montgomery

PennWell Corporation

1421 South Sheridan Road
Tulsa, Oklahoma 74112
U.S.A.
Telephone: (918) 835-3161
Fax: (918) 831-9497
Web site: http://www.pennwell.com

Private Company
Incorporated: 1910 as Petroleum Publishing Company
Employees: 700+
Sales: $100 million (2002 est.)
NAIC: 511120 Periodical Publishers; 511130 Book
Publishers; 561920 Convention and Trade Show
Organizers

For most of the 20th century, PennWell Corporation's principal publication was the *Oil & Gas Journal.* It was not until the 1980s and 1990s that the company diversified into other markets. While the *Oil & Gas Journal* remained the company's flagship publication, PennWell embarked on an aggressive growth strategy in the late 1980s and 1990s that resulted in the company publishing some 44 business-to-business magazines, newsletters, and technical journals. The company also conducts more than 50 conferences and exhibitions and has an extensive line of books, maps, encyclopedias, directories, videos, research reports, and database services. As of 2003 PennWell's overall readership included more than 1.5 million executives, engineers, technical managers, and other professionals worldwide.

Early History: 1902–88

PennWell Corporation, known simply as PennWell, can trace its roots to the first decade of the 20th century, when the U.S. petroleum industry was beginning to emerge. In 1902 *The Oil Investors' Journal* was founded in Beaumont, Texas, by Holland S. Reavis. Reavis was a St. Louis newspaperman who had been drawn to Texas by the Spindletop oil discovery. His journal was devoted initially to financial and investment topics for oil field operators and investors and was focused on development in the Beaumont oil fields. It soon shifted its orientation

to oil company operations and expanded its coverage to the entire U.S. Southwest. The journal adopted a yellow cover in 1907 and acquired the nickname, "The Big Yellow Book," which stuck throughout its history.

Reavis sold *The Oil Investors' Journal* to Patrick C. Boyle in 1910. Boyle was a former oil field scout for John D. Rockefeller. At the time he acquired *The Oil Investors' Journal* Boyle was publisher of the *Oil City Derrick* newspaper in Pennsylvania. Boyle formed the Petroleum Publishing Company, predecessor to the PennWell Corporation, in 1910 when he acquired *The Oil Investors' Journal.* He renamed the semimonthly publication *Oil & Gas Journal* and increased its frequency to weekly. He also moved its main office to Tulsa, Oklahoma, where it remained until it moved to Houston, Texas, in 1989.

Under Boyle's direction, *Oil & Gas Journal* began covering all oil industry operations. Through Boyle's Pennsylvania-based newspaper *Oil & Gas Journal* gained access to a network of experienced oil industry correspondents located throughout the United States.

When Boyle died in 1920, his son-in-law Frank T. Lauinger became president of Petroleum Publishing. He headed the company for about ten years before his sudden death in 1931. He was succeeded by his son, P.C. Lauinger, who had worked with his father throughout the 1920s. P.C. Lauinger ran the company for many years and was active in its management until his death in 1988. Under his leadership the *Oil & Gas Journal* became a technical journal as well as a news magazine. Technical writers, engineers, geologists, and economists were added to the staff, and the magazine expanded its scope internationally. The journal became known as the "bible" of the oil industry.

Petroleum Publishing also expanded under the leadership of P.C. Lauinger. The company began acquiring other periodicals serving other industries. In 1980 it was renamed PennWell Publishing Company during its rapid diversification, with "Penn" representing its roots in Pennsylvania and "Well" its beginnings in the oil fields. The company also began sponsoring trade shows and exhibitions to serve the readers of *Oil & Gas Journal* and other publications.

Company Perspectives:

PennWell is a global information company dedicated to anticipating and exceeding our customers' changing needs. We provide quality, timely information through continuous innovation of our products and services. In each of the high growth strategic markets we serve, PennWell's products cover leading edge developments in technology and management. PennWell has a long history of magazine publishing with roots back to 1910 when the company began publishing an oil journal serving the emerging petroleum industry in the United States. With an aggressive strategy for diversification and a vision for growth, PennWell came from this humble beginning to a company that today serves computer, laser, electronic, municipal, health care, fire and emergency services, energy and environmental fields through business and technical magazines, along with trade shows, conferences, books, maps, database resources and market research for these same markets.

In 1982 PennWell spun off its Tulsa-based printing operation into a new subsidiary, PennWell Printing Co. PennWell Printing operated for 15 years, until 1997, when it was sold to Brown Printing Co., a Minnesota-based subsidiary and joint venture of German media companies Bertelsmann and Gruner + Jahr. At the time of the sale, PennWell Printing had about 200 employees and printed about 100 business and trade magazines.

Developing Aggressive Growth Plans: 1988–2000

When P.C. Lauinger died in 1988, he was succeeded by his son, Philip C. Lauinger, Jr. In 1991 the company's top management developed a ten-year growth plan called Vision 2000, at the urging, in large part, of Robert F. Biolchini. Biolchini, who was P.C. Lauinger's son-in-law, had provided PennWell with business and legal counsel since 1971 and became president and CEO of the company in 2000.

Vision 2000 called for an aggressive growth strategy for PennWell. During the 1990s PennWell made more than 30 acquisitions and launched more than 80 new magazines, conferences, and other information products. The company also expanded into online publishing. It introduced OGJ Online to complement the print version of *Oil & Gas Journal.* OGL Online provided updated news about oil and gas, an electronic version of the current issue of *Oil & Gas Journal,* searchable archives, and an online research center.

PennWell's acquisitions during the 1990s included *Water-World News,* which PennWell acquired in 1991 from the American Water Works Association and renamed *WaterWorld. WaterWorld News* began publication in 1985. In 1995 PennWell acquired *CleanRooms* from Witter Publishing. *CleanRooms* was published monthly for contamination control and maintenance engineers and plant managers. The periodical was first published in 1987. PennWell also acquired *Independent Energy* from Marier Communications Inc. in 1995. The monthly publication for the power industry was first published in 1971.

In 1998 PennWell acquired *Instrumentation & Control Systems* from Reed Elsevier Business Information. First published in 1928, the periodical was the control industry's oldest and most respected publication, providing information on control technology for engineers and engineering management. PennWell renamed the publications *Control Solutions* and included it in its Business and Industrial Division.

PennWell also acquired *Image Processing* magazine from European Technology Publishing Ltd. in 1998. The bimonthly magazine became part of PennWell's Advanced Technology Division. Following the acquisition it continued to be published at ETP's office in Marlborough, England, under the title *Image Processing Europe.* It covered image processing products and technologies and machine vision for imaging and vision systems professionals throughout Europe.

PennWell's periodical publications as well as its conferences and exhibitions were organized into two divisions: Business and Industrial Division and Advanced Technology Division. Both divisions also provided their readers with online publications, research and consulting services, databases, and Internet-based services. In addition, the company's Information Products Group offered a variety of books, software, videos, maps, and more for the petroleum, electric power, fire engineering, dental, and municipal water industries.

The Business and Industrial Division included *Oil & Gas Journal* and other publications for the oil and gas, electric power, fire engineering, dental, and municipal water industries. Dental occupations, for example, were served by *Dental Economics, Dental Equipment & Materials,* and *RDH: Registered Dental Hygienist.*

The Advanced Technology Division, established in 1979, published technically oriented business-to-business periodicals for industries such as global electronics, communications, and information technology. While the Business and Industrial Division was based at the company's corporate headquarters in Tulsa, the Advanced Technology Division operated out of Nashua, New Hampshire.

Among the new publications launched by the Business and Industrial Division in the 1990s were *Power Delivery Product News* in 1991, which was later renamed *Power Delivery.* The bimonthly was aimed at the electric utility industry as well as architect-engineers and system constructors, distributors, wholesalers, and electrical contractors that worked with electric utilities. The division also launched *Power Engineering International* in 1993 and *Dental Equipment & Materials* and *Utility Automation* in 1996.

The Business and Industrial Division also introduced several new trade shows and conferences during the 1990s. The company expanded upon its successful POWER-GEN International conference, first held in 1986, by offering POWER-GEN Asia in 1992, POWER-GEN Europe in 1993, and POWER-GEN Latin America in 1996. PennWell's POWER-GEN International and FDIC (Fire Department Instructors Conference) rank in the top 200 trade shows in the United States in square footage. FDIC, acquired in 1996 and held annually in Indianapolis, is the nation's leading conference and exhibition for training more than 20,000 fire service professionals.

Key Dates:

1902: *Oil Investors' Journal* is founded in Beaumont, Texas, by Holland S. Reavis.

1910: Patrick C. Boyle acquires the *Oil Investors' Journal,* renames it the *Oil & Gas Journal,* and establishes the Petroleum Publishing Company.

1920: Boyle's son-in-law, Frank T. Lauinger, assumes control upon Boyle's death.

1930: Lauinger dies suddenly, and his son P.C. Lauinger takes over the company.

1950: *Oil & Gas Journal* carries more advertising than any other American magazine.

1980: Petroleum Publishing Co. changes its name to PennWell Publishing Co.

1988: Frank T. Lauinger becomes PennWell's chairman following the death of P.C. Lauinger.

1991: PennWell develops Vision 2000, an aggressive plan for growth during the 1990s.

1998: PennWell formulates a new long-term vision and changes its name to PennWell Corporation.

1999: PennWell launches PennEnergy to provide electronic commerce services to the oil and gas and electric power industries.

Advanced Technology publications launched in the 1990s included *Data Storage* in 1994. Originally published bimonthly, it became a monthly publication that focused on trends and developments in data storage technology, new products, and research covering a variety of storage media. The division also acquired *Military & Aerospace Electronics* in 1991 and started *Microlithography World* in 1992, *Cabling Installation & Maintenance* in 1993, *Portable Design* in 1995, *BackOffice Magazine* in 1995, *Vision Systems Design* in 1996, *InfoStor* in 1997, and *Integrated Communications Design* and *WDM (Wavelength-Division-Multiplex) Solutions* in 1999.

New exhibitions and trade shows introduced by the Advanced Technology Division in the 1990s included international versions of the CleanRooms exhibitions for contamination control and maintenance engineers. In the United States, CleanRooms East was first held in 1990 and CleanRooms West in 1993. After PennWell acquired *CleanRooms* magazine in 1995, it introduced CleanRooms Asia in 1997 and CleanRooms Europe in 1998.

PennWell also expanded into online publishing during the 1990s, launching web sites to complement its print publications. *Computer Graphics World* launched its web site, CGW Online, early in 1996. The site included additional articles not found in the print publication as well as extra images, animation, and video clips. It also contained back issues of the magazine, a search engine, an online bookstore, and other features. In 1999 PennWell launched a web site for the water, wastewater, and waste service industries (www.wwinternational.com). The ad-supported site carried editorial content supplied by *WaterWorld* and other PennWell publications.

In 1998 PennWell developed a new long-term plan called Vision New Millennium. The plan resulted in dropping the word "Publishing" from the company's name and a new logo. Although the firm's new name was officially PennWell Corporation, the company continued to be known simply as PennWell.

In 1999 PennWell added conferences and exhibitions and strengthened its position in international markets through acquisitions. In May the company acquired Latcom, Inc., a Miami-based conference and exhibition company that served the Latin American markets in telecommunications, information technology, and energy. The acquisition complemented PennWell's other products and services aimed at the Latin American market, including *Potencia,* a magazine for the Latin American power industry acquired in April 1999; the Latin American edition of *Oil & Gas Journal;* and *Prevencion de la Contaminacion* for water and waste management industries. It also included conferences and exhibitions such as CaribeCom, a communications technology exhibition established in 1982, and CosCom, a telecommunications conference and exhibition for upper management of Central American telephone and power companies.

Later in 1999 PennWell acquired KMI Corporation, a 25-year-old market research and consulting firm based in Newport, Rhode Island, that specialized in fiberoptics and telecommunications. KMI produced a variety of market research reports, newsletters, and maps in addition to providing database and consulting services. It also produced several conferences and exhibitions, including annual conferences on fiberoptics markets and fiberoptic submarine systems. KMI and Latcom both became part of PennWell's Advanced Technology Division.

PennWell ended the decade by acquiring five magazines from IHS Publishing Group, which was in the process of divesting all of its publishing properties. The five magazines— *SMT: Surface Mount Technology, SMT Asia/Pacific, Advanced Packaging, Connector Specifier,* and *Vacuum & ThinFilm*— were acquired in December 1999 and became part of the Advanced Technology Division.

Expansion: 2000–03

In 1999 PennWell launched PennEnergy, a separate company that offered electronic commerce services to the oil and gas and electric power industries. Through its Internet division, PennNet, PennEnergy controlled the Oil & Gas Journal Exchange, a web-based exchange established in 2000 where companies could negotiate for oil and gas properties and sell their used and surplus oilfield and power equipment. The Oil & Gas Journal Exchange also formed a partnership with EBCO, a company that specialized in conducting auctions of oil and gas properties. As part of the partnership PennNet purchased a controlling interest in EBCO, which in its 20-year history had conducted more than $1 billion worth of oil and gas property auction transactions.

Through other key acquisitions, PennWell expanded its presence in electronic commerce in 2000. In March 2000 the company acquired Global Logistics Partners LLC, an Irving, Texas-based broker of used and surplus equipment for the oil, gas, and power industries. In October PennWell bought Madison Energy Advisors Inc., which listed oil and gas properties worth about $250 million. As a result of these acquisitions and other developments, companies using PennEnergy's e-commerce marketplaces conducted annual transactions worth more than $750 million.

In a major restructuring move, PennWell discontinued its in-house subscription fulfillment operation and began using an outside bureau, Omeda Communications, in 2000. The conversion took more than nine months. According to *Circulation Management,* PennWell decided to outsource its fulfillment because its in-house system was incapable of keeping up with the company's growth and technology needs.

Many of PennWell's publications featured international editions that were published in key markets through trademark and content licensing agreements. Most of PennWell's international publications fell within its Advanced Technology Division. In Japan the company had a cross-editorial licensing agreement with Nikkei Business Publications, Inc., Japan's leading business publisher. For the Asia Pacific region, PennWell established Asian and Chinese editions of *CleanRooms* and *SMT Korea* in 2000. They were followed by *Compuprint* in 2001 and *CompoTech China* and *Electronic Application & Design World* in 2002. Other Asian Pacific editions launched in the 1990s included *CompoTech Taiwan* in 1999; *Semiconductor Monthly* in Korea and Chinese and Taiwanese editions of *Solid State Technology* in 1998; *Design Wave* in 1995; and *Taiwan Telecom* in 1994. In Europe PennWell launched *Cabling Installation & Maintenance Europe* in 2000, followed by *Lightwave Europe* in 2002.

In mid-2001 PennWell acquired another market research and management consulting firm, Strategies Unlimited of Mountain View, California. Strategies Unlimited specialized in a variety of leading-edge technologies, including optical networks, optoelectronic components, wireless communications, semiconductors, and similar high-technology industries. In 2002 the Advanced Technology Division introduced *Optical Manufacturing,* a bimonthly magazine that provided global coverage of optoelectronics and photonics manufacturing.

In 2003 PennWell was positioned as a dynamic business-to-business publisher and information provider for a range of industries. Over the years the company has successfully expanded beyond its base of oil, gas, and electric power markets to serve several high technology markets with top quality periodicals, conferences, exhibitions, and other information products. The company's commitment to quality, integrity, and honesty along with an aggressive growth plan have combined to make PennWell a successful company poised for future growth.

Principal Subsidiaries

PennEnergy.

Principal Divisions

Advanced Technology Division; Business and Industrial Division; Information Products Group; Petroleum Division.

Principal Competitors

CMP Media, Inc.; Hart Publications, Inc.; McGraw-Hill Companies; Penton Media, Inc.; Primedia, Inc.; Reed Business Information, Inc.

Further Reading

"Advanstar, PurchasePro Create B-to-B Communities," *Business Marketing,* December 1, 1999, p. 8.

Callahan, Sean, "PennNet Wants to Strike It Rich with Web Auction," *B to B,* June 5, 2000, p. 3.

Cassidy, Neil, "Brown Buys Out PennWell Printing, Sells Division," *Folio: The Magazine for Magazine Management,* November 1, 1997, p. 21.

"Conference & Exhibition Co. Sold to PennWell," *Business Publisher,* May 31, 1999, p. 6.

"Data Storage," *Folio: The Magazine for Magazine Management,* October 1, 1994, p. 72.

"EL&P to Launch New Publication for Power Delivery Marketplace," *Electric Light & Power,* September 1991, p. 1.

Freeman, Laurie, "Oil & Gas Journal," *Business Marketing,* March 1, 1999, p. 24.

"IHS Completes Sale of Publishing Group Assets," *Business Publisher,* December 24, 1999, p. 6.

"Japanese Publisher Reflects on Partnership with Tulsa, Okla. Firm," *Knight-Ridder/Tribune Business News,* June 19, 2001.

" 'Lightwave Europe' from PennWell in March," *Business Publisher,* November 17, 2001, p. 4.

"Lightwave to Publish China Supplement," *Lightwave,* August 2002, p. 33.

"PennWell Acquires Magazine from European Technology Publishing," *Business Publisher,* June 30, 1998.

"PennWell Acquires Market Research & Consulting Firm," *Business Publisher,* July 31, 1999, p. 5.

"PennWell Buys Market Research, Consulting Firm," *Lightwave,* October 2001, p. 54.

"PennWell Completes 42-Title Fulfillment Out-Conversion," *Circulation Management,* April 2000, p. 34.

"PennWell, Ebco Form Partnership," *Oil Daily,* January 28, 2000.

"PennWell Starts 'Cabling Installation & Maintenance Europe'," *Business Publisher,* January 31, 2000, p. 4.

Perin, Monica, "Houston Nets Pair of Energy Auctioneers," *Houston Business Journal,* February 4, 2000, p. 2.

Porter, Stephen M., "CGW Online: Check It Out!," *Computer Graphics World,* February 1996, p. 4.

Schwartz, Matthew, "PennWell Drills into Exchange," *B to B,* February 19, 2001, p. 16.

"Tulsa, Oklahoma-Based PennWell Publishing Company Has Purchased Independent Energy from Marier Communications Inc.," *Folio: The Magazine for Magazine Management,* September 15, 1995, p. 42.

"WaterWorld," *Business Publisher,* January 31, 1999, p. 8.

—David P. Bianco

Peterson American Corporation

21200 Telegraph Road
Southfield, Michigan 48034-4243
U.S.A.
Telephone: (248) 799-5400
Fax: (248) 357-3176
Web site: http://www.pspring.com

Private Company
Incorporated: 1932 as Precision Spring Corporation
Employees: 1,100
Sales: $130 million (2002 est.)
NAIC: 332610 Spring and Wire Product Manufacturing

Peterson American Corporation (PAC) is a leading manufacturer of springs and related products. More than two-thirds of the firm's output is sold to the auto industry, with the rest used in appliances, agricultural equipment, and other products like motorcycles and trampolines. PAC operates more than a dozen manufacturing plants in the United States, Canada, Mexico, and the United Kingdom. The company is owned by the Peterson family and run by fourth-generation descendants of its founder.

Origins

The story of Peterson American Corporation begins with August Christian Peterson, who was born in Norway in 1864. Apprenticed as a blacksmith at a young age, he emigrated in the 1880s to the United States and settled in Chicago. Once there, Peterson began working for the William D. Gibson Company, the largest spring manufacturer in the Midwest. At this time many springs were made by blacksmiths, who wound red-hot metal around a bar to form them.

While working for Gibson, Peterson became an experienced spring maker, and in 1904 he was persuaded to move to Monessen, Pennsylvania to run the spring manufacturing operations of a new steel plant that was being built there. Peterson's 14-year-old son Alfred also was hired as a night watchman to look after the company's furnaces. When this firm went out of business several years later, the family moved to Kenova, West

Virginia to work for another spring producer. That company also folded, however, and the Petersons subsequently moved to Springfield, Ohio.

There, in 1912, August Peterson started his own spring manufacturing company, which was funded by the sale of stock to citizens of the town. The new firm was soon busy supplying the International Harvester company with springs, but this contract proved to be its undoing when the client put pressure on Peterson's investors to sell out. They soon did, and despite a generous offer of $1,000 a month to manage the plant, August Peterson decided to pull up stakes and move again. After considering Toledo, Ohio, he chose to settle in Detroit, an hour's drive north and the home of many of the country's future major automakers.

In 1914 Peterson founded his second company, General Spring and Wire. It was the first mechanical spring manufacturer in Detroit and was soon busy supplying items like valve springs to Continental Motors, who sold engines to a number of carmakers. As had happened in Springfield, the company was doomed ultimately by its reliance on outside investors, who were enticed to sell out by wire and spring maker L.A. Young. Although the Petersons were again offered jobs, they refused and decided to form yet another company, Peterson Spring, which also was located in Detroit. Once again it would be co-owned by the Petersons and a group of investors. Among these were the company's employees, many of whom had followed the family north from Ohio.

This company was successful and soon began to grow, but as had happened twice before a larger firm took notice and stepped in with an offer to buy. This time Eaton Corporation talked the majority of shareholders into selling out, just before the stock market crash of 1929. Alfred Peterson also was forced to sign a noncompetition agreement that forbade him from opening a spring factory for two years. Nonetheless, his three younger brothers Sigurd, Conrad, and Harold formed their own spring making firm, which they called Peterson Brothers. In 1932 that company was absorbed by Precision Spring Corporation, which Alfred had formed upon the completion of his two-year noncompete agreement. This time the Petersons were majority stockholders, assuring that the company would never again be sold to outsiders.

Growth During the Depression

The early 1930s was a difficult time for business in the United States, but there were also opportunities to be found. For someone willing to invest in expansion, there was an abundance of inexpensive used equipment available from companies that had downsized or gone bankrupt. The Petersons took advantage of this and bought two boxcar loads of spring-making machines in New York, renting space for them on Federal Avenue in Detroit. Other equipment for the operation was designed and built by Sigurd Peterson, a talented engineer. Many of the Petersons' employees who had moved to Detroit from Springfield signed on once again to work for the new company, giving it an abundance of pretrained workers.

In 1936 Precision Spring moved into a newly constructed plant on Woodrow Wilson Avenue, which occupied three acres of land. The firm employed more than 300 in the facility, which was considered one of the most modern in the Midwest. Key to the company's success was family involvement, and younger members of the Peterson clan were encouraged to enter the business. One example was Alfred's daughter Thelma, who in 1937 became the first woman to graduate from the University of Michigan's Mechanical Engineering program.

The company's sales grew year by year and, with the exception of a decline in 1938, continued on an upward trend until the start of U.S. involvement in World War II. At that time, with the conversion of auto plants to make vehicles for the war effort, Precision Spring directed its efforts toward this purpose as well.

Following the war the company experienced a surge in demand as the economy boomed and sales of luxury goods and automobiles skyrocketed. The plant was soon operating at full capacity and it became apparent that the firm would need to expand. After looking at sites in nearby Windsor, Ontario and in California, company head Alfred Peterson, Sr., decided to build a plant in Three Rivers, Michigan, about two hours' drive from Detroit and close enough to serve the firm's customers in the auto industry.

Opening a Second Plant in 1951

The facility in Three Rivers was finished in the spring of 1951, and production began there in the summer. Eight key staff members, including plant manager Alfred "Bud" Peterson, Jr., moved to Three Rivers to run the new operation, while Al Peterson, Sr., maintained an office there for monthly visits. Within a few years the new unit began to be seen as a competitor of the Detroit operation, and in 1957 it was spun off to

become a separate corporation known as Peterson Spring. Also in 1957 the company constructed two other plants—Kalamazoo Spring, which was an offshoot of the Three Rivers unit, and Resortes y Productos Metalicos, located in Mexico.

Expansion continued with the acquisition of Lock Rings of Toledo, Ohio in 1962 from the Harper Co. and the opening of Georgia Spring, located in Athens, Georgia, in 1963. That year Alfred Peterson, Sr., passed away and Bud Peterson moved from Three Rivers back to Detroit to help his sister Thelma run the growing group of companies.

Further growth took place after the change of leadership, with Kalamazoo Spring offshoot Greenville Spring and Schoolcraft, Michigan-based Spring Tools opening in 1965. The company entered Europe in 1968 with formation of a joint venture, CIMA Precision Spring Europa of Italy, in conjunction with the Bellazzi family. Also in 1968 Precision Spring of Canada, Ltd. was formed in Kingsville, Ontario. In 1969 the firm purchased a 40 percent stake in a Spanish firm, Industrias Berry.

In 1970 Precision Spring helped form a Japanese joint venture, K.P. Products, with Kato Hatsujo Kaisha. The following year the company bought a firm called Commonwealth Spring and added a plastics division to Precision Spring of Canada. The year 1971 also saw a corporate realignment with the creation of Precision American, a joint venture holding company equally owned by Precision Spring, which was controlled by Thelma and Phyllis Peterson, and Peterson Spring, controlled by Bud Peterson and his children. In 1972 Precision American purchased a company named Spring Products, and in 1975 the firm's Industrias Berry joint venture formed Muvasa, a subsidiary of its own.

On January 1, 1978 Precision American split into two roughly equal halves, with Bud Peterson keeping the former Precision Spring companies, which were renamed Peterson American Corporation (or PAC), and his brother and two sisters taking the remainder, which included Peterson Spring of Canada, Greenville Spring, and an Australian firm, John While. In 1978 as well the company purchased office space in Southfield, Michigan for use as PAC's headquarters, and formed an English subsidiary, Heath Spring. Sales for the year reached $20.8 million.

More growth followed in 1979 when PAC bought California Spring from Ametek and formed joint ventures with Japanese companies to create Muskegon Wire and K.P. American, which would sell Itaya spring machinery in the United States. In 1981 PAC acquired Greenville Spring from Precision Spring.

In 1982 PAC opened Dreison Technic Spring in Detroit and Larmex in Mexico, which was 40 percent owned by the firm. The company also acquired Precision Spring's 26 percent ownership of Resortes of Mexico. An additional 4 percent acquired the next year increased PAC's stake in that company to 80 percent.

Growth continued in the mid-1980s with formation of PAC Fasteners for development of the PAC-Nut, a washer spring nut that was resistant to loosening and could be used in a variety of applications. Other activities included acquisition of the remaining 50 percent of the firm's Muskegon wire mill and the K.P. American unit from PAC's partners; formation of Mattoon Spring in Mattoon, Illinois; acquisition of United Spring Corp.

of Munith, Michigan; and the opening of a new valve spring plant in Windsor, Ontario. The company later moved all of its engine valve spring manufacturing to the latter facility from Three Rivers to reduce costs.

In 1986 Peterson Spring Corporation was merged into PAC, Muskegon Wire was sold, and United Spring was closed. The company also opened a distribution and packaging arm in Three Rivers and made several changes to its international subsidiaries. The firm was now seeing annual revenues of $56 million, nearly triple the figure of a decade earlier.

In 1988 PAC acquired Precision Spring's Kingsville, Ontario plant, bought out the Bellazzi family's stake in CIMA Precision Corp., opened a fastener division in Madison Heights, Michigan to take over production of PAC-Nuts, formed joint venture Norma Products in Canada to make hose clamps, and expanded the company's headquarters in Southfield. The following year a joint venture was formed in Richmond, Indiana, called Sanko Peterson Corporation, to make mass collar rings and other products. PAC would own 45 percent of the operation.

A slowdown in the economy and the increasing market share gains of Japanese automakers were now affecting the company, for whom the auto industry accounted for 70 percent of sales. In 1990 PAC's revenues dropped by 5.1 percent, and the firm closed its Mattoon Spring and California Spring operations. A further decline occurred the following year, which led to the closing of the Kalamazoo plant. The rival Precision Spring was suffering even more, and its last assets were sold to PAC in 1991.

The firm's sales rebounded in 1992, growing by 13 percent to $78.8 million. During the year the company sold its 50 percent stake in CIMA Precision Spring Europa to Gigi Bellazzi. In 1994 the company's PAC-Nut business also was sold to California Industrial Products.

Sales continued to rise during the mid-1990s, and in 1996 topped $100 million for the first time. During that year the firm sold its K.P. American unit to Itaya Engineering at the latter company's request. PAC also sold its 50 percent interest in K.P. Products to Piolax in 1997. In 1999 the firm's English opera-

tions were expanded with the acquisition of A-P Springs of Birmingham.

PAC maintained a research and development laboratory at its headquarters in Southfield, which was becoming more and more sophisticated through the purchase and in-house development of new testing tools. One such item was the Spintron, bought in 1999, which simulated the effects of spring use in high-performance racing engines. Peterson engineers could use it to accurately predict the effects of 500 laps of racing on a set of valve springs, for example, helping the company create springs such as those used by the winner of the 1999 Indianapolis 500. Many years earlier, August Peterson's handmade valve springs had helped Barney Oldfield win one of the first races in that series.

Into the 21st century PAC continued to do the majority of its work for the auto industry, which accounted for more than two thirds of total sales. Less than half of that amount was now attributed to the Big Three American automakers. The remainder of springs produced by the company were used in such products as agricultural equipment, refrigerators, garage doors, lawnmowers, snow blowers, motorcycles, trampolines, and bicycles. PAC was now in the hands of the fourth generation of Petersons, with Bud Peterson's children Alfred "Pete" Peterson III serving as CEO and chairman, and Eric "Rick" Peterson as president. Their sister Gail Lauzzana was vice-president for communications and community relations and corporate secretary, and another sibling, Kristin Peterson, ran the firm's Three Rivers packaging and distribution operations. In early 2002 PAC closed its Three Rivers plant, diverting some of the work done there to other facilities. The Three Rivers packaging and distribution and CIMA Corp. operations were not affected.

After more than 70 years, Peterson American Corporation was a leading maker of springs for the auto industry as well as for a variety of other customers. The firm had plants around the United States and in Mexico, Canada, and the United Kingdom. After four generations of Peterson family stewardship, PAC continued to grow and prosper.

Principal Subsidiaries

Peterson Spring of Canada, Ltd.; Peterson Spring UK Ltd.; Peterson Spring Mexico; Sanko Peterson Corporation.

Principal Competitors

Barnes Group Inc.; Matthew Warren; Grand Rapids Spring & Stamping; Newcomb Spring; Twist, Inc.

Further Reading

Baker, Jack, "Three Rivers, Mich. Automotive Parts Supplier to Close," *South Bend Tribune,* February 14, 2002.

Bodwin, Amy, "Suppliers Cross the Border," *Crain's Detroit Business,* April 25, 1988, p. 1.

MacRae, Shirley McTyre, and Norman MacRae, "Peterson Spring," in *Detroit: The First City of the Midwest,* Carlsbad, Calif.: Heritage Media Corp., 2000.

"Peterson Winds Up Deal on Rival A.P.," *Birmingham Post,* March 30, 1999, p. 30.

—Frank Uhle

Pochet SA

121/123, quai de Valmy
75010 Paris
France
Telephone: (+33) 1-44-72-11-00
Fax: (+33) 1-44-72-11-11

Public Company
Incorporated: 1623 as Verreries du Courval; 1928 as
Pochet
Employees: 2,685
Sales: EUR 319.3 million ($319 million)(2002)
Stock Exchanges: Euronext Paris
Ticker Symbol: PCH.PA
NAIC: 327211 Flat Glass Manufacturing; 327213 Glass
Container Manufacturing

With an activity dating back to the 17th century, Pochet SA has remained a force in France's glass-making industry by focusing on its core product: perfume bottles. Since the 19th century, Pochet (then known under its glass-making arm Verreries du Courval) has been the leading producer of perfume bottles for the world-renowned French perfume industry. The company works closely with top industry designers to fashion the bottles for nearly all of the top perfume names, including Dior, Guerlain, Yves Saint Laurent, Kenzo, Jean-Paul Gaultier, and Calvin Klein. Perfume bottles account for some 54 percent of Pochet's total sales, which neared EUR 320 million in the difficult 2002 year. While bottle-making at the group's historic Verreries du Courval site remains the company's primary focus, Pochet has extended its expertise into two related areas. The first is plastic packaging, through its Qualipac joint venture with Tarkett Sommer, which enables Pochet to offer its perfume clients the possibility of creating integrated accessory lines, including bath care items more appropriately packaged in plastic. Qualipac contributes 19 percent to the company's sales. Pochet acquisition of Lalique in the 1990s has enabled the company to extend itself beyond packaging into the product itself, adding the famed Lalique line of crystal and other luxury products, as well as a globally operating chain of 70 boutiques, half of which are owned outright by Pochet. Lalique adds a further 27 percent to Pochet's sales. France remains Pochet's single largest market, at more than 43 percent of revenues; North America represents 31.5 percent of sales, while the rest of Europe adds another 20 percent to the company's revenues. The company remains quoted on the Euronext Paris Stock Exchange, despite the fact that the Colonna de Giovellina family, which has been the force behind the company since the 1930s, owns more than 98 percent of Pochet's shares. Gabriel Colonna de Giovellina has led Pochet as CEO since the early 1980s.

Perfuming Bottle Specialist in the 19th Century

The modern Pochet represented the combination of two small, family-owned companies, Verreries du Courval and Deroche-Pochet, in the 1930s. The older of the two was Verreries du Courval, founded in the first half of the 17th century in the French glass-making region center of Normandy located in the Bresle valley. That region had originally been chosen by ancient Roman occupiers for its extensive forests, which provided a ready fuel supply for the glass-making process.

Glass-making became a privilege of the French noble class, in part because glass products long remained luxury items reserved for the nation's wealthy. In 1623, the Countess of Eu, an important medieval fortress town in the Bresle valley, granted the nobleman François le Vaillant the right to build a glass-making workshop in Le Courval. In exchange for the right to work glass, le Vaillant agreed to buy the wood needed for his furnace from the Countess d'Eu's lands.

The Verrerie du Courval, as the site became known, originally produced window panes for the houses and castles of the French aristocracy. Le Courval began producing as well a variety of glass bottles in the 18th century. The workshop remained under its noble ownership until the late 18th century. The swelling discontent with France's ruling class that resulted in the revolution of 1789 led ownership of the Le Courval site to be transferred to a local notary and non-noble. The fact that the glass-maker was owned by a commoner allowed the Verrerie du Courval to escape the wrath reserved for other glass-makers still held by the noble class.

Key Dates:

1623: François le Vaillant founds a glass workshop in Le Courval in the Bresle Valley of Normandy.

1780: Pierre Deroche founds a crockery workshop in Paris, which later becomes one of the city's top porcelain and glass painters as Pochet-Deroche, and begins acting as Parisian distributor for Verrerie du Courval.

1853: Verrerie du Courval designs the perfume bottle for Guerlain's "Eau de Cologne Imperiale."

1930: After the Colonna de Giovellina family takes over Pochet-Deroche, it acquires Verrerie du Courval; renamed as Pochet SA, the company now specializes in manufacturing perfume bottles.

1971: Pochet modernizes its Le Courval site, automating its production line.

1983: Gabriel Colonna de Giovellina is named CEO of the company and begins diversifying its operations.

1986: Pochet begins plastic bottling production.

1987: The company opens a subsidiary in the United States.

1994: Pochet acquires a controlling stake in glass designer Lalique.

1996: Pochet goes public on Paris Stock Exchange.

2001: Pochet launches a share buyback offer, boosting Colonna de Giovellina family's stake in the company to more than 98 percent.

2003: Pochet announces it plans to extend the Lalique chain of retail boutiques in the face of slipping sales.

By then, another important name in Pochet's history had begun business. In 1780, Pierre Deroche founded his own crockery workshop in Paris. After the French revolution, however, the Deroche family turned toward the porcelain industry, becoming one of the most prominent porcelain firms in the city during the early 19th century. Deroche, which became known as Pochet-Deroche by the 1830s, soon began to specialize in the painting of porcelain objects, making the company a luxury products specialist. In addition to porcelain painting, Pochet-Deroche began painting glass objects as well. These activities placed the company in contact with Verrerie du Courval, for which Pochet-Deroche became the Parisian distributor.

Deroche continued its porcelain painting activities throughout the 19th century, becoming involved in the earliest years of the photography industry (early photographic efforts were rendered as paintings on glass). Meantime, the Verrerie du Courval had responded to another developing new trend—that of a market for perfume bottles. While France had long been associated with perfumes, the rise of new, industrialized manufacturing techniques, as well as the development of new synthetic ingredients, gave a new boost to the perfume industry in the first half of the 19th century.

The du Courval glass workshop responded to the rising demand for perfumes by producing bottles designed to contain perfumes. This soon became a company specialty; until the late 1850s, however, perfume bottles were fashioned to contain any perfume. Yet the creation of the first "designer" perfume, created by Guerlain for the Empress Eugenie in 1858, launched a new industry—that of the perfume bottle. For his new perfume, called "Eau de Cologne Imperiale," Guerlain called upon du Courval, which created a distinctive bottle for the perfume.

While the Guerlain bottle remained a limited edition, it helped establish the du Courval name as a pre-eminent maker of perfume bottles. Throughout the rest of the 19th century, bottles remained more or less separate from the perfumes themselves. Customers brought their empty bottles to perfumeries and pharmacies to be refilled. Yet the creation of a wealthy middle class, an offshoot of the Industrial Revolution, introduced a new demand in the perfume industry.

The "nouveau riche," eager to show off their wealth, began to look upon the idea of refilling their perfume bottles as miserly. A number of noted designers recognized this trend, and a new breed of perfumes, which featured their own, designer-crafted bottles, was born. Among the first and longest-lasting of the new generation of perfumes was that of famed designer Coco Chanel. Designers and perfume-makers now turned to the du Courval site, which quickly adapted to the demand and began specializing in creating perfume-specific bottles.

Modernizing in the 20th Century

Following World War I, the Pochet-Deroche company came under the control of two brothers of the Colonna de Giovellina, who had served as officers in the French army. Renamed as simply Pochet, the Paris-based company abandoned the porcelain market by the 1930s. Instead, Pochet bought up the Verrerie du Courval. Under the Colonna de Giovellina brothers, Pochet had become a specialist in perfume bottles.

Until the 1930s, the du Courval site had continued producing its glass bottles largely as it had done for some three centuries, that is, blow-molded and by hand. The Colonna de Giovellina family now turned Pochet toward modern manufacturing techniques, in particular by installing new molding machinery. Pochet did not, however, entirely abandon the traditional glass crafting techniques—certain limited editions, large-scale and prototype designs were to remain at least partly hand-made into the next century.

Nonetheless, the new modernized techniques enabled Pochet to grow with the booming demand for designer perfumes in the 20th century. The late 1960s in particular saw enormous growth in the perfume industry as a new wave of clothing designers, including Christian Dior and Yves Saint Laurent, revolutionized the perfume industry. By then, the perfume bottle itself had become one of the most important factors in the marketing of new perfumes, with many consumers buying their perfumes as much for the distinctiveness of the bottle as for the perfume itself.

In 1971, Pochet, which by then had already established itself as one of the leading French perfume bottle makers—and certainly the leading specialist—once again modernized its production facilities, installing new equipment that enabled it to automate the entire bottle production process. Pochet's revamped facilities enabled it to keep pace with the increasing demands of perfume-makers, which, in order to differentiate themselves in an increasingly crowded market, began seeking more and more elaborate bottle designs. In turn, Pochet began investing in research and development in order to introduce new techniques and effects. By the early 1980s, the company's sales had grown to nearly FFr430 million (approximately $65 million).

Diversified for the New Century

Pochet remained firmly under control of the Colonna de Giovellina family. In 1983, a new generation took over the leadership of the company when Gabriel Colonna de Giovellina was named Pochet's CEO. With a background as an engineer, and eight years working for a pharmaceutical company, Colonna de Giovellina began looking for opportunities to expand Pochet's operations. Joined by Hubert Varlet, who was named CEO of Verrerie du Courval in 1985, Colonna de Giovellina now sought to diversify the company beyond its core perfume bottle market.

Yet Pochet remained close to its perfume and bottling specialties. In the mid-1980s, the company recognized a growing trend among perfume makers, which were then beginning to expand their perfume brands across larger lines of bath and beauty accessories. Yet Pochet's glass specialty remained inappropriate for certain applications, especially bath products. In 1986, Pochet extended its molding expertise into plastics. While this operation grew slowly—representing just 3 percent of the company's sales at the beginning of the 1990s—it enabled Pochet to gain experience in the range of plastic materials and also kept it close to the needs of its perfume maker customers. The following year, the company moved closer to the fast-growing North American market, establishing a subsidiary in the United States dedicated to finishing bottles crafted at its Bresle valley facilities.

Pochet remained company-owned until the late 1980s, when a branch of the founding family sought to sell out its shares. In 1989, powerful French conglomerate Compagnie de Navigation Mixte bought up a 30 percent share in Pochet. With its new shareholders deep pockets, Pochet stepped up its expansion. For this, the company looked for partnerships. In 1989, the company joined with luxury goods maker Hermes to form Castille Investissement, which then acquired money-losing Cristalleries de Saint-Louis. Colonna de Giovellina himself took control of the famed crystal maker, bringing it back into profitability after just two years. The success of the Saint-Louis partnership encouraged Hermes and Pochet to add to their partnership. In 1991, Castille Investissement acquired famed Parisian silversmith Puiforcat, which had established an international reputation for its silverware, tea service, and other tableware.

That year also market the start of another important joint-venture for Pochet when the company bought a 50 percent stake in Qualipac, the plastics packaging unit of France's Sommer Allibert. That joint-venture represented Pochet's full entry into the plastics market and grew to represent some 30 percent of the company's revenues by the end of the 1990s.

Pochet's diversification drive enabled it to post strong growth into the mid-1990s, with its sales rising past FFr1.1 billion by the end of 1994. By then, the company had expanded again, this time on its own, eyeing renowned French glass designer Lalique, in which Pochet had held a 9.4 percent since the 1950s. In 1994, Lalique heir Marie Lalique agreed to sell out control of her family's company to Pochet.

Meanwhile, differences in opinion on how to approach Saint-Louis and Puiforcat, both of which had slipped into losses during the difficult economy of the early 1990s, led Pochet and Hermes to end their partnership in 1995. Pochet now regrouped its operations around its core Verrerie du Courval, which produced more than half of the company's revenues, and the Lalique and Qualipac operations. Pochet also went public, listing its shares on the Paris Stock Exchange. The 30 percent of Compagnie de Navigation Mixte came under control of BNP Paribas; Pochet's actual free float never topped 10 percent.

Lalique ran into difficulties in the late 1990s, particularly as the collapse of the Asian and South American economies slashed at a large part of that company's sales. With Lalique slipping into losses, Pochet responded aggressively, expanding Lalique's chain of boutiques, which reached more than 70 stores worldwide at the turn of the century.

Pochet too experienced difficulties at the turn of the century as the collapse of the 1990s stock market boom combined with the September 11, 2001 attacks to force a downturn in the perfume and luxury markets. In response, the Colonna de Giovellina family moved to take back full control of Pochet, launching a share buyback offer. By 2003, the company had succeeded in acquiring more than 98 percent of the company, including the more than 33 percent held by BNP Paribas. By then, however, the continued difficulties of the perfume sector, which contributed to a drop in Pochet's sales from nearly EUR 400 million in 2001 to just under EUR 319 million in 2002, had forced the company to shut down one of its four furnaces. Nonetheless, Pochet maintained a solid position as the world's leading perfume bottle maker—backed by a history stretching back 380 years.

Principal Subsidiaries

Lalique; Verreries Pochet et du Courval; Qualipac (50%).

Principal Competitors

Compagnie de Saint-Gobain; Pilkington plc; Compagnie Financière Richemont AG.

Further Reading

Bialobos, Chantal, "La diva aux 300 millions de flacons," *L'Expansion*, September 3, 1992, p. 92.

Cicco, Anne, "Le longue histoire de Le Courval, berceau du flacon de parfum," *L'Humanité*, December 30, 1998.

"Les familles fondatrices de Pochet veulent reprendre la totalite du capital," *Les Echos,* January 18, 2001, p. 18

Gillet, Philippe, and Fraudreau, Martin, *Les Maîtres du verre et du feu*, Paris: Editions Perrin, 1998.

Leboucq, Valérie, "Le verrier Lalique pèse négativemetn dans les comptes de Pochet," *Les Echos*, April 1, 2003, p. 14.

"Pochet tire un trait sur deux années de vaches maigres," *Le Journal des Finances*, December 16, 2000, p. 20.

"Délaissés par les analystes, les flacons Pochet reprennent leur liberté," *Le Monde*, February 21, 2001.

—M. L. Cohen

Professional Bull Riders Inc.

6 South Tejon Street, Suite 700
Colorado Springs, Colorado 80903-1547
U.S.A.
Telephone: (719) 471-3008
Web site: http://www.pbrnow.com

Private Company
Incorporated: 1992
Employees: 30
Sales: Not available.
NAIC: 711219 Other Spectator Sports

With its headquarters located in Colorado Springs , Colorado, Professional Bull Riders Inc. (PBR) is the governing body for the stand-alone rodeo event of bull riding. According to the rules of the sport, a rider must stay mounted on a bull for eight seconds with the use of just one hand gripping a rope lashed around the animal's belly. PBR's "major league" tour of 29 annual events, culminating in a world championship held in Las Vegas, features the top 45 out of a pool of 700 qualified riders. Events take place in larger urban areas such as Anaheim, Atlanta, Baltimore, New Orleans, Philadelphia, and St. Louis, as well as smaller markets such as Billings, Montana; Guthrie, Oklahoma; Grand Rapids, Michigan; and Worcester, Massachusetts. Most of the competitions are two-day affairs, with all 45 participants making a ride at both Friday and Saturday sessions, and the top 15 scorers advancing to a final round when money is awarded. Scores are determined on a 100-point basis, with 50 points devoted to the rider's performance and another 50 judging how well the animal performed. Should a bull not jump or spin hard enough to give the rider an opportunity to earn a competitive score, the judges may award a re-ride. Bulls and riders are matched at random by use of a computer, and the bulls that are the most difficult to ride are reserved for the "money round." Some of the bulls are pampered celebrities in their own right. Nevertheless, the bulls are dangerous and powerful, some weighing 2,000 pounds, and as a result professional bull riders sustain a high number of injuries, making it one of the most dangerous sports in the world. None of the participants are under contract by the PBR and are responsible for their own expenses. The organization also main-

tains minor league feeder operation. The second tier circuit, the Challenger Tour, sponsors more than 60 events held in smaller markets. After the completion of every five major PBR events, the top five riders in the Challenger Tour replace the five lowest ranked riders in the main tour. Top 45 riders may also participate in Challenger Tour events, and many participate in order to maintain their place on the main tour. A third tour, called Humps N' Horn, provides aspiring bull riders with a chance to compete and learn the sport. PBR has enjoyed steady growth in recent years, prompting some to call it the next NASCAR, the popular stock car racing series.

Bull-Related Sports Origins in the Bronze Age

Sporting contests involving bulls can be traced back to the Minoan-Mycenaean civilization, which evolved on the island of Crete from 3000 to 1100 B.C. Such activities as bull vaulting and bull grappling were conducted as part of religious occasions and have their modern day rodeo counterparts in the antics of the rodeo clown (called "bullfighters" on the bull riding circuit) and the rodeo events of steer wrestling and calf roping. Steer wrestling, in fact, was part of the ancient Greek Olympics. These activities ultimately spread to the Iberian peninsula, resulting in the Spanish tradition of bullfighting, which in the 16th century was brought to Mexico and became popular across all social classes. The Spanish also introduced cattle, horses, and the lariat to the New World, all key elements of the American rodeo. Mexican ranch hands, the most skilled known as charros, displayed impressive riding and roping skills (as well as indulging in elaborate dress). At cattle auctions, fiestas, roundups, and brandings, the charros held contests to show off their skills, one of which was to chase down a bull on horseback, grab it by the tail, and flip it to the ground. As the cattle industry flourished in the southwestern portion of the United States, American cowboys picked up and modified the Mexican tradition and began to hold their own informal meets, called a rodeo (also a word with Spanish origins), where they held trick riding and bronco busting contests. The first organized rodeo, featuring advertised cash prizes and charged admission, was held in Prescott, Arizona, in 1888. Rodeos also became an important part of the Wild West shows that began to tour the country and became cornerstone events at Fourth of July cele-

Company Perspectives:

Professional Bull Riders, Inc., was founded in 1992 by 20 accomplished bull riders who joined together and took a business risk to try to make bull riding—the most popular event in traditional rodeo—into a stand-alone sport.

brations, cattlemen conventions, and annual "stampedes" and Frontier Day celebrations.

Rodeo became organized in the 1920s, and major events were held at Boston Garden and New York City's Madison Square Garden, which led promoters and managers in 1929 to establish the Rodeo Association of America. The contestants remained unorganized until 1936 when, unhappy with prize money, judging, and the way their sport was advertised, they went on strike during the Boston Garden World Championship and formed the Cowboys Turtle Association. The CTA changed its name to the Rodeo Cowboys Association in 1946, then became the Professional Rodeo Cowboys Association in 1975. The PRCA is the chief sanctioning body in rodeo today.

With the advent of World War II, the sport lost a high number of participants to military service, forcing the cancellation of many rodeo events in both the United States and Canada. Yet the war also provided rodeo a chance to be held around the world, essentially wherever American troops were stationed. Rodeo came to be associated with patriotism and American values, major aspects of which are still found today in the presentation of the PBR, as revealed in a 2002 *Los Angeles Times* profile: "The PBR has marketed itself carefully, and tirelessly, and from the beginning eschewed the "Happy Trails" nostalgia of rodeo in favor of speed, noise, patriotism, and dramatics. The big-screen TV overhead plays a video showing U.S. soldiers at attention, then bull riders in front of a flag, then more soldiers, then more riders. The rockets fired from the scaffolding have slammed into the dirt arena, igniting crystallized chemicals. A massive 'USA' sizzles in the soil.''

Aside from women's barrel racing, the five standard rodeo events became bareback riding, steer wrestling, team roping, saddle bronc riding, calf roping, and bull riding. Only bull riding held no plausible connection to cowboy skills. The difference between riding a bucking horse and a bull, however, was dramatic. Horses jumped forward, making it relatively easy for a skilled rider to remain seated, even without a saddle. Both bareback riding and saddle bronc riding became an event based on flair rather than the ability to avoid being thrown off. Rodeo bulls (humpnecked Brahmans mixed with other tighter-skinned breeds) not only jumped, they also spun as well as performed what riders called belly rolls. Moreover, many were massive in size and able to generate a great deal of torque as they attempted to shed the man sitting on their back. While style and the ability to spur the animal were also important elements in bull riding, simply being able to remain seated for eight seconds was a major accomplishment. Moreover, there was an element of danger involved. The power of the bulls caused hard falls, but once on the ground the contestant also had to fear being stepped on or have the bull attempt to gore him. Although horns were

shorn off, they remained potentially lethal. Often a rider would be unable to free his rope hand, become caught up, and was dragged around the pen by a wildly bucking and spinning bull. As a result, rodeo clowns became more protectors than entertainers, their chief function to draw a bull away from a competitor lying on the ground or to rush in to help free a rider caught up in his rope. Out of respect for their value in protecting the health of the bull riders, the clowns increasingly became referred to as bull fighters. In the PBR, they eschewed the makeup and baggy pants that remained a feature of the men working PRCA bull riding events.

Rodeo Grows in the 1980s

Because of the danger and difficulty, bull riding became the most popular rodeo sport and was the last event of the day. Much of the rising success of rodeo was attributed to bull riding, and more and more participants became specialists. In 1985, the annual championships, The National Finals Rodeo, moved from Oklahoma City to Las Vegas, which elevated rodeo to a new level. Bull riders, the stars of the sport, came to believe that they were not receiving their just due. Although a number of bull riding only events were held on occasion, it was not until 1991 that a break-away bull riding circuit was formed to establish an alternative to PRCA events, which charged riders an entrance fee. The company was called Bull Riders Only, founded by former bull rider Shaw P. Sullivan and investment banker Eric Dickson. The first BRO event was held in June 1991 and grossed just $40,000. Four other events were held that year and were successful enough to warrant the production of 11 events in the second season and television coverage by the Prime Network. BRO established the sudden death format of bull riding, with the top 18 out of 30 contestants proceeding to the second round, and the top ten vying for the cash prizes. By the second year, total prize money for each event was $20,000.

The PBR was formed in 1992 in Scottsdale, Arizona, by 20 bull riders, including the top stars. They each invested $1,000 to launch an athlete-owned and operated bull riding tour, which like the PRCA would be headquartered in Colorado Springs, Colorado. Their goal was to increase the opportunity to earn more money as well as to gain some control of their sport. Most riders continued to compete in PRCA events as well as BRO. During its first season in 1994, the PBR conducted eight events with $250,000 in total prize money. Like the PRCA, it held its world championships in Las Vegas, hosted by the MGM Grand Garden. It also secured sponsorship from brewer Anheuser-Busch and its Bud Light brand and sold exclusive broadcast rights to The Nashville Network cable channel through 1999. Although it was far from certain that it would succeed, the PBR grew steadily and began to challenge the BRO for supremacy in the stand-alone sport, despite BRO's head start. In 1994, the BRO circuit included 17 stops and featured essentially the same riders as the PBR, many of whom owned interests in the PBR. In 1995, the PBR grew to 12 events and sought professional management help, hiring Randy Bernard to serve as the chief executive officer. Bernard had several years of experience in the marketing and entertainment department of the California Midstate Fair. By 1997, both BRO and the PBR were producing two dozen events each, although it was becoming clear that the PBR was the stronger of the two rival organizations. BRO one-

---

Key Dates:

1992: Professional Bull Riders (PBR) is established.
1994: PBR completes its first tour of eight events.
1998: The PBR tour now consists of 24 events.
1999: The PBR tour grows to 28 events.
2001: The first major network broadcast of a PBR event.
2002: Humps 'n Horns tour is launched.

---

day events paid $25,000 in prize money and $50,000 for two-day events, while the PBR paid out $75,000 for all of its regular season stops. The market for bull riding, however promising, simply could not support two tours and by the end of the 1997 season BRO went out of business, leaving the PBR as the lone tour. In the meantime, the quality of bull riding in the PRCA greatly deteriorated. While bull riders continued to attend PRCA events in the hopes of make the lucrative National Finals Rodeo, they chose to ride in as few events as possible in hopes of earning just enough money to qualify. The PBR tour, which required participation in all of its events, was becoming the focus of riders, who were now able to make a better living—and lessen the physical toll on their bodies—by devoting their energies to the PBR tour. As a result, PRCA bull riding events often lacked quality fields and resulted in poor performances.

PBR Tour Expands in 1999

In 1998, the PBR conducted 24 events, the minimum amount of prize money now reaching $80,000 per stop, with a total of $4.5 million for the year. Ratings on TNN were growing, and the popularity of bull riding at the Las Vegas championships prompted a new five-year deal which moved the event to the 19,000-seat Thomas and Mack Center located on the campus of the University of Las Vegas. The event headquarters was also switched to Caesars Place. In 1999, the PBR tour expanded to 28 cities, adding former BRO stops Salt Lake City and Phoenix. Its rising popularity was also prompting a comparison to NASCAR, the stock car organization that through savvy marketing grew beyond a regional following to become a national success. The PBR shared a similar demographic to NASCAR, and its fans were also brand loyal to PBR sponsors. It was understandable, therefore, that the PBR would try to emulated NASCAR's success. PBR sponsorships were available at a fraction of the cost of NASCAR, a three- to five-year sponsorship deal in 2000 starting at just $350,000. In 1995, the PBR collected a total of $365,000 in sponsorship revenues. That amount in 2001 would exceed $10 million, as the PBR aggressively pursued all manner of sponsorship opportunities, including signage, on-site inflatables, ring banners, hospitality tables, retail-tie ins, and co-marketing efforts. The PBR gained a major partner in Ford, which launched a sponsorship of the tour, renamed the "BR Built Ford Tough Series," in order to tap into the large truck-buying segment of the sport's demographic.

On November 25, 2001, the PBR received a major boost when NBC televised an event opposite a National Football League game and golf's Skins Game. It garnered surprisingly high ratings, and in the New York City market even outdrew a number of network sporting events that weekend, including golf, a college basketball game, and a National Hockey League game. The strong showing resulted in CBS and NBC deciding to air seven PBR events between them, staring in late 2002 and into 2003. The Outdoor Life Network also began to provide expanded coverage of the PBR on cable and satellite television. Moreover, Spanish language broadcaster Telemundo secured rights to televise PBR events. Ford, pleased with its association with the PBR, extended its commitment in 2002. The tour also launched its PBR Headquarters Program to expand its officially licensed products and make more of it available to western apparel retailers. Key partners included Wrangler, Lucchese Boots, Resistol, Montana Silversmiths, Cripple Creek, Paramount Headwear, and Chambers Belts. In 2003, the PBR launched its Humps 'n Horns tour for aspiring riders to augment its Challenger Tour. All told, the PBR was well positioned to continue its goal of becoming the "next NASCAR." With some of its top riders hailing from Brazil as well as Australia, the PBR held some promise outside of the United States. The next step in the growth of the PBR was the development of superstars. Riders were required to sign autographs after each event and the tour made every effort to promote its personalities, again a fan-friendly approach that worked quite well for NASCAR. No one expected the PBR to produce a Tiger Woods or Michael Jordan, or that the bull riding would begin to rival more established sports, but there was every reason to believe that the PBR could continue to grow on the success of its first ten years and become a popular and profitable entertainment product.

Principal Operating Units

Challenger Series; Humps' n Horns.

Principal Competitors

Professional Rodeo Cowboys Association.

Further Reading

Franscell, Ron, "Professional Bull-Riding Bucking Way into Prime-Time Network Sports," *Denver Post*, March 17, 2002.
Hochman, Paul, "Bull Riding Hits the Mainstream," *Fortune*, July 6, 1998, pp. 40–44.
Hoffman, Brett, "PBR Helps Rodeo Break Through to Big Cities," *Fort Worth Star-Telegram*, October 14, 1998.
Knocke, Ed, "Let's Rodeo," *Texas Monthly*, January 1997, p. 63.
McManes, Chris, "Riders Bullish on Rival Circuits," *Las Vegas Review-Journal*, December 10, 1997.
——, "Bull Rider Bucks for Bucks, Not World Championships," *Las Vegas Review-Journal*, December 14, 1997.
Meadows, Susannah, "X-treme Bull," *Newsweek*, June 25, 2001, pp. 78–79.
Pearson, Demetrius W., and C. Allen Haney, "The Rodeo Cowboy: Cultural Icon, Athlete, or Entrepreneur?," *Journal of Sport and Social Issues*, August 1999, pp. 308–27.
Slater, Eric, "This Ain't Rodeo," *Los Angeles Times*, December 20, 2002, p. A-1.

—Ed Dinger

Public Service of New Hampshire

Public Service Company of New Hampshire

780 North Commercial Street
P.O. Box 330
Manchester, New Hampshire 03105-0330
U.S.A.
Telephone: (603) 669-4000
Toll Free: (800) 662-7764
Fax: (603) 634-2367
Web site: http://www.psnh.com

Wholly Owned Subsidiary of The Northeast Utilities
*   System*
Founded: 1926
Employees: 1,222
Sales: $794.2 million (2002)
NAIC: 221110 Electric Power Generation; 221111
    Hydroelectric Power Generation; 221112 Fossil Fuel
    Power Generation

Public Service Company of New Hampshire (PSNH), the Granite State's largest electric utility, is a wholly owned subsidiary of Connecticut-based Northeast Utilities (NU), which provides energy to customers from Maine to Maryland. PSNH serves more than 447,000 homes and businesses throughout the state with the help of over 1,200 employees who work and live in New Hampshire and contribute in many ways to the communities where they reside. Since its inception in 1926, PSNH has grown to comprise three fossil-fuel-fired generating plants and nine hydroelectric facilities, jointly capable of generating more than 1,110 megawatts of electricity. This ample and diverse supply of energy provides the foundation for the continued economic growth and prosperity of New Hampshire residents. As an integral part of New England's largest electric system, PSNH serves three-quarters of the state in 201 communities. The principal business of the company is the generation, purchase, transmission, distribution, and sale of electricity. PSNH's commitment to safeguarding the environment through reduced emissions, corporate giving, community involvement, and strategic partnerships has earned it numerous awards from state and federal agencies. PSNH accounted for about 41 percent of NU's total consolidated 2002 earnings.

1850–1925: The Forerunners

As in many other states, the forerunners of electricity in New Hampshire were the water wheels powering the grist, lumber, and textile mills that spurred the development of industry. Gas lights and horse-drawn street cars were soon introduced to meet the needs of the people in the towns formed around New Hampshire mills—as well as for the growing population of the Portsmouth shipping center. Then came arc lights and trolley cars. The Nashua Gas Light Company turned on its first gas lights in November 1853 and the Manchester Horse Railroad in 1877 carried its first 16 passengers in ten-foot cars.

By 1882 Thomas A. Edison had put into operation the world's first two commercial electric generators, one in London and another at Pearl Street Station in New York. Meanwhile, the New England Weston Electric Light Company of Boston had arranged to build a generating station in Manchester, New Hampshire, on the property of the Amoskeag Manufacturing Company. Weston Electric turned on the first electric street lights in Manchester on April 23, 1882—two weeks before the start-up of the Pearl Street Station. In 1885 the Manchester Electric Light Company bought all the Weston property in the city and in 1901 merged with the Manchester Traction, Light and Power Company. PSNH records indicate that 39 of the pioneer electric companies that later became part of the company had been in the electric business before 1900 and that another 15 had been incorporated before that date. Two specific developments, the operation of the first alternating-current generator and the industrial use of electric power and alternating current, opened the way for the evolution of PSNH.

1926–32: Founding and Early Years of PSNH

According to Everett B. Sackett, author of *Fifty Years of Service: A History of Public Service Co. of New Hampshire,* investment houses were the buyers and sellers of utility companies. The most active of these investment houses was Samuel Insull's Middle West Utilities (MWU) in Chicago. Insull had bought most of the competing electric companies in the city and set electricity prices low enough to lure customers from the gas companies. Insull's activity increased the volume of sales and thereby created economies of operation, but larger amounts of capital were needed to fund expanded operations. Insull then organized Middle West Utilities (MWU), which functioned as both an operating company and a holding company to raise money ''by selling securities backed in part by the securities of the operating companies and in part by accounting legerdemain,'' wrote Sackett.

At times, to raise new capital, Insull bought companies far removed from his Chicago base of operations. For example, MWU reached out as far east as northern New England to buy the Central Maine Power Company. Eventually Insull combined all his northern New England holdings by forming the New England Public Service Company (NEPSCo) as a holding company that owned all, or nearly all, the common stock of its subsidiaries, one of which was the Public Service Company of New Hampshire (PSNH).

In the early days of the industry, small electric companies emerged almost overnight and then sought to consolidate. PSNH, for instance, had been incorporated in August 1926 as a consolidation of five New Hampshire electric companies. PSNH eventually consolidated Insull's holdings in New Hampshire, thereby acquiring properties in the southern and western parts of the state. Through its contacts with NEPSCo, PSNH could then bring eastern and northern New Hampshire into a statewide system. After its founding and up to December 1943, PSNH acquired the franchises and utility properties of 25 other electric and/or gas companies in New Hampshire. The company then hastened to unify its holdings by lacing the state with utility lines.

One of the ways PSNH promoted the sale of its product was to make central-station power available to rural areas. According to the company's 1928 annual report, many of the newly installed electrical rural lines had been made ''in response to an insistent demand for a higher standard of living and increased comfort on the farm.'' PSNH sold its gas business in 1945.

PSNH also attracted new companies into the state by offering them free trials of electrical applications. According to the company's annual report cited above, if PSNH had ''spare generating and line capacity'' at the time of a company's desire for trial use, granting the request would ''assist in bringing new

industries into the territory.'' A 1929 survey conducted by PSNH and local chambers of commerce found that 18 new industries employed 3,300 employees within the PSNH territory.

To promote domestic use of electricity, PSNH even experimented with an ''active-room'' rate for small houses and apartments: the company billed the customers in proportion to their needs, and at the same low rate applied to larger establishments. Initially PSNH's business included the gas, electric railway, and steam businesses. By 1931, however, the number of gas meters had fallen to 10,960 while electric meters had increased to 51,270; use of the automobile had cut into the street-railway business; and the handful of customers buying steam required the use of only one of the generating plants.

1930s–40s: Meeting Challenges

Insull's Middle West Utilities at first weathered the economic upheaval brought on by the stock-market crash and even came to the aid of the city of Chicago and of some troubled industries. Insull, however, had made some imprudent decisions and could not fend off a group of New York bankers determined to gain control of his $3 billion empire. In 1932 he resigned all his corporate positions. The collapse of the Insull companies occasioned a government investigation of how utility companies were financed and brought about the passing of the Public Utility Holding Company Act of 1935. Thus, NEPSCo was severed from MWU but remained the owner of its regional subsidiaries, which included PSNH.

The year 1936 had been good for New England business, but there was gnawing economic worry about growing competition from southern textile mills. The greatest threat to PSNH's continued growth was the closing of Manchester's Amoskeag Manufacturing Company, the largest cotton mill in the world. With a view to developing the abandoned establishment, PSNH's Schiller and a group of Manchester business leaders formed a new corporation, Amoskeag Industries, Inc. Emboldened by PSNH's purchase of 18 percent of Amoskeag's stock and the offer to pay for waterpower developments and the electrical-distribution system, local industries raised enough additional money to finance renovation of the mill. By year-end 1937, due in large part to PSNH's involvement, 40 companies had bought or leased space in the mill buildings and were employing about 4,000 workers. Thus, PSNH emphasized its continuing concern for creating jobs in New Hampshire.

Over and above dealing with economic storms, in 1936 PSNH also had to cope with ice jams and the worst flood in New England's 300-year history. The hurricane of September 1938 proved so devastating that electric service was interrupted statewide and not fully restored for several weeks. PSNH could cope with these natural disasters because in 1931 it had acquired the Jacona, a government ship converted into a floating power plant anchored at Portsmouth. The Jacona generated steam for about one-sixth of PSNH's total generating capacity. On March 17, 1945 the U.S. government seized the ship for use in the war effort.

From 1929 to 1945, except for a minor setback in 1938, PSNH annually generated and sold an increasing amount of electricity. Residential customers' average use increased with-

Key Dates:

1926: Public Service Company of New Hampshire (PSNH) is formed by consolidating five New Hampshire electric companies.
1929: PSNH begins selling gas and electric appliances.
1935: The Public Utility Holding Company Act is passed.
1946: PSNH goes public.
1950: PSNH's Schiller station becomes the first fully integrated binary cycle plant in the country and is considered the world's most fuel-efficient plant.
1954: PSNH sells the bus lines that grew out of its electric trolley businesses.
1971: PSNH joins the New England PowerPool (NEPOOL).
1989: N.H. Supreme Court rejects PSNH emergency rate increases; the company files bankruptcy; bankruptcy court approves Northeast Utilities' (NU) two-step purchase plan.
1992: PSNH emerges from bankruptcy, becoming a wholly owned NU subsidiary.
2001: The N.H. Deregulation Act and the N.H. Clean Power Act go into effect.
2002: PSNH relocates its headquarters to the old Manchester Steam Plant, which is renovated and renamed Energy Park.

out a break, from 453 KWHs in 1932 to 1,012 KWHs in 1945. The average cost per KWH for domestic consumers moved steadily downward from 7.48 cents in 1932 to 4.45 cents in 1945 (in 1945 dollars).

Postwar Period

By 1966 PSNH's sale of industrial power was 333 times what it had been in 1948, while the gain in domestic use of electricity (due mainly to electrical heating in homes) was twice that much. At year-end 1966, electricity was used to heat 19,276 homes and 1,309 establishments. PSNH slowed down its marketing efforts and discontinued its complimentary wiring of buildings for heat. According to historian Sackett, in 1948 "the company's 31 hydroelectric plants, with a rated capacity of 77,500 KWs, were matched by six fuel-burning plants having a capacity of 76,250 KWs. New England was running out of undeveloped water power." Furthermore, the generating stations situated on New England rivers could not always operate at optimum capacity because of erratic stream flow. For example, the Amoskeag installation at Manchester could run at its maximum level only 17 percent of the time in an average year. Maine still had an undeveloped amount of power, but a 1955 law forbade exportation of power to other states. By 1973, PSNH had retired 41 of its hydroelectric plants.

From 1945–51, the demand for power more than doubled and obliged PSNH to add new generating facilities. In 1948 the company replaced the Jacona with the Resistance, which had been built and used by the government in World War II. After extensive repairs, the Resistance generated 30,000 KWs of electricity, thereby merely replacing the Jacona. PSNH then

planned the construction of a fully integrated 40,000 KW mercury binary-cycle plant that became known as the Schiller Plant. This station, the first of its kind in the country, used a unique mercury-based process to generate power; required only three-fourths of the fuel needed by former methods for producing a comparable amount of electricity; and, according to historian Sackett, "was said to be the most efficient fuel plant in the world." The first unit of the Schiller plant was dedicated in 1950. By 1970 three additional units were also functioning.

Use of electricity increased as fast as PSNH could build additional generating stations and transmission facilities. By 1968 the company was adding new electrical companies and withdrawing its involvement in fields other than electricity. The gas business had been sold in 1945 and the steam business was stopped in 1949. By 1940 the electric-trolley activity, once a major part of PSNH operations, had become unprofitable and the company switched to operating buses. After World II, the lifting of gasoline restrictions led to increased use of automobiles for transportation and PSNH sold its bus lines in 1954.

In 1941 PSNH had registered a 70 percent gain in revenue; however, in 1950 the company was overwhelmed by a 90 percent increase in production costs, especially for the purchase and transportation of coal. Repeatedly, the company implemented rate increases and tried to control costs by joining other utilities to study and implement the use of atomic power. According to PSNH's 1954 annual report, the region's major utilities had organized the Yankee Atomic Electric Company to explore "the unknown and unlimited potentialities of the concentrated energy possessed by atomic fuels." In 1971 PSNH also joined other investor-owned power companies in New England to form the New England Power Pool (NEPOOL) to share the construction and operational costs of developing the "Big 11" power loop. This loop was a network of 345-kilovolt (KV) transmission lines tying together the systems of the 11 pool members. (A kilovolt is a unit of 1,000 volts). Membership in NEPOOL was later opened to all New England utilities, regardless of ownership.

1970s–80s: Escalating Prices and Crises

Since use of nuclear energy was already a proven technology in some parts of New England, as early as 1968 PSNH considered building an 860-megawatt atomic plant at Seabrook, but financial conditions obliged the company to shelve the plans. However, when the newly established Organization of Petroleum Exporting Countries (OPEC) raised the price of oil to previously unknown heights, oil that had cost 4 cents a gallon in October 1970 sold for 27 cents a gallon in 1974. Faced "with the threat of economic starvation and blackmail posed by OPEC," wrote Chris Herbert in the May 1996 issue of *New Hampshire Business Revue*, the U.S. government discouraged the use of fossil fuel and to encourage use of alternate resources, in 1978 Congress passed the Public Utilities Regulatory Policy Act.

By January 1972 PSNH had decided not only to build a nuclear plant at Seabrook but also to have it consist of two 1,150-megawatt units, to be completed in 1979. PSNH was to own 50 percent of the $1.3 billion project and share the remaining investment with other New England utilities. In January 1974 the New Hampshire Site Evaluation Committee, the Public Utilities Commission (PUC) and other regulatory bodies had issued the basic permits, but interveners in the case succeeded in having the New Hampshire Supreme Court overturn these permits. After repeated appeals and rehearings PSNH received its construction permit in July 1976—and experienced its first protest at the planned site.

There followed a decade of other protests at the site, inside regulatory chambers, and in New Hampshire and Washington courtrooms. The 1979 accident at the Three Mile Island nuclear-power plant in Pennsylvania—to name but one event that triggered concern about ecological and safety issues—played a significant role in these protests. So did delays imposed through public intervention, slow regulatory approvals, and two significant labor strikes. PSNH had to borrow money to meet ever-escalating costs. In 1978 the company had been authorized to charge customers for the carrying costs of loans to build the Seabrook plant. New legislation stated that PSNH could not recover any investment in the Seabrook Station until the plant provided electricity to its customers. Deprived of CWIP costs (Construction Works in Progress, known as stranded costs), PSNH had to borrow even more heavily at a time of high interest rates. The N.P. Public Utilities Commission (NHPUC) ordered PSNH to reduce its ownership in the plant from 50 percent to 35.6 percent. In March 1984 the joint owners canceled Seabrook Unit II and formed New Hampshire Yankee, a separate division of PSNH, to manage the construction of Unit I and bring it into operation.

Seabrook Unit I was completed in July 1986 at a cost of $4.5 billion but did not go into full operation until August 19, 1990, at which time PSNH had not yet recovered any of the construction costs. Seabrook's final cost was $6.6 billion and PSNH's share of the debt was $2.9 billion. In May 1986 PSNH asked the NHPUC for a two-step rate increase; however, the agency ruled against the request. In a final effort to remain solvent, PSNH appealed NHPUC's decision by filing for a 15 percent emergency rate increase and asked the New Hampshire Supreme Court to suspend the Anti-CWIP law.

Late 1980s–90s: Bankruptcy and Restructuring

On January 26, 1988, the court ruled that the Anti-CWIP statute was constitutional and prevented PSNH from receiving the emergency rate increase. Two days later, on January 28, PSNH filed for protection under Chapter 11 of the U.S. Bankruptcy Code and became the first investor-owned utility since the Great Depression to declare bankruptcy.

The declaration of bankruptcy ended PSNH's long downward economic spiral but did not win public support for the company or for the station. (PSNH sold the Seabrook plant in 2002. See below, *2000 and Beyond*) Later, in a 1996 editorial printed in *The Keene (N.H.) Sentinel,* Guy MacMillin observed that the decisions—some good, some bad—that brought on the bankruptcy could "be traced to previous generations of New Hampshire politicians and legislators." He pointed out three factors that had contributed to the bankruptcy. First, up until the moment of bankruptcy, state regulators and legislators had encouraged the Seabrook nuclear project. Second, the New Hampshire governor and the legislature, certainly aware that PSNH's electric rates were among the highest in the country, had

accepted the seven-year annual rate increases and the stipulation for recovery of stranded costs that were part of the NU deal. Third, according to MacMillin, state regulators and the legislature had required "that PSNH buy very expensive electricity from small wood-fired and hydroelectric power plants . . . to encourage those technologies and thereby guard against a future oil shortage or nuclear-power collapse."

What ensued after the bankruptcy was a power struggle between the state of New Hampshire, PSNH management, and the Federal Bankruptcy Court. Exercising its exclusive right to reorganize after bankruptcy, in December 1988 PSNH chose to abandon state jurisdiction under NHPUC and restructure under the Federal Energy Regulatory Commission (FERC). According to the PSNH document titled *New Hampshire's Energy Partnership,* the FERC "had a favorable record of allowing utilities to recover costs and increase rates as a result of investments in abandoned generating plants." The state's Anti-CWIP law, on the other hand, would have prevented PSNH and its investors from recovering any investment made in the Seabrook station.

By the spring of 1989 little progress had been made; the state transformed the bankruptcy into an auction open to reorganization plans of other competing utilities and major parties. Connnecticut-based Northeast Utilities (NU), one of the six major bidders, announced its plan in January 1989 and PSNH endorsed it in December of the same year. The plan was based on the revenues of a rate agreement that provided for seven annual rate increases of 5.5 percent from 1990 through 1996. The first 5.5 percent base-rate increase went into effect January 1990. The rate agreement projected that there would be no increase to rates in 1997, 1998, and 1999, and included a special mechanism for adjusting rates up or down, according to the cost for fuel and power purchased during the term of the agreement.

The rate agreement assured the $2.3 billion of new revenue needed to finance NU's two-step plan to reorganize PSNH. As the first investor-owned utility company to fall into bankruptcy since the Great Depression, PSNH started the 1990s in major debt and with a tarnished public image. On May 16, 1991, PSNH completed step one of the NU plan, thereby ending its 39-month bankruptcy. Step two was completed June 5, 1992 and PSNH became a fully owned subsidiary of Northeast Utilities. NU paid approximately $2.3 billion to satisfy the bankruptcy claims of creditors and shareholders of PSNH; acquired responsibility for PSNH's 35.6 percent ownership of Seabrook; and established a new subsidiary, the North Atlantic Energy Corporation (NAEC), which had Seabrook as its only asset. NU then owned all the stock of both PSNH and NAEC.

Throughout the bankruptcy proceedings PSNH had offered uninterrupted service to its customers. PSNH continued to rebuild the trust of its employees and of the general public. Company involvement became central to PSNH's corporate culture; employee volunteers answered to needs across the state. In 1993, PSNH created The Economic and Community Development Division to highlight its focus on the business and ecological needs of the communities it served. PSNH also continued to produce *The New Hampshire Economic Review,* first published in 1970 as a compendium of statistics about the advantages available to businesses in New Hampshire. In 1993, PSNH received the Governor's Volunteerism Award. From

1994 onward, PSNH collaborated with the New Hampshire Department of Resources and Economic Development to increase jobs and commerce opportunities. On an annual basis, the company provided funds for special projects, such as trade shows and the state's Export Marketing Grants program.

PSNH also devoted substantial resources to meeting the requirements of the Clean Air Act. In 1995 PSNH retrofitted its coal-fired Merrimack Station's 320-megawatt Unit 2 in Bow, New Hampshire, with an emissions-cleansing Selective Catalytic Reduction (SCR) system, thereby becoming the first power company in the nation to reduce coal-power plant emissions with SCR pollution equipment. The SCR system, a state-of-the-art technology brought in from Germany, treated the nitrogen oxides before they left the plant by converting them into non-polluting, natural elements. According to a PSNH newsletter, the SCR system "slashed the production of smog-producing . . . nitrogen-oxides emissions by 65 percent, the largest single-source reduction in New England." PSNH's efforts to reduce harmful emissions earned the U.S. EPA's Environmental Merit Award and the Governor's Award for Pollution Prevention. PSNH also formed a landmark alliance with the Audubon Society of New Hampshire, the N.H. Fish and Game Department, and the U.S. Fish and Wildlife Service, to operate the Fishways Learning Center next to the Amoskeag Falls Hydro Station in Manchester, New Hampshire. The Fishways included a fish ladder that, in the Spring, enabled visitors to watch through underwater viewing windows as anadromous fish—such as broodstook Atlantic salmon, river herring, sea lamprey, eels, and American shad—returned to their native waters to spawn. The Center provided year-round environmental educational programs and exhibits on the natural and cultural history of the Merrimack River.

As the deadline for ending the seven-year period of rate adjustments approached, the New Hampshire legislature introduced a bill to reduce PSNH electric rates and to end electric monopolies as early as in 1997. The subsequent law, effective May 21, 1996, directed the NHPUC to develop a statewide plan for restructuring electric utilities. In April and again in October of that year PSNH proposed a plan, dubbed Customers First, "to provide near-term rate relief for all customers and introduce choice of electric-energy suppliers within a reasonable time frame." On February 28, 1997 the NHPUC issued its orders in a document titled *Restructuring New Hampshire's Electric Utility Industry: Final Plan*, which established interim stranded-cost charges for PSNH and set January 1, 1998 as the date by which all customers were to choose an electric company.

In the mid-1990s, more than half the states in the nation—including the New England States, New York, Pennsylvania and California—were considering electric-utility deregulation. Although New Hampshire was "the state that led the charge into electricity deregulation," according to the December 8, 1997 issue of *Asset Sales Report*, PSNH argued with state officials over deregulation because the company insisted that "stranded cost securitization be part of the state's effort to deregulate utilities." If that condition could be met, PSNH said that it could go ahead with deregulation in July 1998. Meanwhile, Hurricane Georges swept across Puerto Rico in September 1998 and knocked out power to 1.3 million customers. Over 60 PSNH employees joined other NU employees who traveled

to Puerto Rico to restore electricity after what was known as "the worst storm to hit that Island in 70 years." By December, electricity had been replaced.

In 1998 the company introduced the Grazing Power Project: more than a thousand sheep were used to reduce vegetation under power line rights-of-way. The four-legged tree-mowers ate the shoots of young trees that could grow up to interfere with power lines at various sites in New Hampshire and then went to Florida to spend winters effectively chomping on the invasive weed known as Kudzu. However—because upcoming deregulation might oblige PSNH to sell some of its facilities—in April 2003 the company opted to leave the sheep in their winter home.

During 1998–99, PSNH continued its commitment to protecting the environment by voluntarily finding additional ways—such as installation of more SCR systems, a new Electrostatic Precipitators (ESPs), new pipelines to burn natural gas—to reduce nitrogen oxide emissions at its three fossil-fuel plants (Merrimack Station, Newington Station, and Schiller Station). PSNH invested over $46 million to virtually eliminate any of the ash particles (the "smoke plume") emitted through its Bow-based Unit Two plant. The ESP system captured the ash particulates remaining after the coal was burned, and deposited them in hoppers, from which they were recycled for use in concrete, construction, and roofing materials. PSNH also supported an agreement between New Hampshire and environmental organizations in the state for setting emission-reduction targets for multiple air-pollution emissions from power plants—especially for sulfur dioxide, nitrogen oxides, carbon dioxide, and mercury. PSNH became the first state in the union to set emission-reduction targets for these four major air pollutants. Under The N.H. Clean Power Act which became effective in 2001, these pollutants were to be capped according to U.S. EPA standards.

2000 and Beyond

In New Hampshire, the topic of deregulation had come to the forefront of public concern in the mid-1990s as customers complained about what they called some of the highest electric rates in the country. Ratepayers also claimed that they had no alternative to buying electricity from PSNH, because that utility had a virtual monopoly in its service areas. The original goal of deregulation was to lower rates by attracting other energy producers into the state to create a competitive climate, to oblige PSNH to sell its power generating plants—including its share of Seabrook Station as well as its fossil-fuel and hydro power generating plants—and to offer consumers a choice of energy providers. (Note: Some people thought that PSNH's ability to generate, transfer, distribute and sell electricity gave it the power to become a monopoly.)

The N.H. Deregulation Bill, supported by both the Legislature and PSNH, was signed in June 2000 by then Governor Jeanne Shaheen and sent to NHPUC for implementation. When the Act went into effect May 1, 2001, customers could choose an alternative energy provider. In a reaction to the effects of California's energy blackouts and price spikes, the Legislature modified the deregulation law so that PSNH's divestiture of its power plants, except Seabrook Station, was delayed until February 2004. In 2002, PSNH sold its share of Seabrook Station to the Florida Power and Light Company and applied part of the proceeds of the sale to the refinancing of existing debt and the continuing reduction of electric retail rates by an average of 16 percent, compared to the cost of electricity in the previous year. The Seabrook sale eliminated the risks of nuclear operation in New Hampshire and enabled PSNH to reduce stranded costs, which would otherwise have been passed on to customers.

Another milestone occurred in December 2002 as Central Vermont Public Service, at the urging of Governor Shaheen, agreed to sell PSNH the assets and customer base of its subsidiary, Connecticut Valley Electric Company (CVEC), which served 13 New Hampshire communities along the Connecticut River in the western area of the state. Pending approval by the FERC, NHPUC and passage of enabling legislation by the N.H. Legislature, the sale was to be effective January 1, 2004. Closure of the sale was to resolve all of CVEC's pending litigation issues over New Hampshire's restructuring plan, provide rate relief to CVEC customers who would be moved to PSNH's lower tariff rates, and enable the recovery of CVEC's stranded costs. This was the first such acquisition by PSNH since its 1972 purchase of the New Ipswich Light Department.

More changes for PSNH occurred as the third millennium got underway. Members of the Legislature in late 2002 introduced legislation to again delay the sale of PSNH's existing power-generation plants. PSNH supported the effort, arguing that the aging but still effective plants would ensure a continued source of low-cost power, compared to the independent market prices to which virtually all other New England utilities were subject. "If we sold the plants, the rates would go up and is that what we want?" PSNH President Gary Long asked during a 2003 interview with *Foster's (Portsmouth) Daily Democrat.* "What [the bill] says is that we don't have to sell for the sake of selling. We would keep those plants as long as they are of economic use to the customers." The law delayed the sale until April 2006 and called for the NHPUC to then decide, based on economic impact on customers, when a sale should take place. Governor Craig Benson signed the bill into law April 23, 2003.

PSNH's history was a microcosm of the evolution of electric utilities. Obliged to restructure under trying circumstances, PSNH showed remarkable resiliency. According to Fitch Ratings, PSNH's credit profile was strengthened by the constructive resolution of electric restructuring issues in New Hampshire, a solid financial performance, and $575 million in total stranded cost securitization proceeds used to improve its balance sheet. PSNH could look ahead to continuing success.

Principal Competitors

Energy East Corporation; National Grid USA.

Further Reading

Frain, William T., Jr., "Customers First: A Plan for New Hampshire," *PSNH Newsletter*, October 1996, pp. 1–7.

Haberman, Steve, "Seabrook Station Sold for $836 M," *Portsmouth Herald*, April 16, 2002.

Hamm, Klaus, "Panel: End Electricity Monopolies," *Concord (N.H.) Monitor*, March 1, 1997, pp. A1, A8.

——, "PSNH and Governor May Negotiate; Utility Wants to Suspend Rate Request," *Concord (N.H.) Monitor,* May 10, 1997, pp. A1, A8.

Herbert, Chris, "An Electric Transformation: How Did N.H. Get to Deregulation in the First Place?," *New Hampshire Business Review,* May 24, 1996, pp. 1+.

Kroll, Heidi L., "Retail Choice: What It Means for PSNH Customers," *New Hampshire Business Review*, January 26, 2001.

"Long-Term Problem Could Exist if PSNH Keeps Its Power Plants," *Portsmouth Herald*, March 6, 2003.

MacMillin, Guy, "The PSNH Offer," *Keene (N.H.) Sentinel*, April 30, 1996, p. 10.

Manning, Colin, "PSNH to Retain Fuel-Burning Plant for Next Three Years," *Foster's/Citizen Online*, April 24, 2003.

Meadows, Donella H., "Deregulation: Lessons Learned," *PSNH Newsletter*, January 1997, p. 3.

Moyer, Judith, *New Hampshire Wired: Electric History Topics*, Manchester, N.H.: PSNH, 2002.

"Public Service of New Hampshire," *Business NH Magazine*, May 1977, p. 14.

Sackett, Everett B., *Fifty Years of Service: A History of Public Service Co. of New Hampshire*, Manchester, N.H.: PSNH, 52 pp.

—Gloria A. Lemieux

Red Spot Paint & Varnish Company

1107 East Louisiana Street
Evansville, Indiana 47711
U.S.A.
Telephone: (812) 428-9100
Toll Free: (800) 457-3544
Fax: (812) 428-9167
Web site: http://www.redspot.com

Private Company
Incorporated: 1903 as Evansville Paint & Varnish Company
Employees: 500
Sales: $100 million (2002)
NAIC: 325510 Paint and Coating Manufacturing

Privately held and family run, Red Spot Paint & Varnish Company is a leading supplier of coatings for plastics. Founded as a hardware retailer in 1903, Red Spot has concentrated on plastics since the 1930s. The company formulates and manufactures paints and primers for sporting equipment, personal electronics, aerospace components, cosmetics packaging, and business machines. The bulk of its business, however, is in the automotive sector, where it supplies an array of coatings that are used on cars—from bumper to bumper, both inside and out. General Motors, Ford Motor Company, DaimlerChrysler, and Toyota are among Red Spot's customers.

Painting Plastic in the Early 1900s

In 1903, Harry D. Bourland founded Evansville Paint & Varnish Co. in Evansville, Indiana. Bourland initially sold hardware and turpentine wholesale to dealers, but the company flourished as he expanded the product offerings and opened his own retail hardware stores in the tri-state area where Indiana, Kentucky, and Illinois meet. Seeking to broaden his company's appeal in the region, Bourland changed its name to Red Spot Paint & Varnish in 1921. The company's bulls-eye logo became a familiar sight in the area.

The family-run business made a significant acquisition in 1927, when Rozaline Bourland (the daughter of Red Spot's founder) married Milton Z. Thorson. Although Thorson started out with Red Spot as a brush cleaner, he would ultimately transform the company from an Indiana-based paint seller to an international force in paints and plastics.

Thorson gradually rose through the company ranks, moving up from brush cleaner to traveling salesman. While out on the road drumming up business for Red Spot paints in the mid-1930s, he was approached by a representative of Hoosier Cardinal, Inc. Hoosier was a plastics manufacturer and was experimenting with a paint that could be applied to the back side of clear plastic, which Hoosier called a "see deep finish." The plastics industry was young, and Hoosier needed someone to manufacture this novel paint. Hoosier's request seemed an odd one, as no one had previously considered mixing plastics and paints. Indeed, when Thorson ran the idea by Red Spot's only researcher, he laughed and told Thorson to focus on furniture coatings. Disregarding this advice, however, Thorson followed his gut and made Red Spot the exclusive paint supplier to Hoosier. Red Spot opened a coating development laboratory and a production facility to accommodate Hoosier's needs. The partnership flourished, and by the late 1930s, the Evansville area was referred to as "Plastics Valley."

World War II and the Maturation of the Plastics Industry

Red Spot's rise was closely linked to that of the plastics industry as a whole. The outbreak of World War II in 1939 created great demand for all sorts of plastic products, particularly those that could substitute for materials—such as rubber—that were in short supply due to the war effort. During the war years, Thorson landed Red Spot contracts for defense supplies. For example, Red Spot provided salt-resistant paints—in the obligatory olive drab combat colors—to Chrysler Corp.'s ammunition plant.

Even beyond the short-term economic opportunities, the war had a profound effect on the plastics industry as a whole. With the tremendous national push for the large-scale production of synthetic rubbers, researchers undertook an extensive examination of the chemistry of polymer formations to figure out how best to achieve this goal. Their findings markedly broadened the industry's understanding of the ways plastics could be created and the range of feasible uses for them. In the decade following the war, plastics producers developed such industry workhorses as polypropylene and high-density polyethylene, which had a range of important applications.

Red Spot was determined to be a part of the expansion of the postwar plastics industry. Using its wartime relationship with Chrysler as a jumping off point, Red Spot spent the immediate postwar years looking for new markets. It courted both appliance and automotive manufacturers, who were incorporating new plastics into their products and needed coatings for these materials. While these efforts bore some fruit during the 1950s, the company's field of vision still did not extend far beyond the tri-state area. Red Spot ended the decade still regarded primarily as a house paint manufacturer and hardware retailer for the Indiana-Illinois-Kentucky region.

Working his way up the company hierarchy, Milton Thorson had a different vision for Red Spot. Recognizing that the plastics business was likely to go global as Europe and Asia continued to rebound from the devastation of the war years, Thorson took his first overseas trip to Paris in 1959 to drum up business for his paints. The company was so shocked by what it perceived to be yet another one of Thorson's quirky ideas that he was forced to pay for his trip out of pocket. Undeterred, Thorson followed up his European tour with trips to the Far East, and by the early 1960s, Red Spot was doing business with Japanese electronics companies. At the same time, Red Spot obtained manufacturing licenses in England and Australia and found sales agents in Japan and Hong Kong. An interesting dichotomy developed, as Red Spot's domestic sales were driven by its house paints and other maintenance coatings, while it built its reputation overseas on industrial coatings. The industrial side of the business would grow rapidly in the coming years.

Dramatic Changes in the 1970s–80s

The plastics industry continued to evolve rapidly. The 1970s saw the introduction of extremely dense plastics—particularly linear low-density polyethylene, released in 1978—which were sufficiently strong and reliable to compete with more "traditional" materials, such as metal, wood, paper, glass, and leather. As large-scale production of this new generation of plastics began, the costs of these materials fell dramatically. Consequently, manufacturers in a variety of industries turned to these high performance and inexpensive new plastics to replace the more expensive natural materials upon which they had previously relied. Seizing this opportunity, plastics producers

began to tinker with alloys and blends of polymers, which made it possible to create individualized plastics capable of satisfying specific performance requirements. This customization further broadened the uses to which these plastics could be put. Automobile manufacturers were particularly interested in these strong, resilient, and comparatively inexpensive new plastics. As they were significantly lighter than traditional materials, they increased fuel efficiency, a notable concern during the energy crisis of the late 1970s.

Car companies had some very particularized requirements, however. They needed specialized coatings for the new materials. They were also extremely concerned that the plastics used in cars did not look or feel like traditional industrial plastics, as consumers were adamant about avoiding coldly "institutional" vehicles. Auto makers turned to coatings manufacturers like Red Spot for color keyed interior auto parts and specialized lacquer coatings. Red Spot in turn developed vacuum metallizing coatings that allowed mirror-bright finishes on plastics, which the auto industry cherished.

Red Spot grew significantly in the 1980s. One key factor in its success was its development of a urethane coating flexible enough to withstand impact on newly developed plastic. In other words, Red Spot produced the first paint that could be used on a plastic car bumper. To boost production, Red Spot expanded its facilities with an eye toward accommodating the needs of the Detroit automotive sector. The company purchased a manufacturing plant in Westland, Michigan, in 1987 and a sales office in Plymouth, Michigan, two years later. Despite its increased attention to production and sales, though, the company remained focused on product development. Nearly one quarter of Red Spot's employees were involved in research and development.

A New Landscape in the 1990s

By the early 1990s, Red Spot was at a crossroads. Its hardware stores, once the core of its business, were struggling to remain profitable, and it was clear that the company's future was in automotive coatings, not consumer paints. In 1991, therefore, the company eliminated its retail division, severing that link with its roots.

The 1990s brought a multitude of changes to the coating industry in the form of more vigilant environmental regulations. The Clean Air Act Amendments of 1990 empowered the Environmental Protection Agency (EPA) to regulate and limit the devastating environmental impact of Volatile Organic Compounds (VOC's), which were a common component of many coatings. Many states, most notably California, adopted even tougher standards. These new restrictions required the coatings industry not only to limit VOC's in the coatings produced but also to change the process by which the coatings were applied. Many of the high-tech coatings developed for the automotive industry in the 1970s and 1980s used solvent solutions to apply the coatings, which were out of compliance with the new environmental laws.

Car manufacturers did not want to have to choose between innovative, high-quality coatings and environmental compliance. The onus thus fell on coatings manufacturers to develop

Key Dates:

1903: H.D. Bourland founds Evansville Paint & Varnish in Evansville, Indiana.
1921: The company is renamed Red Spot Paint & Varnish.
1937: Red Spot develops the first decorative coating for plastic in the world.
1959: Red Spot begins to market its products outside the United States.
2000: Red Spot forms a joint venture with Mays Chemical, as well as a global alliance with Sonneborn & Rieck Ltd. and Fujikara Kasei.

cost-effective and high-tech coatings that met new regulations. Moving away from the lacquers, enamels, and solvent-borne (or solvent-applied) paints that had been the primary coatings used for car makers in the 1960s and 1970s, coatings manufacturers perfected high-solid enamels (which contained fewer VOC's than the earlier enamels), waterborne coatings (instead of solvent-borne), and powder coatings in the 1990s. This change was a dramatic one. "These new products represent a 95 percent turnover in chemistries from just ten years ago," an industry insider told *Industrial Paint and Powder*. This burst of innovation belied the chorus of complaints that had been raised by both automotive and coatings industries about the apocalyptic impact the stricter regulations would have on their businesses. Indeed, Red Spot was particularly well positioned to benefit from the changes necessitated by the new laws. The company had always placed a premium on innovation and new technology rather than on the mass production of basic coatings.

New environmental regulations were not the only dramatic change for the automotive coatings industry in the early 1990s. The globalization of the automotive sector raised the bar for coatings producers still further during this period. Milton Thorson had indeed seen the future when he boarded the plane to Paris to drum up overseas business. As they moved away from their national roots to become multinational conglomerates, car companies wanted relationships with fewer suppliers; they wanted coatings producers who could make all the coatings needed for a given car; they wanted to build partnerships with coatings companies that had a global base. Once again, Red Spot was in an ideal position to benefit from this change. By 1993, Red Spot had rung up $70 million in sales and did about 18 percent of its business in international markets.

In 1994, Red Spot opened a new facility that promised to meet its dual needs, increasing both manufacturing capacity and its research and development base. This $8.3 million, 53,500-square-foot plant was the world's largest facility for the development of automotive plastics. The company planned to use its new facility to create environmentally friendly coatings for plastics used in cars.

But Red Spot was not the only company seeking to make bold technological leaps. In the mid-1990s, Red Spot found itself in a race against rival Morton Automotive Coatings to develop a waterborne "soft-touch" coating. Auto designers were interested in cutting manufacturing costs by limiting the amount of foam and upholstery used on the interior of a car. Rather than layering a soft material on top of plastic, they wanted a coating that would be soft to the touch. In other words, they wanted a paint that felt like velvet for car interiors. The real challenge was to develop this coating without a solvent-borne application. By 1995, Red Spot had prevailed and produced the first waterborne "soft touch" coating, which it named Soft Feel. Two years later, General Motors selected the coating to be used in the interior of the Pontiac Grand Am.

Buoyed by this success, Red Spot opened a 28,000-square-foot Coatings Application Center in Plymouth, Michigan, in 1998. The facility was intended for the development of application systems as well as pioneering new decorative coatings.

New Partnerships in the New Millennium

In an effort to continue to grow its international sales—which had risen to account for over 20 percent of total revenue in 2000—Red Spot focused on establishing additional licenses and sales agents. It also formed several alliances with key international partners. Three of these alliances were cemented in 2000, when Red Spot joined forces with the English coatings manufacturer Sonneborn & Rieck, the Japanese firm Fujikura Kasei, and the American outfit Mays Chemical Company. The alliances with Sonneborn & Rieck and Fujikura Kasei were well chosen because the products manufactured by these companies complemented Red Spot's. For example, Fujikara specialized in the production of the raw acrylics that Red Spot utilized in its coatings.

The most significant partnership, though, was with Mays and involved the creation of a joint venture—Mays + Red Spot Coatings, LLC. The joint venture, which was expected to begin operations in 2002, was intended to handle distribution, customer service, sales, and technical support for product-finishing customers in North America. Mays, a chemical distributor that supplied fluid management services and chemicals to various industries, brought distribution and supply chain expertise to the table, while Red Spot offered its research and development skills, along with its original equipment manufacturers (OEM) product manufacturing capabilities.

Red Spot expanded its reach even further in December 2000 when it acquired the Michigan-based Seibert-Oxidermo, Inc., which specialized in primers for plastics and other coatings used in the transportation industry. Red Spot's president declared that the move provided "further penetration into other areas of the transportation sector and complements our core businesses."

Red Spot's future looked bright. It had diversified its automotive clients so that the company did not rely too heavily on its long-time mainstay Ford Motor Company. In five years, Red Spot cut the portion of its business derived from Ford from 50 percent to 35 percent (General Motors accounted for 32 percent, Chrysler for 13 percent, and Japanese auto manufacturers for 20 percent). Its export sales continued to climb, and the company successfully weathered both the Asian economic crisis and tough financial times in the American automotive industry. Red Spot's 2001 sales topped $95 million.

Principal Competitors

Akzo Nobel N.V.; E.I. du Pont de Nemours and Company; The Valspar Corporation.

Further Reading

Bailey, Jane, "Top Coatings Manufacturers Speak Out," *Industrial Paint and Powder,* June 1, 1994.

Davis, Dan, "The Charge For New Plastic Coatings," *Industrial Paint and Powder*, May 1, 1998.

"Milton Thorson: Paints, Plastics Executive," *Evansville Courier & Press*, December 3, 1999.

"Red Spot, Partner Launch Joint Venture," *Paint & Coatings Industry*, April 1, 2001.

Rose, Robert and Quintanilla, Carl, "More Small U.S. Companies Take Up Exporting, With Much Success," *Asian Wall Street Journal*, December 23, 1996.

Schuch, Linda, "New Wave Waterborne Offers Soft Feel Finish," *Industrial Paint and Powder*, March 1, 1997.

"Seibert-Oxidermo Acquired By Red Spot," *Journal of Coatings Technology*, December 1, 2000.

Triplett, Tim, "Two-Part Coatings Are Star Performers," *Industrial Paint and Powder*, October 1, 1997.

—Rebecca Stanfel

Rockford Products Corporation

707 Harrison Avenue
Rockford, Illinois 61104-7197
U.S.A.
Telephone: (815) 397-6000
Fax: (815) 229-4366
Web site: http://www.rpc-usa.com

Private Company
Incorporated: 1929 as Rockford Screw Products
    Company
Employees: 800
Sales: $15 million (2001 est.)
NAIC: 326199 All Other Plastics Product Manufacturing;
    332722 Bolt, Nut, Screw, Rivet, and Washer
    Manufacturin

Based in Rockford, Illinois, Rockford Products Corporation is a worldwide manufacturer, importer, and distributor of fasteners, cold-formed components, and other industrial products. Although the company had become a multi-million dollar enterprise by the early 2000s, like many manufacturing operations Rockford Products has modest roots and is the result of one man's idea.

Origins

By 1928 the city of Rockford, Illinois, was on its way to becoming one of America's largest manufacturing hubs. It was near the end of that year when Swan Hillman, one of the city's many industrial workers, held a meeting in his home to discuss the possibility of forging a new enterprise. Those at the meeting were receptive to Hillman's idea, and on January 15, 1929, the Rockford Screw Products Company was formed.

With $142,000 in capital, the new manufacturing company began operations in Rockford in a facility on Railroad Avenue. The company's first plant—a 60-year-old brick building—was approximately 12,000 square feet in size and housed ten to 15 workers. Rockford's first board members included President O.G. Nelson, Vice-President Swan Hillman, Secretary-Treasurer Thorwald A. Madsen, and Works Manager David E. Johnson. The latter three men all were former employees of the Rockford-based National Lock Co. Hillman was especially instrumental in Rockford's early success and would provide valuable guidance over the years as the company grew and prospered.

In 1934 Rockford moved its offices and manufacturing operations to a vacant, 45,000-square-foot structure on Ninth Street. As the company prospered during the 1930s, it expanded this facility on several occasions in order to increase capacity. Beginning in 1934, expansions at this plant would occur every year during the 1930s except 1938. Expansion also occurred on Ninth Street in 1940 and 1947.

During the 1940s, with the United States embroiled in World War II, Rockford experienced exceptional growth and prosperity by shifting the lion's share of its efforts to wartime production. Powered by 1,130 employees, the company supplied a consistent stream of screws and bolts for aircraft, trucks, tanks, and a variety of other military equipment. However, the aircraft market was especially lucrative. Rockford enjoyed a three-year stint as the nation's leading aircraft bolt fabricator. According to the company, at one point it rolled out enough daily shipments of aircraft parts to fill two freight carloads.

Following more than ten years of success, Rockford constructed a second plant on Harrison Avenue in 1943. According to a 1955 *Rockford Morning Star* article, construction of the Harrison Avenue facility "was an expression of management's confidence that the post-war years would bring even more business than the war years." Rockford would expand this plant on Harrison Avenue several times to accommodate growth. One of the special features incorporated into the new plant's construction was a railroad spur, which made it possible for the facility to be conveniently serviced by several railroads. At this time, Rockford produced somewhere between 5,000 and 6,000 different kinds of fasteners, the largest of which was a bolt 4.5 inches in diameter requiring a 23-pound nut. Its smallest product was a tiny screw that required a magnifying glass to be seen, 50,000 of which could fill a thimble.

In 1947 Rockford purchased an eight-passenger plane in order to better serve its growing customer base in other areas of the United States. Although the company would continue to prosper, by the close of the 1940s Rockford had temporarily scaled back its workforce to about 800, approximately 125 of

Company Perspectives:

Our basic philosophy is that success doesn't come from brick and mortar and machinery. Success comes from the people. One of our assets, right from day one, was to be fortunate to have people with pride in workmanship who are willing to put forth effort.

whom were women. At this time, Nelson and Hillman still served as president and vice-president, respectively. In 1949 Rockford's manufacturing facility on Ninth Street (Plant I) manufactured a variety of parts including aircraft screws, cap screws, socket-headed cap screws, setscrews, bolts, and pins. Plant II, located on Harrison Avenue, produced other parts including nuts, machine screws, sheet metal screws, and wood screws.

The Postwar Era

During the 1950s Rockford expanded operations outside of its hometown, acquiring a California-based distribution operation and dubbing the new subsidiary Rockford Screw Products Co. of California. Over the years, this operation would aid in the Rockford manufacturer's West Coast distribution efforts.

Growth and prosperity continued as the 1950s progressed. By the time 1955 arrived, the company had devoted about $7 million over a ten-year period to expand operations and purchase new equipment. Rockford opened a third plant in 1954 at Harrison Avenue and Kishwaukee Street, which was mainly used for manufacturing fasteners for the aircraft industry, as well as specialty items. An addition to this structure in 1959 would almost double the plant's size. It also was during this time, in 1954, that a profit-sharing plan for workers was instituted.

In December 1955, Rockford President O.G. Nelson died. Swan Hillman succeeded him as president and chairman. The company had evolved considerably since 1929, and Hillman was the right man to lead the manufacturing operation into a new era. That year, Rockford employed 1,300 workers with a payroll of approximately $7 million and supplied bolts and screws to a myriad of industries. In addition to being used in the manufacture of numerous home appliances, automobiles, electronics, and farm implements, the company's wares were also available to consumers and other end-users via the hardware trade. During this time, Rockford first partnered with the National Auto Parts Association (NAPA) to offer packaged standard fasteners. More than 45 years later, the arrangement, which initially involved 1,128 parts, had grown to include more than 11,000 parts.

1960s–70s: Continued Success

Rockford continued its upward climb in the 1960s. By January 1961, the company employed approximately 1,400 workers. Late in the following year, construction started on a 32,000-square-foot building at Kishwaukee Street and Harrison Avenue that eventually would house the company's administrative offices. The new building marked Rockford's 30th expansion in 33 years. The $800,000 building was completed by March 1964, when 130 executives and office personnel moved from the company's long-time headquarters on 9th Street to

more elaborate surroundings. The new offices included a 150-seat auditorium, air conditioning, and a lobby sporting a decorative rotunda. In addition to the new structure, Rockford was awaiting installation of a $350,000 computer from IBM later that spring. Commenting on the new facility in the March 1, 1964, *Rockford Morning Star*, Hillman remarked: "We have lived in a warehouse for 35 years. This is the apex."

Shortly after the company moved into its new offices, Hillman died. In June 1965, Ward Lidbetter—who had served Rockford as vice-president of operations since 1954 and as assistant president—succeeded Hillman at the helm of Rockford. At the time of his appointment, the company was using 36,000 tons of steel per year to achieve a monthly fastener production level of 325 million units.

By 1967, Rockford ranked among the nation's five largest manufacturers of fasteners. The following year, a wholly owned subsidiary called Rockford Aerospace Products Inc. was established in California. The year 1969 marked 40 years of success for Rockford. The company, which now employed 1,755 workers and had grown to occupy more than one million square feet of space, achieved record sales that year, posting earnings of $1.9 million on $38.9 million in net sales. It also was in 1969 that the company changed its name to Rockford Products Corporation to reflect an expanded array of offerings. In addition, another subsidiary, Rockford International Inc., was formed. Located in the Centex Industrial Center in Elk Grove Village, Illinois, its purpose was to "import, warehouse, package, and sell foreign fasteners to meet growing demands," according to the September 24, 1969, *Rockford Register Republic*.

Rockford Products began the 1970s on a high note. In fiscal 1970, the company recorded net sales of $39 million. With projected increases in the production of defense equipment, as well as spending on capital and consumer durable goods, a healthy market outlook existed for the company's fasteners. By 1972, the firm was supplying nearly 2 percent of all fasteners used in the United States. The company's product mix had changed considerably since 1929, when it mainly produced standard fasteners. By the end of 1972, specialty fasteners made up approximately 80 percent of Rockford Products' output.

During the early 1970s President Ward Lidbetter and other executives spent much of their workdays at metal desks with other general office workers in order to facilitate good communication. In the December 17, 1972 *Rockford Morning Star*, Lidbetter revealed leadership's mantra of the day, explaining: "Our basic philosophy is that success doesn't come from brick and mortar and machinery. Success comes from the people. One of our assets, right from day one, was to be fortunate to have people with pride in workmanship who are willing to put forth effort."

Rockford's annual sales continued to rise as the decade progressed, hitting $53 million in 1973 and $68.3 million in 1974. However, in 1975, slowing economic conditions in such sectors as automotive prompted a series of layoffs at the company. A major change took place the following year when Milwaukee, Wisconsin-based Rexnord Inc. purchased Rockford for $34.6 million. At the time, Rexnord was a *Fortune* 500 company trading on the New York Stock Exchange and posting annual sales of more than $550 million.

Key Dates:

1929: Rockford Screw Products Company is formed.
1934: Rockford moves its offices and manufacturing operations to larger facilities; expansion occurs on a regular basis during the 1930s and 1940s.
1944: The company enjoys a three-year stint as the nation's leading aircraft bolt fabricator.
1954: A profit-sharing plan for workers is instituted.
1955: Rockford partners with the National Auto Parts Association (NAPA) to offer packaged standard fasteners.
1967: The company ranks among the nation's five largest manufacturers of fasteners.
1969: The company's name is changed to Rockford Products Corporation to reflect expanded offerings.
1976: Rexnord Inc. purchases the company for $34.6 million.
1983: In a sagging economy, Rockford workforce is downsized and sales fall.
1985: Seven executives at Rockford Products arrange to buy the firm back from Rexnord.

After achieving sales of $87 million in 1978, Rockford Products ended the decade of the 1970s on another high note, posting sales of $100 million for the first time. However, it also was necessary to lay off a number of workers that year, which had not happened since 1975.

1980s: Economic Challenges

By the early 1980s, Gerald S. Broski had been named president of Rockford. The decade would prove to be a challenging one for the company, as the manufacturing sector was negatively affected by a sagging economy and increasing competition from foreign companies. Early in the decade, the company was forced to lay off employees, issue pay cuts, and replace annual cost-of-living increases with a merit system. By January 1983, staff had been reduced to 1,000 workers and orders had fallen approximately 50 percent below normal levels.

Other changes also were underway. In 1981, Rockford Aerospace Products was sold and operations at Rockford International were moved from Elk Grove Village, Illinois, to Rockford. The following year, Rockford Screw Products of California ceased to exist. By the 1980s Rockford's customer base had changed considerably from past decades, when the aircraft industry represented the firm's top segment. In the early 1980s almost one-third of business was attributed to the automotive industry, along with the automotive aftermarket (10 percent), and companies manufacturing appliances, recreation and farm equipment.

In 1984, John J. Rauh was named president of Rockford Products, and the company announced plans to expand Plant 3 on Harrison Ave. by 33,000 square feet in order to accommodate increased production of automotive front-end assemblies. The expansion was Rockford's first in more than ten years and involved the addition of 30 employees.

By 1985, the company's workforce numbered approximately 850, down from a high of 1,755 during the late 1960s. Late that year, company ownership changed hands once again. Through an employee stock ownership plan, a group of seven executives at Rockford arranged to buy the firm back from Rexnord.

In March 1987, the new board of directors fired President and CEO Jack Rauh. According to the March 7, 1987, *Rockford Register Star*, Rauh was released because "the company was not meeting certain agreements it had made with lenders." Within a week of Rauh's departure, a program to accelerate a $20 million debt payoff related to the Rexnord buyout was announced. It involved pay and benefit cuts that angered workers, causing approximately 75 percent of employees to walk off the job, a situation that was quickly settled. In April, shortly after Rauh was fired, the company appointed R. Ray Wood as its new president and CEO.

From 1990 to 1995, Rockford was able to expand its product line and execute a variety of targeted sales and marketing programs that helped to increase sales. In 1997, the company received ISO 9002 and QS 9000 certifications in recognition of quality. By the early 2000s, Rockford's sales were still far below the levels it had achieved during the late 1970s. However, the company continued to make and import fasteners from its three plants in Rockford, Illinois. The company also began to reach out more internationally, joining Germany's Altenlohn, Brinck & Co. and Japan's Osaka Rashi to create the International Coldforming Alliance (ICA). According to the May 2000 issue of *Appliance Manufacturer,* the alliance allowed each member firm to share knowledge and resources and more effectively compete in the global marketplace.

Although many of the fastener industry's dynamics had changed since Swan Hillman founded the company in 1929, Rockford's 800 workers, each with a stake in the company's success, remained committed to serving the needs of customers in the 21st century.

Principal Competitors

Textron Inc.

Further Reading

Braun, Georgette, "Worker Claims Company Fund Shortchanged," *Rockford Register Star,* May 11, 2002, p. 1E.
Couretas, John, "Nuts, Bolts of Buyouts: Rockford Products Strives for That Lean, Mean Look," *Rockford Register Star,* November 3, 1985, p. 1D.
Couretas, John, "Rockford Products Leaders Start New Chapter," *Rockford Register Star,* November 7, 1985, p. 3D.
"Local Firm Cuts Pay to Finance Heavy Debt," *Rockford Register Star,* March 13, 1987.
Orr, Kathy, "Rockford Products Workers Rebel: Hundreds Walk Off Jobs to Protest Cuts," *Rockford Register Star,* March 14, 1987, p. 1A.
——, "Tumult and Turnaround: Rockford Products Has Fastened Grip On Future," *Rockford Register Star,* February 28, 1988, p. 1H.
Rubendall, Ben, "Rockford Products to Expand," *Rockford Register Star,* July 19, 1984.
"$32 Million Offer for Products Firm," *Rockford Register Star,* August 17, 1976.

—Paul R. Greenland

Tonkin

Ron Tonkin Chevrolet Company

122 North East 122nd Avenue
Portland, Oregon 97230-2103
U.S.A.
Telephone: (503) 255-4100
Toll Free: (800) 460-5328
Fax: (503) 251-5544
Web site: http://www.rontonkin.com

Private Company
Incorporated: 1960
Employees: 76 (est.)
Sales: $66 million (2001 est.)
NAIC: 441110 New Car Dealers; 441310 Automotive
  Parts and Accessories Stores; 811121 Automotive
  Body, Paint, and Interior Repair and Maintenance;
  811111 General Automotive Repair

Ron Tonkin Chevrolet Company has 16 locations in the Portland, Oregon, metropolitan area. Its 11 franchises sell Acura, Chevrolet, Dodge, Ferrari, Honda, Hyundai, Kia, Lincoln-Mercury, Mazda, Nissan, and Toyota vehicles. The company also has two dealerships selling Ducati, Aprilia, Cagiva, and MV Augusta motorcycles and the largest parts warehouse distribution center in the nation.

The 1960s and Early 1970s: The Youngest Chevrolet Dealer in the United States

In 1960, Ronald Barry Tonkin, a native of Portland, became the youngest Chevrolet dealer in the nation. Tonkin had had an early start in the auto industry when, as a boy, he began doing odd jobs at his father's used car lot in Portland, Oregon. After World War II, Edward Tonkin opened one of the first Kaiser-Frazer dealerships in the United States, and Ron Tonkin, who did not yet have his driver's license, learned how to sell cars. "When you cut your teeth on selling Kaisers and Frazers when others are selling Fords and Chevys, you ha[ve] to be a really good salesman," Tonkin expressed in a 1997 *Oregonian* article.

In 1954, Ron Tonkin, then a second lieutenant in the U.S. Army and a graduate of the University of Washington with a B.A.

in business administration, officially joined the family business, following in the footsteps of his brother, Marv. Tonkin became secretary-treasurer and general sales manager of Tonkin Motors Inc. When the brothers learned that Kaiser was going out of business, they shifted to selling AMC Ramblers in 1954. In 1955, they bought out the Lyman Slack Mercury dealership.

Finally, in 1960, Tonkin struck out on his own with a $100,000 loan from First National Bank. Selling his share of Tonkin Motors to Marv, he bought the Gregg-Owens Chevrolet dealership in Portland. He used the loan to buy everything he needed, including the shop, fixtures, equipment, used cars, parts, and accessories. "I decided we were going to be profitable, and we never looked back," he said in a 1997 *Oregonian* article. Sacrificing family time to work until 10:00 at night 364 days a year, Tonkin made sure he met his obligations to employees, creditors, and customers. "I had to put those hours in," he said. "I was driven with ambition to succeed, and I love cars." Tonkin's sales volume quickly soared, and within five years he had outgrown his facilities.

Ron Tonkin Chevrolet moved and took over a five- to six-acre plot on the edge of Portland in 1965. There, Tonkin built the largest automotive center in the Northwest at a cost of somewhere between $500,000 and $600,000. The new location operated on two shifts, remaining open from 6:00 in the morning until 10:00 at night. It stocked 400 cars and trucks, with 250 vehicles prepared for display outside under lights; it had three rotating concrete pads to spotlight vehicles. Nine salesmen roamed the 40,000-square-foot showroom and service building while the newly completed service department serviced up to 50 cars at a time.

The business kept growing, and in 1968, Tonkin expanded his Chevrolet franchise by purchasing another local Chevrolet dealership. When General Motors denied him a Pontiac-GMC franchise in 1969, he turned to Honda Motor, lobbying to become their sole U.S. distributor, and began selling Hondas that year. "Everyone kind of laughed at that first car," Tonkin later recalled, but when the gas shortage hit, the thrifty, no-frills, dependable cars took off. In 1973, Tonkin enlarged his business by adding auto-painting facilities that met pollution authority standards; he was the first dealer to do so in the West.

Tonkin also had begun branching out in a slightly different direction in 1966, selling Ferraris at the Gran Turismo store he

326

opened in Portland. That dealership was less successful than Tonkin's others, until in 1973 the formerly unprofitable luxury car business moved to a different location and began selling Saabs, Alfa Romeos, and a few Maseratis as well. In 1974, Gran Turismo sold more Ferraris than any other dealership in the United States.

The Late 1970s and 1980s:
Riding the Industry's Waves

The late 1970s saw the downsizing of many American cars in response to the gas shortage of 1973 and 1974 and the selling out of some dealerships nationwide. Ron Tonkin's business, however, "never had a bad year," according to Tonkin in a 1979 *Oregonian* article. "In 1976 we doubled the best year we'd had and in 1977 we tripled 1976. In 1978, we almost doubled 1977." In 1979, Tonkin bought two new properties, one for his Gran Turismo dealership and another on which he expanded his car leasing company and established a showroom for luxury cars such as the DeLorean. In addition to selling new and used cars, Tonkin's company did a healthy business in its parts and service departments and body shop.

By the early 1980s, consumers had begun embracing the "new" Japanese cars while Chrysler, Ford, and General Motors experienced heavy losses. Fortunately, for the "big three," however, informal restraints on imports allowed them to direct their attention to product redesign. In addition, efforts by the United Automobile Workers to hold down manufacturing costs, as well as the plunging dollar, wiped out former differences between American and Japanese production costs. But the 1981 to 1982 recession put 5,000 dealers out of business nationwide. Of the remaining 25,000, many, like Tonkin, began the shift to become "megadealerships," businesses that offered many different lines of cars and survived through economies of scale and a better distribution system.

Tonkin continued to prosper. In 1980, the company purchased a Toyota dealership. In the fall of that year, it finished building its $700,000 "world headquarters" in Portland, which included Tonkin's in-house Roto Advertising agency and a home for his Gran Turismo dealership. The Gran Turismo showroom, described by Tonkin in the *Oregon Journal* in 1981 as "a place for big boys' toys, a place for people to have fun," showcased "Cavallino," a sculpture of a horse made by Chi-

cago artist John Kearney out of old automobile bumpers. A heated building with overhead skylights behind the showroom housed the rest of Tonkin's exotic car stock, including vehicles from his personal collection. In 1982, Tonkin Co. ranked 63rd in the list of Oregon's top 100 private businesses with sales in the $40 to $49 million range.

Beginning in 1983 and continuing for the next five years, auto sales were again strong. Throughout this period, Tonkin's business continued to expand. By the mid-1980s, Ron Tonkin enjoyed the reputation of being a shrewd businessman who seldom chose a loser. Tonkin himself attributed his business success to his decision to diversify, which allowed him to compete with higher interest rates and the souring regional economy, and put him in a position to better "cope with adversity than someone with one franchise," as he described it in a 1984 *Business Journal* article. In 1984, Tonkin's company had annual sales volume of more than $50 million—about one-tenth of the total volume in new passenger cars sold in the four-county metro area—putting it at the top of the industry statewide. The business sold nine different makes of cars at six Portland area outlets. Between 1984 and 1986, Ron Tonkin Cos. added several new dealerships, including one of the first Acura franchises nationwide.

Tonkin's sons, Bradley, Edward, and Barry, also joined the business in the mid-1980s when he handed over his Mitsubishi franchise to them. Brad Tonkin became general manager of Tonkin's Honda dealership in 1984, and by 1986, Ed Tonkin had become vice-president and general manager of Tonkin's Chevrolet operations.

Auto sales boomed through the mid- to late 1980s, and dealerships sold for a premium above the value of their assets. But by the late 1980s, car sales had once again begun falling, and by 1988, the car manufacturing industry was dealing with an overcapacity of cars. This situation and the establishment of the megadealer in the 1980s—having somewhat altered the balance of power between manufacturers and dealers—led General Motors to make an unprecedented concession to dealers in 1988, allowing them to sell more than two General Motors lines. Up until that time, the manufacturer had limited franchises to dealers in an effort to ensure that they pushed GM's options.

Yet despite layoffs and plant shutdowns and a 6 percent decline from 1988 total sales for American automakers, 1989 was still the sixth best sales year for motor vehicles in the United States. Dealerships, however, averaged a profit of only about 1 percent of their pretax revenue in the last years of the decade. To capitalize on the auto market downturn, they continued to enlarge. Friction developed between dealers and the auto manufacturers that wanted dealers to bear more of the costs of marketing and devote more attention to their brands.

Tonkin, as the president of the National Automobile Dealers Association (NADA) in 1989, pledged to take the auto manufacturers head-on on critical issues such as dealer profitability, secondary distribution, fleet subsidies offered rental companies, and basic decision making. In *Automotive News* in 1989, he vowed to create "a new awareness of dealers, enhancing their self-esteem and self-worth in the triangle that makes up this industry—the manufacturer, the laborer, and the dealer. [T]oo often our industry has been influenced by what the automakers say and do and by what labor says and does, and the dealers

Key Dates:

1954:   Ron Tonkin joins Tonkin Motors selling Kaiser-Frazer automobiles.
1960:   Tonkin sells his share of Tonkin Motors to his brother and buys the Gregg-Owens Chevrolet dealership in Southwest Portland.
1965:   Ron Tonkin Chevrolet moves and builds the largest automotive center in the Northwest.
1966:   Tonkin begins selling Ferraris at his Gran Turismo store in Portland.
1969:   Tonkin becomes the sole U.S. distributor of Hondas.
1973:   Tonkin enlarges his business by adding auto-painting facilities that meet pollution authority standards; the Gran Turismo store moves to a new location.
1980:   The company adds a Toyota dealership and completes its new "world headquarters."
1982:   Tonkin Co. ranks 63rd in the list of Oregon's top 100 private businesses (sales $40 to $49 million).
1989:   Ron Tonkin becomes president of NADA.
1997:   The company purchases Valencia Acura in Valencia, California.
2002:   The company constructs an 18-acre, 180,000-square-foot centralized parts facility and sheet metal center.

have been at the mercy of whatever decisions are made between those two entities." Tonkin wanted dealers to be able to make a 3 percent profit. He created a dealer group called the Rough Riders to fight automaker practices such as rebate plans, discounts to fleet buyers, and mandatory ad associations. *Automotive News* voted him industry leader of the year in 1989, dealer of the year, and foremost in dealer relations.

By 1990, 2,000 dealers had joined Tonkin's Rough Riders. At the kickoff of the NADA convention that year, Tonkin—who had then completed his term as president—announced that he had filed suit to prevent automakers from selling cars to fleet buyers at prices below those they charged dealers. Tonkin's successor at the NADA lacked his predilection to be a firebrand, however, and the Rough Riders soon disbanded.

The 1990s and Early 21st Century: Continued Success

Stepping out of the spotlight, Tonkin turned his attention once again to his business, and in 1991, the company started Tele-Drive, a copyrighted system whereby prospective buyers called a toll free number for detailed information on the approximately 2,000 cars for sale at any time in the Tonkin dealerships. Customers who determined that the car they wanted was in stock could make an appointment to drive it within half an hour. By 1993, the company was carrying 11 makes of cars, including the Kia, for which it was the only American dealer.

Low interest rates, a strengthening Oregon economy, and pent-up buyer demand fueled sales increases throughout most of 1993 in the auto industry. By 1995, Tonkin's sales had topped $250 million to make its fifth record-breaking year in a row. The Tonkin dealerships sold cars and trucks in nine loca-

tions and employed more than 500 people. It became the first West Coast dealer to sell the Vector M12 sports car and also began to sell an electric-powered bicycle, the EV Warrior, made by Electric Bicycle Company of California.

During the second half of the 1990s, Ron Tonkin began winding down his daily involvement in the family business. But unable to avoid the "gasoline in his veins," he served as chairman of the NADA's Political Action Committee, the eighth largest PAC in the United States. *Automobile News* awarded him the industry's "triple crown" as industry leader of the year, automobile dealer of the year, and the individual who had had the greatest impact on dealer relations. In 1997, the company, under Ed Tonkin's direction, purchased Valencia Acura in Valencia, California.

In 2001, *Oregon Business Magazine* ranked Ron Tonkin Chevrolet Co. third of the 100 best large companies to work for in Oregon. *Ward's Dealer Business* magazine named the business one of its "dealer of the year finalists" for innovation in the industry. Although in 2002 Tonkin dealerships had to pay $12,500 to Oregon's consumer protection and education fund to settle charges of misleading advertising, Edward Tonkin was one of 66 dealers to receive *Time* magazine's quality dealer award in recognition of his exceptional performance in the dealership and community service. In 2002, Tonkin Chevrolet Co. took yet another step forward to become the largest dealer-owned wholesale parts distribution center in the country when it consolidated its wholesale parts dealerships in a newly constructed 18-acre, 180,000-square-foot centralized parts facility and sheet metal center.

Principal Subsidiaries

Ron Tonkin Toyota Inc.; B & E Import Co. (dba Gresham Honda).

Principal Competitors

Braley and Raham Auto Mall; Rey Reece Dealerships.

Further Reading

Brown, Craig, "For Ron Tonkin, There's No Slowing Down," *Oregonian,* June 28, 1997, p. DT01.
Cour, Brian, "Million Dollar Showroom Greets Customers for Exotic Dream Cars," *Oregon Journal,* October 2, 1981, p. 13.
Crick, Rolla J., "Tonkin Readies New Plant," *Oregon Journal,* July 13, 1965, Sec. 3, p. 7.
Friedman, Jack, "Car Megadealer Tonkin Steers for Stock Offering," *Business Journal,* July 22, 1985, p. 1.
McGill, Andrew R., "Ron Tonkin: The Outspoken NADA President-Elect Is Preparing to Make Waves in 1989," *Automotive News,* January 23, 1989, p. E8.
Noles, B.J., "Tonkin Auto Businesses into Third Generation," *Oregonian,* December 5, 1978, A 15.
Olmos, Bob, "Ron Tonkin Says His Auto Sales Brisk," *Oregonian,* August 15, 1979, p. D1.
"Ron Tonkin: NADA's President Sees Another Tough Year Ahead for New Car Dealers," *Automotive News,* November 20, 1989, p. E20.
Treece, James B., "Will the Auto Glut Choke Detroit?," *Business Week,* March 7, 1988, p. 54.

—Carrie Rothburd

Royal & Sun Alliance Insurance Group plc

30 Berkeley Square
London W1J 6EW
United Kingdom
Telephone: (020) 7636-3450
Fax: (020) 7636-3451
Web site: http://www.royalsunalliance.com

Public Company
Incorporated: 1996
Employees: 38,000
Total Assets: £59.95 billion ($96.49 billion) (2002)
Stock Exchanges: London
Ticker Symbol: RSA
NAIC: 524126 Direct Property and Casualty Insurance
Carriers; 551112 Offices of Other Holding Companies

Royal & Sun Alliance Insurance Group plc (RSA) is one of the largest insurance companies based in the United Kingdom. The group concentrates primarily on property and casualty insurance (including automobile and homeowner's insurance) for both individuals and businesses, a sector in which the group holds one of the top positions worldwide. Other RSA operations include risk management and claims administration services, life insurance, pension products, annuities, and mutual funds. Approximately 40 percent of the group's 2002 premium income was generated in the United Kingdom; 31 percent in the Americas; 19 percent in Europe, the Middle East, and Africa; and 10 percent in the Asia-Pacific region. Royal & Sun Alliance is the product of the 1996 merger of Royal Insurance Holdings plc and Sun Alliance Group plc, both of which were themselves the creations of previous amalgamations.

Sun Alliance Group: The Sun

Of the 1996 merger partners, the one with the deeper history was Sun Alliance Group. It represented the amalgamation of four separate British insurance operations, three of them companies and one a chartered corporation. All of them were prominent in the development of the British insurance industry. The most senior of the four, the Sun Insurance Office, retained its separate identity for almost 250 years until its 1959 merger with the most junior, the Alliance Assurance Company, founded in 1824. The other two members of the combination, the London Assurance Corporation and the Phoenix Assurance Company, date from 1720 and 1782, respectively.

The Sun Fire Office, as it was originally known, was founded in 1710. Its founder was the eccentric Charles Povey, whose interest in astronomy may have influenced his choice of name. Financial considerations caused Povey to sell his interests in the concern to the 24 members of the Company of London Insurers in 1710. Thereafter Povey exercised no official control over the infant Sun Fire Office.

The Sun's first decade gave little intimation of its future size and significance. A disparate and shifting body of managers, in the main lacking significant City connections (the City being the London equivalent of Wall Street), coupled with a limited number of staff and types of transactions, held back development. From about 1720, however, there occurred a series of events that were to help set the Sun firmly in the forefront of London's fire offices: a complete reorganization of the firm's capital structure; the appointment of the first of a series of able and honest men to the two principal positions of treasurer and secretary—Colonel Robert Dalzell and Thomas Watts; and a restructuring of the Sun's management.

Control of the Sun's affairs had originally been confined to two bodies—the general meeting of managers and, of more practical importance, the Committee of Management appointed from among them. From about 1720, the latter body took the important step of appointing subcommittees to conduct and report on particular aspects of the office's business. By about 1730 there were four of these, each controlled by a manager and staffed by clerks. These subcommittees were the ancestors of the Sun's modern departmental system.

The Sun's managers were powerful, as shareholders exercised no control over their activities and were not permitted to see accounts, a state of affairs then typical of most British insurance companies and not remedied until the end of the 19th century.

Company Perspectives:

Our business purpose: to help our customers around the world protect themselves against the risks they face in their businesses and daily lives by providing insurance and investment related solutions to meet their individual needs as we have done for nearly 300 years.

The managers themselves underwent transformation during the decades after 1720. From this date we find them to be men of education, real ability, and social distinction, linked with Parliament, the City, the landed aristocracy, and, later in the century, with those entrepreneurs and magnates who engineered the world's first industrial revolution. One such Sun official, William Hamilton—manager from 1809 to 1859, treasurer from 1846 to 1852—recovered the Rosetta Stone from the French in 1801, and in the next year saved the Elgin Marbles from shipwreck.

The period from 1720 to 1790 was one of rapid expansion. By 1786 the Sun had a private firefighting force and over 120 agents in the provinces. By 1790 it could claim a dominant position among the nation's insurance companies, with a gross premium income of over £100,000, much larger than that of its rivals, the Phoenix and Royal Exchange. The four decades that followed, however, were a time of stagnation. By the 1780s, risks had grown extremely complex, actual rates of loss had soared, and established offices, such as the Sun and the London, considered it necessary to raise premium levels again and again, especially on the extremely high-risk mills and distilleries that lined the River Thames in London and had begun to spring up across the land.

This situation was exploited fully by the numerous new insurance ventures that had been founded in response to the country's growing need for insurance services and that now began to offer discounted rates. This led to a destructive rate war, which put many offices out of business altogether and depressed the industry until the 1830s. One such new company, the Phoenix Assurance, set up in 1782 and soon to become an important rival, was acquired by the Sun much later, in 1984.

The Sun survived by entering new types of business and expanding into new geographical areas. Thus 1810 saw the establishment of Sun Life Assurance, and 1836, the creation of a special foreign department to handle foreign business.

The Sun's first foreign ventures were into Europe, initially the Baltic seaboard cities of Germany, later into France and Spain. The experiment met with mixed results—hostility from local insurance companies and the obstructive actions of governmental bureaucracies proved almost as damaging as the disastrous Hamburg fire of 1842 that cost the Sun £117,000 and almost succeeded in driving it from the Continent entirely.

The Sun turned instead to the more promising territories of the British Empire, and over the next 60 years set up agencies in virtually every British colony or dominion. The massive U.S. market was successfully penetrated when the Sun acquired the Watertown Insurance Company of New Jersey in 1882. The Chicago and Boston fires of 1871 and 1872, but more especially the San Francisco disaster of 1906—which cost the Sun £333,000—enabled the Sun to display its solidity and trustworthiness to an admiring American public.

Perhaps because of the cautious nature of its management the Sun had lagged behind its rivals, notably the Phoenix, in establishing foreign operations. It led the way, however, in organizing the major British fire offices in the 1840s into the Association of Tariff Offices, whose function was to prevent a repetition of the rate wars of previous decades.

One perhaps unintended result of the Sun's foreign exposure was its recognition of the need for formal statutes and publicly accessible accounts. These were achieved, in 1891, by the passing of the Sun Insurance Office Act, by which name the Sun Fire Office became known until its merger with the Alliance Assurance Company in 1959.

In 1907 the Sun set up an accident department, reflecting the growth of this type of insurance in the dawning age of mass transport and machines. The department grew rapidly in size, particularly after 1945 when a far greater general level of affluence significantly increased the number of vehicles on British roads.

The outbreak of World War I in 1914 had comparatively little direct influence on the financial position of the Sun because it, in common with most other British insurers, excepted war risks from its coverage. This did not mean it escaped the war years unscathed—naturally a large number of its staff served in the nation's armed services, and a fire at Salonika, Greece, in 1917 caused losses amounting to nearly £300,000. The straitened years of the Depression caused the Sun—and the British insurance industry in general—a reduction in the growth of premium income and an increase in the rate of default on policies, indicating the financial difficulties facing both private individuals and commercial enterprises.

The Sun had entered the field of marine insurance in 1921 and sought, both by its 1931 acquisition of the Elder's Insurance Company of Liverpool and its 1938 agreement with the Royal Exchange to operate a joint marine underwriting account, to establish itself in a field still dominated by the London.

The coming of World War II in 1939 posed no serious financial threat to the Sun, although once again the company lost a large number of its staff to the armed services. Nevertheless, the exigencies of total war demanded, as they had not in World War I, the temporary removal of the Sun's operations from London to the greater safety of the countryside.

In the 1920s, the Sun had several times reorganized its U.S. operations and this process continued in the 1950s, finally resulting in 1958 in a common management structure in the United States for its own operations and for those of the Royal Exchange Assurance and the Atlas Assurance Company.

Sun Alliance Group: The London

The expansion of British trade in the first decades of the 18th century revealed inherent weaknesses in the extant system of maritime insurance in London. In 1719 a wealthy City merchant

Key Dates:

1710: The Sun Fire Office is founded as a fire insurer, based in London.

1720: London Assurance Corporation is incorporated as a marine insurance operation.

1782: Group of sugar refiners form their own fire insurer, the New Fire Office.

1813: The New Fire Office is renamed the Phoenix Assurance Company.

1824: The Alliance Assurance Company is formed to offer both fire and life insurance.

1836: The Liverpool Fire and Life Insurance Company is organized.

1845: The Royal Insurance Company, based in Liverpool, is founded to provide property and casualty insurance, life insurance, and annuities.

1847: Liverpool Fire and Life merges with the London, Edinburgh and Dublin Insurance Company, forming the Liverpool and London Fire and Life Insurance Company.

1864: Liverpool and London Fire and Life acquires the Globe Insurance Company, forming the Liverpool and London and Globe Insurance Company.

1891: Sun Fire Office becomes the Sun Insurance Office.

1919: Royal Insurance acquires Liverpool and London and Globe Insurance.

1959: Sun Insurance and Alliance Assurance merge to form Sun Alliance Insurance.

1965: Sun Alliance merges with London Assurance to form the Sun Alliance and London Insurance plc.

1984: Sun Alliance and London acquires Phoenix Assurance.

1988: Royal Insurance Holdings plc is created as a holding company for the various operating companies of Royal Insurance.

1989: Sun Alliance and London changes its name to Sun Alliance Group plc.

1996: Sun Alliance and Royal Insurance Holdings merge to create Royal & Sun Alliance Insurance Group plc.

1999: Royal & Sun acquires Tyndall Australia Limited, Swedish firm Trygg-Hansa Försäkrings AB, Publikt, and U.S. nonlife insurer Orion Capital Corporation.

2002: Radical survival plan is announced, involving a workforce reduction of 12,000 and the divestment of several businesses, including the Australian and New Zealand insurance units.

named Sir James Lambert, goldsmith and banker Stephen Ram, and broker Philip Helbut, floated the idea of a new marine insurance operation.

A subscription was opened for what was initially known as Ram's Insurance and under the patronage of Lord Chetwynd a petition was presented to King George I arguing that Case Billingsley's concurrent petition for an exclusive charter for maritime business represented an unfair attempt to monopolize marine insurance. Billingsley, a solicitor, had been instrumental in the founding of Lord Onslow's Insurance in 1718, subsequently to become the Royal Exchange Assurance Corporation.

At the same time Lambert and Ram—Helbut by this time having dropped out—persuaded James Colebrook, who had also established a subscription for an insurance company, to unite with them, and all three repetitioned the king. The attorney general decided that neither petition should be rewarded with a charter, and there matters might have rested had not the government made known its requirement for £600,000 for the Civil List—a public fund to support the royal household—whereupon Lambert and Ram each offered £300,000 for a charter. In June 1720 Lord Chetwynd's Insurance was incorporated under the name of the London Assurance Corporation. The transaction of marine insurance was made exclusive to it and to its slightly senior rival, the Royal Exchange Assurance Corporation.

Business began in a City coffeehouse under a governor, two deputies, and a court of directors. The London became associated in the public mind with those numerous ludicrous or fraudulent enterprises that together constituted the notorious South Sea Bubble of 1720, the collapse of which in the autumn of that year ruined thousands of speculators.

The London, distancing itself as best it could from official suspicion, realized that in the chaotic circumstances following the crash it could not keep to the original schedule of payments for its charter, and boldly—and successfully—sought 50 percent remission of the sum. Thus the London survived the perilous days of its infancy. By the end of that tumultuous year marine underwriting was in full swing.

Until the acts of 1806 and 1811 prohibiting the insurance of slave ships and their cargoes, it was a matter of course for those operating in the notorious triangle trade between Britain, West Africa, and the Americas to insure their vessels with City insurers, and the London became heavily involved in this business. As well as covering against shipwreck and "insurrection of negroes," the London also offered insurance against loss due to piracy. Claims for the latter were frequent in the 18th century because of Britain's almost continuous state of war with one or another of the European powers. Between 1744 and 1746 the London hosted the Commission for the Distribution of Reprizals, a body that sought to reimburse shipowners who had genuinely suffered loss at the hands of French or Spanish warships. Despite such circumstances, the London also insured large numbers of foreign vessels, principally Spanish and Portuguese.

The fortunes of the London were not exclusively anchored to the success of maritime business. From the beginning, Lord Chetwynd and the directors had envisaged the London's engagement in the fire insurance business, no doubt stimulated by the example of the Sun Fire Office, set up barely ten years before. Consequently the directors sought and secured another charter in 1721 that empowered the London to underwrite fire business. Almost immediately agents were appointed in all parts of the kingdom. The London followed the Sun in setting up its own corps of firefighters. Curiously, the London set up no agencies for marine business in the major ports until 1829 when its Liverpool agent was instructed to handle this business too.

Like the Sun, the London arrived relatively late in the appointment of foreign representation, partly because business in the core area of marine insurance tended to gravitate toward the City. Not until 1853 were overseas agents appointed, but in that year alone, ten appeared in the Far East, India, and at the Cape of Good Hope. In the next three decades representation spread to South America, Japan, and Australasia. The first U.S. agency for fire business was set up in 1872, followed by a marine operation four years later. By 1881, the London had reached San Francisco and six years later Chicago. This process of foreign expansion had been initiated by J.C. Powell during his governorship, between 1822 and 1846. Powell also carried out a reform of the corporation's internal structure in the 1830s. Powell had a distinguished predecessor in Alexander Aubert, governor from 1787 to 1805, a fellow of the Royal Society, and a noted astronomer.

One of the earliest major losses involving the London was the destruction of its own premises in Cornhill Street in 1748. Losses exceeded premium income threefold and the years to the end of the century were ones of slow recovery. A steady rise in premiums during the 19th century was once again offset by the San Francisco disaster of 1906, which cost the London the then huge sum of £966,750.

The London was also notable during the late 18th and early 19th centuries for the size and frequency of donations it considered patriotic. It voted £200 towards the cost of suppressing the 1797 mutiny in the fleet and £500 toward the relief of dependents of British casualties of the 1815 Waterloo campaign.

In 1824 the Alliance Assurance Company succeeded in having the act of 1720, limiting the transaction of marine insurance to the London and Royal Exchange, repealed despite very considerable opposition from the two corporations. The next ten years were a period of declining profitability for the London. One of its responses was to consolidate its position by a series of mergers and acquisitions, beginning with the Commercial & General Life Assurance Company in 1853 and followed by the Asylum Life Assurance Company four years later. The year 1853 also saw the amalgamation of the Ship and Fire charters by special act of Parliament.

Life insurance for the London, although it had begun as far back as 1721, remained quiescent until the early decades of the 19th century, in contrast to the energetic efforts being made at the Pelican Life Assurance. One reason for this was the London's tardiness in applying the principles of actuarial science to its operations. Consequently, it was not until after 1945 that life premiums exceeded £1 million.

The opening decade of the 20th century was one of slow growth for the London, but World War I stimulated its marine business enormously, with premium income reaching a peak in 1917. The extremely conservative nature of the corporation was modified during the war by its having to employ women on the staff for the first time. The fast rate of expansion in the interwar period—characterized especially by the acquisition or establishment of several large operations in Australasia and the United States—produced a general restructuring of the Lon-

don's management system that split responsibility for home and foreign business and resulted in 1932 in the appointment of the corporation's first general manager.

The Depression, which had begun three years earlier, naturally reduced the rate of growth of premium income and this remained at a comparatively low level until the outbreak of World War II in 1939. The London's directors appear to have regarded the Munich crisis of 1938 as clear warning of the imminence of war and they decided to evacuate the majority of the corporation's staff from London to the greater safety of Somerset and Buckinghamshire, where they remained for the duration of the war and indeed for two years afterward. Once again, under the stimulus of wartime conditions, the London saw its marine business grow rapidly, reaching a high in 1942 at over £2.5 million in premium income, although by this time its fire business had outstripped marine business in size. Although damaged during the blitz of 1940, the London's City headquarters remained structurally intact, so the corporation faced few of the housing difficulties experienced by other less fortunate firms.

Despite an 1891 act of Parliament granting the London the right to conduct accident insurance, it did not, like the other major insurance companies, seriously consider the subject until the passing of the Workmen's Compensation Act of 1906. This stimulated the London, as it did the others, to enter the field in 1907. In the next 50 years accident business grew rapidly, outstripping life in premium income by the 1950s, to rank third behind marine and fire.

Sun Alliance Group: The Phoenix

The punishing premiums levied by the Sun, the London, and the Royal Exchange on the mills and distilleries in the last decades of the 18th century caused a group of "sugarbakers," or distillers, led by the forceful and influential Nathaniel Jarman, to set up its own fire office in 1782, simply and appropriately called the New Fire Office until 1813, when it became the Phoenix Assurance Company.

The New Fire Office provided the first serious competition in the fire business for the veteran offices. Significantly the Sun, most affected by the arrival of this new competitor, early on decided on a policy of limited cooperation with the Phoenix, an unusual measure testifying to the success of the Phoenix's policy of offering discounted premiums if the insured also took out further insurances with the company.

The Phoenix's survival and growth depended at least as much upon the energy and intelligence of its senior management. Notable in this respect were George Griffin Stone-Street, secretary from 1786 to 1802, and his successor Jenkin Jones, secretary from 1802 to 1837. Under their guidance the Phoenix weathered the depression in the insurance industry in the late 18th century and early decades of the 19th century. By 1815 the Phoenix had overtaken the Sun in premium income.

This period also saw the Phoenix establish the Pelican Life Assurance in 1797, acquire several large provincial operations, set up agencies across Britain, and, perhaps most importantly, penetrate the European market from the Baltic Sea to the Iberian Peninsula. Simultaneously the Phoenix established itself in Canada—in Montreal in 1804—although the War of 1812 and the burning of Washington, D.C., by British troops put an end to its first operation in the United States.

These early foreign ventures are indicative of the Phoenix's foremost place in the overseas expansion of British insurance companies. The middle decades of the 19th century were costly for the Phoenix. In the Hamburg fire of 1842 it lost £250,000, more than twice as much as its rival, the Sun, a loss that hit it nearly as hard as did the disastrous 1807 fire at St. Thomas in the Virgin Islands.

The directors of the Phoenix, viewing their widely spread foreign risks, might have used such disasters as good reason for contracting or closing down some of the numerous foreign liabilities. Instead, largely through the farsighted advocacy of Jenkin Jones, they chose to reaffirm their commitment to the foreign enterprises. The wisdom of retaining foreign risks became apparent two generations later when, by the early years of the 20th century, foreign business began to outstrip home earnings.

These decades and the three that followed saw the establishment of agencies in the Far East, the Cape of Good Hope, Australasia, Eastern Europe, and the eastern Mediterranean. In 1879 a New York operation was once again set up, replacing the reinsurance work that the Phoenix had undertaken for other British offices up to that point. The San Francisco disaster of 1906 affected the Phoenix particularly badly—initially, there were doubts about its capacity to survive its liabilities—but, like the other Sun Group companies, the Phoenix settled with an alacrity and generosity that impressed the Americans. Although business in the last two decades of the 19th century was relatively stagnant, legally the era was one of significance for the Phoenix. The 1895 Phoenix Assurance Company Act enabled the Phoenix to add life and accident business to its operations—a provision it chose not to exploit until 1907—and placed the company on a modern footing by requiring it to publish its accounts. In 1901 the Phoenix became a limited liability company.

Until 1907 the Phoenix dealt solely with fire insurance, although it enlarged itself periodically by the acquisition of smaller fire insurance companies. In that year the Phoenix reabsorbed its own offspring, Pelican Life Assurance, at that time known as the Pelican and British Empire Life Office, and thus began its career as a composite insurer. Life business further expanded with the 1909 acquisition of the highly respected Law Life Assurance Society. In 1910 the Phoenix entered marine insurance with the purchase of the Union Marine.

Although the 1906 Workmen's Compensation Act had persuaded the Phoenix to move tentatively into accident insurance, it was not until the 1922 acquisition of the important London Guarantee and Accident Company, with its U.S. interests, that the Phoenix fully established itself in this type of business.

World War I proved financially costly for the company. The Treaty of Versailles failed to provide for the return of the Phoenix's German interests confiscated at the outbreak of hostilities. At a stroke, the Phoenix lost about 7 percent of its total fire premiums. Compounding this loss was the abrupt disappearance of its Russian business as the newly created U.S.S.R. canceled all foreign undertakings in the former Russian Empire. Similarly, the aftereffects of the collapse of the Ottoman Empire and the destruction wrought by the Greco-Turkish War of 1922 destroyed the

Phoenix's position in Turkey. The Phoenix's entry into the expanding aviation insurance market in 1931 helped to offset the effects of the Depression, although it was not until the arrival of jet airliners in the 1950s that the Phoenix appointed its first full-time aviation underwriter. The interwar years were also characterized by the setting-up of branch offices to replace the numerous agencies established during the previous century. E.B. Fergusson, managing director from 1939 to 1957, used the years of World War II as an opportunity to make a series of worldwide journeys, setting up new operations in territories hitherto unexplored by the Phoenix, for example in Ethiopia, Persia—now Iran—and Palestine. The two decades after 1945 were sometimes frustrating for the Phoenix, as newly independent countries either nationalized the Phoenix's operations or, by bureaucratic obfuscation and corruption, rendered them unprofitable. In the home market, in North America, and in Australasia, however, the Phoenix recorded high levels of growth in this period, particularly through the successful marketing of new multiperil property insurance policies that began to replace the straight fire policies common until then.

In 1959 a major rearrangement of the company's capital base took place, increasing authorized capital to £5 million. Nine years later the Continental Insurance Company of New York, the second largest insurance company in the United States, bought one and a half million Phoenix shares, and the two companies pooled senior management and U.S. operations. By this move, the Phoenix sought to increase its capital yet again for expansion into other areas of insurance. Continental benefited from the Phoenix's long established representation in the Commonwealth and the Far East.

The next decade and a half were years of comparative hardships for Britain and for the Phoenix. By the early 1980s senior management had become disillusioned with the performance of the Continental pool, and in 1984 the Phoenix disposed of its 6.25 percent share. Continental simultaneously sold its 24.3 percent shareholding in the Phoenix to the Sun Alliance.

Sun Alliance Group: The Alliance

Despite the depressed conditions in the British insurance industry in the first 30 years of the 19th century, in 1824 two prominent City financiers, Sir Moses Montefiore and Nathan Mayer Rothschild, decided to set up a new insurance company distinguished by a larger share capital and a more influential board than any existing operation. They invited three other men eminent in the spheres of commerce and finance to become copresidents—Samuel Guerney, member of Parliament John Irving, and Francis Baring of the powerful Baring banking family. The subscribed capital was huge by the standards of the time—£5 million divided into 50,000 shares—a measure of the reputation of the founders. The new firm, called the Alliance Assurance Company, was endowed from its inception with a range of contacts and influence in financial and political affairs as well as a capitalization that made it the equal of the already veteran Sun, the London, and the Royal Exchange. The Alliance's first actuary was Benjamin Gompertz, a fellow of the Royal Society, writer of important works on statistical analysis, and a founder of the Institute of Actuaries.

Without delay, the directors proceeded to the appointment of provincial and foreign agents and by 1825 the Alliance had representation in New York, Quebec, Montreal, and the Indian subcontinent. The Alliance's North American ventures proved unsuccessful. It closed its U.S. operation in 1826 and, after a series of fires in Quebec and Montreal, withdrew from Canada in 1850. Not until the final decades of the century did the Alliance reestablish itself in North America.

The checkered history of the Alliance's North American operations was shared by the majority of British insurance companies that tried to enter that lucrative but risky market. The Alliance, however, was unusual in the speed and ruthlessness with which it shut down agencies. After the San Francisco earthquake and fire, which cost it £690,000, the Alliance decided to withdraw from the Pacific coast altogether. This readiness to close, open, and close again was explained by the Alliance's directors as a policy of concentration on quality rather than on quantity of representation.

The Alliance was principally notable for its expansion through the acquisition of established London, provincial, and dominion insurance companies. This process of acquisition began in the 1840s and continued unabated into the first decades of the 20th century, chiefly under the capable leadership of Robert Lewis, managing director from 1912 to 1917, who had begun his insurance career with the Provincial Insurance Company in 1853. The Provincial Insurance Company soon afterward was acquired by the Alliance. Until its 1959 merger with the Sun Insurance Office, the most significant acquisitions were those of the Imperial Fire and Imperial Life companies in 1902.

Already a composite insurance company in that it offered both fire and life insurance from its founding, the Alliance nevertheless had great trouble entering the field of marine insurance. In 1824, on behalf of the Alliance, member of Parliament William Huskisson—a former Sun manager—proposed a bill for the repeal of the 1720 Act which restricted the underwriting of marine business to the Royal Exchange and the London. Huskisson, who later achieved the melancholy distinction of being the first person ever killed by a railway engine, pushed the bill successfully through Parliament, but an Alliance shareholder countered by obtaining an injunction restraining the Alliance from taking on marine business. The Alliance's way out of this impasse was to set up a separate new company, the Alliance Marine, whose shares it finally managed to acquire in 1905.

In common with the other Sun Alliance companies, the Alliance entered the accident business in 1907. It managed to do this, unusually, without needing to acquire an already established accident operation.

Creation of the Sun Alliance Group: 1959–89

The conjunction of these four insurance bodies into the Sun Alliance Insurance Ltd. and the London Insurance Company, predecessor to the Sun Alliance Group, was essentially a result of the post-World War II trend toward the formation of ever larger units in industry and commerce. The Alliance was the first to merge with the Sun Insurance Office, in 1959. The new holding company, called the Sun Alliance Insurance, acquired all the shares in the two operations.

A larger merger, with the London, followed six years later, creating a new group called the Sun Alliance and London

Insurance plc. In January 1989 the group changed its name to Sun Alliance Group plc. The years immediately following the London merger were dominated by the process of integrating the diverse operations of the new group, and by the formation of a central head office administration. The introduction of new types of fire and life coverage and the elimination of unprofitable businesses helped offset the losses that inflation, gathering pace in Britain in the 1970s, the stock market crash of 1974, and the severe drought of 1976, inflicted on the group.

Sun Alliance entered the 1980s with a comfortable asset base, a very high solvency margin—125 percent in 1984—and the ambition to become one of the strongest composite insurance companies in the United Kingdom. All this seemed to point to the Sun Alliance's expansion through a major acquisition. Still, the announcement in July 1984 of its £400 million bid for the remaining equity of the Phoenix Assurance—a price that many analysts considered low, perhaps reflecting the Phoenix's troubled financial state in the preceding years—took the British insurance industry by surprise. Other analysts saw the move as an attempt to make the Sun Alliance safe from foreign predators, expressing surprise that it had not gone for a major U.S. acquisition, to build up its presence in the world's largest insurance market and to forestall any aggressive moves by a U.S. company.

Sun Alliance's initial equity holding in Phoenix had been 24.3 percent, bought from Continental as the price of Phoenix's withdrawal from Continental's pool. This deal marked the first step in a process of disengagement from Continental that ended in 1988 with the selling of Phoenix's Canadian subsidiaries to Continental in exchange for a 75 percent stake in the French Groupe Barthelmey. There followed a period of restructuring as the Sun Alliance digested its huge purchase, especially with regard to the Phoenix's wide foreign representation. A long-running inter-union dispute resulted, because Phoenix staff belonged to a different union than that of Sun Alliance's employees, and Sun Alliance wanted all its staff to belong to one union.

Despite the estimated £155 million that the group lost in the October 1987 hurricane, which devastated parts of southern England—the Sun Alliance still retained a very high share of the U.K. property insurance market—it nevertheless pursued a policy of expansion into new areas of insurance by the careful acquisition of operations already successfully established in the field, two such purchases being First Health, a leader in the area of medical expenses insurance, and Bradford Pennine, a specialist motor subsidiary. The later incorporation of the new holding company, Sun Alliance Group plc, in January 1989, enabling the group to move into non-insurance business, was firm evidence of the company's intention to expand further—by moving into financial services.

Pre-Merger Developments at Sun Alliance: 1989–96

In August 1989, Sun Alliance raised its shareholding in rival Commercial Union plc to 14.5 percent at a cost of £256 million. Sun Alliance explained this move as a defensive measure to prevent a large European insurer—rumored by some analysts to be Allianz of Germany—from gaining a major foothold in the U.K. insurance market. Other analysts, however, remembering Sun Alliance's methods during its successful 1984 bid for the

Phoenix, chose to interpret this as a first step toward another protective acquisition and the creation of a giant U.K. composite capable of withstanding a hostile takeover attempt by any foreign predator. This did not prove to be the case, however, as Sun Alliance sold nearly all of its stake by September 1992, booking a profit of about £280 million in the process.

Sun Alliance's results for 1989 were impressive, despite a 14 percent fall in pretax profits from the 1988 figure. The *Financial Times* called it the United Kingdom's "highest quality financial company," and noted its continuing underlying asset strength and high solvency margin of 119 percent. This was the result of the Sun Alliance's determined defense of its money-making areas, for example U.K. property insurance, and its portfolio of high quality investments.

In the early 1990s, Sun Alliance's fortunes—along with those of the other large British insurers—took a turn for the worse. The global economic downturn, the severely depressed U.K. housing market, bad weather, and a cyclical downturn in the global insurance market coalesced to batter Sun Alliance and the other composite insurers (those that sell both property and casualty and life insurance). Sun Alliance suffered a further blow from its 25 percent share of the domestic mortgage insurance market, which was hit hard by high levels of home repossessions resulting from the poor economy. Sun Alliance posted pretax losses for each of the first three years of the decade—£180.9 million, £466.2 million, and £129.6 million, respectively.

To stem the losses, cost-cutting initiatives were launched, including the elimination of 400 jobs from the company's individual nonlife insurance operations in the United Kingdom in 1991 and another 800 job cuts the following year, along with the elimination of 39 smaller branch outlets. In addition to the sale of its stake in Commercial Union, Sun Alliance made further reductions in its portfolio of equity holdings in 1992: selling its 8 percent stake in London and Manchester, a life insurance group, and reducing its stake in U.S. property and insurance company Chubb Corporation from 9 percent to 5 percent (Chubb also simultaneously reduced its 9 percent cross-holding in Sun Alliance to about 3 percent).

Sun Alliance also completed a string of strategic moves during this period. In 1992 the company merged its nonlife insurance operations in Australia with those of Royal Insurance to form the fourth largest general insurer in Australia, in which Sun held a 60 percent stake. Sun Alliance paid £140 million in 1993 for the insurance and banking subsidiaries of Hafnia, a troubled Danish insurance firm. This deal, which was completed through Codan A/S, a subsidiary 71 percent owned by Sun Alliance, created the largest business-oriented general insurer in Denmark through the combined operations of Hafnia and Codan. Finally, in January 1994 Sun Alliance sold its Canadian property and casualty operations to Royal Insurance, which in turn sold its New Zealand fire and casualty business to Sun Alliance. The latter was the number three general insurance company in New Zealand.

Although continuing to suffer losses from its domestic mortgage insurance operation, Sun Alliance returned to the black in 1993, reporting a sharp turnaround to a pretax profit of £221.7 million. The company stayed profitable for the next two years, setting the stage for the merger with Royal Insurance. In the later months of 1995, Sun Alliance sold Wm. H. McGee & Co. Inc., a U.S.-based underwriting agency subsidiary.

Early History of the Royal

The Royal Insurance Company was established in the major commercial center of Liverpool on May 31, 1845, to provide insurance coverage ". . . against the risk of loss or damage by fire or by storm or by other casualty . . ." on all types of property, and to provide life insurance and annuities. The capital of the company was £2 million, divided into 100,000 shares of £20. Under the leadership of Percy Dove, the first manager and actuary, who had joined the company from the Royal Exchange Assurance, the company immediately embarked on a policy of expansion, taking advantage at home of the fact that from 1853 life insurance premiums became permissible deductions from tax liabilities at all income levels. Overseas widespread industrialization brought with it an increase in the value of property worth insuring and in the income available to insure it.

In the United Kingdom, in marked contrast to its older rivals, the Royal undertook a deliberate policy of aggressive advertising, spending from £20,000 to £30,000 annually to place advertisements in magazines, reviews, railway stations, and public places. By way of contrast, the Pelican Insurance Company was at the same time spending £375 annually on 1,500 railway posters.

Expansion overseas began immediately, and by 1850 agencies had been established in Australia, Canada, Singapore, and South America. The company's operations in the United States, which would have a major effect on its financial position, began in 1851 when the first agency was opened in New York. Baltimore, Maryland; Philadelphia, Pennsylvania; Savannah, Georgia; and Charleston, South Carolina, each had an agency by the end of the year. By the time the company arrived in San Francisco in April 1853, agencies had been established in a total of ten U.S. cities. The U.S. insurance market expanded rapidly as new forms of insurance were devised to meet widening demands, particularly those of businesses. Employers' liability insurance was first introduced in 1885 and automobile liability in 1898. By 1915, blanket bonds of many kinds were being offered to provide comprehensive protection for business and financial institutions. By 1901, the Royal was the leading British company in the U.S. insurance market.

Although beaten to the West Coast of the United States by the Liverpool and London Fire and Life Insurance Company, the Royal was far more adventurous in its policy of overseas expansion than most of its rivals. In the 1850s, it was one of three British companies to establish agencies in Melbourne, Australia. Ten years later, the number of British offices in Australia had risen to ten. By 1863, the Royal and the Sun Fire Office were the only companies offering insurance in the commercial center of Smyrna, Turkey. By the early 1880s, 16 British and six foreign offices were represented there. Not all overseas expansion prospered, however. The company incurred heavy losses from fierce competition in Italy in the 1870s and political instability forced it to withdraw altogether from Spain in 1877. Despite these difficulties, by the end of the 19th century the Royal was one of Britain's greatest exporters of insurance.

Royal's Acquisition of Liverpool and London and Globe: Early 20th Century

An enduring characteristic of the Royal had been its growth through mergers and acquisitions. In 1891 the company absorbed the Queen Insurance Company by exchange of shares. The chairman of the Queen told shareholders that they were to be admitted into partnership with a company second to none in the world, which possessed a magnificent, safe, and progressive business. Ten years later, the Kent Fire, the United Kent Fire, and the Lancashire (fire and life) insurance companies had all been acquired. When the British and Foreign Marine and the British Engine companies were added a few years later, the Royal was in a position to write all classes of nonlife insurance and life insurance. The only exception to this was industrial life business, whereby premiums are collected by a representative of the insurance company, on a weekly, fortnightly, or monthly basis. In 1919, the biggest merger in British insurance history took place when the Royal acquired the enormously successful Liverpool and London and Globe Insurance Company. The latter was established in Liverpool in 1836 as the Liverpool Fire and Life Insurance Company and had risen to an eminent position principally through acquisition. In 1847 it purchased the business of the London, Edinburgh and Dublin Insurance Company and in 1864 it merged with the long-established Globe Insurance Company. The Royal and the Liverpool and London and Globe were the major provincial insurance companies of the late 19th century. The Liverpool had a greater share of the British and colonial markets than the Royal.

The merger of the Royal and the Liverpool was part of a wider trend that gathered pace in the early 20th century, toward the establishment of large composite insurance companies. A major impetus for this trend was provided by the Workmen's Compensation Act of 1906, which extended employers' liability to all workers and provided the opportunity for insurance companies to offer a wider range of services.

Throughout the next 40 years, the Royal expanded its operations both at home and overseas. The number of branches increased from 70 in 1920 to 217 in Britain and Ireland in 1960, 175 in the United States, and 94 branches and offices and an extensive network of agencies elsewhere. In 1951 the company celebrated the centenary of its involvement in the United States. Chairman Colonel Alan Todd remarked that the company had every reason to feel proud of the leading position it occupied in that country. Progress was maintained in all the leading insurance markets. Experience in China provided the only exception: in 1950, after over 100 years' presence, the Royal decided to withdraw.

A new wave of acquisitions began in 1961, when the Royal took over the London and Lancashire Insurance Company to achieve greater economy and efficiency of operations throughout the world. In Canada, two insurance companies, the Western Assurance Company and the British American Insurance Company, were acquired. By the end of the 1960s the Royal, with the greatest total fire and accident premium income, headed the "Big Four" insurance group, followed by Commercial Union, General Accident, and Guardian Royal Exchange.

The 1970s saw further expansion overseas. In 1975 the Royal became the first foreign company for 25 years to be licensed to write business in Japan, and in 1977 it acquired a 20 percent stake in the German insurer Aachen & Munich. Pretax profits continued to rise until 1979. The company identified a number of factors contributing to the fall: an abnormally high level of weather losses, particularly in the United Kingdom, the United States, and the Caribbean; rapid inflation; the strength of sterling against most of the world's currencies; and increases in burglary, vandalism, and arson.

Extensive Restructuring of the Royal: 1980s

The 1980s saw extensive corporate restructuring of the Royal Insurance group. In 1981, two divisions, the general overseas division and the life division, were incorporated as Royal Insurance (Int) Ltd. and Royal Life Insurance Ltd., respectively. Both were to operate as separate companies. The engineering, marine, and aviation businesses were integrated into the appropriate operating companies, and worldwide operations were divided into eight profit centers, all in the form of separately incorporated companies with their own capital and reserves.

Throughout the 1980s, fluctuations in the overseas insurance markets had serious repercussions on the Royal's financial position. In the early 1980s the industry as a whole complained of overcapacity at a time of worldwide economic recession. The Royal cut back its operations in Australia and Canada in 1983 after suffering severe losses, and in 1985 withdrew from workers' compensation in Australia after that business had been nationalized in some states. By 1988 Australia was producing excellent results both in terms of higher insurance profits and premium growth.

Expansion in the United States continued in 1982, when the group acquired the Milbank Insurance Company and a year later the Missouri-based Silvey Corporation and American Overseas Holdings. At this point the United States was the Royal's largest single market, representing 41 percent of its worldwide general insurance premiums. Soaring underwriting losses in 1984 due to severe competition caused the company to increase rates in the United States to restructure the organization to make it more responsive to the needs of the marketplace, and to cut back on expenditure by relocating the head office from New York to Charlotte, North Carolina. This remedial action proved successful as the group recorded a steady recovery in U.S. business from 1985 until 1989, when profits were hit by the effects of Hurricane Hugo, the San Francisco earthquake, and strong competition. A loss of £98 million in 1989 prompted a major strategy review by the company.

The Royal ended the 1980s by creating a new holding company, Royal Insurance Holdings plc, for the group's various operations. The holding company structure was designed to facilitate the moves into non-insurance sectors. The decade closed on a dismal note for the Royal, as pretax profits fell 43 percent as a result of Hurricane Hugo, earthquakes in San Francisco and Australia, and subsidence losses in the United Kingdom.

Difficulties for the Royal: Early 1990s

The Royal was battered in the early 1990s by a combination of forces: the global recession, the severely depressed U.K. housing market, bad weather, and a cyclical downturn in the global insurance market. The housing downturn wreaked havoc on the Royal's expansion into real estate agencies, and the Royal, like Sun Alliance, was a market leader in the domestic mortgage insurance sector, leading to heavy claims resulting from property repossessions. For the first time in its nearly 150-year history, the Royal fell into the red, posting a pretax loss of £187 million ($360.9 million) for 1990. The following year was even worse: a £373 million ($660 million) pretax loss; as part of a cost-saving initiative to improve the group's financial position, there was no final dividend payment that year. The Royal was in the red again in 1992 before returning to profitability.

During this bleak period, a number of steps were taken to cut costs and improve the balance sheet. As part of a broad reorganization, 600 jobs were eliminated from the group's U.K. life insurance operations in late 1991. A number of noncore assets were identified for disposal, including the group's 80 percent stake in the Royal Re reinsurance subsidiary. In April 1991 the Royal reached an agreement to sell the stake to General Re Corporation, but the deal fell apart a few months later. Instead, in February 1993 the Royal announced that it would begin winding down the operations of Royal Re. In December 1991 the Royal raised £249 million from the sale of its stake in Aachen & Munich. Early the following year another £110 million was gained from the sale of the Royal's Dutch operations to Epic, a newly formed joint venture in which the Royal owned a one-third share. In 1992 the Royal merged its nonlife insurance operations in Australia with those of Sun Alliance, taking a 40 percent stake in the newly formed company. Approximately £400 million in cash was raised through a rights issue completed in 1993. Early the following year, the Royal sold its New Zealand fire and casualty business to Sun Alliance. At the same time, the group acquired the Canadian property and casualty operations of Sun Alliance, marking the Royal's first overseas purchase in five years. Most of these moves were spearheaded by Richard Gamble, who had taken over as chief operating officer in early 1991 and then was named chief executive at the beginning of 1992.

Emergence of Royal & Sun Alliance in Late 1990s

In July 1996 the U.K. insurance industry was rocked by the merger of Sun Alliance Group plc and Royal Insurance Holdings plc, a merger that created Royal & Sun Alliance Insurance Group plc (RSA). The new group started off as the largest composite insurance company in the United Kingdom, with a market share of about 16 percent. RSA was also the seventh largest U.K. life insurer. Based on combined 1995 figures, RSA had worldwide premium income of £9.39 billion ($14.1 billion) and pretax profits of £1.03 billion ($1.5 billion). The merger was anticipated to result in savings of £175 million ($262.5 million) per year by 1998 from cost cutting and consolidation, including the dismissal of about 5,000 employees from the initial combined workforce of 45,000. A similar amount, however, would be spent on merger and reorganization expenses. Gamble was named chief executive of the new group, while Roger Taylor, who had been Sun Alliance's chief executive, became executive deputy chairman. The chairman of Sun Alliance, Christopher Benson, initially took the position of nonexecutive chairman, but he was succeeded by Patrick Gillam in March 1997. Gillam, former managing director of the

British Petroleum Company plc, was also chairman of Standard Chartered PLC, a U.K. bank.

One of the main rationales behind the merger was that the combined group would be better positioned to pursue overseas growth opportunities. In fact, from its formation, RSA focused on transforming itself "from a U.K. insurer with overseas operations into a global enterprise headquartered in the United Kingdom." An acquisition spree was soon launched, leading in late 1996 and 1997, to the completion of several deals, the largest helping to bolster the group's fairly small presence in continental Europe. In mid-1997 RSA bought the Italian life insurance and pensions business of Prudential Corporation plc for £46 million. Royal & Sun also purchased the Johnson Corporation, a Canadian life and health insurance company, and paid £75 million in November 1997 for a 40 percent stake in Compañia de Seguros de Vida La Construcción, a Chilean life insurer (two years later, the stake was increased to 51 percent). Late in 1997 RSA announced a shake-up of its boardroom structure, which some analysts had criticized as being cumbersome and confusing. Gamble left the company, while Taylor relinquished his executive responsibilities but stayed onboard as nonexecutive deputy chairman. Robert Mendelsohn, a U.S. citizen who had been in charge of RSA's American operations—and before that had been credited with turning around the fortunes of the Royal's U.S. unit—was named sole chief executive.

During 1998 Royal & Sun became one of the top life insurers in New Zealand through two additional acquisitions: the New Zealand life insurance and investment business of Norwich Union, bought for £53.7 million, and the New Zealand life operation of Guardian Royal Exchange Plc, purchased for £97.6 million. Early the following year, RSA entered into the bidding for the entirety of Guardian Royal, a U.K. composite insurer, but the takeover battle was won by French insurance giant AXA. Also in 1998, RSA became the first British insurer to return to China when it was awarded a potentially lucrative license to begin selling insurance in that huge and rapidly growing market.

Dramatically increasing its appetite, RSA spent a total of £1.82 billion ($2.64 billion) on acquisitions during 1999, completing three major purchases. In May the company acquired Tyndall Australia Limited, a provider of life insurance and retirement and money management services; the purchase made RSA the fourth largest insurance group in the Australasian region. In August the acquisition of the Swedish firm Trygg-Hansa Försäkrings AB, Publikt was completed through Royal & Sun's 72 percent-owned Danish subsidiary, Codan A/S. Trygg-Hansa held the number four position in Sweden in property and casualty insurance. The third major 1999 purchase—Orion Capital Corporation—came in the United States and was consummated in November. Acquired for about £900 million ($1.4 billion), Orion, based in Farmington, Connecticut, was a nonlife insurer focusing on specialty products such as nonstandard automobile insurance; professional liability insurance for engineers, architects, and environmental consultants; and workers' compensation insurance. These specialty areas were attractive because they generated higher margins than general property and casualty business. The deal doubled Royal & Sun's U.S. business to about $3 billion in premiums, making it one of the top 25 U.S. property and casualty insurers. The latter two deals highlighted a recent shift away from life insurance and toward nonlife insurance operations; with the purchase of Orion, nonlife insurance comprised more than three-quarters of RSA's total business.

At the same time that this acquisition spree was underway, Royal & Sun Alliance sought to offload loss-making businesses to shore up the group's finances and improve profits. During 1999, for example, the group sold its U.S. life insurance operations to Swiss Reinsurance Company and also divested its direct automobile insurance operations in France and Germany. Despite these and other disposals, operating profits fell 39 percent in 1998 and another 5.9 percent the next year.

Fighting for Survival in the Early 21st Century

The news from RSA grew even grimmer in the early 21st century. Operating profits fell another 17 percent in 2000 to £462 million. Still more disposals followed in 2001, including the bulk of the group's operations in Italy and Spain as well as its Canadian life insurance unit. Then the destruction of New York's World Trade Center on September 11, 2001, led to £215 million ($300 million) in losses for RSA. The firm also increased its provisions for losses by £371 million to cover potential asbestos-related claims. As a result, operating profits for 2001 plunged to £16 million, while volatility in global stock markets led to large losses from the group's investment portfolio and resulted in a net pretax loss of £1.25 billion.

The embattled Mendelsohn had to contend with a plunging share price and rampant rumors of an impending takeover in addition to the challenge of turning the group's fortunes around. He announced that several more businesses were being placed on the auction block, including the life insurance and asset management businesses in both the United Kingdom and Australia and New Zealand, in a renewed effort to improve the balance sheet. In July 2002 the U.K. asset management unit arm was sold to ISIS Asset Management for £240 million. That same month, Royal & Sun's Isle of Man-based life insurance subsidiary and its entire Benelux operation were also sold off. One month later, unable to sell its U.K. life insurance business, RSA announced that the unit would stop writing new policies and 1,200 jobs would be cut from its workforce. At the same time, Mendelsohn announced that the company was considering implementing a rights issue to garner itself the additional capital it needed; this news sent the company stock plunging 21 percent. Later in the month, the Financial Services Authority, regulator of the City, fined Royal & Sun a record £1.35 million for mis-selling pensions. With the group's troubles snowballing, the board of directors ousted Mendelsohn in September 2002. Bob Gunn, who had been group operating officer, was named acting chief executive.

In November 2002 RSA revealed a radical plan of action for survival. The group would eliminate more than 12,000 employees from the payroll and close down or sell off a number of businesses. Unable to find a buyer for the Australasian operations, RSA said that it would spin off that business through an IPO scheduled for 2003. Early in 2003, in advance of the planned IPO, the Australasian businesses were reorganized under the name Promina Group Limited. In December 2002 RSA completed the sale of the group's German subsidiary, Securitas, to Baloise, a Swiss insurance firm. Also that month, Andy Haste

was named group chief executive, having previously been the head of AXA Sun Life, the U.K. life insurance arm of AXA. John Napier was named to succeed Gillam as chairman, an appointment that took effect in March 2003. Napier was simultaneously serving as chairman of Kelda Group Plc, a U.K. water group. It was now up to Haste and Napier to see the group's survival plan through.

Principal Subsidiaries

Royal International Holdings plc; Royal & Sun Alliance Insurance plc; British Aviation Insurance Company Ltd. (57.1%); FirstAssist Group Ltd.; The Globe Insurance Company Ltd.; Legal Protection Group Holdings Ltd.; The London Assurance; The Marine Insurance Company Ltd.; Phoenix Assurance plc; Royal International Insurance Holdings Ltd.; Royal & Sun Alliance Reinsurance Ltd.; Royal & Sun Alliance Property Services Ltd.; Royal & Sun Alliance Life & Pensions Ltd.; Royal & Sun Alliance Linked Insurances Ltd.; RSA E-Holdings Ltd.; Sun Alliance and London Insurance plc; Sun Alliance and London Assurance Company Ltd.; Royal & Sun Alliance Life Holdings Ltd.; Sun Insurance Office Ltd.; Royal & Sun Alliance Seguros (Argentina) SA; RSA Marketing (Latin America) SA (Argentina); Promina Group Limited (Australia); Royal & Sun Alliance Seguros (Brasil) SA (Brazil); Roins Financial Services Ltd. (Canada); Compagnie d'Assurance du Quebec (Canada; 99.8%); The Johnson Corporation (Canada); Royal & Sun Alliance Insurance Company of Canada; Western Assurance Company (Canada); Royal & Sun Alliance Seguros (Chile) SA (97.5%); Compañia de Seguros de Vida La Construcción (Chile; 51%); Royal & Sun Alliance Seguros (Colombia) SA (86.3%); Royal & Sun Alliance Seguros de Vida (Colombia) SA (86.3%); Codan A/S (Denmark; 71.7%); Codan Forsikring A/S (Denmark; 71.7%); A/S Forsikringsselskabet Codan Liv (Denmark, 71.7%); Insurance Corporation of Channel Islands Ltd. (Guernsey); Royal & Sun Alliance Insurance (Hong Kong) Ltd.; Royal & Sun Alliance Eurolife Ltd. (Ireland); Tower Insurance Company Ltd. (Isle of Man); Royal & Sun Alliance Seguros (Mexico) SA; Royal & Sun Alliance Insurance (Antilles) NV (Netherlands Antilles; 51%); Royal & Sun Alliance—Seguros Fenix (Peru; 64.9%); Royal & Sun Alliance Insurance (Puerto Rico) Inc. (94.3%); Royal & Sun Alliance Insurance (Middle East) Limited E.C. (Saudi Arabia; 50.01%); Royal & Sun Alliance Insurance (Singapore) Ltd.; Trygg-Hansa Försäkrings AB, Publikt (Sweden; 71.7%); Royal & Sun Alliance USA, Inc.; Royal Indemnity Company (U.S.A.); Royal Insurance Company of America (U.S.A.); Orion Capital Corporation (U.S.A.); Security Insurance Company of Hartford (U.S.A.); Guaranty National Insurance Company (U.S.A.); Royal & Sun Alliance Sequros (Uruguay) SA; Royal & Sun Alliance Seguros (Venezuela) SA (99.4%).

Principal Competitors

ING Groep N.V.; AXA; Allianz AG; AEGON N.V.; Aviva plc; Prudential plc; Assicurazioni Generali SpA; Zurich Financial Services; Legal & General Group Plc.

Further Reading

Adams, Christopher, "A Policy of Reducing Costs," *Financial Times*, January 24, 1997, p. 24.

——, "Royal & Sun Chief Departs," *Financial Times,* December 3, 1997, p. 21.

Atkins, Ralph, "U.K. Insurers Agree to £6bn Merger," *Financial Times,* May 4, 1996.

Bolger, Andrew, "Audience Remains Undecided over Mendelsohn's Performance," *Financial Times,* April 20, 2002, p. 14.

——, "Embattled RSA Unveils Radical Survival Strategy," *Financial Times,* November 8, 2002, p. 21.

——, "Invisible Men Move into Hot Seats at RSA," *Financial Times,* December 20, 2002, p. 24.

——, "Legacy of Past Casts Shadow over RSA," *Financial Times,* November 6, 2002, p. 28.

Bolger, Andrew, and Tony Tassell, "Mendelsohn Facing the Music As RSA Scrambles to Raise Capital," *Financial Times,* August 9, 2002, p. 20.

——, "Royal & Sun Fined Record £1.35m," *Financial Times,* August 28, 2002, p. 1.

Boone, Elisabeth, "A Merger Made in Heaven," *Rough Notes,* February 2000, pp. 66–70.

"British Insurance Companies: Light at the End of Their Losses?," *Economist,* February 9, 1991, p. 88.

Bunker, Nick, "How Sun Alliance Brightened Its Image," *Financial Times,* September 8, 1988, p. 26.

——, "The Strength of The Sun Poses a Problem," *Financial Times,* April 11, 1988, p. 20.

The Business of Risk, Royal Insurance Company 1851–1951: The Hundred Year Background of the Royal Insurance Company Limited and the Royal Liverpool Insurance Group in the United States, New York: Royal Insurance Company, 1951.

Cockerell, H.A.L., and Edwin Green, *The British Insurance Business, 1547–1970: An Introduction and Guide to Historical Records in the United Kingdom,* London: Heinemann Educational Books, 1976.

Cosgrave, John N., *We Hold Thee Safe: A History of Royal Insurance in the United States,* Charlotte, N.C.: Royal Insurance, 1986.

Dickson, P.G.M., *The Sun Insurance Office, 1710–1960,* London: Oxford University Press, 1960.

Drew, B., *The London Assurance: A Second Chronicle,* London: London Assuranc, 1949.

Fuhrmans, Vanessa, "Royal & Sun's Unattractiveness Serves As Shield for U.K. Insurer," *Wall Street Journal,* March 3, 2000, p. A16.

——, "U.K.'s Royal & Sun to Take Over Orion Capital in Latest Foray by European Insurer into U.S.," *Wall Street Journal,* July 13, 1999, p. A14.

A History of the Phoenix Assurance Company, London: Phoenix Assurance Company, Ltd., 1975.

Hofmann, Mark A., "Reigning Supreme As Catastrophe King: Royal Has Survived Best amid Worst," *Business Insurance,* September 18, 1995, p. 26.

——, "Remaking Royal: An Insider's View," *Business Insurance,* September 18, 1995, pp. 3+.

——, "Royal Sizes Up Global Market," *Business Insurance,* September 18, 1995, p. 22.

Howard, Lisa A., "Royal SunAlliance's Global Buying Spree," *National Underwriter Life and Health/Financial Services,* April 28, 1997, pp. 45, 48.

Hurren, G., *Phoenix Renascent: A History of the Phoenix Assurance Company,* London: Phoenix Assurance Company, 1973.

Lapper, Richard, "Battered by Storms but Heading for Port," *Financial Times,* March 2, 1992, p. 17.

——, "Royal's Troubles Hit Market's Confidence," *Financial Times,* October 29, 1991, p. 23.

Royal Insurance Profile, London: Royal Insurance, 1989.

"Royal Romance," *Economist,* February 6, 1993, p. 84.

Schooling, Sir W., *The Alliance Assurance Company,* London: Alliance Assurance, 1924.

Short, Eric, "Sun Alliance, Phoenix Plan to Merge into Biggest U.K. Insurer," *Financial Times,* July 12, 1984, p. 1.

Souter, Gavin, "Worst Year Ever for British Insurers," *Business Insurance,* March 11, 1991, pp. 23, 24.

Unsworth, Edwin, "Royal, Sun Merger Rocks U.K.," *Business Insurance,* May 6, 1996, pp. 1, 69.

Zinkewicz, Phil, "Royal Holdings' International Strategy, Begun in 1800s, Continues Today," *Rough Notes,* December 1995, p. 30.

—D. H. O'Leary and Serena Kelly
—update: David E. Salamie

San Francisco Baseball Associates, L.P.

Pacific Bell Park
24 Willie Mays Plaza
San Francisco, California 94107
Telephone: (415) 972-2000
Fax: (415) 947-2800
Web site: http://sanfrancisco.giants.mlb.com

Private Company
Founded: 1883
Employees: 150
Sales: $142 million (2001)
NAIC: 711310 Promoters of Performing Arts, Sports, and
    Similar Events with Facilities; 448150 Clothing
    Accessories Stores.

San Francisco Baseball Associates, L.P. is the company that owns the San Francisco Giants, one of the most storied and successful teams in the history of baseball. Over nearly 125 years of history, they won 20 National League pennants and five World Series championships. The fabled players who have worn Giants colors include Willie Mays, John McGraw, Christy Mathewson, Carl Hubbell, Willie McCovey, Mel Ott, Bill Terry, Juan Marichal, and Frank Robinson. The team has also enjoyed a fair share of controversy over the years, particularly in relation to its decision to leave New York in the 1950s and its subsequent threats to abandon San Francisco. Long cursed to playing in one of the worst ballparks in the history of baseball, as the new century began the Giants moved into a sparkling new stadium that was christened in 2002 by their appearance in the World Series.

Giants' Golden Age: 1880–1960s

The San Francisco Giants trace their lineage back to a professional baseball team founded in Troy New York in the mid-1800s. In 1883, team co-owner John B. Day moved the organization to New York City. Nicknamed the "New York Gothams," the transplanted team was New York's first major league baseball team and began playing at the Polo Grounds. When Jim Mutrie, co-owner along with Day as well as the team's first great manager, began affectionately referring to the players as "my giants," the press and fans also adopted the name, and in 1885 the team was officially renamed.

The Giants were one of the most successful baseball teams anywhere, both financially and competitively. At the turn of the century, an outlaw league drove up player salaries, and the team was sold to Edward Talcott, who turned around and resold it a few years later to Andrew Freedman. By the time Freedman sold the team in 1902, he had hired the manager who for the next 30 years would be synonymous with the team: John J. McGraw. During the 30 years of McGraw's leadership, the Giants won seven pennants and three world championships. Freedman had sold the Giants to John Brush, who renovated the Polo Grounds, hired quality players, and made the team one of the finest in the game. Brush died suddenly in 1912. His family squabbled for years over the ownership of the Giants until in 1919 Charles A. Stoneham took over the team.

The Giants were entering their golden age. With McGraw at the helm and Stoneham spending freely for the best players in baseball, the Giants won four consecutive pennants from 1921 to 1924, including two world championships in 1921 and 1922. However, the Giants were already playing in the shadow of their crosstown rivals, the New York Yankees, then featuring the home run heroics of Babe Ruth. During the 1930s and 1940s, despite occasional pennants, the team began its inexorable slide toward the second division. By the end of World War II, even the Brooklyn Dodgers, once the perennial cellar-dweller of the Senior Circuit, were outdrawing the Giants. By the early 1950s, the Giants had the worst attendance of the three New York City baseball teams.

Meanwhile, San Francisco had been trying without success to get a major league team since the 1930s. It was clear San Francisco could support major league baseball—in 1946 its minor league team, the Seals, was drawing bigger crowds than some major league clubs. Anxious for a big league team, in 1954 the city's voters approved a bond measure for building a new stadium. The New York Giants seemed like the least likely candidate for a move west—the team was enjoying its last hurrah in New York City, beating the Cleveland Indians in the World Series that year. A year later, though, Horace Stoneham, who had inherited the team from his father, was looking to leave New York. Despite pennants in 1951 and 1955, Giants attendance continued to lag far behind that of the Yankees and Dodgers. By 1957, it had the worst attendance in the National League and the second-worst in the majors, a situation attributable in part to New York's three-team market, the decrepit condition of the Polo Grounds, and the decline of the neighborhood in which the stadium was located.

After trying in vain to interest the New York city fathers in building the team a new home, Stoneham made up his mind to leave New York. It was a time when major league baseball was on the move. Teams had left Boston, St. Louis, and Philadelphia for greener pastures—but all resettled east of the continental divide. The first to set his sights on the West Coast was Walter O'Malley, who announced in 1956 that he intended to move his Brooklyn Dodgers to Los Angeles. The entire National League realized that it would make more financial sense to have more than one team on the West Coast. Stoneham entered discussions with San Francisco's mayor, George Christopher. By May 1957, Christopher was convinced that baseball would be profitable in San Francisco and that the city would vote to construct a stadium that met the club's specifications. Stoneham agreed to the move. A complicated deal saw the Giants trade their Minneapolis AAA franchise to the Boston Red Sox for the Seals franchise and the rights to baseball in San Francisco. When Stoneham announced the move, some Giants fans in New York protested. In general, the Giants' move did not cause the outpouring of dismay and bitterness that the Dodgers' move occasioned.

The Giants played their first game in San Francisco on October 15, 1958, beating the Los Angeles Dodgers 8–0. The first two seasons were played in Seals Stadium, the city's old minor league park. In 1958, the city began construction of a much larger stadium on the southern edge of the city next to San Francisco Bay, building on land donated to the city by a local construction magnate on the condition that his company be allowed to build the structure. Construction was rushed into after only perfunctory site studies had been conducted—Stoneham and Mayor Christopher agreed to the site after a single visit at ten o'clock in the morning, when the weather was balmy and pleasant. After construction was well underway, however, the Giants' general manager made an inspection in the early afternoon. Surprised at the heavy winds howling around the half-finished building, he asked one of the workers, "Is it always like this?" "No, it doesn't start blowing like this until about one o'clock."

The new stadium, Candlestick Park, opened on April 12, 1960. By the end of its first season, it was clear to everyone that San Francisco had made a terrible mistake. The powerful, swirl-ing, icy cold winds that blew at the time when most games were being played turned routine pop-ups into home runs, made every fly ball an adventure for fielders, and caused spectators to shiver in their seats. At the first All-Star Game in San Francisco, a pitcher balked when the wind literally blew him off the mound in the middle of his delivery. The Giants installed heating for patrons in reserved seats, but it proved woefully inadequate. One disgusted season ticket holder, who claimed he missed much of each game because he had to leave his seat to get warm, sued the club and won the price of his ticket back. In 1972, stands were extended to enclose the outfield in an attempt to cut down the wind. It only made conditions worse. Over the next four decades the park would be the bane of baseball in San Francisco, despised equally by players and fans.

Problems in the 1970s–80s

Despite their disappointing new ballpark, the Giants were one of the most exciting teams of the 1960s. Sporting a line-up which over the course of the decade included the likes of Willie Mays, Orlando Cepeda, Willie McCovey, Juan Marichal. The Giants went to the World Series in 1961, won the Western Division title in 1971, and were contenders in 1959, 1964–66, and 1969. Starting in 1968, however, the Giants attendance was cut almost in half when an exciting Kansas City Athletics relocated to Oakland, just across the bay from San Francisco. By then, the Giants were usually out of National League contention. By the end of the 1975 season, Giants attendance was once again the worst in the National League. Exasperated, Horace Stoneham threatened to move the team back to the East Coast to Hackensack, New Jersey. He was entertaining offers for the team, one from a Japanese consortium and another from the Toronto, Canada-based Labatt Breweries, Ltd. In 1976, he accepted the Canadian's $13.25 million bid, sweetened by an extra $5.25 million to pay for any legal costs involved in breaking the lease at Candlestick when the team moved to Toronto.

George Moscone, the new mayor of San Francisco, fearful his administration would start with the loss of the city's baseball team, set out to find local investors interested in making a counteroffer. Bob Lurie, one of the Giants' directors, along with Bob Short and a group of other investors, put up $8 million for the team. Among the group's conditions was the renegotiation of the lease on Candlestick Park and the elimination of a 50 cent city tax on baseball tickets. The National League wanted baseball to stay in San Francisco and approved the sale to the local group. By 1978, after two years of internal conflict among the owners, Bob Lurie assumed sole ownership of the team.

The new owner took chances with the team and worked to build a winning club. It hired Frank Robinson as the National League's first black manager from 1981 until 1984. However, the front office's efforts did not alter the fundamental difficulty under which the team labored—that Candlestick Park was the most unpleasant park in major league baseball. Making matters worse, the Giants continued by and large to field losing teams. Fans stayed away. In 1984, the team had its worst finish since arriving in California. Lurie confronted his failing bottom line and decided to sell. The renewed prospect that the city might lose the Giants set the mayor and board of supervisors to work to find a way to save the team. It was clear to all involved that the main liability was Candlestick. Various stadium proposals were devel-

Key Dates:

1883: Troy Trojans move to New York City and become New York Gothams.

1885: The team officially assumes a new nickname, New York Giants.

1902: John McGraw becomes Giants manager.

1919: Charles Stoneham acquires the team.

1921: Giants win the first of two consecutive world championships.

1936: Horace Stoneham inherits the team when Charles Stoneham dies.

1957: Horace Stoneham moves New York Giants to San Francisco.

1960: Candlestick Park opens.

1968: Giants attendance is cut in half when Kansas City Athletics relocate to Oakland.

1975: Attendance at Giants games drops to the worst in the National League.

1976: Giants are sold for $8 million to a group led by Bob Short and Bob Lurie.

1981: Giants hire Frank Robinson as the first black manager in the National League.

1987: San Francisco voters reject a proposal to build a new downtown stadium.

1996: San Francisco voters approve a ballot measure to construct a downtown ballpark with private money.

2000: Pacific Bell Park opens.

2001: Giants' Barry Bonds breaks an all-time, single-season record by hitting 73 home runs.

oped: doming Candlestick, sharing the Oakland Coliseum with the Oakland A's, building a new downtown stadium, even developing a floating stadium on the waters of the bay.

Whatever solution was implemented, it seemed obvious at the time that such a stadium project could only be realized with public monies. However, if San Franciscans wanted to keep the Giants, they did not want to do it by spending their tax dollars on a new ballpark. In November 1989, a proposal to build a new park downtown was rejected by more than 11,000 votes. In reaction, owner Lurie told the *San Francisco Chronicle* he would move the team to "anyplace that wants us." Two years later, a much improved Giants team—still in San Francisco— won the National League pennant. As it headed for the World Series with Bay Area rival Oakland, a new ballpark initiative for a stadium on the downtown waterfront was on the ballot. Voter support for the measure seemed overwhelmingly strong leading up to the election. Then, as game three of the World Series was starting, the Loma Prieta earthquake struck. Abruptly rebuilding devastated areas of San Francisco assumed much higher priority than replacing the stadium that survived the quake. The measure was defeated by a razor thin margin of less than 1,800 votes.

Turmoil and a New Ballpark in the 1990s

Although Bob Lurie was desperate to find a way out of Candlestick, Major League Baseball was committed to keeping the Giants near San Francisco if not in the city. It would only give Lurie the go ahead to look for a new location in the Bay Area. His attempts to move the team to areas south of San Francisco twice failed, first in 1990, when Santa Clara County voted down a stadium measure, and again in January 1992, when voters in the city of San Jose rejected another stadium proposal. In the wake of the San Jose defeat, baseball commissioner Fay Vincent told Lurie he could move wherever he could find a buyer for the team. "I do not like teams moving," Vincent told the *San Francisco Chronicle*, "but in San Francisco, something has to be done. We cannot continue with Candlestick."

Lurie acted quickly. In August 1992, he announced that he had come to an agreement to sell to a group of investors in the Tampa Bay/St. Petersburg, Florida, area for $115 million. Although a Stanford University professor, J. Irving Grousbeck, announced that the team would be losing $10 million within two years if it stayed in Candlestick Park, San Francisco mayor Frank Jordan interested a consortium of local businesspeople, including Safeway grocery chain CEO and former Giants director Peter Magowan, which made an offer for the Giants. The group contacted National League president Bill White just before the League met to vote on the Florida offer. White, an ex-Giant himself, was deeply committed to seeing the Giants remain in San Francisco. On September 8, 1992, although Bob Lurie's agreement with the Florida group looked like a done deal, White announced he would allow the San Franciscans to enter a competitive bid. They offered $100 million for the team, an offer Lurie accepted and the National League approved. The embittered Florida group threatened a lawsuit which was headed off when the National League gave them an expansion team in 1993.

While the sale was in the offing, the Giants had completed the most valuable free agent signing in major league history when it offered Barry Bonds a six-year contract worth $43.7 million. When the National League held its fall meeting without putting the Giants sale on its agenda, though, outgoing owner Lurie refused to sign Bonds's contract, fearing he could be held responsible for paying Bonds. The League finally approved the sale in January 1993, after which Bonds was signed. He was one of the dominant players in the National League for rest of the decade and led the Giants to a pennant in 2002 and a division championship in 1997.

Once the sale went through, Peter Magowan quickly emerged as the senior partner who would be responsible for decision-making on the club. In March 1993, Magowan resigned as the CEO of the Safeway Inc. grocery store chain to devote himself full-time to running the Giants. He announced an effort to attract even more investors willing to put up at least $1 million to $5 million in order to pay of the loan taken out when the team was purchased. More crucially, he put his experience in retailing to work turning the Giants' business around. He improved the food and the service at Candlestick, lowered the price of tickets, and insisted that trash be collected before it could be caught in the park's gusty winds and blown onto the playing field. He added more day games to the schedule. By the middle of the 1993 season, the results were being felt. Giants attendance was increasing despite Candlestick. The millionth fan of 1993 entered the park in early June, the earliest point in the season that this had occurred in club history.

Attendance was not hurt by the fact that the Giants were thick in the pennant race until the last week of the season. The Giants under Magowan also worked hard to improve their image in the community. They sponsored the first AIDS awareness day in the major leagues, a Junior Giants Baseball League for inner-city kids, and a Roberto Clemente Latin American League targeted at Latino youth. The team also made players part of the outreach effort requiring them to take part in community events.

Despite the turnaround in the Giants' fortune, the club's owners never lost sight of the need to replace Candlestick Park. When the team changed hands, Mayor Frank Jordan had promised to do everything in his power to build a new park in time for the 1997 season, and to do it without public funds. It took longer than promised, but in December 1995 a proposal was announced to build a new 42,000-seat, baseball-only stadium in downtown San Francisco. Fifty-five percent of the costs would be paid from park operations. The rest was to come from the sale of the stadium's name, advertising, luxury boxes, and "permanent" rights to about 12,000 premium seats. The funding proposal cut to the heart of public objections to a new park in San Francisco. In March 1996, voters approved the measure by a two-thirds majority.

The go-ahead to build Pacific Bell Park, as the new stadium was named, sent the value of the Giants soaring. In November 1998, the estimated worth of the Giants was almost $200 million, nearly twice what was paid for the team. The appreciation in value came as a surprise to some. A handful of the original investors, including real estate tycoon Walter Shorenstein and securities broker Charles Schwab, sold out within the first couple years. Peter Magowan, on the other hand, had quietly doubled his holdings to 15 percent. Prospects for the future looked rosy as well. In 2000, when Pacific Bell Park finally opened, Magowan predicted that it would double Giants revenues to about $120 million a year. The intimate park somehow captured the beauty of the city. Fans sitting in seats in the infield had a view of San Francisco Bay. Spectators in the outfield had the nearby skyline of San Francisco spread out before them. In addition, there was the game on the field as well. The Giants played super baseball in Pac Bell Park. They ended 2000 with a division title and missed by just two games in 2001. In 2002, the team made it all the way to the World Series.

Principal Competitors

The Athletics Investment Group.

Further Reading

Allen, Lee. *The Giants and the Dodgers*, New York: G.P. Putnam's Sons, 1964.

Beckett, Jamie, "Magowan Bowing Out As Safeway's Chief," *San Francisco Chronicle*, March 9, 1993, p. A1.

Bitker, Steve. *The Original San Francisco Giants: The Giants of '58*, Champaign, Ill.: Sports Publishing, 1998.

Bondy, Flip, "Winds Of Change Welcome At Stick," *New York Daily News*, August 14, 1999, p. 44.

Carlsen, William, "Deal for Giants Wrapped Up," *San Francisco Chronicle*, September 5, 1992.

——, "How Giants Were Saved," *San Francisco Chronicle*, November 12, 1992, p. A1.

Dickey, Glenn, "The Stadium Realities Giants Must Face," *San Francisco Chronicle*, June 12, 1992.

Epstein, Edward, "Critics Sound Off on Giants' Plan For New Ballpark," *San Francisco Chronicle*, April 18, 1997.

"Giants Chronology" *San Francisco Chronicle*, November 11, 1992.

"A History Of The Giants' Stay In San Francisco," *San Francisco Chronicle*, August 8, 1992.

"I Sank the Giants Sale, White Says," *St. Petersburg Times*, April 28, 1994.

Kahn, Roger, *The Era: 1947–1957*, New York: Ticknot & Fields, 1993.

King, Joe, *The San Francisco Giants*, Englewood Cliffs, N.J.: Prentice-Hall, 1958.

Lowitt, Bruce, "A Rich History, from Coast to Coast," *St. Petersburg Times*, August 7, 1992.

Matier, Phillip, and Andrew Ross, "Giants Making All the Right Moves in Their Off-field PR Plays," *San Francisco Chronicle*, July 29, 1994, p. A17.

——, "Giants' New Game Plan," *San Francisco Chronicle*, December 20, 1995.

——, "Giants Trying to Cover All Bases in Ballpark Campaign," *San Francisco Chronicle*, December 22, 1995.

Nevius, C.W., "Peter Magowan—San Francisco's Field of Dreams," *San Francisco Chronicle*, December 7, 1997.

Nolte, Carl, "Giants' Fervor Electrifies S.F.," *San Francisco Chronicle*, March 31, 2000.

Roberts, Jerry, "What a New Stadium Would Mean for S.F.," *San Francisco Chronicle*, February 8, 1996.

Rosenbaum, Art, and Bob Stevens, *The Giants of San Francisco*, New York: Coward-McCann, 1963.

Sandalow, Marc, and April Lynch, "Giants To Stay," *San Francisco Chronicle*, November 11, 1992.

Schulman, Henry, "Magowan Says Pac Bell Park Will Stop Flood of Red Ink," *San Francisco Chronicle*, March 11, 2000.

Swartz, Jon, "Plan Should Pan Out for Gutsy Investors," *San Francisco Chronicle*, September 11, 1998, p. A15.

Sylvester, David A., and Carl Nolte, "San Jose Voters Reject Plan to Build Ballpark," *San Francisco Chronicle*, June 3, 1992, p. A1.

Thomas, Robert, "Yes, the Giants Do Know the Way to San Jose," *New York Times*, January 16, 1992.

Topkin, Marc, Thomas C. Tobin, and Alicia Caldwell, "San Francisco Is Allowed to Bid on Giants," *St. Petersburg Times*, September 10, 1992, p. 1A.

Williams, Peter, *When the Giants Were Giants*, Chapel Hill, N.C.: Algonquin, 1994.

—Gerald E. Brennan

◢SHV

SHV Holdings N.V.

Rijnkade 1
3511 LC Utrecht
The Netherlands
Telephone: (+31) 30-233-8833
Fax: (+31) 30-233-8304
Web site: http://www.shv.nl

Private Company
Incorporated: 1896 as Steenkolen Handels-Vereeniging
Employees: 30,900
Sales: EUR 9.4 billion ($9 billion)(2002)
NAIC: 551112 Offices of Other Holding Companies

SHV Holdings N.V. is one of the Netherlands' private vate companies. The family-owned concern serves a holding company for its interests in liquid petroleum gas, wholesale foods and consumer goods, private equity, recycling materials and products, and oil and gas exploration. Paris-based SHV Gas overseas the company's LPG interests, with operations in 23 countries, under the Primagaz, Calor, and other names. Makro represents the group's interests in the wholesale cash-and-carry market, focused on the Southeast Asian and South American markets (the company sold its European chain to Germany's Metro in the 1990s). NPM Capital is SHV's equity investment arm, with a focus on European venture capital investments. The company also owns one of the world's largest recycling businesses, through U.S.-based David J. Joseph Company and TSR, in Germany, formerly part of the Thyssen group. Lastly, SHV has been involved in the oil and gas exploration business off the Netherlands' coastline through Dyas, a ''non-operator'' that provides investment and partnership to other companies. SHV Holdings is owned by the Fentener van Vlissingen family, which remains committed to the company's privately owned status. The company's exposure to slumping South American currencies caused its sales to drop to EUR 9.4 billion in 2002 (from 10.4 billion in 2001).

Coal Cartel at the Turn of the Century

The Fentener van Vlissingen family was already one of the Netherlands' most prominent coal trading families when, together with eight other Dutch trading families, it formed the Steenkolen Handels-Vereeniging (''Coal Trading Association'') in Utrecht in 1896. A number of the original partners in SHV had been active in the coal trade since the 18th century. In addition to the formation of SHV, the families formed bonds through a number of marriages—this was the case, for example, between the Fentener van Vlissingen and van Beuningen families, which gained control of the SHV by the beginning of World War II.

In 1904, SHV acquired the exclusive trading rights for the coal produced by the Rheinisch-Westfälisches Kohlen Syndikat, which controlled the important Ruhr region coal production. Two years later, the SHV gained the exclusive rights to coal transports along the Netherlands' inland waterways, including the Rhine river, setting up the first of its subsidiary businesses to conduct those operations. SHV inland waterways fleet, later regrouped under the name Nederlandsche Rijnvaart Vereniging, grew into the world's largest by the 1950s.

Much of the growth of SHV came under the leadership of Frederik ''Frits'' Fentener van Vlissingen II, who joined the company in 1904 at the age of 22, taking over from his ailing father. By 1911, the younger Fentener van Vlissingen had been named the company's director. In that same year, Fentener van Vlissingen led the company in a new direction, setting up the Hollandsche Kunstzijde Industrie, a producer of synthetic fabrics, in part because the heavy coal consumption needed by that industry made the new company an important customer for SHV's coal interests. Financial backing for the Hollandsche Kunstzijde came from the German company Vereignigte Glanzstoff, which itself was owned by a member of the SHV partnership.

Under Fenterner van Vlissingen—later called one of the fathers of the Dutch economy—SHV established its own investment capital company, called Unitas, which provided funding for the creation of new companies. As such, SHV became the motor behind the establishment of such major Dutch companies as KLM, Hoogovens, Akzo, and the Nederlandsche Vliegtuigenfabriek, as well as Germany's Vereinigte Stahlwerke.

SHV grew strongly, adding offices in Rotterdam and Amsterdam; in 1913, the company transferred its headquarters to a new office in Utrecht, which was to remain the company's home into the 21st century. The Netherlands' neutral status during World War I enabled it to continue trading, particularly given its close ties with Germany's coal and other industries. In 1917, SHV, through Unitas, itself moved into mining in Germany, setting up Nemos (Netherlandsche Maatschappij tot Ontginning van de Steenkolenvelden) to operate the Sophia Jacoba anthracite mine. That operation led SHV, which had functioned primarily as an importer, to begin exporting coal as well. From its start in 1924, SHV's coal export operation grew to become one of the world's leaders in that market.

The rising importance of oil did not go unnoticed by SHV, however. By the late 1930s, the company had begun trading in that area as well, setting up a fuel facility; the company also took a majority share of the VEM (Verenigde Exploitatiemij) shipping company—a merger of three fishing companies—the trawler fleet of which became an early customer for SHV's oil. Nonetheless, SHV remained reliant on its coal interests into the 1950s, when the rising dominance of petroleum forced it to look elsewhere for its future growth. By then, the Fentener van Vlissingen family had bought out the share in SHV held by the van Beuningen family, becoming the company's sole owner.

Transforming in the 1970s

In adapting to the new market conditions, SHV showed a flexibility that was to become a company hallmark. By the end of the 1950s, SHV had embraced the oil industry, acquiring oil interests in Austria and Italy while building up an important oil bunker business. The company adopted a new trade name for its oil activities, PAM, under which SHV began selling petroleum products. SHV also built up a network of gasoline stations, which extended from the Netherlands into Germany and Austria, under the PAM name. In addition, under a joint venture,

Calpam, SHV began providing heating oil for the home and industrial markets in Belgium, Demark, and Luxembourg.

SHV's fuel interests soon turned toward a new type, however. A large natural gas deposit had been discovered in the Netherland's northern Groningen region at the end of the 1950s. In 1963, SHV set up a new subsidiary, Dyas—taken from the name given to the rock layer beneath which natural gas deposits were often found—to begin exploration activities. Dyas preferred the role of "non-operator," providing financial and other support services to its operator partners. One of the first of these was formed with Amoco and Gelsenkirchen (later Veba), which discovered its first gas deposit in the so-called Bergen Concession, near Amsterdam, in 1964.

That same year, Paul Fentener van Vlissingen joined the company, by then led by brother Frits Fentener van Vlissingen III. The younger Fentener van Vlissingen quickly showed himself an energetic leader and was largely credited with transforming the company after the collapse of the coal industry by leading it on a diversification drive.

This process began in earnest at the end of the 1960s. Electronics became an important new area of interest for SHV with the acquisition of Geveke & Groenpol NV in 1970. SHV split up Geveke & Groenpol into two operations. The first part took over the Geveke & Groenpol installation business, which was placed, alongside other acquisitions, including into a new subsidiary, Group Technical Installation, or GTI. Meanwhile, Geveke & Groenpol's sales and distribution operation were reformed under the name Groenpol Industriële Verkoop, which later became the basis of Geveke Electronics (later known as Getronics).

SHV's foray into electronics lasted only until the early 1980s, when it spun off GTI and Geveke in management buyouts by 1983. Instead, SHV had begun building a number of other growing operations. The first of these was the Makro wholesale cash-and-carry chain, which the company had launched, in partnership with Germany's Metro supermarket group, in 1968. Makro was inspired by the American example of self-service warehouse stores and opened its first branch in Amsterdam.

The concept caught on quickly, and Makro began expanding throughout the Netherlands, then throughout Europe, in conjunction with partner Metro. Makro also entered the South American market in the early 1970s. By the 1980s, Makro had entered the United States as well, although in 1988 SHV sold 51 percent of Makro Inc. to the Kmart Corporation. The success of the Makro concept encouraged SHV to try its hand at other retailing concepts, acquiring, in 1970, the Otto Reichelt chain—which was to form the company's largest retail operation into the mid-1990s—as well as the Netherlands formats Kijkshop and Xenos.

Another diversification area was recycling, which the company entered with the 1975 purchase of the David J. Joseph Company, which had stemmed from a company founded in Ohio in 1863 and which had grown into the largest scrap metal and recycling firm in the United States. At the same time, SHV began building a dry bulk transport and logistics wing, holding interests in such companies as Europees Massagoed Overslagbedrijf, EKOM, and Goudriaan & Co.

Key Dates:

1896: Eight Dutch coal-trading families join together to form Steenkolen Handels-Vereeniging (SHV).

1906: SHV gains an exclusive concession to imports of coal produced by the Rheinisch-Westfälisches Kohlen Syndikat.

1924: SHV begins coal exports, becoming one of the world's leaders in coal shipments.

1950s: The company sets up PAM oil company as the coal market shrinks.

1963: Dyas natural gas exploration company is established.

1968: Makro cash-and-carry chain is launched in partnership with Metro of Germany.

1970: Geveke & Groenpol electronics installation and distribution business is acquired.

1975: David J. Joseph Company of the United States, a scrap metal and recycling firm, is acquired.

1982: The company acquires stake in Primagaz of France.

1983: Geveke operations are spun off in management buyouts.

1987: The company begins acquiring a stake in Calor Gas of the United Kingdom.

1989: Makro enters Southeast Asia with its first stores in Thailand.

1996: SHV acquires full control of Calor Gas.

1997: SHV sells Makro Europe to Metro.

1998: The company acquires 60 percent of Thyssen's scrap metal operations, TSR.

1999: SHV acquires full control of Primagaz and TSR.

2000: SHV acquires NPM Venture Capital, a leading Netherlands' venture capital group.

2001: SHV sells off its last remaining coal trading operations.

2003: The company's sales drop EUR 9.4 billion for 2002.

Re-focusing for the New Century

By the end of the 1980s, SHV had found a new interest. In 1982, the company acquired a major share in France's Primagaz, which had been founded as Société Liotard Frères in 1857. In 1928, that company had the idea of bottling butane—which was a byproduct of the petroleum distillation process—and selling it to households and industries. By 1934, the company had adopted the brand name Primagaz, which became the company's name itself in 1938.

Primagaz had added propane in 1951, and then began an international expansion, spreading throughout most of Europe. The company also developed Liquid Petroleum Gas as a automotive fuel by the end of the 1970s, a market which began in earnest in the mid-1980s.

SHV continued to build up its stake in Primagaz. At the same time, it sought other acquisition targets. A major addition came in the mid-1980s when SHV began building a stake in the United Kingdom's Calor Gas. Formed in 1935, that company spread throughout the United Kingdom by the outbreak World War II. Calor grew strongly in the years following the war,

becoming the country's leading bottled gas provider; it met with more limited success in its own vehicle LPG operations.

SHV initially acquired a nearly 30 percent share in Calor Gas, becoming that company's largest shareholder. In 1987, the company attempted to force a merger between Calor Gas and Burmah Oil, a British oil company. That bid was rejected by Calor Gas, however. Instead, SHV continued to build up its position in Calor Gas, reaching 40 percent by 1988. SHV unsuccessfully tried to marry Burmah and Calor again at the end of the decade and finally gave up on this scheme in 1991.

Instead, SHV used its positions within Primagaz and Calor to take the two companies on an expansion drive into Eastern Europe, setting up partnerships in Poland and Slovakia in 1991 and in Hungary in 1992. SHV also entered the South American market, buying up Brazil's Supergasbras in 1995. Meanwhile, SHV continued to build its interest in Calor, gaining majority control; in 1996, SHV launched an offer to take over full control of Calor Gas. That deal was completed in 1997. Two years later, SHV acquired full control of Primagaz as well.

Makro too had continued to expand, opening its first branches in Southeast Asia in Thailand in 1989, followed by Indonesia in 1992, Malaysia in 1993, and China and the Philippines in 1996. Makro had also significantly expanded its presence in the Brazilian market, with 20 stores by 1990 and 40 stores by the beginning of the next decade.

Yet, faced with bruising competition in Europe, and hampered in its ability to compete by its private status, SHV decided to exit the cash-and-carry market in 1997, selling off its entire Makro Europe operation—by then posting sales of some $8 billion per year—to Germany's Metro. SHV kept its South American and Asian Makro operations. At the same time, the company, which had in the meantime built up a variety of other retailing interests, ranging from office supplies in Beligum to wholesale goods in South Africa, began divesting these operations as well.

Flush with cash from the Makro sale, SHV began eyeing new acquisition candidates. In 1998, the company purchased a 60 percent stake in the scrap metal operations of Germany's Thyssen group, which were renamed TSR. The following year, SHV took full control of TSR.

In 2000, SHV turned to another direction, buying up NPM Venture Capital Group, paying nearly EUR 2 billion for one of the largest venture capital companies in the Netherlands, a move made in part to allow SHV to enter the Internet and e-commerce markets. By 2001, SHV had rebuilt its annual revenues past EUR 10 billion. In that year, the company, which still maintained interests in coal trading, sold off the last of those operations. By the end of 2002, however, the company's exposure to fluctuations in South American currencies pushed its annual sales back to EUR 9.4 million. Nonetheless, SHV remained one of the Netherlands' largest—and most flexible—holding companies.

Principal Subsidiaries

Bizimgaz Ticaret Ve Sanayi A.S. (Turkey); Butan Plin d.d. (Slovenia); Calor Gas Ltd. (United Kingdom); Calor Gas Northern Ireland Ltd (Northern Ireland); Calor Teoranta (United Kingdom); Compagnie des Gaz de Pétrole Primagaz S.A.; CTA Makro Commercial Co., Ltd. (China); Dyas B.V.; Gaspol S.A. (Poland); Guangzhou Chia Tai Makro (JiaJing) Co. Ltd. (China); HKS Metals B.V. (Netherlands); Ipragaz A.S. (Turkey); Joseph Transportation Inc. (United States); Liquigas S.p.A. (Italy); Liquigaz Philippines Corporation (Philippines); Makro Asia Thailand ; Makro Atacadista S.A. (Brazil); Makro Cash & Carry Distribution (M) Sdn. Bhd. (Malaysia); Makro Comercializadora S.A. (Venezuela); Makro de Colombia S.A. (Colombia); Makro Office Centre Limited (Thailand); Makro Taiwan Ltd.; Minasgás S.A. Distribuidora de Gás Combustível (Brazil); Orkam Asia Holding AG (Switzerland); Orkam South America Holding AG (Switzerland); Pilipinas Makro, Inc. (Philippines); Primagas GmbH (Germany); Primagaz Belgium N.V.; Primagaz Central Europe GmbH (Austria); Primagaz Danmark A/S; Primagaz Distribución S.A. (Spain); Primagaz GmbH (Austria); Prímagáz Hungária Rt. (Hungary); Primagaz Nederland B.V.; Primaplyn Spol. s.r.o. (Czech Republic); Probugas a.s. (Slovakia); PT Makro Indonesia (Indonesia); SHV Energy India Ltd (India); SHV Energy Pakistan (Pvt) Ltd. (Pakistan); SHV Gas China (P.R. China); Siam Makro Public Company Limited (Thailand); Supergasbras Distribuidora de Gás S.A. (Brazil); Supermercados Mayoristas Makro S.A. (Argentina); The David J. Joseph Company (United States); Tissir Primagaz (Morocco); TSR Recycling GmbH & Co KG (Germany); World Gas (Thailand) Company Limited (Thailand).

Principal Competitors

Carrefour SA; Wal-Mart Stores, Inc.; TOTAL S.A.; CFF Recycling; Royal Dutch/Shell Group of Companies.

Further Reading

Brinks, Mirjam, "SHV hard op zoek naar uitbreidingsmogelijkheden," *De Telegraaf*, May 11, 2000.

Cramb, Gordon, "SHV to Diversify by Buying NPM Venture Capital Group," *Financial Times*, July 17, 2000, p. 24.

Harverson, Patrick, "SHV in Offer to Buy Rest of Calor," *Financial Times*, October 8, 1996, p. 21.

Smit, Barbara, "How to Put Passion into a Dutch Donkey," *European*, March 21, 1996, p. 25.

——, "Unravelling a Family Empire," *Financial Times*, July 21, 1997, p. 22.

—M. L. Cohen

Low Fat & Fat Free
Ice Cream

Silhouette Brands, Inc.

100 East Highway 34, Suite 113
Matawan, New Jersey 07747
U.S.A.
Telephone: (732) 583-3005
Web site: http://www.skinnycow.com

Public Company:
Incorporated: 1994
Sales: $65 million (2002 est.)
Stock Exchanges: OTC
Ticker Symbol: SIHB
NAIC: 31152 Ice Cream and Frozen Dessert
    Manufacturing

Silhouette Brands, Inc., is a Matawan, New Jersey-based manufacturer of fat-free novelty ice cream products sold under the "Skinny Cow" logo. The company's flagship product is its low-fat, ice cream sandwich, the only hand-made sandwich in the industry. According to Silhouette, hand-made ice cream offers better flavor retention because of its ability to be soft-served at higher temperatures. In addition, Silhouette offers Bongo bars, no-fat ice cream dipped in chocolate and served on a stick, low-fat and fat-free sundae cups, and fat-free fudge bars. Distributed by Dreyers Grade Ice Cream, Skinny Cow items are found in all 50 states and are available through some 150 supermarket chains in more than 18,000 stores.

Early 1990s Origins

Prior to devoting themselves to the low-fat ice cream business, co-founders Saverio Pugliese and Marc Wexler were involved in beer distribution and in the course of business came to know one another. Aside from beer, Pugliese also became involved in the low-calorie ice cream business, establishing a short-lived venture selling a product in the metropolitan New York market called Slender Delight. In the early 1990s, Pugliese attended a food show where he sampled a low-fat, low-calorie soft serve ice cream that he liked a great deal and became convinced that there was a market for it, despite the fact that years of disappointing diet ice creams and frozen yogurts

had disenchanted a large number of consumers and crippled the category. At first, he arranged to go into business with the formulator of the mix but soon carried on alone with nothing more than the basic formula and belief in the product. He then went to Horseman Dairies in Queens, New York, to refine his soft serve recipe. Several months later, he and Wexler became closer friends after attending the Kentucky Derby together. Wexler shared Pugliese's enthusiasm over the ice cream mix, and in 1992 the two men agreed to quit their jobs and go into the ice cream business full time. They scraped together $30,000 in funding, borrowing from banks as well as relatives, and began operating out of Wexler's Matawan home.

At first, Pugliese and Wexler's plan was to sell their soft-serve mix to ice cream and frozen yogurt shops, using the Silhouette brand name that the two men agreed upon. (For a graphic, they came up with a figurine that according to Pugliese looked like an "alien.") Borrowing a van from Pugliese's mother, the partners loaded up gallons of their mix and began to make cold calls at shops in the resort towns of the New Jersey Shore. The soft serve proved popular, and they slowly built up a solid base of customers in New Jersey and the New York metropolitan area. Nevertheless, the two men were still barely able to make a living. In order to expand beyond low-volume, mom-and-pop stores, they decided to develop and market a low-fat, low-calorie ice cream sandwich using their soft serve as a base. Through one of Wexler's contacts from his previous job, they were introduced to a small factory located in the Greenpoint section of Brooklyn that specialized in novelty ice cream products. Wexler and Pugliese, through trial and error and numerous taste tests, settled on the right combination of soft serve and low-fat chocolate wafers. Once satisfied that they had a good product to sell, they produced a supply of ice cream sandwiches, which at first they called The Silhouette Diet Ice Cream Sandwich, and once again loaded up Mrs. Pugliese's van, packed with dry ice, and began to make cold calls to delis and bodegas in the Upper West Side of Manhattan. Their pitch was simple: buy one case (six packages, with six sandwiches in each package), get one case free, no money up front, and the partners would return in a week to see if the items had sold. Invariably, the sandwiches did sell and the stores reordered.

348

Company Perspectives:

Silhoutte Brands is devoted to satisfying the desires of health conscious consumers by providing them with the best tasting, guilt-free alternatives available in the entire ice cream industry. We are dedicated to manufacturing the finest low-fat and fat-free ice cream items.

Silhouette Brands Incorporated in 1994

In conjunction with the launch of a new product, in January 1994 Silhouette Brands was incorporated in the State of Delaware, with Wexler serving as Chairman and Secretary and Pugliese as President and Director. Judging by how well the ice cream sandwich sold despite the lack of any promotion, Wexler and Pugliese knew they had a terrific product, but they were still relegated to selling to mom-and-pop outlets. From their days selling beer, they knew that the key was to gain entry into supermarkets. Sihouette's first major break in entering grocery channels came through a cousin of Pugliese who held a secretarial position with the Mel Weitz Food Towns 16-store, Long Island supermarket chain. She was able to arrange an appointment with the buyer, John Rowan, who was won over by the partners' offer of four cases for the price of two. According to Pugliese, he and Wexler made their first delivery of Skinny Cow sandwiches to a Mel Weitz store in his mother's beat-up van and were immediately intimidated by all the trucks of the major ice cream companies, a feeling only exacerbated when the sliding door of the van immediately fell off. Nevertheless, they made their initial delivery and took up as much shelf space as possible, much to the annoyance of the store manager. They may have lacked experience in the ways of supermarket distribution, yet three days later they were summoned to replenish the freezer case. Again, without promotion of any kind, in store or out, the sandwiches found eager consumers and were sold out.

While continuing to sell soft serve mix to yogurt and ice cream stores, Silhouette marketed its ice cream sandwiches for approximately two years before creating a logo to replace its crude ''alien'' graphic. The partners brainstormed for some time in search of a catchy name, and it was Wexler who was credited with coming up with the Skinny Cow name. In finding an appropriate graphic, the partners reworked its earlier figurine idea, which now turned into a thin cow wearing a bikini. It was ultimately refined into the company's current logo featuring a cow standing in a model's pose. During this same period of time, Silhouette was also able to gain entry into Key Food supermarket chains in Queens and Shop Rites and Dagastino's in the New York metropolitan area, as well as Food Towns in the southern part of New Jersey. When the company reached the point that it was selling more cases of sandwiches a week than Wexler and Pugliese could deliver in their aging van, it had to find an alternate means of distribution. Mattus Ice Cream took on the product and began placing Skinny Cow in a number of other New York metropolitan grocery chains: Waldbaums, A&P, Gristedes, and Associated. The number of cases sold each week grew to 500. A significant reason for the growth of the company was due to members of Weight Watchers who spread the word about Skinny Cow sandwiches, a two-point snack on the organization's point-counting diet system. The product developed a cult-like following among their dieters, creating word-of-mouth advertising that retailers can only dream about. To meet the growing demand for its products, Silhouette opened a small factory in Greenpoint.

The next major step in the development of Silhouette and expansion beyond the New York Metropolitan market was the move to a new distributor, Dreyer's Grand Ice Cream, Inc., one of America's top ice cream manufacturers and distributors. The switch to Dreyer's was not without consequence, as Silhouette was forced to pay a reslotting fee with a number of accounts in order to secure space in grocers' freezer cases. The resulting increase in sales, however, more than covered these initial costs. Sales immediately jumped from 500 cases a week to 2000 and in a short period of time increased to 10,000. In the meantime, Silhouette was entering new markets at a steady rate, carried by major supermarket chains around the country: Randalls in Texas, Farm Fresh in Virginia, and Jewel in Chicago. According to Pugliese, Dreyers was somewhat reluctant at first to aggressively push Skinny Cow into many of these markets and required some prompting from Silhouette's founders. The Weight Watcher's phenomenon continued to grow, fueled to a large degree by Internet discussion boards where Skinny Cow ice cream sandwiches were praised and all but revered. As Silhouette continued to add new customers at an accelerating clip, Dreyers became equally enthusiastic about expanding into new markets. Because its growth outstripped the production capacity of its Brooklyn plant, Silhouette entered into a co-packing arrangement in 1998 with Mr. Cookie Face, Inc., a Lakewood, New Jersey, maker of ice cream novelties that operated a state-of-the-art manufacturing plant. Silhouette's sandwiches were hand served, its Bongo bars hand dipped, and both hand packed by the manufacturer. Quality was maintained by weekly product tests conducted by Mr. Cookie Face personnel.

Annual sales grew from $600,000 in fiscal 1997 to $1.8 million in 1999 and more than $5.5 million in 2000. In the meantime, family members who had lent money to Wexler and Pugliese were repaid, a fact that Wexler told Newark's *The Star Ledger* he was especially proud of. To help support the growth of the business, Silhouette next began to develop a varied line of ice cream sandwiches, adding such traditional flavors as chocolate and strawberry, as well as coffee, mint, and chocolate-peanut. In 2000, Silhouette began to test market in New York a caramel flavored sandwich, ''Dulce De Leche.'' It also offered combination packs of chocolate and vanilla ice cream sandwiches, vanilla and coffee, vanilla and strawberry, and vanilla and mint. In addition, Silhouette developed and introduced entirely new ice cream novelty products. The first was the Bongo ice cream bar, launched in 1998, which came in two versions: vanilla ice cream dipped in reduced-fat milk chocolate and chocolate ice cream dipped in reduced-fat dark chocolate. The item was packaged three to a box. Bongo bars were so successful that in fiscal 1999 it accounted for roughly 28 percent of Silhouette's total sales.

Wal-Mart Distribution Deal in Early 2000s

In 2000, Silhouette entered into distribution deals with a number of major American supermarket chains, including Eagle Food Centers, Genuardi's Family Markets, H-E-Butt

Key Dates:

1992: Saverio Pugliese and Marc Wexler establish an ice cream business.

1994: Silhouette Brands incorporates; ice cream sandwich item is launched.

1998: A co-packing agreement is signed with Mr. Cookie Face.

2001: A distribution agreement signed with Wal-Mart Supercenters.

2002: Sundae cups and fudge bars are introduced.

Grocery Co., and Stop & Shop Supermarkets. By the end of the year, Skinny Cow products were sold in over 3,500 stores, and of that number some 2,100 were locations added in the year 2000 alone. In July 2001, the company announced its most important distribution agreement when it was authorized to sell its ice cream sandwiches to nearly 1,000 Wal-Mart Supercenters located throughout the country. Two months later, Dreyers was able to take Silhouette in depth into the Seattle market, gaining access to 115 Safeways, 79 QFC stores, 25 Brown and Cole Locations, and 21 Haggen stores. The year-end results for fiscal 2001 reflected Silhouette's rapid growth, with revenues increasing from $5.5 million in 2000 to more than $27.7 million in 2001, while net income increased from $129,218 to $433,658. Less successful during this period was the company's attempt to license its name for a store in Rockville Centre, named the ''Silhouette Café,'' with Wexler and Pugliese each owning a 25 percent stake in the business. The concept did not work and the store soon closed.

By the start of 2001, Silhouette's Skinny Cow products were found in 18,000 stores located throughout all 50 states, which represented a quantum leap over the 3,500 stores that distributed Silhouette just two years earlier. In spring 2002, the company launched two new products to further stimulate sales, which were already growing at an impressive rate. One was a four-ounce, fat-free ice cream chocolate fudge bar. The other was a five-ounce sundae cup, which came in low fat and fat free varieties and two flavors: vanilla ice cream with strawberry topping or chocolate ice cream with a chocolate fudge topping.

Business was so good for Silhouette in 2002, in the midst of a troubled economy, that sales more than doubled over the previous year, reaching $65 million. The company was now shipping 60,000 to 65,000 cases of its products each week. Moreover, the cases now carried twelve units instead of six, further emphasizing the company's rapid growth since the mid-1990s, when reaching weekly sales of 2,000 cases containing six units represented a major milestone.

Silhouette played a significant role in revitalizing the low-calorie, low-fat category of novelty ice cream products, which had suffered from years of poor tasting items on the market. Now larger, well financed companies were entering the sector with better products, poised to provide Silhouette with stiff competition. According to *Dairy Foods*, the frozen novelties category offered the greatest opportunity for growth in the frozen dessert market, worth in excess of $20 billion each year, of which 25 percent consisted of frozen novelties. With a solid brand and a strong presence in the marketplace, Silhouette appeared well positioned to continue its impressive growth. Innovation was the key to the future of the category, and the company was pursuing a number of new ideas. In 2003, it introduced single-pack ice cream sandwiches and single-pack fudge bars in the Walgreen's drug store chain. It was also looking to roll out a fat-free Cookies and Cream ice cream bar. From its early years, Silhouette had sold shirts, but now on its Web site it began to market other Skinny Cow branded merchandise, such as bags and coffee mugs. It was the development of new frozen novelty items, however, that would be the key to future growth. In an April 2003 interview, Pugliese talked about the possibility of a Skinny Cow milk shake but was reluctant to talk about any other products in the pipeline.

Principal Competitors

Nabisco Holdings Corp.; ConAgra Foods, Inc.; Unilever.

Further Reading

Hartnett, Michael, ''Consumers Scream for Healthy Ice Cream,'' *Frozen Food Age*, October 1, 2002, p. 1.

Lawlor, Julia, ''Small Business Keep New Jersey's Food Industry on the Front Burner,'' *Star Ledger*, October 27, 1999, p. 73.

—Ed Dinger

Staples, Inc.

500 Staples Drive
Framingham, Massachusetts 01702-4478
U.S.A.
Telephone: (508) 253-5000
Toll Free: (800) 813-1588
Fax: (508) 253-8989
Web site: http://www.staples.com

Public Company
Incorporated: 1985
Employees: 57,816
Sales: $11.6 billion (2002)
Stock Exchanges: NASDAQ
Ticker Symbol: SPLS
NAIC: 453210 Office Supplies and Stationery Stores;
454110 Electronic Shopping and Mail-Order Houses

Staples, Inc. is the country's largest operator of office supplies superstores, offering a vast selection of products at low prices, primarily to small business owners. Staples pioneered this concept in 1986 and grew rapidly after opening its first store in the Boston area. The company subsequently expanded to areas outside the Northeast; by the early 2000s, there were about 1,300 Staples outlets located both in major metropolitan areas and smaller markets in 45 states, the District of Columbia, and 10 Canadian provinces. In addition to the retail operations, the company runs a delivery business that encompasses catalog and Internet businesses under the Staples and Quill names, as well as contract stationery businesses, which deliver office supplies to medium-sized and large companies. Staples' European operations consist of nearly 200 retail outlets, under the Staples name in the United Kingdom and Germany and under the name Office Centre in the Netherlands and Portugal. The firm also runs a number of international mail-order office-products businesses: JPG and Bernard in France and Belgium, Kalamazoo in Spain, Neat Ideas in the United Kingdom, and MondOffice in Italy.

Pioneering the Office Supplies Superstore Concept: 1980s

Staples was founded in November 1985 by Thomas G. Stemberg and Leo Kahn, who had previously competed against each other in the Boston grocery market. Stemberg had worked in the New England food business since graduating from Harvard Business School in 1973. After his employer fired him in 1985 because of "philosophical differences," he used his year's worth of severance pay to explore other business opportunities.

Stemberg was interviewing for a job at a generalized warehouse club retailer when he noticed that the aisle featuring office supplies was in disarray, attesting to the popularity of the products, which moved quickly out of the store. When he learned that this small category of goods accounted for 7 percent of all warehouse store sales, Stemberg recognized a niche market that would provide him with the opportunity he wanted.

In formulating his concept for an office supplies warehouse, Stemberg drew on several demographic factors. As large corporations cut their workforces, small businesses were taking up the slack in the American economy, signaling a quickly expanding, lucrative market. In addition, the service sector of the economy was growing rapidly, and such businesses typically used a good deal of office supplies.

Stemberg's plan called for the elimination of the middleman in office supply distribution. Traditionally, manufacturers of paper and other items sold their goods to one of six major wholesalers around the country. The wholesalers then sold their goods to office supply dealers and stationery stores. The dealers sold supplies to large corporations, while stationers catered to small businesses and individuals. Along the way, however, the two layers of middlemen between the factory and the customer drove up costs dramatically.

With his Staples store, as he planned to call the outlet, Stemberg would collapse those two layers into one. Because supplies would be purchased directly from manufacturers, the store would be able to offer much lower prices than its competitors in the heavily fragmented retail environment. Stemberg hoped with this idea to gain a portion of the office supply market significant enough to justify purchasing in bulk. Stemberg expected that imitators would quickly copy his idea if it proved successful, so he set out to raise a large amount of capital to finance his company, hoping to expand Staples rapidly after its start-up and avoid losing ground to its competitors.

To do so, Stemberg approached his old nemesis Kahn, who invested $500,000. In addition, Stemberg made presentations to venture capitalists in the Boston area and was met with an enthusiastic response. In the first round of financing, the company raised $4 million. With this money, Stemberg set out to recruit a management team. Looking for people who shared his philosophy of how to run a business, he sought out those with a similar background, bringing in people who had worked at the same national grocery chain that he had. By the spring of 1986 everything was in place.

The first Staples Office Superstore opened its doors in May at 1660 Soldiers Field Road in Brighton, Massachusetts, a suburb of Boston. Consisting of one vast, open 14,000-square-foot space, the Staples store had a typical warehouse decor, with concrete floors and an unfinished ceiling. A huge array of goods was stacked on metal shelves, and shopping carts were provided for customers at the front. More than 40 workers were deployed to ring up sales at six cash registers. In an effort to provide customers with one-stop shopping, the store stocked everything that could conceivably be used in an office, from paper and pens, to office furniture, to microwave ovens. Most products were offered at a price half as low as that of Staples' competitors.

To drum up business, Staples gift certificates were sent to 35 local small business office managers, who would be surveyed on their reactions to the store when they made a purchase. After five weeks, only nine of the certificates had been redeemed, and Stemberg learned that he had a sizable marketing task ahead of him.

The marketing push began with an effort to differentiate Staples from other stationery outlets, in order to draw the company's targeted customers into the store. The company invested more than $1 million in several linked minicomputers and a staff of three computer programmers and began amassing a database of small businesses. The database became part of a sophisticated multistep marketing program. Through telemarketing, Staples identified customers and enticed them into the stores. The profiles and buying habits of customers then became part of an extended database, enabling Staples to offer special discounts and encourage repeat business. With these strategies, Staples was able to begin building a solid customer base. In November 1986 the company opened its second store in

Woburn, Massachusetts, another suburb of Boston. A third location emerged in Providence, Rhode Island, the following year, and the company began to plan for its expansion into the New York area.

As Staples broadened its geographical scope throughout the Northeast, the company decided to invest in a centralized distribution facility. Rents tended to be high in the crowded urban areas where Staples stores were located, and the company hoped that this move would allow it to offer a fuller selection in smaller facilities because fewer products would have to be stockpiled onsite at each location. With the distribution center, the company believed that it could replenish its shelves faster than competitors who had to rely on manufacturers for supplies. In addition, the central depot cut down on freight costs, as manufacturers were able to ship large amounts of goods to one location. It also kept payroll costs low. Staples began work on its 136,000-square-foot processing and distribution center in Putnam, Connecticut, in 1987. The decision to proceed with this project aroused controversy among Staples' management because the investment meant that the company would postpone becoming profitable for an even longer period of time.

Late 1980s: Expanding Throughout Northeast, Going Public

In June 1987 Staples made its first foray into the New York market, opening a store in Port Chester. By the end of the year the company had opened a total of nine stores that were clumped in the New York and metropolitan Boston areas. The following year Staples moved into the other major East Coast markets of Philadelphia and Washington, D.C. This was done in conjunction with the opening of the $6 million distribution center.

In the winter of 1988, Staples stepped up its marketing efforts by sending potential customers a special catalog, with a coupon promising a free pen and pencil set with a purchase of $10 or more. Of those who redeemed this offer, company data indicated that more than half would return to make future purchases.

By May 1988 Staples had opened 16 stores, and the company's revenues had risen to $40 million. In its rapid Northeastern expansion, the company sought to lock up prime retail locations throughout the region so that competitors would have difficulty establishing their own stores. To support this rapid growth, Staples solicited three more rounds of financing from the investment banking community, raising a total of $32 million.

The number of Staples stores had grown to 23 by the beginning of 1989. Whenever Staples opened a new store, the company bought a list of all the small businesses located within a 15-minute drive of the outlet. Buyers of office supplies from these firms were then contacted by telemarketers who announced the store's opening and garnered data about the buyers' purchasing habits. In return they received a coupon for free copy paper that would hopefully bring them into the store and spur word-of-mouth advertising.

In addition, the company offered customers a free Staples card that offered discounts on goods purchased. When customers filled out a card application, the company got data about the nature of their businesses. The numeric code on the card also

Key Dates:

1985: Thomas G. Stemberg and Leo Kahn found Staples, Inc.

1986: Founders open the first Staples store—the first office supplies superstore—in Brighton, Massachusetts.

1989: Company raises $37 million through an initial public offering.

1990: First stores in California are opened.

1991: Company establishes first non-U.S. venture, an investment in Canadian office superstore The Business Depot, Ltd.

1992: Staples enters the European market for the first time.

1996: Staples enters into agreement to acquire archrival Office Depot.

1997: Merger with Office Depot is blocked on antitrust grounds.

1998: Quill Corporation is acquired; staples.com is launched.

2002: Staples acquires Medical Arts Press, Inc. and the European mail-order businesses of Guilbert S.A.

enabled Staples to track their purchases precisely. All of this information was collated at the company's headquarters on a daily basis.

In February 1989 Staples introduced its Private Label products—generic office supplies at exceptionally low prices. This strategy was one that Stemberg had first implemented in the grocery business, when he introduced company-label groceries for Star Markets. In April Staples sold stock to the public for the first time, raising $37 million to fund its further expansion. By the end of that month, the company's sales had reached $120 million. Despite this strong growth in revenue, Staples had yet to make any earnings, although the company did turn in its first profitable quarter at the end of January 1989. Overall, losses since Staples' founding had reached $14.1 million.

These losses were caused by the high cost of the company's start-up and expansion as well as the strong competition the company faced. As Stemberg had predicted, Staples had quickly been joined in the office supplies market by a host of imitators around the country. In mid-1989 the company slipped to second place in revenues behind Office Depot Incorporated; Office Club was making a strong showing in California; and retail giants Kmart and Ames were also deliberating a move into the stationery field. To counter these threats, Staples continued its rapid pace of new store openings. By the end of the year the company was operating 38 stores, and it had racked up sales of $182 million.

Early 1990s: Further Growth

Building on these gains, the following year Staples moved to centralize its Northeast delivery operations through a hub-and-spoke system set up with its Putnam facility at the center. This warehouse was augmented with a 32,000-square-foot delivery distribution center. The new system allowed Staples to set up a

toll-free line for orders, which were then shipped for delivery the next day. The operation was dubbed Staples Direct.

In July 1990 the company also commenced operations in a new market, southern California. Staples made its inroad into this competitive field with three stores located in Orange County, California, and a separate California distribution facility. Staples had targeted Orange County because of its high number of small businesses and growing economy, viewing its move into this area as the first step of a planned 34-store California roll-out.

Staples followed its West Coast expansion with the introduction of a new retail concept, called Staples Express. The first of these stores was opened on Court Street in the heart of Boston's financial district. With a space only a third as large as the company's suburban stores, this facility stocked 2,700 items, or half of the usual complement, which were sold at the same low prices. Staples Express was designed to appeal to the small business operator in an urban area and was geared to quick trips and impulse buying on lunch hours and after work. Customer purchases were typically small, being no bigger than what a person could carry.

The unveiling of this prototype was part of the company's strategy to dominate the office supplies market through three distribution channels: the suburban superstore, the urban mini-store, and phone-in direct delivery service. Also in 1990 Staples began to buy its products overseas. To conduct international buying the company formed a subsidiary called Total Global Sourcing, Inc.

By the end of the year, the number of Staples stores had doubled to 74, including nine in California, and the company's sales had nearly reached the $300 million mark. Staples accelerated its California operations the next year when it bought ten Los Angeles stores from defunct superstore operator HQ Office Supplies Warehouse and converted them to Staples stores.

At the same time, Staples entered its first foreign venture, investing in The Business Depot, Ltd., a new Canadian office superstore. In the United States, Staples celebrated the opening of its 100th store, an outlet on Long Island in New York. By the end of the year, sales had risen 83 percent to reach $547 million, and earnings grew by 117 percent.

In June 1992 Staples expanded into another region of the United States with the purchase of Office Mart Holdings Corporation for $3.1 million. This company owned ten WORKplace stores in Florida. Staples had now moved into direct competition with its biggest rival, Florida-based Office Depot.

That year Staples made additional progress in its campaign to expand overseas. The company bought a 48 percent interest in MAXI-Papier, operators of five office superstores in cities around Germany. Staples also signed a partnership agreement with Kingfisher plc to open office superstores in the United Kingdom. Sales at the end of 1992 reached $883 million. In 1993 Staples celebrated the opening of its 200th store, and at that time the company announced plans for an additional 130 store openings over the next two years.

This ambitious schedule was set despite fluctuations in the price of Staples' stock. Wall Street had lost confidence in the company in early 1993 after Staples' two largest rivals embarked upon a rapid string of acquisitions, while Staples demonstrated difficulty rolling out a new line of personal computer products. To redress these problems, Staples pared down the number of machines and software programs it offered, to create a more manageable department. In addition, the company began to make a number of acquisitions of its own. Staples arranged to buy out its Canadian partner in The Business Depot for $32 million in early 1994. The company also signed agreements to buy two contract stationers: New Jersey-based National Office Supply Company, for $99 million; and Spectrum Office Products, of New York, for $23 million. The former company boasted a nationwide distribution system.

Mid-1990s: Still Growing, Despite Blocked Merger with Office Depot

In April 1994 Staples bought seven former Office America stores in Virginia, Arizona, and Kentucky and began to convert them to Staples outlets. In July, the company announced that it would buy D.A. MacIsaac, Inc., a regional contract office supplier, for $15 million. A fourth contract stationer, Philadelphia Stationers, was later bought for $14 million. These moves were all designed to increase Staples' size and penetration of the office supplies business, and they helped the company's revenues surpass the $2 billion mark for the fiscal year ending in January 1995.

Staples next launched a two-year, $240 million program to open an additional 170 new stores, entering still more new markets in the process, and to refurbish all of its existing outlets. The remodeling effort featured wider aisles, bigger in-store signs, and improved lighting. The company also launched a new advertising campaign in 1995, one that featured the tag line "Yeah, we've got that"; the ads, which captured several advertising awards, ran through early 2003. In the meantime, the latest expansion pushed 1995 sales past $3 billion, making Staples only the sixth company in U.S. history to reach that mark within ten years of its founding. The following year the firm opened its 500th store. Also in 1996, Staples bought out its partner in the U.K. and German ventures, Kingfisher, in a £29.4 million deal. By this time there were 34 Staples outlets in the United Kingdom; the MAXI-Papier stores in Germany were subsequently rebranded under the Staples name.

In the boldest move yet in its brief history, Staples reached an agreement in September 1996 to acquire its main rival, Office Depot, for $3.36 billion in stock. The deal had the potential to create the dominant player in the office-supply superstore sector, with 1,100 stores and annual revenues in excess of $10 billion—far eclipsing what would be the number two player, OfficeMax, Inc., which had about 500 stores and sales of just over $3 billion. In an attempt to head off antitrust objections, Stemberg and other officials from Staples and Office Depot tried to emphasize that the superstores did not just compete against each other—they also competed with mass marketers such as Wal-Mart Stores, Inc., warehouse clubs, direct marketers, and others. The Federal Trade Commission (FTC), however, did not buy this argument, with the agency's chief concern being that the merger would significantly reduce competition in a number of markets where the two firms were competitors, leading to price increases as high as 10 percent. The FTC voted to block the deal in March 1997 and one month later rejected the deal again after Staples had reached an agreement to sell 63 stores to OfficeMax. The FTC then sued to stop the deal, and in late June a federal judge granted a preliminary injunction to block the transaction. At this point, Staples and Office Depot abandoned their merger plans, conceding defeat.

Late 1990s: Surpassing the 1,000-Store Mark

In the wake of this setback, Staples lost no time in reasserting its position as the office supplies superstore growth leader. During 1997 the company opened 128 new stores in North America, bringing its store total to more than 740. Revenues for the year topped $5 billion, making Staples the seventh company in U.S. history to reach that mark in a dozen years of operation or fewer. The expansion pace quickened in 1998, as 174 more stores made their debuts. That year, Staples also acquired Quill Corporation for about $685 million in cash and stock as part of its effort to expand beyond retail outlets. The privately held Quill, based in Lincolnshire, Illinois, was a seller of office supplies via catalog and through direct (or "contract") sales to businesses. Quill, which had 1997 revenues of $555 million, continued to operate independently as a Staples subsidiary. Other important developments in 1998 included the launching of the Staples online retail store, staples.com, and the promotion of Ronald L. Sargent from president of North American operations to president and COO of Staples (Stemberg continued to serve as chairman and CEO).

Staples' European operations were bolstered considerably in 1999 with the acquisitions of three companies: Sigma Burowelt of Germany, Office Centre of the Netherlands, and Office Centre of Portugal. Sigma Burowelt operated 15 office supply stores; these were subsequently rebranded under the Staples name, increasing the total in Germany to 41. There were 21 Office Centre outlets in the Netherlands and five in Portugal, as Staples entered those two markets for the first time. The Office Centre stores were conceptually different from the typical Staples outlet—they had more of a business-oriented membership format and were similar to warehouse clubs in the United States. Overall, Staples now had about 120 European stores. Later in 1999 the company opened its 1,000th store worldwide, becoming the first office supplies superstore retailer to do so. Also, the Staples Center opened in Los Angeles that year as the new arena home for the Lakers professional basketball team and the Kings professional hockey team. In this corporate sponsorship deal, Staples, Inc. agreed to pay $100 million over a 20-year period. In the fall of 1999 Staples created a tracking stock for its Internet operations and began selling shares in the stock in private transactions.

Early 2000s: Competing in Uncertain Times

After a remarkably and consistently successful performance since its founding—sales and earnings had increased 30 percent per year for 12 years—Staples finally ran into trouble in the early 2000s. During the latter months of 2000, the retail market for office supplies began foundering. The boom years of the 1990s were over, and the growth of small businesses and home offices—the core of Staples' customer base—was fading away.

Early in 2000 the company announced plans to sell its Internet tracking stock through an initial public offering (IPO), but the bursting of the stock market bubble soon thereafter forced Staples to abandon this plan (the tracking stock was later converted into Staples stock). Furthermore, the firm had made a number of investments in various Internet services that were offered through its web site, which proved to be a money-losing strategy. Staples announced in January 2001 that it would take a $206 million writeoff related to various web investments. As a result, net income for fiscal 2000 totaled just $59.7 million, compared to $315 million for the previous year, although revenues increased 19 percent and surpassed the $10 billion plateau for the first time. Later in 2001, the Internet operations were merged into Staples Direct, the company's thriving catalog unit.

In February 2002 Sargent was promoted to president and CEO, while Stemberg remained chairman. Sargent was charged with leading Staples through its transition from a growth-oriented young retail firm to a more mature company competing in an industry dealing with an increasingly saturated U.S. market. Changes began almost immediately. In March 2002 Staples announced a plan to close 31 underperforming stores, most of which were located in small towns, taking a charge of $50.1 million in the process. The company also considerably slowed its pace of expansion, opening just 72 new stores in North America and 14 in Europe during fiscal 2002, compared to 117 and 19, respectively, the prior year. Furthermore, expansion into new markets was curtailed as well. Many of the new outlets were located in large metropolitan areas where Staples already had a presence. The company also launched a remodeling effort, converting a significant number of stores from the original warehouse design to more of a boutique look, with an open design and lower shelves—all aimed at making it easier and faster for customers to find what they were looking for. The new format was supported through an advertising campaign, launched in early 2003, featuring the new slogan, "That was easy." Finally, under Sargent, Staples eliminated hundreds of items from the store shelves as it sought to shift the chain's focus away from casual shoppers toward small businesses and what were termed "power users." The latter were defined as customers who purchased more than $500 per year of office supplies, and such customers included home-based businesses, persons with home offices, and teachers. Small businesses and power users accounted for 70 percent of Staples' revenues and fully 90 percent of profits.

While overhauling its core North American retailing operations, Staples was also completing acquisitions at home and abroad. The company looked to purchase delivery-based businesses, which tended to have higher profit margins than retailing operations. In July 2002 Staples bought Medical Arts Press, Inc. (MAP) for $383.2 million. Based in Minneapolis with 2001 revenues of $168 million, MAP was a direct marketer of specialized printed office products and practice-related supplies to healthcare offices. MAP became a division of Quill Corporation. Staples in October 2002 spent EUR 806 million (US$788 million) for the European mail-order businesses of Guilbert S.A., a subsidiary of Pinault-Printemps-Redoute S.A. of France. The operations gained through this deal had revenues of about $425 million in 2001, and they sold office supplies and furniture via catalogs and Internet web sites to small businesses under several brands: JPG and Bernard in France and Belgium, Kala-

mazoo in Spain, Neat Ideas in the United Kingdom, and MondOffice in Italy.

Early indications were that Staples' various strategy shifts were paying off. Despite the continuing economic downturn in the United States, Staples managed to post an 8 percent increase in fiscal 2002 sales to $11.6 billion—a jump that enabled the company for the first time to surpass rival Office Depot (which reported 2002 revenues of $11.4 billion). Net income was a record $446.1 million. Staples planned to continue its more modest pace of expansion, opening between 75 and 90 stores in North America during 2003. Another 20 stores were slated to open in Europe that year, including the expansion of the Office Centre concept into Belgium. It appeared that Staples had gotten past the rough patch it encountered earlier in the decade and was ready to enter a new period of industry-leading growth.

Principal Subsidiaries

Hayes Marketing, Inc.; Medical Arts Press, Inc.; Quill Corporation; Smilemakers, Inc.; JPG Benelux SPRL (Belgium); The Business Depot, Ltd. (Canada); JPG SA (France); Reliable France SA; Bernard SA (France); Staples (Deutschland) GmbH (Germany); Mondoffice Srl (Italy); Business Office Supply B.V. (Netherlands); Staples Netherlands B.V.; Sistemas Kalamazoo SA (Spain); Neat Ideas Limited (U.K.); Staples UK Limited.

Principal Operating Units

North American Retail; North American Delivery; European Operations.

Principal Competitors

Office Depot, Inc.; OfficeMax, Inc.; Buhrmann N.V.

Further Reading

Bailey, Steve, and Steven Syre, "It's His Party: Stemberg Marks Down Nasella's Role As Staples Celebrates 10th," *Boston Globe,* April 26, 1996, p. 89.

Barrier, Michael, "Tom Stemberg Calls the Office," *Nation's Business,* July 1990, pp. 42+.

Brumback, Nancy, "New Retailer, Staples, Out to Build Mass Chain of 'Office Superstores,' " *HFD—The Weekly Home Furnishings Newspaper,* December 28, 1987, pp. 57+.

Charm, Robert E., "Thomas G. Stemberg of Staples, Inc.," *New England Business,* May 2, 1988, pp. 17+.

Einhorn, Cheryl Strauss, "Paper Chase," *Barron's,* March 27, 1995, pp. 15–16.

Facenda, Vanessa L., "Staples Writes a New Plan," *Discount Merchandiser,* November 1999, pp. 95+.

Gupta, Udayan, "Retail Start-Up Decides to Start Out Big," *Wall Street Journal,* May 14, 1987.

Hemp, Paul, "Staples Plans a Frontal Assault on the British Market," *Boston Globe,* January 12, 1993, p. 39.

Hirsch, James S., and Eleena de Lisser, "Staples to Acquire Archrival Office Depot," *Wall Street Journal,* September 5, 1996, p. A3.

Hyatt, Josh, "Staples: Gutsy and Growing," *Boston Globe,* June 9, 1992, p. 55.

Klebnikov, Paul, "Hair of the Dog," *Forbes,* April 16, 2001, pp. 74+.

Lanctot, Roger C., "Staples: Homing in on Office Superstores," *HFD—The Weekly Home Furnishings Newspaper,* April 25, 1988, pp. 1+.

Liebeck, Laura, "Staples Plans for Growth," *Discount Store News,* June 22, 1998, pp. 1, 60.

McConville, James A., "Fla. Retail Showdown Looms," *HFD—The Weekly Home Furnishings Newspaper,* March 9, 1992, pp. 73+.

——, "Staples Head Still Sees Growth," *HFD—The Weekly Home Furnishings Newspaper,* October 18, 1993, pp. 103+.

——, "Staples Targets Urban Niche," *HFD—The Weekly Home Furnishings Newspaper,* October 22, 1990, pp. 149+.

McLaughlin, Mark, " 'Category Killer' Office Superstore Uses Blitzkrieg Retailing Approach," *New England Business,* August 4, 1986, pp. 41+.

Miller, Paul, and Shannon Oberndorf, "Staples Buys Quill Corp.," *Catalog Age,* May 1998, pp. 1, 36.

Pereira, Joseph, "Staples Inc. Pulls Back on Its Store-Expansion Plans," *Wall Street Journal,* March 13, 2002, p. B4.

——, "Staples's Shift Boosts Profit," *Wall Street Journal,* March 5, 2003, p. B2.

Savini, Gloria, "Where the Pens Are," *Direct Marketing,* August 1988, pp. 82+.

Selz, Michael, "Office Supply Firms Take Different Paths to Success," *Wall Street Journal,* May 30, 1991, p. B2.

Solomon, Stephen D., "Born to Be Big," *Inc.,* June 1989, pp. 94+.

Stemberg, Tom, "Staples Sets Pace," *Discount Merchandiser,* March 1988, pp. 66+.

Story, Louise, "Staples Expands European Business," *Boston Globe,* August 23, 2002, p. D1.

Strauss, Lawrence, "Back to Business with Staples," *Barron's,* November 18, 2002, p. T8.

Suskind, Ron, "Staples Reacts to a Large New Rival with Confidence," *Wall Street Journal,* December 21, 1992, p. B4.

Teitell, Beth, "Office Supply Supermarkets: A Future Staple?" *Boston Business Journal,* March 17, 1986.

Wilke, John R., and Joseph Pereira, "Office Depot, Staples Deal Is Blocked," *Wall Street Journal,* July 1, 1997, p. A3.

—Elizabeth Rourke
—update: David E. Salamie

Stonyfield Farm, Inc.

10 Burton Drive
Londonderry, New Hampshire 03053
U.S.A.
Telephone: (603} 437-4040
Fax: (603) 437-7594
Toll Free: (800) 776-2697
Web site: http://www.stonyfield.com

Private Company
Incorporated: 1983
Employees: 170
Sales: $90 million (2002)
NAIC: 115200 Manufacturing of All-Natural and Certified
    Organic Yogurt, Ice Cream, and Tofu Products

Stonyfield Farm, Inc., a privately held company based in Londonderry, New Hampshire, is the nation's largest and fastest-growing organic yogurt company. Stonyfield Farm manufactures all-natural and certified organic yogurt, ice cream, and soy products that are distributed nationwide; it is the only leading yogurt company to incorporate six live, active cultures in its products; it ranks first for yogurt sales in natural food stores and fourth for sales in grocery stores. Stonyfield Farm also leads numerous environmental education programs for children and adults. The company was America's first dairy processor to pay farmers for refraining to treat cows with the synthetic bovine growth hormone known as rBGH. Each year, to promote sustainable agricultural practices, the company awards grants to the farmers who produce the organic milk used for its products.

1940–82: Organic History and Company Origins

Development of the organic industry was in large part a reaction to the devastation caused in the 1940s by the use of synthetic pesticides and herbicides in agriculture. Chemical biocides were so effective in destroying foliage and disease-bearing insects that "they were used during World War II to protect troops from malaria," according to Stonyfield Farm's booklet *A Practical Guide to Understanding Organic.* Farmers

and other producers were so impressed by the wartime success of the new technology that they rushed to profligate use of biocides. The emergence of more resistant strains of insects and weeds brought about the use of more powerful chemicals resulting in the destruction of much wildlife and the degradation of formerly healthy ecosystems. "Pesticide use in the United States increased ten-fold from 1945 to 1989, yet total crop loss from pests nearly doubled in that period from 7 percent to 13 percent," according to *A Practical Guide.*

Fortunately, information about the relationship of healthy soil, healthy food, and healthy people began to surface with suggestions for repairing the ongoing damage. For example, in 1922, Austria's Dr. Rudolf Steiner introduced biodynamic farming, a practice that avoided all forms of biocides and consisted in working with the energies that create and maintain life. In America, J.I. Rodale's experiment with methods of growing organic food resulted in his 1947 establishment of the Soil and Health Foundation, forerunner of The Rodale Institute—a worldwide organization dedicated to bringing about a regenerative food system that renewed environmental and human health. In 1962 Rachel Carson published *Silent Spring,* a seminal book in which she emphasized the hazards of chemical agriculture, initiated the move to ban DDT, and spurred revolutionary changes in laws affecting our air, land, and water. In Brooklyn, New York, Samuel Kaymen studied biodynamic agriculture and was active in regional groups that advocated pesticide control and soil conservation; he established the Northeast Organic Farmers Association.

In 1971, Kaymen and his wife Louise founded The Rural Education Center (TREC) as a nonprofit organization in Wilton, New Hampshire. By teaching rural and homesteading skills with an emphasis on organic food production, the Kaymens wanted to revitalize the struggling New England dairy industry and halt the decline of family farms. Their long-range goal was to produce healthy yogurt and educate consumers about the ways business and industry could be both financially and environmentally successful.

In 1982 Samuel invited New Hampshire-native Gary Hirshberg to join TREC's board of trustees. Hirshberg had channeled his passion for safeguarding the environment into

Company Perspectives:

Stonyfield Farm's five-fold mission is: to provide the very highest quality, best-tasting all natural and certified organic products; to educate consumers and producers about the value of protecting the environment and of supporting family farmers and sustainable farming methods; to serve as a model that environmentally and socially responsible businesses can also be profitable; to provide a healthful, productive, and enjoyable work place for all employees—with opportunities to gain new skills and advance personal career goals; to recognize our obligations to stockholders and lenders by providing an excellent return on their investment.

working as a water-pumping specialist and then joining the nonprofit ecological advocacy group known as the New Alchemy Institute, dedicated to spreading information about organic agriculture, aquaculture, and renewable energy systems. However, a 1982 visit to Disney World's Epcot Center modified Hirshberg's thoughts about the role a nonprofit enterprise could play in educating the public about environmental issues.

In a 1999 interview, Hirshberg told writer Courtney Claire Brigham of Londonderry's *Eagle-Tribune* that at Epcot he saw 25,000 people walking through the Kraft artificial cheese exhibit. Struck by the daily attendance at the Kraft exhibit compared to the 25,000 annual visitors of the work done at the nonprofit Alchemy Institute, Hirshberg wondered if an environmentally and socially responsible business could also be profitable. He concluded that "he would not be as effective in spreading environmental awareness in the nonprofit world as he could be in business," Courtney Claire noted. Hirshberg soon had the opportunity to test his conclusion.

1980s–90s: Financial Survival, Ecological Concerns, and Creative Marketing

In April 1983, Kaymen founded Stonyfield Farm in Wilton, New Hampshire, as a TREC nonprofit project; he hoped to expand the farm and make the production of yogurt both an educational and a profitable venture. With his wife and their six children he milked seven Jersey cows and produced a tasty, all-natural yogurt based on a family recipe. From the start, the Kaymens used only the highest quality, all-natural ingredients; their yogurt, made from the premium milk of their own cows, was certified kosher.

Hirshberg agreed to prepare a business plan, and in September accepted the full-time position of president and chief executive director; he obtained a $35,000 loan (which included $30,000 from the Sisters of Mercy) as a start-up fund from the Institute for Community Economics. In September Hirshberg accepted the full-time position of president and executive director of the new company. During 1983 Stonyfield Farm produced 150 cases of whole-milk plain yogurt and realized annual sales of $56,000.

In 1984 Hirshberg drafted the new company's first business plan and—thanks to the fact that his mother, family members, and friends agreed to co-sign loans—secured much needed funds. The production of yogurt in six different flavors propelled 1986 sales to $658,000, but the Stonyfield Farm had outgrown its Wilton facility (an old barn that came with the original property). In 1987 the partners attempted to solve this problem by working with a packing company that shortly fell into bankruptcy. The bank closed down the co-packer, and creditors attached its assets: equipment, cups and lids, ingredients and finished products. Kaymen and Hirshberg spent over $400,000 to recover everything and re-open production. For a whole year—taking turns at working without sleep every other night—they ran the plant three shifts a day, seven days a week. In spite of a weekly loss of $30,000, they managed to keep the company alive, but their troubles were not over. A Vermont dairy firm that had agreed to invest in Stonyfield Farm changed the terms of its offer to what would essentially be a complete takeover of the company.

Refusing to be bought out, Kaymen and Hirshberg began to raise money for a new site for a facility that could not only house their small company but also allow for future growth. Hirshberg obtained a loan guarantee from the U.S. Small Business Administration and won several other investors. The intrepid partners found a landlord willing to give them a lease for 21,000 square feet of land in Londonderry, New Hampshire—a considerable improvement over the 1,500 square feet of the Wilton plant. Construction of the new plant began in 1988; in December the manufacturing and shipping staff relocated to the new custom-designed Stonyfield Farm Yogurt Works in Londonderry, New Hampshire. After many hours of intensive marketing, including distribution of free yogurt in office buildings and supermarkets, the partners knew that the company was still heavily in debt but believed that, with 1988 annual sales of $1.4 million, Stonyfield Farm was finally on its way to better days.

In 1989 Stonyfield Farm launched the Adopt-a-Cow Program (later renamed Have-a-Cow Educational Program) to educate consumers about the value of supporting family farming. The tens of thousands of people who agreed to sponsor a dairy cow were mailed a photograph of "their" Stonyfield Farm cow, updates about life on a modern-day farm, news about farmers' problems, and notes on the value of sustainable farming methods. Moreover, Hirshberg alerted consumers to the dangers of global warming by using the lids of yogurt cups as small billboards. On its yogurt lids, the company printed the slogan "Let's Put a Lid on Global Warming. To find out how, look inside." The underside of each lid carried a printed offer of a free global-warming kit and a suggestion for sending an e-mail to the president of the United States.

Stonyfield Farm significantly decreased the amount of energy needed to produce yogurt by retrofitting the manufacturing process and installing energy-efficient lighting fixtures and hot water heat-recovery systems to capture "waste" heat. The company recycled all cardboard, paper, aluminum, and many plastics. Through recycling and re-use, Stonyfield Farm saved over $70,000 annually and reportedly kept hundreds of tons of waste from going into landfills and incinerators.

After 17 years in the yogurt-making business, co-founder Kaymen retired, retaining a seat on the company's board of directors. Over and above the introduction of manufacturing and packaging efficiencies, Stonyfield Farm continued to re-

Key Dates:

1971: Samuel Kaymen and his wife, Louise, establish The Rural Education Center (TREC) in Wilton, New Hampshire.
1983: TREC spawns Stonyfield Farm, which produces all-natural yogurt; Gary Hirshberg becomes a full-time partner.
1986: The company manufacturers yogurt in six different flavors.
1988: The company relocates to a leased site in Londonderry, New Hampshire.
1996: The company buys the site it had leased.
2000: Stonyfield retrofits its manufacturing processes and minimizes waste through recycling and re-use.
2001: France-based Groupe Danone acquires 40 percent of Stonyfield Farm.
2003: Stonyfield acquires California-based Brown Cow West Corp.

search green packaging and reduced its direct contributions to climate change by investing in carbon-offset projects that either absorbed greenhouse gases from the atmosphere or prevented their generation. Investments since 1997 included the reforestation of riparian habitat in Oregon; construction of an insulated straw-bale house in China to demonstrate how this insulation reduced use of coal by 80 percent; the capture and use of coal-mine methane gas in Ohio and other states; and boiler upgrades in public schools. By offsetting 100 percent of the carbon dioxide emissions from its plant's use of energy, the company became the nation's first ''zero-emissions'' manufacturer and proved that businesses could decrease the impact of their operations on global warming.

More New Products at the Turn of the Century

Stonyfield Farm carried on its environmental activities in tandem with the roll-out of many new products. Among others, these new lines included Yo, Baby! organic yogurt available in six packs of four-ounce cups for infants and toddlers. The company was surprised to find that Yo, Baby! also appealed to grown-ups. For older children, Stonyfield Farm marketed Yo Squeeze (later renamed Squeezers), which consisted of five flavors of fruit blended with yogurt packaged in eight, two-ounce tubes per box; and for grown-ups: nine flavors of organic superpremium (that is, full-fat) ice cream. Such products kept the company on a continuing growth curve. *Prepared Foods*, an industry research and marketing company, named Stonyfield Farm the 2000 New Products Company of the Year.

In 2001 Stonyfield Farm introduced Yo Self, a yogurt that increased calcium absorption. Next, with the introduction of certified organic *Drinkable* Low-Fat Yogurt in five flavors, Stonyfield Farm entered the beverage category. The ten-ounce bottles contained six live active cultures, calcium, protein, and inulin.

For lovers of soy, particularly consumers looking for a non-dairy soy product that didn't taste ''beany,'' Stonyfield Farm introduced O'Soy soy yogurt in strawberry and peach or chocolate and vanilla flavors. O'Soy was the only cultured soy that contained no saturated fat, cholesterol or lactose and offered 30 to 50 million lactose-intolerant Americans a lactose-free alternative to traditional yogurts.

According to Julie Rose in the December 2001 issue of *Fortune Small Business* magazine, Stonyfield Farm moved solidly into the black in 1997, and Hirshberg began to look for a way of giving a return to his 292 stockholders. Mindful that a company's mission and social concern could dissipate under acquisition—as was the case with Anglo-Dutch conglomerate Unilever's acquisition of both Ben & Jerry's Ice Cream and Slimfast—Hirshberg did not want to go public, sell, or lose control of the company. ''Under Hirshberg,'' Julie Rose wrote, ''Stonyfield had tied its fortunes to improving the environment, providing a healthy and enjoyable workplace, educating consumers, being profitable, and yes, giving investors a return.'' Meanwhile, the mission-minded entrepreneur co-founded O'Naturals—a Falmouth, Maine-based ''natural'' fast-food restaurant that he envisioned as the first of a chain.

For months Hirshberg mulled over the possibility of selling Stonyfield Farm equities but when his wife, Meg, was diagnosed with breast cancer, he felt the urgency of coming to a decision about a deal with France-based Groupe Danone SA, owner of Dannon Yogurt in the United States. After many weeks of negotiations, Groupe Danone—the worldwide leader in fresh yogurt products and bottled water—formed a strategic partnership with Stonyfield Farm.

Under the agreement, Hirshberg was to continue as Stonyfield Farm's chairman and CEO. Initially, Danone could buy up to 40 percent of the shares held by the nearly 300 friends and employees whose crucial financial assistance helped Stonyfield Farm during its start-up phase. In 2004, subject to a successful mutual realization of numerous business synergies, Danone could gain majority ownership by purchasing all of Stonyfield Farm's remaining non-employee stock. Moreover, Danone was not to make any changes affecting Stonyfield Farm's employees, operations, or the facility. Stonyfield Farm was to continue buying all its milk from organic dairy farmers; focus on increasing the number of organic family farms in this country; and continue its ''Profits for the Planet'' program.

Hirshberg set aside his initial skepticism about traditional forms of commercial advertising and decided the time had come for his company to solidify its position as a top player in the $2.3 billion national yogurt market. He employed Boston-based eFlicks Media to run a multi-media campaign highlighting Stonyfield Farms' corporate philosophy, products, internet address, and tag line (''Stonyfield Farm: Yogurt on a Mission.'')

By year-end 2002, federally set milk prices had dropped to levels nearing those of 1970; however, for New England dairy farmers, operating and living costs had grown dramatically in these 30 years. In an effort to save New England dairy farmers, St. Albans Co-Op Creamery sent a call-to-action to Stonyfield Farm and its other members. Hirshberg responded immediately with a five-figure contribution and sent a matching appeal to his customers.

2003 and Beyond

Stonyfield Farm began its 20th anniversary year by replacing the plastic lid and plastic inner seal of its small cups of yogurt with a new durable foil seal. This change was estimated to prevent 106 tons of plastic from being thrown into landfills annually. Other savings included the use of 16 percent less energy for manufacturing the foil seals (enough power for more than 180 U.S. households), and the use of 13 percent less water, a saving equal to over 800,000 gallons of water.

Next came the purchase of Antioch, California-based Brown Cow West Corporation, another family-owned producer of natural yogurt. Both Brown Cow and Stonyfield Farm were committed to supporting family farms; they shared similar philosophies about producing yogurt and using only milk from organic dairy farms. Stonyfield Farm planned to set up agreements with western family farmers and to process organic yogurts in California for its western customers. Steve Ford remained at the helm of the new subsidiary. Stonyfield Farm expected that combined 2003 revenues would be about $130 million.

GreenMoney Journal referred to Stonyfield Farm as "one of the top companies in the world reaching toward sustainability." Regarding the company's future, in *Leader to Leader* magazine, Hirshberg wrote, "Stonyfield Farm will continue to inspire individuals, CEOs, and entrepreneurs alike for many years to come. We have often been looked upon as a leading business model that has managed to maximize the company's bottom line while indeed tending to the health of our planet. And yet," he added, "I feel like I am just getting to the starting line."

Principal Subsidiaries

Brown Cow West Corporation.

Principal Competitors

Kraft Foods North America, Inc.; General Mills, Inc.; Groupe Danone.

Further Reading

Brigham, Courtney Claire, "Turning Heads of Giants," *Eagle-Tribune* (Londonderry, N.H.), August 29, 1999.

Carson, Rachel, *Silent Spring*, Boston: Houghton Mifflin Company, 2002, 368 pp.

Dahm, Lori, "Batting a Thousand: Stonyfield Farm Hits Another Home Run With Yo Self," *Dairy Field*, April 2001.

——, "Getting Some Culture: Prebiotics and Probiotics in Yogurt Formulations," *Dairy Field*, January 2001.

Greco, Susan, "Sampling With a Twist," *Inc.,* August 1992, p. 80.

Hirshberg, Gary, "Organics, Stonyfield & O'Naturals in 2012," reprint from *Green Money Journal*, June/July 2002.

——, "Profits With a Conscience," *Leader to Leader*, Winter 2002, pp. 24–28.

Hirshberg, Meg Cadoux, *Stonyfield Farm Cookbook*, New York: Three Rivers Press, 1999, 340 pp.

Kane, Courtney, "Stonyfield Farm Tries Something New: An Old-Fashioned Campaign to Sell Its Yogurt," *New York Times*, April 18, 2002, p. C8.

Peters, James W., "Cause-Related Marketing Strategy Spurs 36 Percent Growth," *BrandPackaging,* June/July 1998, pp. 23–25.

A Practical Guide to Understanding Organic, Londonderry, N.H.: Stonyfield, December 2000.

Quinn, Barbara, "Bottom Line: 'Minimizing Waste is Good Business'," *Pollution Engineering*, July 2001, pp. 26–27.

Rose, Julie, "Stonyfield: Did the Yogurt King Sell His Soul," *Fortune Small Business*, December 13, 2001/January 2002, pp. 39–42.

—Gloria A. Lemieux

Stussy, Inc.

17426 Daimier Street
Irvine, California 92614
U.S.A.
Telephone: (949) 474-3253
Fax: (949) 474-8229
Web site: http://www.stussy.com

Private Company
Incorporated: 1984
Employees: 80
NAIC: 315220 Men's and Boys' Cut and Sew Apparel
Manufacturing; 315230 Women's and Girls' Cut and
Sew Apparel Manufacturing

Stussy, Inc., is an Irvine, California-based apparel company that has managed to stay on the cutting edge of urban street fashion for 20 years, combining a number of influences, including surfer, skatewear, hip hop, reggae, surplus, as well as classic preppy wear. Stussy has a celebrity following and an international reputation, despite spending no money on promotion. From the start, the company has limited its production to a level far below the demand for its products, a strategy that while limiting profits has created an air of exclusivity about its apparel and accessories. Stussy products are found in a variety of outlets, with some sold in skate, surf, and snowboard shops, and other items sold in department and specialty stores. In addition, the company has licensed the Stüssy name to some 50 stores located throughout the world. A handful of boutiques launched in the early 1990s by co-founder Shawn Stussy are owned by the corporation. In recent years, Stussy has expanded beyond men's clothing and now offers a complete line of women's clothing. It also designs and sells such accessories as sunglasses, hats, and backpacks.

Making Surfboards in the 1960s

Stussy, Inc. bears the name of designer Shawn Stussy, who grew up in Southern California. In 1965, when he was ten years old, he took up surfing just as the sport was gaining wide recognition in popular music and movies. By the age of 13,

Stussy began to design and shape his own surfboards in the family garage. He was so talented that as a 15-year-old high school student he was hired by a surfboard manufacturer. After graduating from high school in the early 1970s, he lived a free lifestyle, spending the winters living in a trailer and working as a ski instructor at Mammoth Mountain and summers making surfboards at Laguna Beach. Aside from his interest in surfing and skiing, Stussy was further influenced by his love of punk rock music, which led him to wear orange-spiked hair and affect what he called an "anarchic, do it your own way" attitude that spilled over into his approach to fashion design as well as business practice.

In 1979, when he was 24 years old, Stussy gave up his itinerant ways and settled in Laguna Beach to establish a regular surfboard business. To brand his handiwork he took a large marker and scrawled his signature on the finished boards. It soon became his trademark and logo. In a 1993 interview with *WWD*, Stussy recalled, "It was seen as 'new wave,' anarchic. I had the logo screen-printed on T-shirts and sweatshirts, but it had nothing to do with producing clothes. I was trying to promote the boards." During this early period of his career, Stussy shaped surfboards in his Laguna Canyon studio during the days and at night boxed his T-shirts for sale in area surf shops. He drifted further into the apparel business by simply being involved in finding clothing that he and his friends liked to wear. As he explained to *The Orange County Register* in a 1989 profile, "We've always worn interesting clothes, but it's not like I'm from a garment-family or anything like that." After T-shirts and sweatshirts, Stussy began producing Bermuda shorts, as he explained to *WWD:* "A couple of my buddies and I used to go to the Army-Navy surplus stores and buy size 40 khakis and cut them off way up at the knees. Everybody used to say, 'Those are so fly!'—so we started making them. My mom made a pattern off of them. We started taking orders."

While Stussy may have viewed his clothing ventures as a sideline that helped spur the sale of his surfboards, an old friend named Frank Sinatra, Jr. (no relation to the family of the famous singer) saw greater potential. They had surfed together as teenagers, but now Sinatra was an accountant and possessed the business expertise that Stussy lacked. Sinatra convinced Stussy

---

Company Perspectives:

We are proud that after twenty years of creating what street wear is, we're still recognized and respected by the cultures we flourish from. From skate to surf, to reggae to hip hop, to electronica to preppy, to surplus and everyone in between, Stüssy still makes its mark.

---

that his nascent apparel business held much promise and offered to invest $5,000 to become his partner. In 1983, they joined forces and in 1984 established Stussy Inc. with Stussy handling design and Sinatra shouldering the business responsibilities. It was on March 27, 1986 that the company registered the Stussy trademark in the United States.

As the apparel side of the company began to grow, the surfboard business faded in importance and was ultimately turned over to a licensee for small-scale production. Around two dozen surfboards were produced each month, retailing at a much higher price point than other quality boards—in keeping with the exclusivity approach that Stussy would take in marketing his apparel. Shawn Stussy continued to shape boards in his spare time for himself and friends and was known to cancel a business trip should the wave conditions prove too irresistible, but increasingly the ex-punk rocker, now turned designer, was busy developing a full line of young men's clothing as well as moving beyond the beach market. He drew inspiration from sources around the world rather than the nearby surfing and skating scene, although his clothing was embraced by the skating and beach markets. His approach was to take a classic item and apply a twist. For instance, according to *The Orange County Register*, "A Stussy oxford button-down shirt could pass for Brooks Brothers, except for odd buttons sewn down its front. A knit polo top could be a Ralph Lauren, except for graphic squiggles around the collar." Shawn Stussy's goal was simply to produce a "wearable classic." He described his look as "prep meets punky meets b-boy [beach boy]."

Stussy Hits Europe in 1988

The Stussy formula proved sufficiently successful so that in 1987 the company moved into a 4,000-square-foot office in Irvine, California, while Shawn Stussy also maintained a design studio in the garage of his Laguna Niguel home. In 1988, the company introduced its clothing line in Europe, where it became immediately successful. By the end of the 1980s, the company was generating in the neighborhood of $5 million in annual sales. Its apparel was not only carried in local surf shops but also in upscale stores in New York, England, Australia, and Japan. A designer growing in recognition, Shawn Stussy traveled around the world, connecting with trendsetters and building a following for his clothing.

With the start of the 1990s, the company reached a new level when Shawn Stussy's designs began to reflect a hip-hop influence that was embraced by musicians and their fans, transforming Stussy into "the tag of the moment." Nightclub-goers around the world began to collect Stussy hats, T-shirts, jackets, and anything else that boasted the designer's trademark signature, which also resulted in a market for vintage Stussy designs. Shawn Stussy's approach was very similar to that of many musicians who were building songs by "sampling" bits and pieces of well-known music. Stussy designs drew on images and graphics from a variety of sources, making his apparel seem fresh as well as classic. What started out as beachwear had by now morphed with skatewear, work clothes, surplus, and preppy to produce contemporary street fashion. Regardless of his method, Shawn Stussy and his apparel clearly connected with the youth market. Annual revenues reached an estimated $17 million in 1990 and $24 million in 1991. The appeal of Shawn Stussy's apparel was so strong that it spawned the rise of what *The Los Angeles Times* described as the International Stussy Tribe: " 'Tribe' members include disc jockeys, musicians and artists who begin as fans of Stussy's collections and eventually get to know the designer personally. Consumers who may never become official members of the 'tribe' are still drawn by the basic human instinct to belong to a clique." The company was able to project a strong international presence without resorting to advertising or giving away apparel to celebrities for promotion. Nevertheless, Stussy clothing appeared in music videos and fashion magazines around the world.

Shawn Stussy and Sinatra resisted the temptation to cash in on the Stussy phenomena by increasing production or licensing the Stussy name to any number of products. The partners, uninterested in a quick payout, opted to follow their strategy for maintaining long-term viability based on restricted growth and never supplying the demand for Stussy products. In this way, Stussy items were not seen everywhere and remained fresh to consumers. Aside from the business argument for this approach, it was a question of lifestyle as well. As Shawn Stussy explained to *The Los Angeles Times*, "We have no desire to get bigger, no desire to open new accounts. And we feel we could continue doing business for many more years, sleep at night, enjoy kids growing up and not be a victim of our business. You've got to look 10 or 20 years down the road, and nobody in America does. They just want the money now. They want instant gratification. But then they burn themselves out. This happens especially in the fashion industry."

Emulating other top-notched apparel designers, Shawn Stussy, using his own capital, opened a handful of signature boutiques, taking on sales representatives as partners in joint ventures outside of Stussy Inc. The first shop, 900 square feet in size, was established in the trendy SoHo section of Manhattan in November 1991. It was an immediate downtown hit, its success surpassing the designer's expectations. In the spring of 2002, Stussy opened his second boutique, a 200-square-foot shop located in the unlikely venue of Laguna Beach, chosen because it was close to where he and his girlfriend and partner in the venture, Paula Henry, had just purchased a house. Several weeks later, a Tokyo boutique opened, followed by the October 1992 debut of a 800-square-foot shop located on La Brea Avenue in Los Angeles. Stussy, Inc. also made news in 1992 when its first licensee, Stussy Australia, began to produce a junior clothing line for women called Stussy Sista Gear. (The only other Stussy license was granted to Eyeking Co. in New York for eyewear.) The idea for the women's line came from Australian designers Felicity Rulikowski and Bernadette Wier, who worked in conjunction with Shawn Stussy to develop an initial 25-piece collec-

Key Dates:

1979: Shawn Stussy first signs his name on surfboards, creating a logo that is then transferred to T-shirts.
1984: Stussy, Inc. is created with partner Frank Sinatra.
1991: The company opens a New York boutique.
1993: Stussy Sista line is launched.
1996: Shawn Stussy sells out to Sinatra.
2001: Stussy, Inc. is rumored to be for sale.

tion that featured body-hugging apparel with a retro 1970s flair. As with the menswear, the line had limited distribution both internationally and in the United States, where the clothing was only available in the Stussy boutiques, starting in the spring of 1993. The Stussy Sista idea proved successful, and in October 1998 the company registered the Stussy Sista trademark.

New Leadership in the Mid-1990s

Annual revenues for Stussy, Inc. settled in the $35 million range, which appeared sustainable and apparently satisfactory to both Shawn Stussy and Sinatra. In late 1995, however, rumors began to circulate that Stussy was thinking about retiring from the company that bore his name. In January 1996, it became official when he resigned as president of the company, although he agreed to stay on as a consultant. There appeared to be no acrimony surrounding his departure. As Sinatra told the press, "This is not a hostile thing," further explaining that Stussy's "desire is to enjoy life and be free of the pressures of running a business day to day." Although he planned to spend more time in his home in Hawaii with his wife and son, Shawn Stussy agreed to act as a consultant to Stussy, Inc. He also planned to continue operating the New York and Los Angeles boutiques. Sinatra subsequently bought out his partner's share of the company.

Sinatra planned to continue running Stussy in the same manner as before, although observers questioned whether the company could retain its edge without the original designer's active participation. The brand was well-entrenched in the marketplace, however, and Stussy maintained its niche in the fashion world, generating its usual $35 million in annual revenues. The company continued to eschew traditional marketing and promotion, although in 2000 it decided for the first time to sponsor a

few skateboarders as a way to help strengthen the Stussy brand. In the meantime, Stussy Sista and women's apparel began to take on more importance as it became apparent that fewer women were buying the company's main line of clothing, which was geared more towards 20- to 30-year-old men. As a result, Stussy launched a full-fledged women's collection for fall 2001, designed by Pauline Takahashi, a Los Angeles-born designer who had done previous collections for overseas' retailers under her own name. Rather than the streetwear feel of Stussy's menswear, this new collection, according to a company spokesperson, was "more of a fashion thing," similar in feel to the work of designers Karyl K. and Katayone Adeli.

Also in 2001, rumors circulated that Sinatra was interested in selling the company, with Italian jeanswear company Diesel Jeans SpA named as the most likely buyer. With annual sales roughly ten times the size of Stussy, Diesel was in the market for acquisitions to fuel further growth. Its owner and CEO, Renzo Rosso, made it known that he was a strong believer in owning brands over licensing. The buyout rumors were fueled by Sinatra, who was an infrequent traveler yet flew to Italy to meet with Diesel executives. Moreover, his hiring of a former Diesel designer as well as other moves were seen by observers as window dressing in preparation for a sale. Whether Sinatra came close to selling the company to Diesel is not certain, but in the end he retained ownership of Stussy, which after 20 years in existence maintained its place with youth in worldwide fashion and continued to mix and match elements of standard dress with underground culture.

Principal Competitors

Billabong International Ltd.; Diesel Jeans SpA; Karl Kani Infinity Inc.; Mossimo Inc.; Skechers U.S.A.

Further Reading

Apodaca, Rose, "Sportswear Designer Stussy Is Prospering Partly by Limiting His Outlets," *Los Angeles Times*, July 12, 1992, p. D3.
Dang, Kim-Van, "Stussy: From Surf to Street," *WWD*, September 22, 1993, p. 10.
Lowe, Jennifer, "An Old Surfer From OC Never Dies; He Just Becomes a Clothes Designer," *Orange County Register*, February 24, 1989, p. J1.
Schaben, Susan, "Did You Hear the One About Stussy and Diesel?," *Orange County Business Journal*, March 12–March 18, 2001, p. 7.

—Ed Dinger

Swift & Company

1930 AA Street
Greeley, Colorado 80631-9663
U.S.A.
Telephone: (970) 506-8000
Toll Free: (800) 555-2588
Fax: (970) 506-8307
Web site: http://www.swiftbrands.com

Private Company
Incorporated: 1875
Employees: 21,400
Sales: $7.73 billion (2002.)
NAIC: 311611 Animal (Except Poultry) Slaughtering;
311612 Meat Processed from Carcasses

With headquarters in Greeley, Colorado, and a 265,000 square-foot flagship processing plant in Worthington, Minnesota, Swift & Company is a leading processor of beef, pork, and lamb in both domestic and foreign markets. Swift also maintains plants and other operations at facilities in other locales, notably in Iowa, Kentucky, California, and Australia. Until its 2002 spin off from its status as a division of ConAgra, Inc., most of its products, largely pork, were marketed under the Armour name, another distinguished brand of a company also owned by ConAgra. Swift also supplies other meat processors and the food-service industry with beef and raw pork for such products as bacon, sausage, and ham; it also offers several state-of-the-art product and information systems. A pioneer in vacuum-packaging, the company has an enviable history of providing high quality, fresh meat products worldwide and claims among its international customers companies in Canada, EU (European Union), Hong Kong, Japan, Korea, Mexico, and Taiwan. Two of its plants have been awarded ISO 9002 certification, the only two pork-processing plants in the United States to operate under that status. Although ConAgra retains a large minority interest in Swift, Hicks, Muse, Tate & Furst, in a partnership with Booth Creek Management Corporation, now hold a majority ownership in the business.

1855–1914: From Cape Cod Butcher to Chicago Meat Packer

Swift & Company traces it origins back to 1855 when, on Cape Cod, Massachusetts, 16-year-old Gustavus Franklin Swift, the ninth in a family of 22 children, encouraged by his father, started in business for himself as a slaughterer, packager, and distributor of beef. Until then, he had been working as a butcher in his brother's business, but he had bigger plans for himself and had wanted to try them out in New York City. His father, hoping to keep young Gustavus at home, cut a deal with the lad by offering to buy him his own steer if the new entrepreneur would stay on Cape Cod. His father put up $20, and Gustavus was in business. He bought a mature heifer, butchered it, and packaged it for sale to his neighbors.

Swift stayed in the East until 1875, when he moved to Chicago to become both a cattle dealer and butcher. It was there that he first incorporated his business and bought a shed-like structure to serve as his slaughterhouse. On the first day in the new facility, his fledgling company slaughtered 32 head of cattle. However, part of his plan was to ship live beef to the eastern states via the railroad. At the time Swift made his move to Chicago, western trail-head "cow towns" in Kansas and Nebraska were booming. These were the points where large herds of longhorn steers, bred in Texas but fed out on the northern plains, were rounded up and driven for shipment by rail to Chicago's Union Stockyards. From the Windy City, yet to be butchered, they were shipped to the East.

The Union Stockyards, which were established in 1865 by a group of investors, some of whom were friends of Abraham Lincoln, were processing over two million livestock by the time Swift moved to Chicago. By 1890, the figure had grown to nine million, and the city had been transformed into the largest hog and beef holding pen in the country. Still, the live shipment of cattle from the stockyard was a poor system that was inimical to the cattlemen's interests. For one thing, the live cattle lost up to 15 percent of their weight in transit. The rail service was also very poor and the cattle were often mistreated, given neither sufficient food or water. Some cattle, because of the primitive condition of railcar braking systems, poor rails and roadbeds, and frequent stops, arrived in poor physical health. The upshot

364

Company Perspectives:

For over 150 years, Swift & Company has been providing quality beef and pork products under superior brand names to consumers nationwide. The Swift & Company tradition began with Mr. Gustavus Swift when he purchased a calf for $20.00 and sold the meat to his neighbors. Mr. Swift's innovative thinking was only the beginning. Today, Swift & Company is an industry leader in fresh ideas, products and technology. From our headquarters in Greeley, Colorado, we are proud to offer you high quality products under the Swift Premium and Swift brands. Our commitment to your needs continues as we constantly strive to develop and provide convenient, great tasting fresh beef and pork products.

was that the cattle frequently commanded only low prices in the East, where the western beef was slow to gain popularity.

Swift and a few others helped change the system by slaughtering beef and hogs and packing their meat in Chicago before shipping it to points East. However, through most of the rest of the century, meat processing was pretty much limited to the cold winter months. Not only did the industry lack an adequate distribution system to ship fresh meat to widespread markets, it had no means to prevent the meat from spoiling. Frustrated by this seasonal restriction, Swift tried to get the railroads to build refrigerator cars for transporting meat and dairy products, but the railroads resisted. After all, they had a lot at stake in shipping cattle live, including a great number of stock cars and excellent revenue obtained from their use.

Although he faced rigorous opposition from railroad officials, Swift finally got permission for use of cars on a railroad that permitted them on a roundabout route. Swift bought ten cars and started shipping packaged beef to eastern markets. Soon he started building his own refrigerator cars and secured patents on them, the start of a fleet of cars owned by his company.

1915–81: Swift & Company Grows into Industry Giant

Meanwhile, Swift saw his company grow into one of the nation's main meatpacking companies, with a reach throughout the United States. By 1900, it had also reached beyond national boundaries, opening shops in London, England. At home, the efforts of Swift and others helped transform Chicago into what poet Carl Sandburg styled ''Hog-butcher to the World,'' that is, the world's largest slaughterhouse and meat-processing center.

Modernization was one key to the company's success. For example, in 1915 Swift implemented a ''safety first'' campaign, reducing plant-level industrial accidents by 50 percent. By that time, the company had also developed thriving side-line businesses, and though by 1920, under a consent decree, it was forced to dispose of some of them, it still offered various meat and byproduct items at company-owned outlets across the country. Swift had also diversified, branching out from beef to other meats, notably pork. According to its own 1915 company yearbook, Swift was offering a wide variety of products, including hams, sausage, bacon, chickens, eggs, butter, lard, shortening,

oleomargarine, bouillon cubes, and various soaps (including scented toilet soaps). Despite being legally required to divest some of its sidelines, in 1920 the company still had sales exceeding $1.1 billion, and by 1922 its branch houses were still selling fresh, cured, and smoked meats, meat specialties, poultry, eggs, butter, cheese, oleomargarine, lard, shortening, cooking and salad oils, and soaps.

By 1921, the Union Stockyards in Chicago employed 40,000 workers and occupied more than a square mile of Chicago's South Side; by 1926, Swift's rail carriers had grown into a fleet of over 5,000 refrigerator cars. That was at the virtual height of the industry's development in Chicago, which, during the Great Depression, started into a decline, albeit a slow one. In the worst of the Depression, in 1931, Swift was selling fresh meats under its Select, Premium, and other Swift labels to increasingly brand-conscious consumers.

The Union Stockyards remained one of the nation's great success stories. From 1893 to 1933, there was no year in which less than 15 million head of livestock were unloaded and processed there, and in two years in the 1920s over 18 million head were processed. The industry also garnered infamy during this time, however, for deplorable working conditions, as portrayed in the Upton Sinclair novel *The Jungle*.

Through the period of the Union Stockyards' growth and decline, Swift & Company built plants in several other locales, including, for example, in the Stockyards District of Fort Worth, Texas. The company opened a meat packing plant there in 1902, next to an Armour & Co. plant that opened in that same year. Situated on 14 acres, the Swift & Company plant was adjacent to tracks of the Fort Worth Western Railroad, which carried the plant's products to the East. In their heyday, when they were in full operation, the Swift and Armour plants between them processed up to five million head of cattle per year. In 1971, Swift closed down its operation there, just as, over time, it elsewhere closed many of its plants, partly because for a while it got out of the beef business and partly because the meat industry no longer had to depend on railroads for shipping its products. By that time, however, it had opened large plants in other locations, including, for example, a major operation in Grand Island, Nebraska, in 1965.

In the middle of the century, Swift was a huge operation, much larger than its descendant would be as a subsidiary of ConAgra at the end of the century. In 2002, while still a subsidiary of ConAgra Foods, Swift employed 4,500 workers, a significant figure to be sure, but nothing on the scale it reached when the meat packing industry was in full swing. By 1944, for example, approaching the end of World War II, the company could boast that 20,300 men and women of the Swift organization were in the military and auxiliary services. Despite the fact that many employees went into the military during the conflict, Swift's plants continued to operate at full capacity thanks to war-time demands. In 1943, the company's sales volume reached $1.4 billion.

1982–95: Changes in Ownership

In 1982, Swift underwent another permutation in structure and name, becoming Swift Independent Packing Company

Key Dates:

1855: At 16, and with $20, Gustavus Franklin (G.F.) Swift begins his own meat-market business.

1875: Swift first incorporates his business.

1900: Company opens shops in London, England.

1915: "Safety First" campaign is implemented by the company, reducing plant accidents by 50%.

1920: Company gross sales exceed $1.1 billion; Swift disposes of side line businesses under terms of consent decree.

1931: Swift markets fresh meats under its Select, Premium, and other Swift labels.

1943: Despite Word War II, Swift plants continue to operate at full capacity; G.F. Swift dies.

1953: Swift's Brown 'N Serve sausage products enter the marketplace.

1965: Construction of Swift beef plant in Grand Island, Nebraska, is finished.

1970: Swift's ProTen tender beef becomes the largest dollar sales, branded food item in the world.

1982: Swift is restyled the Swift Independent Packing Company (SIPCO).

1989: ConAgra acquires Swift and merges it with Monfort Inc. to form the Monfort Pork Division in Greeley, Colorado.

1994: ConAgra's Monfort Pork Division is renamed Swift & Company.

2002: ConAgra Food's beef, port, lamb, and Australia Meat Holdings (AMF) are spun off as Swift & Company.

(SIPCO). It held its status as one of the nation's biggest beef and pork packagers. The next year, the company bought what would eventually become its principal plant, an Armour and Company facility in Worthington, Minnesota, that it purchased from Armour's parent, the Greyhound Corporation, At the time, it was a two-story, 95,000 square-foot facility, but eventually it would almost triple in size as Swift's operations there expanded.

By 1984, operating four beef and nine pork meat processing plants, SIPCO had become the second largest producer of fresh meats in the country. By then it was experimenting with case ready beef and was producing vacuum-packed and boneless pork. At its new plant in Worthington, it also introduced its Swift Brands, Swift Tender Lean, and Swift Premium products.

In 1987, ConAgra Foods Inc. acquired a 50 percent interest in SIPCO. Two years later, it bought the remaining shares, adding Swift to a swelling list of subsidiaries that included Monfort, Inc., a Colorado beef packer, which ConAgra had also purchased in 1987, at a cost of $365.5 million. Monfort had its beginnings back in 1930, when it opened a feedlot with 30 head of cattle. It gradually expanded, and in 1960 opened a major meatpacking plant north of Greeley, Colorado. In 1966, Monfort reported annual sales of $85 million with a payroll of $4 million. By 1968, its feedlot in North Greeley grew to process 100,000 cattle, the first single feedlot in the nation to reach that figure. Three years later the company went public. Once acquired by ConAgra, Swift was merged with Monfort

into the Monfort Pork Division, which, in 1995, was renamed Swift & Company.

ConAgra, the parent company, traced its own history back to 1919, when, in Grand Island, Nebraska, it started out as Nebraska Consolidated Mills. It came into existence when four, independent flour mills merged and incorporated. The company became ConAgra (from Latin roots meaning "with" and "land") in 1971, selecting the name to reflect its focus on agricultural products. Over the next several years ConAgra grew into a diversified food producing and marketing giant with an array of products sold under several familiar-brand names: Healthy Choice, Butterball, Banquet, Hunt's, Orville Redenbacher's, Reddi-Whip, Slim Jim, and Armour.

Through the first half of the 1990s, ConAgra's Monfort Pork Division fared well, in part because of a widely disseminated ad campaign suggesting that as "the other white meat" pork was a healthy substitute for beef, and in part because a glutted market drove the cost of hogs down, most notably in 1995, when ConAgra's pork division, by then operating as Swift, enjoyed a very profitable year.

1996 and Beyond: Expansion and Another Ownership Shift

Swift's profits encouraged ConAgra to invest more in its subsidiary's growth. It approved expansion plans that led to both facility improvements and acquisitions. Swift, meanwhile, concentrated on adding value to its products and improving its operational efficiency. Among other things, in 1996 it expanded distribution of its line of Armour Premium branded, case-ready pork products. It also acquired a pork slaughterhouse in Indiana, slated to operate as a value-added processing plant, and improved the capacity of its coolers at its two largest plants. In the following year, 1997, it began building a new up-to-date pork processing plant to replace its outmoded facility in Lexington, Kentucky. The new plant was equipped to produce case-ready products.

In 1998, ConAgra purchased Chicago-based Zoll Foods, a privately held processor and marketer of custom-cut pork ribs and other pork products produced for the food service industry, and made it part of Swift & Co. At the time, Zoll was logging annual sales of about $100 million. Swift's president, David Heggestad, noted that Zoll provided a good fit with Swift's plans to increase its food service presence and grow its value-added line of products. Steven Zoll, president of Zoll Foods, stayed on to manage Zoll Foods, providing the formerly independent company with a high degree of autonomy.

By the decade's end, a significantly part of Swift & Co.'s growth involved its increasing export of pork and pork products. In 1999, the year in which Dennis Henley was named Swift's president and chief operating officer (COO), the company's Worthington, Minnesota, plant became its second pork producing plant to earn ISO 9002 certification—the only ones with that certification in the United States. In order to achieve the very demanding EU certification, the company established a full-service science lab in Minnesota. There, using microbiological and chemical testing, Swift's products were analyzed to safeguard against contaminants.

At the beginning of the new century, Swift & Co. continued to enjoy a reputation for producing high quality products and for its innovations. At its 265,000 square-foot flagship plant in Minnesota, it was slaughtering up to 16,000 hogs a day, and in the process put food safety at the top of its stringent requirements for preparing its pork for the marketplace. The company's position in the ConAgra family certainly seemed secure.

However, in SEC filings made in 2002, that parent announced that an agreement, signed on May 21, would legally transfer a majority interest its fresh beef and pork processing businesses to a new venture. The transaction, valued at about $1.4 billion, took place in August, when a 54 percent ownership of Swift passed to an investor group led by Hicks, Muse, Tate & Furst, Inc. (HMTF), with ConAgra retaining a 46 percent interest. According to a ConAgra news release, its minority stake in its meat processing business would reduce its equity in that segment of its business from over $1 billion to $150 million.

The impact of the deal on Swift was not immediately clear. HMTF and its venture partners, Booth Creek Management Corporation of Vail, Colorado, and George Gillet, took over the managerial reins, however. Also, ConAgra's premier, Pacific-Rim beef processing business headquartered in Brisbane, Australia, also fell under the managerial control of Swift & Company in Greeley and its staff, headed by John Simons, president and COO of the enterprise. In a press release issued when the deal was singed in May 2002, John R. Muse of HMTF stated that the arrangement would "further optimize the performance and build the value of" the operations of Swift & Company. Efforts to focus on the Swift Premium product line, in the form of a $10 million advertising campaign, began in 2003.

Principal Competitors

Farmland Industries, Inc.; Hormel Foods Corporation; Premium Standard Farms, Inc.; Seaboard Corporation; Smithfield Foods, Inc.; Tyson Foods, Inc.

Further Reading

"ConAgra Acquires Zoll Foods," *PR Newswire,* January 14, 1998.

Swift, Louis F., and Arthur Van Vlissingen, *The Yankee of the Yards: The Biography of Gustavus Franklin Smith,* London: A.W. Shaw, 1927.

Reyes, Sonia, "Swift Sautes Plans to Meet Beefy Objectives," *Brandweek,* March 10, 2003, p. 8.

Taylor, Lisa Y., "Old Swift Site in Fort Worth Proposed for Apartments," *Dallas Business Journal,* October 27, 2000, p. 1.

Young, Barbara, "Production Paradigm," *National Provisioner,* February 1, 2001, p. 26.

—John W. Fiero

Tenet Healthcare Corporation

3820 State Street
Santa Barbara, California 93105
U.S.A.
Telephone: (805) 563-7000
Fax: (805) 563-7070
Web site: http://www.tenethealth.com

Public Company
Incorporated: 1968 as National Medical Enterprises, Inc.
Employees: 113,817
Sales: $13.91 billion (2002)
Stock Exchanges: New York
Ticker Symbol: THC
NAIC: 622110 General Medical and Surgical Hospitals

Tenet Healthcare Corporation, formerly National Medical Enterprises, ranks as the second largest hospital chain in the United States. Through its subsidiaries, the company owns or operates 114 acute care hospitals and related businesses in 16 states. These facilities offer a broad range of medical services and support regional healthcare networks designed to provide communities with a full complement of care. Over more than three decades, Tenet has continually adjusted its strategies to accommodate a rapidly changing market. As National Medical Enterprises (NME), the company spent its first decade building and acquiring medical facilities and related services. Industry changes during the mid-1980s prompted NME to shift its emphasis from acute-care to specialty hospitals. The company's Specialty Hospital Group, a division consisting of psychiatric, substance-abuse, and rehabilitation services, was NME's major strength in the late 1980s. After a damaging scandal in the early 1990s, however, NME unloaded its specialty facilities, reconfiguring itself as Tenet, and resuming its focus on acute care facilities. Although the new company realized surging profits in the late 1990s, it was mired in scandal again by the end of 2002.

Growth and Diversification in the 1970s

NME's founder and CEO, Richard K. Eamer, has degrees in accounting and law. Co-founders Leonard Cohen and John Bedrosian are also attorneys. Eamer's interest in the enterprise was piqued by his own work as a financial consultant and hospital attorney. In 1968 he joined forces with Cohen and Bedrosian, although the company is often dated to 1969, when NME acquired its first hospitals in California—four general and three convalescent—and offered public stock. That same year, NME also purchased a medical office building and three potential building sites.

The building, owning, and operating of numerous hospitals allowed NME to develop cost-cutting skills. Attention to both cost management and physician input became trademarks as NME concentrated on building services around community hospitals. Interest in efficiency also led to NME's early diversification into hospital equipment and supplies, a hospital-consulting firm, and even a construction company that specialized in building hospitals. In the early 1970s the focus was on growth. The company launched seven construction projects in 1971, in addition to another hospital purchase, and had tripled in size within a year. In 1973 NME took its first steps outside of California by acquiring a general hospital in Seattle, Washington, and by building another in El Paso, Texas.

By this time, the hospital-management and cost-cutting techniques of NME were already being hired out. There were both domestic and international divisions within NME to oversee management services provided to other hospitals by 1974. Management of non-NME-owned hospitals and healthcare-equipment rental were significant income sources during the company's growth years.

Throughout this period, the central concept was to profit from cost-efficient, well-managed hospitals that satisfied both doctors and patients. NME applied standard business practices in its healthcare ventures. As Eamer told *Forbes,* "in many ways, running a hospital chain is like operating a hotel or retail chain." The first decade was devoted to building a diversified, multi-facility hospital company with an eye on market needs. These efforts culminated in the 1979 purchases of Medfield Corporation and The Hillhaven Corporation. Medfield added five Florida-based hospitals, including one psychiatric institution, to NME; the Tacoma, Washington-based Hillhaven was the nation's third largest chain of nursing homes.

By the end of 1979, NME was the nation's fourth largest publicly owned hospital chain, with the majority of its revenues coming from acute-care hospitals. These two major acquisitions presaged the new decade's changes. Up until this point NME, like the rest of the hospital industry, operated with an eye to the Medicare and Medicaid legislation passed in 1965, which assured reimbursement for medical care of the poor, disabled, or elderly. This assurance spawned enormous growth in the investor-owned hospital industry, a growth which in turn eventuated problems of reimbursement.

Shifting Focus from Acute-Care Hospitals to Specialty Facilities: 1980s

NME began to shift focus from acute-care hospitals to alternative facilities such as nursing homes, and to develop its products-and-services segment, which included healthcare equipment rental for home use and visiting-nurses agencies before the reimbursement problem became widespread. In addition, management-services contracts were booming. In 1980, NME signed a five-year, $150 million contract with Saudi Arabia to help develop healthcare facilities in that country. More international contracts came in 1981, and by the end of that year NME had more than $1 billion in sales.

The healthcare business was the second largest industry in the United States during the early 1980s, second only to food and agriculture. NME acquired National Health Enterprises in 1982, whose 66 additional long-term care facilities made NME the nation's second largest nursing home owner. In order to better manage its own size, NME subdivided into four operating groups; international (largely consultant work), hospital, nursing homes, and medical products and services. In 1983, NME bought the Psychiatric Institutes of America (PIA), one of the nation's largest mental-healthcare providers, based in Washington, D.C.

From 1981 to 1983, corporate revenues doubled. Entry into the private psychiatric industry allowed NME to profit from a sector whose size doubled every two years throughout the 1980s. In 1983, NME further streamlined its specialty interests by forming Recovery Centers of America (RCA), a subsidiary comprised of substance-abuse-recovery operations.

By 1984, the hospital business began a decline, the result of overexpansion and of cost-containment efforts by both government and private healthcare interest groups. NME continued to look to what it considered more stable and promising medical service alternatives. These included its equipment leasing and home care services, and even extended to health insurance and a Miami-based health maintenance organization (HMO) acquired in 1984.

By 1985 NME was the second largest, publicly owned, healthcare services company in the nation, but changes within the industry mandated adjustments and restructuring. The following year, NME sold its recent HMO purchase, as well as a number of unprofitable outpatient clinics and acute-care hospitals. Emphasis was placed on the specialty facilities—especially rehabilitation and substance-abuse centers and psychiatric hospitals—in an effort to bypass nonpayment problems by shifting away from Medicaid- or Medicare-dependent services. The Rehab Hospital Services Corporation (RHSC) of Pennsylvania had been merged with NME in 1985 for this purpose. The company also began developing academic medical center strategies.

As the industry, and NME's stock, wobbled in the late 1980s, the company concentrated on internal reorganization instead of expansion. Restructuring produced the new subdivisions of hospitals, specialty hospitals, long-term care, and retail services in 1986. NME also continued divesting the acute-care hospitals hit by the drop in occupancy rates, shorter stays, and other results of the healthcare cost-containment squeeze. Within one year, the company had unloaded a quarter of its businesses, including ten acute-care hospitals. Many other hospitals were converted to specialty services. NME's specialty hospitals division—consisting of PIA, RHSC, and RCA—became the company's new core business and growth field. NME's specialty hospitals supplanted the acute-care hospitals, which had accounted for 90% of NME's revenues in 1969, and in 1990 NME spun off its long-term care facilities and related operations, as The Hillhaven Corporation.

NME retained a 14 percent equity interest in Hillhaven, and the parent company expected this change to help it avoid the short-term challenges created by healthcare legislation and the recompensation crackdown. At that time, Medicaid accounted for 50 percent of Hillhaven's revenues, but less than 3 percent of the specialty hospitals division's revenues, and less than 6 percent of the general hospitals division's revenues.

Because government programs had not kept pace with the rising cost of healthcare while private insurance rates had, NME began to focus on services that were less dependent on Medicare and Medicaid. With this safeguard and the steady growth in specialty-services industries in the late 1980s, NME seemed to have found its niche.

Still one of the nation's largest healthcare providers, NME held fast to its policy of high-quality, cost-effective care. By concentrating on specialty services such as psychiatric, rehabilitative, and substance-abuse recovery and by limiting itself to profitable acute-care hospitals, NME seemed well-positioned to ride out the changes in U.S. healthcare.

Scandal and Recovery in the 1990s

Indeed, NME's strategy seemed to be working. By 1991, under Eamer's leadership, NME had more than tripled the number of psychiatric facilities it operated. Moreover, of the company's $578 million in operating profits that year, profits from psychiatric care accounted for 40 percent. Unfortunately, however, as a major scandal concerning NME's psychiatric hospitals erupted, this specialty division brought the company to the brink of ruin.

The trouble began in 1991 when the Texas attorney general sued NME for alleged overbilling practices at its psychiatric facilities in that state. Allegations of wrongdoing were compounded that year, as individual patients began to accuse NME of having held them in psychiatric facilities against their will, only releasing them when their insurance coverage was exhausted. Eventually, more than 130 patient suits would be filed. Further, in the summer of 1992, 19 insurance companies, including Metropolitan Life, Aetna, Prudential, and Mutual of Omaha—some of the biggest providers in the country—filed suit accusing NME of an elaborate program of insurance fraud, beginning as early as 1988, whereby NME admitted tens of thousands of patients who did not need inpatient care, paying illegal kickbacks to referring physicians, fabricating trumped-up diagnoses, and charging exorbitant fees to treat them. At its peak, the cost of the fraud was estimated at $750 million.

Although NME would not comment on any of its patient treatment, citing confidentiality restrictions, the company took decisive steps to mitigate the damage of the scandal. In the spring of 1993, amid rumors that the company was facing potential bankruptcy, founders and top executives Richard Eamer and Leonard Cohen were ousted, along with four other board members, and Jeffrey C. Barbakow, former chief executive and president of MGM/UA Communications Company, took over as president and CEO of NME. Barbakow was committed to lifting the company out of its legal quagmire, but his already Herculean task was compounded as NME became a primary target of the Clinton administration's new initiative to crack down on health insurance fraud. In August 1993, 600

FBI and other federal agents raided NME's headquarters and 11 of its psychiatric facilities, seizing hundreds of documents as part of an investigation into possible criminal misconduct. To his credit, Barbakow insisted on full cooperation with the investigations.

The scandals significantly damaged NME's finances as well as its reputation, as operating profits from the psychiatric division fell from $234 million in 1991 to just $3 million in 1993. As for the cost of putting the past behind, by the end of 1993 settlements with only a few of the insurance companies in question had already topped $125 million. Moreover, after spending nearly $65 million in legal fees, NME pled guilty to felony federal charges in 1994 and agreed to pay $379 million to the Justice Department and the Department of Health and Human Services, the largest settlement in history between the U.S. government and a healthcare provider. To offset the cost of these settlements and to excise the source of corruption from its corporate identity, NME sold off all but 10 of its 81 psychiatric facilities for about $200 million in 1994. Also that year, NME sold off 73 rehabilitation hospitals and clinics for $260 million, laying the groundwork for a radical refocusing away from specialty facilities and back to the acute-care business.

Late in 1994, amid other dramatic consolidations in the healthcare industry, NME acquired American Medical Holdings in a $3.3 billion deal, more than doubling its presence in U.S. hospitals. Together, the companies would operate 84 acute-care hospitals with annual revenue in excess of $5.3 billion and become the second largest hospital chain in the country, behind the significantly larger Columbia/HCA Healthcare Corporation. By combining operations, the companies expected to realize a $60 million reduction in annual costs, and other significant efficiencies. NME completed its makeover in May 1995 by reincarnating itself as Tenet Healthcare Corporation, a name that was meant to reflect the company's new, rigorously principled approach to business. Analysts were pleased with the company's clean-up efforts, and projected renewed vitality for Tenet.

Indeed, Tenet's performance improved significantly. Determined to remain large enough to compete with and fend off acquisition from Columbia/RCA, the company sold off its international operations, especially in Asia and Australia, to finance growth in its core U.S. market. The key to success, according to Barbakow, was to concentrate on regional markets where Tenet could create solid networks of hospitals and physicians. Tenet enjoyed a dominant presence in the southern California market, and sought to establish similar positions in south Florida, Louisiana, and Texas, as well as in the Philadelphia area. Strength in regional markets enabled Tenet to exert significant pricing pressure. In addition, the company increased its focus on the most lucrative fields of medicine, including cardiology, neurology, and orthopedics. By 2001, Tenet owned 111 hospitals in the United States, and profits were soaring.

A New Wave of Scandal: 2002

Barbakow hardly had the opportunity to enjoy his success, however, before Tenet was beset by a new wave of scandal. In November 2002, federal agents seized documents at the Redding Medical Center in northern California, one of Tenet's best-performing hospitals, where the director of cardiology and the chairman of cardiac surgery were suspected of performing 25 to 50 percent of their surgeries unnecessarily. While Tenet stressed that it did not participate in doctors' decisions to perform surgery, the allegations raised serious questions about Tenet's aggressive pricing strategies and its hospital management practices, nonetheless. The next month, scrutiny of Tenet intensified when another of its facilities, the Alvarado Hospital Medical Center in San Diego, California, came under investigation for possible violations of anti-kickback laws. Tenet's stock value plummeted 70 percent in just two weeks. At the end of December, trading of its shares was halted altogether due to the investigations. Still a third federal inquiry was launched in January 2003, when Tenet received a subpoena demanding documents from company headquarters and 19 of its hospitals, dating from January 1997 to the present. While the outcome of these investigations remained uncertain, analysts lamented that Tenet's credibility had sustained significant damage. In May 2003, Barbakow resigned as CEO, replaced by Trevor Fetter. Under the latter's leadership until a permanent CEO could be found, the company would likely be weathering this new storm of controversy and internal crises for the foreseeable future.

Principal Subsidiaries

Broadlane, Inc.; Tenet HealthSystem, Inc.

Principal Competitors

Ascension Health; HCA Inc.; Triad Hospitals, Inc.

Further Reading

Abelson, Reed, "Tenet Promises to Take Steps to Reassure Investors," *New York Times*, December 20, 2002, p. C1.

Abelson, Reed, and Andrew Pollack, "More Scrutiny for Big Chain of Hospitals," *New York Times*, November 2, 2002, p. C1.

Brick, Michael, "Investing; A Hospital Chain Rises As Managed Care Suffers," *New York Times*, June 17, 2001, p. C8.

"Chief Executive Officer Resigns from Troubled Tenet Healthcare," *South Florida Sun-Sentinel*, May 28, 2003.

Eamer, Richard K., *The History of National Medical Enterprises, Inc. and the Investor-Owned Hospital Industry*, New York: Newcomen Society in North America, 1989.

Hilzenrath, David S., "Hospital Firm Plans $3 Billion Combination; National Medical Seeks to Alter Its Focus, Shed Taint of Scandal," *Washington Post*, October 12, 1994, p. F1.

Kerr, Peter, "U.S. Raids Hospital Operator," *New York Times*, August 27, 1993, p. D1.

Meier, Barry, "For-Profit Health Care's Human Cost; Tenet Healthcare Tries to Settle Some Old Accounts," *New York Times*, August 8, 1997, p. D1.

Myerson, Allen R., "Hospital Chain Sets Guilty Plea," *New York Times*, June 29, 1994, p. D1.

Pollack, Andrew, "California Patients Talk of Needless Heart Surgeries," *New York Times*, November 4, 2002, p. C1.

Pollack, Andrew, with Reed Abelson, "Chief Faces Problems Again After Restoring Tenet Once," *New York Times*, November 11, 2002, p. C2.

Schine, Eric, "From Scandal to Second Place," *Business Week*, November 27, 1995, p. 124.

Schine, Eric, with Catherine Yang, "Migraines for National Medical," *Business Week*, September 13, 1993, p. 74.

Yang, Catherine, and Eric Schine, " 'Put the Head in the Bed and Keep It There,' " *Business Week*, October 18, 1993, p. 68.

—Carol I. Keeley
—update: Erin Brown

TOKYO GAS

Tokyo Gas Co., Ltd.

5-20 Kaigan, 1-chrome
Minato-ku
Tokyo 105-8527
Japan
Telephone: (03) 5400-7561
Fax: (03) 5472-5385
Web site: http://www.tokyo-gas.co.jp

Public Company
Incorporated: 1885
Employees: 11,967
Sales: ¥1.09 trillion ($8.2 billion) (2002)
Stock Exchanges: Tokyo
Ticker Symbol: 9531
NAIC: 221210 Natural Gas Distribution; 486210 Pipeline
    Transportation of Natural Gas

With nearly nine million customers, Tokyo Gas Co., Ltd. operates as Japan's largest gas company. The firm distributes gas to the Kanto region, the largest region in Japan, which accounts for 40 percent of the country's gross domestic product. The firm imports liquefied natural gas (LNG) from Alaska, Australia, Brunei, Indonesia, Malaysia, and Qatar, receiving it at three major terminals in Negishi, Soedugaura, and Ohgishima. Deregulation of Japan's gas industry began in the late 1990s, forcing Tokyo Gas to cut costs, restructure, and diversify into such areas as the retail electricity market.

Origins

The use of city gas in Japan began in 1871, when a gas-powered street lamp was unveiled in Osaka. Tokyo's first gas lamps appeared three years later, when 85 street lamps were installed as lighting in the vicinity of the Diet (Japan's governmental national assembly) building. One of the main proponents of city gas in Tokyo was Eichi Shibusawa, Japan's leading industrialist at that time. Shibusawa was a central figure in Japan's extremely rapid economic growth following Commodore Perry's mission of 1853–54. Perry threatened to use the fire-power of the U.S. navy unless Japan opened its doors to the West. This event initiated a rapid assimilation of the best of Western culture and technology into Japan via young scholars sent abroad by the newly unified Japanese government. Shibusawa and the national authorities saw gas as a safe replacement for oil lamps common in Japanese cities. These had traditionally been a source of countless blazes. Gas lighting was spectacularly displayed at a technology exhibition in Ueno, Tokyo, in 1887, when a giant chrysanthemum—a symbol of imperial Japan—made of numerous gas power lights was unveiled.

Growth Under Shibusawa: Late 1800s to Early 1900s

Shibusawa was named head of the City of Tokyo's gas board in 1879, and in 1885, when the government sold the business and licenses to supply gas, he became the first chairman of Tokyo Gas. With only 343 customers and 61 employees, Tokyo Gas was very small, but Shibusawa had ambitious plans for the company. The number of users was increasing daily and the company could not meet the demand for gas in northern areas of Tokyo. The initial priority was the installation of a gas pipeline and the construction of a gas production plant. A new factory containing a coal-operated retort began operation in 1889 in what is now the Kogawa part of Tokyo. By 1893, the facility was capable of producing 30,000 cubic feet of city gas per day.

The business was growing to such an extent that in 1895 city authorities set up a gas tax office. Initially, Tokyo Gas was taxed according to the number of gas lamps it operated, and the yearly tax per lamp was set at ¥0.06. Accompanying the increase in the number of customers, the company's tax bill was mushrooming. Shibusawa persuaded the city tax authorities to adopt the more sensible policy of taxing the company on its profits.

Part of Tokyo Gas's strategy was to exploit gas for as many uses as possible. Shibusawa formed Tokyo Gas Railway Company in the hope of building a network of gas-powered trains in the city. The advent of electric power as a far safer and more convenient source of power for trains dashed these plans before they were seriously underway. Shibusawa was, however, instrumental in the spread of electricity into Japan and set up one of the first electric train companies.

Company Perspectives:

The Tokyo Gas Group must aspire to be a company that contributes to socioeconomic advancement, pleasant living, and the mitigation of global environmental problems through its supply of environment-friendly natural gas and other energy, as well as related energy-value added services. Tokyo Gas will thereby continue to move forward on the basis of the solid trust placed in it by its customers, shareholders, and society as a whole.

Victory over China in the 1897 Sino-Japanese War was a key factor in the economic and military development of Japan. The nation joined the Western powers as a major force on the world stage. The war spurred even faster industrial development, and Tokyo Gas was likewise expanding. Company headquarters were moved to a new building in Kanda in central Tokyo. In 1898, a third gas factory was completed in Fukagawa that was capable of producing 250,000 cubic feet of gas per day.

During the late 1890s and early 1900s, electricity was gradually replacing gas as a source of power for lighting. The fastest growing use of gas was as a fuel for cooking and home heating. The company's head of technology, Goro Nakagawa, returned from a fact-finding tour of the United States to report on a range of new cooking devices powered by gas. The decision was made to concentrate marketing efforts in this area. In 1900, the company stated its four main business areas as gas production and supply, gas by-product supply, production and sales of gas appliances, and the development of business related to the gas industry.

In 1906, Japan again experienced victory in a war, this time over Russia, which once more boosted the economy. The demand for gas in Tokyo was booming, and Tokyo Gas opened nine new sales offices around the town. By 1908, 23 years after its founding, the company supplied 100,000 homes with gas, operated 825 kilometers of pipeline, and supplied 1.2 billion cubic feet of gas per year. Of this total, 80 percent was consumed by household customers, with the remainder supplied to industry.

Indeed, business was so good that a rival Tokyo-based gas company, Chiyoda Gas, was started up in 1908. The two companies, in an attempt to attract the same base of customers, began a price war. This price war was a major headache for the management of Tokyo Gas, and in 1911 both companies signed a pricing agreement in order to avoid financial disaster. Chiyoda Gas was so weakened financially that it eventually went bankrupt, and its assets were taken over by Tokyo Gas. By 1913, Tokyo Gas had emerged as the major supplier of city gas in the Kanto region and in that year began supplying gas to the outlying suburbs of the cities of Kawasaki and Saitama.

Depression, Disasters, and War: 1918–40s

Japan experienced an economic depression from 1918 until the late 1920s. Inflation ensued, and Tokyo Gas was forced to raise the price of gas as the price of coal increased. In 1919, the union representing the 560 workers at Tokyo Gas's three production sites in Tokyo demanded higher wages. The number of

new customers was no longer increasing, and many current users could no longer afford to be connected to the gas supply network. To add to this situation, in 1923 the Kanto region of Japan experienced a catastrophic earthquake. Forty-five percent of houses using gas were destroyed, leaving only 130,000 connected. The pipeline network was severely damaged, with many leaks and resultant fires. The city of Tokyo was quick to rebuild, however, and with frantic around-the-clock repair work underway, gas supplies were resumed after two months.

By 1926, the demand for city gas began to increase as Japan emerged from depression, and in that year Tokyo Gas began to expand its marketing activities. A questionnaire was sent to each customer in order to ascertain the public's impression of the service offered by the company's representatives. Sixty-five percent of those asked responded by saying the service was excellent. Rival gas companies were emerging, taking advantage of the devastation of Tokyo Gas's supply network in the 1923 earthquake. The company responded by aiming to attract 100,000 new customers within six years. In fact, it achieved double this figure. The new president, Shoshichi Iwazaki, stressed the importance of service to the company's large customer base, and 200 adding machines from the United States were incorporated into the headquarters and sales offices to make the company's accounting more efficient. Furthermore, after a long safety campaign in the company's three production sites, a 100 percent safety record was achieved in 1935.

During the late 1930s, Japan was again moving toward war, and the increasingly powerful military government began to take control of vital industries, of which gas production was one. By 1938, Tokyo Gas had one million users but on orders from the military was urging its customers to conserve gas and use gas appliances only when necessary. The military were interested in the by-products of coal gas production—coal tar, benzene, and ammonia for industrial use—as well as in using gas to power armaments factories. Coal was also in shorter supply as the nation's steel industry consumed increasing amounts. By 1944, at the height of Japan's war efforts, two of Tokyo Gas's three production facilities were designated military suppliers and were in effect run by a representative of the Imperial Japanese Army. To control Tokyo's gas industry, the military authorities merged all the companies within the Kanto region into a single concern. A similar exercise was carried out in other regions of Japan, and eight main gas companies were formed. On March 10, 1945, the U.S. Air Force sent wave after wave of B-29 bombers to destroy Tokyo, sparing only the Imperial Palace. The result was devastating, with 120,000 dead and 260,000 houses destroyed. Tokyo Gas's headquarters building was saved by the work force, who prevented it from being burned to the ground.

Only 22 years after the Great Kanto Earthquake, Tokyo had succumbed to the military might of the United States. Tokyo Gas's infrastructure was a shambles, with fewer than 1,500 houses receiving gas in August 1945. Once again, the city's inhabitants rebuilt Tokyo with amazing speed. This time they were greatly aided by the United States, which was eager to rebuild Japan as a democratic state. By November 1945, the number of houses supplied with gas had risen to 340,000, a number that was growing daily. In the year following the devastation, work began in earnest to reconnect and resupply the city with gas. By early 1946, 55 percent of the prewar level had been

Key Dates:

1885: Tokyo Gas incorporates.
1913: The company emerges as the major supplier of city gas in the Kanto region.
1945: Tokyo Gas's infrastructure is nearly destroyed during the war effort; the company is run by the American occupation forces.
1949: Gas rationing ends; Tokyo Gas is free to operate as an independent company.
1969: The company begins to procure liquified natural gas (LNG) from Alaska.
1988: Conversion to a 100 percent natural gas supply is complete.
1998: The Ohgishima LNG Terminal begins operation.
1999: The Japanese gas industry starts to deregulate.

achieved. During this time, both the government and industry of Japan was managed by the American occupation forces. General MacArthur formulated the Law for the Elimination of Excessive Concentration of Economic Power to break up the huge Japanese industrial conglomerates that had dominated Japan economically before and during the war. Tokyo Gas came under the management of the occupying powers, with representatives of the U.S. military giving guidance in the early postwar years. In 1949, the gas rationing in place since 1945 came to an end, and Tokyo Gas was free to operate as an independent company.

The Japanese economy recovered swiftly, and by the early 1950s was experiencing rapid growth. Before the war, Japan had relied on Manchuria in China, which was occupied by the Japanese, for a large proportion of her coal. This source became more unreliable and expensive in the postwar years, and the Japanese power companies looked increasingly to crude oil to supply industry needs. Tokyo Gas began a conversion of its Omori coal gas facility to produce gas from oil. In 1954, construction began of a new oil-gas production facility in Toyosu, a project involving the reclamation of land in Tokyo Bay. The huge complex was completed in 1956 and began producing two million cubic meters of gas per day. By 1955, the company was once again supplying one million households. Univac punch-card computers were procured and installed in the headquarters building to monitor customers' consumption. Gas service stations were opened in and around Tokyo, including nine in Yokohama, to accommodate customer enquiries. In 1959, a gas promotion exhibition, entitled Gas in Life, took place to demonstrate how the company produced gas and to display new uses of gas. With the aim of diversifying its sources of raw materials, Tokyo Gas began the purchase of liquid propane gas (LPG) from Saudi Arabia in 1962. In the same year, a 329 kilometer pipeline was constructed to transport 500,000 cubic meters of natural gas daily from a field off Niigata on the west coast of Japan. Unfortunately, the pipeline was severely damaged in an earthquake which hit Niigata two years later.

Japan emerged as an economic superstate in the 1960s. In 1969, Japan's gross national product was second only to that of the United States. A visible contribution made by Tokyo Gas to this success was the completion in 1968 of the world's largest

steel gas-storage tank. With a capacity of 200,000 cubic meters and structure made from steel plates 35 millimeters thick, the tank was designed to hold high-pressure gas.

The Import of LNG Begins in 1969

Around this time, the company was developing a technology that would come to dominate Japan's gas industry—the import of natural gas as a liquid, known as liquefied natural gas (LNG). Natural gas had several major advantages over gas manufactured from oil or coal; for instance, once the transport technology was perfected, it became the cheaper alternative; natural gas is also more environmentally friendly than oil- or coal-manufactured gas, both to produce and to burn. The most important factor in its adoption, however, was that both Tokyo Gas and the Japanese government wanted to reduce the nation's dependence on Middle Eastern oil, which had risen to supply almost 70 percent of the nation's energy needs by 1970.

Motivated by these factors, Tokyo Gas, along with Tokyo Electric Power Company, began negotiations with Phillips Petroleum and Marathon Oil of the United States to procure 96,000 tons of LNG per year from fields off Alaska. Supply began in 1969 with the LNG refrigerator ship *Polar Alaska* docking at the world's first LNG terminal in Negishi in Yokohama. The Sodegaura works on the opposite side of Tokyo Bay began operation as an LNG terminal four years later. Because of the lower energy value of natural gas as compared to manufactured gas (2,000 as opposed to 4,800 kilocalories per cubic meter), it was necessary to convert and inspect the company's network as well as customers' appliances to insure they could adapt to using the new gas. This was done by Tokyo Gas engineers in the early 1970s, and the exercise gave the company the chance to promote and sell its new range of natural gas appliances as well as to inspect its own network.

The oil shock of 1974, which sent the Japanese economy into negative growth, reinforced Tokyo Gas's decision to concentrate on LNG. Sourcing of LNG was expanded to Indonesia, Brunei, and Malaysia, and a computerized loading system was developed for transferring the minus 160 degrees centigrade liquefied gas from ship to storage tank. In 1976, the manufacture of gas from coal at the Toyosu facility was abandoned after 20 years of production.

During the late 1970s and early 1980s, Tokyo Gas sought to present itself as a company that was environmentally aware and concerned with the safety of its factories. In a statement in 1982, it took great pride in the fact that no major accident associated with the transport of the volatile LNG had occurred since the company started using it. The conversion to a 100 percent natural gas supply was completed in 1988. The supply and distribution of LNG was controlled by what the company described as an "intelligent service system" which monitored the gas as it traveled from the supply ship to the consumer's home appliance. Any malfunction was corrected by emergency stations operating around the clock.

Like most other Japanese utility companies, Tokyo Gas had diversified, and the group of companies with Tokyo Gas as the nucleus was informally known as the Tokyo Gas Group. In 1991, 75 percent of the group's sales came from the supply of gas to 7.5 million households in the Kanto region as well as to industrial users. The group's other major business area was gas appliances, which had been manufactured and sold by the company since the early 1900s. In a field related to the refrigeration technology associated with LNG transport, the Tokyo Gas Group was involved in the production of low-temperature chemicals such as liquid oxygen and dry ice, as well as providing a food refrigeration service.

In the early 1990s, the group's profits were reduced by an increase in the price of LNG and rising interest rates. The Tokyo Gas Group continued, however, to be a mainstay of industrial Japan. The firm continued to compete with Tokyo Electric Power as a supplier of energy to the region's population. At the time, Tokyo Gas supplied about a third of Tokyo's residential energy and sought to increase its share through technological developments and the marketing of gas as a source of all home energy needs.

Diversification Amid Deregulation: 1990s and Beyond

In 1993, the company launched a restructuring plan that would reduce the company's workforce while encouraging growth. In order to promote even greater use of natural gas, the firm began providing natural gas production technology to producers in China, a country suffering from significant air pollution due to its high-dependence on coal. Tokyo Gas also teamed up with Petroleum Nasional Bhd (Petronas) in Malaysia to form Gas Malaysia Sdn Bhd, a joint venture designed to develop the country's natural gas supply.

Tokyo Gas closed its Toyosu plant in 1994 and its Tsurumi facility in 1997. Early the following year, a third LNG terminal was launched at Ohgishima. It had the world's first underground LNG storage tank and operated as Japan's first offshore LNG receiving berth.

While Tokyo Gas continued to strengthen its business, the industry around it began to change as a result of deregulation. Starting in 1995, the Japanese government partially liberalized the electric utility industry, allowing independent power producers (IPP's) to sell electric power to the regional companies. Then, in March 2000, these IPP's were allowed to market directly to customers, allowing both foreign and domestic competition in the retail electricity market. At the same time, the gas industry was in the process of deregulating, which in part allowed Tokyo Gas to utilize its profits to diversify (in the past profits were used exclusively to reduce gas rates).

While deregulation brought with it increased opportunities for expansion, it also set the stage for intense competition. In response to its changing business environment, Tokyo Gas launched a new management plan in 1999 entitled Frontier 2007. According to a company press release, Frontier 2007 was based on four goals: business model innovation, construction of the Group's management system, strengthening of the corporate culture, and business expansion into energy-related areas. Management set these goals in place to enable Tokyo Gas to achieve positive financial results and growth as an "energy frontier corporate group."

Deregulation started to significantly change Japan's industry during the early years of the new century. An April 2002 *World Gas Intelligence* article claimed that LNG businesses were "slashing prices, buying fuel more efficiently, tying up with foreign oil companies, and using new pricing methods." In addition, Tokyo Gas and its competitors pursued diversification opportunities made available by industry deregulation. During 2001, the company moved into the electricity retailing sector when it partnered with NTT Facilities Inc. and Osaka Gas Co. Ltd. to launch ENNET Corporation. Tokyo Gas established subsidiary Tokyo Gas Bay Power Co. Ltd. to build a power plant to generate electricity for sale to ENNET. The firm also sought to expand its LNG capacity by landing key contracts. While the company's LNG requirements were currently filled through 2006, Tokyo Gas was actively pursuing contracts for LNG it would need for 2007 and beyond. During this time period, it procured 7.5 million tons of LNG per year from Alaska, Australia, Brunei, Indonesia, Malaysia, and Qatar. In early 2003, Tokyo Gas announced that it planned to add Russia to that list.

By 2003, Tokyo Gas management was confident that deregulation would continue to bring positive changes to the company and the customers it served. As an "energy frontier company," Tokyo Gas was focused on supplying gas, electricity, heat, and energy services, utilizing natural gas as its core energy source. While competition would no doubt remain intense, Tokyo Gas appeared to have a solid strategy in place to remain successful in the years to come.

Principal Subsidiaries

Tokyo Gas Energy Co. Ltd.; Tokyo Gas Chemicals Co. Ltd.; Tokyo Oxygen and Nitrogen Co. Ltd.; Tokyo Gas Urban Development Co. Ltd.; Park Tower Hotel Co. Ltd.; Kanpai Co. Ltd.; Gastar Co. Ltd.; TG Credit Service Co. Ltd.; Chiba Gas Co. Ltd.; Tsukuba Gakuen Gas Co. Ltd.; Tokyo Gas Engineering Co. Ltd.; TG Information Network Co. Ltd.; Tokyo LNG Tanker Co. Ltd.; TG Enterprise Co. Ltd.

Principal Competitors

The Kansai Electric Power Company Inc.; Osaka Gas Co. Ltd.; The Tokyo Electric Power Company Co. Ltd.

Further Reading

Fukuda, Takehiro, "Distributors Aim to Secure Gas Supplies," *Nikkei Weekly*, August 31, 1991, p. 7.

Gray, Tony, "Tokyo Gas Hungry for LNG Deals," *Lloyd's List*, June 19, 2002, p. 2.

"Japan's Deregulation Delivers a Punch," *World Gas Intelligence*, April 16, 2002.

The Story of Tokyo Gas 1885–1985, Tokyo: Tokyo Gas, 1985.

"Tokyo Gas Lining Up Sakhalin LNG," *Nikkei Weekly*, February 10, 2003.

"Tokyo Gas Posts First Profit Gain in Six Years," *Japan Economic Newswire*, May 25, 1992.

"Tokyo Gas to Provide Technology to China," *Nikkei Weekly*, October 24, 1994.

"Tokyo Gas to Supply Malaysia," *Nikkei Weekly*, July 29, 1996, p. 23.

"Tokyo Gas Unveils Long-Range Restructuring Program," *Japan Economic Newswire*, October 8, 1993.

—Dylan Tanner
—update: Christina M. Stansell

The Tussauds Group

Silverglade
Leatherhead Road
Chessington
Surrey KT9 2QL
United Kingdom
Telephone: (+44) 870 429 2300
Fax: (+44) 870 429 5500
Web site: http://www.tussauds.com

*Wholly Owned Subsidiary of Charterhouse Development
   Capital*
Incorporated: 1926
Employees: 2,750
Sales: £178.4 million ($285 million) (2002)
NAIC: 712110 Museums; 713110 Amusement and
   Theme Parks

The Tussauds Group is more than just its famous Madame Tussaud's attraction. The Surrey-based company is Europe's leading owner and operator of theme park attractions, registering more than 15 million visitors per year. The company's Madame Tussaud's attraction remains its most international brand, with sites in London, New York, Las Vegas, Amsterdam, and Hong Kong. In the United Kingdom, Tussauds also owns the Alton Towers theme hotel and park complex, the number one theme park in the UK; Chessington World of Adventures and Thorpe Park, both located in the London region; Warwick Castle; and Germany's Heide Park, acquired in 2002. Tussauds also owns 33 percent of the London Eye, the United Kingdom's number one tourist attraction in terms of visitors; the company operates the attraction and has announced its interest in buying out the 33 percent stake held by partner British Airways. Tussauds has been owned by investment group Charterhouse Development Capital (CDC) since 1998. In 2003, CDC refuted rumors that it planned to sell Tussauds or bring the company public. In 2002, Tussauds Group posted sales of more than £178 million ($285 million).

Molding Amusement History from Wax in the 18th Century

Tussauds history dates back to the late 18th century. Physician Philippe Curtius, originally from Germany, had begun modeling wax figures, principally of internal organs and other structures of the human bodies, but later began preparing wax portraits of notables of the day, which he first placed on exhibition in Berne, Switzerland. Curtius's creations had caught the attention of the French royal family, and Curtius was invited to move his wax workshop to Paris in 1765.

By then, Curtius had hired on a housekeeper, a widow who brought with her a daughter, Marie Grosholtz, who had been born in Strasbourg in 1761, shortly after her father's death. Grosholtz quickly became Curtius's student, and soon became highly regarded for her skills in working with wax. In 1778, Grosholtz completed her first portrait, the subject being Jean-Jacques Rousseau, which was followed by a portrait of Voltaire. These earned Grosholtz an invitation to join the royal court at Versailles, where she was employed as a teacher. Called back to Paris during the French Revolution of 1789, Grosholtz was then given the task of modeling the death masks of her former employers. Meanwhile, Curtius had continued expanding his own waxworks exhibits, notably with a ''Caverne des Grands Voleurs'' (Cave of the Great Thieves), featuring criminals and torture devices.

Grosholtz was named Curitus's heir upon his death in 1794, and she took over the waxworks exhibit and workshop, as well as properties in Paris. The following year, Grosholtz married François Tussaud. The turmoil surrounding the French Revolution had cut interest in Madame Tussaud's exhibit, and in 1802 she made the decision to take the exhibit to England—bringing her eldest son, Joseph, but leaving behind her husband and younger son. In England, Tussaud organized a traveling exhibit of her waxworks. The outbreak of war between France and England prevented Tussaud from returning to France. Instead, She spent the next 33 years traveling throughout the British Isles.

Younger son Francis finally joined his mother in 1826 (Tussaud never saw her husband again, however). In 1835, the Tussaud family finally stopped touring and opened its first permanent exhibition, on London's Baker Street. By then, Tussaud's exhibits had long been one of the Britain's most popular attractions. The ample accommodations of the Baker Street venue permitted the family to expand beyond its traditional touring exhibit. One of the new features introduced during this period was the so-called "Separate Room," itself based on Curtius's "Caverne des Grands Voleurs," placed apart from the main exhibition so as not to offend customer sensibilities. Later known as the "Chamber of Horrors," the room featured portraits of noted murderers as well as instruments of torture and punishment. The exhibit was to remain one of the Tussaud exhibits' most popular attractions.

Madame Tussaud died in 1859. The business remained in the Tussaud family, and Marie Tussaud's grandsons moved it to new, larger quarters on London's Marylebone Road, which became its permanent home. In 1925, most of Madame Tussaud's was destroyed by fire. A number of key pieces, including Marie Tussauds' own death mask, as well as most of the Chamber of Horrors, were rescued and formed the cornerstone of the restored wax museum, which opened in 1928 and now boasted its own restaurant and movie theater. Madame Tussaud's had by then reincorporated as a limited company in 1926.

Diversifying in the 1970s

Much of Tussaud's, including the theater and restaurant, was again destroyed, now by bombing on the first night of the London Blitz of 1940. Yet the museum reopened by the end of that year. Instead of replacing the movie theater, Tussaud's instead sought a different attraction. In 1958, the company opened the London Planetarium, where its cinema had been. The planetarium, which was upgraded in the mid-1960s, was to remain a key attraction at the expanded Tussaud's.

Until the end of the 1960s, Tussauds had remained focused on its single London site. In 1970, however, the company moved beyond London—and the United Kingdom—for the first time, opening a second Madame Tussaud's in Amsterdam that featured a different array of figures from those at the original London location.

The company now sought to diversify beyond its wax figures. In 1973, Tussauds acquired Wookey Hole Caves and Mill, set in the caves of Somerset and featuring a paper mill, and in 1976 it purchased the Tolgus Tin plant in Cornwall, a former tin mine that had been converted into tourist attraction (the company sold the Tolgus site in 1980). Back at Madame Tussaud's, the company was completing a new upgrade to the London Planetarium, debuting a laser-light show, Laserium, in 1977.

Tussauds was itself acquired by S. Pearson & Son (later Pearson Publishing) in 1978. Pearson had also begun to diversify by building up its own attractions wing around the Chessington Zoo. Following its acquisition of Tussauds, control of the zoo was transferred to Tussauds, which then became Pearsons' attractions division. That division grew quickly and in 1978 purchased Warwick Castle. With a history dating back to 914, Warwick Castle was given a thorough facelift by the Tussauds Group, which converted the site into a family-oriented theme park. In 1982, Warwick Castle opened its first major attraction, "A Royal Weekend Party." This was followed in 1986 by the opening of a restored Victorian Rose Garden.

Difficulties in maintaining profits at the Chessington Zoo encouraged the company to transform that site into a theme park in the mid-1980s. The former zoo's animals were maintained as part of the new park, now called the Chessington World of Adventures, which opened in 1987 and quickly tripled the number of its visitors.

Two years later, Tussauds expanded again with the opening in the London Pavilion of the Rock Circus, which centered around a rock and roll theme. In that year, the company sold off the Wookey Hole site in a management buyout, turning its focus instead to larger, more upscale attractions.

The company's next acquisition came in 1990 with the £60 million purchase of the Alton Towers amusement park. Located on a site that dated back to the 12th century, Alton Towers had been redeveloped into one of the United Kingdom's first "American-style" amusement parks in 1980. The site continued to be expanded during the 1980s, yet by the end of the decade had begun to lose its luster. Under Tussauds, however, Alton Towers found new life as a theme park intended to rival the impending opening of Disneyland Paris.

In 1991, Tussauds shut down its Amsterdam site, reopening again in a modern and larger site on that city's main Dam Square. The following year, the Tussauds Group Studios, which had become responsible not only for the development of new attractions at Madame Tussaud's but also for developing attractions at the group's growing list of theme parks and sites, moved to larger facilities.

European Leader in the New Century

Tussauds continued expanding its theme parks in the mid-1990s. The Warwick Castle park added new attractions, such as 1995's "Kingmaker—A Preparation for Battle." Alton Towers also expanded considerably, particularly with the opening of the Alton Towers Hotel in 1996. The £12 million hotel, which featured 125 fully themed rooms, in addition other themed areas, was meant as a direct response to the opening of the Disneyland Paris complex.

By then, Tussauds had entered the European continent as well, taking a 40 percent stake in the new, £300 million theme park Port Aventura in Spain. Tussauds was not only primary shareholder but also operator of the site, which quickly attracted some 2.7 million visitors in its first year.

Meanwhile, the Madame Tussaud's flagship site in London was also undergoing development, notably with the opening of a newly renovated London Planetarium in 1995 and the 1996 debut of a new Chamber of Horrors at a cost of £1 million. Madame Tussaud's then went on the road again, launching a

Key Dates:

1765: Philippe Curtius opens a waxworks exhibit in Paris.

1778: Marie Grosholtz, daughter of Curtius's governess, completes her first portrait, that of Jean-Jacques Rousseau.

1783: Curtius debuts his "Caverne des Grande Voleurs," which later becomes the "Chamber of Horrors" exhibit at the waxworks.

1794: When Curtius dies, Grosholtz (who married and changed her name to Tussaud) inherits the wax exhibit.

1802: Madame Tussaud travels to England, bringing a traveling wax exhibit.

1835: Tussaud's first exhibition site is established on Baker Street, London.

1850: Marie Tussaud dies, and the exhibit is taken over by her sons.

1884: Madame Tussaud's is moved to a new location, on Marylebone Road in London.

1928: Partially destroyed by fire, the Marylebone site is rebuilt and includes a movie theater and restaurant.

1940: Theater and restaurant destroyed in the *Blitzkrieg*.

1970: Madame Tussaud's opens its first international site in Amsterdam.

1973: Wookey Hole Caves and Mill in Somerset are acquired as part of a diversification drive.

1978: S. Pearson & Son buys Tussaud's, which absorbs Pearson-owned Chessington Zoo.

1989: The company inaugurates a rock and roll history-themed Rock Circus.

1990: The company buys Alton Towers amusement park and begins redeveloping the site as a theme park.

1998: Charterhouse Development Capital (CDC) buys Tussaud's from Pearsons.

2000: Madame Tussaud's museum opens in New York.

2001: Madame Tussaud's museum opens in Hong Kong; Rock Circus closes.

2002: The company acquires Heide Park, the largest theme park in Germany.

traveling, limited season exhibition beginning in Melbourne, Australia, in 1997.

Tussauds sold out its stake in Port Aventura in 1998, ending its management of the site as well. Instead, the company looked closer to home for growth, buying Thorpe Park that same year. Foreign expansion remained a company objective, however. In 1998, Madame Tussaud's Touring Attraction moved on to Sydney, while Tussauds began plans to bring its flagship brand to Las Vegas, with an agreement to open a new site in the Venetian hotel and casino complex.

Pearson had begun a streamlining effort in the mid-1990s, and Tussauds turn came in 1998, when the company was sold to investment group Charterhouse Development Capital (CDC). The new owners quickly brought in a new management team, which sought to boost profits while continuing the company's international growth.

Madame Tussaud's opened in Las Vegas in 1999; the success of that site led the company to begin scouting locations for a second U.S. site. In 2000, the company opened Madame Tussaud's New York on that city's 42nd Street. Meanwhile, the travelling exhibit had moved on to Singapore in 1999 before arriving in Hong Kong in 2000. That city's proximity to the vast Chinese mainland, as well as elsewhere in the Asian region, encouraged the company to put down roots. A permanent Madame Tussaud's was opened in Hong Kong's Peak Tower that year.

The year 2000 also marked the opening of the London Eye, operated and controlled at 33 percent by Tussauds in partnership with British Airways. The site quickly became the leading attraction in the United Kingdom. Tussauds shut down the Rock Circus site, which had been unable to reverse declining visitor numbers, in 2001.

Tussauds now began looking for its next acquisition, finding it in Germany when it purchased Heide Park, one of the country's largest, located on a nearly 1,100-acre site in Soltau. That purchase, finalized in 2002, helped boost Tussauds to the top position among Europe's attractions groups.

The company's investment of some £300 million over the previous five years under CDC had enabled it to boost its revenues to nearly £185 million by the end of 2002. By then, Tussauds was rumored to be slated for a sale or public listing by CDC. Although CDC denied the rumors, such a move was seen as fitting into CDC's pattern of investing heavily in order to expand its holdings before selling them again after a period of three to five years. Instead, Tussauds—and parent CDC—appeared prepared to continued its expansion drive, acknowledging its interest in acquiring British Airway's 33 percent stake in the London Eye. The company also announced a £100 million investment program that included the opening of a new £40 million theme hotel, Splash Landings, at Alton Towers in June 2003.

Principal Divisions

Alton Towers; Chessington World of Adventures; Heide Park (Germany); London Eye (33%); Thorpe Park; Warwick Castle.

Principal Competitors

Walt Disney Co.; Viacom Inc.; Busch Entertainment Corporation; Universal Studios Inc.; Euro Disney SCA.

Further Reading

Deckard, Linda, "Tussauds' Herbert Predicts Future of Industry in Europe," *Amusement Business*, December 3, 1990, p. 33.

Gibbs, Geoff, "Wax and Wane: Tussauds Quells Sell-off Speculation," *Guardian*, March 7, 2003.

Koranteng, Juliana, "Tussauds Pumps Up Its Offerings," *Amusement Business*, January 27, 2003, p. 5.

O'Brien, Tim, "Tussauds Properties Reportedly for Sale: 'Record Year' of Growth," *Amusement Business*, March 3, 2003, p. 5

Reece, Damian, "Tussauds Group to Go on Sale with Pounds 500m Price Tag," *Sunday Telegraph*, February 23, 2003, p. 2.

"The Tussauds Group," *Marketing*, February 21, 2002, p. 54.

—M. L. Cohen

Viskase Companies, Inc.

6855 West 65th Street
Chicago, Illinois 60638
U.S.A.
Telephone: (630) 789-4900
Toll Free: (800) 323-8562
Fax: (708) 496-4412
Web site: http://www.viskase.com

Public Company
Incorporated: 1970 as Envirodyne Industries, Inc.
Employees: 1,400
Sales: $189.3 million
Stock Exchanges: OTC
Ticker Symbol: VCIC
NAIC: 325188 All Other Basic Inorganic Chemical Manufacturing

Viskase Companies, Inc. is a Chicago-based corporation that is a world leader in the production of nonedible cellulose and plastic casings and nettings used in the preparation and packaging of processed meat and poultry products. Smaller diameter products like hot dogs, smoked sausages, and beef sticks use the company's NOJAX Casings. Large cellulose casings, which can be smoked, are suitable for medium-sized meat products like bologna, salami, and semi-boneless hams. Fibrous casings can accommodate a variety of sizes for processed meats such as bologna, ham, and salami, as well as poultry products. These food products are also suitable for Viskase's polyamide casings, VISFLEX and VISMAX, which can be used for cooking and shipping. The company's SCOTnet Nettings, made of polyester elastic, are used in both processed meats and poultry products. In addition, Viskase uses regenerated cellulose to produce MEMBRA-CEL, a hydrophilic membrane suitable for dialysis purposes in the laboratory. The company has suffered a number of setbacks in recent years, starting with a leveraged buyout (LBO) in 1989 that saddled it with massive debt and including outbreaks of "Mad Cow" and foot-and-mouth disease that have hurt the sale of beef products around the world. As a result

the company has been forced to shed assets and close plants, while having its stock delisted by the NASDAQ in 2000.

1920s Origins

The history of Viskase began with Erwin O. Freund, who sponsored research to find a substitute for the animal gut casing that was the basis of his Chicago business. For hundreds of years sausages and similar foods had relied on the cleansed intestines of sheep, cows, or pigs, casings that possessed a number of drawbacks. Because the American sausage industry had to rely on other countries to provide it with large numbers of intestine casings, its growth was stunted. Freund's goal was to find an alternative to natural casings, one that relied on a readily available raw material, was strong enough to withstand the pressure of meat forced into it and the cooking process, and could be created in uniform sizes. Freund's researchers latched onto the "viscose" process, which relied on purified cotton cellulose that was processed into filaments. This material was then coated on a pipe, dried, and removed by dipping in a vat of weak acid. The resulting tube was stuffed with meat, linked, and brought to the smokehouse. When smoked the casing sagged, which at first appeared to be a major disappointment, but it was quickly realized that when the casing was removed the meat inside remained intact and firm. Instead of creating a synthetic edible casing, Freund had stumbled upon the Skinless Frankfurter.

Freund organized his new business as the Visking Corporation in 1925 and began producing NOJAX casing for frankfurters in a small building located in the Chicago Union Stockyards. The company continued its research efforts and in 1927 introduced cellulose casings for large sausage products. In 1931 Visking developed a way to print on the casings, to make trademarks and promotional material visible in the meat case, and also brought out the first colored casings. Even stronger cellulose casings were introduced in 1935. In 1941, to spur research efforts, as well as sales, Visking founded the Foods Science and Quality Institute to help the meat and poultry industry to produce new products and make better use of Visking products. During the 1950s Visking developed striped NOJAX casing, fibrous casings called E-Z PEEL, and TASTIJAX, a casing made from algin. Moreover, the com-

Company Perspectives:

Viskase is a customer driven company that excels in delivering technically superior, value-adding solutions to our customers, enhances shareholder value and provides career opportunities to our employees.

pany's research took Visking into areas beyond casings, transforming it into the largest U.S. producer of polyethylene film. It developed Visten, a plastic film for packaging food products, and a transparent plastic film it called Visqueen, which found applications in containers, aprons, shower curtains, aprons, raincoats, and as a moisture barrier building material.

Selling Visking to Union Carbide in 1956

With innovation came prosperity. In 1932 demand for Visking products was strong enough to warrant the building of a new plant in Chicago. In the 1950s, manufacturing facilities were opened in Loudon, Tennessee, and Beauvais, France. In 1956 the company, now a public corporation, recorded net sales of $57.7 million, while earning more than $5 million, or $2.36 per share, prompting a three-for-one stock split. At this point the company chose to shed it independence and join forces with the major supplier of the raw materials it needed to produce polyethylene film—Union Carbide and Carbon Corporation and its resin-producing subsidiary, the Bakelite Company. Union Carbide acquired Visking in 1956, a $91 million stock deal that gave shareholders one share of Union Carbide for every 2.5 shares of Visking, which now began operating as the Visking Co. division of Union Carbide. Six months after Visking shareholders approved the deal, however, the Federal Trade Commission stepped in, filing a compliant that charged Union Carbide with violating antitrust legislation, the first time that the FTC objected to a ''forward vertical'' merger, one in which a supplier acquired a customer. The complaint maintained that Visking was in a position to acquire a monopolistic control over the polyethylene industry, essentially because its corporate parent had the power to manipulate resin prices.

Union Carbide denied the charges but in October 1961 the FTC ruled that the corporation had one year to divest itself of its Visking holdings. The corporation appealed, but finally in 1963 it was forced to sell the polyethylene film operations of Visking, including the Visqueen trademark, to Ethyl Corp. The casing business continued as the Visking division of Union Carbide, then on July 1, 1964, changed its name to the Food Products division, to better reflect the subsidiary's commitment to the food industry. No matter what its name, the old Visking operation continued to develop new products. In the 1960s it introduced SHIRMATIC fibrous casings that worked with high-speed, automatic stuffing equipment that its researchers also developed. It introduced heat shrinkable bags, sold under the brand name PERFLEX, which were used by processed meat and cheese producers to package and preserve their products. The Union Carbide unit now changed its name to the Films Packaging Division, again to better reflect the scope of its activities. Business grew so much that new plants were opened around the world in the 1970s, including Thaon, France;

Pulheim, Germany; Caronno, Italy; as well as an applications laboratory in Beauvais, France. Domestic facilities also were built in Osceola, Arkansas and Kentland, Indiana.

Problems encountered by Union Carbide in the mid-1980s led to a change of ownership for the former Visking business. In December 1984 a Union Carbide pesticide plant in Bhopal, India, suffered one of the largest industrial accidents in history when a cloud of lethal gas escaped, killing 1,757 people and affecting some 300,000 others. Already facing litigation for this incident, Union Carbide experienced a similar, albeit smaller and less tragic, accident at a West Virginia plant, injuring 135 people and resulting in the largest fine, $1.4 million, ever levied by the Occupational Safety and Health Administration. The company's stock plunged in the aftermath of these events, making it an attractive takeover candidate. In 1985 it fought off a hostile takeover bid by GAF Corporation, but as a result of buying back a large number of shares it doubled its debt to an unmanageable $4.5 billion. To reduce this debt Union Carbide was forced to shed assets, primarily its consumer products divisions but also some industrial divisions, including the Films Packaging. In February 1986 the worldwide business was sold to Chicago-based Envirodyne Industries, Inc. for approximately $230 million. New management placed the assets under a new subsidiary incorporated as Viskase Corporation.

Envirodyne was founded in 1970 by Ronald K. Linde and was involved in environmental technology until 1982 when Linde decided to turn to ''relatively mundane businesses where we could add value.'' It entered the plastics industry with the 1983 acquisition of Harvel Industries, which began operating as Clear Shield National Inc., producing such items as plastic flatware and drinking straws. Management displayed a sure hand at building profitability by tightly controlling inventories and accounts receivables. As a result Clear Shield began to grow profits at a clip of 30 percent per year. It was the Union Carbide deal, however, that caught the attention of the investment community. The Viskase assets boosted Envirodyne's sales by 600 percent and profits by 300 percent. Moreover, the price of its stock soared from $8 per share to $32. Envirodyne next bought the Filmco division from RJR Nabisco Inc. for $35 million in cash. The unit manufactured PVC stretch and single-layer plastic under the Filmco name, used to package foods and wrap grocery products. In addition, polypropylene films were used to package European bakery goods, and polystyrene rigid food packaging materials were produced. These assets operated as the Filmco Industries subsidiary before being integrated into Viskase. To achieve its rapid growth, Envirodyne took on considerable debt, equal to about 2.5 times its equity, but management felt confident enough of its cash flow to make yet another significant acquisition in 1988, buying Sandusky Plastics, makers of plastic containers, from The Chariot Group for approximately $27 million.

1989 Takeover Resulting in Crippling Debt

Envirodyne appeared to be a thriving business with its three main subsidiaries performing well, but in 1989 the company attracted the attention of Donald P. Kelly, a well known Chicago dealmaker. He made his mark in the 1980s when as the head of Esmark Inc. he pocketed approximately $15 million by selling the company to Beatrice Cos., then two years later, with

Key Dates:

1925: Erwin O. Freund founds Visking Corporation.
1957: Visking is sold to Union Carbide.
1970: Envirodyne Industries is formed.
1986: Envirodyne acquires former Visking assets, forming Viskase Corporation.
1993: Envirodyne files for bankruptcy protection.
1998: Envirodyne changes its name to Viskase Companies, Inc.
2000: The company is delisted by the NASDAQ due to low market capitalization; the plastic barrier and shrink film business is sold to the Bemis Company for $245 million.

backing from Kohlberg Kravis Roberts, led a $6.2 billion leveraged buyout of Beatrice, and earned close to $100 million by selling the business to American Brands. In his late 60s Kelly appeared to be retired, but in 1989 he mounted a $900 million leveraged buyout of Envirodyne with backing from Salomon Brothers. With only $2 million of his money in the deal, Kelly emerged as chairman and CEO of the corporation.

Already servicing a heavy debt load, Envirodyne quickly reached a tipping point because of the LBO, with its slow-growth businesses unable to keep up with interest payments, resulting in mounting losses. In 1991 alone the company lost $31.8 million. Nevertheless, Kelly and his partners continued to extract their management fees, by 1993 collecting some $7.4 million. In addition, a unit of Salomon Brothers received more than $33 million for investment banking and management service fees incurred from 1989 to 1991. The company was finally forced into Chapter 11 bankruptcy in 1993, but after it emerged it displayed little improvement. Envirodyne posted a net loss of $3.6 million in 1994. The Viskase subsidiary endured a difficult year, due in large part to a baseball strike that hurt the sale of hot dogs. Moreover, it faced new competition in casings with Spain-based Visco SA and British Devro International plc entering the U.S. market. The result was lower costs for casings, and because Viskase costs remained the same, the difference came out of the company's margins.

After Kelly retired as CEO and chairman in 1996, Envirodyne fought off a takeover attempt by energy company Zapata Corp., which was shifting away from the oil and natural gas business. The company continued to lose money, $21.5 million in 1995 and $13.7 million in 1996, leaving management with no choice but to begin selling off assets. In 1997 Viskase sold its PVC flexible film business to Linpac Plastics Ltd., a British firm. The following year Envirodyne took even more radical steps. Sandusky Plastics was sold to Whitely Industries, and Clear Shield went to Solo Cup Co. for $140 million. With Viskase Corp. now Envirodyne's core business, shareholders voted in August 1998 to change the name of the parent corporation to Viskase Companies, Inc. It cut costs by laying off workers and looked to a new, cheaper manufacturing technique it called Nucel to produce less expensive casings. Nevertheless, management also hired New York investment baking firm Donaldson Lufkin & Jenrette Securities Corp to find a buyer for the business. Having failed to turn a profit for close to a decade, Viskase attracted no suitors and the company continued its downward spiral, the situation only exacerbated by incidents of ''Mad Cow'' disease in England that adversely impacted the consumption of meat and in turn the demand for casings.

In early 2000 the price of Viskase stock fell so low that the company had a market capitalization of just $25 million, leading to it being delisted by the NASDAQ and moving to the OTC Bulletin Board. To reduce its remaining debt of $425 million, in July 2000 the company sold its plastic barrier and shrink film business, which accounted for 40 percent of its total revenues, to the Bemis Company for $245 million. Now solely focused on its casings business, Viskase continue to lose money, $17.8 million in 2000, followed by $25.5 million in 2001. Business was especially hurt by mad cow disease spreading to the European continent and an outbreak of foot-and-mouth disease in the United Kingdom. With the American economy struggling as well, Viskase's road to fiscal health appeared uncertain at best.

Principal Subsidiaries

Viskase Corporation; Viskase S.A. (France); Viskase Brasil Embalagens Ltda. (Brazil).

Principal Competitors

Devro plc; Viscofan S.A.

Further Reading

Laderman, Jeffrey M., ''Envirodyne Ain't Glamorous—But Oh, How It Grows,'' *Business Week,* April 27, 1987, p. 100.

Lashinsky, Adam, ''While Envirodyne Sinks, Kelly Gets His Fees,'' *Crain's Chicago Business,* January 25, 1993, p. 3.

Murphy, H. Lee, ''With New Name, Embattled Envirodyne Tries to Find Buyer,'' *Crain's Chicago Business,* September 21, 1998, p. 14.

Palmer, Ann Therese, ''Wiener Woes Dog Envirodyne Industries,'' *Crain's Chicago Business,* June 12, 1995, p. 26.

Rewick, C.J., ''Raiders of the Lost Art: Real Men Use Junk Bonds,'' *Crain's Chicago Business,* June 1, 1998, p. A160.

—Ed Dinger

Warwick Valley Telephone Company

47 Main Street
Warwick, New York 10990
U.S.A.
Telephone: (845) 986-1101
Toll Free: (800) 952-7642
Fax: (845) 986-6699
Web site: http://www.wvtc.com

Public Company
Incorporated: 1902 as Warwick Valley Telephone Co.
Employees: 120
Sales: $27.7 million (2002)
Stock Exchanges: NASDAQ
Ticker Symbol: WWVY
NAIC: 513310 Wired Telecommunications Carriers

Doing business as WVT Communications, Warwick Valley Telephone Company is an independent telecom company serving a mostly rural area of southeastern New York and nearby portions of New Jersey. The Town of Warwick, located 55 miles north of New York City, is comprised of three villages (Warwick, Florida, and Greenwood Lake) and five hamlets (Amity, Bellvale, Edenville, New Milford, and Pine Island). Despite its small size WVT has been in the vanguard of telecoms in adopting new technologies and rolling out new products. WVT converted to all-digital technology and offered cellular service in the late 1980s, then provided internet dialup access in the mid-1990s as well as high-speed ISDN and DSL service later in the decade. With the advent of a new century the company introduced VDSL (very high-speed digital subscriber line), which permits WVT to offer digital TV service to its customers. Internet service is provided by wholly owned subsidiary Hometown Online, Inc., not only operating in Warwick Valley's service area but also in neighboring parts of New York, New Jersey, and Pennsylvania. Another wholly owned subsidiary, Warwick Valley Long Distance Company, resells domestic and international long distance to WVT subscribers. In addition, WVT is involved in a number of joint ventures. It holds a 7.5 percent stake in Ball Atlantic Orange-Poughkeepsie Limited Partnership, a wholesaler of min-

utes to cellular operators, and a 17 percent interest in Zefcom, L.L.C., a reseller of wireless services. WVT also owns an 8.9 percent stake in Hudson Valley DataNet, a company offering high-speed bandwidth in the region.

Founding of Warwick Valley Telephone: 1902

Before the birth of Warwick Valley Telephone in 1902, the entire Town of Warwick was serviced by a single public telephone located in a drugstore on Main Street in the Village of Warwick. Frustrated that the New York Telephone Company was not prepared to offer anything beyond this modest convenience, 25 Warwick residents met in the Village Building on December 1, 1901, to organize their own telephone company. At this preliminary meeting it was agreed that Warwick Valley Telephone Co. would be incorporated with capital stock of $10,000, to be raised by selling 1,000 shares at $10 each. A dozen people subscribed for 120 shares on that first night, providing the new enterprise with $1,200 in immediate funding. In January 1902 nine directors were nominated and the articles of incorporation were filed. By April 1902 the new company initiated telephone service in the Village of Warwick, with a single operator, paid $10 a month, manning a plug-in switchboard. The technology of the day required that a customer turn a crank on the phone to alert the operator, who then placed the call by manually patching callers to the people they wished to reach. Because there was a limited number of lines in the system, customers shared "party lines," with each user assigned a distinctive ring pattern that would indicate an incoming call. Employing technology crude by today's standards, the new telephone company nevertheless played a crucial role in bonding the disparate villages and hamlets that made up the Town of Warwick. By January 1903 WVT had 200 telephones in service, with 134 village customers and another 66 in the country. In order to obtain service, subscribers outside of the village were required to provide their own poles, set apart at prescribed distances. In addition, WVT initiated service in neighboring Vernon Township in New Jersey.

Warwick Valley's next major expansion occurred in 1927 when it paid J.K. Roe $12,500 for the Florida Telephone Co. To this point it had been allowed to use the poles of Orange and

Rockland, the local electric company, at no charge, but to insure further growth Warwick Valley signed a pole rental agreement in 1929. The company then expanded its territory in response to a 1939 petition from Pine Island subscribers of Farmers Union Telephone who requested service, and a year later WVT opened a central office to service that community. By 1943 the company had 1,400 telephones in service. With the country involved in World War II, however, growth slowed somewhat, but picked up significantly following the end of the conflict. In 1949 Warwick Valley moved into a new building, the company's current location, and bought new equipment to become a full-dial operation. By 1950 the company had 3,640 telephones in service, using five exchanges. It was also making further inroads in New Jersey, opening central offices in Highland Lake in 1951 and Upper Greenwood Lake in 1954.

Less Reliance on Operators During 1960s

WVT was still very much dependent on large party-lines but took steps to ease congestion in the 1950s. In 1957 ten-party lines were eliminated in favor of five-party lines, which now became the largest in the system. Technical upgrades continued in the ensuing decade. In 1961 WVT installed North 1+ equipment, which allowed the company to provide Direct Distance Dialing and WATS over the entire system. Operators, who previously had been necessary to place every call, would soon be involved in just 35 percent of all phone traffic. In 1969 0+ dialing was introduced, further reducing the need for operator assistance. Touch-tone dialing was added in 1972, and in 1975 WVT took a major step toward digital switching when it became the first eastern telephone company to install a Stromberg Carlson digital mechanical switch in the Warwick central office. The company also continued in its efforts to eliminate party lines. By 1976 WVT had 15,000 telephones in service (an addition of 10,000 since 1959), of which 82.7 percent were now private lines. The company then launched a promotional effort to market private lines, so that a year later the number of private lines grew to 85 percent and in 1978 totaled 86.8 percent. By 1980 over 90 percent of its customers were on private lines, the same year that WVT switched over from hard-wired telephones to modular instruments.

The 1980s brought developments on a number of fronts, due in large part to the deregulation and the divestiture of AT&T. In 1981 the company began offering calling cards through AT&T. A year later customers were given the option of purchasing their own telephones, rather than renting them ''in place,'' as well as taking responsibility for the wiring and outlets in their homes and offices. By 1985 WVT was the 74th largest independent telephone company operating in the United States, with more than 1,440 access lines in service and just 306 party lines left in operation. In 1988 the entire system became 100 percent digital.

The company took an important step in entering the cellular mobile communication business when in 1986 it became a 15 percent owner of a joint venture, The Orange County MSA Limited Partnership, joining forces with NYNEX Mobile, Highland Telephone, and Continental Telephone. A year later WVT formed a subsidiary, Warwick Valley Mobile Telephone Company, in order to become one of the first in the country to offer retail cellular telephone service and installations. In April 1989 cellular operations commenced when a mobile telephone was installed in the Corvette owned by Warwick resident Frank Seeber. By September 1990 the company had 99 cellular subscribers and lowered prices to attract even greater business.

WVT continued to stay in the forefront of telecom advances in the 1990s. In May 1990 the company began to offer a voice-mail messenger service from Octel Communication. Warwick Valley became an ''equal access'' company in 1991, allowing customers to choose their long distance company from a group of nine competitors. In 1994 it formed subsidiary Warwick Valley Long Distance Company to offer domestic, international, and operator-assisted long distance. In that same year, WVT also began to offer customers prepaid phone cards and advanced calling features such as repeat call, return call, and call trace. The company reached a major turning point in 1995 when for the first time it moved beyond traditional telephone service by establishing Hometown Online to offer toll free, 28.8K Internet service, thereby becoming one of the first telephone companies in the country to offer access to the World Wide Web. WVT had tried to get major online providers AOL and Prodigy to service the community, but when those companies declined, it opted to enter the business itself. At first, service ranged from $12.95 for six hours per month to $74.95 for 24 hours of unlimited usage per month, but soon reduced the cost of unlimited monthly usage to $29.95 and by April 1996 was offering an unlimited monthly access plan for just $19.95. In addition to operating within the service area of Warwick Valley, WVT also did business in outlying areas of New Jersey and Pennsylvania. In December 1995 WVT took the first step in high-speed access when it introduced ISDN (Integrated System Digital Network), a move that was very much in the vanguard of the telecommunications industry. After a year in operation Warwick Online had 1,000 subscribers. WVT launched yet another product when it began offering a pager service in October 1996. Warwick Online then in 1998 became one of the first companies to offer the next generation in high-speed Internet access, DSL (digital subscriber line). Within three years the entire Warwick Valley service area was DSL-capable. Also in 1998 customers received combined billing for their WVT local telephone service and Warwick Online Internet access. A year earlier the company had combined billing for local service with Warwick Valley Mobile.

WVT Listing on NASDAQ: 1998

WVT became a publicly traded company in April 1998 when it listed on the NASDAQ. By now the company had more than 27,000 customers, and subsidiary Warwick Online had more than 15,000 subscribers. Warwick Valley Long Distance was also prospering, surpassing AT&T in the number of local subscribers. WVT assumed control of its directory in 1998, taking over production, sales, and distribution, then in 2001 the

Key Dates:

1902: Warwick Valley Telephone Co. is incorporated.
1927: Florida Telephone Co. is acquired.
1949: System becomes full dial operation.
1972: Touch-tone service is introduced.
1989: First mobile telephone is installed.
1994: Warwick Valley Long Distance Company is formed.
1995: Hometown Online is established.
2001: Company begins doing business as WVT Communications.

production of the directory was taken entirely in-house when a graphic artist was hired. The company also sought new ventures and took steps to ensure continued growth in its core telephone business. In 1998 the company received approval to provide telephone service anywhere in New York State and a year later gained similar approval to provide telephone service throughout New Jersey. WVT also strengthened its commitment to high-speed Internet access, a service which was becoming increasingly more important because of the company's proximity to New York City and northern New Jersey and the rising number of its customers who were becoming telecommuters. In 2000 WVT invested in broadband provider Hudson Valley DataNet, L.L.C. On the wireless side of its business, WVT also invested in Zefcom, Inc., which did business as Tellspire, reselling Sprint PCS wireless services in several urban markets as well as to independent telecoms for resale under their own brands.

In January 2001 Warwick Valley Telephone Company began to do business as WVT Communications, better reflecting the range of its business interests. It remained a small, albeit cutting edge, telephone company, very much trading on its local roots and responsiveness to the community. When technology made the maintenance of an in-house operator service inefficient it was with some reluctance that management ended a 100-year tradition of relying on local operators and opted to outsource the operation to a third-party company, becoming one of the last independents to do so. By the fall of 2001 WVT's entire service area was DSL-ready, but already the company was looking to the next step: VDSL (very high bit rate digital subscriber line). This technology held the potential of allowing WVT to use a fiber-optic network and the existing copper wires in the homes of customers to offer a package of telephone use, high-speed Internet access, and 145 channels of digital television. In February 2002 WVT began testing this package of VDSL services in a resort community of Sussex County, New Jersey. As WVT extended its VDSL capability throughout its coverage area, it began to gain cable TV franchises from the different communities. Although by February 2003 the company still had not received a town-wide franchise, management remained confident that it would succeed, and envisioned that in the near future WVT would be able to offer such products as video-on-demand to its customers. As exciting as the future might be for WVT, however, it faced potential stiff competition from larger digital TV providers such as Cablevision. For a century WVT found a way to prosper while maintaining its hometown image, and there was every reason to believe that it would continue to do so in the foreseeable future.

Principal Subsidiaries

Warwick Valley Long Distance Company; Hometown Online, Inc.

Principal Competitors

AT&T Corp.; Verizon Communications; MCI Communications Corporation.

Further Reading

Hutheesing, Nikhil, "Wireless Windfall," *Forbes,* November 25, 2002, p. 262.
Richardson, Dave, "Hometown Meets High-Tech at Warwick, N.Y., Phone Company," *Times Herald-Record,* February 10, 2003, p. 1.
Ryan, Vincent, "Across the Digital Divide," *Telephony,* July 10, 2000, p. 34.
"Warwick Valley Telephone Co.," *Wall Street Transcript,* August 8, 1995.

—Ed Dinger

Weil, Gotshal & Manges LLP

767 Fifth Avenue
New York, New York 10153
U.S.A.
Telephone: (212) 310-8000
Fax: (212) 310-8007
Web site: http://www.weil.com

Limited Liability Partnership
Founded: 1931
Employees: 800+
Gross Billings: $505.5 million (2002)
NAIC: 541110 Offices of Lawyers

Perhaps best known for its bankruptcy practice, Weil, Gotshal & Manges LLP is one of the world's major law firms, with over 800 lawyers in offices in New York City, Brussels, Budapest, Frankfurt, Dallas, Houston, London, Miami, Prague, Menlo Park, Warsaw, and Washington, D.C., plus associated offices in Cairo, Paris, and Singapore. Established during the Great Depression as a small New York City law firm serving mostly local clients, in 2001 its international practice assists clients in an increasingly globalized economy, helping privatize state industries in Eastern Europe and helping foreign companies invest in that area. Weil, Gotshal & Manges provides legal advice in virtually all areas of domestic and international corporate law, including real estate, taxation, bankruptcy and restructuring, government regulation, intellectual property, trusts and estates, securities and financing, and mergers and acquisitions.

1930s Origins

The law firm that would one day include hundreds of lawyers began in 1931 when Frank L. Weil, Sylvan Gotshal, and Horace S. Manges formed their partnership in New York City. Weil, a native New Yorker, was a graduate of Columbia University, having earned a B.S. degree in 1915 and a law degree in 1917. All three men were established attorneys in their 30s when they combined their expertise to form the partnership. According to Erwin Cherovsky in his *Guide to New York Law*

Firms, Weil Gotshal began as a "small midtown Jewish firm with a substantial base of factoring textile and retail clients."

Although the firm would remain modest in size and scope through the 1940s, its name partners became important community leaders and social welfare organizers. Weil, in particular, distinguished himself as a respected voice in New York's Jewish community, serving as president of the Young Men's Hebrew Association in New York from 1932 through 1940 and co-founding the United Services Organizations. During World War II, Weil served as the president of the National Jewish Welfare Board in addition to his role on the National Advisory Panel to Study Juvenile Delinquency and as a member of the New York State Commission Against Discrimination. In 1946, Weil received a Medal of Merit from President Truman; in 1948 he was tapped by Truman to chair the president's Committee on Religious and Moral Welfare and Character Guidance in the Armed Forces. Among Weil's chief passions, however, was the Boy Scouts of America, where he established the National Jewish Committee on Scouting and on whose board of directors he served until his death in 1957.

Postwar Expansion

The small partnership began its expansion in the 1950s. Among the attorneys leading this effort during this time was Ira M. Millstein. Millstein received his law degree from Columbia University in 1949 and worked for a few years in the Antitrust Division of the U.S. Department of Justice. He joined Weil, Gotshal in 1951, was made partner in 1958, and became the firm's leader in litigation and antitrust work. Todd Lang, the firm's leading corporate specialist, joined the firm in 1948 after receiving his law degree from Yale the year before. Another Columbia University graduate, Harvey R. Miller, was hired in 1970 and became the firm's bankruptcy expert. At that point, according to Cherovsky, the group of "key lawyers needed to galvanize the firm was complete."

Like many other law firms, Weil, Gotshal & Manges grew rapidly in the 1970s and 1980s. The firm added an office in Washington, D.C., in 1975 as its clients requested legal counsel to deal with the newly created Environmental Protection

---

Company Perspectives:

With our global presence and reputation for successfully managing complex legal matters, Weil Gotshal is regularly sought out by clients around the world.

Agency and its new federal laws and regulations. According to one study, the number of lawyers living in Washington, D.C., grew from 11,000 in 1972 to 45,000 in 1987.

Weil, Gotshal added other new offices in Miami in 1981, Houston in 1985, and Dallas in 1987. The firm expanded from 316 lawyers, 61 paralegals, and 470 support staff in 1987 to 391 lawyers, 108 paralegals, and 803 support staff in 1990. Annual gross revenues increased from $120 million in 1986 to $200 million in 1989. Representative clients included General Electric Credit Corporation, TWA, Prudential, Carl Icahn, Odyssey Partners, and Drexel Burnham.

Law firms such as Weil, Gotshal & Manges grew in the 1980s as demand skyrocketed and the industry became more competitive. Firms competed against each other for the best lawyers, who since the late 1970s had gained information about the big law firms from two new periodicals, *The American Lawyer* and *The National Law Review*. With comparative data about law firm finances and management styles, more experienced lawyers switched firms for new opportunities and challenges. Weil Gotshal thus recruited several "lateral hires" in the 1980s, but it also lost some key individuals. For example, Charles Goldstein joined the firm in 1979 and led its booming real estate practice but then in 1984 took most of the firm's real estate lawyers with him when he joined Shea & Gould.

1990s and Beyond

According to the 1994 edition of *The Insider's Guide to Law Firms*, Weil, Gotshal & Manges then consisted of 462 lawyers and its bankruptcy department was "one of the best in the country," citing its representation of York and Olympia in one of the first reorganizations occurring under the laws of two jurisdictions. The law firm's corporate department, with 113 lawyers, was its largest, serving clients such as BMW, American Airlines, Citibank, General Motors, and General Electric. Its business and securities litigation team had succeeded in gaining its clients board membership or control of corporations such as USX, UJB Financial, and National Intergroup. Weil Gotshal attorneys also had worked on well-publicized antitrust cases involving players' associations in professional baseball, football, basketball, and hockey.

In the 1990s Weil, Gotshal & Manges opened its first international offices, including branches in Budapest, Warsaw, and Prague in 1991 and 1992 to take advantage of opportunities after the collapse of communism in Eastern Europe. Many foreign companies needed legal counsel to begin operating, and governments sought advice in privatization ventures. In 1992 the law firm opened its Brussels office.

Although the firm's new European offices helped its financial bottom line, they remained relatively small operations.

However, in 1996 the firm opened a London branch that by 2000 included about 100 lawyers. That move was part of what writer Paul M. Barrett called "a stampede of American law firms heading for major European cities in order to keep up with their increasingly international banking and business clientele." Unlike some American firms that staffed their London offices with mainly American lawyers, Weil Gotshal hired many British lawyers. The decision to open the London office caused internal dissent within the firm's leadership, partly because it cost $15 million to open that office, and it also led to clashes due to different legal cultures in the United States and Britain.

The firm's London office gained work from local clients such as Barclays plc in its leveraged-buyout projects and from Deutsche Bank's London office. It also helped American businesses, such as Hicks, Muse, Tate & Furst Inc., which sought to expand overseas. Chase Manhattan Corporation also provided some work for the London office. In 1997 the London branch accounted for $13 million of the firm's $350 million in annual revenue. The following year it brought in $25 million out of the firm's total of $400 million.

In 2000 Weil Gotshal was one of about ten foreign law firms that for the first time were allowed to operate in Singapore. It formed a strategic alliance with the Singapore law firm of Rajah & Tan in its first involvement in Asia. Intending to create a regional financial center, Singapore's Prime Minister three years earlier had stated that, "In the information age, human talent, not physical resources or financial capital, is the key factor for economic competitiveness and success. We must therefore welcome the infusion of knowledge which foreign talent will bring," according to the September 2000 *International Financial Law Review*.

Weil Gotshal at the turn of the century continued as a leader in representing clients involved in mergers and acquisitions. For example, in 1999 it represented Hannaford Brothers Company when it was acquired by Delhaize America, Inc., a holding company organized formed by Food Lion, Inc. In October 2000 the law firm's client Texaco Inc., which operated in about 150 nations, announced plans to merge with Chevron Corporation to create ChevronTexaco based in San Francisco. In another 2000 merger and acquisition, Weil Gotshal served both companies planning to merge. Its London office provided British law advice to Flextech, while the New York office provided Telewest Communications with American legal advice. The law firm pointed out that the two teams of attorneys worked completely separately to avoid any conflict of interest.

The Lawyer Awards 2000 honored Weil Gotshal as the Corporate Finance Team of the Year for helping Hicks, Muse, Tate & Furst on its bid for Hillsdown Holdings, a public company in the United Kingdom. Such cross-border transactions were quite complicated due to the necessity of meeting legal requirements of both the United States and the United Kingdom.

The firm's practice grew in Central and Eastern Europe as foreign businesses began operating there, local companies expanded, and government-controlled entities became privatized. Its lawyers advised the Hungarian government on developing sound environmental laws. The firm's Warsaw office helped

Key Dates:

1931: The partnership is founded in New York City.
1968: The firm's 47 lawyers move to new offices on Fifth Avenue overlooking Central Park.
1975: An office in Washington, D.C., its first outside New York City, is opened.
1991: The Budapest, Warsaw, and Menlo Park, California, offices are opened.
1996: The partnership expands by opening its London office.
2000: The firm opens its Frankfurt office and forms an alliance with Rajah & Tann in Singapore.

organize Central Europe's first mortgage bank. It also had offices in Budapest and Prague. According to the Weil Gotshal Web site, some of its Central European clients in 2000 were American Airlines, Bankers Trust, Citibank, Coastal Power Corporation, CP Holdings, Dow Chemical, Egis Pharmaceuticals, Estee Lauder, General Electric Capital, Internationale Nederlanden Bank, Rohr Gas, RWE Energie AG, Thyssen AG, the Hungarian telecommunication company MATAV, and MOL, Hungary's national oil company.

Weil Gotshal also increased its international practice by opening in 2000 a branch office in Frankfurt. The new office was started due to more demands on the firm's London office to serve clients in Germany, a key center for private equity, finance, new technology, and mergers and acquisitions.

As the U.S. economy showed signs of a downturn in 2000 and 2001, more companies declared bankruptcy. The American Bankruptcy Institute reported in *The Wall Street Journal* of February 16, 2001 that bankruptcy filings by big public companies in 2000 increased 21 percent from 1999. Those businesses needed legal help, so Weil Gotshal planned to add to the firm's 85 bankruptcy specialists. This development was similar to what happened in previous eras, such as the Great Depression of the 1930s or the slowdown in the early 1990s.

Like many law firms, Weil, Gotshal & Manges provided some legal services on a pro bono basis to needy organizations or individuals. Its lawyers have been involved in cases involving the death penalty, AIDS, and the rights of children, among others. For example, it provided counsel to 45,000 Vietnamese refugees being held in Hong Kong. It also has served the Children's Defense Fund, the ACLU, and the Lawyers Committee for Human Rights on a variety of issues. The www.law.com Web site in 2001 ranked Weil, Gotshal & Manges as number 42 for its pro bono services.

Based on the law firm's 1997 gross revenue of $354 million, *The American Lawyer* ranked it as the United States' tenth largest law firm. The same magazine in November 1998, in cooperation with London's *Legal Business*, used the same financial statistics to rank the firm as number 14 in its first listing of the world's largest law firms. Based on its 661 lawyers, the firm ranked as number 26. It had offices in six countries, and 14 percent of its lawyers were based outside of its home

country. That contrasted with Baker & McKenzie, the most internationalized firm, with offices in 35 nations and 80 percent of its lawyers based outside of its home nation. By 2000, Weil Gotshal had reached the number ten spot in *The American's Lawyer*'s annual rankings of American firms by revenue, up from 11th year before. The firm ranked fifth among New York firms.

As the U.S. economy tanked in the early 2000s, the climate proved highly profitable for Weil Gotshal in the area of bankruptcy representation. Weil Gotshal gained considerable press as lead counsel in the bankruptcy proceedings of client Enron Corporation, which hired the firm in October 2001, a month before the energy giant collapsed. Weil Gotshal's prominent, bankrupt clientele also included WorldCom, Global Crossing, Armstrong World Industries, and Bethlehem Steel. In August 2002, Harvey Miller left the firm after 33 years as head of the firm's bankruptcy department. While Miller's departure caused some analysts to speculate on the continued success of Weil Gotshal's bankruptcy practice, the firm's status as a top-level firm involved in all aspects of corporate law seemed assured.

Principal Operating Units

Business Finance & Restructuring; Business & Securities Litigation; Corporate; Corporate Governance; Litigation; Real Estate; Tax; Trade Practices & Regulatory Law; Trusts & Estates.

Principal Competitors

Simpson Thacher & Bartlett; Skadden, Arps, Slate, Meagher & Flom, LLP; Shearman & Sterling; Sullivan & Cromwell LLP.

Further Reading

"Bankruptcy Specialists at Legal Firms Become Growth Industry in Chilly Times," *Wall Street Journal,* February 16, 2001, p. B10.

Barrett, Paul M., "Legal Eagles: New York Law Firm Goes a Bit Native to Thrive in London," *Wall Street Journal* (European edition), April 27, 1999, p. 1.

Byrne, John A., and Keith Naughton, "The Guru of Good Governance," *Business Week,* April 28, 1997, p. 100.

Cherovsky, Erwin, "Weil Gotshal & Manges," in *The Guide to New York Law Firms,* New York: St. Martin's Press, 1991, pp. 213–16.

Ferguson, Nick, "Singapore Opens Its Doors to Foreign Firms," *International Financial Law Review,* September 2000, p. 55.

"Firm's Lawyers Lived It Up As Enron Went Belly Up," *Houston Chronicle,* September 18, 2002, p. 8.

Koppel, Nathan, "Knee Deep in Debt," *American Lawyer,* May 12, 2003.

Malkani, Sheila V., and Michael F. Walsh, "Weil, Gotshal & Manges," in *The Insider's Guide to Law Firms,* second edition, Boulder, Colo.: Mobius Press, 1994, pp. 435–38.

"Mopping Up: Weil, Gotshal & Manges," *Economist,* July 6, 2002.

"The Morticians Move In," *Business Week,* January 21, 2002, p. 26.

Schmitt, Richard B., "Bankruptcy is a Field of Gold for Weil Gotshal," *Wall Street Journal,* July 23, 2002, p. B1.

"Weil Gotshal Suffers London Losses," *International Financial Law Review,* March 2000, p. 4.

"Weil Gotshal to Open Frankfurt Office," *International Financial Law Review,* May 2000, p. 4.

—David M. Walden

INDEX TO COMPANIES

Index to Companies

Listings in this index are arranged in alphabetical order under the company name. Company names beginning with a letter or proper name such as Eli Lilly & Co. will be found under the first letter of the company name. Definite articles (The, Le, La) are ignored for alphabetical purposes as are forms of incorporation that precede the company name (AB, NV). Company names printed in bold type have full, historical essays on the page numbers appearing in bold. Updates to entries that appeared in earlier volumes are signified by the notation **(upd.)**. Company names in light type are references within an essay to that company, not full historical essays. This index is cumulative with volume numbers printed in bold type.

A & A Die Casting Company, **25** 312
A and A Limousine Renting, Inc., **26** 62
A & C Black Ltd., **7** 165
A&E Plastics, **12** 377
A&E Television Networks, IV 627; **19** 204; **32** 3–7; **46** 232
A. & J. McKenna, **13** 295
A&K Petroleum Company. *See* Kerr-McGee Corporation.
A & M Instrument Co., **9** 323
A&M Records, **23** 389
A&N Foods Co., **II** 553
A&P. *See* The Great Atlantic & Pacific Tea Company, Inc.
A&P Water and Sewer Supplies, Inc., **6** 487
A. and T. McKenna Brass and Copper Works, **13** 295
A & W Brands, Inc., II 595; **25** 3–5
A-dec, Inc., 53 3–5
A-1 Supply. *See* International Game Technology.
A-R Technologies, **48** 275
A.A. Housman & Co., **II** 424; **13** 340
A.A. Mathews. *See* CRSS Inc.
A. Ahlström Oy, **IV** 276–77. *See also* Ahlstrom Corporation.
A.B. Chance Industries Co., Inc., **II** 20; **31** 259
A.B.Dick Company, II 25; **28** 6–8
A.B. Hemmings, Ltd., **13** 51
A.B. Leasing Corp., **13** 111–12
A-B Nippondenso, **III** 593
A.B. Watley Group Inc., 45 3–5
A-BEC Mobility, **11** 487
A.C. Delco, **26** 347, 349
A.C. Moore Arts & Crafts, Inc., 30 3–5
A.C. Nielsen Company, IV 605; **13** 3–5. *See also* ACNielsen Corporation.
A.C. Wickman, **13** 296
A.D. International (Australia) Pty. Ltd., **10** 272
A. Dager & Co., **I** 404
A. Dunkelsbuhler & Co., **IV** 20–21, 65; **7** 122

A/E/C/ Systems International, **27** 362
A.E. Fitkin & Company, **6** 592–93; **50** 37
A.E. Gutman, **16** 486
A.E. LePage, **II** 457
A.E. Lottes, **29** 86
A.G. Becker, **II** 259–60; **11** 318; **20** 260
A.G. Edwards, Inc., 8 3–5; **19** 502; **32** 17–21 (upd.)
A.G. Industries, Inc., **7** 24
A.G. Morris, **12** 427
A.G. Spalding & Bros., Inc., **I** 428–29; **24** 402–03
A.G. Stanley Ltd., **V** 17, 19; **24** 75
A. Gettelman, Co., **I** 269
A. Goertz and Co., **IV** 91
A.H. Belo Corporation, IV 605; **10** 3–5; **28** 367, 369; **30** 13–17 (upd.)
A.H. Robins Co., **10** 70; **12** 188; **16** 438; **50** 538
A. Hirsh & Son, **30** 408
A. Hölscher GmbH, **53** 195
A.I. Credit Corp., **III** 196
A.J. Caley and Son. Ltd., **II** 569
A.J. Oster Co., **III** 681
A. Johnson & Co. *See* Axel Johnson Group.
A.L. Laboratories Inc., **12** 3
A.L. Pharma Inc., 12 3–5. *See also* Alpharma Inc.
A.L. Van Houtte Inc. *See* Van Houtte Inc.
A. Lambert International Inc., **16** 80
A. Leon Capel and Sons, Inc. *See* Capel Incorporated.
A.M. Castle & Co., 25 6–8
A.M. Collins Manufacturing Co., **IV** 286
A. Michel et Cie., **49** 84
A.O. Smith Corporation, 7 139; **22** 181, **11** 3–6; **24** 499; **40** 3–8 (upd.)
A-1 Steak Sauce Co., **I** 259
A-1 Supply, **10** 375
A.P. Green Refractories, **22** 285
A.R. Pechiney, **IV** 173
A. Roger Perretti, **II** 484
A.S. Abell Co., **IV** 678
A.S. Aloe, **III** 443

A.S. Cameron Steam Pump Works, **III** 525
A/S Titan, **III** 418
A.S. Watson & Company, **18** 254
A.S. Yakovlev Design Bureau, 15 3–6
A. Schilling & Company. *See* McCormick & Company, Incorporated.
A. Schulman, Inc., 8 6–8; **49** 3–7 (upd.)
A. Sulka & Co., **29** 457
A.T. Cross Company, 17 3–5; **49** 8–12 (upd.)
A.T. Massey Coal Company, **34** 164
A.T. Mays, **55** 90
A-T-O Inc. *See* Figgie International, Inc.
A.V. Roe & Co., **I** 50, 81; **III** 508; **24** 85
A.W. Bain Holdings, **III** 523
A.W. Baulderstone Holdings Pty. Ltd., **55** 62
A.W. Faber-Castell Unternehmensverwaltung GmbH & Co., 51 3–6
A.W. Shaw Co., **IV** 635
A.W. Sijthoff, **14** 555
A-Z International Companies, **III** 569; **20** 361
AA Development Corp., **I** 91
AA Distributors, **22** 14
AA Energy Corp., **I** 91
AAA Development Corp., **17** 238
Aaardman Animations, **43** 143
Aachener und Münchener Feuer-Versicherungs-Gesellschaft, **III** 376
Aachener und Münchener Gruppe, **III** 349–50
Aachener Union, **II** 385
AAE Ahaus Alstatter Eisenbahn Holding AG, **25** 171
AAF-McQuay Incorporated, 26 3–5
AAI Corporation, **37** 399
Aalborg, **6** 367
Aansworth Shirt Makers, **8** 406
AAON, Inc., 22 3–6
AAPT, **54** 355–57
AAR Corp., III 687; **IV** 60; **28** 3–5
Aargauische Portlandcement-Fabrik Holderbank-Wildegg, **III** 701

Aaron Brothers, Inc., **17** 320, 322
Aaron Rents, Inc., 14 3–5; **33** 368; **35** 3–6 **(upd.)**
AARP, 27 3–5
Aasche Transportation, **27** 404
AASE SARL, **53** 32
Aastrom Biosciences, Inc., **13** 161
AAV Cos., **13** 48; **41** 22
Aavant Health Management Group, Inc., **11** 394
Aavid Thermal Technologies, Inc., 29 3–6
AB Capital & Investment Corporation, **23** 381
AB Ingredients Limited, **41** 32
AB-PT. *See* American Broadcasting-Paramount Theatres, Inc.
ABA. *See* Aktiebolaget Aerotransport.
Abacus Direct Corporation, **46** 156
Abacus Fund, Inc., **II** 445; **22** 405
ABACUS International Holdings Ltd., **26** 429
Abana Pharmaceuticals, **24** 257
Abar Staffing, **25** 434
ABB Asea Brown Boveri Ltd., II 1–4, 13; **III** 427, 466, 631–32; **IV** 66, 109, 204, 300; **15** 483; **22** 7–12 **(upd.)**, 64, 288; **28** 39; **34** 132
ABB Hafo AB. *See* Mitel Corp.
ABB RDM Service, **41** 326
Abba Seafood AB, **18** 396
Abbatoir St.-Valerien Inc., **II** 652
Abbey Business Consultants, **14** 36
Abbey Home Entertainment, **23** 391
Abbey Life Group PLC, **II** 309
Abbey Medical, Inc., **11** 486; **13** 366–67
Abbey National plc, 10 6–8; **39** 3–6 **(upd.)**
Abbey Rents, **II** 572
Abbey Road Building Society, **10** 6–7
Abbott Laboratories, I 619–21, 686, 690, 705; **II** 539; **10** 70, 78, 126; **11** 7–9 **(upd.)**, 91, 494; **12** 4; **14** 98, 389; **22** 75; **25** 55; **36** 38–39; **40** 9–13 **(upd.)**; **46** 394–95; **50** 538
Abbott, Proctor & Paine, **II** 445; **22** 405
ABC Appliance, Inc., 10 9–11
ABC Carpet & Home Co. Inc., 26 6–8
ABC Family Worldwide, Inc., 52 3–6, 84
ABC, Inc., **I** 463–64; **II** 89, 129–33, 151, 156, 170, 173; **III** 188, 214, 251–52; **6** 157–59, 164; **11** 197–98; **17** 150; **XVIII** 65; **19** 201; **21** 25; **24** 516–17; **32** 3; **51** 218–19. *See also* Capital Cities/ABC Inc.
ABC Markets, **17** 558
ABC Rail Products Corporation, 18 3–5
ABC Records, **II** 144
ABC Supply Co., Inc., 22 13–16
ABC Treadco, **19** 455
ABD Securities Corp., **II** 239, 283
ABECOR. *See* Associated Banks of Europe Corp.
Abeille Vie. *See* Aviva.
Abell-Howe Construction Inc., **42** 434
Abercom Holdings, **IV** 92
Abercrombie & Fitch Co., V 116; **15** 7–9; **17** 369; **25** 90; **35** 7–10 **(upd.)**
Aberthaw Cement, **III** 671
Abex Aerospace, **III** 512
Abex Corp., **I** 456; **10** 553; **18** 3
Abex Friction Products, **III** 512
ABF. *See* Associated British Foods PLC.
ABF Freight System, Inc., **16** 39–41

ABI. *See* American Furniture Company, Inc.
Abigail Adams National Bancorp, Inc., 23 3–5
Abilis, **49** 222
Abington Shoe Company. *See* The Timberland Company.
Abiomed, Inc., 47 3–6
Abitec Corporation, **41** 32–33
Abitibi-Consolidated, Inc., 25 9–13 **(upd.)**; **26** 445
Abitibi-Price Inc., IV 245–47, 721; **9** 391
Abko Realty Inc., **IV** 449
ABM Industries Incorporated, 25 14–16 **(upd.)**; **51** 295
ABN. *See* Algemene Bank Nederland N.V.
ABN AMRO Holding, N.V., 39 295; **50** 3–7
Above The Belt, Inc., **16** 37
ABR Foods, **II** 466
Abraham & Straus, **V** 168; **8** 443; **9** 209; **31** 192
Abraham Schaaffhausenscher Bankverein, **IV** 104
Abrams Industries Inc., 23 6–8
Abri Bank Bern, **II** 378
ABS Pump AB, **53** 85
Absolut Company, **31** 458, 460
Abu Dhabi National Oil Company, IV 363–64, 476; **45** 6–9 **(upd.)**
Abu Qir Fertilizer and Chemical Industries Co., **IV** 413
AC Design Inc., **22** 196
AC Humko Corporation, **41** 32–33
AC Roma SpA, **44** 388
ACA Corporation, **25** 368
Academic Press, **IV** 622–23
Academy of Television Arts & Sciences, Inc., 55 3–5
Academy Sports & Outdoors, 27 6–8
Acadia Entities, **24** 456
Acadia Investors, **23** 99
Acadia Partners, **21** 92
Acadian Ambulance & Air Med Services, Inc., 39 7–10
Accel, S.A. de C.V., **51** 115–17
Access Dynamics, Inc., **17** 255
Access Graphics Technology Inc., **13** 128
Access Technology, **6** 225
Accessory Network Group, Inc., **8** 219
Accident and Casualty Insurance Co., **III** 230–31
Acclaim Entertainment Inc., 13 115; **24** 3–8, 538
ACCO World Corporation, 7 3–5; **12** 264; **51** 7–10 **(upd.)**
Accolade Inc., **35** 227
Accor SA, 10 12–14; **13** 364; **27** 9–12 **(upd.)**; **48** 199; **49** 126; **53** 301
Accord Energy, **18** 367; **49** 120
Accountants on Call, **6** 10
Accounting and Tabulating Corporation of Great Britain, **6** 240
Accres Uitgevers B.V., **51** 328
Acctex Information Systems, **17** 468
Accuralite Company, **10** 492
Accurate Forming Co., **III** 643
AccuRead Limited, **42** 165, 167
Accuride Corp., **IV** 179
Accuscan, Inc., **14** 380
AccuStaff Inc. *See* MPS Group, Inc.
ACE Cash Express, Inc., 33 3–6
Ace Comb Company, **12** 216
Ace Electric Co., **I** 156

Ace Hardware Corporation, 12 6–8; **35** 11–14 **(upd.)**
ACE Limited, **45** 109
Ace Medical Company, **30** 164
Ace Novelty Company, **26** 374
Ace Refrigeration Ltd., **I** 315; **25** 81
Acer Inc., 6 244; **10** 257; **16** 3–6; **47** 385
Acer Sertek, **24** 31
Aceralia, **42** 414
Aceros Fortuna S.A. de C.V., **13** 141
Aceto Corp., 38 3–5
ACF Industries, **30** 282
Achatz GmbH Bauunternehmung, **55** 62
Acheson Graphite Corp., **I** 399; **9** 517
ACI. *See* Advance Circuits Inc.
ACI Holdings Inc., **I** 91; **28** 24
ACI Ltd., **29** 478
Aciéries de Ploërmel, **16** 514
Aciéries et Minières de la Sambre, **IV** 52
Aciéries Réunies de Burbach-Eich-Dudelange S.A. *See* ARBED S.A.
Acker Drill Company, **26** 70
Ackerley Communications, Inc., 9 3–5; **50** 95
Acklin Stamping Company, **8** 515
ACLC. *See* Allegheny County Light Company.
ACLI Government Securities Inc., **II** 422
ACM. *See* Advanced Custom Molders, Inc.
Acme Boot, **I** 440–41
Acme Brick Company, **19** 231–32
Acme Can Co., **I** 601; **13** 188
Acme Carton Co., **IV** 333
Acme-Cleveland Corp., I 531; **13** 6–8
Acme Corrugated Cases, **IV** 258
Acme Cotton Products, **13** 366
Acme-Delta Company, **11** 411
Acme Fast Freight Inc., **27** 473
Acme Market. *See* American Stores Company.
Acme Newspictures, **25** 507
Acme Quality Paint Co., **III** 744
Acme Quilting Co., Inc., **19** 304
Acme Road Machinery, **21** 502
Acme Screw Products, **14** 181
ACMI, **21** 118–19
ACNielsen Corporation, 38 6–9 **(upd.)**
Acordis, **41** 10
Acorn Computer, **III** 145
Acorn Financial Corp., **15** 328
Acorn Products, Inc., 55 6–9
Acoustics Development Corporation, **6** 313
Acova S.A., **26** 4
Acquired Systems Enhancement Corporation, **24** 31
ACR. *See* American Capital and Research Corp.
AcroMed Corporation, **30** 164
Acsys, Inc., 44 3–5
ACT Group, **45** 280
ACT Inc, **50** 48
Act III Theatres, **25** 453
Actava Group, **14** 332
Action, **6** 393
Action Furniture by Lane, **17** 183
Action Gaming Inc., **44** 337
Action Labs Inc., **37** 285
Action Performance Companies, Inc., 27 13–15; **32** 344; **37** 319
Action Temporary Services, **29** 273
Active Apparel Group. *See* Everlast Worldwide Inc.
Activenture Corporation, **16** 253; **43** 209

Actividades de Construcción y Servicios S.A. (ACS), **55** 179
Activision, Inc., 24 3; **32 8–11**
Acton Bolt Ltd., **IV** 658
Acuity Brands, Inc., **54** 255
Acumos, **11** 57
Acuson Corporation, 10 15–17; 36 3–6 (upd.)
ACX Technologies, **13** 11; **36** 15
Acxiom Corporation, 35 15–18
Ad Astra Aero, **I** 121
AD-AM Gas Company, **11** 28
Adage Systems International, Inc., **19** 438
Adam, Meldrum & Anderson Company (AM&A), **16** 61–62; **50** 107
Adam Opel AG, 7 6–8; **11** 549; **18** 125; **21 3–7 (upd.)**
Adams Childrenswear, **V** 177
Adams Express Co., **II** 380–81, 395–96; **10** 59–60; **12** 533
Adams Golf, Inc., 37 3–5; 45 76
Adams Industries, **19** 414
Adams/Cates Company, **21** 257
Adanac General Insurance Company, **13** 63
Adaptec, Inc., 11 56; **31 3–6**
Adaptive Data Systems, **25** 531
Adar Associates, Inc. See Scientific-Atlanta, Inc.
ADC of Greater Kansas City, Inc., **22** 443
ADC Telecommunications, Inc., 10 18–21; 30 6–9 (upd.); 44 69
Adco Products, **I** 374
Addison Communications Plc, **45** 272
Addison Corporation, **31** 399
Addison Structural Services, Inc., **26** 433
Addison Wesley, **IV** 659
Addressograph-Multigraph, **11** 494
Adecco S.A., 26 240; **35** 441–42; **36 7–11 (upd.)**
Adelphi Pharmaceutical Manufacturing Co., **I** 496
Adelphia Communications Corporation, 17 6–8; 52 7–10 (upd.)
Ademco. See Alarm Device Manufacturing Company.
Adero Inc., **45** 202
ADESA Corporation, **34** 286
Adesso-Madden, Inc., **37** 372
Adger Assuranceselskab, **III** 310
Adhere Paper Co., **IV** 252; **17** 29
ADI Group Limited. See AHL Services, Inc.
Adia S.A., 6 9–11; **9** 327. See also Adecco S.A.
Adiainvest S.A., **6** 9, 11
adidas AG, 8 392–93; **13** 513; **14 6–9; 17** 244; **22** 202; **23** 472, 474; **25** 205, 207; **36** 344, 346
adidas-Salomon AG, 33 7–11 (upd.)
Adirondack Industries, **24** 403
Adjusters Auto Rental Inc. **16** 380
Adler, **23** 219
Adler and Shaykin, **III** 56; **11** 556–57
Adler Line. See Transatlantische Dampfschiffahrts Gesellschaft.
Adley Express, **14** 567
ADM. See Archer-Daniels-Midland Co.
Administaff, Inc., 52 11–13
Administracion Corporativa y Mercantil, S.A. de C.V., **37** 178
Admiral Co., **II** 86; **III** 573
Admiral Cruise Lines, **6** 368; **27** 91
Adnan Dabbagh, **6** 115

ADNOC. See Abu Dhabi National Oil Company.
Adobe Systems Incorporated, 10 22–24; 15 149; **20** 46, 237; **33 12–16 (upd.); 43** 151
Adolf Würth GmbH & Co. KG, 49 13–15
Adolph Coors Company, I 236–38, 255, 273; **13 9–11 (upd.); 18** 72; **26** 303, 306; **34** 37; **36 12–16 (upd.); 44** 198
Adolphe Lafont, **17** 210
Adonis Radio Corp., **9** 320
Adorence, **16** 482
ADP. See Automatic Data Processing, Inc.
Adria Produtos Alimenticios, Ltd., **12** 411
Adria Steamship Company, **6** 425
Adrian Hope and Company, **14** 46
Adriatico Banco d'Assicurazione, **III** 206, 345–46
Adrienne Vittadini, **15** 291
ADS. See Aerospace Display Systems.
Adsega, **II** 677
Adstaff Associates, Ltd., **26** 240
ADT Ltd., **26** 410; **28** 486
ADT Security Services, Inc., 44 6–9 (upd.)
ADT Security Systems, Inc., 12 9–11
Adtel, Inc., **10** 358
Adtran Inc., 22 17–20
Adtranz **34** 128, 132–33, 136; **42** 45. See also ABB ASEA Brown Boveri Ltd.
Advacel, **18** 20; **43** 17
Advance Chemical Company, **25** 15
Advance Circuits Inc., **49** 234
Advance Foundry, **14** 42
Advance/Newhouse Communications, **42** 114
Advance Publications Inc., **IV 581–84; 13** 178, 180, 429; **19 3–7 (upd.); 31** 376, 378
Advance-Rumely Thresher Co., **13** 16
Advance Transformer Co., **13** 397
Advanced Aerodynamics & Structures Inc. See Mooney Aerospace Group Ltd.
Advanced Casino Systems Corporation, **21** 277
Advanced Communications Engineering. See Scientific-Atlanta, Inc.
Advanced Communications Inc. See Metrocall, Inc.
Advanced Custom Molders, Inc., **17** 533
Advanced Data Management Group S.A., **23** 212
Advanced Entertainment Group, **10** 286
Advanced Fiberoptic Technologies, **30** 267
Advanced Gravis, **28** 244
Advanced Logic Research, Inc., **27** 169
Advanced Marine Enterprises, Inc., **18** 370
Advanced Marketing Services, Inc., 24 354; **34 3–6**
Advanced Medical Technologies, **III** 512
Advanced Metal Technologies Inc., **17** 234
Advanced Metallurgy, Inc., **29** 460
Advanced Micro Devices, Inc., 6 215–17; 9 115; **10** 367; **11** 308; **16** 316; **18** 18–19, 382; **19** 312; **20** 175; **30 10–12 (upd.); 32** 498; **43** 15–16; **47** 384
Advanced MobilComm, **10** 432
Advanced Plasma Systems, Inc., **48** 299
Advanced Structures, Inc., **18** 163
Advanced System Applications, **11** 395
Advanced Technology Laboratories, Inc., 9 6–8

Advanced Telecommunications Corporation, **8** 311
Advanced Tissue Sciences Inc., **41** 377
Advanced Web Technologies, **22** 357
AdvanceMed LLC, **45** 146
Advanstar Communications, **27** 361
Advanta Corporation, 8 9–11; 11 123; **38 10–14 (upd.)**
Advanta Partners, LP, **42** 322
Advantage Company, **8** 311; **27** 306
The Advantage Group, Inc., **25** 185–86
Advantage Health Plans, Inc., **11** 379
Advantage Health Systems, Inc., **25** 383
Advantage Insurers, Inc., **25** 185, 187
Advantage Publishers Group, **34** 5
Advantest Corporation, **39** 350, 353
Advantica Restaurant Group, Inc., 27 16–19 (upd.); 29 150
Advent Corporation, **22** 97
Adventist Health, 53 6–8
Advertising Unlimited, Inc., **10** 461
Advo, Inc., 6 12–14; 53 9–13 (upd.)
Advocat Inc., 46 3–5
AEA. See United Kingdom Atomic Energy Authority.
AEA Investors Inc., **II** 628; **13** 97; **22** 169, 171; **28** 380; **30** 328
AEG A.G., I 151, 193, **409–11; II** 12, 119, 279; **III** 466, 479; **IV** 167; **6** 489; **IX** 11; **14** 169; **15** 142; **22** 28; **23** 495; **34** 131–32
AEG Hausgeräte, **53** 128
Aegis Group plc, 6 15–16
Aegis Insurance Co., **III** 273
AEGON N.V., III 177–79, 201, 273; **33** 418–20; **50 8–12 (upd.); 52** 288. See also Transamerica–An AEGON Company
AEI Music Network Inc., 35 19–21
AEL Ventures Ltd., **9** 512
Aeneas Venture Corp., **26** 502
AEON Group, **V** 96–99; **11** 498–99; **31** 430–31; **37** 227
AEP. See American Electric Power Company.
AEP Industries, Inc., 36 17–19
AEP-Span, **8** 546
Aer Lingus Group plc, 6 59; **12 367–68; 34 7–10; 35** 382–84; **36** 230–31
Aera Energy LLC, **41** 359
Aérazur, **36** 529
Aerial Communications Inc., **31** 452
Aeritalia, **I** 51, 74–75, 467; **24** 86
Aero-Coupling Corp., **III** 641
Aero Engines, **9** 418
Aero International (Regional) SAS, **24** 88
Aero International Inc., **14** 43
Aero Mayflower Transit Company. See Mayflower Group Inc.
Aero O/Y, **6** 87–88
Aero-Portuguesa, **6** 125
Aeroflot—Russian International Airlines, 29 7–10 (upd.)
Aeroflot Soviet Airlines, I 105, 110, 118; **6 57–59; 14** 73; **27** 475
Aerojet, **8** 206, 208
Aerojet-General Corp., **9** 266
Aerolíneas Argentinas S.A., I 107; **6** 97; **33 17–19; 36** 281
Aeroméxico, **20** 168
Aeromotive Systems Co., **55** 31
Aeronautics Leasing, Inc., **39** 33
Aeronca Inc., 46 6–8; 48 274
Aéroports de Paris, 33 20–22

Aeroquip Corporation, III 640–42; V 255; **16** 7–9; **19** 508
Aerospace Avionics, III 509
Aerospace Display Systems, **36** 158
Aerospace International Services, **41** 38
Aerospace Products International, Inc., **49** 141
The Aérospatiale Group, I 41–42, 46, 50, 74, 94; **7** 9–12; **12** 190–91; **14** 72; **21** 8–11 (upd.); **24** 84–86, 88–89; **26** 179. *See also* European Aeronautic Defence and Space Company EADS N.V.
Aerostar, **33** 359–61
The AES Corporation, **10** 25–27; **13** 12–15 (upd.); **24** 359; **53** 14–18 (upd.)
Aetna, Inc., **20** 59; **21** 12–16 (upd.), 95; **22** 139, 142–43; **30** 364
Aetna Life and Casualty Company, II 170–71, 319; III 78, 180–82, 209, 223, 226, 236, 254, 296, 298, 305, 313, 329, 389; IV 123, 703; **10** 75–76; **12** 367; **15** 26; **17** 324; **23** 135; **40** 199
Aetna National Bank, **13** 466
Aetna Oil Co., IV 373; **50** 46
AF Insurance Agency, **44** 33
AFC Enterprises, Inc., **32** 12–16 (upd.); **36** 517, 520; **54** 373
AFCO Industries, Inc., III 241; IV 341
Afcol, I 289; **24** 449–50
AFE Ltd., IV 241
Affiliated Enterprises Inc., I 114
Affiliated Foods Inc., **53** 19–21
Affiliated Hospital Products Inc., **37** 400
Affiliated Music Publishing, **22** 193
Affiliated Paper Companies, Inc., **31** 359, 361
Affiliated Physicians Network, Inc., **45** 194
Affiliated Products Inc., I 622
Affiliated Publications, Inc., **6** 323; **7** 13–16; **19** 285
Affordable Inns, **13** 364
AFG Industries Inc., I 483; **9** 248; **48** 42
AFIA, **22** 143; **45** 104, 108
Afianzadora Insurgentes Serfin, **19** 190
AFL. *See* American Football League.
AFLAC Incorporated, **10** 28–30 (upd.); **38** 15–19 (upd.)
AFP. *See* Australian Forest Products.
AFRA Enterprises Inc., **26** 102
African and European Investment, IV 96
African Coasters, IV 91
African Explosive and Chemical Industries, IV 22
AFT. *See* Advanced Fiberoptic Technologies.
AFW Fabric Corp., **16** 124
AG&E. *See* American Electric Power Company.
Ag-Chem Equipment Company, Inc., **17** 9–11
AG Communication Systems Corporation, **15** 194; **43** 446
AGA, I 358
Agan Chemical Manufacturers Ltd., **25** 266–67
Agar Manufacturing Company, **8** 2
Agatha Christie Ltd., **31** 63 67
AGCO Corp., **13** 16–18
Agefi, **34** 13
AGEL&P. *See* Albuquerque Gas, Electric Light and Power Company.
Agence France-Presse, IV 670; **34** 11–14
Agency, **6** 393
Agency Rent-A-Car, **16** 379

AGF, III 185; **27** 515. *See also* Assurances Generales de France.
AGFA, I 310–11
Agfa-Ansco Corporation, I 337–38; **22** 225–27
Agfa-Gevaert, III 487; **18** 50, 184–86; **26** 540–41; **50** 90
Aggregate Industries plc, **36** 20–22
Aggreko Plc, **45** 10–13
Agiba Petroleum, IV 414
Agilent Technologies Inc., **38** 20–23
Agip SpA, IV 419–21, 454, 466, 472–74, 498; **12** 153
Agiv AG, **39** 40–41; **51** 25
AGLP, IV 618
AGO, III 177, 179, 273, 310
Agor Manufacturing Co., IV 286
Agouron Pharmaceuticals, Inc., **38** 365
AGRAN, IV 505
AGRANA, **27** 436, 439
AgriBank FCB, **8** 489
Agribrands International, Inc., **40** 89
Agrico Chemical Company, IV 82, 84, 576; **7** 188; **31** 470
Agricole de Roquefort et Maria Grimal, **23** 219
Agricultural Insurance Co., III 191
Agricultural Minerals and Chemicals Inc., IV 84; **13** 504
Agrifan, II 355
Agrifull, **22** 380
Agrigenetics, Inc., I 361. *See also* Mycogen Corporation.
Agrilusa, Agro-Industria, **51** 54
Agrippina Versicherungs AG, III 403, 412
Agrobios S.A., **23** 172
Agroferm Hungarian Japanese Fermentation Industry, III 43
Agrologica, **51** 54
Agromán S.A., **40** 218
AGTL. *See* Alberta Gas Trunk Line Company, Ltd.
Agua de la Falda S.A., **38** 231
Agua Pura Water Company, **24** 467
Aguila (Mexican Eagle) Oil Co. Ltd., IV 657
Agusta S.p.A., **46** 66
Agway, Inc., **7** 17–18; **21** 17–19 (upd.); **36** 440
AHL Services, Inc., **26** 149; **27** 20–23; **45** 379
Ahlstrom Corporation, **53** 22–25
Ahmanson. *See* H.F. Ahmanson & Company.
AHMSA. *See* Altos Hornos de México, S.A. de C.V.
Ahold. *See* Koninklijke Ahold NV.
AHP. *See* American Home Products Corporation.
AHS. *See* American Hospital Supply Corporation.
AHSC Holdings Corp., III 9–10
Ahtna AGA Security, Inc., **14** 541
AI Automotive, **24** 204
AIC. *See* Allied Import Company.
AICA, **16** 421; **43** 308
Aichi Bank, II 373
Aichi Kogyo Co., III 415
Aichi Steel Works, III 637
AICPA. *See* The American Institute of Certified Public Accountants.
Aid Auto, **18** 144
Aida Corporation, **11** 504

AIG. *See* American International Group, Inc.
AIG Global Real Estate Investment Corp., III 197; **54** 225
AIG/Lincoln International L.L.C., **54** 225
Aigner. *See* Etienne Aigner AG.
Aiken Stores, Inc., **14** 92
Aikenhead's Home Improvement Warehouse, **18** 240; **26** 306
Aikoku Sekiyu, IV 554
AIL Technologies, **46** 160
AIM Create Co., Ltd., V 127
AIMCO. *See* Apartment Investment and Management Company.
Ainsworth Gaming Technologies, **54** 15
Ainsworth National, **14** 528
AIP. *See* Amorim Investimentos e Participaço.
Air & Water Technologies Corporation, **6** 441–42. *See also* Aqua Alliance Inc.
Air BP, **7** 141
Air Brasil, **6** 134; **29** 496
Air Canada, **6** 60–62; **23** 9–12 (upd.); **29** 302; **36** 230
Air China, **46** 9–11
Air Compak, **12** 182
Air de Cologne, **27** 474
Air Express International Corporation, **13** 19–20; **40** 138; **46** 71
Air France, I 93–94, 104, 110, 120; II 163; **6** 69, 373; **8** 313; **12** 190; **24** 86; **27** 26; **33** 21, 50, 377. *See also* Groupe Air France; Societe Air France.
Air Global International, **55** 30
Air-India Limited, **6** 63–64; **27** 24–26 (upd.); **41** 336–37
Air Inter. *See* Groupe Air France.
Air Jamaica Limited, **54** 3–6
Air La Carte Inc., **13** 48
Air Lanka Catering Services Ltd., **6** 123–24; **27** 464
Air Liberté, **6** 208
Air Liquide. *See* L'Air Liquide SA.
Air London International, **36** 190
Air Methods Corporation, **53** 26–29
Air Micronesia, I 97; **21** 142
Air Midwest, Inc., **11** 299
Air New Zealand Limited, **14** 10–12; **24** 399–400; **27** 475; **38** 24–27 (upd.)
Air Nippon Co., Ltd., **6** 70
Air Pacific, **24** 396, 400
Air Products and Chemicals, Inc., I 297–99, 315, 358, 674; **10** 31–33 (upd.); **11** 403; **14** 125; **54** 10
Air Russia, **24** 400
Air Sea Broker AG, **47** 286–87
Air Southwest Co. *See* Southwest Airlines Co.
Air Spec, Inc., III 643
Air Wisconsin Airlines Corporation, **55** 10–12
Airborne Accessories, II 81
Airborne Freight Corporation, **6** 345–47 345; **13** 19; **14** 517; **18** 177; **34** 15–18 (upd.); **46** 72
Airbus Industrie, **6** 74; **7** 9–11, 504; **9** 418; **10** 164; **13** 356; **21** 8; **24** 84–89; **34** 128, 135; **48** 219. *See also* G.I.E. Airbus Industrie.
AirCal, I 91
Airco, **25** 81–82; **26** 94
Aircraft Marine Products, II 7; **14** 26
Aircraft Modular Products, **30** 73
Aircraft Services International, I 449

Aircraft Transport & Travel Ltd., **I** 92
Aircraft Turbine Center, Inc., **28** 3
Airex Corporation, **16** 337
AirFoyle Ltd., **53** 50
Airgas, Inc., 54 7–10
Airguard Industries, Inc., **17** 104, 106
Airlease International, **II** 422
AirLib. *See* Société d'Exploitation AOM.
Airline Interiors Inc., **41** 368–69
Airlines of Britain Holdings, **34** 398; **38** 105–06
Airlink, **24** 396
Airmark Plastics Corp., **18** 497–98
Airmec-AEI Ltd., **II** 81
Airpax Electronics, Inc., **13** 398
Airport Ground Service Co., **I** 104, 106
Airshop Ltd., **25** 246
Airstream. *See* Thor Industries, Inc.
Airtel, **IV** 640
AirTouch Communications, 11 10–12. *See also* Vodafone Group PLC.
Airtours Plc, II 164; **27 27–29**, 90, 92
AirTran Holdings, Inc., 22 21–23; 28 266; **33** 302; **34** 32; **55 10–11**
AirWair Ltd., **23** 399, 401–02
AirWays Corporation. *See* AirTran Holdings, Inc.
Airways Housing Trust Ltd., **I** 95
Airwick Industries, **II** 567
Aisin Seiki Co., Ltd., III 415–16; 14 64; **48 3–5 (upd.)**
AIT Worldwide, **47** 286–87
Aitken, Inc., **26** 433
AITS. *See* American International Travel Service.
Aiuruoca, **25** 85
Aiwa Co., Ltd., 28 360; **30 18–20**
Ajax, **6** 349
Ajax Iron Works, **II** 16
Ajinomoto Co., Inc., II 463–64, 475; **III** 705; **28 9–11 (upd.)**
Ajman Cement, **III** 760
AJS Auto Parts Inc., **15** 246
AK Steel Holding Corporation, 19 8–9; 41 3–6 (upd.)
Akane Securities Co. Ltd., **II** 443
Akashic Memories, **11** 234
Akemi, **17** 310; **24** 160
Aker RGI, **32** 99
AKH Co. Inc., **20** 63
Akin, Gump, Strauss, Hauer & Feld, L.L.P., 18 366; **33 23–25; 47** 140
AKO Bank, **II** 378
Akorn, Inc., 32 22–24
Akro-Mills Inc., **19** 277–78
Akron Brass Manufacturing Co., **9** 419
Akron Corp., **IV** 290
Akron Extruders Inc., **53** 230
Akroyd & Smithers, **14** 419
Akseli Gallen-Kallela, **IV** 314
Aktiebolaget Aerotransport, **I** 119
Aktiebolaget Electrolux, 22 24–28 (upd.). *See also* Electrolux A.B.
Aktiebolaget SKF, III 622–25; IV 203; **38 28–33 (upd.)**
Aktiengesellschaft für Berg- und Hüttenbetriebe, **IV** 201
Aktiengesellschaft für Maschinenpapier-Zellstoff-Fabrikation, **IV** 323
Aktiv Placering A.B., **II** 352
Akzo Nobel N.V., I 674; **II** 572; **III** 44; **13 21–23**, 545; **14** 27; **15** 436; **16** 69, 462; **21** 466; **41 7–10 (upd.); 51** 223–24; **52** 410

Al Copeland Enterprises, Inc., **7** 26–28; **32** 13–15
Alaadin Middle East-Ersan, **IV** 564
Alabama Bancorp., **17** 152
Alabama Gas Corporation, **21** 207–08
Alabama Power Company, **38** 445, 447–48
Alabama Shipyards Inc., **21** 39–40
Alabaster Co., **III** 762
Aladdin Industries, **16** 487
Aladdin Mills Inc., **19** 276
Aladdin's Castle, **III** 430, 431
Alagasco, **21** 207–08
Alagroup, **45** 337
Alain Afflelou SA, 53 30–32
Alain Manoukian. *See* Groupe Alain Manoukian.
Alais et Camargue, **IV** 173
Alamac Knit Fabrics, Inc., **16** 533–34; **21** 192
Alamito Company, **6** 590
Alamo Engine Company, **8** 514
Alamo Group Inc., 32 25–28
Alamo Rent A Car, Inc., 6 348–50; **24 9–12 (upd.); 25** 93; **26** 409
Alania, **24** 88
ALANTEC Corporation, **25** 162
Alarm Device Manufacturing Company, **9** 413–15
Alaron Inc., **16** 357
Alascom, **6** 325–28; **26** 358
Alaska Air Group, Inc., 6 65–67; 11 50; **29 11–14 (upd.); 48** 219
Alaska Co., **III** 439
Alaska Commercial Company, **12** 363
Alaska Hydro-Train, **6** 382; **9** 510
Alaska Junk Co., **19** 380
Alaska Natural Gas Transportation System, **V** 673, 683
Alaska Pulp Co., **IV** 284, 297, 321
Alaska Steel Co., **19** 381
Alatas Mammoet, **26** 279
Alba Foods, **III** 619–20; **27** 197; **43** 218
Alba-Waldensian, Inc., 30 21–23
Albany and Susquehanna Railroad, **II** 329
Albany Assurance Co., Ltd., **III** 293
Albany Cheese, **23** 219
Albany International Corporation, 8 12–14; 51 11–14 (upd.)
Albemarle Paper Co., **I** 334–35; **10** 289
Albers Brothers Milling Co., **II** 487
Albert E. Reed & Co. Ltd. *See* Reed International PLC.
The Albert Fisher Group plc, 41 11–13
Albert Heijn NV, **II** 641–42; **38** 200, 202
Albert Nipon, Inc., **8** 323
Albert Willcox & Co., **14** 278
Alberta Distillers, **I** 377
Alberta Energy Company Ltd., 16 10–12; 43 3–6 (upd.)
Alberta Gas Trunk Line Company, Ltd., **V** 673–74
Alberta Sulphate Ltd., **IV** 165
Alberto-Culver Company, II 641–42; **8 15–17; 36 23–27 (upd.)**
Albertson's Inc., II 601–03, 604–05, 637; **7 19–22 (upd.); 8** 474; **15** 178, 480; **16** 249; **18** 8; **22** 38; **27** 247, 290, 292; **30 24–28 (upd.); 33** 306; **40** 366
Albi Enterprises, **III** 24
Albion Industries, Inc., **16** 357
Albion Reid Proprietary, **III** 673
Albright & Friel, **I** 313; **10** 154
Albright & Wilson Ltd., **I** 527; **IV** 165; **12** 351; **16** 461; **38** 378, 380; **50** 282

Albuquerque Gas & Electric Company. *See* Public Service Company of New Mexico.
Albuquerque Gas, Electric Light and Power Company, **6** 561–62
Albury Brickworks, **III** 673
Alcan Aluminium Limited, II 415; **IV 9–13**, 14, 59, 154–55; **9** 512; **14** 35; **31 7–12 (upd.); 45** 337
Alcantara and Sores, **II** 582
Alcatel Alsthom Compagnie Générale d'Electricité, II 13, 69, 117; **6** 304; **7** 9; **9 9–11**, 32; **11** 59, 198; **15** 125; **17** 353; **18** 155; **19** 164, 166; **21** 233
Alcatel S.A., 36 28–31 (upd.); 42 375–76; **52** 332, 334; **53** 237; **54** 264
Alchem Capital Corp., **8** 141, 143
Alchem Plastics, **19** 414
Alco Capital Group, Inc., **27** 288
Alco Health Services Corporation, III 9–10. *See also* AmeriSource Health Corporation.
Alco Hydro-Aeroplane, **I** 64
Alco Office Products Inc., **24** 362
Alco Standard Corporation, I 412–13; III 9; **9** 261; **16** 473–74
ALCO Trade Show Services, **26** 102
Alcoa. *See* Aluminum Company of America.
Alcon Laboratories, **II** 547; **7** 382; **10** 46, 48; **30 30–31**
Alcudia, **IV** 528
Alden Merrell Corporation, **23** 169
Aldermac Mines Ltd., **IV** 164
Aldi Group, 11 240; **13 24–26; 17** 125
Aldila Inc., 46 12–14
Aldine Press, **10** 34
Aldiscon, **37** 232
Aldrich Chemical Co., **I** 690
Aldus Corporation, 10 34–36
Aldwarke Main & Car House Collieries, **I** 573
Alenia, **7** 9, 11
Alert Centre Inc., **32** 373
Alert Management Systems Inc., **12** 380
Alessio Tubi, **IV** 228
Alestra, **19** 12
Alex & Ivy, **10** 166–68
Alex Lee Inc., 18 6–9; 44 10–14 (upd.)
Alexander & Alexander Services Inc., III 280; **10 37–39; 13** 476; **22** 318
Alexander & Baldwin, Inc., I 417; **10 40–42; 24** 32; **29** 307; **40 14–19 (upd.)**
Alexander and Lord, **13** 482
Alexander Grant & Co., **I** 481, 656
Alexander Hamilton Life Insurance Co., **II** 420; **29** 256
Alexander Howden Group, **III** 280; **10** 38–39; **22** 318
Alexander Martin Co., **I** 374
Alexander-Schroder Lumber Company, **18** 514
Alexander Smith, Inc., **19** 275
Alexander's, Inc., 10 282; **12** 221; **26** 111; **45 14–16**
Alexandria Petroleum Co., **51** 113
Alexis Lichine, **III** 43
Alfa-Laval AB, III 417–21; IV 203; **8** 376; **53** 328
Alfa Romeo, I 163, 167; **11** 102, 104, 139, 205; **13 27–29**, 218–19; **36 32–35 (upd.)**, 196–97
Alfa, S.A. de C.V., II 262; **11** 386; **19 10–12; 37** 176

Alfa Trading Company, **23** 358
Alfalfa's Markets, **19** 500–02
Alfinal, **III** 420
Alfred A. Knopf, Inc., **13** 428, 429; **31** 376–79
Alfred Bullows & Sons, Ltd., **21** 64
Alfred Dunhill Limited, **19** 369; **27** 487–89
Alfred Hickman Ltd., **III** 751
Alfred Marks Bureau, Ltd., **6** 9–10
Alfred McAlpine plc, **51** 138
Alfred Nobel & Co., **III** 693
Alfred Teves, **I** 193
Alfried Krupp von Bohlen und Halbach Foundation, **IV** 89
ALG. *See* Arkla, Inc.
Alga, **24** 83
Algemeen Burgerlijk Pensioenfonds, **26** 421
Algemeen Dagbald BV, **53** 273
Algemeene Bankvereeniging en Volksbank van Leuven, **II** 304
Algemeene Friesche, **III** 177–79
N.V. Algemeene Maatschappij tot Exploitatie van Verzekeringsmaatschappijen, **III** 199
Algemeene Maatschappij van Levensverzekering en Lijfrente, **III** 178
Algemeene Maatschappij voor Nijverheidskrediet, **II** 304–05
Algemeene Nederlandsche Maatschappij ter begunstiging van de Volksvlijt, **II** 294
Algemene Bank Nederland N.V., **II** 183–84, 185, 239, 527; **III** 200
Algo Group Inc., **24** 13–15
Algoma Steel Corp., **IV** 74; **8** 544–45; **24** 143
Algonquin Energy, Inc., **6** 487
Algonquin Gas Transmission Company, **6** 486; **14** 124–26
ALI. *See* Aeronautics Leasing, Inc.
Alidata, **6** 69
Aligro Inc., **II** 664
Alimenta (USA), Inc., **17** 207
Alimentana S.A., **II** 547
Alimondo, **17** 505
Alitalia–Linee Aeree Italiana, S.p.A., **I** 110, 466–67; **6** 96, 68–69; **24** 311; **29** 15–17 (upd.)
Alken, **II** 474
Oy Alkoholiliike Ab, **IV** 469
Alkor-Oerlikon Plastic GmbH, **7** 141
All American Airways. *See* USAir Group, Inc.
All American Communications Inc., **20** 3–7; **25** 138
All American Gourmet Co., **12** 178, 199
All American Sports Co., **22** 458–59
All British Escarpment Company LTD, **25** 430
All-Clad Metalcrafters Inc., **34** 493, 496–97
The All England Lawn Tennis & Croquet Club, **54** 11–13
All Nippon Airways Co., Ltd., **I** 106, 493; **6** 70–71 118, 427; **16** 168; **24** 326; **33** 50–51; **38** 34–37 (upd.)
All Seasons Vehicles, Inc. *See* ASV, Inc.
All Woods, Inc., **18** 514
Allami Biztosito, **III** 209; **15** 30
Allcom, **16** 392
Alldays plc, 49 16–19
Allders plc, 37 6–8
Alleanza & Unione Mediterranea, **III** 208

Alleanza-Securitas-Esperia, **III** 208
Alleghany Corporation, **II** 398; **IV** 180–81; **10** 43–45; **19** 319; **22** 494
Allegheny Airlines. *See* USAir Group, Inc.; US Airways Group, Inc.
Allegheny Beverage Corp., **7** 472–73
Allegheny County Light Company, **6** 483–84
Allegheny Energy, Inc., 38 38–41 (upd.)
Allegheny International, Inc., **III** 732; **8** 545; **9** 484; **22** 3, 436
Allegheny Ludlum Corporation, **I** 307; **II** 402; **8** 18–20; **9** 484; **21** 489
Allegheny Power System, Inc., V 543–45
Allegheny Steel and Iron Company, **9** 484
Allegiance Life Insurance Company, **22** 268; **50** 122
Allegis, Inc. *See* United Airlines.
Allegmeine Transpotmittel Aktiengesellschaft, **6** 394; **25** 169
Allegretti & Co., **22** 26
Allen & Co., **I** 512, 701; **II** 136; **12** 496; **13** 366; **25** 270
Allen & Ginter, **12** 108
Allen & Hanbury's, **I** 640
Allen-Bradley Co., **I** 80; **II** 110; **III** 593; **11** 429–30; **17** 478; **22** 373; **23** 211
Allen-Liversidge Ltd., **I** 315; **25** 80
Allen Organ Company, 33 26–29
Allen-Stuart Equipment Company, **49** 160
Allen Tank Ltd., **21** 499
Allen's Convenience Stores, Inc., **17** 170
Allergan, Inc., **10** 46–49; **23** 196; **30** 29–33 (upd.)
Allforms Packaging Corp., **13** 442
Allgemeine Deutsche Creditanstalt, **II** 211, 238, 383; **12** 536
Allgemeine Eisenbahn-Versicherungs-Gesellschaft, **III** 399
Allgemeine Elektricitäts-Gesellschaft. *See* AEG A.G.
Allgemeine Handelsgesellschaft der Verbraucher AG. *See* AVA AG.
Allgemeine Rentenstalt Lebens- und Rentenversicherung, **II** 258
Allgemeine Schweizerische Uhrenindustrie, **26** 480
Allgemeine Versicherungs-Gesellschaft Helvetia, **III** 375
Allhabo AB, **53** 85
Allia S.A., **51** 324
Alliance Agro-Alimentaires S.A., **II** 577
Alliance Amusement Company, **10** 319
Alliance Assurance Company, **III** 369–73; **55** 333
Alliance Atlantis Communications Inc., **35** 69; **39** 11–14
Alliance Brothers, **V** 356
Alliance Capital Management Corp., **22** 189
Alliance de Sud, **53** 301
Alliance Entertainment Corp., **17** 12–14; **35** 430
Alliance Gaming Corp., **15** 539; **24** 36
Alliance Insurance Co., **III** 224
Alliance Manufacturing Co., **13** 397
Alliance Marine, **III** 373
Alliance Mortgage Co., **I** 610
Alliance Packaging, **13** 443
Alliance Paper Group, **IV** 316
Alliance Tire and Rubber Co., **II** 47; **25** 267
AllianceWare, Inc., **16** 321
Alliant Energy Corp., **39** 261

Alliant Techsystems Inc., **8** 21–23; **30** 34–37 (upd.)
Allianz AG Holding, **I** 411, 426; **II** 239, 257, 279–80; **III** 183–86, 200, 250, 252, 299–301, 347–48, 373, 377, 393; **IV** 222; **14** 169–70; **15** 10–14 (upd.); **51** 23
Allibert, **III** 614
Allied Bakeries Ltd., **II** 465–66; **13** 52–53
Allied Breweries Ltd., **I** 215; **III** 105; **IV** 712
Allied Chemical, **I** 310, 332, 351–52; **8** 526; **9** 521–22; **13** 76; **22** 5. *See also* General Chemical Corp.
Allied Chemical & Dye Corp., **I** 414; **7** 262; **9** 154; **22** 29
Allied Color Industries, **8** 347
Allied Communications Group, **18** 77; **22** 297
Allied Construction Products, **17** 384
Allied Container Corp., **IV** 345
Allied Corporation, **I** 68, 141, 143, 414, 534; **III** 118, 511; **6** 599; **7** 356; **9** 134; **11** 435; **24** 164; **25** 224; **31** 135. *See also* AlliedSignal Inc.
Allied Crude Vegetable Oil Refining Co., **II** 398; **10** 62
Allied Department Stores, **50** 106
Allied Distributing Co., **12** 106
Allied Domecq PLC, **24** 220; **29** 18–20, 85; **52** 416; **54** 229
Allied Dunbar, **I** 427
Allied Engineering Co., **8** 177
Allied Fibers, **19** 275
Allied Food Markets, **II** 662
Allied Gas Company, **6** 529
Allied Grape Growers, **I** 261
Allied Health and Scientific Products Company, **8** 215
Allied Healthcare Products, Inc., **24** 16–19
Allied Holdings, Inc., **24** 411
Allied Import Company, **V** 96
Allied Irish Banks, plc, **16** 13–15; **43** 7–10 (upd.)
Allied Leisure, **40** 296–98
Allied-Lyons plc, **I** 215–16, 258, 264, 438; **IV** 721; **9** 100, 391; **10** 170; **13** 258; **21** 228, 323; **29** 18, 84; **50** 200
Allied Maintenance Corp., **I** 514
Allied Mills, Inc., **10** 249; **13** 186; **43** 121
Allied Oil Co., **IV** 373; **50** 46
Allied Overseas Trading Ltd., **I** 216
Allied Plywood Corporation, **12** 397
Allied Polymer Group, **I** 429
Allied Products Corporation, **21** 20–22
Allied Radio, **19** 310
Allied Safety, Inc., **V** 215
Allied Shoe Corp., **22** 213
Allied-Signal Corp., **I** 85, 141, 143, 414–16; **III** 511–12; **V** 605; **6** 599–600; **9** 519; **11** 435, 444; **13** 227; **16** 436; **17** 20; **21** 200, 396–97; **40** 35; **43** 320. *See also* AlliedSignal, Inc.
Allied Signal Engines, 9 12–15
Allied Steel and Conveyors, **18** 493
Allied Steel and Wire Ltd., **III** 495
Allied Stores Corporation, **II** 350, 611–12; **V** 25–28; **9** 211; **10** 282; **13** 43; **15** 94, 274; **16** 60; **22** 110; **23** 59–60; **25** 249; **31** 192; **37**
Allied Structural Steel Company, **10** 44
Allied Supermarkets, Inc., **7** 570; **28** 511
Allied Suppliers, **II** 609; **50** 401

Allied Telephone Company. *See* Alltel Corporation.
Allied Tin Box Makers Ltd., **I** 604
Allied Towers Merchants Ltd., **II** 649
Allied Van Lines Inc., **6** 412, 414; **14** 37. *See also* Allied Worldwide, Inc.
Allied Vintners, **I** 215
Allied Waste Industries, Inc., 50 13–16
Allied Worldwide, Inc., 49 20–23
AlliedSignal Inc., 22 29–32 (upd.); 29 408; **31** 154; **37** 158; **50** 234
Allis Chalmers Corporation, **I** 163; **II** 98, 121; **III** 543–44; **9** 17; **11** 104; **12** 545; **13** 16–17, 563; **14** 446; **21** 502–03; **22** 380; **50** 196
Allis-Gleaner Corp. *See* AGCO Corp.
Allison Engine Company, **21** 436
Allison Engineering Company. *See* Rolls-Royce Allison.
Allison Gas Turbine Division, 9 16–19, 417; **10** 537; **11** 473
Allmanna Svenska Elektriska Aktiebolaget. *See* ABB ASEA Brown Boveri Ltd.
Allmänna Telefonaktiebolaget L.M. Ericsson, **V** 334
Allnatt London & Guildhall Properties, **IV** 724
Allnet, **10** 19
Allo Pro, **III** 633
Allor Leasing Corp., **9** 323
Allou Health & Beauty Care, Inc., 28 **12–14**
Alloy & Stainless, Inc., **IV** 228
Alloy, Inc., 55 13–15
Alloys Unlimited, **II** 82
Allparts, Inc., **51** 307
Allserve Inc., **25** 367
Allsport plc., **31** 216, 218
The Allstate Corporation, I 23; **III** 231–32, 259, 294; **V** 180, 182; **6** 12; **10** 50–52; **13** 539; **18** 475; **21** 96–97; **22** 495; **23** 286–87; **25** 155; **27** 30–33 (upd.); **29** 397; **49** 332
ALLTEL Corporation, 6 299–301; **16** 318; **20** 440; **46** 15–19 (upd.); **54** 63, 108
Alltrans Group, **27** 472
Alltrista Corporation, 30 38–41
Allwaste, Inc., 18 10–13
Alma Media Group, **52** 51
Almac Electronics Corporation, **10** 113; **50** 42
Almac's Inc., **17** 558–59
Almacenes de Baja y Media, **39** 201, 204
Almaden Vineyards, **I** 377–78; **13** 134; **34** 89
Almanacksförlaget AB, **51** 328
Almanij NV, 44 15–18. *See also* Algemeene Maatschappij voor Nijverheidskrediet.
Almay, Inc., **III** 54
Almeida Banking House. *See* Banco Bradesco S.A.
Almours Security Co., **IV** 311; **19** 266
Almys, **24** 461
ALNM. *See* Ayres, Lewis, Norris & May.
Aloe Vera of America, **17** 187
Aloha Airlines, Incorporated, I 97; **9** 271–72; **21** 142; **22** 251; **24** 20–22
ALP. *See* Associated London Properties.
Alp Sport Sandals, **22** 173
Alpen-Elektrowerke Aktiengesellschaft, **IV** 230
Alpex Computer Corp., **III** 157

Alpex, S.A. de C.V., **19** 12
Alpha Beta Co., **II** 605, 625, 653; **17** 559
Alpha Engineering Group, Inc., **16** 259–60
Alpha Healthcare Ltd., **25** 455
Alpha Processor Inc., **41** 349
Alpha Technical Systems, **19** 279
Alphaform, **40** 214–15
Alphanumeric Publication Systems, Inc., **26** 518
Alpharma Inc., 35 22–26 (upd.)
Alphonse Allard Inc., **II** 652; **51** 303
Alpina Versicherungs-Aktiengesellschaft, **III** 412
Alpine, **IV** 234
Alpine Electronics, Inc., II 5; **13 30–31**
Alpine Gaming. *See* Century Casinos, Inc.
Alpine Lace Brands, Inc., 18 14–16
Alpine Securities Corporation, **22** 5
Alpre, **19** 192
Alps Electric Co., Ltd., II 5–6; **13** 30; **44** 19–21 (upd.)
Alric Packing, **II** 466
Alsco. *See* Steiner Corporation.
Alsen-Breitenbury, **III** 702
ALSO Holding AG, **29** 419, 422
Alsons Corp., **III** 571; **20** 362
Alsthom, **II** 12
Alsthom-Atlantique, **9** 9
Alta Dena, **25** 83, 85
Alta Electric Company, **25** 15
Alta Gold Co., **IV** 76
ALTA Health Strategies, Inc., **11** 113
Alta Holidays Ltd., **I** 95
Alta Vista Company, **50** 228
Altamil Corp., **IV** 137
Altana AG, **23** 498
AltaSteel Ltd., **51** 352
AltaVista Company, 43 11–13
Alte Leipziger, **III** 242
Altec Electronics, **I** 489–90
ALTEC International, **21** 107–09
Altenburg & Gooding, **22** 428
Altera Corporation, 18 17–20; 43 14–18 (upd.); **47** 384
Alternate Postal Delivery, **6** 14
Alternative Living Services. *See* Alterra Healthcare Corporation.
Alternative Youth Services, Inc., **29** 399–400
Alterra Healthcare Corporation, 42 3–5
Altex, **19** 192–93
Althoff KG, **V** 101
Althouse Chemical Company, **9** 153
Althus Corp, **I** 361
Altman Weil Pensa, **29** 237
Alton & Eastern Railroad Company, **6** 504
Alton Box Board Co., **IV** 295; **19** 225
Alton Towers, **55** 378
Altos Computer Systems, **6** 279; **10** 362
Altos Hornos de México, S.A. de C.V., **13** 144; **19** 220; **39** 188; **42 6–8**
Altran Technologies, 51 15–18
Altron Incorporated, 20 8–10
Altura Energy Ltd., **41** 359
Aluar. *See* Aluminios Argentinos.
Aluma Systems Corp., **9** 512; **22** 14
Alumax Inc., **I** 508; **III** 758; **IV** 18–19; **8** 505–06; **22** 286
Alumina Partners of Jamaica, **IV** 123
Aluminate Sales Corp, **I** 373
Aluminio de Galicia, **IV** 174
Aluminios Argentinos, **26** 433
Aluminium Co. of London, **IV** 69
L'Aluminium Francais, **IV** 173

Aluminium Ltd., **IV** 9–11, 14, 153
Aluminium-Oxid Stade GmbH, **IV** 231
Aluminium Plant and Vessel Co., **III** 419
Aluminum Can Co., **I** 607
Aluminum Company of America, I 373, 599; **II** 315, 402, 422; **III** 490–91, 613; **IV** 9–12, **14–16,** 56, 59, 121–22, 131, 173, 703; **6** 39; **12** 346; **19** 240, 292; **20** 11–14 (upd.); **22** 455; **42** 438; **52** 71
Aluminum Company of Canada Ltd., **II** 345; **IV** 10–12, 154
Aluminum Cooking Utensil Co., **IV** 14
Aluminum Forge Co., **IV** 137
Aluminum Norf GmbH, **IV** 231
Aluminum of Korea, **III** 516
Aluminum Rolling Mills, **17** 280
Aluminum Sales Corporation, **12** 346
Aluminum Seating Corp., **I** 201
Alun Cathcart, **6** 357
Alup-Kompressoren Pressorun, **III** 570; **20** 361
Alupak, A.G., **12** 377
Alusaf, **IV** 92
Alusuisse Lonza Group Ltd., **IV** 12; **31** 11
Alva Jams Pty., **I** 437
Alvic Group, **20** 363
Alvin Ailey Dance Foundation, Inc., 52 **14–17**
Alvis Plc, 47 7–9
Alyeska Pipeline Service Co., **IV** 522, 571; **14** 542; **24** 521; **40** 356
Alyeska Seafoods Co., **II** 578
ALZA Corporation, 10 53–55; 36 36–39 (upd.); **40** 11; **41** 200–01
Alzwerke GmbH, **IV** 230
AM Acquisition Inc., **8** 559–60
AM Cosmetics, Inc., **31** 89
Am-Par Records, **II** 129
Am-Safe, Inc., **16** 357
AM-TEX Corp., Inc., **12** 443
Amagasaki Co., **I** 492; **24** 325
Amagasaki Spinners Ltd., **V** 387
Amagasaki Steel Co., Ltd., **IV** 130
Amalgamaize Co., **14** 18
Amalgamated Chemicals, Ltd., **IV** 401
Amalgamated Dental International, **10** 271–72
Amalgamated Distilled Products, **II** 609
Amalgamated Press, **IV** 666; **7** 244, 342; **17** 397
Amalgamated Roadstone Corp., **III** 752; **28** 449
Amalgamated Sugar Co., **14** 18; **19** 467–68
Amalgamated Weatherware, **IV** 696
Amana Refrigeration Company, **II** 86; **11** 413; **18** 226; **38** 374; **42** 159
Amaray International Corporation, **12** 264
Amarillo Gas Company. *See* Atmos Energy Corporation.
Amarillo Railcar Services, **6** 580
Amarin Plastics, **IV** 290
Amax Gold, **36** 316
AMAX Inc., I 508; **III** 687; **IV** 17–19, 46, 139, 171, 239, 387; **6** 148; **12** 244; **22** 106, 286
Amazon.com, Inc., 25 17–19
Amazône Mineracao SA, **IV** 56
AMB Generali Holding AG, 51 19–23
Ambac Industries, **I** 85
AmBase Corp., **III** 264
Amber's Stores, Inc., **17** 360
Amberg Hospach AG, **49** 436
Amblin Entertainment, 21 23–27; 33 431

AMBRA, Inc., **48** 209
Ambrose Shardlow, **III** 494
AMC Entertainment Inc., 12 12–14; **14** 87; **21** 362; **23** 126; **35** 27–29 **(upd.)**
AMCA International Corporation, **7** 513; **8** 545; **10** 329; **23** 299
AMCC. *See* Applied Micro Circuits Corporation.
Amcell. *See* American Cellular Network.
Amchem Products Inc., **I** 666
AMCO, Inc., **13** 159
Amcor Limited, IV 248–50; **19** 13–16 **(upd.)**
AMCORE Financial Inc., 44 22–26
Amcraft Building Products Co., Inc., **22** 15
AMD. *See* Advanced Micro Devices, Inc.
Amdahl Corporation, III 109–11, 140; **6** 272; **12** 238; **13** 202; **14** 13–16 **(upd.)**; **16** 194, 225–26; **22** 293; **25** 87; **40** 20–25 **(upd.)**; **42** 147. *See also* Fujitsu Limited.
Amdocs Ltd., 47 10–12
AME Finanziaria, **IV** 587; **19** 19; **54** 20
AMEC plc, **I** 568; **36** 322; **49** 65
Amedco, **6** 295
Amedysis, Inc., 53 33–36
Amer Group plc, 24 530; **41** 14–16
Amer Sport, **22** 202
Amerace Corporation, **54** 373
Amerada Hess Corporation, IV 365–67, 400, 454, 522, 571, 658; **11** 353; **21** 28–31 **(upd.)**; **24** 521; **55** 16–20 **(upd.)**
Amerco, 6 351–52
AmerGen Energy LLC, **49** 65, 67
Ameri-Kart Corp., **19** 277, 279
America Japan Sheet Glass Co., **III** 714
America Latina Companhia de Seguros, **III** 289
America Online, Inc., 10 56–58, 237; **13** 147; **15** 54, 265, 321; **18** 24; **19** 41; **22** 52, 519, 522; **26** 16–20 **(upd.)**; **27** 20, 106, 301, 430, 517–18; **29** 143, 227; **32** 163; **33** 254; **34** 361; **35** 304, 306; **38** 269–71; **49** 311–12; **54** 74. *See also* CompuServe Interactive Services, Inc.
America Publishing Company, **18** 213
America Today, **13** 545
America Unplugged, **18** 77
America West Airlines, 6 72–74, 121
America West Express, **32** 334
America West Holdings Corporation, 34 22–26 **(upd.)**
America's Favorite Chicken Company, Inc., 7 26–28. *See also* AFC Enterprises, Inc.
American & Efird, Inc., **12** 501; **23** 260
American Acquisitions, Inc., **49** 279
American Agricultural Chemical Co., **IV** 401
American Air Conditioning, **25** 15
American Air Filter, **26** 3–4
American Airlines, I 30–31, 48, 71, **89–91**, 97, 106, 115, 118, 124–26, 130, 132, 512, 530; **III** 102; **6** 60, 81, **75–77 (upd.)**, 121, 129–31; **9** 271–72; **10** 163; **11** 279; **12** 190, 192, 379, 381, 487, **13** 173; **14** 73; **16** 146; **18** 73; **21** 141, 143; **24** 21, 399–400; **25** 90–91, 403, 421–22; **26** 427–28, 441; **31** 103, 306; **33** 270, 302; **34** 118; **38** 105; **55** 10–11. *See also* AMR Corporation.
American Alliance Co., **III** 191
American Allsafe Co., **8** 386
American Amusements, Inc., **III** 430

American Appliance Co., **II** 85; **11** 411
American Arithmometer Company. *See* Burroughs Corporation.
American Asiatic Underwriters, **III** 195
American Association of Retired Persons, **9** 348. *See also* AARP.
American Austin Quality Foods Inc., **44** 40
American Automar Inc., **12** 29
American Automated, **11** 111
American Automobile Insurance Co., **III** 251
American Aviation and General Insurance Co., **III** 230
American Aviation Manufacturing Corp., **15** 246
American Avitron Inc, **I** 481
American Bakeries Company, **12** 275–76
American Bancorp, **11** 295
American Bancshares, Inc., **11** 457
American Bank, **9** 474–75
American Bank Note, **IV** 599
American Bank of Vicksburg, **14** 41
American Bankcorp, Inc., **8** 188
American Banker/Bond Buyer, **8** 526
American Banknote Corporation, 30 42–45
American Bar Association, 35 30–33
American Barge and Towing Company, **11** 194
American Beauty Cover Company, **12** 472
American Beef Packers, Inc., **16** 473
American Beet Sugar Company, **11** 13–14
American Bell Telephone Company, **V** 259; **14** 336
American Beryllium Co., Inc., **9** 323
American Beverage Corp., **II** 528
American Biltrite Inc., 16 16–18; **18** 116, 118; **43** 19–22 **(upd.)**
American Biodyne Inc., **9** 348
American Biomedical Corporation, **11** 333
American Biscuit Co., **II** 542
American Bottling, **49** 78
American Box Board Company, **12** 376
American Box Co., **IV** 137
American Brake Shoe and Foundry Company, **I** 456. *See also* ABC Rail Products Corporation.
American Brands, Inc., II 468, 477; **IV** 251; **V** 395–97, 398–99, 405; **7** 3–4; **9** 408; **12** 87, 344; **14** 95, 271–72; **16** 108, 110, 242; **19** 168–69; **38** 169; **49** 150–51, 153. *See also* Fortune Brands, Inc.
American Bridge Co., **II** 330; **IV** 572; **7** 549
American Broadcasting Co., **25** 418. *See also* ABC, Inc.; Capital Cities/ABC Inc.
American Builders & Contractors Supply Co. *See* ABC Supply Co., Inc.
American Builders, Inc., **8** 436
American Building Maintenance Industries, Inc., 6 17–19. *See also* ABM Industries Incorporated.
American Bus Lines Inc., **24** 118
American Business Information, Inc., 18 21–25
American Business Interiors. *See* American Furniture Company, Inc.
American Business Products, Inc., 20 15–17
American Cabinet Hardware Corp. *See* Amerock Corporation.
American Cable Systems, Inc. *See* Comcast Corporation.

American Cablesystems, **7** 99
American Cafe, **I** 547
American Can Co., **IV** 36, 290; **8** 476; **10** 130; **11** 29, 197; **12** 408; **13** 255; **15** 127–28; **17** 106; **22** 210; **23** 98; **49** 293. *See also* Primerica Corp.
The American Cancer Society, 24 23–25
American Capital and Research Corp., **28** 201
American Car & Foundry Inc., **21** 503
American Carbide Corporation, **7** 584
American Cash Register Co., **III** 150; **6** 264
American Cast Iron Pipe Company, 50 17–20
American Casualty Co., **III** 230–31, 404
American Casualty Co. of Dallas, **III** 203
American Cellular Network, **7** 91; **24** 122
American Cellulose and Chemical Manufacturing Co., **I** 317
American Cement Co. *See* Giant Cement Holding, Inc.
American Central Insurance Co., **III** 241
American Cereal Co., **II** 558; **12** 409
American Chicle Co., **I** 711; **21** 54; **38** 363–64
American Chocolate & Citrus Co., **IV** 409
American Chrome, **III** 699
American Classic Voyages Company, 22 340, **27** 34–37
American Clay Forming Company, **8** 178
American Clip Company, **7** 3
American Coin Merchandising, Inc., 28 15–17
American Colloid Co., 13 32–35
American Colonial Insurance Company, **44** 356
American Commercial Bank, **II** 336
American Commercial Lines Inc., **22** 164, 166–67
American Commonwealths Power Corporation, **6** 579
American Community Grocers, **II** 670
American Computer Systems. *See* American Software Inc.
American Construction Lending Services, Inc., **39** 380, 382
American Continental Insurance Co., **III** 191–92
American Cotton Cooperative Association, **17** 207; **33** 85
American Cotton Oil Co., **II** 497
American Council on Education, **12** 141
American Courier Express, Inc., **24** 126
American Crayon Company, **12** 115
American Credit Corporation, **II** 236; **20** 59
American Crystal Sugar Company, 7 377; **11** 13–15; **32** 29–33 **(upd.)**
American Cyanamid, I 300–02, 619; **III** 22; **IV** 345, 552; **8** 24–26 **(upd.)**; **10** 269; **11** 494; **13** 231–32; **14** 254, 256; **16** 68; **22** 147; **27** 115–16; **50** 248, 250
American Dairy Queen Corporation, **10** 373
American Data Technology, Inc., **11** 111
American Digital Communications, Inc., **33** 329
American Distilling Co., **I** 226; **10** 180–81
American District Telegraph Co., **III** 644; **12** 9
American Diversified Foods, Inc., **14** 351
American Drew, Inc., **12** 301
American Drug Company, **13** 367

American Eagle Airlines, Inc., **28** 22
American Eagle Fire Insurance Co., **III** 240–41
American Eagle Outfitters, Inc., **14** 427; **24** 26–28; **25** 121; **55** 21–24 (upd.)
American Education Press, **10** 479
American Electric Company, **II** 27; **12** 193; **22** 10; **54** 371–73
American Electric Power Company, **II** 3; **IV** 181; **V** 546–49; **6** 449, 524; **11** 516; **45** 17–21 (upd.)
American Empire Insurance Co., **III** 191
American Emulsions Co., **8** 455
American Encaustic Tiling Co., **22** 170
American Energy Management Inc., **39** 261
American Envelope Co., **III** 40; **16** 303; **28** 251; **43** 257
American Equipment Co., **I** 571
American Export Steamship Lines, **I** 89
American Express Company, **I** 26–27, 480, 614; **II** 108, 176, 309, 380–82, **395–99**, 450–52, 544; **III** 251–52, 319, 340, 389; **IV** 637, 721; **6** 206–07, 409; **8** 118; **9** 335, 343, 391, 468–69, 538; **10** 44–45, **59–64 (upd.);** **11** 41, 416–17, 532; **12** 533; **14** 106; **15** 60, 112, 516, 543; **21** 97, 127; **23** 229; **26** 516; **33** 394–96; **38 42–48 (upd.);** **52** 13
American Factors, Ltd. See Amfac/JMB Hawaii L.L.C.
American Family Corporation, **III** **187–89.** See also AFLAC Inc.
American Family Life Insurance Company, **33** 407
American Family Publishers, **23** 393–94
American Feldmühle Corp., **II** 51; **21** 330
American Filtrona Corp., **IV** 260–61
American Finance Systems, **II** 349
American Financial Corporation, **II** 596; **III 190–92,** 221; **8** 537; **9** 452; **18** 549
American Financial Group Inc., 48 6–10 (upd.)
American Fine Wire, Inc., **33** 248
American First National Supermarkets, **16** 313
American Fitness Centers, **25** 40
American Fitness Products, Inc., **47** 128
American Flange, **30** 397
American Flavor & Fragrance Company, **9** 154
American Flyer Trains, **16** 336–37
American Food Management, **6** 45
American Foods Group, 43 23–27
American Football League, **29** 346
American Fore Group, **III** 241–42
American Foreign Insurance Association, **III** 223, 226. See also AFIA.
American Forest Products Co., **IV** 282; **9** 260
American Freightways Corporation, **42** 141
American Fructose Corp., **14** 18–19
American Fur Company, **25** 220
American Furniture Company, Inc., 12 300; **21 32–34**
American Gage & Machine Company, **I** 472; **51** 190
American Gaming and Electronics, Inc., **43** 461
American Gas & Electric. See American Electric Power Company.
American Gasoline Co., **IV** 540
American General Capital Corp., **I** 614

American General Corporation, **III** 193–94; **10 65–67 (upd.);** **11** 16; **46** 20–23 (upd.); **47** 15
American General Finance Corp., 11 **16–17**
American General Life Insurance Company, **6** 294
American Golf Corporation, 45 22–24
American Gramaphone LLC, 52 18–20
American Graphics, **23** 100
American Greetings Corporation, 7 **23–25; 12** 207–08; **15** 507; **16** 256; **21** 426–28; **22 33–36 (upd.)**
American Grinder and Manufacturing Company, **9** 26
American Hardware & Supply Company. See TruServ Corporation.
American Harvester, **II** 262
American Hawaii Cruises, **27** 34
American Health & Life Insurance Company, **27** 47
American Healthcorp Inc., **48** 25
American Heritage Savings, **II** 420
American Hoechst Corporation. See Hoechst Celanese Corporation.
American Hoist & Derrick Co., **8** 544
American Home Assurance Co., **III** 196–97
American Home Assurance Co. of New York, **III** 203
American Home Mortgage Holdings, Inc., 46 24–26
American Home Patients Centers Inc., **46** 4
American Home Products, I 527, **622–24,** 631, 676–77, 696, 700; **III** 18, 36, 444; **8** 282–83; **10 68–70 (upd.),** 528; **11** 35; **15** 64–65; **16** 191, 438; **21** 466; **24** 288; **25** 477; **36** 87; **38** 365; **49** 349–50. See also Wyeth.
American Home Publishing Co., Inc., **14** 460
American Home Shield, **6** 46; **23** 428, 430
American Home Video, **9** 186
American Homestar Corporation, 18 **26–29; 41 17–20 (upd.)**
American Homeware Inc., **15** 501
American Honda Motor Co., **I** 174; **10** 352
American Hospital Association, **10** 159
American Hospital Supply Co., **I** 627, 629; **III** 80; **10** 141–43; **11** 459, 486; **19** 103; **21** 118; **30** 496; **53** 345
American Hydron, **13** 366; **25** 55
American I.G. Chemical Corporation. See GAF Corporation.
American Impacts Corporation, **8** 464
American Improved Cements. See Giant Cement Holding, Inc.
American Independent Oil Co., **IV** 522, 537. See also Aminoil, Inc.
American Industrial Manufacturing Co., **I** 481
American Information Services, Inc., **11** 111
American Institute of Certified Public Accountants (AICPA), 44 27–30
American Institutional Products, Inc., **18** 246
American Instrument Co., **I** 628; **13** 233
American Insurance Agency, **III** 191, 352
American Insurance Co., **III** 251
American International Airways, Inc., **17** 318; **22** 311
American International Group, Inc., II 422; **III 195–98,** 200; **6** 349; **10** 39; **11**

532–33; **15 15–19 (upd.);** **18** 159; **45** 109; **46** 20; **47 13–19 (upd.);** **48** 219
American International Travel Service, **6** 367; **27** 90
American Iron and Steel Manufacturing Co., **IV** 35; **7** 48
American Isuzu Motors, Inc. See Isuzu Motors, Ltd.
American Italian Pasta Company, 27 **38–40**
American Janitor Service, **25** 15
American Jet Industries, **7** 205
American Ka-Ro, **8** 476
American Knitting Mills of Miami, Inc., **22** 213
American La-France, **10** 296
American Laboratories, **III** 73
American Land Cruiser Company. See Cruise America Inc.
American Lawyer Media Holdings, Inc., **32 34–37**
American Learning Corporation, **7** 168
American Life Insurance Co., **III** 195–96
American Light and Traction. See MCN Corporation.
American Lightwave Systems, Inc., **10** 19
American Limestone Co., **IV** 33
American Limousine Corp., **26** 62
American Linen Supply Company. See Steiner Corporation.
American Linseed Co, **II** 497
American Locker Group Incorporated, **34 19–21**
American Lung Association, 48 11–14
American Machine and Foundry Co., **II** 7; **III** 443; **7** 211–13; **11** 397; **25** 197
American Machine and Metals, **9** 23
American Machinist Press, **IV** 634
American Magnesium Products Co., **I** 404
American Maize-Products Co., 14 **17–20; 23** 464
American Management Systems, Inc., 11 **18–20**
American Manufacturers Mutual Insurance Co., **III** 269, 271; **15** 257
American-Marietta Corp., **I** 68, 405
American Materials & Technologies Corporation, **27** 117
American Media, Inc., 27 41–44
American Medical Association, 39 15–18
American Medical Holdings, **55** 370
American Medical International, Inc., III **73–75,** 79; **14** 232
American Medical Optics, **25** 55
American Medical Response, Inc., 39 **19–22**
American Medical Services, **II** 679–80; **14** 209
American Medicorp, Inc., **III** 81; **6** 191; **14** 432; **24** 230
American Melamine, **27** 317
American Merchandising Associates Inc., **14** 411
American Merchants Union Express Co., **II** 396
American Metal Climax, Inc. See AMAX.
American Metal Co. Ltd. See AMAX.
American Metal Products Company. See Lear Seating Corporation.
American Metal Products Corp., **I** 481
American Metals and Alloys, Inc., **19** 432
American Metals Corp., **III** 569; **20** 361
American Micro Devices, Inc., **16** 549
American Microsystems, **I** 193

American Milk Products Corp., **II** 487

The American Mineral Spirits Company, **8** 99–100

American Motorists Insurance Co., **III** 269, 271; **15** 257

American Motors Corp., I 135–37, 145, 152, 190; **II** 60, 313; **III** 543; **6** 27, 50; **8** 373; **10** 262, 264; **18** 493; **26** 403

American Movie Classics Co., **II** 161

American Multi-Cinema. *See* AMC Entertainment Inc.

American National Bank, **13** 221–22

American National Bank and Trust Co., **II** 286

American National Can Co., **III** 536; **IV** 173, 175; **26** 230; **45** 336

American National Corp., **II** 286

American National Fire Insurance Co., **III** 191

American National General Agencies Inc., **III** 221; **14** 109; **37** 85

American National Insurance Company, 8 27–29; **27** 45–48 **(upd.); 39** 158

American Natural Resources Co., **I** 678; **IV** 395; **13** 416

American Natural Snacks Inc., **29** 480

American Newspaper Publishers Association, **6** 13

American of Philadelphia, **III** 234

American Oil Co., **IV** 369–70; **7** 101; **14** 22

American Olean Tile Company, **III** 424; **22** 48, 170

American Optical Co., **I** 711–12; **III** 607; **7** 436; **38** 363–64

American Overseas Airlines, **12** 380

American Overseas Holdings, **III** 350

American Pad & Paper Company, 20 18–21

American Paging, **9** 494–96

American Paper Box Company, **12** 376

American Patriot Insurance, **22** 15

American Payment Systems, Inc., **21** 514

American Petrofina, Inc., **IV** 498; **7** 179–80; **19** 11

American Pfauter, **24** 186

American Phone Centers, Inc., **21** 135

American Photographic Group, **III** 475; **7** 161

American Physicians Service Group, Inc., **6** 45; **23** 430

American Platinum Works, **IV** 78

American Port Services (Amports), **45** 29

American Postage Meter Co., **III** 156

American Potash and Chemical Corporation, **IV** 95, 446; **22** 302

American Power & Light Co., **6** 545, 596–97; **12** 542; **49** 143

American Power Conversion Corporation, 24 29–31

American Premier Underwriters, Inc., 10 71–74; **48** 9

American Prepaid Professional Services, Inc. *See* CompDent Corporation.

American President Companies Ltd., III 512; **6** 353–55

American President Lines Ltd., **54** 274

American Printing House for the Blind, 26 13–15

American Prospecting Equipment Co., **49** 174

American Protective Mutual Insurance Co. Against Burglary, **III** 230

American Public Automotive Group, **37** 115

American Publishing Co., **IV** 597; **24** 222

American Pure Oil Co., **IV** 497

American Radiator & Standard Sanitary Corp., **III** 663–64

American Railway Express Co., **II** 382, 397; **10** 61

American Railway Publishing Co., **IV** 634

American Re Corporation, III 182; **10** 75–77; **35** 34–37 **(upd.); 46** 303

American Record Corp., **II** 132

American Recreation Company Holdings, Inc., **16** 53; **44** 53–54

American Red Cross, 40 26–29

American Ref-Fuel, **V** 751

American Refrigeration Products S.A, **7** 429

American Republic Assurance Co., **III** 332

American Research and Development Corp., **II** 85; **III** 132; **6** 233; **19** 103

American Residential Mortgage Corporation, 8 30–31

American Residential Services, **33** 141

American Resorts Group, **III** 103

American Retirement Corporation, 42 9–12; **43** 46

American Rice, Inc., 17 161–62; **33** 30–33

American River Transportation Co., **I** 421; **11** 23

American Robot Corp., **III** 461

American Rolling Mill Co., **IV** 28; **8** 176–77

American Royalty Trust Co., **IV** 84; **7** 188

American Rug Craftsmen, **19** 275

American RX Pharmacy, **III** 73

American Safety Equipment Corp., **IV** 136

American Safety Razor Company, III 27–29; **20** 22–24

American Saint-Gobain, **16** 121

American Sales Book Co., Ltd., **IV** 644

American Salt Co., **12** 199

American Satellite Co., **6** 279; **15** 195

American Savings & Loan, **10** 117

American Savings Bank, **9** 276; **17** 528, 531

American Sealants Company. *See* Loctite Corporation.

American Seating Co., **I** 447; **21** 33

American Seaway Foods, Inc, **9** 451

American Service Corporation, **19** 223

American Sheet Steel Co., **IV** 572; **7** 549

American Shipbuilding, **18** 318

American Ships Ltd., **50** 209

American Skiing Company, 28 18–21; **31** 67, 229

American Sky Broadcasting, **27** 305; **35** 156

American Smelting and Refining Co., **IV** 31–33. *See also* ASARCO.

The American Society of Composers, Authors and Publishers (ASCAP), 29 21–24

American Software Inc., 22 214; **25** 20–22

American-South African Investment Co. Ltd., **IV** 79

American Southern Insurance Co., **17** 196

American Standard Companies Inc., 30 46–50 **(upd.)**

American Standard Inc., III 437, 663–65; **19** 455; **22** 4, 6; **28** 486; **40** 452

American States Insurance Co., **III** 276

American States Water Company, 46 27–30

American Steamship Company, **6** 394–95; **25** 168, 170

American Steel & Wire Co., **I** 355; **IV** 572; **7** 549; **13** 97–98; **40** 70, 72

American Steel Foundries, **7** 29–30

American Stock Exchange, **10** 416–17; **54** 242

American Stores Company, II 604–06; **12** 63, 333; **13** 395; **17** 559; **18** 89; **22** 37–40 **(upd.); 25** 297; **27** 290–92; **30** 24, 26–27

American Sugar Refining Company. *See* Domino Sugar Corporation.

American Sumatra Tobacco Corp., **15** 138

American Superconductor Corporation, **41** 141

American Surety Co., **26** 486

American Systems Technologies, Inc., **18** 5

American Teaching Aids Inc., **19** 405

American Technical Services Company. *See* American Building Maintenance Industries, Inc.; ABM Industries Incorporated.

American Telephone and Telegraph Company. *See* AT&T.

American Television and Communications Corp., **I** 534–35; **II** 161; **IV** 596, 675; **7** 528–30; **18** 65

American Textile Co., **III** 571; **20** 362

American Thermos Bottle Company. *See* Thermos Company.

American Threshold, **50** 123

American Tile Supply Company, **19** 233

American Tin Plate Co., **IV** 572; **7** 549

American Tissue Company, **29** 136

American Title Insurance, **III** 242

American Tobacco Co., **I** 12–14, 28, 37, 425; **V** 395–97, 399, 408–09, 417–18, 600; **14** 77, 79; **15** 137–38; **16** 242; **18** 416; **27** 128–29; **33** 82; **43** 126; **50** 116–17, 119, 259–60. *See also* American Brands Inc.; B.A.T. Industries PLC.; Fortune Brands, Inc.

American Tool & Machinery, **III** 420

American Tool Companies, Inc., **52** 270

American Tool Company, **13** 563

American Totalisator Corporation, **10** 319–20

American Tourister, Inc., 10 350; **13** 451, 453; **16** 19–21. *See also* Samsonite Corporation.

American Tower Corporation, 33 34–38

American Tractor Corporation, **10** 379

American Trading and Production Corporation, **7** 101

American Trans Air, **34** 31

American Transport Lines, **6** 384

American Trust and Savings Bank, **II** 261

American Trust Co., **II** 336, 382; **12** 535

American Twist Drill Co., **23** 82

American Ultramar Ltd., **IV** 567

American Vanguard Corporation, 47 20–22

American VIP Limousine, Inc., **26** 62

American Viscose Corp. *See* Avisco.

American Water Works Company, Inc., **V** 543–44; **6** 443–45; **26** 451; **38** 49–52 **(upd.)**

American Window Glass, **16** 120

American Wood Reduction Company, **14** 174

American Woodmark Corporation, 31 13–16
American Woolen, **I** 529
American Yard Products, **22** 26, 28
American Yearbook Company, **7** 255; **25** 252
American-Palestine Trading Corporation, **II** 205–06; **54** 34
American-Strevell Inc., **II** 625
Americana Entertainment Group, Inc., **19** 435
Americana Foods, Inc., **17** 474–75
Americana Healthcare Corp., **15** 522
Americana Hotel, **12** 316
Americana Ships Ltd., **50** 210
AmeriFirst Bank, **11** 258
Amerifirst Federal Savings, **10** 340
AmeriGas Partners, L.P., **12** 498
AmeriGas Propane, Inc., **12** 500
Amerihost Properties, Inc., 30 51–53
AmeriKing Corp., **36** 309
Amerimark Inc., **II** 682
Amerin Corporation. *See* Radian Group Inc.
AmeriServe Food Distribution. *See* Holberg Industries, Inc.
AmeriSource Health Corporation, 37 9–11 (upd.)
Ameristar Casinos, Inc., 33 39–42
AmeriSuites, **52** 281
Amerisystems, **8** 328
Ameritech Corporation, V 265–68; **6** 248; **7** 118; **10** 431; **11** 382; **12** 137; **14** 252–53, 257, 259–61, 364; **15** 197; **18** 30–34 (upd.); **25** 499; **41** 288–90; **43** 447; **44** 49
Ameritech Illinois. *See* Illinois Bell Telephone Company.
Ameritrade Holding Corporation, 34 27–30
Ameritrust Corporation, **9** 476
Ameriwood Industries International Corp., 17 15–17
Amerock Corporation, 13 41; **53 37–40**
Amerotron, **I** 529
Amersham PLC, 50 21–25
Amersil Co., **IV** 78
Ames Department Stores, Inc., V 197–98; **9 20–22**; **10** 497; **15** 88; **19** 449; **30 54–57** (upd.)
Ametek Inc., **9 23–25**; **12** 88; **38** 169
N.V. Amev, **III 199–202**
AMEX. *See* American Stock Exchange.
Amey Plc, 47 23–25; **49** 320
AMF Bowling, Inc., 19 312; **23** 450; **40** 30–33
Amfac Inc., I 417–18, 566; **IV** 703; **10** 42; **23** 320
Amfac/JMB Hawaii L.L.C., 24 32–35 (upd.)
Amfas, **III** 310
AMFM Inc., **35** 221, 245, 248; **37** 104; **41** 384
Amgen, Inc., I 266; **8** 216–17; **10 78–81**; **13** 240; **14** 255; **21** 320; **30 58–61** (upd.); **38** 204; **50** 248, 250, 538; **54** 111
Amherst Coal Co., **IV** 410; **7** 309
AMI. *See* Advanced Metallurgy, Inc.
Amiga Corporation, **7** 96
Aminoil, Inc., **IV** 523. *See also* American Independent Oil Co.
AMISA, **IV** 136

Amisys Managed Care Information Systems, **16** 94
Amitron S.A., **10** 113; **50** 43
Amity Leather Products Company. *See* AR Accessories Group, Inc.
AMK Corporation, **II** 595; **7** 85; **21** 111
Amkor, **23** 17
AMLI Realty Company, **33** 418, 420
Amling Co., **25** 89
Ammirati Puris Lintas, **14** 316; **22** 294
Ammo-Phos, **I** 300; **8** 24
L'Ammoniac Sarro-Lorrain S.a.r.l., **IV** 197
Amnesty International, 50 26–29
Amoco Corporation, I 516, 202; **II** 376; **III** 611; **IV 368–71**, 412, 424–25, 453, 525; **7** 107, 443; **10** 83–84; **11** 441; **12** 18; **14 21–25** (upd.), 494; **18** 365; **19** 297; **26** 369. *See also* BP p.l.c.
Amorim Investimentos e Participaço, **48** 117, 119
Amorim Revestimentos, **48** 118
Amoseas, **IV** 453–54
Amoskeag Company, 6 356; **8 32–33**; **9** 213–14, 217; **22** 54; **31** 199
Amot Controls Corporation, **15** 404; **50** 394
AMP, Inc., II 7–8; **11** 319; **13** 344; **14 26–28** (upd.); **17** 274; **22** 542; **28** 486; **36** 158; **54** 239
Ampad Holding Corporation. *See* American Pad & Paper Company.
AMPAL. *See* American-Palestine Trading Corp.
AMPCO Auto Parks, Inc. *See* American Building Maintenance Industries, Inc.; ABM Industries Incorporated.
Ampeg Company, **48** 353
AMPEP, **III** 625
Ampex Corporation, III 549; **6** 272; **17 18–20**
Amphenol Corporation, 40 34–37
Ampol Petroleum Ltd., **III** 729; **27** 473
Ampro, **25** 504–05
AMR. *See* American Medical Response, Inc.
AMR Combs Inc., **36** 190
AMR Corporation, I 90–91; **6** 76; **8** 315; **22** 252; **26** 427–28; **28 22–26** (upd.); **29** 409; **33** 19; **34** 119; **52 21–26** (upd.); **54** 4
AMR Information Services, **9** 95
Amram's Distributing Limited, **12** 425
AMRE, **III** 211
AMREP Corporation, I 563; **21 35–37**; **24** 78
Amro. *See* Amsterdam-Rotterdam Bank N.V.
Amrop International Australasia, **34** 249
AMS. *See* Advanced Marketing Services, Inc.
AMS Trading Co., **III** 112
Amsco International, **29** 450
Amserve Ltd., **48** 23
AmSouth Bancorporation, 12 15–17; **48 15–18** (upd.)
Amstar Corp., **14** 18
Amstar Sugar Corporation, **II** 582; **7** 466–67; **26** 122
Amsted Industries Incorporated, 7 29–31
Amstel Brewery, **I** 257; **34** 201
Amsterdam-Rotterdam Bank N.V., II 184, **185–86**, 279, 295, 319; **III** 200; **14** 169; **17** 324

Amstrad plc, III 112–14; **48 19–23** (upd.)
AmSurg Corporation, 48 24–27
AMT. *See* American Materials & Technologies Corporation.
Amtech. *See* American Building Maintenance Industries, Inc.; ABM Industries Incorporated.
Amtech Systems Corporation, **11** 65; **27** 405
Amtel, Inc., **8** 545; **10** 136
Amtliches Bayerisches Reisebüro, **II** 163
Amtorg, **13** 365
Amtrak, **II** 2; **10** 73; **19** 141; **26** 440; **52** 168. *See also* National Railroad Passenger Corporation.
Amtran, Inc., 34 31–33
AmTrans. *See* American Transport Lines.
Amvac Chemical Corporation, **47** 20
Amvent Inc., **25** 120
Amway Corporation, III 11–14; **13** **36–39** (upd.); **17** 186; **18** 67, 164; **20** 435; **23** 509; **29** 493; **30 62–66** (upd.); **31** 327
Amylum, **II** 582
ANA. *See* All Nippon Airways Co., Ltd.
Anacomp, Inc., **11** 19
Anaconda Aluminum, **11** 38
Anaconda Co., **III** 644; **IV** 33, 376; **7** 261–63
Anaconda-Jurden Associates, **8** 415
Anadarko Petroleum Corporation, 10 82–84; **52 27–30** (upd.)
Anadex, Inc., **18** 435–36
Anaheim Angels Baseball Club, Inc., 53 41–44
Anaheim Imaging, **19** 336
Analog Devices, Inc., 10 85–87; **18** 20; **19** 67; **38** 54; **43** 17, 311; **47** 384
Analogic Corporation, 23 13–16
Analysts International Corporation, 36 40–42
Analytic Sciences Corporation, 10 88–90; **13** 417
Analytical Nursing Management Corporation (ANMC). *See* Amedisys, Inc.
Analytical Surveys, Inc., 33 43–45
Anam Group, 21 239; **23 17–19**
Anamax Mining Co., **IV** 33
AnAmo Co., **IV** 458
Anarad, Inc., **18** 515
Anaren Microwave, Inc., 33 46–48
ANB Bank, **I** 55
Anchor Bancorp, Inc., 10 91–93
Anchor Brake Shoe, **18** 5
Anchor Brewing Company, 47 26–28
Anchor Corporation, **12** 525
Anchor Gaming, 24 36–39; **41** 216
Anchor Hocking Glassware, I 609–10; **13** 40–42; **14** 483; **26** 353; **49** 253; **53** 39
Anchor Motor Freight, Inc., **12** 309–10
Anchor National Financial Services, Inc., **11** 482
Anchor National Life Insurance Company, **11** 482
Anchor Oil and Gas Co., **IV** 521
Anchor Records, **II** 130
Ancienne Mutuelle, **III** 210
Anders Wilhelmsen & Co., **22** 471
Andersen Consulting, **38** 430
Andersen Corporation, 9 344; **10 94–95**; **11** 305; **22** 346; **39** 324
Andersen Worldwide, 29 25–28 (upd.)

Anderson & Kerr Drilling Co., **IV** 445
Anderson and Campbell, **II** 479
Anderson Box Co., **IV** 342; **8** 267
Anderson Clayton & Co., **II** 560; **12** 411
Anderson, Greenwood & Co., **11** 225–26
Anderson Testing Company, Inc., **6** 441
The Andersons, Inc., 31 17–21
Anderton, **III** 624
Andes Candies, **II** 520–21
Andian National Corp. Ltd., **IV** 415–16
André Courrèges, **III** 47; **8** 342–43
Andreas Christ, **26** 243
Andreas Stihl, 16 22–24
Andrew Corporation, 10 96–98; **32** 38–41 (upd.)
Andrew Jergens Co., **III** 38; **25** 56
Andrew Weir & Co., **III** 273
Andrews, Clark & Company, **IV** 426; **7** 169
Andrews Group, Inc., **10** 402
Andrews McMeel Universal, 40 38–41
Andrews Office Supply and Equipment Co., **25** 500
Andritz AG, 27 269; **51** 24–26
Andrx Corporation, 55 25–27
Anfor, **IV** 249–50
Angele Ghigi, **II** 475
Angelica Corporation, 15 20–22; **43** 28–31 (upd.)
Angelo's Supermarkets, Inc., **II** 674
ANGI Ltd., **11** 28
Angle Steel, **25** 261
Anglian Water Plc, **38** 51
Anglo-American Chewing Gum Ltd., **II** 569
Anglo-American Clays Corp., **III** 691; **IV** 346
Anglo American Corporation of South Africa Limited, I 289, 423; **IV** 20–23, 56–57, 64–68, 79–80, 90, 92, 94–96, 118–20, 191, 239–40; **7** 121–23, 125; **16** 25–30 (upd.), 292; **21** 211, 354; **22** 233; **28** 88, 93; **49** 232–34
Anglo-American Oil Company Limited, **IV** 427; **7** 170
Anglo American Paper Co., **IV** 286
Anglo American PLC, 50 30–36 (upd.)
Anglo-American Telegraph Company Ltd., **IV** 668; **25** 98
Anglo-Belge, **II** 474
Anglo-Canadian, **III** 704
Anglo-Canadian Mining & Refining, **IV** 110
Anglo-Canadian Telephone Company of Montreal. *See* British Columbia Telephone Company.
Anglo-Celtic Watch Company, **25** 430
Anglo Company, Ltd., **9** 363
Anglo-Dutch Unilever group, **9** 317
Anglo-Egyptian D.C.O., **II** 236
Anglo-Egyptian Oilfields, **IV** 412, 414
Anglo-Elementar-Versicherungs-AG, **III** 185
Anglo Energy, Ltd., **9** 364
Anglo-Huronian Ltd., **IV** 164
Anglo-Iranian Oil Co., **IV** 379, 419, 435, 450, 466, 559; **7** 57, 141; **21** 81
Anglo-Lautaro Nitrate Corporation, **9** 363
Anglo Mexican Petroleum Co. Ltd., **IV** 657
Anglo-Palestine Co., **II** 204
Anglo-Persian Oil Co., **IV** 363, 378–79, 381, 429, 450, 466, 515, 524, 531, 557–59; **7** 56–57, 140; **21** 80–81; **45** 47

Anglo-Swiss Condensed Milk Co., **II** 545
Anglo-Thai Corp., **III** 523
Anglo-Transvaal Consolidated, **IV** 534
Anglovaal Industries Ltd., **20** 263
Angus Hill Holdings, **IV** 249
Anheuser-Busch Companies, Inc., 34 34–37 (upd.); **36** 12–15, 163
Anheuser-Busch Company, Inc., I 32, 217–19, 236–37, 254–55, 258, 265, 269–70, 290–91, 598; **IV** 624; **6** 20–21, 48; **9** 100; **10** 99–101 (upd.), 130; **11** 421; **12** 337–38; **13** 5, 10, 258, 366; **15** 429; **17** 256; **18** 65, 70, 72–73, 499, 501; **19** 221, 223; **21** 229, 319–20; **22** 421; **23** 403; **25** 281–82, 368; **26** 432; **29** 84–85; **29** 218; **31** 381, 383
ANIC Gela, **IV** 421
Anikem, **I** 374
Anitec Image Technology Corp., **IV** 287; **15** 229
Anker BV, 53 45–47
ANMC. *See* Amedisys, Inc.
Annabelle's, **II** 480–81; **26** 57
Anne Klein & Co., **15** 145–46; **24** 299; **40** 277–78
Anneplas, **25** 464
AnnTaylor Stores Corporation, V 26–27; **13** 43–45; **15** 9; **25** 120–22; **37** 12–15 (upd.)
Annuaries Marcotte Ltd., **10** 461
Anocout Engineering Co., **23** 82
Anonima Infortunia, **III** 208
ANR Pipeline Co., 17 21–23; **31** 119
Ansa Software, **9** 81
Ansaldo, **II** 191
Ansbacher-Siegle Corp., **13** 460
Anschütz & Co. GmbH, **III** 446
The Anschutz Corporation, 12 18–20; **36** 43–47 (upd.); **37** 312
Anschütz-Kaempfe, **III** 446
Ansell, **I** 215
Ansell Rubber Company, **10** 445
Anselmo L. Morvillo S.A., **19** 336
Ansett Airlines, **6** 73; **14** 11; **27** 475
Ansett Australia, **24** 398, 400; **26** 113
Ansett Transport Industries Limited, **V** 523–25; **27** 473
Ansonia Brass and Battery Co., **IV** 176–77
Ansonia Manufacturing Co., **IV** 176
ANSYS Technologies Inc., **48** 410
Ant Nachrichtentechnik GmbH., **I** 411
Anta Corporation, **6** 188; **25** 308
Antalis, **34** 38, 40
Antar group, **IV** 544, 546
Antares Alliance Group, **14** 15
Antares Capital Corp., **53** 213
Antares Electronics, Inc., **10** 257
Ante Corp., **22** 222
Antenna Company, **32** 40
ANTEX. *See* American National Life Insurance Company of Texas.
Anthem Electronics, Inc., 13 46–47; **17** 276
Anthem P&C Holdings, **15** 257
Anthes Imperial Ltd., **I** 274; **26** 304
Anthes Industries Inc., **9** 512
Anthony Industries Inc. *See* K2 Inc.
Anthony Stumpf Publishing Company, **10** 460
Anthropologie, **14** 524–25
Antillaase Bank-Unie N.V., **II** 184
Antinori. *See* Marchesi Antinori SRL.
The Antioch Company, 40 42–45
Antique Street Lamps, **19** 212

ANTK Tupolev. *See* Aviacionny Nauchno-Tehnicheskii Komplex im. A.N. Tupoleva.
Antoine Saladin, **III** 675
Antonov Design Bureau, 53 48–51
Antwerp Co., **IV** 497
ANZ. *See* Australia and New Zealand Banking Group Limited.
ANZ Securities, **24** 400
Anzon Limited, **III** 681; **44** 118–19
AO Sidanco, **45** 50
AOE Plastic GmbH, **7** 141
Aoki Corporation, **9** 547, 549; **29** 508
AOL. *See* America Online, Inc.
AOL Time Warner Inc., **45** 201; **47** 271
Aon Corporation, III 203–05; **22** 495; **45** 25–28 (upd.); **50** 267, 433
AP. *See* The Associated Press.
AP&L. *See* American Power & Light Co.
AP Bank, Ltd., **13** 439
AP-Dow Jones/Telerate Company, **10** 277
AP Support Services, **25** 13
APAC, Inc., **IV** 374
Apache Corporation, 10 102–04; **11** 28; **18** 366; **32** 42–46 (upd.)
Apache Energy Ltd., **25** 471
APACHE Medical Systems, Inc., **16** 94
Apanage GmbH & Co. KG, **53** 195
Apartment Furniture Rental, **26** 102
Apartment Investment and Management Company, 49 24–26
Apasco S.A. de C.V., 51 27–29
APCOA/Standard Parking. *See* Holberg Industries, Inc.
Apex, **17** 363
Apex Financial Corp., **8** 10
Apex Oil, **37** 310–11
Apex One Inc., **31** 137
Apex Smelting Co., **IV** 18
APH. *See* American Printing House for the Blind.
Apita, **V** 210
APL. *See* American President Companies Ltd.
APL Corporation, **9** 346
APL Ltd., **41** 399
Aplex Industries, Inc., **26** 363
Apline Guild, **12** 173
Aplix, **19** 477
APM Ltd., **IV** 248–49
APN. *See* Affiliated Physicians Network, Inc.
Apogee Enterprises, Inc., 8 34–36; **22** 347
Apollo Advisors L.P., **16** 37; **26** 500, 502; **43** 438
Apollo Apparel Partners, L.P., **12** 431
Apollo Computer, **III** 143; **6** 238; **9** 471; **11** 284
Apollo Group, Inc., 24 40–42
Apollo Heating & Air Conditioning Inc., **15** 411
Apollo Investment Fund Ltd., **31** 211; **39** 174
Apollo Ski Partners LP of New York, **11** 543, 545
Apollo Technologies, **I** 332
Apotekarnes Droghandel A.B., **I** 664–65
Apothekernes Laboratorium A.S., **12** 3–5
Appalachian Computer Services, **11** 112
Appalachian Travel Services, Inc., **25** 185, 187
Appetifrais S.A., **51** 54
Applause Inc., 17 461; **24** 43–46

Apple Computer, Inc., II 6, 62, 103, 107, 124; III 114, **115–16,** 121, 125, 149, 172; **6 218–20 (upd.),** 222, 225, 231, 244, 248, 254–58, 260, 289; **8** 138; **9** 166, 170–71, 368, 464; **10** 22–23, 34, 57, 233, 235, 404, 458–59, 518–19; **11** 45, 50, 57, 62, 490; **12** 139, 183, 335, 449, 455, 470; **13** 90, 388, 482; **16** 195, 367–68, 372, 417–18; **18** 93, 511, 521; **20** 31; **21** 391; **23** 209; **24** 370; **25** 299–300, 348, 530–31; **28** 244–45; **33** 12–14; **34** 512; **36 48–51 (upd.),** 168; **38** 69

Apple Container Corp., III 536; **26** 230

Apple Orthodontix, Inc., **35** 325

Apple South, Inc., **21** 362; **35** 39. *See also* Avado Brands, Inc.

Applebee's International Inc., 14 29–31; **19** 258; **20** 159; **21** 362; **31** 40; **35** **38–41 (upd.)**

Appleton & Cox, III 242

Appleton Papers, I 426

Appleton Wire Works Corp., **8** 13

Appliance Buyers Credit Corp., III 653

Appliance Recycling Centers of America, Inc., 42 13–16

Applica Incorporated, 43 32–36 (upd.)

Les Applications du Roulement, III 623

Applied Beverage Systems Ltd., **21** 339

Applied Biomedical Corp., **47** 4

Applied Bioscience International, Inc., 10 **105–07**

Applied Color Systems, III 424

Applied Communications, Inc., **6** 280; **11** 151; **25** 496; **29** 477–79

Applied Data Research, Inc., **6** 225; **18** 31–32

Applied Digital Data Systems Inc., II 83; **9** 514

Applied Engineering Services, Inc. *See* The AES Corporation.

Applied Films Corporation, 12 121; **35** 148; **48 28–31**

Applied Industrial Materials Corporation, **22** 544, 547

Applied Komatsu Technology, Inc., **10** 109

Applied Laser Systems, **31** 124

Applied Learning International, IV 680

Applied Materials, Inc., 10 108–09; 18 382–84; **46 31–34 (upd.)**

Applied Micro Circuits Corporation, 38 **53–55**

Applied Network Technology, Inc., **25** 162

Applied Power Inc., 9 26–28; 32 47–51 **(upd.)**

Applied Programming Technologies, Inc., **12** 61

Applied Solar Energy, **8** 26

Applied Technology Corp., **11** 87

Applied Thermal Technologies, Inc., **29** 5

Approvisionnement Atlantique, II 652; **51** 303

Appryl, I 303

Apria Healthcare Inc., **43** 266

Aprilia SpA, 17 24–26

APS. *See* Arizona Public Service Company.

APS Healthcare, **17** 166, 168

Apura GmbH, IV 325

APUTCO, **6** 383

Aqua Alliance Inc., 32 52–54 (upd.)

Aqua-Chem, Inc., I 234; **10** 227

Aqua Cool Pure Bottled Water, **52** 188

Aqua Glass, III 570; **20** 362

Aqua Pure Water Co., III 21

Aquafin N.V., **12** 443; **38** 427

Aquarium Supply Co., **12** 230

Aquarius Group, **6** 207

Aquatech, **53** 232

Aquila Energy Corp., **6** 593

Aquila, Inc., IV 486; **50 37–40 (upd.)**

Aquitaine. *See* Société Nationale des Petroles d'Aquitaine.

AR Accessories Group, Inc., 23 20–22

AR-TIK Systems, Inc., **10** 372

ARA Services, II 607–08; 21 507; **25** 181

Arab Contractors, III 753

Arab Japanese Insurance Co., III 296

Arab Petroleum Pipeline Co., IV 412

Arabian American Oil Co., I 570; IV 386, 429, 464–65, 512, 536–39, 552, 553, 559; **7** 172, 352; **14** 492–93; **41** 392. *See also* Saudi Arabian Oil Co.

Arabian Gulf Oil Co., IV 454

Arabian Investment Banking Corp., **15** 94; **26** 53; **47** 361

Arabian Oil Co., IV 451

Aral, IV 487

ARAMARK Corporation, 13 48–50; 16 228; **21** 114–15; **35** 415; **41 21–24**

Aramco. *See* Arabian American Oil Co.; Saudi Arabian Oil Company.

Aramis Inc., **30** 191

Arandell Corporation, 37 16–18

Arapuã. *See* Lojas Arapuã S.A.

Aratex Inc., **13** 49

Aratsu Sekiyu, IV 554

ARBED S.A., IV 24–27, 53; **22 41–45** **(upd.); 26** 83; **42** 414

Arbeitsgemeinschaft der öffentlich-rechtlichen Rundfunkanstalten der Bundesrepublick. *See* ARD.

The Arbitron Company, III 128; **10** 255, 359; **13** 5; **38 56–61**

Arbor Acres, **13** 103

Arbor Drugs Inc., 12 21–23. *See also* CVS Corporation.

Arbor International, **18** 542

Arbor Living Centers Inc., **6** 478

Arbuthnot & Co., III 522

Arby's Inc., II 614; **8** 536–37; **14 32–34,** 351

ARC. *See* American Rug Craftsmen.

ARC International Corporation, **27** 57

ARC Ltd., III 501

ARC Materials Corp., III 688

ARC Propulsion, **13** 462

ARCA. *See* Appliance Recycling Centers of America, Inc.

Arcadia Company, **14** 138

Arcadia Group plc, 28 27–30 (upd.), 95–96

Arcadia Partners, **17** 321

Arcadian Corporation, **18** 433; **27** 317–18

Arcadian Marine Service, Inc., **6** 530

Arcadis NV, 26 21–24

Arcata Corporation, **12** 413

Arcata National Corp., **9** 305

Arcelik, I 478

Arch Mineral Corporation, IV 374; **7** **32–34**

Arch Petroleum Inc., **39** 331

Arch Wireless, Inc., 39 23–26; 41 265, 267

Archbold Container Co., **35** 390

Archbold Ladder Co., **12** 433

Archer-Daniels-Midland Co., I 419–21; IV 373; **7** 432–33, 241 **8** 53; **11 21–23** **(upd.); 17** 207; **22** 85, 426; **23** 384; **25** 241; **31** 234; **32 55–59 (upd.)**

Archer Drug, III 10

Archer Management Services Inc., **24** 360

Archers Gilles & Co., II 187

Archibald Candy Corporation, **36** 309

Archipelago RediBook, **48** 226, 228

Archstone-Smith Trust, 49 27–30

Archway Cookies, Inc., 29 29–31

ArcLight, LLC, **50** 123

ARCO. *See* Atlantic Richfield Company.

ARCO Chemical Company, IV 376–77, 456–57; **10 110–11**

ARCO Comfort Products Co., **26** 4

Arco Electronics, **9** 323

Arco Pharmaceuticals, Inc., **31** 346

Arco Societa Per L'Industria Elettrotecnica, II 82

Arcon Corporation, **26** 287

Arctco, Inc., 12 400–01; **16 31–34; 35** 349, 351

Arctic, III 479

Arctic Alaska Fisheries Corporation, **14** 515; **50** 493–94

Arctic Cat Inc., 40 46–50 (upd.)

Arctic Enterprises, **34** 44

Arctic Slope Regional Corporation, 38 **62–65**

ARD, 41 25–29

Ardal og Sunndal Verk AS, **10** 439

Arden Group, Inc., 29 32–35

Ardent Computer Corp., III 553

Ardent Risk Services, Inc. *See* General Re Corporation.

Areal Technologies, III 715

Argbeit-Gemeinschaft Lurgi und Ruhrchemie, IV 534; **47** 342

Argenbright Security Inc. *See* Securicor Plc.

Argentaria Caja Postal y Banco Hipotecario S.A. *See* Banco Bilbao Vizcaya Argentaria S.A.

Argentine National Bank, **14** 46

Argo Communications Corporation, **6** 300

Argon Medical, **12** 327

Argonaut, I 523–24; **10** 520–22

Argos, I 426; **22** 72; **50** 117

Argos Retail Group, **47** 165, 169

Argos Soditic, **43** 147, 149

Argosy Gaming Company, 21 38–41

Argosy Group LP, **27** 197

Argus Chemical Co., I 405

Argus Corp., IV 22, 272, 611

Argus Energy, **7** 538

Argus Motor Company, **16** 7

Argyle Television Inc., **19** 204

Argyll Group PLC, I 241; II 609–10, 656; **12** 152–53; **24** 418. *See also* Safeway PLC.

Aria Communications, Inc. *See* Ascend Communications, Inc.

Ariba Inc., **38** 432

Ariel Capital Management, **28** 421

Ariens Company, 48 32–34

Aries Technology, **25** 305

Aris Industries, Inc., 15 275; **16 35–38**

Arista Laboratories Inc., **51** 249, 251

Aristech Chemical Corp., **12** 342

Aristocrat Leisure Limited, 54 14–16

Arizona Airways, **22** 219

Arizona Copper Co., IV 177

Arizona Edison Co., **6** 545

Arizona Growth Capital, Inc., **18** 513
AriZona Iced Tea. *See* Ferolito, Vultaggio & Sons.
Arizona One, **24** 455
Arizona Public Service Company, **6** 545–47; **19** 376, 412; **26** 359; **28** 425–26; **54** 290
Arizona Refrigeration Supplies, **14** 297–98
Arjo Wiggins Appleton p.l.c., **13** 458; **27** 513; **34** 38–40
Ark Restaurants Corp., **20** 25–27
Ark Securities Co., **II** 233
Arkady Co., Ltd., **I** 421; **11** 23
Arkansas Best Corporation, **16** 39–41; **19** 455; **42** 410
Arkansas Breeders, **II** 585
Arkansas Chemicals Inc., **I** 341
Arkansas Louisiana Gas Company. *See* Arkla, Inc.
Arkansas Power & Light, **V** 618
Arkay Computer, **6** 224
ARKE, **II** 164
Arkia, **23** 184, 186–87
Arkla, Inc., **V** 550–51; **11** 441
Arla Foods amba, **48** 35–38
Arlesey Lime and Portland Cement Co., **III** 669
Arlington Corporation, **6** 295
Arlington Motor Holdings, **II** 587
Arlington Securities plc, **24** 84, 87–89
Arlon, Inc., **28** 42, 45
Armani. *See* Giorgio Armani S.p.A.
Armaturindistri, **III** 569
Armco Inc., **III** 259, 721; **IV** 28–30, 125, 171; **10** 448; **11** 5, 255; **12** 353; **19** 8; **26** 407; **30** 282–83; **41** 3, 5; **54** 247–48
Armin Corp., **III** 645
Armin Poly Film Corp., **III** 645
Armitage Shanks, **III** 671
Armor All Products Corp., **12** 333; **15** 507; **16** 42–44; **22** 148; **26** 349; **47** 235
Armor Elevator, **11** 5
Armor Holdings, Inc., **27** 49–51
Armour. *See* Tommy Armour Golf Co.
Armour & Company, **8** 144; **12** 198; **13** 21, 506; **23** 173; **55** 365
Armour-Dial, **I** 14; **8** 144; **23** 173–74
Armour Food Co., **I** 449–50, 452; **II** 494, 518; **12** 81, 370; **13** 270; **42** 92
Armour Pharmaceutical Co., **III** 56
Armstrong Advertising Co., **I** 36
Armstrong Air Conditioning Inc. *See* Lennox International Inc.
Armstrong Autoparts, **III** 495
Armstrong Communications, **IV** 640
Armstrong Cork Co., **18** 118
Armstrong Nurseries, **I** 272
Armstrong Rees Ederer Inc., **IV** 290
Armstrong-Siddeley Co., **III** 508
Armstrong Tire Co., **15** 355
Armstrong, Whitworth & Co. Ltd., **I** 50; **III** 508; **IV** 257; **24** 85
Armstrong World Industries, Inc., **III** 422–24; **9** 466; **12** 474–75; **22** 46–50 (upd.), 170–71; **26** 507; **53** 175–76
Armtek, **7** 297
Army and Air Force Exchange Service, **39** 27–29
Army Cooperative Fire Insurance Company, **10** 541
Army Ordnance, **19** 430
Army Signal Corps Laboratories, **10** 96
Arndale, **IV** 696
Arno Press, **IV** 648; **19** 285

Arnold & Porter, **35** 42–44
Arnold Communications, **25** 381
Arnold Electric Company, **17** 213
Arnold Foods Co., **II** 498
Arnold Industries Inc., **35** 297
Arnold, Schwinn & Company. *See* Schwinn Cycle and Fitness L.P.
Arnold Thomas Co., **9** 411
Arnoldo Mondadori Editore S.p.A., **IV** 585–88, 675; **19** 17–21 (upd.); **54** 17–23 (upd.)
Arnotts Ltd., **II** 481; **26** 57–59
Aro Corp., **III** 527; **14** 477, 508; **15** 225
Aromat Corporation, **III** 710; **7** 303
Aromatic Industries, **18** 69
Arpet Petroleum, **III** 740; **IV** 550
Arpic, **III** 426
Arrendadora del Norte, S.A. de C.V., **51** 150
Arrosto Coffee Company, **25** 263
Arrow Air Holdings Corporation, **55** 28–30
Arrow Electronics, Inc., **10** 112–14; **13** 47; **19** 310–11, 313; **29** 414; **30** 175; **50** 41–44 (upd.)
Arrow Food Distributor, **II** 675
Arrow Furniture Co., **21** 32
Arrow Oil Co., **IV** 401
Arrow Oil Tools, **III** 570; **20** 360
Arrow Pacific Plastics, **48** 334
Arrow Pump Co., **I** 185
Arrow Shirt Co., **24** 384
Arrow Specialty Company, **III** 570; **20** 360
Arrowhead Mills Inc., **27** 197–98; **43** 218–19
Arrowsmith & Silver, **I** 428
Arsam Investment Co., **26** 261
A.B. Arsenalen, **II** 352
Arsynco, Inc., **38** 4
The Art Institute of Chicago, **29** 36–38
Art Van Furniture, Inc., **28** 31–33
Artal Luxembourg SA, **33** 446, 449
Artal NV, **40** 51
Artec, **III** 420; **12** 297
Artech Digital Entertainments, Inc., **15** 133
Artek Systems Corporation, **13** 194
Artémis Group, **27** 513
Artesian Manufacturing and Bottling Company, **9** 177
Artesian Resources Corporation, **45** 277
Artesyn Solutions Inc., **48** 369
Artesyn Technologies Inc., **46** 35–38 (upd.)
Artex Enterprises, **7** 256; **25** 167, 253
Arthur Andersen & Company, Société Coopérative, **III** 143; **6** 244; **10** 115–17, 174; **16** 92; **25** 358; **29** 392; **46** 186. *See also* Andersen Worldwide.
Arthur D. Little, Inc., **35** 45–48
Arthur H. Fulton, Inc., **42** 363
Arthur Murray International, Inc., **32** 60–62
Arthur Ovens Motor Freight Co., **6** 371
Arthur Rank Organisation, **25** 328
Arthur Tappan & Co., **IV** 604
Arthur Young & Company, **IV** 119; **10** 386; **19** 311; **33** 235. *See also* Ernst & Young.
Artisan Entertainment Inc., **32** 63–66 (upd.)
Artisan Life Insurance Cooperative, **24** 104
Artisoft, Inc., **18** 143
Artistic Direct, Inc., **37** 108
Artists & Writers Press, Inc., **13** 560

Artists Management Group, **38** 164
ArtMold Products Corporation, **26** 342
Artra Group Inc., **40** 119–20
Arts and Entertainment Network. *See* A&E Television Networks.
Arundel Corp, **46** 196
Arval. *See* PHH Arval.
Arvey Corp., **IV** 287
Arvida Corp., **IV** 703
Arvin Industries, Inc., **8** 37–40. *See also* ArvinMeritor, Inc.
ArvinMeritor, Inc., **54** 24–28 (upd.)
ASA Holdings, **47** 30
ASAB, **III** 480
Asahi Breweries, Ltd., **I** 220–21, 282, 520; **13** 454; **20** 28–30 (upd.); **21** 230, 319–20; **26** 456; **36** 404–05; **50** 201–02; **52** 31–34 (upd.)
Asahi Chemical Industry Co., **I** 221; **III** 760; **IV** 326
Asahi Corporation, **16** 84; **40** 93
Asahi Glass Company, Ltd., **I** 363; **III** 666–68; **11** 234–35; **48** 39–42 (upd.)
Asahi Kasei Industry Co. Ltd., **IV** 476
Asahi Komag Co., Ltd., **11** 234
Asahi Kyoei Co., **I** 221
Asahi Manufacturing, **III** 592
Asahi Medix Co., Ltd., **36** 420
Asahi Milk Products, **II** 538
Asahi National Broadcasting Company, Ltd., **9** 29–31
Asahi Oil, **IV** 542
Asahi Real Estate Facilities Co., Ltd., **6** 427
Asahi Seiko, **III** 595
Asahi Shimbun, **9** 29–30
Asahi Trust & Banking, **II** 323
Asano Group, **III** 718
Asanté Technologies, Inc., **20** 31–33
ASARCO Incorporated, **I** 142; **IV** 31–34; **40** 220–22, 411
ASB Agency, Inc., **10** 92
ASB Air, **47** 286–87
Asbury Associates Inc., **22** 354–55
Asbury Group, **26** 501
ASC, Inc., **55** 31–34
ASCAP. *See* The American Society of Composers, Authors and Publishers.
Ascend Communications, Inc., **24** 47–51; **34** 258
Aschaffenburger Zellstoffwerke AG, **IV** 323–24
ASCO Healthcare, Inc., **18** 195–97
Asco Products, Inc., **22** 413
Ascom AG, **9** 32–34; **15** 125
Ascometal, **IV** 227
Ascotts, **19** 122
ASD, **IV** 228
ASDA Group plc, **II** 611–12, 513, 629; **11** 240; **28** 34–36 (upd.)
ASEA AB. *See* ABB ASEA Brown Boveri Ltd.
Asean Bintulu Fertilizer, **IV** 518
Asepak Corp., **16** 339
A.B. Asesores Bursatiles, **III** 197–98; **15** 18
ASF. *See* American Steel Foundries.
Asgrow Florida Company, **13** 503
Asgrow Seed Co., **29** 435; **41** 306
Ash Company, **10** 271
Ash Resources Ltd., **31** 398–99
Ashanti Goldfields Company Limited, **43** 37–40
Ashbourne PLC, **25** 455

Ashitaka Rinsan Kogyo, **IV** 269
Ashland Inc., 19 22–25; **27** 316, 318; **50** 45–50 (upd.)
Ashland Iron and Mining Co., **IV** 28
Ashland Oil, Inc., I 420; **IV** 71, 198, 366, 372–74, 472, 658; **7** 32–33; **8** 99; **9** 108; **11** 22; **18** 279
Ashley Furniture Industries, Inc., 35 49–51
Ashtead Group plc, 34 41–43
Ashton Joint Venture, **IV** 60, 67
Ashton Mining, **IV** 60
Ashton-Tate Corporation, **9** 81–82; **10** 504–05
Ashworth, Inc., 26 25–28
Asia Life Insurance Co., **III** 195–96
Asia Oil Co., Ltd., **IV** 404, 476; **53** 115
Asia Pulp & Paper, **38** 227
Asia Shuang He Sheng Five Star Beer Co., Ltd., **49** 418
Asia Television, **IV** 718; **38** 320
Asia Terminals Ltd., **IV** 718; **38** 319
AsiaInfo Holdings, Inc., 43 41–44
Asian Football Confederation, **27** 150
Asiana Airlines, Inc., 24 400; **46** 39–42
Asiatic Petroleum Co., **IV** 434, 530
ASICS Corp., **24** 404
Asil çelik, **I** 479
ASK Group, Inc., 9 35–37; **25** 34
Ask Mr. Foster Agency, **22** 127; **26** 308; **55** 90
Asland SA, **III** 705, 740
ASMI. See Acer Semiconductor Manufacturing Inc.
ASML Holding N.V., 50 51–54
Aso Cement, **III** 705
Aspect Telecommunications Corporation, 16 392–93; **22** 51–53
ASPECTA Global Group AG, **53** 162
Aspen Imaging International, Inc., **17** 384
Aspen Mountain Gas Co., **6** 568
Aspen Skiing Company, II 170; **15** 23–26, 234; **43** 438
Aspen Systems, **14** 555
Asplundh Tree Expert Co., 20 34–36
Assam Co. Ltd., **III** 522–23
Assam Oil Co., **IV** 441, 483–84
Asset Management Company, **25** 86
Asset Marketing Inc. See Commercial Financial Services, Inc.
L'Assicuratrice Italiana, **III** 346–47
Assicurazioni Generali SpA, II 192; **III** 206–09, 211, 296, 298; **14** 85; **15** 27–31 (upd.); **51** 19, 23
Assisted Living Concepts, Inc., 43 45–47
Associate Venture Investors, **16** 418
Associated Anglo-Atlantic Corp., **III** 670
Associated Aviation Underwriters, **III** 220
Associated Banks of Europe Corp., **II** 184, 239
Associated Biscuit Co., **II** 631
Associated Book Publishers, **8** 527
Associated Bowater Industries, **IV** 258
Associated Brewing Co., **I** 254
Associated British Foods plc, II 465–66, 565, 609; **11** 526; **13** 51–53 (upd.); **24** 475; **41** 30–33 (upd.)
Associated British Maltsters, **II** 500
Associated British Picture Corporation, **I** 531; **II** 157; **22** 193
Associated British Ports Holdings Plc, 45 29–32
Associated Bulk Carriers Ltd., **38** 345
Associated City Investment Trust, **IV** 696

Associated Communications Companies, **7** 78; **23** 479
Associated Container Transportation, **23** 161
Associated Cooperative Investment Trust Ltd., **IV** 696
Associated Dairies Ltd., **II** 611
Associated Dry Goods Corp., **V** 134; **12** 54–55; **24** 298
Associated Electrical Industries, Ltd., **II** 25; **III** 502
Associated Employers General Agency, **III** 248
Associated Estates Realty Corporation, 25 23–25
Associated Fire Marine Insurance Co., **26** 486
Associated Food Holdings Ltd., **II** 628
Associated Fresh Foods, **II** 611–12; **48** 37
Associated Fuel Pump Systems Corp., **III** 593
Associated Gas & Electric Company, **V** 621, 629–30; **6** 534; **14** 124
Associated Gas Services, Inc., **11** 28
Associated Grocers, Incorporated, 9 38–40; **19** 301; **31** 22–26 (upd.)
Associated Grocers of Arizona, **II** 625
Associated Grocers of Colorado, **II** 670
The Associated Group, **10** 45
Associated Hospital Service of New York, **III** 245–46
Associated Iliffe Press, **IV** 666; **17** 397
Associated Indemnity Co., **III** 251
Associated Inns and Restaurants Company of America, **14** 106; **25** 309; **26** 459
Associated Insurance Cos., **III** 194
Associated International Insurance Co. See Gryphon Holdings, Inc.
Associated Lead Manufacturers Ltd., **III** 679, 680–81
Associated London Properties, **IV** 705; **49** 247
Associated Madison Insurance, **I** 614
Associated Merchandisers, Inc., **27** 246
Associated Merchandising Corp., **16** 215
Associated Milk Producers, Inc., 11 24–26; **48** 43–46 (upd.)
Associated National Insurance of Australia, **III** 309
Associated Natural Gas Corporation, 11 27–28
Associated Newspapers Holdings P.L.C., **IV** 686; **19** 118, 120; **37** 121
Associated Octel Company Limited, **10** 290
Associated Oil Co., **IV** 460
Associated Pipeline Contractors, **III** 559
Associated Piping & Engineering Corp., **III** 535
Associated Portland Cement Manufacturers (1900) Ltd., **III** 669–71
The Associated Press, IV 629, 669–70; **7** 158; **10** 277; **13** 54–56; **25** 506; **31** 27–30 (upd.); **34** 11
Associated Publishing Company, **19** 201
Associated Pulp & Paper Mills, **IV** 328
Associated Sales Agency, **16** 389
Associated Spring Co., **III** 581; **13** 73
Associated Stationers, **14** 521, 523
Associated Television, **7** 78
Associated Timber Exporters of British Columbia Ltd., **IV** 307
Associated TV, **IV** 666; **17** 397

Associates First Capital Corporation, **22** 207
Associates Investment Co., **I** 452
Association des Centres Distributeurs E. Leclerc, 37 19–21
Assubel, **III** 273
Assurances du Groupe de Paris, **III** 211
Assurances Générales de France, **III** 351; **27** 513; **42** 151; **51** 23
AST Holding Corp., **III** 663, 665
AST Research, Inc., 9 41–43; **10** 459, 518–19; **12** 470; **18** 260
Asta Pharma AG, **IV** 71
Asta Werke AG, **IV** 71
Astech, **18** 370
Asteroid, **IV** 97
Astley & Pearce, **10** 277
Aston Brooke Software, **14** 392
Aston Villa plc, 41 34–36
Astor Holdings Inc., **22** 32
Astor Trust Co., **II** 229
Astoria Financial Corporation, 44 31–34; **46** 316
Astra AB, **I** 625–26, 635, 651; **11** 290; **20** 37–40 (upd.); **34** 282, 284
Astra Resources, **12** 543
AstraZeneca PLC, 50 55–60 (upd.); **53** 290; **55** 27
Astrium N.V., **52** 113
Astrolac, **IV** 498
Astrolink International LLC, **54** 406–07
Astronics Corporation, 35 52–54
Astrotech Space Operations, L.P., **11** 429; **37** 365
Astrum International Corp., **12** 88; **13** 453; **16** 20–21; **43** 355
Asur. See Grupo Aeropuerto del Sureste, S.A. de C.V.
ASV, Inc., 34 44–47
ASW. See American Steel & Wire Corp.
Asylum Life Assurance Co., **III** 371
Asylum Records, **23** 33; **26** 150
Asymetrix, **6** 259
AT&E Corp., **17** 430
AT&T Bell Laboratories, Inc., 13 57–59; **22** 17
AT&T Corp., I 462; **II** 13, 54, 61, 66, 80, 88, 120, 125, 252, 403, 430–31, 448; **III** 99, 110–11, 130, 145, 149, 160, 162, 167, 246, 282; **IV** 95, 287; **V** 259–64, 265–68, 269, 272–75, 302–04, 308–12, 318–19, 326–30, 334–36, 339, 341–342, 344–346; **6** 267, 299, 306–07, 326–27, 338–40; **7** 88, 118–19, 146, 288–89, 333; **8** 310–11; **9** 32, 43, 106–07, 138, 320, 321, 344, 478–80, 495, 514; **10** 19, 58, 87, 97, 175, 202–03, 277–78, 286, 431, 433, 455–57; **11** 10, 59, 91, 183, 185, 196, 198, 302, 395, 500–01; **12** 9, 135–36, 162, 544; **13** 212–13, 326, 402, 448; **14** 15, 95, 251–53, 257–61, 318, 336–37, 345, 347, 354, 363–64; **15** 125–26, 228, 455; **16** 223, 318, 368, 467; **18** 30, 32, 74, 76, 111–12, 155, 164–65, 368, 516–18, 569–70; **19** 12, 41; **20** 34, 313; **21** 70, 200–01, 514; **22** 51; **23** 135; **25** 100, 256, 301, 495–99; **26** 187, 225, 431, 520; **27** 363; **28** 242; **29** 59, 39–45 (upd.); **30** 99, 339; **33** 34–35, 37, 91, 93–94; **34** 257–59; **38** 269–70, 416; **42** 224; **43** 50, 222, 443; **44** 47; **46** 373; **47** 319–20; **49** 70, 346–47; **50** 299–300, 318; **54** 29–31, 68–69

AT&T Istel Ltd., 14 35–36
At Home Corporation, 43 48–51
AT&T Wireless Services, Inc., 54 29–32
 (upd.), 313
Ataka & Co., **I** 433; **II** 361
Atari Corporation, II 176; **III** 587; **IV**
 676; **6** 244; **7** 395–96; **9** 44–47; **10** 284,
 482, 485; **13** 472; **23** 23–26 **(upd.); 28**
 319; **32** 8
ATAS International, **26** 527, 530
ATC, **III** 760; **13** 280
Atchison Casting Corporation, 24 144;
 39 30–32
Atchison, Topeka and Santa Fe Railroad, **V**
 507–08; **12** 19–20; **27** 86
ATCO Ltd., **13** 132
ATD Group, **10** 113; **50** 43
ATE Investment, **6** 449
Atelier de Construction Electrique de
 Delle, **9** 9
ATEQ Corp., **III** 533
Atex, Inc., **III** 476; **7** 162; **10** 34; **36** 172,
 174
ATH AG, **IV** 221
Atha Tool Co., **III** 627
Athalon Products, Ltd., **10** 181; **12** 313
Athena Assurances, **27** 513, 515
Athenia Steel Co., **13** 369
Athens National Bank, **III** 190
Athens Piraeus Electricity Co., **IV** 658
Athern, **16** 337
Athlete's Foot Inc., **29** 186; **54** 306, 308
Athletic Attic, **19** 230
Athletic Shoe Company, **17** 243
Athletic Textile Company, Inc., **13** 532
Athletic X-Press, **14** 293
Athleticum Sportmarket, **48** 279
Athol Machine Co., **13** 301
ATI, **IV** 651; **7** 390
ATI Technologies Inc., **54** 269–71
Atlalait, **19** 50
Atlanta Gas Light Company, 6 446–48;
 23 27–30 **(upd.)**
Atlanta-LaSalle Corporation, **43** 54
Atlanta National Bank, **16** 521
Atlanta National League Baseball Club,
 Inc., 43 52–55
Atlanta Paper Co., **IV** 311; **19** 267
Atlantic & Pacific Tea Company (A&P).
 See Great Atlantic & Pacific Tea
 Company, Inc.
Atlantic Acceptance Corporation, **7** 95
Atlantic Aircraft Corp., **I** 34; **17** 197
Atlantic Airways, **52** 167
Atlantic American Corporation, 23 413;
 44 35–37
Atlantic Auto Finance Corp. *See* United
 Auto Group, Inc.
Atlantic Cellular, **43** 341
Atlantic Cement Co., **III** 671
Atlantic Coast Airlines Holdings, Inc., 55
 35–37
Atlantic Coast Carton Company, **19** 77
Atlantic Coast Line Railroad Company. *See*
 CSX Corporation.
Atlantic Computers, **14** 35
Atlantic Container Lines Ltd., **23** 161
Atlantic Energy, Inc., 6 449–50
Atlantic Envelope Company, **54** 251–52,
 255
The Atlantic Group, 23 31–33
Atlantic Gulf and Caribbean Airways, **I**
 115
Atlantic Import, **I** 285

Atlantic Mills, **27** 188
Atlantic Mutual, **41** 65
Atlantic Precision Instrument Company, **13**
 234
Atlantic Precision Works, **9** 72
Atlantic Records, **II** 176; **18** 458; **26** 150
Atlantic Refining Co., **III** 497; **III** 498; **IV**
 375–76, 456, 504, 566, 570; **24** 520–21
Atlantic Research Corporation, **13** 462; **54**
 330–31
Atlantic Richfield Company, I 452; **II** 90,
 425; **III** 740; **IV** 375–77, 379, 435, 454,
 456–57, 467, 494, 522, 536, 571; **7** 57,
 108, 537–38, 558–59; **8** 184, 416; **10**
 110; **13** 13, 341; **19** 175; **24** 521, 524;
 26 4, 372; **31** 31–34 **(upd.); 40** 358; **45**
 49, 55, 252
Atlantic Sea Products, **13** 103
The Atlantic Seaboard Dispatch. *See*
 GATX.
Atlantic Securities Ltd., **II** 223; **III** 98
Atlantic Southeast Airlines, Inc., 26 439;
 47 29–31
Atlantic Southern Properties, Inc., **6**
 449–50
Atlantic Surety Co., **III** 396
Atlantic Transport Company, **19** 198
Atlantic-Union Oil, **IV** 570; **24** 520
Atlantic Wholesalers, **II** 631
Atlantis Energy Inc., **44** 182
Atlantis Group, Inc., **17** 16; **19** 50, 390
Atlantis Ltd., **II** 566
Atlantis Resort and Casino. *See* Sun
 International Hotels Limited.
Atlas Air, Inc., 39 33–35
Atlas America, Inc., **42** 311
Atlas Assurance Co., **III** 370
Atlas Cement Company, **31** 252
Atlas Chemical Industries, **I** 353; **50** 257
Atlas Copco AB, III 425–27, 480; **IV**
 203; **28** 37–41 **(upd.)**
Atlas Corp., **I** 58, 512; **10** 316
Atlas Eléctrica S.A., **22** 27
Atlas Hotels, Inc., **V** 164
Atlas Petroleum Ltd., **IV** 449
Atlas Plastics, **19** 414
Atlas Powder Company, **I** 343–44; **22** 260
Atlas Securities, **47** 160
Atlas Shipping, **I** 285
Atlas Steel Works, **I** 572
Atlas Steels, **IV** 191
Atlas Supply Co., **IV** 369
Atlas Tag & Label, **9** 72
Atlas Van Lines, Inc., 14 37–39
Atlas Ventures, **25** 96
Atlas-Werke AG, **IV** 88
Atlas Works, **I** 531
Atlatec SA de CV, **39** 192
Atle Byrnestad, **6** 368; **27** 92
Atmel Corporation, 17 32–34; **19** 313
Atmos Energy Corporation, 43 56–58
Atmos Lebensmitteltechnik, **III** 420
Atmospherix Ltd. *See* Blyth Industries, Inc.
ATO Chimie, **I** 303; **IV** 560
Atochem S.A., I 303–04, 676; **IV** 525,
 547; **7** 484–85
AtoHaas Americas, **26** 425
Atom-Energi, **II** 2; **22** 9
Atomic Austria GmbH, **41** 14–16
ATR, **7** 9, 11
ATS. *See* Magasins Armand Thiéry et
 Sigrand.
ATT Microelectrica España, **V** 339
Attachmate Corp., **11** 520

ATTC Manufacturing Inc., **48** 5
Atvidabergs Industrier, **25** 463
Atwater McMillian. *See* St. Paul
 Companies, Inc.
Atwood Mobil Products, 53 52–55
Atwood Resources Inc., **17** 372
ATX Technologies, Inc., **32** 374
ATx Telecom Systems Inc., **31** 124
Au Bon Marché, **26** 160
Au Bon Pain Co., Inc., 18 35–38; **44** 327
Au Printemps S.A., V 9–11; **17** 124; **41**
 114. *See also* Pinault-Printemps-Redoute
 S.A.
Aubrey G. Lanston Co., **II** 301
Auchan, 10 205; **23** 230; **27** 94; **37**
 22–24; **39** 183–85; **54** 219–20
AUDI AG, I 202; **IV** 570; **34** 55
Audio Accessories, Inc., **37** 301
Audio Development Company, **10** 18
Audio International Inc., **36** 159
Audio King Corporation, 24 52–54
Audio/Video Affiliates, Inc., **10** 468–69
Audiofina, **44** 377
Audiotronic Holdings, **III** 112
Audiovox Corporation, 34 48–50
Audits & Surveys Worldwide Inc., **28** 501,
 504
Aufina Bank, **II** 378
Aug. Stenman A.B., **III** 493
Augat Inc., **54** 373
Aughton Group, **II** 466
Augsburger Aktienbank, **III** 377
Auguri Mondadori S.p.A., **IV** 586
August Max Woman, **V** 207–08
August Schell's Brewing Co., **22** 421
August Thyssen-Hütte AG, **IV** 221–22
Auguste Metz et Cie, **IV** 24
Ault Incorporated, 34 51–54
Aunor Gold Mines, Ltd., **IV** 164
Aunt Fanny's Bakery, **7** 429
Auntie Anne's, Inc., 35 55–57
Aura Books plc, **34** 5
Aurea Concesiones de Infraestructuras SA,
 55 182
Aurec Information and Directory Systems.
 See Amdocs Ltd.
Aurora Dairy Corporation, **37** 195, 198
Aurora Foods Inc., 26 384; **32** 67–69
Aurora Products, **II** 543
Aurora Systems, Inc., **21** 135
Aurrera S.A., **35** 459
Aurum Corp., **38** 431
Ausilio Generale di Sicurezza, **III** 206
Ausimont N.V., **8** 271
Ausplay, **13** 319
AUSSAT Ltd., **6** 341
Aussedat-Rey, **IV** 288; **23** 366, 368
The Austin Company, 8 41–44
Austin Industries, **25** 402
Austin-Morris, **III** 494
Austin Motor Company, **I** 183; **III** 554; **7**
 458
Austin Nichols, **I** 248, 261, 280–81
Austin Quality Foods, **36** 313
Austin Rover, **14** 321
Austral Waste Products, **IV** 248
Australasian Paper and Pulp Co. Ltd., **IV**
 248
Australasian Sugar Co., **III** 686
Australasian United Steam Navigation Co.,
 III 522
Australia and New Zealand Banking
 Group Limited, II 187–90; **52** 35–40
 (upd.)

Australia Gilt Co. Group, **II** 422
Australia National Bank, Limited, **10** 170
Australian Airlines, **6** 91, 112; **24** 399–400; **27** 475
Australian and Kandos Cement (Holdings) Ltd., **III** 687, 728; **28** 83
Australian and Overseas Telecommunications Corporation, **6** 341–42
Australian Associated Press, **IV** 669
Australian Automotive Air, Pty. Ltd., **III** 593
Australian Blue Asbestos, **III** 687
Australian Consolidated Investments, Limited, **10** 170
Australian Consolidated Press, **27** 42; **54** 299
Australian Forest Products, **I** 438–39
Australian Guarantee Corporation Ltd., **II** 389–90; **48** 427
Australian Gypsum Industries, **III** 673
Australian Iron & Steel Company, **IV** 45; **22** 105
Australian Metal Co., **IV** 139
Australian Mutual Provident Society, **IV** 61, 697
Australian Paper Co., **IV** 248
Australian Petroleum Pty. Ltd., **25** 471
Australian Tankerships Pty. Ltd., **25** 471
Australian Telecommunications Corporation, **6** 342
Australian United Corp., **II** 389
Australian Window Glass, **III** 726
Austria Tabak, **55** 200
Austrian Airlines AG (Österreichische Luftverkehrs AG), 27 26; **33 49–52; 34** 398; **48** 258, 259
Austrian Industries, **IV** 485, 486
Austrian National Bank, **IV** 230
Austrian Star Gastronomie GmbH, **48** 63
Austro-Americana, **6** 425
Austro-Daimler, **I** 138, 206; **11** 31
Authentic Fitness Corp., 16 511; **20 41–43; 46** 450; **51 30–33 (upd.)**
Auto Avio Costruzione, **13** 219
Auto Coil Springs, **III** 581
Auto-Flo Corp., **III** 569; **20** 360
Auto Ordnance Corporation, **19** 430–31
Auto Parts Wholesale, **26** 348
Auto Shack. *See* AutoZone, Inc.
Auto Strop Safety Razor Co., **III** 27–28
Auto-Trol Technology, **14** 15
Auto Union, **I** 150
Auto Value Associates, Inc., 25 26–28
Autobytel Inc., 47 32–34
Autocam Corporation, 51 34–36
Autodesk, Inc., 10 118–20
Autogrill SpA, 24 195; **49 31–33**
Autolite, **I** 29, 142; **III** 555
Autoliv AB, **41** 369
Autologic Information International, Inc., 20 44–46; 26 518–20
Automat, **II** 614
Automated Building Components, **III** 735
Automated Communications, Inc., **8** 311
Automated Design Systems, **25** 348
Automated Loss Prevention Systems, **11** 445
Automated Security (Holdings) PLC, **11** 444
Automated Wagering Systems, **III** 128
Automatic Coil Corp., **33** 359, 361

Automatic Data Processing, Inc., III 117–19; 9 48–51 (upd.), 125, 173; **21** 69; **46** 333; **47 35–39 (upd.)**
Automatic Fire Alarm Co., **III** 644
Automatic Liquid Packaging, **50** 122
Automatic Manufacturing Corporation, **10** 319
Automatic Payrolls, Inc., **III** 117
Automatic Retailers of America, Inc., **II** 607; **13** 48
Automatic Sprinkler Corp. of America. *See* Figgie International, Inc.
Automatic Telephone & Electric, **II** 81
Automatic Toll Systems, **19** 111
Automatic Vaudeville Arcades Co., **II** 154
Automatic Voting Machine Corporation. *See* American Locker Group Incorporated.
Automobile Insurance Co., **III** 181–82
Automobiles Citroen, I 162, 188; **III** 676; **IV** 722; **V** 237; **7 35–38; 11** 103; **16** 121, 420; **50** 195
Automobili Lamborghini Holding S.p.A., 34 55–58 (upd.)
Automobili Lamborghini S.p.A., 13 60–62, 219
Automotive Components Group Worldwide, **10** 325
Automotive Diagnostics, **10** 492
Automotive Group. *See* Lear Seating Corporation.
Automotive Industries Holding Inc., **16** 323
AutoNation, Inc., 41 239; **50 61–64**
Autonet, **6** 435
Autonom Computer, **47** 36
Autophon AG, **9** 32
Autoroutes du Sud de la France SA, 55 38–40
Autosite.com, **47** 34
Autotote Corporation, 20 47–49
AutoTrol Technology, **III** 111
Autoweb.com, **47** 34
AUTOWORKS Holdings, Inc., **24** 205
AutoZone, Inc., 9 52–54; 26 348; **31 35–38 (upd.); 36** 364
AVA AG (Allgemeine Handelsgesellschaft der Verbraucher AG), 33 53–56
Avado Brands, Inc., 31 39–42; 46 234
Avalon Publishing Group. *See* Publishers Group, Inc.
Avana Group, **II** 565
Avantel, **27** 304
Avaya Inc., **41** 287, 289–90
Avco. *See* Aviation Corp. of the Americas.
Avco Corp., **34** 433
Avco Financial Services Inc., 13 63–65
Avco National Bank, **II** 420
Avdel, **34** 433
Avecor Cardiovascular Inc., **8** 347; **22** 360
Aveda Corporation, 24 55–57
Avedis Zildjian Co., 38 66–68
Avendt Group, Inc., **IV** 137
Avenir, **III** 393
Avenor Inc., **25** 13
Aventis, **34** 280, 283–84; **38** 378, 380
Avery Dennison Corporation, IV 251–54; 15 229, 401; **17 27–31 (upd.)**, 445; **49 34–40 (upd.)**
Avesta Steel Works Co., **I** 553–54
AvestaPolarit, **49** 104
Avex Electronics Inc., **40** 68
Avfuel, **11** 538
Avgain Marine A/S, **7** 40; **41** 42

Avia Group International, Inc., **V** 376–77; **26** 397–99
Aviacion y Comercio, **6** 95–96
Aviacionny Nauchno-Tehnicheskii Komplex im. A.N. Tupoleva, 24 58–60
AVIACO. *See* Aviacion y Comercio.
Avianca Aerovías Nacionales de Colombia SA, 36 52–55
Aviation Corp. of the Americas, **I** 48, 78, 89, 115, 530; **III** 66; **6** 75; **9** 497–99; **10** 163; **11** 261, 427; **12** 379, 383; **13** 64
Aviation Inventory Management Co., **28** 5
Aviation Power Supply, **II** 16
Aviation Sales Company, 41 37–39
Aviation Services West, Inc. *See* Scenic Airlines, Inc.
Avid Technology Inc., 38 69–73
Avimo, **47** 7–8
Avion Coach Corporation, **I** 76; **III** 484; **11** 363; **22** 206
Avions Marcel Dassault-Breguet Aviation, I 44–46; **7** 11; **7** 205; **8** 314. *See also* Groupe Dassault Aviation SA.
Avis, Inc., I 30, 446, 463; **II** 468; **III** 502; **IV** 370; **6** 348–49, **356–58**, 392–93; **8** 33; **9** 284; **10** 419; **11** 198; **16** 379–80; **22** 524
Avis Rent A Car, Inc., 22 54–57 (upd.); 24 9; **25** 93, 143, 420–22
Avisco, **I** 317, 365, 442–43; **V** 359; **17** 117
Avisun Corp., **IV** 371
Aviva PLC, 50 65–68 (upd.)
Avnet Electronics Supply Co., **19** 311, 313
Avnet Inc., 9 55–57; 10 112–13; **13** 47; **50** 41
Avon Products, Inc., III 13, **15–16**, 62; **8** 329; **9** 331; **11** 282, 366; **12** 314, 435; **13** 38; **14** 501–02; **17** 186; **19 26–29 (upd.)**, 253; **21** 49, 51; **25** 292; 456; **27** 429; **30** 64, 308–09; **46 43–46 (upd.)**
Avon Publications, Inc., **IV** 627; **19** 201, 204
Avon Rubber plc, **23** 146
Avoncraft Construction Co., **I** 512
Avondale Industries, Inc., I 512–14; **7 39–41; 41 40–43 (upd.)**
Avondale Mills, Inc., **8** 558–60; **9** 466
Avondown Properties Ltd., **IV** 711
Avril Alimentaire SNC, **51** 54
Avro. *See* A.V. Roe & Company.
AVS, **III** 200
Avstar, **38** 72
Avtech Corp., **36** 159
Avtex Fibers Inc., **I** 443; **11** 134
AVX Corporation, **21** 329, 331
AW Bruna Uitgevers BV, **53** 273
AW North Carolina Inc., **48** 5
AWA. *See* America West Holdings Corporation.
AWA Defence Industries (AWADI). *See* British Aerospace Defence Industries.
Award Foods, **II** 528
AwardTrack, Inc., **49** 423
Awesome Transportation, Inc., **22** 549
AXA Colonia Konzern AG, III 209, **210–12; 15** 30; **21** 147; **27 52–55; 49 41–45 (upd.)**
Axe-Houghton Associates Inc., **41** 208
Axel Johnson Group, I 553–55
Axel Springer Verlag AG, IV 589–91; 20 50–53 (upd.); 23 86; **35** 452; **54** 295
Axelrod Foods, **II** 528
Axon Systems Inc., **7** 336

Ayco Corp., **II** 398; **10** 62
Aydin Corp., 19 30–32
Ayerst, **I** 623
Ayr-Way Stores, **27** 452
Ayres, Lewis, Norris & May, Inc., **54** 184
AYS. *See* Alternative Youth Services, Inc.
Ayshire Collieries, **IV** 18
AZA Immobilien AG, **51** 196
Azcon Corporation, 23 34–36
Azerty, **25** 13
Azienda Generale Italiana Petroli. *See* Agip SpA.
Azienda Nazionale Idrogenazione Combustibili, **IV** 419–22
AZL Resources, **7** 538
Aznar International, **14** 225
Azon Limited, **22** 282
AZP Group Inc., **6** 546
Aztar Corporation, 13 66–68
Azteca, **18** 211, 213
Azuma Leather Co. Ltd., **V** 380
Azuma Shiki Manufacturing, **IV** 326
Azusa Valley Savings Bank, **II** 382

B&D. *See* Barker & Dobson.
B&G Foods, Inc., 40 51–54
B & K Steel Fabrications, Inc., **26** 432
B & L Insurance, Ltd., **51** 38
B&M Baked Beans, **40** 53
B & O. *See* Baltimore and Ohio Railroad.
B&Q plc, **V** 106, 108; **24** 266, 269–70
B&S. *See* Binney & Smith Inc.
B&W Diesel, **III** 513
B.A.T. Industries PLC, 14 77; **16** 242; **22 70–73 (upd.); 25** 154–56; **29** 196. *See also* Brown & Williamson Tobacco Corporation
B. B. & R. Knight Brothers, **8** 200; **25** 164
B.B. Foods, **13** 244
B-Bar-B Corp., **16** 340
B.C. Rail Telecommunications, **6** 311
B.C. Sugar, **II** 664
B.C. Ziegler and Co. *See* The Ziegler Companies, Inc.
B. Dalton Bookseller Inc., 10 136; **13** 545; **16** 160; **18** 136; **25 29–31; 30** 68
B-E Holdings, **17** 60
B/E Aerospace, Inc., 30 72–74
B.F. Ehlers, **I** 417; **24** 32
B.F. Goodrich Co. *See* The BFGoodrich Company.
B.F. Walker, Inc., **11** 354
B.I.C. America, **17** 15, 17
B.J.'s Wholesale, **12** 335
The B. Manischewitz Company, LLC, 31 43–46
B. Perini & Sons, Inc., **8** 418
B.R. Simmons, **III** 527
B.S. Bull & Company. *See* Supervalu Inc.
B. Stroh Brewing Co., **I** 290
B.T.I. Chemicals Ltd., **I** 313; **10** 154
B Ticino, **21** 350
B.V. Tabak Export & Import Compagnie, **12** 109
BA. *See* British Airways.
BAA plc, 10 121–23; 29 509, 511; **33 57–61 (upd.); 37** 8
Bålforsens Kraft AB, **28** 444
Baan Company, 25 32–34; 26 496, 498
Babbage's, Inc., 10 124–25
Babcock & Wilcox Co., **III** 465–66, 516, 559–60; **V** 621; **23** 199; **37** 242–45
BABE. *See* British Aerospace plc.
Baby Dairy Products, **48** 438

Baby Furniture and Toy Supermarket, **V** 203
Baby Phat. *See* Phat Fashions LLC.
Baby Superstore, Inc., 15 32–34
Babybird Co., Ltd., **V** 150
BabyCenter.com, **37** 130
Babyliss, S.A., **17** 110
BAC. *See* Barclays American Corp.; British Aircraft Corporation.
Bacardi Limited, 18 39–42
Baccarat, 23 241; **24 61–63; 27** 421, 423
Bache & Company, **III** 340; **8** 349
Bachman Foods, **15** 139
Bachman Holdings, Inc., **14** 165; **34** 144–45
Bachman's Inc., 22 58–60; 24 513
Bachoco. *See* Industrias Bacholo, S.A. de C.V.
Bachrach Advertising, **6** 40
Back Bay Restaurant Group, Inc., 20 54–56
Back Yard Burgers, Inc., 45 33–36
Backer & Spielvogel, **I** 33; **12** 168; **14** 48–49; **22** 296
Backer Spielvogel Bates Worldwide **42** 329. *See also* Bates Worldwide, Inc.
Backroom Systems Group, **II** 317
Bacon & Matheson Drop Forge Co., **I** 185
Bacon's Information, Inc., **55** 289
Bacova Guild, Ltd., **17** 76
Bad Boy Entertainment, **31** 269
Baddour, Inc. *See* Fred's, Inc.
Badger Co., **II** 86
Badger Illuminating Company, **6** 601
Badger Meter, Inc., 22 61–65
Badger Paint and Hardware Stores, **II** 419
Badger Paper Mills, Inc., 15 35–37
Badin-Defforey, **27** 93
Badische Analin & Soda Fabrik A.G., **I** 305
BAe. *See* British Aerospace plc.
BAE Systems, **41** 412; **52** 114
BAFS. *See* Bangkok Aviation Fuel Services Ltd.
Bahia de San Francisco Television, **IV** 621
Bahlsen GmbH & Co. KG, 44 38–41
Bailey, Banks & Biddle, **16** 559
Bailey Controls, **III** 560
Bailey's Pub and Grille. *See* Total Entertainment Restaurant Corporation.
Bain & Company, III 429; **9** 343; **21** 143; **55 41–43**
Bain Capital, Inc., **14** 244–45; **16** 466; **20** 18; **24** 456, 482; **25** 254; **26** 184; **38** 107–09
Baird, **7** 235, 237
Bairnco Corporation, 28 42–45
Bajaj Auto Limited, 39 36–38
BÅKAB. *See* Bålforsens Kraft AB.
Bakelite Corp., **I** 399; **9** 517; **13** 231
Baker. *See* Michael Baker Corporation.
Baker and Botts, L.L.P., 28 46–49
Baker & Co., **IV** 78
Baker & Crane, **II** 318; **17** 323
Baker & Hostetler LLP, 40 55–58
Baker & McKenzie, 10 126–28; 42 17–20 (upd.)
Baker & Taylor Corporation, I 548; **16 45–47; 43 59–62 (upd.); 50** 524
Baker Casing Shoe Co., **III** 429
Baker Cummins Pharmaceuticals Inc., **11** 208
Baker Extract Co., **27** 299

Baker Hughes Incorporated, III 428–29; 11 513; **22 66–69 (upd.); 25** 74
Baker Industries, Inc., **III** 440; **8** 476; **13** 124
Baker International Corp., **III** 428–29
Baker Oil Tools. *See* Baker Hughes Incorporated.
Baker-Raulang Co., **13** 385
Bakers Best Snack Food Corporation, **24** 241
Bakers Square. *See* VICORP Restaurants, Inc.
Bakersfield Savings and Loan, **10** 339
Bakery Products Inc., **IV** 410
Balair Ltd., **I** 122
Balance Bar Company, 32 70–72
Balchem Corporation, 42 21–23
Balco, Inc., **7** 479–80; **27** 415
Balcor Co., **II** 398; **IV** 703
Balcor, Inc., **10** 62
Bald Eagle Corporation, **45** 126
Baldor Electric Company, 21 42–44
Baldwin & Lyons, Inc., 51 37–39
Baldwin-Ehret-Hill Inc., **28** 42
Baldwin Filters, Inc., **17** 104
Baldwin Hardware Manufacturing Co., **III** 570; **20** 361
Baldwin-Montrose Chemical Co., Inc., **31** 110
Baldwin Piano & Organ Company, 16 201; **18 43–46**
Baldwin Rubber Industries, **13** 79
Baldwin Technology Company, Inc., 25 35–39
Baldwin-United Corp., **III** 254, 293; **52** 243–44
Baldwins Ltd., **III** 494
Bålforsens Kraft AB, **IV** 339–40; **28** 444
Balfour Beatty Construction Ltd., III 433–34; **36 56–60 (upd.)**
Balfour Company, L.G., **19** 451–52
Balikpapan Forest Industries, **I** 504
Ball & Young Adhesives, **9** 92
Ball-Bartoe Aircraft Corp., **I** 598; **10** 130
Ball Corporation, I 597–98; **10 129–31 (upd.); 13** 254, 256; **15** 129; **16** 123; **30** 38
The Ball Ground Reps., Inc., **26** 257
Ball Industries, Inc., **26** 539
Ball Stalker Inc., **14** 4
Ballantine & Sons Ltd., **I** 263
Ballantine Beer, **6** 27
Ballantine Books, **13** 429; **31** 376–77, 379
Ballantyne of Omaha, Inc., 27 56–58
Ballard & Ballard Co., **II** 555
Ballard Medical Products, 21 45–48
Ballast Nedam Group, **24** 87–88
Balli Group plc, **26** 527, 530
Bally Entertainment Corp., **19** 205, 207
Bally Gaming International, **15** 539
Bally Manufacturing Corporation, III 430–32; **6** 210; **10** 375, 482; **12** 107; **15** 538–39; **17** 316–17, 443; **41** 214–15; **53** 364–65
Bally Total Fitness Holding Corp., 25 40–42
Bâloise-Holding, 40 59–62
Baltek Corporation, 34 59–61
AB Baltic, **III** 418–19
Baltic Cable, **15** 521
Baltica, **27** 54
Baltimar Overseas Limited, **25** 469
Baltimore & Ohio Railroad, **I** 584; **II** 329. *See also* CSX Corporation.

Baltimore Aircoil Company, **7** 30–31
Baltimore Gas and Electric Company, **V 552–54**; **11** 388; **25 43–46 (upd.)**
Baltimore Paper Box Company, **8** 102
Baltimore Technologies Plc, **42 24–26**
Baltino Foods, **13** 383
Balzaretti-Modigliani, **III** 676; **16** 121
Balzers Process Systems GmbH, **48** 30
Bamberger's of New Jersey, **V** 169; **8** 443
Banamex, **22** 285; **23** 170; **34** 81. *See also* Banco Nacional de Mexico; Grupo Financiero Banamex S.A.
Banana Boat Holding Corp., **15** 359
Banana Brothers, **31** 229
Banana Importers of Ireland, **38** 197
Banana Republic Inc., **V** 61–62; **18** 193–94; **25 47–49**; **31** 51–52; **55** 157
Banc Internacional d'Andorra-Banca Mora, **48** 51
Banc One Corporation, **9** 475; **10 132–34**; **11** 181. *See also* Bank One Corporation.
Banca Brasiliana Italo-Belga, **II** 270
Banca Coloniale di Credito, **II** 271
Banca Commerciale Italiana SpA, **I** 368, 465, 467; **II 191–93**, 242, 271, 278, 295, 319; **III** 207–08, 347; **17** 324; **50** 410
BancA Corp., **11** 305
Banca d'America e d'Italia, **II** 280
Banca Dalmata di Sconto, **II** 271
Banca de Gottardo, **II** 361
Banca di Genova, **II** 270
Banca Internazionale Lombarda, **II** 192
Banca Italiana di Sconto, **II** 191
Banca Italo-Cinese, **II** 270
Banca Italo-Viennese, **II** 270
Banca Jacquet e Hijos, **II** 196
Banca Luis Roy Sobrino, **II** 196
Banca Nazionale de Lavoro, **II** 239
Banca Nazionale dell'Agricoltura, **II** 272
Banca Nazionale di Credito, **II** 271
Banca Serfin. *See* Grupo Financiero Serfin, S.A.
Banca Unione di Credito, **II** 270
Bancard Systems, **24** 395
BancBoston Capital, **48** 412
Bancen. *See* Banco del Centro S.A.
BancFinancial Services Corporation, **25** 187
BancItaly Corp., **II** 226–27, 288, 536; **13** 528
BancMortgage Financial Corp., **25** 185, 187
Banco Aleman-Panameno, **II** 521
Banco Aliança S.A., **19** 34
Banco Azteca, **19** 189
Banco Bilbao Vizcaya Argentaria S.A., **48 47–51 (upd.)**
Banco Bilbao Vizcaya, S.A., **II 194–96**
Banco Bradesco S.A., **13 69–71**; **19** 33
Banco Capitalizador de Monterrey, **19** 189
Banco Central, **II 197–98**. *See also* Banco Santander Central Hispano S.A.
Banco Central de Crédito. *See* Banco Itaú.
Banco Chemical (Portugal) S.A. *See* Chemical Banking Corp.
Banco Comercial, **19** 188
Banco Comercial de Puerto Rico, **41** 311
Banco Comercial Português, SA, **50 69–72**
Banco Credito y Ahorro Ponceno, **41** 312
Banco da América, **19** 34

Banco de Comercio, S.A. *See* Grupo Financiero BBVA Bancomer S.A.
Banco de Credito Local, **48** 51
Banco de Credito y Servicio, **51** 151
Banco de Londres, Mexico y Sudamerica. *See* Grupo Financiero Serfin, S.A.
Banco de Madrid, **40** 147
Banco de Mexico, **19** 189
Banco de Ponce, **41** 313
Banco del Centro S.A., **51** 150
Banco del Norte, **19** 189
Banco di Roma, **I** 465, 467; **II** 191, 257, 271
Banco di Santo Spirito, **I** 467
Banco do Brasil S.A., **II 199–200**
Banco Español de Credito, **II** 195, 198; **IV** 160
Banco Espírito Santo e Comercial de Lisboa S.A., **15 38–40**
Banco Federal de Crédito. *See* Banco Itaú.
Banco Frances y Brasileiro, **19** 34
Banco Industrial de Bilbao, **II** 195
Banco Industrial de Monterrey, **19** 189
Banco Italo-Belga, **II** 270, 271
Banco Italo-Egiziano, **II** 271
Banco Itaú S.A., **19 33–35**
Banco Mercantil del Norte, S.A., **51** 149
Banco Nacional de Cuba, **II** 345
Banco Nacional de Mexico, **9** 333; **19** 188, 193
Banco Pinto de Mahalhães, **19** 34
Banco Popolar, **III** 348; **6** 97. *See also* Popular, Inc.
Banco Português do Brasil S.A., **19** 34
Banco Santander Central Hispano S.A., **36 61–64 (upd.)**; **42** 349
Banco Serfin, **34** 82
Banco Sul Americano S.A., **19** 34
Banco Trento & Bolanzo, **II** 240
Banco União Comercial, **19** 34
Banco Vascongado, **II** 196
BancOhio National Bank in Columbus, **9** 475
Bancomer S.A., **19** 12; **48** 47. *See also* Grupo Financiero BBVA Bancomer S.A.
Bancorp Leasing, Inc., **14** 529
BancorpSouth, Inc., **14** 40–41
Bancrecer. *See* Banco de Credito y Servicio.
Bancroft Racket Co., **III** 24
BancSystems Association Inc., **9** 475, 476
Bandag, Inc., **19 36–38**, 454–56
Bandai Co., Ltd., **23** 388; **25** 488; **38** 415; **55 44–48**
Bando McGlocklin Small Business Lending Corporation, **53** 222–24
Banesto. *See* Banco Español de Credito.
Banexi, **II** 233
Banfi Products Corp., **36 65–67**
Bang & Olufsen Holding A/S, **37 25–28**
Bangkok Airport Hotel, **6** 123–24
Bangkok Aviation Fuel Services Ltd., **6** 123–24
Bangladesh Krishi Bank, **31** 220
Bangor and Aroostook Railroad Company, **8** 33
Bangor Mills, **13** 169
Bangor Punta Alegre Sugar Corp., **30** 425
Bangor Punta Corp., **I** 452, 482; **II** 403
Banister Continental Corp. *See* BFC Construction Corporation.
Bank Austria AG, **23 37–39**
Bank Brussels Lambert, **II 201–03**, 295, 407

Bank Bumiputra, **IV** 519
Bank Central Asia, **18** 181
Bank CIC-Union Européenne A.G., **II** 272
Bank du Louvre, **27** 423
Bank Européene de Credità Moyen Terme, **II** 319; **17** 324
Bank for International Settlements, **II** 368
Bank für Elektrische Unternehmungen. *See* Elektrowatt AG.
Bank für Gemeinwirtschaft, **II** 239
Bank Hapoalim B.M., **II 204–06**; **25** 266, 268; **54 33–37 (upd.)**
Bank Hofmann, **21** 146–47
Bank Leu, **I** 252; **21** 146–47
Bank Leumi Le-Israel, **25** 268
Bank of Adelaide, **II** 189
Bank of America Corporation, **I** 536–37; **II** 252–55, 280, 288–89, 347, 382; **III** 218; **6** 385; **9** 50, 123–24, 333, 536; **12** 106, 466; **14** 170; **18** 516; **22** 542; **25** 432; **26** 486; **46 47–54 (upd.)**; **47** 37
Bank of Antwerp, **IV** 497
Bank of Asheville, **II** 336
Bank of Australasia, **II** 187–89
The Bank of Bishop and Co., Ltd., **11** 114
Bank of Boston Corporation, **II 207–09**; **7** 114; **12** 31; **13** 467; **14** 90
Bank of Brandywine Valley, **25** 542
Bank of Britain, **14** 46–47
Bank of British Columbia, **II** 244, 298
Bank of British Honduras, **II** 344
Bank of British North America, **II** 220
Bank of California, **II** 322, 490. *See also* Union Bank of California.
Bank of Canada, **II** 210, 376
Bank of Central and South America, **II** 344
Bank of Chicago, **III** 270
Bank of China, **II** 298
Bank of Chosen, **II** 338
Bank of Commerce, **II** 331
Bank of Delaware, **25** 542
Bank of England, **II** 217, 235–36, 306–07, 318–19, 333–34, 357, 421–22, 427–28; **III** 234, 280; **IV** 119, 366, 382, 705, 711; **10** 8, 336; **14** 45–46; **17** 324–25; **47** 227
Bank of Finland, **III** 648
Bank of France, **II** 232, 264–65, 354; **III** 391
Bank of Hamilton, **II** 244
Bank of Hindustan, **IV** 699
Bank of Ireland, **16** 13–14; **19** 198; **50 73–76**
Bank of Israel, **II** 206
Bank of Italy, **I** 536; **II** 192, 226, 271–72, 288; **III** 209, 347; **8** 45
The Bank of Jacksonville, **9** 58
Bank of Japan, **I** 519; **II** 291, 325
Bank of Kobe, **II** 371
Bank of Lee County, **14** 40
Bank of Liverpool, **II** 236
Bank of London and South America, **II** 308
Bank of Manhattan Co., **II** 247–48
Bank of Mexico Ltd., **19** 188
The Bank of Milwaukee, **14** 529
Bank of Mississippi, Inc., **14 40–41**
Bank of Montreal, **II 210–12**, 231, 375; **26** 304; **46 55–58 (upd.)**
Bank of Nettleton, **14** 40
Bank of New Brunswick, **II** 221
Bank of New England Corporation, **II 213–15**; **9** 229
Bank of New Orleans, **11** 106

Bank of New Queensland, **II** 188
Bank of New South Wales, **II** 188–89. *See also* Westpac Banking Corporation.
Bank of New York Company, Inc., II 192, **216–19**, 247; **34** 82; **46 59–63** **(upd.)**
Bank of North Mississippi, **14** 41
Bank of Nova Scotia, II 220–23, 345; **IV** 644
Bank of Oklahoma, **22** 4
Bank of Ontario, **II** 210
Bank of Osaka, **II** 360
Bank of Ottawa, **II** 221
Bank of Pasadena, **II** 382
Bank of Queensland, **II** 188
The Bank of Scotland. *See* The Governor and Company of the Bank of Scotland.
Bank of Sherman, **14** 40
Bank of Spain, **II** 194, 197
Bank of the Ohio Valley, **13** 221
Bank of the People, **II** 210
Bank of the United States, **II** 207, 216, 247
Bank of the West, **II** 233
Bank of Tokyo, Ltd., II 224–25, 276, 301, 341, 358; **IV** 151; **12** 138; **16** 496, 498; **24** 358; **50** 498
Bank of Tokyo-Mitsubishi Ltd., 15 41–43 (upd.), 431; **26** 454, 457; **38** 387
Bank of Toronto, **II** 375–76
Bank of Tupelo, **14** 40
Bank of Upper Canada, **II** 210
Bank of Wales, **10** 336, 338
Bank of Western Australia, **II** 187
Bank of Winterthur, **II** 378
Bank One Corporation, 36 68–75 (upd.)
Bank Powszechny Depozytowy, **IV** 119
Bank-R Systems Inc., **18** 517
Bank voor Handel en Nijverheid, **II** 304
BankAmerica Corporation, II 226–28, 436; **8 45–48 (upd.),** 295, 469, 471; **13** 69; **17** 546; **18** 518; **25** 187; **26** 65; **47** 401. *See also* Bank of America
BankBoston. *See* FleetBoston Financial Corporation.
BankCard America, Inc., **24** 394
Bankers and Shippers Insurance Co., **III** 389
Bankers Co., **II** 230
Bankers Corporation, **14** 473
Bankers Investment, **II** 349
Bankers Life and Casualty Co., **10** 247; **16** 207; **33** 110
Bankers Life Co., **III** 328–30
Bankers National Bank, **II** 261
Bankers National Life Insurance Co., **II** 182; **10** 246
Bankers Trust Co., **38** 411
Bankers Trust New York Corporation, I 601; **II** 211, **229–31,** 330, 339; **III** 84–86; **10** 425; **11** 416; **12** 165, 209; **13** 188, 466; **17** 559; **19** 34; **22** 102; **25** 268; 317
Bankhaus IG Herstatt, **II** 242
Banknorth Group, Inc., 55 49–53
Banksia Wines Ltd., **54** 227, 229
BankVermont Corp., **II** 208
BankWatch, **37** 143, 145
Banner Aerospace, Inc., 14 42–44; 37 29–32 (upd.)
Banner International, **13** 20
Banner Life Insurance Company, **III** 273; **24** 284
Banorte. *See* Grupo Financiero Banorte, S.A. de C.V.

Banpais. *See* Grupo Financiero Asemex-Banpais S.A.
BanPonce Corporation, **41** 312
Banque Belge et Internationale en Egypte, **II** 295
Banque Belge pour l'Etranger, **II** 294
Banque Belgo-Zairoise, **II** 294
Banque Bruxelles Lambert. *See* Bank Brussels Lambert.
Banque Commerciale du Maroc, **II** 272
Banque Commerciale-Basle, **II** 270
Banque d'Anvers/Bank van Antwerpen, **II** 294–95
Banque de Bruxelles, **II** 201–02, 239
Banque de Credit et de Depot des Pays Bas, **II** 259
Banque de France, **14** 45–46
Banque de l'Indochine et de Suez, **II** 259
Banque de l'Union Européenne, **II** 94
Banque de l'Union Parisienne, **II** 270; **IV** 497, 557
Banque de la Construction et les Travaux Public, **II** 319; **17** 324
Banque de la Société Générale de Belgique, **II** 294–95
Banque de Louvain, **II** 202
Banque de Paris et des Pays-Bas, **II** 136, 259; **10** 346; **19** 188–89; **33** 179
Banque de Reports et de Depots, **II** 201
Banque du Congo Belge, **II** 294
Banque Européenne pour l'Amerique Latine, **II** 294
Banque Française et Espagnol en Paris, **II** 196
Banque Francaise pour le Commerce et l'Industrie, **II** 232, 270
Banque Génerale des Pays Roumains, **II** 270
Banque Générale du Luxembourg, **II** 294
Banque Indosuez, **II** 429; **52** 361–62
Banque Internationale de Bruxelles, **II** 201–02
Banque Internationale de Luxembourg, **II** 239; **42** 111
Banque Italo-Belge, **II** 294
Banque Italo-Francaise de Credit, **II** 271
Banque Lambert, **II** 201–02
Banque Nationale de Paris S.A., II 232–34, 239; **III** 201, 392–94; **9** 148; **13** 203; **15** 309; **19** 51; **33** 119; **49** 382. *See also* BNP Paribas Group.
Banque Nationale Pour le Commerce et l'Industrie, **II** 232–33
Banque Nordique du Commerce, **II** 366
Banque Orea, **II** 378
Banque Paribas, **II** 192, 260; **IV** 295; **19** 225. *See* BNP Paribas Group.
Banque Rothschild, **IV** 107
Banque Sanpaolo of France, **50** 410
Banque Sino-Belge, **II** 294
Banque Stern, **II** 369
La Banque Suisse et Française. *See* Crédit Commercial de France.
Banque Transatlantique, **II** 271
Banque Worms, **III** 393; **27** 514
Banquet Foods Corp., **II** 90, 494; **12** 81; **42** 91
Banta Corporation, 12 24–26; 19 333; **32 73–77 (upd.)**
Bantam Ball Bearing Company, **13** 522
Bantam Books, Inc., **III** 190–91
Bantam Doubleday Dell Publishing Group, **IV** 594; **13** 429; **15** 51; **27** 222; **31** 375–76, 378

Banyan Systems Inc., 25 50–52
Banyu Pharmaceutical Co., **I** 651; **11** 290; **34** 283
Baoshan Iron and Steel, **19** 220
BAP of New York, Inc., **15** 246
BAPCO, **III** 745
Bar Technologies, Inc., **26** 408
Barat. *See* Barclays PLC.
Barber Dental Supply Inc., **19** 291
Barber-Greene, **21** 502
Barberet & Blanc, **I** 677; **49** 350
Barcel, **19** 192
Barclay Furniture Co., **12** 300
Barclay Group, **I** 335; **10** 290
Barclay White Inc., **38** 436
Barclays Business Credit, **13** 468
Barclays PLC, I 604–05; **II** 202, 204, **235–37,** 239, 244, 308, 319, 333, 383, 422, 429; **III** 516; **IV** 23, 722; **7** 332–33; **8** 118; **11** 29–30; **17** 324–25; **20 57–60 (upd.); 25** 101; **28** 167; **47** 227
BarclaysAmerican Mortgage Corporation, 11 29–30
Barco Manufacturing Co., **16** 8; **26** 541
Barco NV, 44 42–45
Barcolo Manufacturing, **15** 103; **26** 100
Barden Cablevision, **IV** 640; **26** 273
Bardon Group. *See* Aggregate Industries plc.
Bareco Products, **15** 352
Barefoot Inc., **23** 428, 431
Bari Shoes, Inc., **22** 213
Barilla G. e R. Fratelli S.p.A., 17 35–37; 50 77–80 (upd.); 53 243
Baring Brothers & Co., Ltd., **39** 5
Barings PLC, III 699; **14 45–47**
Barker & Dobson, **II** 629; **47** 367
Barker and Company, Ltd., **13** 286
Barlow Rand Ltd., I 288–89, **422–24; IV** 22, 96
Barlow Specialty Advertising, Inc., **26** 341
Barmag AG, 39 39–42
Barmer Bankverein, **II** 238, 241
Barnato Brothers, **IV** 21, 65; **7** 122
Barneda Carton SA, **41** 326
Barnes & Noble, Inc., 10 135–37; 12 172; **13** 494, 545; **14** 61–62; **15** 62; **16** 160; **17** 524; **23** 370; **25** 17, 29–30; **30 67–71 (upd.); 41** 61; **43** 78, 408
Barnes Group, **III** 581
Barnes-Hind, **III** 56, 727
Barnett Banks, Inc., 9 58–60
Barnett Brass & Copper Inc., **9** 543
Barnett Inc., 28 50–52
Barnetts, Hoares, Hanbury and Lloyds, **II** 306
Barney's, Inc., 28 53–55; 36 290, 292
Barnstead/Thermolyne Corporation, **14** 479–80
Baroid, **19** 467–68
Baron Industries Corporation, **53** 298
Baron Philippe de Rothschild S.A., 39 43–46
Barr & Stroud Ltd., **III** 727
Barr Laboratories, Inc., 26 29–31
Barracuda Technologies, **47** 7, 9
Barranquilla Investments, **II** 138; **24** 193
Barratt Developments plc, I 556–57
Barret Fitch North, **II** 445; **22** 405
Barrett Burston, **I** 437
Barrett Business Services, Inc., 16 48–50
The Barrett Co., **I** 414–15; **18** 116; **22** 29
Barricini Foods Inc., **27** 197

Barrick Gold Corporation, 34 62–65; **38** 232

Barris Industries, Inc., **23** 225

Barry & Co., **III** 522

Barry Callebaut AG, 29 46–48

Barry Wright Corporation, **9** 27; **32** 49

Barry's Jewelers. *See* Samuels Jewelers Incorporated.

Barsab Investment Trust. *See* South African Breweries Ltd.

Barsotti's, Inc., **6** 146

Bart Starr, **12** 284

Barth Smelting Corp., **I** 513

Bartlett & Co., **33** 261

Barton & Ludwig, Inc., **21** 96

Barton Beers, Ltd., **29** 219

Barton Brands, **I** 227; **II** 609; **10** 181

Barton, Duer & Koch, **IV** 282; **9** 261

Barton Incorporated, **13** 134; **24** 140; **34** 89

Barton Malow Company, 51 40–43

Barton Protective Services Inc., 53 56–58

Bartow Food Company, **25** 332

Barwig Medizinische Systeme. *See* OEC Medical Systems, Inc.

The Baseball Club of Seattle, LP, 50 81–85

Basel AG, **39** 304

BASF Aktiengesellschaft, I 275, **305–08,** 309, 319, 346–47, 632, 638; **II** 554; **IV** 70–71; **13** 75; **14** 308; **16** 462; **18** **47–51 (upd.),** 186, 234; **21** 544; **24** 75; **26** 305, 368; **27** 22; **28** 194; **41** 45; **50** **86–92 (upd.)**

Bashas' Inc., 33 62–64

Basic American Retirement Communities, **III** 103

Basic Resources, Inc., **V** 725

Basics, **14** 295

BASIS Information Technologies, Inc., **11** 112–13, 132

The Basketball Club of Seattle, LLC, 50 93–97

Basketball Properties Ltd, **53** 166

Baskin-Robbins Ice Cream Co., **I** 215; **7** 128, 372; **17** 474–75; **25** 366; **29** 18

Basle A.G., **I** 632–33, 671–72; **8** 108–09

Basle Air Transport, **I** 121

Basler Bankverein, **II** 368

Bass & Co., **I** 142

Bass Anglers Sportsman Society Inc., **52** 192

Bass Brewers Ltd., **15** 441; **29** 85

Bass Brothers Enterprises Inc., **28** 107; **36** 472

Bass Charington, **29** 84

Bass PLC, I 222–24; **III** 94–95; **9** 99, 425–26; **15** 44–47 **(upd.); 16** 263; **23** 482; **24** 194; **33** 127; **35** 396; **38 74–78** **(upd.); 43** 226

Bass Pro Shops, Inc., 42 27–30

Bassett Boat Company, **30** 303

Bassett Foods, **II** 478

Bassett Furniture Industries, Inc., 18 52–55; 19 275

Bassett-Walker Inc., **V** 390–91; **17** 512

Bassins Food Chain, **II** 649

BAT. *See* British-American Tobacco Co., Ltd.

BAT Industries plc, I 425–27, 605; **II** 628; **III** 66, 185, 522; **9** 312; **23** 427; **30** 273. *See also* British American Tobacco PLC.

Bataafsche Petroleum Maatschappij, **V** 658

Batavia Wine Company, **13** 134

Batchelors Ltd., **I** 315; **25** 81

Bateaux Parisiens, **29** 442

Bateman Eichler Hill Richards, **III** 270

Bates, **16** 545

Bates & Robins, **II** 318; **17** 323

Bates Chemical Company, **9** 154

Bates Manufacturing Company, **10** 314

Bates Worldwide, Inc., 14 48–51; 26 500; **33 65–69 (upd.)**

Batesville Casket Company, **10** 349–50

Bath & Body Works, **11** 41; **24** 237

Bath Industries Inc., **18** 117–18

Bath Iron Works Corporation, 12 27–29; 36 76–79 (upd.)

Bath Plus Inc., **51** 196

Bathurst Bank, **II** 187

Baton Rouge Gas Light Company. *See* Gulf States Utilities Company.

Battelle Laboratories, **25** 260

Battelle Memorial Institute, Inc., 6 288; **10 138–40**

Batten Barton Durstine & Osborn, **I** 25, 28–31, 33; **16** 70; **41** 88

Battle Creek Food Company, **14** 557–58

Battle Creek Toasted Corn Flake Co., **II** 523; **13** 291; **50** 291

Battle Mountain Gold Company, IV 490; **23 40–42**

Battlefield Equipment Rentals, **21** 499, 501

BATUS Inc., **9** 312; **18** 136; **30** 273

Bauborg, **I** 560–61

Baudhuin-Anderson Company, **8** 553

Bauer Audio Visual, Inc., **24** 96

Bauer Nike Hockey Inc., **36** 347

Bauer Publishing Group, 7 42–43; 20 53

Baume & Mercier, **27** 487, 489

Bausch & Lomb Inc., III 446; **7 44–47;** **10** 46–47; **13** 365–66; **25** 22, **53–57** **(upd.),** 183; **30** 30; **42** 66

Bavaria SA, **36** 52

Bavarian Brewing Limited, **25** 280

Bavarian Railway, **II** 241

Bavarian Specialty Foods, **13** 383

Baxter Estates, **II** 649

Baxter Healthcare, **36** 497–98

Baxter International Inc., I 627–29; 9 346; **10 141–43 (upd.),** 198–99; **11** 459–60; **12** 325; **18** 469; **22** 361; **25** 82; **26** 433; **36** 92; **54** 42

Baxter Travenol, **21** 119; **24** 75

The Bay, **16** 216

Bay Area Review Course, Inc., **IV** 623

Bay Cities Transportation Company, **6** 382

Bay City, **21** 502

Bay City Cash Way Company, **V** 222; **25** 534

Bay Colony Life Insurance Co., **III** 254

Bay Harbour Management L.C., **28** 55

Bay Networks, Inc., **20** 33, 69; **26** 276; **36** 352

Bay Petroleum, **I** 526

Bay Ridge Savings Bank, **10** 91

Bay Shipbuilding Corporation, **18** 320

Bay State Gas Company, 38 79–82

Bay State Glass Co., **III** 683

Bay State Iron Manufacturing Co., **13** 16

Bay State Tap and Die Company, **13** 7

Bay West Paper Corporation. *See* Mosinee Paper Corporation.

Bayard SA, 49 46–49

BayBanks, Inc., 12 30–32

Bayer A.G., I 305–06, **309–11,** 319, 346–47, 350; **II** 279; **12** 364; **13 75–77**

(**upd.); 14** 169; **16** 439; **18** 47, 49, 51, 234; **21** 544; **22** 225; **41 44–48 (upd.);** **45** 255

Bayer S.p.A., **8** 179

Bayerische Aluminium AG, **IV** 230

Bayerische Hypotheken- und Wechsel-Bank AG, II 238–40, 241–42; **IV** 323

Bayerische Kraftwerke AG, **IV** 229–30

Bayerische Landesbank, **II** 257–58, 280; **14** 170; **47** 83

Bayerische Motoren Werke A.G., I 73, 75, **138–40,** 198; **II** 5; **III** 543, 556, 591; **11 31–33 (upd.); 13** 30; **17** 25; **21** 441; **27** 20, 203; **38 83–87 (upd.)**

Bayerische Rückversicherung AG, **III** 377

Bayerische Rumpler Werke, **I** 73

Bayerische Stickstoff-Werke AG, **IV** 229–30

Bayerische Vereinsbank A.G., II 239–40, **241–43; III** 401

Bayerische Versicherungsbank, **II** 238; **III** 377

Bayerische Wagnisbeteiligung GmbH, **27** 192

Bayerische Wasserkraftwerke Aktiengesellschaft, **IV** 231

Bayerische Zellstoff, **IV** 325

Bayernwerk AG, IV 231–32, 323; **V** 555–58, 698–700; **23 43–47 (upd.); 39** 57

Bayliner Marine Corporation, **22** 116

Bayou Boeuf Fabricators, **III** 559

Bayou Steel Corporation, IV 234; **31 47–49**

Bayside National Bank, **II** 230

Baystate Corporation, **12** 30

Baytree Investors Inc., **15** 87

Bayview, **III** 673

Bayview Water Company, **45** 277

Bazaar & Novelty. *See* Stuart Entertainment Inc.

Bazar de l'Hotel de Ville, **19** 308

BBA. *See* Bush Boake Allen Inc.

BBAG Osterreichische Brau-Beteiligungs-AG, 38 88–90

BBC. *See* British Broadcasting Corp.

BBC Brown, Boveri Ltd. *See* ABB ASEA Brown Boveri Ltd.

BBDO. *See* Batten Barton Durstine & Osborn.

BBDO Worldwide Network, **22** 394

BBGI. *See* Beasley Broadcast Group, Inc.

BBME. *See* British Bank of the Middle East.

BBN Corp., 19 39–42

BBO & Co., **14** 433

BBVA. *See* Banco Bilbao Vizcaya Argentaria S.A.

BC Development, **16** 481

BC Partners, **51** 322; **53** 138

BC TEL. *See* British Columbia Telephone Company.

BCal. *See* British Caledonian Airways.

BCC, **24** 266, 270

BCE, Inc., V 269–71; 6 307; **7** 333; **12** 413; **18** 32; **36** 351; **44 46–50 (upd.)**

BCI. *See* Banca Commerciale Italiana SpA.

Bcom3 Group, Inc., **40** 142

BCOP. *See* Boise Cascade Office Products.

BCP Corporation, **16** 228–29

BCPA. *See* British Commonwealth Pacific Airways.

BDB. *See* British Digital Broadcasting plc.

BDB Corp., **10** 136

BDDP. *See* Wells Rich Greene BDDP.
Be Free Inc., **49** 434
BEA Systems, Inc., 36 80–83
Beach Hill Investments Pty Ltd., **48** 427
Beach Patrol Inc., **29** 181
BeachviLime Ltd., **IV** 74; **24** 143, 144
Beacon Communications Group, **23** 135
Beacon Education Management LLC. *See* Chancellor Beacon Academies, Inc.
Beacon Manufacturing Company, **I** 377; **19** 304–05
Beacon Oil, **IV** 566
Beacon Participations, **III** 98
Beacon Publishing Co., **IV** 629
Beall-Ladymon, Inc., **24** 458
Bealls, **24** 456
Beamach Group Ltd., **17** 182–83
Beaman Corporation, **16** 96; **25** 390
Bean Fiberglass Inc., **15** 247
Bear Automotive Service Equipment Company, **10** 494
Bear Creek Corporation, 12 444–45; 38 91–94; 39 361
Bear Instruments Inc., **48** 410
Bear Stearns Companies, Inc., II 400–01, 450; **10 144–45 (upd.)**, 382; **20** 313; **24** 272; **52 41–44 (upd.)**
Beard & Stone Electric Co., **I** 451
Bearings, Inc., I 158–59; **13 78–80**
Beasley Broadcast Group, Inc., 51 44–46
Beasley Industries, Inc., **19** 125–26
Beatrice Company, I 353; 440–41; **II 467–69**, 475; **III** 118, 437; **6** 357; **9** 318; **12** 82, 87, 93; **13** 162–63, 452; **14** 149–50; **15** 213–14, 358; **16** 160, 396; **19** 290; **24** 273; **26** 476, 494; **28** 475; **42** 92. *See also* TLC Beatrice International Holdings, Inc.
Beatrice Foods, **21** 322–24, 507, 545; **25** 277–78; **38** 169; **43** 355
Beauharnois Power Company, **6** 502
Beaulieu of America, **19** 276
Beaulieu Winery, **I** 260
Beaumont-Bennett Group, **6** 27
Beauté Prestige International S.A. *See* Shiseido Company Limited.
BeautiControl Cosmetics, Inc., 21 49–52
Beauty Biz Inc., **18** 230
Beaver Lumber Company Limited, **I** 274; **26** 303, 305–06
Beazer Homes USA, Inc., 17 38–41
Beazer Plc., **7** 209
bebe stores, inc., 31 50–52
BEC Group Inc., **22** 35
Bechtel Group, Inc., I 558–59, 563; **III** 248; **IV** 171, 576; **6** 148–49, 556; **13** 13; **24 64–67 (upd.)**; **25** 402; **26** 220; **52** 374
Beck & Gregg Hardware Co., **9** 253
Beck's North America, Inc. *See* Brauerei Beck & Co.
Becker Drill, Inc., **19** 247
Becker Group of Germany, **26** 231
Becker Paribas Futures, **II** 445; **22** 406
Becker Warburg Paribas, **II** 259
Beckett Papers, 23 48–50
Beckley-Cardy Co., **IV** 623–24
Beckman Coulter, Inc., 22 74–77
Beckman Instruments, Inc., I 694; **14 52–54; 16** 94
BECOL. *See* Belize Electric Company Limited.

Becton, Dickinson & Company, I 630–31; 11 34–36 (upd.); 36 84–89 (upd.); 42 182–83; **52** 171
Bed Bath & Beyond Inc., 13 81–83; 14 61; **18** 239; **24** 292; **33** 384; **41 49–52 (upd.)**
Bedcovers, Inc., **19** 304
Beddor Companies, **12** 25
Bedford Chemical, **8** 177
Bedford-Stuyvesant Restoration Corp., **II** 673
Bee Chemicals, **I** 372
Bee Discount, **26** 476
Bee Gee Shoe Corporation, **10** 281
Bee Gee Shrimp, **I** 473
Beech Aircraft Corporation, II 87; **8 49–52**, 313; **11** 411, 413; **27** 98; **38** 375; **46** 354
Beech Holdings Corp., **9** 94
Beech-Nut Nutrition Corporation, I 695; **II** 489; **21 53–56; 46** 290; **51 47–51 (upd.)**
Beecham Group PLC, **I** 626, 640, 668; **II** 331, 543; **III** 18, 65–66; **9** 264; **14** 53; **16** 438
Beechcroft Developments Ltd., **51** 173
Beechwood Insurance Agency, Inc., **14** 472
Beeck-Feinkost GmbH, **26** 59
ZAO BeeOnLine-Portal, **48** 419
Beerman Stores, Inc., **10** 281
Beers Construction Company, **38** 437
Beghin Say S.A., **II** 540
Behr-Manning Company, **8** 396
Behringwerke AG, **14** 255; **50** 249
Beiersdorf AG, 29 49–53; 41 374–77
Beijerinvest Group, **I** 210
Beijing Contact Lens Ltd., **25** 56
Beijing Dentsu, **16** 168
Beijing-Landauer, Ltd., **51** 210
Beijing Liyuan Co., **22** 487
Beijing Machinery and Equipment Corp., **II** 442
Beijing Yanshan Petrochemical Company, **22** 263
Beijing ZF North Drive Systems Technical Co. Ltd., **48** 450
Beirao, Pinto, Silva and Co. *See* Banco Espírito Santo e Comercial de Lisboa S.A.
Bejam Group PLC, **II** 678; **33** 206–07
Beker Industries, **IV** 84
Bekins Company, 15 48–50; 26 197
Bel. *See* Fromageries Bel.
Bel Air Markets, **14** 397
Bel Fuse, Inc., 53 59–62
Belairbus, **I** 42; **12** 191
Belcher New England, Inc., **IV** 394
Belcher Oil Co., **IV** 394
Belco Oil & Gas Corp., 23 219; **40 63–65**
Belcom Holding AG, **53** 323, 325
Belden Inc., II 16; **19 43–45**
Beldis, **23** 219
Beldoch Industries Corp., **17** 137–38
Belfast Banking Co., **II** 318; **17** 323
Belgacom, 6 302–04
Belgian De Vaderlandsche, **III** 309
Belgian Rapid Access to Information Network Services, **6** 304
Belgian Société Internationale Forestière et Minière, **IV** 65
Belglas, **16** 420; **43** 307
Belgo Group plc, **31** 41
Belgochim, **IV** 499

Belize Electric Company Limited, **47** 137
Belize Sugar Industries, **II** 582
Belk Stores Services, Inc., V 12–13; 19 46–48 (upd.)
Bell (Quarry and Concrete), **III** 674
Bell Aerospace, **I** 530; **24** 442; **34** 432–33
Bell Aircraft Company, **I** 529; **11** 267; **13** 267; **34** 431
Bell and Howell Company, I 463; **IV** 642; **9** 33, **61–64; 11** 197; **14** 569; **15** 71; **29 54–58 (upd.)**, 159
Bell Atlantic Corporation, V 272–74; 9 171; **10** 232, 456; **11** 59, 87, 274; **12** 137; **13** 399; **18** 33; **25 58–62 (upd.)**, 91, 497; **27** 22, 365. *See also* Verizon Communications.
Bell Canada Enterprises Inc. *See* BCE, Inc.
Bell Canada International, Inc., V 269, 308–09; **6 305–08; 12** 413; **21** 308; **25** 102
Bell Communications Research, **13** 58; **25** 496
Bell Fibre Products, **12** 377
Bell Helicopter Textron Inc., 46 64–67
Bell Helmets Inc., **22** 458
Bell Industries, Inc., 13 47; **18** 498; **19** 311; **47 40–43**
Bell Laboratories, **II** 33, 60–61, 101, 112; **V** 259–64; **8** 157; **9** 171; **10** 108; **11** 327, 500–01; **12** 61; **14** 52, 281–82; **23** 181; **29** 41, 44; **34** 257–58. *See also* AT&T Bell Labroatories, Inc.
Bell Mountain Partnership, Ltd., **15** 26
Bell-Northern Research, Ltd., **V** 269–71; **15** 131
Bell Pharmacal Labs, **12** 387
Bell Resources, **I** 437–38; **III** 729; **10** 170; **27** 473
Bell Sports Corporation, 16 51–53; 44 51–54 (upd.)
Bell System, **II** 72, 230; **6** 338–40; **7** 99, 333; **11** 500; **16** 392–93
Bell Telephone Company, **I** 409; **6** 332, 334
Bell Telephone Company of Pennsylvania, **I** 585
Bell Telephone Manufacturing, **II** 13
Bell's Asbestos and Engineering, **I** 428
Bellcore. *See* Bell Communications Research.
Belle Alkali Co., **IV** 409; **7** 308
Belledune Fertilizer Ltd., **IV** 165
Bellefonte Insurance Co., **IV** 29
Bellemead Development Corp., **III** 220; **14** 108; **37** 84
Bellofram Corp., **14** 43
BellSouth Corporation, V 276–78; 9 171, 321; **10** 431, 501; **15** 197; **18** 23, 74, 76; **19** 254–55; **22** 19; **27** 20; **29 59–62 (upd.); 43** 447; **45** 390
Bellway Plc, 45 37–39
Belmin Systems, **14** 36
Belmont Electronics, **II** 85–86; **11** 412
Belmont Plaza, **12** 316
Belmont Savings and Loan, **10** 339
Belmont Springs Water Company, Inc., **I** 234; **10** 227
Belo Corporation. *See* A.H. Belo Corporation
Beloit Corporation, 8 243; **14 55–57; 34** 358; **38** 224, 226–28
Beloit Tool Company. *See* Regal-Beloit Corporation.
Beloit Woodlands, **10** 380

Belridge Oil Co., **IV** 541

Belzer Group, **IV** 198–99

Bemis Company, Inc., 8 53–55; **26** 43

Bemrose group, **IV** 650

**Ben & Jerry's Homemade, Inc., 10
146–48; 35 58–62**

Ben Franklin Retail Stores, Inc. *See*
FoxMeyer Health Corporation.

Ben Franklin Savings & Trust, **10** 117

Ben Hill Griffin, **III** 53

Ben Johnson & Co. Ltd., **IV** 661

Ben Line, **6** 398

Ben Myerson Candy Co., Inc., **26** 468

Ben Venue Laboratories Inc., **16** 439; **39**
73

Benchmark Capital, 49 50–52

Benchmark Electronics, Inc., 40 66–69

Benckiser Group, **37** 269

Benckiser N.V. *See* Reckitt Benckiser plc.

Bendicks, **I** 592

Bendix Corporation, I 68, **141–43**, 154,
166, 192, 416; **II** 33; **III** 166, 555; **7**
356; **8** 545; **9** 16–17; **10** 260, 279; **11**
138; **13** 356–57; **15** 284; **17** 564; **21**
416; **22** 31

Beneficial Corporation, II 236; **8 56–58**,
117; **10** 490

Beneficial Finance Company, **27** 428–29

Beneficial National Bank USA, **II** 286

Beneficial Standard Life, **10** 247

Benefit Consultants, Inc., **16** 145

Benefits Technologies, Inc., **52** 382

Benelli Arms S.p.A., **39** 151

Benesse Corporation, **13** 91, 93; **39** 49

Bénéteau SA, 55 54–56

Benetton Group S.p.A., 8 171; **10
149–52**; **15** 369; **18** 193; **25** 56; **49** 31

Benfield Greig Group plc, 53 63–65

Bengal Iron and Steel Co., **IV** 205–06

Benihana, Inc., 18 56–59

Benjamin Allen & Co., **IV** 660

Benjamin Moore and Co., 13 84–87; **38
95–99 (upd.)**

Benlee, Inc., **51** 237

Benlox Holdings PLC, **16** 465

Benn Bros. plc, **IV** 687

Bennett Biscuit Co., **II** 543

Bennett Industries, Inc., **17** 371–73

Bennett's Smokehouse and Saloon, **19** 122;
29 201

Bennigan's, **II** 556–57; **7** 336; **12** 373; **13**
408; **19** 286; **25** 181

Bensdorp, **29** 47

Benson & Hedges, Ltd., **V** 398–99; **15**
137; **19** 171; **49** 151, 153

Benson Wholesale Co., **II** 624

Bentalls, **37** 6, 8

Bentex Holding S.A., **48** 209

Bentley Laboratories, **22** 360

Bentley Mills, Inc., **8** 272

Bentley Motor Ltd., **I** 194; **21** 435

Bentley Systems, **6** 247

Benton & Bowles, **I** 33; **6** 20, 22

Benton International, Inc., **29** 376

Benton Oil and Gas Company, 47 44–46

Benwood Iron Works, **17** 355

Benxi Iron and Steel Corp., **IV** 167

Benzina, **IV** 487

Benzinol, **IV** 487

N.V. Benzit. *See* N.V. Gemeenschappelijk
Benzit van Aandeelen Philips
Gloeilampenfabrieken.

Bercy Management. *See* Elior SA.

Berec Group, **III** 502; **7** 208

Beresford International plc, **24** 335; **27** 159

Beretta. *See* Fabbrica D' Armi Pietro
Beretta S.p.A.

Berg Manufacturing Sales Co., **I** 156

Berg- und Metallbank, **IV** 139–40

Bergdorf Goodman Inc., I 246; **V** 30–31;
25 177; **52 45–48**

Bergedorfer Eisenwerk, **III** 417–20

Bergen Bank, **II** 352

Bergen Brunswig Corporation, I 413; **V
14–16**, 152; **13 88–90 (upd.)**; **18** 97

Berger Associates, Inc., **26** 233

Berger, Jenson and Nicholson, **I** 347; **18**
236

Berger Manufacturing Company, **26** 405

Bergische-Markische Bank, **II** 278

Berglen, **III** 570; **20** 362

Bergmann & Co., **II** 27

Bergstrom Paper Company, **8** 413

Bergswerksgesellschaft Hibernia, **I** 349; **IV**
194

Bergvik & Ala, **IV** 336, 338–39

**Beringer Wine Estates Holdings, Inc., 22
78–81**; **36** 472

Berisford International plc, **19** 492, 494

Berjaya Group, **22** 464–65

Berk Corp., **52** 193

Berkeley Computers, **III** 109; **14** 13

Berkeley Farms, Inc., 46 68–70

Berkey Photo Inc., **I** 447; **III** 475; **36** 171

Berkley Dean & Co., **15** 525

Berkley Petroleum Corporation, **52** 30

Berkline Corp., **17** 183; **20** 363; **39** 267

Berkshire Hathaway Inc., III 213–15; **18
60–63 (upd.)**; **29** 191; **30** 411; **36** 191;
38 98; **40** 196, 199, 398; **39** 232, 235;
42 31–36 (upd.)

Berkshire International, **V** 390–91; **17** 512

Berkshire Partners, **10** 393

**Berkshire Realty Holdings, L.P., 49
53–55**

Berleca Ltd., **9** 395; **42** 269

Berlex Laboratories, **I** 682; **10** 214

Berli Jucker, **18** 180–82

Berlin Exchange, **I** 409

Berlin Göring-Werke, **IV** 233

BerlinDat Gesellschaft für
Informationsverarbeitung und
Systemtechnik GmbH, **39** 57

Berliner Bank, **II** 256

Berliner Bankverein, **II** 278

Berliner Handels- und Frankfurter Bank, **II**
242

Berliner Union, **I** 409

Berlinische Bodengesellschaft, **I** 560

Berlitz International, Inc., IV 643; **7** 286,
312; **13 91–93**; **39 47–50 (upd.)**

Berman Brothers Fur Co., **21** 525

Berman Buckskin, **21** 525

**Bernard C. Harris Publishing Company,
Inc., 39 51–53**

Bernard Chaus, Inc., 27 59–61

Bernard Warschaw Insurance Sales
Agency, Inc., **55** 128

Bernardin Ltd., **30** 39

Berndorf Austria, **44** 206

Berndorf Switzerland, **44** 206

Bernheim-Meyer: A l'Innovation. *See* GIB
Group.

Berni Inns, **I** 247

Bernie Schulman's, **12** 132

Bernina Holding AG, 47 47–50

Bernstein Macauley, Inc., **II** 450

Berrios Enterprises, **14** 236

Berry Bearing Company, **9** 254

Berry Industries, **III** 628

Berry Petroleum Company, 47 51–53

Berry Plastics Corporation, 21 57–59

Bert L. Smokler & Company, **11** 257

Bertea Corp., **III** 603

Bertelsmann A.G., IV 592–94, 614–15;
10 196; **15 51–54 (upd.)**; **17** 399; **19**
285; **22** 194; **26** 19, 43; **30** 67, 70; **31**
375, 378; **43 63–67 (upd.)**, 422; **44** 377;
54 17, 21–22

Bertelsmann Music Group, **52** 428

Bertolini's Authentic Trattorias, **30** 329

Bertram & Graf Gmbh, **28** 45

Bertron Griscom & Company, **V** 641

Bertucci's Inc., 16 54–56, 447

Berwick Industries, Inc., **35** 130–31

Berwind Corp., **14** 18

Beryl Corp., **26** 149

Beryllium Resources, **14** 80

Berzelius Metallhütten Gesellschaft, **IV**
141

Berzelius Umwelt-Service, **III** 625; **IV** 141

Besi, **26** 498

Besnier SA, 19 49–51; **23** 217, 219; **24**
444–45; **25** 83, 85

Bess Mfg., **8** 510

Bessemer Capital Partners L.P., **15** 505

Bessemer Gas Engine Co., **II** 15; **20** 163

Bessemer Limestone & Cement Co., **IV**
409; **31** 454

Bessemer Steamship, **IV** 572; **7** 549

Besser Vibrapac, **III** 673

Best Apparel, **V** 156

Best Buy Co., Inc., 9 65–66; **10** 305; **17**
489; **18** 532–33; **19** 362; **23 51–53
(upd.)**; **24** 52, 502; **29** 120, 123; **30** 464,
466; **38** 315

best energy GmbH, **39** 54, 57

Best Fabric Outlets, **16** 198

Best Holding Corporation. *See* Arkansas
Best Corporation.

Best Manufacturing, **15** 490

Best Power, **24** 29

Best Products Inc., **19** 396–97

Best Read Guides Franchise Corp., **36** 341

Best Western, **14** 106; **25** 308

BestChoice Administrators, Inc., **51**
276–77

Bestfoods, II 496–97; **22 82–86 (upd.)**

Bestform Group Inc., **54** 403

Bestline Products, **17** 227

Bestop Inc., **16** 184

Bestwall Gypsum Co., **IV** 281; **9** 259

Bestway Distribution Services, Inc., **24** 126

Bestway Transportation, **14** 505

Beswick, **II** 17

BET Holdings, Inc., 18 64–66; **22** 224;
25 213; **34** 43

Beta West Properties, **25** 496–97

Bethesda Research Laboratories, Inc., **I**
321; **17** 287, 289

Bethlehem Steel Corporation, IV 35–37,
228, 572–73; **6** 540; **7 48–51 (upd.)**,
447, 549–50; **11** 65; **12** 354; **13** 97, 157;
18 378; **22** 285; **23** 305; **25** 45; **26** 405;
27 62–66 (upd.); **50** 501–02

Beton Union, **III** 738

Betriebs- und Baugesellschaft GmbH, **53**
285

Better Brands Ltd., **32** 518–19

Better Communications, **IV** 597

Betz Laboratories, Inc., I 312–13; **10
153–55 (upd.)**; **15** 536

Bevan and Wedd Durlacher Morduant & Co., **II** 237
Beveridge-Marvellum Company, **8** 483
Beverly Enterprises, Inc., **III** 76–77, 80; **14** 242; **16** 57–59 (**upd.**); **25** 309
Beverly Hills Savings, **II** 420
Beverly Pest Control, **25** 15
Bevis Custom Furniture, Inc., **12** 263
Bevrachtingskantoor, **26** 280
Bewag AG, **38** 449; **39** 54–57
Bezeq, **25** 266
BFC Construction Corporation, **25** 63–65
The BFGoodrich Company, **I** 28, 428, 440; **II** 414; **III** 118, 443; **V** 231–33; **8** 80–81, 290; **9** 12, 96, 133; **10** 438; **11** 158; **19** 52–55 (**upd.**); **20** 260, 262; **21** 260; **22** 114; **23** 170; **25** 70; **30** 158; **31** 135. *See also* Goodrich Corporation.
BFI. *See* Browning-Ferris Industries, Inc.
BFP Holdings Corp. *See* Big Flower Press Holdings, Inc.
BG Freight Line Holding B.V., **30** 318
BG plc, **29** 104
BG&E. *See* Baltimore Gas and Electric Company.
BGC Finance, **II** 420
BGJ Enterprises, Inc. *See* Brown Printing Company.
BH Acquisition Corporation, **22** 439
Bharat Coking Coal Ltd., **IV** 48–49
Bharat Petroleum Ltd., **IV** 441
Bharti Telecom, **16** 84
BHC Communications, Inc., **9** 119; **26** 32–34; **31** 109
BHP. *See* Broken Hill Proprietary Company Ltd.
BHP Steel of Australia, **18** 380
BHPC Marketing, Inc., **45** 41
Bhs plc, **16** 466; **17** 42–44, 334–35
BHV. *See* Bazar de l'Hotel de Ville.
Bi-Lo Inc., **II** 641; **V** 35; **16** 313
Biacore International AB, **25** 377
Bianchi, **13** 27
Bibb Co., **31** 199
BIC Corporation, **III** 29; **8** 59–61; **20** 23; **23** 54–57 (**upd.**)
BICC PLC, **III** 433–34; **11** 520. *See also* Balfour Beatty plc.
BICE Med Grille, **16** 447
Bicoastal Corporation, **II** 9–11
Bidermann Industries, **22** 122; **41** 129
Biederman & Company, **14** 160
Biedermann Motech, **37** 112
Bieffe, **16** 52
Bierbrauerei Wilhelm Remmer, **9** 86
Biesemeyer Manufacturing Corporation, **26** 363
Biffa Waste Services Ltd. *See* Severn Trent PLC.
Big B, Inc., **17** 45–47
Big Bear Stores Co., **13** 94–96
Big Boy, **III** 102–03
Big D Construction Corporation, **42** 432
Big Dog Holdings, Inc., **45** 40–42
Big 5 Sporting Goods Corporation, **12** 477; **55** 57–59
Big Flower Press Holdings, Inc., **21** 60–62; **32** 465–66
Big Foot Cattle Co., **14** 537
Big Guns, Inc., **51** 229
Big Horn Mining Co., **8** 423
Big Idea Productions, Inc., **49** 56–59
Big Lots, Inc., **50** 98–101

Big M, **8** 409–10
Big O Tires, Inc., **20** 61–63
Big Rivers Electric Corporation, **11** 37–39
Big Sky Western Bank, **35** 197, 199
Big Three Industries, **I** 358
Big V Supermarkets, Inc., **25** 66–68
Big Y Foods, Inc., **23** 169; **53** 66–68
Bigelow-Sanford, Inc., **31** 199
BII. *See* Banana Importers of Ireland.
Bike Athletics, **23** 449
BIL, **54** 366–68. *See also* Brierley Investments.
Bilbao Insurance Group, **III** 200
Bilfinger & Berger AG, **I** 560–61; **55** 60–63 (**upd.**)
Bill & Melinda Gates Foundation, **41** 53–55, 119
Bill Acceptance Corporation Ltd., **48** 427
Bill Blass Ltd., **32** 78–80
Bill France Racing, **19** 222
Billabong International Ltd., **44** 55–58
Billboard Publications, Inc., **7** 15
Billerud, **IV** 336
Billing Concepts Corp., **26** 35–38
Billiton International, **IV** 56, 532; **22** 237
Bill's Casino, **9** 426
Bilsom, **40** 96–97
Bilt-Rite Chase-Pitkin, Inc., **41** 416
Biltwell Company, **8** 249
Bimar Foods Inc., **19** 192
Bimbo Bakeries USA, **29** 341
Bimbo, S.A., **36** 162, 164
Bin Zayed Group, **55** 54, 56
Binder Hamlyn, **IV** 685
Binderline Development, Inc., **22** 175
Bindley Western Industries, Inc., **9** 67–69; **50** 123
Bing Crosby Productions, **IV** 595
Bingham Dana LLP, **43** 68–71
Binghamton Container Company, **8** 102
Bingo King. *See* Stuart Entertainment Inc.
Binks Sames Corporation, **21** 63–66
Binney & Smith Inc., **II** 525; **IV** 621; **13** 293; **25** 69–72; **50** 294
Binnie & Partners, **22** 89
Binny & Co. Ltd., **III** 522
Binter Canarias, **6** 97
Bio-Clinic, **11** 486–87
Bio-Dental Technologies Corporation, **46** 466
Bio-Dynamics, Inc., **10** 105, 107; **37** 111
Bio Foods Inc. *See* Balance Bar Company.
Bio Synthetics, Inc., **21** 386
Bio-Toxicological Research Laboratories, **IV** 409
Biodevelopment Laboratories, Inc., **35** 47
Biofermin Pharmaceutical, **I** 704
Biogen Inc., **I** 638, 685; **8** 210; **14** 58–60; **36** 90–93 (**upd.**)
Bioindustrias, **19** 475
Biokyowa, **III** 43; **48** 250
Biological Research, **III** 443
Biological Technology Corp., **IV** 252; **17** 29
Biomedical Reference Laboratories of North Carolina, **11** 424
Biomega Corp., **18** 422
Biomet, Inc., **10** 156–58
Bionaire, Inc., **19** 360
BioSensor A.B., **I** 665
Biotechnica International, **I** 286
Bioteknik-Gruppen, **I** 665
Bioter-Biona, S.A., **II** 493

Bioter S.A., **III** 420
Biotherm, **III** 47
Biovail Corporation, **47** 54–56
Biralo Pty Ltd., **48** 427
Bird & Sons, **22** 14
Bird Corporation, **19** 56–58
Birdair, Inc., **35** 99–100
Birds Eye, **32** 474
Birdsall, Inc., **6** 529, 531
Bireley's, **22** 515
Birfield Ltd., **III** 494
Birkbeck, **10** 6
Birkenstock Footprint Sandals, Inc., **12** 33–35; **42** 37–40 (**upd.**)
Birmingham & Midland Bank. *See* Midland Bank plc.
Birmingham Joint Stock Bank, **II** 307
Birmingham Screw Co., **III** 493
Birmingham Slag Company, **7** 572–73, 575
Birmingham Steel Corporation, **13** 97–98; **18** 379–80; **19** 380; **40** 70–73 (**upd.**)
Birra Moretti, **25** 281–82
Birtman Electric Co., **III** 653; **12** 548
Biscayne Bank. *See* Banco Espírito Santo e Comercial de Lisboa S.A.
Biscayne Federal Savings and Loan Association, **11** 481
Biscuiterie Nantaise, **II** 502; **10** 323
Biscuits Belin, **II** 543
Biscuits Delacre, **II** 480; **26** 56
Biscuits Gondolo, **II** 543
Bishop & Babcock Manufacturing Co., **II** 41
Bishop & Co. Savings Bank, **11** 114
Bishop National Bank of Hawaii, **11** 114
Bishopsgate Insurance, **III** 200
BISSELL, Inc., **9** 70–72; **30** 75–78 (**upd.**)
Bit Software, Inc., **12** 62
Bits & Pieces, **26** 439
Bitumax Proprietary, **III** 672
Bitumen & Oil Refineries (Australia) Ltd., **III** 672–73
Bivac International, **55** 79
BIW. *See* Bath Iron Works.
BIZ Enterprises, **23** 390
BizBuyer.com, **39** 25
Bizimgaz Ticaret Ve Sanayi A.S., **55** 346
Bizmark, **13** 176
BizMart, **6** 244–45; **8** 404–05
BJ Services Company, **15** 534, 536; **25** 73–75
BJ's Pizza & Grill, **44** 85
BJ's Restaurant & Brewhouse, **44** 85
BJ's Wholesale Club, **12** 221; **13** 547–49; **33** 198
BJK&E. *See* Bozell Worldwide Inc.
Björknäs Nya Sågverks, **IV** 338
BK Tag, **28** 157
BK Vision AG, **52** 357
BKW, **IV** 229
BL Ltd., **I** 175; **10** 354
BL Systems. *See* AT&T Istel Ltd.
BL Universal PLC, **47** 168
The Black & Decker Corporation, **I** 667; **III** 435–37, 628, 665; **8** 332, 349; **15** 417–18; **16** 384; **17** 215; **20** 64–68 (**upd.**); **22** 334; **43** 101, 289
Black & Veatch LLP, **22** 87–90
Black Arrow Leasing, **II** 138; **24** 193
Black Box Corporation, **20** 69–71
Black Clawson Company, **24** 478

Black Entertainment Television. *See* BET Holdings, Inc.
Black Flag Co., **I** 622
Black Hawk Broadcasting Group, **III** 188; **10** 29; **38** 17
Black Hills Corporation, 20 72–74
Black Pearl Software, Inc., **39** 396
Black Spread Eagle, **II** 235
BlackBerry. *See* Research in Motion Ltd.
Blackburn Group, **III** 508; **24** 85
Blackhawk Holdings, Inc. *See* PW Eagle Inc.
Blackhorse Agencies, **II** 309; **47** 227
Blackmer Pump Co., **III** 468
Blacks Leisure Group plc, 39 58–60
Blackstone Capital Partners L.P., **V** 223; **6** 378; **17** 366
The Blackstone Group, **II** 434, 444; **IV** 718; **11** 177, 179; **13** 170; **17** 238, 443; **22** 404, 416; **26** 408; **37** 309, 311
Blackstone Hotel Acquisition Co., **24** 195
Blaine Construction Company, **8** 546
Blair and Co., **II** 227
Blair Corporation, 25 76–78; 31 53–55
Blair Paving, **III** 674
Blair Radio, **6** 33
Blakiston Co., **IV** 636
Blane Products, **I** 403
Blanes, S.A. de C.V., **34** 197
Blatz Breweries, **I** 254
Blaupunkt-Werke, **I** 192–93
BLC Insurance Co., **III** 330
BLD Europe, **16** 168
Bleichröder, **II** 191
Blendax, **III** 53; **8** 434; **26** 384
Blessings Corp., 14 550; 19 59–61
Blimpie International, Inc., 15 55–57; 17 501; **32** 444; **49 60–64 (upd.)**
Bliss Manufacturing Co., **17** 234–35
Blitz-Weinhart Brewing, **18** 71–72; **50** 112, 114
Bloch & Guggenheimer, Inc., **40** 51–52
Blochman Lawrence Goldfree, **I** 697
Block Drug Company, Inc., 6 26; **8** **62–64; 27 67–70 (upd.)**
Block Financial Corporation, **17** 265; **29** 227
Block Management, **29** 226
Block Medical, Inc., **10** 351
Blockbuster Entertainment Corporation, **II** 161; **IV** 597; **9 73–75,** 361; **11** 556–58; **12** 43, 515; **13** 494; **18** 64, 66; **19** 417; **22** 161–62; **23** 88, 503; **25** 208–10, 222; **26** 409; **28** 296; **29** 504
Blockbuster Inc., 31 56–60 (upd.), 339–40; **50** 61
Blockson Chemical, **I** 380; **13** 379
Bloedel, Stewart & Welch, **IV** 306–07
Blohm & Voss, **I** 74
Blonder Tongue Laboratories, Inc., 48 **52–55**
Bloomberg L.P., 18 24; **21 67–71**
Bloomingdale's Inc., I 90; **III** 63; **IV** 651, 703; **9** 209, 393; **10** 487; **12 36–38,** 307, 403–04; **16** 328; **23** 210; **25** 257; **31** 190
Blount International, Inc., I 563; **12** **39–41; 24** 78; **26** 117, 119, 363; **48** **56–60 (upd.)**
BLP Group Companies. *See* Boron, LePore & Associates, Inc.
BLT Ventures, **25** 270
Blue Arrow PLC, **II** 334–35; **9** 327; **30** 300
Blue Bell Creameries L.P., 30 79–81

Blue Bell, Inc., **V** 390–91; **12** 205; **17** 512
Blue Bird Corporation, 35 63–66
Blue Bunny Ice Cream. *See* Wells' Dairy, Inc.
Blue Byte, **41** 409
Blue Chip Stamps, **III** 213–14; **30** 412
Blue Circle Industries PLC, III 669–71, 702. *See also* Lafarge Cement UK.
Blue Cross and Blue Shield Association, **10** 159–61; **14** 84
Blue Cross and Blue Shield Mutual of Northern Ohio, **12** 176
Blue Cross and Blue Shield of Colorado, **11** 175
Blue Cross and Blue Shield of Greater New York, **III** 245, 246
Blue Cross and Blue Shield of Ohio, **15** 114
Blue Cross Blue Shield of Michigan, **12** 22
Blue Cross of California, **25** 525
Blue Cross of Northeastern New York, **III** 245–46
Blue Diamond Growers, 28 56–58
Blue Dot Services, **37** 280, 283
Blue Funnel Line, **I** 521; **6** 415–17
Blue Line Distributing, **7** 278–79
Blue Metal Industries, **III** 687; **28** 82
Blue Mountain Arts, Inc., IV 621; **29** **63–66**
Blue Mountain Springs Ltd., **48** 97
Blue Ribbon Beef Pack, Inc., **II** 515–16
Blue Ribbon Sports. *See* Nike, Inc.
Blue Ridge Grocery Co., **II** 625
Blue Ridge Lumber Ltd., **16** 11
Blue Shield of California, **25** 527
Blue Square Israel Ltd., 41 56–58
Blue Tee Corporation, **23** 34, 36
Blue Water Food Service, **13** 244
Bluebird Inc., **10** 443
Bluffton Grocery Co., **II** 668
Blumberg Communications Inc., **24** 96
Blunt Ellis & Loewi, **III** 270
Blyth and Co., **I** 537; **13** 448, 529
Blyth Eastman Dillon & Company, **II** 445; **22** 405–06
Blyth Industries, Inc., 18 67–69
Blyth Merrill Lynch, **II** 448
Blythe Colours BV, **IV** 119
BMC Industries, Inc., 6 275; **17 48–51**
BMC Software, Inc., 14 391; **55 64–67**
BMG/Music, **IV** 594; **15** 51; **37** 192–93. *See also* Bertelsmann Music Group.
BMHC. *See* Building Materials Holding Corporation.
BMI. *See* Broadcast Music Inc.
BMI Ltd., **III** 673
BMI Systems Inc., **12** 174
BMO Corp., **III** 209
BMO Nesbitt Burns, **46** 55
BMW. *See* Bayerische Motoren Werke.
BNA. *See* Banca Nazionale dell'Agricoltura; Bureau of National Affairs, Inc.
BNCI. *See* Banque Nationale Pour le Commerce et l'Industrie.
BNE. *See* Bank of New England Corp.
BNG, Inc., **19** 487
BNP Paribas Group, 36 94–97 (upd.); 42 349
BNS Acquisitions, **26** 247
Boa Shoe Company, **42** 325
BOAC. *See* British Overseas Airways Corp.
Boardwalk Regency, **6** 201

Boart and Hard Metals, **IV** 22
Boart Longyear Company, 26 39–42, 69
Boase Massimi Pollitt, **6** 48
Boatmen's Bancshares Inc., 15 58–60
BoatsDirect.com, **37** 398
Bob Evans Farms, Inc., 9 76–79; 10 259; **35** 83–84
Bobbie Brooks Inc., **17** 384
Bobbs-Merrill, **11** 198
Bobingen A.G., **I** 347
Bobit Publishing Company, 55 68–70
Bobro Products. *See* BWP Distributors.
BOC Group plc, I 314–16, 358; **11** 402; **12** 500; **25 79–82 (upd.)**
Boca Resorts, Inc., 37 33–36
BOCAP Corp., **37** 372
Bochumer Verein für Gusstahlfabrikation, **IV** 88
Bock Bearing Co., **8** 530
Bodcaw Co., **IV** 287; **15** 228
Boddington, **21** 247
Bodegas, **8** 556
Bodeker Drug Company, **16** 399
Bodum Design Group AG, 47 57–59
The Body Shop International plc, 11 **40–42; 53 69–72 (upd.)**
Boehringer Ingelheim GmbH. *See* C.H. Boehringer Sohn.
Boehringer Mannheim Companies, **37** 111–12
The Boeing Company, I 41–43, **47–49,** 50, 55–56, 58, 61, 67–68, 70–72, 74, 77, 82, 84–85, 90, 92–93, 96–97, 100, 102, 104–05, 108, 111–13, 116, 121–22, 126, 128, 130, 195, 489–90, 511, 530; **II** 7, 32–33, 62, 442; **III** 512, 539; **IV** 171, 576; **6** 68, 96, 130, 327; **7** 11, 456, 504; **8** 81, 313, 315; **9** 12, 18, 128, 194, 206, 232, 396, 416–17, 458–60, 498; **10 162–65 (upd.),** 262, 316, 369, 536; **11** 164, 267, 277–79, 363, 427; **12** 180, 190–91, 380; **13** 356–58; **21** 140, 143, 436; **24** 21, 84, 85–86, 88–89, 442; **25** 34, 224, 430–31; **26** 117; **28** 195, 225; **32 81–87 (upd.);** **36** 122, 190; **38** 372; **48** 218–20; **50** 367
Boeke & Huidekooper, **III** 417
Boerenbond, **II** 304
Boettcher & Co., **III** 271
Bofors Nobel Inc., **9** 380–81; **13** 22
Bogen Company, **15** 213
Bohemia, Inc., 13 99–101; 31 467
Bohm-Allen Jewelry, **12** 112
Böhme-Fettchemie, Chemnitz, **III** 32
Bohn Aluminum & Brass, **10** 439
Boise Cascade Corporation, I 142; **III** 499, 648, 664; **IV 255–56,** 333; **6** 577; **7** 356; **8 65–67 (upd.),** 477; **15** 229; **16** 510; **19** 269, 445–46; **22** 154; **31** 13; **32** **88–92 (upd.);** **36** 509; **37** 140; **52** 55
Bokaro Steel Ltd., **IV** 206
Bolands Ltd., **II** 649
Bolar Pharmaceutical Co., **16** 529
Boley G.m.b.H., **21** 123
Boliden Mining, **II** 366
Bolinder-Munktell, **I** 209; **II** 366
Bolitho Bank, **II** 235
Bölkow GmbH, **I** 74
Bolles & Houghton, **10** 355
The Bolsa Chica Company, **8** 300
BolsWessanen N.V. *See* Koninklijke Wessanen nv.
Bolt, Beranek & Newman Inc., **26** 520
Bolt Security, **32** 373

Bolthouse Farms, Inc., **54** 257
BOMAG, **8** 544, 546
Bombadier Defence Services UK, **41** 412
Bombardier Aerospace Group, **36** 190–91
Bombardier, Inc., **12** 400–01; **16** 78; **25** 423; **27** 281, 284; **34** 118–19; **35** 350–51; **42 41–46 (upd.)**
The Bombay Company, Inc., III 581; **10 166–68**; **27** 429
Bon Appetit Holding AG, II 656; **48 61–63**
Bon Dente International Inc., **39** 320
The Bon Marché, Inc., V 25; **9** 209; **19** 88, 306, 309; **23 58–60**; **26** 158, 160
Bon Secours Health System, Inc., 24 68–71
The Bon-Ton Stores, Inc., 16 60–62; **50 106–10 (upd.)**
Bonanza, **7** 336; **10** 331; **15** 361–63
Bonanza Steakhouse, **17** 320
Bonaventura, **IV** 611
Bonaventure Liquor Store Co., **I** 284
Bond Brewing International, **23** 405
Bond Corporation Holdings Limited, I 253, 255; **10 169–71**; **54** 228
Bondex International, **8** 456
Bonduel Pickling Co. Inc., **25** 517
Bonduelle SA, 51 52–54
Bongrain SA, 19 50; **23** 217, 219; **25 83–85**
Boni & Liveright, **13** 428
Bonifiche Siele, **II** 272
Bonimart, **II** 649
Bonneville International Corporation, 29 67–70; **30** 15
Bonneville Power Administration, 50 102–05
Bonnier AB, 52 49–52
Bontrager Bicycles, **16** 495
Bonwit Teller, **13** 43; **17** 43; **54** 304–05
Book-Mart Press, Inc., **41** 111
Book-of-the-Month Club, Inc., IV 661, 675; **7** 529; **13 105–07**
Booker plc, 13 102–04; **31 61–64 (upd.)**
Booker Tate, **13** 102
Booklink Technologies, **26** 19
Bookmasters, **10** 136
Books-A-Million, Inc., 14 61–62; **16** 161; **41 59–62 (upd.)**
Bookstop, **10** 136
Boole & Babbage, Inc., 25 86–88
Booth Bay, Ltd., **16** 37
Booth Creek Ski Holdings, Inc., 31 65–67
Booth Fisheries, **II** 571
Booth, Inc., **II** 420
Booth-Kelly Lumber Co., **IV** 281; **9** 259
Booth Leasing, **I** 449
Bootprint Entertainment, **31** 240
The Boots Company PLC, I 640, 668, 708; **II** 650; **V 17–19**; **8** 548; **19** 122; **24 72–76 (upd.)**
Boots Pharmaceuticals, **18** 51
Booz Allen & Hamilton Inc., 10 172–75
Boral Limited, III 672–74; **43 72–76 (upd.)**
Borax Holdings, **IV** 191
Bordas, **IV** 615
Borden Cabinet Corporation, **12** 296
Borden, Inc., II 470–73, 486, 498, 538, 545; **IV** 569; **7** 127, 129, 380; **11** 173; **15** 490; **16** 43; **17** 56; **22** 84, **91–96 (upd.)**; **24** 273, 288, 520; **27** 38, 40, 316, 318

Border Fine Arts, **11** 95
Border Television, **41** 352
Borders Group, Inc., 9 361; **10** 137; **15 61–62**; **17** 522; **18** 286; **25** 17; **30** 69; **43 77–79 (upd.)**, 408; **47** 211
Borders, Perrin and Norrander, **23** 480
Borealis A/S, **30** 205; **45** 8
Borg Instruments, **23** 494
Borg-Warner Australia, **47** 280
Borg-Warner Automotive, Inc., 14 63–66; **23** 171; **32 93–97 (upd.)**
Borg-Warner Corporation, I 193, 339, 393; **III** 428, **438–41**; **14** 63, 357; **22** 228; **25** 74, 253
Borg-Warner Security Corporation, **13** 123–25; **14** 63, 65, 541; **41** 79
Borland International, Inc., 6 255–56; **9** 80–82; **10** 237, 509, 519, 558; **15** 492; **25** 300–01, 349; **38** 417
Borman's, Inc., **II** 638; **16** 249
Borneo Airways. *See* Malaysian Airlines System BHD.
Borneo Co., **III** 523
Boron, LePore & Associates, Inc., 45 43–45
Borregaard Osterreich AG, **18** 395
Borror Corporation. *See* Dominion Homes, Inc.
Borsheim's, **III** 215; **18** 60
Borun Bros., **12** 477
Bosanquet, Salt and Co., **II** 306
Bosch. *See* Robert Bosch GmbH.
Boschert, **III** 434
Boscov's Department Store, Inc., 31 68–70
Bose Corporation, 13 108–10; **36 98–101 (upd.)**
Bosendorfer, L., Klavierfabrik, A.G., **12** 297
Bosert Industrial Supply, Inc., **V** 215
Boso Condensed Milk, **II** 538
Bossa, **55** 188
Bost Sports Clubs. *See* Town Sports International, Inc.
Bostich, **III** 628
Boston Acoustics, Inc., 22 97–99
Boston and Maine Corporation, **16** 350
The Boston Beer Company, Inc., 18 70–73, 502; **22** 422; **31** 383; **50 111–15 (upd.)**
Boston Casualty Co., **III** 203
Boston Celtics Limited Partnership, 14 67–69
Boston Chicken, Inc., 12 42–44; **23** 266; **29** 170, 172. *See also* Boston Market Corporation.
Boston Co., **II** 451–52
Boston Consulting Group, **I** 532; **9** 343; **18** 70; **22** 193
Boston Corp., **25** 66
Boston Distributors, **9** 453
Boston Edison Company, 12 45–47
Boston Educational Research, **27** 373
Boston Fruit Co., **II** 595
Boston Garden Arena Corporation, **14** 67
Boston Gas Company, **6** 486–88
Boston Globe, **7** 13–16
Boston Herald, **7** 15
Boston Industries Corp., **III** 735
Boston Marine Insurance Co., **III** 242
Boston Market Corporation, 48 64–67 (upd.)
Boston National Bank, **13** 465
Boston News Bureau, **IV** 601

Boston Overseas Financial Corp., **II** 208
Boston Popcorn Co., **27** 197–98; **43** 218
Boston Professional Hockey Association Inc., 39 61–63
Boston Properties, Inc., 22 100–02
Boston Scientific Corporation, 37 37–40
Boston Technology, **43** 117
Boston Ventures Limited Partnership, **17** 444; **27** 41, 393; **54** 334, 337
Boston Whaler, Inc., **V** 376–77; **10** 215–16; **26** 398
Bostrom Seating, Inc., **23** 306
BOTAS, **IV** 563
Botsford Ketchum, Inc., **6** 40
Botswana General Insurance Company, **22** 495
Botto, Rossner, Horne & Messinger, **6** 40
Bottu, **II** 475
BOTWEB, Inc., **39** 95
Bougainville Copper Pty., **IV** 60–61
Boulanger, **37** 22
Boulder Creek Steaks & Saloon, **16** 447
Boulder Natural Gas Company, **19** 411
Boulet Dru DuPuy Petit Group. *See* Wells Rich Greene BDDP.
Boulevard Bancorp, **12** 165
Boulton & Paul Ltd., **31** 398–400
Boundary Gas Inc., **6** 457; **54** 260
Boundary Healthcare, **12** 327
Bouquet, **V** 114
Bourdon, **19** 49
Bourjois, **12** 57
Boussois Souchon Neuvesel, **II** 474; **III** 677; **16** 121–22
Bouverat Industries, **51** 36
Bouygues S.A., I 562–64; **13** 206; **23** 475–76; **24 77–80 (upd.)**; **31** 126, 128; **48** 204
Bouzan Mines Ltd., **IV** 164
Bovaird Seyfang Manufacturing Co., **III** 471
Bovis Construction, **38** 344–45
Bovis Lend Lease, **52** 222
Bovis Ltd., **I** 588
Bow Bangles, **17** 101, 103
Bow Flex of America, Inc. *See* Direct Focus, Inc.
Bow Valley Energy Inc., **47** 397
Bowater PLC, III 501–02; **IV 257–59**; **7** 208; **8** 483–84; **25** 13; **30** 229
Bowdens Media Monitoring Ltd., **55** 289
Bower Roller Bearing Company. *See* Federal-Mogul Corporation.
Bowers and Merena Galleries Inc., **48** 99
Bowery and East River National Bank, **II** 226
Bowery Savings Bank, **II** 182; **9** 173
Bowes Co., **II** 631
Bowling Green Wholesale, Inc. *See* Houchens Industries Inc.
Bowman Gum, Inc., **13** 520
Bowmar Instruments, **II** 113; **11** 506
Bowne & Co., Inc., 18 331–32; **23 61–64**
Bowthorpe plc, 33 70–72
Box Innards Inc., **13** 442
Box Office Attraction Co., **II** 169
BoxCrow Cement Company, **8** 259
The Boy Scouts of America, 34 66–69
Boyd Bros. Transportation Inc., 39 64–66
Boyd Coffee Company, 53 73–75
Boyd Gaming Corporation, 43 80–82
The Boyds Collection, Ltd., 29 71–73
Boyer Brothers, Inc., **14** 17–18

Boyer's International, Inc., **20** 83
Boykin Enterprises, **IV** 136
Boyles Bros. Drilling Company. *See* Christensen Boyles Corporation.
Boys Market, **17** 558–59
Boz, **IV** 697–98
Bozel Électrométallurgie, **IV** 174
Bozell, Jacobs, Kenyon, and Eckhardt Inc. *See* True North Communications Inc.
Bozell Worldwide Inc., 25 89–91
Bozkurt, **27** 188
Bozzuto's, Inc., 13 111–12
BP. *See* British Petroleum Company PLC.
BP Amoco plc, **31** 31, 34; **40** 358
BP Canada. *See* Talisman Energy Inc.
BP p.l.c., 45 46–56 **(upd.),** 409, 412
BPB, **III** 736
BPD, **13** 356
BPI Communications, Inc., **7** 15; **19** 285; **27** 500
BR. *See* British Rail.
Braas, **III** 734, 736
Braathens ASA, 47 60–62
Brabants Dagblad BV, **III** 199, 201; **53** 362
Brabazon, **III** 555
Brach and Brock Confections, Inc., 15 63–65; **29** 47
Brad Foote Gear Works, **18** 453
Bradbury Agnew and Co., **IV** 686
Braden Manufacturing, **23** 299–301
Bradford District Bank, **II** 333
Bradford Exchange Ltd. Inc., **21** 269
Bradford Insulation Group, **III** 687
Bradford Pennine, **III** 373
Bradlees Discount Department Store Company, II 666–67; **12** 48–50; **24** 461
Bradley Lumber Company, **8** 430
Bradley Producing Corp., **IV** 459
Bradstreet Co., **IV** 604–05; **19** 133
Braegen Corp., **13** 127
Bragussa, **IV** 71
BRAINS. *See* Belgian Rapid Access to Information Network Services.
Brake Bros plc, 45 57–59
Bramalea Ltd., 9 83–85; **10** 530–31
Brambles Industries Limited, III 494–95; **24** 400; **42** 47–50
Bramco, **III** 600
Bramwell Gates, **II** 586
Bran & Lübbe, **III** 420
Brand Companies, Inc., **9** 110; **11** 436
Branded Restaurant Group, Inc., **12** 372
Brandeis & Sons, **19** 511
Brandenburgische Motorenwerke, **I** 138
Brandt Zwieback-Biskuits GmbH, **44** 40
Brandywine Asset Management, Inc., **33** 261
Brandywine Holdings Ltd., **45** 109
Brandywine Insurance Agency, Inc., **25** 540
Brandywine Iron Works and Nail Factory, **14** 323
Brandywine Valley Railroad Co., **14** 324
Braniff Airlines, **I** 97, 489, 548; **II** 445; **6** 50, 119–20; **16** 274; **17** 504; **21** 142; **22** 406; **36** 231; **50** 523
Branigar Organization, Inc., **IV** 345
Brannock Device Company, 48 68–70
Brascade Resources, **IV** 308
Brascan Ltd., **II** 456; **IV** 165, 330; **25** 281
Braspetro, **IV** 454, 501–02

Brass Craft Manufacturing Co., **III** 570; **20** 361
Brass Eagle Inc., 34 70–72
Brasseries Kronenbourg, **II** 474–75
Braswell Motor Freight, **14** 567
Braud & Faucheux. *See* Manitou BF S.A.
Brauerei Beck & Co., 9 86–87; **33** 73–76 **(upd.)**
Braun GmbH, III 29; **17** 214–15; **26** 335; **51** 55–58
Braunkohlenwerk Golpa-Jessnitz AG, **IV** 230
Brauns Fashions Corporation. *See* Christopher & Banks Corporation.
Brazcot Limitada, **53** 344
Brazilian Central Bank, **IV** 56
Brazos Gas Compressing, **7** 345
Brazos Sportswear, Inc., 23 65–67
Breakstone Bros., Inc., **II** 533
Breakthrough Software, **10** 507
Breckenridge-Remy, **18** 216
Breco Holding Company, **17** 558, 561
Bredel Exploitatie B.V., **8** 546
Bredell Paint Co., **III** 745
Bredero's Bouwbedrijf of Utrecht, **IV** 707–08, 724; **52** 218, 220–21
BREED Technologies, Inc., **22** 31
Breedband NV, **IV** 133
Brega Petroleum Marketing Co., **IV** 453, 455
Breguet Aviation, **I** 44; **24** 86
Breitenburger Cementfabrik, **III** 701
Bremer Financial Corp., 45 60–63
Bremner Biscuit Co., **II** 562; **13** 426
Brenco Inc., **16** 514
Brenda Mines Ltd., **7** 399
Brennan College Services, **12** 173
Brenntag AG, 8 68–69, 496; **23** 68–70 **(upd.), 23** 453–54
Brent Walker Ltd., **49** 450–51
Brentwood Associates Buyout Fund II LP, **44** 54
Bresler's Industries, Inc., **35** 121
Breslube Enterprises, **8** 464
Bresser Optik, **41** 264
Brewster Lines, **6** 410
Breyers Ice Cream Co. *See* Good Humor-Breyers.
BRI Bar Review Institute, Inc., **IV** 623; **12** 224
BRI International, **21** 425
Brian Mills, **V** 118
Briarpatch, Inc., **12** 109
Briazz, Inc., 53 76–79
Brickwood Breweries, **I** 294
Bricorama, **23** 231
Bricotruc, **37** 259
Bridas S.A., **24** 522
Bridel, **19** 49–50; **25** 85
Bridge Communications Inc., **34** 442–43
The Bridge Group, **55** 41
Bridge Oil Ltd., **I** 438; **50** 200
Bridge Technology, Inc., **10** 395
Bridgeman Creameries, **II** 536
Bridgeport Brass, **I** 377
Bridgeport Machines, Inc., 17 52–54
Bridgestone Corporation, V 234–35; **15** 355; **20** 262; **21** 72–75 **(upd.)**
Bridgestone Liquefied Gas, **IV** 364
Bridgestone/Firestone, **19** 454, 456
Bridgewater Properties, Inc., **51** 229
Bridgeway Plan for Health, **6** 186
Bridgford Company, **13** 382
Bridgford Foods Corporation, 27 71–73

Brier Hill, **IV** 114
Brierly Investment Limited, **19** 156; **24** 399
Briggs & Stratton Corporation, III 597; **8** 70–73; **27** 74–78 **(upd.)**
Briggs and Lundy Lumber Cos., **14** 18
Brigham's Inc., **15** 71
Bright Horizons Family Solutions, Inc., 31 71–73
Bright of America Inc., **12** 426
Bright Star Technologies, **13** 92; **15** 455; **41** 362
Brighter Vision Learning Adventures, **29** 470, 472
Brighton & Hove Bus and Coach Company, **28** 155–56
Brighton Federal Savings and Loan Assoc., **II** 420
Brightpoint, Inc., 18 74–77
Brightwork Development Inc., **25** 348
Briker, **23** 231
Brillion Iron Works Inc., **23** 306
Brimsdown Lead Co., **III** 680
Brin's Oxygen Company Limited. *See* BOC Group plc.
Brinco Ltd., **II** 211
Brink's, Inc., **IV** 180–82; **19** 319
Brinker International, Inc., 10 176–78; **18** 438; **38** 100–03 **(upd.)**
Brinson Partners Inc., **41** 198
BRIntec, **III** 434
Brinton Carpets, **III** 423
BRIO AB, 24 81–83
Brio Technology, **25** 97
Briones Alonso y Martin, **42** 19
Brisbane Gas Co., **III** 673
Brisco Engineering, **41** 412
Bristol Aeroplane, **I** 50, 197; **10** 261; **24** 85
Bristol-BTR, **I** 429
Bristol-Erickson, **13** 297
Bristol Gaming Corporation, **21** 298
Bristol Hotel Company, 23 71–73; **38** 77
Bristol-Myers Squibb Company, I 26, 30, 37, 301, 696, 700, 703; **III** 17–19, 36, 67; **IV** 272; **6** 27; **7** 255; **8** 210, 282–83; **9** 88–91 **(upd.); 10** 70; **11** 289; **12** 126–27; **16** 438; **21** 546; **25** 91, 253, 365; **32** 213; **34** 280, 282, 284; **37** 41–45 **(upd.); 50** 538; **51** 223, 225
Bristol PLC, **IV** 83
Bristol-Siddeley, Ltd., **I** 50; **24** 85
Britannia Airways, **8** 525–26
Britannia Security Group PLC, **12** 10
Britannia Soft Drinks Limited, **38** 77
Britannica Software, **7** 168
Britannica.com, **39** 140, 144
Britches of Georgetowne, **10** 215–16
BRITE. *See* Granada Group PLC.
Brite Voice Systems, Inc., 20 75–78
BriteSmile, Inc., **35** 325
British & Commonwealth Shipping Company, **10** 277
British Aerospace plc, I 42, 46, 50–53, 55, 74, 83, 132, 532; **III** 458, 507; **V** 339; **7** 9, 11, 458–59; **8** 315; **9** 499; **11** 413; **12** 191; **14** 36; **18** 125; **21** 8, 443; **24** 84–90 **(upd.); 27** 474; **48** 81, 274
British Airways plc, I 34, 83, 92–95, 109; **IV** 658; **6** 60, 78–79, 118, 132; **14** 70–74 **(upd.); 18** 80; **22** 52; **24** 86, 311, 396, 399–400; **26** 115; **27** 20–21, 466; **28** 25, 508; **31** 103; **33** 270; **34** 398; **37** 232; **38** 104–05; **39** 137–38; **43** 83–88 **(upd.); 52** 24–25

British Aluminium, Ltd., **II** 422; **IV** 15
British American Cosmetics, **I** 427
British American Financial Services, **42** 450
British American Insurance Co., **III** 350
British American Nickel, **IV** 110
British American Tobacco PLC, V 396, 401–02, 417; **9** 312; **29** 194–95; **34** 39; **49** 367, 369; **50 116–19 (upd.)**
British and Foreign Marine, **III** 350
British and Foreign Steam Navigation Company, **23** 160
British and French Bank, **II** 232–33
British and North American Royal Mail Steam Packet Company. *See* Cunard Line Ltd.
British Bank of North America, **II** 210
British Bank of the Middle East, **II** 298
British-Borneo Oil & Gas PLC, 34 73–75
British Borneo Timber Co., **III** 699
British Broadcasting Corporation Ltd., III 163; **IV** 651; **7 52–55**; **21 76–79 (upd.)**; **24** 192; **39** 198; **42** 114, 116
British Caledonian Airways, **I** 94–95; **6** 79
British Can Co., **I** 604
British Car Auctions, **14** 321
British Celanese Ltd., **I** 317
British Cellulose and Chemical Manufacturing Co., **I** 317
British Chrome, **III** 699
British Coal Corporation, IV 38–40; **50** 282
British Columbia Forest Products Ltd., **IV** 279; **19** 155
British Columbia Packers, **II** 631–32
British Columbia Resources Investment Corp., **IV** 308
British Columbia Telephone Company, IV 308; **6 309–11**
British Commonwealth Insurance, **III** 273
British Commonwealth Pacific Airways, **6** 110; **24** 398
British Continental Airlines, **I** 92
British Credit Trust, **10** 443
British Data Management, Ltd., **33** 212, 214
British Digital Broadcasting plc, **24** 192, 194
British Dyestuffs Corp., **I** 351
British Dynamite Co., **I** 351
British Electric Traction Company. *See* Rentokil Initial Plc.
British Energy Plc, 19 391; **49 65–68**. *See also* British Nuclear Fuels PLC.
British Engine, **III** 350
British European Airways, **I** 93, 466
British Executive and General Aviation, **I** 50; **24** 85
British Fuels, **III** 735
British Gas plc, II 260; **V 559–63**; **6** 478–79; **11** 97; **18** 365–67; **38** 408; **49** 120–21; **50** 178. *See also* Centrica plc.
British Gauge and Instrument Company, **13** 234
British General, **III** 234
British General Post Office, **25 99–100**
British Goodrich Tyre Co., **I** 428
British Home Stores PLC. *See* Storehouse PLC.
British Hovercraft Corp., **I** 120
British Independent Television Enterprises Ltd. *See* Granada Group PLC.

British India and Queensland Agency Co. Ltd., **III** 522
British India Steam Navigation Co., **III** 521–22
British Industrial Solvents Ltd., **IV** 70
British Industry, **III** 335
British Insulated and Helsby Cables Ltd., **III** 433–34
British Interactive Broadcasting Ltd., **20** 79
British Isles Transport Co. Ltd., **II** 564
British Land Plc, 10 6; **47** 168; **54 38–41**
British Leyland Motor Corporation, **I** 175, 186; **III** 516, 523; **13** 286–87; **14** 35–36; **47** 8
British Linen Bank, **10** 336
British Marine Air Navigation, **I** 92
British Metal Corp., **IV** 140, 164
British Midland plc, 34 398; **38 104–06**
British Motor Corporation, **III** 555; **7** 459; **13** 286
British Motor Holdings, **7** 459
British National Films Ltd., **II** 157
British National Oil Corp., **IV** 40
British Newfoundland Corporation, **6** 502
British Nuclear Fuels PLC, I 573; **6 451–54**; **13** 458; **50** 281
British Nylon Spinners (BNS), **17** 118
British Overseas Airways Corp., **I** 51, 93, 120–21; **III** 522; **6** 78–79, 100, 110, 112, 117; **14** 71; **24** 86, 397
British Oxygen Co. *See* BOC Group.
The British Petroleum Company plc, I 241, 303; **II** 449, 563; **IV** 61, 280, 363–64, **378–80**, 381–82, 412–13, 450–54, 456, 466, 472, 486, 497–99, 505, 515, 524–25, 531–32, 557; **6** 304; **7 56–59 (upd.)**, 140–41, 332–33, 516, 559; **9** 490, 519; **11** 538; **13** 449; **14** 317; **16** 394, 461–62; **19** 155, 391; **21 80–84 (upd.)**, 352; **25** 101; **26** 366, 369; **30** 86, 88; **47** 393. *See also* BP p.l.c.
British Plasterboard, **III** 734
British Portland Cement Manufacturers, **III** 669–70
British Printing and Communications Corp., **IV** 623–24, 642; **7** 312; **12** 224
British Prudential Assurance Co., **III** 335
British Rail, **III** 509; **V** 421–24; **10** 122; **27** 474
British Railways, **6** 413
British Railways Board, V 421–24
British Road Services, **6** 413
British Royal Insurance Co., Ltd., **III** 242
British Satellite Broadcasting, **10** 170
British Shoe Corporation, **V** 178
British Sky Broadcasting Group Plc, 20 79–81; **24** 192, 194
British South Africa Co., **IV** 23, 94
British South American Airways, **I** 93
British South American Corporation, **6** 95
British Steel Brickworks, **III** 501; **7** 207
British Steel plc, III 494–95; **IV** 40, **41–43**, 128; **17** 481; **19 62–65 (upd.)**, 391; **24** 302; **49** 98, 101, 104
British Sugar plc, **II** 514, 581–82; **13** 53; **41** 30, 32–33
British Tabulating Machine Company, **6** 240
British Telecommunications plc, I 83, 330; **II** 82; **V 279–82**; **6** 323; **7** 332–33; **8** 153; **9** 32; **11** 59, 185, 547; **15 66–70 (upd.)**, 131; **16** 468; **18** 155, 345; **20** 81; **21** 233; **24** 370; **25** 101–02, 301; **27** 304; **29** 44. *See also* BT Group plc.

British Thermoplastics and Rubber. *See* BTR plc.
British Timken Ltd., **8** 530
British Trimmings Ltd., **29** 133
British Twin Disc Ltd., **21** 504
British Tyre and Rubber Co., **I** 428
British United Airways, **I** 94
British Vita plc, 9 92–93; **19** 413–15; **33 77–79 (upd.)**
British World Airlines Ltd., 18 78–80
British Zaire Diamond Distributors Ltd., **IV** 67
Britoil, **IV** 380; **21** 82
Britt Airways, **I** 118
Britt Lumber Co., Inc., **8** 348
Brittains Bricks, **III** 673
Brittania Sportswear, **16** 509
Britvic Soft Drinks Limited, **38** 74, 77
BritWill Healthcare Corp., **25** 504
BRK Brands, Inc., **28** 134
BRK Electronics, **9** 414
Bro-Well, **17** 56
Broad, Inc., **11** 482
Broad River Power Company, **6** 575
Broadband Networks Inc., **36** 352
Broadbandtalentneet.com, **44** 164
Broadbase Software, Inc., **51** 181
Broadcast Music Inc., 23 74–77; **29** 22–23
Broadcast Technology Systems, Inc., **13** 398
Broadcaster Press, **36** 341
Broadcom Corporation, 34 76–79; **36** 123
Broadcom Eireann Research, **7** 510
Broadcort Capital Corp., **13** 342
Broadgate Property Holdings Limited, **54** 40
The Broadmoor Hotel, 30 82–85
BroadPark, **II** 415
BroadVision Inc., **18** 543; **38** 432
Broadway & Seymour Inc., **17** 264; **18** 112
Broadway-Hale Stores, Inc., **12** 356
Broadway Stores, Inc., **31** 193
Brobeck, Phleger & Harrison, LLP, 31 74–76
Brock Candy Company. *See* Brach and Brock Confections, Inc.
Brock Hotel Corp., **13** 472–73; **31** 94
Brock Residence Inn, **9** 426
Brockway Glass Co., **I** 524; **15** 128
Brockway Standard Holdings Corporation. *See* BWAY Corporation.
Broder Bros. Co., 38 107–09
Broderbund Software, Inc., 10 285; **13 113–16**; **25** 118; **29 74–78 (upd.)**
Les broderies Lesage, **49** 83
Broederlijke Liefdebeurs, **III** 177
Brok SA, **54** 315, 317
Broken Hill Proprietary Company Ltd., I 437–39; **II** 30; **III** 494; **IV 44–47**, 58, 61, 171, 484; **10** 170; **21** 227; **22 103–08 (upd.)**; **26** 248; **50** 199–202
The Bronfman Group, **6** 161, 163; **23** 124–25
Bronson Laboratories, Inc., **34** 460
Bronson Pharmaceuticals, **24** 257
Brooke Bond, **32** 475
Brooke Group Ltd., 15 71–73. *See also* Vector Group Ltd.
Brooke Partners L.P., **11** 275
Brookfield Athletic Shoe Company, **17** 244
Brookfield International Inc., **35** 388
Brooklyn Flint Glass Co., **III** 683

Brooklyn Trust Co., **II** 312
Brooklyn Union Gas, 6 455–57; 27 264–66
Brooks Brothers Inc., V 26–27; **13** 43; **22** **109–12; 24** 313, 316
Brooks Fashion, **29** 164
Brooks Fiber Communications, **41** 289–90
Brooks Fiber Properties, Inc., **27** 301, 307
Brooks, Harvey & Company, Inc., **II** 431; **16** 376
Brooks-Scanlon Lumber Co., **IV** 306
Brooks Shoe Manufacturing Co., **16** 546
Brooks, Shoobridge and Co., **III** 669
Brooks Sports Inc., 32 98–101
Brookshire Grocery Company, 16 63–66
Brookstone, Inc., II 560; **12** 411; **18** 81–83
Brookville Telephone Company, **6** 300
Brookwood Health Services, **III** 73
Brother Industries, Ltd., 13 478; **14** 75–76
Brother International, **23** 212
Brothers Foods, **18** 7
Brothers Gourmet Coffees, Inc., 20 82–85
Brotherton Chemicals, **29** 113
Broughton Foods Co., 17 55–57
Brown & Bigelow, **27** 193
Brown & Brown, Inc., 41 63–66
Brown & Dureau Ltd., **IV** 248–49; **19** 14
Brown & Haley, 23 78–80
Brown & Root, Inc., III 498–99, 559; **13** 117–19; **25** 190–91; **37** 244; **38** 481; **55** 192
Brown & Sharpe Manufacturing Co., 23 81–84
Brown and Williamson Tobacco **Corporation, I** 426; **14** 77–79; **15** 72; **22** 72–73; **33** 80–83 (upd.)
Brown Bibby & Gregory, **I** 605
Brown Boveri. *See* BBC Brown Boveri.
Brown Brothers Harriman & Co., 45 64–67
Brown Co., **I** 452; **IV** 289
Brown Corp., **IV** 286
Brown Cow West Corporation, **55** 360
Brown Drug, **III** 9
Brown-Forman Corporation, I 225–27; **III** 286; **10** 179–82 (upd.); **12** 313; **18** 69; **38** 110–14 (upd.)
Brown Foundation, **III** 498
Brown Group, Inc., V 351–53; **9** 192; **10** 282; **16** 198; **20** 86–89 (upd.)
Brown Institute, **45** 87
Brown Instrument Co., **II** 41
Brown Jordan Co., **12** 301
Brown Oil Tools, **III** 428
Brown Paper Mill Co., **I** 380; **13** 379
Brown Printing Company, 26 43–45
Brown-Service Insurance Company, **9** 507
Brown Shipbuilding Company. *See* Brown & Root, Inc.
Brown, Shipley & Co., Limited, **II** 425; **13** 341; **45** 65
Brown Shoe Co., **V** 351–52; **14** 294
Browne & Nolan Ltd., **IV** 294; **19** 225
Browning-Ferris Industries, Inc., V 749–53; **8** 562; **10** 33; **17** 552; **18** 10; **20** 90–93 (upd.); **23** 491; **33** 382; **46** 456; **50** 13–14
Browning Manufacturing, **II** 19
Browning Telephone Corp., **14** 258

Broyhill Furniture Industries, Inc., III 528, 530; **10** 183–85; **12** 308; **39** 170, 173–74
BRS Ltd., **6** 412–13
Bruce Foods Corporation, 39 67–69
Bruce Power LP, **49** 65, 67
Bruce's Furniture Stores, **14** 235
Bruckmann, Rosser, Sherill & Co., **27** 247; **40** 51
Bruegger's Bagel Bakery, **29** 171
Brufina, **II** 201–02
Brugman, **27** 502
Brummer Seal Company, **14** 64
Brunner Mond and Co., **I** 351
Bruno's Inc., 7 60–62; **13** 404, 406; **23** 261; **26** 46–48 (upd.)
Brunswick Corporation, III 442–44, 599; **9** 67, 119; **10** 262; **17** 453; **21** 291; **22** 113–17 (upd.), 118; **30** 303; **40** 30; **45** 175
Brunswick Pulp & Paper Co., **IV** 282, 311, 329; **9** 260; **19** 266
The Brush Electric Light Company, **11** 387; **25** 44
Brush Electrical Machines, **III** 507–09
Brush Moore Newspaper, Inc., **8** 527
Brush Wellman Inc., 14 80–82
Bryan Bros. Packing, **II** 572
Bryant Heater Co., **III** 471
Bryce & Co., **I** 547
Bryce Brothers, **12** 313
Bryce Grace & Co., **I** 547
Brylane Inc., **29** 106–07
Brymbo Steel Works, **III** 494
Bryn Mawr Stereo & Video, **30** 465
Brynwood Partners, **13** 19
BSA. *See* The Boy Scouts of America.
BSB, **IV** 653; **7** 392
BSC. *See* Birmingham Steel Corporation.
BSC (Industry) Ltd., **IV** 42
BSkyB, **IV** 653; **7** 392; **29** 369, 371; **34** 85
BSN Groupe S.A., II 474–75, 544; **22** 458; **23** 448. *See also* Groupe Danone
BSN Medical, **41** 374, 377
BSR, **II** 82
BT Group plc, 49 69–74 (upd.)
BTG, Inc., 45 68–70
BTI Services, **9** 59
BTM. *See* British Tabulating Machine Company.
BTR Dunlop Holdings, Inc., **21** 432
BTR plc, I 428–30; **III** 185, 727; **8** 397; **24** 88
BTR Siebe plc, 27 79–81. *See also* Invensys PLC.
Bublitz Case Company, **55** 151
Buca, Inc., 38 115–17
Buchanan, **I** 239–40
Buchanan Electric Steel Company, **8** 114
Buck Consultants, Inc., 32 459; **55** 71–73
Buck Knives Inc., 48 71–74
Buckaroo International. *See* Bugle Boy Industries, Inc.
Buckeye Business Products Inc., **17** 384
Buckeye Technologies, Inc., 42 51–54
Buckeye Tractor Ditcher, **21** 502
Buckeye Union Casualty Co., **III** 242
Buckhorn, Inc., **19** 277–78
Buckingham Corp., **I** 440, 468
The Buckle, Inc., 18 84–86
Buckler Broadcast Group, **IV** 597
Buckley/DeCerchio New York, **25** 180
Bucyrus Blades, Inc., **14** 81
Bucyrus-Erie Company, **7** 513

Bucyrus International, Inc., 17 58–61
Bud Bailey Construction, **43** 400
Budapest Bank, **16** 14
The Budd Company, III 568; **IV** 222; **8** 74–76; **20** 359
Buderus AG, III 692, 694–95; **37** 46–49
Budget Group, Inc., 25 92–94
Budget Rent a Car Corporation, I 537; **6** 348–49, 393; **9** 94–95; **13** 529; **22** 524; **24** 12, 409; **25** 143; **39** 370; **41** 402
Budgetel Inn. *See* Marcus Corporation.
Budweiser, **18** 70
Budweiser Japan Co., **21** 320
Buena Vista Distribution, **II** 172; **6** 174; **30** 487
Buena Vista Music Group, **44** 164
Bufete Industrial, S.A. de C.V., 34 80–82
Buffalo Forge Company, **7** 70–71
Buffalo Insurance Co., **III** 208
Buffalo Mining Co., **IV** 181
Buffalo News, **18** 60
Buffalo Paperboard, **19** 78
Buffalo-Springfield, **21** 502
Buffets, Inc., 10 186–87; **22** 465; **32** 102–04 (upd.)
Buffett Partnership, Ltd., **III** 213
Bugaboo Creek Steak House Inc., **19** 342
Bugatti Industries, **14** 321
Bugle Boy Industries, Inc., 18 87–88
Buhrmann NV, 41 67–69; **47** 90–91; **49** 440
Buick Motor Co., **I** 171; **III** 438; **8** 74; **10** 325
Builders Emporium, **13** 169; **25** 535
Builders Square, **V** 112; **9** 400; **12** 345, 385; **14** 61; **16** 210; **31** 20; **35** 11, 13; **47** 209
Building Materials Holding Corporation, 52 53–55
Building One Services Corporation. *See* Encompass Services Corporation.
Building Products of Canada Limited, **25** 232
Buitoni SpA, **II** 548; **17** 36; **50** 78
Bulgari S.p.A., 20 94–97
Bulgarian Oil Co., **IV** 454
Bulgheroni SpA, **27** 105
Bulkships, **27** 473
Bull. *See* Compagnie des Machines Bull S.A.
Bull-GE, **III** 123
Bull HN Information Systems, **III** 122–23
Bull Motors, **11** 5
Bull Run Corp., **24** 404
Bull S.A., **III** 122–23; **43** 89–91 (upd.)
Bull Tractor Company, **7** 534; **16** 178; **26** 492
Bull-Zenith, **25** 531
Bulldog Computer Products, **10** 519
Bulley & Andrews, LLC, 55 74–76
Bullock's, **III** 63; **31** 191
Bulolo Gold Dredging, **IV** 95
Bulova Corporation, I 488; **II** 101; **III** 454–55; **12** 316–17, 453; **13** 120–22; **14** 501; **21** 121–22; **36** 325; **41** 70–73 (upd.)
Bumble Bee Seafoods, Inc., **II** 491, 508, 557; **24** 114
Bumkor-Ramo Corp., **I** 539
Bunawerke Hüls GmbH., **I** 350
Bundy Corporation, 17 62–65, 480
Bunker Ramo Info Systems, **III** 118
Bunte Candy, **12** 427

Bunzl plc, IV 260–62; **12** 264; **31** 77–80 (upd.)
Buquet, **19** 49
Burbank Aircraft Supply, Inc., **14** 42–43; **37** 29, 31
Burberry Ltd., 41 74–76 (upd.); **47** 167, 169
Burberrys Ltd., V 68; **10** 122; **17** 66–68; **19** 181
Burda Holding GmbH. & Co., 20 53; **23** 85–89
Burdines, **9** 209; **31** 192
Bureau de Recherches de Pétrole, **IV** 544–46, 559–60; **7** 481–83; **21** 203–04
The Bureau of National Affairs, Inc., 23 90–93
Bureau Veritas SA, 55 77–79
Burelle S.A., 23 94–96
Burger and Aschenbrenner, **16** 486
Burger Boy Food-A-Rama, **8** 564
Burger Chef, **II** 532
Burger King Corporation, I 21, 278; **II** 556–57, **613–15**, 647; **7** 316; **8** 564; **9** 178; **10** 122; **12** 43, 553; **13** 408–09; **14** 25, 32, 212, 214, 452; **16** 95–97, 396; **17** 69–72 (upd.), 501; **18** 437; **21** 25, 362; **23** 505; **24** 140–41; **25** 228; **26** 284; **33** 240–41; **36** 517, 519
Burgess, Anderson & Tate Inc., **25** 500
Bürhle, **17** 36; **50** 78
Burhmann-Tetterode, **22** 154
Buriot International, Inc., **53** 236
Burke Scaffolding Co., **9** 512
BURLE Industries Inc., **11** 444
Burlesdon Brick Co., **III** 734
Burlington Coat Factory Warehouse Corporation, 10 188–89
Burlington Homes of New England, **14** 138
Burlington Industries, Inc., V 118, **354–55**; **8** 234; **9** 231; **12** 501; **17** **73–76** (upd.), 304–05; **19** 275
Burlington Mills Corporation, **12** 117–18
Burlington Motor Holdings, **30** 114
Burlington Northern, Inc., IV 182; **V** **425–28**; **10** 190–91; **11** 315; **12** 145, 278
Burlington Northern Santa Fe Corporation, 27 82–89 (upd.); **28** 495
Burlington Resources Inc., 10 190–92; **11** 135; **12** 144; **47** 238
Burmah Castrol PLC, IV 378, **381–84**, 440–41, 483–84, 531; **7** 56; **15** 246; **21** 80; **30** **86–91** (upd.); **45** 55
Burmeister & Wain, **III** 417–18
Burn & Co., **IV** 205
Burn Standard Co. Ltd., **IV** 484
Burnards, **II** 677
Burndy, **19** 166
Burnham and Co., **II** 407–08; **6** 599; **8** 388
Burns & Ricker, Inc., **40** 51, 53
Burns & Wilcox Ltd., **6** 290
Burns-Alton Corp., **21** 154–55
Burns Companies, **III** 569; **20** 360
Burns Fry Ltd., **II** 349
Burns International Security Services, III 440; **13** **123–25**; **42** 338. See also Securitas AB.
Burns International Services Corporation, 41 77–80 (upd.)
Burns Philp & Company Limited, **21** 496–98
Burnup & Sims, Inc., **19** 254; **26** 324
Burpee & Co. See W. Atlee Burpee & Co.
Burr & Co., **II** 424; **13** 340

Burr-Brown Corporation, 19 66–68
Burrill & Housman, **II** 424; **13** 340
Burris Industries, **14** 303; **50** 311
Burroughs Corp., **I** 142, 478; **III** 132, 148–49, 152, 165–66; **6** 233, 266, 281–83; **18** 386, 542. See also Unisys Corporation.
Burroughs Mfg. Co., **16** 321
Burroughs Wellcome & Co., **I** 713; **8** 216
Burrows, Marsh & McLennan, **III** 282
Burrups Ltd., **18** 331, 333; **47** 243
Burry, **II** 560; **12** 410
Bursley & Co., **II** 668
Burt Claster Enterprises, **III** 505
Burthy China Clays, **III** 690
Burton-Furber Co., **IV** 180
Burton Group plc, V 20–22. See also Arcadia Group plc.
Burton J. Vincent, Chesley & Co., **III** 271
Burton, Parsons and Co. Inc., **II** 547
Burton Retail, **V** 21
Burton Rubber Processing, **8** 347
Burton Snowboards Inc., 22 118–20, 460
Burtons Gold Medal Biscuits Limited, **II** 466; **13** 53
Burwell Brick, **14** 248
Bury Group, **II** 581
Busch Entertainment Corporation, **34** 36
Bush Boake Allen Inc., IV 346; **30** **92–94**; **38** 247
Bush Brothers & Company, 45 71–73
Bush Hog, **21** 20–22
Bush Industries, Inc., 20 98–100
Bush Terminal Company, **15** 138
Business Communications Group, Inc. See Caribiner International, Inc.
The Business Depot, Ltd., **10** 498; **55** 353
Business Expansion Capital Corp., **12** 42
Business Express Airlines, Inc., **28** 22
Business Information Technology, Inc., **18** 112
Business Men's Assurance Company of America, III 209; **13** 476; **14** **83–85**; **15** 30
Business Objects S.A., 25 95–97
Business Post Group plc, 46 71–73
Business Resources Corp., **23** 489, 491
Business Science Computing, **14** 36
Business Software Association, **10** 35
Business Software Technology, **10** 394
Business Wire, **25** 240
Businessland Inc., **III** 153; **6** 267; **10** 235; **13** 175–76, 277, 482
Busse Broadcasting Corporation, **7** 200; **24** 199
Büssing Automobilwerke AG, **IV** 201
Buster Brown, **V** 351–52
BUT S.A., **24** 266, 270
Butano, **IV** 528
Butler Bros., **21** 96
Butler Cox PLC, **6** 229
Butler Group, Inc., **30** 310–11
Butler Manufacturing Co., 12 51–53; **43** 130
Butler Shoes, **16** 560
Butler Shoes, **16** 560
Butterfield & Butterfield, **32** 162
Butterfield & Swire. See Swire Pacific Ltd.
Butterfield, Wasson & Co., **II** 380, 395; **10** 59; **12** 533
Butterick Co., Inc., 23 97–99
Butterley Company, **III** 501; **7** 207
Butterworth & Co. (Publishers) Ltd., **IV** 641; **7** 311; **17** 398

Buttrey Food & Drug Stores Co., 18 89–91
Butz Thermo-Electric Regulator Co., **II** 40; **12** 246; **50** 231
Butzbacher Weichenbau GmbH & Co. KG, **53** 352
Buxton, **III** 28; **23** 21
buy.com, Inc., 46 74–77
Buzzard Electrical & Plumbing Supply, **9** 399; **16** 186
BVA Investment Corp., **11** 446–47
BVD, **25** 166
BWAY Corporation, 24 91–93
BWP Distributors, **29** 86, 88
Byerly's, Inc. See Lund Food Holdings, Inc.
Byers Machines, **21** 502
Byrnes Long Island Motor Cargo, Inc., **6** 370
Byron Jackson, **III** 428, 439. See also BJ Services Company.
Byron Weston Company, **26** 105
Bytrex, Inc., **III** 643

C&A, 40 74–77 (upd.)
C&A Brenninkmeyer KG, V 23–24
C.&E. Cooper Co., **II** 14
C&E Software, **10** 507
C.&G. Cooper Company, **II** 14; **20** 162
C & G Systems, **19** 442
C & H Distributors, Inc., **27** 177
C&J Clark International Ltd., 52 56–59
C & O. See Chesapeake and Ohio Railway.
C&R Clothiers, **17** 313
C&S Bank, **10** 425–26
C&S Co., Ltd., **49** 425, 427
C&S/Sovran Corporation, **10** 425–27; **18** 518; **26** 453; **46** 52
C & S Wholesale Grocers, Inc., 55 80–83
C&W. See Cable and Wireless plc.
C-COR.net Corp., 38 118–21
C-Cube Microsystems, Inc., 37 50–54; **43** 221–22
C.A. Delaney Capital Management Ltd., **32** 437
C.A. La Electricidad de Caracas, **53** 18
C.A. Pillsbury and Co., **II** 555
C.A. Reed Co., **IV** 353; **19** 498
C.A.S. Sports Agency Inc., **22** 460, 462
C.A. Swanson & Sons. See Vlasic Foods International Inc.
C. Bechstein, **III** 657
C. Brewer, **I** 417; **24** 32
C.D. Haupt, **IV** 296; **19** 226
C.D. Kenny Co., **II** 571
C.D. Magirus AG, **III** 541
C.E. Chappell & Sons, Inc., **16** 61–62; **50** 107
C.E.T. See Club Européen du Tourisme.
C.F. Burns and Son, Inc., **21** 154
C.F. Hathaway Company, **12** 522
C.F. Martin & Co., Inc., 42 55–58; **48** 231
C.F. Mueller Co., **I** 497–98; **12** 332; **47** 234
C.F. Orvis Company. See The Orvis Company, Inc.
C. Francis, Son and Co., **III** 669
C.G. Conn, **7** 286
C.H. Boehringer Sohn, 39 70–73
C.H. Dexter & Co., **I** 320
C.H. Heist Corporation, 24 111–13
C.H. Knorr Company, **II** 497; **22** 83

C.H. Masland & Sons. *See* Masland Corporation.
C.H. Musselman Co., **7** 429
C.H. Robinson, Inc., 8 379–80; **11 43–44; 23** 357
C.H. Robinson Worldwide, Inc., 40 78–81 (upd.)
C-I-L, Inc., **III** 745; **13** 470
C. Itoh & Co., I 431–33, 492, 510; **II** 273, 292, 361, 442, 679; **IV** 269, 326, 516, 543; **7** 529; **10** 500; **17** 124; **24** 324–25; **26** 456. *See also* ITOCHU Corporation.
C.J. Devine, **II** 425
C.J. Lawrence, Morgan Grenfell Inc., **II** 429
C.J. Smith and Sons, **11** 3
C.L. Bencard, **III** 66
C. Lee Cook Co., **III** 467
C.M. Aikman & Co., **13** 168
C.M. Armstrong, Inc., **14** 17
C.M. Barnes Company, **10** 135
C.M. Life Insurance Company, **53** 213
C.M. Page, **14** 112
C-MAC Industries Inc., **48** 369
C.O. Lovette Company, **6** 370
C.O.M.B. Company, **18** 131–33
C/P Utility Services Company, **14** 138
C.P.U., Inc., **18** 111–12
C.R. Anthony Company, **24** 458
C.R. Bard Inc., IV 287; **9 96–98; 22** 360–61
C.R. Eggs, Inc., **25** 332
C. Reichenbach'sche Maschinenfabrik, **III** 561
C. Rowbotham & Sons, **III** 740
C.S. Rolls & Co., **I** 194
C.T. Bowring, **III** 280, 283; **22** 318
C-Tec Corp. *See* Commonwealth Telephone Enterprises, Inc.
C.V. Buchan & Co., **I** 567
C.V. Gebroeders Pel, **7** 429
C.V. Mosby Co., **IV** 677–78
C.W. Acquisitions, **27** 288
C.W. Costello & Associates Inc., **31** 131
C.W. Holt & Co., **III** 450
C.W. Zumbiel Company, **11** 422
C. Wuppesahl & Co. Assekuranzmakler, **25** 538
CAA. *See* Creative Artists Agency LLC.
Cabana (Holdings) Ltd., **44** 318
Cabela's Inc., 26 49–51
Cable & Wireless HKT, 30 95–98 (upd.). *See also* Hong Kong Telecomminications Ltd.
Cable and Wireless plc, IV 695; **V 283–86; 7** 332–33; **11** 547; **15** 69, 521; **17** 419; **18** 253; **25 98–102 (upd.); 26** 332; **27** 307; **49** 70, 73
Cable Communications Operations, Inc., **6** 313
Cable London, **25** 497
Cable Management Advertising Control System, **25** 497
Cable News Network, **II** 166–68; **6** 171–73; **9** 30; **12** 546
Cablec Corp., **III** 433–34
Cableform, **I** 592
Cabletron Systems, Inc., 10 193–94; 10 511; **20** 8; **24** 183; **26** 276
Cablevision Electronic Instruments, Inc., 32 105–07
Cablevision Systems Corporation, 7 63–65; 18 211; **30 99–103 (upd.)**106;

47 421. *See also* Cablevision Electronic Instruments, Inc.
Cabot, Cabot & Forbes, **22** 100
Cabot Corporation, 8 77–79; 29 79–82 (upd.)
Cabot Medical Corporation, **21** 117, 119
Cabot-Morgan Real Estate Co., **16** 159
Cabot Noble Inc., **18** 503, 507; **50** 457
Cabrera Vulcan Shoe Corp., **22** 213
Cache Incorporated, 30 104–06
CACI International Inc., 21 85–87
Cacique, **24** 237
Cadadia, **II** 641–42
Cadbury Schweppes PLC, I 25–26, 220, 288; **II 476–78,** 510, 512, 592; **III** 554; **6** 51–52; **9** 178; **15** 221; **22** 513; **25** 3, 5; **39** 383, 385; **49 75–79 (upd.); 52** 95
CADCAM Technology Inc., **22** 196
Caddell Construction Company, **12** 41
Cademartori, **23** 219
Cadence Design Systems, Inc., 6 247; **10** 118; **11 45–48,** 285, 490–91; **24** 235; **35** 346; **38** 188; **48 75–79 (upd.)**
Cadence Industries Corporation, **10** 401–02
Cadet Uniform Services Ltd., **21** 116
Cadillac Automobile Co., **I** 171; **10** 325
Cadillac Fairview Corp., **IV** 703
Cadillac Plastic, **8** 347
Cadisys Corporation, **10** 119
Cadmus Communications Corporation, 16 531; **23 100–03**
Cadoricin, **III** 47
CAE USA Inc., 8 519; **48 80–82**
Caere Corporation, 20 101–03
Caesar-Wollheim-Gruppe, **IV** 197
Caesars World, Inc., 6 199–202; 17 318
Caf'Casino, **12** 152
Café Express, **47** 443
Café Grand Mère, **II** 520
Caffarel, **27** 105
CAFO, **III** 241
Cagiva Group, 17 24; **30** 172; **39** 37
Cagle's, Inc., 20 104–07
Cahners Business Information, 43 92–95
Cahners Publishing, **IV** 667; **12** 561; **17** 398; **22** 442
CAI Corp., **12** 79
Cailler, **II** 546
Cain Chemical, **IV** 481
Cains Marcelle Potato Chips Inc., **15** 139
Cains Pickles, Inc., **51** 232
Cairo Petroleum Refining Co., **51** 113
Caisse Commericale de Bruxelles, **II** 270
Caisse de dépôt et placement du Quebec, **II** 664
Caisse des Dépôts—Développement (C3D), **6** 206; **48** 107
Caisse National de Crédit Agricole, **II** 264–66
Caisse Nationale de Crédit Agricole, **15** 38–39
Caithness Glass Limited, **38** 402
Caja General de Depositos, **II** 194
Cajun Bayou Distributors and Management, Inc., **19** 301
Cajun Electric Power Cooperative, Inc., **21** 470
CAK Universal Credit Corp., **32** 80
CAL. *See* China Airlines.
Cal Circuit Abco Inc., **13** 387
CAL Corporation, **21** 199, 201
Cal-Dive International Inc., **25** 104–05
Cal-Van Tools. *See* Chemi-Trol Chemical Co.

Cal/Ink, **13** 228
Cala, **17** 558
Calais Railroad Company, **16** 348
Calavo Growers, Inc., 47 63–66
Calcined Coke Corp., **IV** 402
Calcitherm Group, **24** 144
Calco, **I** 300–01
Calculating-Tabulating-Recording Company. *See* International Business Machines Corporation.
Calcutta & Burmah Steam Navigation Co., **III** 521
Caldbeck Macgregor & Co., **III** 523
Calder Race Course, Inc., **29** 118
Caldera Systems Inc., **38** 416, 420
Caldor Inc., 12 54–56, 508; **30** 57
Caledonian Airways. *See* British Caledonian Airways.
Caledonian Bank, **10** 337
Caledonian Paper plc, **IV** 302
Calédonickel, **IV** 107
Calgary Power Company. *See* TransAlta Utilities Corporation.
Calgene, Inc., **29** 330; **41** 155
Calgon Corporation, **6** 27; **16** 387; **34** 281
Calgon Vestal Laboratories, **37** 44
Calgon Water Management, **15** 154; **40** 176
Cali Realty. *See* Mack-Cali Realty Corporation.
California Arabian Standard Oil Co., **IV** 536, 552
California Automated Design, Inc., **11** 284
California Bank, **II** 289
California Bank & Trust, **53** 378
California Charter Inc., **24** 118
California Cheese, **24** 444
California Computer Products, Inc. *See* CalComp Inc.
California Cooler Inc., **I** 227, 244; **10** 181
California Dental Supply Co., **19** 289
California Design Studio, **31** 52
California Federal Bank, **22** 275
California First, **II** 358
California Fruit Growers Exchange. *See* Sunkist Growers, Inc.
California Ink Company, **13** 227
California Institute of Technology, **9** 367
California Insurance Co., **III** 234
California Oilfields, Ltd., **IV** 531, 540
California Pacific, **22** 172
California Perfume Co., **III** 15
California Petroleum Co., **IV** 551–52
California Pizza Kitchen Inc., 15 74–76
California Plant Protection, **9** 408
California Portland Cement Co., **III** 718; **19** 69
California Pro Sports Inc., **24** 404
California Slim, **27** 197
California Steel Industries, **IV** 125
California Telephone and Light, **II** 490
California Test Bureau, **IV** 636
California Texas Oil Co., **III** 672
California Tile, **III** 673
California-Western States Life Insurance Co., **III** 193–94
California Woodfiber Corp., **IV** 266
Caligen, **9** 92
Caligor. *See* Henry Schein Medical.
Call-Chronicle Newspapers, Inc., **IV** 678
Callaghan & Company, **8** 526
Callard and Bowser, **II** 594

Callaway Golf Company, 15 77–79; **16** 109; **19** 430, 432; **23** 267, 474; **37** 4; **45 74–77 (upd.)**; **46** 13

Callaway Wines, **I** 264

Callebaut, **II** 520–21

Callender's Cable and Construction Co. Ltd., **III** 433–34

Callon Petroleum Company, 47 67–69

Calloway's Nursery, Inc., 12 200; **51 59–61**

Calma, **II** 30; **12** 196

Calmar Co., **12** 127

CalMat Co., III 718; **19 69–72**

Calmic Ltd., **I** 715

Calor Gas Ltd., **55** 346

Calor Group, **IV** 383; **53** 166

Caloric Corp., **II** 86

Calpine Corporation, 36 102–04

Calsil Ltd., **III** 674

Calspan SRL Corporation, **54** 395

Caltex Petroleum Corporation, II 53; **III** 672; **IV** 397, 434, 440–41, 479, 484, 492, 519, 527, 536, 545–46, 552, 560, 562, 718; **7** 483; **19 73–75**; **21** 204; **25** 471; **38** 320; **41** 392–93

Calumatic Group, **25** 82

Calumet & Arizona Mining Co., **IV** 177

Calumet Electric Company, **6** 532

Calvert & Co., **I** 293

Calvert Insurance Co. *See* Gryphon Holdings, Inc.

Calvin Bullock Ltd., **I** 472

Calvin Klein, Inc., 9 203; **22 121–24**; **25** 258; **27** 329; **32** 476; **55 84–88 (upd.)**

Calyx & Corolla Inc., **37** 162–63

Camargo Foods, **12** 531

Camas. *See* Aggregate Industries plc.

CamBar. *See* Cameron & Barkley Company.

Camber Corporation, **25** 405

Cambex, **46** 164

Cambrex Corporation, 12 147–48; **16 67–69**; **44 59–62 (upd.)**

Cambria Steel Company, **IV** 35; **7** 48

Cambrian Wagon Works Ltd., **31** 369

Cambridge Applied Nutrition Toxicology and Biosciences Ltd., **10** 105

Cambridge Biotech Corp., **13** 241

Cambridge Electric Co., **14** 124, 126

Cambridge Gas Co., **14** 124

The Cambridge Instrument Company, **35** 272

Cambridge Interactive Systems Ltd., **10** 241

Cambridge SoundWorks, 36 101; Inc., **48 83–86**

Cambridge Steam Corp., **14** 124

Cambridge Technology Partners, Inc., 36 105–08

Cambridge Tool & Mfg. Co. Inc., **48** 268

Cambridge Water, **51** 389

Camco Inc., **IV** 658

Camden Wire Co., Inc., **7** 408; **31** 354–55

CAMECO, **IV** 436

Camelot Barthropp Ltd., **26** 62

Camelot Group plc, **34** 140

Camelot Music, Inc., 26 52–54

Cameron & Barkley Company, 13 79; **28 59–61**

Cameron Ashley Inc., **19** 57

Cameron-Brown Company, **10** 298

Cameron Iron Works, **II** 17

Cameron Oil Co., **IV** 365

CAMI Automotive, **III** 581

Camintonn, **9** 41–42

Camp Manufacturing Co., **IV** 345; **8** 102

Campagnia della Fede Cattolica sotto l'Invocazione di San Paolo, **50** 407

Campbell Box & Tag Co., **IV** 333

Campbell Cereal Company. *See* Malt-O-Meal Company.

Campbell, Cowperthwait & Co., **17** 498

Campbell-Ewald Co., **I** 16–17

Campbell Hausfeld. *See* Scott Fetzer Company.

Campbell Industries, Inc., **11** 534

Campbell-Mithun-Esty, Inc., 13 516; **16 70–72**

Campbell Scientific, Inc., 51 62–65

Campbell Soup Company, I 21, 26, 31, 599, 601; **II 479–81**, 508, 684; **7 66–69 (upd.)**, 340; **10** 382; **11** 172; **18** 58; **25** 516; **26 55–59 (upd.)**; **33** 32; **43** 121; **44** 295

Campbell Taggart, Inc., **I** 219; **19** 135–36, 191; **34** 36

Campeau Corporation, IV 721; **V 25–28**; **9** 209, 211, 391; **12** 36–37; **13** 43; **15** 94; **17** 560; **22** 110; **23** 60; **31** 192; **37** 13

Campo Electronics, Appliances & Computers, Inc., 16 73–75

Campo Lindo, **25** 85

Campofrio Alimentacion, S.A., **18** 247

CAMPSA. *See* Compañia Arrendataria del Monopolio de Petróleos Sociedad Anónima.

Campus Services, Inc., **12** 173

Canada & Dominion Sugar Co., **II** 581

Canada Cable & Wire Company, **9** 11

Canada Cement, **III** 704–05

Canada Cup, **IV** 290

Canada Development Corp., **IV** 252; **17** 29

Canada Dry, **I** 281

Canada, Limited, **24** 143

Canada Packers Inc., II 482–85; **41** 249

Canada Safeway Ltd., **II** 650, 654

Canada Surety Co., **26** 486

Canada Trust. *See* CT Financial Services Inc.

Canada Tungsten Mining Corp., Ltd., **IV** 18

Canada Wire & Cable Company, Ltd., **IV** 164–65; **7** 397–99

Canadair, Inc., I 58; **7** 205; **13** 358; **16 76–78**

Canadian Ad-Check Services Inc., **26** 270

Canadian Airlines International Ltd., **6** 61–62, 101; **12** 192; **23** 10; **24** 400

Canadian Bank of Commerce, **II** 244–45

Canadian British Aluminum, **IV** 11

The Canadian Broadcasting Corporation (CBC), 37 55–58

Canadian Cellucotton Products Ltd., **III** 40; **16** 302; **43** 256

Canadian Copper, **IV** 110

Canadian Copper Refiners, Ltd., **IV** 164

Canadian Dominion Steel and Coal Corp., **III** 508

Canadian Eastern Finance, **IV** 693

Canadian Fina Oil, **IV** 498

Canadian Football League, **12** 457

Canadian Forest Products, **IV** 270. *See also* Canfor Corporation.

Canadian Freightways, Ltd., **48** 113

Canadian Fuel Marketers, **IV** 566

Canadian General Electric Co., **8** 544–45

Canadian Government Merchant Marine, **6** 360–61

Canadian Gridoil Ltd., **IV** 373

Canadian Imperial Bank of Commerce, **II 244–46**; **IV** 693; **7** 26–28; **10** 8; **32** 12, 14

Canadian Industrial Alcohol Company Limited, **14** 141

Canadian International Paper Co., **IV** 286–87; **15** 228

Canadian Keyes Fibre Company, Limited of Nova Scotia, **9** 305

Canadian National Railway System, I 284; **6 359–62**; **12** 278–79; **22** 444; **23** 10

Canadian Niagara Power Company, **47** 137

Canadian Odeon Theatres, **6** 161; **23** 123

Canadian Overseas Telecommunications Corporation, **25** 100

Canadian Pacific Enterprises, **III** 611

Canadian Pacific Limited, V 429–31; **8** 544–46

Canadian Pacific Railway Limited, I 573; **II** 210, 220, 344; **III** 260; **IV** 272, 308, 437; **6** 359–60; **25** 230; **45 78–83 (upd.)**

Canadian Packing Co. Ltd., **II** 482

Canadian Petrofina, **IV** 498

Canadian Radio-Television and Telecommunications Commission, **6** 309

Canadian Steel Foundries, Ltd., **39** 31

Canadian Telephones and Supplies, **6** 310

Canadian Tire Corporation, Limited, **25** 144

Canadian Transport Co., **IV** 308

Canadian Utilities Limited, 13 130–32

Canadian Vickers, **16** 76

Canal Bank, **11** 105

Canal Electric Co., **14** 125–26

Canal Plus, III 48; **7** 392; **10 195–97**, 345, 347; **23** 476; **29** 369, 371; **31** 330; **33** 181; **34 83–86 (upd.)**

CanalSatellite, **29** 369, 371

CanAmera Foods, **7** 82

Canandaigua Brands, Inc., 34 87–91 (upd.)

Canandaigua Wine Company, Inc., 13 133–35

Cananwill, **III** 344

Canary Wharf Group Plc, 30 107–09

Candela Corporation, 48 87–89

Candie's, Inc., 31 81–84

Candle Corporation of America. *See* Blyth Industries, Inc.

Candlewood Hotel Company, Inc., 41 81–83

Candy SpA, **22** 350

Canfor Corporation, IV 321; **17** 540; **42 59–61**

Cannell Communications, **25** 418

Cannon Assurance Ltd., **III** 276

Cannon Express, Inc., 53 80–82

Cannon Mills, Co., **9** 214–16

Cannondale Corporation, 16 494; **21 88–90**; **26** 183, 412

Canon Inc., I 494; **II** 103, 292; **III 120–21**, 143, 172, 575, 583–84; **6** 238, 289; **9** 251; **10** 23; **13** 482; **15** 150; **18 92–95 (upd.)**, 186, 341–42, 383, 386–87; **24** 324; **26** 213; **33** 13; **43** 152, 283–84

Canpet Exploration Ltd., **IV** 566

Canpotex Ltd., **18** 432

Canrad-Hanovia, **27** 57

Cans Inc., **I** 607
Canstar Sports Inc., 15 396–97; **16** 79–81
Canteen Corp., **I** 127; **II** 679–80; **12** 489; **13** 321
Cantel Corp., **11** 184; **18** 32; **20** 76; **30** 388
Canterbury Park Holding Corporation, 42 62–65
Canterra Energy Ltd., **47** 180
Canton Chemical, **I** 323; **8** 147; **50** 160
Canton Railway Corp., **IV** 718; **38** 320
Cantor Fitzgerald Securities Corporation, **10** 276–78
CanWest Global Communications Corporation, 35 67–70; **39** 13
Canyon Cafes, **31** 41
Cap Gemini Ernst & Young, 37 59–61
Cap Rock Energy Corporation, 6 580; **46** 78–81
Capacity of Texas, Inc., **33** 105–06
CAPCO. *See* Central Area Power Coordination Group; Custom Academic Publishing Company.
Capco Energy, Inc., **33** 296
Capcom Co., **7** 396
Cape and Vineyard Electric Co., **14** 124–25
Cape Cod-Cricket Lane, Inc., **8** 289
Cape Cod Potato Chip Company, Inc., **41** 233
Cape Horn Methanol, **III** 512
Cape May Light and Power Company, **6** 449
Cape PLC, **22** 49
Cape Wine and Distillers, **I** 289
Capehart-Farnsworth, **I** 463; **11** 197
Capel Incorporated, 45 84–86
Capex, **6** 224
AB Capital & Investment Corporation, **6** 108; **23** 381
Capital Advisors, Inc., **22** 4
Capital Airlines, **I** 128; **III** 102; **6** 128
Capital and Counties Bank, **II** 307; **IV** 91
Capital Bank N.A., **16** 162
Capital Cities/ABC Inc., II 129–31; **III** 214; **IV** 608–09, 613, 652; **11** 331; **15** 464; **18** 60, 62–63, 329; **30** 490; **42** 31, 33–34. *See also* ABC, Inc.
Capital Concrete Pipe Company, **14** 250
Capital Controls Co., Inc. *See* Severn Trent PLC.
Capital Distributing Co., **21** 37
Capital Factors, Inc., **54** 387
Capital Financial Services, **III** 242
Capital-Gazette Communications, Inc., **12** 302
Capital Grille, **19** 342
Capital Group, **26** 187
Capital Holding Corporation, III 216–19. *See also* Providian Financial Corporation.
Capital Life Insurance Company, **11** 482–83
Capital Management Services. *See* CB Commercial Real Estate Services Group, Inc.
Capital One Financial Corporation, 18 535; **52** 60–63
Capital Radio plc, 35 71–73; **39** 199
Capital Trust Corp., **17** 498
Capitol-EMI, **I** 531–32; **11** 557
Capitol Film + TV International, **IV** 591
Capitol Films, **25** 270
Capitol Pack, Inc., **13** 350

Capitol Printing Ink Company, **13** 227–28
Capitol Publishing, **13** 560
Capitol Radio Engineering Institute, **IV** 636
Capitol Radio Engineering Institute, Inc., **51** 244
Capitol Records, **22** 192–93
Capper Pass, **IV** 191
Capseals, Ltd., **8** 476
CapStar Hotel Company, 21 91–93
Capsugel, **I** 712
Car-lac Electronic Industrial Sales Inc., **9** 420
Car-X, **10** 415
Caracas Petroleum Sociedad Anónima, **IV** 565–66
Caradco, Inc., **45** 216
Caradon plc, 18 561; **20** 108–12 (upd.). *See also* Novar plc.
Carando Foods, **7** 174–75
Carat Group, **6** 15–16
Caratti Sports, Ltd., **26** 184
Caraustar Industries, Inc., 19 76–78; **44** 63–67 (upd.)
Caravali, **13** 493–94
Caravelle Foods, **21** 500
The Carbide/Graphite Group, Inc., 40 82–84
Carbide Router Co., **III** 436
Carbis China Clay & Brick Co., **III** 690
Carbocol, **IV** 417
Carboline Co., **8** 455
CarboMedics, **11** 458–60
Carbon Research Laboratories, **9** 517
Carbone Lorraine S.A., 33 88–90
La Carbonique, **23** 217, 219
Carborundum Company, III 610; **15** 80–82
Cardàpio, **29** 444
Cardboard Containers, **IV** 249
Cardell Corporation, **54** 239
Cardem Insurance Co., **III** 767; **22** 546
Cardiac Pacemakers, Inc., **I** 646; **11** 90; **11** 458; **22** 361
Cardinal Distributors Ltd., **II** 663
Cardinal Freight Carriers, Inc., **42** 365
Cardinal Health, Inc., 18 96–98; **50** 120–23 (upd.)
Cardiotronics Systems, Inc., **21** 47
Cardo AB, 49 156; **53** 83–85
Cardon-Phonocraft Company, **18** 492
Care Advantage, Inc., **25** 383
Care Group, **22** 276
Career Education Corporation, 45 87–89
Career Horizons Inc., **49** 265
CareerCom Corp., **25** 253
CareerStaff Unlimited Inc., **25** 455
Caremark International Inc., 10 143, 198–200; **33** 185
Caremark Rx, Inc., 54 42–45 (upd.)
Carenes, SA, **12** 377
CarePlus, **6** 42
CareTel, Inc., **53** 209
CareUnit, Inc., **15** 123
CareWise, Inc., **36** 365, 367–68
Carey Canada Inc., **III** 766; **22** 546
Carey Diversified LLC. *See* W.P. Carey & Co. LLC.
Carey International, Inc., 26 60–63
Carey-McFall Corp., **V** 379; **19** 421
Carey Straw Mill, **12** 376
S.A. CARFUEL, **12** 152

Cargill, Incorporated, II 494, 517, 616–18; **11** 92; **13** 136–38 (upd.), 186, 351; **18** 378, 380; **21** 290, 500; **22** 85, 426; **25** 332; **31** 17, 20; **40** 85–90 (upd.); **41** 306
Cargill Trust Co., **13** 467
Cargo Express, **16** 198
Cargo Furniture, **31** 436
Cargolux Airlines International S.A., 47 287; **49** 80–82
CARGOSUR, **6** 96
Carhartt, Inc., 30 110–12
Cariani Sausage Co., **II** 518
Caribair, **I** 102
Caribbean Chemicals S.A., **I** 512
Caribe Co., **II** 493
Caribe Shoe Corp., **III** 529
Caribiner International, Inc., 24 94–97
Cariboo Pulp & Paper Co., **IV** 269
Caribou Coffee Company, Inc., 28 62–65
Carintusa Inc., **8** 271
CARIPLO, **III** 347
Carisam International Corp., **29** 511
Carita S.A., **III** 63; **22** 487
Caritas Foundation, **22** 411, 413
Carl Byoir & Associates, **I** 14
Carl Ed. Meyer GmbH, **48** 119
Carl I. Brown and Company, **48** 178
Carl Karcher Enterprises, Inc., **19** 435; **46** 94
Carl Marks & Co., **11** 260–61
Carl-Zeiss-Stiftung, III 445–47, 583; **33** 218; **34** 92–97 (upd.)
Carl's Jr. *See* CKE Restaurants, Inc.
Carl's Superstores, **9** 452
Carlan, **III** 614
Carless Lubricants, **IV** 451
Carleton Financial Computations Inc., **II** 317
Carlin Gold Mining Company, **7** 386–87
Carling O'Keefe Ltd., **I** 218, 229, 254, 269, 438–39; **7** 183; **12** 337; **26** 305
Carlingford, **II** 298
Carlisle Companies Incorporated, 8 80–82
Carlisle Memory Products, **14** 535
Carlo Erba S.p.A., **I** 635
Carlon, **13** 304–06
Carlova, Inc., **21** 54
Carlsberg A/S, I 247; **9** 99–101; **29** 83–85 (upd.)
Carlson Companies, Inc., 6 363–66; **22** 125–29 (upd.); **26** 147, 439–40; **27** 9, 11; **29** 200; **38** 387
Carlson Wagonlit Travel, 55 89–92
Carlton and United Breweries Ltd., I 228–29, 437–39; **7** 182–83
Carlton Cards, **39** 87
Carlton Communications plc, 15 83–85; **23** 111, 113; **24** 194; **50** 124–27 (upd.); **52** 367
Carlton Investments L.P., **22** 514
The Carlyle Group, **11** 364; **14** 43; **16** 47; **21** 97; **30** 472; **43** 60; **49** 444
CarMax, Inc., 26 410; **29** 120, 123; **55** 93–95
Carmeda AB, **10** 439
Carmichael Lynch Inc., 28 66–68
Carmike Cinemas, Inc., 14 86–88; **21** 362; **37** 62–65 (upd.)
Carmine's Prime Meats, Inc., **35** 84

Carnation Company, I 269; II 486–89, 518, 548; 7 339, 383, 429; 10 382; 12 337; 28 311

Carnaud Basse-Indre, IV 228

Carnaud MetalBox, 13 190; 20 111; 32 125–26; 49 295

Carnegie Brothers & Co., Ltd., 9 407

Carnegie Corporation of New York, 35 74–77; 45 403–05

Carnegie Foundation for the Advancement of Teaching, 12 141

Carnegie Group, 41 371–72

Carnegie Steel Co., II 330; IV 572; 7 549; 35 74; 50 500

Carnival Corporation, 27 90–92 (upd.); 36 194

Carnival Cruise Lines, Inc., 6 367–68; 21 106; 22 444–46, 470; 27 27; 52 297–98

Caro Produce and Institutional Foods, 31 359–61

Carol-Braugh-Robinson Co., II 624

Carol Moberg, Inc., 6 40

Carol's Shoe Corp., 22 213

Carolco Pictures Inc., III 48; 10 196

Carolina Biological Supply, 11 424

Carolina Coach Co., 13 397–98

Carolina Coin Caterers Corporation, 10 222

Carolina Energies, Inc., 6 576

Carolina First Corporation, 31 85–87

Carolina First National, II 336

Carolina Freight Corporation, 6 369–72

Carolina Paper Board Corporation. See Caraustar Industries, Inc.

Carolina Power & Light Company, V 564–66; 23 104–07 (upd.)

Carolina Telephone and Telegraph Company, 10 201–03

Carolinas Capital Funds Group, 29 132

Carolinas-Virginia Nuclear Power Association, 27 130

Carpenter Investment and Development Corporation, 31 279

Carpenter Paper Co., IV 282; 9 261

Carpenter Technology Corporation, 13 139–41

CarpetMAX, 25 320

Carpets International Plc., 8 270–71

CARQUEST Corporation, 26 348; 29 86–89

Carr Fowler, III 673

Carr-Gottstein Foods Co., 17 77–80

Carr-Lowrey Glass Co., 13 40

Carr-Union Line, 6 397

Carr's of Carlisle, I 604; II 594

Carrabba's Italian Grill, 12 373–75

Carre Orban International, 34 248

Carrefour SA, II 628; 8 404–05; 10 204–06; 12 153; 19 98, 309; 21 225; 23 230–32; 246–47, 364; 24 475; 27 207, 93–96 (upd.); 34 198; 37 21, 23

Carrera-Optyl Group, 54 319–20

Carrera y Carrera, 52 147, 149

Carreras, Limited, V 411–12; 19 367–69

The Carriage House Companies, Inc., 55 96–98

Carriage Services, Inc., 37 66–68

Carrier Access Corporation, 44 68–73

Carrier Corporation, I 85; III 329; 7 70–73; 13 507; 22 6; 26 4; 29 216

Carrington Laboratories, 33 282

Carrington Viyella, 44 105

Carroll County Electric Company, 6 511

Carroll Reed Ski Shops, Inc., 10 215

Carroll's Foods, Inc., 7 477; 22 368; 43 382; 46 82–85

Carrows, 27 16, 19

Carry Machine Supply, Inc., 18 513

The Carsey-Werner Company, L.L.C., 37 69–72

Carsmart.com, 47 34

Carso Global Telecom S.A. de C.V., 34 362

Carson, Inc., 31 88–90; 46 278

Carson Pirie Scott & Company, II 669; 9 142; 15 86–88; 19 324, 511–12; 41 343–44

Carson Water Company, 19 411

CART. See Championship Auto Racing Teams, Inc.

Carte Blanche, 9 335

CarTemps USA. See Republic Industries, Inc.

Carter & Co., IV 644

Carter Automotive Co., I 159

Carter, Berlind, Potoma & Weill, II 450

Carter Hawley Hale Stores, I 246; V 29–32; 8 160; 12 356; 15 88; 16 466; 17 43, 523; 18 488; 25 177

Carter Holt Harvey Ltd., IV 280; 15 229; 19 155

Carter Lumber Company, 45 90–92

Carter Oil Company, IV 171; 11 353

Carter-Wallace, Inc., 6 27; 8 83–86; 38 122–26 (upd.)

Carteret Savings Bank, III 263–64; 10 340

Carterphone, 22 17

Cartier, 27 329, 487–89

Cartier Monde, IV 93; V 411, 413; 29 90–92

Cartier Refined Sugars Ltd., II 662–63

Cartiera F.A. Marsoni, IV 587

Cartiere Ascoli Piceno, IV 586

Cartiers Superfoods, II 678

Cartillon Importers, Ltd., 6 48

Carton Titan S.A. de C.V., 37 176–77

Cartotech, Inc., 33 44

Carvel Corporation, 35 78–81

Carver Pump Co., 19 36

Carworth Inc., I 630; 11 34

Cary-Davis Tug and Barge Company. See Puget Sound Tug and Barge Company.

CASA. See Construcciones Aeronautics S.A.

Casa Bancária Almeida e Companhia. See Banco Bradesco S.A.

Casa Bonita, II 587

Casa Cuervo, S.A. de C.V., 31 91–93

Casa Ley, S.A. de C.V., 24 416

Casa Saba. See Grupo Casa Saba, S.A. de C.V.

Casablanca Records, 23 390

Casalee, Inc., 48 406

Casarotto Security, 24 510

Cascade Communications Corp., 16 468; 20 8; 24 50

Cascade Fertilizers Ltd., 25 232

Cascade Fiber, 13 99

Cascade Lumber Co., IV 255; 8 65

Cascade Natural Gas Corporation, 6 568; 9 102–04

Cascade Steel Rolling Mills, Inc., 19 380–81

CasChem, Inc. See Cambrex Corporation.

Casco Northern Bank, 14 89–91

Casden Properties, 49 26

Case Corporation. See CNH Global N.V.

Case Manufacturing Corp., I 512

Case, Pomeroy & Co., Inc., IV 76

Case Technologies, Inc., 11 504

Casein Co. of America, II 471

Casey's General Stores, Inc., 19 79–81

Cash America International, Inc., 20 113–15; 33 4

Cash Wise Foods and Liquor, 30 133

Casino, 10 205; 23 231; 26 160; 27 93–94

Casino. See Etablissements Economiques de Casino Guichard, Perrachon et Cie, S.C.A.

Casino America, Inc. See Isle of Capri Casinos, Inc., 41 218

Casino Frozen Foods, Inc., 16 453

Casino Guichard S.A., 37 23

Casino Guichard-Perrachon, 54 306–07. See also Rallye SA.

Casino S.A., 22 515

Casino USA, 16 452

Casinos International Inc., 21 300

CASIO Computer Co., Ltd., III 448–49, 455; IV 599; 10 57; 16 82–84 (upd.); 21 123; 26 18; 40 91–95 (upd.)

Caspian Pipeline Consortium, 47 75

Cassa Generale Ungherese di Risparmio, III 207

Cassa Risparmio Firenze, 50 410

Cassady Broiler Co., II 585

Cassandra Group, 42 272

Cassatt, II 424

Cassco Ice & Cold Storage, Inc., 21 534–35

CAST Inc., 18 20; 43 17

Cast-Matic Corporation, 16 475

Castex, 13 501

Castings, Inc., 29 98

Castle & Cooke, Inc., I 417; II 490–92; 9 175–76; 10 40; 20 116–19 (upd.); 24 32, 115. See also Dole Food Company, Inc.

Castle Brewery, I 287

Castle Cement, 31 400

Castle Communications plc, 17 13

Castle Harlan Investment Partners III, 36 468, 471

Castle Rock Pictures, 23 392

Castle Rubber Co., 17 371

Castle Tretheway Mines Ltd., IV 164

Castlemaine Tooheys, 10 169–70

Castleton Thermostats. See Strix Ltd.

Castorama S.A., 37 258–60. See also Groupe Castorama-Dubois Investissements.

Castro Convertibles. See Krause's Furniture, Inc.

Castrol Ltd., IV 382–83

Castrorama, 10 205; 27 95

Casual Corner Group, Inc., V 207–08; 25 121; 43 96–98; 52 229

Casual Male Retail Group, Inc., 52 64–66

Caswell-Massey Co. Ltd., 51 66–69

CAT Scale Company, 49 329–30

Catalina Lighting, Inc., 43 99–102 (upd.)

Catalina Marketing Corporation, 18 99–102

Catalogue Marketing, Inc., 17 232

Catalyst Telecom, 29 414–15

Catalytica Energy Systems, Inc., 44 74–77

Catamaran Cruisers, 29 442

Catamount Petroleum Corp., 17 121

Cataract, Inc., 34 373

CATCO. *See* Crowley All Terrain Corporation.
Catellus Development Corporation, 24 98–101; 27 88
Caterair International Corporation, **16** 396
Caterpillar Inc., I 147, 181, 186, 422; **III 450–53**, 458, 463, 545–46; **9** 310; **10** 274, 377, 381, 429; **11** 473; **12** 90; **13** 513; **15 89–93 (upd.)**, 225; **16** 180, 309–10; **18** 125; **19** 293; **21** 173, 499–501, 503; **22** 542; **34** 44, 46–47; **52** 213–14
Cathay Insurance Co., **III** 221; **14** 109
Cathay Pacific Airways Limited, I 522; **II** 298; **6** 71, **78–80**; **16** 480–81; **18** 114–15; **34 98–102 (upd.)**
Catherines Stores Corporation, 15 94–97; 38 129
Cathodic Protection Services Co., **14** 325
Catholic Digest, **49** 48
Catholic Order of Foresters, 24 102–05
CatiCentre Ltd. Co, **48** 224
Cato Corporation, 14 92–94
Cato Oil and Grease Company, **IV** 446; **22** 302
Catteau S.A., **24** 475
Cattleman's, Inc., 20 120–22
Cattybrook Brick Company, **14** 249
CATV, **10** 319
Caudill Rowlett Scott. *See* CRSS Inc.
Caudle Engraving, **12** 471
CAV, **III** 554–55
Cavalcade Holdings, Inc., **53** 146
Cavallo Pipeline Company, **11** 441
Cavedon Chemical Co., **I** 341
Cavendish International Holdings, **IV** 695
Cavendish Land, **III** 273
Cavenham Ltd., **7** 202–03; **28** 163
Caves Altovisto, **22** 344
Caves de Roquefort, **19** 51; **24** 445
Cawoods Holdings, **III** 735
Caxton Holdings, **IV** 641
CB Commercial Real Estate Services Group, Inc., 21 94–98
CB&I, **7** 76–77
CB&Q. *See* Chicago, Burlington and Quincy Railroad Company.
CB&T. *See* Synovus Financial Corp.
CBC Film Sales Co., **II** 135
CBE Technologies Inc., **39** 346
CBI Industries, Inc., 7 74–77; 22 228; **48** 323
CBM Realty Corp., **III** 643
CBN. *See* The Christian Broadcasting Network, Inc.
CBN Cable Network, **13** 279–81
CBN Satellite Services, **13** 279
CBOT. *See* Chicago Board of Trade.
CBR-HCI Construction Materials Corp., **31** 253
CBRL Group, Inc., 35 82–85 (upd.)
CBS Corporation, 28 69–73 (upd.); 30 269, 272
CBS Inc., I 29, 488; **II** 61, 89, 102–03, 129–31, **132–34**, 136, 152, 166–67; **III** 55, 188; **IV** 605, 623, 652, 675, 703; **6 157–60 (upd.)**; **11** 327; **12** 75, 561; **16** 201–02; **17** 150, 182; **19** 210, 426, 428; **21** 24; **24** 516–17; **25** 330, 418; **26** 102; **36** 326; **43** 170–71
CBS.MarketWatch.com, **49** 290
CBS Musical Instruments, **16** 201–02; **43** 170–71
CBS Radio Group, **37** 192; **48** 217

CBS Records, **II** 103, 134, 177; **6** 159; **22** 194; **23** 33; **28** 419; **40** 406
CBSI. *See* Complete Business Solutions, Inc.
CBT Corp., **II** 213–14
CBW Inc., **42** 129
CBWL-Hayden Stone, **II** 450
CC Beverage Corporation, **48** 97
CC Soft Drinks Ltd., **I** 248
cc:Mail, Inc., **25** 300
CCA. *See* Container Corporation of America; Corrections Corporation of America.
CCA Industries, Inc., 53 86–89
CCAir Inc., **11** 300
CCB Financial Corp., **33** 293
CCC Franchising Corporation. *See* Primedex Health Systems, Inc.
CCG. *See* The Clark Construction Group, Inc.
CCH Computax, **7** 93–94
CCH Inc., 7 93; **14 95–97**; **33** 461
CCI Asia-Pacific Ltd., **27** 362
CCI Electronique, **10** 113; **50** 43
CCL Industries, Ltd., **15** 129
CCM Inc. *See* The Hockey Company.
CCM Sport Maska, Inc., **15** 396
CCN Group Ltd., **45** 154
CCP Insurance, Inc., **10** 248
CCR, Inc. *See* Rica Foods, Inc.
CCS Automation Systems Inc., **I** 124
CCT. *See* Crowley Caribbean Transport.
CD Titles, Inc., **22** 409
CDC. *See* Canada Development Corporation; Control Data Corporation.
CdF-Chimie, **I** 303; **IV** 174, 198, 525
CDG Books Canada Inc., **27** 224
CDI. *See* Centre de Dechets Industriels Group.
CDI Corporation, 6 139–41; 54 46–49 (upd.)
CDMS. *See* Credit and Data Marketing Services.
CDR. *See* Consortium de Realisation.
CDR International, **13** 228
CDS Holding Corp., **22** 475
CDW Computer Centers, Inc., 16 85–87; 52 67–70 (upd.)
CDX Audio Development, Inc., **18** 208
CE Consulting, **51** 17
CE-Minerals, **IV** 109
CEAG AG, **23** 498
Ceat Ltd., **III** 434; **20** 263
CEC Entertainment, Inc., 31 94–98 (upd.)
Cecil Gee, **51** 253
Ceco Doors, **8** 544–46
Ceco Industries, Inc. *See* Robertson-Ceco Corporation.
CeCorr Inc., **47** 149
CECOS International, Inc., **V** 750
Cedar Engineering, **III** 126
Cedar Fair, L.P., 22 130–32
Cedarapids, Inc., **11** 413; **38** 374, 376; **40** 432
Cedec S.A., **14** 43
Cederroth International AB, **8** 17; **36** 25–26
CEDIS, **12** 153
Cedric Chivers, **35** 243–44
Cegedur, **IV** 174
Cegetel SA, **38** 300
CEIR, **10** 255
Celadon Group Inc., 30 113–16

Celanese Corp., I 317–19, 347; **19** 192; **54** 50, 52. *See also* Hoechst Celanese Corporation.
Celanese Mexicana, S.A. de C.V., 54 50–52
Celebrity Entertainment, Inc., **27** 43
Celebrity, Inc., 22 133–35, 472
Celeron Corporation, **20** 258, 262–63
Celestial Farms, **13** 383
Celestial Seasonings, Inc., II 534; **16 88–91; 49** 336. *See also* The Hain Celestial Group, Inc.
Celestron International, **41** 262–63
Celfor Tool Company. *See* Clark Equipment Company.
Celite Corporation, **III** 706; **7** 291; **10** 43, 45
Celite Mineracao do Nordeste Ltda, **51** 196
Cell Technology, Inc. *See* Air Methods Corporation.
Cell-Tel Monitoring, Inc., **46** 386
Cella Italian Wines, **10** 181
CellAccess Technology, Inc., **25** 162
CellLife International, **49** 280
Cellnet Data Systems, **11** 547; **22** 65
Cellonit-Gesellschaft Dreyfus & Cie., **I** 317
Cellstar Corporation, **18** 74
Cellu-Products Co., **14** 430
Cellular America, **6** 300
Cellular One, **9** 321
Cellular 2000. *See* Rural Cellular Corporation.
CellularOne. *See* Rural Cellular Corporation.
CellularVision, **13** 399
Cellulosa d'Italia, **IV** 272
Cellulose & Chemical Manufacturing Co., **I** 317
Cellulose & Specialties, **8** 434
Cellulose du Pin, **III** 677, 704; **16** 121–22; **19** 226–27
Celotex Corporation, **III** 766–67; **22** 545
Celsius Energy Company, **6** 569
Celtex **I** 388–89. *See also* Pricel.
Cement Products, **46** 196
Cementia, **III** 705
Cementos Apasco, S.A. de C.V., **51** 29
Cementos de Acapulco, S.A. de C.V., **51** 28
Cementos Portland Moctezuma, **21** 261
Cementos Veracruz, S.A. de C.V., **51** 27, 29
Cementownia Chelm, **31** 398, 400
Cemex SA de CV, 20 123–26; 51 27–28
Cemij, **IV** 132
Cemp Investments Ltd., **16** 79–80
Cemsto, **13** 545
CenCall Communications, **10** 433
Cenco, Inc., **6** 188; **10** 262–63; **25** 308; **35** 135
Cencor, **25** 432
Cendant Corporation, **53** 274–75
Cendant Corporation, **48** 234–35
Cendant Corporation, 41 363; **44 78–84 (upd.)**
Cenex Cooperative, **21** 342
Cenex Inc., **II** 536; **19** 160
Cengas, **6** 313
Centaur Communications, **43** 204, 206
Centel Corporation, 6 312–15, 593; **9** 106, 480; **10** 203; **14** 258; **16** 318; **17** 7; **50** 39
Centennial Communications Corporation, 39 74–76

Centennial Technologies Inc., **48** 369

Center Co., Ltd., **48** 182

Center of Insurance, **51** 170

Center Rental & Sales Inc., **28** 387

Centerior Energy Corporation, V 567–68

Centerra Corporation, **24** 79

Centertel, **18** 33

Centex Corporation, 8 87–89, 461; **11** 302; **23** 327; **29 93–96 (upd.)**

Centocor Inc., 14 98–100; **36** 306

CentraBank, **II** 337; **10** 426

Central Alloy Steel Corporation. *See* Republic Engineered Steels, Inc.

Central and South West Corporation, V 569–70; **21** 197–98; **45** 21

Central Area Power Coordination Group, **V** 677

Central Arizona Light & Power Company, **6** 545

Central Asia Gas Pipeline Ltd, **24** 522

Central Bancorp of Cincinnati, **II** 342

Central Bank for Railway Securities, **II** 281

Central Bank of Italy, **II** 403

Central Bank of London, **II** 318; **17** 323

Central Bank of Oman, **IV** 516

Central Bank of Scotland, **10** 337

Central Coalfields Ltd., **IV** 48–49

Central Computer Systems Inc., **11** 65

Central Covenants, **II** 222

Central Detallista, S.A. de C.V., **12** 154; **16** 453

Central Electric & Gas Company. *See* Centel Corporation.

Central Electric and Telephone Company, Inc. *See* Centel Corporation.

Central Elevator Co., **19** 111

Central Fiber Products Company, **12** 376

Central Finance Corporation of Canada, **II** 418; **21** 282

Central Florida Press, **23** 101

Central Foam Corp., **I** 481, 563; **16** 322

Central Freight Lines, Inc., **53** 249

Central Garden & Pet Company, 23 108–10

Central Hankyu Ltd., **V** 71

Central Hardware, **III** 530

Central Hudson Gas And Electricity Corporation, 6 458–60

Central Illinois Public Service Company. *See* CIPSCO Inc.

Central Independent Television, 7 78–80; **15** 84; **23 111–14 (upd.)**; **50** 125

Central India Spinning, Weaving and Manufacturing Co., **IV** 217

Central Indiana Power Company, **6** 556

Central Investment Corp., **12** 184

Central Japan Heavy Industries, **III** 578–79; **7** 348

Central Japan Railway Company, 43 103–06

Central Maine Power, 6 461–64; **14** 126

Central Maloney Transformer, **I** 434

Central Mining and Investment Corp., **IV** 23, 79, 95–96, 524, 565

Central National Bank, **9** 475

Central National Bank & Trust Co., **13** 467

Central National Life Insurance Co., **III** 463; **21** 174

Central Nebraska Packing, **10** 250

Central Newspapers, Inc., 10 207–09

Central Ohio Mobile Power Wash. *See* MPW Industrial Services, Inc.

Central Pacific Railroad, **II** 381; **13** 372

Central Park Bank of Buffalo, **11** 108

Central Parking Corporation, 18 103–05

Central Penn National Corp., **11** 295

Central Planning & Design Institute, **IV** 48

Central Point Software, **10** 509

Central Public Service Corporation, **6** 447; **23** 28

Central Public Utility Corp., **13** 397

Central Research Laboratories, **22** 194

Central Savings and Loan, **10** 339

Central Solvents & Chemicals Company, **8** 100

Central Songs, **22** 193

Central Soya Company, Inc., 7 81–83; **31** 20; **36** 185, 187

Central Sprinkler Corporation, 29 97–99

Central States Indemnity, **18** 62

Central Supply Company. *See* Granite Rock Company.

Central Telephone & Utilities Corporation. *See* Centel Corporation.

Central Terminal Company, **6** 504

Central Textile, **16** 36

Central Transformer, **I** 434

Central Trust Co., **II** 313; **11** 110

Central Union Telephone Company, **14** 251, 257

Central Union Trust Co. of New York, **II** 313

Central Vermont Public Service Corporation, 54 53–56

Central West Public Service Company. *See* Centel Corporation.

Centralab Inc., **13** 398

Centrale Verzorgingsdienst Cotrans N.V., **12** 443

Centran Corp., **9** 475

Centre de Dechets Industriels Group, **IV** 296; **19** 226

Centre Investissements et Loisirs, **48** 107

Centre Lait, **II** 577

Centre Partners Management LLC, **18** 355; **24** 482

Centrepoint Properties Ltd., **54** 116–17

Centrica plc, 29 100–05 (upd.)

Centron DPL Company, Inc., **25** 171

Centronics Corp., **16** 192

Centros Commerciales Pryca, **23** 246, 248

Centrum Communications Inc., **11** 520

CenTrust Federal Savings, **10** 340

Centura Software, **10** 244

Centuri Corporation, 54 57–59

Centurion Brick, **14** 250

Century Aluminum Company, 52 71–74

Century Bakery. *See* Dawn Food Products, Inc.

Century Bank, **II** 312

Century Brewing Company. *See* Rainier Brewing Company.

Century Business Services, Inc., 52 75–78

Century Casinos, Inc., 53 90–93

Century Cellular Network, Inc., **18** 74

Century Communications Corp., 10 210–12; **52** 9

Century Data Systems, Inc., **13** 127

Century Electric Company, **13** 273

Century Finance, **25** 432

Century Hutchinson, Ltd., **13** 429

Century Manufacturing Company, **26** 363

Century Papers, Inc., **16** 387

Century Savings Assoc. of Kansas, **II** 420

Century Supply Corporation, **39** 346

Century Telephone Enterprises, Inc., 9 105–07; **54 60–63 (upd.)**

Century Theatres, Inc., 31 99–101

Century Tool Co., **III** 569; **20** 360

Century 21 Real Estate, **I** 127; **II** 679; **III** 293; **11** 292; **12** 489; **21** 97; **25** 444; **52** 239–40

CenturyTel. *See* Century Telephone Enterprises, Inc.

CEP Industrie, **55** 79

CEPA. *See* Consolidated Electric Power Asia.

CEPAM, **21** 438

CEPCO. *See* Chugoku Electric Power Company Inc.

Cephalon, Inc., 45 93–96

CEPSA. *See* Compañia Española de Petroleos S.A.

Cera Trading Co., **III** 756

Ceramconsult AG, **51** 196

Ceramesh, **11** 361

Ceramic Art Company, **12** 312

Ceramic Supply Company, **8** 177

Ceramic Tile International, Inc., **53** 176

Cerberus Limited, **6** 490

Cereal and Fruit Products, **32** 519

Cereal Industries, **II** 466

Cereal Packaging, Ltd., **13** 294; **50** 294

Cereal Partners Worldwide, **10** 324; **13** 294; **36** 234, 237; **50** 295

Cerebos, **II** 565

Cereol, **36** 185

CERES, **55** 178

Cerestar, **36** 185, 187

Ceresucre, **36** 185

Cerex, **IV** 290

Ceridian Corporation, **10** 257; **38** 58

Cermalloy, **IV** 100

Cerner Corporation, 16 92–94

Cerro Corp., **IV** 11, 136

Cerro de Pasco Corp., **IV** 33; **40** 411

Cerro Metal Products Company, **16** 357

CertainTeed Corporation, III 621, 677–78, 762; **16** 8, 121–22; **19** 58; **35 86–89**

Certanium Alloys and Research Co., **9** 419

Certified Grocers of Florida, Inc., **15** 139

Certified Laboratories, **8** 385

Certified TV and Appliance Company, **9** 120

Certus International Corp., **10** 509

Cerulean, **51** 249, 251

Cerus, **23** 492

Cerveceria Cuahtémoc Moctezuma, **25** 281

Cerveceria Cuauhtemoc, **19** 10

Cerveceria Moctezuma, **23** 170

Cerveceria Polar, I 230–31. *See also* Empresas Polar SA.

Cessna Aircraft Company, III 512; **8 49–51, 90–93**, 313–14; **26** 117; **27 97–101 (upd.)**; **34** 431, 433; **36** 190; **44** 309

CET. *See* Compagnie Européenne de Télésecurité.

Cetelem S.A., 21 99–102

Cetus Corp., **I** 637; **III** 53; **7** 427; **10** 78, 214; **41** 201; **50** 193

CF AirFreight, **6** 390; **25** 149

CF Braun, **13** 119

CF Holding Corporation, **12** 71

CF Industries, **IV** 576

CF&I Steel Corporation, **8** 135
CFC Investment Company, **16** 104
CFM. *See* Compagnie Française du Méthane.
CFP. *See* Compagnie Française des Pétroles.
CFS Continental, Inc., **II** 675; **26** 504
CG&E. *See* Cincinnati Gas & Electric Company.
CGCT, **I** 563
CGE. *See* Alcatel Alsthom.
CGM. *See* Compagnie Générale Maritime.
CGR Management Corporation, **51** 85
CGR-MeV, **III** 635
Chace Precision Metals, Inc., **29** 460–61
Chaco Energy Corporation, **V** 724–25
Chadbourne & Parke, 36 109–12
Chadwick's of Boston, Ltd., V 197–98;
  27 348; **29 106–08**
Chalet Suisse International, Inc., **13** 362
Chalk's International Airlines, **12** 420
Challenge Corp. Ltd. *See* Fletcher Challenge Ltd.
Challenger Airlines, **22** 219
Challenger Minerals Inc., **9** 267
Challenger Series, **55** 312
The Chalone Wine Group, Ltd., 36
  113–16
Chamberlain Group, Ltd., **23** 82
Chambers Corporation, **8** 298; **17** 548–49
Chambosse Brokerage Co., **29** 33
Champ Industries, Inc., **22** 15
Champalimaud, **36** 63
Champcork–Rolhas de Champanhe SA, **48** 118
Champion Engineering Co., **III** 582
Champion Enterprises, Inc., 17 81–84;
  22 207
Champion Forge Co., **41** 366
Champion, Inc., **8** 459; **12** 457
Champion Industries, Inc., 28 74–76
Champion International Corporation,
  III 215; **IV 263–65,** 334; **12** 130; **15**
  229; **18** 62; **20 127–30 (upd.); 22** 352;
  26 444; **47** 189, 191
Champion Modular Restaurant Company, Inc. *See* Checkers Drive-Up Restaurants Inc.
Champion Products Inc., **27** 194
Champion Spark Plug Co., **II** 17; **III** 593
Champion Valley Farms, **II** 480; **26** 56
Championship Auto Racing Teams, Inc.,
  37 73–75
Champlin Petroleum Company, **10** 83
Champps Americana, **27** 480–82
Champs Sports, **14** 293, 295. *See also* Venator Group Inc.
Chance Bros., **III** 724–27
Chance Vought Aircraft Co., **I** 67–68, 84–85, 489–91
Chancellor Beacon Academies, Inc., 53
  94–97
Chancellor Media Corporation, 24
  106–10; 35 247
Chancery Law Publishing Ltd., **17** 272
Chanco Medical Industries, **III** 73
Chandeleur Homes, Inc., **17** 83
The Chandris Group, **11** 377
Chanel SA, 12 57–59; 23 241; **49 83–86**
  (upd.)
Changchun Terumo Medical Products Co. Ltd., **48** 395
Channel Master Corporation, **II** 91; **15** 134

Channel One Communications Corp., **22**
  442
Channel Tunnel Group, **13** 206
Chansam Investments, **23** 388
Chantex Inc., **18** 519
Chantiers de l'Atlantique, **9** 9
Chaparral Steel Co., 8 522–24; **13**
  142–44; 18 379; **19** 380
Chapman Printing Company. *See* Champion Industries, Inc.
Chapman Valve Manufacturing Company, **8** 135
Chappel Music, **23** 389
Charan Industries Inc., **18** 519
Charan Toy Co., Inc., **18** 519
Chargeurs International, 6 373–75, 379;
  20 79; **21 103–06 (upd.); 29** 369, 371
Charise Charles Ltd., **9** 68
Charisma Communications, **6** 323
Charles A. Eaton Co., **III** 24
Charles B. Perkins Co., **II** 667; **24** 461
Charles Barker, plc, **25** 91
Charles D. Burnes Co., Inc. *See* The Holson Burnes Group, Inc.
Charles E. Smith Residential Realty Inc., **49** 29
Charles Hobson, **6** 27
Charles Huston & Sons, **14** 323
Charles Krug Winery, **50** 387
Charles Luckman Assoc., **I** 513
Charles M. Schulz Creative Associates, **39** 95
Charles of the Ritz Group Ltd., **I** 695–97;
  III 56; **23** 237
Charles Pfizer Co., **I** 96
Charles Phillips & Co. Ltd., **II** 677
Charles R. McCormick Lumber Company, **12** 407
Charles River Laboratories
  International, Inc., 25 55; **42 66–69**
The Charles Schwab Corporation, II
  228; **8 94–96; 18** 552; **22** 52; **26 64–67**
  (upd.); 34 407; **38** 430
Charles Scribner's Sons, **7** 166
The Charles Stark Draper Laboratory,
  Inc., 35 90–92
Charlesbank Capital Partners LLC, **44** 54
Charleston Consolidated Railway, Gas and Electric Company, **6** 574
Charlestown Foundry, **III** 690
Charley Brothers, **II** 669
Charley's Eating & Drinking Saloon, **20** 54
Charlie Browns, **24** 269–70
Charlotte Russe Holding, Inc., 35 93–96
Charmin Paper Co., **III** 52; **IV** 329; **8** 433;
  26 383
Charming Shoppes, Inc., 8 97–98; 38
  127–29; 39 287, 289
Charrington & Co., **I** 223
Charrington United Breweries, **38** 76
Chart House Enterprises, Inc., II 556,
  613–14; **17** 70, 71, **85–88**
Chart Industries, Inc., 21 107–09
Charter Bank, **II** 348
Charter Club, **9** 315
Charter Communications, Inc., 33 91–94
Charter Consolidated, **IV** 23, 119–20; **16**
  293; **49** 234
Charter Corp., **III** 254; **14** 460
Charter Golf, Inc. *See* Ashworth, Inc.
Charter Medical Corporation, **31** 356
Charter National Life Insurance Company, **11** 261
Charter Oil Co., **II** 620; **12** 240

Charter Security Life Insurance Cos., **III** 293
Chartered Bank, **II** 357
Chartered Co. of British New Guinea, **III** 698
Chartered Mercantile Bank of India, London and China, **II** 298
Charterhouse Japhet, **24** 269
Charterhouse Petroleum, **IV** 499
ChartHouse International Learning
  Corporation, 49 87–89
Chartwell Associates, **III** 16; **9** 331
Chartwell Investments, **44** 54
Chartwell Land plc, **V** 106; **24** 266, 269
Chas. A. Stevens & Co., **IV** 660
Chas. H. Tompkins Co., **16** 285–86
Chase & Sanborn, **II** 544
Chase Corp., **II** 402
Chase Drier & Chemical Co., **8** 177
Chase, Harris, Forbes, **II** 402
The Chase Manhattan Corporation, I
  123, 334, 451; **II** 202, 227, **247–49,**
  256–57, 262, 286, 317, 385, 397, 402;
  III 104, 248; **IV** 33; **6** 52; **9** 124; **10** 61;
  13 145–48 (upd.), 476; **14** 48, 103; **15**
  38–39; **16** 460; **17** 498; **23** 482; **36** 358;
  46 316. *See* J.P. Morgan Chase & Co.
Chase National Bank, **25** 114
Chastain-Roberts Company, **II** 669; **18**
  504; **50** 454
Chaston Medical & Surgical Products, **13** 366
Chateau Communities, Inc., 37 76–79
Chateau Grower Winery Co., **II** 575
Chateau St. Jean, **22** 80
Chateau Souverain, **22** 80
Chateau Ste. Michelle Winery, **42** 245, 247
Chateaux St. Jacques, **24** 307
Chatfield & Woods Co., **IV** 311; **19** 267
Chatfield Paper Co., **IV** 282; **9** 261
Chatham and Phenix National Bank of New York, **II** 312
Chatham Bank, **II** 312
Chatham Technologies Inc., **38** 189
Chatillon. *See* John Chatillon & Sons Inc.
Chattanooga Gas Company, Inc., **6** 577
Chattanooga Gas Light Company, **6** 448;
  23 30
Chattanooga Medicine Company. *See* Chattem, Inc.
Chattem, Inc., 17 89–92
Chatto, Virago, Bodley Head & Jonathan Cape, Ltd., **13** 429; **31** 376
Chautauqua Airlines, Inc., 38 130–32
Chaux et Ciments de Lafarge et du Teil, **III** 703–04
Chaux et Ciments du Maroc, **III** 703
Check Express, **33** 4–5
Check Point Software Technologies Ltd., **20** 238
Checker Auto Parts. *See* CSK Auto Corporation.
Checker Holding, **10** 370
Checker Motors Corp., **10** 369
Checkers Drive-Up Restaurants Inc., 14
  452; **16 95–98; 46** 98
CheckFree Corporation, **22** 522
Checkpoint Systems, Inc., 39 77–80
The Cheesecake Factory Inc., 17 93–96
Chef-Boy-Ar-Dee Quality Foods Inc., **I** 622
Chef Boyardee, **10** 70; **50** 538
Chef Francisco, **13** 383

Chef Pierre, **II** 572
Chef's Orchard Airline Caterers Inc., **I** 513
Cheil Sugar Co., **I** 515
Cheil Wool Textile Co., **I** 515
Chelan Power Company, **6** 596
Chelsea GCA Realty, Inc., **27** 401
Chelsea Milling Company, 29 109–11
Chem-Nuclear Systems, Inc., **9** 109–10
Chemap, **III** 420
Chemcentral Corporation, 8 99–101
Chemcut, **I** 682
Chemdal Corp., **13** 34
Chemed Corporation, 13 149–50; 15
409–11; **16** 386–87; **49** 307–08
Chemetron Process Equipment, Inc., **8** 545
Chemex Pharmaceuticals, Inc., **8** 63; **27** 69
Chemfab Corporation, 35 97–101
ChemFirst, Inc., **27** 316
Chemgas Holding BV, **41** 340
Chemgrout, **26** 42
Chemi-Trol Chemical Co., 16 99–101
Chemical Banking Corporation, II 234,
250–52, 254; **9** 124, 361; **12** 15, 31; **13**
49, 147, 411; **14 101–04 (upd.); 15** 39;
21 138; **26** 453; **38** 253
Chemical Coatings Co., **I** 321
Chemical Grouting Co. Ltd., **51** 179
Chemical Process Co., **IV** 409; **7** 308
Chemical Products Company, **13** 295
Chemical Specialties Inc., **I** 512
Chemical Waste Management, Inc., V
753; **9 108–10; 11** 435–36
Chemie Linz, **16** 439
Chemins de fer de Paris à Lyon et à la
Méditerranée, **6** 424
Chemins de fer du Midi, **6** 425
Chemins de Fer Fédéraux, **V** 519
Chemisch-Pharmazeutische AG, **IV** 70
Chemische Fabrik auf Actien, **I** 681
Chemische Fabrik Friesheim Elektron AG,
IV 229
Chemische Fabrik vormals Sandoz, **I** 671
Chemische Fabrik Wesseling AG, **IV**
70–71
Chemische Werke Hüls GmbH. *See* Hüls
A.G.
Chemise Lacoste, **9** 157
ChemLawn, **13** 199; **23** 428, 431; **34** 153
Chemmar Associates, Inc., **8** 271
Chemonics Industries–Fire-Trol, **17**
161–62
Chemonics International–Consulting, **17**
161–62
Chempump, **8** 135
Chemurgic Corporation, **6** 148
Chemway Corp., **III** 423
Cheney Bigelow Wire Works, **13** 370
CHEP Pty Ltd., **42** 50
Cheplin Laboratories, **III** 17
Cherokee Inc., 18 106–09
Cherokee Insurance Co., **I** 153; **10** 265
Cherry-Burrell Process Equipment, **8**
544–45
Cherry Company Ltd., **I** 266; **21** 319
Cherry Hill Cheese, **7** 429
Cherry-Levis Co., **26** 172
Chesapeake and Ohio Railroad, **II** 329; **V**
438–40; **10** 43; **13** 372. *See also* CSX
Corporation.
Chesapeake Corporation, 8 102–04; 10
540; **25** 44; **30 117–20 (upd.)**
Chesapeake Microwave Technologies, Inc.,
32 41
Chesapeake Paperboard Company, **44** 66

Chesebrough-Pond's USA, Inc., II 590; **7**
544; **8 105–07; 9** 319; **17** 224–25; **22**
123; **32** 475
Cheshire Wholefoods, **II** 528
Chessington World of Adventures, **55** 378
Chester Engineers, **10** 412
Chester G. Luby, **I** 183
Chester Oil Co., **IV** 368
Cheung Kong (Holdings) Limited, I 470;
IV 693–95; 18 252; **20 131–34 (upd.);**
23 278, 280; **49** 199. *See also* Hutchison
Whampoa Ltd.
Chevignon, **44** 296
Chevrolet, **V** 494; **9** 17; **19** 221, 223; **21**
153; **26** 500
Chevron Corporation, II 143; **IV** 367,
385–87, 452, 464, 466, 479, 484, 490,
523, 531, 536, 539, 563, 721; **9** 391; **10**
119; **12** 20; **17** 121–22; **18** 365, 367; **19**
73, 75, **82–85 (upd.); 25** 444; **29** 385;
40 354, 357–58; **41** 391, 394–95; **49**
121. *See also* ChevronTexaco
Corporation.
Chevron U.K. Ltd., **15** 352
ChevronTexaco Corporation, 47 70–76
(upd.), 343
Chevy Chase Savings Bank, **13** 439
Chevy's, Inc., **33** 140
Chevy's Mexican Restaurants, **27** 226
ChexSystems, **22** 181
Cheyenne Software, Inc., 12 60–62; 25
348–49
CHF. *See* Chase, Harris, Forbes.
Chi-Chi's Inc., 13 151–53; 14 195; **25**
181; **51 70–73 (upd.)**
Chiasso Inc., 53 98–100
Chiat/Day Inc. Advertising, 9 438; **11**
49–52. *See also* TBWA/Chiat/Day.
Chiba Gas Co. Ltd., **55** 375
Chiba Riverment and Cement, **III** 760
Chibu Electric Power Company,
Incorporated, V 571–73
Chic by H.I.S, Inc., 20 135–37; 54 403
Chicago & Calumet Terminal Railroad, **IV**
368
Chicago and Alton Railroad, **I** 456
Chicago and North Western Holdings
Corporation, I 440; **6 376–78**
Chicago and Southern Airlines Inc., **I** 100;
6 81
Chicago Bears Football Club, Inc., IV
703 **33 95–97**
Chicago Board of Trade, 41 84–87
Chicago Bridge & Iron Company, **7** 74–77
Chicago Burlington and Quincy Railroad,
III 282; **V** 425–28
Chicago Chemical Co., **I** 373; **12** 346
Chicago Corp., **I** 526
Chicago Cubs, **IV** 682–83
Chicago Cutlery, **16** 234
Chicago Directory Co., **IV** 660–61
Chicago Edison, **IV** 169
Chicago Faucet Company, **49** 161, 163
Chicago Flexible Shaft Company, **9** 484
Chicago Heater Company, Inc., **8** 135
Chicago Magnet Wire Corp., **13** 397
Chicago Medical Equipment Co., **31** 255
Chicago Motor Club, **10** 126
Chicago Musical Instrument Company, **16**
238
Chicago Pacific Corp., **I** 530; **III** 573; **12**
251; **22** 349; **23** 244; **34** 432
Chicago Pizza & Brewery, Inc., 44
85–88

Chicago Pneumatic Tool Co., **III** 427, 452;
7 480; **21** 502; **26** 41; **28** 40
Chicago Radio Laboratory, **II** 123
Chicago Rawhide Manufacturing Company,
8 462–63
Chicago Rock Island and Peoria Railway
Co., **I** 558
Chicago Rollerskate, **15** 395
Chicago Screw Co., **12** 344
Chicago Shipbuilding Company, **18** 318
Chicago Steel Works, **IV** 113
Chicago Sun-Times Distribution Systems, **6**
14
Chicago Times, **11** 251
Chicago Title and Trust Co., **III** 276; **10**
43–45
Chicago Title Corp., **54** 107
Chicago Tribune. *See* Tribune Company.
Chick-fil-A Inc., 23 115–18
Chicken of the Sea International, 24
114–16 (upd.)
Chico's FAS, Inc., 45 97–99
Chicopee Manufacturing Corp., **III** 35
Chief Auto Parts, **II** 661; **32** 416
Chieftain Development Company, Ltd., **16**
11
Chiers-Chatillon-Neuves Maisons, **IV** 227
Chilcott Laboratories Inc., **I** 710–11
Child World Inc., **13** 166; **18** 524
Childers Products Co., **21** 108
Children's Book-of-the-Month Club, **13**
105
Children's Comprehensive Services, Inc.,
42 70–72
Children's Discovery Centers of America.
See Knowledge Learning Corporation.
Children's Hospitals and Clinics, Inc.,
54 64–67
The Children's Place Retail Stores, Inc.,
37 80–82
Children's Record Guild, **13** 105
Children's Television Workshop, **12** 495;
13 560; **35** 75
Children's World Learning Centers, **II** 608;
V 17, 19; **13** 48; **24** 75
Childtime Learning Centers, Inc., 34
103–06
Chiles Offshore Corporation, 9 111–13
Chili's Grill & Bar, **10** 331; **12** 373–74; **19**
258; **20** 159
Chillicothe Co., **IV** 310; **19** 266
Chilton Corp., **III** 440; **25** 239; **27** 361
Chilton Publications. *See* Cahners Business
Information.
Chiminter, **III** 48
Chimio, **I** 669–70; **8** 451–52
Chimney Rock Winery, **48** 392
China Airlines, 6 71; **34 107–10; 39**
33–34
China Borneo Co., **III** 698
China Canada Investment and
Development Co., **II** 457
China Coast, **10** 322, 324; **16** 156, 158
China.com Corp., **49** 422
China Communications System Company,
Inc. (Chinacom), **18** 34
China Development Corporation, **16** 4
China Eastern Airlines Co. Ltd., 31
102–04; 46 10
China Electric, **II** 67
China Foreign Transportation Corporation,
6 386
China Industries Co., **II** 325
China International Capital Corp., **16** 377

China International Trade and Investment Corporation, **II** 442; **IV** 695; **6** 80; **18** 113, 253; **19** 156; **25** 101; **34** 100. *See also* CITIC Pacific Ltd.

China Light & Power, **6** 499; **23** 278–80

China Merchants International Holdings Co., Ltd., 52 79–82

China Mutual Steam Navigation Company Ltd., **6** 416

China National Automotive Industry Import and Export Corp., **III** 581

China National Aviation Corp., **I** 96; **18** 115; **21** 140

China National Cereals, Oils & Foodstuffs Import and Export Corporation, **24** 359

China National Chemicals Import and Export Corp., **IV** 395; **31** 120

China National Heavy Duty Truck Corporation, **21** 274

China National Machinery Import and Export Corporation, **8** 279

China National Petroleum Corporation, 18 483; **46 86–89**

China Navigation Co., **I** 521; **16** 479–80

China OceanShipping Company, **50** 187

China Orient Leasing Co., **II** 442

China Resources (Shenyang) Snowflake Brewery Co., **21** 320

China Southern Airlines Company Ltd., 31 102; **33 98–100; 46** 10

China Telecom, 50 128–32

China Unicom, **47** 320–21

China Zhouyang Fishery Co. Ltd., **II** 578

Chinese Electronics Import and Export Corp., **I** 535

Chinese Metallurgical Import and Export Corp., **IV** 61

Chinese Petroleum Corporation, IV 388–90, 493, 519; **31 105–108 (upd.)**

Chinese Steel Corp., **IV** 184

The Chinet Company, **30** 397

Chino Mines Co., **IV** 179

Chinon Industries, **III** 477; **7** 163

Chipcom, **16** 392

Chippewa Shoe, **19** 232

CHIPS and Technologies, Inc., 6 217; **9 114–17**

Chiquita Brands International, Inc., II 595–96; **III** 28; **7 84–86; 21 110–13 (upd.); 38** 197

ChiRex, **38** 380

Chiro Tool Manufacturing Corp., **III** 629

Chiron Corporation, 7 427; **10 213–14; 36 117–20 (upd.); 45** 94

Chisholm Coal Company, **51** 352

Chisholm-Mingo Group, Inc., 41 88–90

Chisso Chemical, **II** 301

Chiswick Products, **II** 566

Chita Oil Co., **IV** 476

Chitaka Foods International, **24** 365

Chivers, **II** 477

Chiyoda Bank, **I** 503; **II** 321

Chiyoda Chemical, **I** 433

Chiyoda Fire and Marine, **III** 404

Chiyoda Kogaku Seiko Kabushiki Kaisha, **III** 574–75; **43** 282

Chiyoda Konpo Kogyo Co. Ltd., **V** 536

Chiyoda Mutual, **II** 374

Chloé Chimie, **I** 303

Chloride S.A., **I** 423

Choay, **I** 676–77

Chock Full o'Nuts Corp., 17 97–100; 20 83

Chocoladefabriken Lindt & Sprüngli AG, 27 102–05; 30 220

Chocolat Ibled S.A., **II** 569

Chocolat-Menier S.A., **II** 569

Chocolat Poulait, **II** 478

Chogoku Kogyo, **II** 325

Choice Hotels International Inc., 6 187, 189; **14 105–07; 25** 309–10; **26** 460

ChoiceCare Corporation, **24** 231

ChoicePoint Services, Inc., **31** 358

Chorlton Metal Co., **I** 531

Chorus Line Corporation, 25 247; **30 121–23**

Chosen Sekiyu, **IV** 554

Chotin Transportation Co., **6** 487

Chouinard Equipment. *See* Lost Arrow Inc.

Chow Tai Fook Jewellery Co., **IV** 717

Chris-Craft Industries, Inc., II 176, 403; **III** 599–600; **9 118–19; 26** 32; **31 109–112 (upd.); 46** 313

Christal Radio, **6** 33

Christensen Boyles Corporation, 19 247; **26 68–71**

Christensen Company, **8** 397

Christiaensen, **26** 160

Christian Bourgois, **IV** 614–15

The Christian Broadcasting Network, Inc., 13 279; **52 83–85**

Christian Dalloz SA, 40 96–98

Christian Dior S.A., I 272; **19 86–88; 23** 237, 242; **49 90–93 (upd.)**

Christian Salvesen Plc, 45 10, **100–03**

The Christian Science Publishing Society, 55 99–102

Christian Supply Centers, Inc., **45** 352

Christiana Bank og Kredietklasse, **40** 336

Christie, Mitchell & Mitchell, **7** 344

Christie's International plc, 15 98–101; 39 81–85 (upd.); 49 325

Christofle Orfevrerie, **44** 206

Christofle SA, 40 99–102

Christopher & Banks Corporation, 42 73–75

Christopher Charters, Inc. *See* Kitty Hawk, Inc.

Chromalloy American Corp., **13** 461; **54** 330

Chromalloy Gas Turbine Corp., **13** 462; **54** 331

Chromatic Color, **13** 227–28

Chromcraft Revington, Inc., 15 102–05; 26 100

Chromium Corporation, **52** 103–05

Chrompack, Inc., **48** 410

The Chronicle Publishing Company, Inc., 23 119–22

Chronimed Inc., **26 72–75**

Chronoservice, **27** 475

Chrysalis Group plc, 22 194; **40 103–06**

Chrysler Corporation, I 10, 17, 28, 38, 59, 79, 136, **144–45,** 152, 162–63, 172, 178, 182, 188, 190, 207, 420, 504, 516, 525, 540; **II** 5, 313, 403, 448; **III** 439, 517, 544, 568, 591, 607, 637–38; **IV** 22, 449, 676, 703; **7** 205, 233, 461; **8** 74–75, 315, 505–07; **9** 118, 349–51, 472; **10** 174, 198, 264–65, 290, 317, 353, 430; **11 53–55 (upd.),** 103–04, 429; **13** 28–29, 61, 448, 501, 555; **14** 321, 367, 457; **16** 184, 322, 484; **17** 184; **18** 173–74, 308, 493; **20** 359–60; **22** 52, 55, 175, 330; **23** 352–54; **25** 89–91, 93, 142–44, 329; **26** 403, 501; **31** 130; **36** 34, 242; **38** 480–81; **43** 163–64; **47** 436; **50** 197. *See also* DaimlerChrysler AG

Chrysler Financial Company, LLC, **45** 262

CHT Steel Company Ltd., **51** 352

CH2M Hill Ltd., 22 136–38

Chu Ito & Co., **IV** 476

Chubb Corporation, II 84; **III** 190, **220–22,** 368; **11** 481; **14 108–10 (upd.); 29** 256; **37 83–87 (upd.); 45** 109

Chubb, PLC, 50 133–36

Chubb Security plc, **44** 258

Chubu Electric Power Company, Inc., 46 90–93 (upd.)

Chuck E. Cheese, **13** 472–74; **31** 94

Chugai Boyeki Co. Ltd., **44** 441

Chugai Pharmaceutical Co., Ltd., 8 215–16; **10** 79; **50 137–40**

Chugai Shogyo Shimposha, **IV** 654–55

Chugoku Electric Power Company Inc., V 574–76; 53 101–04 (upd.)

Chunghwa Picture Tubes, **23** 469

Chuo Trust & Banking Co. *See* Yasuda Trust and Banking Company, Limited.

Chupa Chups S.A., 38 133–35

Church & Company, **45** 342, 344

Church & Dwight Co., Inc., 29 112–15

Church and Tower Group, **19** 254

Church, Goodman, and Donnelley, **IV** 660

Church's Fried Chicken, Inc., **I** 260; **7** 26–28; **15** 345; **23** 468; **32** 13–14

Churchill Downs Incorporated, 29 116–19

Churchill Insurance Co. Ltd., **III** 404

Churny Co. Inc., **II** 534

CI Holdings, Limited, **53** 120

Cianbro Corporation, 14 111–13

Cianchette Brothers, Inc. *See* Cianbro Corporation.

Ciba-Geigy Ltd., I 625, **632–34,** 671, 690, 701; **III** 55; **IV** 288; **8** 63, **108–11 (upd.),** 376–77; **9** 153, 441; **10** 53–54, 213; **15** 229; **18** 51; **21** 386; **23** 195–96; **25** 55; **27** 69; **28** 193, 195; **30** 327; **36** 36, 119; **50** 90. *See also* Novartis AG.

CIBC. *See* Canadian Imperial Bank of Commerce.

CIBC Wood Gundy Securities Corp., **24** 482

Ciber, Inc., 18 110–12

Ciby 2000, **24** 79

CICI, **11** 184

CIDLA, **IV** 504–06

Cie Continental d'Importation, **10** 249

Cie des Lampes, **9** 9

Cie Générale d'Electro-Ceramique, **9** 9

Cie.Generale des Eaux S.A., **24** 327

CIENA Corporation, 54 68–71

Cifra, S.A. de C.V., 8 556; **12 63–65; 26** 524; **34** 197–98; **35** 320. *See also* Wal-Mart de Mexico, S.A. de C.V.

Cifunsa. *See* Compania Fundidora del Norte, S.A.

Ciga Group, **54** 345, 347

Cigarrera La Moderna, **21** 260; **22** 73

Cigarros la Tabacelera Mexicana (Cigatam), **21** 259

CIGNA Corporation, III 197, **223–27,** 389; **10** 30; **11** 243; **22 139–44 (upd.),** 269; **38** 18; **45 104–10 (upd.)**

CIGWELD, **19** 442

Cii-HB, **III** 123, 678; **16** 122

Cilag-Chemie, **III** 35–36; **8** 282

Cilbarco, **II** 25

Cilva Holdings PLC, **6** 358

Cima, **14** 224–25
CIMA Precision Spring Europa, **55** 305–06
Cimaron Communications Corp., **38** 54
Cimarron Utilities Company, **6** 580
CIMCO Ltd., **21** 499–501
Cimenteries CBR S.A., **23** 325, 327
Ciments d'Obourg, **III** 701
Ciments de Chalkis Portland Artificiels, **III** 701
Ciments de Champagnole, **III** 702
Ciments de l'Adour, **III** 702
Ciments Français, 40 107–10
Ciments Lafarge France, **III** 704
Ciments Lafarge Quebec, **III** 704
Cimos, **7** 37
Cinar Corporation, 40 111–14
Cincinnati Bell, Inc., 6 316–18; **29** 250, 252
Cincinnati Chemical Works, **I** 633
Cincinnati Electronics Corp., **II** 25
Cincinnati Financial Corporation, 16 102–04; **44 89–92 (upd.)**
Cincinnati Gas & Electric Company, 6 465–68, 481–82
Cincinnati Milacron Inc., 12 66–69. See also Milacron, Inc.
Cincom Systems Inc., 15 106–08
Cine-Groupe, **35** 279
Cineamerica, **IV** 676
Cinecentrum, **IV** 591
Cinema International Corp., **II** 149
Cinemark, **21** 362; **23** 125
Cinemax, **IV** 675; **7** 222–24, 528–29; **23** 276
Cineplex Odeon Corporation, II 145, **6 161–63**; **14** 87; **23 123–26 (upd.)**; **33** 432
Cinnabon Inc., 13 435–37; **23 127–29**; **32** 12, 15
Cinquième Saison, **38** 200, 202
Cinram International, Inc., 43 107–10
Cinsa. See Compania Industrial del Norte, S.A.
Cintas Corporation, 16 228; **21 114–16**, 507; **30** 455; **51 74–77 (upd.)**
Cintel, **II** 158
Cintra. See Concesiones de Infraestructuras de Transportes, S.A.; Corporacion Internacional de Aviacion, S.A. de C.V.
Cinven, **49** 451
Cipal-Parc Astérix, **27** 10
Ciprial S.A., **27** 260
CIPSCO Inc., 6 469–72, 505–06
CIR. See Compagnie Industriali Riunite S.p.A.
Circa Pharmaceuticals, **16** 529
Circle A Ginger Ale Company, **9** 177
Circle International, Inc., **17** 216
The Circle K Company, II 619–20; **V** 210; **7** 113–14, 372, 374; **20 138–40 (upd.)**; **25** 125; **26** 447; **49** 17, 427
Circle Plastics, **9** 323
Circon Corporation, 21 117–20
Circuit City Stores, Inc., 9 65–66, **120–22**; **10** 235, 305–06, 334–35, 468–69; **12** 335; **14** 61; **15** 215; **16** 73, 75; **17** 489; **18** 533; **19** 362; **23** 51–53, 363; **24** 52, 502; **26** 410; **29 120–24 (upd.)**; **30** 464–65; **55** 93, 107
Circus Circus Enterprises, Inc., 6 201, **203–05**; **19** 377, 379
Circus Knie, **29** 126
Circus World, **16** 389–90
Cirque du Soleil Inc., 29 125–28

Cirrus Design Corporation, 44 93–95
Cirrus Logic, Inc., 9 334; **11 56–57**; **25** 117; **48 90–93 (upd.)**
CIS Mortgage Maker Ltd., **51** 89
Cisco Systems, Inc., 11 58–60, 520; **13** 482; **16** 468; **19** 310; **20** 8, 33, 69, 237; **25** 499; **26** 276–77; **34 111–15 (upd.)**, 441, 444; **36** 300; **38** 430; **43** 251
Cise, **24** 79
Cisneros Group of Companies, 47 312; **54 72–75**
CIT Alcatel, **9** 9–10
CIT Financial Corp., **II** 90, 313; **8** 117; **12** 207
CIT Group/Business Credit, Inc., **13** 446
CIT Group/Commercial Services, **13** 536
Citadel Communications Corporation, 35 102–05
Citadel General, **III** 404
Citadel, Inc., **27** 46
CitFed Bancorp, Inc., 16 105–07
CITGO Petroleum Corporation, II 660–61; **IV 391–93**, 508; **7** 491; **31 113–117 (upd.)**; **32** 414, 416–17; **45** 252, 254
Citibanc Group, Inc., **11** 456
Citibank, **II** 227, 230, 248, 250–51, 253–55, 331, 350, 358, 415; **III** 243, 340; **6** 51; **9** 124; **10** 150; **11** 418; **13** 146; **14** 101; **23** 3–4, 482; **25** 180, 542; **50** 6. See also Citigroup Inc
Citibank of Mexico, **34** 82
CITIC Pacific Ltd., 16 481; **18 113–15**; **20** 134. See also China International Trade and Investment Corporation.
Citicasters Inc., **23** 293–94
Citicorp, II 214, **253–55**, 268, 275, 319, 331, 361, 398, 411, 445; **III** 10, 220, 397; **7** 212–13; **8** 196; **9 123–26 (upd.)**, 441; **10** 463, 469; **11** 140; **12** 30, 310, 334; **13** 535; **14** 103, 108, 235; **15** 94, 146, 281; **17** 324, 559; **21** 69, 145; **22** 169, 406; **25** 198, 542
Cities Service Company, **IV** 376, 391–92, 481, 575; **12** 542; **22** 172
Citifor, **19** 156
Citigroup Inc., 30 124–28 (upd.); **42** 332; **46** 316; **54** 143
Citinet. See Hongkong Telecommunications Ltd.
Citivision PLC, **9** 75
Citizen Watch Co., Ltd., III 454–56, 549; **13** 121–22; **21 121–24 (upd.)**; **23** 212; **41** 71–82
Citizen's Electric Light & Power Company, **V** 641
Citizen's Federal Savings Bank, **10** 93
Citizen's Fidelity Corp., **II** 342
Citizen's Industrial Bank, **14** 529
Citizens and Southern Bank, **II** 337; **10** 426
Citizens Bank, **11** 105
Citizens Bank of Hamilton, **9** 475
Citizens Bank of Savannah, **10** 426
Citizens Building & Loan Association, **14** 191
Citizens Federal Savings and Loan Association, **9** 476
Citizens Financial Group, Inc., 12 422; **42 76–80**
Citizens Gas Co., **6** 529
Citizens Gas Fuel Company. See MCN Corporation.
Citizens Gas Light Co., **6** 455

Citizens Gas Supply Corporation, **6** 527
Citizens Mutual Savings Bank, **17** 529–30
Citizens National Bank, **II** 251; **13** 466; **25** 114; **41** 312
Citizens National Gas Company, **6** 527
Citizens Saving and Trust Company, **17** 356
Citizens Savings & Loan Association, **9** 173
Citizens Savings and Loan Society. See Citizens Mutual Savings Bank.
Citizens State Bank, **41** 178, 180
Citizens Telephone Company, **14** 257–58
Citizens Trust Co., **II** 312
Citizens Utilities Company, 7 87–89; **37** 124–27
Citizens' Savings and Loan, **10** 339
Citrix Systems, Inc., 44 96–99
Citroën. See Automobiles Citroen; PSA Peugeot Citroen S.A.
City and St. James, **III** 501
City and Suburban Telegraph Association and Telephonic Exchange, **6** 316–17
City and Village Automobile Insurance Co., **III** 363
City Auto Stamping Co., **I** 201
City Bank Farmers' Trust Co., **II** 254; **9** 124
City Bank of New York, **II** 250, 253
City Brewery, **I** 253
City Capital Associates, **31** 211
City Centre Properties Ltd., **IV** 705–06; **49** 248
City Finance Company, **10** 340; **11** 261
City Ice Delivery, Ltd., **II** 660
City Investing Co., **III** 263; **IV** 721; **9** 391; **13** 363
City Light and Traction Company, **6** 593
City Light and Water Company, **6** 579
City Market Inc., **12** 112
City Mutual Life Assurance Society, **III** 672–73
City National Bank of Baton Rouge, **11** 107
City National Leasing, **II** 457
City of London Real Property Co. Ltd., **IV** 706; **49** 248
City of Seattle Water Department, **12** 443
The City Post Publishing Corp., **12** 359
City Products Corp., **II** 419
City Public Service, 6 473–75
City Savings, **10** 340
City Stores Company, **16** 207
Cityhome Corp., **III** 263
Civic Drugs, **12** 21
Civic Parking LLC, **18** 105
Civil & Civic Contractors, **52** 218–19, 221
Civil & Civic Pty. Ltd., **IV** 707–08; **17** 286
Civil Aviation Administration of China, **31** 102; **33** 98
Civil Service Employees Insurance Co., **III** 214
CJ Banks. See Christopher & Banks Corporation.
CKE Restaurants, Inc., 19 89–93, 433, 435; **25** 389; **27** 19; **29** 203; **37** 349–51; **46 94–99 (upd.)**
CKS Group Inc. See marchFIRST, Inc.
CKS Inc., **23** 479
Clabir Corp., **12** 199
Claeys, **22** 379–80
Claire's Stores, Inc., 17 101–03; **18** 411
Clairol, **III** 17–18; **17** 110

Clairton Steel Co., **IV** 572; **7** 550
Clal Electronic Industries Ltd., **24** 429
Clal Group, **18** 154
CLAM Petroleum, **7** 282
Clancy Paul Inc., **13** 276
Clapp-Eastham Company. *See* GenRad, Inc.
Clara Candy, **15** 65
Clarcor Inc., 17 104–07
Claremont Technology Group Inc., **31** 131
Clares Equipment Co., **I** 252
Clariden Bank, **21** 146–47
Claridge Group, **25** 266, 268
Clarify Corp., **38** 431
Clarion Hotels and Resorts, **25** 309
Clark & Co., **IV** 301
Clark & McKenney Hardware Co. *See* Clarcor Inc.
Clark & Rockefeller, **IV** 426
Clark Bar Candy Company, **53** 304
Clark Bros. Co., **III** 471
The Clark Construction Group, Inc., 8 112–13
Clark, Dietz & Associates-Engineers. *See* CRSS Inc.
Clark Equipment Company, I 153; **7** 513–14; **8** 114–16; **10** 265; **13** 500; **15** 226; **55** 221
Clark Estates Inc., **8** 13
Clark Filter, Inc., **17** 104
Clark Materials Handling Company, **7** 514
Clark Motor Co., **I** 158; **10** 292
Clark Retail Enterprises Inc., **37** 311
Clark-Schwebel, Inc., **28** 195
Clarkins, Inc., **16** 35–36
Clarkson International Tools, **I** 531
CLASSA. *See* Compañía de Líneas Aéreas Subvencionadas S.A.
Classic FM plc, **39** 198–200
Classic Vacation Group, Inc., 46 100–03
Claudel Roustand Galac, **19** 50
Claussen Pickle Co., **12** 371
Claxson Interactive Group, **54** 74
Clayco Construction Company, **41** 225–26
Clayton Brown Holding Company, **15** 232
Clayton Dubilier & Rice Inc., **III** 25; **25** 501; **29** 408; **40** 370; **49** 22
Clayton Homes Incorporated, 13 154–55; 37 77; **54 76–79 (upd.)**
Clayton-Marcus Co., **12** 300
Clayton/National Courier Systems, Inc., **24** 126
CLE. *See* Compagnie Laitière Européenne.
Clean Window Remodelings Co., **III** 757
Cleanaway Ltd., **III** 495
Cleancoal Terminal, **7** 582, 584
Clear Channel Communications, Inc., 23 130–32, 294; **25** 418; **27** 278; **33** 322, 324; **35** 219–21, 233; **36** 422, 424; **37** 104–05
Clear Shield Inc., **17** 157, 159
Clearing Inc., **III** 514
Clearly Canadian Beverage Corporation, 48 94–97
Clearwater Tissue Mills, Inc., **8** 430
Cleary, Gottlieb, Steen & Hamilton, 35 106–09
Cleco Corporation, 37 88–91
Clef, **IV** 125
Clemente Capital Inc., **25** 542
Clements Energy, Inc., **7** 376
Cleo Inc., **12** 207–09; **35** 131
Le Clerc, **21** 225–26
Cletrac Corp., **IV** 366

Cleve-Co Jig Boring Co., **23** 82
Cleveland and Western Coal Company, **7** 369
Cleveland-Cliffs Inc., 13 156–58; 17 355
Cleveland Cotton Products Co., **37** 393
Cleveland Electric Illuminating Company. *See* Centerior Energy Theodor.
Cleveland Fabric Centers, Inc. *See* Fabri-Centers of America Inc.
Cleveland Grinding Machine Co., **23** 82
Cleveland Indians Baseball Company, Inc., 37 92–94
Cleveland Iron Mining Company. *See* Cleveland-Cliffs Inc.
Cleveland Oil Co., **I** 341
Cleveland Paper Co., **IV** 311; **19** 267
Cleveland Pneumatic Co., **I** 457; **III** 512
Cleveland Precision Instruments, Inc., **23** 82
Cleveland Twist Drill Company. *See* Acme-Cleveland Corp.
Clevepak Corporation, **8** 229; **13** 442
Clevite Corporation, **14** 207
CLF Research, **16** 202; **43** 170
Click Messenger Service, Inc., **24** 126
ClickAgents.com, Inc., **49** 433
Clif Bar Inc., 50 141–43
Clifford & Wills, **12** 280–81
Clifford Chance LLP, 38 136–39
Cliffs Corporation, **13** 157; **27** 224
Climax Molybdenum Co., **IV** 17–19
Clinchfield Coal Corp., **IV** 180–81; **19** 320
Clinical Assays, **I** 628
Clinical Partners, Inc., **26** 74
Clinical Pathology Facility, Inc., **26** 391
Clinical Science Research Ltd., **10** 106
Clinique Laboratories, Inc., **30** 191
Clinton Cards plc, 39 86–88
Clinton Pharmaceutical Co., **III** 17; **37** 41
Clipper Group, **12** 439
Clipper, Inc., **IV** 597
Clipper Manufacturing Company, **7** 3
Clipper Seafoods, **II** 587
La Cloche d'Or, **25** 85
Clopay Corp., **34** 195
The Clorox Company, III 20–22, 52; **8** 433; **22 145–48 (upd.)**, 436; **26** 383
Close Brothers Group plc, 39 89–92
The Clothestime, Inc., 20 141–44
Clouterie et Tréfilerie des Flandres, **IV** 25–26
Clover Club, **44** 348
Clover Leaf Creamery, **II** 528
Clover Milk Products Co., **II** 575
Clovis Water Co., **6** 580
Clow Water Systems Co., **55** 266
CLRP. *See* City of London Real Property Company Ltd.
CLSI Inc., **15** 372; **43** 182
Club Aurrera, **8** 556
Club Corporation of America, **26** 27
Club de Hockey Canadien Inc., **26** 305
Club Européen du Tourisme, **6** 207
Club Méditerranée S.A., I 286; **6 206–08; 21 125–28 (upd.); 27** 10
ClubCorp, Inc., 33 101–04
Clubhôtel, **6** 207
Cluett Corporation, **22** 133
Cluett, Peabody & Co., Inc., **II** 414; **8** 567–68
Cluster Consulting, **51** 98
Clyde Iron Works, **8** 545
Clydebank Engineering & Shipbuilding Co., **I** 573

Clydesdale Group, **19** 390
Clyne Maxon Agency, **I** 29
CM&M Equilease, **7** 344
CM&P. *See* Cresap, McCormick and Paget.
CM Industries, **I** 676
CM Research Inc., **51** 244
CMAC Investment Corporation. *See* Radian Group Inc.
CMB Acier, **IV** 228
CMB Packaging SA, **8** 477; **49** 295
CMC. *See* Commercial Metals Company.
CME. *See* Campbell-Mithun-Esty, Inc.
CMGI, Inc., **43** 11, 13, 420, 422
CMI International, Inc., **27** 202, 204
CMIH. *See* China Merchants International Holdings Co., Ltd.
CML Group, Inc., 10 215–18; 22 382, 536; **38** 238
CMP Media Inc., 26 76–80; 28 504
CMP Properties Inc., **15** 122
CMS Energy Corporation, IV 23; **V 577–79; 8** 466; **14 114–16 (upd.)**
CMS Healthcare, **29** 412
CMT Enterprises, Inc., **22** 249
CN. *See* Canadian National Railway System.
CNA Financial Corporation, I 488; **III 228–32**, 339; **12** 317; **36** 325, 327; **38 140–46 (upd.)**
CNA Health Plans, **III** 84
CNB Bancshares Inc., **31** 207
CNBC, Inc., **28** 298
CNC Holding Corp., **13** 166
CNCA. *See* Caisse National de Crédit Agricole.
CNEP. *See* Comptoir National d'Escompte de Paris.
CNET Networks, Inc., 47 77–80
CNF Transportation. *See* Consolidated Freightways, Inc.
CNG. *See* Consolidated Natural Gas Company.
CNH Global N.V., 38 147–56 (upd.)
CNI. *See* Community Networks Inc.
CNN. *See* Cable News Network.
CNP. *See* Compagnie Nationale à Portefeuille.
CNPC. *See* China National Petroleum Corporation.
CNS, Inc., 20 145–47
Co-Axial Systems Engineering Co., **IV** 677
Co-Counsel, Inc., **29** 364
Co. Luxemburgeoise de Banque S.A., **II** 282
Co. of London Insurers, **III** 369
Co-Op Blue Square Consumer Cooperative Society, **41** 56–58
Co-operative Group (CWS) Ltd., 51 86–89
Co-operative Insurance Society Ltd., **51** 89
Co-Steel International Ltd., **8** 523–24; **13** 142–43; **24** 144
Coach and Car Equipment Corp., **41** 369
Coach, Inc., 45 111–15 (upd.); 54 325–26
Coach Leatherware, **10** 219–21; **12** 559
Coach Specialties Co. *See* Fleetwood Enterprises, Inc.
Coach USA, Inc., 24 117–19; 30 431, 433; **55 103–06 (upd.)**
Coachmen Industries Inc., **21** 153; **39** 393
Coal India Ltd., IV 48–50; **44 100–03 (upd.)**
Coalport, **12** 528

Coast American Corporation, **13** 216
Coast Consolidators, Inc., **14** 505
Coast to Coast Hardware. *See* TruServ
  Corporation.
Coast-to-Coast Stores, **II** 419; **12** 8
Coastal Coca-Cola Bottling Co., **10** 223
Coastal Container Line Inc., **30** 318
Coastal Corporation, **IV** 366, **394–95**; **7**
  553–54; **31 118–121 (upd.)**
Coastal Lumber, S.A., **18** 514
Coastal States Corporation, **11** 481
Coastal States Life Insurance Company, **11**
  482
Coastal Valley Canning Co., **I** 260
CoastAmerica Corp., **13** 176
Coastline Distribution, Inc., **52** 399
Coates/Lorilleux, **14** 308
Coating Products, Inc., **III** 643
Coats plc, 44 104–07 (upd.)
Coats Viyella Plc, V 356–58. *See also*
  Coats plc.
CoBank. *See* National Bank for
  Cooperatives.
Cobb & Branham, **14** 257
Cobb, Inc., **II** 585; **14** 515; **50** 492
COBE Laboratories, Inc., 13 159–61; 22
  360; **49** 156
Cobham plc, 30 129–32
Coborn's, Inc., 30 133–35
Cobra Electronics Corporation, 14
  117–19
Cobra Golf Inc., 16 108–10; 23 474
Cobra Ventilation Products, **22** 229
Coburn Optical Industries, **III** 56
Coburn Vision Care, **III** 727
Coca-Cola Bottling Co. Consolidated, **II**
  170, 468; **10 222–24**; **15** 299
Coca-Cola Bottling Company of Northern
  New England, Inc., **21** 319
The Coca-Cola Company, **I** 17, **232–35**,
  244, 248, 278–79, 286, 289, 440, 457;
  II 103, 136–37, 477–78; **III** 215; **IV**
  297; **6** 20–21, 30; **7** 155, 383, 466; **8**
  399; **9** 86, 177; **10** 130, 222–23, **225–28**
  (upd.); **11** 421, 450–51; **12** 74; **13** 284;
  14 18, 453; **15** 428; **16** 480–81; **17** 207;
  18 60, 62–63, 68, 467–68; **19** 391; **21**
  337–39, 401; **23** 418–20; **24** 516; **25**
  183; **27** 21, 150; **28** 271, 473; **29** 85; **31**
  243; **32** 59, **111–16 (upd.)**; **40** 350–52;
  42 31, 34–35; **47** 289, 291; **49** 77–78
Coca-Cola Enterprises, Inc., 10 223; **13**
  162–64; **23** 455–57; **32** 115
Cochrane Corporation, **8** 135
Cochrane Foil Co., **15** 128
Cockburn & Campbell Ltd., **38** 501
Cockburn-Adelaide Cement, **31** 398, 400
Cockerill Sambre Group, **IV** 26–27,
  51–53; **22** 44; **26 81–84 (upd.)**; **42** 416
Coco's, **I** 547; **27** 16, 19
Code Hennessey & Simmons Limited, **39**
  358
Codec, **19** 328
Codelco. *See* Corporacion Nacional del
  Cobre de Chile.
Codex Corp., **II** 61
Codville Distributors Ltd., **II** 649
Coelba. *See* Companhia de Electricidade da
  Bahia.
Coeur d'Alene Mines Corporation, 20
  148–51
Coffee Club Franchise B.V., **53** 221
Coffee People, Inc., **40** 152–54
Cofica, **21** 99

COFINA, **III** 347
COFIRED, **IV** 108
Cofitel SA, **25** 466
Coflexip S.A., 25 103–05
Cofresco Frischhalteprodukte GmbH & Co.
  KG, **53** 221
Cofroma, **23** 219
Cogéma, **IV** 108
COGEMA Canada, **IV** 436
Cogeneracion Prat SA, **41** 325, 327
Cogeneration Development Corp., **42**
  387–88
Cogent Communications Group, Inc., 55
  107–10
Cogent Data Technologies, Inc., **31** 5
Cogentrix Energy, Inc., 10 229–31
Cogetex, **14** 225
Cogifer, S.A., **18** 4; **31** 156, 158
Cognex Corp., **22** 373
CogniSeis Development, Inc., **18** 513, 515
Cognitive Solutions, Inc., **18** 140
Cognos Inc., 11 78; **25** 97; **44 108–11**
Cohasset Savings Bank, **13** 468
Coherent, Inc., 31 122–25
Coherix Corporation, **48** 446
Cohn-Hall-Marx Co. *See* United Merchants
  & Manufacturers, Inc.
Cohoes Bancorp Inc., **41** 212
Cohu, Inc., 32 117–19
Coils Plus, Inc., **22** 4
Coinamatic Laundry Equipment, **II** 650
Coinmach Laundry Corporation, 20
  152–54
Coinstar, Inc., 44 112–14
Coktel Vision, **15** 455
Colas S.A., 31 126–29
Colbert Television Sales, **9** 306
Colchester Car Auctions, **II** 587
Cold Spring Granite Company, 16
  111–14
Coldwater Creek Inc., 21 129–31
Coldwell Banker, **IV** 715, 727; **V** 180,
  182; **11** 292; **12** 97; **18** 475, 478; **27** 32.
  See also CB Commercial Real Estate
  Services Group, Inc.
Cole & Weber Inc., **I** 27
Cole Haan Holdings Incorporated, **36** 346
Cole National Corporation, 13 165–67,
  391
Cole Sewell Corporation, **39** 322, 324
Cole's Craft Showcase, **13** 166
Coleco Industries, Inc., **III** 506; **18** 520; **21**
  375; **43** 229, 232
Coleman & Co., **II** 230
The Coleman Company, Inc., III 485; **9**
  127–29; **22** 207; **26** 119; **28** 135, 247;
  30 136–39 (upd.)
Coleman Outdoor Products Inc., **21** 293
Colemans Ltd., **11** 241
Coles Book Stores Ltd., **7** 486, 488–89
Coles Express Inc., 15 109–11
Coles Myer Ltd., V 33–35; **18** 286; **20**
  155–58 (upd.)
Colex Data, **14** 556
Colgate-Palmolive Company, I 260; **II**
  672; **III 23–26**; **IV** 285; **9** 291; **11** 219,
  317; **14 120–23 (upd.)**, 279; **17** 106; **25**
  365; **27** 212–13, 390; **35 110–15 (upd.)**
Colgens, **22** 193
Collabra Software Inc., **15** 322
Collectors Universe, Inc., 48 98–100
College Construction Loan Insurance
  Assoc., **II** 455; **25** 427

College Entrance Examination Board, **12**
  141
College Survival, Inc., **10** 357
Collegiate Arlington Sports Inc., **II** 652
Collett Dickinson Pearce International
  Group, **I** 33; **16** 168
Collins & Aikman Corporation, **I** 483;
  13 168–70; **25** 535; **41 91–95 (upd.)**
Collins Industries, Inc., 33 105–07
Collins Radio Co., **III** 136; **11** 429
Collins Stewart, **41** 371–72
Colo-Macco. *See* CRSS Inc.
Cologne Re. *See* General Re Corporation;
  Kölnische Rückversicherungs-
  Gesellschaft AG.
Cologne Reinsurance Co., **III** 273, 299
Colombia Graphophone Company, **22** 192
Colombo, **25** 84
Colonia Insurance Company (UK) Ltd., **III**
  273, 394; **49** 43
Colonia Versicherung Aktiengesellschaft.
  See AXA Colonia Konzern AG.
Colonial & General, **III** 359–60
Colonial Air Transport, **I** 89, 115; **12** 379
Colonial Airlines, **I** 102
Colonial Bancorp, **II** 208
Colonial Bank, **II** 236
Colonial Candle of Cape Cod, **18** 69
Colonial Companies Inc., **52** 381
Colonial Container, **8** 359
Colonial Food Stores, **7** 373
Colonial Healthcare Supply Co., **13** 90
Colonial Insurance Co., **IV** 575–76
Colonial Life Assurance Co., **III** 359
Colonial Life Insurance Co. of America,
  III 220–21; **14** 108–09
Colonial Life Insurance Company, **11** 481
Colonial National Bank, **8** 9; **38** 10–12
Colonial National Leasing, Inc., **8** 9
Colonial Packaging Corporation, **12** 150
Colonial Penn Group Insurance Co., **11**
  262; **27** 4
Colonial Penn Life Insurance Co., **V** 624;
  49 144–45
Colonial Rubber Works, **8** 347
Colonial Stores, **II** 397
Colonial Sugar Refining Co. Ltd. *See* CSR
  Limited.
Colonial Williamsburg Foundation, 53
  105–07
Colony Capital, Inc., **27** 201
Colony Communications, **7** 99
Colony Gift Corporation, Ltd., **18** 67, 69
Color-Box, Inc., **8** 103
Color Corporation of America, **8** 553
Color Me Mine, **25** 263
Color Tile, **31** 435
Colorado Belle Casino, **6** 204
Colorado Cooler Co., **I** 292
Colorado Electric Company. *See* Public
  Service Company of Colorado.
Colorado Fuel & Iron (CF&I), **14** 369
Colorado Gaming & Entertainment Co., **21**
  335
Colorado Gathering & Processing
  Corporation, **11** 27
Colorado Interstate Gas Co., **IV** 394
Colorado MEDtech, Inc., 48 101–05
Colorado National Bank, **12** 165
Colorado Technical University, Inc., **41**
  419
Colorcraft, **I** 447
Colorfoto Inc., **I** 447
Coloroll, **44** 148

Colortree. *See* National Envelope Corporation.

ColorTyme, Inc., **45** 367

Colossal Pictures, **10** 286

Colson Co., **III** 96; **IV** 135–36

Colt, **19** 430–31

Colt Industries Inc., I 434–36, 482, 524; **III** 435

Colt Pistol Factory, **9** 416

COLT Telecom Group plc, 41 96–99

Colt's Manufacturing Company, Inc., 12 70–72

Coltec Industries Inc., **30** 158; **32** 96; **46** 213; **52** 158–59

Columbia Administration Software Publishing Corporation, **51** 244

Columbia Artists Management, Inc., **52** 199–200

Columbia Brewery, **25** 281

Columbia Broadcasting System. *See* CBS Corporation.

Columbia Chemical Co. *See* PPG Industries, Inc.

Columbia Electric Street Railway, Light and Power Company, **6** 575

Columbia Forest Products, **IV** 358

Columbia Gas & Electric Company, **6** 466. *See also* Columbia Gas System, Inc.

Columbia Gas Light Company, **6** 574

Columbia Gas of New York, Inc., **6** 536

The Columbia Gas System, Inc., V 580–82; 16 115–18 (upd.)

Columbia Gas Transmission Corporation, **6** 467

Columbia General Life Insurance Company of Indiana, **11** 378

Columbia Hat Company, **19** 94

Columbia House, **IV** 676

Columbia Insurance Co., **III** 214

Columbia News Service, **II** 132

Columbia Paper Co., **IV** 311; **19** 266

Columbia Pictures Entertainment, Inc., II 103, 134, **135–37**, 170, 234, 619; **IV** 675; **10** 227; **12** 73, 455; **21** 360; **22** 193; **25** 139; **28** 71. *See also* Columbia TriStar Motion Pictures Companies.

Columbia Railroad, Gas and Electric Company, **6** 575

Columbia Records, **II** 132; **16** 201; **26** 150

Columbia Records Distribution Corp., **43** 170

Columbia River Packers, **II** 491

Columbia Savings & Loan, **II** 144

Columbia Sportswear Company, 19 94–96; 41 100–03 (upd.)

Columbia Steamship Company, **17** 356

Columbia Steel Co., **IV** 28, 573; **7** 550

Columbia Transportation Co., **17** 357

Columbia TriStar Motion Pictures Companies, 12 73–76 (upd.); 28 71

Columbia TriStar Television Distribution, **17** 149

Columbia/HCA Healthcare Corporation, 13 90; **15 112–14; 22** 409–10; **27** 356

Columbian Carbon Company, **25** 70–71

Columbian Chemicals Co., **IV** 179; **28** 352, 356

Columbian Peanut Co., **I** 421; **11** 23

Columbus & Southern Ohio Electric Company (CSO), **6** 467, 481–82

Columbus Bank & Trust. *See* Synovus Financial Corp.

Columbus McKinnon Corporation, 37 95–98

Columbus-Milpar, **I** 544

Columbus Realty Trust, **26** 378

Columbus Savings and Loan Society, **I** 536; **13** 528

Colwell Systems, **19** 291; **22** 181

Com Dev, Inc., **32** 435

Com Ed. *See* Commonwealth Edison.

Com-Link 21, Inc., **8** 310

Comair Holdings Inc., 13 171–73; 31 420; **34 116–20 (upd.)**

Comalco Fabricators (Hong Kong) Ltd., **III** 758

Comalco Ltd., **IV** 59–61, 122, 191

Comark, **24** 316; **25** 417–18

Comat Services Pte. Ltd., **10** 514

Comau, **I** 163

Combibloc Inc., **16** 339

Combined American Insurance Co. of Dallas, **III** 203

Combined Casualty Co. of Philadelphia, **III** 203

Combined Communications Corp., **II** 619; **IV** 612; **7** 191

Combined Insurance Company of America, **III** 203–04; **45** 25–26

Combined International Corp., **III** 203–04

Combined Mutual Casualty Co. of Chicago, **III** 203

Combined Properties, Inc., **16** 160

Combined Registry Co., **III** 203

Combustion Engineering Group, **22** 11; **25** 534

Combustiveis Industriais e Domésticos. *See* CIDLA.

Comcast Corporation, 7 90–92; 9 428; **10** 432–33; **17** 148; **22** 162; **24 120–24 (upd.); 27** 342, 344; **49** 175

ComCore Semiconductor, Inc., **26** 330

Comdata, **19** 160

Comdial Corporation, 21 132–35

Comdisco, Inc., 9 130–32; 11 47, 86, 484, 490

Comdor Flugdienst GmbH., **I** 111

Comer Motor Express, **6** 370

Comerci. *See* Controladora Comercial Mexicana, S.A. de C.V.

Comercial Mexicana, S.A. *See* Controladora Comercial Mexicana, S.A. de C.V.

Comerco, **III** 21; **22** 147

Comerica Incorporated, 40 115–17

Comet, **II** 139; **V** 106–09; **24** 194, 266, 269–70

Comet American Marketing, **33** 31

Comet Rice, Inc., **33** 31

Cometra Oil, **IV** 576

ComFed Bancorp, **11** 29

COMFORCE Corporation, 40 118–20

Comfort Inns, **21** 362

Comforto GmbH, **8** 252; **39** 206

Cominco Ltd., 37 99–102 55

Comision Federal de Electricidad de Mexico (CFE), **21** 196–97

Comitato Interministriale per la Ricostruzione, **I** 465

Comm-Quip, **6** 313

CommAir. *See* American Building Maintenance Industries, Inc.

Commander Foods, **8** 409

Commander-Larabee Co., **I** 419; **25** 242

Commemorative Brands Inc., **19** 453

Commentry, **III** 676; **16** 120

Commerce and Industry Insurance Co., **III** 196, 203

Commerce Clearing House, Inc., 7 93–94. *See also* CCH Inc.

Commerce Group, **III** 393

Commerce.TV, **42** 323

Commerce Union, **10** 426

The CommerceBank of Washington, **53** 378

Commercial & General Life Assurance Co., **III** 371

Commercial Air Conditioning of Northern California, **25** 15

Commercial Air Lines, Inc., **23** 380

Commercial Alliance Corp. of New York, **II** 289

Commercial Aseguradora Suizo Americana, S.A., **III** 243

Commercial Assurance, **III** 359

Commercial Bank of Australia Ltd., **II** 189, 319, 388–89; **17** 324; **48** 425

Commercial Bank of London, **II** 334

Commercial Bank of Tasmania, **II** 188

Commercial Banking Co. of Sydney, **II** 187–89

Commercial Bureau (Australia) Pty., **I** 438

Commercial Chemical Company, **16** 99

Commercial Credit Company, III 127–28; **8 117–19; 10** 255–56; **15** 464

Commercial Exchange Bank, **II** 254; **9** 124

Commercial Federal Corporation, 12 77–79

Commercial Filters Corp., **I** 512

Commercial Financial Services, Inc., 26 85–89

Commercial Insurance Co. of Newark, **III** 242

Commercial Life, **III** 243

Commercial Life Assurance Co. of Canada, **III** 309

Commercial Metals Company, 15 115–17; 42 81–84 (upd.)

Commercial Motor Freight, Inc., **14** 42

Commercial National Bank, **II** 261; **10** 425

Commercial National Bank & Trust Co., **II** 230

Commercial National Bank of Charlotte, **II** 336

Commercial Realty Services Group, **21** 257

Commercial Ship Repair Co., **I** 185

Commercial Union plc, II 272, 308; **III** 185, **233–35**, 350, 373; **IV** 711

Commerzbank A.G., II 239, 242, **256–58**, 280, 282, 385; **IV** 222; **9** 283; **14** 170; **47 81–84 (upd.); 51** 19, 23

Commerzfilm, **IV** 591

CommLink Corp., **17** 264

Commodity Credit Corp., **11** 24

Commodore Corporation, **8** 229

Commodore International, Ltd., II 6; **III** 112; **6** 243–44; **7 95–97**, 532; **9** 46; **10** 56, 284; **23** 25; **26** 16

Commonwealth & Southern Corporation, **V** 676

Commonwealth Aluminium Corp., Ltd. *See* Comalco Ltd.

Commonwealth Bank, **II** 188, 389

Commonwealth Board Mills, **IV** 248

Commonwealth Brands, Inc., **51** 170

Commonwealth Edison, II 28, 425; **III** 653; **IV** 169; **V 583–85; 6** 505, 529, 531; **12** 548; **13** 341; **15** 422; **48** 163

Commonwealth Energy System, 14 124–26

Commonwealth Hospitality Ltd., **III** 95

Commonwealth Industrial Gases, **25** 82

Commonwealth Industries, **III** 569; **11** 536; **20** 360

Commonwealth Insurance Co., **III** 264

Commonwealth Land Title Insurance Co., **III** 343

Commonwealth Life and Accident Insurance Company, **27** 46–47

Commonwealth Life Insurance Co., **III** 216–19

Commonwealth Limousine Services, Ltd., **26** 62

Commonwealth Mortgage Assurance Co., **III** 344

Commonwealth National Financial Corp., **II** 316; **44** 280

Commonwealth Oil Refining Company, **II** 402; **7** 517; **45** 410

Commonwealth Power Railway and Light Company, **14** 134

Commonwealth Southern Corporation, **14** 134

Commonwealth Telephone Enterprises, Inc., 25 106–08

Commonwealth United Corp., **53** 364

Commtron, Inc., **V** 14, 16; **11** 195; **13** 90

Communication Services Ltd. *See* Hongkong Telecommunications Ltd.

Communications and Systems Specialists, **18** 370

Communications Consultants, Inc., **16** 393

Communications Corp. of America, **25** 418

Communications Data Services, Inc., **IV** 627; **19** 204

Communications Industries Inc., **25** 496

Communications Network Consultants, **29** 400

Communications Properties, Inc., **IV** 677

Communications Solutions Inc., **11** 520

Communications Technology Corp. (CTC), **13** 7–8

Communicorp, **III** 188; **10** 29; **38** 17

Community Coffee Co. L.L.C., 53 108–10

Community Direct, Inc., **7** 16

Community HealthCare Services, **6** 182

Community Hospital of San Gabriel, **6** 149

Community Medical Care, Inc., **III** 245

Community National Bank, **9** 474

Community Networks Inc., **45** 69

Community Newspapers, Inc., **45** 352

Community Power & Light Company, **6** 579–80

Community Psychiatric Centers, 15 118–20

Community Public Service Company, **6** 514

Community Savings and Loan, **II** 317

Comnet Corporation, **9** 347

Comp-U-Card of America, Inc. *See* CUC International Inc.

Compac Corp., **11** 535

Compactom, **I** 588

Compagnia di Assicurazioni, **III** 345

Compagnia di Genova, **III** 347

Compagnia di Participazioni Assicurative ed Industriali S.p.A., **24** 341

Compagnie Auxiliare de Navigation, **IV** 558

Compagnie Bancaire, **II** 259; **21** 99–100

Compagnie Belge pour l'industrie, **II** 202

Compagnie Continentale, **I** 409–10

Compagnie d'Assurances Générales, **III** 391

Compagnie d'assurances Mutuelles contre l'incendie dans les départements de la Seine Inférieure et de l'Eure, **III** 210

Compagnie d'Investissements de Paris, **II** 233

Compagnie de Compteurs, **III** 617; **17** 418

Compagnie de Five-Lille, **IV** 469

Compagnie de Mokta, **IV** 107–08

Compagnie de Navigation Mixte, **III** 185

Compagnie de Reassurance Nord-Atlantique, **III** 276

Compagnie de Recherche et d'Exploitation du Pétrole du Sahara, **IV** 545; **21** 203

Compagnie de Saint-Gobain S.A., II 117, 474–75; **III 675–78,** 704; **8** 395, 397; **15** 80; **16 119–23 (upd.);** **19** 58, 226; **21** 222; **26** 446; **33** 338, 340; **35** 86, 88

Compagnie de Transport Aerien, **I** 122

Compagnie des Alpes, 48 106–08

Compagnie des Cristalleries de Baccarat. *See* Baccarat.

Compagnie des Machines Bull S.A., II 40, 42, 70, 125; **III 122–23,** 154; **IV** 600; **12** 139; **13** 574; **25** 33. *See also* Bull S.A.; Groupe Bull.

Compagnie des Messageries Maritimes, **6** 379

Compagnie des Produits Chimiques et Électrométallurgiques d'Alais, Froges et Camargue, **IV** 173–74

Compagnie du Midi, **III** 209, 211

Compagnie du Nord, **IV** 108

Compagnie Européenne de Publication, **IV** 614–15

Compagnie Européenne de Télésecurité, **32** 374

Compagnie Financier Richemont AG, **19** 367, 369–70

Compagnie Financiere Alcatel, **9** 10

Compagnie Financière Belge des Pétroles. *See* PetroFina S.A.

Compagnie Financière de Paribas, II 192, **259–60;** **III** 185; **21** 99; **27** 138; **33** 339. *See also* BNP Paribas Group.

Compagnie Financière de Richemont AG, **29** 90

Compagnie Financière de Suez. *See* Suez Lyonnaise des Eaux.

Compagnie Financière du Groupe Victoire, **27** 54; **49** 44

Compagnie Financière Richemont AG, 27 487; **29** 91–92; **50 144–47**

Compagnie Française Chaufour Investissement, **27** 100

Compagnie Française de Distribution en Afrique, **IV** 559

Compagnie Française de Manutention, **27** 295

Compagnie Française de Raffinage, **IV** 558–60

Compagnie Française des Lubricants, **I** 341

Compagnie Française des Minerais d'Uranium, **IV** 108

Compagnie Française des Mines de Diamants du Cap, **IV** 64; **7** 121

Compagnie Française des Pétroles. *See* TOTAL S.A.

Compagnie Française des Produits d'Orangina, **I** 281

Compagnie Française du Méthane, **V** 626

Compagnie Française Thomson-Houston, **I** 357; **II** 116. *See also* Thales S.A.

Compagnie Fromagère de la Vallée de l'Ance, **25** 84

Compagnie Générale d'Électricité, I 193; **II 12–13,** 25; **IV** 174, 615; **9** 9–10

Compagnie Generale de Cartons Ondules, **IV** 296; **19** 226

Compagnie Generale de Radiologie, **II** 117

Compagnie Generale de Telegraphie Sans Fils, **II** 116

Compagnie Générale des Eaux, **V** 632–33; **6** 441. *See also* Vivendi SA.

Compagnie Générale des Établissements Michelin, V 236–39; **19** 508; **42 85–89 (upd.)**

Compagnie Générale Maritime et Financière, 6 379–81

Compagnie Industriali Riunite S.p.A., **IV** 587–88; **54** 21

Compagnie Industrielle de Matérials de Manutention, **27** 296

Compagnie Industrielle des Fillers. *See* L'Entreprise Jean Lefebvre.

Compagnie Internationale de l'Informatique, **III** 123

Compagnie Internationale Express, **25** 120

Compagnie Internationale Pirelli S.A., **V** 249

Compagnie Laitière Européenne, **25** 83, 85

Compagnie Luxembourgeoise de Télédiffusion, **15** 54

Compagnie Nationale à Portefeuille, **29** 48

Compagnie Nationale de Navigation, **27** 515

Compagnie Navale Des Pétroles, **IV** 558

Compagnie Parisienne de Garantie, **III** 211

Compagnie Pneumatique Commerciale, **III** 426

Compagnie Tunisienne de Ressorts a Lames, **III** 581

Compagnie Union des Assurances de Paris (UAP), **49** 44

Compal, **47** 152–53

Companhia Brasileira de Aluminio, **IV** 55

Companhia Brasileira de Mineracão e Siderugica, **IV** 54

Companhia de Celulose do Caima, **14** 250

Companhia de Diamantes de Angola, **IV** 21

Companhia de Electricidade da Bahia, **49** 211

Companhia de Minerales y Metales, **IV** 139

Companhia de Pesquisas Mineras de Angola, **IV** 65; **7** 122

Companhia de Seguros Argos Fluminense, **III** 221

Companhia de Seguros Tranquilidade Vida, S.A. *See* Banco Espírito Santo e Comercial de Lisboa S.A.

Companhia Energetica de Minas Gerias (CEMIG), **53** 18

Companhia Industrial de Papel Pirahy, **52** 301

Companhia Siderúrgica de Tubarao, **IV** 125

Companhia Siderúrgica Mannesmann S.A., **III** 565–66

Companhia Siderúrgica Nacional, **II** 199; **43** 112

Companhia Uniao Fabril, **IV** 505

Companhia Vale do Rio Doce, IV 54–57; 43 111–14 (upd.)

Compañia Arrendataria del Monopolio de Petróleos Sociedad Anónima, **IV** 396–97, 527–29

Compañia de Investigacion y Exploitaciones Petrolifera, **IV** 397

Compañia de Líneas Aéreas Subvencionadas S.A., **6** 95

Compañia Española de Petroleos S.A., IV 396–98, 527

Compania Fresnillo, **22** 286

Compania Fundidora del Norte, S.A., **54** 152

Compania General de Aceptaciones. *See* Financiera Aceptaciones.

Compania Hulera Euzkadi, **21** 260; **23** 170

Compania Industrial de San Cristobal, S.A. de C.V., **54** 186

Compania Industrial del Norte, S.A., **54** 152

Compañia Mexicana de Transportación Aérea, **20** 167

Compania Minera de Penoles. *See* Industrias Penoles, S.A. de C.V.

Compañia Minera La India, **IV** 164

Compania Minera Las Torres, **22** 286

Compañia Nacional Minera Petrólia del Táchira, **IV** 507

Compania Siderurgica Huachipato, **24** 209

Compañía Telefónica Nacional de España S.A., **V** 337

Compaq Computer Corporation, II 45; **III** 114, **124–25**; **6** 217, **221–23 (upd.),** 230–31, 235, 243–44; **9** 42–43, 166, 170–71, 472; **10** 87, 232–33, 366, 459, 518–19; **12** 61, 183, 335, 470; **13** 388, 483; **16** 4, 196, 367–68; **17** 274; **21** 123, 391; **22** 288; **25** 184, 239, 498, 531; **26** **90–93 (upd.);** **27** 365; **28** 191; **29** 439; **30** 12; **36** 384; **43** 13; **47** 153. *See also* Hewlett-Packard Company.

Compart, **24** 341

Compass Airlines, **27** 475

Compass Design Automation, **16** 520

Compass Group PLC, 6 193; **24** 194; **27** 482; **34 121–24**

CompDent Corporation, 22 149–51

Compeda, Ltd., **10** 240

Competence ApS, **26** 240

Competition Tire East/West, **V** 494; **19** 292

Competrol Ltd., **22** 189

Compex, **II** 233

CompHealth Inc., 25 109–12

Complete Business Solutions, Inc., 31 130–33

Complete Post, **50** 126

Completion Bond Co., **26** 487

Components Agents Ltd., **10** 113; **50** 43

Composite Craft Inc., **I** 387

Composite Research & Management Co., **17** 528, 530

Comprehensive Care Corporation, 15 121–23

Comprehensive Resources Corp., **IV** 83

Compressed Industrial Gases, **I** 297

Compression Labs Inc., **10** 456; **16** 392, 394; **27** 365

Compressor Controls Corporation, **15** 404; **50** 394

Comptoir d'Escompte de Mulhouse, **II** 232

Comptoir des Textiles Artificielles, **I** 122, 388–89

Comptoir Général de la Photographie. *See* Gaumont SA.

Comptoir Métallurgique Luxembourgeois, **IV** 25

Comptoir National d'Escompte de Paris, **II** 232–33, 270

Comptoirs Modernes S.A., 19 97–99

Compton Communications, **I** 33

Compton Foods, **II** 675

Compton's MultiMedia Publishing Group, Inc., **7** 165

Compton's New Media, Inc., **7** 168

Compu-Notes, Inc., **22** 413

CompuAdd Computer Corporation, 11 61–63

CompuChem Corporation, **11** 425

CompuCom Systems, Inc., 10 232–34, 474; **13** 176

CompuDyne Corporation, 51 78–81

Compugraphic, **III** 168; **6** 284

Compumech Technologies, **19** 312

Compumotor, **III** 603

CompuPharm, Inc., **14** 210

CompUSA, Inc., 10 235–36; 35 116–18 (upd.)

CompuServe Incorporated, 9 268–70; **10** **237–39; 12** 562; **13** 147; **15** 265; **16** 467, 508; **26** 16; **29** 224, 226–27; **34** 361; **50** 329. *See also* America Online, Inc.

CompuServe Interactive Services, Inc., 27 106, **106–08 (upd.),** 301, 307. *See also* America Online, Inc.

Computax, **6** 227–28

Computer Associates International, Inc., 6 224–26; **10** 394; **12** 62; **14** 392; **27** 492; **49 94–97 (upd.)**

Computer City, **12** 470; **36** 387

The Computer Company, **11** 112

Computer Consoles Inc., **III** 164

Computer Data Systems, Inc., 14 127–29

The Computer Department, Ltd., **10** 89

Computer Depot, **6** 243

Computer Discount Corporation. *See* Comdisco, Inc.

Computer Discount Warehouse. *See* CDW Computer Centers, Inc.

Computer Dynamics, Inc., **6** 10

Computer Engineering Associates, **25** 303

Computer Factory, Inc., **13** 176

Computer Learning Centers, Inc., 26 94–96

Computer Network, **20** 237

Computer Peripheral Manufacturers Association, **13** 127

Computer Plaza K.K., **IV** 542–43

Computer Power, **6** 301

Computer Renaissance, Inc., **18** 207–8

Computer Research Corp., **III** 151; **6** 265

Computer Resources Management, Inc., **26** 36

Computer Sciences Corporation, 6 25, **227–29; 13** 462; **15** 474; **18** 370

Computer Shoppe, **V** 191–92

Computer Systems and Applications, **12** 442

Computer Systems Division (CDS), **13** 201

Computer Terminal Corporation, **11** 67–68

ComputerCity, **10** 235

ComputerCraft, **27** 163

Computerized Lodging Systems, Inc., **11** 275

Computerized Waste Systems, **46** 248

ComputerLand Corp., 6 243; **9** 116; **10** 233, 563; **12** 335; **13 174–76,** 277; **33** 341–42

Computervision Corporation, 6 246–47; **7** 498; **10** 240–42; **11** 275; **13** 201; **24** 234

Computing Scale Company of America. *See* International Business Machines Corporation.

Computing-Tabulating-Recording Co., **III** 147

Compuware Corporation, 10 243–45; 30 140–43 (upd.); 38 482

CompX International, Inc., **19** 466, 468

Comsat Corporation, II 425; **12** 19; **13** 341; **23 133–36; 28** 241; **29** 42

Comshare Inc., 23 137–39

Comstock Canada, **9** 301

Comstock Resources, Inc., 47 85–87

Comtec Information Systems Inc., **53** 374

Comtel Electronics, Inc., **22** 409

Comunicaciones Avanzados, S.A. de C.V., **39** 195

Comverse Technology, Inc., 15 124–26; 43 115–18 (upd.)

Comviq GSM AB, **26** 331–33

Con Ed. *See* Consolidated Edison, Inc.

Con-Ferro Paint and Varnish Company, **8** 553

ConAgra, Inc., II 493–95, 517, 585; **7** 432, 525; **8** 53, 499–500; **12 80–82 (upd.); 13** 138, 294, 350, 352; **14** 515; **17** 56, 240–41; **18** 247, 290; **21** 290; **23** 320; **25** 243, 278; **26** 172, 174; **36** 416; **42 90–94 (upd.); 50** 275, 295, 493; **55** 364–65

Conahay & Lyon, **6** 27

Conair Corp., 16 539; **17 108–10; 24** 131; **25** 56

Concept, Inc., **23** 154

Concepts Direct, Inc., 39 93–96

Concepts in Community Living, Inc., **43** 46

Concert Communications Company, **15** 69; **27** 304–05; **49** 72

Concesiones de Infraestructuras de Transportes, S.A., **40** 217

Concession Air, **16** 446

Concha y Toro. *See* Viña Concha y Toro S.A.

Concord Camera Corporation, 41 104–07

Concord EFS, Inc., 52 86–88

Concord Fabrics, Inc., 16 124–26

Concord International, **II** 298

Concord Leasing, Inc., **51** 108

Concord Watch Company, S.A., **28** 291

Concorde Hotels, **27** 421

Concordia, **IV** 497

Concrete Industries (Monier) Ltd., **III** 735

Concretos Apasco, S.A. de C.V., **51** 28–29

Concurrent Logic, **17** 34

The Condé Nast Publications Inc., IV 583–84; **13 177–81; 19** 5; **23** 98

Condor Systems Inc., **15** 530

Cone Communications, **25** 258

Cone Mills Corporation, 8 120–22

Conelectron, **13** 398

Conestoga National Bank, **II** 316

Conexant Systems, Inc., 36 121–25; 43 328

Confectionaire, **25** 283

Confederacion Norte-Centromericana y del Caribe de Futbol, **27** 150

Confederacion Sudamericana de Futbol, **27** 150

Confederation Africaine de Football, **27** 150

Confederation Freezers, **21** 501

Confederation of Engineering Industry, **IV** 484

Confidata Corporation, **11** 111
Confindustria, **I** 162
Confiserie-Group Hofbauer, **27** 105
Congas Engineering Canada Ltd., **6** 478
Congoleum Corp., **12** 28; **16** 18; **18** 116–19; **36** 77–78; **43** 19, 21
Congress Financial Corp., **13** 305–06; **19** 108; **27** 276
Congressional Information Services, **IV** 610
Conic, **9** 324
Conifer Group, **II** 214
Conifer Records Ltd., **52** 429
Conill Corp., **II** 261
Coniston Partners, **I** 130; **II** 680; **III** 29; **6** 130; **10** 302
Conn-Selmer, Inc., **55** 111–14
CONNA Corp., **7** 113; **25** 125
Connect Group Corporation, **28** 242
Connecticut Bank and Trust Co., **II** 213–14
Connecticut General Corporation. *See* CIGNA Corporation.
Connecticut Health Enterprises Network, **22** 425
Connecticut Light and Power Co., **13** 182–84; **21** 514; **48** 305
Connecticut Mutual Life Insurance Company, **III** 225, 236–38, 254, 285
Connecticut National Bank, **13** 467
Connecticut River Banking Company, **13** 467
Connecticut Telephone Company. *See* Southern New England Telecommunications Corporation.
Connecticut Trust and Safe Deposit Co., **II** 213
Connecticut Yankee Atomic Power Company, **21** 513
Connecting Point of America, **6** 244
The Connection Group, Inc., **26** 257
Connectix Corporation, **28** 245
The Connell Company, **29** 129–31
Conner Corp., **15** 327
Conner Peripherals, Inc., **6** 230–32; **10** 403, 459, 463–64, 519; **11** 56, 234; **18** 260
Connie Lee. *See* College Construction Loan Insurance Assoc.
Connoisseur Communications, **37** 104
Connolly Data Systems, **11** 66
Connolly Tool and Machine Company, **21** 215
Connors Brothers, **II** 631–32
Connors Steel Co., **15** 116
Conoco Inc., **I** 286, 329, 346, 402–04; **II** 376; **IV** 365, 382, 389, **399–402**, 413, 429, 454, 476; **6** 539; **7** 346, 559; **8** 152, 154, 556; **11** 97, 400; **16** 127–32 **(upd.)**; **18** 366; **21** 29; **26** 125, 127; **50** 178, 363
Conorada Petroleum Corp., **IV** 365, 400
Conover Furniture Company, **10** 183
ConQuest Telecommunication Services Inc., **16** 319
Conquistador Films, **25** 270
Conrad International Hotels, **III** 91–93
Conrail Inc., **22** 167, 376. *See also* Consolidated Rail Corporation.
Conran Associates, **17** 43
Conrock Co., **19** 70
Conseco Inc., **10** 246–48; **15** 257; **33** 108–12 **(upd.)**

Consgold. *See* Consolidated Gold Fields of South Africa Ltd.; Consolidated Gold Fields PLC.
Conshu Holdings, **24** 450
Conso International Corporation, **29** 132–34
Consodata S.A., **47** 345, 347
Consolidated Aircraft Corporation, **9** 16, 497
Consolidated Aluminum Corp., **IV** 178
Consolidated Asset Management Company, Inc., **25** 204
Consolidated-Bathurst Inc., **IV** 246–47, 334; **25** 11; **26** 445
Consolidated Brands Inc., **14** 18
Consolidated Cable Utilities, **6** 313
Consolidated Cement Corp., **III** 704
Consolidated Cigar Holdings, Inc., **I** 452–53; **15** 137–38; **27** 139–40; **28** 247
Consolidated Coal Co., **IV** 82, 170–71
Consolidated Coin Caterers Corporation, **10** 222
Consolidated Controls, **I** 155
Consolidated Converting Co., **19** 109
Consolidated Copper Corp., **13** 503
Consolidated Delivery & Logistics, Inc., **24** 125–28
Consolidated Denison Mines Ltd., **8** 418
Consolidated Diamond Mines of South-West Africa Ltd., **IV** 21, 65–67; **7** 122–25; **16** 26; **50** 31
Consolidated Distillers Ltd., **I** 263
Consolidated Edison Company of New York, Inc., **I** 28; **V** 586–89; **6** 456; **35** 479
Consolidated Edison, Inc., **45** 116–20 **(upd.)**
Consolidated Electric & Gas, **6** 447; **23** 28
Consolidated Electric Power Asia, **38** 448
Consolidated Electric Supply Inc., **15** 385
Consolidated Electronics Industries Corp. (Conelco), **13** 397–98
Consolidated Foods Corp., **II** 571–73, 584; **III** 480; **12** 159, 494; **22** 27; **29** 132
Consolidated Freightways Corporation, **V** 432–34; **6** 280, 388; **12** 278, 309; **13** 19; **14** 567; **21** 136–39 **(upd.)**; **25** 148–50; **48** 109–13 **(upd.)**
Consolidated Gas Company. *See* Baltimore Gas and Electric Company.
Consolidated Gold Fields of South Africa Ltd., **IV** 94, 96, 118, 565, 566
Consolidated Gold Fields PLC, **II** 422; **III** 501, 503; **IV** 23, 67, 94, 97, 171; **7** 125, 209, 387
Consolidated Grocers Corp., **II** 571
Consolidated Insurances of Australia, **III** 347
Consolidated International, **50** 98
Consolidated Marketing, Inc., **IV** 282; **9** 261
Consolidated Mines Selection Co., **IV** 20, 23
Consolidated Mining and Smelting Co., **IV** 75
Consolidated National Life Insurance Co., **10** 246
Consolidated Natural Gas Company, **V** 590–91; **19** 100–02 **(upd.)**; **54** 83
Consolidated Oatmeal Co., **II** 558
Consolidated Papers, Inc., **8** 123–25; **36** 126–30 **(upd.)**
Consolidated Plantations Berhad, **36** 434–35

Consolidated Power & Light Company, **6** 580
Consolidated Power & Telephone Company, **11** 342
Consolidated Press Holdings, **8** 551; **37** 408–09
Consolidated Products, Inc., **14** 130–32, 352
Consolidated Rail Corporation, **II** 449; **V** 435–37, 485; **10** 44; **12** 278; **13** 449; **14** 324; **29** 360; **35** 291. *See also* Conrail Inc.
Consolidated Rand-Transvaal Mining Group, **IV** 90; **22** 233
Consolidated Rock Products Co., **19** 69
Consolidated Specialty Restaurants, Inc., **14** 131–32
Consolidated Steel, **I** 558; **IV** 570; **24** 520
Consolidated Stores Corp., **13** 543; **29** 311; **35** 254; **50** 98
Consolidated Temperature Controlling Co., **II** 40; **12** 246; **50** 231
Consolidated Theaters, Inc., **14** 87
Consolidated Tire Company, **20** 258
Consolidated Trust Inc., **22** 540
Consolidated Tyre Services Ltd., **IV** 241
Consolidated Vultee, **II** 7, 32
Consolidated Zinc Corp., **IV** 58–59, 122, 189, 191
Consolidation Coal Co., **IV** 401; **8** 154, 346–47
Consolidation Services, **44** 10, 13
Consorcio G Grupo Dina, S.A. de C.V., **36** 131–33
Consortium, **34** 373
Consortium de Realisation, **25** 329
Consortium De Realization SAS, **23** 392
Consoweld Corporation, **8** 124
Constar International Inc., **8** 562; **13** 190; **32** 125
Constellation, **III** 335
Constellation Energy Corporation, **24** 29
Constellation Enterprises Inc., **25** 46
Constellation Insurance Co., **III** 191–92
Constinsouza, **25** 174
Constitution Insurance Company, **51** 143
Construcciones Aeronáuticas SA, **I** 41–42; **7** 9; **12** 190; **24** 88. *See also* European Aeronautic Defence and Space Company EADS N.V.
Construcciones y Contratas, **II** 198
Construction DJL Inc., **23** 332–33
Construtora Moderna SARL, **IV** 505
Consul GmbH, **51** 58
Consul Restaurant Corp., **13** 152
Consumer Access Limited, **24** 95
Consumer Products Company, **30** 39
Consumer Value Stores, **V** 136–37; **9** 67; **18** 199; **24** 290
Consumer's Gas Co., **I** 264
ConsumerNet, **49** 422
Consumers Cooperative Association, **7** 174. *See also* Farmland Industries, Inc.
Consumers Distributing Co. Ltd., **II** 649, 652–53
Consumers Electric Light and Power, **6** 582
The Consumers Gas Company Ltd., **6** 476–79; **43** 154. *See also* Enbridge Inc.
Consumers Mutual Gas Light Company. *See* Baltimore Gas and Electric Company.
Consumers Power Co., **V** 577–79, 593–94; **14** 114–15, **133–36**

Consumers Public Power District, **29** 352
Consumers Union, 26 97–99
**Consumers Water Company, 14 137–39;
39** 329
Contact Software International Inc., **10** 509
Contadina, **II** 488–89
Container Corporation of America, **IV** 295,
465; **V** 147; **7** 353; **8** 476; **19** 225; **26**
446
The Container Store, 36 134–36
Container Transport International, **III** 344
Containers Packaging, **IV** 249
Contaminant Recovery Systems, Inc., **18**
162
CONTAQ Microsystems Inc., **48** 127
Conte S.A., **12** 262
Contech, **10** 493
Contel Corporation, **II** 117; **V** 294–98; **6**
323; **13** 212; **14** 259; **15** 192; **43** 447
Contempo Associates, **14** 105; **25** 307
Contempo Casuals, Inc. *See* The Wet Seal,
Inc.
Contemporary Books, **22** 522
Content Technologies Inc., **42** 24–25
Contex Graphics Systems Inc., **24** 428
Contherm Corp., **III** 420
Conti-Carriers & Terminals Inc., **22** 167
Contico International, L.L.C., **51** 190
ContiCommodity Services, Inc., **10** 250–51
**ContiGroup Companies, Inc., 43 119–22
(upd.)**
Continental Airlines, Inc., I 96–98, 103,
118, 123–24, 129–30; **6** 52, 61, 105,
120–21, 129–30; **12** 381; **20** 84, 262; **21**
140–43 (upd.); 22 80, 220; **25** 420, 423;
26 439–40; **34** 398; **52 89–94 (upd.)**
**Continental Aktiengesellschaft, V
240–43,** 250–51, 256; **8** 212–14; **9** 248;
15 355; **19** 508
Continental American Life Insurance
Company, **7** 102
Continental Assurance Co., **III** 228–30
Continental Baking Co., **I** 463–64; **II**
562–63; **7** 320–21; **11** 198; **12** 276; **13**
427; **19** 192; **27** 309–10; **38** 252
Continental Bancor, **II** 248
Continental Bank and Trust Co., **II** 251; **14**
102
Continental Bank Corporation, I 526; **II
261–63,** 285, 289, 348; **IV** 702; **47** 231
Continental Bio-Clinical Laboratories, **26**
391
Continental Blacks Inc., **I** 403
**Continental Cablevision, Inc., 7 98–100;
17** 148; **19** 201
Continental Can Co., Inc., I 597; **II** 34,
414; **III** 471; **10** 130; **13** 255; **15** 49
293–94**127–30; 24** 428; **26** 117, 449; **32**
125;
Continental-Caoutchouc und Gutta-Percha
Compagnie, **V** 240
Continental Carbon Co., **I** 403–05; **II** 53;
IV 401; **36** 146–48
Continental Care Group, **10** 252–53
Continental Casualty Co., **III** 196, 228–32;
16 204
Continental Cities Corp., **III** 344
Continental Corporation, III 230,
239–44, 273; **10** 561; **12** 318; **15** 30; **38**
142
Continental Cos., **III** 248
Continental Divide Insurance Co., **III** 214
Continental Electronics Corporation, **18**
513–14

Continental Emsco, **I** 490–91; **24** 305
Continental Equipment Company, **13** 225
Continental Express, **11** 299
Continental Fiber Drum, **8** 476
Continental Gas & Electric Corporation, **6**
511
**Continental General Tire Corp., 23
140–42**
**Continental Grain Company, 10 249–51;
13 185–87 (upd.); 30** 353, 355; **40** 87.
See also ContiGroup Companies, Inc.
Continental Group Co., I 599–600,
601–02, 604–05, 607–09, 612–13, 615;
IV 334; **8** 175, 424; **17** 106
Continental Gummi-Werke
Aktiengesellschaft, **V** 241; **9** 248
Continental Hair Products, Inc. *See* Conair
Corp.
Continental Health Affiliates, **17** 307
Continental Homes, **26** 291
Continental Illinois Corp. *See* Continental
Bank Corporation.
Continental Illinois Venture Co., **IV** 702
Continental Insurance Co., **III** 239–42,
372–73, 386
Continental Insurance Cos. of New York,
III 230
Continental Investment Corporation, **9** 507;
12 463; **22** 541; **33** 407
Continental Life Insurance Co., **III** 225
**Continental Medical Systems, Inc., 10
252–54; 11** 282; **14** 233; **25** 111; **33** 185
Continental Milling Company, **10** 250
Continental Modules, Inc., **45** 328
Continental Motors Corp., **I** 199, 524–25;
10 521–22
Continental Mutual Savings Bank, **17** 529
Continental National American Group, **III**
230, 404
Continental National Bank, **II** 261; **11** 119
Continental-National Group, **III** 230
Continental Oil Co., **IV** 39, 365, 382,
399–401, 476, 517, 575–76
Continental Packaging Inc., **13** 255
Continental Plastic Containers, Inc., **25** 512
Continental Radio, **IV** 607
Continental Reinsurance, **11** 533
Continental Research Corporation, **22** 541
Continental Restaurant Systems, **12** 510
Continental Risk Services, **III** 243
Continental Savouries, **II** 500
Continental Scale Works, **14** 229–30
Continental Securities Corporation, **II** 444;
22 404
Continental Telephone Company, **V**
296–97; **9** 494–95; **11** 500; **15** 195
Continental Wood Preservers, Inc., **12** 397
Continentale Allgemeine, **III** 347
ContinueCare Corporation, **25** 41
Contran Corporation, **19** 467
Contrans Acquisitions, Inc., **14** 38
Contred Ltd., **20** 263
Control Data Corporation, **17** 49; **19** 110,
513–15; **25** 496; **30** 338; **38** 58; **46** 35
Control Data Systems, Inc., III 118,
126–28, 129, 131, 149, 152, 165; **6** 228,
252, 266; **8** 117–18, 467; **10 255–57,**
359, 458–59; **11** 469; **16** 137
**Controladora Comercial Mexicana, S.A.
de C.V., 36 137–39**
Controladora PROSA, **18** 516, 518
Controlled Materials and Equipment
Transportation, **29** 354
Controlonics Corporation, **13** 195

Controls Company of America, **9** 67
Controlware GmbH, **22** 53
Convair, **I** 82, 121, 123, 126, 131; **II** 33; **9**
18, 498; **13** 357
Convenient Food Mart Inc., **7** 114; **25** 125
Convergent Technologies, **III** 166; **6** 283;
11 519
Converse Inc., III 528–29; **V** 376; **9
133–36,** 234; **12** 308; **31 134–138
(upd.),** 211; **39** 170, 172–74
Conway Computer Group, **18** 370
Conwest Exploration Company Ltd., **16** 10,
12; **43** 3
Conycon. *See* Construcciones y Contratas.
Conzinc Riotinto of Australia. *See* CRA
Limited.
Cook Bates Inc., **40** 347–48
Cook Data Services, Inc., **9** 73
Cook Industrial Coatings, **I** 307
Cook Standard Tool Co., **13** 369
Cook United, **V** 172
Cooke Engineering Company, **13** 194
**Cooker Restaurant Corporation, 20
159–61; 51 82–85 (upd.)**
Cooking and Crafts Club, **13** 106
Cookson Group plc, III 679–82; 16 290;
44 115–20 (upd.); 49 234–35
**CoolBrands International Inc., 35
119–22**
Coolerator, **I** 463
Coolidge Mutual Savings Bank, **17** 529
**Coop Schweiz Genossenschaftsverband,
48 114–16**
**Cooper Cameron Corporation, 20
162–66 (upd.)**
Cooper Canada Ltd., **16** 80
The Cooper Companies, Inc., 39 97–100
Cooper Industries, Inc., II 14–17; 14
564; **19** 43, 45, 140; **30** 266; **44 121–25
(upd.); 49** 159
Cooper Laboratories, **I** 667, 682
Cooper LaserSonics Inc., **IV** 100
Cooper McDougall & Robertson Ltd., **I**
715
**Cooper Tire & Rubber Company, 8
126–28; 23 143–46 (upd.)**
Cooper-Weymouth, **10** 412
Cooper's, Inc., **12** 283
Cooperative Grange League Federation
Exchange, **7** 17
Coopers & Lybrand, 9 137–38; 12 391;
25 383. *See also*
PricewaterhouseCoopers.
CooperVision, **7** 46; **25** 55
Coordinated Caribbean Transport. *See*
Crowley Caribbean Transport.
Coors Company. *See* Adolph Coors
Company.
Coorsh and Bittner, **7** 430
Coos Bay Lumber Co., **IV** 281; **9** 259
Coosa River Newsprint Co., **III** 40; **16**
303; **43** 257
Coote & Jurgenson, **14** 64
Cooymans, **I** 281
Copart Inc., 23 147–49, 285, 287
Copeland Corp., **II** 20
Copeman Ridley, **13** 103
Copico, **44** 273
Copland Brewing Co., **I** 268; **25** 280
Copley Pharmaceuticals Inc., **13** 264
The Copley Press, Inc., 23 150–52
Copley Real Estate Advisors, **III** 313
Copolymer Corporation, **9** 242

Copper Queen Consolidated Mining Co., IV 176–77

Copper Range Company, IV 76; 7 281–82

Copperweld Steel Co., IV 108–09, 237

The Copps Corporation, 32 120–22

Copycat Ltd., 8 383

Cor Therapeutics, 47 251

Cora Verlag, IV 590

Coral Drilling, I 570

Coral Energy, 41 359

Coral Leisure Group, I 248

Coral Petroleum, IV 395

Corange, Ltd., 37 111–13

Corbett Canyon. See The Wine Group, Inc.

Corbett Enterprises Inc., 13 270

Corbis Corporation, 31 139–42

Corby Distilleries Limited, 14 140–42

Corchos de Mérida S.A., 48 349

Corco. See Commonwealth Oil Refining Company.

Corco, Inc. See Liqui-Box Corporation.

Corcoran & Riggs. See Riggs National Corporation.

Cordiant plc. See Saatchi & Saatchi plc.

Cordis Corporation, 19 103–05; 36 306; 46 104–07 (upd.)

Cordon & Gotch, IV 619

Le Cordon Bleu, II 609; 45 88; 45 88

Cordovan Corp., IV 608

Core Laboratories Inc., I 486; 11 265

Corel Corporation, 15 131–33; 33 113–16 (upd.)

CoreStates Financial Corp, 17 111–15

CoreTek, Inc., 36 353

Corfuerte S.A. de C.V., 23 171

Corimon, 12 218

Corinthian Broadcast Corporation, IV 605; 10 4

Corinthian Colleges, Inc., 39 101–04

Corio Inc., 38 188, 432

Cormetech, III 685

Corn Exchange Bank, II 316

Corn Exchange Bank Trust Co., II 251; 14 102

Corn Exchange National Bank, II 261

Corn Products Company. See Bestfoods.

Corn Sweeteners Inc., I 421; 11 23

Cornelia Insurance Agency. See Advantage Insurers, Inc.

Cornelius Nurseries, Inc., 51 61

Cornell Corrections, 28 255

Cornerstone Direct Marketing, 8 385–86

Cornerstone Propane Partners, L.P., 37 280, 283

Cornerstone Real Estate Advisors Inc., 53 213

Cornerstone Title Company, 8 461

Cornhill Insurance Co., I 429; III 185, 385

Cornhusker Casualty Co., III 213

Corning Asahi Video Products Co., III 667

Corning Clinical Laboratories, 26 390–92

Corning Consumer Products Company, 27 288

Corning Inc., I 609; III 434, 667, 683–85, 720–21; 8 468; 11 334; 13 398; 22 454; 25 254; 30 151–52; 44 126–30 (upd.)

Coro International A.V.V., 39 346

Coronado Corp., II 112

Coronet Industries, Inc., II 90; 14 436

Corporacion Durango, S.A. de C.V., 37 178

Corporacion Estatal Petrolera Ecuatoriana, IV 510–11

Corporación Internacional de Aviación, S.A. de C.V. (Cintra), 20 167–69

Corporación Moctezuma, 21 261

Corporacion Nacional del Cobre de Chile, 38 231; 40 121–23

Corporacion Siderurgica Integral, 22 44

Corporación Venezolana de Petroleo, IV 507

Corporate Childcare Development, Inc. See Bright Horizons Family Solutions, Inc.

Corporate Express, Inc., 22 152–55, 531; 41 67–69; 47 88–92 (upd.); 49 440

Corporate Intelligence, 55 251

Corporate Microsystems, Inc., 10 395

Corporate Partners, 12 391

Corporate Software Inc., 9 139–41

CorporateFamily Solutions. See Bright Horizons Family Solutions, Inc.

Corporation for Public Broadcasting, 14 143–45; 47 259

Corporation of Lloyd's, III 278–79

Corporation Trust Co. See CCH Inc.

Corpoven, IV 508

Corrado Passera, IV 588

Corral Midwest, Inc., 10 333

Correctional Services Corporation, 30 144–46

Corrections Corporation of America, 23 153–55; 28 255

Corrigan-McKinney Steel Company, 13 157

Corrigan's, 16 559

CorrLogic, Inc., 51 81

Corroon & Black. See Willis Corroon Group Plc.

Corrosion Technologies de México SA de C V, 53 285

Corrpro Companies, Inc., 20 170–73

Corrugated Paper, IV 249

CORT Business Services Corporation, 26 100–02

El Corte Inglés Group, 26 128–31 (upd.)

Cortec Corporation, 14 430

Corticeira Amorim, Sociedade Gestora de Participaço es Sociais, S.A., 48 117–20, 349

Corus Group plc, 49 98–105 (upd.)

Corvallis Lumber Co., IV 358

Cory Bros & Co. Ltd., 31 367, 369

Cory Components, 36 158

Cory Corp., II 511

Cory Environmental Ltd., 51 130

Cory Food Services, Inc., II 608

Cory Orchard and Turf. See Chemi-Trol Chemical Co.

Cosco Pacific, 20 313

Cosden Petroleum Corp., IV 498; 26 367

Cosgrove & Co., III 283

Cosi, Inc., 53 111–13

Cosmair Inc., III 47–48; 8 129–32; 342–44; 12 404; 31 418; 46 278

Cosmar Corp., 37 269–71

The Cosmetic Center, Inc., 22 156–58

Cosmetic Technology International, Inc., 22 409

Cosmo Oil Co., Ltd., IV 403–04; 53 114–16 (upd.)

Cosmopolitan Cosmetics GmbH, 48 420, 422

Cosmopolitan Productions, IV 626; 19 203

Cosmos International, Inc., 51 307

Cosmotel, 46 401

Cosorzio Interprovinciale Vini, 10 181

Cost Plus, Inc., 12 393; 27 109–11; 34 337, 340

Cost-U-Less, Inc., 51 90–93

Costa Apple Products, II 480; 26 57

Costa Cruise Lines, 27 29, 90, 92

Costa e Ribeiro Ltd., IV 504

Costa Rica International, Inc., 41 329

Costain Civil Engineering Ltd., III 495; 13 206

Costain Homes, 31 386

Costco Wholesale Corporation, V 36; 10 206; 11 240; 14 393–95; 15 470; 25 235; 27 95; 43 123–25 (upd.)

Costruzioni Meccaniche Nazionalia, 13 218

Côte d'Or, II 521

Cott Corporation, 9 291; 52 95–98

Cottees General Foods, II 477

Cotter & Company, V 37–38; 12 8. See also TruServ Corporation.

Cotter Corporation, 29 488

Cotton Incorporated, 46 108–11

Cotton Producers Association. See Gold Kist Inc.

Coty, Inc., 36 140–42; 37 270

Coudert Brothers, 30 147–50

Coulee Region Organic Produce Pool. See Organic Valley.

Coulter Corporation. See Beckman Coulter, Inc.

Counsel Corp., 46 3

Counselor Co., 14 230

Country Fresh, Inc., 26 449

Country Kitchen Foods, III 21

Country Kitchen International, 22 127

Country Music Television, 11 153

Country Poultry, Inc., II 494

Country Seat Stores, Inc., 15 87

Country Store of Concord, Inc., 10 216

Countrywide Credit Industries, Inc., 16 133–36

County Bank, II 333

County Catering Co., 13 103

County Data Corporation, 18 24

County Fire Insurance Co., III 191

County Market, II 670

County NatWest, II 334–35

County Perfumery, III 65

County Seat Stores Inc., II 669; 9 142–43; 50 455

County Trust Co., II 230

Cour des Comptes, II 233

Courage Brewing Group., I 229, 438–39; III 503

Courcoux-Bouvet, II 260

Courier Corporation, 41 108–12

Courir S.A., 39 183–85

Courrèges Parfums, III 48; 8 343

The Courseware Developers, 11 19

Court Courier Systems, Inc., 24 126

Court House Square, 10 44

Courtaulds plc, I 321; IV 261, 670; V 356–57, 359–61; 12 103; 17 116–19 (upd.); 33 134; 41 9; 52 99, 101; 54 326

Courtney Wines International, II 477

Courtot Investments, II 222

Courts Plc, 45 121–24

Courtyard by Marriott, 9 427

Cousins Mortgage and Equity Investments, 12 393

Coutts & Co., II 333–34

Couvrette & Provost Ltd., II 651

Covance Inc., 30 151–53

Covantage, 11 379

Covenant Life Insurance, III 314

Coventry Climax Engines, Ltd., **13** 286
Coventry Co., **III** 213
Coventry Corporation, **17** 166, 168
Coventry Machinists Company, **7** 458
Coventry Ordnance Works, **I** 573
Coventry Union Banking Co., **II** 318; **17** 323
Covidea, **II** 252
Coville Inc., **16** 353
Covington & Burling, 40 124–27
Cow & Gate Ltd., **II** 586–87
Cowham Engineering, **III** 704
Cowles Media Company, **IV** 613, 648; **7** 191; **19** 285; **23 156–58**; 344
Cox & Co., **II** 236, 307–08
Cox Cable Communications, Inc., **42** 114
Cox Enterprises, Inc., **IV** 246, **595–97**; **6** 32; **7** 327; **9** 74; **17** 148; **22 159–63** **(upd.)**; **24** 120; **30** 217; **38** 307–08
Cox Medical Enterprises, Inc., **21** 47
Cox Newsprint, Inc., **25** 11
Cox Pharmaceuticals, **35** 25
Cox Woodlands Company, **25** 11
Coz Chemical Co., **21** 20, 22
CP. *See* Canadian Pacific Limited.
CP/AAON. *See* AAON, Inc.
CP Air, **6** 60–61
CP National, **6** 300; **19** 412
CP Ships Holding, Inc., **45** 80; **50** 209–10
CPC International Inc., **II** 463, **496–98**; **27** 40. *See also* Bestfoods.
CP8, **43** 89
CPI Corp., **38 157–60**
CPL. *See* Carolina Power & Light Company.
CR2A Holding, **48** 402
CRA Limited, **IV 58–61**, 67, 192; **7** 124. *See also* Rio Tinto plc.
Crabtree & Evelyn Ltd., **51** 67
Crabtree Electricals, **III** 503; **7** 210
Cracker Barrel Old Country Store, Inc., **10 258–59**. *See also* CBRL Group, Inc.
Craft House Corp., **8** 456
Craftique, Inc., **33** 350–51
Craftmade International, Inc., **44 131–33**
Craig Bit Company, **13** 297
Crain Communications, Inc., **12 83–86**; **35 123–27 (upd.)**
Cram Company. *See* The George F. Cram Company, Inc.
Cramer, Berkowitz & Co., **34 125–27**
Cramer Electronics, **10** 112; **50** 41
Cranberry Canners, Inc. *See* Ocean Spray Cranberries, Inc.
Crane & Co., Inc., **26 103–06**; **30** 42
Crane Carton Co., **44** 66
Crane Co., **8 133–36**, 179; **24** 332; **30 154–58 (upd.)**
Crane Packing Company, **19** 311
Crane Supply Company, **8** 135
Cranston Mills, **13** 168
Cranswick plc, 40 128–30
Crate and Barrel, **9 144–46**; **27** 429; **36** 135. *See also* Euromarket Designs Inc.
Cravath, Swaine & Moore, **27** 325; **43 126–28**
Craven Tasker Ltd., **I** 573–74
Crawford and Watson, **IV** 278
Crawford Door Försäljnings AB, **53** 85
Crawford Gosho Co., Ltd., **IV** 442
Crawford Group, Inc., **17** 372
Crawford Supply Company, **6** 392

Cray Research, Inc., **III** 126, 128, **129–31**; **10** 256; **16 137–40 (upd.)**; **21** 391; **22** 428; **29** 440
Crayfish Company, Ltd., **36** 153
Crazy Eddie Inc., **23** 373
Crazy Shirts, Inc., **45** 42
CRC Holdings Corp., **51** 217
CRD Total France, **IV** 560
Cream City Railway Company, **6** 601
Cream of Wheat Corp., **II** 543; **22** 427
Cream Wine Company, **48** 392
Creamola Food Products, **II** 569
Creasy Co., **II** 682
Creative Artists Agency LLC, **10** 228; **22** 297; **23** 512, 514; **32** 115; **38 161–64**
Creative Artists Associates, **43** 235
Creative BioMolecules, Inc., **29** 454
Creative Business Concepts, Inc., **39** 346
Creative Concepts in Advertising, **27** 194
Creative Displays, Inc., **27** 279
Creative Engineering Inc., **13** 472
Creative Food 'N Fun Co., **14** 29
Creative Forming, Inc., **8** 562
Creative Homes, Inc., **IV** 341
Creative Integration and Design Inc., **20** 146
Creative Memories, **40** 44
Creative Technologies Corp., **15** 401
Creative Technology, Inc., **48** 83
Credit & Risk Management Associates, Inc., **18** 170
Credit Acceptance Corporation, **18 120–22**
Crédit Agricole, **II 264–66**, 355; **19** 51
Credit and Data Marketing Services, **V** 118
Credit Clearing House, **IV** 605
Crédit Commercial de France, **25** 173
Crédit Communal de Belgique, **42** 111
Credit du Nord, **II** 260
Crédit Foncier, **II** 264
Crédit Général de Belgique, **II** 304
Credit Immobilier, **7** 538
Crédit Liégeois, **II** 270
Crédit Local de France, **42** 111
Crédit Lyonnais, **II** 242, 257, 354; **6** 396; **7** 12; **9 147–49**; **19** 34, 51, 166; **21** 226; **25** 170, 329; **33 117–21 (upd.)**
Credit Mobilier, **II** 294
Crédit National S.A., **9 150–52**
Credit Service Exchange, **6** 24
Credit Suisse First Boston. *See* Financière Crédit Suisse-First Boston.
Crédit Suisse Group, **II 267–69**, 369–70, 378–79, 402–04; **21 144–47 (upd.)**; **52** 354, 356–358. *See also* Schweizerische Kreditanstalt.
Credit Union Federation, **48** 290
Creditanstalt-Bankverein, **II** 242, 295
CrediThrift Financial, **11** 16
Credithrift Financial of Indiana, **III** 194
Credito de la Union Minera, **II** 194
Credito Italiano, **I** 368, 465, 567; **II** 191, **270–72**; **III** 347
Credito Minero y Mercantil, S.A., **22** 285
Credito Provincial Hipotecario, **19** 189
Creditrust Corp., **42** 259
Cree Inc., **13** 399; **53 117–20**
Crellin Holding, Inc., **8** 477
Crellin Plastics, **8** 13
Crenlo Corp., **16** 180
Creo Inc., **48 121–24**
Creole Petroleum Corporation, **IV** 428; **7** 171
Cresap, McCormick and Paget, **32** 458

Crescendo Productions, **6** 27
Crescent Box & Printing Co., **13** 442
Crescent Capital, **44** 95
Crescent Chemical, **I** 374
Crescent Niagara Corp., **II** 16
Crescent Real Estate Equities Company, **25** 454
Crescent Software Inc., **15** 373
Crescent Vert Company, Ltd., **II** 51; **21** 330
Crescent Washing Machine Company, **8** 298
Crescott, Inc., **15** 501
Cressbrook Dairy Co., **II** 546
Cressey Dockham & Co., **II** 682
Crest Fruit Co., **17** 458
Crest Ridge Homes, Inc., **17** 83
Crest Service Company, **9** 364
Crestbrook Forest Industries Ltd., **IV** 285
Crestmont Financial Corporation, **14** 472
Creusot-Loire, **II** 93–94; **19** 166
Crevettes du Cameroun, **13** 244
CRH plc, **37** 203, 206
Crimson Associates L.P., **26** 48
Crisoba. *See* Compania Industrial de San Cristobal, S.A. de C.V.
Crist Partners, **34** 249
Criterion Casualty Company, **10** 312
Criterion Life Insurance Company, **10** 311
Critical Care Concepts, **50** 123
Critikon, Inc., **III** 36
Crocker National Bank, **II** 226, 317, 319, 383; **13** 535; **17** 324–25
Crocker National Corporation, **12** 536
Crockett Container Corporation, **8** 268
Croda International Plc, **IV** 383; **45 125–28**
Croitex S.A., **26** 374
Crompton & Knowles Corp., **I** 633; **9 153–55**
Crompton Corporation, **36 143–50 (upd.)**; **52** 305
Crop Production Services, Inc., **IV** 576
CROPP. *See* Organic Valley.
Crosby Enterprises, **17** 19
Croscill Home Fashions, **8** 510
Croscill, Inc., **42 95–97**
Crosfield, Lampard & Co., **III** 696
Cross & Trecker Corporation, **10** 330
Cross Company. *See* A.T. Cross Company.
Cross-Continent Auto Retailers, **26** 501
Cross Country Group, **25** 358
Cross Creek Apparel, Inc., **30** 400
Cross Pointe Paper Corporation, **26** 363
Cross/Tessitore & Associates, **16** 259
Cross Timbers Oil Company. *See* XTO Energy, Inc.
Crossair AG. *See* Swiss International Air Lines Ltd.
Crosse and Blackwell, **II** 547
Crossett Lumber Co., **IV** 281; **9** 259
Crossland Capital Corp., **III** 293
Crossley Motors, Ltd., **13** 285
Crothall, **6** 44
Crothers Properties, Ltd., **21** 500
Crouse-Hinds Co., **II** 16; **19** 45
Crow Catchpole, **III** 752; **28** 448
Crowell-Collier Publishing Company, **IV** 310; **7** 286
Crowell Publishing Company, **19** 266
Crowley Foods, Inc., **II** 528
Crowley Maritime Corporation, **6 382–84**; **9** 510–11; **28 77–80 (upd.)**
Crowley, Milner & Company, **19 106–08**

Crown Advertising Agency. *See* King Kullen Grocery Co., Inc.

Crown Aluminum, **I** 544

Crown America Corp., **13** 393

Crown Books Corporation, 14 61; **16** 159–61; **21 148–50; 41** 61

Crown Can Co., **I** 601

Crown Casino, **54** 299

Crown Center Redevelopment Corp., **IV** 621

Crown Central Petroleum Corporation, 7 101–03

Crown, Cork & Seal Company, Inc., I 601–03; 13 188–90 (upd.); **15** 129; **17** 106; **24** 264; **30** 475; **32 123–27** (upd.)

Crown Courier Systems, Inc., **24** 126

Crown Crafts, Inc., 16 141–43

Crown Drugs, **II** 673

Crown Equipment Corporation, 15 134–36

Crown Forest Industries, **IV** 279; **19** 155

Crown House Engineering, **44** 148

Crown Life Insurance Company, **III** 261; **6** 181–82

Crown Media Holdings, Inc., 45 129–32

Crown Oil and Refining Company, **7** 101

Crown Packaging, **19** 155

Crown Pet Foods Ltd., **39** 356

Crown Point Ventures, **49** 316

Crown Publishing Group, **IV** 584; **13** 429; **31** 376, 379

Crown Radio, **17** 123–24; **41** 114

Crown Technical Systems, Inc., **37** 215

Crown Vantage Inc., 29 135–37

Crown Zellerbach Corporation, **IV** 290, 345; **8** 261; **22** 210; **24** 247

Crownx Inc., **6** 181–82

Crowson and Son Ltd., **23** 219

CRSS Inc., 6 142–44; 23 491

CRT, **51** 199

CRTC. *See* Canadian Radio-Television and Telecommunications Commission.

Crucible Steel, **I** 434–35

Crude Oil Pipe Line Co., **IV** 400

Cruden Investments Pty Ltd., **IV** 651; **7** 390

Cruise America Inc., 21 151–53

Cruise Associates, **22** 471

Crum & Forster Holdings, Inc., **II** 448; **III** 172; **6** 290; **13** 448; **26** 546

Crump E & S, **6** 290

Crump Inc., **I** 584

Crupo Camino Real. *See* Real Turismo, S.A. de C.V.

Cruse Bekleidung GmbH & Co. KG, **53** 195

Crush International, **II** 478; **III** 53

Crushed Stone Sales Ltd., **IV** 241

Cruzan Rum Distillery, Ltd., **27** 478

Cruzcampo, **18** 501

Cruzeiro do Sul Airlines, **6** 133

Cryenco Sciences Inc., **21** 109

CryoLife, Inc., 46 112–14

Cryomedics Inc., **I** 667

Crystal Brands, Inc., 9 156–58; 12 431

Crystal Market, **41** 174

Crystal Oil Co., **IV** 180, 548

Crystal Rock Water Co., **51** 396

CS Crable Sportswear Inc., **23** 66

CS First Boston Inc., II 269, **402–04; III** 289; **12** 209; **21** 146. *See also* Credit Suisse Group.

CS Holding. *See* Credit Suisse Group.

CS Life, **21** 146–47

CSA. *See* China Southern Airlines Company Ltd.

CSA Press, **IV** 661

CSC. *See* Computer Sciences Corporation.

CSC Holdings, Inc., **32** 105

CSC Industries, Inc., **IV** 63

CSE Corp., **III** 214

Csemege, **53** 178

CSFB. *See* Financière Crédit Suisse-First Boston; Credit Suisse Group.

CSFBdirect Inc., **46** 55

CSG Information Services, **55** 250–51

CSI Computer Systems, **47** 36

CSK, **10** 482

CSK Auto Corporation, 38 165–67

CSO. *See* Columbus & Southern Ohio Electric Company.

CSR Limited, III 686–88, 728, 735–36; **IV** 46; **22** 106; **28 81–84** (upd.)

CSR Rinker Materials Corp., **46** 197

CSS Industries, Inc., 35 128–31

CST Office Products, **15** 36; **42** 416

CSX Corporation, V 438–40, 485; **6** 340; **9** 59; **13** 462; **22 164–68** (upd.); **29** 360–61

CSY Agri-Processing, **7** 81–82

CT Financial Services Inc., **V** 401–02; **49** 397

CT&T. *See* Carolina Telephone and Telegraph Company.

CTA. *See* Comptoir des Textiles Artificielles.

CTA Makro Commercial Co., Ltd., **55** 347

CTB International Corporation, 43 129–31 (upd.)

CTG, Inc., 11 64–66

CTI. *See* Cosmetic Technology International, Inc.

CTNE, **I** 462

CTR. *See* International Business Machines Corporation.

CTS Corporation, 19 104; **39 105–08**

CTV Network, **35** 69

C2B Technologies, **45** 201

CTX Mortgage Company, **8** 88

Cub Foods, **II** 669–70; **14** 411; **17** 302; **18** 505; **22** 327; **50** 455

Cuban-American Manganese Corp., **IV** 81; **7** 186

Cuban American Nickel Co., **IV** 82; **7** 186

Cuban American Oil Company, **8** 348

Cuban Telephone Co., **I** 462–63

Cubic Corporation, 19 109–11

Cubitts Nigeria, **III** 753

CUC International Inc., 16 144–46. *See also* Cendant Corporation.

Cuckler Steel Span Co., **I** 481

Cudahy Corp., **12** 199

Cuisinart Corporation, 17 110; **24 129–32**

Culbro Corporation, 14 19; **15 137–39**

Culinary Foods, Inc., **14** 516; **50** 493

Cullen/Frost Bankers, Inc., 25 113–16

Culligan International Company, I 373; **II** 468; **12 87–88**, 346; **16** 20

Culligan Water Technologies, Inc., 38 168–70 (upd.)

Cullinet Software Corporation, **6** 225; **14** 390; **15** 108

Cullman Bros. *See* Culbro Corporation.

Cullum Companies, **II** 670

Culp, Inc., 29 138–40

Culter Industries, Inc., **22** 353

Cumberland Farms, Inc., 17 120–22; 26 450

Cumberland Federal Bancorporation, **13** 223; **31** 206

Cumberland Newspapers, **IV** 650; **7** 389

Cumberland Packing Corporation, 26 107–09

Cumberland Paper Board Mills Ltd., **IV** 248

Cumberland Pipeline Co., **IV** 372

Cumberland Property Investment Trust Ltd., **IV** 711

Cummins Cogeneration Co. *See* Cogeneration Development Corp.

Cummins Engine Co., Inc., I 146–48, 186; **III** 545; **IV** 252; **10** 273–74; **12 89–92** (upd.); **16** 297; **17** 29; **19** 293; **21** 503; **26** 256; **40 131–35** (upd.); **42** 387; **52** 213, 216

Cumo Sports, **16** 109

Cumulus Media Inc., 37 103–05

CUNA Mutual Insurance Group, **11** 495

Cunard Line Ltd., I 573; **23 159–62; 27** 90, 92; **36** 323; **38** 341, 344

Cuno Kourten, **13** 353

Cupples Products Co., **IV** 15

CurranCare, LLC, **50** 122

Current, Inc., 37 106–09

Currys Group PLC, **V** 49; **19** 123; **49** 112

Cursenir, **I** 280

Curtice-Burns Foods, Inc., 7 17–18, **104–06; 21** 18, **154–57** (upd.)

Curtin & Pease/Peneco, **27** 361

Curtis Circulation Co., **IV** 619

Curtis Homes, **22** 127

Curtis Industries, **13** 165

Curtis 1000 Inc. *See* American Business Products, Inc.

Curtis Squire Inc., **18** 455

Curtiss Candy Co., **II** 544

Curtiss-Wright Corporation, I 524; **III** 464; **7** 263; **8** 49; **9** 14, 244, 341, 417; **10 260–63; 11** 427; **21** 174; **23** 340; **35 132–37** (upd.)

Curver Group, **III** 614

Curver-Rubbermaid, **III** 615

Curves International, Inc., 54 80–82

Cushman Motor Works, **III** 598

Custom Academic Publishing Company, **12** 174

Custom Building Products of California, Inc., **53** 176

Custom Chrome, Inc., 16 147–49

Custom Electronics, Inc., **9** 120

Custom Expressions, Inc., **7** 24; **22** 35

Custom Hoists, Inc., **17** 458

Custom, Ltd, **46** 197

Custom Metal Products, Inc., **III** 643

Custom Organics, **8** 464

Custom Primers, **17** 288

Custom Products Inc., **III** 643

Custom Publishing Group, **27** 361

Custom Technologies Corp., **19** 152

Custom Thermoform, **24** 512

Custom Tool and Manufacturing Company, **41** 366

Custom Transportation Services, Inc., **26** 62

Custom Woodwork & Plastics Inc., **36** 159

Customized Transportation Inc., **22** 164, 167

AB Custos, **25** 464

Cutisin, **55** 123

Cutler-Hammer Inc., **I** 155; **III** 644–45

Cutter & Buck Inc., 27 112–14
Cutter Laboratories, **I** 310
Cutter Precision Metals, Inc., **25** 7
CVC Capital Partners Limited, **49** 451; **54** 207
CVE Corporation, Inc., **24** 395
CVG Aviation, **34** 118
CVI Incorporated, **21** 108
CVL Inc., **II** 457
CVN Companies, **9** 218
CVPS. *See* Central Vermont Public Service Corporation.
CVS Corporation, 32 166, 170; **34** 285; **45** 133–38 **(upd.)**
CWM. *See* Chemical Waste Management, Inc.
CWP. *See* Custom Woodwork & Plastics Inc.
CWT Farms International Inc., **13** 103
CXT Inc., **33** 257
Cyber Communications Inc., **16** 168
CyberCash Inc., **18** 541, 543
Cybermedia, Inc., 25 117–19, 349
Cybernet Electronics Corp., **II** 51; **21** 330
Cybernex, **10** 463
Cybershield, Inc., **52** 103, 105
CyberSource Corp., **26** 441
CYBERTEK Corporation, **11** 395
CyberTel, **IV** 596–97
CyberTrust Solutions Inc., **42** 24–25
Cybex International, Inc., 49 106–09
Cycle & Carriage Ltd., **20** 313
Cycle Video Inc., **7** 590
Cyclo Chemical Corp., **I** 627
Cyclo Getriebebau Lorenz Braren GmbH, **III** 634
Cyclone Co. of Australia, **III** 673
Cyclops Corporation, **10** 45; **13** 157
Cydsa. *See* Grupo Cydsa, S.A. de C.V.
Cygna Energy Services, **13** 367
Cygne Designs, Inc., 25 120–23; **37** 14
Cymbal Co., Ltd., **V** 150
Cynosure Inc., **11** 88
Cyphernetics Corp., **III** 118
Cypress Amax Minerals Co., **13** 158; **22** 285–86
Cypress Insurance Co., **III** 214
Cypress Semiconductor Corporation, 6 216; **18** 17, 383; **20** 174–76; **43** 14; **48** 125–29 **(upd.)**
Cyprus Amax Coal Company, **35** 367
Cyprus Amax Minerals Company, 21 158–61
Cyprus Minerals Company, 7 107–09
Cyrix Corp., **10** 367; **26** 329
Cyrk Inc., 19 112–14; **21** 516; **33** 416
Cytec Industries Inc., 27 115–17
Czarnikow-Rionda Company, Inc., 32 128–30

D&D Enterprises, Inc., **24** 96
D&F Industries, Inc., **17** 227; **41** 204
D&K Wholesale Drug, Inc., 14 146–48
D&N Systems, Inc., **10** 505
D&O Inc., **17** 363
D & P Studios, **II** 157
D&W Computer Stores, **13** 176
D & W Food Stores, Inc., **8** 482; **27** 314
D.B. Kaplan's, **26** 263
D.B. Marron & Company, **II** 445; **22** 406
D.C. Heath & Co., **II** 86; **11** 413; **36** 273; **38** 374
D.C. National Bancorp, **10** 426
D. Connelly Boiler Company, **6** 145

D. de Ricci-G. Selnet et Associes, **28** 141
d.e.m.o., **28** 345
D.E. Makepeace Co., **IV** 78
D.E. Shaw & Co., **25** 17; **38** 269
D.E. Winebrenner Co., **7** 429
D.G. Calhoun, **12** 112
D.G. Yuengling & Son, Inc., 38 171–73
D. Hald & Co., **III** 417
D.I. Manufacturing Inc., **37** 351
D.K. Gold, **17** 138
D.L. Rogers Group, **37** 363
D.L. Saslow Co., **19** 290
D.M. Nacional, **23** 170
D.M. Osborne Co., **III** 650
D.R. Horton Inc., **25** 217; **26** 291
D.W. Mikesell Co. *See* Mike-Sell's Inc.
Da Gama Textiles Company, **24** 450
Dabney, Morgan & Co., **II** 329
D'Addario & Company, Inc. *See* J. D'Addario & Company, Inc.
Dade Reagents Inc., **19** 103
Dade Wholesale Products, **6** 199
DADG. *See* Deutsch-Australische Dampfschiffs-Gesellschaft.
Dae Won Kang Up Co., **III** 581
Daejin Shipping Company, **6** 98; **27** 271
Daesung Heavy Industries, **I** 516
Daewoo Group, I 516; **II** 53; **III** 457–59, 749; **12** 211; **18** 123–27 **(upd.)**; **30** 185
DAF, **I** 186; **III** 543; **7** 566–67
Daffy's Inc., 26 110–12
NV Dagblad De Telegraaf. *See* N.V. Holdingmaatschappij De Telegraaf.
Dage-Bell, **II** 86
Dagincourt. *See* Compagnie de Saint-Gobain S.A.
D'Agostino Supermarkets Inc., 19 115–17
Dagsbladunie, **IV** 611
DAH. *See* DeCrane Aircraft Holdings Inc.
Dahl Manufacturing, Inc., **17** 106
Dahlberg, Inc., **18** 207–08
Dahlgren, **I** 677
Dahlonega Equipment and Supply Company, **12** 377
Dai-Ichi. *See also listings under* Daiichi.
Dai-Ichi Bank, **I** 507, 511; **IV** 148
Dai-Ichi Kangyo Bank Ltd., II 273–75, 325–26, 360–61, 374; **III** 188
Dai-Ichi Mokko Co., **III** 758
Dai-Ichi Mutual Life Insurance Co., **II** 118; **III** 277, 401; **25** 289; **26** 511; **38** 18
Dai Nippon. *See also listings under* Dainippon.
Dai Nippon Brewery Co., **I** 220, 282; **21** 319
Dai Nippon Ink and Chemicals, Inc., **I** 303; **54** 330
Dai Nippon Mujin, **II** 371
Dai Nippon Printing Co., Ltd., IV 598–600, 631, 679–80
Dai Nippon X-ray Inc., **II** 75
Dai Nippon Yuben Kai, **IV** 631–32
Daido Boeki, **24** 325
Daido Spring Co., **III** 580
Daido Steel Co., Ltd., IV 62–63
Daido Trading, **I** 432, 492; **24** 324
The Daiei, Inc., V 11, 39–40; **17** 123–25 **(upd.)**; **18** 186, 285; **19** 308; **36** 418–19; **41** 113–16 **(upd.)**
Daig Corporation, **43** 349–50
Daignault Rolland, **24** 404

Daihatsu Motor Company, Ltd., 7 110–12; **21** 162–64 **(upd.)**; **38** 415
Daiichi. *See also listings under* Dai-Ichi.
Daiichi Atomic Power Industry Group, **II** 22
Daiichi Bussan Kaisha Ltd., **I** 505, 507
Daiichi Fire, **III** 405
Daijugo Bank, **I** 507
Daiken Company. *See* Marubeni Corporation.
Daikin Industries, Ltd., III 460–61
Daikyo Oil Co., Ltd., **IV** 403–04, 476; **53** 114
Dailey & Associates, **I** 16
Daily Chronicle Investment Group, **IV** 685
Daily Mail and General Trust plc, 19 118–20; **39** 198–99
Daily Mirror, **IV** 665–66; **17** 397
Daily Press Inc., **IV** 684; **22** 522
The Daimaru, Inc., V 41–42, 130; **42** 98–100 **(upd.)**
Daimler Airway, **I** 92
Daimler-Benz Aerospace AG, 16 150–52; **24** 84
Daimler-Benz AG, I 27, 138, **149–51**, 186–87, 192, 194, 198, 411, 549; **II** 257, 279–80, 283; **III** 495, 523, 562, 563, 695, 750; **7** 219; **10** 261, 274; **11** 31; **12** 192, 342; **13** 30, 286, 414; **14** 169; **15** 140–44 **(upd.)**; **20** 312–13; **22** 11; **26** 481, 498
DaimlerChrysler Aerospace AG. *See* European Aeronautic Defence and Space Company EADS N.V.
DaimlerChrysler AG, 34 128–37 **(upd.)**, 306
Dain Bosworth Inc., **15** 231–33, 486
Dain Rauscher Corporation, 35 138–41 **(upd.)**
Daina Seikosha, **III** 620
Daini-Denden Incorporated, **12** 136–37
Daini-Denden Kikaku Company, Ltd., **II** 51. *See also* DDI Corporation.
Dainippon. *See also listings under* Dai-Nippon.
Dainippon Celluloid Company, **I** 509; **III** 486; **18** 183
Dainippon Ink & Chemicals, Inc., **IV** 397; **10** 466–67; **13** 308, 461; **17** 363; **28** 194
Dainippon Shurui, **III** 42
Dainippon Spinning Company, **V** 387
Daio Paper Corporation, IV 266–67, 269
Dairy Crest Group plc, 32 131–33
Dairy Farm Ice and Cold Storage Co., **IV** 700; **47** 176
Dairy Farm Management Services Ltd., **I** 471; **20** 312
Dairy Farmers of America Inc., **48** 45
Dairy Fresh, Inc., **26** 449
Dairy Maid Products Cooperative, **II** 536
Dairy Mart Convenience Stores, Inc., 7 113–15; **17** 501; **25** 124–27 **(upd.)**
Dairy Queen. *See* International Dairy Queen, Inc.
Dairy Queen National Development Company, **10** 372
Dairy Supply Co., **II** 586; **III** 418, 420
Dairyland Food Laboratories, **I** 677
Dairymen, Inc., **11** 24
Daishowa Paper Manufacturing Co., Ltd. II 361; **IV** 268–70, 326, 667; **17** 398
Daisy Manufacturing Company, Inc., **34** 72
Daisy Systems Corp., **11** 46, 284–85, 489

Daisy/Cadnetix Inc., **6** 248; **24** 235
Daisytek International Corporation, **18** 128–30
Daiwa Bank, Ltd., **II** 276–77, 347, 438; **26** 457; **39** 109–11 (upd.)
Daiwa Securities Company, Limited, **II** 276, 300, 405–06, 434; **9** 377
Daiwa Securities Group Inc., **55** 115–18 (upd.)
Daka, Inc. *See* Unique Casual Restaurants, Inc.
Dakin Inc., **24** 44; **33** 415
Dakota Power Company, **6** 580; **20** 73
Dakotah Mills, **8** 558–59; **16** 353
Daksoft, Inc., **20** 74
Daktronics, Inc., **32** 134–37
Dal-Tile International Inc., **22** 46, 49, 169–71; **53** 175–76
Dalberg Co., **II** 61
Dale Carnegie Training, Inc., **28** 85–87
Dale Electronics, **21** 519
Daleville & Middletown Telephone Company, **14** 258
Dalfort Corp., **15** 281
Dalgety PLC, **II** 499–500; **III** 21; **12** 411; **22** 147; **27** 258, 260. *See also* PIC International Group PLC
Dalian, **14** 556
Dalian Cement Factory, **III** 718
Dalian Dali Steel Works Co. Ltd., **53** 173
Dalian International Nordic Tire Co., **20** 263
D'Allaird's, **24** 315–16
Dallas Airmotive, **II** 16
Dallas Ceramic Co. *See* Dal-Tile International Inc.
Dallas Cowboys Football Club, Ltd., **33** 122–25
Dallas-Fort Worth Suburban Newspapers, Inc., **10** 3
Dallas Lumber and Supply Co., **IV** 358
Dallas Power & Light Company, **V** 724
Dallas Semiconductor Corporation, **13** 191–93; **31** 143–46 (upd.)
Dallas Southland Ice Co., **II** 660
Daltex General Agency, Inc., **25** 115
Damar, **IV** 610
Damark International, Inc., **18** 131–34
Damart, **25** 523
Dameron-Pierson Co., **25** 500
Dames & Moore, Inc., **25** 128–31. *See also* URS Corporation.
Dammann Asphalt, **III** 673
Damodar Valley Corp., **IV** 49
Damon, **21** 153
Damon Clinical Laboratories Inc., **26** 392
Damon Corp., **11** 334; **54** 57
Dan River Inc., **35** 142–46
Dan's Supreme, **24** 528
Dana Alexander Inc., **27** 197; **43** 218
Dana Corporation, **I** 152–53; **10** 264–66 (upd.); **23** 170–71; **47** 376
Dana Design Ltd., **16** 297
Danaher Corporation, **7** 116–17
Danair A/S, **I** 120
Danapak Holding Ltd., **11** 422
Danapak Riverwood Multipack A/S, **48** 344
Danat-Bank, **I** 138
Danbury Mint, **34** 370
Danbury Phamacal Inc., **31** 254
Dancer Fitzgerald Sample, **I** 33; **23** 505
Daniel Industries, Inc., **16** 153–55

Daniel International Corp., **I** 570–71; **8** 192
Daniel James Insurance Group, **41** 64
Daniel P. Creed Co., Inc., **8** 386
Daniel's Jewelers, **16** 559
Danieli & C. Officine Meccaniche, **13** 98
Daniels Linseed Co., **I** 419
Daniels Packaging, **12** 25
Daniels Pharmaceuticals, Inc., **24** 257
Danisco A/S, **44** 134–37
Danish Aalborg, **27** 91
Danish Almindelinge Brand-Assurance-Compagni, **III** 299
Danley Machine Corp., **I** 514
Danner Shoe Manufacturing Co., **18** 300
Dannon Co., Inc., **II** 468, 474–75; **14** 149–51
Danone Group, **25** 85; **35** 394, 397
Danray, **12** 135
Dansk Bioprotein, **IV** 406–07
Dansk International Designs Ltd., **10** 179, 181; **12** 313
Dansk Metal and Armaturindistri, **III** 569; **20** 361
Dansk Rejsebureau, **I** 120
Danske Bank Aktieselskab, **50** 148–51
Danskin, Inc., **12** 93–95; **15** 358
Danville Resources, Inc., **13** 502
Danzas Group, **V** 441–43; **40** 136–39 (upd.)
DAP, Inc., **III** 66; **12** 7; **18** 549
DAP Products Inc., **36** 396
Dara Michelle, **17** 101–03
D'Arcy Masius Benton & Bowles, Inc., **I** 233–34; **6** 20–22; **10** 226–27; **26** 187; **28** 137; **32** 138–43 (upd.)
Darden Restaurants, Inc., **16** 156–58; **36** 238; **44** 138–42 (upd.)
Darigold, Inc., **9** 159–61
Darling and Hodgson, **IV** 91
Darling, Brown & Sharpe. *See* Brown & Sharpe Manufacturing Co.
Darmstadter, **II** 282
Darracq, **7** 6
Darrell J. Sekin Transport Co., **17** 218
Dart & Kraft Financial Corp., **II** 534; **III** 610–11; **7** 276; **12** 310; **14** 547
Dart Group Corporation, **II** 645, 656, 667, 674; **12** 49; **15** 270; **16** 159–62; **21** 148; **23** 370; **24** 418; **27** 158; **32** 168
Dart Industries, **II** 533–34; **III** 610; **9** 179–80. *See also* Premark International Inc.
Dart Transit Co., **13** 550
Dart Truck Co., **I** 185
Dartex, **18** 434
Darty S.A., **27** 118–20
Darvel Realty Trust, **14** 126
Darya-Varia Laboratoria, **18** 182
DASA. *See* Daimler-Benz Aerospace AG; Deutsche Aerospace Airbus.
Dashwood Industries, **19** 446
Dassault Aviation SA, **21** 11
Dassault-Breguet. *See* Avions Marcel Dassault-Breguet Aviation.
Dassault Systèmes S.A., **25** 132–34; **26** 179. *See also* Groupe Dassault Aviation SA.
Dassler, **14** 6
Dastek Inc., **10** 464; **11** 234–35
DAT GmbH, **10** 514
Dat Jidosha Seizo Co., **I** 183
Data Acquisition Systems, Inc., **16** 300
Data Architects, **14** 318

Data Base Management Inc., **11** 19
Data-Beam Corp., **25** 301
Data Broadcasting Corporation, **31** 147–50
Data Business Forms, **IV** 640
Data Card Corp., **IV** 680
Data Corp., **IV** 311; **19** 267
Data Documents, **III** 157
Data Force Inc., **11** 65
Data General Corporation, **II** 208; **III** 124, 133; **6** 221, 234; **8** 137–40; **9** 297; **10** 499; **12** 162; **13** 201; **16** 418; **20** 8
Data One Corporation, **11** 111
Data Preparation, Inc., **11** 112
Data Printer, Inc., **18** 435
Data Resources, Inc., **IV** 637
Data Specialties Inc. *See* Zebra Technologies Corporation.
Data Structures Inc., **11** 65
Data Systems Technology, **11** 57; **38** 375
Data Technology Corp., **18** 510
Data 3 Systems, **9** 36
Datac plc, **18** 140
Datachecker Systems, **II** 64–65; **III** 164; **11** 150
Datacraft Corp., **II** 38
DataFocus, Inc., **18** 112
Datamatic Corp., **II** 41, 86; **12** 247; **50** 232
Datapoint Corporation, **11** 67–70
Datapro Research Corp., **IV** 637
Dataquest Inc., **10** 558; **21** 235, 237; **22** 51; **25** 347
Datas Incorporated, **I** 99; **6** 81
Datascope Corporation, **39** 112–14
Dataset Communications Inc., **23** 100
Datastream International Ltd., **IV** 605; **10** 89; **13** 417
DataTimes Corporation, **29** 58
Datavision Inc., **11** 444
Datec, **22** 17
Datek Online Holdings Corp., **32** 144–46; **48** 225–27
Datext, **IV** 596–97
Datran, **11** 468
Datsun. *See* Nissan Motor Company, Ltd.
Datteln, **IV** 141
Datura Corp., **14** 391
Dauphin Deposit Corporation, **14** 152–54
Dauphin Distribution Services. *See* Exel Logistics Ltd.
Daut + Rietz and Connectors Pontarlier, **19** 166
Dave & Buster's, Inc., **33** 126–29
Davenport & Walter, **III** 765
Davenport Mammoet Heavy Transport Inc., **26** 280
The Davey Tree Expert Company, **11** 71–73
The David and Lucile Packard Foundation, **41** 117–19
David B. Smith & Company, **13** 243
David Berg & Co., **14** 537
David Brown & Son. *See* Brown & Sharpe Manufacturing Co.
David Brown, Ltd., **10** 380
David Clark, **30** 357
David Crystal, Inc., **II** 502; **9** 156; **10** 323
David Hafler Company, **43** 323
The David J. Joseph Company, **14** 155–56; **19** 380; **55** 347
David L. Babson & Company Inc., **53** 213
David Lloyd Leisure Ltd., **52** 412, 415–16
David Sandeman Group, **I** 592

David Sassoon & Co., **II** 296
David Williams and Partners, **6** 40
David Wilson Homes Ltd., **45** 442–43
David's Bridal, Inc., 33 130–32; 46 288
David's Supermarkets, **17** 180
Davidson & Associates, **16** 146
Davidson & Leigh, **21** 94
Davidson Automatic Merchandising Co.
   Inc., **II** 607
Davidson Brothers Co., **19** 510
Davies, William Ltd., **II** 482
Davis & Geck, **I** 301; **27** 115
Davis & Henderson Ltd., **IV** 640
Davis Coal & Coke Co., **IV** 180
Davis Estates, **I** 592
Davis Manufacturing Company, **10** 380
Davis Polk & Wardwell, 36 151–54
Davis Service Group PLC, 45 139–41;
   49 374, 377
Davis-Standard Company, **9** 154; **36** 144
Davis Vision, Inc., **27** 209
Davis Wholesale Company, **9** 20
Davison Chemical Corp., **IV** 190
Davlyn Industries, Inc., **22** 487
Davox Corporation, **18** 31
Davy Bamag GmbH, **IV** 142
Davy McKee AG, **IV** 142
DAW Technologies, Inc., 25 135–37
Dawe's Laboratories, Inc., **12** 3
Dawn Food Products, Inc., 17 126–28
Dawnay Day, **III** 501
Dawson Holdings PLC, 43 132–34
Dawson Mills, **II** 536
Day & Zimmermann Inc., 6 579; **9**
   162–64; 31 151–155 (upd.)
Day Brite Lighting, **II** 19
Day-Glo Color Corp., **8** 456
Day International, **8** 347
Day-Lee Meats, **II** 550
Day-N-Nite, **II** 620
Day Runner, Inc., 14 157–58; 41 120–23
   (upd.)
Day-Timers, Inc., **51** 9
Daybridge Learning Centers, **13** 49, 299
Dayco Products, **7** 297
Daylin Corporation, **46** 271
Days Inns of America, Inc., **III** 344; **11**
   178; **13** 362, 364; **21** 362
Daystar International Inc., **11** 44
Daystrom, **III** 617; **17** 418
Daytex, Inc., **II** 669; **18** 505; **50** 455
Dayton Engineering Laboratories, **I** 171; **9**
   416; **10** 325
Dayton Flexible Products Co., **I** 627
Dayton Hudson Corporation, V 43–44; 8
   35; **9** 360; **10** 136, 391–93, 409–10,
   515–16; **13** 330; **14** 376; **16** 176, 559;
   18 108, 135–37 (upd.); **22** 59
Dayton Power & Light Company, **6** 467,
   480–82
Dayton Walther Corp., **III** 650, 652
Daytron Mortgage Systems, **11** 485
Dazey Corp., **16** 384; **43** 289
DB. *See* Deutsche Bundesbahn.
DB Reise & Touristik AG, **37** 250
DBA Holdings, Inc., **18** 24
DBMS Inc., **14** 390
DC Comics Inc., 25 138–41
DCA Advertising, **16** 168
DCA Food Industries, **II** 554; **27** 258–60,
   299
DCE Consultants, **51** 17
DCL BioMedical, Inc., **11** 333
DCMS Holdings Inc., **7** 114; **25** 125

DDB Needham Worldwide, 14 159–61;
   22 394
DDD Energy, Inc., **47** 348, 350
DDI Corporation, 7 118–20; 13 482; **21**
   330–31
NV De Beer and Partners, **45** 386
De Beers Consolidated Mines Limited /
   De Beers Centenary AG, I 107; **IV**
   20–21, 23, 60, **64–68,** 79, 94; **7 121–26**
   (upd.); **16** 25–26, 29; **21** 345–46; **28**
   88–94 (upd.); 50 31, 34
De Bono Industries, **24** 443
De Dietrich & Cie., 31 156–59
De Grenswisselkantoren NV, **III** 201
De Groote Bossche, **III** 200
de Havilland Aircraft Co., **I** 82, 92–93,
   104, 195; **III** 507–08; **7** 11. *See also*
   Bombardier Inc.
de Havilland Holdings, Ltd., **24** 85–86
De La Rue plc, 10 267–69; 34 138–43
   (upd.); 46 251
De Laurentiis Entertainment Group, **III** 84;
   25 317
De Laval Turbine Company, **III** 418–20; **7**
   236–37
De Leuw, Cather & Company, **8** 416
De Nederlandse Bank, **IV** 132
De Paepe, **45** 386
De-sta-Co., **III** 468
De Ster 1905 NV, **III** 200
De Streekkrant-De Weekkrantgroep NV, **48**
   347
De Tomaso Industries, **11** 104; **50** 197
De Trey Gesellschaft, **10** 271
De Vito/Verdi, **26** 111
De Walt, **III** 436
de Wendel, **IV** 226–27
DEA Group, **23** 83
Dead Sea Works Ltd., **55** 229
Dealer Equipment and Services, **10** 492
Dean & Barry Co., **8** 455
Dean & DeLuca, Inc., 36 155–57
Dean-Dempsy Corp., **IV** 334
Dean Foods Company, 7 127–29; 17 56;
   21 157, **165–68, (upd.); 26** 447; **29** 434;
   46 70
Dean Witter, Discover & Co., II 445; **IV**
   186; **V** 180, 182; **7** 213; **12 96–98; 18**
   475; **21** 97; **22** 405–07. *See also*
   Morgan Stanley Dean Witter &
   Company.
Dearborn Publishing Group, **42** 211
Death Row Records, 27 121–23
Deb Shops, Inc., 16 163–65
DeBartolo Realty Corp., **27** 401
Debenhams Plc, V 20–22; 28 29–30,
   95–97; 39 88
Debevoise & Plimpton, 39 115–17
Debis, **26** 498
DeBoles Nutritional Foods Inc., **27**
   197–98; **43** 218–19
Debron Investments Plc., **8** 271
DEC. *See* Digital Equipment Corp.
Decafin SpA, **26** 278, 280
Decathlon S.A., **39** 183–84
Decca Record Company Ltd., **II** 81, 83,
   144; **23** 389
Dechert, 43 135–38
Decision Base Resources, **6** 14
Decision Systems Israel Ltd. (DSI), **21** 239
DecisionQuest, Inc., **25** 130
Decker, Howell & Co., **26** 451
Deckers Outdoor Corporation, 22
   172–74

Deco Industries, Inc., **18** 5
Deco Purchasing Company, **39** 211
Decoflex Ltd., **IV** 645
Decolletage S.A. St.-Maurice, **14** 27
Decora Industries, Inc., 31 160–62
DeCrane Aircraft Holdings Inc., 36
   158–60
Dee and Cee Toy Co., **25** 312
Dee Corporation plc, **I** 549; **II** 628–29,
   642; **24** 269
Deeks McBride, **III** 704
Deep Ocean Services, L.L.C., **44** 203
Deep Oil Technology, **I** 570
Deep Rock Oil Company. *See* Kerr-McGee
   Corporation.
Deep Rock Water Co., **III** 21
DeepFlex Production Partners, L.P., **21** 171
Deepsea Ventures, Inc., **IV** 152; **24** 358
DeepTech International Inc., 21 169–71
Deepwater Light and Power Company, **6**
   449
Deer Park Spring Water Co., **III** 21
Deere & Company, I 181, 527; **III**
   462–64, 651; **10** 377–78, 380, 429; **11**
   472; **13** 16–17, 267; **16** 179; **17** 533; **21**
   172–76 (upd.); 22 542; **26** 492; **42**
   101–06 (upd.)
Deering Harvesting Machinery Company.
   See Navistar.
Deering Milliken & Co., **51** 12. *See also*
   Milliken & Co.
Def Jam Records, Inc., **23** 389, 391; **31**
   269; **33** 373–75
Defense Plant Corp., **IV** 10, 408
Defense Technology Corporation of
   America, **27** 50
Defiance, Inc., 22 175–78
Deflecta-Shield Corporation, **40** 299–300
Deft Software, Inc., **10** 505
DEG. *See* Deutsche Edison Gesellschaft.
Degussa Group, I 303; **IV 69–72,** 118
Degussa-Hüls AG, 32 147–53 (upd.); 34
   209
Deinhard, **I** 281
DEKA Research & Development
   Corporation. *See* Segway LLC.
DeKalb AgResearch Inc., **9** 411; **41**
   304–06
Dekalb Energy Company, **18** 366
DeKalb Farmers Market, **23** 263–64
DeKalb Genetics Corporation, 17
   129–31; 29 330
DeKalb Office Supply, **25** 500
Del Laboratories, Inc., 28 98–100
Del Mar Avionics, **26** 491
Del Monte Corporation, II 595; **7**
   130–32; 12 439; **14** 287; **25** 234
Del Monte Foods Company, 23 163–66
   (upd.); 36 472; **38** 198
Del-Rey Petroleum, **I** 526
Del Webb Corporation, 14 162–64; 17
   186–87; **19** 377–78; **26** 291
Delafield, Harvey, Tabrell, Inc., **17** 498
Delafield Industries, **12** 418
Delagrange, **I** 635
Delaware and Hudson Railway Company,
   Inc., **16** 350; **45** 78
Delaware Charter Guarantee & Trust Co.,
   III 330
Delaware Guarantee and Trust Co. *See*
   Wilmington Trust Company.
Delaware Lackawanna & Western, **I** 584
Delaware Management Holdings, **III** 386

Delaware North Companies Incorporated, 7 133–36
Delbard, **I** 272
Delchamps, Inc., **II** 638; **27** 247
Delco Electronics Corporation, **II** 32–35; **III** 151; **6** 265; **25** 223–24; **45** 142–43
Delek Investment & Properties Ltd., **45** 170
Delhaize "Le Lion" S.A., II 626; **15** 176; **27** 94; **44** 143–46
Delhi Gas Pipeline Corporation, **7** 551
Delhi International Oil Corp., **III** 687; **28** 83
Deli Universal, **13** 545
dELiA*s Inc., 29 141–44
Delicato Vineyards, Inc., 50 152–55
Delicious Foods, **13** 383
Delimaatschappij, **13** 545
Dell Computer Corporation, 9 165–66; **10** 309, 459; **11** 62; **16** 5, 196; **24** 31; **25** 254; **27** 168; **31** 163–166 (upd.); **47** 323; **50** 92
Dell Distributing, **25** 483
Dell Publishing Co., **13** 560
Dellwood Elevator Co., **I** 419
Delmar Chemicals Ltd., **II** 484
Delmar Paper Box Co., **IV** 333
Delmarva Properties, Inc., **8** 103; **30** 118
Delmonico Foods Inc., **II** 511
Delmonico International, **II** 101
Deloitte & Touche, 9 167–69, 423; **24** 29
Deloitte Touche Tohmatsu International, 29 145–48 (upd.)
DeLong Engineering Co., **III** 558
DeLorean Motor Co., **10** 117; **14** 321
DeLorme Publishing Company, Inc., 53 121–23
Delphax, **IV** 252; **17** 29
Delphi Automotive Systems Corporation, 22 52; **36** 243; **25** 223; **37** 429; **45** 142–44
Delphy Industries S.A.S., **53** 221
Delprat, **IV** 58
Delta and Pine Land Company, **21** 386; **33** 133–37
Delta Acceptance Corporation Limited, **13** 63
Delta Air Lines, Inc., I 29, 91, 97, **99–100**, 102, 106, 120, 132; **6** 61, **81–83 (upd.)**, 117, 131–32, 383; **12** 149, 381; **13** 171–72; **14** 73; **21** 141, 143; **22** 22; **25** 420, 422–23; **26** 439; **27** 20, 409; **33** 50–51, 377; **34** 116–17, 119; **39** 118–21 (upd.); **47** 29; **52** 90, 92–93
Delta Biologicals S.r.l., **11** 208
Delta Biotechnology Ltd., **25** 82
Delta Campground Management Corp., **33** 399
Delta Communications, **IV** 610
Delta Education, **29** 470, 472
Delta Faucet Co., **III** 568–69; **39** 263
Delta Health, Inc. See DVI, Inc.
Delta International Machinery Corp., **26** 361–63
Delta Lloyd, **III** 235
Delta Manufacturing, **II** 85
Delta Motors, **III** 580
Delta Play, Ltd., **44** 261
Delta Pride Catfish Inc., **18** 247
Delta Queen Steamboat Company, **27** 34–35
Delta Resources Inc., **26** 519
Delta Savings Assoc. of Texas, **IV** 343

Delta Steamship Lines, **9** 425–26
Delta V Technologies, Inc., **33** 348
Delta Woodside Industries, Inc., 8 141–43; **17** 329; **30** 159–61 (upd.); **42** 118
Deltak, L.L.C., **23** 300; **52** 139
Deltic Timber Corporation, 32 339, 341; **46** 115–17
Deluxe Corporation, 7 137–39; **19** 291; **22** 179–82 (upd.); **37** 107–08
Deluxe Data, **18** 518
DeLuxe Laboratories, **IV** 652
Deluxe Upholstering Ltd., **14** 303
Delvag Luftürsicherungs A.G., **I** 111
Demag AG, **II** 22; **III** 566; **IV** 206
Demerara Company, **13** 102
Deminex, **IV** 413, 424
Deming Company, **8** 135
Demka, **IV** 132–33
Demko, **30** 469
DeMoulas / Market Basket Inc., 23 167–69
Dempsey & Siders Agency, **III** 190
Den Fujita, **9** 74
Den Norske Bank, **22** 275
Den norske Creditbank, **II** 366
Den Norske Stats Oljeselskap AS, IV 405–07, 486
Den-Tal-Ez, **I** 702
Denain-Nord-Est-Longwy, **IV** 227
DenAmerica Corporation, 29 149–51
Denault Ltd., **II** 651
Denby Group plc, 44 147–50
Denison International plc, 46 118–20
Denison Mines, Ltd., **12** 198
Denker & Goodwin, **17** 498
Denki Seikosho, **IV** 62
Denmark Tiscali A/S, **48** 398
Denney-Reyburn, **8** 360
Dennison Manufacturing Company. See Avery Dennison Corporation.
Denny's Restaurants Inc., **II** 680; **III** 103; **V** 88–89; **12** 511; **13** 526; **27** 16–18; **50** 489
Denshi Media Services, **IV** 680
DENSO Corporation, 46 121–26 (upd.)
Dent & Co., **II** 296
Dental Benefits Insurance Company, **51** 276, 278
Dental Capital Corp., **19** 290
Dental Research, **25** 56
DentiCare, Inc., **22** 149
Dentists Management Corporation, **51** 276–78
Dentons Green Brewery, **21** 246
Dentsply International Inc., 10 270–72
Dentsu Inc., I 9–11, 36, 38; **6** 29; **9** 30; **13** 204; **16** 166–69 (upd.); **25** 91; **40** 140–44 (upd.)
Denver & Rio Grande Railroad, **12** 18–19
Denver Chemical Company, **8** 84; **38** 124
Denver Gas & Electric Company. See Public Service Company of Colorado.
Denver Nuggets, 51 94–97
Deocsa, **51** 389
DEP Corporation, 20 177–80; **34** 209
Department 56, Inc., 14 165–67; **22** 59; **34** 144–47 (upd.)
Department Stores International, **I** 426; **22** 72; **50** 117
Deposit Guaranty Corporation, 17 132–35
Deposito and Administratie Bank, **II** 185

Depositors National Bank of Durham, **II** 336
DePree Company, **17** 90–91
DePuy, Inc., 10 156–57; **30** 162–65; **36** 306; **37** 110–13 (upd.)
Der Anker, **III** 177
Derby Commercial Bank, **II** 318; **17** 323
Derby Outdoor, **27** 280
Derbyshire Stone and William Briggs, **III** 752
Deritend Computers, **14** 36
Dermablend, Inc., **31** 89
Deruluft, **6** 57
Derwent Publications, **8** 526
Des Moines Electric Light Company, **6** 504
DESA Industries, **8** 545
Desc, S.A. de C.V., 23 170–72
Desco, **51** 120
Deseret Management Corporation, **29** 67
Deseret National Bank, **11** 118
Deseret Pharmaceutical Company, **21** 45
Desert Partners, **III** 763
Design-Center Southwest, **19** 411
Design Craft Ltd., **IV** 640
Design Trend, Inc., **37** 394
Designcraft Inc. See Sloan's Supermarkets Inc.
Designer Holdings Ltd., 20 181–84; **22** 123
Designs, Inc. See Casual Male Retail Group, Inc.
Desmarais Frères, **IV** 557, 559
DeSoto, Inc., **8** 553; **13** 471
Desoutter Brothers plc, **III** 427; **28** 40
Destec Energy, Inc., 12 99–101; **49** 121
Det Danske/Norske Luftartselskab, **I** 119
Det Danske Rengorings Selskab A/S, **49** 221
Detroit Aircraft Corp., **I** 64; **11** 266
Detroit Automobile Co., **I** 164
Detroit Ball Bearing Co., **13** 78
Detroit Chemical Coatings, **8** 553
Detroit City Gas Company. See MCN Corporation.
Detroit Copper Co., **IV** 176–77
Detroit Diesel Corporation, V 494–95; **9** 18; **10** 273–75; **11** 471; **12** 90–91; **18** 308; **19** 292–94; **21** 503
The Detroit Edison Company, I 164; **V** 592–95; **7** 377–78; **11** 136; **14** 135; **18** 320. See also DTE Energy Co.
Detroit Fire & Marine Insurance Co., **III** 191
Detroit Gear and Machine Co., **III** 439
Detroit-Graphite Company, **8** 553
The Detroit Lions, Inc., 55 119–21
The Detroit Pistons Basketball Company, 41 124–27
Detroit Radiator Co., **III** 663
Detroit Red Wings, **7** 278–79; **24** 293; **37** 207; **46** 127
Detroit Steel Products Co., Inc., **IV** 136; **13** 157; **16** 357
Detroit Stoker Company, **37** 399–401
Detroit Tigers Baseball Club, Inc., 24 293; **37** 207; **46** 127–30
Detroit Toledo & Ironton Railroad, **I** 165
Detroit Vapor Stove Co., **III** 439
Detrola, **II** 60
Dettmers Industries Inc., **36** 159–60
Deutsch-Australische Dampfschiffs-Gesellschaft, **6** 398
Deutsch Erdol A.G., **IV** 552
Deutsch, Inc., 42 107–10

Deutsch-Luxembergische Bergwerks und Hütten AG, **I** 542; **IV** 105
Deutsch-Österreichische Mannesmannröhren-Werke Aktiengesellschaft, **III** 564–65
Deutsch Shea & Evans Inc., **I** 15
Deutsch-Skandinavische Bank, **II** 352
Deutsche Aerospace Airbus, **I** 41–42; **7** 9, 11; **12** 190–91; **21** 8; **52** 113–14
Deutsche Allgemeine Versicherungs-Aktiengesellschaft, **III** 412
Deutsche Anlagen Leasing GmbH, **II** 386
Deutsche-Asiatische Bank, **II** 238, 256
Deutsche BA, **14** 73; **24** 400; **26** 115
Deutsche Babcock AG, **II** 386; **III** **465–66**
Deutsche Bahn AG, **37** 250, 253; **46** **131–35 (upd.)**
Deutsche Bank AG, **I** 151, 409, 549; **II** 98, 191, 239, 241–42, 256–58, **278–80**, 281–82, 295, 319, 385, 427, 429; **III** 154–55, 692, 695; **IV** 91, 141, 229, 232, 378, 557; **V** 241–42; **14** 168–71 (upd.); **15** 13; **16** 364–65; **17** 324; **21** 147, **34** 29; **40** 145–51 (upd.); **47** 81–84; **49** 44
Deutsche Börse, **37** 131–32
Deutsche BP Aktiengesellschaft, **7** **140–43**
Deutsche Bundespost Telekom, **V** **287–90**; **18** 155
Deutsche Bundesbahn, **V** **444–47**; **6** 424–26
Deutsche Edelstahlwerke AG, **IV** 222
Deutsche Edison Gesellschaft, **I** 409–10
Deutsche Erdol Aktiengesellschaft, **7** 140
Deutsche Gold-und Silber-Scheideanstalt vormals Roessler, **IV** 69, 118, 139
Deutsche Grammophon Gesellschaft, **23** 389
Deutsche Herold, **49** 44
Deutsche Hydrierwerke, **III** 32
Deutsche Industriewerke AG, **IV** 230
Deutsche Kreditbank, **14** 170
Deutsche Länderbank, **II** 379
Deutsche Lufthansa Aktiengesellschaft, **I** 94, **110–11**, 120; **6** 59–60, 69, 95–96, 386; **12** 191; **25** 159; **26** 113–16 (upd.); **27** 465; **33** 49; **36** 426; **48** 258
Deutsche Marathon Petroleum, **IV** 487
Deutsche Mineralöl-Explorationsgesellschaft mbH, **IV** 197
Deutsche-Nalco-Chemie GmbH., **I** 373
Deutsche Nippon Seiko, **III** 589
Deutsche Petroleum-Verkaufsgesellschaft mbH, **7** 140
Deutsche Post AG, **29** **152–58**; **40** 138
Deutsche Reichsbahn. *See* Deutsche Bundesbahn.
Deutsche Schiff-und Maschinenbau Aktiengesellschaft "Deschimag," **IV** 87
Deutsche Shell, **7** 140
Deutsche Spezialglas AG, **III** 446
Deutsche Strassen und Lokalbahn A.G., **I** 410
Deutsche Telekom AG, **18** 155; **25** 102; **38** 296; **48** 130–35 (upd.)
Deutsche Texaco, **V** 709
Deutsche Union, **III** 693–94
Deutsche Union-Bank, **II** 278
Deutsche Vermögensberatung AG, **51** 19, 23
Deutsche Wagnisfinanzierung, **II** 258; **47** 83
Deutsche Werke AG, **IV** 230

Deutscher Aero Lloyd, **I** 110
Deutscher Automobil Schutz Allgemeine Rechtsschutz-Versicherung AG, **III** 400
Deutscher Kommunal-Verlag Dr. Naujoks & Behrendt, **14** 556
Deutscher Ring, **40** 61
Deutsches Reisebüro DeR, **II** 163
Deutz AG, **III** 541; **39** **122–26**
Deutz-Allis, **III** 544. *See also* AGCO Corp.
Deutz Farm Equipment, **13** 17
Devanlay SA, **48** 279
Devcon Corporation, **III** 519; **22** 282
Deveaux S.A., **41** **128–30**
Developer's Mortgage Corp., **16** 347
Development Finance Corp., **II** 189
Devenish, **21** 247
DeVilbiss Company, **8** 230
DeVilbiss Health Care, Inc., **11** 488
Deville, **27** 421
Devoe & Raynolds Co., **12** 217
Devoke Company, **18** 362
Devon Energy Corporation, **22** 304
Devro plc, **55** **122–24**
DeVry Incorporated, **9** 63; **29** 56, **159–61**
Dewars Brothers, **I** 239–40
Dewey & Almy Chemical Co., **I** 548
Dewey Ballantine LLP, **48** **136–39**
Dexer Corporation, **41** 10
Dexia Group, **42** **111–13**
The Dexter Corporation, **I** 320–22; **12** **102–04 (upd.)**; **17** 287; **52** 183. *See also* Invitrogen Corporation.
Dexter Lock Company, **45** 269
Dexter Shoe, **18** 60, 63
DFS Dorland Worldwide, **I** 35
DFS Group Ltd., **33** 276
DFW Printing Company, **10** 3
DG Bank, **33** 358
DG&E. *See* Denver Gas & Electric Company.
DH Compounding, **8** 347
DH Technology, Inc., **18** **138–40**
Dharma Juice, **31** 350
DHI Corp., **II** 680
DHJ Industries, Inc., **12** 118
DHL Worldwide Express, **6** **385–87**; **18** 177, 316; **24** 133–36 (upd.); **26** 441; **27** 471, 475; **29** 152
Di Giorgio Corp., **II** 602; **12** **105–07**; **24** 528–29
Di-Rite Company, **11** 534
Dia Prosim, S.A., **IV** 409
Diageo plc, **24** **137–41 (upd.)**; **25** 411; **29** 19; **31** 92; **34** 89; **36** 404; **42** 223
Diagnostic Health Corporation, **14** 233
Diagnostic Imaging Services, Inc., **25** 384
Diagnostic Ventures Inc. *See* DVI, Inc.
Diagnostics Pasteur, **I** 677
Dial-A-Mattress Operating Corporation, **32** 427; **46 136–39**
The Dial Corporation, **8** 144–46; **23** **173–75 (upd.)**; **29** 114; **32** 230; **34** 209
Dial Home Shopping Ltd., **28** 30
Dial-Net Inc., **27** 306
Dialight Corp., **13** 397–98
Dialog Information Services, Inc., **IV** 630
Dialogic Corporation, **18** **141–43**
Diamandis Communications Inc., **IV** 619, 678
Diamang, **IV** 65, 67
Diamedix, **11** 207
Diamond Animal Health, Inc., **39** 216
Diamond Communications, **10** 288

Diamond Corporation Ltd., **IV** 21, 66–67; **7** 123
Diamond Crystal Brands, Inc., **32** 274, 277
Diamond Electronics, **24** 510
Diamond Fields Resources Inc., **27** 457
Diamond Head Resources, Inc. *See* AAON, Inc.
Diamond International Corp., **IV** 290, 295; **13** 254–55; **19** 225; **26** 446
Diamond M Offshore Inc., **12** 318
Diamond Match Company, **14** 163
Diamond Offshore Drilling, Inc., **36** 325; **43** 202
Diamond Oil Co., **IV** 548
Diamond Park Fine Jewelers, **16** 559
Diamond Rug & Carpet Mills, **19** 276
Diamond Savings & Loan, **II** 420
Diamond Shamrock Corporation, **IV** **408–11**, 481; **7** 34, 308–099, 345; **13** 118; **19** 177; **45** 411. *See also* Ultramar Diamond Shamrock Corporation.
Diamond-Star Motors Corporation, **9** 349–51
Diamond Trading Company, **IV** 66–67; **7** 123
Diamond Walnut Growers, **7** 496–97
DiamondCluster International, Inc., **51** **98–101**
Dianatel, **18** 143
Diapositive, **44** 296
Diasonics Ultrasound, Inc., **27** 355
Dibrell Brothers, Incorporated, **12** **108–10**; **13** 492
dick clark productions, inc., **16** **170–73**
Dick Simon Trucking, Inc. *See* Simon Transporation Services Inc.
Dickerman, **8** 366
Dickson Forest Products, Inc., **15** 305
Dickstein Partners, L.P., **13** 261
Dictaphone Corp., **III** 157
Didier Lamarthe, **17** 210
Didier-Werke AG, **IV** 232; **53** 285
Diebold, Incorporated, **7** **144–46**; **22** **183–87 (upd.)**
Diedrich Coffee, Inc., **40** **152–54**
Diehl Manufacturing Co., **II** 9
Diemakers Inc., **IV** 443
Diesel Nacional, S.A. *See* Consorcio G Grupo Dina, S.A. de C.V.
Diesel SpA, **40** **155–57**
Diesel United Co., **III** 533
AB Diesels Motorer, **III** 425–26
Diet Center, **10** 383
Dieter Hein Co., **14** 537
Dieterich Standard Corp., **III** 468
Dietrich & Cie. *See* De Dietrich & Cie.
Dietrich Corp., **II** 512; **15** 221; **51** 158
Dietrich's Bakeries, **II** 631
DiFeo Automotive Group, **26** 500–01
Diffusion Immobilier. *See* Union Financière de France Banque.
DiFranza Williamson, **6** 40
DIG Acquisition Corp., **12** 107
Digex, Inc., **45** 201; **46 140–43**
Digi International Inc., **9** **170–72**; **20** 237
Digicom, **22** 17
Digidesign Inc., **38** 70, 72
DiGiorgio Corporation, **25** 421
Digital Audio Disk Corp., **II** 103
Digital City, Inc., **22** 522
Digital Data Systems Company, **11** 408
Digital Devices, Inc., **III** 643
Digital Directory Assistance, **18** 24
Digital Entertainment Network, **42** 272

Digital Equipment Corporation, **II** 8, 62, 108; **III** 118, 128, **132–35**, 142, 149, 166; **6** 225, **233–36 (upd.)**, 237–38, 242, 246–47, 279, 287; **8** 137–39, 519; **9** 35, 43, 57, 166, 170–71, 514; **10** 22–23, 34, 86, 242, 361, 463, 477; **11** 46, 86–88, 274, 491, 518–19; **12** 147, 162, 470; **13** 127, 202, 482; **14** 318; **15** 108; **16** 394, 418; **18** 143, 345; **19** 310; **21** 123; **25** 499; **26** 90, 93; **34** 441–43; **36** 81, 287; **43** 13; **45** 201; **50** 227

Digital Marketing, Inc., **22** 357

Digital Research in Electronic Acoustics and Music S.A., **17** 34

Digital River, Inc., **50 156–59**

Digitech, **19** 414

Dii Group Inc., **38** 188–89

Diligent Engine Co., **III** 342

Dill & Collins, **IV** 311; **19** 266

Dill Enterprises, Inc., **14** 18

Dillard Department Stores, Inc., **V 45–47**; **10** 488; **11** 349; **12** 64; **13** 544–45; **16 174–77 (upd.)**, 559; **19** 48, 324; **27** 61

Dillard Paper Company, **11 74–76**

Dillingham Construction Corporation, **44 151–54 (upd.)**

Dillingham Corp., **I 565–66**

Dillingham Holdings Inc., **9** 511

Dillon Companies Inc., **II** 645; **12** 111–13; **15** 267; **22** 194

Dillon Paper, **IV** 288

Dillon, Read, and Co., Inc., **I** 144, 559; **III** 151, 389; **6** 265; **11** 53; **20** 259; **24** 66

Dime Bancorp, **44** 32–33; **46** 316

Dime Banking and Loan Association of Rochester, **10** 91

Dime Savings Bank of New York, F.S.B., **9 173–74**

Dimeling, Schrieber & Park, **11** 63; **44** 309

Dimensions in Sport, Ltd., **37** 5

Dimeric Development Corporation, **14** 392

DIMON Inc., **12** 110; **27 124–27**

Dina. *See* Consorcio G Grupo Dina, S.A. de C.V.

Dinamica, S.A., **19** 12

Dine S.A., **23** 170–72

Dineen Mechanical Contractors, Inc., **48** 238

Diners Club, **II** 397; **6** 62; **9** 335; **10** 61

Dinner Bell Foods, Inc., **11** 93

de Dion, **III** 523

Dionex Corporation, **46 144–46**

Dior. *See* Christian Dior S.A.

Dirección General de Correos y Telecomunicaciónes, **V** 337

Dirección Nacional de los Yacimientos Petrolíferos Fiscales, **IV** 577–78

Direct Container Lines, **14** 505

Direct Focus, Inc., **47 93–95**

Direct Friends, **25** 91

Direct Line, **12** 422

Direct Mail Services Pty. Ltd., **10** 461

Direct Marketing Technology Inc., **19** 184

Direct Spanish Telegraph Co., **I** 428

Direct Transit, Inc., **42** 364

Direction Générale des Télécommunications, **V** 471

DirectLine Insurance, **22** 52

Directorate General of Telecommunications, **7 147–49**

DIRECTV, Inc., **21** 70; **35** 156, 158–59; **38 174–77**

Dirr's Gold Seal Meats, **6** 199

Disc Go Round, **18** 207, 209

Disc Manufacturing, Inc., **15** 378

Disclosure, Inc., **18** 24

Disco SA, **V** 11; **19** 308–09

Disconto-Gesellschaft, **II** 238, 279

Discount Auto Parts, Inc., **18 144–46**; **26** 348

Discount Bank, **II** 205

Discount Corporation, **12** 565

Discount Drug Mart, Inc., **14 172–73**

Discount Investment Corporation Ltd., **24** 429

Discount Labels, Inc., **20** 15

Discount Tire Co., **19** 294; **20** 263

Discover, **9** 335; **12** 97

Discovery Communications, Inc., **42 114–17**

Discovery Toys, Inc., **19** 28

Discovery Zone, **31** 97

DiscoVision Associates, **III** 605

Discreet Logic Inc., **20 185–87**

Disctronics, Ltd., **15** 380

Disney Channel, **6** 174–75; **13** 280

Disney Co. *See* The Walt Disney Company.

Disney Studios, **II** 408; **6** 174, 176; **43** 229–30, 233

Disneyland, **6** 175

Disneyland Paris. *See* Euro Disneyland SCA.

Disnorte, **51** 389

Dispatch Communications, **10** 432

Display Components Inc., **II** 110; **17** 479

Displayco Midwest Inc., **8** 103

Disposable Hospital Products, **I** 627

Distillers and Cattle Feeders Trust, **I** 376

Distillers Co. plc, **I 239–41**, 252, 263, 284–85; **II** 429, 609–10; **IV** 70; **43** 214

Distillers Securities, **I** 376

Distinctive Printing and Packaging Co., **8** 103

Distinctive Software Inc., **10** 285

Distribuidora Bega, S.A. de C.V., **31** 92

Distribution Centers Incorporated. *See* Exel Logistics Ltd.

Distribution Services, Inc., **10** 287

Distribution Solutions International, Inc., **24** 126

District Bank, **II** 333

District Cablevision, **II** 160

District News Co., **II** 607

Distrigas, **IV** 425

DITAS, **IV** 563

Ditzler Color Co., **III** 732

DIVAL, **III** 347

Divani & Divani. *See* Industrie Natuzzi S.p.A.

Divco-Wayne Corp., **17** 82

DIVE!, **26** 264

Diversey Corp., **I** 275, 333; **13** 150, 199; **26** 305–06; **32** 476

Diversified Agency Services, **I** 32

Diversified Foods Inc., **25** 179

Diversified Retailing Co., **III** 214

Diversified Services, **9** 95

Diversifoods Inc., **II** 556; **13** 408

Diversity Consultants Inc., **32** 459

DiviCom, **43** 221–22

Dixie Airline, **25** 420

Dixie Bearings, Inc., **13** 78

Dixie Carriers, Inc., **18** 277

Dixie Container Corporation, **12** 377

Dixie Crystals Brands, Inc., **32** 277

The Dixie Group, Inc., **20 188–90**

Dixie Hi-Fi, **9** 120–21

Dixie Home Stores, **II** 683

Dixie-Narco Inc., **III** 573; **22** 349

Dixie Paper, **I** 612–14

Dixie Power & Light Company, **6** 514

Dixie Yarns, Inc., **9** 465; **19** 305

Dixieland Food Stores, **II** 624

Dixon Industries, Inc., **26 117–19**; **48** 59

Dixon Ticonderoga Company, **12 114–16**

Dixons Group plc, **II** 139; **V 48–50**; **9** 65; **10** 45, 306; **19 121–24 (upd.)**; **23** 52; **24** 194, 269–70; **49 110–13 (upd.)**

DIY Home Warehouse, **16** 210

DJ Moldings Corp., **18** 276

DJ Pharma, Inc., **47** 56

Djedi Holding SA, **23** 242

DKB. *See* Dai-Ichi Kangyo Bank Ltd.

DLC. *See* Duquesne Light Company.

DLJ. *See* Donaldson, Lufkin & Jenrette.

DLJ Merchant Banking Partners II, **21** 188; **36** 158–59

DLL. *See* David Lloyd Leisure Ltd.

DM Associates Limited Partnership, **25** 127

DMA, **18** 510

DMB&B. *See* D'Arcy Masius Benton & Bowles.

DMGT. *See* Daily Mail and General Trust.

DMI Furniture, Inc., **44** 132; **46 147–50**

DMP Mineralöl Petrochemie GmbH, **IV** 487

DMV Stainless, **54** 393

DNATA, **39** 137, 139

DNAX Research Institute, **I** 685; **14** 424

DNEL-Usinor, **IV** 227

DNN Galvanizing Limited Partnership, **24** 144

DNP DENMARK A/S, **IV** 600

Do It All, **24** 75

Do it Best Corporation, **30 166–70**

Dobbs House, **21** 54

Dobbs Houses Inc., **I** 696–97; **15** 87

Dobrolet, **6** 57

Dobson Park Industries, **38** 227

Docks de France, **37** 23; **39** 183–84

The Doctors' Company, **55 125–28**

Doctors' Hospital, **6** 191

Documentation Resources, **11** 65

Documentum, Inc., **46 151–53**

DOD Electronics Corp., **15** 215

Dodd, Mead & Co., **14** 498

Dodge & Day. *See* Day & Zimmermann, Inc.

Dodge Corp., **I** 144; **8** 74; **11** 53

The Dodge Group, **11** 78

Dodge Manufacturing Company, **9** 440

Dodge Motor Company, **20** 259

Doduco Corporation, **29** 460–61

Dodwell & Co., **III** 523

Doe Run Company, **12** 244

Doeflex PLC, **33** 79

Dofasco Inc., **IV 73–74**; **24 142–44 (upd.)**

Dogi International Fabrics S.A., **52 99–102**

Doherty Clifford Steers & Sherfield Inc., **I** 31

Doherty, Mann & Olshan. *See* Wells Rich Greene BDDP.

Dolan Design, Inc., **44** 133

Dolby Laboratories Inc., **20 191–93**

Dole Corporation, **44** 152

Dole Food Company, Inc., I 565; II 491–92; **9 175–76**; **20** 116; **31 167–170 (upd.)**
Dolland & Aitchison Group, **V** 399
Dollar Bills, Inc. *See* Dollar Tree Stores, Inc.
Dollar General, **26** 533
Dollar Rent A Car, **6** 349; **24** 10
Dollar Steamship Lines, **6** 353
Dollar Thrifty Automotive Group, Inc., **25** 92, **142–45**
Dollar Tree Stores, Inc., **16** 161; **23 176–78**
Dollfus Mieg & Cie. *See* Groupe DMC.
Dollond & Aitchison Group, **49** 151–52
Dolomite Franchi SpA, **53** 285
Dolphin Book Club, **13** 106
Dolphin Services, Inc., **44** 203
Dom Perignon, **25** 258
Domain Technology, **6** 231
Domaine Carneros, **43** 401
Domaine Chandon, **I** 272
Domaines Barons de Rothschild, **36** 113, 115
Dombrico, Inc., **8** 545
Domco Industries, **19** 407
Dome Laboratories, **I** 654
Dome Petroleum, Ltd., **II** 222, 245, 262, 376; **IV** 371, 401, 494; **12** 364
Domestic Electric Co., **III** 435
Domestic Operating Co., **III** 36
Dominick International Corp., **12** 131
Dominick's Finer Foods, **9** 451; **13** 25, 516; **17** 558, 560–61
Dominion Bank, **II** 375–76
Dominion Bridge Company, Limited, **8** 544
Dominion Cellular, **6** 322
Dominion Dairies, **7** 429
Dominion Engineering Works Ltd., **8** 544
Dominion Far East Line, **I** 469; **20** 311
Dominion Foils Ltd., **17** 280
Dominion Foundries and Steel, Ltd., **IV** 73–74
Dominion Hoist & Shovel Co., **8** 544
Dominion Homes, Inc., **19 125–27**
Dominion Industries Ltd., **15** 229
Dominion Life Assurance Co., **III** 276
Dominion Mushroom Co., **II** 649–50
Dominion Ornamental, **III** 641
Dominion Paper Box Co. Ltd., **IV** 645
Dominion Resources, Inc., **V** 591, **596–99**; **54 83–87 (upd.)**
Dominion Securities, **II** 345; **21** 447
Dominion Steel Castings Company, Ltd. *See* Dofasco Inc.
Dominion Stores Ltd., **II** 650, 652
Dominion Tar & Chemical Co. Ltd., **IV** 271–72
Dominion Terminal Associates, **IV** 171; **7** 582, 584
Dominion Textile Inc., **V** 355; **8** 559–60; **12 117–19**
Domino S.p.A., **51** 324
Domino Sugar Corporation, **26 120–22**; **42** 370
Domino Supermarkets, **24** 528
Domino's Pizza, Inc., **7 150–53**; **9** 74; **12** 123; **15** 344, 346; **16** 447; **21 177–81 (upd.)**; **22** 353; **24** 295; **25** 179–80, 227–28; **26** 177; **33** 388; **37** 208
Domtar Inc., **IV** 271–73, 308
Don Baxter Intravenous Products Co., **I** 627

Don Massey Cadillac, Inc., **37 114–16**
Don's Foods, Inc., **26** 164
Donac Company, **V** 681
Donald L. Bren Co., **IV** 287
Donaldson Company, Inc., **16 178–81**; **49 114–18 (upd.)**
Donaldson, Lufkin & Jenrette, Inc., **II** 422, 451; **III** 247–48; **9** 115, 142, 360–61; **18** 68; **22 188–91**; **26** 348; **35** 247; **41** 197
Donaldson's Department Stores, **15** 274
Doncaster Newspapers Ltd., **IV** 686
Dong-A Motor, **III** 749
Dong-Myung Industrial Co. Ltd., **II** 540
Dongbang Life Insurance Co., **I** 515
Dongguan Shilong Kyocera Optics Co., Ltd., **21** 331
Dongil Frozen Foods Co., **II** 553
Dongsu Industrial Company, **III** 516; **7** 232
Dönkasan, **55** 188
Donn, Inc., **18** 162
Donna Karan Company, **15 145–47**; **24** 299; **25** 294, 523
Donnelley, Gassette & Loyd, **IV** 660
Donnellon McCarthy Inc., **12** 184
Donnelly Coated Corporation, **48** 28
Donnelly Corporation, **12 120–22**; **35 147–50 (upd.)**
Donnkenny, Inc., **17 136–38**
Donohue Inc., **12** 412
Donohue Meehan Publishing Co., **27** 362
Donruss Leaf Inc., **19** 386
Donzi Marine Corp., **III** 600
Dooner Laboratories, **I** 667
Door-to-Door, **6** 14
Dorado Beach Development Inc., **I** 103
Dordrecht, **III** 177–78
Dorenbecher Properties, **19** 381
Doric Corp., **19** 290
Dorling Kindersley Holdings plc, **20 194–96**
Dorman Long & Co. Ltd., **IV** 658
Dorman Products of America, Ltd., **51** 307
Dorman's, Inc., **27** 291
Dorney Park, **22** 130
Dornier GmbH, **I** 46, 74, 151; **15** 142; **34** 131; **52** 113
Dorothy Hamill International, **13** 279, 281
Dorothy Perkins, **V** 21
Dorr-Oliver Inc., **35** 134–35
Dorset Capital, **49** 189
Dorsey & Whitney LLP, **47 96–99**
Dortmunder Union, **II** 240; **IV** 103, 105
Doskocil Companies, Inc., **12 123–25**. *See also* Foodbrands America, Inc.
Dot Wireless Inc., **46** 422
Doty Agency, Inc., **41** 178, 180
Double A Products Co., **23** 82–83
DoubleClick Inc., **46 154–57**; **49** 423, 432
Doubleday Book Shops, Inc., **10** 136; **25** 31; **30** 68
Doubleday-Dell, **IV** 594, 636
Doubletree Corporation, **21 182–85**; **41** 81–82
Doughty Handson, **49** 163
Douglas & Lomason Company, **16 182–85**
Douglas Aircraft Co., **I** 48, 70, 76, 96, 104, 195; **II** 32, 425; **III** 601; **9** 12, 18, 206; **10** 163; **13** 48, 341; **16** 77; **21** 141; **24** 375
Douglas-Dahlin Co., **I** 158–59
Douglas Dynamics L.L.C., **41** 3

Douglas Oil Co., **IV** 401
Doulton Glass Industries Ltd., **IV** 659
Douwe Egberts, **II** 572; **54** 324–25
Dove International, **7** 299–300
Dover Corporation, **III 467–69**; **28 101–05 (upd.)**
Dover Downs Entertainment, Inc., **43 139–41**
Dover Publications Inc., **34 148–50**; **41** 111
Dovrat Shrem, **15** 470
The Dow Chemical Company, **I 323–25**, 334, 341–42, 360, 370–71, 708; **II** 440, 457; **III** 617, 760; **IV** 83, 417; **8 147–50 (upd.)**, 153, 261–62, 548; **9** 328–29, 500–1; **10** 289; **11** 271; **12** 99–100, 254, 364; **14** 114, 217; **16** 99; **17** 418; **18** 279; **21** 387; **28** 411; **38** 187; **50 160–64 (upd.)**
Dow Corning, **II** 54; **III** 683, 685; **44** 129
Dow Jones & Company, Inc., **IV 601–03**, 654, 656, 670, 678; **7** 99; **10** 276–78, 407; **13** 55; **15** 335–36; **19 128–31 (upd.)**, 204; **21** 68–70; **23** 157; **47 100–04 (upd.)**
Dow Jones Telerate, Inc., **10 276–78**
DOW Stereo/Video Inc., **30** 466
Dowdings Ltd., **IV** 349
DowElanco, **21** 385, 387
Dowell Australia Ltd., **III** 674
Dowell Schlumberger. *See* Schlumberger Limited.
Dowidat GmbH, **IV** 197
Dowlais Iron Co., **III** 493
Down River International, Inc., **15** 188
Downe Communications, Inc., **14** 460
Downingtown Paper Company, **8** 476
Downyflake Foods, **7** 429
Dowty Aerospace, **17** 480
Doyle Dane Bernbach, **I** 9, 20, 28, 30–31, 33, 37, 206; **11** 549; **14** 159; **22** 396
DP&L. *See* Dayton Power & Light Company.
DPCE, **II** 139; **24** 194
DPF, Inc., **12** 275; **38** 250–51
DPL Inc., **6 480–82**
DQE, **6 483–85**; **38** 40
Dr. August Oetker KG, **51 102–06**
Dr. Gerhard Mann Pharma, **25** 56
DR Holdings, Inc., **10** 242
Dr. Ing he F. Porsche GmbH, **13** 413–14
Dr. Karl Thomae GmbH, **39** 72–73
Dr. Martens, **23** 399, 401
Dr. Miles' Medical Co., **I** 653
Dr Pepper/Seven Up, Inc., **I** 245; **II** 477; **9 177–78**; **32 154–57 (upd.)**; **49** 78
Dr. Richter & Co., **IV** 70
Dr. Solomon's Software Ltd., **25** 349
Dr. Tigges-Fahrten, **II** 163–64; **44** 432
Drackett Professional Products, **III** 17; **12 126–28**
DraftDirect Worldwide, **22** 297
Draftline Engineering Co., **22** 175
Dragados y Construcciones. *See* Grupo Dragados SA.
Dragon International, **18** 87
Dragonair, **16** 481; **18** 114. *See also* Hong Kong Dragon Airlines.
The Drake, **12** 316
Drake Bakeries, **II** 562
Drake Beam Morin, Inc., **IV** 623; **44 155–57**
Drake Steel Supply Co., **19** 343
Drallos Potato Company, **25** 332

Draper & Kramer, **IV** 724
Draper Corporation, **14** 219; **15** 384
Drathen Co., **I** 220
Dravo Corp., **6** 143
Draw-Tite, Inc., **11** 535
Drayton Corp., **II** 319; **17** 324
DreamWorks SKG, 17 72; **21** 23, 26; **26**
   150, 188; **43 142–46**
The Drees Company, Inc., 41 131–33
Dreher Breweries, **24** 450
Dresdner Bank A.G., I 411; **II** 191,
   238–39, 241–42, 256–57, 279–80,
   281–83, 385; **III** 201, 289, 401; **IV** 141;
   14 169–70; **15** 13; **47** 81–84
Dresdner Feuer-Versicherungs-Gesellschaft,
   III 376
Dresdner RCM Global Investors, **33** 128
The Dress Barn, Inc., 24 145–46
Dresser Industries, Inc., I 486; **III** 429,
   470–73; 499, 527, 545–46; **12** 539; **14**
   325; **15** 225–26, 468; **16** 310; **18** 219;
   24 208; **25** 188, 191; **52** 214–216; **55**
   129–31 (upd.)
Dresser Industries, Inc., **55** 194, 221
Dresser Power, **6** 555
Dressmaster GmbH, **53** 195
Drew Graphics, Inc., **13** 227–28
Drew Industries Inc., 28 106–08
Drewry Photocolor, **I** 447
Drexel Burnham Lambert Incorporated,
   II 167, 329–30, **407–09,** 482; **III** 10,
   253, 254–55, 531, 721; **IV** 334; **6**
   210–11; **7** 305; **8** 327, 349, 388–90,
   568; **9** 346; **12** 229; **13** 169, 299, 449;
   14 43; **15** 71, 281, 464; **16** 535, 561; **20**
   415; **22** 55, 189; **24** 273; **25** 313; **33**
   253. *See also* New Street Capital Inc.
Drexel Heritage Furnishings Inc., III
   571; **11** 534; **12 129–31; 20** 362; **39** 266
Dreyer's Grand Ice Cream, Inc., 10
   147–48; **17 139–41; 30** 81; **35** 59–61
Dreyfus Interstate Development Corp., **11**
   257
DRI. *See* Dominion Resources, Inc.
Dribeck Importers Inc., **9** 87
Drip In Irrigation, **26** 494
Drogueros S.A., **39** 188
Drott Manufacturing Company, **10** 379
Drouot Group, **III** 211
DRS Investment Group, **27** 370
Drug City, **II** 649
Drug Emporium, Inc., 12 132–34, 477
Drug House, **III** 9
Drug, Inc., **III** 17; **37** 42
Drummond Lighterage. *See* Puget Sound
   Tug and Barge Company.
Drummonds' Bank, **12** 422
Druout, **I** 563; **24** 78
Dry Milks Inc., **I** 248
DryClean U.S.A., **14** 25
Dryden and Co., **III** 340
Drypers Corporation, 18 147–49
Drysdale Government Securities, **10** 117
DSC Communications Corporation, 9
   170; **12 135–37**
DSL Group Ltd., **27** 49
DSM Melamine America, **27** 316–18
DSM N.V., I 326–27; III 614; **15** 229
DST Systems Inc., **6** 400–02; **26** 233
DTAG. *See* Dollar Thrifty Automotive
   Group, Inc.
DTE Energy Company, 20 197–201
   (upd.)
Du Bouzet, **II** 233

Du Mont Company, **8** 517
Du Pareil au Même, 43 147–49
Du Pont. *See* E.I. du Pont de Nemours &
   Co.
Du Pont Fabricators, **III** 559
Du Pont Glore Forgan, Inc., **III** 137
Du Pont Photomask, **IV** 600
Duane Reade Holding Corp., 21 186–88
Dublin and London Steam Packet
   Company, **V** 490
Dublin Corporation, **50** 74
DuBois Chemicals Division, **13** 149–50;
   22 188; **26** 306
Ducatel-Duval, **II** 369
Ducati Motor Holding S.p.A., 17 24; **30**
   171–73; 36 472
Duck Head Apparel Company, Inc., 8
   141–43; **30** 159; **42 118–21**
Duckback Products, Inc., **51** 190
Ducks Unlimited, **28** 306
Duckwall-ALCO Stores, Inc., 24 147–49
Duco Ltd., **25** 104–05
Ducommun Incorporated, 30 174–76
Ducon Group, **II** 81
Ducros, **36** 185, 187–88
Dudley Jenkins Group Plc, **53** 362
Dudley Stationery Ltd., **25** 501
Duff & Phelps Credit Rating, **37** 143, 145
Duff Bros., **III** 9–10
Duffy Meats, **27** 259
Duffy-Mott, **II** 477
Duke Energy Corporation, 27 128–31
   (upd.); 40 354, 358
Duke Energy Field Services, Inc., **24** 379;
   40 354, 358
Duke Power Company, V 600–02
Dumes SA, **13** 206
Dumez, **V** 655–57
Dumont Broadcasting Corporation, **7** 335
The Dun & Bradstreet Corporation, I
   540; **IV 604–05,** 643, 661; **8** 526; **9**
   505; **10** 4, 358; **13** 3–4; **19 132–34**
   (upd.); 38 6
Dun & Bradstreet Software Services
   Inc., 11 77–79; 43 183
Dunavant Enterprises, Inc., 54 88–90
Dunbar-Stark Drillings, Inc., **19** 247
Duncan Foods Corp., **I** 234; **10** 227
Duncan Toys Company, 55 132–35
Duncanson & Holt, Inc., **13** 539
Dundee Acquisition Corp., **19** 421
Dundee Bancorp, **36** 314
Dundee Cement Co., **III** 702; **8** 258–59
Dunfey Brothers Capital Group, **12** 368
Dunfey Hotels Corporation, **12** 367
Dunhams Stores Corporation, **V** 111
Dunhill Holdings, **IV** 93; **V** 411
Dunhill Staffing Systems, Inc., **52** 397–98
Dunkin' Donuts, **II** 619; **21** 323; **29** 18–19
Dunlop Coflexip Umbilicals Ltd. *See* Duco
   Ltd.
Dunlop Holdings, **I** 429; **III** 697; **V** 250,
   252–53
Dunlop Ltd., **25** 104
Dunn Bennett, **38** 401
Dunn Bros., **28** 63
Dunn Manufacturing Company, **25** 74
Dunn Paper Co., **IV** 290
Dunning Industries, **12** 109
Dunoyer. *See* Compagnie de Saint-Gobain
   S.A.
Dunwoodie Manufacturing Co., **17** 136
Duo-Bed Corp., **14** 435
Dupey Enterprises, Inc., **17** 320

Dupil-Color, Inc., **III** 745
Duplainville Transport, **19** 333–34
Duplex Products, Inc., 17 142–44, 445
Dupol, **III** 614
Dupont. *See* E.I. du Pont de Nemours &
   Company.
Dupont Chamber Works, **6** 449
Duquesne Light Company, **6** 483–84
Duquesne Systems, **10** 394
Dura Automotive Systems Inc., **53** 55
Dura Convertible Systems, **13** 170
Dura Corp., **I** 476
Dura-Vent, **III** 468
Duracell International Inc., 9 179–81; 12
   559; **13** 433; **17** 31; **24** 274; **39** 336, 339
Durand & Huguenin, **I** 672
Durango-Mapimi Mining Co., **22** 284
Duravit AG, **51** 196
Duray, Inc., **12** 215
Durban Breweries and Distillers, **I** 287
D'Urban, Inc., **41** 169
Durham Chemicals Distributors Ltd., **III**
   699
Durham Raw Materials Ltd., **III** 699
Duriron Company Inc., 17 145–47; 21
   189, 191
Durkee Famous Foods, **II** 567; **7** 314; **8**
   222; **17** 106; **27** 297
Duro-Matic Products Co., **51** 368
Dürr AG, 44 158–61
Durr-Fillauer Medical Inc., **13** 90; **18** 97;
   50 121
Dutch Boy, **II** 649; **III** 745; **10** 434–35
Dutch Crude Oil Company. *See*
   Nederlandse Aardolie Maatschappij.
Dutch East Indies Post, Telegraph and
   Telephone Service, **II** 67
Dutch Nuts Chocoladefabriek B.V., **II** 569
Dutch Pantry, **II** 497
Dutch State Mines. *See* DSM N.V.
Dutchland Farms, **25** 124
Dutton Brewery, **I** 294
Duttons Ltd., **24** 267
Duty Free International, Inc., 11 80–82.
   See also World Duty Free Americas,
   Inc.
Duval Corp., **IV** 489–90; **7** 280; **25** 461
DVI, Inc., 51 107–09
DVM Pharmaceuticals Inc., **55** 233
DWG Corporation. *See* Triarc Companies,
   Inc.
Dyas B.V., **55** 347
Dyckerhoff AG, 35 151–54
Dyersburg Corporation, 21 192–95
Dyke and Dryden, Ltd., **31** 417
Dylex Limited, 29 162–65
Dymed Corporation. *See* Palomar Medical
   Technologies, Inc.
Dynaco Corporation, **III** 643; **22** 409
Dynalectric Co., **45** 146
DynaMark, Inc., **18** 168, 170, 516, 518
Dynamatic Corp., **I** 154
Dynamem Corporation, **22** 409
Dynamic Capital Corp., **16** 80
Dynamic Controls, **11** 202
Dynamic Foods, **53** 148
Dynamic Microprocessor Associated Inc.,
   10 508
Dynamics Corporation of America, **39** 106
Dynamit Nobel AG, **III** 692–95; **16** 364;
   18 559
Dynamix, **15** 455
Dynapar, **7** 116–17

Dynaplast, **40** 214–15
Dynascan AK, **14** 118
Dynasty Footwear, Ltd., **18** 88
Dynatech Corporation, 13 194–96
Dynatron/Bondo Corporation, **8** 456
DynCorp, 45 145–47
Dynegy Inc., 47 70; **49 119–22 (upd.)**
Dynell Electronics, **I** 85
Dyno Industrier AS, **13** 555
Dyonics Inc., **I** 667
DYR, **I** 38; **16** 167
Dystrybucja, **41** 340

E. & B. Carpet Mills, **III** 423
E&B Company, **9** 72
E&B Marine, Inc., **17** 542–43
E & H Utility Sales Inc., **6** 487
E. & J. Gallo Winery, I 27, **242–44**, 260;
    7 154–56 (upd.); **15** 391; **28 109–11**
    (upd.), 223
E&M Laboratories, **18** 514
E & S Retail Ltd. *See* Powerhouse.
E! Entertainment Television Inc., 17
    148–50; **24** 120, 123; **47** 78
E-Stamp Corporation, **34** 474
E-Systems, Inc., I 490; **9 182–85**
E*Trade Group, Inc., 20 206–08; **38** 439;
    45 4
E-II Holdings Inc., **II** 468; **9** 449; **12** 87;
    43 355. *See also* Astrum International
    Corp.
E-Z Haul, **24** 409
E-Z Serve Corporation, 15 270; **17**
    169–71
E.A. Miller, Inc., **II** 494
E.A. Pierce & Co., **II** 424; **13** 340
E A Rosengrens AB, **53** 158
E.A. Stearns & Co., **III** 627
E.B. Badger Co., **11** 413
E.B. Eddy Forest Products, **II** 631
E.C. Snodgrass Company, **14** 112
E.C. Steed, **13** 103
E. de Trey & Sons, **10** 270–71
E.F. Hutton Group, **I** 402; **II** 399, 450–51;
    8 139; **9** 469; **10** 63
E.F. Hutton LBO, **24** 148
E. Gluck Trading Co., **III** 645
E.H. Bindley & Company, **9** 67
E.I. du Pont de Nemours & Company, I
    21, 28, 305, 317–19, 323, **328–30**, 334,
    337–38, 343–44, 346–48, 351–53, 365,
    377, 379, 383, 402–03, 545, 548, 675;
    III 21; **IV** 69, 78, 263, 371, 399,
    401–02, 409, 481, 599; **V** 360; **7** 546; **8**
    151–54 (upd.), 485; **9** 154, 216, 352,
    466; **10** 289; **11** 432; **12** 68, 365,
    416–17; **13** 21, 124; **16** 127, 130, 201,
    439, 461–62; **19** 11, 223; **21** 544; **22**
    147, 260, 405; **24** 111, 388; **25** 152,
    540; **26 123–27 (upd.)**; **34** 80, 283–84;
    37 111; **40** 370; **45** 246
E.J. Brach & Sons, **II** 521. *See also* Brach
    and Brock Confections, Inc.
E.J. Longyear Company. *See* Boart
    Longyear Company.
E. Katz Special Advertising Agency. *See*
    Katz Communications, Inc.
E.L. Phillips and Company, **V** 652–53
E.M. Warburg Pincus & Co., **7** 305; **13**
    176; **16** 319; **25** 313; **29** 262
E. Missel GmbH, **20** 363
E.N.V. Engineering, **I** 154
E.On AG, 50 165–73 (upd.); **51** 217
E.piphany, Inc., 49 123–25

E.R.R. Enterprises, **44** 227
E.R. Squibb, **I** 695; **21** 54–55
E. Rabinowe & Co., Inc., **13** 367
E. Rosen Co., **53** 303–04
E.S. Friedman & Co., **II** 241
E.S. International Holding S.A. *See* Banco
    Espírito Santo e Comercial de Lisboa
    S.A.
E.W. Bliss, **I** 452
E.W. Oakes & Co. Ltd., **IV** 118
The E.W. Scripps Company, IV 606–09;
    7 157–59 (upd.); **24** 122; **25** 507; **28**
    122–26 (upd.)
E.W.T. Mayer Ltd., **III** 681
EADS N.V. *See* European Aeronautic
    Defence and Space Company EADS
    N.V.
EADS SOCATA, 54 91–94
Eagel One Industries, **50** 49
Eagle Airways Ltd., **23** 161
Eagle Credit Corp., **10** 248
Eagle Distributing Co., **37** 351
Eagle Family Foods, Inc., **22** 95
Eagle Floor Care, Inc., **13** 501; **33** 392
Eagle Gaming, L.P., **16** 263; **43** 226
Eagle Hardware & Garden, Inc., 9 399;
    16 186–89; **17** 539–40
Eagle Industries Inc., **8** 230; **22** 282; **25**
    536
Eagle-Lion Films, **II** 147; **25** 328
Eagle Managed Care Corp., **19** 354, 357
Eagle Oil Transport Co. Ltd., **IV** 657
Eagle-Picher Industries, Inc., 8 155–58;
    23 179–83 (upd.)
Eagle Plastics, **19** 414
Eagle Printing Co. Ltd., **IV** 295; **19** 225
Eagle Sentry Inc., **32** 373
Eagle Snacks Inc., **I** 219; **34** 36–37
Eagle Square Manufacturing Co., **III** 627
Eagle Star Insurance Co., **I** 426–27; **III**
    185, 200
Eagle Supermarket, **II** 571
Eagle Thrifty Drug, **14** 397
Eagle Trading, **55** 24
Eagle Travel Ltd., **IV** 241
Earl Scheib, Inc., 32 158–61
Early American Insurance Co., **22** 230
Early Learning Centre, **39** 240, 242
Earth Resources Company, **IV** 459; **17** 320
Earth Wise, Inc., **16** 90
Earth's Best, Inc., **21** 56; **36** 256
The Earthgrains Company, 36 161–65;
    54 326
EarthLink, Inc., 33 92; **36 166–68**; **38**
    269
EAS. *See* Executive Aircraft Services.
Easco Hand Tools, Inc., **7** 117
Eason Oil Company, **6** 578; **11** 198
East African External Communications
    Limited, **25** 100
East Chicago Iron and Forge Co., **IV** 113
East Hartford Trust Co., **13** 467
East India Co., **I** 468; **III** 521, 696; **IV** 48;
    20 309
East Japan Heavy Industries, **III** 578–79; **7**
    348
East Japan Railway Company, V 448–50
East Midlands Electricity, **V** 605
The East New York Savings Bank, **11**
    108–09
East of Scotland, **III** 359
East Texas Pulp and Paper Co., **IV** 342,
    674; **7** 528
East-West Airlines, **27** 475

East-West Federal Bank, **16** 484
East West Motor Express, Inc., **39** 377
Easter Enterprises, **8** 380; **23** 358
Easterday Supply Company, **25** 15
Eastern Air Group Co., **31** 102
Eastern Airlines, I 41, 66, 78, 90, 98–99,
    101–03, 116, 118, 123–25; **III** 102; **6**
    73, 81–82, 104–05; **8** 416; **9** 17–18, 80;
    11 268, 427; **12** 191, 487; **21** 142, 143;
    23 483; **26** 339, 439; **39** 120
Eastern Associated Coal Corp., **6** 487
Eastern Australia Airlines, **24** 396
Eastern Aviation Group, **23** 408
Eastern Bank, **II** 357
Eastern Carolina Bottling Company, **10**
    223
Eastern Coal Corp., **IV** 181
Eastern Coalfields Ltd., **IV** 48–49
The Eastern Company, 48 140–43
Eastern Corp., **IV** 703
Eastern Electricity, **13** 485
Eastern Enterprises, IV 171; **6 486–88**
Eastern Gas and Fuel Associates, **I** 354; **IV**
    171
Eastern Indiana Gas Corporation, **6** 466
Eastern Kansas Utilities, **6** 511
Eastern Machine Screw Products Co., **13** 7
Eastern Market Beef Processing Corp., **20**
    120
Eastern Operating Co., **III** 23
Eastern Pine Sales Corporation, **13** 249
Eastern Software Distributors, Inc., **16** 125
Eastern States Farmers Exchange, **7** 17
Eastern Telegraph Company, **V** 283–84; **25**
    99–100
Eastern Texas Electric. *See* Gulf States
    Utilities Company.
Eastern Tool Co., **IV** 249
Eastern Torpedo Company, **25** 74
Eastern Wisconsin Power, **6** 604
Eastern Wisconsin Railway and Light
    Company, **6** 601
Eastex Pulp and Paper Co., **IV** 341–42
Eastman Chemical Company, 14
    174–75; **25** 22; **38 178–81 (upd.)**
Eastman Christensen Company, **22** 68
Eastman Kodak Company, I 19, 30, 90,
    323, 337–38, 690; **II** 103; **III** 171–72,
    474–77, 486–88, 547–48, 550, 584,
    607–09; **IV** 260–61; **6** 288–89; **7**
    160–64 (upd.), 436–38; **8** 376–77; **9**
    62, 231; **10** 24; **12** 342; **14** 174–75, 534;
    16 168, 449; **18** 184–86, 342, 510; **25**
    153; **29** 370; **36 169–76 (upd.)**; **38**
    178–79; **41** 104, 106; **43** 284; **45** 284
Eastman Radio, **6** 33
Eastmaque Gold Mines, Ltd., **7** 356
Easton Sports, Inc., **51** 163
Eastover Mining, **27** 130
Eastpak, Inc., **30** 138
Eastwynn Theatres, Inc., **37** 63
easyJet Airline Company Limited, 39
    127–29; **52** 330
Eatco, Inc., **15** 246
Eateries, Inc., 33 138–40
Eaton Axle Co., **I** 154
Eaton, Cole & Burnham Company, **8** 134
Eaton Corporation, I 154–55, 186; **III**
    645; **10 279–80 (upd.)**; **12** 547; **27** 100
Eaton Vance Corporation, 18 150–53
EAudio, Inc., **48** 92
Eavey Co., **II** 668
Ebamsa, **II** 474

EBASCO. *See* Electric Bond and Share Company.
Ebasco Services, **III** 499; **V** 612; **IV** 255–56
eBay Inc., 32 162–65; 49 51
EBC Amro Ltd., **II** 186
EBCO, **55** 302
Eberhard Faber, **12** 115
Eberhard Foods, **8** 482
Eberhard Manufacturing Company, **48** 141
EBIC. *See* European Banks' International Co.
Ebiex S.A., **25** 312
EBS. *See* Electric Bond & Share Company; Electronic Bookshelf.
EBSCO Industries, Inc., 17 151–53; 40 158–61 (upd.)
EC Comics, **25** 139
EC Erdolchemie GmbH, **7** 141
ECAD Inc., **48** 75
ECC. *See* Educational Credit Corporation.
ECC Group plc, III 689–91. *See also* English China Clays plc.
ECC International Corp., 42 122–24
Ecce, **41** 129
ECCO. *See* Adecco S.A.
Echigoya Saburobei Shoten, **IV** 292
Echlin Inc., I 156–57; 11 83–85 (upd.); 15 310
Echo Bay Mines Ltd., IV 75–77; 23 40; 38 182–85 (upd.)
Les Echos, **IV** 659
EchoStar Communications Corporation, 35 155–59
EchoStar Satellite Corp., **39** 400
ECI Telecom Ltd., 18 154–56
Eckerd Corporation, 9 186–87; 18 272; **24** 263; **43** 247. *See also* J.C. Penney Company, Inc.
Eckert-Mauchly Corp., **III** 166
Ecko-Ensign Design, **I** 531
Ecko Products, **I** 527
ECL, **16** 238
Eclipse Candles, Ltd., **18** 67, 69
Eclipse Machine Co., **I** 141
Eclipse Telecommunications, Inc., **29** 252
Eco Hotels, **14** 107
Eco SA, **48** 224
Ecolab Inc., I 331–33; 13 197–200 (upd.); 26 306; **34 151–56 (upd.),** 205, 208
Ecology and Environment, Inc., 39 130–33
Econo Lodges of America, **25** 309
Econo-Travel Corporation, **13** 362
Economist Group, **15** 265
Economy Book Store, **10** 135
Economy Fire & Casualty, **22** 495
Economy Grocery Stores Company. *See* The Stop & Shop Companies, Inc.
Ecopetrol. *See* Empresa Colombiana de Petróleos.
EcoSystems Software, Inc., **10** 245; **30** 142
EcoWater Systems, Inc., **16** 357
ECS S.A, 12 138–40
Ecton, Inc., **36** 5
Ecusta Corporation, **8** 414
ed bazinet international, inc., **34** 144–45
Edah, **13** 544–45
Eddie Bauer, Inc., II 503; V 160; 9 188–90; 9 316; 10 324, 489, 491; 11 498; 15 339; 25 48; 27 427, 429–30; 29 278; 36 177–81 (upd.)
Eddy Bakeries, Inc., **12** 198

Eddy Paper Co., **II** 631
Edeka Zentrale A.G., II 621–23; 33 56; **47 105–07 (upd.)**
edel music AG, 44 162–65
Edelbrock Corporation, 37 117–19
Edelhoff AG & Co., **39** 415
Edelstahlwerke Buderus AG, **III** 695
Edenhall Group, **III** 673
Edenton Cotton Mills, **12** 503
EDF. *See* Electricité de France.
Edgars, **I** 289
Edgcomb Metals, **IV** 575–76; **31** 470–71
Edge Research, **25** 301
Edgell Communications Inc., **IV** 624
Edgewater Hotel and Casino, **6** 204–05
EDI, **26** 441
Edina Realty Inc., **13** 348
Edison Brothers Stores, Inc., 9 191–93; 17 369, 409; **33 126–28**
Edison Electric Appliance Co., **II** 28; **12** 194
Edison Electric Co., **I** 368; **II** 330; **III** 433; **6** 572
Edison Electric Illuminating Co., **II** 402; **6** 595, 601; **14** 124
Edison Electric Illuminating Company of Boston, **12** 45
Edison Electric Light & Power, **6** 510
Edison Electric Light Co., **II** 27; **6** 565, 595; **11** 387; **12** 193; **50** 365
Edison General Electric Co., **II** 27, 120, 278; **12** 193; **14** 168; **26** 451
Edison Machine Works, **II** 27
Edison Phonograph, **III** 443
Edison Schools Inc., 37 120–23
Editions Albert Premier, **IV** 614
Editions Bernard Grasset, **IV** 618
Editions Dalloz, **IV** 615
Editions Jean-Baptiste Baillière, **25** 285
Editions Nathan, **IV** 615
Editions Ramsay, **25** 174
Editorial Centro de Estudios Ramón Areces, S.A., **V** 52; **26** 130
Editorial Televisa, **18** 211, 213; **23** 417
Editoriale L'Espresso, **IV** 586–87
Editoriale Le Gazzette, **IV** 587
EdK. *See* Edeka Zentrale A.G.
Edmark Corporation, 14 176–78; 41 134–37 (upd.)
Edmonton City Bakery, **II** 631
EDO Corporation, 46 158–61
Edogawa Oil Co., **IV** 403
EdoWater Systems, Inc., **IV** 137
EDP Group. *See* Electricidade de Portugal, S.A.
Edper Equities, **II** 456
EDS. *See* Electronic Data Systems Corporation.
Education Association Mutual Assurance Company. *See* Horace Mann Educators Corporation.
The Education Finance Group, **33** 418, 420
Education Funds, Inc., **II** 419
Education Loan Processing, **53** 319
Education Management Corporation, 35 160–63
Education Systems Corporation, **7** 256; **25** 253
Educational & Recreational Services, Inc., **II** 607
Educational Broadcasting Corporation, 48 144–47
Educational Computer International, Inc. *See* ECC International Corp.

Educational Credit Corporation, **8** 10; **38** 12
Educational Loan Administration Group, Inc., **33** 420
Educational Publishing Corporation, **22** 519, 522
Educational Supply Company, **7** 255; **25** 252
Educational Testing Service, 12 141–43; 42 209–10, 290
Educorp, Inc., **39** 103
Edumond Le Monnier S.p.A., **54** 22
EduQuest, **6** 245
EduServ Technologies, Inc., **33** 420
Edusoft Ltd., **40** 113
EduTrek International, Inc., **45** 88
Edw. C. Levy Co., 42 125–27
Edward Ford Plate Glass Co., **III** 640–41, 731
Edward J. DeBartolo Corporation, V 116; **8 159–62**
Edward Jones, 30 177–79
Edward Lloyd Ltd., **IV** 258
Edward P. Allis Company, **13** 16
Edward Smith & Company, **8** 553
Edwards & Jones, **11** 360
Edwards Dunlop & Co. Ltd., **IV** 249
Edwards Food Warehouse, **II** 642
Edwards George and Co., **III** 283
Edwards Industries, **IV** 256
Edwards Theatres Circuit, Inc., 31 171–73
Edwardstone Partners, **14** 377
EEC Environmental, Inc., **16** 259
EEGSA. *See* Empresa Eléctrica de Guatemala S.A.
Eerste Nederlandsche, **III** 177–79
Eff Laboratories, **I** 622
Effectenbank, **II** 268; **21** 145
EFM Media Management, **23** 294
Efnadruck GmbH, **IV** 325
Efrat Future Technology Ltd. *See* Comverse Technology, Inc.
EFS National Bank, **52** 87
EFTEC, **32** 257
EG&G Incorporated, 8 163–65; 18 219; **22** 410; **29 166–69 (upd.)**
EGAM, **IV** 422
Egerton Hubbard & Co., **IV** 274
Egg plc, **48** 328
Egghead Inc., 9 194–95; 10 284
Egghead.com, Inc., 31 174–177 (upd.)
EGPC. *See* Egyptian General Petroleum Corporation.
EGUZKIA-NHK, **III** 581
EgyptAir, I 107; **6 84–86; 27 132–35 (upd.)**
Egyptian General Petroleum Corporation, IV 412–14; 32 45; **51 110–14 (upd.)**
EHAPE Einheitspreis Handels Gesellschaft mbH. *See* Kaufhalle AG.
eHow.com, **49** 290
Ehrlich-Rominger, **48** 204
Eidgenössische Bank, **II** 378
Eidgenössische Versicherungs- Aktien-Gesellschaft, **III** 403
Eiffage, 27 136–38
Eiffel Construction Metallique, **27** 138
800-JR Cigar, Inc., 27 139–41
84 Lumber Company, 9 196–97; 39 134–36 (upd.)
Eildon Electronics Ltd., **15** 385
EIMCO, **I** 512

Einstein/Noah Bagel Corporation, 29 170–73; **44** 313

eircom plc, 31 178–181 (upd.)

EIS Automotive Corp., **III** 603

EIS, Inc., **45** 176, 179

Eisai Company, **13** 77

Eisen-und Stahlwerk Haspe AG, **IV** 126

Eisen-und Stahlwerk Hoesch, **IV** 103

Eisenhower Mining Co., **IV** 33

EJ Financial Enterprises Inc., **48** 308–09

EKA AB, **I** 330; **8** 153

Eka Nobel AB, **9** 380

Ekco Group, Inc., 12 377; **16 190–93**

EKT, Inc., **44** 4

El Al Israel Airlines Ltd., I 30; **23 184–87**

El Camino Resources International, Inc., 11 86–88

El Chico Restaurants, Inc., 19 135–38; 36 162–63

El Corte Inglés, S.A., V 51–53; 26 128–31 (upd.)

El Dorado Investment Company, **6** 546–47

El-Mel-Parts Ltd., **21** 499

El Nasr Petroleum Co., **51** 113

El Paso & Southwestern Railroad, **IV** 177

El Paso Electric Company, 21 196–98

El Paso Healthcare System, Ltd., **15** 112; **35** 215

El Paso Natural Gas Company, 10 190; **11** 28; **12 144–46; 19** 411; **27** 86

El Pollo Loco, **II** 680; **27** 16–18

El Taco, **7** 505

Elamex, S.A. de C.V., 51 115–17

ELAN, **IV** 486

Elan Corp. plc, **10** 54

Elan Ski Company, **22** 483

Elanco Animal Health, **47** 112

Elano Corporation, 14 179–81

Elantis, **48** 290

Elastic Reality Inc., **38** 70

Elcat Company, **17** 91

Elco Corporation, **21** 329, 331

Elco Industries Inc., **22** 282

Elco Motor Yacht, **I** 57

Elda Trading Co., **II** 48; **25** 267

Elder-Beerman Stores Corporation, 10 281–83; 19 362

Elder Dempster Line, **6** 416–17

Elder Smith Goldsbrough Mort Ltd., **21** 227

Elder's Insurance Co., **III** 370

Elders IXL Ltd., I 216, 228–29, 264, **437–39**, 592–93; **7** 182–83; **21** 227; **26** 305; **28** 201; **50** 199

Elders Keep, **13** 440

Eldorado Gold Corporation, **22** 237

ele Corporation, **23** 251

Electra Corp., **III** 569; **20** 361–62

Electra/Midland Corp., **13** 398

Electralab Electronics Corp., **III** 643

Electric Boat Co., **I** 57–59, 527; **II** 7; **10** 315

Electric Bond & Share Company, **V** 564–65; **6** 596

Electric Clearinghouse, Inc., **18** 365, 367

Electric Energy, Inc., **6** 470, 505

Electric Fuels Corp., **V** 621; **23** 200

Electric Heat Regulator Co., **II** 40; **12** 246; **50** 231

Electric Iron and Steel, **IV** 162

Electric Light and Power Company, **6** 483

Electric Light Company of Atlantic City. See Atlantic Energy, Inc.

Electric Lightwave, Inc., 37 124–27

Electric Storage Battery Co., **39** 338

Electric Thermostat Co., **II** 40; **12** 246; **50** 231

Electric Transit, Inc., **37** 399–400

Electrical Lamp Service Co. See EMI Group plc.

Electricidade de Portugal, S.A., 47 108–11; 49 211

Electricité de France, I 303; **V 603–05**, 626–28; **41 138–41 (upd.)**

Electro-Alkaline Company. See The Clorox Company.

Electro-Chemische Fabrik Natrium GmbH, **IV** 69–70

Electro Dynamics Corp., **I** 57, 484; **11** 263

Electro-Flo, Inc., **9** 27

Electro-Mechanical Research, **III** 617; **17** 417

Electro Metallurgical Co., **I** 400; **9** 517; **11** 402

Electro-Motive Engineering Company, **10** 273

Electro-Nite International N.V., **IV** 100

Electro-Optical Systems, **III** 172; **6** 289

Electro Refractories and Abrasives Company, **8** 178

Electro String Instrument Corporation, **16** 201; **43** 169

Electrobel, **II** 202

Electrocomponents PLC, 50 174–77

ElectroData Corp., **III** 165; **6** 281

Electrolux AB, 53 124–29 (upd.)

Electrolux Group, II 69, 572; **III** 420, **478–81**; **IV** 338; **6** 69; **11** 439; **12** 158–59, 250; **13** 562, 564; **17** 353; **21** 383. See also Aktiebolaget Electrolux.

Electromagnetic Sciences Inc., 21 199–201

Electromedics, **11** 460

Electronic Arts Inc., 10 284–86; 13 115; **29** 76; **35** 227

Electronic Banking Systems, **9** 173

Electronic Book Technologies, Inc., **26** 216 **29** 427

Electronic Data Systems Corporation, I 172; **II** 65; **III 136–38**, 326; **6** 226; **9** 36; **10** 325, 327; **11** 62, 123, 131; **13** 482; **14** 15, 318; **22** 266; **27** 380; **28 112–16 (upd.)**; **241**; **XXIX** 375; **36** 242; **49** 116, 311, 313. See also Perot Systems Corporation.

Electronic Engineering Co., **16** 393

Electronic Hair Styling, Inc., **41** 228

Electronic Rentals Group PLC, **II** 139; **24** 194

Electronic Tool Company, **16** 100

Electronics Corp. of Israel Ltd. See ECI Telecom Ltd.

Electronics for Imaging, Inc., 15 148–50; 43 150–53 (upd.)

Electrorail, **II** 93; **18** 472

Electrowatt Ltd., **21** 146–47

Electrowerke AG, **IV** 230

Elekom, **31** 176

Elektra. See Grupo Elektra, S.A. de C.V.

Elektra Records, **III** 480; **23** 33

Elektriska Aktiebolaget. See ABB Asea Brown Boveri Ltd.

Elektrizitäts-Gesellschaft Laufenburg, **6** 490

Elektrizitätswerk Wesertal GmbH, **30** 206

Elektrizitätswerk Westfalen AG, **V** 744

ElektroHelios, **III** 479; **22** 26

Elektromekaniska AB, **III** 478

Elektromekano, **II** 1

Elektrowatt AG, 6 489–91

Eleme Petrochemicals Co., **IV** 473

Elementis plc, 40 162–68 (upd.)

Eletropaulo Metropolitana, **53** 18

Eletson Corp., **13** 374

Elettra Broadcasting Corporation, **14** 509

Elettrofinanziaria Spa, **9** 152

Eleventh National Bank, **II** 373

Elf Aquitaine SA, 21 202–06 (upd.); 23 236, 238; **24** 494; **25** 104; **26** 369, 425; **49** 349–51; **50** 179–80, 479, 484. See also Société Nationale Elf Aquitaine.

Elfa International, **36** 134–35

Elgin Blenders, Inc., **7** 128

Elgin Exploration, Inc., **19** 247; **26** 70

Eli Lilly and Company, I 637, **645–47**, 666, 679, 687, 701; **III** 18–19, 60–61; **8** 168, 209; **9** 89–90; **10** 535; **11** 9, **89–91 (upd.)**, 458, 460; **12** 187, 278, 333; **14** 99–100, 259; **17** 437; **18** 420, 422; **19** 105; **21** 387; **26** 31; **32** 212; **44** 175; **45** 382; **47 112–16 (upd.)**, 221, 236; **50** 139

Eli Witt Company, **15** 137, 139; **43** 205

Elias Brothers Restaurants, **III** 103

Elior SA, 49 126–28

Elit Circuits Inc., **I** 330; **8** 153

Elite Microelectronics, **9** 116

Elite Sewing Machine Mfg. Co. Ltd., **III** 415; **48** 5

Elizabeth Arden, Inc., I 646, **III** 48; **8 166–68**, 344; **9** 201–02, 428, 449; **11** 90; **12** 314; **30** 188; **32** 476; **40 169–72 (upd.)**; **47** 113

Eljer Industries, Inc., II 420; **24 150–52**

Elk River Resources, Inc., **IV** 550

Elka, **III** 54

ElkCorp, 52 103–05

Elke Corporation, **10** 514

Elkjop ASA, **49** 113

Elko-Lamoille Power Company, **11** 343

Ellanef Manufacturing Corp., **48** 274

Ellen Tracy, Inc., 55 136–38

Ellenville Electric Company, **6** 459

Ellerbe Becket, 41 142–45

Ellesse International S.p.A., **V** 376; **26** 397–98

Ellett Brothers, Inc., 17 154–56

Ellington Recycling Center, **12** 377

Elliot Group Limited, **45** 139–40

Elliott Automation, **II** 25; **6** 241; **13** 225

Elliott Bay Design Group, **22** 276

Elliott Paint and Varnish, **8** 553

Ellipse Programmes, **48** 164–65

Ellis & Everard, **41** 341

Ellis Adding-Typewriter Co., **III** 151; **6** 265

Ellis Banks, **II** 336

Ellis, Chafflin & Co. See Mead Corporation.

Ellis-Don Ltd., **38** 481

Ellis Paperboard Products Inc., **13** 442

Ellis Park Race Course, **29** 118

Ellisco Co., **35** 130

Ellos A.B., **II** 640

ELMA Electronic, **III** 632

Elmendorf Board, **IV** 343

Elmer's Products, Inc. See Borden, Inc.

Elmer's Restaurants, Inc., 42 128–30

Elmo Semiconductor Corp., **48** 246

Elphinstone, **21** 501

Elrick & Lavidge, **6** 24

Elrick Industries, Inc., **19** 278
Elscint Ltd., 20 202–05
Elsevier NV, IV 610–11, 643, 659; **7** 244; **14** 555–56; **17** 396, 399. *See also* Reed Elsevier.
Elsi, **II** 86
Elsinore Corporation, 36 158; **48 148–51**
ELTO Outboard Motor Co., **III** 597
Eltra Corporation, **I** 416, 524; **22** 31; **31** 135
Eltron International Inc., **53** 374
Elwerath, **IV** 485
ELYO, **42** 387–88
Elyria Telephone Company, **6** 299
Email Ltd., **III** 672–73
EMAP plc, 35 71–72, **164–66**, 242–44
Emballage, **III** 704
Embankment Trust Ltd., **IV** 659
Embassy Book Co., Ltd., **IV** 635
Embassy Hotel Group, **I** 216; **9** 426
Embassy Suites, **9** 425; **24** 253
Embedded Support Tools Corporation, **37** 419, 421
Embers America Restaurants, 30 180–82
Embotelladora Central, S.A., **47** 291
Embraer. *See* Empresa Brasileira de Aeronáutica S.A.
Embry-Riddle, **I** 89
EMC Corporation, 12 147–49; 20 8; **46 162–66 (upd.)**
EMC Technology Services, Inc., **30** 469
Emco, **III** 569; **20** 361
EMD Technologies, **27** 21; **40** 67
Emerald Coast Water Co., **III** 21
Emerald Technology, Inc., **10** 97
Emerson, 46 167–71 (upd.)
Emerson-Brantingham Company, **10** 378
Emerson Drug, **I** 711
Emerson Electric Co., II 18–21, 92; **III** 625; **8** 298; **12** 248; **13** 225; **14** 357; **15** 405–06; **21** 43; **22** 64; **25** 530; **36** 400
Emerson Foote, Inc., **25** 90
Emerson Radio Corp., 30 183–86
Emery Air Freight Corporation, 6 345–46, 386, **388–91; 18** 177. *See also* Emery Worldwide Airlines, Inc.
Emery Group, **I** 377; **III** 33
Emery Worldwide Airlines, Inc., 21 139; **25 146–50 (upd.)**
Emeryville Chemical Co., **IV** 408
Emge Packing Co., Inc., 11 92–93
Emhart Corp., **III** 437; **8** 332; **20** 67
EMI Group plc, I 531; **6** 240; **22 192–95 (upd.); 24** 485; **26** 188, 314; **52** 428. *See also* Thorne EMI plc.
Emil Moestue as, **51** 328
The Emirates Group, 24 400; **39 137–39**
Emmis Communications Corporation, 47 117–21
Empain, **18** 472; **19** 165
Empain-Schneider, **II** 93
Empaques de Carton Titan, **19** 10–11
Empex Hose, **19** 37
Empi, Inc., 27 132–35
Empire Blue Cross and Blue Shield, III 245–46; **6** 195
Empire Brewery, **I** 253
Empire Co., **II** 653
Empire Cos., **IV** 391
Empire District Electric, **IV** 391
Empire Family Restaurants Inc., **15** 362
Empire Gas & Fuel, **IV** 391
Empire Hanna Coal Co., Ltd., **8** 346
Empire Inc., **II** 682

Empire Life and Accident Insurance Co., **III** 217
Empire National Bank, **II** 218
Empire of America, **11** 110
Empire Pencil, **III** 505; **43** 230
Empire Savings, Building & Loan Association, **8** 424
Empire State Group, **IV** 612
Empire State Petroleum, **IV** 374; **50** 47
Empire State Pickling Company, **21** 155
Empire Steel Castings, Inc., **39** 31–32
Empire Stores, **19** 309
Empire Trust Co., **II** 218
Employee Solutions, Inc., 18 157–60
employeesavings.com, **39** 25
Employers' Liability Assurance, **III** 235
Employer's Overload, **25** 432
Employers Reinsurance Corp., **II** 31; **12** 197
Empresa Brasileira de Aeronáutica S.A. (Embraer), 36 182–84
Empresa Colombiana de Petróleos, IV 415–18
Empresa Constructora SA, **55** 182
Empresa de Obras y Montajes Ovalle Moore, S.A., **34** 81
Empresa Eléctrica de Guatemala S.A., **49** 211
Empresa Nacional de Electridad, **I** 459
Empresa Nacional del Petroleo, **IV** 528
Empresa Nacional Electrica de Cordoba, **V** 607
Empresa Nacional Hidro-Electrica del Ribagorzana, **I** 459; **V** 607
Empresa Nacional Hulleras del Norte, **I** 460
Empresas Emel S.A., **41** 316
Empresas Frisco, **21** 259
Empresas ICA, **34** 82
Empresas ICA Sociedad Controladora, S.A. de C.V., 41 146–49
Empresas La Moderna, **21** 413; **29** 435
Empresas Polar SA, 55 139–41 (upd.)
Empresas Tolteca, **20** 123
Emprise Corporation, **7** 134–35
EMS-Chemie Holding AG, **III** 760; **32** 257
EMS Technologies, Inc., **21** 199, 201; **22** 173
Enagas, **IV** 528
Enbridge Inc., 43 154–58
ENCAD, Incorporated, 25 151–53
ENCASO, **IV** 528
ENCI, **IV** 132
Encompass Services Corporation, 33 141–44
Encon Safety Products, Inc., **45** 424
Encor Inc., **47** 396
Encore Computer Corporation, 13 201–02
Encore Distributors Inc., **17** 12–13
Encryption Technology Corporation, **23** 102
Encyclopedia Britannica, Inc., 7 165–68; 12 435, 554–55; **16** 252; **39 140–44 (upd.); 43** 208
Endata, Inc., **11** 112
Endemol Entertainment Holding NV, 46 172–74; 53 154
ENDESA S.A., V 606–08; 46 175–79 (upd.); 49 210–11
Endevco Inc., **11** 28
Endiama, **IV** 67
Endicott Trust Company, **11** 110
Endo Vascular Technologies, Inc., **11** 460

ENDOlap, Inc., **50** 122
Endovations, Inc., **21** 47
ENECO. *See* Empresa Nacional Electrica de Cordoba.
ENEL. *See* Ente Nazionale per l'Energia Elettrica.
Enerchange LLC, **18** 366
Enercon, Inc., **6** 25
Energas Company, **43** 56–57
Energen Corporation, 6 583; **21 207–09**
Energie-Verwaltungs-Gesellschaft, **V** 746
Energieversorgung Ostbayern AG, **23** 47
Energis plc, 44 363; **47 122–25**
Energizer Holdings, Inc., 9 180; **32 171–74; 39** 336, 339
Energy & Minerals, Inc., **42** 354
Energy Absorption Systems, Inc., **15** 378
Energy Biosystems Corp., **15** 352
Energy Coatings Co., **14** 325
Energy Corp. of Louisiana, **V** 619
Energy Film Library, **31** 216, 218
Energy Foundation, **34** 386
The Energy Group, **26** 359
Energy Increments Inc., **19** 411
Energy National, Inc., **27** 485
Energy Resources, **27** 216
Energy Steel Corporation, **19** 472
Energy Systems Group, Inc., **13** 489
Energy Transportation Systems, Inc., **27** 88
Energy Ventures, Inc., **49** 181
Energyline Systems, **26** 5
EnergyOne, **19** 487
Enerplus Resources, **21** 500
Enesco Corporation, 11 94–96; 15 475, 477–78
Enforcer Products, Inc., **54** 254
Engelhard Corporation, II 54; **IV** 23, **78–80; 16** 28; **21 210–14 (upd.); 50** 33
Engen, **IV** 93; **22** 236
Engineered Polymers Co., **I** 202
Engineering Co. of Nigeria, **IV** 473
Engineering Company, **9** 16
Engineering for the Petroleum and Process Industries, **IV** 414
Engineering Plastics, Ltd., **8** 377
Engineering Research Associates, **III** 126, 129
Engineering Systems, Inc., **54** 182
Engineers & Fabricators, Inc., **18** 513
England Corsair Furniture, **14** 302
Englander Co., **I** 400
Engle Homes, Inc., 46 180–82
Engles Management Corp., **26** 448
English China Clays Ltd., III 689–91; **15 151–54 (upd.); 36** 20; **40 173–77 (upd.)**
English Condensed Milk Co., **II** 545
English Electric Co., **I** 50; **II** 25, 81; **6** 241; **24** 85
English Mercantile & General Insurance Co., **III** 376
English Property Corp., **IV** 712
English, Scottish and Australian Bank Ltd., **II** 187–89
Engraph, Inc., 12 150–51
Enhanced Derm Technologies, **50** 122
Enhanced Services Billing, Inc. *See* Billing Concepts Corp.
ENHER. *See* Empresa Nacional Hidro-Electrica del Ribagorzana.
ENI. *See* Ente Nazionale Idrocarburi.
ENI S.p.A., **34** 75
ENIEPSA, **IV** 528
Enimont, **IV** 422, 525
Ennia, **III** 177, 179, 310

Ennis Business Forms, Inc., 21 215–17
Eno Proprietaries, III 65
Enocell Oy, IV 277
The Enoch F. Bills Co., 25 365
Enogex, Inc., 6 539–40
Enova Corporation. See Sempra Energy.
ENPAC Corporation, 18 162
Enpetrol, IV 528
Enquirer/Star Group, Inc., 10 287–88;
  12 358. See also American Media, Inc.
Enrich International, Inc., 33 145–48; 37
  340, 342
Enron Corporation, III 197; V 609–10; 6
  457, 593; 18 365; 19 139–41, 162, 487;
  27 266; 34 82; 46 183–86 (upd.); 49
  121–22; 54 86
Enseco, III 684
Enserch Corp., V 611–13
Ensidesa, I 460
Ensign Oil Company, 9 490
Enskilda S.A., II 352–53
Enso-Gutzeit Oy, IV 274–77; 17 539. See
  also Stora Enso Oyj
ENSTAR Corporation, IV 567; 11 441
Enstar Group Inc., 13 299
Ensys Environmental Products, Inc., 10
  107
ENTASA, IV 528
Ente Gestione Aziende Minerarie, I 466
Ente Nazionale di Energia Elettrica, I 466
Ente Nazionale Idrocarburi, I 369; IV
  412, 419–22, 424, 453, 466, 470, 486,
  546; V 614–17
Ente Nazionale per l'Energia Elettrica,
  V 614–17
Entenmann's Bakery, I 246, 712; 10 551;
  35 415; 38 364
Entercom, 48 272
Entergy Corporation, V 618–20; 6
  496–97; 45 148–51 (upd.)
Enterprise Development Company, 15 413
Enterprise Electronics Corporation, 18
  513–15
Enterprise Federal Savings & Loan, 21 524
Enterprise Integration Technologies, 18 541
Enterprise Leasing, 6 392–93
Enterprise Metals Pty. Ltd., IV 61
Enterprise Oil plc, 11 97–99; 50 178–82
  (upd.)
Enterprise Rent-A-Car, Inc., 16 380; 33
  192
Enterra Corp., 25 546
Entertainment Publications, 16 146
Entertainment UK, 24 266, 269
Entertainment Zone, Inc., 15 212
Entex Information Services, 24 29
Entity Software, 11 469
Entrada Industries Incorporated, 6 568–69;
  26 387
Entravision Communications
  Corporation, 41 150–52
Entré Computer Centers, 6 243–44; 13 175
Entremont, I 676
Entreprise de Recherches et d'Activités
  Pétrolières, IV 453, 467, 544, 560; 7
  481, 483–84
Entreprise Nationale Sonatrach, IV
  423–25; V 626, 692; 10 83–84; 12 145
Entrex, Inc., III 154
Entrust Financial Corp., 16 347
Envergure, 27 421
Envirex, 11 361
Envirodrill Services, Inc., 19 247
Envirodyne Industries, Inc., 17 157–60

EnviroLease, Inc., 25 171
ENVIRON International Corporation, 10
  106
Environmental Defense Fund, 9 305
Environmental Industries, Inc., 31
  182–85
Environmental Mediation, Inc., 47 20
Environmental Planning & Research. See
  CRSS Inc.
Environmental Research and Technology,
  Inc., 23 135
Environmental Systems Corporation, 9 109
Environmental Testing and Certification
  Corporation, 10 106–07
Environmentals Incorporated. See Angelica
  Corporation.
Envirosciences Pty. Ltd., 16 260
Envision Corporation, 24 96
Enwright Environmental Consulting
  Laboratories, 9 110
Enzafruit Worldwide, 38 202
Enzo Biochem, Inc., 41 153–55
Enzyme Bio-Systems, Ltd., 21 386
Enzyme Technologies Corp., I 342; 14 217
Eon Productions, II 147; 25 328
Eon Systems, III 143; 6 238; 38 409
l'Epargne, 12 152
EPE Technologies, 18 473
EPI. See Essentially Pure Ingredients.
EPI Group Limited, 26 137
Epic Express, 48 113
Les Epiceries Presto Limitée, II 651
Epiphone, 16 238–39
Epoch Software, Plc, 49 290
Epoch Systems Inc., 9 140; 12 149
ePOWER International, 33 3, 6
Eppler, Guerin & Turner, Inc., III 330
Eppley, III 99
Epsilon Trading Corporation, 6 81
Epson, 18 386–87, 435
Equant N.V., 52 106–08
Equator Bank, II 298
EQUICOR-Equitable HCA Corp., III 80,
  226; 45 104, 109
Equicor Group Ltd., 29 343
Equifax, Inc., 6 23–25; 25 182, 358; 28
  117–21 (upd.)
Equilink Licensing Group, 22 458
Equilon Enterprises LLC, 41 359, 395
Equistar Chemicals, LP, 45 252, 254
EquiStar Hotel Investors L.P. See CapStar
  Hotel Co.
Equitable Bancorporation, 12 329
Equitable Equipment Company, 7 540
Equitable Life Assurance Society of the
  United States, II 330; III 80, 229, 237,
  247–49, 274, 289, 291, 305–06, 316,
  329, 359; IV 171, 576, 711; 6 23; 13
  539; 19 324, 511; 22 188–90; 23 370,
  482; 27 46
Equitable Resources, Inc., 6 492–94; 54
  95–98 (upd.)
Equitable Trust Co., II 247, 397; 10 61
Equitas, 22 315
Equitec Financial Group, 11 483
Equitex Inc., 16 431
Equity & Law, III 211
Equity Corp. International, 51 332
Equity Corp. Tasman, III 735
Equity Corporation, 6 599; 37 67–68
Equity Group Investment, Inc., 22 339
Equity Marketing, Inc., 26 136–38
Equity Office Properties Trust, 54
  99–102

Equity Residential, 49 55, 129–32; 54
  100
Equity Title Services Company, 13 348
Equivalent Company, 12 421
Equus Capital Corp., 23 65
Equus Computer Systems, Inc., 49
  133–35
Equus II Inc., 18 11
Eram SA, 51 118–20
Eramet, IV 108
ERAP. See Entreprise de Recherches et
  d'Activités Pétrolières.
Erasco Group, II 556; 26 58
EraSoft Technologies, 27 492
Ercea, 41 128–29
ERCO Systems Group, 16 461–63
Ercon Corp., 49 181
ERDA Inc., 36 160
Erdal, II 572
Erdölsproduktions-Gesellschaft AG, IV 485
Erftwerk AG, IV 229
ERGO Versicherungsgruppe AG, 44
  166–69, 443
Ericson Yachts, 10 215
Ericsson, 9 32–33; 11 196, 501; 17 33,
  353; 18 74; 47 321; 53 126–28. See also
  Telefonaktiebolaget LM Ericsson.
Eridania Béghin-Say S.A., 14 17, 19; 36
  185–88
Erie and Pennyslvania, I 584
Erie County Bank, 9 474
Erie Indemnity Company, 35 167–69
Erie Railroad, I 584; II 329; IV 180
Erie Scientific Company, 14 479–80
ERIM International Inc., 54 396
Eritsusha, IV 326
erizon, 36 264
ERKA. See Reichs Kredit-Gesellschaft
  mbH.
ERLY Industries Inc., 17 161–62; 33
  30–31
Ernest Oppenheimer and Sons, IV 21, 79
Ernst & Young, I 412; 9 198–200, 309,
  311; 10 115; 25 358; 29 174–77 (upd.),
  236, 392
Ernst Göhner Foundation, 47 286–87
Ernst, Homans, Ware & Keelips, 37 224
Erol's, 9 74; 11 556
ERPI, 7 167
Ersco Corporation, 17 310; 24 160
Erste Allgemeine, III 207–08
The Ertl Company, 37 318
Erving Distributor Products Co., IV 282; 9
  260
Erving Healthcare, 13 150
Erwin Wasey & Co., I 17, 22
Erzbergbau Salzgitter AG, IV 201
ES&A. See English, Scottish and
  Australian Bank Ltd.
Esanda, II 189
Esaote Biomedica, 29 298
ESB Inc., IV 112; 18 488
Esbjerg Thermoplast, 9 92
Escada AG, 14 467
Escalade, Incorporated, 19 142–44
Escambia Chemicals, I 298
Escan, 22 354
Escanaba Paper Co., IV 311; 19 266
Escaut et Meuse, IV 227
Escher Wyss, III 539, 632
Eschweiler Bergwerks-Verein AG, IV
  25–26, 193
ESCO Electronics Corporation, 17 246,
  248; 24 425

Esco Trading, **10** 482
Escoffier Ltd., **I** 259
Escota SA, **55** 40
Escotel Mobile Communications, **18** 180
Esdon de Castro, **8** 137
ESE Sports Co. Ltd., **V** 376; **26** 397
ESGM. *See* Elder Smith Goldsbrough
   Mort.
ESGO B.V., **49** 222
ESI Energy, Inc., **V** 623–24
Eskay Screw Corporation, **11** 536
Eskilstuna Separator, **III** 419
Eskimo Pie Corporation, 21 218–20; 35
   119, 121
Esmark, Inc., **I** 441; **II** 448, 468–69; **6**
   357; **12** 93; **13** 448; **15** 357; **19** 290; **22**
   55, 513
Esmerk Group, **51** 328
Esperance-Longdoz, **IV** 51–52
Espírito Santo. *See* Banco Espírito Santo e
   Comercial de Lisboa S.A.
ESPN Inc., **II** 131; **IV** 627; **19** 201, 204;
   24 516; **46** 232
Esporta plc, 35 170–72
Esprit de Corp., 8 169–72; 29 178–82
   (upd.)
La Espuela Oil Company, Ltd., **IV** 81–82;
   7 186
Esquire Education Group, **12** 173
Esquire Inc., **I** 453; **IV** 672; **13** 178; **19**
   405
ESS Technology, Inc., 22 196–98
Essanelle Salon Co., **18** 455
Essantee Theatres, Inc., **14** 86
Essef Corporation, 18 161–63
Esselte Leitz GmbH & Co. KG, 48
   152–55
Esselte Pendaflex Corporation, 11
   100–01
Essence Communications, Inc., 24
   153–55
Essener Reisebüro, **II** 164
Essentially Pure Ingredients, **49** 275–76
Essex International Ltd., **19** 452
Essex Outfitters Inc., **9** 394; **42** 268–69
Essilor International, 18 392; **21 221–23**;
   40 96–98
Esso Petroleum, **I** 52; **II** 628; **III** 673; **IV**
   46, 276, 397, 421, 423, 432–33, 439,
   441, 454, 470, 484, 486, 517–19, 531,
   555, 563; **7** 140, 171; **11** 97; **13** 558; **22**
   106; **24** 86; **25** 229, 231–32. *See also*
   Imperial Oil Limited; Standard Oil
   Company of New Jersey.
Essroc Corporation, **40** 108
Estat Telecom Group plc, **31** 180
Estech, Inc., **19** 290
Estee Corp., **27** 197; **43** 218
The Estée Lauder Companies Inc., 30
   187–91 (upd.)
Estée Lauder Inc., I 696; **III** 56; **8** 131; **9**
   201–04; **11** 41; **24** 55
Estel N.V., **IV** 105, 133
Esterline Technologies Corp., 15 155–57;
   53 353
Estes Industries Inc. *See* Centuri
   Corporation.
Eston Chemical, **6** 148
Estronicks, Inc., **19** 290
ETA Systems, Inc., **10** 256–57
Etablissement Mesnel, **I** 202
Etablissement Poulenc-Frères, **I** 388
Etablissements Badin-Defforey, **19** 98

Etablissements Braud. *See* Manitou BF
   S.A.
Etablissements Economiques du Casino
   Guichard, Perrachon et ie, S.C.A., 12
   152–54; 16 452
Etablissements Pierre Lemonnier S.A., **II**
   532
Etablissements Robert Ouvrie S.A., **22** 436
Etam Developpement SA, 35 308; **44**
   170–72
Eteq Microsystems, **9** 116
Ethan Allen Interiors, Inc., III 530–31;
   10 184; **12** 307; **12 155–57; 39 145–48**
   (upd.), 39 173–74
Ethical Personal Care Products, Ltd., **17**
   108
Ethicon, Inc., III 35; **8** 281; **10** 213; **23**
   188–90
Ethyl Corp., I 334–36, 342; **IV** 289; **10**
   289–91 (upd.); 14 217; **52** 349
Etienne Aigner AG, 14 224; **52 109–12**
Etimex Kunstoffwerke GmbH, **7** 141
Etkin Skanska, **38** 437
L'Etoile, **II** 139
Étoile Commerciale S.A., **51** 143
Etos, **II** 641
EToys, Inc., 37 128–30
ETPM Entrêpose, **IV** 468
ETS. *See* Educational Testing Service.
Euclid, **I** 147; **12** 90
Euclid Chemical Co., **8** 455–56
Euclid Crane & Hoist Co., **13** 385
Euralux, **III** 209
Eurasbank, **II** 279–80; **14** 169
The Eureka Company, III 478, 480; **12**
   158–60; 15 416; **22** 26; **53** 126–27. *See*
   also White Consolidated Industries Inc.
Eureka Insurance Co., **III** 343
Eureka Specialty Printing, **IV** 253; **17** 30
Eureka Technology, **18** 20; **43** 17
Eureka Tent & Awning Co., **III** 59
Eureka X-Ray Tube, Inc., **10** 272
Eurex, **41** 84, 87
Euris, **22** 365; **54** 306–07
Euro Disneyland SCA, 6 174, 176; **20**
   209–12
Euro Exhausts, **54** 206
Euro-Pacific Finance, **II** 389
Euro RSCG Worldwide S.A., 10 345,
   347; **13 203–05; 16** 168; **33** 181
Eurobase, **50** 48
Eurobel, **II** 139; **III** 200; **24** 193
Eurobrokers Investment Corp., **II** 457
Eurocan Pulp & Paper Co. Ltd., **III** 648;
   IV 276, 300
Eurocard France, **II** 265
Eurocom S.A. *See* Euro RSCG Worldwide
   S.A.
Eurocopter SA, **7** 9, 11; **21** 8
EuroCross, **48** 381
Eurodis, **46** 71
EuroDollar Rent A Car. *See* Republic
   Industries, Inc.
Eurofighter Jagdflugzeug GmbH, **24** 84
Eurofilter Airfilters Ltd., **17** 106
Eurogroup, **V** 65
Euroimpex, **18** 163
Euromarché SA, **10** 205; **19** 308–09; **23**
   231; **27** 94–95
Euromarket Designs Inc., 9 144; **31**
   186–189 (upd.); 34 324, 327
Euromissile Dynamics Group, **7** 9; **24** 84
Euromoney Publications, **19** 118, 120
Euronda, **IV** 296; **19** 226

Euronext Paris S.A., 37 131–33
Euronova S.R.L., **15** 340
Europa Discount Sud-Ouest, **23** 248
Europa Metalli, **IV** 174
Europaischen Tanklager- und Transport
   AG, **7** 141
Europate, S.A., 36 162–63
Europcar Chauffeur Drive U.K.
   International, **26** 62
Europcar International Corporation,
   Limited, **25** 142, 144, **27** 9, 11
Europcar Interrent, **10** 419
Europe Computer Systems. *See* ECS S.A.
Europe Craft Imports, Inc., **16** 37
Europe Publications, **44** 416
European Acquisition Capital, **53** 46
European Aeronautic Defence and Space
   Company EADS N.V., 34 128, 135; **52**
   113–16 (upd.); 54 91
European-American Bank & Trust
   Company, **14** 169
European-American Banking Corp., **II** 279,
   295
European and African Investments Ltd., **IV**
   21
European Banking Co., **II** 186
European Banks' International Co., **II**
   184–86, 295
European Coal and Steel, **II** 402
European Gas Turbines, **13** 356
European Health Spa, **46** 431
European Investment Bank, **6** 97
European Periodicals, Publicity and
   Advertising Corp., **IV** 641; **7** 311
European Petroleum Co., **IV** 562
European Retail Alliance (ERA), **12**
   152–53
European Silicon Structures, **17** 34
European Software Company, **25** 87
Europeia, **III** 403
Europemballage, **I** 600
Europene du Zirconium (Cezus), **21** 491
Europensiones, **III** 348
Europoligrafico SpA, **41** 326
Europspace Technische Entwicklungen, **51**
   17
Eurosar S.A., **25** 455
Eurotec, **IV** 128
Eurotech BV, **25** 101
Eurotechnique, **III** 678; **16** 122
Eurotunnel Group, 37 134–38 (upd.)
Eurotunnel PLC, 13 206–08
Eurovida, **III** 348
Euthenics Systems Corp. *See* Michael
   Baker Corporation.
Euvia Media AG & Co., **54** 295, 297
EVA Airways Corporation, 13 211; **51**
   121–23
Evac International Ltd, **51** 324
Evaluation Associates, Inc., **III** 306
Evan Picone, **III** 55
Evans, **V** 21
Evans & Sutherland Computer
   Corporation, 19 145–49
Evans-Aristocrat Industries, **III** 570; **20**
   361
Evans Drumhead Company, **48** 232
Evans, Inc., 30 192–94
Evans Products Co., **13** 249–50, 550
Evans Rents, **26** 101
Evansville Paint & Varnish Co. *See* Red
   Spot Paint & Varnish Co.
Evansville Veneer and Lumber Co., **12** 296
Evelyn Haddon, **IV** 91

Evelyn Wood, Inc., **7** 165, 168
Evence Coppée, **III** 704–05
Evenflo Companies, Inc., **19** 144; **54** 73
Evening News Association, **IV** 612; **7** 191
Ever Ready Label Corp., **IV** 253; **17** 30
Ever Ready Ltd., **7** 209; **9** 179–80; **30** 231
Everan Capital Corp., **15** 257
Everest & Jennings, **11** 200
Everett Pulp & Paper Company, **17** 440
Everex Systems, Inc., 12 162; **16 194–96**
Everfresh Beverages Inc., **26** 326
Evergenius, **13** 210
Evergreen Air Cargo Service Co., **51** 123
Evergreen Healthcare, Inc., **14** 210
Evergreen International Aviation, Inc., 53 130–33
Evergreen Marine Corporation (Taiwan) Ltd., 13 209–11; **50 183–89 (upd.)**
Evergreen Media Corporation, **24** 106
Evergreen Resources, Inc., **11** 28
Everlast Worldwide Inc., 47 126–29
Everlaurel, **13** 210
Everready Battery Co., **13** 433; **39** 338
Eversharp, **III** 28
Everyday Learning Corporation, **22** 519, 522
Everything for the Office, **22** 154
Everything Yogurt, **25** 180
Everything's A Dollar Inc. (EAD), **13** 541–43
EVI, Inc., **39** 416
Evian, **6** 47, 49
Evinrude-ELTO, **III** 597
Evinrude Motor Co., **III** 597–99
Evinrude Outboard Motor Company, **27** 75
Evity, Inc., **55** 67
Ewell Industries, **III** 739
Ewo Breweries, **I** 469; **20** 311
Ex-Cell-O Corp., **IV** 297
Ex-Lax Inc., **15** 138–39
Exabyte Corporation, 12 161–63; **26** 256; **40 178–81 (upd.)**
Exacta, **III** 122
Exactis.com Inc., **49** 423
ExamOne World Wide, **48** 256
Exar Corp., 14 182–84
Exatec A/S, **10** 113; **50** 43
Exbud, **38** 437
Excaliber, **6** 205
EXCEL Communications Inc., 18 164–67
Excel Corporation, **11** 92–93; **13** 138, 351; **54** 168
Excel Industries Inc., **53** 55
Excel Mining Systems, Inc., **13** 98
Excelsior Life Insurance Co., **III** 182; **21** 14
Excelsior Printing Company, **26** 105
Excerpta Medica International, **IV** 610
Exchange & Discount Bank, **II** 318; **17** 323
Exchange Bank of Yarmouth, **II** 210
Exchange Oil & Gas Corp., **IV** 282; **9** 260
Excite, Inc., **22** 519; **27** 517. *See also* At Home Corporation.
Exco International, **10** 277
Execu-Fit Health Programs, **11** 379
Executive Aircraft Services, **27** 21
Executive Airlines, Inc., **28** 22
Executive Fund Life Insurance Company, **27** 47
Executive Gallery, Inc., **12** 264
Executive Income Life Insurance Co., **10** 246

Executive Jet, Inc., 36 189–91; **42** 35
Executive Life Insurance Co., **III** 253–55; **11** 483
Executive Risk Inc., **37** 86
Executive Systems, Inc., **11** 18
Executone Information Systems, Inc., 13 212–14; **15** 195
ExecuTrain. *See* International Data Group, Inc.
Executrans, Inc., **21** 96
Exel Logistics Ltd., **6** 412, 414
Exel Ltd., **13** 150
Exel plc, 51 124–30 (upd.)
Exelon Corporation, 48 156–63 (upd.); **49** 65
Exeter & Hampton Electric Company, **37** 406
Exeter Oil Co., **IV** 550
Exide Electronics Group, Inc., 9 10; **20 213–15**; **24** 29
Exmark Manufacturing Company, Inc., **26** 494
Exors. of James Mills, **III** 493
Exp@nets, **37** 280, 283
Expand SA, 48 164–66
Expedia Inc., **46** 101, 103; **47** 421
Expeditors International of Washington Inc., 17 163–65
Expercom, **6** 303
Experian Information Solutions Inc., 28 120; **45 152–55**
Experian Ltd., **47** 165, 168–69
Experience, **III** 359
Exploitasi Tambang Minyak Sumatra Utara, **IV** 492
Explorer Motor Home Corp., **16** 296
Explosive Fabricators Corp., **III** 643
Export & Domestic Can Co., **15** 127
Export-Import Bank, **IV** 33, 184
Express Airlines, Inc., **28** 266
Express Baggage Reclaim Services Limited, **27** 21
Express Foods Inc, **I** 247–48
Express Newspapers plc, **IV** 687; **28** 503
Express Rent-a-Tire, Ltd., **20** 113
Express Scripts Inc., 17 166–68; **44 173–76 (upd.)**
Expression Homes, **22** 205, 207
ExpressJet Holdings Inc., **52** 89, 93
Exsa, **55** 188
ExSample Media BV, **53** 362
Extel Corp., **II** 142; **III** 269–70
Extel Financial Ltd., **IV** 687
Extended Stay America, Inc., 41 156–58
Extendicare Health Services, Inc., III 81; **6 181–83**
Extracorporeal Medical Specialties, **III** 36
Extron International Inc., **16** 538; **43** 33
Exx Inc., **40** 334
Exxon Corporation, I 16–17, 360, 364; **II** 16, 62, 431, 451; **IV** 171, 363, 365, 403, 406, **426–30**, 431–33, 437–38, 454, 466, 506, 508, 512, 515, 522, 537–39, 554; **V** 605; **7 169–73 (upd.)**, 230, 538, 559; **9** 440–41; **11** 353; **14** 24–25, 291, 494; **12** 348; **16** 489, 548; **20** 262; **23** 317; **25** 229–30; **26** 102, 369; **27** 217; **32 175–82 (upd.)**; **45** 54
Exxon Mobil Corporation, **40** 358; **50** 29; **54** 380, 385
Eye Masters Ltd., **23** 329
Eyeful Home Co., **III** 758
Eyelab, **II** 560; **12** 411

Eyes Multimedia Productions Inc., **51** 286–87
EZ Paintr Corporation, **9** 374
EZCORP Inc., 43 159–61
EZPor Corporation, **12** 377

F. & F. Koenigkramer Company, **10** 272
F&G International Insurance, **III** 397
F. & J. Heinz, **II** 507
F & J Meat Packers, Inc., **22** 548–49
F & M Distributors, **12** 132
F. & M. Schaefer Brewing Corporation, **I** 253, 291, **III** 137; **18** 500
F & M Scientific Corp., **III** 142; **6** 237
F&N Foods Ltd., **54** 116–17
F & R Builders, Inc., **11** 257
F.A. Computer Technologies, Inc., **12** 60
F.A. Ensign Company, **6** 38
F.A.I. Insurances, **III** 729
F.A.O. Schwarz. *See* FAO Schwarz
F. Atkins & Co., **I** 604
F.B. McFarren, Ltd., **21** 499–500
F.C. Internazionale Milano SpA, **44** 387
F.E. Compton Company, **7** 167
F. Egger Co., **22** 49
F.F. Dalley Co., **II** 497
F.F. Publishing and Broadsystem Ltd., **IV** 652; **7** 392
F.H. Tomkins Buckle Company Ltd., **11** 525
F. Hoffmann-La Roche & Co. A.G., I 637, 640, **642–44**, 657, 685, 693, 710; **7** 427; **9** 264; **10** 80, 549; **11** 424–25; **14** 406; **32** 211–12; **50 190–93 (upd.)**
F.J. Walker Ltd., **I** 438
F.K.I. Babcock, **III** 466
F. Kanematsu & Co., Ltd. *See* Kanematsu Corporation.
F.L. Industries Inc., **I** 481, 483
F.L. Moseley Co., **III** 142; **6** 237; **50** 223
F.N. Burt Co., **IV** 644
F. Perkins, **III** 651–52
F.S. Smithers, **II** 445; **22** 405
F.W. Dodge Corp., **IV** 636–37
F.W. Means & Company, **11** 337
F.W. Sickles Company, **10** 319
F.W. Williams Holdings, **III** 728
F.W. Woolworth & Co. Ltd. *See* Kingfisher plc.
F.W. Woolworth Co. *See* Woolworth Corporation.
F.X. Matt Brewing Co., **18** 72; **50** 114
Fab-Asia, Inc., **22** 354–55
Fab Industries, Inc., 27 142–44
Fab 9, **26** 431
Fabbrica D' Armi Pietro Beretta S.p.A., 39 149–51
Fabco Automotive Corp., **23** 306; **27** 203
Faber-Castell. *See* A.W. Faber-Castell Unternehmensverwaltung GmbH & Co.
Fabergé, Inc., **II** 590; **III** 48; **8** 168, 344; **11** 90; **32** 475; **47** 114
Fabri-Centers of America Inc., 15 329; **16 197–99**; **18** 223; **43** 291
Fabrica de Cemento El Melan, **III** 671
Fabtek Inc., **48** 59
Facchin Foods Co., **I** 457
Facit, **III** 480; **22** 26
Facom S.A., 32 183–85; **37** 143, 145
Facts on File, Inc., **14** 96–97; **22** 443
FAE Fluid Air Energy SA, **49** 162–63
Fafnir Bearing Company, **13** 523
FAG Kugelfischer Georg Schafer AG, **11** 84; **47** 280

Fagerdala World Foams, **54** 360–61
Fagersta, **II** 366; **IV** 203
Fahr AG, **III** 543
Fahrzeugwerke Eisenach, **I** 138
FAI, **III** 545–46
Failsafe, **14** 35
Fair Grounds Corporation, 44 177–80
Fair, Isaac and Company, 18 168–71,
516, 518
Fairbanks Morse Co., **I** 158, 434–35; **10**
292; **12** 71
Fairchild Aircraft, Inc., 9 205–08, 460;
11 278
Fairchild Camera and Instrument Corp., **II**
50, 63; **III** 110, 141, 455, 618; **6**
261–62; **7** 531; **10** 108; **11** 503; **13**
323–24; **14** 14; **17** 418; **21** 122, 330; **26**
327
Fairchild Communications Service, **8** 328
The Fairchild Corporation, **37** 30
Fairchild Dornier GmbH, 48 167–71
(upd.)
Fairchild Industries, **I** 71, 198; **11** 438; **14**
43; **15** 195; **34** 117
Fairchild Semiconductor Corporation, **II**
44–45, 63–65; **III** 115; **6** 215, 247; **10**
365–66; **16** 332; **24** 235; **41** 201
Fairclough Construction Group plc, I
567–68
Fairey Industries Ltd., **IV** 659
Fairfax, **IV** 650
Fairfield Communities, Inc., 36 192–95
The Fairfield Group, **33** 259–60
Fairfield Manufacturing Co., **14** 43
Fairfield Publishing, **13** 165
Fairmont Foods Co., **7** 430; **15** 139
Fairmont Hotels and Resorts Inc., **45** 80
Fairmont Insurance Co., **26** 487
Fairmount Glass Company, **8** 267
Fairport Machine Shop, Inc., **17** 357
Fairway Marketing Group, Inc., **24** 394
Fairway Outdoor Advertising, Inc., **36** 340,
342
Faiveley S.A., 39 152–54
Falcon Drilling Co. *See* Transocean Sedco
Forex Inc.
Falcon Oil Co., **IV** 396
Falcon Products, Inc., 33 149–51
Falcon Seaboard Inc., **II** 86; **IV** 410; **7** 309
Falconbridge Limited, IV 111, 165–66;
49 136–39
Falconet Corp., **I** 45
Falley’s, Inc., **17** 558, 560–61
Fallon McElligott Inc., 22 199–201
Falls Financial Inc., **13** 223; **31** 206
Falls National Bank of Niagara Falls, **11**
108
Falls Rubber Company, **8** 126
FAME Plastics, Inc., **18** 162
Family Bookstores, **24** 548. *See also*
Family Christian Stores, Inc.
Family Channel. *See* International Family
Entertainment Inc.
Family Christian Stores, Inc., 51 131–34
Family Dollar Stores, Inc., 13 215–17
Family Golf Centers, Inc., 29 183–85
Family Health Program, **6** 184
Family Life Insurance Co., **II** 425; **13** 341
Family Mart Group, **V** 188; **36** 418, 420
Family Restaurants, Inc., **14** 194
Family Steak Houses of Florida, Inc., **15**
420
Famosa Bakery, **II** 543

Famous Amos Chocolate Chip Cookie
Corporation, **27** 332
Famous Atlantic Fish Company, **20** 5
Famous-Barr, **46** 288
Famous Dave’s of America, Inc., 40
182–84 4
Famous Players-Lasky Corp., **I** 451; **II**
154; **6** 161–62; **23** 123
Famous Restaurants Inc., **33** 139–40
FAN, **13** 370
Fancom Holding B.V., **43** 130
Fannie Mae, 45 156–59 (upd.); 54
122–24
Fannie May Candy Shops Inc., **36** 309
Fansteel Inc., 19 150–52
Fantastic Sam’s, **26** 476
Fanthing Electrical Corp., **44** 132
Fantle’s Drug Stores, **16** 160
Fantus Co., **IV** 605
Fanuc Ltd., III 482–83; 17 172–74
(upd.)
Fanzz, **29** 282
FAO Schwarz, I 548; **46** 187–90; **50** 524
Faprena, **25** 85
Far East Airlines, **6** 70
Far East Machinery Co., **III** 581
Far Eastern Air Transport, Inc., **23** 380
Far West Restaurants, **I** 547
Faraday National Corporation, **10** 269
Farah Incorporated, 24 156–58
Farben. *See* I.G. Farbenindustrie AG.
Farbenfabriken Bayer A.G., **I** 309
Farberware, Inc., **27** 287–88
Farbro Corp., **45** 15
Farbwerke Hoechst A.G., **I** 346–47; **IV**
486; **13** 262
Farine Lactée Henri Nestlé, **II** 545
Farinon Corp., **II** 38
Farley Candy Co., **15** 190
Farley Industries, **25** 166
Farley Northwest Industries Inc., I
440–41
Farm Credit Bank of St. Louis/St. Paul, **8**
489–90
Farm Electric Services Ltd., **6** 586
Farm Family Holdings, Inc., 39 155–58
Farm Fresh Catfish Company, **54** 167
Farm Fresh Foods, **25** 332
Farm Journal Corporation, 42 131–34
Farm Power Laboratory, **6** 565; **50** 366
Farmcare Ltd., **51** 89
Farmer Bros. Co., 52 117–19
Farmer Jack, **16** 247; **44** 145
Farmers and Mechanics Bank of
Georgetown, **13** 439
Farmers and Merchants Bank, **II** 349
Farmers Bank of Delaware, **II** 315–16
Farmers Insurance Group of
Companies, 23 286; **25 154–56; 29** 397
Farmers’ Loan and Trust Co., **II** 254; **9**
124
Farmers National Bank & Trust Co., **9** 474
Farmers Petroleum, Inc., **48** 175
Farmers Regional Cooperative, **II** 536
Farmland Foods, Inc., IV 474; **7** 17, **7**
174–75
Farmland Industries, Inc., 39 282; **48**
172–75
Farnam Cheshire Lime Co., **III** 763
Farrar, Straus and Giroux Inc., 15
158–60; 35 451
FAS Acquisition Co., **53** 142
FASC. *See* First Analysis Securities
Corporation.

Fasco Consumer Products, **19** 360
Fasco Industries, **III** 509; **13** 369
Faserwerke Hüls GmbH., **I** 350
Fashion Bar, Inc., **24** 457
Fashion Bug, **8** 97
Fashion Co., **II** 503; **10** 324
Fasquelle, **IV** 618
Fasson. *See* Avery Dennison Corporation.
Fast Air, **31** 305
Fast Fare, **7** 102
Fastenal Company, 14 185–87; 42
135–38 (upd.)
FAT KAT, Inc., **51** 200, 203
Fata European Group, **IV** 187; **19** 348
Fateco Förlag, **14** 556
FATS, Inc., **27** 156, 158
Fatum, **III** 308
Faugere et Jutheau, **III** 283
Faulkner, Dawkins & Sullivan, **II** 450
Faultless Starch/Bon Ami Company, 55
142–45
Fauquet, **25** 85
Favorite Plastics, **19** 414
FAvS. *See* First Aviation Services Inc.
Fawcett Books, **13** 429
Fay’s Inc., 17 175–77
Fayette Tubular Products, **7** 116–17
Faygo Beverages Inc., 55 146–48
Fayva, **13** 359–61
Fazoli’s Systems, Inc., 13 321; **27 145–47**
FB&T Corporation, **14** 154
FBC. *See* First Boston Corp.
FBO. *See* Film Booking Office of America.
FBR. *See* Friedman, Billings, Ramsey
Group, Inc.
FC Holdings, Inc., **26** 363
FCBC, **IV** 174
FCC. *See* Federal Communications
Commission.
FCC National Bank, **II** 286
FCI. *See* Framatome SA.
FDIC. *See* Federal Deposit Insurance Corp.
Fearn International, **II** 525; **13** 293; **50** 293
Feather Fine, **27** 361
Featherlite Inc., 28 127–29
Feature Enterprises Inc., **19** 452
Fechheimer Bros. Co., **III** 215; **18** 60, 62
Fedders Corporation, 18 172–75; 43
162–67 (upd.)
Federal Barge Lines, **6** 487
Federal Bearing and Bushing, **I** 158–59
Federal Bicycle Corporation of America,
11 3
Federal Cartridge, **26** 363
Federal Coca-Cola Bottling Co., **10** 222
Federal Communications Commission, **6**
164–65; **9** 321
Federal Deposit Insurance Corp., **II**
261–62, 285, 337; **12** 30, 79
Federal Electric, **I** 463; **III** 653
Federal Express Corporation, II 620; **V**
451–53; 6 345–46, 385–86, 389; **12**
180, 192; **13** 19; **14** 517; **17** 504–05; **18**
315–17, 368, 370; **24** 22, 133; **25** 148;
26 441; **27** 20, 22, 471, 475; **34** 15, 17;
39 33, 35; **41** 245–47. *See also* FedEx
Corporation.
Federal Home Life Insurance Co., **III** 263;
IV 623
Federal Home Loan Bank, **II** 182
Federal Home Loan Mortgage Corp., **18**
168; **25** 427[see ALSO]Freddie Mac.
Federal Insurance Co., **III** 220–21; **14**
108–109; **37** 83–85

Federal Lead Co., **IV** 32
Federal Light and Traction Company, **6** 561–62
Federal Mining and Smelting Co., **IV** 32
Federal-Mogul Corporation, **I 158–60**; **III** 596; **10 292–94 (upd.)**; **26 139–43 (upd.)**; **47** 279
Federal National Mortgage Association, **II 410–11**; **18** 168; **25** 427. *See also* Fannie Mae.
Federal Pacific Electric, **II** 121; **9** 440
Federal Packaging and Partition Co., **8** 476
Federal Packaging Corp., **19** 78
Federal Paper Board Company, Inc., **I** 524; **8 173–75**; **15** 229; **47** 189
Federal Paper Mills, **IV** 248
Federal Power, **18** 473
Federal Prison Industries, Inc., **34 157–60**
Federal Reserve Bank of New York, **21** 68
Federal Savings and Loan Insurance Corp., **16** 346
Federal Signal Corp., **10 295–97**
Federal Steel Co., **II** 330; **IV** 572; **7** 549; **50** 500
Federal Trade Commission, **6** 260; **9** 370
Federal Yeast Corp., **IV** 410
Federale Mynbou, **IV** 90–93
Federated Department Stores Inc., **IV** 703; **V 25–28**; **9 209–12**; **10** 282; **11** 349; **12** 37, 523; **13** 43, 260; **15** 88; **16** 61, 206; **17** 560; **18** 523; **22** 406; **23** 60; **27** 346–48; **30** 379; **31 190–194 (upd.)**; **35** 368; **36** 201, 204; **37** 13; **50** 107
Federated Development Company, **8** 349
Federated Metals Corp., **IV** 32
Federated Publications, **IV** 612; **7** 191
Federated Timbers, **I** 422
Fédération Internationale de Football Association, **27 148–51**
Federation Nationale d'Achats des Cadres. *See* FNAC.
FedEx Corporation, **18** 128, **176–79 (upd.)**, 535; **33** 20, 22; **34** 474; **42 139–44 (upd.)**; **46** 71
Fedmart, **V** 162
FEE Technology, **29** 461–62
Feed-Rite Controls, Inc., **16** 270
Feffer & Simons, **16** 46
Feikes & Sohn KG, **IV** 325
Feinblech-Contiglühe, **IV** 103
Felco. *See* Farmers Regional Cooperative.
Feld Entertainment, Inc., **32 186–89 (upd.)**
Feldmühle Nobel AG, **II 50–51**; **III 692–95**; **IV** 142, 325, 337; **21** 330; **36** 449
Felixstowe Ltd., **18** 254
Fellowes Manufacturing Company, **28 130–32**
Felten & Guilleaume, **IV** 25
Femsa, **19** 473. *See also* Formento Económico Mexicano, S.A. de C.V.
Femtech, **8** 513
Fendall Company, **40** 96, 98
Fendel Schiffahrts-Aktiengesellschaft, **6** 426
Fender Musical Instruments Company, **16 200–02**; **43 168–72 (upd.)**
Fendi S.p.A., **45** 344
Fenestra Inc., **IV** 136
Fenicia Group, **22** 320
Fenn, Wright & Manson, **25** 121–22
Fenner & Beane, **II** 424

Fenton Hill American Limited, **29** 510
Fenwal Laboratories, **I** 627; **10** 141
Fenway Partners, **47** 361
Fenwick & West LLP, **34 161–63**, 512
Ferembal S.A., **25** 512
Ferfin, **24** 341
Fergus Brush Electric Company, **18** 402
Ferguson Machine Co., **8** 135
Ferguson Manufacturing Company, **25** 164
Ferguson Radio Corp., **I** 531–32
Ferienreise GmbH., **II** 164
Fermec Manufacturing Limited, **40** 432
Fermentaciones Mexicanas S.A. de C.V., **III** 43; **48** 250
Fernando Roqué, **6** 404; **26** 243
Ferngas, **IV** 486
Ferolito, Vultaggio & Sons, **27 152–55**
Ferranti Business Communications, **20** 75
Ferranti Ltd., **II** 81; **6** 240
Ferrari S.p.A., **I** 162; **11** 103; **13 218–20**; **36 196–200 (upd.)**
Ferrellgas Partners, L.P., **35 173–75**
Ferrero SpA, **54 103–05**
Ferrier Hodgson, **10** 170
Ferro Corporation, **III** 536; **8 176–79**; **9** 10; **26** 230
Ferro Engineering Co., **17** 357
Ferrocarril del Noreste, S.A. de C.V. *See* Grupo Transportación Ferroviaria Mexicana, S.A. de C.V.
Ferrovial. *See* Grupo Ferrovail
Ferroxcube Corp. of America, **13** 397
Ferrum Inc., **24** 144
Ferruzzi Agricola Finanziario, **I** 369; **7** 81–83
Ferruzzi Finanziaria S.p.A., **24** 341; **36** 186
Fesca, **III** 417–18
Fetzer Vineyards, **10** 182
FFI Fragrances. *See* Elizabeth Arden, Inc.
FHP International Corporation, **6 184–86**; **17** 166, 168; **44** 174
Fianzas Monterrey, **19** 189
Fiat SpA, **I** 154, 157, **161–63**, 459–60, 466, 479; **II** 280; **III** 206, 543, 591; **IV** 420; **9** 10; **11 102–04 (upd.)**, 139; **13** 17, 27–29, 218–20; **16** 322; **17** 24; **22** 379–81; **36** 32–34, 196–97, 199, 240, 243; **50 194–98 (upd.)**
Fibamex, **17** 106
Fibar, **44** 261
Fiber Chemical Corporation, **7** 308
Fiberglas Canada, **III** 722
Fiberite, Inc., **27** 117; **28** 195
FiberMark, Inc., **37 139–42**; **53** 24
Fibermux Corporation, **10** 19; **30** 7
Fibic Corp., **18** 118
Fibre Containers, **IV** 249
Fibreboard Corporation, **IV** 304; **12** 318; **14** 110; **16 203–05**
FibreChem, Inc., **8** 347
Fibro Tambor, S.A. de C.V., **8** 476
Fichet-Bauche SA, **53** 158
Fichtel & Sachs AG, **III** 566; **14** 328; **38** 299
Fidata Corp., **II** 317
Fidelco Capital Group, **10** 420
Fidelio Software GmbH, **18** 335, 337
Fidelity and Casualty Co. of New York, **III** 242
Fidelity and Guaranty Life Insurance Co., **III** 396–97
Fidelity Exploration & Production Company, **42** 249, 253
Fidelity Federal Savings and Loan, **II** 420

Fidelity Fire Insurance Co., **III** 240
Fidelity Insurance of Canada, **III** 396–97
Fidelity Investments Inc., **II 412–13**; **III** 588; **8** 194; **9** 239; **14 188–90 (upd.)**; **18** 552; **19** 113; **21** 147; **22** 52. *See also* FMR Corp.
Fidelity Leasing Corporation, **42** 312–13
Fidelity Life Association, **III** 269
Fidelity Mutual Insurance Co., **III** 231
Fidelity National Financial Inc., **54 106–08**
Fidelity National Life Insurance Co., **III** 191
Fidelity National Title, **19** 92
Fidelity Oil Group, **7** 324
Fidelity-Phenix Fire Insurance Co., **III** 240–42
Fidelity Title and Trust Co., **II** 315
Fidelity Trust Co., **II** 230; **33** 293
Fidelity Union Life Insurance Co., **III** 185
Fidenas Investment Ltd., **30** 185
Fides Holding, **21** 146
Field Corporation, **18** 355
Field Enterprises Educational Corporation, **16** 252; **26** 15; **43** 208
Field Enterprises, Inc., **IV** 672; **12** 554; **19** 404
Field Group plc, **30** 120
Field Limited Partnership, **22** 441
Field Oy, **10** 113; **50** 43
Fieldale Farms Corporation, **23 191–93**; **25** 185–86
Fieldco Guide Dog Foundation, **42** 207
Fieldcrest Cannon, Inc., **8 32–33**; **9 213–17**; **16** 535; **19** 276, 305; **31 195–200 (upd.)**; **41** 299–301
Fieldstone Cabinetry, **III** 571; **20** 362
Fielmann AG, **31 201–03**
Fiesta Restaurants Inc., **33** 139–40
FIFA. *See* Fédération Internationale de Football Association.
Fifa International, **39** 58
Fifteen Oil, **I** 526
Fifth Generation Systems Inc., **10** 509
Fifth Third Bancorp, **II** 291; **9** 475; **11** 466; **13 221–23**; **31 204–208 (upd.)**
50-Off Stores, **23** 177. *See also* LOT$OFF Corporation.
Figgie International Inc., **7 176–78**; **24** 403–04
Figi's Inc., **9** 218, 220
FII Limited, **38** 197
Fil-Mag Group, **29** 461
Fila Holding S.p.A., **20 216–18**; **39** 60; **52 120–24 (upd.)**
Filene's, **V** 132, 134
Filene's Basement. *See* Value City Department Stores, Inc.
Filergie S.A., **15** 355
Filipacchi Medias S.A. *See* Hachette Filipacchi Medias S.A.
Filiz Lastex, S.A., **15** 386
Filles S.A. de C.V., **7** 115; **25** 126
Film Booking Office of America, **II** 88
Films for the Humanities, Inc., **22** 441
Filofax Inc., **41** 120, 123
Filter Queen-Canada, **17** 234
Filterfresh Corporation, **39** 409
Filtertek, Inc., **24** 425
Filtrol Corp., **IV** 123
Filtrona International Ltd., **31** 77
Filtros Baldwin de Mexico, **17** 106
Filtros Continental, **17** 106
Fimalac S.A., **37 143–45**

Fimaser, **21** 101

Fimestic, **21** 101

Fin. Comit SpA, **II** 192

FINA, Inc., **7 179–81**; **26** 368

Finalrealm Limited, **42** 404

Finance Oil Corp., **49** 304

Financial Computer Services, Inc., **11** 111

Financial Corp. of Indonesia, **II** 257

Financial Data Services, Inc., **11** 111

Financial Investment Corp. of Asia, **III** 197

Financial Network Marketing Company, **11** 482

Financial News Ltd., **IV** 658

Financial News Network, Inc., **25** 507; **31** 147

Financial Security Assurance Inc., **III** 765; **25** 497

Financial Services Corp., **III** 306–07

Financial Services Corporation of Michigan, **11** 163

Financial Systems, Inc., **11** 111

Financial Technologies International, **17** 497

The Financial Times Group, **46** 337

Financiera Aceptaciones, **19** 189

Financière Crédit Suisse-First Boston, **II** 268, 402–04

Financiere de Suez, **II** 295

Financière Saint Dominique, **9** 151–52

FinansSkandic A.B., **II** 352–53

Finast. *See* First National Supermarkets, Inc.

Fincantieri, **I** 466–67

Find-A-Home Service, Inc., **21** 96

Findomestic, **21** 101

Findus, **II** 547; **25** 85

Fine Art Developments Ltd., **15** 340

Fine Fare, **II** 465, 609, 628–29

Fine Fragrances, **22** 213

Finelettrica, **I** 465–66

Finesco, LLC, **37** 200–01

Finevest Services Inc., **15** 526

Fingerhut Companies, Inc., **I** 613; **V** 148; **9 218–20**; **15** 401; **18** 133; **31** 190; **34** 232; **36 201–05 (upd.)**; **37** 130

Fininvest Group, **IV** 587–88

Fininvest S.p.A., **54** 17, 21, 23

The Finish Line, Inc., **29 186–88**

FinishMaster, Inc., **17** 310–11; **24 159–61**

Finland Wood Co., **IV** 275

Finlay Enterprises, Inc., **16 206–08**

Finlay Forest Industries, **IV** 297

Finmare, **I** 465, 467

Finmeccanica S.p.A., **II** 86; **13** 28; **23** 83; **36** 34; **50** 197; **52** 115

Finnair Oy, **I** 120; **6 87–89**; **25 157–60 (upd.)**; **33** 50; **34** 398

Finnforest Oy, **IV** 316

Finnigan Corporation, **11** 513

Finnish Cable Works, **II** 69; **17** 352

Finnish Fiberboard Ltd., **IV** 302

Oy Finnish Peroxides Ab, **IV** 300

Finnish Rubber Works, **II** 69; **17** 352

Oy Finnlines Ltd., **IV** 276

Finsa, **II** 196

FinSer Capital Corporation, **17** 262

Finservizi SpA, **II** 192

Finsider, **I** 465–66; **IV** 125

Firan Motor Coach, Inc., **17** 83

Fire Association of Philadelphia, **III** 342–43

Firearms Training Systems, Inc., **27 156–58**

Fireman's Fund Insurance Company, **I** 418; **II** 398, 457; **III** 214, **250–52**, 263; **10** 62

Firemen's Insurance Co. of Newark, **III** 241–42

Firestone Tire and Rubber Co., **III** 440, 697; **V** 234–35; **8** 80; **9** 247; **15** 355; **17** 182; **18** 320; **20** 259–62; **21** 73–74; **50** 316

Firma Hamburger Kaffee-Import- Geschäft Emil Tengelmann. *See* Tengelmann Group.

Firma Huter Vorfertigung GmbH, **49** 163

FirmLogic, L.P., **52** 423

The First, **10** 340

First Acadiana National Bank, **11** 107

First Albany Companies Inc., **37 146–48**

First Alert, Inc., **28 133–35**

First American. *See* Bremer Financial Corp.

First American Bank Corporation, **8** 188; **41** 178

The First American Corporation, **52 125–27**

First American Media, Inc., **24** 199

First American National Bank, **19** 378

First American National Bank-Eastern, **11** 111

First Analysis Securities Corporation, **22** 5

First and Merchants, **10** 426

First Atlanta Corporation, **16** 523

First Atlantic Capital, Ltd., **28** 340, 342

First Aviation Services Inc., **49 140–42**

First Bancard, Inc., **11** 106

First BanCorporation, **13** 467

First Bank and Trust of Mechanicsburg, **II** 342

First Bank of Savannah, **16** 522

First Bank of the United States, **II** 213, 253

First Bank System Inc., **11** 130; **12 164–66**; **13** 347–48; **24** 393. *See also* U.S. Bancorp

First Boston Corp., **II** 208, 257, 267–69, 402–04, 406–07, 426, 434, 441; **9** 378, 386; **12** 439; **13** 152, 342; **21** 145–46. *See also* CSFB.

First Brands Corporation, **8 180–82**; **16** 44

First Capital Financial, **8** 229

First Carolina Investors Inc., **17** 357

First Chicago Corporation, **II 284–87**. *See also* Bank One Corporation.

First Chicago Venture Capital, **24** 516

First Choice Holidays PLC, **40 185–87**, 284–85

First Cincinnati, Inc., **41** 133

First City Bank of Rosemead, **II** 348

First Colony Farms, **II** 584

First Colony Life Insurance, **I** 334–35; **10** 290

First Commerce Bancshares, Inc., **15 161–63**

First Commerce Corporation, **11 105–07**

First Commercial Savings and Loan, **10** 340

First Consumers National Bank, **10** 491; **27** 429

First Dallas, Ltd., **II** 415

First Data Corporation, **10** 63; **18** 516–18, 537; **24** 393 **30 195–98 (upd.)**; **46** 250; **54** 413

First Data Management Company of Oklahoma City, **11** 112

First Delaware Life Insurance Co., **III** 254

First Deposit Corp., **III** 218–19. *See also* Providian Financial Corporation.

First Empire State Corporation, **11 108–10**

First Engine and Boiler Insurance Co. Ltd., **III** 406

First Executive Corporation, **III 253–55**

First Express, **48** 177

First Federal Savings & Loan Assoc., **IV** 343; **9** 173

First Federal Savings and Loan Association of Crisp County, **10** 92

First Federal Savings and Loan Association of Hamburg, **10** 91

First Federal Savings and Loan Association of Fort Myers, **9** 476

First Federal Savings and Loan Association of Kalamazoo, **9** 482

First Federal Savings Bank of Brunswick, **10** 92

First Fidelity Bank, N.A., New Jersey, **9 221–23**

First Fidelity Bank of Rockville, **13** 440

First Financial Insurance, **41** 178

First Financial Management Corporation, **11 111–13**; **18** 542; **25** 183; **30** 195

First Florida Banks, **9** 59

First Hawaiian, Inc., **11 114–16**

First Health, **III** 373

FIRST HEALTH Strategies, **11** 113

First Healthcare, **14** 242

First Heights, fsa, **8** 437

First Hospital Corp., **15** 122

First Industrial Corp., **II** 41

First Insurance Agency, Inc., **17** 527

First Insurance Co. of Hawaii, **III** 191, 242

First International Trust, **IV** 91

First Interstate Bancorp, **II** 228, **288–90**; **8** 295; **9** 334; **17** 546

First Investment Advisors, **11** 106

First Investors Management Corp., **11** 106

First Jersey National Bank, **II** 334

First Leisure Corporation plc. *See* Esporta plc.

First Liberty Financial Corporation, **11** 457

First Line Insurance Services, Inc., **8** 436

First Madison Bank, **14** 192

First Maryland Bancorp, **16** 14

First Mid America, **II** 445; **22** 406

First Mississippi Corporation, **8 183–86**. *See also* ChemFirst, Inc.

First Mississippi National, **14** 41

First National Bank, **10** 298; **13** 467

First National Bank (Revere), **II** 208

First National Bank and Trust Company, **22** 4

First National Bank and Trust Company of Kalamazoo, **8** 187–88

First National Bank and Trust of Oklahoma City, **II** 289

First National Bank in Albuquerque, **11** 119

First National Bank of Akron, **9** 475

First National Bank of Allentown, **11** 296

First National Bank of Atlanta, **16** 522

First National Bank of Azusa, **II** 382

First National Bank of Boston, **II** 207–08, 402; **12** 310; **13** 446

First National Bank of Carrollton, **9** 475

First National Bank of Chicago, **II** 242, 257, 284–87; **III** 96–97; **IV** 135–36
First National Bank of Commerce, **11** 106
First National Bank of Harrington, Delaware. *See* J.C. Penny National Bank.
First National Bank of Hartford, **13** 466
First National Bank of Hawaii, **11** 114
First National Bank of Highland, **11** 109
First National Bank of Houma, **21** 522
The First National Bank of Lafayette, **11** 107
The First National Bank of Lake Charles, **11** 107
First National Bank of Lake City, **II** 336; **10** 425
First National Bank of Mexico, New York, **II** 231
First National Bank of Minneapolis, **22** 426–27
First National Bank of New York, **II** 254, 330
First National Bank of Raleigh, **II** 336
First National Bank of Salt Lake, **11** 118
First National Bank of Seattle, **8** 469–70
First National Bank of York, **II** 317
First National Bankshares, Inc., **21** 524
First National Boston Corp., **II** 208
First National Casualty Co., **III** 203
First National City Bank, **9** 124; **16** 13
First National City Bank of New York, **II** 254; **9** 124
First National City Corp., **III** 220–21
First National Holding Corporation, **16** 522
First National Insurance Co., **III** 352
First National Life Insurance Co., **III** 218
First National Supermarkets, Inc., **II** 641–42; **9** 452
First Nations Gaming, Ltd., **44** 334
First Nationwide Bank, **8** 30; **14 191–93**
First Nationwide Financial Corp., **I** 167; **11** 139
First Nationwide Holdings Inc., **28** 246
First New England Bankshares Corp., **13** 467
First Nitrogen, Inc., **8** 184
First Nuclear Corporation, **49** 411
First of America Bank Corporation, **8 187–89**
First of America Bank-Monroe, **9** 476
First of Boston, **II** 402–03
First Omni Bank NA, **16** 14; **18** 518; **43** 8
First Options of Chicago, Inc., **51** 148
First Pacific Company Limited, **18 180–82**
First Penn-Pacific Life Insurance Co., **III** 276
First Physician Care, Inc., **36** 367
First Pick Stores, **12** 458
First Quench Retailing Ltd., **52** 416
First Railroad and Banking Company, **11** 111
First Republic Bank of Texas, **II** 336
First Republic Corp., **III** 383; **14** 483
First RepublicBank Corporation, **II** 337; **10** 425–26
First Savings and Loan, **10** 339
First Seattle Dexter Horton National Bank, **8** 470
First Security Bank of Missoula, **35** 197–99
First Security Corporation, **11 117–19**; **38** 491

First Signature Bank and Trust Co., **III** 268
First Sport Ltd., **39** 60
1st State Bank & Trust, **9** 474
First State Bank Southwest Indiana, **41** 178–79
First SunAmerican Life Insurance Company, **11** 482
First Team Sports, Inc., **15** 396–97; **22 202–04**
First Tennessee National Corporation, **11 120–21**; **48 176–79 (upd.)**
First Texas Pharmaceuticals, **I** 678
First Trust and Savings Bank, **II** 284
First Trust Bank, **16** 14
First Union Corporation, **10 298–300**; **24** 482; **37** 148. *See also* Wachovia Corporation.
First Union Trust and Savings Bank, **II** 284–85; **11** 126; **22** 52
First United Financial Services Inc., **II** 286
First USA, Inc., **11 122–24**
First USA Paymentech, **24** 393
First Virginia Banks, Inc., **11 125–26**
First Westchester National Bank of New Rochelle, **II** 236
First Western Bank and Trust Co., **II** 289
First Women's Bank of New York, **23** 3
First Worth Corporation, **19** 232
The First Years Inc., **46 191–94**
FirstAir Inc., **48** 113
Firstamerica Bancorporation, **II** 288–89
Firstar Corporation, **11 127–29**; **33 152–55 (upd.)**
FirstBancorp., **13** 467
FirstGroup plc, **38** 321
FirstMiss, Inc., **8** 185
FirstPage USA Inc., **41** 265
Firth Carpet, **19** 275
Fischbach & Moore, **III** 535
Fischbach Corp., **III** 198; **8** 536–37
FISCOT, **10** 337
Fiserv Inc., **11 130–32**; **33 156–60 (upd.)**
Fish & Neave, **54 109–12**
Fisher & Company, **9** 16
Fisher Body Company, **I** 171; **10** 325
Fisher Broadcasting Co., **15** 164
Fisher-Camuto Corp., **14** 441
Fisher Companies, Inc., **15 164–66**
Fisher Controls International, Inc., **13 224–26**; **15** 405, 407; **29** 330; **46** 171
Fisher Foods, Inc., **II** 602; **9** 451, 452; **13** 237; **41** 11, 13
Fisher Marine, **III** 444; **22** 116
Fisher Nut, **14** 275
Fisher-Price Inc., **II** 559–60; **12 167–69**, 410–11; **13** 317; **25** 314, 380; **32 190–94 (upd.)**; **34** 365
Fisher Scientific International Inc., **III** 511–12; **24 162–66**; **25** 260
Fishers Agricultural Holdings, **II** 466
Fishers Nutrition, **II** 466
Fishers Seed and Grain, **II** 466
Fishery Department of Tamura Kisen Co., **II** 552
Fisk Telephone Systems, **6** 313
Fiskars Corporation, **33 161–64**
Fiskeby Board AB, **48** 344
Fisons plc, **9 224–27**; **23 194–97 (upd.)**
Fitch IBCA Inc., **37** 143, 145
Fitch Lovell PLC, **13** 103
Fitchburg Daily News Co., **IV** 581
Fitchburg Gas and Electric Light, **37** 406
Fitchell and Sachs, **III** 495

Fitel, **III** 491
Fitzsimmons Stores Inc., **16** 452
Fitzwilton Public Limited Company, **12** 529; **34** 496
Five Bros. Inc., **19** 456
Five Star Entertainment Inc., **28** 241
546274 Alberta Ltd., **48** 97
FKM Advertising, **27** 280
FL Industries Holdings, Inc., **11** 516
Flachglass A.G., **II** 474
Flagstar Companies, Inc., **10 301–03**; **29** 150. *See also* Advantica Restaurant Group, Inc.
Flair Corporation, **18** 467
Flair Fold, **25** 11
Flambeau Products Corporation, **55** 132
Flanagan McAdam Resources Inc., **IV** 76
Flapdoodles, **15** 291
Flashes Publishers, Inc., **36** 341
Flatbush Gas Co., **6** 455–56
Flatiron Mandolin Company, **16** 239
Flatow, Moore, Bryan, and Fairburn, **21** 33
Flavors Holdings Inc., **38** 294
Fleck Controls, Inc., **26** 361, 363
Fleer Corporation, **10** 402; **13** 519; **15 167–69**; **19** 386; **34** 447; **37** 295
Fleet Aerospace Corporation. *See* Magellan Aerospace Corporation.
Fleet Call, Inc., **10** 431–32
Fleet Financial Group, Inc., **IV** 687; **9 228–30**; **12** 31; **13** 468; **18** 535; **38** 13, 393
Fleet Holdings, **28** 503
FleetBoston Financial Corporation, **36 206–14 (upd.)**
Fleetway, **7** 244
Fleetwood Enterprises, Inc., **III 484–85**; **13** 155; **17** 83; **21** 153; **22 205–08 (upd.)**; **33** 399
Fleischmann Co., **II** 544; **7** 367
Fleischmann Malting Co., **I** 420–21; **11** 22
Fleming Chinese Restaurants Inc., **37** 297
Fleming Companies, Inc., **II 624–25**, 671; **7** 450; **12** 107, 125; **13** 335–37; **17 178–81 (upd.)**; **18** 506–07; **23** 407; **24** 529; **26** 449; **28** 152, 154; **31** 25; **34** 198; **50** 457
Fleming Foodservice, **26** 504
Fleming Machine Co., **III** 435
Fleming-Wilson Co., **II** 624
Fletcher Challenge Ltd., **III** 687; **IV** 250, 278–80; **19 153–57 (upd.)**; **25** 12
Fleury Michon S.A., **39 159–61**
Fleuve Noir, **IV** 614
Flex Elektrowerkzeuge GmbH, **26** 363
Flex Interim, **16** 421; **43** 308
Flex-O-Lite, **14** 325
Flexi-Van Corporations, **II** 492; **20** 118
Flexible Packaging, **I** 605
Flexsteel Industries Inc., **15 170–72**; **41 159–62 (upd.)**
Flextronics International Ltd., **12** 451; **38 186–89**
Flexys, **16** 462
FLGI Holding Company, **10** 321
Flick Industrial Group, **II** 280, 283; **III** 692–95
Flight One Logistics, Inc., **22** 311
Flight Refuelling Limited. *See* Cobham plc.
Flight Transportation Co., **II** 408
FlightSafety International, Inc., **9 231–33**; **29 189–92 (upd.)**

Flint and Walling Water Systems, III 570; 20 362

Flint Eaton & Co., I 627

Flint Ink Corporation, 13 227–29; 41 163–66 (upd.)

Flip Chip Technologies, LLC, 33 248

Florafax International, Inc., 37 162

Floral City Furniture Company, 14 302–03; 50 309–10

Flori Roberts, Inc., 11 208

Florida Crystals Inc., 35 176–78

Florida Cypress Gardens, Inc., IV 623

Florida Distillers Company, 27 479

Florida East Coast Railway Company, 8 486–87; 12 278

Florida Flavors, 44 137

Florida Frozen Foods, 13 244

Florida Gaming Corporation, 47 130–33

Florida Gas Co., 15 129

Florida Gas Transmission Company, 6 578

Florida National Banks of Florida, Inc., II 252

Florida Panthers Hockey Club, Ltd., 37 33, 35

Florida Power & Light Company. See FPL Group, Inc.

Florida Presbyterian College, 9 187

Florida Progress Corp., V 621–22; 23 198–200 (upd.)

Florida Rock Industries, Inc., 23 326; 46 195–97

Florida Steel Corp., 14 156

Florida Telephone Company, 6 323

Florida's Natural Growers, 45 160–62

FloridaGulf Airlines, 11 300

Florimex Verwaltungsgesellschaft mbH, 12 109

Florists' Transworld Delivery, Inc., 28 136–38

Florsheim Shoe Group Inc., III 528–29; 9 135, 234–36; 12 308; 16 546; 31 209–212 (upd.); 39 170, 172, 174

Flour City International, Inc., 44 181–83

Flow Laboratories, 14 98

Flow Measurement, 26 293

Flower Gate Inc., I 266; 21 320

Flower Time, Inc., 12 179, 200

Flowers Industries, Inc., 12 170–71; 35 179–82 (upd.). See also Keebler Foods Company.

Flowserve Corporation, 33 165–68

Floyd West & Co., 6 290

Fluent, Inc., 29 4–6

Fluf N'Stuf, Inc., 12 425

Fluke Corporation, 15 173–75

Flunch, 37 22

Fluor Corporation, I 569–71, 586; III 248; IV 171, 533, 535, 576; 6 148–49; 8 190–93 (upd.); 12 244; 26 220, 433; 34 164–69 (upd.); 47 340

Fluor Daniel Inc., 41 148

The Fluorocarbon Company. See Furon Company.

Flushing Federal Savings & Loan Association, 16 346

Flushing National Bank, II 230

Flying Colors Toys Inc., 52 193

Flying J Inc., 19 158–60

Flying Tiger Line, V 452; 6 388; 25 146; 39 33

Flymo, III 478, 480; 22 26

FMC Corp., I 442–44, 679; II 513; 11 133–35 (upd.); 14 457; 22 415; 30 471; 47 238

FMR Corp., II 412; 8 194–96; 14 188; 22 413; 30 331; 32 195–200 (upd.)

FMXI, Inc. See Foamex International Inc.

FN Life Insurance Co., III 192

FN Manufacturing Co., 12 71

FNAC, 21 224–26; 26 160

FNC Comercio, III 221

FNCB. See First National City Bank of New York.

FNK. See Finance Oil Corp.

FNMA. See Federal National Mortgage Association.

FNN. See Financial News Network.

Foamex International Inc., 17 182–85; 26 500

Focal Surgery, Inc., 27 355

Focke-Wulf, III 641; 16 7

FOCUS, 44 402

Fodens Ltd., I 186

Fodor's Travel Guides, 13 429

Fogdog Inc., 36 347

Fokker. See N.V. Koninklijke Nederlandse Vliegtuigenfabriek Fokker.

Fokker Aircraft Corporation of America, 9 16

Fokker-VFW, I 41–42; 12 191

Foley & Lardner, 28 139–42

Folgers, III 52

Folksamerica Holding Company, Inc., 48 431

Folland Aircraft, I 50; III 508; 24 85

Follett Corporation, 12 172–74; 16 47; 39 162–65 (upd.); 43 61

Follis DeVito Verdi. See De Vito/Verdi.

Fomento de Valores, S.A. de C.V., 23 170

Fomento Economico Mexicano, S.A. de C.V. See Femsa.

Fonda Group, 36 462

Fondazione Cassa di Risparmio di Venezia, 50 408

Fondiaria Group, III 351

Fonditalia Management, III 347

Font & Vaamonde, 6 27

Font Vella, II 474

FONTAC, II 73

Fontana Asphalt, III 674

Food City, II 649–50

Food Fair, 19 480

Food 4 Less Supermarkets, Inc., II 624; 17 558–61

Food Giant, II 670

Food Ingredients Technologies, 25 367

Food Investments Ltd., II 465

Food King, 20 306

Food Lion, Inc., II 626–27; 7 450; 15 176–78 (upd.), 270; 18 8; 21 508; 33 306; 44 145

Food Machinery Corp. See FMC Corp.

Food Marketing Corp., II 668; 18 504; 50 454

Food Town Inc., II 626–27

Food World, 26 46; 31 372

Foodarama Supermarkets, Inc., 28 143–45

FoodBrands America, Inc., 21 290; 22 510; 23 201–04. See also Doskocil Companies, Inc.

FoodLand Distributors, II 625, 645, 682

Foodmaker, Inc., II 562; 13 152, 426; 14 194–96

Foodstuffs, 9 144

Foodtown, II 626; V 35; 15 177; 24 528

FoodUSA.com, 43 24

Foodways National, Inc., 12 531; 13 383

Foot Locker, V 226; 14 293–95. See also Venator Group Inc.

Footaction. See Footstar, Incorporated.

Foote Cone & Belding Communications Inc., I 12–15, 28, 34; 11 51; 13 517; 22 395; 25 90–91. See also True North Communications Inc.

Foote Mineral Company, 7 386–87

Footquarters, 14 293, 295

Footstar, Incorporated, 24 167–69

Forages et Exploitations Pétrolières. See Forex.

Forbes Inc., 30 199–201

The Ford Foundation, 34 170–72; 52 200–01

Ford Motor Company, I 10, 14, 20–21, 136, 142, 145, 152, 154–55, 162–63, 164–68, 172, 183, 186, 201, 203–04, 280, 297, 337, 354, 423, 478, 484, 540, 693; II 7–8, 33, 60, 86, 143, 415; III 58, 259, 283, 439, 452, 495, 515, 555, 568, 591, 603, 637–38, 651, 725; IV 22, 187, 597, 722; 6 27, 51; 7 377, 461, 520–21; 8 70, 74–75, 117, 372–73, 375, 505–06; 9 94, 118, 126, 190, 283–84, 325, 341–43; 10 32, 241, 260, 264–65, 279–80, 290, 353, 407, 430, 460, 465; 11 53–54, 103–04, 136–40 (upd.), 263, 326, 339, 350, 528–29; 12 68, 91, 294, 311; 13 28, 219, 285, 287, 345, 555; 14 191–92; 15 91, 171, 513, 515; 16 321–22; 17 183, 303–04; 18 112, 308, 319; 19 11, 125, 221, 223, 482, 484; 20 359; 21 153, 200, 503; 22 175, 380–81; 23 143, 339–41, 434; 24 12; 25 90, 93, 142–43, 224, 226, 358; 26 176, 452, 501; 27 20, 202; 29 265; 34 133–34, 136, 303, 305; 36 34, 180, 198, 215–21 (upd.), 242–43; 38 86, 458–59; 40 134; 41 280–81; 54 207

Ford Motor Company, S.A. de C.V., 20 219–21

Ford New Holland, Inc. See New Holland N.V.

Ford Transport Co., I 112; 6 103

Fording Inc., 45 80

Fordyce Lumber Co., IV 281; 9 259

FORE Systems, Inc., 25 161–63; 33 289

Forefront Communications, 22 194

Foreman State Banks, II 285

Foremost Dairies, 47 234–35

Foremost Dairy of California, I 496–97

Foremost-McKesson Inc., I 496–97, III 10; 11 211; 12 332

Foremost Warehouse Corp., 14 372

Forenza, V 116

Forest City Auto Parts, 23 491

Forest City Enterprises, Inc., 16 209–11; 52 128–31 (upd.)

Forest City Ratner Companies, 17 318

Forest E. Olson, Inc., 21 96

Forest Laboratories, Inc., 11 141–43; 47 55; 52 132–36 (upd.)

Forest Oil Corporation, 19 161–63

Forest Products, III 645

Forestry Corporation of New Zealand, 19 156

Företagsfinans, 25 464

Forethought Group, Inc., 10 350

Forever Living Products International Inc., 17 186–88

Forex Chemical Corp., I 341; 14 216; 17 418

Forex-Neptune, III 617

Forge Books. *See* Tom Doherty Associates Inc.
Forges d'Eich–Le Gallais, Metz et Cie, **IV** 24; **22** 42
Forges de la Providence, **IV** 52
Forjas Metalicas, S.A. de C.V. (Formet), **44** 193
Formento Económico Mexicano, S.A. de C.V., **25** 279, 281
Formica Corporation, 10 269; **13 230–32**
Forming Technology Co., **III** 569; **20** 361
Formonix, **20** 101
Formosa Plastics Corporation, 11 159; **14 197–99; 16** 194, 196
Formosa Plastics Group, **31** 108
Formosa Springs, **I** 269; **12** 337
Formulabs, Inc., **52** 307
Formularios y Procedimientos Moore, **IV** 645
Formule 1, **13** 364; **27** 10
Forney Fiber Company, **8** 475
Forrester Research, Inc., 54 113–15
Forsakrings A.B. Volvia, **I** 20
Forstmann Little & Co., I 446, 483; **II** 478, 544; **III** 56; **7** 206; **10** 321; **12** 344, 562; **14** 166; **16** 322; **19** 372–73, 432; **22** 32, 60; **30** 426; **34** 145, 448; **36** 523; **38 190–92; 54** 372
Fort Associates, **I** 418
Fort Bend Utilities Company, **12** 269
Fort Dummer Mills, **III** 213
Fort Garry Brewery, **26** 304
Fort Howard Corporation, 8 197–99; 15 305; **22** 209. *See also* Fort James Corporation.
Fort James Corporation, 22 209–12 (upd.); 29 136
Fort Mill Manufacturing Co., **V** 378
Fort William Power Co., **IV** 246; **25** 10
Forte Plc, **15** 46; **16** 446; **24** 195; **29** 443
Forte's Holdings Ltd., **III** 104–05
Fortis, Inc., 15 179–82; 47 134–37 (upd.); 50 4–6
Fortum Corporation, 30 202–07 (upd.)
Fortun Foods, **26** 59
Fortuna Coffee Co., **I** 451
Fortune Brands, Inc., 19 168; **29 193–97 (upd.); 45** 269; **49** 153; **51** 7
Fortune Enterprises, **12** 60
Fortunoff Fine Jewelry and Silverware Inc., 26 144–46
Forum Cafeterias, **19** 299–300
Forum Hotels, **I** 248
Foseco plc, **IV** 383
Fosgate Electronics, **43** 322
Foss Maritime Co., **9** 509, 511
Fossil, Inc., 17 189–91
Foster & Kleiser, **7** 335; **14** 331
Foster & Marshall, **II** 398; **10** 62
Foster and Braithwaite, **III** 697
Foster Forbes, **16** 123
Foster Grant, **I** 670; **II** 595–96; **12** 214
Foster Management Co., **11** 366–67
Foster Medical Corp., **III** 16; **11** 282
Foster Poultry Farms, 32 201–04
Foster-Probyn Ltd., **38** 501
Foster Sand & Gravel, **14** 112
Foster Wheeler Corporation, I 82; **6 145–47; 23 205–08 (upd.); 25** 82
Foster's Brewing Group Ltd., 7 182–84; 21 227–30 (upd.); 26 303, 305–06; **36** 15
Foster's Group Limited, 50 199–203 (upd.), 261

Fotomat Corp., **III** 549
Fougerolle, **27** 136, 138
Foundation Computer Systems, Inc., **13** 201
Foundation Fieldbus, **22** 373
Foundation Health Corporation, 11 174; **12 175–77**
Founders Equity Inc., **14** 235
Founders of American Investment Corp., **15** 247
Fountain Powerboats Industries, Inc., 28 146–48
Four Media Co., **33** 403
Four-Phase Systems, Inc., **II** 61; **11** 327
Four Queens Hotel and Casino. *See* The Elsinore Corporation.
Four Seasons Hotels Inc., II 531; **9 237–38; 29 198–200 (upd.)**
Four Seasons Nursing Centers, Inc., **6** 188; **25** 308
Four Winds, **21** 153
Fournier Furniture, Inc., **12** 301
4P, **30 396–98**
Fourth Financial Corporation, 11 144–46; 15 60
Foussard Associates, **I** 333
Fowler Road Construction Proprietary, **III** 672
Fowler, Roenau & Geary, LLC, **37** 224
Fowler-Waring Cables Co., **III** 162
Fox and Hound English Pub and Grille. *See* Total Entertainment Restaurant Corporation.
Fox & Jacobs, **8** 87
Fox Broadcasting Company, **II** 156; **IV** 608, 652; **7** 391–92; **9** 428; **21** 25, 360; **24** 517; **25** 174, 417–18; **46** 311
Fox Children's Network, **21** 26
Fox Entertainment Group, Inc., 43 173–76; 52 4–5
Fox Family Worldwide, Inc., 24 170–72. *See also* ABC Family Worldwide, Inc.
Fox Film Corp., **II** 146–47, 154–55, 169; **25** 327–28
Fox, Fowler & Co., **II** 307
Fox Glacier Mints Ltd., **II** 569
Fox Grocery Co., **II** 682
Fox, Inc., **12** 359; **25** 490
Fox Network, **29** 426
Fox Paper Company, **8** 102
Fox Photo, **III** 475; **7** 161
Fox-Vliet Drug Company, **16** 212
Foxboro Company, 13 233–35; 27 81
FoxMeyer Health Corporation, V 152–53; **8** 55; **16 212–14**
Foxmoor, **29** 163
Foxx Hy-Reach, **28** 387
FP&L. *See* Florida Power & Light Co.
FPK LLC, **26** 343
FPL Group, Inc., V 623–25; 45 150; **49 143–46 (upd.)**
FR Corp., **18** 340; **43** 282
Fracmaster Ltd., **55** 294
Fragrance Corporation of America, Ltd., **53** 88
Fragrance Express Inc., **37** 271
Fram Corp., **I** 142, 567
Framatome SA, 9 10; **19 164–67**
Framingham Electric Company, **12** 45
Franc-Or Resources, **38** 231–32
France Cables et Radio, **6** 303
France 5, **6** 374; **21** 105
France-Loisirs, **IV** 615–16, 619
France Quick, **12** 152; **26** 160–61; **27** 10

France Telecom Group, V 291–93, 471; **9** 32; **14** 489; **18** 33; **21 231–34 (upd.); 25** 96, 102; **34** 13; **47** 214; **52** 108
Franchise Associates, Inc., **17** 238
Franchise Business Systems, Inc., **18** 207
Franchise Finance Corp. of America, **19** 159; **37** 351
Francis H. Leggett & Co., **24** 527
Franciscan Vineyards, Inc., **34** 89
Franco-Américaine de Constructions Atomiques, **19** 165
Franco-American Food Co., **I** 428; **II** 479
Frank & Hirsch, **III** 608
Frank & Pignard SA, **51** 35
Frank & Schulte GmbH, **8** 496
Frank Dry Goods Company, **9** 121
Frank H. Nott Inc., **14** 156
Frank Holton Company, **55** 149, 151
Frank J. Rooney, Inc., **8** 87
Frank J. Zamboni & Co., Inc., 34 173–76
Frank Russell Company, 45 316; **46 198–200**
Frank Schaffer Publications, **19** 405; **29** 470, 472
Frank W. Horner, Ltd., **38** 123
Frank's Nursery & Crafts, Inc., 12 178–79; 198–200
Frankel & Co., 39 166–69
Fränkel & Selz, **II** 239
Frankenberry, Laughlin & Constable, **9** 393
Frankford-Quaker Grocery Co., **II** 625
Frankfort Oil Co., **I** 285
Frankfurter Allgemeine Versicherungs-AG, **III** 184
Franklin Assurances, **III** 211
Franklin Baker's Coconut, **II** 531
Franklin Brass Manufacturing Company, **20** 363
Franklin Container Corp., **IV** 312; **19** 267
Franklin Corp., **14** 130; **41** 388
Franklin Covey Company, 37 149–52 (upd.)
Franklin Electric Company, Inc., 43 177–80
Franklin Electronic Publishers, Inc., 23 209–13
Franklin Life Insurance Co., **III** 242–43; **V** 397; **29** 195
Franklin Mint, **IV** 676; **9** 428; **37** 337–38
Franklin Mutual Advisors LLC, **52** 119, 172
Franklin National Bank, **9** 536
Franklin Plastics, **19** 414
Franklin Quest Co., 11 147–49; 41 121. *See also* Franklin Covey Company.
Franklin Rayon Yarn Dyeing Corp., **I** 529
Franklin Research & Development, **11** 41
Franklin Resources, Inc., 9 239–40
Franklin Sports, Inc., **17** 243
Franklin Steamship Corp., **8** 346
Franks Chemical Products Inc., **I** 405
Frans Maas Beheer BV, **14** 568
Franz and Frieder Burda, **IV** 661
Franz Foods, Inc., **II** 584
Franz Ströher AG, **III** 68–69
Franzia. *See* The Wine Group, Inc.
Fraser & Chalmers, **13** 16
Fraser & Neave Ltd., 54 116–18
Fraser Cos. Ltd., **IV** 165
Fratelli Manzoli, **IV** 585
Fratelli Treves, **IV** 585
Fraternal Assurance Society of America, **III** 274

Fray Data International, **14** 319
Frazer & Jones, **48** 141
Fre Kote Inc., **I** 321
Frears, **II** 543
Fred Campbell Auto Supply, **26** 347
Fred Harvey Hotels, **I** 417
Fred Meyer, Inc., II 669; **V 54–56**; **18** 505; **20 222–25 (upd.)**; **35** 370; **50** 455
Fred S. James and Co., **III** 280; **I** 537; **22** 318
Fred Sammons Co., **9** 72
Fred Sammons Company of Chicago, **30** 77
Fred Sands Realtors, **IV** 727
Fred Schmid Appliance & T.V. Co., Inc., **10** 305; **18** 532
Fred Usinger Inc., 54 119–21
The Fred W. Albrecht Grocery Co., 13 236–38
Fred's, Inc., 23 214–16
Freddie Mac, 54 122–25
Fredelle, **14** 295
Frederick & Nelson, **17** 462
Frederick Atkins Inc., 16 215–17
Frederick Bayer & Company, **22** 225
Frederick Gas Company, **19** 487
Frederick Manufacturing Corporation, **26** 119; **48** 59
Frederick Miller Brewing Co., **I** 269
Frederick's of Hollywood Inc., 16 218–20; **25** 521
Free-lance Uitzendburo, **26** 240
Freeborn Farms, **13** 244
Freedom Communications, Inc., 36 222–25
Freedom Group Inc., **42** 10–11
Freedom Technology, **11** 486
Freedom-Valvoline Oil Co., **IV** 373; **19** 23; **50** 46
Freeman, Spogli & Co., **17** 366; **18** 90; **32** 12, 15; **35** 276; **36** 358–59; **47** 142–43
Freemans, **V** 177
FreeMark Communications, **38** 269
Freeport-McMoran Inc., IV 81–84; **7 185–89 (upd.)**; **16** 29; **23** 40
Freeport Power, **38** 448
Freezer House, **II** 398; **10** 62
Freezer Queen Foods, Inc., **21** 509
Freezer Shirt Corporation, **8** 406
Freiberger Papierfabrik, **IV** 323
Freight Car Services, Inc., **23** 306
Freight Outlet, **17** 297
Freightliner, **I** 150; **6** 413
FreightMaster, **III** 498
Frejlack Ice Cream Co., **II** 646; **7** 317
Fremlin Breweries, **I** 294
Fremont Butter and Egg Co., **II** 467
Fremont Canning Company, **7** 196
Fremont Group, **21** 97
Fremont Investors, **30** 268
Fremont Partners, **24** 265
Fremont Savings Bank, **9** 474–75
French and Richards & Co., **I** 692
French Bank of California, **II** 233
French Connection Group plc, 41 167–69
French Fragrances, Inc., 22 213–15; **40** 170. See also Elizabeth Arden, Inc.
French Kier, **I** 568
French Petrofina, **IV** 497
French Quarter Coffee Co., **27** 480–81
Frequency Sources Inc., **9** 324
Fresenius AG, **22** 360; **49** 155–56
Fresh America Corporation, 20 226–28

Fresh Choice, Inc., 20 229–32
Fresh Fields, **19** 501
Fresh Foods, Inc., 25 391; **29 201–03**
Fresh Start Bakeries, **26** 58
Freshbake Foods Group PLC, **II** 481; **7** 68; **25** 518; **26** 57
Fretter, Inc., 9 65; **10** 9–10, **304–06**, 502; **19** 124; **23** 52
Freudenberg & Co., 41 170–73
Frialco, **IV** 165
Frictiontech Inc., **11** 84
Friday's Front Row Sports Grill, **22** 128
Friden, Inc., **II** 10; **30** 418; **53** 237
Fridy-Gauker & Fridy, **I** 313; **10** 154
Fried, Frank, Harris, Shriver & Jacobson, 35 183–86
Fried. Krupp AG Hoesch-Krupp. See Thyssen Krupp AG.
Fried. Krupp GmbH, II 257; **IV** 60, **85–89**, 104, 128, 203, 206, 222, 234
Friedman, Billings, Ramsey Group, Inc., 53 134–37
Friedman's Inc., 29 204–06
Friedrich Flick Industrial Corp., **I** 548; **III** 692; **50** 525
Friedrich Grohe AG & Co. KG, 53 138–41
Friedrich Roessler Söhne, **IV** 69
Friedrichshütte, **III** 694
Friendly Hotels PLC, **14** 107
Friendly Ice Cream Corp., II 511–12; **15** 221; **30 208–10**
Friesch-Groningsche Hypotheekbank, **III** 179
Frigidaire Home Products, III 572; **13** 564; **19** 361; **22** 28, **216–18**, 349
Frigo, **II** 587
Friguia, **IV** 165
Frisby P.M.C. Incorporated, **16** 475
Frisch's Restaurants, Inc., 35 187–89
Frisdranken Industries Winters B.V., **22** 515
Frisia Group, **IV** 197–98
Frito-Lay Company, I 219, 278–79; **III** 136; **22** 95; **32 205–10**; **38** 347; **44** 348
Fritz Companies, Inc., 12 180–82
Fritz Gegauf AG. See Bernina Holding AG.
Fritz Thyssen Stiftung, **IV** 222
Fritz W. Glitsch and Sons, Inc. See Glitsch International, Inc.
Fritzsche Dodge and Ollcott, **I** 307
Froebel-Kan, **IV** 679
Frolic, **16** 545
Fromagerie d'Illoud. See Bongrain SA.
La Fromagerie du Velay, **25** 85
Fromagerie Paul Renard, **25** 85
Fromageries Bel, II 518; **6** 47; **19** 51; **23 217–19**; **25 83–84**
Fromageries des Chaumes, **25** 84
Fromarsac, **25** 84
Frome Broken Hill Co., **IV** 59
Fromm & Sichel, **I** 285
Frontec, **13** 132
Frontenac Co., **24** 45
Frontier Airlines, Inc., I 97–98, 103, 118, 124, 129–30; **6** 129; **11** 298; **21** 141–42; **22 219–21**; **25** 421; **26** 439–40; **39** 33
Frontier Communications, **32** 216, 218
Frontier Corp., 16 221–23; **18** 164
Frontier Electronics, **19** 311
Frontier Expeditors, Inc., **12** 363
Frontier Oil Co., **IV** 373; **50** 46

Frontier Pacific Insurance Company, **21** 263
Frontier Vision Partners L.P., **52** 9
FrontLine Capital Group, **47** 330–31
Frontline Ltd., 45 163–65
Frontstep Inc., **55** 258
Frosch Touristik, **27** 29
Frost & Sullivan, Inc., 53 142–44
Frost National Bank. See Cullen/Frost Bankers, Inc.
Frozen Food Express Industries, Inc., 20 233–35; **27** 404
Fru-Con Holding Corporation, **I** 561; **55** 62
Fruehauf Corp., I 169–70, 480; **II** 425; **III** 652; **7** 259–60, 513–14; **13** 341; **27** 202–03, 251; **40** 432
Fruit of the Loom, Inc., 8 200–02; **16** 535; **25 164–67 (upd.)**; **54** 403
The Frustum Group Inc., **45** 280
Fry's Diecastings, **III** 681
Fry's Food Stores, **12** 112
Fry's Metal Foundries, **III** 681
Frye Copy Systems, **6** 599
Frymaster Corporation, 27 159–62
FSA Corporation, **25** 349
FSI International, Inc., 17 192–94. See also FlightSafety International, Inc.
FSP. See Frank Schaffer Publications.
FTD, **26** 344. See also Florists Transworld Delivery, Inc.
F3 Software Corp., **15** 474
FTP Software, Inc., 20 236–38
Fubu, **29 207–09**
Fuddruckers, **27** 480–82
Fuel Pipeline Transportation Ltd., **6** 123–24; **27** 464
Fuel Resources Development Co., **6** 558–59
Fuel Resources Inc., **6** 457
FuelMaker Corporation, **6** 569
Fuji Bank, Ltd., I 494; **II 291–93**, 360–61, 391, 422, 459, 554; **III** 405, 408–09; **17** 556–57; **24** 324; **26** 455
Fuji Electric Co., Ltd., II 22–23, 98, 103; **III** 139; **13** 356; **18** 511; **22** 373; **42** 145; **48 180–82 (upd.)**
Fuji Gen-Gakki, **16** 202; **43** 171
Fuji Heavy Industries, **I** 207; **III** 581; **9** 294; **12** 400; **13** 499–501; **23** 290; **36** 240, 243
Fuji Iron & Steel Co., Ltd., **I** 493; **II** 300; **IV** 130, 157, 212; **17** 349–50; **24** 325
Fuji Kaolin Co., **III** 691
Fuji Paper, **IV** 320
Fuji Photo Film Co., Ltd., III 172, 476, **486–89**, 549–50; **6** 289; **7** 162; **18** 94, **183–87 (upd.)**, 341–42; **36** 172, 174; **43** 284
Fuji Photo Film USA, Inc., **45** 284
Fuji Seito, **I** 511
Fuji Television, **7** 249; **9** 29
Fuji Xerox. See Xerox Corporation.
Fuji Yoshiten Co., **IV** 292
Fujian Hualong Carburetor, **13** 555
Fujikoshi Kozai, **III** 595
Fujimoto Bill Broker & Securities Co., **II** 405
Fujisawa Pharmaceutical Co., I 635–36; **III** 47; **8** 343
Fujita Airways, **6** 70
Fujitsu-ICL Systems Inc., 11 150–51
Fujitsu Limited, I 455, 541; **II 22–23**, 56, 68, 73, 274; **III 109–11**, 130, **139–41**, 164, 482; **V** 339; **6** 217, 240–42; **10**

238; **11** 308, 542; **13** 482; **14** 13–15, 512; **16** 139, 224–27 (upd.); **17** 172; **21** 390; **27** 107; **40** 20; **145–50 (upd.)**; **43** 285; **50** 156
Fujitsu Takamisawa, **28** 131
Fujiyi Confectionery Co., **II** 569
Fukuin Electric Works, Ltd., **III** 604
Fukuin Shokai Denki Seisakusho, **III** 604
Fukuju Fire, **III** 384
Fukuoka Paper Co., Ltd., **IV** 285
Fukutake Publishing Co., Ltd., **13** 91, 93
Ful-O-Pep, **10** 250
Fulbright & Jaworski L.L.P., 22 4; **47** 138–41
Fulcrum Communications, **10** 19
The Fulfillment Corporation of America, **21** 37
Fulham Brothers, **13** 244
Fullbright & Jaworski, **28** 48
Fuller Brush Co., **II** 572; **15** 475–76, 78
Fuller Co., **6** 395–96; **25** 169–70
Fuller Manufacturing Company **I** 154. *See also* H.B. Fuller Company.
Fuller Smith & Turner P.L.C., 38 193–95
Fulton Bank, **14** 40
Fulton Co., **III** 569; **20** 361
Fulton Insurance Co., **III** 463; **21** 173
Fulton Manufacturing Co., **11** 535
Fulton Municipal Gas Company, **6** 455
Fulton Performance Products, Inc., **11** 535
Funai-Amstrad, **III** 113
Funco, Inc., 20 239–41
Fund American Companies. *See* White Mountains Insurance Group, Ltd.
Fundimensions, **16** 337
Funk & Wagnalls, **IV** 605; **22** 441
Funk Software Inc., **6** 255; **25** 299
Funnel Cake Factory, **24** 241
Funtastic Limited, **52** 193
Fuqua Enterprises, Inc., 17 195–98
Fuqua Industries Inc., I 445–47, 452; **8** 545; **12** 251; **14** 86; **37** 62
Furalco, **IV** 15
Furnishings International Inc., **20** 359, 363; **39** 267
Furniture Brands International, Inc., 31 246, 248; **39** 170–75 (upd.)
The Furniture Center, Inc., **14** 236
Furon Company, 28 149–51
Furr's Restaurant Group, Inc., 53 145–48
Furr's Supermarkets, Inc., II 601; **28** 152–54
Furst Group, **17** 106
Furukawa Electric Co., Ltd., II 22; **III** 139, 490–92; **IV** 15, 26, 153; **15** 514; **22** 44
Fusi Denki, **II** 98
Fuso Marine Insurance Co., **III** 367
Fuso Metal Industries, **IV** 212
Futagi Co., Ltd., **V** 96
Futronix Corporation, **17** 276
Future Diagnostics, Inc., **25** 384
Future Graphics, **18** 387
Future Now, Inc., 6 245; **12** 183–85
FutureCare, **50** 123
Futurestep, Inc., **34** 247, 249
Fuyo Group, **II** 274, 291–93, 391–92, 554
FWD Corporation, **7** 513
FX Coughlin Inc., **51** 130
Fyffes Plc, 38 196–99, 201

G&G Shops, Inc., **8** 425–26

G & H Products, **III** 419
G&K Services, Inc., 16 228–30; **21** 115
G&L Albu, **IV** 90
G&L Inc., **16** 202; **43** 170
G&R Pasta Co., Inc., **II** 512
G. and T. Earle, **III** 669, 670
G.A. Serlachius Oy, **IV** 314–15
G.B. Lewis Company, **8** 359
G. Bruss GmbH and Co. KG, **26** 141
G.C.E. International Inc., **III** 96–97
G.C. Industries, **52** 186
G.C. Murphy Company, **9** 21
G.C. Smith, **I** 423
G.D. Searle & Co., I 365–66, 686–89; **III** 47, 53; **8** 343, 398, 434; **9** 356–57; **10** 54; **12** 186–89 (upd.); **16** 527; **26** 108, 383; **29** 331; **29** 331; **34** 177–82 (upd.)
G. Felsenthal & Sons, **17** 106
G.H. Bass & Co., **15** 406; **24** 383
G.H. Besselaar Associates, **30** 151
G.H. Rinck NV, **V** 49; **19** 122–23; **49** 111
G.H. Wetterau & Sons Grocery Co., **II** 681
G. Heileman Brewing Co., I 253–55, 270; **10** 169–70; **12** 338; **18** 501; **23** 403, 405
G.I.E. Airbus Industrie, I
G.I. Joe's, Inc., **30** 221–23 41–43, 49–52, 55–56, 70, 72, 74–76, 107, 111, 116, 121; **9** 458, 460; **11** 279, 363; **12** 190–92 (upd.)
G-III Apparel Group, Ltd., 22 222–24
G.J. Coles & Coy. Ltd., **20** 155
G.L. Kelty & Co., **13** 168
G.L. Rexroth GmbH, **III** 566; **38** 298, 300
G. Leblanc Corporation, 55 149–52
G.M. Pfaff AG, **30** 419–20
G.P. Group, **12** 358
G.P. Putnam's Sons, **II** 144
G.R. Foods, Inc. *See* Ground Round, Inc.
G.R. Herberger's Department Stores, **19** 324–25; **41** 343–44
G.R. Kinney Corporation, **V** 226, 352; **14** 293; **20** 88
G. Riedel Kälte- und Klimatechnik, **III** 420
G.S. Blodgett Corporation, 15 183–85; **22** 350
G.S. Capital Partners II L.P. *See* Goldman, Sachs & Company.
G. Washington Coffee Refining Co., **I** 622
Gabelli Asset Management Inc., 13 561; **30** 211–14. *See also* Lynch Corporation.
Gable House Properties, **II** 141
Gables Residential Trust, 49 147–49
Gabriel Industries, **II** 532
GAC. *See* The Goodyear Tire & Rubber Company.
GAC Corp., **II** 182; **III** 592
GAC Holdings L.P., **7** 204; **28** 164
Gadzooks, Inc., 18 188–90; **33** 203
GAF, I 337–40, 524–25, 549; **II** 378; **III** 440; **8** 180; **9** 518; **18** 215; **22** 14, 225–29 (upd.); **25** 464
Gage Marketing Group, 26 147–49; **27** 21
Gagliardi Brothers, **13** 383
Gaiam, Inc., 41 174–77
Gail Borden, Jr., and Company. *See* Borden, Inc.
Gain Technology, Inc., **10** 505
Gaines Dog Food Co., **II** 531
Gaines Furniture Manufacturing, Inc., **43** 315
Gainsborough Craftsmen Ltd., **II** 569
Gainsco, Inc., 22 230–32

Gair Paper Co., **I** 599
Galas Harland, S.A., **17** 266, 268
Galavision, Inc., **24** 515–17; **54** 72
Galaxy Carpet Mills, **19** 276
Galaxy Energies Inc., **11** 28
Galbreath Escott, **16** 474
The Gale Group, Inc., **34** 437
Gale Research Inc., **8** 526; **23** 440
Galen Health Care, **15** 112; **35** 215–16
Galen Laboratories, **13** 160
Galerías Preciados, **26** 130
Galeries Lafayette S.A., V 57–59; **23** 220–23 (upd.)
Galesburg Coulter Disc Co., **III** 439–40
Galey & Lord, Inc., 20 242–45
Gallaher Group Plc, 49 150–54 (upd.)
Gallaher Limited, IV 260; **V** 398–400; **19** 168–71 (upd.); **29** 195
Gallatin Bank, **II** 312
Gallatin Steel Company, **18** 380; **24** 144
Galletas, **II** 543
Gallimard, **IV** 618
Gallo Winery. *See* E. & J. Gallo Winery.
Gallop Johnson & Neuman, L.C., **26** 348
The Gallup Organization, 37 153–56; **41** 196–97
Galoob Toys. *See* Lewis Galoob Toys Inc.
Galor, **I** 676
GALP, **IV** 505; **48** 117, 119
Galvanizing Co., **IV** 159
Galveston *Daily News*, **10** 3
Galvin Manufacturing Corp., **II** 60; **11** 326
GALVSTAR, L.P., **26** 530
Galyan's Trading Company, Inc., 47 142–44s
Gamble-Skogmo Inc., **13** 169; **25** 535
The Gambrinus Company, 29 219; **40** 188–90
Gambro AB, 13 159–61, 327–28; **49** 155–57
Gamebusters, **41** 409
Gamesa, **II** 544; **19** 192
GameTime, Inc., **19** 387; **27** 370–71
GAMI. *See* Great American Management and Investment, Inc.
Gamlestaden, **9** 381–82
Gamlestadens Fabriker, **III** 622
Gamma Capital Corp., **24** 3
Gammalink, **18** 143
Gander Mountain, Inc., 20 246–48
Gang-Nail Systems, **III** 735
Gannett Co., Inc., III 159; **IV** 612–13, 629–30; **7** 190–92 (upd.); **9** 3; **18** 63; **23** 157–58, 293; **24** 224; **25** 371; **30** 215–17 (upd.); **32** 354–55; **41** 197–98
Gannett Supply, **17** 282
Gantos, Inc., 17 199–201
The Gap, Inc., V 60–62; **9** 142, 360; **11** 499; **18** 191–94 (upd.); **24** 27; **25** 47–48; **31** 51–52; **55** 153–57 (upd.)
GAR Holdings, **19** 78
Garamond Press, **23** 100
Garan, Inc., 16 231–33
Garantie Mutuelle des Fonctionnaires, **21** 225
Garden Botanika, **11** 41
Garden City Newspapers Inc., **38** 308
Garden Escape, **26** 441
Garden Fresh Restaurant Corporation, 31 213–15
Garden of Eatin' Inc., **27** 198; **43** 218–19
Garden Ridge Corporation, 27 163–65
Garden State BancShares, Inc., **14** 472

Garden State Life Insurance Company, **10** 312; **27** 47–48

Garden State Paper, **38** 307–08

Gardenburger, Inc., 33 169–71

Gardener's Eden, **17** 548–49

Gardenia, **II** 587

Gardner & Harvey Container Corporation, **8** 267

Gardner Advertising. *See* Wells Rich Green BDDP.

Gardner Cryogenics, **13** 140

Gardner Denver, Inc., II 16; **49 158–60**

Gardner Merchant Ltd., **III** 104; **11** 325; **29** 442–44

Gardner Rubber Co. *See* Tillotson Corp.

Garelick Farms, Inc., **26** 449

Garfield Weston, **13** 51

Garfinckel, Brooks Brothers, Miller & Rhodes, Inc., **15** 94; **22** 110

Garfinckels, **37** 12

Garland Publishing, **44** 416

Garland-Compton, **42** 328

Garlock, **I** 435

Garnier, **III** 47

A.B. Garnisonen, **II** 352

Garrard Engineering, **II** 82

Garrett, **9** 18; **11** 472

Garrett & Company, **27** 326

Garrett AiResearch, **9** 18

Garrett-Buchanan, **I** 412

Garrett Poultry Co., **II** 584; **14** 514; **50** 491

Garrick Investment Holdings Ltd., **16** 293

Garrido y Compania, Inc., **26** 448

Gart Sports Company, 24 173–75

Gartner Group, Inc., 21 235–37; 25 22

Gartrell White, **II** 465

Garuda Indonesia, I 107; **6 90–91**

Gary Fisher Mountain Bike Company, **16** 494

Gary Industries, **7** 4

Gary-Wheaton Corp., **II** 286

Gary-Williams Energy Corporation, **19** 177

Gas Authority of India Ltd., **IV** 484

Gas Corp. of Queensland, **III** 673

Gas Energy Inc., **6** 457

Gas Group, **III** 673

Gas Light and Coke Company. *See* British Gas plc.

Gas Light Company. *See* Baltimore Gas and Electric Company.

Gas Machinery Co., **I** 412

Gas Natural, **49** 211

Gas Service Company, **6** 593; **12** 542; **50** 38

Gas Supply Co., **III** 672

Gas Tech, Inc., **11** 513

Gas Utilities Company, **6** 471

Gastar Co. Ltd., **55** 375

Gaston Paper Stock Co., Inc., **8** 476

Gasunie. *See* N.V. Nederlandse Gasunie.

GATC. *See* General American Tank Car Company.

Gate City Company, **6** 446

The Gates Corporation, 9 241–43

Gates Distribution Company, **12** 60

Gates Radio Co., **II** 37

Gates Rubber, **26** 349

Gates/FA Distributing Inc., **29** 413–14

Gateway Books, **14** 61

Gateway Corporation Ltd., II 612, **628–30**, 638, 642; **10** 442; **16** 249; **25** 119. *See also* Somerfield plc.

Gateway Foodmarkets Ltd., **II** 628; **13** 26

Gateway, Inc., 27 166–69 (upd.)

Gateway International Motorsports Corporation, Inc., **43** 139–40

Gateway State Bank, **39** 381–82

Gateway Technologies, Inc., **46** 387

Gateway 2000, Inc., 10 307–09; 11 240; **22** 99; **24** 31; **25** 531

Gatliff Coal Co., **6** 583

Gattini, **40** 215

Gatwick Handling, **28** 157

GATX, 6 394–96; 25 168–71 (upd.); 47 298

Gaultier. *See* Groupe Jean-Paul Gaultier.

Gaumont SA, II 157–58; **25 172–75; 29** 369–71

Gauntlet Developments, **IV** 724

Gavilan Computer Corp., **III** 124; **6** 221

Gaya Motor, P.T. **23** 290

Gaylord Container Corporation, 8 203–05; 24 92

Gaylord Entertainment Company, 11 152–54; 36 226–29 (upd.); 38 456

Gaymer Group, **25** 82

Gaz de France, IV 425; **V 626–28; 38** 407; **40 191–95 (upd.)**

Gazelle Graphics Systems, **28** 244

Gazprom, **18** 50; **30** 205. *See also* OAO Gazprom.

GB Foods Inc., **19** 92

GB-Inno-BM, **II** 658; **V** 63

GB Papers, **IV** 290

GB s.a. *See* GIB Group.

GB Stores, Inc., **14** 427

GBL, **IV** 499

GC Companies, Inc., 25 176–78

GCFC. *See* General Cinema Finance Co.

GD Express Worldwide, **27** 472, 475; **30** 463

GDE Systems, Inc., **17** 492

GDF. *See* Gaz de France.

GDS, **29** 412

GE. *See* General Electric Company.

GE Aircraft Engines, 9 244–46

GE Capital Aviation Services, 36 230–33

GE Capital Corporation, **29** 428, 430

GE Capital Services, **27** 276; **49** 240

GE SeaCo SRL, **29** 428, 431

GEA AG, 27 170–74

GEAC Computer Corporation Ltd., 43 181–85

Geant Casino, **12** 152

Gear Products, Inc., **48** 59

Gearhart Industries Inc., **III** 499; **15** 467

Gearmatic, **I** 185

Geberit AG, 49 161–64

Gebrüder Kiessel GmbH, **IV** 197

Gebrüder Sulzer Aktiengesellschaft. *See* Sulzer Brothers Limited.

Gebrüder Volkart, **III** 402

Gebrueder Ahle GmbH, **III** 581

GEC. *See* General Electric Company.

GECAS. *See* GE Capital Aviation Services.

Gecina SA, 42 151–53

GECO, **III** 618; **17** 419

Geco Mines Ltd., **IV** 165; **7** 398

Gedney. *See* M.A. Gedney Co.

Geer Drug, **III** 9–10

Geerlings & Wade, Inc., 45 166–68

Geest Plc, 38 198, **200–02**

Gefco SA, 54 126–28

Geffen Records Inc., 21 26; **23** 33; **26 150–52; 43** 143

GEGC, **III** 434

GEHE AG, 27 175–78

Gehl Company, 19 172–74

GEICO Corporation, III 214, 248, 252, 273, 448; **10 310–12; 18** 60, 61, 63; **40 196–99 (upd.); 42** 31–34

Gelatin Products Co., **I** 678

Gelco Corporation, **53** 275

Gelco Express, **18** 177

Gelco Truck Services, **19** 293

Gellatly, Hankey and Sewell, **III** 521

Gelsenberg AG, **IV** 454; **7** 141

Gelsenkirchener Bergwerks AG, **I** 542; **IV** 194

Gelson's, **29** 32

Gem State Utilities, **6** 325, 328

GEMA Gesellschaft für Maschinen- und Apparatebau mbH, **IV** 198

Gemaire Distributors, Inc., **52** 398–99

GemChem, Inc., **47** 20

Gemco, **17** 366

Gemcolite Company, **8** 178

N.V. Gemeenschappelijk Benzit van Aandeelen Philips Gloeilampenfabriken, **II** 79; **13** 396

Gemeinhardt Co., **16** 201; **43** 170

Gemey, **III** 47

Gemina S.p.A., **I** 369; **52** 121–22

Gemini Computer Systems, **III** 109; **14** 13; **37** 59–60

Gemini Group Limited Partnership, **23** 10

Gemini Industries, **17** 215

GemPlus, **18** 543

Gemstar-TV Guide International, **43** 431

Gen-Probe, Inc., **50** 138–39

Gen-X Technologies Inc, **53** 285

Genbel Investments Ltd., **IV** 92

GenCare Health Systems, **17** 166–67

Gencor Ltd., I 423; **IV 90–93**, 95; **22 233–37 (upd.); 49** 353

GenCorp Inc., 8 206–08; 9 247–49; 13 381

Gendex Corp., **10** 270, 272

Gene Reid Drilling, **IV** 480

Gene Upton Co., **13** 166

Genencor International Inc., **44** 134, 136

Genender International Incorporated, **31** 52

Genentech Inc., I 628, **637–38; III** 43; **8 209–11 (upd.)**, 216–17; **10** 78, 80, 142, 199; **17** 289; **29** 386; **30** 164; **32 211–15 (upd.); 37** 112; **38** 204, 206; **41** 153, 155

General Accident plc, III 256–57, 350. *See also* Aviva PLC.

General America Corp., **III** 352–53

General American Oil Co., **IV** 523

General American Tank Car Company. *See* GATX Corporation.

General Aniline and Film Corporation. *See* GAF Corporation.

General Aquatics, Inc., **16** 297

General Artificial Silk Co., **IV** 310; **19** 265

General Atlantic Partners, **25** 34; **26** 94

General Automotive Parts Corp., **I** 62; **9** 254

General Aviation Corp., **I** 54; **9** 16

General Battery Corp., **I** 440–41

General Bearing Corporation, 45 169–71

General Binding Corporation, 10 313–14

General Box Corp., **IV** 342

General Brewing Corp., **I** 269

General Bussan Kaisha, Ltd., **IV** 431–32, 555

General Cable Corporation, IV 32; **7** 288; **8** 367; **18** 549; **40 200–03**

General Casualty Co., **III** 258, 343, 352, 404

The General Chemical Group Inc., I 414; **22** 29, 115, 193, 349, 541; **29** 114; **37 157–60**

General Chocolate, **II** 521

General Cigar Company, **43** 204–05. *See also* Culbro Corporation.

General Cigar Holdings, Inc., **27** 139–40

General Cinema Corporation, I 245–46; **II** 478; **IV** 624; **12** 12–13, 226, 356; **14** 87; **19** 362; **26** 468; **27** 481

General Cinema Finance Co., **II** 157–58

General Cinema Theaters. *See* GC Companies, Inc.

General Co. for Life Insurance and Superannuation, **III** 309

General Corporation, **9** 173

General Credit Ltd., **II** 389

General Crude Oil Co., **II** 403; **IV** 287; **15** 228

General DataComm Industries, Inc., 14 200–02

General Diaper Corporation, **14** 550

General Dynamics Corporation, I 55, **57–60**, 62, 71, 74, 77, 482, 525, 527, 597; **6** 79, 229; **7** 520; **8** 51, 92, 315, 338; **9** 206, 323, 417–18, 498; **10 315–18 (upd.)**, 522, 527; **11** 67, 165, 269, 278, 364; **13** 374; **16** 77–78; **18** 62, 554; **27** 100; **30** 471; **36** 76, 78–79; **40 204–10 (upd.)**

General Electric Capital Aviation Services, **48** 218–19

General Electric Capital Corp., **15** 257, 282; **19** 190

General Electric Company, I 41, 52, 82–85, 195, 321, 454, 478, 532, 534, 537; **II** 2, 16, 19, 22, 24, **27–31**, 38–39, 41, 56, 58–59, 66, 82, 86, 88–90, 98–99, 116–17, 119–21, 143, 151–52, 330, 349, 431, 604; **III** 16, 110, 122–23, 132, 149, 152, 154, 170–71, 340, 437, 440, 443, 475, 483, 502, 526, 572–73, 614, 655; **IV** 66, 203, 287, 596, 675; **V** 564; **6** 13, 27, 32, 164–66, 240, 261, 266, 288, 452, 517; **7** 123, 125, 161, 456, 520, 532; **8** 157, 262, 332, 377; **9** 14–18, 27, 128, 162, 244, 246, 352–53, 417–18, 439, 514; **10** 16, 241, 536–37; **11** 46, 313, 318, 422, 472, 490; **12** 68, 190, **193–97 (upd.)**, 237, 247, 250, 252, 484, 544–45, 550; **13** 30, 124, 326, 396, 398, 501, 529, 554, 563–64; **15** 196, 228, 285, 380, 403, 467; **17** 149, 173, 272; **18** 228, 369; **19** 110, 164–66, 210, 335; **20** 8, 152; **22** 37, 218, 406; **23** 104–05, 181; **26** 371; **28** 4–5, 8, 298; **30** 490; **31** 123; **34 183–90 (upd.)**; **41** 366; **43** 447, 466; **45** 17, 19, 117; **47** 351; **50** 233, 392; **51** 184

General Electric Company, PLC, I 411, 423; **II** 3, 12, **24–26**, 31, 58, 72, 80–83; **III** 509; **9** 9–10; **13** 356; **20** 290; **24** 87; **42** 373, 377. *See also* Marconi plc.

General Electric Credit Corporation, **19** 293; **20** 42

General Electric International Mexico, S.A. de C.V., **51** 116

General Electric Mortgage Insurance Company, **52** 244

General Electric Railcar Wheel and Parts Services Corporation, **18** 4

General Electric Venture Capital Corporation, **9** 140; **10** 108

General Electronics Co., **III** 160

General Elevator Corporation, **25** 15

General Europea S.A., **V** 607

General Export Iron and Metals Company, **15** 116

General Felt Industries Inc., **I** 202; **14** 300; **17** 182–83

General Film Distributors Ltd., **II** 157

General Finance Corp., **II** 419; **III** 194, 232; **11** 16

General Finance Service Corp., **11** 447

General Fire and Casualty, **I** 449

General Fire Extinguisher Co. *See* Grinnell Corp.

General Foods Corp., **I** 26, 36, 608, 712; **II** 414, 463, 477, 497, 502, 525, 530–34, 557, 569; **III** 66; **V** 407; **7** 272–74; **10** 323, 551; **12** 167, 372; **13** 293; **18** 416, 419; **25** 517; **26** 251; **36** 236; **44** 341; **50** 293

General Foods, Ltd., **7** 577

General Furniture Leasing. *See* CORT Business Services Corporation.

General Gas Co., **IV** 432

General Glass Corporation, **13** 40

General Growth Properties, **III** 248

General Health Services, **III** 79

General Host Corporation, 7 372; **12** 178–79, **198–200**, 275; **15** 362; **17** 230–31

General Housewares Corporation, 16 234–36; 18 69

General Injectables and Vaccines Inc., **54** 188

General Instrument Corporation, II 5, 112, 160; **10 319–21; 17** 33; **34** 298; **54** 68

General Insurance Co. of America, **III** 352–53

General Jones Processed Food, **I** 438

General Learning Corp., **IV** 675; **7** 528

General Leisure, **16** 33

General Life Insurance Co. of America, **III** 353

General Medical Corp., **18** 469

General Merchandise Company, **V** 91

General Merchandise Services, Inc., **15** 480

General Milk Co., **II** 487; **7** 429

General Milk Products of Canada Ltd., **II** 586

General Mills, Inc., II 493, **501–03**, 525, 556, 576, 684; **III** 505; **7** 547; **8** 53–54; **9** 156, 189–90, 291; **10** 177, **322–24 (upd.)**; **11** 15, 497–98; **12** 80, 167–68, 275; **13** 244, 293–94, 408, 516; **15** 189; **16** 71, 156–58, 337; **18** 225, 523; **22** 337–38; **25** 90, 241, 243, 253; **30** 286; **31** 429–31; **33** 359; **36** 179–80, **234–39 (upd.)**; **44** 138–40; **50** 293–96

General Mining and Finance Corporation. *See* Gencor Ltd.

General Mortgage and Credit Corp., **II** 256

General Motors Acceptance Corporation, **21** 146; **22** 55

General Motors Corporation, I 10, 14, 16–17, 54, 58, 78–80, 85, 101–02, 125, 136, 141, 144–45, 147, 154–55, 162–63, 165–67, **171–73**, 181, 183, 186–87, 203, 205–06, 280, 328–29, 334–35, 360, 448, 464, 481–82, 529, 540; **II** 2, 5, 15, 32–35, 268, 431, 608; **III** 55, 136–38, 292, 442, 458, 482–83, 536, 555, 563, 581, 590–91, 637–38, 640–42, 760; **6** 140, 256, 336, 356, 358; **7** 6–8, 427, 461–64, 513, 565, 567, 599;

8 151–52, 505–07; **9** 16–18, 36, 283, 293–95, 341, 343, 344, 439, 487–89; **10** 198, 232, 262, 264, 273–74, 279–80, 288–89, **325–27 (upd.)**, 419–20, 429, 460, 537; **11** 5, 29, 53, 103–04, 137–39, 339, 350, 427–29, 437–39, 471–72, 528, 530; **12** 90, 160, 309, 311, 487; **13** 109, 124, 179, 344–45, 357; **16** 321–22, 436, 484; **17** 173, 184, 304; **18** 125–26, 168, 308; **19** 293–94, 482, 484; **21** 3, 6, 444; **22** 13, 169, 175, 216; **23** 267–69, 288–91, 340, 459–61; **25** 142–43, 149, 223–24, 300; **29** 375, 407–08; **34** 133–35, 303; **36** 32, **240–44 (upd.)**, 298; **38** 86, 458, 461; **43** 319; **45** 142, 170; **50** 197, 376; **51** 34; **55** 326

General Nucleonics Corp., **III** 643

General Nutrition Companies, Inc., 11 155–57; 24 480; **29 210–14 (upd.); 31** 347; **37** 340, 342; **45** 210

General Office Products Co., **25** 500

General Packing Service, Inc., **19** 78

General Parts Inc., **29** 86

General Petroleum and Mineral Organization of Saudi Arabia, **IV** 537–39

General Petroleum Authority. *See* Egyptian General Petroleum Corporation.

General Petroleum Corp., **IV** 412, 431, 464; **7** 352

General Physics Corporation, **13** 367

General Portland Cement Co., **III** 704–05; **17** 497

General Portland Inc., **28** 229

General Precision Equipment Corp., **II** 10; **30** 418

General Printing and Paper, **II** 624–25

General Printing Ink Corp. *See* Sequa Corp.

General Property Trust, **IV** 708

General Public Utilities Corporation, V 629–31; 6 484, 534, 579–80; **11** 388; **20** 73

General Radio Company. *See* GenRad, Inc.

General Railway Signal Company. *See* General Signal Corporation.

General Re Corporation, III 258–59, 276; **24 176–78 (upd.); 42** 31, 35

General Rent A Car, **6** 349; **25** 142–43

General Research Corp., **14** 98

General Seafoods Corp., **II** 531

General Sekiyu K.K., IV 431–33, 555; **16** 490. *See also* TonenGeneral Sekiyu K.K.

General Signal Corporation, III 645; **9** 250–52; **11** 232

General Spring Products, **16** 321

General Steel Industries Inc., **14** 324

General Supermarkets, **II** 673

General Telephone and Electronics Corp., **II** 47; **V** 295, 345–46; **13** 398; **19** 40; **25** 267

General Telephone Corporation, **V** 294–95; **9** 478, 494

General Time Corporation, **16** 483

General Tire, Inc., 8 206–08, **212–14; 9** 247–48; **20** 260, 262; **22** 219

General Transistor Corporation, **10** 319

General Utilities Company, **6** 555

General Waterworks Corporation, **40** 449

Generale Bank, II 294–95

Générale Biscuit S.A., **II** 475

Générale de Banque, **36** 458

Générale de Mécanique Aéronautique, **I** 46

Générale de Restauration, **49** 126

Générale des Eaux Group, **V** 632–34; **21** 226. *See* Vivendi Universal S.A.
Generale du Jouet, **16** 428
Générale Occidentale, **II** 475; **IV** 614–15
Générale Restauration S.A., **34** 123
Generali. *See* Assicurazioni Generali.
Génération Y2K, **35** 204, 207
GenerComit Gestione SpA, **II** 192
Genesco Inc., **14** 501; **17** 202–06; **27** 59
Genesee & Wyoming Inc., **27** 179–81
Genesee Brewing Co., **18** 72; **50** 114
Genesee Iron Works. *See* Wickes Inc.
Genesis, **II** 176–77
Genesis Health Ventures, Inc., **18** 195–97; **25** 310
Genetic Anomalies, Inc., **39** 395
Genetic Systems Corp., **I** 654; **III** 18; **37** 43
Genetics Institute, Inc., **8** 215–18; **10** 70, 78–80; **50** 538
Geneva Metal Wheel Company, **20** 261
Geneva Pharmaceuticals, Inc., **8** 549; **22** 37, 40
Geneva Rubber Co., **17** 373
Geneva Steel, **7** 193–95
Genex Corp., **I** 355–56; **26** 246
GENEX Services, Inc., **52** 379
GENIX, **V** 152
Genix Group. *See* MCN Corporation.
Genmar Holdings, Inc., **45** 172–75
Genossenschaftsbank Edeka, **II** 621–22
Genosys Biotechnologies, Inc., **36** 431
Genovese Drug Stores, Inc., **18** 198–200; **21** 187; **32** 170; **43** 249
Genpack Corporation, **21** 58
GenRad, Inc., **24** 179–83
GenSet, **19** 442
Genstar, **22** 14; **23** 327
Genstar Gypsum Products Co., **IV** 273
Genstar Stone Products Co., **III** 735; **15** 154; **40** 176
GenTek Inc., **37** 157; **41** 236
Gentex Corporation, **26** 153–57; **35** 148–49
Gentex Optics, **17** 50; **18** 392
GenTrac, **24** 257
Gentry Associates, Inc., **14** 378
Gentry International, **I** 497; **47** 234
Genty-Cathiard, **39** 183–84; **54** 306
Genuardi's Family Markets, Inc., **35** 190–92
Genuin Golf & Dress of America, Inc., **32** 447
Genuine Parts Company, **9** 253–55; **45** 176–79 (upd.)
Genung's, **II** 673
Genus, **18** 382–83
Genzyme Corporation, **13** 239–42; **38** 203–07 (upd.); **47** 4
Genzyme Transgenics Corp., **37** 44
Geo. H. McFadden & Bro., **54** 89
Geo Space Corporation, **18** 513
GEO Specialty Chemicals, Inc., **27** 117
Geo. W. Wheelwright Co., **IV** 311; **19** 266
geobra Brandstätter GmbH & Co. KG, **48** 183–86
Geodynamics Oil & Gas Inc., **IV** 83
Geographics, Inc., **25** 183
Geomarine Systems, **11** 202
The Geon Company, **11** 158–61
Geon Industries, Inc. *See* Johnston Industries, Inc.
Geophysical Service, Inc., **II** 112; **III** 499–500; **IV** 365

GeoQuest Systems Inc., **17** 419
Georesources, Inc., **19** 247
Georg Fischer Foundries Group, **38** 214
George A. Hormel and Company, **II** 504–06; **7** 547; **12** 123–24; **18** 244. *See also* Hormel Foods Corporation.
George A. Touche & Co., **9** 167
George Batten Co., **I** 28
George Booker & Co., **13** 102
George Buckton & Sons Limited, **40** 129
The George F. Cram Company, Inc., **55** 158–60
George Fischer, Ltd., **III** 638
George H. Dentler & Sons, **7** 429
The George Hyman Construction Company, **8** 112–13; **25** 403
George J. Ball, Inc., **27** 507
George K. Baum & Company, **25** 433
George K. Smith & Co., **I** 692
George Kent, **II** 3; **22** 10
George Newnes Company, **IV** 641; **7** 244
George Peabody & Co., **II** 329, 427
George R. Newell Company. *See* Supervalu Inc.
George R. Rich Manufacturing Company. *See* Clark Equipment Company.
George S. May International Company, **55** 161–63
George Smith Financial Corporation, **21** 257
George W. Neare & Co., **III** 224
George Weston Limited, **II** 631–32; **36** 245–48 (upd.); **41** 30, 33
George Wimpey plc, **12** 201–03; **28** 450; **51** 135–38 (upd.)
Georges Renault SA, **III** 427; **28** 40
Georgetown Group, Inc., **26** 187
Georgetown Steel Corp., **IV** 228
Georgia Carpet Outlets, **25** 320
Georgia Cotton Producers Association. *See* Gold Kist Inc.
Georgia Credit Exchange, **6** 24
Georgia Federal Bank, **I** 447; **11** 112–13; **30** 196
Georgia Gulf Corporation, **IV** 282; **9** 256–58, 260
Georgia Hardwood Lumber Co., **IV** 281; **9** 259
Georgia International Life Insurance Co., **III** 218
Georgia Kraft Co., **IV** 312, 342–43; **8** 267–68; **19** 268
Georgia Natural Gas Corporation, **6** 447–48
Georgia-Pacific Corporation, **IV** 281–83, 288, 304, 345, 358; **9** 256–58, **259–62** (upd.); **12** 19, 377; **15** 229; **22** 415, 489; **31** 314; **44** 66; **47** 145–51 (upd.); **51** 284
Georgia Power & Light Co., **V** 621; **6** 447, 537; **23** 28; **27** 20
Georgia Power Company, **38** 446–48; **49** 145
Georgia Railway and Electric Company, **6** 446–47; **23** 28
Georgie Pie, **V** 35
GeoScience Corporation, **18** 515; **44** 422
Geosource Inc., **III** 182; **21** 14; **22** 189
Geotec Boyles Brothers, S.A., **19** 247
Geotecnia y Cimientos SA, **55** 182
Geotek Communications Inc., **21** 238–40
GeoTel Communications Corp., **34** 114
Geothermal Resources International, **11** 271

GeoVideo Networks, **34** 259
Geoworks Corporation, **25** 509
Geraghty & Miller Inc., **26** 23
Gerald Stevens, Inc., **37** 161–63
Gérard, **25** 84
Gerber Products Company, **II** 481; **III** 19; **7** 196–98, 547; **9** 90; **11** 173; **21** 53–55, **241–44** (upd.); **25** 366; **34** 103; **36** 256
Gerber Scientific, Inc., **12** 204–06
Gerbes Super Markets, Inc., **12** 112
Gerbo Telecommunicacoes e Servicos Ltda., **32** 40
Geren Associates. *See* CRSS Inc.
Geriatrics Inc., **13** 49
Gericom AG, **47** 152–54
Gerling-Konzern Versicherungs-Beteiligungs-Aktiengesellschaft, **III** 695; **51** 139–43
Germaine Monteil Cosmetiques Corp., **I** 426; **III** 56
German American Bancorp, **41** 178–80
German-American Car Company. *See* GATX.
German-American Securities, **II** 283
German Cargo Service GmbH., **I** 111
German Mills American Oatmeal Factory, **II** 558; **12** 409
The German Society. *See* The Legal Aid Society.
Germania Refining Co., **IV** 488–89; **50** 351
Germplasm Resource Management, **III** 740
GERPI, **51** 16
Gerresheimer Glas AG, **II** 386; **IV** 232; **43** 186–89
Gerrity Oil & Gas Corporation, **11** 28; **24** 379–80
Gervais Danone, **II** 474
GESA. *See* General Europea S.A.
Gesbancaya, **II** 196
Geschmay Group, **51** 14
Gesellschaft für Chemische Industrie im Basel, **I** 632
Gesellschaft für den Bau von Untergrundbahnen, **I** 410
Gesellschaft für Linde's Eisenmachinen, **I** 581
Gesellschaft für Markt- und Kühlhallen, **I** 581
Gesparal, **III** 47; **8** 342
Gestettner, **II** 159
Gestione Pubblicitaria Editoriale, **IV** 586
GET Manufacturing Inc., **36** 300
Getronics NV, **39** 176–78
Getty Images, Inc., **31** 216–18
Getty Oil Co., **II** 448; **IV** 367, 423, 429, 461, 479, 488, 490, 551, 553; **6** 457; **8** 526; **11** 27; **13** 448; **17** 501; **18** 488; **27** 216; **41** 391, 394–95; **47** 436; **50** 353
Getz Corp., **IV** 137
Geyser Peak Winery, **I** 291
Geysers Geothermal Co., **IV** 84, 523; **7** 188
GFI Informatique SA, **49** 165–68
GfK Aktiengesellschaft, **49** 169–72
GFS. *See* Gordon Food Service Inc.
GFS Realty Inc., **II** 633
GGT Group, **44** 198
GHH, **II** 257
GHI, **28** 155, 157
Ghirardelli Chocolate Company, **24** 480; **27** 105; **30** 218–20
GI Communications, **10** 321

GI Export Corp. *See* Johnston Industries, Inc.
GIAG, **16** 122
Gianni Versace SpA, 22 238-40
Giant Bicycle Inc., **19** 384
Giant Cement Holding, Inc., 23 224-26
Giant Eagle, Inc., **12** 390-91; **13** 237
Giant Food Inc., II 633-35, 656; **13** 282, 284; **15** 532; **16** 313; **22 241-44** (upd.); **24** 462
Giant Industries, Inc., 19 175-77
Giant Resources, **III** 729
Giant Stores, Inc., **7** 113; **25** 124
Giant TC, Inc. *See* Campo Electronics, Appliances & Computers, Inc.
Giant Tire & Rubber Company, **8** 126
Giant Video Corporation, **29** 503
Giant Wholesale, **II** 625
GIB Group, **V** 63-66; **22** 478; **23** 231; **26 158-62** (upd.)
Gibbons, Green, van Amerongen Ltd., **II** 605; **9** 94; **12** 28; **19** 360
Gibbs Automatic Molding Co., **III** 569; **20** 360
Gibbs Construction, **25** 404
GIBCO Corp., **I** 321; **17** 287, 289
Gibraltar Casualty Co., **III** 340
Gibraltar Financial Corp., **III** 270-71
Gibraltar Steel Corporation, 37 164-67
Gibson, Dunn & Crutcher LLP, 36 249-52; 37 292
Gibson Greetings, Inc., 7 24; **12 207-10**; **16** 256; **21** 426-28; **22** 34-35
Gibson Guitar Corp., 16 237-40
Gibson McDonald Furniture Co., **14** 236
GIC. *See* The Goodyear Tire & Rubber Company.
Giddings & Lewis, Inc., 8 545-46; 10 328-30; 23 299; **28** 455
Giftmaster Inc., **26** 439-40
Gil-Wel Manufacturing Company, **17** 440
Gilbane, Inc., 34 191-93
Gilbert & John Greenall Limited, **21** 246
Gilbert-Ash Ltd., **I** 588
Gilbert Lane Personnel, Inc., **9** 326
Gilde-Verlag, **IV** 590
Gilde-Versicherung AG, **III** 400
Gildon Metal Enterprises, **7** 96
Gilead Sciences, Inc., 54 129-31
Gilkey Bros. *See* Puget Sound Tug and Barge Company.
Gill and Duffus, **II** 500
Gill Industries, **II** 161
Gill Interprovincial Lines, **27** 473
Gillett Holdings, Inc., 7 199-201; 11 543, 545; **43** 437-38
The Gillette Company, III 27-30, 114, 215; **IV** 722; **8** 59-60; **9** 381, 413; **17** 104-05; **18** 60, 62, 215, 228; **20 249-53** (upd.); **23** 54-57; **26** 334; **28** 247; **39** 336; **51** 57; **52** 269
Gilliam Furniture Inc., **12** 475
Gilliam Manufacturing Co., **8** 530
Gilman & Co., **III** 523
Gilman Fanfold Corp., Ltd., **IV** 644
Gilman Paper Co., **37** 178
Gilmore Brother's, **I** 707
Gilmore Steel Corporation. *See* Oregon Steel Mills, Inc.
Gilroy Foods, **27** 299
Giltspur, **II** 587
Gimbel Brothers, Inc. *See* Saks Holdings, Inc.

Gimbel's Department Store, **I** 426-27; **8** 59; **22** 72; **50** 117-18
Gindick Productions, **6** 28
Ginn & Co., **IV** 672; **19** 405
Ginnie Mae. *See* Government National Mortgage Association.
Gino's, **III** 103
Gino's East, **21** 362
Ginsber Beer Group, **15** 47; **38** 77
Giorgio Armani S.p.A., 45 180-83
Giorgio Beverly Hills, Inc., **26** 384
Giorgio, Inc., **III** 16; **19** 28
Girard Bank, **II** 315-16; **44** 280
Girbaud, **17** 513; **31** 261
Girl Scouts of the USA, 35 193-96
Girling, **III** 556
Giro Sport Designs International Inc., **16** 53; **44** 53-54
Girod, **19** 50
Girsa S.A., **23** 170
Girvin, Inc., **16** 297
Gist-Brocades Co., **III** 53; **26** 384
The Gitano Group, Inc., 8 219-21; 20 136 **25** 167; **37** 81
Givaudan SA, 43 190-93
GJM International Ltd., **25** 121-22
GK Technologies Incorporated, **10** 547
GKH Partners, **29** 295
GKN plc, III 493-96, 554, 556; **38 208-13** (upd.); **42** 47; **47** 7, 9, 279-80
Glaceries de Saint-Roch, **III** 677; **16** 121
Glaces de Boussois, **II** 474-75
Glacier Bancorp, Inc., 35 197-200
Glacier Park Co., **10** 191
Glacier Water Services, Inc., 47 155-58
Gladieux Corp., **III** 103
Glamar Group plc, **14** 224
Glamis Gold, Ltd., 54 132-35
Glamor Shops, Inc., **14** 93
Glanbia Group, **38** 196, 198
Glasrock Home Health Care, **I** 316; **25** 81
Glass Containers Corp., **I** 609-10
Glass Fibres Ltd., **III** 726
Glass Glover Plc, **52** 419
Glasstite, Inc., **33** 360-61
GlasTec, **II** 420
Glastron. *See* Genmar Holdings, Inc.
Glatfelter Wood Pulp Company, **8** 413
Glaverbel, **III** 667
Glaxo Holdings plc, I 639-41, 643, 668, 675, 693; **III** 66; **6** 346; **9 263-65** (upd.); **10** 551; **11** 173; **20** 39; **26** 31; **34** 284; **38** 365; **50** 56; **54** 130
GlaxoSmithKline plc, 46 201-08 (upd.)
Gleason Corporation, 24 184-87
Glen & Co, **I** 453
Glen Alden Corp., **15** 247
Glen Cove Mutual Insurance Co., **III** 269
Glen-Gery Corporation, **14** 249
Glen Iris Bricks, **III** 673
Glen Line, **6** 416
Glencairn Ltd., **25** 418
Glencore International AG, **52** 71, 73
Glendale Federal Savings, **IV** 29
The Glenlyte Group, **29** 469
Glenlyte Thomas Group LLC, **29** 466
Glenn Advertising Agency, **25** 90
Glenn Pleass Holdings Pty. Ltd., **21** 339
Glens Falls Insurance Co., **III** 242
GLF-Eastern States Association, **7** 17
The Glidden Company, I 353; **8 222-24**; **21** 545
Glimcher Co., **26** 262

Glitsch International, Inc., **6** 146; **23** 206, 208
Global Access, **31** 469
Global Apparel Sourcing Ltd., **22** 223
Global Communications of New York, Inc., **45** 261
Global Crossing Ltd., 32 216-19
Global Energy Group, **II** 345
Global Engineering Company, **9** 266
Global Health Care Partners, **42** 68
Global Industries, Ltd., 37 168-72
Global Information Solutions, **34** 257
Global Interactive Communications Corporation, **28** 242
Global Marine Inc., 9 266-67; 11 87
Global Natural Resources, **II** 401; **10** 145
Global One, **52** 108
Global Outdoors, Inc., 49 173-76
Global Power Equipment Group Inc., 52 137-39
Global Telesystems Ltd. *See* Global Crossing Ltd.
Global Transport Organization, **6** 383
Global Vacations Group. *See* Classic Vacation Group, Inc.
Global Van Lines. *See* Allied Worldwide, Inc.
GlobalCom Telecommunications, Inc., **24** 122
GlobaLex, **28** 141
Globalia, **53** 301
GlobalSantaFe Corporation, 48 187-92 (upd.)
Globalstar Telecommunications Limited, **54** 233
GLOBALT, Inc., **52** 339
Globe & Rutgers Insurance Co., **III** 195-96
Globe Business Furniture, **39** 207
Globe Co. **I** 201
Globe Electric Co., **III** 536
Globe Feather & Down, **19** 304
Globe Files Co., **I** 201
Globe Grain and Milling Co., **II** 555
Globe Industries, **I** 540
Globe Insurance Co., **III** 350
Globe Life Insurance Co., **III** 187; **10** 28; **38** 15
Globe National Bank, **II** 261
Globe Newspaper Co., **7** 15
Globe Pequot Press, **36** 339, 341
Globe Petroleum Ltd., **IV** 401
Globe Steel Abrasive Co., **17** 371
Globe Telegraph and Trust Company, **25** 99
Globe-Union, **III** 536; **26** 229
Globe-Wernicke Co., **I** 201
Globelle Corp., **43** 368
Globetrotter Communications, **7** 199
Globo, **18** 211
Glock Ges.m.b.H., 42 154-56
Gloria Jean's Gourmet Coffees, **20** 83
La Gloria Oil and Gas Company, **7** 102
Gloria Separator GmbH Berlin, **III** 418
Glosser Brothers, **13** 394
Gloster Aircraft, **I** 50; **III** 508; **24** 85
Glotel plc, 53 149-51
Gloucester Cold Storage and Warehouse Company, **13** 243
Glovatorium, **III** 152; **6** 266; **30** 339
Glowlite Corporation, **48** 359
Glycomed Inc., **13** 241; **47** 222
Glyn, Mills and Co., **II** 308; **12** 422
GM. *See* General Motors Corporation.

GM Hughes Electronics Corporation, II 32–36; **10** 325. *See also* Hughes Electronics Corporation.
GMARA, **II** 608
GMFanuc Robotics, **III** 482–83
GMR Properties, **21** 257
GNB International Battery Group, **10** 445
GND Holdings Corp., **7** 204; **28** 164
GNMA. *See* Government National Mortgage Association.
Gnôme & Rhône, **46** 369
The Go-Ahead Group Plc, 28 155–57
Go Fly Ltd., **39** 128
Go-Gro Industries, Ltd., **43** 99
Go Sport. *See* Groupe Go Sport S.A.
Go-Video, Inc. *See* Sensory Science Corporation.
Goal Systems International Inc., **10** 394
Godfather's Pizza Incorporated, II 556–57; **11** 50; **12** 123; **14** 351; **17** 86; **25** 179–81
Godfrey Co., **II** 625
Godfrey L. Cabot, Inc., **8** 77
Godiva Chocolatier, **II** 480; **26** 56
Godo Shusei, **III** 42
Godsell, **10** 277
Godtfred Kristiansen, **13** 310–11
Goebel & Wetterau Grocery Co., **II** 681
Goelitz Confectionary. *See* Herman Goelitz, Inc.
Goering Werke, **II** 282
Göhner AG, **6** 491
Gokey Company, **10** 216; **28** 339
Gold Bond Stamp Company, **6** 363–64; **22** 125
Gold Crust Bakeries, **II** 465
Gold Dust Corp., **II** 497
Gold Exploration and Mining Co. Limited Partnership, **13** 503
Gold Fields of South Africa Ltd., I 423; **IV** 91, 94–97
Gold Kist Inc., 7 432; **17** 207–09; **26** 166–68
Gold Lance Inc., **19** 451–52
Gold Lion, **20** 263
Gold Prospectors' Association of America, **49** 173
Gold Seal, **II** 567
Gold Star Foods Co., **IV** 410
Gold'n Plump Poultry, 54 136–38
Gold's Gym Enterprises, **25** 450
Goldblatt Bros., **IV** 135
Goldblatt's Department Stores, **15** 240–42
Golden Bear International, **33** 103; **42** 433; **45** 300
Golden Belt Manufacturing Co., 16 241–43
Golden Books Family Entertainment, Inc., 28 158–61
Golden Circle Financial Services, **15** 328
Golden Corral Corporation, 10 331–33
Golden Eagle Exploration, **IV** 566–67
Golden Enterprises, Inc., 26 163–65
Golden Gate Airlines, **25** 421
Golden Grain Macaroni Co., **II** 560; **12** 411; **30** 219; **34** 366
Golden Hope Rubber Estate, **III** 697, 699
Golden Moores Finance Company, **48** 286
Golden Nugget, Inc. *See* Mirage Resorts, Incorporated.
Golden Ocean Group, **45** 164
Golden Partners, **10** 333
Golden Peanut Company, **17** 207
Golden Poultry Company, **26** 168

Golden Press, Inc., **13** 559–61
Golden Sea Produce, **10** 439
Golden Skillet, **10** 373
Golden State Bank, **II** 348
Golden State Foods Corporation, 32 220–22
Golden State Newsprint Co. Inc., **IV** 296; **19** 226; **23** 225
Golden State Sanwa Bank, **II** 348
Golden State Vintners, Inc., 33 172–74
Golden Tulip International, **I** 109
Golden West Financial Corporation, 47 159–61
Golden West Homes, **15** 328
Golden West Publishing Corp., **38** 307–08
Golden Wonder, **II** 500; **III** 503
Golden Youth, **17** 227
Goldenberg Group, Inc., **12** 396
Goldenlay Eggs, **II** 500
Goldfield Corp., **12** 198
Goldfine's Inc., **16** 36
Goldkuhl & Broström, **III** 419
Goldline Laboratories Inc., **11** 208
Goldman, Sachs & Co., II 11, 268, 326, 361, 414–16, 432, 434, 448; **III** 80, 531; **IV** 611; **9** 378, 441; **10** 423; **12** 405; **13** 95, 448, 554; **15** 397; **16** 195; **20** 254–57 (upd.), 258; **21** 146; **22** 427–28; **26** 456; **27** 317; **29** 508; **36** 190–91; **38** 289, 291; **51** 358–59, 61. *See also* The Goldman Sachs Group Inc.
The Goldman Sachs Group Inc., 51 144–48 (upd.)
Goldner Hawn Johnson & Morrison Inc., **48** 412
Goldome Savings Bank, **11** 110; **17** 488
Goldsbrough Mort & Co., **I** 437
Goldsmith's, **9** 209
Goldstar Co., Ltd., II 5, 53–54; **III** 517; **7** 233; **12** 211–13; **13** 213; **30** 184; **43** 428
Goldwell, **III** 38
Goldwin Golf, **45** 76
Goldwyn Films. *See* Metro-Goldwyn-Mayer Inc.
Goleta National Bank, **33** 5
Golf Day, **22** 517
The Golub Corporation, 26 169–71
Gomoljak, **14** 250
Gonnella Baking Company, 40 211–13
Good Foods, Inc., **II** 497
The Good Guys!, Inc., 10 334–35; **30** 224–27 (upd.)
The Good Humor-Breyers Ice Cream Company, II 533; **14** 203–05; **15** 222; **17** 140–41; **32** 474, 476
Good Natural Café, **27** 481
Good Times, Inc., **8** 303
Good Vibrations, Inc., **28** 345
Good Weather International Inc., **III** 221; **14** 109
Goodbody & Company, **II** 425; **13** 341; **22** 428
Goodbody James Capel, **16** 14
Goodby, Berlin & Silverstein, **10** 484
Goodebodies, **11** 41
Gooderham and Worts, **I** 216, 263–64
Goodlass, Wall & Co., **III** 680–81
Goodman Bros. Mfg. Co., **14** 436
Goodman Fielder Ltd., II 565; **7** 577; **44** 137; **52** 140–43
Goodman Holding Company, 42 157–60
GoodMark Foods, Inc., 26 172–74
Goodrich Corporation, 46 209–13 (upd.)

Goodrich Oil Co., **IV** 365
Goodrich, Tew and Company, **V** 231
Goodrich Tire Company, **V** 240–41; **6** 27
Goodson Newspaper Group, **29** 262
GoodTimes Entertainment Ltd., 31 238; **48** 193–95
Goodwill Industries International, Inc., 15 511; **16** 244–46
Goodwin & Co., **12** 108
Goodwin, Dannenbaum, Littman & Wingfield, **16** 72
Goody Products, Inc., 12 214–16
Goody's Family Clothing, Inc., 20 265–67
The Goodyear Tire & Rubber Company, I 21; **II** 304; **III** 452; **V** 244–48; **8** 81, 291–92, 339; **9** 324; **10** 445; **15** 91; **16** 474; **19** 221, 223, 455; **20** 259–64 (upd.); **21** 72–74
Google, Inc., 50 204–07
Gordon A. Freisen, International, **III** 73
Gordon B. Miller & Co., **7** 256; **25** 254
Gordon Capital Corp., **II** 245
Gordon Food Service Inc., 8 225–27; **39** 179–82 (upd.)
Gordon Investment Corp., **II** 245
Gordon Jewelry Corporation, **16** 559, 561; **40** 472
Gordon Manufacturing Co., **11** 256
Gordon Publications, **IV** 610
Gordon S. Black Corporation, **41** 197–98
Gordon-Van Cheese Company, **8** 225
Gordy Company, **26** 314
Gore Newspapers Company, **IV** 683; **22** 521
Gorges Foodservice, Inc., **14** 516; **50** 493
Gorham Silver, **12** 313
Gorilla Sports Club, **25** 42
Gorman Eckert & Co., **27** 299
The Gorman-Rupp Company, 18 201–03
Gormully & Jeffrey, **IV** 660
Gorton's, II 502; **10** 323; **13** 243–44
The Gosho Co. *See* Kanematsu Corporation.
Goss Holdings, Inc., 43 194–97
Gotaas-Larsen Shipping Corp., **6** 368; **27** 91
Götabanken, **II** 303, 353
Göteborgs Handelsbank, **II** 351
Göteborgs Handelskompani, **III** 425
Gothenburg Light & Power Company, **6** 580
Gothenburg Tramways Co., **II** 1
Gott Corp., **III** 614; **21** 293
Gottlieb Group, **38** 437
Gottschalks, Inc., 18 204–06; **26** 130
Goulard and Olena, **I** 412
Gould Electronics, Inc., III 745; **11** 45; **13** 127, 201; **14** 206–08; **21** 43
Goulding Industries Ltd., **IV** 295; **19** 225
Goulds Pumps Inc., 24 188–91
Gourmet Award Foods, **29** 480–81
Gourmet Foods, **II** 528
Government Bond Department, **9** 369
Government Employees Insurance Company. *See* GEICO Corporation.
Government National Mortgage Assoc., **II** 410
Government Technology Services Inc., **45** 69
Governor and Company of Adventurers of England. *See* Hudson's Bay Company.

The Governor and Company of the Bank of Scotland, II 422; III 360; V 166; **10 336–38**
Goya Foods Inc., **22 245–47**; 24 516
GP Group Acquisition Limited Partnership, 10 288; 27 41–42
GPAA. *See* Gold Prospectors' Association of America.
GPE. *See* General Precision Equipment Corporation.
GPI. *See* General Parts Inc.
GPI, 53 46
GPM Gas Corporation, 40 357–58
GPS Pool Supply, 29 34
GPT, 15 125
GPU. *See* General Public Utilities Corporation.
GPU, Inc., **27 182–85 (upd.)**
Graber Industries, Inc., V 379; 19 421
Grace. *See* W.R. Grace & Co.
Grace Drilling Company, 9 365
Grace-Sierra Horticultural Products Co., 22 475
Grace Steamship Lines, 50 523
Graco Inc., **19 178–80**
Gradall Industries, Inc., 52 196
Gradco Systems, Inc., 6 290
Gradiaz, Annis & Co., 15 138
Gradmann & Holler, III 283
Graef & Schmidt, III 54
Graf, 23 219
Graf Bertel Dominique/New York, 6 48
Graficas e Instrumentos S.A., 13 234
Graficas Monte Alban S.A., 47 326
Graftek Press, Inc., 26 44
Graham Brothers, 27 267, 269
Graham Container Corp., 8 477
Graham Page, III 568; 20 359
Grahams Builders Merchants, I 429
Gralla, IV 687
Grameen Bank, **31 219–22**
Gramercy Pictures, 23 391
Gramophone Company, 22 192
Grampian Electricity Supply Company, 13 457
Gran Central Corporation, 8 487
Gran Dorado, 48 315
Granada Group PLC, II 70, **138–40**; 17 353; **24 192–95 (upd.)**, 269; 25 270; 32 404; 52 367
Granada Royale Hometels, 9 426
Granaria Holdings B.V., 23 183
GranCare, Inc., **14 209–11**; 25 310
Grand Bazaar Innovations Bon Marché, 13 284; 26 159–60
Grand Casinos, Inc., **20 268–70**; 21 526; 25 386
Grand Department Store, 19 510
Grand Hotel Krasnapolsky N.V., **23 227–29**
Grand Magasin de Nouveautés Fournier d'Annecy, 27 93
Grand Metropolitan plc, I **247–49**, 259, 261; II 555–57, 565, 608, 613–15; 9 99; 13 391, 407, 409; **14 212–15 (upd.)**; 15 72; **17** 69, 71; **20** 452; 21 401; 26 58; 33 276; 34 121; 35 438; 42 223; 43 215. *See also* Diageo plc.
Grand Ole Opry. *See* Gaylord Entertainment Company.
Grand Prix Association of Long Beach, Inc., 43 139–40
Grand Rapids Carpet Sweeper Company, 9 70

Grand Rapids Gas Light Company. *See* MCN Corporation.
Grand Rapids Wholesale Grocery Company, 8 481
Grand Trunk Corp., 6 359–61
Grand Union Company, II 637, 662; 7 **202–04**; 8 410; 13 394; 16 249; 28 **162–65 (upd.)**
Grand Valley Gas Company, 11 28
Grand-Perret, 39 152–53
Grandes Superficies S.A., 23 247
Grandmet USA, I 248
Les Grands Magasins Au Bon Marché, 26 159–60
Grands Magasins L. Tietz, V 103
GrandVision S.A., **43 198–200**
Grandy's, 15 345
Granger Associates, 12 136
Gränges, III 480; 22 27; 53 127–28
Granite Broadcasting Corporation, 42 **161–64**
Granite City Steel Company, 12 353
Granite Furniture Co., 14 235
Granite Rock Company, **26 175–78**
Granite State Bankshares, Inc., 37 **173–75**
Grant Oil Tool Co., III 569; 20 361
Grant Street National Bank, II 317; 44 280
Grantham, Mayo, Van Otterloo & Co. LLC, 24 407
Grantree Corp., 14 4; 33 398
Graphic Controls Corp., IV 678
Graphic Industries Inc., **25 182–84**; 36 508
Graphic Research, Inc., 13 344–45
Graphic Services, III 166; 6 282
Graphics Systems Software, III 169; 6 285; 8 519
Graphite Oil Product Co., I 360
Graphix Zone, 31 238
Grass Valley Group, 8 518, 520
Grasselli Chemical Company, 22 225
Grasselli Dyestuffs Corp., I 337
Grasset, IV 617–18
Grasso Production Management Inc., 37 289
Grattan Plc, V 160; 29 356
The Graver Company, 16 357
Gray Communications Systems, Inc., 24 **196–200**
Gray Dawes & Co., III 522–23
Gray Drug Stores, III 745
Gray Dunn and Co., II 569
Gray Line, 24 118
Gray, Siefert & Co., Inc., 10 44; 33 259–60
Grayarc, III 157
Graybar Electric Company, Inc., 54 **139–42**
Grayrock Capital, I 275
Grays Harbor Mutual Savings Bank, 17 530
Greaseater, Ltd., 8 463–64
Great Alaska Tobacco Co., 17 80
Great American Bagel and Coffee Co., 27 482
Great American Broadcasting Inc., 18 65–66; 22 131; 23 257–58
Great American Cookie Company. *See* Mrs. Fields' Original Cookies, Inc.
Great American Entertainment Company, 13 279; **48** 194
Great American First Savings Bank of San Diego, II 420

Great American Insurance Company, 48 9
Great American Life Insurance Co., III 190–92
Great American Lines Inc., 12 29
Great American Management and Investment, Inc., **8 228–31**; 49 130
Great American Reserve Insurance Co., IV 343; 10 247
Great American Restaurants, 13 321
The Great Atlantic & Pacific Tea Company, Inc., II **636–38**, 629, 655–56, 666; 13 25, 127, 237; 15 259; 16 63–64, **247–50 (upd.)**; 17 106; 18 6; 19 479–80; 24 417; 26 463; 33 434; 55 **164–69 (upd.)**
Great Bagel and Coffee Co., 27 480–81
Great Beam Co., III 690
Great Eastern Railway, 6 424
Great 5¢ Store, V 224
Great Halviggan, III 690
Great Harvest Bread Company, 44 **184–86**
Great Lakes Bancorp, **8 232–33**
Great Lakes Bankgroup, II 457
Great Lakes Carbon Corporation, 12 99
Great Lakes Chemical Corp., I **341–42**; 8 262; **14 216–18 (upd.)**
Great Lakes Corp., IV 136
Great Lakes Energy Corp., 39 261
Great Lakes Pipe Line Co., IV 400, 575; 31 470
Great Lakes Steel Corp., IV 236; 8 346; 12 352; 26 528
Great Lakes Window, Inc., 12 397
Great Land Seafoods, Inc., II 553
Great Northern, III 282
Great Northern Import Co., I 292
Great Northern Nekoosa Corp., IV 282–83, 300; 9 260–61; 47 148
Great Northern Railway Company, 6 596
Great Plains Software Inc., 38 432
Great Plains Transportation, 18 226
Great Shoshone & Twin Falls Water Power Company, 12 265
The Great Universal Stores plc, V **67–69**; 15 83; 17 66, 68; 19 **181–84 (upd.)**; 41 74, 76; 45 152; 50 124. *See also* GUS plc.
Great-West Lifeco Inc., III **260–61**; 21 447. *See also* Power Corporation of Canada.
The Great Western Auction House & Clothing Store, 19 261
Great Western Bank, 47 160
Great Western Billiard Manufactory, III 442
Great Western Financial Corporation, 10 **339–41**
Great Western Foam Co., 17 182
Great Western Railway, III 272
Great World Foods, Inc., 17 93
Greatamerica Corp., I 489; 10 419; 24 303
Greater All American Markets, II 601; 7 19
Greater New York Film Rental Co., II 169
Greater Washington Investments, Inc., 15 248
Greb Industries Ltd., 16 79, 545
Grebner GmbH, 26 21
Grede Foundries, Inc., **38 214–17**
Greeley Beef Plant, 13 350
Greeley Gas Company, 43 56–57
Green Acquisition Co., 18 107
Green Bay Food Company, 7 127

The Green Bay Packers, Inc., 32 223–26
Green Capital Investors L.P., **23** 413–14
Green Cross K.K., **I** 665
Green Giant, **II** 556; **13** 408; **14** 212, 214;
  24 140–41
Green Island Cement (Holdings) Ltd.
  Group, **IV** 694–95
Green Line Investor Services, **18** 553
Green Mountain Coffee, Inc., 31 227–30
Green Power & Light Company. *See*
  UtiliCorp United Inc.
Green River Electric Corporation, **11** 37
Green Siam Air Services Co., Ltd., **51** 123
Green Thumb, **II** 562
Green Tree Financial Corporation, 11
  162–63. *See also* Conseco, Inc.
The Greenalls Group PLC, 21 245–47
The Greenbrier Companies, 19 185–87
Greene King plc, 31 223–26
Greene, Tweed & Company, 55 170–72
Greenfield Healthy Foods, **26** 58
Greenfield Industries Inc., **13** 8
Greenham Construction Materials, **38**
  451–52
Greenleaf Corp., **IV** 203
Greenman Brothers Inc. *See* Noodle
  Kidoodle.
GreenPoint Financial Corp., 28 166–68
Greensboro Life Insurance Company, **11**
  213
Greenville Insulating Board Corp., **III** 763
Greenville Tube Corporation, **21** 108
Greenwell Montagu Gilt-Edged, **II** 319; **17**
  325
Greenwich Associates, **19** 117
Greenwich Capital Markets, **II** 311
Greenwood Mills, Inc., 14 219–21
Greenwood Publishing Group, **IV** 610
Greenwood Trust Company, **18** 478
Gregg Publishing Co., **IV** 636
Greif Bros. Corporation, 15 186–88
Greiner Engineering Inc., **45** 421
Grenfell and Colegrave Ltd., **II** 245
Gresham Insurance Company Limited, **24**
  285
Gresham Life Assurance, **III** 200, 272–73
GretagMacbeth Holdings AG, **18** 291
Gretel's Pretzels, **35** 56
Gretsch & Brenner, **55** 150
Grey Advertising, Inc., I 175, 623; **6**
  26–28; 10 69; **14** 150; **22** 396; **25** 166,
  381
Grey United Stores, **II** 666
Grey Wolf, Inc., 43 201–03
Greyhound Corp., I 448–50; **II** 445; **6**
  27; **8** 144–45; **10** 72; **12** 199; **16** 349;
  22 406, 427; **23** 173–74; **27** 480; **42** 394
Greyhound Lines, Inc., 32 227–31
  (upd.); 48 319
Greyhound Temporary Services, **25** 432
Greylock Mills, **III** 213
GRiD Systems Corp., **II** 107
Griesheim Elektron, **IV** 140
Grieveson, Grant and Co., **II** 422–23
Griffin and Sons, **II** 543
Griffin Bacal, **25** 381
Griffin Land & Nurseries, Inc., 43
  204–06
Griffin Pipe Products Co., **7** 30–31
Griffin Wheel Company, **7** 29–30
Griffon Corporation, 34 194–96
Griffon Cutlery Corp., **13** 166
Grigg, Elliot & Co., **14** 555
Grimes Aerospace, **22** 32

Grindlays Bank, **II** 189
Gringoir/Broussard, **II** 556
Grinnell Corp., III 643–45; **11** 198; **13**
  245–47
Grip Printing & Publishing Co., **IV** 644
Grisewood & Dempsey, **IV** 616
Grist Mill Company, 15 189–91; 22 338
Gristede Brothers, **23** 407; **24** 528–29
Gristede's Sloan's, Inc., 31 231–33
GRM Industries Inc., **15** 247–48
Grocer Publishing Co., **IV** 638
Grocery Store Products Co., **III** 21
Grocery Warehouse, **II** 602
Groen Manufacturing, **III** 468
Grogan-Cochran Land Company, **7** 345
Grohe. *See* Friedrich Grohe AG & Co. KG.
Grolier Inc., IV 619; **16** 251–54; **43**
  207–11 (upd.)
Grolier Interactive, **41** 409
Grolsch. *See* Royal Grolsch NV.
Groot-Noordhollandsche, **III** 177–79
Groovy Beverages, **II** 477
Gross Brothers Laundry. *See* G&K
  Services, Inc.
Gross Townsend Frank Hoffman, **6** 28
Grosset & Dunlap, Inc., **II** 144; **III**
  190–91
Grosskraftwerk Franken AG, **23** 47
Grossman's Inc., 13 248–50
Grossmith Agricultural Industries, **II** 500
Grosvenor Marketing Co., **II** 465
Groton Victory Yard, **I** 661
Ground Round, Inc., 21 248–51
Ground Services Inc., **13** 49
Group Arnault, **32** 146
Group 4 Falck A/S, 42 165–68, 338
Group Health Cooperative, 41 181–84
Group Hospitalization and Medical
  Services, **10** 161
Group Lotus, **13** 357
Group Maeva SA, **48** 316
Group Maintenance America Corp. *See*
  Encompass Services Corporation.
Group 1 Automotive, Inc., 52 144–46
Group Schneider S.A., **20** 214
Groupe AB, **19** 204
Groupe AG, **III** 201–02
Groupe Air France, 6 92–94. *See also*
  Air France; Societe Air France.
Groupe Alain Manoukian, 55 173–75
Groupe Ancienne Mutuelle, **III** 210–11
Groupe André, 17 210–12. *See also*
  Vivarte SA.
Groupe Axime, **37** 232
Groupe Barrière SA, **48** 199
Groupe Barthelmey, **III** 373
Groupe Bisset, **24** 510
Groupe Bollore, **37** 21
Groupe Bruxelles Lambert, **26** 368
Groupe Bull, **10** 563–64; **12** 246; **21** 391;
  34 517. *See also* Compagnie des
  Machines Bull.
Groupe Casino. *See* Etablissements
  Economiques de Casino Guichard,
  Perrachon et Cie, S.C.A.
Groupe Castorama-Dubois
  Investissements, 23 230–32
Groupe Danone, 14 150; **32 232–36**
  (upd.); 55 359
Le Groupe Darty, **24** 266, 270
Groupe Dassault Aviation SA, 26 179–82
  (upd.); 42 373, 376
Groupe de la Cité, IV 614–16, 617
Groupe de la Financière d'Angers, **IV** 108

Groupe DMC (Dollfus Mieg & Cie), 27
  186–88
Groupe Fournier SA, 44 187–89
Groupe Go Sport S.A., 39 183–85; 54
  308
Groupe Guillin SA, 40 214–16
Groupe Jean-Claude Darmon, 44 190–92
Groupe Jean Didier, **12** 413
Groupe Jean-Paul Gaultier, **34** 214
Groupe Lagardère S.A., **15** 293; **21** 265,
  267
Groupe Lapeyre S.A., 33 175–77
Groupe Legris Industries, 23 233–35
Groupe Les Echos, 25 283–85
Groupe Partouche SA, 48 196–99
Groupe Pechiney, **33** 89
Groupe Pinault-Printemps-Redoute, **19** 306,
  309; **21** 224, 226
Groupe Poron, **35** 206
Groupe Promodès S.A., 19 326–28
Groupe Rallye, **39** 183–85
Groupe Rothschild, **22** 365
Groupe Rougier SA, 21 438–40
Groupe Roussin, **34** 13
Groupe Salvat, **IV** 619
Groupe SEB, 35 201–03
Groupe Sidel S.A., 21 252–55
Groupe Soufflet SA, 55 176–78
Groupe Tetra Laval, **53** 327
Groupe Victoire, **III** 394
Groupe Vidéotron Ltée., 20 271–73
Groupe Yves Saint Laurent, 23 236–39
Groupe Zannier S.A., 35 204–07
Groupement des Exploitants Pétroliers, **IV**
  545
Groupement des Mousquetaires. *See* ITM
  Entreprises SA.
Groupement Français pour l'Investissement
  Immobilier, **42** 153
Groupement Laitier du Perche, **19** 50
Groupement pour le Financement de la
  Construction. *See* Gecina SA.
GroupMAC. *See* Encompass Services
  Corporation.
Groux Beverage Corporation, **11** 451
Grove Manufacturing Co., **I** 476–77; **9** 393
Grow Biz International, Inc., 18 207–10
Grow Group Inc., 12 217–19, 387–88
Growing Healthy Inc., **27** 197; **43** 218
Growmark, **I** 421; **11** 23
Growth International, Inc., **17** 371
Grubb & Ellis Company, 21 256–58
Gruene Apotheke, **I** 681
Gruma, S.A. de C.V., 19 192; **31 234–36**
Grumman Corp., I 58–59, **61–63**, 67–68,
  78, 84, 490, 511; **7** 205; **8** 51; **9** 17,
  206–07, 417, 460; **10** 316–17, 536; **11**
  164–67 (upd.), 363–65, 428; **15** 285; **28**
  169
Grün & Bilfinger A.G., **I** 560–61; **55** 60
Grundig AG, I 411; **II** 80, 117; **12** 162;
  13 402–03; **15** 514; **27** 189–92; **48** 383;
  50 299
Grunenthal, **I** 240
Gruner + Jahr AG & Co., **IV** 590, 593; **7**
  245; **15** 51; **20** 53; **22** 442; **23** 85
Gruntal & Co., L.L.C., III 263; **20**
  274–76
Gruntal Financial Corp., **III** 264
Grupo Acerero del Norte, S.A. de C.V., **22**
  286; **42** 6
Grupo Aeropuerto del Sureste, S.A. de
  C.V., 48 200–02

Grupo Banco Bilbao Vizcaya Argentaria S.A., **54** 147
Grupo Bimbo, S.A. de C.V., **31** 236
Grupo Bufete. *See* Bufete Industrial, S.A. de C.V.
Grupo Cabal S.A., **23** 166
Grupo Campi, S.A. de C.V., **39** 230
Grupo Carso, S.A. de C.V., 14 489; **21 259–61**
Grupo Casa Saba, S.A. de C.V., 39 186–89
Grupo Corvi S.A. de C.V., **7** 115; **25** 126
Grupo Cruzcampo S.A., **34** 202
Grupo Cuervo, S.A. de C.V., **31** 91–92
Grupo Cydsa, S.A. de C.V., 39 190–93
Grupo de Ingenieria Ecologica, **16** 260
Grupo Dina. *See* Consorcio G Grupo Dina, S.A. de C.V.
Grupo Dragados SA, 55 179–82
Grupo DST, **41** 405–06
Grupo Editorial Random House Mondadori S.L., **54** 22
Grupo Elektra, S.A. de C.V., 39 194–97
Grupo Empresarial Angeles, **50** 373
Grupo Ferrovial, S.A., 40 217–19
Grupo Financiero Asemex-Banpais S.A., **51** 150
Grupo Financiero Banamex S.A., 27 304; **54 143–46**
Grupo Financiero Banorte, S.A. de C.V., 51 149–51
Grupo Financiero BBVA Bancomer S.A., 54 147–50
Grupo Financiero Inbursa, **21** 259
Grupo Financiero Inverlat, S.A., **39** 188
Grupo Financiero Serfin, S.A., 19 188–90, 474; **36** 63
Grupo Gigante, S.A. de C.V., 34 197–99
Grupo Hecali, S.A., **39** 196
Grupo Herdez, S.A. de C.V., 35 208–10; **54** 167
Grupo Hermes, **24** 359
Grupo ICA, **52** 394
Grupo IMSA, S.A. de C.V., 44 193–96
Grupo Industrial Alfa, S.A. de C.V., **44** 332. *See also* Alfa, S.A. de C.V.
Grupo Industrial Atenquique, S.A. de C.V., **37** 176
Grupo Industrial Bimbo, 19 191–93; 29 338
Grupo Industrial Durango, S.A. de C.V., 37 176–78
Grupo Industrial Maseca S.A. de C.V. (Gimsa). *See* Gruma, S.A. de C.V.
Grupo Industrial Saltillo, S.A. de C.V., 54 151–54
Grupo Irsa, **23** 171
Grupo Lladró S.A., 52 147–49
Grupo Mexico, S.A. de C.V., 40 220–23, 413
Grupo Modelo, S.A. de C.V., 29 218–20
Grupo Nacional Provincial, **22** 285
Grupo Pipsamex S.A., **37** 178
Grupo Protexa, **16** 210
Grupo Pulsar. *See* Pulsar Internacional S.A.
Grupo Quan, **19** 192–93
Grupo Salinas, **39** 196
Grupo Sanborns S.A. de C.V., **35** 118
Grupo Servia, S.A. de C.V., **50** 209
Grupo TACA, 38 218–20
Grupo Televisa, S.A., 9 429; **18 211–14; 19** 10; **24** 515–17; **39** 188, 398; **54 155–58 (upd.)**
Grupo TMM, S.A. de C.V., 50 208–11

Grupo Transportación Ferroviaria Mexicana, S.A. de C.V., 47 162–64
Grupo Tribasa, **34** 82
Grupo Tudor, **IV** 471
Grupo Xtra, **39** 186, 188
Grupo Zeta, **IV** 652–53; **7** 392
Gruppo Banco di Napoli, **50** 410
Gruppo Buffetti S.p.A., **47** 345–46
Gruppo Coin S.p.A., 41 185–87
Gruppo Editoriale L'Espresso S.p.A., **54** 19–21
Gruppo GFT, **22** 123
Gruppo IRI, **V** 325–27
Gryphon Development, **24** 237
Gryphon Holdings, Inc., 21 262–64
GS Financial Services L.P., **51** 148
GSD&M Advertising, 44 197–200
GSG&T, **6** 495
GSG Holdings Ltd., **39** 87
GSI. *See* Geophysical Service, Inc.
GSI Acquisition Co. L.P., **17** 488
GSR, Inc., **17** 338
GSU. *See* Gulf States Utilities Company.
GT Bicycles, 26 183–85, 412
GT Interactive Software, 19 405; **31 237–41.** *See also* Infogrames Entertainment S.A.
GTE Corporation, II 38, 47, 80; **III** 475; **V 294–98;** 9 49, 171, 478–80; **10** 19, 97, 431; **11** 500; **14** 259, 433; **15 192–97 (upd.); 18** 74, 111, 543; **22** 19; **25** 20–21, 91; **26** 520; **27** 302, 305; **46** 373; **50** 299. *See also* British Columbia Telephone Company; Verizon Communications.
GTE Northwest Inc., **37** 124–26
GTECH Holdings, Inc., **27** 381
GTI Corporation, **29** 461–62
GTM-Entrepose, **23** 332
GTM Group, **43** 450, 452; **54** 392
GTO. *See* Global Transport Organization.
GTS Duratek, Inc., **13** 367–68
GTSI. *See* Government Technology Services Inc.
GU Markets, **55** 83
Guangzhou M. C. Packaging, **10** 130
Guangzhou Pearl River Piano Group Ltd., 49 177–79
Guangzhou Railway Corporation, **52** 43
Guaranty Bank & Trust Company, **13** 440
Guaranty Federal Bank, F.S.B., **31** 441
Guaranty Federal Savings & Loan Assoc., **IV** 343
Guaranty Properties Ltd., **11** 258
Guaranty Savings and Loan, **10** 339
Guaranty Trust Co., **II** 329–32, 428; **IV** 20; **16** 25; **22** 110; **36** 152; **50** 30
Guardforce Limited, **45** 378
Guardian, **III** 721
Guardian Bank, **13** 468
Guardian Federal Savings and Loan Association, **10** 91
Guardian Media Group plc, 53 152–55
Guardian Mortgage Company, **8** 460
Guardian National Bank, **I** 165; **11** 137
Guardian Refrigerator Company. *See* Frigidaire Home Products.
Guardian Royal Exchange Plc, III 350; **11 168–70; 33** 319
Gubor Schokoladen, **15** 221
Gucci Group N.V., 45 343–44; **50 212–16 (upd.); 54** 320
Guccio Gucci, S.p.A., 12 281; **15 198–200; 27** 329

GUD Holdings, Ltd., **17** 106
Guelph Dolime, **IV** 74
Guerbet Group, 46 214–16
Guerdon Homes, Inc., **41** 19
Guerlain, 23 240–42; 33 272
Guernsey Banking Co., **II** 333
Guess, Inc., 15 201–03; 17 466; **23** 309; **24** 157; **27** 329
Guest, Keen and Nettlefolds plc. *See* GKN plc.
Guest Supply, Inc., 18 215–17
Gueyraud et Fils Cadet, **III** 703
Guidant Corp., **30** 316; **37** 39; **43** 351
Guideoutdoors.com Inc., **36** 446
Guilbert S.A., 42 169–71; 55 355
Guild Press, Inc., **13** 559
Guild Wineries, **13** 134; **34** 89
Guilford Industries, **8** 270–72
Guilford Mills Inc., 8 234–36; 40 224–27 (upd.)
Guilford of Maine, Inc., **29** 246
Guilford Transportation Industries, Inc., **16** 348, 350
Guillemot Corporation, 41 188–91, 407, 409
Guillin. *See* Groupe Guillin SA
Guinness Mahon, **36** 231
Guinness Overseas Ltd., **25** 281
Guinness Peat Aviation, **10** 277; **36** 426
Guinness plc, I 239, 241, **250–52,** 268, 272, 282; **II** 428–29, 610; **9** 100, 449; **10** 399; **13** 454; **18** 62, 501; **29** 84; **33** 276; **36** 405–06. *See also* Diageo plc.
Guinness/UDV, 43 212–16 (upd.)
Guitar Center, Inc., 29 221–23
Guittard Chocolate Company, 55 183–85
Gujarat State Fertilizer Co., **III** 513
Gulco Industries, Inc., **11** 194
Güldner Aschaffenburg, **I** 582
Gulf + Western Inc., I 418, **451–53,** 540; **II** 147, 154–56, 177; **III** 642, 745; **IV** 289, 672; **7** 64; **10** 482; **13** 121, 169, 470; **22** 210; **24** 33; **25** 328, 535; **33** 3; **41** 71; **51** 165
Gulf + Western Industries, **22** 122. *See also* Paramount Communications.
Gulf Air, **6** 63; **27** 25; **39** 137–38
Gulf Canada Ltd., **I** 216, 262, 264; **IV** 495, 721; **6** 478; **9** 391; **13** 557–58
Gulf Caribbean Marine Lines, **6** 383
Gulf Coast Sportswear Inc., **23** 65
Gulf Energy Development, **22** 107
Gulf Engineering Co. Ltd., **IV** 131
Gulf Exploration Co., **IV** 454
Gulf Island Fabrication, Inc., 44 201–03
Gulf Marine & Maintenance Offshore Service Company, **22** 276
Gulf Mobile and Northern Railroad, **I** 456
Gulf Mobile and Ohio Railroad, **I** 456; **11** 187
Gulf of Suez Petroleum Co., **IV** 412–14
Gulf Oil Chemical Co., **13** 502
Gulf Oil Corp., **I** 37, 584; **II** 315, 402, 408, 448; **III** 225, 231, 259, 497; **IV** 198, 287, 385–87, 392, 421, 450–51, 466, 470, 472–73, 476, 484, 508, 510, 512, 531, 538, 565, 570, 576; **17** 121–22; **21** 494; **24** 521; **25** 444; **33** 253
Gulf Plains Corp., **III** 471
Gulf Power Company, **38** 446, 448
Gulf Public Service Company, Inc, **6** 580; **37** 89
Gulf Resources & Chemical Corp., **15** 464

Gulf States Paper, **IV** 345
Gulf States Steel, **I** 491
Gulf States Utilities Company, 6 495–97; **12** 99
Gulf United Corp., **III** 194
GulfMark Offshore, Inc., 49 180–82
Gulfstream Aerospace Corporation, 7 205–06; **13** 358; **24** 465; **28** 169–72 (upd.); **36** 190–91
Gulfstream Banks, **II** 336
Gulfwind Marine USA, **30** 303
Gulistan Holdings Inc., **28** 219
Gulton Industries Inc., **7** 297; **19** 31
Gummi Werke, **I** 208; **44** 218
Gump's, **7** 286
Gunder & Associates, **12** 553
Gunderson, Inc. See The Greenbrier Companies.
Gunfred Group, **I** 387
Gunite Corporation, 23 306; **51 152–55**
The Gunlocke Company, 12 299; **13** 269; **23 243–45**
Gunnebo AB, 53 156–58
Gunnite, **27** 203
Gunns Ltd., **II** 482
Gunpowder Trust, **I** 379; **13** 379
Gunter Wulff Automaten, **III** 430
Gunther, S.A., **8** 477
Gupta, **15** 492
Gurneys, Birkbeck, Barclay & Buxton, **II** 235
Gurwitch Bristow Products, LLC, **49** 285
GUS plc, 47 165–70 (upd.); 54 38, 40
Gusswerk Paul Saalmann & Sohne, **I** 582
Gustav Schickendanz KG, **V** 165
Gustavus A. Pfeiffer & Co., **I** 710
Gustin-Bacon Group, **16** 8
Gutehoffnungshütte Aktienverein AG, **III** 561, 563; **IV** 104, 201
Guthrie Balfour, **II** 499–500
Guthy-Renker Corporation, 32 237–40
Gutta Percha Co., **I** 428
Gutteridge, Haskins & Davey, **22** 138
Gutzeit. See W. Gutzeit & Co.
Guy Carpenter & Co., **III** 282
Guy Degrenne SA, 44 204–07
Guy Motors, **13** 286
Guy Pease Associates, **34** 248
Guy Salmon Service, Ltd., **6** 349
Guyenne et Gascogne, 23 246–48
Guyomarc'h, **39** 356
GW Utilities Ltd., **I** 264; **6** 478
Gwathmey Siegel & Associates Architects LLC, II 424; **13** 340; **26 186–88**
GWC. See General Waterworks Corporation.
GWK GmbH, **45** 378
GWR Group plc, 39 198–200
Gymboree Corporation, 15 204–06
Gynecare Inc., **23** 190
Gynetics, Inc., **26** 31
Gypsum, Lime, & Alabastine Canada Ltd., **IV** 271

H&D. See Hinde & Dauch Paper Company.
H&H Craft & Floral, **17** 322
H & H Plastics Co., **25** 312
H & R Block, Incorporated, 9 268–70; **25** 434; **27** 106, 307; **29 224–28 (upd.);** **48** 234, 236; **52** 316
H.A. Job, **II** 587
H.B. Claflin Company, **V** 139

H.B. Fenn and Company Ltd., **25** 485
H.B. Fuller Company, 8 237–40; **32** 254–58 (upd.)
H.B. Nickerson & Sons Ltd., **14** 339
H.B. Reese Candy Company, **II** 511; **51** 157
H.B. Tuttle and Company, **17** 355
H.B. Viney Company, Inc., **11** 211
H. Berlind Inc., **16** 388
H.C. Christians Co., **II** 536
H.C. Frick Coke Co., **IV** 573; **7** 550
H.C. Petersen & Co., **III** 417
H.C. Prange Co., **19** 511–12
H Curry & Sons. See Currys Group PLC.
H.D. Lee Company, Inc. See Lee Apparel Company, Inc.
H.D. Pochin & Co., **III** 690
H.D. Vest, Inc., 46 217–19
H. Douglas Barclay, **8** 296
H.E. Butt Grocery Company, 13 251–53; **32 259–62 (upd.); 33** 307
H.E. Moss and Company Tankers Ltd., **23** 161
H.F. Ahmanson & Company, II 181–82; **10 342–44 (upd.); 28** 167; **47** 160
H. Fairweather and Co., **I** 592
H.G. Anderson Equipment Corporation, **6** 441
H.H. Brown Shoe Company, **18** 60, **18** 62
H.H. Cutler Company, **17** 513
H.H. Robertson, Inc., **19** 366
H.H. West Co., **25** 501
H. Hackfeld & Co., **I** 417
H. Hamilton Pty, Ltd., **III** 420
H.I.G. Capital L.L.C., **30** 235
H.I. Rowntree and Co., **II** 568
H.J. Heinz Company, I 30–31, 605, 612; **II** 414, 480, 450, **507–09**, 547; **III** 21; **7** 382, 448, 576, 578; **8** 499; **10** 151; **11** **171–73 (upd.); 12** 411, 529, 531–32; **13** 383; **21** 55, 500–01; **22** 147; **25** 517; **27** 197–98; **33** 446–49; **36 253–57 (upd.);** **43** 217–18
H.J. Justin & Sons. See Justin Industries, Inc.
H.K. Ferguson Company, **7** 355
H.K. Porter Company, Inc., **19** 152
H.L. Green Company, Inc., **9** 448
H.L. Judd Co., **III** 628
H.L. Yoh Company. See Day & Zimmerman, Inc.
H. Lewis and Sons, **14** 294
H. Lundbeck A/S, 44 208–11
H.M. Byllesby & Company, Inc., **6** 539
H.M. Goush Co., **IV** 677–78
H.M. Spalding Electric Light Plant, **6** 592; **50** 37
H. Miller & Sons, Inc., **11** 258
H N Norton Co., **11** 208
H.O. Houghton & Company, **10** 355
H.O. Systems, Inc., **47** 430
H-P. See Hewlett-Packard Co.
H.P. Foods, **II** 475
H.P. Hood, **7** 17–18
H.P. Smith Paper Co., **IV** 290
H.R. MacMillan Export Co., **IV** 306–08
H. Reeve Angel & Co., **IV** 300
H. Salt Fish and Chips, **13** 320
H.T. Cherry Company, **12** 376
H.V. McKay Proprietary, **III** 651
H.W. Heidmann, **I** 542
H.W. Johns Manufacturing Co., **III** 663, 706–08; **7** 291

H.W. Madison Co., **11** 211
H.W.S. Solutions, **21** 37
H.W. Wilson Company, **17** 152; **23** 440
H. Williams and Co., Ltd., **II** 678
Ha-Lo Industries, Inc., 27 193–95
Häagen-Dazs, **II** 556–57, 631; **10** 147; **14** 212, 214; **19** 116; **24** 140, 141
Haake-Beck Brauerei AG, **9** 86
Haas, Baruch & Co. See Smart & Final, Inc.
Haas Corp., **I** 481
Haas Publishing Companies, Inc., **22** 442
Haas Wheat & Partners, **15** 357
Habersham Bancorp, 25 185–87
Habirshaw Cable and Wire Corp., **IV** 177
Habitat for Humanity International, 36 258–61
Habitat/Mothercare PLC. See Storehouse PLC.
Hach Co., **14** 309; **18 218–21**
Hachette Filipacchi Medias S.A., 21 **265–67; 33** 310
Hachette S.A., IV 614–15, **617–19**, 675; **10** 288; **11** 293; **12** 359; **16** 253–54; **17** 399; **21** 266; **22** 441–42; **23** 476; **43** 210. See also Matra-Hachette S.A.
Hachmeister, Inc., **II** 508; **11** 172
Haci Omer Sabanci Holdings A.S., 55 186–89
Hacker-Pschorr Brau, **II** 242; **35** 331
Hackman Oyj Adp, 44 204, **212–15**
Hadco Corporation, 24 201–03
Hadleigh-Crowther, **I** 715
Haemocell, **11** 476
Haemonetics Corporation, 20 277–79
Hafez Insurance Co., **III** 242
Haftpflichtverband der Deutschen Industrie Versicherung auf Gegenseitigkeit V.a.G. See HDI (Haftpflichtverband der Deutschen Industrie Versicherung auf Gegenseitigkeit V.a.G.).
Hagemeyer N.V., 18 180–82; **39 201–04;** **45** 426; **54** 203
Haggar Corporation, 19 194–96; 24 158
Haggen Inc., 38 221–23
Haggie, **IV** 91
Hägglunds Vehicle AB, **47** 7, 9
Hahn Automotive Warehouse, Inc., 24 **204–06**
Hahn Department Stores. See Allied Stores Corp.
Hahn, Inc., **17** 9
Haile Mines, Inc., **12** 253
The Hain Celestial Group, Inc., 43 **217–20 (upd.)**
Hain Food Group, Inc., I 514; **27** **196–98; 36** 256
Hainaut-Sambre, **IV** 52
A.B. Hakon Swenson, **II** 639
Hakuhodo, Inc., 6 29–31, 48–49; **16** 167; **42 172–75 (upd.)**
Hakunetsusha & Company, **12** 483
HAL Inc., 6 104; **9 271–73.** See also Hawaiian Airlines, Inc.
Halcon International, **IV** 456
Hale and Dorr, **31** 75
Haleko Hanseatisches Lebensmittel Kontor GmbH, **29** 500
Halewood, **21** 246
Half Price Books, Records, Magazines Inc., 37 179–82
Halfords Ltd., **IV** 17, 19, 382–83; **24** 75
Halifax Banking Co., **II** 220
Halifax Timber, **I** 335

Halkin Holdings plc, **49** 338–39
Hall & Levine Agency, **I** 14
Hall and Co., **III** 737
Hall and Ham River, **III** 739
Hall Bros. Co., **IV** 620–21; **7** 23
Hall Containers, **III** 739
Hall, Kinion & Associates, Inc., 52 150–52
Hall Laboratories, Inc., **45** 209
Hall-Mark Electronics, **23** 490
Hallamore Manufacturing Co., **I** 481
La Halle aux Chaussures, **17** 210
Haller, Raymond & Brown, Inc., **II** 10
Halliburton Company, II 112; **III** 473, **497–500,** 617; **11** 505; **13** 118–19; **17** 417; **25 188–92 (upd.); 55 190–95 (upd.)**
Hallivet China Clay Co., **III** 690
Hallmark Cards, Inc., IV 620–21; **7** 23–25; **12** 207, 209; **16 255–57 (upd.),** 427; **18** 67, 69, 213; **21** 426–28; **22** 33, 36; **24** 44, 516–17; **25** 69, 71, 368; **28** 160; **29** 64; **39** 87; **40 228–32 (upd.); 45** 131
Hallmark Chemical Corp., **8** 386
Hallmark Holdings, Inc., **51** 190
Hallmark Investment Corp., **21** 92
Hallmark Residential Group, Inc., **45** 221
Halo Lighting, **30** 266
Haloid Company. *See* Xerox Corporation.
Halsam Company, **25** 380
Halsey, Stuart & Co., **II** 431; **III** 276
Halstead Industries, **26** 4; **52** 258
Halter Marine, **22** 276
Hamada Printing Press, **IV** 326
Hamashbir Lata'asiya, **II** 47; **25** 267
Hambrecht & Quist Group, **10** 463, 504; **26** 66; **27** 447; **31** 349
Hambro American Bank & Trust Co., **11** 109
Hambro Countrywide Security, **32** 374
Hambro Life Assurance Ltd., **I** 426; **III** 339
Hambros Bank, **II** 422; **16** 14; **27** 474; **43** 7
Hamburg-Amerikanische-Packetfahrt-Actien-Gesellschaft, **6** 397–98
Hamburg Banco, **II** 351
Hamburg-Amerika, **I** 542
Hamburger Flugzeubau GmbH., **I** 74
Hamelin Group, Inc., **19** 415
Hamer Hammer Service, Inc., **11** 523
Hamersley Holdings, **IV** 59–61
Hamil Textiles Ltd. *See* Algo Group Inc.
Hamilton Aero Manufacturing, **I** 47, 84; **10** 162
Hamilton Beach/Proctor-Silex Inc., 7 369–70; **16** 384; **17 213–15; 24** 435; **43** 289
Hamilton Blast Furnace Co., **IV** 208
Hamilton Brown Shoe Co., **III** 528
Hamilton Group Limited, **15** 478
Hamilton Industries, Inc., **25** 261
Hamilton Malleable Iron Co., **IV** 73; **24** 142
Hamilton National Bank, **13** 465
Hamilton Oil Corp., **IV** 47; **22** 107
Hamilton Standard, **9** 417
Hamilton Steel and Iron Co., **IV** 208
Hamilton/Hall-Mark, **19** 313
Hamish Hamilton, **IV** 659; **8** 526
Hammacher Schlemmer & Company, 21 268–70; 26 439–40
Hammamatsu Commerce Bank, **II** 291

Hammarplast, **13** 493
Hammarsforsens Kraft, **IV** 339
Hammerich & Lesser, **IV** 589
Hammermill Paper Co., **IV** 287; **15** 229; **23** 48–49; **47** 189
Hammers Plastic Recycling, **6** 441
Hammerson plc, 40 233–35
Hammerson Property Investment and Development Corporation PLC, IV 696–98; 26 420
Hammery Furniture Company, **14** 302–03
Hammes Co., **38** 482
Hamming-Whitman Publishing Co., **13** 559
Hammond Corp., **IV** 136
Hammond Lumber Co., **IV** 281; **9** 259
Hammond's, **II** 556
Hammonton Electric Light Company, **6** 449
Hamomag AG, **III** 546
Hampton Industries, Inc., 20 280–82
Hampton Inns, **9** 425–26
Hampton Roads Food, Inc., **25** 389
Hamworthy Engineering Ltd., **31** 367, 369
Han Kook Fertilizer Co., **I** 516
Hanbury, Taylor, Lloyd and Bowman, **II** 306
Hancock Fabrics, Inc., 16 197–99; **18 222–24**
Hancock Holding Company, 15 207–09
Hancock Jaffe Laboratories, **11** 460
Hancock Park Associates. *See* Leslie's Poolmart, Inc.
Hancock Textile Co., Inc., **27** 291
Hand in Hand, **III** 234
Handelsbank of Basel, **III** 375
Handelsfinanz Bank of Geneva, **II** 319; **17** 324
Handelsmaatschappij Montan N.V., **IV** 127
Handelsunion AG, **IV** 222
Handleman Company, 15 210–12
Handley Page Transport Ltd., **I** 50, 92–93; **24** 85
Handspring Inc., 49 183–86
Handy & Harman, 23 249–52
Handy Andy Home Improvement Centers, Inc., **16** 210; **26** 160–61
Handy Dan, **V** 75
Hanes Corp., **II** 572–73; **8** 202, 288; **15** 436; **25** 166
Hanes Holding Company, **11** 256; **48** 267
Hang Chong, **18** 114
Hang Seng Bank, **II** 298; **IV** 717
Hanger Orthopedic Group, Inc., 41 192–95
Haniel & Cie. GmbH, **27** 175
Hanil Development Company, **6** 98
Hanjin Group, **6** 98; **27** 271–72
Hanjin Shipping Co., Ltd., 50 217–21
Hankook Tyre Manufacturing Company, **V** 255–56; **19** 508
Hankuk Glass Industry Co., **III** 715
Hankyu Corporation, V 454–56; 23 253–56 (upd.)
Hankyu Department Stores, Inc., V 70–71
Hanley Brick, **14** 250
Hanmi Citizen Precision Industry, **III** 455
Hanna Andersson Corp., 49 187–90
Hanna-Barbera Cartoons Inc., 7 306; **18** 65; **23 257–59,** 387; **25** 313; **33** 432
Hanna Iron Ore Co., **IV** 236; **26** 528
Hanna Mining Co., **8** 346–47
Hanna Ore Mining Company, **12** 352
Hannaford Bros. Co., 12 220–22

Hannen Brauerei GmbH, **9** 100
Hannifin Corp., **III** 602
HANNOVER International AG für Industrieversicherungen, **53** 162
Hannover Papier, **49** 353
Hannoversche Bank, **II** 278
Hanover Bank, **II** 312–13
Hanover Direct, Inc., 36 262–65
Hanover Foods Corporation, 35 211–14
Hanover House, Inc., **24** 154
Hanovia Co., **IV** 78
Hanrstoffe-und Düngemittelwerk Saar-Lothringen GmbH, **IV** 197
Hans Grohe, **III** 570; **20** 362
Hansa Linie, **26** 279–80
Hanseco Reinsurance Co., **III** 343
Hansen Natural Corporation, 31 242–45
Hanson Industries, **44** 257
Hanson PLC, I 438, 475, 477; **III 501–03,** 506; **IV** 23, 94, 97, 169, 171, 173, 290; **7 207–10 (upd.); 13** 478–79; **17** 39–40, 325; **23** 296–97; **27** 287–88; **30 228–32 (upd.),** 441; **37** 6–7, 205; **39** 345; **45** 332; **50** 57
Hansvedt Industries Inc., **25** 195
Hapag-Lloyd Ag, 6 397–99; **42** 283
Happy Air Exchangers Ltd., **21** 499
Happy Eater Ltd., **III** 106
Happy Kids Inc., 30 233–35
Haralambos Beverage Corporation, **11** 451
Harald Quant Group, **III** 377
Harbert Corporation, 13 98; **14 222–23**
Harbison-Walker Refractories Company, III 472; **24 207–09**
Harbor Group, **41** 262–63
Harbor Tug and Barge Co., **6** 382
Harborlite Corporation, **10** 45
Harbour Group, **24** 16
Harco, Inc., **37** 31
Harcourt Brace and Co., IV 622; **12 223–26**
Harcourt Brace Jovanovich, Inc., II 133–34; **III** 118; **IV** 622–24, 642, 672; **7** 312; **12** 224; **13** 106; **14** 177; **19** 404; **25** 177
Harcourt General, Inc., 12 226; **20 283–87 (upd.); 25** 178; **49** 286
Harcros Chemical Group, **III** 699
Harcros Investment Trust Ltd., **III** 698–99
Hard Rock Cafe International, Inc., 12 227–29; **25** 387; **27** 201; **32 241–45 (upd.); 37** 191; **41** 308
Hardee's Food Systems Inc., **II** 679; **7** 430; **8** 564; **9** 178; **15** 345; **16** 95; **19** 93; **23** 505; **27** 16–18; **46** 98
Hardin Stockton, **21** 96
Harding Lawson Associates Group, Inc., 16 258–60
Hardinge Inc., 25 193–95
Hardison & Stewart Oil, **IV** 569; **24** 519
Hardman Inc., **III** 699
Hardware Wholesalers Inc., **12** 8. *See also* Do it Best Corporation.
Hardwick Stove Company, **III** 573; **22** 349
Hardy Oil & Gas, **34** 75
Hardy Spicer, **III** 595
HARIBO GmbH & Co. KG, 44 216–19
Harima Shipbuilding & Engineering Co., Ltd., **I** 511, 534; **III** 513, 533; **12** 484
Harima Zosenjo, Ltd., **IV** 129
Harken Energy Corporation, **17** 169–70
Harland and Wolff Holdings plc, 19 197–200
Harlem Globetrotters, **7** 199, 335

Harlequin Enterprises Limited, IV 587, 590, 617, 619, 672; **19** 405; **29** 470–71, 473; **52 153–56**

Harley-Davidson, Inc., III 658; **7 211–14**; **13** 513; **16** 147–49; **21** 153; **23** 299–301; **25** 22, **196–200 (upd.)**; **40** 31

Harleysville Group Inc., **37 183–86**

Harlow Metal Co. Ltd., IV 119

Harman International Industries Inc., **15 213–15**; **36** 101

Harmon Industries, Inc., **25 201–04**

Harmon Publishing Company, **12** 231

Harmonic Inc., **43 221–23**

Harmsworth Brothers, **17** 396

Harmsworth Publishing, **19** 118, 120

Harnischfeger Industries, Inc., I 186; **8 241–44**; **14** 56; **26** 355; **38 224–28 (upd.)**

Harold A. Wilson & Co., I 405

Harold's Stores, Inc., **22 248–50**

Harp Lager Ltd., **15** 442; **35** 395, 397

Harper Group Inc., **12** 180; **13** 20; **17 216–19**

Harper House, Inc. *See* Day Runner, Inc.

Harper Robinson and Company, **17** 163

HarperCollins Publishers, IV 652; **7** 389, 391; **14** 555–56; **15 216–18**; **23** 156, 210; **24** 546; **46** 196, 311

Harpers, Inc., **12** 298; **48** 245

Harpo Entertainment Group, **28 173–75**; **30** 270

Harrah's Entertainment, Inc., **9 425–27**; **16 261–63**; **27** 200; **43 224–28 (upd.)**

Harrell International, III 21; **22** 146

Harriman Co., IV 310; **19** 266

Harriman, Ripley and Co., II 407

Harris Abattoir Co., II 482

Harris Adacom Corporation B.V., **21** 239

Harris Bankcorp, II 211; **46** 55

Harris Corporation, II 37–39; **11** 46, 286, 490; **20 288–92 (upd.)**; **27** 364

Harris Daishowa (Australia) Pty., Ltd., IV 268

Harris-Emery Co., **19** 510

Harris Financial, Inc., **11** 482

Harris Interactive Inc., **41 196–99**

Harris Laboratories, II 483; **14** 549

Harris Manufacturing Company, **25** 464

Harris Microwave Semiconductors, **14** 417

Harris Oil Company, **17** 170

Harris Pharmaceuticals Ltd., **11** 208

Harris Publications, **13** 179

Harris Publishing. *See* Bernard C. Harris Publishing Company, Inc.

Harris Queensway, **24** 269

Harris Teeter Inc., **23 260–62**

Harris Transducer Corporation, **10** 319

Harrisburg National Bank and Trust Co., II 315–16

Harrison & Sons (Hanley) Ltd., III 681

Harrisons & Crosfield plc, III 696–700. *See also* Elementis plc.

Harrods Holdings, , **21** 353; **45** 188; **47 171–74**

Harron Communications Corporation, **52** 9

Harrow Stores Ltd., II 677

Harry and David. *See* Bear Creek Corporation.

Harry F. Allsman Co., III 558

Harry Ferguson Co., III 651

Harry N. Abrams, Inc., IV 677; **17** 486

Harry Winston Inc., **45 184–87**

Harry's Farmers Market Inc., **23 263–66**

Harry's Premium Snacks, **27** 197; **43** 218

Harsah Ceramics, **25** 267

Harsco Corporation, **8 245–47**; **11** 135; **30** 471

Harshaw Chemical Company, **9** 154; **17** 363

Harshaw/Filtrol Partnership, IV 80

Hart Glass Manufacturing, III 423

Hart Press, **12** 25

Hart Schaffner & Marx. *See* Hartmarx Corporation.

Hart Son and Co., I 592

Harte & Co., IV 409; **7** 308

Harte-Hanks Communications, Inc., **17 220–22**

Harter Bank & Trust, **9** 474–75

Hartford Container Company, **8** 359

Hartford Electric Light Co., **13** 183

Hartford Financial Services Group, **41** 64

Hartford Fire Insurance, **11** 198

Hartford Insurance Group, I 463–64; **22** 428

Hartford Machine Screw Co., **12** 344

Hartford National Bank and Trust Co., **13** 396

Hartford National Corporation, **13** 464, 466–67

Hartford Trust Co., II 213

Hartley's, II 477

Hartmann & Braun, III 566; **38** 299

Hartmann Fibre, **12** 377

Hartmann Luggage, **12** 313

Hartmarx Corporation, **8 248–50**; **25** 258; **32 246–50 (upd.)**

The Hartstone Group plc, **14 224–26**

The Hartz Mountain Corporation, **12 230–32**; **46 220–23 (upd.)**

Harvard Private Capital Group Inc., **26** 500, 502

Harvard Sports, Inc., **19** 144

Harvard Table Tennis, Inc., **19** 143–44

Harvard Ventures, **25** 358

Harvest Day, **27** 291

Harvest International, III 201

Harvest Partners, Inc., **40** 300; **52** 139

Harvestore, **11** 5

Harvey Aluminum Inc., I 68; **22** 188

Harvey Benjamin Fuller, **8** 237–38

Harvey Group, **19** 312

Harvey Hotel Corporation, **23** 71, 73

Harvey Lumber and Supply Co., III 559

Harveys Casino Resorts, **27 199–201**

Harwood Homes, **31** 386

Harza Engineering Company, **14 227–28**

Has.net, **48** 402

Hasbro, Inc., III 504–06; IV 676; **7** 305, 529; **12** 168–69, 495; **13** 561; **16 264–68 (upd.)**; **17** 243; **18** 520–21; **21** 375; **25** 313, 380–81, 487–89; **28** 159; **34** 369; **43 229–34 (upd.)**; **52** 192–93, 206

Haslemere Estates, **26** 420

Hasler Holding AG, **9** 32

Hassenfeld Brothers Inc., III 504

Hasten Bancorp, **11** 371

Hastings Entertainment, Inc., **29 229–31**

Hastings Filters, Inc., **17** 104

Hastings Manufacturing Company, **17** 106

Hatch Grinding, **29** 86, 88

Hatersley & Davidson, **16** 80

Hatfield Jewelers, **30** 408

Hathaway Manufacturing Co., III 213

Hathaway Shirt Co., I 25–26

Hatteras Yachts Inc., **45** 175

Hattori Seiko Co., Ltd. *See* Seiko Corporation.

HAULOTTE, **51** 295

Hauser, Inc., **46 224–27**

Hausted, Inc., **29** 451

Havas, SA, IV 616; **10** 195–96, **345–48**; **13** 203–04; **33 178–82 (upd.)**; **34** 83. *See also* Vivendi Universal Publishing

Haven Automation International, III 420

Haverty Furniture Companies, Inc., **31 246–49**

Havertys, **39** 174

Haviland Candy Co., **15** 325

Hawaii National Bank, **11** 114

Hawaiian Airlines Inc., **9 271–73**; **22 251–53 (upd.)**; **24** 20–22; **26** 339. *See also* HAL Inc.

Hawaiian Dredging & Construction Co., I 565–66

Hawaiian Electric Industries, Inc., **9 274–77**

Hawaiian Fertilizer Co., II 490

Hawaiian Pineapple Co., II 491

Hawaiian Tug & Barge, **9** 276

Hawaiian Tuna Packers, II 491

Hawk Model Co., **51** 368

Hawker Siddeley Group Public Limited Company, I 41–42, 50, 71, 470; III 507–10; **8** 51; **12** 190; **20** 311; **24** 85–86

Hawkeye Cablevision, II 161

Hawkins Chemical, Inc., **16 269–72**

Hawley & Hazel Chemical Co., III 25

Hawley Group Limited, **12** 10

Hawley Products, **16** 20

Haworth Inc., **8 251–52**; **27** 434; **39 205–08 (upd.)**

Hawthorn Company, **8** 287

Hawthorn-Mellody, I 446; **11** 25

Hawthorne Appliance and Electronics, **10** 9–11

Haxton Foods Inc., **21** 155

Hay Group, I 33; **42** 329–30

Hayakawa Electrical Industries, II 95–96

Hayakawa Metal Industrial Laboratory, II 95; **12** 447

Hayaku Zenjiro, III 408

Hayama Oil, IV 542

Hayashi Kane Shoten, II 578

Hayashikane Shoten K.K., II 578

Hayden Clinton National Bank, **11** 180

Hayden Publications, **27** 499

Hayden Stone, II 450; **9** 468

Hayes Aircraft Corp., **54** 283

Hayes Conyngham & Robinson, **24** 75

Hayes Corporation, **24 210–14**; **53** 381

Hayes Industries Inc., **16** 7

Hayes Lemmerz International, Inc., **27 202–04**

Hayes Microcomputer Products, **9** 515

Hayes Wheel Company, **7** 258

Hayne, Miller & Swearingen, Inc., **22** 202

Hays Petroleum Services, IV 451

Hays Plc, **27 205–07**

Hazard, I 328

HAZCO International, Inc., **9** 110

Hazel-Atlas Glass Co., I 599; **15** 128

Hazel Bishop, III 55

Hazelden Foundation, **28 176–79**

Hazell Sun Ltd., IV 642; **7** 312

Hazeltine, Inc., II 20

Hazlenut Growers of Oregon, **7** 496–97

Hazleton Laboratories Corp., **30** 151

Hazlewood Foods plc, **32 251–53**

Hazzard and Associates, **34** 248
HBO. *See* Home Box Office Inc.
**HCA—The Healthcare Company, 35
215–18 (upd.)**
HCI Direct, Inc., 55 196–98
HCI Holdings, **I** 264
HCL America, **10** 505
HCL Sybase, **10** 505
HCR Manor Care, **25** 306, 310
HCS Technology, **26** 496–97
**HDI (Haftpflichtverband der Deutschen
Industrie Versicherung auf
Gegenseitigkeit V.a.G.), 53 159–63**
HDM Worldwide Direct, **13** 204; **16** 168
HdP. *See* Holding di Partecipazioni
Industriali S.p.A.
HDR Inc., I 563; **48 203–05**
HDS. *See* Heartland Express, Inc.
Head N.V., 55 199–201
Head Sportswear International, **15** 368; **16**
296–97; **43** 374
Headrick Outdoor, **27** 280
Heads and Threads, **10** 43
**Headway Corporate Resources, Inc., 40
236–38**
Headway Technologies, Inc., **49** 392–93
Heal's, **13** 307
Heald Machine Co., **12** 67
Healey & Baker, **IV** 705
Healing Arts Publishing, Inc., **41** 177
Healix Health Services Inc., **48** 310
Health & Tennis Corp., **III** 431; **25** 40
Health and Diet Group, **29** 212
**Health Care & Retirement Corporation,
III** 79; **22 254–56**; **25** 306, 310
Health Care International, **13** 328
Health Development Corp., **46** 432
Health Maintenance Organization of
Pennsylvania. *See* U.S. Healthcare, Inc.
Health Maintenance Organizations, **I** 545
Health Management Center West, **17** 559
Health-Mor Inc. *See* HMI Industries.
**Health O Meter Products Inc., 14
229–31**; **15** 307
Health Plan of America, **11** 379
Health Plan of Virginia, **III** 389
Health Products Inc., **I** 387
**Health Risk Management, Inc., 24
215–17**
Health Services, Inc., **10** 160
**Health Systems International, Inc., 11
174–76**; **25** 527
Health Way, Inc., **II** 538
HealthAmerica Corp., **III** 84
Healthcare, L.L.C., **29** 412
HealthCare USA, **III** 84, 86
HealthCo International, Inc., **19** 290
Healthdyne, Inc., **17** 306–09; **25** 82
Healthmagic, Inc., **29** 412
HealthRider Corporation, **38** 238
HealthRite, Inc., **45** 209
Healthshares L.L.C, **18** 370
Healthsource Inc., **22** 143; **45** 104, 109
**HealthSouth Corporation, 33 183–86
(upd.)**
**HealthSouth Rehabilitation Corporation,
14 232–34**; **25** 111
Healthtex, Inc., 17 223–25, 513
HealthTrust, **III** 80; **15** 112; **35** 215, 217
Healthy Choice, **12** 531
The Hearst Corporation, IV 582, 596,
608, **625–27**; **12** 358–59; **19 201–204
(upd.)**; **21** 404; **22** 161; **32** 3; **46**

228–32 **(upd.)**; **51** 218–20; **54** 17, 22,
74
Hearthstone Insurance Co. of
Massachusetts, **III** 203
Heartland Building Products, **II** 582
Heartland Components, **III** 519; **22** 282
Heartland Express, Inc., 13 550–51; **18
225–27**
Heartland Homes, Inc., **41** 19
Heartland Industrial Partners L.P., **41** 94
Heartland Securities Corp., **32** 145
Heartstream Inc., **18** 423
The Heat Group, 53 164–66
Heat Transfer Pty. Ltd., **III** 420
Heatcraft Inc., **8** 320–22
Heath Co., **II** 124; **13** 573; **34** 516
Heath Steele Mines Ltd., **IV** 18
Heatilator Inc., **13** 269
Heating & Cooling Supply, Inc., **52**
398–99
Heavy Duty Parts, Inc., **19** 37
Hebrew National Kosher Foods, **III** 24
Hechinger Company, 12 233–36; **28** 51
Hecker-H-O Co., **II** 497
Heckett Technology Services Inc., **8**
246–47
Heckler & Koch GmbH, **24** 88
Hecla Mining Company, 17 363; **20** 149,
293–96
Heco Envelope Co., **IV** 282; **9** 261
Hede Nielsen A/S, **47** 219
Heekin Can Inc., 10 130; **13 254–56**
HEFCO, **17** 106
Hefei Rongshida Group Corporation, **22**
350
Hegenscheidt-MFD GmbH & Co. KG, **53**
352
HEI Investment Corp., **9** 276
HEICO Corporation, 15 380; **30 236–38**
Heide Park, **55** 378
Heidelberger Druckmaschinen AG, III
701; **33** 346; **40 239–41**
Heidelberger Zement AG, 23 325–26; **31
250–53**
Heidelburger Drueck, **III** 301
Heidemij. *See* Arcadis NV.
Heidi Bakery, **II** 633
**Heidrick & Struggles International, Inc.,
14** 464; **28 180–82**
Heights of Texas, fsb, **8** 437
Heil Company, **28** 103
Heil-Quaker Corp., **III** 654
Heileman Brewing Co. *See* G. Heileman
Brewing Co.
Heilig-Meyers Company, 14 235–37; **23**
412, 414; **40 242–46 (upd.)**
Heim-Plan Unternehmensgruppe, **25** 455
Heimstatt Bauspar AG, **III** 401
Heineken N.V., I 219, **256–58**, 266, 288;
II 642; **13 257–59 (upd.)**; **14** 35; **17**
256; **18** 72; **21** 319; **25** 21–22; **26** 305;
34 200–04 (upd.)
Heinkel Co., **I** 74
Heinrich Bauer North America, **7** 42–43
Heinrich Bauer Verlag, **23** 85–86
Heinrich Koppers GmbH, **IV** 89
Heinrich Lanz, **III** 463; **21** 173
Heinz Co. *See* H.J. Heinz Company.
Heinz Deichert KG, **11** 95
Heinz Italia S.p.A., **15** 221
Heisers Inc., **I** 185
Heisey Glasswork Company, **19** 210
Heiwa Sogo Bank, **II** 326, 361
Heizer Corp., **III** 109–11; **14** 13–15

HEL&P. *See* Houston Electric Light &
Power Company.
Helados La Menorquina S.A., **22** 515
Helemano Co., **II** 491
Helen of Troy Corporation, 18 228–30
Helen's Arts & Crafts, **17** 321
Helena Rubenstein, Inc., **III** 24, 48; **8**
343–44; **9** 201–02; **14** 121; **30** 188; **35**
111; **46** 277
Helene Curtis Industries, Inc., I 403; **8
253–54**; **18** 217; **22** 487; **28 183–85
(upd.)**; **32** 476
Heliotrope Studios, Inc., **39** 396
Helix Biocore, **11** 458
Hellefors Jernverk, **III** 623
**Heller, Ehrman, White & McAuliffe, 41
200–02**
Heller Financial, Inc., **7** 213; **16** 37; **25** 198
Hellman, Haas & Co. *See* Smart & Final,
Inc.
Hellschreiber, **IV** 669
Helly Hansen ASA, 18 396; **25 205–07**
Helme Products, Inc., **15** 139
Helmerich & Payne, Inc., 18 231–33
Helmsley Enterprises, Inc., 9 278–80; **39
209–12 (upd.)**
Helmut Delhey, **6** 428
Helmuth Hardekopf Bunker GmbH, **7** 141
Help-U-Sell, Inc., **III** 304
Helvetia General, **III** 376
Helvetia Milk Condensing Co., **II** 486; **7**
428
Helvetia Schweizerische
Feuerversicherungs-Gesellschaft St.
Gallen, **III** 375
Hely Group, **IV** 294; **19** 225
Helzberg Diamonds, 18 60, 63; **40
247–49**
Hemelinger Aktienbrauerei, **9** 86
Hemex, **11** 458
Hemlo Gold Mines Inc., 9 281–82; **23** 40,
42
Hemma, **IV** 616
A.B. Hemmings, Ltd., **II** 465
Henderson Brothers Holdings, Inc., **37** 225
Henderson-Union Electric Cooperative, **11**
37
Henderson's Industries, **III** 581
Henijean & Cie, **III** 283
Henkel KGaA, III 21, **31–34**, 45; **IV** 70;
9 382; **13** 197, 199; **22** 145, 257; **30**
291; **34** 153, **205–10 (upd.)**; **51** 223–25
Henkel Manco Inc., 22 257–59
Henkell & Söhnlein Sektkellereien KG, **51**
102, 105
Henley Drilling Company, **9** 364
The Henley Group, Inc., I 416; **III**
511–12; **6** 599–600; **9** 298; **11** 435; **12**
325; **17** 20; **37** 158
Henlys Group plc, **35** 63, 65
Hennes & Mauritz AB, 29 232–34
Hennessy Company, **19** 272
Henney Motor Company, **12** 159
Henredon Furniture Industries, **III** 571; **11**
534; **20** 362; **39** 266
Henri Bendel Inc., **17** 203–04
Henry Broderick, Inc., **21** 96
Henry Denny & Sons, **27** 259
Henry Grant & Co., **I** 604
Henry Holt & Co., **IV** 622–23; **13** 105; **27**
223; **35** 451
Henry I. Siegel Co., **20** 136
Henry J. Kaiser Company, Ltd., **28** 200
Henry J. Tully Corporation, **13** 531

The Henry Jones Co-op Ltd., **7** 577
Henry Jones Foods, **I** 437–38, 592; **7** 182; **11** 212
Henry L. Doherty & Company, **IV** 391; **12** 542
Henry Lee Company, **16** 451, 453
Henry, Leonard & Thomas Inc., **9** 533
Henry Meadows, Ltd., **13** 286
Henry Modell & Company Inc., 32 263–65
Henry Pratt Company, **7** 30–31
Henry S. King & Co., **II** 307
Henry S. Miller Companies, **21** 257
Henry Schein, Inc., 29 298; **31 254–56**
Henry Tate & Sons, **II** 580
Henry Telfer, **II** 513
Henry Waugh Ltd., **I** 469; **20** 311
Henry Willis & Co. See Willis Corroon Group Plc.
Henthy Realty Co., **III** 190
HEPCO. See Hokkaido Electric Power Company Inc.
Hepworth plc, **44** 438
Her Majesty's Stationery Office, 7 215–18
Heraeus Holding GmbH, IV 98–100, 118; **54 159–63 (upd.)**
Herald and Weekly Times, **IV** 650, 652; **7** 389, 391
Herald Publishing Company, **12** 150
Heralds of Liberty, **9** 506
Herbalife International, Inc., 17 226–29; 18 164; **41 203–06 (upd.)**
Herbert Clough Inc., **24** 176
Herbert W. Davis & Co., **III** 344
Herby's Foods, **36** 163
Herco Technology, **IV** 680
Hercofina, **IV** 499
Hercules Filter, **III** 419
Hercules Inc., I 343–45, 347; **III** 241; **19** 11; **22 260–63 (upd.); 28** 195; **30** 36
Hercules Nut Corp., **II** 593
Hercules Offshore Drilling, **28** 347–48
Hereford Paper and Allied Products Ltd., **14** 430
Herff Jones, **II** 488; **25** 254
Heritage Bankcorp, **9** 482
Heritage Communications, **II** 160–61
Heritage Federal Savings and Loan Association of Huntington, **10** 92
Heritage House of America Inc., **III** 81
Heritage Life Assurance, **III** 248
Heritage Media Group, **25** 418
Heritage National Health Plan, **III** 464
Heritage Springfield $$Heritage Springfield, **14** 245
Herley Industries, Inc., 33 187–89
Herman Goelitz, Inc., 28 186–88
Herman Miller, Inc., 8 251–52, **255–57; 39** 205–07
Herman's World of Sports, **I** 548; **II** 628–29; **15** 470; **16** 457; **43** 385; **50** 524
Hermann Pfauter Group, **24** 186
Hermannshütte, **IV** 103, 105
Hermès International S.A., 34 211–14 (upd.); 49 83
Hermes Kreditversicherungsbank, **III** 300
Hermès S.A., 14 238–40
Hermosillo, **51** 389
Herrburger Brooks P.L.C., **12** 297
Herrick, Waddell & Reed. See Waddell & Reed, Inc.
Herring-Hall-Marvin Safe Co. of Hamilton, Ohio, **7** 145

Hersey Products, Inc., **III** 645
Hershey Bank, **II** 342
Hershey Foods Corporation, I 26–27; **II** 478, 508, **510–12,** 569; **7** 300; **11** 15; **12** 480–81; **15** 63–64, **219–22 (upd.),** 323; **27** 38–40; **30** 208–09; **51 156–60 (upd.); 53** 241
Hertel AG, **13** 297
Hertford Industrial Estates, **IV** 724
Hertie Waren- und Kaufhaus GmbH, V 72–74; 19 234, 237
Herts & Beds Petroleum Co., **IV** 566
Herts Pharmaceuticals, **17** 450; **41** 375–76
The Hertz Corporation, I 130; **II** 90; **6** 52, 129, 348–50, 356–57, 392–93; **V** 494; **9 283–85; 10** 419; **11** 494; **16** 379; **21** 151; **22** 54, 56, 524; **24** 9, 409; **25** 143; **33 190–93 (upd.); 36** 215
Hertz-Penske Leasing. See Penske Corporation.
Hervillier, **27** 188
Heska Corporation, 39 213–16
Hespeler Hockey Inc., **22** 204
Hess. See Amerada Hess Corporation.
Hess Department Stores Inc., **16** 61–62; **19** 323–24; **41** 343; **50** 107
Hessische Berg- und Hüttenwerke AG, **III** 695
Hessische Landesbank, **II** 385–86
Hessische Ludwigs-Eisenbahn-Gesellschaft, **6** 424
Hesston Corporation, **13** 17; **22** 380
Hetteen Hoist & Derrick. See Polaris Industries Inc.
Heublein Inc., I 226, 246, 249, **259–61,** 281; **7** 266–67; **10** 180; **14** 214; **21** 314–15; **24** 140; **25** 177; **31** 92; **34** 89
Heuer. See TAG Heuer International SA.
Heuga Holdings B.V., **8** 271
Hewitt & Tuttle, **IV** 426; **17** 355–56
Hewitt Motor Company, **I** 177; **22** 329
Hewlett-Packard Company, II 62; **III** 116, **142–43; 6** 219–20, 225, **237–39 (upd.),** 244, 248, 278–79, 304; **8** 139, 467; **9** 7, 35–36, 57, 115, 471; **10** 15, 34, 86, 232, 257, 363, 404, 459, 499, 501; **11** 46, 234, 274, 284, 382, 491, 518; **12** 61, 147, 162, 183, 470; **13** 128, 326, 501; **14** 354; **15** 125; **16** 5, 139–40, 299, 301, 367, 394, 550; **18** 386–87, 434, 436, 571; **19** 515; **20** 8; **25** 96, 118, 151–53, 499, 531; **26** 177, 520; **27** 221; **28 189–92 (upd.); 33** 15; **36** 3, 81–82, 299–300; **38** 20, 187, 417–19; **41** 117, 288; **43** 294; **50 222–30 (upd.); 51** 150
Hexalon, **26** 420
Hexatec Polymers, **III** 742
Hexcel Corporation, 11 475; **27** 50; **28 193–95**
Heyden Newport Chemical Corp., **I** 526
Heyer-Schulte, **26** 286
Heytesbury Party Ltd., **34** 422
HFC. See Household Finance Corporation.
HFS Inc., **21** 97; **22** 54, 56; **53** 275
HG Hawker Engineering Co. Ltd., **III** 508
HGCC. See Hysol Grafil Composite Components Co.
HH Finch Ltd., **38** 501
HI. See Houston Industries Incorporated.
Hi-Bred Corn Company, **9** 410
Hi-Lo Automotive, Inc., **26** 348–49
Hi-Mirror Co., **III** 715
Hi Tech Consignments, **18** 208

Hi-Tek Polymers, Inc., **8** 554
Hibbett Sporting Goods, Inc., 26 189–91
Hibbing Transportation, **I** 448
Hibernia & Shamrock-Bergwerksgesellschaft zu Berlin, **I** 542–43
Hibernia Bank, **18** 181
Hibernia Corporation, 37 187–90
Hibernian Banking Assoc., **II** 261
Hickman Coward & Wattles, **24** 444
Hickory Farms, Inc., 12 178, 199; **17 230–32**
Hickorycraft, **III** 571; **20** 362
Hicks & Greist, **6** 40
Hicks & Haas, **II** 478
Hicks, Muse, Tate & Furst, Inc., **24** 106; **30** 220; **36** 423; **55** 202
Hicksgas Gifford, Inc., **6** 529
Hidden Creek Industries, Inc., **16** 397; **24** 498
HiFi Buys, **30** 465
Higginson et Hanckar, **IV** 107
Higgs & Young Inc., **I** 412
Higgs International Ltd., **51** 130
High Integrity Systems, **51** 16
High Point Chemical Corp., **III** 38
High Retail System Co., Ltd., **V** 195; **47** 391
Highgate Hotels, Inc., **21** 93
Highland Container Co., **IV** 345
Highland Superstores, **9** 65–66; **10** 9–10, 304–05, 468; **23** 51–52
Highland Telephone Company, **6** 334
Highlander Publications, **38** 307–08
Highlands Insurance Co., **III** 498
Highmark Inc., I 109; **27 208–11**
Highveld Steel and Vanadium Corp., **IV** 22
Higo Bank, **II** 291
Hilbun Poultry, **10** 250
Hilco Technologies, **III** 143; **6** 238
Hildebrandt International, 29 235–38
Hilex Poly Co., Inc., **8** 477
Hill & Knowlton Inc. See WPP Group PLC.
Hill Publishing Co., **IV** 634
Hill-Rom Company, **10** 349–50
Hill Stores, **II** 683
Hill's Pet Nutrition, Inc., 14 123; **26** 207; **27 212–14,** 390. See also Colgate-Palmolive Company.
Hillard Oil and Gas Company, Inc., **11** 523
Hillards, PLC, **II** 678
Hillenbrand Industries, Inc., 6 295; **10 349–51; 16** 20
Hiller Aircraft Company, **9** 205; **48** 167
Hiller Group, **14** 286
Hillerich & Bradsby Company, Inc., 24 403; **51 161–64**
The Hillhaven Corporation, III 76, 87–88; **6** 188; **14 241–43; 16** 57, 515, 517; **25** 307, 456
Hillin Oil, **IV** 658
Hillman, **I** 183
Hillos GmbH, **53** 169
Hills & Dales Railway Co. See Dayton Power & Light Company.
Hills Brothers Inc., **II** 548; **7** 383; **28** 311
Hills Pet Products, **III** 25
Hills Stores Company, 11 228; **13 260–61; 21** 459; **30** 57
Hillsborough Holdings Corporation. See Walter Industries, Inc.
Hillsdale Machine & Tool Company, **8** 514

Hillsdown Holdings, PLC, II 513–14; 24 218–21 (upd.); 28 490; **41** 252
Hillshire Farm, **II** 572
Hillside Industries Inc., **18** 118
Hilo Electric Light Company, **9** 276
Hilti AG, 53 167–69
Hilton, Anderson and Co., **III** 669
Hilton Athletic Apparel, **16** 296–97
Hilton Gravel, **III** 670
Hilton Group plc, 49 191–95 (upd.), 449–50
Hilton Hotels Corporation, II 208; **III 91–93**, 98–99, 102; **IV** 703; **6** 201, 210; **9** 95, 426; **19 205–08 (upd.); 21** 91, 93, 182, 333, 363; **23** 482; **27** 10; **54** 345–46. *See also* Hilton Group plc.
Hilton International Co., **6** 385; **12** 489
Himley Brick, **14** 248
Himolene, Inc., **8** 181
Hinde & Dauch Ltd., **IV** 272
Hinde & Dauch Paper Company, **19** 496
Hindell's Dairy Farmers Ltd., **II** 611–12
Hinds, Hayden & Eldredge, **10** 135
Hindustan Petroleum Corp. Ltd., **IV** 441
Hindustan Shipyard, **IV** 484
Hindustan Steel Ltd., **IV** 205–07
Hines Horticulture, Inc., 49 196–98
Hino Motors, Ltd., 7 219–21; 21 163, **271–74 (upd.); 23** 288
Hinode Life Insurance Co., Ltd., **II** 360; **III** 365
Hinomaru Truck Co., **6** 428
HIP Health Plan, **22** 425
Hip Hing Construction Company Limited, **IV** 717; **38** 319
Hipercor, S.A., **V** 52; **26** 129
Hiram Walker Resources Ltd., I 216, **262–64; IV** 721; **6** 478; **9** 391; **18** 41
Hiram Walker-Consumers' Home Ltd. *See* Consumers' Gas Company Ltd.
Hiram Walker-Gooderham & Worts Ltd., **29** 18
Hire-Purchase Company of Ireland, **16** 13; **43** 7
Hiroshima Yakult Co., **25** 449
The Hirsh Company, **17** 279
Hirth-Krause Company. *See* Wolverine World Wide Inc.
Hirz, **25** 85
Hispanic Broadcasting Corporation, 35 219–22; 41 383, 385
Hispanica de Petroleos, **IV** 424, 527, 546
Hispano Aviacion, **I** 74
HISPANOBRAS, **IV** 55
Hispanoil. *See* Hispanica de Petroleos.
Hispeed Tools, **I** 573
Hisshin-DCA foods, **II** 554
History Book Club, **13** 105–06
Hit de Venezuela, **54** 73
HIT Entertainment PLC, 40 250–52
Hit or Miss, **V** 197–98
Hitachi, Ltd., I 454–55, 494, 534; **II** 5, 30, 59, 64–65, 68, 70, 73, 75, 114, 273–74, 292–91; **III** 130, 140, 143, 464, 482; **IV** 101; **6** 238, 262; **7** 425; **9** 297; **11** 45, 308, 507; **12 237–39 (upd.)**, 484; **14** 201; **16** 139; **17** 353, 556; **18** 383; **19** 11; **21** 174–75, 390; **23** 53; **24** 324; **40 253–57 (upd.)**
Hitachi Metals, Ltd., IV 101–02
Hitachi Zosen Corporation, III 513–14; 8 449; **53 170–73 (upd.)**
Hitchiner Manufacturing Co., Inc., 23 267–70

Hitco, **III** 721–22
Hjalmar Blomqvist A.B., **II** 639
HL&P. *See* Houston Lighting and Power Company.
HLH Products, **7** 229
HMI Industries, Inc., 17 233–35
HMO-PA. *See* U.S. Healthcare, Inc.
HMSHost, **49** 31
HMT Technology Corp., **IV** 102
HMV, **I** 531
Hoan Products Ltd. *See* Lifetime Hoan Corporation.
Hoare Govett Ltd., **II** 349
HOB Entertainment, Inc., 37 191–94
Hobart Corporation, **II** 534; **III** 610–11, 654; **7** 276; **12** 549; **22** 282, 353
Hobart Manufacturing Company, **8** 298
Hobbes Manufacturing, **I** 169–70
Hobby Lobby Stores Inc., **17** 360
Hobson, Bates & Partners, Ltd., **14** 48
Hochschild, Kohn Department Stores, **II** 673
Hochtief AG, 14 298; **17** 376; **24** 88; **33 194–97**
The Hockey Company, 34 215–18
Hocking Glass Company, **13** 40
Hockleys Professional Limited, **55** 281
Hoden Oil, **IV** 478
Hodenpyl-Walbridge & Company, **14** 134
Hodgart Consulting. *See* Hildebrandt International.
Hodgkin, Barnett, Pease, Spence & Co., **II** 307
Hoechst AG, I 305–06, 309, 317, **346–48**, 605, 632, 669–70; **IV** 451; **8** 262, 451–53; **13** 75, 262–64; **18** 47, 49, 51, **234–37 (upd.)**, 401; **21** 544; **22** 32; **25** 376; **34** 284; **35** 455–57; **38** 380; **50** 420
Hoechst Celanese Corporation, 8 562; **11** 436; **12** 118; **13** 118, **262–65; 22** 278; **24** 151; **26** 108; **54** 51–52
Hoeganaes Corporation, **8** 274–75
Hoenig Group Inc., 41 207–09
Hoerner Waldorf Corp., **IV** 264; **20** 129
Hoesch AG, IV 103–06, 128, 133, 195, 228, 232, 323
Hofbräubierzentrale GmbH Saarbrücken, **41** 222
Hoffman Enclosures Inc., **26** 361, 363
Hoffmann-La Roche & Co. *See* F. Hoffmann- La Roche & Co.
Hoffritz, **27** 288
Hofmann Herbold & Partner, **34** 249
Hogan & Hartson L.L.P., 44 220–23; 47 445–46
Högbo Stål & Jernwerks, **IV** 202
Högforsin Tehdas Osakeyhtiö, **IV** 300
Hogue Cellars, **50** 520
Hohner. *See* Matth. Hohner AG.
Hojalata y Laminas S.A., **19** 10
Hojgaard & Schultz, **38** 436
Hokkaido Butter Co., **II** 575
Hokkaido Colonial Bank, **II** 310
Hokkaido Dairy Cooperative, **II** 574
Hokkaido Dairy Farm Assoc., **II** 538
Hokkaido Electric Power Company Inc., V 635–37
Hokkaido Forwarding, **6** 428
Hokkaido Rakuno Kosha Co., **II** 574
Hokkaido Takushoku Bank, **II** 300
Hokoku Cement, **III** 713
Hokoku Fire, **III** 384
Hokuetsu Paper Manufacturing, **IV** 327

Hokuriku Electric Power Company, V 638–40
Hokusin Kai, **IV** 475
Hokuyo Sangyo Co., Ltd., **IV** 285
Holberg Industries, Inc., 36 266–69
Holbrook Grocery Co., **II** 682
Holcemca B.V., **51** 29
Holcim, Ltd., **51** 27, 29
Holco BV, **41** 12
Holcroft & Company, **7** 521
Hold Everything, **17** 548–50
Holden Group, **II** 457
Holderbank Financière Glaris Ltd., III 701–02; 8 258–59, 456; **39** 217. *See also* Holnam Inc
Holding di Partecipazioni Industriali S.p.A., **52** 120, 122
N.V. Holdingmaatschappij De Telegraaf, 23 271–73
Holec Control Systems, **26** 496
Holes-Webway Company, **40** 44
Holga, Inc., **13** 269
Holgate Toys, **25** 379–80
Holiday Corp., 16 263; **22** 418; **38** 76; **43** 226
Holiday Inns, Inc., I 224; **III 94–95**, 99–100; **6** 383; **9** 425–26; **10** 12; **11** 178, 242; **13** 362; **14** 106; **15** 44, 46; **16** 262; **18** 216; **21** 361–62; **23** 71; **24** 253; **25** 386; **27** 21. *See also* The Promus Cos., Inc.
Holiday Magic, Inc., **17** 227
Holiday Mart, **17** 124; **41** 114–15
Holiday Rambler Corporation, **7** 213; **25** 198
Holiday RV Superstores, Incorporated, 26 192–95
Holland & Barrett, **13** 103; **31** 346, 348
Holland & Holland, **49** 84
Holland America Line, **6** 367–68; **26** 279; **27** 90–91
Holland Burgerville USA, 44 224–26
Holland Casino, **23** 229
Holland Electro B.V., **17** 234
Holland Hannen and Cubitts, **III** 753
Holland House, **I** 377–78
Holland Motor Express, **14** 505
Holland Studio Craft, **38** 402
Holland van 1859, **III** 200
Hollandsche Bank-Unie, **II** 184–85
Hollandse Signaalapparaten, **13** 402; **50** 300
Holley Carburetor, **I** 434
Holley Performance Products Inc., 52 157–60
Hollinger International Inc., 24 222–25; 32 358
Hollingsead International, Inc., **36** 158–60
Hollingsworth & Whitney Co., **IV** 329
Hollostone, **III** 673
Holly Corporation, 12 240–42
Holly Farms Corp., **II** 585; **7** 422–24; **14** 515; **23** 376–77; **50** 492
Holly Sugar Company. *See* Imperial Holly Corporation.
Hollywood Casino Corporation, 21 275–77
Hollywood Entertainment Corporation, 25 208–10; 29 504; **31** 339
Hollywood Park, Inc., 20 297–300
Hollywood Park Race Track, **29** 118
Hollywood Pictures, **II** 174; **30** 487
Hollywood Records, **6** 176
Holme Roberts & Owen LLP, 28 196–99

Holmen AB, 52 161–65 (upd.)
Holmen Hygiene, **IV** 315
Holmen S.A., **IV** 325
Holmens Bruk, **IV** 317–18
Holmes Electric Protective Co., **III** 644
Holmes International. *See* Miller Industries, Inc.
Holmsund & Kramfors, **IV** 338
Holnam Inc., III 702; **8** 258–60; **39** 217–20 (upd.)
Holophane Corporation, 19 209–12; **54** 255
Holson Burnes Group, Inc., 14 244–45
Holsten Brauerei AG, **35** 256, 258
Holt Manufacturing Co., **III** 450–51
Holt, Rinehart and Winston, Inc., **IV** 623–24; **12** 224
Holt's Cigar Holdings, Inc., 42 176–78
Holthouse Furniture Corp., **14** 236
Holtzbrinck. *See* Verlagsgruppe Georg von Holtzbrinck.
Holvick Corp., **11** 65
Holvis AG, **15** 229
Holyman Sally Ltd., **29** 431
Holyoke Food Mart Inc., **19** 480
Holzer and Co., **III** 569; **20** 361
Holzverkohlungs-Industrie AG, **IV** 70
Homart Development, **V** 182
Home & Automobile Insurance Co., **III** 214
Home and Community Care, Inc., **43** 46
Home Box Office Inc., II 134, 136, 166–67, 176–77; **IV** 675; **7** 222–24, 528–29; **10** 196; **12** 75; **18** 65; **23** 274–77 (upd.), 500; **25** 498; **28** 71
Home Builders Supply, Inc. *See* Scotty's, Inc.
Home Centers of America, Inc., **18** 286
Home Charm Group PLC, **II** 141
Home Choice Holdings, Inc., **33** 366–67
The Home Depot, Inc., V 75–76; **9** 400; **10** 235; **11** 384–86; **12** 7, 235, 345, 385; **13** 250, 548; **16** 187–88, 457; **17** 366; **18** 238–40 (upd.); **19** 248, 250; **21** 356, 358; **22** 477; **23** 232; **26** 306; **27** 416, 481; **31** 20; **35** 11–13; **39** 134; **43** 385; **44** 332–33
Home Entertainment of Texas, Inc., **30** 466
Home Furnace Co., **I** 481
Home Insurance Company, I 440; **III** 262–64
Home Interiors & Gifts, Inc., 15 475, 477; **55** 202–04
Home Nutritional Services, **17** 308
Home Office Reference Laboratory, Inc., **22** 266
Home Oil Company Ltd., **I** 264; **6** 477–78
Home Products International, Inc., 18 492; **55** 205–07
Home Properties Co., Inc., **21** 95
Home Properties of New York, Inc., 42 179–81
Home Quarters Warehouse, Inc., **12** 233, 235
Home Savings of America, **II** 181–82; **10** 342–43; **16** 346; **28** 167; **47** 160
The Home School, Inc., **41** 111
Home Shopping Network, Inc., V 77–78; **9** 428; **18** 76; **24** 517; **25** 211–15 (upd.); **26** 441; **33** 322
Home Telephone and Telegraph Company, **10** 201
Home Telephone Company. *See* Rochester Telephone Corporation.

Home Vision Entertainment Inc., **31** 339–40
HomeBase, Inc., II 658; **13** 547–48; **33** 198–201 (upd.)
HomeBuyers Preferred, Inc., **51** 210
HomeClub Inc., **13** 547–48; **16** 187; **17** 366. *See also* HomeBase, Inc.
Homécourt, **IV** 226
HomeFed Bank, **10** 340
Homegrocer.com Inc., **38** 223
Homelite, **21** 175
Homemade Ice Cream Company, **10** 371
Homemakers Furniture. *See* John M. Smyth Co.
HomeMax, Inc., **41** 20
Homer McKee Advertising, **I** 22
Homes By Oakwood, Inc., **15** 328
Homeserve.net Ltd., **46** 72
Homestake Mining Company, IV 18, 76; **12** 243–45; **20** 72; **27** 456; **38** 229–32 (upd.)
Hometown Auto Retailers, Inc., 44 227–29
HomeTown Buffet, Inc., **19** 435; **22** 465. *See also* Buffets, Inc
Homette Corporation, **30** 423
Homewood Stores Co., **IV** 573; **7** 550
Homewood Suites, **9** 425–26
Hominal Developments Inc., **9** 512
Hon Industries Inc., 13 266–69; **23** 243–45
Honam Oil Refinery, **II** 53
Honcho Real Estate, **IV** 225; **24** 489
Honda Giken Kogyo Kabushiki Kaisha. *See* Honda Motor Company Limited.
Honda Motor Company Limited, I 9–10, 32, **174–76**, 184, 193; **II** 5; **III** 495, 517, 536, 603, 657–58, 667; **IV** 443; **7** 212–13, 459; **8** 71–72; **9** 294, 340–42; **10** 352–54 (upd.); **11** 33, 49–50, 352; **12** 122, 401; **13** 30; **16** 167; **17** 25; **21** 153; **23** 289–90, 338, 340; **25** 197–99; **27** 76; **29** 239–42 (upd.); **34** 305–06; **36** 243; **55** 326
Hondo Oil & Gas Co., **IV** 375–76
Honeywell Inc., I 63; **II** 30, **40–43**, 54, 68; **III** 122–23, 149, 152, 165, 535, 548–49, 732; **6** 266, 281, 283, 314; **8** 21; **9** 171, 324; **11** 198, 265; **12** 246–49 (upd.); **13** 234, 499; **17** 33; **18** 341; **22** 373, 436; **23** 471; **29** 464; **30** 34; **33** 334, 337; **43** 284; **50** 231–35 (upd.)
Hong Kong Aircraft Engineering Co., **I** 522; **6** 79; **16** 480
Hong Kong Airways, **6** 78–79; **16** 480
Hong Kong and Kowloon Wharf and Godown Co., **I** 470; **IV** 699
Hong Kong Dragon Airlines, **18** 114
Hong Kong Industrial Co., Ltd., **25** 312
Hong Kong Island Line Co., **IV** 718
Hong Kong Mass Transit Railway Corp., **19** 111
Hong Kong Ming Wah Shipping Co., **52** 80
Hong Kong Resort Co., **IV** 718; **38** 320
Hong Kong Telecommunications Ltd., IV 700; **V** 285–86; **6** 319–21; **18** 114; **25** 101–02. *See also* Cable & Wireless HKT.
Hong Kong Telephone Company, **47** 177
Hong Leong Corp., **III** 718
Hong Leong Group Malaysia, **26** 3, 5
Hongkong & Kowloon Wharf & Godown Company, **20** 312

Hongkong and Shanghai Banking Corporation Limited, II 257, 296–99, 320, 358; **III** 289; **17** 325; **18** 253; **25** 12. *See also* HSBC Holdings plc.
Hongkong Electric Company Ltd., 6 498–500; **20** 134
Hongkong Electric Holdings Ltd., 23 278–81 (upd.); **47** 177
Hongkong Land Holdings Ltd., I 470–71; **IV** 699–701; **6** 498–99; **20** 312–13; **23** 280; **47** 175–78 (upd.)
Honig-Copper & Harrington, **I** 14
Honjo Copper Smeltery, **III** 490
Honolua Plantation Land Company, Inc., **29** 308
Honolulu Oil, **II** 491
Honolulu Sugar Refining Co., **II** 490
Honshu Paper Co., Ltd., IV 268, **284–85**, 292, 297, 321, 326
Hood Rubber Company, **15** 488–89
Hood Sailmakers, Inc., **10** 215
Hoogovens. *See* Koninklijke Nederlandsche Hoogovens en Staalfabrieken NV.
Hooiberg, **I** 256
Hook's Drug Stores, **9** 67
Hooker Chemical, **IV** 481
Hooker Corp., **19** 324
Hooker Furniture Corp. *See* Bassett Furniture Industries, Inc.
Hooker Petroleum, **IV** 264
Hooper Holmes, Inc., 22 264–67
Hoosier Insurance Company, **51** 39
Hoosier Park L.P., **29** 118
Hooters of America, Inc., 18 241–43
Hoover Ball and Bearing Co., **III** 589
The Hoover Company, II 7; **III** 478; **12** 158, 250–52; **15** 416, 418; **21** 383; **30** 75, 78; **40** 258–62 (upd.)
Hoover Group Inc., **18** 11
Hoover Industrial, **III** 536; **26** 230
Hoover-NSK Bearings, **III** 589
Hoover Treated Wood Products, Inc., **12** 396
Hopkinton LNG Corp., **14** 126
Hopper Soliday and Co. Inc., **14** 154
Hops Restaurant Bar and Brewery, 31 41; **46** 233–36
Hopwood & Company, **22** 427
Horace Mann Educators Corporation, 22 268–70
Horizon Air Industries, Inc. *See* Alaska Air Group, Inc.
Horizon Bancorp, **II** 252; **14** 103
Horizon Corporation, **8** 348
Horizon Group Inc., **27** 221
Horizon Healthcare Corporation, **25** 456
Horizon Holidays, **14** 36
Horizon Industries, **19** 275
Horizon Lamps, Inc., **48** 299
Horizon Organic Holding Corporation, 37 195–99
Horizon Travel Group, **8** 527
Horizon/CMS Healthcare Corp., **25** 111, 457; **33** 185
Horizons Laitiers, **25** 85
Hormel Foods Corporation, 18 244–47 (upd.); **54** 164–69 (upd.)
Horn & Hardart, **II** 614
Horn Silver Mines Co., **IV** 83; **7** 187
Horn Venture Partners, **22** 464
Hornblower & Co., **II** 450
Hornbrook, Inc., **14** 112
Horne's, **I** 449; **16** 62
Hornsberg Land Co., **I** 553

Horsehead Industries, Inc., 51 165–67
Horsham Corp. *See* TrizecHahn.
Horst Breuer GmbH, **20** 363
Horst Salons Inc., **24** 56
Horten, **II** 622; **47** 107; **50** 117, 119
Horton Homes, Inc., 25 216–18
Hoshino Gakki Co. Ltd., 55 208–11
Hosiery Corporation International. *See* HCI
    Direct, Inc.
Hospal SA, **49** 156
Hospital Corporation of America, II 331;
    III 78–80; **15** 112; **23** 153; **27** 237; **53**
    345. *See also* HCA - The Healthcare
    Company.
Hospital Cost Consultants, **11** 113
Hospital Products, Inc., **10** 534
Hospital Service Association of Pittsburgh,
    III 325
Hospital Specialty Co., **37** 392
Hospitality Franchise Systems, Inc., 11
    177–79; **14** 106; **17** 236. *See also*
    Cendant Corporation.
Hospitality Worldwide Services, Inc., 26
    196–98
Hosposable Products, Inc. *See* Wyant
    Corporation.
Host Communications Inc., **24** 404
Host Marriott Corporation, **21** 366
Host Marriott Services Corp., **III** 103; **16**
    446; **17** 95. *See also* HMSHost
Hot 'n Now, **16** 96–97
Hot Dog Construction Co., **12** 372
Hot Sam Co., **12** 179, 199. *See also* Mrs.
    Fields' Original Cookies, Inc.
Hot Shoppes Inc., **III** 102
Hot Topic, Inc., 33 202–04
Hotchkiss-Brandt, **II** 116; **42** 378
Hoteiya, **V** 209–10
Hotel Corporation of America, **16** 337
Hotel Corporation of India, **27** 26
Hotel Properties Ltd., **30** 107
Hotel Reservations Network, Inc., **47** 420
Hotel Scandinavia K/S, **I** 120
HotRail Inc., **36** 124
HotWired, **45** 200
Houbigant, **37** 270
Houchens Industries Inc., 51 168–70
Houdry Chemicals, **I** 298
Houghton Mifflin Company, 10 355–57;
    26 215; **36 270–74 (upd.)**; **46** 441
Houlihan's Restaurant Group, **25** 546
Housatonic Power Co., **13** 182
House and Land Syndicate, **IV** 710
House of Blues, **32** 241, 244
House of Fabrics, Inc., 16 197–98; **18**
    223; **21 278–80**
House of Fraser PLC, 21 353; **37** 6, 8; **45**
    188–91; **47** 173. *See also* Harrods
    Holdings.
House of Miniatures, **12** 264
House of Windsor, Inc., **9** 533
Household International, Inc., I 31; **II**
    417–20, 605; **7** 569–70; **8** 117; **10** 419;
    16 487–88; **21 281–86 (upd.)**; **22** 38,
    542; **24** 152
Household Products Inc., **I** 622; **10** 68; **50**
    535
Household Rental Systems, **17** 234
Housing Development Finance
    Corporation, **20** 313
Housmex Inc., **23** 171
Houston, Effler & Partners Inc., **9** 135
Houston Electric Light & Power Company,
    44 368

Houston General Insurance, **III** 248
Houston Industries Incorporated, V
    641–44; **7** 376. *See also* Reliant Energy
    Inc.
Houston International Teleport, Inc., **11**
    184
Houston Natural Gas Corp., **IV** 395; **V** 610
Houston Oil & Minerals Corp., **11** 440–41
Houston Oil Co., **IV** 342, 674
Houston Pipe Line Company, **45** 21
Hoveringham Group, **III** 753; **28** 450
Hoving Corp., **14** 501
Hovis-McDougall Co., **II** 565
Hovnanian Enterprises, Inc., 29 243–45
Howaldtswerke-Deutsche Werft AG, **IV**
    201
Howard B. Stark Candy Co., **15** 325
Howard Flint Ink Company, **13** 227
Howard H. Sweet & Son, Inc., **14** 502
Howard Hughes Medical Institute, II 33,
    35; **39 221–24**
Howard Hughes Properties, Ltd., **17** 317
Howard Humphreys, **13** 119
Howard Johnson International, Inc., III
    94, 102–03; **6** 27; **7** 266; **11** 177–78; **15**
    36; **16** 156; **17 236–39**; **25** 309; **52**
    280–81. *See also* Prime Hospitality
    Corporation.
Howard Printing Co., **III** 188; **10** 29
Howard Research and Development
    Corporation, **15** 412, 414
Howard, Smith & Levin, **40** 126
Howard Smith Paper Mills Ltd., **IV**
    271–72
Howden. *See* Alexander Howden Group.
Howdy Company, **9** 177
Howe & Fant, Inc., **23** 82
Howe and Brainbridge Inc., **I** 321
Howe Sound Co., **12** 253
Howe Sound Inc., **IV** 174
Howe Sound Pulp and Paper Ltd., **IV** 321
Howmedica, **29** 455
Howmet Corporation, 12 IV 174;
    253–55; **22** 506
Hoya Corp., **III** 715
Hoyt Archery Company, **10** 216
HPI Health Care Services, **49** 307–08
HQ Global Workplaces, Inc., **47** 331
HQ Office International, **8** 405; **23** 364
HRB Business Services, **29** 227
Hrubitz Oil Company, **12** 244
HSBC Holdings plc, 12 256–58; **17** 323,
    325–26; **26 199–204 (upd.)**
Hsiang-Li Investment Corp., **51** 123
HSN Inc., **25** 411
HSS Hire Service Group PLC, **45** 139–41
HTH, **12** 464
HTM Goedkoop, **26** 278–79; **55** 200
H2O Plus, **11** 41
Hua Bei Oxygen, **25** 82
Huaneng Raw Material Corp., **III** 718
Hub Group, Inc., 26 533; **38 233–35**
Hub Services, Inc., **18** 366
Hubbard Air Transport, **10** 162
Hubbard, Baker & Rice, **10** 126
Hubbard Broadcasting Inc., 24 226–28
Hubbard Construction Co., **23** 332
Hubbard, Westervelt & Motteley, **II** 425;
    13 341
Hubbell Incorporated, 9 286–87; **31**
    257–259 (upd.)
Hubinger Co., **II** 508; **11** 172; **36** 254
Huck Manufacturing Company, **22** 506
Huddart Parker, **III** 672

Hudepohl-Schoenling Brewing Co., **18** 72;
    50 114
Hudnut, **I** 710
The Hudson Bay Mining and Smelting
    Company, Limited, 12 259–61; **13**
    502–03; **16** 29
Hudson Engineering Corp., **III** 559
Hudson Foods Inc., 13 270–72
Hudson Housewares Corp., **16** 389
Hudson Motor Car Co., **I** 135, 158; **III**
    568; **10** 292; **20** 359
Hudson Packaging & Paper Co., **IV** 257
Hudson Pharmaceutical Corp., **31** 347
Hudson River Bancorp, Inc., 41 210–13
Hudson River Railroad, **II** 396
Hudson River Rubber Company, **V** 231
Hudson Scott & Sons, **I** 604
Hudson Software, **13** 481
Hudson Underground Telephone Company,
    6 299
Hudson's. *See* Dayton Hudson Corporation.
Hudson's Bay Company, I 284; **IV**
    400–01, 437; **V 79–81**; **6** 359; **8** 525;
    12 361; **25 219–22 (upd.)**, 230
Hue International, **8** 324
Hueppe Duscha, **III** 571; **20** 362
Huff Daland Dusters, **I** 99; **6** 81
Huffman Manufacturing Company, **7**
    225–26
Huffy Bicycles Co., **19** 383
Huffy Corporation, 7 225–27; **26** 184,
    412; **30 239–42 (upd.)**
Hugerot, **19** 50
Hugh O'Neill Auto Co., **12** 309
Hughes Air West, **25** 421
Hughes Aircraft Corporation, **I** 172, 484,
    539; **III** 428, 539; **7** 426–27; **9** 409; **10**
    327; **11** 263, 540; **13** 356, 398; **15** 528,
    530; **21** 201; **23** 134; **24** 442; **25** 86,
    223; **30** 175. *See also* GM Hughes
    Electronics Corporation.
Hughes Communications, Inc., **13** 398; **18**
    211
Hughes Corp., **18** 535
Hughes Electric Heating Co., **II** 28; **12** 194
Hughes Electronics Corporation, 25
    223–25; **36** 240, 243; **38** 175, 375; **46**
    327; **54** 72, 74
Hughes Helicopter, **26** 431; **46** 65
Hughes Hubbard & Reed LLP, 44
    230–32
Hughes Markets, Inc., 22 271–73
Hughes Network Systems Inc., **21** 239
Hughes Properties, Inc., **17** 317
Hughes Space and Communications
    Company, **33** 47–48
Hughes Supply, Inc., 14 246–47; **39** 360
Hughes Television Network, **11** 184
Hughes Tool Co., **I** 126; **II** 32; **12** 488; **15**
    467; **25** 74; **35** 425. *See also* Baker
    Hughes Incorporated.
Hugo Boss AG, 48 206–09
Hugo Neu Corporation, **19** 381–82
Hugo Stinnes GmbH, **I** 542; **8** 69, 494–95;
    50 168
Huguenot Fenal, **IV** 108
Huhtamaki, **30** 396, 398
The Hull Group, L.L.C., **51** 148
Hulman & Company, 44 233–36; **46** 245
Hüls A.G., I 349–50; **25** 82. *See also*
    Degussa-Hüls AG.
Hulton, **17** 397

Hulton Getty, **31** 216–17
Humana Inc., **III** 79, **81–83**; **6** 28,
191–92, 279; **15** 113; **24** 229–32 **(upd.)**;
35 215–16; **53** 185; **54** 48
**The Humane Society of the United
States**, **54 170–73**
Humanetics Corporation, **29** 213
Humanities Software, **39** 341
Humason Manufacturing Co., **III** 628
Humber, **I** 197
Humberside Sea & Land Services, **31** 367
Humble Oil & Refining Company, **III** 497;
IV 373, 428; **7** 171; **13** 118; **14** 291. *See
also* Exxon.
Humboldt-Deutz-Motoren AG, **III** 541–42,
543; **IV** 126
Hummel, **II** 163–64
Hummel Lanolin Corporation, **45** 126
Hummel-Reise, **44** 432
Hummer, Winblad Venture Partners, **36**
157
Hummingbird, **18** 313
Humongous Entertainment, Inc., **31**
238–40
Humphrey Instruments, **I** 693
Humphrey's Estate and Finance, **IV** 700
Humphreys & Glasgow Ltd., **V** 612
Humps' n Horns, **55** 312
Hunco Ltd., **IV** 640; **26** 273
Hungária Biztositó, **III** 185
Hungarian-Soviet Civil Air Transport Joint
Stock Company. *See* Malæv Plc.
Hungarotex, **V** 166
Hungry Howie's Pizza and Subs, Inc., **25
226–28**
Hunt Consolidated, Inc., **27 215–18**
(upd.)
Hunt Lumber Co., **IV** 358
Hunt Manufacturing Company, **12
262–64**
Hunt Oil Company, **IV** 367, 453–54; **7
228–30**, 378. *See also* Hunt
Consolidated, Inc.
Hunt-Wesson, Inc., **17 240–42**; **25** 278
Hunter-Douglas, **8** 235
Hunter Engineering Co., **IV** 18
Hunter Fan Company, **13 273–75**
Hunter-Hayes Elevator Co., **III** 467
Hunters' Foods, **II** 500
Hunting Aircraft, **I** 50; **24** 85
Huntingdon Life Sciences Group plc, **42
182–85**
Huntington Bancshares Inc., **11 180–82**
Huntington Learning Centers, Inc., **55
212–14**
Huntley and Palmer Foods, **II** 544
Huntley Boorne & Stevens, **I** 604
Hunton & Williams, **35 223–26**
Huntsman Chemical Corporation, **8
261–63**; **9** 305
Hupp Motor Car Company, **III** 601; **8** 74;
10 261
Hurd & Houghton, **10** 355
Hurlburt Paper Co., **IV** 311; **19** 267
Huron Steel Company, Inc., **16** 357
Hurricane Hydrocarbons Ltd., **54
174–77**
Huse Food Group, **14** 352
Husky Energy Inc., **47 179–82**; **49** 203
Husky Oil Ltd., **IV** 454, 695; **V** 673–75;
18 253–54; **19** 159
Husqvarna AB, **53** 126–27
Husqvarna Forest & Garden Company, **III**
480; **13** 564; **22** 26–27

Hussmann Corporation, **I** 457–58; **7**
429–30; **10** 554; **13** 268; **22** 353–54
Hutcheson & Grundy, **29** 286
Hutchinson-Mapa, **IV** 560
Hutchinson Technology Incorporated, **18
248–51**
Hutchinson Wholesale Grocery Co., **II** 624
Hutchison Microtel, **11** 548
Hutchison Whampoa Limited, **I** 470; **IV**
694–95; **18** 114, **252–55**; **20** 131,
312–13; **25** 101; **47** 181; **49 199–204
(upd.)**
Huth Manufacturing Corporation, **10** 414
Hüttenwerk Oberhausen AG, **IV** 222
Hüttenwerk Salzgitter AG, **IV** 201
Huttig Building Products, **31** 398, 400
Huttig Sash & Door Company, **8** 135
Hutton, E.F. *See* E.F. Hutton.
Huyck Corp., **I** 429
Hvide Marine Incorporated, **22 274–76**
HWI. *See* Hardware Wholesalers, Inc.
Hy-Form Products, Inc., **22** 175
Hy-Vee, Inc., **36 275–78**; **42** 432
Hyatt-Clark Industries Inc., **45** 170
Hyatt Corporation, **II** 442; **III** 92, **96–97**;
9 426; **16 273–75 (upd.)**; **22** 101; **23**
482; **48** 148
Hyatt Legal Services, **20** 435; **29** 226
Hyatt Medical Enterprises, **III** 73
Hyatt Roller Bearing Co., **I** 171–72; **9** 17;
10 326
Hybridtech, **III** 18
Hyde Athletic Industries, Inc., **17
243–45**. *See* Saucony Inc.
Hyde Company, A.L., **7** 116–17
Hyder Investments Ltd., **51** 173
Hyder plc, **34 219–21**; **52** 375
Hydra Computer Systems, Inc., **13** 201
Hydrac GmbH, **38** 300
Hydraulic Brake Co., **I** 141
Hydril Company, **46 237–39**
Hydro-Aire Incorporated, **8** 135
Hydro Carbide Corp., **19** 152
Hydro-Carbon Light Company, **9** 127
Hydro Electric, **19** 389–90; **49** 363–64
Hydro-Electric Power Commission of
Ontario, **6** 541; **9** 461
Hydro Med Sciences, **13** 367
Hydro-Québec, **6 501–03**; **32 266–69
(upd.)**
Hydrocarbon Services of Nigeria Co., **IV**
473
Hydroponic Chemical Co., **III** 28
Hydrox Corp., **II** 533
Hyer Boot, **19** 232
Hygeia Sciences, Inc., **8** 85, 512
Hygienic Ice Co., **IV** 722
Hygrade Containers Ltd., **IV** 286
Hygrade Foods, **III** 502; **7** 208; **14** 536
Hygrade Operators Inc., **55** 20
Hyland Laboratories, **I** 627
Hylsa. *See* Hojalata y Laminas S.A.
Hylsamex, S.A. de C.V., **39 225–27**
Hyosung Group, **III** 749
Hyper Shoppes, Inc., **II** 670; **18** 507; **50**
456–57
Hypercom Corporation, **27 219–21**
Hyperion Press, **6** 176
Hyperion Software Corporation, **22
277–79**
Hypermart USA, **8** 555–56
Hyplains Beef, **7** 175
Hypo-Bank. *See* Bayerische Hypotheken-
und Wechsel-Bank AG.

Hypobaruk, **III** 348
Hyponex Corp., **22** 475
Hypro Engineering Inc., **I** 481
Hysol Corp., **I** 321; **12** 103
Hyster Company, **17 246–48**; **33** 364
Hyster-Yale Materials Handling, Inc., **I**
424; **7** 369–71
Hystron Fibers Inc., **I** 347
Hyundai Group, **I** 207, 516; **II** 53–54,
122; **III** 457–59, **515–17**; **7** 231–34
(upd.); **9** 350; **10** 404; **12** 211, 546; **13**
280, 293–94; **18** 124; **23** 353; **25** 469;
29 264, 266
Hyundai Motors, **47** 279

I Can't Believe It's Yogurt, Inc., **17** 474;
35 121
I Pellettieri d'Italia S.p.A., **45** 342
I. Appel, **30** 23
I.B. Kleinert Rubber Company, **37** 399
I.C.H. Corp., **I** 528
I.C. Isaacs & Company, **31 260–62**
I.C. Johnson and Co., **III** 669
I.D. Systems, Inc., **11** 444
I-DIKA Milan SRL, **12** 182
I. Feldman Co., **31** 359
I.G. Farbenindustrie AG, **I** 305–06,
309–11, 337, 346–53, 619, 632–33,
698–99; **II** 257; **III** 677, 694; **IV** 111,
485; **8** 108–09; **11** 7; **13** 75–76, 262; **16**
121; **18** 47; **21** 544; **22** 225–26; **26** 452.
See also BASF A.G.; Bayer A.G.;
Hoechst A.G.
I.J. Stokes Corp., **I** 383
I.M. Pei & Associates, **I** 580; **III** 267; **41**
143
I.M. Singer and Co., **II** 9
I. Magnin Inc., **8** 444; **15** 86; **24** 422; **30**
383; **31** 191, 193
I.N. Kote, **IV** 116; **19** 219
I.N. Tek, **IV** 116; **19** 219
I.R. Maxwell & Co. Ltd., **IV** 641; **7** 311
I-T-E Circuit Breaker, **II** 121
I-X Corp., **22** 416
Iacon, Inc., **49** 299, 301
IAL. *See* International Aeradio Limited.
IAM/Environmental, **18** 11
Iams Company, **26 205–07**; **27** 213
IAWS Group plc, **46** 405; **49 205–08**
IBANCO, **26** 515
Ibanez. *See* Hoshino Gakki Co. Ltd.
IBC Holdings Corporation, **12** 276
IBCA. *See* International Banking and
Credit Analysis.
Iberdrola, S.A., **V** 608; **47** 110; **49
209–12**
Iberia Líneas Aéreas De España S.A., **I**
110; **6 95–97**; **33** 18; **36 279–83 (upd.)**
IBERIABANK Corporation, **37 200–02**
Ibero-Amerika Bank, **II** 521
Iberswiss Catering, **6** 96
Ibex Engineering Co., **III** 420
IBH Holding AG, **7** 513
IBJ. *See* The Industrial Bank of Japan Ltd.
IBM. *See* International Business Machines
Corporation.
IBM Foods, Inc., **51** 280
IBP, Inc., **II 515–17**; **7** 525; **21 287–90
(upd.)**; **23** 201
IBS Conversions Inc., **27** 492
Ibstock Brick Ltd., **37 203–06 (upd.)**
Ibstock plc, **III** 735; **14 248–50**
IC Designs, Inc., **48** 127

IC Industries Inc., I 456–58; III 512; 7 430; **10** 414, 553; **18** 3; **22** 197; **43** 217. *See also* Whitman Corporation.
ICA AB, II 639–40
ICA Fluor Daniel, S. de R.L. de C.V., **41** 148
ICA Mortgage Corporation, **8** 30
ICA Technologies, Ltd., **III** 533
Icahn Capital Corp., **35** 143
Icarus Consulting AG, **29** 376
ICE, **I** 333
ICEE-USA, **24** 240
Iceland Group plc, 33 205–07
Icelandair, 52 166–69
Icelandic Air, **49** 80
ICF Kaiser International, Inc., 28 **200–04**
ICH Corporation, **19** 468
Ichikoh Industries Ltd., **26** 154
ICI. *See* Imperial Chemical Industries plc.
ICI Canada, **22** 436
ICL plc, II 65, 81; **III** 141, 164; **6** **240–42; 11** 150; **16** 226
ICM Mortgage Corporation, **8** 436
ICN Pharmaceuticals, Inc., 52 170–73
ICOA Life Insurance, **III** 253
Icon Health & Fitness, Inc., 38 236–39
Icon International, **24** 445
iConcepts, Inc., **39** 95
Icot Corp., **18** 543
ICS. *See* International Care Services.
ICS, **26** 119
ICX, **IV** 136
ID, Inc., **9** 193
id Software, **31** 237–38; **32** 9
Idaho Frozen Foods, **II** 572–73
Idaho Power Company, 12 265–67
IDB Communications Group, Inc., 11 **183–85; 20** 48; **27** 301, 307
IDC, **25** 101
Ide Megumi, **III** 549
Ideal Basic Industries, **III** 701–02; **8** 258–59; **12** 18
Ideal Corp., **III** 602; **23** 335
Ideal Loisirs Group, **23** 388
IDEC Pharmaceuticals Corporation, **32** 214
Idemitso Petrochemicals, **8** 153
Idemitsu Kosan Co., Ltd., 49 213–16 **(upd.)**
Idemitsu Kosan K.K., II 361; **IV 434–36,** 476, 519
Identification Business, Inc., **18** 140
Identix Inc., 44 237–40
IDEXX Laboratories, Inc., 23 282–84
IDG Books Worldwide, Inc., 27 222–24. *See also* International Data Group, Inc.
IDG Communications, Inc, **7** 238
IDG World Expo Corporation, **7** 239
IDI, **22** 365
IDI Temps, **34** 372
IDO. *See* Nippon Idou Tsushin.
Ido Bathroom Ltd, **51** 324
IDS Ltd., **22** 76
IDT Corporation, 34 222–24
IEC Electronics Corp., 42 186–88
IEL. *See* Industrial Equity Ltd.
IFC Disposables, Inc., **30** 496–98
IFF. *See* International Flavors & Fragrances Inc.
IFI, **I** 161–62; **III** 347
Ifil, **27** 515
IFM, **25** 85
Ifö Sanitär AB, **51** 324
IFS Industries, **6** 294

IG. *See* Integrated Genetics.
IG Farben. *See* I.G. Farbenindustrie AG.
IG Holdings, **27** 430
IGA, **II** 624, 649, 668, 681–82; **7** 451; **15** 479; **18** 6, 9; **25** 234
Iggesund Bruk, **IV** 317–18
Iggesund Paperboard AB, **52** 161, 164
Igloo Products Corp., 21 291–93; 22 116
IGT-International, **10** 375–76
IGT-North America, **10** 375
IHI. *See* Ishikawajima Harima Heavy Industries.
IHI Granitech Corp., **III** 533
IHOP Corporation, 17 249–51; 19 435, 455
Iida & Co., **I** 493; **24** 325
IinteCom, **III** 169
IIS, **26** 441
IISCO-Ujjain Pipe and Foundry Co. Ltd., **IV** 206
IJ Holdings Corp., **45** 173
IK Coach, Ltd., **23** 290
IKEA Group, V 82–84
IKEA International A/S, 26 161, **208–11** **(upd.)**
IKON Office Solutions, Inc., 50 236–39
Il Fornaio (America) Corporation, 27 **225–28**
Il Giornale, **13** 493
Ilacc, **26** 22
ILFC. *See* International Lease Finance Corporation.
Ilitch Holdings Inc., 37 207–210; 46 130
Illco Toy Co. USA, **12** 496
Illinois Bell Telephone Company, IV 660; **14 251–53; 18** 30
Illinois Central Corporation, I 456, 584; **8** 410; **10** 553; **11 186–89**
Illinois Glass Co., **I** 609
Illinois Lock Company, **48** 142
Illinois Merchants Trust Co., **II** 261
Illinois National Bank & Trust Co., **III** 213–14
Illinois Power Company, 6 470, **504–07;** **49** 119, 121
Illinois Steel Co., **IV** 572; **7** 549; **8** 114; **50** 500
Illinois Terminal Company, **6** 504
Illinois Tool Works Inc., III 518–20; 22 **280–83 (upd.); 44** 193
Illinois Traction Company, **6** 504
Illinois Trust and Savings Bank, **II** 261
Illinova Energy Partners, **27** 247
Illuminet Holdings Inc., **47** 430
illycaffè SpA, 50 240–44
Ilmor Engineering of Great Britain, **V** 494
Ilse-Bergbau AG, **IV** 229–30
Ilselder Hütte, **IV** 201
Ilwaco Telephone and Telegraph Company. *See* Pacific Telecom, Inc.
Ilyushin, **24** 60
IMA Bancard, Inc., **24** 395
IMA Holdings Corp., **III** 73–74
Imabari, **25** 469
Image Business Systems Corp., **11** 66
Image Industries, Inc., **25** 320–21
Image Technologies Corporation, **12** 264
Imageline Inc., **25** 348
ImageTag Inc., **49** 290
Imagine Entertainment, **43** 144
Imagine Foods, Inc., 50 245–47
Imagine Manufacturing Solutions Inc., **48** 410
ImagiNet, **41** 97

Imaging Technologies, **25** 183
Imaje, S.A., **28** 104
IMAKE Software and Services, Inc., **49** 423–24
IMall Inc., **26** 441
Imasa Group, **IV** 34
Imasco Limited, I 514; **II** 605; **V 401–02;** **49** 367–68
Imation Corporation, 20 301–04; 33 348. *See also* Minnesota Mining & Manufacturing Company.
Imatra Steel Oy Ab, 55 215–17
Imatran Voima Oy, **IV** 469. *See also* Forum Corporation
Imax Corporation, 21 362; **28 205–08;** **46** 422
IMC. *See* Intertec Marine Corporation.
IMC Drilling Mud, **III** 499
IMC Fertilizer Group, Inc., 8 264–66
Imcera Group, Inc., **8** 264, 266
IMCO Recycling, Incorporated, 32 **270–73**
IMED Corp., **I** 712; **III** 511–12; **10** 551; **38** 364
Imerys S.A., 40 176, **263–66 (upd.)**
Imetal S.A., IV 107–09
IMG. *See* International Management Group.
Imhoff Industrie Holding GmbH, **53** 315
IMI plc, III 593; **9 288–89; 29** 364
Imigest Fondo Imicapital, **III** 347
IMIWeb Bank, **50** 410
Imlo, **26** 22
Immeon Networks LLC, **54** 407
Immersion Corporation, **28** 245
Immobilier Batibail, **42** 152
Immunex Corporation, 8 26; **14 254–56;** **50** 421, **248–53 (upd.),** 538
Immuno Serums, Inc., **V 174–75**
Immuno Therapeutics, Inc., **25** 382
Imo Industries Inc., 7 235–37; 27 229–32 **(upd.)**
IMO Ltd., **III** 539
Impala Platinum Holdings, **IV** 91–93
Impark Limited, **42** 433
IMPATH Inc., 45 192–94
Imperial Airways. *See* British Overseas Airways Corporation.
Imperial and International Communications Limited, **25** 100
Imperial Bank of Canada, **II** 244–45
Imperial Bank of Persia, **II** 298
Imperial British East Africa Co., **III** 522
Imperial Business Forms, **9** 72
Imperial Chemical Industries plc, I 303, **351–53,** 374, 605, 633; **II** 448, 565; **III** 522, 667, 677, 680, 745; **IV** 38, 110, 698; **7** 209; **8** 179, 222, 224; **9** 154, 288; **10** 436; **11** 97, 361; **12** 347; **13** 448, 470; **16** 121; **17** 118; **18** 50; **21** 544; **44** 116–17; **49** 268, 270; **50** 57, 90, 178–79, **50 254–58 (upd.)**
Imperial Feather Company, **19** 304
Imperial Fire Co., **III** 373
Imperial Goonbarrow, **III** 690
Imperial Group Ltd., **II** 513; **III** 503; **7** 209; **17** 238
Imperial Holly Corporation, 12 268–70. *See also* Imperial Sugar Company.
Imperial Japanese Government Steel Works, **17** 349–50
Imperial Life Co., **III** 288, 373
Imperial Marine Insurance Co., **III** 384, 405–06

Imperial Metal Industries Ltd. *See* IMI plc.
Imperial Oil Limited, **IV** 428, **437–39**, 494; **25** 229–33 **(upd.)**; **32** 179–80
Imperial Outdoor, **27** 280
Imperial Packing Co. *See* Beech-Nut Nutrition Corporation.
Imperial Paper, **13** 169
Imperial Pneumatic Tool Co., **III** 525
Imperial Premium Finance, **III** 264
Imperial Savings Association, **8** 30–31
Imperial Smelting Corp., **IV** 58
Imperial Sports, **19** 230
Imperial Sugar Company, **32 274–78 (upd.)**; **54** 168
Imperial Tobacco Company, **I** 425–26, 605; **IV** 260; **V** 401; **49** 153. *See also* B.A.T. Industries PLC.
Imperial Tobacco Group PLC, **50** 116–18, **259–63**
IMPO Import Parfumerien, **48** 116
Imported Auto Parts, Inc., **15** 246
Impressions Software, **15** 455
Imprimis, **8** 467
Impulse, **9** 122
Impulse Designs, **31** 435–36
IMRA America Inc., **48** 5
Imreg, **10** 473–74
IMRS. *See* Hyperion Software Corporation.
IMS International, Inc., **10** 105
In Focus Systems, Inc., **22 287–90**
In Home Health, Inc., **25** 306, 309–10
In-N-Out Burger, **19 213–15**
In-Sink-Erator, **II** 19
INA Corporation, **II** 403; **III** 79, 208, 223–25, 226; **11** 481; **22** 269. *See also* CIGNA Corporation.
INA-Naftaplin, **IV** 454
INA Wälzlager Schaeffler, **III** 595; **47** 278
Inabata & Co., **I** 398
InaCom Corporation, **13** 176, **276–78**; **19** 471
Incasso Bank, **II** 185
Incentive Group, **27** 269
Inchcape PLC, **II** 233; **III 521–24**; **16 276–80 (upd.)**; **50 264–68 (upd.)**; **54** 378
Incheon Iron & Steel Co., **III** 516
Inchon Heavy Industrial Corp., **IV** 183
INCO-Banco Indústria e Comércio de Santa Catarina, **13** 70
Inco Limited, **IV** 75, 78, **110–12**; **39** 338; **45 195–99 (upd.)**
Incola, S.A., **II** 471; **22** 93
Incon Research Inc., **41** 198
InControl Inc., **11** 460
Incredible Universe, **12** 470; **17** 489; **36** 387
Incyte Genomics, Inc., **52 174–77**
Ind Coope, **I** 215
Indemnité, **III** 391
Indemnity Insurance Company. *See* CIGNA Corporation.
Indentimat Corp., **14** 542
Independent Breweries Company, **9** 178
Independent Delivery Services, Inc., **37** 409
Independent Election Corp. of America, **47** 37
Independent Exhibitions Ltd., **27** 362
Independent Grocers Alliance. *See* IGA.
Independent Lock Co., **13** 166
Independent Metal Products Co., **I** 169
Independent Oil & Gas Co., **IV** 521
Independent Petrochemical, **14** 461

Independent Power Generators, **V** 605
Independent Stave Company, **28** 223
Independent Torpedo Company, **25** 73
Independent Warehouses, Inc., **IV** 180
India Exotics, Inc., **22** 133
India General Steam Navigation and Railway Co., **III** 522
India Life Assurance Co., **III** 359
India Rubber, Gutta Percha & Telegraph Works Co., **I** 428
Indian Airlines Corporation. *See* Air-India.
Indian Airlines Ltd., **46 240–42**
Indian Archery and Toy Corp., **19** 142–43
Indian Iron & Steel Co. Ltd., **IV** 49, 205–07
Indian Oil Corporation Ltd., **IV 440–41**, 483; **48 210–13 (upd.)**
Indian Point Farm Supply, Inc., **IV** 458–59
Indiana Bearings, Inc., **13** 78
Indiana Bell Telephone Company, Incorporated, **14 257–61**; **18** 30
Indiana Board and Filler Company, **12** 376
Indiana Electric Corporation, **6** 555
Indiana Energy, Inc., **27 233–36**
Indiana Gaming Company, **21** 40
Indiana Gas & Water Company, **6** 556
Indiana Group, **I** 378
Indiana Oil Purchasing Co., **IV** 370
Indiana Parts and Warehouse, **29** 86, 88
Indiana Power Company, **6** 555
Indiana Protein Technologies, **55** 233
Indiana Refining Co., **IV** 552
Indiana Tube Co., **23** 250
Indianapolis Air Pump Company, **8** 37
Indianapolis Brush Electric Light & Power Company, **6** 508
Indianapolis Cablevision, **6** 508–09
Indianapolis Light and Power Company, **6** 508
Indianapolis Motor Speedway Corporation, **9** 16; **46 243–46**
Indianapolis Power & Light Company, **6** 508–09
Indianapolis Pump and Tube Company, **8** 37
Indianhead Truck Lines, **6** 371
IndianOil Companies. *See* Indian Oil Corporation Ltd.
Indigo NV, **26 212–14**, 540–41
Indo-Asahi Glass Co., Ltd., **III** 667
Indo-China Steam Navigation Co., **I** 469; **20** 311
Indo Mobil Ltd., **48** 212
Indola Cosmetics B.V., **8** 16
Indonesia Petroleum Co., **IV** 516
Indresco, Inc., **22** 285; **52** 215
Induba, S.A. de C.V., **39** 230
Induban, **II** 196
Indura SA Industria Y Commercio, **25** 82
Industri Kapital, **27** 269
Industria Gelati Sammontana, **II** 575
Industria Metalgrafica, **I** 231
Industria Raffinazione Oli Minerali, **IV** 419
Industrial & Trade Shows of Canada, **IV** 639
Industrial Acceptance Bank, **I** 337
Industrial Air Products, **19** 380–81
Industrial Air Tool, **28** 387
Industrial Bancorp, **9** 229
Industrial Bank of Japan, Ltd., **II 300–01**, 310–11, 338, 369, 433, 459; **17** 121
Industrial Bank of Scotland, **10** 337
Industrial Bio-Test Laboratories, **I** 374, 702

Industrial Cartonera, **IV** 295; **19** 226
Industrial Chemical and Equipment, **16** 271
Industrial Circuits, **IV** 680
Industrial Computer Corp., **11** 78
Industrial Development Corp., **IV** 22, 92, 534
Industrial Development Corp. of Zambia Ltd., **IV** 239–41
Industrial Devices Inc., **48** 359
Industrial Engineering, **III** 598
Industrial Engineering Associates, Inc., **II** 112
Industrial Equity Ltd., **I** 438; **17** 357
Industrial Fuel Supply Co., **I** 569
Industrial Gas Equipment Co., **I** 297
Industrial Gases Lagos, **25** 82
Industrial Instrument Company. *See* Foxboro Company.
Industrial Light & Magic, **12** 322; **50** 320
Industrial Mutual Insurance, **III** 264
Industrial National Bank, **9** 229
Industrial Powder Coatings, Inc., **16** 475
Industrial Publishing Company, **9** 413; **27** 361
Industrial Reorganization Corp., **III** 502, 556
Industrial Resources, **6** 144
Industrial Services of America, Inc., **46 247–49**
Industrial Shows of America, **27** 362
Industrial Tectonics Corp., **18** 276
Industrial Trade & Consumer Shows Inc., **IV** 639; **26** 272
Industrial Trust Co. of Wilmington, **25** 540
Industrial Trust Company, **9** 228
Industrial Vehicles Corp. B.V., **III** 543–44
Industrias Bachoco, S.A. de C.V., **39 228–31**
Industrias del Atlantico SA, **47** 291
Industrias Nacobre, **21** 259
Industrias Negromex, **23** 170
Industrias Penoles, S.A. de C.V., **22 284–86**
Industrias Resistol S.A., **23** 170–71
Industrias y Confecciones, S.A. **V** 51; **26** 129
Industrie-Aktiengesellschaft, **IV** 201
Industrie Natuzzi S.p.A., **18 256–58**
Industrie Regionale du Bâtiment, **IV** 108
Industriegas GmbH., **I** 581
Les Industries Ling, **13** 443
Industriförvaltnings AB Kinnevik, **26** 331–33; **36** 335
Industrionics Control, Inc., **III** 643
AB Industrivärden, **II** 366; **32** 397
Induyco. *See* Industrias y Confecciones, S.A.
Indy Lighting, **30** 266
Indy Racing League, **37** 74
Inelco Peripheriques, **10** 459
Inespo, **16** 322
Inexco Oil Co., **7** 282
Infineon Technologies AG, **50 269–73**
Infinity Broadcasting Corporation, **11 190–92**; **22** 97; **23** 510; **28** 72; **35** 232; **48 214–17 (upd.)**
Infinity Enterprises, Inc., **44** 4
Infinity Partners, **36** 160
INFLEX, S.A., **8** 247
Inflight Sales Group Limited, **11** 82; **29** 511
InfoAsia, **28** 241
Infobase Services, **6** 14
Infocom, **32** 8

Infogrames Entertainment S.A., 35 227–30; **41** 407

Infonet Services Corporation, **6** 303; **27** 304

Infoplan, **14** 36

Informatics General Corporation, **III** 248; **11** 468; **25** 86

Informatics Legal Systems, **III** 169; **6** 285

Information Access Company, 12 560–62; **17** 252–55; **34** 438. See also The Thomson Corporation.

Information and Communication Group, **14** 555

Information Associates Inc., **11** 78

Information Builders, Inc., 14 16; **22** 291–93

Information Consulting Group, **9** 345

Information, Dissemination and Retrieval Inc., **IV** 670

Information Holdings Inc., 47 183–86

Information International. See Autologic Information International, Inc.

Information Management Reporting Services. See Hyperion Software Corporation.

Information Management Science Associates, Inc., **13** 174

Information Please LLC, **26** 216

Information Resources, Inc., 10 358–60; **13** 4; **25** 366

Information Unlimited Software, **6** 224

Informix Corporation, 10 361–64, 505; **30** 243–46 (upd.)

Infoseek Corporation, **27** 517; **30** 490

InfoSoft International, Inc. See Inso Corporation.

Infostrada S.p.A., **38** 300

Infosys Technologies Ltd., 38 240–43

Infotech Enterprises, Ltd., **33** 45

Infotechnology Inc., **25** 507–08

Infotel, Inc., **52** 342

Infrasud, **I** 466

Infun, S.A., **23** 269

ING Australia Limited, **52** 35, 39

ING, B.V., **14** 45, 47

Ing. C. Olivetti & C., S.p.A., III 122, **144–46**, 549, 678; **10** 499; **16** 122; **25** 33. See also Olivetti S.p.A

Ingalls Quinn and Johnson, **9** 135

Ingalls Shipbuilding, Inc., I 485; **11** 264–65; **12** 28, **271–73**; **36** 78–79; **41** 42

Ingear, **10** 216

Ingefico, S.A., **52** 301

Ingenico—Compagnie Industrielle et Financière d'Ingénierie, 46 250–52

Ingenious Designs Inc., **47** 420

Ingersoll-Rand Company, III 473, **525–27**; **10** 262; **13** 27, 523; **15** 187, **223–26 (upd.)**; **22** 542; **33** 168; **34** 46; **55** 218–22 (upd.)

Ingka Holding B.V. See IKEA International A/S.

Ingleby Enterprises Inc. See Caribiner International, Inc.

Inglenook Vineyards, **13** 134; **34** 89

Ingles Markets, Inc., 20 305–08

Inglis Ltd., **III** 654; **12** 549

Ingram Book Group, **30** 70

Ingram Corp. Ltd., **III** 559; **IV** 249

Ingram Industries, Inc., 10 518–19; **11** **193–95**; **13** 90, 482; **49** 217–20 (upd.); **52** 178. See also Ingram Micro Inc.

Ingram Micro Inc., 24 29; **52 178–81**

AB Ingredients, **II** 466

Ingredients Technology Corp., **9** 154

Ingres Corporation, **9** 36–37; **25** 87

Ingwerson and Co., **II** 356

INH. See Instituto Nacional de Hidrocarboros.

Inha Works Ltd., **33** 164

Inhalation Therapy Services, **III** 73

INI. See Instituto Nacional de Industria.

Initial Towel Supply. See Rentokil Initial Plc.

Inktomi Corporation, 41 98; **45 200–04**

Inland Container Corporation, IV 311, 341–42, 675; **7** 528; **8 267–69**; **19** 267

Inland Motors Corporation, **18** 291

Inland Paperboard and Packaging, Inc., **31** 438

Inland Pollution Control, **9** 110

Inland Specialty Chemical Corp., **I** 342; **14** 217

Inland Steel Industries, Inc., II 403; **IV** **113–16**, 158, 703; **7** 447; **13** 157; **15** 249–50; **17** 351; **19** 9, **216–20 (upd.)**, 311, 381; **23** 35; **30** 254; **40** 269, 381; **41** 4

Inland Valley, **23** 321

Inmac, Inc., **16** 373

Inmos Ltd., **I** 532; **11** 307; **29** 323

InnCOGEN Limited, **35** 480

InnerCity Foods Joint Venture Company, **16** 97

Inno-BM, **26** 158, 161

Inno-France. See Societe des Grandes Entreprises de Distribution, Inno-France.

Innova International Corporation, **26** 333

Innovacom, **25** 96

Innovation, **26** 158

Innovative Marketing Systems. See Bloomberg L.P.

Innovative Pork Concepts, **7** 82

Innovative Products & Peripherals Corporation, **14** 379

Innovative Software Inc., **10** 362

Innovative Sports Systems, Inc., **15** 396

Innovative Valve Technologies Inc., **33** 167

Innovex Ltd., **21** 425

Inns and Co., **III** 734

Innwerk AG, **IV** 229

Inoue Electric Manufacturing Co., **II** 75–76

Inpaco, **16** 340

Inpacsa, **19** 226

Inprise/Borland Corporation, **33** 115

Input/Output, Inc., **11** 538

INS. See International News Service.

Insa, **55** 189

Insalaco Markets Inc., **13** 394

INSCO, **III** 242

Inserra Supermarkets, 25 234–36

Insight Enterprises, Inc., 18 259–61

Insight Marques SARL IMS SA, **48** 224

Insilco Corporation, I 473; **12** 472; **16** **281–83**; **23** 212; **36** 469–70

Insley Manufacturing Co., **8** 545

Inso Corporation, 26 215–19; **36** 273

Inspiration Resources Corporation, **12** 260; **13** 502–03

Inspirations PLC, **22** 129

Insta-Care Holdings Inc., **16** 59

Insta-Care Pharmacy Services, **9** 186

Instant Auto Insurance, **33** 3, 5

Instant Interiors Corporation, **26** 102

Instant Milk Co., **II** 488

Instapak Corporation, **14** 429

Instinet Corporation, 34 225–27; **48** 227–28

Institut de Sérothérapie Hémopoiétique, **I** 669

Institut für Gemeinwohl, **IV** 139

Institut Merieux, **I** 389

Institut Ronchese, **I** 676

Institute de Development Industriel, **19** 87

Institute for Professional Development, **24** 40

Institute for Scientific Information, **8** 525, 528

Institution Food House. See Alex Lee Inc.

Institutional Financing Services, **23** 491

Instituto Bancario San Paolo di Torino, **50** 407

Instituto Nacional de Hidrocarboros, **IV** 528

Instituto Nacional de Industria, I **459–61**; **V** 606–07; **6** 95–96

Instituto per la Ricostruzione Industriale, **V** 614

Instone Airline, **I** 92

Instromet International, **22** 65

Instrument Systems Corp. See Griffon Corporation.

Instrumentarium Corp., **13** 328; **25** 82

Instrumentation Laboratory Inc., **III** 511–12; **22** 75

Instrumentation Scientifique de Laboratoire, S.A., **15** 404; **50** 394

Insulite Co. of Finland, **IV** 275

Insurance Auto Auctions, Inc., 23 148, **285–87**

Insurance Co. against Fire Damage, **III** 308

Insurance Co. of Scotland, **III** 358

Insurance Co. of the State of Pennsylvania, **III** 196

Insurance Company of North America. See CIGNA Corporation.

Insurance Corp. of Ireland (Life), **III** 335

Insurance Partners L.P., **15** 257

InSync Communications, **42** 425

Intabex Holdings Worldwide, S.A., **27** 126

Intalco Aluminum Corp., **12** 254

Intamin, **17** 443

Intarsia Corp., **38** 187

Intat Precision Inc., **48** 5

INTEC, **6** 428

InteCom Inc., **6** 285

Integon Corp., **IV** 374; **50** 48

Integra-A Hotel and Restaurant Company, **13** 473

Integral Corporation, **14** 381; **23** 446; **33** 331

Integrated Business Information Services, **13** 5

Integrated Computer Systems. See Learning Tree International Inc.

Integrated Data Services Co., **IV** 473

Integrated Defense Technologies,

Integrated Defense Technologies, Inc., 44 423; **54 178–80**

Integrated Genetics, **I** 638; **8** 210; **13** 239; **38** 204, 206

Integrated Health Services, Inc., **11** 282

Integrated Medical Systems Inc., **12** 333; **47** 236

Integrated Resources, Inc., **11** 483; **16** 54; **19** 393

Integrated Silicon Solutions, Inc., **18** 20; **43** 17; **47** 384

Integrated Software Systems Corporation, **6** 224; **11** 469

Integrated Systems Engineering, Inc., **51** 382

Integrated Systems Operations. *See* Xerox Corporation.

Integrated Systems Solutions Corp., **9** 284; **11** 395; **17** 264

Integrated Technology, Inc., **6** 279

Integrated Telecom Technologies, **14** 417

Integris Europe, **49** 382, 384

Integrity Inc., 44 241–43

Integrity Life Insurance, **III** 249

Intel Corporation, II 44–46, 62, 64; **III** 115, 125, 455; **6** 215–17, 222, 231, 233, 235, 257; **9** 42–43, 57, 114–15, 165–66; **10** 365–67 **(upd.),** 477; **11** 62, 308, 328, 490, 503, 518, 520; **12** 61, 449; **13** 47; **16** 139–40, 146, 394; **17** 32–33; **18** 18, 260; **19** 310, 312; **20** 69, 175; **21** 36, 122; **22** 542; **24** 233, 236, 371; **25** 418, 498; **26** 91, 432; **27** 365–66; **30** 10; **34** 441; **36** 123, **284–88 (upd.);** **38** 71, 416; **41** 408; **43** 14–16; **47** 153; **50** 53–54, 225

Intelcom Support Services, Inc., **14** 334

Intelicom Solutions Corp., **6** 229

IntelliCorp, Inc., 9 310; **31** 298; **45** **205–07**

Intelligent Electronics, Inc., 6 243–45; 12 184; **13** 176, 277

Intelligent Interactions Corp., **49** 421

Intelligent Software Ltd., **26** 275

Intelligraphics Inc., **33** 44

Intellimetrics Instrument Corporation, **16** 93

Intellisys, **48** 257

Inter American Aviation, Inc. *See* SkyWest, Inc.

Inter-American Development Bank, **IV** 55

Inter-American Satellite Television Network, **7** 391

Inter-City Gas Ltd., **III** 654; **19** 159

Inter-City Products Corporation, **52** 399

Inter-City Western Bakeries Ltd., **II** 631

Inter-City Wholesale Electric Inc., **15** 385

Inter-Comm Telephone, Inc., **8** 310

Inter-Continental Hotels and Resorts, **38** 77

Inter-Europa Bank in Hungary, **50** 410

Inter IKEA Systems B.V., **V** 82

Inter-Island Airways, Ltd., **22** 251; **24** 20

Inter-Island Steam Navigation Co. *See* Hawaiian Airlines.

Inter Island Telephone, **6** 326, 328

Inter-Mountain Telephone Co., **V** 344

Inter-Ocean Corporation, **16** 103; **44** 90

Inter Parfums Inc., 35 235–38

Inter-Regional Financial Group, Inc., 15 **231–33.** *See also* Dain Rauscher Corporation.

Inter State Telephone, **6** 338

Inter Techniek, **16** 421

Interactive Computer Design, Inc., **23** 489, 491

Interactive Systems, **7** 500

InterAd Holdings Ltd., **49** 422

Interamericana de Talleras SA de CV, **10** 415

Interbake Foods, **II** 631

InterBold, **7** 146; **11** 151

Interbrás, **IV** 503

Interbrew S.A., 16 397; **17 256–58; 25** 279, 282; **26** 306; **34** 202; **38** 74, 78; **50** **274–79 (upd.)**

Interceramic. *See* Internacional de Ceramica, S.A. de C.V.

Interchemical Corp., **13** 460

Intercity Food Services, Inc., **II** 663

Interco Incorporated, III 528–31; 9 133, 135, 192, 234–35; **10** 184; **12** 156, 306–08; **22** 49; **29** 294; **31** 136–37, 210; **39** 146; **51** 120. *See also* Furniture Brands International, Inc.

Intercolonial, **6** 360

Intercomi, **II** 233

Intercontessa AG, **35** 401; **36** 294

Intercontinental Apparel, **8** 249

Intercontinental Breweries, **I** 289

Intercontinental Electronics Corp. *See* IEC Electronics Corp.

Intercontinental Hotels, **I** 248–49

Intercontinental Mortgage Company, **8** 436

Intercontinental Rubber Co., **II** 112

Intercontinentale, **III** 404

Intercord, **22** 194

Intercostal Steel Corp., **13** 97

Interdesign, **16** 421

Interdiscount/Radio TV Steiner AG, **48** 116

Interealty Corp., **43** 184

Interedi-Cosmopolitan, **III** 47

Interep National Radio Sales Inc., 35 **231–34**

Interessen Gemeinschaft Farbenwerke. *See* I.G. Farbenindustrie AG.

Interface Group, **13** 483

Interface, Inc., 8 270–72; 18 112; **29** **246–49 (upd.)**

Interferon Sciences, Inc., **13** 366–67

Interfinancial, **III** 200

InterFirst Bankcorp, Inc., **9** 482

Interfood Ltd., **II** 520–21, 540

Interglas S.A., **22** 515

Intergram, Inc., **27** 21

Intergraph Corporation, 6 246–49; 10 257; **24 233–36 (upd.); 53** 267

Interhandel, **I** 337–38; **II** 378; **22** 226

INTERIM Services, Inc., **9** 268, 270; **25** 434; **29** 224, 227. *See also* Spherion Corporation.

Interinvest S.A., **33** 19

Interlabor, **16** 420–21

Interlabor Interim, **43** 308

The Interlake Corporation, 8 273–75; 38 210

Interlake Steamship Company, **15** 302

Intermaco S.R.L., **43** 368

Intermagnetics General Corp., **9** 10

Intermarché, **35** 398, 401. *See also* ITM Entreprises SA.

Intermark, Inc., **12** 394; **34** 338–39

Intermec Corporation, **29** 414

Intermed, **I** 429

Intermedia, **25** 499

Intermedics, **III** 633; **11** 458–59; **12** 325–26; **40** 66–67

Intermedics Intraocular Inc., **I** 665

Intermet Corporation, 32 279–82

Intermoda, **V** 166

Intermountain Broadcasting and Television Corp., **IV** 674

Intermountain Health Care, Inc., 27 **237–40**

Internacional de Ceramica, S.A. de C.V., **53 174–76**

International Aeradio Limited, **47** 352

International Aero Engines, **9** 418

International Agricultural Corporation, **8** 264–65

International Air Service Co., **24** 21

International Airline Support Group, **Inc., 55 223–25**

International Alliance Services, Inc. *See* Century Business Services, Inc.

International Assurance Co., **III** 195

International Bank, **II** 261

International Bank of Japan, **17** 122

International Bank of Moscow, **II** 242

International Banking and Credit Analysis (IBCA), **37** 144

International Banking Corp., **II** 253; **9** 123

International Banking Technologies, Inc., **11** 113

International Basic Economy Corporation, **13** 103

International Beauty Supply, Ltd. *See* L.L. Knickerbocker Co., Inc.

International Beverage Corporation. *See* Clearly Canadian Beverage Corporation.

International Brewing Holdings Pty., **21** 229; **50** 201

International Brotherhood of Teamsters, **37 211–14**

International Business Directories, Inc., **26** 484

International Business Machines **Corporation, I** 26, 455, 523, 534, 541; **II** 6, 8, 10, 42, 44–45, 56, 62, 68, 70, 73, 86, 99, 107, 113, 134, 159, 211, 274, 326, 379, 397, 432, 440; **III** 9, 109–11, 113–18, 121–28, 130, 132–34, 136, 139–43, 145, **147–49,** 151–52, 154–55, 157, 165–72, 200, 246, 313, 319, 326, 458, 475, 549, 618, 685; **IV** 443, 711; **6** 51, 218–25, 233–35, 237, 240–42, 244–48, **250–53 (upd.),** 254–60, 262, 265, 269–71, 275–77, 279, 281–89, 320, 324, 346, 390, 428; **7** 145–46, 161; **8** 138–39, 466–67; **9** 36, 41–42, 48, 50, 114–15, 131, 139, 165–66, 170–71, 184, 194, 284, 296–97, 310, 327, 463–64; **10** 19, 22–24, 58, 119, 125, 161, 194, 232, 237, 243–44, 255–56, 309, 361–62, 366–67, 394, 456, 463, 474, 500–01, 505, 510, 512–13, 518–19, 542; **11** 19, 45, 50, 59, 61–62, 64–65, 68, 86–88, 150, 273–74, 285, 364, 395, 469, 485, 491, 494, 506, 519; **12** 61, 138–39, 147–49, 161–62, 183, 204, 238, 278, 335, 442, 450, 469–70, 484; **13** 47, 127, 174, 214, 326, 345, 387–88, 403, 482; **14** 13–15, 106, 268–69, 318, 354, 391, 401, 432–33, 446, 533; **15** 106, 440, 454–55, 491–92; **16** 4, 94, 140, 224–26, 301, 367–68, 372; **17** 353, 418, 532–34; **18** 94, 110, 112, 162, 250, 292, 305–07, 344, 434–36; **19** 41, 110, 310, 312, 437; **20** 237, 313; **21** 86, 391; **23** 135, 138, 209, 470; **24** 234; **25** 20–21, 34, 86–87, 96, 133–34, 149, 298–301, 356, 358, 530–32; **26** 90, 187, 275–76, 427, 429, 441, 540, 542; **28** 112, 189; **29** 375, 414; **30 247–51 (upd.),** 140, 300, 337–38; **34** 442–43; **36** 81–82, 171, 480–81; **38** 54–55, 250, 417; **43** 126–27; **46** 165; **47** 153; **49** 94; **50** 223

International Care Services, **6** 182

International Cellucotton Products Co., **III** 40; **16** 302–03; **43** 256–57

International Cementers Inc., **25** 74

International Commercial Bank, **II** 257

International Communication Materials, Inc., **18** 387
International Computers. *See* ICL plc.
International Controls Corporation, 10 368–70
International Corona Corporation, **12** 244
International Creative Management, Inc., 38 161; **43 235–37**
International Credit Card Business Assoc., **II** 436
International Dairy Queen, Inc., 7 266; **10 371–74**; **39 232–36 (upd.)**
International Data Group, Inc., 7 238–40; **12** 561; **25 237–40 (upd.)**; **27** 222
International Development Bank, **IV** 417
International Digital Communications, Inc., **6** 327
International Distillers & Vintners Ltd., **31** 92
International Egyptian Oil Co., **IV** 412
International Engineering Company, Inc., **7** 355
International Epicure, **12** 280
International Equities Corp., **III** 98
International Factoring Corp., **II** 436
International Factors, Limited, **II** 208
International Family Entertainment Inc., 13 279–81; **52** 85
International Finance Corp., **19** 192
International Flavors & Fragrances Inc., 9 290–92; **38 244–48 (upd.)**
International Foods, **II** 468
International Fuel Cells Inc., **39** 394
International Game Technology, 10 375–76; **24** 37 **25** 313; **41 214–16 (upd.)**; **54** 14–15
International Graphics Corp., **IV** 645
International Group, **13** 277
International Harvester Co., **III** 473, 650, 651; **10** 264, 280, 378, 380, 528; **13** 16; **17** 158; **22** 380. *See also* Navistar International Corporation.
International Healthcare, **III** 197
International Home Foods, Inc., **42** 94
International House of Pancakes. *See* IHOP Corporation.
International Hydron, **10** 47; **13** 367
International Imaging Limited, **29** 58
International Income Property, **IV** 708
International Industries, **17** 249
International Insurance Company of Hannover Ltd., **53** 162
International Learning Systems Corp. Ltd., **IV** 641–42; **7** 311
International Lease Finance Corporation, III 198; **6** 67; **36** 231; **48 218–20**
International Light Metals Corp., **IV** 163
International MacGregor, **27** 269
International Management Group, 18 262–65
International Marine Oil Co., **IV** 363
International Marine Services, **22** 276
International Match, **12** 463
International Mercantile Marine Co., **II** 330
International Milling. *See* International Multifoods Corporation.
International Mineral & Chemical, Inc., **8** 265–66
International Minerals and Chemical Corporation, **19** 253
International Multifoods Corporation, II 493; **7 241–43**; **12** 80, 125; **14** 515; **21**

289; **23** 203; **25 241–44 (upd.)**; **28** 238; **50** 493
International Music Co., **16** 202; **43** 171
International News Service, **IV** 626–27; **19** 203; **25** 507
International Nickel Co. of Canada, Ltd. *See* Inco Limited.
International Nutrition Laboratories, **14** 558
International Olympic Committee, 44 244–47
International Organization of Consumers Unions, **26** 98
International Pacific Corp., **II** 389
International Paper Company, I 27; **II** 208, 403; **III** 693, 764; **IV** 16, 245, **286–88**, 289, 326; **8** 267; **11** 76, 311; **15 227–30 (upd.)**; **16** 349; **17** 446; **23** 48–49, 366, 368; **25** 9; **26** 444; **30** 92, 94; **32** 91, 346; **47 187–92 (upd.)**
International Parts Corporation, **10** 414
International Periodical Distributors, **34** 5
International Permalite, **22** 229
International Petroleum Co., Ltd., **IV** 415–16, 438, 478; **25** 230
International Petroleum Corp., **IV** 454, 484
International Pipeline Services, Inc., **51** 248
International Playtex, Inc., **12** 93
International Power PLC, 50 280–85 (upd.)
International Processing Corporation, **50** 123
International Products Corporation. *See* The Terlato Wine Group.
International Proteins Corporation, **21** 248
International Publishing Corp., **IV** 641, 666–67; **7** 343; **17** 397; **23** 350; **49** 407
International Raw Materials, Ltd., **31** 20
International Rectifier Corporation, 31 263–66
International Roofing Company, **22** 13–14
International Sealants Corporation, **8** 333
International Shipholding Corporation, Inc., 27 241–44
International Shoe Co., **III** 528–30
International Silver Company, **I** 30; **12** 472; **14** 482–83
International Specialty Products, Inc., **22** 225, 228–29
International Speedway Corporation, 19 221–23; **32** 439
International Standard Electric, **II** 66–68
International Stores, **I** 427
International Supply Consortium, **13** 79
International Talent Group, **25** 281
International Talent Management, Inc. *See* Motown Records Company L.P.
International Telcell Group, **7** 336
International Telecommunications Satellite Organization, **46** 328
International Telephone & Telegraph Corporation, I 434, 446, **462–64**, 544; **II** 13, 66, 68, 86, 130, 331; **III** 98–99, 162–64, 166, 644–45, 684; **V** 334–35, 337–38; **6** 356; **8** 157; **9** 10–11, 324; **10** 19, 44, 301; **11 196–99 (upd.)**, 337, 516; **12** 18; **13** 246; **14** 332, 488; **19** 131, 205, 208; **22** 55; **25** 100, 432; **46** 412
International Television Corporation Entertainment Group, **23** 391
International Thomson Organisation Ltd. *See* The Thomson Corporation.
International Thomson Organization Ltd., **23** 92

International Time Recording Company. *See* International Business Machines Corporation.
International Total Services, Inc., 37 215–18
International Trust and Investment Corp., **II** 577
International Trust Co., **II** 207
International Utilities Corp., **IV** 75–76; **6** 444
International Western Electric Co., **I** 462; **II** 66; **III** 162; **11** 196
International Wind Systems, **6** 581
International Wine & Spirits Ltd., **9** 533
International Wire Works Corp., **8** 13
International Wireless Inc., **21** 261
Internationale Industriële Beleggung Maatschappij Amsterdam BV, **IV** 128
Internationale Nederlanden Group, **24** 88
Internet Shopping Network, **26** 441
InterNorth, Inc., **II** 16; **V** 610
Interocean Management Corp., **9** 509–11
Interpac Belgium, **6** 303
Interprovincial Pipe Line Ltd., **I** 264; **IV** 439; **25** 231. *See also* Enbridge Inc.
The Interpublic Group of Companies, Inc., I 16–18, 31, 36; **6** 53; **14** 315; **16** 70, 72, 167; **20** 5; **22 294–97 (upd.)**; **23** 478; **28** 66–67; **32** 142; **42** 107; **51** 259
Interra Financial. *See* Dain Rauscher Corporation.
InterRedec, Inc., **17** 196
Interscience, **17** 271
Interscope Communications, Inc., **23** 389, 391; **27** 121
Interscope Music Group, 31 267–69
Intersec, Inc., **27** 21
Intersil Inc., **II** 30; **12** 196; **16** 358
Interstate & Ocean Transport, **6** 577
Interstate Bag, **I** 335
Interstate Bakeries Corporation, 7 320; **12 274–76**; **27** 310; **38 249–52 (upd.)**
Interstate Brick Company, **6** 568–69
Interstate Electric Manufacturing Company. *See* McGraw Electric Company.
Interstate Finance Corp., **11** 16
Interstate Financial Corporation, **9** 475
Interstate Iron and Steel Company. *See* Republic Engineered Steels, Inc.
Interstate Logos, Inc., **27** 278
Interstate Paint Distributors, Inc., **13** 367
Interstate Power Company, **6** 555, 605; **18** 404
Interstate Properties Inc., **45** 15–16
Interstate Public Service Company, **6** 555
Interstate Stores Inc., **V** 203; **15** 469; **18** 522
Interstate Supply Company. *See* McGraw Electric Company.
Interstate United Corporation, **II** 679; **III** 502; **13** 435
Intertec Design, Inc., **34** 371–72
Intertec Publishing Corp., **22** 441
Intertechnique SA, **36** 530
Interturbine Holland, **19** 150
Intertype Corp., **II** 37
Interunfall, **III** 346
Intervideo TV Productions-A.B., **II** 640
Intervision Express, **24** 510
Interweb, **IV** 661
InterWest Partners, **16** 418
Intimate Brands, Inc., 24 237–39' **29** 357
InTouch Systems, Inc., **43** 118
Intrac Handelsgesellschaft mbH, **7** 142

Intradal, **II** 572
Intraph South Africa Ltd., **6** 247
IntraWest Bank, **II** 289
The Intrawest Corporation, **15 234–36**; **31** 67; **43** 438
Intrepid Corporation, **16** 493
IntroGene B.V., **13** 241
Intuit Inc., **13** 147; **14 262–64**; **23** 457; **33 208–11 (upd.)**
Invacare Corporation, **11 200–02**, 486; **47 193–98 (upd.)**
Invenex Laboratories, **17** 287
Invensys PLC, **50 286–90 (upd.)**
Invento Products Corporation, **21** 269
Invep S.p.A., **10** 150
Inveresk Paper Co., **III** 693; **IV** 685
Invergordon Distillers, **III** 509
Inverness Medical Innovations, Inc., **45** 208
Inverness Medical Technology, Inc., **45** 210
Inversale, **9** 92
INVESCO MIM Management Limited, **21** 397
Invesgen S.A., **26** 129
InvestCorp International, **15** 200; **24** 195, 420; **25** 205, 207
Investcorp S.A. See Arabian Investment Banking Corp.
Investimentos Itaú S.A., **19** 33
Investors Bank and Trust Company, **18** 152
Investors Diversified Services, Inc., **II** 398; **6** 199; **8** 348–49; **10** 43–45, 59, 62; **21** 305; **25** 248; **38** 42
Investors Group, **III** 261. See also Power Corporation of Canada.
Investors Management Corp., **10** 331
Investors Overseas Services, **10** 368–69
InvestorsBancorp, **53** 222, 224
Investrónica S.A., **26** 129
Invista Capital Management, **III** 330
Invitrogen Corporation, **52 182–84**
Invivo Corporation, **52 185–87**
The Invus Group, Ltd., **33** 449
Iolab Corp., **III** 36
Iomega Corporation, **18** 509–10; **21 294–97**
IONA Technologies plc, **43 238–41**
Ionics, Incorporated, **52 188–90**
Ionpure Technologies Corporation, **6** 486–88
Iowa Beef Packers, **21** 287
Iowa Beef Processors, **II** 516–17; **IV** 481–82; **13** 351
Iowa Manufacturing, **II** 86
Iowa Mold Tooling Co., Inc., **16** 475
Iowa Public Service Company, **6** 524–25
IP Gas Supply Company, **6** 506
IP Services, Inc., **V** 255
IP Timberlands Ltd., **IV** 288
IP&L. See Illinois Power & Light Corporation.
Ipalco Enterprises, Inc., **6 508–09**; **53** 18
IPC. See International Publishing Corp.
IPC Communications, Inc., **15** 196
IPC Magazines Limited, **IV** 650; **7 244–47**
IPD. See International Periodical Distributors.
IPEC Holdings Ltd., **27** 474–75
Iphotonics Inc., **48** 369
Ipko-Amcor, **14** 225
IPL Energy Inc., **54** 354. See also Enbridge Inc.

IPS Praha a.s., **38** 437
IPS Publishing, **39** 341–42
IPSOA Editore, **14** 555
Ipsos SA, **24** 355; **48 221–24**
Ipswich Bancshares Inc., **55** 52
iQuantic Buck, **55** 73
IQUE, Inc., **21** 194
Iran Air, **6** 101
Iran Pan American Oil Co., **IV** 466
Iranian Oil Exploration and Producing Co., **IV** 466–67
Iraq Petroleum Co., **IV** 363, 386, 429, 450, 464, 558–60
Irby-Gilliland Company, **9** 127
Irdeto, **31** 330
IRI. See Instituto per la Ricostruzione Industriale.
Irideon, Inc., **35** 435
Iridian Asset Management LLC, **52** 172
Iris Associates, Inc., **25** 299, 301
IRIS Holding Co., **III** 347
Irish Agricultural Wholesale Society Ltd. See IAWS Group plc.
Irish Air. See Aer Lingus Group plc.
Irish Life Assurance Company, **16** 14; **43** 7
Irish Paper Sacks Ltd., **IV** 295; **19** 225
Irish Sugar Co., **II** 508
Iron and Steel Corp., **IV** 22, 41, 92, 533–34
Iron and Steel Press Company, **27** 360
Iron Cliffs Mining Company, **13** 156
Iron Mountain Forge, **13** 319
Iron Mountain, Inc., **33 212–14**
Iron Ore Company of Canada, **8** 347
Iroquois Gas Corporation, **6** 526
Irvin Feld & Kenneth Feld Productions, Inc., **15 237–39**. See also Feld Entertainment, Inc.
Irving Bank Corp., **II** 192
Irving Tanning Company, **17** 195
Irving Trust Coompany, **II** 257; **22** 55
Irvington Smelting, **IV** 78
Irwin Lehrhoff Associates, **11** 366
Irwin Toy Limited, **14 265–67**
Isabela Shoe Corporation, **13** 360
Isagro S.p.A., **26** 425
Iscor. See Iron and Steel Corporation.
Isetan Company Limited, **V 85–87**; **36 289–93 (upd.)**
Iseya Tanji Drapery, **V** 85
Ishikawajima-Harima Heavy Industries Co., Ltd., **I** 508, 511, 534; **II** 274; **III 532–33**; **9** 293; **12** 484; **41** 41
Ishizaki Honten, **III** 715
Isis Distributed Systems, Inc., **10** 501
Island Air, **24** 22
The Island ECN, Inc., **48 225–29**
Island Equipment Co., **19** 381
Island Holiday, **I** 417
Island Pictures Corp., **23** 389
Island Records, **23** 389
Islands Restaurants, **17** 85–87
Isle of Capri Casinos, Inc., **33** 41; **41 217–19**
Isolite Insulating Products Co., **III** 714
Isosceles PLC, **II** 628–29; **24** 270; **47** 367–68
Isotec Communications Incorporated, **13** 213
Isover, **III** 676; **16** 121
Ispat Inland Inc., **40 267–72 (upd.)**, 381
Ispat International N.V., **30 252–54**
Israel Chemicals Ltd., **55 226–29**
ISS A/S, **49 221–23**, 376

ISS International Service System, Inc., **8** 271
ISS Securitas, **42** 165, 167
ISSI. See Integrated Silicon Solutions Inc.
Istanbul Fertilizer Industry, **IV** 563
Istante Vesa s.r.l., **22** 239
Istituto Farmacologico Serono S.p.A. See Serono S.A.
Istituto Mobiliare Italiano S.p.A., **50** 407, 409
Istituto per la Ricostruzione Industriale S.p.A., **I** 207, 459, **465–67**; **II** 191–92, 270–71; **IV** 419; **11 203–06**; **13** 28, 218
Isuzu Motors, Ltd., **II** 274; **III** 581, 593; **7** 8, 219; **9 293–95**; **10** 354; **23 288–91 (upd.)**; **36** 240, 243
Isuzu Motors of Japan, **21** 6
IT Group, **28** 203
IT International, **V** 255
IT-Software Companies, **48** 402
Itabira Iron Ore Co. Ltd., **IV** 54; **43** 111
ITABRASCO, **IV** 55
Italcarta, **IV** 339
Italcementi, **IV** 420
Italcimenti Group, **40** 107–08
Italianni's, **22** 128
Italiatour, **6** 69
Italmobiliare, **III** 347
Italstate. See Societa per la Infrastrutture e l'Assetto del Territorio.
Italtel, **V** 326–27
Italware, **27** 94
Itaú. See Banco Itaú S.A.
Itaú Winterthur Seguradura S.A., **III** 404
Itaúsa. See Investimentos Itaú S.A.
Itek Corp., **I** 486; **11** 265
Itel Corporation, **II** 64; **III** 512; **6** 262, 354; **9** 49, **296–99**; **15** 107; **22** 339; **26** 328, 519; **47** 37
Items International Airwalk Inc., **17 259–61**
Ithaca Gas & Electric. See New York State Electric and Gas.
ITI Education Corporation, **29** 472
ITM Entreprises SA, **IV** 239; **36 294–97**
Ito Carnation Co., **II** 518
Ito Food Processing Co., **II** 518
Ito Gofuku Co. Ltd., **V** 129
Ito Meat Processing Co., **II** 518
Ito Processed Food Co., **II** 518
Ito-Yokado Co., Ltd., **II** 661; **V 88–89**; **32** 414, 416–17; **42 189–92 (upd.)**
Itochu and Renown, Inc., **12** 281
ITOCHU Corporation, **19** 9; **32 283–87 (upd.)**; **34** 231; **42** 342
Itochu Housing, **38** 415
Itochu of Japan, **14** 550
Itoh. See C. Itoh & Co.
Itoham Foods Inc., **II 518–19**
Itokin, **III** 48
Itoman & Co., **26** 456
The Itsy Bitsy Entertainment Company, **51** 309
ITT, **21** 200; **24** 188, 405; **30** 101; **47** 103. See also International Telephone and Telegraph Corporation.
ITT Aerospace, **33** 48
ITT Educational Services, Inc., **33 215–17**
ITT Sheraton Corporation, **III 98–101**; **23** 484; **54** 345–47. See also Starwood Hotels & Resorts Worldwide, Inc.
ITT World Directories, **27** 498, 500
iTurf Inc., **29** 142–43

ITW. *See* Illinois Tool Works Inc.
ITW Devcon, **12** 7
IU International, **23** 40
IURA Edition, **14** 556
IV Therapy Associates, **16** 440
IVAC Corp., **I** 646; **11** 90
IVACO Industries Inc., **11** 207
Ivanhoe, Inc., **II** 662, 664
IVAX Corporation, 11 207–09; 41
420–21; **55 230–33 (upd.)**
IVC Industries, Inc., 45 208–11
Iveco, **I** 148; **12** 91
Ives Trains, **16** 336
iVillage Inc., 46 232, 253–56
Ivy Mortgage Corp., **39** 380, 382
Iwai & Co., **I** 492, 509–10; **IV** 151; **24**
325, 358
Iwata Air Compressor, **III** 427
Iwerks Entertainment, Inc., 33 127; 34
228–30
IXC Communications, Inc., **29** 250–52;
37 127
IXI Ltd., **38** 418–19
IYG Holding Company of Japan, **7** 492; **32**
414, 417
The IZOD Gant Corporation, **24** 385
Izod Lacoste, **II** 502–03; **9** 156–57; **10**
324
Izukyu Corporation, **47** 408
Izumi Fudosan, **IV** 726
Izumiya, **V** 477; **36** 418

J&E Davy, **16** 14
J&G Meakin, **12** 529
J&J Colman, **II** 566
J&J Corrugated Box Corp., **IV** 282; **9** 261
J & J Snack Foods Corporation, 24
240–42
J&L Industrial Supply, **13** 297
J&L Steel. *See* Jones & Laughlin Steel
Corp.
J & M Laboratories, **48** 299
J&R Electronics Inc., 26 224–26
J. & W. Seligman and Co., **17** 498
J.A. Baldwin Manufacturing Company, **17**
106
J.A. Jones, Inc., 16 284–86; 17 377
J. Aron & Co., **II** 415; **51** 148
J.B. Hudson & Son, **18** 136
J.B. Hunt Transport Services Inc., 12
277–79; 15 440; **26** 533; **50** 209
J.B. Lippincott & Company, **IV** 652; **14**
554–56; **33** 460
J.B. McLean Publishing Co., Ltd., **IV** 638
J.B. Williams Company, **III** 66; **8** 63
J.B. Wolters Publishing Company, **14** 554
J. Baker, Inc., 13 361; **31 270–73**
J. Beres & Son, **24** 444–45
J Bibby & Sons, **I** 424
J Bibby Agriculture Limited, **13** 53
J. Bulova Company. *See* Bulova
Corporation.
J. Byrons, **9** 186
J.C. Baxter Co., **15** 501
J.C. Hillary's, **20** 54
J.C. Penney Company, Inc., I 516; **V**
90–92; 6 336; **8** 288, 555; **9** 156, 210,
213, 219, 346–94; **10** 409, 490; **11** 349;
12 111, 431, 522; **14** 62; **16** 37, 327–28;
17 124, 175, 177, 366, 460; **18** 108, 136,
168, 200, **269–73 (upd.)**, 373, 478; **19**
300; **21** 24, 527; **25** 91, 254, 368; **26**
161; **27** 346, 429; **31** 260–61; **32** 166,

168–70; **39** 270; **41** 114–15; **43 245–50**
(upd.)
J. Crew Group Inc., 12 280–82; 25 48;
34 231–34 (upd.); 36 472
J.D. Bassett Manufacturing Co. *See* Bassett
Furniture Industries, Inc.
J.D. Edwards & Company, 14 268–70;
38 431
J.D. Power and Associates, 9 166; **32**
297–301
J. D'Addario & Company, Inc., 48
230–33
J.E. Baxter Co., **I** 429
J.E. Nolan, **11** 486
J.E. Sirrine. *See* CRSS Inc.
J.E. Smith Box & Printing Co., **13** 441
J. Edward Connelly Associates, Inc., **22**
438
J. Evershed & Son, **13** 103
J.F. Corporation, **V** 87
J.F. Lauman and Co., **II** 681
J.F. Shea Co., Inc., 55 234–36
J. Fielding & Co., **IV** 249
J.G. McMullen Dredging Co., **III** 558
J. Gadsden Paper Products, **IV** 249
J. George Leyner Engineering Works Co.,
III 525–26
J.H. Heafner Co., **20** 263
J.H. Stone & Sons, **IV** 332
J.H. Whitney & Company, **9** 250; **32** 100
J. Homestock. *See* R.H. Macy & Co.
J. Horner's, **48** 415
J.I. Case Company, I 148, 527; **III** 651;
10 377–81; 13 17; **22** 380. *See also*
CNH Global N.V.
JJ. Farmer Clothing Inc., **51** 320–21
J.J. Kenney Company, Inc., **51** 244
The J. Jill Group, Inc., 35 239–41
J.K. Armsby Co., **7** 130–31
J.K. Starley and Company Ltd, **7** 458
J.L. Clark, Inc. *See* Clarcor Inc.
J.L. Hudson Company. *See* Dayton Hudson
Corporation.
J.L. Kraft & Bros. Co., **II** 532
J.L. Shiely Co., **III** 691
J.L. Wright Company, **25** 379
J. Levin & Co., Inc., **13** 367
J.M. Brunswick & Brothers, **III** 442
J.M. Douglas & Company Limited, **14** 141
J.M. Horton Ice Cream Co., **II** 471
J.M. Huber Corporation, **40** 68
J.M. Jones Co., **II** 668; **18** 504; **50** 454
J.M. Kohler Sons Company, **7** 269
The J.M. Smucker Company, 11 210–12
J.M. Tull Metals Co., Inc., **IV** 116; **15** 250;
19 219
J.M. Voith AG, 33 222–25
J. Mandelbaum & Sons, **19** 510
J-Mar Associates, **31** 435–36
J-Mass, **IV** 289
J. Muirhead Ltd., **I** 315; **25** 81
J.P. Heilwell Industries, **II** 420
J.P. Morgan & Co. Incorporated, II 281,
329–32, 407, 419, 427–28, 430–31,
441; **III** 237, 245, 380; **IV** 20, 180, 400;
9 386; **11** 421; **12** 165; **13** 13; **16** 25,
375; **19** 190; **26** 66, 500; **30 261–65**
(upd.); 33 464; **35** 74; **36** 151–53; **50**
30
J.P. Morgan Chase & Co., 38 253–59
(upd.)

J.P. Stevens Inc., **8** 234; **12** 404; **16**
533–35; **17** 75; **19** 420; **27** 468–69; **28**
218
J.P. Wood, **II** 587
J.R. Brown & Sharpe. *See* Brown &
Sharpe Manufacturing Co.
J.R. Geigy S.A., **I** 632–33, 635, 671; **8**
108–10; **39** 72
J.R. Parkington Co., **I** 280
J.R. Simplot Company, 16 287–89; 21
508; **26** 309
J.R. Wyllie & Sons, **I** 437
J. Ray McDermott & Co., **III** 558–59
J.S. Fry & Sons, **II** 476
J.S. Morgan & Co., **II** 329, 427
J Sainsbury plc, II 657–59, 677–78; **10**
442; **11** 239, 241; **13 282–84 (upd.); 17**
42; **21** 335; **22** 241; **32** 253; **38 260–65**
(upd.)
J. Sanders & Sons, **IV** 711
J. Sears & Company, **V** 177
J. Spiegel and Company. *See* Spiegel, Inc.
J.T. Wing and Co., **I** 158
J.U. Dickson Sawmill Inc. *See* Dickson
Forest Products, Inc.
J.W. Bateson, **8** 87
J.W. Buderus and Sons, **III** 694
J.W. Charles Financial Services Inc., **25**
542
J.W. Childs Associates, L.P., **46** 220
J.W. Childs Equity Partners LP, **40** 274
J.W. Foster and Sons, Inc. *See* Reebok
International Ltd.
J.W. Higman & Co., **III** 690
J.W. Spear, **25** 314
J.W. Wassall Ltd. *See* Wassall PLC.
J. Walter Thompson Co., **I** 9, 17, 25, 37,
251, 354, 623; **10** 69; **11** 51; **12** 168; **16**
167; **48** 442
J. Weingarten Inc., **7** 203; **28** 163
J Wiss & Sons Co., **II** 16
J.Z. Sales Corp., **16** 36
J. Zinmeister Co., **II** 682
Jabil Circuit, Inc., 36 298–301
Jacintoport Corporation, **7** 281
Jack Daniel Distillery, **10** 180
Jack Daniel's. *See* Brown-Forman
Corporation.
Jack Eckerd Corp., **16** 160; **19** 467
Jack Frain Enterprises, **16** 471
Jack Henry and Associates, Inc., 17
262–65
Jack Houston Exploration Company, **7** 345
Jack in the Box, Inc. *See* Foodmaster, Inc.
Jack Schwartz Shoes, Inc., 18 266–68
Jackpot Enterprises Inc., 21 298–300; 24
36
Jackson & Curtis, **II** 444; **22** 405
Jackson & Perkins. *See* Bear Creek
Corporation.
Jackson Box Co., **IV** 311; **19** 267
Jackson Cushion Spring Co., **13** 397
Jackson Furniture of Danville, LLC, **48**
246
Jackson Hewitt, Inc., 48 234–36
Jackson Ice Cream Co., **12** 112
Jackson Marine Corp., **III** 499
Jackson Mercantile Co. *See* Jitney-Jungle
Stores of America, Inc.
Jackson National Life Insurance
Company, III 335–36; **8 276–77; 48**
327
Jackson Purchase Electric Cooperative
Corporation, **11** 37

Jacksonville Shipyards, **I** 170
Jaco Electronics, Inc., 19 311; **30 255–57**
Jacob Holm & Sons A/S, **22** 263
Jacob Leinenkugel Brewing Company,
    12 338; **28 209–11**
Jacobs Brake Manufacturing Company, **7**
    116–17
Jacobs Engineering Group Inc., 6
    148–50; 26 220–23 (upd.)
Jacobs Suchard (AG), **II** 520–22, 540,
    569; **15** 64; **29** 46–47. *See also* Kraft
    Jacobs Suchard AG.
Jacobson Stores Inc., 21 301–03
Jacoby & Meyers, **20** 435
Jacor Communications, Inc., 6 33; **23**
    292–95; 24 108; **27** 339; **35** 220
Jacques Borel International, **II** 641; **10** 12;
    49 126
Jacques Chocolaterie S.A., **53** 315
Jacques Fath Perfumes, **III** 47
Jacuzzi Inc., 7 207, 209; **23 296–98**
Jade Accessories, **14** 224
Jade KK, **25** 349
Jadepoint, **18** 79–80
JAF Pampryl, **I** 281
Jafco Co. Ltd., **49** 433
Jafra Cosmetics, **15** 475, 477
Jagenberg AG, **9** 445–46; **14** 57
Jaguar Cars, Ltd., III 439, 495; **11** 140;
    13 28, 219, **285–87,** 414; **36** 198, 217.
    See also Ford Motor Company.
JAI Parabolic Spring Ltd., **III** 582
JAIX Leasing Company, **23** 306
JAKKS Pacific, Inc., 52 191–94
Ab Jakobstads Cellulosa-Pietarsaaren
    Selluloosa Oy, **IV** 302
JAL. *See* Japan Air Lines.
Jalate Inc., 25 245–47
Jaluzot & Cie. *See* Pinault-Printemps-
    Redoute S.A.
Jamaica Gas Light Co., **6** 455
Jamaica Plain Trust Co., **II** 207
Jamaica Water Supply Company. *See* JWP
    Inc.
Jamba Juice Company, 47 199–202
JAMCO, **III** 589
James A. Ryder Transportation (Jartran), **V**
    505
James Bay Development Corporation, **6**
    502
James Beam Distilling Co., **I** 226; **10** 180
James Beattie plc, 43 242–44
James Burn/American, Inc., **17** 458
James C. Heintz Company, **19** 278
James Ericson, **III** 324
James Felt Realty, Inc., **21** 257
James Fison and Sons. *See* Fisons plc.
James Fleming, **II** 500
James G. Fast Company. *See* Angelica
    Corporation.
James Gulliver Associates, **II** 609
James Hardie Industries Limited, **IV** 249;
    26 494
James Hartley & Son, **III** 724
James Heekin and Company, **13** 254
James Lyne Hancock Ltd., **I** 428
James Magee & Sons Ltd., **IV** 294; **19** 224
James McNaughton Ltd., **IV** 325
James O. Welch Co., **II** 543
James Publishing Group, **17** 272
James R. Osgood & Company, **10** 356
James River Corporation of Virginia, IV
    289–91; 8 483; **22** 209; **29** 136. *See also*
    Fort James Corporation.

James Stedman Ltd., **II** 569
James Talcott, Inc., **11** 260–61
James Thompson, **IV** 22
James Wellbeloved, **39** 354, 356
James Wholesale Company, **18** 7
James Wrigley & Sons, **IV** 257
Jamestown Insurance Co. Ltd., **55** 20
Jamestown Publishers, **22** 522
Jamesway Corporation, **IV** 136; **13** 261; **23**
    177
Jamie Scott, Inc., **27** 348
Jamieson & Co., **22** 428
Jamna Auto Industries Pvt. Ltd., **III** 581
Jämsänkoski Oy, **IV** 347
Jan Bell Marketing Inc., **24** 335. *See also*
    Mayor's Jewelers, Inc.
Janata Bank, **31** 219
Jane Jones Enterprises, **16** 422; **43** 309
Jane's Information Group, **8** 525
Janesville Electric, **6** 604
Janet Frazer, **V** 118
Janin, S.A., **36** 163
Janna Systems Inc., **38** 433
Janson Publications, **22** 522
Janssen-Kyowa, **III** 43
N.V. Janssen M&L, **17** 147
Janssen Pharmaceutica, **III** 36; **8** 282
JANT Pty. Ltd., **IV** 285
Jantzen Inc., **V** 391; **17** 513
Janus Capital Corporation, **6** 401–02; **26**
    233
Japan Acoustics, **II** 118
Japan Advertising Ltd., **16** 166
Japan Air Filter Co., Ltd., **III** 634
Japan Airlines Company, Ltd., I 104–06;
    6 70–71, 118, 123, 386, 427; **24**
    399–400; **27** 464; **32 288–92 (upd.); 49**
    459
Japan Brewery. *See* Kirin Brewery
    Company, Limited.
Japan Broadcasting Corporation, I 586;
    II 66, 101, 118; **7 248–50; 9** 31
Japan-California Bank, **II** 274
Japan Commerce Bank, **II** 291
Japan Copper Manufacturing Co., **II** 104;
    IV 211
Japan Cotton Co., **IV** 150; **24** 357
Japan Creative Tours Co., **I** 106
Japan Credit Bureau, **II** 348
Japan Dairy Products, **II** 538
Japan Day & Night Bank, **II** 292
Japan Development Bank, **II** 300, 403
Japan Dyestuff Manufacturing Co., **I** 397
Japan Elanco Company, Ltd., **17** 437
Japan Electricity Generation and
    Transmission Company (JEGTCO), **V**
    574
Japan Energy Corporation, **13** 202; **14** 206,
    208
Japan Food Corporation, **14** 288
Japan International Bank, **II** 292
Japan International Liquor, **I** 220
Japan Iron & Steel Co., Ltd., **IV** 157; **17**
    349–50
Japan Leasing Corporation, 8 278–80;
    11 87
Japan Medico, **25** 431
Japan National Oil Corp., **IV** 516
Japan National Railway, **V** 448–50; **6** 70
Japan Oil Development Co., **IV** 364
Japan Petroleum Development Corp., **IV**
    461
Japan Petroleum Exploration Co., **IV** 516

Japan Pulp and Paper Company
    Limited, IV 292–93, 680
Japan Reconstruction Finance Bank, **II** 300
Japan Special Steel Co., Ltd., **IV** 63
Japan Steel Manufacturing Co., **IV** 211
Japan Steel Works, **I** 508
Japan Telecom, **7** 118; **13** 482
Japan Telegraphic Communication
    Company (Nihon Denpo-Tsushin Sha),
    16 166
Japan Tobacco Inc., V 403–04; 30 387;
    46 257–60 (upd.)
Japan Trust Bank, **II** 292
Japan Trustee Services Bank Ltd., **53** 322
Japan Try Co., **III** 758
Japan Vilene Company Ltd., **41** 170–72
Japanese and Asian Development Bank, **IV**
    518
Japanese Electronic Computer Co., **III** 140
Japanese Enterprise Co., **IV** 728
Japanese National Railway, **I** 579; **III** 491;
    43 103
Japanese Victor Co., **II** 118
Japex Oman Co., **IV** 516
Japonica Partners, **9** 485
Jara Enterprises, Inc., **31** 276
Jarcho Brothers Inc., **I** 513
Jardinay Manufacturing Corp., **24** 335
Jardine Matheson Holdings Limited, I
    468–71, 521–22, 577, 592; **II** 296; **IV**
    189, 699–700; **16** 479–80; **18** 114; **20**
    309–14 (upd.); 47 175–78
Jartran Inc., **V** 505; **24** 410
Järvenpään Kotelo Oy, **IV** 315
Jarvis plc, 39 237–39
Jas, Hennessy & Co., **I** 272
Jas. I. Miller Co., **13** 491
JASCO Products, **III** 581
Jason Incorporated, 23 299–301; 52 138
Jasper Corporation, **III** 767; **22** 546. *See*
    also Kimball International, Inc.
JAT, **27** 475
Jato, **II** 652
Jauch & Hübener, **14** 279
Java-China-Japan Line, **6** 403–04; **26** 242
Java Software, **30** 453
Javelin Software Corporation, **10** 359
Javex Co., **IV** 272
Jax, **9** 452
Jay Cooke and Co., **III** 237; **9** 370
Jay Jacobs, Inc., 15 243–45
Jay-Ro Services, **III** 419
Jay's Washateria, Inc., **7** 372
Jayco Inc., 13 288–90
Jaywoth Industries, **III** 673
Jazz Basketball Investors, Inc., 55
    237–39
Jazzercise, Inc., 45 212–14
JB Oxford Holdings, Inc., 32 293–96
JBA Holdings PLC, **43** 184
JBL, **22** 97
JCB, **14** 321
JCJL. *See* Java-China-Japan Line.
JD Wetherspoon plc, 30 258–60
JDS Uniphase Corporation, 34 235–37
The Jean Coutu Group (PJC) Inc., 46
    261–65
Jean-Jacques, **19** 50
Jean Lassale, **III** 619–20; **17** 430
Jean Lincet, **19** 50
Jean Nate, **I** 695
Jean Pagées et Fils, **III** 420
Jean-Philippe Fragrances, Inc. *See* Inter
    Parfums, Inc.

Jean Prouvost, **IV** 618
Jeanmarie Creations, Inc., **18** 67, 69
Jeanne Piaubert, **III** 47
Jeanneau SA, **55** 56
Jefferies Group, Inc., 25 248–51
Jefferson Bancorp, Inc., **37** 201
Jefferson Chemical Co., **IV** 552
Jefferson Fire Insurance Co., **III** 239
Jefferson National Life Group, **10** 247
**Jefferson-Pilot Corporation, 11 213–15;
29 253–56 (upd.)**
Jefferson Properties, Inc. *See* JPI.
**Jefferson Smurfit Group plc, IV 294–96;
16 122; 19 224–27 (upd.); 49 224–29
(upd.).** *See also* Smurfit-Stone Container
Corporation.
Jefferson Standard Life Insurance, **11**
213–14
Jefferson Ward, **12** 48–49
Jefferson Warrior Railroad Company, **III**
767; **22** 546
Jeffery Sons & Co. Ltd., **IV** 711
Jeffrey Galion, **III** 472
JEGTCO. *See* Japan Electricity Generation
and Transmission Company (JEGTCO).
Jeld-Wen, Inc., 33 409; 45 215–17
Jell-O Co., **II** 531
Jem Development, **17** 233
Jenaer Glaswerk Schott & Genossen, **III**
445, 447
Jenn-Air Corporation, **III** 573; **22** 349
Jennie-O Foods, **II** 506; **54** 166–67
Jennifer Convertibles, Inc., 31 274–76
**Jenny Craig, Inc., 10 382–84; 12 531; 29
257–60 (upd.)**
Jeno's, **13** 516; **26** 436
Jenoptik AG, 33 218–21; 53 167
Jensen Salsbery, **I** 715
Jenson, Woodward & Lozier, Inc., **21** 96
JEORA Co., **IV** 564
Jeppesen Sanderson, Inc., **IV** 677; **17** 486
Jepson Corporation, **8** 230
Jeri-Jo Knitwear, Inc., **27** 346, 348
Jerome Foods, Inc., **54** 168
Jerome Increase Case Machinery Company.
See J.I. Case Company.
Jerrico Inc., **27** 145
Jerrold Corporation, **10** 319–20
Jerry Bassin Inc., **17** 12–14
Jerry's Famous Deli Inc., 24 243–45
Jerry's Restaurants, **13** 320
Jersey Central Power & Light Company,
27 182
Jersey Paper, **IV** 261
Jersey Standard. *See* Standard Oil Co. of
New Jersey.
Jervis B. Webb Company, 24 246–49
Jesse Jones Sausage Co. *See* GoodMark
Foods, Inc.
Jesse L. Lasky Feature Play Co., **II** 154
Jessup & Moore Paper Co., **IV** 351; **19**
495
Jet America Airlines, **I** 100; **6** 67, 82
Jet Capital Corp., **I** 123
Jet Petroleum, Ltd., **IV** 401
Jet Research Center, **III** 498
Jet Set Corporation, **18** 513
JetBlue Airways Corporation, 44 248–50
**Jetro Cash & Carry Enterprises Inc., 38
266–68**
Jetway Systems, **III** 512
Jeumont-Industrie, **II** 93
Jeumont-Schneider Industries, **II** 93–94; **9**
10; **18** 473

Jevic Transportation, Inc., **45** 448
Jewel Companies, Inc., **II** 605; **6** 531; **12**
63; **18** 89; **22** 38; **26** 476; **27** 291
Jewel Food Stores, **7** 127–28; **13** 25
Jewell Ridge Coal Corp., **IV** 181
JFD-Encino, **24** 243
JG Industries, Inc., 15 240–42
Jheri Redding Products, Inc., **17** 108
JHT, Inc., **39** 377
Jiamusi Combine Harvester Factory, **21**
175
Jiangsu General Ball & Roller Co., Ltd.,
45 170
JIB Group plc, **20** 313
Jiffee Chemical Corporation, **III** 21; **22**
146
Jiffy Auto Rental, **16** 380
Jiffy Convenience Stores, **II** 627
Jiffy Lube International, Inc., **IV** 490; **21**
541; **24** 339; **25** 443–45; **50** 353
Jiffy Mixes, **29** 109–10
Jiffy Packaging, **14** 430
Jiji, **16** 166
Jil Sander A.G., **45** 342, 344
**Jillian's Entertainment Holdings, Inc., 40
273–75**
Jim Beam Brands Co., 14 271–73; 29
196
Jim Cole Enterprises, Inc., **19** 247
**The Jim Henson Company, 23 302–04;
45** 130
The Jim Pattison Group, 37 219–22
Jim Walter Corporation. *See* Walter
Industries, Inc.
Jim Walter Papers, **IV** 282; **9** 261
Jimmy Carter Work Project. *See* Habitat
for Humanity International.
Jintan Taionkei Co. *See* Terumo
Corporation.
**Jitney-Jungle Stores of America, Inc., 27
245–48**
Jitsugyo no Nihon-sha, **IV** 631
Jitsuyo Jidosha Seizo Co., **I** 183
JJB Sports plc, 32 302–04
JLA Credit, **8** 279
JLG Industries, Inc., 52 195–97
JLL. *See* Jones Lang LaSalle Incorporated.
JMB Internacionale S.A., **25** 121
JMB Realty Corporation, IV 702–03.
See also Amfac/JMB Hawaii L.L.C.
Jno. H. Swisher & Son. *See* Swisher
International Group Inc.
JNR. *See* Japan National Railway.
Jo-Ann Fabrics and Crafts, **16** 197
Jo-Gal Shoe Company, Inc., **13** 360
Joanna Cotton Mills, **14** 220
Joannes Brothers, **II** 668
Jobete Music. *See* Motown Records
Company L.P.
JobWorks Agency, Inc., **16** 50
**Jockey International, Inc., 12 283–85; 34
238–42 (upd.)**
Joe Alexander Press, **12** 472; **36** 469
Joe B. Hughes, **III** 498
Joe's American Bar & Grill, **20** 54
Joe's Crab Shack, **15** 279
**The Joffrey Ballet of Chicago, 52
198–202**
Joh. A. Benckiser GmbH, **36** 140
Joh. Parviaisen Tehtaat Oy, **IV** 276
Johann Jakob Rieter & Co., **III** 402
Johannesburg Consolidated Investment Co.
Ltd., **IV** 21–22, 118; **16** 293

John A. Frye Shoe Company, **V** 376; **8** 16;
26 397–98; **36** 24
John A. Pratt and Associates, **22** 181
John Alden Life Insurance, **10** 340
**John B. Sanfilippo & Son, Inc., 14
274–76**
John Bean Spray Pump Co., **I** 442
John Blair & Company, **6** 13
John Brown plc, I 572–74
John Bull, **II** 550
John Carr Group, **31** 398–400
John Chatillon & Sons Inc., **29** 460
John Crane International, **17** 480
John Crosland Company, **8** 88
**The John D. and Catherine T.
MacArthur Foundation, 34 243–46**
John de Kuyper and Son, **I** 377
John Deere. *See* Deere & Company.
John F. Jelke Company, **9** 318
John F. Murray Co., **I** 623; **10** 69
**John Fairfax Holdings Limited, 7
251–54**
John Gardner Catering, **III** 104
John Govett & Co., **II** 349
John Gund Brewing Co., **I** 253
John H. Harland Company, 17 266–69
John H.R. Molson & Bros. *See* The
Molson Companies Limited.
**John Hancock Financial Services, Inc.,
42 193–98 (upd.)**
**John Hancock Mutual Life Insurance
Company, III 265–68,** 291, 313, 332,
400; **IV** 283; **13** 530; **25** 528
John Hill and Son, **II** 569
John Holroyd & Co. of Great Britain, **7**
236
John L. Wortham & Son Agency, **III** 193
John Labatt Ltd., **I** 267; **II** 582; **8** 399; **16**
397; **17** 256–57. *See also* Labatt
Brewing Company Limited.
John Laing plc, I 575–76, 588; **51**
171–73 (upd.)
John Lewis Partnership plc, V 93–95; 13
307; **42 199–203 (upd.)**
John Lucas Co., **III** 745
John Lysaght, **III** 493–95
John M. Hart Company, **9** 304
John M. Smyth Co., **15** 282
John Macfarlane and Sons, **II** 593
John Mackintosh and Sons, **II** 568–69
John McConnell & Co., **13** 102
John McLean and Sons Ltd., **III** 753
John Menzies plc, 39 240–43
John Morrell and Co., **II** 595–96; **21** 111
John Nicholls & Co., **III** 690
**The John Nuveen Company, III 356; 21
304–06; 22** 492, 494–95
John Oster Manufacturing Company. *See*
Sunbeam-Oster.
John Paul Mitchell Systems, 24 250–52
John Pew & Company, **13** 243
**John Q. Hammons Hotels, Inc., 24
253–55**
John R. Figg, Inc., **II** 681
John Rogers Co., **9** 253
John Sands, **22** 35
John Schroeder Lumber Company, **25** 379
John Sexton & Co., **26** 503
John Strange Paper Company, **8** 358
John Swire & Sons Ltd. *See* Swire Pacific
Ltd.
John W. Danforth Company, 48 237–39
John Walker & Sons, **I** 239–40
John Wanamaker, **22** 110

John Wiley & Sons, Inc., 17 270–72
John Williams, **III** 691
John Wyeth & Bro., **I** 713
John Yokley Company, **11** 194
John Zink Company, **22** 3–4; **25** 403
Johnny Rockets Group, Inc., 31 277–81
Johns Manville Corporation, **III** 708; **7** 293; **11** 420; **19** 211–12
Johns Perry, **III** 673
Johnsen, Jorgensen and Wettre, **14** 249
Johnson. *See* Axel Johnson Group.
Johnson & Higgins, 14 277–80
Johnson and Howe Furniture Corporation, **33** 151
Johnson & Johnson, III 18, 35–37; **IV** 285, 722; **7** 45–46; **8 281–83 (upd.)**, 399, 511–12; **9** 89–90; **10** 47, 69, 78, 80, 534–35; **15** 357–58, 360; **16** 168, 440; **17** 104–05, 340, 342–43, 533; **19** 103, 105; **25** 55–56; **34** 280, 283–84; **36 302–07 (upd.)**; **37** 110–11, 113; **41** 154–55; **46** 104; **55** 122–23
Johnson and Patan, **III** 671
Johnson and Sons Smelting Works Ltd., **IV** 119
Johnson Brothers, **12** 528
Johnson, Carruthers & Rand Shoe Co., **III** 528
Johnson Controls, Inc., III 534–37; 13 398; **16** 184, 322; **26 227–32 (upd.)**
Johnson Diversified, Inc., **III** 59
Johnson Engineering Corporation, **37** 365
Johnson Matthey PLC, II 390; **IV** 23, 117–20; **16** 28, 290–94 **(upd.)**, 439; **49 230–35 (upd.)**; **50** 33
Johnson Motor Co., **III** 597–99
Johnson Products Co., Inc., **11** 208; **31** 89
Johnson Publishing Company, Inc., 27 361; **28 212–14**
Johnson Systems, **6** 224
Johnson Wax. *See* S.C. Johnson & Son, Inc.
Johnson Worldwide Associates, Inc., 24 530; **28 215–17**, 412
Johnston Coca-Cola Bottling Company of Chattanooga, **13** 163–64
Johnston Evans & Co., **IV** 704
Johnston Foil Co., **IV** 18
Johnston Harvester Co., **III** 650
Johnston Industries, Inc., 15 246–48
Johnston, Lemon & Co., **53** 134
Johnston Press plc, 35 242–44
Johnstown America Industries, Inc., 23 305–07
Johnstown Sanitary Dairy, **13** 393
Joint Environment for Digital Imaging, **50** 322
Jointless Rim Ltd., **I** 428
Jokisch, **II** 556
Jonathan Backhouse & Co., **II** 235
Jonathan Logan Inc., **13** 536
Jonell Shoe Manufacturing Corporation, **13** 360
Jones & Babson, Inc., **14** 85
Jones & Johnson, **14** 277
Jones & Laughlin Steel Corp., **I** 463, 489–91; **IV** 228; **11** 197
Jones Apparel Group, Inc., 11 216–18; 27 60; **30** 310–11; **39 244–47 (upd.)**, 301, 303
Jones Brothers Tea Co., **7** 202
Jones, Day, Reavis & Pogue, 33 226–29
Jones Environmental, **11** 361

Jones Financial Companies, L.P. *See* Edward Jones.
Jones Intercable, Inc., 14 260; **17** 7; **21 307–09**; **24** 123; **25** 212
Jones Janitor Service, **25** 15
Jones Lang LaSalle Incorporated, 49 236–38
Jones Medical Industries, Inc., 24 256–58; **34** 460
Jones Motor Co., **10** 44
Jones-Rodolfo Corp. *See* Cutter & Buck, Inc.
Jonker Fris, **II** 571
Jonkoping & Vulcan, **12** 462
Jordache Enterprises, Inc., 15 201–02; **23 308–10**
The Jordan Co., **11** 261; **16** 149
Jordan Industries, Inc., 36 308–10
Jordan Marsh, **III** 608; **V** 26; **9** 209
Jordan Valley Electric Cooperative, **12** 265
Jos. A. Bank Clothiers, Inc., II 560; **12** 411; **31 282–85**
Josef Meys, **III** 418
The Joseph & Feiss Company, **48** 209
Joseph Bellamy and Sons Ltd., **II** 569
Joseph Campbell Company. *See* Campbell Soup Company.
Joseph Crosfield, **III** 31
Joseph E. Seagram & Sons Inc., **I** 266, 285; **21** 319
Joseph Garneau Co., **I** 226; **10** 180
Joseph Leavitt Corporation, **9** 20
Joseph Littlejohn & Levy, **27** 204; **53** 241
Joseph Lucas & Son, **III** 554–56
Joseph Lumber Company, **25** 379
Joseph Magnin, **I** 417–18; **17** 124; **41** 114
Joseph Malecki Corp., **24** 444–45
Joseph Nathan & Co., **I** 629–40
Joseph Rank Limited, **II** 564
Joseph Schlitz Brewing Company, **25** 281
Joseph T. Ryerson & Son, Inc., IV 114; **15 249–51**; **19** 217, 381. *See also* Ryerson Tull, Inc.
Joseph Transportation Inc., **55** 347
Josephson International, **27** 392; **43** 235
Joshin Denki, **13** 481
Joshu Railway Company, **6** 431
Joshua's Christian Bookstores, **31** 435–36; **51** 132
Josiah Wedgwood and Sons Limited. *See* Waterford Wedgewood plc..
Jostens, Inc., 7 255–57; 25 252–55 (upd.); **36** 470
Journal Register Company, 29 261–63
Journey's End Corporation, **14** 107
Jovan, **III** 66
Jove Publications, Inc., **II** 144; **IV** 623; **12** 224
Jovi, **II** 652
Joy Manufacturing, **III** 526
Joy Planning Co., **III** 533
Joy Technologies Inc., **II** 17; **26** 70; **38** 227
Joyce International, Inc., **16** 68
JP Foodservice Inc., **24** 445
JP Household Supply Co. Ltd., **IV** 293
JP Information Center Co., Ltd., **IV** 293
JP Planning Co. Ltd., **IV** 293
JPC Co., **IV** 155
JPF Holdings, Inc. *See* U.S. Foodservice.
JPI, 49 239–41
JPS Automotive L.P., **17** 182–84
JPS Textile Group, Inc., 28 218–20
JPT Publishing, **8** 528

JR & F SA, **53** 32
JR Central, **43** 103
Jr. Food Stores, Inc., **51** 170
JR Tokai, **43** 103
JSC MMC Norilsk Nickel, 48 300–02
JT Aquisitions, **II** 661
JTL Corporation, **13** 162–63
JTN Acquisition Corp., **19** 233
JTS Corporation, **23** 23, 26
Jude Hanbury, **I** 294
Judel Glassware Co., Inc., **14** 502
The Judge Group, Inc., 51 174–76
Judson Dunaway Corp., **12** 127
Judson Steel Corp., **13** 97
Jugend & Volk, **14** 556
Jugo Bank, **II** 325
Juice Bowl Products, **II** 480–81; **26** 57
Juice Works, **26** 57
Jujamycn, **24** 439
Jujo Paper Co., Ltd., IV 268, 284–85, 292–93, 297–98, 321, 326, 328, 356
JuJu Media, Inc., **41** 385
Julius Baer Holding AG, 52 203–05
Julius Berger-Bauboag A.G., **I** 560–61; **55** 60
Julius Garfinckel & Co., Inc., **22** 110
Julius Meinl International AG, 53 177–80
Jumping-Jacks Shoes, Inc., **17** 390
Jung-Pumpen, **III** 570; **20** 361
Junghans Uhren, **10** 152
Juniper Networks, Inc., 43 251–55
Junkers Luftverkehr, **I** 110, 197; **6** 87–88
Juno Lighting, Inc., 30 266–68
Juno Online Services, Inc., 38 269–72; 39 25–26
Juovo Pignone, **13** 356
Jupiter National, **15** 247–48; **19** 166
Jupiter Tyndall, **47** 84
Jurgens, **II** 588–89
Jurgensen's, **17** 558
Jurgovan & Blair, **III** 197
Juristförlaget, **14** 556
Jusco Car Life Company, **23** 290
JUSCO Co., Ltd., V 96–99; **11** 498; **36** 419; **43** 386
Jusco Group, **31** 430
Just Born, Inc., 32 305–07
Just For Feet, Inc., 19 228–30
Just Squeezed, **31** 350
Just Toys, Inc., **29** 476
Justin Industries, Inc., 19 231–33
Juventus F.C. S.p.A, 44 387–88; **53 181–83**
JVC. *See* Victor Company of Japan, Ltd.
JW Aluminum Company, **22** 544
JW Bernard & Zn., **39** 203
JWD Group, Inc., **48** 238
JWP Inc., 9 300–02; 13 176
JWT Group Inc., I 9, 19–21, 23; **6** 53. *See also* WPP Group plc.
Jylhävaara, **IV** 348
JZC. *See* John Zink Company.

K&B Inc., 12 286–88; 17 244
K&F Manufacturing. *See* Fender Musical Instruments.
K & G Men's Center, Inc., 21 310–12; 48 286
K&K Insurance Group, **26** 487
K&K Toys, Inc., **23** 176
K&L, **6** 48
K&M Associates L.P., **16** 18; **43** 19
K & R Warehouse Corporation, **9** 20

K-C Aviation, III 41; **16** 304; **43** 258
K-Graphics Inc., **16** 306; **43** 261
K-Group, **27** 261
K-H Corporation, **7** 260
K Shoes Ltd., **52** 57–58
K-Swiss, Inc., 33 243–45
K-tel International, Inc., 21 325–28
K-III Holdings. *See* Primedia Inc.
K.C.C. Holding Co., III 192
K.F. Kline Co., **7** 145; **22** 184
K.H.S. Musical Instrument Co. Ltd., **53** 214
K.H. Wheel Company, **27** 202
K. Hattori & Co., Ltd., III 454–55, 619–20. *See also* Seiko Corporation.
k.k. Staatsbahnen, **6** 419
K Line. *See* Kawasaki Kisen Kaisha, Ltd.
K.O. Lester Co., **31** 359, 361
K.P. American, **55** 305
K.W. Muth Company, **17** 305
KA Teletech, **27** 365
Ka Wah AMEV Insurance, III 200–01
Kabelvision AB, **26** 331–33
Kable News Company. *See* AMREP Corporation.
Kable Printing Co., **13** 559
Kaduna Refining and Petrochemicals Co., IV 473
Kaepa, **16** 546
Kaestner & Hecht Co., II 120
Kafte Inc., **28** 63
Kaga Forwarding Co., **6** 428
Kagami Crystal Works, III 714
Kagle Home Health Care, **11** 282
Kagoshima Central Research Laboratory, **21** 330
Kahan and Lessin, II 624–25
Kahn's Meats, II 572
Kai Tak Land Investment Co., IV 717
Kaiser + Kraft GmbH, **27** 175
Kaiser Aluminum & Chemical Corporation, IV 11–12, 15, 59–60, **121–23**, 191; **6** 148; **12** 377; **8** 348, 350; **22** 455; **50** 104. *See also* ICF Kaiser International, Inc.
Kaiser Cement, III 501, 760; IV 272
Kaiser Company, **6** 184
Kaiser Engineering, IV 218
Kaiser Foundation Health Plan, Inc., 53 184–86
Kaiser Industries, III 760
Kaiser Packaging, **12** 377
Kaiser Permanente Corp., **6** 279; **12** 175; **24** 231; **25** 434, 527; **41** 183. *See also* Kaiser Foundation Health Plan, Inc.
Kaiser Steel, IV 59
Kaiser's Kaffee Geschäft AG, **27** 461
Kaizosha, IV 632
Kajaani Oy, II 302; IV 350
Kajima Corporation, I 577–78; 51 177–79
Kal Kan Foods, Inc., 22 298–300
Kalamazoo Limited, **50** 377
Kalamazoo Paper Co., IV 281; **9** 259
Kalbfleish, I 300
Kaldveer & Associates, **14** 228
Kaliningradnefteprodukt, **48** 378
Kalitta Group, **22** 311
Kalua Koi Corporation, **7** 281
Kalumburu Joint Venture, IV 67
Kamaishi, IV 157; **17** 349
Kaman Corporation, 12 289–92; 16 202; **42 204–08 (upd.); 43** 171
Kamewa Group, **27** 494, 496

Kaminski/Engles Capital Corp. *See* Suiza Foods Corporation.
Kamioka Mining & Smelting Co., Ltd., IV 145, 148
Kammer Valves, A.G., **17** 147
Kampgrounds of America, Inc., 33 230–33
Kamps AG, 44 251–54
Kana Software, Inc., 51 180–83
Kanagawa Bank, II 291
Kanda Shokai, **16** 202; **43** 171
Kanders Florida Holdings, Inc., **27** 50
Kane Financial Corp., III 231
Kane Foods, III 43
Kane Freight Lines, **6** 370
Kane-Miller Corp., **12** 106
Kanebo, Ltd., 53 187–91
Kanebo Spinning Inc., IV 442
Kanegafuchi Shoji, IV 225
Kanematsu Corporation, IV 442–44; 24 259–62 (upd.)
Kangaroo. *See* Seino Transportation Company, Ltd.
Kangol Ltd., IV 136
Kangyo Bank, II 300, 310, 361
Kanhym, IV 91–92
Kanoldt, **24** 75
Kanpai Co. Ltd., **55** 375
Kansai Electric Power Co., Inc., IV 492; V **645–48**
Kansai Seiyu Ltd., V 188
Kansai Sogo Bank, II 361
Kansallis-Osake-Pankki, II 242, **302–03**, 366; IV 349
Kansas City Ingredient Technologies, Inc., **49** 261
Kansas City Power & Light Company, 6 510–12, 592; **12** 541–42; **50** 38
Kansas City Securities Corporation, **22** 541
Kansas City Southern Industries, Inc., 6 400–02; 26 233–36 (upd.); 29 333; **47** 162; **50** 208–09
Kansas City White Goods Company. *See* Angelica Corporation.
Kansas Fire & Casualty Co., III 214
Kansas Power Company, **6** 312
Kansas Public Service Company, **12** 541
Kansas Utilities Company, **6** 580
The Kantar Group, **48** 442
Kanto Steel Co., Ltd., IV 63
Kanzaki Paper Manufacturing Co., IV 285, 293
Kao Corporation, III **38–39**, 48; **16** 168; **20 315–17 (upd.); 51** 223–25
Kaohsiung Refinery, IV 388
Kaolin Australia Pty Ltd., III 691
Kapalua Land Company, Ltd., **29** 307–08
Kaplan Educational Centers, **12** 143
Kaplan, Inc., 42 209–12, 290
Kaplan Musical String Company, **48** 231
Kapok Computers, **47** 153
Kapy, II 139; **24** 194
Karafuto Industry, IV 320
Karan Co. *See* Donna Karan Company.
Karastan Bigelow, **19** 276
Karg'sche Familienstiftung, V 73
Karl Kani Infinity, Inc., 49 242–45
Karlsberg Brauerei GmbH & Co KG, 41 220–23
Karmelkorn Shoppes, Inc., **10** 371, 373; **39** 232, 235
Karrosseriewerke Weinsberg GmbH. *See* ASC, Inc.

Karstadt Aktiengesellschaft, V 100–02; 19 234–37 (upd.)
Karsten Manufacturing Corporation, 51 184–86
Kasado Dockyard, III 760
Kasai Securities, II 434
Kasco Corporation, **28** 42, 45
Kaset Rojananil, **6** 123
Kash n' Karry Food Stores, Inc., 20 318–20; 44 145
Kashi Company, **50** 295
Kasmarov, **9** 18
Kaspare Cohn Commercial & Savings Bank. *See* Union Bank of California.
Kasper A.S.L., Ltd., 40 276–79
Kast Metals, III 452; **15** 92
Kasuga Radio Company. *See* Kenwood Corporation.
Kat-Em International Inc., **16** 125
Katabami Kogyo Co. Ltd., **51** 179
Katalco, I 374
Kataoka Electric Co., II 5
Kate Spade LLC, **49** 285
Katelise Group, III 739–40
Katharine Gibbs Schools Inc., **22** 442
Kathleen Investment (Australia) Ltd., III 729
Kathy's Ranch Markets, **19** 500–01
Katies, V 35
Kativo Chemical Industries Ltd., **8** 239; **32** 256
Katy Industries Inc., I 472–74; 14 483–84; **16** 282; **51 187–90 (upd.)**
Katz Communications, Inc., 6 32–34
Katz Drug, II 604
Katz Media Group, Inc., 35 232, **245–48**
Kauffman-Lattimer, III 9–10
Kaufhalle AG, V 104; **23** 311; **41** 186–87
Kaufhof Holding AG, II 257; V **103–05**
Kaufhof Warenhaus AG, 23 311–14 (upd.)
Kaufman and Broad Home Corporation, 8 284–86; 11 481–83. *See also* KB Home.
Kaufmann Department Stores, Inc., V 132–33; **6** 243; **19** 262
Kaufring AG, 35 249–52
Kaukaan Tehdas Osakeyhtiö, IV 301
Oy Kaukas Ab, IV 300–02; **19** 462
Kaukauna Cheese Inc., **23** 217, 219
Kauppaosakeyhtiö Kymmene Aktiebolag, IV 299
Kauppiaitten Oy, **8** 293
Kautex-Bayern GmbH, IV 128
Kautex-Ostfriedland GmbH, IV 128
Kautex Werke Reinold Hagen AG, IV 128
Kawachi Bank, II 361; **26** 455
Kawamata, **11** 350
Kawasaki Denki Seizo, II 22
Kawasaki Heavy Industries, Ltd., I 75; II 273–74; III 482, 513, 516, **538–40**, 756; IV 124; **7** 232; **8** 72; **23** 290
Kawasaki Kisen Kaisha, Ltd., V 457–60
Kawasaki Steel Corporation, I 432; II 274; III 539, 760; IV 30, **124–25**, 154, 212–13; **13** 324; **19** 8
Kawashimaya Shoten Inc. Ltd., II 433
Kawecki Berylco Industries, **8** 78
Kawneer GmbH., IV 18
Kawsmouth Electric Light Company. *See* Kansas City Power & Light Company.
Kay-Bee Toy Stores, V 137; 15 252–53; 16 389–90; **50** 99. *See also* KB Toys.
Kay County Gas Co., IV 399

Kay Home Products, **17** 372
Kay's Drive-In Food Service, **II** 619
Kaydon Corporation, 18 274–76
Kaye, Scholer, Fierman, Hays & Handler, **47** 436
Kayex, **9** 251
Kaynar Manufacturing Company, **8** 366
Kayser Aluminum & Chemicals, **8** 229
Kayser Roth Corp., **8** 288; **22** 122
Kaysersberg, S.A., **IV** 290
KB Home, 45 218–22 (upd.)
AO KB Impuls, **48** 419
KB Toys, 35 253–55 (upd.)
KBLCOM Incorporated, **V** 644
KC. See Kenneth Cole Productions, Inc.
KC Holdings, Inc., **11** 229–30
KCI Konecranes International, **27** 269
KCPL. See Kansas City Power & Light Company.
KCS Industries, **12** 25–26
KCSI. See Kansas City Southern Industries, Inc.
KCSR. See Kansas City Southern Railway.
KD Acquisition Corporation, **34** 103–04
KD Manitou, Inc. See Manitou BF S.A.
KDT Industries, Inc., **9** 20
Keane Inc., **38** 431
The Keds Corp., **37** 377, 379
Keebler Foods Company, II 594; **35** 181; **36 311–13; 50** 295
Keefe Manufacturing Courtesy Coffee Company, **6** 392
Keegan Management Co., **27** 274
Keen, Robinson and Co., **II** 566
Keene Packaging Co., **28** 43
KEG Productions Ltd., **IV** 640; **26** 272
Keihan JUSCO, **V** 96
Keil Chemical Company, **8** 178
Keio Teito Electric Railway Company, V 461–62
Keisei Electric Railway, **II** 301
Keith-Albee-Orpheum, **II** 88
The Keith Companies Inc., 54 181–84
Keith Prowse Music Publishing, **22** 193
Keithley Instruments Inc., 16 299–301; 48 445
Kelco, **34** 281
Kelda Group plc, 45 223–26
Keller Builders, **43** 400
Keller-Dorian Graveurs, S.A., **17** 458
Kelley & Partners, Ltd., **14** 130
Kelley Drye & Warren LLP, 40 280–83
Kellock, **10** 336
Kellogg Company, I 22–23; **II** 463, 502–03, **523–26**, 530, 560; **10** 323–24; **12** 411; **13** 3, **291–94 (upd.); 15** 189; **18** 65, 225–26; **22** 336, 338; **25** 90; **27** 39; **29** 30, 110; **36** 236–38; **50 291–96 (upd.)**
Kellogg Foundation, **41** 118
Kellwood Company, V 181–82; **8 287–89**
Kelly & Associates, **III** 306
Kelly & Cohen, **10** 468
Kelly, Douglas and Co., **II** 631
Kelly Nason, Inc., **13** 203
Kelly Services, Inc., 6 35–37, 140; **9** 326; **16** 48; **25** 356, 432; **26 237–40 (upd.); 40** 236, 238; **49** 264–65
The Kelly-Springfield Tire Company, 8 290–92; 20 260, 263
Kelsey-Hayes Group of Companies, I 170; **III** 650, 652; **7 258–60; 27 249–52 (upd.)**

Kelso & Co., **III** 663, 665; **12** 436; **19** 455; **21** 490; **30** 48–49; **33** 92
Kelty Pack, Inc., **10** 215
Kelvinator Inc., **17** 487
KemaNobel, **9** 380–81; **13** 22
Kemet Corp., 14 281–83
Kemi Oy, **IV** 316
Kemira, Inc., **III** 760; **6** 152
Kemp's Biscuits Limited, **II** 594
Kemper Corporation, III 269–71, 339; **15 254–58 (upd.); 22** 495; **33** 111; **42** 451
Kemper Financial Services, **26** 234
Kemper Motorenfabrik, **I** 197
Kemper Snowboards, **22** 460
Kemperco Inc., **III** 269–70
Kempinski Group, **II** 258
Kemps Biscuits, **II** 594
Ken-L-Ration, **II** 559
Kendall International, Inc., I 529; **III** 24–25; **IV** 288; **11 219–21; 14** 121; **15** 229; **28** 486
Kendall-Jackson Winery, Ltd., 28 111, **221–23**
Kenetech Corporation, 11 222–24
Kennametal, Inc., IV 203; **13 295–97**
Kennecott Corporation, III 248; **IV** 33–34, 79, 170–71, 179, 192, 288, 576; **7 261–64; 10** 262, 448; **12** 244; **27 253–57 (upd.); 35** 135; **38** 231; **45** 332. See also Rio Tinto PLC.
Kennedy Automatic Products Co., **16** 8
Kenner, **II** 502; **10** 323; **12** 168
Kenner Parker Toys, Inc., **II** 503; **9** 156; **10** 324; **14** 266; **16** 337; **25** 488–89
Kenneth Cole Productions, Inc., 22 223; **25 256–58**
Kenneth O. Lester, Inc., **21** 508
Kenny Rogers' Roasters, **22** 464; **29** 342, 344
Kenroy International, Inc., **13** 274
Kent Drugs Ltd., **II** 640, 650
Kent Electronics Corporation, 17 273–76
Kent Fire, **III** 350
Kent-Moore Corp., **I** 200; **10** 492–93
Kentland-Elkhorn Coal Corp., **IV** 181
Kentrox Industries, **30** 7
Kentucky Bonded Funeral Co., **III** 217
Kentucky Electric Steel, Inc., 31 286–88
Kentucky Fried Chicken, **I** 260–61; **II** 533; **III** 78, 104, 106; **6** 200; **7** 26–28, 433; **8** 563; **12** 42; **13** 336; **16** 97; **18** 8, 538; **19** 92; **21** 361; **22** 464; **23** 384, 504. See also KFC Corporation.
Kentucky Institution for the Education of the Blind. See American Printing House for the Blind.
Kentucky Utilities Company, 6 513–15; 11 37, 236–38; **51** 217
Kenway, **I** 155
Kenwood Corporation, I 532; **19** 360; **23** 53; **31 289–91**
Kenwood Silver Company, Inc., **31** 352
Kenworth Motor Truck Corp., **I** 185–86; **26** 354
Kenyon & Eckhardt Advertising Agency, **25** 89–91
Kenyon Corp., **18** 276
Kenyon Sons and Craven Ltd., **II** 593–94
Kenzo, **25** 122
Keo Cutters, Inc., **III** 569; **20** 360
Keolis SA, 51 191–93
KEPCO. See Kyushu Electric Power Company Inc.

Keramik Holding AG Laufen, 51 194–96
Kerlick, Switzer & Johnson, **6** 48
Kerlyn Oil Co., **IV** 445–46
Kern County Land Co., **I** 527; **10** 379, 527
Kernite SA, **8** 386
Kernkraftwerke Lippe-Ems, **V** 747
Kernridge Oil Co., **IV** 541
Kerr-Addison Mines Ltd., **IV** 165
Kerr Concrete Pipe Company, **14** 250
Kerr Corporation, **14** 481
Kerr Drug Stores, **32** 170
Kerr Group Inc., III 423; **10** 130; **22** 48; **24 263–65; 30** 39
Kerr-McGee Corporation, IV 445–47; 13 118; **22 301–04 (upd.)**
Kerry Group plc, 27 258–60
Kerry Properties Limited, 22 305–08; 24 388
Keski-Suomen Tukkukauppa Oy, **8** 293
Kesko Ltd (Kesko Oy), 8 293–94; 27 261–63 (upd.)
Ketchikan International Sales Co., **IV** 304
Ketchikan Paper Company, **31** 316
Ketchikan Pulp Co., **IV** 304
Ketchum Communications Inc., 6 38–40
Ketner and Milner Stores, **II** 683
Kettle Chip Company (Australia), **26** 58
Kettle Foods Inc., 26 58; **48 240–42**
Kettle Restaurants, Inc., **29** 149
Keumkang Co., **III** 515; **7** 231
Kewanee Public Service Company, **6** 505
Kewaunee Scientific Corporation, 25 259–62
Key Computer Laboratories, Inc., **14** 15
Key Industries, Inc., **26** 342
Key Markets, **II** 628
Key Pharmaceuticals, Inc., **11** 207; **41** 419
Key Tronic Corporation, 14 284–86
KeyCorp, 8 295–97; 11 110; **14** 90
Keyes Fibre Company, 9 303–05
Keypage. See Rural Cellular Corporation.
KeySpan Energy Co., 27 264–66
Keystone Aircraft, **I** 61; **11** 164
Keystone Consolidated Industries, Inc., **19** 467
Keystone Custodian Fund, **IV** 458
Keystone Foods Corporation, **10** 443
Keystone Franklin, Inc., **III** 570; **9** 543; **20** 362
Keystone Frozen Foods, **17** 536
Keystone Gas Co., **IV** 548
Keystone Health Plan West, Inc., **27** 211
Keystone Insurance and Investment Co., **12** 564
Keystone International, Inc., 11 225–27; 28 486
Keystone Life Insurance Co., **III** 389; **33** 419
Keystone Paint and Varnish, **8** 553
Keystone Pipe and Supply Co., **IV** 136
Keystone Portland Cement Co., **23** 225
Keystone Savings and Loan, **II** 420
Keystone Tube Inc., **25** 8
Keytronics, **18** 541
KFC Corporation, 7 265–68; 10 450; **21 313–17 (upd.); 23** 115, 117, 153; **32** 12–14
KFF Management, **37** 350
Khalda Petroleum Co., **IV** 413
KHBB, **16** 72
KHD AG. See Klöckner-Humboldt-Deutz AG.
KHD Konzern, III 541–44
KHL. See Koninklijke Hollandsche Lloyd.

Kia Motors Corporation, I 167; 12 293–95; 29 264–67 (upd.)
Kiabi, 37 22–23
Kian Dai Wools Co. Ltd., 53 344
Kickers Worldwide, 35 204, 207
Kidd, Kamm & Co., 21 482
Kidde Inc., I 475–76; III 503; 7 209; 23 297; 39 344–46
Kidde plc, 44 255–59 (upd.); 50 133–35
Kidder, Peabody & Co., II 31, 207, 430; IV 84; 7 310; 12 197; 13 465–67, 534; 16 322; 22 406
Kidder Press Co., IV 644
Kiddie Products, Inc. See The First Years Inc.
Kids "R" Us, V 203–05; 9 394; 37 81
Kids Foot Locker, 14 293, 295
Kidston Mines, I 438
Kidz Biz Ltd., 52 193
Kiehl's Since 1851, Inc., 52 209–12
Kiekhaefer Corporation, III 443; 22 115
Kien, 13 545
Kienzle Apparate GmbH, III 566; 38 299
Kierulff Electronics, 10 113; 50 42
Kieser Verlag, 14 555
Kiewit Diversified Group Inc., 11 301
Kiewit-Murdock Investment Corp., 15 129
Kijkshop/Best-Sellers, 13 545
Kikkoman Corporation, I 9; 14 287–89; 47 203–06 (upd.)
Kilburn & Co., III 522
Kilgo Motor Express, 6 370
Kilgore Ceramics, III 671
Kilgore Federal Savings and Loan Assoc., IV 343
Killington, Ltd., 28 21
Kilpatrick's Department Store, 19 511
Kilsby Tubesupply, I 570
Kimball International, Inc., 12 296–98; 48 243–47 (upd.)
Kimbell Inc., II 684
Kimberley Central Mining Co., IV 64; 7 121
Kimberly-Clark Corporation, I 14, 413; III 36, 40–41; IV 249, 254, 297–98, 329, 648, 665; 8 282; 15 357; 16 302–05 (upd.); 17 30, 397; 18 147–49; 19 14, 284, 478; 22 209; 43 256–60 (upd.); 52 301–02; 54 185, 187
Kimberly-Clark de México, S.A. de C.V., 54 185–87
Kimco Realty Corporation, 11 228–30
Kimowelt Medien, 39 13
Kincaid Furniture Company, 14 302–03
Kindai Golf Company, 32 447
Kinden Corporation, 7 303
Kinder Morgan, Inc., 45 227–30
KinderCare Learning Centers, Inc., 13 298–300; 34 105; 35 408
Kinear Moodie, III 753
Kineret Acquisition Corp. See The Hain Celestial Group, Inc.
Kinetic Concepts, Inc., 20 321–23
King & Spalding, 23 315–18
The King Arthur Flour Company, 31 292–95
King Bearing, Inc., 13 79
King Cullen, II 644
King Features Syndicate, IV 626; 19 201, 203–04; 46 232
King Folding Box Co., 13 441
King Fook Gold and Jewellery Co., IV 717
King Hickory, 17 183

King Kullen Grocery Co., Inc., 15 259–61; 19 481; 24 528
King Pharmaceuticals, Inc., 54 188–90
King Ranch, Inc., 14 290–92
King-Seeley, II 419; 16 487
King Soopers Inc., 12 112–13
King World Productions, Inc., 9 306–08; 28 174; 30 269–72 (upd.)
King's Lynn Glass, 12 528
Kingbird Media Group LLC, 26 80
Kingfisher plc, V 106–09; 10 498; 19 123; 24 266–71 (upd.); 27 118, 120; 28 34, 36; 49 112–13
Kings, 24 528
Kings County Lighting Company, 6 456
Kings County Research Laboratories, 11 424
Kings Mills, Inc., 13 532
Kings Super Markets, 24 313, 316
Kingsford Corporation, III 21; 22 146
Kingsin Line, 6 397
Kingsport Pulp Corp., IV 310; 19 266
Kingston Technology Corporation, 20 324–26; 38 441
Kinki Nippon Railway Company Ltd., V 463–65
Kinko's Inc., 12 174; 16 306–08; 18 363–64; 43 261–64 (upd.)
Kinnevik. See Industriförvaltnings AB Kinnevik.
Kinney Corporation, 23 32; 24 373
Kinney National Service Inc., II 176; IV 672; 19 404; 25 140
Kinney Services, 6 293
Kinney Shoe Corp., V 226; 11 349; 14 293–95
Kinney Tobacco Co., 12 108
Kinoshita Sansho Steel Co., I 508
Kinpo Electronic, 23 212
Kinross Gold Corporation, 36 314–16
Kinson Resources Inc., 27 38
Kintec Corp., 10 97
Kirby. See Scott Fetzer Company.
Kirby Corporation, 18 277–79; 22 275
Kirby Forest Industries, IV 305
Kirch Gruppe, 10 196; 35 452
KirchMedia GmbH & Co., 54 295–98
Kirchner, Moore, and Co., II 408
KirchPayTV, 46 402
Kirin Brewery Company, Limited, I 220, 258, 265–66, 282; 10 78, 80; 13 258, 454; 20 28; 21 318–21 (upd.); 36 404–05; 52 31–32; 54 227, 229–30
Kirk Stieff Company, 10 181; 12 313
Kirkland Messina, Inc., 19 392, 394
Kirkstall Forge Engineering, III 494
Kirsch Co., II 16
Kirschner Manufacturing Co., 16 296
Kirsten Modedesign GmbH & Co. KG, 53 195
Kishimoto & Co., I 432, 492; 24 325
Kishimoto Shoten Co., Ltd., IV 168
Kistler, Lesh & Co., III 528
Kit Manufacturing Co., 18 280–82
Kita Consolidated, Ltd., 16 142
Kita Karafunto Oil Co., IV 475
Kita Nippon Paper Co., IV 321
Kitagawa & Co. Ltd., IV 442
Kitchell Corporation, 14 296–98
KitchenAid, III 611, 653–54; 8 298–99
Kitchenbell, III 43
Kitchens of Sara Lee, II 571–73
Kittery Electric Light Co., 14 124
Kittinger, 10 324

Kitty Hawk, Inc., 22 309–11
Kiwi International Airlines Inc., 20 327–29
Kiwi Packaging, IV 250
Kiwi Polish Co., 15 507
KJJ. See Klaus J. Jacobs Holdings.
Kjøbenhavns Bandelsbank, II 366
KJPCL. See Royal Interocean Lines.
KKK Shipping, II 274
KKR. See Kohlberg Kravis Roberts & Co.
KLA Instruments Corporation, 11 231–33; 20 8
KLA-Tencor Corporation, 45 231–34 (upd.)
Klaus J. Jacobs Holdings, 29 46–47
Klaus Steilmann GmbH & Co. KG, 53 192–95
KLC/New City Televentures, 25 269
Klein Bicycles, 16 495
Klein Sleep Products Inc., 32 426
Kleiner, Perkins, Caufield & Byers, I 637; 6 278; 10 15, 504; 14 263; 16 418; 27 447; 53 196–98
Kleinwort Benson Group PLC, II 379, 421–23; IV 191; 22 55
Kline Manufacturing, II 16
KLLM Transport Services, 27 404
KLM Royal Dutch Airlines, 26 33924 311, 396–97; 27 474; 29 15, 17; 33 49, 51; 34 397; 47 60–61. See also Koninklijke Luftvaart Maatschappij N.V.
Klöckner-Humboldt-Deutz AG, I 542; III 541–44; IV 126–27; 13 16–17; 50 197
Klöckner-Werke AG, IV 43, 60, 126–28, 201; 19 64; 39 125
Klondike, 14 205
Klopman International, 12 118
Kloth-Senking, IV 201
Klüber Lubrication München KG, 41 170
Kluwer Publishers, IV 611; 14 555
Klynveld Main Goerdeler, 10 387
Klynveld Peat Marwick Goerdeler. See KPMG Worldwide.
KM&G. See Ketchum Communications Inc.
Kmart Canada Co., 25 222
Kmart Corporation, I 516; V 35, 110–12; 6 13; 7 61, 444; 9 361, 400, 482; 10 137, 410, 490, 497, 515–16; 12 48, 54–55, 430, 477–78, 507–08; 13 42, 260–61, 274, 317–18, 444, 446; 14 192, 394; 15 61–62, 210–11, 330–31, 470; 16 35–37, 61, 187, 210, 447, 457; 17 297, 460–61, 523–24; 18 137, 283–87 (upd.); 477; 19 511; 20 155–56; 21 73; 22 258, 328; 23 210, 329; 24 322–23; 25 121; 26 348, 524; 27 313, 429, 451, 481; 32 169; 43 77–78, 293, 385; 47 207–12 (upd.); 48 331; 53 146
Kmart Mexico, 36 139
KMC Enterprises, Inc., 27 274
KMI Corporation, 55 302
KMP Holdings, I 531
KN. See Kühne & Nagel Group.
KN Energy. See Kinder Morgan, Inc.
Kna-Shoe Manufacturing Company, 14 302; 50 309
Knape & Vogt Manufacturing Company, 17 277–79
Knapp & Tubbs, III 423
Knapp Communications Corporation, II 656; 13 180; 24 418
Knapp-Monarch, 12 251
Knauf, III 721, 736

K'Nex Industries, Inc., 52 206–08
KNI Retail A/S, **12** 363
Knickerbocker Toy Co., **III** 505
Knickerbocker Trust Company, **13** 465
Knife River Coal Mining Company, **7** 322–25
Knife River Corporation, **42** 249, 253
Knight Paper Co., **III** 766; **22** 545
Knight-Ridder, Inc., III 190; **IV** 597, 613, **628–30**, 670; **6** 323; **7** 191, 327; **10** 407; **15 262–66 (upd.)**; **18** 323; **30** 216; **38** 307
Knightsbridge Partners, **26** 476
KNILM, **24** 397
Knoff-Bremse, **I** 138
Knogo Corp., **11** 444; **39** 78
Knoll Group Inc., I 202; **14 299–301**
Knoll Pharmaceutical, **I** 682
Knomark, **III** 55
Knorr-Bremse, **11** 31
Knorr Co. See C.H. Knorr Co.
Knorr Foods Co., Ltd., **28** 10
Knott, **III** 98
Knott's Berry Farm, 18 288–90; **22** 130
Knowledge Learning Corporation, 51 197–99; **54** 191
Knowledge Systems Concepts, **11** 469
Knowledge Universe, Inc., 54 191–94, 215–16
KnowledgeWare Inc., 9 309–11; **27** 491; **31 296–298 (upd.)**; **45** 206
Knox County Insurance, **41** 178
Knox Reeves Advertising Agency, **25** 90
Knoxville Glove Co., **34** 159
Knoxville Paper Box Co., Inc., **13** 442
KNP BT. See Buhrmann NV.
KNP Leykam, **49** 352, 354
KNSM. See Koninklijke Nederlandsche Stoomboot Maatschappij.
Knudsen & Sons, Inc., **11** 211
Knudsen Foods, **27** 330
Knutange, **IV** 226
Knutson Construction, **25** 331
KOA. See Kampgrounds of America, Inc.
Koala Corporation, 44 260–62
Kobacker Co., **18** 414–15
Kobayashi Tomijiro Shoten, **III** 44
Kobe Shipbuilding & Engine Works, **II** 57
Kobe Steel, Ltd., I 511; **II** 274; **IV** 16, **129–31**, 212–13; **8** 242; **11 234–35**; **13** 297; **19 238–41 (upd.)**; **38** 225–26
Kobelco America Inc., **19** 241
Kobelco Middle East, **IV** 131
Kobold. See Vorwerk & Co.
Kobrand Corporation, **24** 308; **43** 402
Koç Holding A.S., I 167, **478–80**; **11** 139; **27** 188; **54 195–98 (upd.)**
Koch Enterprises, Inc., 29 215–17
Koch Industries, Inc., IV 448–49; **20 330–32 (upd.)**; **21** 108; **22** 3
Koch-Light Laboratories, **13** 239; **38** 203–04
Kockos Brothers, Inc., **II** 624
Kodak. See Eastman Kodak Company.
Kodansha Ltd., IV 631–33; **38 273–76 (upd.)**
Ködel & Böhn GmbH, **III** 543
Koehring Company, **8** 545; **23** 299
Koehring Cranes & Excavators, **7** 513
Koei Real Estate Ltd., **V** 195; **47** 390
Koenig Plastics Co., **19** 414
Kogaku Co., Ltd., **48** 295
Kohl's Corporation, 9 312–13; **22** 72; **30 273–75 (upd.)**; **50** 117–18

Kohl's Food Stores, Inc., **I** 426–27; **16** 247, 249
Kohlberg & Co., **52** 159
Kohlberg Kravis Roberts & Co., I 566, 609–11; **II** 370, 452, 468, 544, 645, 654, 656, 667; **III** 263, 765–67; **IV** 642–43; **V** 55–56, 408, 410, 415; **6** 357; **7** 130, 132, 200; **9** 53, 180, 230, 469, 522; **10** 75–77, 302; **12** 559; **13** 163, 166, 363, 453; **14** 42; **15** 270; **17** 471; **18** 3; **19** 493; **22** 55, 91, 441, 513, 544; **23** 163; **24** 92, **272–74**, 416, 418; **25** 11, 278; **26** 46, 48, 352; **27** 11; **28** 389, 475; **30** 386; **32** 408; **33** 255; **35** 35; **38** 190; **40** 34, 36, 366; **43** 355; **44** 153; **45** 243; **49** 369
Kohler Bros., **IV** 91
Kohler Company, 7 269–71; **10** 119; **24** 150; **32 308–12 (upd.)**; **53** 176
Kohler Mix Specialties, Inc., **25** 333
Kohner Brothers, **II** 531
Koholyt AG, **III** 693
Koike Shoten, **II** 458
Kojiro Matsukata, **V** 457–58
Kokkola Chemicals Oy, **17** 362–63
Kokomo Gas and Fuel Company, **6** 533
Kokuei Paper Co., Ltd., **IV** 327
Kokura Sekiyu Co. Ltd., **IV** 554
Kokura Steel Manufacturing Co., Ltd., **IV** 212
Kokusai Kisen, **V** 457–58
Kokusaku Kiko Co., Ltd., **IV** 327
Kokusaku Pulp Co., **IV** 327
Kolb-Lena, **25** 85
Kolbenschmidt, **IV** 141
Kolker Chemical Works, Inc., **IV** 409; **7** 308
The Koll Company, 8 300–02; **21** 97; **25** 449
Kollmorgen Corporation, 18 291–94
Kölnische Rückversicherungs- Gesellschaft AG, **24** 178
Komag, Inc., 11 234–35
Komatsu Ltd., III 453, 473, **545–46**; **15** 92; **16 309–11 (upd.)**; **52 213–17 (upd.)**
Kommanditgesellschaft S. Elkan & Co., **IV** 140
Kommunale Energie- Beteiligungsgesellschaft, **V** 746
Kompass Allgemeine Vermögensberatung, **51** 23
Kompro Computer Leasing, **II** 457
Konan Camera Institute, **III** 487
Kone Corporation, 27 267–70
Kongl. Elektriska Telegraf-Verket, **V** 331
Kongo Bearing Co., **III** 595
Konica Corporation, III 547–50; **30 276–81 (upd.)**; **43** 284
König Brauerei GmbH & Co. KG, 35 256–58 (upd.)
Koninklijke Ahold N.V., II 641–42; **12** 152–53; **16 312–14 (upd.)**
Koninklijke Bols Wessanen, N.V., **29** 480–81
Koninklijke Distilleerderijen der Erven Lucas Böls, **I** 226
Koninklijke Grolsch BV. See Royal Grolsch NV.
Koninklijke Hoogovens NV, **26** 527, 530. See also Koninklijke Nederlandsche Hoogovens en Staalfabrieken NV.
Koninklijke Java-China Paketvaart Lijnen. See Royal Interocean Lines.

NV Koninklijke KNP BT. See Buhrmann NV.
Koninklijke KPN N.V. See Royal KPN N.V.
Koninklijke Luchtvaart Maatschappij N.V., I 55, **107–09**, 119, 121; **6** 95, 105, 109–10; **14** 73; **28 224–27 (upd.)**
Koninklijke Nederlandsche Hoogovens en Staalfabrieken NV, IV 105, 123, **132–34**; **49** 98, 101
Koninklijke Nederlandsche Maatschappig Tot Exploitatie van Petroleumbronnen in Nederlandsch-indie, **IV** 530
Koninklijke Nederlandsche Petroleum Maatschappij, **IV** 491
Koninklijke Nederlandsche Stoomboot Maatschappij, **26** 241
N.V. Koninklijke Nederlandse Vliegtuigenfabriek Fokker, I 46, **54–56**, 75, 82, 107, 115, 121–22; **28 327–30 (upd.)**
Koninklijke Nedlloyd Groep N.V., 6 403–05
Koninklijke Nedlloyd N.V., 26 241–44 (upd.)
Koninklijke Numico N.V. See Royal Numico N.V.
Koninklijke Paketvaart Maatschappij, **26** 242
Koninklijke Philips Electronics N.V., 50 297–302 (upd.)
Koninklijke PTT Nederland NV, V 299–301; **27** 471–72, 475. See also Royal KPN NV.
Koninklijke Van Ommeren, **22** 275
Koninklijke Wessanen nv, II 527–29; **54 199–204 (upd.)**
Koninklijke West-Indische Maildienst, **26** 242
Koniphoto Corp., **III** 548
Konishi Honten, **III** 547
Konishi Pharmaceutical, **I** 704
Konishiroku Honten Co., Ltd., **III** 487, 547–49
Konoike Bank, **II** 347
Konrad Hornschuch AG, **31** 161–62
Koo Koo Roo, Inc., 25 263–65
Koop Nautic Holland, **41** 412
Koopman & Co., **III** 419
Koor Industries Ltd., II 47–49; **22** 501; **25 266–68 (upd.)**; **54** 363
Koors Perry & Associates, Inc., **24** 95
Koortrade, **II** 48
Kop-Coat, Inc., **8** 456
Kopin Corp., **13** 399
Köpings Mekaniska Verkstad, **26** 10
Koppel Steel, **26** 407
Koppens Machinenfabriek, **III** 420
Kopper United, **I** 354
Koppers Inc., I 199, **354–56**; **III** 645, 735; **6** 486; **17** 38–39
Koppers Industries, Inc., 26 245–48 (upd.)
Koracorp Industries Inc., **16** 327
Korbel, **I** 226
Korea Automotive Fuel Systems Ltd., **13** 555
Korea Automotive Motor Corp., **16** 436; **43** 319
Korea Development Leasing Corp., **II** 442
Korea Steel Co., **III** 459
Korea Telecommunications Co, **I** 516

Korean Air Lines Co. Ltd., **II** 442; **6** 98–99; **24** 443; **27** 271–73 (upd.); **46** 40
Korean Development Bank, **III** 459
Korean Tungsten Mining Co., **IV** 183
Kori Kollo Corp., **23** 41
Korn/Ferry International, **34** 247–49
Koro Corp., **19** 414
Korrekt Gebäudereinigung, **16** 420; **43** 307
KorrVu, **14** 430
Kortbetalning Servo A.B., **II** 353
Kortgruppen Eurocard-Köpkort A.B., **II** 353
Korvettes, E.J., **14** 426
Koryeo Industrial Development Co., **III** 516; **7** 232
Koryo Fire and Marine Insurance Co., **III** 747
Koss Corporation, **38** 277–79
Kosset Carpets, Ltd., **9** 467
Kotobukiya Co., Ltd., **V** 113–14
Kowa Metal Manufacturing Co., **III** 758
Koyo Seiko, **III** 595–96, 623–24
KPM. *See* Koninklijke Paketvaart Maatschappij.
KPMG International, **29** 176; **33** 234–38 (upd.)
KPMG Worldwide, **7** 266; **10** 115, 385–87
KPN. *See* Koninklijke PTT Nederland N.V.
KPR Holdings Inc., **23** 203
Kraft Foods Inc., **II** 129, 530–34, 556; **V** 407; **III** 610; **7** 272–77 (upd.), 339, 433, 547; **8** 399, 499; **9** 180, 290, 318; **11** 15; **12** 372, 532; **13** 408, 515, 517; **14** 204; **16** 88, 90; **17** 56; **18** 67, 246, 416, 419; **19** 51; **22** 82, 85; **23** 219, 384; **25** 366, 517; **26** 249, 251; **28** 479; **44** 342; **45** 235–44 (upd.); **48** 331
Kraft Foodservice, **26** 504; **31** 359–60
Kraft Jacobs Suchard AG, **26** 249–52 (upd.)
Kraft-Versicherungs-AG, **III** 183
Kraftco Corporation, **II** 533; **14** 204
KraftMaid Cabinetry, Inc., **20** 363; **39** 267
Kraftwerk Union, **I** 411; **III** 466
Kragen Auto Supply Co., **27** 291. *See also* CSK Auto Corporation.
Kramer, **III** 48
Krämer & Grebe, **III** 420
Kramer Guitar, **29** 222
Kramer Machine and Engineering Company, **26** 117
Krames Communications Co., **22** 441, 443
Kransco, **25** 314
Krasnapolsky Restaurant and Wintergarden Company Ltd., **23** 228
Kraus-Anderson, Incorporated, **36** 317–20
Krause Publications, Inc., **35** 259–61
Krause's Furniture, Inc., **27** 274–77
Krauss-Maffei AG, **I** 75; **II** 242; **III** 566, 695; **14** 328; **38** 299
Kravco, **III** 248
Kredietbank N.V., **II** 295, 304–05
Kreditanstalt für Wiederaufbau, **IV** 231–32; **29** 268–72
Kreft, **III** 480; **22** 26
Kreher Steel Co., **25** 8
Krelitz Industries, Inc., **14** 147
Krema Hollywood Chewing Gum Co. S.A., **II** 532
Kremers-Urban, **I** 667
Kresge Foundation, **V** 110

Kreuger & Toll, **IV** 338; **12** 462–63
Kreymborg, **13** 544–45
Kriegschemikalien AG, **IV** 229
Kriegsmetall AG, **IV** 229
Kriegswollbedarfs AG, **IV** 229
Krislex Knits, Inc., **8** 235
Krispy Kitchens, Inc., **II** 584
Krispy Kreme Doughnut Corporation, **21** 322–24
Kroenke Sports Enterprises, **51** 97
Kroeze, **25** 82
The Kroger Company, **II** 605, 632, 643–45, 682; **III** 218; **6** 364; **7** 61; **12** 111–13; **13** 25, 237, 395; **15** 259, 267–70 (upd.), 449; **16** 63–64; **18** 6; **21** 323, 508; **22** 37, 126; **24** 416; **25** 234; **28** 512; **30** 24, 27; **40** 366
Krohn-Fechheimer Shoe Company, **V** 207
Krone AG, **33** 220
Krones A.G., **I** 266; **21** 319
Kronos, Inc., **18** 295–97; **19** 468
Krovtex, **8** 80
Kroy Tanning Company, **17** 195
Krueger Insurance Company, **21** 257
Kruger Inc., **17** 280–82
Kruidvat, **54** 265–67
Krumbhaar Chemical Inc., **14** 308
Krupp, **17** 214; **22** 364; **49** 53–55. *See also* Fried. Krupp GmbH; Thyssen Krupp AG.
Krupp Widia GmbH, **12** 66
Kruse International, **32** 162
The Krystal Company, **33** 239–42
KSSU Group, **I** 107–08, 120–21
KT Contract Services, **24** 118
KTR. *See* Keio Teito Electric Railway Company.
K2 Inc., **16** 295–98; **22** 481, 483; **23** 474; **43** 389
KU Energy Corporation, **6** 513, 515; **11** 236–38
Kubota Corporation, **I** 494; **III** 551–53; **10** 404; **12** 91, 161; **21** 385–86; **24** 324; **39** 37; **40** 134
Kubota, Gonshiro. *See* Gonshiro Oode.
Kudelski Group SA, **44** 263–66
Kuehne & Nagel International AG, **V** 466–69; **53** 199–203 (upd.)
Kuhara Mining Co., **IV** 475
Kuhlman Corporation, **20** 333–35
Kuhlmann, **III** 677; **IV** 174; **16** 121
Kühn + Bayer, **24** 165
Kuhn Loeb, **II** 402–03
Kühne & Nagel International AG, **V** 466–69
Kuitu Oy, **IV** 348
KUK, **III** 577, 712
Kukje Group, **III** 458
Kulicke and Soffa Industries, Inc., **33** 246–48
Kulka Smith Inc., **13** 398
Kulmobelwerk G.H. Walb and Co., **I** 581
Kum-Kleen Products, **IV** 252; **17** 29
Kumagai Gumi Co., **I** 579–80
Kumsung Companies, **III** 747–48
Kunkel Industries, **19** 143
Kunst und Technik Verlag, **IV** 590
Kunz-Holding GmbH & Co., **53** 216
Kuo International Ltd., **I** 566; **44** 153
Kuok Group, **28** 84
Kuoni Travel Holding Ltd., **40** 284–86
The Kuppenheimer Company, **8** 248–50; **32** 247
Kureha Chemical Industry, **I** 675

Kureha Spinning, **24** 325
Kureha Textiles, **I** 432, 492
Kurosawa Construction Co., Ltd., **IV** 155
Kurose, **III** 420
Kurt Möller Verlag, **7** 42
Kurushima Dockyard, **II** 339
Kurzweil Technologies, Inc., **51** 200–04
The Kushner-Locke Company, **25** 269–71
Kuusankoski Aktiebolag, **IV** 299
Kuwait Airways, **27** 135
Kuwait Aviation Fueling Co., **55** 243
Kuwait Investment Office, **II** 198; **IV** 380, 452; **27** 206
Kuwait Petroleum Corporation, **IV** 364, 450–52, 567; **18** 234; **38** 424; **55** 240–43 (upd.)
Kvaerner ASA, **20** 313; **31** 367, 370; **36** 321–23
KW, Inc. *See* Coca-Cola Bottling Company of Northern New England, Inc.
Kwaishinsha Motor Car Works, **I** 183
Kwik Save Group plc, **11** 239–41; **13** 26; **47** 368
Kwik Shop, Inc., **12** 112
Kwik-Fit Holdings plc, **54** 205–07
Kwikasair Ltd., **27** 473
KWIM. *See* Koninklijke West-Indische Maildienst.
KWV, **I** 289
Kygnus Sekiyu K.K., **IV** 555
Kymi Paper Mills Ltd., **IV** 302
Kymmene Corporation, **IV** 276–77, 299–303, 337. *See also* UPM-Kymmene Corporation.
Kyocera Corporation, **II** 50–52; **III** 693; **7** 118; **21** 329–32 (upd.)
Kyodo, **16** 166
Kyodo Dieworks Thailand Co., **III** 758
Kyodo Gyogyo Kaisha, Limited, **II** 552
Kyodo Kako, **IV** 680
Kyodo Kokusan K.K., **21** 271
Kyodo Oil Co. Ltd., **IV** 476
Kyodo Securities Co., Ltd., **II** 433
Kyodo Unyu Kaisha, **I** 502–03, 506; **IV** 713; **V** 481
Kyoei Mutual Fire and Marine Insurance Co., **III** 273
Kyoritsu Pharmaceutical Industry Co., **I** 667
Kyosai Trust Co. *See* Yasuda Trust and Banking Company, Limited.
Kyoto Bank, **II** 291
Kyoto Ceramic Co., Ltd. *See* Kyocera Corporation.
Kyoto Ouchi Bank, **II** 292
Kyowa Hakko Kogyo Co., Ltd., **III** 42–43; **45** 94; **48** 248–50 (upd.)
Kyusha Refining Co., **IV** 403
Kyushu Electric Power Company Inc., **IV** 492; **V** 649–51; **17** 349
Kyushu Oil Refinery Co. Ltd., **IV** 434
Kywan Petroleum Ltd., **13** 556
KYZ International, **9** 427
KZO, **13** 21

L & G, **27** 291
L&H. *See* Lernout and Hauspie.
L. & H. Sales Co., **16** 389
L. and J.G. Stickley, Inc., **50** 303–05
L&W Supply Corp., **III** 764
L E Lundbergföretagen AB, **52** 161, 164
L-3 Communications Holdings, Inc., **48** 251–53; **54** 234

L.A. Darling Co., **IV** 135–36; **16** 357
L.A. Gear, Inc., 8 303–06; 11 349; **31** 413; **32 313–17 (upd.)**
L.A. Mex. *See* Checkers Drive-Up Restaurants Inc.
L.A. T Sportswear, Inc., 26 257–59
L.B. DeLong, **III** 558
L.B. Foster Company, 33 255–58
L. Bamberger & Co., **V** 169; **8** 443
L. Bosendorfer Klavierfabrik, A.G., **12** 297
L.C. Bassford, **III** 653
L.D. Canocéan, **25** 104
The L.D. Caulk Company, **10** 271
L. Fish, **14** 236
L.G. Balfour Company, **12** 472; **19** 451–52; **36** 469
L. Greif & Bro. Inc., **17** 203–05
L. Grossman and Sons. *See* Grossman's Inc.
L.H. Parke Co., **II** 571
L.J. Knowles & Bros., **9** 153
L.J. Melody & Co., **21** 97
L.K. Liggett Company, **24** 74
L. Kellenberger & Co. AG, **25** 194
L.L. Bean, Inc., 9 190, 316; **10 388–90; 12** 280; **19** 333; **21** 131; **22** 173; **25** 48, 206; **29** 278; **36** 180, 420; **38 280–83 (upd.)**
The L.L. Knickerbocker Co., Inc., 25 272–75
L. Luria & Son, Inc., 19 242–44
L.M. Electronics, **I** 489
L.M. Ericsson, **I** 462; **II** 1, 70, 81–82, 365; **III** 479–80; **11** 46, 439; **14** 488. *See also* Telefonaktiebolaget LM Ericsson.
L-N Glass Co., **III** 715
L-N Safety Glass, **III** 715
L-O-F Glass Co. *See* Libbey-Owens-Ford Glass Co.
L. Prang & Co., **12** 207
L.S. DuBois Son and Co., **III** 10
L.S. Starrett Co., 13 301–03
L. Straus and Sons, **V** 168
L.W. Hammerson & Co., **IV** 696
L.W. Pierce Co., Inc. *See* Pierce Leahy Corporation.
L.W. Singer, **13** 429
La Banque Suisse et Française. *See* Crédit Commercial de France.
La Barge Mirrors, **III** 571; **20** 362
La Cerus, **IV** 615
La Choy Food Products Inc., II 467–68; **17** 241; **25 276–78**
La Cinq, **IV** 619
La Cloche d'Or, **25** 85
La Concorde, **III** 208
La Crosse Telephone Corporation, **9** 106
La Cruz del Campo S.A., **9** 100
La Favorita Bakery, **II** 543
La Fromagerie du Velay, **25** 85
La Grange Foundry, Inc., **39** 31
La Halle aux Chaussures, **17** 210
La India Co., **II** 532
La Joya, **51** 389
La Madeleine French Bakery & Café, 33 249–51
La Oroya, **22** 286
La Petite Academy, **13** 299
La Pizza Loca Inc., **44** 86
La Poste, V 270–72;], **47 213–16 (upd.)**
The La Quinta Companies, 42 213–16 (upd.)
La Quinta Inns, Inc., 11 242–44; 21 362
La Redoute S.A., **19** 306, 309

La Rinascente, **12** 153
La-Ru Truck Rental Company, Inc., **16** 386
La Ruche Meridionale, **12** 153
La 7, **47** 345, 347
La Societe Anonyme Francaise Holophane, **19** 211
La Vie Claire, **13** 103
La-Z-Boy Chair Company, 14 302–04; 31 248
La-Z-Boy Incorporated, 50 309–13 (upd.)
Laakirchen, **IV** 339–40; **28** 445
LAB. *See* Lloyd Aereo de Bolivia.
The Lab, Inc., **37** 263
LaB Investing Co. L.L.C, **37** 224
LaBakelite S.A., **I** 387
LaBarge Inc., 41 224–26
Labatt Brewing Company Limited, I 267–68; **18** 72; **25 279–82 (upd.); 26** 303, 306
Labatt U.S.A., **54** 212–14
Labaz, **I** 676; **IV** 546
Labelcraft, Inc., **8** 360
LaBelle Iron Works, **7** 586
LabOne, Inc., 48 254–57
Labor für Impulstechnik, **III** 154
Labor Ready, Inc., 29 273–75
Laboratoire L. Lafon, **45** 94
Laboratoire Michel Robilliard, **IV** 546
Laboratoire Roger Bellon, **I** 389
Laboratoires d'Anglas, **III** 47
Laboratoires de Biologie Végétale Yves Rocher, 35 262–65
Laboratoires Goupil, **III** 48
Laboratoires Roche Posay, **III** 48
Laboratorio Chile S.A., **55** 233
Laboratorios Elmor S.A., **55** 233
Laboratorios Liade S.A., **24** 75
Laboratory Corporation of America Holdings, 42 217–20 (upd.)
Laboratory for Electronics, **III** 168; **6** 284
LaBour Pump, **I** 473
LaBow, Haynes Co., **III** 270
LaBranche & Co. Inc., 37 223–25
Labsphere, Inc., **48** 446
Labtronics, Inc., **49** 307–08
Lachine Rapids Hydraulic and Land Company, **6** 501
Laci Le Beau Tea, **49** 275–76
Lackawanna Steel & Ordnance Co., **IV** 35, 114; **7** 48
Laclede Steel Company, 15 271–73
Lacombe Electric. *See* Public Service Company of Colorado.
Lacquer Products Co., **I** 321
LaCrosse Footwear, Inc., 18 298–301
Lacto Ibérica, **23** 219
Lactos, **25** 85
Lacy Diversified Industries, Ltd., **24** 159–61
Ladbroke Group PLC, II 139, **141–42; 19** 208; **21 333–36 (upd.); 24** 194; **42** 64; **49** 449–50. *See also* Hilton Group plc.
Ladd and Tilton, **14** 527–28
LADD Furniture, Inc., 12 299–301; 23 244
Ladd Petroleum Corp., **II** 30
LADECO, **6** 97; **31** 304; **36** 281
Ladenburg, Thalmann & Co. Inc., **17** 346
Ladenso, **IV** 277
Ladish Co., Inc., 30 282–84
Lady Foot Locker, **V** 226; **14** 293, 295
Lady Lee, **27** 291

Laerdal Medical, **18** 423
Lafarge Cement UK, 54 208–11 (upd.)
Lafarge Coppée S.A., III 702, **703–05,** 736; **8** 258; **10** 422–23; **23** 333
Lafarge Corporation, 24 332; **28 228–31**
Lafayette Manufacturing Co., **12** 296
Lafayette Radio Electronics Corporation, **9** 121–22
Laflin & Rand Powder Co., **I** 328; **III** 525
Lafuma S.A., 39 248–50
LAG&E. *See* Los Angeles Gas and Electric Company.
LaGard Inc., **20** 363
Lagardère Groupe SCA, **16** 254; **24** 84, 88; **34** 83
Lagoven, **IV** 508
Laidlaw Inc., **39** 19, 21
Laidlaw Transportation, Inc., **6** 410; **32** 227, 231
Laing's Properties Ltd. *See* John Laing plc.
L'Air Liquide SA, I 303, **357–59; 11** 402; **47 217–20 (upd.)**
Laitaatsillan Konepaja, **IV** 275
Laiterie Centrale Krompholtz, **25** 84
Laiterie de la Vallée du Dropt, **25** 84
Laiterie Ekabe, **19** 50
SA Laiterie Walhorn Molkerel, **19** 50
Laiteries Prairies de l'Orne, **19** 50
Lake Arrowhead Development Co., **IV** 255
Lake Central Airlines, **I** 131; **6** 131
Lake Erie Screw Corp., **11** 534, 536
Lake Odessa Machine Products, **18** 494
Lake Pacific Partners, LLC, **55** 124
Lake Superior Consolidated Mines Company, **IV** 572; **7** 549; **17** 355–56
Lake Superior Paper Industries, **26** 363
Lakehead Pipe Line Partners, L.P., **43** 155
Lakeland Fire and Casualty Co., **III** 213
Lakeland Industries, Inc., 45 245–48
Läkemedels-Industri Föreningen, **I** 664
Laker Airways, **I** 94; **6** 79; **24** 399
Lakes Entertainment, Inc., 51 205–07
Lakeside Laboratories, **III** 24
The Lakeside Publishing and Printing Co., **IV** 660
Lakestone Systems, Inc., **11** 469
Lalique, **55** 309
Lam Research Corporation, IV 213; **11 245–47; 18** 383; **31 299–302 (upd.)**
Lamar Advertising Company, 27 278–80
The Lamaur Corporation, 41 227–29
Lamb Technicon Corp., **I** 486
Lamb Weston, Inc., I 417; **23 319–21; 24** 33–34
Lambda Electronics Inc., **32** 411
Lambert Brothers, Inc., **7** 573
Lambert Brussels Financial Corporation, **II** 407; **11** 532
Lambert Frères, **33** 339
Lambert Kay Company, **8** 84
Lambert Pharmacal Co., **I** 710–11; **III** 28
Lambert Rivière, **41** 340
Lamborghini. *See* Automobili Lamborghini S.p.A.
Lamkin Brothers, Inc., **8** 386
Lamons Metal Gasket Co., **III** 570; **11** 535; **20** 361
Lamontagne Ltd., **II** 651
Lamonts Apparel, Inc., 15 274–76
Lampadaires Feralux, Inc., **19** 472
Lamson & Sessions Co., 13 304–06
Lamson Bros., **II** 451
Lamson Corporation, **7** 145; **49** 159
Lamson Industries Ltd., **IV** 645

Lamson Store Service Co., **IV** 644
Lan Chile S.A., 31 303–06; **33**
Lanca, **14** 224
Lancashire, **III** 350
Lancaster Caramel Co., **II** 510
Lancaster Colony Corporation, 8 307–09
Lancaster Cork Works, **III** 422
Lancaster Financial Ltd., **14** 472
Lancaster National Bank, **9** 475
Lancaster Press, **23** 102
Lance, Inc., 14 305–07; **41** 230–33 (upd.)
Lancel, **27** 487, 489
Lancer Corporation, 21 337–39
Lanchester Motor Company, Ltd., **13** 286
Lancia, **I** 162; **11** 102
Lancôme, **III** 46–48; **8** 342
Land O'Lakes, Inc., II 535–37; **7** 339; **13** 351; **21** 340–43 (upd.)
Land-O-Sun Dairies, L.L.C., **26** 449
Land Securities PLC, IV 704–06; **49** 246–50 (upd.); **54** 38
Land-Wheelwright Laboratories, **III** 607; **7** 436
Landauer, Inc., 51 208–10
Lander Alarm Co., **III** 740
Lander Company, **21** 54
Länderbank, **II** 282
Landesbank für Westfalen Girozentrale, Münster, **II** 385
Landis International, Inc., **10** 105–06
Landmark Banks, **10** 426
Landmark Communications, Inc., 12 302–05; **22** 442; **52** 401–02; **55** 244–49 (upd.)
Landmark Financial Services Inc., **11** 447
Landmark Target Media, **IV** 597
Landmark Union Trust, **18** 517
Landoll, Inc., **22** 522
Landor Associates, **I** 94
Landry's Seafood Restaurants, Inc., 15 277–79
Lands' End, Inc., 9 314–16; **12** 280; **16** 37; **19** 333; **26** 439; **27** 374, 429; **29** 276–79 (upd.)
Landstar, **26** 533
Lane Bryant, **V** 115–16
The Lane Co., Inc., III 528, 530; **12** 306–08; **39** 170, 173–74
Lane Drug Company, **12** 132
Lane, Piper, and Jaffray, Inc. *See* Piper Jaffray Companies.
Lane Processing Inc., **II** 585
Lane Publishing Co., **IV** 676; **7** 529
Lane Rossi, **IV** 421
Laneco, Inc., **II** 682
Lang Exploratory Drilling, **26** 42
Langdon Rieder Corp., **21** 97
Lange International S.A., **15** 462; **43** 375–76
Lange, Maxwell & Springer, **IV** 641; **7** 311
Langen Packaging Inc., **51** 249, 251
Langenpac NV, **51** 249–50
Langford Labs, **8** 25
Lanier Business Products, Inc., **II** 39; **8** 407; **20** 290
Lanman Companies, Inc., **23** 101
Lannet Data Communications Ltd., **18** 345–46; **26** 275–77
Lano Corp., **I** 446
Lansi-Suomen Osake-Pankki, **II** 303
Lanson Pere et Fils, **II** 475
Lantic Industries, Inc., **II** 664
Lanvin, **I** 696; **III** 48; **8** 343

LAPE. *See* Líneas Aéreas Postales Españolas.
Lapeyre S.A. *See* Groupe Lapeyre S.A.
LaPine Technology, **II** 51; **21** 331
Laporte Industries Ltd., **I** 303; **IV** 300
Lapp, **8** 229
Lara, **19** 192
Larami Corp., **14** 486
Lareco, **26** 22
Largardère Groupe, **43** 210
Largo Entertainment, **25** 329
Largo Music Publishing, **55** 250
Laroche Navarron, **I** 703
Larousse Group, **IV** 614–15
Larrowe Milling Co., **II** 501; **10** 322
Larry Flynt Publishing Inc., 31 307–10
Larry H. Miller Group, 29 280–83
Larry's Food Products, **36** 163
Larsen & Toubro, **IV** 484
Larsen Company, **7** 128
Larson Boats. *See* Genmar Holdings, Inc.
Larson Lumber Co., **IV** 306
Larwin Group, **III** 231
Las Vegas Gas Company, **19** 411
Las Vegas Sands, Inc., 50 306–08
LaSalle Investment Management, Inc., **49** 238
LaSalle Machine Tool, Inc., **13** 7–8
LaSalle National Bank, **II** 184
LaSalle Partners, **49** 28
LaSalle Steel Corporation, **28** 314
LaSalles & Koch Co., **8** 443
Lasco Shipping Co., **19** 380
Laser Tech Color, **21** 60
Lasercharge Pty Ltd, **18** 130
LaserSoft, **24** 349
Oy Läskelä Ab, **IV** 300
Lasky's, **II** 141; **24** 269
Lasmo, **IV** 455, 499
Lason, Inc., 31 311–13
Latcom, Inc., **55** 302
Latham & Watkins, 33 252–54; **37** 292
Latin Communications Group Inc., **41** 151
Latitude Communications, **22** 52
Latrobe Brewing Company, 25 281; **54** 212–14
Latrobe Steel Company, **8** 529–31
Lattice Semiconductor Corp., 16 315–17; **43** 17
Lauda Air Luftfahrt AG, 48 258–60
Lauder Chemical, **17** 363
Laura Ashley Holdings plc, 13 307–09; **37** 226–29 (upd.)
Laura Scudders, **7** 429; **44** 348
Laurel Glen, **34** 3, 5
Laurent-Perrier SA, 42 221–23
Laurentian Group, **48** 290
Laurentien Hotel Co., **III** 99
Lauson Engine Company, **8** 515
LaVista Equipment Supply Co., **14** 545
Lavold, **16** 421; **43** 308
Law Life Assurance Society, **III** 372
Lawn Boy Inc., **7** 535–36; **8** 72; **26** 494
Lawrence Manufacturing Co., **III** 526
Lawrence Warehouse Co., **II** 397–98; **10** 62
Lawrenceburg Gas Company, **6** 466
The Lawson Co., **7** 113; **25** 125
Lawson Inc., **41** 113, 115
Lawson Milk, **II** 572
Lawson Software, 38 284–88
Lawter International Inc., 14 308–10; **18** 220
Lawyers Cooperative, **8** 527–28

Lawyers Trust Co., **II** 230
Layer Five, **43** 252
Layne & Bowler Pump, **11** 5
Layne Christensen Company, 19 245–47; **26** 71
Layton Homes Corporation, **30** 423
Lazard Freres & Co., **II** 268, 402, 422; **IV** 23, 79, 658–59; **6** 356; **7** 287, 446; **10** 399; **12** 165, 391, 547, 562; **21** 145
Lazard LLC, 38 289–92
Lazare Kaplan International Inc., 21 344–47
Lazio. *See* Societá Sportiva Lazio SpA.
LBO Holdings, **15** 459
LBS Communications, **6** 28
LCI International, Inc., 16 318–20
LCIE, **55** 79
LCP Hotels. *See* CapStar Hotel Co.
LDB Corporation, 53 204–06
LDDS-Metro Communications, Inc., 8 310–12
LDDS WorldCom, Inc., **16** 467–68
LDI. *See* Lacy Diversified Industries, Ltd.
LDMA-AU, Inc., **49** 173
LDS Health Services Corporation, **27** 237
LDX NET, Inc., **IV** 576
Le Bon Marché. *See* Bon Marché.
Le Brun and Sons, **III** 291
Le Buffet System-Gastronomie, **V** 74
Le Chameau, **39** 250
Le Clerc, **21** 225–26
Le Courviour S.A., **10** 351
Le Monde S.A., 33 308–10
Le Rocher, Compagnie de Reassurance, **III** 340
Le Touquet's, SA, **48** 197
Lea & Perrins, **II** 475
Lea County Gas Co., **6** 580
Lea Lumber & Plywood Co., **12** 300
Lea Manufacturing, **23** 299
Leach McMicking, **13** 274
Lead Industries Group Ltd., **III** 681; **IV** 108
Leadership Housing Inc., **IV** 136
Leaf North America, **51** 159
Leaf River Forest Products Inc., **IV** 282, 300; **9** 261
Leahy & Co. *See* Pierce Leahy Corporation.
Leamington Priors & Warwickshire Banking Co., **II** 318; **17** 323
Lean Cuisine, **12** 531
LeapFrog Enterprises, Inc., 54 191, 193, 215–18
Lear Corporation, **17** 303, 305
Lear Inc., **II** 61; **8** 49, 51
Lear Romec Corp., **8** 135
Lear Seating Corporation, 16 321–23
Lear Siegler Holdings Corporation, **25** 431
Lear Siegler Inc., I 481–83; **III** 581; **8** 313; **13** 169, 358, 398; **19** 371–72; **30** 426; **44** 308
Learjet Inc., 8 313–16; **9** 242; **27** 281–85 (upd.)
Learning Centers Inc., **51** 198
The Learning Company Inc., 24 275–78, 480; **29** 74, 77; **41** 409
Learning Tree International Inc., 24 279–82
LeaRonal, Inc., 23 322–24
Leasco Data Processing Equipment Corp., **III** 342–44; **IV** 641–42; **7** 311
Lease International SA, **6** 358
Leaseway Personnel Corp., **18** 159

Leaseway Transportation Corp., V 494; **12** 309–11; **19** 293
Leatherback Industries, **22** 229
Leatherman Tool Group, Inc., 51 211–13
Lebhar-Friedman, Inc., 55 250–52
Leblanc Corporation. *See* G. Leblanc Corporation.
LeBoeuf, Lamb, Greene & MacRae, L.L.P., 29 284–86
Lebr Associates Inc., **25** 246
Lech Brewery, **24** 450
Lechmere Inc., 10 391–93
Lechters, Inc., 11 248–50; **39** 251–54 **(upd.)**
Leclerc. *See* Association des Centres Distributeurs E. Leclerc.
LeCroy Corporation, 41 234–37
Lectorum Publications, **29** 426
Ledcor Industries Limited, 46 266–69
Lederle Laboratories, **I** 300–02, 657, 684; **8** 24–25; **14** 254, 256, 423; **27** 115; **50** 248, 250
Lederle Standard Products, **26** 29
Lee Ackerman Investment Company, **18** 513
Lee Apparel Company, Inc., 8 317–19; **17** 512, 514
Lee Brands, **II** 500
Lee Company, **V** 390–92
Lee Cooper Group Ltd., **49** 259
Lee Enterprises, Incorporated, 11 251–53; **47** 120
Lee Hecht Harrison, **6** 10
Lee International, **24** 373
Lee National Corporation, **26** 234
Lee Optical, **13** 390
Lee Rubber and Tire Corp., **16** 8
Lee Telephone Company, **6** 313
Lee Way Holding Co., **14** 42
Lee Way Motor Freight, **I** 278
Leeann Chin, Inc., 30 285–88
Leeds & County Bank, **II** 318; **17** 323
Leeds & Northrup Co., **III** 644–45; **28** 484
Lees Carpets, **17** 76
Leewards Creative Crafts Inc., **17** 322
Lefeldt, **III** 417, 418
Lefrak Organization Inc., 8 357; **26** 260–62
Legacy Homes Ltd., **26** 290
Legal & General Group plc, III 272–73; **IV** 705, 712; **24** 283–85 **(upd.)**; **30** 494; **33** 319
The Legal Aid Society, 48 261–64
Legal Technologies, Inc., **15** 378
Legault and Masse, **II** 664
Legent Corporation, 10 394–96; **14** 392
Legetojsfabrikken LEGO Billund A/S. *See* Lego A/S.
Legg Mason, Inc., 11 493; **33** 259–62
Leggett & Platt, Inc., 9 93; **11** 254–56; **48** 265–68 **(upd.)**
Leggett Stores Inc., **19** 48
Lego A/S, 12 495; **13** 310–13; **40** 287–91 **(upd.)**; **52** 206
Legrand SA, 21 348–50
Lehigh Acquisition Corp., **34** 286
Lehigh Portland Cement Company, 23 325–27; **31** 252
Lehigh Railroad, **III** 258
Lehman Brothers, **I** 78, 125, 484; **II** 192, 259, 398, 448, 450–51; **6** 199; **10** 62–63; **11** 263–64; **13** 448; **14** 145; **22** 445; **25** 301; **38** 411; **48** 59
Lehman Merchant Bank Partners, **19** 324

Lehmer Company. *See* Centel Corporation.
Lehn & Fink, **I** 699
Lehnkering AG, **IV** 140
Lehrman Bros., **III** 419
Lehser Communications, Inc., **15** 265
Leica Camera AG, 35 266–69
Leica Microsystems Holdings GmbH, 35 270–73
Leigh-Mardon Security Group, **30** 44
Leighton Holdings Ltd., **19** 402
Leinenkugel Brewing Company. *See* Jacob Leinenkugel Brewing Company.
Leiner Health Products Inc., 34 250–52
The Leisure Company, **34** 22
Leisure Lodges, **III** 76
Leisure System Inc., **12** 359
Leitz, **III** 583–84
LeMaster Litho Supply, **13** 228
Lemmerz Holding GmbH, **27** 202, 204
Lemmon Co., **54** 363
Lempereur, **13** 297
Lena Goldfields Ltd., **IV** 94
Lenc-Smith, **III** 430
Lend Lease Corporation Limited, IV 707–09; **17** 283–86 **(upd.)**; **47** 410; **52** 218–23 **(upd.)**
Lender's Bagel, **32** 69
Lending Textiles, **29** 132
Lenel Systems International Inc., **24** 510
Lennox Corporation, 11 257–59
Lennon's, **II** 628
Lennox Industries, Inc., **22** 6
Lennox International Inc., 8 320–22; **28** 232–36 **(upd.)**
Lenoir Furniture Corporation, **10** 183
Lenox, Inc., I 227; **10** 179, 181; **12** 312–13; **18** 69; **38** 113
Lens, Inc., **30** 267–68
LensCrafters Inc., V 207–08; **13** 391; **17** 294; **23** 328–30; **43** 199; **52** 227, 229
Lentheric, **I** 426
L'Entreprise Jean Lefebvre, 23 331–33
Leo Burnett Company, Inc., I 22–24, 25, 31, 37; **11** 51, 212; **12** 439; **20** 336–39 **(upd.)**
The Leo Group, **32** 140; **40** 140
Léon Gaumont et Cie. *See* Gaumont SA.
Leonard Bernstein Music Publishing Company, **23** 391
Leonard Development Group, **10** 508
Leonard Express, Inc., **6** 371
Leonard Green & Partners LP, **12** 477–78; **24** 173
Leonard Machinery Corp., **16** 124
Leonard Parker Company, **26** 196
Leonard Silver, **14** 482
Leonardi Manufacturing, **48** 70
Leonardo Editore, **IV** 587
Leonberger Bausparkasse, **II** 258
Lepco Co., **III** 596
Leprino Foods Company, 28 237–39
Lern, Inc., **II** 420
Lerner Plastics, **9** 323
Lerner Stores, **V** 116
Lernout and Hauspie, **51** 202
Leroy Merlin SA, 23 230; **37** 24; **54** 219–21
Les broderies Lesage, **49** 83
Les Chantiers de l'Atlantique, **II** 13
Les Echos. *See* Groupe Les Echos.
Les Grands Magasins Au Bon Marché: Etablissements Vaxelaire-Claes, **26** 159–60
Les Industries Ling, **13** 443

Les Papeteries du Limousin, **19** 227
Les Schwab Tire Centers, 50 314–16
Lesaffre et Compagnie, **52** 305
L'Escaut, **III** 335
Lesco Inc., 19 248–50
The Leslie Fay Companies, Inc., 8 323–25
The Leslie Fay Company, Inc., 39 255–58 **(upd.)**; **40** 276–77
Leslie Paper, **IV** 288
Leslie's Poolmart, Inc., 18 302–04
Lesser-Goldman, **II** 18
Lester B. Knight & Associates, **II** 19
Lester Ink and Coatings Company, **13** 228
Lestrem Group, **IV** 296; **19** 226
Let op Uw Einde, **III** 199
Létang et Rémy, **44** 205
Lettuce Entertain You Enterprises, **38** 103
Leucadia National Corporation, 6 396; **11** ; **25** 170 260–62
Leuna-Werke AG, **7** 142
Leupold & Stevens, Inc., 52 224–26
Level Five Research, Inc., **22** 292
N.V. Levensverzekering Maatschappji Utrecht, **III** 199–200
Lever Brothers Company, I 17, 21, 26, 30, 333; **II** 497, 588–89; **III** 31; **7** 542–43, 545; **9** 291, 317–19; **13** 199; **14** 314. *See also* Unilever.
Leverage Group, **51** 99
Levi Strauss & Co., I 15; **II** 634, 669; **V** 60–61, 362–65; **9** 142; **12** 430; **16** 324–28 **(upd.)**, 509, 511; **17** 512; **18** 191–92; **19** 196; **23** 422; **24** 158; **25** 47
Leviathan Gas Pipeline Company, **21** 171
Levine, Huntley, Vick & Beaver, **6** 28
Leviton Manufacturing Co., Inc., **54** 372
Levitt & Sons, **IV** 728
Levitt Corp., **21** 471
Levitt Homes, **I** 464; **11** 198
Levitt Industries, **17** 331
Levitt Investment Company, **26** 102
Levitz Furniture Inc., 15 280–82; **23** 412, 414
Levolor Hardware Group, **53** 37
Levtex Hotel Ventures, **21** 363
Levy Bakery Goods, **I** 30
Levy Restaurants L.P., 26 263–65
Lew Liberbaum & Co., **27** 197
The Lewin Group, Inc., **21** 425
Lewis and Marks, **IV** 21–22, 96; **16** 27; **50** 32
Lewis Batting Company, **11** 219
Lewis Construction, **IV** 22
Lewis Galoob Toys Inc., 16 329–31
Lewis Grocer Co., **II** 669; **18** 504; **50** 454
Lewis Homes, **45** 221
Lewis-Howe Co., **III** 56
Lewis Refrigeration Company, **21** 500
Lewis's, **V** 178
Lewis's Bank, **II** 308
Lex Electronics, **10** 113; **50** 42
Lex Service plc, **19** 312; **50** 42
Lexecon, Inc., **26** 187
Lexington Broadcast Services, **6** 27
Lexington Furniture Industries, **III** 571; **20** 362
Lexington Ice Company, **6** 514
Lexington Insurance Co., **III** 197
Lexington Utilities Company, **6** 514; **11** 237
LEXIS-NEXIS Group, 17 399; **18** 542; **21** 70; **31** 388, 393; **33** 263–67
Lexitron, **II** 87

Lexmark International, Inc., **9** 116; **10** 519; **18 305–07**; **30** 250
Leybold GmbH, **IV** 71; **48** 30
Leyland and Birmingham Rubber Co., **I** 429
Leyland Motor Corporation, **7** 459
LFC Financial, **10** 339
LFC Holdings Corp. *See* Levitz Furniture Inc.
LFE Corp., **7** 297
LG Chemical Ltd., **26** 425
LG Electronics Inc., **13** 572, 575; **43** 428
LG Group, **18** 124; **34** 514, 517–18
LG&E Energy Corporation, **6 516–18**; **18** 366–67; **50** 172; **51 214–17 (upd.)**
Lhomme S.A., **8** 477
Liaison Agency, **31** 216–17
Lianozovo Dairy, **48** 438
Liaoyang Automotive Spring Factory, **III** 581
Libbey Inc., **49 251–54**
Libbey-Owens-Ford Company, **I** 609; **III** 640–42, 707, 714–15, 725–26, 731; **IV** 421; **7** 292; **16** 7–9; **22** 434; **23** 83; **26** 353; **31** 355
Libby, **II** 547; **7** 382
Libby McNeil & Libby Inc., **II** 489
Libeltex, **9** 92
Liber, **14** 556
Liberty Bank of Buffalo, **9** 229
Liberty Brokerage Investment Company, **10** 278
Liberty Can and Sign Company, **17** 105–06
The Liberty Corporation, **22 312–14**
Liberty Gauge Company, **17** 213
Liberty Hardware Manufacturing Corporation, **20** 363
Liberty House, **I** 417–18
Liberty Life, **IV** 91, 97
Liberty Livewire Corporation, **42 224–27**
Liberty Media Corporation, **18** 66; **19** 282; **25** 214; **34** 224; **42** 114, 224; **47** 414, 416, 418; **50 317–19**
Liberty Mexicana, **III** 415
Liberty Mutual Insurance Group, **I** 28; **11** 379; **48** 271
Liberty Mutual Savings Bank, **17** 530
Liberty National Bank, **II** 229
Liberty National Insurance Holding Company. *See* Torchmark Corporation.
Liberty National Life Insurance Co., **III** 217; **9** 506–07
Liberty Natural Gas Co., **11** 441
Liberty Software, Inc., **17** 264
Liberty Surf UK, **48** 399
Liberty Tax Service, **48** 236
Liberty's, **13** 307
Libra Bank Ltd., **II** 271
Librairie de Jacques-Francois Brétif, **IV** 617
Librairie Fayard, **IV** 618
Librairie Générale Francaise, **IV** 618
Librairie Larousse, **IV** 614–16
Librairie Louis Hachette, **IV** 617–18
Librairie Nathan, **IV** 614, 616
Librairie Victor Lecou, **IV** 617
Librizol India Pvt. Ltd., **48** 212
Libyan Arab Airline, **6** 85
Libyan Arab Foreign Bank, **IV** 454
Libyan National Oil Corporation, **IV 453–55**

Libyan-Turkish Engineering and Consultancy Corp., **IV** 563
Lidköpings Mekaniska Verkstad AB, **III** 623
Lieberman Enterprises, **24** 349
Liebert Corp., **II** 20
Life and Casualty Insurance Co. of Tennessee, **III** 193
Life Assoc. of Scotland, **III** 310
Life Fitness Inc., **III** 431
Life Insurance Co. of Georgia, **III** 310
Life Insurance Co. of Scotland, **III** 358
Life Insurance Co. of Virginia, **III** 204
Life Insurance Securities, Ltd., **III** 288
Life Investors International Ltd., **III** 179; **12** 199
Life of Eire, **III** 273
Life Partners Group, Inc., **33** 111
Life Retail Stores. *See* Angelica Corporation.
Life Savers Corp., **II** 129, 544; **7** 367; **21** 54
Life Science Research, Inc., **10** 105–07
Life Technologies, Inc., **I** 321; **12** 103; **17 287–89**; **52 183–184**
Life Uniform Shops. *See* Angelica Corporation.
Lifecycle, Inc., **III** 431; **25** 40
Lifeline Systems, Inc., **32** 374; **53 207–09**
LifeLink, **11** 378
Lifemark Corp., **III** 74; **14** 232; **33** 183
Lifestyle Fitness Clubs, **46** 432
Lifetime Corp., **29** 363–64
Lifetime Entertainment Services, **IV** 627; **19** 204; **51 218–22**
Lifetime Foam Products, Inc., **12** 439
Lifetime Hoan Corporation, **27 286–89**
Lift Parts Manufacturing, **I** 157
Ligand Pharmaceuticals Incorporated, **10** 48; **47 221–23**
Liggett & Meyers, **V** 396, 405, 417–18; **18** 416; **29** 195
Liggett-Ducat, **49** 153
Liggett Group Inc., **I** 248; **7** 105; **14** 213; **15** 71; **16** 242; **37** 295. *See also* Vector Group Inc.
Light & Power Company, **12** 265
Light Corrugated Box Co., **IV** 332
Light Savers U.S.A., Inc. *See* Hospitality Worldwide Services, Inc.
Light-Servicos de Eletricidade S.A., **II** 456
Lightel Inc., **6** 311
Lighthouse, Ltd., **24** 95
Lighting Corp. of America, **I** 476
LIGHTNET, **IV** 576
Lightwell Co., **III** 634
Lignum Oil Co., **IV** 658
Lil' Champ Food Stores, Inc., **36** 359
LILCO. *See* Long Island Lighting Company.
Lilia Limited, **17** 449
Lille Bonnières et Colombes, **37** 143–44
Lillian Vernon Corporation, **12 314–15**; **35 274–77 (upd.)**
Lillie Rubin, **30** 104–06
Lilliput Group plc, **11** 95; **15** 478
Lilly & Co. *See* Eli Lilly & Co.
Lilly Industries, **22** 437
Lillybrook Coal Co., **IV** 180
Lillywhites Ltd., **III** 105
Lily Tulip Co., **I** 609, 611; **8** 198
Limburger Fabrik und Hüttenverein, **IV** 103

Limhamns Golvindustri AB. *See* Tarkett Sommer AG.
The Limited, Inc., **V 115–16**; **9** 142; **12** 280, 356; **15** 7, 9; **16** 219; **18** 193, 215, 217, 410; **20 340–43 (upd.)**; **24** 237; **25** 120–21, 123; **28** 344; **47** 142–43
Limmer and Trinidad Ltd., **III** 752
LIN Broadcasting Corp., **II** 331; **6** 323; **9 320–22**; **11** 330
Lin Data Corp., **11** 234
Linamar Corporation, **18 308–10**
Lincare Holdings Inc., **43 265–67**
Lincoln American Life Insurance Co., **10** 246
Lincoln Automotive, **26** 363
Lincoln Benefit Life Company, **10** 51
Lincoln Electric Co., **II** 19; **13 314–16**
Lincoln Electric Motor Works, **9** 439
Lincoln Federal Savings, **16** 106
Lincoln First Bank, **II** 248
Lincoln Income Life Insurance Co., **10** 246
Lincoln Liberty Life Insurance Co., **III** 254
Lincoln Marketing, Inc., **18** 518
Lincoln Motor Co., **I** 165
Lincoln National Corporation, **III** 274–77; **6** 195; **10** 44; **22** 144; **25 286–90 (upd.)**
Lincoln Property Company, **8 326–28**; **54 222–26 (upd.)**
Lincoln Savings, **10** 340
Lincoln Savings & Loan, **9** 199
Lincoln Snacks Company, **24 286–88**
Lincoln Telephone & Telegraph Company, **14 311–13**
LinCom Corp., **8** 327
Lindal Cedar Homes, Inc., **29 287–89**
Linde A.G., **I** 297–98, 315, **581–83**; **9** 16, 516; **10** 31–32; **11** 402–03; **25** 81; **48** 323
Lindemann's, **I** 220
Lindemans. *See* Southcorp Limited.
Lindex, **II** 640
Lindsay Manufacturing Co., **20 344–46**
Lindsay Parkinson & Co., **I** 567
Lindt & Sprüngli. *See* Chocoladefabriken Lindt & Sprüngli AG.
Lindustries, **III** 502; **7** 208
Linear Corp., **III** 643
Linear Technology, Inc., **16 332–34**
Líneas Aéreas Postales Españolas, **6** 95
Linens 'n Things, Inc., **13** 81–82; **24 289–92**; **33** 384; **41** 50
Linfood Cash & Carry, **13** 103
Linfood Holdings Ltd., **II** 628–29
Ling Products, **12** 25
Ling-Temco-Vought. *See* LTV Corporation.
Lingerie Time, **20** 143
Linguaphone Group, **43** 204, 206
Linjeflyg, **I** 120
Link-Belt Corp., **I** 443; **IV** 660
Link House Publications PLC, **IV** 687
Link Motor Supply Company, **26** 347
Linmark Westman International Limited, **25** 221–22
Linroz Manufacturing Company L.P., **25** 245
Lintas: Worldwide, **I** 18; **6** 30; **14 314–16**
Lintott Engineering, Ltd., **10** 108
Linz, **16** 559
Lion Corporation, **III 44–45**; **51 223–26 (upd.)**
Lion Manufacturing, **III** 430; **25** 40
Lion Match Company, **24** 450

Lion Nathan Limited, 54 227–30, 342
Lion Oil, **I** 365
Lion's Head Brewery. *See* The Stroh
Brewery Company.
Lionel L.L.C., 12 494; **16 335–38; 18** 524
Lionex Corporation, **13** 46
**Lions Gate Entertainment Corporation,
35 278–81**
Liontech, **16** 337–38
Lippincott & Margulies, **III** 283
Lippincott-Raven Publishers, **14** 556
Lipschutz Bros., Inc., **29** 511
Lipson Alport Glass & Associates, **27** 195
Lipton. *See* Thomas J. Lipton Company.
Liqui-Box Corporation, 16 339–41
Liquid Ag Systems Inc., **26** 494
Liquid Carbonic, **7** 74, 77
Liquid Holdings, Inc., **45** 168
Liquor Barn, **II** 656
Liquorland, **V** 35
Liquorsave, **II** 609–10
LIRCA, **III** 48
Liris, **23** 212
Lisbon Coal and Oil Fuel Co., **IV** 504
Liscaya, **II** 196
Listening Library Inc., **31** 379
Lister, **21** 503
Litco Bancorp., **II** 192
LiTel Communications, Inc., **16** 318
Lithia Motors, Inc., 41 238–40
Litho-Krome Corp., **IV** 621
Lithonia Lighting, Inc., **54** 252, 254–55
LitleNet, **26** 441
Litronix, **III** 455; **21** 122
Littelfuse, Inc., 26 266–69
Little, Brown & Company, **IV** 675; **7** 528;
10 355; **36** 270
**Little Caesar Enterprises, Inc., 24
293–96 (upd.); 27** 481. *See also* Ilitch
Holdings Inc.
**Little Caesar International, Inc., 7
278–79; 7** 278–79; **15** 344, 346; **16** 447;
25 179, 227–28
Little Chef Ltd., **III** 105–06
Little General, **II** 620; **12** 179, 200
Little Giant Pump Company, **8** 515
Little League Baseball, Incorporated, **23**
450
Little Leather Library, **13** 105
Little, Royal, **I** 529–30; **8** 545; **13** 63
Little Switzerland, **19** 451
Little Tikes Co., III 614; **12** 169; **13
317–19**
Littlewoods Financial Services, **30** 494
**Littlewoods Organisation PLC, V
117–19; 24** 316
Littlewoods plc, 42 228–32 (upd.)
Litton Industries Inc., I 85, 452, 476,
484–86, 523–24; **II** 33; **III** 293, 473,
732; **IV** 253; **6** 599; **10** 520–21, 537; **11
263–65 (upd.),** 435; **12** 248, 271–72,
538–40; **15** 287; **17** 30; **19** 31, 110, 290;
21 86; **22** 436; **45** 306; **48** 383. *See also*
Avondale Industries.
Litwin Engineers & Constructors, **8** 546
Livanos, **III** 516
LIVE Entertainment Inc., 18 64, 66; **20
347–49; 24** 349
Liverpool and London and Globe Insurance
Co., **III** 234, 350
Liverpool and London Fire and Life
Insurance Co., **III** 349
Liverpool Daily Post & Echo Ltd., **49** 405

Liverpool Fire and Life Insurance Co., **III**
350
Liverpool Mexico S.A., **16** 216
Livia, **I** 154; **10** 279
Living Arts, Inc., **41** 174
Living Centers of America, **13** 49
Living Videotext, **10** 508
Livingston Communications, **6** 313
Livingston, Fargo and Co., **II** 380, 395; **10**
59
LivingWell Inc., **12** 326
Liz Claiborne, Inc., 8 329–31; 16 37, 61;
25 258, **291–94 (upd.); 55** 136, 138
LKB-Produkter AB, **I** 665
Lloyd A. Fry Roofing, **III** 721
Lloyd Adriatico S.p.A., **III** 377
Lloyd Aereo de Bolivia, **6** 97
Lloyd Creative Staffing, **27** 21
Lloyd George Management, **18** 152
Lloyd Instruments, Ltd., **29** 460–61
Lloyd Italico, **III** 351
Lloyd Thompson Group plc, **20** 313
Lloyd Triestino company, **50** 187
Lloyd-Truax Ltd., **21** 499
Lloyd's Electronics, **14** 118
Lloyd's of London, III 234, **278–81; 9**
297; **10** 38; **11** 533; **22 315–19 (upd.)**
Lloyds Bank PLC, II 306–09 319, 334,
358; **17** 324–25; **48** 373
Lloyds Chemists plc, **27** 177
Lloyds Life Assurance, **III** 351
Lloyds TSB Group plc, 39 6; **47 224–29
(upd.)**
LM Ericsson. *See* Telefonaktiebolaget LM
Ericsson.
LMC Metals, **19** 380
LME. *See* Telefonaktiebolaget LM
Ericsson.
LNG Co., **IV** 473–74
LNM Group, **30** 252
Lo-Cost, **II** 609
Lo-Vaca Gathering Co., **IV** 394; **7** 553
Loadometer Co., **III** 435
Lobitos Oilfields Ltd., **IV** 381–82
**Loblaw Companies Limited, II 631–32;
19** 116; **43 268–72; 51** 301. *See also*
George Weston Limited.
Local Data, Inc., **10** 97
Locations, Inc., **IV** 727
Locke, Lancaster and W.W.&R. Johnson &
Sons, **III** 680
Lockhart Catering, **III** 104
Lockhart Corporation, **12** 564
Lockheed Corporation, I 13, 41, 48, 50,
52, 54, 61, 63, **64–66,** 67–68, 71–72,
74, 76–77, 82, 84, 90, 92–94, 100, 102,
107, 110, 113, 121, 126, 195, 493–94,
529; **II** 19, 32–33; **III** 84, 539, 601; **IV**
15; **6** 71; **9** 12, 17–18, 272, 417,
458–60, 501; **10** 163, 262–63, 317, 536;
11 164, 166, **266–69 (upd.),** 278–79,
363–65; **12** 190; **13** 126, 128; **17** 306;
21 140; **22** 506; **24** 84–85, 87, 311, 326,
375, 397; **25** 303, 316, 347; **34** 371
**Lockheed Martin Corporation, 15
283–86 (upd.); 21** 86; **24** 88; **29** 409;
32 437; **33** 47–48; **38** 372, 376; **45** 306;
48 251; **49** 345, 347; **54** 233
Lockwood Banc Group, Inc., **11** 306
Lockwood Greene Engineers, Inc., **17** 377
Lockwood National Bank, **25** 114
Lockwood Technology, Inc., **19** 179
Lockwoods Foods Ltd., **II** 513

**Loctite Corporation, 8 332–34; 30
289–91 (upd.); 34** 209
Lodding Engineering, **7** 521
Lodestar Group, **10** 19
Lodge-Cottrell, **III** 472
Lodge Plus, Ltd., **25** 430
**LodgeNet Entertainment Corporation,
26** 441; **28 240–42**
The Lodging Group, **12** 297; **48** 245
Loeb Rhoades, Hornblower & Co., **II**
450–51; **9** 469
Loehmann's Inc., 24 297–99
Loening Aeronautical, **I** 61; **11** 164
Loew's Consolidated Enterprises, **II** 154
Loew's, Inc., **31** 99
The Loewen Group, Inc., 16 342–44; 37
67–68; **40 292–95 (upd.)**
Loewenstein Furniture Group, Inc., **21**
531–33
Loewi Financial Cos., **III** 270
Loews Cineplex Entertainment Corp., **37**
64
Loews Corporation, I 245, **487–88; II**
134, 148–49, 169; **III** 228, 231; **12
316–18 (upd.),** 418; **13** 120–21; **19** 362;
22 73; **25** 177, 326–28; **36 324–28
(upd.); 38** 142; **41** 70, 72
LOF Plastics, Inc. *See* Libbey-Owens-Ford.
Loffland Brothers Company, **9** 364
Loft Inc., **I** 276; **10** 451
Logan's Roadhouse, Inc., 19 287–88; **22**
464; **29 290–92; 35** 84
Logged Off Land Co., **IV** 355–56
Logic Modeling, **11** 491
Logica plc, 14 317–19; 37 230–33 (upd.)
Logicon Inc., 20 350–52; 45 68, 310
Logility, **25** 20, 22
Logistics, **III** 431
Logistics Data Systems, **13** 4
Logistics Industries Corporation, **39** 77
Logistics Management Systems, Inc., **8** 33
Logitech International SA, 9 116; **28
243–45**
Logo Athletic, Inc., **35** 363
Logo 7, Inc., **13** 533
Logon, Inc., **14** 377
LoJack Corporation, 48 269–73
Lojas Arapuã S.A., 22 320–22
Loma Linda Foods, **14** 557–58
Lomak Petroleum, Inc., **24** 380
Lomas & Nettleton Financial Corporation,
III 249; **11** 122
Lombard North Central, **II** 442
Lombard Orient Leasing Ltd., **II** 442
London and County Bank, **II** 334
London and Hanseatic Bank, **II** 256
London & Hull, **III** 211
London and Lancashire Insurance Co., **III**
350
London & Leeds Development Corp., **II**
141
London & Midland Bank. *See* Midland
Bank plc.
London & Overseas Freighters plc. *See*
Frontline Ltd.
London & Rhodesia Mining & Land
Company. *See* Lonrho Plc.
London and Scottish Marine Oil, **11** 98
London & Western Trust, **39** 90
London and Westminster Bank, **II** 333–34
London Asiatic, **III** 699
London Assurance Corp., **III** 278, 369–71,
373; **55** 331
London Brick Co., **III** 502; **7** 208; **14** 249

London Brokers Ltd., **6** 290
London Buses Limited, **6** 406
London Cargo Group, **25** 82
London Central, **28** 155–56
London Chartered Bank of Australia, **II** 188
London Clermont Club, **III** 431
London County and Westminster Bank, **II** 334
London County Freehold & Leasehold Properties, **IV** 711
London Drugs Ltd., 46 270–73
London East India Company, **12** 421
London, Edinburgh and Dublin Insurance Co., **III** 350
London Electricity, **12** 443; **41** 141
London Film Productions Ltd., **II** 157; **14** 399
London Fog Industries, Inc., 16 61; **29 293–96**
London General Omnibus Company, **6** 406
London Guarantee and Accident Co., **III** 372
London Insurance Group, **III** 373; **36** 372
London International Group. *See* SSL International plc.
London Joint-Stock Bank, **II** 318, 388; **17** 324
London Life Assoc., **IV** 711
London Life Insurance Co., **II** 456–57
London Precision Machine & Tool, Ltd., **39** 32
London, Provincial and South Western Bank, **II** 235
London Records, **23** 390
London Regional Transport, 6 406–08
London Rubber Co., **49** 380
London South Partnership, **25** 497
London Stock Exchange Limited, 34 253–56; 37 131–33
London Transport, **19** 111
London Weekend Television, **IV** 650–51; **7** 389
Londontown Manufacturing Company. *See* London Fog Industries, Inc.
Lone Star and Crescent Oil Co., **IV** 548
Lone Star Brewing Co., **I** 255
Lone Star Gas Corp., **V** 609, 611
Lone Star Industries, **III** 718, 729, 753; **IV** 304; **23** 326; **28** 450; **35** 154
Lone Star Steakhouse & Saloon, Inc., 21 250; **51 227–29**
Lone Star Steel, **I** 440–41
Lone Star Technologies, Inc., **22** 3
Lonely Planet Publications Pty Ltd., 55 253–55
Long-Airdox Co., **IV** 136
Long Distance Discount Services, Inc., **8** 310; **27** 305
Long Distance/USA, **9** 479
Long Island Airways, **I** 115; **12** 379
Long Island Bancorp, Inc., 16 345–47; 44 33
Long Island Cable Communication Development Company, **7** 63
Long Island Daily Press Publishing Co., **IV** 582–83
Long Island Lighting Company, V 652–54; 6 456; **27** 264
Long Island Power Authority, **27** 265
Long Island Rail Road, **35** 290
Long Island Trust Co., **II** 192, 218
Long John Silver's Restaurants Inc., 13 320–22

Long Lac Mineral Exploration, **9** 282
Long Life Fish Food Products, **12** 230
Long Manufacturing Co., **III** 439; **14** 63
Long-Term Credit Bank of Japan, Ltd., II 301, **310–11**, 338, 369
Long Valley Power Cooperative, **12** 265
The Longaberger Company, 12 319–21; 44 267–70 (upd.)
Longchamps, Inc., **38** 385; **41** 388
LongHorn Steaks Inc., **19** 341
Longines-Wittenauer Watch Co., **II** 121
Longman Group Ltd., **IV** 611, 658
Longmat Foods, **II** 494
Longs Drug Stores Corporation, V 120; 25 295–97 (upd.)
Longview Fibre Company, 8 335–37; 37 234–37 (upd.)
Longwy, **IV** 227
Lonrho Plc, IV 651–52; **10** 170; **21 351–55; 43** 38; **53** 153, 202
Lonsdale Investment Trust, **II** 421
Lonvest Corp., **II** 456–57
Loomis Armored Car Service Limited, **45** 378
Loomis Fargo Group, **42** 338
Loomis, Sayles & Co., **III** 313
Loop One2, **53** 240
Loose Leaf Metals Co., Inc., **10** 314
Lor-Al, Inc., **17** 10
Loral Corporation, II 38; **7** 9; **8 338–40; 9** 323–25; **13** 356; **15** 283, 285; **20** 262; **47** 319
Loral Space & Communications Ltd., 54 231–35 (upd.)
Lord & Taylor, **13** 44; **14** 376; **15** 86; **18** 137, 372; **21** 302
Lord & Thomas, **I** 12–14; **IV** 660
Lord Baltimore Press, Inc., **IV** 286
L'Oréal, II 547; **III 46–49**, 62; **7** 382–83; **8** 129–31; **341–44 (upd.); 11** 41; **23** 238, 242; **31** 418; **46 274–79 (upd.); 52** 211
Lorentzen & Wettre AB, **53** 85
Lorenz, **I** 463
Lorillard Industries, **I** 488; **V** 396, 407, 417; **12** 317; **18** 416; **22** 73; **29** 195; **36** 324, 327
Lorimar Telepictures, **II** 149, 177; **25** 90–91, 329
Loronix Inc., **24** 509
Lorraine-Escaut, **IV** 227
Lorvic Corp., **I** 679
Los Angeles Can Co., **I** 599
Los Angeles Drug Co., **12** 106
Los Angeles Gas and Electric Company, **V** 682; **25** 413
Los Angeles Steamship Co., **II** 490
Los Lagos Corp., **12** 175
Los Nietos Co., **IV** 570; **24** 520
Loss Prevention, Inc., **24** 509
Lost Arrow Inc., 22 323–25
LOT Polish Airlines (Polskie Linie Lotnicze S.A.), 33 268–71
Lothringer Bergwerks- und Hüttenverein Aumetz-Friede AG, **IV** 126
LOT$OFF Corporation, 24 300–01
Lotus Cars Ltd., 14 320–22
Lotus Development Corporation, IV 597; **6** 224–25, 227, **254–56**, 258–60, 270–71, 273; **9** 81, 140; **10** 24, 505; **12** 335; **16** 392, 394; **20** 238; **21** 86; **22** 161; **25 298–302 (upd.); 30** 251; **38** 417
Lotus Publishing Corporation, **7** 239; **25** 239

Lotus Radio, **I** 531
Louart Corporation, **29** 33–34
Loucks, Hoffman & Company, **8** 412
Loudcloud, Inc. *See* Opsware Inc.
Loughead Aircraft Manufacturing Co., **I** 64
Louis Allis, **15** 288
Louis B. Mayer Productions, **II** 148; **25** 326–27
Louis C. Edwards, **II** 609
Louis Cruise Lines, **52** 298–99
Louis Dreyfus Energy Corp., **28** 471
Louis Harris & Associates, Inc., **22** 188
Louis Kemp Seafood Company, **14** 515; **50** 493
Louis Marx Toys, **II** 559; **12** 410
Louis Rich, Inc., **II** 532; **12** 372
Louis Vuitton, I 272; **III** 48; **8** 343; **10 397–99**. *See also* LVMH Moët Hennessy Louis Vuitton SA.
Louisiana & Southern Life Insurance Co., **14** 460
Louisiana Bank & Trust, **11** 106
Louisiana Corporation, **19** 301
Louisiana Energy Services, **27** 130
The Louisiana Land and Exploration Company, IV 76, 365, 367; **7 280–83**
Louisiana-Pacific Corporation, IV 282, **304–05; 9** 260; **16** 203; **22** 491; **31 314–317 (upd.); 32** 91
Louisville Cement Co., **IV** 409
Louisville Gas and Electric Company, **49** 120. *See also* LG&E Energy Corporation.
Louisville Home Telephone Company, **14** 258
Loup River Public Power District, **29** 352
Louthan Manufacturing Company, **8** 178
LoVaca Gathering Company. *See* The Coastal Corporation.
Lovelace Truck Service, Inc., **14** 42
Loveman's, Inc., **19** 323
Lovering China Clays, **III** 690
Lowe Bros. Co., **III** 745
Lowe Group, **22** 294
Lowe's Companies, Inc., V 122–23; 11 384; **12** 234, 345; **18** 239; **21** 324, **356–58 (upd.); 27** 416; **44** 333
Lowell Bearing Co., **IV** 136
Lowell Shoe, Inc., **13** 360
Löwenbräu, **I** 220, 257; **II** 240
Lower Manhattan Development Corporation, **47** 360
Lowes Food Stores. *See* Alex Lee Inc.
Lowney/Moirs, **II** 512
Lowrance Electronics, Inc., 18 311–14
Lowrey's Meat Specialties, Inc., **21** 156
Loyalty Group, **III** 241–43
LPL Investment Group, **40** 35–36
LRL International, **II** 477
LS Management, Inc., **51** 229
LSI. *See* Lear Siegler Inc.
LSI Logic Corporation, 13 323–25; 18 382
LTA Ltd., **IV** 22
LTR Industries, **52** 301–03
LTU Group Holding GmbH, 37 238–41
LTV Aerospace. *See* Vought Aircraft Industries, Inc.
The LTV Corporation, I 62–63, **489–91; 7** 107–08; **8** 157, 315; **10** 419; **11** 166, 364; **12** 124; **17** 357; **18** 110, 378; **19** 466; **24 302–06 (upd.); 26** 406; **45** 306; **52** 254
Luberef, **IV** 538

The Lubrizol Corporation, 30 292–95 (upd.)
Lubrizol Enterprises, Inc., I 360–62; 21 385–87
Luby's Cafeteria's, Inc., 17 290–93; 19 301
Luby's, Inc., 42 233–38 (upd.)
Lucas Bols, II 642
Lucas Digital Ltd., 12 322
Lucas Girling, I 157
Lucas Industries Plc, III 509, 554–57; 27 251
Lucas Ingredients, 27 258
Lucas-Milhaupt, Inc., 23 250
LucasArts Entertainment Company, 32 9
Lucasfilm Ltd., 9 368, 472; 12 322–24; 22 459; 34 350; 38 70; 50 320–23 (upd.)
LucasVarity plc, 27 249, 251
Lucchini, IV 228
Lucent Technologies Inc., 18 154, 180; 20 8; 22 19; 26 275, 277; 29 44, 414; 34 257–60; 36 122, 124; 41 289–90; 44 426; 48 92
Lucille Farms, Inc., 45 249–51
Lucky Brand Dungarees, 18 85
Lucky-Goldstar, II 53–54; III 457; 13 574. See also Goldstar Co., Ltd.
Lucky Lager Brewing Co, I 268; 25 280
Lucky Stores Inc., II 605, 653; 6 355; 8 474; 12 48; 17 369, 559; 22 39; 27 290–93
Lucky Strike, II 143
Ludi Wap S.A., 41 409
Ludlow Corp., III 645
Ludovico, 25 85
Lufkin Rule Co., II 16
Luftag, I 110
Lufthansa. See Deutsche Lufthansa Aktiengesellschaft.
The Luggage Company, 14 224
Lukens Inc., 14 323–25; 27 65
Lukey Mufflers, IV 249
LUKOIL. See OAO LUKOIL.
Lum's, 6 199–200
Lumac B.V., I 387
Lumbermen's Investment Corp., IV 341
Lumbermens Mutual Casualty Co., III 269–71; 15 257
Lumbertown USA, 52 232
Lumex, Inc., 17 197
Lumidor Safety Products, 52 187
La Lumière Economique, II 79
Luminar Plc, 40 296–98
Lummus Crest, IV 469; 26 496
Lumonics Inc., III 635
Lunar Corporation, 29 297–99
Luncheon Voucher, 27 10
Lund Boat Co. See Genmar Holdings, Inc.
Lund Food Holdings, Inc., 22 326–28
Lund International Holdings, Inc., 40 299–301
Lundstrom Jewelers, 24 319
Lunenburg Sea Products Limited, 14 339
Lunevale Products Ltd., I 341
L'Unite Hermetique S.A., 8 515
Lunn Poly, 8 525–26
Luotto-Pankki Oy, II 303
Lurgei, 6 599
LURGI. See Metallurgische Gesellschaft Aktiengesellschaft.
Luria Bros. and Co., I 512–13; 6 151
Lutèce, 20 26
Luther's Bar-B-Q, II 556

Lutheran Brotherhood, 31 318–21
Lux, III 478
Lux Mercantile Co., II 624
Luxair, 49 80
Luxor, II 69; 6 205; 17 353
Luxottica SpA, 17 294–96; 23 328; 43 96; 49 301; 52 227–30 (upd.); 54 320. See also Casual Corner Group, Inc.
LuxSonor Semiconductor Inc., 48 92
Luxury Linens, 13 81–82
LVMH Moët Hennessy Louis Vuitton SA, I 272; 19 86; 24 137, 140; 33 272–77 (upd.); 45 344; 46 277; 49 90, 326; 51 234–35. See also Christian Dior S.A.
LVO Cable Inc., IV 596
LXE Inc., 21 199–201
Lycos, 27 517; 37 384; 47 420. See also Terra Lycos, Inc.
Lydex, I 527
Lykes Corp., I 490–91; 24 303
Lyn Knight Currency Auctions, Inc, 48 100
Lynch Corporation, 43 273–76; 301–02
Lynde Company, 16 269–71
Lynx Express Delivery, 6 412, 414
Lyon & Healy, IV 660
Lyon's Technological Products Ltd., III 745
Lyondell Chemical Company, 45 252–55 (upd.)
Lyondell Petrochemical Company, IV 377, 456–57; 10 110
Lyonnaise Communications, 10 196; 25 497
Lyonnaise des Eaux-Dumez, I 576; V 655–57; 23 332. See also Suez Lyonnaise des Eaux.
Lyons. See J. Lyons & Co. Ltd.
LyphoMed Inc., IV 333; 17 287
Oy Lypsyniemen Konepaja, IV 275–76
Lysaght, 24 143
Lysaght's Canada, Ltd., IV 73
Lystads, I 333
Lytag Ltd., 31 398–99

M & C Saatchi, 42 330
M&F Worldwide Corp., 38 293–95
M and G Fund Management, III 699
M&G Group plc, 48 328
M and H Valve Co., 55 266
M&J Diesel Locomotive Filter Co., 17 106
M&M Limited, 7 299
M and M Manufacturing Company, 23 143
M&M/Mars, 14 48; 15 63–64; 21 219
M & S Computing. See Intergraph Corporation.
M&T Capital Corporation, 11 109
M/A Com Inc., 6 336; 14 26–27
M-Cell Ltd., 31 329
M.A. Gedney Co., 51 230–32
M.A. Hanna Company, 8 345–47; 12 352
M.A.N., III 561–63; IV 86
M.B. McGerry, 21 94
M.D.C., 11 258
M.E.P.C. Ltd., IV 711
M.F. Patterson Dental Supply Co. See Patterson Dental Co.
M.G. Waldbaum Company, 25 332–33
M. Guggenheim's Sons, IV 31
M.H. McLean Wholesaler Grocery Company, 8 380
M.H. Meyerson & Co., Inc., 46 280–83

M. Hensoldt & Söhne Wetzlar Optische Werke AG, III 446
M-I Drilling Fluids Co., III 473; 15 468
M.I. Schottenstein Homes Inc., 19 125–26
M.J. Brock Corporation, 8 460
M.J. Designs, Inc., 17 360
M.L.C. Partners Limited Partnership, 22 459
M. Loeb Ltd., II 652
M. Lowenstein Corp., V 379
M.M. Warburg. See SBC Warburg.
M.P. Burke PLC, 13 485–86
M.P. Pumps, Inc., 8 515
M. Polaner Inc., 10 70; 40 51–52; 50 538
M-R Group plc, 31 312–13
M.S. Carriers, Inc., 42 363, 365
M. Samuel & Co., II 208
M. Shanken Communications, Inc., 50 324–27
M. Sobol, Inc., 28 12
M Stores Inc., II 664
M.T.G.I. Textile Manufacturers Group, 25 121
M.W. Carr, 14 245
M.W. Kellogg Co., III 470; IV 408, 534; 34 81
M-Web Holdings Ltd., 31 329–30
Ma. Ma-Macaroni Co., II 554
Maakauppiaitten Oy, 8 293–94
Maakuntain Keskus-Pankki, II 303
MaasGlas, III 667
Maatschappij tot Exploitatie van de Onderneming Krasnapolsky. See Grand Hotel Krasnapolsky N.V.
Maatschappij tot Exploitatie van Steenfabrieken Udenhout, voorheen Weyers, 14 249
MABAG Maschinen- und Apparatebau GmbH, IV 198
Mabley & Carew, 10 282
Mac Frugal's Bargains - Closeouts Inc., 17 297–99
Mac-Gray Corporation, 44 271–73
Mac Publications LLC, 25 240
Mac Tools, III 628
MacAndrews & Forbes Holdings Inc., II 679; III 56; 9 129; 11 334; 28 246–49; 30 138; 38 293–94
MacArthur Foundation. See The John D. and Catherine T. MacArthur Foundation.
Macau Telephone, 18 114
Maccabees Life Insurance Co., III 350
MacCall Management, 19 158
MacDermid Incorporated, 32 318–21
MacDonald Companies, 15 87
MacDonald Dettwiler and Associates, 32 436
MacDonald, Halsted, and Laybourne, 10 127
Macdonald Hamilton & Co., III 522–23
Macey Furniture Co., 7 493
Macfarlane Lang & Co., II 592–93
Macfield Inc., 12 502
MacFrugal's Bargains Close-Outs Inc., 29 312; 50 98
MacGregor Sporting Goods Inc., III 443; 22 115, 458; 23 449
Mach Performance, Inc., 28 147
Machine Vision International Inc., 10 232
Macintosh. See Apple Computer, Inc.
Mack-Cali Realty Corporation, 42 239–41
Mack Trucks, Inc., I 147, 177–79; 9 416; 12 90; 22 329–32 (upd.)

Mack-Wayne Plastics, **42** 439
Mackay Envelope Corporation, 45 256–59
MacKay-Shields Financial Corp., **III** 316
MacKenzie & Co., **II** 361
Mackenzie Hill, **IV** 724
Mackenzie Mann & Co. Limited, **6** 360
Mackey Airways, **I** 102
Mackie Designs Inc., 30 406; **33 278–81**
Mackinnon Mackenzie & Co., **III** 521–22
Maclaren Power and Paper Co., **IV** 165
Maclean Hunter Limited, III 65; **IV 638–40, 22** 442; **23** 98
Maclean Hunter Publishing Limited, 26 270–74 (upd.); 30 388
Maclin Co., **12** 127
Macluan Capital Corporation, **49** 196
The MacManus Group, **32** 140; **40** 140
MacMark Corp., **22** 459
MacMarr Stores, **II** 654
Macmillan & Co. Ltd., **35** 452
MacMillan Bloedel Limited, IV 165, 272, **306–09,** 721; **9** 391; **19** 444, 446; **25** 12; **26** 445
Macmillan, Inc., IV 637, 641–43; **7 284–86,** 311–12, 343; **9** 63; **12** 226; **13** 91, 93; **17** 399; **18** 329; **22** 441–42; **23** 350, 503; **25** 484; **27** 222–23
Macnaughton Blair, **III** 671
The MacNeal-Schwendler Corporation, 25 303–05
Macneill & Co., **III** 522
Macon Gas Company, **6** 447; **23** 28
Macon Kraft Co., **IV** 311; **11** 421; **19** 267
Maconochie Bros., **II** 569
Macrodata, **18** 87
Macromedia, Inc., 50 328–31
Macwhyte Company, **27** 415
Macy's. See R.H. Macy & Co., Inc.
Macy's California, **21** 129
Mad Dog Athletics, **19** 385
MADD. See Mothers Against Drunk Driving.
Madden's on Gull Lake, 52 231–34
Maddingley Brown Coal Pty Ltd., **IV** 249
Maddux Air Lines, **I** 125; **12** 487
Madeira Wine Company, S.A., 49 255–57
Maderin ECO S.A., **51** 6
Madge Networks N.V., 18 346; **26 275–77**
Madison & Sullivan, Inc., **10** 215
Madison Dearborn Partners LLC, **46** 289; **49** 197; **51** 131, 282, 284
Madison Financial Corp., **16** 145
Madison Foods, **14** 557
Madison Furniture Industries, **14** 436
Madison Gas and Electric Company, 6 605–06; 39 259–62
Madison Resources, Inc., **13** 502
Madison Square Garden, **I** 452
MAEFORT Hungarian Air Transport Joint Stock Company, **24** 310
Maersk Lines, **22** 167
Maes Group Breweries, **II** 475
Maeva Group, **6** 206
Mafco Holdings, Inc., **28** 248; **38** 293–95
Magasins Armand Thiéry et Sigrand, **V** 11; **19** 308
Magazine and Book Services, **13** 48
Magazins Réal Stores, **II** 651
Magcobar, **III** 472
MagCorp, **28** 198
Magdeburg Insurance Group, **III** 377

Magdeburger Versicherungsgruppe, **III** 377
Magee Company, **31** 435–36
Magellan Aerospace Corporation, 46 8; **48 274–76**
Magellan Corporation, **22** 403
Magic Chef Co., **III** 573; **8** 298; **22** 349
Magic City Food Products Company. See Golden Enterprises, Inc.
Magic Marker, **29** 372
Magic Pan, **II** 559–60; **12** 410
Magic Pantry Foods, **10** 382
Magic Years Child Care, **51** 198
Magicsilk, Inc., **22** 133
MagicSoft Inc., **10** 557
Magirus, **IV** 126
Maglificio di Ponzano Veneto dei Fratelli Benetton. See Benetton.
Magma Copper Company, 7 287–90, 385–87; **22** 107
Magma Power Company, 11 270–72
Magna Computer Corporation, **12** 149; **13** 97
Magna Distribuidora Ltda., **43** 368
Magnaflux, **III** 519; **22** 282
Magnavox Co., **13** 398; **19** 393
Magne Corp., **IV** 160
Magnesium Metal Co., **IV** 118
Magnet Cove Barium Corp., **III** 472
MagneTek, Inc., 15 287–89; 41 241–44(upd.)
Magnetic Controls Company, **10** 18
Magnetic Peripherals Inc., **19** 513–14
Magnivision, **22** 35
Magnolia Petroleum Co., **III** 497; **IV** 82, 464
Magnus Co., **I** 331; **13** 197
La Magona d'Italia, **IV** 228
Magor Railcar Co., **I** 170
Magro, **48** 63
MAGroup Inc., **11** 123
Magyar Viscosa, **37** 428
Mahalo Air, **22** 252; **24** 22
Maharam Fabric, **8** 455
Mahir, **I** 37
Mahir & Numan A.S., **48** 154
Mahou, **II** 474
Mai Nap Rt, **IV** 652; **7** 392
MAI PLC, **28** 504
MAI Systems Corporation, 10 242; **11 273–76; 26** 497, 499
Maidenform Worldwide Inc., 20 352–55
Mail Boxes Etc., 18 315–17; 25 500; **41 245–48 (upd.).** See also U.S. Office Products Company.
Mail.com Inc., **38** 271
Mail Coups, Inc., **53** 13
Mail Finance, **53** 239
Mail Marketing Systems Inc., **53** 13
Mail-Well, Inc., 25 184; **28 250–52**
MailCoups, Inc., **53** 9
Mailson Ferreira da Nobrega, **II** 200
Mailtek, Inc., **18** 518
MAIN. See Mid-American Interpool Network.
Main Event Management Corp., **III** 194
Main Plaza Corporation, **25** 115
Main Street Advertising USA, **IV** 597
Maine Central Railroad Company, 16 348–50
Mainline Industrial Distributors, Inc., **13** 79
Mainline Travel, **I** 114
Maison Blanche Department Stores Group, **35** 129
Maison Bouygues, **I** 563

Maison de Schreiber and Aronson, **25** 283
Maison de Valérie, **19** 309
Maison Louis Jadot, 24 307–09
Maizuru Heavy Industries, **III** 514
Majestic Contractors Ltd., **8** 419–20
Majestic Industries, Inc., **43** 459
Majestic Wine Warehouses Ltd., **II** 656
The Major Automotive Companies, Inc., 45 260–62
Major League Baseball, **12** 457
Major SA, **53** 179
Major Video Concepts, **6** 410
Major Video, Inc., **9** 74
MaK Maschinenbau GmbH, **IV** 88
Mak van Waay, **11** 453
Makepeace Preserving Co., **25** 365
Makhteshim Chemical Works Ltd., **II** 47; **25** 266–67
Makita Corporation, III 436; **20** 66; **22 333–35**
Makiyama, **I** 363
Makovsky & Company, **12** 394
Makro Inc., **18** 286
Malama Pacific Corporation, **9** 276
Malapai Resources, **6** 546
Malayan Breweries, **I** 256
Malayan Motor and General Underwriters, **III** 201
Malaysia LNG, **IV** 518–19
Malaysian Airlines System Berhad, 6 71, **100–02,** 117, 415; **29 300–03 (upd.)**
Malaysian International Shipping Co., **IV** 518
Malaysian Sheet Glass, **III** 715
Malbak Ltd., **IV** 92–93
Malcolm Pirnie, Inc., 42 242–44
Malcolm's Diary & Time-Table, **III** 256
Malcus Industri, **III** 624
Malden Mills Industries, Inc., 16 351–53
Malév Plc, 24 310–12; 27 474; **29** 17
Malew Engineering, **51** 354
Malheur Cooperative Electric Association, **12** 265
Malibu, **25** 141
Mall.com, **38** 271
Mallard Bay Drilling, Inc., **28** 347–48
Malleable Iron Works, **II** 34
Mallinckrodt Group Inc., III 16; **IV** 146; **8** 85; **19** 28, **251–53**
Malmö Aviation, **47** 61
Malmö Flygindustri, **I** 198
Malmö Woodworking Factory. See Tarkett Sommer AG.
Malmsten & Bergvalls, **I** 664
Malone & Hyde, Inc., **II** 625, 670–71; **9** 52–53; **14** 147; **18** 506; **50** 456–57
Malrite Communications Group, **IV** 596
Malt-A-Milk Co., **II** 487
Malt-O-Meal Company, 15 189; **22 336–38**
Malterie Soufflet. See Groupe Soufflet SA
Mama's Concept, Inc., **51** 229
Mameco International, **8** 455
Mammoet Transport B.V., 26 241, **278–80**
Man Aktiengesellschaft, III 301, **561–63**
MAN Gutehoffnungshütte AG, **15** 226
Management and Training Corporation, 28 253–56
Management By Information Inc., **48** 307
Management Decision Systems, Inc., **10** 358
Management Engineering and Development Co., **IV** 310; **19** 266

Management Recruiters International, **6** 140

Management Science America, Inc., **11** 77; **25** 20

Manbré and Garton, **II** 582

Manchester and Liverpool District Banking Co., **II** 307, 333

Manchester Board and Paper Co., **19** 77

Manchester Commercial Buildings Co., **IV** 711

Manchester United Football Club plc, 30 296–98; 44 388

Manco, Inc., **13** 166. *See also* Henkel Manco Inc.

Mancuso & Co., **22** 116

Mandabach & Simms, **6** 40

Mandalay Pictures, **35** 278–80

Mandalay Resort Group, 32 322–26 (upd.)

Mandarin, Inc., **33** 128

Mandarin Oriental Hotel Group International Ltd., **I** 471; **IV** 700; **20** 312

Mandarin Oriental International Limited, **47** 177

Mandel Bros., **IV** 660

Manetta Mills, Inc., **19** 304

Manhattan Card Co., **18** 114

Manhattan Co., **II** 217, 247

Manhattan Construction Company. *See* Rooney Brothers Co.

Manhattan Electrical Supply Co., **9** 517

Manhattan Fund, **I** 614

Manhattan International Limousine Network Ltd., **26** 62

Manhattan Trust Co., **II** 229

Manheim Auctions, Inc. *See* Cox Enterprises, Inc.

Manifatture Cotoniere Meridionali, **I** 466

Manischewitz Company. *See* B. Manischewitz Company.

Manistique Papers Inc., **17** 282

Manistique Pulp and Paper Co., **IV** 311; **19** 266

Manitoba Bridge and Engineering Works Ltd., **8** 544

Manitoba Paper Co., **IV** 245–46; **25** 10

Manitoba Rolling Mill Ltd., **8** 544

Manitou BF S.A., 27 294–96

Manitowoc Company, Inc., 18 318–21

Mann Egerton & Co., **III** 523

Mann Theatres Chain, **I** 245; **25** 177

Mann's Wine Company, Ltd., **14** 288

Mann's Wine Pub Co., Ltd., **47** 206

Mannatech Inc., 33 282–85

Manne Tossbergs Eftr., **II** 639

Mannesmann AG, I 411; **III 564–67; IV** 222, 469; **14 326–29 (upd.); 34** 319; **38 296–301 (upd.); 54** 391, 393. *See also* Vodafone Group PLC.

Mannheim Steamroller. *See* American Gramaphone LLC.

Mannheimer Bank, **IV** 558

Manning, Selvage & Lee, **6** 22

Mannstaedt, **IV** 128

Manor AG, **48** 279

Manor Care, Inc., 6 187–90; 14 105–07; **15** 522; **25 306–10 (upd.)**

Manor Healthcare Corporation, **26** 459

Manorfield Investments, **II** 158

Manos Enterprises, **14** 87

Manpower, Inc., 6 10, 140; **9 326–27; 16** 48; **25** 432; **30 299–302 (upd.); 40** 236, 238; **44** 157; **49** 264–65

Mantrec S.A., **27** 296

Mantua Metal Products. *See* Tyco Toys, Inc.

Manufactured Home Communities, Inc., 22 339–41; 46 378

Manufacturers & Merchants Indemnity Co., **III** 191

Manufacturers and Traders Trust Company, **11** 108–09

Manufacturers Casualty Insurance Co., **26** 486

Manufacturers Fire Insurance Co., **26** 486

Manufacturers Hanover Corporation, II 230, 254, **312–14**, 403; **III** 194; **9** 124; **11** 16, 54, 415; **13** 536; **14** 103; **16** 207; **17** 559; **22** 406; **26** 453; **38** 253

Manufacturers National Bank of Brooklyn, **II** 312

Manufacturers National Bank of Detroit, **I** 165; **11** 137; **40** 116

Manufacturers Railway, **I** 219; **34** 36

Manufacturing Management Inc., **19** 381

Manus Nu-Pulse, **III** 420

Manville Corporation, III 706–09, 721; **7 291–95 (upd.); 10** 43, 45; **11** 420–22. *See also* Riverwood International Corporation.

Manweb plc, **19** 389–90; **49** 363–64

MAP. *See* Marathon Ashland Petroleum LLC.

MAPCO Inc., IV 458–59; 26 234; **31** 469, 471

Mapelli Brothers Food Distribution Co., **13** 350

MAPICS, Inc., 55 256–58

Maple Grove Farms of Vermont, Inc., **40** 51–52

Maple Leaf Foods Inc., 41 249–53

Maple Leaf Mills, **II** 513–14; **41** 252

MAPP. *See* Mid-Continent Area Power Planner.

Mapra Industria e Comercio Ltda., **32** 40

MAR Associates, **48** 54

Mar-O-Bar Company, **7** 299

A.B. Marabou, **II** 511

Marantha! Music, **14** 499

Marantz Co., **14** 118

Marathon Ashland Petroleum LLC, **49** 329–30; **50** 49

Marathon Insurance Co., **26** 486

Marathon Oil Co., **IV** 365, 454, 487, 572, 574; **7** 549, 551; **13** 458; **49** 328, 330; **50** 503

Marathon Paper Products, **I** 612, 614

Marauder Company, **26** 433

Maraven, **IV** 508

Marblehead Communications, Inc., **23** 101

Marbodal, **12** 464

Marboro Books, Inc., **10** 136

Marbro Lamp Co., **III** 571; **20** 362

Marc's Big Boy. *See* The Marcus Corporation.

Marcade Group. *See* Aris Industries, Inc.

Marcam Coporation. *See* MAPICS, Inc.

Marceau Investments, **II** 356

March-Davis Bicycle Company, **19** 383

March of Dimes, 31 322–25

March Plasma Systems, Inc., **48** 299

Marchand, **13** 27

Marchesi Antinori SRL, 42 245–48

marchFIRST, Inc., 34 261–64

Marchland Holdings Ltd., **II** 649

Marchon Eyewear, **22** 123

Marciano Investments, Inc., **24** 157

Marcillat, **19** 49

Marcon Coating, Inc., **22** 347

Marconi plc, 33 286–90 (upd.)

Marconi Wireless Telegraph Co. of America, **II** 25, 88

Marconiphone, **I** 531

The Marcus Corporation, 21 359–63

Marcus Samuel & Co., **IV** 530

Marcy Fitness Products, Inc., **19** 142, 144

Mardon Packaging International, **I** 426–27

Mardorf, Peach and Co., **II** 466

Maremont Corporation, **8** 39–40

Margarete Steiff GmbH, 23 334–37

Margarine Unie N.V. *See* Unilever PLC (Unilever N.V.).

Marge Carson, Inc., **III** 571; **20** 362

Margo's La Mode, **10** 281–82; **45** 15

Marico Acquisition Corporation, **8** 448, 450

Marie Brizard & Roger International S.A., 22 342–44

Marie Callender's Restaurant & Bakery, Inc., 13 66; **28 257–59**

Marie-Claire Album, **III** 47

Marigold Foods Inc., **II** 528

Marina Mortgage Company, **46** 25

Marinduque Mining & Industrial Corp., **IV** 146

Marine Bank and Trust Co., **11** 105

Marine Bank of Erie, **II** 342

Marine Computer Systems, **6** 242

Marine Diamond Corp., **IV** 66; **7** 123

Marine-Firminy, **IV** 227

Marine Group, **III** 444; **22** 116

Marine Harvest International, **13** 103

Marine Manufacturing Corporation, **52** 406

Marine Midland Bank, **50** 523

Marine Midland Corp., **I** 548; **II** 298; **9** 475–76; **11** 108; **17** 325

Marine Office of America, **III** 220, 241–42

Marine United Inc., **42** 361

Marinela, **19** 192–93

Marineland Amusements Corp., **IV** 623

MarineMax, Inc., 30 303–05; 37 396

Marion Brick, **14** 249

Marion Foods, Inc., **17** 434

Marion Freight Lines, **6** 370

Marion Laboratories Inc., I 648–49; 8 149; **9** 328–29; **16** 438; **50** 163

Marion Manufacturing, **9** 72

Marion Merrell Dow, Inc., 9 328–29 (upd.)

Marionet Corp., **IV** 680–81

Marionnaud Parfumeries SA, 51 233–35; 54 265–66

Marisa Christina, Inc., 15 290–92; 25 245

Maritime Electric Company, Limited, **15** 182; **47** 136–37

Maritz Inc., 38 302–05

Mark Controls Corporation, **30** 157

Mark Cross, Inc., **17** 4–5

Mark Goldston, **8** 305

Mark Hopkins, **12** 316

Mark IV Industries, Inc., 7 296–98; 21 418; **28 260–64 (upd.)**

Mark Travel Corporation, **30** 448

Mark Trouser, Inc., **17** 338

Markborough Properties, **II** 222; **V** 81; **8** 525; **25** 221

Market Growth Resources, **23** 480

Market Horizons, **6** 27

Market National Bank, **13** 465

Marketime, **V** 55

Marketing Data Systems, Inc., **18** 24

Marketing Equities International, **26** 136
Marketing Information Services, **6** 24
MarketSpan Corp. *See* KeySpan Energy Co.
Markham & Co., **I** 573–74
Marks and Spencer p.l.c., I 588; **II** 513, 678; **V 124–26; 10** 442; **17** 42, 124; **22** 109, 111; **24** 268, 270; **313–17 (upd.),** 474; **28** 96; **35** 308, 310; **41** 114; **42** 231
Marks-Baer Inc., **11** 64
Marks Brothers Jewelers, Inc., 24 318–20
Marland Refining Co., **IV** 399–400
Marlene Industries Corp., **16** 36–37
MarLennan Corp., **III** 283
Marley Co., **19** 360
Marley Holdings, L.P., **19** 246
Marley Tile, **III** 735
Marlin-Rockwell Corp., **I** 539; **14** 510
Marlow Foods, **II** 565
Marman Products Company, **16** 8
The Marmon Group, III 97; **IV 135–38; 16 354–57 (upd.)**
Marmon-Perry Light Company, **6** 508
Marolf Dakota Farms, Inc., **18** 14–15
Marotte, **21** 438
Marquam Commercial Brokerage Company, **21** 257
Marquardt Aircraft, **I** 380; **13** 379
Marquette Electronics, Inc., 13 326–28
Marquette Paper Corporation, **III** 766; **22** 545
Marquis Who's Who, **17** 398
Marriage Mailers, **6** 12
Marriner Group, **13** 175
Marriot Inc., **29** 442
Marriot Management Services, **29** 444
Marriott Corporation, II 173, 608; **III** 92, 94, 99–100, **102–03,** 248; **7** 474–75; **9** 95, 426; **15** 87; **17** 238; **18** 216; **19** 433–34; **21** 91, 364; **22** 131; **23** 436–38; **27** 334; **38** 386; **41** 82
Marriott International, Inc., 21 182, **364–67 (upd.); 29** 403, 406; **41** 156–58; **52** 415
Mars, Incorporated, II 510–11; **III** 114; **7 299–301; 22** 298, 528; **40 302–05 (upd.)**
Marschke Manufacturing Co., **III** 435
Marsene Corp., **III** 440
Marsh & McLennan Companies, Inc., III 280, **282–84; 10** 39; **14** 279; **22** 318; **45** 28, **263–67 (upd.); 53** 64
Marsh Supermarkets, Inc., 17 300–02
Marshalk Company, **I** 16; **22** 294
Marshall Die Casting, **13** 225
Marshall Field & Co., **I** 13, 426; **III** 329; **IV** 660; **V** 43–44; **8** 33; **9** 213; **12** 283; **15** 86; **18** 136–37, 488; **22** 72; **50** 117, 119
Marshall Industries, **19** 311
Marshalls Incorporated, 13 329–31; 14 62
Marship Tankers (Holdings) Ltd., **52** 329
Marsin Medical Supply Co., **III** 9
Marstellar, **13** 204
The Mart, **9** 120
Martank Shipping Holdings Ltd., **52** 329
Marten Transport, **27** 404
Martha, **IV** 486
Martha Lane Adams, **27** 428
Martha Stewart Living Omnimedia, L.L.C., 24 321–23; 47 211
Martin & Pagenstecher GMBH, **24** 208

Martin Band Instrument Company, **55** 149, 151
Martin Bros. Tobacco Co., **14** 19
Martin-Brower Corp., **II** 500; **III** 21; **17** 475
Martin Collet, **19** 50
Martin Dennis Co., **IV** 409
Martin Dunitz, **44** 416
Martin Electric Co., **III** 98
Martin Gillet Co., **55** 96, 98
Martin Guitar Company. *See* C.F. Martin & Co., Inc.
Martin Hilti Foundation, **53** 167
Martin Industries, Inc., 44 274–77
Martin Marietta Corporation, I 47, **67–69,** 71, 102, 112, 142–43, 184, 416; **II** 32, 67; **III** 671; **IV** 60, 163; **7** 356, 520; **8** 315; **9** 310; **10** 162, 199, 484; **11** 166, 277–78, 364; **12** 127, 290; **13** 327, 356; **15** 283; **17** 564; **18** 369; **19** 70; **22** 400; **28** 288. *See also* Lockheed Martin Corporation.
Martin Mathys, **8** 456
Martin Rooks & Co., **I** 95
Martin-Senour Co., **III** 744
Martin Sorrell, **6** 54
Martin Theaters, **14** 86
Martin-Yale Industries, Inc., **19** 142–44
Martin Zippel Co., **16** 389
Martin's, **12** 221
Martindale-Hubbell, **17** 398
Martineau and Bland, **I** 293
Martini & Rossi, **18** 41
Martins Bank, **II** 236, 308
Martinus Nijhoff, **14** 555; **25** 85
Marubeni Corporation, 24 324–27 (upd.)
Marubeni K.K., I 432, **492–95,** 510; **II** 292, 391; **III** 760; **IV** 266, 525; **12** 147; **17** 556
Maruei & Co., **IV** 151; **24** 358
Maruetsu, **17** 124; **41** 114
Marufuku Co., Ltd., **III** 586; **7** 394
Marui Co. Ltd., V 127
Marukuni Kogyo Co., Ltd., **IV** 327
Marusa Co. Ltd., **51** 379
Marutaka Kinitsu Store Ltd., **V** 194; **47** 389
Maruzen Co., Limited, II 348; **IV** 403–04, 476, 554; **18 322–24**
Maruzen Oil Co., Ltd., **53** 114
Marvel Entertainment Group, Inc., 10 400–02; 18 426, 520–21; **21** 404; **25** 141; **34** 449
Marvel Metal Products, **III** 570; **20** 361
Marvel-Schebler Carburetor Corp., **III** 438; **14** 63–64
Marvin & Leonard Advertising, **13** 511–12
Marvin H. Sugarman Productions Inc., **20** 48
Marvin Lumber & Cedar Company, 10 95; **22 345–47**
Marwick, Mitchell & Company, **10** 385
Marwitz & Hauser, **III** 446
Marx, **12** 494
Mary Ann Co. Ltd., **V** 89
Mary Ann Restivo, Inc., **8** 323
Mary Ellen's, Inc., **11** 211
Mary Kathleen Uranium, **IV** 59–60
Mary Kay Corporation, III 16; **9 330–32; 12** 435; **15** 475, 477; **18** 67, 164; **21** 49, 51; **30 306–09 (upd.)**
Maryland Casualty Co., **III** 193, 412
Maryland Cup Company, **8** 197
Maryland Distillers, **I** 285

Maryland Medical Laboratory Inc., **26** 391
Maryland National Corp., **11** 287
Maryland National Mortgage Corporation, **11** 121; **48** 177
Maryland Shipbuilding and Drydock Co., **I** 170
Maryland Steel Co., **IV** 35; **7** 48
Marzotto S.p.A., 20 356–58; 48 206–07
Masayoshi Son, **13** 481–82
Mascan Corp., **IV** 697
Maschinenbauanstalt Humboldt AG, **III** 541
Maschinenfabrik Augsburg-Nürnberg. *See* M.A.N.
Maschinenfabrik Deutschland, **IV** 103
Maschinenfabrik für den Bergbau von Sievers & Co., **III** 541
Maschinenfabrik Gebr. Meer, **III** 565
Maschinenfabrik Sürth, **I** 581
Masco Corporation, III 568–71; 11 385, 534–35; **12** 129, 131, 344; **13** 338; **18** 68; **20 359–63 (upd.); 39 263–68 (upd.)**
Masco Optical, **13** 165
Mascon Toy Co., **III** 569; **20** 360
MASCOR, **14** 13
Mase Westpac Limited, **11** 418
Maserati. *See* Officine Alfieri Maserati S.p.A.
Mashantucket Pequot Gaming Enterprise Inc., 35 282–85
Masinfabriks A.B. Scania, **I** 197
MASkargo Ltd., **6** 101
Masland Corporation, 17 303–05; 19 408
Mason & Hamlin, **III** 656
Mason Best Co., **IV** 343
Masonite Corp., **III** 764; **47** 189
Masonite Holdings, **III** 687
Mass Rapid Transit Corp., **19** 111
Massachusetts Bank, **II** 207
Massachusetts Capital Resources Corp., **III** 314
Massachusetts Electric Company, **51** 265
Massachusetts Mutual Life Insurance Company, III 110, **285–87,** 305; **14** 14; **25** 528; **53 210–13 (upd.)**
Massachusetts Technology Development Corporation, **18** 570
Massachusetts's General Electric Company, **32** 267
Massey Burch Investment Grou Master Boot Polish Co., **II** 566
MasTec, Inc., 55 259–63 (upd.)
Master Builders, **I** 673
Master Electric Company, **15** 134
Master Glass & Color, **24** 159–60
Master Lock Company, 45 268–71
Master Pneumatic Tool Co., **III** 436
Master Processing, **19** 37
Master Products, **14** 162
Master Shield Inc., **7** 116
Master Tank and Welding Company, **7** 541
Master Tek International, Inc., **47** 372
MasterBrand Industries Inc., **12** 344–45
MasterCard International, Inc., 9 333–35; 18 337, 543; **25** 41; **26** 515; **41** 201
Mastercraft Homes, Inc., **11** 257
Mastercraft Industries Corp., **III** 654
Masters-Jackson, **50** 49
Mastex Industries, **29** 132
Maszovlet. *See* Malév Plc.
Matador Records, **22** 194
Matairco, **9** 27
Matalan PLC, 49 258–60

Matane Pulp & Paper Company, **17** 281
Matchbox Toys Ltd., **12** 168
MatchLogic, Inc., **41** 198
Matco Tools, **7** 116
Material Management and Services Inc., **28** 61
Material Sciences Corp., **54** 331
Materials Services Corp., **I** 58
Mathematica, Inc., **22** 291
Mather & Crother Advertising Agency, **I** 25
Mather Co., **I** 159
Mather Metals, **III** 582
Matheson & Co., **IV** 189
Mathews Conveyor Co., **14** 43
Mathieson Chemical Corp., **I** 379–80, 695; **13** 379
Matra, **II** 38, 70; **IV** 617–19; **13** 356; **17** 354; **24** 88
Matra Aerospace Inc., **22** 402
Matra-Hachette S.A., 15 293–97 (upd.); **21** 267. *See also* European Aeronautic Defence and Space Company EADS N.V.
Matria Healthcare, Inc., 17 306–09
Matrix Science Corp., **II** 8; **14** 27
Matson Navigation Company, Inc., **II** 490–91; **10** 40; **41** 399
Matsumoto Medical Instruments, Inc., **11** 476; **29** 455
Matsushita Electric Industrial Co., Ltd., **II** 5, **55–56**, 58, 61, 91–92, 102, 117–19, 361, 455; **III** 476, 710; **6** 36; **7** 163, 302; **10** 286, 389, 403, 432; **11** 487; **12** 448; **13** 398; **18** 18; **20** 81; **26** 511; **33** 432; **36** 399–400, 420
Matsushita Electric Works, Ltd., III **710–11**; **7** 302–03 (upd.); **12** 454; **16** 167; **27** 342
Matsushita Kotobuki Electronics Industries, Ltd., **10** 458–59
Matsuura Trading Co., Ltd., **IV** 327
Matsuzakaya Company, V 129–31
Mattatuck Bank & Trust Co., **13** 467
Mattel, Inc., II 136; **III** 506; **7 304–07**; **12** 74, 168–69, 495; **13** 560–61; **15** 238; **16** 264, 428; **17** 243; **18** 520–21; **25** **311–15 (upd.)**, 381, 488; **27** 20, 373, 375; **28** 159; **29** 74, 78; **32** 187; **34** 369–70; **43** 229, 232–33; **52** 192–93
Matth. Hohner AG, 53 214–17
Matthes & Weber, **III** 32
Matthew Bender & Company, Inc., **IV** 677; **7** 94; **14** 97; **17** 486
Matthews International Corporation, 29 **304–06**
Matthews Paint Co., **22** 437
Maud Foster Mill, **II** 566
Maui Electric Company, **9** 276
Maui Land & Pineapple Company, Inc., **29 307–09**
Maui Tacos International, Inc., **49** 60
Mauna Kea Properties, **6** 129
Maurice H. Needham Co., **I** 31
Maus Frères SA, 19 307; **48 277–79**
Maus-Nordmann, **V** 10; **19** 308
Max & Erma's Restaurants Inc., 19 **258–60**
Max Factor & Co., **III** 54, 56; **6** 51; **12** 314
Max-Grundig-Stiftung, **27** 190–91
Max Klein, Inc., **II** 572
Max Media Properties LLC, **25** 419
Max Television Co., **25** 418

Maxcell Telecom Plus, **6** 323
Maxco Inc., 17 310–11; 24 159, 160
Maxell Corp., **I** 500; **14** 534
Maxi-Papier-Markt, **10** 498; **24** 270
Maxi Vac, Inc., **9** 72
Maxicare Health Plans, Inc., III 84–86; **25 316–19 (upd.); 44** 174
Maxie's of America, **25** 389
The Maxim Group, 25 88, **320–22**
Maxim Integrated Products, Inc., 16 **358–60**
MAXIMUS, Inc., 43 277–80
Maxis Software, **13** 115
Maxoptix Corporation, **10** 404
Maxpro Sports Inc., **22** 458
Maxpro Systems, **24** 509–10
Maxtor Corporation, 6 230; **10 403–05**, 459, 463–64
Maxus Energy Corporation, IV 410; **7** **308–10**; **10** 191; **31** 456
Maxwell Communication Corporation plc, **IV** 605, 611, **641–43**; **7** 286, **311–13 (upd.)**, 343; **10** 288; **13** 91–93; **23** 350; **39** 49; **47** 326; **49** 408
Maxwell Morton Corp, **I** 144, 414
Maxwell Shoe Company, Inc., 30 310–12
Maxwell Travel Inc., **33** 396
MAXXAM Inc., IV 121, 123; **8 348–50**
Maxxim Medical Inc., 12 325–27
May and Baker, **I** 388
May & Speh Inc., **35** 17
The May Department Stores Company, I 540; **II** 414; **V 132–35**; **8** 288; **11** 349; **12** 55, 507–08; **13** 42, 361; **15** 275; **16** 62, 160, 206–07; **18** 414–15; **19 261–64** **(upd.)**; **23** 345; **27** 61, 291, 346, 348; **33** 471, 473; **46 284–88 (upd.)**
May International. *See* George S. May International Company.
Maybelline, **I** 684
Mayer & Schweitzer, **26** 66
Mayer, Brown, Rowe & Maw, 47 **230–32**
Mayfair Foods, **I** 438; **16** 314
Mayfield Dairy Farms, Inc., **7** 128
Mayflower Group Inc., 6 409–11; 15 50
Mayne Nickless Ltd., **IV** 248
Mayo Foundation, 9 336–39; 13 326; **34** **265–69 (upd.)**
Mayor's Jewelers, Inc., 41 254–57
Mays + Red Spot Coatings, LLC, **55** 321
Maytag Corporation, III 572–73; 12 252, 300; **21** 141; **22** 218, **348–51 (upd.); 23** 244; **42** 159; **43** 166
Mayville Metal Products Co., **I** 513
Mazda Motor Corporation, I 520; **II** 4, 361; **III** 603; **9 340–42; 11** 86; **13** 414; **16** 322; **23 338–41 (upd.); 36** 215
Mazel Stores, Inc., 29 310–12
MB Group, **20** 108. *See also* Novar plc.
MBB. *See* Messerschmitt-Bölkow-Blohm.
MBC. *See* Middle East Broadcasting Centre, Ltd.
MBC Holding Company, 40 306–09
MBE. *See* Mail Boxes Etc.
MBNA Corporation, 11 123; **12 328–30;** **33 291–94 (upd.)**
MBPXL Corp., **II** 494
MC Distribution Services, Inc., **35** 298
MCA Inc., II 143–45; 6 162–63; **10** 286; **11** 557; **17** 317; **21** 23, 25–26; **22** 131, 194; **23** 125; **25** 411; **26** 151, 314; **33** 431; **52** 191

Maxcell Telecom Plus, **6** 323
McAfee Associates. *See* Network Associates, Inc.
The McAlpin Company, **19** 272
McAndrew & Forbes Holdings Inc., **23** 407; **26** 119
McArthur Glen Realty, **10** 122; **33** 59
MCC. *See* Maxwell Communications Corporation; Morris Communications Corporation.
McCaffrey & McCall, **I** 33; **11** 496
McCain Feeds Ltd., **II** 484
McCain Foods, **41** 252
McCall Pattern Company, **22** 512; **23** 99
McCall Printing Co., **14** 460
McCall's Corp., **23** 393
McCann-Erickson Worldwide, **I** 10, 14, 16–17, 234; **6** 30; **10** 227; **14** 315; **16** 167; **18** 68; **22** 294; **32** 114
McCann-Erickson Hakuhodo, Ltd., **42** 174
McCarthy Building Companies, Inc., 48 **280–82**
McCarthy Milling, **II** 631; **27** 245–47
McCaughan Dyson and Co., **II** 189
McCaw Cellular Communications, Inc., **II** 331; **6** 274, **322–24; 7** 15; **9** 320–21; **10** 433; **15** 125, 196; **27** 341, 343–44; **29** 44, 61; **36** 514–15; **43** 447; **49** 71–72. *See also* AT&T Wireless Services, Inc.
McClain Industries, Inc., 51 236–38
McClanahan Oil Co., **I** 341; **14** 216
McClatchy Newspapers, Inc., 23 156, 158, **342–44**
McCleary, Wallin and Crouse, **19** 274
McClintic-Marshall, **IV** 36; **7** 49
The McCloskey Corporation, **8** 553
The McClure Syndicate, **25** 138
McColl-Frontenac Petroleum Inc., **IV** 439; **25** 232
McComb Manufacturing Co., **8** 287
McCormack & Dodge, **IV** 605; **11** 77
McCormick & Company, Incorporated, **7 314–16; 17** 104, 106; **21** 497; **27** **297–300 (upd.); 36** 185, 188
McCormick & Schmick's, **31** 41
McCormick Harvesting Machine Co., **I** 180; **II** 330
McCown De Leeuw & Co., **16** 510
McCracken Brooks, **23** 479; **25** 91
McCrory Stores, **II** 424; **9** 447–48; **13** 340
McCulloch Corp., **III** 436; **8** 348–49
McCullough Environmental Services, **12** 443
McDermott International, Inc., III **558–60; 37 242–46 (upd.)**
McDonald Glass Grocery Co. Inc., **II** 669
McDonald's Company (Japan) Ltd., **V** 205
McDonald's Corporation, I 23, 31, 129; **II** 500, 613–15 **646–48; III** 63, 94, 103; **6** 13; **7** 128, 266–67, 316, **317–19** **(upd.)**, 435, 505–06; **8** 261–62, 564; **9** 74, 178, 290, 292, 305; **10** 122; **11** 82, 308; **12** 43, 180, 553; **13** 494; **14** 25, 32, 106, 195, 452–53; **16** 95–97, 289; **17** 69–71; **19** 85, 192, 214; **21** 25, 315, 362; **23** 505; **25** 179, 309, 387; **26** **281–85 (upd.); 31** 278; **32** 442–44; **33** 240; **36** 517, 519–20; **39** 166, 168; **48** 67
McDonnell Douglas Corporation, I 41–43, 45, 48, 50–52, 54–56, 58–59, 61–62, 67–68, **70–72**, 76–77, 82, 84–85, 90, 105, 108, 111, 121–22, 321, 364, 490, 511; **II** 442; **III** 512, 654; **6**

68; **7** 456, 504; **8** 49–51, 315; **9** 18, 183, 206, 231, 271–72, 418, 458, 460; **10** 163–64, 317, 536; **11** 164–65, 267, **277–80 (upd.)**, 285, 363–65; **12** 190–91, 549; **13** 356; **15** 283; **16** 78, 94; **18** 368; **24** 84–85, 87; **28** 225; **32** 81, 83, 85

McDonough Co., **II** 16; **III** 502

McDougal, Littell & Company, **10** 357

McDowell Energy Center, **6** 543

McDowell Furniture Company, **10** 183

McDuff, **10** 305

McElligott Wright Morrison and White, **12** 511

McFadden Holdings L.P., **27** 41

McFadden Industries, **III** 21

McFadden Publishing, **6** 13

McGaughy, Marsha 584, **634–37**, 643, 656, 674; **10** 62; **12** 359; **13** 417; **18** **325–30 (upd.)**; **26** 79; **27** 360

McGaw Inc., **11** 208

McGill Manufacturing, **III** 625

McGraw-Edison Co., **II** 17, 87

McGraw Electric Company. *See* Centel Corporation.

The McGraw-Hill Companies, Inc., **II** 398; **IV** 584, **634–37**, 643, 656, 674; **10** 62; **12** 359; **13** 417; **18** 325–30 **(upd.)**; **26** 79; **27** 360; **51** 239–44 **(upd.)**

McGregor Corporation, **6** 415; **26** 102

McGrew Color Graphics, **7** 430

MCI. *See* Manitou Costruzioni Industriali SRL; Melamine Chemicals, Inc.

MCI Communications Corporation, **II** 408; **III** 13, 149, 684; **V** 302–04; **6** 51–52, 300, 322; **7** 118–19; **8** 310; **9** 171, 478–80; **10** 19, 80, 89, 97, 433, 500; **11** 59, 183, 185, 302, 409, 500; **12** 135–37; **13** 38; **14** 252–53, 260, 364; **15** 222; **16** 318; **18** 32, 112, 164–66, 569–70; **19** 255; **25** 358; **26** 102, 441; **27** 430; **29** 42; **46** 374; **49** 72–73

MCI WorldCom, Inc., **27** 301–08 **(upd.)**

McIlhenny Company, **20** 364–67

McIlwraith McEachern Limited, **27** 474

McJunkin Corp., **13** 79; **28** 61

McKechnie plc, **34** 270–72

McKee Foods Corporation, **7** 320–21; **27** 309–11 **(upd.)**

McKenna Metals Company, **13** 295–96

McKesson Corporation, **I** 413, **496–98**, 713; **II** 652; **III** 10; **6** 279; **8** 464; **9** 532; **11** 91; **12** 331–33 **(upd.)**; **16** 43; **18** 97; **37** 10; **41** 340; **47** 233–37 **(upd.)**

McKesson General Medical, **29** 299

McKinsey & Company, Inc., **I** 108, 144, 437, 497; **III** 47, 85, 670; **9** 343–45; **10** 175; **13** 138; **18** 68; **25** 34, 317; **26** 161

McLain Grocery, **II** 625

McLane America, Inc., **29** 481

McLane Company, Inc., **V** 217; **8** 556; **13** 332–34; **36** 269

McLaren Consolidated Cone Corp., **II** 543; **7** 366

McLaughlin Motor Company of Canada, **I** 171; **10** 325

McLean Clinic, **11** 379

McLeodUSA Incorporated, **32** 327–30; **38** 192

McLouth Steel Products, **13** 158

MCM Electronics, **9** 420

McMahan's Furniture Co., **14** 236

McMan Oil and Gas Co., **IV** 369

McManus, John & Adams, Inc., **6** 21

MCMC. *See* Minneapolis Children's Medical Center.

McMoCo, **IV** 82–83; **7** 187

McMoRan, **IV** 81–83; **V** 739; **7** 185, 187

McMullen & Yee Publishing, **22** 442

McMurtry Manufacturing, **8** 553

MCN Corporation, **6** 519–22; **13** 416; **17** 21–23; **45** 254

McNeil Corporation, **26** 363

McNeil Laboratories, **III** 35–36; **8** 282–83

McNellan Resources Inc., **IV** 76

MCO Holdings Inc., **8** 348–49

MCorp, **10** 134; **11** 122

McPaper AG, **29** 152

McQuay International. *See* AAF-McQuay Incorporated.

McRae's, Inc., **19** 324–25; **41** 343–44

MCS, Inc., **10** 412

MCSi, Inc., **41** 258–60

MCT Dairies, Inc., **18** 14–16

McTeigue & Co., **14** 502

McVitie & Price, **II** 592–93

McWane Corporation, **55** 264–66

McWhorter Inc., **8** 553; **27** 280

MD Distribution Inc., **15** 139

MD Foods (Mejeriselskabet Danmark Foods), **48** 35

MD Pharmaceuticals, **III** 10

MDC. *See* Mead Data Central, Inc.

MDI Co., Ltd., **IV** 327

MDP. *See* Madison Dearborn Partners LLC.

MDS/Bankmark, **10** 247

MDU Resources Group, Inc., **7** 322–25; **42** 249–53 **(upd.)**

Mead & Mount Construction Company, **51** 41

The Mead Corporation, **IV** 310–13, 327, 329, 342–43; **8** 267; **9** 261; **10** 406; **11** 421–22; **17** 399; **19** 265–69 **(upd.)**; **20** 18; **33** 263, 265

Mead Cycle Co., **IV** 660

Mead Data Central, Inc., **IV** 312; **7** 581; **10** 406–08; **19** 268. *See also* LEXIS-NEXIS Group.

Mead John & Co., **19** 103

Mead Johnson, **III** 17

Mead Packaging, **12** 151

Meade County Rural Electric Cooperative Corporation, **11** 37

Meade Instruments Corporation, **41** 261–64

Meadow Gold Dairies, Inc., **II** 473

Meadowcraft, Inc., **29** 313–15

Means Services, Inc., **II** 607

Mears & Phillips, **II** 237

Measurex Corporation, **8** 243; **14** 56; **38** 227

Mebetoys, **25** 312

MEC - Hawaii, UK & USA, **IV** 714

MECA Software, Inc., **18** 363

Mecair, S.p.A., **17** 147

Mecca Bookmakers, **49** 450

Mecca Leisure PLC, **I** 248; **12** 229; **32** 243

Meccano S.A., **52** 207

Mechanics Exchange Savings Bank, **9** 173

Mechanics Machine Co., **III** 438; **14** 63

Mecklermedia Corporation, **24** 328–30; **26** 441; **27** 360, 362

Meconic, **49** 230, 235

Medal Distributing Co., **9** 542

Medallion Pictures Corp., **9** 320

Medar, Inc., **17** 310–11

Medco Containment Services Inc., **9** 346–48; **11** 291; **12** 333; **44** 175

Medcom Inc., **I** 628

Medeco Security Locks, Inc., **10** 350

Medfield Corp., **III** 87

Medford, Inc., **19** 467–68

Medi Mart Drug Store Company. *See* The Stop & Shop Companies, Inc.

Media Arts Group, Inc., **42** 254–57

Media Exchange International, **25** 509

Media General, Inc., **III** 214; **7** 326–28; **18** 61; **23** 225; **38** 306–09 **(upd.)**

Media Groep West B.V., **23** 271

Media News Corporation, **25** 507

Media Play. *See* Musicland Stores Corporation.

MediaBay, **41** 61

Mediacom Inc., **25** 373

Mediamark Research, **28** 501, 504

Mediamatics, Inc., **26** 329

MediaOne Group Inc. *See* U S West, Inc.

Mediaplex, Inc., **49** 433

Mediaset SpA, **50** 332–34

Medic Computer Systems LLC, **16** 94; **45** 279–80

Medical Arts Press, Inc., **55** 353, 355

Medical Care America, Inc., **15** 112, 114; **35** 215–17

Medical China Publishing Limited, **51** 244

Medical Development Corp. *See* Cordis Corp.

Medical Development Services, Inc., **25** 307

Medical Economics Data, **23** 211

Medical Equipment Finance Corporation, **51** 108

Medical Expense Fund, **III** 245

Medical Indemnity of America, **10** 160

Medical Innovations Corporation, **21** 46

Medical Learning Company, **51** 200, 203

Medical Marketing Group Inc., **9** 348

Medical Service Assoc. of Pennsylvania, **III** 325–26

Medical Tribune Group, **IV** 591; **20** 53

Medicare-Glaser, **17** 167

Medicine Bow Coal Company, **7** 33–34

Medicine Shoppe International. *See* Cardinal Health, Inc.

Medicor, Inc., **36** 496

Medicus Intercon International, **6** 22

Medifinancial Solutions, Inc., **18** 370

MedImmune, Inc., **35** 286–89

Medinol Ltd., **37** 39

Mediobanca Banca di Credito Finanziario SpA, **II** 191, 271; **III** 208–09; **11** 205

The Mediplex Group, Inc., **III** 16; **11** 282

Medis Health and Pharmaceuticals Services Inc., **II** 653

Medite Corporation, **19** 467–68

Meditrust, **11** 281–83

Medlabs Inc., **III** 73

MedPartners, Inc., **36** 367. *See also* Caremark Rx, Inc.

Medtech, Ltd., **13** 60–62

Medtronic, Inc., **8** 351–54; **11** 459; **18** 421; **19** 103; **22** 359–61; **26** 132; **30** 313–17 **(upd.)**; **37** 39; **43** 349

Medusa Corporation, **8** 135; **24** 331–33; **30** 156

Mees & Hope, **II** 184

The MEGA Life and Health Insurance Co., **33** 418–20

MEGA Natural Gas Company, **11** 28

MegaBingo, Inc., **41** 273, 275

Megafoods Stores Inc., 13 335–37; **17** 560

Megahouse Corp., **55** 48

MegaKnowledge Inc., **45** 206

Megasong Publishing, **44** 164

Megasource, Inc., **16** 94

Meggitt PLC, 34 273–76; **48** 432, 434

MEGTEC Systems Inc., **54** 331

MEI Diversified Inc., **18** 455

Mei Foo Investments Ltd., **IV** 718; **38** 319

Meier & Frank Co., 23 345–47

Meijer Incorporated, 7 329–31; **15** 449; **17** 302; **27** 312–15 (upd.)

Meiji Commerce Bank, **II** 291

Meiji Fire Insurance Co., **III** 384–85

Meiji Milk Products Company, Limited, II 538–39

Meiji Mutual Life Insurance Company, II 323; **III 288–89**

Meiji Seika Kaisha, Ltd., I 676; **II 540–41**

Meikosha Co., **II** 72

Meinecke Muffler Company, **III** 495; **10** 415

Meineke Discount Muffler Shops, **38** 208

Meis of Illiana, **10** 282

Meisei Electric, **III** 742

Meisel. See Samuel Meisel & Co.

Meisenzahl Auto Parts, Inc., **24** 205

Meissner, Ackermann & Co., **IV** 463; **7** 351

Meister, Lucious and Company, **13** 262

Meiwa Manufacturing Co., **III** 758

N.V. Mekog, **IV** 531

Mel Farr Automotive Group, 20 368–70

Mel Klein and Partners, **III** 74

Melaleuca Inc., 31 326–28

Melamine Chemicals, Inc., 27 316–18

Melbourne Engineering Co., **23** 83

Melbur China Clay Co., **III** 690

Melco, **II** 58; **44** 285

Meldisco. See Footstar, Incorporated.

Melitta Unternehmensgruppe Bentz KG, 53 218–21

Melkunie-Holland, **II** 575

Mellbank Security Co., **II** 316

Mello Smello. See The Miner Group International.

Mellon Bank Corporation, I 67–68, 584; **II 315–17,** 342, 402; **III** 275; **9** 470; **13** 410–11; **18** 112

Mellon Financial Corporation, 42 76; **44 278–82 (upd.); 55** 71

Mellon Indemnity Corp., **III** 258–59; **24** 177

Mellon Stuart Building Services, Inc., **51** 248

Mellon-Stuart Co., I 584–85; **14** 334

Melmarkets, **24** 462

Mélotte, **III** 418

Meloy Laboratories, Inc., **11** 333

Melroe Company, **8** 115–16; **34** 46

Melville Corporation, V 136–38; **9** 192; **13** 82, 329–30; **14** 426; **15** 252–53; **16** 390; **19** 449; **21** 526; **23** 176; **24** 167, 290; **35** 253. See also CVS Corporation.

Melvin Simon and Associates, Inc., 8 355–57; 26 262. See also Simon Property Group, Inc.

Melwire Group, **III** 673

MEM, **37** 270–71

Memco, **12** 48

Memorex Corp., **III** 110, 166; **6** 282–83

Memphis International Motorsports Corporation Inc., **43** 139–40

The Men's Wearhouse, Inc., 17 312–15; **21** 311; **48 283–87 (upd.)**

Menasco Manufacturing Co., **I** 435; **III** 415

Menasha Corporation, 8 358–61

Menck, **8** 544

Mendelssohn & Co., **II** 241

Meneven, **IV** 508

Menka Gesellschaft, **IV** 150; **24** 357

The Mennen Company, **I** 19; **6** 26; **14** 122; **18** 69; **35** 113

Mental Health Programs Inc., **15** 122

The Mentholatum Company Inc., IV 722; **32 331–33**

Mentor Corporation, 26 286–88

Mentor Graphics Corporation, III 143; **8** 519; **11** 46–47, **284–86,** 490; **13** 128

MEPC plc, IV 710–12

Mepco/Electra Inc., **13** 398

MeraBank, **6** 546

MERBCO, Inc., **33** 456

Mercantile Agency, **IV** 604

Mercantile and General Reinsurance Co., **III** 335, 377

Mercantile Bancorporation Inc., **33** 155

Mercantile Bank, **II** 298

Mercantile Bankshares Corp., 11 287–88

Mercantile Credit Co., **16** 13

Mercantile Estate and Property Corp. Ltd., **IV** 710

Mercantile Fire Insurance, **III** 234

Mercantile Mutual, **III** 310

Mercantile Property Corp. Ltd., **IV** 710

Mercantile Security Life, **III** 136

Mercantile Stores Company, Inc., V 139; **19** 270–73 (upd.)

Mercantile Trust Co., **II** 229, 247

Mercator & Noordstar N.V., **40** 61

Mercedes Benz. See Daimler-Benz A.G.

Mercedes Benz of North America, **22** 52

Merchant Bank Services, **18** 516, 518

Merchant Co., **III** 104

Merchant Distributors, Inc., **20** 306

Merchants & Farmers Bank of Ecru, **14** 40

Merchants Bank, **II** 213

Merchants Bank & Trust Co., **21** 524

Merchants Bank of Canada, **II** 210

Merchants Bank of Halifax, **II** 344

Merchants Dispatch, **II** 395–96; **10** 60

Merchants Distributors Inc. See Alex Lee Inc.

Merchants Fire Assurance Corp., **III** 396–97

Merchants Home Delivery Service, **6** 414

Merchants Indemnity Corp., **III** 396–97

Merchants Life Insurance Co., **III** 275

Merchants National Bank, **9** 228; **14** 528; **17** 135

Merchants National Bank of Boston, **II** 213

Merchants Union Express Co., **II** 396; **10** 60

Merchants' Assoc., **II** 261

Merchants' Loan and Trust, **II** 261; **III** 518

Merchants' Savings, Loan and Trust Co., **II** 261

Mercier, **I** 272

Merck & Co., Inc., I 640, 646, **650–52,** 683–84, 708; **II** 414; **III** 42, 60, 66, 299; **8** 154, 548; **10** 213; **11** 9, 90, **289–91 (upd.); 12** 325, 333; **14** 58, 422; **15** 154; **16** 440; **20** 39, 59; **26** 126; **34**

280–85 (upd.); **36** 91, 93, 305; **38** 380; **44** 175; **47** 236; **50** 56, 138–39

Mercury Air Group, Inc., 20 371–73

Mercury Asset Management (MAM), **14** 420; **40** 313

Mercury Communications, Ltd., V 280–82; **7** 332–34; **10** 456; **11** 547–48; **25** 101–02; **27** 365; **49** 70–71, 73

Mercury General Corporation, 25 323–25

Mercury, Inc., **8** 311

Mercury International Ltd., **51** 130

Mercury Mail, Inc., **22** 519, 522

Mercury Records, **13** 397; **23** 389, 391

Mercury Telecommunications Limited, **15** 67, 69

Mercy Air Service, Inc., **53** 29

Meredith and Drew, **II** 593

Meredith Corporation, IV 661–62; **11 292–94; 17** 394; **18** 239; **23** 393; **29 316–19 (upd.)**

Merfin International, **42** 53

Merial, **34** 284

Merico, Inc., **36** 161–64

Merida, **50** 445, 447

Meridian Bancorp, Inc., 11 295–97; 17 111, 114

Meridian Emerging Markets Ltd., **25** 509

Meridian Gold, Incorporated, 47 238–40

Meridian Healthcare, **18** 197

Meridian Insurance Co., **III** 332

Meridian Investment and Development Corp., **22** 189

Meridian Oil Inc., **10** 190–91

Meridian Publishing, Inc., **28** 254

Merillat Industries Inc., III 570; **13 338–39; 20** 362; **39** 266, 268

Merisel, Inc., 10 518–19; **12 334–36; 13** 174, 176, 482

Merit Distribution Services, **13** 333

Merit Medical Systems, Inc., 29 320–22; 36 497

Merit Tank Testing, Inc., **IV** 411

Merita/Cotton's Bakeries, **38** 251

Meritage Corporation, 26 289–92

MeritaNordbanken, **40** 336

Meritor Automotive Inc., **43** 328. See also ArvinMeritor Inc.

Merivienti Oy, **IV** 276

Merix Corporation, 36 329–31

Merkur Direktwerbegesellschaft, **29** 152

Merla Manufacturing, **I** 524

Merlin Gérin, **II** 93–94; **18** 473; **19** 165

Merpati Nusantara Airlines, **6** 90–91

Merrell, **22** 173

Merrell Dow, **16** 438

Merrell Drug, **I** 325

Merrell-Soule Co., **II** 471

Merriam and Morgan Paraffine Co., **IV** 548

Merriam-Webster, Inc., **7** 165, 167; **23** 209–10; **39** 140, 143

Merrill Corporation, 18 331–34; **47 241–44 (upd.)**

Merrill Gas Company, **9** 554

Merrill Lynch & Co., Inc., I 26, 339, 681, 683, 697; **II** 149, 257, 260, 268, 403, 407–08, 412, **424–26,** 441, 445, 449, 451, 456, 654–55, 680; **III** 119, 253, 340, 440; **6** 244; **7** 130; **8** 94; **9** 125, 187, 239, 301, 386; **11** 29, 122, 348, 557; **13** 44, 125, **340–43 (upd.),** 448–49, 512; **14** 65; **15** 463; **16** 195; **17** 137; **21** 68–70, 145; **22** 404–06, 542; **23**

370; **25** 89–90, 329; **29** 295; **32** 14, 168; **40 310–15 (upd.)**; **49** 130; **50** 419

Merrill Lynch Capital Partners, **47** 363

Merrill, Pickard, Anderson & Eyre IV, **11** 490

Merrill Publishing, **IV** 643; **7** 312; **9** 63; **29** 57

Merrimack Services Corp., **37** 303

Merry-Go-Round Enterprises, Inc., 8 362–64; **24** 27

Merry Group, **III** 673

Merry Maids, **6** 46; **23** 428, 430

Merryhill Schools, Inc., **37** 279

The Mersey Docks and Harbour Company, 30 318–20

Mersey Paper Co., **IV** 258

Mersey White Lead Co., **III** 680

Merv Griffin Enterprises, **II** 137; **12** 75; **22** 431

Mervyn's, V 43–44; **10 409–10**; **13** 526; **18** 136–37; **27** 452

Mervyn's California, 39 269–71 (upd.)

Merz + Co., **52** 135

Mesa Air Group, Inc., 32 334–37 (upd.)

Mesa Airlines, Inc., 11 298–300

Mesa LP, **IV** 410, 523; **11** 441; **40** 357

Mesa Petroleum, **IV** 392, 571; **24** 521, 522; **27** 217

Mesaba Holdings, Inc., I 448; **22** 21; **28 265–67**

Messageries du Livre, **IV** 614

Messerschmitt-Bölkow-Blohm GmbH., I 41–42, 46, 51–52, 55, **73–75**, 111; **II** 242; **III** 539; **11** 267; **24** 86; **52** 113

Messner, Vetere, Berger, Carey, Schmetterer, **13** 204

Mesta Machine Co., **22** 415

Mestek, Inc., 10 411–13

Met Food Corp. *See* White Rose Food Corp.

Met-Mex Penoles. *See* Industrias Penoles, S.A. de C.V.

META Group, Inc., **37** 147

Metabio-Joullie, **III** 47

Metaframe Corp., **25** 312

Metal Box plc, I 604–06; **20** 108. *See also* Novar plc.

Metal-Cal. *See* Avery Dennison Corporation.

Metal Casting Technology, Inc., **23** 267, 269

Metal Closures, **I** 615

Metal Industries, **I** 531–32

Metal Manufactures, **III** 433–34

Metal Office Furniture Company, **7** 493

Metales y Contactos, **29** 461–62

Metaleurop S.A., IV 108–09; **21 368–71**

MetalExchange, **26** 530

Metall Mining Corp., **IV** 141; **27** 456

Metallgesellschaft AG, IV 17, **139–42**, 229; **16 361–66 (upd.)**

MetalOptics Inc., **19** 212

MetalPro, Inc., **IV** 168

Metals and Controls Corp., **II** 113

Metals Exploration, **IV** 82

Metalurgica Mexicana Penoles, S.A. *See* Industrias Penoles, S.A. de C.V.

Metaphase Technology, Inc., **10** 257

Metatec International, Inc., 47 245–48

Metcalf & Eddy Companies, Inc., **6** 143, 441; **32** 52

Meteor Film Productions, **23** 391

Meteor Industries Inc., 33 295–97

Methane Development Corporation, **6** 457

Methanex Corporation, 12 365; **19** 155–56; **40 316–19**

Methode Electronics, Inc., 13 344–46

Metinox Steel Ltd., **IV** 203

MetLife. *See* Metropolitan Life Insurance Company.

MetMor Financial, Inc., **III** 293; **52** 239–40

Meto AG, **39** 79

MetPath, Inc., **III** 684; **26** 390

Metra Corporation. *See* Wärtsilä Corporation.

Metra Steel, **19** 381

Metrastock Ltd., **34** 5

Metric Constructors, Inc., **16** 286

Metric Systems Corporation, **18** 513; **44** 420

Metris Companies, **25** 41

Metro AG, 23 311; **50 335–39**

Metro Distributors Inc., **14** 545

Metro Drug Corporation, **II** 649–50; **18** 181

Metro Glass, **II** 533

Metro-Goldwyn-Mayer Inc., 25 173, 253, **326–30 (upd.)**; **33**

Metro Holding AG, **38** 266

Metro Information Services, Inc., 36 332–34

Metro International SA, **36** 335

Metro-Mark Integrated Systems Inc., **11** 469

Metro-North Commuter Railroad Company, **35** 292

Metro Pacific, **18** 180, 182

Metro-Richelieu Inc., **II** 653

Metro Southwest Construction. *See* CRSS Inc.

Metro Support Services, Inc., **48** 171

Metro Vermögensverwaltung GmbH & Co. of Dusseldorf, **V** 104

Metro-Verwegensverwaltung, **II** 257

Metrocall, Inc., 18 77; **39** 25; **41 265–68**

Metrol Security Services, Inc., **32** 373

Metroland Printing, Publishing and Distributing Ltd., **29** 471

Metromail Corp., **IV** 661; **18** 170; **38** 370

Metromedia Companies, II 171; **6** 33, 168–69; **7** 91, **335–37**; **14** 298–300

Metroplex, LLC, **51** 206

Metropolitan Accident Co., **III** 228

Metropolitan Bank, **II** 221, 318; **III** 239; **IV** 644; **17** 323

Metropolitan Baseball Club Inc., 39 272–75

Metropolitan Broadcasting Corporation, **7** 335

Metropolitan Clothing Co., **19** 362

Metropolitan Distributors, **9** 283

Metropolitan District Railway Company, **6** 406

Metropolitan Edison Company, **27** 182

Metropolitan Estate and Property Corp. Ltd., **IV** 710–11

Metropolitan Financial Corporation, 12 165; **13 347–49**

Metropolitan Furniture Leasing, **14** 4

Metropolitan Gas Light Co., **6** 455

Metropolitan Housing Corp. Ltd., **IV** 710

Metropolitan Life Insurance Company, II 679; **III** 265–66, 272, **290–94**, 313, 329, 337, 339–40, 706; **IV** 283; **6** 256; **8** 326–27; **11** 482; **22** 266; **25** 300; **42** 194; **45** 249, 411; **52 235–41 (upd.)**; **54** 223–25

The Metropolitan Museum of Art, 55 267–70

Metropolitan National Bank, **II** 284

Metropolitan Opera Association, Inc., 40 320–23

Metropolitan Petroleum Corp., **IV** 180–81; **19** 319

Metropolitan Railway, **6** 407

Metropolitan Railways Surplus Lands Co., **IV** 711

Metropolitan Reference Laboratories Inc., **26** 391

Metropolitan Tobacco Co., **15** 138

Metropolitan Transportation Authority, 35 290–92

Metropolitan Vickers, **III** 670

METSA, Inc., **15** 363

Metsä-Serla Oy, IV 314–16, 318, 350

Metso Corporation, 30 321–25 (upd.)

Mettler-Toledo International Inc., 30 326–28

Mettler United States Inc., **9** 441

Metwest, **26** 391

Metz Baking Company, **36** 164

Metzdorf Advertising Agency, **30** 80

Metzeler Kautschuk, **15** 354

Mexican Eagle Oil Co., **IV** 365, 531

Mexican Metal Co. *See* Industrias Penoles, S.A. de C.V.

Mexican Original Products, Inc., **II** 585; **14** 515; **50** 492

Mexican Restaurants, Inc., 41 269–71

Mexofina, S.A. de C.V., **IV** 401

Meyer and Charlton, **IV** 90

Meyer Brothers Drug Company, **16** 212

Meyer Corporation, **27** 288

Meyerland Company, **19** 366

Meyers and Co., **III** 9

Meyers & Muldoon, **6** 40

Meyers Motor Supply, **26** 347

Meyers Parking, **18** 104

The Meyne Company, **55** 74

Meyr Melnhof Karton AG, **41** 325–27

Meyrin, **I** 122

MFI, **II** 612

M40 Trains Ltd., **51** 173

MFS Communications Company, Inc., 11 301–03; **14** 253; **27** 301, 307

MG&E. *See* Madison Gas & Electric.

MG Holdings. *See* Mayflower Group Inc.

MG Ltd., **IV** 141

MGD Graphics Systems. *See* Goss Holdings, Inc.

MGIC Investment Corp., 45 320; **52 242–44**

MGM. *See* McKesson General Medical.

MGM Grand Inc., III 431; **6** 210; **17 316–19**; **18** 336–37

MGM Mirage. *See* Mirage Resorts, Incorporated.

MGM Studios, **50** 125

MGM/UA Communications Company, I 286, 487; **II** 103, 135, **146–50**, 155, 161, 167, 169, 174–75, 408; **IV** 676; **6** 172–73; **12** 73, 316, 323, 455; **15** 84; **17** 316. *See also* Metro-Goldwyn-Mayer Inc.

MGN. *See* Mirror Group Newspapers Ltd.

MH Alshaya Group, **28** 96

mh Bausparkasse AG, **III** 377

MH Media Monitoring Limited, **26** 270

MHI Group, Inc., **13** 356; **16** 344

MHS Holding Corp., **26** 101

MHT. *See* Manufacturers Hanover Trust Co.

MI. *See* Masco Corporation.

Miami Computer Supply Corporation. *See* MCSi, Inc.

Miami Power Corporation, **6** 466

Miami Subs Corp., **29** 342, 344

Micamold Electronics Manufacturing Corporation, **10** 319

Mich-Wis. *See* Michigan Wisconsin Pipe Line.

Michael Anthony Jewelers, Inc., 24 334–36

Michael Baker Corporation, 14 333–35; 51 245–48 (upd.)

MICHAEL Business Systems Plc, **10** 257

Michael C. Fina Co., Inc., 52 245–47

Michael Foods, Inc., 25 331–34; 39 319–321

Michael Joseph, **IV** 659

Michael Page International plc, 45 272–74; 52 317–18

Michael Reese Health Plan Inc., **III** 82

Michael's Fair-Mart Food Stores, Inc., **19** 479

Michaels Stores, Inc., 17 320–22, 360; **25** 368

MichCon. *See* MCN Corporation.

Michelin, **III** 697; **7** 36–37; **8** 74; **11** 158, 473; **20** 261–62; **21** 72, 74; **28** 372. *See also* Compagnie Générale des Établissements Michelin.

Michelin et Compagnie, **V** 236

Michiana Merchandising, **III** 10

Michie Co., **IV** 312; **19** 268; **33** 264–65

Michigan Automotive Compressor, Inc., **III** 593, 638–39

Michigan Automotive Research Corporation, **23** 183

Michigan Bell Telephone Co., 14 336–38; 18 30

Michigan Carpet Sweeper Company, **9** 70

Michigan Consolidated Gas Company. *See* MCN Corporation.

Michigan Fruit Canners, **II** 571

Michigan General, **II** 408

Michigan International Speedway, **V** 494

Michigan Livestock Exchange, **36** 442

Michigan Motor Freight Lines, **14** 567

Michigan National Corporation, 11 304–06; 18 517

Michigan Oil Company, **18** 494

Michigan Packaging Company, **15** 188

Michigan Plating and Stamping Co., **I** 451

Michigan Radiator & Iron Co., **III** 663

Michigan Shoe Makers. *See* Wolverine World Wide Inc.

Michigan Spring Company, **17** 106

Michigan State Life Insurance Co., **III** 274

Michigan Steel Corporation, **12** 352

Michigan Tag Company, **9** 72

Michigan Wisconsin Pipe Line, **39** 260

Mick's Inc., **30** 329

Mickey Shorr Mobile Electronics, **10** 9–11

Micro-Circuit, Inc., **III** 645

Micro Contract Manufacturing Inc., **44** 441

Micro D, Inc., **11** 194

Micro Decisionware, Inc., **10** 506

Micro Focus Inc., **27** 491

Micro Magic, Inc., **43** 254

Micro Peripherals, Inc., **18** 138

Micro-Power Corp., **III** 643

Micro Power Systems Inc., **14** 183

Micro Switch, **14** 284

Micro/Vest, **13** 175

Micro Warehouse, Inc., 16 371–73

MicroAge, Inc., 16 367–70; 29 414

Microamerica, **12** 334

Microban Products Company, **27** 288

MicroBilt Corporation, **11** 112

Microcar SA, **55** 54, 56

MicroClean Inc, **50** 49

Microcom, Inc., **26** 93; **50** 227

MicroComputer Accessories, **III** 614

Microcomputer Asset Management Services, **9** 168

Microcomputer Systems, **22** 389

Microdot Inc., I 440; **8 365–68**, 545

Microfal, **I** 341

Microform International Marketing Corp., **IV** 642; **7** 312

Microfral, **14** 216

MicroFridge, **44** 273

Micromass Ltd., **43** 455

Micromedex, **19** 268

Micron Technology, Inc., III 113; **11 307–09; 29 323–26 (upd.)**

Micropolis Corp., **10** 403, 458, 463

MicroPro International Corp., **10** 556. *See also* The Learning Company Inc.

Microprocessor Systems, **13** 235

Microprose Inc., **24** 538

Micros Systems, Inc., 18 335–38

Microseal Corp., **I** 341

Microsensor Systems Inc., **43** 366

Microsoft Corporation, III 116; **6** 219–20, 224, 227, 231, 235, 254–56, **257–60**, 269–71; **9** 81, 140, 171, 195, 472; **10** 22, 34, 57, 87, 119, 237–38, 362–63, 408, 477, 484, 504, 557–58; **11** 59, 77–78, 306, 519–20; **12** 180, 335; **13** 115, 128, 147, 482, 509; **14** 262–64, 318; **15** 132–33, 321, 371, 483, 492, 511; **16** 4, 94, 367, 392, 394, 444; **18** 24, 64, 66, 306–7, 345, 349, 367, 541, 543; **19** 310; **20** 237; **21** 86; **24** 120, 233, 236, 371; **25** 21, 32, 34, 96, 117, 119, 184, 298–301, 498–99, 509; **26** 17, 294–95, 441, 520; **27 319–23 (upd.)**, 448, 517; **28** 245, 301; **29** 65, 439; **30** 391, 450; **33** 115–16, 210; **34** 443, 445, 513; **36** 384; **37** 383; **38** 71, 416; **41** 53–54; **42** 424; **43** 240; **44** 97; **45** 200–02; **47** 419–21; **53** 252, 254; **54** 269–71

Microsoft Network, **38** 270–71

Microtek, Inc., **22** 413

Microtel Limited, **6** 309–10

MicroUnity Systems Engineering Inc., **50** 53

Microware Surgical Instruments Corp., **IV** 137

Microwave Communications, Inc., **V** 302; **27** 302

Mid-America Capital Resources, Inc., **6** 508

Mid-America Dairymen, Inc., II 536; **7 338–40; 11** 24; **21** 342; **22** 95; **26** 448

Mid-America Industries, **III** 495

Mid-America Interpool Network, **6** 506, 602

Mid-America Packaging, Inc., **8** 203

Mid-America Tag & Label, **8** 360

Mid Bus Inc., **33** 107

Mid-Central Fish and Frozen Foods Inc., **II** 675

Mid-Continent Area Power Planner, **V** 672

Mid-Continent Computer Services, **11** 111

Mid-Continent Life Insurance Co., **23** 200

Mid-Continent Telephone Corporation. *See* Alltel Corporation.

Mid-Georgia Gas Company, **6** 448

Mid-Illinois Gas Co., **6** 529

Mid-Pacific Airlines, **9** 271; **24** 21–22

Mid-Packaging Group Inc., **19** 78

Mid-South Towing, **6** 583

Mid-States Development, Inc., **18** 405

Mid-Texas Communications Systems, **6** 313

Mid-Valley Dairy, **14** 397

Mid-West Drive-In Theatres Inc., **I** 245

Mid-West Paper Ltd., **IV** 286

MidAmerican Communications Corporation, **8** 311

Midas International Corporation, I 457–58; **10 414–15**, 554; **24** 337

MIDCO, **III** 340

MidCon, **IV** 481; **25** 363

Middle East Broadcasting Centre, Ltd., **25** 506, 508

Middle East Tube Co. Ltd., **25** 266

Middle South Utilities. *See* Entergy Corporation.

Middle West Corporation, **6** 469–70

Middle West Utilities Company, **V** 583–84; **6** 555–56, 604–05; **14** 227; **21** 468–69

Middle Wisconsin Power, **6** 604

Middleburg Steel and Alloys Group, **I** 423

The Middleby Corporation, 22 352–55

Middlesex Bank, **II** 334

Middlesex Water Company, 45 275–78

Middleton Aerospace, **48** 275

The Middleton Doll Company, 53 222–25

Middleton Packaging, **12** 377

Middleton's Starch Works, **II** 566

Middletown Manufacturing Co., Inc., **16** 321

Middletown National Bank, **13** 467

Midhurst Corp., **IV** 658

Midial, **II** 478

Midland Bank plc, II 208, 236, 279, 295, 298, **318–20**, 334, 383; **9** 505; **12** 257; **14** 169; **17 323–26 (upd.); 19** 198; **26** 202; **33** 395

Midland Brick, **14** 250

Midland Cooperative, **II** 536

Midland Counties Dairies, **II** 587

Midland Electric Coal Co., **IV** 170

Midland Enterprises Inc., **6** 486–88

Midland Gravel Co., **III** 670

Midland Independent Newspaper plc, **23** 351

Midland Industrial Finishes Co., **I** 321

Midland Insurance, **I** 473

Midland International, **8** 56–57

Midland Investment Co., **II** 7

Midland Linseed Products Co., **I** 419

Midland National Bank, **11** 130

Midland Railway Co., **II** 306

Midland-Ross Corporation, **14** 369

Midland Southwest Corp., **8** 347

Midland Steel Products Co., **13** 305–06

Midland United, **6** 556; **25** 89

Midland Utilities Company, **6** 532

Midlands Electricity, **13** 485

Midlands Energy Co., **IV** 83; **7** 188

Midlantic Corp., **13** 411

Midlantic Hotels Ltd., **41** 83

Midrange Performance Group, **12** 149

Midrex Corp., **IV** 130

Midvale Steel and Ordnance Co., **IV** 35, 114; **7** 48

Midway Airlines Corporation, **6** 105, 120–21; **33** 301–03

Midway Games, Inc., **25** 335–38

Midway Manufacturing Company, **III** 430; **15** 539

Midwest Agri-Commodities Company, **11** 15; **32** 29

Midwest Air Charter, **6** 345

Midwest Biscuit Company, **14** 306

Midwest Com of Indiana, Inc., **11** 112

Midwest Dairy Products, **II** 661

Midwest Express Holdings, Inc., **35** 293–95; **43** 258

Midwest Federal Savings & Loan Association, **11** 162–63

Midwest Financial Group, Inc., **8** 188

Midwest Foundry Co., **IV** 137

Midwest Grain Products, Inc., **49** 261–63

Midwest Manufacturing Co., **12** 296

Midwest Realty Exchange, Inc., **21** 257

Midwest Refining Co., **IV** 368

Midwest Resources Inc., **6** 523–25

Midwest Staffing Systems, **27** 21

Midwest Steel Corporation, **13** 157

Midwest Synthetics, **8** 553

Midwinter, **12** 529

Miele & Cie., **III** 418

MIG Realty Advisors, Inc., **25** 23, 25

Miguel Galas S.A., **17** 268

MIH Limited, **31** 329–32

Mikasa, Inc., **28** 268–70

Mike-Sell's Inc., **15** 298–300

Mikemitch Realty Corp., **16** 36

Mikko, **II** 70

Mikko Kaloinen Oy, **IV** 349

Mikohn Gaming Corporation, **39** 276–79

Mikon, Ltd., **13** 345

Milac, **27** 259

Milacron, Inc., **53** 226–30 (upd.)

Milan A.C., S.p.A., **44** 387

Milani Foods, **II** 556; **36** 24

Milbank Insurance Co., **III** 350

Milbank, Tweed, Hadley & McCloy, **27** 324–27

Milbank, Tweed, Hope & Webb, **II** 471

Milcor Steel Co., **IV** 114

Miles Druce & Co., **III** 494

Miles Inc., **22** 148

Miles Kimball Co., **9** 393

Miles Laboratories, **I** 310, 653–55, 674, 678; **6** 50; **13** 76; **14** 558

Miles Redfern, **I** 429

Milgo Electronic Corp., **II** 83; **11** 408

Milgram Food Stores Inc., **II** 682

Milgray Electronics Inc., **19** 311; **47** 41

Milk Producers, Inc., **11** 24

Milk Specialties Co., **12** 199

Mill-Power Supply Company, **27** 129–30

Millbrook Press Inc., **IV** 616

Millennium Chemicals Inc., **30** 231; **45** 252, 254

Millennium Pharmaceuticals, Inc., **47** 249–52

Miller Automotive Group, **52** 146

Miller Brewing Company, **I** 218–19, 236–37, 254–55, 257–58, **269–70**, 283, 290–91, 548; **10** 100; **11** 421; **12** 337–39 (upd.), 372; **13** 10, 258; **15** 429; **17** 256; **18** 70, 72, 418, 499, 501; **21** 230; **22** 199, 422; **26** 303, 306; **27** 374; **28** 209–10; **34** 36–37; **36** 12–15; **44** 342; **50** 202, 523

Miller Chemical & Fertilizer Corp., **I** 412

Miller Companies, **17** 182

Miller Container Corporation, **8** 102

Miller Freeman, Inc., **IV** 687; **27** 362; **28** 501, 504

Miller Group Ltd., **22** 282

Miller Industries, Inc., **26** 293–95

Miller, Mason and Dickenson, **III** 204–05

Miller Plant Farms, Inc., **51** 61

Miller, Tabak, Hirsch & Co., **13** 394; **28** 164

Millet, **39** 250

Millet's Leisure, **V** 177–78

Millicom, **11** 547; **18** 254

Milliken & Co., **V** 366–68; **8** 270–71; **17** 327–30 (upd.); **29** 246

Milliken, Tomlinson Co., **II** 682

Millipore Corporation, **9** 396; **23** 284; **25** 339–43; **43** 454

Mills Clothing, Inc. See The Buckle, Inc.

Millstone Point Company, **V** 668–69

Millville Electric Light Company, **6** 449

Millway Foods, **25** 85

Milne & Craighead, **48** 113

Milne Fruit Products, Inc., **25** 366

Milner, **III** 98

Milnot Company, **46** 289–91; **51** 47

Milsco Manufacturing Co., **23** 299, 300

Milton Bradley Company, **III** 504–06; **16** 267; **17** 105; **21** 372–75; **25** 380; **43** 229, 232

Milton Light & Power Company, **12** 45

Milton Roy Co., **8** 135

Milupa S.A., **37** 341

Milwaukee Brewers Baseball Club, **37** 247–49

Milwaukee Cheese Co. Inc., **25** 517

Milwaukee Electric Manufacturing Co., **III** 534

Milwaukee Electric Railway and Light Company, **6** 601–02, 604–05

Milwaukee Electric Tool, **28** 40

Milwaukee Insurance Co., **III** 242

Milwaukee Mutual Fire Insurance Co., **III** 321

Minatome, **IV** 560

Mindpearl, **48** 381

Mindport, **31** 329

Mindset Corp., **42** 424–25

Mindspring Enterprises, Inc., **36** 168

Mine Safety Appliances Company, **31** 333–35

Minemet Recherche, **IV** 108

The Miner Group International, **22** 356–58

Mineral Point Public Service Company, **6** 604

Minerales y Metales, S.A. See Industrias Penoles, S.A. de C.V.

Minerals & Chemicals Philipp, **IV** 79–80

Minerals & Metals Trading Corporation of India Ltd., **IV** 143–44

Minerals and Resources Corporation Limited, **IV** 23; **13** 502; **50** 34. See also Minorco.

Minerals Technologies Inc., **11** 310–12; **52** 248–51 (upd.)

Minerec Corporation, **9** 363

Minerva, **III** 359

Minerve, **6** 208

Mines et Usines du Nord et de l'Est, **IV** 226

Minet Group, **III** 357; **22** 494–95

Mini Stop, **V** 97

Mining and Technical Services, **IV** 67

Mining Corp. of Canada Ltd., **IV** 164

Mining Development Corp., **IV** 239–40

Mining Trust Ltd., **IV** 32

MiniScribe, Inc., **6** 230; **10** 404

Minister of Finance Inc., **IV** 519

Minitel, **21** 233

Minivator Ltd., **11** 486

Minneapolis Children's Medical Center, **54** 65

Minneapolis General Electric of Minnesota, **V** 670

Minneapolis Heat Regulator Co., **II** 40–41; **12** 246; **50** 231

Minneapolis-Honeywell Regulator Co., **II** 40–41, 86; **8** 21; **12** 247; **22** 427; **50** 232

Minneapolis Millers Association, **10** 322

Minneapolis Steel and Machinery Company, **21** 502

Minnesota Brewing Company. See MBC Holding Company.

Minnesota Cooperative Creamery Association, Inc., **II** 535; **21** 340

Minnesota Linseed Oil Co., **8** 552

Minnesota Mining & Manufacturing Company, **I** 28, 387, **499–501**; **II** 39; **III** 476, 487, 549; **IV** 251, 253–54; **6** 231; **7** 162; **8** 35, **369–71** (upd.); **11** 494; **13** 326; **17** 29–30; **22** 427; **25** 96, 372; **26** 296–99 (upd.)

Minnesota Paints, **8** 552–53

Minnesota Power & Light Company, **11** 313–16

Minnesota Power, Inc., **34** 286–91 (upd.)

Minnesota Sugar Company, **11** 13

Minnesota Valley Canning Co., **I** 22

Minnetonka Corp., **II** 590; **III** 25; **22** 122–23

Minntech Corporation, **22** 359–61

Minn-Dak Farmers Cooperative, **32** 29

Minolta Camera Co., Ltd., **III** 574–76, 583–84

Minolta Co., Ltd., **18** 93, 186, **339–42** (upd.); **43** 281–85 (upd.)

Minorco, **III** 503; **IV** 67–68, 84, 97; **16** 28, 293

Minstar Inc., **11** 397; **15** 49; **45** 174

Minton China, **38** 401

The Minute Maid Company, **I** 234; **10** 227; **28** 271–74, 473; **32** 116

Minute Tapioca, **II** 531

Minuteman International Inc., **46** 292–95

Minyard Food Stores, Inc., **33** 304–07

Mippon Paper, **21** 546; **50** 58

MIPS Computer Systems, **II** 45; **11** 491

Miracle Food Mart, **16** 247, 249–50

Miracle-Gro Products, Inc., **22** 474

Miraflores Designs Inc., **18** 216

Mirage Resorts, Incorporated, **6** 209–12; **15** 238; **28** 275–79 (upd.); **29** 127; **43** 82

Miramar Hotel & Investment Co., **IV** 717; **38** 318

Mirant, **39** 54, 57

Mircali Asset Management, **III** 340

Mircor Inc., **12** 413

Mirrlees Blackstone, **III** 509

Mirror Group Newspapers plc, **IV** 641; **7** 244, 312, **341–43**; **23** 348–51 (upd.); **49** 408

Mirror Printing and Binding House, **IV** 677

Misceramic Tile, Inc., **14** 42

Misr Airwork. *See* AirEgypt.
Misr Bank of Cairo, **27** 132
Misrair. *See* AirEgypt.
Miss Erika, Inc., **27** 346, 348
Miss Selfridge, **V** 177–78
Misset Publishers, **IV** 611
Mission Energy Company, **V** 715
Mission First Financial, **V** 715
Mission Group, **V** 715, 717
Mission Insurance Co., **III** 192
Mission Jewelers, **30** 408
Mississippi Chemical Corporation, 8
183; **IV** 367; **27** 316; **39 280–83**
Mississippi Drug, **III** 10
Mississippi Gas Company, **6** 577
Mississippi Power & Light, **V** 619
Mississippi Power Company, **38** 446–47
Mississippi River Corporation, **10** 44
Mississippi River Recycling, **31** 47, 49
Missoula Bancshares, Inc., **35** 198–99
Missouri Book Co., **10** 136
Missouri Fur Company, **25** 220
Missouri Gaming Company, **21** 39
Missouri Gas & Electric Service Company,
6 593
Missouri-Kansas-Texas Railroad, **I** 472; **IV**
458
Missouri Pacific Railroad, **10** 43–44
Missouri Public Service Company. *See*
UtiliCorp United Inc.
Missouri Utilities Company, **6** 580
Mist Assist, Inc. *See* Ballard Medical
Products.
Mistik Beverages, **18** 71
Mistral Plastics Pty Ltd., **IV** 295; **19** 225
Misys PLC, 45 279–81; 46 296–99
Mitchel & King Skates Ltd., **17** 244
Mitchell Construction, **III** 753
Mitchell Energy and Development
Corporation, 7 344–46
Mitchell Home Savings and Loan, **13** 347
Mitchell Hutchins, Inc., **II** 445; **22** 405–06
Mitchell International, **8** 526
Mitchells & Butler, **I** 223
Mitchum Co., **III** 55
Mitchum, Jones & Templeton, **II** 445; **22**
405
MiTek Industries Inc., **IV** 259
MiTek Wood Products, **IV** 305
Mitel Corporation, 15 131–32; **18**
343–46
MitNer Group, **7** 377
MITRE Corporation, 26 300–02
Mitre Sport U.K., **17** 204–05
MITROPA AG, 37 250–53
Mitsubishi Aircraft Co., **III** 578; **7** 348; **9**
349; **11** 164
Mitsubishi Bank, Ltd., **II** 57, 273–74,
276, **321–22,** 323, 392, 459; **III** 289,
577–78; **7** 348; **15** 41; **16** 496, 498; **50**
498. *See also* Bank of Tokyo-Mitsubishi
Ltd.
Mitsubishi Chemical Industries Ltd., **I**
319, **363–64,** 398; **II** 57; **III** 666, 760;
11 207
Mitsubishi Corporation, **I** 261, 431–32,
492, **502–04,** 505–06, 510, 515,
519–20; **II** 57, 59, 101, 118, 224, 292,
321–25, 374; **III** 577–78; **IV** 285, 518,
713; **6** 499; **7** 82, 233, 590; **9** 294; **12**
340–43 (upd.); **17** 349, 556; **24** 325,
359; **27** 511
Mitsubishi Electric Corporation, **II** 53,
57–59, 68, 73, 94, 122; **III** 577, 586; **7**

347, 394; **18** 18; **23** 52–53; **43** 15; **44**
283–87 (upd.)
Mitsubishi Estate Company, Limited, IV
713–14
Mitsubishi Foods, **24** 114
Mitsubishi Group, **V** 481–82; **7** 377; **21**
390
Mitsubishi Heavy Industries, Ltd., **II** 57,
75, 323, 440; **III** 452–53, 487, 532, 538,
577–79, 685, 713; **IV** 184, 713; **7**
347–50 (upd.); **8** 51; **9** 349–50; **10** 33;
13 507; **15** 92; **24** 359; **40 324–28**
(upd.)
Mitsubishi International Corp., **16** 462
Mitsubishi Kasei Corp., **III** 47–48, 477; **8**
343; **14** 535
Mitsubishi Kasei Industry Co. Ltd., **IV** 476
Mitsubishi Kasei Vinyl Company, **49** 5
Mitsubishi Marine, **III** 385
Mitsubishi Materials Corporation, **III**
712–13; **IV** 554; **38** 463
Mitsubishi Motors Corporation, **III**
516–17, 578–79; **6** 28; **7** 219, 348–49;
8 72, 374; **9 349–51; 23 352–55 (upd.);**
34 128, 136; **40** 326
Mitsubishi Oil Co., Ltd., **IV 460–62,** 479,
492
Mitsubishi Paper Co., **III** 547
Mitsubishi Rayon Co. Ltd., **I** 330; **V**
369–71; 8 153
Mitsubishi Sha Holdings, **IV** 554
Mitsubishi Shipbuilding Co. Ltd., **II** 57; **III**
513, 577–78; **7** 348; **9** 349
Mitsubishi Shokai, **III** 577; **IV** 713; **7** 347
Mitsubishi Trading Co., **IV** 460
Mitsubishi Trust & Banking
Corporation, II 323–24; III 289
Mitsui & Co., Ltd., **I** 282; **IV** 18, 224,
432, 654–55; **V** 142; **6** 346; **7** 303; **13**
356; **24** 325, 488–89; **27** 337; **28**
280–85 (upd.)
Mitsui Bank, Ltd., **II** 273–74, 291,
325–27, 328, 372; **III** 295–97; **IV** 147,
320; **V** 142; **17** 556. *See also* Sumitomo
Mitsui Banking Corporation.
Mitsui Bussan K.K., **I** 363, 431–32, 469,
492, 502–04, **505–08,** 510, 515, 519,
533; **II** 57, 66, 101, 224, 292, 323,
325–28, 392; **III** 295–96, 717–18; **IV**
147, 431; **9** 352–53. *See also* Mitsui &
Co., Ltd.
Mitsui Gomei Kaisha, **IV** 715
Mitsui Group, **9** 352; **16** 84; **20** 310; **21** 72
Mitsui House Code, **V** 142
Mitsui Light Metal Processing Co., **III** 758
Mitsui Marine and Fire Insurance
Company, Limited, III 209, **295–96,**
297
Mitsui Mining & Smelting Co., Ltd., **IV**
145–46, 147–48
Mitsui Mining Company, Limited, IV
145, **147–49**
Mitsui Mutual Life Insurance Company,
III 297–98; 39 284–86 (upd.)
Mitsui-no-Mori Co., Ltd., **IV** 716
Mitsui O.S.K. Lines, Ltd., **I** 520; **IV** 383;
V 473–76; 6 398; **26** 278–80
Mitsui Petrochemical Industries, Ltd., **I**
390, 516; **9 352–54**
Mitsui Real Estate Development Co.,
Ltd., IV 715–16
Mitsui Shipbuilding and Engineering Co.,
III 295, 513
Mitsui Toatsu, **9** 353–54

Mitsui Trading, **III** 636
Mitsui Trust & Banking Company, Ltd.,
II 328; III 297
Mitsukoshi Ltd., **I** 508; **V 142–44; 14**
502; **41** 114; **47** 391
Mitsuya Foods Co., **I** 221
Mitteldeutsche Creditbank, **II** 256
Mitteldeutsche Energieversorgung AG, **V**
747
Mitteldeutsche Privatbank, **II** 256
Mitteldeutsche Stickstoff-Werke Ag, **IV**
229–30
Mitteldeutsches Kraftwerk, **IV** 229
Mity Enterprises, Inc., 38 310–12
Mixconcrete (Holdings), **III** 729
Miyoshi Electrical Manufacturing Co., **II** 6
Mizuno Corporation, 25 344–46
Mizushima Ethylene Co. Ltd., **IV** 476
MJB Coffee Co., **I** 28
MK-Ferguson Company, **7** 356
MLC. *See* Medical Learning Company.
MLC Ltd., **IV** 709; **52** 221–22
MLH&P. *See* Montreal Light, Heat &
Power Company.
MLT Vacations Inc., **30** 446
MM Merchandising Munich, **54** 296–97
MMAR Group Inc., **19** 131
MMC Networks Inc., **38** 53, 55
MML Investors Services, **III** 286; **53** 213
MMS America Corp., **26** 317
MNC Financial. *See* MBNA Corporation.
MNC Financial Corp., **11** 447
MND Drilling, **7** 345
MNet, **11** 122
Mo och Domsjö AB, **IV** 315, **317–19,**
340. *See also* Holmen AB
Moa Bay Mining Co., **IV** 82; **7** 186
Mobay, **I** 310–11; **13** 76
Mobil Corporation, **I** 30, 34, 403, 478; **II**
379; **IV** 93, 295, 363, 386, 401, 403,
406, 423, 428, 454, **463–65,** 466,
472–74, 486, 492, 504–05, 515, 517,
522, 531, 538–39, 545, 554–55, 564,
570–71; **V** 147–48; **6** 530; **7** 171,
351–54 (upd.); 8 552–53; **9** 546; **10**
440; **12** 348; **16** 489; **17** 363, 415; **19**
140, 225, 297; **21 376–80 (upd.); 24**
496, 521; **25** 232, 445; **26** 369; **32** 175,
179, 181; **45** 50; **50** 416
Mobil Oil Australia, **24** 399
Mobile America Housing Corporation. *See*
American Homestar Corporation.
Mobile and Ohio Railroad, **I** 456
Mobile Corporation, **25** 232
Mobile Mini, Inc., **21** 476
Mobile Telecommunications
Technologies Corp., V 277–78; **6** 323;
16 74; **18 347–49**
Mobile Telesystems, **48** 419
Mobilefone, Inc., **25** 108
MobileMedia Corp., **39** 23, 24
MobileStar Network Corp., **26** 429
Mobira, **II** 69; **17** 353
Mobley Chemical, **I** 342
Mobu Company, **6** 431
Mobujidosha Bus Company, **6** 431
MOÇACOR, **IV** 505
Mocatta and Goldsmid Ltd., **II** 357
Mochida Pharaceutical Co. Ltd., **II** 553
Moctezuma Copper Co., **IV** 176–77
Modar, **17** 279
Mode 1 Communications, Inc., **48** 305
Modell's Shoppers World, **16** 35–36

Modell's Sporting Goods. *See* Henry Modell & Company Inc.

Modeluxe Linge Services SA, **45** 139–40

Modem Media, **23** 479

Modern Equipment Co., **I** 412

Modern Furniture Rentals Inc., **14** 4; **27** 163

Modern Handling Methods Ltd., **21** 499

Modern Maid Food Products, **II** 500

Modern Merchandising Inc., **19** 396

Modern Patterns and Plastics, **III** 641

Modern Times Group AB, 36 335–38

Modernistic Industries Inc., **7** 589

Modine Manufacturing Company, 8 372–75

Modis Professional Services. *See* MPS Group, Inc.

MoDo. *See* Mo och Domsjö AB.

MoDo Paper AB, **28** 446; **52** 164

Moen Incorporated, 12 344–45

Moët-Hennessy, I 271–72; **10** 397–98; **23** 238, 240, 242. *See also* LVMH Moët Hennessy Louis Vuitton SA.

Mogen David. *See* The Wine Group, Inc.

Mogul Corp., **I** 321; **17** 287

The Mogul Metal Company. *See* Federal-Mogul Corporation.

Mohasco Corporation, **15** 102; **26** 100–01

Mohawk & Hudson Railroad, **9** 369

Mohawk Airlines, **I** 131; **6** 131

Mohawk Carpet Corp., **26** 101

Mohawk Industries, Inc., 19 274–76; **31** 199

Mohawk Rubber Co. Ltd., **V** 256; **7** 116; **19** 508

Mohegan Tribal Gaming Authority, 37 254–57

Mohr-Value Stores, **8** 555

Moilliet and Sons, **II** 306

Mojave Foods Corporation, **27** 299

Mojo MDA Group Ltd., **11** 50–51; **43** 412

Mokta. *See* Compagnie de Mokta.

MOL. *See* Mitsui O.S.K. Lines, Ltd.

Molecular Biosystems, **III** 61

Molerway Freight Lines, Inc., **53** 250

Molex Incorporated, II 8; **11** 317–19; **14** 27; **54 236–41 (upd.)**

Moline National Bank, **III** 463; **21** 173

Molinera de México S.A. de C.V., **31** 236

Molinos de Puerto Rico, **II** 493

Molinos Nacionales C.A., **7** 242–43; **25** 241

Molins plc, IV 326; **51 249–51**

Molkerie-Zentrak Sud GmbH, **II** 575

Moll Plasticrafters, L.P., **17** 534

Molloy Manufacturing Co., **III** 569; **20** 360

Mölnlycke AB, **IV** 338–39; **28** 443–45; **36** 26

The Molson Companies Limited, I 273–75, 333; **II** 210; **7** 183–84; **12** 338; **13** 150, 199; **21** 320; **23** 404; **25** 279; **26** 303–07 **(upd.)**; **36** 15

Molycorp, **IV** 571; **24** 521

Momentus Group Ltd., **51** 99

Mon-Dak Chemical Inc., **16** 270

Mon-Valley Transportation Company, **11** 194

Mona Meyer McGrath & Gavin, **47** 97

MONACA. *See* Molinos Nacionales C.A.

Monaco Coach Corporation, 31 336–38

Monadnock Paper Mills, Inc., 21 381–84

Monarch Air Lines, **22** 219

Monarch Development Corporation, **38** 451–52

Monarch Food Ltd., **II** 571

Monarch Foods, **26** 503

Monarch Marking Systems, **III** 157

MonArk Boat, **III** 444; **22** 116

Mond Nickel Co., **IV** 110–11

Mondadori. *See* Arnoldo Monadori Editore S.p.A.

Mondex International, **18** 543

Mondi Foods BV, **41** 12

Mondi Paper Co., **IV** 22

Moneris Solutions Corp., **46** 55

Monet Jewelry, **II** 502–03; **9** 156–57; **10** 323–24

Money Access Service Corp., **11** 467

Money Management Associates, Inc., **53** 136

Monfort, Inc., 13 350–52

Monheim Group, **II** 521

Monier Roof Tile, **III** 687, 735

Monis Wineries, **I** 288

Monitor Dynamics Inc., **24** 510

Monitor Group Inc., **33** 257

Monk-Austin Inc., **12** 110

Monmouth Pharmaceuticals Ltd., **16** 439

Monochem, **II** 472; **22** 93

Monogram Aerospace Fasteners, Inc., **11** 536

Monogram Models, **25** 312

Monogramme Confections, **6** 392

Monolithic Memories Inc., **6** 216; **16** 316–17, 549

Monon Corp., **13** 550

Monon Railroad, **I** 472

Monongahela Power, **38** 40

Monoprix, **V** 57–59

Monro Muffler Brake, Inc., 24 337–40

Monroe Auto Equipment, **I** 527

Monroe Calculating Machine Co., **I** 476, 484

Monroe Cheese Co., **II** 471

Monroe Savings Bank, **11** 109

Monrovia Aviation Corp., **I** 544

Monsanto Company, I 310, 363, **365–67,** 402, 631, 666, 686, 688; **III** 741; **IV** 290, 367, 379, 401; **8** 398; **9** 318, **355–57 (upd.),** 466; **12** 186; **13** 76, 225; **16** 460–62; **17** 131; **18** 112; **22** 107; **23** 170–71; **26** 108; **29 327–31 (upd.);** **33** 135; **34** 179; **41** 306; **52** 312; **53** 261

Monsavon, **III** 46–47

Monsoon plc, 39 287–89

Mont Blanc, **17** 5; **27** 487, 489

Montabert S.A., **15** 226

Montan TNT Pty Ltd., **27** 473

Montan Transport GmbH, **IV** 140

Montana-Dakota Utilities Co., **7** 322–23; **37** 281–82; **42** 249–50, 252

Montana Enterprises Inc., **I** 114

Montana Group, **54** 229

The Montana Power Company, 6 566; **7** 322; **11** 320–22; **37** 280, 283; **44 288–92 (upd.);** **50** 367

Montana Refining Company, **12** 240–41

Montana Resources, Inc., **IV** 34

Montaup Electric Co., **14** 125

MontBell America, Inc., **29** 279

Montecatini, **I** 368; **IV** 421, 470, 486

Montedison S.p.A., I 368–69; IV 413, 421–22, 454, 499; **14** 17; **22** 262; **24 341–44 (upd.);** **26** 367; **36** 185–86, 188

Montefibre, **I** 369

Montefina, **IV** 499; **26** 367

Montell N.V., **24** 343

Monterey Homes Corporation. *See* Meritage Corporation.

Monterey Mfg. Co., **12** 439

Monterey's Acquisition Corp., **41** 270

Monterey's Tex-Mex Cafes, **13** 473

Monterrey, Compania de Seguros sobre la Vida. *See* Seguros Monterrey.

Monterrey Group, **19** 10–11, 189

Montfort of Colorado, Inc., **II** 494

Montgomery Elevator Company, **27** 269

Montgomery Ward & Co., Incorporated, **III** 762; **IV** 465; **V 145–48; 7** 353; **8** 509; **9** 210; **10** 10, 116, 172, 305, 391, 393, 490–91; **12** 48, 309, 315, 335, 430; **13** 165; **15** 330, 470; **17** 460; **18** 477; **20** 263, **374–79 (upd.),** 433; **22** 535; **25** 144; **27** 428–30; **43** 292

Montiel Corporation, **17** 321

Montinex, **24** 270

Montreal Bank, **II** 210

Montreal Engineering Company, **6** 585

Montreal Light, Heat & Power Consolidated, **6** 501–02

Montreal Mining Co., **17** 357

Montres Rolex S.A., 8 477; **13 353–55;** **19** 452; **34 292–95 (upd.)**

Montrose Capital, **36** 358

Montrose Chemical Company, **9** 118, 119

Montrose Chrome, **IV** 92

Monument Property Trust Ltd., **IV** 710

Monumental Corp., **III** 179

MONYCo., **III** 306

Moody's Investment Service, **IV** 605; **16** 506; **19** 133; **22** 189

Moog Inc., 13 356–58

Moon-Hopkins Billing Machine, **III** 165

Mooney Aerospace Group Ltd., 52 252–55

Mooney Chemicals, Inc. *See* OM Group, Inc.

Moonlight Mushrooms, Inc. *See* Sylvan, Inc.

Moonstone Mountaineering, Inc., **29** 181

Moore and McCormack Co. Inc., **19** 40

Moore Corporation Limited, IV 644–46, 679; **15** 473; **16** 450; **36** 508

Moore Gardner & Associates, **22** 88

The Moore Group Ltd., **20** 363

Moore-Handley, Inc., IV 345–46; **39 290–92**

Moore McCormack Resources Inc., **14** 455

Moore Medical Corp., 17 331–33

Moorhouse, **II** 477

Moran Group Inc., **II** 682

Moran Health Care Group Ltd., **25** 455

MoRan Oil & Gas Co., **IV** 82–83

Moran Towing Corporation, Inc., 15 301–03

Morana, Inc., **9** 290

Moreland and Watson, **IV** 208

Moretti-Harrah Marble Co., **III** 691

Morgan & Banks Limited, **30** 460

Morgan & Cie International S.A., **II** 431

Morgan Construction Company, **8** 448

Morgan Edwards, **II** 609

Morgan Engineering Co., **8** 545

Morgan Grampian Group, **IV** 687

Morgan Grenfell Group PLC, II 280, 329, **427–29; IV** 21, 712

The Morgan Group, Inc., 46 300–02

Morgan Guaranty International Banking Corp., **II** 331; **9** 124

Morgan Guaranty Trust Co. of New York, **I** 26; **II** 208, 254, 262, 329–32, 339, 428, 431, 448; **III** 80; **10** 150

Morgan Guaranty Trust Company, **11** 421; **13** 49, 448; **14** 297; **25** 541; **30** 261

Morgan, Harjes & Co., **II** 329

Morgan, J.P. & Co. Inc. *See* J.P. Morgan & Co. Incorporated.

Morgan, Lewis & Bockius LLP, 29 332–34

Morgan, Lewis, Githens & Ahn, Inc., **6** 410

Morgan Mitsubishi Development, **IV** 714

Morgan Schiff & Co., **29** 205

Morgan Stanley Dean Witter & Company, 33 311–14 (upd.); 38 289, 291, 411

Morgan Stanley Group, Inc., I 34; **II** 211, 330, 403, 406–08, 422, 428, **430–32**, 441; **IV** 295, 447, 714; **9** 386; **11** 258; **12** 529; **16 374–78 (upd.); 18** 448–49; **20** 60, 363; **22** 404, 407; **25** 542; **30** 353–55; **34** 496; **36** 153

Morgan Yacht Corp., **II** 468

Morgan's Brewery, **I** 287

Mori Bank, **II** 291

Moria Informatique, **6** 229

Morino Associates, **10** 394

Morita & Co., **II** 103

Mormac Marine Group, **15** 302

Morning Star Technologies Inc., **24** 49

Morning Sun, Inc., **23** 66

Morningstar Storage Centers LLC, **52** 311

Morris Air, **24** 455

Morris Communications Corporation, 36 339–42

Morris Motors, **III** 256; **7** 459; **50** 67

Morris Travel Services L.L.C., 26 308–11

Morrison & Co. Ltd., **52** 221

Morrison Homes, Inc., **51** 138

Morrison Industries Ltd., **IV** 278; **19** 153

Morrison Knudsen Corporation, IV 55; **7 355–58; 11** 401, 553; **28 286–90 (upd.); 33** 442; **50** 36350 363. *See also* The Washington Companies.

Morrison Machine Products Inc., **25** 193

Morrison Restaurants Inc., 11 323–25; 18 464

Morse Chain Co., **III** 439; **14** 63

Morse Equalizing Spring Company, **14** 63

Morse Industrial, **14** 64

Morse Shoe Inc., 13 359–61

Morss and White, **III** 643

Morstan Development Co., Inc., **II** 432

Mortgage & Trust Co., **II** 251

Mortgage Associates, **9** 229

Mortgage Guaranty Insurance Corp. *See* MGIC Investment Corp.

Mortgage Insurance Co. of Canada, **II** 222

Mortgage Resources, Inc., **10** 91

Morton Foods, Inc., **II** 502; **10** 323; **27** 258

Morton International Inc., 9 358–59 (upd.), 500–01; **16** 436; **22** 505–06; **43** 319

Morton Thiokol Inc., I 325, **370–72; 19** 508; **28** 253–54. *See also* Thiokol Corporation.

Morton's Restaurant Group, Inc., 28 401; **30 329–31**

Mos Magnetics, **18** 140

MOS Technology, **7** 95

Mosby-Year Book, Inc., **IV** 678; **17** 486

Moseley, Hallgarten, Estabrook, and Weeden, **III** 389

Mosher Steel Company, **7** 540

Mosinee Paper Corporation, 15 304–06

Moskatel's, Inc., **17** 321

Mosler Safe Co., **III** 664–65; **7** 144, 146; **22** 184

Moss Bros Group plc, 51 252–54

Moss-Rouse Company, **15** 412

Mossgas, **IV** 93

Mossimo, Inc., 27 328–30

Mostek Corp., **I** 85; **II** 64; **11** 307–08; **13** 191; **20** 175; **29** 323

Mostjet Ltd. *See* British World Airlines Ltd.

Móstoles Industrial S.A., **26** 129

Mostra Importaciones S.A., **34** 38, 40

Motel 6 Corporation, 10 13; **13 362–64.** *See also* Accor SA

Mother Karen's, **10** 216

Mother's Oats, **II** 558–59; **12** 409

Mothercare Stores, Inc., **16** 466

Mothercare UK Ltd., 17 42–43, **334–36**

Mothers Against Drunk Driving (MADD), 51 255–58

Mothers Work, Inc., 18 350–52

Motif Inc., **22** 288

Motion Designs, **11** 486

Motion Factory, Inc., **38** 72

Motion Picture Association of America, **37** 353–54

Motion Picture Corporation of America, **25** 326, 329

Motiva Enterprises LLC, **41** 359, 395

MotivePower. *See* Wabtec Corporation.

The Motley Fool, Inc., 40 329–31

Moto Photo, Inc., 45 282–84

Moto-Truc Co., **13** 385

Motor Cargo Industries, Inc., 35 296–99

Motor Club of America Insurance Company, **44** 354

Motor Coaches Industries International Inc., **36** 132

Motor Haulage Co., **IV** 181

Motor Parts Industries, Inc., **9** 363

Motor Transit Corp., **I** 448; **10** 72

Motor Wheel Corporation, **20** 261; **27** 202–04

Motorcar Parts & Accessories, Inc., 47 253–55

Motoren-und-Turbinen-Union, **I** 151; **III** 563; **9** 418; **15** 142; **34** 128, 131, 133

Motoren-Werke Mannheim AG, **III** 544

Motorenfabrik Deutz AG, **III** 541

Motorenfabrik Oberursel, **III** 541

Motornetic Corp., **III** 590

Motorola, Inc., I 534; **II** 5, 34, 44–45, 56, **60–62,** 64; **III** 455; **6** 238; **7** 119, 494, 533; **8** 139; **9** 515; **10** 87, 365, 367, 431–33; **11** 45, 308, **326–29 (upd.),** 381–82; **12** 136–37, 162; **13** 30, 356, 501; **17** 33, 193; **18** 18, 74, 76, 260, 382; **19** 391; **20** 8, 439; **21** 123; **22** 17, 19, 288, 542; **26** 431–32; **27** 20, 341–42, 344; **33** 47–48; **34 296–302 (upd.); 38** 188; **43** 15; **44** 97, 357, 359; **45** 346, 348; **47** 318, 320, 385; **48** 270, 272

Motown Records Company L.P., II 145; **22** 194; **23** 389, 391; **26 312–14**

Moulinex S.A., 22 362–65

Mound Metalcraft. *See* Tonka Corporation.

Mount. *See also* Mt.

Mount Hood Credit Life Insurance Agency, **14** 529

Mount Isa Mines, **IV** 61

Mount Vernon Group, **8** 14

Mountain Fuel Supply Company. *See* Questar Corporation.

Mountain Fuel Supply Company, **6** 568–69

Mountain Pass Canning Co., **7** 429

Mountain Safety Research, **18** 445–46

Mountain State Telephone Company, **6** 300

Mountain States Mortgage Centers, Inc., 29 335–37

Mountain States Power Company. *See* PacifiCorp.

Mountain States Telephone & Telegraph Co., **V** 341; **25** 495

Mountain States Wholesale, **II** 602; **30** 25

Mountain Valley Indemnity Co., **44** 356

Mountain West Bank, **35** 197

Mountleigh PLC, **16** 465

Mounts Wire Industries, **III** 673

Mountsorrel Granite Co., **III** 734

Mouvement des Caisses Desjardins, 48 288–91

Movado Group, Inc., 28 291–94

Movado-Zenith-Mondia Holding, **II** 124

Movie Gallery, Inc., 31 339–41

Movie Star Inc., 17 337–39

Movies To Go, Inc., **9** 74; **31** 57

Movil@ccess, S.A. de C.V., **39** 25, 194

Moving Co. Ltd., **V** 127

The Moving Picture Company, **15** 83; **50** 124, 126

The Mowry Co., **23** 102

MP3.com, **43** 109

MPB Corporation, **8** 529, 531

MPI. *See* Michael Page International plc.

MPM, **III** 735

MPS Group, Inc., 49 264–67

MPW Industrial Services Group, Inc., 53 231–33

Mr. Bricolage S.A., 37 258–60

Mr. Coffee, Inc., 14 229–31; **15 307–09; 17** 215; **27** 275; **39** 406

Mr. D's Food Centers, **12** 112

Mr. Donut, **21** 323

Mr. Gasket Inc., 11 84; **15 310–12**

Mr. Gatti's Inc., **15** 345; **53** 204–06

Mr. Goodbuys, **13** 545

Mr. How, **V** 191–92

Mr. M Food Stores, **7** 373

Mr. Maintenance, **25** 15

Mr. Payroll Corp., **20** 113

MRC Bearings, **III** 624

MRD Gaming, **51** 206–07

MRJ Technology Solutions, **54** 396

MRN Radio Network, **19** 223

Mrs. Baird's Bakeries, 29 338–41

Mrs. Fields' Original Cookies, Inc., 27 331–35

Mrs. Paul's Kitchens, **II** 480; **26** 57–58

Mrs. Smith's Frozen Foods, **II** 525; **13** 293–94; **35** 181; **50** 293–94

MS-Relais GmbH, **III** 710; **7** 302–03

MSAS Cargo International, **6** 415, 417

MSE Corporation, **33** 44

MSI Data Corp., **10** 523; **15** 482

M6. *See* Métropole Télévision.

MSL Industries, **10** 44

MSNBC, **28** 301

MSR. *See* Mountain Safety Research.

MSU. *See* Middle South Utilities.

Mt. *See also* Mount.

Mt. Beacon Insurance Co., **26** 486

Mt. Carmel Public Utility Company, **6** 506
Mt. Goldsworthy Mining Associates, **IV** 47
Mt. Lyell Investments, **III** 672–73
Mt. Olive Pickle Company, Inc., 44
293–95
Mt. Summit Rural Telephone Company, **14**
258
Mt. Vernon Iron Works, **II** 14
MTC. *See* Management and Training
Corporation.
MTC Pharmaceuticals, **II** 483
MTel. *See* Mobile Telecommunications
Technologies Corp.
MTG. *See* Modern Times Group AB.
MTM Entertainment Inc., **13** 279, 281
MTR Foods Ltd., 55 271–73
MTS Inc., 37 261–64
MTV, **31** 239
MTV Asia, **23** 390
MTVi Group, **37** 194
Muehlens KG, **48** 422
Mueller Co., **III** 645; **28** 485
Mueller Furniture Company, **8** 252; **39** 206
Mueller Industries, Inc., 7 359–61; **52**
256–60 (upd.)
Mujirushi Ryohin, **V** 188
Mukluk Freight Lines, **6** 383
Mule Battery Manufacturing Co., **III** 643
Mule-Hide Products Co., **22** 15
Mülheimer Bergwerksvereins, **I** 542
Mullen Advertising Inc., 13 513; **51**
259–61
Mullens & Co., **14** 419
Multex Systems, **21** 70
Multi-Color Corporation, 53 234–36
Multi Restaurants, **II** 664
Multibank Inc., **11** 281
Multicom Publishing Inc., **11** 294
Multilink, Inc., **27** 364–65
MultiMed, **11** 379
Multimedia Games, Inc., 41 272–76
Multimedia, Inc., IV 591; **11** 330–32; **30**
217
Multimedia Security Services, Inc., **32** 374
Multiple Access Systems Corp., **III** 109
Multiple Properties, **I** 588
MultiScope Inc., **10** 508
Multitech International. *See* Acer Inc.
Multiview Cable, **24** 121
Münchener Rückversicherungs-
Gesellschaft. *See* Munich Re.
Munford, Inc., **17** 499
Mungana Mines, **I** 438
Munich Re (Münchener
Rückversicherungs-Gesellschaft
Aktiengesellschaft in München), II
239; **III** 183–84, 202, **299–301**,
400–01, 747; **35** 34, 37; **46 303–07**
(upd.)
Municipal Assistance Corp., **II** 448
Munising Paper Co., **III** 40; **13** 156; **16**
303; **43** 257
Munising Woodenware Company, **13** 156
Munksjö, **19** 227
Munksund, **IV** 338
Munsingwear, Inc., **22** 427; **25** 90; **27** 443,
445; **41** 291. *See also* PremiumWear,
Inc.
Munson Transportation Inc., **18** 227
Munster and Leinster Bank Ltd., **16** 13
Mura Corporation, **23** 209
Murata, **37** 347
Murdock Madaus Schwabe, 26 315–19,
470

Murfin Inc., **8** 360
Murmic, Inc., **9** 120
Murphey Favre, Inc., **17** 528, 530
Murphey Family Farms Inc., 7 477; **21**
503; **22 366–68**; **46** 84
Murphy Oil Corporation, 7 362–64; **32**
338–41 (upd.)
Murphy-Phoenix Company, **14** 122
Murphy's Pizza. *See* Papa Murphy's
International, Inc.
Murray Bay Paper Co., **IV** 246; **25** 10
Murray Corp. of America, **III** 443
Murray Goulburn Snow, **II** 575
Murray Inc., **19** 383
Murrayfield, **IV** 696
Murtaugh Light & Power Company, **12**
265
Musashino Railway Company, **V** 510
Muscatine Journal, **11** 251
Muscocho Explorations Ltd., **IV** 76
Muse Air Corporation, **6** 120; **24** 454
Muse, Cordero, Chen, **41** 89
Music and Video Club, **24** 266, 270
Music-Appreciation Records, **13** 105
Music Corporation of America. *See* MCA
Inc.
Music Go Round, **18** 207–09
Music Man, Inc., **16** 202; **43** 170
Music Plus, **9** 75
Musical America Publishing, Inc., **22** 441
Musician's Friend, **29** 221, 223
Musicland Stores Corporation, 9
360–62; **11** 558; **19** 417; **37** 263; **38**
313–17 (upd.)
MusicNet, Inc., **53** 282
Musitek, **16** 202; **43** 170
Muskegon Gas Company. *See* MCN
Corporation.
Muskegon Wire, **55** 305
Musotte & Girard, **I** 553
Mutoh Industries, Ltd., **6** 247; **24** 234
Mutual Benefit Life Insurance Company,
III 243, **302–04**
Mutual Broadcasting System, **23** 509
Mutual Gaslight Company. *See* MCN
Corporation.
Mutual Life Insurance Co. of the State of
Wisconsin, **III** 321
Mutual Life Insurance Company of New
York, II 331; **III** 247, 290, **305–07**,
316, 321, 380
Mutual Marine Office Inc., **41** 284
Mutual Medical Aid and Accident
Insurance Co., **III** 331
Mutual of Omaha, **III** 365; **25** 89–90; **27**
47
Mutual Oil Co., **IV** 399
Mutual Papers Co., **14** 522
Mutual Safety Insurance Co., **III** 305
Mutual Savings & Loan Association, **III**
215; **18** 60
Mutualité Générale, **III** 210
Mutuelle d'Orléans, **III** 210
Mutuelle de l'Ouest, **III** 211
Mutuelle Vie, **III** 210
Mutuelles Unies, **III** 211
Muzak, Inc., 7 90–91; **18 353–56**; **35**
19–20
Muzzy-Lyon Company. *See* Federal-Mogul
Corporation.
MVC. *See* Music and Video Club.
MVR Products Pte Limited, **47** 255
Mwinilunga Canneries Ltd., **IV** 241
MXL Industries, **13** 367

MY Holdings, **IV** 92
Myanmar Oil and Gas Enterprise, **IV** 519
MYCAL Group, **V** 154
Myco-Sci, Inc. *See* Sylvan, Inc.
Mycogen Corporation, 21 385–87
Mycrom, **14** 36
Myer Emporium Ltd., **20** 156
Myers Industries, Inc., 19 277–79
Mygind International, **8** 477
Mylan Laboratories Inc., I 656–57; **20**
380–82 (upd.)
Myllykoski Träsliperi AB, **IV** 347–48
Myokenya, **III** 757
Myrna Knitwear, Inc., **16** 231
Myson Group PLC, **III** 671
Mysore State Iron Works, **IV** 205

N.A. Otto & Cie., **III** 541
N.A. Woodworth, **III** 519; **22** 282
N. Boynton & Co., **16** 534
N.C. Cameron & Sons, Ltd., **11** 95
N.C. Monroe Construction Company, **14**
112
N.E.M., **23** 228
N.H. Geotech. *See* New Holland N.V.
N.K. Fairbank Co., **II** 497
N.L. Industries, **19** 212
N M Electronics, **II** 44
N M Rothschild & Sons Limited, **IV** 64,
712; **24** 267; **39 293–95**
N.M.U. Transport Ltd., **II** 569
N.R.F. Gallimard, **IV** 618
N. Shure Company, **15** 477
N.V. *see under first word of company*
name
N.W. Ayer & Son, **I** 36; **II** 542
N.W. Ayer and Partners, **32** 140
N.Y.P. Holdings Inc., **12** 360
Na Pali, S.A. *See* Quiksilver, Inc.
Naamloze Vennootschap tot Exploitatie
van het Café Krasnapolsky. *See* Grand
Hotel Krasnapolsky N.V.
Nabisco, **24** 358
Nabisco Brands, Inc., II 475, 512,
542–44; **7** 128, 365–67; **12** 167; **25** 366.
See also RJR Nabisco.
Nabisco Foods Group, 7 365–68 (upd.);
9 318; **14** 48. *See also* Kraft Foods Inc.
Nabisco Holdings Corporation, **25** 181; **42**
408; **44** 342
Nabisco Ltd., **24** 288
Nabors Industries, Inc., 9 363–65
Nacamar Internet Services, **48** 398
NACCO Industries, Inc., 7 369–71; **17**
213–15, 246, 248
Nacional de Drogas, S.A. de C.V., **39** 188
Nacional Financiera, **IV** 513
NACO Finance Corp., **33** 398
Naco-Nogales, **51** 389
Nadler Sportswear. *See* Donnkenny, Inc.
Naegele Outdoor Advertising Inc., **36** 340
Naf Naf SA, 44 296–98
NAFI Corp. *See* Chris-Craft Industries, Inc.
Nagano Seiyu Ltd., **V** 188
Nagasaki Shipyard, **I** 502
Nagasakiya Co., Ltd., V 149–51
Nagasco, Inc., **18** 366
Nagase & Company, Ltd., 8 376–78
Nagase-Alfa, **III** 420
Nagase-Landauer, Ltd., **51** 210
Nagel Meat Markets and Packing House, **II**
643
Nagoya Bank, **II** 373
Nagoya Electric Light Co., **IV** 62

NAI. *See* Natural Alternatives International, Inc.; Network Associates, Inc.
Naigai Tsushin Hakuhodo, **6** 29
Naikoku Tsu-un Kabushiki Kaisha, **V** 477
Naiman Co., **25** 449
Nairn Linoleum Co., **18** 116
Nakai Shoten Ltd., **IV** 292
Nakano Vinegar Co. Ltd., **26** 58
Nalco Chemical Corporation, I 373–75; 12 346–48 (upd.)
Nalfloc, **I** 374
Nalge Co., **14** 479–80
NAM. *See* Nederlandse Aardolie Maatschappij.
Namco, **III** 431
Namibia Breweries Ltd., **33** 75
Namkwang Engineering & Construction Co. Ltd., **III** 749
NAMM. *See* North American Medical Management Company, Inc.
Nampack, **I** 423
Namur Re S.A., **51** 143
Nan Ya Plastics Corp., **14** 197–98
NANA Regional Corporation, **7** 558
Nanfang South China Motor Corp., **34** 132
Nankai Kogyo, **IV** 225; **24** 489
Nansei Sekiyu K.K., **IV** 432; **54** 383–84
Nantucket Allserve, Inc., 22 369–71
Nantucket Corporation, **6** 226
Nantucket Mills, **12** 285; **34** 240
Nanyo Bussan, **I** 493; **24** 326
NAPA. *See* National Automotive Parts Association.
NAPC. *See* North American Philips Corp.
Napier, **I** 194
NAPP Systems, Inc., **11** 253
Narmco Industries, **I** 544
Narragansett Electric Company, **51** 265
NAS. *See* National Audubon Society.
NASA. *See* National Aeronautics and Space Administration.
NASCAR. *See* National Association for Stock Car Auto Racing.
NASD, 54 242–46 (upd.)
NASDAQ, **37** 132
Nash DeCamp Company, **23** 356–57
Nash Finch Company, 8 379–81; 11 43; 23 356–58 (upd.); 40 80
Nash-Kelvinator Corp., **I** 135; **12** 158
Nash Motors Co., **I** 135; **8** 75
Nashaming Valley Information Processing, **III** 204
Nashua Corporation, 8 382–84
The Nashville Network, **11** 153
Nashville Speedway USA, Inc., **43** 139–41
Nassau Gas Light Co., **6** 455
Nassco Holdings Inc., **36** 79
NASTECH, **III** 590
Nasu Aluminium Manufacturing Co., **IV** 153
Nasu Nikon Co., Ltd., **48** 295
Nat Robbins, **37** 269–70
Natal Brewery Syndicate, **I** 287
Natco Corp., **I** 445
NaTec Ltd. *See* CRSS Inc.
Nathan's Famous, Inc., 29 342–44
National, **10** 419
The National Academy of Television Arts & Sciences, **55** 3
National Acme Company. *See* Acme-Cleveland Corp.
National Advanced Systems, **II** 64–65
National Advertising Company, **27** 280

National Aeronautics and Space Administration, **II** 139; **6** 227–29, 327; **11** 201, 408; **12** 489; **37** 364–65
National Air Transport Co., **I** 128; **6** 128; **9** 416; **11** 427
National Airlines, **I** 97, 116; **6** 388; **21** 141; **25** 146
National Allied Publications. *See* DC Comics Inc.
National Aluminate Corp., **I** 373; **12** 346
National Aluminum Company, **11** 38
National American Corporation, **33** 399
National American Life Insurance Co. of California, **II** 181
National American Title Insurance Co., **II** 181
National Amusements Inc., 28 295–97
National Aniline & Chemical Coompany, **I** 414; **22** 29
National Association for Stock Car Auto Racing, 32 342–44
National Association of Securities Dealers, Inc., 10 416–18. *See also* NASD.
National Audubon Society, 26 320–23
National Australia Bank, **III** 673
National Auto Credit, Inc., 16 379–81
National Automobile and Casualty Insurance Co., **III** 270
National Automotive Fibers, Inc. *See* Chris-Craft Industries, Inc.
National Automotive Parts Association, **26** 348
National Aviation, **I** 117
National Baby Shop, **V** 203
National Bancard Corporation, **11** 111–13
National Bancorp of Arizona, **12** 565
National Bank, **II** 312
National Bank for Cooperatives, **8** 489–90
National Bank für Deutschland, **II** 270
National Bank of Arizona, **53** 378
National Bank of Belgium, **II** 294
National Bank of Commerce, **II** 331; **9** 536; **11** 105–06; **13** 467
National Bank of Commerce Trust & Savings Association, **15** 161
National Bank of Detroit, **I** 165. *See also* NBD Bancorp, Inc.
National Bank of Egypt, **II** 355
National Bank of Greece, 41 277–79
The National Bank of Jacksonville, **9** 58
National Bank of New Zealand, **II** 308; **19** 155
National Bank of North America, **II** 334
National Bank of South Africa Ltd., **II** 236
National Bank of the City of New York, **II** 312
National Bank of Turkey, **IV** 557
National Bank of Washington, **13** 440
National BankAmericard Inc. *See* Visa International.
National Bankers Express Co., **II** 396; **10** 60
National Basketball Association, **12** 457
National Bell Telephone Company, **V** 259
National-Ben Franklin Insurance Co., **III** 242
National Benefit and Casualty Co., **III** 228
National Benefit Co., **III** 228
National Beverage Corp., 26 324–26; 55 146. *See also* Faygo Beverages Inc.
National Binding Company, **8** 382
National BioSystems, **47** 37

National Biscuit Co., **IV** 152; **22** 336. *See also* Nabisco.
National Bridge Company of Canada, Ltd., **8** 544
National Broach & Machine Co., **I** 481–82
National Broadcasting Company, Inc., II 30, 88–90, 129–33, **151–53,** 170. 173, 487, 543; **III** 188, 329; **IV** 596, 608, 652; **6** 157–59, **164–66 (upd.); 10** 173; **17** 149–50; **19** 201, 210; **21** 24; **23** 120; **28** 69, **298–301 (upd.); 30** 99; **32** 3; **33** 324; **34** 186; **42** 161, 163. *See also* General Electric Company.
National Building Society, **10** 6–7
National Cable & Manufacturing Co., **13** 369
National Cable Television Association, **18** 64
National Can Corp., I 601–02, 607–08; IV 154; **13** 255
National Car Rental System, Inc., I 489; **II** 419–20, 445; **6** 348–49; **10** 373, **419–20; 21** 284; **22** 406, 524; **24** 9; **25** 93, 143. *See also* Republic Industries, Inc.
National Carbon Co., Inc., **I** 400; **9** 516; **11** 402
National Carriers, **6** 413–14
National Cash Register Company. *See* NCR Corporation.
National Cement Co., **35** 419
National Cheerleaders Association, **15** 516–18
National Chemsearch Corp. *See* NCH Corporation.
National Child Care Centers, Inc., **II** 607
National City Bank, **9** 475
National City Bank of New York, **I** 337, 462; **II** 253–54; **III** 380; **IV** 81
National City Co., **II** 254; **9** 124
National City Corp., 9 475; 15 313–16
National Cleaning Contractors, **II** 176
National Coal Board, **IV** 38–40
National Coal Development Corp., **IV** 48
National Comics Publications. *See* DC Comics Inc.
National Commercial Bank, **11** 108; **12** 422; **13** 476
National Components Industries, Inc., **13** 398
National Container Corp., **I** 609
National Convenience Stores Incorporated, 7 372–75; 20 140
National Cranberry Association. *See* Ocean Spray Cranberries, Inc.
National Credit Office, **IV** 604
National CSS, **IV** 605
National Dairy Products Corp., **II** 533; **7** 275; **14** 204
National Data Corporation, **24** 393
National Demographics & Lifestyles Inc., **10** 461
National Development Bank, **IV** 56
National Discount Brokers Group, Inc., 28 302–04
National Disinfectant Company. *See* NCH Corporation.
National Distillers and Chemical Corporation, I 226, 376–78; IV 11; 8 439–41; **9** 231; **10** 181; **30** 441
National Drive-In Grocery Corporation, **7** 372
National Drug Ltd., **II** 652

National Economic Research Associates, III 283

National Education Association, 9 367

National Educational Corporation, 26 95

National Educational Music Co. Ltd., 47 256–58

National Electric Company, 11 388

National Electric Instruments Co., IV 78

National Electric Products Corp., IV 177

National Employers Life Assurance Co. Ltd., 13 539

National Endowment for the Arts, 52 15

National Enquirer, 10 287–88

National Envelope Corporation, 32 345–47

National Executive Service. *See* Carey International, Inc.

National Express Group PLC, 50 340–42

National Express Laboratories, Inc., 10 107

National Family Opinion. *See* NFO Worldwide, Inc.

National Farmers Organization, 53 260

National Fence Manufacturing Co., Inc., 45 327

National Fidelity Life Insurance Co., 10 246

National Fidelity Life Insurance Co. of Kansas, III 194; IV 343

National Finance Corp., IV 22–23

National Fire & Marine Insurance Co., III 213–14; 42 32

National Fire Insurance Co., III 229–30

National Football League, 12 457; 29 345–47; 37 294

National Freight Corporation, 6 412–13

National Fuel Gas Company, 6 526–28

National Gateway Telecom, 6 326–27

National General Corp., III 190–91; 48 7

National Geographic Society, 9 366–68; 30 332–35 (upd.); 42 115, 117

National Golf Properties, Inc. *See* American Golf Corporation

National Grape Co-operative Association, Inc., 20 383–85

National Greyhound Racing Club, II 142

National Grid Company, 50 280–81, 361–362

National Grid Group plc, 11 399–400; 12 349; 13 484; 45 298–99; 47 122

National Grid USA, 51 262–66 (upd.)

National Grocers of Ontario, II 631

National Guardian Corp., 18 33

National Gypsum Company, 8 43; 10 421–24; 13 169; 22 48, 170; 25 535

National Health Enterprises, III 87

National Health Laboratories Incorporated, 11 333–35. *See also* Laboratory Corporation of America Holdings.

National Hockey League, 35 300–03

National Home Centers, Inc., 44 299–301

National Hotel Co., III 91

National Housing Systems, Inc., 18 27

National Hydrocarbon Corp., IV 543

National ICEE Corporation, 24 242

National Import and Export Corp. Ltd., IV 240

National Indemnity Co., III 213–14; 42 32–33

National India Rubber Company, 9 228

National Industries, I 446

National Inking Appliance Company, 14 52

National Instruments Corporation, 22 372–74

National Integrity Life Insurance, III 249

National Intergroup, Inc., IV 237, 574; V 152–53; 12 354; 16 212; 26 529. *See also* FoxMeyer Health Corporation.

National Iranian Oil Company, III 748; IV 370, 374, 466–68, 484, 512, 535; 47 342

National Key Company. *See* Cole National Corporation.

National Kinney Corp., IV 720; 9 391

National Law Publishing Company, Inc., 32 35

National Lead Co., III 681; IV 32; 21 489

National Leisure Group, 47 421

National Liability and Fire Insurance Co., III 214

National Liberty Corp., III 218–19

National Life and Accident Insurance Co., III 194

National Life Insurance Co., III 290

National Life Insurance Co. of Canada, III 243

National Linen Service, 54 251, 254

National Living Centers, 13 49

National Loss Control Service Corp., III 269

National Lumber Co. *See* National Home Centers, Inc.

National Magazine Company Limited, 19 201

National Manufacturing Co., III 150; 6 264; 13 6

National Marine Service, 6 530

National Market System, 9 369

National Media Corporation, 27 336–40

National Medical Care, 22 360

National Medical Enterprises, Inc., III 79, 87–88; 6 188; 10 252; 14 233; 25 307–08; 33 185. *See also* Tenet Healthcare Corporation.

National Minerals Development Corp., IV 143–44

National Mobility Corp., 30 436

National Mortgage Agency of New Zealand Ltd., IV 278; 19 153

National Mortgage Assoc. of Washington, II 410

The National Motor Bearing Company. *See* Federal-Mogul Corporation.

The National Motor Club of America, Inc., 33 418

National Mutual Life Assurance of Australasia, III 249

National Office Furniture, 12 297

National Oil Corp. *See* Libyan National Oil Corporation.

National Oil Distribution Co., IV 524

National Oilwell, Inc., 54 247–50

National Old Line Insurance Co., III 179

National Organization for Women, Inc., 55 274–76

National Packaging, IV 333

National Paper Co., 8 476

National Parks Transportation Company, 25 420–22

National Patent Development Corporation, 7 45; 13 365–68; 25 54

National Periodical Publications. *See* DC Comics Inc.

National Permanent Mutual Benefit Building Society, 10 6

National Petrochemical Co., IV 467

National Petroleum Publishing Co., IV 636

National Petroleum Refiners of South Africa, 47 340

National Pharmacies, 9 346

National Picture & Frame Company, 24 345–47

National Pig Development Co., 46 84

National Postal Meter Company, 14 52

National Potash Co., IV 82; 7 186

National Power PLC, 11 399–400; 12 349–51; 13 458, 484. *See also* International Power PLC.

National Presto Industries, Inc., 16 382–85; 43 286–90 (upd.)

National Processing, Inc., 24 394

National Propane Corporation, 8 535–37

National Provident Institution for Mutual Life Assurance, IV 711

National Provincial Bank, II 319–20, 333–34; IV 722; 17 324

National Public Radio, 19 280–82; 47 259–62 (upd.)

National Publishing Company, 41 110

National Quotation Bureau, Inc., 14 96–97

National R.V. Holdings, Inc., 32 348–51

National Railroad Passenger Corporation, 22 375–78

National Railways of Mexico, IV 512

National Record Mart, Inc., 29 348–50

National Register Publishing Co., 17 399; 23 442

National Regulator Co., II 41

National Reinsurance Corporation. *See* General Re Corporation.

National Rent-A-Car, 6 392–93

National Research Corporation, 8 397

National Restaurants Management, Inc., 38 385–87

National Revenue Corporation, 22 181

National Rifle Association of America, 37 265–68

National Rubber Machinery Corporation, 8 298

National Sanitary Supply Co., 13 149–50; 16 386–87

National Satellite Paging, 18 348

National School Studios, 7 255; 25 252

National Science Foundation, 9 266

National Sea Products Ltd., 14 339–41

National Seal, I 158

National Semiconductor Corporation, II 63–65; III 455, 618, 678; 6 215, 261–63; 9 297; 11 45–46, 308, 463; 16 122, 332; 17 418; 18 18; 19 312; 21 123; 26 327–30 (upd.); 43 15

National Service Industries, Inc., 11 336–38; 54 251–55 (upd.)

National Shoe Products Corp., 16 17

National Slicing Machine Company, 19 359

National-Southwire Aluminum Company, 11 38; 12 353

National Stamping & Electric Works, 12 159

National Standard Co., IV 137; 13 369–71

National Star Brick & Tile Co., III 501; 7 207

National Starch and Chemical Company, II 496; IV 253; 17 30; 32 256–57; 49 268–70

National Steel and Shipbuilding Company, 7 356

National Steel Car Corp., **IV** 73; **24** 143–44

National Steel Corporation, **I** 491; **IV** 74, 163, 236–37, 572; **V** 152–53; **7** 549; **8** 346, 479–80; **11** 315; **12** 352–54; **14** 191; **16** 212; **23** 445; **24** 144; **26** 527–29; **28** 325. *See also* FoxMeyer Health Corporation.

National Student Marketing Corporation, **10** 385–86

National Supply Co., **IV** 29

National Surety Co. of New York, **III** 395

National System Company, **9** 41; **11** 469

National Tanker Fleet, **IV** 502

National Tea, **II** 631–32

National Technical Laboratories, **14** 52

National TechTeam, Inc., **41** 280–83

National Telecommunications of Austin, **8** 311

National Telephone and Telegraph Corporation. *See* British Columbia Telephone Company.

National Telephone Co., **III** 162; **7** 332, 508

National Theatres, Inc., **III** 190

National Trading Manufacturing, Inc., **22** 213

National Transcontinental, **6** 360

National Travelers' Insurance Co., **III** 290

National Trust Life Insurance Co., **III** 218

National Tube Co., **II** 330; **IV** 572; **7** 549

National Union Electric Corporation, **12** 159

National Union Fire Insurance Co. of Pittsburgh, Pa., **III** 195–97

National Union Life and Limb Insurance Co., **III** 290

National Utilities & Industries Corporation, **9** 363

National Westminster Bank PLC, **II** 237, 333–35; **IV** 642; **13** 206

National Wine & Spirits, Inc., **49** 271–74

Nationalbank, **I** 409

Nationale Bank Vereeniging, **II** 185

Nationale-Nederlanden N.V., **III** 179, 200–01, 308–11; **IV** 697; **50** 11

Nationar, **9** 174

NationsBank Corporation, **6** 357; **10** 425–27; **11** 126; **13** 147; **18** 516, 518; **23** 455; **25** 91, 186; **26** 348, 453. *See also* Bank of America Corporation

NationsRent, **28** 388

Nationwide Cellular Service, Inc., **27** 305

Nationwide Credit, **11** 112

Nationwide Group, **25** 155

Nationwide Income Tax Service, **9** 326

Nationwide Logistics Corp., **14** 504

Nationwide Mutual Insurance Co., **26** 488

NATIOVIE, **II** 234

Native Plants, **III** 43

NATM Buying Corporation, **10** 9, 468

Natomas Co., **IV** 410; **6** 353–54; **7** 309; **11** 271

Natref. *See* National Petroleum Refiners of South Africa.

Natrol, Inc., **49** 275–78

Natronag, **IV** 325

Natronzellstoff-und Papierfabriken AG, **IV** 324

NatSteel Electronics Ltd., **48** 369

NatTeknik, **26** 333

Natudryl Manufacturing Company, **10** 271

Natural Alternatives International, Inc., **49** 279–82

Natural Gas Clearinghouse, **11** 355. *See also* NGC Corporation.

Natural Gas Corp., **19** 155

Natural Gas Pipeline Company, **6** 530, 543; **7** 344–45

Natural Gas Service of Arizona, **19** 411

Natural Selection Foods, **54** 256–58

Natural Wonders Inc., **14** 342–44

NaturaLife International, **26** 470

The Nature Company, **10** 215–16; **14** 343; **26** 439; **27** 429; **28** 306

The Nature Conservancy, **26** 323; **28** 305–07, 422

Nature's Sunshine Products, Inc., **15** 317–19; **26** 470; **27** 353; **33** 145

Nature's Way Products Inc., **26** 315

Natuzzi Group. *See* Industrie Natuzzi S.p.A.

NatWest Bancorp, **38** 393

NatWest Bank, **22** 52. *See also* National Westminster Bank PLC.

Naugles, **7** 506

Nautica Enterprises, Inc., **16** 61; **18** 357–60; **25** 258; **27** 60; **44** 302–06 (upd.)

Nautilus International, Inc., **III** 315–16; **13** 532; **25** 40; **30** 161

Nautor Ab, **IV** 302

Navaho Freight Line, **16** 41

Navajo Refining Company, **12** 240

Navajo Shippers, Inc., **42** 364

Navale, **III** 209

Navan Resources, **38** 231

Navarre Corporation, **22** 536; **24** 348–51

Naviera Vizcaina, **IV** 528

Navigant International, Inc., **47** 263–66

Navigation Mixte, **III** 348

Navire Cargo Gear, **27** 269

Navisant, Inc., **49** 424

Navistar International Corporation, **I** 152, 155, 180–82, 186, 525, 527; **II** 330; **10** 280, 428–30 (upd.); **17** 327; **33** 254. *See also* International Harvester Co.

Navy Exchange Service Command, **31** 342–45

Navy Federal Credit Union, **33** 315–17

Naxon Utilities Corp., **19** 359

Naylor, Hutchinson, Vickers & Company. *See* Vickers PLC.

NBC **24** 516–17. *See also* National Broadcasting Company, Inc.

NBC Bankshares, Inc., **21** 524

NBC/Computer Services Corporation, **15** 163

NBD Bancorp, Inc., **9** 476; **11** 339–41, 466. *See also* Bank One Corporation.

NBTY, Inc., **31** 346–48

NCA Corporation, **9** 36, 57, 171

NCB. *See* National City Bank of New York.

NCB Brickworks, **III** 501; **7** 207

NCC L.P., **15** 139

NCH Corporation, **8** 385–87

Nchanga Consolidated Copper Mines, **IV** 239–40

nChip, **38** 187–88

NCNB Corporation, **II** 336–37; **12** 519; **26** 453

NCO Group, Inc., **42** 258–60

NCR Corporation, **I** 540–41; **III** 147–52, 150–53, 157, 165–66; **IV** 298; **V** 263; **6** 250, 264–68 (upd.), 281–82; **9** 416; **11** 62, 151, 542; **12** 162, 148, 246, 484; **16** 65; **29** 44; **30** 336–41 (upd.); **36** 81

NCS. *See* Norstan, Inc.

NCTI (Noise Cancellation Technologies Inc.), **19** 483–84

nCube Corp., **14** 15; **22** 293

ND Marston, **III** 593

NDB. *See* National Discount Brokers Group, Inc.

NDL. *See* Norddeutscher Lloyd.

NEA. *See* Newspaper Enterprise Association.

NEAC Inc., **I** 201–02

Nearly Me, **25** 313

Neatherlin Homes Inc., **22** 547

Nebraska Bell Company, **14** 311

Nebraska Cellular Telephone Company, **14** 312

Nebraska Consolidated Mills Company, **II** 493; **III** 52; **8** 433; **26** 383

Nebraska Furniture Mart, **III** 214–15; **18** 60–61, 63

Nebraska Light & Power Company, **6** 580

Nebraska Power Company, **25** 89

Nebraska Public Power District, **29** 351–54

NEBS. *See* New England Business Services, Inc.

NEC Corporation, **I** 455, 520; **II** 40, 42, 45, 56–57, 66–68, 73, 82, 91, 104, 361; **III** 122–23, 130, 140, 715; **6** 101, 231, 244, 287; **9** 42, 115; **10** 257, 366, 463, 500; **11** 46, 308, 490; **13** 482; **16** 139; **18** 382–83; **19** 391; **21** 388–91 (upd.); **25** 82, 531; **36** 286, 299–300; **47** 320

Neches Butane Products Co., **IV** 552

Neckermann Versand AG, **V** 100–02

Nedbank, **IV** 23

Nederland Line. *See* Stoomvaart Maatschappij Nederland.

Nederlander Organization, **24** 439

Nederlands Talen Institut, **13** 544

Nederlandsche Electriciteits Maatschappij. *See* N.E.M.

Nederlandsche Handel Maatschappij, **26** 242

Nederlandsche Heide Maatschappij, **III** 199

Nederlandsche Heidenmaatschappij. *See* Arcadis NV.

Nederlandsche Kunstzijdebariek, **13** 21

Nederlandsche Nieuw Guinea Petroleum Maatschappij, **IV** 491

Nederlandsche Stoomvart Maatschappij Oceaan, **6** 416

Nederlandse Cement Industrie, **III** 701

Nederlandse Credietbank N.V., **II** 248

Nederlandse Dagbladunie NV, **IV** 610

N.V. Nederlandse Gasunie, **I** 326; **V** 627, 658–61; **38** 407

Nederlandse Handel Maatschappij, **II** 183, 527; **IV** 132–33

Nederlandse Vliegtuigenfabriek, **I** 54

Nedlloyd Group. *See* Koninklijke Nedlloyd N.V.

Nedsual, **IV** 23; **16** 28; **50** 33

Neeco, Inc., **9** 301

Needham Harper Worldwide, **I** 23, 28, 30–33; **13** 203; **14** 159

Needlecraft, **II** 560; **12** 410

Needleworks, Inc., **23** 66

Neenah Paper Co., **III** 40; **16** 303; **43** 257

Neenah Printing, **8** 360

NEES. *See* New England Electric System.

Neff Corp., **32** 352–53

Negromex, **23** 171–72

Neighborhood Restaurants of America, **18** 241

Neilson/Cadbury, **II** 631

Neiman Bearings Co., **13** 78

The Neiman Marcus Group, Inc., **I** 246; **II** 478; **V** 10, 31; **12** 355–57; **15** 50, 86, 291; **17** 43; **21** 302; **25** 177–78; **27** 429; **49** 283–87 **(upd.)**; **52** 45–46

Neisler Laboratories, **I** 400

Neisner Brothers, Inc., **9** 20

Nekoosa Edwards Paper Co., **IV** 282; **9** 261

NEL Equity Services Co., **III** 314

Nelio Chemicals, Inc., **IV** 345

Nelson Bros., **14** 236

Nelson Entertainment Group, **47** 272

Nelson Publications, **22** 442

NEMF. *See* New England Motor Freight, Inc.

Nemuro Bank, **II** 291

Nenuco, **II** 567

Neo Products Co., **37** 401

Neodata, **11** 293

Neopost S.A., **53** 237–40

Neos, **21** 438

Neoterics Inc., **11** 65

Neozyme I Corp., **13** 240

Nepera, Inc., **I** 682; **16** 69

Neptun Maritime Oyj, **29** 431

Neptune Orient Lines Limited, **47** 267–70

NER Auction Group, **23** 148

NERCO, Inc., **V** 689; **7** 376–79

Nesbitt Thomson, **II** 211

Nesco Inc., **28** 6, 8

Nescott, Inc., **16** 36

Nesher Israel Cement Enterprises Ltd., **II** 47; **25** 266

Nespak SpA, **40** 214–15

Neste Oy, **IV** 435, **469–71**, 519. *See also* Fortum Corporation

Nestlé S.A., **I** 15, 17, 251–52, 369, 605; **II** 379, 456, 478, 486–89, 521, **545–49**, 568–70; **III** 47–48; **6** 16; **7** 380–84 **(upd.)**; **8** 131, 342–44, 498–500; **10** 47, 324; **11** 15, 205; **12** 480–81; **13** 294; **14** 214; **15** 63; **16** 168; **19** 50–51; **21** 55–56, 219; **22** 78, 80; **23** 219; **24** 388; **25** 21, 85, 366; **28** 308–13 **(upd.)**; **32** 115, 234; **36** 234, 237; **44** 351; **46** 274; **50** 295

NetCom Systems AB, **26** 331–33

NetCreations, **47** 345, 347

Netherland Bank for Russian Trade, **II** 183

Netherlands Fire Insurance Co. of Tiel, **III** 308, 310

Netherlands India Steam Navigation Co., **III** 521

Netherlands Insurance Co., **III** 179, 308–10

Netherlands Trading Co. *See* Nederlandse Handel Maatschappij.

NetHold B.V., **31** 330

NetLabs, **25** 117

NetMarket Company, **16** 146

NetPlane Systems, **36** 124

Netron, **II** 390

Netscape Communications Corporation, **15** 320–22; **35** 304–07 **(upd.)**; **44** 97; **50** 328–30

NetStar Communications Inc., **24** 49; **35** 69

Nettai Sangyo, **I** 507

Nettingsdorfer, **19** 227

Nettle Creek Corporation, **19** 304

Nettlefolds Ltd., **III** 493

Netto, **11** 240

Net2Phone Inc., **34** 224

NetWest Securities, **25** 450

Network Associates, Inc., **25** 119, **347–49**

Network Communications Associates, Inc., **11** 409

Network Solutions, Inc., **47** 430

Network Ten, **35** 68–69

NetZero Inc., **38** 271

Netzip Inc., **53** 282

Neue Frankfurter Allgemeine Versicherungs-AG, **III** 184

Neue Holding AG, **III** 377

Neuenberger Versicherungs-Gruppe, **III** 404

Neuralgyline Co., **I** 698

Neuro Navigational Corporation, **21** 47

Neutrogena Corporation, **17** 340–44; **36** 305

Nevada Bell Telephone Company, **V** 318–20; **14** 345–47

Nevada Community Bank, **11** 119

Nevada National Bank, **II** 381; **12** 534

Nevada Natural Gas Pipe Line Co., **19** 411

Nevada Power Company, **11** 342–44; **12** 265

Nevada Savings and Loan Association, **19** 412

Nevada Southern Gas Company, **19** 411

Nevada State Bank, **53** 378

Neversink Dyeing Company, **9** 153

Nevex Software Technologies, **42** 24, 26

New Access Communications, **43** 252

New America Publishing Inc., **10** 288

New Asahi Co., **I** 221

New Balance Athletic Shoe, Inc., **17** 245; **25** 350–52; **35** 388

New Bauhinia Limited, **53** 333

New Bedford Gas & Edison Light Co., **14** 124–25

New Broken Hill Consolidated, **IV** 58–61

New Brunswick Scientific Co., Inc., **45** 285–87

New Century Network, **13** 180; **19** 204, 285

New City Releasing, Inc., **25** 269

New Consolidated Canadian Exploration Co., **IV** 96

New Consolidated Gold Fields, **IV** 21, 95–96

New CORT Holdings Corporation. *See* CORT Business Services Corporation.

New Daido Steel Co., Ltd., **IV** 62–63

New Dana Perfumes Company, **37** 269–71

New Departure, **9** 17

New Departure Hyatt, **III** 590

New Dimension Software, Inc., **55** 67

New England Audio Company, Inc. *See* Tweeter Home Entertainment Group, Inc.

New England Business Services, Inc., **18** 361–64

New England Confectionery Co., **15** 323–25

New England CRInc, **8** 562

New England Electric System, **V** 662–64. *See also* National Grid USA.

New England Gas & Electric Association, **14** 124–25

New England Glass Co., **III** 640

New England Life Insurance Co., **III** 261

New England Merchants National Bank, **II** 213–14; **III** 313

New England Motor Freight, Inc., **53** 250

New England Mutual Life Insurance Co., **III** 312–14

New England National Bank of Boston, **II** 213

New England Network, Inc., **12** 31

New England Nuclear Corporation, **I** 329; **8** 152

New England Paper Tube Co., **54** 58

New England Power Association, **V** 662

New England Trust Co., **II** 213

New Fire Office, **III** 371

New Found Industries, Inc., **9** 465

New Galveston Company, Inc., **25** 116

New Guinea Goldfields, **IV** 95

New Halwyn China Clays, **III** 690

New Hampshire Gas & Electric Co., **14** 124

New Hampshire Insurance Co., **III** 196–97

New Hampshire Oak, **III** 512

New Hampton, Inc., **27** 429

New Haven District Telephone Company. *See* Southern New England Telecommunications Corporation.

New Haven Electric Co., **21** 512

New Hokkai Hotel Co., Ltd., **IV** 327

New Holland N.V., **22** 379–81. *See also* CNH Global N.V.

New Horizon Manufactured Homes, Ltd., **17** 83

New Hotel Showboat, Inc. *See* Showboat, Inc.

New Ireland, **III** 393

New Jersey Bell, **9** 321

New Jersey Educational Music Company. *See* National Educational Music Co. Ltd.

New Jersey Hot Water Heating Company, **6** 449

New Jersey Resources Corporation, **54** 259–61

New Jersey Shale, **14** 250

New Jersey Tobacco Co., **15** 138

New Jersey Zinc, **I** 451

New Laoshan Brewery, **49** 418

New Line Cinema, Inc., **47** 271–74

New London City National Bank, **13** 467

New London Ship & Engine, **I** 57

New Look Group plc, **35** 308–10

New Materials Ltd., **48** 344

New Mather Metals, **III** 582

New Mitsui Bussan, **I** 507; **III** 296

New Nippon Electric Co., **II** 67

New Orleans Canal and Banking Company, **11** 105

New Orleans Refining Co., **IV** 540

The New Piper Aircraft, Inc., **44** 307–10

New Plan Realty Trust, **11** 345–47

New Process Company, **25** 76–77

New Process Cork Company Inc., **I** 601; **13** 188

New South Wales Health System, **16** 94

New Street Capital Inc., **8** 388–90 **(upd.)**. *See also* Drexel Burnham Lambert Incorporated.

New Sulzer Diesel, **III** 633

New Times, Inc., **45** 288–90

New Toyo Group, **19** 227

New Trading Company. *See* SBC Warburg.

New United Motor Manufacturing Inc., **I** 205; **38** 461

New UPI Inc., **25** 507

New Valley Corporation, **17** 345–47

New Vanden Borre, **24** 266–70

New World Coffee-Manhattan Bagel, Inc., **32** 15

New World Communications Group, **22** 442; **28** 248

New World Development Company Limited, **IV** 717–19; **8** 500; **38** 318–22 **(upd.)**

New World Entertainment, **17** 149

New World Hotel (Holdings) Ltd., **IV** 717; **13** 66

New World Pasta Company, **53** 241–44

New World Restaurant Group, Inc., **44** 311–14

New York Air, **I** 90, 103, 118, 129; **6** 129

New York Airways, **I** 123–24

New York and Richmond Gas Company, **6** 456

New York and Suburban Savings and Loan Association, **10** 91

New York Biscuit Co., **II** 542

New York Capital Bank, **41** 312

New York Central Railroad Company, **II** 329, 369; **IV** 181; **9** 228; **10** 43–44, 71–73; **17** 496

New York Chemical Manufacturing Co., **II** 250

New York City Off-Track Betting Corporation, **51** 267–70

New York City Transit Authority, **8** 75

New York Condensed Milk Co., **II** 470

New York Daily News, **32** 357–60

New York Electric Corporation. *See* New York State Electric and Gas.

New York Envelope Co., **32** 346

New York Evening Enquirer, **10** 287

New York Fabrics and Crafts, **16** 197

New York Gas Light Company. *See* Consolidated Edison Company of New York.

New York Glucose Co., **II** 496

New York Guaranty and Indemnity Co., **II** 331

New York Harlem Railroad Co., **II** 250

New York Improved Patents Corp., **I** 601; **13** 188

New York, Lake Erie & Western Railroad, **II** 395; **10** 59

New York Life Insurance Company, **II** 217–18, 330; **III** 291, 305, 315–17, 332; **10** 382; **45** 291–95 **(upd.)**

New York Magazine Co., **IV** 651; **7** 390; **12** 359

New York Manufacturing Co., **II** 312

New York Marine and Gotham Insurance, **41** 284

New York Marine Underwriters, **III** 220

New York Quinine and Chemical Works, **I** 496

New York Quotation Company, **9** 370

New York Restaurant Group, Inc., **32** 361–63

New York, Rio and Buenos Aires Airlines, **I** 115

New York Sports Clubs. *See* Town Sports International, Inc.

New York State Board of Tourism, **6** 51

New York State Electric and Gas Corporation, **6** 534–36

New York Stock Exchange, Inc., **9** 369–72; **10** 416–17; **34** 254; **39** 296–300 **(upd.)**; **54** 242

New York Telephone Co., **9** 321

The New York Times Company, **III** 40; **IV** 647–49; **6** 13; **15** 54; **16** 302; **19** 283–85 **(upd.)**; **23** 158; **32** 508; **43** 256

New York Trust Co., **I** 378; **II** 251

New York, West Shore and Buffalo Railroad, **II** 329

New York Zoological Society. *See* Wildlife Conservation Society.

New York's Bankers Trust Co., **12** 107

New York-Newport Air Service Co., **I** 61

New Zealand Aluminum Smelters, **IV** 59

New Zealand Co., **II** 187

New Zealand Countrywide Banking Corporation, **10** 336

New Zealand Forest Products, **IV** 249–50

New Zealand Press Assoc., **IV** 669

New Zealand Sugar Co., **III** 686

New Zealand Wire Ltd., **IV** 279; **19** 154

Newark Electronics Co., **9** 420

Newco Waste Systems, **V** 750

Newcor, Inc., **40** 332–35

Newcrest Mining Ltd., **IV** 47; **22** 107

Newell and Harrison Company. *See* SUPERVALU INC.

Newell Co., **9** 373–76; **12** 216; **13** 40–41; **22** 35; **25** 22

Newell Rubbermaid Inc., **49** 253; **52** 261–71 **(upd.)**; **53** 37, 40

Newey and Eyre, **I** 429

Newfoundland Brewery, **26** 304

Newfoundland Energy, Ltd., **17** 121

Newfoundland Light & Power Co. *See* Fortis, Inc.

Newfoundland Processing Ltd. *See* Newfoundland Energy, Ltd.

Newgateway PLC, **II** 629

Newhall Land and Farming Company, **14** 348–50

Newhouse Broadcasting, **6** 33

Newman's Own, Inc., **37** 272–75

Newmark & Lewis Inc., **23** 373

Newmont Mining Corporation, **III** 248; **IV** 17, 20, 33, 171, 576; **7** 287–89, 385–88; **12** 244; **16** 25; **23** 40; **38** 231–32; **40** 411–12; **50** 30

Newnes, **17** 397

Newport News Shipbuilding and Dry Dock Co., **I** 58, 527; **13** 372–75; **27** 36

Newport News Shipbuilding Inc., **38** 323–27 **(upd.)**; **41** 42; **45** 306

News & Observer Publishing Company, **23** 343

News America Publishing Inc., **12** 358–60; **27** 42; **37** 408

News and Westminster Ltd., **IV** 685

News Communications & Media Plc, **35** 242

News Corporation Limited, **II** 169; **IV** 650–53; **7** 389–93 **(upd.)**; **8** 551; **9** 429; **12** 358–60; **17** 398; **18** 211, 213, 254; **22** 194, 441; **23** 121; **24** 224; **25** 490; **26** 32; **27** 305, 473; **32** 239; **35** 157–58; **37** 408; **43** 174, 433; **46** 308–13 **(upd.)**; **52** 4

News Extracts Ltd., **55** 289

News International Corp., **20** 79

News of the World Organization (NOTW), **46** 309

Newsco NV, **48** 347

Newsfoto Publishing Company, **12** 472; **36** 469

Newspaper Co-op Couponing, **8** 551

Newspaper Enterprise Association, **7** 157–58

Newspaper Proprietors' Assoc., **IV** 669

Newspaper Supply Co., **IV** 607

Newsquest plc, **32** 354–56

Newsweek, Inc., **IV** 688

Newth-Morris Box Co. *See* Rock-Tenn Company.

Newtherm Oil Burners, Ltd., **13** 286

Newton Yarn Mills, **19** 305

Newtown Gas Co., **6** 455

Nexans SA, **54** 262–64

Nexar Technologies, Inc., **22** 409

NEXCOM. *See* Navy Exchange Service Command.

NeXstar Pharmaceuticals Inc., **54** 130

NeXT Incorporated, **III** 116, 121; **6** 219; **18** 93; **34** 348; **36** 49

Next plc, **6** 25; **29** 355–57

Nextel Communications, Inc., **10** 431–33; **21** 239; **26** 389; **27** 341–45 **(upd.)**

Nextera Enterprises, Inc., **54** 191, 193

NEXTLINK Communications, Inc., **38** 192

Neyveli Lignite Corp. Ltd., **IV** 49

NFC plc, **6** 412–14; **14** 547. *See also* Exel plc.

NFL Properties, Inc., **22** 223

NFO Worldwide, Inc., **24** 352–55

NGC Corporation, **18** 365–67. *See also* Dynegy Inc.

NGI International Precious Metals, Ltd., **24** 335

NHK. *See* Japan Broadcasting Corporation.

NHK Spring Co., Ltd., **III** 580–82

NI Industries, **20** 362

Ni-Med, **50** 122

Niagara Corporation, **28** 314–16

Niagara Fire Insurance Co., **III** 241–42

Niagara First Savings and Loan Association, **10** 91

Niagara Insurance Co. (Bermuda) Ltd., **III** 242

Niagara Mohawk Holdings Inc., **45** 296–99 **(upd.)**

Niagara Mohawk Power Corporation, **V** 665–67; **6** 535; **25** 130; **51** 265

Niagara of Wisconsin, **26** 362–63

Niagara Silver Co., **IV** 644

Niagara Sprayer and Chemical Co., **I** 442

NIBRASCO, **IV** 55

Nicaro Nickel Co., **IV** 82, 111; **7** 186

Nice Day, Inc., **II** 539

Nice Systems, **11** 520

NiceCom Ltd., **11** 520

Nichi-Doku Shashinki Shoten, **III** 574; **43** 281

Nichia Steel, **IV** 159

Nichibo, **V** 387

Nichii Co., Ltd., **V** 154–55; **15** 470; **36** 418

Nichimen Corporation, **II** 442; **IV** 150–52, 154; **10** 439; **24** 356–59 **(upd.)**

Nichimo Sekiyu Co. Ltd., **IV** 555; **16** 490

Nicholas Kiwi Ltd., **II** 572; **15** 436

Nicholas Turkey Breeding Farms, **13** 103

Nicholas Ungar, **V** 156

Nichols & Company, **8** 561

Nichols Copper Co., **IV** 164, 177

Nichols-Homeshield, **22** 14

Nichols plc, **44** 315–18

Nichols Research Corporation, **18** 368–70

Nicholson File Co., **II** 16

Nicholson Graham & Jones, **28** 141

Le Nickel. *See* Société Le Nickel.

Nickelodeon, **25** 381

Nickerson Machinery Company Inc., **53** 230
Nicklaus Companies, 45 300–03
Nicolai Pavdinsky Co., **IV** 118
Nicolet Instrument Company, **11** 513
NICOR Inc., 6 529–31
Niederbayerische Celluloswerke, **IV** 324
Niederrheinische Hütte AG, **IV** 222
Niehler Maschinenfabrick, **III** 602
Nielsen, **10** 358
Nielsen & Petersen, **III** 417
Nielsen Marketing Research. *See* A.C. Nielsen Company.
Niemann Chemie, **8** 464
Niese & Coast Products Co., **II** 681
Niesmann & Bischoff, **22** 207
Nieuw Rotterdam, **27** 54
Nieuwe Eerste Nederlandsche, **III** 177–79
Nieuwe HAV-Bank of Schiedam, **III** 200
NIF Ventures Co. Ltd., **55** 118
Nigeria Airways, **I** 107
Nigerian National Petroleum Corporation, IV 472–74
Nigerian Shipping Operations, **27** 473
Nihol Repol Corp., **III** 757
Nihon Denko, **II** 118
Nihon Keizai Shimbun, Inc., IV 654–56
Nihon Kensetsu Sangyo Ltd., **I** 520
Nihon Kohden Corporation, **13** 328
Nihon Lumber Land Co., **III** 758
Nihon Sangyo Co., **I** 183; **II** 118
Nihon Sugar, **I** 511
Nihon Synopsis, **11** 491
Nihon Teppan, **IV** 159
Nihon Timken K.K., **8** 530
Nihon Waters K.K., **43** 456
Nihon Yusen Kaisha, **I** 503, 506; **III** 577, 712
Nihron Yupro Corp., **III** 756
NII. *See* National Intergroup, Inc.
Niitsu Oil, **IV** 542
NIKE, Inc., V 372–74, 376; **8** 303–04, **391–94 (upd.)**; **9** 134–35, 437; **10** 525; **11** 50, 349; **13** 513; **14** 8; **15** 397; **16** 79, 81; **17** 244–45, 260–61; **18** 264, 266–67, 392; **22** 173; **25** 352; **27** 20; **29** 187–88; **31** 413–14; **36 343–48 (upd.)**
Nikka Oil Co., **IV** 150; **24** 357
Nikka Whisky Distilling Co., **I** 220
Nikkei. *See also* Nihon Keizai Shimbun, Inc.
Nikkei Aluminium Co., **IV** 153–55
Nikkei Shimbun Toei, **9** 29
Nikkelverk, **49** 136
Nikken Global Inc., 32 364–67
Nikken Stainless Fittings Co., Ltd., **IV** 160
Nikko Copper Electrolyzing Refinery, **III** 490
Nikko International Hotels, **I** 106
Nikko Kido Company, **6** 431
Nikko Petrochemical Co. Ltd., **IV** 476
The Nikko Securities Company Limited, II 300, 323, 383, **433–35**; **9 377–79 (upd.)**; **12** 536
Nikko Trading Co., **I** 106
Nikolaiev, **19** 49, 51
Nikon Corporation, III 120–21, 575, **583–85**; **9** 251; **12** 340; **18** 93, 186, 340, 342; **43** 282; **48 292–95 (upd.)**
Nile Faucet Corp., **III** 569; **20** 360
Nillmij, **III** 177–79
Nilpeter, **26** 540, 542
Nimas Corp., **III** 570; **20** 362

Nimbus CD International, Inc., 20 386–90
9 Telecom, **24** 79
Nine West Group Inc., 11 348–49; **14** 441; **23** 330; **39** 247, **301–03 (upd.)**
Nineteen Hundred Washer Co., **III** 653; **12** 548
99¢ Only Stores, 25 353–55
Ningbo General Bearing Co., Ltd., **45** 170
Nintendo Co., Ltd., III 586–88; 7 394–96 (upd.); **10** 124–25, 284–86, 483–84; **13** 403; **15** 539; **16** 168, 331; **18** 520; **23** 26; **28 317–21 (upd.)**; **31** 237; **38** 415; **50** 83
Nintendo of America, **24** 4
NIOC. *See* National Iranian Oil Company.
Nippon ARC Co., **III** 715
Nippon Breweries Ltd. *See* Sapporo Breweries Ltd.
Nippon Broilers Co., **II** 550
Nippon Cable Company, **15** 235
Nippon Cargo Airlines, **6** 71
Nippon Chemical Industries, **I** 363
Nippon Credit Bank, II 310, **338–39**; **38** 439
Nippon Del Monte Corporation, **47** 206
Nippon Educational Television (NET). *See* Asahi National Broadcasting Company, Ltd.
Nippon Electric Company, Limited. *See* NEC Corporation.
Nippon Express Co., Ltd., II 273; **V 477–80**
Nippon-Fisher, **13** 225
Nippon Foundation Engineering Co. Ltd., **51** 179
Nippon Fruehauf Co., **IV** 154
Nippon Fukokin Kinyu Koku, **II** 300
Nippon Funtai Kogyo Co., **III** 714
Nippon Gakki Co., Ltd., **III** 656–58; **16** 554, 557
Nippon Ginko, **III** 408
Nippon Global Tanker Co. Ltd., **53** 116
Nippon Gyomo Sengu Co. Ltd., **IV** 555
Nippon Hatsujo Kabushikikaisha. *See* NHK Spring Co., Ltd.
Nippon Helicopter & Aeroplane Transport Co., Ltd., **6** 70
Nippon Hoso Kyokai. *See* Japan Broadcasting Corporation.
Nippon Idou Tsushin, **7** 119–20
Nippon International Container Services, **8** 278
Nippon Interrent, **10** 419–20
Nippon K.K. *See* Nikon Corporation.
Nippon Kairiku Insurance Co., **III** 384
Nippon Kakoh Seishi, **IV** 293
Nippon Kogaku K.K. *See* Nikon Corporation.
Nippon Kogyo Co. Ltd. *See* Nippon Mining Co. Ltd.
Nippon Kokan K.K., **IV** 161–63, 184, 212; **8** 449; **12** 354
Nippon Life Insurance Company, II 374, 451; **III** 273, 288, **318–20**; **IV** 727; **9** 469
Nippon Light Metal Company, Ltd., IV 153–55
Nippon Machinery Trading, **I** 507
Nippon Meat Packers, Inc., II 550–51
Nippon Menka Kaisha. *See* Nichimen Corporation.
Nippon Merck-Banyu, **I** 651; **11** 290

Nippon Mining Co., Ltd., III 759; **IV 475–77**; **14** 207
Nippon Mitsubishi Oil Corporation, **49** 216
Nippon Motorola Manufacturing Co., **II** 62
Nippon New Zealand Trading Co. Ltd., **IV** 327
Nippon Oil Company, Limited, IV 434, 475–76, **478–79**, 554; **19** 74
Nippon Onkyo, **II** 118
Nippon Paint Co., Ltd., **11** 252
Nippon Pelnox Corp., **III** 715
Nippon Phonogram, **23** 390
Nippon Polaroid Kabushiki Kaisha, **III** 608; **7** 437; **18** 570
Nippon Pulp Industries, **IV** 321
Nippon Rayon, **V** 387
Nippon Sangyo Co., Ltd., **IV** 475
Nippon Sanso Corp., **I** 359; **16** 486, 488
Nippon Seiko K.K., III 589–90, 595; **47** 278
Nippon Sekiyu Co. *See* Nippon Oil Company, Limited.
Nippon Sheet Glass Company, Limited, III 714–16
Nippon Shinpan Company, Ltd., II 436–37, 442; **8** 118
Nippon Silica Kogyo Co., **III** 715
Nippon Soda, **II** 301
Nippon Soken, **III** 592
Nippon Steel Chemical Co., **10** 439
Nippon Steel Corporation, I 466, 493–94, 509; **II** 300, 391; **IV** 116, 130, **156–58**, 184, 212, 228, 298; **6** 274; **14** 369; **17 348–51 (upd.)**, 556; **19** 219; **24** 324–25, 370
Nippon Suisan Kaisha, Limited, II 552–53
Nippon Tar, **I** 363
Nippon Telegraph and Telephone Corporation, II 51, 62; **III** 139–40; **V 305–07**; **7** 118–20; **10** 119; **13** 482; **16** 224; **21** 330; **25** 301; **27** 327, 365; **50** 129; **51 271–75 (upd.)**
Nippon Television, **7** 249; **9** 29
Nippon Tire Co., Ltd. *See* Bridgestone Corporation.
Nippon Trust Bank Ltd., **II** 405; **15** 42
Nippon Typewriter, **II** 459
Nippon Victor (Europe) GmbH, **II** 119
Nippon Wiper Blade Co., Ltd., **III** 592
Nippon Yusen Kabushiki Kaisha, IV 713; **V 481–83**; **6** 398
Nippon Yusoki Company, Ltd., **13** 501
Nippondenso Co., Ltd., III 591–94, 637–38. *See also* DENSO Corporation.
NIPSCO Industries, Inc., 6 532–33
Nishi Taiyo Gyogyo Tosei K.K., **II** 578
Nishikawaya Co., Ltd., **V** 209
Nishimbo Industries Inc., **IV** 442
Nishizono Ironworks, **III** 595
NiSource, Inc., **38** 81
Nissan Construction, **V** 154
Nissan Motor Acceptance Corporation, **22** 207
Nissan Motor Co., Ltd., I 9–10, **183–84**, 207, 494; **II** 118, 292–93, 391; **III** 485, 517, 536, 579, 591, 742, 750; **IV** 63; **7** 111, 120, 219; **9** 243, 340–42; **10** 353; **11** 50–51, **350–52 (upd.)**; **16** 167; **17** 556; **23** 338–40, 289; **24** 324; **27** 203; **34** 133, **303–07 (upd.)**
Nissan Trading Company, Ltd., **13** 533
Nisshin Chemical Industries, **I** 397
Nisshin Chemicals Co., **II** 554

Nisshin Flour Milling Company, Ltd., II 554
Nisshin Pharaceutical Co., II 554
Nisshin Steel Co., Ltd., I 432; IV 130, 159–60; 7 588
Nissho Iwai K.K., I 432, 509–11; IV 160, 383; V 373; 6 386; 8 75, 392; 15 373; 25 449; 27 107; 36 345
Nissho Kosan Co., III 715
Nissui. *See* Nippon Suisan Kaisha.
Nitches, Inc., 53 245–47
Nitratos de Portugal, IV 505
Nitroglycerin AB, 13 22
Nitroglycerin Ltd., 9 380
Nittetsu Curtainwall Corp., III 758
Nittetsu Sash Sales Corp., III 758
Nitto Warehousing Co., I 507
Nittoku Metal Industries, Ltd., III 635
Nittsu. *See* Nippon Express Co., Ltd.
Niugini Mining Ltd., 23 42
Nixdorf Computer AG, I 193; II 279; III 109, 154–55; 12 162; 14 13, 169; 26 497
Nixdorf-Krein Industries Inc. *See* Laclede Steel Company.
Nizhny Novgorod Dairy, 48 438
NKK Corporation, IV 74, **161–63**, 212–13; V 152; 24 144; 28 322–26 (upd.); 53 170, 172
NL Industries, Inc., III 681; 10 434–36; 19 466–68
NLG. *See* National Leisure Group.
NLM City-Hopper, I 109
NLM Dutch Airlines, I 108
NLT Corp., II 122; III 194; 10 66; 12 546
NM Acquisition Corp., 27 346
NMC Laboratories Inc., 12 4
NMH Stahlwerke GmbH, IV 128
NMT. *See* Nordic Mobile Telephone.
NNG. *See* Northern Natural Gas Company.
No-Leak-O Piston Ring Company, 10 492
No-Sag Spring Co., 16 321
Noah's New York Bagels, 13 494. *See also* Einstein/Noah Bagel Corporation.
Nobel-Bozel, I 669
Nobel Drilling Corporation, 26 243
Nobel-Hoechst Chimie, I 669
Nobel Industries AB, I 351; 9 380–82; 16 69. *See also* Akzo Nobel N.V.
Nobel Learning Communities, Inc., 37 276–79
Noble Affiliates, Inc., 11 353–55; 18 366
Noble Broadcast Group, Inc., 23 293
Noble Roman's Inc., 14 351–53
Nobles Industries, 13 501
Noblesville Telephone Company, 14 258
Noblitt-Sparks Industries, Inc., 8 37–38
Nobody Beats the Wiz. *See* Cablevision Electronic Instruments, Inc.
Nocibé SA, 54 265–68
Nocona Belt Company, 31 435–36
Nocona Boot Co. *See* Justin Industries, Inc.
Noel Group, Inc., 24 286–88
Noell, IV 201
NOK Corporation, 41 170–72
Nokia Corporation, II 69–71; IV 296; 6 242; 15 125; 17 33, 352–54 (upd.); 18 74, 76; 19 226; 20 439; 38 328–31 (upd.); 47 318–19; 50 510; 52 317; 52 333
NOL Group. *See* Neptune Orient Lines Limited.
Noland Company, 35 311–14
Nolo.com, Inc., 49 288–91

Nolte Mastenfabriek B.V., 19 472
Noma Industries, 11 526
Nomai Inc., 18 510
Nomura Bank of Japan, 34 221
Nomura Holdings, Inc., 49 451
Nomura Securities Company, Limited, II 276, 326, 434, 438–41; 9 377, 383–86 (upd.); 39 109
Nomura Toys Ltd., 16 267; 43 232
Non-Fiction Book Club, 13 105
Non-Stop Fashions, Inc., 8 323
Nonpareil Refining Co., IV 488
Noodle Kidoodle, 16 388–91
Noodles & Company, Inc., 55 277–79
Noordwinning Group, IV 134
NOP Research Group, 28 501, 504
Nopco Chemical Co., IV 409; 7 308
Nopri, V 63–65
Nor-Am Agricultural Products, I 682
Nor-Cal Engineering Co. GmbH, 18 162
Nora Industrier A/S, 18 395
NORAND, 9 411
Noranda Inc., IV 164–66; 7 397–99 (upd.); 9 282; 26 363; 49 136
Norandex, 16 204
Norbro Corporation. *See* Stuart Entertainment Inc.
Norcast Manufacturing Ltd., IV 165
Norcen Energy Resources, Ltd., 8 347
Norcliff Thayer, III 66
Norco Plastics, 8 553
Norcon, Inc., 7 558–59
Norcore Plastics, Inc., 33 361
Nord-Aviation, I 45, 74, 82, 195; 7 10
Nord-Est, 54 391–92
Nordarmatur, I 198
Nordbanken, 9 382
Norddeutsche Affinerie, IV 141
Norddeutsche Bank A.G., II 279
Norddeutscher-Lloyd, I 542; 6 397–98
Nordea AB, 40 336–39
Nordfinanzbank, II 366
Nordic Baltic Holding. *See* Nordea AB.
Nordic Bank Ltd., II 366
Nordic Joint Stock Bank, II 302
Nordic Mobile Telephone, II 70
Nordica S.r.l., 10 151; 15 396–97; 53 24
NordicTrack, 10 215–17; 22 382–84; 38 238. *See also* Icon Health & Fitness, Inc.
Nordland Papier GmbH, IV 300, 302
Nordson Corporation, 11 356–58; 48 296–99 (upd.)
Nordstahl AG, IV 201
Nordstjernan, I 553–54
Nordstrom, Inc., V 156–58; 11 349; 13 494; 14 376; 17 313; 18 371–74 (upd.); 21 302; 22 173
Nordwestdeutsche Kraftwerke AG, III 466; V 698–700
Norelco, 17 110
Norelco Consumer Products Co., 12 439; 26 334–36
Norelec, 27 138
Norex Laboratories, I 699
Norex Leasing, Inc., 16 397
Norfolk Carolina Telephone Company, 10 202
Norfolk Southern Corporation, V 484–86; 6 436, 487; 12 278; 22 167; 29 358–61 (upd.)
Norfolk Steel, 13 97
Norge Co., III 439–40; 18 173–74; 43 163–64
Noric Corporation, 39 332

Norinchukin Bank, II 340–41
NORIS Bank GmbH, V 166
Norlin, 16 238–39
Norm Thompson Outfitters, Inc., 47 275–77
Norma Cie., III 622
Norman BV, 9 93; 33 78
Norman J. Hurll Group, III 673
Normandy Mining Ltd., 23 42
Normark Corporation. *See* Rapala-Normark Group, Ltd.
Norment Security Group, Inc., 51 81
Normond/CMS, 7 117
Norrell Corporation, I 696; 6 46; 23 431; 25 356–59
Norris Cylinder Company, 11 535
Norris Grain Co., 14 537
Norris Oil Company, 47 52
Norshield Corp., 51 81
Norsk Hydro ASA, 10 437–40; 35 315–19 (upd.); 36 322
Norsk Rengjorings Selskap a.s., 49 221
Norstan, Inc., 16 392–94
Norstar Bancorp, 9 229
Nortek, Inc., I 482; 14 482; 22 4; 26 101; 34 308–12; 37 331
Nortel Networks Corporation, 36 349–54 (upd.); 50 130
Nortex International, 7 96; 19 338
North & South Wales Bank, II 318; 17 323
North Advertising, Inc., 6 27
North African Petroleum Ltd., IV 455
North American Aviation, I 48, 71, 78, 81, 101; 7 520; 9 16; 10 163; 11 278, 427
North American Bancorp, II 192
North American Carbon, 19 499
North American Cellular Network, 9 322
North American Coal Corporation, 7 369–71
North American Company, 6 443, 552–53, 601–02
North American Dräger, 13 328
North American Energy Conservation, Inc., 35 480
North American Insurance Co., II 181
North American InTeleCom, Inc., IV 411
North American Life and Casualty Co., III 185, 306
North American Light & Power Company, V 609; 6 504–05; 12 541
North American Managers, Inc., III 196
North American Medical Management Company, Inc., 36 366
North American Mogul Products Co. *See* Mogul Corp.
North American Philips Corporation, II 79–80; 19 393; 21 520
North American Printed Circuit Corp., III 643
North American Printing Ink Company, 13 228
North American Reinsurance Corp., III 377
North American Rockwell Corp., 10 173
North American Systems, 14 230
North American Training Corporation. *See* Rollerblade, Inc.
North American Van Lines, I 278; 14 37. *See also* Allied Worldwide, Inc.
North American Watch Company. *See* Movado Group, Inc.
North Atlantic Energy Corporation, 21 411
North Atlantic Packing, 13 243

North British Insurance Co., **III** 234–35
North British Rubber Company, **20** 258
North Broken Hill Peko, **IV** 61
North Carolina Motor Speedway, Inc., **19** 294
North Carolina National Bank Corporation, **II** 336; **10** 425–27; **18** 518; **46** 52
North Carolina Natural Gas Corporation, **6** 578
North Carolina Shipbuilding Co., **13** 373
North Central Airlines, **I** 132
North Central Finance, **II** 333
North Central Financial Corp., **9** 475
North Central Utilities, Inc., **18** 405
North Cornwall China Clay Co., **III** 690
North East Insurance Company, **44** 356
North Eastern Bricks, **14** 249
North Eastern Coalfields Ltd., **IV** 48
The North Face, Inc., 8 169; **18 375–77**; **25** 206; **41** 103; **54** 400
North Fork Bancorporation, Inc., 44 33; **46 314–17**
North Goonbarrow, **III** 690
North Holland Publishing Co., **IV** 610
North New York Savings Bank, **10** 91
North of Scotland Bank, **II** 318; **17** 324
North of Scotland Hydro-Electric Board, **19** 389
North Pacific Paper Corp., **IV** 298
North Pacific Railroad, **II** 330
North Sea Ferries, **26** 241, 243
North Sea Oil and Gas, **10** 337
North Sea Sun Oil Co. Ltd., **IV** 550
North Shore Gas Company, **6** 543–44
North Shore Land Co., **17** 357
North Shore Medical Centre Pty, Ltd., **IV** 708
North Star Egg Case Company, **12** 376
North Star Marketing Cooperative, **7** 338
North Star Mill, **12** 376
North Star Steel Company, 13 138; **18 378–81**; **19** 380; **40** 87
North Star Transport Inc., **49** 402
North Star Tubes, **54** 391, 393
North Star Universal, Inc., **25** 331, 333
North Supply, **27** 364
The North West Company, Inc., 12 361–63; **25** 219–20
North-West Telecommunications, **6** 327
North West Water Group plc, 11 359–62. *See also* United Utilities PLC.
Northamptonshire Union Bank, **II** 333
Northbrook Corporation, **24** 32
Northbrook Holdings, Inc., **22** 495
Northcliffe Newspapers, **IV** 685; **19** 118
Northeast Airlines Inc., **I** 99–100; **6** 81
Northeast Federal Corp., **13** 468
Northeast Petroleum Industries, Inc., **11** 194; **14** 461
Northeast Savings Bank, **12** 31; **13** 467–68
Northeast Utilities, V 668–69; 13 182–84; **21** 408, 411; **48 303–06 (upd.)**; **55** 313, 316
Northeastern Bancorp of Scranton, **II** 342
Northeastern New York Medical Service, Inc., **III** 246
Northern Aluminum Co. Ltd., **IV** 9–10
Northern and Employers Assurance, **III** 235
Northern Arizona Light & Power Co., **6** 545
Northern Border Pipeline Co., **V** 609–10
Northern California Savings, **10** 340
Northern Crown Bank, **II** 344

Northern Dairies, **10** 441
Northern Development Co., **IV** 282
Northern Drug Company, **14** 147
Northern Electric Company. *See* Northern Telecom Limited.
Northern Energy Resources Company. *See* NERCO, Inc.
Northern Engineering Industries Plc, **21** 436
Northern Fibre Products Co., **I** 202
Northern Foods PLC, I 248; **II** 587; **10 441–43**
Northern Illinois Gas Co., **6** 529–31
Northern Indiana Power Company, **6** 556
Northern Indiana Public Service Company, **6** 532–33
Northern Infrastructure Maintenance Company, **39** 238
Northern Joint Stock Bank, **II** 303
Northern Leisure, **40** 296–98
Northern Light Electric Company, **18** 402–03
Northern National Bank, **14** 90
Northern Natural Gas Co., **V** 609–10; **49** 122
Northern Pacific Corp., **15** 274
Northern Pacific Railroad, **II** 278, 329; **III** 228, 282; **14** 168; **26** 451
Northern Paper, **I** 614
Northern Pipeline Construction Co., **19** 410, 412
Northern Rock plc, 33 318–21
Northern Star Co., **25** 332
Northern States Life Insurance Co., **III** 275
Northern States Power Company, V 670–72; **18** 404; **20 391–95 (upd.)**
Northern Stores, Inc., **12** 362
Northern Sugar Company, **11** 13
Northern Telecom Limited, II 70; **III** 143, 164; **V** 271; **V 308–10**; **6** 242, 307, 310; **9** 479; **10** 19, 432; **11** 69; **12** 162; **14** 259; **16** 392, 468; **17** 353; **18** 111; **20** 439; **22** 51; **25** 34; **27** 342; **47** 318–20. *See also* Nortel Networks Corporation.
Northern Trust Company, III 518; **9** 387–89; **22** 280
Northfield Metal Products, **11** 256
Northgate Computer Corp., **16** 196
Northland. *See* Scott Fetzer Company.
Northland Cranberries, Inc., 38 332–34
Northland Publishing, **19** 231
NorthPrint International, **22** 356
Northrop Corporation, I 47, 49, 55, 59, **76–77**, 80, 84, 197, 525; **III** 84; **9** 416, 418; **10** 162; **11** 164, 166, 269, **363–65 (upd.)**; **25** 316
Northrop Grumman Corporation, 41 43; **45 304–12 (upd.)**; **49** 444
Northrup King Co., **I** 672
NorthStar Computers, **10** 313
Northwest Airlines Inc., I 42, 64, 91, 97, 100, 104, **112–14**, 125, 127; **6** 66, 74, 82 **103–05 (upd.)**, 123; **9** 273; **11** 266, 315; **12** 191, 487; **21** 141, 143; **22** 252; **26 337–40 (upd.)**, 441; **27** 20; **28** 226, 265–66; **30** 447; **31** 419–20; **33** 50–51, 302; **52** 90, 93. *See also* Mesaba Holdings, Inc.
Northwest Benefit Assoc., **III** 228
Northwest Engineering, **21** 502
Northwest Engineering Co. *See* Terex Corporation.
Northwest Express. *See* Bear Creek Corporation.

Northwest Industries, **I** 342; **II** 468 **8** 367; **25** 165–66. *See also* Chicago and North Western Holdings Corporation.
Northwest Instruments, **8** 519
Northwest Linen Co., **16** 228
Northwest Natural Gas Company, 45 313–15
Northwest Outdoor, **27** 280
Northwest Paper Company, **8** 430
Northwest Steel Rolling Mills Inc., **13** 97
Northwest Telecommunications Inc., **6** 598
Northwestern Bell Telephone Co., **V** 341; **25** 495
Northwestern Benevolent Society, **III** 228
NorthWestern Corporation, 37 280–83
Northwestern Engraving, **12** 25
Northwestern Expanded Metal Co., **III** 763
Northwestern Financial Corporation, **11** 29
Northwestern Industries, **III** 263
Northwestern Manufacturing Company, **8** 133
Northwestern Mutual Life Insurance Company, III 321–24, 352; **IV** 333; **45 316–21 (upd.)**; **46** 198; **52** 243–44
Northwestern National Bank, **16** 71
Northwestern National Insurance Co., **IV** 29
Northwestern National Life Insurance Co., **14** 233
Northwestern Public Service Company, **6** 524
Northwestern States Portland Cement Co., **III** 702
Northwestern Telephone Systems, **6** 325, 328
Norton Company, III 678; **8 395–97**; **16** 122; **22** 68; **26** 70
Norton Healthcare Ltd., **11** 208
Norton McNaughton, Inc., 25 245; **27 346–49**
Norton Opax PLC, **IV** 259; **34** 140
Norton Professional Books. *See* W.W. Norton & Company, Inc.
Norton Simon Industries, **I** 446; **IV** 672; **6** 356; **19** 404; **22** 513
Norwales Development Ltd., **11** 239
Norwalk Truck Lines, **14** 567
NORWEB plc, **13** 458; **24** 270
Norwegian Assurance, **III** 258
Norwegian Caribbean Line, **27** 90
Norwegian Globe, **III** 258
Norwegian Petroleum Consultants, **III** 499
Norweld Holding A.A., **13** 316
Norwest Bank, **19** 412
Norwest Corp., **16** 135
Norwest Mortgage Inc., **11** 29; **54** 124
Norwest Publishing, **IV** 661
Norwich & Peterborough Building Society, 55 280–82
Norwich-Eaton Pharmaceuticals, **III** 53; **8** 434; **26** 383
Norwich Pharmaceuticals, **I** 370–71; **9** 358
Norwich Union Fire Insurance Society, Ltd., **III** 242, 273, 404; **IV** 705
Norwich Winterthur Group, **III** 404
Norwood Company, **13** 168
Norwood Promotional Products, Inc., 26 341–43
Nostell Brick & Tile, **14** 249
Notre Capital Ventures II, L.P., **24** 117
Nottingham Manufacturing Co., **V** 357
Nouvelle Compagnie Havraise Pénninsulaire, **27** 514
Nouvelle Elastelle, **52** 100–01

Nouvelles Galeries Réunies, **10** 205; **19** 308; **27** 95

Nouvelles Messageries de la Presse Parisienne, **IV** 618

Nova Corporation, **18** 365–67; **24** 395; **49** 120–21

Nova Corporation of Alberta, **V** 673–75; **12** 364–66

Nova Information Systems, **24** 393

Nova Mechanical Contractors, **48** 238

Nova Pharmaceuticals, **14** 46

Nova Scotia Steel Company, **19** 186

NovaCare, Inc., **11** 366–68; **14** 233; **33** 185; **41** 194

Novacor Chemicals Ltd., **12** 364–66

Novaction Argentina SA, **48** 224

Novagas Clearinghouse Ltd., **18** 367; **49** 120

Novalta Resources Inc., **11** 441

Novamax Technologies Inc., **34** 209

Novanet Semiconductor, **36** 124

Novar plc, **49** 292–96 **(upd.)**

Novartis AG, **18** 51; **34** 284; **39** 304–10 **(upd.)**; **50** 58, 90; **55** 285

Novation, **53** 346–47

Novell, Inc., **6** 255–56, 260, **269–71**; **9** 170–71; **10** 232, 363, 473–74, 558, 565; **11** 59, 519–20; **12** 335; **13** 482; **15** 131, 133, 373, 492; **16** 392, 394; **20** 237; **21** 133–34; **23** 359–62 **(upd.)**; **25** 50–51, 117, 300, 499; **33** 113, 115; **34** 442–43; **36** 80; **38** 418–19

Novello and Co., **II** 139; **24** 193

Novellus Systems, Inc., **18** 382–85

Noven Pharmaceuticals, Inc., **55** 283–85

Novgorodnefteprodukt, **48** 378

Novo Industri A/S, **I** 658–60, 697

Novobord, **49** 353

Novotel. See Accor SA.

NOVUM. See Industrie Natuzzi S.p.A.

NOVUS Financial Corporation, **33** 314

NOW. See National Organization for Women, Inc.

Nowell Wholesale Grocery Co., **II** 681

Nowsco Well Services Ltd., **25** 73

Nox Ltd., **I** 588

Noxell Corporation, **III** 53; **8** 434; **26** 384

NPC International, Inc., **40** 340–42

NPD Group, **13** 4

NPD Trading (USA), Inc., **13** 367

NPR. See National Public Radio, Inc.

NPS Waste Technologies, **13** 366

NRC Handelsblad BV, **53** 273

NRG Energy, Inc., **11** 401; **50** 363

NS. See Norfolk Southern Corporation.

NS Group, **31** 287

NS Petites Inc., **8** 323

NSG Information System Co., **III** 715

NSK. See Nippon Seiko K.K.

NSK Ltd., **42** 384

NSK-Warner, **14** 64

NSMO. See Nederlandsche Stoomvart Maatschappij Oceaan.

NSN Network Services, **23** 292, 294

NSP. See Northern States Power Company.

NSU Werke, **10** 261

NTC Publishing Group, **22** 519, 522

NTCL. See Northern Telecom Limited.

NTN Corporation, **III** 595–96, 623; **28** 241; **47** 278–81 **(upd.)**

NTRON, **11** 486

NTT. See Nippon Telegraph and Telephone Corp.

NTTPC. See Nippon Telegraph and Telephone Public Corporation.

NU. See Northeast Utilities.

Nu-Era Gear, **14** 64

Nu-kote Holding, Inc., **18**

Nu Skin Enterprises, Inc., **27** 350–53; **31** 327 **386–89**

Nuclear Electric, **6** 453; **11** 399–401; **12** 349; **13** 484; **50** 280–81, 361–63

Nuclear Power International, **19** 166

Nucoa Butter Co., **II** 497

Nucor Corporation, **7** 400–02; **13** 143, 423; **14** 156; **18** 378–80; **19** 380; **21** 392–95 **(upd.)**; **26** 407; **52** 326

Nucorp Energy, **II** 262, 620

NUG Optimus Lebensmittel-Einzelhandelgesellschaft mbH, **V** 74

Nugget Polish Co. Ltd., **II** 566

NUMAR Corporation, **25** 192

Numerax, Inc., **IV** 637

NUMMI. See New United Motor Manufacturing, Inc.

Nuovo Pignone, **IV** 420–22

NUR Touristic GmbH, **V** 100–02

Nurad, **III** 468

Nurotoco Inc. See Roto-Rooter Service Company.

Nursefinders, **6** 10

Nutmeg Industries, Inc., **17** 513

Nutraceutical International Corporation, **37** 284–86

NutraSweet Company, **II** 463, 582; **8** 398–400; **26** 108; **29** 331

Nutrena, **II** 617; **13** 137

Nutri-Foods International, **18** 467–68

Nutri/System Inc., **29** 258

Nutrilite Co., **III** 11–12

NutriSystem, **10** 383; **12** 531

Nutrition for Life International Inc., **22** 385–88

Nuveen. See John Nuveen Company.

NV Dagblad De Telegraaf. See N.V. Holdingmaatschappij De Telegraaf.

NVIDIA Corporation, **54** 269–73

NVR L.P., **8** 401–03

NWA, Inc. See Northwest Airlines Corporation.

NWK. See Nordwestdeutsche Kraftwerke AG.

NWL Control Systems, **III** 512

NWS BANK plc, **10** 336–37

Nya AB Atlas, **III** 425–26

NYC OTB Racing Network, **51** 269

Nydqvist & Holm, **III** 426

Nyhamms Cellulosa, **IV** 338

NYK. See Nihon Yusen Kaisha, Nippon Yusen Kabushiki Kaisha; Nippon Yusen Kaisha.

Nyland Mattor, **25** 464

NYLCare Health Plans, **45** 293–94

Nylex Corp., **I** 429

NYLife Care Health Plans, Inc., **17** 166

Nylon de Mexico, S.A., **19** 10, 12

NYMAGIC, Inc., **41** 284–86

Nyman & Schultz Affarsresbyraer A.B., **I** 120

Nymofil, Ltd., **16** 297

NYNEX Corporation, **V** 311–13; **6** 340; **11** 19, 87; **13** 176; **25** 61–62, 102; **26** 520; **43** 445

NYRG. See New York Restaurant Group, Inc.

Nyrop, **I** 113

Nysco Laboratories, **III** 55

NYSE. See New York Stock Exchange.

NYSEG. See New York State Electric and Gas Corporation.

NZI Corp., **III** 257

O&K Rolltreppen, **27** 269

O&Y. See Olympia & York Developments Ltd.

O.B. McClintock Co., **7** 144–45

O.G. Wilson, **16** 560

O. Kraft & Sons, **12** 363

O.N.E. Color Communications L.L.C., **29** 306

O-Pee-Chee, **34** 447–48

O.S. Designs Inc., **15** 396

O.Y.L. Industries Berhad, **26** 3, 5

Oahu Railway & Land Co., **I** 565–66

Oak Creek Homes Inc., **41** 18

Oak Farms Dairies, **II** 660

Oak Harbor Freight Lines, Inc., **53** 248–51

Oak Hill Investment Partners, **11** 490

Oak Hill Sportswear Corp., **17** 137–38

Oak Industries Inc., **III** 512; **21** 396–98

Oak Technology, Inc., **22** 389–93

OakBrook Investments, LLC, **48** 18

Oakley, Inc., **18** 390–93; **49** 297–302 **(upd.)**

OakStone Financial Corporation, **11** 448

Oaktree Capital Management, **30** 185

OakTree Health Plan Inc., **16** 404

Oakville, **7** 518

Oakwood Homes Corporation, **13** 155; **15** 326–28

OAO Gazprom, **42** 261–65

OAO LUKOIL, **40** 343–46

OAO NK YUKOS, **47** 282–85; **49** 304

OAO Siberian Oil Company (Sibneft), **49** 303–06

OAO Tatneft, **45** 322–26

OASIS, **IV** 454

Oasis Group P.L.C., **10** 506

OASYS, Inc., **18** 112

Obayashi Corp., **44** 154

ÖBB. See Österreichische Bundesbahnen GmbH.

Obbola Linerboard, **IV** 339

Oberheim Corporation, **16** 239

Oberland, **16** 122

Oberrheinische Bank, **II** 278

Oberschlesische Stickstoff-Werge AG, **IV** 229

Oberusel AG, **III** 541

Obi, **23** 231

Object Design, Inc., **15** 372

O'Boy Inc. See Happy Kids Inc.

O'Brien Kreitzberg, Inc., **25** 130

Observer AB, **55** 286–89

Obunsha, **9** 29

Occidental Bank, **16** 497; **50** 497

Occidental Chemical Corporation, **19** 414; **45** 254

Occidental Insurance Co., **III** 251

Occidental Life Insurance Company, **I** 536–37; **13** 529; **26** 486–87; **41** 401

Occidental Overseas Ltd., **11** 97; **50** 179

Occidental Petroleum Corporation, **I** 527; **II** 432, 516; **IV** 264, 312, 392, 410, 417, 453–54, 467, **480–82**, 486, 515–16; **7** 376; **8** 526; **12** 100; **19** 268; **25** 360–63 **(upd.)**; **29** 113; **31** 115, 456; **37** 309, 311; **45** 252, 254

Occidental Petroleum Great Britain Inc., **21** 206

Océ N.V., 24 360–63
Ocean, **III** 234
Ocean Combustion Services, **9** 109
Ocean Drilling and Exploration Company. *See* ODECO.
Ocean Group plc, 6 415–17. *See also* Exel plc.
Ocean Pacific Apparel Corporation, **51** 321
Ocean Reef Management, **19** 242, 244
Ocean Salvage and Towage Co., **I** 592
Ocean Scientific, Inc., **15** 380
Ocean Specialty Tankers Corporation, **22** 275
Ocean Spray Cranberries, Inc., 7 403–05; **10** 525; **19** 278; **25** 364–67 (upd.); **38** 334
Ocean Steam Ship Company. *See* Malaysian Airlines System BHD.
Ocean Systems Inc., **I** 400
Ocean Transport & Trading Ltd., **6** 417
Oceania Football Confederation, **27** 150
Oceanic Contractors, **III** 559
Oceanic Properties, **II** 491–92
Oceanic Steam Navigation Company, **19** 197; **23** 160
Oceans of Fun, **22** 130
Ocelet Industries Ltd., **25** 232
O'Charley's Inc., 19 286–88
OCL. *See* Overseas Containers Ltd.
Ocoma Foods, **II** 584
Octagon Group Ltd., **51** 173
Octane Software, **49** 124
Octek, **13** 235
Octel Communications Corp., III 143; **14** 217, **354–56; 16** 394
Octel Messaging, 41 287–90 (upd.)
Octopus Publishing, **IV** 667; **17** 398
Oculinum, Inc., **10** 48
Odakyu Electric Railway Company Limited, V 487–89
Odam's and Plaistow Wharves, **II** 580–81
Odd Job Trading Corp., **29** 311–12
Odd Lot Trading Company, **V** 172–73
Odda Smelteverk A/S, **25** 82
Odeco Drilling, Inc., **7** 362–64; **11** 522; **12** 318; **32** 338, 340
Odegard Outdoor Advertising, L.L.C., **27** 280
Odeon Theatres Ltd., **II** 157–59
Odetics Inc., 14 357–59
Odhams Press Ltd., **IV** 259, 666–67; **7** 244, 342; **17** 397–98
ODL, Inc., 55 290–92
ODM, **26** 490
ODME. *See* Toolex International N.V.
O'Donnell-Usen Fisheries, **II** 494
Odwalla, Inc., 31 349–51
Odyssey Holdings, Inc., **18** 376
Odyssey Partners Group, **II** 679; **V** 135; **12** 55; **13** 94; **17** 137; **28** 218
Odyssey Press, **13** 560
Odyssey Publications Inc., **48** 99
OEC Medical Systems, Inc., 27 354–56
Oelwerken Julius Schindler GmbH, **7** 141
OEN Connectors, **19** 166
Oertel Brewing Co., **I** 226; **10** 180
Oësterreichischer Phönix in Wien, **III** 376
Oetker Group, **I** 219
Off the Rax, **II** 667; **24** 461
Off Wall Street Consulting Group, **42** 313
Office Depot Incorporated, 8 404–05; **10** 235, 497; **12** 335; **13** 268; **15** 331; **18** 24, 388; **22** 154, 412–13; **23** 363–65 (upd.); **27** 95; **34** 198; **43** 293

Office Mart Holdings Corporation, **10** 498
Office National du Crédit Agricole, **II** 264
Office Systems Inc., **15** 407
The Office Works, Inc., **13** 277; **25** 500
OfficeMax Inc., 8 404; **15** 329–31; **18** 286, 388; **20** 103; **22** 154; **23** 364–65; **43** 291–95 (upd.)
Official Airline Guides, Inc., **IV** 605, 643; **7** 312, 343; **17** 399
Officine Alfieri Maserati S.p.A., 11 104; **13** 28, **376–78**
Offset Gerhard Kaiser GmbH, **IV** 325
The Offshore Company, **III** 558; **6** 577; **37** 243
Offshore Food Services Inc., **I** 514
Offshore Logistics, Inc., 37 287–89
Offshore Transportation Corporation, **11** 523
Ogden Corporation, I 512–14, 701; **6** 151–53, 600; **7** 39; **25** 16; **27** 21, 196; **41** 40–41; **43** 217
Ogden Food Products, **7** 430
Ogden Gas Co., **6** 568
Ogden Ground Services, **39** 240, 242
Ogilvie Flour Mills Co., **I** 268; **IV** 245; **25** 9, 281
Ogilvy & Mather, **22** 200
Ogilvy Group Inc., I 20, 25–27, 31, 37, 244; **6** 53; **9** 180. *See also* WPP Group.
Oglebay Norton Company, 17 355–58
Oglethorpe Power Corporation, 6 537–38
O'Gorman and Cozens-Hardy, **III** 725
Ogura Oil, **IV** 479
Oh la la!, **14** 107
Ohbayashi Corporation, I 586–87
The Ohio Art Company, 14 360–62
Ohio Ball Bearing. *See* Bearings Inc.
Ohio Barge Lines, Inc., **11** 194
Ohio Bell Telephone Company, 14 363–65; **18** 30
Ohio Boxboard Company, **12** 376
Ohio Brass Co., **II** 2
Ohio Casualty Corp., III 190; **11** 369–70
Ohio Crankshaft Co. *See* Park-Ohio Industries Inc.
Ohio Edison Company, V 676–78
Ohio Electric Railway Co., **III** 388
Ohio Mattress Co., **12** 438–39
Ohio Oil Co., **IV** 365, 400, 574; **6** 568; **7** 551; **50** 502
Ohio Pizza Enterprises, Inc., **7** 152
Ohio Power Shovel, **21** 502
Ohio Pure Foods Group, **II** 528
Ohio River Company, **6** 487
Ohio-Sealy Mattress Mfg. Co., **12** 438–39
Ohio Valley Electric Corporation, **6** 517
Ohio Ware Basket Company, **12** 319
Ohlmeyer Communications, **I** 275; **26** 305
Ohlsson's Cape Breweries, **I** 287–88; **24** 449
OHM Corp., **17** 553
Ohmeda. *See* BOC Group plc.
Ohmite Manufacturing Co., **13** 397
Ohrbach's Department Store, **I** 30
Ohta Keibin Railway Company, **6** 430
ÖIAG, **IV** 234
Oil Acquisition Corp., **I** 611
Oil and Natural Gas Commission, IV 440–41, **483–84**
Oil and Solvent Process Company, **9** 109
Oil City Oil and Grease Co., **IV** 489
Oil Co. of Australia, **III** 673
Oil Distribution Public Corp., **IV** 434

Oil-Dri Corporation of America, 20 396–99
Oil Drilling, Incorporated, **7** 344
Oil Dynamics Inc., **43** 178
Oil Equipment Manufacturing Company, **16** 8
Oil India Ltd., **IV** 440, 483–84
Oil Shale Corp., **IV** 522; **7** 537
Oilfield Industrial Lines Inc., **I** 477
Oilfield Service Corp. of America, **I** 342
Oita Co., **III** 718
Oji Paper Co., Ltd., I 506, 508; **II** 326; **IV** 268, 284–85, 292–93, 297–98, 320–22, 326–27
OJSC Wimm-Bill-Dann Foods, 48 436–39
OK Bazaars, **I** 289; **24** 450
OK Turbines, Inc., **22** 311
Okadaya Co. Ltd., **V** 96
O'Keefe Marketing, **23** 102
Oki Electric Industry Company, Limited, II 68, 72–74; **15** 125; **21** 390
Okidata, **9** 57; **18** 435
Okinoyama Coal Mine, **III** 759
Oklahoma Airmotive, **8** 349
Oklahoma Entertainment, Inc., **9** 74
Oklahoma Gas and Electric Company, 6 539–40; **7** 409–11
Oklahoma Oil Co., **I** 31
Oklahoma Publishing Company, **11** 152–53; **30** 84
Okonite, **I** 489
Okura & Co., Ltd., I 282; **IV** 167–68
Oland & Sons Limited, **25** 281
Olathe Manufacturing, **26** 494
OLC. *See* Orient Leasing Co., Ltd.
Olcott & McKesson, **I** 496
Old America Stores, Inc., 17 359–61
Old Colony Envelope Co., **32** 345–46
Old Colony Trust Co., **II** 207; **12** 30
Old Country Buffet Restaurant Co. (OCB). *See* Buffets, Inc.
Old Dominion Power Company, **6** 513, 515
Old El Paso, **I** 457; **14** 212; **24** 140–41
Old Harbor Candles, **18** 68
Old Kent Financial Corp., 11 371–72
Old Line Life Insurance Co., **III** 275
Old Mutual, **IV** 23, 535
Old National Bancorp, 14 529; **15** 332–34
Old Navy Clothing Company, **18** 193; **55** 157
Old Quaker Paint Company, **13** 471
Old Republic International Corp., 11 373–75
Old Spaghetti Factory International Inc., 24 364–66
Old Stone Trust Company, **13** 468
Oldach Window Corp., **19** 446
Oldham Estate, **IV** 712
Oldover Corp., **23** 225
Olds Motor Vehicle Co., **I** 171; **10** 325
Olds Oil Corp., **I** 341
Ole's Innovative Sports. *See* Rollerblade, Inc.
Olean Tile Co., **22** 170
Oleochim, **IV** 498–99
OLEX. *See* Deutsche BP Aktiengesellschaft.
Olex Cables Ltd., **10** 445
Olin Corporation, I 318, 330, **379–81**, 434, 695; **III** 667; **IV** 482; **8** 23, 153; **11**

420; **13 379–81 (upd.)**; **16** 68, 297; **32** 319

Olinkraft, Inc., **II** 432; **III** 708–09; **11** 420; **16** 376

Olins Rent-a-Car, **6** 348

Olive Garden Italian Restaurants, **10** 322, 324; **16** 156–58; **19** 258; **35** 83

Oliver Rubber Company, **19** 454, 456

Olivetti S.p.A., 34 316–20 (upd.); **38** 300

Olivine Industries, Inc., **II** 508; **11** 172; **36** 255

Olmstead Products Co., **23** 82

OLN. *See* Outdoor Life Network.

Olofsson, **I** 573

Olohana Corp., **I** 129; **6** 129

Olsen Dredging Co., **III** 558

Olson & Wright, **I** 120; **34** 398

Olsonite Corp., **I** 201

Olsten Corporation, 6 41–43; **9** 327; **29 362–65 (upd.)**; **49** 265. *See also* Adecco S.A.

Olveh, **III** 177–79

Olympia & York Developments Ltd., IV 245, 247, 712, **720–21**; **6** 478; **8** 327; **9 390–92 (upd.)**; **25** 11–12; **30** 108

Olympia Arenas, Inc., **7** 278–79; **24** 294

Olympia Brewing, **I** 260; **11** 50

Olympia Entertainment, **37** 207

Olympia Floor & Tile Co., **IV** 720

Olympiaki, **III** 401

Olympic Airways, **II** 442

Olympic Courier Systems, Inc., **24** 126

Olympic Fastening Systems, **III** 722

Olympic Insurance Co., **26** 486

Olympic Packaging, **13** 443

Olympus Communications L.P., **17** 7

Olympus Optical Company, Ltd., **15** 483

Olympus Sport, **V** 177–78

Olympus Symbol, Inc., **15** 483

OM Group, Inc., 17 362–64

Omaha Cold Store Co., **II** 571

Omaha Public Power District, **29** 353

Oman Oil Refinery Co., **IV** 516

Omega Gas Company, **8** 349

Omega Gold Mines, **IV** 164

Omega Protein Corporation, **25** 546

O'Melveny & Myers, 37 290–93

Omex Corporation, **6** 272

OMI Corporation, **IV** 34; **9** 111–12; **22** 275

Omlon, **II** 75

Ommium Française de Pétroles, **IV** 559

Omnes, **17** 419

Omni Construction Company, Inc., **8** 112–13

Omni Hearing Aid Systems, **I** 667

Omni Hotels Corp., 12 367–69

Omni-Pac, **12** 377

Omni Products International, **II** 420

Omni Services, Inc., **51** 76

Omnibus Corporation, **9** 283

Omnicad Corporation, **48** 75

Omnicare, Inc., 13 150; **49 307–10**

Omnicom Group Inc., I 28–32, 33, 36; **14** 160; **22 394–99 (upd.)**; **23** 478; **43** 410. *See also* TBWA Worldwide.

Omnipoint Communications Inc., **18** 77

OmniSource Corporation, 14 366–67

OmniTech Consulting Group, **51** 99

Omnitel Pronto Italia SpA, **38** 300

Omron Corporation, 28 331–35 (upd.); **53** 46

Omron Tateisi Electronics Company, II 75–77; **III** 549

ÖMV Aktiengesellschaft, IV 234, 454, **485–87**

On Assignment, Inc., 20 400–02

On Command Video Corp., **23** 135

On Cue, **9** 360

On-Line Software International Inc., **6** 225

On-Line Systems. *See* Sierra On-Line Inc.

Onan Corporation, **8** 72

Onbancorp Inc., **11** 110

Once Upon A Child, Inc., **18** 207–8

Oncogen, **III** 18

Ondal Industrietechnik GmbH, **III** 69; **48** 423

Ondulato Imolese, **IV** 296; **19** 226

1-800-FLOWERS, Inc., 26 344–46; **28** 137

1-800-Mattress. *See* Dial-A-Mattress Operating Corporation.

One For All, **39** 405

One Hundred Thirtieth National Bank, **II** 291

One Hundredth Bank, **II** 321

One Price Clothing Stores, Inc., 20 403–05

O'Neal, Jones & Feldman Inc., **11** 142

OneBeacon Insurance Group LLC, **48** 431

Oneida Bank & Trust Company, **9** 229

Oneida County Creameries Co., **7** 202

Oneida Gas Company, **9** 554

Oneida Ltd., 7 406–08; **31 352–355 (upd.)**

ONEOK Inc., 7 409–12

Onex Corporation, 16 395–97; **22** 513; **24** 498; **25** 282; **50** 275

OneZero Media, Inc., **31** 240

Onitsuka Tiger Co., **V** 372; **8** 391; **36** 343–44

Online Distributed Processing Corporation, **6** 201

Online Financial Communication Systems, **11** 112

Only One Dollar, Inc. *See* Dollar Tree Stores, Inc.

Onoda Cement Co., Ltd., I 508; **III 717–19**

Onomichi, **25** 469

OnResponse.com, Inc., **49** 433

Onsale Inc., **31** 177

Onstead Foods, **21** 501

OnTarget Inc., **38** 432

Ontario Hydro Services Company, 6 541–42; **9** 461; **32 368–71 (upd.)**

Ontario Power Generation, **49** 65, 67

Ontel Corporation, **6** 201

OnTrak Systems Inc., **31** 301

Onyx Software Corporation, 53 252–55

Oode Casting Iron Works, **III** 551

O'okiep Copper Company, Ltd., **7** 385–86

Opel. *See* Adam Opel AG.

Open Board of Brokers, **9** 369

Open Cellular Systems, Inc., **41** 225–26

Open Market, Inc., **22** 522

OpenTV, Inc., **31** 330–31

Operadora de Bolsa Serfin. *See* Grupo Financiero Serfin, S.A.

Operon Technologies, Inc., **39** 335

Opinion Research Corporation, 35 47; **46 318–22**

Opp and Micolas Mills, **15** 247–48

Oppenheimer. *See* Ernest Oppenheimer and Sons.

Oppenheimer & Co., **17** 137; **21** 235; **22** 405; **25** 450

Opryland USA, **11** 152–53; **25** 403; **36** 229

Opsware Inc., 49 311–14

Optel Corp., **17** 331

OPTi Computer, **9** 116

Opti-Ray, Inc., **12** 215

Optical Radiation Corporation, **27** 57

Optilink Corporation, **12** 137

Optima Pharmacy Services, **17** 177

Optimum Financial Services Ltd., **II** 457

Option Care Inc., 48 307–10

Optische Werke G. Rodenstock, 44 319–23

OptiSystems Solutions Ltd., **55** 67

Opto-Electronics Corp., **15** 483

Optronics, Inc., **6** 247; **24** 234

Optus Communications, **25** 102

Optus Vision, **17** 150

Opus Group, 34 321–23

OPW, **III** 467–68

Oracle Corporation, 24 367–71 (upd.); **25** 34, 96–97, 499

Oracle Systems Corporation, 6 272–74; **10** 361, 363, 505; **11** 78; **13** 483; **14** 16; **15** 492; **18** 541, 543; **19** 310; **21** 86; **22** 154, 293

Orange and Rockland Utilities, Inc., **45** 116, 120

Orange Glo International, 53 256–59

Orange Julius of America, **10** 371, 373; **39** 232, 293

Orange Line Bus Company, **6** 604

Orange PLC, **24** 89; **38** 300

Orb Books. *See* Tom Doherty Associates Inc.

Orb Estates, **54** 366, 368

Orbis Entertainment Co., **20** 6

Orbis Graphic Arts. *See* Anaheim Imaging.

Orbital Engine Corporation Ltd., **17** 24

Orbital Sciences Corporation, 22 400–03

Orchard Supply Hardware Stores Corporation, 17 365–67; **25** 535

Orcofi, **III** 48

OrderTrust LLP, **26** 440

Ore and Chemical Corp., **IV** 140

Ore-Ida Foods Incorporated, II 508; **11** 172; **12** 531; **13 382–83**; **36** 254, 256

Orebehoved Fanerfabrik, **25** 464

Oregon Ale and Beer Company, **18** 72; **50** 112

Oregon Chai, Inc., 49 315–17

Oregon Craft & Floral Supply, **17** 322

Oregon Cutting Systems, **26** 119

Oregon Dental Service Health Plan, Inc., 51 276–78

Oregon Metallurgical Corporation, 20 406–08

Oregon Pacific and Eastern Railway, **13** 100

Oregon Steel Mills, Inc., 14 368–70; **19** 380

O'Reilly Automotive, Inc., 26 347–49

Orenda Aerospace, **48** 274

Orford Copper Co., **IV** 110

Organic Valley (Coulee Region Organic Produce Pool), 53 260–62

Organización Soriana, S.A. de C.V., 35 320–22

Organon, **I** 665

Orico Life Insurance Co., **48** 328

Oriel Foods, **II** 609

Orient, **21** 122

Orient Express Hotels Inc., **29** 429–30
Orient Glass, **III** 715
Orient Leasing. *See* Orix Corporation.
Orient Overseas, **18** 254
Oriental Brewery Co., Ltd., **21** 320
Oriental Cotton Trading. *See* Tomen
    Corporation.
Oriental Land Co., Ltd., **IV** 715
Oriental Precision Company, **13** 213
Oriental Trading Corp., **22** 213
Oriental Yeast Co., **17** 288
Origin Energy Limited, **43** 75. *See also*
    Boral Limited.
Origin Systems Inc., **10** 285
Origin Technology, **14** 183
Original Arizona Jean Company. *See* J.C.
    Penney Company, Inc.
Original Cookie Co., **13** 166. *See also* Mrs.
    Fields' Original Cookies, Inc.
Original Musical Instrument Company
    (O.M.I.), **16** 239
Original Wassertragers Hummel, **II** 163
Origins Natural Resources Inc., **30** 190
Orinoco Oilfields, Ltd., **IV** 565
Orion, **III** 310
Orion Bank Ltd., **II** 271, 345, 385
Orion Capital Corporation, **55** 331
Orion Healthcare Ltd., **11** 168
Orion Personal Insurances Ltd., **11** 168
Orion Pictures Corporation, **II** 147; **6**
    167–70; **7** 336; **14** 330, 332; **25** 326,
    328–29; **31** 100
Orit Corp., **8** 219–20
ORIX Corporation, **II 442–43**, 259, 348;
    44 324–26 (upd.)
Orkem, **IV** 547, 560; **21** 205
Orkin Pest Control, **11** 431–32, 434
Orkla A/S, 18 394–98; **25** 205–07; **36**
    266
Orlimar Golf Equipment Co., **45** 76
Orm Bergold Chemie, **8** 464
Ormco Corporation, **14** 481
ÖROP, **IV** 485–86
Orowheat Baking Company, **10** 250
La Oroya, **22** 286
ORSCO, Inc., **26** 363
Ortho Diagnostic Systems, Inc., **10** 213; **22**
    75
Ortho Pharmaceutical Corporation, **III** 35;
    8 281; **10** 79–80; **30** 59–60
Orthodontic Centers of America, Inc., 35
    323–26
Orthopedic Services, Inc., **11** 366
Ortloff Engineers, Ltd., **52** 103–05
Orval Kent Food Company, Inc., **7** 430
Orville Redenbacher/Swiss Miss Foods
    Co., **17** 241
The Orvis Company, Inc., 28 336–39
Oryx Energy Company, **IV** 550; **7**
    413–15
Osaka Aluminium Co., **IV** 153
Osaka Beer Brewing Co., **I** 220, 282; **20**
    28
Osaka Electric Tramway, **V** 463
Osaka Gas Co., Ltd., V 679–81
Osaka General Bussan, **IV** 431
Osaka Iron Works, **III** 513
Osaka Marine and Fire Insurance Co., **III**
    367
Osaka Nomura Bank, **II** 276, 438–39
Osaka North Harbor Co. Ltd., **I** 518
Osaka Shinyo Kumiai, **15** 495
Osaka Shosen Kaisha, **I** 503; **V** 473–74,
    481–82

Osaka Spinning Company, **V** 387
Osaka Sumitomo Marine and Fire
    Insurance Co., Ltd., **III** 367
Osaka Textile Co., **I** 506
Osakeyhtiö Gustaf Cederberg & Co., **IV**
    301
Osakeyhtiö T. & J. Salvesen, **IV** 301
Osborn Group Inc., **48** 256
Osborne Books, **IV** 637
Oscar Mayer Foods Corp., **II** 532; **7** 274,
    276; **12** 123, **370–72**
Osco Drug, **II** 604–05
OSF Japan Ltd., **24** 365
Oshawa Group Limited, **II 649–50**
OshKosh B'Gosh, Inc., **9 393–95**; **42**
    266–70 (upd.)
Oshkosh Electric Power, **9** 553
Oshkosh Gas Light Company, **9** 553
Oshkosh Truck Corporation, **7 416–18**;
    14 458
Oshman's Sporting Goods, Inc., **16** 560;
    17 368–70; **27** 7
OSi Specialties, Inc., **16** 543; **36** 148–49
Osiris Holding Company, **16** 344
OSK. *See* Osaka Shosen Kaisha.
Osmonics, Inc., **18 399–401**
Oster. *See* Sunbeam-Oster.
Österreichische Brau-Beteiligungs AG. *See*
    BBAG Österreichische Brau-Beteiligungs
    AG.
Österreichische Bundesbahnen GmbH, **6**
    418–20
Österreichische Creditanstalt-Wiener
    Bankverein, **IV** 230
Österreichische Elektrowerke, **IV** 230
Österreichische Industrieholding AG, **IV**
    486–87
Österreichische Industriekredit AG, **IV** 230
Österreichische Länderbank, **II** 239; **23** 37
Österreichische Luftverkehrs AG. *See*
    Austrian Airlines AG.
Österreichische Mineralölverwaltung AG,
    IV 485
Österreichische Post- und
    Telegraphenverwaltung, **V 314–17**
Österreichische Stickstoffswerke, **IV** 486
Ostrada Yachts, **55** 54, 56
Ostravar A.S., **38** 77
Ostschweizer Zementwerke, **III** 701
O'Sullivan Industries Holdings, Inc., **34**
    313–15
Osuuskunta Metsäliito, **IV** 316
Oswald Tillotson Ltd., **III** 501; **7** 207
Otagiri Mercantile Co., **11** 95
Otake Paper Manufacturing Co., **IV** 327
OTC, **10** 492
Other Options, **29** 400
Otis Company, **6** 579
Otis Elevator Company, Inc., **I** 85, **III**
    467, 663; **13 384–86**; **27** 267, 268; **29**
    422; **39 311–15 (upd.)**
Otis Engineering Corp., **III** 498
Otis Spunkmeyer, Inc., **28 340–42**
Otosan, **I** 167, 479–80; **54** 196–97
OTP, Incorporated, **48** 446
OTR Express, Inc., **25 368–70**
Otsego Falls Paper Company, **8** 358
Ott and Brewer Company, **12** 312
Ottawa Fruit Supply Ltd., **II** 662
Ottaway Newspapers, Inc., **15 335–37**
Otter Tail Power Company, **18 402–05**;
    37 282
Otter-Westelaken, **16** 420; **43** 308

Otto Bremer Foundation. *See* Bremer
    Financial Corp.
Otto-Epoka mbH, **15** 340
Otto Sumisho Inc., **V** 161
Otto Versand GmbH & Co., **V 159–61**;
    10 489–90; **15 338–40 (upd.)**; **27** 427,
    429; **31** 188; **34 324–28 (upd.)**; **36** 177,
    180
Ottumwa Daily Courier, **11** 251
Ourso Investment Corporation, **16** 344
Outback Steakhouse, Inc., **12 373–75**; **34**
    329–32 (upd.)
Outboard Marine Corporation, **III** 329,
    597–600; **8** 71; **16** 383; **20 409–12**
    (upd.); **26** 494; **42** 45; **43** 287; **45** 174
Outdoor Channel, Inc. *See* Global
    Outdoors, Inc.
The Outdoor Group Limited, **39** 58, 60
Outdoor Systems, Inc., **25 371–73**; **27**
    278–80; **48** 217
Outdoor World. *See* Bass Pro Shops, Inc.
The Outdoorsman, Inc., **10** 216
Outlet, **6** 33
Outlet Retail Stores, Inc., **27** 286
Outlook Group Corporation, **37 294–96**
Outlook Window Partnership, **19** 446
Outokumpu Metals Group. *See* OM Group,
    Inc.
Outokumpu Oyj, **IV** 276; **38 335–37**
Ovako Oy, **III** 624
Ovation, **19** 285
OVC, Inc., **6** 313
Overhill Corporation, **10** 382; **51 279–81**
Overland Energy Company, **14** 567
Overland Mail Co., **II** 380–81, 395; **10** 60;
    12 533
Overland Western Ltd., **27** 473
Overnite Transportation Co., **14 371–73**;
    28 492
Overseas Air Travel Ltd., **I** 95
Overseas Containers Ltd., **6** 398, 415–16
Overseas Petroleum and Investment Corp.,
    IV 389
Overseas Shipholding Group, Inc., **11**
    376–77
Overseas Telecommunications
    Commission, **6** 341–42
Overseas Telecommunications, Inc., **27** 304
Ovox Fitness Clubs, **46** 432
Owatonna Tool Co., **I** 200; **10** 493
Owen Healthcare, **50** 122
Owen Owen, **37** 8
Owen Steel Co. Inc., **15** 117
Owens & Minor, Inc., **10** 143; **16**
    398–401
Owens Corning Corporation, **I** 609; **III**
    683, **720–23**; **8** 177; **13** 169; **20 413–17**
    (upd.); **25** 535; **30** 283; **35** 98–99
Owens-Corning Fiberglas, **44** 127
Owens-Illinois Inc., **I** 609–11, 615; **II**
    386; **III** 640, 720–21; **IV** 282, 343; **9**
    261; **16** 123; **22** 254; **24** 92; **26 350–53**
    (upd.); **42** 438; **43** 188; **49** 253
Owens Yacht Company, **III** 443; **22** 115
Owensboro Municipal Utilities, **11** 37
Owosso Corporation, **29 366–68**
Oxdon Investments, **11** 664
Oxfam America, **13** 13
Oxford-AnsCo Development Co., **12** 18
Oxford Biscuit Fabrik, **II** 543
Oxford Bus Company, **28** 155–56
Oxford Chemical Corp., **II** 572
Oxford Financial Group, **22** 456
Oxford Health Plans, Inc., **16 402–04**

Oxford Industries, Inc., 8 406–08; 24 158
Oxford Instruments, **III** 491
Oxford Learning Centres, **34** 105
Oxford Paper Co., **I** 334–35; **10** 289
Oxford Realty Financial Group, Inc., **49** 26
Oxford University Press, **23** 211
Oxirane Chemical Co., **IV** 456
OXO International, **16** 234
Oxy Petrochemicals Inc., **IV** 481
Oxy Process Chemicals, **III** 33
Oxycal Laboratories Inc., **46** 466
OxyChem, **11** 160
Oxygen Media Inc., **28** 175; **51** 220
Ozalid Corporation, **I** 337–38; **IV** 563; **22** 226
Ozark Airlines, **I** 127; **12** 489
Ozark Automotive Distributors, **26** 347–48
Ozark Pipe Line Corp., **IV** 540
Ozark Utility Company, **6** 593; **50** 38
OZM. *See* OneZero Media, Inc.

P&C Foods Inc., 8 409–11; 13 95, 394
P&C Groep N.V., **46** 344
P & F Industries, Inc., 45 327–29
P&F Technologies Ltd., **26** 363
P&G. *See* Procter & Gamble Company.
P&L Coal Holdings Corporation, **45** 333
P & M Manufacturing Company, **8** 386
P & O. *See* Peninsular & Oriental Steam Navigation Company.
P&O Nedlloyd, **26** 241, 243
P.A. Bergner & Company, **9** 142; **15** 87–88
P.A. Geier Company. *See* Royal Appliance Manufacturing Company.
P.A.J.W. Corporation, **9** 111–12
P.A. Rentrop-Hubbert & Wagner Fahrzeugausstattungen GmbH, **III** 582
P.C. Hanford Oil Co., **IV** 368
P.C. Richard & Son Corp., 23 372–74
P. D'Aoust Ltd., **II** 651
P.D. Associated Collieries Ltd., **31** 369
P.D. Kadi International, **I** 580
P.D. Magnetics, **I** 330; **8** 153
P.E.C. Israel Economic Corporation, **24** 429
P.F. Chang's China Bistro, Inc., 37 297–99
P.G. Realty, **III** 340
P.H. Glatfelter Company, 8 412–14; 30 349–52 (upd.)
P.Ink Press, **24** 430
P.L. Porter Co., **III** 580
P.R. Mallory, **9** 179
P.S.L. Food Market, Inc., **22** 549
P. Sharples, **III** 418
P.T. Bridgeport Perkasa Machine Tools, **17** 54
P.T. Dai Nippon Printing Indonesia, **IV** 599
P.T. Darya-Varia Laboratoria, **18** 180
P.T. Gaya Motor, **23** 290
P.T. Muaratewe Spring, **III** 581
P.T. Semen Nusantara, **III** 718
P.T. Unitex, **53** 344
P.W. Huntington & Company, **11** 180
P.W.J. Surridge & Sons, Ltd., **43** 132
Pabst Brewing Company, **I** 217, 255; **10** 99; **18** 502; **50** 114
Pac-Am Food Concepts, **10** 178; **38** 102
Pac-Fab, Inc., **18** 161
PAC Insurance Services, **12** 175; **27** 258

PACCAR Inc., I 155, **185–86; 10** 280; **26 354–56 (upd.); 40** 135
Pace-Arrow, Inc., **III** 484; **22** 206
Pace Companies, **6** 149; **26** 221
PACE Entertainment Corp., **36** 423–24
Pace Express Pty. Ltd., **13** 20
Pace Foods Ltd., **26** 58
Pace Management Service Corp., **21** 91
PACE Membership Warehouse, Inc., **V** 112; **10** 107; **12** 50; **18** 286; **40** 387; **47** 209
Pace Pharmaceuticals, **16** 439
Pacer International, Inc., 54 274–76
Pacer Technology, 40 347–49
Pacer Tool and Mold, **17** 310
Pachena Industries Ltd., **6** 310
Pacific Advantage, **43** 253
Pacific Aero Products Co., **I** 47; **10** 162
Pacific Air Freight, Incorporated, **6** 345
Pacific Air Transport, **I** 47, 128; **6** 128; **9** 416
Pacific Alaska Fuel Services, **6** 383
Pacific and European Telegraph Company, **25** 99
Pacific Bell, **V** 318–20; **11** 59; **12** 137; **21** 285; **22** 19; **37** 126
Pacific Brick Proprietary, **III** 673
Pacific-Burt Co., Ltd., **IV** 644
Pacific Car & Foundry Company. *See* PACCAR Inc.
Pacific Cascade Land Co., **IV** 255
Pacific Coast Co., **IV** 165
Pacific Coast Condensed Milk Co., **II** 486
Pacific Coast Oil Co., **IV** 385
Pacific Communication Sciences, **11** 57
Pacific Dry Dock and Repair Co., **6** 382
Pacific Dunlop Limited, 10 444–46
Pacific Electric Heating Co., **II** 28; **12** 194
Pacific Electric Light Company, **6** 565; **50** 365
Pacific Enterprises, V 682–84; 12 477.
See also Sempra Energy.
Pacific Express Co., **II** 381
Pacific Finance Corp., **I** 537; **9** 536; **13** 529; **26** 486
Pacific Fur Company, **25** 220
Pacific Gamble Robinson, **9** 39
Pacific Gas and Electric Company, I 96; **V** 685–87; **11** 270; **12** 100, 106; **19** 411; **25** 415. *See also* PG&E Corporation.
Pacific Glass Corp., **48** 42
Pacific Guardian Life Insurance Co., **III** 289
Pacific Health Beverage Co., **I** 292
Pacific Home Furnishings, **14** 436
Pacific Indemnity Corp., **III** 220; **14** 108, 110; **16** 204
Pacific Integrated Healthcare, **53** 7
Pacific Lighting Corp., **IV** 492; **V** 682–84; **12** 477; **16** 496; **50** 496. *See also* Sempra Energy.
Pacific Linens, **13** 81–82
Pacific Link Communication, **18** 180
Pacific Lumber Company, **III** 254; **8** 348–50
Pacific Magazines and Printing, **7** 392
Pacific Mail Steamship Company, **6** 353
Pacific Manifolding Book/Box Co., **IV** 644
Pacific Media K.K., **18** 101
Pacific Metal Bearing Co., **I** 159
Pacific Monolothics Inc., **11** 520
Pacific National Bank, **II** 349

Pacific National Insurance Co. *See* TIG Holdings, Inc.
Pacific Natural Gas Corp., **9** 102
Pacific Northern, **6** 66
Pacific Northwest Bell Telephone Co., **V** 341; **25** 495
Pacific Northwest Laboratories, **10** 139
Pacific Northwest Pipeline Corporation, **9** 102–104, 540; **12** 144
Pacific Northwest Power Company, **6** 597
Pacific Pearl, **I** 417
Pacific Petroleums Ltd., **IV** 494; **9** 102
Pacific Plastics, Inc., **48** 334
Pacific Platers Ltd., **IV** 100
Pacific Power & Light Company. *See* PacifiCorp.
Pacific Pride Bakeries, **19** 192
Pacific Recycling Co. Inc., **IV** 296; **19** 226; **23** 225
Pacific Refining Co., **IV** 394–95
Pacific Resources Inc., **IV** 47; **22** 107
Pacific Sentinel Gold Corp., **27** 456
Pacific-Sierra Research, **I** 155
Pacific Silver Corp., **IV** 76
Pacific/Southern Wine & Spirits, **48** 392
Pacific Southwest Airlines Inc., **I** 132; **6** 132
Pacific Steel Ltd., **IV** 279; **19** 154
Pacific Stock Exchange, **48** 226
Pacific Sunwear of California, Inc., 28 343–45; 47 425
Pacific Telecom, Inc., V 689; **6 325–28; 25** 101; **54** 62
Pacific Telesis Group, V 318–20; **6** 324; **9** 321; **11** 10–11; **14** 345, 347; **15** 125; **25** 499; **26** 520; **29** 387; **47** 318
Pacific Teletronics, Inc., **7** 15
Pacific Towboat. *See* Puget Sound Tug and Barge Company.
Pacific Trading Co., Ltd., **IV** 442
Pacific Trail Inc., **17** 462; **29** 293, 295–96
Pacific Western Extruded Plastics Company, **17** 441. *See also* PW Eagle Inc.
Pacific Western Oil Co., **IV** 537
Pacific Wine Co., **18** 71; **50** 112
PacifiCare Health Systems, Inc., III 85; **11 378–80; 25** 318
PacifiCorp, Inc., V 688–90; **6** 325–26, 328; **7** 376–78; **26 357–60 (upd.); 27** 327, 483, 485; **32** 372; **49** 363, 366
Package Products Company, Inc., **12** 150
Packaged Ice, Inc., **21** 338; **26** 449
Packaging Corporation of America, I 526; **12 376–78**, 397; **16** 191; **51 282–85 (upd.)**
Packard Bell Electronics, Inc., I 524; **II** 86; **10** 521, 564; **11** 413; **13 387–89**, 483; **21** 391; **23** 471
Packard Motor Co., **I** 81; **8** 74; **9** 17
Packer's Consolidated Press, **IV** 651
Packerland Packing Company, **7** 199, 201
Pacolet Manufacturing Company, **17** 327
Pact, **50** 175
PacTel. *See* Pacific Telesis Group.
Paddington Corp., **I** 248
Paddock Publications, Inc., 53 263–65
PAFS. *See* Pacific Alaska Fuel Services.
Page, Bacon & Co., **II** 380; **12** 533
Page Boy Inc., **9** 320
PageAhead Software, **15** 492
Pageland Coca-Cola Bottling Works, **10** 222
PageMart Wireless, Inc., **18** 164, 166

Paging Network Inc., 11 381–83; 39
24–25; **41** 266–67
Pagoda Trading Company, Inc., **V** 351,
353; **20** 86
Paid Prescriptions, **9** 346
Paige Publications, **18** 66
PaineWebber Group Inc., I 245; **II**
444–46, 449; **III** 409; **13** 449; **22** 352,
404–07 (upd.), 542; **25** 433
Painter Carpet Mills, **13** 169
Painton Co., **II** 81
PairGain Technologies, **36** 299
Paisley Products, **32** 255
La Paix, **III** 273
Pak-a-Sak, **II** 661
Pak-All Products, Inc., **IV** 345
Pak Arab Fertilizers Ltd., **IV** 364
Pak Mail Centers, **18** 316
Pak-Paino, **IV** 315
Pak Sak Industries, **17** 310; **24** 160
Pak-Well, **IV** 282; **9** 261
Pakhoed Holding, N.V., **9** 532; **26** 420; **41**
339–40
Pakistan International Airlines
Corporation, 46 323–26
Pakkasakku Oy, **IV** 471
Paknet, **11** 548
Pakway Container Corporation, **8** 268
PAL. *See* Philippine Airlines, Inc.
Pal Plywood Co., Ltd., **IV** 327
Palace Station Hotel & Casino. *See* Station
Casinos Inc.
Palais Royal, Inc., **24** 456
Palatine Insurance Co., **III** 234
Palco Industries, **19** 440
Pale Ski & Sports GmbH, **22** 461
Palestine Coca-Cola Bottling Co., **13** 163
PALIC. *See* Pan-American Life Insurance
Company.
Pall Corporation, 9 396–98
Palm Beach Holdings, **9** 157
Palm Harbor Homes, Inc., 39 316–18
Palm, Inc., 34 441, 445; **36 355–57; 38**
433; **49** 184; **54** 312
Palm Shipping Inc., **25** 468–70
Palmafina, **IV** 498–99
Palmax, **47** 153
Palmer Communications, **25** 418
Palmer G. Lewis Co., **8** 135
Palmer Tyre Ltd., **I** 428–29
Palmolive Co. *See* Colgate-Palmolive
Company.
Palo Alto Brewing, **22** 421
Palo Alto Products International, Inc., **29** 6
Palo Alto Research Center, **10** 510
Palomar Medical Technologies, Inc., 22
408–10; 31 124
PAM Group, **27** 462
Pamida Holdings Corporation, 15
341–43
Pamour Porcupine Mines, Ltd., **IV** 164
Pampa OTT, **27** 473
The Pampered Chef, Ltd., 18 406–08
Pamplemousse, **14** 225
Pamplin Corp. *See* R.B. Pamplin Corp.
Pan-Alberta Gas Ltd., **16** 11
Pan American Banks, **II** 336
Pan-American Life Insurance Company,
48 311–13
Pan American Petroleum & Transport Co.,
IV 368–70
Pan American World Airways, Inc., I
20, 31, 44, 64, 67, 89–90, 92, 99,
103–04, 112–13, **115–16,** 121, 124,

126, 129, 132, 248, 452, 530, 547–48;
III 536; **6** 51, 65–66, 71, 74–76, 81–82,
103–05, 110–11, 123, 129–30; **9** 231,
417; **10** 561; **11** 266; **12** 191, **379–81**
(upd.), 419; **13** 19; **14** 73; **24** 397; **29**
189; **36** 52–53; **39** 120; **50** 523
Pan European Publishing Co., **IV** 611
Pan Geo Atlas Corporation, **18** 513
Pan Ocean, **IV** 473
Pan Pacific Fisheries, **24** 114
Panacon Corporation, **III** 766; **22** 545
Panagra, **I** 547–48; **36** 53; **50** 523
Panalpina World Transport (Holding)
Ltd., 47 286–88; 49 81–82
Panama Refining and Petrochemical Co.,
IV 566
Panamerican Beverages, Inc., 47 289–91;
54 74
PanAmSat Corporation, 18 211, 213; **46**
327–29; 54 157
Panarctic Oils, **IV** 494
Panasonic, **9** 180; **10** 125; **12** 470; **43** 427
Panatech Research & Development Corp.,
III 160
Panavia Aircraft GmbH, **24** 84, 86–87
Panavia Consortium, **I** 74–75
Panavision Inc., 24 372–74; 28 249; **38**
295
PanCanadian Petroleum Ltd., **27** 217; **45**
80
Pancho's Mexican Buffet, Inc., 46
330–32
Panda Management Company, Inc., 35
327–29
Pandair, **13** 20
Pandel, Inc., **8** 271
Pandick Press Inc., **23** 63
PanEnergy Corporation, **27** 128, 131
Panera Bread Company, 44 186, **327–29**
Panerai, **27** 489
Panhandle Eastern Corporation, I 377,
569; **IV** 425; **V 691–92; 10** 82–84; **11**
28; **14** 135; **17** 21
Panhandle Oil Corp., **IV** 498
Panhandle Power & Light Company, **6** 580
Panhard, **I** 194
Panhard-Levassor, **I** 149
Panificadora Bimbo, **19** 191
AB Pankakoski, **IV** 274
Panmure Gordon, **II** 337
Pannill Knitting Company, **13** 531
Panocean Storage & Transport, **6** 415, 417
Panola Pipeline Co., **7** 228
Panosh Place, **12** 168
Pansophic Systems Inc., **6** 225
Pantepec Oil Co., **IV** 559, 570; **24** 520
Pantera Energy Corporation, **11** 27
Pantheon Books, **13** 429; **31** 376
Panther, **III** 750
Panther Express International Company, **6**
346
Pantone Inc., 53 266–69
The Pantry, Inc., 36 358–60
Pantry Pride Inc., **I** 668; **II** 670, 674; **III**
56; **23** 407–08
Pants Corral, **II** 634
Papa Aldo's Pizza. *See* Papa Murphy's
International, Inc.
Papa John's International, Inc., 15
344–46; 16 447; **24** 295
Papa Murphy's International, Inc., 54
277–79
Pape and Co., Ltd., **10** 441
Papelera del Besos, **53** 24

Papelera General, S.A. de C.V., **39** 188
Papelera Navarra, **IV** 295; **19** 226
Papeleria Calparsoro S.A., **IV** 325
Papeles Venezolanos C.A., **17** 281
Paper Direct, **37** 107–08
The Paper Factory of Wisconsin, Inc., **12**
209
Paper Magic Group, **35** 130–31
Paper Makers Chemical Corp., **I** 344
Paper Recycling International, **V** 754
Paper Software, Inc., **15** 322
Paper Stock Dealers, Inc., **8** 476
Paperituote Oy, **IV** 347–48
PaperMate, **III** 28; **23** 54
Paperwork Data-Comm Services Inc., **11**
64
Papeterie de Pont Sainte Maxence, **IV** 318
Papeteries Aussedat, **III** 122
Papeteries Boucher S.A., **IV** 300
Les Papeteries de la Chapelle-Darblay, **IV**
258–59, 302, 337
Papeteries de Lancey, 23 366–68
Papeteries de Malaucene S.A.S., **52**
300–01
Les Papeteries du Limousin, **19** 227
Papeteries Navarre, **III** 677; **16** 121
Papetti's Hygrade Egg Products, Inc., 25
332–33; **39 319–21**
Papierfabrik Salach, **IV** 324
Papierwaren Fleischer, **IV** 325
Papierwerke Waldhof-Aschaffenburg AG,
IV 323–24
Papyrus Design Group, **IV** 336; **15** 455
Para-Med Health Services, **6** 181–82
Parachute Press, **29** 426
Parade Gasoline Co., **7** 228
Paradigm Entertainment, **35** 227
Paradise Creations, **29** 373
Paradise Island Resort and Casino. *See* Sun
International Hotels Limited.
Paradise Music & Entertainment, Inc.,
42 271–74
Paradyne, **22** 19
Paragon Communications, **44** 372
Paragon Corporate Holdings, Inc., **IV** 552;
28 6, 8
Paragon Vineyard Company, **36** 114
Paragren Technologies Inc., **38** 432
Parallax Software Inc., **38** 70
Paramax, **6** 281–83
Parametric Technology Corp., 16
405–07
Parametrics Corp., **25** 134
Paramount Communications Inc., **16** 338;
19 403–04; **28** 296
Paramount Fire Insurance Co., **26** 486
Paramount Oil Company, **18** 467
Paramount Paper Products, **8** 383
Paramount Pictures Corporation, I
451–52; **II** 129, 135, 146–47, **154–56,**
171, 173, 175, 177; **IV** 671–72, 675; **7**
528; **9** 119, 428–29; **10** 175; **12** 73, 323;
19 404; **21** 23–25; **23** 503; **24** 327; **25**
88, 311, 327–29, 418; **31** 99; **35** 279
Parashop SA, **48** 279
Parasitix Corporation. *See* Mycogen
Corporation.
Parasole Restaurant Holdings, Inc., **38** 117
Paravision International, **III** 48; **8** 343
Parcelforce, **V** 498
PARCO Co., Ltd., **V** 184–85; **42** 341
Parcor, **I** 676
ParentWatch, **34** 105
Parfums Chanel, **12** 57

Parfums Christian Dior, **I** 272
Parfums Rochas S.A., **I** 670; **III** 68; **8** 452; **48** 422
Parfums Stern, **III** 16
Pargas, **I** 378
Paribas. *See* Banque de Paris et des Pays-Bas, BNP Paribas Group; Compagnie Financiere de Paribas.
Paridoc and Giant, **12** 153
Paris Bourse, **34** 13
Paris Corporation, 22 411–13
Paris Group, **17** 137
Paris Playground Equipment, **13** 319
Parisian, Inc., 14 374–76; 19 324–25; 41 343–44
Park Acquisitions, Inc., **38** 308
Park-Brannock Shoe Company, **48** 69
Park Consolidated Motels, Inc., **6** 187; **14** 105; **25** 306
Park Corp., 22 414–16
Park Drop Forge Co. *See* Park-Ohio Industries Inc.
Park Hall Leisure, **II** 140; **24** 194
Park Inn International, **11** 178
Park-Ohio Industries Inc., 17 371–73
Park Ridge Corporation, **9** 284
Park Tower Hotel Co. Ltd., **55** 375
Park View Hospital, Inc., **III** 78
Parkdale State Bank, **25** 114
Parkdale Wines, **I** 268; **25** 281
Parke-Bernet, **11** 453
Parke, Davis & Co. *See* Warner-Lambert Co.
Parker, **III** 33
Parker Appliance Co., **III** 601–02
Parker Brothers, **II** 502; **III** 505; **10** 323; **16** 337; **21** 375; **25** 489; **43** 229, 232
Parker Drilling Company, 28 346–48
Parker Drilling Company of Canada, **9** 363
Parker-Hannifin Corporation, III 601–03; **21** 108; **24 375–78 (upd.)**
Parker Pattern Works Co., **46** 293
Parker Pen Corp., **III** 218; **9** 326; **52** 287
Parker's Pharmacy, Inc., **15** 524
Parkinson Cowan, **I** 531
Parkmount Hospitality Corp., **II** 142
Parks-Belk Co., **19** 324
Parks Box & Printing Co., **13** 442
Parkway Distributors, **17** 331
Parmalat Finanziaria SpA, 50 343–46
Parr's Bank, **II** 334; **III** 724
Parson and Hyman Co., Inc., **8** 112
Parsons Brinckerhoff, Inc., 34 333–36
The Parsons Corporation, III 749; **8** 415–17
Parsons International Trading Business, **27** 195
Parsons Place Apparel Company, **8** 289
Partech, **28** 346, 348
Partek Corporation, **11** 312; **52** 250
Partex, **IV** 515
Parthénon, **27** 10
Parthenon Insurance Co., **III** 79
Participating Annuity Life Insurance Co., **III** 182; **21** 14
La Participation, **III** 210
Partlow Corporation, **7** 116
Partnership Pacific Ltd., **II** 389
Partouche SA. *See* Groupe Partouche SA.
Parts Industries Corp., **III** 494–95
Parts Plus, **26** 348
Party City Corporation, 54 280–82
PartyLite Gifts, Inc., **18** 67, 69
Pascagoula Lumber Company, **28** 306

Pascale & Associates, **12** 476
Paschen Contractors Inc., **I** 585
Pasha Pillows, **12** 393
Pasminco, **IV** 61
Pasqua Inc., **28** 64
Pass & Seymour, **21** 348–49
Pasta Central, **49** 60
Patagonia, **16** 352; **18** 376; **21** 193; **25** 206. *See also* Lost Arrow Inc.
Patak Spices Ltd., **18** 247
Pataling Rubber Estates Syndicate, **III** 697, 699
Patch Rubber Co., **19** 277–78
Patchoque-Plymouth Co., **IV** 371
PATCO. *See* Philippine Airlines, Inc.
Patent Arms Manufacturing Company, **12** 70
Patent Nut & Bolt Co., **III** 493
Patent Slip and Dock Co., **I** 592
La Paternelle, **III** 210
Paterno Wines International, **48** 392
Paternoster Stores plc, **V** 108; **24** 269
Paterson Candy Ltd., **22** 89
Paterson, Simons & Co., **I** 592
Path-Tek Laboratories, Inc., **6** 41
Pathé Cinéma, **6** 374
Pathe Communications Co., **IV** 676; **7** 529; **25** 329
Pathé Fréres, **IV** 626; **19** 203
Pathé SA, 29 369–71. *See also* Chargeurs International.
Pathmark Stores, Inc., II 672–74; **9** 173; **15** 260; **18** 6; **19** 479, 481; **23 369–71;** **33** 436
PathoGenesis Corporation, **36** 119
Patience & Nicholson, **III** 674
Patient Care, Inc., **13** 150
Patil Systems, **11** 56
Patina Oil & Gas Corporation, 24 379–81
Patino N.V., **17** 380
Patrick Industries, Inc., 30 342–45
Patrick Raulet, S.A., **36** 164
Patricof & Company, **24** 45
Patriot American Hospitality, Inc., **21** 184
Patriot Co., **IV** 582
Patriot Life Insurance Co., **III** 193
PATS Inc., **36** 159
Patterson Dental Co., 19 289–91
Patterson Industries, Inc., **14** 42
Patterson-UTI Energy, Inc., 55 293–95
Pattison & Bowns, Inc., **IV** 180
Patton Electric Company, Inc., **19** 360
Patton Paint Company. *See* PPG Industries, Inc.
Paul A. Brands, **11** 19
Paul Andra KG, **33** 393
Paul Boechat & Cie, **21** 515
Paul C. Dodge Company, **6** 579
Paul Davril, Inc., **25** 258
Paul H. Rose Corporation, **13** 445
Paul Harris Stores, Inc., 15 245; **18** 409–12
Paul, Hastings, Janofsky & Walker LLP, **27** 357–59
Paul Koss Supply Co., **16** 387
Paul Marshall Products Inc., **16** 36
Paul Masson, **I** 285
Paul Ramsay Group, **41** 323
The Paul Revere Corporation, 12 382–83; **52** 379
Paul Revere Insurance, **34** 433
Paul Wahl & Co., **IV** 277

Paul, Weiss, Rifkind, Wharton & **Garrison, 47 292–94**
Paul Williams Copier Corp., **IV** 252; **17** 28
Paul Wurth, **IV** 25
Paulaner Brauerei GmbH & Co. KG, 35 330–33
Pauls Plc, **III** 699
Pavallier, **18** 35
Pavex Construction Company. *See* Granite Rock Company.
Pawnee Industries, Inc., **19** 415
Paxall, Inc., **8** 545
Paxson Communications Corporation, **33 322–26**
Pay 'N Pak Stores, Inc., **9 399–401; 16** 186–88
Pay 'n Save Corp., **12** 477; **15** 274; **17** 366
Pay Less, **II** 601, 604
Paychex, Inc., 15 347–49; 46 333–36 (upd.)
PayConnect Solutions, **47** 39
Payless Cashways, Inc., 11 384–86; 13 274; **44 330–33 (upd.)**
Payless DIY, **V** 17, 19
PayLess Drug Stores, **12** 477–78; **18** 286; **22** 39
Payless ShoeSource, Inc., V 132, 135; **13** 361; **18 413–15; 26** 441
PBF Corp. *See* Paris Corporation.
PBL. *See* Publishing and Broadcasting Ltd.
PBS. *See* Public Broadcasting Stations.
PC Connection, Inc., 37 300–04
PC Globe, Inc., **13** 114
PC Realty, Canada Ltd., **III** 340
PCA. *See* Packaging Corporation of America.
PCA-Budafok Paperboard Ltd., **12** 377
pcBoat.com, **37** 398
PCI Acquisition, **11** 385
PCI/Mac-Pak Group, **IV** 261
PCI NewCo Inc., **36** 159
PCI Services, Inc. *See* Cardinal Health, Inc.
PCL Construction Group Inc., 50 347–49
PCL Industries Ltd., **IV** 296; **19** 226
PCM Uitgevers NV, 53 270–73
PCO, **III** 685
PCS. *See* Potash Corp. of Saskatchewan Inc.
PCS Health Systems Inc., **12** 333; **47** 115, 235–36
PCX. *See* Pacific Stock Exchange.
PDA Engineering, **25** 305
PDA Inc., **19** 290
PDI, Inc., 49 25; **52 272–75**
PDO. *See* Petroleum Development Oman.
PDQ Transportation Inc., **18** 226
PDS Gaming Corporation, 44 334–37
PDV America, Inc., **31** 113
PDVSA. *See* Petróleos de Venezuela S.A.
Peabody Coal Company, I 559; **III** 248; **IV** 47, 169–71, 576; **7** 387–88; **10** 447–49
Peabody Energy Corporation, 45 330–33 (upd.)
Peabody Holding Company, Inc., IV 19, **169–72; 6** 487; **7** 209
Peabody, Riggs & Co., **II** 427
Peace Arch Entertainment Group Inc., **51 286–88**
Peaches Entertainment Corporation, **24** 502
Peachtree Doors, **10** 95

Peachtree Federal Savings and Loan Association of Atlanta, **10** 92
Peachtree Software Inc., **18** 364
Peak Audio Inc., **48** 92
Peak Oilfield Service Company, **9** 364
The Peak Technologies Group, Inc., 14 377–80
Peakstone, **III** 740
Peapod, Inc., 22 522; **30 346–48**
Pearce-Uible Co., **14** 460
Pearl Health Services, **I** 249
Pearl Package Co., Ltd., **IV** 327
Pearle Vision, Inc., I 688; **12** 188; **13 390–92; 14** 214; **23** 329; **24** 140; **34** 179
Pearson plc, IV 611, 652, **657–59; 14** 414; **25** 283, 285; **32** 355; **38** 402; **46 337–41 (upd.)**
Peasant Restaurants Inc., **30** 330
Pease Industries, **39** 322, 324
Peat Marwick. *See* KPMG Peat Marwick.
Peaudouce, **IV** 339
Peavey Electronics Corporation, II 494; **12** 81; **16 408–10**
Peavey Paper Mills, Inc., **26** 362
Pebble Beach Corp., **II** 170
PEC Plastics, **9** 92
Pechelbronn Oil Company, **III** 616; **17** 416–17
Pechenganickel MMC, **48** 300
Pechiney S.A., I 190, 341; **IV** 12, 59, 108, **173–75,** 560; **V** 605; **12** 253–54; **14** 216; **26** 403; **31** 11; **45 334–37 (upd.)**
Péchiney-Saint-Gobain, **I** 389; **III** 677; **16** 121
PECO Energy Company, 11 387–90. *See also* Exelon Corporation.
Pediatric Services of America, Inc., 31 356–58
Pedigree Petfoods, **22** 298
Peebles Inc., 16 411–13; 43 296–99 (upd.)
Peek & Cloppenburg KG, 46 342–45
Peekskill Chemical Works. *See* Binney & Smith Inc.
Peel-Conner Telephone Works, **II** 24
Peerless, **III** 467; **8** 74; **11** 534
Peerless Gear & Machine Company, **8** 515
Peerless Industries, Inc., **III** 569; **20** 360; **39** 264
Peerless Paper Co., **IV** 310; **19** 266
Peerless Pump Co., **I** 442
Peerless Spinning Corporation, **13** 532
Peerless Systems, Inc., **17** 263
Peet's Coffee & Tea, Inc., 13 493; **18** 37; **38 338–40**
Pegulan, **I** 426–27; **25** 464
PEI. *See* Process Engineering Inc.
Peine, **IV** 201
Pekema Oy, **IV** 470–71
Peko-Wallsend Ltd., **13** 97
Pel-Tex Oil Co., **IV** 84; **7** 188
Pelican and British Empire Life Office, **III** 372
Pelican Homestead and Savings, **11** 107
Pelican Insurance Co., **III** 349
Pelican Life Assurance, **III** 371–72
Pelikan Holding AG, **18** 388
Pella Corporation, 10 95; **12 384–86; 22** 346; **39 322–25 (upd.)**
Pelmorex, Inc., **52** 402
Pelto Oil Corporation, **14** 455; **44** 362
PEM International Ltd., **28** 350
Pemco Aviation Group Inc., 54 283–86
Pemex. *See* Petróleos Mexicanos.

Pen Computing Group, **49** 10
Peñarroya, **IV** 107–08
Penauille Polyservices SA, 49 318–21
Penda Corp., **19** 415
Pendexcare Ltd., **6** 181
Pendle Travel Services Ltd. *See* Airtours Plc.
Pendleton Woolen Mills, Inc., 42 275–78
Penford Corporation, 55 296–99
Pengrowth Gas Corp., **25** 232
The Penguin Group, **46** 337
Penguin Publishing Co. Ltd., **IV** 585, 659
Penhaligon's, **24** 237
Peninsula Stores, Ltd. *See* Lucky Stores, Inc.
The Peninsular and Oriental Steam Navigation Company, II 296; **III** 521–22, 712; **V 490–93; 22** 444; **26** 241, 243; **37** 137; **38 341–46 (upd.)**
Peninsular and Oriental Steam Navigation Company (Bovis Division), I 588–89
Peninsular Portland Cement, **III** 704
Peninsular Power, **6** 602
Peninsular Railroad Company, **17** 440
Penn Advertising, **27** 280
Penn-American Refining Co., **IV** 489
Penn Central Corp., **I** 435; **II** 255; **IV** 576; **10** 71, 73, 547; **17** 443
Penn Champ Co., **9** 72
Penn Controls, **III** 535–36; **26** 229
Penn Corp., **13** 561
Penn Cress Ice Cream, **13** 393
Penn Engineering & Manufacturing Corp., 28 349–51
Penn Fuel Co., **IV** 548
Penn Health, **III** 85
Penn National Gaming, Inc., 33 327–29
Penn Square Bank, **II** 248, 262
Penn-Texas Corporation, **I** 434; **12** 71
Penn Traffic Company, 8 409–10; 13 95, 393–95
Penn-Western Gas and Electric, **6** 524
Pennaco Hosiery, Inc., **12** 93
PennEnergy, **55** 302
Penney's. *See* J.C. Penney Company, Inc.
Pennington Drug, **III** 10
Pennon Group Plc, 45 338–41
Pennroad Corp., **IV** 458
Pennsalt Chemical Corp., **I** 383
Pennsylvania Blue Shield, III 325–27
Pennsylvania Coal & Coke Corp., **I** 434
Pennsylvania Coal Co., **IV** 180
Pennsylvania Electric Company, **6** 535; **27** 182
Pennsylvania Farm Bureau Cooperative Association, **7** 17–18
Pennsylvania Gas and Water Company, **38** 51
Pennsylvania General Fire Insurance Assoc., **III** 257
Pennsylvania General Insurance Company, **48** 431
Pennsylvania Glass Sand Co., **I** 464; **11** 198
Pennsylvania House, Inc., **10** 324; **12** 301
Pennsylvania International Raceway, **V** 494
Pennsylvania Life Insurance Company, **27** 47
Pennsylvania Power & Light Company, V 676, **693–94; 11** 388
Pennsylvania Pump and Compressor Co., **II** 16

Pennsylvania Railroad, **I** 456, 472; **II** 329, 490; **6** 436; **10** 71–73; **26** 295
Pennsylvania Refining Co., **IV** 488–89; **50** 351
Pennsylvania Salt Manufacturing Co., **I** 383
Pennsylvania Steel Co., **IV** 35; **7** 48
Pennsylvania Steel Foundry and Machine Co., **39** 32
Pennsylvania Water & Power Company, **25** 44
Pennwalt Corporation, I 382–84; IV 547; **12** 18; **21** 205
PennWell Corporation, 55 300–03
Penny Curtiss Baking Co., Inc., **13** 395
Pennzoil Company, IV 488–90, 551, 553; **10** 190; **14** 491, 493; **20 418–22 (upd.); 23** 40–41; **25** 443, 445; **39** 330; **41** 391, 394; **47** 436
Pennzoil-Quaker State Company, 49 343; **50 350–55 (upd.)**
Penray, **I** 373
Penrod Drilling Corporation, **7** 228, 558
Pension Benefit Guaranty Corp., **III** 255; **12** 489
Penske Corporation, V 494–95; 19 223, **292–94 (upd.); 20** 263
Penske Motorsports, **32** 440
Penske Truck Rental, **24** 445
Pentair, Inc., III 715; **7 419–21; 11** 315; **26 361–64 (upd.)**
Pental Insurance Company, Ltd., **11** 523
Pentane Partners, **7** 518
Pentastar Transportation Group, Inc. *See* Dollar Thrifty Automotive Group, Inc.
Pentaverken A.B., **I** 209
Pentech International, Inc., 14 217; **29 372–74; 52** 193
Pentes Play, Inc., **27** 370, 372
Pentland Group plc, 20 423–25; 35 204, 206–07
Pentland Industries PLC, **V** 375; **26** 396–97
Penton Media, Inc., 9 414; **27 360–62; 33** 335–36
People Express Airlines Inc., I 90, 98, 103, **117–18,** 123–24, 129–30; **6** 129; **21** 142; **22** 220
People That Love (PTL) Television, **13** 279
People's Bank of Halifax, **II** 210
People's Bank of New Brunswick, **II** 210
People's Drug Store, **II** 604–05; **22** 37–38
People's Ice and Refrigeration Company, **9** 274
People's Insurance Co., **III** 368
People's Natural Gas, **IV** 548; **6** 593; **50** 39
People's Radio Network, **25** 508
People's Trust Co. of Brooklyn, **II** 254; **9** 124
People's Trust Company, **49** 412
Peoples, **24** 315–16
Peoples Bancorp, **14** 529
Peoples Bank, **13** 467; **17** 302
Peoples Bank & Trust Co., **31** 207
Peoples Bank of Youngstown, **9** 474
Peoples Energy Corporation, 6 543–44
Peoples Finance Co., **II** 418
Peoples Gas Light & Coke Co., **IV** 169; **6** 529, 543–44
Peoples Gas Light Co., **6** 455; **25** 44
Peoples Heritage Financial Group, Inc. *See* Banknorth Group, Inc.

Peoples Jewelers of Canada, **16** 561; **40** 472

Peoples Life Insurance Co., **III** 218

Peoples National Bank, **41** 178–79

Peoples Natural Gas Company of South Carolina, **6** 576

Peoples Restaurants, Inc., **17** 320–21

Peoples Savings of Monroe, **9** 482

Peoples Security Insurance Co., **III** 219

Peoples Trust of Canada, **49** 411

PeopleServe, Inc., **29** 401

PeopleSoft Inc., **11** 78; **14** 381–83; **33** 330–33 (upd.); **38** 432

The Pep Boys—Manny, Moe & Jack, **11** 391–93; **16** 160; **26** 348; **36** 361–64 (upd.)

PEPCO. *See* Portland Electric Power Company; Potomac Electric Power Company.

Pepe Clothing Co., **18** 85

Pepper Hamilton LLP, **43** 300–03

Pepperell Manufacturing Company, **16** 533–34

Pepperidge Farm, **I** 29; **II** 480–81; **7** 67–68; **26** 56–57, 59

The Pepsi Bottling Group, Inc., **40** 350–53

PepsiCo, Inc., **I** 234, 244–46, 257, 269, **276–79**, 281, 291; **II** 103, 448, 477, 608; **III** 106, 116, 588; **7** 265, 267, 396, 404, 434–35, 466, 505–06; **8** 399; **9** 177, 343; **10** 130, 199, 227, 324, **450–54** (upd.); **11** 421, 450; **12** 337, 453; **13** 162, 284, 448, 494; **15** 72, 75, 380; **16** 96; **18** 65; **19** 114, 221; **21** 143, 313, 315–16, 362, 401, 405, 485–86; **22** 95, 353; **23** 418, 420; **25** 91, 177–78, 366, 411; **28** 271, 473, 476; **31** 243; **32** 59, 114, 205; **36** 234, 237; **38 347–54** (upd.); **40** 340–42, 350–52; **49** 77; **54** 72–73

Pepsodent Company, **I** 14; **9** 318

Perception Technology, **10** 500

Percy Bilton Investment Trust Ltd., **IV** 710

Percy Street Investments Ltd., **IV** 711

Perdigao SA, **52** 276–79

Perdue Farms Inc., **7 422–24**, 432; **23** 375–78 (upd.); **32** 203

Perfect Circle Corp., **I** 152

Perfect Fit Industries, **17** 182–84

Perfect-Ventil GmbH, **9** 413

Performance Contracting, Inc., **III** 722; **20** 415

Performance Food Group Company, **31** 359–62

Performance Technologies, Inc., **10** 395

Perfumania, Inc., **22** 157

Pergamon Holdings, **15** 83; **50** 125

Pergamon Press, **IV** 611, 641–43, 687; **7** 311–12

Perini Corporation, **8 418–21**; **38** 481

Perisem, **I** 281

The Perkin-Elmer Corporation, **III** 455, 727; **7 425–27**; **9** 514; **13** 326; **21** 123

Perkins, **I** 147; **12** 90

Perkins Bacon & Co., **10** 267

Perkins Cake & Steak, **9** 425

Perkins Engines Ltd., **III** 545, 652; **10** 274; **11** 472; **19** 294; **27** 203

Perkins Family Restaurants, L.P., **22** 417–19

Perkins Oil Well Cementing Co., **III** 497

Perkins Products Co., **II** 531

Perl Pillow, **19** 304

Perland Environmental Technologies Inc., **8** 420

Permal Group, **27** 276, 513

Permaneer Corp., **IV** 281; **9** 259. *See also* Spartech Corporation.

Permanent General Companies, Inc., **11** 194

Permanent Pigments Inc., **25** 71

Permanente Cement Company, **I** 565; **44** 152

Permanente Metals Corp., **IV** 15, 121–22

Permian Corporation, **V** 152–53

PERMIGAN, **IV** 492

Permodalan, **III** 699

Pernod Ricard S.A., **I** 248, **280–81**; **21** **399–401** (upd.)

Pernvo Inc., **I** 387

Perot Systems Corporation, **13** 482; **29** 375–78

Perret-Olivier, **III** 676; **16** 120

Perrier, **19** 50

Perrier Corporation of America, **16** 341

Perrier Vittel S.A., **52** 188

Perrigo Company, **12** 218, **387–89**

Perrin, **IV** 614

Perrot Brake Co., **I** 141

Perrow Motor Freight Lines, **6** 370

Perry Brothers, Inc., **24** 149

Perry Capital Corp., **28** 138

Perry Drug Stores Inc., **12** 21; **26** 476

Perry Ellis International, Inc., **16** 37; **41** 291–94

Perry Manufacturing Co., **16** 37

Perry Sports, **13** 545; **13** 545

Perry Tritech, **25** 103–05

Perry's Shoes Inc., **16** 36

Perscombinatie, **IV** 611

Pershing & Co., **22** 189

Personal Care Corp., **17** 235

Personal Performance Consultants, **9** 348

Personal Products Company, **III** 35; **8** 281, 511

Personnel Pool of America, **29** 224, 26–27

Perstorp AB, **I** 385–87; **51 289–92** (upd.)

PERTAMINA, **IV** 383, 461, **491–93**, 517, 567

Pertec Computer Corp., **17** 49; **18** 434

Pertech Computers Ltd., **18** 75

Perusahaan Minyak Republik Indonesia, **IV** 491

Peruvian Corp., **I** 547

Pet Food & Supply, **14** 385

Pet Foods Plus Inc., **39** 355

Pet Incorporated, **I** 457; **II** 486–87; **7** **428–31**; **10** 554; **12** 124; **13** 409; **14** 214; **24** 140; **27** 196; **43** 217; **46** 290

Petaluma Ltd., **54** 227, 229

Petco Animal Supplies, Inc., **29 379–81**

Pete's Brewing Company, **18** 72, 502; **22** 420–22

Peter Bawden Drilling, **IV** 570; **24** 521

Peter, Cailler, Kohler, Chocolats Suisses S.A., **II** 546; **7** 381

Peter Cundill & Associates Ltd., **15** 504

Peter Gast Shipping GmbH, **7** 40; **41** 42

Peter J. Schmitt Co., **13** 394; **24** 444–45

Peter J. Schweitzer, Inc., **III** 40; **16** 303; **43** 257

Peter Jones, **V** 94

Peter Kiewit Sons' Inc., **I** 599–600; **III** 198; **8 422–24**; **15** 18; **25** 512, 514

Peter Norton Computing Group, **10** 508–09

Peter Paul/Cadbury, **II** 477, 512; **15** 221; **51** 158

Peterbilt Motors Co., **I** 185–86; **26** 355

Peters-Revington Corporation, **26** 100. *See also* Chromcraft Revington, Inc.

Peters Shoe Co., **III** 528

Petersen Cos., **52** 192

Petersen Publishing Company, **21** 402–04

Peterson American Corporation, **55** 304–06

Peterson Furniture Company, **51** 9

Peterson, Howell & Heather, **V** 496

Peterson Soybean Seed Co., **9** 411

Petit Bateau, **35** 263

La Petite Academy, **13** 299

Petite Sophisticate, **V** 207–08

Petoseed Co. Inc., **29** 435

Petrie Stores Corporation, **8** 425–27

Petrini's, **II** 653

Petro-Canada Limited, **IV** 367, **494–96**, 499; **13** 557; **50** 172

Petro/Chem Environmental Services, Inc., **IV** 411

Petro-Coke Co. Ltd., **IV** 476

Petro-Lewis Corp., **IV** 84; **7** 188

Petroamazonas, **IV** 511

Petrobas, **21** 31

Petrobel, **IV** 412

Petrobrás. *See* Petróleo Brasileiro S.A.

Petrocarbona GmbH, **IV** 197–98

Petrocel, S.A., **19** 12

Petrochemicals Company, **17** 90–91

Petrochemicals Industry Co., **IV** 451; **55** 243

Petrochemie Danubia GmbH, **IV** 486–87

Petrochim, **IV** 498

PetroChina Company Ltd., **46** 86

Petrocomercial, **IV** 511

Petrocorp. *See* Petroleum Company of New Zealand.

Petroecuador. *See* Petróleos del Ecuador.

Petrofertil, **IV** 501

PetroFina S.A., **IV** 455, 495, **497–500**, 576; **7** 179; **26 365–69** (upd.)

Petrogal. *See* Petróleos de Portugal.

Petroindustria, **IV** 511

Petrol, **IV** 487

Petrol Ofisi Anonim Sirketi, **IV** 564

Petrolane Properties, **17** 558

Petróleo Brasileiro S.A., **IV** 424, **501–03**

Petróleo Mecânica Alfa, **IV** 505

Petróleos de Portugal S.A., **IV** 504–06

Petróleos de Venezuela S.A., **II** 661; **IV** 391–93, **507–09**, 571; **24** 522; **31** 113

Petróleos del Ecuador, **IV** 510–11

Petróleos Mexicanos, **IV** 512–14, 528; **19** 10, **295–98** (upd.); **41** 147

Petroleum and Chemical Corp., **III** 672

Petroleum Authority of Thailand, **IV** 519

Petroleum Company of New Zealand, **IV** 279; **19** 155

Petroleum Development (Qatar) Ltd., **IV** 524

Petroleum Development (Trucial States) Ltd., **IV** 363

Petroleum Development Corp. of the Republic of Korea, **IV** 455

Petroleum Development Oman LLC, **IV** 515–16

Petroleum Helicopters, Inc., **35** 334–36; **37** 288; **39** 8

Petroleum Projects Co., **IV** 414

Petroleum Research and Engineering Co. Ltd., **IV** 473

Petrolgroup, Inc., **6** 441

Petroliam Nasional Bhd. *See* Petronas.
Petrolite Corporation, 15 350–52
Petrolube, **IV** 538
Petromex. *See* Petróleos de Mexico S.A.
Petromin Lubricating Oil Co., **17** 415; **50** 416
Petronas, IV 517–20; 21 501
Petronor, **IV** 514, 528
Petropeninsula, **IV** 511
Petroproduccion, **IV** 511
Petroquímica de Venezuela SA, **IV** 508
Petroquimica Española, **I** 402
Petroquisa, **IV** 501
Petrossian Inc., 54 287–89
PETROSUL, **IV** 504, 506
Petrotransporte, **IV** 511
PETsMART, Inc., 14 384–86; 27 95; **29** 379–80; **41 295–98 (upd.); 45** 42
Petstuff, Inc., **14** 386; **41** 297
Pettibone Corporation, **19** 365
Petzazz, **14** 386
Peugeot S.A., I 163, 187–88; II 13; **III** 508; **11** 104; **26** 11; **50** 197. *See also* PSA Peugeot Citroen S.A.
The Pew Charitable Trusts, 35 337–40
Pez Candy, Inc., 38 355–57
Pfaff-Pegasus of U.S.A. Inc., **15** 385
Pfaltz & Bauer, Inc., **38** 3
The Pfaltzgraff Co. *See* Susquehanna Pfaltzgraff Company.
Pfaudler Vacuum Co., **I** 287
Pfauter-Maag Cutting Tools, **24** 186
PFCI. *See* Pulte Financial Companies, Inc.
PFD Supply, Inc., **47** 304
PFI Acquisition Corp., **17** 184
Pfizer, Hoechst Celanese Corp., **8** 399
Pfizer Inc., I 301, 367, 661–63, 668; 9 356, **402–05 (upd.); 10** 53–54; **11** 207, 310–11, 459; **12** 4; **17** 131; **19** 105; **38 358–67 (upd.); 44** 175
Pflueger Corporation, **22** 483
PG&E Corporation, 26 370–73 (upd.); 27 131. *See also* Portland General Electric.
PGA. *See* The Professional Golfers' Association.
PGH Bricks and Pipes, **III** 735
Phaostron Instruments and Electronic Co., **18** 497–98
Phar-Mor Inc., 12 209, 390–92, 477; 18 507; **21** 459; **22** 157; **50** 457
Pharma Plus Drugmarts, **II** 649–50
PharmaCare Management Services, Inc., **45** 136
Pharmacia & Upjohn Inc., 25 22, **374–78 (upd.); 34** 177, 179
Pharmacia A.B., I 211, 664–65
Pharmaco Dynamics Research, Inc., **10** 106–07
Pharmacom Systems Ltd., **II** 652; **51** 303
Pharmacy Corporation of America, **16** 57
PharmaKinetics Laboratories, Inc., **10** 106
Pharmanex, Inc., **27** 352
Pharmaprix Ltd., **II** 663; **49** 368
Pharmazell GmbH, **IV** 324
Pharmedix, **11** 207
Pharos, **9** 381
Phat Fashions LLC, 49 322–24
Phelan & Collender, **III** 442
Phelan Faust Paint, **8** 553
Phelps Dodge Corporation, IV 33, **176–79**, 216; **7** 261–63, 288; **19** 375; **28 352–57 (upd.); 40** 411
Phenix Bank, **II** 312

Phenix Cheese Corp., **II** 533
Phenix Insurance Co., **III** 240
Phenix Mills Ltd., **II** 662
PHF Life Insurance Co., **III** 263; **IV** 623
PHH Arval, 53 274–76 (upd.)
PHH Corporation, V 496–97; 6 357; **22** 55
PHI. *See* Pizza Hut, Inc.
Phibro Corporation, **II** 447–48; **IV** 80; **13** 447–48; **21** 67
Philadelphia and Reading Corp., **I** 440; **II** 329; **6** 377; **25** 165
Philadelphia Carpet Company, **9** 465
Philadelphia Coke Company, **6** 487
Philadelphia Company, **6** 484, 493
Philadelphia Drug Exchange, **I** 692
Philadelphia Eagles, 37 305–08
Philadelphia Electric Company, V 695–97; 6 450
Philadelphia Life, **I** 527
Philadelphia Smelting and Refining Co., **IV** 31
Philadelphia Sports Clubs. *See* Town Sports International, Inc.
Philadelphia Suburban Corporation, 39 326–29
Philco Corp., **I** 167, 531; **II** 86; **III** 604; **13** 402; **50** 299
Phildar, **37** 22
Phildrew Ventures, **44** 147
Philip Environmental Inc., 16 414–16
Philip Morris Companies Inc., I 23, 269; **II** 530–34; **V** 397, 404, **405–07**, 409, 417; **6** 52; **7** 272, 274, 276, 548; **8** 53; **9** 180; **12** 337, 372; **13** 138, 517; **15** 64, 72–73, 137; **18** 72, **416–19 (upd.); 19** 112, 369; **20** 23; **22** 73, 338; **23** 427; **26** 249, 251; **29** 46–47; **32** 472, 476; **44** 338–43 (upd.); **50** 144; **52** 16. *See also* Kraft Foods Inc.
Philip Smith Theatrical Enterprises. *See* GC Companies, Inc.
Philipp Abm. Cohen, **IV** 139
Philipp Brothers Chemicals, Inc., **II** 447; **IV** 79–0; **25** 82
Philipp Holzmann AG, II 279, 386; **14** 169; **16** 284, 286; **17 374–77**
Philippine Aerospace Development Corporation, **27** 475
Philippine Airlines, Inc., I 107; **6 106–08**, 122–23; **23 379–82 (upd.); 27** 464
Philippine American Life Insurance Co., **III** 195
Philippine Sinter Corp., **IV** 125
Philips, **V** 339; **6** 101; **10** 269; **22** 194
Philips Electronics N.V., 8 153; **9** 75; **10** 16; **12** 475, 549; **13** 396, **400–03 (upd.); 14** 446; **23** 389; **26** 334; **27** 190–92; **32** 373; **34** 258; **37** 121; **47** 383–86. *See also* Koninklijke Philips Electronics N.V.
Philips Electronics North America Corp., 13 396–99; 26 334
N.V. Philips Gloeilampenfabriken, **I** 107, 330; **II** 25, 56, 58, **78–80**, 99, 102, 117, 119; **III** 479, 654–55; **IV** 680; **12** 454. *See also* Philips Electronics N.V.
Philips Medical Systems, **29** 299
Phillip Hawkins, **III** 169; **6** 285
Phillip Securities, **16** 14; **43** 8
Phillippe of California, **8** 16; **36** 24
Phillips & Drew, **II** 379
Phillips & Jacobs, Inc., **14** 486
Phillips Cables, **III** 433

Phillips Carbon Black, **IV** 421
Phillips Colleges Inc., **22** 442; **39** 102
Phillips, de Pury & Luxembourg, 49 325–27
Phillips Manufacturing Company, **8** 464
Phillips Petroleum Company, I 377; **II** 15, 408; **III** 752; **IV** 71, 290, 366, 405, 412, 414, 445, 453, 498, **521–23**, 567, 570–71, 575; **10** 84, 440; **11** 522; **13** 356, 485; **17** 422; **19** 176; **24** 521; **31** 457; **38** 407; **40 354–59 (upd.); 47** 70
Phillips Sheet and Tin Plate Co., **IV** 236
Phillips-Van Heusen Corporation, 24 382–85; 55 87
PHLCorp., **11** 261
PHM Corp., **8** 461
Phoenicia Glass, **25** 266–67
Phoenix Assurance Co., **III** 242, 257, 369, 370–74; **55** 332
Phoenix Financial Services, **11** 115
Phoenix Fire Office, **III** 234
Phoenix Insurance Co., **III** 389; **IV** 711
Phoenix Microsystems Inc., **13** 8
Phoenix Mutual Life Insurance, **16** 207
Phoenix Oil and Transport Co., **IV** 90
Phoenix-Rheinrohr AG, **IV** 222
Phoenix State Bank and Trust Co., **II** 213
Phoenix Technologies Ltd., **13** 482
Phone America of Carolina, **8** 311
Phonogram, **23** 389
PhotoChannel Networks, Inc., **45** 283
Photocircuits Corp., **18** 291–93
PhotoDisc Inc., **31** 216, 218
PHP Healthcare Corporation, 22 423–25
Phuket Air Catering Company Ltd., **6** 123–24; **27** 464
PhyCor, Inc., 36 365–69
Physical Measurements Information, **31** 357
Physician Corporation of America, **24** 231
Physician Sales & Service, Inc., 14 387–89
Physician's Weight Loss Center, **10** 383
Physicians Formula Cosmetics, **8** 512
Physicians Placement, **13** 49
Physio-Control International Corp., 18 420–23; 30 316
Piaget, **27** 487, 489
Piaggio & C. S.p.A., 17 24; **20 426–29**; **36** 472; **39** 36–37
Piam Pty. Ltd., **48** 364
PIC International Group PLC, 24 386–88 (upd.)
Pic 'N' Save, **17** 298–99
PIC Realty Corp., **III** 339
Picard Surgeles, **27** 93
Picault, **19** 50
Piccadilly Cafeterias, Inc., 19 299–302
Pick, **III** 98
Pick-N-Pay, **II** 642; **9** 452
Pick Pay, **48** 63
Pickands Mather, **13** 158
Picker International Corporation, **II** 25; **8** 352; **30** 314
Pickfords Ltd., **6** 412–14
Pickfords Removals, **49** 22
Pickland Mather & Co., **IV** 409
PickOmatic Systems, **8** 135
Pickwick Dress Co., **III** 54
Pickwick International, **I** 613; **9** 360; **38** 315
Piclands Mather, **7** 308

Pico Ski Area Management Company, **28** 21

Picture Classified Network, **IV** 597

PictureTel Corp., 10 455–57; 27 363–66 (upd.)

Piece Goods Shops, **16** 198

Piedmont Airlines, Inc., **6** 132; **12** 490; **28** 507

Piedmont Coca-Cola Bottling Partnership, **10** 223

Piedmont Concrete, **III** 739

Piedmont Natural Gas Company, Inc., 27 367–69

Piedmont Pulp and Paper Co. *See* Westvaco Corporation.

Pier 1 Imports, Inc., 12 179, 200, **393–95; 34 337–41 (upd.); 53** 245

Pierburg GmbH, **9** 445–46

Pierce, **IV** 478

Pierce Brothers, **6** 295

Pierce Leahy Corporation, 24 389–92. *See also* Iron Mountain Inc.

Pierce National Life, **22** 314

Pierce Steam Heating Co., **III** 663

Piercing Pagoda, Inc., 29 382–84; 40 472

Pierre & Vacances SA, 48 314–16

Pierre Foods, **13** 270–72; **29** 203

Pierson, Heldring, and Pierson, **II** 185

Pietrafesa Corporation, **29** 208

Pietro's Pizza Parlors, **II** 480–81; **26** 56–57; **44** 85

Piezo Electric Product, Inc., **16** 239

Pig Improvement Co., **II** 500

Piggly Wiggly Southern, Inc., II 571, 624; **13** 251–52, **404–06; 18** 6, 8; **21** 455; **22** 127; **26** 47; **27** 245; **31** 406, 408; **32** 260

Pignone, **IV** 420

Pike Adding Machine, **III** 165

Pike Corporation of America, **I** 570; **8** 191

Pikrose and Co. Ltd., **IV** 136

Pilgrim Curtain Co., **III** 213

Pilgrim House Group, **50** 134

Pilgrim's Pride Corporation, 7 432–33; 23 383–85 (upd.); 39 203

Pilkington plc, I 429; **II** 475; **III** 56, 641–42, 676–77, 714–15, **724–27; 16** 7, 9, 120–21; **22** 434; **34 342–47 (upd.)**

Pillar Corp., **52** 185

Pillar Holdings, **IV** 191

Pilliod Furniture, Inc., **12** 300

Pillowtex Corporation, 19 303–05; 31 200; **41 299–302 (upd.)**

Pillsbury Company, II 133, 414, 493–94, 511, **555–57,** 575, 613–15; **7** 106, 128, 277, 469, 547; **8** 53–54; **10** 147, 176; **11** 23; **12** 80, 510; **13 407–09 (upd.),** 516; **14** 212, 214; **15** 64; **16** 71; **17** 70–71, 434; **22** 59, 426; **24** 140–41; **25** 179, 241; **27** 196, 287; **29** 433; **32** 32, 67; **38** 100

Pillsbury Madison & Sutro LLP, 29 385–88

Pilot, **I** 531

Pilot Corporation, 49 328–30

Pilot Freight Carriers, **27** 474

Pilot Insurance Agency, **III** 204

Pilsa, **55** 189

Pin 'n' Save, **50** 98

Pinal-Dome Oil, **IV** 569; **24** 520

Pinault-Printemps-Redoute S.A., 15 386; **19 306–09 (upd.); 22** 362; **27** 513; **41** 185–86; **42** 171

Pincus & Co., **7** 305

Pine Tree Casting. *See* Sturm, Ruger & Company, Inc.

Pinecliff Publishing Company, **10** 357

Pinelands, Inc., **9** 119; **26** 33

Pinelands Water Company, **45** 275, 277

Pineville Kraft Corp., **IV** 276

Pinewood Studios, **II** 157

Pinguely-Haulotte SA, 51 293–95

Pininfarina, **I** 188

Pinkerton's Inc., 9 406–09; 13 124–25; **14** 541; **16** 48; **41** 77, 79. *See also* Securitas AB.

Pinnacle Art and Frame, **31** 436

Pinnacle Books, **25** 483

Pinnacle Distribution, **52** 429

Pinnacle Fitness, **25** 42

Pinnacle West Capital Corporation, 6 545–47; 26 359; **54 290–94 (upd.)**

Pinsetter Corp., **III** 443

Pinto Island Metals Company, **15** 116

Pioneer Airlines, **I** 96; **21** 141

Pioneer Asphalt Co., **I** 404; **36** 146–47

Pioneer Asphalts Pty. Ltd., **III** 728

Pioneer Bank, **41** 312

Pioneer Concrete Services Ltd., **III** 728–29

Pioneer Cotton Mill, **12** 503

Pioneer Electronic Corporation, II 103; **III 604–06; 28 358–61 (upd.)**

Pioneer Engineering and Manufacturing Co., **55** 32

Pioneer Federal Savings Bank, **10** 340; **11** 115

Pioneer Financial Corp., **11** 447

Pioneer Food Stores Co-op, **24** 528

Pioneer Hi-Bred International, Inc., 9 410–12; 17 131; **21** 387; **41 303–06 (upd.)**

Pioneer International Limited, III 687, **728–30; 28** 83

Pioneer Life Insurance Co., **III** 274

Pioneer Natural Gas Company, **10** 82

Pioneer Outdoor, **27** 280

Pioneer Plastics Corporation, **31** 399–400

Pioneer Readymixed Concrete and Mortar Proprietary Ltd., **III** 728

Pioneer Saws Ltd., **III** 598

Pioneer-Standard Electronics Inc., 13 47; **19 310–14**

Pipasa, **41** 329

Pipe Line Service Company. *See* Plexco.

Pipeline and Products Marketing Co., **IV** 473

Piper Aircraft Corp., **I** 482; **II** 403; **8** 49–50

Piper Jaffray Companies Inc., 22 426–30, 465. *See also* U.S. Bancorp.

Pirelli S.p.A., IV 174, 420; **V 249–51; 10** 319; **15 353–56 (upd.); 16** 318; **21** 73; **28** 262

Piscataquis Canal and Railroad Company, **16** 348

Pisces Inc., **13** 321

Pispalan Werhoomo Oy, **I** 387

The Piston Ring Company, **I** 199; **10** 492

Pitcairn Aviation, **I** 101

Pitney Bowes, Inc., III 156–58, 159; **19 315–18 (upd.); 47 295–99 (upd.)**

Pittman Company, **28** 350

Pittsburgh & Lake Angeline Iron Company, **13** 156

Pittsburgh & Lake Erie Railroad, **I** 472

Pittsburgh Aluminum Alloys Inc., **12** 353

Pittsburgh Brewing Co., **10** 169–70; **18** 70, 72; **50** 111, 114

Pittsburgh Chemical Co., **IV** 573; **7** 551

Pittsburgh Consolidation Coal Co., **8** 346

Pittsburgh Corning Corp., **III** 683

Pittsburgh Life, **III** 274

Pittsburgh National Bank, **II** 317, 342; **22** 55

Pittsburgh National Corp., **II** 342

Pittsburgh Paint & Glass. *See* PPG Industries, Inc.

Pittsburgh Plate Glass Co. *See* PPG Industries, Inc.

Pittsburgh Railway Company, **9** 413

Pittsburgh Reduction Co., **II** 315; **IV** 9, 14

Pittsburgh Steel Company, **7** 587

Pittsburgh Trust and Savings, **II** 342

The Pittston Company, IV 180–82, 566; **10** 44; **19 319–22 (upd.)**

Pittway Corporation, 9 413–15; 27 361–62; **28 133–34; 33 334–37 (upd.)**

Pivotpoint, Inc., **55** 258

Pixar Animation Studios, 34 348–51

Pixel Semiconductor, **11** 57

Pizitz, Inc., **19** 324

Pizza Dispatch. *See* Dominos's Pizza, Inc.

Pizza Hut Inc., I 221, 278, 294; **II** 614; **7** 152–53, 267, **434–35,** 506; **10** 450; **11** 50; **12** 123; **13** 336, 516; **14** 107; **15** 344–46; **16** 446; **17** 71, 537; **21** 24–25, 315, **405–07 (upd.); 22** 353; **24** 295; **25** 179–80, 227; **28** 238; **33** 388; **40** 340

Pizza Inn, Inc., 46 346–49; 16 447; **25** 179

PizzaCo, Inc., **7** 152

Pizzeria Uno, **25** 178

PJS Publications, **22** 442

PKbanken, **II** 353

Place Two, **V** 156

Placer Cego Petroleum Ltd., **IV** 367

Placer Development Ltd., **IV** 19

Placer Dome Inc., IV 571; **20 430–33; 24** 522; **36** 314

Placid Oil Co., **7** 228

Plaid Holdings Corp., **9** 157

Plain Jane Dress Company, **8** 169

Plains Dairy, **53** 21

Plainwell Paper Co., Inc., **8** 103

Planet Hollywood International, Inc., 18 424–26; 25 387–88; **32** 241, 243–44; **41 307–10 (upd.)**

Planet Insurance Co., **III** 343

Planet Waves, **48** 232

Plank Road Brewery, **I** 269; **12** 337

Plankinton Packing Co., **III** 534

Plant Genetics Inc., **I** 266; **21** 320

Planters Company, **24** 287

Planters Lifesavers, **14** 274–75

Planters Nut & Chocolate Co., **I** 219; **II** 544

Plas-Techs, Inc., **15** 35

Plastic Coating Corporation, **IV** 330; **8** 483

Plastic Containers, Inc., **15** 129; **25** 512

Plastic Engineered Products Company. *See* Ballard Medical Products.

Plastic Parts, Inc., **19** 277

Plasticos Metalgrafica, **I** 231

Plastics, Inc., **13** 41

Plasto Bambola. *See* BRIO AB.

Plastrier. *See* Compagnie de Saint-Gobain S.A.

Plate Glass Group, **24** 450

Plateau Holdings, Inc., **12** 260; **13** 502

Platinum Entertainment, Inc., 35 341–44

PLATINUM Technology, Inc., 14 390–92

Plato Learning, Inc., 44 344–47

Platt & Co., **I** 506
Platt Bros., **III** 636
Platt's Price Service, Inc., **IV** 636–37
Play by Play Toys & Novelties, Inc., 26 **374–76**
Play It Again Sam (PIAS), **44** 164
Play It Again Sports, **18** 207–08
Playboy Enterprises, Inc., 18 427–30; 48 148
PlayCore, Inc., 27 370–72
Players International, Inc., 16 263, 275; **19** 402; **22 431–33; 33** 41; **43** 226–27
Playland, **16** 389
Playmates Toys, 23 386–88
Playmaxx, Inc., **55** 132
Playmobil. *See* geobra Brandstätter GmbH & Co. KG.
Playskool, Inc., III 504, 506; **12** 169; **13** 317; **16** 267; **25 379–81; 43** 229, 232
Playtex Products, Inc., II 448, 468; **8** 511; **13** 448; **15 357–60; 24** 480; **54** 325
Playworld, **16** 389–90
Plaza.Coloso S.A. de C.V., **10** 189
Plaza Medical Group, **6** 184
Plaza Securities, **I** 170
PLC. *See* Prescription Learning Corporation.
Pleasant Company, 25 314; **27 373–75**
Pleasurama PLC, **I** 248; **12** 228; **32** 243
Plessey Company, PLC, II 25, 39, 81–82; **IV** 100; **6** 241; **33** 287–88
Plews Manufacturing Co., **III** 602
Plex Co., Ltd., **55** 48
Plexco, **7** 30–31
Plexus Corporation, 35 345–47
Plezall Wipers, Inc., **15** 502
Plitt Theatres, Inc., **6** 162; **23** 126
Plon et Juillard, **IV** 614
Plough Inc., **I** 684; **49** 356
Plum Associates, **12** 270
Plum Creek Timber Company, Inc., 43 **304–06**
Pluma, Inc., 27 376–78
Plumb Tool, **II** 16
Plus Development Corporation, **10** 458–59
Plus Mark, Inc., **7** 24
Plus System Inc., **9** 537
Plus-Ultra, **II** 196
Plus Vita, **36** 162
Pluto Technologies International Inc., **38** 72
Ply Gem Industries Inc., 12 396–98; 23 225
Plymouth County Electric Co., **14** 124
Plymouth Mills Inc., **23** 66
PMC Contract Research AB, **21** 425
PMC Specialties Group, **III** 745
PMI Corporation, **6** 140. *See also* Physical Measurements Information
The PMI Group, Inc., 49 331–33
PMI Mortgage Insurance Company, **10** 50
PMS Consolidated, **8** 347
PMT Services, Inc., 24 393–95
PN Pertambangan Minyak Dan Gas Bumi Negara, **IV** 492
PNC Bank Corp., 13 410–12 (upd.); 14 103; **18** 63; **53** 135
PNC Financial Corporation, II 317, 342–43; **9** 476; **17** 114
The PNC Financial Services Group Inc., 46 350–53 (upd.)
Pneumo Abex Corp., **I** 456–58; **III** 512; **10** 553–54; **38** 293–94
Pneumo Dynamics Corporation, **8** 409

PNL. *See* Pacific Northwest Laboratories.
PNM Resources Inc., 51 296–300 (upd.)
PNP. *See* Pacific Northwest Power Company.
POAS, **IV** 563
POB Polyolefine Burghausen GmbH, **IV** 487
Pocahontas Foods USA, **31** 359, 361
Pochet SA, 55 307–09
Pocket Books, Inc., **10** 480; **13** 559–60
Poclain Company, **10** 380
Poe & Associates, Inc., **41** 63–64
Pogo Producing Company, I 441; **39** 330–32
Pohang Iron and Steel Company Ltd., IV 183–85; 17 351
Pohjan Sellu Oy, **IV** 316
Pohjoismainen Osakepankki, **II** 302
Pohjola Voima Oy, **IV** 348
Pohjolan Osakepankki, **II** 303
Point Chehalis Packers, **13** 244
Polak & Schwarz Essencefabricken, **9** 290
Poland Spring Natural Spring Water Co., **31** 229
Polar Manufacturing Company, **16** 32
Polar Star Milling Company, **7** 241
Polaris Industries Inc., 12 399–402; 35 **348–53 (upd.); 40** 47, 50
Polaroid Corporation, I 30–31; **II** 412; **III** 475–77, 549, 584, **607–09; IV** 330; **7** 161–62, **436–39 (upd.); 12** 180; **28** **362–66 (upd.); 36** 171–73; **41** 104, 106; **54** 110
Polbeth Packaging Limited, **12** 377
Polenghi, **25** 84
Policy Management Systems **Corporation, 11 394–95**
Poliet S.A., 33 175–77, **338–40; 40** 108
Polioles, S.A. de C.V., **19** 10, 12
Politos, S.A. de C.V., **23** 171
Polk Audio, Inc., 34 352–54
Pollenex Corp., **19** 360
Polo Food Corporation, **10** 250
Polo/Ralph Lauren Corporation, 9 157; **12 403–05; 16** 61; **25** 48
Polser, **19** 49, 51
Polskie Linie Lotnicze S.A. *See* LOT Polish Airlines.
Poly-Glas Systems, Inc., **21** 65
Poly-Hi Corporation, **8** 359
Poly P, Inc., **IV** 458
Poly Version, Inc., **III** 645
Polyblend Corporation, **7** 4
Polycell Holdings, **IV** 666; **17** 397
Polydesign België, **16** 421
Polydesign Nederland, **16** 421
Polydor B.V., **23** 389
Polydor KK, **23** 390
Polydress Plastic GmbH, **7** 141
Polygon Networks Inc., **41** 73
PolyGram N.V., 13 402; **22** 194; **23** **389–92; 25** 411; **26** 152, 314, 394; **31** 269
Polyken Technologies, **11** 220
Polymer Technologies Corporation, **26** 287
Polyphase Corporation. *See* Overhill Corporation.
Polysar Energy & Chemical Corporation of Toronto, **V** 674
Polysius AG, **IV** 89
Pomeroy Computer Resources, Inc., 33 **341–44**
Pomeroy's, **16** 61; **50** 107

Pommersche Papierfabrik Hohenkrug, **III** 692
Pommery et Greno, **II** 475
Ponderosa Steakhouse, 7 336; **12** 373; **14** 331; **15 361–64**
Ponderosa System Inc., **12** 199
Pont-à-Mousson S.A., **III** 675, 677–78, 704; **16** 119, 121–22; **21** 253
Pont Royal SA, **48** 316
Pontiac, **III** 458; **10** 353
Pontificia, **III** 207
Ponto Frio Bonzao, **22** 321
Pony Express, **II** 380–81, 395
Poore Brothers, Inc., 44 348–50
Poorman-Douglas Corporation, **13** 468
Pop.com, **43** 144
Pope and Talbot, Inc., 12 406–08
Pope Cable and Wire B.V., **19** 45
Pope Tin Plate Co., **IV** 236; **26** 527
Popeye's/Church's, **23** 115, 117
Popeyes Famous Fried Chicken and Biscuits, Inc., **7** 26–28; **32** 13
Pophitt Cereals, Inc., **22** 337
Poppe Tyson Inc., **23** 479; **25** 91
Poppin' Fresh Pies, Inc., **12** 510
Popsicle, **II** 573; **14** 205
Popular Aviation Company, **12** 560
Popular Club Plan, **12** 280; **34** 232
Popular, Inc., 41 311–13
Popular Merchandise, Inc., **12** 280
Pori, **IV** 350
Poron Diffusion, **9** 394
Poron, S.A., **42** 268–69
Porsche AG, 13 28, 219, **413–15; 31** **363–366 (upd.); 36** 198
Port Arthur Finance Corp., **37** 309
The Port Authority of New York and **New Jersey, 47** 359; **48 317–20**
Port Blakely Mill Company, **17** 438
Port Dickson Power Sdn. Bhd., **36** 435–36
Port Harcourt Refining Co., **IV** 473
Port of London Authority, **48** 317
Port Stockton Food Distributors, Inc., **16** 451, 453
Portage Industries Corp., **19** 415
Portal Software, Inc., 47 300–03
Portals Water Treatment, **11** 510
Porter-Cable Corporation, **26** 361–63
Porter Chadburn plc, **28** 252
Porter Shoe Manufacturing Company, **13** 360
Portex, **25** 431
Portia Management Services Ltd., **30** 318
Portland General Corporation, 6 548–51
Portland General Electric, **45** 313; **50** 103
Portland Heavy Industries, **10** 369
Portland Plastics, **25** 430–31
Portland Trail Blazers, 50 356–60
Portland-Zementwerke Heidelberg A.G., **23** 326
Portnet, **6** 435
Portsmouth & Sunderland, **35** 242, 244
Portugalia, **46** 398
Portways, **9** 92
Poseidon Exploration Ltd., **IV** 84; **7** 188
Posey, Quest, Genova, **6** 48
Positive Response Television, Inc., **27** 337–38
Post Office Counters, **V** 496
Post Office Group, V 498–501
Post Properties, Inc., 26 377–79
PostBank, **II** 189
La Poste, V 470–72
Posti- Ja Telelaitos, 6 329–31

PostScript, **17** 177
Postum Cereal Company, **II** 497, 523, 530–31; **7** 272–73; **13** 291; **50** 291
Potash Corporation of Saskatchewan Inc., **18** 51, 431–33; **27** 318; **50** 90
Potlatch Corporation, **IV** 282; **8 428–30**; **9** 260; **19** 445; **34 355–59 (upd.)**
Potomac Edison Company, **38** 39–40
Potomac Electric Power Company, **6 552–54**; **25** 46
Potomac Insurance Co., **III** 257
Potomac Leasing, **III** 137
Potter & Brumfield Inc., **11 396–98**
Pottery Barn, **13** 42; **17** 548–50
Potts, **IV** 58
Poulan/Weed Eater. *See* White Consolidated Industries Inc.
Poulsen Wireless, **II** 490
PowCon, Inc., **17** 534
Powell Duffryn plc, **III** 502; **IV** 38; **31 367–70**
Powell Energy Products, **8** 321
Powell Group, **33** 32
Powell River Co. Ltd., **IV** 306–07
Powell's Books, Inc., **37** 181; **40 360–63**
Power Applications & Manufacturing Company, Inc., **6** 441
Power Corporation of Canada, **36 370–74 (upd.)**
Power Financial Corp., **III** 260–61
Power Jets Ltd., **I** 81
Power Parts Co., **7** 358
Power Products, **8** 515
Power Specialty Company, **6** 145
Power Team, **10** 492
PowerBar Inc., **44 351–53**
Powercor. *See* PacifiCorp.
PowerFone Holdings, **10** 433
Powergen PLC, **11 399–401**; **12** 349; **13** 458, 484; **50** 172, 280–81, **361–64 (upd.)**
Powerhouse Technologies, Inc., **13** 485; **27 379–81**
Powers Accounting Machine Company, **6** 240
Powers Regulator, **III** 535
Powers-Samas, **6** 240
PowerSoft Corp., **11** 77; **15** 374
Powertel Inc., **48** 130
Pozzi-Renati Millwork Products, Inc., **8** 135
PP&L. *See* Pennsylvania Power & Light Company.
PP&L Global, Inc., **44** 291
PPG Industries, Inc., **I** 330, 341–42; **III** 21, 641, 667, 676, 722, 725, **731–33**; **8** 153, 222, 224; **16** 120–21; **20** 415; **21** 221, 223; **22** 147, **434–37 (upd.)**; **37** 73; **39** 292
PPI. *See* Precision Pattern Inc.
PPL Corporation, **41 314–17 (upd.)**
PR Holdings, **23** 382
PR Newswire, **35 354–56**
Prac, **I** 281
Practical and Educational Books, **13** 105
Practical Business Solutions, Inc., **18** 112
Prada Holding B.V., **45 342–45**; **50** 215
Pragma Bio-Tech, Inc., **11** 424
Prairie Farmer Publishing Co., **II** 129
Prairie Farms Dairy, Inc., **47 304–07**
Prairie Holding Co., **IV** 571; **24** 522
Prairie Oil and Gas Co., **IV** 368
Prairielands Energy Marketing, Inc., **7** 322, 325

Prakla Seismos, **17** 419
Prandium Inc., **51** 70
Pratt & Whitney, **I** 47, 78, 82–85, 128, 434; **II** 48; **III** 482; **6** 128; **7** 456; **9** 14, 16–18, 244–46, **416–18**; **10** 162; **11** 299, 427; **12** 71; **13** 386; **14** 564; **24** 312; **25** 267; **39** 313
Pratt Holding, Ltd., **IV** 312; **19** 268
Pratt Hotel Corporation, **21** 275; **22** 438
Pratt Properties Inc., **8** 349
Pratta Electronic Materials, Inc., **26** 425
Praxair, Inc., **11 402–04**; **16** 462; **43** 265; **48 321–24 (upd.)**
Praxis Biologics, **8** 26; **27** 115
Praxis Corporation, **30** 499
Pre-Fab Cushioning, **9** 93
Pre-Paid Legal Services, Inc., **20 434–37**
PreAnalytiX, **39** 335
Precept Foods, LLC, **54** 168
Precious Metals Development, **IV** 79
Precise Fabrication Corporation, **33** 257
Precise Imports Corp., **21** 516
Precision Castparts Corp., **15 365–67**
Precision Games, **16** 471
Precision Husky Corporation, **26** 494
Precision Interconnect Corporation, **14** 27
Precision LensCrafters, **13** 391
Precision Moulds, Ltd., **25** 312
Precision Optical Co., **III** 120, 575
Precision Optical Industry Company, Ltd. *See* Canon Inc.
Precision Pattern Inc., **36** 159
Precision Power, Inc., **21** 514
Precision Response Corporation, **47** 420
Precision Software Corp., **14** 319
Precision Spring of Canada, Ltd., **55** 305
Precision Standard Inc. *See* Pemco Aviation Group Inc.
Precision Studios, **12** 529
Precision Tool, Die & Machine Company Inc., **51** 116–17
Precision Tube Formers, Inc., **17** 234
Precoat Metals, **54** 331
Precor, **III** 610–11
Predica, **II** 266
Predicasts Inc., **12** 562; **17** 254
Preferred Medical Products. *See* Ballard Medical Products.
Preferred Products, Inc., **II** 669; **18** 504; **50** 454
PREINCO Holdings, Inc., **11** 532
PREL&P. *See* Portland Railway Electric Light & Power Company.
Prelude Corp., **III** 643
Premark International, Inc., **II** 534; **III 610–12**; **14** 548; **28** 479–80
Premcor Inc., **37 309–11**
Premex A.G., **II** 369
Premier (Transvaal) Diamond Mining Co., **IV** 65–66
Premier & Potter Printing Press Co., Inc., **II** 37
Premier Brands Foods, **II** 514
Premier Consolidated Oilfields PLC, **IV** 383
Premier Cruise Lines, **6** 368; **27** 92
Premier Diamond Mining Company, **7** 122
Premier Health Alliance Inc., **10** 143
Premier Industrial Corporation, **9 419–21**; **19** 311
Premier Insurance Co., **26** 487
Premier Medical Services, **31** 357
Premier Milk Pte Ltd., **54** 117
Premier Milling Co., **II** 465

Premier One Products, Inc., **37** 285
Premier Parks, Inc., **27 382–84**
Premier Radio Networks, Inc., **23** 292, 294
Premier Rehabilitation Centers, **29** 400
Premier Sport Group Inc., **23** 66
Premiere Labels Inc., **53** 236
Premiere Products, **I** 403
Premisteres S.A., **II** 663
Premium Standard Farms, Inc., **30 353–55**
PremiumWear, Inc., **30 356–59**
Prémontré, **III** 676; **16** 120
Prentice Hall Computer Publishing, **10** 24
Prentice Hall Inc., **I** 453; **IV** 672; **19** 405; **23** 503
Prescott Ball & Turben, **III** 271; **12** 60
Prescott Investors, **14** 303; **50** 311
Prescription Learning Corporation, **7** 256; **25** 253
Présence, **III** 211
La Preservatrice, **III** 242
Preserver Group, Inc., **44 354–56**
Preserves and Honey, Inc., **II** 497
President Baking Co., **36** 313
President Casinos, Inc., **22 438–40**
President Riverboat Casino-Mississippi Inc., **21** 300
Presidential Airlines, **I** 117
Presidents Island Steel & Wire Company. *See* Laclede Steel Company.
Presidio Oil Co., **III** 197; **IV** 123
Press Associates, **IV** 669; **19** 334
Press Trust of India, **IV** 669
Presse Pocket, **IV** 614
Pressed Steel Car Co., **6** 395; **25** 169
Presses de la Cité, **IV** 614–15
Presstar Printing, **25** 183
Presstek, Inc., **33 345–48**
Pressware International, **12** 377
Prest-O-Lite Co., Inc., **I** 399; **9** 16, 516; **11** 402
Prestage Farms, **46** 83
Prestige et Collections, **III** 48
Prestige Fragrance & Cosmetics, Inc., **22** 158
The Prestige Group plc., **19** 171
Prestige International, **33** 284
Prestige Leather Creations, **31** 435–36
Prestige Properties, **23** 388
Presto Products, Inc., **II** 609–10; **IV** 187; **19** 348; **50** 401
Preston Corporation, **6 421–23**; **14** 566, 568
Prestone Products Corp., **22** 32; **26** 349
Prestwick Mortgage Group, **25** 187
Pretty Good Privacy, Inc., **25** 349
Pretty Neat Corp., **12** 216
Pretty Paper Inc., **14** 499
Pretty Polly, **I** 429
Pretzel Time. *See* Mrs. Fields' Original Cookies, Inc.
Pretzelmaker. *See* Mrs. Fields' Original Cookies, Inc.
Pretzels Incorporated, **24** 241
Preussag AG, **I** 542–43; **II** 386; **IV** 109, 201, 231; **17 378–82**; **21** 370; **28** 454; **42 279–83 (upd.)**; **44** 432
Preussenelektra Aktiengesellschaft, **I** 542; **V 698–700**; **39** 57
Preval, **19** 49–50
Previews, Inc., **21** 96
PreVision Marketing, Inc., **37** 409
Priam Corporation, **10** 458
Priba, **26** 158, 160

Pribina, **25** 85
Price Chopper Supermarkets. *See* The
    Golub Corporation.
Price Club, **V** 162–64
Price Co., **34** 198
**Price Communications Corporation, 42
    284–86**
Price Company Ltd, II 664; **IV** 246–47;
    V 162–64; 14 393–94; **25** 11
Price Enterprises, Inc., **14** 395
Price, McCormick & Co., **26** 451
Price Rite, **25** 67
Price Waterhouse LLP, III 84, 420, 527;
    9 422–24; 14 245; **26** 439. *See also*
    PricewaterhouseCoopers
PriceCostco, Inc., 14 393–95
Pricel, **6** 373; **21** 103
Pricesearch Ltd Co, **48** 224
**PricewaterhouseCoopers, 29 389–94
    (upd.)**
Prichard and Constance, **III** 65
Pride & Clarke, **III** 523
PRIDE Enterprises. *See* Prison
    Rehabilitative Industries and Diversified
    Enterprises, Inc.
Pride Petroleum Services. *See* DeKalb
    Genetics Corporation.
Priggen Steel Building Co., **8** 545
Primadonna Resorts Inc., **17** 318
Primagas GmbH, **55** 347
Primark Corp., 10 89–90; 13 416–18
Primary Coatings, Inc., **51** 190
Prime Care International, Inc., **36** 367
Prime Computer, Inc. *See* Computervision
    Corporation.
**Prime Hospitality Corporation, 52
    280–83**
Prime Motor Inns Inc., **III** 103; **IV** 718; **11**
    177; **17** 238
The Prime-Mover Co., **13** 267
Prime Service, Inc., **28** 40
Prime Telecommunications Corporation, **8**
    311
PrimeAmerica, **III** 340
**Primedex Health Systems, Inc., 25
    382–85**
Primedia Inc., **7** 286; **12** 306; **21** 403–04;
    22 441–43; **23** 156, 158, 344, 417; **24**
    274
Primergy Corp., **39** 261
Primerica Corporation, I 597, 599–602,
    604, 607–09, **612–14,** 615; **II** 422; **III**
    283 8 118; **9** 218–19, 360–61; **11** 29;
    15 464; **27** 47; **36** 202. *See also*
    American Can Co.
Primerica Financial Services, **30** 124
PriMerit Bank, **19** 412
Primes Régal Inc., **II** 651
PrimeSource, **26** 542
Primestar, **38** 176
PRIMESTAR Partners L.P., **28** 241
Primex Fibre Ltd., **IV** 328
Primo Foods Ltd., **I** 457; **7** 430
Prince Co., **II** 473
Prince Gardner Company, **17** 465; **23** 21
Prince Golf International, Ltd., **23** 450
Prince Holding Corporation, **26** 231
Prince Motor Co. Ltd., **I** 184
Prince of Wales Hotels, PLC, **14** 106; **25**
    308
Prince Sports Group, Inc., 15 368–70
Prince Street Technologies, Ltd., **8** 271
Prince William Bank, **II** 337; **10** 425

Princess Cruise Lines, **IV** 256; **22
    444–46**
Princess Dorothy Coal Co., **IV** 29
Princess Hotel Group, **21** 353
Princess Hotels International Inc., **45** 82
Princess Metropole, **21** 354
Princeton Gas Service Company, **6** 529
Princeton Laboratories Products Company,
    8 84; **38** 124
The Princeton Review, Inc., 12 142; **42**
    210, **287–90**
Princeton Telecommunications Corporation,
    26 38
Princeville Airlines, **24** 22
**Principal Mutual Life Insurance
    Company, III 328–30**
Principles, **V** 21–22
Princor Financial Services Corp., **III** 329
Pringle Barge Line Co., **17** 357
Print Technologies, Inc., **22** 357
Printex Corporation, **9** 363
**Printrak, A Motorola Company, 44
    357–59**
Printronix, Inc., 14 377–78; **18 434–36**
Priority Records, **22** 194
Pripps Ringnes, **18** 394, 396–97
Prism Systems Inc., **6** 310
Prismo Universal, **III** 735
**Prison Rehabilitative Industries and
    Diversified Enterprises, Inc. (PRIDE),
    53 277–79**
Prisunic SA, **V** 9–11; **19** 307–09
Prisunic-Uniprix, **26** 160
Pritchard Corporation. *See* Black &
    Veatch, Inc.
Pritzker & Pritzker, **III** 96–97
Privatbanken, **II** 352
Private Colleges and Universities, Inc., **55**
    15
Pro-Fac Cooperative, Inc., **7** 104–06; **21**
    154–55, 157
Pro-Lawn, **19** 250
Pro-Line Corporation, **36** 26
Pro-optik AG, **31** 203
Probe Exploration Inc., **25** 232
Process Engineering Inc., **21** 108
Process Systems International, **21** 108
Processing Technologies International. *See*
    Food Ingredients Technologies.
Procino-Rossi Corp., **II** 511
Procor Limited, **16** 357
Procordia Foods, **II** 478; **18** 396
Procter & Gamble Company, I 34, 129,
    290, 331, 366; **II** 478, 493, 544, 590,
    684, 616; **III** 20–25, 36–38, 40–41, 44,
    50–53; IV 282, 290, 329–30; **6** 26–27,
    50–52, 129, 363; **7** 277, 300, 419; **8** 63,
    106–07, 253, 282, 344, 399, **431–35**
    (upd.), 477, 511–12; **9** 260, 291,
    317–19, 552; **10** 54, 288; **11** 41, 421; **12**
    80, 126–27, 439; **13** 39, 197, 199, 215;
    14 121–22, 262, 275; **15** 357; **16**
    302–04, 440; **18** 68, 147–49, 217, 229;
    22 146–47, 210; **26 380–85 (upd.); 32**
    208, 474–77; **35** 111, 113; **37** 270; **38**
    365; **42** 51; **43** 257–58; **52** 349
Proctor & Collier, **I** 19
Proctor & Schwartz, **17** 213
Proctor-Silex. *See* Hamilton Beach/Proctor-
    Silex Inc.
Prodega Ltd. *See* Bon Appetit Holding AG.
**Prodigy Communications Corporation,
    10** 237–38; **12** 562; **13** 92; **27** 517; **34
    360–62**

Prodigy Consulting Inc., **51** 198
Product Components, Inc., **19** 415
Production Association
    Kirishinefteorgsintez, **48** 378
Productivity Point International Inc., **54**
    192–93
Productos Ortiz, **II** 594
Produits Chimiques Ugine Kuhlmann, **I**
    303; **IV** 547
Produits Jaeger, **27** 258
Profarmaco Nobel S.r.l., **16** 69
Professional Bull Riders Inc., 55 310–12
Professional Care Service, **6** 42
Professional Computer Resources, Inc., **10**
    513
Professional Detailing, Inc. *See* PDI, Inc.
Professional Education Systems, Inc., **17**
    272; **53** 319
**The Professional Golfers' Association of
    America, 41 318–21**
Professional Health Care Management Inc.,
    14 209
Professional Health-Care Resources, **50**
    123
Professional Research, **III** 73
Professional Underwriters Liability
    Insurance Company, **55** 128
Proffitt's, Inc., 19 323–25, 510, 512. *See
    also* Saks Holdings, Inc.
Profile Extrusion Company, **22** 337
Profimatics, Inc., **11** 66
PROFITCo., **II** 231
Progenx, Inc., **47** 221
Progil, **I** 389
Progress Development Organisation, **10**
    169
**Progress Software Corporation, 15
    371–74**
Progressive Bagel Concepts, Inc. *See*
    Einstein/Noah Bagel Corporation.
**Progressive Corporation, 11 405–07; 29
    395–98 (upd.)**
Progressive Distributions Systems, **44** 334
Progressive Distributors, **12** 220
Progressive Grocery Stores, **7** 202
Progressive Networks, Inc., **37** 193. *See
    also* RealNetworks, Inc.
Progresso, **I** 514; **14** 212
Project Carriers. *See* Hansa Linie.
Projexions Video Supply, Inc., **24** 96
Projiis, **II** 356
ProLab Nutrition, Inc., **49** 275, 277
Prolabo, **I** 388
Proland, **12** 139
Proler International Corp., **13** 98; **19**
    380–81
Promarkt Holding GmbH, **24** 266, 270
Promigas, **IV** 418
Promodès Group, **24** 475; **26** 158, 161; **37**
    21
Promotional Graphics, **15** 474
Promstroybank, **II** 242
Promus Companies, Inc., III 95; **9
    425–27; 15** 46; **16** 263; **22** 537; **38**
    76–77; **43** 225–26
Pronto Pacific, **II** 488
Prontophot Holding Limited, **6** 490
Prontor-Werk Alfred Gauthier GmbH, **III**
    446
Propaganda Films, Inc., **23** 389, 391
Property Automation Software Corporation,
    49 290
Prophecy Ltd., **55** 24
Prophet Foods, **I** 449

Propwix, **IV** 605

ProSiebenSat.1 Media AG, **46** 403; **54 295–98**

Prosim, S.A., **IV** 409

Proskauer Rose LLP, **47 308–10**

ProSource Distribution Services, Inc., **16** 397; **17** 475

Prospect Farms, Inc., **II** 584; **14** 514; **50** 492

The Prospect Group, Inc., **11** 188

Prospect Provisions, Inc. *See* King Kullen Grocery Co., Inc.

Prospectors Airways, **IV** 165

Protan & Fagertun, **25** 464

Protection One, Inc., **32 372–75**

Protective Closures, **7** 296–97

Protective Insurance Company, **51** 37, 39

La Protectrice, **III** 346–47

Protek, **III** 633

Proto Industrial Tools, **III** 628

Protogene Laboratories Inc., **17** 288

Proveedora de Seguridad del Golfo, S.A. de C.V., **45** 425–26

Proventus A.B., **II** 303

Proventus Handels AB, **35** 362

Provi-Soir, **II** 652

Provi-Viande, **II** 652

Provibec, **II** 652

The Providence Journal Company, **28 367–69**; **30** 15

La Providence, **III** 210–11

Providence National Bank, **9** 228

Providence Steam and Gas Pipe Co. *See* Grinnell Corp.

Providencia, **III** 208

Provident Bank, **III** 190

Provident Institution for Savings, **13** 467

Provident Life and Accident Insurance Company of America, **III 331–33**, 404. *See also* UnumProvident Corporation.

Provident National Bank, **II** 342

Provident Services, Inc., **6** 295

Provident Travelers Mortgage Securities Corp., **III** 389

Providian Financial Corporation, **52** 62, **284–90 (upd.)**

Provigo Inc., **II 651–53**; **12** 413; **51 301–04 (upd.)**

Provimi, **36** 185

Les Provinces Réunies, **III** 235

Provincetown-Boston Airlines, **I** 118

Provincial Bank of Ireland Ltd., **16** 13

Provincial Engineering Ltd, **8** 544

Provincial Gas Company, **6** 526

Provincial Insurance Co., **III** 373

Provincial Newspapers Ltd., **IV** 685–86; **28** 502

Provincial Traders Holding Ltd., **I** 437

Provinzial-Hülfskasse, **II** 385

Provost & Provost, **II** 651

PROWA, **22** 89

Proximity Technology, **23** 210

Prudential Assurance Company, **24** 314

Prudential Bache Securities, **9** 441

Prudential-Bache Trade Corporation, **II** 51; **21** 331

Prudential Corporation plc, **II** 319; **III 334–36**; **IV** 711; **8** 276–77. *See also* Prudential plc.

Prudential Insurance Company of America, **I** 19, 334, 402; **II** 103, 456; **III** 79, 92, 249, 259, 265–67, 273, 291–93, 313, 329, **337–41**; **IV** 410, 458; **10** 199; **11** 243; **12** 28, 453, 500; **13**

561; **14** 95, 561; **16** 135, 497; **17** 325; **22** 266; **23** 226; **25** 399; **30** 360–64 (upd.); **36** 77–78; **42** 193, 196; **45** 294; **50** 153, 497; **52** 238–39

Prudential Oil & Gas, Inc., **6** 495–96

Prudential plc, **48 325–29 (upd.)**

Prudential Refining Co., **IV** 400

Prudential Steel, **IV** 74; **24** 143–44

PS Business Parks, Inc., **52** 291

PSA. *See* Pacific Southwest Airlines.

PSA Peugeot Citroen S.A., **7** 35; **28 370–74 (upd.)**; **54** 126

PSB Company, **36** 517

PSCCo. *See* Public Service Company of Colorado.

PSE, Inc., **12** 100

PSF. *See* Premium Standard Farms, Inc.

PSI. *See* Process Systems International.

PSI Resources, **6 555–57**

Psion PLC, **45 346–49**

Psychiatric Institutes of America, **III** 87–88

Psychological Corp., **IV** 623; **12** 223

PT Components, **14** 43

PT PERMINA, **IV** 492, 517

PTI Communications, Inc. *See* Pacific Telecom, Inc.

PTT Nederland N.V., **27** 472; **30** 393–94

PTT Telecom BV, **V** 299–301; **6** 303

PTV. *See* Österreichische Post- und Telegraphenverwaltung.

Pubco Corporation, **17 383–85**

Publi-Graphics, **16** 168

Public Broadcasting Stations, **29** 426; **51** 309

Public/Hacienda Resorts, Inc. *See* Santa Fe Gaming Corporation.

Public Home Trust Co., **III** 104

Public National Bank, **II** 230

Public Savings Insurance Co., **III** 219

Public Service Co., **14** 124

Public Service Company of Colorado, **6 558–60**

Public Service Company of Indiana. *See* PSI Energy.

Public Service Company of New Hampshire, **21 408–12**; **55 313–18 (upd.)**

Public Service Company of New Mexico, **6 561–64**; **27** 486. *See also* PNM Resources Inc.

Public Service Corporation of New Jersey, **44** 360

Public Service Electric and Gas Company, **IV** 366; **V** 701–03; **11** 388

Public Service Enterprise Group Inc., **V 701–03**; **44 360–63 (upd.)**

Public Service Market. *See* The Golub Corporation.

Public Storage, Inc., **21** 476; **52 291–93**, 310–11

Publicaciones Citem, S.A. de C.V., **39** 188

Publicis S.A., **13** 204; **19 329–32**; **21** 265–66; **23** 478, 480; **25** 91; **33** 180; **39** 166, 168; **42** 328, 331

Publicker Industries Inc., **I** 226; **10** 180

PubliGroupe, **49** 424

Publishers Clearing House, **23 393–95**; **27** 20

Publishers Group, Inc., **35 357–59**

Publishers Paper Co., **IV** 295, 677–78; **19** 225

Publishers Press Assoc., **IV** 607; **25** 506

Publishing and Broadcasting Limited, **19** 400–01; **54 299–302**

Publix Super Markets Inc., **II** 155, 627; **7 440–42**; **9** 186; **20** 84, 306; **23** 261; **31 371–374 (upd.)**

Puck Holdings, **35** 474, 476

Puck Lazaroff Inc. *See* The Wolfgang Puck Food Company, Inc.

Pueblo Xtra International, Inc., **47 311–13**; **54** 73–74

Puente Oil, **IV** 385

Puerto Rican Aqueduct and Sewer Authority, **6** 441

Puerto Rican-American Insurance Co., **III** 242

Puerto Rico Electric Power Authority, **47 314–16**

Puget Mill Company, **12** 406–07

Puget Sound Alaska Van Lines. *See* Alaska Hydro-Train.

Puget Sound Energy Inc., **50 365–68 (upd.)**

Puget Sound National Bank, **8** 469–70

Puget Sound Power And Light Company, **6 565–67**; **50** 103

Puget Sound Pulp and Timber Co., **IV** 281; **9** 259

Puget Sound Tug and Barge Company, **6** 382

Pulaski Furniture Corporation, **33 349–52**

Pulitzer Publishing Company, **15 375–77**

Pullman Co., **II** 403; **III** 94, 744

Pullman Savings and Loan Association, **17** 529

Pullman Standard, **7** 540

Pulsar Internacional S.A., **21 413–15**

Pulse Engineering, Inc., **29** 461

Pulte Corporation, **8 436–38**; **22** 205, 207

Pulte Homes, Inc., **42 291–94 (upd.)**

Puma AG Rudolf Dassler Sport, **35 360–63**; **36** 344, 346

AB Pump-Separator, **III** 418–19

Pumpkin Masters, Inc., **48 330–32**

Punchcraft, Inc., **III** 569; **20** 360

Purdue Fredrick Company, **13** 367

Pure-Gar, Inc., **49** 276

Pure Milk Products Cooperative, **11** 24

Pure Oil Co., **III** 497; **IV** 570; **24** 521

Pure Packed Foods, **II** 525; **13** 293; **50** 293

Purex Corporation, **I** 450; **III** 21; **22** 146

Purex Pool Systems, **I** 13, 342; **18** 163

Purfina, **IV** 497

Purina Mills, Inc., **32 376–79**

Puris Inc., **14** 316

Puritan-Bennett Corporation, **13 419–21**

Puritan Chemical Co., **I** 321

Puritan Fashions Corp., **22** 122

Purity Stores, **I** 146

Purity Supreme, Inc., **II** 674; **24** 462

Purle Bros., **III** 735

Purnell & Sons Ltd., **IV** 642; **7** 312

Purodenso Co., **III** 593

Purolator Courier, Inc., **6** 345–46, 390; **16** 397; **18** 177; **25** 148

Purolator Products Company, **III** 593; **21 416–18**; **28** 263

Puros de Villa Gonzales, **23** 465

Purup-Eskofot, **44** 44

Push Records, Inc., **42** 271

Puss 'n Boots, **II** 559

Putnam Investments Inc., **25** 387; **30** 355. *See also* Marsh & McLennan Companies, Inc.
Putnam Management Co., **III** 283
Putnam Reinsurance Co., **III** 198
Putt-Putt Golf Courses of America, Inc., 23 396–98
PW Eagle, Inc., 48 333–36
PWA Group, **IV** 323–25; **28** 446
PWS Holding Corporation, **13** 406; **26** 47
PWT Projects Ltd., **22** 89
PWT Worldwide, **11** 510
PYA/Monarch, **II** 675; **26** 504
Pyramid Breweries Inc., 33 353–55
Pyramid Communications, Inc., **IV** 623
Pyramid Companies, 54 303–05
Pyramid Electric Company, **10** 319
Pyramid Electronics Supply, Inc., **17** 275
Pyramid Technology Corporation, **10** 504; **27** 448
Pytchley Autocar Co. Ltd., **IV** 722
Pyxis. *See* Cardinal Health, Inc.
Pyxis Resources Co., **IV** 182

Q Lube, Inc., **18** 145; **24** 339
Qantas Airways Limited, **I** 92–93; **6** 79, 91, 100, 105, **109–13**, 117; **14** 70, 73; **24 396–401 (upd.)**; **27** 466; **31** 104; **38** 24
Qatar General Petroleum Corporation, IV 524–26
Qiagen N.V., 39 333–35
Qintex Australia Ltd., **II** 150; **25** 329
QMS Ltd., **43** 284
QO Chemicals, Inc., **14** 217
QSP, Inc., **IV** 664
Qtera Corporation, **36** 352
Quad/Graphics, Inc., 19 333–36
Quail Oil Tools, **28** 347–48
Quaker Alloy, Inc., **39** 31–32
Quaker Fabric Corp., 19 337–39
Quaker Oats Company, **I** 30; **II** 558–60, 575, 684; **12** 167, 169, **409–12 (upd.)**; **13** 186; **22** 131, 337–38; **25** 90, 314; **27** 197; **30** 219; **31** 282; **34 363–67 (upd.)**; **38** 349; **43** 121, 218
Quaker State Corporation, **7 443–45**; **21 419–22 (upd.)**; **25** 90; **26** 349. *See also* Pennzoil-Quaker State Company.
QUALCOMM Incorporated, **20 438–41**; **26** 532; **38** 271; **39** 64; **41** 289; **43** 312–13; **46** 410, 422; **47 317–21 (upd.)**
Qualcore, S. de R.L. de C.V., **51** 116
Qualicare, Inc., **6** 192
Qualipac, **55** 309
QualiTROL Corporation, **7** 116–17
Quality Aviation Services, Inc., **53** 132
Quality Bakers of America, **12** 170
Quality Care Inc., **I** 249
Quality Chekd Dairies, Inc., 48 337–39
Quality Courts Motels, Inc., **14** 105. *See also* Choice Hotels International, Inc.
Quality Dining, Inc., 18 437–40
Quality Food Centers, Inc., 17 386–88; **22** 271, 273
Quality Importers, **I** 226; **10** 180
Quality Inns International, **13** 363; **14** 105. *See also* Choice Hotels International, Inc.
Quality Markets, Inc., **13** 393
Quality Oil Co., **II** 624–25
Quality Paperback Book Club (QPB), **13** 105–07
Quality Products, Inc., **18** 162

Qualtec, Inc., **V** 623; **49** 145
Quanex Corporation, 13 422–24
Quanta Computer Inc., 47 322–24
Quanta Systems Corp., **51** 81
Quantex Microsystems Inc., **24** 31
Quantum Chemical Corporation, 8 439–41; **11** 441; **30** 231, 441
Quantum Computer Services, Inc. *See* America Online, Inc.
Quantum Corporation, **6** 230–31; **10** 56, 403, **458–59**, 463; **25** 530; **36** 299–300
Quantum Health Resources, **29** 364
Quantum Marketing International, Inc., **27** 336
Quantum Offshore Contractors, **25** 104
Quantum Overseas N.V., **7** 360
Quantum Restaurant Group, Inc., **30** 330
Quarex Industries, Inc. *See* Western Beef, Inc.
Quark, Inc., 36 375–79
Quarrie Corporation, **12** 554
Quasi-Arc Co., **I** 315; **25** 80
Quebec Bank, **II** 344
Quebec Credit Union League, **48** 290
Quebec Hydro-Electric Commission. *See* Hydro-Québec.
Quebecor Inc., 12 412–14; **19** 333; **26** 44; **29** 471; **47 325–28 (upd.)**
Queen Casuals, **III** 530
Queen City Broadcasting, **42** 162
Queen Insurance Co., **III** 350
Queens Isetan Co., Ltd., **V** 87
Queensborough Holdings PLC, **38** 103
Queensland Alumina, **IV** 59
Queensland and Northern Territories Air Service. *See* Qantas Airways Limited.
Queensland Mines Ltd., **III** 729
Queensland Oil Refineries, **III** 672
Queiroz Pereira, **IV** 504
Quelle Group, V 165–67
Quennessen, **IV** 118
Quesarias Ibéricas, **23** 219
Quesnel River Pulp Co., **IV** 269
Quest Aerospace Education, Inc., **18** 521
Quest Diagnostics Inc., 26 390–92
Quest Education Corporation, **42** 212
Quest Pharmacies Inc., **25** 504–05
Questar Corporation, **6 568–70**; **10** 432; **26 386–89 (upd.)**
Questor Management Co. LLC, **55** 31
Questor Partners, **I** 332; **26** 185
The Quick & Reilly Group, Inc., 18 552; **20 442–44**; **26** 65
QUICK Corp., **IV** 656
Quick Pak Inc., **53** 236
Quick-Shop, **II** 619
Quicken.com. *See* Intuit Inc.
Quickie Designs, **11** 202, 487–88
Quik Stop Markets, Inc., **12** 112
Quiksilver, Inc., 18 441–43; **27** 329
QuikTrip Corporation, 36 380–83
QuikWok Inc., **II** 556; **13** 408
Quill Corporation, 28 375–77; **55** 354
Quillery, **27** 138
Quilter Goodison, **II** 260
Quimica Industrial Huels Do Brasil Ltda., **I** 350
Quimicos Industriales Penoles. *See* Industrias Penoles, S.A. de C.V.
Quincy Compressor Co., **I** 434–35
Quincy Family Steak House, **II** 679; **10** 331; **19** 287; **27** 17, 19
Quintana Roo, Inc., **17** 243, 245; **25** 42
Quintex Australia Limited, **25** 329

Quintiles Transnational Corporation, 21 423–25
Quinton Hazell Automotive, **III** 495; **IV** 382–83
Quintron, Inc., **11** 475
Quintus Computer Systems, **6** 248
Quixote Corporation, 15 378–80
Quixtar Inc., **30** 62
Quixx Corporation, **6** 580
The Quizno's Corporation, 32 444; **42 295–98**
Quoddy Products Inc., **17** 389, 390
Quotron Systems, Inc., **III** 119; **IV** 670; **9** 49, 125; **30** 127; **47** 37
QVC Network Inc., **9** 428–29; **10** 175; **12** 315; **18** 132; **20** 75; **24** 120, 123
Qwest Communications International, Inc., **25** 499; **26** 36; **32** 218; **36** 43–44; **37** 126, 312–17; **49** 312
QwikSilver II, Inc., **37** 119

R&B Falcon Corp. *See* Transocean Sedco Forex Inc.
R&B, Inc., 51 305–07
R & B Manufacturing Co., **III** 569; **20** 361
R&D Systems, Inc., **52** 347
R&O Software-Technik GmbH, **27** 492
R&S Technology Inc., **48** 410
R. and W. Hawaii Wholesale, Inc., **22** 15
R-Anell Custom Homes Inc., **41** 19
R-B. *See* Arby's, Inc.
R-Byte, **12** 162
R-C Holding Inc. *See* Air & Water Technologies Corporation.
R.A. Waller & Co., **III** 282
R.B. Pamplin Corp., 45 350–52
R. Buckland & Son Ltd., **IV** 119
R.C. Bigelow, Inc., 16 90; **49 334–36**
R.C. Willey Home Furnishings, **18** 60
R. Cubed Composites Inc., **I** 387
R.E. Funsten Co., **7** 429
R.G. Barry Corp., 17 389–91; **44 364–67 (upd.)**
R.G. Dun-Bradstreet Corp., **IV** 604–05
R. Griggs Group Limited, 23 399–402; **31** 413–14
R.H. Macy & Co., Inc., **I** 30; **V 168–70**; **8 442–45 (upd.)**; **10** 282; **11** 349; **13** 42; **15** 281; **16** 206–07, 328, 388, 561; **23** 60; **27** 60, 481; **30 379–83 (upd.)**; **31** 190, 192–93; **45** 15
R.H. Squire, **III** 283
R.H. Stengel & Company, **13** 479
R. Hoe & Co., **I** 602; **13** 189
R. Hornibrook (NSW), **I** 592
R.J. Brown Co., **IV** 373; **50** 47
R.J. Reynolds, **I** 259, 261, 363; **II** 542, 544; **III** 16; **IV** 523; **V** 396, 404–05, 407–10, 413, 415, 417–18; **7** 130, 132, 267, 365, 367; **9** 533; **13** 490; **14** 78; **15** 72–73; **16** 242; **18** 416; **19** 369; **21** 315; **27** 125; **29** 195; **32** 344. *See also* RJR Nabisco.
R.J. Reynolds Tobacco Holdings, Inc., 30 384–87 (upd.)
R.J. Tower Corporation. *See* Tower Automotive, Inc.
R.K. Brown, **14** 112
R.L. Crain Limited, **15** 473
R.L. Manning Company, **9** 363–64
R.L. Polk & Co., 10 460–62
R.N. Coate, **I** 216
R-O Realty, Inc., **43** 314
R.O. Hull Co., **I** 361

R.P.M., Inc., **25** 228
R.P. Scherer Corporation, I 678–80; 33 145
R.R. Bowker Co., **17** 398; **23** 440
R.R. Donnelley & Sons Company, IV 660–62, 673; **9 430–32 (upd.); 11** 293; **12** 414, 557, 559; **18** 331; **19** 333; **38 368–71 (upd.)**
R.S.R. Corporation, **31** 48
R.S. Stokvis Company, **13** 499
R. Scott Associates, **11** 57
R. Stock AG, **IV** 198
R-T Investors LC, **42** 323–24
R.T. French USA, **II** 567
R.T. Securities, **II** 457
R.W. Beck, **29** 353
R.W. Harmon & Sons, Inc., **6** 410
R.W. Sears Watch Company, **V** 180
RABA PLC, **10** 274
Rabbit Software Corp., **10** 474
Rabobank Group, 26 419; **33 356–58**
RAC. *See* Ravenswood Aluminum Company.
Racal-Datacom Inc., 11 408–10
Racal Electronics PLC, II 83–84; 11 408, 547; **42** 373, 376; **50** 134
Race Z, Inc. *See* Action Peformance Companies, Inc.
Rachel's Dairy Ltd., **37** 197–98
Racine Hardware Co., **III** 58
Racine Hidraulica, **21** 430
Racine Threshing Machine Works, **10** 377
Racing Champions. *See* Action Performance Companies, Inc.
Racing Champions Corporation, 37 318–20
Racing Collectables Club of America, Inc. *See* Action Performance Companies, Inc.
Rack Rite Distributors, **V** 174
Racket Store. *See* Duckwall-ALCO Stores, Inc.
Rada Corp., **IV** 250
Radian Group Inc., 42 299–301
Radiant Lamp Corp., **13** 398
Radiation Dynamics, **III** 634–35
Radiation, Inc., **II** 37–38
Radiation-Medical Products Corp., **I** 202
Radiator Specialty Co., **III** 570; **20** 362
Radio & Allied Industries, **II** 25
Radio & Television Equipment Company (Radio-Tel), **16** 200–01; **43** 168–69
Radio Austria A.G., **V** 314–16
Radio Cap Company. *See* Norwood Promotional Products, Inc.
Radio City Productions, **30** 102
Radio Corporation of America. *See* RCA Corporation.
Radio Flyer Inc., 34 368–70
Radio-Keith-Orpheum, **II** 32, 88, 135, 146–48, 175; **III** 428; **9** 247; **12** 73; **31** 99
Radio Receptor Company, Inc., **10** 319
Radio Shack, **II** 106–08; **12** 470; **13** 174
Radio Vertrieb Fürth. *See* Grundig AG.
Radiocel, **39** 194
Radiometer A/S, **17** 287
Radiometrics, Inc., **18** 369
RadioShack Canada Inc., **30** 391
RadioShack Corporation, 36 384–88 (upd.)
Radiotelevision Española, **7** 511
Radisson Hotels Worldwide, **22** 126–27
Radium Pharmacy, **I** 704
Radius Inc., 16 417–19

Radix Group, Inc., **13** 20
RadNet Managed Imaging Services, Inc., **25** 382–84
Radnor Venture Partners, LP, **10** 474
Raet, **39** 177
Raf, Haarla Oy, **IV** 349
Raffinerie Tirlemontoise S.A., **27** 436
Raffineriegesellschaft Vohburg/Ingolstadt mbH, **7** 141
RAG AG, 35 364–67
Rag Shops, Inc., 30 365–67
Ragan Outdoor, **27** 280
Ragazzi's, **10** 331
Ragdoll Productions Ltd., 51 308–11
Ragnar Benson Inc., **8** 43–43
RAI, **I** 466
Rail Link, Inc., **27** 181
Rail Van Global Logistics, **54** 276
Railroad Enterprises, Inc., **27** 347
RailTex, Inc., 20 445–47
Railtrack Group PLC, **39** 238; **50 369–72**
Railway Express Agency, **I** 456; **II** 382; **6** 388–89; **25** 146–48
Railway Maintenance Equipment Co., **14** 43
Railway Officials and Employees Accident Assoc., **III** 228
Railway Passengers Assurance Co., **III** 178, 410
Rainbow Crafts, **II** 502; **10** 323
Rainbow Home Shopping Ltd., **V** 160
Rainbow Media, **47** 421
Rainbow Production Corp., **I** 412
Rainbow Programming Holdings, **7** 63–64
Rainbow Resources, **IV** 576
Rainbow Valley Orchards, **54** 257
RainbowBridge Communications, Inc., **25** 162
Raincoast Book Distribution, **34** 5
Rainer Pulp & Paper Company, **17** 439
Rainfair, Inc., **18** 298, 300
Rainforest Café, Inc., 25 386–88; 32 241, 244
Rainier Brewing Company, 23 403–05
Rainier Pulp and Paper Company. *See* Rayonier Inc.
Rainy River Forest Products, Inc., **26** 445
Rajastan Breweries, Ltd., **18** 502
Raky-Danubia, **IV** 485
Ralcorp Holdings, Inc., **13** 293, 425, 427; **15** 189, 235; **21** 53, 56; **22** 337; **36** 238; **43** 438; **50** 294; **55** 96. *See also* Ralston Purina Company.
Raley's Inc., 14 396–98
Ralli International, **III** 502; **IV** 259
Rally's Hamburgers, Inc., 25 389–91; 46 97
Rally's Inc., **14** 452; **15** 345; **16** 96–97; **23** 225
Rallye SA, 12 154; **54 306–09**
Ralph & Kacoo's. *See* Piccadilly Cafeterias, Inc.
Ralph Lauren. *See* Polo/Ralph Lauren Corportion.
The Ralph M. Parsons Company. *See* The Parsons Corporation.
Ralph Wilson Plastics, **III** 610–11
Ralph's Industries, **31** 191
Ralphs Grocery Company, 35 368–70
Ralston Purina Company, I 608, **II** 544, 560, **561–63,** 617; **III** 588; **6** 50–52; **7** 209, 396, 547, 556; **8** 180; **9** 180; **12** 276, 411, 510; **13** 137, 270, 293,

425–27 (upd.); **14** 194–95, 558; **18** 312; **21** 56; **23** 191; **50** 294. *See also* Ralcorp Holdings, Inc.
Ram dis Ticaret, **I** 479
Ram Golf Corp., **III** 24; **32** 447
Ram's Insurance, **III** 370
Ramada International Hotels & Resorts, **II** 142; **III** 99; **IV** 718; **9** 426; **11** 177; **13** 66; **21** 366; **25** 309; **28** 258; **38** 320; **52** 281
Ramazotti, **I** 281
Rambol, **25** 84
Ramo-Woolridge Corp., **I** 539; **14** 510
Ramón Areces Foundation, **V** 52
Rampage Clothing Co., **35** 94
Ramsay Youth Services, Inc., 41 322–24
Ranbar Packing, Inc. *See* Western Beef, Inc.
Ranchers Packing Corp. *See* Western Beef, Inc.
Rand American Investments Limited, **IV** 79; **21** 211
Rand Capital Corp., **35** 52–53
Rand Drill Co., **III** 525
Rand Group, Inc., **6** 247; **24** 234
Rand McNally & Company, 28 378–81; 53 122
Rand Mines Ltd., **I** 422; **IV** 22, 79, 94
Rand Selection Corp. Ltd., **IV** 79
Randall's Food Markets, Inc., 40 364–67
Random House, Inc., II 90; **IV** 583–84, 637, 648; **13** 113, 115, 178, **428–30; 14** 260; **18** 329; **19** 6, 285; **31 375–380 (upd.); 42** 287; **54** 17, 22
Randon Meldkamer, **43** 307
Randstad Holding n.v., 16 420–22; 43 307–10 (upd.)
Randsworth Trust P.L.C., **IV** 703
Range Resources Corporation, 45 353–55
Rank Organisation PLC, II 139, 147, **157–59; III** 171; **IV** 698; **6** 288; **12** 229; **14 399–402 (upd.); 24** 194; **26** 543, 546; **32** 241, 243–44; **34** 140; **40** 296, 298
Ranks Hovis McDougall Limited, II 157, **564–65; 28 382–85 (upd.)**
Ransburg Corporation, **22** 282
Ransom and Randolph Company, **10** 271
Ransom Industries LP, **55** 266
Ransomes America Corp., **III** 600
RAO Unified Energy System of Russia, 45 356–60
Rapala-Normark Group, Ltd., 30 368–71
Rapicom, **III** 159
Rapid American, **I** 440
Rapides Bank & Trust Company, **11** 107
Rapidforms, Inc., **35** 130–31
Rapifax of Canada, **III** 160
Rare Hospitality International Inc., 19 340–42
RAS. *See* Riunione Adriatica di Sicurtà SpA.
Rascal House, **24** 243
Rassini Rheem, **III** 581
Ratin A/S, **49** 376
Rational GmbH, **22** 354
Rational Systems Inc., **6** 255; **25** 299
Ratti Vallensasca, **25** 312
Raufast et Fils, **35** 205
Rauland Corp., **II** 124; **13** 573
Rauma-Repola Oy, **II** 302; **IV** 316, 340, 349–50. *See also* Metso Corporation
Rauscher Pierce Refsnes, Inc., **15** 233

Raven Industries, Inc., 33 359–61
Raven Press, **14** 555
Ravenhead, **16** 120
Ravenna Metal Products Corp., **12** 344
Ravenseft Properties Ltd., **IV** 696, 704–05; **49** 246, 248
Ravenswood Aluminum Company, **52** 72–73
RAVIcad, **18** 20; **43** 17
Rawlings Sporting Goods Co., Inc., 7 177; **23** 449; **24 402–04**
Rawlplug Co. Ltd., **IV** 382–83
Rawls Brothers Co., **13** 369
Rawson, Holdsworth & Co., **I** 464
Ray Industries, **22** 116
Ray Simon, **24** 94
Ray Strauss Unlimited, **22** 123
Ray's Printing of Topeka, **II** 624
Raychem Corporation, III 492; **8 446–47**
Raycom Sports, **6** 33
Raymar Book Corporation, **11** 194
Raymond International Inc., **28** 201
Raymond, Jones & Co., **IV** 647
Raymond, Trice & Company, **14** 40
Raynet Corporation, **8** 447
Rayonese Textile, Inc., **29** 140
Rayonier Inc., 24 405–07
Rayovac Corporation, **13 431–34; 17** 105; **23** 497; **24** 480; **39 336–40 (upd.)**
Raytheon Aircraft Holdings Inc., 46 354–57
Raytheon Company, I 463, 485, 544; **II** 41, 73, **85–87; III** 643; **8** 51, 157; **11** 197, **411–14 (upd.); 12** 46, 247; **14** 223; **17** 419, 553, 564; **21** 200; **23** 181; **24** 88; **25** 223; **36** 190–91; **38 372–77 (upd.); 42** 373, 376; **48** 252; **50** 232
Razel S.A., **55** 62
Razorback Acquisitions, **19** 455
Razorfish, Inc., 37 321–24
RB&W Corp., **17** 372
RBC Dominion Securities, **25** 12
RCA Corporation, I 142, 454, 463; **II** 29–31, 34, 38, 56, 61, 85–86, **88–90**, 96, 102, 117–18, 120, 124, 129, 132–33, 151–52, 313, 609, 645; **III** 118, 122, 132, 149, 152, 165, 171, 569, 653–54; **IV** 252, 583, 594; **6** 164–66, 240, 266, 281, 288, 334; **7** 520; **8** 157; **9** 283; **10** 173; **11** 197, 318, 411; **12** 204, 208, 237, 454, 544, 548; **13** 106, 398, 429, 506, 573; **14** 357, 436; **16** 549; **17** 29; **20** 361; **21** 151; **22** 541; **23** 181; **26** 358, 511; **28** 349; **31** 376; **34** 186, 516; **38** 373
RCA Global Communications, Inc., **27** 304
RCG International, Inc., **III** 344
RCM Technologies, Inc., 34 371–74
RCN Corp., **25** 107
RDMS Direct Marketing BV, **53** 362
RDO Equipment Company, 33 362–65
REA. *See* Railway Express Agency.
Rea & Derick, **II** 605
Rea Construction Company, **17** 377
Rea Magnet Wire Co., **IV** 15
React-Rite, Inc., **8** 271
Read, R.L., **II** 417
Read-Rite Corp., 10 403–04, **463–64; 18** 250
The Reader's Digest Association, Inc., IV 663–64; **17 392–95 (upd.)**
Reader's Garden Inc., **22** 441
Reading & Bates Corp. *See* Transocean Sedco Forex Inc.

Reading Railroad, **9** 407
Ready Mixed Concrete, **III** 687, 737–40; **28** 82
Real Color Displays, **53** 117
Real Decisions, **21** 236
Real Estate Maintenance, **25** 15
Real Fresh, **25** 85
Real Goods Trading Company, **41** 177
Real-Share, Inc., **18** 542
Real Turismo, S.A. de C.V., 50 373–75
RealCom Communications Corporation, **15** 196
Reale Mutuale, **III** 273
Reality Group Limited, **47** 165, 169
The Really Useful Group, 23 390; **26** 393–95; **34** 422
RealNetworks, Inc., 53 280–82
Realty Development Co. *See* King Kullen Grocery Co., Inc.
Realty Investment Group, **25** 127
Realty Parking Properties II L.P., **18** 104
Réassurances, **III** 392
Reavis & McGrath, **47** 139
Rebekah W. Harkness Foundation, **52** 199
Recaro North America Inc., **26** 231
Reckitt & Colman plc, II 566–67; 15 46, 360; **18** 556; **22** 148; **27** 69
Reckitt Benckiser plc, 42 302–06 (upd.)
Reckson Associates Realty Corp., 47 329–31
Reconstruction Bank of Holland, **IV** 707
Reconstruction Finance Bank, **II** 292
Reconstruction Finance Corp., **I** 67, 203; **II** 261; **IV** 10, 333
Record Bar / Licorice Pizza, **9** 361
Record Merchandisers. *See* Entertainment UK.
Record World Inc., **9** 361
Recordati S.p.A., **52** 135
Recording for the Blind & Dyslexic, 51 312–14
Recoton Corp., 15 381–83
Recoupe Recycling Technologies, **8** 104
Recovery Centers of America, **III** 88
Recovery Engineering, Inc., 25 392–94
Recreational Equipment, Inc., 18 444–47; 22 173
Recticel S.A., **III** 581; **17** 182–84
Rectigraph Co., **III** 171
Recubrimientos Interceramic, S.A. de C.V., **53** 175
Recycled Paper Greetings, Inc., 21 426–28
RED, **44** 164
Red & White, **II** 682
The Red Adair Company, **37** 171
Red Ant Entertainment, **17** 14
Red Apple Group, Inc., 23 406–08; 24 528–29; **31** 231
Red Arrow, **II** 138
Red Ball, Inc., **18** 300
Red Brick Systems Inc., **30** 246
Red Bull, **31** 244
Red Carpet Food Systems, **39** 409
Red Chisinau, **51** 389
Red Food Stores, Inc., **19** 327–28
Red Hat, Inc., 45 361–64
Red House Books Ltd., **29** 426
Red Kap, **V** 390–91
Red L Foods, **13** 244
Red Line HealthCare Corporation, **47** 236
Red Lion Entertainment, **29** 503
Red Lobster Inns of America, **16** 156–58

Red Lobster Restaurants, **II** 502–03; **6** 28; **10** 322–24; **19** 258
Red Oak Consulting, **42** 244
Red Owl Stores, Inc., **II** 670; **18** 506; **50** 456
Red Roof Inns, Inc., 13 363; **18 448–49; 21** 362
Red Rooster, **V** 35
Red Sea Insurance Co., **III** 251
Red Spot Paint & Varnish Company, 55 319–22
Red Star Express, **14** 505
Red Star Milling Co., **II** 501; **6** 397; **10** 322
Red Storm, **41** 409
The Red Wing Co., Inc., **28** 382; **55** 96, 98
Red Wing Pottery Sales, Inc., 52 294–96
Red Wing Shoe Company, Inc., 9 433–35; **30 372–75 (upd.)**
Redactron, **III** 166; **6** 282
Redbook Florists Service, **28** 138
Redbook Publishing Co., **14** 460
Reddy Elevator Co., **III** 467
Reddy Ice, **II** 661
Redentza, **IV** 504
Redgate Communications, **26** 19
Redhill Tile Co., **III** 734
Redhook Ale Brewery, Inc., 31 381–84
Redi, **IV** 610
Rediffusion, **II** 139; **24** 194
Reditab S.p.A., **12** 109
Redken Laboratories, **8** 131; **24** 251
Redland Plasterboard, **28** 83
Redland plc, III 495, 688, **734–36; 14** 249, 739; **15** 154; **37** 205
Redlaw Industries Inc., **15** 247
Redman Industries, Inc., **17** 81, 83
Redmond & Co., **I** 376
La Redoute, S.A., **V** 11; **19** 306, 309
Redpath Industries, **II** 581–82
Redrow Group plc, 31 385–87
Redwood Design Automation, **11** 47; **16** 520
Redwood Fire & Casualty Insurance Co., **III** 214
Redwood Systems, **48** 112
Reebok International Ltd., V 375–77; 8 171, 303–04, 393; **9** 134–35, **436–38 (upd.); 11** 50–51, 349; **13** 513; **14** 8; **17** 244–45, 260; **18** 266; **19** 112; **22** 173; **25** 258, 352, 450; **26 396–400 (upd.); 36** 346
Reed & Ellis, **17** 439
Reed & Gamage, **13** 243
Reed Corrugated Containers, **IV** 249
Reed Elsevier plc, 19 268; **23** 271, 273; **31 388–394 (upd.); 32** 354; **33** 263, 265–66, 458; **34** 438; **43** 92–93
Reed International PLC, I 423; **IV** 270, 642, **665–67**, 711; **7** 244–45, 343; **10** 407; **12** 359; **17 396–99 (upd.); 23** 350; **49** 408
Reed Tool Coompany, **III** 429; **22** 68
Reeder Light, Ice & Fuel Company, **6** 592; **50** 38
Reedpack, **IV** 339–40, 667; **28** 445
Reeds Jewelers, Inc., 22 447–49
Reese Finer Foods, Inc., **7** 429
Reese Products, **III** 569; **11** 535; **20** 361
Reeves Banking and Trust Company, **11** 181
Reeves Brothers, **17** 182
Reeves Pulley Company, **9** 440
Refco, Inc., **10** 251; **22** 189

Reference Software International, **10** 558
Refined Sugars, **II** 582
Reflectone Inc. *See* CAE USA Inc.
Reflex Winkelmann & Pannhoff GmbH, **18** 163
Reform Rt, **IV** 652; **7** 392
Refractarios Mexicanos, S.A. de C.V., **22** 285
Refrigeração Paraná S.A., **22** 27
Refrigerantes do Oeste, SA, **47** 291
Regal-Beloit Corporation, **18 450–53**
Regal Drugs, **V** 171
Regal Inns, **13** 364
Regal Manufacturing Co., **15** 385
Regency, **12** 316
Regency Electronics, **II** 101
Regency Health Services Inc., **25** 457
Regency International, **10** 196
Regenerative Environmental Equipment Company, Inc., **6** 441
Regeneron Pharmaceuticals Inc., **10** 80
Regent Canal Co., **III** 272
Regent Carolina Corporation, **37** 226
Regent Communications Inc., **23** 294
Regent Insurance Co., **III** 343
Regent International Hotels Limited, **9** 238; **29** 200
Régie Autonome des Pétroles, **IV** 544–46; **21** 202–04
Régie des Mines de la Sarre, **IV** 196
Régie des Télégraphes et Téléphones. *See* Belgacom.
Régie Nationale des Usines Renault, **I** 136, 145, 148, 178–79, 183, **189–91**, 207, 210; **II** 13; **III** 392, 523; **7** 566–67; **11** 104; **12** 91; **15** 514; **19** 50; **22** 331; **50** 197. *See also* Renault SA.
Regina Verwaltungsgesellschaft, **II** 257
Regional Bell Operating Companies, **15** 125; **18** 111–12, 373
Regis Corporation, **18 454–56**; **22** 157; **26** 475, 477
Register & Tribune Co. *See* Cowles Media Company.
Registered Vitamin Company, **V** 171
Regnecentralen AS, **III** 164
Rego Supermarkets and American Seaway Foods, Inc., **9** 451; **13** 237
Rehab Hospital Services Corp., **III** 88; **10** 252
RehabClinics Inc., **11** 367
Rehrig Manufacturing, **51** 35
REI. *See* Recreational Equipment, Inc.
Reich, Landman and Berry, **18** 263
Reichart Furniture Corp., **14** 236
Reichhold Chemicals, Inc., **I** 386, 524; **8** 554; **10 465–67**
Reichs-Kredit-Gesellschaft mbH, **IV** 230
Reichs-Kredit- und Krontrollstelle GmbH, **IV** 230
Reichswerke AG für Berg- und Hüttenbetriebe Hermann Göring, **IV** 200
Reichswerke AG für Erzbergbau und Eisenhütten, **IV** 200
Reichswerke Hermann Göring, **IV** 233
Reid Bros. & Carr Proprietary, **III** 672–73
Reid Dominion Packaging Ltd., **IV** 645
Reid Ice Cream Corp., **II** 471
Reid, Murdoch and Co., **II** 571
Reid Press Ltd., **IV** 645
Reidman Corporation, **41** 65
Reidsville Fashions, Inc., **13** 532
Reigel Products Corp., **IV** 289
Reimersholms, **31** 458–60

Reims Aviation, **8** 92; **27** 100
Rein Elektronik, **10** 459
Reinsurance Agency, **III** 204–05
Reisebüro Bangemann, **II** 164
Reisholz AG, **III** 693
Reisland GmbH, **15** 340
Reiue Nationale des Usines Renault, **7** 220
Rekkof Restart NV, **28** 327
Relational Courseware, Inc., **21** 235–36
Relational Database Systems Inc., **10** 361–62
Relational Technology Inc., **10** 361
Relationship Marketing Group, Inc., **37** 409
Release Technologies, **8** 484
Reliable Stores Inc., **14** 236
Reliable Tool, **II** 488
Reliance Electric Company, **IV** 429; **9 439–42**
Reliance Group Holdings, Inc., **II** 173; **III 342–44**; **IV** 642
Reliance Life Insurance Co., **III** 275–76
Reliance National Indemnity Company, **18** 159
Reliance Steel & Aluminum Co., **19 343–45**
Reliant Energy Inc., **44 368–73 (upd.)**
ReLife Inc., **14** 233; **33** 185
Relocation Central. *See* CORT Business Services Corporation.
Rembrandt Group Ltd., **50** 144; **I** 289; **IV** 91, 93, 97; **V** 411–13; **19** 367–69; **24** 449
RemedyTemp, Inc., **20 448–50**
Remgro, **IV** 97
Remington Arms Company, Inc., **I** 329; **8** 152; **12 415–17**; **26** 125; **40 368–71 (upd.)**
Remington Products Company, L.L.C., **42 307–10**
Remington Rand, **III** 122, 126, 148, 151, 165–66, 642; **6** 251, 265, 281–82; **10** 255; **12** 416; **19** 430; **30** 337
Remmele Engineering, Inc., **17** 534
Rémy Cointreau S.A., **20 451–53**
Remy Martin, **48** 348–49
REN Corp. USA, Inc., **13** 161
REN Corporation, **49** 156
Renaissance Communications Corp., **22** 522
Renaissance Connects, **16** 394
Renaissance Cosmetics Inc. *See* New Dana Perfumes Co.
Renaissance Energy Ltd., **47** 181
Renaissance Hotel Group N.V., **38** 321
Renaissance Learning Systems, Inc., **39 341–43**
Renal Systems, Inc. *See* Minntech Corporation.
Renault. *See* Régie Nationale des Usines Renault.
Renault S.A., **26** 11, **401–04 (upd.)**; **34** 303, 306
Rendeck International, **11** 66
Rendic International, **13** 228
René Garraud, **III** 68
Renfro Corp., **25** 167
Rengo Co., Ltd., **IV 326**
Renishaw plc, **46 358–60**
RENK AG, **37 325–28**
Rennies Consolidated Holdings, **I** 470; **20** 312
Reno Air Inc., **23 409–11**; **24** 400; **28** 25
Reno de Medici S.p.A., **41 325–27**
Réno-Dépôt Inc., **26** 306

Reno Technologies, **12** 124
Rent-A-Center, Inc., **22** 194; **24** 485; **33** 366, 368; **45 365–67**
Rent-Way, Inc., **33 366–68**
Rental Service Corporation, **28 386–88**
Renters Choice Inc. *See* Rent-A-Center, Inc.
Rentokil Initial Plc, **34** 43; **47 332–35**; **49** 375–77
Rentrak Corporation, **35 371–74**
Rentz, **23** 219
Renwick Technologies, Inc., **48** 286
Reo Products. *See* Lifetime Hoan Corporation.
Repairmaster Canada, Inc., **53** 359
Repco Ltd., **15** 246
REPESA, **IV** 528
Replacement Enterprises Inc., **16** 380
Repligen Inc., **13** 241
Repola Ltd., **19** 465; **30** 325
Repola Oy, **IV** 316, 347, 350
Repsol S.A., **IV** 396–97, 506, 514, **527–29**; **16 423–26 (upd.)**; **49** 211
Repsol-YPF S.A., **40 372–76 (upd.)**
Repubblica, **IV** 587
Republic Aircraft Co., **I** 89
Republic Airlines, **I** 113, 132; **6** 104; **25** 421; **28** 265
Republic Aviation Corporation, **I** 55; **9** 205–07; **48** 167
Republic Broadcasting Corp., **23** 292
Republic Corp., **I** 447
Republic Engineered Steels, Inc., **7 446–47 26 405–08 (upd.)**
Republic Freight Systems, **14** 567
Republic Indemnity Co. of America, **III** 191
Republic Industries, Inc., **24** 12; **26 409–11**, 501
Republic Insurance, **III** 404
Republic National Bank, **19** 466
Republic New York Corporation, **11 415–19**
Republic Pictures, **9** 75
Republic Powdered Metals, Inc., **8** 454
Republic Realty Mortgage Corp., **II** 289
Republic Rubber, **III** 641
Republic Steel Corp., **I** 491; **IV** 114; **7** 446; **12** 353; **13** 169, 157; **14** 155; **24** 304. *See also* Republic Engineered Steels, Inc.
Republic Supply Co. of California, **I** 570
Res-Care, Inc., **29 399–402**
Research Analysis Corporation, **7** 15
Research Cottrell, Inc., **6** 441
Research Genetics, Inc., **52** 183–84
Research in Motion Ltd., **54 310–14**
Research Polymers International, **I** 321; **12** 103
Research Publications, **8** 526
Resecenter, **55** 90
Resem SpA, **I** 387
Reserve Mining Co., **17** 356
Reservoir Productions, **17** 150
Residence Inns, **III** 103; **9** 426
Residential Funding Corporation, **10** 92–93
Resin Exchange, **19** 414
Resinous Products, **I** 392
ResNet Communications Inc., **28** 241
Resolution Systems, Inc., **13** 201
Resolution Trust Corp., **10** 117, 134; **11** 371; **12** 368
Resona Holdings Inc., **53** 322

Resorts International, Inc., I 452; **12** 418–20; **19** 402; **26** 462
Resource America, Inc., 42 311–14
Resource Associates of Alaska, Inc., **7** 376
The Resource Club, **32** 80
Resource Electronics, **8** 385
Resource Group International, **25** 207
ReSource NE, Inc., **17** 553
reSOURCE PARTNER, INC., **22** 95
Respond Industries, Inc., **51** 76
Response Oncology, Inc., 27 385–87
Rest Assured, **I** 429
The Restaurant Company, **22** 417
Restaurant Enterprises Group Inc., **14** 195
Restaurant Franchise Industries, **6** 200
Restaurant Property Master, **19** 468
Restaurants Les Pres Limitée, **II** 652
Restaurants Universal Espana S.A., **26** 374
Restaurants Unlimited, Inc., 13 435–37; **23** 127–29
Restoration Hardware, Inc., 30 376–78
Resurgens Communications Group, **7** 336; **8** 311; **27** 306
Retail Association Pskovnefteprodukt, **48** 378
Retail Concepts Inc., **55** 174
Retail Credit Company. *See* Equifax.
Retail Systems Consulting, Inc., **24** 395
Retail Ventures Inc., **14** 427; **24** 26
Retailers Commercial Agency, Inc., **6** 24
Retequattro, **19** 19
Retirement Care Associates Inc., **25** 457
Retirement Inns of America, Inc., **III** 16; **11** 282
Retirement Systems of Alabama, **52** 387
Reuben H. Donnelley Corp., **IV** 605, 661; **19** 133
Reunion Properties, **I** 470; **20** 311–12
Reuters Holdings PLC, IV 259, 652, 654, 656, **668–70**; **10** 277, 407; **21** 68–70; **22** 450–53 (upd.); **34** 11, 227
Revco D.S., Inc., II 449; **III** 10; **V** 171–73; **9** 67, 187; **12** 4; **13** 449; **16** 560; **19** 357; **32** 169–70; **45** 136
Revell-Monogram Inc., 16 427–29; **25** 71; **27** 14
Revere Copper and Brass Co., **IV** 32. *See also* The Paul Revere Corporation.
Revere Foil Containers, Inc., **12** 377
Revere Furniture and Equipment Company, **14** 105; **25** 307
Revere Ware Corporation, 22 454–56
Revlon Inc., I 29, 449, 620, 633, 668, 677, 693, 696; **II** 498, 679; **III** 29, 46, **54–57**, 727; **6** 27; **8** 131, 341; **9** 202–03, 291; **11** 8, 333–34; **12** 314; **16** 439; **17** 110, **400–04** (upd.); **18** 229; **22** 157; **25** 55; **26** 384; **28** 246–47; **30** 188–89
Revson Bros., **III** 54
Rewe-Beteiligungs-Holding National GmbH, **53** 179; **54** 295–96
Rewe Group, **37** 241
Rewe-Liebbrand, **28** 152
Rex Pulp Products Company, **9** 304
Rex Re Insurance Ltd., **51** 143
REX Stores Corp., 10 468–69; **19** 362
Rexall Drug & Chemical Co., **II** 533–34; **III** 610; **13** 525; **14** 547
Rexall Drug Co., **50** 487
Rexall Sundown, Inc., **37** 340, 342
Rexam PLC, 32 380–85 (upd.); **45** 337; **50** 122
Rexel, Inc., 15 384–87

Rexene Products Co., **III** 760; **IV** 457
Rexham Inc., **IV** 259; **8** 483–84
Rexnord Corporation, I 524; **14** 43; **21** 429–32; **37** 30; **55** 324
Reycan, **49** 104
Reydel Industries, **23** 95–96
Reyes Holdings, Inc., **24** 388
Reymer & Bros., Inc., **II** 508; **11** 172
Reymersholm, **II** 366
The Reynolds and Reynolds Company, 17 142, 144; **50** 376–79
Reynolds Electric Co., **22** 353
Reynolds Metals Company, II 421–22; **IV** 11–12, 15, 59, **186–88**; **IV** 122; **12** 278; **19** 346–48 (upd.); **21** 218; **22** 455; **25** 22
RF Communications, **II** 38
RF Micro Devices, Inc., 43 311–13
RF Monolithics Inc., **13** 193
RFI Group, Inc., **54** 275
RHC Holding Corp., **10** 13; **13** 364; **27** 11
RHD Holdings, **23** 413
Rhee Syngman, **I** 516; **12** 293
Rheem Manufacturing, **25** 368; **52** 398–99
Rhein-Elbe Gelsenkirchener Bergwerks A.G., **IV** 25
Rheinelbe Union, **I** 542
Rheinisch Kalksteinwerke Wulfrath, **III** 738
Rheinisch Oelfinwerke, **I** 306
Rheinisch-Westfalische Bank A.G., **II** 279
Rheinisch-Westfälischer Sprengstoff AG, **III** 694
Rheinisch-Westfälisches Elektrizätätswerke AG, **I** 542–43; **III** 154; **IV** 231; **V** 744; **25** 102
Rheinische Aktiengesellschaft für Braunkohlenbergbau, **V** 708
Rheinische Creditbank, **II** 278
Rheinische Metallwaaren- und Maschinenfabrik AG, **9** 443–44
Rheinische Wasserglasfabrik, **III** 31
Rheinische Zuckerwarenfabrik GmbH, **27** 460
Rheinmetall Berlin AG, 9 443–46
Rheinsche Girozentrale und Provinzialbank, Düsseldorf, **II** 385
Rheinstahl AG, **IV** 222
Rheinstahl Union Brueckenbau, **8** 242
Rheintalische Zementfabrik, **III** 701
Rhenus-Weichelt AG, **6** 424, 426
RHI AG, 53 283–86
RHI Entertainment Inc., **16** 257
Rhino Entertainment Company, 18 457–60; **21** 326
RHM. *See* Ranks Hovis McDougall.
Rhodes & Co., **8** 345
Rhodes Inc., 23 412–14
Rhodesian Anglo American Ltd., **IV** 21, 23; **16** 26; **50** 31
Rhodesian Development Corp., **I** 422
Rhodesian Selection Trust, Ltd., **IV** 17–18, 21
Rhodesian Sugar Refineries, **II** 581
Rhodia SA, 38 378–80
Rhodiaceta, **I** 388–89
Rhokana Corp., **IV** 191
Rhône Moulage Industrie, **39** 152, 154
Rhône-Poulenc S.A., I 303–04, 371, **388–90**, 670, 672, 692; **III** 677; **IV** 174, 487, 547; **8** 153, 452; **9** 358; **10** 470–72 (upd.); **16** 121, 438; **21** 466; **23** 194, 197; **34** 284; **38** 379
Rhymey Breweries, **I** 294

Rhymney Iron Company, **31** 369
Rhythm Watch Co., Ltd., **III** 454; **21** 121
La Riassicuratrice, **III** 346
Rica Foods, Inc., 41 328–30
Ricard, **I** 280
Riccar, **17** 124; **41** 114
Riccardo's Restaurant, **18** 538
Rice Broadcasting Co., Inc., **II** 166
Rice-Stix Dry Goods, **II** 414
Riceland Foods, Inc., **27** 390
Rich Products Corporation, 7 448–49; **38** 381–84 (upd.)
Rich's Inc., **9** 209; **10** 515; **31** 191
Richard A. Shaw, Inc., **7** 128
Richard D. Irwin Inc., **IV** 602–03, 678; **47** 102
Richard Hellman Co., **II** 497
Richard Manufacturing Co., **I** 667
Richard P. Simmons, **8** 19
Richard Shops, **III** 502
Richard Thomas & Baldwins, **IV** 42
Richards & O'Neil LLP, **43** 70
Richards Bay Minerals, **IV** 91
Richardson Company, **36** 147
Richardson Electronics, Ltd., 17 405–07
Richardson-Vicks Company, **III** 53; **8** 434; **26** 383
Richardson's, **21** 246
Richfield Oil Corp., **IV** 375–76, 456
Richfood Holdings, Inc., 7 450–51; **50** 458
Richland Co-op Creamery Company, **7** 592
Richland Gas Company, **8** 349
Richmon Hill & Queens County Gas Light Companies, **6** 455
Richmond American Homes of Florida, Inc., **11** 258
Richmond Carousel Corporation, **9** 120
Richmond Cedar Works Manufacturing Co., **12** 109; **19** 360
Richmond Corp., **I** 600; **15** 129
Richmond Paperboard Corp., **19** 78
Richmond Pulp and Paper Company, **17** 281
Richton International Corporation, 39 344–46
Richway, **10** 515
Richwood Building Products, Inc., **12** 397
Richwood Sewell Coal Co., **17** 357
Ricils, **III** 47
Rickards, Roloson & Company, **22** 427
Rickel Home Centers, **II** 673
Ricky Shaw's Oriental Express, **25** 181
Ricoh Company, Ltd., III 121, 157, **159–61**, 172, 454; **6** 289; **8** 278; **18** 386, 527; **19** 317; **21** 122; **24** 429; **36** 389–93 (upd.)
Ricolino, **19** 192
Riddell Inc., **33** 467
Riddell Sports Inc., 22 457–59; **23** 449
Ridder Publications, **IV** 612–13, 629; **7** 191
Ride, Inc., 22 460–63
Ridge Tool Co., **II** 19
Ridgewell's Inc., **15** 87
Ridgewood Properties Inc., **12** 394
Ridgway Co., **23** 98
Ridgway Color, **13** 227–28
Rieck-McJunkin Dairy Co., **II** 533
Riedel-de Haën AG, **22** 32; **36** 431
Riegel Bag & Paper Co., **IV** 344
Rieke Corp., **III** 569; **11** 535; **20** 361
The Riese Organization, 38 385–88
Rieter Holding AG, 42 315–17

Rieter Machine Works, III 638
Rig Tenders Company, 6 383
Riggin & Robbins, 13 244
Riggs National Corporation, 13 438–40
Right Associates, 27 21; 44 156
**Right Management Consultants, Inc., 42
    318–21**
Right Source, Inc., 24 96
RightPoint, Inc., 49 124
RightSide Up, Inc., 27 21
Rijnhaave Information Systems, 25 21
Rike's, 10 282
Riken Corp., IV 160; 10 493
Riken Kagaku Co. Ltd., 48 250
Riken Kankoshi Co. Ltd., III 159
Riken Optical Co., III 159
Riklis Family Corp., 9 447–50; 12 87; 13
    453; 38 169; 43 355
Riku-un Moto Kaisha, V 477
Rinascente Group, 12 153; 54 220
Ring King Visibles, Inc., 13 269
Ring Ltd., 43 99
Ringier America, 19 333
Ringköpkedjan, II 640
Ringling Bros., Barnum & Bailey Circus,
    25 312–13
Ringnes Bryggeri, 18 396
Rini-Rego Supermarkets Inc., 13 238
Rini Supermarkets, 9 451; 13 237
Rinker Materials Corp., III 688
Rio Grande Industries, Inc., 12 18–19
Rio Grande Oil Co., IV 375, 456
Rio Grande Servaas, S.A. de C.V., 23 145
Rio Grande Valley Gas Co., IV 394
Rio Sportswear Inc., 42 269
Rio Sul Airlines, 6 133
Rio Tinto plc, 19 349–53 (upd.); 27 253;
    42 395; 50 380–85 (upd.)
Rio Tinto-Zinc Corp., II 628; IV 56,
    58–61, 189–91, 380; 21 352
Rioblanco, II 477
Riordan Freeman & Spogli, 13 406
Riordan Holdings Ltd., I 457; 10 554
Riser Foods, Inc., 9 451–54; 13 237–38
Rising Sun Petroleum Co., IV 431, 460,
    542
Risk Management Partners Ltd., 35 36
Risk Planners, II 669
Rit Dye Co., II 497
**Ritchie Bros. Auctioneers Inc., 41
    331–34**
Rite Aid Corporation, V 174–76; 9 187,
    346; 12 221, 333; 16 389; 18 199, 286;
    19 354–57 (upd.); 23 407; 29 213; 31
    232; 32 166, 169–70
Rite-Way Department Store, II 649
Riteway Distributor, 26 183
Rittenhouse and Embree, III 269
Rittenhouse Financial Services, 22 495
Ritter Co. See Sybron Corp.
Ritz Camera Centers, 18 186; 34 375–77
**Ritz-Carlton Hotel Company L.L.C., 9
    455–57; 21 366; 29 403–06 (upd.)**
Ritz Firma, 13 512
**Riunione Adriatica di Sicurtà SpA, III
    185, 206, 345–48**
Riva Group Plc, 53 46
The Rival Company, 17 215; 19 358–60
Rivarossi, 16 337
Rivaud Group, 29 370
River Boat Casino, 9 425–26
River City Broadcasting, 25 418
River North Studios. See Platinum
    Entertainment, Inc.

River Oaks Furniture, Inc., 43 314–16
River-Raisin Paper Co., IV 345
River Ranch Fresh Foods—Salinas, Inc.,
    41 11
River Steam Navigation Co., III 522
River Thames Insurance Co., Ltd., 26 487
Riverdeep Group plc, 41 137
Riverside Chemical Company, 13 502
Riverside Furniture, 19 455
Riverside Insurance Co. of America, 26
    487
Riverside Iron Works, Ltd., 8 544
Riverside National Bank of Buffalo, 11
    108
Riverside Press, 10 355–56
Riverside Publishing Company, 36 272
**Riverwood International Corporation, 7
    294; 11 420–23; 48 340–44 (upd.)**
Riviana Foods, III 24, 25; 27 388–91
Riyadh Armed Forces Hospital, 16 94
Rizzoli Publishing, IV 586, 588; 19 19; 23
    88; 54 19, 21
RJMJ, Inc., 16 37
RJR Nabisco Holdings Corp., I 249, 259,
    261; II 370, 426, 477–78, 542–44; V
    408–10, 415; 7 130, 132, 277, 596; 9
    469; 12 82, 559; 13 342; 14 214, 274;
    17 471; 22 73, 95, 441; 23 163; 24 273;
    30 384; 32 234; 33 228; 36 151, 153; 46
    259; 49 77–78. See also R.J Reynolds
    Tobacco Holdings Inc., Nabisco Brands,
    Inc.; R.J. Reynolds Industries, Inc.
RKO. See Radio-Keith-Orpheum.
RKO-General, Inc., 8 207
RKO Radio Sales, 6 33
RLA Polymers, 9 92
RM Marketing, 6 14
**RMC Group p.l.c., III 734, 737–40; 34
    378–83 (upd.)**
RMF Inc., I 412
RMH Teleservices, Inc., 42 322–24
RMP International, Limited, 8 417
Roadhouse Grill, Inc., 22 464–66
Roadline, 6 413–14
**Roadmaster Industries, Inc., 16 430–33;
    22 116**
Roadmaster Transport Company, 18 27; 41
    18
RoadOne. See Miller Industries, Inc.
Roadway Express, Inc., 25 395–98 (upd.)
Roadway Services, Inc., V 502–03; 12
    278, 309; 14 567; 15 111
Roaman's, V 115
Roan Selection Trust Ltd., IV 18, 239–40
Roanoke Capital Ltd., 27 113–14
**Roanoke Electric Steel Corporation, 45
    368–70**
Roanoke Fashions Group, 13 532
Robb Engineering Works, 8 544
**Robbins & Myers Inc., 13 273; 15
    388–90**
Robbins Co., III 546
Robeco Group, IV 193; 26 419–20
Roberds Inc., 19 361–63
Roberk Co., III 603
Robert Allen Companies, III 571; 20 362
Robert Benson, Lonsdale & Co. Ltd., II
    232, 421–22; IV 191
**Robert Bosch GmbH, I 392–93, 411; III
    554, 555, 591, 593; 13 398; 16 434–37
    (upd.); 22 31; 43 317–21 (upd.)**
Robert E. McKee Corporation, 6 150
Robert Fleming Holdings Ltd., I 471; IV
    79; 11 495

Robert Gair Co., 15 128
Robert Garrett & Sons, Inc., 9 363
Robert Grace Contracting Co., I 584
**Robert Half International Inc., 18
    461–63**
Robert Hall Clothes, Inc., 13 535
Robert Hansen Trucking Inc., 49 402
Robert Johnson, 8 281–82
Robert McLane Company. See McLane
    Company, Inc.
Robert McNish & Company Limited, 14
    141
**Robert Mondavi Corporation, 15
    391–94; 39 45; 50 386–90 (upd.); 54
    343**
Robert R. Mullen & Co., I 20
Robert Skeels & Company, 33 467
Robert Stigwood Organization Ltd., 23 390
Robert W. Baird & Co., III 324; 7 495
Robert Warschauer and Co., II 270
Robert Watson & Co. Ltd., I 568
**Robert Wood Johnson Foundation, 35
    375–78**
Robertet SA, 39 347–49
Roberts Express, V 503
Roberts, Johnson & Rand Shoe Co., III
    528–29
**Roberts Pharmaceutical Corporation, 16
    438–40**
Robertson Building Products, 8 546
**Robertson-Ceco Corporation, 8 546; 19
    364–66**
Robertson, Stephens & Co., 22 465
Robin Hood Flour Mills, Ltd., 7 241–43;
    25 241
Robin International Inc., 24 14
Robinair, 10 492, 494
Robinson & Clark Hardware. See Clarcor
    Inc.
Robinson Clubs, II 163–64
Robinson-Danforth Commission Co., II
    561
**Robinson Helicopter Company, 51
    315–17**
Robinson-Humphrey, II 398; 10 62
Robinson Industries, 24 425
Robinson Radio Rentals, I 531
Robinson Smith & Robert Haas, Inc., 13
    428
Robinson's Japan Co. Ltd., V 89; 42 191
Robinsons Soft Drinks Limited, 38 77
Robot Manufacturing Co., 16 8
Robotic Vision Systems, Inc., 16 68
ROC. See Royal Olympic Cruise Lines Inc.
ROC Communities, Inc., I 272; 22 341
Roccade, 39 177
Roch, S.A., 23 83
**Roche Biomedical Laboratories, Inc., 8
    209–10; 11 424–26.** See also Laboratory
    Corporation of America Holdings.
Roche Bioscience, 14 403–06 (upd.)
Roche Holding AG, 30 164; 32 211,
    213–14; 37 113; 50 421
Roche Products Ltd., I 643
Rocher Soleil, 48 315
Rochester American Insurance Co., III 191
**Rochester Gas And Electric
    Corporation, 6 571–73**
Rochester German Insurance Co., III 191
Rochester Instrument Systems, Inc., 16 357
**Rochester Telephone Corporation, 6
    332–34; 12 136; 16 221**
Röchling Industrie Verwaltung GmbH, 9
    443

Rock Bottom Restaurants, Inc., 25 399–401
Rock Island Oil & Refining Co., **IV** 448–49
Rock Island Plow Company, **10** 378
Rock of Ages Corporation, 37 329–32
Rock Systems Inc., **18** 337
Rock-Tenn Company, IV 312; **13 441–43**; **19** 268
Rockcor Inc., **I** 381; **13** 380
Rockcote Paint Company, **8** 552–53
Rockefeller & Andrews, **IV** 426; **7** 169
The Rockefeller Foundation, 34 384–87; 52 15
Rockefeller Group, **IV** 714
Rocket Chemical Company. *See* WD-40 Company.
Rockford Corporation, 43 322–25
Rockford Drilling Co., **III** 439
Rockford Products Corporation, 55 323–25
Rockhaven Asset Management, LLC, **48** 18
Rocking Horse Child Care Centers of America Inc. *See* Nobel Learning Communities, Inc.
Rockland Corp., **8** 271
Rockland React-Rite, Inc., **8** 270
Rockmoor Grocery, **II** 683
Rockower of Canada Ltd., **II** 649
Rockport Company, **V** 376–77; **26** 397
Rockresorts, Inc., **22** 166
RockShox, Inc., 26 412–14
Rockwell Automation, 43 326–31 (upd.)
Rockwell International Corporation, I 71, 78–80, 154–55, 186; **II** 3, 94, 379; **6** 263; **7** 420; **8** 165; **9** 10; **10** 279–80; **11** 268, 278, **427–30 (upd.)**, 473; **12** 135, 248, 506; **13** 228; **18** 369, 571; **22** 51, 53, 63–64; **32** 81, 84–85; **33** 27; **35** 91; **36** 121–22; **39** 30; **44** 357
Rocky Mountain Bankcard, **24** 393
Rocky Mountain Financial Corporation, **13** 348
Rocky Mountain Pipe Line Co., **IV** 400
Rocky River Power Co. *See* Connecticut Light and Power Co.
Rocky Shoes & Boots, Inc., 26 415–18
Rod's Food Products, **36** 163
Rodale, Inc., 47 336–39 (upd.)
Rodale Press, Inc., 22 443; **23 415–17**; **54** 22
Rodamco N.V., IV 698; **26 419–21**
Rodel, Inc., **26** 425
Röder & Co., **34** 38, 40
Rodeway Inns of America, **II** 142; **III** 94; **11** 242; **25** 309
Rodgers Instrument Corporation, **38** 391
Rodney Square Management Corp., **25** 542
Rodven Records, **23** 391
Roederstein GmbH, **21** 520
Roegelein Co., **13** 271
Roehr Products Co., **III** 443
Roermond, **IV** 276
Roessler & Hasslacher Chemical Co., **IV** 69
Roger Cleveland Golf Company, **15** 462; **43** 375–76
Roger Williams Foods, **II** 682
Rogers & Oling, Inc., **17** 533
Rogers Bros., **I** 672
Rogers CanGuard, Inc., **32** 374

Rogers Communications Inc., 30 388–92 (upd.); **50** 275. *See also* Maclean Hunter Publishing Limited.
Rohde & Schwarz GmbH & Co. KG, 39 350–53
Rohe Scientific Corp., **13** 398
Röhm and Haas Company, I 391–93; **14** 182–83; **26 422–26 (upd.)**
ROHN Industries, Inc., 22 467–69
Rohölgewinnungs AG, **IV** 485
Rohr Gruppe, **20** 100
Rohr Incorporated, I 62; **9 458–60**; **11** 165
Roja, **III** 47
The Rokke Group, **16** 546; **32** 100
Rokuosha, **III** 547
Rol Oil, **IV** 451
Rola Group, **II** 81
Roland Berger & Partner GmbH, 37 333–36
Roland Corporation, 38 389–91
Roland Murten A.G., 7 452–53
Roland NV, **41** 340
Rolex. *See* Montres Rolex S.A.
Roll International Corporation, 37 337–39
Rollalong, **III** 502; **7** 208
Rollerblade, Inc., 15 395–98; **22** 202–03; **34 388–92 (upd.)**
Rolling Stones Records, **23** 33
Rollins Burdick Hunter Company, **III** 204; **45** 27
Rollins Communications, **II** 161
Rollins, Inc., 11 431–34
Rollins Specialty Group, **III** 204
Rollo's, **16** 95
Rolls-Royce Allison, 29 407–09 (upd.)
Rolls-Royce Motors Ltd., I 25–26, 81–82, 166, **194–96**; **III** 652; **9** 16–18, 417–18; **11** 138, 403; **21** 435
Rolls-Royce plc, I 41, 55, 65, **81–83**, 481; **III** 507, 556; **7 454–57 (upd.)**; **9** 244; **11** 268; **12** 190; **13** 414; **21 433–37 (upd.)**; **24** 85; **27** 495–96; **46** 358–59; **47** 7, 9
Rolm Corp., **II** 99; **III** 149; **18** 344; **22** 51; **34** 512
Rolodex Electronics, **23** 209, 212
Rolscreen. *See* Pella Corporation.
Rombas, **IV** 226
Rome Cable and Wire Co., **IV** 15
Rome Network, Inc., **24** 95
Romeike Ltd., **55** 289
Romper Room Enterprises, Inc., **16** 267
Rompetrol, **IV** 454
Ron Nagle, **I** 247
Ron Tonkin Chevrolet Company, 55 326–28
Ronco, Inc., 15 399–401; **21** 327
Rondel's, Inc., **8** 135
Ronel, **13** 274
Roni-Linda Productions, Inc., **27** 347
Ronnebyredds Trävaru, **25** 463
Ronningen-Petter, **III** 468
Ronson PLC, 49 337–39
Ronzoni Foods Corp., **15** 221
Roombar S.A., **28** 241
Rooms To Go Inc., 28 389–92
Rooney Brothers Co., 25 402–04
Roots Canada Ltd., **27** 194; **42 325–27**
Roots-Connersville Blower Corp., **III** 472
Roper Industries, Inc., III 655; **12** 550; **15 402–04**; **25** 89; **50 391–95 (upd.)**
Ropert Group, **18** 67

Ropes & Gray, 40 377–80
RoProperty Services BV. *See* Rodamco N.V.
Rorer Group, I 666–68; **12** 4; **16** 438; **24** 257
Rosaen Co., **23** 82
Rosarita Food Company, **25** 278
Rose & Co., **26** 65
Rose Exterminator Company, **25** 15
Rose Forgrove Ltd., **51** 249, 251
Rose Foundation, **9** 348
Rose's Stores, Inc., 13 261, **444–46**; **23** 215
Rosebud Dolls Ltd., **25** 312
Rosefield Packing Co., **II** 497
Rosehaugh, **24** 269
RoseJohnson Incorporated, **14** 303; **50** 311
Rosemount Estates. *See* Southcorp Limited.
Rosemount Inc., II 20; **13** 226; **15 405–08**; **46** 171
Rosen Enterprises, Ltd., **10** 482
Rosenblads Patenter, **III** 419
Rosenbluth International Inc., 14 407–09
Rosenfeld Hat Company. *See* Columbia Hat Company.
Rosengrens Produktions AB, **53** 158
Rosenmund-Guèdu, **31** 158
Rosenthal A.G., **I** 347; **18** 236; **34** 493, 496
Rosevear, **III** 690
Rosewood Financial, Inc., **24** 383
Roshco, Inc., **27** 288
Roslyn Bancorp, **46** 316
Ross Carrier Company, **8** 115
Ross Clouston, **13** 244
Ross Gear & Tool Co., **I** 539; **14** 510
Ross Hall Corp., **I** 417
Ross Stores, Inc., 17 408–10; **43 332–35 (upd.)**
Rossendale Combining Company, **9** 92
Rossignol Ski Company, Inc. *See* Skis Rossignol S.A.
Rössing Uranium Ltd., **IV** 191
Rossville Union Distillery, **I** 285
Rostocker Brauerei VEB, **9** 87
Roswell Public Service Company, **6** 579
Rota Bolt Ltd., **III** 581
Rotadisk, **16** 7
Rotan Mosle Financial Corporation, **II** 445; **22** 406
Rotary International, 31 395–97
Rotary Lift, **III** 467–68
Rotax, **III** 555–56. *See also* Orbital Engine Corporation Ltd.
Rote. *See* Avery Dennison Corporation.
Rotelcom Data Inc., **6** 334; **16** 222
Rotem Amfert Negev Ltd., **55** 229
Rotex, **IV** 253
Roth, Co., **16** 493
Roth Freres SA, **26** 231
Rothmans International BV, **33** 82
Rothmans International p.l.c., I 438; **IV** 93; **V 411–13**; **27** 488
Rothmans UK Holdings Limited, 19 367–70 (upd.)
Rothschild Financial Corporation, **13** 347
Rothschild Group, **6** 206
Rothschild Investment Trust, **I** 248; **III** 699
Roto-Rooter Corp., 13 149–50; **15 409–11**; **16** 387
Rotodiesel, **III** 556
Rotor Tool Co., **II** 16
Rotork plc, 46 361–64
Rotterdam Bank, **II** 183–85

Rotterdam Beleggings (Investment) Consortium. *See* Robeco.
Rotterdam Lloyd, **6** 403–04; **26** 241–42
The Rottlund Company, Inc., 28 393–95
Rouge et Or, **IV** 614
Rouge Steel Company, 8 448–50
Roughdales Brickworks, **14** 249
Rougier. *See* Groupe Rougier, SA.
Roularta Media Group NV, 48 345–47
Round Hill Foods, **21** 535
Round Table, **16** 447
Roundup Wholesale Grocery Company, **V** 55
Roundy's Inc., 14 410–12
The Rouse Company, II 445; **15 412–15; 22** 406
Roussel Uclaf, I 669–70; 8 451–53 (upd.); **18** 236; **19** 51; **25** 285; **38** 379
Rousselot, **I** 677
Routh Robbins Companies, **21** 96
Roux Séguéla Cayzac & Goudard. *See* Euro RSCG Worldwide S.A.
Rover Group Ltd., I 186; **7 458–60; 11** 31, 33; **14** 36; **21 441–44 (upd.);** **24** 87–88; **38** 83, 85–86
Rowan Companies, Inc., 43 336–39
Rowe & Pitman, **14** 419
Rowe Bros. & Co., **III** 680
Rowe Price-Fleming International, Inc., **11** 495
Rowell Welding Works, **26** 433
Rowenta. *See* Groupe SEB.
Rowland Communications Worldwide, **42** 328, 331
Rowntree and Co., **27** 104
Rowntree Mackintosh PLC, II 476, 511, 521, 548, **568–70; 7** 383; **28** 311
Roxana Petroleum Co., **IV** 531, 540
Roxell, N.V., **43** 129
Roxoil Drilling, **7** 344
Roy and Charles Moore Crane Company, **18** 319
Roy F. Weston, Inc., 33 369–72
Roy Farrell Import-Export Company, **6** 78
Roy Rogers, **III** 102
Royal & Sun Alliance Insurance Group plc, 55 329–39 (upd.)
Royal Ahold. *See* Koninklijke Ahold N.V.
Royal Aluminium Ltd., **IV** 9
Royal Appliance Manufacturing Company, 15 416–18; 17 233
Royal Baking Powder Co., **II** 544; **14** 17
Royal Bank of Australia, **II** 188
The Royal Bank of Canada, II 344–46; 21 445–48 (upd.)
Royal Bank of Ireland Ltd., **16** 13
Royal Bank of Queensland, **II** 188
The Royal Bank of Scotland Group plc, II 298, 358; **10 336–37; 12 421–23; 38** 13, **392–99 (upd.);** **42** 76
Royal Bankgroup of Acadiana, Inc., **37** 201
Royal Brewing Co., **I** 269; **12** 337
Royal Business Machines, **I** 207, 485; **III** 549
Royal Canada, **III** 349
Royal Canin S.A., 39 354–57
Royal Caribbean Cruises Ltd., 6 368; **22** 444–46; **470–73; 27** 29, 91
Royal Copenhagen A/S, **9** 99
Royal Crown Company, Inc., II 468; **6** 21, 50; **8 536–37; 14** 32–33; **23 418–20; 52** 97. *See also* Cott Corporation.

Royal Data, Inc. *See* King Kullen Grocery Co., Inc.
Royal Doulton plc, IV 659; **14 413–15; 34** 497; **38 400–04 (upd.)**
Royal Dutch Harbour Co., **IV** 707
Royal Dutch Paper Co., **IV** 307
Royal Dutch Petroleum Company, IV 530–32, 657; **24** 496. *See also* Shell Transport and Trading Company p.l.c.
Royal Dutch/Shell Group, I 368, 504; **III** 616; **IV** 132–33, 378, 406, 413, 429, 434, 453–54, 460, 491–92, 512, 515, 517–18, 530–32, 540–45, 557–58, 569; **7** 56–57, 172–73, 481–82; **17** 417; **19** 73, 75; **21** 203; **22** 237; **24** 520; **32** 175, 180; **41** 356–57, 359; **45** 47; **49 340–44 (upd.)**
Royal Electric Company, **6** 501
Royal Exchange Assurance Corp., **III** 233–34, 278, 349, 369–71, 373
Royal Farms, **24** 528
Royal Food Distributors, **II** 625
Royal Food Products, **24** 528–29; **36** 163
Royal General Insurance Co., **III** 242
Royal Grolsch NV, 54 315–18
Royal Hawaiian Macadamia Nut Co., **II** 491
Royal Industries, Inc., **19** 371
Royal Insurance Holdings plc, III 349–51
Royal International, **II** 457; **III** 349
Royal Interocean Lines, **6** 404; **26** 243
Royal Jackson, **14** 236
Royal Jordanian, **6** 101
Royal KPN N.V., 30 393–95, 461, 463
Royal London Mutual Insurance, **IV** 697
Royal Mail Group, **V** 498; **6** 416; **19** 198
Royal Nedlloyd. *See* Koninglijke Nedlloyd N.V.
Royal Nepal Airline Corporation, 41 335–38
Royal Netherlands Steamship Company. *See* KNSM.
Royal Numico N.V., 33 145, 147; **37 340–42**
Royal Olympic Cruise Lines Inc., 52 297–99
Royal Orchid Holidays, **6** 122–23
Royal Ordnance plc, **13** 356; **24** 87–88
Royal Packaging Industries Van Leer N.V., 9 305; **30 396–98**
Royal Pakhoed N.V., **9** 532
Royal PTT Post, **30** 463
Royal Re, **III** 349
Royal Sash Manufacturing Co., **III** 757
Royal Securities Company, **6** 585
Royal Securities Corp. of Canada, **II** 425
Royal Sporting House Pte. Ltd., **21** 483
Royal Trust Co., **II** 456–57; **V** 25
Royal Union Life Insurance Co., **III** 275
Royal USA, **III** 349
Royal Vopak NV, 41 339–41
Royal Wessanen, **II** 527
Royale Belge, **III** 177, 200, 394
Royale Inns of America, **25** 307
Royalite, **I** 285
Royce Electronics, **III** 569; **18** 68; **20** 361
Royce Ltd., **I** 194
Royster-Clark, Inc., **13** 504
Rozes, **I** 272
RPC Industries, **III** 635
RPI. *See* Research Polymers International.
RPM Inc., 8 III 598; **454–57; 36 394–98 (upd.);** **51** 369

RSA Security Inc., 46 365–68; 47 430
RSC. *See* Rental Service Corporation.
RSI Corp., **8** 141–42; **30** 160
RSO Records, **23** 390
RSV, **26** 496
RTL Group SA, 41 29; **44 374–78**
RTL-Véeronique, **IV** 611
RTW Air Service(s) Pte. Ltd., **51** 123
RTZ Corporation PLC, IV 189–92; 7 261, 263; **27** 256
RTZ-CRA Group. *See* Rio Tinto plc.
Rubber Latex Limited, **9** 92
Rubbermaid Incorporated, III 613–15; 12 168–69; **13** 317–18; **19** 407; **20** 262, **454–57 (upd.);** **21** 293; **28** 479; **31** 160–61; **34** 369. *See also* Newell Rubbermaid Inc.
Ruberoid Corporation, **I** 339; **22** 227
Rubicon Group plc, **32** 50
Rubio's Restaurants, Inc., 35 379–81
Rubloff Inc., **II** 442
Rubo Lederwaren, **14** 225
Rubry Owen, **I** 154
Ruby, **III** 47
Ruby Tuesday, Inc., 18 464–66
Rubyco, Inc., **15** 386
La Ruche Meridionale, **12** 153
Ruddick Corporation, **23** 260
Rudisill Printing Co., **IV** 661
Rudolf Wolff & Co., **IV** 165
Rudolph Fluor & Brother, **I** 569
Ruel Smith Transportation Services, Inc., **39** 66
Ruff Hewn, **25** 48
Rug Corporation of America, **12** 393
The Rugby Group plc, 31 398–400; 34 380
Ruger Corporation, **19** 431
Ruhr-Zink, **IV** 141
Ruhrgas AG, V 704–06; 7 141; **18** 50; **38 405–09 (upd.);** **42** 263; **50** 90, 172
Ruhrkohle AG, IV 193–95. *See also* RAG AG.
Ruinart Père et Fils, **I** 272
Ruiz Food Products, Inc., 53 287–89
Rumbelows, **I** 532
Runcorn White Lead Co., **III** 680
Runnymede Construction Co., **8** 544
Runo-Everth Treibstoff und Ol AG, **7** 141
Rural Bank, **IV** 279; **19** 155
Rural Cellular Corporation, 43 340–42
Rural/Metro Corporation, 28 396–98; 39 22
Rurhkohle AG, **V** 747
Rush Communications, 33 373–75. *See also* Phat Fashions LLC.
Rush Laboratories, Inc., **6** 41
Russ Berrie and Company, Inc., 12 424–26
Russell & Co., **II** 296
Russell Corporation, 8 458–59; 12 458; **30 399–401 (upd.)**
Russell Electric, **11** 412
Russell Electronics, **II** 85
Russell Kelly Office Services, Inc. *See* Kelly Services Inc.
Russell, Majors & Waddell, **II** 381
Russell Reynolds Associates Inc., 38 410–12
Russell Stover Candies Inc., 12 427–29
Russwerke Dortmund GmbH, **IV** 70
Rust Craft Greeting Cards Incorporated, **12** 561

Rust International Inc., V 754; **6** 599–600; **11 435–36**
Rust-Oleum Corporation, **36** 396
Rustenburg Platinum Co., **IV** 96, 118, 120
Rütgerswerke AG, **IV** 193; **8** 81
Ruth's Chris Steak House, 28 399–401; **37** 297
Rutherford Hill Winery, **48** 392
Ruti Machinery Works, **III** 638
Rutland Plastics, **I** 321; **12** 103
RWE Group, V 707–10; **33** 194, 196; **50 396–400 (upd.)**
RxAmerica, **22** 40; **25** 297
Ryan Aeronautical, **I** 525; **10** 522; **11** 428
Ryan Aircraft Company, **9** 458
Ryan Homes, Inc., **8** 401–02
Ryan Insurance Company, **III** 204; **45** 26
Ryan Milk Company of Kentucky, **7** 128
Ryan's Family Steak Houses, Inc., 15 419–21; **19** 287; **22** 464
Ryanair Holdings plc, 35 382–85
Rycade Corp., **IV** 365, 658
Rydelle-Lion, **III** 45
Ryder System, Inc., V 504–06; **13** 192; **19** 293; **24 408–11 (upd.)**; **25** 93, 144; **28** 3; **41** 37
Ryerson Tull, Inc., **19** 216; **40** 269, **381–84 (upd.)**
Rykoff-Sexton, Inc., **21** 497; **26** 503, 505
The Ryland Group, Inc., 8 460–61; **19** 126; **37 343–45 (upd.)**
Ryobi Ltd., **I** 202
Ryohin Keikaku Co., Ltd., **36** 420
Rypper Corp., **16** 43
Rysher Entertainment, **22** 162; **25** 329
Ryukyu Cement, **III** 760
The Ryvita Company Limited, **II** 466; **13** 52; **41** 31

S&A Restaurant Corp., **7** 336; **10** 176; **14** 331; **15** 363; **38** 100–01
S&C Electric Company, 15 422–24
S&H. *See* Sperry and Hutchinson Co.
S&H Diving Corporation, **6** 578
S&K Famous Brands, Inc., 23 421–23
S&V Screen Inks, **13** 227–28
S. & W. Berisford, **II** 514, 528
S&W Fine Foods, **12** 105
S + T Gesellschaft fur Reprotechnik mbH, **29** 306
S.A. CARFUEL, **12** 152
S.A. Cockerill Sambre. *See* Cockerill Sambre Group.
S.A. de C.V., **29** 461
S.A. des Ateliers d'Aviation Louis Breguet. *See* Groupe Dassault Aviation SA.
s.a. GB-Inno-BM. *See* GIB Group.
S.A. Greetings Corporation, **22** 35
S.A. Innovation—Bon Marché N.V., **26** 160
S.A. Schonbrunn & Co., **14** 18
S.B. Irving Trust Bank Corp., **II** 218
S.B. Penick & Co., **I** 708; **8** 548
S.C. Johnson & Son, Inc., **I** 14; **III** 45, **58–59**; **8** 130; **10** 173; **12** 126–28; **17** 215; **21** 386; **28** 215, **409–12 (upd.)**; **51** 224
S-C-S Box Company, **8** 173
S.D. Cohn & Company, **10** 455; **27** 364
S.D. Warren Co., **IV** 329–30
S-E Bank Group, **II** 351–53
S.E. Massengill, **III** 66
S.E. Rykoff & Co., **26** 503
S.F. Braun, **IV** 451

S.G. Warburg and Co., **II** 232, 259–60, 422, 629; **14** 419; **16** 377. *See also* SBC Warburg.
S. Grumbacher & Son. *See* The Bon-Ton Stores, Inc.
S.H. Benson Ltd., **I** 25–26
S.H. Kress & Co., **17** 203–04
S.I.P., Co., **8** 416
S-K-I Limited, 15 457–59
S.K. Wellman, **14** 81
S. Kuhn & Sons, **13** 221
S.M.A. Corp., **I** 622
S.P. Richards Co., **45** 177–79
S Pearson & Son Ltd., **IV** 657–59; **38** 290
S.R. Dresser Manufacturing Co., **III** 470–71
S.S. Kresge Company. *See* Kmart Corporation.
S.S.V. Inc., **36** 420
S.S. White Dental Manufacturing Co., **I** 383
S. Smith & Sons. *See* Smiths Industries PLC.
S.T. Cooper & Sons, **12** 283
S.T. Dupont Company, **III** 28; **23** 55
S.W.M. Chard, **27** 259
SA Alliance Air, **28** 404
SA Express, **28** 404
Sa SFC NA, **18** 163
Sa SFC NV, **18** 162
SAA. *See* South African Airways.
SAA (Pty) Ltd., 28 402–04
SAAB. *See* Svenska Aeroplan Aktiebolaget.
Saab Automobile AB, 32 386–89 (upd.); **36** 242–43
Saab-Scania A.B., **I** 197–98, 210; **III** 556; V 339; **10** 86; **11 437–39 (upd.)**; **16** 322; **34** 117
Saarberg-Konzern, IV 196–99
Saarstahl AG, **IV** 228
Saatchi & Saatchi plc, **I** 21, 28, **33–35**, 36; **6** 53, 229; **14** 49–50; **16** 72; **21** 236; **22** 296; **33** 65, 67; **328–31 (upd.)**
SAB. *See* South African Breweries Ltd.
SAB WABCO International AB, **53** 85
Sabah Timber Co., **III** 699
Saban Entertainment, **24** 171
Sabanci Group, **54** 197–98
Sabanci Holdings. *See* Haci Omer Sabanci Holdings A.S.
Sabaté Diosos SA, 48 348–50
Sabela Media, Inc., **49** 423
Sabena S.A./N.V., **6** 96; **18** 80; **33** 49, 51, **376–79**; **34** 398
Saber Energy, Inc., **7** 553–54
Saber Software Corp., **25** 348
Sabi International Ltd., **22** 464
Sabian Ltd., **38** 68
SABIM Sable, **12** 152
Sabine Corporation, **7** 229
Sabine Investment Co. of Texas, Inc., **IV** 341
SABO Maschinenfabrik AG, **21** 175
Sabratek Corporation, 29 410–12
SABRE Group Holdings, Inc., **25** 144; **26 427–30**; **28** 22; **52** 23
Sabre Interactive, **46** 434
Sacer, **31** 127–28
Sachs-Dolmer G.m.b.H., **22** 334
Sachsgruppe, **IV** 201
Sacilor, **IV** 174, 226–27. *See also* Usinor-Sacilor
Sackett Plasterboard Co., **III** 762

Sacks Industries, **8** 561
OY Saco AB, **23** 268
SACOR, **IV** 250, 504–06
Sacramento Savings & Loan Association, **10** 43, 45
SADE Ingenieria y Construcciones S.A., **38** 435, 437
SAE Magnetics Ltd., **18** 250
Saeger Carbide Corp., **IV** 203
Saes, **III** 347
SAFECO Corporation, **III** 352–54; **10** 44
Safeguard Scientifics, Inc., **10** 232–34, **473–75**; **27** 338
Safelite Glass Corp., 19 371–73
Safer, Inc., **21** 385–86
Safeskin Corporation, 18 467–70
Safety 1st, Inc., 24 412–15; **46** 192
Safety Fund Bank, **II** 207
Safety-Kleen Corp., 8 462–65
Safety Rehab, **11** 486
Safety Savings and Loan, **10** 339
Safeway Inc., **II** 424, 601, 604–05, 609–10, 628, 632, 637, **654–56**; **6** 364; **7** 61, 569; **9** 39; **10** 442; **11** 239, 241; **12** 113, 209, 559; **13** 90, 336, 340; **16** 64, 160, 249, 452; **22** 37, 126; **24** 273, **416–19 (upd.)**; **25** 296; **27** 292; **28** 510; **30** 24, 27; **33** 305; **40** 366
Safeway PLC, 50 401–06 (upd.)
Saffa SpA, **41** 325–26
Safilo, **40** 155–56
Safilo SpA, 54 319–21
Safmarine, **IV** 22
SAFR. *See* Société Anonyme des Fermiers Reúnis.
Safrap, **IV** 472
Saga Communications, Inc., **II** 608; **III** 103; **IV** 406; **27** 226, **392–94**
Saga Petroleum ASA, **35** 318
Sagami Optical Co., Ltd., **48** 295
Sagamore Insurance Company, **51** 37–39
The Sage Group, 43 343–46
Sagebrush Sales, Inc., **12** 397
Sagebrush Steakhouse, **29** 201
SAGEM S.A., 37 346–48
Saginaw Dock & Terminal Co., **17** 357
Sagitta Arzneimittel, **18** 51; **50** 90
Sagittarius Productions Inc., **I** 286
Sahara Casino Partners L.P., **19** 379
Sahara Resorts. *See* Santa Fe Gaming Corporation.
SAI. *See* Stamos Associates Inc.
Sai Baba, **12** 228
Saia Motor Freight Line, Inc., **6** 421–23; **45** 448
Saibu Gas, **IV** 518–19
SAIC Velcorex, **12** 153; **27** 188
Saiccor, **IV** 92; **49** 353
Sainrapt et Brice, **9** 9
Sainsbury's. *See* J Sainsbury PLC.
St. Alban Boissons S.A., **22** 515
St. Alban's Sand and Gravel, **III** 739
St. Andrews Insurance, **III** 397
St. Charles Manufacturing Co., **III** 654
St. Clair Industries Inc., **I** 482
St. Clair Press, **IV** 570
St. Croix Paper Co., **IV** 281; **9** 259
St. George Reinsurance, **III** 397
Saint-Gobain. *See* Compagnie de Saint Gobain S.A.
St. Helens Crown Glass Co., **III** 724
St. Ives Laboratories Inc., **36** 26
St Ives plc, 34 393–95
St. James Associates, **32** 362–63

The St. Joe Company, 31 422–25
St. Joe Gold, **23** 40
St. Joe Minerals Corp., **I** 569, 571; **8** 192
St. Joe Paper Company, 8 485–88
St. John Knits, Inc., 14 466–68
St. John's Wood Railway Company, **6** 406
St. Joseph Company, **I** 286, 684; **49** 357
St. Jude Medical, Inc., 6 345; **11** 458–61;
43 347–52 (upd.)
St. Laurent Paperboard Inc., **30** 119
St. Lawrence Cement Inc., **III** 702; **8**
258–59
St. Lawrence Corp. Ltd., **IV** 272
St. Lawrence Steamboat Co., **I** 273; **26** 303
St. Louis and Illinois Belt Railway, **6** 504
Saint Louis Bread Company, **18** 35, 37; **44**
327
St. Louis Concessions Inc., **21** 39
St. Louis Music, Inc., 48 351–54
St. Louis Refrigerator Car Co., **I** 219; **34**
36
St. Louis Troy and Eastern Railroad
Company, **6** 504
St. Martin's Press, **25** 484–85; **35** 452
St. Michel-Grellier S.A., **44** 40
St. Paul Bank for Cooperatives, 8
489–90
St. Paul Book and Stationery, Inc., **47** 90
The St. Paul Companies, III 355–57; **15**
257; **21** 305; **22** 154, **492–95** (upd.)
St. Paul Fire and Marine Insurance Co., **III**
355–56
St. Paul Venture Capital Inc., **34** 405–06
Saint-Quirin, **III** 676; **16** 120
St. Regis Corp., **I** 153; **IV** 264, 282; **9** 260;
10 265; **20** 129
St. Regis Paper Co., **IV** 289, 339; **12** 377;
22 209
Sainte Anne Paper Co., **IV** 245–46; **25** 10
Saipem, **IV** 420–22, 453
SAirGroup, **29** 376; **33** 268, 271; **37** 241;
46 398; **47** 287
SAirLogistics, **49** 80–81
Saison Group, **V** 184–85, 187–89; **36**
417–18, 420; **42** 340–41
Saito Ltd., **IV** 268
Saiwa, **II** 543
Sako Ltd., **39** 151
Saks Fifth Avenue, **I** 426; **15** 291; **18** 372;
21 302; **22** 72; **25** 205; **27** 329; **50**
117–19
Saks Holdings, Inc., 24 420–23
Saks Inc., 41 342–45 (upd.)
Sakura Bank, **39** 286. *See also* Sumitomo
Mitsui Banking Corporation.
Sakurai Co., **IV** 327
Salada Foods, **II** 525; **13** 293; **50** 293
Salant Corporation, 12 430–32; **27** 445;
51 318–21 (upd.)
Sale Knitting Company, **12** 501. *See also*
Tultex Corporation.
Salem Broadcasting, **25** 508
Salem Carpet Mills, Inc., **9** 467
Salem Sportswear, **25** 167
Salen Energy A.B., **IV** 563
Salick Health Care, Inc., 21 544, 546; **50**
58; **53** 290–92
Salim Group, **18** 180–81
Salinas Equipment Distributors, Inc., **33**
364
Sallie Mae. *See* SLM Holding Corp.;
Student Loan Marketing Association.
Sally Beauty Company, Inc., **8** 15–17; **36**
23–26

Salmon Carriers, **6** 383
Salmon River Power & Light Company, **12**
265
Salomon Brothers Inc., **28** 164
Salomon Inc., I 630–31; **II** 268, 400, 403,
406, 426, 432, 434, 441, **447–49; III**
221, 215, 721; **IV** 80, 137; **7** 114; **9**
378–79, 386; **11** 35, 371; **13** 331,
447–50 (upd.) Inc.; **18** 60, 62; **19** 293;
21 67, 146; **22** 102; **23** 472–74; **25** 12,
125; **42** 34
Salomon Smith Barney, **30** 124
Salomon Worldwide, 20 458–60; 33 7.
See also adidas-Salomon AG.
Salora, **II** 69; **17** 353
Salsåkers Ångsågs, **IV** 338
Salt River Project, 19 374–76
Salton, Inc., 30 402–04
Saltos del Sil, **II** 197
Salvagnini Company, **22** 6
The Salvation Army USA, 15 510–11; **32**
390–93
Salzgitter AG, IV 128, 198, **200–01; 17**
381
SAM. *See* Sociedad Aeronáutica de
Medellín, S.A.
Sam & Libby Inc., **30** 311
Sam Ash Music Corporation, 30 405–07
Sam Goody, **I** 613; **9** 360–61
Sam's Club, V 216–17; **8** 555–57; **12**
221, 335; **13** 548; **14** 393; **15** 470; **16**
64; **25** 235; **40** 385–87; **41** 254–56
Samancor Ltd., **IV** 92–93
Samaritan Senior Services Inc., **25** 503
Samas-Groep N.V., **47** 91
Sambo's, **12** 510
Sambre-et-Moselle, **IV** 52
Samcor Glass, **III** 685
Samedan Oil Corporation, **11** 353
Sames, S.A., **21** 65–66
Samim, **IV** 422
Samkong Fat Ltd. Co., **III** 747
Sammy Corp., **54** 16
Samna Corp., **6** 256; **25** 300
Sampson's, **12** 220–21
Samson Technologies Corp., **30** 406
Samsonite Corporation, 6 50; **13** 311,
451–53; 16 20–21; **38** 169; **43** 353–57
(upd.)
Samsung-Calex, **17** 483
Samsung Electronics Co., Ltd., 14
416–18; 18 139, 260; **41** 346–49 (upd.)
Samsung Group, I 515–17; **II** 53–54; **III**
143, 457–58, 517, 749; **IV** 519; **7** 233;
12 211–12; **13** 387; **18** 124; **29** 207–08
Samuel Austin & Son Company, **8** 41
Samuel Cabot Inc., 53 293–95
Samuel Meisel & Company, Inc., **11**
80–81; **29** 509, 511
Samuel Montagu & Co., **II** 319; **17**
324–25
Samuel Moore & Co., **I** 155
Samuel Samuel & Co., **IV** 530, 542
Samuel, Son & Co. Ltd., **24** 144
Samuels Jewelers Incorporated, 30
408–10
Samwha Paper Co., **III** 748
San Antonio Public Service Company, **6**
473
San Diego Gas & Electric Company, V
711–14; **6** 590; **11** 272; **25** 416
San Francisco Baseball Associates, L.P.,
55 340–43

San Francisco Mines of Mexico Ltd., **22**
285
San Gabriel Light & Power Company, **16**
496; **50** 496
San Giorgio Macaroni Inc., **II** 511; **53** 242
SAN-MIC Trading Co., **IV** 327
San Miguel Corporation, I 221; **15**
428–30; 23 379
Sanborn Co., **III** 142; **6** 237; **50** 223
Sanborn Hermanos, S.A., 20 461–63; 21
259
Sanborn Manufacturing Company, **30** 138
Sandcastle 5 Productions, **25** 269–70
Sanders Associates, Inc., **9** 324; **13** 127–28
Sanderson & Porter, **I** 376
Sanderson Computers, **10** 500
Sanderson Farms, Inc., 15 425–27
Sandia National Laboratories, 49 345–48
Sandiacre Packaging Machinery Ltd., **51**
249–50
Sandoz Ltd., I 632–33, **671–73,** 675; **7**
315, 452; **8** 108–09, 215; **10** 48, 199; **11**
173; **12** 388; **15** 139; **18** 51; **22** 475; **27**
299; **50** 90. *See also* Novartis AG.
Sandoz Nutrition Corp., **24** 286
SandPoint Corp., **12** 562; **17** 254
Sandusky Plastics, Inc., **17** 157
Sandusky Portland Cement Company, **24**
331
Sandvik AB, III 426–27; **IV** 202–04; **32**
394–98 (upd.)
Sandwell, Inc., **6** 491
Sandwich Chef, Inc. *See* Wall Street Deli,
Inc.
Sandy's Pool Supply, Inc. *See* Leslie's
Poolmart, Inc.
SANFLO Co., Ltd., **IV** 327
Sanford-Brown College, Inc., **41** 419–20
Sangu Express Company, **V** 463
Sanichem Manufacturing Company, **16** 386
Sanitary Farm Dairies, Inc., **7** 372
Sanitas Food Co., **II** 523; **50** 291–92
Sanitation Systems, Inc. *See* HMI
Industries.
Sanitec Corporation, 51 322–24
Sanjushi Bank, **II** 347
Sanka Coffee Corp., **II** 531
Sankin Kai Group, **II** 274
Sanko Kabushiki Kaisha. *See* Marubeni
Corporation.
Sanko Peterson Corporation, **55** 306
Sankyo Company Ltd., I 330, **674–75;**
III 760; **8** 153
Sanlam, **IV** 91, 93, 535; **49** 353
Sano Railway Company, **6** 430
Sanofi Group, I 304, **676–77; III** 18; **IV**
546; **7** 484–85; **21** 205; **23** 236, 238,
242; **35** 262–63, 265
The Sanofi-Synthélabo Group, 49 349–51
(upd.)
SanomaWSOY Corporation, 51 325–28
Sanpaolo IMI S.p.A., 50 407–11
Sanrio Company, Ltd., 38 413–15
Sanseisha Co., **IV** 326
Santa Ana Savings and Loan, **10** 339
Santa Ana Wholesale Company, **16** 451
Santa Barbara Restaurant Group, Inc.,
37 349–52
The Santa Cruz Operation, Inc., 6 244;
38 416–21
Santa Cruz Portland Cement, **II** 490
Santa Fe Gaming Corporation, 19
377–79
Santa Fe Gold Corporation, **38** 232

Santa Fe Industries, **II** 448; **12** 19; **13** 448; **28** 498

Santa Fe International Corporation, IV 451–52; **38 422–24**

Santa Fe Pacific Corporation, V 507–09; **24** 98. *See also* Burlington Northern Santa Fe Corporation.

Santa Fe Railway, **12** 278; **18** 4

Santa Fe Southern Pacific Corp., **III** 512; **IV** 721; **6** 150, 599; **9** 391; **22** 491

Santa Rosa Savings and Loan, **10** 339

Santal, **26** 160

Santiam Lumber Co., **IV** 358

Santone Industries Inc., **16** 327

Sanus Corp. Health Systems, **III** 317

Sanwa Bank, Ltd., II 276, 326, **347–48**, 442, 511; **III** 188, 759; **IV** 150–51; **7** 119; **15** 43, **431–33 (upd.)**; **24** 356, 358

Sanyo Chemical Manufacturing Co., **III** 758

Sanyo Electric Co., Ltd., I 516; **II** 55–56, **91–92**; **III** 569, 654; **6** 101; **14** 535; **20** 361; **36 399–403 (upd.)**

Sanyo Ethylene Co. Ltd., **IV** 476

Sanyo-Kokusaku Pulp Co., Ltd., IV 326, **327–28**

Sanyo Petrochemical Co. Ltd., **IV** 476

Sanyo Railway Co., **I** 506; **II** 325

Sanyo Semiconductor, **17** 33

SAP AG, 11 78; **16 441–44**; **25** 34; **26** 496, 498; **43 358–63 (upd.)**

SAP America Inc., **38** 431–32

SAPAC. *See* Société Parisienne d'Achats en Commun.

Sapeksa, **55** 189

Sapirstein Greeting Card Company. *See* American Greetings Corporation.

Sappi Limited, IV 91–93; **49 352–55**

Sapporo Breweries Limited, I 282–83; **13 454–56 (upd.)**; **20** 28–29; **21** 319–20; **36 404–07 (upd.)**; **52** 32

SAPRA-Landauer Ltd., **51** 210

Sara Lee Corporation, I 15, 30; **II 571–73**, 675; **7** 113 **8** 262; **10** 219–20; **11** 15, 486; **12** 494, 502, 531; **15** 359, **434–37 (upd.)**, 507; **19** 192; **25** 91, 125, 166, 523; **26** 325, 503; **29** 132; **38** 381; **45** 111–12, 114; **49** 10; **52** 99, 101; **54 322–27 (upd.)**

Saracen's Head Brewery, **21** 245

Saratoga Partners, **24** 436

Sarawak Trading, **14** 448

Sargent & Lundy, **6** 556

Sarget S.A., **IV** 71

SARL, **12** 152

Sarma, **III** 623–24; **26** 159–61

Sarmag, **26** 161

Saros Corp., **15** 474

Sarotti A.G., **II** 546

Sarotti GmbH, **53** 315

Sarpe, **IV** 591

Sarrió S.A., **41** 325–26

Sartek Industries Inc., **44** 441

The SAS Group, 34 396–99 (upd.)

SAS Institute Inc., 10 476–78; **38** 432

Saseba Heavy Industries, **II** 274

Saskatchewan Oil and Gas Corporation, **13** 556–57

Sasol Limited, IV 533–35; **47 340–44 (upd.)**

Sason Corporation, **V** 187

SAT. *See* Stockholms Allmänna Telefonaktiebolag.

Satcom Group of Companies, **32** 40

Satellite Business Systems, **III** 182; **21** 14; **23** 135; **27** 304

Satellite Information Services, **II** 141

Satellite Software International, **10** 556

Satellite Television PLC, **IV** 652; **7** 391; **23** 135

Satellite Transmission and Reception Specialist Company, **11** 184

Säteri Oy, **IV** 349

Sato Yasusaburo, **I** 266

Saturday Evening Post Co., **II** 208; **9** 320

Saturn Corporation, III 593, 760; **7 461–64**; **21 449–53 (upd.)**; **22** 154; **36** 242

Saturn Industries, Inc., **23** 489

SATV. *See* Satellite Television PLC.

Saucona Iron Co., **IV** 35; **7** 48

Saucony Inc., 35 386–89

Sauder Woodworking Co., 12 433–34; **35 390–93 (upd.)**

Saudi Arabian Airlines, 6 84, **114–16**; **27** 132, **395–98 (upd.)**

Saudi Arabian Oil Company, IV 536–39; **17 411–15 (upd.)**; **50 412–17 (upd.)**. *See also* Arabian American Oil Co.

Saudi Arabian Parsons Limited, **8** 416

Saudi British Bank, **II** 298

Saudi Consolidated Electric Co., **IV** 538; **17** 414

Saudi Refining Inc., **IV** 539; **17** 414

Saudia. *See* Saudi Arabian Airlines.

Sauer Motor Company, **I** 177; **22** 329

Saul Lerner & Co., **II** 450

Saunders Karp & Co., **26** 190

Saunders, Karp, and Megrue, LP, **28** 258

Saunders-Roe Ltd., **IV** 658

Sauza, **31** 92

Sav-on Drug, **II** 605; **12** 477

Sav-X, **9** 186

Sava Group, **20** 263

Savacentre Ltd., **II** 658; **13** 284

Savage, **19** 430

Savage Shoes, Ltd., **III** 529

Savannah Electric & Power Company, **38** 448

Savannah Foods & Industries, Inc., 7 465–67; **32** 274, 277; **35** 178

Savannah Gas Company, **6** 448; **23** 29

Save & Prosper Group, **10** 277

Save-A-Lot, **II** 682; **11** 228

Save Mart, **14** 397; **27** 292

Save.com, **37** 409

Savia S.A. de C.V., **29** 435

Saviem, **III** 543

Savin, **III** 159; **26** 497

Savings of America, **II** 182

Savio, **IV** 422

Oy Savo-Karjalan Tukkuliike, **8** 293

Savon Sellu Mills, **IV** 315

Savory Milln, **II** 369

Savoy Group, **I** 248; **IV** 705; **24** 195; **49** 247

Savoy Industries, **12** 495

Savoy Pictures Entertainment Inc., **25** 214

Sawdust Pencil Company, **29** 372

Sawgrass Asset Management, LLC, **48** 18

Sawhill Tubular Products, **41** 3

Sawtek Inc., 43 364–66 (upd.)

Sawyer Electrical Manufacturing Company, **11** 4

Sawyer Industries, Inc., **13** 532

Sawyer Research Products, Inc., **14** 81

Saxby, S.A., **13** 385

Saxon and Norman Cement Co., **III** 670

Saxon Oil, **11** 97

Saxon Petroleum, Inc., **19** 162

Sayama Sekiyu, **IV** 554

SB Acquisitions, Inc., **46** 74

SBAR, Inc., **30** 4

Sbarro, Inc., 16 445–47; **19** 435; **27** 146

SBC Communications Inc., 25 498–99; **29** 62; **32 399–403 (upd.)**; **34** 362; **43** 447; **47** 10

SBC Warburg, II 369; **14 419–21**; **15** 197

SBC Warburg Dillon Read, **52** 355

Sberbank, **II** 242

SBK Entertainment World, Inc., **22** 194; **24** 485; **26** 187

SBS Technologies, Inc., 25 405–07

SCA. *See* Svenska Cellulosa AB.

SCA Services, Inc., **V** 754; **9** 109

Scaldia Paper BV, **15** 229

Scali, McCabe & Sloves, **I** 27; **22** 200

Scan Screen, **IV** 600

Scana Corporation, 6 574–76; **19** 499

Scanair, **34** 397–98

Scancem, **38** 437

Scandic Hotels AB, **49** 193

Scandinavian Airlines System, I 107, **119–20**, 121; **6** 96, 122; **25** 159; **26** 113; **27** 26, 463, 474; **31** 305; **33** 50; **38** 105. *See also* The SAS Group.

Scandinavian Bank, **II** 352

Scandinavian Broadcasting System SA, **53** 325

Scandinavian Trading Co., **I** 210

ScanDust, **III** 625

Scania-Vabis. *See* Saab-Scania AB.

ScanSource, Inc., 29 413–15

Scantron Corporation, **17** 266–68

Scarborough Public Utilities Commission, 9 461–62

Scaturro Supermarkets, **24** 528

SCB Computer Technology, Inc., 29 416–18

SCEcorp, **V** 713–14, **715–17**; **6** 590

Scenic Airlines, Inc., **25** 420, 423

Scenographic Designs, **21** 277

Schäfer, **31** 158

Schaffhausenschor Bankverein, **II** 281

Schaper Mfg. Co., **12** 168

Scharff-Koken Manufacturing Co., **IV** 286

Scharnow-Reisen, **II** 163–64; **44** 432

Schaum Publishing Co., **IV** 636

Schauman Wood Oy, **IV** 277, 302

Schawk, Inc., 24 424–26

Schein Pharmaceutical Inc., **13** 77

Schenker-Rhenus Ag, 6 424–26

Schenley Industries Inc., **I** 226, 285; **9** 449; **10** 181; **24** 140

Scherer. *See* R.P. Scherer.

Schering A.G., I 681–82, 684, 701; **10** 214; **14** 60; **16** 543; **36** 92, 148; **50 418–22 (upd.)**

Schering-Plough Corporation, I 682, **683–85**; **II** 590; **III** 45, 61; **11** 142, 207; **14** 58, 60, **422–25 (upd.)**; **36** 91–92; **45** 382; **49 356–62 (upd.)**

Schiavi Homes, Inc., **14** 138

Schibsted ASA, 31 401–05

Schicht Co., **II** 588

Schick Products, **41** 366

Schick Shaving, **I** 711; **III** 55; **38** 363, 365

Schieffelin & Co., **I** 272

Schindler Holding AG, II 122; **12** 546; **27** 267; **29 419–22**

Schlage Lock Co., **III** 526

Schleppschiffahrtsgesellschaft Unterweser, IV 140
Schlesischer Bankverein, II 278
Schlitz Brewing Co., I 218, 255, 268, 270, 291, 600; 10 100; 12 338; 18 500; 23 403
Schlotzsky's, Inc., 36 408–10
Schlumberger Limited, III 429, 499, 616–18; 13 323; 17 416–19 (upd.); 22 64, 68; 25 191; 43 91, 338; 45 418; 49 305
Schmalbach-Lubeca-Werke A.G., 15 128
Schmid, 19 166
Schmidt, I 255
Schmitt Music Company, 40 388–90
Schneider Co., III 113
Schneider et Cie, IV 25; 22 42
Schneider National, Inc., 36 411–13; 47 318–19
Schneider S.A., II 93–94; 18 471–74 (upd.); 19 165–66; 37 39
Schneiderman's Furniture Inc., 28 405–08
Schnitzer Steel Industries, Inc., 19 380–82
Schnoll Foods, 24 528
Schober Direktmarketing, 18 170
Schocken Books, 13 429
Schoeller & Hoesch Group, 30 349, 352
Schoenfeld Industries, 16 511
Scholastic Corporation, 10 479–81; 29 143, 423–27 (upd.)
Scholl Inc., I 685; 14 424; 49 359, 380
Schöller, 27 436, 439
Scholz Homes Inc., IV 115
Schott Corporation, III 445–47; 34 94; 53 296–98
Schottenstein Stores Corp., 14 426–28; 19 108; 24 26; 38 475. See also American Eagle Outfitters, Inc.
Schrader Bellows, III 603
Schreiber Foods, 26 432
Schreiber Frères. See Groupe Les Echos.
Schrock Cabinet Company, 13 564
Schroder Darling & Co., II 389
Schroders plc, 42 332–35
Schroders Ventures, 18 345
Schroeter, White and Johnson, III 204
Schroff Inc., 26 361, 363
Schubach, 30 408
Schubert & Salzer GmbH, 42 316
Schuck's Auto Supply. See CSK Auto Corporation.
Schuff Steel Company, 26 431–34
Schuitema, II 642; 16 312–13
Schuler Chocolates, 15 65
Schuller International, Inc., 11 421
Schultz Sav-O Stores, Inc., 21 454–56; 31 406–08
Schumacher Co., II 624
Schuykill Energy Resources, 12 41
Schwabe-Verlag, 7 42
Schwabel Corporation, 19 453
Schwan's Sales Enterprises, Inc., 7 468–70; 26 435–38 (upd.)
Schwartz Iron & Metal Co., 13 142
Schwarze Pumpe, 38 408
Schweitzer-Mauduit International, Inc., 16 304; 43 258; 52 300–02
Schweiz Allgemeine, III 377
Schweiz Transport-Vericherungs-Gesellschaft, III 410
Schweizer Rück Holding AG, III 377

Schweizerische Bankgesellschaft AG, II 379; V 104
Schweizerische Kreditanstalt, III 375, 410; 6 489
Schweizerische Nordostbahn, 6 424
Schweizerische Post-, Telefon- und Telegrafen-Betriebe, V 321–24
Schweizerische Ruckversicherungs-Gesellschaft. See Swiss Reinsurance Company.
Schweizerische Unfallversicherungs-Actiengesellschaft in Winterthur, III 402
Schweizerische Unionbank, II 368
Schweizerischer Bankverein, II 368
Schweppe, Paul & Gosse, II 476
Schweppes Ltd. See Cadbury Schweppes PLC.
Schwinn Cycle and Fitness L.P., 16 494; 19 383–85; 26 412; 47 95
The Schwinn GT Co., 26 185
Schwitzer, II 420
SCI. See Service Corporation International; Société Centrale d'Investissement.
SCI 169 Rue de Rennes, 53 32
SCI Systems, Inc., 9 463–64; 12 451
Scicon International, 14 317; 49 165
SciCor Inc., 30 152
Science Applications International Corporation, 15 438–40
Scientific-Atlanta, Inc., 6 335–37; 45 371–75 (upd.); 54 406
Scientific Communications, Inc., 10 97
Scientific Data Systems, II 44; III 172; 6 289; 10 365
Scientific Games Holding Corp., III 431; 20 48
Scientific Materials Company, 24 162
SciMed Life Systems, III 18–19; 37 43
Scioto Bank, 9 475
Scitex Corporation Ltd., 15 148, 229; 24 427–32; 26 212; 43 150; 48 123
Scitor, 52 108
SCM Corp., I 29; III 502; IV 330; 7 208; 8 223–24; 17 213
SCO. See Santa Cruz Operation, Inc.
SCOA Industries, Inc., 13 260
Scopus Technology Inc., 38 431
SCOR S.A., III 394; 20 464–66
The Score Board, Inc., 19 386–88
Score! Learning, Inc., 42 211
Scot Bowyers, II 587
Scot Lad Foods, 14 411
Scotch House Ltd., 19 181
Scotia Securities, II 223
Scotiabank. See The Bank of Nova Scotia.
Scotsman Industries, Inc., II 420; 16 397; 20 467–69
Scott-Ballantyne Company. See Ballantyne of Omaha, Inc.
Scott Communications, Inc., 10 97
Scott Fetzer Company, III 214; 12 435–37, 554–55; 17 233; 18 60, 62–63; 42 33
Scott, Foresman, IV 675
Scott Graphics, IV 289; 8 483
Scott Health Care, 28 445
Scott Holdings, 19 384
Scott Lithgow, III 516; 7 232
Scott-McDuff, II 107
Scott Paper Company, III 749; IV 258, 289–90, 311, 325, 327, 329–31; 8 483; 16 302, 304; 17 182; 18 181; 19 266; 22 210; 29 333; 31 409–412 (upd.); 43 258
Scott Transport, 27 473

Scotti Brothers, 20 3
Scottish & Newcastle Breweries PLC, 50 201
Scottish & Newcastle plc, 15 441–44; 35 394–97 (upd.); 50 277
Scottish Amicable plc, 48 328
Scottish Aviation, I 50; 24 85–86
Scottish Brick, 14 250
Scottish Electric, 6 453
Scottish General Fire Assurance Corp., III 256
Scottish Hydro-Electric PLC, 13 457–59
Scottish Inns of America, Inc., 13 362
Scottish Land Development, III 501; 7 207
Scottish Malt Distillers, I 240
Scottish Media Group plc, 32 404–06; 41 350–52
Scottish Mutual plc, 39 5–6
Scottish Nuclear, Ltd., 19 389
Scottish Power plc, 49 363–66 (upd.)
Scottish Radio Holding plc, 41 350–52
Scottish Sealand Oil Services Ltd., 25 171
Scottish Union Co., III 358
Scottish Universal Investments, 45 189
ScottishPower plc, 19 389–91; 27 483, 486
ScottishTelecom plc, 19 389
The Scotts Company, 22 474–76
Scotts Stores, I 289
Scotty's, Inc., 12 234; 22 477–80; 26 160–61
Scovill Fasteners Inc., IV 11; 22 364; 24 433–36
SCP Pool Corporation, 39 358–60
Scranton Corrugated Box Company, Inc., 8 102
Scranton Plastics Laminating Corporation, 8 359
Screen Gems, II 135–36; 12 74; 22 193
Screg Group, I 563; 24 79; 31 128
Scribbans-Kemp Ltd., II 594
Scriha & Deyhle, 10 196
Scripps-Howard, Inc., IV 607–09, 628; 7 64, 157–59. See also The E.W. Scripps Company.
Scrivner Inc., 17 180
SCS Interactive, 44 261
Scudder Kemper Investments. See Zurich Financial Services.
Scudder, Stevens & Clark, II 448; 13 448
Scurlock Oil Co., IV 374; 50 48
SD-Scicon plc, 24 87
SD Warren, 49 352–53
SDA Systems Inc., 48 75
SDB Espan, 51 16
SDC Coatings, III 715
SDGE. See San Diego Gas & Electric Company.
SDK Health Care Information Systems, 16 94
SDK Parks, IV 724
Sea-Alaska Products, II 494
Sea Containers Ltd., 29 428–31
Sea Diamonds Ltd., IV 66; 7 123
Sea Far of Norway, II 484
Sea Insurance Co. Ltd., III 220
Sea-Land Service Inc., I 476; 9 510–11; 22 164, 166
Sea Life Centre Aquariums, 10 439
Sea Ray, III 444
Sea Star Line, 41 399
Sea World, Inc., IV 623–24; 12 224
Seabee Corp., 18 276

Seaboard Air Line Railroad. *See* CSX
Corporation.
Seaboard Corporation, 36 414–16
Seaboard Finance Company, **13** 63
Seaboard Fire and Marine Insurance Co.,
III 242
Seaboard Life Insurance Co., **III** 193
Seaboard Lumber Sales, **IV** 307
Seaboard Oil Co., **IV** 552
Seaboard Surety Company, **III** 357; **22** 494
Seabourn Cruise Lines, **6** 368; **27** 90, 92
Seabrook Farms Co., **24** 527–28
Seabulk Offshore International. *See* Hvide
Marine Incorporated.
Seabury & Smith, **III** 283
Seacat-Zapata Off-Shore Company, **18** 513
Seacoast Products, **III** 502
Seafield Capital Corporation, **27** 385, 387.
See also LabOne, Inc.
Seafield Estate and Consolidated
Plantations Berhad, **14** 448
Seafirst. *See* Seattle First National Bank,
Inc.
SeaFirst Corp., **II** 228; **17** 462
Seagate Technology, Inc., 6 230–31; **8**
466–68; 9 57; **10** 257, 403–04, 459; **11**
56, 234; **13** 483; **18** 250; **25** 530; **34**
400–04 (upd.); 45 429
The Seagram Company Ltd., I 26, 240,
244, **284–86**, 329, 403; **II** 456, 468; **IV**
401; **7** 155; **18** 72; **21** 26, 401; **22** 194;
23 125; **25** 266, 268, 366, **408–12**
(upd.); 26 125, 127, 152; **28** 475; **29**
196; **31** 269; **33** 375, 424, 432; **46** 438;
47 418–20; **50** 114
Seagull Energy Corporation, 11 440–42
Seahawk Services Ltd., **37** 289
Seal Products, Inc., **12** 264
Seal Sands Chemicals, **16** 69
Sealand Petroleum Co., **IV** 400
Sealectro, **III** 434
Sealed Air Corporation, 14 429–31
Sealed Power Corporation, I 199–200;
10 492–94. *See also* SPX Corporation.
SeaLite Sciences, Inc., **52** 171
Sealright Co., Inc., 17 420–23
SealRite Windows, **19** 446
Sealtest, **14** 205
Sealy Inc., 12 438–40; 28 416; **34** 407
Seaman Furniture Company, Inc., 28
389; **32 407–09**
Seamless Rubber Co., **III** 613
Seaquist Manufacturing Corporation, **9**
413–14; **33** 335–36
Searle & Co. *See* G.D. Searle & Co.
Sears Canada Inc., **25** 221
Sears Logistics Services, **18** 225–26
Sears plc, V 177–79
Sears, Roebuck and Co., I 26, 146, 516,
556; **II** 18, 60, 134, 331, 411, 414; **III**
259, 265, 340, 536, 598, 653–55; **V**
180–83; 6 12–13; **7** 166, 479; **8** 224,
287–89; **9** 44, 65–66 156, 210, 213,
219, 235–36, 430–31, 538; **10** 10,
50–52, 199, 236–37, 288, 304–05,
490–91; **11** 62, 349, 393, 498; **12** 54,
96–98, 309, 311, 315, 430–31, 439,
522, 548, 557; **13** 165, 260, 268, 277,
411, 545, 550, 562–63; **14** 62; **15** 402,
470; **16** 73, 75, 160, 327–28, 560; **17**
366, 460, 487; **18** 65, 168, 283, 445,
475–79 (upd.); 19 143, 221, 309, 490;
20 259, 263; **21** 73, 94, 96–97; **23** 23,
52, 210; **25** 221, 357, 535; **27** 30, 32,

163, 347–48, 416, 428–30; **33** 311–12;
36 418; **50** 391; **51** 319, 321
Sears Roebuck de México, S.A. de C.V.,
20 470–72; **21** 259; **34** 340
Seashore Transportation Co., **13** 398
Season-all Industries, **III** 735
SEAT. *See* Sociedad Española de
Automoviles de Turismo.
Seat Pagine Gialle S.p.A., 47 345–47
Seatrain International, **27** 474
Seattle Brewing and Malting Company. *See*
Rainier Brewing Company.
Seattle City Light, 50 423–26
Seattle Coffee Company, **32** 12, 15
Seattle Electric Company, **6** 565; **50**
365–66
Seattle FilmWorks, Inc., 20 473–75
Seattle First National Bank Inc., 8
469–71
Seattle Times Company, 15 445–47
Seaview Oil Co., **IV** 393
Seaway Express, **9** 510
Seaway Food Town, Inc., 9 452; **15**
448–50
SeaWest, **19** 390
SEB-Fastigheter A.B., **II** 352
SEB S.A. *See* Groupe SEB.
Sebastian International, **48** 422
Sebastiani Vineyards, Inc., 28 413–15; 39
421
SECA, **IV** 401
SECDO, **III** 618
SECO Industries, **III** 614
Seco Products Corporation, **22** 354
Secon GmbH, **13** 160
Second Bank of the United States, **II** 213;
9 369
Second Harvest, 29 432–34
Second National Bank, **II** 254
Second National Bank of Bucyrus, **9** 474
Second National Bank of Ravenna, **9** 474
Secoroc, **III** 427
Le Secours, **III** 211
SecPac. *See* Security Pacific Corporation.
Secure Horizons, **11** 378–79
Secure Networks, Inc., **25** 349
Securicor Plc, 11 547; **45 376–79**
Securitas AB, 41 77, 80; **42** 165–66,
336–39
Securitas Esperia, **III** 208
Securities Industry Automation
Corporation, **9** 370
Securities International, Inc., **II** 440–41
Securities Management & Research, Inc.,
27 46
Security Bancorp, **25** 186–87
Security Capital Corporation, 17
424–27; 21 476; **48** 330–31; **49** 28–29
Security Connecticut Life Insurance Co.,
III 276
Security Data Group, **32** 373
Security Dynamics Technologies, Inc., **46**
367
Security Engineering, **III** 472
Security Express, **10** 269
Security First National Bank of Los
Angeles, **II** 349
Security Life and Annuity Company, **11**
213
Security Management Company, **8** 535–36
Security National Bank, **II** 251, 336
Security National Corp., **10** 246
Security Pacific Corporation, II 349–50,
422; **III** 366; **8** 45, 48; **11** 447; **17** 137

Security Trust Company, **9** 229, 388
Security Union Title Insurance Co., **10**
43–44
SED International Holdings, Inc., 43
367–69
Sedat Eldem, **13** 475
SEDCO, **17** 418
Sedgwick Group PLC, **I** 427; **III** 280, 366;
10 38; **22** 318
Sedgwick Sales, Inc., **29** 384
SEDTCO Pty., **13** 61
See's Candies, Inc., III 213; **18** 60–61;
30 411–13
Seeburg Corporation, **II** 22; **III** 430; **15**
538
Seed Restaurant Group Inc., **13** 321; **27**
145
Seed Solutions, Inc., **11** 491
Seeger-Orbis, **III** 624
Seeger Refrigerator Co., **III** 653; **12** 548
Seeman Brothers. *See* White Rose, Inc.
SEEQ Technology, Inc., **9** 114; **13** 47; **17**
32, 34
SEG, **I** 463
Sega Enterprises, Ltd., **28** 320
Sega of America, Inc., 7 396; **10** 124–25,
284–86, **482–85; 18** 520; **50** 157
Sega of Japan, **24** 4
Segespar, **II** 265
Sego Milk Products Company, **7** 428
Seguros Comercial America, **21** 413
Seguros El Corte Inglés, **V** 52
Seguros Monterrey Aetna, **19** 189; **45** 294
Seguros Serfin S.A., **25** 290
Segway LLC, 48 355–57
Seibels, Bruce & Co., **11** 394–95
Seiberling Rubber Company, **V** 244; **20**
259
Seibert-Oxidermo, Inc., **55** 321
Seibu Allstate Life Insurance Company,
Ltd., **27** 31
Seibu Department Stores, Ltd., II 273; **V**
184–86; 42 340–43 (upd.)
Seibu Group, **36** 417–18; **47** 408–09
Seibu Railway Co. Ltd., V 187, **510–11**,
526
Seibu Saison, **6** 207
Seifu Co. Ltd., **48** 250
Seigle's Home and Building Centers,
Inc., 41 353–55
Seijo Green Plaza Co., **I** 283
Seika Co., Ltd., **55** 48
Seikatsu-Soko, **V** 210
Seiko Corporation, I 488; **III** 445,
619–21; 11 46; **12** 317; **13** 122; **16** 168,
549; **17 428–31 (upd.); 21** 122–23; **22**
413; **41** 72
Seiko Instruments USA Inc., **23** 210
Seimi Chemical Co. Ltd., **48** 41
Seine, **III** 391
Seino Transportation Company, Ltd., 6
427–29
Seismograph Service Limited, **II** 86; **11**
413; **17** 419
Seita, 23 424–27
Seitel, Inc., 47 348–50
Seiwa Fudosan Co., **I** 283
The Seiyu, Ltd., V 187–89; 36 417–21
(upd.)
Seizo-sha, **12** 483
Sekisui Chemical Co., Ltd., III 741–43
SEL, **I** 193, 463
Selat Marine Services, **22** 276
Selby Shoe Company, **48** 69

Selden, **I** 164, 300
Select Comfort Corporation, 34 405–08
Select Energy, Inc., **48** 305
Select-Line Industries, **9** 543
Select Theatres Corp. *See* Shubert Organization Inc.
Selection Trust, **IV** 67, 380, 565
Selective Auto and Fire Insurance Co. of America, **III** 353
Selective Insurance Co., **III** 191
Selectour SA, 53 299–301
Selectronics Inc., **23** 210
Selectrons Ltd., **41** 367
Selena Coffee Inc., **39** 409
Selenia, **I** 467; **II** 86; **38** 374
Self Auto, **23** 232
The Self-Locking Carton Company, **14** 163
Self-Service Drive Thru, Inc., **25** 389
Self Service Restaurants, **II** 613
Selfix, Inc. *See* Home Products International, Inc.
Selfridges Plc, V 94, 177–78; **34 409–11**
Selig Chemical Industries, **54** 252, 254
Seligman & Latz, **18** 455
Selkirk Communications Ltd., **26** 273
Selleck Nicholls, **III** 691
Sells-Floto, **32** 186
The Selmer Company, Inc., 19 392–94, 426, 428; **55** 113
Seltel International Inc., **6** 33; **35** 246
Semarca, **11** 523
Sematech, **18** 384, 481
SembCorp Logistics Ltd., **53** 199, 203
Sembler Company, **11** 346
SEMCO Energy, Inc., 44 379–82
Semet-Solvay, **22** 29
Semi-Tech Global, **30** 419–20
Seminis, Inc., 21 413; **29 435–37**
Seminole Electric Cooperative, **6** 583
Seminole Fertilizer, **7** 537–38
Seminole National Bank, **41** 312
Semitic, Inc., **33** 248
Semitool, Inc., 18 480–82
Sempra Energy, 25 413–16 (upd.)
Semrau and Sons, **II** 601
Semtech Corporation, 32 410–13
SEN AG, **IV** 128
Sencel Aero Engineering Corporation, **16** 483
Seneca Foods Corporation, 17 432–34
Senelle-Maubeuge, **IV** 227
Senior Corp., **11** 261
Senshusha, **I** 506
Sensi, Inc., **22** 173
Sensient Technologies Corporation, 52 303–08 (upd.)
Sensormatic Electronics Corp., 11 443–45; 39 77–79
Sensory Science Corporation, 37 353–56
Sentinel Foam & Envelope Corporation, **14** 430
Sentinel Group, **6** 295
Sentinel Savings and Loan, **10** 339
Sentinel-Star Company, **IV** 683; **22** 521
Sentinel Technologies, **III** 38
Sentrust, **IV** 92
Sentry, **II** 624
Sentry Insurance Company, **10** 210
Senyo Kosakuki Kenkyujo, **III** 595
Seohan Development Co., **III** 516; **7** 232
Sepa, **II** 594
Sepal, Ltd., **39** 152, 154
AB Separator, **III** 417–19
SEPECAT, **24** 86

Sephora SA, **51** 234–35; **54** 265–67
SEPIC, **I** 330
Sepracor Inc., 45 380–83
Sept, **IV** 325
Sequa Corporation, 13 460–63; 54 328–32 (upd.)
Séquanaise, **III** 391–92
Sequel Corporation, **41** 193
Sequent Computer Systems Inc., **10** 363
Sequoia Athletic Company, **25** 450
Sequoia Insurance, **III** 270
Sequoia Pharmacy Group, **13** 150
Sera-Tec Biologicals, Inc., **V** 175–76; **19** 355
Seraco Group, **V** 182
Seragen Inc., **47** 223
Serck Group, **I** 429
Serco Group plc, 47 351–53
SEREB, **I** 45; **7** 10
Sereg Valves, S.A., **17** 147
Serewatt AG, **6** 491
Sergeant Drill Co., **III** 525
Sero-Genics, Inc., **V** 174–75
Serono S.A., 47 354–57
Serta, Inc., 28 416–18
Serval Marketing, **18** 393
Servam Corp., **7** 471–73
Servel Inc., **III** 479; **22** 25
Service America Corp., 7 471–73; 27 480–81
Service Bureau Corp., **III** 127
Service Co., Ltd., **48** 182
Service Control Corp. *See* Angelica Corporation.
Service Corporation International, 6 293–95; 16 343–44; **37** 66–68; **51 329–33 (upd.)**
Service Corporation of America, **17** 552
Service Games Company, **10** 482
Service Master L.P., **34** 153
Service Merchandise Company, Inc., V 190–92; 6 287; **9** 400; **19 395–99 (upd.)**
Service Partner, **I** 120
Service Pipe Line Co., **IV** 370
Service Q. General Service Co., **I** 109
Service Systems, **III** 103
ServiceMaster Inc., 23 428–31 (upd.)
Servicemaster Limited Partnership, 6 44–46; 13 199
Services Maritimes des Messageries Impériales. *See* Compagnie des Messageries Maritimes.
ServiceWare, Inc., **25** 118
Servicios Financieros Quadrum S.A., **14** 156
Servisair Plc, **49** 320
Servisco, **II** 608
ServiStar Coast to Coast Corporation. *See* TruServ Corporation.
ServoChem A.B., **I** 387
Servomation Corporation, **7** 472–73
Servomation Wilbur. *See* Service America Corp.
Servoplan, S.A., **8** 272
SES Staffing Solutions, **27** 21
Sesame Street Book Club, **13** 560
Sesamee Mexicana, **48** 142
Sespe Oil, **IV** 569; **24** 519
Sessler Inc., **19** 381
SET, **I** 466
Setagaya Industry Co., Ltd., **48** 295
SETCAR, **14** 458
Seton Scholl. *See* SSL International plc.

Settsu Marine and Fire Insurance Co., **III** 367
Seven Arts Limited, **25** 328
Seven Arts Productions, Ltd., **II** 147, 176
7-Eleven, Inc., 32 414–18 (upd.); 36 358
Seven-Eleven Japan Co., **41** 115. *See also* Ito-Yokado Co., Ltd.
Seven Generation, Inc., **41** 177
Seven Network Limited, **25** 329
Seven-Up Bottling Co. of Los Angeles, **II** 121
Seven-Up Co., **I** 245, 257; **II** 468, 477; **18** 418
SevenOne Media, **54** 297
Sevenson Environmental Services, Inc., 42 344–46
Severn Trent PLC, 12 441–43; 38 425–29 (upd.)
Severonickel Combine, **48** 300
Seversky Aircraft Corporation, **9** 205
Sevin-Rosen Partners, **III** 124; **6** 221
Sewell Coal Co., **IV** 181
Sewell Plastics, Inc., **10** 222
Sextant In-Flight Systems, LLC, **30** 74
Seybold Machine Co., **II** 37; **6** 602
Seymour Electric Light Co., **13** 182
Seymour International Press Distributor Ltd., **IV** 619
Seymour Press, **IV** 619
Seymour Trust Co., **13** 467
SF Bio, **52** 51
SFI Group plc, 51 334–36
SFIC Holdings (Cayman) Inc., **38** 422
SFIM Industries, **37** 348
SFNGR. *See* Nouvelles Galeries Réunies.
SFS Bancorp Inc., **41** 212
SFX Broadcasting Inc., **24** 107
SFX Entertainment, Inc., 36 422–25; 37 383–84
SGC. *See* Supermarkets General Corporation.
SGE. *See* Vinci.
SGI, 29 438–41 (upd.)
SGL Carbon Group, **40** 83; **46** 14
SGLG, Inc., **13** 367
SGS Corp., **II** 117; **11** 46
SGS-Thomson Microelectronics, **54** 269–70
Shaffer Clarke, **II** 594
Shakespeare Company, 16 296; **22 481–84**
Shakey's Pizza, **16** 447
Shaklee Corporation, 12 444–46; 17 186; **38** 93; **39 361–64 (upd.)**
Shalco Systems, **13** 7
Shampaine Industries, Inc., **37** 399
Shamrock Advisors, Inc., **8** 305
Shamrock Broadcasting Inc., **24** 107
Shamrock Capital L.P., **7** 81–82
Shamrock Holdings, **III** 609; **7** 438; **9** 75; **11** 556; **25** 268
Shamrock Oil & Gas Co., **I** 403–04; **IV** 409; **7** 308
Shan-Chih Business Association, **23** 469
Shandwick International, **47** 97
Shanghai Crown Maling Packaging Co. Ltd., **13** 190
Shanghai General Bearing Co., Ltd., **45** 170
Shanghai Hotels Co., **IV** 717
Shanghai International Finance Company Limited, **15** 433
Shanghai Kyocera Electronics Co., Ltd., **21** 331

Shanghai Petrochemical Co., Ltd., 18 483–85; 21 83; 45 50
Shanghai Tobacco, 49 150, 153
Shangri-La Asia Ltd., 22 305
Shanks Group plc, 45 384–87
Shannon Aerospace Ltd., 36 426–28
Shannon Group, Inc., 18 318, 320
Shansby Group, 27 197; 43 218
Share Drug plc, 24 269
Shared Financial Systems, Inc., 10 501
Shared Medical Systems Corporation, 14 432–34
Shared Technologies Inc., 12 71
Shared Use Network Systems, Inc., 8 311
ShareWave Inc., 48 92
Shari Lewis Enterprises, Inc., 28 160
Sharon Steel Corp., I 497; 7 360–61; 8 536; 13 158, 249; 47 234
Sharon Tank Car Corporation, 6 394; 25 169
Sharp & Dohme, Incorporated, I 650; 11 289, 494
Sharp Corporation, I 476; II 95–96; III 14, 428, 455, 480; 6 217, 231; 11 45; 12 447–49 (upd.); 13 481; 16 83; 21 123; 22 197; 40 391–95 (upd.)
The Sharper Image Corporation, 10 486–88; 23 210; 26 439; 27 429
Sharples Co., I 383
Sharples Separator Co., III 418–20
Shasta Beverages. See National Beverage Corp.
Shaw Communications Inc., 26 274; 35 69
The Shaw Group, Inc., 50 427–30
Shaw Industries, Inc., 9 465–67; 19 274, 276; 25 320; 40 396–99 (upd.)
Shaw's Supermarkets, Inc., II 658–59; 23 169
Shawell Precast Products, 14 248
Shawinigan Water and Power Company, 6 501–02
Shawmut National Corporation, II 207; 12 31; 13 464–68
Shea Homes. See J.F. Shea Co., Inc.
Shea's Winnipeg Brewery Ltd., I 268; 25 280
Sheaffer Group, 23 54, 57
Shearman & Sterling, 32 419–22; 35 467
Shearson Hammill & Company, 22 405–06
Shearson Lehman Brothers Holdings Inc., I 202; II 398–99, 450, 478; III 319; 8 118; 9 468–70 (upd.); 10 62–63; 11 418; 12 459; 15 124, 463–64
Shearson Lehman Hutton Group, 49 181
Shearson Lehman Hutton Holdings Inc., II 339, 445, 450–52; III 119; 9 125; 10 59, 63; 17 38–39
Shedd's Food Products Company, 9 318
Sheepbridge Engineering, III 495
Sheffield Banking Co., II 333
Sheffield Exploration Company, 28 470
Sheffield Forgemasters Group Ltd., 39 32
Sheffield Motor Co., I 158; 10 292
Sheffield Twist Drill & Steel Co., III 624
Shekou Container Terminal, 16 481; 38 345
Shelby Insurance Company, 10 44–45
Shelby Steel Processing Co., 51 238
Shelby Steel Tube Co., IV 572; 7 550
Shelby Williams Industries, Inc., 14 435–37
Shelco, 22 146
Sheldahl Inc., 23 432–35

Shelf Life Inc. See King Kullen Grocery Co., Inc.
Shell. See Shell Transport and Trading Company p.l.c.; Shell Oil Company.
Shell Australia Ltd., III 728
Shell BV, IV 518
Shell Canada Limited, 32 45
Shell Chemical Corporation, IV 410, 481, 531–32, 540; 8 415; 24 151
Shell Coal International, IV 532
Shell Forestry, 21 546; 50 58
Shell France, 12 153
Shell Nederland BV, V 658–59
Shell Oil Company, I 20, 26, 569; III 559; IV 392, 400, 531, 540–41; 6 382, 457; 8 261–62; 11 522; 14 25, 438–40 (upd.); 17 417; 19 175–76; 21 546; 22 274; 24 520; 25 96, 232, 469; 26 496; 41 356–60 (upd.), 395; 45 54
Shell Transport and Trading Company p.l.c., I 605; II 436, 459; III 522, 735; IV 363, 378–79, 381–82, 403, 412, 423, 425, 429, 440, 454, 466, 470, 472, 474, 484–86, 491, 505, 508, 530–32, 564; 31 127–28; 50 58, 355. See also Royal Dutch Petroleum Company; Royal Dutch/Shell.
Shell Western E & P, 7 323
Shell Winning, IV 413–14
Sheller-Globe Corporation, I 201–02; 17 182
Shells Seafood Restaurants, Inc., 43 370–72
Shelly Brothers, Inc., 15 65
Shenley Laboratories, I 699
Shepard Warner Elevator Co., III 467
Shepard's Citations, Inc., IV 636–37
Shepherd Hardware Products Ltd., 16 357
Shepherd Neame Limited, 30 414–16
Shepherd Plating and Finishing Company, 13 233
Shepler Equipment Co., 9 512
Sheraton Corp. of America, I 463–64, 487; III 98–99; 11 198; 13 362–63; 21 91
Sherborne Group Inc./NH Holding Inc., 17 20
Sherbrooke Paper Products Ltd., 17 281
Sheridan Bakery, II 633
Sheridan Catheter & Instrument Corp., III 443
Sherix Chemical, I 682
Sherr-Gold, 23 40
Sherritt Gordon Mines, 7 386–87; 12 260
The Sherwin-Williams Company, III 744–46; 8 222, 224; 11 384; 12 7; 13 469–71 (upd.); 19 180; 24 323; 30 474
Sherwood Brands, Inc., 53 302–04
Sherwood Equity Group Ltd. See National Discount Brokers Group, Inc.
Sherwood Medical Group, I 624; III 443–44; 10 70; 50 538
SHI Resort Development Co., III 635
ShianFu Optical Fiber, III 491
Shiara Holdings, Inc., 53 88
Shibaura Seisakusho Works, I 533; 12 483
Shieh Chi Industrial Co., 19 508
Shields & Co., 9 118
Shihlin Electric & Engineering Group, 49 460
Shikoku Drinks Co., IV 297
Shikoku Electric Power Company, Inc., V 718–20
Shikoku Machinery Co., III 634
Shiley, Inc., 38 361

Shillito's, 31 192
Shimizu Construction Company Ltd., 44 153
Shimotsuke Electric Railway Company, 6 431
Shimura Kako, IV 63
Shin-Nihon Glass Co., I 221
Shin Nippon Machine Manufacturing, III 634
Shinano Bank, II 291
Shinko Electric Co., Ltd., IV 129
Shinko Rayon Ltd., I 363; V 369–70
Shinriken Kogyo, IV 63
Shintech, 11 159–60
Shinwa Pharmaceutical Co. Ltd., 48 250
Shinwa Tsushinki Co., III 593
Shiomi Casting, III 551
Shionogi & Co., Ltd., I 646, 651; III 60–61; 11 90, 290; 17 435–37 (upd.)
Ship 'n Shore, II 503; 9 156–57; 10 324
Shipley Co. Inc., 26 425
Shipowners and Merchants Tugboat Company, 6 382
Shipper Group, 16 344
Shipstad & Johnson's Ice Follies, 25 313
Shiro Co., Ltd., V 96
Shirokiya, Ltd., V 199
Shiseido Company, Limited, II 273–74, 436; III 46, 48, 62–64; 8 341, 343; 22 485–88 (upd.)
SHL Systemhouse Inc., 27 305
Shochiku Company Ltd., 28 461
Shockley Electronics, 20 174
Shoe Carnival Inc., 14 441–43
Shoe Corp., I 289
Shoe Supply, Inc., 22 213
Shoe-Town Inc., 23 310
Shoe Works Inc., 18 415
Shohin Kaihatsu Kenkyusho, III 595
Shoman Milk Co., II 538
Shonac Corp., 14 427
Shonco, Inc., 18 438
Shoney's, Inc., 7 474–76; 14 453; 19 286; 23 436–39 (upd.); 29 290–91
Shop & Go, II 620
Shop 'n Bag, II 624
Shop 'n Save, II 669, 682; 12 220–21
Shop Rite Foods Inc., II 672–74; 7 105; 19 479. See also Big V Supermarkets, Inc.
ShopKo Stores Inc., II 669–70; 18 505–07; 21 457–59; 50 455–57
Shoppers Drug Mart Corporation, 49 367–70
Shoppers Food Warehouse Corporation, 16 159, 161
Shoppers World Stores, Inc. See LOT$OFF Corporation.
ShopRite, 24 528. See also Foodarama Supermarkets, Inc.
Shopwell/Food Emporium, II 638; 16 247, 249
ShopWise.com Inc., 53 13
Shore Manufacturing, 13 165
Shorewood Packaging Corporation, 28 419–21; 47 189
Short Aircraft Co., I 50, 55, 92
Short Brothers, 24 85
Shoseido Co., 17 110
Shoshi-Gaisha, IV 320
Shotton Paper Co. Ltd., IV 350
Showa Aircraft Industry Co., I 507–08
Showa Aluminum Corporation, 8 374
Showa Bank, II 291–92

Showa Bearing Manufacturing Co., **III** 595
Showa Cotton Co., Ltd., **IV** 442
Showa Denko, **I** 493–94; **II** 292; **IV** 61;
   24 324–25
Showa Marutsutsu Co. Ltd., **8** 477
Showa Paper Co., **IV** 268
Showa Photo Industry, **III** 548
Showa Products Company, **8** 476
Showa Shell Sekiyu K.K., **II** 459; **IV**
   542–43
ShowBiz Pizza Time, Inc., **12** 123; **13**
   472–74; **15** 73; **16** 447. *See also* CEC
   Entertainment, Inc.
Showboat, Inc., **19 400–02**; **43** 227
Showcase of Fine Fabrics, **16** 197
Showco, Inc., **35** 436
Showerings, **I** 215
Showscan Entertainment Inc., **34** 230
Showscan Film Corporation, **28** 206
Showtime, **II** 173; **7** 222–23; **9** 74; **23**
   274–75, 391, 503; **25** 329–30
Shredded Wheat Co., **II** 543; **7** 366
Shreve and Company, **12** 312
Shreveport Refrigeration, **16** 74
Shrewsbury and Welshpool Old Bank, **II**
   307
Shu Uemura, **III** 43
Shubert Organization Inc., **24 437–39**
Shubrooks International Ltd., **11** 65
Shueisha, **IV** 598
Shuffle Master Inc., **51 337–40**
Shuford Mills, Inc., **14** 430
Shugart Associates, **6** 230; **8** 466; **22** 189
Shull Lumber & Shingle Co., **IV** 306
Shulman Transport Enterprises Inc., **27** 473
Shun Fung Ironworks, **IV** 717
Shunan Shigyo Co., Ltd., **IV** 160
Shurgard Storage Centers, Inc., **21** 476;
   52 293, **309–11**
Shuttleworth Brothers Company. *See*
   Mohawk Industries, Inc.
Shuwa Corp., **22** 101; **36** 292
SHV Holdings N.V., **IV** 383; **14** 156; **55**
   344–47
SI Holdings Inc., **10** 481; **29** 425
SIAS, **19** 192
SIAS-MPA, **I** 281
SIATA S.p.A., **26** 363
SIB Financial Services, **39** 382
Sibco Universal, S.A., **14** 429
Sibel, **48** 350
Siberian Moloko, **48** 438
Sibneft. *See* OAO Siberian Oil Company.
Siboney Shoe Corp., **22** 213
SIBV/MS Holdings, **IV** 295; **19** 226
Sicard Inc., **I** 185
SICC. *See* Univision Communications Inc.
Sichuan Station Wagon Factory, **38** 462
Sick's Brewery, **26** 304
Siclet, **25** 84
Sicma Aero Seat, **36** 529
Siddeley Autocar Co., **III** 508
Sidel. *See* Groupe Sidel S.A.
Sidélor, **IV** 226
Siderbrás, **IV** 125
Siderca S.A.I.C., **41** 405–06
Sidermex, **III** 581
Sidérurgie Maritime, **IV** 26
Sidley Austin Brown & Wood, **40**
   400–03
SIDMAR NV, **IV** 128
Siebe plc, **13** 235. *See also* BTR Siebe plc.
Siebel Group, **13** 544–45
Siebel Marketing Group, **27** 195

Siebel Systems, Inc., **38 430–34**
Siebert Financial Corp., **32 423–25**
Siegas, **III** 480; **22** 26
Siegler Heater Corp., **I** 481
Siemens AG, **I** 74, 192, 409–11, 462, 478,
   542; **II** 22, 25, 38, 80–82, **97–100**, 122,
   257, 279; **III** 139, 154–55, 466, 482,
   516, 724; **6** 215–16; **7** 232; **9** 11, 32,
   44; **10** 16, 363; **11** 59, 196, 235,
   397–98, 460; **12** 546; **13** 402; **14** 169,
   444–47 (upd.); **15** 125; **16** 392; **18** 32;
   19 166, 313; **20** 290; **22** 19, 373–74; **23**
   389, 452, 494–95; **24** 88; **30** 11; **33** 225,
   288
Siemens Solar Industries L.P., **44** 182
The Sierra Club, **28 422–24**
Sierra Designs, Inc., **10** 215–16
Sierra Health Services, Inc., **15 451–53**
Sierra Leone External Telegraph Limited,
   25 100
Sierra Leone Selection Trust, **IV** 66
Sierra On-Line, Inc., **13** 92, 114; **14** 263;
   15 454–56; **16** 146; **29** 75; **41 361–64**
   (upd.)
Sierra Pacific Industries, **22 489–91**
Sierra Precision, **52** 187
Sierrita Resources, Inc., **6** 590
SIFCO Industries, Inc., **41**
Sifo Group AB. *See* Observer AB.
Sight & Sound Entertainment, **35** 21
Sigma-Aldrich Corporation, **I 690–91**;
   36 429–32 (upd.)
Sigma Alimentos, S.A. de C.V., **19** 11–12
Sigma Coatings, **IV** 499
Sigma Network Systems, **11** 464
Sigmor Corp., **IV** 410; **31** 455
Signal Companies, Inc. *See* AlliedSignal
   Inc.
Signal Corporation, **54** 395–96
Signal Galaxies, **13** 127
Signal Oil & Gas Inc., **I** 71, 178; **IV** 382;
   7 537; **11** 278; **19** 175; **22** 331
Signalite, Inc., **10** 319
Signature Bank, **54** 36
Signature Brands USA Inc., **28** 135; **30**
   139
Signature Corporation, **22** 412–13
Signature Flight Support Services
   Corporation, **47** 450
Signature Group, **V** 145
Signature Health Care Corp., **25** 504
Signet Banking Corporation, **11 446–48**
Signet Communications Corp., **16** 195
Signetics Co., **III** 684; **11** 56; **18** 383; **44**
   127
Signode Industries, **III** 519; **22** 282
Sika Finanz AG, **28** 195
SIKEL NV, **IV** 128
Sikes Corporation, **III** 612
Sikorsky Aircraft Corporation, **I** 47, 84,
   115, 530; **III** 458, 602; **9** 416; **10** 162;
   18 125; **24 440–43**; **41** 368; **46** 65
SIL&P. *See* Southern Illinois Light &
   Power Company.
SILA. *See* Swedish Intercontinental
   Airlines.
Silband Sports Corp., **33** 102
Silenka B.V., **III** 733; **22** 436
Silex. *See* Hamilton Beach/Proctor-Silex
   Inc.
Silgan Holdings Inc., **26** 59
Silhouette Brands, Inc., **55 348–50**
Silicon Beach Software, **10** 35
Silicon Compiler Systems, **11** 285

Silicon Engineering, **18** 20; **43** 17
Silicon Graphics Inc., **9 471–73**; **10** 119,
   257; **12** 323; **15** 149, 320; **16** 137, 140;
   20 8; **25** 96; **28** 320; **38** 69; **43** 151; **50**
   322. *See also* SGI.
Silicon Light Machines Corporation, **48**
   128
Silicon Magnetic Systems, **48** 128
Silicon Microstructures, Inc., **14** 183
Silicon Systems Inc., **II** 110
Silk-Epil S.A., **51** 58
Silkies, **55** 196
Silknet Software Inc., **51** 181
Silo Electronics, **16** 73, 75
Silo Holdings, **9** 65; **23** 52
Silo Inc., **V** 50; **10** 306, 468; **19** 123; **49**
   112
Silver & Co., **I** 428
Silver Burdett Co., **IV** 672, 675; **7** 528; **19**
   405
Silver City Airways. *See* British World
   Airlines Ltd.
Silver City Casino, **6** 204
Silver Dollar Mining Company, **20** 149
Silver Dolphin, **34** 3, 5
Silver Furniture Co., Inc., **15** 102, 104
Silver King Communications, **25** 213
Silver King Mines, **IV** 76
Silver Screen Partners, **II** 174
Silver's India Rubber Works & Telegraph
   Cable Co., **I** 428
Silverado Banking, **9** 199
Silverado Partners Acquisition Corp., **22** 80
Silverline, Inc., **16** 33
Silvermans Menswear, Inc., **24** 26
SilverPlatter Information Inc., **23**
   440–43
Silvershoe Partners, **17** 245
Silverstar Ltd. S.p.A., **10** 113; **50** 42
Silverstein Properties, Inc., **47 358–60**;
   48 320
Silvertown Rubber Co., **I** 428
Silvey Corp., **III** 350
Simca, **I** 154, 162; **11** 103; **50** 195
Simco S.A., **37 357–59**
Sime Darby Berhad, **14 448–50**; **36**
   433–36 (upd.)
Simeira Comercio e Industria Ltda., **22** 320
SIMEL S.A., **14** 27
Simer Pump Company, **19** 360
SIMEST, **24** 311
Simi Winery, Inc., **34** 89
Simicon Co., **26** 153
Simkins Industries, Inc., **8** 174–75
Simmons Company, **34** 407; **47 361–64**
Simms, **III** 556
Simon & Schuster Inc., **II** 155; **IV**
   671–72; **13** 559; **19 403–05 (upd.)**; **23**
   503; **28** 158
Simon Adhesive Products, **IV** 253; **17** 30
Simon de Wit, **II** 641
Simon DeBartolo Group Inc., **26** 146; **27**
   401
Simon Engineering, **11** 510
Simon Marketing, Inc., **19** 112, 114
Simon Property Group, Inc., **27**
   399–402; **49** 414
Simon Transportation Services Inc., **27**
   403–06
Simonius'sche Cellulosefabriken AG, **IV**
   324
Simonize, **I** 371
Simons Inc., **26** 412
AB Simpele, **IV** 347

Simple Shoes, Inc., **22** 173
Simplex Industries, Inc., **16** 296
Simplex Technologies Inc., 21 460–63
Simplex Wire and Cable Co., **III** 643–45
Simplicity Pattern Company, **I** 447; **8** 349; **23** 98; **29** 134
Simpson Investment Company, 17 438–41
Simpson Marketing, **12** 553
Simpson Thacher & Bartlett, 27 327; **39 365–68**
Simpson Timber Company. *See* PW Eagle Inc.
Simpsons, **V** 80; **25** 221
Sims Telephone Company, **14** 258
Simsmetal USA Corporation, **19** 380
SimuFlite, **II** 10
Simula, Inc., 41 368–70
Sinai Kosher Foods, **14** 537
Sincat, **IV** 453
Sinclair Broadcast Group, Inc., 25 417–19; **47** 120
Sinclair Coal Co., **IV** 170; **10** 447–48
Sinclair Crude Oil Purchasing Co., **IV** 369
Sinclair Oil Corp., **I** 355, 569; **IV** 376, 394, 456–57, 512, 575
Sinclair Paint Company, **12** 219
Sinclair Petrochemicals Inc., **IV** 456
Sinclair Pipe Line Co., **IV** 368–69
Sinclair Research Ltd., **III** 113
Sindo Ricoh Co., **III** 160
Sinfor Holding, **48** 402
Sing Tao Holdings Ltd., **29** 470–71
Singapore Airlines Ltd., 6 100, **117–18**, 123; **12** 192; **20** 313; **24** 399; **26** 115; **27** 26, **407–09** (upd.), 464, 466; **29** 301; **38** 26
Singapore Alpine Electronics Asia Pte. Ltd., **13** 31
Singapore Candle Company, **12** 393
Singapore Cement, **III** 718
Singapore Petroleum Co., **IV** 452
Singapore Shinei Sangyo Pte Ltd., **48** 369
Singapore Straits Steamship Company, **6** 117
Singapore Telecom, **18** 348
Singapour, **II** 556
Singareni Collieries Ltd., **IV** 48–49
Singer & Friedlander Group plc, I 592; **41 371–73**
Singer Company, **I** 540; **II** 9–11; **6** 27, 241; **9** 232; **11** 150; **13** 521–22; **19** 211; **22** 4; **26** 3; **29** 190. *See also* Bicoastal Corp.
The Singer Company N.V., 30 417–20 (upd.)
Singer Controls, **I** 155
Singer Hardware & Supply Co., **9** 542
Singer Sewing Machine Co., **12** 46
Singer Supermarkets, **25** 235
Single Service Containers Inc., **IV** 286
Singleton Seafood, **II** 494
Singular Software, **9** 80
Sinister Games, **41** 409
Sinkers Inc., **21** 68
Sinochem. *See* China National Chemicals Import and Export Corp.
Sinopec. *See* China National Petroleum Corporation.
Sintel, S.A., **19** 256
Sioux City Gas and Electric Company, **6** 523–24
SIP. *See* Società Italiana per L'Esercizio delle Telecommunicazioni p.A.

Siporex, S.A., **31** 253
Sir Speedy, Inc., 16 448–50; **33** 231
SIRCOMA, **10** 375
SIREM, **23** 95
The Sirena Apparel Group Inc., **25** 245
Sirloin Stockade, **10** 331
Sirrine. *See* CRSS Inc.
Sirrine Environmental Consultants, **9** 110
Sirte Oil Co., **IV** 454
Sisters Chicken & Biscuits, **8** 564
Sisters of Bon Secours USA. *See* Bon Secours Health System, Inc.
SIT-Siemens. *See* Italtel.
SITA Telecommunications Holdings. *See* Equant N.V.
Sitca Corporation, **16** 297
Sithe Energies, Inc., **24** 327
Sitintel, **49** 383
Sitmar Cruises, **22** 445
Sitzmann & Heinlein GmbH, **IV** 198–99
Six Companies, Inc., **IV** 121; **7** 355
Six Continents PLC, **54** 315
Six Flags, Inc., 54 333–40 (upd.)
Six Flags Theme Parks, Inc., III 431; **IV** 676; **17 442–44**
600 Fanuc Robotics, **III** 482–83
Six Industries, Inc., **26** 433
61 Going to the Game!, **14** 293
Sixt AG, 39 369–72
Sizeler Property Investors Inc., **49** 27
Sizes Unlimited, **V** 115
Sizzler International Inc., **15** 361–62. *See also* Worldwide Restaurant Concepts, Inc.
SJB Equities, Inc., **30** 53
The SK Equity Fund, L.P., **23** 177
Skånes Enskilda Bank, **II** 351
Skånska Ättiksfabriken A.B. *See* Perstorp AB.
Skadden, Arps, Slate, Meagher & Flom, 10 126–27; **18 486–88**; **27** 325, 327
Skaggs-Albertson's Properties, **II** 604
Skaggs Companies, **22** 37
Skaggs Drug Centers, Inc., **II** 602–04; **7** 20; **27** 291; **30** 25–27
Skagit Nuclear Power Plant, **6** 566
Skandia Insurance Company, Ltd., 25 85; **50 431–34**
Skandinaviska Enskilda Banken, II 351–53, 365–66; **IV** 203
Skanska AB, IV 204; **25** 463; **32** 396; **38 435–38**
Skanza Mammoet Transport Sdn Bhd, **26** 280
Skechers U.S.A. Inc., 31 413–15
Skelly Oil Co., **IV** 575
Sketchley plc, **19** 124
SKF. *See* Aktiebolaget SKF.
SKF Industries Inc. *See* AB Volvo.
Ski-Doo. *See* Bombardier Inc.
Skidmore, Owings & Merrill, 13 475–76
Skil-Craft Playthings, Inc., **13** 560
Skillern, **16** 560
Skillware, **9** 326
Skinner Macaroni Co., **II** 511
Skis Rossignol S.A., 15 460–62; **43 373–76 (upd.)**
Skoda Auto a.s., 39 373–75
SKODA Group, **37** 399–400
Skönvik, **IV** 338
SKS Group, **20** 363
SKW Nature's Products, Inc., **25** 332
SKW-Trostberg AG, **IV** 232
Sky Channel, **IV** 652

Sky Chefs, Inc., **16** 397
Sky Climber Inc., **11** 436
Sky Courier, **6** 345
Sky Merchant, Inc., **V** 78
Sky Television, **IV** 652–53; **7** 391–92
Skyband, Inc., **IV** 652; **7** 391; **12** 359
SkyBox International Inc., **15** 72–73
Skylight, **25** 508
Skyline Corporation, 30 421–23
Skyline Homes, **17** 82
SkyMall, Inc., 26 439–41; **28** 241
Skypak, **27** 474
Skyservice Airlines Inc., **42** 327
SkyTel Corp., **18** 349; **23** 212
Skywalker Sound, **12** 322; **50** 320
Skyway Airlines, **6** 78; **11** 299; **32** 335; **35** 293–94
SkyWest, Inc., 25 420–24
SL Green Realty Corporation, 44 383–85
SL Holdings. *See* Finlay Enterprises, Inc.
Slade Gorton & Company, **13** 243
Slater Co. Foods, **II** 607
Slater Electric, **21** 349
Slater Systems, Inc., **13** 48
Slautterback Corporation, **48** 299
Slavneft, **49** 306
Sleeman Breweries of Canada, **50** 115
Sleepy's Inc., 32 426–28
SLI, Inc., 48 358–61
Slick Airways, **6** 388; **25** 146
Slim-Fast Nutritional Foods International, Inc., 12 531; **18 489–91**; **27** 196
Slim Jim, Inc. *See* GoodMark Foods, Inc.
Slingerland Drum Company, **16** 239
Slip-X Safety Treads, **9** 72
SLJFB Vedrenne, **22** 344
SLM Holding Corp., 25 425–28 (upd.)
SLM International Inc. *See* The Hockey Company.
SLN-Peñarroya, **IV** 108
Sloan's Supermarkets Inc. *See* Gristede's Sloan's, Inc.
Sloman Neptun Schiffahrts, **26** 279
Slope Indicator Company, **26** 42
Sloss Industries Corporation, **22** 544
Slots-A-Fun, **6** 204
Slough Estates PLC, IV 722–25; **50 435–40 (upd.)**
AB Small Business Investment Co., Inc., **13** 111–12
Small Tube Products, Inc., **23** 517
SMALLCO, **III** 340
Smalley Transportation Company, **6** 421–23
SMAN. *See* Societe Mecanique Automobile du Nord.
Smart & Final, Inc., 12 153–54; **16 451–53**
Smart Communications, **18** 180, 182
Smart Products, **44** 261
Smart Shirts Ltd., **8** 288–89
Smart Talk Network, Inc., **16** 319
SmartCash, **18** 543
SmartForce PLC, 43 377–80
SmarTTarget Marketing, **36** 342
SMBC. *See* Sumitomo Mitsui Banking Corporation.
Smead Manufacturing Co., 17 445–48
Smed International, **39** 207
Smedley's, **II** 513
Smethwick Drop Forgings, **III** 494
SMH. *See* The Swatch Group SA.

SMI Industries, **25** 15
Smiles Holdings Ltd., **38** 501
Smirnoff, **14** 212; **18** 41
Smit International, **26** 241
Smith and Bell Insurance, **41** 178, 180
Smith & Butterfield Co., Inc., **28** 74
Smith & Hawken, **10** 215, 217
Smith & Nephew plc, **17** 449–52; **41**
　374–78 (upd.)
Smith & Wesson Corporation, **30**
　424–27
Smith & Weston, **19** 430
Smith & Wollensky Operating Corp., **32**
　362
Smith Barney Inc., **I** 614; **III** 569; **6** 410;
　10 63; **13** 328; **15** 463–65; **19** 385; **20**
　360; **22** 406
Smith Bros., **I** 711
Smith Corona Corp., **III** 502; **7** 209; **13**
　477–80; **14** 76; **23** 210
Smith-Higgins, **III** 9–10
Smith International, Inc., **III** 429; **15**
　466–68
Smith Mackenzie & Co., **III** 522
Smith McDonell Stone and Co., **14** 97
Smith Meter Co., **11** 4
Smith New Court PLC, **13** 342; **40** 313
Smith Packaging Ltd., **14** 429
Smith Parts Co., **11** 3
Smith Sport Optics Inc., **54** 319–20
Smith Transfer Corp., **II** 607–08; **13** 49
Smith Wall Associates, **32** 145
Smith's Food & Drug Centers, Inc., **8**
　472–74; **17** 558, 561; **24** 36; **26** 432
Smith's Stampings, **III** 494
Smithfield Foods, Inc., **7** 477–78,
　524–25; **22** 509, 511; **43** 25, 381–84
　(upd.); **46** 83
SmithKline Beckman Corporation, **I** 389,
　636, 640, 644, 646, 657, 692–94, 696;
　II 331; **III** 65–66; **14** 46, 53; **26** 391; **30**
　29–31. See also GlaxoSmithKline plc.
SmithKline Beecham plc, **III** 65–67; **8**
　210; **9** 347; **10** 47, 471; **11** 9, 90, 337;
　13 77; **14** 58; **16** 438; **17** 287; **24** 88; **25**
　82; **32** 212–13, 429–34 (upd.); **36** 91;
　38 362. See also GlaxoSmithKline plc.
Smiths Bank, **II** 333
Smiths Food Group, Ltd., **II** 502; **10** 323
Smiths Industries PLC, **III** 555; **25**
　429–31
Smithsonian Institution, **27** 410–13
Smithway Motor Xpress Corporation, **39**
　376–79
Smitty's Super Valu Inc., **II** 663–64; **12**
　391; **17** 560–61
Smittybilt, Incorporated, **40** 299–300
Smoothie Island, **49** 60
SMP Clothing, Inc., **22** 462
SMS, **IV** 226; **7** 401
Smucker. See The J.M. Smucker Company.
Smurfit Companies. See Jefferson Smurfit
　Group plc.
Smurfit-Stone Container Corporation,
　26 442–46 (upd.)
SN Repal. See Société Nationale de
　Recherche de Pétrole en Algérie.
Snack Ventures Europe, **10** 324; **36** 234,
　237
Snake River Sugar Company, **19** 468
Snam Montaggi, **IV** 420
Snam Progetti, **IV** 420, 422
Snap-On, Incorporated, **27** 414–16
　(upd.); **32** 397

Snap-on Tools Corporation, **III** 628; **7**
　479–80; **25** 34
Snapper, **I** 447
Snapple Beverage Corporation, **11**
　449–51; **12** 411; **24** 480; **27** 153; **31**
　243; **34** 366; **39** 383, 386
Snapps Drive-Thru, **25** 389
Snappy Car Rental, Inc., **6** 393; **25**
　142–43. See also Republic Industries,
　Inc.
SNE Enterprises, Inc., **12** 397
SNEA. See Société Nationale Elf
　Aquitaine.
Snecma Group, **17** 482; **46** 369–72
Snell & Wilmer L.L.P., **28** 425–28
Snell Acoustics, **22** 99
Snelling Personnel Services, **52** 150
SNET. See Southern New England
　Telecommunications Corporation.
SNMC Management Corporation, **11** 121;
　48 177
Snoqualmie Falls Plant, **6** 565
Snow Brand Milk Products Company,
　Ltd., **II** 574–75; **48** 362–65 (upd.)
Snow King Frozen Foods, **II** 480; **26** 57
Snow White Dairies Inc. See Dairy Mart
　Convenience Stores, Inc.
Snowy Mountains Hydroelectric Authority,
　IV 707; **13** 118
SNPA, **IV** 453
Snyder Communications, **35** 462, 465
Snyder Oil Company, **24** 379–81; **45** 354
Snyder's of Hanover, **35** 213
SnyderGeneral Corp., **8** 321. See also
　AAF-McQuay Incorporated.
Soap Opera Magazine, **10** 287
Sobrom, **I** 341
Sobu Railway Company, **6** 431
Socal. See Standard Oil Company
　(California).
Socamel-Rescaset, **40** 214, 216
Socar, Incorporated, **IV** 505; **45** 370
Socata. See EADS SOCATA.
Sochiku, **9** 30
Sociade Intercontinental de Compressores
　Hermeticos SICOM, S.A., **8** 515
La Sociale di A. Mondadori & C., **IV** 585
La Sociale, **IV** 585
Sociedad Aeronáutica de Medellín, S.A.,
　36 53
Sociedad Alfa-Laval, **III** 419
Sociedad Bilbaina General de Credito, **II**
　194
Sociedad Española de Automobiles del
　Turismo S.A. (SEAT), **I** 207, 459–60; **6**
　47–48; **11** 550
Sociedad Financiera Mexicana, **19** 189
Sociedade Anónima Concessionária de
　Refinacao em Portugal. See SACOR.
Sociedade de Lubrificantes e Combustiveis,
　IV 505
Sociedade Nacional de Petróleos, **IV** 504
Sociedade Portuguesa de Petroquimica, **IV**
　505
Società Anonima Fabbrica Italiana di
　Automobili, **I** 161
Società Anonima Lombarda Fabbrica
　Automobili, **13** 27
Società Azionaria Imprese Perforazioni, **IV**
　419–21
Società Concessioni e Costruzioni
　Autostrade, **I** 466
Società Edison, **II** 86

Societa Esercizio Fabbriche Automobili e
　Corse Ferrari, **13** 219
Società Finanziaria Idrocarburi, **IV** 421
Società Finanziaria Telefonica per
　Azioni, **I** 465–66; **V** 325–27
Società Generale di Credito Mobiliare, **II**
　191
Società Idrolettrica Piemonte, **I** 465–66
Societa Industria Meccanica Stampaggio
　S.p.A., **24** 500
Societa Italiana Gestione Sistemi Multi
　Accesso, **6** 69
Società Italiana per L'Esercizio delle
　Telecommunicazioni p.A., **I** 466–67; **V**
　325–27
Società Italiana per la Infrastrutture e
　l'Assetto del Territoria, **I** 466
Società Italiana Pirelli, **V** 249
Società Italiana Vetro, **IV** 421
Società Meridionale Finanziaria, **49** 31
Società Nazionale Metanodotti, **IV** 419–21
Società Ravennate Metano, **IV** 420
Società Reale Mutua, **III** 207
Società Sportiva Lazio SpA, **44** 386–88
Société Africaine de Déroulage des Ets
　Rougier, **21** 439
Société Air France, **27** 417–20 (upd.).
　See also Groupe Air France.
Société Alsacienne de Magasins SA, **19**
　308
Societe Anonima Italiana Ing. Nicola
　Romeo & Company, **13** 27
Societe Anonimie Alfa Romeo, **13** 28
Societe Anonyme Automobiles Citroen, **7**
　35–36. See also PSA Peugeot Citroen
　S.A.
Société Anonyme Belge des Magasins
　Prisunic-Uniprix, **26** 159
Société Anonyme de la Manufactures des
　Glaces et Produits Chimiques de Saint-
　Gobain, Chauny et Cirey. See
　Compagnie de Saint-Gobain S.A.
Société Anonyme des Ciments
　Luxembourgeois, **IV** 25
Société Anonyme des Fermiers Reúnis, **23**
　219
Société Anonyme des Hauts Fourneaux et
　Aciéries de Differdange-St. Ingbert-
　Rumelange, **IV** 26
Société Anonyme des Hauts Fourneaux et
　Forges de Dudelange, **22** 42
Société Anonyme des Mines du
　Luxembourg et des Forges de
　Sarrebruck, **IV** 24; **22** 42
La Societe Anonyme Francaise Holophane,
　19 211
Societe Anonyme Francaise Timken, **8** 530
Société Anonyme Telecommunications, **III**
　164
Société, Auxiliaire d'Entrepreses SA, **13**
　206
Société Belge de Banque, **II** 294–95
Société BIC, S.A., **III** 29; **8** 60–61; **23**
　55–57
Société Calédonia, **IV** 107
Société Centrale d'Investissement, **29** 48
Société Centrale Union des Assurances de
　Paris, **III** 391, 393
Société Chimiques des Usines du Rhône, **I**
　388
Société Civil des Mousquetaires. See ITM
　Entreprises SA.
Société Civile Valoptec, **21** 222
Societe Commerciale Citroen, **7** 36

Société Congolaise des Grands Magasins Au Bon Marché, **26** 159
Société d'Emboutissage de Bourgogne. *See* Groupe SEB.
Société d'Exploitation AOM Air Liberté SA (AirLib), 53 305–07
Société d'Investissement de Travaux Publics, **31** 128
Société d'Ougrée-Marihaye, **IV** 51
Société de Collecte des Prodicteirs de Preval, **19** 50
Societe de Construction des Batignolles, **II** 93
Société de Crédit Agricole, **II** 264
Société de Développements et d'Innovations des Marchés Agricoles et Alimentaires, **II** 576
Société de Diffusion de Marques, **II** 576
Société de Diffusion Internationale Agro-Alimentaire, **II** 577
Société de Fiducie du Québec, **48** 289
Société de garantie des Crédits à court terme, **II** 233
Société de l'Oléoduc de la Sarre a.r.l., **IV** 197
Société de Prospection Électrique, **III** 616; **17** 416
La Société de Traitement des Minerais de Nickel, Cobalt et Autres, **IV** 107
Société des Caves de Roquefort, **24** 444
Société des Caves et des Producteurs Reunis de Roquefort, **19** 49
Société des Ciments Français, **33** 339
Société des Eaux d'Evian, **II** 474
Société des Etablissements Gaumont. *See* Gaumont SA.
Société des Fibres de Carbone S.A., **51** 379
Société des Forges d'Eich–Metz et Cie, **IV** 24
Société des Forges et Aciéries du Nord-Est, **IV** 226
Société des Forges et Fonderies de Montataire, **IV** 226
Société des Grandes Entreprises de Distribution, Inno-France, **V** 58
Société des Hauts Fourneaux et Forges de Denain-Anzin, **IV** 226
Société des Immeubles de France, **37** 357, 359
Société des Mines du Luxembourg et de Sarrebruck, **IV** 25
Société des Moteurs Gnôme, **46** 369
Société des Pétroles d'Afrique Equatoriale, **IV** 545; **7** 482
Société des Usines Chimiques des Laboratoires Français, **I** 669
Société des Vins de France, **I** 281
Société du Louvre, 27 421–23
Société Economique de Rennes, **19** 98
Société Électrométallurgique Francaise, **IV** 173
Société European de Semi-Remorques, **7** 513
Société Européenne de Brasseries, **II** 474–75
Société Européenne de Production de L'avion E.C.A.T. *See* SEPECAT.
Société Financière Européenne, **II** 202–03, 233
Societe Financiere pour l caise pour l'Exploitation du Pétrole, **IV** 557
Société Française de Casinos, **48** 198
Société Gélis-Poudenx-Sans, **IV** 108
Société General de Banque, **17** 324

Société Générale, II 233, 266, 295, **354–56**; **9** 148; **13** 203, 206; **19** 51; **33** 118–19; **42 347–51 (upd.)**; **47** 411–12
Société Générale de Banque, **II** 279, 295, 319; **14** 169
Société Générale de Belgique S.A., **II** 270, 294–95; **IV** 26; **10** 13; **22** 44; **26** 368; **27** 11; **36** 456
Société Générale des Entreprises. *See* Vinci.
Société Générale du Telephones, **21** 231
Société Générale pour favoriser l'Industrie nationale, **II** 294
Societe-Hydro-Air S.a.r.L., **9** 27
Société Industrielle Belge des Pétroles, **IV** 498–99
Société Internationale Pirelli S.A., **V** 250
Société Irano-Italienne des Pétroles, **IV** 466
Société Laitière Vendômoise, **23** 219
Société Le Nickel, **IV** 107–08, 110
Societe Mecanique Automobile de l'Est/du Nord, **7** 37
Société Métallurgique, **IV** 25–26, 227
Société Minière de Bakwanga, **IV** 67
Société Minière des Terres Rouges, **IV** 25–26
Société Nationale de Programmes de Télévision Française 1. *See* Télévision Française 1.
Société Nationale de Recherche de Pétrole en Algérie, **IV** 545, 559; **7** 482
Société Nationale de Transport et de Commercialisation des Hydrocarbures, **IV** 423
Société Nationale des Chemins de Fer Français, V 512–15
Société Nationale des Pétroles d'Aquitaine, **21** 203–05
Société Nationale Elf Aquitaine, I 303–04, 670, 676–77; **II** 260; **IV** 174, 397–98, 424, 451, 453–54, 472–74, 499, 506, 515–16, 518, 525, 535, **544–47**, 559–60; **V** 628; **7 481–85 (upd.)**; **8** 452; **11** 97; **12** 153
Société Nationale pour la Recherche, la Production, le Transport, la Transformation et la Commercialisation des Hydrocarbures, **IV** 423–24
Société Nord Africaine des Ciments Lafarge, **III** 703
Société Nouvelle d'Achat de Bijouterie, **16** 207
Société Nouvelle des Etablissements Gaumont. *See* Gaumont SA.
Société Parisienne d'Achats en Commun, **19** 307
Societe Parisienne pour l'Industrie Electrique, **II** 93
Société Parisienne Raveau-Cartier, **31** 128
Société pour l'Eportation de Grandes Marques, **I** 281
Société pour l'Étude et la Realisation d'Engins Balistiques. *See* SEREB.
Société pour L'Exploitation de la Cinquième Chaîne, **6** 374
Société pour le Financement de l'Industrie Laitière, **19** 51
Société Samos, **23** 219
Société Savoyarde des Fromagers du Reblochon, **25** 84
Société Succursaliste S.A. d'Approvisonnements Guyenne et Gascogne. *See* Guyenne et Gascogne.

Société Suisse de Microelectronique & d'Horlogerie. *See* The Swatch Group SA.
Société Tefal. *See* Groupe SEB.
Société Tunisienne de l'Air-Tunisair, 49 371–73
Societe Vendeenne des Embalages, **9** 305
Society Corporation, 9 474–77
Society of Lloyd's, **III** 278–79
SOCO Chemical Inc., **8** 69
Socony. *See* Standard Oil Co. (New York).
Socony Mobil Oil Co., Inc., **IV** 465; **7** 353
Socony-Vacuum Oil Company. *See* Mobil Corporation.
Sodak Gaming, Inc., **9** 427; **41** 216
Sodastream Holdings, **II** 477
Sodexho Alliance SA, 23 154; **29 442–44**; **47** 201
Sodiaal S.A., II 577; **19** 50; **36 437–39 (upd.)**
SODIMA. *See* Sodiaal S.A.
Sodiso, **23** 247
Sodyeco, **I** 673
Soekor, **IV** 93
Soffo, **22** 365
Soficom, **27** 136
SOFIL. *See* Société pour le Financement de l'Industrie Laitière.
Sofimex. *See* Sociedad Financiera Mexicana.
Sofiran, **IV** 467
Sofitam, S.A., **21** 493, 495
Sofitels. *See* Accor SA.
Sofrem, **IV** 174
Soft Lenses Inc., **25** 55
Soft Sheen Products, Inc., 31 416–18; **46** 278
Soft*Switch, **25** 301
Softbank Corp., 12 562; **13 481–83**; **16** 168; **27** 516, 518; **36** 523; **38 439–44 (upd.)**
Softimage Inc., **38** 71–72
SoftKat. *See* Baker & Taylor, Inc.
SoftKey Software Products Inc., **24** 276
Softsel Computer Products, **12** 334–35
SoftSolutions Technology Corporation, **10** 558
Software AG, **11** 18
Software Arts, **6** 254; **25** 299
Software Development Pty., Ltd., **15** 107
Software Dimensions, Inc. *See* ASK Group, Inc.
Software, Etc., **13** 545
The Software Group Inc., **23** 489, 491
Software International, **6** 224
Software Plus, Inc., **10** 514
Software Publishing Corp., **14** 262
Softwood Holdings Ltd., **III** 688
Sogara S.A., **23** 246–48
Sogebra S.A., **I** 257
Sogedis, **23** 219
Sogen International Corp., **II** 355
Sogexport, **II** 355
Soginnove, **II** 355–56
Sogo Co., **42** 342
Sohio Chemical Company, **13** 502
Sohken Kako Co., Ltd., **IV** 327
Soil Teq, Inc., **17** 10
Soilserv, Inc. *See* Mycogen Corporation.
Soinlahti Sawmill and Brick Works, **IV** 300
Sola Holdings, **III** 727
Solair Inc., **14** 43; **37** 30–31

La Solana Corp., **IV** 726
Solar, **IV** 614
Solar Electric Corp., **13** 398
Solaray, Inc., **37** 284–85
Solect Technology Group, **47** 12
Solectron Corporation, **12** 161–62,
    450–52; **38** 186, 189; **46** 38; **48 366–70**
    (upd.)
Solel Boneh Construction, **II** 47; **25**
    266–67
Soletanche Co., **I** 586
Solid Beheer B.V., **10** 514
Solid State Dielectrics, **I** 329; **8** 152
Solite Corp., **23** 224–25
Söll, **40** 96, 98
Sollac, **IV** 226–27; **24** 144; **25** 96
Solley's Delicatessen and Bakery, **24** 243
Solmer, **IV** 227
Solo Serve Corporation, **23** 177; **28**
    429–31
Soloman Brothers, **17** 561
Solomon Smith Barney Inc., **22** 404
Solomon Valley Milling Company, **6** 592;
    50 37
Solon Automated Services, **II** 607
Solsound Industries, **16** 393
Soltam, **25** 266
Solutia Inc., **29** 330; **52 312–15**
Solvay & Cie S.A., **I** 303, **394–96**,
    414–15; **III** 677; **IV** 300; **16** 121; **21**
    254, **464–67 (upd.)**
Solvay Animal Health Inc., **12** 5
Solvent Resource Recovery, Inc., **9** 109
Solvents Recovery Service of New Jersey,
    Inc., **8** 464
SOMABRI, **12** 152
SOMACA, **12** 152
Somali Bank, **31** 220
Someal, **27** 513, 515
Somerfield plc, **47 365–69 (upd.)**
Somerville Electric Light Company, **12** 45
Somerville Packaging Group, **28** 420
Sommer-Allibert S.A., **19 406–09**; **22** 49;
    25 462, 464
Sommers Drug Stores, **9** 186
SONAP, **IV** 504–06
Sonat, Inc., **6 577–78**; **22** 68
Sonatrach. *See* Entreprise Nationale
    Sonatrach.
Sonecor Systems, **6** 340
Sonera Corporation, **50 441–44**
Sonergy, Inc., **49** 280
Sonesson, **I** 211
Sonesta International Hotels
    Corporation, **44 389–91**
Sonet Media AB, **23** 390
Sonic Corp., **37 14 451–53**; **16** 387;
    360–63 (upd.)
Sonic Duo, **48** 419
Sonic Restaurants, **31** 279
Sonneborn Chemical and Refinery Co., **I**
    405
Sonnen Basserman, **II** 475
SonnenBraune, **22** 460
Sonoco Products Company, **8 475–77**; **12**
    150–51; **16** 340
The Sonoma Group, **25** 246
Sonoma Mortgage Corp., **II** 382
Sonometrics Inc., **I** 667
Sonor GmbH, **53** 216
Sony Corporation, **I** 30, 534; **II** 56, 58,
    91–92, **101–03**, 117–19, 124, 134, 137,
    440; **III** 141, 143, 340, 658; **6** 30; **7**
    118; **9** 385; **10** 86, 119, 403; **11** 46,

490–91, 557; **12** 75, 161, 448, **453–56**
    (upd.); **13** 399, 403, 482, 573; **14** 534;
    16 94; **17** 533; **18** 18; **19** 67; **20** 439; **21**
    129; **22** 194; **24** 4; **25** 22; **26** 188, 433,
    489, 511; **28** 241; **30** 18; **31** 239; **40**
    404–10 (upd.); **43** 15; **47** 318–20, 410
Sonzogno, **IV** 585
Soo Line Corporation, **V** 429–30; **24** 533;
    45 80
Soo Line Mills, **II** 631
Sooner Trailer Manufacturing Co., **29** 367
Soparind, **25** 83–85
Sope Creek, **30** 457
SOPEAL, **III** 738
Sophia Jocoba GmbH, **IV** 193
Sophus Berendsen A/S, **49 374–77**
SOPI, **IV** 401
SOPORCEL, **34** 38–39
Sopwith Aviation Co., **III** 507–08
Soravie, **II** 265
Sorbents Products Co. Inc., **31** 20
Sorbus, **6** 242
Sorcim, **6** 224
Soreal, **8** 344
Sorenson Research Company, **36** 496
Sorg Paper Company. *See* Mosinee Paper
    Corporation.
Soriana. *See* Organización Soriana, S.A. de
    C.V.
Soros Fund Management LLC, **27** 198;
    28 432–34; **43** 218
Sorrento, Inc., **19** 51; **24 444–46**; **26** 505
SOS Co., **II** 531
SOS Staffing Services, **25 432–35**
Sosa, Bromley, Aguilar & Associates, **6** 22
Soterra, Inc., **15** 188
Sotheby's Holdings, Inc., **11 452–54**; **15**
    98–100; **29 445–48 (upd.)**; **32** 164; **39**
    81–84; **49** 325
Soufflet SA. *See* Groupe Soufflet SA.
Sound Advice, Inc., **41 379–82**
Sound of Music Inc. *See* Best Buy Co.,
    Inc.
Sound Trek, **16** 74
Sound Video Unlimited, **16** 46; **43** 60
Sound Warehouse, **9** 75
Souplantation Incorporated. *See* Garden
    Fresh Restaurant Corporation.
Source One Mortgage Services Corp., **12**
    79
Source Perrier, **7** 383; **24** 444
Souriau, **19** 166
South African Airways Ltd., **6** 84, 433,
    435; **27** 132
The South African Breweries Limited, **I**
    287–89, 422; **24 447–51 (upd.)**; **26** 462
South African Coal, Oil and Gas Corp., **IV**
    533
South African Railways, **6** 434–35
South African Torbanite Mining and
    Refining Co., **IV** 534
South African Transport Services, **6** 433,
    435
South American Cable Co., **I** 428
South Asia Tyres, **20** 263
South Australian Brewing Company, **54**
    228, 341
South Bend Toy Manufacturing Company,
    25 380
South Carolina Electric & Gas Company, **6**
    574–76
South Carolina Industries, **IV** 333
South Carolina National Corporation, **16**
    523, 526

South Carolina Power Company, **38**
    446–47
South Central Bell Telephone Co. **V**
    276–78
South Central Railroad Co., **14** 325
South China Morning Post (Holdings) Ltd.,
    II 298; **IV** 652; **7** 392
South Coast Gas Compression Company,
    Inc., **11** 523
South Coast Terminals, Inc., **16** 475
South Dakota Public Service Company, **6**
    524
South Fulton Light & Power Company, **6**
    514
South Improvement Co., **IV** 427
South Jersey Industries, Inc., **42 352–55**
South Manchuria Railroad Co. Ltd., **IV**
    434
South of Scotland Electricity Board, **19**
    389–90
South Overseas Fashion Ltd., **53** 344
South Penn Oil Co., **IV** 488–89; **50** 352
South Puerto Rico Sugar Co., **I** 452
South Puerto Rico Telephone Co., **I** 462
South Sea Textile, **III** 705
South Texas Stevedore Co., **IV** 81
South Wales Electric Company, **34** 219
South West Water Plc. *See* Pennon Group
    Plc.
South Western Electricity plc, **38** 448; **41**
    316
South-Western Publishing Co., **8** 526–28
Southam Inc., **7 486–89**; **15** 265; **24** 223;
    36 374
Southco, **II** 602–03; **7** 20–21; **30** 26
Southcorp Holdings Ltd., **17** 373; **22** 350
Southcorp Limited, **54 341–44**
Southdown, Inc., **14 454–56**
Southeast Bank of Florida, **11** 112
Southeast Banking Corp., **II** 252; **14** 103
Southeast Public Service Company, **8** 536
Southeastern Freight Lines, Inc., **53** 249
Southeastern Personnel. *See* Norrell
    Corporation.
Southeastern Power and Light Company, **6**
    447; **23** 28
Southeastern Telephone Company, **6** 312
Southern and Phillips Gas Ltd., **13** 485
Southern Australia Airlines, **24** 396
Southern Bank, **10** 426
Southern Bearings Co., **13** 78
Southern Bell, **10** 202
Southern Biscuit Co., **II** 631
Southern Blvd. Supermarkets, Inc., **22** 549
Southern Box Corp., **13** 441
Southern California Edison Co., **II** 402; **V**
    711, 713–15, 717; **11** 272; **12** 106; **35**
    479
Southern California Financial Corporation,
    27 46
Southern California Fruit Growers
    Exchange. *See* Sunkist Growers, Inc.
Southern California Gas Co., **I** 569; **25**
    413–14, 416
Southern Casualty Insurance Co., **III** 214
Southern Clay Products, **III** 691
Southern Clays Inc., **IV** 82
Southern Co., **24** 525
Southern Colorado Power Company, **6** 312
Southern Comfort Corp., **I** 227
The Southern Company, **38 445–49**
    (upd.)
Southern Connecticut Newspapers Inc., **IV**
    677

Southern Cooker Limited Partnership, **51** 85

Southern Cotton Co., **IV** 224; **24** 488

Southern Cotton Oil Co., **I** 421; **11** 23

Southern Cross Paints, **38** 98

Southern Discount Company of Atlanta, **9** 229

Southern Electric PLC, 13 484–86

Southern Electric Supply Co., **15** 386

Southern Electronics Corp. *See* SED International Holdings, Inc.

Southern Equipment & Supply Co., **19** 344

Southern Extract Co., **IV** 310; **19** 266

Southern Forest Products, Inc., **6** 577

Southern Gage, **III** 519; **22** 282

Southern Graphic Arts, **13** 405

Southern Guaranty Cos., **III** 404

Southern Idaho Water Power Company, **12** 265

Southern Illinois Light & Power Company, **6** 504

Southern Indiana Gas and Electric Company, 13 487–89

Southern Japan Trust Bank, **V** 114

Southern Kraft Corp., **IV** 286

Southern Lumber Company, **8** 430

Southern Manufacturing Company, **8** 458

Southern Minnesota Beet Sugar Cooperative, **32** 29

Southern National Bankshares of Atlanta, **II** 337; **10** 425

Southern Natural Gas Co., **III** 558; **6** 447–48, 577

Southern Nevada Power Company, **11** 343

Southern Nevada Telephone Company, **6** 313; **11** 343

Southern New England Telecommunications Corporation, 6 338–40

Southern Nitrogen Co., **IV** 123

Southern Oregon Broadcasting Co., **7** 15

Southern Pacific Communications Corporation, **9** 478–79

Southern Pacific Rail Corp., **12** 18–20. *See also* Union Pacific Corporation.

Southern Pacific Railroad, **I** 13; **II** 329, 381, 448; **IV** 625; **19** 202

Southern Pacific Transportation Company, V 516–18; **12** 278; **26** 235; **37** 312

Southern Peru Copper Corp.,

Southern Peru Copper Corporation, IV 3; **40** 220, 222, **411–13**

Southern Phenix Textiles Inc., **15** 247–48

Southern Pine Lumber Co., **IV** 341

Southern Power Company. *See* Duke Energy Corporation.

Southern Railway Company, **V** 484–85; **29** 359

Southern Recycling Inc., **51** 170

Southern Science Applications, Inc., **22** 88

Southern States Cooperative Incorporated, 36 440–42

Southern States Trust Co., **II** 336

Southern Sun Hotel Corporation. *See* South African Breweries Ltd.; Sun International Hotels Limited.

Southern Surety Co., **III** 332

Southern Telephone Company, **14** 257

Southern Television Corp., **II** 158; **IV** 650; **7** 389

Southern Union Company, 12 542; **27** **424–26**

Southern Utah Fuel Co., **IV** 394

Southern Video Partnership, **9** 74

Southern Water plc, **19** 389–91; **49** 363, 365–66

Southgate Medical Laboratory System, **26** 391

Southington Savings Bank, **55** 52

The Southland Corporation, II 449, 620, **660–61; IV** 392, 508; **V** 89; **7** 114, 374, **490–92 (upd.); 9** 178; **13** 333, 449, 525; **23** 406–07; **25** 125; **26** 447; **31** 115, 231; **42** 191; **50** 487. *See also* 7- Eleven, Inc.

Southland Mobilcom Inc., **15** 196

Southland Paper, **13** 118

Southland Royal Company, **27** 86

Southland Royalty Co., **10** 190

Southlife Holding Co., **III** 218

Southmark Corp., **11** 483; **33** 398

Southport, Inc., **44** 203

Southtrust Corporation, 11 455–57

Southview Pulp Co., **IV** 329

Southwest Airlines Co., I 106; **6** 72–74, **119–21; 21** 143; **22** 22; **24 452–55 (upd.); 25** 404; **26** 308, 439–40; **33** 301–02; **35** 383; **44** 197, 248; **52** 167

Southwest Airmotive Co., **II** 16

Southwest Convenience Stores, LLC, **26** 368

Southwest Converting, **19** 414

Southwest Enterprise Associates, **13** 191

Southwest Forest Industries, **IV** 287, 289, 334

Southwest Gas Corporation, 19 410–12

Southwest Hide Co., **16** 546

Southwest Potash Corp., **IV** 18; **6** 148–49

Southwest Property Trust Inc., **52** 370

Southwest Sports Group, **51** 371, 374

Southwest Water Company, 47 370–73

Southwestern Bell Corporation, V 328–30; **6** 324; **10** 431, 500; **14** 489; **17** 110; **18** 22. *See also* SBC Communications Inc.

Southwestern Bell Publications, **26** 520

Southwestern Electric Power Co., 21 468–70

Southwestern Gas Pipeline, **7** 344

Southwestern Illinois Coal Company, **7** 33

Southwestern Life Insurance, **I** 527; **III** 136

Southwestern Pipe, **III** 498

Southwestern Public Service Company, 6 579–81

Southwestern Refining Company, Inc., **IV** 446; **22** 303

Southwestern Textile Company, **12** 393

Southwire Company, Inc., 8 478–80; **12** 353; **23 444–47 (upd.)**

Souvall Brothers, **8** 473

Sovereign Corp., **III** 221; **14** 109; **37** 84

Sovran Financial, **10** 425–26

SovTransavto, **6** 410

Soyland Power Cooperative, **6** 506

SP Pharmaceuticals, LLC, **50** 123

SP Reifenwerke, **V** 253

SP Tyres, **V** 253

Space Control GmbH, **28** 243–44

Space Craft Inc., **9** 463

Space Data Corporation, **22** 401

Space Systems Corporation. *See* Orbital Sciences Corporation.

Space Systems/Loral, **9** 325

Spacehab, Inc., 37 364–66

Spacemakers Inc., **IV** 287

Spaghetti Warehouse, Inc., 25 436–38

Spagnesi, **18** 258

Spago. *See* The Wolfgang Puck Food Company, Inc.

Spalding & Evenflo, **24** 530

Spalding, Inc., **17** 243; **23** 449; **54** 73

Spangler Candy Company, 44 392–95

Spanish Broadcasting System, Inc., 41 383–86

Spanish International Communications Corp. *See* Univision Communications Inc.

Spanish River Pulp and Paper Mills, **IV** 246; **25** 10

SPAO, **39** 184

Spar Aerospace Limited, 32 435–37

SPAR Handels AG, 35 398–401; 36 296

Sparbanken Bank, **18** 543

SPARC International, **7** 499

Spare Change, **10** 282

Sparklets Ltd., **I** 315; **25** 80

Sparks Computerized Car Care Centers, **25** 445

Sparks Family Hospital, **6** 191

Sparks-Withington Company. *See* Sparton Corporation.

Sparrow Records, **22** 194

Sparta, Inc., **18** 369

Sparta Surgical Corporation, **33** 456

Spartan Communications, **38** 308–09

Spartan Industries, Inc., **45** 15

Spartan Insurance Co., **26** 486

Spartan Motors Inc., 14 457–59

Spartan Stores Inc., I 127; **II** 679–80; **8** **481–82; 10** 302; **12** 489; **14** 412

Spartech Corporation, 9 92; **19 413–15; 33** 78–79

Sparton Corporation, 18 492–95

SPCM, Inc., **14** 477

Spear, Leeds & Kellogg, L.P., **51** 148

Spec's Music, Inc., 19 416–18

Spécia, **I** 388

Special Agent Investigators, Inc., **14** 541

Special Foods, **14** 557

Special Light Alloy Co., **IV** 153

Special Zone Limited, **26** 491

Specialized Bicycle Components Inc., 19 384; **50 445–48**

Specialty Brands Inc., **25** 518

Specialty Coatings Inc., 8 483–84

Specialty Equipment Companies, Inc., 25 439–42

Specialty Foods Corporation, **29** 29, 31

Specialty Papers Co., **IV** 290

Specialty Products Co., **8** 386

Specialty Retailers, Inc., **24** 456

Spectra-Physics AB, **9** 380–81

Spectra Star, Inc., **18** 521

Spectradyne, **28** 241

Spectral Dynamics Corporation. *See* Scientific- Atlanta, Inc.

Spectron MicroSystems, **18** 143

Spectrum Club, **25** 448–50

Spectrum Communications Holdings International Limited, **24** 95

Spectrum Concepts, **10** 394–95

Spectrum Data Systems, Inc., **24** 96

Spectrum Dyed Yarns of New York, **8** 559

Spectrum Health Care Services, **13** 48

Spectrum Medical Technologies, Inc., **22** 409

Spectrum Technology Group, Inc., **7** 378; **18** 112

Spectrumedia, **21** 361

Speed-O-Lac Chemical, **8** 553

SpeeDee Marts, **II** 661
SpeeDee Oil Change and Tune-Up, 25 443–47
Speedway Motorsports, Inc., 32 438–41
Speedway SuperAmerica LLC, **49** 330
Speedy Auto Glass, **30** 501
Speedy Europe, **54** 207
Speedy Muffler King, **10** 415; **24** 337, 339
Speidel Newspaper Group, **IV** 612; **7** 191
Speizman Industries, Inc., 44 396–98
Spelling Entertainment, 14 460–62; **35** 402–04 (upd.)
Spencer & Spencer Systems, Inc., **18** 112
Spencer Beef, **II** 536
Spencer Gifts, Inc., **II** 144; **15** 464
Spencer Stuart and Associates, Inc., 14 463–65
Spenco Medical Corp., **III** 41; **16** 303; **43** 257
Sperry & Hutchinson Co., **12** 299; **23** 243–44
Sperry Aerospace Group, **II** 40, 86; **6** 283; **12** 246, 248; **50** 233
Sperry Corporation, **I** 101, 167; **III** 165, 642; **6** 281–82; **8** 92; **11** 139; **12** 39; **13** 511; **18** 386, 542; **22** 379; **36** 481. *See also* Unisys Corporation.
Sperry Milling Co., **II** 501; **10** 322
Sperry New Holland. *See* New Holland N.V.
Sperry Rand Corp., **II** 63, 73; **III** 126, 129, 149, 166, 329, 642; **6** 241, 261, 281–82; **16** 137
Sperry Top-Sider, Inc., **37** 377, 379
Sphere Inc., **8** 526; **13** 92
Sphere SA, **27** 9
Spherion Corporation, 45 272, 274; **52** 316–18
Spicer Manufacturing Co., **I** 152; **III** 568; **20** 359; **23** 170–71
Spider Software, Inc., **46** 38
Spie Batignolles SA, **I** 563; **II** 93–94; **13** 206; **18** 471–73; **24** 79
Spiegel, Inc., III 598; **V** 160; **8** 56–58; **10** 168, **489–91; 11** 498; **9** 190, 219; **13** 179; **15** 339; **27** 427–31 (upd.); **34** 232, 324, 326; **36** 177, 180
SPIEGEL-Verlag Rudolf Augstein GmbH & Co. KG, 44 399–402
Spillers, **II** 500
Spin Physics, **III** 475–76; **7** 163
SpinCircuit Inc., **38** 188
Spinelli Coffee Co., **51** 385
Spinnaker Industries, Inc., **43** 276
Spinnaker Software Corp., **24** 276
SPIRE Corporation, **14** 477
Spire, Inc., **25** 183
Spirella Company of Great Britain Ltd., **V** 356; **44** 105
Spirit Airlines, Inc., 31 419–21
Spirit Cruises, **29** 442–43
Spliethoff, **26** 280
Spoerle Electronic, **10** 113; **50** 42
Spokane Falls Electric Light and Power Company. *See* Edison Electric Illuminating Company.
Spokane Falls Water Power Company, **6** 595
Spokane Gas and Fuel, **IV** 391
Spokane Natural Gas Company, **6** 597
Spokane Street Railway Company, **6** 595
Spokane Traction Company, **6** 596
Spom Japan, **IV** 600
Spon Press, **44** 416

Spoor Behrins Campbell and Young, **II** 289
Spoornet, **6** 435
Sporis, **27** 151
Sporloisirs S.A., **9** 157
Sport Chalet, Inc., 16 454–56
Sport Developpement SCA, **33** 10
Sport Supply Group, Inc., 22 458–59; **23** 448–50; **30** 185
Sporting Dog Specialties, Inc., **14** 386
Sporting News Publishing Co., **IV** 677–78
Sportland, **26** 160
Sportmagazine NV, **48** 347
Sportmart, Inc., 15 469–71. *See also* Gart Sports Company.
Sports & Co. *See* Hibbett Sporting Goods, Inc.
Sports & Recreation, Inc., 15 470; **17** 453–55
The Sports Authority, Inc., 15 470; **16** 457–59; **17** 453; **18** 286; **24** 173; **43** 385–88 (upd.)
The Sports Club Company, 25 448–51
Sports Experts Inc., **II** 652
Sports Holdings Corp., **34** 217
Sports Inc., **14** 8; **33** 10
Sports Plus, **44** 192
Sports-Tech Inc., **21** 300
Sports Traders, Inc., **18** 208
Sportservice Corporation, **7** 133–35
The Sportsman's Guide, Inc., 36 443–46
Sportstown, Inc., **15** 470
Sportsystems Corporation, **7** 133, 135
Sprague Co., **I** 410
Sprague Devices, Inc., **11** 84
Sprague Electric Company, **6** 261
Sprague Electric Railway and Motor Co., **II** 27; **12** 193
Sprague Technologies, **21** 520
Sprague, Warner & Co., **II** 571
Spray-Rite, **I** 366
Sprayon Products, **III** 745
Spraysafe, **29** 98
Sprecher & Schuh, **9** 10
Spreckels Sugar Company, Inc., **32** 274, 277
Spring Co., **21** 96, 246
Spring Forge Mill, **8** 412
Spring Group plc, **54** 191–93
Spring Grove Services, **45** 139–40
Spring Industries, Inc., V 378–79
Spring Valley Brewery. *See* Kirin Brewery Company, Limited.
Springbok Editions, **IV** 621
Springer Verlag GmbH & Co., **IV** 611, 641
Springfield Bank, **9** 474
Springfield Gas Light Company, **38** 81
Springhouse Corp., **IV** 610
Springhouse Financial Corp., **III** 204
Springmaid International, Inc., **19** 421
Springs Industries, Inc., 19 419–22 (upd.); **29** 132; **31** 199
Sprint Canada Inc., **44** 49
Sprint Communications Company, L.P., 9 478–80; **10** 19, 57, 97, 201–03; **11** 183, 185, 500–01; **18** 32, 164–65, 569–70; **22** 19, 162; **24** 120, 122; **25** 102; **26** 17; **27** 365; **36** 167. *See also* Sprint Corporation; US Sprint Communications.
Sprint Corporation, 46 373–76 (upd.)
Sprint PCS, **33** 34, 36–37; **38** 433
Sprocket Systems, **50** 320

Sprout Group, **37** 121
Sprout-Matador A.S., **51** 25
Spruce Falls Power and Paper Co., **III** 40; **IV** 648; **16** 302, 304; **19** 284; **43** 256
SPS Technologies, Inc., 30 428–30
Spun Yarns, Inc., **12** 503
Spur Oil Co., **7** 362
SPX Corporation, 10 492–95; **47** 374–79 (upd.)
SPZ, Inc., **26** 257
SQ Software, Inc., **10** 505
SQL Solutions, Inc., **10** 505
Square D Company, **18** 473
Square Industries, **18** 103, 105
Squibb Beech-Nut. *See* Beech-Nut Nutrition Corp.
Squibb Corporation, **I** 380–81, 631, 651, 659, 675, **695–97; III** 17, 19, 67; **8** 166; **9** 6–7; **13** 379–80; **16** 438–39[see aslo]Bristol-Myers Squibb Company.
Squire Fashions Inc. *See* Norton McNaughton of Squire, Inc.
SR. *See* Southern Railway.
SR Beteiligungen Aktiengesellschaft, **III** 377
SRI International, **10** 139
SRI Strategic Resources Inc., **6** 310
SS Cars, Ltd. *See* Jaguar Cars, Ltd.
SS Lazio. *See* Societá Sportiva Lazio SpA.
SSA. *See* Stevedoring Services of America Inc.
Ssangyong Cement Industrial Co., Ltd., III 747–50; **IV** 536–37, 539
Ssangyong Motor Company, **34** 132
SSC&B-Lintas, **I** 16–17; **14** 315
SSC Benelux & Company, **52** 310–11
SSDS, Inc., **18** 537; **43** 433
SSI Medical Services, Inc., **10** 350
SSL International plc, 49 378–81
SSMC Inc., **II** 10
SSP Company, Inc., **17** 434
St. *See under* Saint
Staal Bankiers, **13** 544
Stackpole Fibers, **37** 427
Stadia Colorado Corporation, **18** 140
Stadt Corporation, **26** 109
Städtische Elecktricitäts-Werke A.G., **I** 410
Staefa Control System Limited, **6** 490
Staff International, **40** 157
StaffAmerica, Inc., **16** 50
Stafford-Lowdon, **31** 435
Stafford Old Bank, **II** 307
Stag Cañon Fuel Co., **IV** 177
Stage Stores, Inc., 24 456–59
Stagecoach Holdings plc, 30 431–33; **55** 103
Stags' Leap Winery, **22** 80
Stahl-Urban Company, **8** 287–88
Stahlwerke Peine-Salzgitter AG, **IV** 201
Stahlwerke Röchling AG, **III** 694–95
Stahlwerke Südwestfalen AG, **IV** 89
Stakis plc, **49** 193
Stal-Astra GmbH, **III** 420
Staley Continental, **II** 582
Stamford Drug Group, **9** 68
Stamford FHI Acquisition Corp., **27** 117
Stamos Associates Inc., **29** 377
Stamps.com Inc., **34** 474
Stanadyne Automotive Corporation, 37 367–70
Stanadyne, Inc., **7** 336; **12** 344
Standard & Poor's Corp., **IV** 29, 482, 636–37; **12** 310; **25** 542
Standard Accident Co., **III** 332

Standard Aero, **III** 509

Standard Aircraft Equipment, **II** 16

Standard Alaska, **7** 559

Standard Bank, **17** 324

Standard Bank of Canada, **II** 244

Standard Box Co., **17** 357

Standard Brands, **I** 248; **II** 542, 544; **7** 365, 367; **18** 538

Standard Car Truck, **18** 5

Standard Chartered plc, **II** 298, 309, 319, **357–59**, 386; **10** 170; **47** 227; **48** **371–74 (upd.)**

Standard Chemical Products, **III** 33

Standard Commercial Corporation, **12** 110; **13 490–92**; **27** 126

Standard Drug Co., **V** 171

Standard Electric Time Company, **13** 233

Standard Electrica, **II** 13

Standard Elektrik Lorenz A.G., **II** 13, 70; **17** 353

Standard Equities Corp., **III** 98

Standard Federal Bank, 9 481–83

Standard Fire Insurance Co., **III** 181–82

Standard Fruit and Steamship Co. of New Orleans, **II** 491; **31** 168

Standard Gauge Manufacturing Company, **13** 233

Standard General Insurance, **III** 208

Standard Gypsum Corp., **19** 77

Standard Industrial Group Ltd., **IV** 658

Standard Insert Co., **28** 350

Standard Insulation Co., **I** 321

Standard Insurance Co. of New York, **III** 385

Standard Investing Corp., **III** 98

Standard Kollsman Industries Inc., **13** 461

Standard Life & Accident Insurance Company, **27** 47–48

Standard Life Assurance Company, **III** **358–61**; **IV** 696–98

Standard Life Insurance Company, **11** 481

Standard Magnesium & Chemical Co., **IV** 123

Standard Metals Corp., **IV** 76

Standard Microsystems Corporation, **11** **462–64**

Standard Milling Co., **II** 497

Standard Motor Co., **III** 651

Standard Motor Products, Inc., **40** **414–17**

Standard of America Life Insurance Co., **III** 324

Standard of Georgia Insurance Agency, Inc., **10** 92

Standard Oil Co., **III** 470, 513; **IV** 46, 372, 399, 426–29, 434, 463, 478, 488–89, 530–31, 540, 542, 551, 574, 577–78, 657; **V** 590, 601; **6** 455; **7** 169–72, 263, 351, 414, 551; **8** 415; **10** 110, 289; **14** 21, 491–92; **25** 230; **27** 129; **50** 350. *See also* Exxon Corporation.

Standard Oil Co. (California), **II** 448; **IV** 18–19, 385–87, 403, 429, 464, 536–37, 545, 552, 560, 578; **6** 353; **7** 172, 352, 483; **13** 448

Standard Oil Co. (Illinois), **IV** 368

Standard Oil Co. (Indiana), **II** 262; **IV** 366, 368–71, 466–67; **7** 443; **10** 86; **14** 222

Standard Oil Co. (Minnesota), **IV** 368

Standard Oil Co. (New York), **IV** 428–29, 431, 460, 463–65, 485, 504, 537, 549, 558; **7** 171, 351–52

Standard Oil Co. of Iowa, **IV** 385

Standard Oil Co. of Kentucky, **IV** 387

Standard Oil Co. of New Jersey, **I** 334, 337, 370; **II** 16, 496; **IV** 378–79, 385–86, 400, 415–16, 419, 426–29, 431–33, 438, 460, 463–64, 488, 522, 531, 537–38, 544, 558, 565, 571; **V** 658–59; **7** 170–72, 253, 351; **13** 124; **17** 412–13; **24** 521

Standard Oil Co. of Ohio, **IV** 373, 379, 427, 452, 463, 522, 571; **7** 57, 171, 263; **12** 309; **21** 82; **24** 521

Standard Oil Development Co., **IV** 554

Standard Oil Trust, **IV** 31, 368, 375, 385–86, 427, 463

Standard Pacific Corporation, **52 319–22**

Standard Plastics, **25** 312

Standard Printing Company, **19** 333

Standard Process & Engraving, Inc., **26** 105

Standard Products Company, **19** 454

Standard Rate & Data Service, **IV** 639; **7** 286

Standard Register Co., **15 472–74**

Standard Sanitary, **III** 663–64

Standard Screw Co., **12** 344

Standard Shares, **9** 413–14

Standard Steel Propeller, **I** 47, 84; **9** 416; **10** 162

Standard Telephone and Radio, **II** 13

Standard Telephones and Cables, Ltd., **III** 162–63; **6** 242

Standard Tin Plate Co., **15** 127

Standard-Vacuum Oil Co., **IV** 431–32, 440, 460, 464, 491–92, 554–55; **7** 352

Standex International Corporation, **16** 470–71; **17 456–59**; **44 403–06 (upd.)**

Stanhome Inc., **9** 330; **11** 94–96; **15** **475–78**

Stanhome Worldwide Direct Selling, **35** 262, 264

STANIC, **IV** 419, 421

Stanko Fanuc Service, **III** 483

Stanley Electric Manufacturing Co., **II** 28; **12** 194

Stanley Furniture Company, Inc., **34** **412–14**

Stanley Home Products, Incorporated. *See* Stanhome Inc.

Stanley Mining Services, Ltd., **19** 247

The Stanley Works, **III** 626–29; **7** 480; **9** 543; **13** 41; **20 476–80 (upd.)**

StanMont, Inc., **24** 425

Stanolind Oil & Gas Co., **III** 498; **IV** 365, 369–70

Stant Corporation, **15** 503, 505

Staples, Inc., **8** 404–05; **10 496–98**; **18** 24, 388; **20** 99; **22** 154; **23** 363, 365; **24** 270; **55 351–56 (upd.)**

Star, **10** 287–88

Star Air Service. *See* Alaska Air Group, Inc.

Star Alliance, **26** 113; **33** 51; **38** 36

Star Banc Corporation, **11 465–67**; **13** 222; **31** 206. *See also* Firstar Corporation.

Star Building Systems, Inc., **19** 366

Star Engraving, **12** 471

Star Enterprise, **IV** 536, 539, 553

Star Enterprises, Inc., **6** 457

Star Finishing Co., **9** 465

Star Laboratories Inc., **24** 251

Star Markets Company, Inc., **23** 169

Star Medical Technologies, Inc., **22** 409; **31** 124

Star Paper Ltd., **IV** 300

Star Paper Tube, Inc., **19** 76–78

Star Sportwear Manufacturing Corp., **29** 294

Star Systems, Inc., **52** 88

Star Video, Inc., **6** 313

Starber International, **12** 181

Starbucks Corporation, **13** 493–94; **18** 37; **22** 370; **25** 178, 501; **28** 63; **34** **415–19 (upd.)**; **36** 156–57; **37** 181; **38** 340; **40** 152–53; **44** 313; **50** 97

Starcraft Corporation, **III** 444; **13** 113; **22** 116; **30 434–36**

Stardent Computer Inc., **III** 553; **26** 256

Starfish Software, **23** 212

Stark Record and Tape Service. *See* Camelot Music, Inc.

Starkey Laboratories, Inc., **52 323–25**

StarKist Foods, **II** 508; **11** 172; **36** 254–55

Starlawerken, **I** 527

Starlen Labs, Ltd., **31** 346

Starlight Networks, Inc., **27** 366

Starline Optical Corp., **22** 123

StarMed Staffing Corporation, **6** 10

Starpointe Savings Bank, **9** 173

Starrett Corporation, **21 471–74**

Star's Discount Department Stores, **16** 36

Startech Semiconductor Inc., **14** 183

Startel Corp., **15** 125

Starter Corp., **12 457–458**

Starwood Capital, **29** 508

Starwood Hotels & Resorts Worldwide, Inc., **33** 217; **54 345–48**

The Stash Tea Company, **50 449–52**

State Bank of Albany, **9** 228

State Farm Insurance Companies, **27** 30; **29** 397; **39** 155

State Farm Mutual Automobile Insurance Company, **III 362–64**; **10** 50; **22** 266; **23** 286; **25** 155; **41** 313; **51** **341–45 (upd.)**

State Finance and Thrift Company, **14** 529

State Financial Services Corporation, **51** **346–48**

State Leed, **13** 367

State Metal Works, **III** 647

State-o-Maine, **18** 357–59

State-Record Co., **IV** 630

State Savings Bank and Trust Co., **11** 180; **42** 429

State Street Boston Corporation, **8** **491–93**

State Trading Corp. of India Ltd., **IV** 143

Staten Island Advance Corp., **IV** 581–82; **19** 4

Staten Island Bancorp, Inc., **39 380–82**

Stater Brothers, **17** 558

Statex Petroleum, Inc., **19** 70

Static, Inc., **14** 430

Static Snowboards, Inc., **51** 393

Station Casinos Inc., **25 452–54**

Stationers Distributing Company, **14** 523

Stationers, Inc., **28** 74

Statler Hotel Co., **III** 92, 98; **19** 206

Statoil. *See* Den Norske Stats Oljeselskap AS.

Statoil Energy Inc., **54** 97

StatScript Management Services, **26** 73

Statter, Inc., **6** 27

Staubli International, **II** 122; **12** 546

Stauffer Chemical Company, **8** 105–07; **21** 545

Stauffer Communications, Inc., **36** 339–41

Stauffer-Meiji, **II** 540

Stax Records, **23** 32

STC PLC, III 141, **162–64**; **25** 497; **36** 351

Stead & Miller, 13 169

Steag AG, **IV** 193

Steak & Ale, **II** 556–57; **7** 336; **12** 373; **13** 408–09

The Steak n Shake Company, 14 130–31; **41 387–90**

Steam and Gas Pipe Co., **III** 644

Steam Boiler Works, **18** 318

Steamboat Ski and Resort Corporation, **28** 21

Stearman, **I** 47, 84; **9** 416; **10** 162

Stearns & Foster, **12** 439

Stearns Catalytic World Corp., **II** 87; **11** 413

Stearns Coal & Lumber, **6** 514

Stearns, Inc., 43 389–91

Stearns Manufacturing Co., **16** 297

Steaua-Romana, **IV** 557

Steego Auto Paints, **24** 160

Steel and Tube Co. of America, **IV** 114

Steel Authority of India Ltd., IV 205–07

Steel Ceilings and Aluminum Works, **IV** 22

Steel Co. of Canada Ltd., **IV** 208

Steel Dynamics, Inc., 18 380; **26** 530; **52 326–28**

Steel Mills Ltd., **III** 673

Steel Products Engineering Co., **I** 169

Steel Stamping Co., **III** 569; **20** 360

Steelcase Inc., 7 493–95; **8** 251–52, 255, 405; **25** 500; **27 432–35 (upd.)**; **39** 205–07

Steelmade Inc., **I** 513

Steely, **IV** 109

Steen Production Services, Inc., **51** 248

Steenfabriek De Ruiterwaard, **14** 249

Steenkolen Handelsvereniging NV, **IV** 132; **39** 176; **50** 335

Steering Aluminum, **I** 159

Stefany, **12** 152

Stegbar Pty Ltd., **31** 398–400

Steger Furniture Manufacturing Co., **18** 493

Steiff. *See* Margarete Steiff GmbH.

Steil, Inc., **8** 271

Steilman Group. *See* Klaus Steilmann GmbH & Co. KG.

Stein Mart Inc., 19 423–25

Stein Printing Company, **25** 183

Stein Robaire Helm, **22** 173

Steinbach Inc., **IV** 226; **14** 427

Steinbach Stores, Inc., **19** 108

Steinberg Incorporated, II 652–53, **662–65**; **V** 163

Steinberger, **16** 239

Steiner Corporation (Alsco), 53 308–11

Steinheil Optronik GmbH, **24** 87

Steinman & Grey, **6** 27

Steinmüller Verwaltungsgesellschaft, **V** 747

Steinway & Sons, **16** 201; **43** 170

Steinway Musical Properties, Inc., 19 392, 394, **426–29**; **55** 111, 114

Stelco Inc., IV 208–10; **24** 144; **51 349–52 (upd.)**

Stella Bella Corporation, **19** 436

Stella D'Oro Company, **7** 367

Stellar Systems, Inc., **III** 553; **14** 542

Stellenbosch Farmers Winery, **I** 288

Stelmar Shipping Ltd., 52 329–31

Stelux Manufacturing Company, **13** 121; **41** 71

Stelwire Ltd., **51** 352

Stena AB, **25** 105; **29** 429–30

Stena Line AB, **38** 345

Stena-Sealink, **37** 137

Stens Corporation, **48** 34

Stensmölla Kemiska Tekniska Industri, **I** 385

Stentor Canadian Network Management, **6** 310

Stenval Sud, **19** 50

Stepan Company, 30 437–39

Stephen F. Whitman & Son, Inc., **7** 429

Stephens Inc., **III** 76; **16** 59; **18** 223

Stephenson Clarke and Company, **31** 368–69

Sterchi Bros. Co., **14** 236

Steria SA, 49 382–85

Stericycle Inc., 33 380–82

STERIS Corporation, 29 449–52

Sterling Chemicals, Inc., 16 460–63; **27** 117

Sterling Drug Inc., I 309–10, **698–700**; **III** 477; **7** 163; **13** 76–77; **36** 173; **41** 45

Sterling Electronics Corp., 18 496–98; **19** 311

Sterling Engineered Products, **III** 640, 642; **16** 9

Sterling Forest Corp., **III** 264

Sterling House Corp., **42** 4

Sterling Industries, **13** 166

Sterling Information Services, Ltd., **IV** 675; **7** 528

Sterling Manhattan, **7** 63

Sterling Oil, **I** 526

Sterling Oil & Development, **II** 490

Sterling Organics Ltd., **12** 351; **50** 282

Sterling Plastics, **III** 642

Sterling Plastics Inc., **16** 9

Sterling Products Inc., **I** 622; **10** 68; **50** 535

Sterling Remedy Co., **I** 698

Sterling Software, Inc., 11 468–70; **31** 296

Sterling Stores Co. Inc., **24** 148

Sterling Winthrop, **7** 164; **36** 174; **49** 351

Stern & Stern Textiles, **11** 261

Stern-Auer Shoe Company, **V** 207

Stern Bros. Investment Bank, **V** 362–65; **19** 359

Stern Bros., LLC, **37** 224

Stern Publishing, **38** 478

Stern's, **9** 209

Sternco Industries, **12** 230–31

STET. *See* Società Finanziaria Telefonica per Azioni.

Steuben Glass, **III** 683

Stevcoknit Fabrics Company, **8** 141–43

Stevedoring Services of America Inc., 28 435–37; **50** 209–10

Steven Madden, Ltd., 37 371–73

Stevens Linen Associates, Inc., **8** 272

Stevens Park Osteopathic Hospital, **6** 192

Stevens Sound Proofing Co., **III** 706; **7** 291

Stevens, Thompson & Runyan, Inc. *See* CRSS Inc.

Stevens Water Monitoring Systems, **52** 226

Steve's Ice Cream, **16** 54–55

Steward Esplen and Greenhough, **II** 569

Stewards Foundation, **6** 191

Stewart and Richey Construction Co., **51** 170

Stewart & Stevenson Services Inc., 11 471–73

Stewart Bolling Co., **IV** 130

Stewart Cash Stores, **II** 465

Stewart Enterprises, Inc., 16 344; **20 481–83**; **37** 67

Stewart P. Orr Associates, **6** 224

Stewart Systems, Inc., **22** 352–53

Stewart's Beverages, 39 383–86

Steyr Walzlager, **III** 625

Stichting Continuiteit AMEV, **III** 202

Stickley. *See* L. and J.G. Stickley, Inc.

Stieber Rollkupplung GmbH, **14** 63

Stihl Inc. *See* Andreas Stihl.

Stilcraft, **24** 16

Stillwater Mining Company, 47 380–82

Stimson & Valentine, **8** 552

Stimsonite Corporation, **49** 38

Stinnes AG, 6 424, 426; **8** 68–69, **494–97**; **23** 68–70, **451–54 (upd.)**; **33** 195

Stirling Readymix Concrete, **III** 737–38

STM Systems Corp., **11** 485

STMicroelectronics NV, 52 332–35

Stock, **IV** 617–18

Stock Clearing Corporation, **9** 370

Stock Yards Packing Co., Inc., 37 374–76

Stockholder Systems Inc., **11** 485

Stockholm Southern Transportation Co., **I** 553

Stockholms Allmänna Telefonaktiebolag, **V** 334

Stockholms Enskilda Bank, **II** 1, 351, 365–66; **III** 419, 425–26

Stockholms Intecknings Garanti, **II** 366

Stockpack Ltd., **44** 318

Stockton and Hartlepool Railway, **III** 272

Stockton Wheel Co., **III** 450

Stoelting Brothers Company, **10** 371

Stokely Van Camp, **II** 560, 575; **12** 411; **22** 338

Stokvis/De Nederlandsche Kroon Rijwiefabrieken, **13** 499

Stoll-Moss Theatres Ltd., 34 420–22

Stollwerck AG, 53 312–15

Stolt-Nielsen S.A., 42 356–59; **54** 349–50

Stolt Sea Farm Holdings PLC, 54 349–51

Stone & Webster, Inc., 13 495–98

Stone and Kimball, **IV** 660

Stone-Consolidated Corporation, **25** 9, 12

Stone Container Corporation, IV 332–34; **8** 203–04; **15** 129; **17** 106; **25** 12. *See also* Smurfit-Stone Container Corporation.

Stone Exploration Corp., **IV** 83; **7** 187

Stone Manufacturing Company, 14 469–71; **43 392–96 (upd.)**

Stonega Coke & Coal Co. *See* Westmoreland Coal Company.

Stoner Associates. *See* Severn Trent PLC.

Stonewall Insurance Co., **III** 192

Stonington Partners, **19** 318

StonyBrook Services Inc., **24** 49

Stonyfield Farm, Inc., 55 357–60

Stoody Co., **19** 440

Stoof, **26** 278–79

Stoomvaart Maatschappij Nederland, **6** 403–04; **26** 241

The Stop & Shop Companies, Inc., II 666–67; **9** 451, 453; **12** 48–49; **16** 160, 314; **23** 169; **24 460–62 (upd.)**

Stop N Go, **7** 373; **25** 126

Stoppenbauch Inc., **23** 202

Stora Enso Oyj, 36 128, **447–55 (upd.)**

Stora Kopparbergs Bergslags AB, III 693, 695; **IV 335-37**, 340; **12** 464; **28** 445-46
Storage Dimensions Inc., **10** 404
Storage Technology Corporation, III 110; **6 275-77**; **12** 148, 161; **16** 194; **28** 198
Storage USA, Inc., 21 475-77
Storebor Brux Company, **52** 406
Storebrand Insurance Co., III 122
Storehouse PLC, II 658; **13** 284; **16 464-66**; **17** 42-43, 335; **24** 75
Storer Communications, II 161; **IV** 596; **7** 91-92, 200-1; **24** 122
Storer Leasing Inc., **I** 99; **6** 81
Storm Technology, **28** 245
Storz Instruments Co., **I** 678; **25** 56; **27** 115
Stouffer Corp., **I** 485; II 489, 547; **6** 40; **7** 382; **8 498-501**
Stouffer Foods Corporation, **28** 238
Stout Air Services, **I** 128; **6** 128
Stout Airlines, **I** 47, 84; **9** 416; **10** 162
Stout Metal Airplane Co., **I** 165
Stowe Machine Co., Inc., **30** 283
Stowe Woodward, **I** 428-29
STP, **19** 223; **26** 349
STRAAM Engineers. *See* CRSS Inc.
Straits Steamship Co. *See* Malaysian Airlines System.
Stran, **8** 546
Strata Energy, Inc., **IV** 29
StrataCom, Inc., **11** 59; **16 467-69**; **34** 113
Strategic Implications International, Inc., **45** 44
Strategix Solutions, **43** 309
Stratford Corporation, **15** 103; **26** 100
Strathmore Consolidated Investments, **IV** 90
Stratos Boat Co., Ltd., III 600
Stratton Oakmont Inc., **37** 372-73; **46** 282
Stratton Ski Corporation, **15** 235
Stratus Computer, Inc., **6** 279; **10 499-501**
Straus-Frank Company, **29** 86, 88
Strauss Turnbull and Co., II 355
Strawberries, **30** 465
Strawbridge & Clothier's, **6** 243
Strayer Education, Inc., 53 316-19
Stream International Inc., **48** 369
Stream Machine Co., **48** 92
Streamline Holdings, **39** 237-38
StreamScapes Media, **51** 286, 288
De Streekkrant-De Weekkrantgroep NV, **48** 347
Street & Smith Publications, Inc., **IV** 583; **13** 178
The Stride Rite Corporation, **8 502-04**; **9** 437; **33** 244; **37 377-80 (upd.)**
Strix Ltd., 51 353-55
Stroehmann Bakeries, II 631
Stroh and Co., **IV** 486
The Stroh Brewery Company, **I** 32, 255, **290-92**; **13** 10-11, 455; **18** 72, **499-502** (upd.); **22** 422; **23** 403, 405; **36** 14-15
Strömberg, **IV** 300; **27** 267, 268
Stromberg Carburetor Co., **I** 141
Stromberg-Carlson, II 82
Stromeyer GmbH, **7** 141
Strong Brewery, **I** 294
Strong Electric Corporation, **19** 211
Strong International, **27** 57

Stroock & Stroock & Lavan LLP, 40 418-21
Strother Drug, III 9-10
Strouds, Inc., 33 383-86
Structural Dynamics Research Corporation, **10** 257
Structural Fibers, Inc. *See* Essef Corporation.
Structural Iberica S.A., **18** 163
Struebel Group, **18** 170
Strydel, Inc., **14** 361
Stryker Corporation, **10** 351; **11 474-76**; **29 453-55 (upd.)**
Stuart & Sons Ltd., **34** 493, 496
Stuart Co., **I** 584
Stuart Entertainment Inc., 16 470-72
Stuart Hall Co., **17** 445
Stuart Medical, Inc., **10** 143; **16** 400
Stuart Perlman, **6** 200
Stuckey's, Inc., **7** 429
Studebaker Co., **I** 141-42, 451; **8** 74; **9** 27
Studebaker-Packard, **9** 118; **10** 261
Studebaker Wagon Co., **IV** 660
Student Loan Marketing Association, II **453-55**. *See also* SLM Holding Corp.
Studiengesellschaft, **I** 409
StudioCanal, **48** 164-65
Studley Products Inc., **12** 396
Stuffit Co., **IV** 597
Stuller Settings, Inc., 35 405-07
Sturbridge Yankee Workshop, Inc., **10** 216
Sturgeon Bay Shipbuilding and DryDock Company, **18** 320
Sturm, Ruger & Company, Inc., 19 430-32
Stussy, Inc., 55 361-63
Stuttgart Gas Works, **I** 391
Stuttgarter Verein Versicherungs-AG, III 184
Stuyvesant Insurance Group, II 182
Style Magazine BV, **48** 347
Styleclick.com, Inc., **47** 420
Stylus Writing Instruments, **27** 416
Stymer Oy, **IV** 470-71
SU214, **28** 27, 30
Suave Shoe Corporation. *See* French Fragrances, Inc.
Sub-Zero Freezer Co., Inc., 31 426-28
Subaru, **6** 28; **23** 290
Suber Suisse S.A., **48** 350
The SubLine Company, Inc., **53** 340
SubLogic, **15** 455
Submarine Boat Co., **I** 57
Submarine Signal Co., II 85-86; **11** 412
SUBperior Distribution Systems, Inc., **53** 340
Suburban Cablevision, **IV** 640
Suburban Coastal Corporation, **10** 92
Suburban Cos., **IV** 575-76
Suburban Light and Power Company, **12** 45
Suburban Propane Partners, L.P., **I** 378; **30 440-42[ro**
Suburban Savings and Loan Association, **10** 92
Subway, **15** 56-57; **32 442-44**
Successories, Inc., 30 443-45[ro
Suchard Co., II 520
Sud-Aviation, **I** 44-45; **7** 10; **8** 313
Sudbury Inc., **16 473-75**; **17** 373
Sudbury River Consulting Group, **31** 131
Suddeutsche Bank A.G., II 279
Süddeutsche Donau- Dampfschiffahrts-Gesellschaft, **6** 425

Süddeutsche Kalkstickstoffwerke AG, **IV** 229, 232
Sudler & Hennessey, **I** 37
Südpetrol, **IV** 421
Südzucker AG, 27 436-39
Suez Bank, **IV** 108
Suez Canal Co., **IV** 530
Suez Lyonnaise des Eaux, 36 456-59 (upd.); **38** 321; **40** 447, 449; **42** 386, 388; **45** 277; **47** 219
Suez Oil Co., **IV** 413-14
Suez Oil Processing Co., **51** 113
Suffolk County Federal Savings and Loan Association, **16** 346
Sugar Entertainment, **51** 288
Sugar Land State Bank, **25** 114
Sugar Mount Capital, LLC, **33** 355
Sugarland Industries. *See* Imperial Holly Corporation.
SugarLoaf Creations, Inc. *See* American Coin Merchandising, Inc.
Sugarloaf Mountain Corporation, **28** 21
The Suit Company, **51** 253
Suita Brewery, **I** 220
Suito Sangyo Co., Ltd. *See* Seino Transportation Company, Ltd.
SUITS. *See* Scottish Universal Investments.
Suiza Foods Corporation, **25** 512, 514; **26 447-50**; **37** 197; **38** 381
Sukhoi Design Bureau Aviation Scientific-Industrial Complex, 24 463-65
Sullair Co., **I** 435
Sullivan & Cromwell, **26 451-53**; **27** 327; **47** 437
Sullivan-Schein Dental Products Inc., **31** 256
Sullivan, Stauffer, Colwell & Bayles, **14** 314
Sullivan Systems, III 420
Sulpetro Limited, **25** 232
Sulphide Corp., **IV** 58
Sulzbach, **I** 409
Sulzer Brothers Limited, III 402, 516, **630-33**, 638
Sumergrade Corporation, **19** 304; **41** 300
Suminoe Textile Co., **8** 235
Sumisei Secpac Investment Advisors, III 366
Sumisho Electronics Co. Ltd., **18** 170
Sumitomo Bank, Limited, **I** 587; II 104, 224, 273-74, 347, **360-62**, 363, 392, 415; **IV** 269, 726; **9** 341-42; **18** 170; **23** 340; **26 454-57 (upd.)**
Sumitomo Chemical Company Ltd., **I** 363, **397-98**; II 361; III 715; **IV** 432
Sumitomo Corporation, **I** 431-32, 492, 502, 504-05, 510-11, 515, **518-20**; III 43, 365; **V** 161; **7** 357; **11 477-80 (upd.)**, 490; **15** 340; **17** 556; **18** 170; **24** 325; **28** 288; **36** 420; **45** 115
Sumitomo Electric Industries, **I** 105; II **104-05**; III 490, 684; **IV** 179; **V** 252
Sumitomo Heavy Industries, Ltd., III 533, **634-35**; **10** 381; **42 360-62 (upd.)**
Sumitomo Life Insurance Co., II 104, 360, 422; III 288, **365-66**
Sumitomo Marine and Fire Insurance Company, Limited, III **367-68**
Sumitomo Metal Industries, Ltd., **I** 390; II 104, 361; **IV** 130, **211-13**, 216; **10** 463-64; **11** 246; **24** 302
Sumitomo Metal Mining Co., Ltd., **IV 214-16**; **9** 340; **23** 338

Sumitomo Mitsui Banking Corporation, 51 356–62 (upd.)
Sumitomo Realty & Development Co., Ltd., IV 726–27
Sumitomo Rubber Industries, Ltd., V 252–53; 20 263
Sumitomo Trading, 45 8
The Sumitomo Trust & Banking Company, Ltd., II 104, 363–64; IV 726; 53 320–22 (upd.)
Sumitomo Wire Company, 16 555
Summa Corporation, 9 266; 17 317; 50 306
Summer Paper Tube, 19 78
SummerGate Inc., 48 148
Summers Group Inc., 15 386
The Summit Bancorporation, 14 472–74
Summit Constructors. See CRSS Inc.
Summit Engineering Corp., I 153
Summit Family Restaurants Inc., 19 89, 92, 433–36
Summit Gear Company, 16 392–93
Summit Management Co., Inc., 17 498
Summit Screen Inks, 13 228
Summit Systems Inc., 45 280
Summit Technology Inc., 30 485
Sumolis, 54 315, 317
Sun Aire, 25 421–22
Sun Alliance Group PLC, III 296, 369–74, 400; 37 86. See also Royal & Sun Alliance Insurance Group plc.
Sun Apparel Inc., 39 247
Sun Chemical Corp. See Sequa Corp.
Sun Communities Inc., 46 377–79
Sun Company, Inc., I 286, 631; IV 449, 548–50; 7 114, 414; 11 484; 12 459; 17 537; 25 126
Sun Country Airlines, I 114; 30 446–49
Sun-Diamond Growers of California, 7 496–97
Sun Distributors L.P., 12 459–461
Sun Electric, 15 288
Sun Electronics, 9 116
Sun Equities Corporation, 15 449
Sun-Fast Color, 13 227
Sun Federal, 7 498
Sun Federal Savings and Loan Association of Tallahassee, 10 92
Sun Financial Group, Inc., 25 171
Sun Fire Coal Company, 7 281
Sun Fire Office, III 349, 369–71
Sun Foods, 12 220–21
Sun Gro Horticulture Inc., 49 196, 198
Sun Healthcare Group Inc., 25 455–58
Sun International Hotels Limited, 12 420; 26 462–65; 37 254–55
Sun Kyowa, III 43
Sun Life Assurance Co. of Canada, IV 165
Sun Life Group of America, 11 482
Sun-Maid Growers of California, 7 496–97
Sun Mark, Inc., 21 483
Sun Media, 27 280; 29 471–72; 47 327
Sun Men's Shop Co., Ltd., V 150
Sun Microsystems, Inc., II 45, 62; III 125; 6 222, 235, 238, 244; 7 498–501; 9 36, 471; 10 118, 242, 257, 504; 11 45–46, 490–91, 507; 12 162; 14 15–16, 268; 15 321; 16 140, 195, 418–19; 18 537; 20 175, 237; 21 86; 22 154; 23 471; 25 348, 499; 26 19; 27 448; 30 450–54 (upd.); 36 80–81; 38 416, 418; 43 238–40; 44 97; 45 200; 49 124; 50 329; 53 57
Sun Newspapers, III 213–14

Sun Oil Co., III 497; IV 371, 424, 548–50; 7 413–14; 11 35; 18 233; 19 162; 36 86–87. See also Sunoco, Inc.
Sun Optical Co., Ltd., V 150
Sun Pac Foods, 45 161
Sun-Pat Products, II 569
Sun Pharmaceuticals, 24 480
Sun Shades 501 Ltd., 21 483
Sun Ship, IV 549
Sun Sportswear, Inc., 17 460–63; 23 65–66
Sun State Marine Services, Inc. See Hvide Marine Incorporated.
Sun Techno Services Co., Ltd., V 150
Sun Technology Enterprises, 7 500
Sun Television & Appliances Inc., 10 502–03; 19 362
Sun Valley Equipment Corp., 33 363
SunAir, 11 300
SunAmerica Inc., 11 481–83
Sunbeam-Oster Co., Inc., 9 484–86; 14 230; 16 488; 17 215; 19 305; 22 3; 28 135, 246; 30 136; 42 309
Sunbelt Beverage Corporation, 32 520
Sunbelt Coca-Cola, 10 223
Sunbelt Nursery Group, Inc., 12 179, 200, 394
Sunbelt Rentals Inc., 34 42
Sunbird, III 600; V 150
Sunburst Hospitality Corporation, 26 458–61
Sunburst Technology Corporation, 36 273
Sunburst Yarns, Inc., 13 532
Sunciti Manufacturers Ltd., III 454; 21 122
Sunclipse Inc., IV 250
Sunco N.V., 22 515
Suncoast Motion Picture Company, 9 360
SunCor Development Company, 6 546–47
Suncor Energy Inc., 33 167; 54 352–54
Sundance Publishing, IV 609; 12 559
Sunday Pictorial, IV 665–66; 17 397
Sundheim & Doetsch, IV 189
Sundor Group, 54 213
Sunds Defibrator AG, IV 338–40, 350; 28 444
Sundstrand Corporation, 7 502–04; 21 478–81 (upd.)
Sundt Corp., 24 466–69
Sundwig Eisenhütte Maschinenfabrik GmbH & Co., 51 25
SunGard Data Systems Inc., 11 484–85
Sunglass Hut International, Inc., 18 393; 21 482–84; 52 227, 230
Sunglee Electronics Co. Ltd., III 748–49
Sunila Oy, IV 348–49
Sunkiss Thermoreactors, 21 65
Sunkist Growers, Inc., 7 496; 25 366; 26 466–69; 47 63
Sunkist Soft Drinks Inc., I 13
Sunkus & Associates, 49 427
Sunkus Co. Ltd., V 150
Sunlight Services Group Limited, 45 139
Sunlit Industries, 44 132
Sunnybrook Farms, 25 124
Sunoco, Inc., 28 438–42 (upd.)
SunQuest HealthCare Corp. See Unison HealthCare Corporation.
Sunquest Information Systems Inc., 45 279, 281
Sunray DX Oil Co., IV 550, 575; 7 414
The Sunrider Corporation, 26 316, 470–74; 27 353
SunRise Imaging, 44 358

Sunrise Inc., 55 48
Sunrise Medical Inc., 11 202, 486–88
Sunrise Test Systems, 11 491
Sunsations Sunglass Company, 21 483
Sunshine Biscuit Co., 35 181; 36 313
Sunshine Bullion Co., 25 542
Sunshine Jr. Stores, Inc., 17 170
Sunshine Mining Company, 20 149
SunSoft Inc., 7 500; 43 238
Sunstate, 24 396
Sunsweet Growers, 7 496
Suntory Ltd., 13 454; 21 320; 36 404
SunTrust Banks Inc., 23 455–58; 33 293
Sunward Technologies, Inc., 10 464
Supasnaps, V 50
Supelco, Inc., 36 431
Super Bazars, 26 159
Super D Drugs, 9 52
Super Dart. See Dart Group Corporation.
Super 8 Motels, Inc., 11 178
Super Food Services, Inc., 15 479–81; 18 8
Super Oil Seals & Gaskets Ltd., 16 8
Super 1 Stores. See Brookshire Grocery Company.
Super-Power Company, 6 505
Super Quick, Inc., 7 372
Super Rite Foods, Inc., V 176; 19 356
Super Sagless Spring Corp., 15 103
Super Sol Ltd., 41 56–57
Super Store Industries, 14 397
Super Valu Stores, Inc., II 632, 668–71; 6 364; 7 450; 8 380; 14 411; 17 180; 22 126; 23 357–58. See also SUPERVALU INC.
SuperAmerica Group, Inc., IV 374
Superbrix, 14 248
Supercomputer Systems, Inc., III 130; 16 138
Supercuts Inc., 26 475–78
Superdrug plc, V 175; 24 266, 269–70
Superenvases Envalic, I 231
Superior Bearings Company. See Federal-Mogul Corporation.
Superior Foam and Polymers, Inc., 44 261
Superior Healthcare Group, Inc., 11 221
Superior Industries International, Inc., 8 505–07
Superior Oil Co., III 558; IV 400, 465, 524; 7 353; 49 137
Superior Recycled Fiber Industries, 26 363
Superior Transfer, 12 309
Superior Uniform Group, Inc., 30 455–57
SuperMac Technology Inc., 16 419
Supermarchés GB, 26 159
Supermarchés Montréal, II 662–63
Supermarkets General Holdings Corporation, II 672–74; 16 160; 23 369–71
Supermart Books, 10 136
Supersaver Wholesale Clubs, 8 555
Supersnaps, 19 124
SuperStation WTBS, 6 171
Supertest Petroleum Corporation, 9 490
SUPERVALU INC., 18 503–08 (upd.); 21 457–57; 22 327; 50 453–59 (upd.)
Supervalue Corp., 13 393
Supervised Investors Services, III 270
SupeRx, II 644
Supplyon AG, 48 450
Suprema Specialties, Inc., 27 440–42
Supreme International Corporation, 27 443–46; 30 358; 41 291

Supreme Life Insurance Company of America, **28** 212
Supreme Sugar Co., **I** 421; **11** 23
Supron Energy Corp., **15** 129
Surety Life Insurance Company, **10** 51
SureWay Air Traffic Corporation, **24** 126
Surgical Health Corporation, **14** 233
Surgical Mechanical Research Inc., **I** 678
Surgical Plastics, **25** 430–31
Surgikos, Inc., **III** 35
Surgitool, **I** 628
OAO Surgutneftegaz, **48** 375–78
Suroflex GmbH, **23** 300
Surpass Software Systems, Inc., **9** 81
Surplus Software, **31** 176
Surrey Free Inns plc. *See* SFI Group plc.
Surridge Dawson Ltd. *See* Dawson Holdings PLC.
Survey Research Group, **10** 360
SurVivaLink, **18** 423
Susan Bristol, **16** 61
Susan Kay Cosmetics. *See* The Cosmetic Center, Inc.
SuSE Linux AG, **45** 363
Susie's Casuals, **14** 294
Susquehanna Pfaltzgraff Company, **8 508–10**
Sussex Group, **15** 449
Sussex Trust Company, **25** 541
Sutherland Lumber Co., **19** 233
Sutter Corp., **15** 113
Sutter Health, **12** 175–76
Sutter Home Winery Inc., **16 476–78**
Sutton & Towne, Inc., **21** 96
Sutton Laboratories, **22** 228
Suunto Oy, **41** 14, 16
Suwa Seikosha, **III** 620
Suzaki Hajime, **V** 113–14
Suzannah Farms, **7** 524
Suze, **I** 280
Suzhou Elevator Company, **29** 420
Suzuki & Co., **I** 509–10; **IV** 129; **9** 341–42; **23** 340
Suzuki Motor Corporation, **III** 581, 657; **7** 110; **8** 72; **9 487–89**; **23** 290, **459–62** (upd.); **36** 240, 243; **39** 38
Suzuki Shoten Co., **V** 380, 457–58
Suzy Shier, **18** 562
Svea Choklad A.G., **II** 640
AB Svensk Färgämnesindustri, **50** 55
Svensk Fastighetskredit A.B., **II** 352
Svensk Filmindustrie, **52** 49, 51
Svensk Golvindustri, **25** 463
Svenska A.B. Humber & Co., **I** 197
Svenska Aeroplan Aktiebolaget. *See* Saab-Scania AB.
Svenska Cellulosa Aktiebolaget SCA, **II** 365–66; **IV** 295–96, 325, 336, **338–40**, 667; **17** 398; **19** 225–26; **28 443–46** (upd.); **52** 163
Svenska Centrifug AB, **III** 418
Svenska Elektron, **III** 478
A.B. Svenska Flaktfabriken, **II** 2; **22** 8
Svenska Flygmotor A.B., **I** 209; **26** 10
Svenska Handelsbanken AB, **II** 353, **365–67**; **IV** 338–39; **28** 443–44; **50 460–63** (upd.)
Svenska Järnvagsverkstäderna A.B., **I** 197
Svenska Kullagerfabriken A.B., **I** 209; **III** 622; **7** 565; **26** 9. *See also* AB Volvo.
Svenska Oljeslageri AB, **IV** 318
Svenska Stålpressnings AB, **26** 11
Svenska Varv, **6** 367
Svenska Varv, **27** 91

Svenskt Stål AB, **IV** 336
Sverdrup Corporation, **14 475–78**
Sverker Martin-Löf, **IV** 339
SVF. *See* Société des Vins de France.
SVIDO, **17** 250
Sviluppo Iniziative Stradali Italiene, **IV** 420
SVPW, **I** 215
SWA. *See* Southwest Airlines.
Swallow Airplane Company, **8** 49; **27** 98
Swallow Sidecar and Coach Building Company, **13** 285
Swan, **10** 170
Swan Electric Light Co., **I** 410
Swan's Down Cake Flour, **II** 531
Swank Inc., **17 464–66**
Swann Corp., **I** 366
Swarovski International Holding AG, **40 422–25**
The Swatch Group SA, **7** 532–33; **25** 481; **26 479–81**
Swearingen Aircraft Company, **9** 207; **48** 169
SwedeChrome, **III** 625
Swedish Ericsson Group, **17** 353
Swedish Furniture Research Institute, **V** 82
Swedish Intercontinental Airlines, **I** 119; **34** 396
Swedish Match AB, **39 387–90** (upd.)
Swedish Match S.A., **IV** 336–37; **9** 381; **12 462–64**; **23** 55; **25** 464
Swedish Ordnance-FFV/Bofors AB, **9** 381–82
Swedish Telecom, **V 331–33**
SwedishAmerican Health System, **51 363–66**
Sweedor, **12** 464
Sweeney Specialty Restaurants, **14** 131
Sweeney's, **16** 559
Sweet & Maxwell, **8** 527
Sweet Life Foods Inc., **18** 507; **50** 457
Sweet Traditions LLC, **21** 323
Sweetheart Cup Company, Inc., **36 460–64**
Swenson Granite Company, Inc., **37** 331
Swett & Crawford Group, **III** 357; **22** 494
Swift & Company, **II** 447, 550; **13** 351, 448; **17** 124; **41** 114; **55 364–67**
Swift Adhesives, **10** 467
Swift-Armour S.A., **II** 480
Swift-Armour S.A. Argentina, **25** 517; **26** 57
Swift-Eckrich, **II** 467
Swift Independent Packing Co., **II** 494; **13** 350, 352; **42** 92
Swift Textiles, Inc., **12** 118; **15** 247
Swift Transportation Co., Inc., **26** 533; **33** 468; **42 363–66**
Swinerton Inc., **43 397–400**
Swing-N-Slide, Inc. *See* PlayCore, Inc.
Swingline, Inc., **7** 3–5
Swire Group, **34** 100
Swire Pacific Ltd., **I** 469–70, **521–22**; **6** 78; **16 479–81** (upd.); **18** 114; **20** 310, 312
Swisher International Group Inc., **14** 17–19; **23 463–65**; **27** 139
Swiss Air Transport Company Ltd., **I** 107, 119, **121–22**; **24** 312; **27** 409; **33** 49, 51, 271
Swiss-American Corporation, **II** 267; **21** 145
Swiss Banca de Gottardo, **26** 456
Swiss Banca della Svizzera Italiano, **II** 192

Swiss Bank Corporation, **II** 267, **368–70**, 378–79; **14** 419–20; **21** 145–46; **52** 354. *See also* UBS AG.
Swiss Barry Callebaut AG, **53** 315
Swiss Broadcasting Corporation, **53** 325
Swiss Cement-Industrie-Gesellschaft, **III** 701
Swiss Colony Wines, **I** 377
Swiss Drilling Co., **IV** 372; **19** 22; **50** 45
Swiss Federal Railways (Schweizerische Bundesbahnen), **V 519–22**
Swiss General Chocolate Co., **II** 545–46; **7** 380–81
Swiss International Air Lines Ltd., **48 379–81**
Swiss Life, **52** 357–58
Swiss Locomotive and Machine Works, **III** 631–32
Swiss Oil Co., **IV** 372–73
Swiss Reinsurance Company (Schweizerische Rückversicherungs-Gesellschaft), **III** 299, 301, 335, **375–78**; **15** 13; **21** 146; **45** 110; **46 380–84** (upd.)
Swiss Saurer AG, **39** 39, 41
Swiss Time Australia Pty Ltd, **25** 461
Swiss Volksbank, **21** 146–47
Swissair Associated Co., **I** 122; **6** 60, 96, 117; **34** 397–98; **36** 426
Swissair Group, **47** 286–87; **49** 80–81
SwissCargo, **49** 81
Switchboard Inc., **25** 52
SXI Limited, **17** 458
Sybase, Inc., **6** 255, 279; **10** 361, **504–06**; **11** 77–78; **15** 492; **25** 96, 299; **27 447–50** (upd.)
SyberVision, **10** 216
Sybra, Inc., **19** 466–68
Sybron International Corp., **14 479–81**; **19** 289–90
Sycamore Networks, Inc., **45 388–91**
SYCOM, Inc., **18** 363
Sydney Electricity, **12** 443
Sydney Paper Mills Ltd., **IV** 248
Sydney Ross Co., **I** 698–99
Sydsvenska Kemi AB, **51** 289
Syfrets Trust Co., **IV** 23
Sykes Enterprises, Inc., **45 392–95**
Sylacauga Calcium Products, **III** 691
Syllogic B.V., **29** 376
Sylvan, Inc., **22 496–99**
Sylvan Lake Telephone Company, **6** 334
Sylvan Learning Systems, Inc., **13** 299; **34** 439; **35 408–11**; **55** 213
Sylvania Companies, **I** 463; **II** 63; **III** 165, 475; **V** 295; **7** 161; **8** 157; **11** 197; **13** 402; **23** 181; **50** 299
Sylvia Paperboard Co., **IV** 310; **19** 266
Symantec Corporation, **10 507–09**; **25** 348–49
Symbian Ltd., **45** 346, 348
Symbios Logic Inc., **19** 312; **31** 5
Symbiosis Corp., **10** 70; **50** 538
Symbol Technologies, Inc., **10** 363, 523–24; **15 482–84**
Symington-Wayne, **III** 472
Symphony International, **14** 224
Syms Corporation, **29 456–58**
Symtron Systems Inc., **37** 399–400
Symtronix Corporation, **18** 515
Syn-Optics, Inc., **29** 454
Synbiotics Corporation, **23** 284
Syncordia Corp., **15** 69
Syncro Ltd., **51** 89

Syncrocom, Inc., **10** 513
Syncrude Canada Limited, **25** 232
Synercom Technology Inc., **14** 319
Synercon Corporation, **25** 538
Synergen Inc., **13** 241
Synergy Dataworks, Inc., **11** 285
Synergy Software Inc., **31** 131
Synetic, Inc., **16** 59
Synfloor SA, **25** 464
Synopsis, Inc., 11 489–92; 18 20; **43** 17
SynOptics Communications, Inc., 10 194,
    510–12; **11** 475; **16** 392; **22** 52
Synovus Financial Corp., 12 465–67; 18
    516–17; **52 336–40 (upd.)**
Syntax Ophthalmic Inc., **III** 727
Syntex Corporation, I 512, **701–03; III**
    18, 53; **8** 216–17, 434, 548; **10** 53; **12**
    322; **26** 384; **50** 321
Syntex Pharmaceuticals Ltd., **21** 425
Synthecolor S.A., **8** 347
Synthélabo, **III** 47–48
Synthetic Blood Corp., **15** 380
Synthetic Pillows, Inc., **19** 304
Synthomer. *See* Yule Catto & Company
    plc.
Syntron, Inc., **18** 513–15
SyQuest Technology, Inc., 18 509–12
Syracuse China, **8** 510
Syratech Corp., 14 482–84; 27 288
Syrian Airways, **6** 85; **27** 133
Syroco, **14** 483–84
SYSCO Corporation, II 675–76; 9 453;
    16 387; **18** 67; **24 470–72 (upd.),** 528;
    26 504; **47** 457
SYSCO Security Systems, Inc., **51** 81
Syscon Corporation, **38** 227
Sysorex Information Systems, **11** 62
SysScan, **V** 339
Systech Environmental Corporation, **28**
    228–29
System Designers plc. *See* SD-Scicon plc.
System Development Co., **III** 166; **6** 282
System Fuels, Inc., **11** 194
System Integrators, Inc., **6** 279
System Parking West, **25** 16
System Software Associates, Inc., 10
    513–14
Systematic Business Services, Inc., **48**
    256–57
Systematics Inc., **6** 301; **11** 131
Systemax, Inc., 52 341–44
Systembolaget, **31** 459–60
Systems & Computer Technology Corp.,
    19 437–39
Systems and Services Company. *See*
    SYSCO Corporation.
Systems Center, Inc., **6** 279; **11** 469
Systems Construction Ltd., **II** 649
Systems Development Corp., **25** 117
Systems Engineering and Manufacturing
    Company, **11** 225
Systems Engineering Labs (SEL), **11** 45;
    13 201
Systems Exploration Inc., **10** 547
Systems Magnetic Co., **IV** 101
Systems Marketing Inc., **12** 78
Systronics, **13** 235
Sytner Group plc, 45 396–98
Syufy Enterprises. *See* Century Theatres,
    Inc.
Szabo, **II** 608

T. and J. Brocklebank Ltd., **23** 160
T&N PLC, **26** 141

T-Fal. *See* Groupe SEB.
T-Netix, Inc., 46 385–88
T.G.I. Friday's, **10** 331; **19** 258; **20** 159;
    21 250; **22** 127; **44** 349
T.J. Falgout, **11** 523
T.J. Maxx, **V** 197–98; **13** 329–30; **14** 62
T. Kobayashi & Co., Ltd., **III** 44
T.L. Smith & Company, **21** 502
T/Maker, **9** 81
T. Mellon & Sons, **II** 315
T. Rowe Price Associates, Inc., 10 89; **11**
    493–96; 34 423–27 (upd.)
T.S. Farley, Limited, **10** 319
T-Shirt Brokerage Services, Inc., **26** 257
T-Tech Industries, **26** 363
T. Wear Company S.r.l., **25** 121
TA Associates Inc., **10** 382; **32** 146; **54**
    361
TA Logistics, **49** 402
TA Media AG, **15** 31
TA Triumph-Adler AG, 48 382–85
TAB Products Co., 17 467–69
Tabacalera, S.A., **V** 414–16; **15** 139; **17**
    470–73 (upd.)
TABCORP Holdings Limited, 44 407–10
Table Supply Stores, **II** 683
Tabulating Machine Company. *See*
    International Business Machines
    Corporation.
TACA. *See* Grupo TACA.
Taco Bell Corp., I 278; **7** 267, **505–07; 9**
    178; **10** 450; **13** 336, 494; **14** 453; **15**
    486; **16** 96–97; **17** 537; **21** 315, **485–88**
    (upd.); 25 178; **37** 349, 351
Taco Cabana, Inc., 23 466–68
Taco John's International Inc., 15
    485–87
Taco Kid, **7** 506
Tadiran Telecommunications Ltd., **II** 47;
    25 266–67
Taehan Cement, **III** 748
Taft Broadcasting Co. *See* Great American
    Broadcasting Inc.
TAG Heuer International SA, 7 554; **25**
    459–61
TAG Pharmaceuticals, Inc., **22** 501; **54** 363
Taguchi Automobile. *See* Seino
    Transportation Company, Ltd.
Tahoe Joe's, Inc., **32** 102 **32** 249
TAI, Ltd., **34** 397
Taiba Corporation, **8** 250
Taiheiyo Bank, **15** 495
Taiko Trading Co. Ltd., **51** 179
Taikoo Dockyard Co., **I** 521; **16** 480
Taikoo Sugar Refinery, **I** 521; **16** 480
Taio Paper Mfg. Co., Ltd. *See* Daio Paper
    Co., Ltd.
Taisho America, **III** 295
Taisho Marine and Fire Insurance Co.,
    Ltd., **III** 209, 295–96
Taisho Pharmaceutical, **I** 676; **II** 361
Taittinger S.A., 27 421; **43 401–05**
Taiwan Aerospace Corp., **11** 279; **24** 88
Taiwan Auto Glass, **III** 715
Taiwan Power Company, **22** 89
Taiwan Semiconductor Manufacturing
    Company Ltd., 18 20; **22** 197; **43** 17;
    47 383–87
Taiway, **III** 596
Taiyo Bussan, **IV** 225; **24** 489
Taiyo Fishery Company, Limited, II
    578–79
Taiyo Kobe Bank, Ltd., II 326, **371–72**
Taiyo Kogyo Corporation, **35** 98, 100

Taiyo Metal Manufacturing Co., **III** 757
Takada & Co., **IV** 151; **24** 358
Takanashi Milk Products Ltd., **37** 197
Takara, **25** 488
Takaro Shuzo, **III** 42
Takashimaya Company, Limited, V
    193–96; 41 114; **47 388–92 (upd.)**
Take-Two Interactive Software, Inc., 46
    389–91
Takeda Chemical Industries, Ltd., I
    704–06; III 760; **46 392–95 (upd.)**
Takeda Riken, **11** 504
Takeuchi Mining Co., **III** 545
Takihyo, **15** 145
Takkyubin, **V** 537
Tako Oy, **IV** 314
Talanx AG, **53** 162
The Talbots, Inc., II 503; **10** 324; **11**
    497–99; 12 280; **31 429–432 (upd.)**
Talcott National Corporation, **11** 260–61
Talegen Holdings Inc., **26** 546
Talent Net Inc., **44** 164
Taliq Corp., **III** 715
Talisman Energy Inc., 9 490–93; 47
    393–98 (upd.)
TALK Corporation, **34** 48
Talk Radio Network, Inc., **23** 294
Talley Industries, Inc., 10 386; **16**
    482–85
Tally Corp., **18** 434
Talmadge Farms, Inc., **20** 105
Taltex Ltd., **51** 379
TAM Ceramics Inc., **III** 681; **44** 118–19
Tama. *See* Hoshino Gakki Co. Ltd.
Tamar Bank, **II** 187
Tamarkin Co., **12** 390
Tambrands Inc., III 40; **8 511–13; 12**
    439; **15** 359–60, 501; **16** 303; **26** 384;
    37 394
Tamco, **12** 390; **19** 380
Tamedia AG, 53 323–26
TAMET, **IV** 25
Tamglass Automotive OY, **22** 436
Tampa Electric Company, **6** 582–83
Tampax Inc. *See* Tambrands Inc.
Oy Tampella Ab, **II** 47; **III** 648; **IV** 276;
    25 266
Tampere Paper Board and Roofing Felt
    Mill, **IV** 314
Tampereen Osake-Pankki, **II** 303
Tampimex Oil, **11** 194
TAMSA. *See* Tubos de Acero de Mexico,
    S.A.
Tamura Kisan Co., **II** 552
Tanaka, **6** 71
Tanaka Kikinzoku Kogyo KK, **IV** 119
Tanaka Matthey KK, **IV** 119
Tandem Computers, Inc., 6 278–80; 10
    499; **11** 18; **14** 318; **26** 93; **29 477–79;**
    50 227
Tandon, **25** 531
Tandy Corporation, II 70, **106–08; 6**
    257–58; **9** 43, 115, 165; **10** 56–57,
    166–67, 236; **12 468–70 (upd.); 13** 174;
    14 117; **16** 84; **17** 353–54; **24** 502; **25**
    531; **26** 18; **34** 198; **49** 183. *See also*
    RadioShack Corporation.
Tandycrafts, Inc., 31 433–37
Tangent Industries, **15** 83; **50** 124
Tangent Systems, **6** 247–48
Tanger Factory Outlet Centers, Inc., 49
    386–89
Tangiers International. *See* Algo Group
    Inc.

Tangram Rehabilitation Network, Inc., **29** 401

Tanimura & Antle, **54** 257

Tanjong Pagar Dock Co., **I** 592

Tanks Oil and Gas, **11** 97; **50** 178

Tanne-Arden, Inc., **27** 291

Tanner-Brice Company, **13** 404

Tantalum Mining Corporation, **29** 81

TAP—Air Portugal Transportes Aéreos Portugueses S.A., 46 396–99 (upd.)

Tapiola Insurance, **IV** 316

Tapis-St. Maclou, **37** 22

Tappan. *See* White Consolidated Industries Inc.

Tara Exploration and Development Ltd., **IV** 165

Tara Foods, **II** 645

Target Marketing and Promotions, Inc., **55** 15

Target Rock Corporation, **35** 134–36

Target Stores, V 35, 43–44; **10** 284, **515–17; 12** 508; **13** 261, 274, 446; **14** 398; **15** 275; **16** 390; **17** 460–61; **18** 108, 137, 283, 286; **20** 155; **22** 328; **27** 315, **451–54 (upd.); 39** 269, 271; **55** 159

Tarkett Sommer AG, 12 464; **25 462–64**

Tarmac plc, III 734, **751–54; 14** 250; **28 447–51 (upd.); 36** 21

TarMacadam (Purnell Hooley's Patent) Syndicate Ltd., **III** 751

Tarragon Oil and Gas Ltd., **24** 522

Tarragon Realty Investors, Inc., 45 399–402

Tarslag, **III** 752

TASC. *See* Analytical Sciences Corp.

Tashima Shoten, **III** 574

Tasman Pulp and Paper Co. Ltd. *See* Fletcher Challenge Ltd.

Tasman U.E.B., **IV** 249

Tasmanian Fibre Containers, **IV** 249

Tastee Freeze, **39** 234

Tasty Baking Company, 14 485–87; 35 412–16 (upd.)

TAT European Airlines, **14** 70, 73; **24** 400

Tata Airlines. *See* Air-India Limited.

Tata Enterprises, **III** 43

Tata Industries, **20** 313; **21** 74

Tata Iron & Steel Co. Ltd., IV 48, 205–07, **217–19; 44 411–15 (upd.)**

Tate & Lyle PLC, II 514, **580–83; 7** 466–67; **13** 102; **26** 120; **42 367–72 (upd.)**

Tatebayashi Flour Milling Co., **II** 554

Tateisi Electric Manufacturing, **II** 75

Tateisi Medical Electronics Manufacturing Co., **II** 75

Tatham Corporation, **21** 169, 171

Tatham/RSCG, **13** 204

Tati SA, 25 465–67

Tatneft. *See* OAO Tatneft.

Tattered Cover Book Store, 43 406–09

Tatung Co., III 482; **13** 387; **23 469–71**

Taurus Exploration, **21** 208

Taurus Programming Services, **10** 196

TaurusHolding GmbH & Co. KG, 46 400–03

Tax Management, Inc., **23** 92

Taylor & Francis Group plc, 44 416–19

Taylor Aircraft Corporation, **44** 307

Taylor Corporation, 36 465–67; 37 108

Taylor Diving and Salvage Co., **III** 499

Taylor-Evans Seed Co., **IV** 409

Taylor Guitars, 48 386–89

Taylor Made Golf Co., 23 270, **472–74; 33** 7

Taylor Material Handling, **13** 499

Taylor Medical, **14** 388

Taylor Nelson Sofres plc, 34 428–30; 37 144

Taylor Petroleum, Inc., **17** 170

Taylor Publishing Company, 12 471–73; 25 254; **36 468–71 (upd.)**

Taylor Rental Corp., **III** 628

Taylor Wines Co., **I** 234; **10** 227

Taylor Woodrow plc, I 590–91; III 739; **13** 206; **38 450–53 (upd.)**

Taylors and Lloyds, **II** 306

Tayto Ltd., **22** 515

Tazo Tea Company, **50** 450

Tazuke & Co., **IV** 151; **24** 358

TBC Corp., **20** 63

TBS. *See* Turner Broadcasting System, Inc.

TBWA Advertising, Inc., 6 47–49; 22 394

TBWA Worldwide, **42** 175; **43** 412

TBWA\Chiat\Day, 43 410–14 (upd.)

TC Advertising. *See* Treasure Chest Advertising, Inc.

TC Debica, **20** 264

TCA. *See* Air Canada.

TCBC. *See* Todays Computers Business Centers.

TCBY Enterprises Inc., 17 474–76

TCF. *See* Tokyo City Finance.

TCF Financial Corporation, 47 399–402

TCF Holdings, Inc., **II** 170–71

TCH Corporation, **12** 477

TCI. *See* Tele-Communications, Inc.

TCI Communications, **29** 39

TCI Inc., **33** 92–93

TCI International Inc., **43** 48

TCM Investments, Inc., **49** 159

TCPL. *See* TransCanada PipeLines Ltd.

TCS Management Group, Inc., **22** 53

TCW Capital, **19** 414–15

TD Bank. *See* The Toronto-Dominion Bank.

TDK Corporation, I 500; **II** 109–11; **IV** 680; **17 477–79 (upd.); 49 390–94 (upd.)**

TDL Group Ltd., 46 404–06

TDL Infomedia Ltd., **47** 347

TDS. *See* Telephone and Data Systems, Inc.

Teaberry Electronics Corp., **III** 569; **20** 361

Teachers Insurance and Annuity Association, III 379–82; 22 268; **35** 75; **47** 331; **49** 413

Teachers Insurance and Annuity Association-College Retirement Equities Fund, 45 403–07 (upd.)

Teachers Service Organization, Inc., **8** 9–10

Team America, **9** 435

Team Penske, **V** 494

Team Rental Group. *See* Budget Group, Inc.

Teams, Inc., **37** 247

Teamsters Central States Pension Fund, **19** 378

Teamsters Union, **13** 19

TearDrop Golf Company, 32 445–48

Tebel Maschinefabrieken, **III** 420

Tebel Pneumatiek, **III** 420

Tech Data Corporation, 10 518–19

Tech/Ops Landauer, Inc. *See* Landauer, Inc.

Tech Pacific International, **18** 180; **39** 201, 203

Tech-Sym Corporation, 18 513–15; 44 420–23 (upd.)

Tech Textiles, USA, **15** 247–48

Techalloy Co., **IV** 228

Techgistics, **49** 403

Technair Packaging Laboratories, **18** 216

TECHNE Corporation, 52 345–48

Technical Ceramics Laboratories, Inc., **13** 141

Technical Coatings Co., **13** 85; **38** 96–97

Technical Materials, Inc., **14** 81

Technical Olympic USA, **46** 180

Technical Publishing, **IV** 605

Technicare, **11** 200

Technicolor Inc., **28** 246

Technicon Instruments Corporation, **III** 56; **11** 333–34; **22** 75

Technifax, **8** 483

Techniques d'Avant-Garde. *See* TAG Heuer International SA.

Technisch Bureau Visser, **16** 421

Technitrol, Inc., 29 459–62

Techno-Success Company, **V** 719

AB Technology, **II** 466

Technology Management Group, Inc., **18** 112

Technology Resources International Ltd., **18** 76

Technology Venture Investors, **11** 490; **14** 263

Technophone Ltd., **17** 354

TechTeam Europe, Ltd., **41** 281

Teck Corporation, 9 282; **27 455–58**

Tecnacril Ltda, **51** 6

Tecnamotor S.p.A., **8** 72, 515

Tecneco, **IV** 422

Tecnifax Corp., **IV** 330

Tecnipublicaciones, **14** 555

Tecnost S.p.a., **34** 319

TECO Energy, Inc., 6 582–84

Tecom Industries, Inc., **18** 513–14

Tecomar S.A., **50** 209

Tecsa, **55** 182

Tecstar, Inc., **30** 436

Tectrix Fitness Equipment, Inc., **49** 108

Tecumseh Products Company, 8 72, **514–16**

Ted Bates, Inc., **I** 33, 623; **10** 69; **16** 71–72; **50** 537

Teddy's Shoe Store. *See* Morse Shoe Inc.

Tedelex, **IV** 91–92

Teekay Shipping Corporation, 25 468–71

Teepak International, **55** 123

Tees and Hartlepool, **31** 367, 369

Tefal. *See* Groupe SEB.

TEFSA, **17** 182

TEIC. *See* B.V. Tabak Export & Import Compagnie.

Teijin Limited, I 511; **V 380–82**

Teikoku Bank, **I** 507; **II** 273, 325–26

Teikoku Hormone, **I** 704

Teikoku Jinken. *See* Teijin Limited.

Teikoku Sekiyu Co. Ltd., **IV** 475

Teikoku Shiki, **IV** 326

Teito Electric Railway, **V** 461

Teito Transport Co. Ltd., **V** 536

Tejas Gas Co., **41** 359

Tejas Snacks LP, **44** 349

Tejon Ranch Company, 35 417–20

Teklogix International, **45** 346, 348
Tekmunc A/S, **17** 288
Teknekron Infoswitch Corporation, **22** 51
Teknika Electronics Corporation, **43** 459
Tekrad, Inc. *See* Tektronix, Inc.
Tekton Corp., **IV** 346
Tektronix, Inc., **II** 101; **8 517–21**; **10** 24;
   11 284–86; **12** 454; **36** 331; **38** 71; **39**
   350, 353; **41** 235
Tel-A-Data Limited, **11** 111
TelAutograph Corporation, **29** 33–34
Telcon. *See* Telegraph Construction and
   Maintenance Company.
Tele-Communications, Inc., **II 160–62**,
   167; **10** 484, 506; **11** 479; **13** 280; **15**
   264–65; **17** 148; **18** 64–66, 211, 213,
   535; **19** 282; **21** 307, 309; **23** 121, 502;
   24 6, 120; **25** 213–14; **26** 33; **28** 241;
   38 120; **42** 114–15; **43** 433; **50** 317
Tele Consulte, **14** 555
Télé Luxembourg, **44** 376
Tele-Response and Support Services, Inc.,
   53 209
Telebook, **25** 19
Telec Centre S.A., **19** 472
TeleCheck Services, **18** 542
TeleCheck Services, Inc., **11** 113
TeleChef, **33** 387, 389
Teleclub, **IV** 590
Teleco Oilfield Services Inc., **6** 578; **22** 68
TeleColumbus, **11** 184
Telecom Australia, **6 341–42**
Telecom Canada. *See* Stentor Canadian
   Network Management.
**Telecom Corporation of New Zealand
   Limited**, **54 355–58**
Telecom Eireann, **7 508–10**. *See also*
   eircom plc.
Telecom Italia S.p.A., **15** 355; **24** 79; **34**
   316, 319; **43 415–19**; **47** 345–46
Telecom New Zealand, **18** 33
Telecom One, Inc., **29** 252
Telecom*USA, **27** 304
Telecommunications of Jamaica Ltd., **25**
   101
Telecomputing Corp., **I** 544
Telecredit, Inc., **6** 25
Telectronic Pacing Systems, **10** 445
Teledyne Inc., **I** 486, **523–25**; **II** 33, 44;
   10 262–63, 365, **520–22 (upd.)**; **11** 265;
   13 387; **17** 109; **18** 369; **29** 400; **35** 136
Teleflora Inc., **28** 1 8–90; **19** 12; **21** 259
Teleflora LLC, **37** 337
Telefonaktiebolaget LM Ericsson, **V
   334–36**; **46 407–11 (upd.)**
Telefónica de España, S.A., **V 337–40**;
   43 422
Telefónica S.A., **46** 172, **412–17 (upd.)**
Telefonos de Mexico S.A. de C.V., **14
   488–90**
Téléfrance, **25** 174
Telefunken Fernseh & Rundfunk GmbH., **I**
   411; **II** 117
telegate AG, **18** 155; **47** 345, 347
Teleglobe Inc., **14** 512
Telegraph Condenser Co., **II** 81
Telegraph Construction and Maintenance
   Company, **25** 98–100
Telegraph Manufacturing Co., **III** 433
Telegraph Works, **III** 433
Telegraphic Service Company, **16** 166
Telekomunikacja Polska SA, **18** 33; **50
   464–68**
Telelistas Editors Ltda., **26** 520

TeleMarketing Corporation of Louisiana, **8**
   311
Telemarketing Investments, Ltd., **8** 311
Telematics International Inc., **18** 154, 156
Télémécanique, **II** 94; **18** 473; **19** 166
Telemundo Group, Inc., **III** 344; **24** 516
Telenet Communications, **18** 32
Telenet Information Services, **47** 37
Telenor, **31** 221
Telenorma, **I** 193
Telenova, **III** 169; **6** 285
Teleos Communications Inc., **26** 277
Telephone and Data Systems, Inc., **9
   494–96**, 527–529; **31** 449
Telephone Company of Ireland, **7** 508
Telephone Exchange Company of
   Indianapolis, **14** 257
Telephone Management Corporation, **8** 310
Telephone Utilities, Inc. *See* Pacific
   Telecom, Inc.
Telephone Utilities of Washington, **6** 325,
   328
Telepictures, **II** 177
TelePizza S.A., **33 387–89**
Teleport Communications Group, **14** 253;
   24 122
Teleprompter Corp., **II** 122; **7** 222; **10** 210;
   18 355
Telerate Systems Inc., **IV** 603, 670; **10**
   276–78; **21** 68; **47** 102–03
Teleregister Corp., **I** 512
Telerent Europe. *See* Granada Group PLC.
TeleRep, **IV** 596
Telesat Cable TV, Inc., **23** 293
Telesis Oil and Gas, **6** 478
Telesistema, **18** 212
Telesistema Mexico. *See* Grupo Televisa.
TeleSite, U.S.A., Inc., **44** 442
Telesphere Network, Inc., **8** 310
Telesystems SLW Inc., **10** 524
Telettra S.p.A., **V** 326; **9** 10; **11** 205
Tele2 AB, **26** 331–33
Teletype Corp., **14** 569
Televimex, S.A., **18** 212
Television de Mexico, S.A., **18** 212
Television Española, S.A., **7 511–12**; **18**
   211
Télévision Française 1, **23 475–77**
Television Sales and Marketing Services
   Ltd., **7** 79–80
Teleway Japan, **7** 118–19; **13** 482
Telex Corporation, **II** 87; **13** 127
TeleZüri AG, **53** 324
Telfin, **V** 339
Telia AB, **54** 406
Telia Mobitel, **11** 19; **26** 332
Telihoras Corporation, **10** 319
Telinfo, **6** 303
Telinq Inc., **10** 19
Telios Pharmaceuticals, Inc., **11** 460; **17**
   288
Tellabs, Inc., **11 500–01**; **40 426–29**
   (upd.); **45** 390; **54** 69
Telmex. *See* Teléfonos de México S.A. de
   C.V.
Telpar, Inc., **14** 377
Telport, **14** 260
Telrad Telecommunications Ltd., **II** 48; **25**
   266–67
Telstra Corporation Limited, **50 469–72**
Telxon Corporation, **10 523–25**
Tembec, Inc., **IV** 296; **19** 226
Temco Electronics and Missile Co., **I** 489
Temenggong of Jahore, **I** 592

Temerlin McClain, **23** 479; **25** 91
TEMIC TELEFUNKEN, **34** 128, 133, 135
Temp Force, **16** 421–22; **43** 308
Temp World, Inc., **6** 10
Temple, Barker & Sloan/Strategic Planning
   Associates, **III** 283
Temple Frosted Foods, **25** 278
Temple Inks Company, **13** 227
Temple-Inland Inc., **IV** 312, **341–43**, 675;
   8 267–69; **19** 268; **31 438–442 (upd.)**
Temple Press Ltd., **IV** 294–95; **19** 225
Templeton, **II** 609
TEMPO Enterprises, **II** 162
Tempo-Team, **16** 420; **43** 307
Tempur-Pedic Inc., **54 359–61**
Tempus Expeditions, **13** 358
Tempus Group plc, **48** 442
TemTech Ltd., **13** 326
10 Sen Kinitsu Markets, **V** 194
Ten Speed Press, **27** 223
Tenacqco Bridge Partnership, **17** 170
Tenby Industries Limited, **21** 350
Tencor Instruments, Inc. *See* KLA-Tencor
   Corporation.
Tenet Healthcare Corporation, **55
   368–71 (upd.)**
TenFold Corporation, **35 421–23**
Tengelmann Group, **II 636–38**; **16**
   249–50; **27 459–62**; **35** 401; **55** 164
Tengelmann Warenhandelsgesellschaft
   OHG, **47** 107
Tengen Inc., **III** 587; **7** 395
Tennant Company, **13 499–501**; **33
   390–93 (upd.)**
Tenneco Inc., **I** 182, **526–28**; **IV** 76, 152,
   283, 371, 499; **6** 531; **10** 379–80, 430,
   526–28 (upd.); **11** 440; **12** 91, 376; **13**
   372–73; **16** 191, 461; **19** 78, 483; **21**
   170; **22** 275, 380; **24** 358; **38** 325, 380;
   40 134; **45** 354; **51** 282–84
Tennessee Book Company, **11** 193
Tennessee Coal, Iron and Railroad Co., **IV**
   573; **7** 550
Tennessee Eastman Corporation, **III** 475; **7**
   161. *See also* Eastman Chemical
   Company.
Tennessee Electric Power Co., **III** 332
Tennessee Gas Pipeline Co., **14** 126
Tennessee Gas Transmission Co., **I** 526; **13**
   496; **14** 125
Tennessee Insurance Company, **11** 193–94
Tennessee Paper Mills Inc. *See* Rock-Tenn
   Company.
Tennessee Restaurant Company, **9** 426; **30**
   208–9
Tennessee River Pulp & Paper Co., **12**
   376–77; **51** 282–83
Tennessee Trifting, **13** 169
Tennessee Valley Authority, **II** 2–3, 121;
   IV 181; **22** 10; **38** 447; **50 473–77**
Tennessee Woolen Mills, Inc., **19** 304
Tenngasco, **I** 527
Teollisuusosuuskunta Metsä-Saimaa, **IV**
   315
TEP. *See* Tucson Electric Power Company.
Tequila Sauza, **31** 91
Tequilera de Los Altos, **31** 92
TeraBeam Networks Inc., **41** 261, 263–64
Teradata Corporation, **6** 267; **30** 339–40
Teradyne, Inc., **11 502–04**
Terex Corporation, **7 513–15**; **8** 116; **40**
   430–34 (upd.)
Teril Stationers Inc., **16** 36
The Terlato Wine Group, **48 390–92**

Terminal Transfer and Storage, Inc., **6** 371
Terminix International, **6** 45–46; **11** 433; **23** 428, 430; **25** 16
Terra Industries, Inc., 13 277, **502–04**
Terra Lycos, Inc., 43 420–25; **46** 416
Terrace Park Dairies, **II** 536
Terracor, **11** 260–61
Terragrafics, **14** 245
Terrain King, **32** 26
Terre Haute Electric, **6** 555
Terre Lune, **25** 91
Territorial Hotel Co., **II** 490
Territory Ahead, Inc., **29** 279
Territory Enterprises Ltd., **IV** 59
Terry Coach Industries, Inc., **III** 484; **22** 206
Terry's of York, **II** 594
Terumo Corporation, 48 393–95
Tesa, S.A., **23** 82
TESC. *See* The European Software Company.
Tesco PLC, II 513, **677–78; 10** 442; **11** 239, 241; **24 473–76 (upd.); 54** 38, 40
Tesoro Bolivia Petroleum Company, **25** 546
Tesoro Petroleum Corporation, 7 **516–19; 45 408–13 (upd.)**
Tesseract Inc., **11** 78; **33** 331
Tessman Seed, Inc., **16** 270–71
The Testor Corporation, 8 455; **51** **367–70**
TETI, **I** 466
Tetley Inc., **I** 215; **14** 18
Tetra Pak International SA, 53 327–29
Tetra Plastics Inc., **V** 374; **8** 393
Tetra Tech, Inc., 29 463–65
Tettemer & Associates. *See* The Keith Companies.
Teutonia National Bank, **IV** 310; **19** 265
Teva Pharmaceutical Industries Ltd., 22 **500–03; 47** 55; **54 362–65 (upd.)**
Tex-Mex Partners L.C., **41** 270
Tex-Star Oil & Gas Corp., **IV** 574; **7** 551
Texaco Canada Inc., **25** 232
Texaco Inc., I 21, 360; **II** 31, 313, 448; **III** 760; **IV** 386, 403, 418, 425, 429, 439, 461, 464, 466, 472–73, 479–80, 484, 488, 490, 510–11, 530–31, 536–39, 545, **551–53,** 560, 565–66, 570, 575; **7** 172, 280, 483; **9** 232; **10** 190; **12** 20; **13** 448; **14 491–94 (upd.); 17** 412; **18** 488; **41** 359, **391–96 (upd.) 19** 73, 75, 176; **24** 521; **27** 481; **28** 47; **47** 72, 436; **50** 353. *See also* ChevronTexaco Corporation.
Texada Mines, Ltd., **IV** 123
Texas Air Corporation, I 97, 100, 103, 118, **123–24,** 127, 130; **6** 82, 129; **12** 489; **21** 142–43; **35** 427
Texas Almanac, **10** 3
Texas Bus Lines, **24** 118
Texas Butadiene and Chemical Corp., **IV** 456
Texas Co., **III** 497; **IV** 386, 400, 464, 536, 551–52; **7** 352
Texas Commerce Bankshares, **II** 252
Texas Eastern Corp., **6** 487; **11** 97, 354; **14** 126; **50** 179
Texas Eastern Transmission Company, **11** 28
Texas Eastman, **III** 475; **7** 161
Texas Electric Service Company, **V** 724
Texas Gas Resources Corporation, **IV** 395; **22** 166

Texas Gypsum, **IV** 341
Texas Homecare, **21** 335
Texas Industries, Inc., 8 522–24; **13** 142–43
Texas Instruments Incorporated, I 315, 482, 523, 620; **II** 64, **112–15; III** 120, 124–25, 142, 499; **IV** 130, 365, 681; **6** 216, 221–22, 237, 241, 257, 259; **7** 531; **8** 157; **9** 43, 116, 310; **10** 22, 87, 307; **11** 61, 308, 490, 494, **505–08 (upd.); 12** 135, 238; **14** 42–43; **16** 4, 333; **17** 192; **18** 18, 436; **21** 123; **23** 181, 210; **25** 81, 96, 531; **38** 375; **43** 15; **46 418–23 (upd.)**
Texas International Airlines, **I** 117, 123; **II** 408; **IV** 413; **21** 142
Texas Life Insurance Co., **III** 293
Texas Metal Fabricating Company, **7** 540
Texas-New Mexico Utilities Company, **6** 580
Texas Oil & Gas Corp., **IV** 499, 572, 574; **7** 549, 551
Texas Overseas Petroleum Co., **IV** 552
Texas Pacific Coal and Oil Co., **I** 285–86
Texas Pacific Group Inc., 22 80; **23** 163, 166; **30** 171; **34** 231; **36 472–74**
Texas Pacific Oil Co., **IV** 550
Texas Pipe Line Co., **IV** 552
Texas Power & Light Company, **V** 724
Texas Public Utilities, **II** 660
Texas Rangers Baseball, 51 371–74
Texas Super Duper Markets, Inc., **7** 372
Texas Timberjack, Inc., **51** 279–81
Texas Trust Savings Bank, **8** 88
Texas United Insurance Co., **III** 214
Texas Utilities Company, V 724–25; **12** 99; **25 472–74 (upd.); 35** 479
Texasgulf Inc., **IV** 546–47; **13** 557; **18** 433
Texboard, **IV** 296; **19** 226
Texize, **I** 325, 371
Texkan Oil Co., **IV** 566
Texstar Petroleum Company, **7** 516
Texstyrene Corp., **IV** 331
Textile Diffusion, **25** 466
Textile Paper Tube Company, Ltd., **8** 475
Textile Rubber and Chemical Company, **15** 490
Textron Inc., I 186, **529–30; II** 420; **III** 66, 628; **8** 93, 157, 315, 545; **9** 497, 499; **11** 261; **12** 251, 382–83, 400–01; **13** 63–64; **17** 53; **21** 175; **22** 32; **27** 100; **34 431–34 (upd.); 35** 350–51; **46** 65
Textron Lycoming Turbine Engine, 9 **497–99**
Texwood Industries, Inc., **20** 363
TF-I, **I** 563
TFC. *See* Times Fiber Communications, Inc.
TFM. *See* Grupo Transportación Ferroviaria Mexicana, S.A. de C.V.
TFN Group Communications, Inc., **8** 311
TF1 **24** 79. *See also* Télévision Française 1
TFP, Inc., **44** 358–59
TG Credit Service Co. Ltd., **55** 375
TGEL&PCo. *See* Tucson Gas, Electric Light & Power Company.
Th. Pilter, **III** 417
TH:s Group, **10** 113; **50** 43
Thai Airways International Ltd., I 119; **II** 442; **6 122–24**
Thai Airways International Public **Company Limited, 27 463–66 (upd.)**
Thai Aluminium Co. Ltd., **IV** 155

Thai Nylon Co. Ltd., **53** 344
Thai Union International Inc., **24** 116
Thalassa International, **10** 14; **27** 11
Thales S.A., 42 373–76; 47 9; **49** 165, 167
Thalhimer Brothers, **V** 31
Thames Board Ltd., **IV** 318
Thames Television Ltd., **I** 532
Thames Trains, **28** 157
Thames Water plc, 11 509–11; 22 89
Thameslink, **28** 157
Tharsis Co., **IV** 189–90
Thatcher Glass, **I** 610
THAW. *See* Recreational Equipment, Inc.
Thayer Laboratories, **III** 55
Theatrical Syndicate, **24** 437
Thelem SA, **54** 267
Theo H. Davies & Co., **I** 470; **20** 311
Theo Hamm Brewing Co., **I** 260
Théraplix, **I** 388
Therm-o-Disc, **II** 19
Therm-X Company, **8** 178
Thermacote Welco Company, **6** 146
Thermadyne Holding Corporation, 19 **440–43**
Thermal Dynamics, **19** 441
Thermal Energies, Inc., **21** 514
Thermal Power Company, **11** 270
Thermal Snowboards, Inc., **22** 462
Thermal Transfer Ltd., **13** 485
ThermaStor Technologies, Ltd., **44** 366
Thermo BioAnalysis Corp., 25 475–78
Thermo Electron Corporation, 7 520–22; 11 512–13; **13** 421; **24** 477; **25** 475–76; **52** 389
Thermo Fibertek, Inc., 24 477–79
Thermo Instrument Systems Inc., 11 **512–14; 25** 475–77
Thermo King Corporation, 13 505–07
Thermodynamics Corp., **III** 645
Thermoforming USA, **16** 339
Thermogas Co., **IV** 458–59; **35** 175
Thermolase Corporation, **22** 410
Thermoplast und Apparatebau GmbH, **IV** 198
Thermos Company, 16 486–88
TheStreet.com, **34** 125
THHK Womenswear Limited, **53** 333
ThiemeMeulenhoff BV, **53** 273
Thies Companies, **13** 270
Thiess, **III** 687
Thiess Dampier Mitsui, **IV** 47
Things Remembered, **13** 165–66
Think Entertainment, **II** 161
Think Technologies, **10** 508
Thiokol Corporation, I 370; **8** 472; **9** 358–59, **500–02 (upd.); 12** 68; **22** **504–07 (upd.)**
Third Coast Capital, Inc., **51** 109
Third National Bank. *See* Fifth Third Bancorp.
Third National Bank of Dayton, **9** 475
Third National Bank of New York, **II** 253
Third Wave Publishing Corp. *See* Acer Inc.
ThirdAge.com, **49** 290
Thirteen/WNET. *See* Educational Broadcasting Corporation.
Thistle Group, **9** 365
Thistle Hotels PLC, 54 366–69
Thom McAn, **V** 136–37; **11** 349
Thomas & Betts Corporation, II 8; **11** **515–17; 14** 27; **54 370–74 (upd.)**
Thomas and Hochwalt, **I** 365
Thomas & Howard Co., **II** 682; **18** 8
Thomas and Judith Pyle, **13** 433

Thomas Barlow & Sons Ltd., **I** 288, 422;
IV 22
Thomas Bros. Maps, **28** 380
Thomas Cook Group Ltd., **17** 325
Thomas Cook Travel Inc., **6** 84; **9**
503–05; **27** 133; **33** 394–96 (upd.); **42**
282
Thomas De La Rue and Company, Ltd., **44**
357–58
Thomas Firth & Sons, **I** 573
Thomas H. Lee Co., **11** 156, 450; **14**
230–31; **15** 309; **19** 371, 373; **24**
480–83; **25** 67; **28** 134; **30** 219; **32** 362;
52 95
Thomas Industries Inc., **29** 466–69
Thomas J. Lipton Company, **II** 609, 657;
11 450; **14** 495–97; **16** 90; **32** 474
Thomas Jefferson Life Insurance Co., **III**
397
Thomas Kinkade Galleries. *See* Media Arts
Group, Inc.
Thomas Linnell & Co. Ltd., **II** 628
Thomas Nationwide Transport. *See* TNT.
Thomas Nationwide Transport Limited. *See*
TNT Post Group N.V.
Thomas Nelson Inc., **8** 526; **14** 498–99;
24 548; **38** 454–57 (upd.)
Thomas Publishing Company, **26** 482–85
Thomas Tilling plc, **I** 429
Thomas Y. Crowell, **IV** 605
Thomaston Mills, Inc., **27** 467–70
Thomasville Furniture Industries, Inc.,
III 423; **12** 474–76; **22** 48; **28** 406; **31**
248; **39** 170, 174
Thompson and Formby, **16** 44
Thompson Aircraft Tire Corp., **14** 42
Thompson-Hayward Chemical Co., **13** 397
Thompson Medical Company. *See* Slim-
Fast Nutritional Foods International Inc.
Thompson Nutritional Products, **37** 286
Thompson PBE Inc., **24** 160–61
Thompson Products Co., **I** 539
Thompson-Ramo-Woolridge, **I** 539
Thompson-Werke, **III** 32
Thomson BankWatch Inc., **19** 34
Thomson-Bennett, **III** 554
Thomson-Brandt, **I** 411; **II** 13, 116–17; **9**
9
The Thomson Corporation, **IV** 651, 686;
7 390; **8** 525–28; **10** 407; **12** 361, 562;
17 255; **22** 441; **34** 435–40 (upd.); **44**
155
Thomson-CSF, **II** 116–17; **III** 556. *See
also* Thales S.A.
Thomson-Houston Electric Co., **II** 27, 116,
330; **12** 193
Thomson International, **37** 143
Thomson-Jenson Energy Limited, **13** 558
Thomson-Lucas, **III** 556
THOMSON multimedia S.A., **18** 126; **36**
384; **42** 377–80 (upd.)
Thomson-Ramo-Woolridge. *See* TRW Inc.
Thomson S.A., **I** 411; **II** 31, 116–17; **7** 9;
13 402; **50** 300. *See also* THOMSON
multimedia S.A.
Thomson T-Line, **II** 142
Thomson Travel Group, **27** 27
Thonet Industries Inc., **14** 435–36
Thor Industries, Inc., **39** 391–94
Thorn Apple Valley, Inc., **7** 523–25; **12**
125; **22** 508–11 (upd.); **23** 203
Thorn EMI plc, **I** 52, 411, 531–32; **II**
117, 119; **III** 480; **19** 390; **22** 27,
192–94; **24** 87, 484–85; **26** 151; **40** 105

Thorn plc, 24 484–87
Thorncraft Inc., **25** 379
Thorndike, Doran, Paine and Lewis, Inc.,
14 530
Thornton, **III** 547
Thornton & Co., **II** 283
Thornton Stores, **14** 235
Thorntons plc, 46 424–26
Thoroughgood, **II** 658
Thorpe Park, **55** 378
Thorsen Realtors, **21** 96
Thos. & Wm. Molson & Company. *See*
The Molson Companies Limited.
Thousand Trails, Inc., **13** 494; **33** 397–99
Thousands Springs Power Company, **12**
265
THQ, Inc., **39** 395–97; **52** 191
Threads for Life, **49** 244
Threadz, **25** 300
Three-Diamond Company. *See* Mitsubishi
Shokai.
The 3DO Company, **10** 286; **43** 426–30
3 Guys, **II** 678, **V** 35
3-in-One Oil Co., **I** 622
3 Maj, **25** 469
Three Ring Asia Pacific Beer Co., Ltd., **49**
418
Three Rivers Pulp and Paper Company, **17**
281
Three Score, **23** 100
3 Suisses International, **12** 281
3Com Corporation, **III** 143; **6** 238, 269;
10 237; **11** 518–21; **20** 8, 33; **26** 276;
34 441–45 (upd.); **36** 122, 300, 357; **49**
184. *See also* Palm, Inc.
3D Planet SpA, **41** 409
3dfx Interactive Inc., **54** 269–71
3M. *See* Minnesota Mining &
Manufacturing Co.
3S Systems Support Services Ltd., **6** 310
360 Youth Inc., **55** 15
360networks inc., **46** 268
Threlfall Breweries, **I** 294
Threshold Entertainment, **25** 270
Thrif D Discount Center, **V** 174
Thrift Drug, **V** 92
Thrift Mart, **16** 65
ThriftiCheck Service Corporation, **7** 145
Thriftimart Inc., **12** 153; **16** 452
Thriftway Food Drug, **21** 530
Thriftway Foods, **II** 624
Thrifty Corporation, **25** 413, 415–16; **55**
58
Thrifty PayLess, Inc., **V** 682, 684; **12**
477–79; **18** 286; **19** 357; **25** 297
Thrifty Rent-A-Car, **6** 349; **24** 10; **44** 355.
See also Dollar Thrifty Automotive
Group, Inc.
Throwing Corporation of America, **12** 501
Thrustmaster S.A., **41** 190
Thummel Schutze & Partner, **28** 141
Thunder Bay Press, **34** 3–5
Thüringer Schokoladewerk GmbH, **53** 315
Thuringia Insurance Co., **III** 299
Thurmond Chemicals, Inc., **27** 291
Thurston Motor Lines Inc., **12** 310
Thy-Marcinelle, **IV** 52
Thyssen AG, **II** 279; **III** 566; **IV** 195,
221–23, 228; **8** 75–76; **14** 169, 328
Thyssen Krupp AG, **28** 104, 452–60
(upd.); **42** 417
Thyssen-Krupp Stahl AG, **26** 83
Thyssengas, **38** 406–07
TI. *See* Texas Instruments.

TI Corporation, **10** 44
TI Group plc, **17** 480–83
TIAA-CREF. *See* Teachers Insurance and
Annuity Association-College Retirement
Equities Fund.
Tianjin Agricultural Industry and
Commerce Corp., **II** 577
Tianjin Automobile Industry Group, **21** 164
Tianjin Bohai Brewing Company, **21** 230;
50 202
Tibbals Floring Co., **III** 611
Tibbett & Britten Group plc, **32** 449–52
Tiber Construction Company, **16** 286
Tichenor Media System Inc., **35** 220
Ticino Societa d'Assicurazioni Sulla Vita,
III 197
Ticketmaster Corp., **13** 508–10; **25** 214;
36 423–24
Ticketmaster Group, Inc., **37** 381–84
(upd.); **47** 419, 421
Ticketron, **13** 508–09; **24** 438; **37** 381–82
Tichnor & Fields, **10** 356
Tickometer Co., **III** 157
Ticor Title Insurance Co., **10** 45
Tidel Systems, **II** 661; **32** 416
Tidewater Inc., **11** 522–24; **37** 385–88
(upd.)
Tidewater Oil Co., **IV** 434, 460, 489, 522
Tidewater Utilities, Inc., **45** 275, 277
Tidi Wholesale, **13** 150
Tidy House Products Co., **II** 556
TIE. *See* Transport International Express.
Tiel Utrecht Fire Insurance Co., **III**
309–10
Tien Wah Press (Pte.) Ltd., **IV** 600
Le Tierce S.A., **II** 141
Tierco Group, Inc., **27** 382
Tierney & Partners, **23** 480
Tiffany & Co., **III** 16; **12** 312; **14**
500–03; **15** 95; **19** 27; **26** 145; **27** 329;
41 256
TIG Holdings, Inc., **26** 486–88
Tiger Accessories, **18** 88
Tiger International, Inc., **17** 505; **18** 178;
42 141
Tiger Management Associates, **13** 158, 256
Tiger Oats, **I** 424
TigerDirect, Inc., **52** 342–44
Tigon Corporation, **V** 265–68; **41** 288
Tilcon, **I** 429
Tilden Interrent, **10** 419
Tile & Coal Company, **14** 248
Tilgate Pallets, **I** 592
Tillie Lewis Foods Inc., **I** 513–14
Tillinghast, Nelson & Warren Inc., **32** 459
Tillotson Corp., **14** 64; **15** 488–90
Tim-Bar Corp., **IV** 312; **19** 267
Tim Horton's Restaurants, **23** 507; **47** 443.
See also TDL Group Ltd.
Timber Lodge Steakhouse, Inc., **37** 351–52
Timber Realization Co., **IV** 305
The Timberland Company, **11** 349; **13**
511–14; **17** 245; **19** 112; **22** 173; **25**
206; **54** 375–79 (upd.)
Timberline Software Corporation, **15**
491–93
TIMCO. *See* Triad International
Maintenance Corp.
Time Distribution Services, **13** 179
Time Electronics, **19** 311
Time Industries, **IV** 294; **19** 225; **26** 445
Time-Life Books, Inc. **44** 447, 449. *See
also* Time Warner Inc.
Time Life Music, **44** 242

Time-O-Stat Controls Corp., **II** 41; **12** 247; **50** 232
Time Saver Stores, Inc., **12** 112; **17** 170
Time-Sharing Information, **10** 357
Time Warner Inc., **II** 155, 161, 168, 175–177, 252, 452; **III** 245; **IV** 341–42, 636, **673–76**; **6** 293; **7** 63, 222–24, 396, **526–30 (upd.)**; **8** 267–68, 527; **9** 119, 469, 472; **10** 168, 286, 484, 488, 491; **12** 531; **13** 105–06, 399; **14** 260; **15** 51, 54; **16** 146, 223; **17** 148, 442–44; **18** 66, 535; **19** 6, 336; **22** 52, 194, 522; **23** 31, 33, 257, 274, 276, 393; **24** 321–22; **25** 141, 498–99; **26** 33, 151, 441; **27** 121, 429–30; **43** 55; **54** 334, 336–37
Timely Brands, **I** 259
Timeplex, **III** 166; **6** 283; **9** 32
Times Fiber Communications, Inc., **40** 35–36
Times Media Ltd., **IV** 22
The Times Mirror Company, **I** 90; **IV** 583, 630, **677–78**; **14** 97; **17** 484–86 **(upd.)**; **21** 404; **22** 162, 443; **26** 446; **35** 419
Times Newspapers, **8** 527
Times-Picayune Publishing Co., **IV** 583
Times Publishing Group, **54** 116, 118
TIMET. *See* Titanium Metals Corporation.
Timex Corporation, **25** 479–82 **(upd.)**
Timex Enterprises Inc., **III** 455; **7** **531–33**; **10** 152; **12** 317; **21** 123; **25** 22
The Timken Company, **III** 596; **7** 447; **8** **529–31**; **15** 225; **42** 381–85 **(upd.)**; **55** 221–22
Timothy Whites, **24** 74
Timpte Industries, **II** 488
Tioga Gas Plant Inc., **55** 20
Tioxide Group plc, **III** 680; **44** 117, 119
Tip Corp., **I** 278
Tip Top Drugstores plc, **24** 269
Tip Top Tailors, **29** 162
TIPC Network. *See* Gateway 2000.
Tiphook PLC, **13** 530
Tipton Centers Inc., **V** 50; **19** 123; **49** 112
Tiroler Hauptbank, **II** 270
Tiscali SpA, **48 396–99**
TISCO. *See* Tata Iron & Steel Company Ltd.
Tishman Realty and Construction, **III** 248
Tishman Speyer Properties, L.P., **47** **403–06**
Tissue Papers Ltd., **IV** 260
Tissue Technologies, Inc., **22** 409
Titan Acquisition Corporation, **51** 34, 36
The Titan Corporation, **36 475–78**; **45** 68, 70
Titan Manufacturing Company, **19** 359
Titan Sports, Inc., **52** 192
Titanium Metals Corporation, **10** 434; **21** **489–92**
Titanium Technology Corporation, **13** 140
Titianium Enterprises, **IV** 345
TITISA, **9** 109
Title Guarantee & Trust Co., **II** 230
Titmus Optical Inc., **III** 446
Titmuss Sainer Dechert. *See* Dechert.
Tivoli Audio, **48** 85
Tivoli Systems, Inc., **14** 392
TJ International, Inc., **19 444–47**
The TJX Companies, Inc., **V 197–98**; **13** 548; **14** 426; **19 448–50 (upd.)**; **29** 106
TKD Electronics Corp., **II** 109
TKM Foods, **II** 513
TKR Cable Co., **15** 264

TKT. *See* Transkaryotic Therapies Inc.
TLC Associates, **11** 261
TLC Beatrice International Holdings, Inc., **22 512–15**
TLC Gift Company, **26** 375
TLC Group, **II** 468
TLO, **25** 82
TMB Industries, **24** 144
TMC Industries Ltd., **22** 352
TML Information Services Inc., **9** 95
TMP Worldwide Inc., **30 458–60**
TMS, Inc., **7** 358
TMS Marketing, **26** 440
TMS Systems, Inc., **10** 18
TMT. *See* Trailer Marine Transport.
TMW Capital Inc., **48** 286
TN Technologies Inc., **23** 479
TNT Crust, Inc., **23** 203
TNT Freightways Corporation, **IV** 651; **14 504–06**
TNT Grading Inc., **50** 348
TNT Limited, **V 523–25**; **6** 346
TNT Post Group N.V., **27 471–76 (upd.)**; **30** 393, 461–63 **(upd.)**
Toa Airlines, **I** 106; **6** 427
Toa Fire & Marine Reinsurance Co., **III** 385
Toa Kyoseki Co. Ltd., **IV** 476
Toa Medical Electronics Ltd., **22** 75
Toa Nenryo Kogyo, **IV** 432
Toa Oil Co. Ltd., **IV** 476, 543
Toa Tanker Co. Ltd., **IV** 555
Toasted Corn Flake Co., **II** 523; **13** 291; **50** 292
Toastmaster, **17** 215; **22** 353
Tobacco Group PLC, **30** 231
Tobacco Products Corporation, **18** 416
Tobata Imaon Co., **I** 183
Tobias, **16** 239
Tobler Co., **II** 520–21
Tobu Railway Co Ltd, **6 430–32**
TOC Retail Inc., **17** 170
Tocom, Inc., **10** 320
Today's Man, Inc., **20 484–87**; **21** 311
Todays Computers Business Centers, **6** 243–44
Todays Temporary, **6** 140
The Todd-AO Corporation, **33 400–04**. *See also* Liberty Livewire Corporation.
Todd Shipyards Corporation, **IV** 121; **7** 138; **14 507–09**
Todhunter International, Inc., **27 477–79**
Todito.com, S.A. de C.V., **39** 194, 196
Todorovich Agency, **III** 204
Toei Co. Ltd., **9** 29–30; **28** 462
Tofaş, **I** 479–80; **54** 196–97
Toggenburger Bank, **II** 378
Togo's Eatery, **29** 19
Toho Co., Ltd., **I** 363; **IV** 403; **24** 327; **28** 461–63
Tohoku Alps, **II** 5
Tohoku Pulp Co., **IV** 297
Tohokushinsha Film Corporation, **18** 429
Tohuku Electric Power Company, Inc., **V** 724, 732
Tojo Railway Company, **6** 430
Tokai Aircraft Co., Ltd., **III** 415
The Tokai Bank, Limited, **II** 373–74; **15** **494–96 (upd.)**
Tokai Kogyo Co. Ltd., **I** 615; **48** 42
Tokai Paper Industries, **IV** 679
Tokheim Corporation, **21 493–95**
Tokio Marine and Fire Insurance Co., Ltd., **II** 323; **III** 248, 289, 295, **383–86**

Tokos Medical Corporation, **17** 306, 308–09
Tokushima Ham Co., **II** 550
Tokushima Meat Processing Factory, **II** 550
Tokushu Seiko, Ltd., **IV** 63
Tokuyama Soda, **I** 509
Tokuyama Teppan Kabushikigaisha, **IV** 159
Tokyo Broadcasting System, **7** 249; **9** 29; **16** 167
Tokyo Car Manufacturing Co., **I** 105
Tokyo City Finance, **36** 419–20
Tokyo Confectionery Co., **II** 538
Tokyo Corporation, **V** 199
Tokyo Dairy Industry, **II** 538
Tokyo Denki Kogaku Kogyo, **II** 109
Tokyo Dento Company, **6** 430
Tokyo Disneyland, **IV** 715; **6** 123, 176
Tokyo Electric Company, Ltd., **I** 533; **12** 483
Tokyo Electric Express Railway Co., **IV** 728
Tokyo Electric Light Co., **IV** 153
Tokyo Electric Power Company, **IV** 167, 518; **V 729–33**
Tokyo Electronic Corp., **11** 232
Tokyo Express Highway Co., Ltd., **IV** 713–14
Tokyo Express Railway Company, **V** 510, 526
Tokyo Fire Insurance Co. Ltd., **III** 405–06, 408
Tokyo Food Products, **I** 507
Tokyo Fuhansen Co., **I** 502, 506
Tokyo Gas and Electric Industrial Company, **9** 293
Tokyo Gas Co., Ltd., **IV** 518; **V 734–36**; **55 372–75 (upd.)**
Tokyo Ishikawajima Shipbuilding and Engineering Company, **III** 532; **9** 293
Tokyo Maritime Insurance Co., **III** 288
Tokyo Motors. *See* Isuzu Motors, Ltd.
Tokyo Sanyo Electric, **II** 91–92
Tokyo Shibaura Electric Company, Ltd., **I** 507, 533; **12** 483
Tokyo Steel Works Co., Ltd., **IV** 63
Tokyo Stock Exchange, **34** 254
Tokyo Tanker Co., Ltd., **IV** 479
Tokyo Telecommunications Engineering Corp. *See* Tokyo Tsushin Kogyo K.K.
Tokyo Trust & Banking Co., **II** 328
Tokyo Tsushin Kogyo K.K., **II** 101, 103
Tokyo Yokohama Electric Railways Co., Ltd., **V** 199
Tokyu Corporation, **IV** 728; **V** 199, **526–28**; **47 407–10 (upd.)**
Tokyu Department Store Co., Ltd., **V** **199–202**; **32 453–57 (upd.)**
Toledo Edison Company. *See* Centerior Energy Corporation.
Toledo Milk Processing, Inc., **15** 449
Toledo Scale Corp., **9** 441; **30** 327
Toledo Seed & Oil Co., **I** 419
Toll Brothers Inc., **15 497–99**
Tollgrade Communications, Inc., **44** **424–27**
Tom Bowling Lamp Works, **III** 554
Tom Brown, Inc., **37 389–91**
Tom Doherty Associates Inc., **25 483–86**
Tom Huston Peanut Co., **II** 502; **10** 323
Tom Piper Ltd., **I** 437
Tom Snyder Productions, **29** 470, 472
Tom Thumb, **40** 365–66

Tom Thumb-Page, **16** 64
Tom's of Maine, Inc., 45 414–16
Tomakomai Paper Co., Ltd., **IV** 321
Toman Corporation, **19** 390
Tombstone Pizza Corporation, 13 515–17
Tomcan Investments Inc., **53** 333
Tomei Fire and Marine Insurance Co., **III** 384–85
Tomen Corporation, IV 224–25; **19** 256; **24 488–91 (upd.)**
Tomen Transportgerate, **III** 638
Tomkins-Johnson Company, 16 8
Tomkins plc, 11 525–27; 28 382, 384; **30** 424, 426; **44 428–31 (upd.)**
Tomlee Tool Company, **7** 535; **26** 493
Tommy Armour Golf Co., **32** 446–47
Tommy Hilfiger Corporation, 16 61; **20 488–90; 25** 258; **53 330–33 (upd.)**
Tomoe Trading Co., **III** 595
Tonami Transportation Company, **6** 346
Tone Brothers, Inc., 21 496–98
Tone Coca-Cola Bottling Company, Ltd., **14** 288; **47** 206
Tonen Corporation, IV 554–56; 16 489–92 (upd.)
TonenGeneral Sekiyu K.K., 54 380–86 (upd.)
Tong Yang Group, **III** 304
Toni Co., **III** 28; **9** 413
Tonka Corporation, 12 169; **14** 266; **16** 267; **25** 380, **487–89; 43** 229, 232
Tonkin, Inc., **19** 114
Tony Lama Company Inc., **19** 233
Tony Roma's, A Place for Ribs Inc., **40** 340–41
Tony Stone Images, **31** 216–17
Toohey, **10** 170
Toolex International N.V., 26 489–91
Tootal Group, **V** 356–57
Tootsie Roll Industries Inc., 12 480–82; 15 323
Top End Wheelchair Sports, **11** 202
Top Green International, **17** 475
Top Man, **V** 21
Top Shop, **V** 21
Top Tool Company, Inc., **25** 75
Top Value Stamp Co., **II** 644–45; **6** 364; **22** 126
Topco Associates, **17** 78
Topkapi, **17** 101–03
Toppan Printing Co., Ltd., IV 598–99, **679–81**
Topps Company, Inc., 13 518–20; 19 386; **34 446–49 (upd.)**
Topps Markets, **16** 314
Tops Appliance City, Inc., 17 487–89
TopTip, **48** 116
Topy Industries, Limited, **8** 506–07
Tor Books. *See* Tom Doherty Associates Inc.
Toray Industries, Inc., V 380, **383; 17** 287; **51 375–79 (upd.)**
Torbensen Gear & Axle Co., **I** 154
Torchmark Corporation, III 194; **9 506–08; 10** 66; **11** 17; **22** 540–43; **33 405–08 (upd.)**
Torfeaco Industries Limited, **19** 304
Torise Ham Co., **II** 550
Tornator Osakeyhtiö, **IV** 275–76
Toro Assicurazioni, **III** 347
The Toro Company, III 600; **7 534–36; 26 492–95 (upd.)**
Toromont Industries, Ltd., 21 499–501

Toronto and Scarborough Electric Railway, **9** 461
The Toronto-Dominion Bank, II 319, **375–77,** 456; **16** 13–14; **17** 324; **18** 551–53; **21** 447; **43** 7; **49 395–99 (upd.)**
Toronto Electric Light Company, **9** 461
Toronto Sun Publishing Company. *See* Sun Media.
Torpshammars, **IV** 338
Torrey Canyon Oil, **IV** 569; **24** 519
The Torrington Company, III 526, 589–90; **13 521–24**
Torrington National Bank & Trust Co., **13** 467
Torstar Corporation, IV 672; **7 488–89; 19** 405; **29 470–73; 52** 155. *See also* Harlequin Enterprises Limited.
Tosa Electric Railway Co., **II** 458
Toscany Co., **13** 42
Tosco Corporation, 7 537–39; 12 240; **20** 138; **24** 522; **36** 359; **40** 358
Toshiba Corporation, I 221, 507–08, **533–35; II** 5, 56, 59, 62, 68, 73, 99, 102, 118, 122, 326, 440; **III** 298, 461, 533, 604; **6** 101, 231, 244, 287; **7** 529; **9** 7, 181; **10** 518–19; **11** 46, 328; **12** 454, **483–86 (upd.),** 546; **13** 324, 399, 482; **14** 117, 446; **16** 5, 167; **17** 533; **18** 18, 260; **21** 390; **22** 193, 373; **23** 471; **40 435–40 (upd.); 43** 15;
Toshiba Corporation, **47** 153–54
Toshin Kaihatsu Ltd., **V** 195; **47** 390
Toshin Paper Co., Ltd., **IV** 285
Tostem. *See* Toyo Sash Co., Ltd.
Total Audio Visual Services, **24** 95
Total Beverage Corporation, **16** 159, 161
Total Compagnie Française des Pétroles S.A., I 303; **II** 259; **III** 673; **IV** 363–64, 423–25, 466, 486, 498, 504, 515, 525, 544–47, **557–61; V** 628; **7** 481–84; **13** 557; **21** 203
Total Entertainment Restaurant Corporation, 46 427–29
Total Exploration S.A., **11** 537
Total Fina Elf S.A., 47 342, 365, 368; **50 478–86 (upd.)**
Total Global Sourcing, Inc., **10** 498
Total Home Entertainment (THE), **39** 240, 242
Total Petroleum Corporation, **21** 500
TOTAL S.A., 24 492–97 (upd.), 522; **25** 104; **26** 369
Total System Services, Inc., 12 465–66; 18 168, 170, **516–18; 52** 336
Totem Resources Corporation, 9 509–11
Totino's Finer Foods, **II** 556; **13** 516; **26** 436
Toto Bank, **II** 326
TOTO LTD., III 755–56; 28 464–66 (upd.)
Totsu Co., **I** 493; **24** 325
Touch America Inc., **37** 127; **44** 288
Touch-It Corp., **22** 413
Touche Remnant Holdings Ltd., **II** 356
Touche Ross. *See* Deloitte Touche Tohmatsu International.
Touchstone Films, **II** 172–74; **6** 174–76; **30** 487
Le Touquet's, SA, **48** 197
Tour d'Argent, **II** 518
Tourang Limited, **7** 253
Touristik Union International GmbH. and Company K.G., II 163–65; 46 460

Touron y Cia, **III** 419
Touropa, **II** 163–64; **44** 432
Toval Japon, **IV** 680
Towa Nenryo Kogyo Co. Ltd., **IV** 554–55
Towa Optical Manufacturing Company, **41** 261–63
Tower Air, Inc., 28 467–69
Tower Automotive, Inc., 24 498–500
Tower Records, **9** 361; **10** 335; **11** 558; **30** 224. *See also* MTS Inc.
Towers, **II** 649
Towers Perrin, 32 458–60
Towle Manufacturing Co., **14** 482–83; **18** 69
Town & City, **IV** 696
Town & Country Corporation, 7 372; **16** 546; **19 451–53; 25** 254
Town Investments, **IV** 711
Town Sports International, Inc., 46 430–33
Townsend Hook, **IV** 296, 650, 652; **19** 226
Toxicol Laboratories, Ltd., **21** 424
Toy Biz, Inc., 10 402; **18 519–21; 54** 58
Toy Liquidators, **13 541–43; 50** 99
Toy Park, **16** 390
Toyad Corp., **7** 296
Toymax International, Inc., 29 474–76; 52 193
Toyo Bearing Manufacturing, **III** 595
Toyo Cotton Co., **IV** 224–25
Toyo Ink Manufacturing, **26** 213
Toyo Kogyo, **I** 167; **II** 361; **11** 139
Toyo Marine and Fire, **III** 385
Toyo Menka Kaisha Ltd. *See* Tomen Corporation.
Toyo Microsystems Corporation, **11** 464
Toyo Oil Co., **IV** 403
Toyo Pulp Co., **IV** 322
Toyo Rayon. *See* Toray Industries, Inc.
Toyo Sash Co., Ltd., III 757–58
Toyo Seikan Kaisha Ltd., I 615–16
Toyo Soda, **II** 301
Toyo Tire & Rubber Co., **V** 255–56; **9** 248
Toyo Toki Co., Ltd., **III** 755
Toyo Tozo Co., **I** 265; **21** 319
Toyo Trust and Banking Co., **II** 347, 371; **17** 349
Toyoda Automatic Loom Works, Ltd., I 203; **III** 591, 593, 632, **636–39**
Toyokawa Works, **I** 579
Toyoko Co., Ltd., **V** 199
Toyoko Kogyo, **V** 199
Toyomenka (America) Inc., **IV** 224
Toyomenka (Australia) Pty., Ltd., **IV** 224
Toyota Gossei, **I** 321
Toyota Industrial Equipment, **27** 294, 296
Toyota Motor Corporation, I 9–10, 174, 184, **203–05,** 507–08, 587; **II** 373; **III** 415, 495, 521, 523, 536, 579, 581, 591–93, 624, 636–38, 667, 715, 742; **IV** 702; **6** 514; **7** 111, 118, 212, 219–21; **8** 315; **9** 294, 340–42; **10** 353, 407; **11** 351, 377, 487, **528–31 (upd.); 14** 321; **15** 495; **21** 162, 273; **23** 289–90, 338–40; **25** 198; **34** 303, 305–06; **38 458–62 (upd.); 50** 264, 266–68
Toyota Tsusho America, Inc., **13** 371
Toys 'R' Us, Inc., III 588; **V 203–06; 7** 396; **10** 235, 284, 484; **12** 178; **13** 166; **14** 61; **15** 469; **16** 389–90, 457; **18 522–25 (upd.); 24** 412; **25** 314; **31** 477–78; **37** 129; **43** 385
Tozer Kemsley & Milbourn, **II** 208
TP Transportation, **39** 377

TPA. *See* Aloha Airlines Incorporated.
TPCR Corporation, **V** 163; **14** 394
TPG. *See* TNT Post Group N.V.
Trac Inc., **44** 355
Trace International Holdings, Inc., **17** 182–83; **26** 502
Tracey Bros., **IV** 416
Tracey-Locke, **II** 660
Tracinda Corporation, **25** 329–30
Tracker Marine. *See* Bass Pro Shops, Inc.
Tracker Services, Inc., **9** 110
Traco International N.V., **8** 250; **32** 249
Tracor Inc., 10 547; **17 490–92; 26** 267
Tractebel S.A., 20 491–93. *See also* Suez Lyonnaise des Eaux.
Tractor Supply Corp., **I** 446
Tradax, **II** 617; **13** 137
Trade Assoc. of Bilbao, **II** 194
Trade Development Bank, **11** 415–17
Trade Source International, **44** 132
Trade Waste Incineration, Inc., **9** 109
Trade Winds Campers, **III** 599
TradeARBED, **IV** 25
Trader Joe's Company, 13 525–27; 41 422; **50 487–90 (upd.)**
Trader Media Group, **53** 152
Trader Publications, Inc., **IV** 597
Trader Publishing Company, **12** 302
Traders & General Insurance, **III** 248
Traders Bank of Canada, **II** 344
Traders Group Ltd., **11** 258
Tradesmens National Bank of Philadelphia, **II** 342
The Trading Service, **10** 278
Traex Corporation, **8** 359
Trafalgar House Investments Ltd., **I** 248–49, 572–74; **IV** 259, 711; **20** 313; **23** 161; **24** 88; **36** 322
Trafalgar House PLC, **47** 178
Trafford Park Printers, **53** 152
Trafiroad NV, **39** 239
Trailer Bridge, Inc., 41 397–99
Trailer Marine Transport, **6** 383
Trailways Lines, Inc., **I** 450; **9** 425; **32** 230
Trak Auto Corporation, **16** 159–62
TRAK Communications Inc., **44** 420
TRAK Microwave Corporation, **18** 497, 513
Trammell Crow Company, IV 343; **8** 326–28, **532–34; 49** 147–48; **54** 222–24
Tran Telecommunications Corp., **III** 110; **14** 14
Trane Company, **III** 663, 665; **10** 525; **21** 107; **22** 6; **26** 4; **30** 46, 48–49
Trans Air System, **6** 367; **27** 90
Trans-Arabian Pipe Line Co., **IV** 537, 552
Trans-Australia Airlines, **6** 110–12
Trans-Canada Air Lines. *See* Air Canada.
Trans Colorado, **11** 299
Trans-Continental Leaf Tobacco Company, (TCLTC), **13** 491
Trans Continental Records, **52** 430
Trans Freight Lines, **27** 473–74
Trans International Airlines, **I** 537; **13** 529; **41** 402
Trans Louisiana Gas Company, **43** 56–57
Trans-Lux Corporation, 51 380–83
Trans-Mex, Inc. S.A. de C.V., **42** 365
Trans-Natal Coal Corp., **IV** 93
Trans Ocean Products, **II** 578; **8** 510
Trans-Pacific Airlines, **22** 251. *See also* Aloha Airlines Incorporated.
Trans Rent-A-Car, **6** 348
Trans-Resources Inc., **13** 299

Trans Union Corp., **IV** 137; **6** 25; **28** 119
Trans Western Publishing, **25** 496
Trans World Airlines, Inc., I 58, 70, 90, 97, 99–100, 102, 113, 121, 123–24, **125–27,** 132, 466; **II** 32–33, 142, 425, 679; **III** 92, 428; **6** 50, 68, 71, 74, 76–77, 81–82, 114, 130; **9** 17, 232; **10** 301–03, 316; **11** 277, 427; **12** 381, **487–90 (upd.);** **13** 341; **14** 73; **15** 419; **21** 141–42; **22** 22, 219; **26** 439; **29** 190; **35 424–29 (upd.); 52** 21, 90, 168
Trans-World Corp., **19** 456; **47** 231
Trans World Entertainment Corporation, 24 501–03
Trans World International, **18** 262–63
Trans World Life Insurance Company, **27** 46–47
Trans World Music, **9** 361
Trans World Seafood, Inc., **13** 244
Transaction Systems Architects, Inc., 29 477–79
Transaction Technology, **12** 334
TransAlta Utilities Corporation, 6 585–87
Transamerica—An AEGON Company, 41 400–03 (upd.)
Transamerica Corporation, I 536–38; II 147–48, 227, 288–89, 422; **III** 332, 344; **7** 236–37; **8** 46; **11** 273, 533; **13 528–30 (upd.);** **21** 285; **25** 328; **27** 230; **46** 48. *See also* TIG Holdings, Inc.
Transamerica Pawn Holdings. *See* EZCORP Inc.
TransAmerican Waste Industries Inc., **41** 414
Transat. *See* Compagnie Générale Transatlantique (Transat).
Transatlantic Holdings, Inc., III 198; **11 532–33; 15** 18
Transatlantische Dampfschiffahrts Gesellschaft, **6** 397
Transatlantische Gruppe, **III** 404
TransBrasil S/A Linhas Aéreas, 6 134; **29** 495; **31 443–45; 46** 398
TransCanada PipeLines Limited, I 264; **V** 270–71, **737–38; 17** 22–23
Transco Energy Company, IV 367; **V** 739–40; **6** 143; **18** 366
Transcontinental Air Transport, **I** 125; **9** 17; **11** 427; **12** 487
Transcontinental and Western Air Lines, **9** 416; **12** 487
Transcontinental Gas Pipe Line Corporation, **V** 739; **6** 447
Transcontinental Pipeline Company, **6** 456–57
Transcontinental Services Group N.V., **16** 207
TransCor America, Inc., **23** 154
Transelco, Inc., **8** 178
TransEuropa, **II** 164
Transfer Drivers, Inc., **46** 301
Transflash, **6** 404; **26** 243
Transfracht, **6** 426
Transiciel SA, 48 400–02
Transinternational Life, **II** 422
Transit Homes of America, Inc., **46** 301
Transit Mix Concrete and Materials Company, **7** 541
Transitions Optical Inc., **21** 221, 223
Transitron, **16** 332
Transkaryotic Therapies Inc., **54** 111
Transking Inc. *See* King Kullen Grocery Co., Inc.

Transkrit Corp., **IV** 640; **26** 273
Translite, **III** 495
Transmanche-Link, **13** 206–08; **37** 135
Transmedia Network Inc., 20 494–97
Transmedica International, Inc., **41** 225
Transmisiones y Equipos Mecanicos, S.A. de C.V., **23** 171
Transmitter Equipment Manufacturing Co., **13** 385
TransMontaigne Inc., 28 470–72
Transmontane Rod and Gun Club, **43** 435–36
Transnet Ltd., 6 433–35
TransOcean Oil, **III** 559
Transocean Sedco Forex Inc., 45 417–19
Transpac, **IV** 325
Transport Corporation of America, Inc., 49 400–03
Transport Management Co., **III** 192
Transport- und Unfall-Versicherungs-Aktiengesellschaft Zürich, **III** 411
Transportacion Ferroviaria Mexicana, **50** 209
Transportacion Maritima Mexicana S.A. de C.V., **12** 279; **26** 236; **47** 162; **50** 208
Transportation Insurance Co., **III** 229
Transportation Technologies Industries Inc., **51** 155
Transportation.com, **45** 451
Transportes Aéreas Centro-Americanos. *See* Grupo TACA.
Transportes Aereos Portugueses, S.A., 6 125–27. *See also* TAP—Air Portugal Transportes Aéreos Portugueses S.A.
Transportes Aeromar, **39** 188
Transrack S.A., **26** 363
Transtar, **6** 120–21; **24** 454
Transue & Williams Steel Forging Corp., **13** 302
Transvaal Silver and Base Metals, **IV** 90
Transway International Corp., **10** 369
Transworld Communications, **35** 165
Transworld Corp., **14** 209
Transworld Drilling Company Limited. *See* Kerr-McGee Corporation.
The Tranzonic Companies, 8 512; **15 500–02; 37 392–95**
Trapper's, **19** 286
Trasgo, S.A. de C.V., **14** 516; **50** 493
Trausch Baking Co., **I** 255
Trävaru Svartvik, **IV** 338
Travel Air Manufacturing Company, **8** 49; **27** 97
Travel Automation Services Ltd., **I** 95
Travel Inc., **26** 309
Travel Information Group, **17** 398
Travel Ports of America, Inc., 17 493–95
Travelers Bank & Trust Company, **13** 467
Travelers Book Club, **13** 105
Travelers Corporation, I 37, 545; **III** 313, 329, **387–90,** 707–08; **6** 12; **15** 463 124. *See also* Citigroup Inc.
Travelers/Aetna Property Casualty Corp., **21** 15
Traveller's Express, **I** 449
Travelocity.com, Inc., 46 434–37
TraveLodge, **III** 94, 104–06
Travenol Laboratories, **I** 627–28; **10** 141–43
Travers Morgan Ltd., **42** 183
Travis Boats & Motors, Inc., 37 396–98
Travis Perkins plc, 34 450–52
Travocéan, **25** 104
Trayco, **III** 570; **20** 362

Traylor Engineering & Manufacturing Company, **6** 395; **25** 169
TRC. *See* Tennessee Restaurant Company.
TRC Companies, Inc., 32 461–64
TRE Corp., **23** 225
Treadco, Inc., 16 39; **19** 38, **454–56**
Treasure Chest Advertising Company, Inc., 21 60; **32 465–67**
Treasure House Stores, Inc., **17** 322
Treatment Centers of America, **11** 379
Trebuhs Realty Co., **24** 438
Trechmann, Weekes and Co., **III** 669
Tredegar Corporation, 10 291; **52 349–51**
Tree of Life, Inc., II 528; **29 480–82**
Tree Sweet Products Corp., **12** 105; **26** 325
Tree Tavern, Inc., **27** 197
TrefilARBED, **IV** 26
Tréfimétaux, **IV** 174
Trefoil Capital Investors, L.P., **8** 305
Trek, **IV** 90, 92–93
Trek Bicycle Corporation, 16 493–95; 19 384–85
Trelleborg A.B., **III** 625; **IV** 166
Tremec. *See* Transmisiones y Equipos Mecanicos, S.A. de C.V.
Tremletts Ltd., **IV** 294; **19** 225
Tremont Corporation, **21** 490
Trencherwood Plc, **45** 443
Trend International Ltd., **13** 502
Trend-Lines, Inc., 22 516–18
Trends Magazine NV, **48** 347
Trendwest Resorts, Inc., 12 439; **33 409–11**. *See also* Jeld-Wen, Inc.
Trent Tube, **I** 435
Trenton Foods, **II** 488
TrentonWorks Limited. *See* The Greenbrier Companies.
Tresco, **8** 514
Trethowal China Clay Co., **III** 690
Tri-City Federal Savings and Loan Association, **10** 92
Tri-City Utilities Company, **6** 514
Tri-County National Bank, **9** 474
Tri-Marine International Inc., **24** 116
Tri-Miller Packing Company, **7** 524
Tri-Sonics, Inc., **16** 202; **43** 170
Tri-State Baking, **53** 21
Tri-State Improvement Company, **6** 465–66
Tri-State Publishing & Communications, Inc., **22** 442
Tri-State Recycling Corporation, **15** 117
Tri-State Refining Co., **IV** 372; **50** 46
Tri-Union Seafoods LLC, **24** 116
Tri Valley Growers, 32 468–71
Triad, **14** 224
Triad Artists Inc., **23** 514
Triad International Maintenance Corp., **13** 417
Triad Nitrogen, Inc., **27** 316, 318
Triad Systems Corp., **38** 96
Triangle Auto Springs Co., **IV** 136
The Triangle Group, **16** 357
Triangle Industries Inc., **I** 602, 607–08, 614; **II** 480–81; **14** 43
Triangle Manufacturing, **26** 57
Triangle Pharmaceuticals, Inc., **54** 131
Triangle Portfolio Associates, **II** 317
Triangle Publications, Inc., **IV** 652; **7** 391; **12** 359–60
Triangle Refineries, **IV** 446; **22** 302
Triangle Sheet Metal Works, Inc., **45** 327

Triarc Companies, Inc., 8 535–37; 13 322; **14** 32–33; **34 453–57 (upd.); 39** 383, 385
Triathlon Leasing, **II** 457
Tribe Computer Works. *See* Zoom Technologies, Inc.
Tribune Company, III 329; **IV 682–84; 10** 56; **11** 331; **22 519–23 (upd.); 26** 17; **32** 358–59; **38** 306; **42** 133
Trical Resources, **IV** 84
Tricity Cookers, **I** 531–32
Trick & Murray, **22** 153
Trico Products Corporation, I 186; **15 503–05**
Tricon Global Restaurants, Inc., **21** 313, 317, 405, 407, 485; **40** 342
Tridel Enterprises Inc., 9 512–13
Trident Data Systems, **54** 396
Trident NGL Holdings Inc., **18** 365, 367
Trident Seafoods, **II** 494
Trifari, Krussman & Fishel, Inc., **9** 157
Trigen Energy Corporation, 6 512; **42 386–89**
Trigon Industries, **13** 195; **14** 431
Trilan Developments Ltd., **9** 512
Trilogy Fabrics, Inc., **16** 125
Trilon Financial Corporation, II 456–57; IV 721; **9** 391
Trimac Ltd., **25** 64
TriMas Corp., III 571; **11 534–36; 20** 359, 362; **39** 266
Trimble Navigation Limited, 40 441–43
Trimel Corp., **47** 54
Trinidad and Tobago External Telecommunications Company, **25** 100
Trinidad Oil Co., **IV** 95, 552
Trinidad-Tesoro Petroleum Company Limited, **7** 516, 518
Trinity Beverage Corporation, **11** 451
Trinity Broadcasting, **13** 279
Trinity Capital Opportunity Corp., **17** 13
Trinity Distributors, **15** 139
Trinity Industries, Incorporated, 7 540–41
Trinity Mirror plc, 49 404–10 (upd.)
Trinkaus und Burkhardt, **II** 319; **17** 324
TRINOVA Corporation, III 640–42; 731; 13 8; **16** 7, 9
Trintex, **6** 158
Triology Corp., **III** 110
Triple Five Group Ltd., 49 411–15
Triple P N.V., 26 496–99
Triplex, **6** 279
Triplex (Northern) Ltd., **III** 725
Trippe Manufacturing Co., **10** 474; **24** 29
Triquet Paper Co., **IV** 282; **9** 261
TriStar Pictures, **I** 234; **II** 134, 136–37; **6** 158; **10** 227; **12** 75, 455; **23** 275; **28** 462; **32** 114. *See also* Columbia TriStar Motion Pictures Companies.
Triton Bioscience, **III** 53; **26** 384
Triton Cellular Partners, L.P., **43** 341
Triton Energy Corporation, 11 537–39; 55 20
Triton Group Ltd., **I** 447; **31** 287; **34** 339
Triton Oil, **IV** 519
Triton Systems Corp., **22** 186
Triumph-Adler, **I** 485; **III** 145; **11** 265. *See also* TA Triumph-Adler AG.
Triumph American, Inc., **12** 199
Triumph Films, **25** 174
Triumph, Finlay, and Philips Petroleum, **11** 28
Triumph Group, Inc., 21 153; **31 446–48**

Triumph Motorcycles Ltd., 53 334–37
Trivest, Inc., **II** 457; **21** 531–32
Trizec Corporation Ltd., 9 84–85; **10 529–32**
TrizecHahn, **37** 311
TRM Copy Centers Corporation, 18 526–28
Trojan, **III** 674
Troll, **13** 561
Trolley Barn Brewery Inc., **25** 401
Trona Corp., **IV** 95
Tropical Marine Centre, **40** 128–29
Tropical Oil Co., **IV** 415–16
Tropical Shipping, Inc., **6** 529, 531
Tropical Sportswear Int'l Corporation, **42** 120
Tropicana Products, Inc., II 468, 525; **13** 293; **25** 366; **28** 271, **473–77; 38** 349; **45** 160–62; **50** 294
Trotter, Inc., **49** 108
Trotter-Yoder & Associates, **22** 88
Troxel Cycling, **16** 53
Troy & Nichols, Inc., **13** 147
Troy Design Group, **55** 32
Troy Metal Products. *See* KitchenAid.
Troyfel Ltd., **III** 699
TRT Communications, Inc., **6** 327; **11** 185
Tru-Run Inc., **16** 207
Tru-Stitch, **16** 545
Tru-Trac Therapy Products, **11** 486
Truck Components Inc., **23** 306
Trudeau Marketing Group, Inc., **22** 386
True Form Boot Co., **V** 177
True North Communications Inc., 23 478–80; 25 91
True Temper Hardware Co., **30** 241–42
True Value Hardware Stores, **V** 37–38; **30** 168. *See also* TruServ Corporation.
Trugg-Hansa Holding AB, **III** 264
TruGreen, **23** 428, 430
Truitt Bros., **10** 382
Truman Dunham Co., **III** 744
Truman Hanburg, **I** 247
Trumball Asphalt, **III** 721
Trümmer-Verwertungs-Gesellschaft, **IV** 140
Trump Organization, 16 262; **23 481–84; 43** 225
Trunkline Gas Company, **6** 544; **14** 135
Trunkline LNG Co., **IV** 425
Trus Joist Corporation. *See* TJ International, Inc.
TruServ Corporation, 24 504–07
Trussdeck Corporation. *See* TJ International, Inc.
Trust Company of the West, **19** 414; **42** 347
Trustcorp, Inc., **9** 475–76
Trusted Information Systems, Inc., **25** 349
Trustees, Executors and Agency Co. Ltd., **II** 189
Trusthouse Forte PLC, I 215; **III 104–06; 16** 446
TRW Inc., I 539–41; II 33; **6** 25; **8** 416; **9** 18, 359; **10** 293; **11** 68, **540–42 (upd.); 12** 238; **14 510–13 (upd.); 16** 484; **17** 372; **18** 275; **19** 184; **23** 134; **24** 480; **26** 141; **28** 119; **32** 437; **33** 47; **34** 76; **43** 311, 313; **45** 152
TRW Vehicle Safety Systems Inc., **41** 369
Tryart Pty. Limited, **7** 253
TSA. *See* Transaction Systems Architects, Inc.

Tsai Management & Research Corp., **III** 230–31

TSB Group plc, 12 491–93; 16 14

TSI Inc., **38** 206

TSI Soccer Corporation, **29** 142–43

Tsingtao Brewery Group, 49 416–20

TSMC. *See* Taiwan Semiconductor Manufacturing Company Ltd.

TSO. *See* Teacher's Service Organization, Inc.

TSO Financial Corp., **II** 420; **8** 10

Tsogo Sun Gaming & Entertainment, **17** 318

TSP. *See* Tom Snyder Productions.

TSR Inc., **24** 538

Tsuang Hine Co., **III** 582

Tsubakimoto-Morse, **14** 64

Tsukumo Shokai, **I** 502; **III** 712

Tsumeb Corp., **IV** 17–18

Tsurumi Steelmaking and Shipbuilding Co., **IV** 162

Tsurusaki Pulp Co., Ltd., **IV** 285

Tsutsunaka Plastic Industry Co., **III** 714; **8** 359

TSYS. *See* Total System Services, Inc.

TTK. *See* Tokyo Tsushin Kogyo K.K.

TTX Company, 6 436–37

Tubby's, Inc., 53 338–40

Tube Fab Ltd., **17** 234

Tube Forming, Inc., **23** 517

Tube Investments, **II** 422; **IV** 15

Tube Reducing Corp., **16** 321

Tube Service Co., **19** 344

Tubed Chemicals Corporation, **27** 299

Tuborg, **9** 99

Tubos de Acero de Mexico, S.A. (TAMSA), 41 404–06

Tuboscope, **42** 420

Tucker, Lynch & Coldwell. *See* CB Commercial Real Estate Services Group, Inc.

TUCO, Inc., **8** 78

Tucson Electric Power Company, V 713; **6 588–91; 42** 388

Tucson Gas & Electric, **19** 411–12

Tuesday Morning Corporation, 18 529–31

Tuff Stuff Publications, **23** 101

TUI. *See* Touristik Union International GmbH. and Company K.G.

TUI Group GmbH, 42 283; **44 432–35**

Tuileries et Briqueteries d'Hennuyeres et de Wanlin, **14** 249

TUJA, **27** 21

Tully's Coffee Corporation, 51 384–86

Tultex Corporation, 13 531–33

Tumbleweed, Inc., 33 412–14

Tunhems Industri A.B., **I** 387

Tunisair. *See* Société Tunisienne de l'Air-Tunisair.

Tupolev Aviation and Scientific Technical Complex, 24 58–60

Tupperware Corporation, I 29; **II** 534; **III** 610–12;, **15** 475, 477; **17** 186; **18** 67; **28 478–81**

Turbinbolaget, **III** 419

Turbine Engine Asset Management LLC, **28** 5

TurboLinux Inc., **45** 363

Turcot Paperboard Mills Ltd., **17** 281

Turkish Engineering, Consultancy and Contracting Corp., **IV** 563

Turkish Petroleum Co. *See* Türkiye Petrolleri Anonim Ortakliği.

Türkiye Garanti Bankasi, **I** 479

Türkiye Petrolleri Anonim Ortakliği, IV 464, 557–58, **562–64; 7** 352

Turnbull, **III** 468

Turner Broadcasting System, Inc., II 134, 149, 161 **166–68; IV** 676; **6 171–73 (upd.); 7** 64, 99, 306, 529; **23** 33, 257; **25** 313, 329, 498; **28** 71; **30** 100; **47** 272

The Turner Corporation, 8 538–40; 23 485–88 (upd.); 25 402; **33** 197

Turner Entertainment Co., **18** 459

Turner Glass Company, **13** 40

Turner Network Television, **21** 24

Turner's Turkeys, **II** 587

Turnstone Systems, **44** 426

TURPAS, **IV** 563

Turtle Wax, Inc., 15 506–09; 16 43; **26** 349

Tuscarora Inc., 17 155; **29 483–85**

The Tussauds Group, IV 659; **55 376–78**

Tutt Bryant Industries PLY Ltd., **26** 231

Tuttle, Oglebay and Company. *See* Oglebay Norton Company.

TV & Stereo Town, **10** 468

TV Asahi, **7** 249

TV Azteca, S.A. de C.V., 39 194–95, **398–401**

TV Food Network, **22** 522

TV Guide, Inc., 43 431–34 (upd.)

TVA. *See* Tennessee Valley Authority.

TVE. *See* Television Española, S.A.

TVE Holdings, **22** 307

TVH Acquisition Corp., **III** 262, 264

TVI, Inc., 15 510–12

TVN Entertainment Corporation, **32** 239

TVS Entertainment PLC, **13** 281

TVW Enterprises, **7** 78

TVX, **II** 449; **13** 449

TW Kutter, **III** 420

TW Services, Inc., II 679–80; 10 301–03

TWA. *See* Trans World Airlines; Transcontinental & Western Airways.

TWC. *See* The Weather Channel, Inc.

Tweco Co., **19** 441

Tweeds, **12** 280

Tweeter Home Entertainment Group, Inc., 30 464–66; 41 379, 381

Twen-Tours International, **II** 164

Twentieth Century Fox Film Corporation, II 133, 135, 146, 155–56, **169–71**, 175; **IV** 652; **7** 391–92; **12** 73, 322, 359; **15** 23, 25, 234; **25** 327, 490–94 (upd.); **43** 173; **46** 311

Twentsche Bank, **II** 183

"21" International Holdings, **17** 182

21 Invest International Holdings Ltd., **14** 322

21st Century Food Products. *See* Hain Food Group, Inc.

21st Century Mortgage, **18** 28

Twenty-Second National Bank, **II** 291

Twenty-third Publications, **49** 48

24/7 Real Media, Inc., 49 421–24

TWI. *See* Trans World International.

Twin City Wholesale Drug Company, **14** 147

Twin Disc, Inc., 21 502–04

Twin Hill Acquisition Company, Inc., **48** 286

Twining Crosfield Group, **II** 465; **13** 52

Twinings' Foods International, **II** 465–66; **III** 696

Twinings Tea, **41** 31

Twinlab Corporation, 34 458–61

Twinpak, **IV** 250

Two Guys, **12** 49

2-in-1 Shinola Bixby Corp., **II** 497

2ndhead Oy, **51** 328

21st Century Mortgage, **41** 18, 20

TWW Plc, **26** 62

TXEN, Inc., **18** 370

TXL Oil Corp., **IV** 552

TXP Operation Co., **IV** 367

TxPort Inc., **13** 8

Ty-D-Bol, **III** 55

Ty Inc., 33 415–17

Tyco International Ltd., 21 462; **28 482–87 (upd.); 30** 157; **44** 6; **50** 135; **54** 236, 239, 373

Tyco Laboratories, Inc., III 643–46; 13 245–47

Tyco Submarine Systems Ltd., **32** 217

Tyco Toys, Inc., 12 494–97; 13 312, 319; **18** 520–21; **25** 314

Tyler Corporation, 23 489–91

Tymnet, **18** 542

Tyndall Fund-Unit Assurance Co., **III** 273

Typhoo Tea, **II** 477

Typpi Oy, **IV** 469

Tyrolean Airways, **9** 233; **33** 50

Tyrvään Oy, **IV** 348

Tyskie Brewery, **24** 450

Tyson Foods, Inc., II 584–85; 7 422–23, 432; **14 514–16 (upd.); 21** 535; **23** 376, 384; **26** 168; **39** 229; **50 491–95 (upd.)**

U.C.L.A.F. *See* Roussel-Uclaf.

U-Haul International Inc. *See* Amerco.

U.K. Corrugated, **IV** 296; **19** 226

U.S. *See also* US.

U.S. Aggregates, Inc., 42 390–92

U.S. Appliances, **26** 336

U.S. Bancorp, 12 165; **14 527–29; 36 489–95 (upd.)**

U.S. Bank of Washington, **14** 527

U.S. Banknote Company, **30** 43

U.S. Bearings Company. *See* Federal-Mogul Corporation.

U.S. Billing, Inc. *See* Billing Concepts Corp.

U.S. Biomedicals Corporation, **27** 69

U.S. Bioscience, Inc., **35** 286, 288

U.S. Borax, Inc., 42 393–96

U.S. Brass., **24** 151

U.S. Can Corporation, 30 474–76

U.S. Cellular Corporation, 31 449–452 (upd.)

U.S. Computer of North America Inc., **43** 368

U.S. Delivery Systems, Inc., 22 153, **531–33; 47** 90. *See also* Velocity Express Corporation.

U.S. Electrical Motors, **II** 19

U.S. Elevator Corporation, **19** 109–11

U.S. Envelope, **19** 498

U.S. Food Products Co., **I** 376

U.S. Foodservice, 26 503–06; 37 374, 376

U.S.G. Co., **III** 762

U.S. Generating Company, **26** 373

U.S. Geological Survey, **9** 367

U.S. Graphite. *See* Wickes Inc.

U.S. Guarantee Co., **III** 220; **14** 108

U.S. Healthcare, Inc., 6 194–96; 21 16

U.S. Home Corporation, 8 541–43

U.S. Industries, Inc., **7** 208; **18** 467; **23** 296; **24** 150; **27** 288

U.S. Intec, **22** 229

U.S. International Reinsurance, **III** 264
U.S. Investigations Services Inc., **35** 44
U.S. Land Co., **IV** 255
U.S. Lawns, **31** 182, 184
U.S. Life Insurance, **III** 194
U.S. Lines, **I** 476; **III** 459; **11** 194
U.S. Lock Corporation, **9** 543; **28** 50–52
U.S. Long Distance Corp. *See* Billing
   Concepts Corp.
U.S. Marine Corp., **III** 444
U.S. News and World Report Inc., 30
   477–80
U.S. Office Products Company, 25
   500–02; 41 69, 247; **47** 91
U.S. Overall Company, **14** 549
U.S. Plywood Corp. *See* United States
   Plywood Corp.
U.S. Realty and Improvement Co., **III** 98
U.S. RingBinder Corp., **10** 313–14
U.S. Robotics Inc., 9 514–15; **20** 8, 69;
   22 17; **24** 212; **34** 444; **36** 122, 357; **48**
   369; **49** 184
U.S. Rubber Company, **I** 478; **10** 388
U.S. Satellite Broadcasting Company,
   Inc., 20 505–07
U.S. Satellite Systems, **III** 169; **6** 285
U.S. Shoe Corporation, **43** 98; **44** 365
U.S. Smelting Refining and Mining, **7** 360
U.S. Software Inc., **29** 479
U.S. Steel Corp. *See* United States Steel
   Corp.
U.S. Telephone Communications, **9** 478
U.S. Tile Co., **III** 674
U.S. Timberlands Company, L.P., 42
   397–400
U.S. Time Corporation, **13** 120
U.S. Trust Co. of New York, **II** 274
U.S. Trust Corp., 17 496–98
U.S. Vanadium Co., **9** 517
U.S. Venture Partners, **15** 204–05
U.S. Vitamin & Pharmaceutical Corp., **III**
   55
U S West, Inc., **V** 341–43; **11** 12, 59,
   547; **25** 101, 495–99 (upd.); **32** 218; **36**
   43; **37** 124–27
U.S. Windpower, **11** 222–23
U.S. Xpress Enterprises, Inc., **18** 159
U-Tote'M, **II** 620; **7** 372
UA. *See* Metro- Goldwyn-Mayer Inc.,
   MGM/UA Communications Company;
   United Artists Corp.
UAA. *See* EgyptAir.
UAL Corporation, 34 462–65 (upd.); **52**
   22, 25
UAL, Inc. *See* United Airlines.
UAP. *See* Union des Assurances de Paris.
UAP Inc., **45** 179
UARCO Inc., **15** 473–74
UAT. *See* UTA.
Ub Iwerks, **6** 174
Ube Industries, Ltd., III 759–61; **38**
   463–67 (upd.)
Uberseebank A.G., **III** 197
Ubi Soft Entertainment S.A., 41 188–89,
   407–09
Ubique Ltd, **25** 301
UBL Educational Loan Center, **42** 211
UBS AG, 52 352–59 (upd.)
Ucabail, **II** 265
UCAR International, Inc., **40** 83
UCC-Communications Systems, Inc., **II** 38
Uccel, **6** 224
Uchiyama, **V** 727
UCI, **IV** 92; **25** 173

UCPMI, **IV** 226
Uddeholm and Bohler, **IV** 234
Udet Flugzeugwerke, **I** 73
Udo Fischer Co., **8** 477
UDRT. *See* United Dominion Realty Trust,
   Inc.
UE Automotive Manufacturing, **III** 580
Ueda Kotsu Company, **47** 408
UETA Inc., **29** 510–11
Ufa Sports, **44** 190
Ugg Holdings, Inc., **22** 173
UGI. *See* United Gas Improvement.
UGI Corporation, 12 498–500
Ugine-Kuhlmann, **IV** 108, 174
Ugine S.A., IV 174; **20** 498–500
Ugine Steels, **IV** 227
Ugly Duckling Corporation, 22 524–27
Uhlmans Inc., **24** 458
UI International, **6** 444
UIB. *See* United Independent Broadcasters,
   Inc.
UICI, 33 418–21
Uinta Co., **6** 568
Uintah National Corp., **11** 260
UIS Co., **13** 554–55; **15** 324
Uitgeversmaatschappij Elsevier, **IV** 610
Uitzendbureau Amstelveen. *See* Randstad
   Holding n.v.
UJB Financial Corp., **14** 473
UK Paper, **IV** 279; **19** 155
UKF. *See* Unie van Kunstmestfabrieken.
Ukrop's Super Market's, Inc., 39 402–04
UL. *See* Underwriters Laboratories, Inc.
Ullrich Copper, Inc., **6** 146
Ullstein AV Produktions-und
   Vertriebsgesellschaft, **IV** 590
Ullstein Langen Müller, **IV** 591
Ullstein Tele Video, **IV** 590
ULN. *See* Union Laitière Normande.
ULPAC, **II** 576
Ulstein Holding ASA, **27** 494
Ulster Bank, **II** 334
Ultimate Electronics, Inc., 18 532–34; **21**
   33; **24** 52, 269
Ultra Bancorp, **II** 334
Ultra High Pressure Units Ltd., **IV** 66; **7**
   123
Ultra Mart, **16** 250
Ultra Pac, Inc., 24 512–14
Ultra Radio & Television, **I** 531
UltraCam. *See* Ultrak Inc.
UltraCare Products, **18** 148
Ultrak Inc., 24 508–11
Ultralar, **13** 544
Ultramar Diamond Shamrock
   Corporation, 31 453–457 (upd.)
Ultramar PLC, IV 565–68
Ultrametl Mfg. Co., **17** 234
Ultronic Systems Corp., **IV** 669
UM Technopolymer, **III** 760
Umacs of Canada Inc., **9** 513
Umberto's of New Hyde Park Pizzeria, **16**
   447
Umbro Holdings Ltd., **43** 392. *See also*
   Stone Manufacturing Company.
UMC. *See* United Microelectronics Corp.
UMG. *See* Universal Music Group.
UMI Company, **29** 58
NV Umicore SA, 47 411–13
Umm-al-Jawabi Oil Co., **IV** 454
Umpqua River Navigation Company, **13**
   100
Unadulterated Food Products, Inc., **11** 449
UNAT, **III** 197–98

Unbrako Socket Screw Company Ltd., **30**
   429
Uncas-Merchants National Bank, **13** 467
Uncle Ben's Inc., 22 528–30
Under Sea Industries, **III** 59
Underground Group, **6** 407
Underwood, **III** 145; **24** 269
Underwriter for the Professions Insurance
   Company, **55** 128
Underwriters Adjusting Co., **III** 242
Underwriters Laboratories, Inc., 30
   467–70
Underwriters Reinsurance Co., **10** 45
Unefon, S.A., **39** 194, 196
UNELCO. *See* Union Electrica de Canarias
   S.A.
Unelec, Inc., **13** 398
Unfall, **III** 207
Ungermann-Bass, Inc., **6** 279
Uni-Cardan AG, **III** 494
Uni-Cast. *See* Sturm, Ruger & Company,
   Inc.
Uni-Charm, **III** 749
Uni Europe, **III** 211
Uni-Marts, Inc., 17 499–502
Uni-President Group, **49** 460
Uni-Sankyo, **I** 675
Unibail SA, 40 444–46
Unibank, **40** 336; **50** 149–50
Unic, **V** 63
Unicapital, Inc., **15** 281
Unicare Health Facilities, **6** 182; **25** 525
Unicco Security Services, **27** 22
Unicel. *See* Rural Cellular Corporation.
Unicer, **9** 100
Unichem, **25** 73
Unichema International, **13** 228
Unicoa, **I** 524
Unicom Corporation, 29 486–90 (upd.).
   See also Exelon Corporation.
Unicomi, **II** 265
Unicon Producing Co., **10** 191
Unicoolait, **19** 51
UNICOR. *See* Federal Prison Industries,
   Inc.
Unicord, **24** 115
Unicorn Shipping Lines, **IV** 91
UniCorp, **8** 228
Unicorp Financial, **III** 248
Unicredit, **II** 265
UniCredito Italiano, **50** 410
Uniden, **14** 117
Unidrive, **47** 280
UniDynamics Corporation, **8** 135
Unie van Kunstmestfabrieken, **I** 326
Uniface Holding B.V., **10** 245; **30** 142
Unifi, Inc., 12 501–03
Unified Energy System of Russia. *See*
   RAO Unified Energy System of Russia.
Unified Management Corp., **III** 306
Unified Western Grocers, **31** 25
UniFirst Corporation, 16 228; **21** 115,
   505–07
Uniflex Corporation, **53** 236
Uniforce Services Inc., **40** 119
Unigate PLC, II 586–87; **28** 488–91
   (upd.); 29 150. *See also* Uniq Plc.
Unigep Group, **III** 495
Unigesco Inc., **II** 653
Uniglory, **13** 211
Unigroup, **15** 50
UniHealth America, **11** 378–79
Unijoh Sdn, Bhd, **47** 255
Unik S.A., **23** 170–171

Unilab Corp., **26** 391
Unilac Inc., **II** 547
Unilever PLC/Unilever N.V., **I** 369, 590, 605; **II** 547, **588–91**; **III** 31–32, 46, 52, 495; **IV** 532; **7** 382, **542–45 (upd.)**, 577; **8** 105–07, 166, 168, 341, 344; **9** 449; **11** 205, 421; **13** 243–44; **14** 204–05; **18** 395, 397; **19** 193; **21** 219; **22** 123; **23** 242; **26** 306; **28** 183, 185; **30** 396–97; **32 472–78 (upd.)**; **36** 237; **49** 269
Unilife Assurance Group, **III** 273
UniLife Insurance Co., **22** 149
Unilog SA, **42 401–03**
Uniloy Milacron Inc., **53** 230
UniMac Companies, **11** 413
Unimat, **II** 265
Unimation, **II** 122
Unimetal, **IV** 227; **30** 252
Uninsa, **I** 460
Union, **III** 391–93
Union & NHK Auto Parts, **III** 580
Union Acceptances Ltd., **IV** 23
Unión Aérea Española, **6** 95
Union Aéromaritime de Transport. *See* UTA.
Union Assurance, **III** 234
Union Bag–Camp Paper Corp., **IV** 344–45
Union Bancorp of California, **II** 358
Union Bank. *See* State Street Boston Corporation.
Union Bank of Australia, **II** 187–89
Union Bank of Birmingham, **II** 318; **17** 323
Union Bank of California, **16 496–98**. *See also* UnionBanCal Corporation.
Union Bank of Canada, **II** 344
Union Bank of England, **II** 188
Union Bank of Finland, **II** 302, 352
Union Bank of Halifax, **II** 344
Union Bank of London, **II** 235
Union Bank of New London, **II** 213
Union Bank of New York, **9** 229
Union Bank of Scotland, **10** 337
Union Bank of Switzerland, **II** 257, 267, 334, 369, 370, **378–79**; **21** 146. *See also* UBS AG.
Union Battery Co., **III** 536
Union Bay Sportswear, **17** 460
Union Camp Corporation, **IV 344–46**; **8** 102; **39** 291; **47** 189
Union-Capitalisation, **III** 392
Union Carbide Corporation, **I** 334, 339, 347, 374, 390, **399–401**, 582, 666; **II** 103, 313, 562; **III** 742, 760; **IV** 92, 374, 379, 521; **7** 376; **8** 180, 182, 376; **9** 16, **516–20 (upd.)**; **10** 289, 472; **11** 402–03; **12** 46, 347; **13** 118; **14** 281–82; **16** 461; **17** 159; **18** 235; **22** 228, 235; **43** 265–66; **48** 321; **50** 47; **55** 380
Union Cervecera, **9** 100
Union Colliery Company, **V** 741
Union Commerce Corporation, **11** 181
Union Commerciale, **19** 98
Union Corporation. *See* Gencor Ltd.
Union d'Etudes et d'Investissements, **II** 265
Union des Assurances de Paris, **II** 234; **III** 201, **391–94**
Union des Coopératives Bressor, **25** 85
Union des Cooperatives Laitières. *See* Unicoolait.
Union des Mines, **52** 362
Union des Transports Aériens. *See* UTA.

Union Electric Company, **V** 741–43; **6** 505–06; **26** 451
Unión Electrica de Canarias S.A., **V** 607
Unión Electrica Fenosa. *See* Unión Fenosa S.A.
Union Equity Co-Operative Exchange, **7** 175
Union et Prévoyance, **III** 403
Unión Fenosa, S.A., **51 387–90**
Union Fertilizer, **I** 412
Union Fidelity Corporation, **III** 204; **45** 26
Union Financiera, **19** 189
Union Financière de France Banque SA, **52 360–62**
Union Fork & Hoe Company. *See* Acorn Products, Inc.
Union Gas & Electric Co., **6** 529
Union Générale de Savonnerie, **III** 33
l'Union Générale des Pétroles, **IV** 545–46, 560; **7** 482–83
Union Glass Co., **III** 683
Union Hardware, **III** 443; **22** 115
Union Hop Growers, **I** 287
Union Laitière Normande, **19** 50. *See also* Compagnie Laitière Européenne.
Union Levantina de Seguros, **III** 179
Union Light, Heat & Power Company, **6** 466
Union Marine, **III** 372
Union Minière. *See* NV Umicore SA.
Union Mutual Life Insurance Company. *See* UNUM Corp.
Union National Bank, **II** 284; **10** 298
Union National Bank of Wilmington, **25** 540
Union of European Football Association, **27** 150
Union of Food Co-ops, **II** 622
Union of London, **II** 333
Union Oil Associates, **IV** 569
Union Oil Co., **9** 266
Union Oil Co. of California, **I** 13; **IV** 385, 400, 403, 434, 522, 531, 540, 569, 575; **11** 271. *See also* Unocal Corporation.
Union Pacific Corporation, **I** 473; **II** 381; **III** 229; **V 529–32**; **12** 18–20, 278; **14** 371–72; **28 492–500 (upd.)**; **36** 43–44
Union Pacific Resources Group, **52** 30
Union Pacific Tea Co., **7** 202
Union Paper Bag Machine Co., **IV** 344
Union Petroleum Corp., **IV** 394
Union Planters Corporation, **54 387–90**
L'Union pour le Developement Régional, **II** 265
Union Power Company, **12** 541
Union Rückversicherungs-Gesellschaft, **III** 377
Union Savings, **II** 316
Union Savings and Loan Association of Phoenix, **19** 412
Union Savings Bank, **9** 173
Union Savings Bank and Trust Company, **13** 221
Union Steam Ship Co., **IV** 279; **19** 154
Union Steamship Co. of New Zealand Ltd., **27** 473
Union Steel Co., **IV** 22, 572; **7** 550
Union Sugar, **II** 573
Union Suisse des Coopératives de Consommation. *See* Coop Schweiz.
Union Sulphur Co., **IV** 81; **7** 185
Union Supply Co., **IV** 573; **7** 550
Union Tank Car Co., **IV** 137
Union Telecard Alliance, LLC, **34** 223

Union Telephone Company, **14** 258
Union Texas Petroleum Holdings, Inc., **I** 415; **7** 379; **9 521–23**; **22** 31
Union-Transport, **6** 404; **26** 243
Union Trust Co., **II** 284, 313, 315–16, 382; **9** 228; **13** 222
The Union Underwear Company, **I** 440–41; **8** 200–01; **25** 164–66
Union Wine, **I** 289
Unionamerica, Inc., **III** 243; **16** 497; **50** 497
UnionBanCal Corporation, **50 496–99 (upd.)**
UnionBay Sportswear Co., **27** 112
Unione Manifatture, S.p.A., **19** 338
Uniphase Corporation. *See* JDS Uniphase Corporation.
Uniplex Business Software, **41** 281
Uniq Plc, **52** 418, 420
Unique Casual Restaurants, Inc., **27 480–82**
Uniroy of Hempstead, Inc. *See* Aris Industries, Inc.
Uniroyal Chemical Corporation, **36** 145
Uniroyal Corp., **I** 30–31; **II** 472; **V** 242; **8** 503; **11** 159; **20** 262
Uniroyal Goodrich, **42** 88
Uniroyal Holdings Ltd., **21** 73
Unishops, Inc. *See* Aris Industries, Inc.
Unison HealthCare Corporation, **25 503–05**
Unisource Worldwide, Inc., **I** 413, **47** 149
Unistar Radio Networks, **23** 510
Unisys Corporation, **II** 42; **III 165–67**; **6 281–83 (upd.)**; **8** 92; **9** 32, 59; **12** 149, 162; **17** 11, 262; **18** 345, 386, 434, 542; **21** 86; **36 479–84 (upd.)**
The Unit Companies, Inc., **6** 394, 396; **25** 170
Unit Group plc, **8** 477
Unitech plc, **27** 81
United Acquisitions, **7** 114; **25** 125
United Advertising Periodicals, **12** 231
United Agri Products, **II** 494
United AgriSeeds, Inc., **21** 387
United Air Express. *See* United Parcel Service of America Inc.
United Air Fleet, **23** 408
United Aircraft and Transportation Co., **I** 48, 76, 78, 85–86, 96, 441, 489; **9** 416, 418; **10** 162, 260; **12** 289; **21** 140
United Airlines, **I** 23, 47, 71, 84, 90, 97, 113, 116, 118, 124, **128–30**; **II** 142, 419, 680; **III** 225; **6** 71, 75–77, 104, 121, 123, **128–30 (upd.)**, 131, 388–89; **9** 271–72, 283, 416, 549; **10** 162, 199, 301, 561; **11** 299; **12** 192, 381; **14** 73; **21** 141; **22** 199, 220; **24** 21, 22; **25** 146, 148, 421–23; **26** 113, 338–39, 440; **27** 20; **29** 507; **38** 105; **52** 386; **55** 10–11. *See also* UAL Corporation.
United Alaska Drilling, Inc., **7** 558
United Alkalai Co., **I** 351
United Alloy Steel Company, **26** 405
United-American Car, **13** 305
United American Insurance Company of Dallas, **9** 508; **33** 407
United American Lines, **6** 398
United Arab Airlines. *See* EgyptAir.
United Artists Corp., **I** 537; **II** 135, 146–48, 149, 157–58, 160, 167, 169; **III** 721; **IV** 676; **6** 167; **9** 74; **12** 13, 73; **13** 529; **14** 87, 399; **21** 362; **23** 389; **26** 487; **36** 47; **41** 402. *See also* MGM/UA

Communications Company; Metro-Goldwyn-Mayer Inc.
United Artists Theatre Circuit, Inc., **37** 63–64
United Auto Group, Inc., **45** 261
United Auto Group, Inc., 26 500–02
United Bank of Arizona, **II** 358
United Biscuits (Holdings) plc, II 466, 540, **592–94**; **III** 503; **26** 59; **36** 313; **42** **404–09 (upd.)**
United Brands Company, II 595–97; **III** 28; **7** 84–85; **12** 215; **21** 110, 112; **25** 4
United Breweries Ltd. **I** 221, 223, 288; **24** 449. *See also* Carlsberg A/S.
United Broadcasting Corporation Public Company Ltd., **31** 330
United Business Media plc, 52 363–68 **(upd.)**
United Cable Television Corporation, **II** 160; **9** 74; **18** 65; **43** 431
United California Bank, **II** 289
United Car, **I** 540; **14** 511
United Carbon Co., **IV** 373; **50** 47
United Central Oil Corporation, **7** 101
United Cigar Manufacturers Company, **II** 414. *See also* Culbro Corporation.
United Cities Gas Company, **43** 56, 58
United City Property Trust, **IV** 705
United Co., **I** 70
United Communications Systems, Inc. **V** 346
United Computer Services, Inc., **11** 111
United Consolidated Industries, **24** 204
United Corp., **10** 44
United County Banks, **II** 235
United Dairies, **II** 586–87
United Dairy Farmers, **III** 190
United Defense, L.P., 30 471–73
United Distiller & Vintners, **43** 215. *See also* Diageo plc.
United Distillers Glenmore, Inc., **34** 89
United Dominion Corp., **III** 200
United Dominion Industries Limited, IV 288; **8 544–46**; **16 499–502 (upd.)**; **47** 378
United Dominion Realty Trust, Inc., 52 **369–71**
United Drapery Stores, **III** 502; **7** 208
United Drug Co., **II** 533
United Electric Light and Water Co., **13** 182
United Engineering Steels, **III** 495
United Engineers & Constructors, **II** 86; **11** 413
United Express, **11** 299
United Factors Corp., **13** 534–35
United Features Syndicate, Inc., **IV** 607–08
United Federal Savings and Loan of Waycross, **10** 92
United Financial Corporation, **12** 353
United Financial Group, Inc., **8** 349
United 5 and 10 Cent Stores, **13** 444
United Foods, Inc., 21 508–11
United Fruit Co., **I** 529, 566; **II** 120, 595; **IV** 308; **7** 84–85; **21** 110–11; **44** 152
United Funds, Inc., **22** 540–41
United Gas and Electric Company of New Albany, **6** 555
United Gas and Improvement Co., **13** 182
United Gas Corp., **IV** 488–90
United Gas Improvement Co., **IV** 549; **V** 696; **6** 446, 523; **11** 388
United Gas Industries, **III** 502; **7** 208
United Gas Pipe Line Co., **IV** 489–90

United Geophysical Corp., **I** 142
United Graphics, **12** 25
United Grocers, **II** 625
United Guaranty Corp., **III** 197
United Health Maintenance, Inc., **6** 181–82
United HealthCare Corporation, 9 **524–26**; **24** 229, 231. *See also* Humana Inc.
The United Illuminating Company, 21 **512–14**
United Image Entertainment, **18** 64, 66
United Independent Broadcasters, Inc., **II** 132
United Industrial Corporation, 37 **399–402**
United Industrial Syndicate, **8** 545
United Information Systems, Inc., **V** 346
United Insurance Co., **I** 523
Oy United International, **IV** 349
United International Holdings Inc., **28** 198
United International Pictures, **II** 155
United Investors Life Insurance Company, **22** 540; **33** 407
United Iron & Metal Co., **14** 156
United Jewish Communities, 33 422–25
United Kent Fire, **III** 350
United Kingdom Atomic Energy Authority, **6** 451–52
United Knitting, Inc., **21** 192, 194
United Liberty Life Insurance Co., **III** 190–92
United Life & Accident Insurance Co., **III** 220–21; **14** 109
United Life Insurance Company, **12** 541
United Light & Railway Co., **V** 609
United Light and Power, **6** 511
United Machinery Co., **15** 127
United Match Factories, **12** 462
United Media, **22** 442
United Medical Service, Inc., **III** 245–46
United Merchandising Corp., **12** 477
United Merchants & Manufacturers, **Inc., 13 534–37**; **31** 160
United Meridian Corporation, **8** 350
United Metals Selling Co., **IV** 31
United Microelectronics Corporation, **22** 197; **47** 384, 386
United Micronesian, **I** 97; **21** 142
United Molasses, **II** 582
United Mortgage Servicing, **16** 133
United Natural Foods, Inc., 32 479–82
United Natural Gas Company, **6** 526
United Netherlands Navigation Company. *See* Vereenigde Nederlandsche Scheepvaartmaatschappij.
United News & Media plc, 28 501–05 **(upd.)**; **35** 354. *See also* United Business Media plc.
United Newspapers plc, IV 685–87
United of Omaha, **III** 365
United Office Products, **11** 64
United Oil Co., **IV** 399
United Optical, **10** 151
United Pacific Financial Services, **III** 344
United Pacific Insurance Co., **III** 343
United Pacific Life Insurance Co., **III** 343–44
United Pacific Reliance Life Insurance Co. of New York, **III** 343
United Packages, **IV** 249
United Pan-Europe Communications **NV, 47 414–17**
United Paper Mills Ltd., II 302; **IV** 316, **347–50**

United Paramount Network, **25** 418–19; **26** 32; **31** 109
United Paramount Theatres, **II** 129
United Parcel Service of America Inc., V **533–35**; **6** 345–46, 385–86, 390; **11** 11; **12** 309, 334; **13** 19, 416; **14** 517; **17** **503–06 (upd.)**; **18** 82, 177, 315–17; **24** 22, 133; **25** 148, 150, 356; **27** 471, 475; **34** 15, 17, 473; **39** 33; **41** 245; **42** 140; **49** 460
United Pipeline Co., **IV** 394
United Power and Light Corporation, **6** 473; **12** 541
United Presidential Life Insurance Company, **12** 524, 526
United Press International, Inc., IV 607, 627, 669–70; **7** 158–59; **16** 166; **19** 203; **22** 453; **25 506–09**
United Railways & Electric Company, **25** 44
United Refining Co., **23** 406, 408
United Rentals, Inc., 28 386, 388; **34** **466–69**; **48** 272
United Resources, Inc., **21** 514
United Retail Group Inc., 33 426–28
United Retail Merchants Stores Inc., **9** 39
United Roasters, **III** 24; **14** 121
United Satellite Television, **10** 320
United Savings of Texas, **8** 349
United Scientific Holdings, **47** 8
United Servomation, **7** 471–72
United Shipping & Technology, Inc., **49** 440
United Shirt Shops, Inc. *See* Aris Industries, Inc.
United Skates of America, **8** 303
United Software Consultants Inc., **11** 65
United States Aluminum Co., **17** 213
United States Aviation Underwriters, Inc., **24** 176
United States Baking Co., **II** 542
United States Can Co., **15** 127, 129
United States Cellular Corporation, 9 494–96, **527–29**. *See also* U.S. Cellular Corporation.
United States Department of Defense, **6** 327
United States Distributing Corp., **IV** 180–82
United States Electric and Gas Company, **6** 447
United States Electric Light and Power Company, **25** 44
The United States Electric Lighting Company, **11** 387
United States Export-Import Bank, **IV** 55
United States Express Co., **II** 381, 395–96; **10** 59–60; **12** 534
United States Fidelity and Guaranty Co., **III** 395
United States Filter Corporation, I 429; **IV** 374; **20 501–04**; **38** 168, 170; **50** 48; **52** 189
United States Foil Co., **IV** 186; **19** 346
United States Football League, **29** 347
United States Glucose Co., **II** 496
United States Graphite Company, **V** 221–22
United States Gypsum Co., **III** 762–64
United States Health Care Systems, Inc. *See* U.S. Healthcare, Inc.
United States Independent Telephone Company, **6** 332
United States Leasing Corp., **II** 442

United States Mail Steamship Co., **23** 160

United States Medical Finance Corp., **18** 516, 518

United States Mortgage & Trust Company, **II** 251; **14** 102

United States National Bancshares, **25** 114

United States National Bank of Galveston. *See* Cullen/Frost Bankers, Inc.

United States National Bank of Oregon, **14** 527

The United States National Bank of Portland, **14** 527–28

United States National Bank of San Diego, **II** 355

United States Pipe and Foundry Co., **III** 766; **22** 544–45

United States Plywood Corp., **IV** 264, 282, 341; **9** 260; **13** 100; **20** 128

United States Postal Service, 10 60; **14 517–20; 34 470–75 (upd.); 42** 140

United States Realty-Sheraton Corp., **III** 98

United States Satellite Broadcasting Company Inc., **24** 226; **38** 176

United States Security Trust Co., **13** 466

United States Shoe Corporation, V 207–08; 17 296, 390; **23** 328; **39** 301; **52** 229

United States Steel Corporation, I 298, 491; **II** 129, 330; **III** 282, 326, 379; **IV** 35, 56, 110, 158, 572–74; **6** 514; **7** 48, 70–73, 401–02, 549–51; **10** 32; **11** 194; **12** 353–54; **17** 350, 356; **18** 378; **26** 405, 451; **50 500–04 (upd.); 54** 247–48

United States Sugar Refining Co., **II** 496

United States Surgical Corporation, 10 533–35; 13 365; **21** 119–20; **28** 486; **34 476–80 (upd.)**

United States Tobacco Company, **9** 533

United States Trucking Corp., **IV** 180–81

United States Trust Co. of New York. *See* U.S. Trust Corp.

United States Underseas Cable Corp., **IV** 178

United States Zinc Co., **IV** 32

United Stationers Inc., 14 521–23; 25 13; **36** 508

United Steel, **III** 494

United Steel Mills Ltd., **25** 266

United Supers, **II** 624

United Technologies Automotive Inc., 15 513–15

United Technologies Corporation, I 68, **84–86,** 143, 411, 530, 559; **II** 64, 82; **III** 74; **9** 18, 418; **10 536–38 (upd.); 11** 308; **12** 289; **13** 191, 384–86; **22** 6; **34** 371–72, 432, **481–85 (upd.); 39** 311, 313

United Telecommunications, Inc., V 344–47; 8 310; **9** 478–80; **10** 202; **12** 541

United Telephone Company, **7** 508; **14** 257

United Telephone Company of the Carolinas, **10** 202

United Telephone of Indiana, **14** 259

United Telephone System, Inc., **V** 346

United Telespectrum, **6** 314

United Television, Inc., **9** 119; **26** 32

United Television Programs, **II** 143

United Thermal Corp., **42** 388

United Transportation Co., **6** 382

United Truck Lines, **14** 505

United Utilities, Inc., **V** 344; **10** 202

United Utilities PLC, 52 372–75 (upd.)

United Van Lines, **14** 37; **15** 50

United Verde Copper Co., **IV** 178

United Video Satellite Group, 18 535–37. *See also* TV Guide, Inc.

United Vintners, **I** 243, 260–61

United Water Resources, Inc., 40 447–50; 45 277

United Way of America, 36 485–88

United Westburne Inc., **19** 313

United Westphalia Electricity Co., **IV** 127

Unitek Corp., **III** 18

Unitel Communications Inc., **6** 311; **44** 49; **46** 401; **47** 136

Unitika Ltd., V 387–89; 53 341–44 (upd.)

Unitil Corporation, 37 403–06

Unitog Co., **16** 228; **19 457–60; 21** 115; **51** 76

Unitransa, **27** 474

Unitrin Inc., 16 503–05

Unitron Medical Communications, **29** 412

Unity Cellular Systems, Inc. *See* Rural Cellular Corporation.

Unity Financial Corp., **19** 411

Unity Joint-Stock Bank, **II** 334

UNIVAC, **III** 133, 152, 313; **6** 233, 240, 266

Univar Corporation, 8 99; **9 530–32; 12** 333; **41** 340; **55** 297

Univas, **13** 203 **23** 171

Univasa, **39** 229

Univel Inc., **38** 418

Universal Adding Machine, **III** 165

Universal American, **I** 452

Universal Atlas Cement Co., **IV** 573–74; **7** 550–51; **50** 502

Universal Belo Productions, **10** 5

Universal Cheerleaders Association. *See* Varsity Spirit Corp.

Universal Cigar Corp., **14** 19

Universal Consumer Products Group, **30** 123

Universal Containers, **IV** 249

Universal Controls, Inc., **10** 319

Universal Cooler Corp., **8** 515

Universal Corporation, V 417–18; 48 403–06 (upd.)

Universal Data Systems, **II** 61; **22** 17

Universal Electronics Inc., 39 405–08

Universal Foods Corporation, 7 546–48; 21 498. *See also* Sensient Technologies Corporation.

Universal Footcare Products Inc., **31** 255

Universal Forest Products Inc., 10 539–40

Universal Frozen Foods, **23** 321

Universal Furniture, **III** 571; **20** 362

Universal Genève, **13** 121

Universal Guaranty Life Insurance Company, **11** 482

Universal Health Services, Inc., 6 191–93

Universal Highways, **III** 735

Universal Industries, Inc., **10** 380; **13** 533

Universal Instruments Corp., **III** 468

Universal International, Inc., 25 353, 355, **510–11**

Universal Juice Co., **21** 55

Universal Leaf Tobacco Company. *See* Universal Corporation.

Universal Manufacturing, **I** 440–41; **25** 167

Universal Marking Systems, **25** 331

Universal Match, **12** 464

Universal Matchbox Group, **12** 495

Universal Matthey Products Ltd., **IV** 119

Universal Music Group, **22** 194; **26** 152; **37** 193

Universal Paper Bag Co., **IV** 345

Universal Pictures, **II** 102, 135, 144, 154–55, 157; **10** 196; **14** 399; **25** 271. *See also* Universal Studios, Inc.

Universal Press Syndicate, **10** 4; **40** 38

Universal Records, **27** 123

Universal Resources Corporation, **6** 569; **26** 388

Universal Shoes, Inc., **22** 213

Universal Stamping Machine Co., **III** 156

Universal Studios Florida, **14** 399

Universal Studios, Inc., II 143–44; **12** 73; **21** 23–26; **25** 411; **33 429–33; 47** 419–21

Universal Tea Co., Inc., **50** 449

Universal Telephone, **9** 106

Universal Television, **II** 144

Universal Textured Yarns, **12** 501

Universal Transfers Co. Ltd., **IV** 119

University Computing Corp., **II** 38; **11** 468; **17** 320; **25** 87

University HealthSystem Consortium, **53** 346

University Microfilms, **III** 172; **6** 289

University of Phoenix, **24** 40

Univisa, **24** 516

Univision Communications Inc., IV 621; **18** 213; **24 515–18; 41** 150–52; **54** 72–73, 158

Unix System Laboratories Inc., **6** 225; **25** 20–21; **38** 418

UNM. *See* United News & Media plc.

Uno-e Bank, **48** 51

Uno Restaurant Corporation, 16 447; **18** 465, **538–40**

Uno-Ven, **IV** 571; **24** 522

Unocal Corporation, IV 508, **569–71; 24 519–23 (upd.)**

UNR Industries, Inc. *See* ROHN Industries, Inc.

Unterberg Harris, **25** 433

UNUM Corp., III 236; **13 538–40**

UnumProvident Corporation, 52 376–83 (upd.)

Uny Co., Ltd., II 619; **V 209–10,** 154; **13** 545; **36** 419; **49 425–28 (upd.)**

UPC. *See* United Pan-Europe Communications NV.

UPI. *See* United Press International.

Upjohn Company, I 675, 684, 686, 700, **707–09; III** 18, 53; **6** 42; **8 547–49 (upd.); 10** 79; **12** 186; **13** 503; **14** 423; **16** 440; **29** 363. *See also* Pharmacia & Upjohn Inc.

UPM-Kymmene Corporation, 19 461–65; 25 12; **30** 325; **50 505–11 (upd.)**

UPN. *See* United Paramount Network.

Upper Deck Company, LLC, **34** 448; **37** 295

Upper Peninsula Power Co., **53** 369

UPS. *See* United Parcel Service of America Inc.

UPSHOT, **27** 195

Upton Machine Company, **12** 548

Uraga Dock Co., **II** 361; **III** 634

Uraga Heavy Industries, **III** 634

Urbaine, **III** 391–92

Urban Investment and Development Co., **IV** 703

Urban Outfitters, Inc., 14 524–26

Urban Systems Development Corp., **II** 121

Urbaser SA, **55** 182
Urenco, **6** 452
URS Corporation, 45 420–23
Urwick Orr, **II** 609
US. *See also* U.S.
US Airways Express, **32** 334; **38** 130
US Airways Group, Inc., 28 506–09 (upd.); **33** 303; **52** 24–25, **384–88 (upd.)**
US Industrial Chemicals, Inc., **I** 377; **8** 440
US Industries Inc., **30** 231
US Monolithics, **54** 407
US 1 Industries, **27** 404
US Order, Inc., **10** 560, 562
US Sprint Communications Company, **V** 295–96, 346–47; **6** 314; **8** 310; **9** 32; **10** 543; **11** 302; **12** 136, 541; **14** 252–53; **15** 196; **16** 318, 392; **25** 101; **29** 44; **43** 447. *See also* Sprint Communications Company, L.P.
US Telecom, **9** 478–79
US West Communications Services, Inc., **19** 255; **21** 285; **29** 39, 45, 478; **37** 312, 315–16. *See also* Regional Bell Operating Companies.
USA Cafes, **14** 331
USA Floral Products Inc., **27** 126
USA Interactive, Inc., 47 418–22 (upd.)
USA Networks Inc., **25** 330, 411; **33** 432; **37** 381, 383–84; **43** 422
USA Security Systems, Inc., **27** 21
USA Truck, Inc., 42 410–13
USAA, 10 541–43
USAir Group, Inc., I 55, **131–32**; **III** 215; **6** 121, **131–32 (upd.)**; **11** 300; **14** 70, 73; **18** 62; **21** 143; **24** 400; **26** 429; **42** 34. *See also* US Airways Group, Inc.
USANA, Inc., 27 353; **29 491–93**
USCC. *See* United States Cellular Corporation.
USCP-WESCO Inc., **II** 682
Usego AG., **48** 63
USF&G Corporation, III 395–98; 11 494–95; **19** 190
USFL. *See* United States Football League.
USFreightways Corporation, **27** 475; **49** 402
USG Corporation, III 762–64; 26 507–10 (upd.)
USH. *See* United Scientific Holdings.
Usines de l'Espérance, **IV** 226
Usines Métallurgiques de Hainaut, **IV** 52
Usinger's Famous Sausage. *See* Fred Usinger Inc.
Usinor SA, 42 414–17 (upd.)
Usinor Sacilor, IV 226–28; **22** 44; **24** 144; **26** 81, 84; **54** 393
USLD Communications Corp. *See* Billing Concepts Corp.
USLIFE, **III** 194
USM, **10** 44
Usource LLC, **37** 406
USPS. *See* United States Postal Service.
USSC. *See* United States Surgical Corporation.
USSI. *See* U.S. Software Inc.
UST Inc., 9 533–35; 42 79; **50 512–17 (upd.)**
UST Wilderness Management Corporation, **33** 399
Usutu Pulp Company, **49** 353
USV Pharmaceutical Corporation, **11** 333
USWeb/CKS. *See* marchFIRST, Inc.

USX Corporation, I 466; **IV** 130, 228, **572–74**; **7** 193–94, **549–52 (upd.)**. *See also* United States Steel Corporation.
UT Starcom, **44** 426
UTA, **I** 119, 121; **6** 373–74, 93; **34** 397
Utag, **11** 510
Utah Construction & Mining Co., **I** 570; **IV** 146; **14** 296
Utah Federal Savings Bank, **17** 530
Utah Gas and Coke Company, **6** 568
Utah Group Health Plan, **6** 184
Utah International, **II** 30; **12** 196
Utah Medical Products, Inc., 36 496–99
Utah Mines Ltd., **IV** 47; **22** 107
Utah Oil Refining Co., **IV** 370
Utah Power and Light Company, 9 536; **12** 266; **27 483–86**. *See also* PacifiCorp.
UTI Energy, Inc. *See* Patterson-UTI Energy, Inc.
Utilicom, **6** 572
Utilicorp United Inc., 6 592–94. *See also* Aquilla, Inc.
UtiliTech Solutions, **37** 88
Utilities Power & Light Corporation, **I** 512; **6** 508
Utility Constructors Incorporated, **6** 527
Utility Engineering Corporation, **6** 580
Utility Fuels, **7** 377
Utility Service Affiliates, Inc., **45** 277
Utility Services, Inc., **42** 249, 253
Utility Supply Co. *See* United Stationers Inc.
AB Utra Wood Co., **IV** 274
Utrecht Allerlei Risico's, **III** 200
UUNET, 38 468–72
UV Industries, Inc., **7** 360; **9** 440

V & V Cos., **I** 412
V&S Variety Stores, **V** 37
V.A.W. of America Inc., **IV** 231
V.L. Churchill Group, **10** 493
VA Linux Systems, **45** 363
VA TECH ELIN EBG GmbH, 49 429–31
Vabis, **I** 197
Vacheron Constantin, **27** 487, 489
Vaco, **38** 200, 202
Vaculator Division. *See* Lancer Corporation.
Vacuum Metallurgical Company, **11** 234
Vacuum Oil Co., **IV** 463–64, 504, 549; **7** 351–52
Vadic Corp., **II** 83
Vadoise Vie, **III** 273
VAE Nortrak Cheyenne Inc., **53** 352
Vagnfabriks A.B., **I** 197
Vail Associates, Inc., 11 543–46; **31** 65, 67
Vail Resorts, Inc., 43 435–39 (upd.)
Vaillant GmbH, 44 436–39
Val Corp., **24** 149
Val-Pak Direct Marketing Systems, Inc., **22** 162
Val Royal LaSalle, **II** 652
Valassis Communications, Inc., 8 550–51; 37 407–10 (upd.)
Valcambi S.A., **II** 268; **21** 145
Valcom, **13** 176
ValCom Inc. *See* InaCom Corporation.
Valdi Foods Inc., **II** 663–64
Valdosta Drug Co., **III** 9–10
Vale do Rio Doce Navegacao SA— Docenave, **43** 112
Vale Harmon Enterprises, Ltd., **25** 204

Vale Power Company, **12** 265
Valentine & Company, **8** 552–53
Valeo, III 593; **23 492–94**
Valero Energy Corporation, IV 394; **7 553–55**; **19** 140; **31** 119
Valhi, Inc., 10 435–36; 19 466–68
Valid Logic Systems Inc., **11** 46, 284; **48** 77
Valio-Finnish Co-operative Dairies' Assoc., **II** 575
Valke Oy, **IV** 348
Vallen Corporation, 45 424–26
Valley Bank of Helena, **35** 197, 199
Valley Bank of Maryland, **46** 25
Valley Bank of Nevada, **19** 378
Valley Crest Tree Company, **31** 182–83
Valley Deli Inc., **24** 243
Valley East Medical Center, **6** 185
Valley Falls Co., **III** 213
Valley Fashions Corp., **16** 535
Valley Federal of California, **11** 163
Valley Fig Growers, **7** 496–97
Valley Forge Life Insurance Co., **III** 230
Valley Media Inc., 35 430–33
Valley National Bank, **II** 420
Valley-Todeco, Inc., **13** 305–06
Valley Transport Co., **II** 569
Valleyfair, **22** 130
Vallourec SA, IV 227; **54 391–94**
Valmac Industries, **II** 585
Valmet Corporation, I 198; **III 647–49**; **IV** 276, 350, 471
Valmet Oy. *See* Metso Corporation.
Valmont Industries, Inc., 13 276; **19** 50, **469–72**
Valores Industriales S.A., 19 10, 12, 189, **473–75**; **29** 219
The Valspar Corporation, 8 552–54; 32 483–86 (upd.)
Valtec Industries, **III** 684
Valtek International, Inc., **17** 147
Valtur, **6** 207; **48** 316
Value America, **29** 312
Value City Department Stores,
Value City Department Stores, Inc., 29 311; **38 473–75**
Value Foods Ltd., **11** 239
Value Giant Stores, **12** 478
Value House, **II** 673
Value Investors, **III** 330
Value Line, Inc., 16 506–08
Value Merchants Inc., 13 541–43
Value Rent-A-Car, **9** 350; **23** 354
ValueClick, Inc., 49 432–34
Valueland, **8** 482
ValueVision International, Inc., 22 534–36; **27** 337
ValuJet, Inc. *See* AirTran Holdings, Inc.
Valvoline, Inc., **I** 291; **IV** 374
Valvtron, **11** 226
Van Ameringen-Haebler, Inc., **9** 290
Van Brunt Manufacturing Co., **III** 462; **21** 173
Van Camp Seafood Company, Inc., II 562–63; **7 556–57**; **13** 426. *See also* Chicken of the Sea International.
Van Cleef & Arpels Inc., **26** 145
Van de Kamp's, Inc., **II** 556–57; **7** 430; **32** 67
Van den Bergh Foods, **II** 588; **9** 319
Van der Horst Corp. of America, **III** 471
Van der Moolen Holding NV, **37** 224
Van Dorn Company, **13** 190
Van Dorn Electric Tool Co., **III** 435

Van Gend and Loos, **6** 404; **26** 241, 243
Van Houton, **II** 521
Van Houtte Inc., **39 409–11**
Van Kirk Chocolate, **7** 429
Van Kok-Ede, **II** 642
Van Leer Containers Inc., **30** 397
Van Leer Holding, Inc., **9** 303, 305
Van Leer N.V. *See* Royal Packaging
    Industries Van Leer N.V.
Van Mar, Inc., **18** 88
Van Munching & Company, Inc., **I** 256; **13**
    257, 259; **34** 202
Van Nostrand Reinhold, **8** 526
Van Ommeren, **41** 339–40
Van Ryn Gold Mines Estate, **IV** 90
Van Schaardenburg, **II** 528
Van Sickle, **IV** 485
Van Waters & Rogers, **8** 99; **41** 340
Van Wezel, **26** 278–79
Van Wijcks Waalsteenfabrieken, **14** 249
Vanadium Alloys Steel Company
    (VASCO), **13** 295–96
Vanant Packaging Corporation, **8** 359
Vance International Airways, **8** 349
Vancouver Pacific Paper Co., **IV** 286
Vanderbilt Mortgage and Finance, **13** 154
Vanderlip-Swenson-Tilghman Syndicate,
    IV 81; **7** 185
Vanessa and Biffi, **11** 226
The Vanguard Group, Inc., **34 486–89**
    (upd.)
The Vanguard Group of Investment
    Companies, **9** 239; **14 530–32**
Vanguard International Semiconductor
    Corp., **47** 385
Vanity Fair Mills, Inc., **V** 390–91
Vanity Fair Paper Mills, **IV** 281; **9** 259
Vans, Inc., **16 509–11**; **17** 259–61; **47**
    423–26 (upd.)
Vansickle Industries, **III** 603
Vanstar, **13** 176
Vantage Analysis Systems, Inc., **11** 490
Vantive Corporation, **33** 333; **38** 431–32
Vantona Group Ltd., **V** 356; **44** 105
Vantress Pedigree, Inc., **II** 585
Vapor Corp., **III** 444
Varco International, Inc., **42 418–20**
Varco-Pruden, Inc., **8** 544–46
Vare Corporation, **8** 366
Vari-Lite International, Inc., **35 434–36**
Variable Annuity Life Insurance Co., **III**
    193–94
Varian Associates Inc., **12 504–06**
Varian, Inc., **48 407–11 (upd.)**
Varibus Corporation, **6** 495
Variflex, Inc., **51 391–93**
Variform, Inc., **12** 397
VARIG S.A. (Viação Aérea Rio-
    Grandense), **6 133–35**; **26** 113; **29**
    494–97 (upd.); **31** 443–45; **33** 19
Varity Corporation, **III 650–52**; **7** 258,
    260; **19** 294; **27** 203, 251
Varlen Corporation, **16 512–14**
Varney Air Lines, **I** 47, 128; **6** 128; **9** 416
Varney Speed Lines. *See* Continental
    Airlines, Inc.
Varo, **7** 235, 237
Varsity Spirit Corp., **15 516–18**; **22** 459
Varta AG, **III** 536; **9** 180–81; **23 495–99**;
    26 230
Vasco Metals Corp., **I** 523; **10** 520, 522
Vascoloy-Ramet, **13** 295
VASP (Viaçao Aérea de Sao Paulo), **6**
    134; **29** 495; **31** 444–45

Vasset, S.A., **17** 362–63
Vast Solutions, **39** 24
Vastar Resources, Inc., **24 524–26**; **38**
    445, 448
Vaughan Harmon Systems Ltd., **25** 204
Vaughan Printers Inc., **23** 100
Vaungarde, Inc., **22** 175
Vauxhall, **19** 391
VAW Leichtmetall GmbH, **IV** 231
VBB Viag-Bayernwerk-Beteiligungs-
    Gesellschaft mbH, **IV** 232; **50** 170
VDM Nickel-Technologie AG, **IV** 89
VEB Londa, **III** 69
Veba A.G., **I** 349–50, **542–43**; **III** 695;
    IV 194–95, 199, 455, 508; **8** 69,
    494–495; **15 519–21 (upd.)**; **23** 69, 451,
    453–54; **24** 79; **25** 102; **26** 423; **32** 147.
    See also E.On AG.
Vebego International BV, **49 435–37**
VECO International, Inc., **7 558–59**
Vector Automotive Corporation, **13** 61
Vector Casa de Bolsa, **21** 413
Vector Gas Ltd., **13** 458
Vector Group Ltd., **35 437–40 (upd.)**
Vector Video, Inc., **9** 74
Vectra Bank Colorado, **53** 378
Veda International, **54** 395–96
Vedelectric, **13** 544
Vedior NV, **35 441–43**; **44** 5
Veeco Instruments Inc., **32 487–90**
Veeder-Root Company, **7** 116–17
VeggieTales. *See* Big Idea Productions,
    Inc.
Veit Companies, **43 440–42**
Vel-Tex Chemical, **16** 270
Velcarta S.p.A., **17** 281
Velcro Industries N.V., **19 476–78**
Velda Farms, Inc., **26** 448
Vellumoid Co., **I** 159
VeloBind, Inc., **10** 314
Velocity Express Corporation, **49 438–41**
Velsicol, **I** 342, 440
Velva-Sheen Manufacturing Co., **23** 66
Vemar, **7** 558
Venator Group Inc., **35 444–49 (upd.)**
Vencemos, **20** 124
Vencor, Inc., **IV** 402; **14** 243; **16 515–17**;
    25 456
Vendex International N.V., **10** 136–37;
    13 544–46; **26** 160; **46** 187, 189
Vendôme Luxury Group plc, **27 487–89**;
    29 90, 92
Vendors Supply of America, Inc., **7**
    241–42; **25** 241
Venetian Casino Resort, LLC, **47**
    427–29
Venevision, **54** 72–73, 75
Venevision, **24** 516, 517
Vennootschap Nederland, **III** 177–78
Ventshade Company, **40** 299–300
Ventura, **29** 356–57
Venture Out RV, **26** 193
Venture Stores Inc., **V** 134; **12 507–09**
Ventures Limited, **49** 137
Venturi, Inc., **9** 72
Vepco. *See* Virginia Electric and Power
    Company.
Vera Cruz Electric Light, Power and
    Traction Co. Ltd., **IV** 658
Vera Imported Parts, **11** 84
Verafumos Ltd., **12** 109
Veragon Corporation. *See* Drypers
    Corporation.
Veratex Group, **13** 149–50

Veravision, **24** 510
Verbatim Corporation, **III** 477; **7** 163; **14**
    533–35; **36** 173
Verbundnetz Gas AG, **38** 408
Verd-A-Fay, **13** 398
Vereenigde Nederlandsche
    Scheepvaartmaatschappij, **6** 404; **26** 242
Vereeniging Refractories, **IV** 22
Vereeniging Tiles, **III** 734
Verein für Chemische Industrie, **IV** 70
Vereinigte Aluminium Werke AG, **IV**
    229–30, 232
Vereinigte Deutsche Metallwerke AG, **IV**
    140
Vereinigte Elektrizitäts und Bergwerke
    A.G., **I** 542
Vereinigte Elektrizitätswerke Westfalen
    AG, **IV** 195; **V 744–47**
Vereinigte Energiewerke AG, **V** 709
Vereinigte Flugtechnische Werke GmbH., **I**
    42, 55, 74–75
Vereinigte Glanzstoff-Fabriken, **13** 21
Vereinigte Industrie-Unternehmungen
    Aktiengesellschaft, **IV** 229–30
Vereinigte Leichtmetall-Werke GmbH, **IV**
    231
Vereinigte Papierwarenfabriken GmbH, **IV**
    323
Vereinigte Papierwerke Schickedanz AG,
    26 384
Vereinigte Stahlwerke AG, **III** 565; **IV** 87,
    104–05, 132, 221; **14** 327
Vereinigte Versicherungsgruppe, **III** 377
Vereinigten Westdeutsche Waggonfabriken
    AG, **III** 542–43
Vereinsbank Wismar, **II** 256
Vereinte Versicherungen, **III** 377
Verenigde Bedrijven Bredero, **26** 280
N.V. Verenigde Fabrieken Wessanen and
    Laan, **II** 527
Verenigde Nederlandse Uitgeverijen. *See*
    VNU N.V.
Verenigde Spaarbank Groep. *See* VSB
    Groep.
Veridian Corporation, **54 395–97**
Verienigte Schweizerbahnen, **6** 424
Verifact Inc. (IVI), **46** 251
VeriFone, Inc., **15** 321; **18 541–44**; **27**
    219–21; **28** 191; **50** 227
Verilyte Gold, Inc., **19** 452
VeriSign, Inc., **47 430–34**
Veritas Capital Fund L.P., **44** 420, 423
Veritas Capital Management, L.L.C., **54**
    178
Veritas Capital Partners, **26** 408
Veritas Software Corporation, **45**
    427–31
Veritec Technologies, Inc., **48** 299
Veritus Inc., **27** 208–09
Verizon Communications, **43 443–49**
    (upd.)
Verizon Wireless, Inc., **42** 284
Verlagsgruppe Georg von Holtzbrinck
    GmbH, **15** 158, 160; **25** 485; **35 450–53**
Vermeer Manufacturing Company, **17**
    507–10
Vermont General Insurance Company, **51**
    248
Vermont Pure Holdings, Ltd., **51 394–96**
The Vermont Teddy Bear Co., Inc., **36**
    500–02
Verneuil Holding Co, **21** 387
Vernitron Corporation, **18** 293

Vernon and Nelson Telephone Company. *See* British Columbia Telephone Company.
Vernon Graphics, **III** 499
Vernon Paving, **III** 674
Vernon Savings & Loan, **9** 199
Vernons, **IV** 651
Vernors, Inc., **25** 4
Vero, **III** 434
La Verrerie Souchon-Neuvesel, **II** 474
Verreries Champenoises, **II** 475
Verreries Pochet et du Courval, **55** 309
Versace. *See* Gianni Versace SpA.
Versatec Inc., **13** 128
Versatile Farm and Equipment Co., **22** 380
Versax, S.A. de C.V., **19** 12
Versicherungs-Verein, **III** 402, 410–11
Verson Allsteel Press Co., **21** 20, 22
Vert Baudet, **19** 309
Vertex Data Science Limited, **52** 372, 374–75
Vertical Technology Industries, **14** 571
Verticom, **25** 531
Verve Records, **23** 389
Vessel Management Services, Inc., **28** 80
Vestar Capital Partners, **42** 309
Vestek Systems, Inc., **13** 417
Vestro, **19** 309
Vesuvius Crucible Co., **III** 681
Vesuvius USA Corporation, **8** 179
Veszpremtej, **25** 85
Veterinary Cos. of America, **III** 25
VEW AG, **IV** 234; **39 412–15**
Vexlar, **18** 313
VF Corporation, **V 390–92**; **12** 205; **13** 512; **17** 223, 225, **511–14 (upd.)**; **25** 22; **31** 261; **54 398–404 (upd.)**
VFW-Fokker B.V., **I** 41, 55, 74–75
VHA Inc., **53 345–47**
VHA Long Term Care, **23** 431
VH1 Inc., **23** 503
VI-Jon Laboratories, Inc., **12** 388
Via Cariane. *See* Keolis SA.
Via-Générale de Transport et d'Industrie SA, **28** 155
VIA/Rhin et Moselle, **III** 185
Viacao Aerea Rio Grandense of South America. *See* VARIG, SA.
Viacom Enterprises, **6** 33; **7** 336
Viacom Inc., **23** 274–76, **500–03 (upd.)**; **24** 106, 327; **26** 32; **28** 295; **30** 101; **31** 59, 109; **35** 402; **48** 214; **51** 218–19. *See also* National Amusements Inc.
Viacom International Inc., **7** 222–24, 530, **560–62**; **9** 429; **10** 175; **19** 403
Viag AG, **IV 229–32**, 323; **25** 332; **32** 153; **43** 188–89. *See also* E.On AG.
Viajes El Corte Inglés, S.A., **26** 129
VIASA, **I** 107; **6** 97; **36** 281
ViaSat, Inc., **54 405–08**
Viasoft Inc., **27 490–93**
VIASYS Healthcare, Inc., **52 389–91**
Viatech Continental Can Company, Inc., **25 512–15 (upd.)**
Vichy, **III** 46
Vickers-Armstrong Ltd., **I** 50, 57, 82; **24** 85
Vickers Inc., **III** 640, 642; **13** 8; **23** 83
Vickers plc, **I** 194–95; **II** 3; **III** 555, 652, 725; **16** 9; **21** 435; **27 494–97**; **47** 9
VICOM, **48** 415
Vicon Industries, Inc., **44 440–42**
Vicoreen Instrument Co., **I** 202

VICORP Restaurants, Inc., **12 510–12**; **48 412–15 (upd.)**
Vicra Sterile Products, **I** 628
Vicsodrive Japan, **III** 495
Victor Company, **10** 483
Victor Company of Japan, Ltd., **I** 411; **II** 55–56, 91, 102, **118–19**; **III** 605; **IV** 599; **12** 454; **26 511–13 (upd.)**
Victor Comptometer, **I** 676; **III** 154
Victor Equipment Co., **19** 440
Victor Manufacturing and Gasket Co., **I** 152
Victor Musical Industries Inc., **II** 119; **10** 285
Victor Talking Machine Co., **II** 88, 118
Victor Value, **II** 678
Victoria, **III** 308
Victoria & Co., **39** 247
Victoria & Legal & General, **III** 359
Victoria Coach Station, **6** 406
Victoria Creations Inc., **13** 536
Victoria Group, **44 443–46 (upd.)**
VICTORIA Holding AG, **III 399–401**. *See also* Victoria Group.
Victoria Paper Co., **IV** 286
Victoria Sugar Co., **III** 686
Victoria Wine Co., **I** 216
Victoria's Secret, **V** 115–16; **11** 498; **12** 557, 559; **16** 219; **18** 215; **24** 237; **25** 120–22, 521
Victorinox AG, **21 515–17**
Victory Fire Insurance Co., **III** 343
Victory Insurance, **III** 273
Victory Oil Co., **IV** 550
Victory Refrigeration Company, **22** 355
Victory Savings and Loan, **10** 339
Victory Supermarket. *See* Big V Supermarkets, Inc.
Vidal Sassoon, **17** 110
Video Concepts, **9** 186
Video Independent Theatres, Inc., **14** 86
Video Library, Inc., **9** 74
Video News International, **19** 285
Video Superstores Master Limited Partnership, **9** 74
Videoconcepts, **II** 107
VideoFusion, Inc., **16** 419
Videotex Network Japan, **IV** 680
Videotron, **25** 102
VideV, **24** 509
La Vie Claire, **13** 103
Vielle Montaign, **22** 285
Vienna Sausage Manufacturing Co., **14 536–37**
Viessmann Werke GmbH & Co., **37 411–14**
View-Master/Ideal Group, **12** 496
Viewdata Corp., **IV** 630; **15** 264
Viewer's Edge, **27** 429
Viewlogic, **11** 490
ViewStar Corp., **20** 103
Viewtel, **14** 36
ViewTrade Holding Corp., **46** 282
Vigilance-Vie, **III** 393
Vigilant Insurance Co., **III** 220; **14** 108; **37** 83
Vigoro, **22** 340
Vigortone, **II** 582
Viiala Oy, **IV** 302
Viking, **II** 10; **IV** 659
Viking Brush, **III** 614
Viking Building Products, **22** 15
Viking Computer Services, Inc., **14** 147

Viking Consolidated Shipping Corp, **25** 470
Viking Direct Limited, **10** 545
Viking Foods, Inc., **8** 482; **14** 411
Viking Industries, **39** 322, 324
Viking Office Products, Inc., **10 544–46**
Viking Penguin, **IV** 611
Viking Press, **12** 25
Viking Pump Company, **21** 499–500
Viking Star Shipping, Inc. *See* Teekay Shipping Corporation.
Viktor Achter, **9** 92
Village Inn. *See* VICORP Restaurants, Inc.
Village Super Market, Inc., **7 563–64**
Village Voice Media, Inc., **38 476–79**
Villager, Inc., **11** 216; **39** 244
Villazon & Co., **27** 139
Villeroy & Boch AG, **37 415–18**
VILPAC, S.A., **26** 356
AO VimpelCom, **48 416–19**
Vimto. *See* Nichols plc.
Vin & Spirit AB, **31 458–61**
Viña Concha y Toro S.A., **45 432–34**
Vinci, **27** 54; **43 450–52**; **49** 44
Vincor International Inc., **50 518–21**
Vine Products Ltd., **I** 215
Viner Bros., **16** 546
Vinewood Companies, **53** 232
Vingaarden A/S, **9** 100
Vingresor A.B., **I** 120
Vining Industries, **12** 128
Viniprix SA, **10** 205; **19** 309; **27** 95
Vinita Rock Company, **50** 49
Vinland Web-Print, **8** 360
Vinson & Elkins L.L.P., **28** 48; **30 481–83**; **47** 139–40, 447
Vintage Petroleum, Inc., **42 421–23**
Vintners International, **34** 89
Vinyl Maid, Inc., **IV** 401
Vipont Pharmaceutical, **III** 25; **14** 122
VIPS, **11** 113
Viratec Thin Films, Inc., **22** 347
Virco Manufacturing Corporation, **17 515–17**
Virgin Atlantic Airlines. *See* Virgin Group PLC.
Virgin Express, **35** 384
Virgin Group PLC, **12 513–15**; **14** 73; **18** 80; **22** 194; **24** 486; **29** 302; **32 491–96 (upd.)**; **50** 125
The Virgin Islands Telephone Co., **19** 256
Virgin Music Group Worldwide, **52** 429
Virgin Retail Group Ltd., **9** 75, 361; **37** 262
Virginia Eastern Shore Sustainable Development Corporation, **28** 307
Virginia Electric and Power Company, **V** 596–98
Virginia Fibre Corporation, **15** 188
Virginia Folding Box Company, **IV** 352; **19** 497
Virginia Laminating, **10** 313
Virginia Mason Medical Center, **41** 183
Virginia National Bankshares, **10** 426
Virginia Railway and Power Company (VR&P), **V** 596
Virginia Trading Corp., **II** 422
Viridor Waste Limited, **45** 338
Viromedics, **25** 382
Visa. *See* Valores Industriales S.A.
Visa International, **II** 200; **9** 333–35, **536–38**; **18** 543; **20** 59; **26 514–17 (upd.)**; **41** 200–01
Visco Products Co., **I** 373; **12** 346

Viscodrive GmbH, **III** 495

Viscount Industries Limited, **6** 310

Vishay Intertechnology, Inc., **11** 516; **21** **518–21**

VisiCorp, **6** 254; **25** 298

Vision Centers, **I** 688; **12** 188

Vision Hardware Group. *See* Acorn Products, Inc.

Vision Technology Group Ltd., **19** 124; **49** 113

Visionware Ltd., **38** 419

Visionworks, **9** 186

Viskase Companies, Inc., **17** 157, 159; **55** **379–81**

Visking Co., **I** 400

Visnews Ltd., **IV** 668, 670

VisQueen, **I** 334

Vista Bakery Inc., **14** 306

Vista Chemical Company, **I** **402–03;** **V** 709

Vista Concepts, Inc., **11** 19

Vista Resources, Inc., **17** 195

Vista 2000, Inc., **36** 444

Vistana, Inc., **22** **537–39;** **26** 464

Visual Action Holdings plc, **24** 96, 374

Visual Information Technologies, **11** 57

Visual Technology, **6** 201

VISX, Incorporated, **30** **484–86**

Vita-Achter, **9** 92

Vita Lebensversicherungs-Gesellschaft, **III** 412

Vita Liquid Polymers, **9** 92

Vitafoam Incorporated, **9** 93; **33** 78

Vital Health Corporation, **13** 150

Vital Processing Services LLC, **18** 516, 518

Vitalink Communications Corp., **11** 520; **34** 444

Vitalink Pharmacy Services, Inc., **15** **522–24;** **25** 309–10

Vitalscheme, **38** 426

Vitamin World, **31** 346–48

Vitesse Semiconductor Corporation, **32** **497–500**

Vitex Foods, **10** 382

Vitoria-Minas Railroad, **43** 111

Vitramon, Inc., **54** 371–72

Vitro Corp., **8** 178; **10** **547–48;** **17** 492

Vitro Corporativo S.A. de C.V., **34** **490–92**

Vitro S.A., **19** 189

VIVA, **23** 390

Viva Home Co., **III** 757

Vivarte SA, **54** **409–12 (upd.)**

Vivendi Universal S.A., **29** 369, 371; **32** 52, 54; **33** 178, 181; **34** 83, 85; **38** 168, 170; **40** 408; **41** 361; **43** 450, 452; **44** 190; **46** **438–41 (upd.);** **47** 420–21; **48** 164–65

Vivendia, **40** 449

Vivesvata Iron and Steel Ltd., **IV** 207

Viviane Woodard Cosmetic Corp., **II** 531

Vivra, Inc., **15** 119; **18** **545–47**

VK Mason Construction Ltd., **II** 222

VKI Technologies Inc., **39** 409

Vladivostok Dairy, **48** 438

Vlasic Foods International Inc., **II** 480–81; **7** 67–68; **25** **516–19;** **26** 56, 59

VLN Corp., **I** 201

VLSI Technology, Inc., **11** 246; **16** **518–20;** **31** 300

VMG Products. *See* Drypers Corporation.

VMX Inc., **14** 355; **41** 289

VND, **III** 593

Vnesheconobank, **II** 242

VNG. *See* Verbundnetz Gas AG.

VNS. *See* Vereenigde Nederlandsche Scheepvaartmaatschappij.

VNU N.V., **27** 361, **498–501;** **38** 8

VNU/Claritas, **6** 14

Vobis Microcomputer, **20** 103; **23** 311

VocalTec, Inc., **18** 143

Vodac, **11** 548

Vodacom World Online Ltd, **48** 399

Vodafone Group Plc, **II** 84; **11** **547–48;** **34** 85; **36** **503–06 (upd.);** **38** 296, 300

Vodapage, **11** 548

Vodata, **11** 548

Vodavi Technology Corporation, **13** 213

Voest-Alpine Stahl AG, **IV** **233–35;** **31** 47–48

Vogel Peterson Furniture Company, **7** 4–5

Vogoro Corp., **13** 503

Voice Data Systems, **15** 125

Voice Powered Technology International, Inc., **23** 212

Voice Response, Inc., **11** 253

VoiceStream Wireless Corporation, **48** 130

Voith Sulzer Papiermaschinen GmbH. *See* J.M. Voith AG.

Vokes, **I** 429

Volition, Inc., **39** 395

Volkert Stampings, **III** 628

Volkswagen Aktiengesellschaft, **I** 30, 32, 186, 192, **206–08,** 460; **II** 279; **IV** 231; **7** 8; **10** 14; **11** 104, **549–51 (upd.);** **13** 413; **14** 169; **16** 322; **19** 484; **26** 12; **27** 11, 496; **31** 363–65; **32** **501–05 (upd.);** **34** 55, 130; **39** 373–74

Volt Information Sciences Inc., **26** **518–21**

Volta Aluminium Co., Ltd., **IV** 122

Volume Distributors. *See* Payless ShoeSource, Inc.

Volume Service Company. *See* Restaurants Unlimited, Inc.

Volume Shoe Corporation. *See* Payless ShoeSource,Inc.

Voluntary Hospitals of America, **6** 45

Volunteer Leather Company, **17** 202, 205

Volunteer State Life Insurance Co., **III** 221; **37** 84

AB Volvo, **I** 186, 192, 198, **209–11;** **II** 5, 366; **III** 543, 591, 623, 648; **IV** 336; **7** **565–68 (upd.);** **9** 283–84, 350, 381; **10** 274; **12** 68, 342; **13** 30, 356; **14** 321; **15** 226; **16** 322; **18** 394; **23** 354; **26** **9–12 (upd.),** 401, 403; **33** 191, 364; **39** 126. *See also* Ford Motor Company.

Volvo-Penta, **21** 503

von Roll, **6** 599

Von Ruden Manufacturing Co., **17** 532

von Weise Gear Co., **III** 509

Von's Grocery Co., **II** 419; **8** 474; **17** 559

The Vons Companies, Incorporated, **II** 655; **7** **569–71;** **12** 209; **24** 418; **28** **510–13 (upd.);** **35** 328

VOP Acquisition Corporation, **10** 544

Vornado Realty Trust, **20** **508–10;** **39** 211; **45** 14–16; **47** 360

Voroba Hearing Systems, **25** 56

Vortex Management, Inc., **41** 207

Vorwerk & Co., **27** **502–04**

Vosper Thornycroft Holding plc, **41** **410–12**

Vossloh AG, **53** **348–52**

Votainer International, **13** 20

Vought Aircraft Industries, Inc., **11** 364; **45** 309; **49** **442–45**

Voxson, **I** 531; **22** 193

Voyage Conseil, **II** 265

Voyager Communications Inc., **24** 5

Voyager Energy, **IV** 84

Voyager Ltd., **12** 514

Voyager Petroleum Ltd., **IV** 83; **7** 188

Voyageur Travel Insurance Ltd., **21** 447

VR&P. *See* Virginia Railway and Power Company.

Vratislavice A.S., **38** 77

VRG International. *See* Roberts Pharmaceutical Corporation.

Vriesco Plastics B.V., **53** 221

Vroom & Dreesmann, **13** 544–46

Vrumona B.V., **I** 257

VS Services, **13** 49

VSA. *See* Vendors Supply of America, Inc.

VSB Groep, **III** 199, 201

VSD Communications, Inc., **22** 443

VSEL, **24** 88

VSM. *See* Village Super Market, Inc.

VST. *See* Vision Technology Group Ltd.

Vtel Corporation, **10** 456; **27** 365

VTR Incorporated, **16** 46; **43** 60

Vu-Tech Communications, Inc., **48** 54

Vulcan Materials Company, **7** **572–75;** **12** 39; **25** 266; **41** 147, 149; **52** **392–96 (upd.)**

Vulcan Ventures Inc., **32** 145; **43** 144

Vulcraft, **7** 400–02

VVM, **III** 200

VW&R. *See* Van Waters & Rogers.

VWR Textiles & Supplies, Inc., **11** 256

VWR United Company, **9** 531

Vycor Corporation, **25** 349

Vyvx, **31** 469

W&A Manufacturing Co., LLC, **26** 530

W&F Fish Products, **13** 103

W. & G. Turnbull & Co., **IV** 278; **19** 153

W & J Sloane Home Furnishings Group, **35** 129

W. & M. Duncan, **II** 569

W.A. Bechtel Co., **I** 558

W.A. Harriman & Co., **III** 471

W.A. Krueger Co., **19** 333–35

W.A. Whitney Company, **53** **353–56**

W. Atlee Burpee & Co., **II** 532; **11** 198; **27** **505–08**

W.B. Constructions, **III** 672

W.B. Doner & Company, **10** 420; **12** 208; **28** 138

W.B. Saunders Co., **IV** 623–24

W.C. Bradley Company, **18** 516

W.C.G. Sports Industries Ltd. *See* Canstar Sports Inc.

W.C. Heraeus GmbH, **IV** 100

W.C. Norris, **III** 467

W.C. Platt Co., **IV** 636

W.C. Ritchie & Co., **IV** 333

W.C. Smith & Company Limited, **14** 339

W. Duke & Sons, **V** 395, 600

W. Duke Sons & Company, **27** 128

W.E. Andrews Co., Inc., **25** 182

W.E. Dillon Company, Ltd., **21** 499

W.F. Linton Company, **9** 373

W. Gunson & Co., **IV** 278; **19** 153

W. Gutzeit & Co., **IV** 274–77

W.H. Brady Co., **17** **518–21**

W.H. Gunlocke Chair Co. *See* Gunlocke Company.

W.H. McElwain Co., **III** 528

W.H. Morton & Co., **II** 398; **10** 62
W.H. Smith & Son (Alacra) Ltd., **15** 473
W H Smith Group PLC, **V** 211–13
W.J. Noble and Sons, **IV** 294; **19** 225
W.L. Gore & Associates, Inc., **14** 538–40; **26** 417
W.M. Bassett Furniture Co. *See* Bassett Furniture Industries, Inc.
W.M. Ritter Lumber Co., **IV** 281; **9** 259
W.O. Daley & Company, **10** 387
W.P. Carey & Co. LLC, **49** 446–48
W.R. Bean & Son, **19** 335
W.R. Berkley Corp., **III** 248; **15** 525–27
W.R. Breen Company, **11** 486
W.R. Case & Sons Cutlery Company, **18** 567
W.R. Grace & Company, **I** 547–50; **III** 525, 695; **IV** 454; **11** 216; **12** 337; **13** 149, 502, 544; **14** 29; **16** 45–47; **17** 308, 365–66; **21** 213, 507, 526; **22** 188, 501; **25** 535; **35** 38, 40; **43** 59–60; **49** 307; **50** 78, **522–29 (upd.)**; **54** 363
W. Rosenlew, **IV** 350
W.S. Barstow & Company, **6** 575
W.T. Grant Co., **16** 487
W.T. Rawleigh, **17** 105
W.T. Young Foods, **III** 52; **8** 433; **26** 383
W. Ullberg & Co., **I** 553
W.V. Bowater & Sons, Ltd., **IV** 257–58
W.W. Cargill and Brother, **II** 616; **13** 136
W.W. Grainger, Inc., **V** 214–15; **13** 297; **26** **537–39 (upd.)**
W.W. Kimball Company, **12** 296; **18** 44
W.W. Norton & Company, Inc., **28** 518–20
Waban Inc., **V** 198; **13** 547–49; **19** 449. *See also* HomeBase, Inc.
Wabash National Corp., **13** 550–52
Wabash Valley Power Association, **6** 556
Wabtec Corporation, **40** 451–54
Wabush Iron Co., **IV** 73; **24** 143
Wachbrit Insurance Agency, **21** 96
Wachovia Bank of Georgia, N.A., **16** 521–23
Wachovia Bank of South Carolina, N.A., **16** 524–26
Wachovia Corporation, **II** 336; **10** 425; **12** 16, **516–20**; **16** 521, 524, 526; **23** 455; **46** **442–49 (upd.)**
Wachtell, Lipton, Rosen & Katz, **47** 435–38
The Wackenhut Corporation, **13** 124–25; **14** 541–43; **28** 255; **41** 80
Wacker-Chemie GmbH, **35** 454–58
Wacker Oil Inc., **11** 441
Waco Aircraft Company, **27** 98
Wacoal Corp., **25** 520–24
Waddell & Reed, Inc., **22** 540–43; **33** 405, 407
Wade Smith, **28** 27, 30
Wadsworth Inc., **8** 526
WaferTech, **18** 20; **43** 17; **47** 385
Waffle House Inc., **14** 544–45
Wagenseller & Durst, **25** 249
Waggener Edstrom, **42** 424–26
The Wagner & Brown Investment Group, **9** 248
Wagner Castings Company, **16** 474–75
Wagner Litho Machinery Co., **13** 369–70
Wagner Spray Tech, **18** 555
Wagonlit Travel, **22** 128; **55** 90
Wagons-Lits, **27** 11; **29** 443; **37** 250–52
Wah Chang Corp., **I** 523–24; **10** 520–21
AB Wahlbecks, **25** 464

Wahlstrom & Co., **23** 480
Waialua Agricultural Co., **II** 491
Waitaki International Biosciences Co., **17** 288
Waite Amulet Mines Ltd., **IV** 164
Waitrose Ltd. *See* John Lewis Partnership plc.
Wakefern Food Corporation, **II** 672; **7** 563–64; **18** 6; **25** 66, 234–35; **28** 143; **33** 434–37
Wako Shoji Co. Ltd. *See* Wacoal Corp.
Wakodo Co., **I** 674
Wal-Mart de Mexico, S.A. de C.V., **35** 322, **459–61 (upd.)**
Wal-Mart Stores, Inc., **II** 108; **V** 216–17; **6** 287; **7** 61, 331; **8** 33, 295, **555–57 (upd.)**; **9** 187, 361; **10** 236, 284, 515–16, 524; **11** 292; **12** 48, 53–55, 63–64, 97, 208–09, 221, 277, 333, 477, 507–08; **13** 42, 215–17, 260–61, 274, 332–33, 444, 446; **14** 235; **15** 139, 275; **16** 61–62, 65, 390; **17** 297, 321, 460–61; **18** 108, 137, 186, 283, 286; **19** 511; **20** 263; **21** 457–58; **22** 224, 257, 328; **23** 214; **24** 148, 149, 334; **25** 221–22, 254, 314; **26** **522–26 (upd.)**, 549; **27** 286, 313, 315, 416, 451; **29** 230, 314, 318; **32** 169, 338, 341; **33** 307; **34** 198; **37** 64; **41** 61, 115; **45** 408, 412
Walbridge Aldinger Co., **38** 480–82
Walbro Corporation, **13** 553–55
Walchenseewerk AG, **23** 44
Waldbaum, Inc., **II** 638; **15** 260; **16** 247, 249; **19** 479–81; **24** 528
Walden Book Company Inc., **V** 112; **10** 136–37; **16** 160; **17** 522–24; **25** 30; **47** 209
Waldes Truarc Inc., **III** 624
Oy Waldhof AB, **IV** 324
Wales & Company, **14** 257
Walgreen Co., **V** 218–20; **9** 346; **18** 199; **20** 511–13 **(upd.)**; **21** 186; **24** 263; **32** 166, 170; **45** 133, 137
Walk Haydel & Associates, Inc., **25** 130
Walk Softly, Inc., **25** 118
Walker & Lee, **10** 340
Walker Cain, **I** 215
Walker Dickson Group Limited, **26** 363
Walker Interactive Systems, **11** 78; **25** 86
Walker Manufacturing Company, **I** 527; **19** 482–84
Walker McDonald Manufacturing Co., **III** 569; **20** 361
Walkers Parker and Co., **III** 679–80
Walki GmbH, **IV** 349
AB Walkiakoski, **IV** 347
Walkins Manufacturing Corp., **III** 571; **20** 362
Walkup's Merchant Express Inc., **27** 473
Wall Drug Store, Inc., **40** 455–57
Wall Paper Manufacturers, **IV** 666; **17** 397
Wall Street Deli, Inc., **33** 438–41
Wall Street Leasing, **III** 137
Wallace & Tiernan Group, **I** 383; **11** 361; **52** 374
The Wallace Berrie Company. *See* Applause Inc.
Wallace Computer Services, Inc., **36** 507–10
Wallace International Silversmiths, **I** 473; **14** 482–83
Wallace Murray Corp., **II** 420
Wallbergs Fabriks A.B., **8** 14

Wallens Dairy Co., **II** 586
Wallin & Nordstrom, **V** 156
Wallingford Bank and Trust Co., **II** 213
Wallis, **V** 177
Wallis Arnold Enterprises, Inc., **21** 483
Wallis Tin Stamping Co., **I** 605
Wallis Tractor Company, **21** 502
Walrus, Inc., **18** 446
Walsin-Lihwa, **13** 141
Walston & Co., **II** 450; **III** 137
Walt Disney Company, **II** 102, 122, 129, 156, **172–74**; **III** 142, 504, 586; **IV** 585, 675, 703; **6** 15, **174–77 (upd.)**, 368; **7** 305; **8** 160; **10** 420; **12** 168, 208, 229, 323, 495–96; **13** 551; **14** 260; **15** 197; **16** 143, 336; **17** 243, 317, 442–43; **21** 23–26, 360–61; **23** 257–58, 303, 335, 476, 514; **25** 172, 268, 312–13; **27** 92, 287; **30** **487–91 (upd.)**; **34** 348; **43** 142, 447; **50** 322, 389; **51** 218, 220; **52** 3, 5, 84; **53** 41; **54** 333, 335–37
Walt Disney World, **6** 82, 175–76; **18** 290
Walter Baker's Chocolate, **II** 531
Walter Bau, **27** 136, 138
Walter E. Heller, **17** 324
Walter Herzog GmbH, **16** 514
Walter Industries, Inc., **III** 765–67; **22** **544–47 (upd.)**
Walter Kidde & Co., **I** 475, 524; **27** 287
Walter Pierce Oil Co., **IV** 657
Walter Wilson, **49** 18
Walter Wright Mammoet, **26** 280
Walton Manufacturing, **11** 486
Walton Monroe Mills, Inc., **8** 558–60
Wander Ltd., **I** 672
Wanderer Werke, **III** 154
Wang Global, **39** 176–78
Wang Laboratories, Inc., **II** 208; **III** 168–70; **6** **284–87 (upd.)**; **8** 139; **9** 171; **10** 34; **11** 68, 274; **12** 183; **18** 138; **19** 40; **20** 237
Wanishi, **IV** 157; **17** 349
WAP, **26** 420
Waples-Platter Co., **II** 625
War Damage Corp., **III** 353, 356; **22** 493
War Emergency Tankers Inc., **IV** 552
Warbasse-Cogeneration Technologies Partnership, **35** 479
Warburg, Pincus Capital Corp., **6** 13; **9** 524; **14** 42; **24** 373
Warburg USB, **38** 291
Warburtons Bakery Cafe, Inc., **18** 37
Ward Manufacturing Inc., **IV** 101
Ward's Communications, **22** 441
Wardley Ltd., **II** 298
Wards. *See* Circuit City Stores, Inc.
Waring and LaRosa, **12** 167
The Warnaco Group Inc., **9** 156; **12** **521–23**; **22** 123; **25** 122, 523; **46** **450–54 (upd.)**; **51** 30. *See also* Authentic Fitness Corp.
Warner & Swasey Co., **III** 168; **6** 284; **8** 545
Warner Brothers, **25** 327–28; **26** 102
Warner Communications Inc., **II** 88, 129, 135, 146–47, 154–55, 169–70, **175–77**, 208, 452; **III** 443, 505; **IV** 623, 673, 675–76; **7** 526, 528–30 **8** 527; **9** 44–45, 119, 469; **10** 196; **11** 557; **12** 73, 495–96; **17** 65, 149, 442–43; **21** 23–25, 360; **22** 519, 522; **23** 23–24, 390, 501; **24** 373; **25** 418–19, 498; **26** 151. *See also* Time Warner Inc.
Warner Cosmetics, **III** 48; **8** 129

Warner Gear Co., **III** 438–39; **14** 63–64
Warner-Lambert Co., I 643, 674, 679, 696, **710–12**; **7** 596; **8** 62–63; **10** 549–52 **(upd.)**; **12** 480, 482; **13** 366; **16** 439; **20** 23; **25** 55, 366; **34** 284; **38** 366
Warner Records, **II** 177
Warner Sugar Refining Co., **II** 496
Warrantech Corporation, 53 357–59
Warren Apparel Group Ltd., **39** 257
Warren Bancorp Inc., **55** 52
Warren Bank, **13** 464
Warren, Gorham & Lamont, **8** 526
Warren Oilfield Services, **9** 363
Warren Petroleum, **18** 365, 367; **49** 121
Warri Refining and Petrochemicals Co., **IV** 473
Warrick Industries, **31** 338
Warringah Brick, **III** 673
Warrington Products Ltd. *See* Canstar Sports Inc.
Warrior River Coal Company, **7** 281
Wartsila Marine Industries Inc., **III** 649
Warwick Chemicals, **13** 461
Warwick Electronics, **III** 654
Warwick International Ltd., **13** 462
Warwick Valley Telephone Company, 55 382–84
Wasa, **I** 672–73
Wasag-Chemie AG, **III** 694
Wasatch Gas Co., **6** 568
Wascana Energy Inc., 13 556–58
Washburn Crosby Co., **II** 501, 555; **10** 322
Washburn Graphics Inc., **23** 100
The Washington Companies, 33 442–45
Washington Duke Sons & Co., **12** 108
Washington Federal, Inc., 17 525–27
Washington Football, Inc., 35 462–65
Washington Gas Light Company, 19 485–88
Washington Inventory Service, **30** 239
Washington Mills Company, **13** 532
Washington Mutual, Inc., 17 528–31
Washington National Corporation, 11 482; **12 524–26**
Washington Natural Gas Company, 9 539–41
The Washington Post Company, III 214; **IV 688–90**; **6** 323; **11** 331; **18** 60, 61, 63; **20 515–18 (upd.)**; **23** 157–58; **42** 31, 33–34, 209–10
Washington Public Power Supply System, **50** 102
Washington Railway and Electric Company, **6** 552–53
Washington Scientific Industries, Inc., 17 532–34
Washington Specialty Metals Corp., **14** 323, 325
Washington Sports Clubs. *See* Town Sports International, Inc.
Washington Steel Corp., **14** 323, 325
Washington Water Power Company, 6 566, **595–98**; **50** 103–04, 366
Washtenaw Gas Company. *See* MCN Corporation.
Wassall Plc, 18 548–50
Wasserstein Perella Partners, **II** 629; **III** 512, 530–31; **V** 223; **17** 366
Waste Connections, Inc., 46 455–57
Waste Control Specialists LLC, **19** 466, 468
Waste Holdings, Inc., 41 413–15

Waste Management, Inc., V 749–51, **752–54**; **6** 46, 600; **9** 73, 108–09; **11** 435–36; **18** 10; **20** 90; **23** 430; **50** 61
Water Engineering, **11** 360
Water Pik Technologies, Inc., I 524–25; **34 498–501**
Water Products Group, **6** 487–88
Water Street Corporate Recovery Fund, **10** 423
The Waterbury Companies, **16** 482
Waterford Wedgwood Holdings PLC, IV 296; **12 527–29**
Waterford Wedgwood plc, 34 493–97 (upd.); **38** 403
Waterhouse Investor Services, Inc., 18 551–53; **49** 397
Waterloo Gasoline Engine Co., **III** 462; **21** 173
Waterlow and Sons, **10** 269
Waterman Marine Corporation, **27** 242
The Waterman Pen Company. *See* BIC Corporation.
WaterPro Supplies Corporation, **6** 486, 488
Waters Corporation, 43 453–57
Waterstone's, **42** 444
Waterstreet Inc., **17** 293
Watertown Insurance Co., **III** 370
Watkins-Johnson Company, 15 528–30
Watkins Manufacturing Co., **I** 159
Watkins-Strathmore Co., **13** 560
Watmough and Son Ltd., **II** 594
Watney Mann and Truman Brewers, **I** 228, 247; **9** 99
Watsco Inc., 52 397–400
Watson & Philip. *See* Alldays plc.
Watson Group, **55** 52
Watson-Haas Lumber Company, **33** 257
Watson Pharmaceuticals Inc., 16 527–29
Watson-Triangle, **16** 388, 390
Watson-Wilson Transportation System, **V** 540; **14** 567
Watson Wyatt Worldwide, 42 427–30
Watt & Shand, **16** 61; **50** 107
Watt AG, **6** 491
Watt Electronic Products, Limited, **10** 319
The Watt Stopper, **21** 348, 350
Wattie Industries, **52** 141
Wattie Pict Ltd., **I** 437
Wattie's Ltd., 7 576–78; **11** 173
Watts Industries, Inc., 19 489–91
Watts/Silverstein, Inc., **24** 96
Waukesha Engine Servicenter, **6** 441
Waukesha Foundry Company, **11** 187
Waukesha Motor Co., **III** 472
Wausau Paper Mills, **15** 305
Wausau Sulphate Fibre Co. *See* Mosinee Paper Corporation.
Wavelength Corporate Communications Pty Limited, **24** 95
Waverly, Inc., 10 135; **16** 530–32; **19** 358
Waverly Oil Works, **I** 405
Waverly Pharmaceutical Limited, **11** 208
Wawa Inc., 17 535–37
Waxman Industries, Inc., III 570; **9** 542–44; **20** 362; **28** 50–51
Wayco Foods, **14** 411
Waycross-Douglas Coca-Cola Bottling, **10** 222
Wayfinder Group Inc., **51** 265
Waymaker Oy, **55** 289
Wayne Home Equipment. *See* Scott Fetzer Company.
Wayne Oakland Bank, **8** 188
WB. *See* Warner Communications Inc.

WBI Holdings, Inc., **42** 249, 253
WCI Holdings Corporation, **V** 223; **13** 170; **41** 94
WCK, Inc., **14** 236
WCPS Direct, Inc., **53** 359
WCRS Group plc, **6** 15
WCT Live Communication Limited, **24** 95
WD-40 Company, 18 554–57
We Energies. *See* Wisconsin Energy Corporation.
Wear-Ever, **17** 213
WearGuard, **13** 48
Wearne Brothers, **6** 117
The Weather Channel Companies, 52 401–04; **55** 244. *See also* Landmark Communications, Inc.
The Weather Department, Ltd., **10** 89
Weather Guard, **IV** 305
Weatherford International, Inc., 39 416–18
Weathers-Lowin, Leeam, **11** 408
Weaver, **III** 468
Webb & Knapp, **10** 43
Webb Corbett and Beswick, **38** 402
Webber Gage Co., **13** 302
WeBco International LLC, **26** 530
Webco Securities, Inc., **37** 225
Weber, **16** 488
Weber Aircraft Inc., **41** 369
Weber Metal, **30** 283–84
Weber-Stephen Products Co., 40 458–60
Webers, **I** 409
Weblock, **I** 109
WebLogic Inc., **36** 81
Webster Publishing Co., **IV** 636
Webtron Corp., **10** 313
Webvan Group Inc., **38** 223
Wedgwood. *See* Waterford Wedgewood Holdings PLC.
Week's Dairy, **II** 528
Weeres Industries Corporation, 52 405–07
Wegener NV, 53 360–62
Wegert Verwaltungs-GmbH and Co. Beteiligungs-KG, **24** 270
Wegmans Food Markets, Inc., 9 545–46; **24** 445; **41 416–18 (upd.)**
Weichenwerk Brandenburg GmbH, **53** 352
Weidemann Brewing Co., **I** 254
Weider Health and Fitness, Inc., **38** 238
Weider Nutrition International, Inc., 29 498–501; **33** 146–47; **34** 459
Weider Sporting Goods, **16** 80
Weifang Power Machine Fittings Ltd., **17** 106
Weight Watchers Gourmet Food Co., **43** 218
Weight Watchers International Inc., II 508; **10** 383; **11** 172; **12** 530–32; **13** 383; **27** 197; **33 446–49 (upd.)**; **36** 255–56
Weil Ceramics & Glass, **52** 148
Weil, Gotshal & Manges LLP, 55 385–87
Weiner's Stores, Inc., 33 450–53
Weirton Steel Corporation, I 297; **IV 236–38**; **7** 447, 598; **8** 346, 450; **10** 31–32; **12** 352, 354; **26** 407, **527–30 (upd.)**
Weis Markets, Inc., 15 531–33
The Weitz Company, Inc., 42 431–34
Welbecson, **III** 501
Welbilt Corp., 19 492–94; **27** 159
Welborn Transport Co., **39** 64, 65

Welch's, **25** 366
Welcome Wagon International Inc., **III** 28; **16** 146
Weldless Steel Company, **8** 530
Welex Jet Services, **III** 498–99
Wella AG, 48 420–23 (upd.)
Wella Group, III 68–70
Welland Pipe Ltd., **51** 352
Wellby Super Drug Stores, **12** 220
Wellcome Foundation Ltd., I 638, **713–15; 8** 210, 452; **9** 265; **10** 551; **32** 212
Wellcome Trust, **41** 119
Weller Electric Corp., **II** 16
Wellington, **II** 457
Wellington Management Company, **14** 530–31; **23** 226
Wellington Sears Co., **15** 247–48
Wellman, Inc., 8 561–62; 21 193; **52 408–11 (upd.)**
Wellmark, Inc., **10** 89
Wellness Co., Ltd., **IV** 716
WellPoint Health Networks Inc., 25 525–29
Wellrose Limited, **53** 333
Wells Aircraft, **12** 112
Wells Fargo & Company, II 380–84, 319, 395; **III** 440; **10** 59–60; **12** 165, **533–37 (upd.); 17** 325; **18** 60, 543; **19** 411; **22** 542; **25** 434; **27** 292; **32** 373; **38** 44, **483–92 (upd.); 41** 200–01; **46** 217; **54** 124. *See also* American Express Company.
Wells Fargo HSBC Trade Bank, **26** 203
Wells-Gardner Electronics Corporation, 43 458–61
Wells Lamont, **IV** 136
Wells Rich Greene BDDP, 6 48, **50–52**
Wells' Dairy, Inc., 36 511–13
Wellspring Associates L.L.C., **16** 338
Wellspring Resources LLC, **42** 429
Welsbach Mantle, **6** 446
Welsh Associated Collieries Ltd., **31** 369
Welsh Water. *See* Hyder plc.
Weltkunst Verlag GmbH, **IV** 590
Wendy's International, Inc., II 614–15, 647; **7** 433; **8 563–65; 9** 178; **12** 553; **13** 494; **14** 453; **16** 95, 97; **17** 71, 124; **19** 215; **23** 384, **504–07 (upd.); 26** 284; **33** 240; **36** 517, 519; **41** 114; **46** 404–05; **47 439–44 (upd.)**
Wenger S.A., **III** 419; **21** 515
Wenlock Brewery Co., **I** 223
Wenmac Corp., **51** 368
Wenner Media, Inc., 32 506–09
Wenstroms & Granstoms Electriska Kraftbolag, **II** 1
Werco, Inc., **54** 7
Werkhof GmbH, **13** 491
Werknet, **16** 420; **43** 308
Werner Baldessarini Design GmbH, **48** 209
Werner Enterprises, Inc., 26 531–33
Werner International, **III** 344; **14** 225
Wernicke Co., **I** 201
Wertheim Schroder & Company, **17** 443
Weru Aktiengesellschaft, 18 558–61; 49 295
Wesco Financial Corp., **III** 213, 215; **18** 62; **42** 32–34
Wesco Food Co., **II** 644
Wescot Decision Systems, **6** 25
Weserflug, **I** 74
Wesper Co., **26** 4
Wesray and Management, **17** 213

Wesray Capital Corporation, **6** 357; **13** 41; **17** 443; **47** 363
Wesray Corporation, **22** 55
Wesray Holdings Corp., **13** 255
Wesray Transportation, Inc., **14** 38
Wessanen. *See* Koninklijke Wessanen nv.
Wessanen USA, **II** 528; **29** 480
Wessanen's Koninklijke Fabrieken N.V., **II** 527
Wesson/Peter Pan Foods Co., **17** 241
West Australia Land Holdings, Limited, **10** 169
West Bend Co., III 610–11; **14 546–48; 16** 384; **43** 289
West Coast Entertainment Corporation, 29 502–04
West Coast Grocery Co., **II** 670; **18** 506; **50** 456
West Coast Machinery, **13** 385
West Coast of America Telegraph, **I** 428
West Coast Power Company, **12** 265
West Coast Restaurant Enterprises, **25** 390
West Coast Savings and Loan, **10** 339
West Coast Telecom, **III** 38
West Company, **53** 298
West Corporation, 42 435–37
West End Family Pharmacy, Inc., **15** 523
West Fraser Timber Co. Ltd., IV 276; **17 538–40**
West Georgia Coca-Cola Bottlers, Inc., **13** 163
West Group, 34 438, **502–06 (upd.)**
West Ham Gutta Percha Co., **I** 428
West Harrison Gas & Electric Company, **6** 466
West India Oil Co., **IV** 416, 428
West Japan Heavy Industries, **III** 578–79; **7** 348
West Jersey Electric Company, **6** 449
West Lynn Creamery, Inc., **26** 450
West Marine, Inc., 17 541–43; 37 398
West Missouri Power Company. *See* UtiliCorp United Inc.; Aquila, Inc.
West Newton Savings Bank, **13** 468
West Newton Telephone Company, **14** 258
West of England, **III** 690
West of England Sack Holdings, **III** 501; **7** 207
West One Bancorp, 11 552–55; 36 491
West Penn Electric. *See* Allegheny Power System, Inc.
West Penn Power Company, **38** 38–40
West Pharmaceutical Services, Inc., 42 438–41
West Point-Pepperell, Inc., 8 566–69; 9 466; **15** 247; **25** 20; **28** 218. *See also* WestPoint Stevens Inc.; JPS Textile Group, Inc.
West Publishing Co., IV 312; **7 579–81; 10** 407; **19** 268; **33** 264–65. *See also* The West Group.
West Rand Consolidated Mines, **IV** 90
West Rand Investment Trust, **IV** 21; **16** 27; **50** 32
West Richfield Telephone Company, **6** 299
West Side Bank, **II** 312
West Side Printing Co., **13** 559
West Surrey Central Dairy Co. Ltd., **II** 586
West TeleServices Corporation. *See* West Corporation.
West Texas Utilities Company, **6** 580
West Union Corporation, **22** 517
West Virginia Bearings, Inc., **13** 78

West Virginia Pulp and Paper Co. *See* Westvaco Corporation.
West Witwatersrand Areas Ltd., **IV** 94–96
West Yorkshire Bank, **II** 307
West's Holderness Corn Mill, **II** 564
Westaff Inc., 33 454–57
WestAir Holding Inc., **11** 300; **25** 423; **32** 336
Westamerica Bancorporation, 17 544–47
Westbrae Natural, Inc., **27** 197–98; **43** 218
Westburne Group of Companies, **9** 364
Westchester County Savings & Loan, **9** 173
Westchester Specialty Group, Inc., **26** 546
Westclox Seth Thomas, **16** 483
Westcott Communications Inc., **22** 442
Westdeutsche Landesbank Girozentrale, II 257–58, **385–87; 33** 395; **46 458–61 (upd.); 47** 83
Westec Corporation. *See* Tech-Sym Corporation.
Western Aerospace Ltd., **14** 564
Western Air Express, **I** 125; **III** 225; **9** 17
Western Air Lines, **I** 98, 100, 106; **6** 82; **21** 142; **25** 421–23
Western Alaska Fisheries, **II** 578
Western American Bank, **II** 383
Western Assurance Co., **III** 350
Western Atlas Inc., III 473; **12 538–40; 17** 419
Western Australian Specialty Alloys Proprietary Ltd., **14** 564
Western Auto, **19** 223
Western Auto Supply Co., **8** 56; **11** 392
Western Automatic Machine Screw Co., **12** 344
Western Bancorporation, **I** 536; **II** 288–89; **13** 529
Western Bank, **17** 530
Western Beef, Inc., 22 548–50
Western Bingo, **16** 471
Western California Canners Inc., **I** 513
Western Canada Airways, **II** 376
Western Coalfields Ltd., **IV** 48–49
Western Company of North America, 15 534–36; 25 73, 75
Western Condensing Co., **II** 488
Western Copper Mills Ltd., **IV** 164
Western Corrugated Box Co., **IV** 358
Western Crude, **11** 27
Western Dairy Products, **I** 248
Western Data Products, Inc., **19** 110
Western Digital Corp., 10 403, 463; **11** 56, 463; **25 530–32**
Western Edison, **6** 601
Western Electric Co., **II** 57, 66, 88, 101, 112; **III** 162–63, 440; **IV** 181, 660; **V** 259–64; **VII** 288; **11** 500–01; **12** 136; **13** 57; **49** 346
Western Electric Manufacturing Company, **54** 139
Western Empire Construction. *See* CRSS Inc.
Western Equities, Inc. *See* Tech-Sym Corporation.
Western Family Foods, **47** 457; **53** 21
Western Federal Savings & Loan, **9** 199
Western Fire Equipment Co., **9** 420
Western Gas Resources, Inc., 45 435–37
Western Geophysical, **I** 485; **11** 265; **12** 538–39
Western Glucose Co., **14** 17
Western Grocers, Inc., **II** 631, 670

Western Hotels Inc. *See* Westin Hotels and Resorts Worldwide.
Western Illinois Power Cooperative, **6** 506
Western Inland Lock Navigation Company, **9** 228
Western International Communications, **35** 68
Western International Hotels, **I** 129; **6** 129
Western International Media, **22** 294
Western International University, **24** 40
Western Kentucky Gas Company, **43** 56–57
Western Kraft Corp., **IV** 358; **8** 476
Western Life Insurance Co., **III** 356; **22** 494
Western Light & Telephone Company. *See* Western Power & Gas Company.
Western Light and Power. *See* Public Service Company of Colorado.
Western Massachusetts Co., **13** 183
Western Medical Services, **33** 456
Western Merchandise, Inc., **8** 556
Western Merchandisers, Inc., **29** 229–30
Western Mining Corp., **IV** 61, 95
Western-Mobile, **III** 735
Western Mortgage Corporation, **16** 497; **50** 497
Western National Life Company, **10** 246; **14** 473
Western Natural Gas Company, **7** 362
Western New York State Lines, Inc., **6** 370
Western Newell Manufacturing Company. *See* Newell Co.
Western Nuclear, Inc., **IV** 179
Western Offset Publishing, **6** 13
Western Offshore Drilling and Exploration Co., **I** 570
Western Pacific, **22** 220
Western Pacific Industries, **10** 357
Western Paper Box Co., **IV** 333
Western Pioneer, Inc., **18** 279
Western Piping and Engineering Co., **III** 535
Western Platinum, **21** 353
Western Playing Card Co., **13** 559
Western Powder Co., **I** 379; **13** 379
Western Power & Gas Company. *See* Centel Corporation.
Western Printing and Lithographing Company, **19** 404
Western Public Service Corporation, **6** 568
Western Publishing Group, Inc., IV 671; **13** 114, **559–61**; **15** 455; **25** 254, 313; **28** 159; **29** 76
Western Reflections LLC, **55** 291
Western Reserve Bank of Lake County, **9** 474
Western Reserve Telephone Company. *See* Alltel Corporation.
Western Reserves, **12** 442
Western Resources, Inc., 12 541–43; **27** 425; **32** 372–75
Western Rosin Company, **8** 99
Western Sizzlin', **10** 331; **19** 288
Western Slope Gas, **6** 559
Western Steel Group, **26** 407
Western Steer Family Restaurant, **10** 331; **18** 8
Western Sugar Co., **II** 582; **42** 371
Western Telegraph Company, **25** 99
Western Telephone Company, **14** 257
Western Union Corporation, **I** 512; **III** 644; **6** 227–28, 338, 386; **9** 536; **10** 263;

12 9; **14** 363; **15** 72; **17** 345–46; **21** 25; **24** 515
Western Union Financial Services, Inc., 54 413–16
Western Union Insurance Co., **III** 310
Western Vending, **13** 48; **41** 22
Western Veneer and Plywood Co., **IV** 358
Western Wireless Corporation, 36 514–16
Westfair Foods Ltd., **II** 649
Westfalenbank of Bochum, **II** 239
Westfalia AG, **III** 418–19
Westfalia Dinnendahl Gröppel AG, **III** 543
Westfälische Transport AG, **6** 426
Westfälische Verbands- Elektrizitätswerk, **V** 744
Westgate House Investments Ltd., **IV** 711
Westimex, **II** 594
Westin Hotel Co., I 129–30; **6** 129; **9** 283, **547–49**; **21** 91; **54** 345–47
Westin Hotels and Resorts Worldwide, 29 505–08 (upd.)
Westinghouse Air Brake Company. *See* Wabtec Corporation.
Westinghouse Brake & Signal, **III** 509
Westinghouse Cubic Ltd., **19** 111
Westinghouse Electric Corporation, I 4, 7, 19, 22, 28, 33, 82, 84–85, 524; **II** 57–58, 59, 80, 86, 88, 94, 98–99, **120–22**, 151; **III** 440, 467, 641; **IV** 59, 401; **6** 39, 164, 261, 452, 483, 556; **9** 12, 17, 128, 162, 245, 417, 439–40, 553; **10** 280, 536; **11** 318; **12** 194, **544–47 (upd.)**; **13** 230, 398, 402, 506–07; **14** 300–01; **16** 8; **17** 488; **18** 320, 335–37, 355; **19** 164–66, 210; **21** 43; **26** 102; **27** 269; **28** 69; **33** 253; **36** 327; **41** 366; **45** 306; **48** 217; **50** 299. *See also* CBS Radio Group.
WestJet Airlines Ltd., 38 493–95
Westland Aircraft Ltd., **I** 50, 573; **IV** 658; **24** 85
WestLB. *See* Westdeutsche Landesbank Girozentrale.
Westmark Mortgage Corp., **13** 417
Westmark Realty Advisors, **21** 97
Westmark Systems, Inc., **26** 268
Westmill Foods, **II** 466
Westminster Bank Ltd., **II** 257, 319, 320, 333–34; **17** 324
Westminster Press Ltd., **IV** 658
Westminster Trust Ltd., **IV** 706
Westmoreland Coal Company, 7 582–85
Westmount Enterprises, **I** 286
Weston and Mead, **IV** 310
Weston Bakeries, **II** 631
Weston Engineering, **53** 232
Weston Foods Inc. *See* George Weston Limited.
Weston Pharmaceuticals, **V** 49; **19** 122–23; **49** 111–12
Weston Presidio, **49** 189
Weston Resources, **II** 631–32
Westpac Banking Corporation, II 388–90; **17** 285; **48 424–27 (upd.)**
Westphalian Provinzialbank-Hülfskasse, **II** 385
WestPoint Stevens Inc., 16 533–36; **21** 194; **28** 219. *See also* JPS Textile Group, Inc.
Westport Woman, **24** 145
Westvaco Corporation, I 442; **IV** 351–54; **19 495–99 (upd.)**
The Westwood Group, **20** 54

Westwood One, Inc., 17 150; **23 508–11**
Westwood Pharmaceuticals, **III** 19
Westwools Holdings, **I** 438
Westworld Resources Inc., **23** 41
Westwynn Theatres, **14** 87
The Wet Seal, Inc., 18 562–64; **49** 285
Wetterau Incorporated, II 645, **681–82**; **7** 450; **18** 507; **32** 222; **50** 457
Wexpro Company, **6** 568–69
Weyco Group, Incorporated, 32 510–13
Weyerhaeuser Company, I 26; **IV** 266, 289, 298, 304, 308, **355–56**, 358; **8** 428, 434; **9 550–52 (upd.)**; **19** 445–46, 499; **22** 489; **26** 384; **28 514–17 (upd.)**; **31** 468; **32** 91; **42** 397; **49** 196–97
Weyman-Burton Co., **9** 533
WFSC. *See* World Fuel Services Corporation.
WGM Safety Corp., **40** 96–97
WH Smith PLC, 42 442–47 (upd.)
Whalstrom & Co., **I** 14
Wharf Holdings Limited, **12** 367–68; **18** 114
Whatman plc, 46 462–65
Wheat, First Securities, **19** 304–05
Wheaton Industries, 8 570–73
Wheatsheaf Investment, **27** 94
Wheel Horse, **7** 535
Wheel Restaurants Inc., **14** 131
Wheelabrator Technologies, Inc., I 298; **II** 403; **III** 511–12; **V** 754; **6 599–600**; **10** 32; **11** 435
Wheeled Coach Industries, Inc., **33** 105–06
Wheeler Condenser & Engineering Company, **6** 145
Wheeler, Fisher & Co., **IV** 344
Wheeling-Pittsburgh Corp., 7 586–88
Wheelock Marden, **I** 470; **20** 312
Whemco, **22** 415
Whemo Denko, **I** 359
Wherehouse Entertainment Incorporated, 9 361; **11 556–58**; **29** 350; **35** 431–32
WHI Inc., **14** 545
Whippet Motor Lines Corporation, **6** 370
Whippoorwill Associates Inc., **28** 55
Whirl-A-Way Motors, **11** 4
Whirlpool Corporation, I 30; **II** 80; **III** 572, 573, **653–55**; **8** 298–99; **11** 318; **12** 252, 309, **548–50 (upd.)**; **13** 402–03, 563; **15** 403; **18** 225–26; **22** 218, 349; **23** 53; **25** 261; **50** 300, 392
Whirlwind, Inc., **6** 233; **7** 535
Whiskey Trust, **I** 376
Whistler Corporation, **13** 195
Whitaker-Glessner Company, **7** 586
Whitaker Health Services, **III** 389
Whitall Tatum, **III** 423
Whitbread PLC, I 288, **293–94**; **18** 73; **20 519–22 (upd.)**; **29** 19; **35** 395; **42** 247; **50** 114; **52 412–17 (upd.)**
Whitby Pharmaceuticals, Inc., **10** 289
White & Case LLP, 35 466–69
White Automotive, **10** 9, 11
White Brand, **V** 97
White Brothers, **39** 83, 84
White Bus Line, **I** 448
White Castle System, Inc., 12 551–53; **33** 239; **36 517–20 (upd.)**
White Consolidated Industries Inc., II 122; **III** 480, 654, 573; **8** 298; **12** 252, 546; **13 562–64**; **22** 26–28, 216–17, 349; **53** 127
White Discount Department Stores, **16** 36

White Eagle Oil & Refining Co., **IV** 464; **7** 352

White Fuel Corp., **IV** 552

White Industrial Power, **II** 25

White Miller Construction Company, **14** 162

White Motor Co., **II** 16

White Mountain Freezers, **19** 360

White Mountains Insurance Group, Ltd., **48 428–31**

White-New Idea, **13** 18

White Oil Corporation, **7** 101

White Rock Corp., **I** 377; **27** 198; **43** 218

White-Rodgers, **II** 19

White Rose, Inc., 12 106; **24 527–29**

White Star Line, **23** 161

White Stores, **II** 419–20

White Swan Foodservice, **II** 625

White Tractor, **13** 17

White Wave, 43 462–64

White Weld, **II** 268; **21** 145

White-Westinghouse. *See* White Consolidated Industries Inc.

Whiteaway Laidlaw, **V** 68

Whitehall Canadian Oils Ltd., **IV** 658

Whitehall Company Jewellers, **24** 319

Whitehall Electric Investments Ltd., **IV** 658

Whitehall Labs, **8** 63

Whitehall Petroleum Corp. Ltd., **IV** 657–58

Whitehall Securities Corp., **IV** 658

Whitehall Trust Ltd., **IV** 658

Whitewater Group, **10** 508

Whitewear Manufacturing Company. *See* Angelica Corporation.

Whitman Corporation, 7 430; **10** 414–15, **553–55 (upd.); 11** 188; **22** 353–54; **27** 196; **43** 217

Whitman Education Group, Inc., 41 **419–21**

Whitman Publishing Co., **13** 559–60

Whitman's Chocolates, **I** 457; **7** 431; **12** 429

Whitmire Distribution. *See* Cardinal Health, Inc.

Whitney Communications Corp., **IV** 608

Whitney Group, **40** 236–38

Whitney Holding Corporation, 21 **522–24**

Whitney National Bank, **12** 16

Whitney Partners, L.L.C., **40** 237

Whittaker Corporation, I 544–46; **III** 389, 444; **34** 275; **48 432–35 (upd.)**

Whittar Steel Strip Co., **IV** 74; **24** 143

Whitteways, **I** 215

Whittle Communications L.P., **IV** 675; **7** 528; **13** 403; **22** 442

Whittman-Hart Inc. *See* marchFIRST, Inc.

Whitworth Brothers Company, **27** 360

Whole Foods Market, Inc., 19 501–02; **20 523–27; 41** 422–23; **47** 200; **50 530–34 (upd.)**

Wholesale Cellular USA. *See* Brightpoint, Inc.

The Wholesale Club, Inc., **8** 556

Wholesale Depot, **13** 547

Wholesale Food Supply, Inc., **13** 333

Wholesome Foods, L.L.C., **32** 274, 277

Wholly Harvest, **19** 502

WHSC Direct, Inc., **53** 359

Whyte & Mackay Distillers Ltd., **V** 399; **19** 171; **49** 152

Wicanders Group, **48** 119

Wicat Systems, **7** 255–56; **25** 254

Wichita Industries, **11** 27

Wickes Companies, Inc., I 453, 483; **II** 262; **III** 580, 721; **V 221–23; 10** 423; **13** 169–70; **15** 281; **17** 365–66; **19** 503–04; **20** 415; **41** 93

Wickes Inc. 25 533–36 (upd.)

Wickman-Wimet, **IV** 203

Wicor, Inc., **54** 419

Widows and Orphans Friendly Society, **III** 337

Wielkopolski Bank Kredytowy, **16** 14

Wien Air Alaska, **II** 420

Wienerwald Holding, **17** 249

Wiesner, Inc., **22** 442

Wifstavarfs, **IV** 325

Wiggins Teape Ltd., **I** 426; **IV** 290

Wild by Nature. *See* King Cullen Grocery Co., Inc.

Wild Leitz G.m.b.H., **23** 83

Wild Oats Markets, Inc., 19 500–02; 29 213; **41 422–25 (upd.)**

WildBlue Communications Inc., **54** 406

Wildlife Conservation Society, 31 462–64

Wildlife Land Trust, **54** 172

Wildwater Kingdom, **22** 130

Wiles Group Ltd., **III** 501; **7** 207

Wiley Manufacturing Co., **8** 545

Oy Wilh. Schauman AB, **IV** 300–02; **19** 463

Wilhelm Fette GmbH, **IV** 198–99

Wilhelm Weber GmbH, **22** 95

Wilhelm Wilhelmsen Ltd., **7** 40; **41** 42

Wilkins Department Store, **19** 510

Wilkinson, Gaddis & Co., **24** 527

Wilkinson Sword Co., **III** 23, 28–29; **12** 464; **38** 365

Willamette Falls Electric Company. *See* Portland General Corporation.

Willamette Industries, Inc., IV 357–59; **13** 99, 101; **16** 340; **28** 517; **31 465–468 (upd.)**

Willcox & Gibbs Sewing Machine Co., **15** 384

Willetts Manufacturing Company, **12** 312

William A. Rogers Ltd., **IV** 644

William B. Tanner Co., **7** 327

William Barnet and Son, Inc., **III** 246

William Barry Co., **II** 566

William Benton Foundation, **7** 165, 167

William Bonnel Co., **I** 334; **10** 289

The William Brooks Shoe Company. *See* Rocky Shoes & Boots, Inc.

William Burdon, **III** 626

William Byrd Press Inc., **23** 100

William Carter Company, **17** 224

William Colgate and Co., **III** 23

William Collins & Sons, **II** 138; **IV** 651–52; **7** 390–91; **24** 193

William Cory & Son Ltd., **6** 417

William Crawford and Sons, **II** 593

William Douglas McAdams Inc., **I** 662; **9** 403

William Duff & Sons, **I** 509

William E. Pollack Government Securities, **II** 390

William E. Wright Company, **9** 375

William Esty Company, **16** 72

William Gaymer and Son Ltd., **I** 216

William George Company, **32** 519

William Grant Company, **22** 343

William H. Rorer Inc., **I** 666

William Hancock & Co., **I** 223

William Hewlett, **41** 117

William Hill Organization Limited, **49** **449–52**

William Hodges & Company, **33** 150

William Hollins & Company Ltd., **44** 105

William J. Hough Co., **8** 99–100

William Lyon Homes, **III** 664

William M. Mercer Cos. Inc., **III** 283; **32** 459

William Mackinnon & Co., **III** 522

William McDonald & Sons, **II** 593

William Morris Agency, Inc., III 554; **23** **512–14; 43** 235–36

William Morrow & Company, **19** 201

William Neilson, **II** 631

William Odhams Ltd., **7** 244

William P. Young Contruction, **43** 400

William Penn Cos., **III** 243, 273

William Penn Life Insurance Company of New York, **24** 285

William Press, **I** 568

William R. Warner & Co., **I** 710

William S. Kimball & Co., **12** 108

William Southam and Sons, **7** 487

William T. Blackwell & Company, **V** 395

William Underwood Co., **I** 246, 457; **7** 430

William Varcoe & Sons, **III** 690

William Zinsser & Co., **8** 456

Williams & Connolly LLP, 47 445–48

Williams & Glyn's Bank Ltd., **12** 422

Williams & Wilkins. *See* Waverly, Inc.

Williams Brother Offshore Ltd., **I** 429

Williams Communications Group, Inc., 6 340; **25** 499; **34 507–10**

The Williams Companies, Inc., III 248; **IV** 84, 171, **575–76; 27** 307; **31** **469–472 (upd.)**

Williams Deacon's Bank, **12** 422

Williams, Donnelley and Co., **IV** 660

Williams Electronics, **III** 431; **12** 419

Williams Electronics Games, Inc., **15** 539

Williams Gold Refining Co., **14** 81

The Williams Manufacturing Company, **19** 142–43

Williams/Nintendo Inc., **15** 537

Williams Oil-O-Matic Heating Corporation, **12** 158; **21** 42

Williams plc, **44** 255

Williams Printing Company. *See* Graphic Industries Inc.

Williams-Sonoma, Inc., 13 42; **15** 50; **17** **548–50; 27** 225, 429; **44 447–50 (upd.)**

Williamsburg Gas Light Co., **6** 455

Williamsburg Restoration, Incorporated, **53** 106

Williamson-Dickie Manufacturing Company, 14 549–50; **45 438–41 (upd.)**

Willie G's, **15** 279

Willis Corroon Group plc, III 280, 747; **22** 318; **25 537–39**

Willis Stein & Partners, **21** 404

Williston Basin Interstate Pipeline Company, **7** 322, 324. *See also* WBI Holdings, Inc.

Willor Manufacturing Corp., **9** 323

Willys-Overland, **I** 183; **8** 74

Wilmington Coca-Cola Bottling Works, Inc., **10** 223

Wilmington Trust Corporation, 25 **540–43**

Wilsdorf & Davis, **13** 353–54

Wilshire Real Estate Investment Trust Inc., **30** 223

Wilshire Restaurant Group Inc., **13** 66; **28** 258

Wilson & Co., **I** 490

Wilson Bowden Plc, 45 442–44

Wilson Brothers, **8** 536

Wilson Foods Corp., **I** 489, 513; **II** 584–85; **12** 124; **14** 515; **22** 510; **50** 492

Wilson Jones Company, **7** 4–5

Wilson Learning Group, **17** 272

Wilson-Maeulen Company, **13** 234

Wilson Pharmaceuticals & Chemical, **I** 489

Wilson Sonsini Goodrich & Rosati, 34 511–13

Wilson Sporting Goods Company, I 278, 489; **13** 317; **16** 52; **23** 449; **24** 403, **530–32**; **25** 167; **41** 14–16

Wilson's Motor Transit, **6** 370

Wilson's Supermarkets, **12** 220–21

Wilsons The Leather Experts Inc., 21 525–27

WilTel Network Services, **27** 301, 307

Wilts and Dorset Banking Co., **II** 307

Wiltshire United Dairies, **II** 586

Wimbledon Tennis Championships. *See* The All England Lawn Tennis & Croquet Club.

Wimpey International Ltd., **13** 206

Wimpey's plc, **I** 315, 556

Win-Chance Foods, **II** 508; **36** 255

Win Schuler Foods, **II** 480; **25** 517; **26** 57

Wincanton plc, II 586–87; **52 418–20**

Winchell's Donut Shops, **II** 680

Winchester Arms, **I** 379–81, 434; **13** 379

Wind River Systems, Inc., 37 419–22

Windmere Corporation, 16 537–39. *See also* Applica Incorporated.

Windmere-Durable Holdings, Inc., **30** 404

WindowVisions, Inc., **29** 288

Windsong Exports, **52** 429

Windsor Forestry Tools, Inc., **48** 59

Windsor Manufacturing Company, **13** 6

Windsor Trust Co., **13** 467

Windstar Sail Cruises, **6** 368; **27** 90–91

Windsurfing International, **23** 55

Windward Capital Partners, **28** 152, 154

The Wine Group, Inc., 39 419–21

Wine World, Inc., **22** 78, 80

Winfire, Inc., **37** 194

Wingate Partners, **14** 521, 523

Wings & Wheels, **13** 19

Wings Luggage, Inc., **10** 181

WingspanBank.com, **38** 270

Winkelman Stores, Inc., **8** 425–26

Winkler-Grimm Wagon Co., **I** 141

Winlet Fashions, **22** 223

Winmar Co., **III** 353

Winn-Dixie Stores, Inc., II 626–27, 670, **683–84**; **7** 61; **11** 228; **15** 178; **16** 314; **18** 8; **21 528–30 (upd.)**; **34** 269

Winnebago Industries Inc., 7 589–91; 22 207; **27 509–12 (upd.)**

Winners Apparel Ltd., **V** 197

Winning International, **21** 403

Winschermann group, **IV** 198

WinsLoew Furniture, Inc., 21 531–33

Winston & Newell Company. *See* Supervalu Inc.

Winston & Strawn, 35 470–73

Winston Furniture Company, Inc., **21** 531–33

Winston Group, **10** 333

Winston, Harper, Fisher Co., **II** 668

Winter Hill Frozen Foods and Services, **55** 82

WinterBrook Corp., **26** 326

Winterflood Securities Limited, **39** 89, 91

Wintershall AG, **I** 306; **IV** 485; **18** 49; **38** 408

Winterthur Insurance, **21** 144, 146–47

Winterthur Schweizerische Versicherungs-Gesellschaft, III 343, **402–04**

Winthrop Laboratories, **I** 698–99

Winthrop Lawrence Corporation, **25** 541

Winton Engines, **10** 273

Winton Motor Car Company, **V** 231

Winyah Concrete & Block, **50** 49

Wipro Limited, 43 465–68

Wire and Cable Specialties Corporation, **17** 276

Wire and Plastic Products PLC. *See* WPP Group PLC.

Wireless Hong Kong. *See* Hong Kong Telecommunications Ltd.

Wireless LLC, **18** 77

Wireless Management Company, **11** 12

Wireless Speciality Co., **II** 120

Wirtz Productions Ltd., **15** 238

Wisaforest Oy AB, **IV** 302

Wisconsin Bell, Inc., 14 551–53; 18 30

Wisconsin Central Transportation Corporation, 12 278; **24 533–36**

Wisconsin Dairies, 7 592–93

Wisconsin Energy Corporation, 6 601–03, 605; **54 417–21 (upd.)**

Wisconsin Gas Company, **17** 22–23

Wisconsin Knife Works, **III** 436

Wisconsin Power and Light, **22** 13; **39** 260

Wisconsin Public Service Corporation, 6 604–06; **9 553–54.** *See also* WPS Resources Corporation.

Wisconsin Steel, **10** 430; **17** 158–59

Wisconsin Tissue Mills Inc., **8** 103

Wisconsin Toy Company. *See* Value Merchants Inc.

Wisconsin Wire and Steel, **17** 310; **24** 160

Wise Foods, Inc., **22** 95

Wiser's De Luxe Whiskey, **14** 141

Wishnick-Tumpeer Chemical Co., **I** 403–05

Wispark Corporation, **6** 601, 603

Wisser Service Holdings AG, **18** 105

Wisvest Corporation, **6** 601, 603

Witco Corporation, I 403, **404–06**; **16 540–43 (upd.)**

Wite-Out Products, Inc., **23** 56–57

Witech Corporation, **6** 601, 603

Withington Company. *See* Sparton Corporation.

Wittington Investments Ltd., **13** 51

The Wiz. *See* Cablevision Electronic Instruments, Inc.

Wizards of the Coast Inc., 24 537–40; 43 229, 233

WizardWorks Group, Inc., **31** 238–39

WLIW-TV. *See* Educational Broadcasting Corporation.

WLR Foods, Inc., 14 516; **21 534–36; 50** 494

WM Investment Company, **34** 512

Wm. Morrison Supermarkets PLC, 38 496–98

Wm. Underwood Company, **40** 53

Wm. Wrigley Jr. Company, 7 594–97

WMC, Limited, 43 469–72

WMS Industries, Inc., III 431; **15 537–39; 41** 215–16; **53 363–66 (upd.)**

WMX Technologies Inc., 11 435–36; **17 551–54**; **26** 409

Woermann and German East African Lines, **I** 542

Wöhlk, **III** 446

Wolf Furniture Enterprises, **14** 236

Wolfe & Associates, **25** 434

Wolfe Industries, Inc., **22** 255

Wolff Printing Co., **13** 559

The Wolfgang Puck Food Company, Inc., 26 534–36

Wolohan Lumber Co., 19 503–05; 25 535

Wolters Kluwer NV, IV 611; **14 554–56; 31** 389, 394; **33 458–61 (upd.)**

Wolvercote Paper Mill, **IV** 300

Wolverine Die Cast Group, **IV** 165

Wolverine Insurance Co., **26** 487

Wolverine Tube Inc., 23 515–17

Wolverine World Wide Inc., 16 544–47; 17 390; **32** 99; **44** 365

Womack Development Company, **11** 257

Womacks Saloon and Gaming Parlor, **53** 91

Womble Carlyle Sandridge & Rice, PLLC, 52 421–24

Women's Specialty Retailing Group. *See* Casual Corner Group, Inc.

Women's World, **15** 96

Wometco Coca-Cola Bottling Co., **10** 222

Wometco Coffee Time, **I** 514

Wometco Enterprises, **I** 246, 514

Wonderware Corp., **22** 374

Wong International Holdings, **16** 195

Wood Fiberboard Co., **IV** 358

Wood Gundy, **II** 345; **21** 447

Wood Hall Trust plc, I 438, 592–93; **50** 200

Wood-Metal Industries, Inc. *See* Wood-Mode, Inc.

Wood-Mode, Inc., 23 518–20

Wood River Oil and Refining Company, **11** 193

Wood Shovel and Tool Company, **9** 71

Wood, Struthers & Winthrop, Inc., **22** 189

Wood Wyant Inc., **30** 496–98

Woodall Industries, **III** 641; **14** 303; **50** 310

Woodard-Walker Lumber Co., **IV** 358

Woodbridge Winery, **50** 388

Woodbury Co., **19** 380

Woodcock, Hess & Co., **9** 370

Woodfab, **IV** 295; **19** 225

Woodhaven Gas Light Co., **6** 455

Woodhill Chemical Sales Company, **8** 333

Woodland Publishing, Inc., **37** 286

Woodlands, **7** 345–46

Woods and Co., **II** 235

Woods Equipment Company, **32** 28

Woodside Travel Trust, **26** 310

Woodville Appliances, Inc., **9** 121

Woodward-Clyde Group Inc., **45** 421

Woodward Corp., **IV** 311; **19** 267

Woodward Governor Company, 13 565–68; 49 453–57 (upd.)

Woodworkers Warehouse, **22** 517

Woolco Department Stores, **II** 634; **7** 444; **V** 107, 225–26; **14** 294; **22** 242

Woolverton Motors, **I** 183

The Woolwich plc, 30 492–95

Woolworth Corporation, II 414; **6** 344; **V** 106–09, **224–27**; **8** 509; **14** 293–95; **17** 42, 335; **20 528–32 (upd.)**; **25** 22. *See also* Venator Group Inc.

Woolworth Holdings, **II** 139; **V** 108; **19** 123; **24** 194
Woolworth's Ltd., **II** 656. *See also* Kingfisher plc.
Wooster Preserving Company, **11** 211
Wooster Rubber Co., **III** 613
Worcester City and County Bank, **II** 307
Worcester Gas Light Co., **14** 124
Worcester Wire Works, **13** 369
Word, Inc., **14** 499; **38** 456
Word Processors Personnel Service, **6** 10
WordPerfect Corporation, **6** 256; **10** 519, **556–59**; **12** 335; **25** 300; **41** 281. *See also* Corel Corporation.
WordStar International, **15** 149; **43** 151. *See also* The Learning Company Inc.
Work Wear Corp., **II** 607; **16** 229
Working Assets Funding Service, **43** **473–76**
Working Title Films, **23** 389
Workscape Inc., **42** 430
World Air Network, Ltd., **6** 71
World Airways, **10** 560–62; **28** 404
World Bank Group, **33** **462–65**
World Book Group. *See* Scott Fetzer Company.
World Book, Inc., **IV** 622; **12** **554–56**
World Championship Wrestling (WCW), **32** 516
World Color Press Inc., **12** **557–59**; **19** 333; **21** 61
World Commerce Corporation, **25** 461
World Communications, Inc., **11** 184
World Duty Free Americas, Inc., **29** **509–12 (upd.)**
World Duty Free plc, **33** 59
World Film Studio, **24** 437
World Financial Network National Bank, **V** 116
World Flight Crew Services, **10** 560
World Foot Locker, **14** 293
World Fuel Services Corporation, **47** **449–51**
World Gift Company, **9** 330
World International Holdings Limited, **12** 368
World Journal Tribune Inc., **IV** 608
World Machinery Company, **45** 170–71
World Online, **48** 398–39
World Poker Tour, LLC, **51** 205, 207
World Publishing Co., **8** 423
World Savings and Loan, **19** 412; **47** 159–60
World Service Life Insurance Company, **27** 47
World Trade Corporation. *See* International Business Machines Corporation.
World Trans, Inc., **33** 105
World-Wide Shipping Group, **II** 298; **III** 517
World Wrestling Federation Entertainment, Inc., **32** **514–17**
World Yacht Enterprises, **22** 438
World's Finest Chocolate Inc., **39** **422–24**
WorldCom, Inc., **14** 330, 332; **18** 33, 164, 166; **29** 227; **38** 269–70, 468; **46** 376. *See also* MCI WorldCom, Inc.
WorldCorp, Inc., **10** **560–62**
WorldGames, **10** 560
WorldMark, The Club, **33** 409
Worlds of Fun, **22** 130
Worlds of Wonder, Inc., **25** 381; **26** 548

Worldview Systems Corporation, **26** 428; **46** 434
WorldWay Corporation, **16** 41
Worldwide Fiber Inc., **46** 267
Worldwide Insurance Co., **48** 9
Worldwide Logistics, **17** 505
Worldwide Restaurant Concepts, Inc., **47** **452–55**
Worldwide Semiconductor Manufacturing Co., **47** 386
Worldwide Underwriters Insurance Co., **III** 218–19
Wormald International Ltd., **13** 245, 247
Worms et Cie, **27** 275–76, **513–15**
Wormser, **III** 760
Worth Corp., **27** 274
Wortham, Gus Sessions, **III** 193; **10** 65
Worthen Banking Corporation, **15** 60
Worthington & Co., **I** 223
Worthington Corp., **I** 142
Worthington Foods, Inc., **I** 653; **14** **557–59**; **33** 170
Worthington Industries, Inc., **7** **598–600**; **8** 450; **21** **537–40 (upd.)**
Worthington Telephone Company, **6** 312
Woven Belting Co., **8** 13
WPL Holdings, **6** **604–06**
WPM. *See* Wall Paper Manufacturers.
WPP Group plc, **I** 21; **6** 53–54; **22** 201, 296; **23** 480; **48** **440–42 (upd.)**. *See also* Ogilvy Group Inc.
WPS Resources Corporation, **53** **367–70 (upd.)**
Wrather Corporation, **18** 354
Wrenn Furniture Company, **10** 184
WRG. *See* Wells Rich Greene BDDP.
Wright & Company Realtors, **21** 257
Wright Aeronautical, **9** 16
Wright Airplane Co., **III** 151; **6** 265
Wright and Son, **II** 593
Wright Company, **9** 416
Wright Engine Company, **11** 427
Wright Group, **22** 519, 522
Wright Manufacturing Company, **8** 407
Wright Plastic Products, **17** 310; **24** 160
Wright, Robertson & Co. *See* Fletcher Challenge Ltd.
Wright Stephenson & Co., **IV** 278
Wrightson Limited, **19** 155
Write Right Manufacturing Co., **IV** 345
WS Atkins Plc, **45** **445–47**
WSGC Holdings, Inc., **24** 530
WSI. *See* Weather Services International.
WSI Corporation, **10** 88–89
WSM Inc., **11** 152
WSMC. *See* Worldwide Semiconductor Manufacturing Co.
WSMP, Inc., **29** 202
WTC Airlines, Inc., **IV** 182
WTD Industries, Inc., **20** **533–36**
Wührer, **II** 474
Wunderlich Ltd., **III** 687
Wunderman, Ricotta & Kline, **I** 37
Wurlitzer Co., **17** 468; **18** 45
Württembergische Landes- Elektrizitäts AG, **IV** 230
WVPP. *See* Westvaco Corporation.
WVT Communications. *See* Warwick Valley Telephone Company.
WWG Industries, Inc., **22** 352–53
WWTV, **18** 493
Wyandotte Chemicals Corporation, **18** 49
Wyandotte Corp., **I** 306
Wyant Corporation, **30** **496–98**

Wycombe Bus Company, **28** 155–56
Wyeth, 50 535–39 (upd.)
Wyeth-Ayerst Laboratories, **25** 477; **27** 69
Wyeth Laboratories, **I** 623; **10** 69
Wyle Electronics, **14** **560–62**; **19** 311
Wyly Corporation, **11** 468
Wyman-Gordon Company, **14** **563–65**; **30** 282–83; **41** 367
Wymore Oil Co., **IV** 394
Wynkoop Brewing Company, **43** 407
Wynn's International, Inc., **22** 458; **33** **466–70**
Wynncor Ltd., **IV** 693
Wyoming Mineral Corp., **IV** 401
Wyse Technology, Inc., **10** 362; **15** **540–42**

X-Acto, **12** 263
X-Chem Oil Field Chemicals, **8** 385
X-Rite, Inc., **48** **443–46**
XA Systems Corporation, **10** 244
Xaos Tools, Inc., **10** 119
Xcelite, **II** 16
Xcor International, **III** 431; **15** 538; **53** 364–65
Xeikon NV, **26** **540–42**
Xenell Corporation, **48** 358
Xenia National Bank, **9** 474
Xenotech, **27** 58
Xerox Corporation, **I** 31–32, 338, 490, 693; **II** 10, 117, 157, 159, 412, 448; **III** 110, 116, 120–21, 157, 159, **171–73**, 475; **IV** 252, 703; **6** 244, **288–90 (upd.)**, 390; **7** 45, 161; **8** 164; **10** 22, 139, 430, 510–11; **11** 68, 494, 518; **13** 127, 448; **14** 399; **17** 28–29, 328–29; **18** 93, 111–12; **22** 411–12; **25** 54–55, 148, 152; **26** 213, 540, 542, **543–47 (upd.)**; **28** 115; **36** 171; **40** 394; **41** 197; **46** 151
Xiamen Airlines, **33** 99
Xilinx, Inc., **16** 317, **548–50**; **18** 17, 19; **19** 405; **43** 15–16
Xing Technology Corp., **53** 282
XMR, Inc., **42** 361
XP, **27** 474
Xpect First Aid Corp., **51** 76
Xpert Recruitment, Ltd., **26** 240
Xpress Automotive Group, Inc., **24** 339
XR Ventures LLC, **48** 446
XRAL Storage and Terminaling Co., **IV** 411
Xros, Inc., **36** 353
XTO Energy Inc., **52** **425–27**
XTRA Corp., **18** 67
Xtra Limited New Zealand, **54** 355–57
XTX Corp., **13** 127
Xynetics, **9** 251
Xytek Corp., **13** 127

Y & S Candies Inc., **II** 511
Yacimientos Petrolíferos Fiscales Sociedad Anónima, **IV** 578
Yageo Corporation, **16** **551–53**
Yahoo! Inc., **25** 18; **27** **516–19**; **38** 439; **45** 201
Yakovlev, **24** 60
Yale & Towne Manufacturing Co., **I** 154–55; **10** 279
Yale and Valor, PLC, **50** 134–35
Yamabun Oil Co., **IV** 403
Yamagata Enterprises, **26** 310
Yamaguchi Bank, **II** 347
Yamaha Corporation, **III** 366, 599, 656–59; **11** 50; **12** 401; **16** 410, **554–58**

(upd.); **17** 25; **18** 250; **19** 428; **22** 196; **33** 28; **40 461–66 (upd.)**; **49** 178

Yamaha Musical Instruments, **16** 202; **43** 170

Yamaichi Capital Management, **42** 349

Yamaichi Securities Company, Limited, **II** 300, 323, 434, **458–59**; **9** 377

Yamamotoyama Co., Ltd., **50** 449

Yamano Music, **16** 202; **43** 171

Yamanouchi Consumer Inc., **39** 361

Yamanouchi Pharmaceutical Co., Ltd., **12** 444–45; **38** 93

Yamatame Securities, **II** 326

Yamato Transport Co. Ltd., **V 536–38**; **49 458–61 (upd.)**

Yamazaki Baking Co., **II** 543; **IV** 152; **24** 358

Yanbian Industrial Technology Training Institute, **12** 294

Yangzhou Motor Coach Manufacturing Co., **34** 132

The Yankee Candle Company, Inc., **37 423–26**; **38** 192

Yankee Energy Gas System, Inc., **13** 184

Yankee Gas Services Company, **48** 305

YankeeNets LLC, 35 474–77

Yankton Gas Company, **6** 524

Yarmouth Group, Inc., **17** 285

Yaryan, **I** 343

Yashica Co., Ltd., **II** 50–51; **21** 330

Yasuda Fire and Marine Insurance Company, Limited, **II** 292, 391; **III 405–07,** 408; **45** 110

Yasuda Mutual Life Insurance Company, **II** 292, 391, 446; **III** 288, 405, **408–09**; **22** 406–07; **39 425–28 (upd.)**

The Yasuda Trust and Banking Company, Limited, **II** 273, 291, **391–92**; **17 555–57 (upd.)**

Yates-Barco Ltd., **16** 8

Yates Circuit Foil, **IV** 26

Yawata Iron & Steel Co., Ltd., **I** 493, 509; **II** 300; **IV** 130, 157, 212; **17** 350; **24** 325

Year Book Medical Publishers, **IV** 677–78

Yearbooks, Inc., **12** 472

Yeargin Construction Co., **II** 87; **11** 413

Yellow Cab Co., **I** 125; **V** 539; **10** 370; **12** 487; **24** 118

Yellow Corporation, 14 566–68; 45 448–51 (upd.)

Yellow Freight System, Inc. of Deleware, **V** 503, **539–41**; **12** 278

Yeomans & Foote, **I** 13

Yeomans & Partners Ltd., **I** 588

YES! Entertainment Corporation, 10 306; **26 548–50**

Yesco Audio Environments, **18** 353, 355

Yeti Cycles Inc., **19** 385

Yeung Chi Shing Estates, **IV** 717

YGK Inc., **6** 465, 467

Yhtyneet Paperitehtaat Oy. *See* United Paper Mills Ltd.

Yili Food Co., **II** 544

YKK, **19** 477

YMCA of the USA, 31 473–76

Ymos A.G., **IV** 53; **26** 83

YOCREAM International, Inc., 47 456–58

Yogen Fruz World-Wide, Inc. *See* CoolBrands International Inc.

Yokado Clothing Store, **V** 88

Yokogawa Electric Corp., **III** 142–43, 536; **26** 230

Yokogawa Electric Works, Limited, **6** 237; **13** 234

Yokohama Bottle Plant, **21** 319

Yokohama Cooperative Wharf Co., **IV** 728

Yokohama Electric Cable Manufacturing Co., **III** 490

The Yokohama Rubber Co., Ltd., **V 254–56**; **19 506–09 (upd.)**

Yokohama Specie Bank, **I** 431; **II** 224

Yokohama Tokyu Deppartment Store Co., Ltd., **32** 457

Yoosung Enterprise Co., Ltd., **23** 269

Yoplait S.A. *See* Sodiaal S.A.

York & London, **III** 359

The York Bank and Trust Company, **16** 14; **43** 8

York-Benimaru, **V** 88

York Corp., **III** 440

York Developments, **IV** 720

The York Group, Inc., 50 540–43

York International Corp., 13 569–71; 22 6

York Research Corporation, 35 478–80

York Manufacturing Co $$York Manufacturing Co., **13** 385

York Safe & Lock Company, **7** 144–45; **22** 184

York Steak House, **16** 157

York Wastewater Consultants, Inc., **6** 441

Yorkshire and Pacific Securities Ltd., **IV** 723

Yorkshire Energies, **45** 21

Yorkshire Insurance Co., **III** 241–42, 257

Yorkshire Paper Mills Ltd., **IV** 300

Yorkshire Post Newspapers, **IV** 686; **28** 503

Yorkshire Television Ltd., **IV** 659

Yorkshire-Tyne Tees Television, **24** 194

Yorkshire Water Services Ltd. *See* Kelda Group plc.

Yorkville Group, **IV** 640

Yosemite Park & Curry Co., **II** 144

Yoshikazu Taguchi, **6** 428

Yoshitomi Pharmaceutical, **I** 704

Young & Co.'s Brewery, P.L.C., 38 499–502

Young & Rubicam Inc., **I** 9–11, 25, **36–38**; **II** 129; **6** 14, 47; **9** 314; **13** 204; **16** 166–68; **22 551–54 (upd.)**; **41** 89–90, 198; **48** 442

Young & Selden, **7** 145

Young & Son, **II** 334

Young Broadcasting Inc., 40 467–69; **42** 163

Young Chang Akki Company, **51** 201

Young Innovations, Inc., 44 451–53

Young Readers of America, **13** 105

Young's Engineering Company Limited, **IV** 717; **38** 319

Young's Market Company, LLC, 32 518–20

Youngblood Truck Lines, **16** 40

Youngs Drug Products Corporation, **8** 85; **38** 124

Youngstown, **IV** 114

Youngstown Pressed Steel Co., **III** 763

Youngstown Sheet & Tube, **I** 490–91; **13** 157

Younkers, Inc., 19 324–25, **510–12**; **41** 343–44

Yount-Lee Oil Co., **IV** 369

Your Communications Limited, **52** 372, 374

Youth Centre Inc., **16** 36

Youth Services International, Inc., 21 541–43; **30** 146

Youthtrack, Inc., **29** 399–400

Yoxall Instrument Company, **13** 234

Yoyoteiki Cargo Co., Ltd., **6** 428

YPF Sociedad Anónima, IV 577–78. *See also* Repsol-YPF S.A.

Yside Investment Group, **16** 196

YTT. *See* Yorkshire-Tyne Tees Television.

Yuasa Battery Co., **III** 556

Yuba Heat Transfer Corp., **I** 514

The Yucaipa Cos., 17 558–62; **22** 39; **32** 222; **35** 369

Yugraneft, **49** 306

Yukon Pacific Corporation, **22** 164, 166

YUKOS, **49** 305–06. *See also* OAO NK YUKOS.

Yule Catto & Company plc, 54 422–25

Yurakucho Seibu Co., Ltd., **V** 185

Yutaka Co., Ltd., **55** 48

Yutani Heavy Industries, Ltd., **IV** 130

Yves Rocher. *See* Laboratoires de Biologie Végétale Yves Rocher.

Yves Saint Laurent, **I** 697; **12** 37

Yves Soulié, **II** 266

YWCA of the U.S.A., 45 452–54

Z Media, Inc., **49** 433

Z-Spanish Media Corp., **35** 220; **41** 151

Z.C. Mines, **IV** 61

Zaadunie B.V., **I** 672

Zagara's Inc., **35** 190–91

Zahnfabrik Weinand Sohne & Co. G.m.b.H., **10** 271

Zahnradfabrik Friedrichshafen, **III** 415

Zale Corporation, 16 206, **559–61**; **17** 369; **19** 452; **23** 60; **40 470–74 (upd.)**

Zambezi Saw Mills (1968) Ltd., **IV** 241

Zambia Breweries, **25** 281

Zambia Industrial and Mining Corporation Ltd., IV 239–41

Zamboni. *See* Frank J. Zamboni & Co., Inc.

Zander & Ingeström, **III** 419

Zanders Feinpapiere AG, **IV** 288; **15** 229

Zanussi, **III** 480; **22** 27; **53** 127

Zany Brainy, Inc., 31 477–79; **36** 502

Zap, Inc., **25** 546

Zapata Corporation, 17 157, 160; **25 544–46**

Zapata Drilling Co., **IV** 489

Zapata Gulf Marine Corporation, **11** 524

Zapata Offshore Co., **IV** 489

Zapata Petroleum Corp., **IV** 489; **50** 351

Zaring Premier Homes, **41** 133

Zausner, **25** 83

Zayre Corp., **V** 197–98; **9** 20–21; **13** 547–48; **19** 448; **29** 106; **30** 55–56; **33** 198

ZCMI. *See* Zion's Cooperative Mercantile Institution.

ZDF, **41** 28–29

ZDNet, **36** 523

Zealand Mines S.A., **23** 41

Zebco, **22** 115

Zebra Technologies Corporation, 14 378, **569–71**; **53 371–74 (upd.)**

Zecco, Inc., **III** 443; **6** 441

Zee Medical, Inc., **47** 235

Zehrmart, **II** 631

Zeiss Ikon AG, **III** 446

Zell Bros., **16** 559
Zell/Chilmark Fund LP, **12** 439; **19** 384
Zellers, **V** 80; **25** 221
Zellstoff AG, **III** 400
Zellstoffabrik Waldhof AG, **IV** 323–24
Zellweger Telecommunications AG, **9** 32
Zeneca Group PLC, **21** 544–46. *See also*
  AstraZeneca PLC.
Zengine, Inc., **41** 258–59
Zenit Bank, **45** 322
Zenith Data Systems, Inc., **II** 124–25; **III**
  123; **6** 231; **10** 563–65; **36** 299
Zenith Electronics Corporation, **II** 102,
  123–25; **10** 563; **11** 62, 318; **12** 183,
  454; **13** 109, 398, **572–75 (upd.)**; **18**
  421; **34 514–19 (upd.)**
Zenith Media, **42** 330–31
Zentec Corp., **I** 482
Zentralsparkasse und Kommerzialbank
  Wien, **23** 37
Zentronics, **19** 313
Zep Manufacturing Company, **54** 252, 254
Zeppelin Luftschifftechnik GmbH, **48** 450
Zerex, **50** 48
Zergo Holdings, **42** 24–25
Zero Corporation, **17 563–65**
Zero Plus Dialing, Inc. *See* Billing
  Concepts Corp.
Zetor s.p., **21** 175
Zeus Components, Inc., **10** 113; **50** 43
Zewawell AG, **IV** 324
ZF Friedrichshafen AG, **48 447–51**
Zhenjiang Zhengmao Hitachi Zosen
  Machinery Co. Ltd., **53** 173
Zhongbei Building Material Products
  Company, **26** 510
Zhongde Brewery, **49** 417
Ziebart International Corporation, **30**
  499–501
The Ziegler Companies, Inc., **24 541–45**
Ziff Communications Company, **7**
  239–40; **12** 359, **560–63**; **13** 483; **16**
  371; **17** 152, 253; **25** 238, 240; **41** 12
Ziff Davis Media Inc., **36 521–26 (upd.)**;
  47 77, 79. *See also* CNET Networks,
  Inc.
Ziff-Davis Publishing Co., **38** 441
Zijlker, **IV** 491
Zila, Inc., **46 466–69**
Zilber Ltd., **13** 541
Zildjian. *See* Avedis Zildjian Co.
Zilkha & Company, **12** 72
Zilog, Inc., **15 543–45**; **16** 548–49; **22**
  390
Zimbabwe Sugar Refineries, **II** 581
Zimmer AG, **IV** 142
Zimmer Holdings, Inc., **45 455–57**
Zimmer Inc., **10** 156–57; **11** 475
Zimmer Manufacturing Co., **III** 18; **37**
  110, 113
Zinc Corp., **IV** 58–59, 61
Zinc Products Company, **30** 39
Zion Foods, **23** 408
Zion's Cooperative Mercantile
  Institution, **33 471–74**
Zions Bancorporation, **12 564–66**; **24**
  395; **53 375–78 (upd.)**
Zippo Manufacturing Company, **18**
  565–68
Zipps Drive-Thru, Inc., **25** 389
Zippy Mart, **7** 102
Zircotube, **IV** 174
Zivnostenska, **II** 282
Zodiac S.A., **36 527–30**

Zody's Department Stores, **9** 120–22
Zoecon, **I** 673
Zoll Foods, **55** 366
Zoll Medical, **18** 423
Zoloto Mining Ltd., **38** 231
Zoltek Companies, Inc., **37 427–30**
Zomba Records Ltd., **52 428–31**
The Zondervan Corporation, **51** 131
Zondervan Publishing House, **14** 499; **24**
  546–49
Zoom Technologies, Inc., **53 379–82**
  (upd.). *See also* Zoom Technologies,
  Inc.
Zoom Telephonics, Inc., **18 569–71**
Zortech Inc., **10** 508
Zotos International, Inc., **III** 63; **17** 110; **22**
  487; **41** 228
ZPT Radom, **23** 427
ZS Sun Limited Partnership, **10** 502
Zuari Cement, **40** 107, 109
Zuellig Group N.A., Inc., **46** 226
Zuid Nederlandsche Handelsbank, **II** 185
Zuka Juice, **47** 201
Zumtobel AG, **50 544–48**
Zürcher Bankverein, **II** 368
Zurich Financial Services, **40** 59, 61; **42**
  448–53 (upd.)
Zurich Insurance Group, **15** 257; **25** 154,
  156
Zürich Versicherungs-Gesellschaft, **III**
  194, 402–03, **410–12**. *See also* Zurich
  Financial Services
Zurn Industries, Inc., **24** 150
Zwarovski, **16** 561
Zweckform Büro-Produkte G.m.b.H., **49** 38
Zycad Corp., **11** 489–91
Zycon Corporation, **24** 201
Zygo Corporation, **42 454–57**
Zymaise, **II** 582
ZyMOS Corp., **III** 458
Zytec Corporation, **19 513–15**. *See also*
  Artesyn Technologies Inc.

INDEX TO INDUSTRIES

Index to Industries

ACCOUNTING

American Institute of Certified Public Accountants (AICPA), 44
Andersen Worldwide, 29 (upd.)
Automatic Data Processing, Inc., 47 (upd.)
Deloitte & Touche, 9
Deloitte Touche Tohmatsu International, 29 (upd.)
Ernst & Young, 9; 29 (upd.)
KPMG International, 33 (upd.)
L.S. Starrett Co., 13
McLane Company, Inc., 13
NCO Group, Inc., 42
Paychex, Inc., 46 (upd.)
Price Waterhouse, 9
PricewaterhouseCoopers, 29 (upd.)
Robert Wood Johnson Foundation, 35
Univision Communications Inc., 24

ADVERTISING & OTHER BUSINESS SERVICES

A.C. Nielsen Company, 13
ABM Industries Incorporated, 25 (upd.)
Ackerley Communications, Inc., 9
ACNielsen Corporation, 38 (upd.)
Acsys, Inc., 44
Adecco S.A., 36 (upd.)
Adia S.A., 6
Administaff, Inc., 52
Advo, Inc., 6; 53 (upd.)
Aegis Group plc, 6
AHL Services, Inc., 27
Alloy, Inc., 55
Amdocs Ltd., 47
American Building Maintenance Industries, Inc., 6
The American Society of Composers, Authors and Publishers (ASCAP), 29
Amey Plc, 47
Analysts International Corporation, 36
The Arbitron Company, 38
Armor Holdings, Inc., 27
Ashtead Group plc, 34
The Associated Press, 13
Bain & Company, 55
Barrett Business Services, Inc., 16
Barton Protective Services Inc., 53
Bates Worldwide, Inc., 14; 33 (upd.)
Bearings, Inc., 13
Berlitz International, Inc., 13
Big Flower Press Holdings, Inc., 21
Boron, LePore & Associates, Inc., 45
Bozell Worldwide Inc., 25
Bright Horizons Family Solutions, Inc., 31
Broadcast Music Inc., 23
Buck Consultants, Inc., 55
Bureau Veritas SA, 55
Burns International Services Corporation, 13; 41 (upd.)
Cambridge Technology Partners, Inc., 36
Campbell-Mithun-Esty, Inc., 16
Career Education Corporation, 45
Carmichael Lynch Inc., 28

CDI Corporation, 54 (upd.)
Central Parking Corporation, 18
Century Business Services, Inc., 52
Chancellor Beacon Academies, Inc., 53
ChartHouse International Learning Corporation, 49
Chiat/Day Inc. Advertising, 11
Chicago Board of Trade, 41
Chisholm-Mingo Group, Inc., 41
Christie's International plc, 15; 39 (upd.)
Cintas Corporation, 21
COMFORCE Corporation, 40
Computer Learning Centers, Inc., 26
Corporate Express, Inc., 47 (upd.)
CORT Business Services Corporation, 26
Cox Enterprises, Inc., 22 (upd.)
Creative Artists Agency LLC, 38
Cyrk Inc., 19
Dale Carnegie Training, Inc., 28
D'Arcy Masius Benton & Bowles, Inc., 6; 32 (upd.)
Dawson Holdings PLC, 43
DDB Needham Worldwide, 14
Deluxe Corporation, 22 (upd.)
Dentsu Inc., I; 16 (upd.); 40 (upd.)
Deutsch, Inc., 42
Deutsche Post AG, 29
DoubleClick Inc., 46
Drake Beam Morin, Inc., 44
Earl Scheib, Inc., 32
EBSCO Industries, Inc., 17
Ecology and Environment, Inc., 39
Edison Schools Inc., 37
Education Management Corporation, 35
Employee Solutions, Inc., 18
Ennis Business Forms, Inc., 21
Equifax Inc., 6; 28 (upd.)
Equity Marketing, Inc., 26
ERLY Industries Inc., 17
Euro RSCG Worldwide S.A., 13
Fallon McElligott Inc., 22
Fiserv, Inc., 33 (upd.)
FlightSafety International, Inc., 29 (upd.)
Florists' Transworld Delivery, Inc., 28
Foote, Cone & Belding Communications, Inc., I
Forrester Research, Inc., 54
Frankel & Co., 39
Franklin Covey Company, 37 (upd.)
Frost & Sullivan, Inc., 53
Gage Marketing Group, 26
The Gallup Organization, 37
George S. May International Company, 55
GfK Aktiengesellschaft, 49
Glotel plc, 53
Grey Advertising, Inc., 6
Group 4 Falck A/S, 42
Groupe Jean-Claude Darmon, 44
GSD&M Advertising, 44
Gwathmey Siegel & Associates Architects LLC, 26
Ha-Lo Industries, Inc., 27
Hakuhodo, Inc., 6; 42 (upd.)
Hall, Kinion & Associates, Inc., 52

Handleman Company, 15
Havas SA, 33 (upd.)
Hays Plc, 27
Headway Corporate Resources, Inc., 40
Heidrick & Struggles International, Inc., 28
Hildebrandt International, 29
IKON Office Solutions, Inc., 50
Interep National Radio Sales Inc., 35
International Brotherhood of Teamsters, 37
International Management Group, 18
International Total Services, Inc., 37
The Interpublic Group of Companies, Inc., I; 22 (upd.)
Ipsos SA, 48
Iron Mountain, Inc., 33
ITT Educational Services, Inc., 33
J.D. Power and Associates, 32
Jackson Hewitt, Inc., 48
Japan Leasing Corporation, 8
Jostens, Inc., 25 (upd.)
JWT Group Inc., I
Katz Communications, Inc., 6
Katz Media Group, Inc., 35
Kelly Services Inc., 6; 26 (upd.)
Ketchum Communications Inc., 6
Kinko's Inc., 16; 43 (upd.)
Korn/Ferry International, 34
Labor Ready, Inc., 29
Lamar Advertising Company, 27
Learning Tree International Inc., 24
Leo Burnett Company Inc., I; 20 (upd.)
Lintas: Worldwide, 14
Mail Boxes Etc., 18; 41 (upd.)
Manpower, Inc., 30 (upd.)
marchFIRST, Inc., 34
Maritz Inc., 38
MAXIMUS, Inc., 43
Mediaset SpA, 50
MPS Group, Inc., 49
Mullen Advertising Inc., 51
National Media Corporation, 27
Neopost S.A., 53
New England Business Services, Inc., 18
New Valley Corporation, 17
NFO Worldwide, Inc., 24
Nobel Learning Communities, Inc., 37
Norrell Corporation, 25
Norwood Promotional Products, Inc., 26
Observer AB, 55
The Ogilvy Group, Inc., I
Olsten Corporation, 6; 29 (upd.)
Omnicom Group, I; 22 (upd.)
On Assignment, Inc., 20
1-800-FLOWERS, Inc., 26
Opinion Research Corporation, 46
Outdoor Systems, Inc., 25
Paris Corporation, 22
Paychex, Inc., 15
PDI, Inc., 52
Penauille Polyservices SA, 49
Phillips, de Pury & Luxembourg, 49
Pierce Leahy Corporation, 24
Pinkerton's Inc., 9
PMT Services, Inc., 24

ADVERTISING & OTHER BUSINESS SERVICES (continued)

Publicis S.A., 19
Publishers Clearing House, 23
Randstad Holding n.v., 16; 43 (upd.)
RemedyTemp, Inc., 20
Rental Service Corporation, 28
Rentokil Initial Plc, 47
Right Management Consultants, Inc., 42
Ritchie Bros. Auctioneers Inc., 41
Robert Half International Inc., 18
Roland Berger & Partner GmbH, 37
Ronco, Inc., 15
Russell Reynolds Associates Inc., 38
Saatchi & Saatchi, I; 42 (upd.)
Securitas AB, 42
ServiceMaster Limited Partnership, 6
Shared Medical Systems Corporation, 14
Sir Speedy, Inc., 16
Skidmore, Owings & Merrill, 13
SmartForce PLC, 43
SOS Staffing Services, 25
Sotheby's Holdings, Inc., 11; 29 (upd.)
Spencer Stuart and Associates, Inc., 14
Spherion Corporation, 52
Steiner Corporation (Alsco), 53
Strayer Education, Inc., 53
Superior Uniform Group, Inc., 30
Sykes Enterprises, Inc., 45
Sylvan Learning Systems, Inc., 35
TA Triumph-Adler AG, 48
Taylor Nelson Sofres plc, 34
TBWA Advertising, Inc., 6
TBWA\Chiat\Day, 43 (upd.)
Thomas Cook Travel Inc., 33 (upd.)
Ticketmaster Group, Inc., 13; 37 (upd.)
TMP Worldwide Inc., 30
TNT Post Group N.V., 30
Towers Perrin, 32
Transmedia Network Inc., 20
Treasure Chest Advertising Company, Inc., 32
TRM Copy Centers Corporation, 18
True North Communications Inc., 23
24/7 Real Media, Inc., 49
Tyler Corporation, 23
U.S. Office Products Company, 25
UniFirst Corporation, 21
United Business Media plc, 52 (upd.)
United News & Media plc, 28 (upd.)
Unitog Co., 19
Valassis Communications, Inc., 37 (upd.)
ValueClick, Inc., 49
Vebego International BV, 49
Vedior NV, 35
The Wackenhut Corporation, 14
Waggener Edstrom, 42
Warrantech Corporation, 53
Wells Rich Greene BDDP, 6
Westaff Inc., 33
Whitman Education Group, Inc., 41
William Morris Agency, Inc., 23
WPP Group plc, 6; 48 (upd.)
Young & Rubicam, Inc., I; 22 (upd.)

AEROSPACE

A.S. Yakovlev Design Bureau, 15
Aeronca Inc., 46
The Aerospatiale Group, 7; 21 (upd.)
Alliant Techsystems Inc., 30 (upd.)
Antonov Design Bureau, 53
Aviacionny Nauchno-Tehnicheskii Komplex im. A.N. Tupoleva, 24
Avions Marcel Dassault-Breguet Aviation, I
B/E Aerospace, Inc., 30
Banner Aerospace, Inc., 14

Beech Aircraft Corporation, 8
Bell Helicopter Textron Inc., 46
The Boeing Company, I; 10 (upd.); 32 (upd.)
Bombardier Inc., 42 (upd.)
British Aerospace plc, I; 24 (upd.)
CAE USA Inc., 48
Canadair, Inc., 16
Cessna Aircraft Company, 8
Cirrus Design Corporation, 44
Cobham plc, 30
Daimler-Benz Aerospace AG, 16
DeCrane Aircraft Holdings Inc., 36
Ducommun Incorporated, 30
EADS SOCATA, 54
Empresa Brasileira de Aeronáutica S.A. (Embraer), 36
European Aeronautic Defence and Space Company EADS N.V., 52 (upd.)
Fairchild Aircraft, Inc., 9
Fairchild Dornier GmbH, 48 (upd.)
First Aviation Services Inc., 49
G.I.E. Airbus Industrie, I; 12 (upd.)
General Dynamics Corporation, I; 10 (upd.); 40 (upd.)
GKN plc, 38 (upd.)
Goodrich Corporation, 46 (upd.)
Groupe Dassault Aviation SA, 26 (upd.)
Grumman Corporation, I; 11 (upd.)
Grupo Aeropuerto del Sureste, S.A. de C.V., 48
Gulfstream Aerospace Corporation, 7; 28 (upd.)
HEICO Corporation, 30
International Lease Finance Corporation, 48
N.V. Koninklijke Nederlandse Vliegtuigenfabriek Fokker, I; 28 (upd.)
Learjet Inc., 8; 27 (upd.)
Lockheed Corporation, I; 11 (upd.)
Lockheed Martin Corporation, 15 (upd.)
Loral Space & Communications Ltd., 54 (upd.)
Magellan Aerospace Corporation, 48
Martin Marietta Corporation, I
McDonnell Douglas Corporation, I; 11 (upd.)
Meggitt PLC, 34
Messerschmitt-Bölkow-Blohm GmbH., I
Moog Inc., 13
Mooney Aerospace Group Ltd., 52
The New Piper Aircraft, Inc., 44
Northrop Grumman Corporation, I; 11 (upd.); 45 (upd.)
Orbital Sciences Corporation, 22
Pemco Aviation Group Inc., 54
Pratt & Whitney, 9
Raytheon Aircraft Holdings Inc., 46
Robinson Helicopter Company, 51
Rockwell International Corporation, I; 11 (upd.)
Rolls-Royce Allison, 29 (upd.)
Rolls-Royce plc, I; 7 (upd.); 21 (upd.)
Sequa Corp., 13
Shannon Aerospace Ltd., 36
Sikorsky Aircraft Corporation, 24
Smiths Industries PLC, 25
Snecma Group, 46
Société Air France, 27 (upd.)
Spacehab, Inc., 37
Spar Aerospace Limited, 32
Sukhoi Design Bureau Aviation Scientific-Industrial Complex, 24
Sundstrand Corporation, 7; 21 (upd.)
Textron Lycoming Turbine Engine, 9
Thales S.A., 42
Thiokol Corporation, 9; 22 (upd.)

United Technologies Corporation, I; 10 (upd.)
Vought Aircraft Industries, Inc., 49
Whittaker Corporation, 48 (upd.)
Woodward Governor Company, 49 (upd.)
Zodiac S.A., 36

AIRLINES

Aer Lingus Group plc, 34
Aeroflot—Russian International Airlines, 6; 29 (upd.)
Aerolíneas Argentinas S.A., 33
Air Canada, 6; 23 (upd.)
Air China, 46
Air Jamaica Limited, 54
Air New Zealand Limited, 14; 38 (upd.)
Air Wisconsin Airlines Corporation, 55
Air-India Limited, 6; 27 (upd.)
AirTran Holdings, Inc., 22
Alaska Air Group, Inc., 6; 29 (upd.)
Alitalia-Linee Aeree Italiana, S.p.A., 6; 29 (upd.)
All Nippon Airways Company Limited, 6; 38 (upd.)
Aloha Airlines, Incorporated, 24
America West Holdings Corporation, 6; 34 (upd.)
American Airlines, I; 6 (upd.)
AMR Corporation, 28 (upd.); 52 (upd.)
Amtran, Inc., 34
Arrow Air Holdings Corporation, 55
Asiana Airlines, Inc., 46
Atlantic Coast Airlines Holdings, Inc., 55
Atlantic Southeast Airlines, Inc., 47
Atlas Air, Inc., 39
Austrian Airlines AG (Österreichische Luftverkehrs AG), 33
Aviacionny Nauchno-Tehnicheskii Komplex im. A.N. Tupoleva, 24
Avianca Aerovías Nacionales de Colombia SA, 36
Banner Aerospace, Inc., 37 (upd.)
Braathens ASA, 47
British Airways PLC, I; 14 (upd.); 43 (upd.)
British Midland plc, 38
British World Airlines Ltd., 18
Cargolux Airlines International S.A., 49
Cathay Pacific Airways Limited, 6; 34 (upd.)
Chautauqua Airlines, Inc., 38
China Airlines, 34
China Eastern Airlines Co. Ltd., 31
China Southern Airlines Company Ltd., 33
Comair Holdings Inc., 13; 34 (upd.)
Continental Airlines, Inc., I; 21 (upd.); 52 (upd.)
Corporación Internacional de Aviación, S.A. de C.V. (Cintra), 20
Delta Air Lines, Inc., I; 6 (upd.); 39 (upd.)
Deutsche Lufthansa Aktiengesellschaft, I; 26 (upd.)
Eastern Airlines, I
easyJet Airline Company Limited, 39
EgyptAir, 6; 27 (upd.)
El Al Israel Airlines Ltd., 23
The Emirates Group, 39
EVA Airways Corporation, 51
Finnair Oy, 6; 25 (upd.)
Frontier Airlines, Inc., 22
Garuda Indonesia, 6
Groupe Air France, 6
Grupo TACA, 38
HAL Inc., 9
Hawaiian Airlines, Inc., 22 (upd.)
Iberia Líneas Aéreas de España S.A., 6; 36 (upd.)

Icelandair, 52
Indian Airlines Ltd., 46
Japan Air Lines Company Ltd., I; 32 (upd.)
JetBlue Airways Corporation, 44
Kitty Hawk, Inc., 22
Kiwi International Airlines Inc., 20
Koninklijke Luchtvaart Maatschappij, N.V.
  (KLM Royal Dutch Airlines), I; 28 (upd.)
Korean Air Lines Co., Ltd., 6; 27 (upd.)
Lan Chile S.A., 31
Lauda Air Luftfahrt AG, 48
LOT Polish Airlines (Polskie Linie
  Lotnicze S.A.), 33
LTU Group Holding GmbH, 37
Malév Plc, 24
Malaysian Airlines System Berhad, 6; 29
  (upd.)
Mesa Air Group, Inc., 32 (upd.)
Mesa Airlines, Inc., 11
Mesaba Holdings, Inc., 28
Midway Airlines Corporation, 33
Midwest Express Holdings, Inc., 35
Northwest Airlines Corporation, I; 6 (upd.);
  26 (upd.)
Offshore Logistics, Inc., 37
Pakistan International Airlines Corporation,
  46
Pan American World Airways, Inc., I; 12
  (upd.)
Panalpina World Transport (Holding) Ltd.,
  47
People Express Airlines, Inc., I
Petroleum Helicopters, Inc., 35
Philippine Airlines, Inc., 6; 23 (upd.)
Preussag AG, 42 (upd.)
Qantas Airways Limited, 6; 24 (upd.)
Reno Air Inc., 23
Royal Nepal Airline Corporation, 41
Ryanair Holdings plc, 35
SAA (Pty) Ltd., 28
Sabena S.A./N.V., 33
The SAS Group, 34 (upd.)
Saudi Arabian Airlines, 6; 27 (upd.)
Scandinavian Airlines System, I
Singapore Airlines Ltd., 6; 27 (upd.)
SkyWest, Inc., 25
Société d'Exploitation AOM Air Liberté
  SA (AirLib), 53
Société Tunisienne de l'Air-Tunisair, 49
Southwest Airlines Co., 6; 24 (upd.)
Spirit Airlines, Inc., 31
Sun Country Airlines, 30
Swiss Air Transport Company, Ltd., I
Swiss International Air Lines Ltd., 48
TAP—Air Portugal Transportes Aéreos
  Portugueses S.A., 46
Texas Air Corporation, I
Thai Airways International Public
  Company Limited, 6; 27 (upd.)
Tower Air, Inc., 28
Trans World Airlines, Inc., I; 12 (upd.); 35
  (upd.)
TransBrasil S/A Linhas Aéreas, 31
Transportes Aereos Portugueses, S.A., 6
TV Guide, Inc., 43 (upd.)
UAL Corporation, 34 (upd.)
United Airlines, I; 6 (upd.)
US Airways Group, Inc., 28 (upd.); 52
  (upd.)
USAir Group, Inc., I; 6 (upd.)
VARIG S.A. (Viação Aérea Rio-
  Grandense), 6; 29 (upd.)
WestJet Airlines Ltd., 38

AUTOMOTIVE

AB Volvo, I; 7 (upd.); 26 (upd.)
Adam Opel AG, 7; 21 (upd.)

Aisin Seiki Co., Ltd., 48 (upd.)
Alfa Romeo, 13; 36 (upd.)
Alvis Plc, 47
American Motors Corporation, I
Applied Power Inc., 32 (upd.)
Arvin Industries, Inc., 8
ArvinMeritor, Inc., 54 (upd.)
ASC, Inc., 55
Autocam Corporation, 51
Automobiles Citroen, 7
Automobili Lamborghini Holding S.p.A.,
  13; 34 (upd.)
AutoNation, Inc., 50
Bajaj Auto Limited, 39
Bayerische Motoren Werke AG, I; 11
  (upd.); 38 (upd.)
Bendix Corporation, I
Blue Bird Corporation, 35
Bombardier Inc., 42 (upd.)
Borg-Warner Automotive, Inc., 14; 32
  (upd.)
The Budd Company, 8
CarMax, Inc., 55
CARQUEST Corporation, 29
Chrysler Corporation, I; 11 (upd.)
CNH Global N.V., 38 (upd.)
Consorcio G Grupo Dina, S.A. de C.V., 36
CSK Auto Corporation, 38
Cummins Engine Company, Inc., I; 12
  (upd.); 40 (upd.)
Custom Chrome, Inc., 16
Daihatsu Motor Company, Ltd., 7; 21
  (upd.)
Daimler-Benz A.G., I; 15 (upd.)
DaimlerChrysler AG, 34 (upd.)
Dana Corporation, I; 10 (upd.)
Deere & Company, 42 (upd.)
Delphi Automotive Systems Corporation,
  45
Don Massey Cadillac, Inc., 37
Donaldson Company, Inc., 49 (upd.)
Douglas & Lomason Company, 16
Ducati Motor Holding S.p.A., 30
Eaton Corporation, I; 10 (upd.)
Echlin Inc., I; 11 (upd.)
Edelbrock Corporation, 37
Federal-Mogul Corporation, I; 10 (upd.);
  26 (upd.)
Ferrari S.p.A., 13; 36 (upd.)
Fiat SpA, I; 11 (upd.); 50 (upd.)
FinishMaster, Inc., 24
Ford Motor Company, I; 11 (upd.); 36
  (upd.)
Ford Motor Company, S.A. de C.V., 20
Fruehauf Corporation, I
General Motors Corporation, I; 10 (upd.);
  36 (upd.)
Gentex Corporation, 26
Genuine Parts Company, 9; 45 (upd.)
GKN plc, 38 (upd.)
Group 1 Automotive, Inc., 52
Harley-Davidson Inc., 7; 25 (upd.)
Hayes Lemmerz International, Inc., 27
The Hertz Corporation, 33 (upd.)
Hino Motors, Ltd., 7; 21 (upd.)
Holley Performance Products Inc., 52
Hometown Auto Retailers, Inc., 44
Honda Motor Company Limited (Honda
  Giken Kogyo Kabushiki Kaisha), I; 10
  (upd.); 29 (upd.)
Insurance Auto Auctions, Inc., 23
Isuzu Motors, Ltd., 9; 23 (upd.)
Kelsey-Hayes Group of Companies, 7; 27
  (upd.)
Kia Motors Corporation, 12; 29 (upd.)
Kwik-Fit Holdings plc, 54
Lear Seating Corporation, 16

Les Schwab Tire Centers, 50
Lithia Motors, Inc., 41
Lotus Cars Ltd., 14
Lund International Holdings, Inc., 40
Mack Trucks, Inc., I; 22 (upd.)
The Major Automotive Companies, Inc., 45
Masland Corporation, 17
Mazda Motor Corporation, 9; 23 (upd.)
Mel Farr Automotive Group, 20
Metso Corporation, 30 (upd.)
Midas International Corporation, 10
Mitsubishi Motors Corporation, 9; 23
  (upd.)
Monaco Coach Corporation, 31
Monro Muffler Brake, Inc., 24
National R.V. Holdings, Inc., 32
Navistar International Corporation, I; 10
  (upd.)
Nissan Motor Co., Ltd., I; 11 (upd.); 34
  (upd.)
O'Reilly Automotive, Inc., 26
Officine Alfieri Maserati S.p.A., 13
Oshkosh Truck Corporation, 7
Paccar Inc., I
PACCAR Inc., 26 (upd.)
Pennzoil-Quaker State Company, IV; 20
  (upd.); 50 (upd.)
Penske Corporation, 19 (upd.)
The Pep Boys—Manny, Moe & Jack, 11;
  36 (upd.)
Peugeot S.A., I
Piaggio & C. S.p.A., 20
Porsche AG, 13; 31 (upd.)
PSA Peugeot Citroen S.A., 28 (upd.)
R&B, Inc., 51
Regie Nationale des Usines Renault, I
Renault S.A., 26 (upd.)
Republic Industries, Inc., 26
The Reynolds and Reynolds Company, 50
Robert Bosch GmbH., I; 16 (upd.); 43
  (upd.)
RockShox, Inc., 26
Rockwell Automation, 43 (upd.)
Rolls-Royce plc, I; 21 (upd.)
Ron Tonkin Chevrolet Company, 55
Rover Group Ltd., 7; 21 (upd.)
Saab Automobile AB, 32 (upd.)
Saab-Scania A.B., I; 11 (upd.)
Safelite Glass Corp., 19
Saturn Corporation, 7; 21 (upd.)
Sealed Power Corporation, I
Sheller-Globe Corporation, I
Sixt AG, 39
Skoda Auto a.s., 39
Spartan Motors Inc., 14
SpeeDee Oil Change and Tune-Up, 25
SPX Corporation, 10; 47 (upd.)
Standard Motor Products, Inc., 40
Superior Industries International, Inc., 8
Suzuki Motor Corporation, 9; 23 (upd.)
Syner Group plc, 45
Tower Automotive, Inc., 24
Toyota Motor Corporation, I; 11 (upd.); 38
  (upd.)
Triumph Motorcycles Ltd., 53
TRW Inc., 14 (upd.)
Ugly Duckling Corporation, 22
United Auto Group, Inc., 26
United Technologies Automotive Inc., 15
Valeo, 23
Volkswagen Aktiengesellschaft, I; 11
  (upd.); 32 (upd.)
Walker Manufacturing Company, 19
Winnebago Industries Inc., 7; 27 (upd.)
Woodward Governor Company, 49 (upd.)
ZF Friedrichshafen AG, 48
Ziebart International Corporation, 30

BEVERAGES

A & W Brands, Inc., 25
Adolph Coors Company, I; 13 (upd.); 36 (upd.)
Allied Domecq PLC, 29
Allied-Lyons PLC, I
Anchor Brewing Company, 47
Anheuser-Busch Companies, Inc., I; 10 (upd.); 34 (upd.)
Asahi Breweries, Ltd., I; 20 (upd.); 52 (upd.)
Bacardi Limited, 18
Banfi Products Corp., 36
Baron Philippe de Rothschild S.A., 39
Bass PLC, I; 15 (upd.); 38 (upd.)
BBAG Osterreichische Brau-Beteiligungs-AG, 38
Beringer Wine Estates Holdings, Inc., 22
The Boston Beer Company, Inc., 18; 50 (upd.)
Brauerei Beck & Co., 9; 33 (upd.)
Brown-Forman Corporation, I; 10 (upd.); 38 (upd.)
Cadbury Schweppes PLC, 49 (upd.)
Canandaigua Brands, Inc., 34 (upd.)
Canandaigua Wine Company, Inc., 13
Carlsberg A/S, 9; 29 (upd.)
Carlton and United Breweries Ltd., I
Casa Cuervo, S.A. de C.V., 31
Cerveceria Polar, I
The Chalone Wine Group, Ltd., 36
Clearly Canadian Beverage Corporation, 48
Coca Cola Bottling Co. Consolidated, 10
The Coca-Cola Company, I; 10 (upd.); 32 (upd.)
Corby Distilleries Limited, 14
Cott Corporation, 52
D.G. Yuengling & Son, Inc., 38
Dean Foods Company, 21 (upd.)
Delicato Vineyards, Inc., 50
Distillers Company PLC, I
Dr Pepper/Seven Up, Inc., 9; 32 (upd.)
E. & J. Gallo Winery, I; 7 (upd.); 28 (upd.)
Empresas Polar SA, 55 (upd.)
Faygo Beverages Inc., 55
Ferolito, Vultaggio & Sons, 27
Florida's Natural Growers, 45
Foster's Brewing Group Ltd., 7; 21 (upd.)
Foster's Group Limited, 50 (upd.)
Fuller Smith & Turner P.L.C., 38
G. Heileman Brewing Company Inc., I
The Gambrinus Company, 40
Geerlings & Wade, Inc., 45
General Cinema Corporation, I
Golden State Vintners, Inc., 33
Grand Metropolitan PLC, I
Green Mountain Coffee, Inc., 31
The Greenalls Group PLC, 21
Greene King plc, 31
Grupo Modelo, S.A. de C.V., 29
Guinness/UDV, I; 43 (upd.)
The Hain Celestial Group, Inc., 43 (upd.)
Hansen Natural Corporation, 31
Heineken N.V, I; 13 (upd.); 34 (upd.)
Heublein, Inc., I
Hiram Walker Resources, Ltd., I
illycaffè SpA, 50
Imagine Foods, Inc., 50
Interbrew S.A., 17; 50 (upd.)
Jacob Leinenkugel Brewing Company, 28
JD Wetherspoon plc, 30
Karlsberg Brauerei GmbH & Co KG, 41
Kendall-Jackson Winery, Ltd., 28
Kikkoman Corporation, 14
Kirin Brewery Company, Limited, I; 21 (upd.)

König Brauerei GmbH & Co. KG, 35 (upd.)
Labatt Brewing Company Limited, I; 25 (upd.)
Latrobe Brewing Company, 54
Laurent-Perrier SA, 42
Lion Nathan Limited, 54
Madeira Wine Company, S.A., 49
Maison Louis Jadot, 24
Marchesi Antinori SRL, 42
Marie Brizard & Roger International S.A., 22
MBC Holding Company, 40
Miller Brewing Company, I; 12 (upd.)
The Minute Maid Company, 28
Moët-Hennessy, I
The Molson Companies Limited, I, 26 (upd.)
National Beverage Corp., 26
National Grape Cooperative Association, Inc., 20
National Wine & Spirits, Inc., 49
Nichols plc, 44
Ocean Spray Cranberries, Inc., 25 (upd.)
Odwalla, Inc., 31
Oregon Chai, Inc., 49
Panamerican Beverages, Inc., 47
Parmalat Finanziaria SpA, 50
Paulaner Brauerei GmbH & Co. KG, 35
Peet's Coffee & Tea, Inc., 38
The Pepsi Bottling Group, Inc., 40
PepsiCo, Inc., I; 10 (upd.); 38 (upd.)
Pernod Ricard S.A., I; 21 (upd.)
Pete's Brewing Company, 22
Philip Morris Companies Inc., 18 (upd.)
Pyramid Breweries Inc., 33
R.C. Bigelow, Inc., 49
Rainier Brewing Company, 23
Redhook Ale Brewery, Inc., 31
Rémy Cointreau S.A., 20
Robert Mondavi Corporation, 15; 50 (upd.)
Royal Crown Company, Inc., 23
Royal Grolsch NV, 54
Sapporo Breweries Limited, I; 13 (upd.); 36 (upd.)
Scottish & Newcastle plc, 15; 35 (upd.)
The Seagram Company Ltd., I; 25 (upd.)
Sebastiani Vineyards, Inc., 28
Shepherd Neame Limited, 30
Snapple Beverage Corporation, 11
The South African Breweries Limited, I; 24 (upd.)
Southcorp Limited, 54
Starbucks Corporation, 13; 34 (upd.)
The Stash Tea Company, 50
Stewart's Beverages, 39
The Stroh Brewery Company, I; 18 (upd.)
Sutter Home Winery Inc., 16
Taittinger S.A., 43
The Terlato Wine Group, 48
Todhunter International, Inc., 27
Triarc Companies, Inc., 34 (upd.)
Tsingtao Brewery Group, 49
Tully's Coffee Corporation, 51
Van Houtte Inc., 39
Vermont Pure Holdings, Ltd., 51
Vin & Spirit AB, 31
Viña Concha y Toro S.A., 45
Vincor International Inc., 50
Whitbread and Company PLC, I
The Wine Group, Inc., 39
Young & Co.'s Brewery, P.L.C., 38

BIOTECHNOLOGY

Amersham PLC, 50
Amgen, Inc., 10; 30 (upd.)
Biogen Inc., 14; 36 (upd.)

Cambrex Corporation, 44 (upd.)
Centocor Inc., 14
Charles River Laboratories International, Inc., 42
Chiron Corporation, 10; 36 (upd.)
Covance Inc., 30
CryoLife, Inc., 46
Delta and Pine Land Company, 33
Dionex Corporation, 46
Enzo Biochem, Inc., 41
Genentech, Inc., 32 (upd.)
Genzyme Corporation, 38 (upd.)
Gilead Sciences, Inc., 54
Howard Hughes Medical Institute, 39
Huntingdon Life Sciences Group plc, 42
IDEXX Laboratories, Inc., 23
Immunex Corporation, 14; 50 (upd.)
IMPATH Inc., 45
Incyte Genomics, Inc., 52
Invitrogen Corporation, 52
The Judge Group, Inc., 51
Life Technologies, Inc., 17
Medtronic, Inc., 30 (upd.)
Millipore Corporation, 25
Minntech Corporation, 22
Mycogen Corporation, 21
New Brunswick Scientific Co., Inc., 45
Qiagen N.V., 39
Quintiles Transnational Corporation, 21
Seminis, Inc., 29
Sigma-Aldrich Corporation, 36 (upd.)
Starkey Laboratories, Inc., 52
STERIS Corporation, 29
TECHNE Corporation, 52
Waters Corporation, 43
Whatman plc, 46
Wyeth, 50 (upd.)

CHEMICALS

A. Schulman, Inc., 8
Aceto Corp., 38
Air Products and Chemicals, Inc., I; 10 (upd.)
Airgas, Inc., 54
Akzo Nobel N.V., 13
AlliedSignal Inc., 22 (upd.)
American Cyanamid, I; 8 (upd.)
American Vanguard Corporation, 47
ARCO Chemical Company, 10
Atochem S.A., I
Baker Hughes Incorporated, 22 (upd.)
Balchem Corporation, 42
BASF Aktiengesellschaft, I; 18 (upd.); 50 (upd.)
Bayer A.G., I; 13 (upd.); 41 (upd.)
Betz Laboratories, Inc., I; 10 (upd.)
The BFGoodrich Company, 19 (upd.)
BOC Group plc, I; 25 (upd.)
Brenntag AG, 8; 23 (upd.)
Burmah Castrol PLC, 30 (upd.)
Cabot Corporation, 8; 29 (upd.)
Cambrex Corporation, 16
Catalytica Energy Systems, Inc., 44
Celanese Corporation, I
Celanese Mexicana, S.A. de C.V., 54
Chemcentral Corporation, 8
Chemi-Trol Chemical Co., 16
Church & Dwight Co., Inc., 29
Ciba-Geigy Ltd., I; 8 (upd.)
The Clorox Company, 22 (upd.)
Croda International Plc, 45
Crompton & Knowles, 9
Crompton Corporation, 36 (upd.)
Cytec Industries Inc., 27
Degussa-Hüls AG, 32 (upd.)
DeKalb Genetics Corporation, 17
The Dexter Corporation, I; 12 (upd.)

Dionex Corporation, 46
The Dow Chemical Company, I; 8 (upd.); 50 (upd.)
DSM, N.V, I
E.I. du Pont de Nemours & Company, I; 8 (upd.); 26 (upd.)
Eastman Chemical Company, 14; 38 (upd.)
Ecolab Inc., I; 13 (upd.); 34 (upd.)
Elementis plc, 40 (upd.)
English China Clays Ltd., 15 (upd.); 40 (upd.)
ERLY Industries Inc., 17
Ethyl Corporation, I; 10 (upd.)
Ferro Corporation, 8
First Mississippi Corporation, 8
Formosa Plastics Corporation, 14
Fort James Corporation, 22 (upd.)
G.A.F., I
The General Chemical Group Inc., 37
Georgia Gulf Corporation, 9
Givaudan SA, 43
Great Lakes Chemical Corporation, I; 14 (upd.)
Guerbet Group, 46
H.B. Fuller Company, 32 (upd.)
Hauser, Inc., 46
Hawkins Chemical, Inc., 16
Henkel KGaA, 34 (upd.)
Hercules Inc., I; 22 (upd.)
Hoechst A.G., I; 18 (upd.)
Hoechst Celanese Corporation, 13
Huls A.G., I
Huntsman Chemical Corporation, 8
IMC Fertilizer Group, Inc., 8
Imperial Chemical Industries PLC, I; 50 (upd.)
International Flavors & Fragrances Inc., 9; 38 (upd.)
Israel Chemicals Ltd., 55
Koppers Industries, Inc., I; 26 (upd.)
L'Air Liquide SA, I; 47 (upd.)
Lawter International Inc., 14
LeaRonal, Inc., 23
Loctite Corporation, 30 (upd.)
Lubrizol Corporation, I; 30 (upd.)
Lyondell Chemical Company, 45 (upd.)
M.A. Hanna Company, 8
MacDermid Incorporated, 32
Mallinckrodt Group Inc., 19
MBC Holding Company, 40
Melamine Chemicals, Inc., 27
Methanex Corporation, 40
Minerals Technologies Inc., 52 (upd.)
Mississippi Chemical Corporation, 39
Mitsubishi Chemical Industries, Ltd., I
Mitsui Petrochemical Industries, Ltd., 9
Monsanto Company, I; 9 (upd.); 29 (upd.)
Montedison SpA, I
Morton International Inc., 9 (upd.)
Morton Thiokol, Inc., I
Nagase & Company, Ltd., 8
Nalco Chemical Corporation, I; 12 (upd.)
National Distillers and Chemical Corporation, I
National Sanitary Supply Co., 16
National Starch and Chemical Company, 49
NCH Corporation, 8
NL Industries, Inc., 10
Nobel Industries AB, 9
Norsk Hydro ASA, 35 (upd.)
Novacor Chemicals Ltd., 12
NutraSweet Company, 8
Olin Corporation, I; 13 (upd.)
OM Group, Inc., 17
Penford Corporation, 55
Pennwalt Corporation, I

Perstorp AB, I; 51 (upd.)
Petrolite Corporation, 15
Pioneer Hi-Bred International, Inc., 41 (upd.)
Praxair, Inc., 11
Quantum Chemical Corporation, 8
Reichhold Chemicals, Inc., 10
Rhodia SA, 38
Rhône-Poulenc S.A., I; 10 (upd.)
Robertet SA, 39
Rohm and Haas Company, I; 26 (upd.)
Roussel Uclaf, I; 8 (upd.)
RPM, Inc., 36 (upd.)
RWE AG, 50 (upd.)
The Scotts Company, 22
SCP Pool Corporation, 39
Sequa Corp., 13
Shanghai Petrochemical Co., Ltd., 18
Sigma-Aldrich Corporation, 36 (upd.)
Solutia Inc., 52
Solvay & Cie S.A., I; 21 (upd.)
Stepan Company, 30
Sterling Chemicals, Inc., 16
Sumitomo Chemical Company Ltd., I
Takeda Chemical Industries, Ltd., 46 (upd.)
Terra Industries, Inc., 13
Teva Pharmaceutical Industries Ltd., 22
Total Fina Elf S.A., 50 (upd.)
TOTAL S.A., 24 (upd.)
Ube Industries, Ltd., 38 (upd.)
Union Carbide Corporation, I; 9 (upd.)
Univar Corporation, 9
The Valspar Corporation, 32 (upd.)
Vista Chemical Company, I
Witco Corporation, I; 16 (upd.)
Yule Catto & Company plc, 54
Zeneca Group PLC, 21

CONGLOMERATES

Accor SA, 10; 27 (upd.)
AEG A.G., I
Alcatel Alsthom Compagnie Générale d'Electricité, 9
Alco Standard Corporation, I
Alexander & Baldwin, Inc., 40 (upd.)
Alfa, S.A. de C.V., 19
Allied Domecq PLC, 29
Allied-Signal Inc., I
AMFAC Inc., I
The Anschutz Corporation, 36 (upd.)
Aramark Corporation, 13
ARAMARK Corporation, 41
Archer-Daniels-Midland Company, I; 11 (upd.)
Arkansas Best Corporation, 16
Associated British Ports Holdings Plc, 45
BAA plc, 33 (upd.)
Barlow Rand Ltd., I
Bat Industries PLC, I
Berkshire Hathaway Inc., 42 (upd.)
Bond Corporation Holdings Limited, 10
BTR PLC, I
Bunzl plc, 31 (upd.)
Burlington Northern Santa Fe Corporation, 27 (upd.)
Business Post Group plc, 46
C. Itoh & Company Ltd., I
Cargill, Incorporated, 13 (upd.); 40 (upd.)
CBI Industries, Inc., 7
Chemed Corporation, 13
Chesebrough-Pond's USA, Inc., 8
China Merchants International Holdings Co., Ltd., 52
Cisneros Group of Companies, 54
CITIC Pacific Ltd., 18
Colt Industries Inc., I
Compagnie Financiere Richemont AG, 50

The Connell Company, 29
CSR Limited, 28 (upd.)
Daewoo Group, 18 (upd.)
De Dietrich & Cie., 31
Deere & Company, 21 (upd.)
Delaware North Companies Incorporated, 7
Desc, S.A. de C.V., 23
The Dial Corp., 8
Dr. August Oetker KG, 51
EBSCO Industries, Inc., 40 (upd.)
El Corte Inglés Group, 26 (upd.)
Elders IXL Ltd., I
Engelhard Corporation, 21 (upd.)
Farley Northwest Industries, Inc., I
Fimalac S.A., 37
First Pacific Company Limited, 18
Fisher Companies, Inc., 15
Fletcher Challenge Ltd., 19 (upd.)
FMC Corporation, I; 11 (upd.)
Fortune Brands, Inc., 29 (upd.)
Fraser & Neave Ltd., 54
Fuqua Industries, Inc., I
General Electric Company, 34 (upd.)
GIB Group, 26 (upd.)
Gillett Holdings, Inc., 7
Grand Metropolitan PLC, 14 (upd.)
Great American Management and Investment, Inc., 8
Greyhound Corporation, I
Grupo Carso, S.A. de C.V., 21
Grupo Industrial Bimbo, 19
Grupo Industrial Saltillo, S.A. de C.V., 54
Gulf & Western Inc., I
Haci Omer Sabanci Holdings A.S., 55
Hagemeyer N.V., 39
Hankyu Corporation, 23 (upd.)
Hanson PLC, III; 7 (upd.)
Hitachi Zosen Corporation, 53 (upd.)
Hitachi, Ltd., I; 12 (upd.); 40 (upd.)
Hutchison Whampoa Limited, 18; 49 (upd.)
IC Industries, Inc., I
Ilitch Holdings Inc., 37
Inchcape PLC, 16 (upd.); 50 (upd.)
Ingram Industries, Inc., 11; 49 (upd.)
Instituto Nacional de Industria, I
International Controls Corporation, 10
International Telephone & Telegraph Corporation, I; 11 (upd.)
Istituto per la Ricostruzione Industriale, I
ITOCHU Corporation, 32 (upd.)
Jardine Matheson Holdings Limited, I; 20 (upd.)
Jason Incorporated, 23
Jefferson Smurfit Group plc, 19 (upd.)
The Jim Pattison Group, 37
Jordan Industries, Inc., 36
Justin Industries, Inc., 19
Kanematsu Corporation, 24 (upd.)
Kao Corporation, 20 (upd.)
Katy Industries, Inc., I
Kesko Ltd. (Kesko Oy), 8; 27 (upd.)
Kidde plc, I; 44 (upd.)
Knowledge Universe, Inc., 54
Koç Holding A.S., I; 54 (upd.)
Koninklijke Nedlloyd N.V., 26 (upd.)
Koor Industries Ltd., 25 (upd.)
K2 Inc., 16
The L.L. Knickerbocker Co., Inc., 25
Lancaster Colony Corporation, 8
Larry H. Miller Group, 29
Lear Siegler, Inc., I
Lefrak Organization Inc., 26
Leucadia National Corporation, 11
Litton Industries, Inc., I; 11 (upd.)
Loews Corporation, I; 12 (upd.); 36 (upd.)
Loral Corporation, 8

CONGLOMERATES (*continued*)

LTV Corporation, I
LVMH Moët Hennessy Louis Vuitton SA, 33 (upd.)
Marubeni Corporation, I; 24 (upd.)
MAXXAM Inc., 8
McKesson Corporation, I
Melitta Unternehmensgruppe Bentz KG, 53
Menasha Corporation, 8
Metallgesellschaft AG, 16 (upd.)
Metromedia Co., 7
Minnesota Mining & Manufacturing Company (3M), I; 8 (upd.); 26 (upd.)
Mitsubishi Corporation, I; 12 (upd.)
Mitsubishi Heavy Industries, Ltd., 40 (upd.)
Mitsui & Co., Ltd., 28 (upd.)
Mitsui Bussan K.K., I
The Molson Companies Limited, I; 26 (upd.)
Montedison S.p.A., 24 (upd.)
NACCO Industries, Inc., 7
National Service Industries, Inc., 11; 54 (upd.)
New World Development Company Limited, 38 (upd.)
Nichimen Corporation, 24 (upd.)
Nissho Iwai K.K., I
Norsk Hydro A.S., 10
Novar plc, 49 (upd.)
Ogden Corporation, I
Onex Corporation, 16
Orkla A/S, 18
Park-Ohio Industries Inc., 17
Pentair, Inc., 7
Philip Morris Companies Inc., 44 (upd.)
Poliet S.A., 33
Powell Duffryn plc, 31
Power Corporation of Canada, 36 (upd.)
Preussag AG, 17
Pubco Corporation, 17
Pulsar Internacional S.A., 21
R.B. Pamplin Corp., 45
The Rank Organisation Plc, 14 (upd.)
Red Apple Group, Inc., 23
Roll International Corporation, 37
Rubbermaid Incorporated, 20 (upd.)
Samsung Group, I
San Miguel Corporation, 15
Sara Lee Corporation, 15 (upd.); 54 (upd.)
Schindler Holding AG, 29
Sea Containers Ltd., 29
Seaboard Corporation, 36
Sequa Corporation, 54 (upd.)
ServiceMaster Inc., 23 (upd.)
SHV Holdings N.V., 55
Sime Darby Berhad, 14; 36 (upd.)
Société du Louvre, 27
Standex International Corporation, 17; 44 (upd.)
Stinnes AG, 23 (upd.)
Sudbury Inc., 16
Sumitomo Corporation, I; 11 (upd.)
Swire Pacific Ltd., I; 16 (upd.)
Talley Industries, Inc., 16
Tandycrafts, Inc., 31
TaurusHolding GmbH & Co. KG, 46
Teledyne, Inc., I; 10 (upd.)
Tenneco Inc., I; 10 (upd.)
Textron Inc., I; 34 (upd.)
Thomas H. Lee Co., 24
Thorn Emi PLC, I
Thorn plc, 24
TI Group plc, 17
Time Warner Inc., IV; 7 (upd.)
Tokyu Corporation, 47 (upd.)
Tomen Corporation, 24 (upd.)

Tomkins plc, 11; 44 (upd.)
Toshiba Corporation, I; 12 (upd.); 40 (upd.)
Tractebel S.A., 20
Transamerica–An AEGON Company, I; 13 (upd.); 41 (upd.)
The Tranzonic Cos., 15
Triarc Companies, Inc., 8
Triple Five Group Ltd., 49
TRW Inc., I; 11 (upd.)
Unilever, II; 7 (upd.); 32 (upd.)
Unión Fenosa, S.A., 51
United Technologies Corporation, 34 (upd.)
Universal Studios, Inc., 33
Valhi, Inc., 19
Valores Industriales S.A., 19
Veba A.G., I; 15 (upd.)
Vendôme Luxury Group plc, 27
Viacom Inc., 23 (upd.)
Virgin Group, 12; 32 (upd.)
W.R. Grace & Company, I; 50
The Washington Companies, 33
Watsco Inc., 52
Wheaton Industries, 8
Whitbread PLC, 20 (upd.)
Whitman Corporation, 10 (upd.)
Whittaker Corporation, I
WorldCorp, Inc., 10
Worms et Cie, 27
Yamaha Corporation, 40 (upd.)

CONSTRUCTION

A. Johnson & Company H.B., I
ABC Supply Co., Inc., 22
Abrams Industries Inc., 23
AMREP Corporation, 21
ASV, Inc., 34
The Austin Company, 8
Autoroutes du Sud de la France SA, 55
Balfour Beatty plc, 36 (upd.)
Baratt Developments PLC, I
Barton Malow Company, 51
Beazer Homes USA, Inc., 17
Bechtel Group, Inc., I; 24 (upd.)
Bellway Plc, 45
BFC Construction Corporation, 25
Bilfinger & Berger AG, 55 (upd.)
Bilfinger & Berger Bau A.G., I
Bird Corporation, 19
Black & Veatch LLP, 22
Boral Limited, 43 (upd.)
Bouygues S.A., I; 24 (upd.)
Brown & Root, Inc., 13
Bufete Industrial, S.A. de C.V., 34
Building Materials Holding Corporation, 52
Bulley & Andrews, LLC, 55
CalMat Co., 19
Centex Corporation, 8; 29 (upd.)
Cianbro Corporation, 14
The Clark Construction Group, Inc., 8
Colas S.A., 31
Day & Zimmermann, Inc., 31 (upd.)
Dillingham Construction Corporation, I; 44 (upd.)
Dominion Homes, Inc., 19
The Drees Company, Inc., 41
Edw. C. Levy Co., 42
Eiffage, 27
Ellerbe Becket, 41
Empresas ICA Sociedad Controladora, S.A. de C.V., 41
Encompass Services Corporation, 33
Engle Homes, Inc., 46
Environmental Industries, Inc., 31
Eurotunnel PLC, 13
Fairclough Construction Group PLC, I
Fleetwood Enterprises, Inc., 22 (upd.)

Fluor Corporation, I; 8 (upd.); 34 (upd.)
Forest City Enterprises, Inc., 52 (upd.)
George Wimpey plc, 12; 51 (upd.)
Gilbane, Inc., 34
Granite Rock Company, 26
Grupo Dragados SA, 55
Grupo Ferrovial, S.A., 40
Habitat for Humanity International, 36
Hillsdown Holdings plc, 24 (upd.)
Hochtief AG, 33
Horton Homes, Inc., 25
Hospitality Worldwide Services, Inc., 26
Hovnanian Enterprises, Inc., 29
J.A. Jones, Inc., 16
J.F. Shea Co., Inc., 55
Jarvis plc, 39
JLG Industries, Inc., 52
John Brown PLC, I
John Laing plc, I; 51 (upd.)
John W. Danforth Company, 48
Kajima Corporation, I; 51 (upd.)
Kaufman and Broad Home Corporation, 8
KB Home, 45 (upd.)
Kitchell Corporation, 14
The Koll Company, 8
Komatsu Ltd., 16 (upd.)
Kraus-Anderson, Incorporated, 36
Kumagai Gumi Company, Ltd., I
L'Entreprise Jean Lefebvre, 23
Ledcor Industries Limited, 46
Lennar Corporation, 11
Lincoln Property Company, 8
Lindal Cedar Homes, Inc., 29
Linde A.G., I
MasTec, Inc., 55
McCarthy Building Companies, Inc., 48
Mellon-Stuart Company, I
Michael Baker Corp., 14
Morrison Knudsen Corporation, 7; 28 (upd.)
New Holland N.V., 22
NVR L.P., 8
Ohbayashi Corporation, I
Opus Group, 34
PCL Construction Group Inc., 50
The Peninsular & Oriental Steam Navigation Company (Bovis Division), I
Perini Corporation, 8
Peter Kiewit Sons' Inc., 8
Philipp Holzmann AG, 17
Post Properties, Inc., 26
Pulte Homes, Inc., 8; 42 (upd.)
Pyramid Companies, 54
Redrow Group plc, 31
RMC Group p.l.c., 34 (upd.)
Rooney Brothers Co., 25
The Rottlund Company, Inc., 28
The Ryland Group, Inc., 8; 37 (upd.)
Sandvik AB, 32 (upd.)
Schuff Steel Company, 26
Shorewood Packaging Corporation, 28
Simon Property Group, Inc., 27
Skanska AB, 38
Standard Pacific Corporation, 52
Sundt Corp., 24
Swinerton Inc., 43
Taylor Woodrow plc, I; 38 (upd.)
Thyssen Krupp AG, 28 (upd.)
Toll Brothers Inc., 15
Trammell Crow Company, 8
Tridel Enterprises Inc., 9
The Turner Corporation, 8; 23 (upd.)
U.S. Aggregates, Inc., 42
U.S. Home Corporation, 8
VA TECH ELIN EBG GmbH, 49
Veit Companies, 43
Walbridge Aldinger Co., 38

Walter Industries, Inc., 22 (upd.)
The Weitz Company, Inc., 42
Wilson Bowden Plc, 45
Wood Hall Trust PLC, I

CONTAINERS

Ball Corporation, I; 10 (upd.)
BWAY Corporation, 24
Clarcor Inc., 17
Continental Can Co., Inc., 15
Continental Group Company, I
Crown Cork & Seal Company, Inc., I; 13
  (upd.); 32 (upd.)
Gaylord Container Corporation, 8
Golden Belt Manufacturing Co., 16
Greif Bros. Corporation, 15
Grupo Industrial Durango, S.A. de C.V.,
  37
Hanjin Shipping Co., Ltd., 50
Inland Container Corporation, 8
Kerr Group Inc., 24
Keyes Fibre Company, 9
Libbey Inc., 49
Liqui-Box Corporation, 16
The Longaberger Company, 12
Longview Fibre Company, 8
The Mead Corporation, 19 (upd.)
Metal Box PLC, I
Molins plc, 51
National Can Corporation, I
Owens-Illinois, Inc., I; 26 (upd.)
Packaging Corporation of America, 51
  (upd.)
Primerica Corporation, I
Reynolds Metals Company, 19 (upd.)
Royal Packaging Industries Van Leer N.V.,
  30
Sealright Co., Inc., 17
Shurgard Storage Centers, Inc., 52
Smurfit-Stone Container Corporation, 26
  (upd.)
Sonoco Products Company, 8
Thermos Company, 16
Toyo Seikan Kaisha, Ltd., I
U.S. Can Corporation, 30
Ultra Pac, Inc., 24
Viatech Continental Can Company, Inc., 25
  (upd.)
Vitro Corporativo S.A. de C.V., 34

DRUGS/PHARMACEUTICALS

A.L. Pharma Inc., 12
Abbott Laboratories, I; 11 (upd.); 40 (upd.)
Akorn, Inc., 32
Alpharma Inc., 35 (upd.)
ALZA Corporation, 10; 36 (upd.)
American Home Products, I; 10 (upd.)
Amersham PLC, 50
Amgen, Inc., 10
Andrx Corporation, 55
Astra AB, I; 20 (upd.)
AstraZeneca PLC, 50 (upd.)
Barr Laboratories, Inc., 26
Bayer A.G., I; 13 (upd.)
Biovail Corporation, 47
Block Drug Company, Inc., 8
Bristol-Myers Squibb Company, III; 9
  (upd.); 37 (upd.)
C.H. Boehringer Sohn, 39
Caremark Rx, Inc., 10; 54 (upd.)
Carter-Wallace, Inc., 8; 38 (upd.)
Cephalon, Inc., 45
Chiron Corporation, 10
Chugai Pharmaceutical Co., Ltd., 50
Ciba-Geigy Ltd., I; 8 (upd.)
D&K Wholesale Drug, Inc., 14

Eli Lilly and Company, I; 11 (upd.); 47
  (upd.)
Express Scripts Inc., 44 (upd.)
F. Hoffmann-La Roche Ltd., I; 50 (upd.)
Fisons plc, 9; 23 (upd.)
Forest Laboratories, Inc., 52 (upd.)
FoxMeyer Health Corporation, 16
Fujisawa Pharmaceutical Company Ltd., I
G.D. Searle & Co., I; 12 (upd.); 34 (upd.)
GEHE AG, 27
Genentech, Inc., I; 8 (upd.)
Genetics Institute, Inc., 8
Genzyme Corporation, 13
Glaxo Holdings PLC, I; 9 (upd.)
GlaxoSmithKline plc, 46 (upd.)
Groupe Fournier SA, 44
H. Lundbeck A/S, 44
Hauser, Inc., 46
Heska Corporation, 39
Huntingdon Life Sciences Group plc, 42
ICN Pharmaceuticals, Inc., 52
IVAX Corporation, 55 (upd.)
Johnson & Johnson, III; 8 (upd.)
Jones Medical Industries, Inc., 24
The Judge Group, Inc., 51
King Pharmaceuticals, Inc., 54
Kyowa Hakko Kogyo Co., Ltd., 48 (upd.)
Leiner Health Products Inc., 34
Ligand Pharmaceuticals Incorporated, 47
Marion Merrell Dow, Inc., I; 9 (upd.)
McKesson Corporation, 12; 47 (upd.)
MedImmune, Inc., 35
Merck & Co., Inc., I; 11 (upd.)
Miles Laboratories, I
Millennium Pharmaceuticals, Inc., 47
Monsanto Company, 29 (upd.)
Moore Medical Corp., 17
Murdock Madaus Schwabe, 26
Mylan Laboratories Inc., I; 20 (upd.)
National Patent Development Corporation,
  13
Natrol, Inc., 49
Natural Alternatives International, Inc., 49
Novartis AG, 39 (upd.)
Noven Pharmaceuticals, Inc., 55
Novo Industri A/S, I
Omnicare, Inc., 49
Pfizer Inc., I; 9 (upd.); 38 (upd.)
Pharmacia & Upjohn Inc., I; 25 (upd.)
Quintiles Transnational Corporation, 21
R.P. Scherer, I
Roberts Pharmaceutical Corporation, 16
Roche Bioscience, 14 (upd.)
Rorer Group, I
Roussel Uclaf, I; 8 (upd.)
Sandoz Ltd., I
Sankyo Company, Ltd., I
The Sanofi-Synthélabo Group, I; 49 (upd.)
Schering AG, I; 50 (upd.)
Schering-Plough Corporation, I; 14 (upd.);
  49 (upd.)
Sepracor Inc., 45
Serono S.A., 47
Shionogi & Co., Ltd., 17 (upd.)
Sigma-Aldrich Corporation, I; 36 (upd.)
SmithKline Beckman Corporation, I
SmithKline Beecham plc, 32 (upd.)
Squibb Corporation, I
Sterling Drug, Inc., I
The Sunrider Corporation, 26
Syntex Corporation, I
Takeda Chemical Industries, Ltd., I
Teva Pharmaceutical Industries Ltd., 22; 54
  (upd.)
The Upjohn Company, I; 8 (upd.)
Vitalink Pharmacy Services, Inc., 15
Warner-Lambert Co., I; 10 (upd.)

Watson Pharmaceuticals Inc., 16
The Wellcome Foundation Ltd., I
Zila, Inc., 46

ELECTRICAL & ELECTRONICS

ABB ASEA Brown Boveri Ltd., II; 22
  (upd.)
Acer Inc., 16
Acuson Corporation, 10; 36 (upd.)
ADC Telecommunications, Inc., 30 (upd.)
Adtran Inc., 22
Advanced Micro Devices, Inc., 30 (upd.)
Advanced Technology Laboratories, Inc., 9
Agilent Technologies Inc., 38
Aiwa Co., Ltd., 30
Akzo Nobel N.V., 41 (upd.)
Alliant Techsystems Inc., 30 (upd.)
AlliedSignal Inc., 22 (upd.)
Alpine Electronics, Inc., 13
Alps Electric Co., Ltd., II
Altera Corporation, 18; 43 (upd.)
Altron Incorporated, 20
Amdahl Corporation, 40 (upd.)
American Power Conversion Corporation,
  24
AMP Incorporated, II; 14 (upd.)
Amphenol Corporation, 40
Amstrad plc, 48 (upd.)
Analog Devices, Inc., 10
Analogic Corporation, 23
Anam Group, 23
Anaren Microwave, Inc., 33
Andrew Corporation, 10; 32 (upd.)
Apple Computer, Inc., 36 (upd.)
Applied Power Inc., 32 (upd.)
Arrow Electronics, Inc., 10; 50 (upd.)
Ascend Communications, Inc., 24
Astronics Corporation, 35
Atari Corporation, 9; 23 (upd.)
Atmel Corporation, 17
Audiovox Corporation, 34
Ault Incorporated, 34
Autodesk, Inc., 10
Avnet Inc., 9
Bang & Olufsen Holding A/S, 37
Barco NV, 44
Benchmark Electronics, Inc., 40
Bicoastal Corporation, II
Blonder Tongue Laboratories, Inc., 48
Bose Corporation, 13; 36 (upd.)
Boston Acoustics, Inc., 22
Bowthorpe plc, 33
Braun GmbH, 51
Broadcom Corporation, 34
Bull S.A., 43 (upd.)
Burr-Brown Corporation, 19
C-COR.net Corp., 38
Cabletron Systems, Inc., 10
Cadence Design Systems, Inc., 48 (upd.)
Cambridge SoundWorks, Inc., 48
Canon Inc., 18 (upd.)
Carbone Lorraine S.A., 33
Carl-Zeiss-Stiftung, 34 (upd.)
CASIO Computer Co., Ltd., 16 (upd.); 40
  (upd.)
CDW Computer Centers, Inc., 52 (upd.)
Checkpoint Systems, Inc., 39
Chubb, PLC, 50
Cirrus Logic, Inc., 48 (upd.)
Cisco Systems, Inc., 34 (upd.)
Citizen Watch Co., Ltd., 21 (upd.)
Cobham plc, 30
Cobra Electronics Corporation, 14
Coherent, Inc., 31
Cohu, Inc., 32
Compagnie Générale d'Électricité, II
Conexant Systems, Inc., 36

ELECTRICAL & ELECTRONICS
(*continued*)

Cooper Industries, Inc., II
Cray Research, Inc., 16 (upd.)
Cree Inc., 53
CTS Corporation, 39
Cubic Corporation, 19
Cypress Semiconductor Corporation, 20; 48
  (upd.)
Daktronics, Inc., 32
Dallas Semiconductor Corporation, 13; 31
  (upd.)
De La Rue plc, 34 (upd.)
Dell Computer Corporation, 31 (upd.)
DH Technology, Inc., 18
Digi International Inc., 9
Discreet Logic Inc., 20
Dixons Group plc, 19 (upd.)
Dolby Laboratories Inc., 20
Dynatech Corporation, 13
E-Systems, Inc., 9
Electronics for Imaging, Inc., 15; 43 (upd.)
Emerson, II; 46 (upd.)
Emerson Radio Corp., 30
ENCAD, Incorporated, 25
Equant N.V., 52
Equus Computer Systems, Inc., 49
ESS Technology, Inc., 22
Everex Systems, Inc., 16
Exabyte Corporation, 40 (upd.)
Exar Corp., 14
Exide Electronics Group, Inc., 20
Flextronics International Ltd., 38
Fluke Corporation, 15
Foxboro Company, 13
Fuji Electric Co., Ltd., II; 48 (upd.)
Fujitsu Limited, 16 (upd.); 42 (upd.)
General Dynamics Corporation, 40 (upd.)
General Electric Company, II; 12 (upd.)
General Electric Company, PLC, II
General Instrument Corporation, 10
General Signal Corporation, 9
GenRad, Inc., 24
GM Hughes Electronics Corporation, II
Goldstar Co., Ltd., 12
Gould Electronics, Inc., 14
Grundig AG, 27
Guillemot Corporation, 41
Hadco Corporation, 24
Hamilton Beach/Proctor-Silex Inc., 17
Harman International Industries Inc., 15
Harris Corporation, II; 20 (upd.)
Hayes Corporation, 24
Herley Industries, Inc., 33
Hewlett-Packard Company, 28 (upd.); 50
  (upd.)
Holophane Corporation, 19
Honeywell Inc., II; 12 (upd.); 50 (upd.)
Hubbell Incorporated, 9; 31 (upd.)
Hughes Supply, Inc., 14
Hutchinson Technology Incorporated, 18
Hypercom Corporation, 27
IEC Electronics Corp., 42
Imax Corporation, 28
In Focus Systems, Inc., 22
Indigo NV, 26
Ingram Micro Inc., 52
Integrated Defense Technologies, Inc., 54
Intel Corporation, II; 10 (upd.)
International Business Machines
  Corporation, 30 (upd.)
International Rectifier Corporation, 31
Itel Corporation, 9
Jabil Circuit, Inc., 36
Jaco Electronics, Inc., 30
JDS Uniphase Corporation, 34
Juno Lighting, Inc., 30

Katy Industries, Inc., 51 (upd.)
Keithley Instruments Inc., 16
Kemet Corp., 14
Kent Electronics Corporation, 17
Kenwood Corporation, 31
Kimball International, Inc., 48 (upd.)
Kingston Technology Corporation, 20
KitchenAid, 8
KLA-Tencor Corporation, 45 (upd.)
KnowledgeWare Inc., 9
Kollmorgen Corporation, 18
Konica Corporation, 30 (upd.)
Koninklijke Philips Electronics N.V., 50
  (upd.)
Koor Industries Ltd., II
Koss Corporation, 38
Kudelski Group SA, 44
Kulicke and Soffa Industries, Inc., 33
Kyocera Corporation, II
LaBarge Inc., 41
Lattice Semiconductor Corp., 16
LeCroy Corporation, 41
Legrand SA, 21
Linear Technology, Inc., 16
Littelfuse, Inc., 26
Loral Corporation, 9
Lowrance Electronics, Inc., 18
LSI Logic Corporation, 13
Lucent Technologies Inc., 34
Lucky-Goldstar, II
Lunar Corporation, 29
Mackie Designs Inc., 33
MagneTek, Inc., 15; 41 (upd.)
Marconi plc, 33 (upd.)
Marquette Electronics, Inc., 13
Matsushita Electric Industrial Co., Ltd., II
Maxim Integrated Products, Inc., 16
Merix Corporation, 36
Methode Electronics, Inc., 13
Mitel Corporation, 18
MITRE Corporation, 26
Mitsubishi Electric Corporation, II; 44
  (upd.)
Molex Incorporated, 54 (upd.)
Motorola, Inc., II; 11 (upd.); 34 (upd.)
National Instruments Corporation, 22
National Presto Industries, Inc., 16; 43
  (upd.)
National Semiconductor Corporation, II; 26
  (upd.)
NEC Corporation, II; 21 (upd.)
Nexans SA, 54
Nintendo Co., Ltd., 28 (upd.)
Nokia Corporation, II; 17 (upd.); 38 (upd.)
Nortel Networks Corporation, 36 (upd.)
Northrop Grumman Corporation, 45 (upd.)
Oak Technology, Inc., 22
Oki Electric Industry Company, Limited, II
Omron Corporation, II; 28 (upd.)
Otter Tail Power Company, 18
Palm, Inc., 36
Palomar Medical Technologies, Inc., 22
The Peak Technologies Group, Inc., 14
Peavey Electronics Corporation, 16
Philips Electronics N.V., II; 13 (upd.)
Philips Electronics North America Corp.,
  13
Pioneer Electronic Corporation, 28 (upd.)
Pioneer-Standard Electronics Inc., 19
Pitney Bowes Inc., 47 (upd.)
Pittway Corporation, 9
The Plessey Company, PLC, II
Plexus Corporation, 35
Polk Audio, Inc., 34
Potter & Brumfield Inc., 11
Premier Industrial Corporation, 9
Protection One, Inc., 32

Quanta Computer Inc., 47
Racal Electronics PLC, II
RadioShack Corporation, 36 (upd.)
Radius Inc., 16
Raychem Corporation, 8
Rayovac Corporation, 13
Raytheon Company, II; 11 (upd.); 38
  (upd.)
RCA Corporation, II
Read-Rite Corp., 10
Reliance Electric Company, 9
Research in Motion Ltd., 54
Rexel, Inc., 15
Richardson Electronics, Ltd., 17
Ricoh Company, Ltd., 36 (upd.)
The Rival Company, 19
Rockford Corporation, 43
S&C Electric Company, 15
SAGEM S.A., 37
St. Louis Music, Inc., 48
Sam Ash Music Corporation, 30
Samsung Electronics Co., Ltd., 14; 41
  (upd.)
SANYO Electric Co., Ltd., II; 36 (upd.)
ScanSource, Inc., 29
Schneider S.A., II; 18 (upd.)
SCI Systems, Inc., 9
Scientific-Atlanta, Inc., 45 (upd.)
Scitex Corporation Ltd., 24
Seagate Technology, Inc., 34 (upd.)
Semtech Corporation, 32
Sensormatic Electronics Corp., 11
Sensory Science Corporation, 37
SGI, 29 (upd.)
Sharp Corporation, II; 12 (upd.); 40 (upd.)
Sheldahl Inc., 23
Siemens A.G., II; 14 (upd.)
Silicon Graphics Incorporated, 9
Smiths Industries PLC, 25
Solectron Corporation, 12; 48 (upd.)
Sony Corporation, II; 12 (upd.); 40 (upd.)
SPX Corporation, 47 (upd.)
Sterling Electronics Corp., 18
STMicroelectronics NV, 52
Strix Ltd., 51
Sumitomo Electric Industries, Ltd., II
Sun Microsystems, Inc., 30 (upd.)
Sunbeam-Oster Co., Inc., 9
SyQuest Technology, Inc., 18
Tandy Corporation, II; 12 (upd.)
Tatung Co., 23
TDK Corporation, II; 17 (upd.); 49 (upd.)
Tech-Sym Corporation, 18
Technitrol, Inc., 29
Tektronix, Inc., 8
Telxon Corporation, 10
Teradyne, Inc., 11
Texas Instruments Inc., II; 11 (upd.); 46
  (upd.)
Thales S.A., 42
Thomas & Betts Corporation, 54 (upd.)
THOMSON multimedia S.A., II; 42 (upd.)
The Titan Corporation, 36
Tops Appliance City, Inc., 17
Toromont Industries, Ltd., 21
Trans-Lux Corporation, 51
Trimble Navigation Limited, 40
Tweeter Home Entertainment Group, Inc.,
  30
Ultrak Inc., 24
Universal Electronics Inc., 39
Varian Associates Inc., 12
Veeco Instruments Inc., 32
VIASYS Healthcare, Inc., 52
Vicon Industries, Inc., 44
Victor Company of Japan, Limited, II; 26
  (upd.)

Vishay Intertechnology, Inc., 21
Vitesse Semiconductor Corporation, 32
Vitro Corp., 10
VLSI Technology, Inc., 16
Wells-Gardner Electronics Corporation, 43
Westinghouse Electric Corporation, II; 12
  (upd.)
Wyle Electronics, 14
Yageo Corporation, 16
York Research Corporation, 35
Zenith Data Systems, Inc., 10
Zenith Electronics Corporation, II; 13
  (upd.); 34 (upd.)
Zoom Telephonics, Inc., 18
Zumtobel AG, 50
Zytec Corporation, 19

**ENGINEERING &
MANAGEMENT SERVICES**

AAON, Inc., 22
Aavid Thermal Technologies, Inc., 29
Alliant Techsystems Inc., 30 (upd.)
Altran Technologies, 51
Amey Plc, 47
Analytic Sciences Corporation, 10
Arcadis NV, 26
Arthur D. Little, Inc., 35
The Austin Company, 8
Balfour Beatty plc, 36 (upd.)
Brown & Root, Inc., 13
Bufete Industrial, S.A. de C.V., 34
C.H. Heist Corporation, 24
CDI Corporation, 6
CH2M Hill Ltd., 22
The Charles Stark Draper Laboratory, Inc.,
  35
Coflexip S.A., 25
Corrections Corporation of America, 23
CRSS Inc., 6
Dames & Moore, Inc., 25
DAW Technologies, Inc., 25
Day & Zimmermann Inc., 9; 31 (upd.)
Donaldson Co. Inc., 16
EG&G Incorporated, 8; 29 (upd.)
Eiffage, 27
Essef Corporation, 18
Fluor Corporation, 34 (upd.)
Forest City Enterprises, Inc., 52 (upd.)
Foster Wheeler Corporation, 6; 23 (upd.)
Framatome SA, 19
Gilbane, Inc., 34
Grupo Dragados SA, 55
Halliburton Company, 25 (upd.)
Harding Lawson Associates Group, Inc., 16
Harza Engineering Company, 14
HDR Inc., 48
ICF Kaiser International, Inc., 28
Jacobs Engineering Group Inc., 6; 26
  (upd.)
The Judge Group, Inc., 51
JWP Inc., 9
The Keith Companies Inc., 54
Kvaerner ASA, 36
Layne Christensen Company, 19
The MacNeal-Schwendler Corporation, 25
Malcolm Pirnie, Inc., 42
McDermott International, Inc., 37 (upd.)
McKinsey & Company, Inc., 9
Michael Baker Corporation, 51 (upd.)
Ogden Corporation, 6
Opus Group, 34
Parsons Brinckerhoff, Inc., 34
The Parsons Corporation, 8
RCM Technologies, Inc., 34
Renishaw plc, 46
Rosemount Inc., 15
Roy F. Weston, Inc., 33

Royal Vopak NV, 41
Rust International Inc., 11
Sandia National Laboratories, 49
Sandvik AB, 32 (upd.)
Science Applications International
  Corporation, 15
Serco Group plc, 47
Stone & Webster, Inc., 13
Susquehanna Pfaltzgraff Company, 8
Sverdrup Corporation, 14
Tech-Sym Corporation, 44 (upd.)
Tetra Tech, Inc., 29
Thyssen Krupp AG, 28 (upd.)
Towers Perrin, 32
Tracor Inc., 17
TRC Companies, Inc., 32
Underwriters Laboratories, Inc., 30
United Dominion Industries Limited, 8; 16
  (upd.)
URS Corporation, 45
VA TECH ELIN EBG GmbH, 49
VECO International, Inc., 7
Vinci, 43
WS Atkins Plc, 45

ENTERTAINMENT & LEISURE

A&E Television Networks, 32
ABC Family Worldwide, Inc., 52
Academy of Television Arts & Sciences,
  Inc., 55
Acclaim Entertainment Inc., 24
Activision, Inc., 32
AEI Music Network Inc., 35
Airtours Plc, 27
All American Communications Inc., 20
The All England Lawn Tennis & Croquet
  Club, 54
Alliance Entertainment Corp., 17
Alvin Ailey Dance Foundation, Inc., 52
Amblin Entertainment, 21
AMC Entertainment Inc., 12; 35 (upd.)
American Golf Corporation, 45
American Gramaphone LLC, 52
American Skiing Company, 28
Ameristar Casinos, Inc., 33
AMF Bowling, Inc., 40
Anaheim Angels Baseball Club, Inc., 53
Anchor Gaming, 24
Applause Inc., 24
Aprilia SpA, 17
Argosy Gaming Company, 21
Aristocrat Leisure Limited, 54
The Art Institute of Chicago, 29
Artisan Entertainment Inc., 32 (upd.)
Asahi National Broadcasting Company,
  Ltd., 9
Aspen Skiing Company, 15
Aston Villa plc, 41
Atlanta National League Baseball Club,
  Inc., 43
The Atlantic Group, 23
Autotote Corporation, 20
Aztar Corporation, 13
Baker & Taylor Corporation, 16; 43 (upd.)
Bally Total Fitness Holding Corp., 25
The Baseball Club of Seattle, LP, 50
The Basketball Club of Seattle, LLC, 50
Bertelsmann A.G., 15 (upd.); 43 (upd.)
Bertucci's Inc., 16
Big Idea Productions, Inc., 49
Blockbuster Inc., 9; 31 (upd.)
Boca Resorts, Inc., 37
Bonneville International Corporation, 29
Booth Creek Ski Holdings, Inc., 31
Boston Celtics Limited Partnership, 14
Boston Professional Hockey Association
  Inc., 39

The Boy Scouts of America, 34
British Broadcasting Corporation Ltd., 7;
  21 (upd.)
British Sky Broadcasting Group Plc, 20
Cablevision Systems Corporation, 7
Callaway Golf Company, 45 (upd.)
Canterbury Park Holding Corporation, 42
Capital Cities/ABC Inc., II
Carlson Companies, Inc., 22 (upd.)
Carlson Wagonlit Travel, 55
Carmike Cinemas, Inc., 14; 37 (upd.)
Carnival Corporation, 27 (upd.)
Carnival Cruise Lines, Inc., 6
The Carsey-Werner Company, L.L.C., 37
CBS Inc., II; 6 (upd.)
Cedar Fair, L.P., 22
Central Independent Television, 7; 23
  (upd.)
Century Casinos, Inc., 53
Century Theatres, Inc., 31
Championship Auto Racing Teams, Inc.,
  37
Chicago Bears Football Club, Inc., 33
Chris-Craft Industries, Inc., 31 (upd.)
Chrysalis Group plc, 40
Churchill Downs Incorporated, 29
Cinar Corporation, 40
Cineplex Odeon Corporation, 6; 23 (upd.)
Cinram International, Inc., 43
Cirque du Soleil Inc., 29
Classic Vacation Group, Inc., 46
Cleveland Indians Baseball Company, Inc.,
  37
ClubCorp, Inc., 33
Colonial Williamsburg Foundation, 53
Columbia Pictures Entertainment, Inc., II
Columbia TriStar Motion Pictures
  Companies, 12 (upd.)
Comcast Corporation, 7
Compagnie des Alpes, 48
Continental Cablevision, Inc., 7
Corporation for Public Broadcasting, 14
Cox Enterprises, Inc., 22 (upd.)
Crown Media Holdings, Inc., 45
Cruise America Inc., 21
Cunard Line Ltd., 23
Dallas Cowboys Football Club, Ltd., 33
Dave & Buster's, Inc., 33
Death Row Records, 27
Denver Nuggets, 51
The Detroit Lions, Inc., 55
The Detroit Pistons Basketball Company,
  41
Detroit Tigers Baseball Club, Inc., 46
dick clark productions, inc., 16
DIRECTV, Inc., 38
Dover Downs Entertainment, Inc., 43
DreamWorks SKG, 43
E! Entertainment Television Inc., 17
edel music AG, 44
Educational Broadcasting Corporation, 48
Edwards Theatres Circuit, Inc., 31
Elsinore Corporation, 48
Endemol Entertainment Holding NV, 46
Equity Marketing, Inc., 26
Esporta plc, 35
Euro Disneyland SCA, 20
Fair Grounds Corporation, 44
Family Golf Centers, Inc., 29
FAO Schwarz, 46
Fédération Internationale de Football
  Association, 27
Feld Entertainment, Inc., 32 (upd.)
First Choice Holidays PLC, 40
First Team Sports, Inc., 22
Fisher-Price Inc., 32 (upd.)
Florida Gaming Corporation, 47

ENTERTAINMENT & LEISURE
(continued)

Fox Entertainment Group, Inc., 43
Fox Family Worldwide, Inc., 24
Gaumont SA, 25
Gaylord Entertainment Company, 11; 36
  (upd.)
GC Companies, Inc., 25
Geffen Records Inc., 26
Gibson Guitar Corp., 16
Girl Scouts of the USA, 35
Global Outdoors, Inc., 49
GoodTimes Entertainment Ltd., 48
Granada Group PLC, II; 24 (upd.)
Grand Casinos, Inc., 20
The Green Bay Packers, Inc., 32
Groupe Partouche SA, 48
Grupo Televisa, S.A., 54 (upd.)
Hallmark Cards, Inc., 40 (upd.)
Hanna-Barbera Cartoons Inc., 23
Hard Rock Cafe International, Inc., 32
  (upd.)
Harpo Entertainment Group, 28
Harrah's Entertainment, Inc., 16; 43 (upd.)
Harveys Casino Resorts, 27
Hasbro, Inc., 43 (upd.)
Hastings Entertainment, Inc., 29
The Hearst Corporation, 46 (upd.)
The Heat Group, 53
Hilton Group plc, III; 19 (upd.); 49 (upd.)
HIT Entertainment PLC, 40
HOB Entertainment, Inc., 37
Hollywood Casino Corporation, 21
Hollywood Entertainment Corporation, 25
Hollywood Park, Inc., 20
Home Box Office Inc., 7; 23 (upd.)
Imax Corporation, 28
Indianapolis Motor Speedway Corporation,
  46
Infinity Broadcasting Corporation, 48
  (upd.)
Infogrames Entertainment S.A., 35
Integrity Inc., 44
International Creative Management, Inc.,
  43
International Family Entertainment Inc., 13
International Game Technology, 41 (upd.)
International Olympic Committee, 44
International Speedway Corporation, 19
Interscope Music Group, 31
The Intrawest Corporation, 15
Irvin Feld & Kenneth Feld Productions,
  Inc., 15
Isle of Capri Casinos, Inc., 41
iVillage Inc., 46
Iwerks Entertainment, Inc., 34
Jackpot Enterprises Inc., 21
Japan Broadcasting Corporation, 7
Jazz Basketball Investors, Inc., 55
Jazzercise, Inc., 45
Jillian's Entertainment Holdings, Inc., 40
The Jim Henson Company, 23
The Joffrey Ballet of Chicago, 52
Juventus F.C. S.p.A, 53
K'Nex Industries, Inc., 52
Kampgrounds of America, Inc. (KOA), 33
King World Productions, Inc., 9; 30 (upd.)
Knott's Berry Farm, 18
Kuoni Travel Holding Ltd., 40
The Kushner-Locke Company, 25
Ladbroke Group PLC, II; 21 (upd.)
Lakes Entertainment, Inc., 51
Las Vegas Sands, Inc., 50
Lego A/S, 13; 40 (upd.)
Liberty Livewire Corporation, 42
Liberty Media Corporation, 50
Lifetime Entertainment Services, 51

Lionel L.L.C., 16
Lions Gate Entertainment Corporation, 35
LIVE Entertainment Inc., 20
LodgeNet Entertainment Corporation, 28
Lucasfilm Ltd., 12; 50 (upd.)
Luminar Plc, 40
Manchester United Football Club plc, 30
Mandalay Resort Group, 32 (upd.)
The Marcus Corporation, 21
Mashantucket Pequot Gaming Enterprise
  Inc., 35
MCA Inc., II
Media General, Inc., 7
Mediaset SpA, 50
Metro-Goldwyn-Mayer Inc., 25 (upd.)
Metromedia Companies, 14
Métropole Télévision, 33
Metropolitan Baseball Club Inc., 39
The Metropolitan Museum of Art, 55
Metropolitan Opera Association, Inc., 40
MGM Grand Inc., 17
MGM/UA Communications Company, II
Midway Games, Inc., 25
Mikohn Gaming Corporation, 39
Milwaukee Brewers Baseball Club, 37
Mizuno Corporation, 25
Mohegan Tribal Gaming Authority, 37
Motown Records Company L.P., 26
Movie Gallery, Inc., 31
Multimedia Games, Inc., 41
Muzak, Inc., 18
National Amusements Inc., 28
National Association for Stock Car Auto
  Racing, 32
National Broadcasting Company, Inc., II; 6
  (upd.)
National Football League, 29
National Hockey League, 35
National Public Radio, Inc., 19; 47 (upd.)
National Rifle Association of America, 37
Navarre Corporation, 24
Navigant International, Inc., 47
New Line Cinema, Inc., 47
New York City Off-Track Betting
  Corporation, 51
News Corporation Limited, 46 (upd.)
Nicklaus Companies, 45
Nintendo Co., Ltd., 28 (upd.)
O'Charley's Inc., 19
Orion Pictures Corporation, 6
Paradise Music & Entertainment, Inc., 42
Paramount Pictures Corporation, II
Pathé SA, 29
PDS Gaming Corporation, 44
Peace Arch Entertainment Group Inc., 51
Penn National Gaming, Inc., 33
Philadelphia Eagles, 37
Pierre & Vacances SA, 48
Pixar Animation Studios, 34
Platinum Entertainment, Inc., 35
Play by Play Toys & Novelties, Inc., 26
Players International, Inc., 22
PolyGram N.V., 23
Portland Trail Blazers, 50
Powerhouse Technologies, Inc., 27
Premier Parks, Inc., 27
President Casinos, Inc., 22
Preussag AG, 42 (upd.)
Princess Cruise Lines, 22
Professional Bull Riders Inc., 55
The Professional Golfers' Association of
  America, 41
Promus Companies, Inc., 9
ProSiebenSat.1 Media AG, 54
Publishing and Broadcasting Limited, 54
Putt-Putt Golf Courses of America, Inc., 23
Ragdoll Productions Ltd., 51

Rainforest Cafe, Inc., 25
Rank Organisation PLC, II
Rawlings Sporting Goods Co., Inc., 24
The Really Useful Group, 26
Rentrak Corporation, 35
Rhino Entertainment Company, 18
Ride, Inc., 22
Rollerblade, Inc., 34 (upd.)
Roularta Media Group NV, 48
Royal Caribbean Cruises Ltd., 22
Royal Olympic Cruise Lines Inc., 52
RTL Group SA, 44
Rush Communications, 33
S-K-I Limited, 15
Salomon Worldwide, 20
San Francisco Baseball Associates, L.P., 55
Santa Fe Gaming Corporation, 19
Schwinn Cycle and Fitness L.P., 19
Scottish Radio Holding plc, 41
Seattle FilmWorks, Inc., 20
Sega of America, Inc., 10
Selectour SA, 53
SFX Entertainment, Inc., 36
Showboat, Inc., 19
Shubert Organization Inc., 24
Shuffle Master Inc., 51
Six Flags, Inc., 17; 54 (upd.)
Smithsonian Institution, 27
Società Sportiva Lazio SpA, 44
Sony Corporation, 40 (upd.)
Speedway Motorsports, Inc., 32
Spelling Entertainment Group, Inc., 14
The Sports Club Company, 25
Station Casinos Inc., 25
Stoll-Moss Theatres Ltd., 34
Stuart Entertainment Inc., 16
TABCORP Holdings Limited, 44
Take-Two Interactive Software, Inc., 46
Tele-Communications, Inc., II
Television Española, S.A., 7
Texas Rangers Baseball, 51
Thomas Cook Travel Inc., 9
The Thomson Corporation, 8
Thousand Trails, Inc., 33
THQ, Inc., 39
Ticketmaster Corp., 13
The Todd-AO Corporation, 33
Toho Co., Ltd., 28
The Topps Company, Inc., 34 (upd.)
Touristik Union International GmbH. and
  Company K.G., II
Town Sports International, Inc., 46
Toy Biz, Inc., 18
Trans World Entertainment Corporation, 24
Travelocity.com, Inc., 46
TUI Group GmbH, 44
Turner Broadcasting System, Inc., II; 6
  (upd.)
The Tussauds Group, 55
Twentieth Century Fox Film Corporation,
  II; 25 (upd.)
Ubi Soft Entertainment S.A., 41
United Pan-Europe Communications NV,
  47
Universal Studios, Inc., 33
Univision Communications Inc., 24
USA Interactive, Inc., 47 (upd.)
Vail Resorts, Inc., 11; 43 (upd.)
Venetian Casino Resort, LLC, 47
Viacom, Inc., 7; 23 (upd.)
Vivendi Universal S.A., 46 (upd.)
Walt Disney Company, II; 6 (upd.); 30
  (upd.)
Warner Communications Inc., II
Washington Football, Inc., 35
West Coast Entertainment Corporation, 29

Wherehouse Entertainment Incorporated, 11
Whitbread PLC, 52 (upd.)
Wildlife Conservation Society, 31
William Hill Organization Limited, 49
Wilson Sporting Goods Company, 24
Wizards of the Coast Inc., 24
WMS Industries, Inc., 53 (upd.)
World Wrestling Federation Entertainment, Inc., 32
YankeeNets LLC, 35
YES! Entertainment Corporation, 26
YMCA of the USA, 31
Young Broadcasting Inc., 40
Zomba Records Ltd., 52

FINANCIAL SERVICES: BANKS

Abbey National plc, 10; 39 (upd.)
Abigail Adams National Bancorp, Inc., 23
ABN AMRO Holding, N.V., 50
Algemene Bank Nederland N.V., II
Allied Irish Banks, plc, 16; 43 (upd.)
Almanij NV, 44
AMCORE Financial Inc., 44
American Residential Mortgage Corporation, 8
AmSouth Bancorporation, 12; 48 (upd.)
Amsterdam-Rotterdam Bank N.V., II
Anchor Bancorp, Inc., 10
Astoria Financial Corporation, 44
Australia and New Zealand Banking Group Limited, II; 52 (upd.)
Banc One Corporation, 10
Banca Commerciale Italiana SpA, II
Banco Bilbao Vizcaya Argentaria S.A., II; 48 (upd.)
Banco Bradesco S.A., 13
Banco Central, II
Banco Comercial Português, SA, 50
Banco do Brasil S.A., II
Banco Espírito Santo e Comercial de Lisboa S.A., 15
Banco Itaú S.A., 19
Banco Santander Central Hispano S.A., 36 (upd.)
Bank Austria AG, 23
Bank Brussels Lambert, II
Bank Hapoalim B.M., II; 54 (upd.)
Bank of America Corporation, 46 (upd.)
Bank of Boston Corporation, II
Bank of Ireland, 50
Bank of Mississippi, Inc., 14
Bank of Montreal, II; 46 (upd.)
Bank of New England Corporation, II
The Bank of New York Company, Inc., II; 46 (upd.)
The Bank of Nova Scotia, II
Bank of Tokyo-Mitsubishi Ltd., II; 15 (upd.)
Bank One Corporation, 36 (upd.)
BankAmerica Corporation, II; 8 (upd.)
Bankers Trust New York Corporation, II
Banknorth Group, Inc., 55
Banque Nationale de Paris S.A., II
Barclays PLC, II; 20 (upd.)
BarclaysAmerican Mortgage Corporation, 11
Barings PLC, 14
Barnett Banks, Inc., 9
BayBanks, Inc., 12
Bayerische Hypotheken- und Wechsel-Bank AG, II
Bayerische Vereinsbank A.G., II
Beneficial Corporation, 8
BNP Paribas Group, 36 (upd.)
Boatmen's Bancshares Inc., 15
Bremer Financial Corp., 45

Brown Brothers Harriman & Co., 45
Canadian Imperial Bank of Commerce, II
Carolina First Corporation, 31
Casco Northern Bank, 14
The Chase Manhattan Corporation, II; 13 (upd.)
Chemical Banking Corporation, II; 14 (upd.)
Citicorp, II; 9 (upd.)
Citigroup Inc., 30 (upd.)
Citizens Financial Group, Inc., 42
Close Brothers Group plc, 39
Commercial Credit Company, 8
Commercial Federal Corporation, 12
Commerzbank A.G., II; 47 (upd.)
Compagnie Financiere de Paribas, II
Continental Bank Corporation, II
CoreStates Financial Corp, 17
Countrywide Credit Industries, Inc., 16
Crédit Agricole, II
Crédit Lyonnais, 9; 33 (upd.)
Crédit National S.A., 9
Credit Suisse Group, II; 21 (upd.)
Credito Italiano, II
Cullen/Frost Bankers, Inc., 25
The Dai-Ichi Kangyo Bank Ltd., II
The Daiwa Bank, Ltd., II; 39 (upd.)
Danske Bank Aktieselskab, 50
Dauphin Deposit Corporation, 14
Deposit Guaranty Corporation, 17
Deutsche Bank AG, II; 14 (upd.); 40 (upd.)
Dexia Group, 42
Dime Savings Bank of New York, F.S.B., 9
Donaldson, Lufkin & Jenrette, Inc., 22
Dresdner Bank A.G., II
Fifth Third Bancorp, 13; 31 (upd.)
First Bank System Inc., 12
First Chicago Corporation, II
First Commerce Bancshares, Inc., 15
First Commerce Corporation, 11
First Empire State Corporation, 11
First Fidelity Bank, N.A., New Jersey, 9
First Hawaiian, Inc., 11
First Interstate Bancorp, II
First Nationwide Bank, 14
First of America Bank Corporation, 8
First Security Corporation, 11
First Tennessee National Corporation, 11; 48 (upd.)
First Union Corporation, 10
First Virginia Banks, Inc., 11
Firstar Corporation, 11; 33 (upd.)
Fleet Financial Group, Inc., 9
FleetBoston Financial Corporation, 36 (upd.)
Fourth Financial Corporation, 11
The Fuji Bank, Ltd., II
Generale Bank, II
German American Bancorp, 41
Glacier Bancorp, Inc., 35
Golden West Financial Corporation, 47
The Governor and Company of the Bank of Scotland, 10
Grameen Bank, 31
Granite State Bankshares, Inc., 37
Great Lakes Bancorp, 8
Great Western Financial Corporation, 10
GreenPoint Financial Corp., 28
Grupo Financiero Banamex S.A., 54
Grupo Financiero Banorte, S.A. de C.V., 51
Grupo Financiero BBVA Bancomer S.A., 54
Grupo Financiero Serfin, S.A., 19
H.F. Ahmanson & Company, II; 10 (upd.)
Habersham Bancorp, 25

Hancock Holding Company, 15
Hibernia Corporation, 37
The Hongkong and Shanghai Banking Corporation Limited, II
HSBC Holdings plc, 12; 26 (upd.)
Hudson River Bancorp, Inc., 41
Huntington Bancshares Inc., 11
IBERIABANK Corporation, 37
The Industrial Bank of Japan, Ltd., II
J Sainsbury plc, 38 (upd.)
J.P. Morgan & Co. Incorporated, II; 30 (upd.)
J.P. Morgan Chase & Co., 38 (upd.)
Japan Leasing Corporation, 8
Julius Baer Holding AG, 52
Kansallis-Osake-Pankki, II
KeyCorp, 8
Kredietbank N.V., II
Kreditanstalt für Wiederaufbau, 29
Lloyds Bank PLC, II
Lloyds TSB Group plc, 47 (upd.)
Long Island Bancorp, Inc., 16
Long-Term Credit Bank of Japan, Ltd., II
Manufacturers Hanover Corporation, II
MBNA Corporation, 12
Mellon Bank Corporation, II
Mellon Financial Corporation, 44 (upd.)
Mercantile Bankshares Corp., 11
Meridian Bancorp, Inc., 11
Metropolitan Financial Corporation, 13
Michigan National Corporation, 11
Midland Bank PLC, II; 17 (upd.)
The Mitsubishi Bank, Ltd., II
The Mitsubishi Trust & Banking Corporation, II
The Mitsui Bank, Ltd., II
The Mitsui Trust & Banking Company, Ltd., II
Mouvement des Caisses Desjardins, 48
N M Rothschild & Sons Limited, 39
National Bank of Greece, 41
National City Corp., 15
National Westminster Bank PLC, II
NationsBank Corporation, 10
NBD Bancorp, Inc., 11
NCNB Corporation, II
Nippon Credit Bank, II
Nordea AB, 40
Norinchukin Bank, II
North Fork Bancorporation, Inc., 46
Northern Rock plc, 33
Northern Trust Company, 9
NVR L.P., 8
Old Kent Financial Corp., 11
Old National Bancorp, 15
PNC Bank Corp., II; 13 (upd.)
The PNC Financial Services Group Inc., 46 (upd.)
Popular, Inc., 41
Pulte Corporation, 8
Rabobank Group, 33
Republic New York Corporation, 11
Riggs National Corporation, 13
The Royal Bank of Canada, II; 21 (upd.)
The Royal Bank of Scotland Group plc, 12; 38 (upd.)
The Ryland Group, Inc., 8
St. Paul Bank for Cooperatives, 8
Sanpaolo IMI S.p.A., 50
The Sanwa Bank, Ltd., II; 15 (upd.)
SBC Warburg, 14
Seattle First National Bank Inc., 8
Security Capital Corporation, 17
Security Pacific Corporation, II
Shawmut National Corporation, 13
Signet Banking Corporation, 11
Singer & Friedlander Group plc, 41

FINANCIAL SERVICES: BANKS
(*continued*)

Skandinaviska Enskilda Banken, II
Société Générale, II; 42 (upd.)
Society Corporation, 9
Southtrust Corporation, 11
Standard Chartered plc, II; 48 (upd.)
Standard Federal Bank, 9
Star Banc Corporation, 11
State Financial Services Corporation, 51
State Street Boston Corporation, 8
Staten Island Bancorp, Inc., 39
The Sumitomo Bank, Limited, II; 26 (upd.)
Sumitomo Mitsui Banking Corporation, 51
  (upd.)
The Sumitomo Trust & Banking Company,
  Ltd., II; 53 (upd.)
The Summit Bancorporation, 14
SunTrust Banks Inc., 23
Svenska Handelsbanken AB, II; 50 (upd.)
Swiss Bank Corporation, II
Synovus Financial Corp., 12; 52 (upd.)
The Taiyo Kobe Bank, Ltd., II
TCF Financial Corporation, 47
The Tokai Bank, Limited, II; 15 (upd.)
The Toronto-Dominion Bank, II; 49 (upd.)
TSB Group plc, 12
U.S. Bancorp, 14; 36 (upd.)
U.S. Trust Corp., 17
UBS AG, 52 (upd.)
Union Bank of California, 16
Union Bank of Switzerland, II
Union Financière de France Banque SA, 52
Union Planters Corporation, 54
UnionBanCal Corporation, 50 (upd.)
Wachovia Bank of Georgia, N.A., 16
Wachovia Bank of South Carolina, N.A.,
  16
Washington Mutual, Inc., 17
Wells Fargo & Company, II; 12 (upd.); 38
  (upd.)
West One Bancorp, 11
Westamerica Bancorporation, 17
Westdeutsche Landesbank Girozentrale, II;
  46 (upd.)
Westpac Banking Corporation, II; 48 (upd.)
Whitney Holding Corporation, 21
Wilmington Trust Corporation, 25
The Woolwich plc, 30
World Bank Group, 33
The Yasuda Trust and Banking Company,
  Ltd., II; 17 (upd.)
Zions Bancorporation, 12; 53 (upd.)

FINANCIAL SERVICES:
NON-BANKS

A.B. Watley Group Inc., 45
A.G. Edwards, Inc., 8; 32 (upd.)
ACE Cash Express, Inc., 33
ADVANTA Corp., 8
Advanta Corporation, 38 (upd.)
American Express Company, II; 10 (upd.);
  38 (upd.)
American General Finance Corp., 11
American Home Mortgage Holdings, Inc.,
  46
Ameritrade Holding Corporation, 34
Arthur Andersen & Company, Société
  Coopérative, 10
Avco Financial Services Inc., 13
Aviva PLC, 50 (upd.)
Bear Stearns Companies, Inc., II; 10
  (upd.); 52 (upd.)
Benchmark Capital, 49
Bill & Melinda Gates Foundation, 41
Bozzuto's, Inc., 13
Capital One Financial Corporation, 52

Carnegie Corporation of New York, 35
Cash America International, Inc., 20
Cendant Corporation, 44 (upd.)
Cetelem S.A., 21
The Charles Schwab Corporation, 8; 26
  (upd.)
Citfed Bancorp, Inc., 16
Coinstar, Inc., 44
Comerica Incorporated, 40
Commercial Financial Services, Inc., 26
Concord EFS, Inc., 52
Coopers & Lybrand, 9
Cramer, Berkowitz & Co., 34
Credit Acceptance Corporation, 18
CS First Boston Inc., II
Dain Rauscher Corporation, 35 (upd.)
Daiwa Securities Company, Limited, II
Daiwa Securities Group Inc., 55 (upd.)
Datek Online Holdings Corp., 32
The David and Lucile Packard Foundation,
  41
Dean Witter, Discover & Co., 12
Dow Jones Telerate, Inc., 10
Drexel Burnham Lambert Incorporated, II
DVI, Inc., 51
E*Trade Group, Inc., 20
Eaton Vance Corporation, 18
Edward Jones, 30
Euronext Paris S.A., 37
Experian Information Solutions Inc., 45
Fair, Isaac and Company, 18
Fannie Mae, 45 (upd.)
Federal National Mortgage Association, II
Fidelity Investments Inc., II; 14 (upd.)
First Albany Companies Inc., 37
First Data Corporation, 30 (upd.)
First USA, Inc., 11
FMR Corp., 8; 32 (upd.)
Forstmann Little & Co., 38
Fortis, Inc., 15
Frank Russell Company, 46
Franklin Resources, Inc., 9
Freddie Mac, 54
Friedman, Billings, Ramsey Group, Inc., 53
Gabelli Asset Management Inc., 30
The Goldman Sachs Group Inc., 51 (upd.)
Goldman, Sachs & Co., II; 20 (upd.)
Grede Foundries, Inc., 38
Green Tree Financial Corporation, 11
Gruntal & Co., L.L.C., 20
H & R Block, Incorporated, 9; 29 (upd.)
H.D. Vest, Inc., 46
Hoenig Group Inc., 41
Household International, Inc., II; 21 (upd.)
Ingenico—Compagnie Industrielle et
  Financière d'Ingénierie, 46
Instinet Corporation, 34
Inter-Regional Financial Group, Inc., 15
The Island ECN, Inc., 48
Istituto per la Ricostruzione Industriale
  S.p.A., 11
JB Oxford Holdings, Inc., 32
Jefferies Group, Inc., 25
John Hancock Financial Services, Inc., 42
  (upd.)
The John Nuveen Company, 21
Jones Lang LaSalle Incorporated, 49
Kansas City Southern Industries, Inc., 26
  (upd.)
Kleiner, Perkins, Caufield & Byers, 53
Kleinwort Benson Group PLC, II
Kohlberg Kravis Roberts & Co., 24
KPMG Worldwide, 10
La Poste, 47 (upd.)
LaBranche & Co. Inc., 37
Lazard LLC, 38
Legg Mason, Inc., 33

London Stock Exchange Limited, 34
M.H. Meyerson & Co., Inc., 46
MacAndrews & Forbes Holdings Inc., 28
MasterCard International, Inc., 9
MBNA Corporation, 33 (upd.)
Merrill Lynch & Co., Inc., II; 13 (upd.); 40
  (upd.)
Morgan Grenfell Group PLC, II
Morgan Stanley Dean Witter & Company,
  II; 16 (upd.); 33 (upd.)
Mountain States Mortgage Centers, Inc., 29
NASD, 54 (upd.)
National Association of Securities Dealers,
  Inc., 10
National Auto Credit, Inc., 16
National Discount Brokers Group, Inc., 28
Navy Federal Credit Union, 33
New Street Capital Inc., 8
New York Stock Exchange, Inc., 9; 39
  (upd.)
The Nikko Securities Company Limited, II;
  9 (upd.)
Nippon Shinpan Company, Ltd., II
Nomura Securities Company, Limited, II; 9
  (upd.)
Norwich & Peterborough Building Society,
  55
Orix Corporation, II
ORIX Corporation, 44 (upd.)
PaineWebber Group Inc., II; 22 (upd.)
The Pew Charitable Trusts, 35
Piper Jaffray Companies Inc., 22
Pitney Bowes Inc., 47 (upd.)
Providian Financial Corporation, 52 (upd.)
The Prudential Insurance Company of
  America, 30 (upd.)
The Quick & Reilly Group, Inc., 20
Resource America, Inc., 42
Safeguard Scientifics, Inc., 10
Salomon Inc., II; 13 (upd.)
SBC Warburg, 14
Schroders plc, 42
Shearson Lehman Brothers Holdings Inc.,
  II; 9 (upd.)
Siebert Financial Corp., 32
SLM Holding Corp., 25 (upd.)
Smith Barney Inc., 15
Soros Fund Management LLC, 28
State Street Boston Corporation, 8
Student Loan Marketing Association, II
T. Rowe Price Associates, Inc., 11; 34
  (upd.)
Teachers Insurance and Annuity
  Association-College Retirement Equities
  Fund, 45 (upd.)
Texas Pacific Group Inc., 36
Total System Services, Inc., 18
Trilon Financial Corporation, II
United Jewish Communities, 33
The Vanguard Group, Inc., 14; 34 (upd.)
VeriFone, Inc., 18
Visa International, 9; 26 (upd.)
Wachovia Corporation, 12; 46 (upd.)
Waddell & Reed, Inc., 22
Washington Federal, Inc., 17
Waterhouse Investor Services, Inc., 18
Watson Wyatt Worldwide, 42
Western Union Financial Services, Inc., 54
Working Assets Funding Service, 43
Yamaichi Securities Company, Limited, II
The Ziegler Companies, Inc., 24
Zurich Financial Services, 42 (upd.)

FOOD PRODUCTS

Agway, Inc., 7
Ajinomoto Co., Inc., II; 28 (upd.)
The Albert Fisher Group plc, 41

Alberto-Culver Company, 8
Aldi Group, 13
Alpine Lace Brands, Inc., 18
American Crystal Sugar Company, 11; 32 (upd.)
American Foods Group, 43
American Italian Pasta Company, 27
American Maize-Products Co., 14
American Rice, Inc., 33
Amfac/JMB Hawaii L.L.C., 24 (upd.)
Archer-Daniels-Midland Company, 32 (upd.)
Archway Cookies, Inc., 29
Arla Foods amba, 48
Associated British Foods plc, II; 13 (upd.); 41 (upd.)
Associated Milk Producers, Inc., 11; 48 (upd.)
Aurora Foods Inc., 32
B&G Foods, Inc., 40
The B. Manischewitz Company, LLC, 31
Bahlsen GmbH & Co. KG, 44
Balance Bar Company, 32
Baltek Corporation, 34
Barilla G. e R. Fratelli S.p.A., 17; 50 (upd.)
Bear Creek Corporation, 38
Beatrice Company, II
Beech-Nut Nutrition Corporation, 21; 51 (upd.)
Ben & Jerry's Homemade, Inc., 10; 35 (upd.)
Berkeley Farms, Inc., 46
Besnier SA, 19
Bestfoods, 22 (upd.)
Blue Bell Creameries L.P., 30
Blue Diamond Growers, 28
Bonduelle SA, 51
Bongrain SA, 25
Booker PLC, 13; 31 (upd.)
Borden, Inc., II; 22 (upd.)
Boyd Coffee Company, 53
Brach and Brock Confections, Inc., 15
Brake Bros plc, 45
Bridgford Foods Corporation, 27
Brothers Gourmet Coffees, Inc., 20
Broughton Foods Co., 17
Brown & Haley, 23
Bruce Foods Corporation, 39
BSN Groupe S.A., II
Burger King Corporation, 17 (upd.)
Bush Boake Allen Inc., 30
Bush Brothers & Company, 45
C.H. Robinson Worldwide, Inc., 40 (upd.)
Cadbury Schweppes PLC, II; 49 (upd.)
Cagle's, Inc., 20
Calavo Growers, Inc., 47
Calcot Ltd., 33
Campbell Soup Company, II; 7 (upd.); 26 (upd.)
Canada Packers Inc., II
Cargill Inc., 13 (upd.)
Carnation Company, II
The Carriage House Companies, Inc., 55
Carroll's Foods, Inc., 46
Carvel Corporation, 35
Castle & Cooke, Inc., II; 20 (upd.)
Cattleman's, Inc., 20
Celestial Seasonings, Inc., 16
Central Soya Company, Inc., 7
Chelsea Milling Company, 29
Chicken of the Sea International, 24 (upd.)
Chiquita Brands International, Inc., 7; 21 (upd.)
Chock Full o'Nuts Corp., 17
Chocoladefabriken Lindt & Sprüngli AG, 27

Chupa Chups S.A., 38
Clif Bar Inc., 50
The Clorox Company, 22 (upd.)
Coca-Cola Enterprises, Inc., 13
Community Coffee Co. L.L.C., 53
ConAgra Foods, Inc., 42 (upd.)
Conagra, Inc., II; 12 (upd.)
The Connell Company, 29
ContiGroup Companies, Inc., 43 (upd.)
Continental Grain Company, 10; 13 (upd.)
CoolBrands International Inc., 35
CPC International Inc., II
Cranswick plc, 40
Cumberland Packing Corporation, 26
Curtice-Burns Foods, Inc., 7; 21 (upd.)
Czarnikow-Rionda Company, Inc., 32
Dairy Crest Group plc, 32
Dalgety, PLC, II
Danisco A/S, 44
Dannon Co., Inc., 14
Darigold, Inc., 9
Dawn Food Products, Inc., 17
Dean Foods Company, 7; 21 (upd.)
DeKalb Genetics Corporation, 17
Del Monte Foods Company, 7; 23 (upd.)
Di Giorgio Corp., 12
Diageo plc, 24 (upd.)
Dole Food Company, Inc., 9; 31 (upd.)
Domino Sugar Corporation, 26
Doskocil Companies, Inc., 12
Dreyer's Grand Ice Cream, Inc., 17
The Earthgrains Company, 36
Emge Packing Co., Inc., 11
Empresas Polar SA, 55 (upd.)
Eridania Béghin-Say S.A., 36
ERLY Industries Inc., 17
Eskimo Pie Corporation, 21
Farmland Foods, Inc., 7
Farmland Industries, Inc., 48
Ferrero SpA, 54
Fieldale Farms Corporation, 23
Fleer Corporation, 15
Fleury Michon S.A., 39
Florida Crystals Inc., 35
Flowers Industries, Inc., 12; 35 (upd.)
FoodBrands America, Inc., 23
Foster Poultry Farms, 32
Fred Usinger Inc., 54
Fresh America Corporation, 20
Fresh Foods, Inc., 29
Frito-Lay Company, 32
Fromageries Bel, 23
Fyffes Plc, 38
Gardenburger, Inc., 33
Geest Plc, 38
General Mills, Inc., II; 10 (upd.); 36 (upd.)
George A. Hormel and Company, II
George Weston Limited, 36 (upd.)
Gerber Products Company, 7; 21 (upd.)
Ghirardelli Chocolate Company, 30
Givaudan SA, 43
Gold Kist Inc., 17; 26 (upd.)
Gold'n Plump Poultry, 54
Golden Enterprises, Inc., 26
Gonnella Baking Company, 40
Good Humor-Breyers Ice Cream Company, 14
Goodman Fielder Ltd., 52
GoodMark Foods, Inc., 26
Gorton's, 13
Goya Foods Inc., 22
Great Harvest Bread Company, 44
Grist Mill Company, 15
Groupe Danone, 32 (upd.)
Groupe Soufflet SA, 55
Gruma, S.A. de C.V., 31
Grupo Herdez, S.A. de C.V., 35

Guittard Chocolate Company, 55
H.J. Heinz Company, II; 11 (upd.); 36 (upd.)
The Hain Celestial Group, Inc., 27; 43 (upd.)
Hanover Foods Corporation, 35
HARIBO GmbH & Co. KG, 44
The Hartz Mountain Corporation, 12
Hazlewood Foods plc, 32
Herman Goelitz, Inc., 28
Hershey Foods Corporation, II; 15 (upd.); 51 (upd.)
Hill's Pet Nutrition, Inc., 27
Hillsdown Holdings plc, II; 24 (upd.)
Horizon Organic Holding Corporation, 37
Hormel Foods Corporation, 18 (upd.); 54 (upd.)
Hudson Foods Inc., 13
Hulman & Company, 44
Hunt-Wesson, Inc., 17
Iams Company, 26
IAWS Group plc, 49
IBP, Inc., II; 21 (upd.)
Iceland Group plc, 33
Imagine Foods, Inc., 50
Imperial Holly Corporation, 12
Imperial Sugar Company, 32 (upd.)
Industrias Bachoco, S.A. de C.V., 39
International Multifoods Corporation, 7; 25 (upd.)
Interstate Bakeries Corporation, 12; 38 (upd.)
Itoham Foods Inc., II
J & J Snack Foods Corporation, 24
The J.M. Smucker Company, 11
J.R. Simplot Company, 16
Jacobs Suchard A.G., II
Jim Beam Brands Co., 14
John B. Sanfilippo & Son, Inc., 14
Julius Meinl International AG, 53
Just Born, Inc., 32
Kal Kan Foods, Inc., 22
Kamps AG, 44
Keebler Foods Company, 36
Kellogg Company, II; 13 (upd.); 50 (upd.)
Kerry Group plc, 27
Kettle Foods Inc., 48
Kikkoman Corporation, 14; 47 (upd.)
The King Arthur Flour Company, 31
King Ranch, Inc., 14
Koninklijke Wessanen nv, II; 54 (upd.)
Kraft Foods Inc., 45 (upd.)
Kraft General Foods Inc., II; 7 (upd.)
Kraft Jacobs Suchard AG, 26 (upd.)
Krispy Kreme Doughnut Corporation, 21
La Choy Food Products Inc., 25
Lamb Weston, Inc., 23
Lance, Inc., 14; 41 (upd.)
Land O'Lakes, Inc., II; 21 (upd.)
Leprino Foods Company, 28
Lincoln Snacks Company, 24
Lucille Farms, Inc., 45
M.A. Gedney Co., 51
Malt-O-Meal Company, 22
Maple Leaf Foods Inc., 41
Mars, Incorporated, 7; 40 (upd.)
Maui Land & Pineapple Company, Inc., 29
McCormick & Company, Incorporated, 7; 27 (upd.)
McIlhenny Company, 20
McKee Foods Corporation, 7; 27 (upd.)
Meiji Milk Products Company, Limited, II
Meiji Seika Kaisha, Ltd., II
Michael Foods, Inc., 25
Mid-America Dairymen, Inc., 7
Midwest Grain Products, Inc., 49
Mike-Sell's Inc., 15

FOOD PRODUCTS (*continued*)

Milnot Company, 46
Monfort, Inc., 13
Mrs. Baird's Bakeries, 29
Mt. Olive Pickle Company, Inc., 44
MTR Foods Ltd., 55
Murphy Family Farms Inc., 22
Nabisco Foods Group, II; 7 (upd.)
Nantucket Allserve, Inc., 22
Nathan's Famous, Inc., 29
National Presto Industries, Inc., 43 (upd.)
National Sea Products Ltd., 14
Natural Selection Foods, 54
Nestlé S.A., II; 7 (upd.); 28 (upd.)
New England Confectionery Co., 15
New World Pasta Company, 53
Newhall Land and Farming Company, 14
Newman's Own, Inc., 37
Nippon Meat Packers, Inc., II
Nippon Suisan Kaisha, Limited, II
Nisshin Flour Milling Company, Ltd., II
Northern Foods PLC, 10
Northland Cranberries, Inc., 38
Nutraceutical International Corporation, 37
NutraSweet Company, 8
Ocean Spray Cranberries, Inc., 7; 25 (upd.)
OJSC Wimm-Bill-Dann Foods, 48
Ore-Ida Foods Incorporated, 13
Organic Valley (Coulee Region Organic
    Produce Pool), 53
Oscar Mayer Foods Corp., 12
Otis Spunkmeyer, Inc., 28
Overhill Corporation, 51
Papetti's Hygrade Egg Products, Inc., 39
Parmalat Finanziaria SpA, 50
Penford Corporation, 55
PepsiCo, Inc., I; 10 (upd.); 38 (upd.)
Perdigao SA, 52
Perdue Farms Inc., 7; 23 (upd.)
Pet Incorporated, 7
Petrossian Inc., 54
Pez Candy, Inc., 38
Philip Morris Companies Inc., 18 (upd.)
PIC International Group PLC, 24 (upd.)
Pilgrim's Pride Corporation, 7; 23 (upd.)
Pillsbury Company, II; 13 (upd.)
Pioneer Hi-Bred International, Inc., 9
Pizza Inn, Inc., 46
Poore Brothers, Inc., 44
PowerBar Inc., 44
Prairie Farms Dairy, Inc., 47
Premium Standard Farms, Inc., 30
The Procter & Gamble Company, III; 8
    (upd.); 26 (upd.)
Purina Mills, Inc., 32
Quaker Oats Company, II; 12 (upd.); 34
    (upd.)
Quality Chekd Dairies, Inc., 48
Ralston Purina Company, II; 13 (upd.)
Ranks Hovis McDougall Limited, II; 28
    (upd.)
Reckitt & Colman PLC, II
Reckitt Benckiser plc, 42 (upd.)
Rica Foods, Inc., 41
Rich Products Corporation, 7; 38 (upd.)
Riviana Foods Inc., 27
Roland Murten A.G., 7
Rowntree Mackintosh, II
Royal Numico N.V., 37
Ruiz Food Products, Inc., 53
Russell Stover Candies Inc., 12
Sanderson Farms, Inc., 15
Sara Lee Corporation, II; 15 (upd.); 54
    (upd.)
Savannah Foods & Industries, Inc., 7
Schlotzsky's, Inc., 36
Schwan's Sales Enterprises, Inc., 7

See's Candies, Inc., 30
Seminis, Inc., 29
Sensient Technologies Corporation, 52
    (upd.)
Silhouette Brands, Inc., 55
Smithfield Foods, Inc., 7; 43 (upd.)
Snow Brand Milk Products Company, Ltd.,
    II; 48 (upd.)
Sodiaal S.A., 36 (upd.)
SODIMA, II
Sorrento, Inc., 24
Spangler Candy Company, 44
Stock Yards Packing Co., Inc., 37
Stollwerck AG, 53
Stolt Sea Farm Holdings PLC, 54
Stolt-Nielsen S.A., 42
Stonyfield Farm, Inc., 55
Stouffer Corp., 8
Südzucker AG, 27
Suiza Foods Corporation, 26
Sun-Diamond Growers of California, 7
Sunkist Growers, Inc., 26
Supervalu Inc., 18 (upd.); 50 (upd.)
Suprema Specialties, Inc., 27
Swift & Company, 55
Sylvan, Inc., 22
Taiyo Fishery Company, Limited, II
Tasty Baking Company, 14; 35 (upd.)
Tate & Lyle PLC, II; 42 (upd.)
TCBY Enterprises Inc., 17
TDL Group Ltd., 46
Thomas J. Lipton Company, 14
Thorn Apple Valley, Inc., 7; 22 (upd.)
Thorntons plc, 46
TLC Beatrice International Holdings, Inc.,
    22
Tombstone Pizza Corporation, 13
Tone Brothers, Inc., 21
Tootsie Roll Industries Inc., 12
Tri Valley Growers, 32
Tropicana Products, Inc., 28
Tyson Foods, Inc., II; 14 (upd.); 50 (upd.)
U.S. Foodservice, 26
Uncle Ben's Inc., 22
Unigate PLC, II; 28 (upd.)
United Biscuits (Holdings) plc, II; 42
    (upd.)
United Brands Company, II
United Foods, Inc., 21
Universal Foods Corporation, 7
Van Camp Seafood Company, Inc., 7
Vienna Sausage Manufacturing Co., 14
Vlasic Foods International Inc., 25
Wattie's Ltd., 7
Wells' Dairy, Inc., 36
White Wave, 43
Wimm-Bill-Dann Foods, 48
Wisconsin Dairies, 7
WLR Foods, Inc., 21
Wm. Wrigley Jr. Company, 7
World's Finest Chocolate Inc., 39
Worthington Foods, Inc., 14
YOCREAM International, Inc., 47

FOOD SERVICES & RETAILERS

Advantica Restaurant Group, Inc., 27
    (upd.)
AFC Enterprises, Inc., 32 (upd.)
Affiliated Foods Inc., 53
Albertson's Inc., II; 7 (upd.); 30 (upd.)
Aldi Group, 13
Alex Lee Inc., 18; 44 (upd.)
America's Favorite Chicken Company,
    Inc., 7
American Stores Company, II
Applebee's International, Inc., 14; 35
    (upd.)

ARA Services, II
Arby's Inc., 14
Arden Group, Inc., 29
Argyll Group PLC, II
Ark Restaurants Corp., 20
Asahi Breweries, Ltd., 20 (upd.)
Asda Group PLC, II
ASDA Group plc, 28 (upd.)
Associated Grocers, Incorporated, 9; 31
    (upd.)
Association des Centres Distributeurs E.
    Leclerc, 37
Au Bon Pain Co., Inc., 18
Auchan, 37
Auntie Anne's, Inc., 35
Autogrill SpA, 49
Avado Brands, Inc., 31
Back Bay Restaurant Group, Inc., 20
Back Yard Burgers, Inc., 45
Bashas' Inc., 33
Bear Creek Corporation, 38
Benihana, Inc., 18
Big Bear Stores Co., 13
Big V Supermarkets, Inc., 25
Big Y Foods, Inc., 53
Blimpie International, Inc., 15; 49 (upd.)
Bob Evans Farms, Inc., 9
Bon Appetit Holding AG, 48
Boston Chicken, Inc., 12
Boston Market Corporation, 48 (upd.)
Briazz, Inc., 53
Brinker International, Inc., 10; 38 (upd.)
Brookshire Grocery Company, 16
Bruno's, Inc., 7; 26 (upd.)
Buca, Inc., 38
Buffets, Inc., 10; 32 (upd.)
Burger King Corporation, II
C & S Wholesale Grocers, Inc., 55
C.H. Robinson, Inc., 11
California Pizza Kitchen Inc., 15
Cargill, Inc., II
Caribou Coffee Company, Inc., 28
Carlson Companies, Inc., 22 (upd.)
Carr-Gottstein Foods Co., 17
Casey's General Stores, Inc., 19
CBRL Group, Inc., 35 (upd.)
CEC Entertainment, Inc., 31 (upd.)
Chart House Enterprises, Inc., 17
Checkers Drive-Up Restaurants Inc., 16
The Cheesecake Factory Inc., 17
Chi-Chi's Inc., 13; 51 (upd.)
Chicago Pizza & Brewery, Inc., 44
Chick-fil-A Inc., 23
Cinnabon Inc., 23
The Circle K Corporation, II
CKE Restaurants, Inc., 19; 46 (upd.)
Coborn's, Inc., 30
Compass Group PLC, 34
Comptoirs Modernes S.A., 19
Consolidated Products Inc., 14
Controladora Comercial Mexicana, S.A. de
    C.V., 36
Cooker Restaurant Corporation, 20; 51
    (upd.)
The Copps Corporation, 32
Cosi, Inc., 53
Cost-U-Less, Inc., 51
Cracker Barrel Old Country Store, Inc., 10
D'Agostino Supermarkets Inc., 19
Dairy Mart Convenience Stores, Inc., 7; 25
    (upd.)
Darden Restaurants, Inc., 16; 44 (upd.)
Dean & DeLuca, Inc., 36
Delhaize "Le Lion" S.A., 44
DeMoulas / Market Basket Inc., 23
DenAmerica Corporation, 29
Diedrich Coffee, Inc., 40

Domino's Pizza, Inc., 7; 21 (upd.)
Eateries, Inc., 33
Edeka Zentrale A.G., II; 47 (upd.)
Einstein/Noah Bagel Corporation, 29
El Chico Restaurants, Inc., 19
Elior SA, 49
Elmer's Restaurants, Inc., 42
Embers America Restaurants, 30
Etablissements Economiques du Casino
   Guichard, Perrachon et Cie, S.C.A., 12
Famous Dave's of America, Inc., 40
Fazoli's Systems, Inc., 27
Flagstar Companies, Inc., 10
Fleming Companies, Inc., II
Food Lion, Inc., II; 15 (upd.)
Foodarama Supermarkets, Inc., 28
Foodmaker, Inc., 14
The Fred W. Albrecht Grocery Co., 13
Fresh Choice, Inc., 20
Fresh Foods, Inc., 29
Friendly Ice Cream Corp., 30
Frisch's Restaurants, Inc., 35
Fuller Smith & Turner P.L.C., 38
Furr's Restaurant Group, Inc., 53
Furr's Supermarkets, Inc., 28
Garden Fresh Restaurant Corporation, 31
The Gateway Corporation Ltd., II
Genuardi's Family Markets, Inc., 35
George Weston Limited, II; 36 (upd.)
Ghirardelli Chocolate Company, 30
Giant Food Inc., II; 22 (upd.)
Godfather's Pizza Incorporated, 25
Golden Corral Corporation, 10
Golden State Foods Corporation, 32
The Golub Corporation, 26
Gordon Food Service Inc., 8; 39 (upd.)
The Grand Union Company, 7; 28 (upd.)
The Great Atlantic & Pacific Tea
   Company, Inc., II; 16 (upd.); 55 (upd.)
Gristede's Sloan's, Inc., 31
Ground Round, Inc., 21
Groupe Promodès S.A., 19
Guyenne et Gascogne, 23
H.E. Butt Grocery Co., 13; 32 (upd.)
Haggen Inc., 38
Hannaford Bros. Co., 12
Hard Rock Cafe International, Inc., 12
Harris Teeter Inc., 23
Harry's Farmers Market Inc., 23
Hickory Farms, Inc., 17
Holberg Industries, Inc., 36
Holland Burgerville USA, 44
Hooters of America, Inc., 18
Hops Restaurant Bar and Brewery, 46
Houchens Industries Inc., 51
Hughes Markets, Inc., 22
Hungry Howie's Pizza and Subs, Inc., 25
Hy-Vee, Inc., 36
ICA AB, II
Iceland Group plc, 33
IHOP Corporation, 17
Il Fornaio (America) Corporation, 27
In-N-Out Burger, 19
Ingles Markets, Inc., 20
Inserra Supermarkets, 25
International Dairy Queen, Inc., 10; 39
   (upd.)
ITM Entreprises SA, 36
Ito-Yokado Co., Ltd., 42 (upd.)
J Sainsbury plc, II; 13 (upd.); 38 (upd.)
Jamba Juice Company, 47
JD Wetherspoon plc, 30
Jerry's Famous Deli Inc., 24
Jitney-Jungle Stores of America, Inc., 27
John Lewis Partnership plc, 42 (upd.)
Johnny Rockets Group, Inc., 31
KFC Corporation, 7; 21 (upd.)

King Kullen Grocery Co., Inc., 15
Koninklijke Ahold N.V. (Royal Ahold), II;
   16 (upd.)
Koo Koo Roo, Inc., 25
The Kroger Company, II; 15 (upd.)
The Krystal Company, 33
Kwik Save Group plc, 11
La Madeleine French Bakery & Café, 33
Landry's Seafood Restaurants, Inc., 15
LDB Corporation, 53
Leeann Chin, Inc., 30
Levy Restaurants L.P., 26
Little Caesar Enterprises, Inc., 7; 24 (upd.)
Loblaw Companies Limited, 43
Logan's Roadhouse, Inc., 29
Lone Star Steakhouse & Saloon, Inc., 51
Long John Silver's Restaurants Inc., 13
Luby's, Inc., 17; 42 (upd.)
Lucky Stores, Inc., 27
Lund Food Holdings, Inc., 22
Madden's on Gull Lake, 52
Marie Callender's Restaurant & Bakery,
   Inc., 28
Marsh Supermarkets, Inc., 17
Max & Erma's Restaurants Inc., 19
McDonald's Corporation, II; 7 (upd.); 26
   (upd.)
Megafoods Stores Inc., 13
Meijer Incorporated, 7
Metromedia Companies, 14
Mexican Restaurants, Inc., 41
The Middleby Corporation, 22
Minyard Food Stores, Inc., 33
MITROPA AG, 37
Morrison Restaurants Inc., 11
Morton's Restaurant Group, Inc., 30
Mrs. Fields' Original Cookies, Inc., 27
Nash Finch Company, 8; 23 (upd.)
Nathan's Famous, Inc., 29
National Convenience Stores Incorporated,
   7
New World Restaurant Group, Inc., 44
New York Restaurant Group, Inc., 32
Noble Roman's Inc., 14
Noodles & Company, Inc., 55
NPC International, Inc., 40
O'Charley's Inc., 19
Old Spaghetti Factory International Inc., 24
The Oshawa Group Limited, II
Outback Steakhouse, Inc., 12; 34 (upd.)
P&C Foods Inc., 8
P.F. Chang's China Bistro, Inc., 37
Pancho's Mexican Buffet, Inc., 46
Panda Management Company, Inc., 35
Panera Bread Company, 44
Papa John's International, Inc., 15
Papa Murphy's International, Inc., 54
Pathmark Stores, Inc., 23
Peapod, Inc., 30
Penn Traffic Company, 13
Performance Food Group Company, 31
Perkins Family Restaurants, L.P., 22
Petrossian Inc., 54
Piccadilly Cafeterias, Inc., 19
Piggly Wiggly Southern, Inc., 13
Pizza Hut Inc., 7; 21 (upd.)
Planet Hollywood International, Inc., 18;
   41 (upd.)
Players International, Inc., 22
Ponderosa Steakhouse, 15
Provigo Inc., II; 51 (upd.)
Publix Super Markets Inc., 7; 31 (upd.)
Pueblo Xtra International, Inc., 47
Quality Dining, Inc., 18
Quality Food Centers, Inc., 17
The Quizno's Corporation, 42
Rally's Hamburgers, Inc., 25

Ralphs Grocery Company, 35
Randall's Food Markets, Inc., 40
Rare Hospitality International Inc., 19
Restaurants Unlimited, Inc., 13
Richfood Holdings, Inc., 7
The Riese Organization, 38
Riser Foods, Inc., 9
Roadhouse Grill, Inc., 22
Rock Bottom Restaurants, Inc., 25
Rubio's Restaurants, Inc., 35
Ruby Tuesday, Inc., 18
Ruth's Chris Steak House, 28
Ryan's Family Steak Houses, Inc., 15
Safeway Inc., II; 24 (upd.)
Safeway PLC, 50 (upd.)
Santa Barbara Restaurant Group, Inc., 37
Sbarro, Inc., 16
Schlotzsky's, Inc., 36
Schultz Sav-O Stores, Inc., 21
Schwan's Sales Enterprises, Inc., 26 (upd.)
Seaway Food Town, Inc., 15
Second Harvest, 29
See's Candies, Inc., 30
Seneca Foods Corporation, 17
Service America Corp., 7
SFI Group plc, 51
Shells Seafood Restaurants, Inc., 43
Shoney's, Inc., 7; 23 (upd.)
ShowBiz Pizza Time, Inc., 13
Smart & Final, Inc., 16
Smith's Food & Drug Centers, Inc., 8
Sodexho Alliance SA, 29
Somerfield plc, 47 (upd.)
Sonic Corporation, 14; 37 (upd.)
The Southland Corporation, II; 7 (upd.)
Spaghetti Warehouse, Inc., 25
SPAR Handels AG, 35
Spartan Stores Inc., 8
The Steak n Shake Company, 41
Steinberg Incorporated, II
The Stop & Shop Companies, Inc., II
Subway, 32
Super Food Services, Inc., 15
Supermarkets General Holdings
   Corporation, II
Supervalu Inc., II; 18 (upd.); 50 (upd.)
SYSCO Corporation, II; 24 (upd.)
Taco Bell Corp., 7; 21 (upd.)
Taco Cabana, 23
Taco John's International Inc., 15
TelePizza S.A., 33
Tesco PLC, II
Total Entertainment Restaurant
   Corporation, 46
Trader Joe's Company, 13; 50 (upd.)
Travel Ports of America, Inc., 17
Tree of Life, Inc., 29
Triarc Companies, Inc., 34 (upd.)
Tubby's, Inc., 53
Tully's Coffee Corporation, 51
Tumbleweed, Inc., 33
TW Services, Inc., II
Ukrop's Super Market's, Inc., 39
Unique Casual Restaurants, Inc., 27
United Natural Foods, Inc., 32
Uno Restaurant Corporation, 18
Vail Resorts, Inc., 43 (upd.)
VICORP Restaurants, Inc., 12; 48 (upd.)
Village Super Market, Inc., 7
The Vons Companies, Incorporated, 7; 28
   (upd.)
Waffle House Inc., 14
Wakefern Food Corporation, 33
Waldbaum, Inc., 19
Wall Street Deli, Inc., 33
Wawa Inc., 17
Wegmans Food Markets, Inc., 9; 41 (upd.)

FOOD SERVICES & RETAILERS
(*continued*)

Weis Markets, Inc., 15
Wendy's International, Inc., 8; 23 (upd.); 47 (upd.)
Wetterau Incorporated, II
White Castle System, Inc., 12; 36 (upd.)
White Rose, Inc., 24
Whole Foods Market, Inc., 50 (upd.)
Wild Oats Markets, Inc., 19; 41 (upd.)
Winn-Dixie Stores, Inc., II; 21 (upd.)
Wm. Morrison Supermarkets PLC, 38
The Wolfgang Puck Food Company, Inc., 26
Worldwide Restaurant Concepts, Inc., 47
Young & Co.'s Brewery, P.L.C., 38
Yucaipa Cos., 17

HEALTH & PERSONAL CARE PRODUCTS

Akorn, Inc., 32
Alberto-Culver Company, 8
Alco Health Services Corporation, III
Allergan, Inc., 10; 30 (upd.)
American Safety Razor Company, 20
American Stores Company, 22 (upd.)
Amway Corporation, III; 13 (upd.)
Aveda Corporation, 24
Avon Products, Inc., III; 19 (upd.); 46 (upd.)
Bally Total Fitness Holding Corp., 25
Bausch & Lomb Inc., 7; 25 (upd.)
Baxter International Inc., I; 10 (upd.)
BeautiControl Cosmetics, Inc., 21
Becton, Dickinson & Company, I; 11 (upd.)
Beiersdorf AG, 29
Big B, Inc., 17
Bindley Western Industries, Inc., 9
Block Drug Company, Inc., 8; 27 (upd.)
The Body Shop International plc, 53 (upd.)
The Boots Company PLC, 24 (upd.)
Bristol-Myers Squibb Company, III; 9 (upd.)
C.R. Bard Inc., 9
Candela Corporation, 48
Cardinal Health, Inc., 18; 50 (upd.)
Carson, Inc., 31
Carter-Wallace, Inc., 8
Caswell-Massey Co. Ltd., 51
CCA Industries, Inc., 53
Chattem, Inc., 17
Chesebrough-Pond's USA, Inc., 8
Chronimed Inc., 26
Cintas Corporation, 51 (upd.)
The Clorox Company, III
CNS, Inc., 20
Colgate-Palmolive Company, III; 14 (upd.); 35 (upd.)
Conair Corp., 17
Cordis Corp., 19
Cosmair, Inc., 8
Coty, Inc., 36
Cybex International, Inc., 49
Datascope Corporation, 39
Del Laboratories, Inc., 28
DEP Corporation, 20
DePuy, Inc., 30
The Dial Corp., 23 (upd.)
Direct Focus, Inc., 47
Drackett Professional Products, 12
Elizabeth Arden, Inc., 8; 40 (upd.)
Empi, Inc., 26
Enrich International, Inc., 33
The Estée Lauder Companies Inc., 9; 30 (upd.)

Ethicon, Inc., 23
Forest Laboratories, Inc., 11
Forever Living Products International Inc., 17
French Fragrances, Inc., 22
Gambro AB, 49
General Nutrition Companies, Inc., 11; 29 (upd.)
Genzyme Corporation, 13
The Gillette Company, III; 20 (upd.)
Groupe Yves Saint Laurent, 23
Guerlain, 23
Guest Supply, Inc., 18
Hanger Orthopedic Group, Inc., 41
Helen of Troy Corporation, 18
Helene Curtis Industries, Inc., 8; 28 (upd.)
Henkel KGaA, III
Henry Schein, Inc., 31
Herbalife International, Inc., 17; 41 (upd.)
Inter Parfums Inc., 35
Invacare Corporation, 11
IVAX Corporation, 11
IVC Industries, Inc., 45
The Jean Coutu Group (PJC) Inc., 46
John Paul Mitchell Systems, 24
Johnson & Johnson, III; 8 (upd.); 36 (upd.)
Kanebo, Ltd., 53
Kao Corporation, III
Kendall International, Inc., 11
Kimberly-Clark Corporation, III; 16 (upd.); 43 (upd.)
Kyowa Hakko Kogyo Co., Ltd., III
L'Oréal SA, III; 8 (upd.); 46 (upd.)
Laboratoires de Biologie Végétale Yves Rocher, 35
The Lamaur Corporation, 41
Lever Brothers Company, 9
Lion Corporation, III; 51 (upd.)
Luxottica SpA, 17
Mannatech Inc., 33
Mary Kay Corporation, 9; 30 (upd.)
Maxxim Medical Inc., 12
Medco Containment Services Inc., 9
Medtronic, Inc., 8
Melaleuca Inc., 31
The Mentholatum Company Inc., 32
Mentor Corporation, 26
Merck & Co., Inc., 34 (upd.)
Merit Medical Systems, Inc., 29
Nature's Sunshine Products, Inc., 15
NBTY, Inc., 31
Neutrogena Corporation, 17
New Dana Perfumes Company, 37
Nikken Global Inc., 32
Nutrition for Life International Inc., 22
OEC Medical Systems, Inc., 27
Patterson Dental Co., 19
Perrigo Company, 12
Physician Sales & Service, Inc., 14
Playtex Products, Inc., 15
The Procter & Gamble Company, III; 8 (upd.); 26 (upd.)
Revlon Inc., III; 17 (upd.)
Roche Biomedical Laboratories, Inc., 11
S.C. Johnson & Son, Inc., III
Safety 1st, Inc., 24
Schering-Plough Corporation, 14 (upd.)
Shaklee Corporation, 39 (upd.)
Shionogi & Co., Ltd., III
Shiseido Company, Limited, III; 22 (upd.)
Slim-Fast Nutritional Foods International, Inc., 18
Smith & Nephew plc, 17
SmithKline Beecham PLC, III
Soft Sheen Products, Inc., 31
Sunrise Medical Inc., 11
Tambrands Inc., 8

Terumo Corporation, 48
Tom's of Maine, Inc., 45
The Tranzonic Companies, 37
Turtle Wax, Inc., 15
United States Surgical Corporation, 10; 34 (upd.)
USANA, Inc., 29
Utah Medical Products, Inc., 36
VHA Inc., 53
VIASYS Healthcare, Inc., 52
VISX, Incorporated, 30
Water Pik Technologies, Inc., 34
Weider Nutrition International, Inc., 29
Wella AG, III; 48 (upd.)
West Pharmaceutical Services, Inc., 42
Wyeth, 50 (upd.)
Zila, Inc., 46
Zimmer Holdings, Inc., 45

HEALTH CARE SERVICES

Acadian Ambulance & Air Med Services, Inc., 39
Adventist Health, 53
Advocat Inc., 46
Alterra Healthcare Corporation, 42
Amedysis, Inc., 53
The American Cancer Society, 24
American Lung Association, 48
American Medical Association, 39
American Medical International, Inc., III
American Medical Response, Inc., 39
American Red Cross, 40
AmeriSource Health Corporation, 37 (upd.)
AmSurg Corporation, 48
Applied Bioscience International, Inc., 10
Assisted Living Concepts, Inc., 43
Beverly Enterprises, Inc., III; 16 (upd.)
Bon Secours Health System, Inc., 24
Caremark Rx, Inc., 10; 54 (upd.)
Children's Comprehensive Services, Inc., 42
Children's Hospitals and Clinics, Inc., 54
Chronimed Inc., 26
COBE Laboratories, Inc., 13
Columbia/HCA Healthcare Corporation, 15
Community Psychiatric Centers, 15
CompDent Corporation, 22
CompHealth Inc., 25
Comprehensive Care Corporation, 15
Continental Medical Systems, Inc., 10
Express Scripts Incorporated, 17
Extendicare Health Services, Inc., 6
FHP International Corporation, 6
Genesis Health Ventures, Inc., 18
GranCare, Inc., 14
Group Health Cooperative, 41
Hazelden Foundation, 28
HCA - The Healthcare Company, 35 (upd.)
Health Care & Retirement Corporation, 22
Health Risk Management, Inc., 24
Health Systems International, Inc., 11
HealthSouth Corporation, 14; 33 (upd.)
Highmark Inc., 27
The Hillhaven Corporation, 14
Hooper Holmes, Inc., 22
Hospital Corporation of America, III
Howard Hughes Medical Institute, 39
Humana Inc., III; 24 (upd.)
Intermountain Health Care, Inc., 27
Jenny Craig, Inc., 10; 29 (upd.)
Kinetic Concepts, Inc. (KCI), 20
LabOne, Inc., 48
Laboratory Corporation of America Holdings, 42 (upd.)
Lifeline Systems, Inc., 53
Lincare Holdings Inc., 43
Manor Care, Inc., 6; 25 (upd.)

March of Dimes, 31
Matria Healthcare, Inc., 17
Maxicare Health Plans, Inc., III; 25 (upd.)
Mayo Foundation, 9; 34 (upd.)
Merit Medical Systems, Inc., 29
National Health Laboratories Incorporated, 11
National Medical Enterprises, Inc., III
NovaCare, Inc., 11
Option Care Inc., 48
Orthodontic Centers of America, Inc., 35
Oxford Health Plans, Inc., 16
PacifiCare Health Systems, Inc., 11
Palomar Medical Technologies, Inc., 22
Pediatric Services of America, Inc., 31
PHP Healthcare Corporation, 22
PhyCor, Inc., 36
Primedex Health Systems, Inc., 25
Quest Diagnostics Inc., 26
Ramsay Youth Services, Inc., 41
Res-Care, Inc., 29
Response Oncology, Inc., 27
Rural/Metro Corporation, 28
Sabratek Corporation, 29
St. Jude Medical, Inc., 11; 43 (upd.)
Salick Health Care, Inc., 53
Sierra Health Services, Inc., 15
Smith & Nephew plc, 41 (upd.)
The Sports Club Company, 25
SSL International plc, 49
Stericycle Inc., 33
Sun Healthcare Group Inc., 25
SwedishAmerican Health System, 51
Tenet Healthcare Corporation, 55 (upd.)
Twinlab Corporation, 34
U.S. Healthcare, Inc., 6
Unison HealthCare Corporation, 25
United HealthCare Corporation, 9
United Way of America, 36
Universal Health Services, Inc., 6
Vencor, Inc., 16
VISX, Incorporated, 30
Vivra, Inc., 18
WellPoint Health Networks Inc., 25
YWCA of the U.S.A., 45

HOTELS

Amerihost Properties, Inc., 30
Aztar Corporation, 13
Bass PLC, 38 (upd.)
Boca Resorts, Inc., 37
Boyd Gaming Corporation, 43
Bristol Hotel Company, 23
The Broadmoor Hotel, 30
Caesars World, Inc., 6
Candlewood Hotel Company, Inc., 41
Carlson Companies, Inc., 22 (upd.)
Castle & Cooke, Inc., 20 (upd.)
Cedar Fair, L.P., 22
Cendant Corporation, 44 (upd.)
Choice Hotels International Inc., 14
Circus Circus Enterprises, Inc., 6
Club Méditerranée S.A., 6; 21 (upd.)
Doubletree Corporation, 21
Extended Stay America, Inc., 41
Fibreboard Corporation, 16
Four Seasons Hotels Inc., 9; 29 (upd.)
Fuller Smith & Turner P.L.C., 38
Gables Residential Trust, 49
Gaylord Entertainment Company, 11; 36 (upd.)
Granada Group PLC, 24 (upd.)
Grand Casinos, Inc., 20
Grand Hotel Krasnapolsky N.V., 23
Helmsley Enterprises, Inc., 9
Hilton Group plc, III; 19 (upd.); 49 (upd.)
Holiday Inns, Inc., III

Hospitality Franchise Systems, Inc., 11
Howard Johnson International, Inc., 17
Hyatt Corporation, III; 16 (upd.)
ITT Sheraton Corporation, III
JD Wetherspoon plc, 30
John Q. Hammons Hotels, Inc., 24
The La Quinta Companies, 11; 42 (upd.)
Ladbroke Group PLC, 21 (upd.)
Las Vegas Sands, Inc., 50
Madden's on Gull Lake, 52
Mandalay Resort Group, 32 (upd.)
Manor Care, Inc., 25 (upd.)
The Marcus Corporation, 21
Marriott International, Inc., III; 21 (upd.)
Mirage Resorts, Incorporated, 6; 28 (upd.)
Motel 6 Corporation, 13
Omni Hotels Corp., 12
Park Corp., 22
Players International, Inc., 22
Preussag AG, 42 (upd.)
Prime Hospitality Corporation, 52
Promus Companies, Inc., 9
Real Turismo, S.A. de C.V., 50
Red Roof Inns, Inc., 18
Resorts International, Inc., 12
Ritz-Carlton Hotel Company L.L.C., 9; 29 (upd.)
Santa Fe Gaming Corporation, 19
The SAS Group, 34 (upd.)
SFI Group plc, 51
Showboat, Inc., 19
Sonesta International Hotels Corporation, 44
Starwood Hotels & Resorts Worldwide, Inc., 54
Sun International Hotels Limited, 26
Sunburst Hospitality Corporation, 26
Thistle Hotels PLC, 54
Trusthouse Forte PLC, III
Vail Resorts, Inc., 43 (upd.)
Westin Hotels and Resorts Worldwide, 9; 29 (upd.)
Whitbread PLC, 52 (upd.)
Young & Co.'s Brewery, P.L.C., 38

INFORMATION TECHNOLOGY

A.B. Watley Group Inc., 45
Acxiom Corporation, 35
Adaptec, Inc., 31
Adobe Systems Incorporated, 10; 33 (upd.)
Advanced Micro Devices, Inc., 6
Agence France-Presse, 34
Agilent Technologies Inc., 38
Aldus Corporation, 10
AltaVista Company, 43
Amdahl Corporation, III; 14 (upd.); 40 (upd.)
Amdocs Ltd., 47
America Online, Inc., 10 ; 26 (upd.)
American Business Information, Inc., 18
American Management Systems, Inc., 11
American Software Inc., 25
Amstrad PLC, III
Analytic Sciences Corporation, 10
Analytical Surveys, Inc., 33
Anker BV, 53
Apollo Group, Inc., 24
Apple Computer, Inc., III; 6 (upd.)
The Arbitron Company, 38
Asanté Technologies, Inc., 20
AsiaInfo Holdings, Inc., 43
ASK Group, Inc., 9
ASML Holding N.V., 50
AST Research Inc., 9
At Home Corporation, 43
AT&T Bell Laboratories, Inc., 13
AT&T Corporation, 29 (upd.)

AT&T Istel Ltd., 14
Autologic Information International, Inc., 20
Automatic Data Processing, Inc., III; 9 (upd.)
Autotote Corporation, 20
Avid Technology Inc., 38
Aydin Corp., 19
Baan Company, 25
Baltimore Technologies Plc, 42
Banyan Systems Inc., 25
Battelle Memorial Institute, Inc., 10
BBN Corp., 19
BEA Systems, Inc., 36
Bell and Howell Company, 9; 29 (upd.)
Bell Industries, Inc., 47
Billing Concepts Corp., 26
Bloomberg L.P., 21
BMC Software, Inc., 55
Boole & Babbage, Inc., 25
Booz Allen & Hamilton Inc., 10
Borland International, Inc., 9
Bowne & Co., Inc., 23
Brite Voice Systems, Inc., 20
Broderbund Software, 13; 29 (upd.)
BTG, Inc., 45
Bull S.A., 43 (upd.)
Business Objects S.A., 25
C-Cube Microsystems, Inc., 37
CACI International Inc., 21
Cadence Design Systems, Inc., 11
Caere Corporation, 20
Cahners Business Information, 43
CalComp Inc., 13
Cambridge Technology Partners, Inc., 36
Canon Inc., III
Cap Gemini Ernst & Young, 37
Caribiner International, Inc., 24
Catalina Marketing Corporation, 18
CDW Computer Centers, Inc., 16
Cerner Corporation, 16
Cheyenne Software, Inc., 12
CHIPS and Technologies, Inc., 9
Ciber, Inc., 18
Cincom Systems Inc., 15
Cirrus Logic, Incorporated, 11
Cisco Systems, Inc., 11
Citizen Watch Co., Ltd., 21 (upd.)
Citrix Systems, Inc., 44
CNET Networks, Inc., 47
Cogent Communications Group, Inc., 55
Cognos Inc., 44
Commodore International Ltd., 7
Compagnie des Machines Bull S.A., III
Compaq Computer Corporation, III; 6 (upd.); 26 (upd.)
Complete Business Solutions, Inc., 31
CompuAdd Computer Corporation, 11
CompuCom Systems, Inc., 10
CompUSA, Inc., 35 (upd.)
CompuServe Incorporated, 10
CompuServe Interactive Services, Inc., 27 (upd.)
Computer Associates International, Inc., 6; 49 (upd.)
Computer Data Systems, Inc., 14
Computer Sciences Corporation, 6
Computervision Corporation, 10
Compuware Corporation, 10; 30 (upd.)
Comshare Inc., 23
Conner Peripherals, Inc., 6
Control Data Corporation, III
Control Data Systems, Inc., 10
Corbis Corporation, 31
Corel Corporation, 15; 33 (upd.)
Corporate Software Inc., 9
Cray Research, Inc., III

INFORMATION TECHNOLOGY
(*continued*)

CTG, Inc., 11
Cybermedia, Inc., 25
Dassault Systèmes S.A., 25
Data Broadcasting Corporation, 31
Data General Corporation, 8
Datapoint Corporation, 11
Dell Computer Corp., 9
Dialogic Corporation, 18
DiamondCluster International, Inc., 51
Digex, Inc., 46
Digital Equipment Corporation, III; 6 (upd.)
Digital River, Inc., 50
Documentum, Inc., 46
The Dun & Bradstreet Corporation, IV; 19 (upd.)
Dun & Bradstreet Software Services Inc., 11
DynCorp, 45
E.piphany, Inc., 49
EarthLink, Inc., 36
ECS S.A, 12
Edmark Corporation, 14; 41 (upd.)
Egghead Inc., 9
El Camino Resources International, Inc., 11
Electronic Arts Inc., 10
Electronic Data Systems Corporation, III; 28 (upd.)
Electronics for Imaging, Inc., 43 (upd.)
EMC Corporation, 12; 46 (upd.)
Encore Computer Corporation, 13
Evans & Sutherland Computer Corporation, 19
Exabyte Corporation, 12
Experian Information Solutions Inc., 45
First Financial Management Corporation, 11
Fiserv Inc., 11
FlightSafety International, Inc., 9
FORE Systems, Inc., 25
Franklin Electronic Publishers, Inc., 23
FTP Software, Inc., 20
Fujitsu Limited, III; 42 (upd.)
Fujitsu-ICL Systems Inc., 11
Future Now, Inc., 12
Gartner Group, Inc., 21
Gateway 2000, Inc., 10
Gateway, Inc., 27 (upd.)
GEAC Computer Corporation Ltd., 43
Gericom AG, 47
Getronics NV, 39
GFI Informatique SA, 49
Google, Inc., 50
GT Interactive Software, 31
Guthy-Renker Corporation, 32
Handspring Inc., 49
Hewlett-Packard Company, III; 6 (upd.)
Hyperion Software Corporation, 22
ICL plc, 6
Identix Inc., 44
IKON Office Solutions, Inc., 50
Imation Corporation, 20
Infineon Technologies AG, 50
Information Access Company, 17
Information Builders, Inc., 22
Information Resources, Inc., 10
Informix Corporation, 10; 30 (upd.)
Infosys Technologies Ltd., 38
Ing. C. Olivetti & C., S.p.a., III
Inktomi Corporation, 45
Inso Corporation, 26
Intel Corporation, 36 (upd.)
IntelliCorp, Inc., 45
Intelligent Electronics, Inc., 6
Intergraph Corporation, 6; 24 (upd.)

International Business Machines Corporation, III; 6 (upd.); 30 (upd.)
Intuit Inc., 14; 33 (upd.)
Iomega Corporation, 21
IONA Technologies plc, 43
J.D. Edwards & Company, 14
Jack Henry and Associates, Inc., 17
The Judge Group, Inc., 51
Juniper Networks, Inc., 43
Juno Online Services, Inc., 38
Kana Software, Inc., 51
KLA Instruments Corporation, 11
KnowledgeWare Inc., 31 (upd.)
Komag, Inc., 11
Kronos, Inc., 18
Kurzweil Technologies, Inc., 51
Lam Research Corporation, 11
Landauer, Inc., 51
Lason, Inc., 31
Lawson Software, 38
The Learning Company Inc., 24
Learning Tree International Inc., 24
Legent Corporation, 10
LEXIS-NEXIS Group, 33
Logica plc, 14; 37 (upd.)
Logicon Inc., 20
Logitech International SA, 28
LoJack Corporation, 48
Lotus Development Corporation, 6; 25 (upd.)
The MacNeal-Schwendler Corporation, 25
Macromedia, Inc., 50
Madge Networks N.V., 26
MAI Systems Corporation, 11
MAPICS, Inc., 55
Maxtor Corporation, 10
Mead Data Central, Inc., 10
Mecklermedia Corporation, 24
Mentor Graphics Corporation, 11
Merisel, Inc., 12
Metatec International, Inc., 47
Metro Information Services, Inc., 36
Micro Warehouse, Inc., 16
Micron Technology, Inc., 11; 29 (upd.)
Micros Systems, Inc., 18
Microsoft Corporation, 6; 27 (upd.)
Misys plc, 45; 46
MITRE Corporation, 26
The Motley Fool, Inc., 40
National Semiconductor Corporation, 6
National TechTeam, Inc., 41
Navarre Corporation, 24
NCR Corporation, III; 6 (upd.); 30 (upd.)
Netscape Communications Corporation, 15; 35 (upd.)
Network Associates, Inc., 25
Nextel Communications, Inc., 10
NFO Worldwide, Inc., 24
Nichols Research Corporation, 18
Nimbus CD International, Inc., 20
Nixdorf Computer AG, III
Novell, Inc., 6; 23 (upd.)
NVIDIA Corporation, 54
Océ N.V., 24
Odetics Inc., 14
Onyx Software Corporation, 53
Opsware Inc., 49
Oracle Corporation, 6; 24 (upd.)
Packard Bell Electronics, Inc., 13
Parametric Technology Corp., 16
PC Connection, Inc., 37
PeopleSoft Inc., 14; 33 (upd.)
Perot Systems Corporation, 29
Pitney Bowes Inc., III
PLATINUM Technology, Inc., 14
Policy Management Systems Corporation, 11

Portal Software, Inc., 47
Primark Corp., 13
The Princeton Review, Inc., 42
Printrak, A Motorola Company, 44
Printronix, Inc., 18
Prodigy Communications Corporation, 34
Progress Software Corporation, 15
Psion PLC, 45
Quantum Corporation, 10
Quark, Inc., 36
Racal-Datacom Inc., 11
Razorfish, Inc., 37
RCM Technologies, Inc., 34
RealNetworks, Inc., 53
Red Hat, Inc., 45
Renaissance Learning Systems, Inc., 39
Reuters Holdings PLC, 22 (upd.)
The Reynolds and Reynolds Company, 50
Ricoh Company, Ltd., III
RSA Security Inc., 46
SABRE Group Holdings, Inc., 26
The Sage Group, 43
The Santa Cruz Operation, Inc., 38
SAP AG, 16; 43 (upd.)
SAS Institute Inc., 10
SBS Technologies, Inc., 25
SCB Computer Technology, Inc., 29
Schawk, Inc., 24
Seagate Technology, Inc., 8
Siebel Systems, Inc., 38
Sierra On-Line, Inc., 15; 41 (upd.)
SilverPlatter Information Inc., 23
SmartForce PLC, 43
Softbank Corp., 13; 38 (upd.)
Standard Microsystems Corporation, 11
STC PLC, III
Steria SA, 49
Sterling Software, Inc., 11
Storage Technology Corporation, 6
Stratus Computer, Inc., 10
Sun Microsystems, Inc., 7; 30 (upd.)
SunGard Data Systems Inc., 11
Sybase, Inc., 10; 27 (upd.)
Sykes Enterprises, Inc., 45
Symantec Corporation, 10
Symbol Technologies, Inc., 15
Synopsis, Inc., 11
System Software Associates, Inc., 10
Systems & Computer Technology Corp., 19
Tandem Computers, Inc., 6
TenFold Corporation, 35
Terra Lycos, Inc., 43
The Thomson Corporation, 34 (upd.)
3Com Corporation, 11; 34 (upd.)
The 3DO Company, 43
Timberline Software Corporation, 15
Transaction Systems Architects, Inc., 29
Transiciel SA, 48
Triple P N.V., 26
Ubi Soft Entertainment S.A., 41
Unilog SA, 42
Unisys Corporation, III; 6 (upd.); 36 (upd.)
United Business Media plc, 52 (upd.)
UUNET, 38
Verbatim Corporation, 14
Veridian Corporation, 54
VeriFone, Inc., 18
VeriSign, Inc., 47
Veritas Software Corporation, 45
Viasoft Inc., 27
Volt Information Sciences Inc., 26
Wang Laboratories, Inc., III; 6 (upd.)
West Group, 34 (upd.)
Western Digital Corp., 25
Wind River Systems, Inc., 37
Wipro Limited, 43

Wolters Kluwer NV, 33 (upd.)
WordPerfect Corporation, 10
Wyse Technology, Inc., 15
Xerox Corporation, III; 6 (upd.); 26 (upd.)
Xilinx, Inc., 16
Yahoo! Inc., 27
Zapata Corporation, 25
Ziff Davis Media Inc., 36 (upd.)
Zilog, Inc., 15

INSURANCE

AEGON N.V., III; 50 (upd.)
Aetna, Inc., III; 21 (upd.)
AFLAC Incorporated, 10 (upd.); 38 (upd.)
Alexander & Alexander Services Inc., 10
Alleghany Corporation, 10
Allianz Aktiengesellschaft Holding, III; 15 (upd.)
The Allstate Corporation, 10; 27 (upd.)
AMB Generali Holding AG, 51
American Family Corporation, III
American Financial Corporation, III
American Financial Group Inc., 48 (upd.)
American General Corporation, III; 10 (upd.); 46 (upd.)
American International Group, Inc., III; 15 (upd.); 47 (upd.)
American National Insurance Company, 8; 27 (upd.)
American Premier Underwriters, Inc., 10
American Re Corporation, 10; 35 (upd.)
N.V. AMEV, III
Aon Corporation, III; 45 (upd.)
Assicurazioni Generali SpA, III; 15 (upd.)
Atlantic American Corporation, 44
Aviva PLC, 50 (upd.)
Axa, III
AXA Colonia Konzern AG, 27; 49 (upd.)
B.A.T. Industries PLC, 22 (upd.)
Baldwin & Lyons, Inc., 51
Bâloise-Holding, 40
Benfield Greig Group plc, 53
Berkshire Hathaway Inc., III; 18 (upd.)
Blue Cross and Blue Shield Association, 10
Brown & Brown, Inc., 41
Business Men's Assurance Company of America, 14
Capital Holding Corporation, III
Catholic Order of Foresters, 24
The Chubb Corporation, III; 14 (upd.); 37 (upd.)
CIGNA Corporation, III; 22 (upd.); 45 (upd.)
Cincinnati Financial Corporation, 16; 44 (upd.)
CNA Financial Corporation, III; 38 (upd.)
Commercial Union PLC, III
Connecticut Mutual Life Insurance Company, III
Conseco Inc., 10; 33 (upd.)
The Continental Corporation, III
The Doctors' Company, 55
Empire Blue Cross and Blue Shield, III
Enbridge Inc., 43
Engle Homes, Inc., 46
The Equitable Life Assurance Society of the United States Fireman's Fund Insurance Company, III
ERGO Versicherungsgruppe AG, 44
Erie Indemnity Company, 35
Farm Family Holdings, Inc., 39
Farmers Insurance Group of Companies, 25
Fidelity National Financial Inc., 54
The First American Corporation, 52
First Executive Corporation, III
Foundation Health Corporation, 12

Gainsco, Inc., 22
GEICO Corporation, 10; 40 (upd.)
General Accident PLC, III
General Re Corporation, III; 24 (upd.)
Gerling-Konzern Versicherungs-Beteiligungs-Aktiengesellschaft, 51
Great-West Lifeco Inc., III
Gryphon Holdings, Inc., 21
Guardian Royal Exchange Plc, 11
Harleysville Group Inc., 37
HDI (Haftpflichtverband der Deutschen Industrie Versicherung auf Gegenseitigkeit V.a.G.), 53
The Home Insurance Company, III
Horace Mann Educators Corporation, 22
Household International, Inc., 21 (upd.)
Jackson National Life Insurance Company, 8
Jefferson-Pilot Corporation, 11; 29 (upd.)
John Hancock Financial Services, Inc., III; 42 (upd.)
Johnson & Higgins, 14
Kaiser Foundation Health Plan, Inc., 53
Kemper Corporation, III; 15 (upd.)
Legal & General Group plc, III; 24 (upd.)
The Liberty Corporation, 22
Lincoln National Corporation, III; 25 (upd.)
Lloyd's of London, III; 22 (upd.)
The Loewen Group Inc., 40 (upd.)
Lutheran Brotherhood, 31
Marsh & McLennan Companies, Inc., III; 45 (upd.)
Massachusetts Mutual Life Insurance Company, III; 53 (upd.)
The Meiji Mutual Life Insurance Company, III
Mercury General Corporation, 25
Metropolitan Life Insurance Company, III; 52 (upd.)
MGIC Investment Corp., 52
Mitsui Marine and Fire Insurance Company, Limited, III
Mitsui Mutual Life Insurance Company, III; 39 (upd.)
Munich Re (Münchener Rückversicherungs-Gesellschaft Aktiengesellschaft in München), III; 46 (upd.)
The Mutual Benefit Life Insurance Company, III
The Mutual Life Insurance Company of New York, III
Nationale-Nederlanden N.V., III
New England Mutual Life Insurance Company, III
New York Life Insurance Company, III; 45 (upd.)
Nippon Life Insurance Company, III
Northwestern Mutual Life Insurance Company, III; 45 (upd.)
NYMAGIC, Inc., 41
Ohio Casualty Corp., 11
Old Republic International Corp., 11
Oregon Dental Service Health Plan, Inc., 51
Pan-American Life Insurance Company, 48
The Paul Revere Corporation, 12
Pennsylvania Blue Shield, III
The PMI Group, Inc., 49
Preserver Group, Inc., 44
Principal Mutual Life Insurance Company, III
The Progressive Corporation, 11; 29 (upd.)
Provident Life and Accident Insurance Company of America, III
Prudential Corporation PLC, III

The Prudential Insurance Company of America, III; 30 (upd.)
Prudential plc, 48 (upd.)
Radian Group Inc., 42
Reliance Group Holdings, Inc., III
Riunione Adriatica di Sicurtà SpA, III
Royal & Sun Alliance Insurance Group plc, 55 (upd.)
Royal Insurance Holdings PLC, III
SAFECO Corporaton, III
The St. Paul Companies, Inc., III; 22 (upd.)
SCOR S.A., 20
Skandia Insurance Company, Ltd., 50
The Standard Life Assurance Company, III
State Farm Mutual Automobile Insurance Company, III; 51 (upd.)
State Financial Services Corporation, 51
Sumitomo Life Insurance Company, III
The Sumitomo Marine and Fire Insurance Company, Limited, III
Sun Alliance Group PLC, III
SunAmerica Inc., 11
Svenska Handelsbanken AB, 50 (upd.)
Swiss Reinsurance Company (Schweizerische Rückversicherungs-Gesellschaft), III; 46 (upd.)
Teachers Insurance and Annuity Association-College Retirement Equities Fund, III; 45 (upd.)
Texas Industries, Inc., 8
TIG Holdings, Inc., 26
The Tokio Marine and Fire Insurance Co., Ltd., III
Torchmark Corporation, 9; 33 (upd.)
Transatlantic Holdings, Inc., 11
The Travelers Corporation, III
UICI, 33
Union des Assurances de Pans, III
Unitrin Inc., 16
UNUM Corp., 13
UnumProvident Corporation, 52 (upd.)
USAA, 10
USF&G Corporation, III
Victoria Group, 44 (upd.)
VICTORIA Holding AG, III
W.R. Berkley Corp., 15
Washington National Corporation, 12
White Mountains Insurance Group, Ltd., 48
Willis Corroon Group plc, 25
"Winterthur" Schweizerische Versicherungs-Gesellschaft, III
The Yasuda Fire and Marine Insurance Company, Limited, III
The Yasuda Mutual Life Insurance Company, III; 39 (upd.)
"Zürich" Versicherungs-Gesellschaft, III

LEGAL SERVICES

Akin, Gump, Strauss, Hauer & Feld, L.L.P., 33
American Bar Association, 35
American Lawyer Media Holdings, Inc., 32
Amnesty International, 50
Arnold & Porter, 35
Baker & Hostetler LLP, 40
Baker & McKenzie, 10; 42 (upd.)
Baker and Botts, L.L.P., 28
Bingham Dana LLP, 43
Brobeck, Phleger & Harrison, LLP, 31
Cadwalader, Wickersham & Taft, 32
Chadbourne & Parke, 36
Cleary, Gottlieb, Steen & Hamilton, 35
Clifford Chance LLP, 38
Coudert Brothers, 30
Covington & Burling, 40
Cravath, Swaine & Moore, 43
Davis Polk & Wardwell, 36

LEGAL SERVICES (continued)

Debevoise & Plimpton, 39
Dechert, 43
Dewey Ballantine LLP, 48
Dorsey & Whitney LLP, 47
Fenwick & West LLP, 34
Fish & Neave, 54
Foley & Lardner, 28
Fried, Frank, Harris, Shriver & Jacobson, 35
Fulbright & Jaworski L.L.P., 47
Gibson, Dunn & Crutcher LLP, 36
Heller, Ehrman, White & McAuliffe, 41
Hildebrandt International, 29
Hogan & Hartson L.L.P., 44
Holme Roberts & Owen LLP, 28
Hughes Hubbard & Reed LLP, 44
Hunton & Williams, 35
Jones, Day, Reavis & Pogue, 33
Kelley Drye & Warren LLP, 40
King & Spalding, 23
Latham & Watkins, 33
LeBoeuf, Lamb, Greene & MacRae, L.L.P., 29
The Legal Aid Society, 48
Mayer, Brown, Rowe & Maw, 47
Milbank, Tweed, Hadley & McCloy, 27
Morgan, Lewis & Bockius LLP, 29
O'Melveny & Myers, 37
Paul, Hastings, Janofsky & Walker LLP, 27
Paul, Weiss, Rifkind, Wharton & Garrison, 47
Pepper Hamilton LLP, 43
Pillsbury Madison & Sutro LLP, 29
Pre-Paid Legal Services, Inc., 20
Proskauer Rose LLP, 47
Ropes & Gray, 40
Shearman & Sterling, 32
Sidley Austin Brown & Wood, 40
Simpson Thacher & Bartlett, 39
Skadden, Arps, Slate, Meagher & Flom, 18
Snell & Wilmer L.L.P., 28
Stroock & Stroock & Lavan LLP, 40
Sullivan & Cromwell, 26
Vinson & Elkins L.L.P., 30
Wachtell, Lipton, Rosen & Katz, 47
Weil, Gotshal & Manges LLP, 55
White & Case LLP, 35
Williams & Connolly LLP, 47
Wilson Sonsini Goodrich & Rosati, 34
Winston & Strawn, 35
Womble Carlyle Sandridge & Rice, PLLC, 52

MANUFACTURING

A-dec, Inc., 53
A. Schulman, Inc., 49 (upd.)
A.B.Dick Company, 28
A.O. Smith Corporation, 11; 40 (upd.)
A.T. Cross Company, 17; 49 (upd.)
A.W. Faber-Castell
  Unternehmensverwaltung GmbH & Co., 51
AAF-McQuay Incorporated, 26
AAON, Inc., 22
AAR Corp., 28
ABC Rail Products Corporation, 18
Abiomed, Inc., 47
ACCO World Corporation, 7; 51 (upd.)
Acme-Cleveland Corp., 13
Acorn Products, Inc., 55
Acuson Corporation, 36 (upd.)
Adams Golf, Inc., 37
Adolf Würth GmbH & Co. KG, 49
AEP Industries, Inc., 36
Ag-Chem Equipment Company, Inc., 17

AGCO Corp., 13
Ahlstrom Corporation, 53
Airgas, Inc., 54
Aisin Seiki Co., Ltd., III
AK Steel Holding Corporation, 41 (upd.)
Aktiebolaget Electrolux, 22 (upd.)
Aktiebolaget SKF, III; 38 (upd.)
Alamo Group Inc., 32
Alberto-Culver Company, 36 (upd.)
Aldila Inc., 46
Alfa-Laval AB, III
Allen Organ Company, 33
Alliant Techsystems Inc., 8; 30 (upd.)
Allied Healthcare Products, Inc., 24
Allied Products Corporation, 21
Allied Signal Engines, 9
AlliedSignal Inc., 22 (upd.)
Allison Gas Turbine Division, 9
Alltrista Corporation, 30
Alps Electric Co., Ltd., 44 (upd.)
Alvis Plc, 47
Amer Group plc, 41
American Biltrite Inc., 43 (upd.)
American Business Products, Inc., 20
American Cast Iron Pipe Company, 50
American Homestar Corporation, 18; 41 (upd.)
American Locker Group Incorporated, 34
American Standard Companies Inc., 30 (upd.)
American Tourister, Inc., 16
American Woodmark Corporation, 31
Ameriwood Industries International Corp., 17
Amerock Corporation, 53
AMETEK, Inc., 9
AMF Bowling, Inc., 40
Ampex Corporation, 17
Amway Corporation, 30 (upd.)
Analogic Corporation, 23
Anchor Hocking Glassware, 13
Andersen Corporation, 10
The Andersons, Inc., 31
Andreas Stihl, 16
Andritz AG, 51
Anthem Electronics, Inc., 13
Apasco S.A. de C.V., 51
Applica Incorporated, 43 (upd.)
Applied Films Corporation, 48
Applied Materials, Inc., 10; 46 (upd.)
Applied Micro Circuits Corporation, 38
Applied Power Inc., 9; 32 (upd.)
ARBED S.A., 22 (upd.)
Arctco, Inc., 16
Arctic Cat Inc., 40 (upd.)
Ariens Company, 48
Armor All Products Corp., 16
Armstrong World Industries, Inc., III; 22 (upd.)
Artesyn Technologies Inc., 46 (upd.)
ArvinMeritor, Inc., 54 (upd.)
Asahi Glass Company, Ltd., 48 (upd.)
Ashley Furniture Industries, Inc., 35
ASML Holding N.V., 50
Astronics Corporation, 35
ASV, Inc., 34
Atlas Copco AB, III; 28 (upd.)
Atwood Mobil Products, 53
Avedis Zildjian Co., 38
Avery Dennison Corporation, 17 (upd.); 49 (upd.)
Avondale Industries, 7; 41 (upd.)
Badger Meter, Inc., 22
Baker Hughes Incorporated, III
Baldor Electric Company, 21
Baldwin Piano & Organ Company, 18
Baldwin Technology Company, Inc., 25

Balfour Beatty plc, 36 (upd.)
Ballantyne of Omaha, Inc., 27
Ballard Medical Products, 21
Bally Manufacturing Corporation, III
Baltek Corporation, 34
Bandai Co., Ltd., 55
Barmag AG, 39
Barnes Group Inc., 13
Barry Callebaut AG, 29
Bassett Furniture Industries, Inc., 18
Bath Iron Works, 12; 36 (upd.)
Beckman Coulter, Inc., 22
Beckman Instruments, Inc., 14
Becton, Dickinson & Company, 36 (upd.)
Beiersdorf AG, 29
Bel Fuse, Inc., 53
Belden Inc., 19
Bell Sports Corporation, 16; 44 (upd.)
Beloit Corporation, 14
Bénéteau SA, 55
Benjamin Moore & Co., 13; 38 (upd.)
Bernina Holding AG, 47
Berry Plastics Corporation, 21
BIC Corporation, 8; 23 (upd.)
BICC PLC, III
Billabong International Ltd., 44
Binks Sames Corporation, 21
Binney & Smith Inc., 25
Biomet, Inc., 10
BISSELL Inc., 9; 30 (upd.)
The Black & Decker Corporation, III; 20 (upd.)
Blount International, Inc., 12; 48 (upd.)
Blyth Industries, Inc., 18
BMC Industries, Inc., 17
Bodum Design Group AG, 47
Boral Limited, 43 (upd.)
Borden, Inc., 22 (upd.)
Borg-Warner Automotive, Inc., 14
Borg-Warner Corporation, III
Boston Scientific Corporation, 37
The Boyds Collection, Ltd., 29
Brannock Device Company, 48
Brass Eagle Inc., 34
Bridgeport Machines, Inc., 17
Briggs & Stratton Corporation, 8; 27 (upd.)
BRIO AB, 24
British Vita plc, 33 (upd.)
Brother Industries, Ltd., 14
Brown & Sharpe Manufacturing Co., 23
Brown-Forman Corporation, 38 (upd.)
Broyhill Furniture Industries, Inc., 10
Brunswick Corporation, III; 22 (upd.)
BTR Siebe plc, 27
Buck Knives Inc., 48
Buckeye Technologies, Inc., 42
Bucyrus International, Inc., 17
Bugle Boy Industries, Inc., 18
Building Materials Holding Corporation, 52
Bulgari S.p.A., 20
Bulova Corporation, 13; 41 (upd.)
Bundy Corporation, 17
Burelle S.A., 23
Burton Snowboards Inc., 22
Bush Boake Allen Inc., 30
Bush Industries, Inc., 20
Butler Manufacturing Co., 12
C&J Clark International Ltd., 52
C.F. Martin & Co., Inc., 42
Callaway Golf Company, 15; 45 (upd.)
Campbell Scientific, Inc., 51
Cannondale Corporation, 21
Caradon plc, 20 (upd.)
The Carbide/Graphite Group, Inc., 40
Carbone Lorraine S.A., 33
Cardo AB, 53
Carl-Zeiss-Stiftung, III; 34 (upd.)

Carrier Corporation, 7
CASIO Computer Co., Ltd., III; 40 (upd.)
Catalina Lighting, Inc., 43 (upd.)
Caterpillar Inc., III; 15 (upd.)
Central Sprinkler Corporation, 29
Centuri Corporation, 54
Century Aluminum Company, 52
Cessna Aircraft Company, 27 (upd.)
Champion Enterprises, Inc., 17
Chanel, 12
Chanel SA, 49 (upd.)
Chart Industries, Inc., 21
Chris-Craft Industries, Inc., 31 (upd.)
Christian Dalloz SA, 40
Christofle SA, 40
Chromcraft Revington, Inc., 15
Ciments Français, 40
Cincinnati Milacron Inc., 12
Cinram International, Inc., 43
Circon Corporation, 21
Cirrus Design Corporation, 44
Citizen Watch Co., Ltd., III
Clarcor Inc., 17
Clark Equipment Company, 8
Clayton Homes Incorporated, 13; 54 (upd.)
The Clorox Company, 22 (upd.)
CNH Global N.V., 38 (upd.)
Coach, Inc., 45 (upd.)
Cobra Golf Inc., 16
Cockerill Sambre Group, 26 (upd.)
Cohu, Inc., 32
Colas S.A., 31
The Coleman Company, Inc., 30 (upd.)
Collins & Aikman Corporation, 41 (upd.)
Collins Industries, Inc., 33
Colorado MEDtech, Inc., 48
Colt's Manufacturing Company, Inc., 12
Columbia Sportswear Company, 19
Columbus McKinnon Corporation, 37
CompuDyne Corporation, 51
Concord Camera Corporation, 41
Congoleum Corp., 18
Conn-Selmer, Inc., 55
Conso International Corporation, 29
Consorcio G Grupo Dina, S.A. de C.V., 36
Converse Inc., 9
The Cooper Companies, Inc., 39
Cooper Industries, Inc., 44 (upd.)
Cordis Corporation, 46 (upd.)
Corning Inc., 44 (upd.)
Corrpro Companies, Inc., 20
Corticeira Amorim, Sociedade Gestora de
   Participaço es Sociais, S.A., 48
Crane Co., 8; 30 (upd.)
Creo Inc., 48
Crown Equipment Corporation, 15
CTB International Corporation, 43 (upd.)
Cuisinart Corporation, 24
Culligan Water Technologies, Inc., 12; 38
   (upd.)
Cummins Engine Company, Inc., 40 (upd.)
Curtiss-Wright Corporation, 10; 35 (upd.)
Cutter & Buck Inc., 27
Cybex International, Inc., 49
Daewoo Group, III
Daikin Industries, Ltd., III
Danaher Corporation, 7
Daniel Industries, Inc., 16
Danisco A/S, 44
Day Runner, Inc., 41 (upd.)
Decora Industries, Inc., 31
DeCrane Aircraft Holdings Inc., 36
Deere & Company, III; 42 (upd.)
Defiance, Inc., 22
Denby Group plc, 44
Denison International plc, 46
DENSO Corporation, 46 (upd.)

Department 56, Inc., 14
DePuy Inc., 37 (upd.)
Detroit Diesel Corporation, 10
Deutsche Babcock A.G., III
Deutz AG, 39
Devro plc, 55
Dial-A-Mattress Operating Corporation, 46
Diebold, Incorporated, 7; 22 (upd.)
Diesel SpA, 40
Dixon Industries, Inc., 26
Dixon Ticonderoga Company, 12
DMI Furniture, Inc., 46
Donaldson Company, Inc., 49 (upd.)
Donnelly Corporation, 12; 35 (upd.)
Douglas & Lomason Company, 16
Dover Corporation, III; 28 (upd.)
Dresser Industries, Inc., III
Drew Industries Inc., 28
Drexel Heritage Furnishings Inc., 12
Drypers Corporation, 18
Ducommun Incorporated, 30
Duncan Toys Company, 55
Duracell International Inc., 9
Durametallic, 21
Duriron Company Inc., 17
Dürr AG, 44
EADS SOCATA, 54
Eagle-Picher Industries, Inc., 8; 23 (upd.)
The Eastern Company, 48
Eastman Kodak Company, III; 7 (upd.); 36
   (upd.)
ECC International Corp., 42
Ecolab Inc., 34 (upd.)
Eddie Bauer Inc., 9
EDO Corporation, 46
EG&G Incorporated, 29 (upd.)
Ekco Group, Inc., 16
Elamex, S.A. de C.V., 51
Elano Corporation, 14
Electrolux AB, III; 53 (upd.)
Eljer Industries, Inc., 24
Elscint Ltd., 20
Encompass Services Corporation, 33
Energizer Holdings, Inc., 32
Enesco Corporation, 11
English China Clays Ltd., 40 (upd.)
Escalade, Incorporated, 19
Esselte Leitz GmbH & Co. KG, 48
Essilor International, 21
Esterline Technologies Corp., 15
Ethan Allen Interiors, Inc., 12; 39 (upd.)
The Eureka Company, 12
Everlast Worldwide Inc., 47
Fabbrica D' Armi Pietro Beretta S.p.A., 39
Facom S.A., 32
Faiveley S.A., 39
Falcon Products, Inc., 33
Fanuc Ltd., III; 17 (upd.)
Farah Incorporated, 24
Farmer Bros. Co., 52
Fastenal Company, 42 (upd.)
Faultless Starch/Bon Ami Company, 55
Featherlite Inc., 28
Fedders Corporation, 18; 43 (upd.)
Federal Prison Industries, Inc., 34
Federal Signal Corp., 10
Fellowes Manufacturing Company, 28
Fender Musical Instruments Company, 16;
   43 (upd.)
Figgie International Inc., 7
Firearms Training Systems, Inc., 27
First Alert, Inc., 28
First Brands Corporation, 8
The First Years Inc., 46
Fisher Controls International, Inc., 13
Fisher Scientific International Inc., 24
Fisher-Price Inc., 12; 32 (upd.)

Fiskars Corporation, 33
Fisons plc, 9
Fleetwood Enterprises, Inc., III; 22 (upd.)
Flexsteel Industries Inc., 15; 41 (upd.)
Flextronics International Ltd., 38
Flint Ink Corporation, 41 (upd.)
Florsheim Shoe Company, 9
Flour City International, Inc., 44
Flowserve Corporation, 33
Fort James Corporation, 22 (upd.)
Fountain Powerboats Industries, Inc., 28
Foxboro Company, 13
Framatome SA, 19
Frank J. Zamboni & Co., Inc., 34
Franklin Electric Company, Inc., 43
Freudenberg & Co., 41
Friedrich Grohe AG & Co. KG, 53
Frigidaire Home Products, 22
Frymaster Corporation, 27
FSI International, Inc., 17
Fuji Photo Film Co., Ltd., III; 18 (upd.)
Fuqua Enterprises, Inc., 17
Furniture Brands International, Inc., 39
   (upd.)
Furon Company, 28
The Furukawa Electric Co., Ltd., III
G. Leblanc Corporation, 55
G.S. Blodgett Corporation, 15
Gardner Denver, Inc., 49
The Gates Corporation, 9
GE Aircraft Engines, 9
GEA AG, 27
Geberit AG, 49
Gehl Company, 19
GenCorp Inc., 8; 9 (upd.)
General Bearing Corporation, 45
General Cable Corporation, 40
General Dynamics Corporation, 40 (upd.)
General Housewares Corporation, 16
Genmar Holdings, Inc., 45
geobra Brandstätter GmbH & Co. KG, 48
The George F. Cram Company, Inc., 55
Gerber Scientific, Inc., 12
Gerresheimer Glas AG, 43
Giddings & Lewis, Inc., 10
The Gillette Company, 20 (upd.)
GKN plc, III; 38 (upd.)
Gleason Corporation, 24
The Glidden Company, 8
Global Power Equipment Group Inc., 52
Glock Ges.m.b.H., 42
Goodman Holding Company, 42
Goodrich Corporation, 46 (upd.)
Goody Products, Inc., 12
The Gorman-Rupp Company, 18
Goss Holdings, Inc., 43
Goulds Pumps Inc., 24
Graco Inc., 19
Greene, Tweed & Company, 55
Griffon Corporation, 34
Grinnell Corp., 13
Groupe André, 17
Groupe Guillin SA, 40
Groupe Legis Industries, 23
Groupe SEB, 35
Grow Group Inc., 12
Grupo Cydsa, S.A. de C.V., 39
Grupo IMSA, S.A. de C.V., 44
Grupo Industrial Saltillo, S.A. de C.V., 54
Grupo Lladró S.A., 52
Guangzhou Pearl River Piano Group Ltd.,
   49
Gulf Island Fabrication, Inc., 44
Gunite Corporation, 51
The Gunlocke Company, 23
Guy Degrenne SA, 44
H.B. Fuller Company, 8; 32 (upd.)

MANUFACTURING (*continued*)

Hach Co., 18
Hackman Oyj Adp, 44
Haemonetics Corporation, 20
Halliburton Company, III
Hallmark Cards, Inc., 40 (upd.)
Hanson PLC, 30 (upd.)
Hardinge Inc., 25
Harland and Wolff Holdings plc, 19
Harmon Industries, Inc., 25
Harnischfeger Industries, Inc., 8; 38 (upd.)
Harsco Corporation, 8
Hartmarx Corporation, 32 (upd.)
The Hartz Mountain Corporation, 46 (upd.)
Hasbro, Inc., III; 16 (upd.)
Hawker Siddeley Group Public Limited
    Company, III
Haworth Inc., 8; 39 (upd.)
Head N.V., 55
Health O Meter Products Inc., 14
Heekin Can Inc., 13
HEICO Corporation, 30
Heidelberger Druckmaschinen AG, 40
Henkel Manco Inc., 22
The Henley Group, Inc., III
Heraeus Holding GmbH, 54 (upd.)
Herman Miller, Inc., 8
Hermès International S.A., 34 (upd.)
Hillenbrand Industries, Inc., 10
Hillerich & Bradsby Company, Inc., 51
Hillsdown Holdings plc, 24 (upd.)
Hilti AG, 53
Hitachi Zosen Corporation, III
Hitchiner Manufacturing Co., Inc., 23
HMI Industries, Inc., 17
Holnam Inc., 8
Holson Burnes Group, Inc., 14
Home Products International, Inc., 55
HON INDUSTRIES Inc., 13
The Hoover Company, 12; 40 (upd.)
Hoshino Gakki Co. Ltd., 55
Huffy Corporation, 7; 30 (upd.)
Hunt Manufacturing Company, 12
Hunter Fan Company, 13
Hydril Company, 46
Hyster Company, 17
Hyundai Group, III; 7 (upd.)
Icon Health & Fitness, Inc., 38
Igloo Products Corp., 21
Illinois Tool Works Inc., III; 22 (upd.)
Imatra Steel Oy Ab, 55
IMI plc, 9
Imo Industries Inc., 7; 27 (upd.)
Inchcape PLC, III; 16 (upd.); 50 (upd.)
Industrie Natuzzi S.p.A., 18
Infineon Technologies AG, 50
Ingalls Shipbuilding, Inc., 12
Ingersoll-Rand Company, III; 15 (upd.)
Ingersoll-Rand Company Ltd., 55 (upd.)
Insilco Corporation, 16
Interco Incorporated, III
Interface, Inc., 8
The Interlake Corporation, 8
Internacional de Ceramica, S.A. de C.V.,
    53
International Controls Corporation, 10
International Flavors & Fragrances Inc., 38
    (upd.)
International Game Technology, 10
Invacare Corporation, 47 (upd.)
Invensys PLC, 50 (upd.)
Invivo Corporation, 52
Ionics, Incorporated, 52
Irwin Toy Limited, 14
Ishikawajima-Harima Heavy Industries Co.,
    Ltd., III
J. D'Addario & Company, Inc., 48

J.I. Case Company, 10
J.M. Voith AG, 33
Jabil Circuit, Inc., 36
Jacuzzi Inc., 23
JAKKS Pacific, Inc., 52
Japan Tobacco Inc., 46 (upd.)
Jayco Inc., 13
Jeld-Wen, Inc., 45
Jenoptik AG, 33
Jervis B. Webb Company, 24
JLG Industries, Inc., 52
Johnson Controls, Inc., III; 26 (upd.)
Johnson Matthey PLC, 49 (upd.)
Johnson Worldwide Associates, Inc., 28
Johnstown America Industries, Inc., 23
Jones Apparel Group, Inc., 11
Jostens, Inc., 7; 25 (upd.)
K'Nex Industries, Inc., 52
Kaman Corporation, 12; 42 (upd.)
Karsten Manufacturing Corporation, 51
Kasper A.S.L., Ltd., 40
Katy Industries, Inc., 51 (upd.)
Kawasaki Heavy Industries, Ltd., III
Kaydon Corporation, 18
KB Toys, 35 (upd.)
Keramik Holding AG Laufen, 51
Kerr Group Inc., 24
Kewaunee Scientific Corporation, 25
Key Tronic Corporation, 14
Keystone International, Inc., 11
KHD Konzern, III
Kimball International, Inc., 12; 48 (upd.)
Kit Manufacturing Co., 18
Knape & Vogt Manufacturing Company,
    17
Knoll Group Inc., 14
Koala Corporation, 44
Kobe Steel, Ltd., IV; 19 (upd.)
Koch Enterprises, Inc., 29
Kohler Company, 7; 32 (upd.)
Komatsu Ltd., III; 16 (upd.); 52 (upd.)
Kone Corporation, 27
Konica Corporation, III
Kubota Corporation, III; 26 (upd.)
Kuhlman Corporation, 20
Kyocera Corporation, 21 (upd.)
L-3 Communications Holdings, Inc., 48
L. and J.G. Stickley, Inc., 50
L.B. Foster Company, 33
La-Z-Boy Incorporated, 14; 50 (upd.)
LADD Furniture, Inc., 12
Ladish Co., Inc., 30
Lafarge Cement UK, 54 (upd.)
Lafarge Corporation, 28
Lafuma S.A., 39
Lakeland Industries, Inc., 45
Lam Research Corporation, 31 (upd.)
Lamson & Sessions Co., 13
Lancer Corporation, 21
The Lane Co., Inc., 12
LeapFrog Enterprises, Inc., 54
Leatherman Tool Group, Inc., 51
Leggett & Platt, Inc., 11; 48 (upd.)
Leica Camera AG, 35
Leica Microsystems Holdings GmbH, 35
Lennox International Inc., 8; 28 (upd.)
Lenox, Inc., 12
Leupold & Stevens, Inc., 52
Lexmark International, Inc., 18
Linamar Corporation, 18
Lincoln Electric Co., 13
Lindal Cedar Homes, Inc., 29
Lindsay Manufacturing Co., 20
Little Tikes Co., 13
Loctite Corporation, 8
Logitech International SA, 28
The Longaberger Company, 12; 44 (upd.)

Louis Vuitton, 10
Lucas Industries PLC, III
Luxottica SpA, 52 (upd.)
Lynch Corporation, 43
M&F Worldwide Corp., 38
MacAndrews & Forbes Holdings Inc., 28
Mackay Envelope Corporation, 45
Mail-Well, Inc., 28
Makita Corporation, 22
MAN Aktiengesellschaft, III
Manitou BF S.A., 27
Manitowoc Company, Inc., 18
Mannesmann AG, III; 14 (upd.)
Margarete Steiff GmbH, 23
Marisa Christina, Inc., 15
Mark IV Industries, Inc., 7; 28 (upd.)
The Marmon Group, 16 (upd.)
Martin Industries, Inc., 44
Marvin Lumber & Cedar Company, 22
Mary Kay, Inc., 30 (upd.)
Masco Corporation, III; 20 (upd.); 39
    (upd.)
Master Lock Company, 45
Mattel, Inc., 7; 25 (upd.)
Matth. Hohner AG, 53
Matthews International Corporation, 29
Maxco Inc., 17
Maxwell Shoe Company, Inc., 30
Maytag Corporation, III; 22 (upd.)
McClain Industries, Inc., 51
McDermott International, Inc., III
McKechnie plc, 34
McWane Corporation, 55
Meade Instruments Corporation, 41
Meadowcraft, Inc., 29
Meggitt PLC, 34
Merck & Co., Inc., 34 (upd.)
Merillat Industries Inc., 13
Mestek, Inc., 10
Metso Corporation, 30 (upd.)
Mettler-Toledo International Inc., 30
Michael Anthony Jewelers, Inc., 24
Microdot Inc., 8
The Middleton Doll Company, 53
Midwest Grain Products, Inc., 49
Mikasa, Inc., 28
Mikohn Gaming Corporation, 39
Milacron, Inc., 53 (upd.)
Miller Industries, Inc., 26
Milton Bradley Company, 21
Mine Safety Appliances Company, 31
Minolta Co., Ltd., III; 18 (upd.); 43 (upd.)
Minuteman International Inc., 46
Mitsubishi Heavy Industries, Ltd., III; 7
    (upd.)
Mity Enterprises, Inc., 38
Modine Manufacturing Company, 8
Moen Incorporated, 12
Mohawk Industries, Inc., 19
Molex Incorporated, 11
Montres Rolex S.A., 13; 34 (upd.)
Motorcar Parts & Accessories, Inc., 47
Moulinex S.A., 22
Movado Group, Inc., 28
Mr. Coffee, Inc., 15
Mr. Gasket Inc., 15
Mueller Industries, Inc., 7; 52 (upd.)
Multi-Color Corporation, 53
Nashua Corporation, 8
National Envelope Corporation, 32
National Gypsum Company, 10
National Oilwell, Inc., 54
National Picture & Frame Company, 24
National Standard Co., 13
National Starch and Chemical Company,
    49
Natrol, Inc., 49

Natural Alternatives International, Inc., 49
NCR Corporation, 30 (upd.)
Neopost S.A., 53
New Balance Athletic Shoe, Inc., 25
New Holland N.V., 22
Newcor, Inc., 40
Newell Rubbermaid Inc., 9; 52 (upd.)
Newport News Shipbuilding Inc., 13; 38 (upd.)
Nexans SA, 54
NHK Spring Co., Ltd., III
NIKE, Inc., 36 (upd.)
Nikon Corporation, III; 48 (upd.)
Nintendo Co., Ltd., III; 7 (upd.)
Nippon Seiko K.K., III
Nippondenso Co., Ltd., III
NKK Corporation, 28 (upd.)
NordicTrack, 22
Nordson Corporation, 11; 48 (upd.)
Nortek, Inc., 34
Norton Company, 8
Norton McNaughton, Inc., 27
Novellus Systems, Inc., 18
NTN Corporation, III; 47 (upd.)
Nu-kote Holding, Inc., 18
O'Sullivan Industries Holdings, Inc., 34
Oak Industries Inc., 21
Oakley, Inc., 49 (upd.)
Oakwood Homes Corporation, 15
ODL, Inc., 55
The Ohio Art Company, 14
Oil-Dri Corporation of America, 20
Oneida Ltd., 7; 31 (upd.)
Optische Werke G. Rodenstock, 44
Orange Glo International, 53
Osmonics, Inc., 18
Otis Elevator Company, Inc., 13; 39 (upd.)
Outboard Marine Corporation, III; 20 (upd.)
Owens Corning Corporation, 20 (upd.)
Owosso Corporation, 29
P & F Industries, Inc., 45
Pacer Technology, 40
Pacific Dunlop Limited, 10
Pall Corporation, 9
Palm Harbor Homes, Inc., 39
Panavision Inc., 24
Park Corp., 22
Parker-Hannifin Corporation, III; 24 (upd.)
Patrick Industries, Inc., 30
Pechiney SA, IV; 45 (upd.)
Pella Corporation, 12; 39 (upd.)
Penn Engineering & Manufacturing Corp., 28
Pentair, Inc., 26 (upd.)
Pentech International, Inc., 29
The Perkin-Elmer Corporation, 7
Peterson American Corporation, 55
Phillips-Van Heusen Corporation, 24
Physio-Control International Corp., 18
Pilkington plc, 34 (upd.)
Pinguely-Haulotte SA, 51
Pioneer Electronic Corporation, III
Pitney Bowes, Inc., 19
Pittway Corporation, 33 (upd.)
PlayCore, Inc., 27
Playmates Toys, 23
Playskool, Inc., 25
Pleasant Company, 27
Ply Gem Industries Inc., 12
Pochet SA, 55
Polaris Industries Inc., 12; 35 (upd.)
Polaroid Corporation, III; 7 (upd.); 28 (upd.)
PPG Industries, Inc., 22 (upd.)
Prada Holding B.V., 45
Praxair, Inc., 48 (upd.)

Precision Castparts Corp., 15
Premark International, Inc., III
Presstek, Inc., 33
Prince Sports Group, Inc., 15
Printronix, Inc., 18
Pulaski Furniture Corporation, 33
Pumpkin Masters, Inc., 48
Puritan-Bennett Corporation, 13
Purolator Products Company, 21
PW Eagle, Inc., 48
Quixote Corporation, 15
R. Griggs Group Limited, 23
Racing Champions Corporation, 37
Radio Flyer Inc., 34
Rapala-Normark Group, Ltd., 30
Raven Industries, Inc., 33
Raychem Corporation, 8
Rayovac Corporation, 39 (upd.)
Recovery Engineering, Inc., 25
Red Spot Paint & Varnish Company, 55
Red Wing Pottery Sales, Inc., 52
Red Wing Shoe Company, Inc., 9
Regal-Beloit Corporation, 18
Reichhold Chemicals, Inc., 10
Remington Arms Company, Inc., 12; 40 (upd.)
Remington Products Company, L.L.C., 42
RENK AG, 37
Revell-Monogram Inc., 16
Revere Ware Corporation, 22
Rexam PLC, 32 (upd.)
Rexnord Corporation, 21
RF Micro Devices, Inc., 43
Rheinmetall Berlin AG, 9
RHI AG, 53
Riddell Sports Inc., 22
Rieter Holding AG, 42
River Oaks Furniture, Inc., 43
RMC Group p.l.c., 34 (upd.)
Roadmaster Industries, Inc., 16
Robbins & Myers Inc., 15
Robertson-Ceco Corporation, 19
Rockford Products Corporation, 55
RockShox, Inc., 26
Rockwell Automation, 43 (upd.)
Rohde & Schwarz GmbH & Co. KG, 39
ROHN Industries, Inc., 22
Rohr Incorporated, 9
Roland Corporation, 38
Rollerblade, Inc., 15; 34 (upd.)
Ronson PLC, 49
Roper Industries, Inc., 15; 50 (upd.)
Rotork plc, 46
Royal Appliance Manufacturing Company, 15
Royal Canin S.A., 39
Royal Doulton plc, 14; 38 (upd.)
RPM, Inc., 8; 36 (upd.)
Rubbermaid Incorporated, III
Russ Berrie and Company, Inc., 12
S.C. Johnson & Son, Inc., 28 (upd.)
Sabaté Diosos SA, 48
Safeskin Corporation, 18
Safilo SpA, 54
Salant Corporation, 12; 51 (upd.)
Salton, Inc., 30
Samsonite Corporation, 13; 43 (upd.)
Samuel Cabot Inc., 53
Sandvik AB, 32 (upd.)
Sanitec Corporation, 51
Sanrio Company, Ltd., 38
Sauder Woodworking Company, 12; 35 (upd.)
Sawtek Inc., 43 (upd.)
Schindler Holding AG, 29
Schlumberger Limited, III
Schott Corporation, 53

Scotsman Industries, Inc., 20
Scott Fetzer Company, 12
The Scotts Company, 22
Scovill Fasteners Inc., 24
Sealed Air Corporation, 14
Sealy Inc., 12
Segway LLC, 48
Seiko Corporation, III; 17 (upd.)
Select Comfort Corporation, 34
The Selmer Company, Inc., 19
Semitool, Inc., 18
Sequa Corp., 13
Serta, Inc., 28
Shakespeare Company, 22
The Shaw Group, Inc., 50
Shelby Williams Industries, Inc., 14
Sherwood Brands, Inc., 53
Shorewood Packaging Corporation, 28
Shuffle Master Inc., 51
Shurgard Storage Centers, Inc., 52
SIFCO Industries, Inc., 41
Simmons Company, 47
Simula, Inc., 41
The Singer Company N.V., 30 (upd.)
Skis Rossignol S.A., 15; 43 (upd.)
Skyline Corporation, 30
SLI, Inc., 48
Smead Manufacturing Co., 17
Smith & Wesson Corporation, 30
Smith Corona Corp., 13
Smith International, Inc., 15
Smiths Industries PLC, 25
Snap-On, Incorporated, 7; 27 (upd.)
Sparton Corporation, 18
Specialized Bicycle Components Inc., 50
Specialty Equipment Companies, Inc., 25
Speizman Industries, Inc., 44
SPS Technologies, Inc., 30
SPX Corporation, 47 (upd.)
Stanadyne Automotive Corporation, 37
Standex International Corporation, 17
Stanley Furniture Company, Inc., 34
The Stanley Works, III; 20 (upd.)
Stearns, Inc., 43
Steel Dynamics, Inc., 52
Steelcase, Inc., 7; 27 (upd.)
Steinway Musical Properties, Inc., 19
Stelco Inc., 51 (upd.)
Stewart & Stevenson Services Inc., 11
STMicroelectronics NV, 52
Stryker Corporation, 11; 29 (upd.)
Sturm, Ruger & Company, Inc., 19
Sub-Zero Freezer Co., Inc., 31
Sudbury Inc., 16
Sulzer Brothers Limited (Gebruder Sulzer Aktiengesellschaft), III
Sumitomo Heavy Industries, Ltd., III; 42 (upd.)
Susquehanna Pfaltzgraff Company, 8
Swank Inc., 17
Swarovski International Holding AG, 40
The Swatch Group SA, 26
Swedish Match AB, 12; 39 (upd.)
Sweetheart Cup Company, Inc., 36
Sybron International Corp., 14
Syratech Corp., 14
Systemax, Inc., 52
TAB Products Co., 17
TAG Heuer International SA, 25
Taiwan Semiconductor Manufacturing Company Ltd., 47
Tarkett Sommer AG, 25
Taylor Guitars, 48
Taylor Made Golf Co., 23
TDK Corporation, 49 (upd.)
TearDrop Golf Company, 32
Tecumseh Products Company, 8

MANUFACTURING (*continued*)

Tektronix, Inc., 8
Tempur-Pedic Inc., 54
Tennant Company, 13; 33 (upd.)
Terex Corporation, 7; 40 (upd.)
The Testor Corporation, 51
Tetra Pak International SA, 53
Thales S.A., 42
Thermadyne Holding Corporation, 19
Thermo BioAnalysis Corp., 25
Thermo Electron Corporation, 7
Thermo Fibertek, Inc., 24
Thermo Instrument Systems Inc., 11
Thermo King Corporation, 13
Thiokol Corporation, 22 (upd.)
Thomas & Betts Corp., 11
Thomas Industries Inc., 29
Thomasville Furniture Industries, Inc., 12
Thor Industries, Inc., 39
Thyssen Krupp AG, 28 (upd.)
Timex Corporation, 7; 25 (upd.)
The Timken Company, 8; 42 (upd.)
TJ International, Inc., 19
Todd Shipyards Corporation, 14
Tokheim Corporation, 21
Tonka Corporation, 25
Toolex International N.V., 26
Topps Company, Inc., 13
Toray Industries, Inc., 51 (upd.)
The Toro Company, 7; 26 (upd.)
The Torrington Company, 13
TOTO LTD., 28 (upd.)
Town & Country Corporation, 19
Toymax International, Inc., 29
Toyoda Automatic Loom Works, Ltd., III
Tredegar Corporation, 52
Trek Bicycle Corporation, 16
Trico Products Corporation, 15
TriMas Corp., 11
Trinity Industries, Incorporated, 7
TRINOVA Corporation, III
Triumph Group, Inc., 31
Tubos de Acero de Mexico, S.A. (TAMSA), 41
Tultex Corporation, 13
Tupperware Corporation, 28
Twin Disc, Inc., 21
Ty Inc., 33
Tyco International Ltd., III; 28 (upd.)
Tyco Toys, Inc., 12
U.S. Robotics Inc., 9
Ube Industries, Ltd., 38 (upd.)
United Defense, L.P., 30
United Dominion Industries Limited, 8; 16 (upd.)
United Industrial Corporation, 37
United States Filter Corporation, 20
Unitika Ltd., 53 (upd.)
Unitog Co., 19
Utah Medical Products, Inc., 36
VA TECH ELIN EBG GmbH, 49
Vaillant GmbH, 44
Vallourec SA, 54
Valmet Corporation (Valmet Oy), III
Valmont Industries, Inc., 19
The Valspar Corporation, 8
Vari-Lite International, Inc., 35
Varian, Inc., 48 (upd.)
Variflex, Inc., 51
Varity Corporation, III
Varlen Corporation, 16
Varta AG, 23
Velcro Industries N.V., 19
Vermeer Manufacturing Company, 17
Vickers plc, 27
Victorinox AG, 21
Viessmann Werke GmbH & Co., 37

Villeroy & Boch AG, 37
Virco Manufacturing Corporation, 17
Viskase Companies, Inc., 55
Vitro Corporativo S.A. de C.V., 34
Vorwerk & Co., 27
Vosper Thornycroft Holding plc, 41
Vossloh AG, 53
W.A. Whitney Company, 53
W.H. Brady Co., 17
W.L. Gore & Associates, Inc., 14
W.W. Grainger, Inc., 26 (upd.)
Wabash National Corp., 13
Wabtec Corporation, 40
Walbro Corporation, 13
Washington Scientific Industries, Inc., 17
Wassall Plc, 18
Waterford Wedgwood plc, 12; 34 (upd.)
Waters Corporation, 43
Watts Industries, Inc., 19
WD-40 Company, 18
Weber-Stephen Products Co., 40
Weeres Industries Corporation, 52
Welbilt Corp., 19
Wellman, Inc., 8; 52 (upd.)
Weru Aktiengesellschaft, 18
West Bend Co., 14
Western Digital Corp., 25
Whirlpool Corporation, III; 12 (upd.)
White Consolidated Industries Inc., 13
Williamson-Dickie Manufacturing Company, 45 (upd.)
Wilson Sporting Goods Company, 24
Windmere Corporation, 16
WinsLoew Furniture, Inc., 21
WMS Industries, Inc., 15; 53 (upd.)
Wolverine Tube Inc., 23
Wood-Mode, Inc., 23
Woodward Governor Company, 13; 49 (upd.)
Wyant Corporation, 30
Wyman-Gordon Company, 14
Wynn's International, Inc., 33
X-Rite, Inc., 48
Yamaha Corporation, III; 16 (upd.)
The York Group, Inc., 50
York International Corp., 13
Young Innovations, Inc., 44
Zebra Technologies Corporation, 53 (upd.)
Zero Corporation, 17
Zippo Manufacturing Company, 18
Zodiac S.A., 36
Zygo Corporation, 42

MATERIALS

AK Steel Holding Corporation, 19
American Biltrite Inc., 16
American Colloid Co., 13
American Standard Inc., III
Ameriwood Industries International Corp., 17
Apasco S.A. de C.V., 51
Apogee Enterprises, Inc., 8
Asahi Glass Company, Limited, III
Bairnco Corporation, 28
Bayou Steel Corporation, 31
Blessings Corp., 19
Blue Circle Industries PLC, III
Boral Limited, III
British Vita PLC, 9
Cameron & Barkley Company, 28
Carborundum Company, 15
Carl-Zeiss-Stiftung, 34 (upd.)
Carlisle Companies Incorporated, 8
Cemex SA de CV, 20
Century Aluminum Company, 52
CertainTeed Corporation, 35
Chargeurs International, 21 (upd.)

Chemfab Corporation, 35
Compagnie de Saint-Gobain S.A., III; 16 (upd.)
Cookson Group plc, III; 44 (upd.)
Corning Incorporated, III
CSR Limited, III
Dal-Tile International Inc., 22
The David J. Joseph Company, 14
The Dexter Corporation, 12 (upd.)
Dyckerhoff AG, 35
ECC Group plc, III
Edw. C. Levy Co., 42
84 Lumber Company, 9; 39 (upd.)
ElkCorp, 52
English China Clays Ltd., 15 (upd.); 40 (upd.)
Envirodyne Industries, Inc., 17
Feldmuhle Nobel A.G., III
Fibreboard Corporation, 16
Florida Rock Industries, Inc., 46
Foamex International Inc., 17
Formica Corporation, 13
GAF Corporation, 22 (upd.)
The Geon Company, 11
Giant Cement Holding, Inc., 23
Gibraltar Steel Corporation, 37
Granite Rock Company, 26
Groupe Sidel S.A., 21
Harbison-Walker Refractories Company, 24
Harrisons & Crosfield plc, III
Heidelberger Zement AG, 31
Hexcel Corporation, 28
"Holderbank" Financière Glaris Ltd., III
Holnam Inc., 39 (upd.)
Howmet Corp., 12
Ibstock Brick Ltd., 14; 37 (upd.)
Imerys S.A., 40 (upd.)
Internacional de Ceramica, S.A. de C.V., 53
Joseph T. Ryerson & Son, Inc., 15
Lafarge Coppée S.A., III
Lafarge Corporation, 28
Lehigh Portland Cement Company, 23
Manville Corporation, III; 7 (upd.)
Matsushita Electric Works, Ltd., III; 7 (upd.)
Medusa Corporation, 24
Mitsubishi Materials Corporation, III
Nippon Sheet Glass Company, Limited, III
OmniSource Corporation, 14
Onoda Cement Co., Ltd., III
Owens-Corning Fiberglass Corporation, III
Pilkington plc, III; 34 (upd.)
Pioneer International Limited, III
PPG Industries, Inc., III
Redland plc, III
RMC Group p.l.c., III
Rock of Ages Corporation, 37
The Rugby Group plc, 31
Schuff Steel Company, 26
Sekisui Chemical Co., Ltd., III
Shaw Industries, 9
The Sherwin-Williams Company, III; 13 (upd.)
Simplex Technologies Inc., 21
Solutia Inc., 52
Sommer-Allibert S.A., 19
Southdown, Inc., 14
Spartech Corporation, 19
Ssangyong Cement Industrial Co., Ltd., III
Sun Distributors L.P., 12
Tarmac PLC, III
Tarmac plc, 28 (upd.)
TOTO LTD., III; 28 (upd.)
Toyo Sash Co., Ltd., III
Tuscarora Inc., 29
U.S. Aggregates, Inc., 42

Ube Industries, Ltd., III
United States Steel Corporation, 50 (upd.)
USG Corporation, III; 26 (upd.)
Vulcan Materials Company, 7; 52 (upd.)
Wacker-Chemie GmbH, 35
Walter Industries, Inc., III
Waxman Industries, Inc., 9
Zoltek Companies, Inc., 37

MINING & METALS

A.M. Castle & Co., 25
Aggregate Industries plc, 36
Aktiebolaget SKF, 38 (upd.)
Alcan Aluminium Limited, IV; 31 (upd.)
Alleghany Corporation, 10
Allegheny Ludlum Corporation, 8
Altos Hornos de México, S.A. de C.V., 42
Aluminum Company of America, IV; 20
  (upd.)
AMAX Inc., IV
Amsted Industries Incorporated, 7
Anglo American Corporation of South
  Africa Limited, IV; 16 (upd.)
Anglo American PLC, 50 (upd.)
ARBED S.A., IV, 22 (upd.)
Arch Mineral Corporation, 7
Armco Inc., IV
ASARCO Incorporated, IV
Ashanti Goldfields Company Limited, 43
Atchison Casting Corporation, 39
Barrick Gold Corporation, 34
Battle Mountain Gold Company, 23
Bethlehem Steel Corporation, IV; 7 (upd.);
  27 (upd.)
Birmingham Steel Corporation, 13; 40
  (upd.)
Boart Longyear Company, 26
Boral Limited, 43 (upd.)
British Coal Corporation, IV
British Steel plc, IV; 19 (upd.)
Broken Hill Proprietary Company Ltd., IV,
  22 (upd.)
Brush Wellman Inc., 14
Buderus AG, 37
Carpenter Technology Corporation, 13
Chaparral Steel Co., 13
Christensen Boyles Corporation, 26
Cleveland-Cliffs Inc., 13
Coal India Ltd., IV; 44 (upd.)
Cockerill Sambre Group, IV; 26 (upd.)
Coeur d'Alene Mines Corporation, 20
Cold Spring Granite Company, 16
Cominco Ltd., 37
Commercial Metals Company, 15; 42
  (upd.)
Companhia Vale do Rio Doce, IV; 43
  (upd.)
Corporacion Nacional del Cobre de Chile,
  40
Corus Group plc, 49 (upd.)
CRA Limited, IV
Cyprus Amax Minerals Company, 21
Cyprus Minerals Company, 7
Daido Steel Co., Ltd., IV
De Beers Consolidated Mines Limited/De
  Beers Centenary AG, IV; 7 (upd.); 28
  (upd.)
Degussa Group, IV
Dofasco Inc., IV; 24 (upd.)
Echo Bay Mines Ltd., IV; 38 (upd.)
Engelhard Corporation, IV
Falconbridge Limited, 49
Fansteel Inc., 19
Fluor Corporation, 34 (upd.)
Freeport-McMoRan Inc., IV; 7 (upd.)
Fried. Krupp GmbH, IV
Gencor Ltd., IV, 22 (upd.)

Geneva Steel, 7
Glamis Gold, Ltd., 54
Gold Fields of South Africa Ltd., IV
Grupo Mexico, S.A. de C.V., 40
Handy & Harman, 23
Hanson PLC, 30 (upd.)
Hecla Mining Company, 20
Hemlo Gold Mines Inc., 9
Heraeus Holding GmbH, IV
Hitachi Metals, Ltd., IV
Hoesch AG, IV
Homestake Mining Company, 12; 38 (upd.)
Horsehead Industries, Inc., 51
The Hudson Bay Mining and Smelting
  Company, Limited, 12
Hylsamex, S.A. de C.V., 39
IMCO Recycling, Incorporated, 32
Imerys S.A., 40 (upd.)
Imetal S.A., IV
Inco Limited, IV; 45 (upd.)
Industrias Penoles, S.A. de C.V., 22
Inland Steel Industries, Inc., IV; 19 (upd.)
Intermet Corporation, 32
Ispat Inland Inc., 40 (upd.)
Ispat International N.V., 30
Johnson Matthey PLC, IV; 16 (upd.)
JSC MMC Norilsk Nickel, 48
Kaiser Aluminum & Chemical Corporation,
  IV
Kawasaki Steel Corporation, IV
Kennecott Corporation, 7; 27 (upd.)
Kentucky Electric Steel, Inc., 31
Kerr-McGee Corporation, 22 (upd.)
Kinross Gold Corporation, 36
Klockner-Werke AG, IV
Kobe Steel, Ltd., IV; 19 (upd.)
Koninklijke Nederlandsche Hoogovens en
  Staalfabrieken NV, IV
Laclede Steel Company, 15
Layne Christensen Company, 19
Lonrho Plc, 21
The LTV Corporation, 24 (upd.)
Lukens Inc., 14
Magma Copper Company, 7
The Marmon Group, IV; 16 (upd.)
MAXXAM Inc., 8
Meridian Gold, Incorporated, 47
Metaleurop S.A., 21
Metallgesellschaft AG, IV
Minerals and Metals Trading Corporation
  of India Ltd., IV
Minerals Technologies Inc., 11; 52 (upd.)
Mitsui Mining & Smelting Co., Ltd., IV
Mitsui Mining Company, Limited, IV
Mueller Industries, Inc., 52 (upd.)
National Steel Corporation, 12
NERCO, Inc., 7
Newmont Mining Corporation, 7
Niagara Corporation, 28
Nichimen Corporation, IV
Nippon Light Metal Company, Ltd., IV
Nippon Steel Corporation, IV; 17 (upd.)
Nisshin Steel Co., Ltd., IV
NKK Corporation, IV; 28 (upd.)
Noranda Inc., IV; 7 (upd.)
North Star Steel Company, 18
Nucor Corporation, 7; 21 (upd.)
Oglebay Norton Company, 17
Okura & Co., Ltd., IV
Oregon Metallurgical Corporation, 20
Oregon Steel Mills, Inc., 14
Outokumpu Oyj, 38
Park Corp., 22
Peabody Coal Company, 10
Peabody Energy Corporation, 45 (upd.)
Peabody Holding Company, Inc., IV
Pechiney SA, IV; 45 (upd.)

Peter Kiewit Sons' Inc., 8
Phelps Dodge Corporation, IV; 28 (upd.)
The Pittston Company, IV; 19 (upd.)
Placer Dome Inc., 20
Pohang Iron and Steel Company Ltd., IV
Potash Corporation of Saskatchewan Inc.,
  18
Quanex Corporation, 13
RAG AG, 35
Reliance Steel & Aluminum Co., 19
Republic Engineered Steels, Inc., 7; 26
  (upd.)
Reynolds Metals Company, IV
Rio Tinto PLC, 19 (upd.); 50 (upd.)
RMC Group p.l.c., 34 (upd.)
Roanoke Electric Steel Corporation, 45
Rouge Steel Company, 8
The RTZ Corporation PLC, IV
Ruhrkohle AG, IV
Ryerson Tull, Inc., 40 (upd.)
Saarberg-Konzern, IV
Salzgitter AG, IV
Sandvik AB, IV
Schnitzer Steel Industries, Inc., 19
Southern Peru Copper Corporation, 40
Southwire Company, Inc., 8; 23 (upd.)
Steel Authority of India Ltd., IV
Stelco Inc., IV
Stillwater Mining Company, 47
Sumitomo Metal Industries, Ltd., IV
Sumitomo Metal Mining Co., Ltd., IV
Tata Iron & Steel Co. Ltd., IV; 44 (upd.)
Teck Corporation, 27
Texas Industries, Inc., 8
Thyssen AG, IV
The Timken Company, 8; 42 (upd.)
Titanium Metals Corporation, 21
Tomen Corporation, IV
Total Fina Elf S.A., 50 (upd.)
U.S. Borax, Inc., 42
Ugine S.A., 20
NV Umicore SA, 47
Usinor SA, IV; 42 (upd.)
Usinor Sacilor, IV
VIAG Aktiengesellschaft, IV
Voest-Alpine Stahl AG, IV
Vulcan Materials Company, 52 (upd.)
Walter Industries, Inc., 22 (upd.)
Weirton Steel Corporation, IV; 26 (upd.)
Westmoreland Coal Company, 7
Wheeling-Pittsburgh Corp., 7
WMC, Limited, 43
Worthington Industries, Inc., 7; 21 (upd.)
Zambia Industrial and Mining Corporation
  Ltd., IV

PAPER & FORESTRY

Abitibi-Consolidated, Inc., 25 (upd.)
Abitibi-Price Inc., IV
Albany International Corporation, 51 (upd.)
Amcor Limited, IV; 19 (upd.)
American Pad & Paper Company, 20
Arjo Wiggins Appleton p.l.c., 34
Asplundh Tree Expert Co., 20
Avery Dennison Corporation, IV
Badger Paper Mills, Inc., 15
Beckett Papers, 23
Bemis Company, Inc., 8
Bohemia, Inc., 13
Boise Cascade Corporation, IV; 8 (upd.);
  32 (upd.)
Bowater PLC, IV
Bunzl plc, IV
Canfor Corporation, 42
Caraustar Industries, Inc., 19; 44 (upd.)
Carter Lumber Company, 45

PAPER & FORESTRY (continued)

Champion International Corporation, IV; 20 (upd.)
Chesapeake Corporation, 8; 30 (upd.)
Consolidated Papers, Inc., 8; 36 (upd.)
Crane & Co., Inc., 26
Crown Vantage Inc., 29
CSS Industries, Inc., 35
Daio Paper Corporation, IV
Daishowa Paper Manufacturing Co., Ltd., IV
Deltic Timber Corporation, 46
Dillard Paper Company, 11
Domtar Inc., IV
Enso-Gutzeit Oy, IV
Esselte Pendaflex Corporation, 11
Federal Paper Board Company, Inc., 8
FiberMark, Inc., 37
Fletcher Challenge Ltd., IV
Fort Howard Corporation, 8
Fort James Corporation, 22 (upd.)
Georgia-Pacific Corporation, IV; 9 (upd.); 47 (upd.)
Groupe Rougier SA, 21
Guilbert S.A., 42
Holmen AB, 52 (upd.)
Honshu Paper Co., Ltd., IV
International Paper Company, IV; 15 (upd.); 47 (upd.)
James River Corporation of Virginia, IV
Japan Pulp and Paper Company Limited, IV
Jefferson Smurfit Group plc, IV; 49 (upd.)
Jujo Paper Co., Ltd., IV
Kimberly-Clark Corporation, 16 (upd.); 43 (upd.)
Kimberly-Clark de México, S.A. de C.V., 54
Kruger Inc., 17
Kymmene Corporation, IV
Longview Fibre Company, 8; 37 (upd.)
Louisiana-Pacific Corporation, IV; 31 (upd.)
MacMillan Bloedel Limited, IV
The Mead Corporation, IV; 19 (upd.)
Metsa-Serla Oy, IV
Mo och Domsjö AB, IV
Monadnock Paper Mills, Inc., 21
Mosinee Paper Corporation, 15
Nashua Corporation, 8
National Envelope Corporation, 32
NCH Corporation, 8
Oji Paper Co., Ltd., IV
P.H. Glatfelter Company, 8; 30 (upd.)
Packaging Corporation of America, 12
Papeteries de Lancey, 23
Plum Creek Timber Company, Inc., 43
Pope and Talbot, Inc., 12
Potlatch Corporation, 8; 34 (upd.)
PWA Group, IV
Rayonier Inc., 24
Rengo Co., Ltd., IV
Reno de Medici S.p.A., 41
Rexam PLC, 32 (upd.)
Riverwood International Corporation, 11; 48 (upd.)
Rock-Tenn Company, 13
St. Joe Paper Company, 8
Sanyo-Kokusaku Pulp Co., Ltd., IV
Sappi Limited, 49
Schweitzer-Mauduit International, Inc., 52
Scott Paper Company, IV; 31 (upd.)
Sealed Air Corporation, 14
Sierra Pacific Industries, 22
Simpson Investment Company, 17
Specialty Coatings Inc., 8
Stone Container Corporation, IV

Stora Enso Oyj, 36 (upd.)
Stora Kopparbergs Bergslags AB, IV
Svenska Cellulosa Aktiebolaget SCA, IV; 28 (upd.)
Temple-Inland Inc., IV; 31 (upd.)
TJ International, Inc., 19
U.S. Timberlands Company, L.P., 42
Union Camp Corporation, IV
United Paper Mills Ltd. (Yhtyneet Paperitehtaat Oy), IV
Universal Forest Products Inc., 10
UPM-Kymmene Corporation, 19; 50 (upd.)
West Fraser Timber Co. Ltd., 17
Westvaco Corporation, IV; 19 (upd.)
Weyerhaeuser Company, IV; 9 (upd.); 28 (upd.)
Wickes Inc., 25 (upd.)
Willamette Industries, Inc., IV; 31 (upd.)
WTD Industries, Inc., 20

PERSONAL SERVICES

AARP, 27
ADT Security Services, Inc., 12; 44 (upd.)
American Retirement Corporation, 42
Arthur Murray International, Inc., 32
Berlitz International, Inc., 39 (upd.)
Carriage Services, Inc., 37
CDI Corporation, 54 (upd.)
Childtime Learning Centers, Inc., 34
Chubb, PLC, 50
Corinthian Colleges, Inc., 39
Correctional Services Corporation, 30
CUC International Inc., 16
Curves International, Inc., 54
Davis Service Group PLC, 45
DeVry Incorporated, 29
Educational Testing Service, 12
The Ford Foundation, 34
Franklin Quest Co., 11
Goodwill Industries International, Inc., 16
Gunnebo AB, 53
The Humane Society of the United States, 54
Huntington Learning Centers, Inc., 55
Jazzercise, Inc., 45
The John D. and Catherine T. MacArthur Foundation, 34
Kaplan, Inc., 42
KinderCare Learning Centers, Inc., 13
Knowledge Learning Corporation, 51
The Loewen Group Inc., 16; 40 (upd.)
Management and Training Corporation, 28
Manpower, Inc., 9
Michael Page International plc, 45
Mothers Against Drunk Driving (MADD), 51
National Organization for Women, Inc., 55
Prison Rehabilitative Industries and Diversified Enterprises, Inc. (PRIDE), 53
Recording for the Blind & Dyslexic, 51
Regis Corporation, 18
The Rockefeller Foundation, 34
Rollins, Inc., 11
Rosenbluth International Inc., 14
Rotary International, 31
The Salvation Army USA, 32
Service Corporation International, 6; 51 (upd.)
SOS Staffing Services, 25
Stewart Enterprises, Inc., 20
Supercuts Inc., 26
Weight Watchers International Inc., 12; 33 (upd.)
The York Group, Inc., 50
Youth Services International, Inc., 21
YWCA of the U.S.A., 45

PETROLEUM

Abu Dhabi National Oil Company, IV; 45 (upd.)
Agway, Inc., 21 (upd.)
Alberta Energy Company Ltd., 16; 43 (upd.)
Amerada Hess Corporation, IV; 21 (upd.); 55 (upd.)
Amoco Corporation, IV; 14 (upd.)
Anadarko Petroleum Corporation, 10; 52 (upd.)
ANR Pipeline Co., 17
Anschutz Corp., 12
Apache Corporation, 10; 32 (upd.)
Arctic Slope Regional Corporation, 38
Ashland Inc., 19; 50 (upd.)
Ashland Oil, Inc., IV
Atlantic Richfield Company, IV; 31 (upd.)
Baker Hughes Incorporated, 22 (upd.)
Belco Oil & Gas Corp., 40
Benton Oil and Gas Company, 47
Berry Petroleum Company, 47
BJ Services Company, 25
BP p.l.c., 45 (upd.)
The British Petroleum Company plc, IV; 7 (upd.); 21 (upd.)
British-Borneo Oil & Gas PLC, 34
Broken Hill Proprietary Company Ltd., 22 (upd.)
Burlington Resources Inc., 10
Burmah Castrol PLC, IV; 30 (upd.)
Callon Petroleum Company, 47
Caltex Petroleum Corporation, 19
Chevron Corporation, IV; 19 (upd.)
ChevronTexaco Corporation, 47 (upd.)
Chiles Offshore Corporation, 9
China National Petroleum Corporation, 46
Chinese Petroleum Corporation, IV; 31 (upd.)
CITGO Petroleum Corporation, IV; 31 (upd.)
The Coastal Corporation, IV; 31 (upd.)
Compañia Española de Petróleos S.A., IV
Comstock Resources, Inc., 47
Conoco Inc., IV; 16 (upd.)
Cooper Cameron Corporation, 20 (upd.)
Cosmo Oil Co., Ltd., IV; 53 (upd.)
Crown Central Petroleum Corporation, 7
DeepTech International Inc., 21
Den Norske Stats Oljeselskap AS, IV
Deutsche BP Aktiengesellschaft, 7
Diamond Shamrock, Inc., IV
Dynegy Inc., 49 (upd.)
E.On AG, 50 (upd.)
Egyptian General Petroleum Corporation, IV; 51 (upd.)
Elf Aquitaine SA, 21 (upd.)
Empresa Colombiana de Petróleos, IV
Enbridge Inc., 43
Energen Corporation, 21
Enron Corporation, 19
Ente Nazionale Idrocarburi, IV
Enterprise Oil PLC, 11; 50 (upd.)
Entreprise Nationale Sonatrach, IV
Equitable Resources, Inc., 54 (upd.)
Exxon Corporation, IV; 7 (upd.); 32 (upd.)
Ferrellgas Partners, L.P., 35
FINA, Inc., 7
Flying J Inc., 19
Forest Oil Corporation, 19
OAO Gazprom, 42
General Sekiyu K.K., IV
Giant Industries, Inc., 19
Global Industries, Ltd., 37
Global Marine Inc., 9
GlobalSantaFe Corporation, 48 (upd.)
Grey Wolf, Inc., 43

Halliburton Company, 25 (upd.); 55 (upd.)
Helmerich & Payne, Inc., 18
Holly Corporation, 12
Hunt Consolidated, Inc., 27 (upd.)
Hunt Oil Company, 7
Hurricane Hydrocarbons Ltd., 54
Husky Energy Inc., 47
Idemitsu Kosan Co., Ltd., 49 (upd.)
Idemitsu Kosan K.K., IV
Imperial Oil Limited, IV; 25 (upd.)
Indian Oil Corporation Ltd., IV; 48 (upd.)
Kanematsu Corporation, IV
Kerr-McGee Corporation, IV; 22 (upd.)
Kinder Morgan, Inc., 45
King Ranch, Inc., 14
Koch Industries, Inc., IV; 20 (upd.)
Koppers Industries, Inc., 26 (upd.)
Kuwait Petroleum Corporation, IV; 55 (upd.)
Libyan National Oil Corporation, IV
The Louisiana Land and Exploration Company, 7
OAO LUKOIL, 40
Lyondell Petrochemical Company, IV
MAPCO Inc., IV
Maxus Energy Corporation, 7
McDermott International, Inc., 37 (upd.)
Meteor Industries Inc., 33
Mitchell Energy and Development Corporation, 7
Mitsubishi Oil Co., Ltd., IV
Mobil Corporation, IV; 7 (upd.); 21 (upd.)
Murphy Oil Corporation, 7; 32 (upd.)
Nabors Industries, Inc., 9
National Iranian Oil Company, IV
Neste Oy, IV
NGC Corporation, 18
Nigerian National Petroleum Corporation, IV
Nippon Oil Company, Limited, IV
OAO NK YUKOS, 47
Noble Affiliates, Inc., 11
OAO Gazprom, 42
OAO LUKOIL, 40
OAO NK YUKOS, 47
OAO Siberian Oil Company (Sibneft), 49
OAO Surgutneftegaz, 48
OAO Tatneft, 45
Occidental Petroleum Corporation, IV; 25 (upd.)
Oil and Natural Gas Commission, IV
ÖMV Aktiengesellschaft, IV
Oryx Energy Company, 7
Parker Drilling Company, 28
Patina Oil & Gas Corporation, 24
Patterson-UTI Energy, Inc., 55
Pennzoil-Quaker State Company, IV; 20 (upd.); 50 (upd.)
PERTAMINA, IV
Petro-Canada Limited, IV
PetroFina S.A., IV; 26 (upd.)
Petróleo Brasileiro S.A., IV
Petróleos de Portugal S.A., IV
Petróleos de Venezuela S.A., IV
Petróleos del Ecuador, IV
Petróleos Mexicanos, IV; 19 (upd.)
Petroleum Development Oman LLC, IV
Petronas, IV
Phillips Petroleum Company, IV; 40 (upd.)
Pogo Producing Company, 39
Premcor Inc., 37
Qatar General Petroleum Corporation, IV
Quaker State Corporation, 7; 21 (upd.)
Range Resources Corporation, 45
Repsol S.A., IV; 16 (upd.)
Repsol-YPF S.A., 40 (upd.)
Resource America, Inc., 42

Rowan Companies, Inc., 43
Royal Dutch Petroleum Company/ The "Shell" Transport and Trading Company p.l.c., IV
Royal Dutch/Shell Group, 49 (upd.)
RWE AG, 50 (upd.)
Santa Fe International Corporation, 38
Sasol Limited, IV; 47 (upd.)
Saudi Arabian Oil Company, IV; 17 (upd.); 50 (upd.)
Schlumberger Limited, 17 (upd.)
Seagull Energy Corporation, 11
Seitel, Inc., 47
Shanghai Petrochemical Co., Ltd., 18
Shell Oil Company, IV; 14 (upd.); 41 (upd.)
Showa Shell Sekiyu K.K., IV
OAO Siberian Oil Company (Sibneft), 49
Société Nationale Elf Aquitaine, IV; 7 (upd.)
Suburban Propane Partners, L.P., 30
Sun Company, Inc., IV
Suncor Energy Inc., 54
Sunoco, Inc., 28 (upd.)
OAO Surgutneftegaz, 48
Talisman Energy Inc., 9; 47 (upd.)
OAO Tatneft, 45
Tesoro Petroleum Corporation, 7; 45 (upd.)
Texaco Inc., IV; 14 (upd.); 41 (upd.)
Tidewater Inc., 37 (upd.)
Tom Brown, Inc., 37
Tonen Corporation, IV; 16 (upd.)
TonenGeneral Sekiyu K.K., 54 (upd.)
Tosco Corporation, 7
TOTAL S.A., IV; 24 (upd.)
TransMontaigne Inc., 28
Transocean Sedco Forex Inc., 45
Travel Ports of America, Inc., 17
Triton Energy Corporation, 11
Türkiye Petrolleri Anonim Ortakliği, IV
Ultramar Diamond Shamrock Corporation, IV; 31 (upd.)
Union Texas Petroleum Holdings, Inc., 9
Unocal Corporation, IV; 24 (upd.)
USX Corporation, IV; 7 (upd.)
Valero Energy Corporation, 7
Varco International, Inc., 42
Vastar Resources, Inc., 24
Vintage Petroleum, Inc., 42
Wascana Energy Inc., 13
Weatherford International, Inc., 39
Western Atlas Inc., 12
Western Company of North America, 15
Western Gas Resources, Inc., 45
The Williams Companies, Inc., IV; 31 (upd.)
World Fuel Services Corporation, 47
XTO Energy Inc., 52
YPF Sociedad Anonima, IV

PUBLISHING & PRINTING

A.B.Dick Company, 28
A.H. Belo Corporation, 10; 30 (upd.)
Advance Publications Inc., IV; 19 (upd.)
Advanced Marketing Services, Inc., 34
Affiliated Publications, Inc., 7
Agence France-Presse, 34
American Banknote Corporation, 30
American Greetings Corporation, 7, 22 (upd.)
American Media, Inc., 27
American Printing House for the Blind, 26
Andrews McMeel Universal, 40
The Antioch Company, 40
Arandell Corporation, 37
Arnoldo Mondadori Editore S.p.A., IV; 19 (upd.); 54 (upd.)

The Associated Press, 31 (upd.)
The Atlantic Group, 23
Axel Springer Verlag AG, IV; 20 (upd.)
Banta Corporation, 12; 32 (upd.)
Bauer Publishing Group, 7
Bayard SA, 49
Berlitz International, Inc., 13
Bernard C. Harris Publishing Company, Inc., 39
Bertelsmann A.G., IV; 15 (upd.); 43 (upd.)
Big Flower Press Holdings, Inc., 21
Blue Mountain Arts, Inc., 29
Bobit Publishing Company, 55
Bonnier AB, 52
Book-of-the-Month Club, Inc., 13
Bowne & Co., Inc., 23
Broderbund Software, 13; 29 (upd.)
Brown Printing Company, 26
Burda Holding GmbH. & Co., 23
The Bureau of National Affairs, Inc., 23
Butterick Co., Inc., 23
Cadmus Communications Corporation, 23
Cahners Business Information, 43
CCH Inc., 14
Central Newspapers, Inc., 10
Champion Industries, Inc., 28
The Christian Science Publishing Society, 55
The Chronicle Publishing Company, Inc., 23
Chrysalis Group plc, 40
CMP Media Inc., 26
Commerce Clearing House, Inc., 7
Concepts Direct, Inc., 39
The Condé Nast Publications Inc., 13
Consumers Union, 26
The Copley Press, Inc., 23
Courier Corporation, 41
Cowles Media Company, 23
Cox Enterprises, Inc., IV; 22 (upd.)
Crain Communications, Inc., 12; 35 (upd.)
Current, Inc., 37
Dai Nippon Printing Co., Ltd., IV
Daily Mail and General Trust plc, 19
Dawson Holdings PLC, 43
Day Runner, Inc., 14
DC Comics Inc., 25
De La Rue plc, 10; 34 (upd.)
DeLorme Publishing Company, Inc., 53
Deluxe Corporation, 7; 22 (upd.)
Dorling Kindersley Holdings plc, 20
Dover Publications Inc., 34
Dow Jones & Company, Inc., IV; 19 (upd.); 47 (upd.)
The Dun & Bradstreet Corporation, IV; 19 (upd.)
Duplex Products Inc., 17
The E.W. Scripps Company, IV; 7 (upd.); 28 (upd.)
Edmark Corporation, 14
Electronics for Imaging, Inc., 43 (upd.)
Elsevier N.V., IV
EMAP plc, 35
EMI Group plc, 22 (upd.)
Encyclopaedia Britannica, Inc., 7; 39 (upd.)
Engraph, Inc., 12
Enquirer/Star Group, Inc., 10
Entravision Communications Corporation, 41
Essence Communications, Inc., 24
Farm Journal Corporation, 42
Farrar, Straus and Giroux Inc., 15
Flint Ink Corporation, 13
Follett Corporation, 12; 39 (upd.)
Forbes Inc., 30
Franklin Electronic Publishers, Inc., 23
Freedom Communications, Inc., 36

PUBLISHING & PRINTING (*continued*)

Gannett Co., Inc., IV; 7 (upd.); 30 (upd.)
Gibson Greetings, Inc., 12
Golden Books Family Entertainment, Inc., 28
Goss Holdings, Inc., 43
Graphic Industries Inc., 25
Gray Communications Systems, Inc., 24
Grolier Incorporated, 16; 43 (upd.)
Groupe de la Cite, IV
Groupe Les Echos, 25
Grupo Televisa, S.A., 54 (upd.)
Guardian Media Group plc, 53
Hachette, IV
Hachette Filipacchi Medias S.A., 21
Hallmark Cards, Inc., IV; 16 (upd.); 40 (upd.)
Harcourt Brace and Co., 12
Harcourt Brace Jovanovich, Inc., IV
Harcourt General, Inc., 20 (upd.)
Harlequin Enterprises Limited, 52
HarperCollins Publishers, 15
Harris Interactive Inc., 41
Harte-Hanks Communications, Inc., 17
Havas SA, 10; 33 (upd.)
Hazelden Foundation, 28
The Hearst Corporation, IV; 19 (upd.); 46 (upd.)
Her Majesty's Stationery Office, 7
N.V. Holdingmaatschappij De Telegraaf, 23
Hollinger International Inc., 24
Houghton Mifflin Company, 10; 36 (upd.)
IDG Books Worldwide, Inc., 27
Information Holdings Inc., 47
International Data Group, Inc., 7; 25 (upd.)
IPC Magazines Limited, 7
John Fairfax Holdings Limited, 7
John H. Harland Company, 17
John Wiley & Sons, Inc., 17
Johnson Publishing Company, Inc., 28
Johnston Press plc, 35
Jostens, Inc., 25 (upd.)
Journal Register Company, 29
Kaplan, Inc., 42
Kinko's, Inc., 43 (upd.)
Knight-Ridder, Inc., IV; 15 (upd.)
Kodansha Ltd., IV; 38 (upd.)
Krause Publications, Inc., 35
Landmark Communications, Inc., 12; 55 (upd.)
Larry Flynt Publishing Inc., 31
Le Monde S.A., 33
Lebhar-Friedman, Inc., 55
Lee Enterprises, Incorporated, 11
LEXIS-NEXIS Group, 33
Lonely Planet Publications Pty Ltd., 55
M. Shanken Communications, Inc., 50
Maclean Hunter Publishing Limited, IV; 26 (upd.)
Macmillan, Inc., 7
Martha Stewart Living Omnimedia, L.L.C., 24
Marvel Entertainment Group, Inc., 10
Matra-Hachette S.A., 15 (upd.)
Maxwell Communication Corporation plc, IV; 7 (upd.)
McClatchy Newspapers, Inc., 23
The McGraw-Hill Companies, Inc., IV; 18 (upd.); 51 (upd.)
Mecklermedia Corporation, 24
Media General, Inc., 38 (upd.)
Meredith Corporation, 11; 29 (upd.)
Merrill Corporation, 18; 47 (upd.)
The Miner Group International, 22
Mirror Group Newspapers plc, 7; 23 (upd.)
Moore Corporation Limited, IV

Morris Communications Corporation, 36
Multimedia, Inc., 11
National Audubon Society, 26
National Geographic Society, 9; 30 (upd.)
New Times, Inc., 45
New York Daily News, 32
The New York Times Company, IV; 19 (upd.)
News America Publishing Inc., 12
News Corporation Limited, IV; 7 (upd.)
Newsquest plc, 32
Nihon Keizai Shimbun, Inc., IV
Nolo.com, Inc., 49
Ottaway Newspapers, Inc., 15
Outlook Group Corporation, 37
Pantone Inc., 53
PCM Uitgevers NV, 53
Pearson plc, IV; 46 (upd.)
PennWell Corporation, 55
Penton Media, Inc., 27
Petersen Publishing Company, 21
Plato Learning, Inc., 44
Playboy Enterprises, Inc., 18
Pleasant Company, 27
PR Newswire, 35
Primedia Inc., 22
The Providence Journal Company, 28
Publishers Group, Inc., 35
Publishing and Broadcasting Limited, 54
Pulitzer Publishing Company, 15
Quad/Graphics, Inc., 19
Quebecor Inc., 12; 47 (upd.)
R.L. Polk & Co., 10
R.R. Donnelley & Sons Company, IV; 9 (upd.); 38 (upd.)
Rand McNally & Company, 28
Random House Inc., 13; 31 (upd.)
The Reader's Digest Association, Inc., IV; 17 (upd.)
Recycled Paper Greetings, Inc., 21
Reed Elsevier plc, 31 (upd.)
Reed International PLC, IV; 17 (upd.)
Reuters Holdings PLC, IV; 22 (upd.)
Rodale Press, Inc., 23
Rodale, Inc., 47 (upd.)
Rogers Communications Inc., 30 (upd.)
St Ives plc, 34
SanomaWSOY Corporation, 51
Schawk, Inc., 24
Schibsted ASA, 31
Scholastic Corporation, 10; 29 (upd.)
Scott Fetzer Company, 12
Scottish Media Group plc, 32
Seat Pagine Gialle S.p.A., 47
Seattle Times Company, 15
The Sierra Club, 28
Simon & Schuster Inc., IV; 19 (upd.)
Sir Speedy, Inc., 16
SkyMall, Inc., 26
Softbank Corp., 13
Southam Inc., 7
SPIEGEL-Verlag Rudolf Augstein GmbH & Co. KG, 44
Standard Register Co., 15
Tamedia AG, 53
Taylor & Francis Group plc, 44
Taylor Corporation, 36
Taylor Publishing Company, 12; 36 (upd.)
Thomas Nelson, Inc., 14; 38 (upd.)
Thomas Publishing Company, 26
The Thomson Corporation, 8; 34 (upd.)
The Times Mirror Company, IV; 17 (upd.)
Tom Doherty Associates Inc., 25
Toppan Printing Co., Ltd., IV
The Topps Company, Inc., 34 (upd.)
Torstar Corporation, 29
Tribune Company, IV, 22 (upd.)

Trinity Mirror plc, 49 (upd.)
U.S. News and World Report Inc., 30
United Business Media plc, 52 (upd.)
United News & Media plc, 28 (upd.)
United Newspapers plc, IV
United Press International, Inc., 25
Valassis Communications, Inc., 8
Value Line, Inc., 16
Verlagsgruppe Georg von Holtzbrinck GmbH, 35
Village Voice Media, Inc., 38
VNU N.V., 27
Volt Information Sciences Inc., 26
W.W. Norton & Company, Inc., 28
Wallace Computer Services, Inc., 36
The Washington Post Company, IV; 20 (upd.)
Waverly, Inc., 16
Wegener NV, 53
Wenner Media, Inc., 32
West Group, 7; 34 (upd.)
Western Publishing Group, Inc., 13
WH Smith PLC, V; 42 (upd.)
Wolters Kluwer NV, 14; 33 (upd.)
World Book, Inc., 12
World Color Press Inc., 12
Xeikon NV, 26
Zebra Technologies Corporation, 14
Ziff Communications Company, 12
Ziff Davis Media Inc., 36 (upd.)
Zondervan Publishing House, 24

REAL ESTATE

Alexander's, Inc., 45
Amfac/JMB Hawaii L.L.C., 24 (upd.)
Apartment Investment and Management Company, 49
Archstone-Smith Trust, 49
Associated Estates Realty Corporation, 25
Berkshire Realty Holdings, L.P., 49
Boston Properties, Inc., 22
Bramalea Ltd., 9
British Land Plc, 54
Canary Wharf Group Plc, 30
CapStar Hotel Company, 21
Castle & Cooke, Inc., 20 (upd.)
Catellus Development Corporation, 24
CB Commercial Real Estate Services Group, Inc., 21
Chateau Communities, Inc., 37
Cheung Kong (Holdings) Limited, IV; 20 (upd.)
Clayton Homes Incorporated, 54 (upd.)
Del Webb Corporation, 14
The Edward J. DeBartolo Corporation, 8
Equity Office Properties Trust, 54
Equity Residential, 49
Fairfield Communities, Inc., 36
Forest City Enterprises, Inc., 16; 52 (upd.)
Gecina SA, 42
Griffin Land & Nurseries, Inc., 43
Grubb & Ellis Company, 21
The Haminerson Property Investment and Development Corporation plc, IV
Hammerson plc, 40
Harbert Corporation, 14
Helmsley Enterprises, Inc., 39 (upd.)
Home Properties of New York, Inc., 42
Hongkong Land Holdings Limited, IV; 47 (upd.)
Hyatt Corporation, 16 (upd.)
J.F. Shea Co., Inc., 55
JMB Realty Corporation, IV
Jones Lang LaSalle Incorporated, 49
JPI, 49
Kaufman and Broad Home Corporation, 8
Kerry Properties Limited, 22

Kimco Realty Corporation, 11
The Koll Company, 8
Land Securities PLC, IV; 49 (upd.)
Lefrak Organization Inc., 26
Lend Lease Corporation Limited, IV; 17 (upd.); 52 (upd.)
Lincoln Property Company, 8; 54 (upd.)
The Loewen Group Inc., 40 (upd.)
Mack-Cali Realty Corporation, 42
Manufactured Home Communities, Inc., 22
Maui Land & Pineapple Company, Inc., 29
Maxco Inc., 17
Meditrust, 11
Melvin Simon and Associates, Inc., 8
MEPC plc, IV
Meritage Corporation, 26
The Middleton Doll Company, 53
Mitsubishi Estate Company, Limited, IV
Mitsui Real Estate Development Co., Ltd., IV
The Nature Conservancy, 28
New Plan Realty Trust, 11
New World Development Company Ltd., IV
Newhall Land and Farming Company, 14
Olympia & York Developments Ltd., IV; 9 (upd.)
Park Corp., 22
Perini Corporation, 8
Post Properties, Inc., 26
Public Storage, Inc., 52
Railtrack Group PLC, 50
Reckson Associates Realty Corp., 47
Rodamco N.V., 26
The Rouse Company, 15
Shubert Organization Inc., 24
The Sierra Club, 28
Silverstein Properties, Inc., 47
Simco S.A., 37
SL Green Realty Corporation, 44
Slough Estates PLC, IV; 50 (upd.)
Starrett Corporation, 21
Storage USA, Inc., 21
Sumitomo Realty & Development Co., Ltd., IV
Sun Communities Inc., 46
Tanger Factory Outlet Centers, Inc., 49
Tarragon Realty Investors, Inc., 45
Taylor Woodrow plc, 38 (upd.)
Tejon Ranch Company, 35
Tishman Speyer Properties, L.P., 47
Tokyu Land Corporation, IV
Trammell Crow Company, 8
Trendwest Resorts, Inc., 33
Tridel Enterprises Inc., 9
Trizec Corporation Ltd., 10
Trump Organization, 23
Unibail SA, 40
United Dominion Realty Trust, Inc., 52
Vistana, Inc., 22
Vornado Realty Trust, 20
W.P. Carey & Co. LLC, 49

RETAIL & WHOLESALE

A.C. Moore Arts & Crafts, Inc., 30
A.T. Cross Company, 49 (upd.)
Aaron Rents, Inc., 14; 35 (upd.)
ABC Appliance, Inc., 10
ABC Carpet & Home Co. Inc., 26
Abercrombie & Fitch Co., 15
Academy Sports & Outdoors, 27
Ace Hardware Corporation, 12; 35 (upd.)
Action Performance Companies, Inc., 27
Alain Afflelou SA, 53
Alba-Waldensian, Inc., 30
Alberto-Culver Company, 36 (upd.)
Alldays plc, 49

Allders plc, 37
Allou Health & Beauty Care, Inc., 28
Amazon.com, Inc., 25
American Coin Merchandising, Inc., 28
American Eagle Outfitters, Inc., 24; 55 (upd.)
American Furniture Company, Inc., 21
American Stores Company, 22 (upd.)
AmeriSource Health Corporation, 37 (upd.)
Ames Department Stores, Inc., 9; 30 (upd.)
Amway Corporation, 13; 30 (upd.)
The Andersons, Inc., 31
AnnTaylor Stores Corporation, 13; 37 (upd.)
Appliance Recycling Centers of America, Inc., 42
Arbor Drugs Inc., 12
Arcadia Group plc, 28 (upd.)
Army and Air Force Exchange Service, 39
Art Van Furniture, Inc., 28
ASDA Group plc, 28 (upd.)
Ashworth, Inc., 26
Au Printemps S.A., V
Audio King Corporation, 24
Authentic Fitness Corporation, 20; 51 (upd.)
Auto Value Associates, Inc., 25
Autobytel Inc., 47
AutoNation, Inc., 50
AutoZone, Inc., 9; 31 (upd.)
AVA AG (Allgemeine Handelsgesellschaft der Verbraucher AG), 33
Aveda Corporation, 24
Aviation Sales Company, 41
B. Dalton Bookseller Inc., 25
Babbage's, Inc., 10
Baby Superstore, Inc., 15
Baccarat, 24
Bachman's Inc., 22
Banana Republic Inc., 25
Barnes & Noble, Inc., 10; 30 (upd.)
Barnett Inc., 28
Barney's, Inc., 28
Bass Pro Shops, Inc., 42
Bear Creek Corporation, 38
Bearings, Inc., 13
bebe stores, inc., 31
Bed Bath & Beyond Inc., 13; 41 (upd.)
Belk Stores Services, Inc., V; 19 (upd.)
Bergdorf Goodman Inc., 52
Bergen Brunswig Corporation, V; 13 (upd.)
Bernard Chaus, Inc., 27
Best Buy Co., Inc., 9; 23 (upd.)
Bhs plc, 17
Big Dog Holdings, Inc., 45
Big 5 Sporting Goods Corporation, 55
Big Lots, Inc., 50
Big O Tires, Inc., 20
Birkenstock Footprint Sandals, Inc., 42 (upd.)
Black Box Corporation, 20
Blacks Leisure Group plc, 39
Blair Corporation, 25; 31 (upd.)
Bloomingdale's Inc., 12
Blue Square Israel Ltd., 41
Blyth Industries, Inc., 18
The Body Shop International PLC, 11
The Bombay Company, Inc., 10
The Bon Marché, Inc., 23
The Bon-Ton Stores, Inc., 16; 50 (upd.)
Books-A-Million, Inc., 14; 41 (upd.)
The Boots Company PLC, V; 24 (upd.)
Borders Group, Inc., 15; 43 (upd.)
Boscov's Department Store, Inc., 31
Bozzuto's, Inc., 13
Bradlees Discount Department Store Company, 12

Brambles Industries Limited, 42
Broder Bros. Co., 38
Brooks Brothers Inc., 22
Brookstone, Inc., 18
The Buckle, Inc., 18
Buhrmann NV, 41
Building Materials Holding Corporation, 52
Burlington Coat Factory Warehouse Corporation, 10
The Burton Group plc, V
Buttrey Food & Drug Stores Co., 18
buy.com, Inc., 46
C&A, V; 40 (upd.)
C&J Clark International Ltd., 52
Cabela's Inc., 26
Cablevision Electronic Instruments, Inc., 32
Cache Incorporated, 30
Caldor Inc., 12
Calloway's Nursery, Inc., 51
Camelot Music, Inc., 26
Campeau Corporation, V
Campo Electronics, Appliances & Computers, Inc., 16
Carrefour SA, 10; 27 (upd.)
Carson Pirie Scott & Company, 15
Carter Hawley Hale Stores, Inc., V
Carter Lumber Company, 45
Cartier Monde, 29
Casual Corner Group, Inc., 43
Casual Male Retail Group, Inc., 52
Catherines Stores Corporation, 15
Cato Corporation, 14
CDW Computer Centers, Inc., 16
Celebrity, Inc., 22
Central Garden & Pet Company, 23
Chadwick's of Boston, Ltd., 29
Charlotte Russe Holding, Inc., 35
Charming Shoppes, Inc., 38
ChevronTexaco Corporation, 47 (upd.)
Chiasso Inc., 53
The Children's Place Retail Stores, Inc., 37
Christian Dior S.A., 49 (upd.)
Christopher & Banks Corporation, 42
Cifra, S.A. de C.V., 12
The Circle K Company, 20 (upd.)
Circuit City Stores, Inc., 9; 29 (upd.)
Clinton Cards plc, 39
The Clothestime, Inc., 20
CML Group, Inc., 10
Co-operative Group (CWS) Ltd., 51
Coach, Inc., 45 (upd.)
Coborn's, Inc., 30
Coinmach Laundry Corporation, 20
Coldwater Creek Inc., 21
Cole National Corporation, 13
Coles Myer Ltd., V; 20 (upd.)
Collectors Universe, Inc., 48
Comdisco, Inc., 9
CompUSA, Inc., 10
Computerland Corp., 13
Concepts Direct, Inc., 39
The Container Store, 36
Controladora Comercial Mexicana, S.A. de C.V., 36
Coop Schweiz Genossenschaftsverband, 48
Corby Distilleries Limited, 14
Corporate Express, Inc., 22; 47 (upd.)
The Cosmetic Center, Inc., 22
Cost Plus, Inc., 27
Costco Wholesale Corporation, V; 43 (upd.)
Cotter & Company, V
County Seat Stores Inc., 9
Courts Plc, 45
CPI Corp., 38
Crate and Barrel, 9
Croscill, Inc., 42

RETAIL & WHOLESALE (*continued*)

Crowley, Milner & Company, 19
Crown Books Corporation, 21
Cumberland Farms, Inc., 17
CVS Corporation, 45 (upd.)
Daffy's Inc., 26
The Daiei, Inc., V; 17 (upd.); 41 (upd.)
The Daimaru, Inc., V; 42 (upd.)
Dairy Mart Convenience Stores, Inc., 25 (upd.)
Daisytek International Corporation, 18
Damark International, Inc., 18
Dart Group Corporation, 16
Darty S.A., 27
David's Bridal, Inc., 33
Dayton Hudson Corporation, V; 18 (upd.)
Deb Shops, Inc., 16
Debenhams Plc, 28
dELiA*s Inc., 29
Department 56, Inc., 34 (upd.)
Designer Holdings Ltd., 20
Deveaux S.A., 41
Diesel SpA, 40
Digital River, Inc., 50
Dillard Department Stores, Inc., V; 16 (upd.)
Dillon Companies Inc., 12
Discount Auto Parts, Inc., 18
Discount Drug Mart, Inc., 14
Dixons Group plc, V; 19 (upd.); 49 (upd.)
Do it Best Corporation, 30
Dollar Tree Stores, Inc., 23
The Dress Barn, Inc., 24; 55 (upd.)
Drug Emporium, Inc., 12
Du Pareil au Même, 43
Duane Reade Holding Corp., 21
Duckwall-ALCO Stores, Inc., 24
Duty Free International, Inc., 11
Dylex Limited, 29
E-Z Serve Corporation, 17
Eagle Hardware & Garden, Inc., 16
eBay Inc., 32
Eckerd Corporation, 9; 32 (upd.)
Eddie Bauer, Inc., 36 (upd.)
Egghead.com, Inc., 31 (upd.)
El Corte Inglés Group, V
Elder-Beerman Stores Corporation, 10
Electrocomponents PLC, 50
Ellett Brothers, Inc., 17
EMI Group plc, 22 (upd.)
Ethan Allen Interiors, Inc., 39 (upd.)
EToys, Inc., 37
Euromarket Designs Inc., 31 (upd.)
Evans, Inc., 30
EZCORP Inc., 43
Family Christian Stores, Inc., 51
Family Dollar Stores, Inc., 13
Fastenal Company, 14; 42 (upd.)
Faultless Starch/Bon Ami Company, 55
Fay's Inc., 17
Federated Department Stores, Inc., 9; 31 (upd.)
Fielmann AG, 31
Fila Holding S.p.A., 20; 52 (upd.)
Fingerhut Companies, Inc., 9; 36 (upd.)
The Finish Line, Inc., 29
Finlay Enterprises, Inc., 16
Fleming Companies, Inc., 17 (upd.)
Florsheim Shoe Group Inc., 9; 31 (upd.)
FNAC, 21
Follett Corporation, 12
Footstar, Incorporated, 24
Fortunoff Fine Jewelry and Silverware Inc., 26
Frank's Nursery & Crafts, Inc., 12
Fred Meyer, Inc., V; 20 (upd.)
Fred's, Inc., 23

Frederick Atkins Inc., 16
Fretter, Inc., 10
Friedman's Inc., 29
Funco, Inc., 20
G.I. Joe's, Inc., 30
Gadzooks, Inc., 18
Gaiam, Inc., 41
Galeries Lafayette S.A., V; 23 (upd.)
Galyan's Trading Company, Inc., 47
Gander Mountain, Inc., 20
Gantos, Inc., 17
The Gap, Inc., V; 18 (upd.); 55 (upd.)
Garden Ridge Corporation, 27
Gart Sports Company, 24
GEHE AG, 27
General Binding Corporation, 10
General Host Corporation, 12
Genesco Inc., 17
Genovese Drug Stores, Inc., 18
Genuine Parts Company, 45 (upd.)
Gerald Stevens, Inc., 37
Giant Food Inc., 22 (upd.)
GIB Group, V; 26 (upd.)
Glacier Water Services, Inc., 47
The Good Guys, Inc., 10; 30 (upd.)
Goodwill Industries International, Inc., 16
Goody's Family Clothing, Inc., 20
Gottschalks, Inc., 18
GrandVision S.A., 43
Graybar Electric Company, Inc., 54
The Great Universal Stores plc, V; 19 (upd.)
Griffin Land & Nurseries, Inc., 43
Grossman's Inc., 13
Groupe Alain Manoukian, 55
Groupe Castorama-Dubois Investissements, 23
Groupe DMC (Dollfus Mieg & Cie), 27
Groupe Go Sport S.A., 39
Groupe Lapeyre S.A., 33
Groupe Zannier S.A., 35
Grow Biz International, Inc., 18
Grupo Casa Saba, S.A. de C.V., 39
Grupo Elektra, S.A. de C.V., 39
Grupo Gigante, S.A. de C.V., 34
Gruppo Coin S.p.A., 41
GT Bicycles, 26
Gucci Group N.V., 50 (upd.)
Guccio Gucci, S.p.A., 15
Guilbert S.A., 42
Guitar Center, Inc., 29
GUS plc, 47 (upd.)
Hahn Automotive Warehouse, Inc., 24
Half Price Books, Records, Magazines Inc., 37
Hallmark Cards, Inc., 40 (upd.)
Hammacher Schlemmer & Company, 21
Hancock Fabrics, Inc., 18
Hankyu Department Stores, Inc., V
Hanna Andersson Corp., 49
Hanover Direct, Inc., 36
Harold's Stores, Inc., 22
Harrods Holdings, 47
Harry Winston Inc., 45
Hasbro, Inc., 43 (upd.)
Haverty Furniture Companies, Inc., 31
Hechinger Company, 12
Heilig-Meyers Company, 14; 40 (upd.)
Helzberg Diamonds, 40
Hennes & Mauritz AB, 29
Henry Modell & Company Inc., 32
Hertie Waren- und Kaufhaus GmbH, V
Hibbett Sporting Goods, Inc., 26
Hills Stores Company, 13
Hines Horticulture, Inc., 49
The Hockey Company, 34
Holiday RV Superstores, Incorporated, 26

Holt's Cigar Holdings, Inc., 42
The Home Depot, Inc., V; 18 (upd.)
Home Interiors & Gifts, Inc., 55
Home Shopping Network, Inc., V; 25 (upd.)
HomeBase, Inc., 33 (upd.)
Hot Topic, Inc., 33
House of Fabrics, Inc., 21
House of Fraser PLC, 45
Hudson's Bay Company, V; 25 (upd.)
IKEA International A/S, V; 26 (upd.)
InaCom Corporation, 13
Insight Enterprises, Inc., 18
International Airline Support Group, Inc., 55
Intimate Brands, Inc., 24
Isetan Company Limited, V; 36 (upd.)
Ito-Yokado Co., Ltd., V; 42 (upd.)
J&R Electronics Inc., 26
J. Baker, Inc., 31
The J. Jill Group, Inc., 35
J.C. Penney Company, Inc., V; 18 (upd.); 43 (upd.)
Jack Schwartz Shoes, Inc., 18
Jacobson Stores Inc., 21
Jalate Inc., 25
James Beattie plc, 43
Jay Jacobs, Inc., 15
Jennifer Convertibles, Inc., 31
Jetro Cash & Carry Enterprises Inc., 38
JG Industries, Inc., 15
JJB Sports plc, 32
John Lewis Partnership plc, V; 42 (upd.)
JUSCO Co., Ltd., V
Just For Feet, Inc., 19
K & B Inc., 12
K & G Men's Center, Inc., 21
Karstadt Aktiengesellschaft, V; 19 (upd.)
Kash n' Karry Food Stores, Inc., 20
Kasper A.S.L., Ltd., 40
Kaufhof Warenhaus AG, V; 23 (upd.)
Kaufring AG, 35
Kay-Bee Toy Stores, 15
Kiehl's Since 1851, Inc., 52
Kingfisher plc, V; 24 (upd.)
Kinney Shoe Corp., 14
Kmart Corporation, V; 18 (upd.); 47 (upd.)
Knoll Group Inc., 14
Kohl's Corporation, 9; 30 (upd.)
Kotobukiya Co., Ltd., V
Krause's Furniture, Inc., 27
L. and J.G. Stickley, Inc., 50
L. Luria & Son, Inc., 19
L.A. T Sportswear, Inc., 26
L.L. Bean, Inc., 38 (upd.)
La-Z-Boy Incorporated, 14; 50 (upd.)
Lamonts Apparel, Inc., 15
Lands' End, Inc., 9; 29 (upd.)
Laura Ashley Holdings plc, 37 (upd.)
Lazare Kaplan International Inc., 21
Lechmere Inc., 10
Lechters, Inc., 11; 39 (upd.)
LensCrafters Inc., 23
Leroy Merlin SA, 54
Lesco Inc., 19
Leslie's Poolmart, Inc., 18
Leupold & Stevens, Inc., 52
Levitz Furniture Inc., 15
Lewis Galoob Toys Inc., 16
Lifetime Hoan Corporation, 27
Lillian Vernon Corporation, 12; 35
The Limited, Inc., V; 20 (upd.)
Linens 'n Things, Inc., 24
Littlewoods plc, V; 42 (upd.)
Liz Claiborne, Inc., 25 (upd.)
Loehmann's Inc., 24

Lojas Arapuã S.A., 22
London Drugs Ltd., 46
Longs Drug Stores Corporation, V; 25 (upd.)
Lost Arrow Inc., 22
LOT$OFF Corporation, 24
Lowe's Companies, Inc., V; 21 (upd.)
Luxottica SpA, 52 (upd.)
Mac Frugal's Bargains - Closeouts Inc., 17
Mac-Gray Corporation, 44
MarineMax, Inc., 30
Marionnaud Parfumeries SA, 51
Marks and Spencer p.l.c., V; 24 (upd.)
Marks Brothers Jewelers, Inc., 24
Marshalls Incorporated, 13
Marui Co., Ltd., V
Maruzen Co., Limited, 18
Mary Kay, Inc., 30 (upd.)
Matalan PLC, 49
Matsuzakaya Company Limited, V
Maus Frères SA, 48
The Maxim Group, 25
The May Department Stores Company, V; 19 (upd.); 46 (upd.)
Mayor's Jewelers, Inc., 41
Mazel Stores, Inc., 29
McKesson Corporation, 47 (upd.)
McLane Company, Inc., 13
MCSi, Inc., 41
Media Arts Group, Inc., 42
Meier & Frank Co., 23
Meijer Incorporated, 27 (upd.)
Melville Corporation, V
The Men's Wearhouse, Inc., 17; 48 (upd.)
Menard, Inc., 34
Mercantile Stores Company, Inc., V; 19 (upd.)
Merry-Go-Round Enterprises, Inc., 8
Mervyn's California, 10; 39 (upd.)
Metro AG, 50
Michael C. Fina Co., Inc., 52
Michaels Stores, Inc., 17
Micro Warehouse, Inc., 16
MicroAge, Inc., 16
Mitsukoshi Ltd., V
Monsoon plc, 39
Montgomery Ward & Co., Incorporated, V; 20 (upd.)
Moore-Handley, Inc., 39
Morse Shoe Inc., 13
Moss Bros Group plc, 51
Mothers Work, Inc., 18
Moto Photo, Inc., 45
Mr. Bricolage S.A., 37
MTS Inc., 37
Musicland Stores Corporation, 9; 38 (upd.)
Nagasakiya Co., Ltd., V
National Educational Music Co. Ltd., 47
National Home Centers, Inc., 44
National Intergroup, Inc., V
National Record Mart, Inc., 29
National Wine & Spirits, Inc., 49
Natural Wonders Inc., 14
Navy Exchange Service Command, 31
Neff Corp., 32
The Neiman Marcus Group, Inc., 12; 49 (upd.)
New Look Group plc, 35
Next plc, 29
Nichii Co., Ltd., V
NIKE, Inc., 36 (upd.)
Nine West Group Inc., 11
99¢ Only Stores, 25
Nocibé SA, 54
Noland Company, 35
Noodle Kidoodle, 16
Nordstrom, Inc., V; 18 (upd.)

Norelco Consumer Products Co., 26
Norm Thompson Outfitters, Inc., 47
The North West Company, Inc., 12
Norton McNaughton, Inc., 27
Nu Skin Enterprises, Inc., 27
Oakley, Inc., 49 (upd.)
Office Depot Incorporated, 8; 23 (upd.)
OfficeMax, Inc., 15; 43 (upd.)
Old America Stores, Inc., 17
One Price Clothing Stores, Inc., 20
Orchard Supply Hardware Stores Corporation, 17
Organización Soriana, S.A. de C.V., 35
The Orvis Company, Inc., 28
OshKosh B'Gosh, Inc., 42 (upd.)
Oshman's Sporting Goods, Inc., 17
Otto Versand (GmbH & Co.), V; 15 (upd.); 34 (upd.)
Owens & Minor, Inc., 16
P.C. Richard & Son Corp., 23
Pamida Holdings Corporation, 15
The Pampered Chef, Ltd., 18
The Pantry, Inc., 36
Parisian, Inc., 14
Party City Corporation, 54
Paul Harris Stores, Inc., 18
Pay 'N Pak Stores, Inc., 9
Payless Cashways, Inc., 11; 44 (upd.)
Payless ShoeSource, Inc., 18
Pearle Vision, Inc., 13
Peebles Inc., 16; 43 (upd.)
Peet's Coffee & Tea, Inc., 38
Petco Animal Supplies, Inc., 29
Petrie Stores Corporation, 8
PETsMART, Inc., 14; 41 (upd.)
Phar-Mor Inc., 12
Pier 1 Imports, Inc., 12; 34 (upd.)
Piercing Pagoda, Inc., 29
Pilot Corporation, 49
Pinault-Printemps Redoute S.A., 19 (upd.)
Pomeroy Computer Resources, Inc., 33
Powell's Books, Inc., 40
The Price Company, V
PriceCostco, Inc., 14
Proffitt's, Inc., 19
Provigo Inc., 51 (upd.)
Purina Mills, Inc., 32
Quelle Group, V
QuikTrip Corporation, 36
Quill Corporation, 28
R.H. Macy & Co., Inc., V; 8 (upd.); 30 (upd.)
RadioShack Corporation, 36 (upd.)
Rag Shops, Inc., 30
Raley's Inc., 14
Rallye SA, 54
Rapala-Normark Group, Ltd., 30
RDO Equipment Company, 33
Reckitt Benckiser plc, 42 (upd.)
Recoton Corp., 15
Recreational Equipment, Inc., 18
Reeds Jewelers, Inc., 22
Rent-A-Center, Inc., 45
Rent-Way, Inc., 33
Restoration Hardware, Inc., 30
Revco D.S., Inc., V
REX Stores Corp., 10
Rhodes Inc., 23
Richton International Corporation, 39
Riklis Family Corp., 9
Rite Aid Corporation, V; 19 (upd.)
Ritz Camera Centers, 34
Roberds Inc., 19
Rocky Shoes & Boots, Inc., 26
Rogers Communications Inc., 30 (upd.)
Rooms To Go Inc., 28
Roots Canada Ltd., 42

Rose's Stores, Inc., 13
Ross Stores, Inc., 17; 43 (upd.)
Roundy's Inc., 14
S&K Famous Brands, Inc., 23
Saks Holdings, Inc., 24
Saks Inc., 41 (upd.)
Sam Ash Music Corporation, 30
Sam's Club, 40
Samuels Jewelers Incorporated, 30
Sanborn Hermanos, S.A., 20
SanomaWSOY Corporation, 51
Schmitt Music Company, 40
Schneiderman's Furniture Inc., 28
Schottenstein Stores Corp., 14
Schultz Sav-O Stores, Inc., 31
The Score Board, Inc., 19
Scotty's, Inc., 22
SCP Pool Corporation, 39
Seaman Furniture Company, Inc., 32
Sears plc, V
Sears Roebuck de México, S.A. de C.V., 20
Sears, Roebuck and Co., V; 18 (upd.)
SED International Holdings, Inc., 43
Seibu Department Stores, Ltd., V; 42 (upd.)
Seigle's Home and Building Centers, Inc., 41
The Seiyu, Ltd., V; 36 (upd.)
Selfridges Plc, 34
Service Merchandise Company, Inc., V; 19 (upd.)
7-Eleven, Inc., 32 (upd.)
Shaklee Corporation, 12
The Sharper Image Corporation, 10
Shoe Carnival Inc., 14
ShopKo Stores Inc., 21
Shoppers Drug Mart Corporation, 49
SkyMall, Inc., 26
Sleepy's Inc., 32
Solo Serve Corporation, 28
Sophus Berendsen A/S, 49
Sound Advice, Inc., 41
Southern States Cooperative Incorporated, 36
Spec's Music, Inc., 19
Spiegel, Inc., 10; 27 (upd.)
Sport Chalet, Inc., 16
Sport Supply Group, Inc., 23
Sportmart, Inc., 15
Sports & Recreation, Inc., 17
The Sports Authority, Inc., 16; 43 (upd.)
The Sportsman's Guide, Inc., 36
Stage Stores, Inc., 24
Stanhome Inc., 15
Staples, Inc., 10; 55 (upd.)
Starbucks Corporation, 34 (upd.)
Starcraft Corporation, 30
Stein Mart Inc., 19
Stinnes AG, 8
The Stop & Shop Companies, Inc., 24 (upd.)
Storehouse PLC, 16
Stride Rite Corporation, 8
Strouds, Inc., 33
Stuller Settings, Inc., 35
Successories, Inc., 30
Sun Television & Appliances Inc., 10
Sunglass Hut International, Inc., 21
Supreme International Corporation, 27
Swarovski International Holding AG, 40
Syms Corporation, 29
Systemax, Inc., 52
Takashimaya Company, Limited, V; 47 (upd.)
The Talbots, Inc., 11; 31 (upd.)
Target Stores, 10; 27 (upd.)

RETAIL & WHOLESALE (*continued*)

Tati SA, 25
Tattered Cover Book Store, 43
Tech Data Corporation, 10
Tengelmann Group, 27
Tesco PLC, 24 (upd.)
Thrifty PayLess, Inc., 12
Tiffany & Co., 14
The Timberland Company, 54 (upd.)
The TJX Companies, Inc., V; 19 (upd.)
Today's Man, Inc., 20
Tokyu Department Store Co., Ltd., V; 32 (upd.)
Tops Appliance City, Inc., 17
Total Fina Elf S.A., 50 (upd.)
Toys ''R'' Us, Inc., V; 18 (upd.)
Travis Boats & Motors, Inc., 37
Travis Perkins plc, 34
Trend-Lines, Inc., 22
TruServ Corporation, 24
Tuesday Morning Corporation, 18
Tupperware Corporation, 28
TVI, Inc., 15
Tweeter Home Entertainment Group, Inc., 30
Ultimate Electronics, Inc., 18
Ultramar Diamond Shamrock Corporation, 31 (upd.)
Uni-Marts, Inc., 17
United Rentals, Inc., 34
The United States Shoe Corporation, V
United Stationers Inc., 14
Universal International, Inc., 25
Uny Co., Ltd., V; 49 (upd.)
Urban Outfitters, Inc., 14
Vallen Corporation, 45
Valley Media Inc., 35
Value City Department Stores, Inc., 38
Value Merchants Inc., 13
ValueVision International, Inc., 22
Vans, Inc., 47 (upd.)
Venator Group Inc., 35 (upd.)
Vendex International N.V., 13
Venture Stores Inc., 12
The Vermont Teddy Bear Co., Inc., 36
VF Corporation, 54 (upd.)
Viking Office Products, Inc., 10
Vivarte SA, 54 (upd.)
Vorwerk & Co., 27
W. Atlee Burpee & Co., 27
W.W. Grainger, Inc., V
Waban Inc., 13
Wacoal Corp., 25
Wal-Mart de Mexico, S.A. de C.V., 35 (upd.)
Wal-Mart Stores, Inc., V; 8 (upd.); 26 (upd.)
Walden Book Company Inc., 17
Walgreen Co., V; 20 (upd.)
Wall Drug Store, Inc., 40
Weiner's Stores, Inc., 33
West Marine, Inc., 17
Western Beef, Inc., 22
The Wet Seal, Inc., 18
Weyco Group, Incorporated, 32
WH Smith PLC, V; 42 (upd.)
Whole Foods Market, Inc., 20
Wickes Inc., V; 25 (upd.)
Williams-Sonoma, Inc., 17; 44 (upd.)
Wilsons The Leather Experts Inc., 21
Wolohan Lumber Co., 19
Woolworth Corporation, V; 20 (upd.)
World Duty Free Americas, Inc., 29 (upd.)
The Yankee Candle Company, Inc., 37
Young's Market Company, LLC, 32
Younkers, Inc., 19
Zale Corporation, 16; 40 (upd.)

Zany Brainy, Inc., 31
Ziebart International Corporation, 30
Zion's Cooperative Mercantile Institution, 33

RUBBER & TIRE

Aeroquip Corporation, 16
Bandag, Inc., 19
The BFGoodrich Company, V
Bridgestone Corporation, V; 21 (upd.)
Carlisle Companies Incorporated, 8
Compagnie Générale des Établissements Michelin, V; 42 (upd.)
Continental Aktiengesellschaft, V
Continental General Tire Corp., 23
Cooper Tire & Rubber Company, 8; 23 (upd.)
Elementis plc, 40 (upd.)
General Tire, Inc., 8
The Goodyear Tire & Rubber Company, V; 20 (upd.)
The Kelly-Springfield Tire Company, 8
Les Schwab Tire Centers, 50
Myers Industries, Inc., 19
Pirelli S.p.A., V; 15 (upd.)
Safeskin Corporation, 18
Sumitomo Rubber Industries, Ltd., V
Tillotson Corp., 15
Treadco, Inc., 19
Ube Industries, Ltd., 38 (upd.)
The Yokohama Rubber Co., Ltd., V; 19 (upd.)

TELECOMMUNICATIONS

A.H. Belo Corporation, 30 (upd.)
Acme-Cleveland Corp., 13
ADC Telecommunications, Inc., 10
Adelphia Communications Corporation, 17; 52 (upd.)
Adtran Inc., 22
AEI Music Network Inc., 35
AirTouch Communications, 11
Alcatel S.A., 36 (upd.)
Alliance Atlantis Communications Inc., 39
ALLTEL Corporation, 6; 46 (upd.)
American Telephone and Telegraph Company, V
American Tower Corporation, 33
Ameritech Corporation, V; 18 (upd.)
Amstrad plc, 48 (upd.)
AO VimpelCom, 48
Arch Wireless, Inc., 39
ARD, 41
Ascom AG, 9
Aspect Telecommunications Corporation, 22
AT&T Bell Laboratories, Inc., 13
AT&T Corporation, 29 (upd.)
AT&T Wireless Services, Inc., 54 (upd.)
BCE Inc., V; 44 (upd.)
Beasley Broadcast Group, Inc., 51
Belgacom, 6
Bell Atlantic Corporation, V; 25 (upd.)
Bell Canada, 6
BellSouth Corporation, V; 29 (upd.)
BET Holdings, Inc., 18
BHC Communications, Inc., 26
Bonneville International Corporation, 29
Bouygues S.A., 24 (upd.)
Brightpoint, Inc., 18
Brite Voice Systems, Inc., 20
British Columbia Telephone Company, 6
British Telecommunications plc, V; 15 (upd.)
BT Group plc, 49 (upd.)
C-COR.net Corp., 38
Cable & Wireless HKT, 30 (upd.)

Cable and Wireless plc, V; 25 (upd.)
Cablevision Systems Corporation, 30 (upd.)
The Canadian Broadcasting Corporation (CBC), 37
Canal Plus, 10; 34 (upd.)
CanWest Global Communications Corporation, 35
Capital Radio plc, 35
Carlton Communications PLC, 15; 50 (upd.)
Carolina Telephone and Telegraph Company, 10
Carrier Access Corporation, 44
CBS Corporation, 28 (upd.)
Centel Corporation, 6
Centennial Communications Corporation, 39
Century Communications Corp., 10
Century Telephone Enterprises, Inc., 9; 54 (upd.)
Chancellor Media Corporation, 24
Charter Communications, Inc., 33
China Telecom, 50
Chris-Craft Industries, Inc., 9
The Christian Broadcasting Network, Inc., 52
Chrysalis Group plc, 40
CIENA Corporation, 54
Cincinnati Bell, Inc., 6
Citadel Communications Corporation, 35
Clear Channel Communications, Inc., 23
Cogent Communications Group, Inc., 55
COLT Telecom Group plc, 41
Comcast Corporation, 24 (upd.)
Comdial Corporation, 21
Commonwealth Telephone Enterprises, Inc., 25
Comsat Corporation, 23
Comverse Technology, Inc., 15; 43 (upd.)
Corning Inc., 44 (upd.)
Craftmade International, Inc., 44
Cumulus Media Inc., 37
DDI Corporation, 7
Deutsche Bundespost TELEKOM, V
Deutsche Telekom AG, 48 (upd.)
Dialogic Corporation, 18
Directorate General of Telecommunications, 7
DIRECTV, Inc., 38
Discovery Communications, Inc., 42
DSC Communications Corporation, 12
EchoStar Communications Corporation, 35
ECI Telecom Ltd., 18
eircom plc, 31 (upd.)
Electric Lightwave, Inc., 37
Electromagnetic Sciences Inc., 21
Emmis Communications Corporation, 47
Energis plc, 47
Entravision Communications Corporation, 41
Equant N.V., 52
EXCEL Communications Inc., 18
Executone Information Systems, Inc., 13
Expand SA, 48
Fox Family Worldwide, Inc., 24
France Télécom Group, V; 21 (upd.)
Frontier Corp., 16
Gannett Co., Inc., 30 (upd.)
General DataComm Industries, Inc., 14
Geotek Communications Inc., 21
Getty Images, Inc., 31
Global Crossing Ltd., 32
Granite Broadcasting Corporation, 42
Gray Communications Systems, Inc., 24
Groupe Vidéotron Ltée., 20
Grupo Televisa, S.A., 18; 54 (upd.)
GTE Corporation, V; 15 (upd.)

Guthy-Renker Corporation, 32
GWR Group plc, 39
Harmonic Inc., 43
Havas, SA, 10
Hispanic Broadcasting Corporation, 35
Hong Kong Telecommunications Ltd., 6
Hubbard Broadcasting Inc., 24
Hughes Electronics Corporation, 25
IDB Communications Group, Inc., 11
IDT Corporation, 34
Illinois Bell Telephone Company, 14
Indiana Bell Telephone Company,
    Incorporated, 14
Infineon Technologies AG, 50
Infinity Broadcasting Corporation, 11
IXC Communications, Inc., 29
Jacor Communications, Inc., 23
Jones Intercable, Inc., 21
Koninklijke PTT Nederland NV, V
Landmark Communications, Inc., 55 (upd.)
LCI International, Inc., 16
LDDS-Metro Communications, Inc., 8
LIN Broadcasting Corp., 9
Lincoln Telephone & Telegraph Company,
    14
LodgeNet Entertainment Corporation, 28
Loral Space & Communications Ltd., 54
    (upd.)
Mannesmann AG, 38
MasTec, Inc., 19; 55 (upd.)
McCaw Cellular Communications, Inc., 6
MCI WorldCom, Inc., V; 27 (upd.)
McLeodUSA Incorporated, 32
Mercury Communications, Ltd., 7
Metrocall, Inc., 41
Metromedia Companies, 14
Métropole Télévision, 33
MFS Communications Company, Inc., 11
Michigan Bell Telephone Co., 14
MIH Limited, 31
MITRE Corporation, 26
Mobile Telecommunications Technologies
    Corp., 18
Modern Times Group AB, 36
The Montana Power Company, 44 (upd.)
Multimedia, Inc., 11
National Broadcasting Company, Inc., 28
    (upd.)
National Grid USA, 51 (upd.)
NCR Corporation, 30 (upd.)
NetCom Systems AB, 26
Nevada Bell Telephone Company, 14
New Valley Corporation, 17
Nexans SA, 54
Nextel Communications, Inc., 27 (upd.)
Nippon Telegraph and Telephone
    Corporation, V; 51 (upd.)
Norstan, Inc., 16
Nortel Networks Corporation, 36 (upd.)
Northern Telecom Limited, V
NYNEX Corporation, V
Octel Messaging, 14; 41 (upd.)
Ohio Bell Telephone Company, 14
Olivetti S.p.A., 34 (upd.)
Österreichische Post- und
    Telegraphenverwaltung, V
Pacific Telecom, Inc., 6
Pacific Telesis Group, V
Paging Network Inc., 11
PanAmSat Corporation, 46
Paxson Communications Corporation, 33
PictureTel Corp., 10; 27 (upd.)
Posti- ja Telelaitos, 6
Price Communications Corporation, 42
ProSiebenSat.1 Media AG, 54
Publishing and Broadcasting Limited, 54
QUALCOMM Incorporated, 20; 47 (upd.)

QVC Network Inc., 9
Qwest Communications International, Inc.,
    37
Research in Motion Ltd., 54
RMH Teleservices, Inc., 42
Rochester Telephone Corporation, 6
Rogers Communications Inc., 30 (upd.)
Royal KPN N.V., 30
Rural Cellular Corporation, 43
Saga Communications, Inc., 27
Sawtek Inc., 43 (upd.)
SBC Communications Inc., 32 (upd.)
Schweizerische Post-, Telefon- und
    Telegrafen-Betriebe, V
Scientific-Atlanta, Inc., 6; 45 (upd.)
Seat Pagine Gialle S.p.A., 47
Securicor Plc, 45
Sinclair Broadcast Group, Inc., 25
Società Finanziaria Telefonica per Azioni,
    V
Sonera Corporation, 50
Southern New England
    Telecommunications Corporation, 6
Southwestern Bell Corporation, V
Spanish Broadcasting System, Inc., 41
Spelling Entertainment, 35 (upd.)
Sprint Corporation, 9; 46 (upd.)
StrataCom, Inc., 16
Swedish Telecom, V
Sycamore Networks, Inc., 45
SynOptics Communications, Inc., 10
T-Netix, Inc., 46
Telecom Australia, 6
Telecom Corporation of New Zealand
    Limited, 54
Telecom Eireann, 7
Telecom Italia S.p.A., 43
Telefonaktiebolaget LM Ericsson, V; 46
    (upd.)
Telefónica de España, S.A., V
Telefónica S.A., 46 (upd.)
Telefonos de Mexico S.A. de C.V., 14
Telekomunikacja Polska SA, 50
Telephone and Data Systems, Inc., 9
Télévision Française 1, 23
Tellabs, Inc., 11; 40 (upd.)
Telstra Corporation Limited, 50
Tiscali SpA, 48
The Titan Corporation, 36
Tollgrade Communications, Inc., 44
TV Azteca, S.A. de C.V., 39
U.S. Satellite Broadcasting Company, Inc.,
    20
U S West, Inc., V; 25 (upd.)
U.S. Cellular Corporation, 9; 31 (upd.)
United Pan-Europe Communications NV,
    47
United Telecommunications, Inc., V
United Video Satellite Group, 18
USA Interactive, Inc., 47 (upd.)
Verizon Communications, 43 (upd.)
ViaSat, Inc., 54
Vivendi Universal S.A., 46 (upd.)
Vodafone Group PLC, 11; 36 (upd.)
Watkins-Johnson Company, 15
The Weather Channel Companies, 52
West Corporation, 42
Western Union Financial Services, Inc., 54
Western Wireless Corporation, 36
Westwood One, Inc., 23
Williams Communications Group, Inc., 34
The Williams Companies, Inc., 31 (upd.)
Wipro Limited, 43
Wisconsin Bell, Inc., 14
Working Assets Funding Service, 43
Young Broadcasting Inc., 40
Zoom Technologies, Inc., 53 (upd.)

TEXTILES & APPAREL

Abercrombie & Fitch Co., 35 (upd.)
adidas-Salomon AG, 14; 33 (upd.)
Alba-Waldensian, Inc., 30
Albany International Corp., 8
Algo Group Inc., 24
American Safety Razor Company, 20
Amoskeag Company, 8
Angelica Corporation, 15; 43 (upd.)
AR Accessories Group, Inc., 23
Aris Industries, Inc., 16
Authentic Fitness Corporation, 20; 51
    (upd.)
Banana Republic Inc., 25
Benetton Group S.p.A., 10
Bill Blass Ltd., 32
Birkenstock Footprint Sandals, Inc., 12
Blair Corporation, 25
Brazos Sportswear, Inc., 23
Brooks Brothers Inc., 22
Brooks Sports Inc., 32
Brown Group, Inc., V; 20 (upd.)
Bugle Boy Industries, Inc., 18
Burberry Ltd., 17; 41 (upd.)
Burlington Industries, Inc., V; 17 (upd.)
Calcot Ltd., 33
Calvin Klein, Inc., 22; 55 (upd.)
Candie's, Inc., 31
Canstar Sports Inc., 16
Capel Incorporated, 45
Carhartt, Inc., 30
Cato Corporation, 14
Chargeurs International, 21 (upd.)
Charming Shoppes, Inc., 8
Cherokee Inc., 18
Chic by H.I.S, Inc., 20
Chico's FAS, Inc., 45
Chorus Line Corporation, 30
Christian Dior S.A., 19; 49 (upd.)
Christopher & Banks Corporation, 42
Cintas Corporation, 51 (upd.)
Claire's Stores, Inc., 17
Coach Leatherware, 10
Coats plc, 44 (upd.)
Coats Viyella Plc, V
Collins & Aikman Corporation, 13
Columbia Sportswear Company, 19; 41
    (upd.)
Concord Fabrics, Inc., 16
Cone Mills Corporation, 8
Converse Inc., 31 (upd.)
Cotton Incorporated, 46
Courtaulds plc, V; 17 (upd.)
Croscill, Inc., 42
Crown Crafts, Inc., 16
Crystal Brands, Inc., 9
Culp, Inc., 29
Cygne Designs, Inc., 25
Dan River Inc., 35
Danskin, Inc., 12
Deckers Outdoor Corporation, 22
Delta Woodside Industries, Inc., 8; 30
    (upd.)
Designer Holdings Ltd., 20
The Dixie Group, Inc., 20
Dogi International Fabrics S.A., 52
Dominion Textile Inc., 12
Donna Karan Company, 15
Donnkenny, Inc., 17
Duck Head Apparel Company, Inc., 42
Dunavant Enterprises, Inc., 54
Dyersburg Corporation, 21
Edison Brothers Stores, Inc., 9
Ellen Tracy, Inc., 55
Eram SA, 51
Esprit de Corp., 8; 29 (upd.)
Etam Developpement SA, 44

TEXTILES & APPAREL (*continued*)

Etienne Aigner AG, 52
Evans, Inc., 30
Fab Industries, Inc., 27
Fabri-Centers of America Inc., 16
Fieldcrest Cannon, Inc., 9; 31 (upd.)
Fila Holding S.p.A., 20
Florsheim Shoe Group Inc., 31 (upd.)
Fossil, Inc., 17
Frederick's of Hollywood Inc., 16
French Connection Group plc, 41
Fruit of the Loom, Inc., 8; 25 (upd.)
Fubu, 29
G&K Services, Inc., 16
G-III Apparel Group, Ltd., 22
Galey & Lord, Inc., 20
Garan, Inc., 16
Gianni Versace SpA, 22
Giorgio Armani S.p.A., 45
The Gitano Group, Inc. 8
Greenwood Mills, Inc., 14
Groupe DMC (Dollfus Mieg & Cie), 27
Groupe Yves Saint Laurent, 23
Gucci Group N.V., 50 (upd.)
Guccio Gucci, S.p.A., 15
Guess, Inc., 15
Guilford Mills Inc., 8; 40 (upd.)
Gymboree Corporation, 15
Haggar Corporation, 19
Hampton Industries, Inc., 20
Happy Kids Inc., 30
Hartmarx Corporation, 8
The Hartstone Group plc, 14
HCI Direct, Inc., 55
Healthtex, Inc., 17
Helly Hansen ASA, 25
Hermès S.A., 14
The Hockey Company, 34
Hugo Boss AG, 48
Hyde Athletic Industries, Inc., 17
I.C. Isaacs & Company, 31
Interface, Inc., 8; 29 (upd.)
Irwin Toy Limited, 14
Items International Airwalk Inc., 17
J. Crew Group, Inc., 12; 34 (upd.)
Jockey International, Inc., 12; 34 (upd.)
Johnston Industries, Inc., 15
Jones Apparel Group, Inc., 39 (upd.)
Jordache Enterprises, Inc., 23
Jos. A. Bank Clothiers, Inc., 31
JPS Textile Group, Inc., 28
K-Swiss, Inc., 33
Karl Kani Infinity, Inc., 49
Kellwood Company, 8
Kenneth Cole Productions, Inc., 25
Kinney Shoe Corp., 14
Klaus Steilmann GmbH & Co. KG, 53
L.A. Gear, Inc., 8; 32 (upd.)
L.L. Bean, Inc., 10; 38 (upd.)
LaCrosse Footwear, Inc., 18
Laura Ashley Holdings plc, 13
Lee Apparel Company, Inc., 8
The Leslie Fay Company, Inc., 8; 39 (upd.)
Levi Strauss & Co., V; 16 (upd.)
Liz Claiborne, Inc., 8
London Fog Industries, Inc., 29
Lost Arrow Inc., 22
Maidenform Worldwide Inc., 20
Malden Mills Industries, Inc., 16
Marzotto S.p.A., 20
Milliken & Co., V; 17 (upd.)
Mitsubishi Rayon Co., Ltd., V
Mossimo, Inc., 27
Mothercare UK Ltd., 17
Movie Star Inc., 17
Naf Naf SA, 44
Nautica Enterprises, Inc., 18; 44 (upd.)

New Balance Athletic Shoe, Inc., 25
Nike, Inc., V; 8 (upd.)
Nine West Group, Inc., 39 (upd.)
Nitches, Inc., 53
The North Face, Inc., 18
Oakley, Inc., 18
OshKosh B'Gosh, Inc., 9; 42 (upd.)
Oxford Industries, Inc., 8
Pacific Sunwear of California, Inc., 28
Peek & Cloppenburg KG, 46
Pendleton Woolen Mills, Inc., 42
Pentland Group plc, 20
Perry Ellis International, Inc., 41
Phat Fashions LLC, 49
Pillowtex Corporation, 19; 41 (upd.)
Pluma, Inc., 27
Polo/Ralph Lauren Corporation, 12
Prada Holding B.V., 45
PremiumWear, Inc., 30
Puma AG Rudolf Dassler Sport, 35
Quaker Fabric Corp., 19
Quiksilver, Inc., 18
R.G. Barry Corporation, 17; 44 (upd.)
Recreational Equipment, Inc., 18
Red Wing Shoe Company, Inc., 30 (upd.)
Reebok International Ltd., V; 9 (upd.); 26 (upd.)
Rieter Holding AG, 42
Rollerblade, Inc., 15
Russell Corporation, 8; 30 (upd.)
St. John Knits, Inc., 14
Salant Corporation, 51 (upd.)
Saucony Inc., 35
Shaw Industries, Inc., 40 (upd.)
Shelby Williams Industries, Inc., 14
Skechers U.S.A. Inc., 31
Sophus Berendsen A/S, 49
Springs Industries, Inc., V; 19 (upd.)
Starter Corp., 12
Steiner Corporation (Alsco), 53
Steven Madden, Ltd., 37
Stone Manufacturing Company, 14; 43 (upd.)
The Stride Rite Corporation, 8; 37 (upd.)
Stussy, Inc., 55
Sun Sportswear, Inc., 17
Superior Uniform Group, Inc., 30
Teijin Limited, V
Thomaston Mills, Inc., 27
The Timberland Company, 13; 54 (upd.)
Tommy Hilfiger Corporation, 20; 53 (upd.)
Toray Industries, Inc., V
Tultex Corporation, 13
Unifi, Inc., 12
United Merchants & Manufacturers, Inc., 13
United Retail Group Inc., 33
Unitika Ltd., V
Vans, Inc., 16; 47 (upd.)
Varsity Spirit Corp., 15
VF Corporation, V; 17 (upd.); 54 (upd.)
Walton Monroe Mills, Inc., 8
The Warnaco Group Inc., 12; 46 (upd.)
Wellman, Inc., 8; 52 (upd.)
West Point-Pepperell, Inc., 8
WestPoint Stevens Inc., 16
Weyco Group, Incorporated, 32
Williamson-Dickie Manufacturing Company, 14
Wolverine World Wide Inc., 16

TOBACCO

American Brands, Inc., V
B.A.T. Industries PLC, 22 (upd.)
British American Tobacco PLC, 50 (upd.)
Brooke Group Ltd., 15

Brown & Williamson Tobacco Corporation, 14; 33 (upd.)
Culbro Corporation, 15
Dibrell Brothers, Incorporated, 12
DIMON Inc., 27
800-JR Cigar, Inc., 27
Gallaher Group Plc, 49 (upd.)
Gallaher Limited, V; 19 (upd.)
Holt's Cigar Holdings, Inc., 42
Imasco Limited, V
Imperial Tobacco Group PLC, 50
Japan Tobacco Incorporated, V
Philip Morris Companies Inc., V; 18 (upd.)
R.J. Reynolds Tobacco Holdings, Inc., 30 (upd.)
RJR Nabisco Holdings Corp., V
Rothmans UK Holdings Limited, V; 19 (upd.)
Seita, 23
Standard Commercial Corporation, 13
Swisher International Group Inc., 23
Tabacalera, S.A., V; 17 (upd.)
Universal Corporation, V; 48 (upd.)
UST Inc., 9; 50 (upd.)
Vector Group Ltd., 35 (upd.)

TRANSPORT SERVICES

Aéroports de Paris, 33
Air Express International Corporation, 13
Airborne Freight Corporation, 6; 34 (upd.)
Alamo Rent A Car, Inc., 6; 24 (upd.)
Alexander & Baldwin, Inc., 10
Allied Worldwide, Inc., 49
Amerco, 6
American Classic Voyages Company, 27
American President Companies Ltd., 6
Anschutz Corp., 12
Aqua Alliance Inc., 32 (upd.)
Atlas Van Lines, Inc., 14
Avis Rent A Car, Inc., 6; 22 (upd.)
BAA plc, 10
Bekins Company, 15
Boyd Bros. Transportation Inc., 39
Brambles Industries Limited, 42
British Railways Board, V
Broken Hill Proprietary Company Ltd., 22 (upd.)
Budget Group, Inc., 25
Budget Rent a Car Corporation, 9
Burlington Northern Santa Fe Corporation, V; 27 (upd.)
C.H. Robinson Worldwide, Inc., 40 (upd.)
Canadian National Railway System, 6
Canadian Pacific Railway Limited, V; 45 (upd.)
Cannon Express, Inc., 53
Carey International, Inc., 26
Carlson Companies, Inc., 6
Carolina Freight Corporation, 6
Celadon Group Inc., 30
Central Japan Railway Company, 43
Chargeurs, 6
Chicago and North Western Holdings Corporation, 6
Christian Salvesen Plc, 45
Coach USA, Inc., 24; 55 (upd.)
Coles Express Inc., 15
Compagnie Générale Maritime et Financière, 6
Consolidated Delivery & Logistics, Inc., 24
Consolidated Freightways Corporation, V; 21 (upd.); 48 (upd.)
Consolidated Rail Corporation, V
Crowley Maritime Corporation, 6; 28 (upd.)
CSX Corporation, V; 22 (upd.)
Danzas Group, V; 40 (upd.)

Deutsche Bahn AG, 46 (upd.)
Deutsche Bundesbahn, V
DHL Worldwide Express, 6; 24 (upd.)
Dollar Thrifty Automotive Group, Inc., 25
East Japan Railway Company, V
Emery Air Freight Corporation, 6
Emery Worldwide Airlines, Inc., 25 (upd.)
Enterprise Rent-A-Car Company, 6
Eurotunnel Group, 37 (upd.)
EVA Airways Corporation, 51
Evergreen International Aviation, Inc., 53
Evergreen Marine Corporation (Taiwan)
    Ltd., 13; 50 (upd.)
Executive Jet, Inc., 36
Exel plc, 51 (upd.)
Expeditors International of Washington
    Inc., 17
Federal Express Corporation, V
FedEx Corporation, 18 (upd.); 42 (upd.)
Fritz Companies, Inc., 12
Frontline Ltd., 45
Frozen Food Express Industries, Inc., 20
GATX Corporation, 6; 25 (upd.)
GE Capital Aviation Services, 36
Gefco SA, 54
Genesee & Wyoming Inc., 27
The Go-Ahead Group Plc, 28
The Greenbrier Companies, 19
Greyhound Lines, Inc., 32 (upd.)
Grupo TMM, S.A. de C.V., 50
Grupo Transportación Ferroviaria
    Mexicana, S.A. de C.V., 47
GulfMark Offshore, Inc., 49
Hanjin Shipping Co., Ltd., 50
Hankyu Corporation, V; 23 (upd.)
Hapag-Lloyd AG, 6
Harland and Wolff Holdings plc, 19
Harper Group Inc., 17
Heartland Express, Inc., 18
The Hertz Corporation, 9
Holberg Industries, Inc., 36
Hospitality Worldwide Services, Inc., 26
Hub Group, Inc., 38
Hvide Marine Incorporated, 22
Illinois Central Corporation, 11
International Shipholding Corporation, Inc.,
    27
J.B. Hunt Transport Services Inc., 12
John Menzies plc, 39
Kansas City Southern Industries, Inc., 6; 26
    (upd.)
Kawasaki Kisen Kaisha, Ltd., V
Keio Teito Electric Railway Company, V
Keolis SA, 51
Kinki Nippon Railway Company Ltd., V
Kirby Corporation, 18
Koninklijke Nedlloyd Groep N.V., 6
Kuehne & Nagel International AG, V; 53
    (upd.)
La Poste, V; 47 (upd.)
Leaseway Transportation Corp., 12
London Regional Transport, 6
Maine Central Railroad Company, 16
Mammoet Transport B.V., 26
Mayflower Group Inc., 6
Mercury Air Group, Inc., 20
The Mersey Docks and Harbour Company,
    30
Metropolitan Transportation Authority, 35
Miller Industries, Inc., 26
Mitsui O.S.K. Lines, Ltd., V
Moran Towing Corporation, Inc., 15
The Morgan Group, Inc., 46
Morris Travel Services L.L.C., 26
Motor Cargo Industries, Inc., 35
National Car Rental System, Inc., 10
National Express Group PLC, 50

National Railroad Passenger Corporation,
    22
Neptune Orient Lines Limited, 47
NFC plc, 6
Nippon Express Co., Ltd., V
Nippon Yusen Kabushiki Kaisha, V
Norfolk Southern Corporation, V; 29 (upd.)
Oak Harbor Freight Lines, Inc., 53
Ocean Group plc, 6
Odakyu Electric Railway Company
    Limited, V
Oglebay Norton Company, 17
Österreichische Bundesbahnen GmbH, 6
OTR Express, Inc., 25
Overnite Transportation Co., 14
Overseas Shipholding Group, Inc., 11
Pacer International, Inc., 54
The Peninsular and Oriental Steam
    Navigation Company, V; 38 (upd.)
Penske Corporation, V
PHH Arval, V; 53 (upd.)
The Port Authority of New York and New
    Jersey, 48
Post Office Group, V
Preston Corporation, 6
RailTex, Inc., 20
Railtrack Group PLC, 50
Roadway Express, Inc., 25 (upd.)
Roadway Services, Inc., V
Royal Olympic Cruise Lines Inc., 52
Royal Vopak NV, 41
Ryder System, Inc., V; 24 (upd.)
Santa Fe Pacific Corporation, V
Schenker-Rhenus AG, 6
Schneider National, Inc., 36
Securicor Plc, 45
Seibu Railway Co. Ltd., V
Seino Transportation Company, Ltd., 6
Simon Transportation Services Inc., 27
Smithway Motor Xpress Corporation, 39
Société Nationale des Chemins de Fer
    Français, V
Southern Pacific Transportation Company,
    V
Stagecoach Holdings plc, 30
Stelmar Shipping Ltd., 52
Stevedoring Services of America Inc., 28
Stinnes AG, 8
Stolt-Nielsen S.A., 42
Sunoco, Inc., 28 (upd.)
Swift Transportation Co., Inc., 42
The Swiss Federal Railways
    (Schweizerische Bundesbahnen), V
Teekay Shipping Corporation, 25
Tibbett & Britten Group plc, 32
Tidewater Inc., 11; 37 (upd.)
TNT Freightways Corporation, 14
TNT Post Group N.V., V; 27 (upd.); 30
    (upd.)
Tobu Railway Co Ltd, 6
Tokyu Corporation, V
Totem Resources Corporation, 9
Trailer Bridge, Inc., 41
Transnet Ltd., 6
Transport Corporation of America, Inc., 49
TTX Company, 6
U.S. Delivery Systems, Inc., 22
Union Pacific Corporation, V; 28 (upd.)
United Parcel Service of America Inc., V;
    17 (upd.)
United States Postal Service, 14; 34 (upd.)
USA Truck, Inc., 42
Velocity Express Corporation, 49
Werner Enterprises, Inc., 26
Wincanton plc, 52
Wisconsin Central Transportation
    Corporation, 24

Yamato Transport Co. Ltd., V; 49 (upd.)
Yellow Corporation, 14; 45 (upd.)
Yellow Freight System, Inc. of Delaware,
    V

UTILITIES

AES Corporation, 10; 13 (upd.); 53 (upd.)
Aggreko Plc, 45
Air & Water Technologies Corporation, 6
Alberta Energy Company Ltd., 16; 43
    (upd.)
Allegheny Energy, Inc., V; 38 (upd.)
American Electric Power Company, Inc.,
    V; 45 (upd.)
American States Water Company, 46
American Water Works Company, Inc., 6;
    38 (upd.)
Aquila, Inc., 50 (upd.)
Arkla, Inc., V
Associated Natural Gas Corporation, 11
Atlanta Gas Light Company, 6; 23 (upd.)
Atlantic Energy, Inc., 6
Atmos Energy Corporation, 43
Baltimore Gas and Electric Company, V;
    25 (upd.)
Bay State Gas Company, 38
Bayernwerk AG, V; 23 (upd.)
Bewag AG, 39
Big Rivers Electric Corporation, 11
Black Hills Corporation, 20
Bonneville Power Administration, 50
Boston Edison Company, 12
Bouygues S.A., 24 (upd.)
British Energy Plc, 49
British Gas plc, V
British Nuclear Fuels plc, 6
Brooklyn Union Gas, 6
Calpine Corporation, 36
Canadian Utilities Limited, 13
Cap Rock Energy Corporation, 46
Carolina Power & Light Company, V; 23
    (upd.)
Cascade Natural Gas Corporation, 9
Centerior Energy Corporation, V
Central and South West Corporation, V
Central Hudson Gas and Electricity
    Corporation, 6
Central Maine Power, 6
Central Vermont Public Service
    Corporation, 54
Centrica plc, 29 (upd.)
Chubu Electric Power Company, Inc., V;
    46 (upd.)
Chugoku Electric Power Company Inc., V;
    53 (upd.)
Cincinnati Gas & Electric Company, 6
CIPSCO Inc., 6
Citizens Utilities Company, 7
City Public Service, 6
Cleco Corporation, 37
CMS Energy Corporation, V, 14
The Coastal Corporation, 31 (upd.)
Cogentrix Energy, Inc., 10
The Coleman Company, Inc., 9
The Columbia Gas System, Inc., V; 16
    (upd.)
Commonwealth Edison Company, V
Commonwealth Energy System, 14
Connecticut Light and Power Co., 13
Consolidated Edison, Inc., V; 45 (upd.)
Consolidated Natural Gas Company, V; 19
    (upd.)
Consumers Power Co., 14
Consumers Water Company, 14
Consumers' Gas Company Ltd., 6
Destec Energy, Inc., 12
The Detroit Edison Company, V

UTILITIES (*continued*)

Dominion Resources, Inc., V; 54 (upd.)
DPL Inc., 6
DQE, Inc., 6
DTE Energy Company, 20 (upd.)
Duke Energy Corporation, V; 27 (upd.)
E.On AG, 50 (upd.)
Eastern Enterprises, 6
El Paso Electric Company, 21
El Paso Natural Gas Company, 12
Electricidade de Portugal, S.A., 47
Electricité de France, V; 41 (upd.)
Elektrowatt AG, 6
Enbridge Inc., 43
ENDESA S.A., V; 46 (upd.)
Enron Corporation, V; 46 (upd.)
Enserch Corporation, V
Ente Nazionale per L'Energia Elettrica, V
Entergy Corporation, V; 45 (upd.)
Equitable Resources, Inc., 6; 54 (upd.)
Exelon Corporation, 48 (upd.)
Florida Progress Corporation, V; 23 (upd.)
Fortis, Inc., 15; 47 (upd.)
Fortum Corporation, 30 (upd.)
FPL Group, Inc., V; 49 (upd.)
Gaz de France, V; 40 (upd.)
General Public Utilities Corporation, V
Générale des Eaux Group, V
GPU, Inc., 27 (upd.)
Gulf States Utilities Company, 6
Hawaiian Electric Industries, Inc., 9
Hokkaido Electric Power Company Inc., V
Hokuriku Electric Power Company, V
Hongkong Electric Holdings Ltd., 6; 23 (upd.)
Houston Industries Incorporated, V
Hyder plc, 34
Hydro-Québec, 6; 32 (upd.)
Iberdrola, S.A., 49
Idaho Power Company, 12
Illinois Bell Telephone Company, 14
Illinois Power Company, 6
Indiana Energy, Inc., 27
International Power PLC, 50 (upd.)
IPALCO Enterprises, Inc., 6
The Kansai Electric Power Co., Inc., V
Kansas City Power & Light Company, 6
Kelda Group plc, 45
Kenetech Corporation, 11
Kentucky Utilities Company, 6
KeySpan Energy Co., 27
KU Energy Corporation, 11
Kyushu Electric Power Company Inc., V
LG&E Energy Corporation, 6; 51 (upd.)
Long Island Lighting Company, V
Lyonnaise des Eaux-Dumez, V
Madison Gas and Electric Company, 39
Magma Power Company, 11
MCN Corporation, 6
MDU Resources Group, Inc., 7; 42 (upd.)
Middlesex Water Company, 45
Midwest Resources Inc., 6
Minnesota Power, Inc., 11; 34 (upd.)
The Montana Power Company, 11; 44 (upd.)
National Fuel Gas Company, 6
National Grid USA, 51 (upd.)
National Power PLC, 12
Nebraska Public Power District, 29
N.V. Nederlandse Gasunie, V
Nevada Power Company, 11
New England Electric System, V
New Jersey Resources Corporation, 54
New York State Electric and Gas, 6
Niagara Mohawk Holdings Inc., V; 45 (upd.)
NICOR Inc., 6

NIPSCO Industries, Inc., 6
North West Water Group plc, 11
Northeast Utilities, V; 48 (upd.)
Northern States Power Company, V; 20 (upd.)
Northwest Natural Gas Company, 45
NorthWestern Corporation, 37
Nova Corporation of Alberta, V
Oglethorpe Power Corporation, 6
Ohio Edison Company, V
Oklahoma Gas and Electric Company, 6
ONEOK Inc., 7
Ontario Hydro Services Company, 6; 32 (upd.)
Osaka Gas Co., Ltd., V
Otter Tail Power Company, 18
Pacific Enterprises, V
Pacific Gas and Electric Company, V
PacifiCorp, V; 26 (upd.)
Panhandle Eastern Corporation, V
PECO Energy Company, 11
Pennon Group Plc, 45
Pennsylvania Power & Light Company, V
Peoples Energy Corporation, 6
PG&E Corporation, 26 (upd.)
Philadelphia Electric Company, V
Philadelphia Suburban Corporation, 39
Piedmont Natural Gas Company, Inc., 27
Pinnacle West Capital Corporation, 6; 54 (upd.)
PNM Resources Inc., 51 (upd.)
Portland General Corporation, 6
Potomac Electric Power Company, 6
Powergen PLC, 11; 50 (upd.)
PPL Corporation, 41 (upd.)
PreussenElektra Aktiengesellschaft, V
PSI Resources, 6
Public Service Company of Colorado, 6
Public Service Company of New Hampshire, 21; 55 (upd.)
Public Service Company of New Mexico, 6
Public Service Enterprise Group Inc., V; 44 (upd.)
Puerto Rico Electric Power Authority, 47
Puget Sound Energy Inc., 50 (upd.)
Puget Sound Power and Light Company, 6
Questar Corporation, 6; 26 (upd.)
RAO Unified Energy System of Russia, 45
Reliant Energy Inc., 44 (upd.)
Rochester Gas and Electric Corporation, 6
Ruhrgas AG, V; 38 (upd.)
RWE AG, V; 50 (upd.)
Salt River Project, 19
San Diego Gas & Electric Company, V
SCANA Corporation, 6
Scarborough Public Utilities Commission, 9
SCEcorp, V
Scottish Hydro-Electric PLC, 13
Scottish Power plc, 19; 49 (upd.)
Seattle City Light, 50
SEMCO Energy, Inc., 44
Sempra Energy, 25 (upd.)
Severn Trent PLC, 12; 38 (upd.)
Shikoku Electric Power Company, Inc., V
Sonat, Inc., 6
South Jersey Industries, Inc., 42
The Southern Company, V; 38 (upd.)
Southern Electric PLC, 13
Southern Indiana Gas and Electric Company, 13
Southern Union Company, 27
Southwest Gas Corporation, 19
Southwest Water Company, 47
Southwestern Electric Power Co., 21
Southwestern Public Service Company, 6
Suez Lyonnaise des Eaux, 36 (upd.)

TECO Energy, Inc., 6
Tennessee Valley Authority, 50
Texas Utilities Company, V; 25 (upd.)
Thames Water plc, 11
Tohoku Electric Power Company, Inc., V
The Tokyo Electric Power Company, Incorporated, V
Tokyo Gas Co., Ltd., V; 55 (upd.)
TransAlta Utilities Corporation, 6
TransCanada PipeLines Limited, V
Transco Energy Company, V
Trigen Energy Corporation, 42
Tucson Electric Power Company, 6
UGI Corporation, 12
Unicom Corporation, 29 (upd.)
Union Electric Company, V
The United Illuminating Company, 21
United Utilities PLC, 52 (upd.)
United Water Resources, Inc., 40
Unitil Corporation, 37
Utah Power and Light Company, 27
UtiliCorp United Inc., 6
Vereinigte Elektrizitätswerke Westfalen AG, V
VEW AG, 39
Warwick Valley Telephone Company, 55
Washington Gas Light Company, 19
Washington Natural Gas Company, 9
Washington Water Power Company, 6
Western Resources, Inc., 12
Wheelabrator Technologies, Inc., 6
Wisconsin Energy Corporation, 6; 54 (upd.)
Wisconsin Public Service Corporation, 9
WPL Holdings, Inc., 6
WPS Resources Corporation, 53 (upd.)

WASTE SERVICES

Allied Waste Industries, Inc., 50
Allwaste, Inc., 18
Appliance Recycling Centers of America, Inc., 42
Azcon Corporation, 23
Brambles Industries Limited, 42
Browning-Ferris Industries, Inc., V; 20 (upd.)
Chemical Waste Management, Inc., 9
Copart Inc., 23
E.On AG, 50 (upd.)
Ecology and Environment, Inc., 39
Industrial Services of America, Inc., 46
Ionics, Incorporated, 52
ISS A/S, 49
Kelda Group plc, 45
MPW Industrial Services Group, Inc., 53
Pennon Group Plc, 45
Philip Environmental Inc., 16
Roto-Rooter Corp., 15
Safety-Kleen Corp., 8
Sevenson Environmental Services, Inc., 42
Severn Trent PLC, 38 (upd.)
Shanks Group plc, 45
Stericycle Inc., 33
TRC Companies, Inc., 32
Veit Companies, 43
Waste Connections, Inc., 46
Waste Holdings, Inc., 41
Waste Management, Inc., V
WMX Technologies Inc., 17

GEOGRAPHIC INDEX

Geographic Index

Algeria

Entreprise Nationale Sonatrach, IV

Argentina

Aerolíneas Argentinas S.A., 33
YPF Sociedad Anonima, IV

Australia

Amcor Limited, IV; 19 (upd.)
Aristocrat Leisure Limited, 54
Australia and New Zealand Banking Group
  Limited, II; 52 (upd.)
Billabong International Ltd., 44
Bond Corporation Holdings Limited, 10
Boral Limited, III; 43 (upd.)
Brambles Industries Limited, 42
Broken Hill Proprietary Company Ltd., IV;
  22 (upd.)
Carlton and United Breweries Ltd., I
Coles Myer Ltd., V; 20 (upd.)
CRA Limited, IV
CSR Limited, III; 28 (upd.)
Elders IXL Ltd., I
Foster's Group Limited, 7; 21 (upd.); 50
  (upd.)
Goodman Fielder Ltd., 52
John Fairfax Holdings Limited, 7
Lend Lease Corporation Limited, IV; 17
  (upd.); 52 (upd.)
Lion Nathan Limited, 54
Lonely Planet Publications Pty Ltd., 55
News Corporation Limited, IV; 7 (upd.);
  46 (upd.)
Pacific Dunlop Limited, 10
Pioneer International Limited, III
Publishing and Broadcasting Limited, 54
Qantas Airways Limited, 6; 24 (upd.)
Southcorp Limited, 54
TABCORP Holdings Limited, 44
Telecom Australia, 6
Telstra Corporation Limited, 50
Westpac Banking Corporation, II; 48 (upd.)
WMC, Limited, 43

Austria

Andritz AG, 51
Austrian Airlines AG (Österreichische
  Luftverkehrs AG), 33
Bank Austria AG, 23
BBAG Osterreichische Brau-Beteiligungs-
  AG, 38
Gericom AG, 47
Glock Ges.m.b.H., 42
Julius Meinl International AG, 53
Lauda Air Luftfahrt AG, 48
ÖMV Aktiengesellschaft, IV
Österreichische Bundesbahnen GmbH, 6
Österreichische Post- und
  Telegraphenverwaltung, V
RHI AG, 53
VA TECH ELIN EBG GmbH, 49
Voest-Alpine Stahl AG, IV

Zumtobel AG, 50

Bahamas

Sun International Hotels Limited, 26
Teekay Shipping Corporation, 25

Bangladesh

Grameen Bank, 31

Belgium

Almanij NV, 44
Bank Brussels Lambert, II
Barco NV, 44
Belgacom, 6
C&A, 40 (upd.)
Cockerill Sambre Group, IV; 26 (upd.)
Delhaize "Le Lion" S.A., 44
Generale Bank, II
GIB Group, V; 26 (upd.)
Interbrew S.A., 17; 50 (upd.)
Kredietbank N.V., II
PetroFina S.A., IV; 26 (upd.)
Roularta Media Group NV, 48
Sabena S.A./N.V., 33
Solvay & Cie S.A., I; 21 (upd.)
Tractebel S.A., 20
NV Umicore SA, 47
Xeikon NV, 26

Bermuda

Bacardi Limited, 18
Frontline Ltd., 45
Jardine Matheson Holdings Limited, I; 20
  (upd.)
Sea Containers Ltd., 29
Tyco International Ltd., III; 28 (upd.)
White Mountains Insurance Group, Ltd., 48

Brazil

Banco Bradesco S.A., 13
Banco Itaú S.A., 19
Companhia Vale do Rio Doce, IV; 43
  (upd.)
Empresa Brasileira de Aeronáutica S.A.
  (Embraer), 36
Lojas Arapua S.A., 22
Perdigao SA, 52
Petróleo Brasileiro S.A., IV
TransBrasil S/A Linhas Aéreas, 31
VARIG S.A. (Viação Aérea Rio-
  Grandense), 6; 29 (upd.)

Canada

Abitibi-Consolidated, Inc., V; 25 (upd.)
Abitibi-Price Inc., IV
Air Canada, 6; 23 (upd.)
Alberta Energy Company Ltd., 16; 43
  (upd.)
Alcan Aluminium Limited, IV; 31 (upd.)
Algo Group Inc., 24
Alliance Atlantis Communications Inc., 39
Bank of Montreal, II; 46 (upd.)

Bank of Nova Scotia, The, II
Barrick Gold Corporation, 34
BCE Inc., V; 44 (upd.)
Bell Canada, 6
BFC Construction Corporation, 25
Biovail Corporation, 47
Bombardier Inc., 42 (upd.)
Bramalea Ltd., 9
British Columbia Telephone Company, 6
Campeau Corporation, V
Canada Packers Inc., II
Canadair, Inc., 16
Canadian Broadcasting Corporation (CBC),
  The, 37
Canadian Imperial Bank of Commerce, II
Canadian National Railway System, 6
Canadian Pacific Railway Limited, V; 45
  (upd.)
Canadian Utilities Limited, 13
Canfor Corporation, 42
Canstar Sports Inc., 16
CanWest Global Communications
  Corporation, 35
Cinar Corporation, 40
Cineplex Odeon Corporation, 6; 23 (upd.)
Cinram International, Inc., 43
Cirque du Soleil Inc., 29
Clearly Canadian Beverage Corporation, 48
Cognos Inc., 44
Cominco Ltd., 37
Consumers' Gas Company Ltd., 6
CoolBrands International Inc., 35
Corby Distilleries Limited, 14
Corel Corporation, 15; 33 (upd.)
Cott Corporation, 52
Creo Inc., 48
Discreet Logic Inc., 20
Dofasco Inc., IV; 24 (upd.)
Dominion Textile Inc., 12
Domtar Inc., IV
Dylex Limited, 29
Echo Bay Mines Ltd., IV; 38 (upd.)
Enbridge Inc., 43
Extendicare Health Services, Inc., 6
Falconbridge Limited, 49
Fortis, Inc., 15; 47 (upd.)
Four Seasons Hotels Inc., 9; 29 (upd.)
GEAC Computer Corporation Ltd., 43
George Weston Limited, II; 36 (upd.)
Great-West Lifeco Inc., III
Groupe Vidéotron Ltée., 20
Harlequin Enterprises Limited, 52
Hemlo Gold Mines Inc., 9
Hiram Walker Resources, Ltd., I
Hockey Company, The, 34
Hudson Bay Mining and Smelting
  Company, Limited, The, 12
Hudson's Bay Company, V; 25 (upd.)
Hurricane Hydrocarbons Ltd., 54
Husky Energy Inc., 47
Hydro-Québec, 6; 32 (upd.)
Imasco Limited, V
Imax Corporation, 28
Imperial Oil Limited, IV; 25 (upd.)

Canada (*continued*)

Inco Limited, IV; 45 (upd.)
Intrawest Corporation, The, 15
Irwin Toy Limited, 14
Jean Coutu Group (PJC) Inc., The, 46
Jim Pattison Group, The, 37
Kinross Gold Corporation, 36
Kruger Inc., 17
Labatt Brewing Company Limited, I; 25
   (upd.)
Ledcor Industries Limited, 46
Linamar Corporation, 18
Lions Gate Entertainment Corporation, 35
Loblaw Companies Limited, 43
Loewen Group, Inc., The, 16; 40 (upd.)
London Drugs Ltd., 46
Maclean Hunter Publishing Limited, IV; 26
   (upd.)
MacMillan Bloedel Limited, IV
Magellan Aerospace Corporation, 48
Maple Leaf Foods Inc., 41
Methanex Corporation, 40
Mitel Corporation, 18
Molson Companies Limited, The, I; 26
   (upd.)
Moore Corporation Limited, IV
Mouvement des Caisses Desjardins, 48
National Sea Products Ltd., 14
Noranda Inc., IV; 7 (upd.)
Nortel Networks Corporation, 36 (upd.)
North West Company, Inc., The, 12
Northern Telecom Limited, V
Nova Corporation of Alberta, V
Novacor Chemicals Ltd., 12
Olympia & York Developments Ltd., IV; 9
   (upd.)
Onex Corporation, 16
Ontario Hydro Services Company, 6; 32
   (upd.)
Oshawa Group Limited, The, II
PCL Construction Group Inc., 50
Peace Arch Entertainment Group Inc., 51
Petro-Canada Limited, IV
Philip Environmental Inc., 16
Placer Dome Inc., 20
Potash Corporation of Saskatchewan Inc.,
   18
Power Corporation of Canada, 36 (upd.)
Provigo Inc., II; 51 (upd.)
Quebecor Inc., 12; 47 (upd.)
Research in Motion Ltd., 54
Ritchie Bros. Auctioneers Inc., 41
Rogers Communications Inc., 30 (upd.)
Roots Canada Ltd., 42
Royal Bank of Canada, The, II; 21 (upd.)
Scarborough Public Utilities Commission,
   9
Seagram Company Ltd., The, I; 25 (upd.)
Shoppers Drug Mart Corporation, 49
Southam Inc., 7
Spar Aerospace Limited, 32
Steinberg Incorporated, II
Stelco Inc., IV; 51 (upd.)
Suncor Energy Inc., 54
Talisman Energy Inc., 9; 47 (upd.)
TDL Group Ltd., 46
Teck Corporation, 27
Thomson Corporation, The, 8; 34 (upd.)
Toromont Industries, Ltd., 21
Toronto-Dominion Bank, The, II; 49 (upd.)
Torstar Corporation, 29
TransAlta Utilities Corporation, 6
TransCanada PipeLines Limited, V
Tridel Enterprises Inc., 9
Trilon Financial Corporation, II
Triple Five Group Ltd., 49
Trizec Corporation Ltd., 10

Van Houtte Inc., 39
Varity Corporation, III
Vincor International Inc., 50
Wascana Energy Inc., 13
West Fraser Timber Co. Ltd., 17
WestJet Airlines Ltd., 38

Chile

Corporacion Nacional del Cobre de Chile,
   40
Lan Chile S.A., 31
Viña Concha y Toro S.A., 45

China

Air China, 46
Asia Info Holdings, Inc., 43
China Eastern Airlines Co. Ltd., 31
China National Petroleum Corporation, 46
China Southern Airlines Company Ltd., 33
China Telecom, 50
Chinese Petroleum Corporation, IV; 31
   (upd.)
Guangzhou Pearl River Piano Group Ltd.,
   49
Shanghai Petrochemical Co., Ltd., 18
Tsingtao Brewery Group, 49

Colombia

Avianca Aerovías Nacionales de Colombia
   SA, 36
Empresa Colombiana de Petróleos, IV

Czech Republic

Skoda Auto a.s., 39

Denmark

Arla Foods amba, 48
Bang & Olufsen Holding A/S, 37
Carlsberg A/S, 9; 29 (upd.)
Danisco A/S, 44
Danske Bank Aktieselskab, 50
Group 4 Falck A/S, 42
H. Lundbeck A/S, 44
IKEA International A/S, V; 26 (upd.)
ISS A/S, 49
Lego A/S, 13; 40 (upd.)
Novo Industri A/S, I
Sophus Berendsen A/S, 49

Ecuador

Petróleos del Ecuador, IV

Egypt

EgyptAir, 6; 27 (upd.)
Egyptian General Petroleum Corporation,
   IV; 51 (upd.)

El Salvador

Grupo TACA, 38

Finland

Ahlstrom Corporation, 53
Amer Group plc, 41
Enso-Gutzeit Oy, IV
Finnair Oy, 6; 25 (upd.)
Fiskars Corporation, 33
Fortum Corporation, 30 (upd.)
Hackman Oyj Adp, 44
Imatra Steel Oy Ab, 55
Kansallis-Osake-Pankki, II
Kesko Ltd. (Kesko Oy), 8; 27 (upd.)
Kone Corporation, 27
Kymmene Corporation, IV

Metsa-Serla Oy, IV
Metso Corporation, 30 (upd.)
Neste Oy, IV
Nokia Corporation, II; 17 (upd.); 38 (upd.)
Outokumpu Oyj, 38
Posti- ja Telelaitos, 6
Sanitec Corporation, 51
SanomaWSOY Corporation, 51
Sonera Corporation, 50
Stora Enso Oyj, 36 (upd.)
United Paper Mills Ltd. (Yhtyneet
   Paperitehtaat Oy), IV
UPM-Kymmene Corporation, 19; 50 (upd.)
Valmet Corporation (Valmet Oy), III

France

Accor SA, 10; 27 (upd.)
Aéroports de Paris, 33
Aerospatiale Group, The, 7; 21 (upd.)
Agence France-Presse, 34
Alain Afflelou SA, 53
Alcatel Alsthom Compagnie Générale
   d'Electricité, 9
Alcatel S.A., 36 (upd.)
Altran Technologies, 51
Association des Centres Distributeurs E.
   Leclerc, 37
Atochem S.A., I
Au Printemps S.A., V
Auchan, 37
Automobiles Citroen, 7
Autoroutes du Sud de la France SA, 55
Avions Marcel Dassault-Breguet Aviation,
   I
Axa, III
Baccarat, 24
Banque Nationale de Paris S.A., II
Baron Philippe de Rothschild S.A., 39
Bayard SA, 49
Bénéteau SA, 55
Besnier SA, 19
BNP Paribas Group, 36 (upd.)
Bonduelle SA, 51
Bongrain SA, 25
Bouygues S.A., I; 24 (upd.)
BSN Groupe S.A., II
Bull S.A., 43 (upd.)
Bureau Veritas SA, 55
Burelle S.A., 23
Business Objects S.A., 25
Canal Plus, 10; 34 (upd.)
Cap Gemini Ernst & Young, 37
Carbone Lorraine S.A., 33
Carrefour SA, 10; 27 (upd.)
Cetelem S.A., 21
Chanel, 12
Chanel SA, 49 (upd.)
Chargeurs International, 6; 21 (upd.)
Christian Dalloz SA, 40
Christian Dior S.A., 19; 49 (upd.)
Christofle SA, 40
Ciments Français, 40
Club Mediterranée S.A., 6; 21 (upd.)
Coflexip S.A., 25
Colas SA, 31
Compagnie de Saint-Gobain S.A., III; 16
   (upd.)
Compagnie des Alpes, 48
Compagnie des Machines Bull S.A., III
Compagnie Financiere de Paribas, II
Compagnie Générale d'Électricité, II
Compagnie Générale des Établissements
   Michelin, V; 42 (upd.)
Compagnie Générale Maritime et
   Financière, 6
Comptoirs Modernes S.A., 19
Crédit Agricole, II

Crédit Lyonnais, 9; 33 (upd.)
Crédit National S.A., 9
Darty S.A., 27
Dassault Systèmes S.A., 25
De Dietrich & Cie., 31
Deveaux S.A., 41
Dexia Group, 42
Du Pareil au Même, 43
EADS SOCATA, 54
ECS S.A., 12
Eiffage, 27
Electricité de France, V; 41 (upd.)
Elf Aquitaine SA, 21 (upd.)
Elior SA, 49
Eram SA, 51
Eridania Béghin-Say S.A., 36
Essilor International, 21
Etablissements Economiques du Casino
  Guichard, Perrachon et Cie, S.C.A., 12
Etam Developpement SA, 44
Euro Disneyland SCA, 20
Euro RSCG Worldwide S.A., 13
Euronext Paris S.A., 37
Expand SA, 48
Facom S.A., 32
Faiveley S.A., 39
Fimalac S.A., 37
Fleury Michon S.A., 39
FNAC, 21
Framatome SA, 19
France Télécom Group, V; 21 (upd.)
Fromageries Bel, 23
G.I.E. Airbus Industrie, I; 12 (upd.)
Galeries Lafayette S.A., V; 23 (upd.)
Gaumont SA, 25
Gaz de France, V; 40 (upd.)
Gecina SA, 42
Gefco SA, 54
Générale des Eaux Group, V
GFI Informatique SA, 49
GrandVision S.A., 43
Groupe Air France, 6
Groupe Alain Manoukian, 55
Groupe André, 17
Groupe Castorama-Dubois Investissements,
  23
Groupe Danone, 32 (upd.)
Groupe Dassault Aviation SA, 26 (upd.)
Groupe de la Cite, IV
Groupe DMC (Dollfus Mieg & Cie), 27
Groupe Fournier SA, 44
Groupe Go Sport S.A., 39
Groupe Guillin SA, 40
Groupe Jean-Claude Darmon, 44
Groupe Lapeyre S.A., 33
Groupe Legris Industries, 23
Groupe Les Echos, 25
Groupe Partouche SA, 48
Groupe Promodès S.A., 19
Groupe Rougier SA, 21
Groupe SEB, 35
Groupe Sidel S.A., 21
Groupe Soufflet SA, 55
Groupe Yves Saint Laurent, 23
Groupe Zannier S.A., 35
Guerbet Group, 46
Guerlain, 23
Guilbert S.A., 42
Guillemot Corporation, 41
Guy Degrenne SA, 44
Guyenne et Gascogne, 23
Hachette, IV
Hachette Filipacchi Medias S.A., 21
Havas, SA, 10; 33 (upd.)
Hermès International S.A., 14; 34 (upd.)
Imerys S.A., 40 (upd.)
Imetal S.A., IV

Infogrames Entertainment S.A., 35
Ingenico—Compagnie Industrielle et
  Financière d'Ingénierie, 46
ITM Entreprises SA, 36
Keolis SA, 51
L'Air Liquide SA, I; 47 (upd.)
L'Entreprise Jean Lefebvre, 23
L'Oréal SA, III; 8 (upd.); 46 (upd.)
La Poste, V; 47 (upd.)
Laboratoires de Biologie Végétale Yves
  Rocher, 35
Lafarge Coppée S.A., III
Lafuma S.A., 39
Laurent-Perrier SA, 42
Lazard LLC, 38
Le Monde S.A., 33
Legrand SA, 21
Leroy Merlin SA, 54
LVMH Möet Hennessy Louis Vuitton SA,
  10; 33 (upd.)
Lyonnaise des Eaux-Dumez, V
Maison Louis Jadot, 24
Manitou BF S.A., 27
Marie Brizard & Roger International S.A.,
  22
Marionnaud Parfumeries SA, 51
Matra-Hachette S.A., 15 (upd.)
Metaleurop S.A., 21
Métropole Télévision, 33
Moët-Hennessy, I
Moulinex S.A., 22
Mr. Bricolage S.A., 37
Naf Naf SA, 44
Neopost S.A., 53
Nexans SA, 54
Nocibé SA, 54
Papeteries de Lancey, 23
Pathé SA, 29
Pechiney SA, IV; 45 (upd.)
Penauille Polyservices SA, 49
Pernod Ricard S.A., I; 21 (upd.)
Peugeot S.A., I
Pierre & Vacances SA, 48
Pinault-Printemps Redoute S.A., 19 (upd.)
Pinguely-Haulotte SA, 51
Pochet SA, 55
Poliet S.A., 33
PSA Peugeot Citroen S.A., 28 (upd.)
Publicis S.A., 19
Rallye SA, 54
Regie Nationale des Usines Renault, I
Rémy Cointreau S.A., 20
Renault S.A., 26 (upd.)
Rhodia SA, 38
Rhône-Poulenc S.A., I; 10 (upd.)
Robertet SA, 39
Roussel Uclaf, I; 8 (upd.)
Royal Canin S.A., 39
Sabaté Diosos SA, 48
SAGEM S.A., 37
Salomon Worldwide, 20
Sanofi-Synthélabo Group, The, I; 49 (upd.)
Schneider S.A., II; 18 (upd.)
SCOR S.A., 20
Seita, 23
Selectour SA, 53
Simco S.A., 37
Skis Rossignol S.A., 15; 43 (upd.)
Snecma Group, 46
Société Air France, 27 (upd.)
Société d'Exploitation AOM Air Liberté
  SA (AirLib), 53
Société du Louvre, 27
Société Générale, II; 42 (upd.)
Société Nationale des Chemins de Fer
  Français, V

Société Nationale Elf Aquitaine, IV; 7
  (upd.)
Sodexho Alliance SA, 29
Sodiaal S.A., 36 (upd.)
SODIMA, II
Sommer-Allibert S.A., 19
Steria SA, 49
Suez Lyonnaise des Eaux, 36 (upd.)
Taittinger S.A., 43
Tati SA, 25
Télévision Française 1, 23
Thales S.A., 42
THOMSON multimedia S.A., II; 42 (upd.)
Total Fina Elf S.A., 50 (upd.)
TOTAL S.A., IV; 24 (upd.)
Transiciel SA, 48
Ubi Soft Entertainment S.A., 41
Ugine S.A., 20
Unibail SA, 40
Unilog SA, 42
Union des Assurances de Pans, III
Union Financière de France Banque SA, 52
Usinor SA, IV; 42 (upd.)
Valeo, 23
Vallourec SA, 54
Vinci, 43
Vivarte SA, 54 (upd.)
Vivendi Universal S.A., 46 (upd.)
Worms et Cie, 27
Zodiac S.A., 36

Germany

A.W. Faber-Castell
  Unternehmensverwaltung GmbH & Co.,
  51
Adam Opel AG, 7; 21 (upd.)
adidas-Salomon AG, 14; 33 (upd.)
Adolf Würth GmbH & Co. KG, 49
AEG A.G., I
Aldi Group, 13
Allianz Aktiengesellschaft Holding, III; 15
  (upd.)
AMB Generali Holding AG, 51
Andreas Stihl, 16
ARD, 41
AVA AG (Allgemeine Handelsgesellschaft
  der Verbraucher AG), 33
AXA Colonia Konzern AG, 27; 49 (upd.)
Axel Springer Verlag AG, IV; 20 (upd.)
Bahlsen GmbH & Co. KG, 44
Barmag AG, 39
BASF Aktiengesellschaft, I; 18 (upd.); 50
  (upd.)
Bauer Publishing Group, 7
Bayer A.G., I; 13 (upd.); 41 (upd.)
Bayerische Hypotheken- und Wechsel-
  Bank AG, II
Bayerische Motoren Werke AG, I; 11
  (upd.); 38 (upd.)
Bayerische Vereinsbank A.G., II
Bayernwerk AG, V; 23 (upd.)
Beiersdorf AG, 29
Bertelsmann A.G., IV; 15 (upd.); 43 (upd.)
Bewag AG, 39
Bilfinger & Berger AG, 55 (upd.)
Bilfinger & Berger Bau A.G., I
Brauerei Beck & Co., 9; 33 (upd.)
Braun GmbH, 51
Brenntag AG, 8; 23 (upd.)
Buderus AG, 37
Burda Holding GmbH. & Co., 23
C&A Brenninkmeyer KG, V
C.H. Boehringer Sohn, 39
Carl-Zeiss-Stiftung, III; 34 (upd.)
Commerzbank A.G., II; 47 (upd.)
Continental Aktiengesellschaft, V
Daimler-Benz A.G., I; 15 (upd.)

Germany (*continued*)

Daimler-Benz Aerospace AG, 16
DaimlerChrysler AG, 34 (upd.)
Degussa Group, IV
Degussa-Huls AG, 32 (upd.)
Deutsche Babcock A.G., III
Deutsche Bahn AG, 46 (upd.)
Deutsche Bank AG, II; 14 (upd.); 40 (upd.)
Deutsche BP Aktiengesellschaft, 7
Deutsche Bundesbahn, V
Deutsche Bundespost TELEKOM, V
Deutsche Lufthansa Aktiengesellschaft, I;
    26 (upd.)
Deutsche Post AG, 29
Deutsche Telekom AG, 48 (upd.)
Deutz AG, 39
Dr. August Oetker KG, 51
Dresdner Bank A.G., II
Dürr AG, 44
Dyckerhoff AG, 35
E.On AG, 50 (upd.)
Edeka Zentrale A.G., II; 47 (upd.)
edel music AG, 44
ERGO Versicherungsgruppe AG, 44
Esselte Leitz GmbH & Co. KG, 48
Etienne Aigner AG, 52
Fairchild Dornier GmbH, 48 (upd.)
Feldmuhle Nobel A.G., III
Fielmann AG, 31
Freudenberg & Co., 41
Fried. Krupp GmbH, IV
Friedrich Grohe AG & Co. KG, 53
GEA AG, 27
GEHE AG, 27
geobra Brandstätter GmbH & Co. KG, 48
Gerling-Konzern Versicherungs-
    Beteiligungs-Aktiengesellschaft, 51
Gerresheimer Glas AG, 43
GfK Aktiengesellschaft, 49
Grundig AG, 27
Hapag-Lloyd AG, 6
HARIBO GmbH & Co. KG, 44
HDI (Haftpflichtverband der Deutschen
    Industrie Versicherung auf
    Gegenseitigkeit V.a.G.), 53
Heidelberger Druckmaschinen AG, 40
Heidelberger Zement AG, 31
Henkel KGaA, III; 34 (upd.)
Heraeus Holding GmbH, IV; 54 (upd.)
Hertie Waren- und Kaufhaus GmbH, V
Hochtief AG, 33
Hoechst A.G., I; 18 (upd.)
Hoesch AG, IV
Hugo Boss AG, 48
Huls A.G., I
Infineon Technologies AG, 50
J.M. Voith AG, 33
Jenoptik AG, 33
Kamps AG, 44
Karlsberg Brauerei GmbH & Co KG, 41
Karstadt Aktiengesellschaft, V; 19 (upd.)
Kaufhof Warenhaus AG, V; 23 (upd.)
Kaufring AG, 35
KHD Konzern, III
Klaus Steilmann GmbH & Co. KG, 53
Klockner-Werke AG, IV
König Brauerei GmbH & Co. KG, 35
    (upd.)
Kreditanstalt für Wiederaufbau, 29
Leica Camera AG, 35
Leica Microsystems Holdings GmbH, 35
Linde A.G., I
LTU Group Holding GmbH, 37
MAN Aktiengesellschaft, III
Mannesmann AG, III; 14 (upd.); 38 (upd.)
Margarete Steiff GmbH, 23
Matth. Hohner AG, 53

Melitta Unternehmensgruppe Bentz KG, 53
Messerschmitt-Bölkow-Blohm GmbH., I
Metallgesellschaft AG, IV; 16 (upd.)
Metro AG, 50
MITROPA AG, 37
Munich Re (Münchener
    Rückversicherungs-Gesellschaft
    Aktiengesellschaft in München), III; 46
    (upd.)
Nixdorf Computer AG, III
Optische Werke G. Rodenstock, 44
Otto Versand GmbH & Co., V; 15 (upd.);
    34 (upd.)
Paulaner Brauerei GmbH & Co. KG, 35
Peek & Cloppenburg KG, 46
Philipp Holzmann AG, 17
Porsche AG, 13; 31 (upd.)
Preussag AG, 17; 42 (upd.)
PreussenElektra Aktiengesellschaft, V
ProSiebenSat.1 Media AG, 54
Puma AG Rudolf Dassler Sport, 35
PWA Group, IV
Qiagen N.V., 39
Quelle Group, V
RAG AG, 35
RENK AG, 37
Rheinmetall Berlin AG, 9
Robert Bosch GmbH, I; 16 (upd.); 43
    (upd.)
Rohde & Schwarz GmbH & Co. KG, 39
Roland Berger & Partner GmbH, 37
Ruhrgas AG, V; 38 (upd.)
Ruhrkohle AG, IV
RWE AG, V; 50 (upd.)
Saarberg-Konzern, IV
Salzgitter AG, IV
SAP AG, 16; 43 (upd.)
Schenker-Rhenus AG, 6
Schering AG, I; 50 (upd.)
Siemens A.G., II; 14 (upd.)
Sixt AG, 39
SPAR Handels AG, 35
SPIEGEL-Verlag Rudolf Augstein GmbH
    & Co. KG, 44
Stinnes AG, 8; 23 (upd.)
Stollwerck AG, 53
Südzucker AG, 27
TA Triumph-Adler AG, 48
Tarkett Sommer AG, 25
TaurusHolding GmbH & Co. KG, 46
Tengelmann Group, 27
Thyssen Krupp AG, IV; 28 (upd.)
Touristik Union International GmbH. and
    Company K.G., II
TUI Group GmbH, 44
Vaillant GmbH, 44
Varta AG, 23
Veba A.G., I; 15 (upd.)
Vereinigte Elektrizitätswerke Westfalen
    AG, V
Verlagsgruppe Georg von Holtzbrinck
    GmbH, 35
VEW AG, 39
VIAG Aktiengesellschaft, IV
Victoria Group, 44 (upd.)
VICTORIA Holding AG, III
Viessmann Werke GmbH & Co., 37
Villeroy & Boch AG, 37
Volkswagen Aktiengesellschaft, I; 11
    (upd.); 32 (upd.)
Vorwerk & Co., 27
Vossloh AG, 53
Wacker-Chemie GmbH, 35
Wella AG, III; 48 (upd.)
Weru Aktiengesellschaft, 18
Westdeutsche Landesbank Girozentrale, II;
    46 (upd.)

ZF Friedrichshafen AG, 48

Ghana

Ashanti Goldfields Company Limited, 43

Greece

National Bank of Greece, 41
Royal Olympic Cruise Lines Inc., 52
Stelmar Shipping Ltd., 52

Hong Kong

Cable & Wireless HKT, 30 (upd.)
Cathay Pacific Airways Limited, 6; 34
    (upd.)
Cheung Kong (Holdings) Limited, IV; 20
    (upd.)
China Merchants International Holdings
    Co., Ltd., 52
CITIC Pacific Ltd., 18
First Pacific Company Limited, 18
Hong Kong Telecommunications Ltd., 6
Hongkong and Shanghai Banking
    Corporation Limited, The, II
Hongkong Electric Holdings Ltd., 6; 23
    (upd.)
Hongkong Land Holdings Limited, IV; 47
    (upd.)
Hutchison Whampoa Limited, 18; 49
    (upd.)
Kerry Properties Limited, 22
New World Development Company
    Limited, IV; 38 (upd.)
Playmates Toys, 23
Singer Company N.V., The, 30 (upd.)
Swire Pacific Ltd., I; 16 (upd.)
Tommy Hilfiger Corporation, 20; 53 (upd.)

Hungary

Malév Plc, 24

Iceland

Icelandair, 52

India

Air-India Limited, 6; 27 (upd.)
Bajaj Auto Limited, 39
Coal India Limited, IV; 44 (upd.)
Indian Airlines Ltd., 46
Indian Oil Corporation Ltd., IV; 48 (upd.)
Infosys Technologies Ltd., 38
Minerals and Metals Trading Corporation
    of India Ltd., IV
MTR Foods Ltd., 55
Oil and Natural Gas Commission, IV
Steel Authority of India Ltd., IV
Tata Iron & Steel Co. Ltd., IV; 44 (upd.)
Wipro Limited, 43

Indonesia

Garuda Indonesia, 6
PERTAMINA, IV

Iran

National Iranian Oil Company, IV

Ireland

Aer Lingus Group plc, 34
Allied Irish Banks, plc, 16; 43 (upd.)
Baltimore Technologies Plc, 42
Bank of Ireland, 50
eircom plc, 31 (upd.)
Fyffes Plc, 38
Harland and Wolff Holdings plc, 19

IAWS Group plc, 49
IONA Technologies plc, 43
Jefferson Smurfit Group plc, IV; 19 (upd.); 49 (upd.)
Kerry Group plc, 27
Ryanair Holdings plc, 35
Shannon Aerospace Ltd., 36
Telecom Eireann, 7
Waterford Wedgwood plc, 34 (upd.)

Isle Of Man

Strix Ltd., 51

Israel

Amdocs Ltd., 47
Bank Hapoalim B.M., II; 54 (upd.)
Blue Square Israel Ltd., 41
ECI Telecom Ltd., 18
El Al Israel Airlines Ltd., 23
Elscint Ltd., 20
Israel Chemicals Ltd., 55
Koor Industries Ltd., II; 25 (upd.)
Scitex Corporation Ltd., 24
Teva Pharmaceutical Industries Ltd., 22; 54 (upd.)

Italy

Alfa Romeo, 13; 36 (upd.)
Alitalia-Linee Aeree Italiana, S.p.A., 6; 29 (upd.)
Aprilia SpA, 17
Arnoldo Mondadori Editore S.p.A., IV; 19 (upd.); 54 (upd.)
Assicurazioni Generali SpA, III; 15 (upd.)
Autogrill SpA, 49
Automobili Lamborghini Holding S.p.A., 13; 34 (upd.)
Banca Commerciale Italiana SpA, II
Barilla G. e R. Fratelli S.p.A., 17; 50 (upd.)
Benetton Group S.p.A., 10
Bulgari S.p.A., 20
Credito Italiano, II
Diesel SpA, 40
Ducati Motor Holding S.p.A., 30
Ente Nazionale Idrocarburi, IV
Ente Nazionale per L'Energia Elettrica, V
Fabbrica D' Armi Pietro Beretta S.p.A., 39
Ferrari S.p.A., 13; 36 (upd.)
Ferrero SpA, 54
Fiat SpA, I; 11 (upd.); 50 (upd.)
Fila Holding S.p.A., 20; 52 (upd.)
Gianni Versace SpA, 22
Giorgio Armani S.p.A., 45
Gruppo Coin S.p.A., 41
Guccio Gucci, S.p.A., 15
illycaffè SpA, 50
Industrie Natuzzi S.p.A., 18
Ing. C. Olivetti & C., S.p.a., III
Istituto per la Ricostruzione Industriale S.p.A., I; 11
Juventus F.C. S.p.A., 53
Luxottica SpA, 17; 52 (upd.)
Marchesi Antinori SRL, 42
Marzotto S.p.A., 20
Mediaset SpA, 50
Montedison SpA, I; 24 (upd.)
Officine Alfieri Maserati S.p.A., 13
Olivetti S.p.A., 34 (upd.)
Parmalat Finanziaria SpA, 50
Piaggio & C. S.p.A., 20
Pirelli S.p.A., V; 15 (upd.)
Reno de Medici S.p.A., 41
Riunione Adriatica di Sicurtè SpA, III
Safilo SpA, 54
Sanpaolo IMI S.p.A., 50

Seat Pagine Gialle S.p.A., 47
Società Finanziaria Telefonica per Azioni, V
Società Sportiva Lazio SpA, 44
Telecom Italia S.p.A., 43
Tiscali SpA, 48

Jamaica

Air Jamaica Limited, 54

Japan

Aisin Seiki Co., Ltd., III; 48 (upd.)
Aiwa Co., Ltd., 30
Ajinomoto Co., Inc., II; 28 (upd.)
All Nippon Airways Co., Ltd., 6; 38 (upd.)
Alpine Electronics, Inc., 13
Alps Electric Co., Ltd., II; 44 (upd.)
Asahi Breweries, Ltd., I; 20 (upd.); 52 (upd.)
Asahi Glass Company, Ltd., III; 48 (upd.)
Asahi National Broadcasting Company, Ltd., 9
Bandai Co., Ltd., 55
Bank of Tokyo-Mitsubishi Ltd., II; 15 (upd.)
Bridgestone Corporation, V; 21 (upd.)
Brother Industries, Ltd., 14
C. Itoh & Company Ltd., I
Canon Inc., III; 18 (upd.)
CASIO Computer Co., Ltd., III; 16 (upd.); 40 (upd.)
Central Japan Railway Company, 43
Chubu Electric Power Company, Inc., V; 46 (upd.)
Chugai Pharmaceutical Co., Ltd., 50
Chugoku Electric Power Company Inc., V; 53 (upd.)
Citizen Watch Co., Ltd., III; 21 (upd.)
Cosmo Oil Co., Ltd., IV; 53 (upd.)
Dai Nippon Printing Co., Ltd., IV
Dai-Ichi Kangyo Bank Ltd., The, II
Daido Steel Co., Ltd., IV
Daiei, Inc., The, V; 17 (upd.); 41 (upd.)
Daihatsu Motor Company, Ltd., 7; 21 (upd.)
Daikin Industries, Ltd., III
Daimaru, Inc., The, V; 42 (upd.)
Daio Paper Corporation, IV
Daishowa Paper Manufacturing Co., Ltd., IV
Daiwa Bank, Ltd., The, II; 39 (upd.)
Daiwa Securities Company, Limited, II
Daiwa Securities Group Inc., 55 (upd.)
DDI Corporation, 7
DENSO Corporation, 46 (upd.)
Dentsu Inc., I; 16 (upd.); 40 (upd.)
East Japan Railway Company, V
Fanuc Ltd., III; 17 (upd.)
Fuji Bank, Ltd., The, II
Fuji Electric Co., Ltd., II; 48 (upd.)
Fuji Photo Film Co., Ltd., III; 18 (upd.)
Fujisawa Pharmaceutical Company Ltd., I
Fujitsu Limited, III; 16 (upd.); 42 (upd.)
Furukawa Electric Co., Ltd., The, III
General Sekiyu K.K., IV
Hakuhodo, Inc., 6; 42 (upd.)
Hankyu Corporation, V; 23 (upd.)
Hino Motors, Ltd., 7; 21 (upd.)
Hitachi, Ltd., I; 12 (upd.); 40 (upd.)
Hitachi Metals, Ltd., IV
Hitachi Zosen Corporation, III; 53 (upd.)
Hokkaido Electric Power Company Inc., V
Hokuriku Electric Power Company, V
Honda Motor Company Limited, I; 10 (upd.); 29 (upd.)
Honshu Paper Co., Ltd., IV
Hoshino Gakki Co. Ltd., 55

Idemitsu Kosan Co., Ltd., IV; 49 (upd.)
Industrial Bank of Japan, Ltd., The, II
Isetan Company Limited, V; 36 (upd.)
Ishikawajima-Harima Heavy Industries Co., Ltd., III
Isuzu Motors, Ltd., 9; 23 (upd.)
Ito-Yokado Co., Ltd., V; 42 (upd.)
ITOCHU Corporation, 32 (upd.)
Itoham Foods Inc., II
Japan Airlines Company, Ltd., I; 32 (upd.)
Japan Broadcasting Corporation, 7
Japan Leasing Corporation, 8
Japan Pulp and Paper Company Limited, IV
Japan Tobacco Inc., V; 46 (upd.)
Jujo Paper Co., Ltd., IV
JUSCO Co., Ltd., V
Kajima Corporation, I; 51 (upd.)
Kanebo, Ltd., 53
Kanematsu Corporation, IV; 24 (upd.)
Kansai Electric Power Co., Inc., The, V
Kao Corporation, III; 20 (upd.)
Kawasaki Heavy Industries, Ltd., III
Kawasaki Kisen Kaisha, Ltd., V
Kawasaki Steel Corporation, IV
Keio Teito Electric Railway Company, V
Kenwood Corporation, 31
Kikkoman Corporation, 14; 47 (upd.)
Kinki Nippon Railway Company Ltd., V
Kirin Brewery Company, Limited, I; 21 (upd.)
Kobe Steel, Ltd., IV; 19 (upd.)
Kodansha Ltd., IV; 38 (upd.)
Komatsu Ltd., III; 16 (upd.); 52 (upd.)
Konica Corporation, III; 30 (upd.)
Kotobukiya Co., Ltd., V
Kubota Corporation, III; 26 (upd.)
Kumagai Gumi Company, Ltd., I
Kyocera Corporation, II; 21 (upd.)
Kyowa Hakko Kogyo Co., Ltd., III; 48 (upd.)
Kyushu Electric Power Company Inc., V
Lion Corporation, III; 51 (upd.)
Long-Term Credit Bank of Japan, Ltd., II
Makita Corporation, 22
Marubeni Corporation, I; 24 (upd.)
Marui Co., Ltd., V
Maruzen Co., Limited, 18
Matsushita Electric Industrial Co., Ltd., II
Matsushita Electric Works, Ltd., III; 7 (upd.)
Matsuzakaya Company Limited, V
Mazda Motor Corporation, 9; 23 (upd.)
Meiji Milk Products Company, Limited, II
Meiji Mutual Life Insurance Company, The, III
Meiji Seika Kaisha, Ltd., II
Minolta Co., Ltd., III; 18 (upd.); 43 (upd.)
Mitsubishi Bank, Ltd., The, II
Mitsubishi Chemical Industries, Ltd., I
Mitsubishi Corporation, I; 12 (upd.)
Mitsubishi Electric Corporation, II; 44 (upd.)
Mitsubishi Estate Company, Limited, IV
Mitsubishi Heavy Industries, Ltd., III; 7 (upd.); 40 (upd.)
Mitsubishi Materials Corporation, III
Mitsubishi Motors Corporation, 9; 23 (upd.)
Mitsubishi Oil Co., Ltd., IV
Mitsubishi Rayon Co., Ltd., V
Mitsubishi Trust & Banking Corporation, The, II
Mitsui & Co., Ltd., 28 (upd.)
Mitsui Bank, Ltd., The, II
Mitsui Bussan K.K., I

Japan (*continued*)

Mitsui Marine and Fire Insurance Company, Limited, III
Mitsui Mining & Smelting Co., Ltd., IV
Mitsui Mining Company, Limited, IV
Mitsui Mutual Life Insurance Company, III; 39 (upd.)
Mitsui O.S.K. Lines, Ltd., V
Mitsui Petrochemical Industries, Ltd., 9
Mitsui Real Estate Development Co., Ltd., IV
Mitsui Trust & Banking Company, Ltd., The, II
Mitsukoshi Ltd., V
Mizuno Corporation, 25
Nagasakiya Co., Ltd., V
Nagase & Company, Ltd., 8
NEC Corporation, II; 21 (upd.)
NHK Spring Co., Ltd., III
Nichii Co., Ltd., V
Nichimen Corporation, IV; 24 (upd.)
Nihon Keizai Shimbun, Inc., IV
Nikko Securities Company Limited, The, II; 9 (upd.)
Nikon Corporation, III; 48 (upd.)
Nintendo Co., Ltd., III; 7 (upd.); 28 (upd.)
Nippon Credit Bank, II
Nippon Express Co., Ltd., V
Nippon Life Insurance Company, III
Nippon Light Metal Company, Ltd., IV
Nippon Meat Packers, Inc., II
Nippon Oil Company, Limited, IV
Nippon Seiko K.K., III
Nippon Sheet Glass Company, Limited, III
Nippon Shinpan Company, Ltd., II
Nippon Steel Corporation, IV; 17 (upd.)
Nippon Suisan Kaisha, Limited, II
Nippon Telegraph and Telephone Corporation, V; 51 (upd.)
Nippon Yusen Kabushiki Kaisha, V
Nippondenso Co., Ltd., III
Nissan Motor Company Ltd., I; 11 (upd.); 34 (upd.)
Nisshin Flour Milling Company, Ltd., II
Nisshin Steel Co., Ltd., IV
Nissho Iwai K.K., I
NKK Corporation, IV; 28 (upd.)
Nomura Securities Company, Limited, II; 9 (upd.)
Norinchukin Bank, II
NTN Corporation, III; 47 (upd.)
Odakyu Electric Railway Company Limited, V
Ohbayashi Corporation, I
Oji Paper Co., Ltd., IV
Oki Electric Industry Company, Limited, II
Okura & Co., Ltd., IV
Omron Corporation, II; 28 (upd.)
Onoda Cement Co., Ltd., III
Orix Corporation, II
ORIX Corporation, 44 (upd.)
Osaka Gas Co., Ltd., V
Pioneer Electronic Corporation, III; 28 (upd.)
Rengo Co., Ltd., IV
Ricoh Company, Ltd., III; 36 (upd.)
Roland Corporation, 38
Sankyo Company, Ltd., I
Sanrio Company, Ltd., 38
Sanwa Bank, Ltd., The, II; 15 (upd.)
SANYO Electric Company, Ltd., II; 36 (upd.)
Sanyo-Kokusaku Pulp Co., Ltd., IV
Sapporo Breweries, Ltd., I; 13 (upd.); 36 (upd.)
Seibu Department Stores, Ltd., V; 42 (upd.)

Seibu Railway Co. Ltd., V
Seiko Corporation, III; 17 (upd.)
Seino Transportation Company, Ltd., 6
Seiyu, Ltd., The, V; 36 (upd.)
Sekisui Chemical Co., Ltd., III
Sharp Corporation, II; 12 (upd.); 40 (upd.)
Shikoku Electric Power Company, Inc., V
Shionogi & Co., Ltd., III; 17 (upd.)
Shiseido Company, Limited, III; 22 (upd.)
Showa Shell Sekiyu K.K., IV
Snow Brand Milk Products Company, Ltd., II; 48 (upd.)
Softbank Corp., 13; 38 (upd.)
Sony Corporation, II; 12 (upd.); 40 (upd.)
Sumitomo Bank, Limited, The, II; 26 (upd.)
Sumitomo Chemical Company Ltd., I
Sumitomo Corporation, I; 11 (upd.)
Sumitomo Electric Industries, Ltd., II
Sumitomo Heavy Industries, Ltd., III; 42 (upd.)
Sumitomo Life Insurance Company, III
Sumitomo Marine and Fire Insurance Company, Limited, The, III
Sumitomo Metal Industries, Ltd., IV
Sumitomo Metal Mining Co., Ltd., IV
Sumitomo Mitsui Banking Corporation, 51 (upd.)
Sumitomo Realty & Development Co., Ltd., IV
Sumitomo Rubber Industries, Ltd., V
Sumitomo Trust & Banking Company, Ltd., The, II; 53 (upd.)
Suzuki Motor Corporation, 9; 23 (upd.)
Taiyo Fishery Company, Limited, II
Taiyo Kobe Bank, Ltd., The, II
Takashimaya Company, Limited, V; 47 (upd.)
Takeda Chemical Industries, Ltd., I; 46 (upd.)
TDK Corporation, II; 17 (upd.); 49 (upd.)
Teijin Limited, V
Terumo Corporation, 48
Tobu Railway Co Ltd, 6
Toho Co., Ltd., 28
Tohoku Electric Power Company, Inc., V
Tokai Bank, Limited, The, II; 15 (upd.)
Tokio Marine and Fire Insurance Co., Ltd., The, III
Tokyo Electric Power Company, Incorporated, The, V
Tokyo Gas Co., Ltd., V; 55 (upd.)
Tokyu Corporation, V; 47 (upd.)
Tokyu Department Store Co., Ltd., V; 32 (upd.)
Tokyu Land Corporation, IV
Tomen Corporation, IV; 24 (upd.)
TonenGeneral Sekiyu K.K., IV; 16 (upd.); 54 (upd.)
Toppan Printing Co., Ltd., IV
Toray Industries, Inc., V; 51 (upd.)
Toshiba Corporation, I; 12 (upd.); 40 (upd.)
TOTO LTD., III; 28 (upd.)
Toyo Sash Co., Ltd., III
Toyo Seikan Kaisha, Ltd., I
Toyoda Automatic Loom Works, Ltd., III
Toyota Motor Corporation, I; 11 (upd.); 38 (upd.)
Ube Industries, Ltd., III; 38 (upd.)
Unitika Ltd., V; 53 (upd.)
Uny Co., Ltd., V; 49 (upd.)
Victor Company of Japan, Limited, II; 26 (upd.)
Wacoal Corp., 25
Yamaha Corporation, III; 16 (upd.); 40 (upd.)

Yamaichi Securities Company, Limited, II
Yamato Transport Co. Ltd., V; 49 (upd.)
Yasuda Fire and Marine Insurance Company, Limited, The, III
Yasuda Mutual Life Insurance Company, The, III; 39 (upd.)
Yasuda Trust and Banking Company, Ltd., The, II; 17 (upd.)
Yokohama Rubber Co., Ltd., The, V; 19 (upd.)

Korea

Anam Group, 23
Asiana Airlines, Inc., 46
Daewoo Group, III; 18 (upd.)
Electronics Co., Ltd., 14
Goldstar Co., Ltd., 12
Hanjin Shipping Co., Ltd., 50
Hyundai Group, III; 7 (upd.)
Kia Motors Corporation, 12; 29 (upd.)
Korean Air Lines Co., Ltd., 6; 27 (upd.)
Lucky-Goldstar, II
Pohang Iron and Steel Company Ltd., IV
Samsung Electronics Co., Ltd., I; 41 (upd.)
Ssangyong Cement Industrial Co., Ltd., III

Kuwait

Kuwait Petroleum Corporation, IV; 55 (upd.)

Liechtenstein

Hilti AG, 53

Luxembourg

ARBED S.A., IV; 22 (upd.)
Cargolux Airlines International S.A., 49
RTL Group SA, 44

Lybia

Libyan National Oil Corporation, IV

Madeira

Madeira Wine Company, S.A., 49

Malaysia

Malaysian Airlines System Berhad, 6; 29 (upd.)
Petronas, IV
Sime Darby Berhad, 14; 36 (upd.)

Mexico

Alfa, S.A. de C.V., 19
Altos Hornos de México, S.A. de C.V., 42
Apasco S.A. de C.V., 51
Bufete Industrial, S.A. de C.V., 34
Casa Cuervo, S.A. de C.V., 31
Celanese Mexicana, S.A. de C.V., 54
Cemex SA de CV, 20
Cifra, S.A. de C.V., 12
Consorcio G Grupo Dina, S.A. de C.V., 36
Controladora Comercial Mexicana, S.A. de C.V., 36
Corporación Internacional de Aviación, S.A. de C.V. (Cintra), 20
Desc, S.A. de C.V., 23
Empresas ICA Sociedad Controladora, S.A. de C.V., 41
Ford Motor Company, S.A. de C.V., 20
Gruma, S.A. de C.V., 31
Grupo Aeropuerto del Sureste, S.A. de C.V., 48
Grupo Carso, S.A. de C.V., 21
Grupo Casa Saba, S.A. de C.V., 39
Grupo Cydsa, S.A. de C.V., 39

Grupo Elektra, S.A. de C.V., 39
Grupo Financiero Banamex S.A., 54
Grupo Financiero Banorte, S.A. de C.V.,
  51
Grupo Financiero BBVA Bancomer S.A.,
  54
Grupo Financiero Serfin, S.A., 19
Grupo Gigante, S.A. de C.V., 34
Grupo Herdez, S.A. de C.V., 35
Grupo IMSA, S.A. de C.V., 44
Grupo Industrial Bimbo, 19
Grupo Industrial Durango, S.A. de C.V.,
  37
Grupo Industrial Saltillo, S.A. de C.V., 54
Grupo Mexico, S.A. de C.V., 40
Grupo Modelo, S.A. de C.V., 29
Grupo Televisa, S.A., 18; 54 (upd.)
Grupo TMM, S.A. de C.V., 50
Grupo Transportación Ferroviaria
  Mexicana, S.A. de C.V., 47
Hylsamex, S.A. de C.V., 39
Industrias Bachoco, S.A. de C.V., 39
Industrias Penoles, S.A. de C.V., 22
Internacional de Ceramica, S.A. de C.V.,
  53
Kimberly-Clark de México, S.A. de C.V.,
  54
Organización Soriana, S.A. de C.V., 35
Petróleos Mexicanos, IV; 19 (upd.)
Pulsar Internacional S.A., 21
Real Turismo, S.A. de C.V., 50
Sanborn Hermanos, S.A., 20
Sears Roebuck de México, S.A. de C.V.,
  20
Telefonos de Mexico S.A. de C.V., 14
Tubos de Acero de Mexico, S.A.
  (TAMSA), 41
TV Azteca, S.A. de C.V., 39
Valores Industriales S.A., 19
Vitro Corporativo S.A. de C.V., 34
Wal-Mart de Mexico, S.A. de C.V., 35
  (upd.)

Nepal

Royal Nepal Airline Corporation, 41

The Netherlands

ABN AMRO Holding, N.V., 50
AEGON N.V., III; 50 (upd.)
Akzo Nobel N.V., 13; 41 (upd.)
Algemene Bank Nederland N.V., II
Amsterdam-Rotterdam Bank N.V., II
Arcadis NV, 26
ASML Holding N.V., 50
Baan Company, 25
Buhrmann NV, 41
CNH Global N.V., 38 (upd.)
DSM, N.V, I
Elsevier N.V., IV
Endemol Entertainment Holding NV, 46
Equant N.V., 52
European Aeronautic Defence and Space
  Company EADS N.V., 52 (upd.)
Getronics NV, 39
Grand Hotel Krasnapolsky N.V., 23
Gucci Group N.V., 50
Hagemeyer N.V., 39
Head N.V., 55
Heineken N.V., I; 13 (upd.); 34 (upd.)
Indigo NV, 26
Ispat International N.V., 30
Koninklijke Ahold N.V. (Royal Ahold), II;
  16 (upd.)
Koninklijke Luchtvaart Maatschappij, N.V.
  (KLM Royal Dutch Airlines), I; 28 (upd.)
Koninklijke Nederlandsche Hoogovens en
  Staalfabrieken NV, IV

Koninklijke Nedlloyd N.V., 6; 26 (upd.)
Koninklijke Philips Electronics N.V., 50
  (upd.)
Koninklijke PTT Nederland NV, V
Koninklijke Wessanen nv, II; 54 (upd.)
KPMG International, 10; 33 (upd.)
Mammoet Transport B.V., 26
MIH Limited, 31
N.V. AMEV, III
N.V. Holdingmaatschappij De Telegraaf,
  23
N.V. Koninklijke Nederlandse
  Vliegtuigenfabriek Fokker, I; 28 (upd.)
N.V. Nederlandse Gasunie, V
Nationale-Nederlanden N.V., III
New Holland N.V., 22
Océ N.V., 24
PCM Uitgevers NV, 53
Philips Electronics N.V., II; 13 (upd.)
PolyGram N.V., 23
Prada Holding B.V., 45
Qiagen N.V., 39
Rabobank Group, 33
Randstad Holding n.v., 16; 43 (upd.)
Rodamco N.V., 26
Royal Dutch/Shell Group, IV; 49 (upd.)
Royal Grolsch NV, 54
Royal KPN N.V., 30
Royal Numico N.V., 37
Royal Packaging Industries Van Leer N.V.,
  30
Royal Vopak NV, 41
SHV Holdings N.V., 55
TNT Post Group N.V., V, 27 (upd.); 30
  (upd.)
Toolex International N.V., 26
Triple P N.V., 26
Unilever N.V., II; 7 (upd.); 32 (upd.)
United Pan-Europe Communications NV,
  47
Vebego International BV, 49
Vedior NV, 35
Velcro Industries N.V., 19
Vendex International N.V., 13
VNU N.V., 27
Wegener NV, 53
Wolters Kluwer NV, 14; 33 (upd.)

New Zealand

Air New Zealand Limited, 14; 38 (upd.)
Fletcher Challenge Ltd., IV; 19 (upd.)
Telecom Corporation of New Zealand
  Limited, 54
Wattie's Ltd., 7

Nigeria

Nigerian National Petroleum Corporation,
  IV

Norway

Braathens ASA, 47
Den Norse Stats Oljeselskap AS, IV
Helly Hansen ASA, 25
Kvaerner ASA, 36
Norsk Hydro ASA, 10; 35 (upd.)
Orkla A/S, 18
Schibsted ASA, 31
Stolt Sea Farm Holdings PLC, 54

Oman

Petroleum Development Oman LLC, IV

Pakistan

Pakistan International Airlines Corporation,
  46

Panama

Panamerican Beverages, Inc., 47

Peru

Southern Peru Copper Corporation, 40

Philippines

Philippine Airlines, Inc., 6; 23 (upd.)
San Miguel Corporation, 15

Poland

LOT Polish Airlines (Polskie Linie
  Lotnicze S.A.), 33
Telekomunikacja Polska SA, 50

Portugal

Banco Comercial Português, SA, 50
Banco Espírito Santo e Comercial de
  Lisboa S.A., 15
Corticeira Amorim, Sociedade Gestora de
  Participaço es Sociais, S.A., 48
Electricidade de Portugal, S.A., 47
Petróleos de Portugal S.A., IV
TAP—Air Portugal Transportes Aéreos
  Portugueses S.A., 46
Transportes Aereos Portugueses, S.A., 6

Puerto Rico

Puerto Rico Electric Power Authority, 47

Qatar

Qatar General Petroleum Corporation, IV

Russia

A.S. Yakovlev Design Bureau, 15
Aeroflot—Russian International Airlines, 6;
  29 (upd.)
AO VimpelCom, 48
Aviacionny Nauchno-Tehnicheskii
  Komplex im. A.N. Tupoleva, 24
JSC MMC Norilsk Nickel, 48
OAO Gazprom, 42
OAO LUKOIL, 40
OAO NK YUKOS, 47
OAO Siberian Oil Company (Sibneft), 49
OAO Surgutneftegaz, 48
OAO Tatneft, 45
OJSC Wimm-Bill-Dann Foods, 48
RAO Unified Energy System of Russia, 45
Sukhoi Design Bureau Aviation Scientific-
  Industrial Complex, 24

Saudi Arabia

Saudi Arabian Airlines, 6; 27 (upd.)
Saudi Arabian Oil Company, IV; 17 (upd.);
  50 (upd.)

Scotland

Distillers Company PLC, I
General Accident PLC, III
Governor and Company of the Bank of
  Scotland, The, 10
Royal Bank of Scotland Group plc, The,
  12
Scottish & Newcastle plc, 15
Scottish Hydro-Electric PLC, 13
Scottish Media Group plc, 32
ScottishPower plc, 19
Stagecoach Holdings plc, 30
Standard Life Assurance Company, The,
  III

Singapore

Flextronics International Ltd., 38
Fraser & Neave Ltd., 54
Neptune Orient Lines Limited, 47
Singapore Airlines Ltd., 6; 27 (upd.)

South Africa

Anglo American Corporation of South
  Africa Limited, IV; 16 (upd.)
Barlow Rand Ltd., I
De Beers Consolidated Mines Limited/De
  Beers Centenary AG, IV; 7 (upd.); 28
  (upd.)
Gencor Ltd., IV; 22 (upd.)
Gold Fields of South Africa Ltd., IV
SAA (Pty) Ltd., 28
Sappi Limited, 49
Sasol Limited, IV; 47 (upd.)
South African Breweries Limited, The, I;
  24 (upd.)
Transnet Ltd., 6

Spain

Banco Bilbao Vizcaya Argentaria S.A., II;
  48 (upd.)
Banco Central, II
Banco do Brasil S.A., II
Banco Santander Central Hispano S.A., 36
  (upd.)
Chupa Chups S.A., 38
Compañia Española de Petróleos S.A., IV
Dogi International Fabrics S.A., 52
El Corte Inglés Group, V; 26 (upd.)
ENDESA S.A., V; 46 (upd.)
Grupo Dragados SA, 55
Grupo Ferrovial, S.A., 40
Grupo Lladró S.A., 52
Iberdrola, S.A., 49
Iberia Líneas Aéreas de España S.A., 6; 36
  (upd.)
Instituto Nacional de Industria, I
Repsol-YPF S.A., IV; 16 (upd.); 40 (upd.)
Tabacalera, S.A., V; 17 (upd.)
Telefónica S.A., V; 46 (upd.)
TelePizza S.A., 33
Television Española, S.A., 7
Terra Lycos, Inc., 43
Unión Fenosa, S.A., 51

Sweden

A. Johnson & Company H.B., I
AB Volvo, I; 7 (upd.); 26 (upd.)
Aktiebolaget Electrolux, 22 (upd.)
Aktiebolaget SKF, III; 38 (upd.)
Alfa-Laval AB, III
Astra AB, I; 20 (upd.)
Atlas Copco AB, III; 28 (upd.)
Bonnier AB, 52
BRIO AB, 24
Cardo AB, 53
Electrolux AB, III; 53 (upd.)
Gambro AB, 49
Gunnebo AB, 53
Hennes & Mauritz AB, 29
Holmen AB, 52 (upd.)
ICA AB, II
Mo och Domsjö AB, IV
Modern Times Group AB, 36
NetCom Systems AB, 26
Nobel Industries AB, 9
Nordea AB, 40
Observer AB, 55
Perstorp AB, I; 51 (upd.)
Saab Automobile AB, 32 (upd.)
Saab-Scania A.B., I; 11 (upd.)
Sandvik AB, IV; 32 (upd.)

SAS Group, The, 34 (upd.)
Scandinavian Airlines System, I
Securitas AB, 42
Skandia Insurance Company, Ltd., 50
Skandinaviska Enskilda Banken, II
Skanska AB, 38
Stora Kopparbergs Bergslags AB, IV
Svenska Cellulosa Aktiebolaget SCA, IV;
  28 (upd.)
Svenska Handelsbanken AB, II; 50 (upd.)
Swedish Match AB, 39 (upd.)
Swedish Telecom, V
Telefonaktiebolaget LM Ericsson, V; 46
  (upd.)
Vin & Spirit AB, 31

Switzerland

ABB ASEA Brown Boveri Ltd., II; 22
  (upd.)
Adecco S.A., 36 (upd.)
Adia S.A., 6
Arthur Andersen & Company, Société
  Coopérative, 10
Ascom AG, 9
Bâloise-Holding, 40
Barry Callebaut AG, 29
Bernina Holding AG, 47
Bodum Design Group AG, 47
Bon Appetit Holding AG, 48
Chocoladefabriken Lindt & Sprüngli AG,
  27
Ciba-Geigy Ltd., I; 8 (upd.)
Compagnie Financiere Richemont AG, 50
Coop Schweiz Genossenschaftsverband, 48
Credit Suisse Group, II; 21 (upd.)
Danzas Group, V; 40 (upd.)
De Beers Consolidated Mines Limited/De
  Beers Centenary AG, IV; 7 (upd.); 28
  (upd.)
Elektrowatt AG, 6
F. Hoffmann-La Roche Ltd., I; 50 (upd.)
Fédération Internationale de Football
  Association, 27
Geberit AG, 49
Givaudan SA, 43
Holderbank Financière Glaris Ltd., III
International Olympic Committee, 44
Jacobs Suchard A.G., II
Julius Baer Holding AG, 52
Keramik Holding AG Laufen, 51
Kraft Jacobs Suchard AG, 26 (upd.)
Kudelski Group SA, 44
Kuehne & Nagel International AG, V; 53
  (upd.)
Kuoni Travel Holding Ltd., 40
Logitech International SA, 28
Maus Frères SA, 48
Mettler-Toledo International Inc., 30
Montres Rolex S.A., 13; 34 (upd.)
Nestlé S.A., II; 7 (upd.); 28 (upd.)
Novartis AG, 39 (upd.)
Panalpina World Transport (Holding) Ltd.,
  47
Rieter Holding AG, 42
Roland Murten A.G., 7
Sandoz Ltd., I
Schindler Holding AG, 29
Schweizerische Post-, Telefon- und
  Telegrafen-Betriebe, V
Serono S.A., 47
STMicroelectronics NV, 52
Sulzer Brothers Limited (Gebruder Sulzer
  Aktiengesellschaft), III
Swarovski International Holding AG, 40
Swatch Group SA, The, 26
Swedish Match S.A., 12
Swiss Air Transport Company, Ltd., I

Swiss Bank Corporation, II
Swiss Federal Railways (Schweizerische
  Bundesbahnen), The, V
Swiss International Air Lines Ltd., 48
Swiss Reinsurance Company
  (Schweizerische Rückversicherungs-
  Gesellschaft), III; 46 (upd.)
TAG Heuer International SA, 25
Tamedia AG, 53
Tetra Pak International SA, 53
UBS AG, 52 (upd.)
Union Bank of Switzerland, II
Victorinox AG, 21
Winterthur Schweizerische Versicherungs-
  Gesellschaft, III
Zurich Financial Services, 42 (upd.)
Zürich Versicherungs-Gesellschaft, III

Taiwan

Acer Inc., 16
China Airlines, 34
Directorate General of
  Telecommunications, 7
EVA Airways Corporation, 51
Evergreen Marine Corporation (Taiwan)
  Ltd., 13; 50 (upd.)
Formosa Plastics Corporation, 14
Quanta Computer Inc., 47
Taiwan Semiconductor Manufacturing
  Company Ltd., 47
Tatung Co., 23
Yageo Corporation, 16

Thailand

Thai Airways International Public
  Company Limited, 6; 27 (upd.)

Tunisia

Société Tunisienne de l'Air-Tunisair, 49

Turkey

Haci Omer Sabanci Holdings A.S., 55
Koç Holding A.S., I; 54 (upd.)
Türkiye Petrolleri Anonim Ortakliği, IV

Ukraine

Antonov Design Bureau, 53

United Arab Emirates

Abu Dhabi National Oil Company, IV; 45
  (upd.)
Emirates Group, The, 39

United Kingdom

Abbey National plc, 10; 39 (upd.)
Aegis Group plc, 6
Aggregate Industries plc, 36
Aggreko Plc, 45
Airtours Plc, 27
Albert Fisher Group plc, The, 41
All England Lawn Tennis & Croquet Club,
  The, 54
Alldays plc, 49
Allders plc, 37
Allied Domecq PLC, 29
Allied-Lyons PLC, I
Alvis Plc, 47
Amersham PLC, 50
Amey Plc, 47
Amnesty International, 50
Amstrad plc, III; 48 (upd.)
Anglo American PLC, 50 (upd.)
Anker BV, 53
Arcadia Group plc, 28 (upd.)

Argyll Group PLC, II
Arjo Wiggins Appleton p.l.c., 34
ASDA Group plc, II; 28 (upd.)
Ashtead Group plc, 34
Associated British Foods plc, II; 13 (upd.);
    41 (upd.)
Associated British Ports Holdings Plc, 45
Aston Villa plc, 41
AstraZeneca PLC, 50 (upd.)
AT&T Istel Ltd., 14
Aviva PLC, 50 (upd.)
B.A.T. Industries PLC, I; 22 (upd.)
BAA plc, 10; 33 (upd.)
Balfour Beatty plc, 36 (upd.)
Barclays PLC, II; 20 (upd.)
Barings PLC, 14
Barratt Developments PLC, I
Bass PLC, I; 15 (upd.); 38 (upd.)
Bat Industries PLC, I; 20 (upd.)
Bellway Plc, 45
Benfield Greig Group plc, 53
Bhs plc, 17
BICC PLC, III
Blacks Leisure Group plc, 39
Blue Circle Industries PLC, III
BOC Group plc, I; 25 (upd.)
Body Shop International plc, The, 11; 53
    (upd.)
Booker plc, 13; 31 (upd.)
Boots Company PLC, The, V; 24 (upd.)
Bowater PLC, IV
Bowthorpe plc, 33
BP p.l.c., 45 (upd.)
Brake Bros plc, 45
British Aerospace plc, I; 24 (upd.)
British Airways PLC, I; 14 (upd.); 43
    (upd.)
British American Tobacco PLC, 50 (upd.)
British Broadcasting Corporation Ltd., 7;
    21 (upd.)
British Coal Corporation, IV
British Energy Plc, 49
British Gas plc, V
British Land Plc, 54
British Midland plc, 38
British Nuclear Fuels plc, 6
British Petroleum Company plc, The, IV; 7
    (upd.); 21 (upd.)
British Railways Board, V
British Sky Broadcasting Group Plc, 20
British Steel plc, IV; 19 (upd.)
British Telecommunications plc, V; 15
    (upd.)
British Vita plc, 9; 33 (upd.)
British World Airlines Ltd., 18
British-Borneo Oil & Gas PLC, 34
BT Group plc, 49 (upd.)
BTR PLC, I
BTR Siebe plc, 27
Bunzl plc, IV; 31 (upd.)
Burberry Ltd., 17; 41 (upd.)
Burmah Castrol PLC, IV; 30 (upd.)
Burton Group plc, The, V
Business Post Group plc, 46
C&J Clark International Ltd., 52
Cable and Wireless plc, V; 25 (upd.)
Cadbury Schweppes PLC, II; 49 (upd.)
Canary Wharf Group Plc, 30
Capital Radio plc, 35
Caradon plc, 20 (upd.)
Carlton Communications PLC, 15; 50
    (upd.)
Cartier Monde, 29
Central Independent Television, 7; 23
    (upd.)
Centrica plc, 29 (upd.)
Christian Salvesen Plc, 45

Christie's International plc, 15; 39 (upd.)
Chrysalis Group plc, 40
Chubb, PLC, 50
Clifford Chance LLP, 38
Clinton Cards plc, 39
Close Brothers Group plc, 39
Co-operative Group (CWS) Ltd., 51
Coats plc, 44 (upd.)
Coats Viyella Plc, V
Cobham plc, 30
COLT Telecom Group plc, 41
Commercial Union PLC, III
Compass Group PLC, 34
Cookson Group plc, III; 44 (upd.)
Corus Group plc, 49 (upd.)
Courtaulds plc, V; 17 (upd.)
Courts Plc, 45
Cranswick plc, 40
Croda International Plc, 45
Daily Mail and General Trust plc, 19
Dairy Crest Group plc, 32
Dalgety, PLC, II
Davis Service Group PLC, 45
Dawson Holdings PLC, 43
De La Rue plc, 10; 34 (upd.)
Debenhams Plc, 28
Denby Group plc, 44
Denison International plc, 46
Devro plc, 55
Diageo plc, 24 (upd.)
Dixons Group plc, V; 19 (upd.); 49 (upd.)
Dorling Kindersley Holdings plc, 20
easyJet Airline Company Limited, 39
ECC Group plc, III
Electrocomponents PLC, 50
Elementis plc, 40 (upd.)
EMAP plc, 35
EMI Group plc, 22 (upd.)
Energis plc, 47
English China Clays Ltd., 15 (upd.); 40
    (upd.)
Enterprise Oil PLC, 11; 50 (upd.)
Esporta plc, 35
Eurotunnel Group, 13; 37 (upd.)
Exel plc, 51 (upd.)
Fairclough Construction Group PLC, I
First Choice Holidays PLC, 40
Fisons plc, 9; 23 (upd.)
French Connection Group plc, 41
Fuller Smith & Turner P.L.C., 38
Gallaher Group Plc, 49 (upd.)
Gallaher Limited, V; 19 (upd.)
Gateway Corporation Ltd., The, II
Geest Plc, 38
General Electric Company PLC, II
George Wimpey PLC, 12; 51 (upd.)
GKN plc, III; 38 (upd.)
Glaxo Holdings PLC, I; 9 (upd.)
GlaxoSmithKline plc, 46 (upd.)
Glotel plc, 53
Go-Ahead Group Plc, The, 28
Granada Group PLC, II; 24 (upd.)
Grand Metropolitan PLC, I; 14 (upd.)
Great Universal Stores plc, The, V; 19
    (upd.)
Greenalls Group PLC, The, 21
Greene King plc, 31
Guardian Media Group plc, 53
Guardian Royal Exchange Plc, 11
Guinness/UDV, I; 43 (upd.)
GUS plc, 47 (upd.)
GWR Group plc, 39
Hammerson plc, 40
Hammerson Property Investment and
    Development Corporation plc, The, IV
Hanson PLC, III; 7 (upd.); 30 (upd.)
Harrisons & Crosfield plc, III

Harrods Holdings, 47
Hartstone Group plc, The, 14
Hawker Siddeley Group Public Limited
    Company, III
Hays Plc, 27
Hazlewood Foods plc, 32
Her Majesty's Stationery Office, 7
Hillsdown Holdings plc, II; 24 (upd.)
Hilton Group plc, 49 (upd.)
HIT Entertainment PLC, 40
House of Fraser PLC, 45
HSBC Holdings plc, 12; 26 (upd.)
Huntingdon Life Sciences Group plc, 42
Ibstock Brick Ltd., 14; 37 (upd.)
ICL plc, 6
IMI plc, 9
Imperial Chemical Industries PLC, I; 50
    (upd.)
Imperial Tobacco Group PLC, 50
Inchcape PLC, III; 16 (upd.); 50 (upd.)
International Power PLC, 50 (upd.)
Invensys PLC, 50 (upd.)
IPC Magazines Limited, 7
J Sainsbury plc, II; 13 (upd.); 38 (upd.)
James Beattie plc, 43
Jarvis plc, 39
JD Wetherspoon plc, 30
JJB Sports plc, 32
John Brown PLC, I
John Laing plc, I; 51 (upd.)
John Lewis Partnership plc, V; 42 (upd.)
John Menzies plc, 39
Johnson Matthey PLC, IV; 16 (upd.); 49
    (upd.)
Johnston Press plc, 35
Kelda Group plc, 45
Kennecott Corporation, 7; 27 (upd.)
Kidde plc, 44 (upd.)
Kingfisher plc, V; 24 (upd.)
Kleinwort Benson Group PLC, II
Kvaerner ASA, 36
Kwik-Fit Holdings plc, 54
Ladbroke Group PLC, II; 21 (upd.)
Lafarge Cement UK, 54 (upd.)
Land Securities PLC, IV; 49 (upd.)
Laura Ashley Holdings plc, 13; 37 (upd.)
Legal & General Group plc, III; 24 (upd.)
Littlewoods plc, V; 42 (upd.)
Lloyd's of London, III; 22 (upd.)
Lloyds Bank PLC, II
Lloyds TSB Group plc, 47 (upd.)
Logica plc, 14; 37 (upd.)
London Regional Transport, 6
London Stock Exchange Limited, 34
Lonrho Plc, 21
Lotus Cars Ltd., 14
Lucas Industries PLC, III
Luminar Plc, 40
Madge Networks N.V., 26
Manchester United Football Club plc, 30
Marconi plc, 33 (upd.)
Marks and Spencer p.l.c., V; 24 (upd.)
Matalan PLC, 49
Maxwell Communication Corporation plc,
    IV; 7 (upd.)
McKechnie plc, 34
Meggitt PLC, 34
MEPC plc, IV
Mercury Communications, Ltd., 7
Mersey Docks and Harbour Company, The,
    30
Metal Box PLC, I
Michael Page International plc, 45
Midland Bank PLC, II; 17 (upd.)
Mirror Group Newspapers plc, 7; 23 (upd.)
Misys plc, 45; 46
Molins plc, 51

United Kingdom (continued)

Monsoon plc, 39
Morgan Grenfell Group PLC, II
Moss Bros Group plc, 51
Mothercare UK Ltd., 17
N M Rothschild & Sons Limited, 39
National Express Group PLC, 50
National Power PLC, 12
National Westminster Bank PLC, II
New Look Group plc, 35
Newsquest plc, 32
Next plc, 29
NFC plc, 6
Nichols plc, 44
North West Water Group plc, 11
Northern Foods PLC, 10
Northern Rock plc, 33
Norwich & Peterborough Building Society, 55
Novar plc, 49 (upd.)
Ocean Group plc, 6
Pearson plc, IV; 46 (upd.)
Peninsular & Oriental Steam Navigation Company (Bovis Division), The, I
Peninsular and Oriental Steam Navigation Company, The, V; 38 (upd.)
Pennon Group Plc, 45
Pentland Group plc, 20
PIC International Group PLC, 24 (upd.)
Pilkington plc, III; 34 (upd.)
Plessey Company, PLC, The, II
Post Office Group, V
Powell Duffryn plc, 31
Powergen PLC, 11; 50 (upd.)
Prudential plc, 48 (upd.)
Psion PLC, 45
R. Griggs Group Limited, 23
Racal Electronics PLC, II
Ragdoll Productions Ltd., 51
Railtrack Group PLC, 50
Rank Organisation Plc, The, II; 14 (upd.)
Ranks Hovis McDougall Limited, II; 28 (upd.)
Really Useful Group, The, 26
Reckitt Benckiser plc, II; 42 (upd.)
Redland plc, III
Redrow Group plc, 31
Reed Elsevier plc, IV; 17 (upd.); 31 (upd.)
Renishaw plc, 46
Rentokil Initial Plc, 47
Reuters Holdings PLC, IV; 22 (upd.)
Rexam PLC, 32 (upd.)
Rio Tinto PLC, 19 (upd.); 50 (upd.)
RMC Group p.l.c., III ; 34 (upd.)
Rolls-Royce Motors Ltd., I
Rolls-Royce plc, I; 7 (upd.); 21 (upd.)
Ronson PLC, 49
Rothmans International p.l.c., V
Rothmans UK Holdings Limited, 19 (upd.)
Rotork plc, 46
Rover Group Ltd., 7; 21 (upd.)
Rowntree Mackintosh, II
Royal & Sun Alliance Insurance Group plc, 55 (upd.)
Royal Bank of Scotland Group plc, The, 38 (upd.)
Royal Doulton plc, 14; 38 (upd.)
Royal Dutch Petroleum Company/ The Shell Transport and Trading Company p.l.c., IV
Royal Insurance Holdings PLC, III
RTZ Corporation PLC, The, IV
Rugby Group plc, The, 31
Saatchi & Saatchi PLC, I
Safeway PLC, 50 (upd.)
Sage Group, The, 43
SBC Warburg, 14

Schroders plc, 42
Scottish & Newcastle plc, 35 (upd.)
Scottish Power plc, 49 (upd.)
Scottish Radio Holding plc, 41
Sea Containers Ltd., 29
Sears plc, V
Securicor Plc, 45
Selfridges Plc, 34
Serco Group plc, 47
Severn Trent PLC, 12; 38 (upd.)
SFI Group plc, 51
Shanks Group plc, 45
Shepherd Neame Limited, 30
Singer & Friedlander Group plc, 41
Slough Estates PLC, IV; 50 (upd.)
Smith & Nephew plc, 17;41 (upd.)
SmithKline Beecham plc, III; 32 (upd.)
Smiths Industries PLC, 25
Somerfield plc, 47 (upd.)
Southern Electric PLC, 13
SSL International plc, 49
St Ives plc, 34
Standard Chartered plc, II; 48 (upd.)
STC PLC, III
Stoll-Moss Theatres Ltd., 34
Stolt-Nielsen S.A., 42
Storehouse PLC, 16
Sun Alliance Group PLC, III
Sytner Group plc, 45
Tarmac plc, III; 28 (upd.)
Tate & Lyle PLC, II; 42 (upd.)
Taylor & Francis Group plc, 44
Taylor Nelson Sofres plc, 34
Taylor Woodrow plc, I; 38 (upd.)
Tesco PLC, II; 24 (upd.)
Thames Water plc, 11
Thistle Hotels PLC, 54
Thorn Emi PLC, I
Thorn plc, 24
Thorntons plc, 46
TI Group plc, 17
Tibbett & Britten Group plc, 32
Tomkins plc, 11; 44 (upd.)
Travis Perkins plc, 34
Trinity Mirror plc, 49 (upd.)
Triumph Motorcycles Ltd., 53
Trusthouse Forte PLC, III
TSB Group plc, 12
Tussauds Group, The, 55
Ultramar PLC, IV
Unigate PLC, II; 28 (upd.)
Unilever PLC, II; 7 (upd.); 32 (upd.)
United Biscuits (Holdings) plc, II; 42 (upd.)
United Business Media plc, 52 (upd.)
United News & Media plc, 28 (upd.)
United Newspapers plc, IV
United Utilities PLC, 52 (upd.)
Vendôme Luxury Group plc, 27
Vickers plc, 27
Virgin Group, 12; 32 (upd.)
Vodafone Group PLC, 11; 36 (upd.)
Vosper Thornycroft Holding plc, 41
Wassall Plc, 18
Waterford Wedgwood Holdings PLC, 12
Watson Wyatt Worldwide, 42
Wellcome Foundation Ltd., The, I
WH Smith PLC, V, 42 (upd.)
Whatman plc, 46
Whitbread PLC, I; 20 (upd.); 52 (upd.)
William Hill Organization Limited, 49
Willis Corroon Group plc, 25
Wilson Bowden Plc, 45
Wincanton plc, 52
Wm. Morrison Supermarkets PLC, 38
Wood Hall Trust PLC, I
Woolwich plc, The, 30

WPP Group plc, 6; 48 (upd.)
WS Atkins Plc, 45
Young & Co.'s Brewery, P.L.C., 38
Yule Catto & Company plc, 54
Zeneca Group PLC, 21
Zomba Records Ltd., 52

United States

A & E Television Networks, 32
A & W Brands, Inc., 25
A-dec, Inc., 53
A. Schulman, Inc., 8; 49 (upd.)
A.B. Watley Group Inc., 45
A.B.Dick Company, 28
A.C. Moore Arts & Crafts, Inc., 30
A.G. Edwards, Inc., 8; 32
A.H. Belo Corporation, 10; 30 (upd.)
A.L. Pharma Inc., 12
A.M. Castle & Co., 25
A.O. Smith Corporation, 11; 40 (upd.)
A.T. Cross Company, 17; 49 (upd.)
AAF-McQuay Incorporated, 26
AAON, Inc., 22
AAR Corp., 28
Aaron Rents, Inc., 14; 35 (upd.)
AARP, 27
Aavid Thermal Technologies, Inc., 29
Abbott Laboratories, I; 11 (upd.); 40 (upd.)
ABC Appliance, Inc., 10
ABC Carpet & Home Co. Inc., 26
ABC Family Worldwide, Inc., 52
ABC Rail Products Corporation, 18
ABC Supply Co., Inc., 22
Abercrombie & Fitch Co., 15; 35 (upd.)
Abigail Adams National Bancorp, Inc., 23
Abiomed, Inc., 47
ABM Industries Incorporated, 25 (upd.)
Abrams Industries Inc., 23
Academy of Television Arts & Sciences, Inc., 55
Academy Sports & Outdoors, 27
Acadian Ambulance & Air Med Services, Inc., 39
Acclaim Entertainment Inc., 24
ACCO World Corporation, 7; 51 (upd.)
ACE Cash Express, Inc., 33
Ace Hardware Corporation, 12; 35 (upd.)
Aceto Corp., 38
Ackerley Communications, Inc., 9
Acme-Cleveland Corp., 13
ACNielsen Corporation, 13; 38 (upd.)
Acorn Products, Inc., 55
Acsys, Inc., 44
Action Performance Companies, Inc., 27
Activision, Inc., 32
Acuson Corporation, 10; 36 (upd.)
Acxiom Corporation, 35
Adams Golf, Inc., 37
Adaptec, Inc., 31
ADC Telecommunications, Inc., 10; 30 (upd.)
Adelphia Communications Corporation, 17; 52 (upd.)
Administaff, Inc., 52
Adobe Systems Inc., 10; 33 (upd.)
Adolph Coors Company, I; 13 (upd.); 36 (upd.)
ADT Security Services, Inc., 12; 44 (upd.)
Adtran Inc., 22
Advance Publications Inc., IV; 19 (upd.)
Advanced Marketing Services, Inc., 34
Advanced Micro Devices, Inc., 6; 30 (upd.)
Advanced Technology Laboratories, Inc., 9
Advanta Corporation, 8; 38 (upd.)
Advantica Restaurant Group, Inc., 27 (upd.)
Adventist Health, 53

Advo, Inc., 6; 53 (upd.)
Advocat Inc., 46
AEI Music Network Inc., 35
AEP Industries, Inc., 36
Aeronca Inc., 46
Aeroquip Corporation, 16
AES Corporation, The, 10; 13 (upd.); 53 (upd.)
Aetna, Inc., III; 21 (upd.)
AFC Enterprises, Inc., 32
Affiliated Foods Inc., 53
Affiliated Publications, Inc., 7
AFLAC Incorporated, 10 (upd.); 38 (upd.)
Ag-Chem Equipment Company, Inc., 17
AGCO Corp., 13
Agilent Technologies Inc., 38
Agway, Inc., 7; 21 (upd.)
AHL Services, Inc., 27
Air & Water Technologies Corporation, 6
Air Express International Corporation, 13
Air Methods Corporation, 53
Air Products and Chemicals, Inc., I; 10 (upd.)
Air Wisconsin Airlines Corporation, 55
Airborne Freight Corporation, 6; 34 (upd.)
Airgas, Inc., 54
AirTouch Communications, 11
AirTran Holdings, Inc., 22
AK Steel Holding Corporation, 19; 41 (upd.)
Akin, Gump, Strauss, Hauer & Feld, L.L.P., 33
Akorn, Inc., 32
Alamo Group Inc., 32
Alamo Rent A Car, Inc., 6; 24 (upd.)
Alaska Air Group, Inc., 6; 29 (upd.)
Alba-Waldensian, Inc., 30
Albany International Corporation, 8; 51 (upd.)
Alberto-Culver Company, 8; 36 (upd.)
Albertson's Inc., II; 7 (upd.); 30 (upd.)
Alco Health Services Corporation, III
Alco Standard Corporation, I
Aldila Inc., 46
Aldus Corporation, 10
Alex Lee Inc., 18; 44 (upd.)
Alexander & Alexander Services Inc., 10
Alexander & Baldwin, Inc., 10; 40 (upd.)
Alexander's, Inc., 45
All American Communications Inc., 20
Alleghany Corporation, 10
Allegheny Energy, Inc., 38 (upd.)
Allegheny Ludlum Corporation, 8
Allegheny Power System, Inc., V
Allen Organ Company, 33
Allergan, Inc., 10; 30 (upd.)
Alliance Entertainment Corp., 17
Alliant Techsystems Inc., 8; 30 (upd.)
Allied Healthcare Products, Inc., 24
Allied Products Corporation, 21
Allied Signal Engines, 9
Allied Waste Industries, Inc., 50
Allied Worldwide, Inc., 49
AlliedSignal Inc., I; 22 (upd.)
Allison Gas Turbine Division, 9
Allou Health & Beauty Care, Inc., 28
Alloy, Inc., 55
Allstate Corporation, The, 10; 27 (upd.)
ALLTEL Corporation, 6; 46 (upd.)
Alltrista Corporation, 30
Allwaste, Inc., 18
Aloha Airlines, Incorporated, 24
Alpharma Inc., 35 (upd.)
Alpine Lace Brands, Inc., 18
AltaVista Company, 43
Altera Corporation, 18; 43 (upd.)
Alterra Healthcare Corporation, 42

Altron Incorporated, 20
Aluminum Company of America, IV; 20 (upd.)
Alvin Ailey Dance Foundation, Inc., 52
ALZA Corporation, 10; 36 (upd.)
AMAX Inc., IV
Amazon.com, Inc., 25
Amblin Entertainment, 21
AMC Entertainment Inc., 12; 35 (upd.)
AMCORE Financial Inc., 44
Amdahl Corporation, III; 14 (upd.); 40 (upd.)
Amdocs Ltd., 47
Amedysis, Inc., 53
Amerada Hess Corporation, IV; 21 (upd.); 55 (upd.)
Amerco, 6
America Online, Inc., 10 ; 26 (upd.)
America West Holdings Corporation, 6; 34 (upd.)
America's Favorite Chicken Company, Inc., 7
American Airlines, I; 6 (upd.)
American Banknote Corporation, 30
American Bar Association, 35
American Biltrite Inc., 16; 43 (upd.)
American Brands, Inc., V
American Building Maintenance Industries, Inc., 6
American Business Information, Inc., 18
American Business Products, Inc., 20
American Cancer Society, The, 24
American Cast Iron Pipe Company, 50
American Classic Voyages Company, 27
American Coin Merchandising, Inc., 28
American Colloid Co., 13
American Crystal Sugar Company, 9; 32 (upd.)
American Cyanamid, I; 8 (upd.)
American Eagle Outfitters, Inc., 24; 55 (upd.)
American Electric Power Company, Inc., V; 45 (upd.)
American Express Company, II; 10 (upd.); 38 (upd.)
American Family Corporation, III
American Financial Group Inc., III; 48 (upd.)
American Foods Group, 43
American Furniture Company, Inc., 21
American General Corporation, III; 10 (upd.); 46 (upd.)
American General Finance Corp., 11
American Golf Corporation, 45
American Gramaphone LLC, 52
American Greetings Corporation, 7; 22 (upd.)
American Home Mortgage Holdings, Inc., 46
American Home Products, I; 10 (upd.)
American Homestar Corporation, 18; 41 (upd.)
American Institute of Certified Public Accountants (AICPA), 44
American International Group, Inc., III; 15 (upd.); 47 (upd.)
American Italian Pasta Company, 27
American Lawyer Media Holdings, Inc., 32
American Locker Group Incorporated, 34
American Lung Association, 48
American Maize-Products Co., 14
American Management Systems, Inc., 11
American Media, Inc., 27
American Medical Association, 39
American Medical International, Inc., III
American Medical Response, Inc., 39
American Motors Corporation, I

American National Insurance Company, 8; 27 (upd.)
American Pad & Paper Company, 20
American Power Conversion Corporation, 24
American Premier Underwriters, Inc., 10
American President Companies Ltd., 6
American Printing House for the Blind, 26
American Re Corporation, 10; 35 (upd.)
American Red Cross, 40
American Residential Mortgage Corporation, 8
American Retirement Corporation, 42
American Rice, Inc., 33
American Safety Razor Company, 20
American Skiing Company, 28
American Society of Composers, Authors and Publishers (ASCAP), The, 29
American Software Inc., 25
American Standard Companies Inc., III; 30 (upd.)
American States Water Company, 46
American Stores Company, II; 22 (upd.)
American Telephone and Telegraph Company, V
American Tourister, Inc., 16
American Tower Corporation, 33
American Vanguard Corporation, 47
American Water Works Company, Inc., 6; 38 (upd.)
American Woodmark Corporation, 31
Amerihost Properties, Inc., 30
AmeriSource Health Corporation, 37 (upd.)
Ameristar Casinos, Inc., 33
Ameritech Corporation, V; 18 (upd.)
Ameritrade Holding Corporation, 34
Ameriwood Industries International Corp., 17
Amerock Corporation, 53
Ames Department Stores, Inc., 9; 30 (upd.)
AMETEK, Inc., 9
AMF Bowling, Inc., 40
Amfac/JMB Hawaii L.L.C., I; 24 (upd.)
Amgen, Inc., 10; 30 (upd.)
Amoco Corporation, IV; 14 (upd.)
Amoskeag Company, 8
AMP Incorporated, II; 14 (upd.)
Ampex Corporation, 17
Amphenol Corporation, 40
AMR Corporation, 28 (upd.); 52 (upd.)
AMREP Corporation, 21
AmSouth Bancorporation, 12; 48 (upd.)
Amsted Industries Incorporated, 7
AmSurg Corporation, 48
Amtran, Inc., 34
Amway Corporation, III; 13 (upd.); 30 (upd.)
Anadarko Petroleum Corporation, 10; 52 (upd.)
Anaheim Angels Baseball Club, Inc., 53
Analog Devices, Inc., 10
Analogic Corporation, 23
Analysts International Corporation, 36
Analytic Sciences Corporation, 10
Analytical Surveys, Inc., 33
Anaren Microwave, Inc., 33
Anchor Bancorp, Inc., 10
Anchor Brewing Company, 47
Anchor Gaming, 24
Anchor Hocking Glassware, 13
Andersen Corporation, 10
Andersen Worldwide, 29 (upd.)
Andersons, Inc., The, 31
Andrew Corporation, 10; 32 (upd.)
Andrews McMeel Universal, 40
Andrx Corporation, 55
Angelica Corporation, 15; 43 (upd.)

United States (*continued*)

Anheuser-Busch Companies, Inc., I; 10 (upd.); 34 (upd.)

AnnTaylor Stores Corporation, 13; 37 (upd.)

ANR Pipeline Co., 17

Anschutz Corporation, The, 12; 36 (upd.)

Anthem Electronics, Inc., 13

Antioch Company, The, 40

Aon Corporation, III; 45 (upd.)

Apache Corporation, 10; 32 (upd.)

Apartment Investment and Management Company, 49

Apogee Enterprises, Inc., 8

Apollo Group, Inc., 24

Applause Inc., 24

Apple Computer, Inc., III; 6 (upd.); 36 (upd.)

Applebee's International Inc., 14; 35 (upd.)

Appliance Recycling Centers of America, Inc., 42

Applica Incorporated, 43 (upd.)

Applied Bioscience International, Inc., 10

Applied Films Corporation, 48

Applied Materials, Inc., 10; 46 (upd.)

Applied Micro Circuits Corporation, 38

Applied Power, Inc., 9; 32 (upd.)

Aqua Alliance Inc., 32 (upd.)

Aquila, Inc., 50 (upd.)

AR Accessories Group, Inc., 23

ARA Services, II

ARAMARK Corporation, 13; 41 (upd.)

Arandell Corporation, 37

Arbitron Company, The, 38

Arbor Drugs Inc., 12

Arby's Inc., 14

Arch Mineral Corporation, 7

Arch Wireless, Inc., 39

Archer-Daniels-Midland Company, I; 11 (upd.); 32 (upd.)

Archstone-Smith Trust, 49

Archway Cookies, Inc., 29

ARCO Chemical Company, 10

Arctco, Inc., 16

Arctic Cat Inc., 40 (upd.)

Arctic Slope Regional Corporation, 38

Arden Group, Inc., 29

Argosy Gaming Company, 21

Ariens Company, 48

Aris Industries, Inc., 16

Ark Restaurants Corp., 20

Arkansas Best Corporation, 16

Arkla, Inc., V

Armco Inc., IV

Armor All Products Corp., 16

Armor Holdings, Inc., 27

Armstrong World Industries, Inc., III; 22 (upd.)

Army and Air Force Exchange Service, 39

Arnold & Porter, 35

Arrow Air Holdings Corporation, 55

Arrow Electronics, Inc., 10; 50 (upd.)

Art Institute of Chicago, The, 29

Art Van Furniture, Inc., 28

Artesyn Technologies Inc., 46 (upd.)

Arthur D. Little, Inc., 35

Arthur Murray International, Inc., 32

Artisan Entertainment Inc., 32 (upd.)

ArvinMeritor, Inc., 8; 54 (upd.)

Asanté Technologies, Inc., 20

ASARCO Incorporated, IV

ASC, Inc., 55

Ascend Communications, Inc., 24

Ashland Inc., 19; 50 (upd.)

Ashland Oil, Inc., IV

Ashley Furniture Industries, Inc., 35

Ashworth, Inc., 26

ASK Group, Inc., 9

Aspect Telecommunications Corporation, 22

Aspen Skiing Company, 15

Asplundh Tree Expert Co., 20

Assisted Living Concepts, Inc., 43

Associated Estates Realty Corporation, 25

Associated Grocers, Incorporated, 9; 31 (upd.)

Associated Milk Producers, Inc., 11; 48 (upd.)

Associated Natural Gas Corporation, 11

Associated Press, The, 13; 31 (upd.)

AST Research Inc., 9

Astoria Financial Corporation, 44

Astronics Corporation, 35

ASV, Inc., 34

At Home Corporation, 43

AT&T Bell Laboratories, Inc., 13

AT&T Corporation, 29 (upd.)

AT&T Wireless Services, Inc., 54 (upd.)

Atari Corporation, 9; 23 (upd.)

Atchison Casting Corporation, 39

Atlanta Gas Light Company, 6; 23 (upd.)

Atlanta National League Baseball Club, Inc., 43

Atlantic American Corporation, 44

Atlantic Coast Airlines Holdings, Inc., 55

Atlantic Energy, Inc., 6

Atlantic Group, The, 23

Atlantic Richfield Company, IV; 31 (upd.)

Atlantic Southeast Airlines, Inc., 47

Atlas Air, Inc., 39

Atlas Van Lines, Inc., 14

Atmel Corporation, 17

Atmos Energy Corporation, 43

Atwood Mobil Products, 53

Au Bon Pain Co., Inc., 18

Audio King Corporation, 24

Audiovox Corporation, 34

Ault Incorporated, 34

Auntie Anne's, Inc., 35

Aurora Foods Inc., 32

Austin Company, The, 8

Authentic Fitness Corporation, 20; 51 (upd.)

Auto Value Associates, Inc., 25

Autobytel Inc., 47

Autocam Corporation, 51

Autodesk, Inc., 10

Autologic Information International, Inc., 20

Automatic Data Processing, Inc., III; 9 (upd.); 47 (upd.)

AutoNation, Inc., 50

Autotote Corporation, 20

AutoZone, Inc., 9; 31 (upd.)

Avado Brands, Inc., 31

Avco Financial Services Inc., 13

Aveda Corporation, 24

Avedis Zildjian Co., 38

Avery Dennison Corporation, IV; 17 (upd.); 49 (upd.)

Aviation Sales Company, 41

Avid Technology Inc., 38

Avis Rent A Car, Inc., 6; 22 (upd.)

Avnet Inc., 9

Avon Products, Inc., III; 19 (upd.); 46 (upd.)

Avondale Industries, 7; 41 (upd.)

Aydin Corp., 19

Azcon Corporation, 23

Aztar Corporation, 13

B&G Foods, Inc., 40

B. Dalton Bookseller Inc., 25

B. Manischewitz Company, LLC, The, 31

B/E Aerospace, Inc., 30

Babbage's, Inc., 10

Baby Superstore, Inc., 15

Bachman's Inc., 22

Back Bay Restaurant Group, Inc., 20

Back Yard Burgers, Inc., 45

Badger Meter, Inc., 22

Badger Paper Mills, Inc., 15

Bain & Company, 55

Bairnco Corporation, 28

Baker & Hostetler LLP, 40

Baker & McKenzie, 10; 42 (upd.)

Baker & Taylor Corporation, 16; 43 (upd.)

Baker and Botts, L.L.P., 28

Baker Hughes Incorporated, III; 22 (upd.)

Balance Bar Company, 32

Balchem Corporation, 42

Baldor Electric Company, 21

Baldwin & Lyons, Inc., 51

Baldwin Piano & Organ Company, 18

Baldwin Technology Company, Inc., 25

Ball Corporation, I; 10 (upd.)

Ballantyne of Omaha, Inc., 27

Ballard Medical Products, 21

Bally Manufacturing Corporation, III

Bally Total Fitness Holding Corp., 25

Baltek Corporation, 34

Baltimore Gas and Electric Company, V; 25 (upd.)

Banana Republic Inc., 25

Banc One Corporation, 10

Bandag, Inc., 19

Banfi Products Corp., 36

Bank of America Corporation, 46 (upd.)

Bank of Boston Corporation, II

Bank of Mississippi, Inc., 14

Bank of New England Corporation, II

Bank of New York Company, Inc., The, II; 46 (upd.)

Bank One Corporation, 36 (upd.)

BankAmerica Corporation, II; 8 (upd.)

Bankers Trust New York Corporation, II

Banknorth Group, Inc., 55

Banner Aerospace, Inc., 14; 37 (upd.)

Banta Corporation, 12; 32 (upd.)

Banyan Systems Inc., 25

BarclaysAmerican Mortgage Corporation, 11

Barnes & Noble, Inc., 10; 30 (upd.)

Barnes Group Inc., 13

Barnett Banks, Inc., 9

Barnett Inc., 28

Barney's, Inc., 28

Barr Laboratories, Inc., 26

Barrett Business Services, Inc., 16

Barton Malow Company, 51

Barton Protective Services Inc., 53

Baseball Club of Seattle, LP, The, 50

Bashas' Inc., 33

Basketball Club of Seattle, LLC, The, 50

Bass Pro Shops, Inc., 42

Bassett Furniture Industries, Inc., 18

Bates Worldwide, Inc., 14; 33 (upd.)

Bath Iron Works, 12; 36 (upd.)

Battelle Memorial Institute, Inc., 10

Battle Mountain Gold Company, 23

Bausch & Lomb Inc., 7; 25 (upd.)

Baxter International Inc., I; 10 (upd.)

Bay State Gas Company, 38

BayBanks, Inc., 12

Bayou Steel Corporation, 31

BBN Corp., 19

BEA Systems, Inc., 36

Bear Creek Corporation, 38

Bear Stearns Companies, Inc., II; 10 (upd.); 52 (upd.)

Bearings, Inc., 13

Beasley Broadcast Group, Inc., 51

Beatrice Company, II
BeautiControl Cosmetics, Inc., 21
Beazer Homes USA, Inc., 17
bebe stores, inc., 31
Bechtel Group, Inc., I; 24 (upd.)
Beckett Papers, 23
Beckman Coulter, Inc., 22
Beckman Instruments, Inc., 14
Becton, Dickinson & Company, I; 11 (upd.); 36 (upd.)
Bed Bath & Beyond Inc., 13; 41 (upd.)
Beech Aircraft Corporation, 8
Beech-Nut Nutrition Corporation, 21; 51 (upd.)
Bekins Company, 15
Bel Fuse, Inc., 53
Belco Oil & Gas Corp., 40
Belden Inc., 19
Belk Stores Services, Inc., V; 19 (upd.)
Bell and Howell Company, 9; 29 (upd.)
Bell Atlantic Corporation, V; 25 (upd.)
Bell Helicopter Textron Inc., 46
Bell Industries, Inc., 47
Bell Sports Corporation, 16; 44 (upd.)
BellSouth Corporation, V; 29 (upd.)
Beloit Corporation, 14
Bemis Company, Inc., 8
Ben & Jerry's Homemade, Inc., 10; 35 (upd.)
Benchmark Capital, 49
Benchmark Electronics, Inc., 40
Bendix Corporation, I
Beneficial Corporation, 8
Benihana, Inc., 18
Benjamin Moore & Co., 13; 38 (upd.)
Benton Oil and Gas Company, 47
Bergdorf Goodman Inc., 52
Bergen Brunswig Corporation, V; 13 (upd.)
Beringer Wine Estates Holdings, Inc., 22
Berkeley Farms, Inc., 46
Berkshire Hathaway Inc., III; 18 (upd.); 42 (upd.)
Berkshire Realty Holdings, L.P., 49
Berlitz International, Inc., 13; 39 (upd.)
Bernard C. Harris Publishing Company, Inc., 39
Bernard Chaus, Inc., 27
Berry Petroleum Company, 47
Berry Plastics Corporation, 21
Bertucci's Inc., 16
Best Buy Co., Inc., 9; 23 (upd.)
Bestfoods, 22 (upd.)
BET Holdings, Inc., 18
Bethlehem Steel Corporation, IV; 7 (upd.); 27 (upd.)
Betz Laboratories, Inc., I; 10 (upd.)
Beverly Enterprises, Inc., III; 16 (upd.)
BFGoodrich Company, The, V; 19 (upd.)
BHC Communications, Inc., 26
BIC Corporation, 8; 23 (upd.)
Bicoastal Corporation, II
Big B, Inc., 17
Big Bear Stores Co., 13
Big Dog Holdings, Inc., 45
Big 5 Sporting Goods Corporation, 55
Big Flower Press Holdings, Inc., 21
Big Idea Productions, Inc., 49
Big Lots, Inc., 50
Big O Tires, Inc., 20
Big Rivers Electric Corporation, 11
Big V Supermarkets, Inc., 25
Big Y Foods, Inc., 53
Bill & Melinda Gates Foundation, 41
Bill Blass Ltd., 32
Billing Concepts Corp., 26
Bindley Western Industries, Inc., 9
Bingham Dana LLP, 43

Binks Sames Corporation, 21
Binney & Smith Inc., 25
Biogen Inc., 14; 36 (upd.)
Biomet, Inc., 10
Bird Corporation, 19
Birkenstock Footprint Sandals, Inc., 12; 42 (upd.)
Birmingham Steel Corporation, 13; 40 (upd.)
BISSELL Inc., 9; 30 (upd.)
BJ Services Company, 25
Black & Decker Corporation, The, III; 20 (upd.)
Black & Veatch LLP, 22
Black Box Corporation, 20
Black Hills Corporation, 20
Blair Corporation, 25; 31
Blessings Corp., 19
Blimpie International, Inc., 15; 49 (upd.)
Block Drug Company, Inc., 8; 27 (upd.)
Blockbuster Inc., 9; 31 (upd.)
Blonder Tongue Laboratories, Inc., 48
Bloomberg L.P., 21
Bloomingdale's Inc., 12
Blount International, Inc., 48 (upd.)
Blount, Inc., 12
Blue Bell Creameries L.P., 30
Blue Bird Corporation, 35
Blue Cross and Blue Shield Association, 10
Blue Diamond Growers, 28
Blue Mountain Arts, Inc., 29
Blyth Industries, Inc., 18
BMC Industries, Inc., 17
BMC Software, Inc., 55
Boart Longyear Company, 26
Boatmen's Bancshares Inc., 15
Bob Evans Farms, Inc., 9
Bobit Publishing Company, 55
Boca Resorts, Inc., 37
Boeing Company, The, I; 10 (upd.); 32 (upd.)
Bohemia, Inc., 13
Boise Cascade Corporation, IV; 8 (upd.); 32 (upd.)
Bombay Company, Inc., The, 10
Bon Marché, Inc., The, 23
Bon Secours Health System, Inc., 24
Bon-Ton Stores, Inc., The, 16; 50 (upd.)
Bonneville International Corporation, 29
Bonneville Power Administration, 50
Book-of-the-Month Club, Inc., 13
Books-A-Million, Inc., 14; 41 (upd.)
Boole & Babbage, Inc., 25
Booth Creek Ski Holdings, Inc., 31
Booz Allen & Hamilton, Inc., 10
Borden, Inc., II; 22 (upd.)
Borders Group, Inc., 15; 43 (upd.)
Borg-Warner Automotive, Inc., 14; 32 (upd.)
Borg-Warner Corporation, III
Borland International, Inc., 9
Boron, LePore & Associates, Inc., 45
Boscov's Department Store, Inc., 31
Bose Corporation, 13; 36 (upd.)
Boston Acoustics, Inc., 22
Boston Beer Company, Inc., The, 18; 50 (upd.)
Boston Celtics Limited Partnership, 14
Boston Chicken, Inc., 12
Boston Edison Company, 12
Boston Market Corporation, 48 (upd.)
Boston Professional Hockey Association Inc., 39
Boston Properties, Inc., 22
Boston Scientific Corporation, 37
Bowne & Co., Inc., 23

Boy Scouts of America, The, 34
Boyd Bros. Transportation Inc., 39
Boyd Coffee Company, 53
Boyd Gaming Corporation, 43
Boyds Collection, Ltd., The, 29
Bozell Worldwide Inc., 25
Bozzuto's, Inc., 13
Brach and Brock Confections, Inc., 15
Bradlees Discount Department Store Company, 12
Brannock Device Company, 48
Brass Eagle Inc., 34
Brazos Sportswear, Inc., 23
Bremer Financial Corp., 45
Briazz, Inc., 53
Bridgeport Machines, Inc., 17
Bridgford Foods Corporation, 27
Briggs & Stratton Corporation, 8; 27 (upd.)
Bright Horizons Family Solutions, Inc., 31
Brightpoint, Inc., 18
Brinker International, Inc., 10; 38 (upd.)
Bristol Hotel Company, 23
Bristol-Myers Squibb Company, III; 9 (upd.); 37 (upd.)
Brite Voice Systems, Inc., 20
Broadcast Music Inc., 23
Broadcom Corporation, 34
Broadmoor Hotel, The, 30
Brobeck, Phleger & Harrison, LLP, 31
Broder Bros. Co., 38
Broderbund Software, Inc., 13; 29 (upd.)
Brooke Group Ltd., 15
Brooklyn Union Gas, 6
Brooks Brothers Inc., 22
Brooks Sports Inc., 32
Brookshire Grocery Company, 16
Brookstone, Inc., 18
Brothers Gourmet Coffees, Inc., 20
Broughton Foods Co., 17
Brown & Brown, Inc., 41
Brown & Haley, 23
Brown & Root, Inc., 13
Brown & Sharpe Manufacturing Co., 23
Brown & Williamson Tobacco Corporation, 14; 33 (upd.)
Brown Brothers Harriman & Co., 45
Brown Group, Inc., V; 20 (upd.)
Brown Printing Company, 26
Brown-Forman Corporation, I; 10 (upd.); 38 (upd.)
Browning-Ferris Industries, Inc., V; 20 (upd.)
Broyhill Furniture Industries, Inc., 10
Bruce Foods Corporation, 39
Bruno's, Inc., 7; 26 (upd.)
Brunswick Corporation, III; 22 (upd.)
Brush Wellman Inc., 14
BTG, Inc., 45
Buca, Inc., 38
Buck Consultants, Inc., 55
Buck Knives Inc., 48
Buckeye Technologies, Inc., 42
Buckle, Inc., The, 18
Bucyrus International, Inc., 17
Budd Company, The, 8
Budget Group, Inc., 25
Budget Rent a Car Corporation, 9
Buffets, Inc., 10; 32 (upd.)
Bugle Boy Industries, Inc., 18
Building Materials Holding Corporation, 52
Bulley & Andrews, LLC, 55
Bulova Corporation, 13; 41 (upd.)
Bundy Corporation, 17
Bureau of National Affairs, Inc., The 23
Burger King Corporation, II; 17 (upd.)
Burlington Coat Factory Warehouse Corporation, 10

United States (*continued*)

Burlington Industries, Inc., V; 17 (upd.)
Burlington Northern Santa Fe Corporation, V; 27 (upd.)
Burlington Resources Inc., 10
Burns International Services Corporation, 13; 41 (upd.)
Burr-Brown Corporation, 19
Burton Snowboards Inc., 22
Bush Boake Allen Inc., 30
Bush Brothers & Company, 45
Bush Industries, Inc., 20
Business Men's Assurance Company of America, 14
Butler Manufacturing Co., 12
Butterick Co., Inc., 23
Buttrey Food & Drug Stores Co., 18
buy.com, Inc., 46
BWAY Corporation, 24
C & S Wholesale Grocers, Inc., 55
C-COR.net Corp., 38
C-Cube Microsystems, Inc., 37
C.F. Martin & Co., Inc., 42
C.H. Heist Corporation, 24
C.H. Robinson Worldwide, Inc., 11; 40 (upd.)
C.R. Bard Inc., 9
Cabela's Inc., 26
Cabletron Systems, Inc., 10
Cablevision Electronic Instruments, Inc., 32
Cablevision Systems Corporation, 7; 30 (upd.)
Cabot Corporation, 8; 29 (upd.)
Cache Incorporated, 30
CACI International Inc., 21
Cadence Design Systems, Inc., 11; 48 (upd.)
Cadmus Communications Corporation, 23
Cadwalader, Wickersham & Taft, 32
CAE USA Inc., 48
Caere Corporation, 20
Caesars World, Inc., 6
Cagle's, Inc., 20
Cahners Business Information, 43
Calavo Growers, Inc., 47
CalComp Inc., 13
Calcot Ltd., 33
Caldor Inc., 12
California Pizza Kitchen Inc., 15
Callaway Golf Company, 15; 45 (upd.)
Callon Petroleum Company, 47
Calloway's Nursery, Inc., 51
CalMat Co., 19
Calpine Corporation, 36
Caltex Petroleum Corporation, 19
Calvin Klein, Inc., 22; 55 (upd.)
Cambrex Corporation, 16; 44 (upd.)
Cambridge SoundWorks, Inc., 48
Cambridge Technology Partners, Inc., 36
Camelot Music, Inc., 26
Cameron & Barkley Company, 28
Campbell Scientific, Inc., 51
Campbell Soup Company, II; 7 (upd.); 26 (upd.)
Campbell-Mithun-Esty, Inc., 16
Campo Electronics, Appliances & Computers, Inc., 16
Canandaigua Brands, Inc., 13; 34 (upd.)
Candela Corporation, 48
Candie's, Inc., 31
Candlewood Hotel Company, Inc., 41
Cannon Express, Inc., 53
Cannondale Corporation, 21
Canterbury Park Holding Corporation, 42
Cap Rock Energy Corporation, 46
Capel Incorporated, 45
Capital Cities/ABC Inc., II

Capital Holding Corporation, III
Capital One Financial Corporation, 52
CapStar Hotel Company, 21
Caraustar Industries, Inc., 19; 44 (upd.)
Carbide/Graphite Group, Inc., The, 40
Carborundum Company, 15
Cardinal Health, Inc., 18; 50 (upd.)
Career Education Corporation, 45
Caremark Rx, Inc., 10; 54 (upd.)
Carey International, Inc., 26
Cargill, Incorporated, II; 13 (upd.); 40 (upd.)
Carhartt, Inc., 30
Caribiner International, Inc., 24
Caribou Coffee Company, Inc., 28
Carlisle Companies Incorporated, 8
Carlson Companies, Inc., 6; 22 (upd.)
Carlson Wagonlit Travel, 55
CarMax, Inc., 55
Carmichael Lynch Inc., 28
Carmike Cinemas, Inc., 14; 37 (upd.)
Carnation Company, II
Carnegie Corporation of New York, 35
Carnival Corporation, 6; 27 (upd.)
Carolina First Corporation, 31
Carolina Freight Corporation, 6
Carolina Power & Light Company, V; 23 (upd.)
Carolina Telephone and Telegraph Company, 10
Carpenter Technology Corporation, 13
CARQUEST Corporation, 29
Carr-Gottstein Foods Co., 17
Carriage House Companies, Inc., The, 55
Carriage Services, Inc., 37
Carrier Access Corporation, 44
Carrier Corporation, 7
Carroll's Foods, Inc., 46
Carsey-Werner Company, L.L.C., The, 37
Carson Pirie Scott & Company, 15
Carson, Inc., 31
Carter Hawley Hale Stores, Inc., V
Carter Lumber Company, 45
Carter-Wallace, Inc., 8; 38 (upd.)
Carvel Corporation, 35
Cascade Natural Gas Corporation, 9
Casco Northern Bank, 14
Casey's General Stores, Inc., 19
Cash America International, Inc., 20
Castle & Cooke, Inc., II; 20 (upd.)
Casual Corner Group, Inc., 43
Casual Male Retail Group, Inc., 52
Caswell-Massey Co. Ltd., 51
Catalina Lighting, Inc., 43 (upd.)
Catalina Marketing Corporation, 18
Catalytica Energy Systems, Inc., 44
Catellus Development Corporation, 24
Caterpillar Inc., III; 15 (upd.)
Catherines Stores Corporation, 15
Catholic Order of Foresters, 24
Cato Corporation, 14
Cattleman's, Inc., 20
CB Commercial Real Estate Services Group, Inc., 21
CBI Industries, Inc., 7
CBRL Group, Inc., 35 (upd.)
CBS Corporation, II; 6 (upd.); 28 (upd.)
CCA Industries, Inc., 53
CCH Inc., 14
CDI Corporation, 6; 54 (upd.)
CDW Computer Centers, Inc., 16; 52 (upd.)
CEC Entertainment, Inc., 31 (upd.)
Cedar Fair, L.P., 22
Celadon Group Inc., 30
Celanese Corporation, I
Celebrity, Inc., 22

Celestial Seasonings, Inc., 16
Cendant Corporation, 44 (upd.)
Centel Corporation, 6
Centennial Communications Corporation, 39
Centerior Energy Corporation, V
Centex Corporation, 8; 29 (upd.)
Centocor Inc., 14
Central and South West Corporation, V
Central Garden & Pet Company, 23
Central Hudson Gas and Electricity Corporation, 6
Central Maine Power, 6
Central Newspapers, Inc., 10
Central Parking Corporation, 18
Central Soya Company, Inc., 7
Central Sprinkler Corporation, 29
Central Vermont Public Service Corporation, 54
Centuri Corporation, 54
Century Aluminum Company, 52
Century Business Services, Inc., 52
Century Casinos, Inc., 53
Century Communications Corp., 10
Century Telephone Enterprises, Inc., 9; 54 (upd.)
Century Theatres, Inc., 31
Cephalon, Inc., 45
Cerner Corporation, 16
CertainTeed Corporation, 35
Cessna Aircraft Company, 8; 27 (upd.)
Chadbourne & Parke, 36
Chadwick's of Boston, Ltd., 29
Chalone Wine Group, Ltd., The, 36
Champion Enterprises, Inc., 17
Champion Industries, Inc., 28
Champion International Corporation, IV; 20 (upd.)
Championship Auto Racing Teams, Inc., 37
Chancellor Beacon Academies, Inc., 53
Chancellor Media Corporation, 24
Chaparral Steel Co., 13
Charles River Laboratories International, Inc., 42
Charles Schwab Corporation, The, 8; 26 (upd.)
Charles Stark Draper Laboratory, Inc., The, 35
Charlotte Russe Holding, Inc., 35
Charming Shoppes, Inc., 8; 38
Chart House Enterprises, Inc., 17
Chart Industries, Inc., 21
Charter Communications, Inc., 33
ChartHouse International Learning Corporation, 49
Chase Manhattan Corporation, The, II; 13 (upd.)
Chateau Communities, Inc., 37
Chattem, Inc., 17
Chautauqua Airlines, Inc., 38
Checkers Drive-Up Restaurants Inc., 16
Checkpoint Systems, Inc., 39
Cheesecake Factory Inc., The, 17
Chelsea Milling Company, 29
Chemcentral Corporation, 8
Chemed Corporation, 13
Chemfab Corporation, 35
Chemi-Trol Chemical Co., 16
Chemical Banking Corporation, II; 14 (upd.)
Chemical Waste Management, Inc., 9
Cherokee Inc., 18
Chesapeake Corporation, 8; 30 (upd.)
Chesebrough-Pond's USA, Inc., 8
Chevron Corporation, IV; 19 (upd.)
ChevronTexaco Corporation, 47 (upd.)

Cheyenne Software, Inc., 12
Chi-Chi's Inc., 13; 51 (upd.)
Chiasso Inc., 53
Chiat/Day Inc. Advertising, 11
Chic by H.I.S, Inc., 20
Chicago and North Western Holdings
  Corporation, 6
Chicago Bears Football Club, Inc., 33
Chicago Board of Trade, 41
Chick-fil-A Inc., 23
Chicken of the Sea International, 24 (upd.)
Chico's FAS, Inc., 45
Children's Comprehensive Services, Inc.,
  42
Children's Hospitals and Clinics, Inc., 54
Children's Place Retail Stores, Inc., The,
  37
Childtime Learning Centers, Inc., 34
Chiles Offshore Corporation, 9
CHIPS and Technologies, Inc., 9
Chiquita Brands International, Inc., 7; 21
  (upd.)
Chiron Corporation, 10; 36 (upd.)
Chisholm-Mingo Group, Inc., 41
Chock Full o' Nuts Corp., 17
Choice Hotels International Inc., 14
Chorus Line Corporation, 30
Chris-Craft Industries, Inc., 9; 31 (upd.)
Christensen Boyles Corporation, 26
Christian Broadcasting Network, Inc., The,
  52
Christian Science Publishing Society, The,
  55
Christopher & Banks Corporation, 42
Chromcraft Revington, Inc., 15
Chronicle Publishing Company, Inc., The,
  23
Chronimed Inc., 26
Chrysler Corporation, I; 11 (upd.)
CH2M Hill Ltd., 22
Chubb Corporation, The, III; 14 (upd.); 37
  (upd.)
Church & Dwight Co., Inc., 29
Churchill Downs Incorporated, 29
Cianbro Corporation, 14
Ciber, Inc., 18
CIENA Corporation, 54
CIGNA Corporation, III; 22 (upd.); 45
  (upd.)
Cincinnati Bell, Inc., 6
Cincinnati Financial Corporation, 16; 44
  (upd.)
Cincinnati Gas & Electric Company, 6
Cincinnati Milacron Inc., 12
Cincom Systems Inc., 15
Cinnabon Inc., 23
Cintas Corporation, 21; 51 (upd.)
CIPSCO Inc., 6
Circle K Company, The, II; 20 (upd.)
Circon Corporation, 21
Circuit City Stores, Inc., 9; 29 (upd.)
Circus Circus Enterprises, Inc., 6
Cirrus Design Corporation, 44
Cirrus Logic, Inc., 11; 48 (upd.)
Cisco Systems, Inc., 11; 34 (upd.)
Citadel Communications Corporation, 35
Citfed Bancorp, Inc., 16
CITGO Petroleum Corporation, IV; 31
  (upd.)
Citicorp, II; 9 (upd.)
Citigroup Inc., 30 (upd.)
Citizens Financial Group, Inc., 42
Citizens Utilities Company, 7
Citrix Systems, Inc., 44
City Public Service, 6
CKE Restaurants, Inc., 19; 46 (upd.)
Claire's Stores, Inc., 17

Clarcor Inc., 17
Clark Construction Group, Inc., The, 8
Clark Equipment Company, 8
Classic Vacation Group, Inc., 46
Clayton Homes Incorporated, 13; 54 (upd.)
Clear Channel Communications, Inc., 23
Cleary, Gottlieb, Steen & Hamilton, 35
Cleco Corporation, 37
Cleveland Indians Baseball Company, Inc.,
  37
Cleveland-Cliffs Inc., 13
Clif Bar Inc., 50
Clorox Company, The, III; 22 (upd.)
Clothestime, Inc., The, 20
ClubCorp, Inc., 33
CML Group, Inc., 10
CMP Media Inc., 26
CMS Energy Corporation, V, 14
CNA Financial Corporation, III; 38 (upd.)
CNET Networks, Inc., 47
CNS, Inc., 20
Coach USA, Inc., 24; 55 (upd.)
Coach, Inc., 10; 45 (upd.)
Coastal Corporation, The, IV, 31 (upd.)
COBE Laboratories, Inc., 13
Coborn's, Inc., 30
Cobra Electronics Corporation, 14
Cobra Golf Inc., 16
Coca Cola Bottling Co. Consolidated, 10
Coca-Cola Company, The, I; 10 (upd.); 32
  (upd.)
Coca-Cola Enterprises, Inc., 13
Coeur d'Alene Mines Corporation, 20
Cogent Communications Group, Inc., 55
Cogentrix Energy, Inc., 10
Coherent, Inc., 31
Cohu, Inc., 32
Coinmach Laundry Corporation, 20
Coinstar, Inc., 44
Cold Spring Granite Company, 16
Coldwater Creek Inc., 21
Cole National Corporation, 13
Coleman Company, Inc., The, 9; 30 (upd.)
Coles Express Inc., 15
Colgate-Palmolive Company, III; 14 (upd.);
  35 (upd.)
Collectors Universe, Inc., 48
Collins & Aikman Corporation, 13; 41
  (upd.)
Collins Industries, Inc., 33
Colonial Williamsburg Foundation, 53
Colorado MEDtech, Inc., 48
Colt Industries Inc., I
Colt's Manufacturing Company, Inc., 12
Columbia Gas System, Inc., The, V; 16
  (upd.)
Columbia Pictures Entertainment, Inc., II
Columbia Sportswear Company, 19; 41
  (upd.)
Columbia TriStar Motion Pictures
  Companies, 12 (upd.)
Columbia/HCA Healthcare Corporation, 15
Columbus McKinnon Corporation, 37
Comair Holdings Inc., 13; 34 (upd.)
Comcast Corporation, 7; 24 (upd.)
Comdial Corporation, 21
Comdisco, Inc., 9
Comerica Incorporated, 40
COMFORCE Corporation, 40
Commerce Clearing House, Inc., 7
Commercial Credit Company, 8
Commercial Federal Corporation, 12
Commercial Financial Services, Inc., 26
Commercial Metals Company, 15; 42
  (upd.)
Commodore International Ltd., 7
Commonwealth Edison Company, V

Commonwealth Energy System, 14
Commonwealth Telephone Enterprises,
  Inc., 25
Community Coffee Co. L.L.C., 53
Community Psychiatric Centers, 15
Compaq Computer Corporation, III; 6
  (upd.); 26 (upd.)
CompDent Corporation, 22
CompHealth Inc., 25
Complete Business Solutions, Inc., 31
Comprehensive Care Corporation, 15
CompuAdd Computer Corporation, 11
CompuCom Systems, Inc., 10
CompuDyne Corporation, 51
CompUSA, Inc., 10; 35 (upd.)
CompuServe Interactive Services, Inc., 10;
  27 (upd.)
Computer Associates International, Inc., 6;
  49 (upd.)
Computer Data Systems, Inc., 14
Computer Learning Centers, Inc., 26
Computer Sciences Corporation, 6
Computerland Corp., 13
Computervision Corporation, 10
Compuware Corporation, 10; 30 (upd.)
Comsat Corporation, 23
Comshare Inc., 23
Comstock Resources, Inc., 47
Comverse Technology, Inc., 15; 43 (upd.)
ConAgra Foods, Inc., II; 12 (upd.); 42
  (upd.)
Conair Corp., 17
Concepts Direct, Inc., 39
Concord Camera Corporation, 41
Concord EFS, Inc., 52
Concord Fabrics, Inc., 16
Condé Nast Publications Inc., The, 13
Cone Mills Corporation, 8
Conexant Systems, Inc., 36
Congoleum Corp., 18
Conn-Selmer, Inc., 55
Connecticut Light and Power Co., 13
Connecticut Mutual Life Insurance
  Company, III
Connell Company, The, 29
Conner Peripherals, Inc., 6
Conoco Inc., IV; 16 (upd.)
Conseco, Inc., 10; 33 (upd.)
Conso International Corporation, 29
Consolidated Delivery & Logistics, Inc., 24
Consolidated Edison, Inc., V; 45 (upd.)
Consolidated Freightways Corporation, V;
  21 (upd.); 48 (upd.)
Consolidated Natural Gas Company, V; 19
  (upd.)
Consolidated Papers, Inc., 8; 36 (upd.)
Consolidated Products Inc., 14
Consolidated Rail Corporation, V
Consumers Power Co., 14
Consumers Union, 26
Consumers Water Company, 14
Container Store, The, 36
ContiGroup Companies, Inc., 43 (upd.)
Continental Airlines, Inc., I; 21 (upd.); 52
  (upd.)
Continental Bank Corporation, II
Continental Cablevision, Inc., 7
Continental Can Co., Inc., 15
Continental Corporation, The, III
Continental General Tire Corp., 23
Continental Grain Company, 10; 13 (upd.)
Continental Group Company, I
Continental Medical Systems, Inc., 10
Control Data Corporation, III
Control Data Systems, Inc., 10
Converse Inc., 9; 31 (upd.)

United States (*continued*)

Cooker Restaurant Corporation, 20; 51 (upd.)
Cooper Cameron Corporation, 20 (upd.)
Cooper Companies, Inc., The, 39
Cooper Industries, Inc., II; 44 (upd.)
Cooper Tire & Rubber Company, 8; 23 (upd.)
Coopers & Lybrand, 9
Copart Inc., 23
Copley Press, Inc., The, 23
Copps Corporation, The, 32
Corbis Corporation, 31
Cordis Corporation, 19; 46 (upd.)
CoreStates Financial Corp, 17
Corinthian Colleges, Inc., 39
Corning Inc., III; 44 (upd.)
Corporate Express, Inc., 22; 47 (upd.)
Corporate Software Inc., 9
Corporation for Public Broadcasting, 14
Correctional Services Corporation, 30
Corrections Corporation of America, 23
Corrpro Companies, Inc., 20
CORT Business Services Corporation, 26
Cosi, Inc., 53
Cosmair, Inc., 8
Cosmetic Center, Inc., The, 22
Cost Plus, Inc., 27
Cost-U-Less, Inc., 51
Costco Wholesale Corporation, V; 43 (upd.)
Cotter & Company, V
Cotton Incorporated, 46
Coty, Inc., 36
Coudert Brothers, 30
Countrywide Credit Industries, Inc., 16
County Seat Stores Inc., 9
Courier Corporation, 41
Covance Inc., 30
Covington & Burling, 40
Cowles Media Company, 23
Cox Enterprises, Inc., IV; 22 (upd.)
CPC International Inc., II
CPI Corp., 38
Cracker Barrel Old Country Store, Inc., 10
Craftmade International, Inc., 44
Crain Communications, Inc., 12; 35 (upd.)
Cramer, Berkowitz & Co., 34
Crane & Co., Inc., 26
Crane Co., 8; 30 (upd.)
Crate and Barrel, 9
Cravath, Swaine & Moore, 43
Cray Research, Inc., III; 16 (upd.)
Creative Artists Agency LLC, 38
Credit Acceptance Corporation, 18
Cree Inc., 53
Crompton Corporation, 9; 36 (upd.)
Croscill, Inc., 42
Crowley Maritime Corporation, 6; 28 (upd.)
Crowley, Milner & Company, 19
Crown Books Corporation, 21
Crown Central Petroleum Corporation, 7
Crown Crafts, Inc., 16
Crown Equipment Corporation, 15
Crown Media Holdings, Inc., 45
Crown Vantage Inc., 29
Crown, Cork & Seal Company, Inc., I; 13; 32 (upd.)
CRSS Inc., 6
Cruise America Inc., 21
CryoLife, Inc., 46
Crystal Brands, Inc., 9
CS First Boston Inc., II
CSK Auto Corporation, 38
CSS Industries, Inc., 35
CSX Corporation, V; 22 (upd.)

CTB International Corporation, 43 (upd.)
CTG, Inc., 11
CTS Corporation, 39
Cubic Corporation, 19
CUC International Inc., 16
Cuisinart Corporation, 24
Culbro Corporation, 15
Cullen/Frost Bankers, Inc., 25
Culligan Water Technologies, Inc., 12; 38 (upd.)
Culp, Inc., 29
Cumberland Farms, Inc., 17
Cumberland Packing Corporation, 26
Cummins Engine Company, Inc., I; 12 (upd.); 40 (upd.)
Cumulus Media Inc., 37
Cunard Line Ltd., 23
Current, Inc., 37
Curtice-Burns Foods, Inc., 7; 21 (upd.)
Curtiss-Wright Corporation, 10; 35 (upd.)
Curves International, Inc., 54
Custom Chrome, Inc., 16
Cutter & Buck Inc., 27
CVS Corporation, 45 (upd.)
Cybermedia, Inc., 25
Cybex International, Inc., 49
Cygne Designs, Inc., 25
Cypress Semiconductor Corporation, 20; 48 (upd.)
Cyprus Amax Minerals Company, 21
Cyprus Minerals Company, 7
Cyrk Inc., 19
Cytec Industries Inc., 27
Czarnikow-Rionda Company, Inc., 32
D&K Wholesale Drug, Inc., 14
D'Agostino Supermarkets Inc., 19
D'Arcy Masius Benton & Bowles, Inc., VI; 32 (upd.)
D.G. Yuengling & Son, Inc., 38
Daffy's Inc., 26
Dain Rauscher Corporation, 35 (upd.)
Dairy Mart Convenience Stores, Inc., 7; 25 (upd.)
Daisytek International Corporation, 18
Daktronics, Inc., 32
Dal-Tile International Inc., 22
Dale Carnegie Training, Inc., 28
Dallas Cowboys Football Club, Ltd., 33
Dallas Semiconductor Corporation, 13; 31 (upd.)
Damark International, Inc., 18
Dames & Moore, Inc., 25
Dan River Inc., 35
Dana Corporation, I; 10 (upd.)
Danaher Corporation, 7
Daniel Industries, Inc., 16
Dannon Co., Inc., 14
Danskin, Inc., 12
Darden Restaurants, Inc., 16; 44 (upd.)
Darigold, Inc., 9
Dart Group Corporation, 16
Data Broadcasting Corporation, 31
Data General Corporation, 8
Datapoint Corporation, 11
Datascope Corporation, 39
Datek Online Holdings Corp., 32
Dauphin Deposit Corporation, 14
Dave & Buster's, Inc., 33
Davey Tree Expert Company, The, 11
David and Lucile Packard Foundation, The, 41
David J. Joseph Company, The, 14
David's Bridal, Inc., 33
Davis Polk & Wardwell, 36
DAW Technologies, Inc., 25
Dawn Food Products, Inc., 17
Day & Zimmermann Inc., 9; 31 (upd.)

Day Runner, Inc., 14; 41 (upd.)
Dayton Hudson Corporation, V; 18 (upd.)
DC Comics Inc., 25
DDB Needham Worldwide, 14
Dean & DeLuca, Inc., 36
Dean Foods Company, 7; 21 (upd.)
Dean Witter, Discover & Co., 12
Death Row Records, 27
Deb Shops, Inc., 16
Debevoise & Plimpton, 39
Dechert, 43
Deckers Outdoor Corporation, 22
Decora Industries, Inc., 31
DeCrane Aircraft Holdings Inc., 36
DeepTech International Inc., 21
Deere & Company, III; 21 (upd.); 42 (upd.)
Defiance, Inc., 22
DeKalb Genetics Corporation, 17
Del Laboratories, Inc., 28
Del Monte Foods Company, 7; 23 (upd.)
Del Webb Corporation, 14
Delaware North Companies Incorporated, 7
dELiA*s Inc., 29
Delicato Vineyards, Inc., 50
Dell Computer Corporation, 9; 31 (upd.)
Deloitte Touche Tohmatsu International, 9; 29 (upd.)
DeLorme Publishing Company, Inc., 53
Delphi Automotive Systems Corporation, 45
Delta Air Lines, Inc., I; 6 (upd.); 39 (upd.)
Delta and Pine Land Company, 33
Delta Woodside Industries, Inc., 8; 30 (upd.)
Deltic Timber Corporation, 46
Deluxe Corporation, 7; 22 (upd.)
DeMoulas / Market Basket Inc., 23
DenAmerica Corporation, 29
Denison International plc, 46
Dentsply International Inc., 10
Denver Nuggets, 51
DEP Corporation, 20
Department VVI, Inc., 14; 34 (upd.)
Deposit Guaranty Corporation, 17
DePuy Inc., 30; 37 (upd.)
Designer Holdings Ltd., 20
Destec Energy, Inc., 12
Detroit Diesel Corporation, 10
Detroit Edison Company, The, V
Detroit Lions, Inc., The, 55
Detroit Pistons Basketball Company, The, 41
Detroit Tigers Baseball Club, Inc., 46
Deutsch, Inc., 42
DeVry Incorporated, 29
Dewey Ballantine LLP, 48
Dexter Corporation, The, I; 12 (upd.)
DH Technology, Inc., 18
DHL Worldwide Express, 6; 24 (upd.)
Di Giorgio Corp., 12
Dial Corp., The, 8; 23 (upd.)
Dial-A-Mattress Operating Corporation, 46
Dialogic Corporation, 18
Diamond Shamrock, Inc., IV
DiamondCluster International, Inc., 51
Dibrell Brothers, Incorporated, 12
dick clark productions, inc., 16
Diebold, Incorporated, 7; 22 (upd.)
Diedrich Coffee, Inc., 40
Digex, Inc., 46
Digi International Inc., 9
Digital Equipment Corporation, III; 6 (upd.)
Digital River, Inc., 50
Dillard Department Stores, Inc., V; 16 (upd.)

Dillard Paper Company, 11
Dillingham Construction Corporation, I; 44 (upd.)
Dillon Companies Inc., 12
Dime Savings Bank of New York, F.S.B., 9
DIMON Inc., 27
Dionex Corporation, 46
Direct Focus, Inc., 47
DIRECTV, Inc., 38
Discount Auto Parts, Inc., 18
Discount Drug Mart, Inc., 14
Discovery Communications, Inc., 42
Dixie Group, Inc., The, 20
Dixon Industries, Inc., 26
Dixon Ticonderoga Company, 12
DMI Furniture, Inc., 46
Do it Best Corporation, 30
Doctors' Company, The, 55
Documentum, Inc., 46
Dolby Laboratories Inc., 20
Dole Food Company, Inc., 9; 31 (upd.)
Dollar Thrifty Automotive Group, Inc., 25
Dollar Tree Stores, Inc., 23
Dominion Homes, Inc., 19
Dominion Resources, Inc., V; 54 (upd.)
Domino Sugar Corporation, 26
Domino's Pizza, Inc., 7; 21 (upd.)
Don Massey Cadillac, Inc., 37
Donaldson Company, Inc., 16; 49 (upd.)
Donaldson, Lufkin & Jenrette, Inc., 22
Donna Karan Company, 15
Donnelly Corporation, 12; 35 (upd.)
Donnkenny, Inc., 17
Dorsey & Whitney LLP, 47
Doskocil Companies, Inc., 12
DoubleClick Inc., 46
Doubletree Corporation, 21
Douglas & Lomason Company, 16
Dover Corporation, III; 28 (upd.)
Dover Downs Entertainment, Inc., 43
Dover Publications Inc., 34
Dow Chemical Company, The, I; 8 (upd.); 50 (upd.)
Dow Jones & Company, Inc., IV; 19 (upd.); 47 (upd.)
Dow Jones Telerate, Inc., 10
DPL Inc., 6
DQE, 6
Dr Pepper/Seven Up, Inc., 9; 32 (upd.)
Drackett Professional Products, 12
Drake Beam Morin, Inc., 44
DreamWorks SKG, 43
Drees Company, Inc., The, 41
Dress Barn, Inc., The, 24; 55 (upd.)
Dresser Industries, Inc., III
Drew Industries Inc., 28
Drexel Burnham Lambert Incorporated, II
Drexel Heritage Furnishings Inc., 12
Dreyer's Grand Ice Cream, Inc., 17
Drug Emporium, Inc., 12
Drypers Corporation, 18
DSC Communications Corporation, 12
DTE Energy Company, 20 (upd.)
Duane Reade Holding Corp., 21
Duck Head Apparel Company, Inc., 42
Duckwall-ALCO Stores, Inc., 24
Ducommun Incorporated, 30
Duke Energy Corporation, V; 27 (upd.)
Dun & Bradstreet Corporation, The, IV; 19 (upd.)
Dun & Bradstreet Software Services Inc., 11
Dunavant Enterprises, Inc., 54
Duncan Toys Company, 55
Duplex Products Inc., 17
Duracell International Inc., 9

Durametallic, 21
Duriron Company Inc., 17
Duty Free International, Inc., 11
DVI, Inc., 51
Dyersburg Corporation, 21
Dynatech Corporation, 13
DynCorp, 45
Dynegy Inc., 49 (upd.)
E! Entertainment Television Inc., 17
E*Trade Group, Inc., 20
E. & J. Gallo Winery, I; 7 (upd.); 28 (upd.)
E.I. du Pont de Nemours & Company, I; 8 (upd.); 26 (upd.)
E.piphany, Inc., 49
E.W. Scripps Company, The, IV; 7 (upd.); 28 (upd.)
Eagle Hardware & Garden, Inc., 16
Eagle-Picher Industries, Inc., 8; 23 (upd.)
Earl Scheib, Inc., 32
Earthgrains Company, The, 36
EarthLink, Inc., 36
Eastern Airlines, I
Eastern Company, The, 48
Eastern Enterprises, 6
Eastman Chemical Company, 14; 38 (upd.)
Eastman Kodak Company, III; 7 (upd.); 36 (upd.)
Eateries, Inc., 33
Eaton Corporation, I; 10 (upd.)
Eaton Vance Corporation, 18
eBay Inc., 32
EBSCO Industries, Inc., 17; 40 (upd.)
ECC International Corp., 42
Echlin Inc., I; 11 (upd.)
EchoStar Communications Corporation, 35
Eckerd Corporation, 9; 32 (upd.)
Ecolab, Inc., I; 13 (upd.); 34 (upd.)
Ecology and Environment, Inc., 39
Eddie Bauer, Inc., 9; 36 (upd.)
Edelbrock Corporation, 37
Edison Brothers Stores, Inc., 9
Edison Schools Inc., 37
Edmark Corporation, 14; 41 (upd.)
EDO Corporation, 46
Education Management Corporation, 35
Educational Broadcasting Corporation, 48
Educational Testing Service, 12
Edw. C. Levy Co., 42
Edward J. DeBartolo Corporation, The, 8
Edward Jones, 30
Edwards Theatres Circuit, Inc., 31
EG&G Incorporated, 8; 29 (upd.)
Egghead Inc., 9
Egghead.com, Inc., 31 (upd.)
84 Lumber Company, 9; 39 (upd.)
800-JR Cigar, Inc., 27
Einstein/Noah Bagel Corporation, 29
Ekco Group, Inc., 16
El Camino Resources International, Inc., 11
El Chico Restaurants, Inc., 19
El Paso Electric Company, 21
El Paso Natural Gas Company, 12
Elamex, S.A. de C.V., 51
Elano Corporation, 14
Elder-Beerman Stores Corporation, 10
Electric Lightwave, Inc., 37
Electromagnetic Sciences Inc., 21
Electronic Arts Inc., 10
Electronic Data Systems Corporation, III; 28 (upd.)
Electronics for Imaging, Inc., 15; 43 (upd.)
Eli Lilly and Company, I; 11 (upd.); 47 (upd.)
Elizabeth Arden, Inc., 8; 40 (upd.)
Eljer Industries, Inc., 24
ElkCorp, 52
Ellen Tracy, Inc., 55

Ellerbe Becket, 41
Ellett Brothers, Inc., 17
Elmer's Restaurants, Inc., 42
Elsinore Corporation, 48
Embers America Restaurants, 30
EMC Corporation, 12; 46 (upd.)
Emerson, II; 46 (upd.)
Emerson Radio Corp., 30
Emery Worldwide Airlines, Inc., 6; 25 (upd.)
Emge Packing Co., Inc., 11
Emmis Communications Corporation, 47
Empi, Inc., 26
Empire Blue Cross and Blue Shield, III
Employee Solutions, Inc., 18
ENCAD, Incorporated, 25
Encompass Services Corporation, 33
Encore Computer Corporation, 13
Encyclopaedia Britannica, Inc., 7; 39 (upd.)
Energen Corporation, 21
Energizer Holdings, Inc., 32
Enesco Corporation, 11
Engelhard Corporation, IV; 21 (upd.)
Engle Homes, Inc., 46
Engraph, Inc., 12
Ennis Business Forms, Inc., 21
Enquirer/Star Group, Inc., 10
Enrich International, Inc., 33
Enron Corporation, V; 19; 46 (upd.)
Enserch Corporation, V
Entergy Corporation, V; 45 (upd.)
Enterprise Rent-A-Car Company, 6
Entravision Communications Corporation, 41
Envirodyne Industries, Inc., 17
Environmental Industries, Inc., 31
Enzo Biochem, Inc., 41
Equifax Inc., 6; 28 (upd.)
Equitable Life Assurance Society of the United States, III
Equitable Resources, Inc., 6; 54 (upd.)
Equity Marketing, Inc., 26
Equity Office Properties Trust, 54
Equity Residential, 49
Equus Computer Systems, Inc., 49
Erie Indemnity Company, 35
ERLY Industries Inc., 17
Ernst & Young, 9; 29 (upd.)
Escalade, Incorporated, 19
Eskimo Pie Corporation, 21
Esprit de Corp., 8; 29 (upd.)
ESS Technology, Inc., 22
Essef Corporation, 18
Esselte Pendaflex Corporation, 11
Essence Communications, Inc., 24
Estée Lauder Companies Inc., The, 9; 30 (upd.)
Esterline Technologies Corp., 15
Ethan Allen Interiors, Inc., 12; 39 (upd.)
Ethicon, Inc., 23
Ethyl Corporation, I; 10 (upd.)
EToys, Inc., 37
Eureka Company, The, 12
Euromarket Designs Inc., 31 (upd.)
Evans & Sutherland Computer Corporation, 19
Evans, Inc., 30
Everex Systems, Inc., 16
Evergreen International Aviation, Inc., 53
Everlast Worldwide Inc., 47
Exabyte Corporation, 12; 40 (upd.)
Exar Corp., 14
EXCEL Communications Inc., 18
Executive Jet, Inc., 36
Executone Information Systems, Inc., 13
Exelon Corporation, 48 (upd.)
Exide Electronics Group, Inc., 20

United States (*continued*)

Expeditors International of Washington Inc., 17

Experian Information Solutions Inc., 45

Express Scripts Inc., 17; 44 (upd.)

Extended Stay America, Inc., 41

Exxon Corporation, IV; 7 (upd.); 32 (upd.)

EZCORP Inc., 43

E-Systems, Inc., 9

E-Z Serve Corporation, 17

Fab Industries, Inc., 27

Fabri-Centers of America Inc., 16

Fair Grounds Corporation, 44

Fair, Isaac and Company, 18

Fairchild Aircraft, Inc., 9

Fairfield Communities, Inc., 36

Falcon Products, Inc., 33

Fallon McElligott Inc., 22

Family Christian Stores, Inc., 51

Family Dollar Stores, Inc., 13

Family Golf Centers, Inc., 29

Famous Dave's of America, Inc., 40

Fannie Mae, 45 (upd.)

Fansteel Inc., 19

FAO Schwarz, 46

Farah Incorporated, 24

Farley Northwest Industries, Inc., I

Farm Family Holdings, Inc., 39

Farm Journal Corporation, 42

Farmer Bros. Co., 52

Farmers Insurance Group of Companies, 25

Farmland Foods, Inc., 7

Farmland Industries, Inc., 48

Farrar, Straus and Giroux Inc., 15

Fastenal Company, 14; 42 (upd.)

Faultless Starch/Bon Ami Company, 55

Fay's Inc., 17

Faygo Beverages Inc., 55

Fazoli's Systems, Inc., 27

Featherlite Inc., 28

Fedders Corporation, 18; 43 (upd.)

Federal Express Corporation, V

Federal National Mortgage Association, II

Federal Paper Board Company, Inc., 8

Federal Prison Industries, Inc., 34

Federal Signal Corp., 10

Federal-Mogul Corporation, I; 10 (upd.); 26 (upd.)

Federated Department Stores Inc., 9; 31 (upd.)

FedEx Corporation, 18 (upd.); 42 (upd.)

Feld Entertainment, Inc., 32 (upd.)

Fellowes Manufacturing Company, 28

Fender Musical Instruments Company, 16; 43 (upd.)

Fenwick & West LLP, 34

Ferolito, Vultaggio & Sons, 27

Ferrellgas Partners, L.P., 35

Ferro Corporation, 8

FHP International Corporation, 6

FiberMark, Inc., 37

Fibreboard Corporation, 16

Fidelity Investments Inc., II; 14 (upd.)

Fidelity National Financial Inc., 54

Fieldale Farms Corporation, 23

Fieldcrest Cannon, Inc., 9; 31 (upd.)

Fifth Third Bancorp, 13; 31 (upd.)

Figgie International Inc., 7

FINA, Inc., 7

Fingerhut Companies, Inc., 9; 36 (upd.)

Finish Line, Inc., The, 29

FinishMaster, Inc., 24

Finlay Enterprises, Inc., 16

Firearms Training Systems, Inc., 27

Fireman's Fund Insurance Company, III

First Albany Companies Inc., 37

First Alert, Inc., 28

First American Corporation, The 52

First Aviation Services Inc., 49

First Bank System Inc., 12

First Brands Corporation, 8

First Chicago Corporation, II

First Commerce Bancshares, Inc., 15

First Commerce Corporation, 11

First Data Corporation, 30 (upd.)

First Empire State Corporation, 11

First Executive Corporation, III

First Fidelity Bank, N.A., New Jersey, 9

First Financial Management Corporation, 11

First Hawaiian, Inc., 11

First Interstate Bancorp, II

First Mississippi Corporation, 8

First Nationwide Bank, 14

First of America Bank Corporation, 8

First Security Corporation, 11

First Team Sports, Inc., 22

First Tennessee National Corporation, 11; 48 (upd.)

First Union Corporation, 10

First USA, Inc., 11

First Virginia Banks, Inc., 11

First Years Inc., The, 46

Firstar Corporation, 11; 33 (upd.)

Fiserv Inc., 11; 33 (upd.)

Fish & Neave, 54

Fisher Companies, Inc., 15

Fisher Controls International, Inc., 13

Fisher Scientific International Inc., 24

Fisher-Price Inc., 12; 32 (upd.)

Flagstar Companies, Inc., 10

Fleer Corporation, 15

FleetBoston Financial Corporation, 9; 36 (upd.)

Fleetwood Enterprises, Inc., III; 22 (upd.)

Fleming Companies, Inc., II; 17 (upd.)

Flexsteel Industries Inc., 15; 41 (upd.)

FlightSafety International, Inc., 9; 29 (upd.)

Flint Ink Corporation, 13; 41 (upd.)

Florida Crystals Inc., 35

Florida Gaming Corporation, 47

Florida Progress Corporation, V; 23 (upd.)

Florida Rock Industries, Inc., 46

Florida's Natural Growers, 45

Florists' Transworld Delivery, Inc., 28

Florsheim Shoe Group Inc., 9; 31 (upd.)

Flour City International, Inc., 44

Flowers Industries, Inc., 12; 35 (upd.)

Flowserve Corporation, 33

Fluke Corporation, 15

Fluor Corporation, I; 8 (upd.); 34 (upd.)

Flying J Inc., 19

FMC Corporation, I; 11 (upd.)

FMR Corp., 8; 32 (upd.)

Foamex International Inc., 17

Foley & Lardner, 28

Follett Corporation, 12; 39 (upd.)

Food Lion, Inc., II; 15 (upd.)

Foodarama Supermarkets, Inc., 28

FoodBrands America, Inc., 23

Foodmaker, Inc., 14

Foote, Cone & Belding Communications, Inc., I

Footstar, Incorporated, 24

Forbes Inc., 30

Ford Foundation, The, 34

Ford Motor Company, I; 11 (upd.); 36 (upd.)

FORE Systems, Inc., 25

Forest City Enterprises, Inc., 16; 52 (upd.)

Forest Laboratories, Inc., 11; 52 (upd.)

Forest Oil Corporation, 19

Forever Living Products International Inc., 17

Formica Corporation, 13

Forrester Research, Inc., 54

Forstmann Little & Co., 38

Fort Howard Corporation, 8

Fort James Corporation, 22 (upd.)

Fortune Brands, Inc., 29 (upd.)

Fortunoff Fine Jewelry and Silverware Inc., 26

Fossil, Inc., 17

Foster Poultry Farms, 32

Foster Wheeler Corporation, 6; 23 (upd.)

Foundation Health Corporation, 12

Fountain Powerboats Industries, Inc., 28

Fourth Financial Corporation, 11

Fox Entertainment Group, Inc., 43

Fox Family Worldwide, Inc., 24

Foxboro Company, 13

FoxMeyer Health Corporation, 16

FPL Group, Inc., V; 49 (upd.)

Frank J. Zamboni & Co., Inc., 34

Frank Russell Company, 46

Frank's Nursery & Crafts, Inc., 12

Frankel & Co., 39

Franklin Covey Company, 11; 37 (upd.)

Franklin Electric Company, Inc., 43

Franklin Electronic Publishers, Inc., 23

Franklin Resources, Inc., 9

Fred Meyer, Inc., V; 20 (upd.)

Fred Usinger Inc., 54

Fred W. Albrecht Grocery Co., The, 13

Fred's, Inc., 23

Freddie Mac, 54

Frederick Atkins Inc., 16

Frederick's of Hollywood Inc., 16

Freedom Communications, Inc., 36

Freeport-McMoRan Inc., IV; 7 (upd.)

French Fragrances, Inc., 22

Fresh America Corporation, 20

Fresh Choice, Inc., 20

Fresh Foods, Inc., 29

Fretter, Inc., 10

Fried, Frank, Harris, Shriver & Jacobson, 35

Friedman's Inc., 29

Friedman, Billings, Ramsey Group, Inc., 53

Friendly Ice Cream Corp., 30

Frigidaire Home Products, 22

Frisch's Restaurants, Inc., 35

Frito-Lay Company, 32

Fritz Companies, Inc., 12

Frontier Airlines, Inc., 22

Frontier Corp., 16

Frost & Sullivan, Inc., 53

Frozen Food Express Industries, Inc., 20

Fruehauf Corporation, I

Fruit of the Loom, Inc., 8; 25 (upd.)

Frymaster Corporation, 27

FSI International, Inc., 17

FTP Software, Inc., 20

Fubu, 29

Fujitsu-ICL Systems Inc., 11

Fulbright & Jaworski L.L.P., 47

Funco, Inc., 20

Fuqua Enterprises, Inc., 17

Fuqua Industries, Inc., I

Furniture Brands International, Inc., 39 (upd.)

Furon Company, 28

Furr's Restaurant Group, Inc., 53

Furr's Supermarkets, Inc., 28

Future Now, Inc., 12

G&K Services, Inc., 16

G-III Apparel Group, Ltd., 22

G. Heileman Brewing Company Inc., I

G. Leblanc Corporation, 55

G.A.F., I

G.D. Searle & Company, I; 12 (upd.); 34 (upd.)
G.I. Joe's, Inc., 30
G.S. Blodgett Corporation, 15
Gabelli Asset Management Inc., 30
Gables Residential Trust, 49
Gadzooks, Inc., 18
GAF Corporation, 22 (upd.)
Gage Marketing Group, 26
Gaiam, Inc., 41
Gainsco, Inc., 22
Galey & Lord, Inc., 20
Gallup Organization, The, 37
Galyan's Trading Company, Inc., 47
Gambrinus Company, The, 40
Gander Mountain, Inc., 20
Gannett Co., Inc., IV; 7 (upd.); 30 (upd.)
Gantos, Inc., 17
Gap, Inc., The, V; 18 (upd.); 55 (upd.)
Garan, Inc., 16
Garden Fresh Restaurant Corporation, 31
Garden Ridge Corporation, 27
Gardenburger, Inc., 33
Gardner Denver, Inc., 49
Gart Sports Company, 24
Gartner Group, Inc., 21
Gates Corporation, The, 9
Gateway, Inc., 10; 27 (upd.)
GATX Corporation, 6; 25 (upd.)
Gaylord Container Corporation, 8
Gaylord Entertainment Company, 11; 36 (upd.)
GC Companies, Inc., 25
GE Aircraft Engines, 9
GE Capital Aviation Services, 36
Geerlings & Wade, Inc., 45
Geffen Records Inc., 26
Gehl Company, 19
GEICO Corporation, 10; 40 (upd.)
GenCorp Inc., 8; 9
Genentech, Inc., I; 8 (upd.); 32 (upd.)
General Bearing Corporation, 45
General Binding Corporation, 10
General Cable Corporation, 40
General Chemical Group Inc., The, 37
General Cinema Corporation, I
General DataComm Industries, Inc., 14
General Dynamics Corporation, I; 10 (upd.); 40 (upd.)
General Electric Company, II; 12 (upd.); 34 (upd.)
General Host Corporation, 12
General Housewares Corporation, 16
General Instrument Corporation, 10
General Mills, Inc., II; 10 (upd.); 36 (upd.)
General Motors Corporation, I; 10 (upd.); 36 (upd.)
General Nutrition Companies, Inc., 11; 29 (upd.)
General Public Utilities Corporation, V
General Re Corporation, III; 24 (upd.)
General Signal Corporation, 9
General Tire, Inc., 8
Genesco Inc., 17
Genesee & Wyoming Inc., 27
Genesis Health Ventures, Inc., 18
Genetics Institute, Inc., 8
Geneva Steel, 7
Genmar Holdings, Inc., 45
Genovese Drug Stores, Inc., 18
GenRad, Inc., 24
Gentex Corporation, 26
Genuardi's Family Markets, Inc., 35
Genuine Parts Company, 9; 45 (upd.)
Genzyme Corporation, 13; 38 (upd.)
Geon Company, The, 11
George A. Hormel and Company, II

George F. Cram Company, Inc., The, 55
George S. May International Company, 55
Georgia Gulf Corporation, 9
Georgia-Pacific Corporation, IV; 9 (upd.); 47 (upd.)
Geotek Communications Inc., 21
Gerald Stevens, Inc., 37
Gerber Products Company, 7; 21 (upd.)
Gerber Scientific, Inc., 12
German American Bancorp, 41
Getty Images, Inc., 31
Ghirardelli Chocolate Company, 30
Giant Cement Holding, Inc., 23
Giant Food Inc., II; 22 (upd.)
Giant Industries, Inc., 19
Gibraltar Steel Corporation, 37
Gibson Greetings, Inc., 12
Gibson Guitar Corp., 16
Gibson, Dunn & Crutcher LLP, 36
Giddings & Lewis, Inc., 10
Gilbane, Inc., 34
Gilead Sciences, Inc., 54
Gillett Holdings, Inc., 7
Gillette Company, The, III; 20 (upd.)
Girl Scouts of the USA, 35
Gitano Group, Inc., The, 8
Glacier Bancorp, Inc., 35
Glacier Water Services, Inc., 47
Glamis Gold, Ltd., 54
Gleason Corporation, 24
Glidden Company, The, 8
Global Crossing Ltd., 32
Global Industries, Ltd., 37
Global Marine Inc., 9
Global Outdoors, Inc., 49
Global Power Equipment Group Inc., 52
GlobalSantaFe Corporation, 48 (upd.)
GM Hughes Electronics Corporation, II
Godfather's Pizza Incorporated, 25
Gold Kist Inc., 17; 26 (upd.)
Gold'n Plump Poultry, 54
Golden Belt Manufacturing Co., 16
Golden Books Family Entertainment, Inc., 28
Golden Corral Corporation, 10
Golden Enterprises, Inc., 26
Golden State Foods Corporation, 32
Golden State Vintners, Inc., 33
Golden West Financial Corporation, 47
Goldman Sachs Group Inc., The, II; 20 (upd.); 51 (upd.)
Golub Corporation, The, 26
Gonnella Baking Company, 40
Good Guys, Inc., The, 10; 30 (upd.)
Good Humor-Breyers Ice Cream Company, 14
Goodman Holding Company, 42
GoodMark Foods, Inc., 26
Goodrich Corporation, 46 (upd.)
GoodTimes Entertainment Ltd., 48
Goodwill Industries International, Inc., 16
Goody Products, Inc., 12
Goody's Family Clothing, Inc., 20
Goodyear Tire & Rubber Company, The, V; 20 (upd.)
Google, Inc., 50
Gordon Food Service Inc., 8; 39 (upd.)
Gorman-Rupp Company, The, 18
Gorton's, 13
Goss Holdings, Inc., 43
Gottschalks, Inc., 18
Gould Electronics, Inc., 14
Goulds Pumps Inc., 24
Goya Foods Inc., 22
GPU, Inc., 27 (upd.)
Graco Inc., 19
GranCare, Inc., 14

Grand Casinos, Inc., 20
Grand Union Company, The, 7; 28 (upd.)
Granite Broadcasting Corporation, 42
Granite Rock Company, 26
Granite State Bankshares, Inc., 37
Graphic Industries Inc., 25
Gray Communications Systems, Inc., 24
Graybar Electric Company, Inc., 54
Great American Management and Investment, Inc., 8
Great Atlantic & Pacific Tea Company, Inc., The, II; 16 (upd.); 55 (upd.)
Great Harvest Bread Company, 44
Great Lakes Bancorp, 8
Great Lakes Chemical Corporation, I; 14 (upd.)
Great Western Financial Corporation, 10
Grede Foundries, Inc., 38
Green Bay Packers, Inc., The, 32
Green Mountain Coffee, Inc., 31
Green Tree Financial Corporation, 11
Greenbrier Companies, The, 19
Greene, Tweed & Company, 55
GreenPoint Financial Corp., 28
Greenwood Mills, Inc., 14
Greif Bros. Corporation, 15
Grey Advertising, Inc., 6
Grey Wolf, Inc., 43
Greyhound Lines, Inc., I; 32 (upd.)
Griffin Land & Nurseries, Inc., 43
Griffon Corporation, 34
Grinnell Corp., 13
Grist Mill Company, 15
Gristede's Sloan's, Inc., 31
Grolier Incorporated, 16; 43 (upd.)
Grossman's Inc., 13
Ground Round, Inc., 21
Group 1 Automotive, Inc., 52
Group Health Cooperative, 41
Grow Biz International, Inc., 18
Grow Group Inc., 12
Grubb & Ellis Company, 21
Grumman Corporation, I; 11 (upd.)
Gruntal & Co., L.L.C., 20
Gryphon Holdings, Inc., 21
GSD&M Advertising, 44
GT Bicycles, 26
GT Interactive Software, 31
GTE Corporation, V; 15 (upd.)
Guangzhou Pearl River Piano Group Ltd., 49
Guccio Gucci, S.p.A., 15
Guess, Inc., 15
Guest Supply, Inc., 18
Guilford Mills Inc., 8; 40 (upd.)
Guitar Center, Inc., 29
Guittard Chocolate Company, 55
Gulf & Western Inc., I
Gulf Island Fabrication, Inc., 44
Gulf States Utilities Company, 6
GulfMark Offshore, Inc., 49
Gulfstream Aerospace Corporation, 7; 28 (upd.)
Gunite Corporation, 51
Gunlocke Company, The, 23
Guthy-Renker Corporation, 32
Gwathmey Siegel & Associates Architects LLC, 26
Gymboree Corporation, 15
H & R Block, Incorporated, 9; 29 (upd.)
H.B. Fuller Company, 8; 32 (upd.)
H.D. Vest, Inc., 46
H.E. Butt Grocery Company, 13; 32 (upd.)
H.F. Ahmanson & Company, II; 10 (upd.)
H.J. Heinz Company, II; 11 (upd.); 36 (upd.)
Ha-Lo Industries, Inc., 27

United States (*continued*)

Habersham Bancorp, 25
Habitat for Humanity International, 36
Hach Co., 18
Hadco Corporation, 24
Haemonetics Corporation, 20
Haggar Corporation, 19
Haggen Inc., 38
Hahn Automotive Warehouse, Inc., 24
Hain Celestial Group, Inc., The, 27; 43 (upd.)
HAL Inc., 9
Half Price Books, Records, Magazines Inc., 37
Hall, Kinion & Associates, Inc., 52
Halliburton Company, III; 25 (upd.); 55 (upd.)
Hallmark Cards, Inc., IV; 16 (upd.); 40 (upd.)
Hamilton Beach/Proctor-Silex Inc., 17
Hammacher Schlemmer & Company, 21
Hampton Industries, Inc., 20
Hancock Fabrics, Inc., 18
Hancock Holding Company, 15
Handleman Company, 15
Handspring Inc., 49
Handy & Harman, 23
Hanger Orthopedic Group, Inc., 41
Hanna Andersson Corp., 49
Hanna-Barbera Cartoons Inc., 23
Hannaford Bros. Co., 12
Hanover Direct, Inc., 36
Hanover Foods Corporation, 35
Hansen Natural Corporation, 31
Happy Kids Inc., 30
Harbert Corporation, 14
Harbison-Walker Refractories Company, 24
Harcourt Brace and Co., 12
Harcourt Brace Jovanovich, Inc., IV
Harcourt General, Inc., 20 (upd.)
Hard Rock Cafe International, Inc., 12; 32 (upd.)
Harding Lawson Associates Group, Inc., 16
Hardinge Inc., 25
Harley-Davidson Inc., 7; 25 (upd.)
Harleysville Group Inc., 37
Harman International Industries Inc., 15
Harmon Industries, Inc., 25
Harmonic Inc., 43
Harnischfeger Industries, Inc., 8; 38 (upd.)
Harold's Stores, Inc., 22
Harper Group Inc., 17
HarperCollins Publishers, 15
Harpo Entertainment Group, 28
Harrah's Entertainment, Inc., 16; 43 (upd.)
Harris Corporation, II; 20 (upd.)
Harris Interactive Inc., 41
Harris Teeter Inc., 23
Harry Winston Inc., 45
Harry's Farmers Market Inc., 23
Harsco Corporation, 8
Harte-Hanks Communications, Inc., 17
Hartmarx Corporation, 8; 32 (upd.)
Hartz Mountain Corporation, The, 12; 46 (upd.)
Harveys Casino Resorts, 27
Harza Engineering Company, 14
Hasbro, Inc., III; 16 (upd.); 43 (upd.)
Hastings Entertainment, Inc., 29
Hauser, Inc., 46
Haverty Furniture Companies, Inc., 31
Hawaiian Airlines, Inc., 22 (upd.)
Hawaiian Electric Industries, Inc., 9
Hawkins Chemical, Inc., 16
Haworth Inc., 8; 39 (upd.)
Hayes Corporation, 24
Hayes Lemmerz International, Inc., 27

Hazelden Foundation, 28
HCA - The Healthcare Company, 35 (upd.)
HCI Direct, Inc., 55
HDR Inc., 48
Headway Corporate Resources, Inc., 40
Health Care & Retirement Corporation, 22
Health O Meter Products Inc., 14
Health Risk Management, Inc., 24
Health Systems International, Inc., 11
HealthSouth Corporation, 14; 33 (upd.)
Healthtex, Inc., 17
Hearst Corporation, The, IV; 19 (upd.); 46 (upd.)
Heartland Express, Inc., 18
Heat Group, The, 53
Hechinger Company, 12
Hecla Mining Company, 20
Heekin Can Inc., 13
HEICO Corporation, 30
Heidrick & Struggles International, Inc., 28
Heilig-Meyers Company, 14; 40 (upd.)
Helen of Troy Corporation, 18
Helene Curtis Industries, Inc., 8; 28 (upd.)
Heller, Ehrman, White & McAuliffe, 41
Helmerich & Payne, Inc., 18
Helmsley Enterprises, Inc., 9; 39 (upd.)
Helzberg Diamonds, 40
Henkel Manco Inc., 22
Henley Group, Inc., The, III
Henry Modell & Company Inc., 32
Henry Schein, Inc., 31
Herbalife International, Inc., 17; 41 (upd.)
Hercules Inc., I; 22 (upd.)
Herley Industries, Inc., 33
Herman Goelitz, Inc., 28
Herman Miller, Inc., 8
Hershey Foods Corporation, II; 15 (upd.); 51 (upd.)
Hertz Corporation, The, 9; 33 (upd.)
Heska Corporation, 39
Heublein, Inc., I
Hewlett-Packard Company, III; 6 (upd.); 28 (upd.); 50 (upd.)
Hexcel Corporation, 28
Hibbett Sporting Goods, Inc., 26
Hibernia Corporation, 37
Hickory Farms, Inc., 17
Highmark Inc., 27
Hildebrandt International, 29
Hill's Pet Nutrition, Inc., 27
Hillenbrand Industries, Inc., 10
Hillerich & Bradsby Company, Inc., 51
Hillhaven Corporation, The, 14
Hills Stores Company, 13
Hilton Hotels Corporation, III; 19 (upd.)
Hines Horticulture, Inc., 49
Hispanic Broadcasting Corporation, 35
Hitchiner Manufacturing Co., Inc., 23
HMI Industries, Inc., 17
HOB Entertainment, Inc., 37
Hoechst Celanese Corporation, 13
Hoenig Group Inc., 41
Hogan & Hartson L.L.P., 44
Holberg Industries, Inc., 36
Holiday Inns, Inc., III
Holiday RV Superstores, Incorporated, 26
Holland Burgerville USA, 44
Holley Performance Products Inc., 52
Hollinger International Inc., 24
Holly Corporation, 12
Hollywood Casino Corporation, 21
Hollywood Entertainment Corporation, 25
Hollywood Park, Inc., 20
Holme Roberts & Owen LLP, 28
Holnam Inc., 8; 39 (upd.)
Holophane Corporation, 19
Holson Burnes Group, Inc., 14

Holt's Cigar Holdings, Inc., 42
Home Box Office Inc., 7; 23 (upd.)
Home Depot, Inc., The, V; 18 (upd.)
Home Insurance Company, The, III
Home Interiors & Gifts, Inc., 55
Home Products International, Inc., 55
Home Properties of New York, Inc., 42
Home Shopping Network, Inc., V; 25 (upd.)
HomeBase, Inc., 33 (upd.)
Homestake Mining Company, 12; 38 (upd.)
Hometown Auto Retailers, Inc., 44
HON INDUSTRIES Inc., 13
Honda Motor Company Limited, I; 10 (upd.); 29 (upd.)
Honeywell Inc., II; 12 (upd.); 50 (upd.)
Hooper Holmes, Inc., 22
Hooters of America, Inc., 18
Hoover Company, The, 12; 40 (upd.)
Hops Restaurant Bar and Brewery, 46
Horace Mann Educators Corporation, 22
Horizon Organic Holding Corporation, 37
Hormel Foods Corporation, 18 (upd.); 54 (upd.)
Horsehead Industries, Inc., 51
Horton Homes, Inc., 25
Hospital Corporation of America, III
Hospitality Franchise Systems, Inc., 11
Hospitality Worldwide Services, Inc., 26
Hot Topic, Inc., 33
Houchens Industries Inc., 51
Houghton Mifflin Company, 10; 36 (upd.)
House of Fabrics, Inc., 21
Household International, Inc., II; 21 (upd.)
Houston Industries Incorporated, V
Hovnanian Enterprises, Inc., 29
Howard Hughes Medical Institute, 39
Howard Johnson International, Inc., 17
Howmet Corp., 12
Hub Group, Inc., 38
Hubbard Broadcasting Inc., 24
Hubbell Incorporated, 9; 31 (upd.)
Hudson Foods Inc., 13
Hudson River Bancorp, Inc., 41
Huffy Corporation, 7; 30 (upd.)
Hughes Electronics Corporation, 25
Hughes Hubbard & Reed LLP, 44
Hughes Markets, Inc., 22
Hughes Supply, Inc., 14
Hulman & Company, 44
Humana Inc., III; 24 (upd.)
Humane Society of the United States, The, 54
Hungry Howie's Pizza and Subs, Inc., 25
Hunt Consolidated, Inc., 27 (upd.)
Hunt Manufacturing Company, 12
Hunt Oil Company, 7
Hunt-Wesson, Inc., 17
Hunter Fan Company, 13
Huntington Bancshares Inc., 11
Huntington Learning Centers, Inc., 55
Hunton & Williams, 35
Huntsman Chemical Corporation, 8
Hutchinson Technology Incorporated, 18
Hvide Marine Incorporated, 22
Hy-Vee, Inc., 36
Hyatt Corporation, III; 16 (upd.)
Hyde Athletic Industries, Inc., 17
Hydril Company, 46
Hypercom Corporation, 27
Hyperion Software Corporation, 22
Hyster Company, 17
I.C. Isaacs & Company, 31
Iams Company, 26
IBERIABANK Corporation, 37
IBP, Inc., II; 21 (upd.)
IC Industries, Inc., I

ICF Kaiser International, Inc., 28
ICN Pharmaceuticals, Inc., 52
Icon Health & Fitness, Inc., 38
Idaho Power Company, 12
IDB Communications Group, Inc., 11
Identix Inc., 44
IDEXX Laboratories, Inc., 23
IDG Books Worldwide, Inc., 27
IDT Corporation, 34
IEC Electronics Corp., 42
Igloo Products Corp., 21
IHOP Corporation, 17
IKON Office Solutions, Inc., 50
Il Fornaio (America) Corporation, 27
Ilitch Holdings Inc., 37
Illinois Bell Telephone Company, 14
Illinois Central Corporation, 11
Illinois Power Company, 6
Illinois Tool Works Inc., III; 22 (upd.)
Imagine Foods, Inc., 50
Imation Corporation, 20
IMC Fertilizer Group, Inc., 8
IMCO Recycling, Incorporated, 32
Immunex Corporation, 14; 50 (upd.)
Imo Industries Inc., 7; 27 (upd.)
IMPATH Inc., 45
Imperial Holly Corporation, 12
Imperial Sugar Company, 32 (upd.)
In Focus Systems, Inc., 22
In-N-Out Burger, 19
InaCom Corporation, 13
Incyte Genomics, Inc., 52
Indiana Bell Telephone Company,
    Incorporated, 14
Indiana Energy, Inc., 27
Indianapolis Motor Speedway Corporation,
    46
Industrial Services of America, Inc., 46
Infinity Broadcasting Corporation, 11; 48
    (upd.)
Information Access Company, 17
Information Builders, Inc., 22
Information Holdings Inc., 47
Information Resources, Inc., 10
Informix Corporation, 10; 30 (upd.)
Ingalls Shipbuilding, Inc., 12
Ingersoll-Rand Company, III; 15 (upd.)
Ingersoll-Rand Company Ltd., 55 (upd.)
Ingles Markets, Inc., 20
Ingram Industries, Inc., 11; 49 (upd.)
Ingram Micro Inc., 52
Inktomi Corporation, 45
Inland Container Corporation, 8
Inland Steel Industries, Inc., IV; 19 (upd.)
Inserra Supermarkets, 25
Insight Enterprises, Inc., 18
Insilco Corporation, 16
Inso Corporation, 26
Instinet Corporation, 34
Insurance Auto Auctions, Inc., 23
Integrated Defense Technologies, Inc., 54
Integrity Inc., 44
Intel Corporation, II; 10 (upd.); 36 (upd.)
IntelliCorp, Inc., 45
Intelligent Electronics, Inc., 6
Inter Parfums Inc., 35
Inter-Regional Financial Group, Inc., 15
Interco Incorporated, III
Interep National Radio Sales Inc., 35
Interface, Inc., 8; 29 (upd.)
Intergraph Corporation, 6; 24 (upd.)
Interlake Corporation, The, 8
Intermet Corporation, 32
Intermountain Health Care, Inc., 27
International Airline Support Group, Inc.,
    55
International Brotherhood of Teamsters, 37

International Business Machines
    Corporation, III; 6 (upd.); 30 (upd.)
International Controls Corporation, 10
International Creative Management, Inc.,
    43
International Dairy Queen, Inc., 10; 39
    (upd.)
International Data Group, Inc., 7; 25 (upd.)
International Family Entertainment Inc., 13
International Flavors & Fragrances Inc., 9;
    38 (upd.)
International Game Technology, 10; 41
    (upd.)
International Lease Finance Corporation,
    48
International Management Group, 18
International Multifoods Corporation, 7; 25
    (upd.)
International Paper Company, IV; 15
    (upd.); 47 (upd.)
International Rectifier Corporation, 31
International Shipholding Corporation, Inc.,
    27
International Speedway Corporation, 19
International Telephone & Telegraph
    Corporation, I; 11 (upd.)
International Total Services, Inc., 37
Interpublic Group of Companies, Inc., The,
    I; 22 (upd.)
Interscope Music Group, 31
Interstate Bakeries Corporation, 12; 38
    (upd.)
Intimate Brands, Inc., 24
Intuit Inc., 14; 33 (upd.)
Invacare Corporation, 11; 47 (upd.)
Invitrogen Corporation, 52
Invivo Corporation, 52
Iomega Corporation, 21
Ionics, Incorporated, 52
IPALCO Enterprises, Inc., 6
Iron Mountain, Inc., 33
Irvin Feld & Kenneth Feld Productions,
    Inc., 15
Island ECN, Inc., The, 48
Isle of Capri Casinos, Inc., 41
Ispat Inland Inc., 40 (upd.)
Itel Corporation, 9
Items International Airwalk Inc., 17
ITT Educational Services, Inc., 33
ITT Sheraton Corporation, III
IVAX Corporation, 11; 55 (upd.)
IVC Industries, Inc., 45
iVillage Inc., 46
Iwerks Entertainment, Inc., 34
IXC Communications, Inc., 29
J & J Snack Foods Corporation, 24
J&R Electronics Inc., 26
J. Baker, Inc., 31
J. Crew Group Inc., 12; 34 (upd.)
J. D'Addario & Company, Inc., 48
J. Jill Group, Inc., The, 35
J.A. Jones, Inc., 16
J.B. Hunt Transport Services Inc., 12
J.C. Penney Company, Inc., V; 18 (upd.);
    43 (upd.)
J.D. Edwards & Company, 14
J.D. Power and Associates, 32
J.F. Shea Co., Inc., 55
J.I. Case Company, 10
J.M. Smucker Company, The, 11
J.P. Morgan & Co. Incorporated, II; 30
    (upd.)
J.P. Morgan Chase & Co., 38 (upd.)
J.R. Simplot Company, 16
Jabil Circuit, Inc., 36
Jack Henry and Associates, Inc., 17
Jack Schwartz Shoes, Inc., 18

Jackpot Enterprises Inc., 21
Jackson Hewitt, Inc., 48
Jackson National Life Insurance Company,
    8
Jaco Electronics, Inc., 30
Jacob Leinenkugel Brewing Company, 28
Jacobs Engineering Group Inc., 6; 26
    (upd.)
Jacobson Stores Inc., 21
Jacor Communications, Inc., 23
Jacuzzi Inc., 23
JAKKS Pacific, Inc., 52
Jalate Inc., 25
Jamba Juice Company, 47
James River Corporation of Virginia, IV
Jason Incorporated, 23
Jay Jacobs, Inc., 15
Jayco Inc., 13
Jazz Basketball Investors, Inc., 55
Jazzercise, Inc., 45
JB Oxford Holdings, Inc., 32
JDS Uniphase Corporation, 34
Jefferies Group, Inc., 25
Jefferson-Pilot Corporation, 11; 29 (upd.)
Jeld-Wen, Inc., 45
Jennifer Convertibles, Inc., 31
Jenny Craig, Inc., 10; 29 (upd.)
Jerry's Famous Deli Inc., 24
Jervis B. Webb Company, 24
JetBlue Airways Corporation, 44
Jetro Cash & Carry Enterprises Inc., 38
JG Industries, Inc., 15
Jillian's Entertainment Holdings, Inc., 40
Jim Beam Brands Co., 14
Jim Henson Company, The, 23
Jitney-Jungle Stores of America, Inc., 27
JLG Industries, Inc., 52
Jockey International, Inc., 12; 34 (upd.)
Joffrey Ballet of Chicago, The 52
John B. Sanfilippo & Son, Inc., 14
John D. and Catherine T. MacArthur
    Foundation, The, 34
John H. Harland Company, 17
John Hancock Financial Services, Inc., III;
    42 (upd.)
John Nuveen Company, The, 21
John Paul Mitchell Systems, 24
John Q. Hammons Hotels, Inc., 24
John W. Danforth Company, 48
John Wiley & Sons, Inc., 17
Johnny Rockets Group, Inc., 31
Johnson & Higgins, 14
Johnson & Johnson, III; 8 (upd.); 36 (upd.)
Johnson Controls, Inc., III; 26 (upd.)
Johnson Publishing Company, Inc., 28
Johnson Worldwide Associates, Inc., 28
Johnston Industries, Inc., 15
Johnstown America Industries, Inc., 23
Jones Apparel Group, Inc., 11; 39 (upd.)
Jones, Day, Reavis & Pogue, 33
Jones Intercable, Inc., 21
Jones Lang LaSalle Incorporated, 49
Jones Medical Industries, Inc., 24
Jordache Enterprises, Inc., 23
Jordan Industries, Inc., 36
Jos. A. Bank Clothiers, Inc., 31
Joseph T. Ryerson & Son, Inc., 15
Jostens, Inc., 7; 25 (upd.)
Journal Register Company, 29
JPI, 49
JPS Textile Group, Inc., 28
Judge Group, Inc., The, 51
Juniper Networks, Inc., 43
Juno Lighting, Inc., 30
Juno Online Services, Inc., 38
Just Born, Inc., 32

United States (*continued*)

Just For Feet, Inc., 19
Justin Industries, Inc., 19
JWP Inc., 9
JWT Group Inc., I
K & B Inc., 12
K & G Men's Center, Inc., 21
K'Nex Industries, Inc., 52
K-Swiss, Inc., 33
K-tel International, Inc., 21
Kaiser Aluminum & Chemical Corporation, IV
Kaiser Foundation Health Plan, Inc., 53
Kal Kan Foods, Inc., 22
Kaman Corporation, 12; 42 (upd.)
Kampgrounds of America, Inc. 33
Kana Software, Inc., 51
Kansas City Power & Light Company, 6
Kansas City Southern Industries, Inc., 6; 26 (upd.)
Kaplan, Inc., 42
Karl Kani Infinity, Inc., 49
Karsten Manufacturing Corporation, 51
Kash n' Karry Food Stores, Inc., 20
Kasper A.S.L., Ltd., 40
Katy Industries, Inc., I; 51 (upd.)
Katz Communications, Inc., 6
Katz Media Group, Inc., 35
Kaufman and Broad Home Corporation, 8
Kaydon Corporation, 18
KB Home, 45 (upd.)
KB Toys, 15; 35 (upd.)
Keebler Foods Company, 36
Keith Companies Inc., The, 54
Keithley Instruments Inc., 16
Kelley Drye & Warren LLP, 40
Kellogg Company, II; 13 (upd.); 50 (upd.)
Kellwood Company, 8
Kelly Services Inc., 6; 26 (upd.)
Kelly-Springfield Tire Company, The, 8
Kelsey-Hayes Group of Companies, 7; 27 (upd.)
Kemet Corp., 14
Kemper Corporation, III; 15 (upd.)
Kendall International, Inc., 11
Kendall-Jackson Winery, Ltd., 28
Kenetech Corporation, 11
Kenneth Cole Productions, Inc., 25
Kent Electronics Corporation, 17
Kentucky Electric Steel, Inc., 31
Kentucky Utilities Company, 6
Kerr Group Inc., 24
Kerr-McGee Corporation, IV; 22 (upd.)
Ketchum Communications Inc., 6
Kettle Foods Inc., 48
Kewaunee Scientific Corporation, 25
Key Tronic Corporation, 14
KeyCorp, 8
Keyes Fibre Company, 9
KeySpan Energy Co., 27
Keystone International, Inc., 11
KFC Corporation, 7; 21 (upd.)
Kidde, Inc., I
Kiehl's Since 1851, Inc., 52
Kikkoman Corporation, 47 (upd.)
Kimball International, Inc., 12; 48 (upd.)
Kimberly-Clark Corporation, III; 16 (upd.); 43 (upd.)
Kimco Realty Corporation, 11
Kinder Morgan, Inc., 45
KinderCare Learning Centers, Inc., 13
Kinetic Concepts, Inc. (KCI), 20
King & Spalding, 23
King Arthur Flour Company, The, 31
King Kullen Grocery Co., Inc., 15
King Pharmaceuticals, Inc., 54
King Ranch, Inc., 14

King World Productions, Inc., 9; 30 (upd.)
Kingston Technology Corporation, 20
Kinko's, Inc., 16; 43 (upd.)
Kinney Shoe Corp., 14
Kirby Corporation, 18
Kit Manufacturing Co., 18
Kitchell Corporation, 14
KitchenAid, 8
Kitty Hawk, Inc., 22
Kiwi International Airlines Inc., 20
KLA-Tencor Corporation, 11; 45 (upd.)
Kleiner, Perkins, Caufield & Byers, 53
Kmart Corporation, V; 18 (upd.); 47 (upd.)
Knape & Vogt Manufacturing Company, 17
Knight-Ridder, Inc., IV; 15 (upd.)
Knoll Group Inc., 14
Knott's Berry Farm, 18
Knowledge Learning Corporation, 51
Knowledge Universe, Inc., 54
KnowledgeWare Inc., 9; 31 (upd.)
Koala Corporation, 44
Koch Enterprises, Inc., 29
Koch Industries, Inc., IV; 20 (upd.)
Kohl's Corporation, 9; 30 (upd.)
Kohlberg Kravis Roberts & Co., 24
Kohler Company, 7; 32 (upd.)
Koll Company, The, 8
Kollmorgen Corporation, 18
Komag, Inc., 11
Koo Koo Roo, Inc., 25
Koppers Industries, Inc., I; 26 (upd.)
Korn/Ferry International, 34
Koss Corporation, 38
Kraft Foods Inc., II; 7 (upd.); 45 (upd.)
Kraus-Anderson, Incorporated, 36
Krause Publications, Inc., 35
Krause's Furniture, Inc., 27
Krispy Kreme Doughnut Corporation, 21
Kroger Company, The, II; 15 (upd.)
Kronos, Inc., 18
Krystal Company, The, 33
K2 Inc., 16
KU Energy Corporation, 11
Kuhlman Corporation, 20
Kulicke and Soffa Industries, Inc., 33
Kurzweil Technologies, Inc., 51
Kushner-Locke Company, The, 25
L-3 Communications Holdings, Inc., 48
L. and J.G. Stickley, Inc., 50
L. Luria & Son, Inc., 19
L.A. Gear, Inc., 8; 32 (upd.)
L.A. T Sportswear, Inc., 26
L.B. Foster Company, 33
L.L. Bean, Inc., 10; 38 (upd.)
L.L. Knickerbocker Co., Inc., The, 25
L.S. Starrett Co., 13
La Choy Food Products Inc., 25
La Madeleine French Bakery & Café, 33
La Quinta Companies, The, 11; 42 (upd.)
La-Z-Boy Incorporated, 14; 50 (upd.)
LaBarge Inc., 41
LabOne, Inc., 48
Labor Ready, Inc., 29
Laboratory Corporation of America Holdings, 42 (upd.)
LaBranche & Co. Inc., 37
Laclede Steel Company, 15
LaCrosse Footwear, Inc., 18
LADD Furniture, Inc., 12
Ladish Co., Inc., 30
Lafarge Corporation, 28
Lakeland Industries, Inc., 45
Lakes Entertainment, Inc., 51
Lam Research Corporation, 11; 31 (upd.)
Lamar Advertising Company, 27
Lamaur Corporation, The, 41

Lamb Weston, Inc., 23
Lamonts Apparel, Inc., 15
Lamson & Sessions Co., 13
Lancaster Colony Corporation, 8
Lance, Inc., 14; 41 (upd.)
Lancer Corporation, 21
Land O'Lakes, Inc., II; 21 (upd.)
Landauer, Inc., 51
Landmark Communications, Inc., 12; 55 (upd.)
Landry's Seafood Restaurants, Inc., 15
Lands' End, Inc., 9; 29 (upd.)
Lane Co., Inc., The, 12
Larry Flynt Publishing Inc., 31
Larry H. Miller Group, 29
Las Vegas Sands, Inc., 50
Lason, Inc., 31
Latham & Watkins, 33
Latrobe Brewing Company, 54
Lattice Semiconductor Corp., 16
Lawson Software, 38
Lawter International Inc., 14
Layne Christensen Company, 19
Lazare Kaplan International Inc., 21
LCI International, Inc., 16
LDB Corporation, 53
LDDS-Metro Communications, Inc., 8
LeapFrog Enterprises, Inc., 54
Lear Seating Corporation, 16
Lear Siegler, Inc., I
Learjet Inc., 8; 27 (upd.)
Learning Company Inc., The, 24
Learning Tree International Inc., 24
LeaRonal, Inc., 23
Leaseway Transportation Corp., 12
Leatherman Tool Group, Inc., 51
Lebhar-Friedman, Inc., 55
LeBoeuf, Lamb, Greene & MacRae, L.L.P., 29
Lechmere Inc., 10
Lechters, Inc., 11; 39 (upd.)
LeCroy Corporation, 41
Lee Apparel Company, Inc., 8
Lee Enterprises, Incorporated, 11
Leeann Chin, Inc., 30
Lefrak Organization Inc., 26
Legal Aid Society, The, 48
Legent Corporation, 10
Legg Mason, Inc., 33
Leggett & Platt, Inc., 11; 48 (upd.)
Lehigh Portland Cement Company, 23
Leiner Health Products Inc., 34
Lennar Corporation, 11
Lennox International Inc., 8; 28 (upd.)
Lenox, Inc., 12
LensCrafters Inc., 23
Leo Burnett Company Inc., I; 20 (upd.)
Leprino Foods Company, 28
Les Schwab Tire Centers, 50
Lesco Inc., 19
Leslie Fay Companies, Inc., The, 8; 39 (upd.)
Leslie's Poolmart, Inc., 18
Leucadia National Corporation, 11
Leupold & Stevens, Inc., 52
Lever Brothers Company, 9
Levi Strauss & Co., V; 16 (upd.)
Levitz Furniture Inc., 15
Levy Restaurants L.P., 26
Lewis Galoob Toys Inc., 16
LEXIS-NEXIS Group, 33
Lexmark International, Inc., 18
LG&E Energy Corporation, 6; 51 (upd.)
Libbey Inc., 49
Liberty Corporation, The, 22
Liberty Livewire Corporation, 42
Liberty Media Corporation, 50

Life Technologies, Inc., 17
Lifeline Systems, Inc., 53
Lifetime Entertainment Services, 51
Lifetime Hoan Corporation, 27
Ligand Pharmaceuticals Incorporated, 47
Lillian Vernon Corporation, 12; 35 (upd.)
Limited, Inc., The, V; 20 (upd.)
LIN Broadcasting Corp., 9
Lincare Holdings Inc., 43
Lincoln Electric Co., 13
Lincoln National Corporation, III; 25
    (upd.)
Lincoln Property Company, 8; 54 (upd.)
Lincoln Snacks Company, 24
Lincoln Telephone & Telegraph Company,
    14
Lindal Cedar Homes, Inc., 29
Lindsay Manufacturing Co., 20
Linear Technology, Inc., 16
Linens 'n Things, Inc., 24
Lintas: Worldwide, 14
Lionel L.L.C., 16
Liqui-Box Corporation, 16
Lithia Motors, Inc., 41
Littelfuse, Inc., 26
Little Caesar Enterprises, Inc., 7; 24 (upd.)
Little Tikes Co., 13
Litton Industries, Inc., I; 11 (upd.)
LIVE Entertainment Inc., 20
Liz Claiborne, Inc., 8; 25 (upd.)
Lockheed Martin Corporation, I; 11 (upd.);
    15 (upd.)
Loctite Corporation, 8; 30 (upd.)
LodgeNet Entertainment Corporation, 28
Loehmann's Inc., 24
Loews Corporation, I; 12 (upd.); 36 (upd.)
Logan's Roadhouse, Inc., 29
Logicon Inc., 20
LoJack Corporation, 48
London Fog Industries, Inc., 29
Lone Star Steakhouse & Saloon, Inc., 51
Long Island Bancorp, Inc., 16
Long Island Lighting Company, V
Long John Silver's Restaurants Inc., 13
Longaberger Company, The, 12; 44 (upd.)
Longs Drug Stores Corporation, V; 25
    (upd.)
Longview Fibre Company, 8; 37 (upd.)
Loral Space & Communications Ltd., 8; 9;
    54 (upd.)
Lost Arrow Inc., 22
LOT$OFF Corporation, 24
Lotus Development Corporation, 6; 25
    (upd.)
Louisiana Land and Exploration Company,
    The, 7
Louisiana-Pacific Corporation, IV; 31
    (upd.)
Lowe's Companies, Inc., V; 21 (upd.)
Lowrance Electronics, Inc., 18
LSI Logic Corporation, 13
LTV Corporation, The, I; 24 (upd.)
Lubrizol Corporation, I; 30 (upd.)
Luby's, Inc., 17; 42 (upd.)
Lucasfilm Ltd., 12; 50 (upd.)
Lucent Technologies Inc., 34
Lucille Farms, Inc., 45
Lucky Stores, Inc., 27
Lukens Inc., 14
Lunar Corporation, 29
Lund Food Holdings, Inc., 22
Lund International Holdings, Inc., 40
Lutheran Brotherhood, 31
Lynch Corporation, 43
Lyondell Chemical Company, IV; 45
    (upd.)
M&F Worldwide Corp., 38

M. Shanken Communications, Inc., 50
M.A. Gedney Co., 51
M.A. Hanna Company, 8
M.H. Meyerson & Co., Inc., 46
Mac Frugal's Bargains - Closeouts Inc., 17
Mac-Gray Corporation, 44
MacAndrews & Forbes Holdings Inc., 28
MacDermid Incorporated, 32
Mack Trucks, Inc., I; 22 (upd.)
Mack-Cali Realty Corporation, 42
Mackay Envelope Corporation, 45
Mackie Designs Inc., 33
Macmillan, Inc., 7
MacNeal-Schwendler Corporation, The, 25
Macromedia, Inc., 50
Madden's on Gull Lake, 52
Madison Gas and Electric Company, 39
Magma Copper Company, 7
Magma Power Company, 11
MagneTek, Inc., 15; 41 (upd.)
MAI Systems Corporation, 11
Maidenform Worldwide Inc., 20
Mail Boxes Etc., 18; 41 (upd.)
Mail-Well, Inc., 28
Maine Central Railroad Company, 16
Major Automotive Companies, Inc., The,
    45
Malcolm Pirnie, Inc., 42
Malden Mills Industries, Inc., 16
Mallinckrodt Group Inc., 19
Malt-O-Meal Company, 22
Management and Training Corporation, 28
Mandalay Resort Group, 32 (upd.)
Manitowoc Company, Inc., 18
Mannatech Inc., 33
Manor Care, Inc., 6; 25 (upd.)
Manpower, Inc., 9; 30 (upd.)
Manufactured Home Communities, Inc., 22
Manufacturers Hanover Corporation, II
Manville Corporation, III; 7 (upd.)
MAPCO Inc., IV
MAPICS, Inc., 55
March of Dimes, 31
marchFIRST, Inc., 34
Marcus Corporation, The, 21
Marie Callender's Restaurant & Bakery,
    Inc., 28
MarineMax, Inc., 30
Marion Laboratories, Inc., I
Marisa Christina, Inc., 15
Maritz Inc., 38
Mark IV Industries, Inc., 7; 28 (upd.)
Marks Brothers Jewelers, Inc., 24
Marmon Group, The, IV; 16 (upd.)
Marquette Electronics, Inc., 13
Marriott International, Inc., III; 21 (upd.)
Mars, Incorporated, 7; 40 (upd.)
Marsh & McLennan Companies, Inc., III;
    45 (upd.)
Marsh Supermarkets, Inc., 17
Marshalls Incorporated, 13
Martha Stewart Living Omnimedia, L.L.C.,
    24
Martin Industries, Inc., 44
Martin Marietta Corporation, I
Marvel Entertainment Group, Inc., 10
Marvin Lumber & Cedar Company, 22
Mary Kay Corporation, 9; 30 (upd.)
Masco Corporation, III; 20 (upd.); 39
    (upd.)
Mashantucket Pequot Gaming Enterprise
    Inc., 35
Masland Corporation, 17
Massachusetts Mutual Life Insurance
    Company, III; 53 (upd.)
MasTec, Inc., 19; 55 (upd.)
Master Lock Company, 45

MasterCard International, Inc., 9
Matria Healthcare, Inc., 17
Mattel, Inc., 7; 25 (upd.)
Matthews International Corporation, 29
Maui Land & Pineapple Company, Inc., 29
Max & Erma's Restaurants Inc., 19
Maxco Inc., 17
Maxicare Health Plans, Inc., III; 25 (upd.)
Maxim Group, The, 25
Maxim Integrated Products, Inc., 16
MAXIMUS, Inc., 43
Maxtor Corporation, 10
Maxus Energy Corporation, 7
Maxwell Shoe Company, Inc., 30
MAXXAM Inc., 8
Maxxim Medical Inc., 12
May Department Stores Company, The, V;
    19 (upd.); 46 (upd.)
Mayer, Brown, Rowe & Maw, 47
Mayflower Group Inc., 6
Mayo Foundation, 9; 34 (upd.)
Mayor's Jewelers, Inc., 41
Maytag Corporation, III; 22 (upd.)
Mazel Stores, Inc., 29
MBC Holding Company, 40
MBNA Corporation, 12; 33 (upd.)
MCA Inc., II
McCarthy Building Companies, Inc., 48
McCaw Cellular Communications, Inc., 6
McClain Industries, Inc., 51
McClatchy Newspapers, Inc., 23
McCormick & Company, Incorporated, 7;
    27 (upd.)
McDermott International, Inc., III; 37
    (upd.)
McDonald's Corporation, II; 7 (upd.); 26
    (upd.)
McDonnell Douglas Corporation, I; 11
    (upd.)
McGraw-Hill Companies, Inc., The, IV; 18
    (upd.); 51 (upd.)
MCI WorldCom, Inc., V; 27 (upd.)
McIlhenny Company, 20
McKee Foods Corporation, 7; 27 (upd.)
McKesson Corporation, I; 12; 47 (upd.)
McKinsey & Company, Inc., 9
McLane Company, Inc., 13
McLeodUSA Incorporated, 32
MCN Corporation, 6
MCSi, Inc., 41
McWane Corporation, 55
MDU Resources Group, Inc., 7; 42 (upd.)
Mead Corporation, The, IV; 19 (upd.)
Mead Data Central, Inc., 10
Meade Instruments Corporation, 41
Meadowcraft, Inc., 29
Mecklermedia Corporation, 24
Medco Containment Services Inc., 9
Media Arts Group, Inc., 42
Media General, Inc., 7; 38 (upd.)
MedImmune, Inc., 35
Meditrust, 11
Medtronic, Inc., 8; 30 (upd.)
Medusa Corporation, 24
Megafoods Stores Inc., 13
Meier & Frank Co., 23
Meijer Incorporated, 7; 27 (upd.)
Mel Farr Automotive Group, 20
Melaleuca Inc., 31
Melamine Chemicals, Inc., 27
Mellon Bank Corporation, II
Mellon Financial Corporation, 44 (upd.)
Mellon-Stuart Company, I
Melville Corporation, V
Melvin Simon and Associates, Inc., 8
Men's Wearhouse, Inc., The, 17; 48 (upd.)
Menard, Inc., 34

United States (*continued*)

Menasha Corporation, 8
Mentholatum Company Inc., The, 32
Mentor Corporation, 26
Mentor Graphics Corporation, 11
Mercantile Bankshares Corp., 11
Mercantile Stores Company, Inc., V; 19
  (upd.)
Merck & Co., Inc., I; 11 (upd.); 34 (upd.)
Mercury Air Group, Inc., 20
Mercury General Corporation, 25
Meredith Corporation, 11; 29 (upd.)
Meridian Bancorp, Inc., 11
Meridian Gold, Incorporated, 47
Merillat Industries Inc., 13
Merisel, Inc., 12
Merit Medical Systems, Inc., 29
Meritage Corporation, 26
Merix Corporation, 36
Merrell Dow, Inc., I; 9 (upd.)
Merrill Corporation, 18; 47 (upd.)
Merrill Lynch & Co., Inc., II; 13 (upd.); 40
  (upd.)
Merry-Go-Round Enterprises, Inc., 8
Mervyn's California, 10; 39 (upd.)
Mesa Air Group, Inc., 11; 32 (upd.)
Mesaba Holdings, Inc., 28
Mestek Inc., 10
Metatec International, Inc., 47
Meteor Industries Inc., 33
Methode Electronics, Inc., 13
Metro Information Services, Inc., 36
Metro-Goldwyn-Mayer Inc., 25 (upd.)
Metrocall, Inc., 41
Metromedia Co., 7; 14
Metropolitan Baseball Club Inc., 39
Metropolitan Financial Corporation, 13
Metropolitan Life Insurance Company, III;
  52 (upd.)
Metropolitan Museum of Art, The, 55
Metropolitan Opera Association, Inc., 40
Metropolitan Transportation Authority, 35
Mexican Restaurants, Inc., 41
MFS Communications Company, Inc., 11
MGIC Investment Corp., 52
MGM Grand Inc., 17
MGM/UA Communications Company, II
Michael Anthony Jewelers, Inc., 24
Michael Baker Corporation, 14; 51 (upd.)
Michael C. Fina Co., Inc., 52
Michael Foods, Inc., 25
Michaels Stores, Inc., 17
Michigan Bell Telephone Co., 14
Michigan National Corporation, 11
Micro Warehouse, Inc., 16
MicroAge, Inc., 16
Microdot Inc., 8
Micron Technology, Inc., 11; 29 (upd.)
Micros Systems, Inc., 18
Microsoft Corporation, 6; 27 (upd.)
Mid-America Dairymen, Inc., 7
Midas International Corporation, 10
Middleby Corporation, The, 22
Middlesex Water Company, 45
Middleton Doll Company, The, 53
Midway Airlines Corporation, 33
Midway Games, Inc., 25
Midwest Express Holdings, Inc., 35
Midwest Grain Products, Inc., 49
Midwest Resources Inc., 6
Mikasa, Inc., 28
Mike-Sell's Inc., 15
Mikohn Gaming Corporation, 39
Milacron, Inc., 53 (upd.)
Milbank, Tweed, Hadley & McCloy, 27
Miles Laboratories, I
Millennium Pharmaceuticals, Inc., 47

Miller Brewing Company, I; 12 (upd.)
Miller Industries, Inc., 26
Milliken & Co., V; 17 (upd.)
Millipore Corporation, 25
Milnot Company, 46
Milton Bradley Company, 21
Milwaukee Brewers Baseball Club, 37
Mine Safety Appliances Company, 31
Miner Group International, The, 22
Minerals Technologies Inc., 11; 52 (upd.)
Minnesota Mining & Manufacturing
  Company (3M), I; 8 (upd.); 26 (upd.)
Minnesota Power, Inc., 11; 34 (upd.)
Minntech Corporation, 22
Minute Maid Company, The, 28
Minuteman International Inc., 46
Minyard Food Stores, Inc., 33
Mirage Resorts, Incorporated, 6; 28 (upd.)
Mississippi Chemical Corporation, 39
Mitchell Energy and Development
  Corporation, 7
MITRE Corporation, 26
Mity Enterprises, Inc., 38
Mobil Corporation, IV; 7 (upd.); 21 (upd.)
Mobile Telecommunications Technologies
  Corp., 18
Modine Manufacturing Company, 8
Moen Incorporated, 12
Mohawk Industries, Inc., 19
Mohegan Tribal Gaming Authority, 37
Molex Incorporated, 11; 54 (upd.)
Monaco Coach Corporation, 31
Monadnock Paper Mills, Inc., 21
Monfort, Inc., 13
Monro Muffler Brake, Inc., 24
Monsanto Company, I; 9 (upd.); 29 (upd.)
Montana Power Company, The, 11; 44
  (upd.)
Montgomery Ward & Co., Incorporated, V;
  20 (upd.)
Moog Inc., 13
Mooney Aerospace Group Ltd., 52
Moore Medical Corp., 17
Moore-Handley, Inc., 39
Moran Towing Corporation, Inc., 15
Morgan Group, Inc., The, 46
Morgan Stanley Dean Witter & Company,
  II; 16 (upd.); 33 (upd.)
Morgan, Lewis & Bockius LLP, 29
Morris Communications Corporation, 36
Morris Travel Services L.L.C., 26
Morrison Knudsen Corporation, 7; 28
  (upd.)
Morrison Restaurants Inc., 11
Morse Shoe Inc., 13
Morton International Inc., 9 (upd.)
Morton Thiokol, Inc., I
Morton's Restaurant Group, Inc., 30
Mosinee Paper Corporation, 15
Mossimo, Inc., 27
Motel 6 Corporation, 13
Mothers Against Drunk Driving (MADD),
  51
Mothers Work, Inc., 18
Motley Fool, Inc., The, 40
Moto Photo, Inc., 45
Motor Cargo Industries, Inc., 35
Motorcar Parts & Accessories, Inc., 47
Motorola, Inc., II; 11 (upd.); 34 (upd.)
Motown Records Company L.P., 26
Mountain States Mortgage Centers, Inc., 29
Movado Group, Inc., 28
Movie Gallery, Inc., 31
Movie Star Inc., 17
MPS Group, Inc., 49
MPW Industrial Services Group, Inc., 53
Mr. Coffee, Inc., 15

Mr. Gasket Inc., 15
Mrs. Baird's Bakeries, 29
Mrs. Fields' Original Cookies, Inc., 27
Mt. Olive Pickle Company, Inc., 44
MTS Inc., 37
Mueller Industries, Inc., 7; 52 (upd.)
Mullen Advertising Inc., 51
Multi-Color Corporation, 53
Multimedia Games, Inc., 41
Multimedia, Inc., 11
Murdock Madaus Schwabe, 26
Murphy Family Farms Inc., 22
Murphy Oil Corporation, 7; 32 (upd.)
Musicland Stores Corporation, 9; 38 (upd.)
Mutual Benefit Life Insurance Company,
  The, III
Mutual Life Insurance Company of New
  York, The, III
Muzak, Inc., 18
Mycogen Corporation, 21
Myers Industries, Inc., 19
Mylan Laboratories Inc., I; 20 (upd.)
Nabisco Foods Group, II; 7 (upd.)
Nabors Industries, Inc., 9
NACCO Industries, Inc., 7
Nalco Chemical Corporation, I; 12 (upd.)
Nantucket Allserve, Inc., 22
NASD, 54 (upd.)
Nash Finch Company, 8; 23 (upd.)
Nashua Corporation, 8
Nathan's Famous, Inc., 29
National Amusements Inc., 28
National Association for Stock Car Auto
  Racing, 32
National Association of Securities Dealers,
  Inc., 10
National Audubon Society, 26
National Auto Credit, Inc., 16
National Beverage Corp., 26
National Broadcasting Company, Inc., II; 6
  (upd.); 28 (upd.)
National Can Corporation, I
National Car Rental System, Inc., 10
National City Corp., 15
National Convenience Stores Incorporated,
  7
National Discount Brokers Group, Inc., 28
National Distillers and Chemical
  Corporation, I
National Educational Music Co. Ltd., 47
National Envelope Corporation, 32
National Football League, 29
National Fuel Gas Company, 6
National Geographic Society, 9; 30 (upd.)
National Grape Cooperative Association,
  Inc., 20
National Grid USA, 51 (upd.)
National Gypsum Company, 10
National Health Laboratories Incorporated,
  11
National Hockey League, 35
National Home Centers, Inc., 44
National Instruments Corporation, 22
National Intergroup, Inc., V
National Media Corporation, 27
National Medical Enterprises, Inc., III
National Oilwell, Inc., 54
National Organization for Women, Inc., 55
National Patent Development Corporation,
  13
National Picture & Frame Company, 24
National Presto Industries, Inc., 16; 43
  (upd.)
National Public Radio, Inc., 19; 47 (upd.)
National R.V. Holdings, Inc., 32
National Railroad Passenger Corporation,
  22

Potter & Brumfield Inc., 11
Powell's Books, Inc., 40
PowerBar Inc., 44
Powerhouse Technologies, Inc., 27
PPG Industries, Inc., III; 22 (upd.)
PPL Corporation, 41 (upd.)
PR Newswire, 35
Prairie Farms Dairy, Inc., 47
Pratt & Whitney, 9
Praxair, Inc., 11; 48 (upd.)
Pre-Paid Legal Services, Inc., 20
Precision Castparts Corp., 15
Premark International, Inc., III
Premcor Inc., 37
Premier Industrial Corporation, 9
Premier Parks, Inc., 27
Premium Standard Farms, Inc., 30
PremiumWear, Inc., 30
Preserver Group, Inc., 44
President Casinos, Inc., 22
Presstek, Inc., 33
Preston Corporation, 6
Price Communications Corporation, 42
Price Company, The, V
PriceCostco, Inc., 14
PricewaterhouseCoopers, 9; 29 (upd.)
Primark Corp., 13
Prime Hospitality Corporation, 52
Primedex Health Systems, Inc., 25
Primedia Inc., 22
Primerica Corporation, I
Prince Sports Group, Inc., 15
Princess Cruise Lines, 22
Princeton Review, Inc., The, 42
Principal Mutual Life Insurance Company,
    III
Printrak, A Motorola Company, 44
Printronix, Inc., 18
Prison Rehabilitative Industries and
    Diversified Enterprises, Inc. (PRIDE), 53
Procter & Gamble Company, The, III; 8
    (upd.); 26 (upd.)
Prodigy Communications Corporation, 34
Professional Bull Riders Inc., 55
Professional Golfers' Association of
    America, The, 41
Proffitt's, Inc., 19
Progress Software Corporation, 15
Progressive Corporation, The, 11; 29 (upd.)
Promus Companies, Inc., 9
Proskauer Rose LLP, 47
Protection One, Inc., 32
Providence Journal Company, The, 28
Provident Life and Accident Insurance
    Company of America, III
Providian Financial Corporation, 52 (upd.)
Prudential Insurance Company of America,
    The, III; 30 (upd.)
PSI Resources, 6
Pubco Corporation, 17
Public Service Company of Colorado, 6
Public Service Company of New
    Hampshire, 21; 55 (upd.)
Public Service Company of New Mexico, 6
Public Service Enterprise Group Inc., V;
    44 (upd.)
Public Storage, Inc., 52
Publishers Clearing House, 23
Publishers Group, Inc., 35
Publix Supermarkets Inc., 7; 31 (upd.)
Pueblo Xtra International, Inc., 47
Puget Sound Energy Inc., 6; 50 (upd.)
Pulaski Furniture Corporation, 33
Pulitzer Publishing Company, 15
Pulte Corporation, 8
Pulte Homes, Inc., 42 (upd.)
Pumpkin Masters, Inc., 48

Purina Mills, Inc., 32
Puritan-Bennett Corporation, 13
Purolator Products Company, 21
Putt-Putt Golf Courses of America, Inc., 23
PW Eagle, Inc., 48
Pyramid Breweries Inc., 33
Pyramid Companies, 54
Quad/Graphics, Inc., 19
Quaker Fabric Corp., 19
Quaker Oats Company, The, II; 12 (upd.);
    34 (upd.)
Quaker State Corporation, 7; 21 (upd.)
QUALCOMM Incorporated, 20; 47 (upd.)
Quality Chekd Dairies, Inc., 48
Quality Dining, Inc., 18
Quality Food Centers, Inc., 17
Quanex Corporation, 13
Quantum Chemical Corporation, 8
Quantum Corporation, 10
Quark, Inc., 36
Quest Diagnostics Inc., 26
Questar Corporation, 6; 26 (upd.)
Quick & Reilly Group, Inc., The, 20
Quiksilver, Inc., 18
QuikTrip Corporation, 36
Quill Corporation, 28
Quintiles Transnational Corporation, 21
Quixote Corporation, 15
Quizno's Corporation, The, 42
QVC Network Inc., 9
Qwest Communications International, Inc.,
    37
R&B, Inc., 51
R.B. Pamplin Corp., 45
R.C. Bigelow, Inc., 49
R.G. Barry Corporation, 17; 44 (upd.)
R.H. Macy & Co., Inc., V; 8 (upd.); 30
    (upd.)
R.J. Reynolds Tobacco Holdings, Inc., 30
    (upd.)
R.L. Polk & Co., 10
R.P. Scherer, I
R.R. Donnelley & Sons Company, IV; 9
    (upd.); 38 (upd.)
Racal-Datacom Inc., 11
Racing Champions Corporation, 37
Radian Group Inc., 42
Radio Flyer Inc., 34
RadioShack Corporation, 36 (upd.)
Radius Inc., 16
Rag Shops, Inc., 30
RailTex, Inc., 20
Rainforest Cafe, Inc., 25
Rainier Brewing Company, 23
Raley's Inc., 14
Rally's Hamburgers, Inc., 25
Ralphs Grocery Company, 35
Ralston Purina Company, II; 13 (upd.)
Ramsay Youth Services, Inc., 41
Rand McNally & Company, 28
Randall's Food Markets, Inc., 40
Random House, Inc., 13; 31 (upd.)
Range Resources Corporation, 45
Rapala-Normark Group, Ltd., 30
Rare Hospitality International Inc., 19
Raven Industries, Inc., 33
Rawlings Sporting Goods Co., Inc., 24
Raychem Corporation, 8
Rayonier Inc., 24
Rayovac Corporation, 13; 39 (upd.)
Raytheon Aircraft Holdings Inc., 46
Raytheon Company, II; 11 (upd.); 38
    (upd.)
Razorfish, Inc., 37
RCA Corporation, II
RCM Technologies, Inc., 34
RDO Equipment Company, 33

Read-Rite Corp., 10
Reader's Digest Association, Inc., The, IV;
    17 (upd.)
RealNetworks, Inc., 53
Reckson Associates Realty Corp., 47
Recording for the Blind & Dyslexic, 51
Recoton Corp., 15
Recovery Engineering, Inc., 25
Recreational Equipment, Inc., 18
Recycled Paper Greetings, Inc., 21
Red Apple Group, Inc., 23
Red Hat, Inc., 45
Red Roof Inns, Inc., 18
Red Spot Paint & Varnish Company, 55
Red Wing Pottery Sales, Inc., 52
Red Wing Shoe Company, Inc., 9; 30
    (upd.)
Redhook Ale Brewery, Inc., 31
Reebok International Ltd., V; 9 (upd.); 26
    (upd.)
Reeds Jewelers, Inc., 22
Regal-Beloit Corporation, 18
Regis Corporation, 18
Reichhold Chemicals, Inc., 10
Reliance Electric Company, 9
Reliance Group Holdings, Inc., III
Reliance Steel & Aluminum Co., 19
Reliant Energy Inc., 44 (upd.)
RemedyTemp, Inc., 20
Remington Arms Company, Inc., 12; 40
    (upd.)
Remington Products Company, L.L.C., 42
Renaissance Learning Systems, Inc., 39
Reno Air Inc., 23
Rent-A-Center, Inc., 45
Rent-Way, Inc., 33
Rental Service Corporation, 28
Rentrak Corporation, 35
Republic Engineered Steels, Inc., 7; 26
    (upd.)
Republic Industries, Inc., 26
Republic New York Corporation, 11
Res-Care, Inc., 29
Resorts International, Inc., 12
Resource America, Inc., 42
Response Oncology, Inc., 27
Restaurants Unlimited, Inc., 13
Restoration Hardware, Inc., 30
Revco D.S., Inc., V
Revell-Monogram Inc., 16
Revere Ware Corporation, 22
Revlon Inc., III; 17 (upd.)
REX Stores Corp., 10
Rexel, Inc., 15
Rexnord Corporation, 21
Reynolds and Reynolds Company, The, 50
Reynolds Metals Company, IV; 19 (upd.)
RF Micro Devices, Inc., 43
Rhino Entertainment Company, 18
Rhodes Inc., 23
Rica Foods, Inc., 41
Rich Products Corporation, 7; 38 (upd.)
Richardson Electronics, Ltd., 17
Richfood Holdings, Inc., 7
Richton International Corporation, 39
Riddell Sports Inc., 22
Ride, Inc., 22
Riese Organization, The, 38
Riggs National Corporation, 13
Right Management Consultants, Inc., 42
Riklis Family Corp., 9
Riser Foods, Inc., 9
Rite Aid Corporation, V; 19 (upd.)
Ritz Camera Centers, 34
Ritz-Carlton Hotel Company L.L.C., 9; 29
    (upd.)
Rival Company, The, 19

United States (*continued*)

River Oaks Furniture, Inc., 43
Riverwood International Corporation, 11; 48 (upd.)
Riviana Foods Inc., 27
RJR Nabisco Holdings Corp., V
RMH Teleservices, Inc., 42
Roadhouse Grill, Inc., 22
Roadmaster Industries, Inc., 16
Roadway Express, Inc., V; 25 (upd.)
Roanoke Electric Steel Corporation, 45
Robbins & Myers Inc., 15
Roberds Inc., 19
Robert Half International Inc., 18
Robert Mondavi Corporation, 15; 50 (upd.)
Robert Wood Johnson Foundation, 35
Roberts Pharmaceutical Corporation, 16
Robertson-Ceco Corporation, 19
Robinson Helicopter Company, 51
Roche Bioscience, 11; 14 (upd.)
Rochester Gas and Electric Corporation, 6
Rochester Telephone Corporation, 6
Rock Bottom Restaurants, Inc., 25
Rock of Ages Corporation, 37
Rock-Tenn Company, 13
Rockefeller Foundation, The, 34
Rockford Corporation, 43
Rockford Products Corporation, 55
RockShox, Inc., 26
Rockwell Automation, 43 (upd.)
Rockwell International Corporation, I; 11 (upd.)
Rocky Shoes & Boots, Inc., 26
Rodale Press, Inc., 23
Rodale, Inc., 47 (upd.)
Rohm and Haas Company, I; 26 (upd.)
ROHN Industries, Inc., 22
Rohr Incorporated, 9
Roll International Corporation, 37
Rollerblade, Inc., 15; 34 (upd.)
Rollins, Inc., 11
Rolls-Royce Allison, 29 (upd.)
Ron Tonkin Chevrolet Company, 55
Ronco, Inc., 15
Rooms To Go Inc., 28
Rooney Brothers Co., 25
Roper Industries, Inc., 15; 50 (upd.)
Ropes & Gray, 40
Rorer Group, I
Rose's Stores, Inc., 13
Rosemount Inc., 15
Rosenbluth International Inc., 14
Ross Stores, Inc., 17; 43 (upd.)
Rotary International, 31
Roto-Rooter Corp., 15
Rottlund Company, Inc., The, 28
Rouge Steel Company, 8
Roundy's Inc., 14
Rouse Company, The, 15
Rowan Companies, Inc., 43
Roy F. Weston, Inc., 33
Royal Appliance Manufacturing Company, 15
Royal Caribbean Cruises Ltd., 22
Royal Crown Company, Inc., 23
RPM, Inc., 8; 36 (upd.)
RSA Security Inc., 46
Rubbermaid Incorporated, III; 20 (upd.)
Rubio's Restaurants, Inc., 35
Ruby Tuesday, Inc., 18
Ruiz Food Products, Inc., 53
Rural Cellular Corporation, 43
Rural/Metro Corporation, 28
Rush Communications, 33
Russ Berrie and Company, Inc., 12
Russell Corporation, 8; 30 (upd.)
Russell Reynolds Associates Inc., 38

Russell Stover Candies Inc., 12
Rust International Inc., 11
Ruth's Chris Steak House, 28
Ryan's Family Steak Houses, Inc., 15
Ryder System, Inc., V; 24 (upd.)
Ryerson Tull, Inc., 40 (upd.)
Ryland Group, Inc., The, 8; 37 (upd.)
S&C Electric Company, 15
S&K Famous Brands, Inc., 23
S-K-I Limited, 15
S.C. Johnson & Son, Inc., III; 28 (upd.)
Saatchi & Saatchi, 42 (upd.)
Sabratek Corporation, 29
SABRE Group Holdings, Inc., 26
SAFECO Corporaton, III
Safeguard Scientifics, Inc., 10
Safelite Glass Corp., 19
Safeskin Corporation, 18
Safety 1st, Inc., 24
Safety-Kleen Corp., 8
Safeway Inc., II; 24 (upd.)
Saga Communications, Inc., 27
St. Joe Company, The, 31
St. Joe Paper Company, 8
St. John Knits, Inc., 14
St. Jude Medical, Inc., 11; 43 (upd.)
St. Louis Music, Inc., 48
St. Paul Bank for Cooperatives, 8
St. Paul Companies, Inc., The, III; 22 (upd.)
Saks Inc., 24; 41 (upd.)
Salant Corporation, 12; 51 (upd.)
Salick Health Care, Inc., 53
Salomon Inc., II; 13 (upd.)
Salt River Project, 19
Salton, Inc., 30
Salvation Army USA, The, 32
Sam Ash Music Corporation, 30
Sam's Club, 40
Samsonite Corporation, 13; 43 (upd.)
Samuel Cabot Inc., 53
Samuels Jewelers Incorporated, 30
San Diego Gas & Electric Company, V
Sanderson Farms, Inc., 15
Sandia National Laboratories, 49
Santa Barbara Restaurant Group, Inc., 37
Santa Cruz Operation, Inc., The, 38
Santa Fe Gaming Corporation, 19
Santa Fe International Corporation, 38
Santa Fe Pacific Corporation, V
Sara Lee Corporation, II; 15 (upd.); 54 (upd.)
SAS Institute Inc., 10
Saturn Corporation, 7; 21 (upd.)
Saucony Inc., 35
Sauder Woodworking Company, 12; 35 (upd.)
Savannah Foods & Industries, Inc., 7
Sawtek Inc., 43 (upd.)
Sbarro, Inc., 16
SBC Communications Inc., 32 (upd.)
SBS Technologies, Inc., 25
SCANA Corporation, 6
ScanSource, Inc., 29
SCB Computer Technology, Inc., 29
SCEcorp, V
Schawk, Inc., 24
Schering-Plough Corporation, I; 14 (upd.); 49 (upd.)
Schlotzsky's, Inc., 36
Schlumberger Limited, III; 17 (upd.)
Schmitt Music Company, 40
Schneider National, Inc., 36
Schneiderman's Furniture Inc., 28
Schnitzer Steel Industries, Inc., 19
Scholastic Corporation, 10; 29 (upd.)
Schott Corporation, 53

Schottenstein Stores Corp., 14
Schuff Steel Company, 26
Schultz Sav-O Stores, Inc., 21; 31 (upd.)
Schwan's Sales Enterprises, Inc., 7; 26 (upd.)
Schweitzer-Mauduit International, Inc., 52
Schwinn Cycle and Fitness L.P., 19
SCI Systems, Inc., 9
Science Applications International Corporation, 15
Scientific-Atlanta, Inc., 6; 45 (upd.)
Score Board, Inc., The, 19
Scotsman Industries, Inc., 20
Scott Fetzer Company, 12
Scott Paper Company, IV; 31 (upd.)
Scotts Company, The, 22
Scotty's, Inc., 22
Scovill Fasteners Inc., 24
SCP Pool Corporation, 39
Seaboard Corporation, 36
Seagate Technology, Inc., 8; 34 (upd.)
Seagull Energy Corporation, 11
Sealed Air Corporation, 14
Sealed Power Corporation, I
Sealright Co., Inc., 17
Sealy Inc., 12
Seaman Furniture Company, Inc., 32
Sears, Roebuck and Co., V; 18 (upd.)
Seattle City Light, 50
Seattle FilmWorks, Inc., 20
Seattle First National Bank Inc., 8
Seattle Times Company, 15
Seaway Food Town, Inc., 15
Sebastiani Vineyards, Inc., 28
Second Harvest, 29
Security Capital Corporation, 17
Security Pacific Corporation, II
SED International Holdings, Inc., 43
See's Candies, Inc., 30
Sega of America, Inc., 10
Segway LLC, 48
Seigle's Home and Building Centers, Inc., 41
Seitel, Inc., 47
Select Comfort Corporation, 34
Selmer Company, Inc., The, 19
SEMCO Energy, Inc., 44
Seminis, Inc., 29
Semitool, Inc., 18
Sempra Energy, 25 (upd.)
Semtech Corporation, 32
Seneca Foods Corporation, 17
Sensient Technologies Corporation, 52 (upd.)
Sensormatic Electronics Corp., 11
Sensory Science Corporation, 37
Sepracor Inc., 45
Sequa Corporation, 13; 54 (upd.)
Serta, Inc., 28
Service America Corp., 7
Service Corporation International, 6; 51 (upd.)
Service Merchandise Company, Inc., V; 19 (upd.)
ServiceMaster Inc., 6; 23 (upd.)
7-11, Inc., 32 (upd.)
Sevenson Environmental Services, Inc., 42
SFX Entertainment, Inc., 36
SGI, 29 (upd.)
Shakespeare Company, 22
Shaklee Corporation, 12; 39 (upd.)
Shared Medical Systems Corporation, 14
Sharper Image Corporation, The, 10
Shaw Group, Inc., The, 50
Shaw Industries, Inc., 9; 40 (upd.)
Shawmut National Corporation, 13
Shearman & Sterling, 32

Shearson Lehman Brothers Holdings Inc., II; 9 (upd.)
Shelby Williams Industries, Inc., 14
Sheldahl Inc., 23
Shell Oil Company, IV; 14 (upd.); 41 (upd.)
Sheller-Globe Corporation, I
Shells Seafood Restaurants, Inc., 43
Sherwin-Williams Company, The, III; 13 (upd.)
Sherwood Brands, Inc., 53
Shoe Carnival Inc., 14
Shoney's, Inc., 7; 23 (upd.)
ShopKo Stores Inc., 21
Shorewood Packaging Corporation, 28
ShowBiz Pizza Time, Inc., 13
Showboat, Inc., 19
Shubert Organization Inc., 24
Shuffle Master Inc., 51
Shurgard Storage Centers, Inc., 52
Sidley Austin Brown & Wood, 40
Siebel Systems, Inc., 38
Siebert Financial Corp., 32
Sierra Club, The, 28
Sierra Health Services, Inc., 15
Sierra On-Line, Inc., 15; 41 (upd.)
Sierra Pacific Industries, 22
SIFCO Industries, Inc., 41
Sigma-Aldrich Corporation, I; 36 (upd.)
Signet Banking Corporation, 11
Sikorsky Aircraft Corporation, 24
Silhouette Brands, Inc., 55
Silicon Graphics Incorporated, 9
SilverPlatter Information Inc., 23
Silverstein Properties, Inc., 47
Simmons Company, 47
Simon & Schuster Inc., IV; 19 (upd.)
Simon Property Group, Inc., 27
Simon Transportation Services Inc., 27
Simplex Technologies Inc., 21
Simpson Investment Company, 17
Simpson Thacher & Bartlett, 39
Simula, Inc., 41
Sinclair Broadcast Group, Inc., 25
Sir Speedy, Inc., 16
Six Flags, Inc., 17; 54 (upd.)
Skadden, Arps, Slate, Meagher & Flom, 18
Skechers USA Inc., 31
Skidmore, Owings & Merrill, 13
Skyline Corporation, 30
SkyMall, Inc., 26
SkyWest, Inc., 25
SL Green Realty Corporation, 44
Sleepy's Inc., 32
SLI, Inc., 48
Slim-Fast Nutritional Foods International, Inc., 18
SLM Holding Corp., 25 (upd.)
Smart & Final, Inc., 16
SmartForce PLC, 43
Smead Manufacturing Co., 17
Smith & Wesson Corporation, 30
Smith Barney Inc., 15
Smith Corona Corp., 13
Smith International, Inc., 15
Smith's Food & Drug Centers, Inc., 8
Smithfield Foods, Inc., 7; 43 (upd.)
SmithKline Beckman Corporation, I
Smithsonian Institution, 27
Smithway Motor Xpress Corporation, 39
Smurfit-Stone Container Corporation, 26 (upd.)
Snap-On, Incorporated, 7; 27 (upd.)
Snapple Beverage Corporation, 11
Snell & Wilmer L.L.P., 28
Society Corporation, 9
Soft Sheen Products, Inc., 31

Solectron Corporation, 12; 48 (upd.)
Solo Serve Corporation, 28
Solutia Inc., 52
Sonat, Inc., 6
Sonesta International Hotels Corporation, 44
Sonic Corp., 14; 37 (upd.)
Sonoco Products Company, 8
Soros Fund Management LLC, 28
Sorrento, Inc., 24
SOS Staffing Services, 25
Sotheby's Holdings, Inc., 11; 29 (upd.)
Sound Advice, Inc., 41
South Jersey Industries, Inc., 42
Southdown, Inc., 14
Southern Company, The, V; 38 (upd.)
Southern Indiana Gas and Electric Company, 13
Southern New UK Telecommunications Corporation, 6
Southern Pacific Transportation Company, V
Southern States Cooperative Incorporated, 36
Southern Union Company, 27
Southland Corporation, The, II; 7 (upd.)
Southtrust Corporation, 11
Southwest Airlines Co., 6; 24 (upd.)
Southwest Gas Corporation, 19
Southwest Water Company, 47
Southwestern Bell Corporation, V
Southwestern Electric Power Co., 21
Southwestern Public Service Company, 6
Southwire Company, Inc., 8; 23 (upd.)
Spacehab, Inc., 37
Spaghetti Warehouse, Inc., 25
Spangler Candy Company, 44
Spanish Broadcasting System, Inc., 41
Spartan Motors Inc., 14
Spartan Stores Inc., 8
Spartech Corporation, 19
Sparton Corporation, 18
Spec's Music, Inc., 19
Specialized Bicycle Components Inc., 50
Specialty Coatings Inc., 8
Specialty Equipment Companies, Inc., 25
SpeeDee Oil Change and Tune-Up, 25
Speedway Motorsports, Inc., 32
Speizman Industries, Inc., 44
Spelling Entertainment, 14; 35 (upd.)
Spencer Stuart and Associates, Inc., 14
Spherion Corporation, 52
Spiegel, Inc., 10; 27 (upd.)
Spirit Airlines, Inc., 31
Sport Chalet, Inc., 16
Sport Supply Group, Inc., 23
Sportmart, Inc., 15
Sports & Recreation, Inc., 17
Sports Authority, Inc., The, 16; 43 (upd.)
Sports Club Company, The, 25
Sportsman's Guide, Inc., The, 36
Springs Industries, Inc., V; 19 (upd.)
Sprint Corporation, 9; 46 (upd.)
SPS Technologies, Inc., 30
SPX Corporation, 10; 47 (upd.)
Squibb Corporation, I
Stage Stores, Inc., 24
Stanadyne Automotive Corporation, 37
Standard Commercial Corporation, 13
Standard Federal Bank, 9
Standard Microsystems Corporation, 11
Standard Motor Products, Inc., 40
Standard Pacific Corporation, 52
Standard Register Co., 15
Standex International Corporation, 17; 44 (upd.)
Stanhome Inc., 15

Stanley Furniture Company, Inc., 34
Stanley Works, The, III; 20 (upd.)
Staples, Inc., 10; 55 (upd.)
Star Banc Corporation, 11
Starbucks Corporation, 13; 34 (upd.)
Starcraft Corporation, 30
Starkey Laboratories, Inc., 52
Starrett Corporation, 21
Starter Corp., 12
Starwood Hotels & Resorts Worldwide, Inc., 54
Stash Tea Company, The, 50
State Farm Mutual Automobile Insurance Company, III; 51 (upd.)
State Financial Services Corporation, 51
State Street Boston Corporation, 8
Staten Island Bancorp, Inc., 39
Station Casinos Inc., 25
Steak n Shake Company, The, 41
Stearns, Inc., 43
Steel Dynamics, Inc., 52
Steelcase, Inc., 7; 27 (upd.)
Stein Mart Inc., 19
Steiner Corporation (Alsco), 53
Steinway Musical Properties, Inc., 19
Stepan Company, 30
Stericycle Inc., 33
STERIS Corporation, 29
Sterling Chemicals, Inc., 16
Sterling Drug, Inc., I
Sterling Electronics Corp., 18
Sterling Software, Inc., 11
Stevedoring Services of America Inc., 28
Steven Madden, Ltd., 37
Stewart & Stevenson Services Inc., 11
Stewart Enterprises, Inc., 20
Stewart's Beverages, 39
Stillwater Mining Company, 47
Stock Yards Packing Co., Inc., 37
Stone & Webster, Inc., 13
Stone Container Corporation, IV
Stone Manufacturing Company, 14; 43 (upd.)
Stonyfield Farm, Inc., 55
Stop & Shop Companies, Inc., The, II; 24 (upd.)
Storage Technology Corporation, 6
Storage USA, Inc., 21
Stouffer Corp., 8
StrataCom, Inc., 16
Stratus Computer, Inc., 10
Strayer Education, Inc., 53
Stride Rite Corporation, The, 8; 37 (upd.)
Stroh Brewery Company, The, I; 18 (upd.)
Stroock & Stroock & Lavan LLP, 40
Strouds, Inc., 33
Stryker Corporation, 11; 29 (upd.)
Stuart Entertainment Inc., 16
Student Loan Marketing Association, II
Stuller Settings, Inc., 35
Sturm, Ruger & Company, Inc., 19
Stussy, Inc., 55
Sub-Zero Freezer Co., Inc., 31
Suburban Propane Partners, L.P., 30
Subway, 32
Successories, Inc., 30
Sudbury Inc., 16
Suiza Foods Corporation, 26
Sullivan & Cromwell, 26
Summit Bancorporation, The, 14
Summit Family Restaurants, Inc. 19
Sun Communities Inc., 46
Sun Company, Inc., IV
Sun Country Airlines, 30
Sun Distributors L.P., 12
Sun Healthcare Group Inc., 25
Sun Microsystems, Inc., 7; 30 (upd.)

United States (continued)

Sun Sportswear, Inc., 17
Sun Television & Appliances Inc., 10
Sun-Diamond Growers of California, 7
SunAmerica Inc., 11
Sunbeam-Oster Co., Inc., 9
Sunburst Hospitality Corporation, 26
Sundstrand Corporation, 7; 21 (upd.)
Sundt Corp., 24
SunGard Data Systems Inc., 11
Sunglass Hut International, Inc., 21
Sunkist Growers, Inc., 26
Sunoco, Inc., 28 (upd.)
Sunrider Corporation, The, 26
Sunrise Medical Inc., 11
SunTrust Banks Inc., 23
Super Food Services, Inc., 15
Supercuts Inc., 26
Superior Industries International, Inc., 8
Superior Uniform Group, Inc., 30
Supermarkets General Holdings
    Corporation, II
SUPERVALU Inc., II; 18 (upd.); 50 (upd.)
Suprema Specialties, Inc., 27
Supreme International Corporation, 27
Susquehanna Pfaltzgraff Company, 8
Sutter Home Winery Inc., 16
Sverdrup Corporation, 14
Swank Inc., 17
SwedishAmerican Health System, 51
Sweetheart Cup Company, Inc., 36
Swift & Company, 55
Swift Transportation Co., Inc., 42
Swinerton Inc., 43
Swisher International Group Inc., 23
Sybase, Inc., 10; 27 (upd.)
Sybron International Corp., 14
Sycamore Networks, Inc., 45
Sykes Enterprises, Inc., 45
Sylvan Learning Systems, Inc., 35
Sylvan, Inc., 22
Symantec Corporation, 10
Symbol Technologies, Inc., 15
Syms Corporation, 29
Synopsis, Inc., 11
SynOptics Communications, Inc., 10
Synovus Financial Corp., 12; 52 (upd.)
Syntex Corporation, I
SyQuest Technology, Inc., 18
Syratech Corp., 14
SYSCO Corporation, II; 24 (upd.)
System Software Associates, Inc., 10
Systemax, Inc., 52
Systems & Computer Technology Corp.,
    19
T-Netix, Inc., 46
T. Rowe Price Associates, Inc., 11; 34
    (upd.)
TAB Products Co., 17
Taco Bell Corp., 7; 21 (upd.)
Taco Cabana, Inc., 23
Taco John's International Inc., 15
Take-Two Interactive Software, Inc., 46
Talbots, Inc., The, 11; 31 (upd.)
Talley Industries, Inc., 16
Tambrands Inc., 8
Tandem Computers, Inc., 6
Tandy Corporation, II; 12 (upd.)
Tandycrafts, Inc., 31
Tanger Factory Outlet Centers, Inc., 49
Target Stores, 10; 27 (upd.)
Tarragon Realty Investors, Inc., 45
Tasty Baking Company, 14; 35 (upd.)
Tattered Cover Book Store, 43
Taylor Corporation, 36
Taylor Guitars, 48
Taylor Made Golf Co., 23

Taylor Publishing Company, 12; 36 (upd.)
TBWA\Chiat\Day, 6; 43 (upd.)
TCBY Enterprises Inc., 17
TCF Financial Corporation, 47
Teachers Insurance and Annuity
    Association-College Retirement Equities
    Fund, III; 45 (upd.)
TearDrop Golf Company, 32
Tech Data Corporation, 10
Tech-Sym Corporation, 18; 44 (upd.)
TECHNE Corporation, 52
Technitrol, Inc., 29
TECO Energy, Inc., 6
Tecumseh Products Company, 8
Tejon Ranch Company, 35
Tektronix, Inc., 8
Tele-Communications, Inc., II
Teledyne, Inc., I; 10 (upd.)
Telephone and Data Systems, Inc., 9
Tellabs, Inc., 11; 40 (upd.)
Telxon Corporation, 10
Temple-Inland Inc., IV; 31 (upd.)
Tempur-Pedic Inc., 54
Tenet Healthcare Corporation, 55 (upd.)
TenFold Corporation, 35
Tennant Company, 13; 33 (upd.)
Tenneco Inc., I; 10 (upd.)
Tennessee Valley Authority, 50
Teradyne, Inc., 11
Terex Corporation, 7; 40 (upd.)
Terlato Wine Group, The, 48
Terra Industries, Inc., 13
Tesoro Petroleum Corporation, 7; 45 (upd.)
Testor Corporation, The, 51
Tetra Tech, Inc., 29
Texaco Inc., IV; 14 (upd.); 41 (upd.)
Texas Air Corporation, I
Texas Industries, Inc., 8
Texas Instruments Inc., II; 11 (upd.); 46
    (upd.)
Texas Pacific Group Inc., 36
Texas Rangers Baseball, 51
Texas Utilities Company, V; 25 (upd.)
Textron Inc., I; 34 (upd.)
Textron Lycoming Turbine Engine, 9
Thermadyne Holding Corporation, 19
Thermo BioAnalysis Corp., 25
Thermo Electron Corporation, 7
Thermo Fibertek, Inc., 24
Thermo Instrument Systems Inc., 11
Thermo King Corporation, 13
Thermos Company, 16
Thiokol Corporation, 9; 22 (upd.)
Thomas & Betts Corporation, 11; 54 (upd.)
Thomas Cook Travel Inc., 9; 33 (upd.)
Thomas H. Lee Co., 24
Thomas Industries Inc., 29
Thomas J. Lipton Company, 14
Thomas Nelson, Inc., 14; 38 (upd.)
Thomas Publishing Company, 26
Thomaston Mills, Inc., 27
Thomasville Furniture Industries, Inc., 12
Thor Industries, Inc., 39
Thorn Apple Valley, Inc., 7; 22 (upd.)
Thousand Trails, Inc., 33
THQ, Inc., 39
3Com Corporation, 11; 34 (upd.)
3DO Company, The, 43
Thrifty PayLess, Inc., 12
Ticketmaster Group, Inc., 13; 37 (upd.)
Tidewater Inc., 11; 37 (upd.)
Tiffany & Co., 14
TIG Holdings, Inc., 26
Tillotson Corp., 15
Timberland Company, The, 13; 54 (upd.)
Timberline Software Corporation, 15
Time Warner Inc., IV; 7 (upd.)

Times Mirror Company, The, IV; 17 (upd.)
Timex Corporation, 7; 25 (upd.)
Timken Company, The, 8; 42 (upd.)
Tishman Speyer Properties, L.P., 47
Titan Corporation, The, 36
Titanium Metals Corporation, 21
TJ International, Inc., 19
TJX Companies, Inc., The, V; 19 (upd.)
TLC Beatrice International Holdings, Inc.,
    22
TMP Worldwide Inc., 30
TNT Freightways Corporation, 14
Today's Man, Inc., 20
Todd Shipyards Corporation, 14
Todd-AO Corporation, The, 33
Todhunter International, Inc., 27
Tokheim Corporation, 21
Toll Brothers Inc., 15
Tollgrade Communications, Inc., 44
Tom Brown, Inc., 37
Tom Doherty Associates Inc., 25
Tom's of Maine, Inc., 45
Tombstone Pizza Corporation, 13
Tone Brothers, Inc., 21
Tonka Corporation, 25
Tootsie Roll Industries Inc., 12
Topps Company, Inc., The, 13; 34 (upd.)
Tops Appliance City, Inc., 17
Torchmark Corporation, 9; 33 (upd.)
Toro Company, The, 7; 26 (upd.)
Torrington Company, The, 13
Tosco Corporation, 7
Total Entertainment Restaurant
    Corporation, 46
Total System Services, Inc., 18
Totem Resources Corporation, 9
Tower Air, Inc., 28
Tower Automotive, Inc., 24
Towers Perrin, 32
Town & Country Corporation, 19
Town Sports International, Inc., 46
Toy Biz, Inc., 18
Toymax International, Inc., 29
Toys "R" Us, Inc., V; 18 (upd.)
Tracor Inc., 17
Trader Joe's Company, 13; 50 (upd.)
Trailer Bridge, Inc., 41
Trammell Crow Company, 8
Trans World Airlines, Inc., I; 12 (upd.); 35
    (upd.)
Trans World Entertainment Corporation, 24
Trans-Lux Corporation, 51
Transaction Systems Architects, Inc., 29
Transamerica–An AEGON Company, I; 13
    (upd.); 41 (upd.)
Transatlantic Holdings, Inc., 11
Transco Energy Company, V
Transmedia Network Inc., 20
TransMontaigne Inc., 28
Transocean Sedco Forex Inc., 45
Transport Corporation of America, Inc., 49
Tranzonic Companies, The, 37
Travel Ports of America, Inc., 17
Travelers Corporation, The, III
Travelocity.com, Inc., 46
Travis Boats & Motors, Inc., 37
TRC Companies, Inc., 32
Treadco, Inc., 19
Treasure Chest Advertising Company, Inc.,
    32
Tredegar Corporation, 52
Tree of Life, Inc., 29
Trek Bicycle Corporation, 16
Trend-Lines, Inc., 22
Trendwest Resorts, Inc., 33
Tri Valley Growers, 32
Triarc Companies, Inc., 8; 34 (upd.)

Tribune Company, IV; 22 (upd.)
Trico Products Corporation, 15
Trigen Energy Corporation, 42
TriMas Corp., 11
Trimble Navigation Limited, 40
Trinity Industries, Incorporated, 7
TRINOVA Corporation, III
Triple Five Group Ltd., 49
Triton Energy Corporation, 11
Triumph Group, Inc., 31
TRM Copy Centers Corporation, 18
Tropicana Products, Inc., 28
True North Communications Inc., 23
Trump Organization, 23
TruServ Corporation, 24
TRW Inc., I; 11 (upd.); 14 (upd.)
TTX Company, 6
Tubby's, Inc., 53
Tucson Electric Power Company, 6
Tuesday Morning Corporation, 18
Tully's Coffee Corporation, 51
Tultex Corporation, 13
Tumbleweed, Inc., 33
Tupperware Corporation, 28
Turner Broadcasting System, Inc., II; 6
  (upd.)
Turner Corporation, The, 8; 23 (upd.)
Turtle Wax, Inc., 15
Tuscarora Inc., 29
TV Guide, Inc., 43 (upd.)
TVI, Inc., 15
TW Services, Inc., II
Tweeter Home Entertainment Group, Inc.,
  30
Twentieth Century Fox Film Corporation,
  II; 25 (upd.)
24/7 Real Media, Inc., 49
Twin Disc, Inc., 21
Twinlab Corporation, 34
Ty Inc., 33
Tyco Toys, Inc., 12
Tyler Corporation, 23
Tyson Foods, Inc., II; 14 (upd.); 50 (upd.)
U S West, Inc., V; 25 (upd.)
U.S. Aggregates, Inc., 42
U.S. Bancorp, 14; 36 (upd.)
U.S. Borax, Inc., 42
U.S. Can Corporation, 30
U.S. Cellular Corporation, 31 (upd.)
U.S. Delivery Systems, Inc., 22
U.S. Foodservice, 26
U.S. Healthcare, Inc., 6
U.S. Home Corporation, 8
U.S. News and World Report Inc., 30
U.S. Office Products Company, 25
U.S. Robotics Inc., 9
U.S. Satellite Broadcasting Company, Inc.,
  20
U.S. Timberlands Company, L.P., 42
U.S. Trust Corp., 17
UAL Corporation, 34 (upd.)
UGI Corporation, 12
Ugly Duckling Corporation, 22
UICI, 33
Ukrop's Super Market's, Inc., 39
Ultimate Electronics, Inc., 18
Ultra Pac, Inc., 24
Ultrak Inc., 24
Ultramar Diamond Shamrock Corporation,
  31 (upd.)
Uncle Ben's Inc., 22
Underwriters Laboratories, Inc., 30
Uni-Marts, Inc., 17
Unicom Corporation, 29 (upd.)
Unifi, Inc., 12
UniFirst Corporation, 21
Union Bank of California, 16

Union Camp Corporation, IV
Union Carbide Corporation, I; 9 (upd.)
Union Electric Company, V
Union Pacific Corporation, V; 28 (upd.)
Union Planters Corporation, 54
Union Texas Petroleum Holdings, Inc., 9
UnionBanCal Corporation, 50 (upd.)
Unique Casual Restaurants, Inc., 27
Unison HealthCare Corporation, 25
Unisys Corporation, III; 6 (upd.); 36 (upd.)
United Airlines, I; 6 (upd.)
United Auto Group, Inc., 26
United Brands Company, II
United Defense, L.P., 30
United Dominion Industries Limited, 8; 16
  (upd.)
United Dominion Realty Trust, Inc., 52
United Foods, Inc., 21
United HealthCare Corporation, 9
United Illuminating Company, The, 21
United Industrial Corporation, 37
United Jewish Communities, 33
United Merchants & Manufacturers, Inc.,
  13
United Natural Foods, Inc., 32
United Parcel Service of America Inc., V;
  17 (upd.)
United Press International, Inc., 25
United Rentals, Inc., 34
United Retail Group Inc., 33
United States Cellular Corporation, 9
United States Filter Corporation, 20
United States Postal Service, 14; 34 (upd.)
United States Shoe Corporation, The, V
United States Steel Corporation, 50 (upd.)
United States Surgical Corporation, 10; 34
  (upd.)
United Stationers Inc., 14
United Technologies Automotive Inc., 15
United Technologies Corporation, I; 10
  (upd.); 34 (upd.)
United Telecommunications, Inc., V
United Video Satellite Group, 18
United Water Resources, Inc., 40
United Way of America, 36
Unitil Corporation, 37
Unitog Co., 19
Unitrin Inc., 16
Univar Corporation, 9
Universal Corporation, V; 48 (upd.)
Universal Electronics Inc., 39
Universal Foods Corporation, 7
Universal Forest Products Inc., 10
Universal Health Services, Inc., 6
Universal International, Inc., 25
Universal Studios, Inc., 33
Univision Communications Inc., 24
Uno Restaurant Corporation, 18
Unocal Corporation, IV; 24 (upd.)
UNUM Corp., 13
UnumProvident Corporation, 52 (upd.)
Upjohn Company, The, I; 8 (upd.)
Urban Outfitters, Inc., 14
URS Corporation, 45
US Airways Group, Inc., 28 (upd.); 52
  (upd.)
USA Interactive, Inc., 47 (upd.)
USA Truck, Inc., 42
USAA, 10
USAir Group, Inc., I; 6 (upd.)
USANA, Inc., 29
USF&G Corporation, III
USG Corporation, III; 26 (upd.)
UST Inc., 9; 50 (upd.)
USX Corporation, IV; 7 (upd.)
Utah Medical Products, Inc., 36
Utah Power and Light Company, 27

UtiliCorp United Inc., 6
UUNET, 38
Vail Resorts, Inc., 11; 43 (upd.)
Valassis Communications, Inc., 8; 37
  (upd.)
Valero Energy Corporation, 7
Valhi, Inc., 19
Vallen Corporation, 45
Valley Media Inc., 35
Valmont Industries, Inc., 19
Valspar Corporation, The, 8; 32 (upd.)
Value City Department Stores, Inc., 38
Value Line, Inc., 16
Value Merchants Inc., 13
ValueClick, Inc., 49
ValueVision International, Inc., 22
Van Camp Seafood Company, Inc., 7
Vanguard Group, Inc., The, 14; 34 (upd.)
Vans, Inc., 16; 47 (upd.)
Varco International, Inc., 42
Vari-Lite International, Inc., 35
Varian Associates Inc., 12
Varian, Inc., 48 (upd.)
Variflex, Inc., 51
Varlen Corporation, 16
Varsity Spirit Corp., 15
Vastar Resources, Inc., 24
VECO International, Inc., 7
Vector Group Ltd., 35 (upd.)
Veeco Instruments Inc., 32
Veit Companies, 43
Velocity Express Corporation, 49
Vencor, Inc., 16
Venetian Casino Resort, LLC, 47
Venture Stores Inc., 12
Verbatim Corporation, 14
Veridian Corporation, 54
VeriFone, Inc., 18
VeriSign, Inc., 47
Veritas Software Corporation, 45
Verizon Communications, 43 (upd.)
Vermeer Manufacturing Company, 17
Vermont Pure Holdings, Ltd., 51
Vermont Teddy Bear Co., Inc., The, 36
VF Corporation, V; 17 (upd.); 54 (upd.)
VHA Inc., 53
Viacom Inc., 7; 23 (upd.)
ViaSat, Inc., 54
Viasoft Inc., 27
VIASYS Healthcare, Inc., 52
Viatech Continental Can Company, Inc., 25
  (upd.)
Vicon Industries, Inc., 44
VICORP Restaurants, Inc., 12; 48 (upd.)
Vienna Sausage Manufacturing Co., 14
Viking Office Products, Inc., 10
Village Super Market, Inc., 7
Village Voice Media, Inc., 38
Vinson & Elkins L.L.P., 30
Vintage Petroleum, Inc., 42
Virco Manufacturing Corporation, 17
Visa International, 9; 26 (upd.)
Vishay Intertechnology, Inc., 21
Viskase Companies, Inc., 55
Vista Chemical Company, I
Vistana, Inc., 22
VISX, Incorporated, 30
Vitalink Pharmacy Services, Inc., 15
Vitesse Semiconductor Corporation, 32
Vitro Corp., 10
Vivra, Inc., 18
Vlasic Foods International Inc., 25
VLSI Technology, Inc., 16
Volt Information Sciences Inc., 26
Vons Companies, Incorporated, The, 7; 28
  (upd.)

United States (continued)

Vornado Realty Trust, 20
Vought Aircraft Industries, Inc., 49
Vulcan Materials Company, 7; 52 (upd.)
W. Atlee Burpee & Co., 27
W.A. Whitney Company, 53
W.H. Brady Co., 17
W.L. Gore & Associates, Inc., 14
W.P. Carey & Co. LLC, 49
W.R. Berkley Corp., 15
W.R. Grace & Company, I; 50 (upd.)
W.W. Grainger, Inc., V; 26 (upd.)
W.W. Norton & Company, Inc., 28
Waban Inc., 13
Wabash National Corp., 13
Wabtec Corporation, 40
Wachovia Bank of Georgia, N.A., 16
Wachovia Bank of South Carolina, N.A., 16
Wachovia Corporation, 12; 46 (upd.)
Wachtell, Lipton, Rosen & Katz, 47
Wackenhut Corporation, The, 14
Waddell & Reed, Inc., 22
Waffle House Inc., 14
Waggener Edstrom, 42
Wakefern Food Corporation, 33
Wal-Mart Stores, Inc., V; 8 (upd.); 26 (upd.)
Walbridge Aldinger Co., 38
Walbro Corporation, 13
Waldbaum, Inc., 19
Walden Book Company Inc., 17
Walgreen Co., V; 20 (upd.)
Walker Manufacturing Company, 19
Wall Drug Store, Inc., 40
Wall Street Deli, Inc., 33
Wallace Computer Services, Inc., 36
Walt Disney Company, The, II; 6 (upd.); 30 (upd.)
Walter Industries, Inc., II; 22 (upd.)
Walton Monroe Mills, Inc., 8
Wang Laboratories, Inc., III; 6 (upd.)
Warnaco Group Inc., The, 12; 46 (upd.)
Warner Communications Inc., II
Warner-Lambert Co., I; 10 (upd.)
Warrantech Corporation, 53
Warwick Valley Telephone Company, 55
Washington Companies, The, 33
Washington Federal, Inc., 17
Washington Football, Inc., 35
Washington Gas Light Company, 19
Washington Mutual, Inc., 17
Washington National Corporation, 12
Washington Natural Gas Company, 9
Washington Post Company, The, IV; 20 (upd.)
Washington Scientific Industries, Inc., 17
Washington Water Power Company, 6
Waste Connections, Inc., 46
Waste Holdings, Inc., 41
Waste Management, Inc., V
Water Pik Technologies, Inc., 34
Waterhouse Investor Services, Inc., 18
Waters Corporation, 43
Watkins-Johnson Company, 15
Watsco Inc., 52
Watson Pharmaceuticals Inc., 16
Watson Wyatt Worldwide, 42
Watts Industries, Inc., 19
Waverly, Inc., 16
Wawa Inc., 17
Waxman Industries, Inc., 9
WD-40 Company, 18
Weather Channel Companies, The 52
Weatherford International, Inc., 39
Weber-Stephen Products Co., 40
Weeres Industries Corporation, 52

Wegmans Food Markets, Inc., 9; 41 (upd.)
Weider Nutrition International, Inc., 29
Weight Watchers International Inc., 12; 33 (upd.)
Weil, Gotshal & Manges LLP, 55
Weiner's Stores, Inc., 33
Weirton Steel Corporation, IV; 26 (upd.)
Weis Markets, Inc., 15
Weitz Company, Inc., The, 42
Welbilt Corp., 19
Wellman, Inc., 8; 52 (upd.)
WellPoint Health Networks Inc., 25
Wells Fargo & Company, II; 12 (upd.); 38 (upd.)
Wells Rich Greene BDDP, 6
Wells' Dairy, Inc., 36
Wells-Gardner Electronics Corporation, 43
Wendy's International, Inc., 8; 23 (upd.); 47 (upd.)
Wenner Media, Inc., 32
Werner Enterprises, Inc., 26
West Bend Co., 14
West Coast Entertainment Corporation, 29
West Corporation, 42
West Group, 34 (upd.)
West Marine, Inc., 17
West One Bancorp, 11
West Pharmaceutical Services, Inc., 42
West Point-Pepperell, Inc., 8
West Publishing Co., 7
Westaff Inc., 33
Westamerica Bancorporation, 17
Western Atlas Inc., 12
Western Beef, Inc., 22
Western Company of North America, 15
Western Digital Corp., 25
Western Gas Resources, Inc., 45
Western Publishing Group, Inc., 13
Western Resources, Inc., 12
Western Union Financial Services, Inc., 54
Western Wireless Corporation, 36
Westin Hotels and Resorts Worldwide, 9; 29 (upd.)
Westinghouse Electric Corporation, II; 12 (upd.)
Westmoreland Coal Company, 7
WestPoint Stevens Inc., 16
Westvaco Corporation, IV; 19 (upd.)
Westwood One, Inc., 23
Wet Seal, Inc., The, 18
Wetterau Incorporated, II
Weyco Group, Incorporated, 32
Weyerhaeuser Company, IV; 9 (upd.); 28 (upd.)
Wheaton Industries, 8
Wheelabrator Technologies, Inc., 6
Wheeling-Pittsburgh Corp., 7
Wherehouse Entertainment Incorporated, 11
Whirlpool Corporation, III; 12 (upd.)
White & Case LLP, 35
White Castle System, Inc., 12; 36 (upd.)
White Consolidated Industries Inc., 13
White Rose, Inc., 24
Whitman Corporation, 10 (upd.)
Whitman Education Group, Inc., 41
Whitney Holding Corporation, 21
Whittaker Corporation, I; 48 (upd.)
Whole Foods Market, Inc., 20; 50 (upd.)
Wickes Inc., V; 25 (upd.)
Wild Oats Markets, Inc., 19; 41 (upd.)
Wildlife Conservation Society, 31
Willamette Industries, Inc., IV; 31 (upd.)
William Morris Agency, Inc., 23
Williams & Connolly LLP, 47
Williams Communications Group, Inc., 34

Williams Companies, Inc., The, IV; 31 (upd.)
Williams-Sonoma, Inc., 17; 44 (upd.)
Williamson-Dickie Manufacturing Company, 14; 45 (upd.)
Wilmington Trust Corporation, 25
Wilson Sonsini Goodrich & Rosati, 34
Wilson Sporting Goods Company, 24
Wilsons The Leather Experts Inc., 21
Wind River Systems, Inc., 37
Windmere Corporation, 16
Wine Group, Inc., The, 39
Winn-Dixie Stores, Inc., II; 21 (upd.)
Winnebago Industries Inc., 7; 27 (upd.)
WinsLoew Furniture, Inc., 21
Winston & Strawn, 35
Wisconsin Bell, Inc., 14
Wisconsin Central Transportation Corporation, 24
Wisconsin Dairies, 7
Wisconsin Energy Corporation, 6; 54 (upd.)
Wisconsin Public Service Corporation, 9
Witco Corporation, I; 16 (upd.)
Wizards of the Coast Inc., 24
WLR Foods, Inc., 21
Wm. Wrigley Jr. Company, 7
WMS Industries, Inc., 15; 53 (upd.)
WMX Technologies Inc., 17
Wolfgang Puck Food Company, Inc., The, 26
Wolohan Lumber Co., 19
Wolverine Tube Inc., 23
Wolverine World Wide Inc., 16
Womble Carlyle Sandridge & Rice, PLLC, 52
Wood-Mode, Inc., 23
Woodward Governor Company, 13; 49 (upd.)
Woolworth Corporation, V; 20 (upd.)
WordPerfect Corporation, 10
Working Assets Funding Service, 43
World Bank Group, 33
World Book, Inc., 12
World Color Press Inc., 12
World Duty Free Americas, Inc., 29 (upd.)
World Fuel Services Corporation, 47
World Wrestling Federation Entertainment, Inc., 32
World's Finest Chocolate Inc., 39
WorldCorp, Inc., 10
Worldwide Restaurant Concepts, Inc., 47
Worthington Foods, Inc., 14
Worthington Industries, Inc., 7; 21 (upd.)
WPL Holdings, Inc., 6
WPS Resources Corporation, 53 (upd.)
WTD Industries, Inc., 20
Wyant Corporation, 30
Wyeth, 50 (upd.)
Wyle Electronics, 14
Wyman-Gordon Company, 14
Wynn's International, Inc., 33
Wyse Technology, Inc., 15
X-Rite, Inc., 48
Xerox Corporation, III; 6 (upd.); 26 (upd.)
Xilinx, Inc., 16
XTO Energy Inc., 52
Yahoo! Inc., 27
Yankee Candle Company, Inc., The, 37
YankeeNets LLC, 35
Yellow Corporation, 14; 45 (upd.)
Yellow Freight System, Inc. of Delaware, V
YES! Entertainment Corporation, 26
YMCA of the USA, 31
YOCREAM International, Inc., 47
York Group, Inc., The, 50

York International Corp., 13
York Research Corporation, 35
Young & Rubicam, Inc., I; 22 (upd.)
Young Broadcasting Inc., 40
Young Innovations, Inc., 44
Young's Market Company, LLC, 32
Younkers, Inc., 19
Youth Services International, Inc., 21
Yucaipa Cos., 17
YWCA of the United States, 45
Zale Corporation, 16; 40 (upd.)
Zany Brainy, Inc., 31
Zapata Corporation, 25
Zebra Technologies Corporation, 14; 53
   (upd.)
Zenith Data Systems, Inc., 10
Zenith Electronics Corporation, II; 13
   (upd.); 34 (upd.)
Zero Corporation, 17
Ziebart International Corporation, 30
Ziegler Companies, Inc., The, 24
Ziff Communications Company, 12
Ziff Davis Media Inc., 36 (upd.)
Zila, Inc., 46
Zilog, Inc., 15
Zimmer Holdings, Inc., 45
Zion's Cooperative Mercantile Institution,
   33
Zions Bancorporation, 12; 53 (upd.)
Zippo Manufacturing Company, 18
Zoltek Companies, Inc., 37
Zondervan Publishing House, 24
Zoom Technologies, Inc., 53 (upd.)
Zoom Telephonics, Inc., 18
Zygo Corporation, 42
Zytec Corporation, 19

Venezuela

Cerveceria Polar, I
Cisneros Group of Companies, 54
Empresas Polar SA, 55 (upd.)
Petróleos de Venezuela S.A., IV

Wales

Hyder plc, 34
Iceland Group plc, 33
Kwik Save Group plc, 11

Zambia

Zambia Industrial and Mining Corporation
   Ltd., IV

NOTES ON CONTRIBUTORS

Notes on Contributors

BIANCO, David. Writer, editor, and publishing consultant.

BRENNAN, Gerald E. Writer based in California specializing in business, government, and political science issues.

BROWN, Erin. Writer on business topics.

COHEN, M. L. Novelist and writer living in Paris.

COVELL, Jeffrey L. Seattle-based writer.

DINGER, Ed. Bronx-based writer and editor.

FIERO, John W. Writer, researcher, and consultant.

GASBARRE, April Dougal. Michigan-based writer specializing in international business.

GREENLAND, Paul R. Illinois-based writer and researcher; author of two books and former senior editor of a national business magazine; contributor to *The Encyclopedia of Chicago History* (University of Chicago Press) and *Company Profiles for Students.*

HAUSER, Evelyn. Researcher, writer and marketing specialist based in Arcata, California; expertise includes historical and trend research in such topics as globalization, emerging industries and lifestyles, future scenarios, biographies, and the history of organizations.

HENRY, Elizabeth. Writer and editor based in Maine.

INGRAM, Frederick C. Utah-based business writer who has contributed to *GSA Business, Appalachian Trailway News,* the *Encyclopedia of Business,* the *Encyclopedia of Global Industries,* the *Encyclopedia of Consumer Brands,* and other regional and trade publications.

LEMIEUX, Gloria A. Writer and editor living in Nashua, New Hampshire.

MONTGOMERY, Bruce P. Curator and director of historical collection, University of Colorado at Boulder.

ROTHBURD, Carrie. Writer and editor specializing in corporate profiles, academic texts, and academic journal articles.

SALAMIE, David E. Part-owner of InfoWorks Development Group, a reference publication development and editorial services company.

STANFEL, Rebecca. Writer and editor based in Montana.

STANSELL, Christina M. Writer, researcher, and editor based in Farmington Hills, Michigan.

TRADII, Mary. Writer based in Denver, Colorado.

UHLE, Frank. Ann Arbor-based writer; movie projectionist, disc jockey, and staff member of *Psychotronic Video* magazine.

WALDEN, David M. Business writer and historian in Salt Lake City.

WOODWARD, A. Writer on business topics.